VOLUME III

THE COMPETITION RESULTS
RÉSULTATS DES COMPÉTITIONS

THE OFFICIAL REPORT OF THE CENTENNIAL OLYMPIC GAMES
RAPPORT OFFICIEL DES JEUX OLYMPIQUES DU CENTENAIRE

Atlanta 1996®

THE ATLANTA COMMITTEE FOR THE OLYMPIC GAMES
COMITÉ D'ATLANTA POUR LES JEUX OLYMPIQUES

THE OFFICIAL REPORT OF THE CENTENNIAL OLYMPIC GAMES
RAPPORT OFFICIEL DES JEUX OLYMPIQUES DU CENTENAIRE

VOLUME I PLANNING AND ORGANIZING
PLANIFICATION ET ORGANISATION

This volume is comprised of a prologue, which covers the history of the bid process, and 28 chapters, organized by program and functional area, which address in detail the preparations for the 1996 Olympic Games. For the benefit of future organizing committees, each chapter contains conclusions and recommendations.

Ce volume comprend un prologue, qui couvre tout le processus de soumission de la candidature d'Atlanta, et 28 chapitres, classés en fonction des programmes et domaines fonctionnels concernés, et indiquant en détail comment les Jeux Olympiques de 1996 ont été préparés. Chaque chapitre comprend des conclusions et recommandations destinées aux futurs organisateurs.

VOLUME II THE CENTENNIAL OLYMPIC GAMES
JEUX OLYMPIQUES DU CENTENAIRE

This volume is comprised of a prologue and three major sections. The prologue provides a description of the city of Atlanta and its history. Section One begins with the arrival of the Olympic Torch to Los Angeles, California, on 27 April 1996, and progresses as the Torch Relay moves across the US reaching Atlanta 19 July, the day of the Opening Ceremony. This Torch Relay description is juxtaposed with Atlanta's preparations for the Centennial Olympic Games during spring and summer 1996 and highlights of Cultural Olympiad exhibitions and events prior to the start of the Games. Section Two is a day-by-day account of the Games, 19 July–4 August, with highlights of athletic achievements and descriptions of cultural events, as well as details of Games-time operations. Section Three provides information on the competition of each sport in the programme of the 1996 Olympic Games.

Ce volume comprend un prologue, qui décrit Atlanta et raconte son histoire, et trois grands chapitres. Le premier débute par l'arrivée de la flamme olympique à Los Angeles, en Californie, le 27 avril 1996, et retrace le relais du flambeau à travers les Etats-Unis jusqu'à son arrivée à Atlanta le 19 juillet, jour de la cérémonie d'ouverture des Jeux. Cette narration est juxtaposée aux préparatifs menés par Atlanta au printemps et pendant l'été de 1996 en vue des Jeux Olympiques du Centenaire, et indique les grands moments de l'Olympiade culturelle avant le début des Jeux. Le deuxième raconte les Jeux, jour par jour, du 19 juillet au 4 août, et donne les moments forts des épreuves sportives et des manifestations culturelles. Il donne aussi des détails sur l'aspect administratif des Jeux. Le troisième fournit des informations sur les épreuves de chaque sport inscrit au programme des Jeux Olympiques de 1996.

VOLUME III THE COMPETITION RESULTS
RÉSULTATS DES COMPÉTITIONS

This volume is comprised of the detailed results for all athletes in all events. Also included as a reference is a section on medal winners and record-setting performances arranged by sport and discipline, as well as a section of venue maps for the major locations used during the 1996 Olympic Games.

Ce volume donne les résultats détaillés de toutes les épreuves sportives. Il comprend aussi, en tant que référence, les médailles et les records par discipline sportive, ainsi qu'un chapitre consacré aux plans des principaux sites utilisés pendant les Jeux Olympiques de 1996.

VOLUME III

THE COMPETITION RESULTS
RÉSULTATS DES COMPÉTITIONS

THE OFFICIAL REPORT OF THE CENTENNIAL OLYMPIC GAMES
RAPPORT OFFICIEL DES JEUX OLYMPIQUES DU CENTENAIRE

PEACHTREE
ATLANTA

COLOPHON

The Official Report of the Centennial Olympic Games employs the typography and look developed for the 1996 Olympic Games by The Atlanta Committee for the Olympic Games (ACOG). The text type is Stone Serif. Univers is used for sidebar and tabular material. Display type is Copperplate Gothic. The Quilt of Leaves motif serves as a decorative element throughout the three volumes, in combination with the ACOG color palette in volumes I and II.

The typographer for this volume was Robin Sherman. Four-color film was created by Bright Arts, Ltd., Hong Kong, with coordination by Imago, USA, Inc., New York.

Le rapport officiel des Jeux Olympiques du Centenaire emploie la typographie et l'apparence développées pour les Jeux Olympiques de 1996 par le Comité d'Atlanta pour les Jeux Olympiques (ACOG). La police de caractères du texte est Stone Serif. Univers est utilisé pour les matériaux des sidebars et de tabulation. La police de caractères de l'étalage est Copperplate Gothic. Le motif de la courtepointe de feuilles s'emploie comme élement décoratif à travers les trois tomes, en combinaison avec la palette à couleurs d'ACOG dans les tomes I et II.

Le typographe pour ce tome était Robin Sherman. Le film à quatre couleurs était créé par Bright Arts, Ltd., Hongkong, avec la coordination d'Imago, USA, Inc., New York.

Published by
PEACHTREE PUBLISHERS
494 Armour Circle NE
Atlanta, GA 30324

Manufactured in Singapore
Fabriqué à Singapour

First printing
Premier tirage

Library of Congress Cataloguing in Publication Data

Atlanta Committee for the Olympic Games.
     The official report of the Centennial Olympic Games / the Atlanta
Committee for the Olympic Games.
          p. cm.
     Includes indexes.
     Contents: v. 1. Planning and organizing -- v. 2. The Centennial Olympic
games -- v. 3. the competition results.
     ISBN 1-56145-150-9 (set). -- ISBN 1-56145-168-1 (v. 1). -- ISBN 1-56145-151-7 (v. 2). -- ISBN
1-56145-169-X (v. 3)
     1. Olympic Games (26th : 1996 : Atlanta, Ga.) 2. Atlanta
Committee for the Olympic Games. I. Title.
GV722 1996.A86 1997
796.48--DC21   97-23578
                                                                      CIP

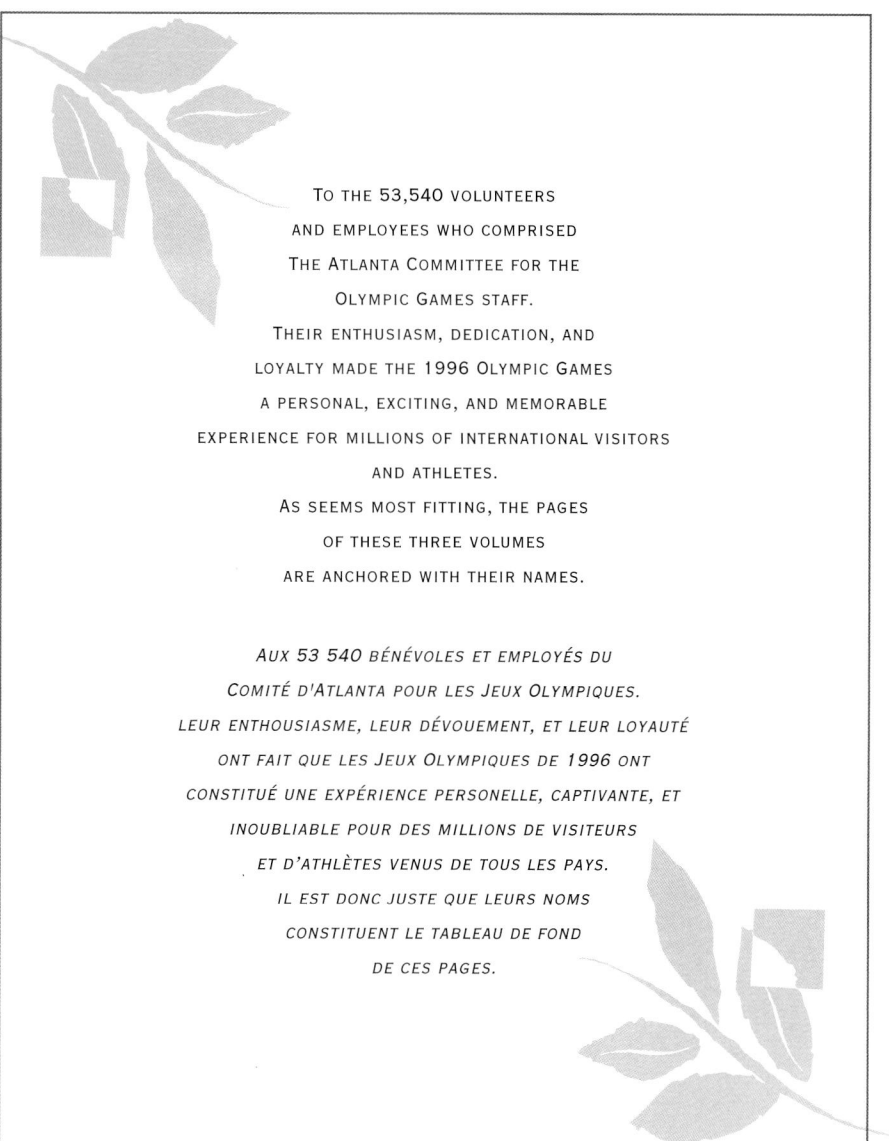

To the 53,540 volunteers
and employees who comprised
The Atlanta Committee for the
Olympic Games staff.
Their enthusiasm, dedication, and
loyalty made the 1996 Olympic Games
a personal, exciting, and memorable
experience for millions of international visitors
and athletes.
As seems most fitting, the pages
of these three volumes
are anchored with their names.

*Aux 53 540 bénévoles et employés du
Comité d'Atlanta pour les Jeux Olympiques.
Leur enthousiasme, leur dévouement, et leur loyauté
ont fait que les Jeux Olympiques de 1996 ont
constitué une expérience personelle, captivante, et
inoubliable pour des millions de visiteurs
et d'athlètes venus de tous les pays.
Il est donc juste que leurs noms
constituent le tableau de fond
de ces pages.*

TABLE OF CONTENTS

National Olympic Committee Abbreviations / *Abréviations des comités nationaux olympiques* .viii

Preface / *Préface* x

Medals Awarded and Olympic and World Records Established / *Médailles remises et records olympiques et du monde établis* 1

Aquatics—Diving / *Natation — Plongeon*
3 m Springboard, Men / *Tremplin de 3 m, Messieurs* 16
3 m Springboard, Women / *Tremplin de 3 m, Dames* .16
10 m Platform, Men / *Haut vol de 10 m, Messieurs* 17
10 m Platform, Women / *Haut vol de 10 m, Dames* .17

Aquatics—Swimming / *Natation — Natation*
50 m Freestyle, Men / *50 m nage libre, Messieurs* 20
50 m Freestyle, Women / *50 m nage libre, Dames* .20
100 m Freestyle, Men / *100 m nage libre, Messieurs* 21
100 m Freestyle, Women / *100 m nage libre, Dames* .22
200 m Freestyle, Men / *200 m nage libre, Messieurs* 23
200 m Freestyle, Women / *200 m nage libre, Dames* .23
400 m Freestyle, Men / *400 m nage libre, Messieurs* 24
400 m Freestyle, Women / *400 m nage libre, Dames* .24
800 m Freestyle, Women / *800 m nage libre, Dames* .25
1,500 m Freestyle, Men / *1 500 m nage libre, Messieurs* 25
100 m Backstroke, Men / *100 m dos, Messieurs* 26
100 m Backstroke, Women / *100 m dos, Dames* .27
200 m Backstroke, Men / *200 m dos, Messieurs* 27
200 m Backstroke, Women / *200 m dos, Dames* .28
100 m Breaststroke, Men / *100 m brasse, Messieurs* 28
100 m Breaststroke, Women / *100 m brasse, Dames* .29
200 m Breaststroke, Men / *200 m brasse, Messieurs* 30
200 m Breaststroke, Women / *200 m brasse, Dames* .30
100 m Butterfly, Men / *100 m papillon, Messieurs* 31
100 m Butterfly, Women / *100 m papillon, Dames* .32
200 m Butterfly, Men / *200 m papillon, Messieurs* 32
200 m Butterfly, Women / *200 m papillon, Dames* .33
200 m Individual Medley, Men / *200 m quatre nages, Messieurs* 33
200 m Individual Medley, Women / *200 m quatre nages, Dames* 34
400 m Individual Medley, Men / *400 m quatre nages, Messieurs* 35
400 m Individual Medley, Women / *400 m quatre nages, Dames* 35
4 x 100 m Freestyle Relay, Men / *4 x 100 m relais nage libre, Messieurs* 35
4 x 100 m Freestyle Relay, Women / *4 x 100 m relais nage libre, Dames* 36
4 x 200 m Freestyle Relay, Men / *4 x 200 m relais nage libre, Messieurs* 36
4 x 200 m Freestyle Relay, Women / *4 x 200 m relais nage libre, Dames* 37
4 x 100 m Medley Relay, Men / *4 x 100 m relais quatre nages, Messieurs* 37
4 x 100 m Medley Relay, Women / *4 x 100 m relais quatre nages, Dames* 38

Aquatics—Synchronized Swimming / *Natation — Natation synchronisée*
Team, Women / *Epreuve par équipes, Dames* .40

Aquatics—Water Polo / *Natation — Water-polo*
Men / *Messieurs* .42

Archery / *Tir à l'arc*
Individual, Men / *Epreuve individuelle, Messieurs* 60
Individual, Women / *Epreuve individuelle, Dames* 62
Team, Men / *Epreuve par équipes, Messieurs* 64
Team, Women / *Epreuve par équipes, Dames* 65

Athletics / *Athlétisme*
100 m, Men / *100 m, Messieurs* 68
100 m, Women / *100 m, Dames* 69
200 m, Men / *200 m, Messieurs* 70
200 m, Women / *200 m, Dames* 71
400 m, Men / *400 m, Messieurs* 72
400 m, Women / *400 m, Dames* 73
800 m, Men / *800 m, Messieurs* 74
800 m, Women / *800 m, Dames* 75
1,500 m, Men / *1 500 m, Messieurs* 76
1,500 m, Women / *1 500 m, Dames* 77
5,000 m, Men / *5 000 m, Messieurs* 78
5,000 m, Women / *5 000 m, Dames* 79
10,000 m, Men / *10 000 m, Messieurs* 80
10,000 m, Women / *10 000 m, Dames* 81
110 m Hurdles, Men / *110 m haies, Messieurs* 82
100 m Hurdles, Women / *100 m haies, Dames* 83
400 m Hurdles, Men / *400 m haies, Messieurs* 84
400 m Hurdles, Women / *400 m haies, Dames* 84
3,000 m Steeplechase, Men / *3 000 m steeple, Messieurs* 85
4 x 100 m Relay, Men / *Relais 4 x 100 m, Messieurs* 86
4 x 100 m Relay, Women / *Relais 4 x 100 m, Dames* 86
4 x 400 m Relay, Men / *Relais 4 x 400 m, Messieurs* 87
4 x 400 m Relay, Women / *Relais 4 x 400 m, Dames* 88
High Jump, Men / *Saut en hauteur, Messieurs* 88
HighJump, Women / *Saut en hauteur, Dames* 89
Pole Vault, Men / *Saut à la perche, Messieurs* 89
Long Jump, Men / *Saut en longueur, Messieurs* 90
Long Jump, Women / *Saut en longueur, Dames* 91
Triple Jump, Men / *Triple saut, Messieurs* 91
Triple Jump, Women / *Triple saut, Dames* . . .92
Hammer Throw, Men / *Marteau, Messieurs* 93
Shot Put, Men / *Poids, Messieurs* 93
Shot Put, Women / *Poids, Dames* 94
Discus Throw, Men / *Disque, Messieurs* 94
Discus Throw, Women / *Disque, Dames* 95
Javelin Throw, Men / *Javelot, Messieurs* 95
Javelin Throw, Women / *Javelot, Dames* 96
Decathlon, Men / *Décathlon, Messieurs* 96
Heptathlon, Women / *Heptathlon, Dames* 101
10 km Race Walk, Women / *10 km marche, Dames* 105
20 km Race Walk, Men / *20 km marche, Messieurs* 105
50 km Race Walk, Men / *50 km marche, Messieurs* 106
Marathon, Men / *Marathon, Messieurs* 106
Marathon, Women / *Marathon, Dames* 107
1,500 m Wheelchair, Men / *1 500 m fauteuil roulant, Messieurs* 107
800 m Wheelchair, Women / *800 m fauteuil roulant, Dames* 107
Marathon and Race Walk Courses / *Parcours du marathon et de la marche* 108

Badminton / *Badminton*
Singles, Men / *Simples, Messieurs* 110

Singles, Women / *Simples, Dames* 111
Doubles, Men / *Doubles, Messieurs* 112
Doubles, Women / *Doubles, Dames* 113
Doubles, Mixed / *Doubles, Mixtes* 114

Baseball / *Baseball*
Men / *Messieurs* 116

Basketball / *Basketball*
Men / *Messieurs* 128
Women / *Dames* 140

Boxing / *Boxe*
Light Flyweight, 48 kg (106 lb), Men / *Mi-mouche, 48 kg, Messieurs* 154
Flyweight, 51 kg (112 lb), Men / *Mouche, 51 kg, Messieurs* 154
Bantamweight, 54 kg (119 lb), Men / *Coq, 54 kg, Messieurs* 155
Featherweight, 57 kg (125 lb), Men / *Plume, 57 kg, Messieurs* 155
Lightweight, 60 kg (132 lb), Men / *Léger, 60 kg, Messieurs* 156
Light Welterweight, 63.5 kg (139 lb), Men / *Mi-welter, 63,5 kg, Messieurs* 156
Welterweight, 67 kg (147 lb), Men / *Welter, 67 kg, Messieurs* 157
Light Middleweight, 71 kg (156 lb), Men / *Mi-moyen, 71 kg, Messieurs* 157
Middleweight, 75 kg (165 lb), Men / *Moyen, 75 kg, Messieurs* 158
Light Heavyweight, 81 kg (178 lb), Men / *Mi-lourd, 81 kg, Messieurs* 158
Heavyweight, 91 kg (201 lb), Men / *Lourd, 91 kg, Messieurs* 159
Super Heavyweight, +91 kg (+201 lb), Men / *Super-lourd, +91 kg, Messieurs* 159

Canoe / Kayak—Slalom / *Canoë / Kayak — Slalom*
Kayak Single, Men / *Kayak simple, Messieurs* 162
Kayak Single, Women / *Kayak simple, Dames* 162
Canoe Single, Men / *Canoë simple, Messieurs* 163
Canoe Double, Men / *Canoë double, Messieurs* 163
Canoe / Kayak—Slalom Venue Map / *Plan du site de Canoë / Kayak — Slalom* 164

Canoe / Kayak—Sprint / *Canoë / Kayak — Sprint*
500 m Kayak Single, Men / *500 m kayak simple, Messieurs* 166
500 m Kayak Single, Women / *500 m kayak simple, Dames* 166
500 m Kayak Double, Men / *500 m kayak double, Messieurs* 167
500 m Kayak Double, Women / *500 m kayak double, Dames* 168
500 m Kayak Fours, Women / *500 m kayak à quatre, Dames* 168
1,000 m Kayak Single, Men / *1 000 m kayak simple, Messieurs* 169
1,000 m Kayak Double, Men / *1 000 m kayak double, Messieurs* 170
1,000 m Kayak Fours, Men / *1 000 m kayak à quatre, Messieurs* 171
500 m Canoe Single, Men / *500 m canoë simple, Messieurs* 172
500 m Canoe Double, Men / *500 m canoë double, Messieurs* 172
1,000 m Canoe Single, Men / *1 000 m canoë simple, Messieurs* 173
1,000 m Canoe Double, Men / *1 000 m canoë double, Messieurs* 173

Cycling—Mountain Bike / *Cyclisme — VTT*
Cross Country, Men / *Cross-country, Messieurs* 176
Cross Country, Women / *Cross-country, Dames* 176

Cycling—Road / *Cyclisme — Route*
Road Race, Men / *Course sur route, Messieurs* 177
Road Race, Women / *Course sur route, Dames* 178
Individual Time Trial, Men / *Course individuelle contre la montre, Messieurs* 178
Individual Time Trial, Women / *Course individuelle contre la montre, Dames* 179

Cycling—Track / *Cyclisme — Piste*
1 km Time Trial, Men / *Course de 1 km contre la montre, Messieurs* 180
Sprint, Men / *Sprint, Messieurs* 180
Sprint, Women / *Sprint, Dames* 181
Individual Pursuit, Men / *Poursuite individuelle, Messieurs* 182
Individual Pursuit, Women / *Poursuite individuelle, Dames* 183
Team Pursuit, Men / *Poursuite par équipes, Messieurs* 183
Point Race, Men / *Course aux points, Messieurs* 184
Point Race, Women / *Course aux points, Dames* 184

Equestrian / *Sports équestres*
Individual 3-Day Event / *Concours complet individuel* 186
Team 3-Day Event / *Concours complet par équipes* 187
Individual Dressage / *Dressage individuel* 188
Team Dressage / *Dressage par équipes* 190
Individual Jumping / *Saut d'obstacles individuel* 191
Team Jumping / *Saut d'obstacles par équipes* 192

Fencing / *Escrime*
Individual Epée, Men / *Epée individuelle, Messieurs* 194
Individual Epée, Women / *Epée individuelle, Dames* 195
Team Epée, Men / *Epée par équipes, Messieurs* 196
Team Epée, Women / *Epée par équipes, Dames* 196
Individual Foil, Men / *Fleuret individuel, Messieurs* 197
Individual Foil, Women / *Fleuret individuel, Dames* 198
Team Foil, Men / *Fleuret par équipes, Messieurs* 199
Team Foil, Women / *Fleuret par équipes, Dames* 199
Individual Sabre, Men / *Sabre individuel, Messieurs* 200
Team Sabre, Men / *Sabre par équipes, Messieurs* 201

Football / *Football*
Men / *Messieurs* 204
Women / *Dames* 220

Gymnastics—Artistic / *Gymnastique — Artistique*
Team, Men / *Concours général par équipes, Messieurs* 230
Team, Women / *Concours général par équipes, Dames* 234
Individual All-Around, Men / *Concours général individuel, Messieurs* 238
Individual All-Around, Women / *Concours général individuel, Dames* 238
Individual Apparatus, Men / *Par engin, Messieurs* 239
Individual Apparatus, Women / *Par engin, Dames* 239

Gymnastics—Rhythmic / *Gymnastique — Rythmique*
Individual All-Around, Women / *Concours général individuel, Dames* 242
Team, Women / *Concours d'ensemble, Dames* 242

Handball / *Handball*
Men / *Messieurs* 244
Women / *Dames* 257

Hockey / *Hockey*
Men / *Messieurs* 266
Women / *Dames* 281

Judo / *Judo*
Extra Lightweight, 60 kg, Men / *Super-léger, 60 kg, Messieurs* 294
Extra Lightweight, 48 kg, Women / *Super-léger, 48 kg, Dames* 296
Half-Lightweight, 65 kg, Men / *Mi-léger, 65 kg, Messieurs* 297
Half-Lightweight, 52 kg, Women / *Mi-léger, 52 kg, Dames* 299
Lightweight, 71 kg, Men / *Léger, 71 kg, Messieurs* 300
Lightweight, 56 kg, Women / *Léger, 56 kg, Dames* 302
Half-Middleweight, 78 kg, Men / *Mi-moyen, 78 kg, Messieurs* 303
Half-Middleweight, 61 kg, Women / *Mi-moyen, 61 kg, Dames* 305
Middleweight, 86 kg, Men / *Moyen, 86 kg, Messieurs* 306
Middleweight, 66 kg, Women / *Moyen, 66 kg, Dames* 308
Half-Heavyweight, 95 kg, Men / *Mi-lourd, 95 kg, Messieurs* 309
Half-Heavyweight, 72 kg, Women / *Mi-lourd, 72 kg, Dames* 311
Heavyweight, +95 kg, Men / *Lourd, plus de 95 kg, Messieurs* 312
Heavyweight, +72 kg, Women / *Lourd, plus de 72 kg, Dames* 314

Modern Pentathlon / *Pentathlon moderne*
Men / *Messieurs* 316

Rowing / *Aviron*
Single Sculls, Men / *Skiff, Messieurs* 320
Single Sculls, Women / *Skiff, Dames* 321
Double Sculls, Men / *Deux rameurs en couple, Messieurs* 322
Double Sculls, Women / *Deux rameuses en couple, Dames* 323
Lightweight Double Sculls, Men / *Deux rameurs en couple poids léger, Messieurs* 325
Lightweight Double Sculls, Women / *Deux rameuses en couple poids léger, Dames* 326
Quadruple Sculls, Men / *Quatre rameurs en couple sans barreur, Messieurs* 328
Quadruple Sculls, Women / *Quatre rameuses en couple sans barreuse, Dames* 330
Coxless Pair, Men / *Deux rameurs en pointe sans barreur, Messieurs* 331
Coxless Pair, Women / *Deux rameuses en pointe sans barreuse, Dames* 332
Coxless Four, Men / *Quatre rameurs en pointe sans barreur, Messieurs* 333
Lightweight Coxless Four, Men / *Quatre rameurs en pointe sans barreur poids léger, Messieurs* 335
Eight, Men / *Huit, Messieurs* 338
Eight, Women / *Huit, Dames* 340

Shooting / *Tir*
50 m Free Pistol, Men / *Pistolet libre à 50 m, Messieurs* 344
25 m Rapid Fire Pistol, Men / *Pistolet de tir rapide à 25 m, Messieurs* 344
25 m Sport Pistol, Women / *Pistolet sport à 25 m, Dames* 345
10 m Air Pistol, Men / *Pistolet à air comprimé à 10 m, Messieurs* 345
10 m Air Pistol, Women / *Pistolet à air comprimé à 10 m, Dames* 346
10 m Air Rifle, Men / *Carabine à air comprimé à 10 m, Messieurs* 346
10 m Air Rifle, Women / *Carabine à air comprimé à 10 m, Dames* 347
50 m Free Rifle 3 Position, Men / *Carabine libre 3 positions à 50 m, Messieurs* 347
50 m Standard Rifle 3 Position, Women / *Carabine standard 3 positions à 50 m, Dames* 348
50 m Free Rifle Prone, Men / *Carabine libre position couchée à 50 m, Messieurs* 348
Trap, Men / *Fosse olympique, Messieurs* 349
Double Trap, Men / *Double trap, Messieurs* 349
Double Trap, Women / *Double trap, Dames* 350
Skeet, Men / *Skeet, Messieurs* 350
10 m Running Target, Men / *Cible mobile à 10 m, Messieurs* 351

Softball / *Softball*
Women / *Dames* 354

Table Tennis / *Tennis de table*
Singles, Men / *Simples, Messieurs* 366
Singles, Women / *Simples, Dames* 367
Doubles, Men / *Doubles, Messieurs* 369
Doubles, Women / *Doubles, Dames* 370

Tennis / *Tennis*
Singles, Men / *Simples, Messieurs* 372
Singles, Women / *Simples, Dames* 373
Doubles, Men / *Doubles, Messieurs* 374
Doubles, Women / *Doubles, Dames* 375

Volleyball / *Volleyball*
Volleyball—Beach, Men / *Volleyball — De plage, Messieurs* 377
Volleyball—Beach, Women / *Volleyball — De plage, Dames* 386
Volleyball—Indoor, Men / *Volleyball — En salle, Messieurs* 394
Volleyball—Indoor, Women / *Volleyball — En salle, Dames* 405

Weightlifting / *Haltérophilie*
54 kg, Men / *54 kg, Messieurs* 418
59 kg, Men / *59 kg, Messieurs* 418
64 kg, Men / *64 kg, Messieurs* 418
70 kg, Men / *70 kg, Messieurs* 419
76 kg, Men / *76 kg, Messieurs* 419
83 kg, Men / *83 kg, Messieurs* 419
91 kg, Men / *91 kg, Messieurs* 420
99 kg, Men / *99 kg, Messieurs* 420
108 kg, Men / *108 kg, Messieurs* 420
108+ kg, Men / *Plus de 108 kg, Messieurs* 421

Wrestling / *Lutte*
Freestyle, 48 kg (105.5 lb), Men / *Libre, 48 kg, Messieurs* 424
Freestyle, 52 kg (114.5 lb), Men / *Libre, 52 kg, Messieurs* 424
Freestyle, 57 kg (125.5 lb), Men / *Libre, 57 kg, Messieurs* 425
Freestyle, 62 kg (136.5 lb), Men / *Libre, 62 kg, Messieurs* 425
Freestyle, 68 kg (149.5 lb), Men / *Libre, 68 kg, Messieurs* 426
Freestyle, 74 kg (163 lb), Men / *Libre, 74 kg, Messieurs* 426
Freestyle, 82 kg (180.5 lb), Men / *Libre, 82 kg, Messieurs* 427
Freestyle, 90 kg (198 lb), Men / *Libre, 90 kg, Messieurs* 427
Freestyle, 100 kg (220 lb), Men / *Libre, 100 kg, Messieurs* 428
Freestyle, 130 kg (286 lb), Men / *Libre, 130 kg, Messieurs* 428
Greco-Roman, 48 kg (105.5 lb), Men / *Gréco-romaine, 48 kg, Messieurs* 429
Greco-Roman, 52 kg (114.5 lb), Men / *Gréco-romaine, 52 kg, Messieurs* 429
Greco-Roman, 57 kg (125.5 lb), Men / *Gréco-romaine, 57 kg, Messieurs* 430
Greco-Roman, 62 kg (136.5 lb), Men / *Gréco-romaine, 62 kg, Messieurs* 430
Greco-Roman, 68 kg (149.5 lb), Men / *Gréco-romaine, 68 kg, Messieurs* 431
Greco-Roman, 74 kg (163 lb), Men / *Gréco-romaine, 74 kg, Messieurs* 431
Greco-Roman, 82 kg (180.5 lb), Men / *Gréco-romaine, 82 kg, Messieurs* 432
Greco-Roman, 90 kg (198 lb), Men / *Gréco-romaine, 90 kg, Messieurs* 432
Greco-Roman, 100 kg (220 lb), Men / *Gréco-romaine, 100 kg, Messieurs* 433
Greco-Roman, 130 kg (286 lb), Men / *Gréco-romaine, 130 kg, Messieurs* 433

Yachting / *Yachting*
Board (IMCO One-Design: Mistral), Men / *Planche à voile (IMCO/Mistral), Messieurs* 436
Board (IMCO One-Design: Mistral), Women / *Planche à voile (IMCO/Mistral), Dames* 437
Single-Handed Dinghy (Finn), Men / *Dériveur solitaire (Finn), Messieurs* 438
Single-Handed Dinghy (Europe), Women / *Dériveur solitaire (Europe), Dames* 439
Double-Handed Dinghy (470), Men / *Dériveur à deux places (470), Messieurs* 440
Double-Handed Dinghy (470), Women / *Dériveur à deux places (470), Dames* 442
Dinghy (Laser), Mixed / *Dériveur (Laser), Mixte* 442
Multihull (Tornado), Mixed / *Multicoque (Tornado), Mixte* 444
Two-Person Keelboat (Star), Mixed / *Quillard à deux places (Star), Mixte* 445
Fleet/Match Race Keelboat (Soling), Mixed / *Quillard match/racing (Soling), Mixte* 446

Venue Maps / *Plan des sites* 448

NATIONAL OLYMPIC COMMITTEE ABBREVIATIONS
ABRÉVIATIONS DES COMITÉS NATIONAUX OLYMPIQUES

AFG	Afghanistan *Afghanistan*	CAM	Cambodia *Cambodge*	GBR	Great Britain *Grande-Bretagne*
AHO	Netherlands Antilles *Antilles néerlandaises*	CAN	Canada *Canada*	GBS	Guinea-Bissau *Guinée-Bissau*
ALB	Albania *Albanie*	CAY	Cayman Islands *les Caïmans*	GEO	Georgia *Géorgie*
ALG	Algeria *Algérie*	CGO	Congo *République du Congo*	GEQ	Equatorial Guinea *Guinée équatoriale*
AND	Andorra *Andorre*	CHA	Chad *Tchad*	GER	Germany *Allemagne*
ANG	Angola *Angola*	CHI	Chile *Chili*	GHA	Ghana *Ghana*
ANT	Antigua and Barbuda *Antigua-et-Barbuda*	CHN	People's Republic of China *République populaire de Chine*	GRE	Greece *Grèce*
ARG	Argentina *Argentine*	CIV	Ivory Coast *Côte d'Ivoire*	GRN	Grenada *Grenade*
ARM	Armenia *Arménie*	CMR	Cameroon *Cameroun*	GUA	Guatemala *Guatemala*
ARU	Aruba *Aruba*	COK	Cook Islands *Iles Cook*	GUI	Guinea *Guinée*
ASA	American Samoa *Samoa américaines*	COL	Colombia *Colombie*	GUM	Guam *Guam*
AUS	Australia *Australie*	COM	Comoros *Comores*	GUY	Guyana *Guyana*
AUT	Austria *Autriche*	CPV	Cape Verde *Cap-Vert*	HAI	Haiti *Haïti*
AZE	Azerbaijan *Azerbaïdjan*	CRC	Costa Rica *Costa Rica*	HKG	Hong Kong *Hong-Kong*
BAH	Bahamas *Bahamas*	CRO	Croatia *Croatie*	HON	Honduras *Honduras*
BAN	Bangladesh *Bangladesh*	CUB	Cuba *Cuba*	HUN	Hungary *Hongrie*
BAR	Barbados *Barbade*	CYP	Cyprus *Chypre*	INA	Indonesia *Indonésie*
BDI	Burundi *Burundi*	CZE	Czech Republic *République tchèque*	IND	India *Inde*
BEL	Belgium *Belgique*	DEN	Denmark *Danemark*	IRI	Islamic Republic of Iran *République islamique d'Iran*
BEN	Benin *Bénin*	DJI	Djibouti *Djibouti*	IRL	Ireland *Irlande*
BER	Bermuda *Bermudes*	DMA	Dominica *Dominique*	IRQ	Iraq *Iraq*
BHU	Bhutan *Bhoutan*	DOM	Dominican Republic *République dominicaine*	ISL	Iceland *Islande*
BIH	Bosnia and Herzegovina *Bosnie-Herzégovine*	ECU	Ecuador *Equateur*	ISR	Israel *Israël*
BIZ	Belize *Belize*	EGY	Egypt *Egypte*	ISV	Virgin Islands *Iles Vierges*
BLR	Belarus *Bélarus*	ESA	El Salvador *El Salvador*	ITA	Italy *Italie*
BOL	Bolivia *Bolivie*	ESP	Spain *Espagne*	IVB	British Virgin Islands *Iles Vierges britanniques*
BOT	Botswana *Botswana*	EST	Estonia *Estonie*	JAM	Jamaica *Jamaïque*
BRA	Brazil *Brésil*	ETH	Ethiopia *Ethiope*	JOR	Jordan *Jordanie*
BRN	Bahrain *Bahrein*	FIJ	Fiji *Fidji*	JPN	Japan *Japon*
BRU	Brunei Darussalam *Brunéi Darussalam*	FIN	Finland *Finlande*	KAZ	Kazakhstan *Kazakhstan*
BUL	Bulgaria *Bulgarie*	FRA	France *France*	KEN	Kenya *Kenya*
BUR	Burkina Faso *Burkina Faso*	GAB	Gabon *Gabon*	KGZ	Kyrgyzstan *Kirghizistan*
CAF	Central African Republic *République Centrafricaine*	GAM	Gambia *Gambie*	KOR	Korea *Corée*

KSA	Saudi Arabia / *Arabie Saoudite*	NIG	Niger / *Niger*	SUD	Sudan / *Soudan*
KUW	Kuwait / *Koweït*	NOR	Norway / *Norvège*	SUI	Switzerland / *Suisse*
LAO	Lao People's Democratic Republic / *République démocratique populaire Lao*	NRU	Nauru / *Nauru*	SUR	Suriname / *Suriname*
LAT	Latvia / *Lettonie*	NZL	New Zealand / *Nouvelle-Zélande*	SVK	Slovakia / *Slovaquie*
LBA	Libyan Arab Jamahiriya / *Jamahiriya arabe libyenne*	OMA	Oman / *Oman*	SWE	Sweden / *Suède*
LBR	Liberia / *Libéria*	PAK	Pakistan / *Pakistan*	SWZ	Swaziland / *Swaziland*
LCA	Saint Lucia / *Sainte-Lucie*	PAN	Panama / *Panama*	SYR	Syrian Arab Republic / *République arabe syrienne*
LES	Lesotho / *Lesotho*	PAR	Paraguay / *Paraguay*	TAN	United Republic of Tanzania / *République unie de Tanzanie*
LIB	Lebanon / *Liban*	PER	Peru / *Pérou*	TGA	Tonga / *Tonga*
LIE	Liechtenstein / *Liechtenstein*	PHI	Philippines / *Philippines*	THA	Thailand / *Thaïlande*
LTU	Lithuania / *Lituanie*	PLE	Palestine / *Palestine*	TJK	Tajikistan / *Tadjikistan*
LUX	Luxembourg / *Luxembourg*	PNG	Papua New Guinea / *Papouasie-Nouvelle-Guinée*	TKM	Turkmenistan / *Turkménistan*
MAD	Madagascar / *Madagascar*	POL	Poland / *Pologne*	TOG	Togo / *Togo*
MAR	Morocco / *Maroc*	POR	Portugal / *Portugal*	TPE	Chinese Taipei / *Chinese Taipei*
MAS	Malaysia / *Malaisie*	PRK	Democratic People's Republic of Korea / *République démocratique populaire de Corée*	TRI	Trinidad and Tobago / *Trinité-et-Tobago*
MAW	Malawi / *Malawi*	PUR	Puerto Rico / *Porto Rico*	TUN	Tunisia / *Tunisie*
MDA	Republic of Moldova / *République de Moldova*	QAT	Qatar / *Qatar*	TUR	Turkey / *Turquie*
MDV	Maldives / *Maldives*	ROM	Romania / *Roumanie*	UAE	United Arab Emirates / *Emirats arabes unis*
MEX	Mexico / *Mexique*	RSA	South Africa / *Afrique du Sud*	UGA	Uganda / *Ouganda*
MGL	Mongolia / *Mongolie*	RUS	Russian Federation / *Fédération de Russie*	UKR	Ukraine / *Ukraine*
MKD	Former Yugoslav Republic of Macedonia / *Ex-République yougoslave de Macédoine*	RWA	Rwanda / *Rwanda*	URU	Uruguay / *Uruguay*
MLI	Mali / *Mali*	SAM	Western Samoa / *Samoa occidentales*	USA	United States of America / *Etats-Unis d'Amérique*
MLT	Malta / *Malte*	SEN	Senegal / *Sénégal*	UZB	Uzbekistan / *Ouzbékistan*
MON	Monaco / *Monaco*	SEY	Seychelles / *Seychelles*	VAN	Vanuatu / *Vanuatu*
MOZ	Mozambique / *Mozambique*	SIN	Singapore / *Singapour*	VEN	Venezuela / *Venezuela*
MRI	Mauritius / *Maurice*	SKN	Saint Kitts and Nevis / *Saint-Kitts-et-Nevis*	VIE	Vietnam / *Vietnam*
MTN	Mauritania / *Mauritanie*	SLE	Sierra Leone / *Sierra Leone*	VIN	Saint Vincent and The Grenadines / *Saint-Vincent-et-les-Grenadines*
MYA	Myanmar / *Myanmar*	SLO	Slovenia / *Slovénie*	YEM	Yemen / *Yémen*
NAM	Namibia / *Namibie*	SMR	San Marino / *Saint-Marin*	YUG	Yugoslavia / *Yougoslavie*
NCA	Nicaragua / *Nicaragua*	SOL	Solomon Islands / *Iles Salomon*	ZAI	Zaire / *Zaïre*
NED	Netherlands / *Pays-Bas*	SOM	Somalia / *Somalie*	ZAM	Zambia / *Zambie*
NEP	Nepal / *Népal*	SRI	Sri Lanka / *Sri Lanka*	ZIM	Zimbabwe / *Zimbabwe*
NGR	Nigeria / *Nigéria*	STP	Sao Tome and Principe / *Sao Tomé-et-Principe*		

PREFACE / *PRÉFACE*

THE OFFICIAL REPORT of the Centennial Olympic Games is strongly influenced by historical precedence and IOC requirements. The organizers and authors of this Report have tried to provide as much detail as possible to assist Olympic scholars and future organizing committees.

This third and final volume contains the competition results from all events of the Programme of the 1996 Olympic Games. Every athlete who participated in the Games is named in this volume. The results are organized by their respective sports, which are listed alphabetically.

One organizational change in the presentation of the results of the 1996 Olympic Games concerns the order of the listing of men's and women's events. We have chosen to juxtapose men's and women's events that are the same or comparable for each sport.

We have endeavored to provide an accurate record of the competition results and have relied on both the Official Results books that were produced for each sport after the Games and authorized by the governing International Federations as well as additional research.

Note on Designations of New Records

The statistics in this volume indicate World and Olympic records set during the 1996 Olympic Games as determined by the governing International Federation for each sport. The records are shown—by a "W" for a new World record and an "O" for a new Olympic record—within the results of each sport, with the exception of Weightlifting (see below).

World records are also Olympic records. Other types of records (such as national and area) as well as World and Olympic records that were equaled but not broken are not identified here.

For five sports, the International Federations define which performances qualify for new records when an event is without Olympic precedent or produces a tie. Decisions are made based on the following criteria:

■ *Aquatics–Swimming.* In the Women's 4 x 200 m Relay, which was a new event for these Games, the Olympic record is shown to have been broken more than once as the event progressed.

■ *Archery.* The format for all events was changed, so many new records were set in these Games. The best individual scores and combined scores at the completion of each event are denoted as Olympic records.

■ *Athletics.* In the Women's 5,000 m and the Women's Triple Jump, which were new events, only the best result at the completion of each of these events is designated as an Olympic record. In the Pole Vault, three athletes tied in setting an Olympic record height. Because all three vaults occurred in the same round, all three athletes are shown as having set an Olympic record.

■ *Shooting.* There were many new shooting events in these Olympic Games. Only the best score at the completion of each new event is denoted as an Olympic record. There were ties in both the Men's Trap and the Men's 50 m Free Rifle 3 Position events. Because the tying scores occurred within the same match, both athletes in each event are shown as having set an Olympic record.

■ *Weightlifting.* All weight divisions were changed for the 1996 Games. Olympic records were broken more than once in some divisions as events progressed. Records are shown in a separate table immediately following the Weightlifting results.

L E RAPPORT OFFICIEL des Jeux Olympiques du Centenaire est fortement influencé par l'historique et les exigences du C.I.O. Les organisateurs et les auteurs de ce Rapport se sont efforcés de fournir autant de détails que possible afin d'aider les érudits de l'Olympisme et les comité d'organisation à venir.

Ce troisième et dernier volume contient les résultats des compétitions de toutes les épreuves figurant au programme des Jeux Olympiques de 1996. Le nom de chaque athlète ayant participé aux Jeux apparaît dans ce volume. Les résultats sont organisés en fonction de chaque sport, par énumérations alphabétique suivant la langue anglaise.

Un changement organisationnel dans la présentation des résultats des Jeux de 1996 concerne l'ordre d'énumération des épreuves masculines et féminines. Nous avons décidé de juxtaposer les épreuves masculines et féminines semblables ou comparables dans chaque sport.

Nous avons tenté de donner un compte précis des résultats des compétitions. Nous nous sommes servis à cet effet des livres des Résultats officiels produits pour chaque sport pendant les Jeux et autorisés par des Fédérations Internationales. Nous avons également effectué des recherches supplémentaires le cas échéant.

Les Nouveaux Records

Le présent volume contient des statistiques qui reflètent les records du monde et olympiques établis lors des Jeux Olympiques de 1996, conformément à la Fédération Internationale qui est l'organe directeur de chaque sport. Ils figurent parmi les résultats avec la mention "W" pour un nouveau record du monde, et "O" pour un record olympique, et ce pour tous les sports, à l'exception de l'haltérophilie (Voir ci-dessous). Tous les records du monde sont aussi des records olympiques. Les autres (nationaux et régionaux) et ceux qui ont été égalés mais non battus ne sont pas identifiés dans ces statistiques.

Dans le cas de cinq sports, les F.I. déterminent ce qui constitue un nouveau record s'il n'y a pas eu d'épreuve olympique précédente ou en cas d'ex aequo. Les décisions sont prises en fonction des critères suivants :

■ *Natation — Natation* : Dans le relais 4 fois 200 m féminin, épreuve nouvelle pour les Jeux, le record olympique a été battu à plusieurs reprises au fur et à mesure de la progression de la compétition.

■ *Tir à l'arc* : Le format de toutes les épreuves a été modifié, de sorte que de nombreux records ont été établis lors de ces Jeux. Les meilleurs scores individuels et combinés dans chaque épreuve constituent des records olympiques.

■ *Athlétisme* : Dans le 5 000 m et le triple saut féminins, qui sont des épreuves nouvelles, seul le meilleur résultat obtenu dans chaque discipline est considéré comme un record olympique. Dans le saut à la perche, trois athlètes ont établi un nouveau record olympique. Etant donné que les trois sauts victorieux ont eu lieu lors du même essai, les trois athlètes sont considérés comme ayant établi le nouveau record.

■ *Tir* : De nombreuses épreuves nouvelles ont été disputées lors de ces Jeux. Seuls les meilleurs scores enregistrés à la fin de chacune sont considérés comme des records olympiques. Il y a eu ex aequo à la fosse olympique et à la carabine libre 3 positions à 50 m messieurs. Etant donné que ces résultats ont été enregistrés au cours du même match, les deux athlètes sont considérés comme ayant battu le record olympique.

■ *Haltérophilie* : Toutes les catégories de poids ont été changées pour les Jeux de 1996. Les records olympiques ont été battus plus d'une fois dans certaines, au fur et à mesure de la progression de la compétition. Les records sont indiqués dans un tableau distinct qui suit immédiatement les résultats de ce sport.

• FREDDIE A MCKEITHEN JR • JAMES E MCKELVEY • JOE M MCKELVEY • MARY J MCKELVEY • BRUCE G MCKELVY • GEORGE M MCKELVY • SHARON MCKENNA • HEATHER MCKENNEY • JULIE A MCKENNEY • JOYCE E MCKENNIE • JAMES H MCKENRICK JR • ANNE W MCKENZIE • BETTY A MCKENZIE • DAN G MCKENZIE • DIONNE MCKENZIE • JANICE M MCKENZIE • KAREN MCKENZIE • KENNETH M MCKENZIE • LEZLIE J MCKENZIE • THRILLIA C MCKENZIE • WANDA L MCKENZIE • WANDA L MCKENZIE • DEBBIE MCKENZIE WILLSON • HELEN S MCKEON • KELLY A MCKEONE •

xi

JACQUELINE S MCKERSON • SUSAN A
MCKESSY • MICHAEL A MCKIBBEN • JAMES P
MCKILLOP • DONALD B MCKIM • MEREDITH J
MCKIM • ANNETTE G MCKIMMEY • HOWARD MCKIN-
LEY • JENNIFER J MCKINLEY • KEVIN L MCKINLEY •
MICHAEL D MCKINLEY • RUTH MCKINLEY • SALLY L
MCKINLEY • WILLIAM H MCKINLEY • BARBARA
MCKINNEY • BETSY E MCKINNEY • CAROL H MCK-
INNEY • CAROLYN L MCKINNEY • DIANNE H MCKIN-
NEY • DONNELL MCKINNEY • ERIN M MCKINNEY
• JAMES A MCKINNEY • JAN B MCKINNEY •
KENDALL C MCKINNEY • MARK A MCKINNEY •
NANCY R MCKINNEY • SHELIA Q MCKINNEY •
SUSAN G MCKINNEY • SUZANNE P MCKINNEY •
TIFFANY B MCKINNEY • WENDELL O MCKINNEY
• BARRIE F MCKINNEY-VOROBIEV • LINDA H
MCKINNIE • DENISE C MCKINNON • JEFFERY T
MCKINNON • SUSAN A MCKINNON • CRAIG C
MCKIRGAN • ARLENE MCKNIGHT • ASHLEY R
MCKNIGHT • CEZAR E MCKNIGHT • ELIZABETH R
MCKNIGHT • GEORGE MCKNIGHT • LISA Y MCK-
NIGHT • LLOYD M MCKNIGHT • LOUISE J MCK-
NIGHT • MARQUETTE MCKNIGHT • MARQUETTE
MCKNIGHT • MARTHA M MCKNIGHT • PATRICK S
MCKNIGHT • ROBERT H MCKNIGHT • SUSAN L
MCKNIGHT • XAVIER R MCKNIGHT • ZELLA M MCK-
NIGHT • WILLIAM R MCKNIGHT MT • CONNIE A
MCKOY • DAVID MCKOY • DEBORAH L MCLAIN •
LINDA M MCLAIN • FREDRICK C MCLAM •
WILLIAM F MCLANE • LAURIE S MCLAREN •
CALVIN W MCLARIN • DOUGLAS E MCLARNAN •
TARA T MCLARNON • BRAD A MCLARTY • JUDY F
MCLARTY • LAMONTA J MCLARTY • ANDREW H
MCLAUGHLIN • BARBARA G MCLAUGHLIN •
BERNARD J MCLAUGHLIN • JAMES F MCLAUGH-
LIN • JESSICA A MCLAUGHLIN • KATHLEEN M
MCLAUGHLIN • KRISTIN T MCLAUGHLIN • LISA A
MCLAUGHLIN • MARK B MCLAUGHLIN • ROBERT
E MCLAUGHLIN • SARAH E MCLAUGHLIN •
MICHELLE A MCLAURIN • MARY N MCLAURINE •
J MARSH MCLAWHORN • CAMILA C MCLEAN •
CAROLINE W MCLEAN • DAN MCLEAN • DONALD
C MCLEAN • GAYLA A MCLEAN • GERALDINE J
MCLEAN • LAURA J MCLEAN • BARBARA
MCLEAN RN MN CNP • BERT H MCLEES • ALI-
SON C MCLEISH • SUSAN M MCLEISH • FLO-
RENCE M MCLELLAND • LANE B MCLELLAND •
MIRIAM S MCLEMORE • TODD L MCLEMORE •
LISA R MCLEN • BRENDA J MCLENDON • JANE
MCLENDON • JOEY M MCLENDON • MARY K MCLEN-
DON • SANDRA L MCLENDON • VERSEY H MCLEN-
DON • DANIEL M MCLEOD • DAVID G MCLEOD •
HUGH C MCLEOD • J. HADIAH MCLEOD • JAMES E
MCLEOD • LESLIE D MCLEOD • MACK N MCLEOD •
HENRY G MCLEROY • JAMES H MCLEROY • JANICE
B MCLEROY • JANICE R MCLEROY • JUDITH A
MCLEROY • WANICE W MCLEROY • MARILYN M
MCLINSKEY • GEORGE B MCMAHAN • KELLIE E.
MCMAHAN • MARY MARCIA MCMAHAN • RACHEL
J MCMAHAN • THEODORE C MCMAHAN JR • AMY
M MCMAHON • CHRIS W MCMAHON • GAYLE F
MCMAHON • JEFF MCMAHON • JENNIFER L
MCMAHON • KATHLEEN MCMAHON • MICHAEL G
MCMAHON • MOLLY A MCMAHON • STEPHANIE L
MCMAHON • WILLIAM R MCMAHON • FRANCIS J
MCMAHON JR • PATRICK J MCMANAMY • ANN L
MCMANUS • BARBARA J MCMANUS • CON-
STANCE MCMANUS • HEATHER MCMANUS •
JEANNETTE L MCMANUS • RICK MCMANUS • SU-
SAN L MCMANUS • DONALD D MCMANUS EMT •
WILLIAM A MCMANUS MD • DANIEL A MCMASTER
• LEONA W MCMEANS • ERIN M MCMEEL ATC • CA-
ROLE H MCMENAMY • KIMBERLY Y MCMICHAEL •
TINA R MCMICHEN • AMANDA G MCMILLAN • MOL-
LY A MCMILLAN • STEVEN W MCMILLAN • TRACY E
MCMILLAN • VIRGINIA B MCMILLAN • BETTIE
MCMILLAN-YORK • IRA BRUCE MCMILLIAN • SH-
ERYL D MCMILLIAN • CHARLOTTE K MCMILLION
• RAY E MCMILLION • DEBRA K MCMINN • BRIAN
F MCMINN • SERETHA MCMOORE • THOMAS F
MCMORROW JR • CHARLES G MCMULLEN •
ERMA E MCMULLEN • NOEL M MCMULLEN • AU-
DRIA E MCMULLINS • THOMAS L MCMURDO •
BRETT B MCMURPHY • REBECCA L MCMURRAY •
JAMES D MCNABB • LELAND J MCNABB •
NATHAN C MCNABB • RODNEY D MCNABB • WL-
LLIAM S MCNABB • CHERYL L MCNAIR • ERNES-
TINE MCNAIR • EDWARD D MCNALLY • MARY M
MCNALLY • SEAN W MCNALLY • PETER J MCNA-
MARA • BARBARA G MCNAMEE • ROBERT G MC-
NAMEE • TOM M MCNAMEE • KEVIN J MCNANNA
• KIRSTIN E MCNARY • JIM H MCNATT • LINDA K
MCNATT • CATHERINE E MCNEAL • CLOIE E MC-
NEAL • JIMMIE L MCNEAL • KENYA A MCNEAL •
LA CHAIN L MCNEAL • VICKEY MCNEAL • WEN-
DELL D MCNEAL • CHARLES D MCNEAR • SU-
SANNAH J MCNEAR • THOMAS J MCNEELEY •
DEBORAH A MCNEELY • CYNTHIA R MCNEES •
ELLEN G MCNEES • ALEXANDER E MCNEIL •
DANIEL H MCNEIL • DEBORAH L MCNEIL • EDDIE
W MCNEIL • MICHEL R MCNEIL • STEVEN P MC-
NEIL • JAMES B MCNEIL JR • JOSEPH MCNEIL JR
• JAMES D MCNEILL • JULIE B MCNEILL • MARI-
ON G MCNEILL • PATRICIA A MCNEILL • WILLIAM
M MCNEILL • ANN MCNEMAR • MELISSA J MC-
NEW • SHAWN P MCNEW • ELIZABETH A MCNI-
CHOL • ALOISE E MCNICHOLS • JOHN J MCNI-
CHOLS • MARY J MCNICHOLS • RACHAEL L
MCNICHOLS • JUDITH A MCNIFF • CHUCK R MC-
NITT • ANGELA N MCNULTY • CHRISTOPHER C
MCNULTY • DENNIS R MCNULTY • LOUIS MC-
NULTY • TARA L MCNULTY • MAXINE E MCNUTT
• KEVIN P MCOWEN • MEGAN MCPEAKE • BRIAN C
MCPHERSON • DANA A MCPHERSON • DONALD T
MCPHERSON • EDWIN M MCPHERSON • HARVEY C
MCPHERSON • JANICE A MCPHERSON • JUDITH A
MCPHERSON • JUSTIN R MCPHERSON • RAE L
MCPHERSON • WALTER A MCPHERSON •
JOANNE E MCPIKE • DONALD A MCQUADE •
ROBERTA A MCQUADE • CHARRISSA L MC-
QUAIG • BIRGIT E MCQUEEN • DAVID V MC-
QUEEN • KIRK D MCQUEEN • LINDA C MCQUEEN
• PATRICK M MCQUEEN • SANDRA M MCQUEEN •
YVETTE M MCQUEEN • JAMES A MCQUILLAN •
JOYCE H MCRAE • MEREDITH A MCRAE • KRIS-
TINE L MCROBERTS • FARA MCSPADDEN • GUY
P MCSWEENEY • NANCY K MCSWEENEY • AN-
GELA MCTIER • SHANNON G MCTIGHE • MERITA
L MCTOY • CYNTHIA G MCTYRE • BETTY L MC-
VAIGH • MATTHEW W MCVETTA • ELIZABETH A
MCVEY • W ERIC MCVEY • DEBORAH L MCVIN-
NIE • JAMES R MCWHORTER JR • BLONDEAN P
MCWILLIAMS • ROY L MCWILLIAMS • VIVIAN G
MCWILLIAMS • EDDIE C MEACHAM JR • VIVIAN F
MEACHEM • MICHAEL G MEAD • CATHERINE L
MEADE • DARCY M MEADERS • DELAYNE MEAD-
ERS • KELLI L MEADERS • PATRICIA H MEADORS •
JOSEPH P MEADOWCROFT • ANITA C MEADOWS •
CAROLYN N MEADOWS • CASEY L MEADOWS •
CHARLES L MEADOWS • DAVID G MEADOWS • DE
LAINE B MEADOWS • ERIC J MEADOWS • ROGER D
MEADOWS • ROSEMARIE MEADOWS • SHIRLEY C
MEADOWS • TODD T MEADOWS • VELVET L
MEADOWS-LANE • ELIZABETH R MEAGHER •
RYAN P MEAGHER • TEDDI M MEAGHER •
THOMAS J MEAGHER • TAFAJAL H MEAH • KEN-
NETH M MEAKINS • LOUISA J MEALS-ANDERSON •
JOAN E MEALY • JOSEPH E MEANEY • SALLY J
MEANEY • JACQUELYN B MEANS • MARY FRANCIS
MEANS • MICHAEL Q MEANS • TONEY E MEANS •
ALFRED I MEANS JR • DIANE MEARS • DOROTHY A
MEARS • ELANA E MEARS • RICHARD K MEARS •
WESLEY MEARS • ROBERT E MEARSE • MICHAEL
G MEATYARD • ROBERT L MEDCALF • JOHN G
MEDEIROS • JUDITH A MEDEIROS • NILSON C
MEDEIROS • ROXANA MEDIAVILLA • ERNEST MED-
INA • JACQUELINE J MEDINA • JANET MEDINA •
JEANNE P MEDINA • JOSE A MEDINA • MARILYN
KAY MEDINA • TABO MEDINA • WAYNE P MEDING •
TROY R MEDLER • DENNIS R MEDLIN • LAURA A
MEDLIN • PAT L MEDLIN • JOANNE B MEDLOCK •
MIA MEDLOCK • MICHAEL P MEDLOCK • SHAN-
NON MEDLOCK • THOMAS W MEDLOCK •
MONIQUE D MEDLOCK-ROSS • ROBERTA L MED-
NANSKY • AMANDA MEDROW • JOANNE V MEE-
GAN • CASSANDRA MEEHAN • GENEVA M MEE-
HAN • MARTIN R MEEHAN • PATRICK J MEEHAN
• AMY R MEEKER • DANIELLA E MEEKER • GLO-
RIA J MEEKER • RALPH W MEEKER • BURRELLE
S MEEKS • CAROL B MEEKS • CATHERINE R
MEEKS • EARL L MEEKS • JEANETTE S MEEKS •
JEFFREY M MEEKS • JEREMY B MEEKS • PHILLIP
O MEEKS • WILLIAM H MEEKS • BRADLEY S
MEELER • NANCY M MEERS • JEWEL S
MEERTENS • WILLIAM L MEGATHLIN JR • JEAN S
MEGENITY • AMYN MEGHANI • IMRAN M MEGHJI
• MANOJ MEHTA • MEGHANI D MEHTA • RASHMI
MEHTA • HANS A MEIER • MARGARET MEIER •
OLIVER MEIER • SHARON K MEIER • THOMAS J
MEIER • KAREN S MEIFERT • DELUORINE A
MEIGHAN • JAMES C MEIGS • JUDY H MEIGS •
ELLY A MEIJER • DAVID C MEILANDER • KRISTA
M MEINERSMANN • TEDD G MEINERSMANN • DI-
ANE C MEISKEY ATC • PATRICIA M MEISMER •
HARVEY M MEISNER • PAUL MEISNER • STEVE M
MEISSEL • BRETT D MEISTER • LEIGH A MEIS-
TER • STEVEN J MEISTER • ROBIN K MEJIA • DI-
ANE L MELANSON • RUSSELL G MELANSON •
KEVIN A MELARKEY • LAURI A MELBOURNE •
GREG MELCHIOR • VONDA M MELCHIOR •
MICHELLE ANN MELCHOR • RUBI MELCHOR •
THOMAS A MELEGA • GLORIA I MELENDEZ • LIL-
IA MELENDEZ • BRENDA S MELHADO • ERIN C
MELICK • JAN E MELIOUS • JAMES R MELL • LOR-
RAINE K MELL • MONICA MELLADO • RALPH E
MELLANBY • ANNE G MELLEN • ABBY L
MELLINGER • JANETTE MELLO • JEFFREY J MEL-
LO • HAROLD J MELLOY • THEODORE B MELNICK
• ROBERT J MELO • GLADYS C MELSEN • CAROL G
MELSHEIMER • WILLIAM C MELSHEIMER • AN-
NETTE M MELTON • BILL MELTON • BRENDA C
MELTON • CAROLYN S MELTON • JAMES D
MELTON • M SUSAN MELTON • MICHELLE K
MELTON • NORMAN R MELTON • PETER MELTON •
ROBERT D MELTON • THERESA MELTON • WAL-
LACE W MELTON • BETSY MELVIN • CAROL S
MELVIN • LINDA S MELVIN • JOHN H MELZER •
DAVID J MEMMOLI • MELODY A MENA • MABEL C
MENADIER MT • GLENN E MENARD • JILL
MENARD • NADINA E MENARD • KIMBERLY L
MENCER • MARTIN J MENCER • ENRIQUE J MEN-
CHACA • FAYE MENDELSOHN • LILLY MENDEL-
SOHN • ANNE MENDEN • CATHY L MENDEN-
HALL • JOSEPH H MENDENHALL • WILLIAM H
MENDENHALL • HOLLIS M MENDES •
STEPHANIE M MENDES • VINCENT J MENDES JR
• ALEXANDRA MENDEZ • DANIELA M MENDOZA
• FELIPE M MENDOZA • LOURDES G MENDOZA •
MERCELENA MENDOZA • OSCAR MENDOZA •
VIRGINIA P MENDOZA • ALINA I MENDOZA-
BROOKS • GEORGE T MENDROS • MICHAEL T
MENDROS • ROBERT S MENEELY • SUSAN D
MENEFIELD • SILVIA-EDITH MENENDEZ GALLEGO
• VIRGINIA N MENES • MICHAEL J MENEZES •
ROBERTO A MENEZES • WILLIAM J MENG • NANCY
F MENKE • PATRICK A MENKE • DR DAVID MENNA •
MICHAEL V MENON • FRANK MENONI • STANLEY C
MENSINGER • MICHAEL A MENTCH • NANCY A
MENTES • ANTONIO MENTIS • KAREN A MENTON
• CHRISTINE J MENTZER • DIANE M MENZER •
VIRGINIA C MENZIES • JUAN MERCADO • MARI-
AN L MERCADO BOYLE • MARIE L MERCALDO •
KAY MERCE-VARELA • ANTHONY MERCED •
AMANDA N MERCER • BETTY J MERCER • DAVID
W MERCER • DESIRAE R MERCER • JIM T MER-
CER • SUZANNE S MERCER • FAISAL M MER-
CHANT • MELISSA A MERCHANT • BETTY B
MERCIER • DONNA C MERCK • CEASER MERCK-
SON • SILVIO C MERCURI • DEBORAH R MERCY •
DAVID MEREDITH • JAIME K MEREDITH • RHAE A
MEREDITH • THOMAS P MEREDITH • CECELIA E
MEREDITH MT • PETER M MERENA • CAROLYN S
MERIDETH • ARIS MERIJANIAN • GOHAR MERI-
JANIAN • BARBARA R MERIN • NANCY L MERIN •
ROBERT G MERIN • LOTTIE J MERIWEATHER • PAT
E MERKEL • JENNIFER D MERKLE • PATRICIA G
MERKNER • RONALD E MERKNER • MANUELA
MERLO • MARK MERMELSTEIN • JOHN A MERNA •
BARRON L MERRELL • CHARLES R MERRELL •
JUDY A MERRELL • JOHN G MERRIAM • MENILYN T
MERRICK • RICHARD E MERRIFIELD • GRANT B
MERRILL • KEITH MERRILL • KEYRUN R MERRILL
• NANCY H MERRILL • PATI C MERRILL • TODD A
MERRILL • ANTHONY MERRILLES • KAREN K
MERRILLES • DEBORAH M MERRIMAN • JOSHUA
R MERRIMAN • AMY W MERRITT • ANDRENISE C
MERRITT • BARBARA MERRITT • CLAUDE L MER-
RITT • CONNIE L MERRITT • DAVID A MERRITT •
DEBORAH A MERRITT • DIANNE W MERRITT •
GWENDOLYN MERRITT • JAMES C. MERRITT •
KARA M MERRITT • PATRICIA MERRITT • PATRICIA
B MERRITT • RAMON MERRITT • RUTH E MERRITT
• TIM MERRITT • TOMMIE B MERRITT • ROSALYN
MERRITT-STANSBERRY • MELINDA G MERRITT
SMITH • DAVID M MERRITT SR • KIMBERLY M MER-
RIWEATHER • ANNA J MERSHON • BARBARA A
MERTZ • SCOTT A MERTZLUFFT • FERNANDO J
MESA • RENEE PAIGE MESAROS • SHEILA A
MESCAL • KATHLEEN A MESHULA • JULIA L MES-
MER • DONITA M MESSENGER • JERRELL R MES-
SENGER • LARRY E MESSENGER • STEPHEN R
MESSER • GEORGE U MESSNER • LORI J MESS-
NER • RICHARD MACNEILL MESSNER • REUBEN J
MESTAS • MARY E MESTER • MARK RICHARD MET-
ALLO • BERNARD METAYER • ELIZABETH J MET-
CALF • JAN M METCALF • JEFF W METCALF •
KATHY D METCALF • MELISSA METCALF •
RICHARD W METCALF • SUSAN K METCALF • TIM
METCALF • ADRIAN P METCALFE • ANNIE M
METCALFE • LEO METELICA • ERIC R METER •
LISA M METKO • FELICIA M METOYER • KEVIN M
METROCAVAGE • DONALD J METTHE • THOMAS
J METTHE • MARGARET K METTS • DAMON S
METZ • ELLEN L METZ • RICHARD A METZ • JAN-
ICE L METZEL • AMY M METZGER • BRIDGET L
METZGER • MERCEDITA METZGER • DONALD E
METZGER 2 ATC • MIKE W METZLER • JERRY D
MEUSCHKE • CARUCHA L MEUSE • LA NOVIA N
MEUSE • THOMAS J MEW • DEBBIE K MEWBORN
• JAMES W MEWBORN • LYDIA MEWBOURN •
RUTH A MEWHIRTER • JOAN V MEYBERG • ORIN
R MEYBOHN • ALEXA MEYER • ANNETTE C MEY-
ER • BRIAN A MEYER • DONALD E MEYER • DOU-
GLAS A MEYER • ERICA Y MEYER • ERIN H MEY-
ER • EVA L MEYER • FOY MEYER • GEORGE A
MEYER • GEORGE W MEYER • JULIE MEYER •
KENNY J MEYER • LINDA J MEYER • LYNDSAY E
MEYER • M E MEYER • MARGARET E MEYER •
MARTIN MEYER • MELINDA A MEYER • MICHAEL
A MEYER • PATRICIA MEYER • PAULA M MEYER •
PEGGY J MEYER • ROBERT E MEYER • SALLY
MEYER • SUSAN B MEYER • SUSAN M MEYER • PE-
TER A MEYER III • MARGUERITE MEYER MT • ERIC
MEYERHOFF • HARRIET MEYERHOFF • AARON H
MEYERS • ALAN M MEYERS • BRUCE I MEYERS •
JANET L MEYERS • JUNE R MEYERS • KAREN J
MEYERS • LISA A MEYERS • MICHELLE K MEYERS •
NICHOLAS J MEYERS • SHERON MEYERS •
THOMAS B MEYERS • TIMOTHY MEYERS • HENRY V
MEYERS III • MARK MEYERSON • STEFANIE MEYLE
• DONNA M MEYNARD • BONNIE L MEYO • FRANCIS
J MEYO • LOIS A MEYTHALER • PAUL J MEZNARICH
• BETH A MEZULIS • CHELU K MFALILA • FAISAL I
MIAN • IHSAN R MIAN • SHAHZAD I MIAN • RICK MI-
ANULLI • FRANCIS MIAWAMA • DAVID M MICAHNIK
• MARY E MICALE • CHARLES R MICALLEF • ANN
MARIE MICHAEL • BRIAN S MICHAEL • DIANE S
MICHAEL • JAMES F MICHAEL • JULIA D MICHAEL •
KATHERINE A MICHAEL • LINSLEY A MICHAEL •
TANYA B MICHAEL • TERRY A MICHAEL • CHARLES
F MICHAELS • KATHARINE ANNE MICHAELS •
SCOTT S. MICHAELS • DEBRA M MICHALAK • JOHN
J MICHALAK • DOUGLAS W MICHALKE • CAMILLE E
MICHALLET • JOYLYNN R MICHALS • TODD N
MICHALS • DEBORAH J MICHAUD • DIANA E
MICHAUD • JOHN R MICHAUD • LARRY MICHAUD •
STEVE T MICHAUD • DIANE A MICHEL • JESSICA L
MICHEL • TERRY L MICHEL • WOLTECHE MICHEL •
JOYCE A MICHELETTI • RAYMOND W MICHELETTI •
TRACY L MICHELETTI • FRAN MICHELMAN • DARIN
N MICHELS • VINCENT C MICHELS • PAL ERIK M
MICHELSEN • ANNETTE M MICHO • BELLA ANN G
MICK • CYNTHIA T MICKELBURY • LISA J MICKEL-
SON • LESTER M MICKENS • JUDITH H MICKLE •
JULIE MICKLE • MABEL L MICKLE • MARGARET G
MIDDIONE • DONITA F MIDDLEBROOKS • HER-
BERT MIDDLEBROOKS • LUCILLE K MIDDLE-
BROOKS • VALERIE G MIDDLEBROOKS • VALERIE
G MIDDLEBROOKS • JENNIFER S MIDDLECOFT •
AMANDA M MIDDLEMAS • WILLIAM R MIDDLEMAS •
BENJAMIN L MIDDLETON • GORDON D MIDDLE-
TON • JAMES A MIDDLETON • LEANNE S MIDDLE-
TON • MARTHA K MIDDLETON • MARY MIDDLETON
• MICHEAL J MIDDLETON • RUTH L MIDDLETON •
TIM I MIDDLETON • VANN MIDDLETON • VERNON C
MIDDLETON • WILLIAM R MIDDLETON • LINDA L
MIDGETT • MARLIANNE MIDYETTE • JUDITH
MIELE • JOHN R MIGDAL • VLADAN MIHAJOVIC •
LADISLAW P MIHAL • RHONDA G MIHALIK • PA-
TRICIA J MIHALKO • PATRICK MIHM • ALICE B MI-
JANOVICH • ANN B MIJANOVICH • GLEN MIJARES

MEDALS AWARDED AND
OLYMPIC AND WORLD RECORDS ESTABLISHED
MÉDAILLES REMISES
ET RECORDS OLYMPIQUES ET DU MONDE ÉTABLIS

Medal	**Médaille**
Gold	Or
Silver	Argent
Bronze	Bronze

Aquatics—Diving / *Natation — Plongeon*

Medals Awarded / *Médailles remises* : 12

3 m Springboard, Men
Tremplin de 3 m, Messieurs

Gold:	Ni Xiong	CHN
Silver:	Zhuocheng Yu	CHN
Bronze:	Mark Lenzi	USA

3 m Springboard, Women
Tremplin de 3 m, Dames

Gold:	Mingxia Fu	CHN
Silver:	Irina Lashko	RUS
Bronze:	Annie Pelletier	CAN

10 m Platform, Men
Haut vol de 10 m, Messieurs

Gold:	Dmitri Saoutine	RUS
Silver:	Jan Hempel	GER
Bronze:	Hailiang Xiao	CHN

10 m Platform, Women
Haut vol de 10 m, Dames

Gold:	Mingxia Fu	CHN
Silver:	Annika Walter	GER
Bronze:	Mary Ellen Clark	USA

Aquatics—Swimming / *Natation — Natation*   *Athlete competed in round other than final / *Athlète n'ayant pas participé aux finales*

Medals Awarded / *Médailles remises* : 96

50 m Freestyle, Men
50 m nage libre, Messieurs

Gold:	Aleksander Popov	RUS
Silver:	Gary Hall, Jr.	USA
Bronze:	Fernando de Queiroz Scherer	BRA

50 m Freestyle, Women
50 m nage libre, Dames

Gold:	Amy Van Dyken	USA
Silver:	Jingyi Le	CHN
Bronze:	Sandra Voelker	GER

100 m Freestyle, Men
100 m nage libre, Messieurs

Gold:	Aleksander Popov	RUS
Silver:	Gary Hall, Jr.	USA
Bronze:	Gustavo França Borges	BRA

100 m Freestyle, Women
100 m nage libre, Dames

Gold:	Jingyi Le	CHN
Silver:	Sandra Voelker	GER
Bronze:	Angel Martino	USA

200 m Freestyle, Men
200 m nage libre, Messieurs

Gold:	Danyon Loader	NZL
Silver:	Gustavo França Borges	BRA
Bronze:	Daniel Kowalski	AUS

200 m Freestyle, Women
200 m nage libre, Dames

Gold:	Claudia Poll	CRC
Silver:	Franziska van Almsick	GER
Bronze:	Dagmar Hase	GER

400 m Freestyle, Men
400 m nage libre, Messieurs

Gold:	Danyon Loader	NZL
Silver:	Paul Palmer	GBR
Bronze:	Daniel Kowalski	AUS

400 m Freestyle, Women
400 m nage libre, Dames

Gold:	Michelle Smith	IRL
Silver:	Dagmar Hase	GER
Bronze:	Kirsten Vlieghuis	NED

800 m Freestyle, Women
800 m nage libre, Dames

Gold:	Brooke Bennett	USA
Silver:	Dagmar Hase	GER
Bronze:	Kirsten Vlieghuis	NED

1,500 m Freestyle, Men
1 500 m nage libre, Messieurs

Gold:	Kieren Perkins	AUS
Silver:	Daniel Kowalski	AUS
Bronze:	Graeme Smith	GBR

100 m Backstroke, Men
100 m dos, Messieurs

Gold:	Jeff Rouse	USA
Silver:	Rodolfo Falcon	CUB
Bronze:	Neisser Bent	CUB

100 m Backstroke, Women
100 m dos, Dames

Gold:	Beth Botsford	USA
Silver:	Whitney Hedgepeth	USA
Bronze:	Marianne Kriel	RSA

200 m Backstroke, Men
200 m dos, Messieurs

Gold:	Brad Bridgewater	USA
Silver:	Tripp Schwenk	USA
Bronze:	Emanuele Merisi	ITA

200 m Backstroke, Women
200 m dos, Dames

Gold:	Krisztina Egerszegi	HUN
Silver:	Whitney Hedgepeth	USA
Bronze:	Cathleen Rund	GER

100 m Breaststroke, Men
100 m brasse, Messieurs

Gold:	Fred Deburghgraeve	BEL
Silver:	Jeremy Linn	USA
Bronze:	Mark Warnecke	GER

100 m Breaststroke, Women
100 m brasse, Dames

Gold:	Penelope Heyns	RSA
Silver:	Amanda Beard	USA
Bronze:	Samantha Riley	AUS

200 m Breaststroke, Men
200 m brasse, Messieurs

Gold:	Norbert Rózsa	HUN
Silver:	Károly Güttler	HUN
Bronze:	Andrey Korneyev	RUS

200 m Breaststroke, Women
200 m brasse, Dames

Gold:	Penelope Heyns	RSA
Silver:	Amanda Beard	USA
Bronze:	Agnes Kovács	HUN

100 m Butterfly, Men
100 m papillon, Messieurs

Gold:	Denis Pankratov	RUS
Silver:	Scott Miller	AUS
Bronze:	Vladislav Kulikov	RUS

100 m Butterfly, Women
100 m papillon, Dames

Gold:	Amy Van Dyken	USA
Silver:	Limin Liu	CHN
Bronze:	Angel Martino	USA

200 m Butterfly, Men
200 m papillon, Messieurs

Gold:	Denis Pankratov	RUS
Silver:	Tom Malchow	USA
Bronze:	Scott Goodman	AUS

200 m Butterfly, Women
200 m papillon, Dames

Gold:	Susan O'Neill	AUS
Silver:	Petria Thomas	AUS
Bronze:	Michelle Smith	IRL

200 m Individual Medley, Men
200 m quatre nages, Messieurs

Gold:	Attila Czene	HUN
Silver:	Jani Sievinen	FIN
Bronze:	Curtis Myden	CAN

200 m Individual Medley, Women
200 m quatre nages, Dames

Gold:	Michelle Smith	IRL
Silver:	Marianne Limpert	CAN
Bronze:	Li Lin	CHN

400 m Individual Medley, Men
400 m quatre nages, Messieurs

Gold:	Tom Dolan	USA
Silver:	Eric Namesnik	USA
Bronze:	Curtis Myden	CAN

400 m Individual Medley, Women
400 m quatre nages, Dames

Gold:	Michelle Smith	IRL
Silver:	Allison Wagner	USA
Bronze:	Krisztina Egerszegi	HUN

4 x 100 m Freestyle Relay, Men
4 x 100 m relais nage libre, Messieurs

Gold:	Josh Davis	USA
	David Fox*	
	Gary Hall, Jr.	
	Jon Olsen	
	Bradley Schumacher	
	Scott Tucker*	
Silver:	Aleksander Popov	RUS
	Vladimir Predkin	
	Vladimir Pyshnenko	
	Roman Yegorov	

Bronze:	Mark Pinger	GER
	Christian Troeger	
	Bengt Zikarsky	
	Bjoern Zikarsky	

4 x 100 m Freestyle Relay, Women
4 x 100 m relais nage libre, Dames

Gold:	Catherine Fox	USA
	Lisa Jacob*	
	Angel Martino	
	Jenny Thompson	
	Melanie Valerio*	
	Amy Van Dyken	
Silver:	Na Chao	CHN
	Jingyi Le	
	Yun Nian	
	Ying Shan	
Bronze:	Antje Buschschulte	GER
	Simone Osygus	
	Franziska van Almsick	
	Sandra Voelker	

4 x 200 m Freestyle Relay, Men
4 x 200 m relais nage libre, Messieurs

Gold:	Ryan Berube	USA
	Josh Davis	
	Joe Hudepohl	
	Jon Olsen*	
	Bradley Schumacher	
Silver:	Lars Frolander	SWE
	Anders Holmertz	
	Anders Lyrbring	
	Christer Wallin	
Bronze:	Aimo Heilmann	GER
	Christian Keller	
	Christian Troeger	
	Steffen Zesner	

4 x 200 m Freestyle Relay, Women
4 x 200 m relais nage libre, Dames

Gold:	Trina Jackson	USA
	Lisa Jacob*	
	Annette Salmeen*	
	Sheila Taormina	
	Cristina Teuscher	
	Jenny Thompson	
	Ashley Whitney*	
Silver:	Franziska van Almsick	GER
	Meike Freitag*	
	Dagmar Hase	
	Kerstin Kielgass	
	Simone Osygus*	
	Anke Scholz	
Bronze:	Julia Greville	AUS
	Emma Johnson	
	Lise Mackie*	
	Susan O'Neill	
	Nicole Stevenson	

4 x 100 m Medley Relay, Men
4 x 100 m relais quatre nages, Messieurs

Gold:	Josh Davis*	USA
	Kurt Grote*	
	Gary Hall, Jr.	
	John Hargis*	
	Mark Henderson	
	Jeremy Linn	
	Jeff Rouse	
	Tripp Schwenk*	
Silver:	Roman Ivanovskiy*	RUS
	Vladislav Kulikov*	
	Stanislav Lopukhov	
	Denis Pankratov	
	Aleksander Popov	
	Vladimir Selkov	
	Roman Yegorov*	

Bronze:	Steven Dewick	AUS
	Toby Haenen*	
	Michael Klim	
	Scott Miller	
	Philip Rogers	

4 x 100 m Medley Relay, Women
4 x 100 m relais quatre nages, Dames

Gold:	Amanda Beard	USA
	Beth Botsford	
	Catherine Fox*	
	Whitney Hedgepeth*	
	Angel Martino	
	Kristine Quance*	
	Jenny Thompson*	
	Amy Van Dyken	
Silver:	Helen Denman*	AUS
	Angela Kennedy*	
	Susan O'Neill	
	Samantha Riley	
	Sarah Ryan	
	Nicole Stevenson	
Bronze:	Huijue Cai	CHN
	Yan Chen	
	Xue Han	
	Ying Shan	

Olympic Records / *Records olympiques* : 14

100 m Freestyle, Women
100 m nage libre, Dames

54.50	Jingyi Le	CHN

100 m Breaststroke, Men
100 m brasse, Messieurs

1:00.60	Fred Deburghgraeve	BEL

100 m Breaststroke, Women
100 m brasse, Dames

1:07.02	Penelope Heyns	RSA

200 m Breaststroke, Women
200 m brasse, Dames

2:26.63	Penelope Heyns	RSA
2:25.41	Penelope Heyns	RSA

100 m Butterfly, Men
100 m papillon, Messieurs

52.89	Scott Miller	USA
52.27	Denis Pankratov	RUS

200 m Individual Medley, Men
200 m quatre nages, Messieurs

1:59.91	Attila Czene	HUN

4 x 100 m Freestyle Relay, Men
4 x 100 m relais nage libre, Messieurs

3:15.41	Jon Olsen	USA
	Josh Davis	
	Bradley Shumacher	
	Gary Hall, Jr.	

4 x 100 m Freestyle Relay, Women
4 x 100 m relais nage libre, Dames

3:39.29	Angel Martino	USA
	Amy Van Dyken	
	Catherine Fox	
	Jenny Thompson	

4 x 200 m Freestyle Relay, Women
4 x 200 m relais nage libre, Dames

8:09.46	Eri Yamanoi	JPN
	Naoko Imoto	
	Aiko Miyake	
	Suzu Chiba	
8:04.99	Lisa Jacob	USA
	Ashley Whitney	
	Sheila Taormina	
	Annette Salmeen	

Continued on next page
Continué à la page suivante

Aquatics—Swimming / *Natation — Natation* continued from previous page / *suite de la page précédente*

7:59.87	Trina Jackson	USA
	Cristina Teuscher	
	Sheila Taormina	
	Jenny Thompson	

4 x 100 m Medley Relay, Men
4 x 100 m relais quatre nages, Messieurs

3:34.84	Jeff Rouse	USA
	Jeremy Linn	
	Mark Henderson	
	Gary Hall, Jr.	

World Records / *Records du monde* : 4

100 m Breaststroke, Men
100 m brasse, Messieurs

| 1:00.60 | Fred Deburghgraeve | BEL |

100 m Breaststroke, Women
100 m brasse, Dames

| 1:07.02 | Penelope Heyns | RSA |

100 m Butterfly, Men
100 m papillon, Messieurs

| 52.27 | Denis Pankratov | RUS |

4 x 100 m Medley Relay, Men
4 x 100 m relais quatre nages, Messieurs

3:34.84	Jeff Rouse	USA
	Jeremy Linn	
	Mark Henderson	
	Gary Hall, Jr.	

Aquatics—Synchronized Swimming / *Natation — Natation synchronisée*

Medals Awarded / *Médailles remises* : 3

Women
Dames

Gold:	Suzannah Bianco	USA
	Tammy Cleland	
	Becky Dyroen-Lancer	
	Emily Porter LeSueur	

Silver:	Heather Pease	CAN
	Jill Savery	
	Nathalie Schneyder	
	Heather Simmons-Carrasco	
	Jill Sudduth	
	Margot Thien	
	Lisa Alexander	
	Janice Bremner	

(Silver team, CAN):
Karen Clark
Karen Fonteyne
Sylvie Frechette
Valerie Hould-Marchand
Kasia Kulesza
Christine Larsen
Cari Read
Erin Woodley

Bronze:	Raika Fujii	JPN
	Mayuko Fujiki	
	Rei Jimbo	
	Miho Kawabe	
	Akiko Kawase	
	Riho Nakajima	
	Miya Tachibana	
	Kaori Takahashi	
	Miho Takeda	
	Junko Tanaka	

Aquatics—Water Polo / *Natation — Water-polo*

Medals Awarded / *Médailles remises* : 3

Men
Messieurs

Gold:	Jose Maria Abarca	ESP
	Angel Andreo	
	Daniel Ballart	
	Manuel Estiarte	
	Pedro Garcia	
	Salvador Gomez	
	Ivan Moro	

Silver:	Miguel Oca	CRO
	Jorge Paya	
	Sergi Pedrerol	
	Jesus Rollan	
	Jordi Sans	
	Carlos Sanz	
	Maro Balic	
	Perica Bukic	
	Damir Glavan	
	Igor Hinic	
	Vjekoslav Kobescak	

(Silver team continued):
Josko Krekovic
Ognjen Krzic
Dubravko Simenc
Sinisa Skolnekovic
Ratko Stritof
Tino Vegar
Renato Vrbicic
Zdeslav Vrdoljak

Bronze:	Alberto Angelini	ITA
	Francesco Attolico	
	Fabio Bencivenga	

(Bronze team, ITA):
Alessandro Bovo
Alessandro Calcaterra
Roberto Calcaterra
Marco Gerini
Alberto Ghibellini
Luca Giustolisi
Amedeo Pomilio
Francesco Postiglione
Carlo Silipo
Leonardo Sottani

Archery / *Tir à l'arc*

Medals Awarded / *Médailles remises* : 12

Individual, Men
Epreuve individuelle, Messieurs

Gold:	Justin Huish	USA
Silver:	Magnus Petersson	SWE
Bronze:	Kyo-Moon Oh	KOR

Individual, Women
Epreuve individuelle, Dames

Gold:	Kyung-Wook Kim	KOR
Silver:	Ying He	CHN
Bronze:	Olena Sadovnycha	UKR

Team, Men
Epreuve par équipes, Messieurs

Gold:	Justin Huish	USA
	Richard Johnson	
	Rod White	
Silver:	Yong-Ho Jang	KOR
	Bo-Ram Kim	
	Kyo-Moon Oh	
Bronze:	Matteo Bisiani	ITA
	Michele Frangilli	
	Andrea Parenti	

Team, Women
Epreuve par équipes, Dames

Gold:	Jo-Sun Kim	KOR
	Kyung-Wook Kim	
	Hye-Young Yoon	
Silver:	Barbara Mensing	GER
	Cornelia Pfohl	
	Sandra Wagner	
Bronze:	Iwona Dzieciol	POL
	Katarzyna Klata	
	Joanna Nowicka	

Olympic Records / *Records olympiques* : 15

Individual, Men
Epreuve individuelle, Messieurs
72 Arrow Ranking Round
Tour de classement de 72 flèches

| 684 | Michele Frangilli | ITA |

18 Arrow Match
Match de 18 flèches

| 170 | Michele Frangilli | ITA |

12 Arrow Match
Match de 12 flèches

| 115 | Kyo-Moon Oh | KOR |

1/16th, 1/8th Combined
1/16, 1/8 combinés

| 336 | Kyo-Moon Oh | KOR |

36 Arrow Finals Combined
Finale combinée de 36 flèches

| 338 | Kyo-Moon Oh | KOR |

Individual, Women
Epreuve individuelle, Dames
72 Arrow Ranking Round
Tour de classement de 72 flèches

| 673 | Lina Herasymenko | UKR |

18 Arrow Match
Match de 18 flèches

| 168 | Natalia Nasaridze | TUR |

1/16th, 1/8th Combined
1/16, 1/8 combinés

| 331 | Hye-Young Yoon | KOR |

36 Arrow Finals
Finale de 36 flèches

| 330 | Kyung-Wook Kim | KOR |

Team, Men
Epreuve par équipes, Messieurs
216 Arrow Ranking Round
Tour de classement de 216 flèches

2031	Yong-Ho Jang	KOR
	Bo-Ram Kim	
	Kyo-Moon Oh	

27 Arrow Match
Match de 27 flèches

253	Simon Fairweather	AUS
	Jackson Fear	
	Matthew Gray	

54 Arrow Finals Combined
Finale combinée de 54 flèches

502	Justin Huish	USA
	Richard Johnson	
	Rod White	

Team, Women
Epreuve par équipes, Dames
216 Arrow Ranking Round
Tour de classement de 216 flèches

1984	Jo-Sun Kim	KOR
	Kyung-Wook Kim	
	Hye-Young Yoon	

27 Arrow Match
Match de 27 flèches

249	Jo-Sun Kim	KOR
	Kyung-Wook Kim	
	Hye-Young Yoon	

54 Arrow Finals Combined
Finale combinée de 54 flèches

490	Jo-Sun Kim	KOR
	Kyung-Wook Kim	
	Hye-Young Youn	

World Records / *Records du monde* : 4

Individual, Men
Epreuve individuelle, Messieurs
36 Arrow Finals Combined
Finale combinée de 36 flèches

| 338 | Kyo-Moon Oh | KOR |

Team, Men
Epreuve par équipes, Messieurs
216 Arrow Ranking Round
Tour de classement de 216 flèches

2031	Yong-Ho Jang	KOR
	Bo-Ram Kim	
	Kyo-Moon Oh	

Team, Women
Epreuve par équipes, Dames
216 Arrow Ranking Round
Tour de classement de 216 flèches

1984	Jo-Sun Kim	KOR
	Kyung-Wook Kim	
	Hye-Young Yoon	

54 Arrow Finals Combined
Finale combinée de 54 flèches

490	Jo-Sun Kim	KOR
	Kyung-Wook Kim	
	Hye-Young Yoon	

Medals Awarded / *Médailles remises* : 138

100 m, Men
100 m, Messieurs

Gold:	Donovan Bailey	CAN
Silver:	Frank Fredericks	NAM
Bronze:	Ato Boldon	TRI

100 m, Women
100 m, Dames

Gold:	Gail Devers	USA
Silver:	Merlene Ottey	JAM
Bronze:	Gwen Torrence	USA

200 m, Men
200 m, Messieurs

Gold:	Michael Johnson	USA
Silver:	Frank Fredericks	NAM
Bronze:	Ato Boldon	TRI

200 m, Women
200 m, Dames

Gold:	Marie-Jose Perec	FRA
Silver:	Merlene Ottey	JAM
Bronze:	Mary Onyali	NGR

400 m, Men
400 m, Messieurs

Gold:	Michael Johnson	USA
Silver:	Roger Black	GBR
Bronze:	Davis Kamoga	UGA

400 m, Women
400 m, Dames

Gold:	Marie-Jose Perec	FRA
Silver:	Catherine Freeman	AUS
Bronze:	Falilat Ogunkoya	NGR

800 m, Men
800 m, Messieurs

Gold:	Vebjørn Rodal	NOR
Silver:	Hezekiel Sepeng	RSA
Bronze:	Fred Onyancha	KEN

800 m, Women
800 m, Dames

Gold:	Svetlana Masterkova	RUS
Silver:	Ana Fidelia Quirot	CUB
Bronze:	Maria Lurdes Mutola	MOZ

1,500 m, Men
1 500 m, Messieurs

Gold:	Noureddine Morceli	ALG
Silver:	Fermin Cacho	ESP
Bronze:	Stephen Kipkorir	KEN

1,500 m, Women
1 500 m, Dames

Gold:	Svetlana Masterkova	RUS
Silver:	Gabriela Szabo	ROM
Bronze:	Theresia Kiesl	AUT

5,000 m, Men
5 000 m, Messieurs

Gold:	Venuste Niyongabo	BDI
Silver:	Paul Bitok	KEN
Bronze:	Khalid Boulami	MAR

5,000 m, Women
5 000 m, Dames

Gold:	Junxia Wang	CHN
Silver:	Pauline Konga	KEN
Bronze:	Roberta Brunet	ITA

10,000 m, Men
10 000 m, Messieurs

Gold:	Haile Gebreselassie	ETH
Silver:	Paul Tergat	KEN
Bronze:	Salah Hissou	MAR

10,000 m, Women
10 000 m, Dames

Gold:	Fernanda Ribeiro	POR
Silver:	Junxia Wang	CHN
Bronze:	Gete Wami	ETH

110 m Hurdles, Men
110 m haies, Messieurs

Gold:	Allen Johnson	USA
Silver:	Mark Crear	USA
Bronze:	Florian Schwarthoff	GER

100 m Hurdles, Women
100 m haies, Dames

Gold:	Ludmila Engquist	SWE
Silver:	Brigita Bukovec	SLO
Bronze:	Patricia Girard-Leno	FRA

400 m Hurdles, Men
400 m haies, Messieurs

Gold:	Derrick Adkins	USA
Silver:	Samuel Matete	ZAM
Bronze:	Calvin Davis	USA

400 m Hurdles, Women
400 m haies, Dames

Gold:	Deon Hemmings	JAM
Silver:	Kim Batten	USA
Bronze:	Tonja Buford-Bailey	USA

3,000 m Steeplechase, Men
3 000 m steeple, Messieurs

Gold:	Joseph Keter	KEN
Silver:	Moses Kiptanui	KEN
Bronze:	Alessandro Lambruschini	ITA

4 x 100 m Relay, Men
Relais 4 x 100 m, Messieurs

Gold:	Donovan Bailey	CAN
	Carlton Chambers*	
	Robert Esmie	
	Glenroy Gilbert	
	Bruny Surin	
Silver:	Jon Drummond	USA
	Tim Harden	
	Michael Marsh	
	Dennis Mitchell	
	Tim Montgomery*	
Bronze:	Edson Luciano Ribeiro	BRA
	André Domingos da Silva	
	Arnaldo de Oliveira da Silva	
	Robson Caetano da Silva	

4 x 100 m Relay, Women
Relais 4 x 100 m, Dames

Gold:	Gail Devers	USA
	Chryste Gaines	
	Carlette Guidry*	
	Inger Miller	
	Gwen Torrence	
Silver:	Eldece Clarke	BAH
	Pauline Davis	
	Debbie Ferguson*	
	Sevetheda Fynes	
	Chandra Sturrup	
Bronze:	Juliet Cuthbert	JAM
	Michelle Freeman	
	Andria Lloyd*	
	Nikole Mitchell	
	Merlene Ottey	
	Gillian Russell*	

4 x 400 m Relay, Men
Relais 4 x 400 m, Messieurs

Gold:	Alvin Harrison	USA
	Anthuan Maybank	
	Derek Mills	
	Jason Rouser*	
	LaMont Smith	
Silver:	Jamie Baulch	GBR
	Roger Black	
	Mark Hylton*	
	Du'aine Ladejo*	
	Mark Richardson	
	Iwan Thomas	
Bronze:	Dennis Blake*	JAM
	Davian Clarke	
	Gregory Haughton	
	Roxbert Martin	
	Michael McDonald	
	Garth Robinson*	

4 x 400 m Relay, Women
Relais 4 x 400 m, Dames

Gold:	Kim Graham	USA
	Maicel Malone	
	Jearl Miles	
	Rochelle Stevens	
	Linetta Wilson*	
Silver:	Bisi Afolabi	NGR
	Falilat Ogunkoya	
	Charity Opara	
	Fatima Yusuf	
Bronze:	Grit Breuer	GER
	Linda Kisabaka	
	Uta Rohlaender	
	Anja Rucker	

High Jump, Men
Saut en hauteur, Messieurs

Gold:	Charles Austin	USA
Silver:	Artur Partyka	POL
Bronze:	Steve Smith	GBR

High Jump, Women
Saut en hauteur, Dames

Gold:	Stefka Kostadinova	BUL
Silver:	Niki Bakogianni	GRE
Bronze:	Inha Babakova	UKR

Pole Vault, Men
Saut à la perche, Messieurs

Gold:	Jean Galfione	FRA
Silver:	Igor Trandenkov	RUS
Bronze:	Andrei Tivontchik	GER

Long Jump, Men
Saut en longueur, Messieurs

Gold:	Carl Lewis	USA
Silver:	James Beckford	JAM
Bronze:	Joe Greene	USA

Long Jump, Women
Saut en longueur, Dames

Gold:	Chioma Ajunwa	NGR
Silver:	Fiona May	ITA
Bronze:	Jackie Joyner-Kersee	USA

Triple Jump, Men
Triple saut, Messieurs

Gold:	Kenny Harrison	USA
Silver:	Jonathan Edwards	GBR
Bronze:	Yoelbi Quesada	CUB

Triple Jump, Women
Triple saut, Dames

Gold:	Inessa Kravets	UKR
Silver:	Inna Lasovskaya	RUS
Bronze:	Sarka Kasparkova	CZE

Hammer Throw, Men
Marteau, Messieurs

Gold:	Balázs Kiss	HUN
Silver:	Lance Deal	USA
Bronze:	Oleksiy Krykun	UKR

Shot Put, Men
Poids, Messieurs

Gold:	Randy Barnes	USA
Silver:	John Godina	USA
Bronze:	Oleksandr Bagach	UKR

Shot Put, Women
Poids, Dames

Gold:	Astrid Kumbernuss	GER
Silver:	Xinmei Sui	CHN
Bronze:	Irina Khudorozhkina	RUS

Discus Throw, Men
Disque, Messieurs

Gold:	Lars Riedel	GER
Silver:	Vladimir Dubrovshchik	BLR
Bronze:	Vasiliy Kaptyukh	BLR

Discus Throw, Women
Disque, Dames

Gold:	Ilke Wyludda	GER
Silver:	Natalya Sadova	RUS
Bronze:	Elyna Zvereva	BLR

Javelin Throw, Men
Javelot, Messieurs

Gold:	Jan Zelezny	CZE
Silver:	Steve Backley	GBR
Bronze:	Seppo Raty	FIN

Javelin Throw, Women
Javelot, Dames

Gold:	Heli Rantanen	FIN
Silver:	Louise McPaul	AUS
Bronze:	Elsa Katrine Hattestad	NOR

Decathlon, Men
Décathlon, Messieurs

Gold:	Dan O'Brien	USA
Silver:	Frank Busemann	GER
Bronze:	Tomas Dvorak	CZE

Heptathlon, Women
Heptathlon, Dames

Gold:	Ghada Shouaa	SYR
Silver:	Natalya Sazanovich	BLR
Bronze:	Denise Lewis	GBR

10 km Race Walk, Women
10 km marche, Dames

Gold:	Yelena Nikolayeva	RUS
Silver:	Elisabetta Perrone	ITA
Bronze:	Yan Wang	CHN

20 km Race Walk, Men
20 km marche, Messieurs

Gold:	Jefferson Pérez	ECU
Silver:	Ilya Markov	RUS
Bronze:	Bernardo Segura	MEX

50 km Race Walk, Men
50 km marche, Messieurs

Gold:	Robert Korzeniowski	POL
Silver:	Mikhail Shchennikov	RUS
Bronze:	Valentin Massana	ESP

Marathon, Men
Marathon, Messieurs

Gold:	Josia Thugwane	RSA
Silver:	Bong-Ju Lee	KOR
Bronze:	Eric Wainaina	KEN

Marathon, Women
Marathon, Dames

Gold:	Fatuma Roba	ETH
Silver:	Valentina Yegorova	RUS
Bronze:	Yuko Arimori	JPN

1,500 m Wheelchair, Men
1 500 m fauteuil roulant, Messieurs

Gold:	Claude Issorat	FRA
Silver:	Scot Hollonbeck	USA
Bronze:	Franz Nietlispach	SUI

800 m Wheelchair, Women
800 m fauteuil roulant, Dames

Gold:	Louise Sauvage	AUS
Silver:	Jean Driscoll	USA
Bronze:	Cheri Becerra	USA

Olympic Records / *Records olympiques* : 17

100 m, Men
100 m, Messieurs

9.84	Donovan Bailey	CAN

200 m, Men
200 m, Messieurs

19.32	Michael Johnson	USA

400 m, Men
400 m, Messieurs

43.49	Michael Johnson	USA

400 m, Women
400 m, Dames

48.25	Marie-Jose Perec	FRA

800 m, Men
800 m, Messieurs

1:42.58	Vebjørn Rodal	NOR

5,000 m, Women
5 000 m, Dames

14:59.88	Junxia Wang	CHN

10,000 m, Men
10 000 m, Messieurs

27:07.34	Haile Gebreselassie	ETH

10,000 m, Women
10 000 m, Dames

31:01.63	Fernanda Ribeiro	POR

110 m Hurdles, Men
110 m haies, Messieurs

12.95	Allen Johnson	USA

400 m Hurdles, Women
400 m haies, Dames

52.82	Deon Hemmings	JAM

High Jump, Men
Saut en hauteur, Messieurs

2.39 m	Charles Austin	USA

High Jump, Women
Saut en hauteur, Dames

2.05 m	Stefka Kostadinova	BUL

Pole Vault, Men
Saut à la perche, Messieurs

5.92 m	Jean Galfione	
	Andrei Tivontchik	
	Igor Trandenkov	RUS

Triple Jump, Men
Triple saut, Messieurs

18.09 m	Kenny Harrison	USA

Continued on next page
Continué à la page suivante

Athletics / *Athlétisme* continued from previous page / suite de la page précédente

Triple Jump, Women *Triple saut, Dames*			Discus Throw, Men *Disque, Messieurs*			World Records / *Records du monde : 2*			200 m, Men *200 m, Messieurs*		
15.33 m	Inessa Kravets	UKR	69.40 m	Lars Riedel	GER	**100 m, Men** *100 m, Messieurs*			19.32	Michael Johnson	USA
			10 km Race Walk, Women *10 km marche, Dames*			9.84	Donovan Bailey	CAN			
			41:49	Yelena Nikolayeva	RUS						

Badminton / *Badminton*

Medals Awarded / *Médailles remises : 15*

Singles, Men
Simples, Messieurs
Gold: Poul-Erik Hoyer Larsen — DEN
Silver: Jiong Dong — CHN
Bronze: Rashid Sidek — MAS

Singles, Women
Simples, Dames
Gold: Soo Hyun Bang — KOR
Silver: Mia Audina — INA
Bronze: Susi Susanti — INA

Doubles, Men
Doubles, Messieurs
Gold: Rexy Mainaky / Ricky Subagja — INA
Silver: Soon Kit Cheah / Kim Hock Yap — MAS
Bronze: Antonius Ariantho / Denny Kantano — INA

Doubles, Women
Doubles, Dames
Gold: Fei Ge / Jun Gu — CHN
Silver: Young Ah Gil / Hye Ock Jang — KOR
Bronze: Yiyuan Qin / Yongshu Tang — CHN

Doubles, Mixed
Doubles, Mixtes
Gold: Young Ah Gil / Dong Moon Kim — KOR
Silver: Joo-Bong Park / Kyung Min Ra — KOR
Bronze: Jianjun Liu / Man Sun — CHN

Baseball / *Baseball*

Medals Awarded / *Médailles remises : 3*

Men
Messieurs
Gold: Omar Ajete — CUB
Miguel Caldes
Jose Ariel Contreras
Jose Estrada
Jorge Fumero
Alberto Hernandez
Rey Isaac
Orestes Kindelan
Pedro Luis Lazo
Omar Linares
Omar Luis
Juan Manrique
Eliecer Montes de Oca
Antonio Pacheco
Juan Padilla
Eduardo Paret
Osmany Romero
Antonio Scull
Luis Ulacia
Lazaro Vargas

Silver: Kosuke Fukudome — JPN
Tadahito Iguchi
Makoto Imaoka
Takeo Kawamura
Jutaro Kimura
Takashi Kurosu
Takao Kuwamoto
Nobuhiko Matsunaka
Koichi Misawa
Masahiko Mori
Masao Morinaka
Daishin Nakamura
Masahiro Nojima
Hideaki Okubo
Hitoshi Ono
Yasuyuki Saigo
Tomoaki Sato
Masanori Sugiura
Takayuki Takabayashi
Yoshitomo Tani

Bronze: Chad Allen — USA
Kris Benson
R. A. Dickey
Troy Glaus
Chad Green
Seth Greisinger
Kip Harkrider
A. J. Hinch
Jacque Jones
Billy Koch
Mark Kotsay
Matt LeCroy
Travis Lee
Braden Looper
Brian Loyd
Warren Morris
Augie Ojeda
Jim Parque
Jeff Weaver
Jason Williams

Basketball / *Basketball*

Medals Awarded / *Médailles remises : 6*

Men
Messieurs
Gold: Charles Barkley — USA
Anfernee Hardaway
Grant Hill
Karl Malone
Reggie Miller
Shaquille O'Neal
Hakeem Olajuwon
Gary Payton
Scottie Pippen
Mitch Richmond
David Robinson
John Stockton

Silver: Miroslav Beric — YUG
Dejan Bodiroga
Predrag Danilovic
Vlade Divac
Aleksandar Djordjevic
Nikola Loncar
Sasa Obradovic
Zarko Paspalj
Zeljko Rebraca
Zoran Savic
Dejan Tomasevic
Milenko Topic

Bronze: Gintaras Einikis — LTU
Arturas Karnisovas
Rimas Kurtinaitis
Darius Lukminas
Sarunas Marciulionis
Tomas Pacesas
Arvydas Sabonis
Saulius Stombergas
Rytis Vaisvila
Eurelijus Zukauskas
Mindaugas Zukauskas

Women
Dames
Gold: Jennifer Azzi — USA
Ruthie Bolton
Teresa Edwards
Venus Lacey
Lisa Leslie
Rebecca Lobo
Katrina McClain
Nikki McCray
Carla McGhee
Dawn Staley
Katy Steding
Sheryl Swoopes

Silver: Janeth dos Santos Arcain — BRA
Roseli do Carmo Gustavo
Silvia Andrea Santos Luz
Hortência de Fátima Marcari Oliva
Alessandra Santos de Oliveira
Claudia Maria Pastor
Ariana Aparecida dos Santos
Cintia Silva dos Santos
Maria Angélica Gonçalves da Silva
Maria Paula Gonçalves da Silva
Leila de Souza Sobral
Marta de Souza Sobral

Bronze: Carla Boyd — AUS
Michelle Brogan
Sandy Brondello
Michelle Chandler
Allison Cook
Trisha Fallon
Robyn Maher
Fiona Robinson
Shelley Sandie
Rachael Sporn
Michele Timms
Jennifer Whittle

Boxing / *Boxe*

Light Flyweight, 48 kg (106 lb), Men
Mi-mouche, 48 kg, Messieurs

Gold:	Daniel Petrov Bojilov	BUL
Silver:	Mansueto Velasco	PHI
Bronze:	Oleg Kiryukhin	UKR
	Rafael Lozano	ESP

Flyweight, 51 kg (112 lb), Men
Mouche, 51 kg, Messieurs

Gold:	Maikro Romero	CUB
Silver:	Boulat Djoumadilov	KAZ
Bronze:	Zoltan Lunka	GER
	Albert Pakeev	RUS

Bantamweight, 54 kg (119 lb), Men
Coq, 54 kg, Messieurs

Gold:	István Kovács	HUN
Silver:	Arnaldo Mesa	CUB
Bronze:	Vichairachanon Khadpo	THA
	Raimkul Malakhbekov	RUS

Featherweight, 57 kg (125 lb), Men
Plume, 57 kg, Messieurs

Gold:	Somrot Kamsing	THA
Silver:	Serafim Todorov	BUL
Bronze:	Pablo Julio Chacón	ARG
	Floyd Mayweather	USA

Lightweight, 60 kg (132 lb), Men
Léger, 60 kg, Messieurs

Gold:	Hocine Soltani	ALG
Silver:	Tontcho Tontchev	BUL
Bronze:	Terrance Cauthen	USA
	Leonard Doroftei	ROM

Light Welterweight, 63.5 kg (139 lb), Men
Mi-welter, 63,5 kg, Messieurs

Gold:	Hector Vinent	CUB
Silver:	Oktay Urkal	GER
Bronze:	Fathi Missaoui	TUN
	Bolat Niazymbetov	KAZ

Welterweight, 67 kg (147 lb), Men
Welter, 67 kg, Messieurs

Gold:	Oleg Saitov	RUS
Silver:	Juan Hernandez	CUB
Bronze:	Daniel Santos	PUR
	Marian Simion	ROM

Light Middleweight, 71 kg (156 lb), Men
Mi-moyen, 71 kg, Messieurs

Gold:	David Reid	USA
Silver:	Alfredo Duvergel	CUB
Bronze:	Ermakhan Ibraimov	KAZ
	Karim Tulaganov	UZB

Middleweight, 75 kg (165 lb), Men
Moyen, 75 kg, Messieurs

Gold:	Ariel Hernandez	CUB
Silver:	Malik Beyleroglu	TUR
Bronze:	Mohamed Bahari	ALG
	Rhoshii Wells	USA

Light Heavyweight, 81 kg (178 lb), Men
Mi-lourd, 81 kg, Messieurs

Gold:	Vasilli Jirov	KAZ
Silver:	Seung-Bae Lee	KOR
Bronze:	Antonio Tarver	USA
	Thomas Ulrich	GER

Heavyweight, 91 kg (201 lb), Men
Lourd, 91 kg, Messieurs

Gold:	Felix Savon	CUB
Silver:	David Defiagbon	CAN
Bronze:	Nate Jones	USA
	Luan Krasniqi	GER

Super Heavyweight, +91 kg (+201 lb), Men
Super-lourd, +91 kg, Messieurs

Gold:	Volodymyr Klychko	UKR
Silver:	Paea Wolfgram	TGA
Bronze:	Duncan Dokiwari	NGR
	Alexei Lezin	RUS

Canoe/Kayak—Slalom / *Canoë/Kayak — Slalom*

Kayak Single, Men
Kayak simple, Messieurs

Gold:	Oliver Fix	GER
Silver:	Andraz Vehovar	SLO
Bronze:	Thomas Becker	GER

Kayak Single, Women
Kayak simple, Dames

Gold:	Stepanka Hilgertova	CZE
Silver:	Dana Chladek	USA
Bronze:	Myriam Fox-Jerusalmi	FRA

Canoe Single, Men
Canoë simple, Messieurs

Gold:	Michal Martikan	SVK
Silver:	Lukas Pollert	CZE
Bronze:	Patrice Estanguet	FRA

Canoe Double, Men
Canoë double, Messieurs

Gold:	Frank Adisson	FRA
	Wilfrid Forgues	
Silver:	Jiri Rohan	CZE
	Miroslav Simek	
Bronze:	Andre Ehrenberg	GER
	Michael Senft	

Canoe/Kayak—Sprint / *Canoë/Kayak — Sprint*

500 m Kayak Single, Men
500 m kayak simple, Messieurs

Gold:	Antonio Rossi	ITA
Silver:	Knut Holmann	NOR
Bronze:	Piotr Markiewicz	POL

500 m Kayak Single, Women
500 m kayak simple, Dames

Gold:	Rita Kóbán	HUN
Silver:	Caroline Brunet	CAN
Bronze:	Josefa Idem	ITA

500 m Kayak Double, Men
500 m kayak double, Messieurs

Gold:	Kay Bluhm	GER
	Torsten Gutsche	
Silver:	Beniamino Bonomi	ITA
	Daniele Scarpa	
Bronze:	Daniel Collins	AUS
	Andrew Trim	

500 m Kayak Double, Women
500 m kayak double, Dames

Gold:	Agneta Andersson	SWE
	Susanne Gunnarsson	
Silver:	Birgit Fischer	GER
	Ramona Portwich	
Bronze:	Katrin Borchert	AUS
	Anna Wood	

500 m Kayak Fours, Women
500 m kayak à quatre, Dames

Gold:	Birgit Fischer	GER
	Manuela Mucke	
	Ramona Portwich	
	Anett Schuck	
Silver:	Daniela Baumer	SUI
	Sabine Eichenberger	
	Ingrid Haralamow	
	Garbiela Müller	
Bronze:	Agneta Andersson	SWE
	Ingela Ericsson	
	Anna Olsson	
	Susanne Rosenqvist	

1,000 m Kayak Single, Men
1 000 m kayak simple, Messieurs

Gold:	Knut Holmann	NOR
Silver:	Beniamino Bonomi	ITA
Bronze:	Clint Robinson	AUS

1,000 m Kayak Double, Men
1 000 m kayak double, Messieurs

Gold:	Antonio Rossi	ITA
	Daniele Scarpa	
Silver:	Kay Bluhm	GER
	Torsten Gutsche	
Bronze:	Andrian Dushev	BUL
	Milko Kazanov	

1,000 m Kayak Fours, Men
1 000 m kayak à quatre, Messieurs

Gold:	Detlef Hofman	GER
	Thomas Reineck	
	Olaf Winter	
	Mark Zabel	
Silver:	Attila Adrovicz	HUN
	Ferenc Csipes	
	Gábor Horváth	
	András Rajna	
Bronze:	Oleg Gorobiy	RUS
	Anatoliy Tishchenko	
	Georgiy Tsybulnikov	
	Sergey Verlin	

500 m Canoe Single, Men
500 m canoë simple, Messieurs

Gold:	Martin Doktor	CZE
Silver:	Slavomir Knazovicky	SVK
Bronze:	Imre Pulai	HUN

500 m Canoe Double, Men
500 m canoë double, Messieurs

Gold:	Csaba Horváth	HUN
	György Kolonics	
Silver:	Nikolai Juravschi	MDA
	Victor Reneischi	
Bronze:	Gheorghe Andriev	ROM
	Grigore Obreja	

1,000 m Canoe Single, Men
1 000 m canoë simple, Messieurs

Gold:	Martin Doktor	CZE
Silver:	Ivan Klementjevs	LAT
Bronze:	György Zala	HUN

1,000 m Canoe Double, Men
1 000 m canoë double, Messieurs

Gold:	Andreas Dittmer	GER
	Gunar Kirchbach	
Silver:	Antonel Borsan	ROM
	Marcel Glavan	
Bronze:	Csaba Horváth	HUN
	György Kolonics	

Cycling / *Cyclisme*

Medals Awarded / *Médailles remises* : 42

Mountain Bike / *VTT*
Cross Country, Men
Cross-country, Messieurs
Gold:	Bart Brentjens	NED
Silver:	Thomas Frischknecht	SUI
Bronze:	Miguel Martinez	FRA

Cross Country, Women
Cross-country, Dames
Gold:	Paola Pezzo	ITA
Silver:	Alison Sydor	CAN
Bronze:	Susan DeMattei	USA

Road / *Route*
Road Race, Men
Course sur route, Messieurs
Gold:	Pascal Richard	SUI
Silver:	Rolf Sorensen	DEN
Bronze:	Maximilian Scjandri	GBR

Road Race, Women
Course sur route, Dames
Gold:	Jeannie Longo-Ciprelli	FRA
Silver:	Imelda Chiappa	ITA
Bronze:	Clara Hughes	CAN

Individual Time Trial, Men
Course individuelle contre la montre, Messieurs
Gold:	Miguel Indurain	ESP
Silver:	Abraham Olano	ESP
Bronze:	Chris Boardman	GBR

Individual Time Trial, Women
Course individuelle contre la montre, Dames
Gold:	Zulfiya Zabirova	RUS
Silver:	Jeannie Longo-Ciprelli	FRA
Bronze:	Clara Hughes	CAN

Track / *Piste*
1 km Time Trial, Men
Course de 1 km contre la montre, Messieurs
Gold:	Florian Rousseau	FRA
Silver:	Erin Hartwell	USA
Bronze:	Takanobu Jumonji	JPN

Sprint, Men
Sprint, Messieurs
Gold:	Jens Fiedler	GER
Silver:	Marty Nothstein	USA
Bronze:	Curt Harnett	CAN

Sprint, Women
Sprint, Dames
Gold:	Felicia Ballanger	FRA
Silver:	Michelle Ferris	AUS
Bronze:	Ingrid Haringa	NED

Individual Pursuit, Men
Poursuite individuelle, Messieurs
Gold:	Andrea Collinelli	ITA
Silver:	Philippe Ermenault	FRA
Bronze:	Bradley McGee	AUS

Individual Pursuit, Women
Poursuite individuelle, Dames
Gold:	Antonella Bellutti	ITA
Silver:	Marion Clignet	FRA
Bronze:	Judith Arndt	GER

Team Pursuit, Men
Poursuite par équipes, Messieurs
Gold:	Christophe Capelle	FRA
	Philippe Ermenault	
	Jean-Michel Monin	
	Francis Moreau	
	Anton Chantyr	
Silver:	Eduard Gritsun	RUS
	Nikolay Kuznetsov	
	Aleksey Markov	
Bronze:	Brett Aitkin*	AUS
	Bradley McGee	
	Stuart O'Grady	
	Timothy O'Shannessey	
	Dean Woods	

Point Race, Men
Course aux points, Messieurs
Gold:	Silvio Martinello	ITA
Silver:	Brian Walton	CAN
Bronze:	Stuart O'Grady	AUS

Point Race, Women
Course aux points, Dames
Gold:	Nathalie Lancien	FRA
Silver:	Ingrid Haringa	NED
Bronze:	Lucy Tyler-Sharman	AUS

Olympic Records / *Records olympiques* : 13

Track / *Piste*
1 km Time Trial, Men
Course de 1 km contre la montre, Messieurs
1:02.712	Florian Rousseau	FRA

Sprint, Men
Sprint, Messieurs
10.129	Gary Neiwand	AUS

Sprint, Women
Sprint, Dames
11.212	Michelle Ferris	AUS

Individual Pursuit, Men
Poursuite individuelle, Messieurs
4:21.295	Philippe Ermenault	FRA
4:19.699	Andrea Collinelli	ITA
4:19.153	Andrea Collinelli	ITA

Individual Pursuit, Women
Poursuite individuelle, Dames
3:40.335	Judith Arndt	GER
3:35.774	Marion Clignet	FRA
3:34.130	Antonella Bellutti	ITA
3:32.371	Antonella Bellutti	ITA

Team Pursuit, Men
Poursuite par équipes, Messieurs
4:08.785	Russian Federation	
4:06.880	France	
4:05.930	France	

World Records / *Records du monde* : 2

Track / *Piste*
Individual Pursuit, Men
Poursuite individuelle, Messieurs
4:19.699	Andrea Collinelli	ITA
4:19.153	Andrea Collinelli	ITA

Equestrian / *Sports équestres*

Medals Awarded / *Médailles remises* : 18

Individual 3-Day Event
Concours complet individuel
Gold:	Blyth Tait	NZL
Silver:	Sally Clark	NZL
Bronze:	Kerry Millikin	USA

Team 3-Day Event
Concours complet par équipes
Gold:	Phillip Dutton	AUS
	Andrew Hoy	
	Gillian Rolton	
	Wendy Schaeffer	
Silver:	Bruce Davidson	USA
	Jill Henneberg	
	David O'Connor	
	Karen O'Connor	
Bronze:	Vaughn Jefferis	NZL
	Victoria Latta	
	Andrew Nicholson	
	Blyth Tait	

Individual Dressage
Dressage individuel
Gold:	Isabell Werth	GER
Silver:	Anky van Grunsven	NED
Bronze:	Sven Rothenberger	NED

Team Dressage
Dressage par équipes
Gold:	Klaus Balkenhol	GER
	Martin Schaudt	
	Monica Theodorescu	
	Isabell Werth	
Silver:	Tineke Bartels-de Vries	NED
	Anky van Grunsven	
	Gonnelien Rothenberger	
	Sven Rothenberger	
Bronze:	Robert Dover	USA
	Michelle Gibson	
	Steffen Peters	
	Guenter Seidel	

Individual Jumping
Saut d'obstacles individuel
Gold:	Ulrich Kirchhoff	GER
Silver:	Willi Melliger	SUI
Bronze:	Alexandra Ledermann	FRA

Team Jumping
Saut d'obstacles par équipes
Gold:	Ludger Beerbaum	GER
	Ulrich Kirchhoff	
	Lars Nieberg	
	Franke Sloothaak	
Silver:	Leslie Burr-Howard	USA
	Anne Kursinski	
	Peter Leone	
	Michael Matz	
Bronze:	Álvaro Affonso de Miranda Neto	BRA
	André Bier Johannpeter	
	Luiz Felipe de Azevedo	
	Rodrigo de Paula Pessoa	

Fencing / *Escrime* *Athlete competed in round other than final / *Athlète n'ayant pas participé aux finales*

Medals Awarded / *Médailles remises* : 30

Individual Epée, Men
Epée individuelle, Messieurs
Gold:	Aleksandr Beketov	RUS
Silver:	Ivan Trevejo Perez	CUB
Bronze:	Géza Imre	HUN

Individual Epée, Women
Epée individuelle, Dames
Gold:	Laura Flessel	FRA
Silver:	Valerie Barlois	FRA
Bronze:	Gyöngyi Szalay	HUN

Team Epée, Men
Epée par équipes, Messieurs
Gold:	Sandro Cuomo	ITA
	Angelo Mazzoni	
	Maurizio Randazzo	
Silver:	Aleksandr Beketov	RUS
	Pavel Kolobkov	
	Valeriy Zakharevich	
Bronze:	Jean-Michel Henry	FRA
	Robert Leroux	
	Eric Srecki	

Team Epée, Women
Epée par équipes, Dames
Gold:	Valerie Barlois	FRA
	Laura Flessel	
	Sophie Moresee-Pichot	
Silver:	Laura Chiesa	ITA
	Elisa Uga	
	Margherita Zalaffi	
Bronze:	Karina Aznavuryan	RUS
	Yuliya Garayeva	
	Mariya Mazina	

Individual Foil, Men
Fleuret individuel, Messieurs
Gold:	Alessandro Puccini	ITA
Silver:	Lionel Plumenail	FRA
Bronze:	Franck Boidin	FRA

Individual Foil, Women
Fleuret individuel, Dames
Gold:	Laura Badea	ROM
Silver:	Valentina Vezzali	ITA
Bronze:	Giovanna Trillini	ITA

Team Foil, Men
Fleuret par équipes, Messieurs
Gold:	Ilgar Mamedov	RUS
	Vladislav Pavlovich	
	Dmitriy Shevchenko	
Silver:	Piotr Kielpikowski*	POL
	Adam Krzesinski	
	Jaroslaw Rodzewicz	
	Ryszard Sobczak	
Bronze:	Oscar Manuel Garcia Perez	CUB
	Elvis Gregory	
	Rolando Samuel Tucker Leon	

Team Foil, Women
Fleuret par équipes, Dames
Gold:	Francesca Bortolozzi Borella	ITA
	Giovanna Trillini	
	Valentina Vezzali	
Silver:	Laura Badea	ROM
	Roxana Scarlat	
	Reka Szabo-Lazar	
Bronze:	Sabine Bau	GER
	Anja Fichtel-Nauritz	
	Monika Weber-Koszto	

Individual Sabre, Men
Sabre individuel, Messieurs
Gold:	Stanislav Pozdnyakov	RUS
Silver:	Sergey Sharikov	RUS
Bronze:	Damien Touya	FRA

Team Sabre, Men
Sabre par équipes, Messieurs
Gold:	Grigoriy Kiriyenko	RUS
	Stanislav Pozdnyakov	
	Sergey Sharikov	
Silver:	Csaba Köves	HUN
	József Navarrete	
	Bence Szabó	
Bronze:	Raffaello Caserta	ITA
	Luigi Tarantino	
	Tonhi Terenzi	

Football / *Football*

Medals Awarded / *Médailles remises* : 6

Men
Messieurs

Gold:	Daniel Amokachi	NGR
	Emmanuel Amunike	
	Tijani Babangida	
	Celestine Babayaro	
	Emmanuel Babayaro	
	Joseph Dosu	
	Teslim Fatusi	
	Victor Ikpeba	
	Nwankwo Kanu	
	Garba Lawal	
	Abiodon Obafemi	
	Mobi Obaraku	
	Kingsley Obiekwu	
	Augustine Okocha	
	Sunday Oliseh	
	Wilson Oruma	
	Okechukwu Uche	
	Taribo West	
Silver:	Matias Jesus Almeyda	ARG
	Roberto Fabián Ayala	
	Christian Gustavo Bassedas	
	Carlos Gustavo Bossio	
	Pablo Oscar Cavallero	
	José Antonio Chamot	
	Hernán Jorge Crespo	
	Marcelo Alejandro Delgado	
	Marcelo Daniel Gallardo	
	Claudio Javier López	
	Gustavo Adrián López	
	Hugo Alberto Morales	
	Arnaldo Ariel Ortega	
	Pablo Ariel Paz	
	Hector Mauricio Pineda	
	Roberto Nestor Sensini	
	Diego Pablo Simeone	
	Javier Adelmar Zanetti	
Bronze:	Flávio da Conceição	BRA
	José Marcelo Ferreira	
	Rivaldo Victor Borba Ferreira	
	Oswaldo Giroldo Junior	
	Luiz Carlos Goulart	
	Ronaldo Guiaro	
	Danrlei de Deus Hinterhloz	
	Ronaldo Luiz Nazario Lima	
	Alexandre da Silva Mariano	
	José Elias Moedim Junior	
	André Luiz Moreira	
	José Roberto Gama Oliveira	
	Sávio Bortolini Pimentel	
	Aldair Nascimento Santos	
	Narciso dos Santos	
	Nelson de Jesus Silva	
	Roberto Carlos Silva	
	Marcelo José de Souza	

Women
Dames

Gold:	Michelle Akers	USA
	Brandi Chastain	
	Joy Fawcett	
	Julie Foudy	
	Carin Gabarra	
	Mia Hamm	
	Mary Harvey	
	Kristine Lilly	
	Shannon MacMillan	
	Tiffeny Milbrett	
	Carla Overbeck	
	Cindy Parlow	
	Tiffany Roberts	
	Briana Scurry	
	Tisha Venturini	
	Staci Wilson	
Silver:	Yufeng Chen	CHN
	Yunjie Fan	
	Hong Gao	
	Ailing Liu	
	Ying Liu	
	Guihong Shi	
	Qingxia Shui	
	Qingmei Sun	
	Wen Sun	
	Liping Wang	
	Haiying Wei	
	Lirong Wen	
	Huilin Xie	
	Hongqi Yu	
	Lihong Zhao	
	Honglian Zhong	
Bronze:	Ann Kristin Aarones	NOR
	Agnete Carlsen	
	Gro Espeseth	
	Tone Günn Früstol	
	Tone Haugen	
	Linda Medalen	
	Merete Myklebüst	
	Bente Nordby	
	Anne Nymark Andersen	
	Nina Nymark Andersen	
	Marianne Pettersen	
	Hege Riise	
	Brit Sandaune	
	Reidun Seth	
	Tina Svensson	
	Trine Tangeraas	

Gymnastics—Artistic / *Gymnastique — Artistique*

Medals Awarded / *Médailles remises* : 45

Team, Men
Concours général par équipes, Messieurs

Gold:	Sergei Charkov	RUS
	Nikolay Krukov	
	Alexei Nemov	
	Eugeni Podgorni	
	Dmitriy Trush	
	Dmitri Vasilenko	
	Alexei Voropaev	
Silver:	Bin Fan	CHN
	Hongbin Fan	
	Huadong Huang	
	Liping Huang	
	Xiaoshuang Li	
	Jian Shen	
	Jinjing Zhang	
Bronze:	Igor Korobchinski	UKR
	Oleg Kosiak	
	Grigory Misutin	
	Vladimir Shamenko	
	Rustam Sharipov	
	Alexandre Svetlichnyi	
	Yuri Yermakov	

Team, Women
Concours général par équipes, Dames

Gold:	Amanda Borden	USA
	Amy Chow	
	Dominique Dawes	
	Shannon Miller	
	Dominique Moceanu	
	Jaycie Phelps	
	Kerri Strug	
Silver:	Svetlana Chorkina	RUS
	Elena Dolgopolova	
	Rozalia Galiyeva	
	Elena Grosheva	
	Dina Kochetkova	
	Eugenia Kuznetsova	
	Oksana Liapina	
Bronze:	Simona Amanar	ROM
	Gina Gogean	
	Lavinia Milosovici	
	Ionela Loaies	
	Alexandra Marinescu	
	Mirela Tugurlan	

Individual All-Around, Men
Concours général individuel, Messieurs

Gold:	Xiaoshuang Li	CHN
Silver:	Alexei Nemov	RUS
Bronze:	Vitaly Scherbo	BLR

Individual All-Around, Women
Concours général individuel, Dames

Gold:	Lilia Podkopayeva	UKR
Silver:	Gina Gogean	ROM
Bronze:	Simona Amanar	ROM

	Lavinia Milosovici	ROM

Individual Apparatus, Men
Par engin, Messieurs

Floor
Sol

Gold:	Ioannis Melissanidis	GRE
Silver:	Xiaoshuang Li	CHN
Bronze:	Alexei Nemov	RUS

Pommel Horse
Cheval d'arçons

Gold:	Donghua Li	SUI
Silver:	Marius Urzica	ROM
Bronze:	Alexei Nemov	RUS

Rings
Anneaux

Gold:	Yuri Chechi	ITA
Silver:	Szilveszter Csollány	HUN
	Dan Burinca	ROM

Vault
Saut de cheval

Gold:	Alexei Nemov	RUS
Silver:	Hong-Chul Yeo	KOR
Bronze:	Vitaly Scherbo	BLR

Parallel Bars
Barres parallèles

Gold:	Rustam Sharipov	UKR
Silver:	Jair Lynch	USA

Bronze:	Vitaly Scherbo	BLR

Horizontal Bar
Barre fixe

Gold:	Andreas Wecker	GER
Silver:	Krasimir Dounev	BUL
Bronze:	Bin Fan	CHN
	Alexei Nemov	RUS
	Vitaly Scherbo	BLR

Individual Apparatus, Women
Par engin, Dames

Floor
Sol

Gold:	Lilia Podkopayeva	UKR
Silver:	Simona Amanar	ROM
Bronze:	Dominique Dawes	USA

Balance Beam
Poutre

Gold:	Shannon Miller	USA
Silver:	Lilia Podkopayeva	UKR
Bronze:	Gina Gogean	ROM

Vault
Saut de cheval

Gold:	Simona Amanar	ROM
Silver:	Huilan Mo	CHN
Bronze:	Gina Gogean	ROM

Uneven Bars
Barres asymétriques

Gold:	Svetlana Chorkina	RUS
Silver:	Wenjing Bi	CHN
	Amy Chow	USA

Gymnastics—Rhythmic / *Gymnastique — Rythmique*

Medals Awarded / *Médailles remises* : 6

Individual All-Around, Women
Concours général individuel, Dames

Gold:	Kateryna Serebryanska	UKR
Silver:	Ianina Batrychinko	RUS
Bronze:	Olena Vitrichenko	UKR

Team, Women
Concours d'ensemble, Dames

Gold:	Marta Baldo	ESP
	Nuria Cabanillas	
	Estela Gimenez	
	Lorena Gurendez	
	Tania Lamarca	
	Estibaliz Martinez	

Silver:	Ina Deltcheva	BUL
	Valentina Kevlian	
	Maria Koleva	
	Maya Tabakova	
	Ivelina Taleva	
	Vjara Vatachka	

Bronze:	Evguenia Botchkareva	RUS
	Olga Chtyrenko	
	Irina Dziouba	
	Angelina Iouchkova	
	Ioulia Ivanova	
	Elena Krivochei	

Handball / *Handball*

Medals Awarded / *Médailles remises* : 6

Men
Messieurs

Gold: Patrik Cavar — CRO
Valner Frankovic
Slavko Goluza
Bruno Gudelj
Vladimir Jelcic
Bozidar Jovic
Nenad Kljaic
Venio Losert
Valter Matosevic
Zoran Mikulic
Alvaro Nacinovic
Goran Perkovac
Iztok Puc
Zlatko Saracevic
Irfan Smajlagic
Vladimir Sujster

Silver: Magnus Andersson — SWE
Robert Andersson
Per Carlen
Martin Frandesjo
Erik Hajas
Robert Hedin
Andreas Larsson
Ola Lindgren
Stefan Lövgren
Mats Olsson
Staffan Olsson
Johan Peterson
Thomas Sivertsson
Thomas Svensson
Pierre Thorsson
Magnus Wislander

Bronze: Talant Dujshebaev — ESP
Salvador Esquer
Aitor Etxaburu
Jesus Fernandez
Jaume Fort
Mateo Garralda
Raul Gonzalez
Rafael Guijosa
Fernando Hernandez
Jose Hombrados
Demetrio Lozano
Jordi Nunez
Jesus Olalla
Juan Perez
Inaki Urdangarin
Alberto Urdiales

Women
Dames

Gold: Anja Jul Andersen — DEN
Camilla Andersen
Kristine Andersen
Heidi Astrup
Tina Bottzau
Marianne Florman
Conny Hamann
Anja Byrial Hansen
Anette Hoffman
Tonje Kjaergaard
Janne Kolling
Susanne Lauritsen
Gitte Madsen
Lene Rantala
Gitte Sunesen
Anne Dorthe Tanderup

Silver: Eun-Hee Cho — KOR
Sun-Hee Han
Jeong-Ho Hong
Soon-Young Huh
Cheong-Shim Kim
Eun-Mi Kim
Jeong-Mi Kim
Mi-Sim Kim
Rang Kim
Hye-Jeong Kwag
Sang-Eun Lee
O-Kyeong Lim
Hyang-Ja Moon
Seong-Ok Oh
Yong-Ran Oh
Jeong-Rim Park

Bronze: Éva Erdös — HUN
Andrea Farkas
Beáta Hoffmann
Anikó Kántor
Erzsebét Kocsis
Beatrix Kökény
Eszter Mátféi
Auguszta Mátyás
Anikó Meksz
Anikó Nagy
Helga Németh
Ildikó Pádár
Beáta Siti
Anna Szantó
Katalin Szilágyi
Beatrix Tóth

Hockey / *Hockey*

Medals Awarded / *Médailles remises* : 6

Men
Messieurs

Gold: Floris Jan Bovelander — NED
Jacques Brinkman
Maurits Crucq
Marc Delissen
Jeroen Delmee
Leo Klein Gebbink
Taco van den Honert
Ronald Jansen
Erik Jazet
Bram Lomans
Tycho van Meer
Teun de Nooijer
Wouter van Pelt
Stephan Veen
Guus Vogels
Remco van Wijk

Silver: Jaime Amat — ESP
Pablo Amat
Javier Arnau
Jordi Arnau
Oscar Barrena
Ignacio Cobos
Juan Dinares
Juan Escarre
Xavier Escude
Juantxo Garcia-Maurino
Antonio Gonzalez
Ramon Jufresa
Joaquin Malgosa
Victor Pujol
Ramon Sala
Pablo Usoz

Bronze: Stuart Carruthers — AUS
Baeden Choppy
Stephen Davies
Damon Diletti
Lachlan Dreher
Lachlan Elmer
Brendan Garard
Paul Gaudoin
Mark Hager
Paul Lewis
Grant Smith
Matthew Smith
Daniel Sproule
Jason Stacy
Kenneth Wark
Michael York

Women
Dames

Gold: Michelle Andrews — AUS
Alyson Annan
Louise Dobson
Renita Farrell
Juliet Haslam
Rechelle Hawkes
Clover Maitland
Karen Marsden
Jennifer Morris
Jacqueline Pereira
Nova Peris-Kneebone
Katrina Powell
Lisa Powell
Danielle Roche
Kate Starre
Liane Tooth

Silver: Eun-Jung Chang — KOR
Eun-Jung Cho
Eun-Kyung Choi
Mi-Soon Choi
Young-Sun Jeon
Deok-San Jin
Myung-Ok Kim
Soo-Hyun Kown
Chang-Sook Kwon
Eun-Kyung Lee
Eun-Young Lee
Ji-Young Lee
Jeong-Sook Lim
Seung-Shin Oh
Hyun-Jung Woo
Jae-Sook You

Bronze: Stella de Heij — NED
Wietske de Ruiter
Fleur van de Kieft
Dillianne van den Boogaard
Suzan van der Wielen
Myntje Donners
Willemijn Duyster
Noor Holsboer
Nicky Koolen
Ellen Kuipers
Jeannette Lewin
Suzanne Plesman
Florentine Steenberghe
Margje Teeuwen
Carole Thate
Jacqueline Toxopeus

Judo / *Judo*

Medals Awarded / *Médailles remises* : 56

Extra Lightweight, 60 kg, Men
Super-léger, 60 kg, Messieurs

Gold:	Tadahiro Nomura	JPN
Silver:	Girolamo Giovinazzo	ITA
Bronze:	Dorjpalam Narmandakh	MGL
	Richard Trautmann	GER

Extra Lightweight, 48 kg, Women
Super-léger, 48 kg, Dames

Gold:	Sun Hui Kye	PRK
Silver:	Ryoko Tamura	JPN
Bronze:	Amarilis Savon	CUB
	Yolanda Soler	ESP

Half-Lightweight, 65 kg, Men
Mi-léger, 65 kg, Messieurs

Gold:	Udo Quellmalz	GER
Silver:	Yukimasa Nakamura	JPN
Bronze:	Henrique Carlos Guimarães	BRA
	Israel Hernandez Plana	CUB

Half-Lightweight, 52 kg, Women
Mi-léger, 52 kg, Dames

Gold:	Marie-Claire Restoux	FRA
Silver:	Sook-Hee Hyun	KOR
Bronze:	Noriko Sugawara	JPN
	Legna Verdecia	CUB

Lightweight, 71 kg, Men
Léger, 71 kg, Messieurs

Gold:	Kenzo Nakamura	JPN
Silver:	Dae-Sung Kwak	KOR
Bronze:	Christophe Gagliano	FRA
	James Pedro	USA

Lightweight, 56 kg, Women
Léger, 56 kg, Dames

Gold:	Driulis Gonzalez	CUB
Silver:	Sun-Yong Jung	KOR
Bronze:	Isabel Fernandez	ESP
	Marisabel Lomba	BEL

Half-Middleweight, 78 kg, Men
Mi-moyen, 78 kg, Messieurs

Gold:	Djamel Bouras	FRA
Silver:	Toshihiko Koga	JPN
Bronze:	In-Chul Cho	KOR
	Soso Liparteliani	GEO

Half-Middleweight, 61 kg, Women
Mi-moyen, 61 kg, Dames

Gold:	Yuko Emoto	JPN
Silver:	Gella Vandecaveye	BEL
Bronze:	Jenny Gal	NED
	Sung-Sook Jung	KOR

Middleweight, 86 kg, Men
Moyen, 86 kg, Messieurs

Gold:	Ki-Young Jeon	KOR
Silver:	Armen Bagdasarov	UZB
Bronze:	Mark Huizinga	NED
	Marko Spittka	GER

Middleweight, 66 kg, Women
Moyen, 66 kg, Dames

Gold:	Min-Sun Cho	KOR
Silver:	Aneta Szczepanska	POL
Bronze:	Xianbo Wang	CHN
	Claudia Zwiers	NED

Half-Heavyweight, 95 kg, Men
Mi-lourd, 95 kg, Messieurs

Gold:	Pawel Nastula	POL
Silver:	Min-Soo Kim	KOR
Bronze:	Aurélio Fernandes Miguel	BRA
	Stephane Traineau	FRA

Half-Heavyweight, 72 kg, Women
Mi-lourd, 72 kg, Dames

Gold:	Ulla Werbrouck	BEL
Silver:	Yoko Tanabe	JPN
Bronze:	Diadenis Luna Castellano	CUB
	Ylenia Scapin	ITA

Heavyweight, +95 kg, Men
Lourd, plus de 95 kg, Messieurs

Gold:	David Douillet	FRA
Silver:	Ernesto Perez	ESP
Bronze:	Frank Moeller	GER
	Harry Van Barneveld	BEL

Heavyweight, +72 kg, Women
Lourd, plus de 72 kg, Dames

Gold:	Fuming Sun	CHN
Silver:	Estela Rodriguez	CUB
Bronze:	Christine Cicot	FRA
	Johanna Hagn	GER

Modern Pentathlon / *Pentathlon moderne*

Medals Awarded / *Médailles remises* : 3

Men
Messieurs

Gold:	Alexandre Paryguin	KAZ
Silver:	Eduard Zenovka	RUS
Bronze:	János Martinek	HUN

Rowing / *Aviron*

Medals Awarded / *Médailles remises* : 42

Single Sculls, Men
Skiff, Messieurs

Gold:	Xeno Muller	SUI
Silver:	Derek Porter	CAN
Bronze:	Thomas Lange	GER

Single Sculls, Women
Skiff, Dames

Gold:	Ekaterina Khodotovich	BLR
Silver:	Silken Laumann	CAN
Bronze:	Trine Hansen	DEN

Double Sculls, Men
Deux rameurs en couple, Messieurs

Gold:	Agostino Abbagnale	ITA
	Davide Tizzano	
Silver:	Steffen Skår Størseth	NOR
	Kjetil Undset	
Bronze:	Samuel Barathay	FRA
	Frederic Kowal	

Double Sculls, Women
Deux rameuses en couple, Dames

Gold:	Kathleen Heddle	CAN
	Marnie McBean	
Silver:	Mianying Cao	CHN
	Xiuyun Zhang	
Bronze:	Irene Eijs	NED
	Eeke van Nes	

Lightweight Double Sculls, Men
Deux rameurs en couple poids léger, Messieurs

Gold:	Markus Gier	SUI
	Michael Gier	
Silver:	Pepijn Aardewijn	NED
	Maarten van der Linden	
Bronze:	Anthony Edwards	AUS
	Bruce Hick	

Lightweight Double Sculls, Women
Deux rameuses en couple poids léger, Dames

Gold:	Constanta Burcica	ROM
	Camelia Macoviciuc	
Silver:	Teresa Z. Bell	USA
	Lindsay Burns	
Bronze:	Rebecca Joyce	AUS
	Virginia Lee	

Quadruple Sculls, Men
Quatre rameurs en couple sans barreur, Messieurs

Gold:	Andreas Hajek	GER
	Andre Steiner	
	Stephan Volkert	
	Andre Willms	
Silver:	Jason Gailes	USA
	Brian Jamieson	
	Eric Mueller	
	Tim Young	
Bronze:	Duncan Free	AUS
	Boden Hanson	
	Janusz Hooker	
	Ronald Snook	

Quadruple Sculls, Women
Quatre rameuses en couple sans barreuse, Dames

Gold:	Kathrin Boron	GER
	Kerstin Koeppen	
	Katrin Rutschow	
	Jana Sorgers	
Silver:	Inna Frolova	UKR
	Svitlana Maziy	
	Dina Myftakhutdinova	
	Olena Ronzhina	
Bronze:	Laryssa Biesenthal	CAN
	Kathleen Heddle	
	Marnie McBean	
	Diane O'Grady	

Coxless Pair, Men
Deux rameurs en pointe sans barreur, Messieurs

Gold:	Matthew Pinsent	GBR
	Steven Redgrave	
Silver:	Robert Scott	AUS
	David Weightman	
Bronze:	Michel Andrieux	FRA
	Jean-Christophe Rolland	

Coxless Pair, Women
Deux rameuses en pointe sans barreuse, Dames

Gold:	Kate Slatter	AUS
	Megan Still	
Silver:	Karen Kraft	USA
	Missy Schwen	
Bronze:	Helene Cortin	FRA
	Christine Gosse	

Coxless Four, Men
Quatre rameurs en pointe sans barreur, Messieurs

Gold:	Drew Ginn	AUS
	Nicholas Green	
	Michael McKay	
	James Tomkins	
Silver:	Gilles Bosquet	FRA
	Daniel Fauche	
	Olivier Moncelet	
	Bertrand Vecten	
Bronze:	Timothy Foster	GBR
	Rupert Obholzer	
	Greg Searle	
	Jonny Searle	

Lightweight Coxless Four, Men
Quatre rameurs en pointe sans barreur poids léger, Messieurs

Gold:	Eskild Ebbesen	DEN
	Victor Feddersen	
	Niels Laulund Henriksen	
	Thomas Poulsen	
Silver:	David Boyes	CAN
	Gavin Hassett	
	Jeffrey Lay	
	Brian Peaker	
Bronze:	William Carlucci	USA
	David Collins	
	Jeff Pfaendtner	
	Marc Schneider	

Eight, Men
Huit, Messieurs

Gold:	Michiel Bartman	NED
	Jeroen Duyster	
	Ronald Florijn	
	Koos Maasdijk	
	Nico Rienks	
	Diederik Simon	
	Niels van der Zwan	
	Niels van Steenis	
	Henk-Jan Zwolle	
Silver:	Roland Baar	GER
	Wolfram Huhn	
	Detlef Kirchhoff	
	Mark Kleinschmidt	
	Frank Richter	
	Thorsten Streppelhoff	
	Peter Thiede	
	Ulrich Viefers	
	Marc Weber	
Bronze:	Nikolay Aksyonov	RUS
	Anton Chermashentsev	
	Andrey Glukhov	
	Aleksandr Lukyanov	
	Sergey Matveyev	
	Pavel Melnikov	
	Roman Monchenko	
	Dmitriy Rozinkevich	
	Vladimir Volodenkov	

Eight, Women
Huit, Dames

Gold:	Vera Cochelea	ROM
	Liliana Gafencu	
	Elena Georgescu	
	Doina Ignat	
	Elisabeta Lipa	
	Ioana Olteanu	
	Marioara Popescu	
	Doina Spircu	
	Anca Tanase	
Silver:	Alison Korn	CAN
	Theresa Luke	
	Maria Maunder	
	Heather McDermid	
	Jessica Monroe	
	Emma Robinson	
	Lesley Thompson	
	Tosha Tsang	
	Anna van der Kamp	
Bronze:	Tamara Davydenko	BLR
	Natalya Lavrinenko	
	Yelena Mikulich	
	Aleksandra Pankina	
	Yaroslava Pavlovich	
	Valentina Skrabatun	
	Natalya Stasyuk	
	Natalya Volchek	
	Marina Znak	

Shooting / *Tir*

Medals Awarded / *Médailles remises* : 45

50 m Free Pistol, Men
Pistolet libre à 50 m, Messieurs
Gold:	Boris Kokorev	RUS
Silver:	Igor Basinski	BLR
Bronze:	Roberto di Donna	ITA

25 m Rapid Fire Pistol, Men
Pistolet de tir rapide à 25 m, Messieurs
Gold:	Ralf Schumann	GER
Silver:	Emil Milev	BUL
Bronze:	Vladimir Vokhmyanin	KAZ

25 m Sport Pistol, Women
Pistolet sport à 25 m, Dames
Gold:	Duihong Li	CHN
Silver:	Diana Jorgova	BUL
Bronze:	Marina Logvinenko	RUS

10 m Air Pistol, Men
Pistolet à air comprimé à 10 m, Messieurs
Gold:	Roberto di Donna	ITA
Silver:	Yifu Wang	CHN
Bronze:	Tanu Kiriakov	BUL

10 m Air Pistol, Women
Pistolet à air comprimé à 10 m, Dames
Gold:	Olga Klochneva	RUS
Silver:	Marina Logvinenko	RUS
Bronze:	Mariya Grozdeva	BUL

10 m Air Rifle, Men
Carabine à air comprimé à 10 m, Messieurs
Gold:	Artem Khadzhibekov	RUS
Silver:	Wolfram Waibel, Jr.	AUT
Bronze:	Jean-Pierre Amat	FRA

10 m Air Rifle, Women
Carabine à air comprimé à 10 m, Dames
Gold:	Renata Mauer	POL
Silver:	Petra Horneber	GER
Bronze:	Aleksandra Ivosev	YUG

50 m Free Rifle 3 Position, Men
Carabine libre 3 positions à 50 m, Messieurs
Gold:	Jean-Pierre Amat	FRA
Silver:	Sergey Belyayev	KAZ
Bronze:	Wolfram Waibel, Jr.	AUT

50 m Standard Rifle 3 Position, Women
Carabine standard 3 positions à 50 m, Dames
Gold:	Aleksandra Ivosev	YUG
Silver:	Irina Gerasimenok	RUS
Bronze:	Renata Mauer	POL

50 m Free Rifle Prone, Men
Carabine libre position couchée à 50 m, Messieurs
Gold:	Christian Klees	GER
Silver:	Sergey Belyayev	KAZ
Bronze:	Jozef Gonci	SVK

Trap, Men
Fosse olympique, Messieurs
Gold:	Michael Diamond	AUS
Silver:	Josh Lakatos	USA
Bronze:	Lance Bade	USA

Double Trap, Men
Double trap, Messieurs
Gold:	Russell Mark	AUS
Silver:	Albano Pera	ITA
Bronze:	Bing Zhang	CHN

Double Trap, Women
Double trap, Dames
Gold:	Kim Rhode	USA
Silver:	Susanne Kiermayer	GER
Bronze:	Deserie Huddleston	AUS

Skeet, Men
Skeet, Messieurs
Gold:	Ennio Falco	ITA
Silver:	Miroslaw Rzepkowski	POL
Bronze:	Andrea Benelli	ITA

10 m Running Target, Men
Cible mobile à 10 m, Messieurs
Gold:	Ling Yang	CHN
Silver:	Jun Xiao	CHN
Bronze:	Miroslav Janus	CZE

Olympic Records / *Records olympiques* : 27

50 m Free Pistol - Final, Men
Pistolet libre à 50 m - Finale, Messieurs
666.4	Boris Kokorev	RUS

25 m Rapid Fire Pistol, Men
Pistolet de tir rapide à 25 m, Messieurs
596	Ralf Schumann	GER

25 m Rapid Fire Pistol - Final, Men
Pistolet de tir rapide à 25 m - Finale, Messieurs
698.0	Ralf Schumann	GER

25 m Sport Pistol, Women
Pistolet sport à 25 m, Dames
589	Duihong Li	CHN

25 m Sport Pistol - Final, Women
Pistolet sport à 25 m - Finale, Dames
687.9	Duihong Li	CHN

10 m Air Pistol, Men
Pistolet à air comprimé à 10 m, Messieurs
587	Yifu Wang	CHN

10 m Air Pistol, Women
Pistolet à air comprimé à 10 m, Dames
390	Marina Logvinenko	RUS

10 m Air Pistol - Final, Women
Pistolet à air comprimé à 10 m - Finale, Dames
490.1	Olga Klochneva	RUS

10 m Air Rifle, Men
Carabine à air comprimé à 10 m, Messieurs
596	Wolfram Waibel, Jr.	AUT

10 m Air Rifle - Final, Men
Carabine à air comprimé à 10 m - Finale, Messieurs
695.7	Artem Khadzhibekov	RUS

10 m Air Rifle, Women
Carabine à air comprimé à 10 m, Dames
397	Petra Horneber	GER

50 m Free Rifle 3 Position, Men
Carabine libre 3 positions à 50 m, Messieurs
1175	Jean-Pierre Amat	FRA
1175	Sergey Belyayev	KAZ

50 m Free Rifle 3 Position - Final, Men
Carabine libre 3 positions à 50 m - Finale, Messieurs
1273.9	Jean-Pierre Amat	FRA

50 m Standard Rifle 3 Position, Women
Carabine standard 3 positions à 50 m, Dames
589	Renata Mauer	POL

50 m Standard Rifle 3 Position - Final, Women
Carabine standard 3 positions à 50 m - Finale, Dames
686.1	Aleksandra Ivosev	YUG

50 m Free Rifle Prone, Men
Carabine libre position couchée à 50 m, Messieurs
600	Christian Klees	GER

50 m Free Rifle Prone - Final, Men
Carabine libre position couchée à 50 m - Finale, Messieurs
704.8	Christian Klees	GER

Trap, Men
Fosse olympique, Messieurs
124	Michael Diamond	AUS

Trap - Final, Men
Fosse olympique - Finale, Messieurs
149	Michael Diamond	AUS

Double Trap, Men
Double trap, Messieurs
141	Russell Mark	AUS
141	I-Chien Huang	TPE

Double Trap - Final, Men
Double trap - Finale, Messieurs
189	Russell Mark	AUS

Double Trap, Women
Double trap, Dames
108	Kim Rhode	USA

Double Trap - Final, Women
Double trap - Finale, Dames
141	Kim Rhode	USA

Skeet, Men
Skeet, Messieurs
125	Ennio Falco	ITA

Skeet - Final, Men
Skeet - Finale, Messieurs
149	Ennio Falco	ITA

10 m Running Target, Men
Cible mobile à 10 m, Messieurs
585	Ling Yang	CHN

10 m Running Target - Final, Men
Cible mobile à 10 m - Finale, Messieurs
685.8	Ling Yang	CHN

World Records / *Records du monde* : 1

50 m Free Rifle Prone, Men
Carabine libre position couchée à 50 m, Messieurs
704.8	Christian Klees	GER

Softball / *Softball*

Medals Awarded / *Médailles remises* : 3

Women
Dames

Gold:	Laura Berg	USA
	Gillian Boxx	
	Sheila Cornell	
	Lisa Fernandez	
	Michele Granger	
	Lori Harrigan	
	Dionna Harris	
	Kim Ly Maher	
	Leah O'Brien	
	Dorothy Richardson	
	Julie Smith	
	Michele Smith	
	Shelly Stokes	
	Danielle Tyler	
	Christa Lee Williams	
Silver:	Zhongxin An	CHN
	Hong Chen	
	Liping He	
	Li Lei	
	Xuqing Liu	
	Yaju Liu	
	Ying Ma	
	Jingbai Ou	
	Hua Tao	
	Lihong Wang	
	Ying Wang	
	Qiang Wei	
	Jian Xu	
	Fang Yan	
	Chunfang Zhang	
Bronze:	Joanne Brown	AUS
	Kim Cooper	
	Carolyn Crudgington	
	Kerry Dienelt	
	Peta Edebone	
	Tanya Harding	
	Jennifer Holliday	
	Jocelyn Lester	
	Sally McDermid	
	Francine McRae	
	Haylea Petrie	
	Nicole Richardson	
	Melanie Roche	
	Natalie Ward	
	Brooke Wilkins	

Table Tennis / *Tennis de table*

Medals Awarded / *Médailles remises* : 12

Singles, Men
Simples, Messieurs
Gold:	Guoliang Liu	CHN
Silver:	Tao Wang	CHN
Bronze:	Joerg Rosskopf	GER

Singles, Women
Simples, Dames
Gold:	Yaping Deng	CHN
Silver:	Jing Chen	TPE
Bronze:	Hong Qiao	CHN

Doubles, Men
Doubles, Messieurs
Gold:	Linghui Kong	CHN
	Guoliang Liu	
Silver:	Lin Lu	CHN
	Tao Wang	
Bronze:	Chul-Seung Lee	KOR
	Nam-Kyu Yoo	

Doubles, Women
Doubles, Dames
Gold:	Yaping Deng	CHN
	Hong Qiao	
Silver:	Wei Liu	CHN
	Yunping Qiao	
Bronze:	Hae-Jung Park	KOR
	Ji-Hae Ryu	

Medals Awarded and Olympic and World Records Established / *Médailles remises et records olympiques et du monde établis*   **11**

PETER B MILLICHAP • JOAN R MILLIGAN • KERRY G MILLIGAN • LARRI M MILLIGAN • STEPHEN L MILLIGAN • TANISHA M MILLIGAN • VALENCIA A MILLIGAN • ANNE W MILLIKEN • CHARLES MILLIKEN • KAY MILLINER • FREDRICK M MILLING • THOMAS V MILLINGTON • WILLIAM J MILLION • CAROL P MILLIRON • DAVID F MILLMAN • JEFFERY M MILLON • EARL MILLOY • ARCHIE C MILLS • BERLIN H MILLS • BETTY K MILLS • CARLYLE MILLS • CARRIE L MILLS • CHARLES L MILLS • DAVID S MILLS • GAYLA S MILLS • JAMES H MILLS • JANE E MILLS • JANE L MILLS • JESSE W MILLS

Tennis / *Tennis*

Medals Awarded / *Médailles remises* : 12

Singles, Men
Simples, Messieurs

Gold:	Andre Agassi	USA
Silver:	Sergi Bruguera	ESP
Bronze:	Leander Paes	IND

Singles, Women
Simples, Dames

Gold:	Lindsay Davenport	USA
Silver:	Arantxa Sanchez Vicario	ESP
Bronze:	Jana Novotna	CZE

Doubles, Men
Doubles, Messieurs

Gold:	Todd Woodbridge	AUS
	Mark Woodforde	
Silver:	Neil Broad	GBR
	Tim Henman	
Bronze:	Marc-Kevin Goellner	GER
	David Prinosil	

Doubles, Women
Doubles, Dames

Gold:	Gigi Fernandez	USA
	Mary Joe Fernandez	
Silver:	Jana Novotna	CZE
	Helena Sukova	
Bronze:	Conchita Martinez	ESP
	Arantxa Sanchez Vicario	

Volleyball / *Volleyball*

Medals Awarded / *Médailles remises* : 6

Volleyball—Beach
Volleyball — De plage
Men
Messieurs

Gold:	Karch Kiraly	USA
	Kent Steffes	
Silver:	Michael Dodd	USA
	Mike Whitmarsh	
Bronze:	John Child	CAN
	Mark Heese	

Women
Dames

Gold:	Sandra Tavares Pires	BRA
	Jacqueline Louise Cruz Silva	
Silver:	Mônica Rodrigues	BRA
	Adriana Ramos Samuel	
Bronze:	Natalie Cook	AUS
	Kerri Ann Pottharst	

Medals Awarded / *Médailles remises* : 6

Volleyball—Indoor
Volleyball — En salle
Men
Messieurs

Gold:	Peter Blange	NED
	Guido Görtzen	
	Rob Grabert	
	Henk-Jan Held	
	Misha Latuhihin	
	Jan Posthuma	
	Brecht Rodenburg	
	Richard Schuil	
	Bas van de Goor	
	Mike van de Goor	
	Olof van der Meulen	
	Ron Zwerver	
Silver:	Lorenzo Bernardi	ITA
	Vigor Bovolenta	
	Marco Bracci	
	Luca Cantagalli	
	Andrea Gardini	
	Andrea Giani	
	Pasquale Gravina	
	Marco Meoni	
	Samuele Papi	
	Andrea Sartoretti	
	Paolo Tofoli	
	Andrea Zorzi	

Bronze:	Vladimir Batez	YUG
	Dejan Brdjovic	
	Djorde Djuric	
	Andrija Geric	
	Nikola Grbic	
	Vladimir Grbic	
	Rajko Jokanovic	
	Slobodan Kovac	
	Djula Mester	
	Zarko Petrovic	
	Zeljko Tanaskovic	
	Goran Vujevic	

Women
Dames

Gold:	Taismari Aguero	CUB
	Regla Bell	
	Magalys Carvajal	
	Marleny Costa	
	Ana Ibis Fernandez	
	Mirka Francia	
	Idalmis Gato	
	Lilia Izquierdo	
	Luis Mireya	
	Raiza O'Farrill	
	Yumilka Ruiz	
	Regla Torres	

Silver:	Yongmei Cui	CHN
	Qi He	
	Yawen Lai	
	Yan Li	
	Xiaoning Liu	
	Wenli Pan	
	Yue Sun	
	Lina Wang	
	Yi Wang	
	Ziling Wang	
	Yongmei Wu	
	Yunying Zhu	
Bronze:	Ana Margarida Vieira Alvares	BRA
	Leila Gomes de Barros	
	Ericléia Bodzick	
	Hilma Aparecida Caldeiras	
	Ana Paula Rodrigues Connelly	
	Marcia Regina Cunha	
	Virna Cristine Dantas Dias	
	Ana Beatriz Moser	
	Ana Flávia Chritaro Sanglard	
	Helia Rogério de Souza	
	Sandra Maria Lima Suruagy	
	Fernanda Porto Venturini	

Weightlifting / *Haltérophilie*

Medals Awarded / *Médailles remises* : 30

54 kg, Men
54 kg, Messieurs
Gold:	Halil Mutlu	TUR
Silver:	Xiangsen Zhang	CHN
Bronze:	Sevdalin Minchev	BUL

59 kg, Men
59 kg, Messieurs
Gold:	Lingsheng Tang	CHN
Silver:	Leonidas Sabanis	GRE
Bronze:	Nikolai Pechalov	BUL

64 kg, Men
64 kg, Messieurs
Gold:	Naim Süleymanoglu	TUR
Silver:	Valerios Leonidis	GRE
Bronze:	Jiangang Xiao	CHN

70 kg, Men
70 kg, Messieurs
Gold:	Xugang Zhan	CHN
Silver:	Myong Nam Kim	PRK
Bronze:	Attila Feri	HUN

76 kg, Men
76 kg, Messieurs
Gold:	Pablo Lara	CUB
Silver:	Yoto Yotov	BUL
Bronze:	Chol Ho Jon	PRK

83 kg, Men
83 kg, Messieurs
Gold:	Pyrros Dimas	GRE
Silver:	Marc Huster	GER
Bronze:	Andrzej Cofalik	POL

91 kg, Men
91 kg, Messieurs
Gold:	Alexei Petrov	RUS
Silver:	Leonidas Kokas	GRE
Bronze:	Oliver Caruso	GER

99 kg, Men
99 kg, Messieurs
Gold:	Akakios Kakiasvilis	GRE
Silver:	Anatoliy Khrapatyy	KAZ
Bronze:	Denis Gotfrid	UKR

108 kg, Men
108 kg, Messieurs
Gold:	Timur Taymazov	UKR
Silver:	Sergey Syrtsov	RUS
Bronze:	Nicu Vlad	ROM

+108 kg, Men
Plus de 108 kg, Messieurs
Gold:	Andrey Chemerkin	RUS
Silver:	Ronny Weller	GER
Bronze:	Stefan Botev	AUS

Olympic Records / *Records olympiques* : 25

54 kg Snatch Weight, Men
54 kg poids arraché, Messieurs
| 130.0 kg | Halil Mutlu | TUR |
| 132.5 kg | Halil Mutlu | TUR |

54 kg Total, Men
54 kg total, Messieurs
| 287.5 kg | Halil Mutlu | TUR |

59 kg Clean and Jerk Weight, Men
59 kg poids épaulé-jeté, Messieurs
| 170.0kg | Lingsheng Tang | CHN |

59 kg Total, Men
59 kg total, Messieurs
| 305.0 kg | Lingsheng Tang | CHN |
| 307.5 kg | Lingsheng Tang | CHN |

64 kg Clean and Jerk Weight, Men
64 kg poids épaulé-jeté, Messieurs
| 185.0 kg | Naim Süleymanoglu | TUR |
| 187.5 kg | Valerios Leonidis | GRE |

64 kg Total, Men
64 kg total, Messieurs
| 332.5 kg | Naim Süleymanoglu | TUR |
| 335.0 kg | Naim Süleymanoglu | TUR |

70 kg Snatch Weight, Men
70 kg poids arraché, Messieurs
| 162.5 kg | Xugang Zhan | CHN |

70 kg Clean and Jerk Weight, Men
70 kg poids épaulé-jeté, Messieurs
| 195.0 kg | Xugang Zhan | CHN |

70 kg Total, Men
70 kg total, Messieurs
| 352.5 kg | Xugang Zhan | CHN |
| 357.5 kg | Xugang Zhan | CHN |

83 kg Snatch Weight, Men
83 kg poids arraché, Messieurs
| 180.0 kg | Pyrros Dimas | GRE |

83 kg Clean and Jerk Weight, Men
83 kg poids épaulé-jeté, Messieurs
| 213.5 kg | Marc Huster | GER |

83 kg Total, Men
83 kg total, Messieurs
| 387.5 kg | Pyrros Dimas | GRE |
| 392.5 kg | Pyrros Dimas | GRE |

91 kg Snatch Weight, Men
91 kg poids arraché, Messieurs
| 187.5 kg | Aleksey Petrov | RUS |

99 kg Clean and Jerk Weight, Men
99 kg poids épaulé-jeté, Messieurs
| 235.0 kg | Akakios Kakiasvilis | GRE |

99 kg Total, Men
99 kg total, Messieurs
| 420.0 kg | Akakios Kakiasvilis | GRE |

108 kg Clean and Jerk Weight, Men
108 kg poids épaulé-jeté, Messieurs
| 235.0 kg | Timur Taimazov | UKR |

+108 kg Clean and Jerk Weight, Men
+108 kg poids épaulé-jeté, Messieurs
| 255.0 kg | Ronny Weller | GER |
| 260.0 kg | Andrey Chemerkin | RUS |

+108 kg Total, Men
+108 kg total, Messieurs
| 457.5 kg | Andrey Chemerkin | RUS |

World Records / *Records du monde* : 19

54 kg Snatch Weight, Men
54 kg poids arraché, Messieurs
| 132.5 kg | Halil Mutlu | TUR |

59 kg Total, Men
59 kg total, Messieurs
| 307.5 kg | Lingsheng Tang | CHN |

64 kg Clean and Jerk Weight, Men
64 kg poids épaulé-jeté, Messieurs
| 185.0 kg | Naim Süleymanoglu | TUR |
| 187.5 kg | Valerios Leonidis | GRE |

64 kg Total, Men
64 kg total, Messieurs
| 332.5 kg | Naim Süleymanoglu | TUR |
| 335.0 kg | Naim Süleymanoglu | TUR |

70 kg Snatch Weight, Men
70 kg poids arraché, Messieurs
| 162.5 kg | Xugang Zhan | CHN |

70 kg Clean and Jerk Weight, Men
70 kg poids épaulé-jeté, Messieurs
| 195.0 kg | Xugang Zhan | CHN |

70 kg Total, Men
70 kg total, Messieurs
| 357.5 kg | Xugang Zhan | CHN |

83 kg Snatch Weight, Men
83 kg poids arraché, Messieurs
| 180.0 kg | Pyrros Dimas | GRE |

83 kg Clean and Jerk Weight, Men
83 kg poids épaulé-jeté, Messieurs
| 213.0 kg | Pyrros Dimas | GRE |
| 213.5 kg | Marc Huster | GER |

83 kg Total, Men
83 kg total, Messieurs
| 392.5 kg | Pyrros Dimas | GRE |

91 kg Snatch Weight, Men
91 kg poids arraché, Messieurs
| 187.5 kg | Aleksey Petrov | RUS |

99 kg Clean and Jerk Weight, Men
99 kg poids épaulé-jeté, Messieurs
| 235.0 kg | Akakios Kakiasvilis | GRE |

99 kg Total, Men
99 kg total, Messieurs
| 420.0 kg | Akakios Kakiasvilis | GRE |

108 kg Clean and Jerk Weight, Men
108 kg poids épaulé-jeté, Messieurs
| 235.0 kg | Timur Taymazov | UKR |

+108 kg Clean and Jerk Weight, Men
+108 kg poids épaulé-jeté, Messieurs
| 255.0 kg | Ronny Weller | GER |
| 260.0 kg | Andrey Chemerkin | RUS |

Wrestling / *Lutte*

Medals Awarded / *Médailles remises* : 60

Freestyle, 48 kg (105.5 lb), Men
Libre, 48 kg, Messieurs
Gold:	Il Kim	PRK
Silver:	Armen Mkrchyan	ARM
Bronze:	Alexis Vila Perdomo	CUB

Freestyle, 52 kg (114.5 lb), Men
Libre, 52 kg, Messieurs
Gold:	Valentin Dimitrov Jordanov	BUL
Silver:	Namik Abdullayev	AZE
Bronze:	Maulen Mamyrov	KAZ

Freestyle, 57 kg (125.5 lb), Men
Libre, 57 kg, Messieurs
Gold:	Kendall Cross	USA
Silver:	Giuvi Sissaouri	CAN
Bronze:	Yong Sam Ri	PRK

Freestyle, 62 kg (136.5 lb), Men
Libre, 62 kg, Messieurs
Gold:	Tom Brands	USA
Silver:	Jae-Sung Jang	KOR
Bronze:	Elbrus Tedeyev	UKR

Freestyle, 68 kg (149.5 lb), Men
Libre, 68 kg, Messieurs
Gold:	Vadim Bogiyev	RUS
Silver:	Townsend Saunders	USA
Bronze:	Zaza Zazirov	UKR

Freestyle, 74 kg (163 lb), Men
Libre, 74 kg, Messieurs
Gold:	Buvaysa Saytyev	RUS
Silver:	Jang-Soon Park	KOR
Bronze:	Takuya Ota	JPN

Freestyle, 82 kg (180.5 lb), Men
Libre, 82 kg, Messieurs
Gold:	Khadzhimurad Magomedov	RUS
Silver:	Hyun-Mo Yang	KOR
Bronze:	Amir Reza Khadem Azghadi	IRI

Freestyle, 90 kg (198 lb), Men
Libre, 90 kg, Messieurs
Gold:	Rasull Khadem Azghadi	IRI
Silver:	Makharbek Khadartsev	RUS
Bronze:	Eldari Kurtanidze	GEO

Freestyle, 100 kg (220 lb), Men
Libre, 100 kg, Messieurs
Gold:	Kurt Angle	USA
Silver:	Abbas Jadidi	IRI
Bronze:	Arawat Sabejew	GER

Freestyle, 130 kg (286 lb), Men
Libre, 130 kg, Messieurs
Gold:	Mahmut Demir	TUR
Silver:	Aleksey Medvedev	BLR
Bronze:	Bruce Baumgartner	USA

Greco-Roman, 48 kg (105.5 lb), Men
Gréco-romaine, 48 kg, Messieurs
Gold:	Kwon-Ho Sim	KOR
Silver:	Aleksandr Pavlov	BLR
Bronze:	Zafar Gulyov	RUS

Greco-Roman, 52 kg (114.5 lb), Men
Gréco-romaine, 52 kg, Messieurs
Gold:	Armen Nazaryan	ARM
Silver:	Brandon Paulson	USA
Bronze:	Andriy Kalashnikov	UKR

Greco-Roman, 57 kg (125.5 lb), Men
Gréco-romaine, 57 kg, Messieurs
Gold:	Yuriy Melnichenko	KAZ
Silver:	Dennis Hall	USA
Bronze:	Zetian Sheng	CHN

Greco-Roman, 62 kg (136.5 lb), Men
Gréco-romaine, 62 kg, Messieurs
Gold:	Wlodzimierz Zawadzki	POL
Silver:	Juan Luis Maren Delis	CUB
Bronze:	Mehmet Akif Pirim	TUR

Greco-Roman, 68 kg (149.5 lb), Men
Gréco-romaine, 68 kg, Messieurs
Gold:	Ryszard Wolny	POL
Silver:	Ghani Yolouz	FRA
Bronze:	Aleksandr Tretyakov	RUS

Greco-Roman, 74 kg (163 lb), Men
Gréco-romaine, 74 kg, Messieurs
Gold:	Feliberto Ascuy Aguilera	CUB
Silver:	Marko Asell	FIN
Bronze:	Jozef Tracz	POL

Greco-Roman, 82 kg (180.5 lb), Men
Gréco-romaine, 82 kg, Messieurs
Gold:	Hamza Yerlikaya	TUR
Silver:	Thomas Zander	GER
Bronze:	Valeriy Tsilent	BLR

Greco-Roman, 90 kg (198 lb), Men
Gréco-romaine, 90 kg, Messieurs
Gold:	Vyacheslav Oliynyk	UKR
Silver:	Jacek Fafinski	POL
Bronze:	Maik Bullmann	GER

Greco-Roman, 100 kg (220 lb), Men
Gréco-romaine, 100 kg, Messieurs
Gold:	Andrzej Wronski	POL
Silver:	Sergey Lishtvan	BLR
Bronze:	Mikael Ljungberg	SWE

Greco-Roman, 130 kg (286 lb), Men
Gréco-romaine, 130 kg, Messieurs
Gold:	Aleksandr Karelin	RUS
Silver:	Matt Ghaffari	USA
Bronze:	Serguei Moureiko	MDA

Yachting / *Yachting*

Medals Awarded / *Médailles remises* : 30

Board (IMCO One-Design: Mistral), Men
Planche à voile (IMCO/Mistral), Messieurs
Gold:	Nikolaos Kaklamanakis	GRE
Silver:	Carlos Mauricio Espinola	ARG
Bronze:	Gal Fridman	ISR

Board (IMCO One-Design: Mistral), Women
Planche à voile (IMCO/Mistral), Dames
Gold:	Lai Shan Lee	HKG
Silver:	Barbara Kendall	NZL
Bronze:	Alessandra Sensini	ITA

Single-Handed Dinghy (Finn), Men
Dériveur solitaire (Finn), Messieurs
Gold:	Mateusz Kusznierewicz	POL
Silver:	Sebastien Godefroid	BEL
Bronze:	Roy Heiner	NED

Single-Handed Dinghy (Europe), Women
Dériveur solitaire (Europe), Dames
Gold:	Kristine Roug	DEN
Silver:	Margriet Matthijsse	NED
Bronze:	Courtenay Becker-Dey	USA

Double-Handed Dinghy (470), Men
Dériveur à deux places (470), Messieurs
Gold:	Yevhen Braslavets Ihor Matviyenko	UKR
Silver:	John Merricks Ian Walker	GBR
Bronze:	Nuno Barreto Hugo Rocha	POR

Double-Handed Dinghy (470), Women
Dériveur à deux places (470), Dames
Gold:	Begona Via Dufresne Theresa Zabell	ESP
Silver:	Alicia Kinoshita Yumiko Shige	JPN
Bronze:	Olena Pakholchik Ruslana Taran	UKR

Dinghy (Laser), Mixed
Dériveur (Laser), Mixte
Gold:	Robert Scheidt	BRA
Silver:	Ben Ainslie	GBR
Bronze:	Peer Moberg	NOR

Multihull (Tornado), Mixed
Multicoque (Tornado), Mixte
Gold:	Jose Luis Ballester Fernando Leon	ESP
Silver:	Mitchell Booth Andrew Landenberger	AUS
Bronze:	Lars Schmidt Grael Henrique Pellicano	BRA

Two-Person Keelboat (Star), Mixed
Quillard à deux places (Star), Mixte
Gold:	Marcelo Bastos Ferreira Torben Schmidt Grael	BRA
Silver:	Bobbie Lohse Hans Wallen	SWE
Bronze:	Colin Beashel David Giles	AUS

Fleet/Match Race Keelboat (Soling), Mixed
Quillard match/racing (Soling), Mixte
Gold:	Thomas Flach Bernd Jaekel Jochen Schuemann	GER
Silver:	Dmitriy Shabanov Georgiy Shayduko Igor Skalin	RUS
Bronze:	Jim Barton Jeff Madrigali Kent Massey	USA

AQUATICS—DIVING
NATATION—PLONGEON

Abbreviations and terms used in Diving results tables
Abréviations et termes employés dans les tableaux de résultats de plongeon

Term	English	Français
B	Bronze Medal	Médaille de bronze
continued	continued	continué
Ctry	Country	Pays
Final	Final	Finale
G	Gold Medal	Médaille d'or
Name	Name	Nom
Preliminaries	Preliminaries	Eliminatoires
Pts Behind	Points Behind	Ecart en points
Q	Qualified	Qualifié
Rnk	Rank	Classement
S	Silver Medal	Médaille d'argent
Semifinals	Semifinals	Demi-finales
Total Pts	Total Points	Total des points

International Amateur Swimming Federation (FINA)
Fédération Internationale de Natation Amateur
**Avenue de Beaumont 9
1012 Lausanne
Switzerland**

• KATHY L MINNIEWEATHER • VERONICA H MINNIFIELD • CAROLYN MINNIFIELD WESSON • MICHAEL L MINNIS • ANGELA M MINOR • GAY L MINOR • MICHELLE L MINOR • WENDY K MINOR • WILLIE E MINOR • BILL MINTER • CHARLES K MINTER • CAROL E MINTON • CAROLYN J MINTON • CHOLLY P MINTON • JOHN W MINTON • ALLISAN T MINTZ • DALE R MINTZ • ELYSE L MINTZ • MARK L MINTZ • STEPHANIE MINTZ • STEPHEN ALLEN MINTZ • PETER A MIR • ROGER A MIR • JOHN J MIRABILE • IRIS C MIRACLE • KATHLEEN D MIRACLE • STEVEN MIRACLE •

15

Aquatics—Diving / *Natation—Plongeon*
3 m Springboard, Men / *Tremplin de 3 m, Messieurs*

PRELIMINARIES

Rnk	Name	Ctry	Total Pts	Pts Behind	
1	XIONG, Ni	CHN	463.02	0.00	Q
2	YU, Zhuocheng	CHN	438.93	24.09	Q
3	MURPHY, Michael	AUS	419.13	43.89	Q
4	DONIE, Scott	USA	414.03	48.99	Q
5	WELS, Andreas	GER	405.33	57.69	Q
6	SAOUTINE, Dmitri	RUS	391.74	71.28	Q
7	SEMENIOUK, Andrei	BLR	385.32	77.70	Q
8	PLATAS, Fernando	MEX	382.83	80.19	Q
9	LENZI, Mark	USA	372.03	90.99	Q
10	FRECE, Richard	AUT	365.73	97.29	Q
11	STEWART, Evan	ZIM	361.53	101.49	Q
12	VOLOD'KOV, Roman	UKR	359.85	103.17	Q
13	HEMPEL, Jan	GER	358.26	104.76	Q

PRELIMINARIES - *continued*

Rnk	Name	Ctry	Total Pts	Pts Behind	
14	COMTOIS, Philippe	CAN	357.75	105.27	Q
15	STATSENKO, Valeri	RUS	357.18	105.84	Q
16	LORENZINI, Davide	ITA	356.55	106.47	Q
17	LENGYEL, Imre	HUN	346.74	116.28	Q
18	ALI, Antonio	GBR	345.33	117.69	Q
19	BEDARD, David	CAN	342.33	120.69	
20	SJODIN, Jimmy	SWE	339.93	123.09	
21	KHAMOULKINE, Viatcheslav	BLR	331.86	131.16	
22	ANDERSSON, Joakim	SWE	331.83	131.19	
23	LAPYN, Maksym	UKR	328.23	134.79	
24	MORGAN, Bob	GBR	318.69	144.33	
25	di FAZIO, Dario	VEN	317.04	145.98	
26	SIRANIDIS, Nikolaos	GRE	316.50	146.52	

PRELIMINARIES - *continued*

Rnk	Name	Ctry	Total Pts	Pts Behind
27	IGLESIAS, Tony	BOL	307.83	155.19
28	BUTLER, Russell	AUS	305.79	157.23
29	SANDIN, Ramon	PUR	302.55	160.47
30	RODRIGUEZ, Joel	MEX	296.91	166.11
31	GIL, Jose Miguel	ESP	295.47	167.55
32	LEE, Jong-Hee	KOR	293.52	169.50
33	al-HASAN, Ali	KUW	272.40	190.62
34	PICHI, Suchat	THA	257.13	205.89
35	BIYANWILA, Janaka	SRI	247.44	215.58
36	ALVAREZ, Rafael	ESP	208.83	254.19
37	CHEN, Han-Hung	TPE	194.13	268.89
38	ZUGIC, Sinisa	YUG	181.17	281.85
39	ORINE, Serguei	TJK	162.66	300.36

SEMIFINALS

Rnk	Name	Ctry	Total Pts	Pts Behind	
1	XIONG, Ni	CHN	694.47	0.00	Q
2	YU, Zhuocheng	CHN	662.34	32.13	Q
3	MURPHY, Michael	AUS	639.21	55.26	Q
4	DONIE, Scott	USA	637.89	56.58	Q
5	SAOUTINE, Dmitri	RUS	621.48	72.99	Q
6	WELS, Andreas	GER	612.54	81.93	Q

SEMIFINALS - *continued*

Rnk	Name	Ctry	Total Pts	Pts Behind	
7	LENZI, Mark	USA	601.77	92.70	Q
8	PLATAS, Fernando	MEX	600.45	94.02	Q
9	SEMENIOUK, Andrei	BLR	587.55	106.92	Q
10	HEMPEL, Jan	GER	578.25	116.22	Q
11	STATSENKO, Valeri	RUS	574.71	119.76	Q
12	VOLOD'KOV, Roman	UKR	570.15	124.32	Q

SEMIFINALS - *continued*

Rnk	Name	Ctry	Total Pts	Pts Behind
13	STEWART, Evan	ZIM	567.96	126.51
14	FRECE, Richard	AUT	563.64	130.83
15	LORENZINI, Davide	ITA	559.35	135.12
16	COMTOIS, Philippe	CAN	551.28	143.19
17	LENGYEL, Imre	HUN	551.25	143.22
18	ALI, Antonio	GBR	548.79	145.68

FINAL

Rnk	Name	Ctry	Total Pts	Pts Behind	
1	XIONG, Ni	CHN	701.46	0.00	G
2	YU, Zhuocheng	CHN	690.93	10.53	S
3	LENZI, Mark	USA	686.49	14.97	B
4	DONIE, Scott	USA	666.93	34.53	

FINAL - *continued*

Rnk	Name	Ctry	Total Pts	Pts Behind
5	SAOUTINE, Dmitri	RUS	644.67	56.79
6	MURPHY, Michael	AUS	640.95	60.51
7	HEMPEL, Jan	GER	622.32	79.14
8	PLATAS, Fernando	MEX	619.98	81.48

FINAL - *continued*

Rnk	Name	Ctry	Total Pts	Pts Behind
9	STATSENKO, Valeri	RUS	597.69	103.77
10	SEMENIOUK, Andrei	BLR	595.56	105.90
11	VOLOD'KOV, Roman	UKR	593.13	108.33
12	WELS, Andreas	GER	583.56	117.90

Aquatics—Diving / *Natation—Plongeon*
3 m Springboard, Women / *Tremplin de 3 m, Dames*

PRELIMINARIES

Rnk	Name	Ctry	Total Pts	Pts Behind	
1	ILYINA, Vera	RUS	308.88	0.00	Q
2	LINDBERG, Anna	SWE	292.02	16.86	Q
3	ZHUPYNA, Olena	UKR	286.47	22.41	Q
4	FU, Mingxia	CHN	284.28	24.60	Q
5	BOCKNER, Claudia	GER	281.31	27.57	Q
6	MOSES, Melisa	USA	279.75	29.13	Q
7	VYGOUZOVA, Irina	KAZ	276.45	32.43	Q
8	LASHKO, Irina	RUS	271.92	36.96	Q
9	KEIM, Jenny	USA	270.48	38.40	Q
10	PISSAREVA, Iryna	UKR	269.43	39.45	

PRELIMINARIES - *continued*

Rnk	Name	Ctry	Total Pts	Pts Behind	
11	MOTOBUCHI, Yuki	JPN	262.71	46.17	Q
12	ALCALA, Maria Jose	MEX	257.01	51.87	Q
13	ROMERO, Maria Elena	MEX	252.84	56.04	Q
14	ALEXEEVA, Svetlana	BLR	246.27	62.61	Q
15	ROGERS, Jodie	AUS	242.19	66.69	Q
16	KOCH, Simona	GER	239.91	68.97	Q
17	PELLETIER, Annie	CAN	236.58	72.30	Q
18	IVANOVA, Elena	KAZ	235.50	73.38	Q
19	TOURKY, Loudy	AUS	229.11	79.77	
20	GYULBUDAKIAN, Arus	ARM	228.72	80.16	

PRELIMINARIES - *continued*

Rnk	Name	Ctry	Total Pts	Pts Behind
21	BULMER, Eryn	CAN	226.74	82.14
22	RI, Ok Rim	PRK	219.63	89.25
23	TAN, Shuping	CHN	212.49	96.39
24	d'ORIANO, Francesca	ITA	208.77	100.11
25	PINTER, Orsolya	HUN	206.52	102.36
26	CRUZ, Julia	ESP	205.32	103.56
27	ALBERTY, Vivian	PUR	195.18	113.70
28	KAZARASHVILI, Nana	GEO	191.49	117.39
29	CHLEMOVA, Natalia	TJK	180.54	128.34
30	HERNANDEZ, Daphne	CRC	151.11	157.77

SEMIFINALS

Rnk	Name	Ctry	Total Pts	Pts Behind	
1	ILYINA, Vera	RUS	539.07	0.00	Q
2	LINDBERG, Anna	SWE	512.31	26.76	Q
3	LASHKO, Irina	RUS	506.43	32.64	Q
4	FU, Mingxia	CHN	505.77	33.30	Q
5	ZHUPYNA, Olena	UKR	496.02	43.05	Q
6	MOSES, Melisa	USA	491.70	47.37	Q

SEMIFINALS - *continued*

Rnk	Name	Ctry	Total Pts	Pts Behind	
7	KEIM, Jenny	USA	481.65	57.42	Q
8	BOCKNER, Claudia	GER	481.50	57.57	Q
9	PISSAREVA, Iryna	UKR	480.66	58.41	Q
10	VYGOUZOVA, Irina	KAZ	479.31	59.76	Q
11	MOTOBUCHI, Yuki	JPN	472.71	66.36	Q
12	PELLETIER, Annie	CAN	455.34	83.73	Q

SEMIFINALS - *continued*

Rnk	Name	Ctry	Total Pts	Pts Behind
13	ALCALA, Maria Jose	MEX	450.63	88.44
14	ALEXEEVA, Svetlana	BLR	446.64	92.43
15	ROGERS, Jodie	AUS	446.37	92.70
16	KOCH, Simona	GER	444.90	94.17
17	ROMERO, Maria Elena	MEX	440.19	98.88
18	IVANOVA, Elena	KAZ	422.70	116.37

FINAL

Rnk	Name	Ctry	Total Pts	Pts Behind	
1	FU, Mingxia	CHN	547.68	0.00	G
2	LASHKO, Irina	RUS	512.19	35.49	S
3	PELLETIER, Annie	CAN	509.64	38.04	B
4	MOSES, Melisa	USA	507.99	39.69	

FINAL - *continued*

Rnk	Name	Ctry	Total Pts	Pts Behind
5	ZHUPYNA, Olena	UKR	507.27	40.41
6	MOTOBUCHI, Yuki	JPN	506.04	41.64
7	ILYINA, Vera	RUS	493.56	54.12
8	LINDBERG, Anna	SWE	489.81	57.87

FINAL - *continued*

Rnk	Name	Ctry	Total Pts	Pts Behind
9	KEIM, Jenny	USA	486.63	61.05
10	VYGOUZOVA, Irina	KAZ	475.92	71.76
11	BOCKNER, Claudia	GER	455.70	91.98
12	PISSAREVA, Iryna	UKR	448.02	99.66

Aquatics—Diving / *Natation—Plongeon*
10 m Platform, Men / *Haut vol de 10 m, Messieurs*

PRELIMINARIES

Rnk	Name	Ctry	Total Pts	Pts Behind	
1	SAOUTINE, Dmitri	RUS	452.82	0.00	Q
2	XIAO, Hailiang	CHN	445.86	6.96	Q
3	TIAN, Liang	CHN	425.73	27.09	Q
4	TIMOSHININ, Vladimir	RUS	425.43	27.39	Q
5	JEFFREY, Patrick	USA	406.74	46.08	Q
6	PICHLER, David	USA	394.59	58.23	Q
7	HEMPEL, Jan	GER	394.17	58.65	Q
8	PLATAS, Fernando	MEX	392.31	60.51	Q
9	TERAUCHI, Ken	JPN	381.51	71.31	Q
10	KOUDREVITCH, Serguei	BLR	375.90	76.92	Q
11	KUEHNE, Michael	GER	375.27	77.55	Q
12	FRECE, Richard	AUT	373.41	79.41	Q
13	CHOE, Hyong Gil	PRK	353.40	99.42	Q

PRELIMINARIES - *continued*

Rnk	Name	Ctry	Total Pts	Pts Behind	
14	SJODIN, Jimmy	SWE	352.74	100.08	Q
15	KVOTCHINSKI, Andrei	BLR	349.14	103.68	Q
16	AKHMETBEKOV, Daniar	KAZ	346.62	106.20	Q
17	MORGAN, Bob	GBR	343.20	109.62	Q
18	TAYLOR, Leon	GBR	341.70	111.12	Q
19	KANETO, Keita	JPN	339.18	113.64	
20	VOLOD'KOV, Roman	UKR	335.97	116.85	
21	MOURATOV, Samat	KAZ	335.43	117.39	
22	ACOSTA, Alberto	MEX	322.47	130.35	
23	PAVON, Daniel	ESP	312.78	140.04	
24	CHERECHES, Gabriel	ROM	309.30	143.52	
25	di FAZIO, Dario	VEN	307.02	145.80	

PRELIMINARIES - *continued*

Rnk	Name	Ctry	Total Pts	Pts Behind
26	YANCHENKO, Oleh	UKR	301.92	150.90
27	DJABRAILOV, Emil	AZE	294.93	157.89
28	LAWSON, Tony	AUS	294.75	158.07
29	PICHI, Suchat	THA	290.64	162.18
30	IGLESIAS, Tony	BOL	290.16	162.66
31	KWON, Kyung-Min	KOR	276.27	176.55
32	AVTANDILYAN, Hovannes	ARM	275.64	177.18
33	NG, Sui	HKG	273.30	179.52
34	GAKHARIA, Gocha	GEO	256.68	196.14
35	al-MATROUK, Abdul	KUW	239.79	213.03
36	CHUAN, Hung-Ping	TPE	220.89	231.93
37	VULETIC, Vukan	YUG	187.17	265.65

SEMIFINALS

Rnk	Name	Ctry	Total Pts	Pts Behind	
1	SAOUTINE, Dmitri	RUS	647.46	0.00	Q
2	XIAO, Hailiang	CHN	625.41	22.05	Q
3	TIAN, Liang	CHN	611.49	35.97	Q
4	TIMOSHININ, Vladimir	RUS	594.90	52.56	Q
5	HEMPEL, Jan	GER	591.39	56.07	Q
6	JEFFREY, Patrick	USA	581.16	66.30	Q

SEMIFINALS - *continued*

Rnk	Name	Ctry	Total Pts	Pts Behind	
7	PLATAS, Fernando	MEX	570.21	77.25	Q
8	PICHLER, David	USA	570.12	77.34	Q
9	KOUDREVITCH, Serguei	BLR	556.53	90.93	Q
10	TERAUCHI, Ken	JPN	555.90	91.56	Q
11	KUEHNE, Michael	GER	544.38	103.08	Q
12	FRECE, Richard	AUT	521.76	125.70	Q

SEMIFINALS - *continued*

Rnk	Name	Ctry	Total Pts	Pts Behind	
13	MORGAN, Bob	GBR	519.84	127.62	
14	SJODIN, Jimmy	SWE	517.74	129.72	
15	CHOE, Hyong Gil	PRK	516.66	130.80	
16	KVOTCHINSKI, Andrei	BLR	509.64	137.82	
17	AKHMETBEKOV, Daniar	KAZ	505.20	142.26	
18	TAYLOR, Leon	GBR	483.57	163.89	

FINAL

Rnk	Name	Ctry	Total Pts	Pts Behind	
1	SAOUTINE, Dmitri	RUS	692.34	0.00	G
2	HEMPEL, Jan	GER	663.27	29.07	S
3	XIAO, Hai Liang	CHN	658.20	34.14	B
4	TIAN, Liang	CHN	648.18	44.16	

FINAL - *continued*

Rnk	Name	Ctry	Total Pts	Pts Behind
5	TIMOSHININ, Vladimir	RUS	628.59	63.75
6	PICHLER, David	USA	607.11	85.23
7	PLATAS, Fernando	MEX	603.03	89.31
8	KUEHNE, Michael	GER	583.98	108.36

FINAL - *continued*

Rnk	Name	Ctry	Total Pts	Pts Behind
9	JEFFREY, Patrick	USA	560.22	132.12
10	TERAUCHI, Ken	JPN	559.89	132.45
11	KOUDREVITCH, Serguei	BLR	528.00	164.34
12	FRECE, Richard	AUT	503.64	188.70

Aquatics—Diving / *Natation—Plongeon*
10 m Platform, Women / *Haut vol de 10 m, Dames*

PRELIMINARIES

Rnk	Name	Ctry	Total Pts	Pts Behind	
1	FU, Mingxia	CHN	329.25	0.00	Q
2	RUEHL, Becky	USA	323.91	5.34	Q
3	VYGOUZOVA, Irina	KAZ	319.11	10.14	Q
4	GUO, Jingjing	CHN	315.39	13.86	Q
5	WALTER, Annika	GER	298.11	31.14	Q
6	CIOCAN, Clara	ROM	281.52	47.73	Q
7	ZHUPYNA, Olena	UKR	280.11	49.14	Q
8	KHRISTOFOROVA, Olga	RUS	268.65	60.60	Q
9	CHIKINA, Natalya	KAZ	267.18	62.07	Q
10	RICHTER, Anja	AUT	266.13	63.12	Q
11	WETZIG, Ute	GER	258.93	70.32	Q

PRELIMINARIES - *continued*

Rnk	Name	Ctry	Total Pts	Pts Behind	
12	CLARK, Mary Ellen	USA	253.89	75.36	Q
13	ALCALA, Maria Jose	MEX	252.36	76.89	Q
14	ALLEN, Hayley	GBR	251.73	77.52	Q
15	CHOE, Myong Hwa	PRK	248.10	81.15	Q
16	GUEORGUIEVA, Radoslava	BUL	246.06	83.19	Q
17	WARD, Lesley	GBR	244.98	84.27	Q
18	SERBINA, Svitlana	UKR	244.05	85.20	Q
19	ARLOW, Vyninka	AUS	243.57	85.68	
20	TIMOSHININA, Svetlana	RUS	242.76	86.49	
21	GORDON, Paige	CAN	242.13	87.12	
22	OPRIEA, Anisoara	ROM	233.34	95.91	

PRELIMINARIES - *continued*

Rnk	Name	Ctry	Total Pts	Pts Behind
23	RI, Ok Rim	PRK	230.16	99.09
24	MONTMINY, Anne	CAN	229.32	99.93
25	BAKER, Vanessa	AUS	225.84	103.41
26	HERNANDEZ, Daphne	CRC	217.77	111.48
27	SAEZ DE IBARRA, Dolores	ESP	216.36	112.89
28	d'ORIANO, Francesca	ITA	202.86	126.39
29	DANAUX, Julie	FRA	201.27	127.98
30	ITZAINA, Ana Carolina	URY	191.40	137.85
31	IM, Youn-Gi	KOR	180.15	149.10
32	KIM, Yeo-Young	KOR	166.56	162.69
33	TOMMAOROS, Sukrutai	THA	115.44	213.81

SEMIFINALS

Rnk	Name	Ctry	Total Pts	Pts Behind	
1	FU, Mingxia	CHN	509.19	0.00	Q
2	GUO, Jingjing	CHN	492.69	16.50	Q
3	RUEHL, Becky	USA	487.29	21.90	Q
4	VYGOUZOVA, Irina	KAZ	477.51	31.68	Q
5	WALTER, Annika	GER	464.25	44.94	Q
6	ZHUPYNA, Olena	UKR	451.35	57.84	Q

SEMIFINALS - *continued*

Rnk	Name	Ctry	Total Pts	Pts Behind	
7	CIOCAN, Clara	ROM	438.93	70.26	Q
8	KHRISTOFOROVA, Olga	RUS	435.72	73.47	Q
9	CLARK, Mary Ellen	USA	428.76	80.43	Q
10	RICHTER, Anja	AUT	426.96	82.23	Q
11	WETZIG, Ute	GER	410.37	98.82	Q
12	ALLEN, Hayley	GBR	410.16	99.03	Q

SEMIFINALS - *continued*

Rnk	Name	Ctry	Total Pts	Pts Behind	
13	CHOE, Myong Hwa	PRK	409.35	99.84	
14	SERBINA, Svitlana	UKR	409.11	100.08	
15	CHIKINA, Natalya	KAZ	405.78	103.41	
16	GUEORGUIEVA, Radoslava	BUL	402.54	106.65	
17	ALCALA, Maria Jose	MEX	400.35	108.84	
18	WARD, Lesley	GBR	395.97	113.22	

FINAL

Rnk	Name	Ctry	Total Pts	Pts Behind	
1	FU, Mingxia	CHN	521.58	0.00	G
2	WALTER, Annika	GER	479.22	42.36	S
3	CLARK, Mary Ellen	USA	472.95	48.63	B
4	RUEHL, Becky	USA	455.19	66.39	

FINAL - *continued*

Rnk	Name	Ctry	Total Pts	Pts Behind
5	GUO, Jingjing	CHN	447.21	74.37
6	ZHUPYNA, Olena	UKR	437.01	84.57
7	VYGOUZOVA, Irina	KAZ	432.60	88.98
8	KHRISTOFOROVA, Olga	RUS	426.12	95.46

FINAL - *continued*

Rnk	Name	Ctry	Total Pts	Pts Behind
9	ALLEN, Hayley	GBR	418.11	103.47
10	CIOCAN, Clara	ROM	413.46	108.12
11	RICHTER, Anja	AUT	408.45	113.13
12	WETZIG, Ute	GER	367.35	154.23

CHARLES A MITCHELL • CHARLES S MITCHELL • CLARA J MITCHELL • CLYDE K MITCHELL • COLLEEN D MITCHELL • CURTISS H MITCHELL • DARROL L MITCHELL • DAVID J MITCHELL • DEBORAH M MITCHELL • DEBRA D MITCHELL • DIANE T MITCHELL • DREXEL D MITCHELL • EDITH C MITCHELL • ELIZABETH S MITCHELL • ELNETTA D MITCHELL • ERIK D MITCHELL • ERYLENE MITCHELL • FRACHETTE C MITCHELL • GREGORY C MITCHELL • GRETA F MITCHELL • HAL MITCHELL • HAROLD E MITCHELL • HOWARD C MITCHELL • JACQULELINE MITCHELL • JAMES E MITCHELL • JAN Q MITCHELL • JANE B MITCHELL • JEFFREY S MITCHELL • JOE E MITCHELL • JOSIE MITCHELL • JUDY A MITCHELL • JUSTINE K MITCHELL • KAREN A MITCHELL • KAREN B MITCHELL • KATHRYN J MITCHELL • KAY M MITCHELL • KHARI MITCHELL • LARISA L MITCHELL • LARRY B MITCHELL • LAURA A MITCHELL • LEBREAN MITCHELL • LORRAINE K MITCHELL • MAGDALENE MITCHELL • MALCOLM L MITCHELL • MARC K MITCHELL • MATTHEW B MITCHELL • MATTHEW S MITCHELL • MATTHEW W MITCHELL • MELINDA A MITCHELL • MICHELLE R MITCHELL • MILDRED M MITCHELL • OMAR MITCHELL • PAMELA D MITCHELL • PAUL M MITCHELL • REGINALD MITCHELL • RELISA E MITCHELL • RICHARD D MITCHELL • RICHARD L MITCHELL • RUFUS J MITCHELL • RUTH E MITCHELL • SAMUEL J MITCHELL • SANDIE M MITCHELL • SANDRA MITCHELL • SANDRA G MITCHELL • SEBASTIAN MITCHELL • SHARON MITCHELL • SHARON A MITCHELL • SHARON R MITCHELL • SHURHEA MITCHELL • SID E MITCHELL • STEPHANIE M MITCHELL • SUBIRA D MITCHELL • SUE MITCHELL • SUSAN I MITCHELL • SUSAN M MITCHELL • TANGELA MITCHELL • TARA L MITCHELL • THERESA A MITCHELL • THOMAS J MITCHELL • THOMAS J MITCHELL • TRACY LEON MITCHELL • URSULA F MITCHELL • VALENCIA Y MITCHELL • VICKIE D MITCHELL • VICTORIA V MITCHELL • WILLIAM MITCHELL • WILLIAM P MITCHELL • IDA M MITCHELL-HINTON • CLAUDETTE MITCHELL ALI • PHILLIP D MITCHELLJHORDAN • RICHARD A MITCHEM • JANICE H MITCHENER • SARAH JANE MITCHUM • SAMARENDRANATH MITRA • JEVON C MITSUOKA • SINHAN E MITTLEIDER • JENNIFER MITZEL • KAZUHIDE MIURA • JOSE MIURA-LOPEZ • JUNKO MIWA • DELIA S MIXON • GRETCHEN M MIXON • JOE H MIXON • ROBERT W MIXON • TERRY B MIXSON • TAKASHI MIYAMOTO • YORIKO MIYAO • AMBREY L MIZE • CHRISTINE J MIZE • ELIZABETH H MIZE • LAVONNE S MIZELL • MICHAEL E MIZELL • NICOLE M MIZELL • SARA L MIZELL • SHANNON MIZELL • THOMAS J MIZELL • DAVID L MIZELLE • DEBRA A MIZERAK • MIRIAM MIZRAHI • KUMI MIZUNO • JANUSZ K MLYNARZ • SHARON LEE MNICH • MARY L MOAK • CHARLES L MOATES • VADAREE H MOATES • STEVE M MOATS • FARNAZ MOAZZAM • BERTHE MOBASSER • SEYED MEHDI MOBINI • ALAN B MOBLEY • CAROLYN A MOBLEY • CHANDA N MOBLEY • DAN H MOBLEY • DEBORAH B MOBLEY • ELIZABETH P MOBLEY • JOHN L MOBLEY • LISA A MOBLEY • MANDY L MOBLEY • MARY A MOBLEY • MICHAEL K MOBLEY • MICHAEL W MOBLEY • MIKE MOBLEY • VIRGINIA L MOBLEY • WILLIAM E MOBLEY • NAOKO MOCHIZUKI • GARY MOCK • JENNIE C MOCK • SUSAN MOCK • WILLIAM H MOCK • BOBBI K MOCK SAT • DAVID M MOCKETT • MARCIA J MODAY • NIA MODESTE • TRENT D MODGLIN • JACK C MODLIN • SUSAN E MODRAK • BEIJOO V MODY • SHALIN H MODY • IMKE MOEBUS • JAMES MOED • NELL A MOELING • BRAD M MOELLER • CHRISTINA MOELLER • CLIFTON W MOELLER • DAVID B MOELLER • DORIS H MOELLER • ERIK MOELLER • JAYNE S MOELLER • JEAN S MOELLER • KRISTEN L MOELLER • L. HOMER MOELLER • PATRICK E MOELLER • JARAH MOESCH • PETER M MOESCHEN • NATALIE J MOESS • GREGORY K MOFFATT • LESLIE L MOFFATT • STACEY G MOFFATT • CONNIE A MOFFETT • DIANE S MOFFETT • DANI M MOFFIT • KELLY A MOG • IDAH L MOGANETSI • WUBESHT MOGES • PIETRO E MOGIANESI • CINDY R MOGIL • MICHELE T MOGILSKI • MILTON A MOGREN • BENEDETH U MOH • OMER A MOHAMED • ZIAD M MOHAMED • HANI H MOHAMMED • ARUN V MOHAN • JOHN R MOHAR • EDWARD MOHME • NANCY M MOHME • CRISSY J MOHR • ELIZABETH N MOHR • JOHN H MOHR • KIMBERLY D MOHRMANN • CHRISTIANE MOHRSTEDT • JAMES A MOHS • PHILIP MOISE • DERRICK L MOITE • DANIEL S MOJAHEDI • AMLAN KISHOR MOJUMDAR • SANHITA MOJUMDAR • MOHSEN M MOKHLESI • RIDHA MOKNI PHD • REBECCA N MOKOTO • RENE MOLBORN • GONZALO MOLINA • MARIROSA MOLINA • MONICA MOLINA • SUSAN V MOLINARO • GIANIRA M MOLINARY • DIANE MOLINE • GARY L MOLINE • JILL MOLINE • KERRY E MOLINELLI • MELISSA C MOLINERO • PAUL MOLL • WILLIAM R MOLL • DORERLINE E MOLL-PERSON • THAD W MOLLANDS • JAMES C MOLLEN • AMY J MOLLER • DALE R MOLLER • LISA M MOLLICHELLA • BETH A MOLLINEAUX • ANNE C MOLLOY • EBEN MOLLOY • BROOKE E MOLNAR • CHARLENE R MOLNAR • CHRISTIAN C MOLNAR • CHRISTINE A MOLNAR • FREDERICK J MOLNAR • NINA B MOLNAR •

SARA E MOLNAR • STEPHEN F MOLNAR • JO F MOLOCK • KEVIN D MOLONEY • CATHERINE B MOLONY • BRENDA S MOLTON • SARA MOMPART • ANNE P MONAGHAN • HILDA MONAGHAN • MARY E MONAGHAN • MARY E MONAGHAN • PATRICK D MONAGHAN • JAMES C MONAGHAN JR • DAN MONAHAN • DEANA A MONAHAN • SHARLENE S MONAHAN • KEITUMETSE D MONAISA • RUTH T. MONCHIL • PAMELA M MONCREE • CLARENCE L MONCRIEF • GAY A MONCRIEF • MYRA A MONCRIEF • JAMES V MONCUS • DOUGLAS E MONDA • ROSE K MONDAY • SHARON H MONDAY • DAVID P MONDECAR • ANNE S MONEY • JEFFREY PAUL MONEY • SUZANNE S MONEY • MIRIAM M MONGES • JOHN C MONGEY • SHAWN MONIER • CHRISTOPHER B MONK • JANET P MONK • JENNIFER MONK • MELISSA MONK • RUBY I MONK • SARAH C MONK • JOE C MONKS • STACEY R MONN • KATHERINE L MONNIER • SIRIBOA A MONRO • ASHLEY D MONROE • CORETTA L MONROE • DIANE H MONROE • GARY B MONROE • GERALD T MONROE • RONALD L MONROE • STEPHAN S MONROE • JEFFREY S MONROE ATC • ROBIN A MONSKY • CARL D MONSON • RENE S MONTAIGNE • ADA M MONTALVO • IVETTE S MONTALVO • JAIME E MONTALVO • LAREE H MONTALVO • RICHARD MONTALVO • MELANIE N MONTANARI • SUSAN A MONTANARO • ROBERTO MONTANEZ • LENORA M MONTAVON MT • KEVIN MONTE DE RAMOS • JORGE A MONTEAGUDO • ENRIQUE MONTERO • MANUEL ROBERTO MONTERO • EDGAR R MONTERROSO • THERESE M MONTESI • MICKEY Y MONTEVIDEO • YAHNICA C MONTFORD • ANN F MONTGOMERY • CAROL A MONTGOMERY • CAROL T MONTGOMERY • CAROL W MONTGOMERY • DAVID K MONTGOMERY • ERIKA P MONTGOMERY • JAMES C MONTGOMERY • JAMES D MONTGOMERY • JAMES M MONTGOMERY • JOHN C MONTGOMERY • JOHN C MONTGOMERY • JULIE P MONTGOMERY • LADELL MONTGOMERY • LAURA A MONTGOMERY • LEIGH H MONTGOMERY • LINDA K MONTGOMERY • LINDA S MONTGOMERY • LORI A MONTGOMERY • MAGGIE A MONTGOMERY • MARY R MONTGOMERY • MERCEDES F MONTGOMERY • MERCY B MONTGOMERY • MILLICENT W MONTGOMERY • PAMELA A MONTGOMERY • PAT J MONTGOMERY • PATRICIA MONTGOMERY • SHERON R MONTGOMERY • TERRACITA F MONTGOMERY • THERESA C MONTGOMERY • THERESA L MONTGOMERY • TIFFANY M MONTGOMERY • TODD C MONTGOMERY • WILLIAM D MONTGOMERY • MICHAEL W MONTGOMERY ATC • BONITA MONTGOMERY TAYLOR • DIANE B MONTI • ROBERT A MONTI JR • GESSICA MONTICONE • STACEY L MONTOOTH • CLAUDIA L MONTOYA • BRENDA L MONYER • JOHN C MOODIE • ALFONZO O MOODY • BEVERLY A MOODY • CURTIS B MOODY • EDNA M MOODY • EMORY MOODY • HORACE W MOODY • JONATHAN M MOODY • KATHY L MOODY • KAYE G MOODY • MARY J MOODY • NANCY E MOODY • PAUL H MOODY • PAULA S MOODY • ROXANN MOODY • STEPHEN W MOODY • TARA L MOODY • THOMAS W MOODY • WILLIAM L MOODY • RENEE MOOG • DAVID J MOOK • CHRISTINE K MOOMEY • BEVERLY A MOON • CHARLES A MOON • CINDY K MOON • DAVID L MOON • DAVID S MOON • DELBERT E MOON • ELIZABETH P MOON • GIZELLA K MOON • HAESUN MOON • JEONG H MOON • JOSEPH C MOON • JUDY F MOON • JULIE S MOON • JUNG LAN L MOON • MELISSA Z MOON • RODNEY G MOON • SUNGHWAN MOON • TERRY L MOON • WILLIAM J MOON • BARBARA J MOONEY • CHARLES E MOONEY • CLIFFORD T MOONEY • MEGAN MOONEY • NANCY B MOONEY • WILLIAM G MOONEY • SHELIA A MOONEY WELTON • ALICE M MOORE • ALICIA K MOORE • ANGELA MOORE • ANTHONY MOORE • BARBARA A MOORE • BARBARAANN MOORE • BARRY E MOORE • BELINDA G MOORE • BELINDA R MOORE • BEN G MOORE • BENJAMIN F MOORE • BERNARD MOORE • BERNICE G MOORE • BETH S MOORE • BETTY A MOORE • BETTY E MOORE • BEVERLY C MOORE • BONITA L MOORE • BRIAN L MOORE • BRITT H MOORE • CAROL A MOORE • CAROL A MOORE • CAROL H MOORE • CAROL SUE MOORE • CARY MOORE • CASSANDRA G MOORE • CELIA W MOORE • CHARLES A MOORE • CHARLES C MOORE • CHARLES E MOORE • CHARLES E MOORE • CHARLES L MOORE • CHARLES W MOORE • CHRISTOPHER H MOORE • CHRISTOPHER J MOORE • CLARENCE J MOORE • CLIFTON E MOORE • CONNIE L MOORE • COURTNEY F MOORE • CURTIS A MOORE • CYNTHIA A MOORE • CYNTHIA L MOORE • CYNTHIA L MOORE • CYNTHIA W MOORE • DANIEL C MOORE • DAVID B MOORE • DAVID C MOORE • DAVID L MOORE • DAVID S MOORE • DEBRA D MOORE • DELLA F MOORE • DENISE MOORE • DENISE MOORE • DENISE K MOORE • DIANA K MOORE • DOLORES M MOORE • DONNA L MOORE • DONNA M MOORE • DOROTHY A MOORE • DOROTHY C MOORE • DOUGLASS M MOORE • E.J. MOORE • EDGAR F MOORE • ERIC N MOORE • ERICA L MOORE • EUGENE I MOORE • EVANDA G MOORE • EVERLINE MOORE • FANNIE L MOORE • FAYE B MOORE • FRANCES D MOORE • FRANKIE MOORE • GLENDA M MOORE • GLENN V MOORE • GWEN M MOORE • HAROLD E MOORE • HOWARD L MOORE • HULON S MOORE • IOULIA A MOORE • JACK MOORE • JACK E MOORE • JAMES H MOORE • JAMES H MOORE • JAMES N MOORE • JAMES P MOORE • JAN MOORE • JANE A MOORE • JANE C MOORE • JEANNETTE L MOORE • JEFF F MOORE • JEFFREY H MOORE • JENNIFER B MOORE

• JENNIFER K MOORE • JERE N MOORE • JEREMIAH MOORE • JERLYN V MOORE • JERRY W MOORE • JIMMIE J MOORE • JOE W MOORE • JOHN F MOORE • JOHN S MOORE • JOHN W MOORE • JOHN WHITMAN MOORE • JOHNITA M MOORE • JOHNNY L MOORE • JON S MOORE • JONATHAN W MOORE • JOY B MOORE • JUDITH R MOORE • JUDY E MOORE • JUDY J MOORE • JULIA M MOORE • JULIE C MOORE • KAREN C MOORE • KATHY K MOORE • KELLEY D MOORE • KELLY L MOORE • KENDALE A MOORE • KEVIN A MOORE • KIMBERLEE A MOORE • KOHLEN L MOORE • KRISTEN MOORE • LESLEE A MOORE • LINDA F MOORE • LINDA K MOORE • LINDSEY MOORE • LORI A MOORE • LUEGENIA D MOORE • M DAVID MOORE • MARCUS MOORE • MARCUS O MOORE • MARGARET A MOORE • MARGARET C MOORE • MARGARET M MOORE • MARILYN B MOORE • MARILYN T MOORE • MARK A MOORE • MARK S MOORE • MARTHA L MOORE • MARY MOORE • MARY A MOORE • MATHEW S MOORE • MATT W MOORE • MATTHEW J MOORE • MELINDA A MOORE • MELISSA MOORE • MELVIN R MOORE • MICHAEL A MOORE • MICHAEL K MOORE • MICHEL A MOORE • MICHELLE D MOORE • MILFORD A MOORE • MONIQUE M MOORE • NADINE D MOORE • NANCY B MOORE • NANCY B MOORE • NEILL A MOORE • NICHELLE I MOORE • OTIS L MOORE • PATRICIA A MOORE • PATTI A MOORE • PEGGY A MOORE • PHILIP M MOORE • REBECCA D MOORE • RICHARD M MOORE • ROBERT T MOORE • ROBIN M MOORE • ROBYN K MOORE • RONALD E MOORE • RUAL R MOORE • RUDOLPH MOORE • RUTH M MOORE • SAMUEL J MOORE • SHARON D MOORE • SHARON G MOORE • SHAWN R MOORE • SHERRY A MOORE • STEPHANIE E MOORE • STEPHEN L MOORE • SUSAN A MOORE • SUSAN E MOORE • SUSAN H MOORE • SUZANNE H MOORE • TAMIKA MOORE • TERRA A MOORE • TERRI L MOORE • VALERIE J MOORE • VALERIE M MOORE • VANESSA G MOORE • VICKIE M MOORE • VICTORIA E MOORE • VIRGINIA MOORE • VIVIAN J MOORE • WINFRED G MOORE • MARGARET A. MOORE-JACKSON • JAN MOORE-KIRKLAND • JEANNE M MOORE-SHAMLEY • KENNETH B MOORE ATC • REBECCA G MOORE ATC • RODERICK G MOORE CATC • ROZALYN K MOORE CATC • HENRY B MOORE JR • JAMES MOORE JR • PAUL M MOORE JR • THOMAS J MOORE MD • PAMELA E MOORE SAT • CHARLOTTE A MOOREHEAD • DONALD M MOOREHEAD JR • ARLETTE C MOORER • DANA L MOORHEAD • DARA M MOORHEAD • JAMES L MOORHEAD • BANKS A MOORMAN • DAVID MOORMAN • FRANCIS D MOORMAN • JEANETTE E MOORMAN • MICHELLE R MOORMAN • JAMES N MOOTREY • SHERIE L MOR • CHARLES H MORA • MARY M MORADI • TOM MORAETES • ALEXIS MORAITAKIS • AMANDA MORALES • BRIAN A MORALES • EFRAIN H MORALES • KATHLEEN A MORALES • LINDA M MORALES • EDWENNA MORALES-RODRIGUEZ • ANA C MORALES COTO • CONSUELO N MORALETA • ALLEN L MORAN • BARBARA MORAN • BARBARA L MORAN • CHRISTIAN MORAN • DONNA MORAN • JAMES T MORAN • JANET M MORAN • MARK E MORAN • MAUREEN MORAN • RICHARD A MORAN • SEAN R MORAN • SHARON L MORAN • JEAN L MORAN MT • GARY W MORAND • WANDA B MORANT • GOKTUG MORCOL • DALE T MORDEN • HAROLD MOREAU • MARY M MOREHEAD • ROWENA E MOREHOUSE • ANA N MOREIRA • ANDREA S MOREIRA • SUSANA B MOREIRA • MICHAEL E MOREL • STEVEN C MORELAND • JOHN A MORELAND III • ROGER W MORELL • MATTHEW J MORELLI ATC • BETH P MOREMAN • LORI E MORENCY • GEORGE L MORENO • GERRY S MORENO • MATTHEW G MORENO • SAMUEL MORENO • SANDRA MORENO • BRYAN S MORENS • SHEILA N MORENS • BETHANY E MORETON • MARIJANE MORETTI • KIMBERLY W MORETZ • SANDRA L MORETZ • ALEXANDER MORGAN • ANDREA MORGAN • ANTHONY W MORGAN • ARIADNE MORGAN • ARLYN D MORGAN • BARBARA R MORGAN • BARRY S MORGAN • BERNARD MORGAN • BOBBIE J MORGAN • CHRISTINE E MORGAN • DANIEL J MORGAN • DAVID C MORGAN • DAVID L MORGAN • DAVID L MORGAN • DEBBIE D MORGAN • DENNIS L MORGAN • DREW A MORGAN • DUANE E MORGAN • ERIS V MORGAN • EVA J MORGAN • FREDERICK W MORGAN • GINGER L MORGAN • GLORIA R MORGAN • GWEN MORGAN • JAMES F MORGAN • JAMES T MORGAN • JANE MORGAN • JENE MORGAN • JENNIFER J MORGAN • JOHN E MORGAN • JOHN E MORGAN • JULIET M MORGAN • KELLY A MORGAN • LARK A MORGAN • LEANNA R MORGAN • LEIGH L MORGAN • LINDA F MORGAN • MAGGIE A MORGAN • MARC MORGAN • MARIANNE P MORGAN • MARK J MORGAN • MARTHA M MORGAN • MICHAEL MORGAN • MICHELE L MORGAN • MONIQUE J MORGAN • MYRTLE J MORGAN • NATHANIEL MORGAN • PATRICIA A MORGAN • PAUL D MORGAN • PHILLIP S MORGAN • POLLY V MORGAN • RANDALL D MORGAN • RENITA F MORGAN • ROBERT DALE MORGAN • ROBERT G MORGAN • SANDRA A MORGAN • SCOTT MORGAN • SCOTT R MORGAN • SUSAN R MORGAN • THOMAS L MORGAN • THOMASINE C MORGAN • VIVA A MORGAN • WAYMAN L MORGAN • YVONNE A MORGAN • SANDRA D MORGAN-HILL • WILBERT G MORGAN JR • ALLA B MORGULYAN • RUMIKO MORI • MARCIA M MORI SUSMILCH • JOHN R MORIARITY • TOMOKO MORIKAWA • DENITA J MORIN • DOMINIQUE J MORIN • MARC A MORIN • MICHAEL A MORIN • PAULINE T MORIN • A.K. MORISON • GAY S MORISON • GORDON C MORISON • JAMES A MORISON • MARY V MORISON • CHAD MORITZ •

AQUATICS—SWIMMING
NATATION—NATATION

Abbreviations and terms used in Swimming results tables
Abréviations et termes employés dans les tableaux de résultats de natation

Term	English	Français
B	Bronze Medal	Médaille de bronze
Ctry	Country	Pays
DNS	Did Not Start	Absent au départ
DQ	Disqualified	Disqualifié
Final	Final	Finale
G	Gold Medal	Médaille d'or
Heat	Heat	Série
Ln	Lane	Couloir
Name	Name	Nom
O	Olympic Record	Record olympique
Result	Result	Résultat
Rnk	Rank	Classement
S	Silver Medal	Médaille d'argent
W	World Record	Record du monde

International Amateur Swimming Federation (FINA)
Fédération Internationale de Natation Amateur
Avenue de Beaumont 9
1012 Lausanne
Switzerland

Aquatics—Swimming / *Natation—Natation*

50 m Freestyle, Men / *50 m nage libre, Messieurs*

HEAT 1

Rnk	Ln	Name	Ctry	Result
1	4	LAWRENCE, Woody	DMA	27.88
2	5	NAZIM, Moosa	MDV	28.37
3	3	MAKOSSO, Rene	CGO	30.00

HEAT 2

Rnk	Ln	Name	Ctry	Result
1	6	RIVERA, Khemo	ISV	24.62
2	3	HINDS, Howard	AHO	24.63
3	5	HUANG, Chih-Yung	TPE	24.89
4	2	CARRILLO CANELA, Alfredo	PAR	24.91
5	1	COLLIER, Michael	SLE	34.21
	4	BAKARE, Musa	NGR	DNS

HEAT 3

Rnk	Ln	Name	Ctry	Result
1	3	TONGUE, Nick	NZL	23.73
2	4	LI, Arthur	HKG	23.77
3	5	CAZMIRCIUC, Maxim	MDA	23.78
4	6	BOLLINGER, Darrick	GUM	23.97
5	2	BERBEROGLU, Kaan	TUR	24.37
6	1	KEREKJARTO, Tamas	HUN	24.67
7	8	SNG, Ju Wei	SIN	25.04
8	7	GULIYEV, Emil	AZE	25.23

HEAT 4

Rnk	Ln	Name	Ctry	Result
1	8	MATSUSHITA, Yukihiro	JPN	23.60
2	4	ILES, Salim	ALG	23.61
2	5	BLOMQVIST, Janne	FIN	23.61
4	3	NACHAYEV, Ravil	UZB	23.93
5	6	ZINHOM, Tamer	EGY	24.02
6	7	XAVIER, Sebastian	IND	24.15
7	2	LONCAR, Alen	CRO	24.17
8	1	VASILEV, Vitaliy	KGZ	24.54

HEAT 5

Rnk	Ln	Name	Ctry	Result
1	5	BRINN, Sion	JAM	23.35
2	8	MIHAELIDES, Stavros	CYP	23.37
3	6	LINSCHEER, Enrico	SUR	23.45
4	4	LEGAULT, Hugues	CAN	23.63
5	1	TRINDADE, Paulo	POR	23.73
6	7	BERA, Richard	INA	23.80
7	3	O'HARE, Nicholas	IRL	24.03
	2	IOANOVICI, Alexandru	ROM	DQ

HEAT 6

Rnk	Ln	Name	Ctry	Result
1	1	BUSQUETS, Ricardo	PUR	22.61
2	4	DELGADO, Felipe	ECU	23.26
3	2	BORISENKO, Sergey	KAZ	23.29
3	8	SEI, Indrek	EST	23.29
5	7	KIZIEROWSKI, Bartosz	POL	23.34
6	6	BENAVIDES, Juan	ESP	23.36
7	3	LINDSTROM, Par	SWE	23.47
8	5	GIZIOTIS, George	GRE	23.56

HEAT 7

Rnk	Ln	Name	Ctry	Result
1	1	JIANG, Chengji	CHN	22.55
2	3	ZIKARSKY, Bengt	GER	22.68
2	8	SANCHEZ, Francisco	VEN	22.68
4	6	GUSPERTI, Rene	ITA	22.85
5	2	KHNYKIN, Pavlo	UKR	22.91
6	7	MAZUOLIS, Raimundas	LTU	22.98
7	5	LUDERITZ, Alexander	GER	23.06
8	4	MEOLANS, Jose	ARG	23.21

HEAT 8

Rnk	Ln	Name	Ctry	Result
1	4	HALL, Gary, Jr.	USA	22.36
2	2	DEDEKIND, Brendon	RSA	22.60
3	5	de QUIROZ SCHERER, Fernando	BRA	22.68
4	6	FOSTER, Mark	GBR	22.73
5	1	VLASOV, Yuriy	UKR	22.77
6	3	KALFAYAN, Christophe	FRA	22.83
7	7	PREDKIN, Vladimir	RUS	23.03
8	8	KALINOVSKIY, Dmitriy	BLR	23.61

HEAT 9

Rnk	Ln	Name	Ctry	Result
1	4	POPOV, Aleksander	RUS	22.22
2	5	FOX, David	USA	22.64
3	8	MURRAY, Allan	BAH	22.75
4	2	van den HOOGENBAND, Pieter	NED	22.82
5	3	BORGES, Gustavo Franca	BRA	22.86
6	6	FYDLER, Chris	AUS	22.98
7	1	RUKHLEVICH, Oleg	BLR	23.12
8	7	BRUCK, Yoav	ISR	23.22

FINAL B

Rnk	Ln	Name	Ctry	Result
1	2	van den HOOGENBAND, Pieter	NED	22.67
2	4	ZIKARSKY, Bengt	GER	22.73
3	6	VLASOV, Yuriy	UKR	22.82
4	3	MURRAY, Allan	BAH	22.92
4	8	BORGES, Gustavo Franca	BRA	22.92
6	1	GUSPERTI, Rene	ITA	22.96
6	7	KALFAYAN, Christophe	FRA	22.96
8	5	FOSTER, Mark	GBR	23.01

FINAL A

Rnk	Ln	Name	Ctry	Result
1	4	POPOV, Aleksander	RUS	22.13 G
2	5	HALL, Gary, Jr.	USA	22.26 S
3	1	de QUIROZ SCHERER, Fernando	BRA	22.29 B
4	3	JIANG, Chengji	CHN	22.33
5	6	DEDEKIND, Brendon	RSA	22.59
6	7	FOX, David	USA	22.68
7	8	SANCHEZ, Francisco	VEN	22.72
8	2	BUSQUETS, Ricardo	PUR	22.73

Aquatics—Swimming / *Natation—Natation*

50 m Freestyle, Women / *50 m nage libre, Dames*

HEAT 1

Rnk	Ln	Name	Ctry	Result
1	5	POPCHENKO, Yelena	BLR	27.18
2	3	PURI, Sangeeta	IND	28.02
3	2	PRONO TONANEZ, Veronica	PAR	28.40
4	4	RIZZO, Gail	MLT	28.43
5	6	VO TRAN TRUONG, An	VIE	29.02
6	7	LOUIS, Ingrid	MRI	29.56
7	1	BAKALE, Monika	CGO	34.43
8	8	GURUNG, Nishma	NEP	41.45

HEAT 2

Rnk	Ln	Name	Ctry	Result
1	4	FITCH, Alison	NZL	26.74
2	1	SEO, So-Yung	KOR	27.30
3	2	LAKOS, Gyongyver	HUN	27.34
4	5	MOODIE, Teresa	ZIM	27.38
5	8	RADAN, Duska	YUG	27.62
6	3	UJCIC, Gabrijela	CRO	27.63
7	7	OZOLINA, Agnese	LAT	27.65
8	6	THOMSON, Gillian	PHI	28.51

HEAT 3

Rnk	Ln	Name	Ctry	Result
1	8	DIEZI, Dominique	SUI	26.57
2	2	COPARROPA ALEMAN, Eileen	PAN	26.67
3	4	SALMELA, Minna	FIN	26.72
4	1	DAHL, Monica	NAM	26.76
5	6	SIGURDARDOTTIR, Elin	ISL	26.90
6	5	ALVAREZ, Valeria	ARG	27.12
7	3	YEO, Joscelin	SIN	27.51
	7	MAHAIRA, Antonia	GRE	DNS

50 m Freestyle, Women / *50 m nage libre, Dames*

HEAT 4

Rnk	Ln	Name	Ctry	Result
1	4	PETRUTYTE, Laura	LTU	26.13
2	2	JOHANSEN, Vibeke	NOR	26.22
3	6	DRAXLER, Judith	AUT	26.34
4	5	CERON, Blanca	ESP	26.39
5	7	SPARAVEC, Metka	SLO	26.43
6	3	DESSUREAULT, Martine	CAN	26.44
7	8	NIELSEN, Mette	DEN	26.50
8	1	LEGLER, Casey	FRA	26.52

HEAT 5

Rnk	Ln	Name	Ctry	Result
1	4	MARTINO, Angel	USA	25.47
2	5	SHAN, Ying	CHN	25.71
3	6	MARTINDALE, Leah	BAR	25.76
4	3	van WIRDUM, Karin	AUS	25.88
5	7	YERMAKOVA, Yevgeniya	KAZ	25.97
6	2	RYAN, Sarah	AUS	26.34
7	1	KRIEL, Marianne	RSA	26.42
8	8	ZELVIENE, Dita	LTU	26.55

HEAT 6

Rnk	Ln	Name	Ctry	Result
1	4	VAN DYKEN, Amy	USA	25.12
2	5	VOLKER, Sandra	GER	25.45
3	3	OLOFSSON, Linda	SWE	25.84
4	6	MUIS, Marianne	GER	25.93
5	2	OSYGUS, Simone	GER	26.00
6	1	ROLPH, Susan	GBR	26.39
7	7	DOBRESCU, Liliana	ROM	26.47
8	8	LIN, Chien-Ju	TPE	27.00

HEAT 7

Rnk	Ln	Name	Ctry	Result
1	4	LE, Jingyi	CHN	25.10
2	5	MESHCHERYAKOVA, Natalya	RUS	25.73
3	3	MINAMOTO, Sumika	JPN	25.89
4	6	POSTMA, Angela	NED	26.00
5	7	FRANCO, Claudia	ESP	26.17
6	1	ELWANI, Rania	EGY	26.26
7	8	CROPPER, Siobhan	TRI	26.29
8	2	NICHOLLS, Laura	CAN	26.52

FINAL B

Rnk	Ln	Name	Ctry	Result
1	3	MUIS, Marianne	NED	25.74
2	2	POSTMA, Angela	NED	25.82
3	8	FRANCO, Claudia	ESP	26.04
4	5	MINAMOTO, Sumika	JPN	26.05
5	6	YERMAKOVA, Yevgeniya	KAZ	26.06
6	7	OSYGUS, Simone	GER	26.16
7	4	VAN WIRDUM, Karin	AUS	26.17
8	1	PETRUTYTE, Laura	LTU	26.36

FINAL A

Rnk	Ln	Name	Ctry	Result	
1	5	VAN DYKEN, Amy	USA	24.87	G
2	4	LE, Jingyi	CHN	24.90	S
3	3	VOELKER, Sandra	GER	25.14	B
4	6	MARTINO, Angel	USA	25.31	
5	1	MARTINDALE, Leah	BAR	25.49	
6	8	OLOFSSON, Linda	SWE	25.63	
7	2	SHAN, Ying	CHN	25.70	
8	7	MESHCHERYAKOVA, Natalya	RUS	25.88	

Aquatics—Swimming / *Natation—Natation*

100 m Freestyle, Men / *100 m nage libre, Messieurs*

HEAT 1

Rnk	Ln	Name	Ctry	Result
1	4	BOLLINGER, Darrick	GUM	52.68
2	5	ROBERTS, Kenny	SEY	52.89
3	6	MULARONI, Diego	SMR	57.11
4	3	al-DHAHERI, Khuwaiter	UAE	57.70
	2	al GAZALI, Ali	YEM	DNS

HEAT 2

Rnk	Ln	Name	Ctry	Result
1	1	MAZUOLIS, Raimundas	LTU	50.27
2	3	GOJKOVIC, Janko	BIH	51.28
3	2	YIZIOTIS, Georgios	GRE	52.04
4	7	KOH, Yun-Ho	KOR	52.56
5	4	KALABIC, Nikola	YUG	52.98
6	6	PERDOMO CUENCA, Diego	COL	53.01
7	8	SNG, Ju Wei	SIN	53.50
8	5	BOCANEGRA SCHALL, Juan Luis	GUA	54.05

HEAT 3

Rnk	Ln	Name	Ctry	Result
1	1	ASHIHMIN, Sergey	KGZ	51.07
2	6	LINSCHEER, Giovanni	SUR	51.82
3	8	LI, Arthur	HKG	51.84
4	4	ISAZA CHU, Jose	PAN	51.86
5	3	TSVETKOVSKIY, Oleg	UZB	52.39
6	2	MIHAELIDES, Stavros	CYP	52.65
7	5	CAZMIRCIUC, Maxim	MDA	53.18
8	7	HUANG, Chih-Yung	TPE	53.47

HEAT 4

Rnk	Ln	Name	Ctry	Result
1	4	BRINN, Sion	JAM	50.38
2	1	SEI, Indrek	EST	51.19
3	7	BENAVIDES, Juan	ESP	51.20
4	5	DELGADO, Felipe	ECU	51.38
5	3	ZHAO, Lifeng	CHN	51.70
6	6	KANJER, Marijan	CRO	51.76
7	8	VARONEN, Kalle	FIN	52.00
8	2	ZINHOM, Tamer	EGY	52.16

HEAT 5

Rnk	Ln	Name	Ctry	Result
1	8	BUSQUETS, Ricardo	PUR	49.61
2	1	KIZIEROWSKI, Bartosz	POL	50.18
3	5	RUKHLEVICH, Oleg	BLR	50.42
4	4	YEGOROV, Aleksey	KAZ	50.49
5	3	GRUSON, Nicolas	FRA	50.71
6	2	DEDEKIND, Brendon	RSA	50.95
7	6	McCARTHY, Earl	IRL	50.99
8	7	ITO, Shunsuke	JPN	51.29

HEAT 6

Rnk	Ln	Name	Ctry	Result
1	4	HALL, Gary, Jr.	USA	48.90
2	3	SANCHEZ, Francisco	VEN	49.59
3	5	KHNYKIN, Pavlo	UKR	49.69
4	2	van den HOOGENBAND, Pieter	NED	49.73
5	7	TROGER, Christian	GER	50.06
6	6	ZUBOR, Attila	HUN	50.43
7	1	BRAY, Trent	NZL	51.18
8	8	BERA, Richard	INA	51.25

HEAT 7

Rnk	Ln	Name	Ctry	Result
1	1	CLARKE, Stephen	CAN	50.14
2	4	OLSEN, Jon	USA	50.17
3	5	FYDLER, Chris	AUS	50.27
4	6	ZIKARSKY, Bjorn	GER	50.38
5	8	BRUCK, Yoav	ISR	50.61
6	2	IVAN, Nicolae	ROM	51.14
7	7	SZABADOS, Bela	HUN	51.26
8	3	MEOLANS, Jose	ARG	52.02

HEAT 8

Rnk	Ln	Name	Ctry	Result
1	4	POPOV, Aleksander	RUS	48.74
2	3	BORGES, Gustavo Franca	BRA	49.17
3	5	SCHERER, Fernando	BRA	49.79
4	6	FROLANDER, Lars	SWE	49.91
5	2	SVANIDZE, Rostyslav	UKR	50.31
6	1	PREDKIN, Vladimir	RUS	50.75
7	8	ILES, Salim	ALG	50.87
8	7	SHACKELL, Nicholas	GBR	51.03

100 m Freestyle, Men / *100 m nage libre, Messieurs*

<table>
<tr><td colspan="5">FINAL B</td><td colspan="5">FINAL A</td></tr>
<tr><td>Rnk</td><td>Ln</td><td>Name</td><td>Ctry</td><td>Result</td><td>Rnk</td><td>Ln</td><td>Name</td><td>Ctry</td><td>Result</td></tr>
<tr><td>1</td><td>3</td><td>OLSEN, Jon</td><td>USA</td><td>49.80</td><td>1</td><td>4</td><td>POPOV, Aleksander</td><td>RUS</td><td>48.74 G</td></tr>
<tr><td>2</td><td>4</td><td>TROGER, Christian</td><td>GER</td><td>49.90</td><td>2</td><td>5</td><td>HALL, Gary, Jr.</td><td>USA</td><td>48.81 S</td></tr>
<tr><td>3</td><td>8</td><td>ZIKARSKY, Bjorn</td><td>GER</td><td>49.91</td><td>3</td><td>3</td><td>BORGES, Gustavo Franca</td><td>BRA</td><td>49.02 B</td></tr>
<tr><td>4</td><td>1</td><td>BRINN, Sion</td><td>JAM</td><td>50.09</td><td>4</td><td>1</td><td>van den HOOGENBAND, Pieter</td><td>NED</td><td>49.13</td></tr>
<tr><td>5</td><td>2</td><td>FYDLER, Chris</td><td>AUS</td><td>50.31</td><td>5</td><td>8</td><td>SCHERER, Fernando</td><td>BRA</td><td>49.57</td></tr>
<tr><td>6</td><td>7</td><td>SVANIDZE, Rostyslav</td><td>UKR</td><td>50.43</td><td>6</td><td>7</td><td>KHNYKIN, Pavlo</td><td>UKR</td><td>49.65</td></tr>
<tr><td>7</td><td>5</td><td>CLARKE, Stephen</td><td>CAN</td><td>50.45</td><td>7</td><td>2</td><td>BUSQUETS, Ricardo</td><td>PUR</td><td>49.68</td></tr>
<tr><td>8</td><td>6</td><td>KIZIEROWSKI, Bartosz</td><td>POL</td><td>50.51</td><td>8</td><td>6</td><td>SANCHEZ, Francisco</td><td>VEN</td><td>49.84</td></tr>
</table>

Aquatics—Swimming / *Natation — Natation*
100 m Freestyle, Women / *100 m nage libre, Dames*

<table>
<tr><td colspan="5">HEAT 1</td><td colspan="5">HEAT 2</td><td colspan="5">HEAT 3</td></tr>
<tr><td>Rnk</td><td>Ln</td><td>Name</td><td>Ctry</td><td>Result</td><td>Rnk</td><td>Ln</td><td>Name</td><td>Ctry</td><td>Result</td><td>Rnk</td><td>Ln</td><td>Name</td><td>Ctry</td><td>Result</td></tr>
<tr><td>1</td><td>3</td><td>NYIRY, Anna</td><td>HUN</td><td>57.82</td><td>1</td><td>1</td><td>CROPPER, Siobhan</td><td>TRI</td><td>57.30</td><td>1</td><td>6</td><td>SALMELA, Minna</td><td>FIN</td><td>57.15</td></tr>
<tr><td>2</td><td>5</td><td>MOODIE, Teresa</td><td>ZIM</td><td>58.59</td><td>2</td><td>2</td><td>DRAXLER, Judith</td><td>AUT</td><td>57.34</td><td>2</td><td>2</td><td>ROSE, Gabrielle</td><td>BRA</td><td>57.16</td></tr>
<tr><td>3</td><td>4</td><td>ALVAREZ, Valeria</td><td>ARG</td><td>59.26</td><td>3</td><td>4</td><td>MAHAIRA, Antonia</td><td>GRE</td><td>57.92</td><td>3</td><td>4</td><td>VIANINI, Cecilia</td><td>ITA</td><td>57.17</td></tr>
<tr><td>4</td><td>7</td><td>POLEJAEVA, Viktoria</td><td>KGZ</td><td>59.40</td><td>4</td><td>3</td><td>KYNEROVA, Kristyna</td><td>CZE</td><td>58.03</td><td>4</td><td>7</td><td>SPARAVEC, Metka</td><td>SLO</td><td>57.66</td></tr>
<tr><td>5</td><td>2</td><td>UJCIC, Gabrijela</td><td>CRO</td><td>59.92</td><td>5</td><td>7</td><td>PAQUIER, Sandrine</td><td>SUI</td><td>58.38</td><td>5</td><td>1</td><td>DAHL, Monica</td><td>NAM</td><td>57.95</td></tr>
<tr><td>6</td><td>6</td><td>RADAN, Duska</td><td>YUG</td><td>1:00.34</td><td>6</td><td>8</td><td>ZHIDKO, Svetlana</td><td>BLR</td><td>58.64</td><td>6</td><td>3</td><td>MULLER, Helene</td><td>RSA</td><td>57.98</td></tr>
<tr><td>7</td><td>1</td><td>PICKERING, Caroline</td><td>FIJ</td><td>1:00.51</td><td>7</td><td>5</td><td>TSAI, Shu-Min</td><td>TPE</td><td>58.65</td><td>7</td><td>8</td><td>LEE, Bo-Eun</td><td>KOR</td><td>58.27</td></tr>
<tr><td>8</td><td>8</td><td>RIZZO, Gail</td><td>MLT</td><td>1:02.19</td><td>8</td><td>6</td><td>YERMAKOVA, Yevgeniya</td><td>KAZ</td><td>59.12</td><td>8</td><td>5</td><td>YEO, Joscelin</td><td>SIN</td><td>58.87</td></tr>
</table>

<table>
<tr><td colspan="5">HEAT 4</td><td colspan="5">HEAT 5</td><td colspan="5">HEAT 6</td></tr>
<tr><td>Rnk</td><td>Ln</td><td>Name</td><td>Ctry</td><td>Result</td><td>Rnk</td><td>Ln</td><td>Name</td><td>Ctry</td><td>Result</td><td>Rnk</td><td>Ln</td><td>Name</td><td>Ctry</td><td>Result</td></tr>
<tr><td>1</td><td>4</td><td>VOELKER, Sandra</td><td>GER</td><td>55.55</td><td>1</td><td>4</td><td>LE, Jingyi</td><td>CHN</td><td>54.90</td><td>1</td><td>3</td><td>MARTINO, Angel</td><td>USA</td><td>55.44</td></tr>
<tr><td>2</td><td>5</td><td>VAN DYKEN, Amy</td><td>USA</td><td>55.94</td><td>2</td><td>5</td><td>BRIENESSE, Karin</td><td>NED</td><td>55.81</td><td>2</td><td>5</td><td>van ALMSICK, Franziska</td><td>GER</td><td>55.80</td></tr>
<tr><td>3</td><td>6</td><td>DOBRESCU, Liliana</td><td>ROM</td><td>56.27</td><td>3</td><td>2</td><td>RYAN, Sarah</td><td>AUS</td><td>56.07</td><td>3</td><td>6</td><td>JACOBSEN, Mette</td><td>DEN</td><td>56.06</td></tr>
<tr><td>4</td><td>3</td><td>ROLPH, Susan</td><td>GBR</td><td>56.62</td><td>4</td><td>6</td><td>MESHCHERYAKOVA, Natalya</td><td>RUS</td><td>56.33</td><td>4</td><td>4</td><td>SHAN, Ying</td><td>CHN</td><td>56.10</td></tr>
<tr><td>5</td><td>7</td><td>SHAKESPEARE, Shannon</td><td>CAN</td><td>56.63</td><td>5</td><td>3</td><td>PICKERING, Karen</td><td>GBR</td><td>56.40</td><td>5</td><td>1</td><td>MARTINDALE, Leah</td><td>BAR</td><td>56.13</td></tr>
<tr><td>6</td><td>8</td><td>FIGUES, Solennes</td><td>FRA</td><td>56.90</td><td>6</td><td>1</td><td>ELWANI, Rania</td><td>EGY</td><td>56.89</td><td>6</td><td>2</td><td>MORAVCOVA, Martina</td><td>SVK</td><td>56.20</td></tr>
<tr><td>7</td><td>2</td><td>MINAMOTO, Sumika</td><td>JPN</td><td>57.25</td><td>7</td><td>7</td><td>FRANCO, Claudia</td><td>ESP</td><td>57.00</td><td>7</td><td>7</td><td>OLOFSSON, Linda</td><td>SWE</td><td>56.56</td></tr>
<tr><td>8</td><td>1</td><td>ZELVIENE, Dita</td><td>LTU</td><td>58.57</td><td>8</td><td>8</td><td>FITCH, Alison</td><td>NZL</td><td>57.71</td><td>8</td><td>8</td><td>JOHANSEN, Vibeke</td><td>NOR</td><td>56.88</td></tr>
</table>

<table>
<tr><td colspan="5">FINAL B</td><td colspan="5">FINAL A</td></tr>
<tr><td>Rnk</td><td>Ln</td><td>Name</td><td>Ctry</td><td>Result</td><td>Rnk</td><td>Ln</td><td>Name</td><td>Ctry</td><td>Result</td></tr>
<tr><td>1</td><td>4</td><td>SHAN, Ying</td><td>CHN</td><td>55.74</td><td>1</td><td>4</td><td>LE, Jingyi</td><td>CHN</td><td>54.50 O G</td></tr>
<tr><td>2</td><td>1</td><td>OLOFSSON, Linda</td><td>SWE</td><td>55.83</td><td>2</td><td>3</td><td>VOELKER, Sandra</td><td>GER</td><td>54.88 S</td></tr>
<tr><td>3</td><td>6</td><td>DOBRESCU, Liliana</td><td>ROM</td><td>55.98</td><td>3</td><td>5</td><td>MARTINO, Angel</td><td>USA</td><td>54.93 B</td></tr>
<tr><td>4</td><td>5</td><td>MARTINDALE, Leah</td><td>BAR</td><td>56.03</td><td>4</td><td>7</td><td>VAN DYKEN, Amy</td><td>USA</td><td>55.11</td></tr>
<tr><td>5</td><td>2</td><td>MESHCHERYAKOVA, Natalya</td><td>RUS</td><td>56.17</td><td>5</td><td>6</td><td>van ALMSICK, Franziska</td><td>GER</td><td>55.59</td></tr>
<tr><td>6</td><td>7</td><td>PICKERING, Karen</td><td>GBR</td><td>56.32</td><td>6</td><td>8</td><td>RYAN, Sarah</td><td>AUS</td><td>55.85</td></tr>
<tr><td>7</td><td>3</td><td>MORAVCOVA, Martina</td><td>SVK</td><td>56.47</td><td>7</td><td>1</td><td>JACOBSEN, Mette</td><td>DEN</td><td>56.01</td></tr>
<tr><td>8</td><td>8</td><td>ROLPH, Susan</td><td>GBR</td><td>56.58</td><td>8</td><td>2</td><td>BRIENESSE, Karin</td><td>NED</td><td>56.12</td></tr>
</table>

Aquatics—Swimming / *Natation—Natation*

200 m Freestyle, Men / *200 m nage libre, Messieurs*

HEAT 1				
Rnk	Ln	Name	Ctry	Result
1	4	SANTANDER, Carlos	VEN	1:53.13
2	3	PROBERT, Carl	FIJ	1:56.33
3	5	ALSHAMROUKH, Thamer S.A.M.	KUW	2:13.75

HEAT 2				
Rnk	Ln	Name	Ctry	Result
1	6	ISAZA CHU, Jose	PAN	1:54.58
2	3	BUCAR, Jure	SLO	1:54.75
3	1	PAPA, Raymond	PHI	1:54.77
4	4	SIKORA, Bartosz	POL	1:55.33
5	5	SNG, Ju Wei	SIN	1:55.51
6	2	LAPINE, Dmitri	KGZ	1:55.52
7	8	DELGADO, Felipe	ECU	1:57.10
8	7	ZAVHORODNIY, Denys	UKR	1:58.67

HEAT 3				
Rnk	Ln	Name	Ctry	Result
1	3	VUCETIC, Miroslav	CRO	1:51.26
2	1	KOH, Yun-Ho	KOR	1:52.80
3	7	KABANOV, Vyacheslav	UZB	1:53.36
4	5	McCARTHY, Earl	IRL	1:53.67
5	4	MANGANAS, Dimitrios	GRE	1:53.84
6	6	ILES, Salim	ALG	1:54.10
7	8	SETHSOTHORN, Torlarp	THA	1:54.73
8	2	ZAKHAROV, Andrei	MDA	1:57.47

HEAT 4				
Rnk	Ln	Name	Ctry	Result
1	4	LOADER, Danyon	NZL	1:48.48
2	1	BORGES, Gustavo Franca	BRA	1:49.00
3	2	PALMER, Paul	GBR	1:49.05
3	5	SIEVINEN, Jani	FIN	1:49.05
5	7	HEILMANN, Aimo	GER	1:49.57
6	6	PYSHNENKO, Vladimir	RUS	1:49.79
7	8	BUTACU, Nicolae	ROM	1:50.83
8	3	CZENE, Attila	HUN	1:51.59

HEAT 5				
Rnk	Ln	Name	Ctry	Result
1	3	HOLMERTZ, Anders	SWE	1:48.41
2	4	DAVIS, Josh	USA	1:48.63
3	2	ROSOLINO, Massimiliano	ITA	1:48.80
4	6	SICILIANO, Piermaria	ITA	1:49.88
5	5	PIERSMA, John	USA	1:50.59
6	8	ITO, Shunsuke	JPN	1:51.97
7	1	BORDEAU, Christophe	FRA	1:52.17
8	7	KOLLAR, Miklos	HUN	1:52.19

HEAT 6				
Rnk	Ln	Name	Ctry	Result
1	5	van den HOOGENBAND, Pieter	NED	1:48.68
2	3	KOWALSKI, Daniel	AUS	1:48.92
3	4	KLIM, Michael	AUS	1:49.17
4	6	KASVIO, Antti	FIN	1:50.55
5	1	CARSTENSEN, Jacob	DEN	1:50.79
6	7	CLAYTON, Andrew	GBR	1:51.06
7	2	BRAY, Trent	NZL	1:51.59
8	8	YEGOROV, Aleksey	KAZ	1:51.66

FINAL B				
Rnk	Ln	Name	Ctry	Result
1	5	HEILMANN, Aimo	GER	1:48.81
2	4	KLIM, Michael	AUS	1:49.50
3	3	PYSHNENKO, Vladimir	RUS	1:49.55
4	2	PIERSMA, John	USA	1:49.90
5	6	SICILIANO, Piermaria	ITA	1:50.07
6	7	CARSTENSEN, Jacob	DEN	1:50.54
7	8	CLAYTON, Andrew	GBR	1:50.59
8	1	BUTACU, Nicolae	ROM	1:51.46

FINAL A					
Rnk	Ln	Name	Ctry	Result	
1	5	LOADER, Danyon	NZL	1:47.63	G
2	1	BORGES, Gustavo Franca	BRA	1:48.08	S
3	7	KOWALSKI, Daniel	AUS	1:48.25	B
4	6	van den HOOGENBAND, Pieter	NED	1:48.36	
5	4	HOLMERTZ, Anders	SWE	1:48.42	
6	2	ROSOLINO, Massimiliano	ITA	1:48.50	
7	3	DAVIS, Josh	USA	1:48.54	
8	8	PALMER, Paul	GBR	1:49.39	

Aquatics—Swimming / *Natation—Natation*

200 m Freestyle, Women / *200 m nage libre, Dames*

HEAT 1				
Rnk	Ln	Name	Ctry	Result
1	5	MOODIE, Teresa	ZIM	2:08.23
2	4	PETRUTYTE, Laura	LTU	2:09.78
3	3	ZARMAS, Marina	CYP	2:10.85

HEAT 2				
Rnk	Ln	Name	Ctry	Result
1	4	CAM, Sandra	BEL	2:04.90
2	1	ADEL, Carolyn	SUR	2:05.04
3	5	MULLER, Helene	RSA	2:05.59
4	6	INTPORN-UDOM, Ravee	THA	2:05.77
5	3	LEE, Jie-Hyun	KOR	2:05.78
6	2	BORODICH, Inga	BLR	2:05.85
7	7	CHIAWAY, Maritza	PER	2:07.80

HEAT 3				
Rnk	Ln	Name	Ctry	Result
1	2	MAHAIRA, Antonia	GRE	2:03.21
2	4	HARMOKIVI, Paula	FIN	2:03.54
3	8	MADINE, Marion	IRL	2:04.92
4	1	ALEGRIA, Ana	POR	2:05.16
5	5	ELWANI, Rania	EGY	2:06.94
6	6	CHANG, Wei-Cha	TPE	2:06.97
7	3	STRASSER, Chantal	SUI	2:07.98
8	7	YEO, Joscelin	SIN	2:08.10

HEAT 4				
Rnk	Ln	Name	Ctry	Result
1	6	O'NEILL, Susan	AUS	2:00.89
2	3	MORAVCOVA, Martina	SVK	2:00.99
3	4	CHIBA, Suzu	JPN	2:01.11
4	1	BAINBRIDGE, Dionne	NZL	2:02.69
5	2	MALAR, Joanne	CAN	2:03.53
6	8	KYNEROVA, Kristyna	CZE	2:03.63
7	7	IMOTO, Naoko	JPN	2:03.78
8	5	SHAN, Ying	CHN	2:04.29

HEAT 5				
Rnk	Ln	Name	Ctry	Result
1	4	POLL, Claudia	CRC	1:59.87
2	5	JACKSON, Trina	USA	2:00.29
3	3	HASE, Dagmar	GER	2:00.38
4	6	GREVILLE, Julia	AUS	2:00.44
5	7	DOBRESCU, Liliana	ROM	2:00.85
6	1	FIGUES, Solennes	FRA	2:02.74
7	8	LAPUNOVA, Olena	UKR	2:04.07
8	2	NILSSON, Malin	SWE	2:04.39

HEAT 6				
Rnk	Ln	Name	Ctry	Result
1	4	van ALMSICK, Franziska	GER	1:59.40
2	5	TEUSCHER, Cristina	USA	2:00.57
3	2	JOHNCKE, Louise	SWE	2:01.13
4	7	PICKERING, Karen	GBR	2:01.46
5	3	CHEN, Yan	CHN	2:03.32
6	1	LITOVCHENKO, Tatyana	RUS	2:04.09
7	6	DIACONESCU, Ioana	ROM	2:04.59
8	8	MUUSFELDT, Mia	DEN	2:07.29

200 m Freestyle, Women / *200 m nage libre, Dames*

FINAL B

Rnk	Ln	Name	Ctry	Result
1	4	MORAVCOVA, Martina	SVK	2:00.96
2	5	CHIBA, Suzu	JPN	2:01.00
3	3	JOHNCKE, Louise	SWE	2:01.37
4	7	FIGUES, Solennes	FRA	2:01.47
5	6	PICKERING, Karen	GBR	2:02.58
6	1	MAHAIRA, Antonia	GRE	2:03.19
7	2	BAINBRIDGE, Dionne	NZL	2:03.20
8	8	MALAR, Joanne	CAN	2:03.79

FINAL A

Rnk	Ln	Name	Ctry	Result	
1	5	POLL, Claudia	CRC	1:58.16	G
2	4	van ALMSICK, Franziska	GER	1:58.57	S
3	6	HASE, Dagmar	GER	1:59.56	B
4	3	JACKSON, Trina	USA	1:59.57	
5	8	O'NEILL, Susan	AUS	1:59.87	
6	7	TEUSCHER, Cristina	USA	2:00.79	
7	2	GREVILLE, Julia	AUS	2:01.46	
8	1	DOBRESCU, Liliana	ROM	2:01.63	

Aquatics—Swimming / *Natation—Natation*
400 m Freestyle, Men / *400 m nage libre, Messieurs*

HEAT 1

Rnk	Ln	Name	Ctry	Result
1	4	KVASSOV, Andrei	KGZ	4:00.69
2	5	FIORILLI, Agustin	ARG	4:02.53
3	3	DALLAL, Omar	JOR	4:41.12

HEAT 2

Rnk	Ln	Name	Ctry	Result
1	1	BERMUDEZ, Alejandro	COL	3:57.45
2	4	VUCETIC, Miroslav	CRO	3:59.20
3	7	MONASTERIO, Ricardo	VEN	4:00.44
4	5	ERGENEKAN, Can	TUR	4:02.39
5	6	KWOK, Mark	HKG	4:02.68
6	2	ZAKHAROV, Andrei	MDA	4:09.30
7	8	SNG, Ju Wei	SIN	4:12.24
	3	KASVIO, Antti	FIN	DNS

HEAT 3

Rnk	Ln	Name	Ctry	Result
1	4	KOWALSKI, Daniel	AUS	3:51.67
2	5	HOLMERTZ, Anders	SWE	3:52.27
3	3	WIESE, Sebastian	GER	3:53.55
4	2	MANGANAS, Dimitrios	GRE	3:54.85
5	6	AKATYEV, Aleksey	RUS	3:56.40
6	7	LIMA, Luiz	BRA	3:56.43
7	1	BUCAR, Jure	SLO	3:57.36
8	8	WOO, Cheol	KOR	4:03.11

HEAT 4

Rnk	Ln	Name	Ctry	Result
1	6	BREMBILLA, Emiliano	ITA	3:49.35
2	5	ROSOLINO, Massimiliano	ITA	3:51.05
3	3	HOFFMANN, Jorg	GER	3:51.26
4	4	PIERSMA, John	USA	3:53.58
5	7	de FABRIQUE, Yann	FRA	3:55.42
6	1	SETHSOTHORN, Torlarp	THA	3:57.08
7	2	SZABADOS, Bela	HUN	3:59.36
8	8	MASRY, Hicham	SYR	4:10.23

HEAT 5

Rnk	Ln	Name	Ctry	Result
1	5	LOADER, Danyon	NZL	3:51.54
2	3	PALMER, Paul	GBR	3:51.98
3	2	CARSTENSEN, Jacob	DEN	3:52.62
4	4	DOLAN, Tom	USA	3:53.91
5	6	ALLEN, Malcolm	AUS	3:54.34
6	8	SNITKO, Ihor	UKR	3:55.67
7	7	NEETHLING, Ryk	RSA	3:56.19
8	1	YASUI, Hisato	JPN	4:00.19

FINAL B

Rnk	Ln	Name	Ctry	Result
1	5	PIERSMA, John	USA	3:50.69
2	4	WIESE, Sebastian	GER	3:52.37
3	1	NEETHLING, Ryk	RSA	3:54.34
4	7	SNITKO, Ihor	UKR	3:54.63
5	3	ALLEN, Malcolm	AUS	3:55.48
6	8	AKATYEV, Aleksey	RUS	3:55.72
7	2	de FABRIQUE, Yann	FRA	3:56.46
8	6	MANGANAS, Dimitrios	GRE	3:57.39

FINAL A

Rnk	Ln	Name	Ctry	Result	
1	6	LOADER, Danyon	NZL	3:47.97	G
2	7	PALMER, Paul	GBR	3:49.00	S
3	2	KOWALSKI, Daniel	AUS	3:49.39	B
4	4	BREMBILLA, Emiliano	ITA	3:49.87	
5	1	HOLMERTZ, Anders	SWE	3:50.68	
6	5	ROSOLINO, Massimiliano	ITA	3:51.04	
7	3	HOFFMANN, Jorg	GER	3:52.15	
8	8	CARSTENSEN, Jacob	DEN	3:54.45	

Aquatics—Swimming / *Natation—Natation*
400 m Freestyle, Women / *400 m nage libre, Dames*

HEAT 1

Rnk	Ln	Name	Ctry	Result
1	6	CHOUX, Leatitia	FRA	4:21.39
2	4	RAABY, Britt	DEN	4:21.46
3	7	INTPORN-UDOM, Ravee	THA	4:21.93
4	1	NEMEC, Martina	AUT	4:23.72
5	5	MAHAIRA, Antonia	GRE	4:24.05
6	3	CHIAWAY, Maritza	PER	4:27.11
7	2	KISS, Judit	HUN	4:29.80
8	8	ZARMAS, Marina	CYP	4:32.15

HEAT 2

Rnk	Ln	Name	Ctry	Result
1	1	BOSEVSKA, Mirjana	MKD	4:21.27
2	4	CHEMEZOVA, Nadezhda	RUS	4:21.33
3	3	BARRANCOS, Alicia	ARG	4:22.11
4	8	ADEL, Carolyn	SUR	4:22.66
5	6	JEONG, Eun-Na	KOR	4:23.35
6	2	HARMOKIVI, Paula	FIN	4:23.84
7	7	STRASSER, Chantal	SUI	4:24.49
8	5	ALEGRIA, Ana	POR	4:27.19

HEAT 3

Rnk	Ln	Name	Ctry	Result
1	4	POLL, Claudia	CRC	4:12.07
2	5	EVANS, Janet	USA	4:13.60
3	2	JOHNSON, Emma	AUS	4:14.13
4	6	CHIBA, Suzu	JPN	4:16.07
5	3	LEWIS, Hayley	AUS	4:17.02
6	7	LIN, Chi-Chan	TPE	4:17.18
7	8	SCHWARTZ, Andrea	CAN	4:19.46
8	1	MORAVCOVA, Martina	SVK	4:22.10

400 m Freestyle, Women / *400 m nage libre, Dames*

HEAT 4

Rnk	Ln	Name	Ctry	Result
1	6	VLIEGHUIS, Kirsten	NED	4:11.04
2	4	HASE, Dagmar	GER	4:11.17
3	5	GEURTS, Carla Louise	NED	4:11.18
4	3	TEUSCHER, Cristina	USA	4:12.20
5	7	HARDCASTLE, Sarah	GBR	4:14.50
6	8	ESPARZA, Maria	ESP	4:19.45
7	1	SPLICHALOVA, Olga	CZE	4:20.04
	2	NILSSON, Malin	SWE	DNS

HEAT 5

Rnk	Ln	Name	Ctry	Result
1	5	KIELGASS, Kerstin	GER	4:08.99
2	4	SMITH, Michelle	IRL	4:09.00
3	3	YAMANOI, Eri	JPN	4:13.40
4	8	BAINBRIDGE, Dionne	NZL	4:16.47
5	7	NEGREA, Carla	ROM	4:16.89
6	1	CAM, Sandra	BEL	4:17.35
7	2	DALBY, Irene	NOR	4:19.34
8	6	CHEN, Yan	CHN	4:22.55

FINAL B

Rnk	Ln	Name	Ctry	Result
1	5	HARDCASTLE, Sarah	GBR	4:14.13
2	8	CAM, Sandra	BEL	4:14.94
3	1	LIN, Chi-Chan	TPE	4:15.74
4	4	JOHNSON, Emma	AUS	4:15.79
5	3	CHIBA, Suzu	JPN	4:16.60
6	6	BAINBRIDGE, Dionne	NZL	4:16.79
7	7	LEWIS, Hayley	AUS	4:16.92
8	2	NEGREA, Carla	ROM	4:17.08

FINAL A

Rnk	Ln	Name	Ctry	Result	
1	5	SMITH, Michelle	IRL	4:07.25	G
2	6	HASE, Dagmar	GER	4:08.30	S
3	3	VLIEGHUIS, Kirsten	NED	4:08.70	B
4	4	KIELGASS, Kerstin	GER	4:09.83	
5	7	POLL, Claudia	CRC	4:10.00	
6	2	GEURTS, Carla Louise	NED	4:10.06	
7	8	YAMANOI, Eri	JPN	4:11.68	
8	1	TEUSCHER, Cristina	USA	4:14.21	

Aquatics—Swimming / *Natation — Natation*

800 m Freestyle, Women / *800 m nage libre, Dames*

HEAT 1

Rnk	Ln	Name	Ctry	Result
1	5	INTPORN-UDOM, Ravee	THA	9:01.14
2	4	SUH, Hyun-Soo	KOR	9:03.22
3	6	CHIAWAY, Maritza	PER	9:09.12
4	3	KOROTAEVA, Olga	KGZ	9:21.20
5	2	MENEGON, Daniela	SWZ	10:12.46

HEAT 2

Rnk	Ln	Name	Ctry	Result
1	3	HARDCASTLE, Sarah	GBR	8:37.54
2	6	DALBY, Irene	NOR	8:37.73
3	4	EVANS, Janet	USA	8:38.08
4	2	GEURTS, Carla Louise	NED	8:39.85
5	1	CAM, Sandra	BEL	8:48.33
6	7	ESPARZA, Itziar	ESP	8:50.22
7	8	KOVACS, Rita	HUN	9:06.97
	5	CHEN, Yan	CHN	DNS

HEAT 3

Rnk	Ln	Name	Ctry	Result
1	4	BENNETT, Brooke	USA	8:32.38
2	3	HASE, Dagmar	GER	8:33.55
3	6	KIELGASS, Kerstin	GER	8:36.33
4	5	VLIEGHUIS, Kirsten	NED	8:39.73
5	7	DRYDEN, Nicole	CAN	8:47.19
6	2	SPLICHALOVA, Olga	CZE	8:47.68
7	1	RICHARDSON, Stephanie	CAN	8:52.61
8	8	BOSEVSKA, Mirjana	MKD	8:57.52

HEAT 4

Rnk	Ln	Name	Ctry	Result
1	6	LIN, Chi-Chan	TPE	8:40.31
2	7	YAMANOI, Eri	JPN	8:40.47
3	5	GARTRELL, Stacey	AUS	8:42.39
4	3	PU, Yiqi	CHN	8:45.32
5	4	LEWIS, Hayley	AUS	8:45.79
6	1	BARRANCOS, Alicia	ARG	8:48.54
7	8	NEGREA, Carla	ROM	8:54.19
8	2	MIYAKE, Aiko	JPN	8:55.77

FINAL

Rnk	Ln	Name	Ctry	Result	
1	4	BENNETT, Brooke	USA	8:27.89	G
2	5	HASE, Dagmar	GER	8:29.91	S
3	1	VLIEGHUIS, Kirsten	NED	8:30.84	B
4	3	KIELGASS, Kerstin	GER	8:31.06	
5	2	DALBY, Irene	NOR	8:38.34	
6	7	EVANS, Janet	USA	8:38.91	
7	8	GEURTS, Carla Louise	NED	8:40.43	
8	6	HARDCASTLE, Sarah	GBR	8:41.75	

Aquatics—Swimming / *Natation — Natation*

1,500 m Freestyle, Men / *1 500 m nage libre, Messieurs*

HEAT 1

Rnk	Ln	Name	Ctry	Result
1	4	VALLE, Ramon	HON	16:14.76
2	3	REZAKHANI TALEGHANI, Hamed	IRI	17:22.86
3	5	al-MA'SHARI, Rashid Salim	OMA	18:11.59

HEAT 2

Rnk	Ln	Name	Ctry	Result
1	2	MIKHNOVETS, Sergey	BLR	15:41.80
2	4	MONASTERIO, Ricardo	VEN	15:42.39
3	5	CARSTENSEN, Jacob	DEN	15:43.75
4	7	FIORILLI, Agustin	ARG	15:51.85
5	3	CAMERON, Scott	NZL	15:56.60
6	6	MANGANAS, Dimitrios	GRE	16:15.94
7	1	FERREIRA, Pedro	POR	16:34.55

HEAT 3

Rnk	Ln	Name	Ctry	Result
1	4	SMITH, Graeme	GBR	15:14.81
2	7	NEETHLING, Ryk	RSA	15:19.98
3	3	PALMER, Paul	GBR	15:22.65
4	5	BRUNER, Carlton	USA	15:25.82
5	6	SNITKO, Ihor	UKR	15:31.40
6	1	HVIID, Frederik	ESP	15:42.40
7	2	ZAVHORODNIY, Denys	UKR	15:46.79
8	8	LEE, Gyu-Chang	KOR	15:47.92

1,500 m Freestyle, Men / *1 500 m nage libre, Messieurs*

HEAT 4

Rnk	Ln	Name	Ctry	Result
1	4	KOWALSKI, Daniel	AUS	15:12.55
2	5	HOFFMANN, Jorg	GER	15:18.61
3	7	LIMA, Luiz	BRA	15:24.16
4	3	WRIGHT, Peter	USA	15:25.43
5	6	BUTSENIN, Aleksey	RUS	15:31.27
6	8	SETHSOTHORN, Torlarp	THA	15:40.04
7	1	de FABRIQUE, Yann	FRA	15:40.49
8	2	MAJCEN, Igor	SLO	16:10.81

HEAT 5

Rnk	Ln	Name	Ctry	Result
1	5	AKATYEV, Aleksey	RUS	15:16.47
2	1	BREMBILLA, Emiliano	ITA	15:16.72
3	2	HIRANO, Masato	JPN	15:19.48
4	4	PERKINS, Kieren	AUS	15:21.42
5	6	ZESNER, Steffen	GER	15:21.65
6	3	FORMENTINI, Marco	ITA	15:41.14
7	7	YASUI, Hisato	JPN	15:43.66
8	8	MASRY, Hicham	SYR	16:42.35

FINAL

Rnk	Ln	Name	Ctry	Result	
1	8	PERKINS, Kieren	AUS	14:56.40	G
2	4	KOWALSKI, Daniel	AUS	15:02.43	S
3	5	SMITH, Graeme	GBR	15:02.48	B
4	6	BREMBILLA, Emiliano	ITA	15:08.58	
5	1	NEETHLING, Ryk	RSA	15:14.63	
6	7	HIRANO, Masato	JPN	15:17.28	
7	2	HOFFMANN, Jorg	GER	15:18.86	
8	3	AKATYEV, Aleksey	RUS	15:21.68	

Aquatics—Swimming / *Natation — Natation*
100 m Backstroke, Men / *100 m dos, Messieurs*

HEAT 1

Rnk	Ln	Name	Ctry	Result
1	4	LIM, Alex	MAS	57.68
2	5	PRIAHIN, Konstantin	KGZ	1:00.26
3	3	JORGE, Leandro	MOZ	1:03.86
4	6	SHAHI, Sitaram	NEP	1:14.58

HEAT 2

Rnk	Ln	Name	Ctry	Result
1	2	NECKLES, Nicholas	BAR	57.91
2	3	PHUANGTHONG, Dulyarit	THA	58.32
3	6	KIM, Min-Suk	KOR	58.43
4	5	USHKALOV, Sergey	KAZ	58.61
5	7	RAJCEVICH, Nicolas	CHI	59.90
6	8	KOH, Gerald	SIN	1:00.29
7	4	FUNG A WING, Mike	SUR	1:01.24
8	1	ALOTAIBI, Fahad S. A. B. S.	KUW	1:04.27

HEAT 3

Rnk	Ln	Name	Ctry	Result
1	7	URBACH, Eithan	ISR	56.74
2	3	PAPA, Raymond	PHI	57.67
3	4	MACHOVIC, Miroslav	SVK	57.78
4	5	KARLO, Tomislav	CRO	57.89
5	1	BIZUB, Rastislav	CZE	58.29
6	2	KRIST JANSSON, Logi Jes	ISL	58.53
7	6	O'CONNOR, Adrian	IRL	58.56
8	8	ELIZAROV, Artur	MDA	59.24

HEAT 4

Rnk	Ln	Name	Ctry	Result
1	4	GRIGALIONIS, Darius	LTU	56.20
2	6	NIKOLAYCHUK, Volodymyr	UKR	56.71
2	8	BUYUKUNCU, Derya	TUR	56.71
4	2	ROMERO, Rogerio	BRA	56.94
5	3	ZHAO, Yi	CHN	57.17
6	1	ARENA, Carlos	MEX	57.40
7	5	LAURENTINO, Nuno	POR	57.59
8	7	ADAMIDIS, Panagiotis	GRE	58.12

HEAT 5

Rnk	Ln	Name	Ctry	Result
1	1	BENT, Neisser	CUB	54.83
2	2	LOPEZ-ZUBERO, Martin	ESP	55.36
3	6	SCHOTT, Franck	FRA	55.77
4	5	SELKOV, Vladimir	RUS	55.87
5	4	WILLEY, Neil	GBR	56.27
6	8	BUTACU, Nicolae	ROM	56.73
7	7	WINTER, Jonathan	NZL	56.92
8	3	DEUTSCH, Tamas	HUN	56.96

HEAT 6

Rnk	Ln	Name	Ctry	Result
1	5	FALCON, Rodolfo	CUB	55.29
2	4	SCHWENK, Tripp	USA	55.71
3	8	BRAKNIS, Robert	CAN	56.14
4	2	ITOI, Hajime	JPN	56.22
5	7	THELOKE, Ster	GER	56.26
6	3	DEWICK, Steven	AUS	56.35
7	1	RENAUD, Chris	CAN	56.52
	6	SIEVINEN, Jani	FIN	DNS

HEAT 7

Rnk	Ln	Name	Ctry	Result
1	4	ROUSE, Jeff	USA	54.20
2	1	BRAUN, Ralf	GER	55.73
3	3	MERISI, Emanuele	ITA	55.82
4	6	SIEMBIDA, Mariusz	POL	56.16
5	2	KONNAI, Keitaro	JPN	56.35
6	5	HARRIS, Martin	GBR	57.17
7	8	SPOKAS, Mindaugas	LTU	57.20
	7	POPOV, Aleksandr	RUS	DNS

FINAL B

Rnk	Ln	Name	Ctry	Result
1	8	KONNAI, Keitaro	JPN	55.74
2	7	WILLEY, Neil	GBR	56.07
3	6	ITOI, Hajime	JPN	56.23
4	5	SIEMBIDA, Mariusz	POL	56.31
5	3	GRIGALIONIS, Darius	LTU	56.33
6	2	THELOKE, Stev	GER	56.63
7	1	DEWICK, Steven	AUS	56.82
8	4	BRAKNIS, Robert	CAN	57.00

FINAL A

Rnk	Ln	Name	Ctry	Result	
1	4	ROUSE, Jeff	USA	54.10	G
2	3	FALCON, Rodolfo	CUB	54.98	S
3	5	BENT, Neisser	CUB	55.02	B
4	6	LOPEZ-ZUBERO, Martin	ESP	55.22	
5	2	SCHWENK, Tripp	USA	55.30	
6	8	MERISI, Emanuele	ITA	55.53	
7	7	BRAUN, Ralf	GER	55.56	
8	1	SCHOTT, Franck	FRA	55.76	

Aquatics—Swimming / *Natation—Natation*

100 m Backstroke, Women / *100 m dos, Dames*

HEAT 1

Rnk	Ln	Name	Ctry	Result
1	4	KISS, Annamaria	HUN	1:07.38
2	6	RIZZO, Gail	MLT	1:07.61
3	3	ESCALERA, Ximena	BOL	1:11.70
4	5	RAZAFINDRAMAHATRA, Harijesy	MAD	1:13.83

HEAT 2

Rnk	Ln	Name	Ctry	Result
1	4	LEE, Ji-Hyun	KOR	1:03.96
2	3	MINPRAPHAL, Praphalsai	THA	1:04.61
3	7	KUBALCIKOVA, Marcela	CZE	1:05.48
4	1	GERVY, Yseult	BEL	1:05.72
5	2	KLEPKOU, Aikaterini	GRE	1:05.94
6	5	HEREA, Florina	ROM	1:06.12
6	6	THOMSON, Gillian	PHI	1:06.12
8	8	TSAI, Shu-Min	TPE	1:11.44

HEAT 3

Rnk	Ln	Name	Ctry	Result
1	5	STEVENSON, Nicole	AUS	1:02.50
2	3	CHEN, Yan	CHN	1:02.62
3	2	BUSCHSCHULTE, Antje	GER	1:02.68
4	4	ZHIVANEVSKAYA, Nina	RUS	1:02.94
5	7	RICARDO, Helene	FRA	1:04.03
6	1	PINERA, Eva	ESP	1:04.41
7	6	HE, Cihong	CHN	1:05.87
8	8	ALVAREZ, Valeria	ARG	1:06.38

HEAT 4

Rnk	Ln	Name	Ctry	Result
1	3	KRIEL, Marianne	RSA	1:02.33
2	5	NAKAMURA, Mai	JPN	1:02.35
3	4	NAKAO, Miki	JPN	1:02.90
4	6	KOCHETKOVA, Olga	RUS	1:03.17
5	7	LIPSCOMBE, Lydia	NZL	1:03.61
6	2	ALSHAMMAR, Therese	SWE	1:03.79
7	8	KOIVISTO, Anu	FIN	1:05.25
8	1	KOMOROWICZ, Dagmara	POL	1:06.70

HEAT 5

Rnk	Ln	Name	Ctry	Result
1	4	HEDGEPETH, Whitney	USA	1:01.70
2	5	BOTSFORD, Beth	USA	1:02.00
3	7	SCHOLZ, Anke	GER	1:03.05
4	3	JACOBSEN, Mette	DEN	1:03.14
5	6	HOWARD, Julie	CAN	1:03.84
6	2	OVERTON, Elli	AUS	1:03.88
7	1	SLATTER, Helen	GBR	1:03.89
8	8	SANTOS, Maria	POR	1:04.84

FINAL B

Rnk	Ln	Name	Ctry	Result
1	4	ZHIVANEVSKAYA, Nina	RUS	1:02.38
2	5	SCHOLZ, Anke	GER	1:02.85
3	6	LIPSCOMBE, Lydia	NZL	1:03.30
4	3	KOCHETKOVA, Olga	RUS	1:03.52
5	8	SLATTER, Helen	GBR	1:03.61
6	1	OVERTON, Elli	AUS	1:03.69
7	7	HOWARD, Julie	CAN	1:04.01
8	2	ALSHAMMAR, Therese	SWE	1:04.15

FINAL A

Rnk	Ln	Name	Ctry	Result	
1	5	BOTSFORD, Beth	USA	1:01.19	G
2	4	HEDGEPETH, Whitney	USA	1:01.47	S
3	3	KRIEL, Marianne	RSA	1:02.12	B
4	6	NAKAMURA, Mai	JPN	1:02.33	
5	7	CHEN, Yan	CHN	1:02.50	
6	1	BUSCHSCHULTE, Antje	GER	1:02.52	
7	2	STEVENSON, Nicole	AUS	1:02.70	
8	8	NAKAO, Miki	JPN	1:02.78	

Aquatics—Swimming / *Natation—Natation*

200 m Backstroke, Men / *200 m dos, Messieurs*

HEAT 1

Rnk	Ln	Name	Ctry	Result
1	4	NECKLES, Nicholas	BAR	2:05.88
2	5	LIM, Alex	MAS	2:06.17
3	3	KOH, Gerald	SIN	2:09.86
4	6	TRUONG NGOC, Tuan	VIE	2:12.05

HEAT 2

Rnk	Ln	Name	Ctry	Result
1	4	SAVICKAS, Arunas	LTU	2:04.38
2	7	PHUANGTHONG, Dulyarit	THA	2:05.26
3	8	RAJCEVICH, Nicolas	CHI	2:05.79
4	5	ARENA, Carlos	MEX	2:05.96
5	1	ELIZAROV, Artur	MDA	2:07.86
6	3	O'CONNOR, Adrian	IRL	2:08.90
7	6	ADAMIDIS, Panagiotis	GRE	2:10.22
	2	ALOTAIBI, Fahad S.A.B.S.	KUW	DNS

HEAT 3

Rnk	Ln	Name	Ctry	Result
1	6	STRAHIJA, Marko	CRO	2:01.95
2	4	ROMERO, Rogerio	BRA	2:03.49
3	1	MACHOVIC, Miroslav	SVK	2:04.15
4	2	BUYUKUNCU, Derya	TUR	2:04.28
5	3	BIZUB, Rastislav	CZE	2:04.55
6	7	PAPA, Raymond	PHI	2:05.09
7	8	LAURENTINO, Nuno	POR	2:05.95
	5	NIKOLAYCHUK, Volodymyr	UKR	DNS

HEAT 4

Rnk	Ln	Name	Ctry	Result
1	4	SCHWENK, Tripp	USA	1:59.58
2	6	LOPEZ-ZUBERO, Martin	ESP	2:00.77
3	2	SIKORA, Bartosz	POL	2:00.99
4	3	RUCKWOOD, Adam	GBR	2:01.35
5	1	AGH, Oliver	HUN	2:01.84
6	7	OSTAPCHUK, Sergey	RUS	2:03.50
7	8	ZHAO, Yi	CHN	2:13.31
	5	DEUTSCH, Tamas	HUN	DNS

HEAT 5

Rnk	Ln	Name	Ctry	Result
1	5	BRIDGEWATER, Brad	USA	1:59.04
2	2	MAZZARI, Mirko	ITA	1:59.95
3	3	FALCON CABRERA, Rodolfo	CUB	2:01.20
4	4	SELKOV, Vladimir	RUS	2:01.32
5	7	JI, Sang-Joon	KOR	2:01.39
6	6	RENAUD, Chris	CAN	2:02.48
7	1	BENT, Neisser	CUB	2:04.23
	8	THELOKE, Stev	GER	DNS

HEAT 6

Rnk	Ln	Name	Ctry	Result
1	4	MERISI, Emanuele	ITA	2:00.01
2	7	ITOI, Hajime	JPN	2:00.43
3	5	BRAUN, Ralf	GER	2:01.50
4	6	HORII, Ryuji	JPN	2:02.33
5	1	DEWICK, Steven	AUS	2:04.46
6	8	HARRIS, Martin	GBR	2:07.75
7	3	BUTACU, Nicolae	ROM	2:08.59
	2	SIEVINEN, Jani	FIN	DNS

200 m Backstroke, Men / *200 m dos, Messieurs*

FINAL B

Rnk	Ln	Name	Ctry	Result
1	2	HORII, Ryuji	JPN	2:01.54
2	7	RENAUD, Chris	CAN	2:01.70
3	6	STRAHIJA, Marko	CRO	2:01.84
4	3	AGH, Oliver	HUN	2:02.17
5	4	RUCKWOOD, Adam	GBR	2:02.40
6	5	JI, Sang-Joon	KOR	2:02.68
7	1	ROMERO, Rogerio	BRA	2:03.20
8	8	OSTAPCHUK, Sergey	RUS	2:03.91

FINAL A

Rnk	Ln	Name	Ctry	Result
1	4	BRIDGEWATER, Brad	USA	1:58.54 G
2	5	SCHWENK, Tripp	USA	1:58.99 S
3	6	MERISI, Emanuele	ITA	1:59.18 B
4	1	SIKORA, Bartosz	POL	2:00.05
5	2	ITOI, Hajime	JPN	2:00.10
6	7	LOPEZ-ZUBERO, Martin	ESP	2:00.74
7	3	MAZZARI, Mirko	ITA	2:01.27
8	8	FALCON CABRERA, Rodolfo	CUB	2:08.14

Aquatics—Swimming / *Natation—Natation*
200 m Backstroke, Women / *200 m dos, Dames*

HEAT 1

Rnk	Ln	Name	Ctry	Result
1	5	GROZDANIC, Maja	YUG	2:20.65
2	4	MINPRAPHAL, Praphalsai	THA	2:21.82
3	3	KVESIC, Dijana	BIH	2:23.78

HEAT 2

Rnk	Ln	Name	Ctry	Result
1	4	HOWARD, Julie	CAN	2:17.25
2	2	KOIVISTO, Anu	FIN	2:19.58
3	6	CHAVES, Petra	POR	2:20.49
4	5	THOMSON, Gillian	PHI	2:21.36
5	3	KLEPKOU, Aikaterini	GRE	2:22.83
6	7	LIN, Chi-Chan	TPE	2:24.50

HEAT 3

Rnk	Ln	Name	Ctry	Result
1	5	ZHIVANEVSKAYA, Nina	RUS	2:13.32
2	3	VIGARANI, Lorenza	ITA	2:13.58
3	4	BOTSFORD, Beth	USA	2:14.16
4	2	RICARDO, Helene	FRA	2:14.18
4	7	LEE, Chang-Ha	KOR	2:14.18
6	1	BURCZYK, Izabela	POL	2:16.91
7	8	MARIA, Ivette	ESP	2:18.72
8	6	WU, Yanyan	CHN	2:20.89

HEAT 4

Rnk	Ln	Name	Ctry	Result
1	3	HEDGEPETH, Whitney	USA	2:11.63
2	6	SCHOLZ, Anke	GER	2:12.73
3	4	NAKAO, Miki	JPN	2:12.92
4	7	CASARU, Catalina	ROM	2:15.92
5	2	KRIEL, Marianne	RSA	2:15.99
6	1	JACOBSEN, Mette	DEN	2:16.68
7	5	STEVENSON, Nicole	AUS	2:16.71
8	8	GERVY, Yseult	BEL	2:18.69

HEAT 5

Rnk	Ln	Name	Ctry	Result
1	4	EGERSZEGI, Krisztina	HUN	2:09.18
2	5	RUND, Cathleen	GER	2:13.58
3	2	SIMCIC, Anna	NZL	2:13.74
4	6	CHEN, Yan	CHN	2:14.74
5	3	NAKAMURA, Mai	JPN	2:15.05
6	1	DEAKINS, Joanne	GBR	2:15.12
7	8	PIVONKOVA, Katerina	CZE	2:18.20
8	7	LIPSCOMBE, Lydia	NZL	2:19.54

FINAL B

Rnk	Ln	Name	Ctry	Result
1	2	NAKAMURA, Mai	JPN	2:13.40
2	4	BOTSFORD, Beth	USA	2:13.48
3	6	CHEN, Yan	CHN	2:14.37
4	7	DEAKINS, Joanne	GBR	2:14.50
5	5	LEE, Chang-Ha	KOR	2:14.55
6	1	CASARU, Catalina	ROM	2:15.15
7	3	RICARDO, Helene	FRA	2:16.29
8	8	KRIEL, Marianne	RSA	2:18.41

FINAL A

Rnk	Ln	Name	Ctry	Result
1	4	EGERSZEGI, Krisztina	HUN	2:07.83 G
2	5	HEDGEPETH, Whitney	USA	2:11.98 S
3	7	RUND, Cathleen	GER	2:12.06 B
4	3	SCHOLZ, Anke	GER	2:12.90
5	6	NAKAO, Miki	JPN	2:13.57
6	8	SIMCIC, Anna	NZL	2:14.04
7	1	VIGARANI, Lorenza	ITA	2:14.56
8	2	ZHIVANEVSKAYA, Nina	RUS	2:14.59

Aquatics—Swimming / *Natation—Natation*
100 m Breaststroke, Men / *100 m brasse, Messieurs*

HEAT 1

Rnk	Ln	Name	Ctry	Result
1	3	ARIAS, Jorge	PER	1:06.03
2	6	RAZAKARIVONY, Jean	MAD	1:07.34
3	5	DESMARAIS, Bernard	MRI	1:09.05
4	2	RAHMAN, Karar	BAN	1:11.47
5	4	ALOTAIBI, S. A. B. S. Sultan	KUW	1:12.65

HEAT 2

Rnk	Ln	Name	Ctry	Result
1	4	TATAROV, Vadim	MDA	1:04.87
2	3	MORENO CASTILLO, Mauricio	COL	1:05.22
3	7	MADRIGAL, Juan Jose	CRC	1:05.47
4	2	LINDEMEIER, Jorg	NAM	1:05.50
5	6	VERDINO, Christophe	MON	1:05.66
6	5	SURIANO, Francisco	ESA	1:05.82
7	8	KOH, Desmond	SIN	1:06.97
8	1	PETRACHOV, Evgeni	KGZ	1:07.44

HEAT 3

Rnk	Ln	Name	Ctry	Result
1	1	GONZALEZ MONTESINOS, Mario	CUB	1:03.05
2	3	SIRISANONT, Ratapong	THA	1:03.81
3	4	KRIVENTSOV, Aleksey	BLR	1:04.20
4	5	BEIGA, Nerijus	LTU	1:04.45
5	8	CHIA, Elvin	MAS	1:04.46
6	7	MORK, Borge	NOR	1:04.92
7	2	HUANG, Chih-Yung	TPE	1:05.26
8	6	SAVITSKIY, Aleksandr	KAZ	1:05.85

100 m Breaststroke, Men / *100 m brasse, Messieurs*

HEAT 4

Rnk	Ln	Name	Ctry	Result
1	3	LINN, Jeremy	USA	1:01.53
2	5	GROTE, Kurt	USA	1:02.01
3	4	DZHABURIYA, Oleksandr	UKR	1:02.70
4	6	KENT, Paul	NZL	1:02.76
5	7	MADEN, Richard	GBR	1:02.78
6	2	ALEKSEYEV, Vadim	ISR	1:02.92
7	8	CHO, Kwang-Jea	KOR	1:03.39
8	1	KRAWCZYK, Marek	POL	1:03.57

HEAT 5

Rnk	Ln	Name	Ctry	Result
1	3	WARNECKE, Mark	GER	1:01.79
2	4	GUTTLER, Karoly	HUN	1:01.80
2	5	ROGERS, Philip	AUS	1:01.80
4	2	ZENG, Qiliang	CHN	1:02.26
5	1	MALEK, Daniel	CZE	1:02.46
6	6	HAYASHI, Akira	JPN	1:02.63
7	8	CAPDEVILLA, Marc	ESP	1:02.69
8	7	TORRES, Todd	PUR	1:03.08

HEAT 6

Rnk	Ln	Name	Ctry	Result
1	4	DEBURGHGRAEVE, Fred	BEL	1:00.60 W
2	6	LOPUKHOV, Stanislav	RUS	1:02.00
3	5	IVANOVSKIY, Roman	RUS	1:02.69
4	3	ROZSA, Norbert	HUN	1:02.72
5	2	LATOCHA, Vladimir	FRA	1:02.80
6	1	KUIPERS, Benno Gerrit	NED	1:02.92
7	7	MIYAZAKI, Yoshinobu	JPN	1:03.13
8	8	CLEVELAND, Jonathan	CAN	1:03.14

FINAL B

Rnk	Ln	Name	Ctry	Result
1	8	LATOCHA, Vladimir	FRA	1:02.28
2	4	MALEK, Daniel	CZE	1:02.39
3	1	MADEN, Richard	GBR	1:02.51
4	5	HAYASHI, Akira	JPN	1:02.75
5	2	DZHABURIYA, Oleksandr	UKR	1:02.91
6	7	KENT, Paul	NZL	1:03.05
7	3	CAPDEVILLA, Marc	ESP	1:03.51
	6	IVANOVSKIY, Roman	RUS	DQ

FINAL A

Rnk	Ln	Name	Ctry	Result
1	4	DEBURGHGRAEVE, Fred	BEL	1:00.65 G
2	5	LINN, Jeremy	USA	1:00.77 S
3	3	WARNECKE, Mark	GER	1:01.33 B
4	2	GUTTLER, Karoly	HUN	1:01.49
5	6	ROGERS, Philip	AUS	1:01.64
6	1	GROTE, Kurt	USA	1:01.69
7	8	ZENG, Qiliang	CHN	1:02.01
8	7	LOPUKHOV, Stanislav	RUS	1:02.13

Aquatics—Swimming / *Natation — Natation*
100 m Breaststroke, Women / *100 m brasse, Dames*

HEAT 1

Rnk	Ln	Name	Ctry	Result
1	3	BYUN, Hye-Young	KOR	1:12.85
2	6	TAY, Li Leng	MAS	1:14.17
3	5	CEBALLOS, Isabel Cristina	COL	1:14.75
4	4	PANG, Wan Yiu Snowie	HKG	1:16.02
5	2	MANUKYAN, Anush	ARM	1:20.70
6	7	HEM, Reaksmey	CAM	1:44.68

HEAT 2

Rnk	Ln	Name	Ctry	Result
1	3	MANHALOVA, Lenka	CZE	1:12.72
2	6	HAGMAN, Mia	FIN	1:13.01
3	4	SOUTINHO, Joana	POR	1:13.73
4	2	KODAJOVA, Natalia	SVK	1:14.24
5	5	MOU, Ying-Hsin	TPE	1:14.82
6	1	SANTA CRUZ, Maria	ARG	1:16.19
7	8	CRUZ, Nadia Vanda	ANG	1:16.62
8	7	GIBBES, Cerian	TRI	1:16.99

HEAT 3

Rnk	Ln	Name	Ctry	Result
1	6	PECZAK, Alicja	POL	1:10.70
2	5	DUMITRU, Kathrin	GER	1:11.92
3	7	LANDIK, Olga	RUS	1:12.55
4	2	OLAY, Maria	ESP	1:12.58
5	3	WILSON, Anna	NZL	1:12.93
6	8	RUDKOVSKAYA, Yelena	BLR	1:13.71
7	4	LACUSTA, Larisa	ROM	1:13.91
8	1	YEO, Joscelin	SIN	1:14.90

HEAT 4

Rnk	Ln	Name	Ctry	Result
1	6	KOVACS, Agnes	HUN	1:09.05
2	7	LISCHKA, Vera	AUT	1:09.68
3	4	BONDARENKO, Svitlana	UKR	1:09.79
4	3	HAN, Xue	CHN	1:10.40
5	5	DENMAN, Helen	AUS	1:10.64
6	1	JALTNER, Hanna	SWE	1:10.69
7	2	IWASAKI, Kyoko	JPN	1:11.33
8	8	OSTLING, Maria	SWE	1:11.58

HEAT 5

Rnk	Ln	Name	Ctry	Result
1	4	BEARD, Amanda	USA	1:09.04
2	3	RILEY, Samantha	AUS	1:09.37
3	5	CLOUTIER, Guylaine	CAN	1:09.72
4	2	TANAKA, Masami	JPN	1:09.89
5	6	FLOOD, Lisa	CAN	1:10.26
6	7	KING, Jaime	GBR	1:10.83
7	1	RUSSELL, Julia	RSA	1:10.87
8	8	BREMOND, Karine	FRA	1:11.80

HEAT 6

Rnk	Ln	Name	Ctry	Result
1	4	HEYNS, Penelope	RSA	1:07.02 W
2	5	BECUE, Brigitte	BEL	1:09.83
3	1	AUSTEVOLL, Elin	NOR	1:09.96
4	7	dalla VALLE, Manuela	ITA	1:10.25
5	3	QUANCE, Kristine	USA	1:10.92
6	2	MILLER, Terrie	NOR	1:11.09
7	8	BAANS, Madelon	NED	1:11.17
8	6	YUAN, Yuan	CHN	1:11.65

FINAL B

Rnk	Ln	Name	Ctry	Result
1	2	HAN, Xue	CHN	1:09.90
2	6	FLOOD, Lisa	CAN	1:10.21
3	7	DENMAN, Helen	AUS	1:10.26
4	5	AUSTEVOLL, Elin	NOR	1:10.27
5	4	TANAKA, Masami	JPN	1:10.43
6	8	PECZAK, Alicja	POL	1:10.44
7	3	dalla VALLE, Manuela	ITA	1:11.19
8	1	JALTNER, Hanna	SWE	1:11.41

FINAL A

Rnk	Ln	Name	Ctry	Result
1	4	HEYNS, Penelope	RSA	1:07.73 G
2	5	BEARD, Amanda	USA	1:08.09 S
3	6	RILEY, Samantha	AUS	1:09.18 B
4	1	BONDARENKO, Svitlana	UKR	1:09.21
5	2	LISCHKA, Vera	AUT	1:09.24
6	7	CLOUTIER, Guylaine	CAN	1:09.40
7	3	KOVACS, Agnes	HUN	1:09.55
8	8	BECUE, Brigitte	BEL	1:09.79

Aquatics—Swimming / *Natation—Natation*

200 m Breaststroke, Men / *200 m brasse, Messieurs*

HEAT 1

Rnk	Ln	Name	Ctry	Result
1	5	BONILLA ABRIL, Roberto	GUA	2:21.86
2	4	SURIANO, Francisco	ESA	2:25.57
3	3	HUANG, Chih-Yung	TPE	2:25.96
	6	KOH, Desmond	SIN	DNS

HEAT 2

Rnk	Ln	Name	Ctry	Result
1	5	KALMIKOVS, Valerijs	LAT	2:17.07
2	8	COUTO, Jose	POR	2:17.28
3	6	GUKOV, Aleksandr	BLR	2:17.49
4	3	CHIA, Elvin	MAS	2:20.39
5	2	VERDINO, Christophe	MON	2:20.77
6	4	TATAROV, Vadim	MDA	2:21.34
7	1	TORRES, Todd	PUR	2:22.66
8	7	BEIGA, Nerijus	LTU	2:23.40

HEAT 3

Rnk	Ln	Name	Ctry	Result
1	5	ROZSA, Norbert	HUN	2:14.66
2	6	GILLINGHAM, Nick	GBR	2:14.96
3	3	MITCHELL, Ryan	AUS	2:15.31
4	4	HAYASHI, Akira	JPN	2:15.37
5	7	FERNANDEZ, Joaquin	ESP	2:16.05
6	8	GONZALEZ MONTESINOS, Mario	CUB	2:16.15
7	1	MALEK, Daniel	CZE	2:17.08
8	2	WANG, Yiwu	CHN	2:19.13

HEAT 4

Rnk	Ln	Name	Ctry	Result
1	4	GUTTLER, Karoly	HUN	2:13.89
2	3	ROGERS, Philip	AUS	2:14.97
3	2	SARNIN, Jean	FRA	2:15.27
4	5	DEBURGHGRAEVE, Fred	BEL	2:16.10
5	1	SIRISANONT, Ratapong	THA	2:17.32
6	6	PERROT, Stephan	FRA	2:18.58
7	7	MORK, Borge	NOR	2:20.42
8	8	ALEKSEYEV, Vadim	ISR	2:20.47

HEAT 5

Rnk	Ln	Name	Ctry	Result
1	4	KORNEYEV, Andrey	RUS	2:14.11
2	5	GROTE, Kurt	USA	2:14.63
3	2	KRAWCZYK, Marek	POL	2:15.17
4	6	WUNDERLICH, Eric	USA	2:15.18
5	3	IVANOV, Andrey	RUS	2:15.56
6	7	CLEVELAND, Jonathan	CAN	2:16.08
7	1	IVANUSA, Dmytro	UKR	2:17.54
8	8	KENT, Paul	NZL	DNS

FINAL B

Rnk	Ln	Name	Ctry	Result
1	6	IVANOV, Andrey	RUS	2:14.37
2	1	GONZALEZ MONTESINOS, Mario	CUB	2:15.11
3	5	MITCHELL, Ryan	AUS	2:15.63
4	2	FERNANDEZ, Joaquin	ESP	2:16.05
5	8	KALMIKOVS, Valerijs	LAT	2:16.23
6	4	SARNIN, Jean	FRA	2:16.26
7	7	CLEVELAND, Jonathan	CAN	2:16.39
8	3	HAYASHI, Akira	JPN	2:16.69

FINAL A

Rnk	Ln	Name	Ctry	Result	
1	6	ROZSA, Norbert	HUN	2:12.57	G
2	4	GUTTLER, Károly	HUN	2:13.03	S
3	5	KORNEYEV, Andrey	RUS	2:13.17	B
4	2	GILLINGHAM, Nick	GBR	2:14.37	
5	7	ROGERS, Philip	AUS	2:14.79	
6	1	KRAWCZYK, Marek	POL	2:14.84	
7	8	WUNDERLICH, Eric	USA	2:15.69	
8	3	GROTE, Kurt	USA	2:16.05	

Aquatics—Swimming / *Natation—Natation*

200 m Breaststroke, Women / *200 m brasse, Dames*

HEAT 1

Rnk	Ln	Name	Ctry	Result
1	3	GRAF, Erika	URU	2:42.97
2	5	CHEREVKO, Aksana	KGZ	2:57.65
	4	VESTERGAARD, Britta	DEN	DNS

HEAT 2

Rnk	Ln	Name	Ctry	Result
1	4	BREMOND, Karine	FRA	2:36.26
2	6	CEBALLOS, Isabel Cristina	COL	2:36.94
3	7	KALMIKOVA, Margarita	LAT	2:39.63
4	3	MOU, Ying-Hsin,	TPE	2:43.94
5	2	CRUZ, Nadia Vanda	ANG	2:44.24
6	1	KODAJOVA, Natalia	SVK	2:45.21
7	5	GIBBES, Cerian	TRI	2:45.87

HEAT 3

Rnk	Ln	Name	Ctry	Result
1	5	KEJZAR, Alenka	SLO	2:33.34
2	6	BECERRA, Lourdes	ESP	2:33.80
3	4	FISCHER, Elvira	AUT	2:33.89
4	1	HAGMAN, Mia	FIN	2:36.11
5	7	ROH, Joo-Hee	KOR	2:36.20
6	2	DUMITRU, Kathrin	GER	2:37.07
7	8	SANTA CRUZ, Maria	ARG	2:37.85
	3	WILSON, Anna	NZL	DNS

HEAT 4

Rnk	Ln	Name	Ctry	Result
1	4	HEYNS, Penelope	RSA	2:26.63 O
2	3	IWASAKI, Kyoko	JPN	2:30.84
3	7	ERIKSSON, Lena	SWE	2:31.65
4	2	BONDARENKO, Svitlana	UKR	2:32.42
5	1	RUSSELL, Julia	RSA	2:32.44
6	8	AUSTEVOLL, Elin	NOR	2:32.48
7	6	MANTS, Riley	CAN	2:32.97
8	5	YUAN, Yuan	CHN	2:33.89

HEAT 5

Rnk	Ln	Name	Ctry	Result
1	4	BEARD, Amanda	USA	2:28.10
2	3	KOVACS, Agnes	HUN	2:29.58
3	6	NEUMANN, Nadine	AUS	2:29.91
4	7	LIN, Li	CHN	2:30.64
5	5	SIROKY, Jilen	USA	2:31.57
6	2	MANHALOVA, Lenka	CZE	2:32.14
7	1	MAKAROVA, Yelena	RUS	2:33.74
8	8	dalla VALLE, Manuela	ITA	2:34.76

HEAT 6

Rnk	Ln	Name	Ctry	Result
1	4	RILEY, Samantha	AUS	2:28.30
2	3	TANAKA, Masami	JPN	2:29.36
3	5	BECUE, Brigitte	BEL	2:29.62
4	6	PETELSKI, Christin	CAN	2:30.30
5	2	PECZAK, Alicja	POL	2:30.64
6	1	HARDIMAN, Marie	GBR	2:31.12
7	7	OSTLING, Maria	SWE	2:33.44
8	8	LACUSTA, Larisa	ROM	2:38.08

200 m Breaststroke, Women / *200 m brasse, Dames*

FINAL B

Rnk	Ln	Name	Ctry	Result
1	7	ERIKSSON, Lena	SWE	2:28.87
2	3	IWASAKI, Kyoko	JPN	2:29.32
3	1	MANHALOVA, Lenka	CZE	2:29.96
4	8	RUSSELL, Julia	RSA	2:30.38
5	5	PECZAK, Alicja	POL	2:30.99
6	6	HARDIMAN, Marie	GBR	2:31.39
7	2	SIROKY, Jilen	USA	2:33.43
8	4	LIN, Li	CHN	2:33.45

FINAL A

Rnk	Ln	Name	Ctry	Result	
1	4	HEYNS, Penelope	RSA	2:25.41	O G
2	5	BEARD, Amanda	USA	2:25.75	S
3	2	KOVACS, Agnes	HUN	2:26.57	B
4	3	RILEY, Samantha	AUS	2:27.91	
5	6	TANAKA, Masami	JPN	2:28.05	
6	1	NEUMANN, Nadine	AUS	2:28.34	
7	7	BECUE, Brigitte	BEL	2:28.36	
8	8	PETELSKI, Christin	CAN	2:31.45	

Aquatics—Swimming / *Natation — Natation*

100 m Butterfly, Men / *100 m papillon, Messieurs*

HEAT 1

Rnk	Ln	Name	Ctry	Result
1	4	FILIPOVSKI, Kire	MKD	56.13
2	5	YANG, Dae-Chul	KOR	57.05
3	3	BRUZAS, Mindaugas	LTU	57.10
4	6	MASUD, Kamal	PAK	58.59
5	2	PEREYRA, David	BOL	1:01.63

HEAT 2

Rnk	Ln	Name	Ctry	Result
1	3	PINEDA, Ruben	ESA	56.01
2	4	NACHAYEV, Ravil	UZB	56.61
3	6	JAKOVLEVS, Arturs	LAT	56.62
4	1	LI, Arthur	HKG	56.92
5	7	THUM, Ping Tjin	SIN	57.07
6	2	ISAZA CHU, Jose	PAN	57.62
7	8	SERGILE, Alain	HAI	58.23
	5	ILES, Salim	ALG	DNS

HEAT 3

Rnk	Ln	Name	Ctry	Result
1	4	TEIXEIRA, Andre	BRA	55.23
2	3	LINSCHEER, Giovanni	SUR	56.09
3	6	GOJKOVIC, Janko	BIH	56.11
4	1	DELGADO, Roberto	ECU	56.29
5	5	ANG, Anthony	MAS	56.41
6	7	CAZMIRCIUC, Maxim	MDA	56.46
7	8	SAGISI, Patrick	GUM	56.93
	2	SEI, Indrek	EST	DNS

HEAT 4

Rnk	Ln	Name	Ctry	Result
1	3	SANCHEZ, Francisco	VEN	53.90
1	5	BUSQUETS, Ricardo	PUR	53.90
3	4	BUYUKUNCU, Derya	TUR	54.89
4	2	MARKOVIC, Vladan	YUG	54.90
5	1	GOLOVCHENKO, Javier	URU	55.26
6	8	PETCU, Razvan	ROM	55.50
7	7	POPOTAS, Georgios	GRE	56.16
8	6	ZINHOM, Tamer	EGY	56.46

HEAT 5

Rnk	Ln	Name	Ctry	Result
1	6	GAVRILOV, Andrey	KAZ	54.56
2	4	MILOSEVIC, Milos	CRO	54.62
3	1	HANSKI, Vesa	FIN	54.73
4	2	GONZALEZ, Jesus	MEX	54.94
5	8	KUTLER, Dan	ISR	55.11
6	7	LOADER, Danyon	NZL	55.39
7	3	MANKOC, Peter	SLO	55.59
8	5	ORIANA, Andrea	ITA	56.04

HEAT 6

Rnk	Ln	Name	Ctry	Result
1	2	CLARKE, Stephen	CAN	53.41
2	4	KULIKOV, Vladislav	RUS	53.54
3	3	ESPOSITO, Franck	FRA	53.77
4	5	HARGIS, John	USA	54.06
5	6	FROLANDER, Lars	SWE	54.37
6	7	LAMPE, Oliver	GER	54.56
7	1	PERDOMO CUENCA, Diego	COL	55.08
	8	LOPEZ-ZUBERO, Martin	ESP	DNS

HEAT 7

Rnk	Ln	Name	Ctry	Result
1	4	MILLER, Scott	AUS	52.89 O
2	7	KHNYKIN, Pavlo	UKR	53.25
3	5	KLIM, Michael	AUS	53.42
4	3	HENDERSON, Mark	USA	53.58
5	6	HICKMAN, James	GBR	53.73
6	2	YAMAMOTO, Takashi	JPN	53.95
7	1	PARENTI, Edward	CAN	54.03
8	8	KALCHEV, Denislav	BUL	54.81

HEAT 8

Rnk	Ln	Name	Ctry	Result
1	4	PANKRATOV, Denis	RUS	52.96
2	2	JIANG, Chengji	CHN	53.40
3	3	SZUKALA, Rafal	POL	53.41
4	6	HORVATH, Peter	HUN	53.69
5	5	SYLANTYEV, Denys	UKR	54.33
6	8	MATSUSHITA, Yukihiro	JPN	54.50
7	1	AARTSEN, Stefan	NED	54.62
8	7	MEOLANS, Jose	ARG	56.02

FINAL B

Rnk	Ln	Name	Ctry	Result
1	3	HICKMAN, James	GBR	53.23
1	4	HENDERSON, Mark	USA	53.23
3	5	HORVATH, Peter	HUN	53.48
4	2	BUSQUETS, Ricardo	PUR	53.65
5	7	YAMAMOTO, Takashi	JPN	53.98
6	6	ESPOSITO, Franck	FRA	54.02
7	1	PARENTI, Edward	CAN	54.19
8	8	HARGIS, John	USA	54.29

FINAL A

Rnk	Ln	Name	Ctry	Result	
1	5	PANKRATOV, Denis	RUS	52.27	W G
2	4	MILLER, Scott	AUS	52.53	S
3	8	KULIKOV, Vladislav	RUS	53.13	B
4	6	JIANG, Chengji	CHN	53.20	
5	2	SZUKALA, Rafal	POL	53.29	
6	1	KLIM, Michael	AUS	53.30	
7	7	CLARKE, Stephen	CAN	53.33	
8	3	KHNYKIN, Pavlo	UKR	53.58	

Aquatics—Swimming / *Natation—Natation*

100 m Butterfly, Women / *100 m papillon, Dames*

HEAT 1

Rnk	Ln	Name	Ctry	Result
1	5	PEREYRA, Maria	ARG	1:03.98
2	3	ZELVIENE, Dita	LTU	1:04.63
3	4	PARK, Woo-Hee	KOR	1:05.36
	6	DAHL, Monica	NAM	DNS

HEAT 2

Rnk	Ln	Name	Ctry	Result
1	5	FRANCISCO, Ana	POR	1:02.98
2	3	KUBALCIKOVA, Marcela	CZE	1:03.82
3	7	BARANOVSKAYA, Natalya	BLR	1:04.09
4	8	ZUHAL, Nida	TUR	1:04.11
5	2	MESKOVSKA, Natasha	MKD	1:04.25
6	4	HSIEH, Shu-Ting	TPE	1:04.39
7	1	KARYSTINOU, Marina	GRE	1:05.05
8	6	UJCIC, Gabrijela	CRO	1:06.85

HEAT 3

Rnk	Ln	Name	Ctry	Result
1	7	ZOLOTUKHINA, Natalya	UKR	1:02.18
2	5	URYNIUK, Anna	POL	1:02.39
3	3	PARSSINEN, Marja	FIN	1:02.53
4	8	MINPRAPHAL, Praphalsai	THA	1:03.35
5	1	KONRADSDOTTIR, Eydis	ISL	1:03.41
6	2	LOOTS, Amanda	RSA	1:03.53
7	6	KLOCKER, Edit	HUN	1:03.61
8	4	MADINE, Marion	IRL	1:03.80

HEAT 4

Rnk	Ln	Name	Ctry	Result
1	4	KASHIMA, Hitomi	JPN	1:00.85
2	5	CAI, Huijue	CHN	1:00.89
3	3	JACOBSEN, Mette	DEN	1:00.91
4	2	ROSE, Gabrielle	BRA	1:01.22
5	7	VOITOVITSCH, Julia	GER	1:01.47
6	6	JEANSON, Cecile	FRA	1:01.58
7	8	ZISU, Loredana	ROM	1:02.66
8	1	YEO, Joscelin	SIN	1:02.71

HEAT 5

Rnk	Ln	Name	Ctry	Result
1	4	MARTINO, Angel	USA	59.31
2	5	O'NEILL, Susan	AUS	1:00.55
3	2	SJOBERG, Johanna	SWE	1:01.01
4	7	SKOU, Sophia	DEN	1:01.25
5	1	NAZEMNOVA, Yelena	RUS	1:01.54
6	6	TOCCHINI, Ilaria	ITA	1:01.83
7	3	KENNEDY, Angela	AUS	1:01.89
8	8	FOOT, Caroline	GBR	1:03.04

HEAT 6

Rnk	Ln	Name	Ctry	Result
1	3	VAN DYKEN, Amy	USA	1:00.04
2	5	LIU, Limin	CHN	1:00.18
3	4	AOYAMA, Ayari	JPN	1:00.20
4	6	POZDEYEVA, Svetlana	RUS	1:01.29
5	2	EVANETZ, Sarah	CAN	1:01.32
6	7	PELAEZ, Maria	ESP	1:01.99
7	8	AMEY, Jessica	CAN	1:02.81
	1	VOLKER, Sandra	GER	DNS

FINAL B

Rnk	Ln	Name	Ctry	Result
1	4	SJOBERG, Johanna	SWE	1:00.76
2	1	NAZEMNOVA, Yelena	RUS	1:00.93
3	3	SKOU, Sophia	DEN	1:00.95
4	7	VOITOVITSCH, Julia	GER	1:01.14
5	8	JEANSON, Cecile	FRA	1:01.20
6	5	ROSE, Gabrielle	BRA	1:01.39
7	2	EVANETZ, Sarah	CAN	1:01.44
8	6	POZDEYEVA, Svetlana	RUS	1:01.62

FINAL A

Rnk	Ln	Name	Ctry	Result
1	5	VAN DYKEN, Amy	USA	59.13 G
2	3	LIU, Limin	CHN	59.14 S
3	4	MARTINO, Angel	USA	59.23 B
4	7	KASHIMA, Hitomi	JPN	1:00.11
5	2	O'NEILL, Susan	AUS	1:00.17
6	6	AOYAMA, Ayari	JPN	1:00.18
7	1	CAI, Huijue	CHN	1:00.46
8	8	JACOBSEN, Mette	DEN	1:00.76

Aquatics—Swimming / *Natation—Natation*

200 m Butterfly, Men / *200 m papillon, Messieurs*

HEAT 1

Rnk	Ln	Name	Ctry	Result
1	4	KWOK, Mark	HKG	2:04.01
2	5	SOZA TORUNO, Walter	NCA	2:04.66
3	3	OSORIO MARTI, Aitor	AND	2:12.59

HEAT 2

Rnk	Ln	Name	Ctry	Result
1	2	ANG, Anthony	MAS	2:03.01
2	6	BRUZAS, Mindaugas	LTU	2:03.76
3	1	INTHARAPICHAI, Niti	THA	2:03.88
4	4	LEE, Jung-Hyung	KOR	2:04.53
5	7	GOLOVCHENKO, Javier	URU	2:04.96
6	3	PANKOV, Dmitriy	UZB	2:05.36
7	8	VASCONCELLOS, Andres	ECU	2:05.98
	5	GONZALEZ, Jesus	MEX	DNS

HEAT 3

Rnk	Ln	Name	Ctry	Result
1	3	GALIC, Dominik	CRO	2:01.17
2	1	MALENKO, Aleksandar	MKD	2:01.46
3	4	MADEIRA, Diogo	POR	2:01.58
4	7	ANDRIOUCHINE, Konstantin	KGZ	2:01.59
5	6	MARKOVIC, Vladan	YUG	2:01.80
6	5	BALLESTER, Jose Luis	ESP	2:02.69
7	8	HORKY, Josef	CZE	2:02.84
8	2	POPOTAS, Georgios	GRE	2:06.00

HEAT 4

Rnk	Ln	Name	Ctry	Result
1	7	SYLANTYEV, Denys	UKR	1:58.04
2	4	MALCHOW, Tom	USA	1:58.69
3	1	HORVATH, Peter	HUN	1:58.76
4	5	ESPOSITO, Franck	FRA	1:58.79
5	2	BARRETT, Casey	CAN	2:00.28
6	3	ABRARD, David	FRA	2:00.60
7	6	YAMAMOTO, Takashi	JPN	2:00.87
8	8	ERGENEKAN, Can	TUR	2:01.65

HEAT 5

Rnk	Ln	Name	Ctry	Result
1	4	GOODMAN, Scott	AUS	1:57.77
2	5	MILLER, Scott	AUS	1:58.97
3	1	AARTSEN, Stefan	NED	2:00.04
4	3	BREMER, Chris-Carol	GER	2:00.48
5	6	CZENE, Attila	HUN	2:00.50
6	7	ORIANA, Andrea	ITA	2:00.67
7	2	KOLESNIKOV, Aleksey	RUS	2:00.77
8	8	MORA, Nelson	VEN	2:01.50

HEAT 6

Rnk	Ln	Name	Ctry	Result
1	3	HICKMAN, James	GBR	1:58.16
2	4	PANKRATOV, Denis	RUS	1:58.28
3	1	HANSKI, Vesa	FIN	1:59.73
4	7	LAMPE, Oliver	GER	1:59.87
5	2	GALKA, Konrad	POL	1:59.97
6	6	LOADER, Danyon	NZL	2:00.81
7	5	CAREY, Ray	USA	2:01.10
8	8	THUM, Ping Tjin	SIN	2:07.00

200 m Butterfly, Men / *200 m papillon, Messieurs*

FINAL B

Rnk	Ln	Name	Ctry	Result	
1	1	CZENE, Attila	HUN	1:58.99	
2	4	HANSKI, Vesa	FIN	1:59.64	
3	2	BARRETT, Casey	CAN	1:59.72	
4	5	LAMPE, Oliver	GER	2:00.08	
5	6	AARTSEN, Stefan	NED	2:00.41	
6	3	GALKA, Konrad	POL	2:00.91	
7	8	ABRARD, David	FRA	2:01.25	
8	7	BREMER, Chris-Carol	GER	2:01.62	

FINAL A

Rnk	Ln	Name	Ctry	Result	
1	6	PANKRATOV, Denis	RUS	1:56.51	G
2	2	MALCHOW, Tom	USA	1:57.44	S
3	4	GOODMAN, Scott	AUS	1:57.48	B
4	1	ESPOSITO, Franck	FRA	1:58.10	
5	8	MILLER, Scott	AUS	1:58.28	
6	5	SYLANTYEV, Denys	UKR	1:58.37	
7	3	HICKMAN, James	GBR	1:58.47	
8	7	HORVATH, Peter	HUN	1:59.12	

Aquatics—Swimming / *Natation—Natation*
200 m Butterfly, Women / *200 m papillon, Dames*

HEAT 1

Rnk	Ln	Name	Ctry	Result
1	4	PARK, Woo-Hee	KOR	2:22.99
2	5	MATA, Melissa	CRC	2:23.89
3	3	ALVAREZ, Sonia	PUR	2:25.24

HEAT 2

Rnk	Ln	Name	Ctry	Result
1	6	ZOLOTUKHINA, Natalya	UKR	2:16.68
2	5	MESKOVSKA, Natasha	MKD	2:17.90
3	8	ZUHAL, Nida	TUR	2:18.46
4	4	KUBALCIKOVA, Marcela	CZE	2:19.38
5	2	PEREYRA, Maria	ARG	2:19.57
6	3	KARYSTINOU, Marina	GRE	2:20.57
7	1	LOOTS, Amanda	RSA	2:20.73
8	7	DANCEVIC, Tinka	CRO	2:20.74

HEAT 3

Rnk	Ln	Name	Ctry	Result
1	3	THOMAS, Petria	AUS	2:10.64
2	4	QU, Yun	CHN	2:11.35
3	6	DEGLAU, Jessica	CAN	2:12.48
4	5	JACKSON, Trina	USA	2:12.69
5	2	SKOU, Sophia	DEN	2:13.59
6	7	TOCCHINI, Ilaria	ITA	2:16.10
7	1	FRANCISCO, Ana	POR	2:17.61
8	8	KLOCKER, Edit	HUN	2:17.90

HEAT 4

Rnk	Ln	Name	Ctry	Result
1	5	HARUNA, Mika	JPN	2:12.59
2	2	JEANSON, Cecile	FRA	2:13.58
3	7	PELAEZ, Maria	ESP	2:13.85
4	6	URYNIUK, Anna	POL	2:13.90
5	4	KASHIMA, Hitomi	JPN	2:16.04
6	1	HSIEH, Shu-Tzu	TPE	2:16.27
7	8	HERBST, Sabine	GER	2:16.66
	3	JACOBSEN, Mette	DEN	DNS

HEAT 5

Rnk	Ln	Name	Ctry	Result
1	4	O'NEILL, Susan	AUS	2:09.46
2	3	SMITH, Michelle	IRL	2:10.03
3	5	LIU, Limin	CHN	2:13.12
4	2	SCHWARTZ, Andrea	CAN	2:13.33
5	7	FRANCO, Barbara	ESP	2:13.34
6	6	SALMEEN, Annette	USA	2:14.69
7	1	ZISU, Loredana	ROM	2:17.56
8	8	MINPRAPHAL, Praphalsai	THA	2:18.19

FINAL B

Rnk	Ln	Name	Ctry	Result
1	6	SKOU, Sophia	DEN	2:12.41
2	3	JEANSON, Cecile	FRA	2:12.99
3	2	PELAEZ, Maria	ESP	2:13.05
4	1	SALMEEN, Annette	USA	2:13.64
4	7	URYNIUK, Anna	POL	2:13.64
6	8	KASHIMA, Hitomi	JPN	2:13.97
7	4	SCHWARTZ, Andrea	CAN	2:14.07
8	5	FRANCO, Barbara	ESP	2:14.16

FINAL A

Rnk	Ln	Name	Ctry	Result	
1	4	O'NEILL, Susan	AUS	2:07.76	G
2	3	THOMAS, Petria	AUS	2:09.82	S
3	5	SMITH, Michelle	IRL	2:09.91	B
4	6	QU, Yun	CHN	2:10.26	
5	8	LIU, Limin	CHN	2:10.70	
6	2	DEGLAU, Jessica	CAN	2:11.40	
7	7	HARUNA, Mika	JPN	2:11.93	
8	1	JACKSON, Trina	USA	2:11.96	

Aquatics—Swimming / *Natation—Natation*
200 m Individual Medley, Men / *200 m quatre nages, Messieurs*

HEAT 1

Rnk	Ln	Name	Ctry	Result
1	4	SOZA TORUNO, Walter	NCA	2:06.15
2	7	SAVITSKIY, Aleksandr	KAZ	2:08.78
3	2	SERRANO, Armando	COL	2:09.67
4	5	FILIPOVSKI, Kire	MKD	2:11.90
5	3	ABDULLAH, Wan	MAS	2:12.11
6	6	ALOTAIBI, S.A.B.S. Sultan	KUW	2:19.77
	1	HEM, Lumphat	CAM	DQ

HEAT 2

Rnk	Ln	Name	Ctry	Result
1	4	MARINIOUK, Serguei	MDA	2:04.99
2	5	HORKY, Josef	CZE	2:05.45
3	3	KALMIKOVS, Valerijs	LAT	2:06.16
4	2	PUKHNATIY, Oleg	UZB	2:06.39
5	6	CAC, Kresimir	CRO	2:06.97
6	7	KIM, Bang-Hyun	KOR	2:06.99
7	1	LOPEZ, Arsenio	PUR	2:07.09
8	8	KWOK, Mark	HKG	2:07.61

HEAT 3

Rnk	Ln	Name	Ctry	Result
1	2	WOUDA, Marcel	NED	2:01.21
2	5	DUNN, Matthew	AUS	2:01.44
3	4	CZENE, Attila	HUN	2:02.10
4	6	KINUGASA, Tatsuya	JPN	2:03.42
5	3	THELOKE, Stev	GER	2:04.23
6	7	ZUBOR, Attila	HUN	2:06.24
7	1	SERHEYEV, Serhiy	UKR	2:06.30
	8	MANKOC, Peter	SLO	DQ

200 m Individual Medley, Men / *200 m quatre nages, Messieurs*

HEAT 4

Rnk	Ln	Name	Ctry	Result
1	4	DOLAN, Tom	USA	2:01.99
2	6	MARCHAND, Xavier	FRA	2:03.17
3	7	van der SPOEL, Martin	NED	2:03.75
4	5	KELLER, Christian	GER	2:03.82
5	2	YOSHIMI, Jo	JPN	2:04.49
6	3	COOMBS, Simon	AUS	2:07.31
7	8	KALCHEV, Denislav	BUL	2:08.16
8	1	KOH, Gerald	SIN	2:11.76

HEAT 5

Rnk	Ln	Name	Ctry	Result
1	4	SIEVINEN, Jani	FIN	2:01.05
2	5	MYDEN, Curtis	CAN	2:01.50
3	3	BURGESS, Greg	USA	2:01.93
4	6	SACCHI, Luca	ITA	2:03.24
5	8	SIRISANONT, Ratapong	THA	2:05.18
6	2	MALINSKI, Marcin	POL	2:05.42
7	7	LEHTINEN, Jyri	FIN	2:05.51
8	1	KOH, Desmond	SIN	2:08.99

FINAL B

Rnk	Ln	Name	Ctry	Result
1	6	KELLER, Christian	GER	2:02.90
2	3	van der SPOEL, Martin	NED	2:03.01
3	4	SACCHI, Luca	ITA	2:03.49
4	2	THELOKE, Stev	GER	2:03.94
5	1	MARINIOUK, Serguei	MDA	2:04.11
6	5	KINUGASA, Tatsuya	JPN	2:04.59
7	8	SIRISANONT, Ratapong	THA	2:05.02
8	7	YOSHIMI, Jo	JPN	2:05.42

FINAL A

Rnk	Ln	Name	Ctry	Result	
1	1	CZENE, Attila	HUN	1:59.91	O G
2	4	SIEVINEN, Jani	FIN	2:00.13	S
3	6	MYDEN, Curtis	CAN	2:01.13	B
4	5	WOUDA, Marcel	NED	2:01.45	
5	3	DUNN, Matthew	AUS	2:01.57	
6	2	BURGESS, Greg	USA	2:02.56	
7	7	DOLAN, Tom	USA	2:03.89	
8	8	MARCHAND, Xavier	FRA	2:04.29	

Aquatics—Swimming / *Natation—Natation*

200 m Individual Medley, Women / *200 m quatre nages, Dames*

HEAT 1

Rnk	Ln	Name	Ctry	Result
1	4	BOGATYREVA, Olga	KGZ	2:26.42
2	5	SABATE, Meritxell	AND	2:37.38
3	3	GHNIEM, Mira	JOR	2:56.99

HEAT 2

Rnk	Ln	Name	Ctry	Result
1	5	AUSTEVOLL, Elin	NOR	2:19.81
2	3	ADEL, Carolyn	SUR	2:21.54
3	4	CHAVES, Petra	POR	2:22.03
4	7	LEE, Jie-Hyun	KOR	2:22.97
5	1	ALVAREZ, Sonia	PUR	2:25.57
6	2	THOMSON, Gillian	PHI	2:25.87
7	6	UJHELYI, Beata	HUN	2:26.77
8	8	TSAI, Shu-Min	TPE	2:28.71

HEAT 3

Rnk	Ln	Name	Ctry	Result
1	4	COADA, Beatrice	ROM	2:16.80
2	2	PARERA, Silvia	ESP	2:17.67
3	8	KEJZAR, Alenka	SLO	2:18.39
4	6	SARAKATSANI, Aikaterini	GRE	2:19.74
5	7	RUSSELL, Julia	RSA	2:20.40
6	5	NEMEC, Martina	AUT	2:21.10
7	1	MINPRAPHAL, Praphalsai	THA	2:22.34
8	3	CLITON, Nadege	FRA	2:25.25

HEAT 4

Rnk	Ln	Name	Ctry	Result
1	3	LIMPERT, Marianne	CAN	2:15.12
2	5	MALAR, Joanne	CAN	2:16.34
3	7	MORAVCOVA, Martina	SVK	2:16.50
4	4	QUANCE, Kristine	USA	2:17.48
5	1	VESTERGAARD, Britta	DEN	2:18.35
6	6	ROSE, Gabrielle	BRA	2:18.99
7	2	WILSON, Anna	NZL	2:19.97
8	8	LAPUNOVA, Olena	UKR	2:20.76

HEAT 5

Rnk	Ln	Name	Ctry	Result
1	3	SMIT, Minouche	NED	2:16.30
2	4	WAGNER, Allison	USA	2:16.32
3	5	SMITH, Michelle	IRL	2:16.35
4	1	KARLSSON, Louise	SWE	2:16.37
5	7	HERBST, Sabine	GER	2:18.00
6	6	ROLPH, Susan	GBR	2:18.81
7	8	SHMELYOVA, Darya	RUS	2:20.34
8	2	KUROTORI, Fumie	JPN	2:20.58

HEAT 6

Rnk	Ln	Name	Ctry	Result
1	5	OVERTON, Elli	AUS	2:15.81
2	3	LIN, Li	CHN	2:16.31
3	4	WU, Yanyan	CHN	2:16.55
4	2	JOHNSON, Emma	AUS	2:17.02
5	1	PECZAK, Alicja	POL	2:17.48
6	6	BECUE, Brigitte	BEL	2:18.28
7	7	MANHALOVA, Lenka	CZE	2:18.43
8	8	YEO, Joscelin	SIN	2:21.76

FINAL B

Rnk	Ln	Name	Ctry	Result
1	6	QUANCE, Kristine	USA	2:15.24
2	5	WU, Yanyan	CHN	2:16.61
3	1	HERBST, Sabine	GER	2:16.68
4	3	COADA, Beatrice	ROM	2:16.75
5	4	MORAVCOVA, Martina	SVK	2:17.40
6	8	VESTERGAARD, Britta	DEN	2:17.95
7	2	PECZAK, Alicja	POL	2:18.21
8	7	PARERA, Silvia	ESP	2:19.92

FINAL A

Rnk	Ln	Name	Ctry	Result	
1	1	SMITH, Michelle	IRL	2:13.93	G
2	4	LIMPERT, Marianne	CAN	2:14.35	S
3	6	LIN, Li	CHN	2:14.74	B
4	7	MALAR, Joanne	CAN	2:15.30	
5	5	OVERTON, Elli	AUS	2:16.04	
6	2	WAGNER, Allison	USA	2:16.43	
7	3	SMIT, Minouche	NED	2:16.73	
8	8	KARLSSON, Louise	SWE	2:17.25	

Aquatics—Swimming / *Natation—Natation*
400 m Individual Medley, Men / *400 m quatre nages, Messieurs*

HEAT 1

Rnk	Ln	Name	Ctry	Result
1	5	SOZA TORUNO, Walter	NCA	4:32.11
2	3	LOPEZ, Arsenio	PUR	4:34.81
3	4	ABDULLAH, Wan	MAS	4:38.95

HEAT 2

Rnk	Ln	Name	Ctry	Result
1	4	NAMESNIK, Eric	USA	4:16.21
2	5	SACCHI, Luca	ITA	4:19.63
3	6	MARINIOUK, Serguei	MDA	4:20.24
4	2	HVIID, Frederik	ESP	4:23.67
5	3	KURASAWA, Toshiaki	JPN	4:24.83
6	1	BERMUDEZ, Alejandro	COL	4:27.97
7	8	KWOK, Mark	HKG	4:31.13
8	7	CAC, Kresimir	CRO	4:34.02

HEAT 3

Rnk	Ln	Name	Ctry	Result
1	5	DUNN, Matthew	AUS	4:19.51
2	4	SIEVINEN, Jani	FIN	4:23.13
3	3	STEED, Trent	AUS	4:24.39
4	2	KINUGASA, Tatsuya	JPN	4:26.73
5	6	BATHAZI, Istvan	HUN	4:27.37
6	7	KALMIKOVS, Valerijs	LAT	4:28.04
7	1	MALENKO, Aleksandar	MKD	4:34.06
8	8	KOH, Desmond	SIN	4:36.87

HEAT 4

Rnk	Ln	Name	Ctry	Result
1	6	WOUDA, Marcel	NED	4:17.30
2	4	DOLAN, Tom	USA	4:17.66
3	3	MALINSKI, Marcin	POL	4:18.34
4	5	MYDEN, Curtis	CAN	4:18.43
5	7	HORKY, Josef	CZE	4:26.58
6	1	SIRISANONT, Ratapong	THA	4:26.99
7	2	KISS, Gergo	HUN	4:28.05
8	8	KIM, Bang-Hyun	KOR	4:31.16

FINAL B

Rnk	Ln	Name	Ctry	Result
1	4	HVIID, Frederik	ESP	4:22.47
2	3	KURASAWA, Toshiaki	JPN	4:23.36
3	2	KINUGASA, Tatsuya	JPN	4:24.25
4	7	SIRISANONT, Ratapong	THA	4:26.35
5	8	BERMUDEZ, Alejandro	COL	4:26.64
6	6	HORKY, Josef	CZE	4:28.39
7	5	STEED, Trent	AUS	4:29.35
	1	BATHAZI, Istvan	HUN	DQ

FINAL A

Rnk	Ln	Name	Ctry	Result	
1	3	DOLAN, Tom	USA	4:14.90	G
2	4	NAMESNIK, Eric	USA	4:15.25	S
3	2	MYDEN, Curtis	CAN	4:16.28	B
4	7	DUNN, Matthew	AUS	4:16.66	
5	5	WOUDA, Marcel	NED	4:17.71	
6	1	SACCHI, Luca	ITA	4:18.31	
7	6	MALINSKI, Marcin	POL	4:20.50	
8	8	MARINIOUK, Serguei	MDA	4:21.15	

Aquatics—Swimming / *Natation—Natation*
400 m Individual Medley, Women / *400 m quatre nages, Dames*

HEAT 1

Rnk	Ln	Name	Ctry	Result
1	4	GERVY, Yseult	BEL	4:53.11
2	7	ADEL, Carolyn	SUR	4:55.48
3	5	BOSEVSKA, Mirjana	MKD	4:55.57
4	1	SARAKATSANI, Aikaterini	GRE	4:56.32
5	3	MINPRAPHAL, Praphalsai	THA	4:58.33
6	2	LEE, Ji-Hyun	KOR	4:59.52
7	6	HSIEH, Shu-Tzu	TPE	5:01.70

HEAT 2

Rnk	Ln	Name	Ctry	Result
1	3	HERBST, Sabine	GER	4:45.36
2	7	BECERRA, Lourdes	ESP	4:45.54
3	5	MALAR, Joanne	CAN	4:47.85
4	6	OVERTON, Elli	AUS	4:49.82
5	4	WU, Yanyan	CHN	4:54.07
6	2	WILSON, Anna	NZL	4:55.72
7	8	NEMEC, Martina	AUT	5:02.52
8	1	CLITON, Nadege	FRA	5:06.46

HEAT 3

Rnk	Ln	Name	Ctry	Result
1	5	SMITH, Michelle	IRL	4:43.79
2	2	METZLER, Whitney	USA	4:44.74
3	3	KUROTORI, Fumie	JPN	4:48.51
4	7	HIRANAKA, Hideko	JPN	4:49.32
5	1	CHRASTOVA, Pavla	CZE	4:51.35
6	4	CHEN, Yan	CHN	4:53.87
7	8	VESTERGAARD, Britta	DEN	4:55.03
8	6	RUND, Cathleen	GER	4:55.30

HEAT 4

Rnk	Ln	Name	Ctry	Result
1	4	EGERSZEGI, Krisztina	HUN	4:43.09
2	3	JOHNSON, Emma	AUS	4:43.45
3	5	WAGNER, Allison	USA	4:44.06
4	1	COADA, Beatrice	ROM	4:44.66
5	7	SWEETNAM, Nancy	CAN	4:48.56
6	2	CERNA, Hana	CZE	4:49.43
7	8	HARDCASTLE, Sarah	GBR	4:54.64
8	6	SHMELYOVA, Darya	RUS	4:57.06

FINAL B

Rnk	Ln	Name	Ctry	Result
1	4	MALAR, Joanne	CAN	4:46.34
2	2	CERNA, Hana	CZE	4:46.78
3	3	SWEETNAM, Nancy	CAN	4:47.55
4	5	KUROTORI, Fumie	JPN	4:47.98
5	6	HIRANAKA, Hideko	JPN	4:48.72
6	7	OVERTON, Elli	AUS	4:50.73
7	8	GERVY, Yseult	BEL	4:52.89
8	1	CHRASTOVA, Pavla	CZE	4:56.23

FINAL A

Rnk	Ln	Name	Ctry	Result	
1	3	SMITH, Michelle	IRL	4:39.18	G
2	6	WAGNER, Allison	USA	4:42.03	S
3	4	EGERSZEGI, Krisztina	HUN	4:42.53	B
4	1	HERBST, Sabine	GER	4:43.78	
5	5	JOHNSON, Emma	AUS	4:44.02	
6	2	COADA, Beatrice	ROM	4:44.91	
7	8	BECERRA, Lourdes	ESP	4:45.17	
8	7	METZLER, Whitney	USA	4:46.20	

Aquatics—Swimming / *Natation—Natation*
4 x 100 m Freestyle Relay, Men / *4 x 100 m relais nage libre, Messieurs*

HEAT 1

Rnk	Ln	Ctry	Names	Result
1	4	GER	PINGER, Mark / LUDERITZ, Alexander / ZIKARSKY, Bengt / ZIKARSKY, Bjoern	3:19.27
2	5	SWE	LETSLER, Fredrik / FROLANDER, Lars / WALLIN, Christer / WALLBERG, Johan	3:20.74
3	3	GBR	SHACKELL, Nicholas / RAPLEY, Alan / STEVENS, Mark / FIBBENS, Michael	3:21.34
4	6	CRO	VUCETIC, Miroslav / MILOSEVIC, Milos / LONCAR, Alen / KANJER, Marijan	3:26.02
5	7	PUR	GONZALEZ, Eduardo / GONZALEZ, Jose / LOPEZ, Arsenio / BUSQUETS, Ricardo	3:28.27
	2	KAZ	YEGOROV, Aleksey / USHKALOV, Sergey / KHOVRIN, Aleksey / BORISENKO, Sergey	DQ

HEAT 2

Rnk	Ln	Ctry	Names	Result
1	3	NED	GEELEN, Pie / VEENS, Mark Hermanus / van der SPOEL, Martin / van den HOOGENBAND, Pieter	3:20.16
2	5	BRA	SCHERER, Fernando / MASSURA, Alexandre / CORDEIRO, Andre / BORGES, Gustavo	3:20.21
3	4	AUS	KLIM, Michael / VANDER-WAL, Ian / LOGAN, Scott / FYDLER, Chris	3:20.88
4	6	ROM	IVAN, Nicolae / PETCU, Razvan / BADITA, Horatiu / IOANOVICI, Alexandru	3:21.66
5	2	FIN	SIEVINEN, Jani / KASVIO, Antti / BLOMQVIS, Janne / VARONEN, Kalle	3:22.99
6	7	ECU	SANTOS, Julio / DELGADO, Felipe / DELGADO, Roberto / SANTOS, Javier	3:27.77

4 x 100 m Freestyle Relay, Men / *4 x 100 m relais nage libre, Messieurs*

HEAT 3

Rnk	Ln	Ctry	Names	Result
1	4	USA	FOX, David / TUCKER, Scott / SCHUMACHER, Bradley / DAVIS, Josh	3:18.40
2	5	RUS	YEGOROV, Roman / PIMANKOV, Denis / USHKOV, Konstantin / PYSHNENKO, Vladimir	3:20.39
3	3	NZL	STEEL, John / TONGUE, Walter / LOADER, Danyon / BRAY, Trent	3:21.65
4	6	FRA	DEPICKERE, Ludovic / GRUSON, Nicolas / CHAVATTE, Peirrick / LEFEVRE, Frederic	3:21.79
5	2	VEN	HENAO, Diego / SANTANDER, Carlos / CARRIZO, Alejandro / SANCHEZ, Francisco	3:23.04
6	7	UZB	NACHAYEV, Ravil / TSVETKOVSKIY, Oleg / PUKHNATIY, Oleg / KABANOV, Vyacheslav	3:28.33
7	1	KGZ	ASHIHMIN, Sergey / KVASSOV, Andrei / LAPINE, Dmitri / VASILEV, Vitaliy	3:30.62

FINAL

Rnk	Ln	Ctry	Names	Result	
1	4	USA	OLSEN, Jon / DAVIS, Josh / SCHUMACHER, Bradley / HALL, Gary, Jr.	3:15.41	O G
2	2	RUS	YEGOROV, Roman / POPOV, Aleksander / PREDKIN, Vladimir / PYSHNENKO, Vladimir	3:17.06	S
3	5	GER	TROEGER, Christian / ZIKARSKY, Bengt / ZIKARSKY, Bjoern / PINGER, Mark	3:17.20	B
4	6	BRA	SCHERER, Fernando / MASSURA, Alexandre / CORDEIRO, Andre / BORGES, Gustavo	3:18.30	
5	3	NED	VEENS, Mark Hermanus / GEELEN, Pie / van der SPOEL, Martin / van den HOOGENBAND, Pieter	3:19.02	
6	1	AUS	KLIM, Michael / DUNN, Matthew / LOGAN, Scott / FYDLER, Chris	3:20.13	
7	7	SWE	FROLANDER, Lars / LETSLER, Fredrik / HOLMERTZ, Anders / WALLIN, Christer	3:20.16	
8	8	GBR	SHACKELL, Nicholas / RAPLEY, Alan / STEVENS, Mark / FIBBENS, Michael	3:21.52	

Aquatics—Swimming / *Natation—Natation*
4 x 100 m Freestyle Relay, Women / *4 x 100 m relais nage libre, Dames*

HEAT 1

Rnk	Ln	Ctry	Names	Result
1	5	RUS	LESHUKOVA, Svetlana / SOROKINA, Natalya / NAZEMNOVA, Yelena / MESHCHERYAKOVA, Natalya	3:47.33
2	4	AUS	WINDSOR, Anna / RYAN, Sarah / MACKIE, Lise / GREVILLE, Julia	3:47.94
3	3	GBR	ROLPH, Susan / SHEPPARD, Alison / WILLMOTT, Carrie / PICKERING, Karen	3:48.26
4	6	FRA	FIGUES, Solennes / DELORD, Jacqueline / LEGLER, Casey / LE VERGE, Marianne	3:48.30
5	2	FIN	SALMELA, Minna / HARMOKIVI, Paula / PARSSINEN, Marja / HEIKKILA, Marja	3:50.33
6	7	KOR	LEE, Bo-Eun / SEO, So-Yung / LEE, Jie-Hyun / JEONG, Eun-Na	3:57.83

HEAT 2

Rnk	Ln	Ctry	Names	Result
1	4	USA	THOMPSON, Jenny / FOX, Catherine / JACOB, Lisa / VALERIO, Melanie	3:42.36
2	2	NED	MUIS, Marianne / MASSEURS, Manon / van HOFWEGEN, Willemina / SMIT, Minouche	3:43.63
3	3	SWE	JOHNCKE, Louise / SJOBERG, Johanna / KARLSSON, Louise / OLOFSSON, Linda	3:45.39
4	6	ROM	DIACONESCU, Ioana / HEREA, Florina / TRUFASU, Andreea / DOBRESCU, Liliana	3:48.43
5	5	JPN	MINAMOTO, Sumika / IMOTO, Naoko / YAMANOI, Eri / CHIBA, Suzu	3:48.77
6	7	SUI	DIEZI, Dominique / ZAHND, Nicole / PREACCO, Lara / PAQUIER, Sandrine	3:53.30

HEAT 3

Rnk	Ln	Ctry	Names	Result
1	4	CHN	SHAN, Ying / CHAO, Na / NIAN, Yun / LE, Jingyi	3:44.06
2	5	GER	OSYGUS, Simone / BUSCHSCHULTE, Antje / FREITAG, Meike / van ALMSICK, Franziska	3:44.17
3	3	CAN	SHAKESPEARE, Shannon / HOWARD, Julie / MOODY, Andrea / LIMPERT, Marianne	3:45.66
4	6	DEN	NIELSEN, Mette / JACOBSEN, Mette / EGDAL, Karen / JENSEN, Ditte	3:48.93
5	2	ESP	CERON, Blanca / MADRID, Fatima / GARABATOS, Susana / FRANCO, Claudia	3:49.47
6	1	BLR	ZHIDKO, Svetlana / BORODICH, Inga / BARANOVSKAYA, Natalya / POPCHENKO, Yelena	3:50.22
7	7	TPE	CHANG, Wei-Chia / TSAI, Shu-Min / LIN, Chien-Ju / LIN, Chi-Chan	3:56.39

FINAL

Rnk	Ln	Ctry	Names	Result	
1	4	USA	MARTINO, Angel / VAN DYKEN, Amy / FOX Catherine / THOMPSON, Jenny	3:39.29	O G
2	3	CHN	LE, Jingyi / CHAO, Na / NIAN, Yun / SHAN, Ying	3:40.48	S
3	6	GER	VOELKER, Sandra / OSYGUS, Simone / BUSCHSCHULTE, Antje / van ALMSICK, Franziska	3:41.48	B
4	5	NED	MUIS, Marianne / SMIT, Minouche / van HOFWEGEN, Willemina / BRIENESSE, Karin	3:42.40	
5	2	SWE	OLOFSSON, Linda / JOHNCKE, Louise / KARLSSON, Louise / SJOBERG, Johanna	3:44.91	
6	8	AUS	RYAN, Sarah / GREVILLE, Julia / MACKIE, Lise / O'NEILL, Susan	3:45.31	
7	7	CAN	SHAKESPEARE, Shannon / HOWARD, Julie / MOODY, Andrea / LIMPERT, Marianne	3:46.27	
	1	RUS	NAZEMNOVA, Yelena / LESHUKOVA, Svetlana / MESHCHERYAKOVA, Natalya / SOROKINA, Natalya	DQ	

Aquatics—Swimming / *Natation—Natation*
4 x 200 m Freestyle Relay, Men / *4 x 200 m relais nage libre, Messieurs*

HEAT 1

Rnk	Ln	Ctry	Names	Result
1	5	GBR	SALTER, James / CLAYTON, Andrew / STEVENS, Mark / PALMER, Paul	7:21.92
2	4	GER	DUBROVIN, Konstantin / KELLER, Christian / LAMPE, Oliver / ZESNER, Steffen	7:22.17
3	3	BRA	LEAL, Cassiano / LIMA, Luiz / SAEZ, Fernando / TEIXEIRA, Andre	7:28.82
4	2	VEN	SANCHEZ, Francisco / SANTANDER, Carlos / HENAO, Diego / MANZANO, Rafael	7:32.63
5	6	CRO	KOZULJ, Gordan / VUCETIC, Miroslav / KANJER, Marijan / STRAHIJA, Marko	7:43.69

HEAT 2

Rnk	Ln	Ctry	Names	Result
1	5	ITA	BREMBILLA, Emiliano / IDINI, Emanuele / SICILIANO, Piermaria / ROSOLINO, Massimiliano	7:22.69
2	4	AUS	PERKINS, Kieren / HOUSMAN, Glen / VANDER-WAL, Ian / ALLEN, Malcolm	7:23.24
3	3	NZL	BRAY, Trent / BURDAN, Murray / CAMERON, Scott / LOADER, Danyon	7:24.35
4	6	UZB	KABANOV, Vyacheslav / AGAFONOV, Aleksandr / PANKOV, Dmitriy / TSVETKOVSKIY, Oleg	7:40.60
5	7	ECU	DELGADO, Roberto / SANTOS, Julio / SANTOS, Javier / VASCONCELLOS, Andres	7:54.37
6	2	KGZ	ASHIHMIN, Sergey / KVASSOV, Andrei / LAPINE, Dmitri / VASILEV, Vitaliy	8:00.00

HEAT 3

Rnk	Ln	Ctry	Names	Result
1	4	USA	BERUBE, Ryan / HUDEPOHL, Joe / SCHUMACHER, Bradley / OLSEN, Jon	7:18.28
2	5	SWE	WALLIN, Christer / FROLANDER, Lars / LYRBRING, Anders / HOLMERTZ, Anders	7:20.61
3	3	FRA	de FABRIQUE, Yann / POIROT, Lionel / ORSONI, Bruno / BORDEAU, Christophe	7:22.98
4	6	NED	van den HOOGENBAND, Pieter / HOEIJMANS, Tim / van der SPOEL, Martin / van der ZIJDEN, Mark	7:23.39
5	2	KOR	KOH, Yun-Ho / LEE, Gyu-Chang / WOO, Cheol / KIM, Min-Suk	7:45.98
6	7	SIN	SNG, Ju Wei / KOH, Gerald / KOH, Desmond / THUM, Ping Tjin	7:54.19

FINAL

Rnk	Ln	Ctry	Names	Result	
1	4	USA	DAVIS, Josh / HUDEPOHL, Joe / SCHUMACHER, Bradley / BERUBE, Ryan	7:14.84	G
2	5	SWE	WALLIN, Christer / HOLMERTZ, Anders / FROLANDER, Lars / LYRBRING, Anders	7:17.56	S
3	6	GER	HEILMANN, Aimo / KELLER, Christian / TROEGER, Christian / ZESNER, Steffen	7:17.71	B
4	1	AUS	KOWALSKI, Daniel / KLIM, Michael / ALLEN, Malcolm / DUNN, Matthew	7:18.47	
5	3	GBR	PALMER, Paul / CLAYTON, Andrew / STEVENS, Mark / SALTER, James	7:18.74	
6	2	ITA	ROSOLINO, Massimiliano / IDINI, Emanuele / MERISI, Emanuele / SICILIANO, Piermaria	7:19.92	
7	8	NED	WOUDA, Marcel / van der ZIJDEN, Mark / van der SPOEL, Martin / van den HOOGENBAND, Pieter	7:21.96	
8	7	FRA	de FABRIQUE, Yann / POIROT, Lionel / ORSONI, Bruno / BORDEAU, Christophe	7:24.85	

Aquatics—Swimming / *Natation — Natation*

4 x 200 m Freestyle Relay, Women / *4 x 200 m relais nage libre, Dames*

HEAT 1

Rnk	Ln	Ctry	Names	Result
1	5	JPN	YAMANOI, Eri / IMOTO, Naoko / MIYAKE, Aiko / CHIBA, Suzu	8:09.46 O
2	3	NED	SMIT, Minouche / STOKKERS, Patricia / BRIENESSE, Karin / GEURTS, Carla Louise	8:12.78
3	4	CHN	CHEN, Yan / PU, Yiqi / WANG, Luna / NIAN, Yun	8:13.29
4	6	FRA	LE VERGE, Marianne / RICARDO, Helene / CHOUX, Leatitia / FIGUES, Solennes	8:18.90
5	2	SUI	PAQUIER, Sandrine / DIEZI, Dominique / ZAHND, Nicole / STRASSER, Chantal	8:21.55
6	7	BLR	ZHIDKO, Svetlana / BORODICH, Inga / BARANOVSKAYA, Natalya / POPCHENKO, Yelena	8:21.70
7	1	ARG	PEREYRA, Maria / BARRANCOS, Alicia / ALVAREZ, Valeria / BERTELLOTTI, Maria	8:46.36

HEAT 2

Rnk	Ln	Ctry	Names	Result
1	4	USA	JACOB, Lisa / WHITNEY, Ashley / TAORMINA, Sheila / SALMEEN, Annette	8:04.99 O
2	5	CAN	MALAR, Joanne / SIMARD, Sophie / LIMPERT, Marianne / DEGLAU, Jessica	8:12.03
3	3	SWE	JOHNCKE, Louise / SJOBERG, Johanna / LILLHAGE, Josefin / SANDLUND, Asa	8:13.64
4	6	GBR	HUDDART, Claire / HORNER, Victoria / BELTON, Janine / PICKERING, Karen	8:14.92
5	2	NZL	CATHERWOOD, Sarah / FITCH, Alison / WILSON, Anna / BAINBRIDGE, Dionne	8:14.98
6	1	KOR	JEONG, Eun-Na / LEE, Bo-Eun / LEE, Jie-Hyun / SEO, So-Yung	8:22.90
7	8	TPE	TSAI, Shu-Min / CHANG, Wei-Chia / HSIEH, Shu-Ting / LIN, Chi-Chan	8:27.61

HEAT 3

Rnk	Ln	Ctry	Names	Result
1	4	GER	OSYGUS, Simone / FREITAG, Meike / SCHOLZ, Anke / van ALMSICK, Franziska	8:08.58
2	5	AUS	GREVILLE, Julia / MACKIE, Lise / JOHNSON, Emma / O'NEILL, Susan	8:09.33
3	6	ROM	DOBRESCU, Liliana / ZISU, Loredana / DIACONESCU, Ioana / NEGREA, Carla	8:10.77
4	2	RUS	LITOVCHENKO, Tatyana / YAYTSKAYA, Inna / NAZEMNOVA, Yelena / CHEMEZOVA, Nadezhda	8:16.06
5	3	DEN	JENSEN, Ditte / VESTERGAARD, Britta / RAABY, Britt / PUGGAARD, Berit	8:16.32
6	1	CZE	CERNA, Hana / KYNEROVA, Kristyna / CHRASTOVA, Pavla / SPLICHALOVA, Olga	8:21.19
7	7	KGZ	POLEJAEVA, Viktoria / TITOVA, Olga / KOROTAEVA, Olga / BOGATYREVA, Olga	8:45.76

FINAL

Rnk	Ln	Ctry	Names	Result
1	4	USA	JACKSON, Trina / TEUSCHER, Cristina / TAORMINA, Sheila / THOMPSON, Jenny	7:59.87 O G
2	5	GER	van ALMSICK, Franziska / KIELGASS, Kerstin / SCHOLZ, Anke / HASE, Dagmar	8:01.55 S
3	3	AUS	GREVILLE, Julia / STEVENSON, Nicole / JOHNSON, Emma / O'NEILL, Susan	8:05.47 B
4	6	JPN	YAMANOI, Eri / IMOTO, Naoko / MIYAKE, Aiko / CHIBA, Suzu	8:07.46
5	7	CAN	LIMPERT, Marianne / SHAKESPEARE, Shannon / SCHWARTZ, Andrea / DEGLAU, Jessica	8:08.16
6	1	NED	GEURTS, Carla Louise / STOKKERS, Patricia / SMIT, Minouche / VLIEGHUIS, Kirsten	8:08.48
7	2	ROM	DOBRESCU, Liliana / ZISU, Loredana / DIACONESCU, Ioana / NEGREA, Carla	8:10.02
8	8	CHN	NIAN, Yun / WANG, Luna / CHEN, Yan / SHAN, Ying	8:15.38

Aquatics—Swimming / *Natation — Natation*

4 x 100 m Medley Relay, Men / *4 x 100 m relais quatre nages, Messieurs*

HEAT 1

Rnk	Ln	Ctry	Names	Result
1	5	UKR	NIKOLAYCHUK, Volodymyr / DZHABURIYA, Oleksandr / SYLANTYEV, Denys / KHNYKIN, Pavlo	3:42.29
2	4	KAZ	USHKALOV, Sergey / SAVITSKIY, Aleksandr / GAVRILOV, Andrey / YEGOROV, Aleksey	3:49.51
3	3	MAS	LIM, Alex / CHIA, Elvin / ANG, Anthony / ABDULLAH, Wan	3:52.58

HEAT 2

Rnk	Ln	Ctry	Names	Result
1	4	AUS	HAENEN, Toby / ROGERS, Philip / MILLER, Scott / KLIM, Michael	3:41.30
2	5	JPN	KONNAI, Keitaro / HAYASHI, Akira / YAMAMOTO, Takashi / ITO, Shunsuke	3:41.78
3	3	FRA	SCHOTT, Franck / LATOCHA, Vladimir / ESPOSITO, Franck / GRUSON, Nicolas	3:42.94
4	7	LTU	GRIGALIONIS, Darius / BEIGA, Nerijus / BRUZAS, Mindaugas / MAZUOLIS, Raimundas	3:51.31
5	1	PUR	BODEGA, Carlos / TORRES, Todd / BUSQUETS, Ricardo / GONZALEZ, Jose	3:52.04
6	8	KGZ	PRIAHIN, Konstantin / PETRACHOV, Evgeni / ANDRIOUCHINE, Konstantin / ASHIHMIN, Sergey	3:56.24

HEAT 3

Rnk	Ln	Ctry	Names	Result
1	5	GER	THELOKE, Stev / WARNECKE, Mark / LAMPE, Oliver / ZIKARSKY, Bengt	3:41.10
2	4	RUS	POPOV, Aleksander / IVANOVSKIY, Roman / KULIKOV, Vladislav / YEGOROV, Roman	3:41.49
3	3	POL	SIEMBIDA, Mariusz / KRAWCZYK, Marek / SZUKALA, Rafal / KIZIEROWSKI, Bartosz	3:41.72
4	2	ISR	URBACH, Eithan / ALEKSEYEV, Vadim / KUTLER, Dan / BRUCK, Yoav	3:42.24
5	6	NZL	WINTER, Jonathan / KENT, Paul / LOADER, Danyon / BRAY, Trent	3:45.80
6	7	CRO	KARLO, Tomislav / CAC, Kresimir / MILOSEVIC, Milos / VUCETIC, Miroslav	3:50.09
7	1	KOR	KIM, Min-Suk / CHO, Kwang-Jea / YANG, Dae-Chu / KOH, Yun-Ho	3:50.84
8	8	SIN	KOH, Gerald / KOH, Desmond / THUM, Ping Tjin / SNG, Ju Wei	3:59.51

HEAT 4

Rnk	Ln	Ctry	Names	Result
1	4	USA	SCHWENK, Tripp / GROTE, Kurt / HARGIS, John / DAVIS, Josh	3:39.93
2	5	HUN	DEUTSCH, Tamas / GUTTLER, Karoly / HORVATH, Peter / ZUBOR, Attila	3:41.05
3	7	NED	van der SPOEL, Martin / KUIPERS, Benno Gerrit / AARTSEN, Stefan / van den HOOGENBAND, Pieter	3:42.42
4	6	CAN	BRAKNIS, Robert / CLEVELAND, Jonathan / PARENTI, Edward / CLARKE, Stephen	3:42.95
5	2	CHN	ZHAO, Yi / ZENG, Qiliang / JIANG, Chengji / ZHAO, Lifeng	3:43.50
6	1	THA	PHUANGTHONG, Dulyarit / SIRISANONT, Ratapong / INTHARAPICHAI, Niti / SETHSOTHORN, Torlarp	3:56.80
	3	GBR	WILLEY, Neil / MADEN, Richard / HICKMAN, James / SHACKELL, Nicholas	DQ
	8	POR	LAURENTINO, Nuno / COUTO, Jose / CABRITA, Miguel / MACHADO, Miguel	DQ

FINAL

Rnk	Ln	Ctry	Names	Result
1	4	USA	ROUSE, Jeff / LINN, Jeremy / HENDERSON, Mark / HALL, Gary, Jr.	3:34.84 W G
2	2	RUS	SELKOV, Vladimir / LOPUKHOV, Stanislav / PANKRATOV, Denis / POPOV, Aleksander	3:37.55 S
3	6	AUS	DEWICK, Steven / ROGERS, Philip / MILLER, Scott / KLIM, Michael	3:39.56 B
4	3	GER	BRAUN, Ralf / WARNECKE, Mark / KELLER, Christian / ZIKARSKY, Bjorn	3:39.64
5	1	JPN	KONNAI, Keitaro / HAYASHI, Akira / YAMAMOTO, Takashi / ITO, Shunsuke	3:40.51
6	5	HUN	DEUTSCH, Tamas / GUTTLER, Karoly / HORVATH, Peter / CZENE, Attila	3:40.84
7	7	POL	SIEMBIDA, Mariusz / KRAWCZYK, Marek / SZUKALA, Rafal / KIZIEROWSKI, Bartosz	3:41.94
8	8	ISR	URBACK, Eithan / ALEKSEYEV, Vadim / KUTLER, Dan / BRUCK, Yoav	3:42.90

Aquatics—Swimming / *Natation — Natation*

4 x 100 m Medley Relay, Women / *4 x 100 m relais quatre nages, Dames*

HEAT 1

Rnk	Ln	Ctry	Names	Result
1	4	CHN	CHEN, Yan / HAN, Xue / CAI, Huijue / SHAN, Ying	4:09.23
2	5	RUS	ZHIVANEVSKAYA, Nina / MAKAROVA, Yelena / POZDEYEVA, Svetlana / MESHCHERYAKOVA, Natalya	4:10.65
3	3	HUN	EGERSZEGI, Krisztina / KOVACS, Agnes / KLOCKER, Edit / NYIRY, Anna	4:10.92
4	7	NED	STARINK, Brenda / BAANS, Madelon / van HOFWEGEN, Willemina / BRIENESSE, Karin	4:11.64
5	2	FIN	KOIVISTO, Anu / HAGMAN, Mia / PARSSINEN, Marja / SALMELA, Minna	4:14.14
6	6	FRA	RICARDO, Helene / BREMOND, Karine / JEANSON, Cecile / FIGUES, Solennes	4:15.69
7	8	ARG	ALVAREZ, Valeria / SANTA CRUZ, Maria / PEREYRA, Maria / BERTELLOTTI, Maria	4:27.99
8	1	TPE	LIN, Chien-Ju / MOU, Ying-Hsin / HSIEH, Shu-Ting / TSAI, Shu-Min	4:38.90

HEAT 2

Rnk	Ln	Ctry	Names	Result
1	4	USA	HEDGEPETH, Whitney / QUANCE, Kristine / THOMPSON, Jenny / FOX, Catherine	4:05.80
2	5	CAN	HOWARD, Julie / CLOUTIER, Guylaine / EVANETZ, Sarah / SHAKESPEARE, Shannon	4:09.50
3	3	SWE	ALSHAMMAR, Therese / JALTNER, Hanna / SJOBERG, Johanna / JOHNCKE, Louise	4:10.88
4	6	GBR	SLATTER, Helen / KING, Jaime / FOOT, Caroline / PICKERING, Karen	4:13.75
5	2	ESP	PINERA, Eva / OLAY, Maria / PELAEZ, Maria / FRANCO, Claudia	4:15.63
6	7	ROM	CASARU, Catalina / COADA, Beatrice / ZISU, Loredana / DOBRESCU, Liliana	4:16.18
7	1	KOR	LEE, Ji-Hyun / BYUN, Hye-Young / PARK, Woo-Hee / LEE, Bo-Eun	4:18.98
8	8	CZE	PIVONKOVA, Katerina / MANHALOVA, Lenka / KUBALCIKOVA, Marcela / KYNEROVA, Kristyna	4:21.05

HEAT 3

Rnk	Ln	Ctry	Names	Result
1	4	AUS	STEVENSON, Nicole / DENMAN, Helen / KENNEDY, Angela / RYAN, Sarah	4:08.87
2	3	GER	BUSCHSCHULTE, Antje / DUMITRU, Kathrin / van ALMSICK, Franziska / VOLKER, Sandra	4:08.95
3	6	RSA	KRIEL, Marianne / HEYNS, Penelope / LOOTS, Amanda / MULLER, Helene	4:09.47
4	2	ITA	VIGARANI, Lorenza / dalla VALLE, Manuela / TOCCHINI, Ilaria / VIANINI, Cecilia	4:10.57
5	5	JPN	NAKAMURA, Mai / TANAKA, Masami / AOYAMA, Ayari / CHIBA, Suzu	4:10.71
6	7	NZL	LIPSCOMBE, Lydia / WILSON, Anna / SIMCIC, Anna / FITCH, Alison	4:19.83
7	1	POR	SANTOS, Maria / SOUTINHO, Joana / FRANCISCO, Ana / ALEGRIA, Ana	4:21.61
8	8	GRE	KLEPKOU, Aikaterini / SARAKATSANI, Aikaterini / KARYSTINOU, Marina / MAHAIRA, Antonia	4:24.80

FINAL

Rnk	Ln	Ctry	Names	Result	
1	4	USA	BOTSFORD, Beth / BEARD, Amanda / MARTINO, Angel / VAN DYKEN, Amy	4:02.88	G
2	5	AUS	STEVENSON, Nicole / RILEY, Samantha / O'NEILL, Susan / RYAN, Sarah	4:05.08	S
3	6	CHN	CHEN, Yan / HAN, Xue / CAI, Huijue / SHAN, Ying	4:07.34	B
4	2	RSA	KRIEL, Marianne / HEYNS, Penelope / LOOTS, Amanda / MULLER, Helene	4:08.16	
5	7	CAN	HOWARD, Julie / CLOUTIER, Guylaine / EVANETZ, Sarah / SHAKESPEARE, Shannon	4:08.29	
6	3	GER	BUSCHSCHULTE, Antje / DUMITRU, Kathrin / van ALMSICK, Franziska / VOLKER, Sandra	4:09.22	
7	8	RUS	ZHIVANEVSKAYA, Nina / MAKAROVA, Yelena / NAZEMNOVA, Yelena / MESHCHERYAKOVA, Natalya	4:10.56	
8	1	ITA	VIGARANI, Lorenza / dalla VALLE, Manuela / TOCCHINI, Ilaria / VIANINI, Cecilia	4:10.59	

AQUATICS—SYNCHRONIZED SWIMMING
NATATION—NATATION SYNCHRONISÉE

Abbreviations and terms used in Synchronized Swimming results tables
Abréviations et termes employés dans les tableaux de résultats de natation synchronisée

Term	English	Français
B	Bronze Medal	Médaille de bronze
Ctry	Country	Pays
Final	Final	Finale
Free Routine	Free routine	Programme libre
G	Gold Medal	Médaille d'or
Names	Names	Noms
Points	Points	Points
Pts Behind	Points Behind	Ecart en points
Rnk	Rank	Classement
S	Silver Medal	Médaille d'argent
Technical Routine	Technical Routine	Programme technique
Total Pts	Total Points	Total des points

International Amateur Swimming Federation (FINA)
Fédération Internationale de Natation Amateur
Avenue de Beaumont 9
1012 Lausanne
Switzerland

• DANIEL J MURPHY • DARIN R MURPHY • DEANA K MURPHY • DENICE L MURPHY • DIANE E MURPHY • EDWARD J MURPHY • ELBERT MURPHY • ELIZABETH R MURPHY • ERYN MURPHY • GAIL S MURPHY • GRACE M MURPHY • JANICE L MURPHY • JOHN K MURPHY • JOSEPH F MURPHY • JOSEPH M MURPHY • JUDITH M MURPHY • JULIA C MURPHY • JULIA M MURPHY • KAREN P MURPHY • KATHLEEN MURPHY • KATHLEEN C MURPHY • KATHLEEN L MURPHY • KELLY A MURPHY • KENT S MURPHY • KERRY J MURPHY • KEVIN J MURPHY • KIMBERLY P MURPHY •

39

Aquatics—Synchronized Swimming / *Natation—Natation synchronisée*

Team, Women / *Epreuve par équipes, Dames*

TECHNICAL ROUTINE

Rnk	Ctry	Names	Points	(35%)	Pts behind
1	USA	DYROEN-LANCER, Becky / LeSUEUR, Emily Porter / SCHNEYDER, Nathalie / CLELAND, Tammy / SAVERY, Jill / THIEN, Margot / PEASE, Heather / SUDDUTH, Jill	99.200	34.720	0.000
2	CAN	CLARK, Karen / FRECHETTE, Sylvie / BREMNER, Janice / FONTEYNE, Karen / HOULD-MARCHAND, Valerie / WOODLEY, Erin / READ, Cari / ALEXANDER, Lisa	97.933	34.277	0.442
3	JPN	TACHIBANA, Miya / KAWASE, Akiko / JIMBO, Rei / TAKEDA, Miho / TAKAHASHI, Kaori / FUJII, Raika / TANAKA, Junko / NAKAJIMA, Riho	97.667	34.183	0.536
4	RUS	AZAROVA, Elena / ANTONOVA, Elena / BROUSNIKINA, Olga / KISSELEVA, Maria / MAXIMOVA, Gana / NOVOKSHCHENOVA, Olga / PANKRATOVA, Youlia / SEDAKOVA, Olga	97.000	33.950	0.769
5	FRA	AESCHBACHER, Marianne / DEDIEU, Virginie / FABRE, Julie / LIGNOT, Myriam / MARECHAL, Delphine / MASSARDIER, Charlotte / RATHIER, Magali / RIFFET, Eva	95.600	33.460	1.260
6	CHN	LONG, Yan / LI, Min / LI, Yuanyuan / WU, Chunlan / CHEN, Xuan / GUO, Cui / FU, Yuling / PAN, Yan	94.600	33.110	1.610
7	MEX	GONZALEZ, Olivia / AGUILAR, Wendy / REICH, Aline / REICH, Ingrid / LEAL, Lilian / VILA, Patricia / MEDINA, Ariadna / LEAL, Erika	94.400	33.040	1.680
8	ITA	BALLAN, Giada / BIANCHI, Serena / BRUNETTI, Mara / CARNINI, Manuela / CARRAFELLI, Brunella / CECCONI, Maurizia / CELLI, Paola / NUZZO, Letizia	93.733	32.807	1.913

FREE ROUTINE / FINAL

Rnk	Ctry	Names	Technical			Free			Total pts	Pts behind
			Points	(35%)	Rnk	Points	(65%)	Rnk		
1	USA	CLELAND, Tammy / BIANCO, Suzannah / PEASE, Heather / LeSUEUR, Emily Porter / DYROEN-LANCER, Becky / SUDDUTH, Jill / SCHNEYDER, Nathalie / SIMMONS-CARRASCO, Heather / SAVERY, Jill / THIEN, Margot	99.200	34.720	1	100.000	65.000	1	99.720	0.000 G
2	CAN	CLARK, Karen / LARSEN, Christine / BREMNER, Janice / FRECHETTE, Sylvie / HOULD-MARCHAND, Valerie / FONTEYNE, Karen / KULESZA, Kasia / READ, Cari / WOODLEY, Erin / ALEXANDER, Lisa	97.933	34.277	2	98.600	64.090	2	98.367	1.353 S
3	JPN	KAWASE, Akiko / TACHIBANA, Miya / TAKAHASHI, Kaori / TAKEDA, Miho / JIMBO, Rei / FUJII, Raika / KAWABE, Miho / NAKAJIMA, Riho / TANAKA, Junko / FUJIKI, Mayuko	97.667	34.183	3	97.800	63.570	3	97.753	1.967 B
4	RUS	AZAROVA, Elena / IOURIAEVA, Anna / KISSELEVA, Maria / BROUSNIKINA, Olga / ANTONOVA, Elena / LOBOVA, Marina / PANKRATOVA, Youlia / NOVOKSHCHENOVA, Olga / MAXIMOVA, Gana / SEDAKOVA, Olga	97.000	33.950	4	97.400	63.310	4	97.260	2.460
5	FRA	DEDIEU, Virginie / AESCHBACHER, Marianne / LIGNOT, Myriam / LEVEQUE, Celine / FABRE, Julie / MANABLE, Isabelle / RATHIER, Magali / MASSARDIER, Charlotte / MARECHAL, Delphine / RIFFET, Eva	95.600	33.460	5	96.333	62.616	5	96.076	3.644
6	ITA	BIANCHI, Serena / BALLAN, Giada / CARNINI, Manuela / BRUNETTI, Mara / BURLANDO, Giovanna / CARRAFELLI, Brunella / FARINELLI, Roberta / CELLI, Paola / CECCONI, Maurizia / NUZZO, Letizia	93.733	32.807	8	94.533	61.446	6	94.253	5.467
7	CHN	LI, Min / LONG, Yan / CHEN, Xuan / WU, Chunlan / LI, Yuanyuan / JIN, Na / FU, Yuling / LI, Fei / GUO, Cui / PAN, Yan	94.600	33.110	6	93.867	61.014	7	94.124	5.596
8	MEX	AGUILAR, Wendy / GONZALEZ, Olivia / LEAL, Lilian / REICH, Ingrid / REICH, Aline / VILA, Patricia / MEDINA, Ariadna / GUZMAN, Berenice / RAMIREZ, Perla / LEAL, Erika	94.400	33.040	7	93.533	60.796	8	93.836	5.884

AQUATICS—WATER POLO
NATATION — WATER-POLO

Abbreviations and terms used in Water Polo results tables
Abréviations et termes employés dans les tableaux de résultats de water-polo

Term	English	Français
% Eff	% Efficiency	% Efficacité
1st Referee	1st Referee	Premier arbitre
2nd Referee	2nd Referee	Deuxième arbitre
Against	Against	Contre
Assistant Coach	Assistant Coach	Entraîneur adjoint
Assists	Assists	Passes décisives
Attempted	Attempted	Tenté
Blocks	Blocks	Contres
Bronze	Bronze Medal	Médaille de bronze
Center Shots	Center Shots	Tirs du centre en retrait
Classification	Classification	Classement
Coach	Coach	Entraîneur
Diff	Difference	Différence
Drawn	Drawn	Egalité
Extramen Shots	Extramen Shots	Tirs en supériorité numérique
Final Classification	Final Classification	Classement final
Final Summary	Final Summary	Sommaire finale
Final	Final	Finale
For	For	Pour
Fouls	Fouls	Fautes
Goalkeeper	Goalkeeper	Gardien de but
Goals	Goals	Buts
Gold	Gold Medal	Médaille d'or
Group	Group	Groupe
Lost	Lost	Perdu
Mandown Shots	Mandown Shots	Tirs en infériorité numérique
Matches	Matches	Matchs
Name	Name	Nom
Natural Shots	Natural Shots	Tirs à égalité numérique
OT	Overtime	Prolongation
Penalty Shots	Penalty Shots	Coups de pénalités
Played	Played	Joué
Points	Points	Points
Preliminaries	Preliminaries	Eliminatoires
Qtr	Quarter	Période
Quarterfinals	Quarterfinals	Quarts de finale
Rnk	Rank	Classement
Semifinals	Semifinals	Demi-finales
Shots Made	Shots Made	Marqués
Shots Saved	Shots Saved	Arrêts
Silver	Silver Medal	Médaille d'argent
Steals	Steals	Interceptions
Team	Team	Equipe
Total Shots	Total Shots	Total des tirs
Turnovers	Turnovers	Pertes du ballon
Won	Won	Gagné

International Amateur Swimming Federation (FINA)
Fédération Internationale de Natation Amateur
**Avenue de Beaumont 9
1012 Lausanne
Switzerland**

Water Polo / *Water-polo*
Men / *Messieurs*

PRELIMINARIES - GROUP A

NED 8 - 11 YUG

	Qtr 1	Qtr 2	Qtr 3	Qtr 4
	2-3	2-4	2-3	2-1

Netherlands			Yugoslavia	
4/12	33.3%	Natural shots	4/10	40.0%
0/3	0.0%	Center shots	0/1	0.0%
4/8	50.0%	Extramen shots	5/11	45.5%
0/0	0.0	Mandown shots	0/0	0.0%
0/0	0.0	Penalty shots	2/2	100.0%
8/21	38.1%	Total shots	11/23	47.8%
	2	Assists	4	
	7	Turnovers	6	
	4	Steals	3	
	2	Blocks	0	
	18	Fouls	8	

1st Referee: FRA DEMEY, Jean
2nd Referee: ROM TIMOC, Radu

TEAM: NED Netherlands
Coach: van ZEELAND, Hans

Names	Shots Made	Attempted	% Eff
van de BUNT, Arie	0	2	0.0%
de VRIES, Wyco	1	2	50.0%
ISSARD, Koos	0	1	0.0%
van der MEER, Harry	4	9	44.4%
HAVENGA, Arno			
STOFFELS, Joeri	0	1	0.0%
de JONG, Bas	1	2	50.0%
KUNZ, Marco			
URI, Eelco			
NIEUWENBURG, Hans			
VERMEULEN, Wim			
de GROOT, Gert	1	2	50.0%
van der KOLK, Niels	1	2	50.0%
Goalkeeper	Shots Saved	Attempted	% Eff
van de BUNT, Arie	9	19	47.4%

TEAM: YUG Yugoslavia
Coach: ANDRIC, Dragan
Assistant Coach: PAVLOVIC, Vladimir

Names	Shots Made	Attempted	% Eff
SOSTAR, Aleksandar			
TRBOJEVIC, Petar	3	4	75.0%
SUBOTIC, Vaso	0	1	0.0%
ZIMONJIC, Predrag	1	2	50.0%
MILANOVIC, Igor	0	2	0.0%
SAPIC, Aleksandar	0	1	0.0%
VICEVIC, Mirko	3	4	75.0%
USKOKOVIC, Veljko	1	2	50.0%
SAVIC, Dejan	0	2	0.0%
JELENIC, Viktor	0	1	0.0%
VUJASINOVIC, Vladimir	3	4	75.0%
PEROVIC, Ranko			
TADIC, Milan			
Goalkeeper	Shots Saved	Attempted	% Eff
SOSTAR, Aleksandar	10	16	62.5%

PRELIMINARIES - GROUP A

HUN 8 - 7 RUS

	Qtr 1	Qtr 2	Qtr 3	Qtr 4
	1-2	1-3	4-1	2-1

Hungary			Russian Federation	
5/13	38.5%	Natural shots	5/16	31.3%
0/3	0.0%	Center shots	1/1	100.0%
3/12	25.0%	Extramen shots	1/4	25.0%
0/0	0.0%	Mandown shots	0/0	0.0%
0/0	0.0%	Penalty shots	0/0	0.0%
8/28	28.6%	Total shots	7/21	33.3%
	7	Assists	5	
	2	Turnovers	13	
	0	Steals	7	
	4	Blocks	3	
	38	Fouls	36	

1st Referee: AUS KERR, Peter
2nd Referee: ITA MEROLA, Salvatore

TEAM: HUN Hungary
Coach: HORKAI, Gyorgy
Assistant Coach: GERENDAS, Gyorgy

Names	Shots Made	Attempted	% Eff
KOSZ, Zoltan			
TOTH, Frank	1	3	33.3%
MONOSTORI, Attila	1	4	25.0%
VARGA, Zsolt	1	3	33.3%
KASAS, Tamas	2	3	66.7%
TOTH, Laszlo			
DALA, Tamas	1	2	50.0%
BENEDEK, Tibor	2	5	40.0%
FODOR, Rajmund	0	2	0.0%
VINCZE, Balazs	0	4	0.0%
GYONGYOSI, Andras	0	1	0.0%
KUNA, Peter			
NEMETH, Zsolt	0	1	0.0%
Goalkeeper	Shots Saved	Attempted	% Eff
KOSZ, Zoltan	8	15	53.3%

TEAM: RUS Russian Federation
Coach: KABANOV, Alexandre
Assistant Coach: OUKHOV, Boris

Names	Shots Made	Attempted	% Eff
MAXIMOV, Nikolai			
PANFILI, Alexei	2	3	66.7%
EVSTIGNEEV, Serguei			
KOZLOV, Nikolai	2	7	28.6%
GARBOUZOV, Serguei	0	2	0.0%
ERYCHOV, Alexandre			
APANASSENKO, Maxim	0	1	0.0%
IVLEV, Serguei	0	2	0.0%
GORCHKOV, Dmitrii	2	5	40.0%
KONSTANTINOV, Ilia			
SMOLOVOI, Iouri			
KARABOUTOV, Vladimir	1	1	100.0%
DOUGUINE, Dmitri			
Goalkeeper	Shots Saved	Attempted	% Eff
MAXIMOV, Nikolai	9	17	52.9%

PRELIMINARIES - GROUP A

ESP 9 - 3 GER

	Qtr 1	Qtr 2	Qtr 3	Qtr 4
	3-0	1-2	2-1	3-0

Spain			Germany	
2/10	20.0%	Natural shots	1/12	8.3%
1/3	33.3%	Center shots	0/2	0.0%
6/13	46.2%	Extramen shots	1/11	9.1%
0/0	0.0%	Mandown shots	0/0	0.0%
0/1	0.0%	Penalty shots	1/1	100.0%
9/27	33.3%	Total shots	3/26	11.5%
	7	Assists	0	
	6	Turnovers	8	
	5	Steals	2	
	3	Blocks	4	
	16	Fouls	65	

1st Referee: CAN LEGARE, Daniel
2nd Referee: USA BERNARD, Bret

TEAM: ESP Spain
Coach: JANE, Juan
Assistant Coach: FERNANDEZ de CUEVAS, Santiago

Names	Shots Made	Attempted	% Eff
ROLLAN, Jesus			
ABARCA, Jose Maria			
PEDREROL, Sergi	0	1	0.0%
ANDREO, Angel			
ESTIARTE, Manuel	1	4	25.0%
BALLART, Daniel	0	3	0.0%
PAYA, Jorge			
MORO, Ivan	1	2	50.0%
SANS, Jordi	1	2	50.0%
GOMEZ, Salvador	2	6	33.3%
OCA, Miguel	2	4	50.0%
SANZ, Carlos	1	2	50.0%
GARCIA, Pedro	1	3	33.3%
Goalkeeper	Shots Saved	Attempted	% Eff
ROLLAN, Jesus	10	13	76.9%

TEAM: GER Germany
Coach: FIROIU, Niculae

Names	Shots Made	Attempted	% Eff
BORGMANN, Ingo			
DRESEL, Torsten	1	2	50.0%
BUKOWSKI, Peter	0	1	0.0%
ERJAVEC, Davor	0	4	0.0%
ILGNER, Michael			
KLINGENBERG, Dirk	0	2	0.0%
de la PENA, Raul	1	6	16.7%
STERZIK, Uwe	0	4	0.0%
VOSS, Daniel			
REIMANN, Rene	0	3	0.0%
TOMANEK, Lars	0	1	0.0%
DRESEL, Jorg	1	3	33.3%
DAHLER, Oliver			
Goalkeeper	Shots Saved	Attempted	% Eff
BORGMANN, Ingo	5	14	35.7%

Men / *Messieurs*

PRELIMINARIES - GROUP A

YUG 9 - 9 RUS

	Qtr 1	Qtr 2	Qtr 3	Qtr 4
	3-3	1-1	4-2	1-3

Yugoslavia				Russian Federation
2/10	20.0%	Natural shots	6/13	46.2%
1/1	100.0%	Center shots	0/2	0.0%
6/8	75.0%	Extramen shots	3/8	37.5%
0/0	0.0%	Mandown shots	0/0	0.0%
0/0	0.0%	Penalty shots	0/0	0.0%
9/19	47.4%	Total shots	9/23	39.1%
	8	Assists	8	
	9	Turnovers	5	
	6	Steals	6	
	2	Blocks	3	
	26	Fouls	51	

1st Referee: GRE ILIADIS, Dimitrios
2nd Referee: NED KEMAN, Wilhelm

TEAM: YUG Yugoslavia

Coach: ANDRIC, Dragan
Assistant Coach: PAVLOVIC, Vladimir

Names	Shots Made	Attempted	% Eff
SOSTAR, Aleksandar			
TRBOJEVIC, Petar	1	2	50.0%
SUBOTIC, Vaso	0	2	0.0%
ZIMONJIC, Predrag	0	2	0.0%
MILANOVIC, Igor			
SAPIC, Aleksandar	2	2	100.0%
VICEVIC, Mirko	1	3	33.3%
USKOKOVIC, Veljko	1	2	50.0%
SAVIC, Dejan	0	1	0.0%
JELENIC, Viktor	2	3	66.7%
VUJASINOVIC, Vladimir	2	2	100.0%
PEROVIC, Ranko			
TADIC, Milan			
Goalkeeper	Shots Saved	Attempted	% Eff
SOSTAR, Aleksandar	7	16	43.8%

TEAM: RUS Russian Federation

Coach: KABANOV, Alexandre
Assistant Coach: OUKHOV, Boris

Names	Shots Made	Attempted	% Eff
MAXIMOV, Nikolai	0	1	0.0%
PANFILI, Alexei	1	1	100.0%
EVSTIGNEEV, Serguei	0	1	0.0%
KOZLOV, Nikolai	1	4	25.0%
GARBOUZOV, Serguei			
ERYCHOV, Alexandre	1	4	25.0%
APANASSENKO, Maxim	0	2	0.0%
IVLEV, Serguei			
GORCHKOV, Dmitrii	4	5	80.0%
KONSTANTINOV, Ilia	1	2	50.0%
SMOLOVOI, Iouri	0	1	0.0%
KARABOUTOV, Vladimir	1	2	50.0%
DOUGUINE, Dmitri			
Goalkeepers	Shots Saved	Attempted	% Eff
MAXIMOV, Nikolai	1	3	33.3%
DOUGUINE, Dmitri	2	9	22.2%

PRELIMINARIES - GROUP A

GER 8 - 9 HUN

	Qtr 1	Qtr 2	Qtr 3	Qtr 4	OT
	1-3	3-3	3-1	1-2	0-0

Germany				Hungary
2/8	25.0%	Natural shots	1/9	11.1%
2/4	50.0%	Center shots	1/2	50.0%
4/15	26.7%	Extramen shots	7/12	58.3%
0/0	0.0%	Mandown shots	0/0	0.0%
0/0	0.0%	Penalty shots	0/1	0.0%
8/26	30.8%	Total shots	9/24	37.5%
	3	Assists	5	
	12	Turnovers	7	
	8	Steals	2	
	4	Blocks	5	
	39	Fouls	40	

1st Referee: CRO KLARIC, Zeljko
2nd Referee: FRA DEMEY, Jean

TEAM: GER Germany

Coach: FIROIU, Niculae

Names	Shots Made	Attempted	% Eff
BORGMANN, Ingo			
DRESEL, Torsten			
BUKOWSKI, Peter	1	3	33.3%
ERJAVEC, Davor	3	7	42.9%
ILGNER, Michael			
KLINGENBERG, Dirk	0	3	0.0%
de la PENA, Raul	0	2	0.0%
STERZIK, Uwe			
VOSS, Daniel			
REIMANN, Rene	1	2	50.0%
TOMANEK, Lars	1	4	25.0%
DRESEL, Jorg	1	4	25.0%
DAHLER, Oliver	1	1	100.0%
Goalkeeper	Shots Saved	Attempted	% Eff
BORGMANN, Ingo	4	13	30.8%

TEAM: HUN Hungary

Coach: HORKAI, Gyorgy
Assistant Coach: GERENDAS, Gyorgy

Names	Shots Made	Attempted	% Eff
KOSZ, Zoltan			
TOTH, Frank	0	1	0.0%
MONOSTORI, Attila	0	1	0.0%
VARGA, Zsolt			
KASAS, Tamas	3	7	42.9%
TOTH, Laszlo	0	1	0.0%
DALA, Tamas	2	3	66.7%
BENEDEK, Tibor	2	4	50.0%
FODOR, Rajmund	0	1	0.0%
VINCZE, Balazs	0	2	0.0%
GYONGYOSI, Andras	1	1	100.0%
KUNA, Peter			
NEMETH, Zsolt	1	3	33.3%
Goalkeeper	Shots Saved	Attempted	% Eff
KOSZ, Zoltan	9	16	56.3%

PRELIMINARIES - GROUP A

NED 7 - 8 ESP

	Qtr 1	Qtr 2	Qtr 3	Qtr 4
	1-2	0-2	3-2	3-2

Netherlands				Spain
4/11	36.4%	Natural shots	5/18	27.8%
1/3	33.3%	Center shots	1/6	16.7%
2/5	40.0%	Extramen shots	2/6	33.3%
0/0	0.0%	Mandown shots	0/0	0.0%
0/0	0.0%	Penalty shots	0/0	0.0%
7/19	36.8%	Total shots	8/30	26.7%
	5	Assists	3	
	7	Turnovers	2	
	7	Steals	7	
	2	Blocks	3	
	25	Fouls	19	

1st Referee: UKR BELEVTSOV, Vyacheslav
2nd Referee: AUS KERR, Peter

TEAM: NED Netherlands

Coach: van ZEELAND, Hans

Names	Shots Made	Attempted	% Eff
van de BUNT, Arie			
de VRIES, Wyco	1	2	50.0%
ISSARD, Koos	0	1	0.0%
van der MEER, Harry	2	6	33.3%
HAVENGA, Arno	1	3	33.3%
STOFFELS, Joeri	0	2	0.0%
de JONG, Bas			
KUNZ, Marco	2	3	66.7%
URI, Eelco			
NIEUWENBURG, Hans			
VERMEULEN, Wim			
de GROOT, Gert	1	2	50.0%
van der KOLK, Niels			
Goalkeeper	Shots Saved	Attempted	% Eff
van de BUNT, Arie	10	18	55.6%

TEAM: ESP Spain

Coach: JANE, Juan
Assistant Coach: FERNANDEZ de CUEVAS, Santiago

Name	Shots Made	Attempted	% Eff
ROLLAN, Jesus			
ABARCA, Jose Maria	0	1	0.0%
PEDREROL, Sergi	0	1	0.0%
ANDREO, Angel			
ESTIARTE, Manuel	3	4	75.0%
BALLART, Daniel			
PAYA, Jorge			
MORO, Ivan	0	1	0.0%
SANS, Jordi	2	4	50.0%
GOMEZ, Salvador	1	10	10.0%
OCA, Miguel	1	2	50.0%
SANZ, Carlos	0	2	0.0%
GARCIA, Pedro	1	5	20.0%
Goalkeeper	Shots Saved	Attempted	% Eff
ROLLAN, Jesus	5	12	41.7%

PRELIMINARIES - GROUP A

RUS 10 - 8 GER

	Qtr 1	Qtr 2	Qtr 3	Qtr 4
	3-2	3-3	2-1	2-2

Russian Federation			Germany	
4/16	25.0%	Natural shots	1/8	12.5%
2/3	66.7%	Center shots	1/1	100.0%
2/4	50.0%	Extramen shots	6/16	37.5%
0/0	0.0%	Mandown shots	0/0	0.0%
2/2	100.0%	Penalty shots	0/0	0.0%
10/25	40.0%	Total shots	8/25	32.0%
	7	Assists	7	
	8	Turnovers	4	
	6	Steals	8	
	1	Blocks	7	
	48	Fouls	35	

1st Referee:	BEL	SIMONS, Francois
2nd Referee:	ITA	MEROLA, Salvatore

TEAM: RUS Russian Federation

Coach: KABANOV, Alexandre
Assistant Coach: OUKHOV, Boris

Names	Shots Made	Attempted	% Eff
MAXIMOV, Nikolai			
PANFILI, Alexei	1	3	33.3%
EVSTIGNEEV, Serguei	0	2	0.0%
KOZLOV, Nikolai	2	5	40.0%
GARBOUZOV, Serguei	4	5	80.0%
ERYCHOV, Alexandre	0	2	0.0%
APANASSENKO, Maxim			
IVLEV, Serguei			
GORCHKOV, Dmitrii	0	2	0.0%
KONSTANTINOV, Ilia	1	3	33.3%
SMOLOVOI, Iouri	1	2	50.0%
KARABOUTOV, Vladimir	1	1	100.0%
DOUGUINE, Dmitri			

Goalkeeper	Shots Saved	Attempted	% Eff
MAXIMOV, Nikolai	9	17	52.9%

TEAM: GER Germany

Coach: FIROIU, Niculae

Names	Shots Made	Attempted	% Eff
BORGMANN, Ingo			
DRESEL, Torsten	0	1	0.0%
BUKOWSKI, Peter	0	2	0.0%
ERJAVEC, Davor	2	4	50.0%
ILGNER, Michael			
KLINGENBERG, Dirk	0	3	0.0%
de la PENA, Raul	2	5	40.0%
STERZIK, Uwe			
VOSS, Daniel			
REIMANN, Rene	2	5	40.0%
TOMANEK, Lars	0	3	0.0%
DRESEL, Jorg	2	2	100.0%
DAHLER, Oliver			

Goalkeeper	Shots Saved	Attempted	% Eff
BORGMANN, Ingo	5	15	33.3%

PRELIMINARIES - GROUP A

ESP 7 - 9 YUG

	Qtr 1	Qtr 2	Qtr 3	Qtr 4
	1-2	1-3	2-2	3-2

Spain			Yugoslavia	
2/9	22.2%	Natural shots	4/9	44.4%
0/0	0.0%	Center shots	0/1	0.0%
5/14	35.7%	Extramen shots	5/8	62.5%
0/0	0.0%	Mandown shots	0/0	0.0%
0/1	0.0%	Penalty shots	0/0	0.0%
7/24	29.2%	Total shots	9/18	50.0%
	7	Assists	5	
	9	Turnovers	5	
	9	Steals	5	
	2	Blocks	4	
	38	Fouls	27	

1st Referee:	CUB	MARTINEZ, Eugenio
2nd Referee:	GRE	ILIADIS, Dimitrios

TEAM: ESP Spain

Coach: JANE, Juan
Assistant Coach: FERNANDEZ de CUEVAS, Santiago

Names	Shots Made	Attempted	% Eff
ROLLAN, Jesus			
ABARCA, Jose Maria			
PEDREROL, Sergi	0	3	0.0%
ANDREO, Angel			
ESTIARTE, Manuel	2	4	50.0%
BALLART, Daniel	0	1	0.0%
PAYA, Jorge			
MORO, Ivan	0	2	0.0%
SANS, Jordi	1	1	100.0%
GOMEZ, Salvador	1	2	50.0%
OCA, Miguel	2	6	33.3%
SANZ, Carlos			
GARCIA, Pedro	1	5	20.0%

Goalkeeper	Shots Saved	Attempted	% Eff
ROLLAN, Jesus	4	13	30.8%

TEAM: YUG Yugoslavia

Coach: ANDRIC, Dragan
Assistant Coach: PAVLOVIC, Vladimir

Names	Shots Made	Attempted	% Eff
SOSTAR, Aleksandar			
TRBOJEVIC, Petar	1	3	33.3%
SUBOTIC, Vaso	2	2	100.0%
ZIMONJIC, Predrag	0	2	0.0%
MILANOVIC, Igor			
SAPIC, Aleksandar	2	2	100.0%
VICEVIC, Mirko	0	2	0.0%
USKOKOVIC, Veljko	1	2	50.0%
SAVIC, Dejan	1	2	50.0%
JELENIC, Viktor	0	1	0.0%
VUJASINOVIC, Vladimir	2	2	100.0%
PEROVIC, Ranko			
TADIC, Milan			

Goalkeeper	Shots Saved	Attempted	% Eff
SOSTAR, Aleksandar	8	15	53.3%

PRELIMINARIES - GROUP A

HUN 10 - 8 NED

	Qtr 1	Qtr 2	Qtr 3	Qtr 4
	2-2	3-2	3-2	2-2

Hungary			Netherlands	
4/16	25.0%	Natural shots	3/12	25.0%
3/7	42.9%	Center shots	0/0	0.0%
3/8	37.5%	Extramen shots	4/10	40.0%
0/0	0.0%	Mandown shots	0/0	0.0%
0/1	0.0%	Penalty shots	1/1	100.0%
10/32	31.3%	Total shots	8/23	34.8%
	5	Assists	2	
	4	Turnovers	12	
	4	Steals	1	
	5	Blocks	3	
	43	Fouls	15	

1st Referee:	CAN	LEGARE, Daniel
2nd Referee:	KAZ	PRIKHODKO, Vladimir

TEAM: HUN Hungary

Coach: HORKAI, Gyorgy
Assistant Coach: GERENDAS, Gyorgy

Names	Shots Made	Attempted	% Eff
KOSZ, Zoltan			
TOTH, Frank	0	3	0.0%
MONOSTORI, Attila	0	2	0.0%
VARGA, Zsolt	4	8	50.0%
KASAS, Tamas	1	4	25.0%
TOTH, Laszlo	1	2	50.0%
DALA, Tamas			
BENEDEK, Tibor	4	7	57.1%
FODOR, Rajmund	0	3	0.0%
VINCZE, Balazs			
GYONGYOSI, Andras	0	1	0.0%
KUNA, Peter			
NEMETH, Zsolt	0	2	0.0%

Goalkeeper	Shots Saved	Attempted	% Eff
KUNA, Peter	8	14	57.1%

TEAM: NED Netherlands

Coach: van ZEELAND, Hans

Names	Shots Made	Attempted	% Eff
van de BUNT, Arie			
de VRIES, Wyco			
ISSARD, Koos	1	1	100.0%
van der MEER, Harry	4	7	57.1%
HAVENGA, Arno	0	4	0.0%
STOFFELS, Joeri	0	1	0.0%
de JONG, Bas	0	1	0.0%
KUNZ, Marco	2	3	66.7%
URI, Eelco			
NIEUWENBURG, Hans			
VERMEULEN, Wim			
de GROOT, Gert	1	5	20.0%
van der KOLK, Niels	0	1	0.0%

Goalkeeper	Shots Saved	Attempted	% Eff
van de BUNT, Arie	14	24	58.3%

Men / *Messieurs*

PRELIMINARIES - GROUP A

YUG 9 - 8 GER

	Qtr 1	Qtr 2	Qtr 3	Qtr 4
	2-1	1-3	5-2	1-2

Yugoslavia				Germany
0/4	0.0%	Natural shots	4/12	33.3%
1/2	50.0%	Center shots	1/1	100.0%
7/14	50.0%	Extramen shots	2/14	14.3%
0/0	0.0%	Mandown shots	0/0	0.0%
1/1	100.0%	Penalty shots	1/1	100.0%
9/21	42.9%	Total shots	8/28	28.6%
5		Assists		5
12		Turnovers		4
3		Steals		4
4		Blocks		2
19		Fouls		85

1st Referee: USA BERNARD, Bret
2nd Referee: KAZ PRIKHODKO, Vladimir

TEAM: YUG Yugoslavia
Coach: ANDRIC, Dragan
Assistant Coach: PAVLOVIC, Vladimir

Names	Shots Made	Attempted	% Eff
SOSTAR, Aleksandar			
TRBOJEVIC, Petar			
SUBOTIC, Vaso	1	3	33.3%
ZIMONJIC, Predrag			
MILANOVIC, Igor	1	3	33.3%
SAPIC, Aleksandar	0	2	0.0%
VICEVIC, Mirko	3	5	60.0%
USKOKOVIC, Veljko	1	2	50.0%
SAVIC, Dejan			
JELENIC, Viktor	1	2	50.0%
VUJASINOVIC, Vladimir	2	4	50.0%
PEROVIC, Ranko			
TADIC, Milan			
Goalkeepers	Shots Saved	Attempted	% Eff
SOSTAR, Aleksandar	6	12	50.0%
TADIC, Milan	0	2	0.0%

TEAM: GER Germany
Coach: FIROIU, Niculae

Names	Shots Made	Attempted	% Eff
BORGMANN, Ingo			
DRESEL, Torsten	1	2	50.0%
BUKOWSKI, Peter	0	1	0.0%
ERJAVEC, Davor	1	3	33.3%
ILGNER, Michael			
KLINGENBERG, Dirk	1	4	25.0%
de la PENA, Raul	1	3	33.3%
STERZIK, Uwe			
VOSS, Daniel			
REIMANN, Rene	2	9	22.2%
TOMANEK, Lars	0	2	0.0%
DRESEL, Jorg	2	4	50.0%
DAHLER, Oliver			
Goalkeeper	Shots Saved	Attempted	% Eff
BORGMANN, Ingo	4	13	30.8%

PRELIMINARIES - GROUP A

NED 5 - 10 RUS

	Qtr 1	Qtr 2	Qtr 3	Qtr 4
	2-2	0-3	1-2	2-3

Netherlands				Russian Federation
2/8	25.0%	Natural shots	6/20	30.0%
1/3	33.3%	Center shots	0/1	0.0%
2/14	14.3%	Extramen shots	4/5	80.0%
0/0	0.0%	Mandown shots	0/0	0.0%
0/0	0.0%	Penalty shots	0/0	0.0%
5/25	20.0%	Total shots	10/26	38.5%
4		Assists		6
8		Turnovers		6
6		Steals		6
1		Blocks		3
12		Fouls		37

1st Referee: CRO KLARIC, Zeljko
2nd Referee: CUB MARTINEZ, Eugenio

TEAM: NED Netherlands
Coach: van ZEELAND, Hans

Names	Shots Made	Attempted	% Eff
van de BUNT, Arie			
de VRIES, Wyco	1	3	33.3%
ISSARD, Koos	0	4	0.0%
van der MEER, Harry	1	6	16.7%
HAVENGA, Arno	0	2	0.0%
STOFFELS, Joeri			
de JONG, Bas			
KUNZ, Marco	0	2	0.0%
URI, Eelco	1	2	50.0%
NIEUWENBURG, Hans	1	1	100.0%
VERMEULEN, Wim			
de GROOT, Gert	1	2	50.0%
van der KOLK, Niels	0	3	0.0%
Goalkeeper	Shots Saved	Attempted	% Eff
van de BUNT, Arie	10	20	50.0%

TEAM: RUS Russian Federation
Coach: KABANOV, Alexandre
Assistant Coach: OUKHOV, Boris

Names	Shots Made	Attempted	% Eff
MAXIMOV, Nikolai			
PANFILI, Alexei	1	1	100.0%
EVSTIGNEEV, Serguei	2	2	100.0%
KOZLOV, Nikolai	2	5	40.0%
GARBOUZOV, Serguei	1	4	25.0%
ERYCHOV, Alexandre	0	2	0.0%
APANASSENKO, Maxim			
IVLEV, Serguei	0	1	0.0%
GORCHKOV, Dmitrii	2	5	40.0%
KONSTANTINOV, Ilia	0	3	0.0%
SMOLOVOI, Iouri	2	3	66.7%
KARABOUTOV, Vladimir			
DOUGUINE, Dmitri			
Goalkeeper	Shots Saved	Attempted	% Eff
MAXIMOV, Nikolai	13	18	72.2%

PRELIMINARIES - GROUP A

ESP 7 - 8 HUN

	Qtr 1	Qtr 2	Qtr 3	Qtr 4
	2-2	2-3	1-1	2-2

Spain				Hungary
3/13	23.1%	Natural shots	2/14	14.3%
0/0	0.0%	Center shots	1/1	100.0%
4/17	23.5%	Extramen shots	5/9	55.6%
0/0	0.0%	Mandown shots	0/0	0.0%
0/1	0.0%	Penalty shots	0/0	0.0%
7/31	22.6%	Total shots	8/24	33.3%
4		Assists		7
7		Turnovers		6
5		Steals		2
5		Blocks		3
18		Fouls		65

1st Referee: ROM TIMOC, Radu
2nd Referee: UKR BELEVTSOV, Vyacheslav

TEAM: ESP Spain
Coach: JANE, Juan
Assistant Coach: FERNANDEZ de CUEVAS, Santiago

Names	Shots Made	Attempted	% Eff
ROLLAN, Jesus			
ABARCA, Jose Maria			
PEDREROL, Sergi	0	3	0.0%
ANDREO, Angel			
ESTIARTE, Manuel	2	6	33.3%
BALLART, Daniel	1	2	50.0%
PAYA, Jorge	1	1	100.0%
MORO, Ivan	0	3	0.0%
SANS, Jordi	0	3	0.0%
GOMEZ, Salvador	1	3	33.3%
OCA, Miguel	0	3	0.0%
SANZ, Carlos	1	4	25.0%
GARCIA, Pedro	1	3	33.3%
Goalkeeper	Shots Saved	Attempted	% Eff
ROLLAN, Jesus	5	13	38.5%

TEAM: HUN Hungary
Coach: HORKAI, Gyorgy
Assistant Coach: GERENDAS, Gyorgy

Names	Shots Made	Attempted	% Eff
KOSZ, Zoltan			
TOTH, Frank	3	6	50.0%
MONOSTORI, Attila			
VARGA, Zsolt	2	4	50.0%
KASAS, Tamas	0	1	0.0%
TOTH, Laszlo	0	1	0.0%
DALA, Tamas	0	3	0.0%
BENEDEK, Tibor	1	2	50.0%
FODOR, Rajmund	0	2	0.0%
VINCZE, Balazs	0	2	0.0%
GYONGYOSI, Andras	1	1	100.0%
KUNA, Peter			
NEMETH, Zsolt	1	2	50.0%
Goalkeeper	Shots Saved	Attempted	% Eff
KOSZ, Zoltan	12	19	63.2%

PRELIMINARIES - GROUP A

HUN 12 - 8 YUG

	Qtr 1	Qtr 2	Qtr 3	Qtr 4
	4-2	3-1	4-3	1-2

Hungary				Yugoslavia
4/8	50.0%	Natural shots	0/7	0.0%
2/5	40.0%	Center shots	1/3	33.3%
5/11	45.5%	Extramen shots	6/11	54.5%
0/0	0.0%	Mandown shots	0/0	0.0%
1/1	100.0%	Penalty shots	1/1	100.0%
12/25	48.0%	Total shots	8/22	36.4%
8		Assists	4	
7		Turnovers	7	
11		Steals	7	
4		Blocks	2	
51		Fouls	39	

1st Referee: BEL SIMONS, Francois
2nd Referee: ITA MEROLA, Salvatore

TEAM: HUN Hungary

Coach: HORKAI, Gyorgy
Assistant Coach: GERENDAS, Gyorgy

Names	Shots Made	Attempted	% Eff
KOSZ, Zoltan			
TOTH, Frank			
MONOSTORI, Attila	1	1	100.0%
VARGA, Zsolt	3	6	50.0%
KASAS, Tamas	2	2	100.0%
TOTH, Laszlo	1	5	20.0%
DALA, Tamas			
BENEDEK, Tibor	3	4	75.0%
FODOR, Rajmund	0	1	0.0%
VINCZE, Balazs	0	1	0.0%
GYONGYOSI, Andras	1	2	50.0%
KUNA, Peter			
NEMETH, Zsolt	1	3	33.3%
Goalkeeper	**Shots Saved**	**Attempted**	**% Eff**
KOSZ, Zoltan	6	14	42.9%

TEAM: YUG Yugoslavia

Coach: ANDRIC, Dragan
Assistant Coach: PAVLOVIC, Vladimir

Names	Shots Made	Attempted	% Eff
SOSTAR, Aleksandar			
TRBOJEVIC, Petar	0	2	0.0%
SUBOTIC, Vaso			
ZIMONJIC, Predrag	1	4	25.0%
MILANOVIC, Igor	1	3	33.3%
SAPIC, Aleksandar	2	5	40.0%
VICEVIC, Mirko	2	2	100.0%
USKOKOVIC, Veljko	2	3	66.7%
SAVIC, Dejan	0	1	0.0%
JELENIC, Viktor			
VUJASINOVIC, Vladimir	0	2	0.0%
PEROVIC, Ranko			
TADIC, Milan			
Goalkeepers	**Shots Saved**	**Attempted**	**% Eff**
SOSTAR, Aleksandar	4	15	26.7%
TADIC, Milan	0	1	0.0%

PRELIMINARIES - GROUP A

RUS 6 - 8 ESP

	Qtr 1	Qtr 2	Qtr 3	Qtr 4
	3-2	0-2	3-3	0-1

Russian Federation				Spain
3/17	17.6%	Natural shots	0/7	0.0%
0/3	0.0%	Center shots	2/5	40.0%
2/13	15.4%	Extramen shots	6/11	54.5%
0/0	0.0%	Mandown shots	0/0	0.0%
1/1	100.0%	Penalty shots	0/0	0.0%
6/34	17.6%	Total shots	8/23	34.8%
4		Assists	7	
7		Turnovers	5	
4		Steals	1	
1		Blocks	10	
79		Fouls	12	

1st Referee: NED KEMAN, Wilhelm
2nd Referee: USA BERNARD, Bret

TEAM: RUS Russian Federation

Coach: KABANOV, Alexandre
Assistant Coach: OUKHOV, Boris

Names	Shots Made	Attempted	% Eff
MAXIMOV, Nikolai	0	1	0.0%
PANFILI, Alexei	0	2	0.0%
EVSTIGNEEV, Serguei	1	3	33.3%
KOZLOV, Nikolai	0	4	0.0%
GARBOUZOV, Serguei	1	2	50.0%
ERYCHOV, Alexandre	1	4	25.0%
APANASSENKO, Maxim	1	5	20.0%
IVLEV, Serguei	0	2	0.0%
GORCHKOV, Dmitrii	0	2	0.0%
KONSTANTINOV, Ilia	1	2	50.0%
SMOLOVOI, Iouri	0	4	0.0%
KARABOUTOV, Vladimir	1	3	33.3%
DOUGUINE, Dmitri			
Goalkeeper	**Shots Saved**	**Attempted**	**% Eff**
MAXIMOV, Nikolai	10	18	55.6%

TEAM: ESP Spain

Coach: JANE, Juan
Assistant Coach: FERNANDEZ de CUEVAS, Santiago

Names	Shots Made	Attempted	% Eff
ROLLAN, Jesus			
ABARCA, Jose Maria			
PEDREROL, Sergi	0	2	0.0%
ANDREO, Angel			
ESTIARTE, Manuel	0	2	0.0%
BALLART, Daniel	2	3	66.7%
PAYA, Jorge			
MORO, Ivan	0	1	0.0%
SANS, Jordi	0	1	0.0%
GOMEZ, Salvador	2	6	33.3%
OCA, Miguel	3	4	75.0%
SANZ, Carlos			
GARCIA, Pedro	1	4	25.0%
Goalkeeper	**Shots Saved**	**Attempted**	**% Eff**
ROLLAN, Jesus	11	17	64.7%

PRELIMINARIES - GROUP A

NED 8 - 9 GER

	Qtr 1	Qtr 2	Qtr 3	Qtr 4
	2-2	0-4	5-2	1-1

Netherlands				Germany
5/14	35.7%	Natural shots	2/10	20.0%
0/3	0.0%	Center shots	1/5	20.0%
3/7	42.9%	Extramen shots	6/12	50.0%
0/0	0.0%	Mandown shots	0/0	0.0%
0/0	0.0%	Penalty shots	0/0	0.0%
8/24	33.3%	Total shots	9/27	33.3%
5		Assists	7	
5		Turnovers	4	
5		Steals	5	
2		Blocks	0	
31		Fouls	25	

1st Referee: FRA DEMEY, Jean
2nd Referee: ALG HAMICI, Salah

TEAM: NED Netherlands

Coach: van ZEELAND, Hans

Names	Shots Made	Attempted	% Eff
van de BUNT, Arie			
de VRIES, Wyco	0	1	0.0%
ISSARD, Koos	0	3	0.0%
van der MEER, Harry	0	1	0.0%
HAVENGA, Arno	4	5	80.0%
STOFFELS, Joeri	0	1	0.0%
de JONG, Bas	1	1	100.0%
KUNZ, Marco	2	6	33.3%
URI, Eelco	1	1	100.0%
NIEUWENBURG, Hans	0	1	0.0%
VERMEULEN, Wim			
de GROOT, Gert	0	1	0.0%
van der KOLK, Niels	0	3	0.0%
Goalkeeper	**Shots Saved**	**Attempted**	**% Eff**
van de BUNT, Arie	10	19	52.6%

TEAM: GER Germany

Coach: FIROIU, Niculae

Names	Shots Made	Attempted	% Eff
BORGMANN, Ingo			
DRESEL, Torsten			
BUKOWSKI, Peter	0	3	0.0%
ERJAVEC, Davor	3	9	33.3%
ILGNER, Michael			
KLINGENBERG, Dirk	1	3	33.3%
de la PENA, Raul	0	2	0.0%
STERZIK, Uwe	0	1	0.0%
VOSS, Daniel			
REIMANN, Rene	2	4	50.0%
TOMANEK, Lars			
DRESEL, Jorg	2	4	50.0%
DAHLER, Oliver	1	1	100.0%
Goalkeeper	**Shots Saved**	**Attempted**	**% Eff**
BORGMANN, Ingo	12	20	60.0%

Men / *Messieurs*

PRELIMINARIES - GROUP B

CRO 8 - 5 GRE

	Qtr 1	Qtr 2	Qtr 3	Qtr 4
	3-1	1-1	2-1	2-2

Croatia				Greece
3/7	42.9%	Natural shots	1/11	9.1%
2/8	25.0%	Center shots	0/2	0.0%
3/5	60.0%	Extramen shots	4/13	30.8%
0/0	0.0%	Mandown shots	0/0	0.0%
0/0	0.0%	Penalty shots	0/0	0.0%
8/20	40.0%	Total shots	5/26	19.2%
	2	Assists	2	
	8	Turnovers	3	
	2	Steals	2	
	4	Blocks	2	
	33	Fouls	26	

1st Referee: NED KEMAN, Wilhelm
2nd Referee: GER LUDECKE, Rolf

TEAM: CRO Croatia

Coaches: SILIC, Bruno   NOLA, Fabjan
Assistant Coach: JEH, Vlado

Names	Shots Made	Attempted	% Eff
SKOLNEKOVIC, Sinisa			
VRDOLJAK, Zdeslav	0	1	0.0%
KREKOVIC, Josko	1	3	33.3%
SIMENC, Dubravko	3	4	75.0%
KRZIC, Ognjen			
STRITOF, Ratko	1	2	50.0%
VRBICIC, Renato	2	5	40.0%
GLAVAN, Damir			
VEGAR, Tino	0	1	0.0%
BUKIC, Perica			
HINIC, Igor	1	4	25.0%
BALIC, Maro			
KOBESCAK, Vjekoslav			

Goalkeeper	Shots Saved	Attempted	% Eff
SKOLNEKOVIC, Sinisa	10	15	66.7%

TEAM: GRE Greece

Coach: IOSIFIDIS, Kyriakos
Assistant Coach: MICHALOS, Panagiotis

Names	Shots Made	Attempted	% Eff
VOLTYRAKIS, Gerasimos			
KAIAFAS, Filippos	2	5	40.0%
CHATZITHEODOROU, Theodoros	0	3	0.0%
LOUDIS, Konstantinos	1	2	50.0%
MAVROTAS, Georgios	0	1	0.0%
PAPANASTASIOU, Anastasios	1	2	50.0%
PSYCHOS, Georgios	0	2	0.0%
KALAKONAS, Theodoros	0	3	0.0%
AFROUDAKIS, Georgios	1	4	25.0%
LORANTOS, Theodoros	0	3	0.0%
CHATZIS, Thomas			
GEORGARAS, Simeon	0	1	0.0%
PATRAS, Evangelos			

Goalkeeper	Shots Saved	Attempted	% Eff
VOLTYRAKIS, Gerasimos	7	15	46.7%

PRELIMINARIES - GROUP B

UKR 6 - 6 ROM

	Qtr 1	Qtr 2	Qtr 3	Qtr 4
	0-1	2-1	0-2	4-2

Ukraine				Romania
5/10	50.0%	Natural shots	4/9	44.4%
0/1	0.0%	Center shots	0/0	0.0%
0/7	0.0%	Extramen shots	2/10	20.0%
0/0	0.0%	Mandown shots	0/0	0.0%
1/1	100.0%	Penalty shots	0/0	0.0%
6/19	31.6%	Total shots	6/19	31.6%
	4	Assists	3	
	7	Turnovers	4	
	16	Steals	4	
	4	Blocks	1	
	60	Fouls	37	

1st Referee: CUB MARTINEZ, Eugenio
2nd Referee: HUN KOSZTOLANCZY, Gyorgy

TEAM: UKR Ukraine

Coaches: DROZIN, Yuriy   GAYDAYENKO, Yuriy

Names	Shots Made	Attempted	% Eff
YEGOROV, Oleks	0	1	0.0%
ANDREYEV, Dima	0	1	0.0%
STRATAN, Dima	0	2	0.0%
VLADYMYROV, Oleg			
POTULNYTSKY, Aleks	1	4	25.0%
SOLODUN, Tolik	0	3	0.0%
SKURATOV, Vadym	0	1	0.0%
KHALCHYTSKY, Vitaliy			
KEBALO, Vadym			
KOVALENKO, Andriy	4	4	100.0%
KOSTANDA, Slava			
HORBACH, Igor	1	1	100.0%
ROZHDESTVENSKY, Vadym	0	2	0.0%

Goalkeeper	Shots Saved	Attempted	% Eff
YEGOROV, Oleks	7	13	53.8%

TEAM: ROM Romania

Coach: RUS, Viorel
Assistant Coach: MARINESCU, Gheorghe

Names	Shots Made	Attempted	% Eff
LISAC, Gelu			
DINU, Robert			
TOTOLICI, Liviu	1	2	50.0%
BONCA, Florin			
SABAU, Radu	0	2	0.0%
FULGEANU, Nicolae	1	1	100.0%
HAGIU, Vlad	1	7	14.3%
SANDA, Petre	0	1	0.0%
STEMATE, Dinel			
MOLDVAI, Istvan	1	1	100.0%
RATH, Bogdan	1	4	25.0%
RADU, Catalin	1	1	100.0%
ANDREI, Edward			

Goalkeeper	Shots Saved	Attempted	% Eff
LISAC, Gelu	8	14	57.1%

PRELIMINARIES - GROUP B

ITA 10 - 7 USA

	Qtr 1	Qtr 2	Qtr 3	Qtr 4
	3-1	1-3	2-0	4-3

Italy				United States
3/16	18.8%	Natural shots	2/7	28.6%
3/6	50.0%	Center shots	0/3	0.0%
4/9	44.4%	Extramen shots	5/16	31.3%
0/0	0.0%	Mandown shots	0/0	0.0%
0/0	0.0%	Penalty shots	0/0	0.0%
10/31	32.3%	Total shots	7/26	26.9%
	9	Assists	8	
	7	Turnovers	11	
	1	Steals	5	
	1	Blocks	2	
	46	Fouls	51	

1st Referee: BEL SIMONS, Francois
2nd Referee: KAZ PRIKHODKO, Vladimir

TEAM: ITA Italy

Coach: RUDIC, Ratko
Assistant Coach: CASTELLUCCI, Giuseppe

Names	Shots Made	Attempted	% Eff
ATTOLICO, Francesco			
POSTIGLIONE, Francesco	1	2	50.0%
BOVO, Alessandro	0	1	0.0%
BENCIVENGA, Fabio	0	2	0.0%
CALCATERRA, Alessandro	2	5	40.0%
CALCATERRA, Roberto	2	4	50.0%
GIUSTOLISI, Luca	1	2	50.0%
ANGELINI, Alberto			
POMILIO, Amedeo	2	7	28.6%
GERINI, Marco			
SOTTANI, Leonardo			
SILIPO, Carlo	1	4	25.0%
GHIBELLINI, Alberto	1	4	25.0%

Goalkeeper	Shots Saved	Attempted	% Eff
ATTOLICO, Francesco	9	19	47.4%

TEAM: USA United States of America

Coach: CORSO, Richard
Assistant Coaches: AZEVEDO, Rick   VARGAS, John

Names	Shots Made	Attempted	% Eff
DUPLANTY, Chris	0	1	0.0%
HACKETT, Dan			
LASTER, Jeremy	1	3	33.3%
KOPP, Kyle	0	1	0.0%
OEDING, Chris	1	2	50.0%
ARROYO, Gavin			
ROUSSEAU, Alex	0	1	0.0%
McNAIR, Rick	2	3	66.7%
EVERIST, Kirk			
HUMBERT, Chris	1	6	16.7%
EVANS, Mike	1	5	20.0%
BARNHART, Troy, Jr.			
WIGO, Wolf	1	4	25.0%

Goalkeeper	Shots Saved	Attempted	% Eff
DUPLANTY, Chris	9	19	47.4%

PRELIMINARIES - GROUP B

ROM 6 - 11 CRO

	Qtr 1	Qtr 2	Qtr 3	Qtr 4
	2-5	2-1	0-2	2-3

Romania				Croatia
1/11	9.1%	Natural shots	1/6	16.7%
0/1	0.0%	Center shots	3/5	60.0%
4/11	36.4%	Extramen shots	7/10	70.0%
0/0	0.0%	Mandown shots	0/0	0.0%
1/1	100.0%	Penalty shots	0/0	0.0%
6/24	25.0%	Total shots	11/21	52.4%
	4	Assists	8	
	6	Turnovers	6	
	3	Steals	8	
	2	Blocks	3	
	47	Fouls	38	

1st Referee: NED TELLEGEN, Robert
2nd Referee: RUS AFANASIEV, Andrei

TEAM: ROM Romania
Coach: RUS, Viorel
Assistant Coach: MARINESCU, Gheorghe

Names	Shots Made	Attempted	% Eff
LISAC, Gelu			
DINU, Robert			
TOTOLICI, Liviu	0	2	0.0%
BONCA, Florin			
SABAU, Radu			
FULGEANU, Nicolae	1	4	25.0%
HAGIU, Vlad	3	5	60.0%
SANDA, Petre	0	1	0.0%
STEMATE, Dinel	0	6	0.0%
MOLDVAI, Istvan	1	1	100.0%
RATH, Bogdan	1	3	33.3%
RADU, Catalin	0	2	0.0%
ANDREI, Edward			
Goalkeeper	**Shots Saved**	**Attempted**	**% Eff**
LISAC, Gelu	5	16	31.3%

TEAM: CRO Croatia
Coaches: SILIC, Bruno   NOLA, Fabjan
Assistant Coach: JEH, Vlado

Names	Shots Made	Attempted	% Eff
SKOLNEKOVIC, Sinisa			
VRDOLJAK, Zdeslav	1	1	100.0%
KREKOVIC, Josko	0	2	0.0%
SIMENC, Dubravko	0	1	0.0%
KRZIC, Ognjen	1	2	50.0%
STRITOF, Ratko	0	1	0.0%
VRBICIC, Renato	2	3	66.7%
GLAVAN, Damir	0	1	0.0%
VEGAR, Tino	1	2	50.0%
BUKIC, Perica	3	3	100.0%
HINIC, Igor	1	2	50.0%
BALIC, Maro			
KOBESCAK, Vjekoslav	2	3	66.7%
Goalkeeper	**Shots Saved**	**Attempted**	**% Eff**
SKOLNEKOVIC, Sinisa	12	18	66.7%

PRELIMINARIES - GROUP B

ITA 8 - 6 UKR

	Qtr 1	Qtr 2	Qtr 3	Qtr 4
	2-2	4-1	1-1	1-2

Italy				Ukraine
6/12	50.0%	Natural shots	4/8	50.0%
0/2	0.0%	Center shots	0/1	0.0%
2/12	16.7%	Extramen shots	1/6	16.7%
0/0	0.0%	Mandown shots	0/0	0.0%
0/1	0.0%	Penalty shots	1/1	100.0%
8/27	29.6%	Total shots	6/16	37.5%
	6	Assists	3	
	5	Turnovers	9	
	7	Steals	5	
	1	Blocks	3	
	50	Fouls	30	

1st Referee: YUG RADENOVIC, Miroslav
2nd Referee: CAN LEGARE, Daniel

TEAM: ITA Italy
Coach: RUDIC, Ratko
Assistant Coach: CASTELLUCCI, Giuseppe

Names	Shots Made	Attempted	% Eff
ATTOLICO, Francesco			
POSTIGLIONE, Francesco	1	1	100.0%
BOVO, Alessandro	0	3	0.0%
BENCIVENGA, Fabio	2	2	100.0%
CALCATERRA, Alessandro	0	2	0.0%
CALCATERRA, Roberto	0	1	0.0%
GIUSTOLISI, Luca	1	1	100.0%
ANGELINI, Alberto	1	4	25.0%
POMILIO, Amedeo	0	4	0.0%
GERINI, Marco			
SOTTANI, Leonardo	1	2	50.0%
SILIPO, Carlo	2	6	33.3%
GHIBELLINI, Alberto	0	1	0.0%
Goalkeeper	**Shots Saved**	**Attempted**	**% Eff**
ATTOLICO, Francesco	5	11	45.5%

TEAM: UKR Ukraine
Coaches: DROZIN, Yuriy   GAYDAYENKO, Yuriy

Names	Shots Made	Attempted	% Eff
YEGOROV, Oleks	0	1	0.0%
ANDREYEV, Dima	1	1	100.0%
STRATAN, Dima	0	1	0.0%
VLADYMYROV, Oleg			
POTULNYTSKY, Aleks	2	4	50.0%
SOLODUN, Tolik			
SKURATOV, Vadym	1	3	33.3%
KHALCHYTSKY, Vitaliy			
KEBALO, Vadym			
KOVALENKO, Andriy	2	5	40.0%
KOSTANDA, Slava			
HORBACH, Igor			
ROZHDESTVENSKY, Vadym	0	1	0.0%
Goalkeeper	**Shots Saved**	**Attempted**	**% Eff**
YEGOROV, Oleks	7	15	46.7%

PRELIMINARIES - GROUP B

USA 9 - 7 GRE

	Qtr 1	Qtr 2	Qtr 3	Qtr 4
	4-2	3-1	1-2	1-2

United States				Greece
4/13	30.8%	Natural shots	4/17	23.5%
2/4	50.0%	Center shots	0/1	0.0%
3/5	60.0%	Extramen shots	3/9	33.3%
0/0	0.0%	Mandown shots	0/0	0.0%
0/0	0.0%	Penalty shots	0/0	0.0%
9/22	40.9%	Total shots	7/27	25.9%
	6	Assists	5	
	4	Turnovers	4	
	7	Steals	5	
	2	Blocks	1	
	43	Fouls	21	

1st Referee: ESP FERNANDEZ, Joaquin
2nd Referee: CUB MARTINEZ, Eugenio

TEAM: USA United States of America
Coach: CORSO, Richard
Assistant Coaches: AZEVEDO, Rick   VARGAS, John

Names	Shots Made	Attempted	% Eff
DUPLANTY, Chris	0	2	0.0%
HACKETT, Dan			
LASTER, Jeremy	0	2	0.0%
KOPP, Kyle	0	1	0.0%
OEDING, Chris			
ARROYO, Gavin	2	3	66.7%
ROUSSEAU, Alex	0	1	0.0%
McNAIR, Rick	0	2	0.0%
EVERIST, Kirk	0	2	0.0%
HUMBERT, Chris	4	4	100.0%
EVANS, Mike	0	2	0.0%
BARNHART, Troy, Jr.			
WIGO, Wolf	3	3	100.0%
Goalkeeper	**Shots Saved**	**Attempted**	**% Eff**
DUPLANTY, Chris	12	19	63.2%

TEAM: GRE Greece
Coach: IOSIFIDIS, Kyriakos
Assistant Coach: MICHALOS, Panagiotis

Names	Shots Made	Attempted	% Eff
VOLTYRAKIS, Gerasimos			
KAIAFAS, Filippos	2	6	33.3%
CHATZITHEODOROU, Theodoros			
LOUDIS, Konstantinos	1	3	33.3%
MAVROTAS, Georgios	0	3	0.0%
PAPANASTASIOU, Anastasios	0	2	0.0%
PSYCHOS, Georgios	0	4	0.0%
KALAKONAS, Theodoros			
AFROUDAKIS, Georgios			
LORANTOS, Theodoros	2	4	50.0%
CHATZIS, Thomas	2	3	66.7%
GEORGARAS, Simeon	0	2	0.0%
PATRAS, Evangelos			
Goalkeeper	**Shots Saved**	**Attempted**	**% Eff**
VOLTYRAKIS, Gerasimos	6	15	40.0%

Men / *Messieurs*

PRELIMINARIES - GROUP B

GRE 8 - 5 ROM

	Qtr 1	Qtr 2	Qtr 3	Qtr 4
	3-1	2-1	2-2	1-1

Greece				Romania
1/7	14.3%	Natural shots	2/12	16.7%
2/3	66.7%	Center shots	0/1	0.0%
4/9	44.4%	Extramen shots	3/10	30.0%
0/0	0.0%	Mandown shots	0/0	0.0%
1/2	50.0%	Penalty shots	0/1	0.0%
8/21	38.1%	Total shots	5/24	20.8%
	6	Assists	4	
	5	Turnovers	5	
	9	Steals	4	
	2	Blocks	2	
	9	Fouls	33	

1st Referee:	FRA	DEMEY, Jean
2nd Referee:	HUN	KOSZTOLANCZY, Gyorgy

PRELIMINARIES - GROUP B

CRO 8 - 10 ITA

	Qtr 1	Qtr 2	Qtr 3	Qtr 4
	1-3	2-2	2-2	3-3

Croatia				Italy
0/7	0.0%	Natural shots	3/9	33.3%
0/2	0.0%	Center shots	0/1	0.0%
8/14	57.1%	Extramen shots	7/15	46.7%
0/0	0.0%	Mandown shots	0/0	0.0%
0/0	0.0%	Penalty shots	0/0	0.0%
8/23	34.8%	Total shots	10/25	40.0%
	5	Assists	6	
	6	Turnovers	11	
	2	Steals	4	
	3	Blocks	2	
	43	Fouls	52	

1st Referee:	ESP	FERNANDEZ, Joaquin
2nd Referee:	AUS	KERR, Peter

PRELIMINARIES - GROUP B

UKR 7 - 9 USA

	Qtr 1	Qtr 2	Qtr 3	Qtr 4
	1-1	2-1	3-5	1-2

Ukraine				United States
3/13	23.1%	Natural shots	2/16	12.5%
0/2	0.0%	Center shots	2/4	50.0%
4/9	44.4%	Extramen shots	5/13	38.5%
0/0	0.0%	Mandown shots	0/0	0.0%
0/0	0.0%	Penalty shots	0/0	0.0%
7/24	29.2%	Total shots	9/33	27.3%
	5	Assists	9	
	6	Turnovers	8	
	3	Steals	7	
	7	Blocks	3	
	65	Fouls	29	

1st Referee:	NED	KEMAN, Wilhelm
2nd Referee:	NED	TELLEGEN, Robert

TEAM: GRE Greece

Coach: IOSIFIDIS, Kyriakos

Assistant Coach: MICHALOS, Panagiotis

Names	Shots Made	Attempted	% Eff
VOLTYRAKIS, Gerasimos			
KAIAFAS, Filippos	1	1	100.0%
CHATZITHEODOROU, Theodoros			
LOUDIS, Konstantinos	2	3	66.7%
MAVROTAS, Georgios	0	3	0.0%
PAPANASTASIOU, Anastasios	2	3	66.7%
PSYCHOS, Georgios	0	1	0.0%
KALAKONAS, Theodoros	0	1	0.0%
AFROUDAKIS, Georgios	1	4	25.0%
LORANTOS, Theodoros	1	4	25.0%
CHATZIS, Thomas	1	1	100.0%
GEORGARAS, Simeon			
PATRAS, Evangelos			

Goalkeeper	Shots Saved	Attempted	% Eff
VOLTYRAKIS, Gerasimos	12	17	70.6%

TEAM: CRO Croatia

Coaches: SILIC, Bruno   NOLA, Fabjan

Assistant Coach: JEH, Vlado

Names	Shots Made	Attempted	% Eff
SKOLNEKOVIC, Sinisa			
VRDOLJAK, Zdeslav	0	2	0.0%
KREKOVIC, Josko	2	5	40.0%
SIMENC, Dubravko	2	2	100.0%
KRZIC, Ognjen	0	3	0.0%
STRITOF, Ratko	0	1	0.0%
VRBICIC, Renato	1	2	50.0%
GLAVAN, Damir	0	1	0.0%
VEGAR, Tino	1	2	50.0%
BUKIC, Perica	2	3	66.7%
HINIC, Igor	0	1	0.0%
BALIC, Maro			
KOBESCAK, Vjekoslav	0	1	0.0%

Goalkeeper	Shots Saved	Attempted	% Eff
SKOLNEKOVIC, Sinisa	7	17	41.2%

TEAM: UKR Ukraine

Coaches: DROZIN, Yuriy   GAYDAYENKO, Yuriy

Names	Shots Made	Attempted	% Eff
YEGOROV, Oleks			
ANDREYEV, Dima	0	1	0.0%
STRATAN, Dima	0	2	0.0%
VLADYMYROV, Oleg	0	1	0.0%
POTULNYTSKY, Aleks	1	4	25.0%
SOLODUN, Tolik	1	2	50.0%
SKURATOV, Vadym	1	5	20.0%
KHALCHYTSKY, Vitaliy			
KEBALO, Vadym			
KOVALENKO, Andriy	3	6	50.0%
KOSTANDA, Slava			
HORBACH, Igor	1	2	50.0%
ROZHDESTVENSKY, Vadym	0	1	0.0%

Goalkeeper	Shots Saved	Attempted	% Eff
VLADYMYROV, Oleg	6	15	40.0%

TEAM: ROM Romania

Coach: RUS, Viorel

Assistant Coach: MARINESCU, Gheorghe

Names	Shots Made	Attempted	% Eff
LISAC, Gelu			
DINU, Robert			
TOTOLICI, Liviu	2	7	28.6%
BONCA, Florin	0	1	0.0%
SABAU, Radu			
FULGEANU, Nicolae	0	1	0.0%
HAGIU, Vlad			
SANDA, Petre	0	4	0.0%
STEMATE, Dinel	1	3	33.3%
MOLDVAI, Istvan	0	1	0.0%
RATH, Bogdan	2	6	33.3%
RADU, Catalin	0	1	0.0%
ANDREI, Edward			

Goalkeeper	Shots Saved	Attempted	% Eff
LISAC, Gelu	6	14	42.9%

TEAM: ITA Italy

Coach: RUDIC, Ratko

Assistant Coach: CASTELLUCCI, Giuseppe

Names	Shots Made	Attempted	% Eff
ATTOLICO, Francesco			
POSTIGLIONE, Francesco	1	3	33.3%
BOVO, Alessandro			
BENCIVENGA, Fabio	0	1	0.0%
CALCATERRA, Alessandro	0	1	0.0%
CALCATERRA, Roberto	2	3	66.7%
GIUSTOLISI, Luca	1	1	100.0%
ANGELINI, Alberto	2	3	66.7%
POMILIO, Amedeo	1	3	33.3%
GERINI, Marco			
SOTTANI, Leonardo	0	1	0.0%
SILIPO, Carlo	2	6	33.3%
GHIBELLINI, Alberto	1	3	33.3%

Goalkeeper	Shots Saved	Attempted	% Eff
ATTOLICO, Francesco	6	14	42.9%

TEAM: USA United States of America

Coach: CORSO, Richard

Assistant Coaches: AZEVEDO, Rick   VARGAS, John

Names	Shots Made	Attempted	% Eff
DUPLANTY, Chris			
HACKETT, Dan			
LASTER, Jeremy	0	3	0.0%
KOPP, Kyle	2	3	66.7%
OEDING, Chris	2	3	66.7%
ARROYO, Gavin	1	2	50.0%
ROUSSEAU, Alex	1	4	25.0%
McNAIR, Rick	0	7	0.0%
EVERIST, Kirk	0	1	0.0%
HUMBERT, Chris	3	5	60.0%
EVANS, Mike	0	3	0.0%
BARNHART, Troy, Jr.	0	2	0.0%
WIGO, Wolf			

Goalkeeper	Shots Saved	Attempted	% Eff
DUPLANTY, Chris	7	14	50.0%

PRELIMINARIES - GROUP B

ITA 10 - 8 GRE

	Qtr 1	Qtr 2	Qtr 3	Qtr 4
	1-2	2-1	4-3	3-2

Italy			Greece	
6/18	33.3%	Natural shots	1/8	12.5%
0/4	0.0%	Center shots	0/2	0.0%
4/6	66.7%	Extramen shots	5/9	55.6%
0/0	0.0%	Mandown shots	0/0	0.0%
0/0	0.0%	Penalty shots	2/2	100.0%
10/28	35.7%	Total shots	8/21	38.1%
10		Assists	6	
3		Turnovers	11	
6		Steals	6	
4		Blocks	4	
63		Fouls	14	

1st Referee: RUS AFANASIEV, Andrei
2nd Referee: BEL SIMONS, Francois

TEAM: ITA Italy

Coach: RUDIC, Ratko
Assistant Coach: CASTELLUCCI, Giuseppe

Names	Shots Made	Attempted	% Eff
ATTOLICO, Francesco			
POSTIGLIONE, Francesco	1	1	100.0%
BOVO, Alessandro	2	5	40.0%
BENCIVENGA, Fabio	2	4	50.0%
CALCATERRA, Alessandro	2	3	66.7%
CALCATERRA, Roberto	0	3	0.0%
GIUSTOLISI, Luca			
ANGELINI, Alberto	0	4	0.0%
POMILIO, Amedeo	0	2	0.0%
GERINI, Marco			
SOTTANI, Leonardo	2	2	100.0%
SILIPO, Carlo	1	4	25.0%
GHIBELLINI, Alberto			
Goalkeeper	**Shots Saved**	**Attempted**	**% Eff**
ATTOLICO, Francesco	6	14	42.9%

TEAM: GRE Greece

Coach: IOSIFIDIS, Kyriakos
Assistant Coach: MICHALOS, Panagiotis

Names	Shots Made	Attempted	% Eff
VOLTYRAKIS, Gerasimos			
KAIAFAS, Filippos	2	3	66.7%
CHATZITHEODOROU, Theodoros			
LOUDIS, Konstantinos	2	2	100.0%
MAVROTAS, Georgios	2	5	40.0%
PAPANASTASIOU, Anastasios	0	1	0.0%
PSYCHOS, Georgios	0	1	0.0%
KALAKONAS, Theodoros	0	1	0.0%
AFROUDAKIS, Georgios	1	4	25.0%
LORANTOS, Theodoros	1	4	25.0%
CHATZIS, Thomas			
GEORGARAS, Simeon			
PATRAS, Evangelos			
Goalkeeper	**Shots Saved**	**Attempted**	**% Eff**
VOLTYRAKIS, Gerasimos	7	17	41.2%

PRELIMINARIES - GROUP B

UKR 8 - 16 CRO

	Qtr 1	Qtr 2	Qtr 3	Qtr 4
	0-3	1-3	1-4	6-6

Ukraine			Croatia	
4/13	30.8%	Natural shots	6/21	28.6%
1/4	25.0%	Center shots	2/4	50.0%
2/6	33.3%	Extramen shots	8/11	72.7%
0/0	0.0%	Mandown shots	0/0	0.0%
1/2	50.0%	Penalty shots	0/1	0.0%
8/25	32.0%	Total shots	16/37	43.2%
5		Assists	9	
7		Turnovers	6	
2		Steals	5	
1		Blocks	5	
34		Fouls	23	

1st Referee: GER LUDECKE, Rolf
2nd Referee: JPN WAKABAYASHI, Kazuhito

TEAM: UKR Ukraine

Coaches: DROZIN, Yuriy GAYDAYENKO, Yuriy

Names	Shots Made	Attempted	% Eff
YEGOROV, Oleks			
ANDREYEV, Dima	1	4	25.0%
STRATAN, Dima	1	2	50.0%
VLADYMYROV, Oleg			
POTULNYTSKY, Aleks	1	4	25.0%
SOLODUN, Tolik	0	1	0.0%
SKURATOV, Vadym	3	4	75.0%
KHALCHYTSKY, Vitaliy	0	1	0.0%
KEBALO, Vadym			
KOVALENKO, Andriy	1	6	16.7%
KOSTANDA, Slava	1	2	50.0%
HORBACH, Igor			
ROZHDESTVENSKY, Vadym	0	1	0.0%
Goalkeeper	**Shots Saved**	**Attempted**	**% Eff**
YEGOROV, Oleks	10	26	38.5%

TEAM: CRO Croatia

Coaches: SILIC, Bruno NOLA, Fabjan
Assistant Coach: JEH, Vlado

Names	Shots Made	Attempted	% Eff
SKOLNEKOVIC, Sinisa			
VRDOLJAK, Zdeslav	2	5	40.0%
KREKOVIC, Josko	0	3	0.0%
SIMENC, Dubravko	1	3	33.3%
KRZIC, Ognjen	3	4	75.0%
STRITOF, Ratko	1	2	50.0%
VRBICIC, Renato	2	4	50.0%
GLAVAN, Damir	1	1	100.0%
VEGAR, Tino	2	5	40.0%
BUKIC, Perica	2	2	100.0%
HINIC, Igor	1	4	25.0%
BALIC, Maro			
KOBESCAK, Vjekoslav	1	4	25.0%
Goalkeeper	**Shots Saved**	**Attempted**	**% Eff**
SKOLNEKOVIC, Sinisa	11	19	57.9%

PRELIMINARIES - GROUP B

USA 10 - 5 ROM

	Qtr 1	Qtr 2	Qtr 3	Qtr 4
	2-0	4-1	3-1	1-3

United States			Romania	
7/18	38.9%	Natural shots	2/11	18.2%
1/3	33.3%	Center shots	1/1	100.0%
2/6	33.3%	Extramen shots	2/7	28.6%
0/0	0.0%	Mandown shots	0/0	0.0%
0/0	0.0%	Penalty shots	0/0	0.0%
10/27	37.0%	Total shots	5/19	26.3%
7		Assists	4	
7		Turnovers	3	
12		Steals	3	
4		Blocks	1	
50		Fouls	41	

1st Referee: YUG RADENOVIC, Miroslav
2nd Referee: ALG HAMICI, Salah

TEAM: USA United States of America

Coach: CORSO, Richard
Assistant Coaches: AZEVEDO, Rick VARGAS, John

Names	Shots Made	Attempted	% Eff
DUPLANTY, Chris	0	1	0.0%
HACKETT, Dan			
LASTER, Jeremy	1	1	100.0%
KOPP, Kyle	1	2	50.0%
OEDING, Chris	1	4	25.0%
ARROYO, Gavin	1	1	100.0%
ROUSSEAU, Alex	1	2	50.0%
McNAIR, Rick	0	3	0.0%
EVERIST, Kirk	0	1	0.0%
HUMBERT, Chris	1	2	50.0%
EVANS, Mike	3	6	50.0%
BARNHART, Troy, Jr.	0	1	0.0%
WIGO, Wolf	1	3	33.3%
Goalkeepers	**Shots Saved**	**Attempted**	**% Eff**
DUPLANTY, Chris	4	7	57.1%
HACKETT, Dan	1	3	33.3%

TEAM: ROM Romania

Coach: RUS, Viorel
Assistant Coach: MARINESCU, Gheorghe

Names	Shots Made	Attempted	% Eff
LISAC, Gelu	0	1	0.0%
DINU, Robert			
TOTOLICI, Liviu	1	4	25.0%
BONCA, Florin			
SABAU, Radu	0	1	0.0%
FULGEANU, Nicolae			
HAGIU, Vlad	2	5	40.0%
SANDA, Petre	0	2	0.0%
STEMATE, Dinel	0	1	0.0%
MOLDVAI, Istvan	1	1	100.0%
RATH, Bogdan	0	1	0.0%
RADU, Catalin	1	3	33.3%
ANDREI, Edward			
Goalkeepers	**Shots Saved**	**Attempted**	**% Eff**
LISAC, Gelu	2	9	22.2%
DINU, Robert	3	6	50.0%

Men / *Messieurs*

PRELIMINARIES - GROUP B

GRE 9 - 6 UKR

	Qtr 1	Qtr 2	Qtr 3	Qtr 4
	0-0	2-1	4-1	3-4

Greece				Ukraine
0/3	0.0%	Natural shots	2/15	13.3%
2/3	66.7%	Center shots	1/2	50.0%
6/10	60.0%	Extramen shots	2/8	25.0%
0/0	0.0%	Mandown shots	0/0	0.0%
1/1	100.0%	Penalty shots	1/1	100.0%
9/17	52.9%	Total shots	6/26	23.1%
	6	Assists	3	
	11	Turnovers	6	
	6	Steals	5	
	6	Blocks	1	
	7	Fouls	75	

1st Referee: AUS KERR, Peter
2nd Referee: HUN KOSZTOLANCZY, Gyorgy

TEAM: GRE Greece

Coach: IOSIFIDIS, Kyriakos
Assistant Coach: MICHALOS, Panagiotis

Names	Shots Made	Attempted	% Eff
VOLTYRAKIS, Gerasimos			
KAIAFAS, Filippos	0	2	0.0%
CHATZITHEODOROU, Theodoros			
LOUDIS, Konstantinos	0	3	0.0%
MAVROTAS, Georgios	3	4	75.0%
PAPANASTASIOU, Anastasios	1	1	100.0%
PSYCHOS, Georgios	1	2	50.0%
KALAKONAS, Theodoros			
AFROUDAKIS, Georgios	2	2	100.0%
LORANTOS, Theodoros	2	3	66.7%
CHATZIS, Thomas			
GEORGARAS, Simeon			
PATRAS, Evangelos			

Goalkeeper	Shots Saved	Attempted	% Eff
VOLTYRAKIS, Gerasimos	8	14	57.1%

TEAM: UKR Ukraine

Coaches: DROZIN, Yuriy GAYDAYENKO, Yuriy

Names	Shots Made	Attempted	% Eff
YEGOROV, Oleks	0	1	0.0%
ANDREYEV, Dima	0	3	0.0%
STRATAN, Dima	1	1	100.0%
VLADYMYROV, Oleg			
POTULNYTSKY, Aleks	1	8	12.5%
SOLODUN, Tolik	1	4	25.0%
SKURATOV, Vadym	1	2	50.0%
KHALCHYTSKY, Vitaliy	0	1	0.0%
KEBALO, Vadym	0	2	0.0%
KOVALENKO, Andriy	2	2	100.0%
KOSTANDA, Slava	0	2	0.0%
HORBACH, Igor			
ROZHDESTVENSKY, Vadym			

Goalkeeper	Shots Saved	Attempted	% Eff
YEGOROV, Oleks	3	12	25.0%

PRELIMINARIES - GROUP B

ITA 10 - 9 ROM

	Qtr 1	Qtr 2	Qtr 3	Qtr 4
	2-2	3-3	3-1	2-3

Italy				Romania
5/14	35.7%	Natural shots	2/10	20.0%
0/1	0.0%	Center shots	0/2	0.0%
4/10	40.0%	Extramen shots	7/12	58.3%
0/0	0.0%	Mandown shots	0/0	0.0%
1/1	100.0%	Penalty shots	0/0	0.0%
10/26	38.5%	Total shots	9/24	37.5%
	4	Assists	5	
	8	Turnovers	9	
	5	Steals	4	
	4	Blocks	4	
	74	Fouls	54	

1st Referee: ESP FERNANDEZ, Joaquin
2nd Referee: JPN WAKABAYASHI, Kazuhito

TEAM: ITA Italy

Coach: RUDIC, Ratko
Assistant Coach: CASTELLUCCI, Giuseppe

Names	Shots Made	Attempted	% Eff
ATTOLICO, Francesco			
POSTIGLIONE, Francesco	0	2	0.0%
BOVO, Alessandro	1	3	33.3%
BENCIVENGA, Fabio	0	1	0.0%
CALCATERRA, Alessandro	0	2	0.0%
CALCATERRA, Roberto	0	1	0.0%
GIUSTOLISI, Luca			
ANGELINI, Alberto	2	3	66.7%
POMILIO, Amedeo	2	4	50.0%
GERINI, Marco			
SOTTANI, Leonardo	1	4	25.0%
SILIPO, Carlo	2	3	66.7%
GHIBELLINI, Alberto	2	3	66.7%

Goalkeeper	Shots Saved	Attempted	% Eff
GERINI, Marco	6	15	40.0%

TEAM: ROM Romania

Coach: RUS, Viorel
Assistant Coach: MARINESCU, Gheorghe

Names	Shots Made	Attempted	% Eff
LISAC, Gelu			
DINU, Robert			
TOTOLICI, Liviu	3	6	50.0%
BONCA, Florin	1	1	100.0%
SABAU, Radu	0	3	0.0%
FULGEANU, Nicolae	1	1	100.0%
HAGIU, Vlad	3	7	42.9%
SANDA, Petre	0	1	0.0%
STEMATE, Dinel			
MOLDVAI, Istvan	1	4	25.0%
RATH, Bogdan	0	1	0.0%
RADU, Catalin			
ANDREI, Edward			

Goalkeepers	Shots Saved	Attempted	% Eff
LISAC, Gelu	0	2	0.0%
DINU, Robert	4	12	33.3%

PRELIMINARIES - GROUP B

CRO 8 - 10 USA

	Qtr 1	Qtr 2	Qtr 3	Qtr 4
	2-2	2-2	1-4	3-2

Croatia				United States
4/19	21.1%	Natural shots	6/12	50.0%
1/4	25.0%	Center shots	1/1	100.0%
3/14	21.4%	Extramen shots	2/7	28.6%
0/0	0.0%	Mandown shots	0/0	0.0%
0/0	0.0%	Penalty shots	1/1	100.0%
8/37	21.6%	Total shots	10/21	47.6%
	5	Assists	4	
	6	Turnovers	7	
	6	Steals	4	
	3	Blocks	4	
	35	Fouls	28	

1st Referee: KAZ PRIKHODKO, Vladimir
2nd Referee: NED TELLEGEN, Robert

TEAM: CRO Croatia

Coaches: SILIC, Bruno NOLA, Fabjan
Assistant Coach: JEH, Vlado

Names	Shots Made	Attempted	% Eff
SKOLNEKOVIC, Sinisa			
VRDOLJAK, Zdeslav	1	3	33.3%
KREKOVIC, Josko	0	6	0.0%
SIMENC, Dubravko	4	5	80.0%
KRZIC, Ognjen	0	3	0.0%
STRITOF, Ratko	0	1	0.0%
VRBICIC, Renato	1	5	20.0%
GLAVAN, Damir			
VEGAR, Tino	0	1	0.0%
BUKIC, Perica	2	5	40.0%
HINIC, Igor	0	4	0.0%
BALIC, Maro			
KOBESCAK, Vjekoslav	0	4	0.0%

Goalkeeper	Shots Saved	Attempted	% Eff
SKOLNEKOVIC, Sinisa	4	14	28.6%

TEAM: USA United States of America

Coach: CORSO, Richard
Assistant Coaches: AZEVEDO, Rick VARGAS, John

Names	Shots Made	Attempted	% Eff
DUPLANTY, Chris			
HACKETT, Dan			
LASTER, Jeremy	2	5	40.0%
KOPP, Kyle	1	1	100.0%
OEDING, Chris	1	3	33.3%
ARROYO, Gavin	0	1	0.0%
ROUSSEAU, Alex			
McNAIR, Rick	1	4	25.0%
EVERIST, Kirk	2	2	100.0%
HUMBERT, Chris	1	3	33.3%
EVANS, Mike	1	1	100.0%
BARNHART, Troy, Jr.			
WIGO, Wolf	1	1	100.0%

Goalkeeper	Shots Saved	Attempted	% Eff
DUPLANTY, Chris	20	28	71.4%

Men / *Messieurs*

FINAL SUMMARY - GROUP A

Rnk	Team	Played	Won	Drawn	Lost	For	Against	Diff	Points
1	HUN	5	5	0	0	47	38	9	10
2	YUG	5	3	1	1	46	44	2	7
3	ESP	5	3	0	2	39	33	6	6
4	RUS	5	2	1	2	42	38	4	5
5	GER	5	1	0	4	36	45	-9	2
6	NED	5	0	0	5	36	48	-12	0

FINAL SUMMARY - GROUP B

Rnk	Team	Played	Won	Drawn	Lost	For	Against	Diff	Points
1	ITA	5	5	0	0	48	38	10	10
2	USA	5	4	0	1	45	37	8	8
3	CRO	5	3	0	2	51	39	12	6
4	GRE	5	2	0	3	37	38	-1	4
5	ROM	5	0	1	4	31	45	-14	1
6	UKR	5	0	1	4	33	48	-15	1

CLASSIFICATION

GER 10 - 4 UKR

	Qtr 1	Qtr 2	Qtr 3	Qtr 4
	3-0	3-1	1-1	3-2

Germany				Ukraine
4/18	22.2%	Natural shots	2/13	15.4%
3/3	100.0%	Center shots	0/0	0.0%
2/5	40.0%	Extramen shots	1/8	12.5%
0/0	0.0%	Mandown shots	0/0	0.0%
1/2	50.0%	Penalty shots	1/1	100.0%
10/29	34.5%	Total shots	4/22	18.2%
4		Assists	2	
6		Turnovers	10	
3		Steals	5	
3		Blocks	2	
16		Fouls	12	

1st Referee: CRO KLARIC, Zeljko
2nd Referee: YUG RADENOVIC, Miroslav

CLASSIFICATION

NED 10 - 8 ROM

	Qtr 1	Qtr 2	Qtr 3	Qtr 4
	3-2	2-1	4-1	1-4

Netherlands				Romania
6/9	66.7%	Natural shots	4/15	26.7%
0/0	0.0%	Center shots	0/0	0.0%
3/17	17.6%	Extramen shots	4/10	40.0%
0/0	0.0%	Mandown shots	0/0	0.0%
1/1	100.0%	Penalty shots	0/0	0.0%
10/27	37.0%	Total shots	8/25	32.0%
8		Assists	6	
8		Turnovers	4	
5		Steals	4	
3		Blocks	3	
24		Fouls	37	

1st Referee: RUS AFANASIEV, Andrei
2nd Referee: GRE ILIADIS, Dimitrios

TEAM: GER Germany
Coach: FIROIU, Niculae

Names	Shots Made	Attempted	% Eff
BORGMANN, Ingo			
DRESEL, Torsten			
BUKOWSKI, Peter	1	2	50.0%
ERJAVEC, Davor	2	3	66.7%
ILGNER, Michael	0	1	0.0%
KLINGENBERG, Dirk	2	5	40.0%
de la PENA, Raul	1	2	50.0%
STERZIK, Uwe	1	4	25.0%
VOSS, Daniel			
REIMANN, Rene	1	5	20.0%
TOMANEK, Lars	1	3	33.3%
DRESEL, Jorg	1	3	33.3%
DAHLER, Oliver	0	1	0.0%
Goalkeeper	Shots Saved	Attempted	% Eff
BORGMANN, Ingo	9	13	69.2%

TEAM: UKR Ukraine
Coaches: DROZIN, Yuriy GAYDAYENKO, Yuriy

Names	Shots Made	Attempted	% Eff
YEGOROV, Oleks			
ANDREYEV, Dima			
STRATAN, Dima	2	7	28.6%
VLADYMYROV, Oleg			
POTULNYTSKY, Aleks	0	1	0.0%
SOLODUN, Tolik	1	3	33.3%
SKURATOV, Vadym			
KHALCHYTSKY, Vitaliy	0	1	0.0%
KEBALO, Vadym			
KOVALENKO, Andriy	0	3	0.0%
KOSTANDA, Slava	0	2	0.0%
HORBACH, Igor	0	4	0.0%
ROZHDESTVENSKY, Vadym	1	1	100.0%
Goalkeeper	Shots Saved	Attempted	% Eff
YEGOROV, Oleks	12	20	60.0%

TEAM: NED Netherlands
Coach: van ZEELAND, Hans

Names	Shots Made	Attempted	% Eff
van de BUNT, Arie			
de VRIES, Wyco	1	2	50.0%
ISSARD, Koos	1	1	100.0%
van der MEER, Harry	2	4	50.0%
HAVENGA, Arno	1	5	20.0%
STOFFELS, Joeri	1	1	100.0%
de JONG, Bas	0	1	0.0%
KUNZ, Marco	1	4	25.0%
URI, Eelco	2	3	66.7%
NIEUWENBURG, Hans			
VERMEULEN, Wim			
de GROOT, Gert	1	4	25.0%
van der KOLK, Niels	0	2	0.0%
Goalkeeper	Shots Saved	Attempted	% Eff
van de BUNT, Arie	8	16	50.0%

TEAM: ROM Romania
Coach: RUS, Viorel
Assistant Coach: MARINESCU, Gheorghe

Names	Shots Made	Attempted	% Eff
LISAC, Gelu			
DINU, Robert			
TOTOLICI, Liviu	4	7	57.1%
BONCA, Florin	0	2	0.0%
SABAU, Radu	0	1	0.0%
FULGEANU, Nicolae	1	1	100.0%
HAGIU, Vlad	2	4	50.0%
SANDA, Petre	0	2	0.0%
STEMATE, Dinel	0	1	0.0%
MOLDVAI, Istvan	1	1	100.0%
RATH, Bogdan	0	3	0.0%
RADU, Catalin	0	3	0.0%
ANDREI, Edward			
Goalkeepers	Shots Saved	Attempted	% Eff
LISAC, Gelu	5	12	41.7%
DINU, Robert	3	6	50.0%

Men / *Messieurs*

CLASSIFICATION

GER 9 - 6 NED

	Qtr 1	Qtr 2	Qtr 3	Qtr 4
	1-0	2-3	3-1	3-2

Germany			Netherlands	
2/12	16.7%	Natural shots	3/24	12.5%
0/0	0.0%	Center shots	0/2	0.0%
7/17	41.2%	Extramen shots	1/4	25.0%
0/0	0.0%	Mandown shots	0/0	0.0%
0/0	0.0%	Penalty shots	2/2	100.0%
9/29	31.0%	Total shots	6/32	18.8%
4		Assists	2	
6		Turnovers	9	
3		Steals	7	
7		Blocks	2	
21		Fouls	39	

1st Referee: ESP FERNANDEZ, Joaquin
2nd Referee: USA BERNARD, Bret

TEAM: GER Germany

Coach: FIROIU, Niculae

Names	Shots Made	Attempted	% Eff
BORGMANN, Ingo			
DRESEL, Torsten	1	2	50.0%
BUKOWSKI, Peter	2	5	40.0%
ERJAVEC, Davor	2	8	25.0%
ILGNER, Michael	0	3	0.0%
KLINGENBERG, Dirk	3	6	50.0%
de la PENA, Raul	0	1	0.0%
STERZIK, Uwe	0	1	0.0%
VOSS, Daniel			
REIMANN, Rene			
TOMANEK, Lars	1	3	33.3%
DRESEL, Jorg			
DAHLER, Oliver			
Goalkeeper	Shots Saved	Attempted	% Eff
BORGMANN, Ingo	7	13	53.8%

TEAM: NED Netherlands

Coach: van ZEELAND, Hans

Names	Shots Made	Attempted	% Eff
van de BUNT, Arie			
de VRIES, Wyco	0	2	0.0%
ISSARD, Koos	1	2	50.0%
van der MEER, Harry	2	6	33.3%
HAVENGA, Arno	0	3	0.0%
STOFFELS, Joeri	0	1	0.0%
de JONG, Bas			
KUNZ, Marco	1	6	16.7%
URI, Eelco	0	6	0.0%
NIEUWENBURG, Hans	0	1	0.0%
VERMEULEN, Wim			
de GROOT, Gert	0	1	0.0%
van der KOLK, Niels	2	4	50.0%
Goalkeeper	Shots Saved	Attempted	% Eff
van de BUNT, Arie	13	22	59.1%

CLASSIFICATION

ROM 11 - 8 UKR

	Qtr 1	Qtr 2	Qtr 3	Qtr 4
	2-0	4-3	3-2	2-3

Romania			Ukraine	
2/10	20.0%	Natural shots	1/8	12.5%
0/1	0.0%	Center shots	1/1	100.0%
8/9	88.9%	Extramen shots	6/14	42.9%
0/0	0.0%	Mandown shots	0/0	0.0%
1/1	100.0%	Penalty shots	0/1	0.0%
11/21	52.4%	Total shots	8/24	33.3%
10		Assists	7	
8		Turnovers	7	
5		Steals	3	
1		Blocks	2	
48		Fouls	58	

1st Referee: HUN KOSZTOLANCZY, Gyorgy
2nd Referee: ITA MEROLA, Salvatore

TEAM: ROM Romania

Coach: RUS, Viorel
Assistant Coach: MARINESCU, Gheorghe

Names	Shots Made	Attempted	% Eff
LISAC, Gelu			
DINU, Robert			
TOTOLICI, Liviu	0	2	0.0%
BONCA, Florin	1	2	50.0%
SABAU, Radu			
FULGEANU, Nicolae	1	1	100.0%
HAGIU, Vlad	4	6	66.7%
SANDA, Petre	0	1	0.0%
STEMATE, Dinel			
MOLDVAI, Istvan	2	4	50.0%
RATH, Bogdan	1	3	33.3%
RADU, Catalin	1	1	100.0%
ANDREI, Edward	1	1	100.0%
Goalkeeper	Shots Saved	Attempted	% Eff
LISAC, Gelu	6	14	42.9%

TEAM: UKR Ukraine

Coaches: DROZIN, Yuriy GAYDAYENKO, Yuriy

Names	Shots Made	Attempted	% Eff
YEGOROV, Oleks			
ANDREYEV, Dima	0	1	0.0%
STRATAN, Dima			
VLADYMYROV, Oleg			
POTULNYTSKY, Aleks	1	6	16.7%
SOLODUN, Tolik	2	6	33.3%
SKURATOV, Vadym			
KHALCHYTSKY, Vitaliy			
KEBALO, Vadym	1	2	50.0%
KOVALENKO, Andriy	1	3	33.3%
KOSTANDA, Slava			
HORBACH, Igor	1	2	50.0%
ROZHDESTVENSKY, Vadym	2	4	50.0%
Goalkeeper	Shots Saved	Attempted	% Eff
YEGOROV, Oleks	7	18	38.9%

CLASSIFICATION

NED 9 - 9 UKR

	Qtr 1	Qtr 2	Qtr 3	Qtr 4
	1-2	5-1	2-3	1-3

Netherlands			Ukraine	
7/18	38.9%	Natural shots	3/11	27.3%
0/1	0.0%	Center shots	0/3	0.0%
2/8	25.0%	Extramen shots	4/6	66.7%
0/0	0.0%	Mandown shots	0/0	0.0%
0/1	0.0%	Penalty shots	2/2	100.0%
9/28	32.1%	Total shots	9/22	40.9%
7		Assists	6	
2		Turnovers	10	
8		Steals	7	
5		Blocks	4	
23		Fouls	16	

1st Referee: CAN LEGARE, Daniel
2nd Referee: JPN WAKABAYASHI, Kazuhito

TEAM: NED Netherlands

Coach: van ZEELAND, Hans

Names	Shots Made	Attempted	% Eff
van de BUNT, Arie	0	1	0.0%
de VRIES, Wyco	0	2	0.0%
ISSARD, Koos	0	2	0.0%
van der MEER, Harry	1	3	33.3%
HAVENGA, Arno	3	6	50.0%
STOFFELS, Joeri	1	2	50.0%
de JONG, Bas	0	1	0.0%
KUNZ, Marco	1	4	25.0%
URI, Eelco	1	3	33.3%
NIEUWENBURG, Hans			
VERMEULEN, Wim			
de GROOT, Gert	1	2	50.0%
van der KOLK, Niels	1	2	50.0%
Goalkeeper	Shots Saved	Attempted	% Eff
van de BUNT, Arie	7	16	43.8%

TEAM: UKR Ukraine

Coaches: DROZIN, Yuriy GAYDAYENKO, Yuriy

Names	Shots Made	Attempted	% Eff
YEGOROV, Oleks			
ANDREYEV, Dima			
STRATAN, Dima	1	5	20.0%
VLADYMYROV, Oleg			
POTULNYTSKY, Aleks	2	3	66.7%
SOLODUN, Tolik	3	5	60.0%
SKURATOV, Vadym			
KHALCHYTSKY, Vitaliy			
KEBALO, Vadym	0	2	0.0%
KOVALENKO, Andriy	1	1	100.0%
KOSTANDA, Slava			
HORBACH, Igor	2	5	40.0%
ROZHDESTVENSKY, Vadym	0	1	0.0%
Goalkeeper	Shots Saved	Attempted	% Eff
YEGOROV, Oleks	6	15	40.0%

CLASSIFICATION

GER 10 - 6 ROM

	Qtr 1	Qtr 2	Qtr 3	Qtr 4
	2-2	2-0	3-2	3-2

Germany			Romania	
2/7	28.6%	Natural shots	3/14	21.4%
2/5	40.0%	Center shots	1/1	100.0%
6/10	60.0%	Extramen shots	2/8	25.0%
0/0	0.0%	Mandown shots	0/0	0.0%
0/1	0.0%	Penalty shots	0/0	0.0%
10/23	43.5%	Total shots	6/23	26.1%
	9	Assists	5	
	3	Turnovers	9	
	12	Steals	9	
	4	Blocks	1	
	45	Fouls	31	

1st Referee: RUS   AFANASIEV, Andrei
2nd Referee: ALG   HAMICI, Salah

TEAM: GER Germany
Coach: FIROIU, Niculae

Names	Shots Made	Attempted	% Eff
BORGMANN, Ingo	0	1	0.0%
DRESEL, Torsten	0	1	0.0%
BUKOWSKI, Peter	0	1	0.0%
ERJAVEC, Davor	2	4	50.0%
ILGNER, Michael	0	1	0.0%
KLINGENBERG, Dirk	1	1	100.0%
de la PENA, Raul	2	5	40.0%
STERZIK, Uwe			
VOSS, Daniel			
REIMANN, Rene	1	2	50.0%
TOMANEK, Lars	1	1	100.0%
DRESEL, Jorg	2	5	40.0%
DAHLER, Oliver	1	1	100.0%
Goalkeepers	**Shots Saved**	**Attempted**	**% Eff**
BORGMANN, Ingo	5	10	50.0%
VOSS, Daniel	2	3	66.7%

TEAM: ROM Romania
Coach: RUS, Viorel
Assistant Coach: MARINESCU, Gheorghe

Names	Shots Made	Attempted	% Eff
LISAC, Gelu	0	2	0.0%
DINU, Robert			
TOTOLICI, Liviu	2	4	50.0%
BONCA, Florin	0	2	0.0%
SABAU, Radu	0	3	0.0%
FULGEANU, Nicolae			
HAGIU, Vlad	2	4	50.0%
SANDA, Petre	0	2	0.0%
STEMATE, Dinel			
MOLDVAI, Istvan	1	1	100.0%
RATH, Bogdan	1	2	50.0%
RADU, Catalin	0	2	0.0%
ANDREI, Edward	0	1	0.0%
Goalkeeper	**Shots Saved**	**Attempted**	**% Eff**
LISAC, Gelu	9	19	47.4%

FINAL SUMMARY - CLASSIFICATION

		Matches				Goals		
Rnk	Team	Played	Won	Drawn	Lost	For	Against	Diff	Points
1	GER	3	3	0	0	29	16	13	6
2	NED	3	1	1	1	25	26	-1	3
3	ROM	3	1	0	2	25	28	-3	2
4	UKR	3	0	1	2	21	30	-9	1

QUARTERFINALS

HUN 12 - 8 GRE

	Qtr 1	Qtr 2	Qtr 3	Qtr 4
	3-2	4-2	2-2	3-2

Hungary			Greece	
5/13	38.5%	Natural shots	2/7	28.6%
2/4	50.0%	Center shots	1/2	50.0%
5/14	35.7%	Extramen shots	4/16	25.0%
0/0	0.0%	Mandown shots	0/0	0.0%
0/0	0.0%	Penalty shots	1/1	100.0%
12/31	38.7%	Total shots	8/26	30.8%
	10	Assists	5	
	5	Turnovers	12	
	3	Steals	3	
	4	Blocks	5	
	48	Fouls	8	

1st Referee: KAZ   PRIKHODKO, Vladimir
2nd Referee: UKR   BELEVTSOV, Vyacheslav

TEAM: HUN Hungary
Coach: HORKAI, Gyorgy
Assistant Coach: GERENDAS, Gyorgy

Names	Shots Made	Attempted	% Eff
KOSZ, Zoltan			
TOTH, Frank	1	4	25.0%
MONOSTORI, Attila	0	1	0.0%
VARGA, Zsolt	2	4	50.0%
KASAS, Tamas	1	5	20.0%
TOTH, Laszlo	1	1	100.0%
DALA, Tamas	2	5	40.0%
BENEDEK, Tibor	1	4	25.0%
FODOR, Rajmund			
VINCZE, Balazs	2	3	66.7%
GYONGYOSI, Andras	0	1	0.0%
KUNA, Peter			
NEMETH, Zsolt	2	3	66.7%
Goalkeeper	**Shots Saved**	**Attempted**	**% Eff**
KOSZ, Zoltan	8	16	50.0%

TEAM: GRE Greece
Coach: IOSIFIDIS, Kyriakos
Assistant Coach: MICHALOS, Panagiotis

Names	Shots Made	Attempted	% Eff
VOLTYRAKIS, Gerasimos			
KAIAFAS, Filippos	2	9	22.2%
CHATZITHEODOROU, Theodoros			
LOUDIS, Konstantinos			
MAVROTAS, Georgios	3	4	75.0%
PAPANASTASIOU, Anastasios	2	4	50.0%
PSYCHOS, Georgios	0	2	0.0%
KALAKONAS, Theodoros			
AFROUDAKIS, Georgios	1	3	33.3%
LORANTOS, Theodoros	0	1	0.0%
CHATZIS, Thomas	0	2	0.0%
GEORGARAS, Simeon	0	1	0.0%
PATRAS, Evangelos			
Goalkeepers	**Shots Saved**	**Attempted**	**% Eff**
VOLTYRAKIS, Gerasimos	2	8	25.0%
PATRAS, Evangelos	1	7	14.3%

Men / *Messieurs*

QUARTERFINALS

YUG 6 - 8 CRO

	Qtr 1	Qtr 2	Qtr 3	Qtr 4
	1-3	1-2	2-1	2-2

Yugoslavia			Croatia	
2/7	28.6%	Natural shots	4/13	30.8%
0/4	0.0%	Center shots	0/1	0.0%
4/13	30.8%	Extramen shots	4/8	50.0%
0/0	0.0%	Mandown shots	0/0	0.0%
0/0	0.0%	Penalty shots	0/0	0.0%
6/24	25.0%	Total shots	8/22	36.4%
	4	Assists	4	
	9	Turnovers	5	
	6	Steals	6	
	0	Blocks	2	
	35	Fouls	29	

1st Referee: FRA DEMEY, Jean
2nd Referee: AUS KERR, Peter

TEAM: YUG Yugoslavia

Coach: ANDRIC, Dragan
Assistant Coach: PAVLOVIC, Vladimir

Names	Shots Made	Attempted	% Eff
SOSTAR, Aleksandar			
TRBOJEVIC, Petar	0	1	0.0%
SUBOTIC, Vaso	0	2	0.0%
ZIMONJIC, Predrag			
MILANOVIC, Igor	0	5	0.0%
SAPIC, Aleksandar	1	1	100.0%
VICEVIC, Mirko	2	5	40.0%
USKOKOVIC, Veljko	2	3	66.7%
SAVIC, Dejan	1	3	33.3%
JELENIC, Viktor	0	1	0.0%
VUJASINOVIC, Vladimir	0	3	0.0%
PEROVIC, Ranko			
TADIC, Milan			
Goalkeeper	**Shots Saved**	**Attempted**	**% Eff**
SOSTAR, Aleksandar	10	18	55.6%

TEAM: CRO Croatia

Coaches: SILIC, Bruno   NOLA, Fabjan
Assistant Coach: JEH, Vlado

Names	Shots Made	Attempted	% Eff
SKOLNEKOVIC, Sinisa	0	1	0.0%
VRDOLJAK, Zdeslav	1	2	50.0%
KREKOVIC, Josko	1	2	50.0%
SIMENC, Dubravko	3	4	75.0%
KRZIC, Ognjen			
STRITOF, Ratko	0	1	0.0%
VRBICIC, Renato	0	1	0.0%
GLAVAN, Damir			
VEGAR, Tino	1	3	33.3%
BUKIC, Perica	2	4	50.0%
HINIC, Igor	0	1	0.0%
BALIC, Maro			
KOBESCAK, Vjekoslav	0	3	0.0%
Goalkeeper	**Shots Saved**	**Attempted**	**% Eff**
SKOLNEKOVIC, Sinisa	9	15	60.0%

QUARTERFINALS

ESP 5 - 4 USA

	Qtr 1	Qtr 2	Qtr 3	Qtr 4
	2-0	2-1	1-0	0-3

Spain			United States	
1/9	11.1%	Natural shots	2/20	10.0%
1/3	33.3%	Center shots	0/2	0.0%
3/8	37.5%	Extramen shots	2/6	33.3%
0/0	0.0%	Mandown shots	0/0	0.0%
0/0	0.0%	Penalty shots	0/0	0.0%
5/20	25.0%	Total shots	4/28	14.3%
	5	Assists	4	
	5	Turnovers	4	
	3	Steals	9	
	4	Blocks	5	
	8	Fouls	56	

1st Referee: NED TELLEGEN, Robert
2nd Referee: CUB MARTINEZ, Eugenio

TEAM: ESP Spain

Coach: JANE, Juan
Assistant Coach: FERNANDEZ de CUEVAS, Santiago

Names	Shots Made	Attempted	% Eff
ROLLAN, Jesus			
ABARCA, Jose Maria			
PEDREROL, Sergi			
ANDREO, Angel			
ESTIARTE, Manuel	2	6	33.3%
BALLART, Daniel	0	2	0.0%
PAYA, Jorge	0	1	0.0%
MORO, Ivan	0	1	0.0%
SANS, Jordi	1	2	50.0%
GOMEZ, Salvador	1	3	33.3%
OCA, Miguel	0	2	0.0%
SANZ, Carlos			
GARCIA, Pedro	1	3	33.3%
Goalkeeper	**Shots Saved**	**Attempted**	**% Eff**
ROLLAN, Jesus	11	15	73.3%

TEAM: USA United States of America

Coach: CORSO, Richard
Assistant Coaches: AZEVEDO, Rick   VARGAS, John

Names	Shots Made	Attempted	% Eff
DUPLANTY, Chris			
HACKETT, Dan			
LASTER, Jeremy	1	5	20.0%
KOPP, Kyle	0	2	0.0%
OEDING, Chris	2	5	40.0%
ARROYO, Gavin	1	4	25.0%
ROUSSEAU, Alex			
McNAIR, Rick	0	4	0.0%
EVERIST, Kirk			
HUMBERT, Chris	0	2	0.0%
EVANS, Mike	0	4	0.0%
BARNHART, Troy, Jr.	0	1	0.0%
WIGO, Wolf	0	1	0.0%
Goalkeeper	**Shots Saved**	**Attempted**	**% Eff**
DUPLANTY, Chris	9	14	64.3%

QUARTERFINALS

RUS 9 - 11 ITA

	Qtr 1	Qtr 2	Qtr 3	Qtr 4
	4-4	3-2	1-3	1-2

Russian Federation			Italy	
2/8	25.0%	Natural shots	1/6	16.7%
1/3	33.3%	Center shots	1/3	33.3%
5/14	35.7%	Extramen shots	9/18	50.0%
0/0	0.0%	Mandown shots	0/0	0.0%
1/1	100.0%	Penalty shots	0/0	0.0%
9/26	34.6%	Total shots	11/27	40.7%
	5	Assists	8	
	5	Turnovers	6	
	4	Steals	1	
	3	Blocks	6	
	84	Fouls	62	

1st Referee: GER LUDECKE, Rolf
2nd Referee: BEL SIMONS, Francois

TEAM: RUS Russian Federation

Coach: KABANOV, Alexandre
Assistant Coach: OUKHOV, Boris

Names	Shots Made	Attempted	% Eff
MAXIMOV, Nikolai			
PANFILI, Alexei	1	2	50.0%
EVSTIGNEEV, Serguei			
KOZLOV, Nikolai	0	3	0.0%
GARBOUZOV, Serguei	0	1	0.0%
ERYSHOV, Alexandre	3	6	50.0%
APANASSENKO, Maxim	1	3	33.3%
IVLEV, Serguei	1	1	100.0%
GORCHKOV, Dmitrii	1	2	50.0%
KONSTANTINOV, Ilia	2	3	66.7%
SMOLOVOI, Iouri	0	2	0.0%
KARABOUTOV, Vladimir	0	3	0.0%
DOUGUINE, Dmitri			
Goalkeeper	**Shots Saved**	**Attempted**	**% Eff**
MAXIMOV, Nikolai	8	19	42.1%

TEAM: ITA Italy

Coach: RUDIC, Ratko
Assistant Coach: CASTELLUCCI, Giuseppe

Names	Shots Made	Attempted	% Eff
ATTOLICO, Francesco			
POSTIGLIONE, Francesco			
BOVO, Alessandro	2	2	100.0%
BENCIVENGA, Fabio	0	1	0.0%
CALCATERRA, Alessandro	1	3	33.3%
CALCATERRA, Roberto	1	4	25.0%
GIUSTOLISI, Luca	2	4	50.0%
ANGELINI, Alberto	2	3	66.7%
POMILIO, Amedeo	0	1	0.0%
GERINI, Marco			
SOTTANI, Leonardo	1	2	50.0%
SILIPO, Carlo	2	6	33.3%
GHIBELLINI, Alberto	0	1	0.0%
Goalkeeper	**Shots Saved**	**Attempted**	**% Eff**
ATTOLICO, Francesco	7	16	43.8%

Men / *Messieurs*

SEMIFINALS

GRE 7 - 6 USA

	Qtr 1	Qtr 2	Qtr 3	Qtr 4
	1-1	3-0	1-4	2-1

Greece			United States	
2/7	28.6%	Natural shots	3/12	25.0%
2/3	66.7%	Center shots	1/2	50.0%
2/10	20.0%	Extramen shots	1/5	20.0%
0/0	0.0%	Mandown shots	0/0	0.0%
1/2	50.0%	Penalty shots	1/1	100.0%
7/22	31.8%	Total shots	6/20	30.0%
	3	Assists	4	
	5	Turnovers	8	
	3	Steals	5	
	0	Blocks	2	
	6	Fouls	59	

1st Referee: ROM TIMOC, Radu
2nd Referee: CRO KLARIC, Zeljko

TEAM: GRE Greece

Coach: IOSIFIDIS, Kyriakos
Assistant Coach: MICHALOS, Panagiotis

Names	Shots Made	Attempted	% Eff
VOLTYRAKIS, Gerasimos			
KAIAFAS, Filippos	0	3	0.0%
CHATZITHEODOROU, Theodoros			
LOUDIS, Konstantinos	2	5	40.0%
MAVROTAS, Georgios	1	1	100.0%
PAPANASTASIOU, Anastasios	2	3	66.7%
PSYCHOS, Georgios	0	1	0.0%
KALAKONAS, Theodoros			
AFROUDAKIS, Georgios	1	4	25.0%
LORANTOS, Theodoros	1	4	25.0%
CHATZIS, Thomas			
GEORGARAS, Simeon	0	1	0.0%
PATRAS, Evangelos			
Goalkeeper	**Shots Saved**	**Attempted**	**% Eff**
VOLTYRAKIS, Gerasimos	9	15	60.0%

TEAM: USA United States of America

Coach: CORSO, Richard
Assistant Coaches: AZEVEDO, Rick   VARGAS, John

Names	Shots Made	Attempted	% Eff
DUPLANTY, Chris			
HACKETT, Dan			
LASTER, Jeremy	1	2	50.0%
KOPP, Kyle			
OEDING, Chris	1	3	33.3%
ARROYO, Gavin	0	1	0.0%
ROUSSEAU, Alex			
McNAIR, Rick	2	3	66.7%
EVERIST, Kirk	0	2	0.0%
HUMBERT, Chris	2	4	50.0%
EVANS, Mike	0	3	0.0%
BARNHART, Troy, Jr.	0	1	0.0%
WIGO, Wolf	0	1	0.0%
Goalkeeper	**Shots Saved**	**Attempted**	**% Eff**
DUPLANTY, Chris	8	15	53.3%

SEMIFINALS

YUG 15 - 16 RUS

Qtr 1	Qtr 2	Qtr 3	Qtr 4	OT	OT	OT
5-4	1-2	3-3	3-3	1-2	2-1	0-1

Yugoslavia			Russian Federation	
6/17	35.3%	Natural shots	2/11	18.2%
2/5	40.0%	Center shots	0/1	0.0%
6/14	42.9%	Extramen shots	12/18	66.7%
0/0	0.0%	Mandown shots	0/0	0.0%
1/1	100.0%	Penalty shots	2/2	100.0%
15/37	40.5%	Total shots	16/32	50.0%
	8	Assists	12	
	5	Turnovers	6	
	4	Steals	2	
	4	Blocks	5	
	40	Fouls	50	

1st Referee: NED TELLEGEN, Robert
2nd Referee: BEL SIMONS, Francois

TEAM: YUG Yugoslavia

Coach: ANDRIC, Dragan
Assistant Coach: PAVLOVIC, Vladimir

Names	Shots Made	Attempted	% Eff
SOSTAR, Aleksandar			
TRBOJEVIC, Petar	1	1	100.0%
SUBOTIC, Vaso			
ZIMONJIC, Predrag	0	4	0.0%
MILANOVIC, Igor			
SAPIC, Aleksandar	0	4	0.0%
VICEVIC, Mirko	2	5	40.0%
USKOKOVIC, Veljko	4	9	44.4%
SAVIC, Dejan	2	2	100.0%
JELENIC, Viktor	3	5	60.0%
VUJASINOVIC, Vladimir	3	6	50.0%
PEROVIC, Ranko	0	1	0.0%
TADIC, Milan			
Goalkeepers	**Shots Saved**	**Attempted**	**% Eff**
SOSTAR, Aleksandar	6	16	37.5%
TADIC, Milan	2	8	25.0%

TEAM: RUS Russian Federation

Coach: KABANOV, Alexandre
Assistant Coach: OUKHOV, Boris

Names	Shots Made	Attempted	% Eff
MAXIMOV, Nikolai			
PANFILI, Alexei			
EVSTIGNEEV, Serguei	0	2	0.0%
KOZLOV, Nikolai	1	4	25.0%
GARBOUZOV, Serguei			
ERYSHOV, Alexandre	3	6	50.0%
APANASSENKO, Maxim	4	6	66.7%
IVLEV, Serguei	2	4	50.0%
GORCHKOV, Dmitrii	2	4	50.0%
KONSTANTINOV, Ilia	1	2	50.0%
SMOLOVOI, Iouri	2	2	100.0%
KARABOUTOV, Vladimir	1	2	50.0%
DOUGUINE, Dmitri			
Goalkeeper	**Shots Saved**	**Attempted**	**% Eff**
MAXIMOV, Nikolai	8	23	34.8%

SEMIFINALS

HUN 6 - 7 ESP

	Qtr 1	Qtr 2	Qtr 3	Qtr 4
	2-2	2-1	1-1	1-3

Hungary			Spain	
2/12	16.7%	Natural shots	3/10	30.0%
1/2	50.0%	Center shots	1/3	33.3%
2/12	16.7%	Extramen shots	3/11	27.3%
0/0	0.0%	Mandown shots	0/0	0.0%
1/1	100.0%	Penalty shots	0/0	0.0%
6/27	22.2%	Total shots	7/24	29.2%
	2	Assists	4	
	6	Turnovers	6	
	5	Steals	3	
	4	Blocks	5	
	82	Fouls	14	

1st Referee: NED KEMAN, Wilhelm
2nd Referee: GER LUDECKE, Rolf

TEAM: HUN Hungary

Coach: HORKAI, Gyorgy
Assistant Coach: GERENDAS, Gyorgy

Names	Shots Made	Attempted	% Eff
KOSZ, Zoltan			
TOTH, Frank	0	1	0.0%
MONOSTORI, Attila	0	2	0.0%
VARGA, Zsolt	0	1	0.0%
KASAS, Tamas	1	4	25.0%
TOTH, Laszlo	1	3	33.3%
DALA, Tamas	0	3	0.0%
BENEDEK, Tibor	2	2	100.0%
FODOR, Rajmund	0	1	0.0%
VINCZE, Balazs	1	4	25.0%
GYONGYOSI, Andras	0	3	0.0%
KUNA, Peter			
NEMETH, Zsolt	1	3	33.3%
Goalkeeper	**Shots Saved**	**Attempted**	**% Eff**
KOSZ, Zoltan	7	14	50.0%

TEAM: ESP Spain

Coach: JANE, Juan
Assistant Coach: FERNANDEZ de CUEVAS, Santiago

Names	Shots Made	Attempted	% Eff
ROLLAN, Jesus			
ABARCA, Jose Maria			
PEDREROL, Sergi	1	1	100.0%
ANDREO, Angel			
ESTIARTE, Manuel	0	2	0.0%
BALLART, Daniel	0	1	0.0%
PAYA, Jorge			
MORO, Ivan	1	5	20.0%
SANS, Jordi	0	3	0.0%
GOMEZ, Salvador	4	7	57.1%
OCA, Miguel	0	3	0.0%
SANZ, Carlos	1	2	50.0%
GARCIA, Pedro			
Goalkeeper	**Shots Saved**	**Attempted**	**% Eff**
ROLLAN, Jesus	8	14	57.1%

Men / *Messieurs*

SEMIFINALS

CRO 7 - 6 ITA

Qtr 1	Qtr 2	Qtr 3	Qtr 4	OT	OT
0-1	2-1	1-0	1-2	1-2	2-0

Croatia			Italy	
0/5	0.0%	Natural shots	0/12	0.0%
0/4	0.0%	Center shots	0/2	0.0%
5/8	62.5%	Extramen shots	6/18	33.3%
0/0	0.0%	Mandown shots	0/0	0.0%
2/2	100.0%	Penalty shots	0/0	0.0%
7/19	36.8%	Total shots	6/32	18.8%
	4	Assists	5	
	12	Turnovers	12	
	3	Steals	9	
	2	Blocks	4	
	77	Fouls	94	

1st Referee: KAZ PRIKHODKO, Vladimir
2nd Referee: CUB MARTINEZ, Eugenio

TEAM: CRO Croatia
Coaches: SILIC, Bruno   NOLA, Fabjan
Assistant Coach: JEH, Vlado

Names	Shots Made	Attempted	% Eff
SKOLNEKOVIC, Sinisa			
VRDOLJAK, Zdeslav	0	1	0.0%
KREKOVIC, Josko	4	7	57.1%
SIMENC, Dubravko	1	2	50.0%
KRZIC, Ognjen	1	1	100.0%
STRITOF, Ratko	0	1	0.0%
VRBICIC, Renato	1	4	25.0%
GLAVAN, Damir			
VEGAR, Tino	0	2	0.0%
BUKIC, Perica			
HINIC, Igor	0	1	0.0%
BALIC, Maro			
KOBESCAK, Vjekoslav			
Goalkeeper	**Shots Saved**	**Attempted**	**% Eff**
SKOLNEKOVIC, Sinisa	16	22	72.7%

TEAM: ITA Italy
Coach: RUDIC, Ratko
Assistant Coach: CASTELLUCCI, Giuseppe

Names	Shots Made	Attempted	% Eff
ATTOLICO, Francesco			
POSTIGLIONE, Francesco	1	1	100.0%
BOVO, Alessandro	1	5	20.0%
BENCIVENGA, Fabio	0	1	0.0%
CALCATERRA, Alessandro			
CALCATERRA, Roberto	1	3	33.3%
GIUSTOLISI, Luca	0	1	0.0%
ANGELINI, Alberto	0	3	0.0%
POMILIO, Amedeo	2	7	28.6%
GERINI, Marco			
SOTTANI, Leonardo	0	1	0.0%
SILIPO, Carlo	0	5	0.0%
GHIBELLINI, Alberto	1	5	20.0%
Goalkeeper	**Shots Saved**	**Attempted**	**% Eff**
ATTOLICO, Francesco	7	14	50.0%

FINAL 7 - 8

USA 12 - 8 YUG

Qtr 1	Qtr 2	Qtr 3	Qtr 4
2-1	5-2	2-2	3-3

United States			Yugoslavia	
6/14	42.9%	Natural shots	1/9	11.1%
0/3	0.0%	Center shots	1/3	33.3%
4/5	80.0%	Extramen shots	6/11	54.5%
0/0	0.0%	Mandown shots	0/0	0.0%
2/2	100.0%	Penalty shots	0/0	0.0%
12/24	50.0%	Total shots	8/23	34.8%
	9	Assists	7	
	4	Turnovers	4	
	6	Steals	3	
	2	Blocks	2	
	27	Fouls	34	

1st Referee: HUN KOSZTOLANCZY, Gyorgy
2nd Referee: ESP FERNANDEZ, Joaquin

TEAM: USA United States of America
Coach: CORSO, Richard
Assistant Coaches: AZEVEDO, Rick   VARGAS, John

Names	Shots Made	Attempted	% Eff
DUPLANTY, Chris			
HACKETT, Dan			
LASTER, Jeremy	1	1	100.0%
KOPP, Kyle	0	2	0.0%
OEDING, Chris	3	3	100.0%
ARROYO, Gavin	1	3	33.3%
ROUSSEAU, Alex	0	1	0.0%
McNAIR, Rick	1	1	100.0%
EVERIST, Kirk	0	2	0.0%
HUMBERT, Chris	2	4	50.0%
EVANS, Mike	0	2	0.0%
BARNHART, Troy, Jr.	2	3	66.7%
WIGO, Wolf	2	2	100.0%
Goalkeeper	**Shots Saved**	**Attempted**	**% Eff**
DUPLANTY, Chris	8	16	50.0%

TEAM: YUG Yugoslavia
Coach: ANDRIC, Dragan
Assistant Coach: PAVLOVIC, Vladimir

Names	Shots Made	Attempted	% Eff
SOSTAR, Aleksandar			
TRBOJEVIC, Petar	0	2	0.0%
SUBOTIC, Vaso	0	1	0.0%
ZIMONJIC, Predrag	0	2	0.0%
MILANOVIC, Igor			
SAPIC, Aleksandar	1	1	100.0%
VICEVIC, Mirko	0	1	0.0%
USKOKOVIC, Veljko	1	2	50.0%
SAVIC, Dejan	3	5	60.0%
JELENIC, Viktor	1	3	33.3%
VUJASINOVIC, Vladimir	2	5	40.0%
PEROVIC, Ranko	0	1	0.0%
TADIC, Milan			
Goalkeeper	**Shots Saved**	**Attempted**	**% Eff**
SOSTAR, Aleksandar	8	20	40.0%

FINAL 5 - 6

GRE 8 - 10 RUS

Qtr 1	Qtr 2	Qtr 3	Qtr 4	OT	OT
2-2	1-1	1-2	3-2	1-2	0-1

Greece			Russian Federation	
1/7	14.3%	Natural shots	7/17	41.2%
2/6	33.3%	Center shots	1/5	20.0%
4/11	36.4%	Extramen shots	2/6	33.3%
0/0	0.0%	Mandown shots	0/0	0.0%
1/1	100.0%	Penalty shots	0/0	0.0%
8/25	32.0%	Total shots	10/28	35.7%
	7	Assists	7	
	5	Turnovers	11	
	4	Steals	10	
	3	Blocks	2	
	19	Fouls	90	

1st Referee: FRA DEMEY, Jean
2nd Referee: ITA MEROLA, Salvatore

TEAM: GRE Greece
Coach: IOSIFIDIS, Kyriakos
Assistant Coach: MICHALOS, Panagiotis

Names	Shots Made	Attempted	% Eff
VOLTYRAKIS, Gerasimos			
KAIAFAS, Filippos	1	4	25.0%
CHATZITHEODOROU, Theodoros	0	1	0.0%
LOUDIS, Konstantinos	2	3	66.7%
MAVROTAS, Georgios	1	2	50.0%
PAPANASTASIOU, Anastasios	0	3	0.0%
PSYCHOS, Georgios			
KALAKONAS, Theodoros			
AFROUDAKIS, Georgios	3	8	37.5%
LORANTOS, Theodoros	1	3	33.3%
CHATZIS, Thomas	0	1	0.0%
GEORGARAS, Simeon			
PATRAS, Evangelos			
Goalkeeper	**Shots Saved**	**Attempted**	**% Eff**
VOLTYRAKIS, Gerasimos	13	23	56.5%

TEAM: RUS Russian Federation
Coach: KABANOV, Alexandre
Assistant Coach: OUKHOV, Boris

Names	Shots Made	Attempted	% Eff
MAXIMOV, Nikolai			
PANFILI, Alexei	0	3	0.0%
EVSTIGNEEV, Serguei	1	2	50.0%
KOZLOV, Nikolai	2	6	33.3%
GARBOUZOV, Serguei	1	2	50.0%
ERYSHOV, Alexandre	2	2	100.0%
APANASSENKO, Maxim			
IVLEV, Serguei	1	1	100.0%
GORCHKOV, Dmitrii	1	2	50.0%
KONSTANTINOV, Ilia	1	5	20.0%
SMOLOVOI, Iouri	0	4	0.0%
KARABOUTOV, Vladimir	1	1	100.0%
DOUGUINE, Dmitri			
Goalkeeper	**Shots Saved**	**Attempted**	**% Eff**
DOUGUINE, Dmitri	4	12	33.3%

FINAL - BRONZE

HUN 18 - 20 ITA

Qtr 1	Qtr 2	Qtr 3	Qtr 4	OT	OT
4-3	4-4	3-2	5-7	0-3	2-1

Hungary			Italy	
4/8	50.0%	**Natural shots**	9/15	60.0%
1/1	100.0%	**Center shots**	1/2	50.0%
11/21	52.4%	**Extramen shots**	9/17	52.9%
0/0	0.0%	**Mandown shots**	0/0	0.0%
2/2	100.0%	**Penalty shots**	1/1	100.0%
18/32	56.3%	**Total shots**	20/35	57.1%
	12	**Assists**	14	
	9	**Turnovers**	4	
	8	**Steals**	8	
	0	**Blocks**	4	
	66	**Fouls**	97	

1st Referee: YUG   RADENOVIC, Miroslav
2nd Referee: CRO   KLARIC, Zeljko

TEAM: HUN Hungary

Coach: HORKAI, Gyorgy
Assistant Coach: GERENDAS, Gyorgy

Names	Shots Made	Attempted	% Eff
KOSZ, Zoltan			
TOTH, Frank	1	2	50.0%
MONOSTORI, Attila	1	4	25.0%
VARGA, Zsolt	1	2	50.0%
KASAS, Tamas	3	5	60.0%
TOTH, Laszlo			
DALA, Tamas	1	2	50.0%
BENEDEK, Tibor	4	7	57.1%
FODOR, Rajmund	2	2	100.0%
VINCZE, Balazs	2	4	50.0%
GYONGYOSI, Andras	2	2	100.0%
KUNA, Peter			
NEMETH, Zsolt	1	2	50.0%
Goalkeeper	**Shots Saved**	**Attempted**	**% Eff**
KOSZ, Zoltan	7	27	25.9%

TEAM: ITA Italy

Coach: RUDIC, Ratko
Assistant Coach: CASTELLUCCI, Giuseppe

Names	Shots Made	Attempted	% Eff
ATTOLICO, Francesco			
POSTIGLIONE, Francesco	2	3	66.7%
BOVO, Alessandro			
BENCIVENGA, Fabio	0	1	0.0%
CALCATERRA, Alessandro	0	1	0.0%
CALCATERRA, Roberto	3	5	60.0%
GIUSTOLISI, Luca	1	1	100.0%
ANGELINI, Alberto	4	6	66.7%
POMILIO, Amedeo	3	4	75.0%
GERINI, Marco			
SOTTANI, Leonardo	3	3	100.0%
SILIPO, Carlo	4	7	57.1%
GHIBELLINI, Alberto	0	4	0.0%
Goalkeeper	**Shots Saved**	**Attempted**	**% Eff**
ATTOLICO, Francesco	4	22	18.2%

FINAL - GOLD

ESP 7 - 5 CRO

Qtr 1	Qtr 2	Qtr 3	Qtr 4
0-1	1-2	4-2	2-0

Spain			Croatia	
0/6	0.0%	**Natural shots**	3/15	20.0%
1/1	100.0%	**Center shots**	0/0	0.0%
5/13	38.5%	**Extramen shots**	2/9	22.2%
0/0	0.0%	**Mandown shots**	0/0	0.0%
1/1	100.0%	**Penalty shots**	0/0	0.0%
7/21	33.3%	**Total shots**	5/24	20.8%
	5	**Assists**	3	
	13	**Turnovers**	6	
	4	**Steals**	2	
	3	**Blocks**	2	
	20	**Fouls**	73	

1st Referee: GER   LUDECKE, Rolf
2nd Referee: KAZ   PRIKHODKO, Vladimir

TEAM: ESP Spain

Coach: JANE, Juan
Assistant Coach: FERNANDEZ de CUEVAS, Santiago

Names	Shots Made	Attempted	% Eff
ROLLAN, Jesus			
ABARCA, Jose Maria			
PEDREROL, Sergi	0	2	0.0%
ANDREO, Angel			
ESTIARTE, Manuel	3	5	60.0%
BALLART, Daniel	0	1	0.0%
PAYA, Jorge			
MORO, Ivan			
SANS, Jordi	2	2	100.0%
GOMEZ, Salvador	0	1	0.0%
OCA, Miguel	1	3	33.3%
SANZ, Carlos	0	1	0.0%
GARCIA, Pedro	1	6	16.7%
Goalkeeper	**Shots Saved**	**Attempted**	**% Eff**
ROLLAN, Jesus	8	13	61.5%

TEAM: CRO Croatia

Coaches: SILIC, Bruno   NOLA, Fabjan
Assistant Coach: JEH, Vlado

Names	Shots Made	Attempted	% Eff
SKOLNEKOVIC, Sinisa			
VRDOLJAK, Zdeslav	0	4	0.0%
KREKOVIC, Josko	1	6	16.7%
SIMENC, Dubravko	0	1	0.0%
KRZIC, Ognjen	0	1	0.0%
STRITOF, Ratko	0	1	0.0%
VRBICIC, Renato	1	2	50.0%
GLAVAN, Damir	1	2	50.0%
VEGAR, Tino	1	3	33.3%
BUKIC, Perica	1	2	50.0%
HINIC, Igor			
BALIC, Maro			
KOBESCAK, Vjekoslav	0	2	0.0%
Goalkeeper	**Shots Saved**	**Attempted**	**% Eff**
SKOLNEKOVIC, Sinisa	8	15	53.3%

FINAL CLASSIFICATION

Rnk	Ctry	
1	Spain	**Gold**
2	Croatia	**Silver**
3	Italy	**Bronze**
4	Hungary	
5	Russian Federation	
6	Greece	
7	United States of America	
8	Yugoslavia	

ARCHERY
TIR À L'ARC

Abbreviations and terms used in Archery results tables
Abréviations et termes employés dans les tableaux de résultats de tir à l'arc

Term	English	Français
1/32 Round	1/32 Round	1/32 Tour
1/16 Round	1/16 Round	1/16 Tour
1/8 Elimination	1/8 Elimination	1/8 Elimination
1/8 Round	1/8 Round	1/8 Tour
1st Half	First Half	Première moitié
2nd Half	Second Half	Deuxième moitié
9's	Nines	Neuf
10's	Tens	Dix
Bronze	Bronze Medal	Médaille de bronze
Bronze Medal	Bronze Medal	Médaille de bronze
BYE	Bye	Exemption
Continued	Continued	Continué
Ctry	Country	Pays
Final Classification	Final Classification	Classement final
First Half	First Half	Première moitié
Gold	Gold Medal	Médaille d'or
Gold Medal	Gold Medal	Médaille d'or
Hits	Hits	Impacts
Indvl Total	Individual Total	Total individuel
Medal Round	Medal Round	Tour pour les médailles
Name	Name	Nom
O	Olympic Record	Record olympique
Q	Qualified	Qualifié
Quarterfinals	Quarterfinals	Quarts de finale
Ranking Round	Ranking Round	Tour de classement
Rnk	Rank	Classement
Score	Score	Résultat
Second Half	Second Half	Deuxième moitié
Semifinals	Semifinals	Demi-finales
Silver	Silver Medal	Médaille d'argent
Silver Medal	Silver Medal	Médaille d'argent
Total	Total	Total
W	World Record	Record du monde

International Archery Federation (FITA)
Fédération Internationale de Tir à l'Arc
Avenue de Cour 135
CH-1007 Lausanne
Switzerland

Archery / Tir à l'arc

Individual, Men / Epreuve individuelle, Messieurs

RANKING ROUND

Rnk	Name	Ctry	1st half	2nd half	Score	Hits	10's	9's	
1	FRANGILLI, Michele	ITA	344/1	340/3	684 O	72	39	30	Q
2	JANG, Yong-Ho	KOR	343/2	339/6	682	72	38	30	Q
3	OH, Kyo-Moon	KOR	339/3	342/1	681	72	37	31	Q
4	CHIKAREV, Vadim	KAZ	338/6	339/5	677	72	34	33	Q
5	LIPPONEN, Jari	FIN	338/5	338/7	676	72	34	33	Q
6	TSIREMPILOV, Baljinima	RUS	336/8	339/4	675	72	36	28	Q
7	PETERSSON, Magnus	SWE	331/19	341/2	672	72	31	35	Q
8	FEAR, Jackson	AUS	334/12	337/8	671	72	28	39	Q
9	HUISH, Justin	USA	336/10	334/14	670	72	29	37	Q
10	BISIANI, Matteo	ITA	338/4	331/22	669	72	34	25	Q
11	KIM, Bo-Ram	KOR	332/15	336/9	668	72	28	36	Q
12	WHITE, Rod	USA	336/9	330/31	666	72	28	34	Q
13	YAMAMOTO, Hiroshi	JPN	337/7	328/36	665	72	24	41	Q
14	TANG, Hua	CHN	332/14	332/18	664	72	31	28	Q
15	JOHNSON, Richard	USA	330/20	334/13	664	72	30	30	Q
16	ZABRODSKY, Stanislav	UKR	331/16	333/15	664	72	29	34	Q
17	HALLARD, Steven	GBR	334/11	330/28	664	72	28	34	Q
18	GRAY, Matthew	AUS	331/17	332/19	663	72	30	27	Q
19	GROV, Martinus	NOR	333/13	330/29	663	72	27	34	Q
20	FAIRWEATHER, Simon	AUS	331/18	329/32	660	72	28	31	Q
21	VERMEIREN, Paul	BEL	329/21	330/24	659	72	30	27	Q
22	LARSSON, Mikael	SWE	328/23	331/23	659	72	29	31	Q
23	YEVETSKY, Valeriy	UKR	326/25	333/16	659	72	27	33	Q
24	HARDINGES, Gary	GBR	328/24	330/25	658	72	27	33	Q
25	MATSUSHITA, Takayoshi	JPN	325/32	332/17	657	72	27	31	Q
26	LETULLE, Damien	FRA	326/26	331/21	657	72	27	31	Q
27	SALLY, Kevin	CAN	325/33	332/20	657	72	24	33	Q
28	MEDVED, Samo	SLO	326/28	330/30	656	72	23	35	Q
29	ANCHONDO, Jose	MEX	319/46	334/11	653	72	26	30	Q
30	SZYMCZAK, Pawel	POL	323/37	330/26	653	72	23	32	Q
31	KOPRIVNIKAR, Peter	SLO	329/22	323/46	652	72	24	32	Q
32	CHHANGTE, Lalremsanga	IND	315/56	335/10	650	72	25	29	Q

RANKING ROUND - *continued*

Rnk	Name	Ctry	1st half	2nd half	Score	Hits	10's	9's	
33	LINDSAY, Andrew	NZL	323/36	327/37	650	72	24	32	Q
34	HANLON, Keith	IRL	325/30	325/43	650	72	22	36	Q
35	POMBO, Nuno	POR	322/40	328/34	650	72	20	35	Q
36	KIVILO, Raul	EST	315/55	334/12	649	72	25	27	Q
37	YATSENKO, Aleksandr	UKR	320/43	329/33	649	72	23	33	Q
38	POIKOLAINEN, Tomi	FIN	322/38	326/39	648	72	22	34	Q
39	PARENTI, Andrea	ITA	323/35	324/44	647	72	27	24	Q
40	BJERENDAL, Goran	SWE	324/34	322/48	646	72	25	25	Q
41	CHO, Sheng-Ling	TPE	325/31	321/49	646	72	23	32	Q
42	WU, Tsung-Yi	TPE	315/54	330/27	645	72	22	31	Q
43	RUSNOV, Rob	CAN	322/39	323/45	645	72	21	35	Q
44	RAM, Limba	IND	319/45	325/40	644	72	25	28	Q
45	TORRES, Lionel	FRA	319/44	325/42	644	72	23	28	Q
46	FLUTE, Sebastien	FRA	321/42	323/47	644	72	19	36	Q
47	SHEN, Jun	CHN	317/50	327/38	644	72	18	33	Q
48	TUOVILA, Tommi	FIN	316/51	328/35	644	72	17	35	Q
49	JUBZHANG, Jubzhang	BHU	318/49	325/41	643	72	24	27	Q
50	KRUMPESTAR, Matevz	SLO	325/29	318/56	643	72	21	28	Q
51	PODLAZOV, Andrey	RUS	319/47	321/52	640	72	18	36	Q
52	GONZALEZ, Adolfo	MEX	315/52	321/51	636	72	19	32	Q
53	BADENOV, Bair	RUS	319/48	316/57	635	71	15	41	Q
54	ROBITAILLE, Jeannot	CAN	315/53	319/55	634	72	17	34	Q
55	DORJE, Skalzang	IND	326/27	308/59	634	72	16	35	Q
56	MARTYNOV, Sergei	KAZ	312/58	320/54	632	72	15	33	Q
57	HSIEH, Sheng-Feng	TPE	309/60	321/50	630	72	20	27	Q
58	LUO, Hengyu	CHN	312/57	315/58	627	72	17	32	Q
59	SHIN, Vitaliy	KAZ	306/62	320/53	626	72	20	24	Q
60	VAZQUEZ, Antonio	ESP	322/41	299/62	621	72	15	30	Q
61	KUCUKKAYALAR, Okyay	TUR	310/59	308/61	618	71	13	30	Q
62	MLIAKOV, Stefan	BUL	309/61	308/60	617	72	12	28	Q
63	TURA, Paolo	SMR	295/63	297/63	592	72	16	20	Q
64	REBELO, Dominic	KEN	264/64	254/64	518	70	11	11	Q

1/32 ROUND | 1/16 ROUND | 1/8 ROUND | QUARTERFINALS | SEMIFINALS | MEDAL ROUND

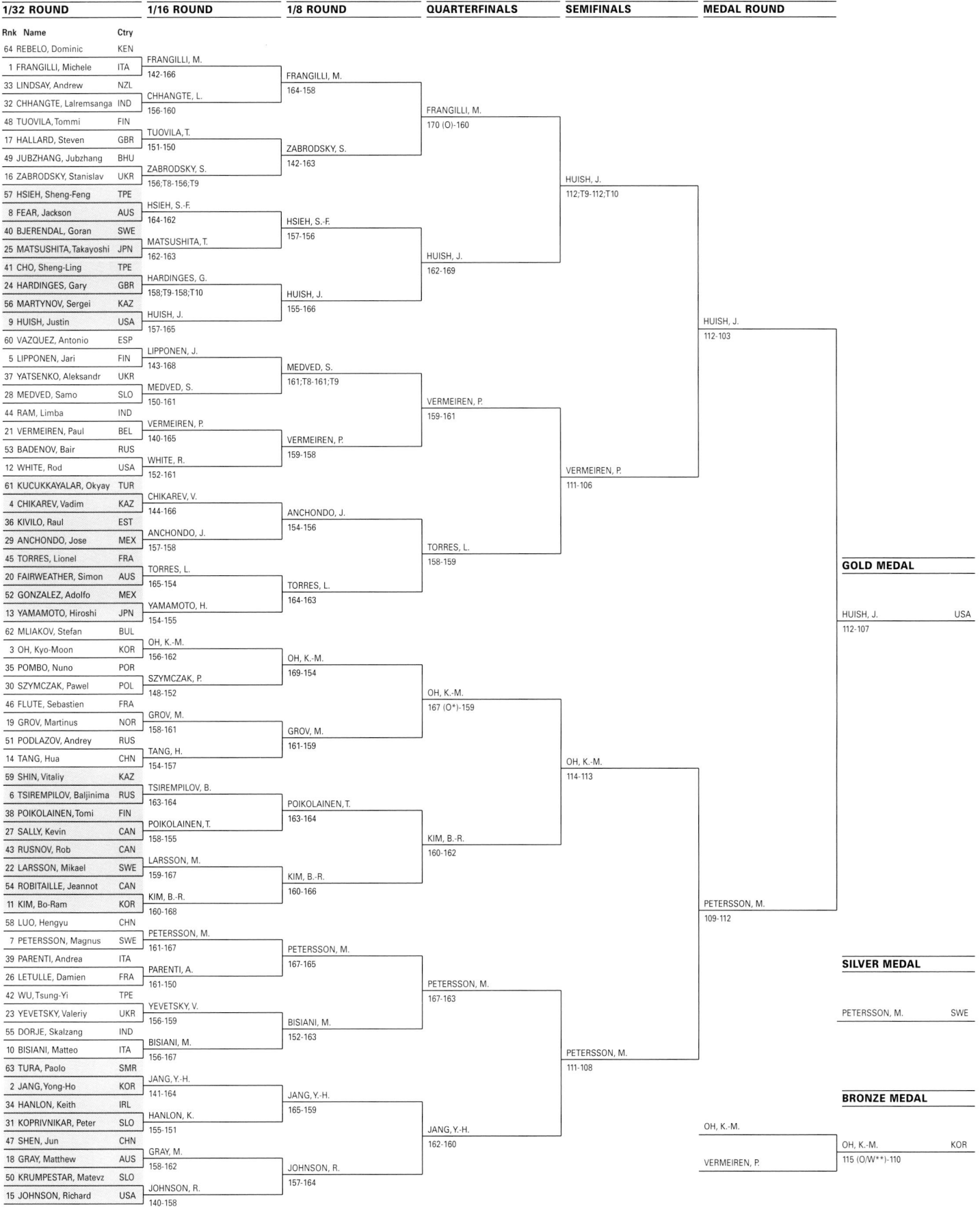

1/32 ROUND

Rnk	Name	Ctry
64	REBELO, Dominic	KEN
1	FRANGILLI, Michele	ITA
33	LINDSAY, Andrew	NZL
32	CHHANGTE, Lalremsanga	IND
48	TUOVILA, Tommi	FIN
17	HALLARD, Steven	GBR
49	JUBZHANG, Jubzhang	BHU
16	ZABRODSKY, Stanislav	UKR
57	HSIEH, Sheng-Feng	TPE
8	FEAR, Jackson	AUS
40	BJERENDAL, Goran	SWE
25	MATSUSHITA, Takayoshi	JPN
41	CHO, Sheng-Ling	TPE
24	HARDINGES, Gary	GBR
56	MARTYNOV, Sergei	KAZ
9	HUISH, Justin	USA
60	VAZQUEZ, Antonio	ESP
5	LIPPONEN, Jari	FIN
37	YATSENKO, Aleksandr	UKR
28	MEDVED, Samo	SLO
44	RAM, Limba	IND
21	VERMEIREN, Paul	BEL
53	BADENOV, Bair	RUS
12	WHITE, Rod	USA
61	KUCUKKAYALAR, Okyay	TUR
4	CHIKAREV, Vadim	KAZ
36	KIVILO, Raul	EST
29	ANCHONDO, Jose	MEX
45	TORRES, Lionel	FRA
20	FAIRWEATHER, Simon	AUS
52	GONZALEZ, Adolfo	MEX
13	YAMAMOTO, Hiroshi	JPN
62	MLIAKOV, Stefan	BUL
3	OH, Kyo-Moon	KOR
35	POMBO, Nuno	POR
30	SZYMCZAK, Pawel	POL
46	FLUTE, Sebastien	FRA
19	GROV, Martinus	NOR
51	PODLAZOV, Andrey	RUS
14	TANG, Hua	CHN
59	SHIN, Vitaliy	KAZ
6	TSIREMPILOV, Baljinima	RUS
38	POIKOLAINEN, Tomi	FIN
27	SALLY, Kevin	CAN
43	RUSNOV, Rob	CAN
22	LARSSON, Mikael	SWE
54	ROBITAILLE, Jeannot	CAN
11	KIM, Bo-Ram	KOR
58	LUO, Hengyu	CHN
7	PETERSSON, Magnus	SWE
39	PARENTI, Andrea	ITA
26	LETULLE, Damien	FRA
42	WU, Tsung-Yi	TPE
23	YEVETSKY, Valeriy	UKR
55	DORJE, Skalzang	IND
10	BISIANI, Matteo	ITA
63	TURA, Paolo	SMR
2	JANG, Yong-Ho	KOR
34	HANLON, Keith	IRL
31	KOPRIVNIKAR, Peter	SLO
47	SHEN, Jun	CHN
18	GRAY, Matthew	AUS
50	KRUMPESTAR, Matevz	SLO
15	JOHNSON, Richard	USA

1/16 ROUND

FRANGILLI, M. 142-166
CHHANGTE, L. 156-160
TUOVILA, T. 151-150
ZABRODSKY, S. 156;T8-156;T9
HSIEH, S.-F. 164-162
MATSUSHITA, T. 162-163
HARDINGES, G. 158;T9-158;T10
HUISH, J. 157-165
LIPPONEN, J. 143-168
MEDVED, S. 150-161
VERMEIREN, P. 140-165
WHITE, R. 152-161
CHIKAREV, V. 144-166
ANCHONDO, J. 157-158
TORRES, L. 165-154
YAMAMOTO, H. 154-155
OH, K.-M. 156-162
SZYMCZAK, P. 148-152
GROV, M. 158-161
TANG, H. 154-157
TSIREMPILOV, B. 163-164
POIKOLAINEN, T. 158-155
LARSSON, M. 159-167
KIM, B.-R. 160-168
PETERSSON, M. 161-167
PARENTI, A. 161-150
YEVETSKY, V. 156-159
BISIANI, M. 156-167
JANG, Y.-H. 141-164
HANLON, K. 155-151
GRAY, M. 158-162
JOHNSON, R. 140-158

1/8 ROUND

FRANGILLI, M. 164-158
ZABRODSKY, S. 142-163
HSIEH, S.-F. 157-156
HUISH, J. 155-166
MEDVED, S. 161;T8-161;T9
VERMEIREN, P. 159-158
ANCHONDO, J. 154-156
TORRES, L. 164-163
OH, K.-M. 169-154
GROV, M. 161-159
POIKOLAINEN, T. 163-164
KIM, B.-R. 160-166
PETERSSON, M. 167-165
BISIANI, M. 152-163
JANG, Y.-H. 165-159
JOHNSON, R. 157-164

QUARTERFINALS

FRANGILLI, M. 170 (O)-160
HUISH, J. 162-169
VERMEIREN, P. 159-161
TORRES, L. 158-159
OH, K.-M. 167 (O*)-159
KIM, B.-R. 160-162
PETERSSON, M. 167-163
JANG, Y.-H. 162-160

SEMIFINALS

HUISH, J. 112;T9-112;T10
VERMEIREN, P. 111-106
OH, K.-M. 114-113
PETERSSON, M. 111-108

MEDAL ROUND

HUISH, J. 112-103
PETERSSON, M. 109-112

GOLD MEDAL
HUISH, J. USA 112-107

SILVER MEDAL
PETERSSON, M. SWE

BRONZE MEDAL
OH, K.-M.
VERMEIREN, P.
OH, K.-M. KOR 115 (O/W**)-110

FINAL CLASSIFICATION

Rnk	Name	Ctry	
1	HUISH, Justin	USA	Gold
2	PETERSSON, Magnus	SWE	Silver
3	OH, Kyo-Moon	KOR	Bronze
4	VERMEIREN, Paul	BEL	

FINAL CLASSIFICATION - *continued*

Rnk	Name	Ctry
5	KIM, Bo-Ram	KOR
6	FRANGILLI, Michele	ITA
7	JANG, Yong-Ho	KOR
8	TORRES, Lionel	FRA

*Olympic Record for 1/16, 1/8 Combined, Men (Score: 336).
Record olympique pour 1/16, 1/8 combinés, Messieurs (Score : 336).
**World Record for 36 Arrow Finals Combined, Men (Score: 338).
*Record du monde pour finale combinée de 36
flèches, Messieurs (Score : 338).*

Archery / *Tir à l'arc* **61**

Archery / *Tir à l'arc*

Individual, Women / *Epreuve individuelle, Dames*

RANKING ROUND

Rnk	Name	Ctry	1st half	2nd half	Score		Hits	10's	9's	
1	HERASYMENKO, Lina	UKR	332/2	341/1	673	O	72	31	35	Q
2	HE, Ying	CHN	333/1	336/3	669		72	30	33	Q
3	NASARIDZE, Natalia	TUR	331/3	336/2	667		72	28	37	Q
4	KIM, Jo-Sun	KOR	328/9	335/4	663		72	33	24	Q
5	SADOVNYCHA, Olena	UKR	329/7	334/5	663		72	30	27	Q
6	ALTINKAYNAK, Elif	TUR	329/6	334/6	663		72	28	31	Q
7	VALEEVA, Natalia	MDA	329/8	333/7	662		72	27	34	Q
8	KIM, Kyung-Wook	KOR	329/5	332/8	661		72	28	29	Q
9	YOON, Hye-Young	KOR	330/4	330/12	660		72	24	38	Q
10	MOZHAR, Anna	KAZ	326/11	327/16	653		72	28	27	Q
11	ARZHANNIKOVA, Ljudmila	NED	328/10	324/20	652		72	26	26	Q
12	NOWICKA, Joanna	POL	324/14	327/15	651		72	27	27	Q
13	MURZAYEVA, Makhlukhanum	RUS	318/30	332/9	650		72	23	33	Q
14	ALDEGANI, Giovanna	ITA	326/12	324/22	650		72	19	38	Q
15	WILLIAMSON, Alison	GBR	322/19	326/17	648		72	25	27	Q
16	YANG, Jianping	CHN	317/35	331/10	648		72	22	33	Q
17	DYKMAN, Janet	USA	316/36	330/13	646		72	18	37	Q
18	ZABUGINA, Olga	BLR	321/24	324/19	645		72	24	27	Q
19	LIN, Yi-Yin	TPE	322/20	322/24	644		72	24	29	Q
20	GALINOVSKAYA, Rita	RUS	323/16	321/26	644		72	24	28	Q
21	LANGSTON, Lindsay	USA	323/18	320/28	643		72	21	32	Q
22	SJOVALL, Jenny	SWE	318/32	325/18	643		72	16	39	Q
23	TUTATCHIKOVA, Elena	RUS	325/13	316/40	641		72	21	33	Q
24	WAGNER, Sandra	GER	317/33	323/23	640		72	19	30	Q
25	DAMANHURI, Hamdiah	INA	319/28	320/30	639		72	20	32	Q
26	LEWIS, Kirstin	RSA	317/34	322/25	639		72	19	31	Q
27	VERSTEGEN, Christel	NED	319/29	320/29	639		72	17	40	Q
28	KLATA, Katarzyna	POL	322/22	317/36	639		72	17	34	Q
29	BRETON, Marisol	MEX	308/48	330/11	638		71	21	33	Q
30	PERSSON, Kristina	SWE	315/39	321/27	636		72	19	31	Q
31	HESS, Wenche-Lin	NOR	324/15	312/47	636		72	16	32	Q
32	WANG, Xiaozhu	CHN	322/21	314/45	636		72	16	32	Q

RANKING ROUND - *continued*

Rnk	Name	Ctry	1st half	2nd half	Score	Hits	10's	9's	
33	FANTATO, Paola	ITA	306/50	329/14	635	72	21	25	Q
34	LEONOVA, Irina	KAZ	321/23	314/44	635	72	18	33	Q
35	YAKUSHEVA, Olga	BLR	318/31	317/38	635	72	15	35	Q
36	di BLASI, Giuseppina	ITA	319/26	315/43	634	72	19	29	Q
37	KVRIVISHVILI, Khatuna	GEO	319/25	315/42	634	72	19	29	Q
38	EKSI, Elif	TUR	309/46	324/21	633	72	20	25	Q
39	KOVACS, Judit	HUN	323/17	310/48	633	72	18	30	Q
40	BONAL, Severine	FRA	315/37	317/35	632	72	22	22	Q
41	LIN, Ya-Hua	TPE	314/40	318/33	632	72	19	27	Q
42	MENSING, Barbara	GER	313/42	319/32	632	72	15	34	Q
43	OUCHI, Ai	JPN	315/38	316/41	631	72	17	29	Q
44	YANG, Chun-Chi	TPE	313/41	317/37	630	72	18	29	Q
45	OTGON, Jargal	MGL	312/43	318/34	630	72	15	35	Q
46	TOUNIIANTSE, Yana	KAZ	305/52	316/39	621	72	21	23	Q
47	PFOHL, Cornelia	GER	319/27	302/56	621	72	20	28	Q
48	BACKMAN, Christa	SWE	309/47	308/51	617	72	11	33	Q
49	MATTHEWS, Myfanwy	AUS	303/54	313/46	616	72	11	27	Q
50	BRIDGER, Deonne	AUS	309/45	306/53	615	72	11	28	Q
51	DAHLIANA, Danahuri	INA	310/44	305/54	615	72	11	27	Q
52	KODAMA, Kinue	JPN	294/57	319/31	613	72	15	24	Q
53	ADAMS, Judi	USA	300/55	306/52	606	72	10	26	Q
54	BILUKHA, Natalya	UKR	296/56	309/49	605	72	9	30	Q
55	LANTANG, Nurfitriyana	INA	307/49	293/60	600	72	14	18	Q
56	HENDRICKS, Leanda	RSA	303/53	297/58	600	72	12	21	Q
57	DZIECIOL, Iwona	POL	306/51	293/61	599	71	12	25	Q
58	KOIDE, Misato	JPN	275/62	308/50	583	71	12	20	Q
59	KISS, Timea	HUN	288/58	294/59	582	72	9	19	Q
60	UGYEN, Ugyen	BHU	282/59	298/57	580	72	10	17	Q
61	PALOVANDOVA, Nadejda	MDA	276/61	304/55	580	70	10	24	Q
62	BORRESEN, Jill	RSA	277/60	290/62	567	71	9	18	Q
63	REYES, Maria	PUR	267/63	268/64	535	72	6	16	Q
64	MBUTA, Jennifer	KEN	220/64	280/63	500	71	6	12	Q

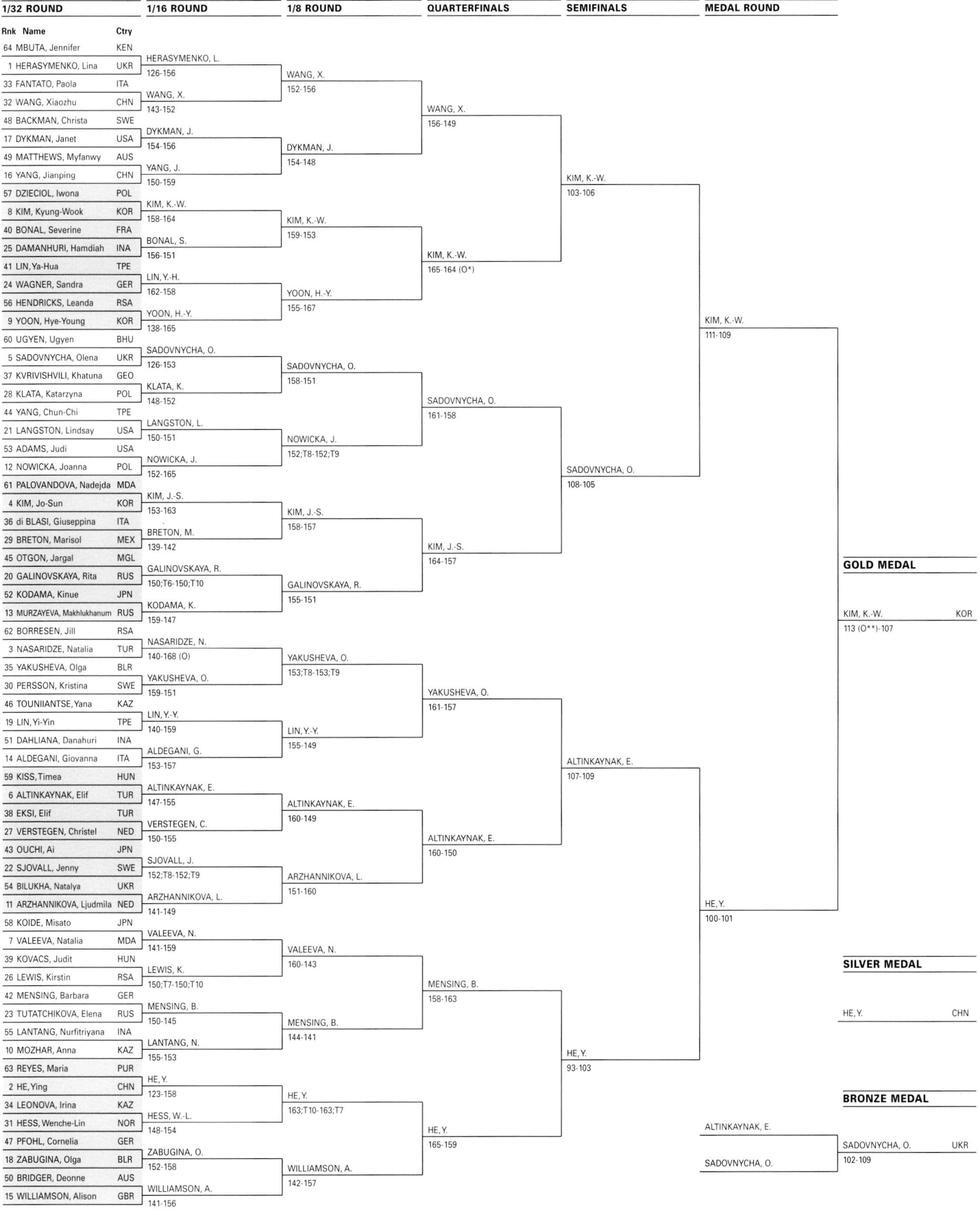

1/32 ROUND	1/16 ROUND	1/8 ROUND	QUARTERFINALS	SEMIFINALS	MEDAL ROUND

Rnk Name Ctry

64 MBUTA, Jennifer KEN
1 HERASYMENKO, Lina UKR — HERASYMENKO, L. 126-156
33 FANTATO, Paola ITA
32 WANG, Xiaozhu CHN — WANG, X. 143-152 — WANG, X. 152-156
48 BACKMAN, Christa SWE
17 DYKMAN, Janet USA — DYKMAN, J. 154-156 — WANG, X. 156-149
49 MATTHEWS, Myfanwy AUS
16 YANG, Jianping CHN — YANG, J. 150-159 — DYKMAN, J. 154-148
57 DZIECIOL, Iwona POL
8 KIM, Kyung-Wook KOR — KIM, K.-W. 158-164 — KIM, K.-W. 103-106
40 BONAL, Severine FRA — BONAL, S. 156-151 — KIM, K.-W. 159-153
25 DAMANHURI, Hamdiah INA
41 LIN, Ya-Hua TPE
24 WAGNER, Sandra GER — LIN, Y.-H. 162-158 — KIM, K.-W. 165-164 (O*)
56 HENDRICKS, Leanda RSA
9 YOON, Hye-Young KOR — YOON, H.-Y. 138-165 — YOON, H.-Y. 155-167
60 UGYEN, Ugyen BHU
5 SADOVNYCHA, Olena UKR — SADOVNYCHA, O. 126-153
37 KVRIVISHVILI, Khatuna GEO — KLATA, K. 148-152 — SADOVNYCHA, O. 158-151
28 KLATA, Katarzyna POL
44 YANG, Chun-Chi TPE — SADOVNYCHA, O. 161-158
21 LANGSTON, Lindsay USA — LANGSTON, L. 150-151 — KIM, K.-W. 111-109
53 ADAMS, Judi USA — NOWICKA, J. 152;T8-152;T9
12 NOWICKA, Joanna POL — NOWICKA, J. 152-165
61 PALOVANDOVA, Nadejda MDA — SADOVNYCHA, O. 108-105
4 KIM, Jo-Sun KOR — KIM, J.-S. 153-163
36 di BLASI, Giuseppina ITA — KIM, J.-S. 158-157
29 BRETON, Marisol MEX — BRETON, M. 139-142
45 OTGON, Jargal MGL — KIM, J.-S. 164-157
20 GALINOVSKAYA, Rita RUS — GALINOVSKAYA, R. 150;T6-150;T10
52 KODAMA, Kinue JPN — GALINOVSKAYA, R. 155-151
13 MURZAYEVA, Makhlukhanum RUS — KODAMA, K. 159-147
62 BORRESEN, Jill RSA
3 NASARIDZE, Natalia TUR — NASARIDZE, N. 140-168 (O)
35 YAKUSHEVA, Olga BLR — YAKUSHEVA, O. 153;T8-153;T9
30 PERSSON, Kristina SWE — YAKUSHEVA, O. 159-151
46 TOUNIIANTSE, Yana KAZ — YAKUSHEVA, O. 161-157
19 LIN, Yi-Yin TPE — LIN, Y.-Y. 140-159
51 DAHLIANA, Danahuri INA — LIN, Y.-Y. 155-149
14 ALDEGANI, Giovanna ITA — ALDEGANI, G. 153-157
59 KISS, Timea HUN — ALTINKAYNAK, E. 107-109
6 ALTINKAYNAK, Elif TUR — ALTINKAYNAK, E. 147-155
38 EKSI, Elif TUR — ALTINKAYNAK, E. 160-149
27 VERSTEGEN, Christel NED — VERSTEGEN, C. 150-155
43 OUCHI, Ai JPN — ALTINKAYNAK, E. 160-150
22 SJOVALL, Jenny SWE — SJOVALL, J. 152;T8-152;T9
54 BILUKHA, Natalya UKR — ARZHANNIKOVA, L. 151-160
11 ARZHANNIKOVA, Ljudmila NED — ARZHANNIKOVA, L. 141-149
58 KOIDE, Misato JPN — HE, Y. 100-101
7 VALEEVA, Natalia MDA — VALEEVA, N. 141-159
39 KOVACS, Judit HUN — VALEEVA, N. 160-143
26 LEWIS, Kirstin RSA — LEWIS, K. 150;T7-150;T10
42 MENSING, Barbara GER — MENSING, B. 158-163
23 TUTATCHIKOVA, Elena RUS — MENSING, B. 150-145
55 LANTANG, Nurfitriyana INA — MENSING, B. 144-141
10 MOZHAR, Anna KAZ — LANTANG, N. 155-153
63 REYES, Maria PUR — HE, Y. 93-103
2 HE, Ying CHN — HE, Y. 123-158
34 LEONOVA, Irina KAZ — HE, Y. 163;T10-163;T7
31 HESS, Wenche-Lin NOR — HESS, W.-L. 148-154
47 PFOHL, Cornelia GER — HE, Y. 165-159
18 ZABUGINA, Olga BLR — ZABUGINA, O. 152-158
50 BRIDGER, Deonne AUS — WILLIAMSON, A. 142-157
15 WILLIAMSON, Alison GBR — WILLIAMSON, A. 141-156

GOLD MEDAL

KIM, K.-W. KOR
113 (O**)-107

SILVER MEDAL

HE, Y. CHN

BRONZE MEDAL

ALTINKAYNAK, E.
SADOVNYCHA, O.
SADOVNYCHA, O. UKR
102-109

FINAL CLASSIFICATION

Rnk	Name	Ctry	
1	KIM, Kyung-Wook	KOR	Gold
2	HE, Ying	CHN	Silver
3	SADOVNYCHA, Olena	UKR	Bronze
4	ALTINKAYNAK, Elif	TUR	

FINAL CLASSIFICATION - continued

Rnk	Name	Ctry
5	YAKUSHEVA, Olga	BLR
6	KIM, Jo-Sun	KOR
7	WANG, Xiaozhu	CHN
8	MENSING, Barbara	GER

*Olympic Record for 1/16, 1/8 Combined, Women (Score: 331).
Record olympique pour 1/16, 1/8 combinés, Dames (Score : 331).
**Olympic Record for 36 Arrow Finals Combined, Women (Score: 330).
Record olympique pour finale combinée de 36 flèches, Dames (Score : 330).

Archery / *Tir à l'arc*

Team, Men / *Epreuve par équipes, Messieurs*

RANKING ROUND

Rnk	Ctry	Names	First half	Second half	Indvl total	Total
1	KOR	JANG, Yong-Ho	343	339	682	
		KIM, Bo-Ram	332	336	668	
		OH, Kyo-Moon	339	342	681	2031 W
2	ITA	BISIANI, Matteo	338	331	669	
		FRANGILLI, Michele	344	340	684	
		PARENTI, Andrea	323	324	647	2000
3	USA	HUISH, Justin	336	334	670	
		JOHNSON, Richard	330	334	664	
		WHITE, Rod	336	330	666	2000
4	AUS	FAIRWEATHER, Simon	331	329	660	
		FEAR, Jackson	334	337	671	
		GRAY, Matthew	331	332	663	1994
5	SWE	BJERENDAL, Goran	324	322	646	
		LARSSON, Mikael	328	331	659	
		PETERSSON, Magnus	331	341	672	1977
6	UKR	YATSENKO, Aleksandr	320	329	649	
		YEVETSKY, Valeriy	326	333	659	
		ZABRODSKY, Stanislav	331	333	664	1972
7	FIN	LIPPONEN, Jari	338	338	676	
		POIKOLAINEN, Tomi	322	326	648	
		TUOVILA, Tommi	316	328	644	1968
8	SLO	KOPRIVNIKAR, Peter	329	323	652	
		KRUMPESTAR, Matevz	325	318	643	
		MEDVED, Samo	326	330	656	1951

RANKING ROUND - *continued*

Rnk	Ctry	Names	First half	Second half	Indvl total	Total
9	RUS	BADENOV, Bair	319	316	635	
		PODLAZOV, Andrey	319	321	640	
		TSIREMPILOV, Baljinima	336	339	675	1950
10	FRA	FLUTE, Sebastien	321	323	644	
		LETULLE, Damien	326	331	657	
		TORRES, Lionel	319	325	644	1945
11	CAN	ROBITAILLE, Jeannot	315	319	634	
		RUSNOV, Rob	322	323	645	
		SALLY, Kevin	325	332	657	1936
12	KAZ	CHIKAREV, Vadim	338	339	677	
		MARTYNOV, Sergei	312	320	632	
		SHIN, Vitaliy	306	320	626	1935
13	CHN	LUO, Hengyu	312	315	627	
		SHEN, Jun	317	327	644	
		TANG, Hua	332	332	664	1935
14	IND	CHHANGTE, Lalremsanga	315	335	650	
		DORJE, Skalzang	326	308	634	
		RAM, Limba	319	325	644	1928
15	TPE	CHO, Sheng-Ling	325	321	646	
		HSIEH, Sheng-Feng	309	321	630	
		WU, Tsung-Yi	315	330	645	1921

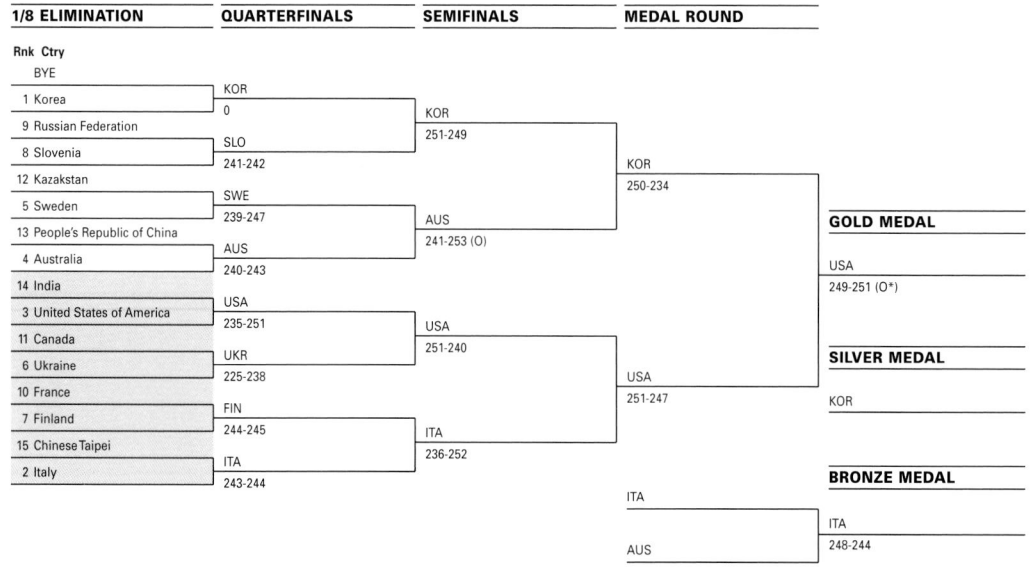

1/8 ELIMINATION — **QUARTERFINALS** — **SEMIFINALS** — **MEDAL ROUND**

Rnk Ctry

- BYE
- 1 Korea
- 9 Russian Federation
- 8 Slovenia
- 12 Kazakstan
- 5 Sweden
- 13 People's Republic of China
- 4 Australia
- 14 India
- 3 United States of America
- 11 Canada
- 6 Ukraine
- 10 France
- 7 Finland
- 15 Chinese Taipei
- 2 Italy

Quarterfinals:
- KOR 0
- SLO 241-242
- SWE 239-247
- AUS 240-243
- USA 235-251
- UKR 225-238
- FIN 244-245
- ITA 243-244

Semifinals:
- KOR 251-249
- AUS 241-253 (O)
- USA 251-240
- ITA 236-252

Medal Round:
- KOR 250-234
- USA 251-247
- ITA 248-244 / AUS

GOLD MEDAL
USA 249-251 (O*)

SILVER MEDAL
KOR

BRONZE MEDAL
ITA 248-244

Olympic Record for 54 Arrow Finals Combined, Team, Men (Score: 502).

**Olympic Record for 54 Arrow Finals Combined, Team, Men (Score: 502).*
Record olympique pour finale combinée de 54 flèches, epreuve par équipes, Messieurs (Score : 502).

FINAL CLASSIFICATION

Rnk	Ctry	
1	United States of America	Gold
2	Korea	Silver
3	Italy	Bronze
4	Australia	
5	Slovenia	
6	Sweden	
7	Ukraine	
8	Finland	

Archery / *Tir à l'arc*

Team, Women / *Epreuve par équipes, Dames*

RANKING ROUND

Rnk	Ctry	Names	First half	Second half	Indvl total	Total
1	KOR	KIM, Jo-Sun	328	335	663	
		KIM, Kyung-Wook	329	332	661	
		YOON, Hye-Young	330	330	660	1984 W
2	TUR	ALTINKAYNAK, Elif	329	334	663	
		EKSI, Elif	309	324	633	
		NASARIDZE, Natalia	331	336	667	1963
3	CHN	HE, Ying	333	336	669	
		WANG, Xiaozhu	322	314	636	
		YANG, Jianping	317	331	348	1953
4	UKR	BILUKHA, Natalya	296	309	605	
		HERASYMENKO, Lina	332	341	673	
		SADOVNYCHA, Olena	329	334	663	1941
5	RUS	GALINOVSKAYA, Rita	323	321	644	
		MURZAYEVA, Makhlukhanum	318	332	650	
		TUTATCHIKOVA, Elena	325	316	641	1935
6	ITA	ALDEGANI, Giovanna	326	324	650	
		di BLASI, Giuseppina	319	315	634	
		FANTATO, Paola	306	329	635	1919
7	KAZ	LEONOVA, Irina	321	314	635	
		MOZHAR, Anna	326	327	653	
		TOUNIIANTSE, Yana	305	316	621	1909
8	TPE	LIN, Ya-Hua	314	318	632	
		LIN, Yi-Yin	322	322	644	
		YANG, Chun-Chi	313	317	630	1906

RANKING ROUND - *continued*

Rnk	Ctry	Names	First half	Second half	Indvl total	Total
9	SWE	BACKMAN, Christa	309	308	617	
		PERSSON, Kristina	315	321	636	
		SJOVALL, Jenny	318	325	643	1896
10	USA	ADAMS, Judi	300	306	606	
		DYKMAN, Janet	316	330	646	
		LANGSTON, Lindsay	323	320	643	1895
11	GER	MENSING, Barbara	313	319	632	
		PFOHL, Cornelia	319	302	621	
		WAGNER, Sandra	317	323	640	1893
12	POL	DZIECIOL, Iwona	306	293	599	
		KLATA, Katarzyna	322	317	639	
		NOWICKA, Joanna	324	327	651	1889
13	INA	DAHLIANA, Danahuri	310	305	615	
		DAMANHURI, Hamdiah	319	320	639	
		LANTANG, Nurfitriyana	307	293	600	1854
14	JPN	KODAMA, Kinue	294	319	613	
		KOIDE, Misato	275	308	583	
		OUCHI, Ai	315	316	631	1827
15	RSA	BORRESEN, Jill	277	290	567	
		HENDRICKS, Leanda	303	297	600	
		LEWIS, Kirstin	317	322	639	1806

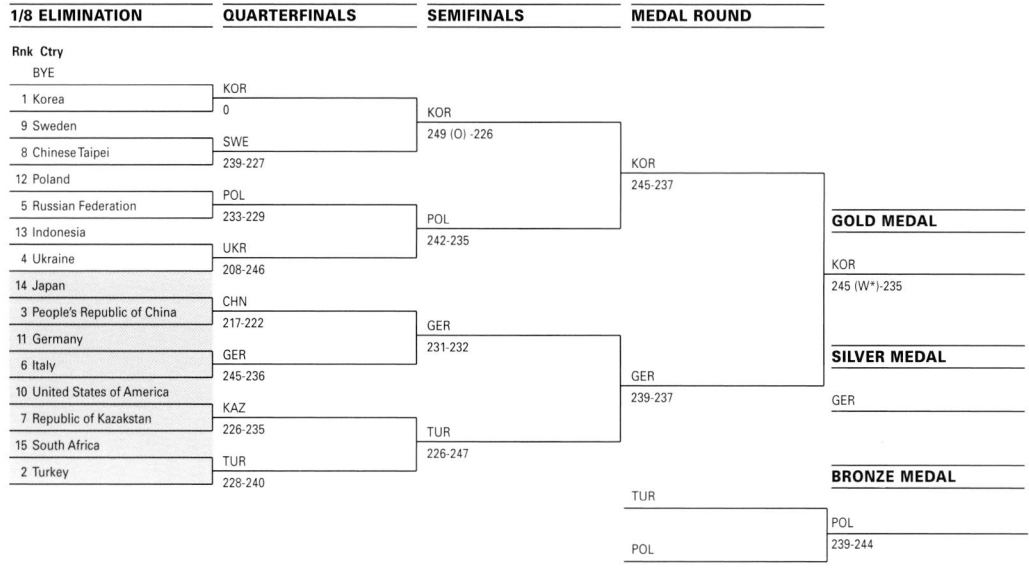

*World Record for 54 Arrow Finals Combined, Team, Women (Score: 490).

*Record du monde pour finale combinée de 54 flèches, epreuve par équipes, Dames (Score : 490).

FINAL CLASSIFICATION

Rnk	Ctry	
1	Korea	Gold
2	Germany	Silver
3	Poland	Bronze
4	Turkey	
5	Ukraine	
6	People's Republic of China	
7	Sweden	
8	Republic of Kazakstan	

• JANA B NEWTON • KAREN B NEWTON • LUCY B
NEWTON • MYRON L NEWTON • NANCY NEW-
TON • ROBERT D NEWTON • STEPHEN R NEW-
TON • TOM NEWTON MD • CHUNG WA NG • CYN-
THIA NG • PHOUNG-TRANG T NGO • MARIA
NGONG • CHINH H NGUYEN • CUONG T NGUYEN
• HUNGANH P NGUYEN • LESLIE K NGUYEN •
NHU H NGUYEN • QUYNH DAO T NGUYEN •
THANH D NGUYEN • TRANG Q NGUYEN • TRUNG
Q NGUYEN • TUYEN H NGUYEN • VAN T NGUYEN
• MABRASA E NHEKAIRO • JIAN NI • SYED I NIAZI
• RENEE NICCOLLAI • JOHN NICELY • DANIEL C
NICHITA • MARGARET A NICHOL • ANNA R
NICHOLAS-MACKENZIE • NANCY NICHOLL-HAS-
SON • LAWRENCE D NICHOLLS • LISA NICHOLLS
• PETER J NICHOLLS • ROBERT P NICHOLLS •
BRENDA NICHOLS • CARL L NICHOLS • DARRELL
C NICHOLS • DONNA M NICHOLS • DOROTHY M
NICHOLS • ELIZABETH J NICHOLS • HEATHER H
NICHOLS • HOPE E NICHOLS • JAMES A NICHOLS
• JEFF D NICHOLS • JUANITA NICHOLS • KATHER-
INE L NICHOLS • KATHLEEN S NICHOLS • LISA A
NICHOLS • MARGARET F NICHOLS • MARY JO NICHOLS
• MICHAEL C NICHOLS • MICHAEL T NICHOLS •
MICHELLE NICHOLS • NIKKI L NICHOLS • RON
NICHOLS • ROSA L NICHOLS • SCOTTI NICHOLS •
SHELLEY R NICHOLS • TIMOTHY NICHOLS • VICKI D
NICHOLS • MARY E NICHOLS-THOMAS • RANDOLPH G
NICHOLS JR • BETTY J NICHOLSON • BRIAN T NICHOL-
SON • CHAD C NICHOLSON • DAVID P NICHOLSON •
KELLY N NICHOLSON • LYNDA J NICHOLSON • MARY M
NICHOLSON • NIKKI N NICHOLSON • PEGGY L NICHOL-
SON • RAY NICHOLSON • SUSANNA R NICHOLSON •
VERNON T NICHOLSON • WILLIAM G NICHOLSON •
WILLIAM M NICHOLSON JR • DONALD J
NICHTER • CAROLE L NICK • WARREN L NICK-
ELL • JEFFREY L NICKELS • JASON E NICKEL-
SON • DELBERT M NICKERSON • DENISE L
NICKERSON • JAMES K NICKERSON • LUCY A
NICKERSON • TRACY E NICKERSON • JACK
NICKLES • BARBARA J NICLAUS • ADRIAN D
NICOL • ALAN M NICOL • JOHN NICOL • KIM L
NICOL • RAY M NICOLA • SWAN S NICOLSON •
KIRSTEN L NIDIFFER • ANGELIKA NIDO • JUNGE
NIE • ALPHONSUS P NIEC • MARIE I NIEC •
ROBERT L NIEDERGERKE • ANDRIS NIEDRA •
KARYN NIEHAUS • KARISSA NIEHOFF • JILL M
NIELAND • CLARA K NIELSEN • DAN NIELSEN •
FANNY E NIELSEN • JOHNNY G. NIELSEN •
RALPH R NIELSEN • ROGER L NIELSEN • JILL M
NIELSON • SILKE NIEMANN • CHARLES J
NIEMEYER • JERRY R NIEMEYER • MARION D
NIEMI • NEIL A NIEMI • JAMES W NIEMIEC • TIM-
OTHY J NIEMIEC • JAMES M NIEMIRA • DAVID J
NIENHUIS • GREGORIA NIEVES • JOHN NIEVES
• RUBEN A NIEVES • DEBRA M NIEZGODSKI •
ARJA NIGGELIE • JOYCE W NIGGLEY • DEBRA J.
NIGH • OLIVIA NIGH • ELIANE R NIKERLE • KEI-
TH M NIKITIN • KONSTANTINOS NIKODINOVIC •
MICHAEL J NIKOLAUS • ASHEESH NIKORE •
LAURA NILES • LORIEANNE D NILES •
SHARONNE D NILES • JUDY L NILSEN • VALERIA
NILSEN • SREEHARI NIMMALA • DONALD F
NIMS • PATRICIA A NINNIE • NATALIE L NISBET •
SAM N NISHI • JAMIE E NISHINO • ARLYN K NIS-
LY • ANNA M NISONGER • BRIAN K NITTA • MAN-
ABU NITTA • PENNY D NITTOLO • MADALYN L
NIVER • ANDY D NIX • DIANE M NIX • EDWARD J
NIX • JAMES ELLIS NIX • JAY V NIX • JOHNEEN M
NIX • MACKIE M NIX • MARIE NIX • SUSAN B NIX
• GAYNELL W NIXON • LEA P NIXON • MINNIE M
NIXON • RAY A NIXON • ROSEMARY C NIXON •
CINDIELLA NIXON RN • PATRICIA J NIZIOLEK •
JULIA F NJIE • PA MODOU NJIE • BEVERLY I
NKEMDICHE • VUSUMUZI J NKOSI • KENNETH U
NNAEMEKA • KUN H NO • LYNDA L NOACK •
HENRY L NOAH • DEANNE H NOBERINI • DEVON
N NOBIS • CESAR I NOBLE • DAVID S NOBLE •
DOROTHY S NOBLE • EDWIN C NOBLE • HOY-
LENE H NOBLE • LAWRENCE C NOBLE •
MICHAEL E NOBLE • PATRICIA NOBLE • ROSLYN
C NOBLE • BESSIE L NOBLES • SARAH F NO-
BLES • STEVEN L NOBLES • SAKAGUCHI
NOBORU • ANTONIO CLAUDIO L NOBREGA •
ELIZABETH R NOCAS • JOVITA E NOCULA • JIL-
LIAN NODLAND • CAROLYN J NOEL • INKE A
NOEL • LESSELY NOEL • MARK MC DOWELL
NOEL • MICHAEL E NOEL • SEDRUOLA NOEL •
VICKI A NOETHLING • CYNTHIA M NOFI • ERIC C
NOFSINGER • STEPHEN K NOGI • GUILHERME R
NOGUEIRA JORGE • CARMEN T NOGUERAS • CA-
ROLE F NOLAN • FARRAH K NOLAN • GINA A
NOLAN • JOHN F NOLAN • SANDRA Y NOLAN •
TERRENCE R NOLAN • WILLIAM P NOLAN •
SARA K NOLAND • EBERHARD NOLL • PATRICIA
LOUISE NOLL • VELMA D NOLLEY • FREDERICK
J NOLTE • MARILYN H NOLTE • HIROSHI NOMA •
RURIKO NOMURA • NOMANDA L NONGAUZA •
PEGGI LYN NOON • ANNE C NOONAN • GUDRUN
NOONAN • SHAHAB NOOROMID • SITTHICHOKE
NOPCHINABUTR • KERRI R NORCROSS •
JANELLE A NORD • PETER G NORD • RANDELL K
NORD • CECILIE S NORDBACK • DESIREE B
NORDIN • MALENA A NORDIN • JEANNE B
NORDSTROM • JULIE A NORED • JEFF A NOREM
• VERN M NOREN • FRANCINE NORFLEET •
KAREN P NORHEIM • SRINIVAS V NORI • PAUL W
NORINE • SUSAN A NORKUS ATC • JALANE M
NORLUND • GUPPY N NORMA • ADELLE NOR-
MAN • ANTHONY L NORMAN • CHARLOTTE J
NORMAN • CINDY S NORMAN • DEANNE K NOR-
MAN • EDWARD L NORMAN • ERIC S NORMAN •
FRIDA A NORMAN • GLENN M NORMAN • LA-
JUAN D NORMAN • MARGARET M NORMAN •
MARY-MARGARET NORMAN • MELANIE NOR-
MAN • MELISSA L NORMAN • MICHELE K NORMAN
• PETER M NORMAN • ROBERT S NORMAN •

RODERIC E NORMAN • THOMAS H NORMAN •
TOMMY M NORMAN • VELISA A NORMAN •
CLARA NORMAN RN • KAREN B NORMANDY •
ROGER E NORMES • BARBARA G NORNES •
JOHN M NORRAY • RUTH S NORRAY • PATRICIA
R NORRELL • ANGELA L NORRIS • BARBARA J
NORRIS • BEVERLY J NORRIS • CARRIE F NOR-
RIS • DIANE R NORRIS • GEORGE C NORRIS •
HELEN M NORRIS • JAMES G NORRIS • JANE
NORRIS • JESSICA E NORRIS • JOYCE A NORRIS
• KAREN K NORRIS • KELLY A NORRIS • LASHAN-
DA N NORRIS • MARGARET M NORRIS • MAR-
GARET V NORRIS • MELVIN S NORRIS • REBEC-
CA NORRIS • STEPHANIE E NORRIS • STEVEN R
NORRIS • VELMA M NORRIS • WILLIAM T NOR-
RIS • WENDY C NORRIS ATC • ANGELA E NOR-
SWORTHY • GRETA G NORTH • JUDY NORTH •
ROBB B NORTH • ROBERT R NORTH • SCOTT G
NORTH • TERESA D NORTH • DAVID J
NORTHART • CAROL NORTHEN • DEBORAH L
NORTHERN • NANCY P NORTHERN • HOLLY M
NORTHEY • ANDY NORTON • BARBARA D NOR-
TON • BOBBIE C NORTON • CATHERINE M NOR-
TON • DIANE K NORTON • DURAND NORTON •
JONATHAN M NORTON • JUDY S NORTON •
KATHRYN JILL NORTON • LESTER C NORTON •
LISA M NORTON • LYNN E NORTON • MARC M
NORTON • MARIE K NORTON • MARTHA H NOR-
TON • MARY F NORTON • MATTHEW A NORTON •
MICHELLE D NORTON • NATALIE A NORTON •
ROD NORTON • WAYNE E NORTON • WENDY M
NORTON • JAMES E NORVILL • DEANTHONY M
NORWOOD • DEVORIN K NORWOOD • ELIZA-
BETH ANNE NORWOOD • FAY C NORWOOD •
GENEVA ROSE NORWOOD • KEVIN D NORWOOD
• LESTER NORWOOD • LUCIA B NORWOOD •
PHILIP D NORWOOD • RACHEL J NORWOOD •
SUSAN M NORWOOD • ROBERT J NOSS • JAMES
M NOSSAMAN • JENNIFER L NOTHEIS • ANTHO-
NY F NOTO • ELIZABETH S NOTT • TARA L NOTT
• ANGELA J NOTTINGHAM • PAM S NOUD • VIR-
GINIA E NOURIE • STEVE J NOURY • CHRISTINE
P NOVAC • MICHAEL F NOVAC • JANA M NOVAK •
MARIAN J NOVAK • PETER A NOVAK • TERESA A
NOVAK • MICHELLE E NOVELLO • CARMINE L
NOVEMBRE • SHERI R NOVIELLO • MICHAEL A
NOVOSEL • CHARLES P NOWAK • DENIS C
NOWAK • MARSHA K NOWAKOWSKI • PATRICIA E
NOWAKOWSKI • MARK A NOWELL • ROBERT J
NOWICKI • ROBERT G NOWITZKE • WILLIAM E
NOYCE • JILLIAN W NOYES • JULIE W NOYES •
PAUL PHELE P NTLATLENG • KOSITA C
NTUKOGU • JEAN G NUCCI • BOOKER T NUCK-
LES • CAROLINE NUCKOLLS • GEORGE R.
NUCKOLLS • CAROLYN D NUGENT • DANIEL A
NUGENT • JOHN E NUGENT • BERENDINA M NU-
MAN • ALEXANDRE V NUNES • KARINE NUNES •
TILLOU V NUNES III • ANGEL L NUNEZ •
JOSEPHINE C NUNEZ-GROSS • SHEILA B
NUNGESSER • ROGER H NUNLEY • JAMES C
NUNN • JANET S NUNN • STEWART E NUNN •
WILLIAM D NUNNALLY • MARGARET N NUNNEL-
LEY • VININEATH N NUON • AZIZEH NURIDDIN •
HELI M NURKKALA • JOANNE R NURSS • NAIK-
WA NURULLAH • KERI L NUSBAUM • CHARLTON
E NUSSMEYER • WILLIAM E NUTT • STEPHEN P
NUTTALL • BRUCE D NUTTER • GREG W NUTTER
• JOANN D NUZZULO • CHRISTINE U NWANKWO
• GRACE NWANKWO • PAMELA M NWAQBAKA-
DENZMORE • VERONICA L NWOKE • BETSY D
NWOKOCHA • MICHAEL NYAGUZE • PIA M NY-
BERG • BRIAN M NYBY • TARA L NYE • KIM A NYE
ATC • MICHAEL A NYLAND • KAREN A NYROP •
ELVIS U NZEPUOME • AMY R O BRIEN • JOAN A O
BRIEN • PATRICIA A O BRIEN • CORNELIUS J O
CONNOR • JOAN L O CONNOR • JOHN J O CON-
NOR • CATHERINE W O DILLON • JAMES M O DIL-
LON • ELLEN O KEEFE • PAUL J O KEEFFE •
GABRIELLE O MEARA • AUDRENTHIA A O NEAL •
CAROLYN P O NEAL • GENA M O NEAL • MICHAEL
S O NEAL • VALERIE J O REILLY • GLORIA J O RI-
LEY • TARA ANN O SHAUGHNESSY • TAFFEE J
OAKES • DAVID OAKLEY • DAVID E OAKLEY •
JAMES M OAKLEY • LAURA A OAKLEY • ADAM C
OAS • DIANE C OATES • ANNETTE L OBANION •
STEVEN J OBAROWSKI • KEN M O'BARR •
OLIVET OBASEKI • BARBARA A OBAZEE •
VLADIMIR OBELIC • AMY L OBENOUR • BEN-
NETT H OBERFELD • PAUL S OBERMAN • TERRI
A OBERT • LORRINE G OBI • SYLVIE J OBIDOWS-
KI • EDDIE V OBLETON • SANDRA D OBOROKU-
MO • BRYAN C OBRA • THOMAS A O'BRA • ALE-
JANDRO OBREGON • BETTY S OBREGON •
VIVIANA A OBREGON • KATHERINE M OBREMSKEY
• SANDRA S OBREMSKEY • DANIEL P. OBRIEN •
DEANNA F OBRIEN • DIANE J OBRIEN • FRANCIS T
OBRIEN • JACQUELINE OBRIEN • JASON C
OBRIEN • JOHN P OBRIEN • MATTHEW L OBRIEN •
SHAWN K OBRIEN • ERIN L O'BRIEN • BECKY R
O'BRIEN • BRENDAN O'BRIEN • CATHY J O'BRIEN
• COLLEEN M O'BRIEN • DAVID P O'BRIEN • ELLEN
M O'BRIEN • ERIN E O'BRIEN • JOSEPH O'BRIEN •
MEGAN L O'BRIEN • ROBERT L O'BRIEN •
STEPHEN T O'BRIEN • TIMOTHY J O'BRIEN •
WILLIAM R O'BRIEN • MARY ANNE E O'BRIEN RN •
DENISE D OBRIEN-BOURG • MAUREEN T OBRIEN-
HUMPHRIES • VINCENT J OBRIEN CATC •
CHARLES J OBRIEN III • DENISE L OBRONT •
CINDY L O'BRYANT • THEODORE P O'CALLAGHAN
• BRITT A OCLEARY • DAVID O'CONNEL • JAMES H
OCONNELL • JOHN M OCONNELL • JOHN R
OCONNELL • JONN R OCONNELL • MARGARET
OCONNELL • PETER J OCONNELL • TRUDY B OCON-
NELL • JAN K O'CONNELL • TIMOTHY NELSON O'-
CONNELL • MURIEL C O'CONNER • CAROL A OCON-
NOR • JOHN W OCONNOR • LAUREL E OCONNOR
• MARY HELEN OCONNOR • RICHARD P OCON-

NOR • SHANNON N OCONNOR • AIDAN H O'-
CONNOR • AILISH M O'CONNOR • CHRISTINE L
O'CONNOR • CIARA M O'CONNOR • E ANNE O'CON-
NOR • FRANK E O'CONNOR • JAMES C O'CONNOR •
JOHN L O'CONNOR • KAREN I O'CONNOR • KELLY A
O'CONNOR • LARA A. O'CONNOR • LYDIA B O'CON-
NOR • PATRICIA W O'CONNOR • RALPH C O'CON-
NOR • ROBERT N O'CONNOR • RODERICK S O'-
CONNOR • RORY L O'CONNOR • TAEKO ODA •
EMMANUEL ODAI • RYAN A ODDO • WARREN A
ODDO • PATRICK O'DEA • LISA W ODELL • DAVID
M O'DELL • DEE O'DELL • GEORGE W O'DELL •
LISA A ODEN • MARY R ODEN • THERESA M
ODEN • BIRDIE L ODEN JR • JOSEPH E ODER •
PAT R ODER • ZEPHANIAH O ODIEMBO • BONNIE
MARCELLA ODLE • SHERYL M ODLEVAK • AN-
DREW B ODOM • ANTHONY G ODOM • BRADLEY
E ODOM • CHRISTINA M ODOM • FRANK T ODOM
• KATHY ANN ODOM • LORETTA D ODOM • MAY-
NARD V ODOM • TIFFANY ODOM • JOSEPH B
ODOM II • DIANNE A ODOMES • ELIZABETH M
ODONNELL • JAMES F ODONNELL • BILL O'-
DONNELL • BRENNAN M O'DONNELL • JAMES H
O'DONNELL • JOHN R O'DONNELL • LESLIE A
O'DONNELL • COLLEEN ODONNELL ATC •
PATRICK E O'DONOHUE • MEGAN ODRISCOLL •
NICOLE E ODROSKE • EDNA E O'DROSKE • EM-
MANUEL A ODUAH • TOLA O ODUSANYA • JOYCE
A OEHRLE • JOHN W OEI • KEITH M OELKE •
SHIRLEY P OELSCHIG • CATHERINE D OERTING
• DEBRA L OESTREICHER • GARY G OETGEN •
KELLEY S OETGEN • R. ERIC OETGEN • SYDNEY
G OETGEN • JOE A O'FARRELL • REBECCA J OF-
FENBACHER • JOSIE OFFUTT • RYAN L OFFUTT •
KAYCE N OFODILE • SOLOMON W OGADO •
JOAN L OGANOWSKI • MASAYO OGAWA • ALLI-
SON M OGBURN • CRAIG E OGDEN • DANIEL L
OGDEN • EULALIE A OGDEN • JACKIE OGDEN •
JOHNS A OGDEN • KENNETH R OGDEN •
WILLIAM F OGDEN • KRISTIN A OGDON • AMY E
OGGEL • JAMES C OGIER • TAMARA M OGIER •
CHRISANN OGILVIE • SEAN P OGILVIE • DEBRA
M OGLE • RICHARD L OGLE • WAYNE G OGLE •
DAVID OGLES • MICHAEL D. OGLES • BARRY T
OGLESBY • ELLIS OGLESBY • EVERETT OGLES-
BY • REBECCA N OGLESBY • ASHLEY M OGLE-
TREE • CARY T OGLETREE • CHRISTY S OGLE-
TREE • ELIZABETH A OGLETREE • SAMUEL P
OGNIBENE • LISA OGONOWSKI • MAUREEN A
OGRADY • TIMOTHY J O'GRADY • STAN A OGULA
• ILAUNA A OGUNLOYE • CHUNG-HWA OH • IL
YOUNG OH • RAYNA B OH • ROCHELLE P O'HA-
GAN • JONATHAN H O'HAIRE • MICHELLE L
O'HALLORAN • ROBERT P O'HALLORAN • HEN-
RY OHANIAN • CAROLINE M OHARA • CLAUDE M
OHARA • KATHLEEN M OHARA • KENDRA E
OHARA • DANIEL P O'HARA • JULIE A O'HARA •
MISSY O'HAVER • NORMA J OHBERG • PATRICK
M OHEARN • LYNN M OHL • JENNIFER OHLSON
• TOMMY OHLUND • LINDA L OHMART • JOANN
OHMSIEDER • BRADY N OHR • RYUHJI OHTAKE •
YUKI OISHI • JOYCE A OJALA • PAULA K OJALA •
LINUS O OJIMMA • NADINE OKA • CHINEDUM M
OKAFOR • TORU OKAMOTO • MANABU OKAWA •
REBECCA E O'KEEFE • CHARLOTTE C O'KEEFE •
ROBERT O'KEEFE • ROBIN K O'KEEFE • ROBERT
O'KEEFE III • WILLIAM J O'KEEFFE • NKEMDILIM
N OKEKE • JAMES W OKELLEY • KARMAN M OKEL-
LEY • JOHN O'KELLEY • KEN M O'KELLEY • WILDA
OKEN • LESLIE A OKIN • GEORGE P OKOLO •
CHRISTY OKON • EKAETTE V OKONMKPAETO • AN-
GELA C OKPARA • YONCA OKTAY • ANNA G OKULA •
SOPHIA O OLAITAN • ERIN OLANDER • NICHOLAS
R OLANDER • JACQUELINE T. O'LAUGHLIN • JEN-
NIFER F OLAVESON • NELSSY S OLAYA • FAYE L OL-
BERT • MATTHEW OLBRYCH • CHARLES OLCKERS
• STEVEN M OLDENBOURG • MARION G OLDER-
MAN • ROB G OLDFIELD • VALERIE L OLDFIELD •
DAN F OLDHAM • RUTH A OLDHAM • SANDRA E
OLDHAM • CHRISTOPHER L OLDS • JEAN E
OLEARY • PATRICIA M OLEARY • TERRI A OLEARY •
BRIGID G O'LEARY • ROSEMARY O'LEARY • BRUCE
W OLECKI • EDIE B OLECKI • LORI A OLEJNICZAK •
BARBARA B OLESON • WILLIAM A OLESON •
SCOTT M OLIARO ATC • ANN G OLIM • MARTHA C
OLIN • JOHN B OLINGER • BEVERLY A OLIS •
DEANA M OLIVA • JOHN F OLIVA • DARREN J
OLIVE • MARCIA R OLIVEIRA • BERNADETTE M
OLIVER • BRIAN C OLIVER • CHARLES OLIVER •
ELIZABETH D OLIVER • HAROLD W OLIVER •
HUGH D OLIVER • JACK H OLIVER • JANICE W
OLIVER • JEREMIAH W OLIVER • JOHN A OLIVER
• KAREN E OLIVER • KATHLEEN Q OLIVER •
KISHA OLIVER • KYLE M OLIVER • PATRICIA
OLIVER • PATRICIA M OLIVER • PHYLLIS C OLIV-
ER • SHANNON M OLIVER • SOFIA A OLIVER •
SONYA A OLIVER • THOMAS L OLIVER • WESLEY
W OLIVER • WILLIAM E OLIVER • L CLIFTON
OLIVER II • LEE P OLIVER III EMT • PRISCILLA
OLIVER PH.D • SIMON G OLIVERO • ADEBAYO
OLIYIDE • OLUREMI O OLIYIDE • BERNARD OL-
LANOVE • GAYLE S OLLANOVE • MICHAEL OL-
LANOVE • CARRIE S OLLAR • GEORGE OLLEY •
IRENE E OLLEY • AMANDA L OLLIFF • WILLIAM C
OLLIFF • IVAN JR OLMO • L DREW OLMSTEAD •
GLORIA K OLMSTEAD • JONATHAN T OLMSTEAD
• ROBERT D OLMSTEAD • SARAH C OLMSTEAD •
GEORGE W OLNEY • DOUGLAS N OLSEN • JANET
H OLSEN • JUDITH C OLSEN • LAURIE I OLSEN •
RONALD J OLSEN • THOMAS V OLSEN • ANNIKA
L OLSON • BARBARA L OLSON • BRADFORD G
OLSON • CHRIS OLSON • DONNA J OLSON • ERI-
KA C OLSON • JEFF OLSON • KARI OLSON •
KRISTEN A OLSON • LEE M OLSON • LESLIE C
OLSON • MAUREEN L OLSON • MICHAEL D OL-
SON • ROY W OLSON • RUTH W OLSON • SUSAN
P OLSON • TAYLOR A OLSON • DAVID L OLT •

ATHLETICS
ATHLÉTISME

Abbreviations and terms used in Athletics results tables
Abréviations et termes employés dans les tableaux de résultats d'athlétisme

Term	English	Français
*	False Start	Faux départ
B	Bronze Medal	Médaille de bronze
Best Intermediate Time	Best Intermediate Time	Meilleur temps intermédiaire
Continued	Continued	Continué
Ctry	Country	Pays
DNF	Did Not Finish	Abandon
DNS	Did Not Start	Absent au départ
DQ	Disqualified	Disqualifié
Discus Throw	Discus Throw	Disque
Final	Final	Finale
Final Time	Final Time	Temps final
G	Gold Medal	Médaille d'or
Group	Group	Groupe
High Jump	High Jump	Saut en hauteur
Heat	Heat	Série
Hurdles	Hurdles	Haies
Javelin Throw	Javelin Throw	Javelot
Long Jump	Long Jump	Saut en longueur
Ln	Lane	Couloir
NC Pts	Noncumulative Points	Points non cumulés
NH	No Height	Non franchi
NM	No Mark	Aucun résultat
Name	Name	Nom
O	Olympic Record	Record olympique
Or	Order	Ordre
Pole Vault	Pole Vault	Saut à la perche
Q	Qualified By Right	Qualifié de droit
q	Qualified By Time	Qualifié sur temps
Qualification	Qualification	Qualification
Qualifying Round	Qualifying Round	Tour de qualification
Result	Result	Résultat
Rnk	Rank	Classement
Round	Round	Tour
S	Silver Medal	Médaille d'argent
Semifinal	Semifinal	Demi-finale
Shot Put	Shot Put	Poids
X, O	Failed, Cleared	Manqué, Franchi
W	World Record	Record du monde

International Amateur Athletic Federation (IAAF)
Fédération Internationale Amateur d'Athlétisme
**17, rue Princesse Florestine
BP 359,98007
Monte Carlo
Monaco**

LOREEN C OLUFSON • JOSEPH OLVERA • MARGARITO OLVERA • ROSALIO OLVERA • JULIUS H OLZER • ROBERT C OMALLEY ATC • CHRISTEN O'MARA • FRANCES M O'MEARA • L. RYAN O'MEARA • MICHAEL J O'MEARA • SCOTT D O'MEARA • JOSEPH W OMER • KEELY A OMER • WILLIAM A OMMEN • SUSUMU OMORI • THOMAS F OMORRISSEY • ACELA V ONATE • ANTHONY W ONDRUS • PHILLIP R ONEACRE • BERNARD F ONEAL • CHRISTOPHER J ONEAL • CHRISTOPHER S ONEAL • DEMARIO R ONEAL • FYPHINE N ONEAL • JEAN C ONEAL • LAWANDA ONEAL • PATRICK ONEAL • SANDRA M ONEAL

67

ROUND 1, HEAT 1

Rnk	Ln	Name	Ctry	Result	
1	6	TUFFOUR, Emmanuel	GHA	10.15	Q
2	5	SURIN, Bruny	CAN	10.18	Q
3	2	FEDORIV, Andrey	RUS	10.39	Q
4	1*	WELLS, Renward	BAH	10.48	
5	3	DE SOYZA, Chinthaka	SRI	10.55	
6	7	CUNHA, Luis	POR	10.65	
7	9	MOCCI RAOUMBE, Patrick	GAB	10.87	
8	8	OULD MENIRA, Nordine	MTN	• 10.95	
9	4	EDU, Bonifacio	GEQ	11.87	

ROUND 1, HEAT 2

Rnk	Ln	Name	Ctry	Result	
1	1	EZINWA, Davidson	NGR	10.03	Q
2	2	DRUMMOND, Jon	USA	10.08	Q
3	9	WYMEERSCH, Erik	BEL	10.24	Q
4	5	GORDON, Leon	JAM	10.48	
5	6	BURKART, Stefan	SUI	10.48	
6	7	JOLICOEUR, Barnabe	MRI	10.57	
7	4	TARAFDAR, Bimal	BAN	10.98	
8	3	GHAFOOR, Abdul	AFG	12.20	
	8	TYNES, Andrew	BAH	DNS	

ROUND 1, HEAT 3

Rnk	Ln	Name	Ctry	Result	
1	5	BOLDON, Ato	TRI	10.06	Q
2	7*	MARKOULLIDES, Anninos	CYP	10.26	Q
3	2	COLLINS, Kim	SKN	10.27	Q
4	8	NKETIA, Gus	NZL	10.34	q
5	4	STEWART, Raymond	JAM	10.38	q
6	9	TILLI, Stefano	ITA	10.38	
7	6	AL-SAFFAR, Jamal	KSA	10.44	
8	3	ALMEIDA, Amarildo	GBS	10.85	
9	1	BACAR, Mohamed	COM	11.02	

ROUND 1, HEAT 4

Rnk	Ln	Name	Ctry	Result	
1	7	GREEN, Michael	JAM	10.16	Q
2	9	STEVENS, Patrick	BEL	10.21	Q
3	8	OSOVYCH, Serhiy	UKR	10.29	Q
4	1	MADONIA, Ezio	ITA	10.33	q
5	2	RIBEIRO, Edson	BRA	10.39	
6	3	DONALDSON, Chris	NZL	10.39	
7	5	STRENIUS, Patrik	SWE	10.48	
8	4	KOULA, Tolutau	TGA	10.71	
9	6	CHERNOBAY, Vladislav	KGZ	10.88	

ROUND 1, HEAT 5

Rnk	Ln	Name	Ctry	Result	
1	2	ALIU, Deji	NGR	10.34	Q
2	8	DIARRA, Ousmane	MLI	10.34	Q
3	3	CHEN, Wenzhong	CHN	10.37	Q
4	6*	BORREGA, Manuel	ESP	10.52	
5	7	TSUCHIE, Hiroyasu	JPN	10.58	
6	9	BENITEZ, Ruben	ESA	10.74	
7	1	MEDVEDEV, Vitaliy	KAZ	10.90	
8	4	PETERS, Mitchell	ISV	11.12	
9	5	KIMBA, Boureima	NIG	11.24	

ROUND 1, HEAT 6

Rnk	Ln	Name	Ctry	Result	
1	4	MITCHELL, Dennis	USA	10.24	Q
2	7	MACKIE, Ian	GBR	10.27	Q
3	3	BLUME, Marc	GER	10.33	Q
4	9	TERZIAN, Alexandros	GRE	10.48	
5	1	AMEGNIGAN, Franck	TOG	10.51	
6	6	MAPSTONE, Rod	AUS	10.56	
7	8	COOPER, Sayon	LBR	10.58	
8	2	GAI, Pa Modou	GAM	10.72	
9	5	CASTELLON, Jorge	BOL	10.74	

ROUND 1, HEAT 7

Rnk	Ln	Name	Ctry	Result	
1	1	THOMPSON, Obadele	BAR	10.33	Q
2	5	RURAK, Kostya	UKR	10.37	Q
3	9	THEOPHILE, Pascal	FRA	10.41	Q
4	2	GATS, Carlos	ARG	10.57	
5	3	MASCOLL, Joel	VIN	10.64	
6	6	KUCHMURADOV, Anvar	UZB	10.71	
7	4	AKHUNDOV, Arif	AZE	11.11	
8	8	OTHMAN, Khaled	LBA	11.65	
9	7	ZIRIGNON, Jean-Olivier	CIV	22.69	

ROUND 1, HEAT 8

Rnk	Ln	Name	Ctry	Result	
1	7	MARSH, Michael	USA	10.14	Q
2	8	BRAITHWAITE, Darren	GBR	10.29	Q
3	9	CUMMINS, Kirk	BAR	10.47	Q
4	5	ERIKSSON, Torbjorn	SWE	10.49	
5	6	HENDERSON, Paul	AUS	10.52	
6	3	MENDEZ, Alberto	DOM	10.60	
7	2*	SILVA, Arnaldo	BRA	10.62	
8	1	BONELLO, Mario	MLT	10.89	
9	4	da COSTA, Odair	STP	11.05	

ROUND 1, HEAT 9

Rnk	Ln	Name	Ctry	Result	
1	8	SILVA, Andre	BRA	10.25	Q
2	5	CHRISTIE, Linford	GBR	10.26	Q
3	6	ZISIMIDES, Yiannis	CYP	10.32	Q
4	1	JOSE, Venancio	ESP	10.34	q
5	9*	DOUHOU, Hamed	CIV	10.53	
6	7	DENNIS, Robert	LBR	10.65	
7	2	ONCHIRI, Donald	KEN	10.66	
8	3	JIN, Sun-Kuk	KOR	10.73	
9	4	PULU, Peter	PNG	10.76	

ROUND 1, HEAT 10

Rnk	Ln	Name	Ctry	Result	
1	5	NKANSAH, Eric	GHA	10.26	Q
2	2	GUIMS, Needy	FRA	10.39	Q
3	1	ADENIKEN, Olapade	NGR	10.41	Q
4	7	DELAI, Jone	FIJ	10.42	
5	8	SAVIN, Vitaliy	KAZ	10.52	
6	9	NYAMBEK, Watson	MAS	10.55	
7	6	RYAN, Neil	IRL	10.78	
8	3	VERNE, Javier	PER	10.91	
9	4	LAM HAI, Van	VIE	11.14	

ROUND 1, HEAT 11

Rnk	Ln	Name	Ctry	Result	
1	3	BAILEY, Donovan	CAN	10.24	Q
2	1	ASAHARA, Nobuharu	JPN	10.28	Q
3	2*	KARLSSON, Peter	SWE	10.35	Q
4	6	TURAY, Sanusi	SLE	10.39	
5	9	INSAKOVS, Sergejs	LAT	10.42	
6	8	PAPADIAS, Haralambos	GRE	10.46	
7	7	HUANG, Hsin-Ping	TPE	10.70	
8	4	AGUEH, Eric	BEN	10.98	
	5	EMBALO, Alfayaya	CPV	DNS	

ROUND 1, HEAT 12

Rnk	Ln	Name	Ctry	Result	
1	4	FREDERICKS, Frank	NAM	10.32	Q
2	1	GILBERT, Glenroy	CAN	10.34	Q
3	3	YENOVELIS, Alexandros	GRE	10.39	Q
4	6	FEO, Frutos	ESP	10.56	
5	8	SIRIMOU, Benjamin	CMR	10.58	
6	7	SADEQ, Hamed	KUW	10.81	
7	9	BEAN, Devon	BER	10.89	
8	5	LOUA, Robert	GUI	11.21	
9	2*	SHERWIN, Mark	COK	11.41	

ROUND 2, HEAT 1

Rnk	Ln	Name	Ctry	Result	
1	5	BOLDON, Ato	TRI	9.95	Q
2	3	ASAHARA, Nobuharu	JPN	10.19	Q
3	6	NKANSAH, Eric	GHA	10.24	Q
4	4	ALIU, Deji	NGR	10.26	
5	7	GILBERT, Glenroy	CAN	10.28	
6	8	BLUME, Marc	GER	10.33	
7	1	FEDORIV, Andrey	RUS	10.34	
8	2	NKETIA, Gus	NZL	10.35	

ROUND 2, HEAT 2

Rnk	Ln	Name	Ctry	Result	
1	6	CHRISTIE, Linford	GBR	10.03	Q
2	5	BAILEY, Donovan	CAN	10.05	Q
3	3	DRUMMOND, Jon	USA	10.17	Q
4	4	TUFFOUR, Emmanuel	GHA	10.18	q
5	2	WYMEERSCH, Erik	BEL	10.37	
6	7	ADENIKEN, Olapade	NGR	10.38	
7	8*	GUIMS, Needy	FRA	10.43	
8	1	MADONIA, Ezio	ITA	10.43	

ROUND 2, HEAT 3

Rnk	Ln	Name	Ctry	Result	
1	5	FREDERICKS, Frank	NAM	9.93	Q
2	3	EZINWA, Davidson	NGR	10.08	Q
3	4	THOMPSON, Obadele	BAR	10.14	Q
4	8	STEWART, Raymond	JAM	10.18	
5	7	KARLSSON, Peter	SWE	10.24	
6	6	BRAITHWAITE, Darren	GBR	10.27	
7	2	CHEN, Wenzhong	CHN	10.29	
8	1	DIARRA, Ousmane	MLI	10.38	

100 m, Men / *100 m, Messieurs*

ROUND 2, HEAT 4

Rnk	Ln	Name	Ctry	Result	
1	6	MITCHELL, Dennis	USA	10.09	Q
2	3	GREEN, Michael	JAM	10.11	Q
3	4	MARKOULLIDES, Anninos	CYP	10.23	Q
4	5	STEVENS, Patrick	BEL	10.31	
5	2	COLLINS, Kim	SKN	10.34	
6	1	THEOPHILE, Pascal	FRA	10.38	
7	7	OSOVYCH, Serhiy	UKR	10.38	
8	8	CUMMINS, Kirk	BAR	10.45	

ROUND 2, HEAT 5

Rnk	Ln	Name	Ctry	Result	
1	6	MARSH, Michael	USA	10.04	Q
2	4	SURIN, Bruny	CAN	10.13	Q
3	5	MACKIE, Ian	GBR	10.25	Q
4	3	SILVA, Andre	BRA	10.26	
5	2	YENOVELIS, Alexandros	GRE	10.31	
6	1	JOSE, Venancio	ESP	10.46	
7	7	RURAK, Kostya	UKR	10.47	
8	8	ZISIMIDES, Yiannis	CYP	10.47	

SEMIFINAL 1

Rnk	Ln	Name	Ctry	Result	
1	5	FREDERICKS, Frank	NAM	9.94	Q
2	3*	BAILEY, Donovan	CAN	10.00	Q
3	6	MARSH, Michael	USA	10.08	Q
4	4	GREEN, Michael	JAM	10.11	Q
5	1	ASAHARA, Nobuharu	JPN	10.16	
6	8	THOMPSON, Obadele	BAR	10.16	
7	2	TUFFUOR, Emmanuel	GHA	10.22	
8	7	MARKOULLIDES, Anninos	CYP	10.36	

SEMIFINAL 2

Rnk	Ln	Name	Ctry	Result	
1	3	BOLDON, Ato	TRI	9.93	Q
2	5	MITCHELL, Dennis	USA	10.00	Q
3	6	CHRISTIE, Linford	GBR	10.04	Q
4	4	EZINWA, Davidson	NGR	10.04	Q
5	1	SURIN, Bruny	CAN	10.13	
6	2	DRUMMOND, Jon	USA	10.16	
7	8	NKANSAH, Eric	GHA	10.26	
	7	MACKIE, Ian	GBR	DNS	

FINAL

Rnk	Ln	Name	Ctry	Result		
1	6	BAILEY, Donovan	CAN	9.84	W	G
2	5	FREDERICKS, Frank	NAM	9.89		S
3	3*	BOLDON, Ato	TRI	9.90		B
4	4	MITCHELL, Dennis	USA	9.99		
5	1	MARSH, Michael	USA	10.00		
6	7	EZINWA, Davidson	NGR	10.14		
7	8	GREEN, Michael	JAM	10.16		
2**		CHRISTIE, Linford	GBR	DQ		

Athletics / *Athlétisme*
100 m, Women / *100 m, Dames*

ROUND 1, HEAT 1

Rnk	Ln	Name	Ctry	Result	
1	7	STURRUP, Chandra	BAH	11.24	Q
2	8	RAKOTONDRABE, Rivosoa	MAD	11.36	Q
3	9	PRIVALOVA, Irina	RUS	11.42	Q
4	5	GEORGIEVA, Zlatka	BUL	11.74	Q
5	1	VOROBYOVA, Natalya	KAZ	11.91	
6	2	DMITRIADI, Lyudmila	UZB	12.04	
7	6	OUK, Chanthan	CAM	14.82	

ROUND 1, HEAT 2

Rnk	Ln	Name	Ctry	Result	
1	8	PINTUSEVYCH, Zhanna	UKR	11.20	Q
2	4	PASCHKE, Melanie	GER	11.27	Q
3	1	SIDIBE, Odiah	FRA	11.40	Q
4	3	TOMBIRI-SHIREY, Mary	NGR	11.50	Q
5	2	JOSEPH, Hermin	DMA	11.56	
6	6	AMARAL, Cleide	BRA	11.76	
7	5	MANI, Leonie	CMR	11.76	
8	7	DZHABBAROVA, Elvira	AZE	11.96	

ROUND 1, HEAT 3

Rnk	Ln	Name	Ctry	Result	
1	6	OTTEY, Merlene	JAM	11.13	Q
2	2	JAYASINGHE, Susanthika	SRI	11.18	Q
3	9	THANOU, Ekaterini	GRE	11.35	Q
4	3	PUKHA, Iryna	UKR	11.36	Q
5	7	SAMUEL, Heather	ANT	11.44	q
6	5	YAN, Jiankui	CHN	11.46	
7	8	BROCK, Mirtha	COL	11.83	
8	1	da SILVA PIRES, Sortelina	STP	13.31	

ROUND 1, HEAT 4

Rnk	Ln	Name	Ctry	Result	
1	4	CUTHBERT, Juliet	JAM	11.06	Q
2	7	HILL, D'Andre	USA	11.11	Q
3	2	LICHTENHAGEN, Silke	GER	11.30	Q
4	9	CLARKE, Eldece	BAH	11.33	Q
5	5	PENDAREVA, Petya	BUL	11.59	
6	1	MOTHERSILLE, Cydonie	CAY	11.61	
7	3	BAPTISTE, Michelle	LCA	11.92	
8	8	MARTINDALE, Natalie	VIN	12.25	

ROUND 1, HEAT 5

Rnk	Ln	Name	Ctry	Result	
1	6	TRANDENKOVA, Marina	RUS	11.20	Q
2	9	AJUNWA, Chioma	NGR	11.25	Q
3	7*	MAYBERRY, Myra	PUR	11.51	Q
4	4	DOUGLAS, Stephi	GBR	11.61	Q
5	5	BORRERO, Zandra	COL	11.62	
6	1	PERC, Jerneja	SLO	11.63	
7	8	McDONALD, Beverly	JAM	12.08	
8	2	da FREDERICO, Ismenia	CPV	13.03	

ROUND 1, HEAT 6

Rnk	Ln	Name	Ctry	Result	
1	9	TORRENCE, Gwen	USA	11.11	Q
2	5	VORONOVA, Natalya	RUS	11.22	Q
3	4	JARDIM, Lucrecia	POR	11.32	Q
4	3	KOFFA, Katerina	GRE	11.33	Q
5	2	HERNESNIEMI, Sanna	FIN	11.39	q
6	1	RICHARDSON, Marcia	GBR	11.42	q
7	7	WANG, Huei-Chen	TPE	11.70	
8	8	GENIWALA'A, Nester	SOL	13.74	
9	6	OBIONG, Juliana	GEQ	13.88	

ROUND 1, HEAT 7

Rnk	Ln	Name	Ctry	Result	
1	5	DEVERS, Gail	USA	10.92	Q
2	7	ONYALI, Mary	NGR	11.17	Q
3	3	PHILIPP, Andrea	GER	11.32	Q
4	9	FERGUSON, Debbie	BAH	11.33	Q
5	4	JACOBS, Simmone	GBR	11.39	q
6	6	DONDERS, Mireille	SUI	11.67	
7	2	LEE, Young-Sook	KOR	11.88	
8	1	CHAVEZ, Pastora	HON	12.10	

ROUND 2, HEAT 1

Rnk	Ln	Name	Ctry	Result	
1	4	TORRENCE, Gwen	USA	11.11	Q
2	5	TRANDENKOVA, Marina	RUS	11.15	Q
3	3	AJUNWA, Chioma	NGR	11.24	Q
4	1	SIDIBE, Odiah	FRA	11.38	Q
5	7	KOFFA, Katerina	GRE	11.38	
6	6	RAKOTONDRABE, Rivosoa	MAD	11.43	
7	2	SAMUEL, Heather	ANT	11.60	
8	8	DOUGLAS, Stephi	GBR	11.75	

ROUND 2, HEAT 2

Rnk	Ln	Name	Ctry	Result	
1	3	DEVERS, Gail	USA	10.94	Q
2	4	ONYALI, Mary	NGR	11.08	Q
3	7	FERGUSON, Debbie	BAH	11.26	Q
4	6	JARDIM, Lucrecia	POR	11.37	Q
5	2	PHILIPP, Andrea	GER	11.38	
6	8	PUKHA, Iryna	UKR	11.42	
7	1	RICHARDSON, Marcia	GBR	11.55	
	5	JAYASINGHE, Susanthika	SRI	DNF	

100 m, Women / *100 m, Dames*

ROUND 2, HEAT 3

Rnk	Ln	Name	Ctry	Result	
1	4	CUTHBERT, Juliet	JAM	11.20	Q
2	6	STURRUP, Chandra	BAH	11.21	Q
3	5	HILL, D'Andre	USA	11.21	Q
4	2	PRIVALOVA, Irina	RUS	11.40	Q
5	1	JACOBS, Simmone	GBR	11.47	
6	8	THANOU, Ekaterini	GRE	11.48	
7	3	LICHTENHAGEN, Silke	GER	11.53	
8	7	TOMBIRI-SHIREY, Mary	NGR	11.56	

ROUND 2, HEAT 4

Rnk	Ln	Name	Ctry	Result	
1	6	OTTEY, Merlene	JAM	11.02	Q
2	4	PINTUSEVYCH, Zhanna	UKR	11.14	Q
3	5	VORONOVA, Natalya	RUS	11.17	Q
4	3	PASCHKE, Melanie	GER	11.18	Q
5	1	CLARKE, Eldece	BAH	11.47	
6	7	HERNESNIEMI, Sanna	FIN	11.49	
7	8	MAYBERRY, Myra	PUR	11.66	
8	2	GEORGIEVA, Zlatka	BUL	11.99	

SEMIFINAL 1

Rnk	Ln	Name	Ctry	Result	
1	4	OTTEY, Merlene	JAM	10.93	Q
2	6	TORRENCE, Gwen	USA	10.97	Q
3	3	TRANDENKOVA, Marina	RUS	11.07	Q
4	5	PINTUSEVYCH, Zhanna	UKR	11.14	Q
5	8	AJUNWA, Chioma	NGR	11.14	
6	2	HILL, D'Andre	USA	11.20	
7	1	FERGUSON, Debbie	BAH	11.28	
8	7	SIDIBE, Odiah	FRA	11.35	

SEMIFINAL 2

Rnk	Ln	Name	Ctry	Result	
1	6	DEVERS, Gail	USA	11.00	Q
2	3	ONYALI, Mary	NGR	11.04	Q
3	2	VORONOVA, Natalya	RUS	11.07	Q
4	5	STURRUP, Chandra	BAH	11.07	Q
5	4	CUTHBERT, Juliet	JAM	11.07	
6	8	PASCHKE, Melanie	GER	11.14	
7	1	PRIVALOVA, Irina	RUS	11.31	
8	7	JARDIM, Lucrecia	POR	11.32	

FINAL

Rnk	Ln	Name	Ctry	Result	
1	3	DEVERS, Gail	USA	10.94	G
2	4	OTTEY, Merlene	JAM	10.94	S
3	6	TORRENCE, Gwen	USA	10.96	B
4	8	STURRUP, Chandra	BAH	11.00	
5	2	TRANDENKOVA, Marina	RUS	11.06	
6	1	VORONOVA, Natalya	RUS	11.10	
7	5	ONYALI, Mary	NGR	11.13	
8	7	PINTUSEVYCH, Zhanna	UKR	11.14	

Athletics / *Athlétisme*
200 m, Men / *200 m, Messieurs*

ROUND 1, HEAT 1

Rnk	Ln	Name	Ctry	Result	
1	5	MARSH, Michael	USA	20.27	Q
2	8	INSAKOVS, Sergejs	LAT	20.41	Q
3	7	DOUGLAS, Troy	BER	20.41	Q
4	4	BRIMACOMBE, Steve	AUS	20.45	q
5	3	VISAGIE, Alfred	RSA	21.10	
6	6	al-HOOTI, Mohamed	OMA	21.10	
7	2	MAZUKA, Takahiro	JPN	21.13	

ROUND 1, HEAT 2

Rnk	Ln	Name	Ctry	Result	
1	3	GARCIA, Ivan	CUB	20.49	Q
2	8	AGYEMANG, Albert	GHA	20.69	Q
3	4	CAWLEY, Elston	JAM	20.73	Q
4	1	DAKO, Owusu	GBR	20.83	
5	7*	SBOKOS, Thomas	GRE	20.88	
6	5	IVANOV, Anton	BUL	21.20	
7	6	WILSON, David	GUM	21.85	
8	2	BRAHIM, Mohamed	MTN	22.71	

ROUND 1, HEAT 3

Rnk	Ln	Name	Ctry	Result	
1	8	BOLDON, Ato	TRI	20.26	Q
2	6	THOMPSON, Obadele	BAR	20.42	Q
3	4	MARKOULLIDES, Anninos	CYP	20.57	Q
4	3	GATS, Carlos	ARG	20.82	q
5	2	GIKONYO, Joseph	KEN	20.88	
6	5	DONALDSON, Chris	NZL	20.96	
7	7	TAO, Wu-Shiun	TPE	21.25	

ROUND 1, HEAT 4

Rnk	Ln	Name	Ctry	Result	
1	7	JOHNSON, Michael	USA	20.55	Q
2	5	WYMEERSCH, Erik	BEL	20.68	Q
3	2	SPENCER, Percival	JAM	20.73	Q
4	4	WAOTA, Franck	CIV	20.78	q
5	8	SIRIMOU, Benjamin	CMR	21.00	
6	6	BOUSSOMBO, Antoine	GAB	21.06	
	3	JOSE, Venancio	ESP	DNS	

ROUND 1, HEAT 5

Rnk	Ln	Name	Ctry	Result	
1	2	OBIKWELU, Francis	NGR	20.62	Q
2	5	RIBEIRO, Edson	BRA	20.69	Q
3	4	REGIS, John	GBR	20.78	Q
4	7	LISK, Pierre	SLE	20.86	
5	8	HEDNER, Lars	SWE	20.97	
6	1	GRIESSER, Thomas	AUT	21.20	
7	3	DANGBO, Pascal	BEN	21.65	
8	6	DJAFFAR, Hadhari	COM	22.68	

ROUND 1, HEAT 6

Rnk	Ln	Name	Ctry	Result	
1	4	STEVENS, Patrick	BEL	20.60	Q
2	5	MAYORAL, Jordi	ESP	20.65	Q
3	1	da SILVA, Claudinei	BRA	20.80	Q
4	3	LOUA, Joseph	GUI	20.81	q
5	6	LAWSON, Boevi	TOG	20.99	
6	7	VILIEN, Anderson	HAI	21.62	
7	8	OGILVIE, Peter	CAN	22.00	
8	2	ENVELA, Gustavo	GEQ	22.09	

ROUND 1, HEAT 7

Rnk	Ln	Name	Ctry	Result	
1	6	CHRISTIE, Linford	GBR	20.64	Q
2	4	MACKOWIAK, Robert	POL	20.67	Q
3	7	PANAYIOTOPOULOS, George	GRE	20.69	Q
4	5	MOEN, Geir	NOR	20.78	q
5	3	GIBBONS, O'Brian	CAN	20.79	q
6	8	FEDORIV, Andrey	RUS	20.95	
7	2	ABDOULAYE, Brahim	CHA	21.67	

ROUND 1, HEAT 8

Rnk	Ln	Name	Ctry	Result	
1	5	de SILVA, Neil	TRI	20.54	Q
2	3	da SILVA, Robson	BRA	20.61	Q
3	7	LOUM, Oumar	SEN	20.69	Q
4	2	CAPOBIANCO, Dean	AUS	20.76	q
5	4	COAD, Matthew	NZL	21.25	
6	8	ALI, Amos	PNG	21.37	
7	6	JACK, Laurence	VAN	21.94	
	1	ADENIKEN, Olapade	NGR	DNS	

ROUND 1, HEAT 9

Rnk	Ln	Name	Ctry	Result	
1	4	WILLIAMS, Jeff	USA	20.37	Q
2	7	DOLOGODIN, Slava	UKR	20.57	Q
3	5	NAVARRO, Francisco	ESP	20.87	Q
4	6	REIMANN, Alain	SUI	20.99	
5	2	DIARRA, Ousmane	MLI	21.20	
6	8	al-ASWAD, Mohd	UAE	21.77	
	3	ISMAIL, Ibrahim	QAT	DNS	

200 m, Men / *200 m, Messieurs*

ROUND 1, HEAT 10					
Rnk	Ln	Name	Ctry	Result	
1	5	ITO, Koji	JPN	20.56	Q
2	7	ERIKSSON, Torbjorn	SWE	20.77	Q
3	4	TUFFUOR, Emmanuel	GHA	20.85	Q
4	2	KEDDELL, Mark	NZL	20.93	
5	8	DIPEBA, Justice	BOT	21.09	
6	6	CHAMBERS, Carlton	CAN	21.32	
7	3	JANSSEN, Miguel	ARU	21.72	

ROUND 1, HEAT 11					
Rnk	Ln	Name	Ctry	Result	
1	7	FREDERICKS, Frank	NAM	20.59	Q
2	2	OGUNKOYA, Seun	NGR	20.78	Q
3	6	RYAN, Gary	IRL	20.78	Q
4	4	KEITEL, Sebastian	CHI	20.96	
5	5	POESTINGER, Christoph	AUT	20.98	
6	3	FLORIS, Sandro	ITA	21.01	
7	8	CHEN, Wenzhong	CHN	21.05	

ROUND 2, HEAT 1					
Rnk	Ln	Name	Ctry	Result	
1	4	FREDERICKS, Frank	NAM	20.38	Q
2	3	WILLIAMS, Jeff	USA	20.47	Q
3	5	THOMPSON, Obadele	BAR	20.53	Q
4	6*	WYMEERSCH, Erik	BEL	20.59	
5	8	SPENCER, Percival	JAM	20.59	
6	7	DOUGLAS, Troy	BER	20.63	
7	1	NAVARRO, Francisco	ESP	21.06	
	2	GIBBONS, O'Brian	CAN	DNS	

ROUND 2, HEAT 2					
Rnk	Ln	Name	Ctry	Result	
1	6	JOHNSON, Michael	USA	20.37	Q
2	8	MOEN, Geir	NOR	20.48	Q
3	3	de SILVA, Neil	TRI	20.62	Q
4	4	da SILVA, Robson	BRA	20.65	
5	5	MAYORAL, Jordi	ESP	20.68	
6	7	PANAYIOTOPOULOS, George	GRE	20.86	
7	1	CAPOBIANCO, Dean	AUS	21.03	
8	2	LOUM, Oumar	SEN	21.31	

ROUND 2, HEAT 3					
Rnk	Ln	Name	Ctry	Result	
1	4	GARCIA, Ivan	CUB	20.36	Q
2	6	ITO, Koji	JPN	20.47	Q
3	8	BRIMACOMBE, Steve	AUS	20.53	Q
4	5	MACKOWIAK, Robert	POL	20.61	
5	1	MARKOULLIDES, Anninos	CYP	20.63	
6	3	DOLOGODIN, Slava	UKR	20.65	
7	7	CAWLEY, Elston	JAM	20.75	
8	2	WAOTA, Franck	CIV	21.14	

ROUND 2, HEAT 4					
Rnk	Ln	Name	Ctry	Result	
1	6	MARSH, Michael	USA	20.39	Q
2	5*	STEVENS, Patrick	BEL	20.43	Q
3	8	REGIS, John	GBR	20.56	Q
4	4	INSAKOVS, Sergejs	LAT	20.58	q
5	3	AGYEMANG, Albert	GHA	20.87	
6	7	OGUNKOYA, Seun	NGR	21.00	
7	2	LOUA, Joseph	GUI	21.01	
	1	da SILVA, Claudinei	BRA	DNF	

ROUND 2, HEAT 5					
Rnk	Ln	Name	Ctry	Result	
1	6	BOLDON, Ato	TRI	20.25	Q
2	5	OBIKWELU, Francis	NGR	20.49	Q
3	2	TUFFUOR, Emmanuel	GHA	20.49	Q
4	3	CHRISTIE, Linford	GBR	20.59	
5	4	RIBEIRO, Edson	BRA	20.60	
6	7	ERIKSSON, Torbjorn	SWE	20.83	
7	8	GATS, Carlos	ARG	20.84	
8	1	RYAN, Gary	IRL	20.89	

SEMIFINAL 1					
Rnk	Ln	Name	Ctry	Result	
1	4	JOHNSON, Michael	USA	20.27	Q
2	6	GARCIA, Ivan	CUB	20.34	Q
3	3	WILLIAMS, Jeff	USA	20.39	Q
4	5	STEVENS, Patrick	BEL	20.46	Q
5	7	OBIKWELU, Francis	NGR	20.56	
6	8	REGIS, John	GBR	20.58	
7	2	TUFFUOR, Emmanuel	GHA	20.61	
8	1	de SILVA, Neil	TRI	21.26	

SEMIFINAL 2					
Rnk	Ln	Name	Ctry	Result	
1	5	FREDERICKS, Frank	NAM	19.98	Q
2	4	BOLDON, Ato	TRI	20.05	Q
3	3	MARSH, Michael	USA	20.26	Q
4	2	THOMPSON, Obadele	BAR	20.32	Q
5	7	BRIMACOMBE, Steve	AUS	20.38	
6	6	ITO, Koji	JPN	20.45	
7	8	INSAKOVS, Sergejs	LAT	20.48	
8	1	MOEN, Geir	NOR	20.96	

FINAL					
Rnk	Ln	Name	Ctry	Result	
1	3	JOHNSON, Michael	USA	19.32 W	G
2	5	FREDERICKS, Frank	NAM	19.68	S
3	6	BOLDON, Ato	TRI	19.80	B
4	8	THOMPSON, Obadele	BAR	20.14	
5	2	WILLIAMS, Jeff	USA	20.17	
6	4	GARCIA, Ivan	CUB	20.21	
7	7	STEVENS, Patrick	BEL	20.27	
8	1	MARSH, Michael	USA	20.48	

Athletics / *Athlétisme*
200 m, Women / *200 m, Dames*

ROUND 1, HEAT 1					
Rnk	Ln	Name	Ctry	Result	
1	5	GUIDRY, Carlette	USA	22.37	Q
2	8	ONYALI, Mary	NGR	22.42	Q
3	3	PASCHKE, Melanie	GER	22.93	Q
4	2	RODRIGUEZ, Patricia	COL	23.13	Q
5	1	YAN, Jiankui	CHN	23.21	q
6	7	MAYBERRY, Myra	PUR	23.23	q
7	4	GEORGIEVA, Zlatka	BUL	24.05	
8	6	KUETEY, Laure	BEN	25.57	

ROUND 1, HEAT 2					
Rnk	Ln	Name	Ctry	Result	
1	2	YOUNG, Dannette	USA	22.65	Q
2	7	GAINSFORD-TAYLOR, Melinda	AUS	22.70	Q
3	5	JARDIM, Lucrecia	POR	22.95	Q
4	1	FOMENKO, Viktoriya	UKR	23.18	Q
5	6	MYERS, Sandra	ESP	23.18	q
6	3	UBAH, Calister	NGR	23.34	q
7	4	KYRIAKOU, Dora	CYP	23.85	
8	8*	TOURE, M'Mah	GUI	26.64	

ROUND 1, HEAT 3					
Rnk	Ln	Name	Ctry	Result	
1	6	CUTHBERT, Juliet	JAM	23.03	Q
2	2	PRIVALOVA, Irina	RUS	23.16	Q
3	1	FREEMAN, Cathy	AUS	23.25	Q
4	7	HERNESNIEMI, Sanna	FIN	23.35	Q
5	8	DONDERS, Mireille	SUI	23.52	
6	5	AZARASHVILI, Maia	GEO	23.63	
7	4	PALACIOS, Felipa	COL	24.12	
8	3	SHOAI, Lineo	LES	26.25	

200 m, Women / *200 m, Dames*

ROUND 1, HEAT 4

Rnk	Ln	Name	Ctry	Result	
1	7	OTTEY, Merlene	JAM	22.92	Q
2	1	MERRY, Katharine	GBR	23.14	Q
3	6	GACHEVSKA, Monika	BUL	23.30	Q
4	5	SAMUEL, Heather	ANT	23.34	Q
5	4	BELLO, Ameerah	ISV	23.45	q
6	3	DU, Xiujie	CHN	23.69	
7	8	CRUZ, Guilhermina	ANG	24.92	
	2	TRANDENKOVA, Marina	RUS	DNS	

ROUND 1, HEAT 5

Rnk	Ln	Name	Ctry	Result	
1	1	MALCHUGINA, Galina	RUS	22.63	Q
2	7	STURRUP, Chandra	BAH	22.63	Q
3	6	McDONALD, Beverly	JAM	23.04	Q
4	5	PINTUSEVYCH, Zhanna	UKR	23.15	Q
5	2	JACOBS, Simmone	GBR	23.36	q
6	3	PERRY, Tara	CAN	23.46	
7	4	ZIVKOVIC, Marina	YUG	23.51	
8	8	KALTOUMA, Nadjina	CHA	24.47	

ROUND 1, HEAT 6

Rnk	Ln	Name	Ctry	Result	
1	5	PEREC, Marie-Jose	FRA	22.62	Q
2	3	MILLER, Inger	USA	22.74	Q
3	7	BIKAR, Alenka	SLO	22.88	Q
4	4	KOFFA, Katerina	GRE	23.09	Q
5	8	SAFRONNIKOVA, Natalya	BLR	23.14	q
6	2	FYNES, Sevatheda	BAH	23.39	q
7	1	NKOMA, Georgette	CMR	23.68	
8	6	DMITRIADI, Lyudmila	UZB	24.88	

ROUND 2, HEAT 1

Rnk	Ln	Name	Ctry	Result	
1	3	GUIDRY, Carlette	USA	22.51	Q
2	6	STURRUP, Chandra	BAH	22.81	Q
3	4	GAINSFORD-TAYLOR, Melinda	AUS	22.91	Q
4	2	SAFRONNIKOVA, Natalya	BLR	23.15	Q
5	1	HERNESNIEMI, Sanna	FIN	23.38	
6	8	GACHEVSKA, Monika	BUL	23.44	
7	7	BELLO, Ameerah	ISV	23.66	
	5	McDONALD, Beverly	JAM	DNS	

ROUND 2, HEAT 2

Rnk	Ln	Name	Ctry	Result	
1	4	OTTEY, Merlene	JAM	22.61	Q
2	3	MALCHUGINA, Galina	RUS	22.69	Q
3	5	PASCHKE, Melanie	GER	22.84	Q
4	7	KOFFA, Katerina	GRE	23.04	Q
5	6	MERRY, Katharine	GBR	23.17	
6	8	FYNES, Sevatheda	BAH	23.26	
7	1	YAN, Jiankui	CHN	23.30	
8	2	FOMENKO, Viktoriya	UKR	23.44	

ROUND 2, HEAT 3

Rnk	Ln	Name	Ctry	Result	
1	3	PEREC, Marie-Jose	FRA	22.24	Q
2	5	ONYALI, Mary	NGR	22.37	Q
3	6	MILLER, Inger	USA	22.57	Q
4	1	FREEMAN, Cathy	AUS	22.74	Q
5	4	JARDIM, Lucrecia	POR	22.88	
6	7	JACOBS, Simmone	GBR	22.96	
7	2	MYERS, Sandra	ESP	23.20	
8	8	SAMUEL, Heather	ANT	23.54	

ROUND 2, HEAT 4

Rnk	Ln	Name	Ctry	Result	
1	6	YOUNG, Dannette	USA	22.53	Q
2	4	CUTHBERT, Juliet	JAM	22.62	Q
3	3	PRIVALOVA, Irina	RUS	22.82	Q
4	5	BIKAR, Alenka	SLO	22.89	Q
5	8	MAYBERRY, Myra	PUR	23.48	
6	1	RODRIGUEZ, Patricia	COL	23.50	
7	7	UBAH, Calister	NGR	23.62	
8	2	PINTUSEVYCH, Zhanna	UKR	23.68	

SEMIFINAL 1

Rnk	Ln	Name	Ctry	Result	
1	4	PEREC, Marie-Jose	FRA	22.07	Q
2	3	ONYALI, Mary	NGR	22.16	Q
3	5	CUTHBERT, Juliet	JAM	22.24	Q
4	7	MILLER, Inger	USA	22.33	Q
5	6*	YOUNG, Dannette	USA	22.49	
6	2	FREEMAN, Cathy	AUS	22.78	
7	1	SAFRONNIKOVA, Natalya	BLR	22.98	
	8	PRIVALOVA, Irina	RUS	DNS	

SEMIFINAL 2

Rnk	Ln	Name	Ctry	Result	
1	4	OTTEY, Merlene	JAM	22.08	Q
2	6	MALCHUGINA, Galina	RUS	22.35	Q
3	5	STURRUP, Chandra	BAH	22.54	Q
4	3	GUIDRY, Carlette	USA	22.56	Q
5	2	GAINSFORD-TAYLOR, Melinda	AUS	22.76	
6	7	PASCHKE, Melanie	GER	22.81	
7	8	BIKAR, Alenka	SLO	22.82	
8	1	KOFFA, Katerina	GRE	23.20	

FINAL

Rnk	Ln	Name	Ctry	Result	
1	3	PEREC, Marie-Jose	FRA	22.12	G
2	5	OTTEY, Merlene	JAM	22.24	S
3	4	ONYALI, Mary	NGR	22.38	B
4	7	MILLER, Inger	USA	22.41	
5	6	MALCHUGINA, Galina	RUS	22.45	
6	8	STURRUP, Chandra	BAH	22.54	
7	1	CUTHBERT, Juliet	JAM	22.60	
8	2	GUIDRY, Carlette	USA	22.61	

Athletics / *Athlétisme*
400 m, Men / *400 m, Messieurs*

ROUND 1, HEAT 1

Rnk	Ln	Name	Ctry	Result	
1	3	BLACK, Roger	GBR	45.28	Q
2	2	de SILVA, Neil	TRI	45.34	Q
3	1	BALOSAK, Stefan	SVK	45.86	Q
4	6	MONYE, Jude	NGR	46.10	q
5	7	JOUBERT, Michael	AUS	46.30	
6	5	AKOTO, Kossi	TOG	46.94	
	8	ABDELNASER, Mustafa	LBA	DQ	
	4	HECINI, Amar	ALG	DQ	

ROUND 1, HEAT 2

Rnk	Ln	Name	Ctry	Result	
1	5	CLARKE, Davian	JAM	45.54	Q
2	7	PARRELA, Sanderlei	BRA	45.60	Q
3	1	DOUGLAS, Troy	BER	45.61	Q
4	6	GITONGA, Charles	KEN	45.62	q
5	2	RYSIUKIEWICZ, Piotr	POL	46.07	q
6	3	al-BESHI, Mohammed	KSA	46.82	
7	8	JEAN-MARIE, Ivan	LCA	47.13	
8	4	ABDOU, Hassani	COM	50.17	

ROUND 1, HEAT 3

Rnk	Ln	Name	Ctry	Result	
1	6	HARRISON, Alvin	USA	44.69	Q
2	5	ISMAIL, Ibrahim	QAT	45.61	Q
3	2	GREENE, Paul	AUS	46.12	Q
4	8	OMORI, Shigekazu	JPN	46.30	
5	3	CLERC, Laurent	SUI	46.42	
6	4	SHON, Ju-Il	KOR	46.74	
7	7	BABO, Subul	PNG	48.15	
	1	DIPEBA, Justice	BOT	DNS	

400 m, Men / *400 m, Messieurs*

ROUND 1, HEAT 4					
Rnk	Ln	Name	Ctry	Result	
1	6	COOMBS, Eswort	VIN	45.84	Q
2	5	RAPNOUIL, Jean-Louis	FRA	45.93	Q
3	3	LADEJO, Du'aine	GBR	46.27	Q
4	2	McINTOSH, Troy	BAH	46.42	
5	7	da SILVA, Valdinei	BRA	46.61	
6	1	JONES, Richard	GUY	46.69	
7	4	MOROBE, Mpho	LES	47.54	
8	8	AMIR, Mohamed	MDV	49.67	

ROUND 1, HEAT 5					
Rnk	Ln	Name	Ctry	Result	
1	8	THILAKARATNE, Sugath	SRI	45.79	Q
2	3	JOHNSON, Michael	USA	45.80	Q
3	6	CARDENAS, Alejandro	MEX	45.85	Q
4	1	PHIRI, Bobang	RSA	45.94	q
5	5	OCHIENG, Kennedy	KEN	45.99	q
6	2*	DEMOSTHENOUS, Evripides	CYP	46.76	
7	4	RUBAYIZA, Emmanuel	RWA	49.20	
	7	OGOLA, Francis	UGA	DNF	

ROUND 1, HEAT 6					
Rnk	Ln	Name	Ctry	Result	
1	7	REYNOLDS, Butch	USA	45.42	Q
2	3	MALHERBE, Arnaud	RSA	45.75	Q
3	6	CHIWIRA, Tawanda	ZIM	45.89	Q
4	5	RUSTERHOLZ, Mathias	SUI	45.92	q
5	1	JALLOW, Dawda	GAM	46.73	
6	4	FARRELL, Eugene	IRL	47.18	
7	2	NZE, Casimiro	GEQ	50.14	
	8	HASSAN, Ibrahim	GHA	DNF	

ROUND 1, HEAT 7					
Rnk	Ln	Name	Ctry	Result	
1	1	CHUKWU, Clement	NGR	45.18	Q
2	8	KITUR, Samson	KEN	45.39	Q
3	5	McDONALD, Michael	JAM	45.50	Q
4	6	MOKGANYETSI, Hendrik	RSA	45.89	q
5	4	dos SANTOS, Osmar	BRA	46.16	
6	2	GUY, Robert	TRI	46.80	
7	7	BIGUET, Martial	CAF	48.92	
8	3	ALI, Anwar	YEM	50.81	

ROUND 1, HEAT 8					
Rnk	Ln	Name	Ctry	Result	
1	2	BADA, Sunday	NGR	45.19	Q
2	7	THOMAS, Iwan	GBR	45.22	Q
3	1*	KAMOGA, Davis	UGA	45.56	Q
4	5	MARTIN, Roxbert	JAM	46.01	q
5	8	LADBROOK, Mark	AUS	46.28	
6	6	OLIVER, Carl	BAH	47.41	
7	3	BIYAGO, Kimitene	CHA	48.88	
	4	OUEDRAOGO, Ibrahim	BUR	DNS	

ROUND 2, HEAT 1					
Rnk	Ln	Name	Ctry	Result	
1	3	BADA, Sunday	NGR	44.88	Q
2	4	CLARKE, Davian	JAM	44.98	Q
3	6	KITUR, Samson	KEN	45.03	Q
4	2	DOUGLAS, Troy	BER	45.26	Q
5	5	MALHERBE, Arnaud	RSA	45.26	
6	7	CHIWIRA, Tawanda	ZIM	45.38	
7	8	RUSTERHOLZ, Mathias	SUI	45.72	
8	1	RYSIUKIEWICZ, Piotr	POL	46.19	

ROUND 2, HEAT 2					
Rnk	Ln	Name	Ctry	Result	
1	3	BLACK, Roger	GBR	44.72	Q
2	4	ISMAIL, Ibrahim	QAT	44.96	Q
3	5	REYNOLDS, Butch	USA	45.21	Q
4	8	BALOSAK, Stefan	SVK	45.32	Q
5	7	CARDENAS, Alejandro	MEX	45.33	
6	1	PHIRI, Bobang	RSA	45.51	
7	6	PARRELA, Sanderlei	BRA	45.72	
8	2	OCHIENG, Kennedy	KEN	45.72	

ROUND 2, HEAT 3					
Rnk	Ln	Name	Ctry	Result	
1	6	JOHNSON, Michael	USA	44.62	Q
2	7	MARTIN, Roxbert	JAM	44.74	Q
3	8	KAMOGA, Davis	UGA	44.82	Q
4	4	de SILVA, Neil	TRI	45.02	Q
5	3	CHUKWU, Clement	NGR	45.24	
6	2	LADEJO, Du'aine	GBR	45.62	
7	5	THILAKARATNE, Sugath	SRI	45.78	
8	1	GREENE, Paul	AUS	46.22	

ROUND 2, HEAT 4					
Rnk	Ln	Name	Ctry	Result	
1	4	HARRISON, Alvin	USA	44.79	Q
2	6	THOMAS, Iwan	GBR	45.04	Q
3	7	McDONALD, Michael	JAM	45.26	Q
4	5	COOMBS, Eswort	VIN	45.43	Q
5	3	RAPNOUIL, Jean-Louis	FRA	45.74	
6	1	MOKGANYETSI, Hendrik	RSA	46.48	
	2	MONYE, Jude	NGR	DNF	
	8	GITONGA, Charles	KEN	DNS	

SEMIFINAL 1					
Rnk	Ln	Name	Ctry	Result	
1	4	BLACK, Roger	GBR	44.69	Q
2	3	CLARKE, Davian	JAM	44.87	Q
3	6	ISMAIL, Ibrahim	QAT	45.02	Q
4	5	HARRISON, Alvin	USA	45.04	Q
5	2	KITUR, Samson	KEN	45.17	
6	7	BALOSAK, Stefan	SVK	45.59	
7	8	DOUGLAS, Troy	BER	46.33	
	1	REYNOLDS, Butch	USA	DNF	

SEMIFINAL 2					
Rnk	Ln	Name	Ctry	Result	
1	5	JOHNSON, Michael	USA	44.59	Q
2	6	MARTIN, Roxbert	JAM	44.81	Q
3	1	KAMOGA, Davis	UGA	44.85	Q
4	3	THOMAS, Iwan	GBR	45.01	Q
5	4	BADA, Sunday	NGR	45.30	
6	8	COOMBS, Eswort	VIN	45.36	
7	2	McDONALD, Michael	JAM	45.48	
8	7	de SILVA, Neil	TRI	45.56	

FINAL						
Rnk	Ln	Name	Ctry	Result		
1	4	JOHNSON, Michael	USA	43.49	O	G
2	3	BLACK, Roger	GBR	44.41		S
3	2	KAMOGA, Davis	UGA	44.53		B
4	1	HARRISON, Alvin	USA	44.62		
5	8	THOMAS, Iwan	GBR	44.70		
6	5	MARTIN, Roxbert	JAM	44.83		
7	6	CLARKE, Davian	JAM	44.99		
	7	ISMAIL, Ibrahim	QAT	DNF		

Athletics / *Athlétisme*

400 m, Women / *400 m, Dames*

ROUND 1, HEAT 1					
Rnk	Ln	Name	Ctry	Result	
1	3	DAVIS, Pauline	BAH	51.00	Q
2	1	GONCHARENKO, Svetlana	RUS	51.07	Q
3	8	SMITH, Phylis	GBR	51.29	Q
4	5	POETSCHKA, Renee	AUS	51.55	Q
5	4	KYRIAKOU, Dora	CYP	52.09	q
6	2	BIRUNGI, Grace	UGA	53.12	
7	7	HAOULATA, Ahamada	COM	1:03.44	

ROUND 1, HEAT 2					
Rnk	Ln	Name	Ctry	Result	
1	3	MALONE, Maicel	USA	51.28	Q
2	2	CAMPBELL, Juliet	JAM	51.57	Q
3	1	DINKINS, Grace-Ann	LBR	51.83	Q
4	4	KOTLYAROVA, Olga	RUS	51.90	Q
5	6	BENESOVA, Hana	CZE	52.28	q
6	5	MANUYLOVA, Yana	UKR	52.51	q
7	8	BELLO, Ameerah	ISV	53.40	

ROUND 1, HEAT 3					
Rnk	Ln	Name	Ctry	Result	
1	5	GRAHAM, Kim	USA	51.70	Q
2	7	FUCHSOVA, Helena	CZE	51.71	Q
3	2	YUSUF, Fatima	NGR	52.25	Q
4	1	NAYLOR, Lee	AUS	52.53	Q
5	3	RURAK, Olena	UKR	52.92	
6	6	ZIVKOVIC, Marina	YUG	53.10	
7	4	MANSARAY, Melrose	SLE	54.37	

ROUND 1, HEAT 4					
Rnk	Ln	Name	Ctry	Result	
1	5	de ANGELI, Virna	ITA	51.68	Q
2	7	RICHARDS, Sandie	JAM	51.79	Q
3	3	PEREC, Marie-Jose	FRA	51.82	Q
4	6	ANTOINE, LaDonna	CAN	51.99	Q
5	2	MWANAMWAMBWA, Ngozi	ZAM	54.12	
6	1	ADDY, Mercy	GHA	54.92	
	4	RESTREPO, Ximena	COL	DNF	

ROUND 1, HEAT 5					
Rnk	Ln	Name	Ctry	Result	
1	2	MILES, Jearl	USA	51.96	Q
2	6	BREUER, Grit	GER	52.20	Q
3	1	FRAZER, Merlene	JAM	52.20	Q
4	7	FIGUEIREDO, Maria Magnolia	BRA	52.41	Q
5	5	FRANCIS, Diane	SKN	52.48	q
6	3	STRAKER, Melissa	BAR	52.92	
7	8	CRUZ, Guilhermina	ANG	55.42	

ROUND 1, HEAT 6					
Rnk	Ln	Name	Ctry	Result	
1	5	MYERS, Sandra	ESP	52.54	Q
2	2	OGUNKOYA, Falilat	NGR	52.65	Q
3	3	FRASER, Donna	GBR	52.78	Q
4	8	KOSTOVALOVA, Nadezda	CZE	53.03	Q
5	1	BODRITSKAYA, Svetlana	KAZ	53.24	
6	4	DU, Xiujie	CHN	53.95	
7	7	FRANCO, Arely	ESA	1:01.38	

400 m, Women / *400 m, Dames*

ROUND 1, HEAT 7

Rnk	Ln	Name	Ctry	Result	
1	8	AFOLABI, Bisi	NGR	51.80	Q
2	4	FREEMAN, Catherine	AUS	51.99	Q
3	6	KOZAK, Anna	BLR	52.39	Q
4	1	SPURI, Patrizia	ITA	52.45	Q
5	3	STEWART, Zoila	CRC	52.66	
6	2	SIMASOTCHI, Corinne	SUI	53.69	
7	7	OUABANGUI, Denise	CAF	55.74	

ROUND 2, HEAT 1

Rnk	Ln	Name	Ctry	Result	
1	3	FREEMAN, Catherine	AUS	50.43	Q
2	4	BREUER, Grit	GER	50.57	Q
3	6	GRAHAM, Kim	USA	50.96	Q
4	5	AFOLABI, Bisi	NGR	51.07	Q
5	7	BENESOVA, Hana	CZE	51.30	
6	2	KOTLYAROVA, Olga	RUS	51.36	
7	8	FRASER, Donna	GBR	51.58	
8	1	KYRIAKOU, Dora	CYP	52.26	

ROUND 2, HEAT 2

Rnk	Ln	Name	Ctry	Result	
1	3	PEREC, Marie-Jose	FRA	51.00	Q
2	5	DAVIS, Pauline	BAH	51.08	Q
3	4	CAMPBELL, Juliet	JAM	51.17	Q
4	6	GONCHARENKO, Svetlana	RUS	51.35	Q
5	2	FIGUEIREDO, Maria Magnolia	BRA	51.98	
6	8	ANTOINE, LaDonna	CAN	52.03	
7	7	DINKINS, Grace-Ann	LBR	52.53	
8	1	MANUYLOVA, Yana	UKR	52.82	

ROUND 2, HEAT 3

Rnk	Ln	Name	Ctry	Result	
1	5	OGUNKOYA, Falilat	NGR	50.65	Q
2	6	MILES, Jearl	USA	50.84	Q
3	4	RICHARDS, Sandie	JAM	51.22	Q
4	2	POETSCHKA, Renee	AUS	51.33	Q
5	3	de ANGELI, Virna	ITA	51.77	
6	8	KOZAK, Anna	BLR	52.14	
7	7	FRANCIS, Diane	SKN	52.24	
8	1	KOSTOVALOVA, Nadezda	CZE	53.21	

ROUND 2, HEAT 4

Rnk	Ln	Name	Ctry	Result	
1	6	MALONE, Maicel	USA	51.16	Q
2	1	YUSUF, Fatima	NGR	51.27	Q
3	3	MYERS, Sandra	ESP	51.53	Q
4	7	FRAZER, Merlene	JAM	51.57	Q
5	5	FUCHSOVA, Helena	CZE	51.70	
6	4	SMITH, Phylis	GBR	52.16	
7	8	SPURI, Patrizia	ITA	52.78	
8	2	NAYLOR, Lee	AUS	53.75	

SEMIFINAL 1

Rnk	Ln	Name	Ctry	Result	
1	3	FREEMAN, Catherine	AUS	50.32	Q
2	6	YUSUF, Fatima	NGR	50.36	Q
3	8	RICHARDS, Sandie	JAM	50.74	Q
4	4	BREUER, Grit	GER	50.75	Q
5	2	GRAHAM, Kim	USA	51.13	
6	5	MALONE, Maicel	USA	51.16	
7	1	FRAZER, Merlene	JAM	51.18	
8	7	AFOLABI, Bisi	NGR	51.40	

SEMIFINAL 2

Rnk	Ln	Name	Ctry	Result	
1	5	PEREC, Marie-Jose	FRA	49.19	Q
2	4	OGUNKOYA, Falilat	NGR	49.57	Q
3	3	DAVIS, Pauline	BAH	49.85	Q
4	6	MILES, Jearl	USA	50.21	Q
5	7	GONCHARENKO, Svetlana	RUS	50.84	
6	8	MYERS, Sandra	ESP	51.42	
7	2	POETSCHKA, Renee	AUS	51.49	
8	1	CAMPBELL, Juliet	JAM	51.65	

FINAL

Rnk	Ln	Name	Ctry	Result		
1	3	PEREC, Marie-Jose	FRA	48.25	O	**G**
2	4	FREEMAN, Catherine	AUS	48.63		**S**
3	5	OGUNKOYA, Falilat	NGR	49.10		**B**
4	2	DAVIS, Pauline	BAH	49.28		
5	8	MILES, Jearl	USA	49.55		
6	6	YUSUF, Fatima	NGR	49.77		
7	7	RICHARDS, Sandie	JAM	50.45		
8	1	BREUER, Grit	GER	50.71		

Athletics / *Athlétisme*
800 m, Men / *800 m, Messieurs*

ROUND 1, HEAT 1

Rnk	Or	Name	Ctry	Result	
1	5	RODAL, Vebjorn	NOR	1:45.30	Q
2	3	ROBB, Curtis	GBR	1:45.85	Q
3	1	BARBOSA, Jose Luiz	BRA	1:46.58	q
4	7	MATTHEWS, David	IRL	1:46.76	q
5	4	DEHMEL, Joachim	GER	1:47.12	
6	6	RAKOTOARIMANANA, Joseph	MAD	1:47.33	
7	2	ASINGA, Tommy	SUR	1:48.29	

Best Intermediate Time

	Name	Ctry	Result
400 m	BARBOSA, Jose Luiz	BRA	50.79

ROUND 1, HEAT 2

Rnk	Or	Name	Ctry	Result	
1	2	KIBITOK, Philip	KEN	1:45.34	Q
2	6	MOTCHEBON, Nico	GER	1:45.82	Q
3	5	KONCZYLO, Bruno	FRA	1:46.04	q
4	7	HECINI, Adem	ALG	1:47.23	
5	3	ABDULLA, Abdulrahman	QAT	1:48.52	
6	4	GODOY, Flavio	BRA	1:48.91	
7	1	AIDARA, Cherif	MTN	1:56.20	

Best Intermediate Time

	Name	Ctry	Result
400 m	ABDULLA, Abdulrahman	QAT	52.03

ROUND 1, HEAT 3

Rnk	Or	Name	Ctry	Result	
1	2	TELLEZ, Norberto	CUB	1:47.24	Q
2	7	WINROW, Craig	GBR	1:47.41	Q
3	1	SOUKUP, Pavel	CZE	1:47.67	
4	5	DIAZ, Andres	ESP	1:47.86	
5	6	DOUGLAS, Atle	NOR	1:48.60	
6	3	HARRIS, Cedric	DMA	1:51.46	
7	4	ARLETE, Fernando	GBS	2:00.07	

Best Intermediate Time

	Name	Ctry	Result
400 m	DIAZ, Andres	ESP	53.66

ROUND 1, HEAT 4

Rnk	Or	Name	Ctry	Result	
1	3	KIPTOO, David	KEN	1:45.11	Q
2	5	d'URSO, Giuseppe	ITA	1:45.27	Q
3	6	BOTHA, Johan	RSA	1:45.63	q
4	4	JEAN-JOSEPH, Jimmy	FRA	1:45.64	q
5	7	ADEN, Ibrahim	SOM	1:47.31	
6	8	NKAZAMYAMPI, Charles	BDI	1:47.95	
7	1	KAILES, Tavakalo	VAN	1:55.07	
8	2	ISMAIL, Naseer	MDV	1:58.70	

Best Intermediate Time

	Name	Ctry	Result
400 m	JEAN-JOSEPH, Jimmy	FRA	51.59

ROUND 1, HEAT 5

Rnk	Or	Name	Ctry	Result	
1	3	GRAY, Johnny	USA	1:45.87	Q
2	6	TUPURITIS, Einars	LAT	1:45.88	Q
3	4	NGIDHI, Savieri	ZIM	1:46.46	q
4	5	KORANYI, Balazs	HUN	1:46.63	q
5	2	ABRANTES, Antonio	POR	1:47.73	
6	7	TERRELONGE, Clive	JAM	1:48.29	
7	1	MAKHANYA, Themba	SWZ	1:59.02	

Best Intermediate Time

	Name	Ctry	Result
400 m	GRAY, Johnny	USA	50.63

ROUND 1, HEAT 6

Rnk	Or	Name	Ctry	Result	
1	2	HATUNGIMANA, Arthemon	BDI	1:47.10	Q
2	5	BENVENUTI, Andrea	ITA	1:47.45	Q
3	4	van HEERDEN, Marius	RSA	1:47.46	
4	3	STRANG, David	GBR	1:47.96	
5	1	KAVESHNIKOV, Boris	KGZ	1:48.88	
6	7	PARRILLA, Jose	USA	1:49.99	
7	6	TERAP ADOUM, Yaya	CHA	1:52.68	

Best Intermediate Time

	Name	Ctry	Result
400 m	van HEERDEN, Marius	RSA	53.36

800 m, Men / *800 m, Messieurs*

ROUND 1, HEAT 7

Rnk	Or	Name	Ctry	Result	
1	3	LAHLOU, Benyounes	MAR	1:45.85	Q
2	4	ONYANCHA, Fred	KEN	1:46.07	Q
3	1	BYRNE, Paul	AUS	1:47.05	q
4	7	MORGAN, Alex	JAM	1:47.40	
5	2	BABIKER, Mohamed	SUD	1:48.50	
6	6	MOLINARI, Manlio	SMR	1:56.08	
	5	PARRA, Roberto	ESP	DNS	

Best Intermediate Time

	Name	Ctry	Result
400 m	BABIKER, Mohamed	SUD	52.65

ROUND 1, HEAT 8

Rnk	Or	Name	Ctry	Result	
1	6	SEPENG, Hezekiel	RSA	1:46.45	Q
2	4	BUCHER, Andre	SUI	1:46.85	Q
3	3	GIOCONDI, Andrea	ITA	1:47.26	
4	5	ROCK, Brandon	USA	1:48.47	
5	2	DESTINE, Jean	HAI	1:48.82	
6	1	BASWEIDAN, Saeed	YEM	1:49.35	
7	7	RHYMER, Greg	IVB	1:50.03	

Best Intermediate Time

	Name	Ctry	Result
400 m	Information Not Available		

SEMIFINAL 1

Rnk	Or	Name	Ctry	Result	
1	5	SEPENG, Hezekiel	RSA	1:45.16	Q
2	6	MOTCHEBON, Nico	GER	1:45.40	Q
3	3	KIBITOK, Philip	KEN	1:45.58	
4	2	BUCHER, Andre	SUI	1:46.41	
5	4	d'URSO, Giuseppe	ITA	1:46.97	
6	7	BYRNE, Paul	AUS	1:47.58	
7	1	KONCZYLO, Bruno	FRA	1:48.02	
8	8	WINROW, Craig	GBR	1:48.57	

Best Intermediate Time

	Name	Ctry	Result
400 m	KONCZYLO, Bruno	FRA	52.96

SEMIFINAL 2

Rnk	Or	Name	Ctry	Result	
1	5	LAHLOU, Benyounes	MAR	1:43.99	Q
2	3	GRAY, Johnny	USA	1:44.00	Q
3	4	ONYANCHA, Fred	KEN	1:44.02	q
4	6	HATUNGIMANA, Arthemon	BDI	1:44.92	
5	7	NGIDHI, Savieri	ZIM	1:46.78	
6	2	ROBB, Curtis	GBR	1:47.48	
7	1	BOTHA, Johan	RSA	1:48.06	
8	8	BARBOSA, Jose Luiz	BRA	1:50.33	

Best Intermediate Time

	Name	Ctry	Result
400 m	GRAY, Johnny	USA	50.72

SEMIFINAL 3

Rnk	Or	Name	Ctry	Result	
1	4	TELLEZ, Norberto	CUB	1:43.79	Q
2	3	KIPTOO, David	KEN	1:43.90	Q
3	6	RODAL, Vebjorn	NOR	1:43.96	q
4	5	TUPURITIS, Einars	LAT	1:46.41	
5	8	MATTHEWS, David	IRL	1:47.83	
6	1	JEAN-JOSEPH, Jimmy	FRA	1:48.50	
7	7	KORANYI, Balazs	HUN	1:50.30	
	2	BENVENUTI, Andrea	ITA	DNF	

Best Intermediate Time

	Name	Ctry	Result
400 m	KIPTOO, David	KEN	51.65

FINAL

Rnk	Or	Name	Ctry	Result	
1	1	RODAL, Vebjorn	NOR	1:42.58	O G
2	6	SEPENG, Hezekiel	RSA	1:42.74	S
3	7	ONYANCHA, Fred	KEN	1:42.79	B
4	4	TELLEZ, Norberto	CUB	1:42.85	
5	8	MOTCHEBON, Nico	GER	1:43.91	
6	5	KIPTOO, David	KEN	1:44.19	
7	2	GRAY, Johnny	USA	1:44.21	
8	3	LAHLOU, Benyounes	MAR	1:45.52	

Best Intermediate Time

	Name	Ctry	Result
400 m	GRAY, Johnny	USA	49.55

Athletics / *Athlétisme*
800 m, Women / *800 m, Dames*

ROUND 1, HEAT 1

Rnk	Or	Name	Ctry	Result	
1	3	MASTERKOVA, Svetlana	RUS	1:59.67	Q
2	5	VRIESDE, Laetitia	SUR	1:59.71	Q
3	4	MENDES, Luciana	BRA	2:00.25	
4	1	BENIDA, Noria	ALG	2:02.44	
5	2	ZHANG, Jian	CHN	2:04.17	
6	6	TSIBA, Leontine	CGO	2:08.58	
7	8	GARCIA, Sharette	BIZ	2:13.52	
	7	PAULINO, Tina	MOZ	DNS	

Best Intermediate Time

	Name	Ctry	Result
400 m	MENDES, Luciana	BRA	57.74

ROUND 1, HEAT 2

Rnk	Or	Name	Ctry	Result	
1	5	MUTOLA, Maria Lurdes	MOZ	1:58.98	Q
2	6	AFANASYEVA, Yelena	RUS	1:59.18	Q
3	3	KISABAKA, Linda	GER	1:59.56	q
4	1	DORSILE, Viviane	FRA	2:00.02	q
5	7	COELHO, Eduarda	POR	2:03.22	
6	8	ORELLANA, Marta	ARG	2:04.99	
	2	MODAHL, Diane	GBR	DNF	

Best Intermediate Time

	Name	Ctry	Result
400 m	MODAHL, Diane	GBR	58.23

ROUND 1, HEAT 3

Rnk	Or	Name	Ctry	Result	
1	6	DUKHNOVA, Natasha	BLR	1:59.23	Q
2	2	HODGKINSON, Toni	NZL	1:59.35	Q
3	7	WILLIAMS, Dawn	DMA	1:59.65	q
4	5	RAINEY, Meredith	USA	1:59.96	q
5	4	TSYOMA, Lyubov	RUS	2:00.18	q
6	8	CROOKS, Charmaine	CAN	2:00.27	
7	1	NASHEEDA, Yaznee	MDV	2:36.85	
	3	MENENDEZ, Ana	ESP	DNF	

Best Intermediate Time

	Name	Ctry	Result
400 m	CROOKS, Charmaine	CAN	57.43

ROUND 1, HEAT 4

Rnk	Or	Name	Ctry	Result	
1	2	QUIROT, Ana Fidelia	CUB	1:59.98	Q
2	4	JONGMANS, Stella	NED	2:00.26	Q
3	3	CLARK, Joetta	USA	2:00.38	
4	7	EWERLOF, Malin	SWE	2:01.61	
5	5	STRASHILOVA, Petya	BUL	2:02.13	
6	8	LIGHTFOOT, Lisa	AUS	2:02.88	
7	6	JOSEPH, Restituta	TAN	2:08.31	

Best Intermediate Time

	Name	Ctry	Result
400 m	QUIROT, Ana Fidelia	CUB	58.52

ROUND 1, HEAT 5

Rnk	Or	Name	Ctry	Result	
1	8	HOLMES, Kelly	GBR	1:58.80	Q
2	7	DJATE-TAILLARD, Patricia	FRA	1:58.98	Q
3	2	FORMANOVA, Ludmila	CZE	1:59.37	q
4	3	HAMILTON, Suzy	USA	2:00.47	
5	5	TURNER, Inez	JAM	2:01.48	
6	4	DULECHA, Kutre	ETH	2:04.80	
	1	N'JIE, Adama	GAM	DNF	

Best Intermediate Time

	Name	Ctry	Result
400m	DJATE-TAILLARD, Patricia	FRA	59.11

800 m, Women / *800 m, Dames*

SEMIFINAL 1

Rnk	Or	Name	Ctry	Result	
1	6	MASTERKOVA, Svetlana	RUS	1:57.95	Q
2	4	QUIROT, Ana Fidelia	CUB	1:57.99	Q
3	3	HOLMES, Kelly	GBR	1:58.49	Q
4	5	DUKHNOVA, Natasha	BLR	1:58.67	Q
5	7	WILLIAMS, Dawn	DMA	1:59.06	
6	1	KISABAKA, Linda	GER	1:59.23	
7	2	DORSILE, Viviane	FRA	2:00.68	
	8	JONGMANS, Stella	NED	DNF	

Best Intermediate Time

	Name	Ctry	Result
400 m	QUIROT, Ana Fidelia	CUB	56.62

SEMIFINAL 2

Rnk	Or	Name	Ctry	Result	
1	6	MUTOLA, Maria Lurdes	MOZ	1:57.62	Q
2	2	AFANASYEVA, Yelena	RUS	1:57.77	Q
3	3	DJATE-TAILLARD, Patricia	FRA	1:57.93	Q
4	1	HODGKINSON, Toni	NZL	1:58.25	Q
5	5	VRIESDE, Laetitia	SUR	1:58.29	
6	8	FORMANOVA, Ludmila	CZE	1:59.28	
7	4	RAINEY, Meredith	USA	1:59.36	
8	7	TSYOMA, Lyubov	RUS	2:02.50	

Best Intermediate Time

	Name	Ctry	Result
400 m	Information Not Available		

FINAL

Rnk	Or	Name	Ctry	Result	
1	3	MASTERKOVA, Svetlana	RUS	1:57.73	G
2	6	QUIROT, Ana Fidelia	CUB	1:58.11	S
3	5	MUTOLA, Maria Lurdes	MOZ	1:58.71	B
4	2	HOLMES, Kelly	GBR	1:58.81	
5	4	AFANASYEVA, Yelena	RUS	1:59.57	
6	8	DJATE-TAILLARD, Patricia	FRA	1:59.61	
7	7	DUKHNOVA, Natasha	BLR	2:00.32	
8	1	HODGKINSON, Toni	NZL	2:00.54	

Best Intermediate Time

	Name	Ctry	Result
400m	MASTERKOVA, Svetlana	RUS	58.43

Athletics / *Athlétisme*

1,500 m, Men / *1 500 m, Messieurs*

ROUND 1, HEAT 1

Rnk	Or	Name	Ctry	Result	
1	1	ROTICH, Laban	KEN	3:35.88	Q
2	10	KOERS, Marko	NED	3:36.18	Q
3	3	BRUTON, Niall	IRL	3:37.42	Q
4	11	McKAY, Kevin	GBR	3:38.02	Q
5	8	OLTEANU, Ovidiu	ROM	3:38.33	
6	7	SHABUNIN, Vyacheslav	RUS	3:38.56	
7	6	de OLIVEIRA, Edgar	BRA	3:40.70	
8	4	AGAR, Steve	DMA	3:43.02	
9	5	HYDE, Brian	USA	3:48.20	
10	9	BULKOVSKIY, Andriy	UKR	3:53.30	
11	2	KEIRUAN, Tawai	VAN	4:02.78	

Best Intermediate Times

	Name	Ctry	Result
400 m	de OLIVEIRA, Edgar	BRA	57.01
800 m	de OLIVEIRA, Edgar	BRA	1:56.58
1200 m	ROTICH, Laban	KEN	2:55.33

ROUND 1, HEAT 2

Rnk	Or	Name	Ctry	Result	
1	7	MORCELI, Noureddine	ALG	3:41.95	Q
2	9	MAYOCK, John	GBR	3:42.31	Q
3	3	BILE, Abdi	SOM	3:42.32	Q
4	4	ESTEVEZ, Reyes	ESP	3:42.48	Q
5	5	el BASIR, Rachid	MAR	3:42.85	
6	2	ACHON, Julius	UGA	3:43.08	
7	8	JESUS, Luis	POR	3:44.65	
8	1	CRUZ, Joaquim	BRA	3:45.32	
9	6	N'TYAMBA, Joao	ANG	3:46.41	
10	10	IBRAHIM, Ali	DJI	3:46.62	
11	11	GOTTSCHALK, Michael	GER	3:56.46	

Best Intermediate Times

	Name	Ctry	Result
400 m	CRUZ, Joaquim	BRA	1:01.85
800 m	IBRAHIM, Ali	DJI	2:05.16
1200 m	MORCELI, Noureddine	ALG	3:01.37

ROUND 1, HEAT 3

Rnk	Or	Name	Ctry	Result	
1	11	HAKIMI, Ali	TUN	3:36.58	Q
2	2	KIPKORIR, Stephen	KEN	3:36.70	Q
3	1	TOLGYESI, Balazs	HUN	3:36.71	Q
4	10	MAAZOUZI, Driss	MAR	3:37.08	Q
5	8	HEALY, Shane	IRL	3:37.28	q
6	12	ZORKO, Branko	CRO	3:37.35	q
7	6	SULEIMAN, Mohammed	QAT	3:37.70	q
8	7	DAMIAN, Mickael	FRA	3:39.21	
9	4	PYRAH, Jason	USA	3:39.91	
10	5	TRAVASSOS, Antonio	POR	3:42.01	
11	3	JOHNS, Martin	NZL	3:44.91	
12	9	RIYAZ, Hussain	MDV	4:15.14	

Best Intermediate Times

	Name	Ctry	Result
400 m	TOLGYESI, Balazs	HUN	56.41
800 m	KIPKORIR, Stephen	KEN	1:56.65
1200 m	KIPKORIR, Stephen	KEN	2:55.00

ROUND 1, HEAT 4

Rnk	Or	Name	Ctry	Result	
1	11	el GUERROUJ, Hicham	MAR	3:37.66	Q
2	6	TANUI, William	KEN	3:37.72	Q
3	4	CHEKHEMANI, Kader	FRA	3:37.81	Q
4	10	VICIOSA, Isaac	ESP	3:37.93	Q
5	8	FEITEIRA, Luis	POR	3:38.09	q
6	2	O'SULLIVAN, Marcus	IRL	3:38.16	
7	9	PHILIPP, Peter	SUI	3:41.60	
8	7	EDLER-MUHR, Werner	AUT	3:45.02	
9	5	SHARANGABO, Alexis	RWA	3:46.42	
10	3	EZAYEDI, Ali Mabruk	LBA	3:51.49	
	1	HOOD, Graham	CAN	DNF	

Best Intermediate Times

	Name	Ctry	Result
400 m	TANUI, William	KEN	57.96
800 m	el GUERROUJ, Hicham	MAR	1:58.84
1200 m	el GUERROUJ, Hicham	MAR	2:56.69

ROUND 1, HEAT 5

Rnk	Or	Name	Ctry	Result	
1	12	CACHO, Fermin	ESP	3:39.84	Q
2	9	McMULLEN, Paul	USA	3:39.94	Q
3	3	IMPENS, Christophe	BEL	3:40.16	Q
4	6	WHITEMAN, Anthony	GBR	3:40.74	Q
5	7	LOGINOV, Andrey	RUS	3:40.99	
6	1	KWIZERA, Dieudonne	BDI	3:41.45	
7	10	KRAMA, Ahmed	ALG	3:42.09	
8	5	PRASAD, Bahadur	IND	3:46.16	
9	11	DUBUS, Eric	FRA	3:47.01	
10	2	EBNER, Thomas	AUT	3:48.38	
11	4	CLEARY, Paul	AUS	3:52.85	
12	8	KOLE, Selwyn	SOL	4:03.44	

Best Intermediate Times

	Name	Ctry	Result
400 m	EBNER, Thomas	AUT	1:00.65
800 m	EBNER, Thomas	AUT	2:02.45
1200 m	CACHO, Fermin	ESP	2:59.20

1,500 m, Men / *1 500 m, Messieurs*

SEMIFINAL 1

Rnk	Or	Name	Ctry	Result	
1	10	MORCELI, Noureddine	ALG	3:32.88	Q
2	1	CACHO, Fermin	ESP	3:33.12	Q
3	2	BILE, Abdi	SOM	3:33.30	Q
4	4	TANUI, William	KEN	3:33.57	Q
5	12	ROTICH, Laban	KEN	3:33.73	Q
6	9	MAAZOUZI, Driss	MAR	3:34.35	q
7	6	MAYOCK, John	GBR	3:34.55	q
8	7	CHEKHEMANI, Kader	FRA	3:34.84	
9	8	ZORKO, Branko	CRO	3:35.14	
10	3	TOLGYESI, Balazs	HUN	3:35.57	
11	11	FEITEIRA, Luis	POR	3:40.31	
12	5	BRUTON, Niall	IRL	3:42.88	

Best Intermediate Times

	Name	Ctry	Result
400 m	TOLGYESI, Balazs	HUN	54.92
800 m	TOLGYESI, Balazs	HUN	1:54.06
1200 m	TANUI, William	KEN	2:52.55

SEMIFINAL 2

Rnk	Or	Name	Ctry	Result	
1	12	el GUERROUJ, Hicham	MAR	3:35.29	Q
2	1	KIPKORIR, Stephen	KEN	3:35.53	Q
3	2	HAKIMI, Ali	TUN	3:35.91	Q
4	5	SULEIMAN, Mohammed	QAT	3:36.01	Q
5	8	KOERS, Marko	NED	3:36.06	Q
6	11	VICIOSA, Isaac	ESP	3:36.11	
7	6	WHITEMAN, Anthony	GBR	3:36.11	
8	4	IMPENS, Christophe	BEL	3:37.64	
9	10	McMULLEN, Paul	USA	3:37.81	
10	3	ESTEVEZ, Reyes	ESP	3:39.44	
11	7	HEALY, Shane	IRL	3:39.81	
12	9	McKAY, Kevin	GBR	3:43.61	

Best Intermediate Times

	Name	Ctry	Result
400 m	KIPKORIR, Stephen	KEN	58.75
800 m	KIPKORIR, Stephen	KEN	1:58.41
1200 m	el GUERROUJ, Hicham	MAR	2:54.60

FINAL

Rnk	Or	Name	Ctry	Result	
1	2	MORCELI, Noureddine	ALG	3:35.78	G
2	3	CACHO, Fermin	ESP	3:36.40	S
3	1	KIPKORIR, Stephen	KEN	3:36.72	B
4	11	ROTICH, Laban	KEN	3:37.39	
5	10	TANUI, William	KEN	3:37.42	
6	4	BILE, Abdi	SOM	3:38.03	
7	6	KOERS, Marko	NED	3:38.18	
8	9	HAKIMI, Ali	TUN	3:38.19	
9	7	SULEIMAN, Mohammed	QAT	3:38.26	
10	5	MAAZOUZI, Driss	MAR	3:39.65	
11	12	MAYOCK, John	GBR	3:40.18	
12	8	el GUERROUJ, Hicham	MAR	3:40.75	

Best Intermediate Times

	Name	Ctry	Result
400 m	KIPKORIR, Stephen	KEN	1:01.03
800 m	KIPKORIR, Stephen	KEN	2:01.63
1200 m	MORCELI, Noureddine	ALG	2:55.12

Athletics / *Athlétisme*
1,500 m, Women / *1 500 m, Dames*

ROUND 1, HEAT 1

Rnk	Or	Name	Ctry	Result	
1	3	KIESL, Theresia	AUT	4:09.24	Q
2	1	MASTERKOVA, Svetlana	RUS	4:09.88	Q
3	10	BOULMERKA, Hassiba	ALG	4:09.96	Q
4	11	WUESTENHAGEN, Carmen	GER	4:10.06	Q
5	9	DELAHUNTY, Sinead	IRL	4:10.20	Q
6	5	GRIFFITHS, Gwen	RSA	4:10.80	Q
7	2	BRZEZINSKA, Anna	POL	4:11.06	q
8	6	PELLS, Leah	CAN	4:13.17	q
9	7	QUENTIN, Frederique	FRA	4:15.95	
10	8	HENNER, Juli	USA	4:27.14	
11	4	HTWE, Khin Khin	MYA	4:30.64	

Best Intermediate Times

	Name	Ctry	Result
400 m	QUENTIN, Frederique	FRA	1:02.92
800 m	QUENTIN, Frederique	FRA	2:18.36
1200 m	KIESL, Theresia	AUT	3:23.72

ROUND 1, HEAT 2

Rnk	Or	Name	Ctry	Result	
1	3	BORISOVA, Lyudmila	RUS	4:13.29	Q
2	5	MUGO, Naomi	KEN	4:13.35	Q
3	8	SACRAMENTO, Carla	POR	4:13.57	Q
4	9	GHEORGHIU, Catalina	ROM	4:13.82	Q
5	2	BITZNER-DUCRET, Blandine	FRA	4:13.83	Q
6	11	ZUNIGA, Maite	ESP	4:14.05	Q
7	4	KUHNEMUND, Sylvia	GER	4:14.35	q
8	1	DUKHNOVA, Natasha	BLR	4:14.75	q
9	10	HUBER, Vicki	USA	4:14.82	
10	6	O'SULLIVAN, Sonia	IRL	4:19.77	
11	7	STRASHILOVA, Petya	BUL	4:26.66	

Best Intermediate Times

	Name	Ctry	Result
400 m	KUHNEMUND, Sylvia	GER	1:07.32
800 m	GHEORGHIU, Catalina	ROM	2:18.53
1200 m	GHEORGHIU, Catalina	ROM	3:27.59

ROUND 1, HEAT 3

Rnk	Or	Name	Ctry	Result	
1	2	SZABO, Gabriela	ROM	4:07.32	Q
2	6	HOLMES, Kelly	GBR	4:07.36	Q
3	5	JACOBS, Regina	USA	4:07.41	Q
4	3	CROWLEY, Margaret	AUS	4:07.51	Q
5	7	RYDZ, Malgorzata	POL	4:07.51	Q
6	4	ROGACHOVA, Lyudmila	RUS	4:07.61	Q
7	8	DULECHA, Kutre	ETH	4:07.69	q
8	9	EWERLOF, Malin	SWE	4:09.06	q
9	10	DOMINGUEZ, Marta	ESP	4:15.00	
10	1	SCHNURR, Paula	CAN	4:29.67	

Best Intermediate Times

	Name	Ctry	Result
400 m	EWERLOF, Malin	SWE	1:06.66
800 m	EWERLOF, Malin	SWE	2:14.93
1200 m	EWERLOF, Malin	SWE	3:21.47

SEMIFINAL 1

Rnk	Or	Name	Ctry	Result	
1	10	KIESL, Theresia	AUT	4:09.44	Q
2	11	SZABO, Gabriela	ROM	4:09.83	Q
3	1	MASTERKOVA, Svetlana	RUS	4:10.35	Q
4	3	RYDZ, Malgorzata	POL	4:10.77	Q
5	5	GRIFFITHS, Gwen	RSA	4:11.12	Q
6	6	DUKHNOVA, Natasha	BLR	4:11.43	
7	4	WUESTENHAGEN, Carmen	GER	4:11.47	
8	9	BITZNER-DUCRET, Blandine	FRA	4:12.27	
9	7	DELAHUNTY, Sinead	IRL	4:12.52	
10	8	ZUNIGA, Maite	ESP	4:14.10	
11	12	ROGACHOVA, Lyudmila	RUS	4:14.54	
12	2	BOULMERKA, Hassiba	ALG	4:23.86	

Best Intermediate Times

	Name	Ctry	Result
400 m	SZABO, Gabriela	ROM	1:10.86
800 m	DELAHUNTY, Sinead	IRL	2:18.74
1200 m	DELAHUNTY, Sinead	IRL	3:24.93

SEMIFINAL 2

Rnk	Or	Name	Ctry	Result	
1	3	HOLMES, Kelly	GBR	4:05.88	Q
2	8	JACOBS, Regina	USA	4:06.13	Q
3	12	CROWLEY, Margaret	AUS	4:06.21	Q
4	6	PELLS, Leah	CAN	4:06.26	Q
5	7	SACRAMENTO, Carla	POR	4:06.70	Q
6	4	BORISOVA, Lyudmila	RUS	4:06.89	q
7	1	BRZEZINSKA, Anna	POL	4:07.17	q
8	9	DULECHA, Kutre	ETH	4:09.03	
9	2	EWERLOF, Malin	SWE	4:13.85	
10	5	KUEHNEMUND, Sylvia	GER	4:16.85	
11	10	MUGO, Naomi	KEN	4:20.01	q
	11	GHEORGHIU, Catalina	ROM	DQ	

Best Intermediate Times

	Name	Ctry	Result
400 m	GHEORGHIU, Catalina	ROM	1:06.68
800 m	EWERLOF, Malin	SWE	2:14.12
1200 m	JACOBS, Regina	USA	3:20.37

FINAL

Rnk	Or	Name	Ctry	Result	
1	10	MASTERKOVA, Svetlana	RUS	4:00.83	G
2	11	SZABO, Gabriela	ROM	4:01.54	S
3	5	KIESL, Theresia	AUT	4:03.02	B
4	7	PELLS, Leah	CAN	4:03.56	
5	2	CROWLEY, Margaret	AUS	4:03.79	
6	1	SACRAMENTO, Carla	POR	4:03.91	
7	4	BORISOVA, Lyudmila	RUS	4:05.90	
8	12	RYDZ, Malgorzata	POL	4:05.92	
9	3	GRIFFITHS, Gwen	RSA	4:06.33	
10	13	JACOBS, Regina	USA	4:07.21	
11	6	HOLMES, Kelly	GBR	4:07.46	
12	8	BRZEZINSKA, Anna	POL	4:08.27	
	9	MUGO, Naomi	KEN	DNS	

Best Intermediate Times

	Name	Ctry	Result
400 m	HOLMES, Kelly	GBR	1:02.66
800 m	HOLMES, Kelly	GBR	2:10.55
1200 m	HOLMES, Kelly	GBR	3:16.63

Athletics / *Athlétisme*

5,000 m, Men / *5 000 m, Messieurs*

ROUND 1, HEAT 1

Rnk	Or	Name	Ctry	Result	
1	8	SGHIR, Smail	MAR	14:02.71	Q
2	7	KORORIA, Shem	KEN	14:02.75	Q
3	6	BENZINE, Reda	ALG	14:03.06	Q
4	4	di NAPOLI, Genny	ITA	14:03.56	Q
5	13	CREIGHTON, Shaun	AUS	14:04.08	Q
6	9	HOFF, Shadrack	RSA	14:05.97	Q
7	5	JIMENEZ, Anacleto	ESP	14:16.57	Q
8	10	RAMOS, Jose	POR	14:17.26	Q
9	2	GIUSTO, Matt	USA	14:30.76	
10	12	ROLDAN, William	COL	14:39.50	
11	11	OULD MOHAMEDOU, Sidi Ahmed	MTN	15:29.16	
	1	GEBRSELASSIE, Haile	ETH	DNS	
	3	QUINTANILLA, Armando	MEX	DNS	

Best Intermediate Times

	Name	Ctry	Result
1000 m	ROLDAN, William	COL	2:50.73
2000 m	ROLDAN, William	COL	5:40.78
3000 m	ROLDAN, William	COL	8:35.70
4000 m	KORORIA, Shem	KEN	11:27.44

ROUND 1, HEAT 2

Rnk	Or	Name	Ctry	Result	
1	14	BAYISSA, Fita	ETH	13:50.61	Q
2	5	LAHLAFI, Brahim	MAR	13:51.25	Q
3	9	NYARIKI, Tom	KEN	13:51.47	Q
4	11	MOLINA, Enrique	ESP	13:51.55	Q
5	10	BELAOUT, Aissa	ALG	13:51.96	Q
6	12	BAUMANN, Dieter	GER	13:52.00	Q
7	1	NUTTALL, John	GBR	13:52.16	Q
8	7	WYATT, Jonathan	NZL	13:52.56	Q
9	6	SPIVEY, Jim	USA	13:53.16	q
10	13	FINNERTY, Cormac	IRL	13:54.01	q
11	3	PAYNTER, Julian	AUS	14:00.25	q
12	2	GARCIA, Adalberto	BRA	14:28.64	
13	4	MOYO, Henry	MAW	14:30.53	
	8	NIZIGAMA, Aloys	BDI	DNS	

Best Intermediate Times

	Name	Ctry	Result
1000 m	WYATT, Jonathan	NZL	2:54.66
2000 m	WYATT, Jonathan	NZL	5:46.39
3000 m	PAYNTER, Julian	AUS	8:36.11
4000 m	WYATT, Jonathan	NZL	11:22.79

ROUND 1, HEAT 3

Rnk	Or	Name	Ctry	Result	
1	13	MORAPEDI, John	RSA	13:54.30	Q
2	9	BITOK, Paul	KEN	13:54.45	Q
3	6	NIYONGABO, Venuste	BDI	13:54.53	Q
4	4	KENNEDY, Bob	USA	13:54.57	Q
5	7	BOULAMI, Khalid	MAR	13:54.72	Q
6	10	VANKO, Miroslav	SVK	13:54.88	Q
7	5	MEZGEBU, Assefa	ETH	13:54.89	Q
8	1	BALDINI, Stefano	ITA	13:55.41	Q
9	8	PANCORBO, Manuel	ESP	13:57.42	q
10	11	FRANKE, Stephane	GER	14:06.34	q
11	14	JESUS, Luis	POR	14:08.87	q
12	3	SEIF ELDIN, Khmees Abdalla	SUD	14:15.21	
13	2	ADANI, Abukar	SOM	15:19.80	
	12	al-QAHTANI, Alyan	KSA	DNS	

Best Intermediate Times

	Name	Ctry	Result
1000 m	JESUS, Luis	POR	2:53.25
2000 m	JESUS, Luis	POR	5:42.09
3000 m	MORAPEDI, John	RSA	8:33.99
4000 m	VANKO, Miroslav	SVK	11:24.06

SEMIFINAL 1

Rnk	Or	Name	Ctry	Result	
1	1	KORORIA, Shem	KEN	13:27.50	Q
2	10	BITOK, Paul	KEN	13:27.61	Q
3	2	LAHLAFI, Brahim	MAR	13:27.73	Q
4	15	KENNEDY, Bob	USA	13:27.90	Q
5	11	di NAPOLI, Genny	ITA	13:28.80	Q
6	5	BOULAMI, Khalid	MAR	13:29.72	Q
7	12	BAYISSA, Fita	ETH	13:30.88	q
8	6	BENZINE, Reda	ALG	13:37.52	q
9	8	FRANKE, Stephane	GER	13:40.94	q
10	9	WYATT, Jonathan	NZL	13:47.81	
11	3	JIMENEZ, Anacleto	ESP	13:50.90	
12	7	VANKO, Miroslav	SVK	13:51.45	
13	13	MORAPEDI, John	RSA	13:54.43	
14	14	CREIGHTON, Shaun	AUS	13:55.23	
15	4	RAMOS, Jose	POR	14:24.81	

Best Intermediate Times

	Name	Ctry	Result
1000 m	BITOK, Paul	KEN	2:51.20
2000 m	LAHLAFI, Brahim	MAR	5:37.78
3000 m	LAHLAFI, Brahim	MAR	8:16.45
4000 m	LAHLAFI, Brahim	MAR	10:53.95

SEMIFINAL 2

Rnk	Or	Name	Ctry	Result	
1	5	NYARIKI, Tom	KEN	14:03.21	Q
2	14	NIYONGABO, Venuste	BDI	14:03.48	Q
3	1	BAUMANN, Dieter	GER	14:03.75	Q
4	3	MOLINA, Enrique	ESP	14:04.08	Q
5	11	SGHIR, Smail	MAR	14:04.23	Q
6	6	BELAOUT, Aissa	ALG	14:04.56	Q
7	8	MEZGEBU, Assefa	ETH	14:05.48	
8	10	BALDINI, Stefano	ITA	14:06.45	
9	4	NUTTALL, John	GBR	14:08.39	
10	2	FINNERTY, Cormac	IRL	14:08.88	
11	12	HOFF, Shadrack	RSA	14:16.14	
12	13	PAYNTER, Julian	AUS	14:23.60	
13	7	SPIVEY, Jim	USA	14:27.72	
14	9	PANCORBO, Manuel	ESP	14:39.64	
	15	JESUS, Luis	POR	DNS	

Best Intermediate Times

	Name	Ctry	Result
1000 m	FINNERTY, Cormac	IRL	2:58.88
2000 m	FINNERTY, Cormac	IRL	6:04.75
3000 m	SPIVEY, Jim	USA	8:56.20
4000 m	FINNERTY, Cormac	IRL	11:35.54

FINAL

Rnk	Or	Name	Ctry	Result	
1	11	NIYONGABO, Venuste	BDI	13:07.96	G
2	14	BITOK, Paul	KEN	13:08.16	S
3	8	BOULAMI, Khalid	MAR	13:08.37	B
4	13	BAUMANN, Dieter	GER	13:08.81	
5	5	NYARIKI, Tom	KEN	13:12.29	
6	7	KENNEDY, Bob	USA	13:12.35	
7	2	MOLINA, Enrique	ESP	13:12.91	
8	12	LAHLAFI, Brahim	MAR	13:13.26	
9	4	KORORIA, Shem	KEN	13:14.63	
10	6	BAYISSA, Fita	ETH	13:18.30	
11	1	SGHIR, Smail	MAR	13:22.89	
12	3	di NAPOLI, Genny	ITA	13:28.36	
13	15	BENZINE, Reda	ALG	13:42.34	
14	9	FRANKE, Stephane	GER	13:44.64	
15	10	BELAOUT, Aissa	ALG	14:06.52	

Best Intermediate Times

	Name	Ctry	Result
1000 m	NYARIKI, Tom	KEN	2:45.40
2000 m	KORORIA, Shem	KEN	5:20.87
3000 m	KORORIA, Shem	KEN	8:00.05
4000 m	NYARIKI, Tom	KEN	10:40.42

Athletics / *Athlétisme*
5,000 m, Women / *5 000 m, Dames*

ROUND 1, HEAT 1

Rnk	Or	Name	Ctry	Result	
1	6	O'SULLIVAN, Sonia	IRL	15:15.80	Q
2	14	FIDATOV, Elena	ROM	15:17.89	Q
3	1	JENNINGS, Lynn	USA	15:19.66	Q
4	4	WEYERMANN, Anita	SUI	15:19.91	Q
5	11	WEDLUND, Sara	SWE	15:20.61	q
6	7	HARE, Anne	NZL	15:22.31	q
7	5	WASSILUK, Petra	GER	15:37.73	
8	13	YANG, Siju	CHN	15:40.41	
9	10	MACHADO, Roseli	BRA	15:41.63	
10	16	CHEROMEI, Lydia	KEN	15:49.85	
11	15	HIROYAMA, Harumi	JPN	15:50.43	
12	2	MARTINEZ, Isabel	ESP	15:59.42	
13	8	YISHAK, Luchia	ETH	16:04.29	
14	12	ANDERSON, Kate	AUS	16:17.83	
15	3	WYETH, Alison	GBR	16:24.74	
16	9	MAHAMANE, Rachida	NIG	19:17.87	

Best Intermediate Times

	Name	Ctry	Result
1000 m	MACHADO, Roseli	BRA	3:02.05
2000 m	WEDLUND, Sara	SWE	6:05.50
3000 m	WEDLUND, Sara	SWE	9:09.80
4000 m	WEDLUND, Sara	SWE	12:18.06

ROUND 1, HEAT 2

Rnk	Or	Name	Ctry	Result	
1	16	BRUNET, Roberta	ITA	15:22.58	Q
2	2	SHIMIZU, Michiko	JPN	15:23.56	Q
3	13	RADCLIFFE, Paula	GBR	15:23.90	Q
4	15	WANG, Junxia	CHN	15:24.28	Q
5	3	CHERUIYOT, Rose	KEN	15:26.87	q
6	7	LOKAR, Claudia	GER	15:28.35	
7	9	SLANEY, Mary	USA	15:41.30	
8	12	BUTLER, Kathy	CAN	15:47.50	
9	8	DENBOBA, Merima	ETH	15:48.35	
10	5	CHRISTIANSEN, Nina	DEN	15:56.38	
11	10	DIAS, Ana	POR	15:57.35	
12	1	OLTEANU, Stela	ROM	15:58.28	
13	11	CELNOVA, Jelena	LAT	15:59.00	
14	14	McMAHON, Marie	IRL	15:59.12	
15	4	HARVEY, Natalie	AUS	16:06.45	
	6	GRIFFITHS, Gwen	RSA	DNS	

Best Intermediate Times

	Name	Ctry	Result
1000 m	BRUNET, Roberta	ITA	3:09.29
2000 m	CHERUIYOT, Rose	KEN	6:16.93
3000 m	CHERUIYOT, Rose	KEN	9:24.93
4000 m	CHERUIYOT, Rose	KEN	12:30.89

ROUND 1, HEAT 3

Rnk	Or	Name	Ctry	Result	
1	12	KONGA, Pauline	KEN	15:07.01	Q
2	7	WORKU, Ayelech	ETH	15:21.59	Q
3	16	RUDOLPH, Amy	USA	15:21.90	Q
4	13	ROMANOVA, Yelena	RUS	15:23.37	Q
5	10	WEI, Li	CHN	15:33.49	
6	15	SOMMAGGIO, Silvia	ITA	15:33.63	
7	8	SZABO, Gabriela	ROM	15:42.35	
8	1	PETITE, Cristina	ESP	15:48.63	
9	11	OUAZIZ, Zohra	MAR	15:55.03	
10	14	McCANDLESS, Katy	IRL	15:55.66	
11	5	MIKITENKO, Irina	KAZ	15:57.67	
12	2	ICHIKAWA, Yoshiko	JPN	15:58.90	
13	6	McGEORGE, Sonia	GBR	16:01.92	
14	3	MEAGHER, Robyn	CAN	16:24.49	
15	4	PORTOBLANCO, Marta	NCA	18:42.78	
	9	SCHUWALOW, Carolyn	AUS	DNS	

Best Intermediate Times

	Name	Ctry	Result
1000 m	OUAZIZ, Zohra	MAR	3:03.91
2000 m	KONGA, Pauline	KEN	6:05.48
3000 m	KONGA, Pauline	KEN	9:00.94
4000 m	KONGA, Pauline	KEN	12:03.51

FINAL

Rnk	Or	Name	Ctry	Result	
1	4	WANG, Junxia	CHN	14:59.88 O	G
2	13	KONGA, Pauline	KEN	15:03.49	S
3	12	BRUNET, Roberta	ITA	15:07.52	B
4	15	SHIMIZU, Michiko	JPN	15:09.05	
5	2	RADCLIFFE, Paula	GBR	15:13.11	
6	1	ROMANOVA, Yelena	RUS	15:14.09	
7	7	FIDATOV, Elena	ROM	15:16.71	
8	3	CHERUIYOT, Rose	KEN	15:17.33	
9	8	JENNINGS, Lynn	USA	15:17.50	
10	10	RUDOLPH, Amy	USA	15:19.77	
11	5	WEDLUND, Sara	SWE	15:22.98	
12	11	WORKU, Ayelech	ETH	15:28.81	
13	6	HARE, Anne	NZL	15:29.11	
14	14	WEYERMANN, Anita	SUI	15:44.40	
	9	O'SULLIVAN, Sonia	IRL	DNF	

Best Intermediate Times

	Name	Ctry	Result
1000 m	KONGA, Pauline	KEN	3:06.15
2000 m	HARE, Anne	NZL	6:08.76
3000 m	KONGA, Pauline	KEN	9:08.02
4000 m	KONGA, Pauline	KEN	12:05.25

Athletics / *Athlétisme*
10,000 m, Men / *10 000 m, Messieurs*

ROUND 1, HEAT 1

Rnk	Or	Name	Ctry	Result	
1	18	BIKILA, Worku	ETH	27:50.57	Q
2	21	TERGAT, Paul	KEN	27:50.66	Q
3	24	NTAWULIKURA, Mathias	RWA	27:51.69	Q
4	4	NIZIGAMA, Aloys	BDI	27:53.21	Q
5	23	HISSOU, Salah	MAR	27:53.32	Q
6	15	BALDINI, Stefano	ITA	27:55.79	Q
7	7	ANTON, Abel	ESP	27:56.26	Q
8	2	de la TORRE, Carlos	ESP	28:04.14	Q
9	22	KALDY, Zoltan	HUN	28:13.49	q
10	13	HHAWU, Marko	TAN	28:14.08	q
11	6	EVANS, Paul	GBR	28:24.39	q
12	3	JOHNSTON, Robbie	NZL	28:40.60	
13	14	HANADA, Katsuhiko	JPN	28:52.22	
14	10	STEFKO, Robert	SVK	29:03.80	
15	5	PATRICIO, Carlos	POR	29:15.41	
16	20	da COSTA, Ronaldo	BRA	29:26.58	
17	8	MIDDLEMAN, Dan	USA	29:50.72	
18	16	EZZHER, Mohamed	FRA	29:55.34	
19	19	PITAYO, Martin	MEX	30:32.20	
20	12	VASQUEZ, Herder	COL	33:26.15	
21	1	ABU MARAHEEL, Majed	PLE	34:40.50	
	11	ZEROUAL, Larbi	MAR	DNF	
	17	PAYNTER, Julian	AUS	DNS	
	9	WATANABE, Yasuyuki	JPN	DNS	

Best Intermediate Times

	Name	Ctry	Result
1000 m	NIZIGAMA, Aloys	BDI	2:51.63
2000 m	NIZIGAMA, Aloys	BDI	5:36.09
3000 m	NIZIGAMA, Aloys	BDI	8:21.29
4000 m	NIZIGAMA, Aloys	BDI	11:06.98
5000 m	NIZIGAMA, Aloys	BDI	13:53.98
6000 m	NIZIGAMA, Aloys	BDI	16:42.99
7000 m	NTAWULIKURA, Mathias	RWA	19:33.11
8000 m	NTAWULIKURA, Mathias	RWA	22:19.38
9000 m	NTAWULIKURA, Mathias	RWA	25:07.94

ROUND 1, HEAT 2

Rnk	Or	Name	Ctry	Result	
1	23	GEBRSELASSIE, Haile	ETH	28:14.20	Q
2	16	MACHUKA, Josphat	KEN	28:14.27	Q
3	18	KOECH, Paul	KEN	28:17.48	Q
4	3	BROWN, Jon	GBR	28:19.85	Q
5	8	al-QAHTANI, Alyan	KSA	28:22.35	Q
6	21	SKAH, Khalid	MAR	28:23.21	Q
7	12	FRANKE, Stephane	GER	28:24.30	Q
8	17	QUINTANILLA, Armando	MEX	28:27.28	Q
9	1	GOMEZ, Alejandro	ESP	28:28.16	q
10	10	GUERRA, Silvio	ECU	28:30.15	
11	5	ASSEFA, Abraham	ETH	28:32.24	
12	7	TAKAOKA, Toshinari	JPN	28:38.18	
13	24	CREIGHTON, Shaun	AUS	28:44.29	
14	14	BRAZ, Alfredo	POR	28:50.28	
15	13	RAMAALA, Hendrick	RSA	29:07.81	
16	15	BARQUIST, Brad	USA	29:11.20	
17	19	MULINGA, Charles	ZAM	29:14.99	
18	11	VANKO, Miroslav	SVK	29:17.53	
19	6	DOLLMAN, Sean	IRL	29:19.03	
20	9	SADJADI, Hamid	IRI	29:22.65	
21	22	SCHIEBLER, Jeff	CAN	29:47.79	
	20	BEHAR, Abdellah	FRA	DNF	
	4	GUERRA, Paulo	POR	DNF	
	2	WILLIAMS, Todd	USA	DNF	

Best Intermediate Times

	Name	Ctry	Result
1000 m	VANKO, Miroslav	SVK	2:54.63
2000 m	VANKO, Miroslav	SVK	5:44.76
3000 m	VANKO, Miroslav	SVK	8:37.92
4000 m	ASSEFA, Abraham	ETH	11:30.02
5000 m	ASSEFA, Abraham	ETH	14:24.62
6000 m	KOECH, Paul	KEN	17:14.58
7000 m	QUINTANILLA, Armando	MEX	20:01.22
8000 m	KOECH, Paul	KEN	22:45.72
9000 m	KOECH, Paul	KEN	25:34.40

FINAL

Rnk	Or	Name	Ctry	Result		
1	8	GEBRSELASSIE, Haile	ETH	27:07.34	O	G
2	1	TERGAT, Paul	KEN	27:08.17		S
3	9	HISSOU, Salah	MAR	27:24.67		B
4	20	NIZIGAMA, Aloys	BDI	27:33.79		
5	5	MACHUKA, Josphat	KEN	27:35.08		
6	15	KOECH, Paul	KEN	27:35.19		
7	11	SKAH, Khalid	MAR	27:46.98		
8	17	NTAWULIKURA, Mathias	RWA	27:50.73		
9	2	FRANKE, Stephane	GER	27:59.08		
10	10	BROWN, Jon	GBR	27:59.72		
11	19	QUINTANILLA, Armando	MEX	28:09.46		
12	13	HHAWU, Marko	TAN	28:20.58		
13	12	ANTON, Abel	ESP	28:29.37		
14	18	de la TORRE, Carlos	ESP	28:32.11		
15	14	GOMEZ, Alejandro	ESP	28:39.11		
16	4	KALDY, Zoltan	HUN	28:45.48		
17	3	BIKILA, Worku	ETH	28:59.15		
18	6	BALDINI, Stefano	ITA	29:07.77		
	7	al-QAHTANI, Alyan	KSA	DNF		
	16	EVANS, Paul	GBR	DNF		

Best Intermediate Times

	Name	Ctry	Result
1000 m	BALDINI, Stefano	ITA	2:48.32
2000 m	NIZIGAMA, Aloys	BDI	5:31.26
3000 m	NIZIGAMA, Aloys	BDI	8:16.87
4000 m	NIZIGAMA, Aloys	BDI	11:06.63
5000 m	NIZIGAMA, Aloys	BDI	13:55.22
6000 m	KOECH, Paul	KEN	16:35.48
7000 m	MACHUKA, Josphat	KEN	19:18.36
8000 m	TERGAT, Paul	KEN	22:01.98
9000 m	TERGAT, Paul	KEN	24:35.88

Athletics / *Athlétisme*

10,000 m, Women / *10 000 m, Dames*

<table>
<tr><td colspan="5">ROUND 1, HEAT 1</td></tr>
<tr><td>Rnk</td><td>Or</td><td>Name</td><td>Ctry</td><td>Result</td></tr>
<tr><td>1</td><td>8</td><td>WAMI, Gete</td><td>ETH</td><td>32:20.92 Q</td></tr>
<tr><td>2</td><td>3</td><td>ADERE, Birhane</td><td>ETH</td><td>32:21.09 Q</td></tr>
<tr><td>3</td><td>7</td><td>VAQUERO, Julia</td><td>ESP</td><td>32:27.05 Q</td></tr>
<tr><td>4</td><td>9</td><td>LOROUPE, Tecla</td><td>KEN</td><td>32:28.73 Q</td></tr>
<tr><td>5</td><td>16</td><td>KAWAKAMI, Yuko</td><td>JPN</td><td>32:31.69 Q</td></tr>
<tr><td>6</td><td>1</td><td>McKIERNAN, Catherina</td><td>IRL</td><td>32:32.10 Q</td></tr>
<tr><td>7</td><td>2</td><td>WANG, Junxia</td><td>CHN</td><td>32:36.53 Q</td></tr>
<tr><td>8</td><td>17</td><td>de REUCK, Colleen</td><td>RSA</td><td>32:39.19 Q</td></tr>
<tr><td>9</td><td>15</td><td>FONSHELL, Kate</td><td>USA</td><td>32:48.05</td></tr>
<tr><td>10</td><td>6</td><td>CARROLL, Nyla</td><td>NZL</td><td>32:50.64</td></tr>
<tr><td>11</td><td>11</td><td>SOMMAGGIO, Silvia</td><td>ITA</td><td>32:59.40</td></tr>
<tr><td>12</td><td>4</td><td>KASHAPOVA, Klara</td><td>RUS</td><td>33:28.34</td></tr>
<tr><td>13</td><td>10</td><td>WESSEL, Kathrin</td><td>GER</td><td>33:31.67</td></tr>
<tr><td>14</td><td>5</td><td>FERREIRA, Conceicao</td><td>POR</td><td>33:40.76</td></tr>
<tr><td>15</td><td>13</td><td>FATES, Farida</td><td>FRA</td><td>34:38.49</td></tr>
<tr><td></td><td>14</td><td>JEITZINER, Ursula</td><td>SUI</td><td>DNF</td></tr>
<tr><td></td><td>12</td><td>RISK, Kylie</td><td>AUS</td><td>DNF</td></tr>
</table>

Best Intermediate Times

	Name	Ctry	Result
1000 m	CARROLL, Nyla	NZL	3:28.03
2000 m	KAWAKAMI, Yuko	JPN	6:49.48
3000 m	KAWAKAMI, Yuko	JPN	10:09.61
4000 m	KAWAKAMI, Yuko	JPN	13:27.29
5000 m	VAQUERO, Julia	ESP	16:47.66
6000 m	de REUCK, Colleen	RSA	19:58.76
7000 m	VAQUERO, Julia	ESP	23:03.53
8000 m	de REUCK, Colleen	RSA	26:17.43
9000 m	VAQUERO, Julia	ESP	29:28.25

<table>
<tr><td colspan="5">ROUND 1, HEAT 2</td></tr>
<tr><td>Rnk</td><td>Or</td><td>Name</td><td>Ctry</td><td>Result</td></tr>
<tr><td>1</td><td>13</td><td>TULU, Derartu</td><td>ETH</td><td>31:35.90 Q</td></tr>
<tr><td>2</td><td>11</td><td>BARSOSIO, Sally</td><td>KEN</td><td>31:36.00 Q</td></tr>
<tr><td>3</td><td>2</td><td>RIBEIRO, Fernanda</td><td>POR</td><td>31:36.32 Q</td></tr>
<tr><td>4</td><td>17</td><td>CHIBA, Masako</td><td>JPN</td><td>31:37.03 Q</td></tr>
<tr><td>5</td><td>10</td><td>NEGURA, Iulia</td><td>ROM</td><td>31:40.16 Q</td></tr>
<tr><td>6</td><td>9</td><td>SANDELL, Annemari</td><td>FIN</td><td>31:40.42 Q</td></tr>
<tr><td>7</td><td>5</td><td>SUZUKI, Hiromi</td><td>JPN</td><td>31:54.89 Q</td></tr>
<tr><td>8</td><td>14</td><td>GUIDA, Maria</td><td>ITA</td><td>31:55.35 Q</td></tr>
<tr><td>9</td><td>1</td><td>PETROVA, Lyudmila</td><td>RUS</td><td>31:58.84 q</td></tr>
<tr><td>10</td><td>16</td><td>WANG, Mingxia</td><td>CHN</td><td>32:10.26 q</td></tr>
<tr><td>11</td><td>3</td><td>YANG, Siju</td><td>CHN</td><td>32:22.77 q</td></tr>
<tr><td>12</td><td>4</td><td>HOBSON, Susan</td><td>AUS</td><td>32:25.13 q</td></tr>
<tr><td>13</td><td>6</td><td>NESBIT, Joan</td><td>USA</td><td>32:33.48</td></tr>
<tr><td>14</td><td>18</td><td>SULTANOVA, Firiya</td><td>RUS</td><td>32:40.91</td></tr>
<tr><td>15</td><td>15</td><td>DALLENBACH, Chantal</td><td>FRA</td><td>33:22.35</td></tr>
<tr><td>16</td><td>7</td><td>NAUER, Daria</td><td>SUI</td><td>33:56.95</td></tr>
<tr><td>17</td><td>12</td><td>APPELL, Olga</td><td>USA</td><td>34:12.54</td></tr>
<tr><td>18</td><td>8</td><td>NAHIMANA, Justine</td><td>BDI</td><td>35:58.51</td></tr>
</table>

Best Intermediate Times

	Name	Ctry	Result
1000 m	NESBIT, Joan	USA	3:04.91
2000 m	NESBIT, Joan	USA	6:18.30
3000 m	CHIBA, Masako	JPN	9:25.51
4000 m	CHIBA, Masako	JPN	12:33.80
5000 m	CHIBA, Masako	JPN	15:42.64
6000 m	CHIBA, Masako	JPN	18:51.87
7000 m	CHIBA, Masako	JPN	22:04.48
8000 m	RIBEIRO, Fernanda	POR	25:17.66
9000 m	RIBEIRO, Fernanda	POR	28:30.10

<table>
<tr><td colspan="6">FINAL</td></tr>
<tr><td>Rnk</td><td>Or</td><td>Name</td><td>Ctry</td><td>Result</td><td></td></tr>
<tr><td>1</td><td>18</td><td>RIBEIRO, Fernanda</td><td>POR</td><td>31:01.63 O</td><td>G</td></tr>
<tr><td>2</td><td>20</td><td>WANG, Junxia</td><td>CHN</td><td>31:02.58</td><td>S</td></tr>
<tr><td>3</td><td>2</td><td>WAMI, Gete</td><td>ETH</td><td>31:06.65</td><td>B</td></tr>
<tr><td>4</td><td>13</td><td>TULU, Derartu</td><td>ETH</td><td>31:10.46</td><td></td></tr>
<tr><td>5</td><td>10</td><td>CHIBA, Masako</td><td>JPN</td><td>31:20.62</td><td></td></tr>
<tr><td>6</td><td>5</td><td>LOROUPE, Tecla</td><td>KEN</td><td>31:23.22</td><td></td></tr>
<tr><td>7</td><td>17</td><td>KAWAKAMI, Yuko</td><td>JPN</td><td>31:23.23</td><td></td></tr>
<tr><td>8</td><td>14</td><td>NEGURA, Iulia</td><td>ROM</td><td>31:26.46</td><td></td></tr>
<tr><td>9</td><td>9</td><td>VAQUERO, Julia</td><td>ESP</td><td>31:27.07</td><td></td></tr>
<tr><td>10</td><td>11</td><td>BARSOSIO, Sally</td><td>KEN</td><td>31:53.38</td><td></td></tr>
<tr><td>11</td><td>12</td><td>McKIERNAN, Catherina</td><td>IRL</td><td>32:00.38</td><td></td></tr>
<tr><td>12</td><td>3</td><td>SANDELL, Annemari</td><td>FIN</td><td>32:14.66</td><td></td></tr>
<tr><td>13</td><td>4</td><td>de REUCK, Colleen</td><td>RSA</td><td>32:14.69</td><td></td></tr>
<tr><td>14</td><td>8</td><td>PETROVA, Lyudmila</td><td>RUS</td><td>32:25.89</td><td></td></tr>
<tr><td>15</td><td>6</td><td>WANG, Mingxia</td><td>CHN</td><td>32:38.98</td><td></td></tr>
<tr><td>16</td><td>15</td><td>SUZUKI, Hiromi</td><td>JPN</td><td>32:43.39</td><td></td></tr>
<tr><td>17</td><td>16</td><td>HOBSON, Susan</td><td>AUS</td><td>32:47.71</td><td></td></tr>
<tr><td>18</td><td>7</td><td>ADERE, Birhane</td><td>ETH</td><td>32:57.35</td><td></td></tr>
<tr><td>19</td><td>19</td><td>YANG, Siju</td><td>CHN</td><td>33:15.29</td><td></td></tr>
<tr><td></td><td>1</td><td>GUIDA, Maria</td><td>ITA</td><td>DNS</td><td></td></tr>
</table>

Best Intermediate Times

	Name	Ctry	Result
1000 m	McKIERNAN, Catherina	IRL	3:07.50
2000 m	McKIERNAN, Catherina	IRL	6:11.66
3000 m	McKIERNAN, Catherina	IRL	9:17.21
4000 m	RIBEIRO, Fernanda	POR	12:26.23
5000 m	RIBEIRO, Fernanda	POR	15:35.83
6000 m	BARSOSIO, Sally	KEN	18:42.91
7000 m	VAQUERO, Julia	ESP	21:55.16
8000 m	VAQUERO, Julia	ESP	25:03.31
9000 m	RIBEIRO, Fernanda	POR	28:11.64

110 m Hurdles, Men / *110 m haies, Messieurs*

ROUND 1, HEAT 1

Rnk	Ln	Name	Ctry	Result	
1	5	KOVAC, Igor	SVK	13.62	Q
2	8	McKOY, Mark	AUT	13.70	Q
3	1	KISLYKH, Andrey	RUS	13.74	Q
4	6*	EDORH, Claude	GER	13.74	q
5	3	CHEN, Yanhao	CHN	13.76	
6	4	DVORAK, Tomas	CZE	13.78	
7	2	SOTO, Mickey	PUR	13.94	
8	7	LEFOU, Judex	MRI	14.69	

ROUND 1, HEAT 2

Rnk	Ln	Name	Ctry	Result	
1	7	SCHWARTHOFF, Florian	GER	13.39	Q
2	8	BATTE, Erick	CUB	13.47	Q
3	3	TULLOCH, Andy	GBR	13.56	Q
4	5	LISABETH, Johan	BEL	13.72	q
5	2	ALBIHN, Claes	SWE	13.79	
6	1	OYIKI, Moses	NGR	14.04	
7	4	CAHILL, Sean	IRL	14.28	
8	6	ARISTOV, Yuriy	UZB	15.04	

ROUND 1, HEAT 3

Rnk	Ln	Name	Ctry	Result	
1	1	CREAR, Mark	USA	13.44	Q
2	6	GARCIA, Anier	CUB	13.56	Q
3	8*	PIETERS, Sven	BEL	13.56	Q
4	3	BOROI, George	ROM	13.66	q
5	5	PERIN, Emerson	BRA	13.76	
6	2	MARSEILLE, Wagner	HAI	13.95	
7	7*	ROTTL, Herwig	AUT	14.08	
8	4*	ISMAEELL, Fawaz	BRN	14.32	

ROUND 1, HEAT 4

Rnk	Ln	Name	Ctry	Result	
1	8	JACKSON, Colin	GBR	13.36	Q
2	5	KAISER, Erik	GER	13.64	Q
3	3	PEDERS, Guntis	LAT	13.72	Q
4	4	MENSAH, Frank	GHA	13.87	
5	7*	ERESE, William	NGR	13.98	
6	6	NAIVALU, Joe	FIJ	14.23	
	2	MAJID, Nur Herman	MAS	DNS	
	1	YOUNG, Curt	PAN	DNS	

ROUND 1, HEAT 5

Rnk	Ln	Name	Ctry	Result	
1	6	JOHNSON, Allen	USA	13.66	Q
2	4	MEHLICH, Krzysztof	POL	13.81	Q
3	3	de SOUZA, Walmes	BRA	13.82	Q
4	8	BISBAS, Stelios	GRE	13.85	
5	5	HAAPAKOSKI, Antti	FIN	13.90	
6	7	de los SANTOS, Miguel	ESP	14.01	
7	1	ADEGBITE, Steve	NGR	14.06	
	2	ANDRADE, Henry	CPV	DNF	

ROUND 1, HEAT 6

Rnk	Ln	Name	Ctry	Result	
1	7	JARRETT, Tony	GBR	13.47	Q
2	1	CLARICO, Vincent	FRA	13.52	Q
3	8	KEARNS, T. J.	IRL	13.67	Q
4	6	CHIAMULERA, Pedro	BRA	13.70	q
5	5	PECHONKIN, Yevgeniy	RUS	13.86	
6	2	LICHTENEGGER, Elmar	AUT	14.03	
7	4	KATSANTONIS, Prodromos	CYP	14.34	
8	3*	MAZOU, Hakim	CGO	14.52	

ROUND 1, HEAT 7

Rnk	Ln	Name	Ctry	Result	
1	5	VANDER-KUYP, Kyle	AUS	13.32	Q
2	8	VALLE, Emilio	CUB	13.35	Q
3	6*	NSENGA, Jonathan	BEL	13.61	Q
4	4*	KAZANOVS, Igors	LAT	13.74	q
5	2	KROEKER, Tim	CAN	13.74	q
6	7	FONT, Jesus	ESP	13.90	
7	3	PERERA, Mahesh	SRI	14.24	
8	1	RIESCO, Jose	PER	14.29	

ROUND 1, HEAT 8

Rnk	Ln	Name	Ctry	Result	
1	2	SWIFT, Eugene	USA	13.36	Q
2	3	LI, Tong	CHN	13.57	Q
3	6	FOSTER, Robert	JAM	13.58	Q
4	7*	CSILLAG, Levente	HUN	13.64	q
5	5	ROMARY, Emmanuel	FRA	13.68	q
6	4	SALA, Carlos	ESP	13.94	
7	8	SHOROKHOV, Yeniya	KGZ	14.29	
8	1	TUCKER, Paul	GUY	14.65	

ROUND 2, HEAT 1

Rnk	Ln	Name	Ctry	Result	
1	6	SWIFT, Eugene	USA	13.37	Q
2	7	FOSTER, Robert	JAM	13.51	Q
3	8	LISABETH, Johan	BEL	13.53	Q
4	5	CLARICO, Vincent	FRA	13.57	Q
5	2	PEDERS, Guntis	LAT	13.59	
6	1	CHIAMULERA, Pedro	BRA	13.77	
	3	KAISER, Erik	GER	DNF	q
	4*	JARRETT, Tony	GBR	DQ	

ROUND 2, HEAT 2

Rnk	Ln	Name	Ctry	Result	
1	5	CREAR, Mark	USA	13.14	Q
2	4	SCHWARTHOFF, Florian	GER	13.27	Q
3	1	KAZANOVS, Igors	LAT	13.42	Q
4	6	LI, Tong	CHN	13.43	Q
5	2	KEARNS, T. J.	IRL	13.55	
6	3	GARCIA, Anier	CUB	13.58	
7	8	NSENGA, Jonathan	BEL	13.63	
8	7	ROMARY, Emmanuel	FRA	13.81	

ROUND 2, HEAT 3

Rnk	Ln	Name	Ctry	Result	
1	3	JACKSON, Colin	GBR	13.33	Q
2	8	PIETERS, Sven	BEL	13.36	Q
3	4	BATTE, Erick	CUB	13.46	Q
4	2	BOROI, George	ROM	13.56	Q
5	6	McKOY, Mark	AUT	13.64	
6	1	EDORH, Claude	GER	13.64	
7	5*	KOVAC, Igor	SVK	13.70	
8	7	KISLYKH, Andrey	RUS	13.74	

ROUND 2, HEAT 4

Rnk	Ln	Name	Ctry	Result	
1	3	JOHNSON, Allen	USA	13.27	Q
2	5	VALLE, Emilio	CUB	13.29	Q
3	4	VANDER-KUYP, Kyle	AUS	13.49	Q
4	6	MEHLICH, Krzysztof	POL	13.51	Q
5	8	CSILLAG, Levente	HUN	13.61	
6	2	TULLOCH, Andy	GBR	13.68	
7	1	de SOUZA, Walmes	BRA	14.12	
8	7	KROEKER, Tim	CAN	14.14	

SEMIFINAL 1

Rnk	Ln	Name	Ctry	Result	
1	5	JOHNSON, Allen	USA	13.10	Q
2	6	JACKSON, Colin	GBR	13.17	Q
3	4	VALLE, Emilio	CUB	13.18	Q
4	7	VANDER-KUYP, Kyle	AUS	13.38	Q
5	8	MEHLICH, Krzysztof	POL	13.55	
6	1	BOROI, George	ROM	13.57	
7	3	PIETERS, Sven	BEL	13.59	
8	9	KAISER, Erik	GER	13.59	
9	2	LI, Tong	CHN	13.60	

SEMIFINAL 2

Rnk	Ln	Name	Ctry	Result	
1	6	SCHWARTHOFF, Florian	GER	13.13	Q
2	4	SWIFT, Eugene	USA	13.21	Q
3	3	CREAR, Mark	USA	13.22	Q
4	8	BATTE, Erick	CUB	13.26	Q
5	2	CLARICO, Vincent	FRA	13.43	
6	5	FOSTER, Robert	JAM	13.49	
7	1	KAZANOVS, Igors	LAT	14.13	
	7	LISABETH, Johan	BEL	DNF	

FINAL

Rnk	Ln	Name	Ctry	Result	
1	6	JOHNSON, Allen	USA	12.95	O G
2	8	CREAR, Mark	USA	13.09	S
3	3	SCHWARTHOFF, Florian	GER	13.17	B
4	5	JACKSON, Colin	GBR	13.19	
5	7	VALLE, Emilio	CUB	13.20	
6	4	SWIFT, Eugene	USA	13.23	
7	2	VANDER-KUYP, Kyle	AUS	13.40	
8	1	BATTE, Erick	CUB	13.43	

100 m Hurdles, Women / *100 m haies, Dames*

ROUND 1, HEAT 1

Rnk	Ln	Name	Ctry	Result	
1	4	ANDERSON, Katie	CAN	12.86	Q
2	3	DICKEY, Cheryl	USA	12.92	Q
3	8	LOPEZ, Aliuska	CUB	13.06	Q
4	1	KULAWANSA, Sriyani	SRI	13.09	Q
5	5*	WOLF, Birgit	GER	13.16	q
6	6	SHEKHODANOVA, Natalya	RUS	13.24	q
7	7	AGYEPONG, Jacqui	GBR	13.24	
8	2*	CHAN, Sau Ying	HKG	13.63	

ROUND 1, HEAT 2

Rnk	Ln	Name	Ctry	Result	
1	4	FREEMAN, Michelle	JAM	12.76	Q
2	6	GIRARD-LENO, Patricia	FRA	12.84	Q
3	2	RAMALALANIRINA, Nicole	MAD	12.90	Q
4	3	DIMITROVA, Svetla	BUL	12.92	Q
5	8	KANAZAWA, Yvonne	JPN	13.30	
6	5	NSIAH, Vida	GHA	13.34	
7	7	TASHLIN, Lesley	CAN	13.61	

ROUND 1, HEAT 3

Rnk	Ln	Name	Ctry	Result	
1	3	ENGQUIST, Ludmila	SWE	12.66	Q
2	8	ATEDE, Angela	NGR	12.88	Q
3	7	MARDOMINGO, Maria Jose	ESP	12.91	Q
4	6	TOURRET, Monique	FRA	13.12	Q
5	4	SOLLI REIMANN, Lena	NOR	13.13	
6	2	GRIGORYEVA, Natalya	UKR	13.16	q
7	5	PAQUETTE, Sonia	CAN	13.29	

ROUND 1, HEAT 4

Rnk	Ln	Name	Ctry	Result	
1	7	BAUMANN, Julie	SUI	12.86	Q
2	5	THORP, Angie	GBR	12.93	Q
3	4	GOODE, Lynda	USA	12.97	Q
4	1	PATZWAHL, Kristin	GER	12.98	Q
5	2	RESHETNIKOVA, Tatyana	RUS	13.01	q
6	6	CINELU, Cecile	FRA	13.05	q
7	8	VU, Bich Huong	VIE	13.85	
8	3	CAMARA, Aminata	MLI	14.94	

ROUND 1, HEAT 5

Rnk	Ln	Name	Ctry	Result	
1	5	BUKOVEC, Brigita	SLO	12.72	Q
2	3	ROSE, Dione	JAM	12.81	Q
3	7	ALADEFA, Taiwo	NGR	13.06	Q
4	4	YURKOVA, Lidiya	BLR	13.20	Q
5	8	BODROVA, Nadiya	UKR	13.22	q
6	2	ROGERS, Rachel	FIJ	14.07	
	6	ANGHEL, Elisabeta	ROM	DNF	

ROUND 1, HEAT 6

Rnk	Ln	Name	Ctry	Result	
1	2	DEVERS, Gail	USA	12.73	Q
2	5	RUSSELL, Gillian	JAM	12.85	Q
3	8	GRAUDYN, Yuliya	RUS	12.95	Q
4	4	AKPAN, Ime	NGR	13.11	Q
5	7	OVCHAROVA, Olena	UKR	13.23	q
6	6	LINSTER, Veronique	LUX	13.47	
	3	TUZZI, Carla	ITA	DNF	

ROUND 2, HEAT 1

Rnk	Ln	Name	Ctry	Result	
1	5	BUKOVEC, Brigita	SLO	12.66	Q
2	3	ROSE, Dione	JAM	12.76	Q
3	4*	GRAUDYN, Yuliya	RUS	12.77	Q
4	2	DIMITROVA, Svetla	BUL	12.84	Q
5	6	ATEDE, Angela	NGR	12.85	
6	1	CINELU, Cecile	FRA	13.06	
7	7	YURKOVA, Lidiya	BLR	13.07	
	8	BODROVA, Nadiya	UKR	DNF	

ROUND 2, HEAT 2

Rnk	Ln	Name	Ctry	Result	
1	5	ENGQUIST, Ludmila	SWE	12.47	Q
2	7	LOPEZ, Aliuska	CUB	12.67	Q
3	3*	GIRARD-LENO, Patricia	FRA	12.72	Q
4	6	GOODE, Lynda	USA	12.78	Q
5	4	RUSSELL, Gillian	JAM	12.78	
6	1*	RESHETNIKOVA, Tatyana	RUS	13.01	
7	2	AKPAN, Ime	NGR	13.02	
8	8	OVCHAROVA, Olena	UKR	13.16	

ROUND 2, HEAT 3

Rnk	Ln	Name	Ctry	Result	
1	5	FREEMAN, Michelle	JAM	12.57	Q
2	7	SHEKHODANOVA, Natalya	RUS	12.68	Q
3	6	RAMALALANIRINA, Nicole	MAD	12.90	Q
4	8*	PATZWAHL, Kristin	GER	12.91	Q
5	2	KULAWANSA, Sriyani	SRI	12.91	
6	4	DICKEY, Cheryl	USA	12.92	
7	1	GRIGORYEVA, Natalya	UKR	12.96	
8	3	ANDERSON, Katie	CAN	13.17	

ROUND 2, HEAT 4

Rnk	Ln	Name	Ctry	Result	
1	4	DEVERS, Gail	USA	12.83	Q
2	3	BAUMANN, Julie	SUI	12.98	Q
3	5	THORP, Angie	GBR	12.99	Q
4	6	MARDOMINGO, Maria Jose	ESP	13.05	Q
5	8	WOLF, Birgit	GER	13.08	
6	2	ALADEFA, Taiwo	NGR	13.11	
7	7	TOURRET, Monique	FRA	13.17	
8	1	SOLLI REIMANN, Lena	NOR	13.30	

SEMIFINAL 1

Rnk	Ln	Name	Ctry	Result	
1	5	FREEMAN, Michelle	JAM	12.61	Q
2	4	BUKOVEC, Brigita	SLO	12.63	Q
3	3	SHEKHODANOVA, Natalya	RUS	12.67	Q
4	2	GOODE, Lynda	USA	12.77	Q
5	8	THORP, Angie	GBR	12.80	
6	6	BAUMANN, Julie	SUI	12.90	
7	1*	RAMALALANIRINA, Nicole	MAD	13.01	
8	7*	PATZWAHL, Kristin	GER	13.05	

SEMIFINAL 2

Rnk	Ln	Name	Ctry	Result	
1	5	ENGQUIST, Ludmila	SWE	12.51	Q
2	2	GIRARD-LENO, Patricia	FRA	12.59	Q
3	6	DEVERS, Gail	USA	12.62	Q
4	3	ROSE, Dione	JAM	12.64	Q
5	4	LOPEZ, Aliuska	CUB	12.70	
6	7	GRAUDYN, Yuliya	RUS	12.74	
7	1	MARDOMINGO, Maria Jose	ESP	12.89	
	8	DIMITROVA, Svetla	BUL	DNF	

FINAL

Rnk	Ln	Name	Ctry	Result	
1	6	ENGQUIST, Ludmila	SWE	12.58	G
2	3	BUKOVEC, Brigita	SLO	12.59	S
3	5	GIRARD-LENO, Patricia	FRA	12.65	B
4	8	DEVERS, Gail	USA	12.66	
5	2	ROSE, Dione	JAM	12.74	
6	4	FREEMAN, Michelle	JAM	12.76	
7	7	SHEKHODANOVA, Natalya	RUS	12.80	
8	1	GOODE, Lynda	USA	13.11	

Athletics / *Athlétisme*

400 m Hurdles, Men / *400 m haies, Messieurs*

ROUND 1, HEAT 1

Rnk	Ln	Name	Ctry	Result	
1	7	FAYE, Ibou	SEN	48.84	Q
2	8	MORI, Fabrizio	ITA	48.90	Q
3	5	YAMAZAKI, Kazuhiko	JPN	49.07	
4	6	MORGAN, Dinsdale	JAM	49.16	
5	4	ALADEFA, Kehinde	NGR	49.60	
6	3	CRAMPTON, Peter	GBR	49.78	
7	1	HASHAN, Gilbert	MRI	49.94	
8	2	VILA, Salvador	ESP	50.55	

ROUND 1, HEAT 2

Rnk	Ln	Name	Ctry	Result	
1	2	de ARAUJO, Eronilde	BRA	48.52	Q
2	1	OTTOZ, Laurent	ITA	48.92	Q
3	7	SILVA, Carlos	POR	49.09	
4	3	FARAJ, Mubarak	QAT	49.27	
5	4	KOCUVAN, Miro	SLO	49.66	
6	8	BRUWIER, Jean-Paul	BEL	49.69	
7	5	KINYOR, Barnabas	KEN	49.82	
8	6	MATEESCU, Mugur	ROM	49.97	

ROUND 1, HEAT 3

Rnk	Ln	Name	Ctry	Result	
1	5	MATETE, Samuel	ZAM	48.21	Q
2	2	ROBINSON, Rohan	AUS	48.89	Q
3	3	KETER, Erick	KEN	49.03	
4	6	ZADOINOV, Vadim	MDA	49.73	
5	7	SOMAYLI, Hadi	KSA	49.94	
6	8	MBAYE, Hamadou	SEN	50.30	
7	4	HERBERT, Llewellyn	RSA	51.13	

ROUND 1, HEAT 4

Rnk	Ln	Name	Ctry	Result	
1	5	BRONSON, Bryan	USA	49.06	Q
2	6	KOVACS, Dusan	HUN	49.23	Q
3	3	JANUSZEWSKI, Pawel	POL	49.63	
4	4	KAWAMURA, Hideaki	JPN	49.88	
5	8	MASVANISE, Julius	ZIM	50.16	
6	2	KUCEJ, Jozef	SVK	50.31	
7	1	SY SAVANE, Amadou	GUI	50.90	
8	7	HOLLINGSWORTH, Simon	AUS	52.16	

ROUND 1, HEAT 5

Rnk	Ln	Name	Ctry	Result	
1	1	RIDGEON, Jon	GBR	49.31	Q
2	8	DOLLENDORF, Marc	BEL	49.49	Q
3	3	MASHCHENKO, Ruslan	RUS	49.94	
4	5	TEBELIS, Egils	LAT	50.73	
5	6	CORDERO, Domingo	PUR	51.20	
6	4	SCHELBERT, Marcel	SUI	51.20	
7	2	YOUNG, Curt	PAN	55.20	
	7	GRAHAM, Winthrop	JAM	DNF	

ROUND 1, HEAT 6

Rnk	Ln	Name	Ctry	Result	
1	2	DAVIS, Calvin	USA	48.94	Q
2	8	NYLANDER, Sven	SWE	49.54	Q
3	6	SABER, Ashraf	ITA	49.71	
4	5	BIWOTT, Gideon	KEN	49.74	
5	1	McGUIRK, Tom	IRL	50.76	
6	7	SILVA, Cleverson	BRA	51.23	
7	4	PITILLAS, Oscar	ESP	51.35	
8	3	GITTENS, Lancelot	GUY	54.79	

ROUND 1, HEAT 7

Rnk	Ln	Name	Ctry	Result	
1	6	ADKINS, Derrick	USA	48.46	Q
2	8	TEIXEIRA, Everson	BRA	48.52	Q
3	3	HARNDEN, Ken	ZIM	48.54	q
4	7	GARDNER, Neil	JAM	48.59	q
5	1	KARUBE, Shunji	JPN	48.96	
6	4	JENNINGS, Gary	GBR	50.41	
7	2	MONREAL, Inigo	ESP	52.23	
8	5	WAKIT, Ivan	PNG	53.42	

SEMIFINAL 1

Rnk	Ln	Name	Ctry	Result	
1	3	ADKINS, Derrick	USA	47.76	Q
2	1	NYLANDER, Sven	SWE	48.21	Q
3	2	MORI, Fabrizio	ITA	48.43	Q
4	6	de ARAUJO, Eronilde	BRA	48.45	Q
5	8	KOVACS, Dusan	HUN	48.57	
6	7	HARNDEN, Ken	ZIM	48.61	
7	4	RIDGEON, Jon	GBR	49.43	
8	5	BRONSON, Bryan	USA	50.32	

SEMIFINAL 2

Rnk	Ln	Name	Ctry	Result	
1	3	DAVIS, Calvin	USA	47.91	Q
2	4	TEIXEIRA, Everson	BRA	48.28	Q
3	6	MATETE, Samuel	ZAM	48.28	Q
4	7	ROBINSON, Rohan	AUS	48.28	Q
5	1	GARDNER, Neil	JAM	48.30	
6	2	OTTOZ, Laurent	ITA	48.52	
7	5	FAYE, Ibou	SEN	48.84	
8	8	DOLLENDORF, Marc	BEL	48.91	

FINAL

Rnk	Ln	Name	Ctry	Result	
1	6	ADKINS, Derrick	USA	47.54	G
2	1	MATETE, Samuel	ZAM	47.78	S
3	5	DAVIS, Calvin	USA	47.96	B
4	4	NYLANDER, Sven	SWE	47.98	
5	8	ROBINSON, Rohan	AUS	48.30	
6	7	MORI, Fabrizio	ITA	48.41	
7	3	TEIXEIRA, Everson	BRA	48.57	
8	2	de ARAUJO, Eronilde	BRA	48.78	

Athletics / *Athlétisme*

400 m Hurdles, Women / *400 m haies, Dames*

ROUND 1, HEAT 1

Rnk	Ln	Name	Ctry	Result	
1	1	ARNARDOTTIR, Gudrun	ISL	54.88	Q
2	7	FARMER-PATRICK, Sandra	USA	55.55	Q
3	2	PARRIS, Debbie	JAM	55.64	Q
4	8	SCHENK, Michele	SUI	55.70	q
5	5	LEDOVSKAYA, Tanya	BLR	55.82	q
6	4	de ANGELI, Virna	ITA	57.12	
7	6	KAPALU, Mary Estelle	VAN	58.68	
8	3	HSU, Pei-Chin	TPE	58.80	

ROUND 1, HEAT 2

Rnk	Ln	Name	Ctry	Result	
1	2	BUFORD-BAILEY, Tonja	USA	55.23	Q
2	8	GUNNELL, Sally	GBR	55.29	Q
3	3	RIEGER, Silvia	GER	55.33	Q
4	7	EDEH, Rosey	CAN	55.64	q
5	4	TORCHINA, Natalia	KAZ	55.94	
6	6	STOOP, Martina	SUI	56.32	
7	5	ALONSO, Miriam	ESP	56.53	
8	1	AKINREMI, Lade	NGR	56.83	

ROUND 1, HEAT 3

Rnk	Ln	Name	Ctry	Result	
1	7	BATTEN, Kim	USA	54.92	Q
2	2	TERESHCHUK, Tetyana	UKR	55.82	Q
3	3	MERCKEN, Ann	BEL	55.88	Q
4	4	KNOROZ, Anna	RUS	56.21	
5	8	SCOTT-POMALES, Catherine	JAM	56.21	
6	6	van der VEEN, Karen	RSA	57.00	
7	5	KUROCHKINA, Tanya	BLR	57.28	

400 m Hurdles, Women / *400 m haies, Dames*

ROUND 1, HEAT 4

Rnk	Ln	Name	Ctry	Result	
1	8	HEMMINGS, Deon	JAM	54.70	Q
2	5	MEISSNER, Heike	GER	55.05	Q
3	2	SMITH, Susan	IRL	55.22	Q
4	3	TIRLEA, Ionela	ROM	55.42	q
5	4	JEKABSONE, Lana	LAT	56.18	
6	7	VORONKOVA, Nelli	BLR	56.97	
7	6	PANIAGUA, Eva	ESP	58.10	

SEMIFINAL 1

Rnk	Ln	Name	Ctry	Result		
1	3	HEMMINGS, Deon	JAM	52.99	O	Q
2	6	BUFORD-BAILEY, Tonja	USA	53.38		Q
3	4	MEISSNER, Heike	GER	54.27		Q
4	2	TIRLEA, Ionela	ROM	54.41		Q
5	8	SMITH, Susan	IRL	54.93		
6	1	MERCKEN, Ann	BEL	54.95		
7	7	LEDOVSKAYA, Tanya	BLR	54.99		
8	5	TERESHCHUK, Tetyana	UKR	55.34		

SEMIFINAL 2

Rnk	Ln	Name	Ctry	Result	
1	6	BATTEN, Kim	USA	53.65	Q
2	7	RIEGER, Silvia	GER	54.27	Q
3	2	EDEH, Rosey	CAN	54.49	Q
4	1	PARRIS, Debbie	JAM	54.72	Q
5	5	FARMER-PATRICK, Sandra	USA	54.73	
6	4	ARNARDOTTIR, Gudrun	ISL	54.81	
7	8	SCHENK, Michele	SUI	55.96	
	3	GUNNELL, Sally	GBR	DNF	

FINAL

Rnk	Ln	Name	Ctry	Result		
1	5	HEMMINGS, Deon	JAM	52.82	O	G
2	6	BATTEN, Kim	USA	53.08		S
3	4	BUFORD-BAILEY, Tonja	USA	53.22		B
4	2	PARRIS, Debbie	JAM	53.97		
5	1	MEISSNER, Heike	GER	54.03		
6	7	EDEH, Rosey	CAN	54.39		
7	8	TIRLEA, Ionela	ROM	54.40		
8	3	RIEGER, Silvia	GER	54.57		

Athletics / *Athlétisme*
3,000 m Steeplechase, Men / *3 000 m steeple, Messieurs*

ROUND 1, HEAT 1

Rnk	Or	Name	Ctry	Result	
1	8	KETER, Joseph	KEN	8:30.23	Q
2	4	SIAMUSIYE, Godfrey	ZAM	8:30.56	Q
3	2	IONESCU, Florin	ROM	8:31.34	Q
4	9	LAMBRUSCHINI, Alessandro	ITA	8:31.69	Q
5	1	BOUAOUICHE, Hicham	MAR	8:31.97	Q
6	3	STREGE, Martin	GER	8:32.76	Q
7	7	HASSAN, Jamal	QAT	8:36.99	q
8	11	HENRIQUES, Eduardo	POR	8:38.58	
9	6	de la TORRE, Elisardo	ESP	8:42.75	
10	12	DUVAL, Spencer	GBR	8:46.76	
11	10	GARY, Robert	USA	8:49.68	
	5	HIGA, Primo	SOL	DNF	

Best Intermediate Times

	Name	Ctry	Result
1000 m	IONESCU, Florin	ROM	2:51.99
2000 m	IONESCU, Florin	ROM	5:43.59

ROUND 1, HEAT 2

Rnk	Or	Name	Ctry	Result	
1	1	SAHERE, Abdelaziz	MAR	8:26.79	Q
2	11	BIRIR, Matthew	KEN	8:27.09	Q
3	6	CROGHAN, Mark	USA	8:27.91	Q
4	4	BOURGEOIS, Joel	CAN	8:28.14	Q
5	12	CHASTON, Justin	GBR	8:28.32	Q
6	3	PRONIN, Vladimir	RUS	8:29.49	Q
7	9	BOSCH, Nadir	FRA	8:31.65	q
8	7	BAUERMEISTER, Kim	GER	8:36.86	q
9	2	VERA, Ricardo	URU	8:40.78	
10	10	NIEVES, Nestor	VEN	8:47.34	
11	5	ALMEIDA, Vitor	POR	8:48.16	
12	8	do CARMO, Clodoaldo	BRA	8:51.78	

Best Intermediate Times

	Name	Ctry	Result
1000 m	CROGHAN, Mark	USA	2:46.51
2000 m	BIRIR, Matthew	KEN	5:39.02

ROUND 1, HEAT 3

Rnk	Or	Name	Ctry	Result	
1	3	CAROSI, Angelo	ITA	8:30.83	Q
2	11	KIPTANUI, Moses	KEN	8:30.87	Q
3	4	BOULAMI, Brahim	MAR	8:30.97	Q
4	10	BRAND, Steffen	GER	8:31.18	Q
5	8	DAVIS, Marc	USA	8:31.25	Q
6	7	CULLEN, Keith	GBR	8:31.26	Q
7	1	SVENOY, Jim	NOR	8:31.30	q
8	5	UNTHANK, Chris	AUS	8:31.86	q
9	2	GOLYAS, Vladimir	RUS	8:35.50	q
10	9	MOGOTSI, Shadrack	RSA	8:46.24	
11	6	YAHYA, Ibrahim	KSA	8:46.37	

Best Intermediate Times

	Name	Ctry	Result
1000 m	CULLEN, Keith	GBR	2:52.40
2000 m	KIPTANUI, Moses	KEN	5:41.77

SEMIFINAL 1

Rnk	Or	Name	Ctry	Result	
1	3	DAVIS, Marc	USA	8:26.76	Q
2	5	BIRIR, Matthew	KEN	8:27.16	Q
3	4	LAMBRUSCHINI, Alessandro	ITA	8:27.32	Q
4	10	BOUAOUICHE, Hicham	MAR	8:27.76	Q
5	1	STREGE, Martin	GER	8:27.99	Q
6	7	IONESCU, Florin	ROM	8:28.77	
7	2	BOURGEOIS, Joel	CAN	8:31.45	
8	6	SAHERE, Abdelaziz	MAR	8:33.90	
9	12	GOLYAS, Vladimir	RUS	8:36.85	
10	8	SIAMUSIYE, Godfrey	ZAM	8:37.41	
11	11	CULLEN, Keith	GBR	8:46.74	
12	9	BAUERMEISTER, Kim	GER	8:51.83	

Best Intermediate Times

	Name	Ctry	Result
1000 m	BAUERMEISTER, Kim	GER	2:52.58
2000 m	DAVIS, Marc	USA	5:43.15

SEMIFINAL 2

Rnk	Or	Name	Ctry	Result	
1	4	KETER, Joseph	KEN	8:18.90	Q
2	5	KIPTANUI, Moses	KEN	8:18.91	Q
3	6	BRAND, Steffen	GER	8:19.11	Q
4	11	SVENOEY, Jim	NOR	8:19.79	Q
5	3	BOULAMI, Brahim	MAR	8:20.43	Q
6	7	CROGHAN, Mark	USA	8:21.01	q
7	8	CAROSI, Angelo	ITA	8:21.86	q
8	9	UNTHANK, Chris	AUS	8:25.59	
9	10	CHASTON, Justin	GBR	8:28.50	
10	2	PRONIN, Vladimir	RUS	8:34.79	
11	12	HASSAN, Jamal	QAT	8:36.40	
12	1	BOSCH, Nadir	FRA	8:47.31	

Best Intermediate Times

	Name	Ctry	Result
1000 m	CROGHAN, Mark	USA	2:45.69
2000 m	CROGHAN, Mark	USA	5:34.75

FINAL

Rnk	Or	Name	Ctry	Result	
1	9	KETER, Joseph	KEN	8:07.12	G
2	10	KIPTANUI, Moses	KEN	8:08.33	S
3	11	LAMBRUSCHINI, Alessandro	ITA	8:11.28	B
4	2	BIRIR, Matthew	KEN	8:17.18	
5	6	CROGHAN, Mark	USA	8:17.84	
6	4	BRAND, Steffen	GER	8:18.52	
7	1	BOULAMI, Brahim	MAR	8:23.13	
8	3	SVENOEY, Jim	NOR	8:23.39	
9	7	CAROSI, Angelo	ITA	8:29.67	
10	12	STREGE, Martin	GER	8:30.31	
11	5	BOUAOUICHE, Hicham	MAR	8:46.22	
12	8	DAVIS, Marc	USA	9:51.96	

Best Intermediate Times

	Name	Ctry	Result
1000 m	KIPTANUI, Moses	KEN	2:44.38
2000 m	KIPTANUI, Moses	KEN	5:29.15

Athletics / *Athlétisme*
4 x 100 m Relay, Men / *Relais 4 x 100 m, Messieurs*

ROUND 1, HEAT 1

Rnk	Ln	Ctry	Names	Result
1	7	UKR	RURAK, Kostya / OSOVYCH, Serhiy / KRAMARENKO, Oleh / DOLOGODIN, Slava	38.90 Q
2	5	BRA	SILVA, Arnaldo de O. / SILVA, Robson C. da / RIBEIRO, Edson L. / SILVA, Andre D. da	38.97 Q
3	1	GHA	AZIZ, Zakari / NSIAH, Christian / AGYEMANG, Albert / TUFFUOR, Emmanuel	39.47 q
4	4	NGR	ALIU, Deji / EZINWA, Osmond / OBIKWELU, Francis / EZINWA, Davidson	39.47 q
5	3	CMR	MOUSSAMBANI, A. / SIRIMOU, B. / NTHEPE, A. I. / TOUKENE-GUEBOGO, C.	39.81
6	6	VIN	SAMPSON, Erasto / MASCOLL, Joel / COOMBS, Eswort / CATO, Kahlil	40.54
7	2	MRI	CASQUETTE, Arnaud / MEYEPA, Dominique / POTANAH, Bruno / JOLICOEUR, Barnabe	40.92
8	8	LAO	PHENGTHALANGSY, P. / AMNOUAYPHONE, T. / VONGPHARKDY, S. / KETKEOLATSAMI, S.	44.14

ROUND 1, HEAT 2

Rnk	Ln	Ctry	Names	Result
1	5	CAN	CHAMBERS, Carlton / GILBERT, Glenroy / SURIN, Bruny / BAILEY, Donovan	38.68 Q
2	7	GER	HUKE, Michael / BLUME, Marc / RUTH, Andreas / SCHWARTHOFF, Florian	38.77 Q
3	6	SLE	LISK, Pierre / GANDA, Tom / THOMAS, Josephus / TURAY, Sanusi	38.98 q
4	8	SKN	LIDDIE, Ricardo / HAYNES, Bertram / COLLINS, Kim / ISAIAH, Alain Maxime	40.12
5	1	GEQ	MBOMIO, Ponciano / NZE, Casimiro / EDU, Bonifacio / ENVELA, Gustavo	45.63
	3	PNG	AKIA, Allan / PULU, Peter / ALI, Amos / BABO, Subul	DNF
	4	NZL	DONALDSON, Chris / KEDDELL, Mark / NKETIA, Gus / COAD, Matthew	DNS
	2	JPN	TSUCHIE, Hiroyasu / ITO, Koji / INOUE, Satoru / ASAHARA, Nobuharu	DQ

ROUND 1, HEAT 3

Rnk	Ln	Ctry	Names	Result
1	3	USA	DRUMMOND, Jon / HARDEN, Tim / MONTGOMERY, Tim / MITCHELL, Dennis	38.58 Q
2	7	SWE	KARLSSON, Peter / ERIKSSON, Torbjorn / HEDNER, Lars / STRENIUS, Patrik	39.02 Q
3	6	BAH	WELLS, Renward / STYLES, Joseph / LEWIS, Iram / TYNES, Andrew	39.38 q
4	4	THA	NAMWONG, Sayan / VECHAPHUT, Worasit / NATENEE, Kongdech / JANTHANA, Ekkachai	39.80
5	2	FIJ	BOLE, Solomone / DELAI, Jone / SEMITI, Henry / NAKAUNICINA, Soloveni	40.23
	5	GBR	JARRETT, Tony / BRAITHWAITE, Darren / CAMPBELL, Darren / DAKO, Owusu	DNF
	8	QAT		DNS

ROUND 1, HEAT 4

Rnk	Ln	Ctry	Names	Result
1	6	JAM	SPENCER, Percival / GREEN, Michael / GORDON, Leon / STEWART, Raymond	39.21 Q
2	4	ESP	FEO, Frutos / JOSE, Venancio / MAYORAL, Jordi / NAVARRO, Francisco	39.35 Q
3	8	CIV	WAOTA, Franck / DOUHOU, Hamed / NDRI, Eric / MEITE, Ibrahim	39.43 q
4	5	TOG	FOLLIGAN, Teko / LAWSON, Boevi / AYASSOU, Justin / AKOTO, Kossi	39.56
5	3	GAB	MOCCI RAOUMBE, Patrick / BOUSSOMBO, Antoine / TAYOT, Charles / EBANG, Eric	39.97
6	1	BEN	FANOU, Arcadius / DANGBO, Pascal / ALASSANE OUSSENI, Issa / AGUEH, Eric	40.79
7	7	GAM	SARR, Momodou / JALLOW, Dawda / SOWE, Cherno / GAI, Pa Modou	41.80
	2	ITA	PUGGIONI, Giovanni / MADONIA, Ezio / CIPOLLONI, Angelo / FLORIS, Sandro	DNF

ROUND 1, HEAT 5

Rnk	Ln	Ctry	Names	Result
1	4	AUS	HENDERSON, Paul / JACKSON, Tim / BRIMACOMBE, Steve / MAPSTONE, Rod	38.93 Q
2	2	FRA	LOMBA, Hermann / GROISARD, Regis / THEOPHILE, Pascal / GUIMS, Needy	39.00 Q
3	3	CUB	ISASI, Joel / LAMELA, Joel / GARCIA, Ivan / PEREZ, Luis Alberto	39.14 q
4	8	AUT	SCHUTZENAUER, M. / LACHKOVICS, M. / GRIESSER, Thomas / POESTINGER, Christoph	39.80
5	5	CYP	SPYROU, L. / MARKOULLIDES, A. / KATSANTONIS, Prodromos / ZISIMIDES, Yiannis	40.06
6	1	LBR	MAWENH, Kouty / COOPER, Sayon / NEUFVILLE, Edward Dosa-WeA / DENNIS, Robert	40.18
7	7	IVB	VARLACK, Ralston / CLINE, Keita / TODMAN, Willys / TODMAN, Mario	41.26
	6	GRE	YENOVELIS, A. / SBOKOS, Thomas / PANAYIOTOPOULOS, George / ALEXOPOULOS, A.	DQ

SEMIFINAL 1

Rnk	Ln	Ctry	Names	Result
1	3	CAN	CHAMBERS, Carlton / GILBERT, Glenroy / SURIN, Bruny / BAILEY, Donovan	38.36 Q
2	6	BRA	SILVA, Arnaldo de O. / SILVA, Robson C. da / RIBEIRO, Edson L. / SILVA, Andre D. da	38.42 Q
3	5	UKR	RURAK, Kostya / OSOVYCH, Serhiy / KRAMARENKO, Oleh / DOLOGODIN, Slava	38.56 Q
4	7	GHA	AZIZ, Zakari / NKANSAH, Eric / AGYEMANG, Albert / TUFFUOR, Emmanuel	38.62 Q
5	1	SLE	LISK, Pierre / GANDA, Tom / THOMAS, Josephus / TURAY, Sanusi	38.91
6	2	ESP	FEO, Frutos / JOSE, Venancio / MAYORAL, Jordi / NAVARRO, Francisco	38.91
7	8	CIV	WAOTA, Franck / DOUHOU, Hamed / NDRI, Eric / MEITE, Ibrahim	38.99
	4	GER	HUKE, Michael / BLUME, Marc / BLUME, Holger / SCHWARTHOFF, Florian	DNF

SEMIFINAL 2

Rnk	Ln	Ctry	Names	Result
1	3	USA	DRUMMOND, Jon / HARDEN, Tim / MONTGOMERY, Tim / MITCHELL, Dennis	37.96 Q
2	7	CUB	ISASI, Joel / LAMELA, Joel / GARCIA, Ivan / PEREZ, Luis Alberto	38.55 Q
3	1	SWE	KARLSSON, Peter / MARTENSSON, Torbjorn / HEDNER, Lars / STRENIUS, Patrik	38.63 Q
4	5	FRA	LOMBA, Hermann / GROISARD, Regis / THEOPHILE, Pascal / GUIMS, Needy	38.82 Q
	8	NGR	ALIU, Deji / EZINWA, Osmond / OBIKWELU, Francis / EZINWA, Davidson	DNF
	4	AUS	HENDERSON, Paul / JACKSON, Tim / BRIMACOMBE, Steve / MAPSTONE, Rod	DQ
	2	BAH	WELLS, Renward / FERGUSON, Dwight / LEWIS, Iram / TYNES, Andrew	DQ
	6	JAM	GORDON, Leon / GREEN, Michael / SPENCER, Percival / STEWART, Raymond	DQ

FINAL

Rnk	Ln	Ctry	Names	Result
1	6	CAN	ESMIE, Robert / GILBERT, Glenroy / SURIN, Bruny / BAILEY, Donovan	37.69 G
2	4	USA	DRUMMOND, Jon / HARDEN, Tim / MARSH, Michael / MITCHELL, Dennis	38.05 S
3	3	BRA	SILVA, Arnaldo de O. / SILVA, Robson C. da / RIBEIRO, Edson L. / SILVA, Andre D. da	38.41 B
4	7	UKR	RURAK, Kostya / OSOVYCH, Serhiy / KRAMARENKO, Oleh / DOLOGODIN, Slava	38.55
5	2	SWE	KARLSSON, Peter / MARTENSSON, Torbjorn / HEDNER, Lars / STRENIUS, Patrik	38.67
6	5	CUB	SIMON, Andres / LAMELA, Joel / ISASI, Joel / PEREZ, Luis Alberto	39.39
	8	FRA	LOMBA, Hermann / GROISARD, Regis / THEOPHILE, Pascal / GUIMS, Needy	DNF
	1	GHA	AZIZ, Zakari / NSIAH, Christian / AGYEMANG, Albert / TUFFUOR, Emmanuel	DNS

Athletics / *Athlétisme*
4 x 100 m Relay, Women / *Relais 4 x 100 m, Dames*

ROUND 1, HEAT 1

Rnk	Ln	Ctry	Names	Result
1	3	USA	GAINES, Chryste / GUIDRY, Carlette / MILLER, Inger / TORRENCE, Gwen	42.49 Q
2	7	BAH	CLARKE, Eldece / FYNES, Sevetheda / FERGUSON, Debbie / DAVIS, Pauline	43.14 Q
3	5	AUS	CRIPPS, Sharon / HANIGAN, Kylie / HEWITT, Lauren / LAMBERT, Jodi	43.75 q
4	8	COL	BROCK, Mirtha / PALACIOS, Felipa / RODRIGUEZ, Patricia / BORRERO, Zandra	44.16
5	1	CUB	HECHAVARRIA, Idalia / LOPEZ, Aliuska / PEREZ, Dainelkis / ALLEN, Liliana	44.32
6	6	ISV	NOEL, Maria / BELLO, Ameerah / PATRICK, Jilma / THOMAS, Rochelle	46.09
	4	CMR	MANI, Leonie / NKOMA, Georgette / ABENA FOUDA, Edwige / MBALLA ELOUNDOU, S.	DNF
	2	ANT	WILLIAMS, Sonia / POTTER, Dine / THOMAS, Charmaine / SAMUEL, Heather	DQ

ROUND 1, HEAT 2

Rnk	Ln	Ctry	Names	Result
1	5	JAM	FREEMAN, Michelle / RUSSELL, Gillian / MITCHELL, Nikole / LLOYD, Andria	43.36 Q
2	4	NGR	AJUNWA, Chioma / TOMBIRI-SHIREY, M. / OPARA-THOMPSON, Christy / ONYALI, Mary	43.54 Q
3	8	GBR	THORP, Angie / RICHARDSON, Marcia / JACOBS, Simmone / MERRY, Katharine	43.88 q
4	2	THA	KAWRUNGRUANG, Sunisa / INCHAREON, Kwuanfah / SRICHURE, S. / HUBSON, S.	45.62
	3	GER	PHILIPP, Andrea / LICHTENHAGEN, Silke / PASCHKE, Melanie / KNOLL, Silke	DNF
	7	MAD	RAMALALANIRINA, L. / RAKOTONDRABE, R. / RAMALALANIRINA, N. / RAVAONIRINA, L.	DNF
	6	LES	SELLO, Sebongile / TS'EHLO, 'm'apotlaki / KOAEANA, Nteboheleng / SHOAI, Lineo	DQ

4 x 100 m Relay, Women / *Relais 4 x 100 m, Dames*

<table>
<tr><th colspan="5">ROUND 1, HEAT 3</th></tr>
<tr><th>Rnk</th><th>Ln</th><th>Ctry</th><th>Names</th><th>Result</th></tr>
<tr><td>1</td><td>3</td><td>RUS</td><td>LESHCHOVA, Yekaterina / MALCHUGINA, Galina / VORONOVA, Natalya / PRIVALOVA, I.</td><td>43.00 Q</td></tr>
<tr><td>2</td><td>7</td><td>FRA</td><td>CITTE, Sandra / SIDIBE, Odiah / COMBE, Delphine / GIRARD-LENO, Patricia</td><td>43.09 Q</td></tr>
<tr><td>3</td><td>8</td><td>BUL</td><td>DIMITROVA, Dessislava / PENDAREVA, Petya / GEORGIEVA, Zlatka / GACHEVSKA, M.</td><td>44.19</td></tr>
<tr><td>4</td><td>2</td><td>FIN</td><td>MANNINEN, Johanna / HERNESNIEMI, Sanna / SUOMI, Heidi / PIRTTIMAA, Anu</td><td>44.21</td></tr>
<tr><td>5</td><td>5</td><td>CAN</td><td>ANDERSON, Katie / PERRY, Tara / ANTOINE, Ladonna / TASHLIN, Lesley</td><td>44.34</td></tr>
<tr><td></td><td>6</td><td>SKN</td><td>PRENTICE, Bernadeth / MORTON, Bernice / FRANCIS, Elricia / BASS, Valma</td><td>DNF</td></tr>
<tr><td></td><td>4</td><td>SLE</td><td>BARBER, Eunice / KAMANOR, Sia / FORNAH, Sama / MANSARAY, Melrose</td><td>DQ</td></tr>
</table>

<table>
<tr><th colspan="5">FINAL</th></tr>
<tr><th>Rnk</th><th>Ln</th><th>Ctry</th><th>Names</th><th>Result</th></tr>
<tr><td>1</td><td>5</td><td>USA</td><td>GAINES, Chryste / DEVERS, Gail / MILLER, Inger / TORRENCE, Gwen</td><td>41.95 G</td></tr>
<tr><td>2</td><td>2</td><td>BAH</td><td>CLARKE, Eldece / STURRUP, Chandra / FYNES, Sevetheda / DAVIS, Pauline</td><td>42.14 S</td></tr>
<tr><td>3</td><td>6</td><td>JAM</td><td>FREEMAN, Michelle / CUTHBERT, Juliet / MITCHELL, Nikole / OTTEY, Merlene</td><td>42.24 B</td></tr>
<tr><td>4</td><td>4</td><td>RUS</td><td>LESHCHOVA, Yekaterina / MALCHUGINA, Galina / VORONOVA, Natalya / PRIVALOVA, I.</td><td>42.27</td></tr>
<tr><td>5</td><td>7</td><td>NGR</td><td>AJUNWA, Chioma / TOMBIRI-SHIREY, Mary / OPARA-THOMPSON, Christy / ONYALI, M.</td><td>42.56</td></tr>
<tr><td>6</td><td>3</td><td>FRA</td><td>CITTE, Sandra / SIDIBE, Odiah / GIRARD-LENO, Patricia / PEREC, Marie-Jose</td><td>42.76</td></tr>
<tr><td>7</td><td>8</td><td>AUS</td><td>CRIPPS, Sharon / HANIGAN, Kylie / HEWITT, Lauren / LAMBERT, Jodi</td><td>43.70</td></tr>
<tr><td>8</td><td>1</td><td>GBR</td><td>THORP, Angie / RICHARDSON, Marcia / JACOBS, Simmone / MERRY, Katharine</td><td>43.93</td></tr>
</table>

Athletics / *Athlétisme*
4 x 400 m Relay, Men / *Relais 4 x 400 m, Messieurs*

<table>
<tr><th colspan="5">ROUND 1, HEAT 1</th></tr>
<tr><th>Rnk</th><th>Ln</th><th>Ctry</th><th>Names</th><th>Result</th></tr>
<tr><td>1</td><td>6</td><td>GBR</td><td>LADEJO, Du'aine / BAULCH, Jamie / HYLTON, Mark / RICHARDSON, Mark</td><td>3:01.79 Q</td></tr>
<tr><td>2</td><td>2</td><td>POL</td><td>RYSIUKIEWICZ, Piotr / JANUSZEWSKI, Pawel / MACKOWIAK, Robert / HACZEK, Piotr</td><td>3:01.92 Q</td></tr>
<tr><td>3</td><td>4</td><td>BRA</td><td>TEIXEIRA, Everson / da SILVA, Valdinei / dos SANTOS, Osmar / PARRELA, Sanderlei</td><td>3:02.51</td></tr>
<tr><td>4</td><td>8</td><td>AUS</td><td>LADBROOK, Mark / JOUBERT, Michael / GREENE, Paul / MacKENZIE, Cameron</td><td>3:03.73</td></tr>
<tr><td>5</td><td>5</td><td>LCA</td><td>JOHNSON, Dominic / JEAN-MARIE, Ivan / CHARLEMAGNE, Maxime / SEALES, Max</td><td>3:10.51</td></tr>
<tr><td>6</td><td>3</td><td>FIJ</td><td>NAKAUNICINA, Soloveni / SEMITI, Henry / BOLE, Solomone / NAIKELEKELEVESI, I.</td><td>3:10.67</td></tr>
<tr><td>7</td><td>7</td><td>SLE</td><td>SILLAH, Foday / KORJIE, Haroun / TURAY, Frank / AMARA, Prince</td><td>3:11.65</td></tr>
</table>

<table>
<tr><th colspan="5">ROUND 1, HEAT 2</th></tr>
<tr><th>Rnk</th><th>Ln</th><th>Ctry</th><th>Names</th><th>Result</th></tr>
<tr><td>1</td><td>5</td><td>USA</td><td>SMITH, LaMont / ROUSER, Jason / MILLS, Derek / MAYBANK, Anthuan</td><td>3:00.56 Q</td></tr>
<tr><td>2</td><td>3</td><td>RUS</td><td>ZHAROV, Innokentiy / VDOVIN, Mikhail / MASHCHENKO, Ruslan / KOSOV, Dmitriy</td><td>3:04.73 Q</td></tr>
<tr><td>3</td><td>2</td><td>GHA</td><td>AMEGATCHER, Solomon / DUAH, Abu / SEDAME, Julius / ALI, Ahmed</td><td>3:05.53</td></tr>
<tr><td>4</td><td>6</td><td>CUB</td><td>MENA, Omar / CRUSELLAS, Jorge / VERA, Georkis / HERNANDEZ, Roberto</td><td>3:05.75</td></tr>
<tr><td>5</td><td>8</td><td>QAT</td><td>FARAJ, Mubarak / DOKA, Ali / al-ABDULLA, Sami / al-DOSARI, Hamad</td><td>3:08.25</td></tr>
<tr><td>6</td><td>7</td><td>ANT</td><td>BARNES, N'kosie / TERRY, Michael / BROWNE, Mitchell / LINDSAY, Howard</td><td>3:09.46</td></tr>
<tr><td>7</td><td>4</td><td>LES</td><td>SEATILE, Isaac / MASEELA, Motlatsi / MAHANETSA, Makoekoe / MOROBE, Mpho</td><td>3:15.67</td></tr>
</table>

<table>
<tr><th colspan="5">ROUND 1, HEAT 3</th></tr>
<tr><th>Rnk</th><th>Ln</th><th>Ctry</th><th>Names</th><th>Result</th></tr>
<tr><td>1</td><td>7</td><td>KEN</td><td>YEGO, Samson / KEMBOI, Simon / OCHIENG, Kennedy / CHEPKWONY, Julius</td><td>3:02.52 Q</td></tr>
<tr><td>2</td><td>3</td><td>SEN</td><td>DIARRA, Moustapha / DIA, Aboubakry / NDIAYE, Hachim / FAYE, Ibou</td><td>3:02.61 Q</td></tr>
<tr><td>3</td><td>8</td><td>NGR</td><td>EKPEYONG, Udeme / CHUKWU, Clement / MACHEM, Ayuba / BADA, Sunday</td><td>3:02.73</td></tr>
<tr><td>4</td><td>5</td><td>SUI</td><td>CLERC, Laurent / WIDMER, Kevin / ROHR, Alain / RUSTERHOLZ, Mathias</td><td>3:03.05</td></tr>
<tr><td>5</td><td>6</td><td>VIN</td><td>COOMBS, Eswort / DICKSON, Thomas / LINLEY, Eversley / SAMPSON, Erasto</td><td>3:06.52</td></tr>
<tr><td>6</td><td>4</td><td>IVB</td><td>TODMAN, Mario / AUGUSTINE, Steve / RHYMER, Greg / VARLACK, Ralston</td><td>3:17.30</td></tr>
<tr><td>7</td><td>2</td><td>PNG</td><td>BAI, Samuel / WAKIT, Ivan / ALI, Amos / BABO, Subul</td><td>3:19.92</td></tr>
</table>

<table>
<tr><th colspan="5">ROUND 1, HEAT 4</th></tr>
<tr><th>Rnk</th><th>Ln</th><th>Ctry</th><th>Names</th><th>Result</th></tr>
<tr><td>1</td><td>5</td><td>JAM</td><td>HAUGHTON, Gregory / BLAKE, Dennis / MARTIN, Roxbert / ROBINSON, Garth</td><td>3:02.81 Q</td></tr>
<tr><td>2</td><td>3</td><td>ITA</td><td>VACCARI, Marco / AIMAR, Alessandro / NUTI, Andrea / SABER, Ashraf</td><td>3:03.60 Q</td></tr>
<tr><td>3</td><td>7</td><td>RSA</td><td>VISAGIE, Alfred / MALHERBE, Arnaud / MOKGANYETSI, Hendrik / PHIRI, Bobang</td><td>3:03.79</td></tr>
<tr><td>4</td><td>6</td><td>MRI</td><td>HASHAN, Gilbert / PIERRE-LOUIS, Desire / TIRVENGADUM, Rudy / MILAZAR, Jean</td><td>3:08.17</td></tr>
<tr><td>5</td><td>2</td><td>ZIM</td><td>MASVANISE, Julius / CHIWIRA, Tawanda / NGIDHI, Savieri / HARNDEN, Ken</td><td>3:13.35</td></tr>
<tr><td>6</td><td>4</td><td>MDV</td><td>SHAGEEF, Ahmed / AMIR, Mohamed / ISMAIL, Naseer / RIYAZ, Hussain</td><td>3:24.88</td></tr>
<tr><td></td><td>8</td><td>GRN</td><td>BRITTON, Richard / JONES, Rufus / FRANCIQUE, Alleyne / WILLIAMS, Clint</td><td>DQ</td></tr>
</table>

<table>
<tr><th colspan="5">ROUND 1, HEAT 5</th></tr>
<tr><th>Rnk</th><th>Ln</th><th>Ctry</th><th>Names</th><th>Result</th></tr>
<tr><td>1</td><td>8</td><td>JPN</td><td>KARUBE, Shunji / OSAKADA, Jun / OMORI, Shigekazu / TABATA, Kenji</td><td>3:02.82 Q</td></tr>
<tr><td>2</td><td>5</td><td>BAH</td><td>McINTOSH, Troy / MUNNINGS, Timothy / COOPER, Theron / DARLING, Dennis</td><td>3:04.09 Q</td></tr>
<tr><td>3</td><td>4</td><td>KSA</td><td>al-BESHI, Mohammed / al-SHARFA, Hashim / al-SAYDAN, Saleh / SOMAYLI, Hadi</td><td>3:04.67</td></tr>
<tr><td>4</td><td>3</td><td>GER</td><td>LIEDER, Rico / HEIN, Andreas / KARSTEN, Kai / SCHOENLEBE, Thomas</td><td>3:05.16</td></tr>
<tr><td>5</td><td>2</td><td>BOT</td><td>MATSHAMEKO, Aggripa / BALOSENG, Keteng / MOSWEU, Rampa / KUBISA, Johnson</td><td>3:06.62</td></tr>
<tr><td></td><td>6</td><td>GAM</td><td>JALLOW, Dawda / DRAMMEH, Momodou / DRAMMEH, Lamin / JOHN, Assan</td><td>DNF</td></tr>
<tr><td></td><td>7</td><td>GUY</td><td>HARRY, Andrew / GILL, Roger / GITTENS, Lancelot / JONES, Richard</td><td>DQ</td></tr>
</table>

<table>
<tr><th colspan="5">SEMIFINAL 1</th></tr>
<tr><th>Rnk</th><th>Ln</th><th>Ctry</th><th>Names</th><th>Result</th></tr>
<tr><td>1</td><td>6</td><td>GBR</td><td>THOMAS, Iwan / BAULCH, Jamie / LADEJO, Du'aine / RICHARDSON, Mark</td><td>3:01.36 Q</td></tr>
<tr><td>2</td><td>4</td><td>SEN</td><td>DIARRA, Moustapha / DIA, Aboubakry / NDIAYE, Hachim / FAYE, Ibou</td><td>3:01.72 Q</td></tr>
<tr><td>3</td><td>3</td><td>KEN</td><td>KITUR, Samson / YEGO, Samson / KEMBOI, Simon / CHEPKWONY, Julius</td><td>3:01.73 Q</td></tr>
<tr><td>4</td><td>5</td><td>POL</td><td>RYSIUKIEWICZ, Piotr / JEDRUSIK, Tomasz / MACKOWIAK, Robert / HACZEK, Piotr</td><td>3:02.29 Q</td></tr>
<tr><td>5</td><td>8</td><td>RSA</td><td>VISAGIE, Alfred / MALHERBE, Arnaud / MOKGANYETSI, Hendrik / PHIRI, Bobang</td><td>3:02.96</td></tr>
<tr><td>6</td><td>7</td><td>BRA</td><td>PARRELA, Sanderlei / da SILVA, Valdinei / TEIXEIRA, Everson / de ARAUJO, Eronilde</td><td>3:03.46</td></tr>
<tr><td>7</td><td>2</td><td>AUS</td><td>LADBROOK, Mark / JOUBERT, Michael / GREENE, Paul / MacKENZIE, Cameron</td><td>3:04.55</td></tr>
<tr><td>8</td><td>1</td><td>RUS</td><td>ZHAROV, Innokentiy / VDOVIN, Mikhail / MASHCHENKO, Ruslan / KOSOV, Dmitriy</td><td>3:05.63</td></tr>
</table>

<table>
<tr><th colspan="5">SEMIFINAL 2</th></tr>
<tr><th>Rnk</th><th>Ln</th><th>Ctry</th><th>Names</th><th>Result</th></tr>
<tr><td>1</td><td>5</td><td>USA</td><td>SMITH, LaMont / ROUSER, Jason / MILLS, Derek / MAYBANK, Anthuan</td><td>2:57.87 Q</td></tr>
<tr><td>2</td><td>6</td><td>JAM</td><td>McDONALD, Michael / BLAKE, Dennis / HAUGHTON, Gregory / MARTIN, Roxbert</td><td>2:58.42 Q</td></tr>
<tr><td>3</td><td>4</td><td>JPN</td><td>KARUBE, Shunji / OSAKADA, Jun / OMORI, Shigekazu / ITO, Koji</td><td>3:01.92 Q</td></tr>
<tr><td>4</td><td>8</td><td>BAH</td><td>McINTOSH, Troy / MUNNINGS, Timothy / COOPER, Theron / DARLING, Dennis</td><td>3:02.17 Q</td></tr>
<tr><td>5</td><td>3</td><td>ITA</td><td>MORI, Fabrizio / AIMAR, Alessandro / NUTI, Andrea / SABER, Ashraf</td><td>3:02.56</td></tr>
<tr><td>6</td><td>2</td><td>SUI</td><td>CLERC, Laurent / WIDMER, Kevin / ROHR, Alain / RUSTERHOLZ, Mathias</td><td>3:05.36</td></tr>
<tr><td>7</td><td>1</td><td>KSA</td><td>al-SAYDAN, Saleh / al-BESHI, Mohammed / al-SHARFA, Hashim / SOMAYLI, Hadi</td><td>3:07.18</td></tr>
<tr><td></td><td>7</td><td>NGR</td><td>EKPEYONG, Udeme / CHUKWU, Clement / MACHEM, Ayuba / BADA, Sunday</td><td>DQ</td></tr>
</table>

<table>
<tr><th colspan="5">FINAL</th></tr>
<tr><th>Rnk</th><th>Ln</th><th>Ctry</th><th>Names</th><th>Result</th></tr>
<tr><td>1</td><td>5</td><td>USA</td><td>SMITH, LaMont / HARRISON, Alvin / MILLS, Derek / MAYBANK, Anthuan</td><td>2:55.99 G</td></tr>
<tr><td>2</td><td>6</td><td>GBR</td><td>THOMAS, Iwan / BAULCH, Jamie / RICHARDSON, Mark / BLACK, Roger</td><td>2:56.60 S</td></tr>
<tr><td>3</td><td>4</td><td>JAM</td><td>McDONALD, Michael / MARTIN, Roxbert / HAUGHTON, Gregory / CLARKE, Davian</td><td>2:59.42 B</td></tr>
<tr><td>4</td><td>3</td><td>SEN</td><td>DIARRA, Moustapha / DIA, Aboubakry / NDIAYE, Hachim / FAYE, Ibou</td><td>3:00.64</td></tr>
<tr><td>5</td><td>7</td><td>JPN</td><td>KARUBE, Shunji / ITO, Koji / OSAKADA, Jun / OMORI, Shigekazu</td><td>3:00.76</td></tr>
<tr><td>6</td><td>8</td><td>POL</td><td>RYSIUKIEWICZ, Piotr / JEDRUSIK, Tomasz / HACZEK, Piotr / MACKOWIAK, Robert</td><td>3:00.96</td></tr>
<tr><td>7</td><td>2</td><td>BAH</td><td>OLIVER, Carl / McINTOSH, Troy / DARLING, Dennis / MUNNINGS, Timothy</td><td>3:02.71</td></tr>
<tr><td></td><td>1</td><td>KEN</td><td></td><td>DNS</td></tr>
</table>

Athletics / *Athlétisme*

4 x 400 m Relay, Women / *Relais 4 x 400 m, Dames*

ROUND 1, HEAT 1

Rnk	Ln	Ctry	Names	Result
1	2	USA	STEVENS, Rochelle / WILSON, Linetta / GRAHAM, Kim / MALONE, Maicel	3:22.71 Q
2	5	NGR	AFOLABI, Bisi / YUSUF, Fatima / OPARA, Charity / OGUNKOYA, Falilat	3:23.24 Q
3	8	FRA	LANDRE, Francine / DORSILE, Viviane / ELIEN, Evelyne / de VASSOIGNE, Elsa	3:28.07 Q
4	7	GBR	SMITH, Phylis / CURBISHLEY, Allison / FRASER, Donna / OLADAPO, Georgina	3:28.13
5	3	UKR	FOMENKO, Viktoriya / KOSHCHEY, Lyudmyla / MANUYLOVA, Yana / MOROZ, Olha	3:28.16
6	1	ANT	POTTER, Dine / WILLIAMS, Sonia / THOMAS, Charmaine / SAMUEL, Heather	3:44.98
	6	ISV		DNS
	4	IND	K MATHEW, B. / KUNNATH CHACKO, Rosakutty / SIKDAR, Jyotirmoyee / WILSON, Shiny	DQ

ROUND 1, HEAT 2

Rnk	Ln	Ctry	Names	Result
1	4	GER	ROHLAENDER, Uta / KISABAKA, Linda / RUCKER, Anja / BREUER, Grit	3:24.08 Q
2	5	CUB	BONNE, Idalmis / DUPORTY, Julia / MORALES, Surella / QUIROT, Ana Fidelia	3:24.23 Q
3	2	RUS	CHEBYKINA, Tatyana / KOTLYAROVA, O. / KULIKOVA, Yekaterina / GONCHARENKO, S.	3:24.86 Q
4	6	JAM	CAMPBELL, Juliet / BARNES, Tracey / FRAZER, Merlene / TURNER, Inez	3:25.33 q
5	7	CZE	KOSTOVALOVA, Nadezda / FORMANOVA, Ludmila / FUCHSOVA, H. / BENESOVA, H.	3:26.82 q
6	3	AUS	NAYLOR, Lee / HANIGAN, Kylie / GAINSFORD-TAYLOR, Melinda / POETSCHKA, Renee	3:33.78
7	8	SKN	PRENTICE, Bernadeth / FRANCIS, Diane / BASS, Valma / WIGLEY, Tamara	3:35.12

FINAL

Rnk	Ln	Ctry	Names	Result
1	3	USA	STEVENS, Rochelle / MALONE, Maicel / GRAHAM, Kim / MILES, Jearl	3:20.91 G
2	6	NGR	AFOLABI, Bisi / YUSUF, Fatima / OPARA, Charity / OGUNKOYA, Falilat	3:21.04 S
3	5	GER	ROHLAENDER, Uta / KISABAKA, Linda / RUCKER, Anja / BREUER, Grit	3:21.14 B
4	8	JAM	FRAZER, Merlene / RICHARDS, Sandie / CAMPBELL, Juliet / HEMMINGS, Deon	3:21.69
5	2	RUS	CHEBYKINA, Tatyana / GONCHARENKO, Svetlana / KULIKOVA, Y. / KOTLYAROVA, Olga	3:22.22
6	4	CUB	BONNE, Idalmis / DUPORTY, Julia / MORALES, Surella / QUIROT, Ana Fidelia	3:25.85
7	7	CZE	KOSTOVALOVA, N. / FORMANOVA, Ludmila / FUCHSOVA, Helena / BENESOVA, Hana	3:26.99
8	1	FRA	LANDRE, Francine / DORSILE, Viviane / ELIEN, Evelyne / de VASSOIGNE, Elsa	3:28.46

Athletics / *Athlétisme*

High Jump, Men / *Saut en hauteur, Messieurs*

QUALIFYING ROUND - GROUP A

Rnk	Name	Ctry	2.10	2.15	2.20	2.24	2.26	2.28	Result
1	AUSTIN, Charles	USA			O		O	O	2.28 Q
2	HOEN, Steinar	NOR		O	O	O	XXO	O	2.28 Q
3	KEMP, Troy	BAH		O		O	O	XO	2.28 Q
3	KOTEWICZ, Jaroslaw	POL		O		O	O	XO	2.28 Q
3	PAPAKOSTAS, Lambros	GRE			O	O	O	XO	2.28 Q
6	LEE, Jin-Taek	KOR		O	XO	O	O	XO	2.28 Q
7	SMITH, Steve	GBR		O		XO	XO	XO	2.28 Q
8	JANKU, Tomas	CZE	O	O	O	O	XO	XXO	2.28 Q
8	RADKIEWICZ, Przemyslaw	POL		O	O	XO	O	XXO	2.28 Q
10	LEFRANCOIS, Charles	CAN		O	O	O	O	XXX	2.26
11	MANDY, Mark	IRL	O	O	O	XXX			2.20
12	LUCIANO, Julio	DOM	O	XO	XO	XXX			2.20
13	WRIGHT, Cameron	USA	O	O	XXO	XXX			2.20
14	ANDERSON, Chris	AUS	O	O	XXX				2.15
14	NOMURA, Tomohiro	JPN	O	O	XXX				2.15
14	ZORIC, Stevan	YUG		O	XXX				2.15
17	KIM, Tae-Hoi	KOR	XO	XXO	XXX				2.15
	MUNOZ, Hugo	PER	XXX						NH
	WONG, Yew Tong	SIN	XXX						NH

QUALIFYING ROUND - GROUP B

Rnk	Name	Ctry	2.10	2.15	2.20	2.24	2.26	2.28	Result
1	FORSYTH, Tim	AUS			O	O	O	O	2.28 Q
1	PARTYKA, Artur	POL			O		O	O	2.28 Q
1	TOPIC, Dragutin	YUG			O	O	O	O	2.28 Q
4	SOTOMAYOR, Javier	CUB			O		XO	XO	2.28 Q
5	KREISSIG, Wolfgang	GER		O	XO	XO	O	XO	2.28 Q
6	TYRTYSHNIK, Vyacheslav	UKR	O	O	O	XO	O	XXX	2.26
7	MATOUSSEVICH, Konstantin	ISR		XO	O	XXO	O	XXX	2.26
8	ORTIZ, Arturo	ESP		O	O	XO	XO	XXX	2.26
9	GRANT, Dalton	GBR	O	O	XO	XO	XO	XXX	2.26
10	THOMPSON, Ian	BAH		O		XO	XXO	XXX	2.26
11	MAYO, Gilmar	COL		O	XO	XO	XXO	XXX	2.26
12	TURBAN, Marko	EST		XO	O	O	XXX		2.24
13	NAIKO, Khemraj	MRI	O	O	XO	XXX			2.20
14	LOO, Kum Zee	MAS	XO	O	XXX				2.15
15	BROXTERMAN, Ed	USA	XXO	O	XXX				2.15
16	CHO, Hyun-Wook	KOR	O	XXX					2.10
17	GOR, Fakhr Al-Dien	JOR	XXO	XXX					2.10
	SANOU, Oliver	BUR	XXX						NH
	SJOBERG, Patrik	SWE							DNS

FINAL

Rnk	Name	Ctry	2.15	2.20	2.25	2.29	2.32	2.35	2.37	2.39	2.41	2.46	Result
1	AUSTIN, Charles	USA	O		O		O	O	XX	O		XXX	2.39 O G
2	PARTYKA, Artur	POL		O		O		O	XO	X	XX		2.37 S
3	SMITH, Steve	GBR			XO		O	XO	XX	X			2.35 B
4	TOPIC, Dragutin	YUG		O	O	O	O	XX	X				2.32
5	HOEN, Steinar	NOR		O	O	XO	O	XX	X				2.32
6	PAPAKOSTAS, Lambros	GRE		O	O	O	XO	XX	X				2.32
7	FORSYTH, Tim	AUS		O	O	O	XXO	XX	X				2.32
8	LEE, Jin-Taek	KOR		XO	O	O	XXX						2.29
9	KREISSIG, Wolfgang	GER		XO	XO	O	XXX						2.29
10	RADKIEWICZ, Przemyslaw	POL		XO	XO	XO	XXX						2.29
11	KOTEWICZ, Jaroslaw	POL	O		O	XXX							2.25
11	SOTOMAYOR, Javier	CUB			O	XXX							2.25
13	KEMP, Troy	BAH			XO	X	XX						2.25
14	JANKU, Tomas	CZE	XO	XO	XO	XXX							2.25

Athletics / *Athlétisme*
High Jump, Women / *Saut en hauteur, Dames*

QUALIFYING ROUND - GROUP A

Rnk	Name	Ctry	1.75	1.80	1.85	1.90	1.93	Result	
1	BABAKOVA, Inha	UKR		O	O	O	O	1.93	q
1	BAKOGIANNI, Niki	GRE		O	O	O	O	1.93	q
1	BEVILACQUA, Antonella	ITA		O	O	O	O	1.93	q
1	GULYAYEVA, Yelena	RUS		O	O	O	O	1.93	q
1	KOSTADINOVA, Stefka	BUL		O	O	O	O	1.93	q
1	WALLER, Tisha	USA	O	O	O	O	O	1.93	q
1	ZALEVSKAYA, Svetlana	KAZ		O	O	O	O	1.93	q
8	BOLSHOVA, Olga	MDA		O	XO	O	XO	1.93	q
9	TEABERRY, Connie	USA	O	XO	O	XXO	XXX	1.90	
10	CADUSCH, Sieglinde	SUI	O	O	O	XXX		1.85	
10	MARTI, Debbie	GBR	O	O	O	XXX		1.85	
12	ALLEYNE, Natasha	TRI	O	XO	XXO	XXX		1.85	
13	ROSARIO, Juana	DOM	O	O	XXX			1.80	
14	MUNKOVA, Svetlana	UZB	O	XXO	XXX			1.80	
15	TIENDREBEOGO, Irene	BUR	XXO	XXO	XXX			1.80	
	CLINE, Coralea	IVB						DNS	
	KIRCHMANN, Sigrid	AUT						DNS	

QUALIFYING ROUND - GROUP B

Rnk	Name	Ctry	1.75	1.80	1.85	1.90	1.93	Result	
1	ASTAFEI, Alina	GER		O	O	O	O	1.93	q
1	HAUGLAND, Hanne	NOR		O	O	O	O	1.93	q
1	MOTKOVA, Tatyana	RUS	O	O	O	O	O	1.93	q
1	ZILINSKIENE, Nele	LTU		O	O	O	O	1.93	q
5	BILAC, Britta	SLO		O	O	O	XO	1.93	q
6	KOVACIKOVA, Zuzana	CZE	O	O	XO	XO	XXO	1.93	q
7	KHRAMOVA, Tatyana	BLR		O	O	O	XXX	1.90	
8	BERGQVIST, Kajsa	SWE	O	O	XO	O	XXX	1.90	
9	HAGGETT, Lea	GBR		XO	O	XO	XXX	1.90	
10	QUINTERO, Ioamnet	CUB		O	O	XXO	XXX	1.90	
11	LYAKHOVA, Yuliya	RUS		O	O	XXX		1.85	
11	STYOPINA, Vita	UKR		O	O	XXX		1.85	
13	GLIZNUTSA, Inna	MDA	O	XO	O	XXX		1.85	
14	ACUFF, Amy	USA	O	O	XO	XX		1.85	
14	JAVAD, Alica	SVK		O	XO	XXX		1.85	
16	VENEVA, Venelina	BUL	XXO	XXO	XXX			1.80	
	INVERARITY, Alison	AUS			XXX			NH	

FINAL

Rnk	Name	Ctry	1.80	1.85	1.90	1.93	1.96	1.99	2.01	2.03	2.05	2.10	Result	
1	KOSTADINOVA, Stefka	BUL		O	O	O	O	O	O	O	XO	XXX	2.05	O G
2	BAKOGIANNI, Niki	GRE	O	O	XO	O	O	XO	XO	XXO	XXX		2.03	S
3	BABAKOVA, Inha	UKR		O	O	O	O	O	O	XXX			2.01	B
4	BEVILACQUA, Antonella	ITA	O	O	O	O	O	O	XXX				1.99	
5	GULYAYEVA, Yelena	RUS		O	O	O	XO	XO	XXX				1.99	
6	ASTAFEI, Alina	GER		O	O	O	O	X	XX				1.96	
6	MOTKOVA, Tatyana	RUS		O	O	O	O	X	XX				1.96	
6	ZILINSKIENE, Nele	LTU	O	O	O	O	O	XXX					1.96	
9	HAUGLAND, Hanne	NOR		O	XXO	XO	O	XXX					1.96	
10	BILAC, Britta	SLO	O	O	O	O	XXX						1.93	
10	WALLER, Tisha	USA	O	O	O	O	XXX						1.93	
12	BOLSHOVA, Olga	MDA	O	O	XO	XO	XXX						1.93	
12	KOVACIKOVA, Zuzana	CZE	O	XO	O	XO	XXX						1.93	
14	ZALEVSKAYA, Svetlana	KAZ	O	O	XO	XXO	XXX						1.93	

Athletics / *Athlétisme*
Pole Vault, Men / *Saut à la perche, Messieurs*

QUALIFYING ROUND - GROUP A

Rnk	Name	Ctry	5.20	5.40	5.60	5.70	Result	
1	ANDJI, Alain	FRA		O	O	O	5.70	q
1	LOBINGER, Tim	GER		O	O	O	5.70	q
3	HARTWIG, Jeff	USA		O	XO	O	5.70	q
4	TRANDENKOV, Igor	RUS			XXO	O	5.70	q
5	POTAPOVICH, Igor	KAZ			O	XO	5.70	q
6	STOLLE, Michael	GER	XO	XO	O	XXO	5.70	q
7	MARKOV, Dmitriy	BLR		O	O	XXX	5.60	q
8	MILLER, Jim	AUS		XO	XO	XXX	5.60	
9	CHISTYAKOV, Viktor	RUS		XXO	XO	XXX	5.60	
10	FERNANDES, Nuno	POR	XO	O	XXO	XXX	5.60	
11	SEMYONOV, Konstantin	ISR		O	X	XX	5.40	
12	LOOIJE, Laurens	NED	XXO	O	XXX		5.40	
13	WINTER, Neil	GBR	O	XO	XXX		5.40	
14	DIAZ, Edgardo	PUR	XO	XXO	XXX		5.40	
15	YONEKURA, Teruyasu	JPN	XXO	XXX			5.20	
	BRITS, Okkert	RSA			XXX		NH	
	BUBKA, Vasiliy	UKR		XXX			NH	
	CONCEPCION, Juan Gabriel	ESP		XXX			NH	
	GARDENNE, Kersley	MRI	XXX				NH	

QUALIFYING ROUND - GROUP B

Rnk	Name	Ctry	5.20	5.40	5.60	5.70	Result	
1	BOCHKARYOV, Pyotr	RUS			O	O	5.70	q
1	BOTHA, Riaan	RSA		O	O	O	5.70	q
3	GALFIONE, Jean	FRA		XO	O	O	5.70	q
4	TIVONTCHIK, Andrei	GER			O	XXO	5.70	q
5	JOHNSON, Lawrence	USA		XO	XXO	XXO	5.70	q
6	HUFFMAN, Scott	USA		O	O	XXX	5.60	q
6	KRASNOV, Danny	ISR		O	O	XXX	5.60	q
8	ARCOS, Jose Manuel	ESP		XXO	O	XXX	5.60	
9	VAARANIEMI, Heikki	FIN		XO	XXO	X	5.60	
10	BUCKFIELD, Nick	GBR		O	XXX		5.40	
10	GARCIA, Javier	ESP		O	XXX		5.40	
12	KIM, Chul-Kyun	KOR	O	XO	XXX		5.40	
13	VOSS, Martin	DEN	XO	XO	X	XX	5.40	
14	OBIZAJEVS, Aleksandrs	LAT		XXO	XXX		5.40	
15	JUCOV, Alexandru	MDA	O	XXX			5.20	
	ARKELL, Simon	AUS		XXX			NH	
	BUKREJEV, Valeri	EST		XXX			NH	
	JOHNSON, Dominic	LCA	XXX				NH	
	BUBKA, Sergey	UKR					DNS	

Pole Vault, Men / *Saut à la perche, Messieurs*

FINAL

Rnk	Name	Ctry	5.40	5.60	5.70	5.80	5.86	5.92	5.97	6.02	Result
1	GALFIONE, Jean	FRA		O		XO	O	O	X	XX	5.92 O **G**
2	TRANDENKOV, Igor	RUS			O		XX	O		XXX	5.92 O **S**
3	TIVONTCHIK, Andrei	GER		XO		XO	XO	XO	XXX		5.92 O **B**
4	POTAPOVICH, Igor	KAZ			O		O	X	XX		5.86
5	BOCHKARYOV, Pyotr	RUS		XO		XO	O	XX	X		5.86
6	MARKOV, Dmitriy	BLR	O	O	XO	XXO	XO	XXX			5.86
7	LOBINGER, Tim	GER		O	O	O	X	XX			5.80
8	JOHNSON, Lawrence	USA	O	O	O	XXX					5.70
9	ANDJI, Alain	FRA	O	O	XXO	XXX					5.70
9	STOLLE, Michael	GER	O	O	XXO	XXX					5.70
11	HARTWIG, Jeff	USA	O	O	XXX						5.60
11	KRASNOV, Danny	ISR	O	O	XXX						5.60
13	HUFFMAN, Scott	USA	XO	O	XXX						5.60
14	BOTHA, Riaan	RSA	O	XO		XXX					5.60

Athletics / *Athlétisme*
Long Jump, Men / *Saut en longueur, Messieurs*

QUALIFYING ROUND - GROUP A

Rnk	Name	Ctry	1	2	3	Result	
1	POWELL, Mike	USA	8.20			8.20	Q
2	NIJS, Erik	BEL	7.80	X	8.16	8.16	Q
3	HUANG, Geng	CHN	7.70	8.12		8.12	Q
4	BECKFORD, James	JAM	X	8.02	X	8.02	q
4	SUNNEBORN, Mattias	SWE	8.02			8.02	q
6	CANKAR, Gregor	SLO	X	X	8.00	8.00	q
7	OWUSU, Andrew	GHA	7.91	7.88	X	7.91	
8	NAI, Hui-Fang	TPE	7.81	7.48	7.91	7.91	
9	TUDOR, Bogdan	ROM	7.88	7.72	7.87	7.88	
10	GOMBALA, Milan	CZE	7.88	X	X	7.88	
11	KOUKODIMOS, Kostas	GRE	7.82	X	X	7.82	
12	CALADO, Carlos	POR	7.36	7.81	X	7.81	
13	KYRYLENKO, Vitaliy	UKR	7.77	X	7.62	7.77	
14	FERREIRA, Nelson	BRA	7.76	7.69		7.76	
15	JEFFERSON, Jaime	CUB	7.61	7.47	7.65	7.65	
16	PETRUKHNOV, Aleksey	RUS	X	7.25	7.50	7.50	
17	LIMO, Remmy	KEN	X	7.46	X	7.46	
18	FOUCHE, Francois	RSA	7.29	7.30	7.44	7.44	
19	LEWIS, Kenny	GRN	7.41	7.22	X	7.41	
20	CLINE, Keita	IVB	X	X	7.26	7.26	
21	SHABANGU, Victor	SWZ	6.79	X	X	6.79	
	ERGOTIC, Sinisa	CRO	X	X	X	NM	
	FERNANDO, Benny	SRI	X	X	X	NM	
	LOTT, Hans-Peter	GER	X	X	X	NM	
	SUNG, Hee-Jun	KOR	X	X	X	NM	
	ZIO, Franck	BUR	X	X	X	NM	

QUALIFYING ROUND - GROUP B

Rnk	Name	Ctry	1	2	3	Result	
1	LEWIS, Carl	USA	7.93	X	8.29	8.29	Q
2	GREENE, Joe	USA	8.28			8.28	Q
3	NAUMKIN, Yuriy	RUS	7.83	8.21		8.21	Q
4	BANGUE, Emmanuel	FRA	7.88	X	8.09	8.09	Q
5	GLOVATSKIY, Aleksandr	BLR	7.90	8.07		8.07	Q
6	PEDROSO, Ivan	CUB	8.05			8.05	Q
7	IGNATOV, Andrey	RUS	X	X	8.00	8.00	q
8	VASDEKIS, Spyros	GRE	7.98	7.90	7.96	7.98	
9	TARUS, Bogdan	ROM	X	7.96	7.93	7.96	
10	TOURE, Cheikh Tidiane	SEN	7.91	X	7.76	7.91	
11	ACKERMANN, Georg	GER	X	X	7.86	7.86	
12	UZSOKI, Janos	HUN	X	X	7.82	7.82	
13	BIANCHI, Simone	ITA	X	X	7.79	7.79	
14	EMMIYAN, Robert	ARM	7.76	7.52	X	7.76	
15	CHEN, Jing	CHN	X	7.70	X	7.70	
16	CHAO, Chih-Kuo	TPE	7.67	X	X	7.67	
17	OLIVAN, Jesus	ESP	7.59	7.64	X	7.64	
18	de SOUZA, Douglas	BRA	7.59	X	7.61	7.61	
19	DUNCAN, Richard	CAN	7.51	7.56	7.61	7.61	
20	ASAHARA, Nobuharu	JPN	5.49	7.46	X	7.46	
21	MARINKOVIC, Andreja	YUG	X	7.17	X	7.17	
22	da CRUZ, Marcio	BRA	7.12	X	X	7.12	
	MALYAVIN, Vladimir	TKM	X	X	X	NM	
	MANUEL, Ellsworth	AHO	X	X		NM	
	MLADENOV, Ivaylo	BUL	X	X		NM	
	SALLAH, Ousman	GAM	X	X	X	NM	
	HEPBURN, Craig	BAH				DNS	

FINAL

Rnk	Name	Ctry	1	2	3	4	5	6	Result
1	LEWIS, Carl	USA	X	8.14	8.50		8.06	X	8.50 **G**
2	BECKFORD, James	JAM	X	8.02	8.13	X	X	8.29	8.29 **S**
3	GREENE, Joe	USA	7.80	7.79	8.24	X	X	X	8.24 **B**
4	BANGUE, Emmanuel	FRA	8.19	8.10	X	7.88	6.46	6.87	8.19
5	POWELL, Mike	USA	7.89	8.17	7.99	X	X	X	8.17
6	CANKAR, Gregor	SLO	X	X	8.11	X	X	5.33	8.11
7	GLOVATSKIY, Aleksandr	BLR	8.07	X	8.07	X	X	X	8.07
8	SUNNEBORN, Mattias	SWE	7.89	7.97	8.06	8.04	8.03	7.75	8.06
9	HUANG, Geng	CHN	7.99	7.87	7.89				7.99
10	NAUMKIN, Yuriy	RUS	7.96	7.88	7.95				7.96
11	IGNATOV, Andrey	RUS	X	7.83	7.58				7.83
12	PEDROSO, Ivan	CUB	X	7.57	7.75				7.75
13	NIJS, Erik	BEL	7.59	X	7.72				7.72

Athletics / *Athlétisme*
Long Jump, Women / *Saut en longueur, Dames*

QUALIFYING ROUND - GROUP A

Rnk	Name	Ctry	1	2	3	Result	
1	MAY, Fiona	ITA	6.58	6.85		6.85	Q
2	AJUNWA, Chioma	NGR	6.64	6.81		6.81	Q
3	JAKLOFSKY, Sharon	NED	X	6.69	6.75	6.75	Q
4	VASZI, Tunde	HUN	6.41	6.73		6.73	Q
5	CHEKHOVTSOVA, Iryna	UKR	6.44	6.70		6.70	Q
6	JOYNER-KERSEE, Jackie	USA	6.70			6.70	Q
6	KARCZMAREK, Agata	POL	6.70			6.70	Q
8	BOEGMAN, Nicole	AUS	X	X	6.67	6.67	q
9	XANTHOU, Niki	GRE	X	X	6.60	6.60	q
10	CUZA, Lisette	CUB	6.45	6.56	6.39	6.56	
11	PERSHINA, Yelena	KAZ	6.50	X	X	6.50	
12	VELTMAN, Marieke	USA	6.43	6.49	X	6.49	
13	RUBLYOVA, Olga	RUS	6.47	X		6.47	
14	CARDENAS, Regla	CUB	6.36	6.21	6.42	6.42	
15	PREDIKAKA, Ksenija	SLO	X	6.37	X	6.37	
16	NAERIS, Virge	EST	X	6.26	6.17	6.26	
17	GOTOVSKA, Valentina	LAT	X	X	6.08	6.08	
18	AVILA, Andrea	ARG	X	5.92	6.00	6.00	
19	ATROSCHENKO, Anzhela	BLR	X	X	5.94	5.94	
20	YASMIN, Nilufar	BAN	5.19	4.65	5.24	5.24	
21	LARAME, Beryl	SEY	X	3.88	X	3.88	
	GHEORGHIU, Mihaela	ROM	X			NM	
	NIELSEN, Renata	DEN	X	X	X	NM	
	BAPTISTE, Michelle	LCA				DNS	
	ROSE, Dione	JAM				DNS	

QUALIFYING ROUND - GROUP B

Rnk	Name	Ctry	1	2	3	Result	
1	PRANDZHEVA, Iva	BUL	6.58	6.62	X	6.62	q
2	BRUNNER, Chantal	NZL	X	6.47	6.62	6.62	q
3	PATOULIDOU, Voula	GRE	6.58	6.09	6.13	6.58	q
4	HYACINTH, Flora	ISV	X	X	6.58	6.58	
5	EDWARDS, Jackie	BAH	6.44	6.55	6.27	6.55	
6	MONTALVO, Niurka	CUB	6.48	X	X	6.48	
7	BARBER, Eunice	SLE	6.20	6.20	6.45	6.45	
8	CISTJAKOVA, Galina	SVK	6.33	X	6.26	6.33	
9	LEWIS, Denise	GBR	X	X	6.33	6.33	
10	SINCHUKOVA, Yelena	RUS	X	6.31	X	6.31	
11	GUTHRIE-GRESHAM, Diane	JAM	6.27	X	X	6.27	
12	LIKU, Ana	TGA	X	X	6.06	6.06	
13	MUROS, Elma	PHI	5.98	6.04	5.99	6.04	
14	INANCSI, Rita	HUN	6.02	X	X	6.02	
15	AKHTAR, Shabana	PAK	5.72	5.70	5.80	5.80	
16	DEVONISH, Nicole	CAN	5.74	5.59	X	5.74	
17	KOSHCHEYEVA, Yelena	KAZ	X	5.49	5.55	5.55	
	GALKINA, Lyudmila	RUS	X	X	X	NM	
	GOLDING, Lacena	JAM	X	X	X	NM	
	KOIVULA, Heli	FIN	X	X	X	NM	
	KRAVETS, Inessa	UKR	X	X	X	NM	
	NINOVA, Ljudmila	AUT	X	X	X	NM	
	SAZANOVICH, Natasha	BLR	X			NM	
	VERSHYNINA, Viktoriya	UKR	X	X	X	NM	
	WILLIAMS, Shana	USA	X	X	X	NM	

FINAL

Rnk	Name	Ctry	1	2	3	4	5	6	Result	
1	AJUNWA, Chioma	NGR	7.12	6.99	6.85	6.84		X	7.12	G
2	MAY, Fiona	ITA	6.68	7.02	6.78	6.73	6.76	6.88	7.02	S
3	JOYNER-KERSEE, Jackie	USA	6.55	6.75	6.86	X	6.52	7.00	7.00	B
4	XANTHOU, Niki	GRE	X	6.97	X	6.67	6.95	6.85	6.97	
5	CHEKHOVTSOVA, Iryna	UKR	6.84	6.88	X	6.97	X	X	6.97	
6	KARCZMAREK, Agata	POL	6.90	X	X	X	X	6.65	6.90	
7	PRANDZHEVA, Iva	BUL	X	X	6.81	X	6.82	X	6.82	
8	BOEGMAN, Nicole	AUS	6.73	X	X	X	6.55	6.23	6.73	
9	VASZI, Tunde	HUN	6.60	X	X				6.60	
10	BRUNNER, Chantal	NZL	6.45	6.49	6.45				6.49	
11	PATOULIDOU, Voula	GRE	X	6.26	6.37				6.37	
	JAKLOFSKY, Sharon	NED	X	X	X				NM	

Athletics / *Athlétisme*
Triple Jump, Men / *Triple saut, Messieurs*

QUALIFYING ROUND - GROUP A

Rnk	Name	Ctry	1	2	3	Result	
1	HARRISON, Kenny	USA	17.58			17.58	Q
2	QUESADA, Yoelbi	CUB	17.19			17.19	Q
3	WELLMAN, Brian	BER	17.10			17.10	Q
4	HOWARD, Robert	USA	16.83	16.76	16.92	16.92	q
5	SOTNIKOV, Viktor	RUS	16.86	X	16.19	16.86	q
6	ROMAIN, Jerome	DMA	16.80	X	X	16.80	q
7	RUTHERFORD, Frank	BAH	X	16.38	16.73	16.73	q
8	AGYEPONG, Francis	GBR	16.71	16.68	X	16.71	
9	SILVA, Anisio	BRA	16.38	16.67	16.08	16.67	
10	CALADO, Carlos	POR	16.43	16.65	X	16.65	
11	ASADOV, Vasif	AZE	X	X	16.21	16.21	

QUALIFYING ROUND - GROUP A - *continued*

Rnk	Name	Ctry	1	2	3	Result
12	KATONON, Jacob	KEN	16.08	16.17	X	16.17
13	TSONOV, Stoyko	BUL	16.00	16.15	X	16.15
14	ORDINA, Tibor	HUN	16.04	X	X	16.04
15	MURPHY, Andrew	AUS	15.97	X	16.00	16.00
16	IGBINOGHENE, Festus	NGR	15.95	X	15.72	15.95
17	ARZAMASOV, Sergey	KAZ	15.91	X		15.91
18	SMETANIN, Maksim	KGZ	15.83	15.90	X	15.90
19	JASIM, Ihsan	IRQ	15.19	15.27	X	15.27
20	MDHLONGWA, Ndabe	ZIM	14.47	X	X	14.47
21	SASSI, Karim	TUN	X	X	14.25	14.25
	BRUZIKS, Maris	LAT				DNS

Triple Jump, Men / *Triple saut, Messieurs*

QUALIFYING ROUND - GROUP B

Rnk	Name	Ctry	1	2	3	Result	
1	CONLEY, Mike	USA	17.20			17.20	Q
2	GEORGIEV, Galin	BUL	17.02			17.02	Q
3	EDWARDS, Jonathan	GBR	16.93	16.96		16.96	q
4	KRAVCHENKO, Volodymyr	UKR	16.71	16.90	X	16.90	q
5	MARTIROSYAN, Armen	ARM	15.71	16.68	16.74	16.74	q
6	FRIEDEK, Charles	GER	X	16.71	16.58	16.71	
7	URRUTIA, Aliecer	CUB	16.71	16.54	X	16.71	
8	SOKOV, Vasiliy	RUS	X	16.68	X	16.68	
9	NACHUM, Rogel	ISR	15.86	16.67	16.53	16.67	
10	GARCIA, Yoel	CUB	15.94	X	16.62	16.62	
11	ZOU, Sixin	CHN	16.13	16.44	16.53	16.53	
12	BAPTISTA, Messias Jose	BRA	16.02	16.45	16.13	16.45	
13	RAIZGYS, Audrius	LTU	16.38	X	16.06	16.38	
14	CZINGLER, Zsolt	HUN	16.22	16.35	X	16.35	
15	al-AHMADY, Salem	KSA	X	15.97	16.30	16.30	
16	DODOO, Francis	GHA	X	X	16.24	16.24	
17	NJERVE, Sigurd	NOR	15.22	X	16.15	16.15	
18	FATYANOV, Aleksey	AZE	16.14	X	16.13	16.14	
19	SAUTKIN, Igor	RUS	X	X	16.06	16.06	
20	PETIN, Yevgeniy	UZB	X	15.58	15.89	15.89	
21	NIOZE, Paul	SEY	15.63	15.43	X	15.63	
22	LOVELACE, Kawan	BIZ	15.40	X	14.97	15.40	

FINAL

Rnk	Name	Ctry	1	2	3	4	5	6	Result	
1	HARRISON, Kenny	USA	17.99	X		18.09		X	18.09	O G
2	EDWARDS, Jonathan	GBR	X	X	17.13	17.88	X	X	17.88	S
3	QUESADA, Yoelbi	CUB	17.04	17.29	X	17.44	X	X	17.44	B
4	CONLEY, Mike	USA	17.08	X	16.17	17.40	X	X	17.40	
5	MARTIROSYAN, Armen	ARM	16.85	X	16.97	16.48	X	16.34	16.97	
6	WELLMAN, Brian	BER	16.95	X	16.82	X	X	X	16.95	
7	GEORGIEV, Galin	BUL	16.85	X	X	X	X	16.92	16.92	
8	HOWARD, Robert	USA	16.72	16.83	16.90	X	16.44	16.52	16.90	
9	SOTNIKOV, Viktor	RUS	16.84	16.53	16.56				16.84	
10	KRAVCHENKO, Volodymyr	UKR	16.35	15.92	16.62				16.62	
11	RUTHERFORD, Frank	BAH	16.38	X	16.36				16.38	
	ROMAIN, Jerome	DMA	X						NM	

Athletics / *Athlétisme*

Triple Jump, Women / *Triple saut, Dames*

QUALIFYING ROUND - GROUP A

Rnk	Name	Ctry	1	2	3	Result	
1	PRANDZHEVA, Iva	BUL	X	14.61		14.61	Q
2	GOVOROVA, Olena	UKR	X	14.60		14.60	Q
3	REN, Ruiping	CHN	X	X	14.56	14.56	Q
4	VASDEKI, Olga	GRE	14.13	14.48		14.48	Q
5	KHLUSOVYCH, Olena	UKR	14.38			14.38	Q
6	BLAZEVICA, Jelena	LAT	14.24			14.24	Q
7	BIRYUKOVA, Anna	RUS	13.81	13.94	14.19	14.19	
8	CISTJAKOVA, Galina	SVK	14.08	14.14	13.54	14.14	
9	NAERIS, Virge	EST	13.94	13.95	14.00	14.00	
10	RHODES, Cynthea	USA	X	13.95	13.88	13.95	
11	LAH, Barbara	ITA	X	13.74	X	13.74	
12	GRIFFITH, Michelle	GBR	13.38	X	13.70	13.70	
13	LEE, Suzette	JAM	13.64	13.65	X	13.65	
14	MARTIAL, Nicola	GUY	12.75	X	12.91	12.91	
15	BITANJI, Vera	ALB	12.55	12.82	X	12.82	
	ORRANGE, Diana	USA	X	X	X	NM	

QUALIFYING ROUND - GROUP B

Rnk	Name	Ctry	1	2	3	Result	
1	LASOVSKAYA, Inna	RUS	14.75			14.75	Q
2	KRAVETS, Inessa	UKR	14.57			14.57	Q
3	HANSEN, Ashia	GBR	14.55			14.55	Q
4	KASPARKOVA, Sarka	CZE	14.42			14.42	Q
5	HUDSON, Sheila	USA	14.26			14.26	Q
6	MATEESCU, Rodica	ROM	13.85	14.22		14.22	Q
7	SPROGE, Gundega	LAT	13.67	X	X	13.67	
8	KAYUKOVA, Natalya	RUS	13.35	X	13.54	13.54	
9	de SOUZA, Maria Aparecida	BRA	13.12	13.38	13.13	13.38	
10	WANG, Xiangrong	CHN	X	13.06	13.32	13.32	
11	KOIVULA, Heli	FIN	12.43	X	13.25	13.25	
12	GILHARRY, Althea	BIZ	X	12.78	12.75	12.78	
13	OUOBA, Chantal	BUR	12.40	12.19	12.24	12.40	
	BALINT, Zita	HUN	X	X	X	NM	
	LOBINGER, Petra	GER	X	X	X	NM	
	PAREDES, Conchi	ESP	X	X	X	NM	
	ALDAMA, Yamile	CUB				DNS	

FINAL

Rnk	Name	Ctry	1	2	3	4	5	6	Result	
1	KRAVETS, Inessa	UKR	X	14.40	14.84	X	15.33	14.75	15.33	O G
2	LASOVSKAYA, Inna	RUS	X	14.98	X	14.66	14.70	14.21	14.98	S
3	KASPARKOVA, Sarka	CZE	X	14.45	14.98	14.69	X	14.48	14.98	B
4	PRANDZHEVA, Iva	BUL	X	X	14.84	14.39	X	14.92	14.92	
5	HANSEN, Ashia	GBR	13.61	14.49	13.75	14.35	14.24	14.30	14.49	
6	VASDEKI, Olga	GRE	13.94	14.44	14.39	X	14.17	14.33	14.44	
7	REN, Ruiping	CHN	14.30	14.11	13.80	13.70	13.75	13.91	14.30	
8	MATEESCU, Rodica	ROM	X	13.92	14.21	14.07	13.68	X	14.21	
9	BLAZEVICA, Jelena	LAT	13.98	14.12	13.88				14.12	
10	GOVOROVA, Olena	UKR	X	14.04	14.09				14.09	
11	HUDSON, Sheila	USA	14.02	13.91	13.69				14.02	
12	KHLUSOVYCH, Olena	UKR	13.81	13.65					13.81	

Athletics / *Athlétisme*
Hammer Throw, Men / *Marteau, Messieurs*

QUALIFYING ROUND - GROUP A

Rnk	Name	Ctry	1	2	3	Result	
1	KISS, Balazs	HUN	X	78.34		78.34	Q
2	WEIS, Heinz	GER	75.16	77.84		77.84	Q
3	ZIOLKOWSKI, Szymon	POL	77.64			77.64	Q
4	SIDORENKO, Vasiliy	RUS	76.64			76.64	Q
5	KRYKUN, Oleksiy	UKR	73.82	75.78	75.70	75.78	q
6	ALAY, Sergey	BLR	74.94	73.60	75.10	75.10	q
7	DETHLOFF, Claus	GER	74.60	73.68	72.68	74.60	
8	PAPADIMITRIOU, Alexandros	GRE	74.42	X	74.46	74.46	
9	EPALLE, Christophe	FRA	74.22	73.42	73.98	74.22	
10	DUPRAY, Gilles	FRA	X	70.92	74.04	74.04	
11	SEDLACEK, Pavel	CZE	72.60	73.98	X	73.98	
12	McMAHON, Kevin	USA	73.10	73.46	72.78	73.46	
13	TAMM, Juri	EST	72.14	73.16	X	73.16	
14	PAOLUZZI, Loris	ITA	71.38	71.68	72.82	72.82	
15	ANNUS, Adrian	HUN	68.68	72.26	72.58	72.58	
16	GUSTAFSSON, Tore	SWE	70.36	71.02	X	71.02	
17	BIELECKI, Jan	DEN	X	X	69.40	69.40	
18	LINSCHEID, Roman	IRL	X	68.14	66.90	68.14	

QUALIFYING ROUND - GROUP B

Rnk	Name	Ctry	1	2	3	Result	
1	DEAL, Lance	USA	75.10	76.34	78.56	78.56	Q
2	ASTAPKOVICH, Igor	BLR	76.00	78.52		78.52	Q
3	SKVARUK, Andriy	UKR	73.52	77.48		77.48	Q
4	SGRULLETTI, Enrico	ITA	77.36			77.36	Q
5	PIOLANTI, Raphael	FRA	75.46	X	76.44	76.44	q
6	KONOVALOV, Ilya	RUS	74.84	75.10	75.08	75.10	q
7	SANCHEZ, Alberto	CUB	73.16	74.22	74.82	74.82	
8	KHERSONTSEV, Vadim	RUS	73.62	74.00	74.48	74.48	
9	KOBS, Karsten	GER	72.04	X	74.20	74.20	
10	KRASKO, Aleksandr	BLR	71.82	73.74	X	73.74	
11	NEMETH, Zsolt	HUN	41.64	72.24	73.68	73.68	
12	WAHLMAN, Marko	FIN	72.60	73.50	X	73.50	
13	CARLIN, Sean	AUS	73.32	72.00	X	73.32	
14	POPEJOY, Ken	USA	72.08	72.46	X	72.46	
15	SMITH, David	GBR	X	X	69.32	69.32	
16	ABBAS, Aqarab	PAK	65.60	X	64.34	65.60	
17	CHARADIA, Andres	ARG	65.26	X	X	65.26	
18	KHOZHATELYOV, Vitaliy	UZB	64.52	X	X	64.52	
	POLYHRONIOU, Hristos	GRE	X	X	X	NM	

FINAL

Rnk	Name	Ctry	1	2	3	4	5	6	Result	
1	KISS, Balazs	HUN	79.28	80.50	81.24	78.60	79.82	X	81.24	G
2	DEAL, Lance	USA	X	X	76.94	75.62	77.26	81.12	81.12	S
3	KRYKUN, Oleksiy	UKR	76.24	77.64	79.44	X	78.14	80.02	80.02	B
4	SKVARUK, Andriy	UKR	74.24	X	79.92	75.80	76.56	X	79.92	
5	WEIS, Heinz	GER	78.78	79.30	X	78.10	78.98	79.78	79.78	
6	KONOVALOV, Ilya	RUS	76.44	77.48	77.44	77.70	76.52	78.72	78.72	

FINAL - *continued*

Rnk	Name	Ctry	1	2	3	4	5	6	Result
7	ASTAPKOVICH, Igor	BLR	76.38	78.20	X	76.62	77.38	X	78.20
8	ALAY, Sergey	BLR	75.46	76.68	77.38	76.50	76.38	75.78	77.38
9	SGRULLETTI, Enrico	ITA	76.34	76.94	75.22	76.88	74.78	76.98	76.98
10	ZIOLKOWSKI, Szymon	POL	76.30	74.90	76.64				76.64
11	PIOLANTI, Raphael	FRA	74.34	75.24	X				75.24
12	SIDORENKO, Vasiliy	RUS	73.62	X	74.68				74.68

Athletics / *Athlétisme*
Shot Put, Men / *Poids, Messieurs*

QUALIFYING ROUND - GROUP A

Rnk	Name	Ctry	1	2	3	Result	
1	,BUDER, Oliver-Sven	GER	19.76	20.43		20.43	Q
2	BARNES, Randy	USA	X	19.70	20.42	20.42	Q
3	VIRASTYUK, Roman	UKR	19.81			19.81	Q
4	PERIC, Dragan	YUG	19.61	X	19.61	19.61	q
5	GONCHARUK, Dmitriy	BLR	19.57	X	19.17	19.57	q
6	FANTINI, Corrado	ITA	18.63	19.40	19.00	19.40	q
7	MARTINEZ, Manuel	ESP	19.12	18.93	18.90	19.12	
8	MERTENS, Michael	GER	18.57	18.90	19.07	19.07	
9	LARSSON, Kent	SWE	18.60	18.86	19.05	19.05	
10	HARJU, Arsi	FIN	18.56	19.01	X	19.01	
11	VENTURI, Giorgio	ITA	18.60	18.98	18.52	18.98	
12	LOUCA, Elias	CYP	18.48	17.98	X	18.48	
13	UGWU, Chima	NGR	18.39	18.35	18.33	18.39	
14	SHIDLOVSKIY, Aleksey	RUS	17.84	18.34	18.37	18.37	
15	KLEIZA, Saulius	LTU	18.08	18.21	18.18	18.21	
16	LEIATO, Anthony	ASA	12.28	X	13.02	13.02	
	KOCZIAN, Jeno	HUN	X	X	X	NM	
	RUBTSOV, Sergey	KAZ	X			NM	

QUALIFYING ROUND - GROUP B

Rnk	Name	Ctry	1	2	3	Result	
1	dal SOGLIO, Paolo	ITA	19.43	20.58		20.58	Q
2	GODINA, John	USA	20.54			20.54	Q
3	BAGACH, Oleksandr	UKR	20.23			20.23	Q
4	HUNTER, C. J.	USA	19.95			19.95	Q
5	KLYMENKO, Oleksandr	UKR	19.11	19.45	X	19.45	q
6	MUBARAK, Bilal Saad	QAT	19.39	19.23	19.28	19.39	q
7	URBAN, Dirk	GER	19.39	18.82	19.23	19.39	
8	HALVARI, Mika	FIN	19.37	X	18.78	19.37	
9	PALCHIKOV, Yevgeniy	RUS	18.75	18.83	18.96	18.96	
10	MENC, Miroslav	CZE	18.69	18.13	18.42	18.69	
11	WEIL, Gert	CHI	18.64	18.67	18.58	18.67	
12	MEDINA, Yojer	VEN	X	18.49	18.53	18.53	
13	PICKERING, Shaun	GBR	18.29	18.23	17.45	18.29	
14	LOUCA, Mihalis	CYP	18.23	18.03	18.12	18.23	
15	al-KHALIDI, Khalid	KSA	18.22	X	17.83	18.22	
16	SNYDER, Brad	CAN	17.98	X	X	17.98	
17	BULAT, Viktor	BLR	16.70	16.67	17.29	17.29	
18	KOT, Sergey	UZB	16.51	X	16.05	16.51	

FINAL

Rnk	Name	Ctry	1	2	3	4	5	6	Result	
1	BARNES, Randy	USA	19.46	20.44	X	20.26	20.32	21.62	21.62	G
2	GODINA, John	USA	X	19.91	19.98	20.64	20.79	X	20.79	S
3	BAGACH, Oleksandr	UKR	20.41	20.50	20.29	X	X	20.75	20.75	B
4	dal SOGLIO, Paolo	ITA	20.12	20.65	19.92	20.74	20.60	X	20.74	
5	BUDER, Oliver-Sven	GER	20.16	19.92	20.37	20.13	20.51	19.71	20.51	
6	VIRASTYUK, Roman	UKR	19.46	19.86	20.32	20.21	20.45	X	20.45	

FINAL - *continued*

Rnk	Name	Ctry	1	2	3	4	5	6	Result
7	HUNTER, C. J.	USA	19.99	20.09	20.39	X	20.25	20.35	20.39
8	PERIC, Dragan	YUG	19.66	19.75	19.98	X	X	20.07	20.07
9	GONCHARUK, Dmitriy	BLR	X	19.79	X				19.79
10	MUBARAK, Bilal Saad	QAT	19.11	19.33	X				19.33
11	FANTINI, Corrado	ITA	19.30	X	X				19.30
	KLYMENKO, Oleksandr	UKR	X	X	X				NM

Athletics / *Athlétisme*
Shot Put, Women / *Poids, Dames*

QUALIFYING ROUND - GROUP A

Rnk	Name	Ctry	1	2	3	Result	
1	KUMBERNUSS, Astrid	GER	19.93			19.93	Q
2	PRICE-SMITH, Connie	USA	18.79	X	19.08	19.08	Q
3	PAVLYSH, Vita	UKR	17.49	19.04		19.04	Q
4	KORZHANENKO, Irina	RUS	X	18.92		18.92	Q
5	CUMBA, Yumileidis	CUB	18.44	18.55	18.47	18.55	
6	LI, Meisu	CHN	17.88	X	18.39	18.39	
7	KRIVELYOVA, Svetlana	RUS	18.23	17.60	17.86	18.23	
8	ALTHOUSE, Valeyta	USA	17.62	17.54	18.16	18.16	
9	URUSOVA, Elvira	GEO	16.61	17.27	17.69	17.69	
10	LUNDAHL, Karoliina	FIN	17.14	16.97	X	17.14	
11	BALTABAYEVA, Yelena	KAZ	16.40	X	15.35	16.40	
12	MACHADO, Teresa	POR	15.91	15.62	15.60	15.91	
	HUANG, Zhihong	CHN				DNS	

QUALIFYING ROUND - GROUP B

Rnk	Name	Ctry	1	2	3	Result	
1	SUI, Xinmei	CHN	19.36			19.36	Q
2	STORP, Stephanie	GER	19.29			19.29	Q
3	FEDYUSHYNA, Valentyna	UKR	19.22			19.22	Q
4	KHUDOROZHKINA, Irina	RUS	X	17.73	19.03	19.03	Q
5	NEIMKE, Kathrin	GER	19.02			19.02	q
6	LAZA, Belsis	CUB	18.15	18.61	18.58	18.61	q
7	OAKES, Judy	GBR	18.37	18.56	18.45	18.56	q
8	PAGEL, Ramona	USA	17.61	18.55	18.48	18.55	q
9	MITKOVA, Svetla	BUL	17.41	17.48	17.30	17.48	
10	LEE, Myung-Sun	KOR	15.90	16.92	16.64	16.92	
11	ADRIANO, Elisangela	BRA	X	16.49	14.61	16.49	
12	KAWAR, Nada	JOR	15.28	X	14.73	15.28	
13	MISIPEKA, Lisa	ASA	13.40	13.72	13.74	13.74	
	de BRUIN, Corrie	NED				DNS	

FINAL

Rnk	Name	Ctry	1	2	3	4	5	6	Result	
1	KUMBERNUSS, Astrid	GER	20.56	X	19.67	X	X	20.47	20.56	G
2	SUI, Xinmei	CHN	19.06	18.95	19.88	19.24	19.21	19.43	19.88	S
3	KHUDOROZHKINA, Irina	RUS	19.35	X	X	X			19.35	B
4	PAVLYSH, Vita	UKR	17.30	18.20	19.30	18.21	19.23	X	19.30	
5	PRICE-SMITH, Connie	USA	18.44	18.61	19.22	X	X	X	19.22	
6	STORP, Stephanie	GER	18.91	X	X	18.06	18.25	19.06	19.06	

FINAL - *continued*

Rnk	Name	Ctry	1	2	3	4	5	6	Result
7	NEIMKE, Kathrin	GER	17.87	18.40	18.92	X	18.62	18.65	18.92
8	KORZHANENKO, Irina	RUS	18.43	X	18.55	18.65	18.50	18.68	18.68
9	PAGEL, Ramona	USA	16.57	18.48	17.55				18.48
10	LAZA, Belsis	CUB	X	18.40	18.40				18.40
11	OAKES, Judy	GBR	18.34	18.10	18.18				18.34
12	FEDYUSHYNA, Valentyna	UKR	X	X	17.99				17.99

Athletics / *Athlétisme*
Discus Throw, Men / *Disque, Messieurs*

QUALIFYING ROUND - GROUP A

Rnk	Name	Ctry	1	2	3	Result	
1	RIEDEL, Lars	GER	64.66			64.66	Q
2	DUBROVSHCHIK, Vladimir	BLR	63.22			63.22	Q
3	HORVATH, Attila	HUN	58.94	62.90		62.90	Q
4	KIDYKAS, Vaclovas	LTU	59.64	62.74		62.74	Q
5	SCHULT, Juergen	GER	62.58			62.58	Q
6	SETLIFF, Adam	USA	62.36	58.42	60.06	62.36	q
7	SWEENEY, Nick	IRL	58.82	62.04	61.06	62.04	
8	WEIR, Bob	GBR	61.64	60.54	X	61.64	
9	OLUKOJU, Adewale	NGR	X	60.98	59.32	60.98	
10	FORTUNA, Diego	ITA	57.78	59.30	60.08	60.08	
11	VALVIK, Svein Inge	NOR	59.34	58.34	59.60	59.60	
12	MOYA, Roberto	CUB	59.22	57.60	X	59.22	
13	MAKHASHIRI, Dashdendev	MGL	59.16	54.18	X	59.16	
14	PRIMC, Igor	SLO	59.12	56.40	57.62	59.12	
15	GRASU, Costel	ROM	58.30	X	58.56	58.56	
16	KOKHANOVSKIY, Andriy	UKR	57.90	X	X	57.90	
17	PUGLIESE, Marcelo	ARG	56.72	X	X	56.72	
18	BORICHEVSKIY, Aleksandr	RUS	X	56.46	55.18	56.46	
19	POLTORATSKIY, Roman	UZB	X	X	51.96	51.96	
20	ZITNANSKY, Jaroslav	SVK	X	50.94	51.50	51.50	

QUALIFYING ROUND - GROUP B

Rnk	Name	Ctry	1	2	3	Result	
1	ALEKNA, Virgilijus	LTU	64.50			64.50	Q
2	WASHINGTON, Anthony	USA	63.66			63.66	Q
3	SIDOROV, Vitaliy	UKR	X	57.60	63.42	63.42	Q
4	LYAKHOV, Sergey	RUS	59.62	62.42		62.42	q
5	ELIZALDE, Alexis	CUB	60.98	62.22	61.44	62.22	q
6	KAPTYUKH, Vasiliy	BLR	57.28	61.14	62.22	62.22	q
7	GODINA, John	USA	61.82	59.88	57.46	61.82	
8	JIMENEZ-GAONA, Ramon	PAR	58.18	61.36	X	61.36	
9	LI, Shaojie	CHN	58.54	60.06	60.20	60.20	
10	BILEK, Marek	CZE	59.86	58.42	58.62	59.86	
11	TAMMERT, Aleksander	EST	58.84	X	59.04	59.04	
12	MUSTAPIC, Dragan	CRO	X	57.94	56.62	57.94	
13	SINGH, Shakti	IND	53.72	56.58	54.30	56.58	
14	HAFSTEINSSON, Vesteinn	ISL	53.94	52.14	56.30	56.30	
15	TUNKS, Jason	CAN	X	X	55.58	55.58	
16	CONJUNGO, Mickael	CAF	X	X	55.34	55.34	
17	MOELLENBECK, Michael	GER	X	55.18	55.06	55.18	
18	SMITH, Glen	GBR	54.88	X	X	54.88	
19	MENE, Chris	SAM	49.22	51.28	50.24	51.28	
	MARTINEZ, David	ESP	X	X	X	NM	

FINAL

Rnk	Name	Ctry	1	2	3	4	5	6	Result	
1	RIEDEL, Lars	GER	X	X	65.40	63.10	69.40	69.24	69.40	O G
2	DUBROVSHCHIK, Vladimir	BLR	64.86	66.60	64.38	59.68	X	X	66.60	S
3	KAPTYUKH, Vasiliy	BLR	63.24	64.00	65.80	X	63.82	65.08	65.80	B
4	WASHINGTON, Anthony	USA	65.42	X	X	61.34	X	62.50	65.42	
5	ALEKNA, Virgilijus	LTU	62.28	65.30	64.50	X	64.54	63.74	65.30	
6	SCHULT, Juergen	GER	62.82	64.42	62.62	64.62	64.38	63.78	64.62	

FINAL - *continued*

Rnk	Name	Ctry	1	2	3	4	5	6	Result
7	SIDOROV, Vitaliy	UKR	63.44	X	X	62.76	63.78	62.82	63.78
8	KIDYKAS, Vaclovas	LTU	61.48	57.52	62.78	X	61.68	61.88	62.78
9	ELIZALDE, Alexis	CUB	60.52	60.36	62.70				62.70
10	HORVATH, Attila	HUN	60.66	62.28	59.72				62.28
11	LYAKHOV, Sergey	RUS	60.62	59.90	X				60.62
12	SETLIFF, Adam	USA	X	56.30	X				56.30

Athletics / *Athlétisme*
Discus Throw, Women / *Disque, Dames*

QUALIFYING ROUND - GROUP A

Rnk	Name	Ctry	1	2	3	Result	
1	WYLUDDA, Ilke	GER	66.78			66.78	Q
2	CHERNYAVSKAYA, Olga	RUS	60.36	59.62	63.02	63.02	Q
3	GRASU, Nicole	ROM	63.00			63.00	Q
4	ZVEREVA, Elyna	BLR	61.86	62.74		62.74	Q
5	MACHADO, Teresa	POR	59.14	62.02		62.02	Q
6	COSTIAN, Daniela	AUS	61.66	X	61.24	61.66	
7	MARTEN, Maritza	CUB	59.70	57.80	60.08	60.08	
8	ANGELOVA, Atanaska	BUL	59.82	X	X	59.82	
9	KELESIDOU, Anastasia	GRE	59.60	58.44	58.56	59.60	
10	SILHAVA, Zdenka	CZE	59.24	57.98	57.14	59.24	
11	VOGOLI, Katerina	GRE	58.24	55.48	58.70	58.70	
12	KATEWICZ, Renata	POL	X	X	58.24	58.24	
13	KARI, Monia	TUN	X	53.02	58.02	58.02	
14	BARNES MILEHAM, Lacy	USA	X	57.48	56.32	57.48	
15	MAFFEIS, Agnese	ITA	X	X	56.54	56.54	
16	HILL, Aretha	USA	56.04	55.20	55.14	56.04	
17	MARTINELLI, Liliana	ARG	51.46	55.68	X	55.68	
18	de BRUIN, Corrie	NED	X	X	55.48	55.48	
19	FILIMONOVA, Lyudmila	BLR	X	53.30	X	53.30	
20	TRAORE, Oumou	MLI	X	39.70	37.16	39.70	

QUALIFYING ROUND - GROUP B

Rnk	Name	Ctry	1	2	3	Result	
1	XIAO, Yanling	CHN	59.56	59.60	65.10	65.10	Q
2	DIETZSCH, Franka	GER	63.94			63.94	Q
3	GUENDLER, Anja	GER	53.10	61.72	63.80	63.80	Q
4	VIZANIARI, Lisa-Marie	AUS	63.00			63.00	Q
5	SADOVA, Natalya	RUS	59.50	61.36	62.28	62.28	Q
6	BERGMANN, Mette	NOR	59.60	62.24		62.24	Q
7	YATCHENKO, Ira	BLR	59.60	62.04		62.04	Q
8	HECHEVARRIA, Barbara	CUB	56.74	61.38	61.98	61.98	
9	MATEJKOVA, Alice	CZE	60.72	59.40	X	60.72	
10	McKERNAN, Jacqui	GBR	53.74	58.88	57.60	58.88	
11	GOORMACHTIGH, Jacqueline	NED	55.70	56.94	58.74	58.74	
12	FAUMUINA, Beatrice	NZL	57.30	X	58.40	58.40	
13	IVANOVA, Valentina	RUS	58.30	58.38	58.32	58.38	
14	RUNNE, Eha	EST	X	X	58.24	58.24	
15	BOIT, Cristina	ROM	58.10	X	X	58.10	
16	ANTONOVA, Olena	UKR	57.56	57.92	54.82	57.92	
17	TSIKOUNA, Stella	GRE	X	53.62	56.66	56.66	
18	POWELL, Suzy	USA	55.06	56.24	53.98	56.24	
19	DEVALUEZ, Isabelle	FRA	55.08	X	53.92	55.08	

FINAL

Rnk	Name	Ctry	1	2	3	4	5	6	Result	
1	WYLUDDA, Ilke	GER	68.02	69.66	66.70	67.86	67.34	X	69.66	G
2	SADOVA, Natalya	RUS	62.04	65.66	63.34	66.48	65.72	65.82	66.48	S
3	ZVEREVA, Elyna	BLR	63.96	65.64	65.64	63.02	64.10	64.84	65.64	B
4	DIETZSCH, Franka	GER	64.22	65.48	63.90	63.56	X	X	65.48	
5	XIAO, Yanling	CHN	56.90	63.34	63.72	60.86	64.72	X	64.72	
6	CHERNYAVSKAYA, Olga	RUS	64.70	64.06	X	64.20	61.40	X	64.70	

FINAL - continued

Rnk	Name	Ctry	1	2	3	4	5	6	Result
7	GRASU, Nicole	ROM	61.12	63.28	X	59.92	62.78	63.26	63.28
8	VIZANIARI, Lisa-Marie	AUS	62.48	X	59.62	60.32	X	59.96	62.48
9	BERGMANN, Mette	NOR	59.48	X	62.28				62.28
10	MACHADO, Teresa	POR	61.38	60.48	60.02				61.38
11	GUENDLER, Anja	GER	61.16	60.76	59.48				61.16
12	YATCHENKO, Ira	BLR	X	57.76	60.46				60.46

Athletics / *Athlétisme*
Javelin Throw, Men / *Javelot, Messieurs*

QUALIFYING ROUND - GROUP A

Rnk	Name	Ctry	1	2	3	Result	
1	GATSIOUDIS, Kostas	GRE	87.12			87.12	Q
2	MAKAROV, Sergey	RUS	85.88			85.88	Q
3	RATY, Seppo	FIN	83.66			83.66	Q
4	HECHT, Raymond	GER	83.24			83.24	Q
5	BLANK, Peter	GER	82.68	X		82.68	q
6	KINNUNEN, Kimmo	FIN	78.82	X	80.98	80.98	q
7	HILL, Mick	GBR	77.12	X	80.48	80.48	q
8	FAGERNES, Paal Arne	NOR	78.38	X	79.78	79.78	
9	STEPHENS, Dave	USA	77.98	79.18	79.18	79.18	
10	GONZALEZ, Emeterio	CUB	X	77.94	74.42	77.94	
11	BAUMANN, Edgar	PAR	X	75.90	77.74	77.74	
12	LOVEGROVE, Gavin	NZL	X	77.12	X	77.12	
13	VOYNOV, Sergey	UZB	75.58	76.30	68.50	76.30	
14	WENNLUND, Dag	SWE	75.24	X	X	75.24	
15	McHUGH, Terry	IRL	69.72	X	72.84	72.84	
16	CHU, Ki-Young	KOR	X	70.30	71.42	71.42	
17	THOMPSON, Kirt	TRI	68.02	X	64.12	68.02	

QUALIFYING ROUND - GROUP B

Rnk	Name	Ctry	1	2	3	Result	
1	ZELEZNY, Jan	CZE	86.52			86.52	Q
2	PUKSTYS, Tom	USA	80.70	81.34	84.70	84.70	Q
3	BACKLEY, Steve	GBR	84.14			84.14	Q
4	HENRY, Boris	GER	83.22			83.22	Q
5	ZHANG, Lianbiao	CHN	76.24	76.76	79.88	79.88	q
6	HAKKARAINEN, Harri	FIN	77.96	79.34	X	79.34	
7	OVCHINNIKOV, Vladimir	RUS	74.88	76.12	78.20	78.20	
8	RIECH, Todd	USA	X	76.68	78.02	78.02	
9	POLYMEROU, Dimitrios	GRE	76.98	X	77.82	77.82	
10	CURREY, Andrew	AUS	71.34	76.58	77.28	77.28	
11	MORUYEV, Andrey	RUS	X	76.96	77.20	77.20	
12	NIELAND, Nick	GBR	69.54	X	75.74	75.74	
13	PARFYONOV, Vladimir	UZB	68.54	73.96	73.28	73.96	
14	LUACES, Isbel	CUB	73.84	73.20	X	73.84	
15	SILD, Donald-Aik	EST	72.54	X	68.28	72.54	
16	BAZIGHE, Pius	NGR	68.02	70.78	65.70	70.78	
	SASIMOVICH, Vladimir	BLR				NM	

FINAL

Rnk	Name	Ctry	1	2	3	4	5	6	Result	
1	ZELEZNY, Jan	CZE	X	88.16	82.68	83.86	86.02	86.12	88.16	G
2	BACKLEY, Steve	GBR	87.44	85.66	X	80.74	80.88	85.64	87.44	S
3	RATY, Seppo	FIN	83.44	86.66	76.52	84.52	81.70	86.98	86.98	B
4	HECHT, Raymond	GER	83.88	86.88	X	83.10	X	85.10	86.88	
5	HENRY, Boris	GER	81.24	85.68	X	82.58	83.94	84.08	85.68	
6	MAKAROV, Sergey	RUS	82.72	85.30	81.12	X	82.28	83.78	85.30	

FINAL - continued

Rnk	Name	Ctry	1	2	3	4	5	6	Result
7	KINNUNEN, Kimmo	FIN	82.72	80.26	X	84.02	81.98	X	84.02
8	PUKSTYS, Tom	USA	78.48	80.90	83.58	81.28	82.18	81.68	83.58
9	BLANK, Peter	GER	76.66	81.82	X				81.82
10	GATSIOUDIS, Kostas	GRE	X	79.08	81.46				81.46
11	ZHANG, Lianbiao	CHN	80.28	78.86	80.96				80.96
12	HILL, Mick	GBR	78.58	X	X				78.58

Athletics / *Athlétisme*
Javelin Throw, Women / *Javelot, Dames*

QUALIFYING ROUND - GROUP A

Rnk	Name	Ctry	1	2	3	Result	
1	HATTESTAD, Elsa Katrine	NOR	64.52			64.52	Q
2	SHIKOLENKO, Natasha	BLR	X	50.10	62.32	62.32	q
3	LI, Lei	CHN	59.54	61.48	X	61.48	q
4	LOPEZ, Isel	CUB	60.12	61.40	X	61.40	q
5	NERIUS, Steffi	GER	X	56.82	60.98	60.98	q
6	INGBERG, Mikaela	FIN	53.52	X	60.46	60.46	q
7	SANDERSON, Tessa	GBR	58.86	56.80	56.64	58.86	
8	LEE, Young-Sun	KOR	54.62	57.94	58.66	58.66	
9	STONE, Joanna	AUS	52.30	49.16	58.54	58.54	
10	TAS, Aysel	TUR	55.32	56.20	57.86	57.86	
11	UPPA, Taina	FIN	57.74	56.80	X	57.74	
12	STRASEK, Renata	SLO	54.72	51.46	57.04	57.04	
13	JEPPESEN, Jette	DEN	55.24	54.52	56.16	56.16	
14	MANJANI, Mirela	ALB	X	X	55.64	55.64	
15	WHEELER, Erica	USA	53.34	49.54	52.72	53.34	
16	SUANIU, Iloai	SAM	X	38.08	X	38.08	
	RADICHEVA, Sonya	BUL				DNS	

QUALIFYING ROUND - GROUP B

Rnk	Name	Ctry	1	2	3	Result	
1	TILEA, Felicia	ROM	58.84	X	66.94	66.94	Q
2	RANTANEN, Heli	FIN	66.54			66.54	Q
3	McPAUL, Louise	AUS	62.32			62.32	q
4	PALMA, Odelmys	CUB	62.30	54.76	X	62.30	q
5	RIVERO, Xiomara	CUB	X	52.84	61.32	61.32	q
6	FORKEL, Karen	GER	60.84	59.48	X	60.84	q
7	RENK, Silke	GER	58.88	59.10	59.70	59.70	
8	EVE, Laverne	BAH	52.92	X	58.48	58.48	
9	OVCHINNIKOVA, Oksana	RUS	X	57.28	X	57.28	
10	RAMANAUSKAITE, Rita	LTU	X	56.38	56.94	56.94	
11	TOMECKOVA, Nikola	CZE	55.02	52.48	X	55.02	
12	CARROLL, Nicole	USA	53.46	54.74	52.18	54.74	
13	HOLROYD, Shelley	GBR	53.46	52.72	54.72	54.72	
14	ARAMENDIZ MEJIA, Zuleima	COL	53.86	X	54.24	54.24	
15	MIYAJIMA, Akiko	JPN	49.58	53.18	53.98	53.98	
16	AUZEIL, Nadine	FRA	52.76	52.66	50.84	52.76	

FINAL

Rnk	Name	Ctry	1	2	3	4	5	6	Result	
1	RANTANEN, Heli	FIN	67.94	64.72	63.84	62.60	63.82	59.18	67.94	G
2	McPAUL, Louise	AUS	61.72	62.74	64.18	59.76	63.34	65.54	65.54	S
3	HATTESTAD, Elsa Katrine	NOR	61.42	60.78	X	58.66	62.74	64.98	64.98	B
4	LOPEZ, Isel	CUB	X	63.50	57.98	X	64.68	X	64.68	
5	RIVERO, Xiomara	CUB	X	61.94	62.76	X	64.48	61.60	64.48	
6	FORKEL, Karen	GER	56.50	59.20	64.18	58.70	62.04	62.42	64.18	

FINAL - *continued*

Rnk	Name	Ctry	1	2	3	4	5	6	Result
7	INGBERG, Mikaela	FIN	X	61.52	X	60.30	X	X	61.52
8	LI, Lei	CHN	X	56.96	60.74	59.56	58.52	60.12	60.74
9	NERIUS, Steffi	GER	57.88	60.20	59.78				60.20
10	TILEA, Felicia	ROM	56.02	57.28	59.94				59.94
11	PALMA, Odelmye	CUB	X	59.70	57.50				59.70
12	SHIKOLENKO, Natasha	BLR	58.56	X	X				58.56

Athletics / *Athlétisme*
Decathlon, Men / *Décathlon, Messieurs*

100 m - HEAT 1

Rnk	Ln	Name	Ctry	Result	NC Pts
1	7	HOUSTON, Victor	BAR	10.76	915
2	2	DOST, Marcel	NED	10.87	890
3	3	POSERINA, Beniamino	ITA	11.05	850
4	1	HUBER, Philipp	SUI	11.06	847
5	6	KASAPOGLU, Alper	TUR	11.07	845
6	8	KURTOSI, Zsolt	HUN	11.09	841
7	4	FERRIER, Scott	AUS	11.26	804
8	5	AFANASYEV, Nikolay	RUS	11.44	765

100 m - HEAT 2

Rnk	Ln	Name	Ctry	Result	NC Pts
1	4	GANIYEV, Ramil	UZB	10.84	897
2	3	WINTER, Peter	AUS	10.85	894
3	6	SZABO, Dezso	HUN	10.94	874
4	2*	PENALVER, Antonio	ESP	10.95	872
5	1*	NAZAROV, Andrei	EST	11.04	852
6	8*	ROSENDAAL, Jack	NED	11.24	808
7	5	CHMARA, Sebastian	POL	11.28	799
8	7	PIZIKS, Rojs	LAT	11.40	774

100 m - HEAT 3

Rnk	Ln	Name	Ctry	Result	NC Pts
1	2	ZMELIK, Robert	CZE	10.83	899
2	8	PIRINI, Doug	NZL	10.89	885
3	6	FRITZ, Steve	USA	10.90	883
4	3	MULLER, Frank	GER	10.95	872
5	4	KOLPAKOV, Vitaliy	UKR	11.15	827
6	1	LEVICQ, Sebastien	FRA	11.17	823
7	7	KRUGER, Alex	GBR	11.38	778
8	5	KASEORG, Indrek	EST	11.40	774

100 m - HEAT 4

Rnk	Ln	Name	Ctry	Result	NC Pts
1	8	HUFFINS, Chris	USA	10.47	982
2	7	PAJONK, Dirk-Achim	GER	10.67	935
3	6	MAGNUSSON, Jon Arnar	ISL	10.67	935
4	4*	BALANQUE, Eugenio	CUB	10.71	926
5	1	PLAZIAT, Christian	FRA	10.85	894
6	3	DAMASEK, Kamil	CZE	10.86	892
7	5*	VERETELNIKOV, Oleg	UZB	11.06	847
8	2	DUANY, Raul	CUB	11.20	817

100 m - HEAT 5

Rnk	Ln	Name	Ctry	Result	NC Pts
1	8	O'BRIEN, Dan	USA	10.50	975
2	7	BUSEMANN, Frank	GER	10.60	952
3	5	DVORAK, Tomas	CZE	10.64	942
4	1	NOOL, Erki	EST	10.65	940
5	4	HAMALAINEN, Eduard	BLR	10.85	894
5	2	LOBODYN, Lev	UKR	10.85	894
7	6	BENET, Francisco	ESP	10.95	872
8	3	SMITH, Michael	CAN	11.08	843

Decathlon, Men / *Décathlon, Messieurs*

LONG JUMP - GROUP A

Rnk	Name	Ctry	1	2	3	Result	NC Pts
1	BUSEMANN, Frank	GER	8.07			8.07	1079
2	PLAZIAT, Christian	FRA	7.82	7.44		7.82	1015
3	FRITZ, Steve	USA	7.77	7.60	7.49	7.77	1002
4	CHMARA, Sebastian	POL	7.75	7.44		7.75	997
5	GANIYEV, Ramil	UZB	X	7.32	7.61	7.61	962
6	DVORAK, Tomas	CZE	7.60	X	X	7.60	960
7	O'BRIEN, Dan	USA	7.55	X	7.57	7.57	952
8	KOLPAKOV, Vitaliy	UKR	7.53	X	X	7.53	942
9	HAMALAINEN, Eduard	BLR	X	6.11	7.48	7.48	930
10	SMITH, Michael	CAN	7.38	7.47	X	7.47	927
11	ROSENDAAL, Jack	NED	6.83	6.97	7.33	7.33	893
12	MAGNUSSON, Jon Arnar	ISL	7.28	X	5.88	7.28	881
13	PENALVER, Antonio	ESP	7.27	7.25	7.11	7.27	878
14	KASEORG, Indrek	EST	7.26	X	7.21	7.26	876
15	DAMASEK, Kamil	CZE	7.21	7.10	7.22	7.22	866
16	FERRIER, Scott	AUS	X	6.44	6.61	6.61	723
17	KRUGER, Alex	GBR	6.55		4.50	6.55	709
18	BALANQUE, Eugenio	CUB	6.30	6.36	6.34	6.36	666
	NAZAROV, Andrei	EST	X	X		NM	
	SZABO, Dezso	HUN	X	X	X	NM	

LONG JUMP - GROUP B

Rnk	Name	Ctry	1	2	3	Result	NC Pts
1	NOOL, Erki	EST	7.88	7.55	7.55	7.88	1030
2	ZMELIK, Robert	CZE	X	7.45	7.64	7.64	970
3	HOUSTON, Victor	BAR	X	7.18	7.53	7.53	942
4	PAJONK, Dirk-Achim	GER	7.50	7.35	7.24	7.50	935
5	HUFFINS, Chris	USA	X	7.49	X	7.49	932
6	LOBODYN, Lev	UKR	X	X	7.35	7.35	898
7	PIRINI, Doug	NZL	7.01	7.29	7.33	7.33	893
8	DUANY, Raul	CUB	7.30	7.25	6.94	7.30	886
9	VENET, Francisco	ESP	6.87	7.30	7.22	7.30	886
10	MUELLER, Frank	GER	7.25	X	X	7.25	874
11	VERETELNIKOV, Oleg	UZB	6.94	7.24	7.06	7.24	871
12	KASAPOGLU, Alper	TUR	7.22	X	7.09	7.22	866
13	DOST, Marcel	NED	7.19	X	7.21	7.21	864
14	LEVICQ, Sebastien	FRA	7.06	X	7.16	7.16	852
15	HUBER, Philipp	SUI	7.15	6.57	X	7.15	850
16	KURTOSI, Zsolt	HUN	6.73	6.99	7.05	7.05	826
17	POSERINA, Beniamino	ITA	6.98	6.95	X	6.98	809
18	PIZIKS, Rojs	LAT	6.79	4.68	6.86	6.86	781
19	AFANASYEV, Nikolay	RUS	6.35	6.74	6.59	6.74	753
	WINTER, Peter	AUS	X	X	X	NM	

SHOT PUT - GROUP A

Rnk	Name	Ctry	1	2	3	Result	NC Pts
1	SMITH, Michael	CAN	16.95	16.97	16.69	16.97	911
2	PENALVER, Antonio	ESP	16.66	16.91	X	16.91	907
3	HAMALAINEN, Eduard	BLR	15.93	X	16.32	16.32	871
4	DVORAK, Tomas	CZE	15.08	15.82	15.50	15.82	840
5	O'BRIEN, Dan	USA	14.86	15.66	15.36	15.66	830
6	MAGNUSSON, Jon Arnar	ISL	15.28	15.52	X	15.52	822
7	DAMASEK, Kamil	CZE	15.24	15.51	X	15.51	821
8	FRITZ, Steve	USA	14.93	15.12	15.31	15.31	809
9	PLAZIAT, Christian	FRA	14.85	X	X	14.85	780
10	GANIYEV, Ramil	UZB	14.71	14.44	X	14.71	772
11	CHMARA, Sebastian	POL	14.51	14.10	14.32	14.51	760
12	KOLPAKOV, Vitaliy	UKR	X	14.33	X	14.33	749
13	BALANQUE, Eugenio	CUB	14.11	13.95	13.96	14.11	735
14	BUSEMANN, Frank	GER	13.49	13.60	13.08	13.60	704
15	ROSENDAAL, Jack	NED	13.59	13.11	X	13.59	703
16	KASEORG, Indrek	EST	12.46	12.44	13.11	13.11	674
17	FERRIER, Scott	AUS	12.05	12.57	12.12	12.57	641
	KRUGER, Alex	GBR				DNS	
	NAZAROV, Andrei	EST				DNS	
	SZABO, Dezso	HUN				DNS	

SHOT PUT - GROUP B

Rnk	Name	Ctry	1	2	3	Result	NC Pts
1	LOBODYN, Lev	UKR	14.76	15.25	15.57	15.57	825
2	HUFFINS, Chris	USA	X	13.75	15.57	15.57	825
3	PIRINI, Doug	NZL	14.75	X	X	14.75	774
4	MUELLER, Frank	GER	14.69	X	X	14.69	771
5	PIZIKS, Rojs	LAT	14.60	X	X	14.60	765
6	PAJONK, Dirk-Achim	GER	14.30	14.46	14.36	14.46	757
7	KURTOSI, Zsolt	HUN	14.29	X	X	14.29	746
8	LEVICQ, Sebastien	FRA	14.05	13.92	13.99	14.05	731
9	NOOL, Erki	EST	14.01	X	13.87	14.01	729
10	DOST, Marcel	NED	13.81	X	13.91	13.91	723
11	BENET, Francisco	ESP	13.91	13.79	13.72	13.91	723
12	DUANY, Raul	CUB	13.78	13.11	13.21	13.78	715
13	ZMELIK, Robert	CZE	13.53	X	X	13.53	700
14	WINTER, Peter	AUS	13.43	X	X	13.43	693
15	AFANASYEV, Nikolay	RUS	13.38	X	12.79	13.38	690
16	HUBER, Philipp	SUI	12.61	13.34	12.74	13.34	688
17	KASAPOGLU, Alper	TUR	12.46	12.89	12.59	12.89	661
18	VERETELNIKOV, Oleg	UZB	12.66	X	X	12.66	647
19	HOUSTON, Victor	BAR	11.82	11.97	11.42	11.97	605
	POSERINA, Beniamino	ITA	X	X	X	NM	

HIGH JUMP - GROUP A

Rnk	Name	Ctry	1.80	1.83	1.86	1.89	1.92	1.95	1.98	2.01	2.04	2.07	2.10	2.13	2.16	Result	NC Pts
1	GANIYEV, Ramil	UZB						O		O	XO	O	XO	O	XXX	2.13	925
2	CHMARA, Sebastian	POL					O		O		O	XO	O	XXX		2.10	896
3	O'BRIEN, Dan	USA	O			O		O		O	O	O	XXX			2.07	868
4	PENALVER, Antonio	ESP			O		O	O	O	O	XO	O	XXX			2.07	868
5	KASEORG, Indrek	EST				O	O	O	O	XO	O	XO	XXX			2.07	868
6	KOLPAKOV, Vitaliy	UKR						O		O	XO	XXO	XXX			2.07	868
7	BUSEMANN, Frank	GER				O		O		O	O	XX				2.04	840
7	PLAZIAT, Christian	FRA						O		O	O	XXX				2.04	840
9	FRITZ, Steve	USA				O		O	XO	XO	XO	XXX				2.04	840
10	DAMASEK, Kamil	CZE			O		O	O	O	XO	XXX					2.01	813
11	NOOL, Erki	EST				O	XXO	O	XO	XO	XXX					2.01	813
12	DVORAK, Tomas	CZE			O	O	XXO	O	O	XXX						1.98	785
13	HAMALAINEN, Eduard	BLR	O				XO		XO		XXX					1.98	785
14	MAGNUSSON, Jon Arnar	ISL			O		XO	O	XXX							1.95	758
15	SMITH, Michael	CAN				O	XO	XXO	XXX							1.95	758
16	BALANQUE, Eugenio	CUB		XO		XO	XXX									1.89	705
	FERRIER, Scott	AUS														DNS	
	KRUGER, Alex	GBR														DNS	
	NAZAROV, Andrei	EST														DNS	
	SZABO, Dezso	HUN														DNS	

Decathlon, Men / *Décathlon, Messieurs*

HIGH JUMP - GROUP B

Rnk	Name	Ctry	1.71	1.74	1.77	1.80	1.83	1.86	1.89	1.92	1.95	1.98	2.01	2.04	2.07	2.10	2.13	2.16	2.19	Result	NC Pts
1	PIZIKS, Rojs	LAT									O		O	O	XXO	XO	XXO	XO	XXX	2.16	953
2	ROSENDAAL, Jack	NED							O		O			XXO	XXO					2.07	868
3	DUANY, Raul	CUB		O				XXO	O	O	XO	O	XO	O	XXO	XXX				2.07	868
4	HUFFINS, Chris	USA						O		O				O	XXX					2.04	840
5	KURTOSI, Zsolt	HUN						O		O	XO	XXO	XO	XXX						2.01	813
6	AFANASYEV, Nikolay	RUS							O			XO	XXX							1.98	785
6	POSERINA, Beniamino	ITA						O		O		XO	XXX							1.98	785
8	BENET, Francisco	ESP				O	O	O	O	O		XXO	XXX							1.98	785
9	DOST, Marcel	NED			O		O	O	O	O	O	XXX								1.95	758
9	HOUSTON, Victor	BAR									O		XXX							1.95	758
11	PAJONK, Dirk-Achim	GER						O	XO	O	O	XXX								1.95	758
12	LOBODYN, Lev	UKR									XO		XXX							1.95	758
12	MUELLER, Frank	GER						O			XO	XXX								1.95	758
14	VERETELNIKOV, Oleg	UZB						O	O	XO	XXO	XXX								1.95	758
15	ZMELIK, Robert	CZE								XXO	XXO	XXX								1.95	758
16	LEVICQ, Sebastien	FRA						O	XXO	O	XXX									1.92	731
17	KASAPOGLU, Alper	TUR						O	O	XO	XXX									1.92	731
18	PIRINI, Doug	NZL		O			O	O	O	XXX										1.89	705
19	HUBER, Philipp	SUI				O	XXO	XXO	XXX											1.86	679
	WINTER, Peter	AUS																		DNS	

400 m - HEAT 1

Rnk	Ln	Name	Ctry	Result	NC Pts
1	7	DOST, Marcel	NED	48.19	900
2	4	HUBER, Philipp	SUI	48.72	875
3	1	POSERINA, Beniamino	ITA	49.52	837
4	6	KASAPOGLU, Alper	TUR	49.61	833
5	2	KURTOSI, Zsolt	HUN	50.43	795
6	3	AFANASYEV, Nikolay	RUS	50.83	777
	8	FERRIER, Scott	AUS	DNS	
	5	HOUSTON, Victor	BAR	DNS	

400 m - HEAT 2

Rnk	Ln	Name	Ctry	Result	NC Pts
1	6	CHMARA, Sebastian	POL	48.75	873
2	5	GANIYEV, Ramil	UZB	49.14	855
3	3	PENALVER, Antonio	ESP	50.41	796
4	2	ROSENDAAL, Jack	NED	50.93	772
5	7	PIZIKS, Rojs	LAT	51.48	748
	4	NAZAROV, Andrei	EST	DNS	
	1	SZABO, Dezso	HUN	DNS	
	8	WINTER, Peter	AUS	DNS	

400 m - HEAT 3

Rnk	Ln	Name	Ctry	Result	NC Pts
1	1	BALANQUE, Eugenio	CUB	47.46	935
2	3	KOLPAKOV, Vitaliy	UKR	48.12	903
3	7	PIRINI, Doug	NZL	48.56	882
4	4	KASEORG, Indrek	EST	49.03	860
5	2	MUELLER, Frank	GER	49.05	859
6	6	ZMELIK, Robert	CZE	49.55	835
7	8	FRITZ, Steve	USA	50.13	809
8	5	LEVICQ, Sebastien	FRA	50.55	789

400 m - HEAT 4

Rnk	Ln	Name	Ctry	Result	NC Pts
1	8	MAGNUSSON, Jon Arnar	ISL	47.17	950
2	7	DAMASEK, Kamil	CZE	47.35	941
3	6	PAJONK, Dirk-Achim	GER	48.81	870
4	2	HUFFINS, Chris	USA	48.83	869
5	4	PLAZIAT, Christian	FRA	49.07	858
6	1	VERETELNIKOV, Oleg	UZB	49.65	831
7	3	DUANY, Raul	CUB	50.50	792
	5	KRUGER, Alex	GBR	DNS	

400 m - HEAT 5

Rnk	Ln	Name	Ctry	Result	NC Pts
1	2	O'BRIEN, Dan	USA	46.82	967
2	7	HAMALAINEN, Eduard	BLR	46.91	963
3	3	NOOL, Erki	EST	47.26	945
4	1	DVORAK, Tomas	CZE	48.29	895
5	6	BUSEMANN, Frank	GER	48.34	893
6	5	BENET, Francisco	ESP	48.67	877
7	4	LOBODYN, Lev	UKR	48.96	863
8	8	SMITH, Michael	CAN	51.97	726

110 m HURDLES - HEAT 1

Rnk	Ln	Name	Ctry	Result	NC Pts
1	4	BALANQUE, Eugenio	CUB	14.07	965
2	6	ROSENDAAL, Jack	NED	14.46	916
3	3	KASEORG, Indrek	EST	14.53	907
4	8	KASAPOGLU, Alper	TUR	14.55	905
5	5	POSERINA, Beniamino	ITA	14.68	889
6	7	AFANASYEV, Nikolay	RUS	14.79	875
7	2	PIZIKS, Rojs	LAT	15.20	825
	1	VERETELNIKOV, Oleg	UZB	DNS	

110 m HURDLES - HEAT 2

Rnk	Ln	Name	Ctry	Result	NC Pts
1	6*	KOLPAKOV, Vitaliy	UKR	14.30	936
2	2	LEVICQ, Sebastien	FRA	14.50	911
3	1	DOST, Marcel	NED	14.52	908
4	8*	KURTOSI, Zsolt	HUN	14.64	894
5	4*	DUANY, Raul	CUB	14.84	869
6	3*	MUELLER, Frank	GER	14.86	867
7	7	PIRINI, Doug	NZL	14.88	864
8	5	HUBER, Philipp	SUI	15.08	840

110 m HURDLES - HEAT 3

Rnk	Ln	Name	Ctry	Result	NC Pts
1	7*	HUFFINS, Chris	USA	14.10	962
2	4	MAGNUSSON, Jon Arnar	ISL	14.22	946
3	3	BENET, Francisco	ESP	14.36	929
4	9	CHMARA, Sebastian	POL	14.59	900
5	1	SMITH, Michael	CAN	14.78	876
6	2	PAJONK, Dirk-Achim	GER	14.79	875
7	8	GANIYEV, Ramil	UZB	14.88	864
8	6	DAMASEK, Kamil	CZE	14.94	857
9	5*	NOOL, Erki	EST	15.03	846

110 m HURDLES - HEAT 4

Rnk	Ln	Name	Ctry	Result	NC Pts
1	2	BUSEMANN, Frank	GER	13.47	1044
2	1	DVORAK, Tomas	CZE	13.79	1002
3	7	O'BRIEN, Dan	USA	13.87	991
4	4	HAMALAINEN, Eduard	BLR	13.95	981
5	3	FRITZ, Steve	USA	13.97	978
6	8	ZMELIK, Robert	CZE	14.17	953
7	5	PENALVER, Antonio	ESP	14.35	930
8	9	PLAZIAT, Christian	FRA	14.52	908
	6	LOBODYN, Lev	UKR	DNS	

Decathlon, Men / *Décathlon, Messieurs*

DISCUS THROW - GROUP A

Rnk	Name	Ctry	1	2	3	Result	
1	FRITZ, Steve	USA	49.08	49.84	X	49.84	867
2	HAMALAINEN, Eduard	BLR	49.62	X	X	49.62	862
3	SMITH, Michael	CAN	X	49.54	X	49.54	861
4	PENALVER, Antonio	ESP	45.46	47.30	48.92	48.92	848
5	O'BRIEN, Dan	USA	47.82	43.60	48.78	48.78	845
6	DVORAK, Tomas	CZE	45.44	44.94	46.28	46.28	793
7	PLAZIAT, Christian	FRA	45.34	43.94	X	45.34	774
8	BUSEMANN, Frank	GER	45.04	44.34	X	45.04	768
9	LEVICQ, Sebastien	FRA	43.92	45.00	44.90	45.00	767
10	GANIYEV, Ramil	UZB	31.46	42.98	44.86	44.86	764
11	MAGNUSSON, Jon Arnar	ISL	35.38	43.78	X	43.78	742
12	ZMELIK, Robert	CZE	43.44	42.66	X	43.44	735
13	NOOL, Erki	EST	35.98	X	42.98	42.98	725
14	CHMARA, Sebastian	POL	42.60	X	X	42.60	718
15	DOST, Marcel	NED	39.66	40.04	41.92	41.92	704
16	BALANQUE, Eugenio	CUB	39.76	41.64	41.22	41.64	698
	LOBODYN, Lev	UKR				DNS	

DISCUS THROW - GROUP B

Rnk	Name	Ctry	1	2	3	Result	
1	HUFFINS, Chris	USA	48.48	48.72	X	48.72	844
2	PIZIKS, Rojs	LAT	44.78	X	45.90	45.90	785
3	MUELLER, Frank	GER	44.04	X	45.90	45.90	785
4	KOLPAKOV, Vitaliy	UKR	45.54	X	45.66	45.66	780
5	PIRINI, Doug	NZL	45.34	45.20	44.26	45.34	774
6	BENET, Francisco	ESP	X	44.30	X	44.30	752
7	POSERINA, Beniamino	ITA	43.42	X	42.22	43.42	734
8	HUBER, Philipp	SUI	43.32	39.68	X	43.32	732
9	KURTOSI, Zsolt	HUN	43.22	42.76	40.62	43.22	730
10	AFANASYEV, Nikolay	RUS	41.82	43.08	42.56	43.08	727
11	DAMASEK, Kamil	CZE	42.66	X	X	42.66	719
12	PAJONK, Dirk-Achim	GER	38.90	40.72	41.94	41.94	704
13	ROSENDAAL, Jack	NED	40.62	X	41.24	41.24	690
14	KASAPOGLU, Alper	TUR	40.64	40.18	X	40.64	678
15	KASEORG, Indrek	EST	39.46	39.44	X	39.46	654
16	DUANY, Raul	CUB	36.22	37.10	38.56	38.56	635
	VERETELNIKOV, Oleg	UZB				DNS	

POLE VAULT - GROUP A

Rnk	Name	Ctry	4.20	4.30	4.40	4.50	4.60	4.70	4.80	4.90	5.00	5.10	5.20	5.30	5.40	5.50	Result	NC Pts
1	LEVICQ, Sebastien	FRA					XO			O		XO		O	O	XXX	5.40	1035
2	ZMELIK, Robert	CZE					O		O		O		XO	XXO	O	XXX	5.40	1035
3	NOOL, Erki	EST									O		O		XXO	XXX	5.40	1035
4	DOST, Marcel	NED					O		O		O	O	O	XXX			5.20	972
5	GANIYEV, Ramil	UZB					XXO	O	O	O		XO	XXX				5.20	972
6	FRITZ, Steve	USA	XXO		O	XO	O	XO	O	XXO	XXO						5.10	941
7	SMITH, Michael	CAN					XO		XO		O	XXX					5.00	910
8	HAMALAINEN, Eduard	BLR							O		XO		XXX				5.00	910
8	O'BRIEN, Dan	USA			O	O			O		XO	XXX					5.00	910
10	CHMARA, Sebastian	POL				O		XO		O	XXX						4.90	880
11	PLAZIAT, Christian	FRA					XO		XO	XO	XXX						4.90	880
12	BUSEMANN, Frank	GER	O			XO	O	O	XO	XXX							4.80	849
13	MAGNUSSON, Jon Arnar	ISL			O		O	O	XXO	XXX							4.80	849
14	DVORAK, Tomas	CZE		O		O	O	O	XXX								4.70	819
15	PENALVER, Antonio	ESP	O		O	XXO	XO	O	XXX								4.70	819
16	BALANQUE, Eugenio	CUB			O		O	XO	XXX								4.70	819
	LOBODYN, Lev	UKR															DNS	

POLE VAULT - GROUP B

Rnk	Name	Ctry	4.00	4.10	4.20	4.30	4.40	4.50	4.60	4.70	4.80	4.90	5.00	5.10	5.20	Result	NC Pts
1	MUELLER, Frank	GER					O			XO		XO	XO	O	XXX	5.10	941
2	PIZIKS, Rojs	LAT						XO		O	O	XO	XXO	XXX		5.00	910
3	DAMASEK, Kamil	CZE					O		XO	O	XO	O	XXX			4.90	880
4	BENET, Francisco	ESP					O		XO	O	O	XXX				4.80	849
5	KOLPAKOV, Vitaliy	UKR					XO		O	XO	XO	XXX				4.80	849
6	KASAPOGLU, Alper	TUR					O		XXO		XXO	XXX				4.80	849
7	POSERINA, Beniamino	ITA			O		XXO		XXO		XXO		XXX			4.80	849
8	HUFFINS, Chris	USA				O		O		O	XXX					4.70	819
9	ROSENDAAL, Jack	NED			O		XO		O	XXO	XXX					4.70	819
10	HUBER, Philipp	SUI					O		O	XXX						4.60	790
11	KURTOSI, Zsolt	HUN			XO		O		O	XXX						4.60	790
12	PIRINI, Doug	NZL		XO		O		XO	O	XXX						4.60	790
13	PAJONK, Dirk-Achim	GER			O		XO	XO	XXX							4.50	760
14	DUANY, Raul	CUB	XXO	O	O	XXO	O	XXX								4.40	731
	AFANASYEV, Nikolay	RUS						XXX								NH	
	KASEORG, Indrek	EST														DNS	
	VERETELNIKOV, Oleg	UZB														DNS	

Decathlon, Men / *Décathlon, Messieurs*

JAVELIN THROW - GROUP A

Rnk	Name	Ctry	1	2	3	Result	NC Pts
1	DVORAK, Tomas	CZE	70.16	63.70		70.16	892
2	BUSEMANN, Frank	GER	66.86	61.88	64.70	66.86	842
3	DUANY, Raul	CUB	62.86	62.40	X	62.86	781
4	MAGNUSSON, Jon Arnar	ISL	X	60.60	61.10	61.10	754
5	BALANQUE, Eugenio	CUB	57.56	59.92	58.80	59.92	737
6	PIRINI, Doug	NZL	58.02	X	X	58.02	708
7	PENALVER, Antonio	ESP	56.34	57.08	54.62	57.08	694
8	AFANASYEV, Nikolay	RUS	50.88	52.32	55.12	55.12	665
9	CHMARA, Sebastian	POL	48.08	49.02	54.84	54.84	661
10	KURTOSI, Zsolt	HUN	49.96	51.40	54.80	54.80	660
11	PAJONK, Dirk-Achim	GER	50.28	50.68	54.16	54.16	650
12	PLAZIAT, Christian	FRA	50.44	52.12	52.18	52.18	621
13	HUBER, Philipp	SUI	50.08	51.96	X	51.96	618

JAVELIN THROW - GROUP B

Rnk	Name	Ctry	1	2	3	Result	NC Pts
1	ZMELIK, Robert	CZE	62.90	67.20	64.60	67.20	847
2	O'BRIEN, Dan	USA	64.62	64.32	66.90	66.90	842
3	MUELLER, Frank	GER	62.48	66.10	64.88	66.10	830
4	FRITZ, Steve	USA	64.18	65.70	X	65.70	824
5	NOOL, Erki	EST	65.48	61.30	X	65.48	821
6	LEVICQ, Sebastien	FRA	64.42	60.64	59.48	64.42	805
7	SMITH, Michael	CAN	62.24	63.94	64.34	64.34	803
8	ROSENDAAL, Jack	NED	60.98	57.40	63.80	63.80	795
9	HUFFINS, Chris	USA	55.58	60.62		60.62	747
10	BENET, Francisco	ESP	58.56	59.44	58.84	59.44	729
11	PIZIKS, Rojs	LAT	54.26	55.28	58.40	58.40	714
12	DOST, Marcel	NED	57.76			57.76	704
13	HAMALAINEN, Eduard	BLR	57.66	53.64	54.14	57.66	703
14	POSERINA, Beniamino	ITA	56.78			56.78	690
15	DAMASEK, Kamil	CZE	X	55.84	55.10	55.84	675
16	GANIYEV, Ramil	UZB	51.34	53.70	52.96	53.70	644
17	KOLPAKOV, Vitaliy	UKR	53.58	51.28		53.58	642
18	KASAPOGLU, Alper	TUR	45.24	X	44.60	45.24	518

1500 m - HEAT 1

Rnk	Or	Name	Ctry	Result	NC Pts
1	3	HUBER, Philipp	SUI	4:18.15	824
2	2	PAJONK, Dirk-Achim	GER	4:21.62	801
3	8	ROSENDAAL, Jack	NED	4:25.98	771
4	9	DUANY, Raul	CUB	4:35.59	708
5	6	KASAPOGLU, Alper	TUR	4:38.69	689
6	4	BALANQUE, Eugenio	CUB	4:38.97	687
7	1	PIRINI, Doug	NZL	4:39.09	686
8	5	AFANASYEV, Nikolay	RUS	4:41.00	674
9	7	KURTOSI, Zsolt	HUN	4:43.21	660

1500 m - HEAT 2

Rnk	Or	Name	Ctry	Result	NC Pts
1	1	DAMASEK, Kamil	CZE	4:26.86	765
2	6	CHMARA, Sebastian	POL	4:26.96	765
3	8	LEVICQ, Sebastien	FRA	4:29.50	748
4	7	PIZIKS, Rojs	LAT	4:30.88	739
5	10	PLAZIAT, Christian	FRA	4:35.00	712
6	4	BENET, Francisco	ESP	4:36.04	705
7	5	MUELLER, Frank	GER	4:37.50	696
8	12	PENALVER, Antonio	ESP	4:37.71	695
9	11	DOST, Marcel	NED	4:38.81	688
10	3	SMITH, Michael	CAN	4:43.81	656
11	2	POSERINA, Beniamino	ITA	4:58.28	570
12	9	KOLPAKOV, Vitaliy	UKR	5:05.41	529

1500 m - HEAT 3

Rnk	Or	Name	Ctry	Result	NC Pts
1	9	DVORAK, Tomas	CZE	4:31.25	736
2	4	BUSEMANN, Frank	GER	4:31.41	735
3	6	HAMALAINEN, Eduard	BLR	4:34.68	714
4	2	FRITZ, Steve	USA	4:38.26	691
5	1	ZMELIK, Robert	CZE	4:38.45	690
6	7	GANIYEV, Ramil	UZB	4:42.74	663
7	8	NOOL, Erki	EST	4:43.36	659
8	5	O'BRIEN, Dan	USA	4:45.89	644
9	3	MAGNUSSON, Jon Arnar	ISL	4:46.97	637
10	10	HUFFINS, Chris	USA	5:14.36	480

FINAL

Rnk	Name	Ctry	100 m	Long Jump	Shot Put	High Jump	400 m	110 m Hurdles	Discus	Pole Vault	Javelin	1500 m	Total Pts
1	O'BRIEN, Dan	USA	10.50	7.57	15.66	2.07	46.82	13.87	48.78	5.00	66.90	4:45.89	
			975	952	830	868	967	991	845	910	842	644	8824 G
2	BUSEMANN, Frank	GER	10.60	8.07	13.60	2.04	48.34	13.47	45.04	4.80	66.86	4:31.41	
			952	1079	704	840	893	1044	768	849	842	735	8706 S
3	DVORAK, Tomas	CZE	10.64	7.60	15.82	1.98	48.29	13.79	46.28	4.70	70.16	4:31.25	
			942	960	840	785	895	1002	793	819	892	736	8664 B
4	FRITZ, Steve	USA	10.90	7.77	15.31	2.04	50.13	13.97	49.84	5.10	65.70	4:38.26	
			883	1002	809	840	809	978	867	941	824	691	8644
5	HAMALAINEN, Eduard	BLR	10.85	7.48	16.32	1.98	46.91	13.95	49.62	5.00	57.66	4:34.68	
			894	930	871	785	963	981	862	910	703	714	8613
6	NOOL, Erki	EST	10.65	7.88	14.01	2.01	47.26	15.03	42.98	5.40	65.48	4:43.36	
			940	1030	729	813	945	846	725	1035	821	659	8543
7	ZMELIK, Robert	CZE	10.83	7.64	13.53	1.95	49.55	14.17	43.44	5.40	67.20	4:38.45	
			899	970	700	758	835	953	735	1035	847	690	8422
8	GANIYEV, Ramil	UZB	10.84	7.61	14.71	2.13	49.14	14.88	44.86	5.20	53.70	4:42.74	
			897	962	772	925	855	864	764	972	644	663	8318
9	PENALVER, Antonio	ESP	10.95	7.27	16.91	2.07	50.41	14.35	48.92	4.70	57.08	4:37.71	
			872	878	907	868	796	930	848	819	694	695	8307
10	HUFFINS, Chris	USA	10.47	7.49	15.57	2.04	48.83	14.10	48.72	4.70	60.62	5:14.36	
			982	932	825	840	869	962	844	819	747	480	8300
11	PLAZIAT, Christian	FRA	10.85	7.82	14.85	2.04	49.07	14.52	45.34	4.90	52.18	4:35.00	
			894	1015	780	840	858	908	774	880	621	712	8282
12	MAGNUSSON, Jon Arnar	ISL	10.67	7.28	15.52	1.95	47.17	14.22	43.78	4.80	61.10	4:46.97	
			935	881	822	758	950	946	742	849	754	637	8274

continued on next page / continué à la page suivante

Decathlon, Men / *Décathlon, Messieurs*

FINAL - *continued*

Rnk	Name	Ctry	100 m	Long Jump	Shot Put	High Jump	400 m	110 m Hurdles	Discus	Pole Vault	Javelin	1500 m	Total Pts
13	SMITH, Michael	CAN	11.08	7.47	16.97	1.95	51.97	14.78	49.54	5.00	64.34	4:43.81	
			843	927	911	758	726	876	861	910	803	656	8271
14	MUELLER, Frank	GER	10.95	7.25	14.69	1.95	49.05	14.86	45.90	5.10	66.10	4:37.50	
			872	874	771	758	859	867	785	941	830	696	8253
15	CHMARA, Sebastian	POL	11.28	7.75	14.51	2.10	48.75	14.59	42.60	4.90	54.84	4:26.96	
			799	997	760	896	873	900	718	880	661	765	8249
16	DAMASEK, Kamil	CZE	10.86	7.22	15.51	2.01	47.35	14.94	42.66	4.90	55.84	4:26.86	
			892	866	821	813	941	857	719	880	675	765	8229
17	LEVICQ, Sebastien	FRA	11.17	7.16	14.05	1.92	50.55	14.50	45.00	5.40	64.42	4:29.50	
			823	852	731	731	789	911	767	1035	805	748	8192
18	DOST, Marcel	NED	10.87	7.21	13.91	1.95	48.19	14.52	41.92	5.20	57.76	4:38.81	
			890	864	723	758	900	908	704	972	704	688	8111
19	BENET, Francisco	ESP	10.95	7.30	13.91	1.98	48.67	14.36	44.30	4.80	59.44	4:36.04	
			872	886	723	785	877	929	752	849	729	705	8107
20	PAJONK, Dirk-Achim	GER	10.67	7.50	14.46	1.95	48.81	14.79	41.94	4.50	54.16	4:21.62	
			935	935	757	758	870	875	704	760	650	801	8045
21	ROSENDAAL, Jack	NED	11.24	7.33	13.59	2.07	50.93	14.46	41.24	4.70	63.80	4:25.98	
			808	893	703	868	772	916	690	819	795	771	8035
22	KOLPAKOV, Vitaliy	UKR	11.15	7.53	14.33	2.07	48.12	14.30	45.66	4.80	53.58	5:05.41	
			827	942	749	868	903	936	780	849	642	529	8025
23	PIZIKS, Rojs	LAT	11.40	6.86	14.60	2.16	51.48	15.20	45.90	5.00	58.40	4:30.88	
			774	781	765	953	748	825	785	910	714	739	7994
24	PIRINI, Doug	NZL	10.89	7.33	14.75	1.89	48.56	14.88	45.34	4.60	58.02	4:39.09	
			885	893	774	705	882	864	774	790	708	686	7961
25	BALANQUE, Eugenio	CUB	10.71	6.36	14.11	1.89	47.46	14.07	41.64	4.70	59.92	4:38.97	
			926	666	735	705	935	965	698	819	737	687	7873
26	DUANY, Raul	CUB	11.20	7.30	13.78	2.07	50.50	14.84	38.56	4.40	62.86	4:35.59	
			817	886	715	868	792	869	635	731	781	708	7802
27	KURTOSI, Zsolt	HUN	11.09	7.05	14.29	2.01	50.43	14.64	43.22	4.60	54.80	4:43.21	
			841	826	746	813	795	894	730	790	660	660	7755
28	HUBER, Philipp	SUI	11.06	7.15	13.34	1.86	48.72	15.08	43.32	4.60	51.96	4:18.15	
			847	850	688	679	875	840	732	790	618	824	7743
29	KASAPOGLU, Alper	TUR	11.07	7.22	12.89	1.92	49.61	14.55	40.64	4.80	45.24	4:38.69	
			845	866	661	731	833	905	678	849	518	689	7575
30	POSERINA, Beniamino	ITA	11.05	6.98	NM	1.98	49.52	14.68	43.42	4.80	56.78	4:58.28	
			850	809	0	785	837	889	734	849	690	570	7013
31	AFANASYEV, Nikolay	RUS	11.44	6.74	13.38	1.98	50.83	14.79	43.08	NH	55.12	4:41.00	
			765	753	690	785	777	875	727	0	665	674	6711

Athletics / *Athlétisme*

Heptathlon, Women / *Heptathlon, Dames*

100 m HURDLES - HEAT 1

Rnk	Ln	Name	Ctry	Result	NC Pts
1	4	GARCIA, Magalys	CUB	13.30	1080
2	1*	BOND-MILLS, Catherine	CAN	13.66	1027
3	7	LEBEDENKO, Yelena	RUS	13.70	1021
4	3	ATROSCHENKO, Anzhela	BLR	14.27	941
5	5	CLOPES, Inma	ESP	14.30	936
6	6	KAZANINA, Svetlana	KAZ	14.69	883
	2	SPADA, Giuliana	ITA	DNF	

100 m HURDLES - HEAT 2

Rnk	Ln	Name	Ctry	Result	NC Pts
1	8	STEIGAUF, Mona	GER	13.22	1091
2	1	WLODARCZYK, Urszula	POL	13.48	1053
3	6	BLAIR, Kelly	USA	13.62	1033
4	7	MOSKALETS, Svetlana	RUS	13.70	1021
5	3	SHOUAA, Ghada	SYR	13.72	1018
6	5	HAUTALA, Tiia	FIN	13.72	1018
7	2	NADLER, Patricia	SUI	13.81	1005
8	4*	INANCSI, Rita	HUN	13.95	985

100 m HURDLES - HEAT 3

Rnk	Ln	Name	Ctry	Result	NC Pts
1	6	JOYNER-KERSEE, Jackie	USA	13.24	1089
2	7	LEWIS, Denise	GBR	13.45	1058
3	5	BARBER, Eunice	SLE	13.50	1050
4	4	BRAUN, Sabine	GER	13.55	1043
5	2	SAZANOVICH, Natalya	BLR	13.56	1041
6	1	NAZAROVIENE, Remigija	LTU	13.59	1037
7	3	GUTHRIE-GRESHAM, Diane	JAM	14.17	954

100 m HURDLES - HEAT 4

Rnk	Ln	Name	Ctry	Result	NC Pts
1	4	HANSON, Sharon	USA	13.34	1074
2	2*	NASTASE, Liliana	ROM	13.37	1069
3	6	BEER, Peggy	GER	13.52	1047
4	3	CARDENAS, Regla	CUB	13.89	994
5	7	TYUKHAY, Irina	RUS	13.90	993
6	1*	MARXER, Manuela	LIE	13.90	993
7	5	JAMIESON, Jane	AUS	14.57	899

Heptathlon, Women / *Heptathlon, Dames*

HIGH JUMP - GROUP A

Rnk	Name	Ctry	1.62	1.65	1.68	1.71	1.74	1.77	1.80	1.83	1.86	1.89	Result	NC Pts
1	SHOUAA, Ghada	SYR					O		O	XO	O	XXX	1.86	1054
2	WLODARCZYK, Urszula	POL			O	O	O	O	XO	XXO	XXX		1.86	1054
3	INANCSI, Rita	HUN			O	O	O	XO	XO	XXX			1.83	1016
4	BRAUN, Sabine	GER					O	O	XXO	XXO	XXX		1.83	1016
5	MOSKALETS, Svetlana	RUS		O	O		XO	O	XXX				1.80	978
5	SAZANOVICH, Natalya	BLR		O	O	O	XO	O	XXX				1.80	978
7	GUTHRIE-GRESHAM, Diane	JAM		O		O	O	XO	XXX				1.80	978
8	JAMIESON, Jane	AUS	O		O	O	O	XXO	XXO	XXX			1.80	978
9	LEBEDENKO, Yelena	RUS		O	O	O	XO	O	XXX				1.77	941
10	STEIGAUF, Mona	GER				O	O	XO	XXX				1.77	941
11	LEWIS, Denise	GBR		XO	O	O	XO	XXX					1.77	941
12	CARDENAS, Regla	CUB	O	XO	XO	O	XO	XXX					1.77	941
13	TYUKHAY, Irina	RUS		O	O	O	O	XXO	XXX				1.77	941
	JOYNER-KERSEE, Jackie	USA											DNS	

HIGH JUMP - GROUP B

Rnk	Name	Ctry	1.50	1.53	1.56	1.59	1.62	1.65	1.68	1.71	1.74	1.77	1.80	1.83	1.86	1.89	Result	NC Pts
1	KAZANINA, Svetlana	KAZ					O	O	O	XO	O	O	XXO	XO	XXO	XXX	1.86	1054
2	BOND-MILLS, Catherine	CAN								O	O	XO	XO	XXO	XXX		1.83	1016
3	BLAIR, Kelly	USA						O		O	O	O	XXX				1.80	978
4	CLOPES, Inma	ESP					O	O	O	XO	XO	XXX					1.77	941
4	HAUTALA, Tiia	FIN						O	O	XO	XO	XXX					1.77	941
6	HANSON, Sharon	USA				O	O	O	XO	XXO	XXO	XO	XXX				1.77	941
7	BARBER, Eunice	SLE						O	O	O	XXO	XXX					1.77	941
8	NAZAROVIENE, Remigija	LTU					O	O	O	O	XXX						1.74	903
9	ATROSCHENKO, Anzhela	BLR					O	O	O	O	XO	XXX					1.74	903
10	BEER, Peggy	GER						XXO	XO	XXO	XXX						1.74	903
11	GARCIA, Magalys	CUB					O	O	O	O	XXX						1.71	867
12	NADLER, Patricia	SUI		O	O		O	XO	XXO	XXX							1.68	830
13	NASTASE, Liliana	ROM		O	O		XO	XO	XXX								1.65	795
14	MARXER, Manuela	LIE		O	O		XXO	XXX									1.62	759
	SPADA, Giuliana	ITA															DNS	

SHOT PUT - GROUP A

Rnk	Name	Ctry	1	2	3	Result	NC Pts
1	SHOUAA, Ghada	SYR	15.42	15.95		15.95	925
2	INANCSI, Rita	HUN	14.02	14.69	X	14.69	840
3	BRAUN, Sabine	GER	14.48	13.88	14.14	14.48	826
4	WLODARCZYK, Urszula	POL	14.36	14.33	14.33	14.36	818
5	TYUKHAY, Irina	RUS	13.98	13.35	14.16	14.16	805
6	LEBEDENKO, Yelena	RUS	12.14	13.72	13.54	13.72	775
7	NASTASE, Liliana	ROM	13.15	12.70	13.30	13.30	747
8	HAUTALA, Tiia	FIN	13.22	12.49	X	13.22	742
9	GARCIA, Magalys	CUB	13.03	12.86	12.58	13.03	729
10	BOND-MILLS, Catherine	CAN	12.86	X	X	12.86	718
11	KAZANINA, Svetlana	KAZ	10.27	12.09	12.50	12.50	694
12	NADLER, Patricia	SUI	12.34	X	X	12.34	684
13	ATROSCHENKO, Anzhela	BLR	12.21	12.31	12.04	12.31	682
14	BLAIR, Kelly	USA	12.05	12.29	12.10	12.29	680

SHOT PUT - GROUP B

Rnk	Name	Ctry	1	2	3	Result	NC Pts
1	SAZANOVICH, Natalya	BLR	14.52	14.41	14.42	14.52	829
2	MOSKALETS, Svetlana	RUS	14.23	13.98	X	14.23	809
3	CARDENAS, Regla	CUB	14.01	14.14	X	14.14	803
4	LEWIS, Denise	GBR	13.79	13.92	13.61	13.92	789
5	NAZAROVIENE, Remigija	LTU	13.83	13.35	13.74	13.83	783
6	BEER, Peggy	GER	13.65	12.52	12.76	13.65	771
7	JAMIESON, Jane	AUS	13.30	13.63	13.64	13.64	770
8	MARXER, Manuela	LIE	12.93	X	13.46	13.46	758
9	HANSON, Sharon	USA	11.93	13.45	12.50	13.45	757
10	CLOPES, Inma	ESP	13.05	12.87	X	13.05	731
11	GUTHRIE-GRESHAM, Diane	JAM	12.76	12.88	X	12.88	719
12	BARBER, Eunice	SLE	12.60	12.87	X	12.87	719
13	STEIGAUF, Mona	GER	12.29	X	12.35	12.35	684

200 m - HEAT 1

Rnk	Ln	Name	Ctry	Result	NC Pts
1	5	GARCIA, Magalys	CUB	24.04	977
2	3	ATROSCHENKO, Anzhela	BLR	24.59	925
3	7	LEBEDENKO, Yelena	RUS	24.67	917
4	2	BOND-MILLS, Catherine	CAN	24.90	896
5	4	KAZANINA, Svetlana	KAZ	25.15	873
6	6	CLOPES, Inma	ESP	25.87	809

200 m - HEAT 2

Rnk	Ln	Name	Ctry	Result	NC Pts
1	3	SHOUAA, Ghada	SYR	23.85	995
2	2	WLODARCZYK, Urszula	POL	24.27	955
3	5*	BLAIR, Kelly	USA	24.49	934
4	8	STEIGAUF, Mona	GER	24.50	933
5	1	NADLER, Patricia	SUI	24.88	898
6	4	INANCSI, Rita	HUN	24.92	894
7	7	MOSKALETS, Svetlana	RUS	25.04	883
8	6*	HAUTALA, Tiia	FIN	25.33	857

200 m - HEAT 3

Rnk	Ln	Name	Ctry	Result	NC Pts
1	7	SAZANOVICH, Natalya	BLR	23.72	1008
2	3	LEWIS, Denise	GBR	24.44	939
3	2	NAZAROVIENE, Remigija	LTU	24.51	932
4	5	BARBER, Eunice	SLE	24.67	917
5	4	BRAUN, Sabine	GER	24.89	897
6	6	GUTHRIE-GRESHAM, Diane	JAM	25.12	876

Heptathlon, Women / *Heptathlon, Dames*

200 m - HEAT 4

Rnk	Ln	Name	Ctry	Result	NC Pts
1	6	CARDENAS, Regla	CUB	24.04	977
2	7	HANSON, Sharon	USA	24.42	941
3	4	BEER, Peggy	GER	24.64	920
4	2	NASTASE, Liliana	ROM	24.96	890
5	8	TYUKHAY, Irina	RUS	24.98	889
6	3	MARXER, Manuela	LIE	25.05	882
7	5	JAMIESON, Jane	AUS	25.70	824

LONG JUMP - GROUP A

Rnk	Name	Ctry	1	2	3	Result	NC Pts
1	CARDENAS, Regla	CUB	6.52	6.33	6.41	6.52	1014
2	LEBEDENKO, Yelena	RUS	X	6.33	6.33	6.33	953
3	NAZAROVIENE, Remigija	LTU	6.14	6.26	6.33	6.33	953
4	BEER, Peggy	GER	X	6.09	5.93	6.09	877
5	NASTASE, Liliana	ROM	6.09	X	X	6.09	877
6	KAZANINA, Svetlana	KAZ	5.65	5.98	X	5.98	843
7	HANSON, Sharon	USA	5.96	5.79	5.85	5.96	837
8	JAMIESON, Jane	AUS	5.93	5.91	X	5.93	828
9	HAUTALA, Tiia	FIN	5.63	5.70	5.85	5.85	804
10	NADLER, Patricia	SUI	5.82	5.79	5.80	5.82	795
11	CLOPES, Inma	ESP	5.74	X	5.69	5.74	771
12	ATROSCHENKO, Anzhela	BLR	X	X	5.63	5.63	738
	BOND-MILLS, Catherine	CAN	X	X	X	NM	
	MARXER, Manuela	LIE				DNS	

LONG JUMP - GROUP B

Rnk	Name	Ctry	1	2	3	Result	NC Pts
1	SAZANOVICH, Natalya	BLR	6.45	6.70	6.18	6.70	1072
2	GUTHRIE-GRESHAM, Diane	JAM	X	6.38	6.57	6.57	1030
3	BARBER, Eunice	SLE	6.57	X	X	6.57	1030
4	MOSKALETS, Svetlana	RUS	6.56	6.48	6.44	6.56	1027
5	STEIGAUF, Mona	GER	6.29	6.47	X	6.47	997
6	BLAIR, Kelly	USA	X	6.16	6.32	6.32	949
7	INANCSI, Rita	HUN	6.32	X	X	6.32	949
7	LEWIS, Denise	GBR	X	6.32	X	6.32	949
9	WLODARCZYK, Urszula	POL	6.21	6.30	X	6.30	943
10	SHOUAA, Ghada	SYR	X	6.26	6.23	6.26	930
11	BRAUN, Sabine	GER	6.11	6.14	6.21	6.21	915
12	TYUKHAY, Irina	RUS	5.97	6.07	6.07	6.07	871
13	GARCIA, Magalys	CUB	5.68	5.47	5.71	5.71	762

JAVELIN THROW - GROUP A

Rnk	Name	Ctry	1	2	3	Result	NC Pts
1	SHOUAA, Ghada	SYR	53.22	55.70	55.00	55.70	971
2	LEWIS, Denise	GBR	45.90	50.10	54.82	54.82	954
3	GARCIA, Magalys	CUB	51.22	X	X	51.22	884
4	BLAIR, Kelly	USA	50.32	49.66	46.96	50.32	866
5	BRAUN, Sabine	GER	46.64	48.72	X	48.72	835
6	INANCSI, Rita	HUN	46.46	43.40	45.32	46.46	792
7	SAZANOVICH, Natalya	BLR	46.00	44.58	X	46.00	783
8	BARBER, Eunice	SLE	41.08	X	45.26	45.26	768
9	WLODARCZYK, Urszula	POL	42.16	43.28	40.74	43.28	730
10	MOSKALETS, Svetlana	RUS	42.64	X	40.96	42.64	718
11	STEIGAUF, Mona	GER	42.40	X	X	42.40	713
12	GUTHRIE-GRESHAM, Diane	JAM	38.86	X	40.32	40.32	673
13	TYUKHAY, Irina	RUS	37.58	40.08	X	40.08	669

JAVELIN THROW - GROUP B

Rnk	Name	Ctry	1	2	3	Result	NC Pts
1	HANSON, Sharon	USA	X	44.38	46.98	46.98	802
2	BEER, Peggy	GER	X	46.72	44.76	46.72	797
3	LEBEDENKO, Yelena	RUS	45.02	X		45.02	764
4	JAMIESON, Jane	AUS	43.18	41.46	44.58	44.58	755
5	NADLER, Patricia	SUI	31.94	43.84	43.08	43.84	741
6	KAZANINA, Svetlana	KAZ	43.00	X	43.80	43.80	740
7	NAZAROVIENE, Remigija	LTU	39.86	41.92	42.68	42.68	719
8	CARDENAS, Regla	CUB	41.72	40.58	41.08	41.72	700
9	BOND-MILLS, Catherine	CAN	38.66	40.56	39.46	40.56	678
10	CLOPES, Inma	ESP	39.50	40.42	39.76	40.42	675
11	HAUTALA, Tiia	FIN	38.92	X	38.98	38.98	648
12	NASTASE, Liliana	ROM	37.98	X	38.66	38.66	642
	ATROSCHENKO, Anzhela	BLR				DNS	

800 m - HEAT 1

Rnk	Or	Name	Ctry	Result	NC Pts
1	4	BOND-MILLS, Catherine	CAN	2:14.50	900
2	6	HAUTALA, Tiia	FIN	2:16.09	877
3	1	NADLER, Patricia	SUI	2:18.06	850
4	3	NASTASE, Liliana	ROM	2:19.73	827
5	7	CLOPES, Inma	ESP	2:26.35	739

800 m - HEAT 2

Rnk	Or	Name	Ctry	Result	NC Pts
1	1	BEER, Peggy	GER	2:13.15	919
2	4	KAZANINA, Svetlana	KAZ	2:13.42	915
3	7	GUTHRIE-GRESHAM, Diane	JAM	2:17.55	857
4	8	JAMIESON, Jane	AUS	2:18.60	843
5	5	GARCIA, Magalys	CUB	2:21.03	810
6	3	TYUKHAY, Irina	RUS	2:26.69	735

800 m - HEAT 3

Rnk	Or	Name	Ctry	Result	NC Pts
1	1	HANSON, Sharon	USA	2:11.67	940
2	7	NAZAROVIENE, Remigija	LTU	2:12.61	927
3	6	BARBER, Eunice	SLE	2:13.27	917
4	4	STEIGAUF, Mona	GER	2:15.44	887
5	5	CARDENAS, Regla	CUB	2:20.48	817
6	2	LEBEDENKO, Yelena	RUS	2:28.58	711

800 m - HEAT 4

Rnk	Or	Name	Ctry	Result	NC Pts
1	6	WLODARCZYK, Urszula	POL	2:12.35	931
2	3	SHOUAA, Ghada	SYR	2:15.43	887
3	8	BLAIR, Kelly	USA	2:16.87	867
4	7	INANCSI, Rita	HUN	2:17.37	860
5	4	LEWIS, Denise	GBR	2:17.41	859
6	5	SAZANOVICH, Natalya	BLR	2:17.92	852
7	1	BRAUN, Sabine	GER	2:22.87	785
8	2	MOSKALETS, Svetlana	RUS	2:30.89	682

Heptathlon, Women / *Heptathlon, Dames*

FINAL

Rnk	Name	Ctry	100 m Hurdles	High Jump	Shot Put	200 m	Long Jump	Javelin Throw	800 m	Total Pts
1	SHOUAA, Ghada	SYR	13.72	1.86	15.95	23.85	6.26	55.70	2:15.43	
			1018	1054	925	995	930	971	887	6780 **G**
2	SAZANOVICH, Natalya	BLR	13.56	1.80	14.52	23.72	6.70	46.00	2:17.92	
			1041	978	829	1008	1072	783	852	6563 **S**
3	LEWIS, Denise	GBR	13.45	1.77	13.92	24.44	6.32	54.82	2:17.41	
			1058	941	789	939	949	954	859	6489 **B**
4	WLODARCZYK, Urszula	POL	13.48	1.86	14.36	24.27	6.30	43.28	2:12.35	
			1053	1054	818	955	943	730	931	6484
5	BARBER, Eunice	SLE	13.50	1.77	12.87	24.67	6.57	45.26	2:13.27	
			1050	941	719	917	1030	768	917	6342
6	INANCSI, Rita	HUN	13.95	1.83	14.69	24.92	6.32	46.46	2:17.37	
			985	1016	840	894	949	792	860	6336
7	BRAUN, Sabine	GER	13.55	1.83	14.48	24.89	6.21	48.72	2:22.87	
			1043	1016	826	897	915	835	785	6317
8	BLAIR, Kelly	USA	13.62	1.80	12.29	24.49	6.32	50.32	2:16.87	
			1033	978	680	934	949	866	867	6307
9	HANSON, Sharon	USA	13.34	1.77	13.45	24.42	5.96	46.98	2:11.67	
			1074	941	757	941	837	802	940	6292
10	NAZAROVIENE, Remigija	LTU	13.59	1.74	13.83	24.51	6.33	42.68	2:12.61	
			1037	903	783	932	953	719	927	6254
11	STEIGAUF, Mona	GER	13.22	1.77	12.35	24.50	6.47	42.40	2:15.44	
			1091	941	684	933	997	713	887	6246
12	CARDENAS, Regla	CUB	13.89	1.77	14.14	24.04	6.52	41.72	2:20.48	
			994	941	803	977	1014	700	817	6246
13	BEER, Peggy	GER	13.52	1.74	13.65	24.64	6.09	46.72	2:13.15	
			1047	903	771	920	877	797	919	6234
14	MOSKALETS, Svetlana	RUS	13.70	1.80	14.23	25.04	6.56	42.64	2:30.89	
			1021	978	809	883	1027	718	682	6118
15	GARCIA, Magalys	CUB	13.30	1.71	13.03	24.04	5.71	51.22	2:21.03	
			1080	867	729	977	762	884	810	6109
16	GUTHRIE-GRESHAM, Diane	JAM	14.17	1.80	12.88	25.12	6.57	40.32	2:17.55	
			954	978	719	876	1030	673	857	6087
17	LEBEDENKO, Yelena	RUS	13.70	1.77	13.72	24.67	6.33	45.02	2:28.58	
			1021	941	775	917	953	764	711	6082
18	KAZANINA, Svetlana	KAZ	14.69	1.86	12.50	25.15	5.98	43.80	2:13.42	
			883	1054	694	873	843	740	915	6002
19	TYUKHAY, Irina	RUS	13.90	1.77	14.16	24.98	6.07	40.08	2:26.69	
			993	941	805	889	871	669	735	5903
20	JAMIESON, Jane	AUS	14.57	1.80	13.64	25.70	5.93	44.58	2:18.60	
			899	978	770	824	828	755	843	5897
21	HAUTALA, Tiia	FIN	13.72	1.77	13.22	25.33	5.85	38.98	2:16.09	
			1018	941	742	857	804	648	877	5887
22	NASTASE, Liliana	ROM	13.37	1.65	13.30	24.96	6.09	38.66	2:19.73	
			1069	795	747	890	877	642	827	5847
23	NADLER, Patricia	SUI	13.81	1.68	12.34	24.88	5.82	43.84	2:18.06	
			1005	830	684	898	795	741	850	5803
24	CLOPES, Inma	ESP	14.30	1.77	13.05	25.87	5.74	40.42	2:26.35	
			936	941	731	809	771	675	739	5602
25	BOND-MILLS, Catherine	CAN	13.66	1.83	12.86	24.90	NM	40.56	2:14.50	
			1027	1016	718	896	0	678	900	5235

Athletics / *Athlétisme*
10 km Race Walk, Women / *10 km marche, Dames*

FINAL

Rnk	Name	Ctry	2 km (Rnk)	4 km (Rnk)	6 km (Rnk)	8 km (Rnk)	Final Time
1	NIKOLAYEVA, Yelena	RUS	8:40 (2)	16:49 (1)	25:00 (1)	33:24 (1)	41:49 O **G**
2	PERRONE, Elisabetta	ITA	8:40 (2)	16:54 (3)	25:19 (2)	33:51 (2)	42:12 **S**
3	WANG, Yan	CHN	8:50 (17)	17:13 (7)	25:36 (5)	34:04 (4)	42:19 **B**
4	GU, Yan	CHN	8:49 (10)	17:14 (11)	25:38 (7)	34:12 (6)	42:34
5	GIORDANO, Rossella	ITA	8:40 (2)	16:56 (5)	25:25 (3)	34:04 (4)	42:43
6	KARDAPOLTSEVA, Olya	BLR	8:48 (9)	17:13 (7)	25:45 (10)	34:27 (8)	43:02
7	RADTKE, Katarzyna	POL	8:50 (17)	17:14 (11)	25:47 (11)	34:30 (10)	43:05
8	TSYBULSKAYA, Valya	BLR	8:49 (10)	17:14 (11)	25:40 (9)	34:23 (7)	43:21
9	URBANIKNE ROZSA, Maria	HUN	8:49 (10)	17:20 (15)	26:01 (13)	34:50 (11)	43:32
10	GRUZINOVA, Yelena	RUS	8:49 (10)	17:22 (16)	26:08 (14)	35:03 (14)	43:50
11	SIDOTI, Annarita	ITA	8:40 (2)	17:13 (7)	25:59 (12)	35:00 (13)	43:57
12	SAXBY-JUNNA, Kerry	AUS	8:40 (2)	17:00 (6)	25:38 (7)	34:55 (12)	43:59
13	FEITOR, Susana	POR	8:50 (17)	17:38 (18)	26:36 (17)	35:32 (15)	44:24
14	ROHL, Michelle	USA	8:51 (20)	17:49 (20)	26:42 (18)	35:36 (16)	44:29
15	BOYDE, Kathrin	GER	9:04 (29)	17:53 (21)	26:43 (19)	35:44 (18)	44:50
16	ESSAYAH, Sari	FIN	8:43 (8)	17:15 (14)	26:22 (15)	35:51 (19)	45:02
17	MISYULYA, Natalya	BLR	8:52 (21)	17:39 (19)	26:48 (20)	36:06 (20)	45:11
18	MENDOZA, Graciela	MEX	9:04 (29)	18:01 (31)	27:06 (24)	36:13 (21)	45:13
19	MANNING, Anne	AUS	9:05 (33)	17:58 (28)	27:01 (21)	36:15 (22)	45:27
20	LAWRENCE, Debbie	USA	9:04 (29)	18:00 (30)	27:02 (22)	36:23 (24)	45:32
21	TOLSTAYA, Svetlana	KAZ	8:59 (25)	17:54 (23)	27:04 (23)	36:18 (23)	45:35
22	LIEPINA, Anita	LAT	9:04 (29)	17:57 (25)	27:06 (24)	36:23 (24)	45:35
23	GALLAGHER, Deirdre	IRL	9:10 (37)	18:27 (40)	27:47 (37)	36:58 (33)	45:47
24	RAJ, Annastasia	MAS	9:05 (33)	18:12 (36)	27:25 (30)	36:47 (28)	45:47
25	McCAFFREY, Janice	CAN	8:58 (23)	17:57 (25)	27:06 (24)	36:29 (26)	45:47
26	SAVILLE, Jane	AUS	9:10 (37)	18:20 (37)	27:30 (32)	36:47 (28)	45:56
27	SZEBENZKY, Aniko	HUN	9:05 (33)	18:08 (33)	27:29 (31)	36:52 (31)	45:57
28	VASCO, Maria	ESP	8:58 (23)	17:53 (21)	27:09 (27)	36:44 (27)	46:09
29	CIMPEAN, Norica	ROM	8:49 (10)	17:58 (28)	27:22 (29)	36:49 (30)	46:19
30	RAGOZINA, Tatyana	UKR	8:53 (22)	17:55 (24)	27:15 (28)	36:52 (31)	46:25
31	FORTAIN, Nathalie	FRA	9:10 (37)	18:20 (37)	27:42 (35)	37:17 (35)	46:43
32	POITRAS, Tina	CAN	8:59 (25)	17:57 (25)	27:30 (32)	37:16 (34)	46:51
33	LUPTON, Vicky	GBR	9:11 (42)	18:26 (39)	27:51 (39)	37:28 (36)	47:05
34	IRUSTA, Geovanna	BOL	9:05 (33)	18:08 (33)	27:41 (34)	37:29 (37)	47:13
35	SAZONOVA, Maya	KAZ	8:59 (25)	18:04 (32)	27:47 (37)	37:49 (38)	47:33
36	NADAUD-LEVEQUE, Valerie	FRA	9:10 (37)	18:40 (42)	28:23 (41)	38:10 (39)	47:49
37	MILUSAUSKAITE, Sonata	LTU	9:10 (37)	18:29 (41)	28:15 (40)	38:13 (40)	48:05
38	DELIC, Kada	BIH	9:29 (44)	19:11 (44)	29:06 (43)	39:01 (41)	48:47
	GRANADOS, Encarna	ESP	9:01 (28)	18:08 (33)	27:43 (36)		DNF
	GAO, Hongmiao	CHN	8:49 (10)	17:13 (7)	25:37 (6)	34:00 (3)	DQ
	GUMMELT, Beate	GER	8:39 (1)	16:55 (4)	25:33 (4)	34:28 (9)	DQ
	HERAZO, Victoria	USA	9:17 (43)	18:51 (43)	28:27 (42)		DQ
	MITSUMORI, Yuka	JPN	8:49 (10)	17:22 (16)	26:22 (15)	35:36 (16)	DQ
	STANKINA, Irina	RUS	8:40 (2)	16:49 (1)			DQ

Athletics / *Athlétisme*
20 km Race Walk, Men / *20 km marche, Messieurs*

FINAL

Rnk	Name	Ctry	4 km (Rnk)	8 km (Rnk)	12 km (Rnk)	16 km (Rnk)	Final Time
1	PEREZ QUEZADA, Jefferson L.	ECU	16:49 (17)	32:59 (11)	48:57 (5)	1:04:45 (2)	1:20:07 **G**
2	MARKOV, Ilya	RUS	16:47 (4)	32:57 (3)	48:56 (2)	1:04:45 (2)	1:20:16 **S**
3	SEGURA, Bernardo	MEX	16:47 (4)	32:59 (11)	48:57 (5)	1:04:45 (2)	1:20:23 **B**
4	A'HERN, Nick	AUS	16:50 (23)	33:00 (18)	48:57 (5)	1:04:45 (2)	1:20:31
5	SHAFIKOV, Rishat	RUS	16:47 (4)	32:56 (1)	48:41 (1)		1:20:41
6	FADEJEVS, Aigars	LAT	16:51 (28)	32:59 (11)	48:57 (5)	1:04:45 (2)	1:20:47
7	SHCHENNIKOV, Mikhail	RUS	16:49 (17)	32:57 (3)	48:56 (2)	1:04:52 (7)	1:21:09
8	KORZENIOWSKI, Robert	POL	16:48 (9)	33:00 (18)	49:02 (13)	1:05:10 (8)	1:21:13
9	MISYULYA, Yevgeniy	BLR	16:49 (17)	32:59 (11)	49:03 (15)	1:05:10 (8)	1:21:16
10	TOUTAIN, Thierry	FRA	16:48 (9)	32:57 (3)	49:02 (13)	1:05:27 (12)	1:21:56
11	PLAZA, Daniel	ESP	16:47 (4)	32:59 (11)	48:58 (11)	1:05:18 (11)	1:22:05
12	KHMELNITSKIY, Mikhail	BLR	16:53 (32)	33:10 (26)	49:23 (19)	1:05:48 (14)	1:22:17
13	URBANIK, Sandor	HUN	16:48 (9)	32:57 (3)	48:57 (5)	1:05:17 (10)	1:22:18
14	LANGLOIS, Denis	FRA	16:53 (32)	33:09 (24)	49:16 (18)		1:23:08
15	DAIMER, Nischan	GER	16:54 (36)	33:09 (24)	49:41 (22)		1:23:23
16	PERRICELLI, Giovanni	ITA	16:53 (32)	33:28 (34)	50:23 (32)	1:07:12 (17)	1:23:41
17	IHLY, Robert	GER	16:58 (40)	33:31 (36)	50:14 (31)		1:23:47
18	BORISOV, Valeriy	KAZ	16:50 (23)	33:00 (18)	49:43 (24)	1:06:40 (16)	1:23:52
19	GARCIA, Daniel	MEX	16:50 (23)	33:01 (22)	48:57 (5)	1:05:40 (13)	1:24:10
20	MASSANA, Valentin	ESP	16:46 (2)	32:58 (8)	49:27 (20)		1:24:14
21	YU, Guohui	CHN	16:50 (23)	33:16 (30)	50:01 (27)		1:24:30
22	IKESHIMA, Daisuke	JPN	16:49 (17)	33:17 (31)	49:59 (25)		1:24:54
23	KIMTAI, David	KEN	16:49 (17)	32:58 (8)	49:41 (22)		1:25:01
24	ERM, Andreas	GER	16:55 (37)	33:19 (32)	50:06 (29)		1:25:08
25	MALYSA, Jiri	CZE	16:50 (23)	33:12 (27)	50:00 (26)		1:25:13
26	GALDINO, Sergio	BRA	16:48 (9)	33:03 (23)	50:36 (34)		1:25:14
27	de BENEDICTIS, Giovanni	ITA	16:53 (32)	33:14 (29)	50:05 (28)		1:25:22
28	LI, Zewen	CHN	16:47 (4)	32:56 (1)	49:09 (17)		1:25:28
29	JORGENSEN, Claus	DEN	17:02 (47)	33:48 (43)	50:40 (36)		1:25:28
30	STAF, Jan	SWE	17:02 (47)	33:34 (37)	50:37 (35)		1:25:30
31	URBANO, Jose	POR	17:01 (43)	33:45 (40)	50:45 (38)	1:08:11 (19)	1:25:32
32	NELSON, Scott	NZL	16:46 (2)	33:29 (35)	50:35 (33)	1:08:13 (20)	1:25:50
33	GHOULA, Hatem	TUN	16:48 (9)	32:58 (8)	49:31 (21)		1:25:52
34	DIDONI, Michele	ITA	16:52 (29)	33:13 (28)	50:09 (30)	1:08:10 (18)	1:26:02
35	BROSSEAU, Jean-Olivier	FRA	17:05 (52)	33:59 (50)	51:05 (41)	1:08:40 (22)	1:26:29
36	ST. PIERRE, Martin	CAN	17:05 (52)	33:57 (48)	51:14 (44)	1:08:52 (24)	1:26:37
37	BENI DAOUD, Mohieddine	TUN	16:56 (38)	33:53 (46)	51:35 (47)	1:09:53 (29)	1:27:15
38	VALICEK, Robert	SVK	17:00 (41)	33:56 (47)	51:11 (43)	1:09:02 (25)	1:27:27
39	VAZQUEZ, Fernando	ESP	17:00 (41)	33:57 (48)	50:55 (39)	1:08:42 (23)	1:27:35
40	KAVULANYA, Justus	KEN	16:48 (9)	33:48 (43)	51:20 (45)	1:09:27 (27)	1:27:49
41	CIUMACENCO, Fedosei	MDA	17:04 (50)	33:45 (40)	51:51 (48)	1:09:48 (28)	1:27:57
42	HUERTA, Arturo	CAN	17:01 (43)	33:34 (37)	50:44 (37)	1:09:16 (26)	1:28:23
43	GARCIA, Luis	GUA	16:52 (29)	33:41 (39)	50:56 (40)	1:08:32 (21)	1:28:28
44	KAZLAUSKAS, Valdas	LTU	17:01 (43)	33:48 (43)	51:27 (46)	1:10:04 (30)	1:28:33
45	BALAN, Costica	ROM	17:04 (50)	34:36 (55)	52:34 (51)	1:10:47 (31)	1:28:36
46	BLAZEK, Pavol	SVK	17:24 (57)	34:56 (57)	52:44 (55)	1:10:47 (31)	1:29:41
47	RUSSELL, Dion	AUS	17:02 (47)	34:33 (54)	52:43 (53)	1:11:17 (34)	1:30:04
48	KRATOCHVIL, Tomas	CZE	17:05 (52)	34:15 (52)	52:15 (49)	1:11:03 (33)	1:30:11
49	BERTOLINO, Claudio	BRA	17:06 (55)	34:20 (53)	52:38 (52)	1:11:30 (35)	1:31:04
50	CLAUSEN, Curt	USA	17:07 (56)	34:39 (56)	52:43 (53)	1:11:59 (37)	1:31:30
51	McDONALD, Jimmy	IRL	18:03 (58)	37:06 (58)	55:12 (56)	1:13:35 (38)	1:32:11
52	SONNEK, Hubert	CZE	16:57 (39)	34:10 (51)	52:24 (50)	1:11:56 (36)	1:32:42
53	HTAY, Myint	MYA	19:18 (59)	40:14 (59)	1:01:17 (57)	1:22:00 (39)	1:42:28
	MORENO, Hector	COL					DNF
	AOUANOUK, Moussa	ALG					DNS
	KOLLAR, Igor	SVK	16:34 (1)	32:57 (3)	49:01 (12)	1:05:59 (15)	DQ
	LI, Mingcai	CHN	17:01 (43)	33:45 (40)	51:06 (42)		DQ
	MARTINEZ, Julio	GUA	16:48 (9)	32:59 (11)	49:06 (16)		DQ
	OSCAL, Roberto	GUA	16:49 (17)	33:27 (33)			DQ
	RODRIGUEZ, Miguel Angel	MEX	16:49 (17)	32:59 (11)	48:56 (2)	1:04:44 (1)	DQ
	SAWE, Julius	KEN	16:48 (9)	33:00 (18)			DQ

Athletics / *Athlétisme*
50 km Race Walk, Men / *50 km marche, Messieurs*

FINAL

Rnk	Name	Ctry	10 km (Rnk)	20 km (Rnk)	30 km (Rnk)	40 km (Rnk)	Final Time
1	KORZENIOWSKI, Robert	POL	46:20 (4)	1:31:37 (3)	2:16:12 (3)	3:00:06 (1)	3:43:30 G
2	SHCHENNIKOV, Mikhail	RUS	46:44 (27)	1:32:14 (16)	2:16:48 (11)	3:00:34 (6)	3:43:46 S
3	MASSANA, Valentin	ESP	45:44 (1)	1:31:10 (1)	2:16:12 (3)	3:00:07 (2)	3:44:19 B
4	di MEZZA, Arturo	ITA	46:33 (16)	1:32:47 (22)	2:18:06 (17)	3:02:30 (10)	3:44:52
5	GINKO, Viktor	BLR	46:20 (4)	1:31:38 (4)	2:16:11 (2)	3:00:13 (5)	3:45:27
6	ZAMUDIO, Ignacio	MEX	46:20 (4)	1:31:38 (4)	2:16:13 (5)	3:00:07 (2)	3:46:07
7	KONONEN, Valentin	FIN	46:20 (4)	1:31:42 (14)	2:16:14 (10)	3:00:39 (7)	3:47:40
8	KOREPANOV, Sergey	KAZ	46:34 (17)	1:32:38 (20)	2:18:02 (16)	3:02:31 (11)	3:48:42
9	GARCIA, Daniel	MEX	46:21 (11)	1:31:40 (10)	2:16:13 (5)	3:00:08 (4)	3:50:05
10	BERRETT, Tim	CAN	46:21 (11)	1:31:38 (4)	2:16:10 (1)	3:02:07 (9)	3:51:28
11	RAKOVIC, Aleksandar	YUG	46:46 (30)	1:32:59 (30)	2:18:44 (23)	3:04:38 (14)	3:51:31
12	NOACK, Axel	GER	46:44 (27)	1:32:47 (22)	2:18:12 (19)	3:04:46 (15)	3:51:55
13	PERRICELLI, Giovanni	ITA	46:34 (17)	1:32:47 (22)	2:18:31 (22)	3:05:17 (17)	3:52:31
14	ZHANG, Huiqiang	CHN	46:44 (27)	1:32:33 (19)	2:18:10 (18)	3:03:15 (12)	3:53:10
15	WALLSTAB, Thomas	GER	47:24 (34)	1:34:17 (36)	2:21:17 (28)	3:08:05 (21)	3:54:48
16	MORENO, Hector	COL	47:44 (40)	1:34:39 (38)	2:21:26 (31)	3:08:48 (22)	3:54:57
17	URIAS, Julio	GUA	46:20 (4)	1:31:41 (12)	2:18:14 (20)	3:06:46 (18)	3:56:27
18	SANCHEZ, German	MEX	46:34 (17)	1:31:38 (4)	2:16:13 (5)	3:01:01 (8)	3:57:47
19	PILLER, Rene	FRA	46:34 (17)	1:32:47 (22)	2:19:12 (24)	3:07:06 (19)	3:58:00
20	MRAZEK, Roman	SVK	47:07 (33)	1:35:19 (42)	2:22:50 (33)	3:10:11 (25)	3:58:20
21	MALIK, Stefan	SVK	47:47 (42)	1:34:14 (35)	2:20:30 (27)	3:07:40 (20)	3:58:40
22	BARROSO, Jaime	ESP	46:35 (22)	1:32:49 (29)	2:21:18 (29)	3:11:11 (27)	4:01:09
23	LIEPINS, Modris	LAT	47:24 (34)	1:33:22 (31)	2:17:06 (12)	3:04:59 (16)	4:01:12
24	JAMES, Allen	USA	47:39 (38)	1:34:38 (37)	2:21:25 (30)	3:10:34 (26)	4:01:18
25	MATYUKHIN, Nikolay	RUS	46:43 (26)	1:32:15 (18)	2:18:20 (21)	3:09:45 (24)	4:01:49
26	CHYLINSKI, Andrzej	USA	48:53 (49)	1:37:13 (48)	2:25:04 (39)	3:13:31 (30)	4:03:13

FINAL - *continued*

Rnk	Name	Ctry	10 km (Rnk)	20 km (Rnk)	30 km (Rnk)	40 km (Rnk)	Final Time
27	HOLUSA, Milos	CZE	46:34 (17)	1:32:48 (26)	2:19:34 (25)	3:09:43 (23)	4:03:16
28	FESSELIER, Martial	FRA	48:32 (46)	1:36:53 (47)	2:25:01 (38)	3:12:24 (28)	4:04:42
29	KOSAKA, Tadahiro	JPN	47:24 (34)	1:34:39 (38)	2:22:49 (32)	3:13:01 (29)	4:05:57
30	LINDMAN, Antero	FIN	47:24 (34)	1:34:39 (38)	2:22:57 (35)	3:14:08 (32)	4:07:58
31	CHARRIERE, Pascal	SUI	48:21 (44)	1:36:25 (43)	2:26:17 (41)	3:18:49 (35)	4:10:20
32	TICHY, Peter	SVK	48:32 (46)	1:36:43 (45)	2:24:24 (37)	3:13:38 (31)	4:10:55
33	BARRETT, Craig	NZL	46:19 (3)	1:31:39 (9)	2:17:36 (14)	3:15:32 (33)	4:15:15
34	MADDOCKS, Chris	GBR	46:53 (32)	1:34:06 (32)	2:23:31 (36)	3:20:19 (36)	4:18:41
35	ZUJUS, Daugvinas	LTU	48:32 (46)	1:37:36 (49)	2:29:20 (42)	3:23:48 (37)	4:23:35
36	MAGALHAES, Jose	POR	48:54 (50)	1:38:34 (50)	2:30:58 (43)	3:28:32 (38)	4:27:37
	COUSINS, Duane	AUS	47:45 (41)	1:34:48 (41)	2:22:54 (34)	3:17:02 (34)	4:02:16
	de BENEDICTIS, Giovanni	ITA	46:22 (15)	1:31:45 (15)	2:17:09 (13)		DNF
	GARCIA, Jesus Angel	ESP	45:44 (1)	1:31:34 (2)	2:16:13 (5)	3:04:33 (13)	DNF
	LEHTINEN, Jani	FIN	48:03 (43)	1:36:26 (44)	2:26:12 (40)		DNF
	MISYULYA, Yevgeniy	BLR	46:39 (24)	1:32:14 (16)	2:17:41 (15)		DNF
	PLOTNIKOV, Andrey	RUS	46:38 (23)	1:32:38 (20)			DNF
	POPOVYCH, Vitaliy	UKR	46:21 (11)	1:31:41 (12)			DNF
	SONNEK, Hubert	CZE	48:31 (45)	1:36:46 (46)			DNF
	WEIGEL, Ronald	GER	46:34 (17)	1:32:48 (26)			DNF
	CIUMACENCO, Fedosei	MDA					DNS
	BAKER, Simon	AUS	46:40 (25)	1:32:48 (26)	2:19:37 (26)		DQ
	LOPEZ, Hugo	GUA	46:52 (31)	1:34:06 (32)			DQ
	MAO, Xinyuan	CHN	47:39 (38)	1:34:06 (32)			DQ
	NELSON, Herman	USA	48:54 (50)				DQ
	TOUTAIN, Thierry	FRA	46:20 (4)	1:31:38 (4)	2:16:13 (5)		DQ
	ZHAO, Yongsheng	CHN	46:21 (11)	1:31:40 (10)			DQ

Athletics / *Athlétisme*
Marathon, Men / *Marathon, Messieurs*

FINAL

Rnk	Name	Ctry	Result
1	THUGWANE, Josia	RSA	2:12:36 G
2	LEE, Bong-Ju	KOR	2:12:39 S
3	WAINAINA, Eric	KEN	2:12:44 B
4	FIZ, Martin	ESP	2:13:20
5	NERURKAR, Richard	GBR	2:13:39
6	SILVA, German	MEX	2:14:29
7	MONEGHETTI, Steve	AUS	2:14:35
8	PAREDES, Benjamin	MEX	2:14:55
9	GOFFI, Danilo	ITA	2:15:08
10	dos SANTOS, Luis Antonio	BRA	2:15:55
11	GRISALES, Carlos	COL	2:15:56
12	KIM, Yi-Yong	KOR	2:16:17
13	CHIMUSASA, Tendai	ZIM	2:16:31
14	PINTO, Antonio	POR	2:16:41
15	CERON, Dionicio	MEX	2:16:48
16	KALOMBO, Mwenze	ZAI	2:17:01
17	BEBLO, Leszek	POL	2:17:04
18	JUZDADO, Alberto	ESP	2:17:24
19	TANIGUCHI, Hiromi	JPN	2:17:26
20	BETTIOL, Salvatore	ITA	2:17:27
21	FONSECA, Peter	CAN	2:17:28
22	VERA, Rolando	ECU	2:17:40
23	de HIGHDEN, Rod	AUS	2:17:42
24	MOLINA, Jose Luis	CRC	2:17:49
25	CASTRO, Domingos	POR	2:18:03
26	MANSOURI, Tahar	TUN	2:18:06
27	PEU, Lawrence	RSA	2:18:09
28	BRANTLY, Keith	USA	2:18:17
29	RALEKHETLA, Thabiso	LES	2:18:26
30	STEFANOV, Khristo	BUL	2:18:29
31	KEMPAINEN, Bob	USA	2:18:38
32	HANNINEN, Harri	FIN	2:18:41
33	THYS, Gert	RSA	2:18:55
34	QUILTY, Sean	AUS	2:19:35

FINAL - *continued*

Rnk	Name	Ctry	Result
35	NELSON, Carey	CAN	2:19:39
36	ANDRIOPOULOS, Spyridon	GRE	2:19:41
37	STRIZHAKOV, Oleg	RUS	2:19:51
38	KIM, Jung-Won	PRK	2:19:54
39	DEACON, Bruce	CAN	2:19:56
40	KIM, Jong-Su	PRK	2:20:19
41	COOGAN, Mark	USA	2:20:27
42	SALAH, Ahmed	DJI	2:20:33
43	SARAFYNYUK, Petro	UKR	2:20:37
44	el MOUAZIZ, Abdelkader	MAR	2:20:39
45	van VLAANDEREN, Bert	NED	2:20:48
46	MATIAS, Manuel	POR	2:20:58
47	de LIMA, Vanderlei	BRA	2:21:01
48	DOBLER, Konrad	GER	2:21:12
49	DEVIC, Borislav	YUG	2:21:22
50	MILESI, Davide	ITA	2:21:45
51	PROKOPCHUK, Aleksandr	LAT	2:21:50
52	AGUTA, Lameck	KEN	2:22:04
53	GARCIA, Diego	ESP	2:22:11
54	OYA, Masaki	JPN	2:22:13
55	WHITEHEAD, Peter	GBR	2:22:37
56	BITOK, Ezequiel	KEN	2:23:03
57	HSU, Gi-Sheng	TPE	2:23:04
58	LOSKUTOV, Pavel	EST	2:23:14
59	MAZA, Ruben	VEN	2:23:24
60	BRACE, Steve	GBR	2:23:28
61	GAJDUS, Grzegorz	POL	2:23:41
62	SIMELANE, Isaac	SWZ	2:23:43
63	AKYLBEKOV, Nazirdin	KGZ	2:23:59
64	SZALKAI, Anders	SWE	2:24:27
65	MWATHIWA, John	MAW	2:24:45
66	SHVETSOV, Leonid	RUS	2:24:49
67	HELLEBUYCK, Eddy	BEL	2:25:04
68	SALIH, Ahmed	SUD	2:25:12

FINAL - *continued*

Rnk	Name	Ctry	Result
69	SALIM, Ikaji	TAN	2:25:29
70	FEDORENKO, Pavelas	LTU	2:25:41
71	MALLQUI, Miguel	PER	2:25:56
72	HUDSON, Ethel	INA	2:26:02
73	dos SANTOS, Diamantino	BRA	2:26:53
74	BOGATI, Tika	NEP	2:27:04
75	HOLASSIE, Ronnie	TRI	2:27:20
76	TJITUNGA, Joseph	NAM	2:27:52
77	VLAS, Valeri	MDA	2:28:36
78	SIBANDZE, Daniel	SWZ	2:28:49
79	COTELO, Waldemar	URU	2:28:50
80	STEFANOV, Petko	BUL	2:29:06
81	MEKONNEN, Abebe	ETH	2:29:45
82	MARTINEZ, Luis	GUA	2:29:55
83	WADE, Sean	NZL	2:30:35
84	BENREDOUANE, Abderrahim	MAR	2:30:49
85	MONZO, Abdou	NIG	2:30:57
86	BARRIENTOS, Marcelo	CHI	2:31:05
87	BERNADO, Toni	AND	2:31:28
88	ADILI, Adel	LBA	2:32:12
89	TARAZONA, Carlos	VEN	2:32:35
90	GASHAKA, Tharcisse	BDI	2:32:55
91	CALIZAYA, Policarpio	BOL	2:33:08
92	QAMUNGA, Simon	TAN	2:33:11
93	JITSUI, Kenjiro	JPN	2:33:27
94	ZEFERINO, Antonio	CPV	2:34:13
95	BALLANTYNE, Pamenos	VIN	2:34:16
96	MUTOKE, Kaleka	ZAI	2:34:40
97	NDISSIPOU, Ernest	CAF	2:35:55
98	ETTOUNSI, Ali	MAR	2:36:01
99	AGUIRRE, William	NCA	2:37:02
100	VENCE, Roy	PHI	2:37:10
101	al SAADI, M.	YEM	2:40:41
102	HERNANDEZ, Julio	COL	2:41:56

FINAL - *continued*

Rnk	Name	Ctry	Result
103	CHUTTOO, Ajay	MRI	2:42:07
104	ANTONIO, Nils	JAM	2:44:10
105	TO, Rithya	CAM	2:47:01
106	OLIVERAS, Maximo	PUR	2:47:15
107	DJUGUM, Islam	BIH	2:47:38
108	WILLIAMS, Marlon	ISV	2:48:26
109	MUSLAR, Eugene	BIZ	2:51:41
110	ISAK, Abdi	SOM	2:59:55
111	WASIQI, A Baser	AFG	4:24:17
	DINSAMO, Belayneh	ETH	DNF
	FREIGANG, Stephan	GER	DNF
	ISHYAKA, Patrick	RWA	DNF
	KELEKETU, Benjamin	BOT	DNF
	KIM, Wan-Ki	KOR	DNF
	KUNDROTAS, Ceslovas	LTU	DNF
	OMAR, Moussa	DJI	DNF
	RAZAFINDRAKOTO, Victor	MAD	DNF
	SILIO, Antonio	ARG	DNF
	SUMAYE, Julius	TAN	DNF
	TUMO, Turbo	ETH	DNF
	ULMALA, Risto	FIN	DNF
	VIRBICKAS, Dainius	LTU	DNF

Best Intermediate Times

	Name	Ctry	Result
5k	FONSECA, Peter	CAN	16:14
10k	GAJDUS, Grzegorz	POL	31:50
15k	CHIMUSASA, Tendai	ZIM	47:36
20k	BEBLO, Leszek	POL	1:04:06
Half	DINSAMO, Belayneh	ETH	1:07:36
25k	CHIMUSASA, Tendai	ZIM	1:19:54
30k	CASTRO, Domingos	POR	1:35:24
35k	THUGWANE, Josia	RSA	1:50:35
40k	THUGWANE, Josia	RSA	2:06:08

Athletics / *Athlétisme*

Marathon, Women / *Marathon, Dames*

FINAL			
Rnk	Name	Ctry	Result
1	ROBA, Fatuma	ETH	2:26:05 **G**
2	YEGOROVA, Valentina	RUS	2:28:05 **S**
3	ARIMORI, Yuko	JPN	2:28:39 **B**
4	DOERRE-HEINIG, Katrin	GER	2:28:45
5	RIOS, Rocio	ESP	2:30:50
6	SIMON, Lidia	ROM	2:31:04
7	MACHADO, Maria	POR	2:31:11
8	KROLIK, Sonja	GER	2:31:16
9	REN, Xiujuan	CHN	2:31:21
10	LAUCK, Anne Marie	USA	2:31:30
11	SOBANSKA, Malgorzata	POL	2:31:52
12	MAKI, Izumi	JPN	2:32:35
13	FERRARA, Ornella	ITA	2:33:09
14	PONT, Monica	ESP	2:33:27
15	KANANA, Angeline	KEN	2:34:19
16	McCOLGAN, Liz	GBR	2:34:30
17	ASARI, Junko	JPN	2:34:31
18	ROCHAT-MOSER, Franziska	SUI	2:34:48
19	GONZALEZ, Griselda	ARG	2:35:12
20	JONG, Song Ok	PRK	2:35:31
21	BOGACHOVA, Irina	KGZ	2:35:44
22	GONZALEZ, Inglandini	COL	2:35:45
23	AKTAS, Serap	TUR	2:36:14
24	MAZOVKA, Yelena	BLR	2:36:22
25	RENDERS, Marleen	BEL	2:36:27

FINAL - *continued*			
Rnk	Name	Ctry	Result
26	KIM, Chang Ok	PRK	2:36:31
27	DIAS, Albertina	POR	2:36:39
28	McCANN, Kerryn	AUS	2:36:41
29	NIKIEL, Aniela	POL	2:36:44
30	OH, Mi-Ja	KOR	2:36:54
31	SOMERS, Linda	USA	2:36:58
32	BARTOSZEK, Danuta	CAN	2:37:06
33	DIAZ, Mari Carmen	MEX	2:37:14
34	GLAUSER, Nelly	SUI	2:37:19
35	BURANGULOVA, Ramilya	RUS	2:38:04
36	FOLDINGNE NAGY, Judit	HUN	2:38:43
37	OLIVERA, Erika	CHI	2:39:06
38	DANSON, Yvonne	SIN	2:39:18
39	NARLOCH, Marcia	BRA	2:39:33
40	STATKUVIENE, Stefanija	LTU	2:39:51
41	van SCHUPPEN, Antje	NED	2:40:46
42	POLYZOU, Maria	GRE	2:41:33
43	LOMA, Guadaloupe	MEX	2:41:56
44	CATUNA, Anuta	ROM	2:42:01
45	MACLEOD, Karen	GBR	2:42:08
46	MOLLER, Lorraine	NZL	2:42:21
47	MACHADO, Albertina	POR	2:43:44
48	HAAKENSTAD, Anita	NOR	2:43:58
49	ALONSO, Ana Isabel	ESP	2:44:12

FINAL - *continued*			
Rnk	Name	Ctry	Result
50	GALUSHKO, Natasha	BLR	2:44:21
51	FERNANDEZ, Adriana	MEX	2:44:23
52	ALLISON, May	CAN	2:44:38
53	JAVORNIK, Helena	SLO	2:46:58
54	SALAZAR, Marilu	PER	2:48:58
55	CIRIC, Suzana	YUG	2:49:30
56	PRASAD, Nadia	FRA	2:50:05
57	MALAXOS, Sue	AUS	2:50:46
58	RIGG, Suzanne	GBR	2:52:09
59	MONGUDHI, Elizabeth	NAM	2:56:19
60	de SOUZA, Solange	BRA	2:56:23
61	DADABAYEVA, Guylsara	TJK	3:09:08
62	RANAMAGAR, Bimala	NEP	3:16:19
63	DAVAAJARGAL, Erhemsaihan	MGL	3:19:06
64	KETAVONG, Sirivanh	LAO	3:25:16
65	BENITO, Marie	GUM	3:27:28
	BIKTAGIROVA, Madina	BLR	DNF
	CHEPCHUMBA, Joyce	KEN	DNF
	CHIRCHIR, Salina	KEN	DNF
	CURATOLO, Maria	ITA	DNF
	de OLIVEIRA, Carmen	BRA	DNF
	GALEA, Carol	MLT	DNF
	GRADUS, Kamila	POL	DNF
	KANG, Soon-Duk	KOR	DNF

FINAL - *continued*			
Rnk	Name	Ctry	Result
	KARLSHOJ, Gitte	DEN	DNF
	KLOCHKO, Lyubov	UKR	DNF
	LEE, Mi-Kyung	KOR	DNF
	MEYER, Elana	RSA	DNF
	ONDIEKI, Lisa	AUS	DNF
	PIPPIG, Uta	GER	DNF
	POMACU, Cristina	ROM	DNF
	RAUTA, Kirsi	FIN	DNF
	SALUMAE, Jane	EST	DNF
	SPANGLER, Jenny	USA	DNF
	TENORIO, Martha	ECU	DNF
	VICECONTE, Maura	ITA	DNF
	ZHILYAYEVA, Alla	RUS	DNF

Best Intermediate Times			
	Name	Ctry	Result
5k	PIPPIG, Uta	GER	17:30
10k	PIPPIG, Uta	GER	34:09
15k	PIPPIG, Uta	GER	51:18
20k	ROBA, Fatuma	ETH	1:08:45
Half	ROBA, Fatuma	ETH	1:12:31
25k	ROBA, Fatuma	ETH	1:25:50
30k	ROBA, Fatuma	ETH	1:42:57
35k	ROBA, Fatuma	ETH	2:00:46
40k	ROBA, Fatuma	ETH	2:18:40

Athletics / *Athlétisme*

1,500 m Wheelchair, Men / *1 500 m fauteuil roulant, Messieurs*

FINAL				
Rnk	Or	Name	Ctry	Result
1	2	ISSORAT, Claude	FRA	3:15.18 **G**
2	4	HOLLONBECK, Scot	USA	3:15.30 **S**
3	5	NIETLISPACH, Franz	SUI	3:16.41 **B**
4	7	COUPRIE, Philippe	FRA	3:16.45
5	6	MENDOZA, Saul	MEX	3:16.58
6	3	LUNA, Jorge	MEX	3:16.78
7	1	WIGGINS, Paul	AUS	3:16.86
8	8	HEILVEIL, Jacob	USA	3:16.90

Athletics / *Athlétisme*

800 m Wheelchair, Women / *800 m fauteuil roulant, Dames*

FINAL				
Rnk	Or	Name	Ctry	Result
1	5	SAUVAGE, Louise	AUS	1:54.90 **G**
2	4	DRISCOLL, Jean	USA	1:55.19 **S**
3	8	BECERRA, Cheri	USA	1:55.49 **B**
4	7	GREY, Tanni	GBR	1:55.55
5	1	PETITCLERC, Chantal	CAN	1:55.61
6	3	SHANNON, Leann	USA	1:55.82
7	2	WETTERSTROM, Monica	SWE	1:56.83
8	6	ANGGRENY, Lily	GER	2:05.33

VENUE MAP
PLAN DU SITE

Marathon Race Course
Parcours du marathon
Race Walk Course
Parcours de la marche
Atlanta / *Atlanta*

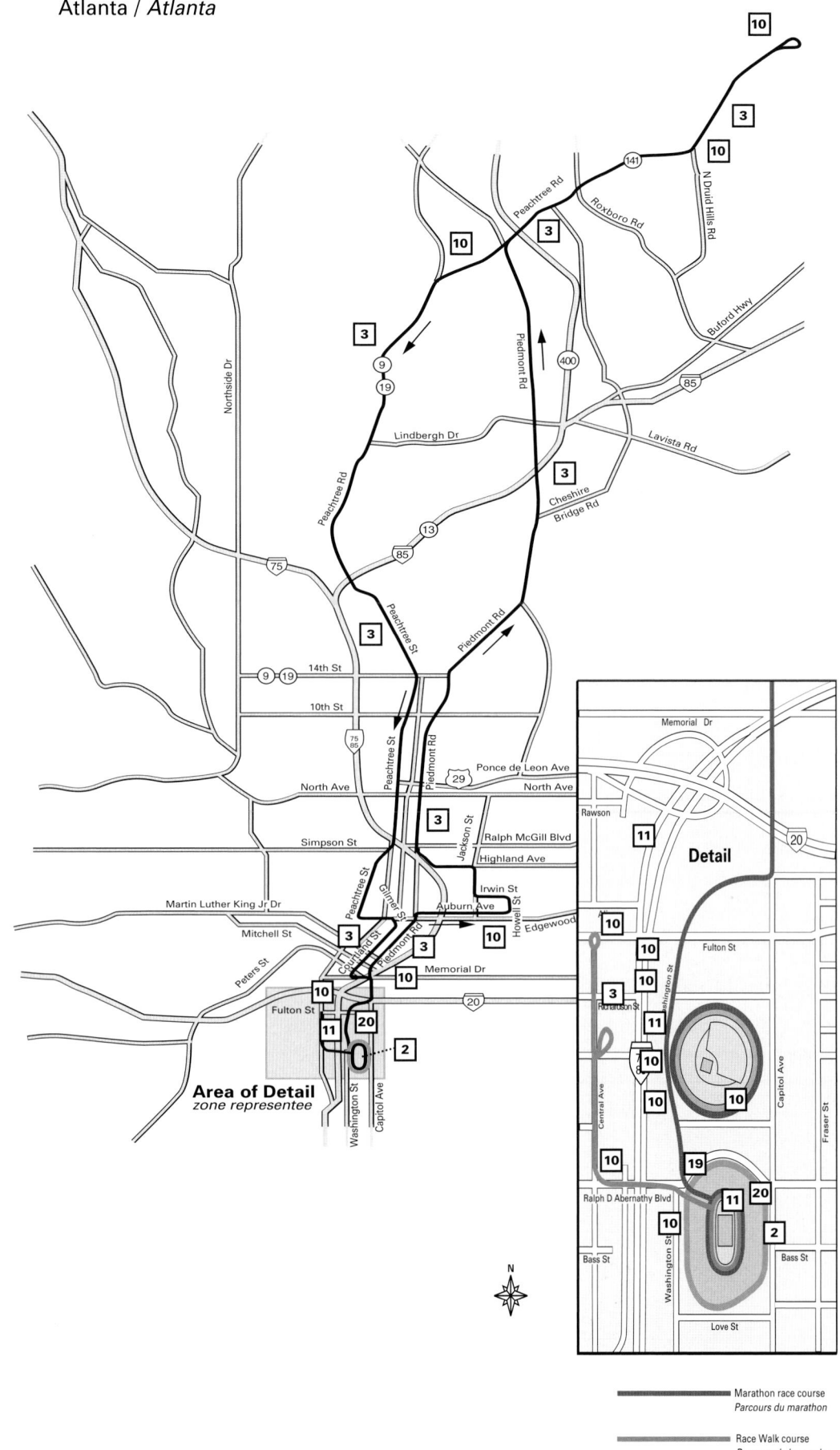

LEGEND

This legend represents the major functional areas located at each Olympic venue. The numbers below correspond to the numbers shown on the venue maps.

1	Accreditation
2	Ceremonies
3	Competition area
4	Competition related area
5	Event seating
6	ACOG management
7	Sports administration federation services
8	Material acquisition/ distribution
9	Press
10	Broadcasters
11	Health services and medical control
12	Spectator services
13	Olympic Family services
14	Security
15	Technology
16	Food services
17	Transportation
18	Ticketing
19	Spectator entrance
20	Athlete entrance

LÉGENDE

Les principaux domaines fonctionnels en place sur chaque site figurent dans cette légende. Les chiffres correspondent à ceux que l'on trouve sur les cartes des sites.

1	*Accréditation*
2	*Cérémonies*
3	*Aire de compétition*
4	*Aire des services liés aux compétitions*
5	*Places*
6	*Direction du site*
7	*Services administratifs des fédérations sportives*
8	*Acquisition/distribution du matériel*
9	*Presse*
10	*Diffuseurs*
11	*Services et contrôles médicaux*
12	*Services aux spectateurs*
13	*Services à la Famille olympique*
14	*Sécurité*
15	*Technologie*
16	*Alimentation*
17	*Transports*
18	*Billetterie*
19	*Entrée réservée aux spectateurs*
20	*Entrée réservée aux athlètes*

Marathon race course
Parcours du marathon

Race Walk course
Parcours de la marche

BADMINTON
BADMINTON

Abbreviations and terms used in Badminton results tables
Abréviations et termes employés dans les tableaux de résultats de badminton

Term	English	Français
Bronze Medal	Bronze Medal	Médaille de bronze
BYE	Bye	Exemption
Ctry	Country	Pays
Final Classification	Final Classification	Classement final
First Round	First Round	Premier tour
Gold Medal	Gold Medal	Médaille d'or
Medal Round	Medal Round	Tour pour les médailles
Name	Name	Nom
Quarterfinals	Quarterfinals	Quarts de finale
Rnk	Rank	Classement
Second Round	Second Round	Deuxième tour
Semifinals	Semifinals	Demi-finales
Silver Medal	Silver Medal	Médaille d'argent
Third Round	Third Round	Troisième tour

International Badminton Federation (IBF)
Fédération Internationale de Badminton
Manor Park
Mackenzie Way, Cheltenham
Gloucestershire GL 51 9TX
England

PA • ATSMON PAZ • GENE N PAZ • JENNIFER M PAZIAN • KRISTIN L PAZIAN • BRIAN A PEABODY • KIMBERLY A PEACE • KIMBERLY J PEACE • LAUREL M PEACE • JASON M PEACH • LEANN P PEACH • SUZANNE S PEACHIN • ANTONY PEACOCK • BARBARA R PEACOCK • BILL C PEACOCK • BILLY J PEACOCK • CAROLYN A PEACOCK • JAMES D PEACOCK • JOEL A PEACOCK • MARY FRANCES PEACOCK • MICHAEL F PEACOCK • MARLENE E PEARAH • CAREY H PEARCE • DAVID A PEARCE • JAYNE E PEARCE • JENNIFER J PEARCE • NEAL P PEARCE • PATRICK Z PEARCE • WILLIAM H PEARCE •

109

Badminton / *Badminton*

Singles, Men / *Simples, Messieurs*

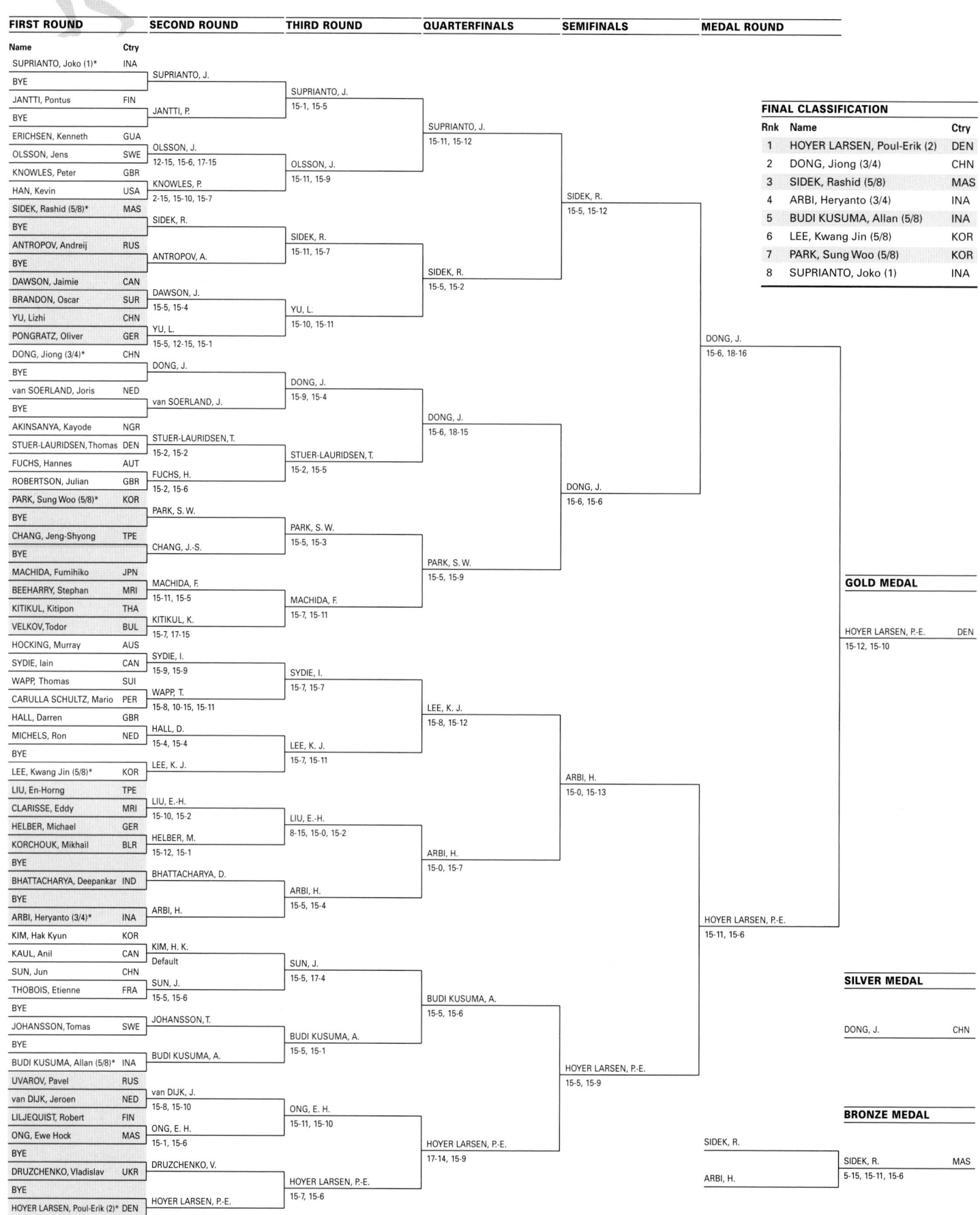

FIRST ROUND		SECOND ROUND	THIRD ROUND	QUARTERFINALS	SEMIFINALS	MEDAL ROUND
Name	Ctry					
SUPRIANTO, Joko (1)*	INA	SUPRIANTO, J.				
BYE			SUPRIANTO, J.			
JANTTI, Pontus	FIN	JANTTI, P.	15-1, 15-5			
BYE				SUPRIANTO, J.		
ERICHSEN, Kenneth	GUA	OLSSON, J.		15-11, 15-12		
OLSSON, Jens	SWE	12-15, 15-6, 17-15	OLSSON, J.			
KNOWLES, Peter	GBR	KNOWLES, P.	15-11, 15-9			
HAN, Kevin	USA	2-15, 15-10, 15-7			SIDEK, R.	
SIDEK, Rashid (5/8)*	MAS	SIDEK, R.			15-5, 15-12	
BYE			SIDEK, R.			
ANTROPOV, Andreij	RUS	ANTROPOV, A.	15-11, 15-7			
BYE				SIDEK, R.		
DAWSON, Jaimie	CAN	DAWSON, J.		15-5, 15-2		
BRANDON, Oscar	SUR	15-5, 15-4	YU, L.			
YU, Lizhi	CHN	YU, L.	15-10, 15-11			
PONGRATZ, Oliver	GER	15-5, 12-15, 15-1				DONG, J.
DONG, Jiong (3/4)*	CHN	DONG, J.				15-6, 18-16
BYE			DONG, J.			
van SOERLAND, Joris	NED	van SOERLAND, J.	15-9, 15-4			
BYE				DONG, J.		
AKINSANYA, Kayode	NGR	STUER-LAURIDSEN, T.		15-6, 18-15		
STUER-LAURIDSEN, Thomas	DEN	15-2, 15-2	STUER-LAURIDSEN, T.			
FUCHS, Hannes	AUT	FUCHS, H.	15-2, 15-5			
ROBERTSON, Julian	GBR	15-2, 15-6			DONG, J.	
PARK, Sung Woo (5/8)*	KOR	PARK, S. W.			15-6, 15-6	
BYE			PARK, S. W.			
CHANG, Jeng-Shyong	TPE	CHANG, J.-S.	15-5, 15-3			
BYE				PARK, S. W.		
MACHIDA, Fumihiko	JPN	MACHIDA, F.		15-5, 15-9		
BEEHARRY, Stephan	MRI	15-11, 15-5	MACHIDA, F.			
KITIKUL, Kitipon	THA	KITIKUL, K.	15-7, 15-11			
VELKOV, Todor	BUL	15-7, 17-15				
HOCKING, Murray	AUS	SYDIE, I.				
SYDIE, Iain	CAN	15-9, 15-9	SYDIE, I.			
WAPP, Thomas	SUI	WAPP, T.	15-7, 15-7			
CARULLA SCHULTZ, Mario	PER	15-8, 10-15, 15-11		LEE, K. J.		
HALL, Darren	GBR	HALL, D.		15-8, 15-12		
MICHELS, Ron	NED	15-4, 15-4	LEE, K. J.			
BYE			15-7, 15-11			
LEE, Kwang Jin (5/8)*	KOR	LEE, K. J.			ARBI, H.	
LIU, En-Horng	TPE	LIU, E.-H.			15-0, 15-13	
CLARISSE, Eddy	MRI	15-10, 15-2	LIU, E.-H.			
HELBER, Michael	GER	HELBER, M.	8-15, 15-0, 15-2			
KORCHOUK, Mikhail	BLR	15-12, 15-1		ARBI, H.		
BYE				15-0, 15-7		
BHATTACHARYA, Deepankar	IND	BHATTACHARYA, D.				
BYE			ARBI, H.			
ARBI, Heryanto (3/4)*	INA	ARBI, H.	15-5, 15-4			
KIM, Hak Kyun	KOR	KIM, H. K.				HOYER LARSEN, P.-E.
KAUL, Anil	CAN	Default	SUN, J.			15-11, 15-6
SUN, Jun	CHN	SUN, J.	15-5, 17-4			
THOBOIS, Etienne	FRA	15-5, 15-6		BUDI KUSUMA, A.		
BYE				15-5, 15-6		
JOHANSSON, Tomas	SWE	JOHANSSON, T.				
BYE			BUDI KUSUMA, A.			
BUDI KUSUMA, Allan (5/8)*	INA	BUDI KUSUMA, A.	15-5, 15-1			
UVAROV, Pavel	RUS	van DIJK, J.			HOYER LARSEN, P.-E.	
van DIJK, Jeroen	NED	15-8, 15-10			15-5, 15-9	
LILJEQUIST, Robert	FIN	ONG, E. H.	ONG, E. H.			
ONG, Ewe Hock	MAS	15-1, 15-6	15-11, 15-10			
BYE				HOYER LARSEN, P.-E.		
DRUZCHENKO, Vladislav	UKR	DRUZCHENKO, V.		17-14, 15-9		
BYE			HOYER LARSEN, P.-E.			
HOYER LARSEN, Poul-Erik (2)*	DEN	HOYER LARSEN, P.-E.	15-7, 15-6			

FINAL CLASSIFICATION

Rnk	Name	Ctry
1	HOYER LARSEN, Poul-Erik (2)	DEN
2	DONG, Jiong (3/4)	CHN
3	SIDEK, Rashid (5/8)	MAS
4	ARBI, Heryanto (3/4)	INA
5	BUDI KUSUMA, Allan (5/8)	INA
6	LEE, Kwang Jin (5/8)	KOR
7	PARK, Sung Woo (5/8)	KOR
8	SUPRIANTO, Joko (1)	INA

GOLD MEDAL

HOYER LARSEN, P.-E.   DEN
15-12, 15-10

SILVER MEDAL

DONG, J.   CHN

BRONZE MEDAL

SIDEK, R.   MAS
5-15, 15-11, 15-6

ARBI, H.

*Player's seed is indicated by the number in parentheses after a player's name.

*La tête de série de l'athlète est indiquée par le chiffre entre parenthèses après le nom.

Badminton / *Badminton*
Singles, Women / *Simples, Dames*

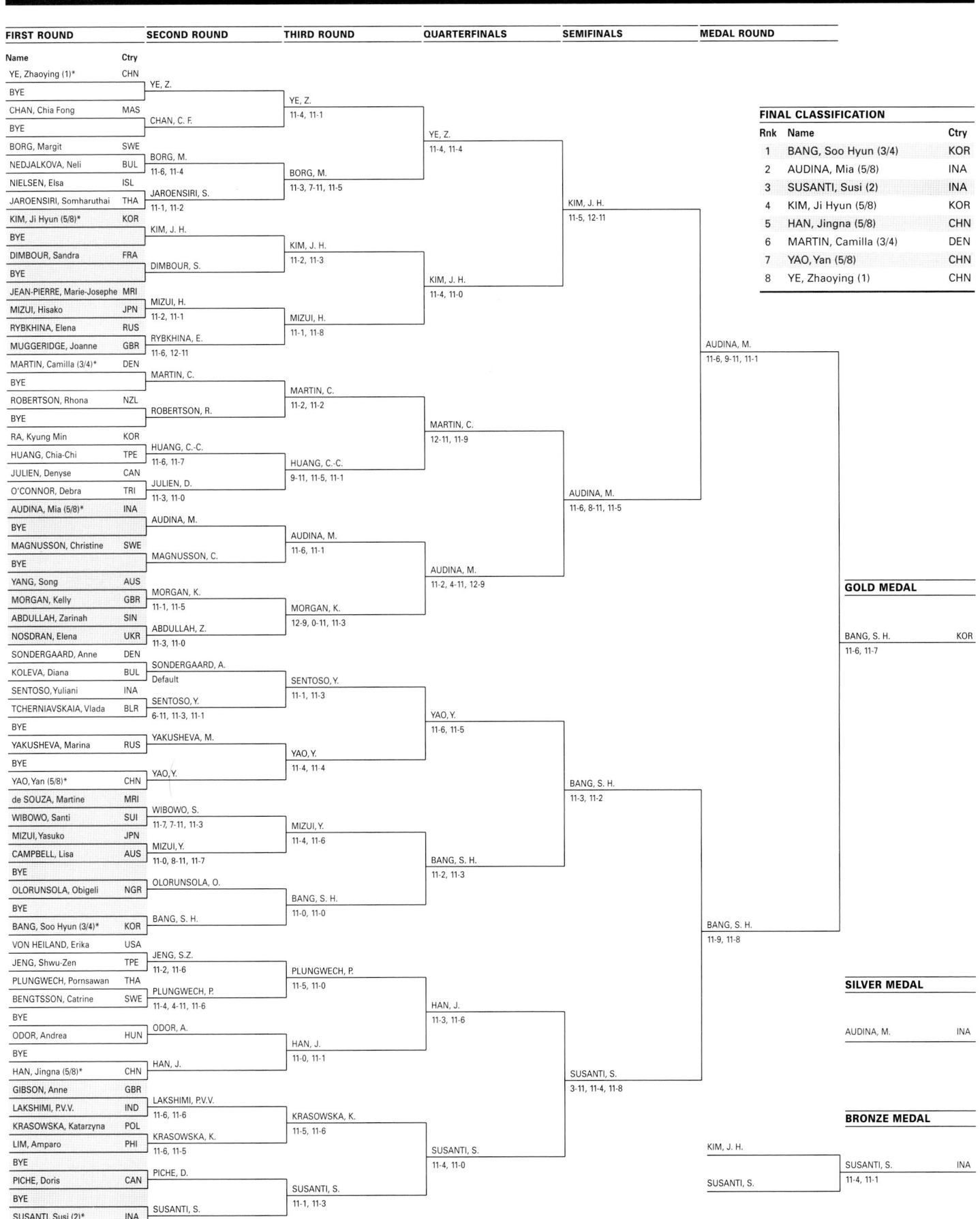

*Player's seed is indicated by the number in parentheses after a player's name.

*La tête de série de l'athlète est indiquée par le chiffre entre parenthèses après le nom.

Badminton / *Badminton*
Doubles, Men / *Doubles, Messieurs*

FIRST ROUND	SECOND ROUND	QUARTERFINALS	SEMIFINALS	MEDAL ROUND

Name	Ctry
MAINAKY, Rexy / SUBAGJA, Ricky (1)*	INA
BYE	
SOGAARD, Michael / SVARRER, Henrik	DEN
KIM, Dong Moon / YOO, Yong Sung	KOR
HUANG, Zhanzhong / JIANG, Xin (5/8)*	CHN
BYE	
BEEHARRY, Stephan / CLARISSE, Eddy	MRI
BLACKBURN, Peter / STAIGHT, Paul	AUS
GUNAWAN / SUPRIANTO, Bambang (3/4)*	INA
BYE	
KAUL, Anil / SYDIE, Iain	CAN
SOO, Beng Kiang / TAN, Kim Her	MAS
TEERAWIWATANA, Pramote / THONGSARI, Sakrapee (5/8)*	THA
BYE	
ARCHER, Simon / HUNT, Chris	GBR
CHAN, Siu Kwong / HE, Tim	HKG
PONTING, Nick / ROBERTSON, Julian	GBR
ANTROPOV, Andreij / ZUEV, Nickolaj	RUS
HELBER, Michael / KECK, Michael	GER
AXELSSON, Peter / JONSSON, Par-Gunnar (5/8)*	SWE
DAWSON, Jaimie / YUNG, Darryl	CAN
ERIKSEN, Jens / JAKOBSEN, Christian	DEN
BYE	
ARIANTHO, Antonius / KANTONO, Denny (3/4)*	INA
HA, Tae Kwon / KANG, Kyung Jin	KOR
SIRIPOOL, Siripong / SUDHISODHI, Khunakorn	THA
BYE	
HOLST-CHRISTENSEN, Jon / LUND, Thomas (5/8)*	DEN
HALL, Darren / KNOWLES, Peter	GBR
GE, Cheng / TAO, Xiaoqiang	CHN
BYE	
CHEAH, Soon Kit / YAP, Kim Hock (2)*	MAS

SECOND ROUND

MAINAKY, R. / SUBAGJA, R.

SOGAARD, M. / SVARRER, H.
15-11, 5-15, 18-15

HUANG, Z. / JIANG, X.

BLACKBURN, P. / STAIGHT, P.
15-3, 15-8

GUNAWAN / SUPRIANTO, B.

SOO, B. K. / TAN, K. H.
15-7, 15-3

TEERAWIWATANA, P. / THONGSARI, S.

ARCHER, S. / HUNT, C.
15-11, 15-12

ANTROPOV, A. / ZUEV, N.
18-13, 7-15, 15-4

HELBER, M. / KECK, M.
15-8, 15-13

ERIKSEN, J. / JAKOBSEN, C.
15-10, 17-14

ARIANTHO, A. / KANTONO, D.

HA, T. K. / KANG, K. J.
15-8, 15-5

HOLST-CHRISTENSEN, J. / LUND, T.

GE, C. / TAO, X.
15-2, 15-3

CHEAH, S. K. / YAP, K. H.

QUARTERFINALS

MAINAKY, R. / SUBAGJA, R.
15-10, 15-7

HUANG, Z. / JIANG, X.
15-7, 15-9

SOO, B. K. / TAN, K. H.
18-13, 4-15, 15-6

ARCHER, S. / HUNT, C.
18-14, 15-11

ANTROPOV, A. / ZUEV, N.
15-1, 15-7

ARIANTHO, A. / KANTONO, D.
15-8, 15-12

HA, T. K. / KANG, K. J.
15-11, 14-17, 15-11

CHEAH, S. K. / YAP, K. H.
15-8, 15-2

SEMIFINALS

MAINAKY, R. / SUBAGJA, R.
15-7, 15-7

SOO, B. K. / TAN, K. H.
15-5, 15-12

ARIANTHO, A. / KANTONO, D.
15-5, 15-1

CHEAH, S. K. / YAP, K. H.
18-17, 15-8

MEDAL ROUND

MAINAKY, R. / SUBAGJA, R.
15-3, 15-5

CHEAH, S. K. / YAP, K. H.
15-10, 15-4

GOLD MEDAL

MAINAKY, R. / SUBAGJA, R.   INA
5-15, 15-13, 15-12

SILVER MEDAL

CHEAH, S. K. / YAP, K. H.   MAS

BRONZE MEDAL

SOO, B. K. / TAN, K. H.

ARIANTHO, A. / KANTONO, D.   INA

ARIANTHO, A. / KANTONO, D.
15-4, 12-15, 15-8

*Player's seed is indicated by the number in parentheses after a player's name.

*La tête de série de l'athlète est indiquée par le chiffre entre parenthèses après le nom.

FINAL CLASSIFICATION

Rnk	Name	Ctry
1	MAINAKY, Rexy / SUBAGJA, Ricky (1)	INA
2	CHEAH, Soon Kit / YAP, Kim Hock (2)	MAS
3	ARIANTHO, Antonius / KANTONO, Denny (3/4)	INA
4	SOO, Beng Kiang / TAN, Kim Her	MAS
5	ANTROPOV, Andreij / ZUEV, Nickolaj	RUS
5	ARCHER, Simon / HUNT, Chris	GBR
5	HA, Tae Kwon / KANG, Kyung Jin	KOR
5	HUANG, Zhanzhong / JIANG, Xin (5/8)	CHN

Badminton / *Badminton*

Doubles, Women / *Doubles, Dames*

FIRST ROUND	SECOND ROUND	QUARTERFINALS	SEMIFINALS	MEDAL ROUND

Name	Ctry
GIL, Young Ah / JANG, Hye Ock (1)*	KOR
BYE	
MATSUO, Tomomi / SAKAMOTO, Masako	JPN
KOLEVA, Diana / NEDJALKOVA, Neli	BUL
BRADBURY, Julie / WRIGHT, Joanne (5/8)*	GBR
BYE	
JORGENSEN, Ann / OLSEN, Lotte	DEN
RYBKHINA, Elena / YAKUSHEVA, Marina	RUS
QIN, Yiyuan / TANG, Yongshu (3/4)*	CHN
BYE	
FINARSIH / TAMPI, Lili	INA
CATOR, Rhonda / HARDY, Amanda	AUS
STUER-LAURIDSEN, Lisbet / THOMSEN, Marlene (5/8)*	DEN
FRENCH, Linda / VON HEILAND, Erika	USA
CHUNG, Jae Hee / PARK, Soo Yun	KOR
CHEN, Li-Chin / TSAI, Huey-Min	TPE
MORGAN, Kelly / MUGGERIDGE, Joanne	GBR
COENE, Eline / van den HEUVEL, Erica	NED
EVTOUSHENKO, Victoria / NOSDRAN, Elena	UKR
CHEN, Ying / PENG, Xingyong (5/8)*	CHN
KIM, Mee-Hyang / KIM, Shin Young	KOR
MIYAMURA, Aikiko / MIYAMURA, Aiko	JPN
BYE	
KIRKEGAARD, Helene / OLSEN, Rikke (3/4)*	DEN
JENKINS, Tammy / ROBERTSON, Rhona	NZL
DENG, Sian / JULIEN, Denyse	CAN
BENGTSSON, Maria / BORG, Margit	SWE
ELIZA / ZELIN, Rosiana (5/8)*	INA
de SOUZA, Martine / JEAN-PIERRE, Marie-Josephe	MRI
SCHMIDT, Katrin / UBBEN, Kerstin	GER
BYE	
GE, Fei / GU, Jun (2)*	CHN

SECOND ROUND

GIL, Y. A. / JANG, H. O.

MATSUO, T. / SAKAMOTO, M.
15-0, 15-4

BRADBURY, J. / WRIGHT, J.

JORGENSEN, A. / OLSEN, L.
15-13, 15-10

QIN, Y. / TANG, Y.

FINARSIH / TAMPI, L.
15-9, 15-4

STUER-LAURIDSEN, L. / THOMSEN, M.
15-4, 15-1

CHUNG, J. H. / PARK, S. Y.
15-7, 15-6

COENE, E. / van den HEUVEL, E.
15-10, 15-5

CHEN, Y. / PENG, X.
15-2, 11-15, 15-1

KIM, M.-H. / KIM, S. Y.
15-12, 18-13

KIRKEGAARD, H. / OLSEN, R.

JENKINS, T. / ROBERTSON, R.
15-7, 15-4

ELIZA / ZELIN, R.
15-6, 15-13

SCHMIDT, K. / UBBEN, K.
15-1, 15-2

GE, F. / GU, J.

QUARTERFINALS

GIL, Y. A. / JANG, H. O.
15-7, 15-6

JORGENSEN, A. / OLSEN, L.
15-4, 15-5

QIN, Y. / TANG, Y.
15-1, 4-15, 15-6

STUER-LAURIDSEN, L. / THOMSEN, M.
15-8, 13-15, 15-9

CHEN, Y. / PENG, X.
15-8, 15-13

KIRKEGAARD, H. / OLSEN, R.
15-8, 15-8

ELIZA / ZELIN, R.
15-9, 15-2

GE, F. / GU, J.
15-3, 15-6

SEMIFINALS

GIL, Y. A. / JANG, H. O.
15-9, 15-9

QIN, Y. / TANG, Y.
15-8, 15-3

KIRKEGAARD, H. / OLSEN, R.
15-6, 8-15, 15-5

GE, F. / GU, J.
15-7, 15-3

MEDAL ROUND

GIL, Y. A. / JANG, H. O.
15-12, 10-15, 18-16

GE, F. / GU, J.
15-8, 15-2

GOLD MEDAL

GE, F. / GU, J.   CHN
15-5, 15-5

SILVER MEDAL

GIL, Y. A. / JANG, H. O.   KOR

BRONZE MEDAL

QIN, Y. / TANG, Y.   CHN
7-15, 15-4, 15-8

QIN, Y. / TANG, Y.

KIRKEGAARD, H. / OLSEN, R.

*Player's seed is indicated by the number in parentheses after a player's name.
*La tête de série de l'athlète est indiquée par le chiffre entre parenthèses après le nom.

FINAL CLASSIFICATION

Rnk	Name	Ctry
1	GE, Fei / GU, Jun	CHN
2	GIL, Young Ah / JANG, Hye Ock (1)	KOR
3	QIN, Yiyuan / TANG, Yongshu (3/4)	CHN
4	KIRKEGAARD, Helene / OLSEN, Rikke (3/4)	DEN
5	CHEN, Ying / PENG, Xingyong (5/8)	CHN
5	ELIZA / ZELIN, Rosiana (5/8)	INA
5	JORGENSEN, Ann / OLSEN, Lotte	DEN
5	STUER-LAURIDSEN, Lisbet / THOMSEN, Marlene (5/8)	DEN

Badminton / *Badminton*

Doubles, Mixed / *Doubles, Mixtes*

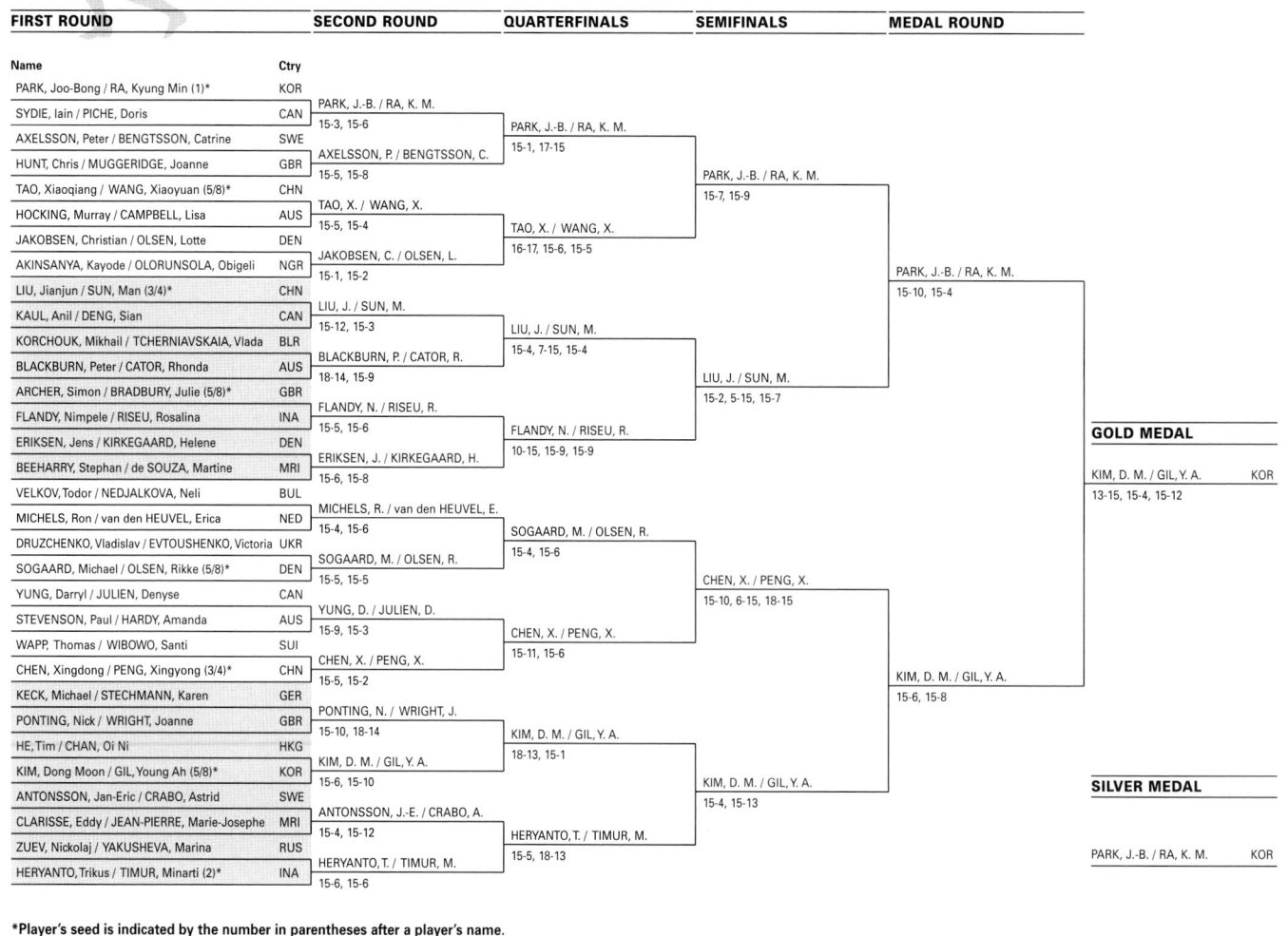

FIRST ROUND		SECOND ROUND	QUARTERFINALS	SEMIFINALS	MEDAL ROUND

Name / **Ctry**

PARK, Joo-Bong / RA, Kyung Min (1)* — KOR
SYDIE, Iain / PICHE, Doris — CAN
> PARK, J.-B. / RA, K. M.
> 15-3, 15-6

AXELSSON, Peter / BENGTSSON, Catrine — SWE
HUNT, Chris / MUGGERIDGE, Joanne — GBR
> AXELSSON, P. / BENGTSSON, C.
> 15-5, 15-8

> > PARK, J.-B. / RA, K. M.
> > 15-1, 17-15

TAO, Xiaoqiang / WANG, Xiaoyuan (5/8)* — CHN
HOCKING, Murray / CAMPBELL, Lisa — AUS
> TAO, X. / WANG, X.
> 15-5, 15-4

JAKOBSEN, Christian / OLSEN, Lotte — DEN
AKINSANYA, Kayode / OLORUNSOLA, Obigeli — NGR
> JAKOBSEN, C. / OLSEN, L.
> 15-1, 15-2

> > TAO, X. / WANG, X.
> > 16-17, 15-6, 15-5

> > > PARK, J.-B. / RA, K. M.
> > > 15-7, 15-9

LIU, Jianjun / SUN, Man (3/4)* — CHN
KAUL, Anil / DENG, Sian — CAN
> LIU, J. / SUN, M.
> 15-12, 15-3

KORCHOUK, Mikhail / TCHERNIAVSKAIA, Vlada — BLR
BLACKBURN, Peter / CATOR, Rhonda — AUS
> BLACKBURN, P. / CATOR, R.
> 18-14, 15-9

> > LIU, J. / SUN, M.
> > 15-4, 7-15, 15-4

ARCHER, Simon / BRADBURY, Julie (5/8)* — GBR
FLANDY, Nimpele / RISEU, Rosalina — INA
> FLANDY, N. / RISEU, R.
> 15-5, 15-6

ERIKSEN, Jens / KIRKEGAARD, Helene — DEN
BEEHARRY, Stephan / de SOUZA, Martine — MRI
> ERIKSEN, J. / KIRKEGAARD, H.
> 15-6, 15-8

> > FLANDY, N. / RISEU, R.
> > 10-15, 15-9, 15-9

> > > LIU, J. / SUN, M.
> > > 15-2, 5-15, 15-7

> > > > PARK, J.-B. / RA, K. M.
> > > > 15-10, 15-4

VELKOV, Todor / NEDJALKOVA, Neli — BUL
MICHELS, Ron / van den HEUVEL, Erica — NED
> MICHELS, R. / van den HEUVEL, E.
> 15-4, 15-6

DRUZCHENKO, Vladislav / EVTOUSHENKO, Victoria — UKR
SOGAARD, Michael / OLSEN, Rikke (5/8)* — DEN
> SOGAARD, M. / OLSEN, R.
> 15-5, 15-5

> > SOGAARD, M. / OLSEN, R.
> > 15-4, 15-6

YUNG, Darryl / JULIEN, Denyse — CAN
STEVENSON, Paul / HARDY, Amanda — AUS
> YUNG, D. / JULIEN, D.
> 15-9, 15-3

WAPP, Thomas / WIBOWO, Santi — SUI
CHEN, Xingdong / PENG, Xingyong (3/4)* — CHN
> CHEN, X. / PENG, X.
> 15-5, 15-2

> > CHEN, X. / PENG, X.
> > 15-11, 15-6

> > > CHEN, X. / PENG, X.
> > > 15-10, 6-15, 18-15

> > > > KIM, D. M. / GIL, Y. A.
> > > > 15-6, 15-8

KECK, Michael / STECHMANN, Karen — GER
PONTING, Nick / WRIGHT, Joanne — GBR
> PONTING, N. / WRIGHT, J.
> 15-10, 18-14

HE, Tim / CHAN, Oi Ni — HKG
KIM, Dong Moon / GIL, Young Ah (5/8)* — KOR
> KIM, D. M. / GIL, Y. A.
> 15-6, 15-10

> > KIM, D. M. / GIL, Y. A.
> > 18-13, 15-1

ANTONSSON, Jan-Eric / CRABO, Astrid — SWE
CLARISSE, Eddy / JEAN-PIERRE, Marie-Josephe — MRI
> ANTONSSON, J.-E. / CRABO, A.
> 15-4, 15-12

ZUEV, Nickolaj / YAKUSHEVA, Marina — RUS
HERYANTO, Trikus / TIMUR, Minarti (2)* — INA
> HERYANTO, T. / TIMUR, M.
> 15-6, 15-6

> > HERYANTO, T. / TIMUR, M.
> > 15-5, 18-13

> > > KIM, D. M. / GIL, Y. A.
> > > 15-4, 15-13

GOLD MEDAL

KIM, D. M. / GIL, Y. A. — KOR
13-15, 15-4, 15-12

SILVER MEDAL

PARK, J.-B. / RA, K. M. — KOR

BRONZE MEDAL

LIU, J. / SUN, M.
CHEN, X. / PENG, X.
> LIU, J. / SUN, M. — CHN
> 13-15, 17-15, 15-4

*Player's seed is indicated by the number in parentheses after a player's name.

*La tête de série de l'athlète est indiquée par le chiffre entre parenthèses après le nom.

FINAL CLASSIFICATION

Rnk	Name	Ctry
1	KIM, Dong Moon / GIL, Young Ah (5/8)	KOR
2	PARK, Joo-Bong / RA, Kyung Min (1)	KOR
3	LIU, Jianjun / SUN, Man (3/4)	CHN
4	CHEN, Xingdong / PENG, Xingyong (3/4)	CHN
5	FLANDY, Nimpele / RISEU, Rosalina	INA
5	HERYANTO, Trikus / TIMUR, Minarti (2)	INA
5	SOGAARD, Michael / OLSEN, Rikke (5/8)	DEN
5	TAO, Xiaoqiang / WANG, Xiaoyuan (5/8)	CHN

BASEBALL
BASEBALL

Abbreviations and terms used in Baseball results tables
Abréviations et termes employés dans les tableaux de résultats de baseball

Term	English	Français
1B	First Base	Première base
2B	Second Base	Seconde base
3B	Third Base	Troisième base
A	Assists	Assistances
AB	At Bat	A la batte
Against	Against	Contre
Asst. Coach	Assistant Coach	Entraîneur adjoint
BB	Bases On Balls	Bases sur balles
Batters	Batters	Frappeurs
Bronze	Bronze Medal	Médaille de bronze
C	Catcher	Receveur
CF	Center Field	Champ centre
Coach	Coach	Entraîneur
DH	Designated Hitter	Frappeur désigné
E	Errors	Erreurs
ER	Earned Runs	Points mérités
Final	Final	Finale
Final-Bronze	Final-Bronze	Finale-Bronze
Final-Gold	Final-Gold	Finale-Or
Final Team Standings	Final Team Standings	Classement final par équipes
For	For	Pour
G Behind	Games behind	Matchs en arrière
Games	Games	Matchs
Gold	Gold Medal	Médaille d'or
H	Hits	Coups sûrs
HP	Home Plate	Plaque de but
IP	Innings Pitched	Manches lancées
L	Losses	Pertes
LF	Left Field	Champ gauche
Losses	Losses	Pertes
Lost	Lost	Perdu
P	Pitcher	Lanceur
PH	Pinch Hitter	Frappeur d'urgence
PO	Put Outs	Retraits
POS	Field position	Position
PR	Pinch Runner	Coureur d'urgence
Pitcher	Pitcher	Lanceur
Played	Played	Joué
Preliminaries	Preliminaries	Eliminatoires
R	Runs	Points
RBI	Runs Batted In	Points produits
RF	Right Field	Champ droit
Rnk	Rank	Classement
Round Robin Team Standings	Round Robin Team Standings	Round robin classement par équipes
Runs	Runs	Points
S	Saves	Sauvetages
SO	Strike Outs	Elimination à la batte
SS	Short Stop	Arrêt court
Semifinals	Semifinals	Demi-finales
Silver	Silver Medal	Médaille d'argent
Team	Team	Equipe
Umpires	Umpires	Arbitres
W	Wins	Victoires
W/L/S	Wins/Losses/Saves	Victoires/Pertes/Sauvetages
W/L Avg	Win/Loss Average	Moyenne victoire/perte
Wins	Wins	Victoires
Won	Won	Gagné

International Baseball Association (IBA)
Association Internationale de Baseball
Avenue Mon-Repos 24
Case Postale 131
1000 Lausanne 5
Switzerland

Baseball / *Baseball*

Men / *Messieurs*

PRELIMINARIES — USA 4 — NCA 1

Team	1	2	3	4	5	6	7	8	9	R	H	E
USA	0	0	0	0	2	2	0	0	0	4	6	0
NCA	1	0	0	0	0	0	0	0	0	1	7	1

TEAM: USA United States of America

Coach: BERTMAN, J.　　Asst. Coach: POLK, Ronald

Batters	POS	AB	R	H	RBI	BB	SO	PO	A
WILLIAMS, Jason	SS	4	0	1	1	0	1	0	1
OJEDA, Augie	SS	0	0	0	0	0	0	0	1
KOTSAY, Mark	LF	3	0	0	0	2	0	4	0
JONES, Jacque	CF	4	0	1	1	1	1	1	0
LEE, Travis	1B	4	0	1	0	0	0	10	0
GLAUS, Troy	3B	3	1	0	0	1	1	0	1
ALLEN, Chad	RF	4	1	2	0	0	2	1	0
LeCROY, Matt	DH	3	1	1	0	1	0	0	0
HINCH, A. J.	C	2	1	0	1	0	0	10	1
MORRIS, Warren	2B	2	0	0	1	1	1	1	2
HARKRIDER, Kip	2B	0	0	0	0	0	0	0	2
BENSON, Kris	P	0	0	0	0	0	0	0	3
LOOPER, Braden	P	0	0	0	0	0	0	0	0
Totals		29	4	6	4	6	6	27	11

Pitchers	W/L/S	IP	H	R	ER	BB	SO
BENSON, Kris	W	8	7	1	1	2	7
LOOPER, Braden	S	1	0	0	0	0	2
Totals		9	7	1	1	2	9

TEAM: NCA Nicaragua

Coach: SANCHEZ REYNOSA, Julio　　Asst. Coach: TORRES, Alejandro

Batters	POS	AB	R	H	RBI	BB	SO	PO	A
MORENO, Sandy	CF	2	1	1	0	1	1	4	0
ZAMORA, Fredy	PH	1	0	0	0	0	1	0	0
	CF	0	0	0	0	0	0	0	0
AVELLAN, Jorge Luis	2B	4	0	0	0	0	1	2	1
PORRAS, Nemesio	1B	4	0	0	0	0	0	4	2
ROA, Henry	3B	4	0	1	1	0	1	2	3
BACA, Erasmo	DH	4	0	0	0	0	1	0	0
VEGA, Anibal	LF	4	0	1	0	0	1	2	0
PADILLA, Jose Ramon	RF	3	0	2	0	1	1	1	0
OSEJO, Julio Cesar	C	3	0	0	0	0	2	9	2
CARDOZE, Norman	PH	1	0	0	0	0	0	0	0
	C	0	0	0	0	0	0	0	0
DAVILA MONTIEL, Bayardo	SS	3	0	2	0	0	0	2	3
FLORES, Asdrudes	P	0	0	0	0	0	0	0	0
OBANDO VARELA, Omar	P	0	0	0	0	0	0	1	0
MAIRENA, Oswaldo	P	0	0	0	0	0	0	0	0
Totals		33	1	7	1	2	9	27	11

Pitchers	W/L/S	IP	H	R	ER	BB	SO
FLORES, Asdrudes	L	5 1/3	3	4	4	4	5
OBANDO VARELA, Omar		3	3	0	0	1	1
MAIRENA, Oswaldo		2/3	0	0	0	0	0
Totals		9	6	4	4	6	6

UMPIRES

HP	TANAKA, Yoshikazu	JPN
1B	BENITO, Hensley	AHO
2B	DIAZ BLANCO, Nelson	CUB
3B	HERNANDEZ REYES, Jose	MEX

PRELIMINARIES — CUB 19 — AUS 8

Team	1	2	3	4	5	6	7	8	9	R	H	E
CUB	2	0	3	3	0	8	0	3		19	20	2
AUS	0	4	0	4	0	0	0	0		8	12	5

TEAM: CUB Cuba

Coach: FUENTES FLEITAS, Jorge　　Asst. Coach: GONZALEZ ALMO, Luis

Batters	POS	AB	R	H	RBI	BB	SO	PO	A
ESTRADA, Jose	CF	7	0	2	0	0	0	0	0
ULACIA, Luis	LF	4	2	1	0	1	0	0	1
CALDES, Miguel	PR	1	1	0	0	0	0	0	0
	LF	0	0	0	0	0	0	0	0
LINARES, Omar	3B	5	5	3	0	1	1	1	3
KINDELAN, Orestes	DH	6	4	4	6	0	1	0	0
PACHECO, Antonio	2B	5	4	4	7	1	0	2	2
PADILLA, Juan	2B	0	0	0	0	0	0	0	0
ISAAC, Rey	RF	4	1	2	0	1	0	1	0
VARGAS, Lazaro	1B	4	0	2	0	1	0	7	1
HERNANDEZ, Alberto	C	5	1	1	3	0	1	13	0
PARET, Eduardo	SS	5	1	1	2	1	2	0	2
MONTES de OCA, Eliecer	P	0	0	0	0	0	0	0	0
ROMERO, Osmany	P	0	0	0	0	0	0	0	1
CONTRERAS, Jose Ariel	P	0	0	0	0	0	0	0	3
Totals		46	19	20	18	6	5	24	13

Pitchers	W/L/S	IP	H	R	ER	BB	SO
MONTES de OCA, Eliecer	W	1 1/3	4	3	3	3	2
ROMERO, Osmany		2	6	5	4	1	4
CONTRERAS, Jose Ariel	S	4 2/3	2	0	0	0	6
Totals		8	12	8	7	4	12

TEAM: AUS Australia

Coach: KNAPP, Donald　　Asst. Coach: DERKSEN, Robert

Batters	POS	AB	R	H	RBI	BB	SO	PO	A
HEWITT, Jason	2B	3	2	3	0	1	0	2	3
	3B	0	0	0	0	0	0	0	0
HINTON, Steven	SS	5	2	2	1	0	1	2	1
THOMPSON, Stuart	DH	4	1	1	1	1	3	0	0
SCOTT, Andrew	1B	4	0	2	2	0	1	5	1
VAGG, Richard	PH	1	0	0	0	0	0	0	0
HYNES, David	LF	3	1	3	1	1	0	1	0
SHELDON-COLLINS, Matthew	PH	1	0	0	0	0	0	0	0
MOORE, John	C	4	0	0	1	0	3	5	0
McDONALD, Grant	CF	4	1	1	2	0	1	5	0
VOGLER, Peter	RF	3	1	0	0	1	0	4	0
DOUBLEDAY, Mark	3B	3	0	0	0	0	2	0	2
TUNKIN, Scott	PH	1	0	0	0	0	1	0	0
	2B	0	0	0	0	0	0	0	0
WILLIAMS, Jeffrey	P	0	0	0	0	0	0	0	1
McNALLY, Andrew	P	0	0	0	0	0	0	0	0
NAKAMURA, Michael	P	0	0	0	0	0	0	0	0
LINDBERG, Sten	P	0	0	0	0	0	0	0	0
HOWELL, Stuart	P	0	0	0	0	0	0	0	0
TONKIN, Shane	P	0	0	0	0	0	0	0	0
Totals		36	8	12	8	4	12	24	8

Pitchers	W/L/S	IP	H	R	ER	BB	SO
WILLIAMS, Jeffrey		3 1/3	8	6	5	1	1
McNALLY, Andrew		2/3	2	2	1	1	1
NAKAMURA, Michael	L	1 1/3	2	4	4	2	2
LINDBERG, Sten		1 2/3	4	4	4	2	0
HOWELL, Stuart		2/3	4	3	3	0	1
TONKIN, Shane		1/3	0	0	0	0	0
Totals		8	20	19	16	6	5

UMPIRES

HP	LIM, Kyung-Ko	KOR
1B	ALEXANDER, Richard	USA
2B	van GRONINGEN SCHINKEL, Fred	NED
3B	BONILLA BARBERENA, Alberto Jose	NCA

PRELIMINARIES — JPN 12 — NED 2

Team	1	2	3	4	5	6	7	8	9	R	H	E
JPN	1	1	1	0	1	2	6			12	17	0
NED	0	1	0	0	0	0	1			2	6	4

TEAM: JPN Japan

Coach: KAWASHIMA, Katsuji　　Asst. Coach: OTAGAKI, Kozo

Batters	POS	AB	R	H	RBI	BB	SO	PO	A
TAKABAYASHI, Takayuki	RF	4	3	2	2	1	1	1	0
	CF	0	0	0	0	0	0	0	0
NAKAMURA, Daishin	CF	4	1	1	0	0	1	1	0
SAIGO, Yasuyuki	PH	1	1	1	2	0	0	0	0
	RF	0	0	0	0	0	0	0	0
TANI, Yoshitomo	LF	5	2	2	2	0	1	0	0
MATSUNAKA, Nobuhiko	1B	4	0	1	1	0	1	4	0
OKUBO, Hideaki	C	4	3	3	1	1	0	11	0
IGUCHI, Tadahito	SS	4	1	2	1	0	0	1	1
KUWAMOTO, Takao	2B	4	1	1	1	0	0	2	2
SATO, Tomoaki	DH	3	1	2	1	1	0	0	0
FUKUDOME, Kosuke	3B	4	1	2	0	0	0	1	0
IMAOKA, Makoto	3B	0	0	0	0	0	0	0	0
MISAWA, Koichi	P	0	0	0	0	0	0	0	2
MORI, Masahiko	P	0	0	0	0	0	0	0	1
Totals		37	12	17	11	3	4	21	6

Pitchers	W/L/S	IP	H	R	ER	BB	SO
MISAWA, Koichi	W	6	3	1	1	0	9
MORI, Masahiko		1	3	1	1	2	2
Totals		7	6	2	2	2	11

TEAM: NED Netherlands

Coach: LEURS, Jan Dick　　Asst. Coach: MAAT, Boudewijn

Batters	POS	AB	R	H	RBI	BB	SO	PO	A
CRANSTON, Jeffrey	CF	4	0	1	0	0	1	1	0
BALENTINA, Randolph	C	3	0	0	0	0	2	4	0
ten BOSCH, Giel	3B	3	0	0	0	0	3	0	1
JOOST, Marcel	RF	3	1	1	1	0	1	2	0
MARTIS, Edsel	DH	3	1	2	1	0	0	0	0
KRUYT, Marcel	LF	2	0	0	0	0	0	4	0
KEMP, Adonis	LF	0	0	0	0	1	0	0	0
de BRUIN, Eric	1B	3	0	2	0	0	0	7	0
't HOEN, Evert-Jan	SS	2	0	0	0	0	2	2	1
WARD, Ruben	PH	0	0	0	0	1	0	0	0
DIX, Eddie	2B	3	0	0	0	0	2	1	4
KOHL, Geoffry	P	0	0	0	0	0	0	0	0
NANNE, Tom	P	0	0	0	0	0	0	0	0
JANSEN, Eelco	P	0	0	0	0	0	0	0	0
WOUT, Daniel	P	0	0	0	0	0	0	0	0
Totals		26	2	6	2	2	11	21	6

Pitchers	W/L/S	IP	H	R	ER	BB	SO
KOHL, Geoffry	L	5	8	4	4	2	3
NANNE, Tom		1	2	2	1	1	1
JANSEN, Eelco		1/3	6	6	6	0	0
WOUT, Daniel		2/3	1	0	0	0	0
Totals		7	17	12	11	3	4

UMPIRES

HP	JOHNSON, Glen	CAN
1B	TANCRED, Gerard	AUS
2B	JACQUES, Leon	USA
3B	ROSARIO, Anibal	USA

Men / *Messieurs*

Team	1	2	3	4	5	6	7	8	9	R	H	E
KOR	1	0	0	0	0	0	0	0	0	1	5	1
ITA	1	0	0	1	0	0	0	0	-	2	6	1

TEAM: KOR Korea

Coach: KIM, Choong-Nam   Asst. Coach: CHO, Doo-Bok

Batters	POS	AB	R	H	RBI	BB	SO	PO	A
LEE, Byoung-Kyu	RF	4	1	1	0	0	0	1	0
CHOI, Man-Ho	CF	2	0	0	1	1	1	3	0
KANG, Hyuk	1B	4	0	1	0	0	1	4	0
KANG, Pil-Sun	3B	4	0	0	0	0	2	0	2
JIN, Kab-Yong	C	4	0	2	0	0	0	11	2
AN, Hee-Bong	DH	4	0	0	0	0	0	0	0
LEE, Dong	2B	2	0	1	0	1	0	0	0
CHO, Kyung-Hwam	LF	2	0	0	0	1	0	1	0
CHO, In-Sung	PH	1	0	0	0	0	0	0	0
CHEA, Jong-Kook	SS	3	0	0	0	0	1	4	1
BACK, Jae-Ho	PH	1	0	0	0	0	0	0	0
MUN, Dong-Hwan	P	0	0	0	0	0	0	0	0
Totals		31	1	5	1	3	5	24	5

Pitcher	W/L/S	IP	H	R	ER	BB	SO
MUN, Dong-Hwan	L	8	6	2	2	1	11
Totals		8	6	2	2	1	11

TEAM: ITA Italy

Coach: AMBROSIONI, Silvano   Asst. Coach: VARRIALE, Salvatore

Batters	POS	AB	R	H	RBI	BB	SO	PO	A
LIVERZIANI, Claudio	RF	4	0	2	0	0	2	4	0
VECCHI, Enrico	CF	3	0	0	0	0	0	7	0
CARROZZA, Luigi	C	4	1	1	0	0	2	5	0
CASOLARI, Francesco	DH	4	0	1	1	0	2	0	0
d'AURIA, Alberto	2B	3	0	0	0	0	1	1	3
UBANI, Marco	LF	3	1	1	0	0	0	2	0
ILLUMINATI, Pier Paolo	1B	3	0	1	1	0	1	7	0
BAGIALEMANI, Ruggero	3B	2	0	0	0	1	1	1	3
EVANGELISTI, Andrea	SS	3	0	0	0	0	2	0	1
CABALISTI, Roberto	P	0	0	0	0	0	0	0	2
Totals		29	2	6	2	1	11	27	9

Pitcher	W/L/S	IP	H	R	ER	BB	SO
CABALISTI, Roberto	W	9	5	1	1	3	5
Totals		9	5	1	1	3	5

UMPIRES

HP	YEAST, Davis	USA
1B	HERNANDEZ, Robert	NCA
2B	TANAKA, Yoshikazu	JPN
3B	DIAZ BLANCO, Nelson	CUB

Team	1	2	3	4	5	6	7	8	9	10	R	H	E
Japan	0	1	0	0	1	4	0	0	0	1	7	6	0
Cuba	3	3	0	0	0	0	0	0	0	2	8	12	1

TEAM: JPN Japan

Coach: KAWASHIMA, Katsuji   Asst. Coach: OTAGAKI, Kozo

Batters	POS	AB	R	H	RBI	BB	SO	PO	A
TAKABAYASHI, Takayuki	CF	4	0	0	0	0	1	4	0
SAIGO, Yasuyuki	RF	4	1	1	0	0	1	1	0
TANI, Yoshitomo	LF	4	0	0	0	0	3	3	0
IMAOKA, Makoto	PH	0	0	0	0	1	0	0	0
NAKAMURA, Daishin	PR	0	1	0	0	0	0	0	0
	LF	0	0	0	0	0	0	0	0
MATSUNAKA, Nobuhiko	1B	3	1	1	0	1	1	7	0
OKUBO, Hideaki	C	5	1	1	1	0	0	12	0
IGUCHI, Tadahito	SS	4	1	0	0	0	2	0	1
KUWAMOTO, Takao	2B	2	0	0	0	0	2	0	0
NOJIMA, Masahiro	2B	2	0	1	1	0	1	1	3
SATO, Tomoaki	DH	4	1	1	1	0	2	0	0
FUKUDOME, Kosuke	3B	4	1	1	1	0	1	0	4
ONO, Hitoshi	P	0	0	0	0	0	0	0	0
KIMURA, Jutaro	P	0	0	0	0	0	0	0	0
MORINAKA, Masao	P	0	0	0	0	0	0	0	0
MORI, Masahiko	P	0	0	0	0	0	0	1	0
Totals		36	7	6	4	2	14	28	8

Pitchers	W/L/S	IP	H	R	ER	BB	SO
ONO, Hitoshi		1 1/3	4	5	5	1	0
KIMURA, Jutaro		3 2/3	3	1	1	0	5
MORINAKA, Masao	L	4	3	2	2	1	6
MORI, Masahiko		1/3	2	0	0	0	1
Totals		9 1/3	12	8	8	2	12

TEAM: CUB Cuba

Coach: FUENTES FLEITAS, Jorge   Asst. Coach: GONZALEZ ALMO, Luis

Batters	POS	AB	R	H	RBI	BB	SO	PO	A
ESTRADA, Jose	CF	5	2	2	2	0	2	0	0
ISAAC, Rey	RF	4	1	3	2	0	1	0	0
LINARES, Omar	3B	5	2	2	1	0	2	1	2
KINDELAN, Orestes	DH	5	1	2	2	0	1	0	0
PACHECO, Antonio	2B	5	0	0	0	0	3	0	6
CALDES, Miguel	LF	5	0	1	1	0	0	1	0
VARGAS, Lazaro	1B	3	1	1	0	1	0	11	0
HERNANDEZ, Alberto	C	4	1	1	0	0	2	14	1
PARET, Eduardo	SS	2	0	0	0	1	1	3	2
LAZO, Pedro Luis	P	0	0	0	0	0	0	0	1
AJETE, Omar	P	0	0	0	0	0	0	0	1
LUIS, Omar	P	0	0	0	0	0	0	0	0
Totals		38	8	12	8	2	12	30	13

Pitchers	W/L/S	IP	H	R	ER	BB	SO
LAZO, Pedro Luis		5 1/3	5	6	4	1	9
AJETE, Omar		4 1/3	1	1	1	1	4
LUIS, Omar	W	1/3	0	0	0	0	1
Totals		10	6	7	5	2	14

UMPIRES

HP	HODGDON, Michael	USA
1B	ROSARIO, Anibal	PUR
2B	MARCHI, Roberto	ITA
3B	JOHNSON, Glen	CAN

Team	1	2	3	4	5	6	7	8	9	R	H	E
NED	8	2	0	0	0	4	0	2		16	18	1
AUS	0	2	0	0	0	4	0	0		6	7	2

TEAM: NED Netherlands

Coach: LEURS, Jan Dick   Asst. Coach: MAAT, Boudewijn

Batters	POS	AB	R	H	RBI	BB	SO	PO	A
CRANSTON, Jeffrey	CF	6	1	2	3	0	2	4	0
BALENTINA, Randolph	C	6	1	3	1	0	0	4	0
ten BOSCH, Giel	3B	6	1	1	0	0	0	1	0
JOOST, Marcel	RF	6	2	4	2	0	0	2	0
KRUYT, Marcel	DH	3	2	1	0	2	1	0	0
KEMP, Adonis	LF	4	2	1	3	1	1	1	0
de BRUIN, Eric	1B	3	3	2	0	2	0	8	1
't HOEN, Evert-Jan	SS	5	2	3	3	0	0	1	3
DIX, Eddie	2B	4	2	1	2	1	1	2	2
CORDEMANS, Rob	P	0	0	0	0	0	0	1	0
NANNE, Tom	P	0	0	0	0	0	0	0	0
NANNE, Paul	P	0	0	0	0	0	0	0	1
Totals		43	16	18	14	6	5	24	7

Pitchers	W/L/S	IP	H	R	ER	BB	SO
CORDEMANS, Rob	W	5 1/3	6	5	5	5	4
NANNE, Tom		0	1	1	1	2	0
NANNE, Paul		2 2/3	0	0	0	1	0
Totals		8	7	6	6	8	4

TEAM: AUS Australia

Coach: KNAPP, Donald   Asst. Coach: DERKSEN, Robert

Batters	POS	AB	R	H	RBI	BB	SO	PO	A
HEWITT, Jason	3B	5	1	1	1	0	1	0	1
HINTON, Steven	SS	3	0	0	0	2	0	1	4
THOMPSON, Stuart	DH	3	0	1	1	2	1	0	0
SCOTT, Andrew	1B	4	0	1	1	0	0	8	0
HYNES, David	LF	4	1	1	1	0	0	2	0
	RF	0	0	0	0	0	0	0	0
McDONALD, Grant	CF	3	1	0	0	1	1	2	0
TUNKIN, Scott	2B	2	1	1	1	2	0	2	0
MOORE, John	C	3	1	1	0	1	1	4	0
	LF	0	0	0	0	0	0	1	0
VOGLER, Peter	RF	2	0	0	0	0	3	0	0
SHELDON-COLLINS, Matthew	PH	2	1	1	1	0	0	0	0
	C	0	0	0	0	0	1	0	0
SHELDON-COLLINS, Simon	P	0	0	0	0	0	0	0	0
NAKAMURA, Michael	P	0	0	0	0	0	0	0	0
LINDBERG, Sten	P	0	0	0	0	0	0	0	0
McNALLY, Andrew	P	0	0	0	0	0	0	0	0
HOWELL, Stuart	P	0	0	0	0	0	0	0	1
Totals		31	6	7	6	8	4	24	6

Pitchers	W/L/S	IP	H	R	ER	BB	SO
SHELDON-COLLINS, Simon	L	1/3	4	5	5	1	0
NAKAMURA, Michael		1/3	3	3	3	1	0
LINDBERG, Sten		5	6	5	3	3	4
McNALLY, Andrew		1 1/3	4	3	2	1	1
HOWELL, Stuart		1	1	0	0	0	0
Totals		8	18	16	13	6	5

UMPIRES

HP	BENITO, Hensley	AHO
1B	JACQUES, Leon	USA
2B	YEAST, Davis	USA
3B	LIM, Kyung-Ko	KOR

Men / *Messieurs*

PRELIMINARIES ITA 2 NCA 7

Team	1	2	3	4	5	6	7	8	9	R	H	E
ITA	1	0	1	0	0	0	0	0	0	2	10	1
NCA	3	0	4	0	0	0	0	0	-	7	5	2

TEAM: ITA Italy

Coach: AMBROSIONI, Silvano   Asst. Coach: VARRIALE, Salvatore

Batters	POS	AB	R	H	RBI	BB	SO	PO	A
LIVERZIANI, Claudio	RF	5	2	2	1	0	1	3	0
VECCHI, Enrico	CF	3	0	0	0	2	1	2	0
CARROZZA, Luigi	C	4	0	2	0	0	2	3	0
CASOLARI, Francesco	DH	4	0	1	0	0	2	0	0
d'AURIA, Alberto	2B	4	0	0	0	0	1	3	2
UBANI, Marco	LF	4	0	3	0	0	0	1	0
ILLUMINATI, PierPaolo	1B	2	0	0	0	0	1	7	1
CECCAROLI, Paolo	PH	1	0	0	0	1	1	0	0
	1B	0	0	0	0	0	0	4	0
BAGIALEMANI, Ruggero	3B	2	0	0	0	0	2	0	4
RIGOLI, David	PH	1	0	1	0	1	0	0	0
	3B	0	0	0	0	0	0	0	2
EVANGELISTI, Andrea	SS	4	0	1	0	0	1	0	0
FOCHI, Massimo	P	0	0	0	0	0	0	0	1
CRETIS, Rolando	P	0	0	0	0	0	0	1	0
MASIN, Massimiliano	P	0	0	0	0	0	0	0	0
Totals		34	2	10	1	4	12	24	10

Pitchers	W/L/S	IP	H	R	ER	BB	SO
FOCHI, Massimo	L	3	4	7	7	3	1
CRETIS, Rolando		4	1	0	0	1	1
MASIN, Massimiliano		1	0	0	0	0	1
Totals		8	5	7	7	4	3

TEAM: NCA Nicaragua

Coach: SANCHEZ REYNOSA, Julio   Asst. Coach: TORRES, Alejandro

Batters	POS	AB	R	H	RBI	BB	SO	PO	A
MORENO, Sandy	CF	4	0	0	0	0	0	3	0
AVELLAN, Jorge Luis	SS	3	1	0	0	1	0	4	2
PORRAS, Nemesio	1B	2	1	1	0	2	0	5	0
ROA, Henry	3B	4	2	1	1	0	0	0	0
BACA, Erasmo	DH	3	2	2	2	1	0	0	0
VEGA, Anibal	LF	3	1	1	3	0	0	1	0
ZAMORA, Fredy	PH	1	0	0	0	0	1	0	0
	LF	0	0	0	0	0	0	0	0
PADILLA, Jose Ramon	RF	4	0	0	0	0	1	0	0
CARDOZE, Norman	2B	3	0	0	0	0	1	2	2
OSEJO, Julio Cesar	C	3	0	0	0	0	0	12	3
COREA, Fredy	P	0	0	0	0	0	0	0	1
MIRANDA, Luis Daniel	P	0	0	0	0	0	0	0	0
Totals		30	7	5	6	4	3	27	8

Pitchers	W/L/S	IP	H	R	ER	BB	SO
COREA, Fredy	W	8	9	2	1	3	12
MIRANDA, Luis Daniel		1	1	0	0	1	0
Totals		9	10	2	1	4	12

UMPIRES

HP	ALEXANDER, Richard	USA
1B	HODGDON, Michael	USA
2B	TANCRED, Gerard	AUS
3B	TANAKA, Yoshikazu	JPN

PRELIMINARIES KOR 2 USA 7

Team	1	2	3	4	5	6	7	8	9	R	H	E
Korea	0	0	0	1	0	1	0	0	0	2	8	4
USA	1	0	0	3	1	0	1	1	-	7	10	3

TEAM: KOR Korea

Coach: KIM, Choong-Nam   Asst. Coach: CHO, Doo-Bok

Batters	POS	AB	R	H	RBI	BB	SO	PO	A
LEE, Byoung-Kyu	LF	4	0	0	0	1	0	2	0
LEE, Dong	3B	4	0	1	0	0	1	0	2
KANG, Hyuk	RF	4	2	2	1	0	1	1	0
AN, Hee-Bong	DH	3	0	0	0	1	1	0	0
JIN, Kab-Yong	1B	3	0	2	0	1	0	8	0
CHO, In-Sung	C	3	0	1	1	0	0	9	1
BACK, Jae-Ho	2B	3	0	0	0	0	0	2	6
KANG, Pil-Sun	PH	1	0	0	0	0	0	0	0
CHEA, Jong-Kook	SS	3	0	1	0	0	0	1	1
CHO, Kyung-Hwam	PH	1	0	1	0	0	0	0	0
CHOI, Man-Ho	CF	2	0	0	0	1	0	1	0
SON, Min-Han	P	0	0	0	0	0	0	0	1
CHO, Jin-Ho	P	0	0	0	0	0	0	0	0
Totals		31	2	8	2	4	3	24	11

Pitchers	W/L/S	IP	H	R	ER	BB	SO
SON, Min-Han	L	7	8	6	4	2	6
CHO, Jin-Ho		1	2	1	1	0	2
Totals		8	10	7	5	2	8

TEAM: USA United States of America

Coach: BERTMAN, J.   Asst. Coach: POLK, Ronald

Batters	POS	AB	R	H	RBI	BB	SO	PO	A
WILLIAMS, Jason	SS	4	1	2	0	0	0	1	3
OJEDA, Augie	PR	1	1	0	0	0	1	0	0
	SS	0	0	0	0	0	0	0	1
KOTSAY, Mark	LF	4	0	1	0	0	0	0	1
JONES, Jacque	CF	3	0	0	0	0	1	4	0
LEE, Travis	1B	4	1	1	2	0	1	12	1
GLAUS, Troy	3B	4	0	0	0	0	2	3	6
ALLEN, Chad	RF	4	1	1	1	0	1	0	1
LeCROY, Matt	DH	2	1	1	0	1	0	0	0
GREEN, Chad	PR	1	0	0	0	0	1	0	0
	DH	0	0	0	0	0	0	0	0
HINCH, A. J.	C	4	1	2	0	0	1	4	2
MORRIS, Warren	2B	2	1	1	3	1	0	3	1
HARKRIDER, Kip	2B	1	0	1	0	0	0	0	3
GREISINGER, Seth	P	0	0	0	0	0	0	0	1
WEAVER, Jeff	P	0	0	0	0	0	0	0	0
Totals		34	7	10	6	2	8	27	20

Pitchers	W/L/S	IP	H	R	ER	BB	SO
GREISINGER, Seth	W	6	7	2	2	3	2
WEAVER, Jeff	S	3	1	0	0	1	1
Totals		9	8	2	2	4	3

UMPIRES

HP	HERNANDEZ REYES, Jose	MEX
1B	BONILLA BARBERENA, Alberto Jose	NCA
2B	van GRONINGEN SCHINKEL, Fred	NED
3B	MARCHI, Roberto	ITA

PRELIMINARIES NED 2 CUB 18

Team	1	2	3	4	5	6	7	8	9	R	H	E
NED	0	1	0	0	0	1	0			2	4	0
CUB	2	0	2	1	6	7	-			18	17	0

TEAM: NED Netherlands

Coach: LEURS, Jan Dick   Asst. Coach: MAAT, Boudewijn

Batters	POS	AB	R	H	RBI	BB	SO	PO	A
CRANSTON, Jeffrey	CF	3	0	0	0	0	2	2	0
BALENTINA, Randolph	C	2	0	0	0	0	1	3	1
FLUONIA, Marlon	PH	0	0	0	0	0	0	0	0
	C	0	0	0	0	0	0	3	0
de BRUIN, Eric	1B	2	0	0	0	0	0	7	0
NANNE, Paul	PH	1	0	0	0	0	0	0	0
	1B	0	0	0	0	0	0	0	0
JOOST, Marcel	RF	3	1	1	1	0	0	1	0
MARTIS, Edsel	DH	2	0	1	0	1	1	0	0
KEMP, Adonis	LF	3	0	0	0	0	1	0	0
't HOEN, Evert-Jan	SS	3	0	1	0	0	2	0	3
WARD, Ruben	3B	2	1	1	1	1	0	0	1
DIX, Eddie	2B	1	0	0	0	0	1	2	2
ten BOSCH, Giel	PH	1	0	0	0	1	1	0	0
	2B	0	0	0	0	0	0	0	0
CALLENBACH, Peter	P	0	0	0	0	0	0	0	0
van MARIS, Andreas	P	0	0	0	0	0	0	0	0
WOUT, Daniel	P	0	0	0	0	0	0	0	0
Totals		23	2	4	2	3	9	18	7

Pitchers	W/L/S	IP	H	R	ER	BB	SO
CALLENBACH, Peter	L	41/3	11	11	11	3	3
van MARIS, Andreas		1	4	5	5	2	1
WOUT, Daniel		2/3	2	2	2	1	2
Totals		6	17	18	18	6	6

TEAM: CUB Cuba

Coach: FUENTES FLEITAS, Jorge   Asst. Coach: GONZALEZ ALMO, Luis

Batters	POS	AB	R	H	RBI	BB	SO	PO	A
ESTRADA, Jose	CF	5	2	2	3	0	0	1	0
ISAAC, Rey	RF	5	1	3	2	0	0	1	1
LINARES, Omar	3B	3	3	2	2	1	1	0	1
SCULL, Antonio	PH	1	0	0	0	0	1	0	0
	1B	0	0	0	0	0	0	1	0
KINDELAN, Orestes	DH	4	3	2	2	1	2	0	0
PACHECO, Antonio	2B	4	1	1	0	0	1	1	5
PADILLA, Juan	2B	0	0	0	0	0	0	0	0
CALDES, Miguel	LF	3	2	1	1	1	0	0	0
VARGAS, Lazaro	1B	2	2	1	2	2	0	7	0
	3B	0	0	0	0	0	0	0	1
MANRIQUE, Juan	C	4	3	3	4	0	1	9	0
PARET, Eduardo	SS	3	1	2	2	1	0	1	1
LUIS, Omar	P	0	0	0	0	0	0	0	0
MONTES de OCA, Eliecer	P	0	0	0	0	0	0	0	0
Totals		34	18	17	18	6	6	21	9

Pitchers	W/L/S	IP	H	R	ER	BB	SO
LUIS, Omar	W	6	3	2	2	1	8
MONTES de OCA, Eliecer		1	1	0	0	2	1
Totals		7	4	2	2	3	9

UMPIRES

HP	MARCHI, Roberto	ITA
1B	LIM, Kyung-Ko	KOR
2B	HERNANDEZ, Robert	NCA
3B	ALEXANDER, Richard	USA

Men / *Messieurs*

Team	1	2	3	4	5	6	7	8	9	R	H	E
NCA	0	1	1	5	1	0	0	0	0	8	14	4
KOR	0	0	1	0	0	0	1	1	0	3	8	1

TEAM: NCA Nicaragua
Coach: SANCHEZ REYNOSA, Julio   Asst. Coach: TORRES, Alejandro

Batters	POS	AB	R	H	RBI	BB	SO	PO	A
BERRIOS, Carlos Alberto	RF	5	1	1	3	0	2	1	0
CARDOZE, Norman	2B	4	1	1	0	1	1	2	3
PORRAS, Nemesio	1B	4	0	1	1	1	0	5	0
ROA, Henry	3B	5	1	3	0	0	0	0	0
BACA, Erasmo	DH	5	0	3	0	0	1	0	0
VEGA, Anibal	LF	2	2	2	0	2	0	0	0
MORENO, Sandy	PR	0	0	0	0	1	0	0	0
	CF	0	0	0	0	0	0	2	0
ZAMORA, Fredy	CF	3	1	0	1	1	1	1	0
	LF	0	0	0	0	0	0	1	0
DAVILA MONTIEL, Bayardo	SS	5	1	2	2	0	0	4	4
OSEJO, Julio Cesar	C	4	1	1	1	0	0	10	2
QUIROZ, Jose Luis	P	0	0	0	0	0	0	1	2
OBANDO VARELA, Omar	P	0	0	0	0	0	0	0	0
Totals		37	8	14	8	6	5	27	11

Pitchers	W/L/S	IP	H	R	ER	BB	SO
QUIROZ, Jose Luis	W	6 1/3	7	2	1	4	7
OBANDO VARELA, Omar		2 2/3	1	1	1	1	3
Totals		9	8	3	2	5	10

TEAM: KOR Korea
Coach: KIM, Choong-Nam   Asst. Coach: CHO, Doo-Bok

Batters	POS	AB	R	H	RBI	BB	SO	PO	A
LEE, Byoung-Kyu	LF	5	2	4	1	0	0	1	0
	RF	0	0	0	0	0	0	2	0
LEE, Dong	3B	3	0	0	0	1	0	3	2
	2B	0	0	0	0	0	0	0	1
KANG, Hyuk	1B	5	0	2	2	0	1	7	3
JIN, Kab-Yong	RF	2	0	0	0	0	0	2	0
CHO, Kyung-Hwam	LF	2	0	0	0	0	2	1	0
CHO, In-Sung	C	4	0	0	0	1	2	5	2
AN, Hee-Bong	DH	4	0	1	0	0	1	0	0
BACK, Jae-Ho	2B	1	0	0	0	2	0	1	3
KANG, Pil-Sun	PH	1	0	0	0	0	0	0	0
	3B	0	0	0	0	0	0	0	0
CHEA, Jong-Kook	SS	3	1	1	0	0	2	2	3
CHOI, Man-Ho	CF	3	0	0	0	1	2	1	0
KIM, Sun-Woo	P	0	0	0	0	0	0	0	1
MUN, Dong-Hwan	P	0	0	0	0	0	0	1	0
OH, Chul-Min	P	0	0	0	0	0	0	1	1
Totals		33	3	8	3	5	10	27	16

Pitchers	W/L/S	IP	H	R	ER	BB	SO
KIM, Sun-Woo	L	3	4	4	4	3	2
MUN, Dong-Hwan		2	6	4	4	0	0
OH, Chul-Min		4	4	0	0	3	3
Totals		9	14	8	8	6	5

UMPIRES

HP	JACQUES, Leon	USA
1B	DIAZ BLANCO, Nelson	CUB
2B	ROSARIO, Anibal	PUR
3B	BENITO, Hensley	AHO

Team	1	2	3	4	5	6	7	8	9	R	H	E
AUS	0	1	0	0	1	7	0	0	0	9	14	0
JPN	2	0	0	0	0	1	0	0	3	6	11	3

TEAM: AUS Australia
Coach: KNAPP, Donald   Asst. Coach: DERKSEN, Robert

Batters	POS	AB	R	H	RBI	BB	SO	PO	A
HEWITT, Jason	3B	5	1	2	1	0	1	0	2
	2B	0	0	0	0	0	0	4	2
HINTON, Steven	SS	5	0	1	1	0	2	1	4
THOMPSON, Stuart	DH	5	1	1	3	0	1	0	0
SCOTT, Andrew	1B	4	2	2	0	1	2	9	1
HYNES, David	LF	5	1	1	1	0	0	1	0
MOORE, John	LF	0	0	0	0	0	0	1	0
TUNKIN, Scott	2B	3	1	3	1	0	0	0	3
DOUBLEDAY, Mark	3B	1	0	0	0	0	0	1	0
McDONALD, Grant	CF	4	0	1	1	0	1	4	0
DAWES, Scott	C	4	1	1	0	0	2	5	0
VOGLER, Peter	RF	4	2	2	0	0	0	0	0
TONKIN, Shane	P	0	0	0	0	0	0	1	0
WILLIAMS, Jeffrey	P	0	0	0	0	0	0	0	0
McNALLY, Andrew	P	0	0	0	0	0	0	0	0
Totals		40	9	14	8	1	9	27	12

Pitchers	W/L/S	IP	H	R	ER	BB	SO
TONKIN, Shane		4 2/3	5	2	2	2	2
WILLIAMS, Jeffrey	W	4	6	4	4	2	3
McNALLY, Andrew	S	1/3	0	0	0	0	0
Totals		9	11	6	6	4	5

TEAM: JPN Japan
Coach: KAWASHIMA, Katsuji   Asst. Coach: OTAGAKI, Kozo

Batters	POS	AB	R	H	RBI	BB	SO	PO	A
TAKABAYASHI, Takayuki	CF	5	1	2	1	0	1	2	0
SAIGO, Yasuyuki	RF	3	1	2	0	2	1	0	0
TANI, Yoshitomo	LF	4	1	2	0	1	0	1	1
MATSUNAKA, Nobuhiko	1B	4	0	0	1	0	1	10	2
IMAOKA, Makoto	PH	1	1	0	0	0	0	0	0
OKUBO, Hideaki	C	5	1	3	3	0	0	10	0
IGUCHI, Tadahito	SS	4	1	2	1	1	0	1	4
KUWAMOTO, Takao	2B	3	0	0	0	0	0	1	2
NOJIMA, Masahiro	2B	1	0	0	0	0	0	1	1
NAKAMURA, Daishin	PH	1	0	0	0	0	0	0	0
SATO, Tomoaki	DH	3	0	0	0	0	1	0	0
FUKUDOME, Kosuke	3B	4	0	0	0	0	1	0	4
KAWAMURA, Takeo	P	0	0	0	0	0	0	0	0
MORINAKA, Masao	P	0	0	0	0	0	0	0	0
MORI, Masahiko	P	0	0	0	0	0	0	0	0
KIMURA, Jutaro	P	0	0	0	0	0	0	1	0
Totals		38	6	11	6	4	5	27	14

Pitchers	W/L/S	IP	H	R	ER	BB	SO
KAWAMURA, Takeo	L	5	9	5	4	1	4
MORINAKA, Masao		2/3	4	4	0	0	2
MORI, Masahiko		2 1/3	1	0	0	0	1
KIMURA, Jutaro		1	0	0	0	0	2
Totals		9	14	9	4	1	9

UMPIRES

HP	van GRONINGEN SCHINKEL, Fred	NED
1B	HERNANDEZ REYES, Jose	MEX
2B	JOHNSON, Glen	CAN
3B	YEAST, Davis	USA

Team	1	2	3	4	5	6	7	8	9	R	H	E
USA	6	0	5	2	0	2	0			15	11	0
Italy	3	0	0	0	0	0	0			3	6	2

TEAM: USA United States of America
Coach: BERTMAN, J.   Asst. Coach: POLK, Ronald

Batters	POS	AB	R	H	RBI	BB	SO	PO	A
WILLIAMS, Jason	SS	4	3	2	1	0	2	0	1
	3B	0	0	0	0	0	0	0	1
KOTSAY, Mark	LF	4	3	3	4	1	0	1	0
	RF	0	0	0	0	0	0	0	0
JONES, Jacque	CF	4	1	2	2	1	1	2	0
LEE, Travis	1B	3	1	0	0	2	1	7	1
GLAUS, Troy	3B	3	1	0	0	2	1	1	2
OJEDA, Augie	SS	0	0	0	0	0	0	0	1
ALLEN, Chad	RF	2	1	1	0	2	0	2	0
GREEN, Chad	PH	1	0	0	0	0	1	0	0
	LF	0	0	0	0	0	0	0	0
LeCROY, Matt	DH	5	1	1	2	0	2	0	0
LOYD, Brian	C	5	2	1	2	0	2	5	0
MORRIS, Warren	2B	2	2	1	0	2	1	1	2
HARKRIDER, Kip	2B	1	0	0	0	0	0	1	1
DICKEY, R. A.	P	0	0	0	0	0	0	0	0
KOCH, Billy	P	0	0	0	0	0	0	1	0
Totals		34	15	11	11	10	11	21	9

Pitchers	W/L/S	IP	H	R	ER	BB	SO
DICKEY, R. A.	W	5	6	3	3	2	3
KOCH, Billy		2	0	0	0	1	2
Totals		7	6	3	3	3	5

TEAM: ITA Italy
Coach: AMBROSIONI, Silvano   Asst. Coach: VARRIALE, Salvatore

Batters	POS	AB	R	H	RBI	BB	SO	PO	A
RIGOLI, David	3B	4	1	2	0	0	0	0	4
LIVERZIANI, Claudio	RF	4	1	1	1	0	2	1	0
CARROZZA, Luigi	C	2	1	2	1	0	0	4	0
BARBONI, Marco	C	1	0	0	0	0	1	5	0
CASOLARI, Francesco	DH	3	0	1	1	0	0	0	0
UBANI, Marco	LF	0	0	0	0	3	0	1	0
ILLUMINATI, Pier Paolo	1B	3	0	0	0	0	1	7	0
d'AURIA, Alberto	2B	3	0	0	0	0	0	0	2
de FRANCESCHI, Roberto	CF	3	0	0	0	0	1	3	0
EVANGELISTI, Andrea	SS	2	0	0	0	0	0	1	3
BAGIALEMANI, Ruggero	PH	1	0	0	0	0	0	0	0
PASSERINI, Paolo	P	0	0	0	0	0	0	0	0
CARBINI, Dante	P	0	0	0	0	0	0	0	0
BETTO, Fabio	P	0	0	0	0	0	0	0	0
MASIN, Massimiliano	P	0	0	0	0	0	0	0	0
FOCHI, Massimo	P	0	0	0	0	0	0	0	0
CECCAROLI, Paolo	P	0	0	0	0	0	0	0	0
Totals		26	3	6	3	3	5	21	6

Pitchers	W/L/S	IP	H	R	ER	BB	SO
PASSERINI, Paolo	L	2/3	3	5	5	2	1
CARBINI, Dante		1 2/3	3	5	3	4	2
BETTO, Fabio		1	2	3	2	3	2
MASIN, Massimiliano		1 2/3	1	0	0	0	3
FOCHI, Massimo		1	2	2	2	1	2
CECCAROLI, Paolo		1	0	0	0	0	1
Totals		7	11	15	12	10	11

UMPIRES

HP	LIM, Kyung-Ko	KOR
1B	TANAKA, Yoshikazu	JPN
2B	BONILLA BARBERENA, Alberto Jose	NCA
3B	TANCRED, Gerard	AUS

Men / *Messieurs*

PRELIMINARIES — CUB 14 KOR 11

Team	1	2	3	4	5	6	7	8	9	R	H	E
CUB	0	1	1	4	0	3	2	3	0	14	20	0
KOR	0	0	0	2	0	3	1	0	5	11	17	2

TEAM: CUB Cuba
Coach: FUENTES FLEITAS, Jorge   Asst. Coach: GONZALEZ ALMO, Luis

Batters	POS	AB	R	H	RBI	BB	SO	PO	A
ESTRADA, Jose	CF	6	1	1	3	0	1	2	0
ISAAC, Rey	RF	1	1	1	0	1	0	0	0
SCULL, Antonio	1B	3	1	1	0	0	0	7	1
LINARES, Omar	3B	5	1	2	1	1	2	0	1
	RF	0	0	0	0	0	0	1	0
KINDELAN, Orestes	DH	6	1	2	1	0	1	0	0
PACHECO, Antonio	2B	5	1	3	1	0	1	0	5
PADILLA, Juan	PR	1	1	1	0	0	0	0	0
	2B	0	0	0	0	0	0	0	0
CALDES, Miguel	LF	5	1	1	1	1	1	2	0
VARGAS, Lazaro	1B	5	2	4	2	0	0	4	0
	3B	0	0	0	0	0	0	0	1
MANRIQUE, Juan	C	4	2	2	4	0	1	8	0
PARET, Eduardo	SS	5	2	2	1	0	1	2	4
ROMERO, Osmany	P	0	0	0	0	0	0	0	0
CONTRERAS, Jose Ariel	P	0	0	0	0	0	0	1	0
MONTES de OCA, Eliecer	P	0	0	0	0	0	0	0	0
FUMERO, Jorge	P	0	0	0	0	0	0	0	0
Totals		46	14	20	14	3	8	27	12

Pitchers	W/L/S	IP	H	R	ER	BB	SO
ROMERO, Osmany	W	5	6	5	5	1	3
CONTRERAS, Jose Ariel		3 2/3	9	6	6	1	4
MONTES de OCA, Eliecer		0	2	0	0	0	0
FUMERO, Jorge	S	1/3	0	0	0	0	1
Totals		9	17	11	11	2	8

TEAM: KOR Korea
Coach: KIM, Choong-Nam   Asst. Coach: CHO, Doo-Bok

Batters	POS	AB	R	H	RBI	BB	SO	PO	A
LEE, Byoung-Kyu	LF	6	1	2	2	0	0	1	0
LEE, Dong	SS	3	2	3	0	0	0	2	1
CHEA, Jong-Kook	SS	0	0	0	0	0	0	0	0
CHO, Kyung-Hwam	PH	2	1	1	0	0	1	0	0
KANG, Hyuk	RF	4	3	3	2	1	0	3	0
JIN, Kab-Yong	1B	5	0	0	0	0	3	5	0
AN, Hee-Bong	DH	3	1	2	3	1	0	0	0
CHO, In-Sung	C	4	1	1	1	0	0	8	1
KANG, Pil-Sun	3B	5	0	1	1	0	3	0	3
BACK, Jae-Ho	2B	2	0	0	0	0	0	3	2
KIM, Soo-Kwan	PH	3	1	1	1	0	0	0	0
	2B	0	0	0	0	0	0	1	0
CHOI, Man-Ho	CF	5	1	3	1	0	1	4	0
JEON, Seung-Nam	P	0	0	0	0	0	0	0	0
KIM, Sun-Woo	P	0	0	0	0	0	0	0	0
OH, Chul-Min	P	0	0	0	0	0	0	0	1
LIM, Sun-Dong	P	0	0	0	0	0	0	0	0
KIM, Young-Soo	P	0	0	0	0	0	0	0	1
Totals		42	11	17	11	2	8	27	9

Pitchers	W/L/S	IP	H	R	ER	BB	SO
JEON, Seung-Nam	L	2 2/3	4	2	2	1	2
KIM, Sun-Woo		2/3	4	4	4	0	2
OH, Chul-Min		2	5	3	3	1	2
LIM, Sun-Dong		1 2/3	5	5	4	1	2
KIM, Young-Soo		2	2	0	0	0	2
Totals		9	20	14	13	3	8

UMPIRES
HP	BENITO, Hensley	AHO
1B	JOHNSON, Glen	CAN
2B	HERNANDEZ REYES, Jose	MEX
3B	HODGDON, Michael	USA

PRELIMINARIES — NCA 5 NED 0

Team	1	2	3	4	5	6	7	8	9	R	H	E
NCA	1	0	4	0	0	0				5	10	0
NED	0	0	0	0	0	0				0	5	1

TEAM: NCA Nicaragua
Coach: SANCHEZ REYNOSA, Julio   Asst. Coach: TORRES, Alejandro

Batters	POS	AB	R	H	RBI	BB	SO	PO	A
MORENO, Sandy	CF	3	2	2	1	0	0	2	0
AVELLAN, Jorge Luis	2B	3	1	2	1	0	0	1	1
PORRAS, Nemesio	1B	2	1	2	0	1	0	7	0
ROA, Henry	3B	3	0	0	1	0	0	0	1
BACA, Erasmo	DH	3	0	0	0	0	0	0	0
VEGA, Anibal	LF	2	0	1	1	0	1	0	0
ZAMORA, Fredy	LF	1	0	0	0	0	0	0	0
PADILLA, Jose Ramon	RF	2	0	0	1	1	1	0	0
DAVILA MONTIEL, Bayardo	SS	3	0	2	0	0	0	1	3
OSEJO, Julio Cesar	C	3	1	1	0	0	0	7	3
FLORES, Asdrudes	P	0	0	0	0	0	0	0	1
Totals		25	5	10	4	2	2	18	9

Pitcher	W/L/S	IP	H	R	ER	BB	SO
FLORES, Asdrudes	W	6	5	0	0	1	8
Totals		6	5	0	0	1	8

TEAM: NED Netherlands
Coach: LEURS, Jan Dick   Asst. Coach: MAAT, Boudewijn

Batters	POS	AB	R	H	RBI	BB	SO	PO	A
CRANSTON, Jeffrey	CF	3	0	1	0	0	1	2	0
BALENTINA, Randolph	C	3	0	1	0	0	1	4	0
ten BOSCH, Giel	3B	3	0	2	0	0	0	0	1
JOOST, Marcel	RF	3	0	1	0	0	2	1	0
KRUYT, Marcel	DH	1	0	0	0	1	1	0	0
KEMP, Adonis	LF	2	0	0	0	0	1	2	0
de BRUIN, Eric	1B	2	0	0	0	0	1	6	0
't HOEN, Evert-Jan	SS	2	0	0	0	0	0	2	4
DIX, Eddie	2B	2	0	0	0	0	1	1	3
KOHL, Geoffry	P	0	0	0	0	0	0	0	0
WOUT, Daniel	P	0	0	0	0	0	0	0	0
Totals		21	0	5	0	1	8	18	8

Pitchers	W/L/S	IP	H	R	ER	BB	SO
KOHL, Geoffry	L	2 2/3	8	5	3	1	2
WOUT, Daniel		3 1/3	2	0	0	1	0
Totals		6	10	5	3	2	2

UMPIRES
HP	TANCRED, Gerard	AUS
1B	MARCHI, Roberto	ITA
2B	HODGDON, Michael	USA
3B	JACQUES, Leon	USA

PRELIMINARIES — ITA 12 AUS 8

Team	1	2	3	4	5	6	7	8	9	R	H	E
ITA	3	2	2	2	2	0	0	1	0	12	15	3
AUS	0	2	1	2	1	0	0	2	0	8	12	3

TEAM: ITA Italy
Coach: AMBROSIONI, Silvano   Asst. Coach: VARRIALE, Salvatore

Batters	POS	AB	R	H	RBI	BB	SO	PO	A
RIGOLI, David	SS	3	4	2	1	2	0	2	1
UBANI, Marco	LF	4	3	4	3	0	0	1	0
LIVERZIANI, Claudio	RF	3	0	2	2	2	0	2	1
CARROZZA, Luigi	C	5	2	2	0	0	13	0
CASOLARI, Francesco	DH	5	1	2	3	0	2	0	0
ILLUMINATI, Pier Paolo	1B	0	0	0	0	0	0	1	0
BAGIALEMANI, Ruggero	3B	5	1	1	0	0	1	0	2
d'AURIA, Alberto	2B	5	0	0	0	0	0	1	2
CECCAROLI, Paolo	1B	5	0	1	1	0	3	4	0
	P	0	0	0	0	0	0	0	0
VECCHI, Enrico	CF	5	1	1	0	0	1	3	0
CRETIS, Rolando	P	0	0	0	0	0	0	0	0
CABALISTI, Roberto	P	0	0	0	0	0	0	0	0
MASIN, Massimiliano	DH	0	0	0	0	0	0	0	0
	P	0	0	0	0	0	0	0	0
Totals		40	12	15	10	4	7	28	6

Pitchers	W/L/S	IP	H	R	ER	BB	SO
CRETIS, Rolando		3	6	5	4	4	4
CABALISTI, Roberto	W	4 2/3	6	3	2	2	7
MASIN, Massimiliano		0	0	0	0	1	0
CECCAROLI, Paolo	S	1 1/3	0	0	0	0	2
Totals		9	12	8	6	7	13

TEAM: AUS Australia
Coach: KNAPP, Donald   Asst. Coach: DERKSEN, Robert

Batters	POS	AB	R	H	RBI	BB	SO	PO	A
HEWITT, Jason	2B	5	1	1	0	1	2	3	1
	3B	0	0	0	0	0	0	0	0
HINTON, Steven	SS	6	2	2	0	0	2	0	3
THOMPSON, Stuart	DH	4	0	0	1	2	0	0	0
SCOTT, Andrew	1B	5	2	1	2	0	2	7	3
HYNES, David	LF	5	0	3	0	0	0	1	1
	RF	0	0	0	0	0	0	0	0
McDONALD, Grant	CF	5	1	2	1	0	2	2	0
DAWES, Scott	C	4	1	1	2	1	2	8	1
VAGG, Richard	3B	3	1	1	0	1	2	2	1
TUNKIN, Scott	PH	0	0	0	1	0	0	0	0
	2B	0	0	0	0	0	0	1	0
VOGLER, Peter	RF	3	0	1	0	1	0	2	1
MOORE, John	PH	1	0	0	0	0	1	0	0
	LF	0	0	0	0	0	0	0	0
NAKAMURA, Michael	P	0	0	0	0	0	0	1	0
SHELDON-COLLINS, Simon	P	0	0	0	0	0	0	0	0
LINDBERG, Sten	P	0	0	0	0	0	0	1	0
HOWELL, Stuart	P	0	0	0	0	0	0	0	1
TONKIN, Shane	P	0	0	0	0	0	0	0	0
Totals		41	8	12	6	7	13	27	14

Pitchers	W/L/S	IP	H	R	ER	BB	SO
NAKAMURA, Michael	L	2	4	5	5	2	2
SHELDON-COLLINS, Simon		2/3	5	4	2	0	1
LINDBERG, Sten		4	4	3	3	2	3
HOWELL, Stuart		1 1/3	2	0	0	0	0
TONKIN, Shane		2/3	0	0	0	0	1
Totals		9	15	12	10	4	7

UMPIRES
HP	ROSARIO, Anibal	PUR
1B	YEAST, Davis	USA
2B	TANAKA, Yoshikazu	JPN
3B	HERNANDEZ, Robert	USA

Men / *Messieurs*

PRELIMINARIES — USA 15 JPN 5

Team	1	2	3	4	5	6	7	8	9	R	H	E
USA	7	0	0	0	7	1	0			15	14	0
JPN	2	0	2	1	0	0	0			5	6	1

TEAM: USA United States of America
Coach: BERTMAN, J.　　　Asst. Coach: POLK, Ronald

Batters	POS	AB	R	H	RBI	BB	SO	PO	A
WILLIAMS, Jason	SS	3	2	1	3	0	2	2	3
OJEDA, Augie	SS	1	0	1	0	0	0	0	1
KOTSAY, Mark	LF	5	2	2	0	0	0	1	0
	RF	0	0	0	0	0	0	1	0
JONES, Jacque	CF	5	2	3	4	0	1	0	0
LEE, Travis	1B	4	0	0	0	0	0	7	0
LeCROY, Matt	DH	4	2	2	1	0	0	0	0
ALLEN, Chad	RF	2	2	2	2	1	0	1	0
GREEN, Chad	PH	1	0	0	0	0	1	0	0
	LF	0	0	0	0	0	0	0	0
GLAUS, Troy	3B	3	2	1	1	1	0	1	1
HINCH, A. J.	C	4	2	1	2	0	1	6	0
MORRIS, Warren	2B	3	1	1	1	0	2	1	2
HARKRIDER, Kip	2B	1	0	0	0	0	0	1	2
BENSON, Kris	P	0	0	0	0	0	0	0	0
PARQUE, Jim	P	0	0	0	0	0	0	0	0
LOOPER, Braden	P	0	0	0	0	0	0	0	0
Totals		36	15	14	14	2	7	21	9

Pitchers	W/L/S	IP	H	R	ER	BB	SO
BENSON, Kris	W	5	5	5	5	2	5
PARQUE, Jim		1	1	0	0	1	1
LOOPER, Braden		1	0	0	0	0	0
Totals		7	6	5	5	3	6

TEAM: JPN Japan
Coach: KAWASHIMA, Katsuji　　　Asst. Coach: OTAGAKI, Kozo

Batters	POS	AB	R	H	RBI	BB	SO	PO	A
TAKABAYASHI, Takayuki	CF	2	1	1	2	1	0	1	0
	RF	0	0	0	0	0	0	1	0
SAIGO, Yasuyuki	RF	3	1	1	0	0	1	1	0
	LF	0	0	0	0	0	0	0	0
TANI, Yoshitomo	LF	3	1	2	0	0	0	2	0
	CF	0	0	0	0	0	0	2	0
OKUBO, Hideaki	C	2	0	0	1	1	0	7	0
MATSUNAKA, Nobuhiko	1B	3	1	1	1	0	1	6	0
IGUCHI, Tadahito	SS	2	0	0	1	1	1	1	2
SATO, Tomoaki	DH	2	0	0	0	1	0	0	0
KUROSU, Takashi	PH	1	0	0	0	0	0	0	0
FUKUDOME, Kosuke	3B	2	0	0	0	0	2	0	1
KUWAMOTO, Takao	PH	1	0	0	0	0	0	0	0
IMAOKA, Makoto	2B	2	1	1	0	0	0	0	2
NAKAMURA, Daishin	PH	1	0	0	0	0	0	0	0
MISAWA, Koichi	P	0	0	0	0	0	0	0	0
KIMURA, Jutaro	P	0	0	0	0	0	0	0	0
MORINAKA, Masao	P	0	0	0	0	0	0	0	0
MORI, Masahiko	P	0	0	0	0	0	0	0	0
ONO, Hitoshi	P	0	0	0	0	0	0	0	0
Totals		24	5	6	4	3	6	21	5

Pitchers	W/L/S	IP	H	R	ER	BB	SO
MISAWA, Koichi	L	2/3	3	4	4	0	0
KIMURA, Jutaro		0	3	3	3	0	0
MORINAKA, Masao		4	5	7	2	2	6
MORI, Masahiko		1 1/3	2	1	1	0	1
ONO, Hitoshi		1	1	0	0	0	0
Totals		7	14	15	10	2	7

UMPIRES
HP	DIAZ BLANCO, Nelson	CUB
1B	BONILLA BARBERENA, Alberto Jose	NCA
2B	BENITO, Hensley	AHO
3B	HERNANDEZ REYES, Jose	MEX

PRELIMINARIES — JPN 13 NCA 6

Team	1	2	3	4	5	6	7	8	9	R	H	E
JPN	6	2	0	0	2	0	0	2	1	13	13	1
NCA	0	2	0	2	0	0	2	0	0	6	11	2

TEAM: JPN Japan
Coach: KAWASHIMA, Katsuji　　　Asst. Coach: OTAGAKI, Kozo

Batters	POS	AB	R	H	RBI	BB	SO	PO	A
TAKABAYASHI, Takayuki	RF	5	1	0	1	1	0	2	1
SAIGO, Yasuyuki	LF	1	2	0	0	4	0	1	0
NAKAMURA, Daishin	PR	1	1	0	0	0	0	0	0
	CF	0	0	0	0	0	0	1	0
TANI, Yoshitomo	CF	4	1	2	2	0	0	3	0
	LF	0	0	0	0	0	0	1	0
MATSUNAKA, Nobuhiko	1B	3	1	2	4	2	0	7	1
OKUBO, Hideaki	C	4	1	0	1	1	0	7	0
SATO, Tomoaki	DH	5	1	3	2	0	1	0	0
IGUCHI, Tadahito	SS	5	2	2	0	0	1	2	2
IMAOKA, Makoto	2B	5	1	3	0	0	1	1	2
FUKUDOME, Kosuke	3B	5	2	1	3	0	0	1	3
SUGIURA, Masanori	P	0	0	0	0	0	0	0	0
KIMURA, Jutaro	P	0	0	0	0	0	0	0	0
KAWAMURA, Takeo	P	0	0	0	0	0	0	1	0
Totals		38	13	13	13	8	3	27	9

Pitchers	W/L/S	IP	H	R	ER	BB	SO
SUGIURA, Masanori		3	6	4	4	2	3
KIMURA, Jutaro	W	3 1/3	5	2	2	0	2
KAWAMURA, Takeo		2 2/3	0	0	0	1	2
Totals		9	11	6	6	3	7

TEAM: NCA Nicaragua
Coach: SANCHEZ REYNOSA, Julio　　　Asst. Coach: TORRES, Alejandro

Batters	POS	AB	R	H	RBI	BB	SO	PO	A
MORENO, Sandy	CF	5	1	1	0	0	1	2	0
BERRIOS, Carlos Alberto	RF	3	0	0	0	0	2	2	0
ZAMORA, Fredy	PH	2	0	0	0	0	1	0	0
	RF	0	0	0	0	0	0	0	0
PORRAS, Nemesio	1B	5	0	2	2	0	1	8	1
ROA, Henry	3B	4	2	2	0	0	0	1	0
BACA, Erasmo	DH	3	2	1	0	1	0	0	0
VEGA, Anibal	LF	3	0	1	1	1	0	1	1
CARDOZE, Norman	2B	3	0	1	0	1	1	4	5
DAVILA MONTIEL, Bayardo	SS	4	0	2	3	0	1	3	3
OSEJO, Julio Cesar	C	2	0	0	0	0	0	4	1
ALEMAN, Martin	PH	2	1	1	0	0	0	0	0
	C	0	0	0	0	0	0	1	0
COREA, Fredy	P	0	0	0	0	0	0	0	0
BOJORGE, Eduardo	P	0	0	0	0	0	0	1	0
MIRANDA, Luis Daniel	P	0	0	0	0	0	0	0	0
MAIRENA, Oswaldo	P	0	0	0	0	0	0	0	0
OBANDO VARELA, Omar	P	0	0	0	0	0	0	0	0
Totals		36	6	11	6	3	7	27	11

Pitchers	W/L/S	IP	H	R	ER	BB	SO
COREA, Fredy	L	1/3	2	5	5	3	0
BOJORGE, Eduardo		6 2/3	8	5	5	4	2
MIRANDA, Luis Daniel		1/3	0	2	0	1	0
MAIRENA, Oswaldo		2/3	1	0	0	0	1
OBANDO VARELA, Omar		1	2	1	0	0	0
Totals		9	13	13	10	8	3

UMPIRES
HP	YEAST, Davis	USA
1B	ROSARIO, Anibal	PUR
2B	ALEXANDER, Richard	USA
3B	LIM, Kyung-Ko	KOR

PRELIMINARIES — ITA 6 CUB 20

Team	1	2	3	4	5	6	7	8	9	R	H	E
ITA	0	0	0	0	4	0	2			6	11	7
CUB	0	4	5	5	4	2	0			20	19	0

TEAM: ITA Italy
Coach: AMBROSIONI, Silvano　　　Asst. Coach: VARRIALE, Salvatore

Batters	POS	AB	R	H	RBI	BB	SO	PO	A
RIGOLI, David	3B	3	1	1	0	1	1	1	4
UBANI, Marco	LF	2	0	0	1	0	1	0	0
VECCHI, Enrico	LF	0	1	0	0	1	0	0	0
LIVERZIANI, Claudio	RF	4	1	2	0	0	2	5	1
CASOLARI, Francesco	DH	4	0	3	2	0	1	0	0
FOCHI, Massimo	2B	3	0	1	2	0	0	2	1
CECCAROLI, Paolo	1B	4	0	0	0	0	3	5	0
de FRANCESCHI, Roberto	CF	3	1	1	0	1	0	2	0
BARBONI, Marco	C	1	1	1	0	1	0	0	0
ILLUMINATI, Pier Paolo	C	2	0	0	0	0	0	3	0
EVANGELISTI, Andrea	SS	3	1	2	1	0	0	0	1
MASIN, Massimiliano	P	0	0	0	0	0	0	0	0
CARBINI, Dante	P	0	0	0	0	0	0	0	0
BETTO, Fabio	P	0	0	0	0	0	0	0	0
PASSERINI, Paolo	P	0	0	0	0	0	0	0	0
Totals		29	6	11	6	4	8	18	7

Pitchers	W/L/S	IP	H	R	ER	BB	SO
MASIN, Massimiliano	L	2 2/3	6	9	4	2	0
CARBINI, Dante		2/3	6	5	5	0	0
BETTO, Fabio		1 2/3	4	4	4	2	2
PASSERINI, Paolo		1	3	2	2	0	0
Totals		6	19	20	15	4	2

TEAM: CUB Cuba
Coach: FUENTES FLEITAS, Jorge　　　Asst. Coach: GONZALEZ ALMO, Luis

Batters	POS	AB	R	H	RBI	BB	SO	PO	A
ESTRADA, Jose	CF	4	1	1	3	1	0	2	0
VARGAS, Lazaro	1B	4	0	1	0	1	0	4	0
LINARES, Omar	3B	5	2	2	0	0	1	0	1
KINDELAN, Orestes	DH	4	3	3	2	1	0	0	0
PACHECO, Antonio	2B	5	4	2	3	0	0	2	2
MANRIQUE, Juan	C	5	3	3	1	0	0	8	0
CALDES, Miguel	LF	3	3	2	4	1	1	2	0
ULACIA, Luis	RF	3	1	2	2	0	0	1	0
SCULL, Antonio	PR	1	2	1	3	0	0	0	0
	RF	0	0	0	0	0	0	0	0
PARET, Eduardo	SS	4	1	2	1	0	0	2	1
FUMERO, Jorge	P	0	0	0	0	0	0	0	1
MONTES de OCA, Eliecer	P	0	0	0	0	0	0	0	0
Totals		38	20	19	19	4	2	21	5

Pitchers	W/L/S	IP	H	R	ER	BB	SO
FUMERO, Jorge	W	6	10	6	6	4	7
MONTES de OCA, Eliecer		1	1	0	0	0	1
Totals		7	11	6	6	4	8

UMPIRES
HP	BONILLA BARBERENA, Alberto Jose	NCA
1B	van GRONINGEN SCHINKEL, Fred	NED
2B	HERNANDEZ, Robert	USA
3B	HODGDON, Michael	USA

Men / *Messieurs*

PRELIMINARIES — AUS 5 / USA 15

Team	1	2	3	4	5	6	7	8	9	R	H	E
AUS	1	2	2	0	0	0	0			5	9	1
USA	7	0	2	6	0	0	-			15	13	0

TEAM: AUS Australia
Coach: KNAPP, Donald   Asst. Coach: DERKSEN, Robert

Batters	POS	AB	R	H	RBI	BB	SO	PO	A
HEWITT, Jason	3B	3	1	1	0	0	0	1	0
VAGG, Richard	3B	1	0	0	0	0	0	0	0
HINTON, Steven	SS	3	1	1	0	0	0	1	0
DOUBLEDAY, Mark	SS	1	0	0	0	0	0	0	0
THOMPSON, Stuart	DH	4	1	1	1	0	0	0	0
SCOTT, Andrew	1B	3	0	2	1	0	1	2	0
	LF	0	0	0	0	0	0	0	0
HYNES, David	LF	3	0	1	0	0	1	0	0
	RF	0	0	0	0	0	0	1	0
TUNKIN, Scott	2B	3	0	1	0	0	1	2	1
McDONALD, Grant	CF	2	1	0	1	0	0	1	0
SHELDON-COLLINS, Matthew	PH	1	0	0	0	0	0	0	0
	1B	0	0	0	0	0	0	0	0
DAWES, Scott	C	2	1	1	2	0	0	8	1
MOORE, John	PH	1	0	0	0	0	0	0	0
	C	0	0	0	0	0	0	0	0
VOGLER, Peter	RF	3	0	1	0	0	0	1	0
	CF	0	0	0	0	0	0	2	0
McNALLY, Andrew	P	0	0	0	0	0	0	0	0
HOWELL, Stuart	P	0	0	0	0	0	0	0	0
SHELDON-COLLINS, Simon	P	0	0	0	0	0	0	0	0
NAKAMURA, Michael	P	0	0	0	0	0	0	0	0
Totals		30	5	9	5	0	4	18	2

Pitchers	W/L/S	IP	H	R	ER	BB	SO
McNALLY, Andrew	L	1/3	4	6	6	2	1
HOWELL, Stuart		2 2/3	6	5	5	0	2
SHELDON-COLLINS, Simon		1	3	4	2	1	2
NAKAMURA, Michael		2	0	0	0	0	3
Totals		6	13	15	13	3	8

TEAM: USA United States of America
Coach: BERTMAN, J.   Asst. Coach: POLK, Ronald

Batters	POS	AB	R	H	RBI	BB	SO	PO	A
WILLIAMS, Jason	SS	3	0	1	1	0	2	1	3
OJEDA, Augie	SS	1	0	0	0	0	0	0	1
KOTSAY, Mark	LF	3	2	2	1	1	0	1	0
	RF	0	0	0	0	0	0	0	0
JONES, Jacque	CF	4	2	2	3	0	2	1	0
LEE, Travis	1B	2	2	1	0	1	0	11	0
LeCROY, Matt	DH	4	1	1	1	0	1	0	0
ALLEN, Chad	RF	3	2	2	0	0	1	1	0
GREEN, Chad	PH	1	0	0	0	0	1	0	0
	LF	0	0	0	0	0	0	0	0
GLAUS, Troy	3B	3	3	2	2	1	1	0	2
LOYD, Brian	C	3	1	1	3	0	0	4	0
MORRIS, Warren	2B	2	2	1	3	0	0	2	3
HARKRIDER, Kip	2B	1	0	0	0	0	0	0	1
GREISINGER, Seth	P	0	0	0	0	0	0	0	0
WEAVER, Jeff	P	0	0	0	0	0	0	0	1
PARQUE, Jim	P	0	0	0	0	0	0	0	0
Totals		30	15	13	14	3	8	21	11

Pitchers	W/L/S	IP	H	R	ER	BB	SO
GREISINGER, Seth	W	5	9	5	5	0	0
WEAVER, Jeff		1	0	0	0	0	0
PARQUE, Jim		1	0	0	0	0	0
Totals		7	9	5	5	0	4

UMPIRES
HP	MARCHI, Roberto	ITA
1B	JOHNSON, Glen	CAN
2B	HERNANDEZ REYES, Jose	MEX
3B	BENITO, Hensley	AHO

PRELIMINARIES — NED 3 / KOR 11

Team	1	2	3	4	5	6	7	8	9	R	H	E
NED	0	1	1	0	0	0	1	0	0	3	10	0
KOR	0	3	2	1	5	0	0	0	-	11	16	1

TEAM: NED Netherlands
Coach: LEURS, Jan Dick   Asst. Coach: MAAT, Boudewijn

Batters	POS	AB	R	H	RBI	BB	SO	PO	A
CRANSTON, Jeffrey	CF	2	0	0	0	1	1	1	0
KEMP, Adonis	PH	2	1	1	0	0	1	0	0
	CF	0	0	0	0	0	0	0	0
BALENTINA, Randolph	C	4	0	3	0	1	1	5	1
ten BOSCH, Giel	2B	5	0	0	1	0	1	3	2
JOOST, Marcel	RF	3	0	1	0	2	1	2	0
MARTIS, Edsel	DH	5	1	0	0	0	1	0	0
KRUYT, Marcel	LF	3	1	3	0	1	0	1	0
de BRUIN, Eric	1B	4	0	2	2	0	0	8	1
't HOEN, Evert-Jan	SS	4	0	0	0	0	1	3	3
WARD, Ruben	3B	4	0	0	0	0	2	1	3
CALLENBACH, Peter	P	0	0	0	0	0	0	0	0
JANSEN, Eelco	P	0	0	0	0	0	0	0	0
NANNE, Tom	P	0	0	0	0	0	0	0	0
NANNE, Paul	P	0	0	0	0	0	0	0	0
Totals		36	3	10	3	5	9	24	10

Pitchers	W/L/S	IP	H	R	ER	BB	SO
CALLENBACH, Peter	L	2	5	4	4	1	1
JANSEN, Eelco		2	4	3	3	0	1
NANNE, Tom		2/3	3	4	4	1	0
NANNE, Paul		3 1/3	4	0	0	0	3
Totals		8	16	11	11	2	5

TEAM: KOR Korea
Coach: KIM, Choong-Nam   Asst. Coach: CHO, Doo-Bok

Batters	POS	AB	R	H	RBI	BB	SO	PO	A
CHOI, Man-Ho	CF	5	3	3	3	0	1	1	0
LEE, Byoung-Kyu	LF	5	0	4	3	0	0	1	0
KANG, Hyuk	1B	5	1	2	0	0	0	4	0
AN, Hee-Bong	DH	4	1	1	0	0	0	0	0
JIN, Kab-Yong	C	5	1	3	0	0	0	9	1
CHO, Kyung-Hwan	RF	4	2	1	0	0	0	4	0
BACK, Jae-Ho	SS	3	0	1	2	0	1	3	3
KANG, Pil-Sun	3B	4	1	1	3	0	3	1	0
KIM, Soo-Kwan	2B	2	2	0	0	2	0	3	3
CHO, Jin-Ho	P	0	0	0	0	0	0	1	0
KIM, Young-Soo	P	0	0	0	0	0	0	0	0
JEON, Seung-Nam	P	0	0	0	0	0	0	0	1
Totals		37	11	16	11	2	5	27	8

Pitchers	W/L/S	IP	H	R	ER	BB	SO
CHO, Jin-Ho		2 2/3	5	2	2	3	5
KIM, Young-Soo	W	2 1/3	0	0	0	2	1
JEON, Seung-Nam	S	4	5	1	1	0	3
Totals		9	10	3	3	5	9

UMPIRES
HP	TANAKA, Yoshikazu	JPN
1B	JACQUES, Leon	USA
2B	DIAZ BLANCO, Nelson	CUB
3B	BONILLA BARBERENA, Alberto Jose	NCA

PRELIMINARIES — CUB 10 / USA 8

Team	1	2	3	4	5	6	7	8	9	R	H	E
CUB	4	0	0	0	0	6	0	0	0	10	13	0
USA	1	0	0	0	1	0	3	2	1	8	13	2

TEAM: CUB Cuba
Coach: FUENTES FLEITAS, Jorge   Asst. Coach: GONZALEZ ALMO, Luis

Batters	POS	AB	R	H	RBI	BB	SO	PO	A
ESTRADA, Jose	CF	5	1	1	1	0	0	1	0
ULACIA, Luis	RF	5	1	2	1	0	1	2	0
LINARES, Omar	3B	5	2	2	3	0	0	0	1
KINDELAN, Orestes	DH	5	1	2	0	0	0	0	0
PACHECO, Antonio	2B	4	1	1	0	1	1	1	3
PADILLA, Juan	PR	0	0	0	0	0	0	0	0
	2B	0	0	0	0	0	0	0	0
VARGAS, Lazaro	1B	5	1	2	0	0	0	8	0
MANRIQUE, Juan	C	4	1	0	0	1	1	12	0
CALDES, Miguel	LF	5	1	2	5	0	1	1	0
PARET, Eduardo	SS	3	1	1	0	1	0	2	3
LUIS, Omar	P	0	0	0	0	0	0	0	0
AJETE, Omar	P	0	0	0	0	0	0	0	0
LAZO, Pedro Luis	P	0	0	0	0	0	0	0	0
Totals		41	10	13	10	3	4	27	7

Pitchers	W/L/S	IP	H	R	ER	BB	SO
LUIS, Omar	W	6 1/3	5	3	3	2	5
AJETE, Omar		1 1/3	6	4	3	0	4
LAZO, Pedro Luis	S	1 1/3	2	1	1	1	3
Totals		9	13	8	7	3	12

TEAM: USA United States of America
Coach: BERTMAN, J.   Asst. Coach: POLK, Ronald

Batters	POS	AB	R	H	RBI	BB	SO	PO	A
WILLIAMS, Jason	SS	3	2	1	0	0	1	0	8
KOTSAY, Mark	LF	4	0	1	0	1	2	1	0
JONES, Jacque	CF	5	1	1	1	0	2	3	0
LEE, Travis	1B	4	0	3	2	1	0	15	1
LeCROY, Matt	DH	5	0	2	0	0	2	0	0
GREEN, Chad	PR	0	0	0	0	0	0	0	0
ALLEN, Chad	RF	5	1	1	1	0	1	0	0
GLAUS, Troy	3B	4	1	1	1	1	2	0	3
HINCH, A. J.	C	4	0	0	0	0	2	4	0
MORRIS, Warren	2B	4	3	3	2	0	0	2	4
KOCH, Billy	P	0	0	0	0	0	0	1	1
PARQUE, Jim	P	0	0	0	0	0	0	1	0
WEAVER, Jeff	P	0	0	0	0	0	0	0	0
LOOPER, Braden	P	0	0	0	0	0	0	0	0
Totals		38	8	13	7	3	12	27	17

Pitchers	W/L/S	IP	H	R	ER	BB	SO
KOCH, Billy	L	5	8	8	6	3	1
PARQUE, Jim		1	3	2	2	0	0
WEAVER, Jeff		1	0	0	0	0	0
LOOPER, Braden		2	2	0	0	0	3
Totals		9	13	10	8	3	4

UMPIRES
HP	ROSARIO, Anibal	PUR
1B	BENITO, Hensley	AHO
2B	HERNANDEZ REYES, Jose	MEX
3B	JOHNSON, Glen	CAN

PRELIMINARIES — AUS 0 NCA 10

Team	1	2	3	4	5	6	7	8	9	R	H	E
AUS	0	0	0	0	0	0	0	0		0	5	2
NCA	0	3	1	1	0	0	0	5		10	13	0

TEAM: AUS Australia
Coach: KNAPP, Donald   Asst. Coach: DERKSEN, Robert

Batters	POS	AB	R	H	RBI	BB	SO	PO	A
HEWITT, Jason	3B	3	0	0	0	1	2	1	2
SHELDON-COLLINS, Matthew	1B	3	0	0	0	0	3	9	1
McDONALD, Grant	PH	1	0	1	0	0	0	0	0
	CF	0	0	0	0	0	0	1	0
THOMPSON, Stuart	DH	3	0	1	0	1	0	0	0
SCOTT, Andrew	LF	4	0	0	0	0	1	1	0
	1B	0	0	0	0	0	0	1	0
HYNES, David	RF	2	0	1	0	1	0	2	0
	LF	0	0	0	0	0	0	0	0
TUNKIN, Scott	2B	1	0	1	0	0	0	1	3
DAWES, Scott	C	3	0	0	0	0	0	4	0
VOGLER, Peter	CF	3	0	1	0	0	1	1	0
	RF	0	0	0	0	0	0	1	0
DOUBLEDAY, Mark	SS	3	0	0	0	0	0	1	3
WILLIAMS, Jeffrey	P	0	0	0	0	0	0	1	1
LINDBERG, Sten	P	0	0	0	0	0	0	0	0
Totals		26	0	5	0	3	7	23	10

Pitchers	W/L/S	IP	H	R	ER	BB	SO
WILLIAMS, Jeffrey	L	7 1/3	10	8	8	2	4
LINDBERG, Sten		1/3	3	2	2	1	0
Totals		7 2/3	13	10	10	3	4

TEAM: NCA Nicaragua
Coach: SANCHEZ REYNOSA, Julio   Asst. Coach: TORRES, Alejandro

Batters	POS	AB	R	H	RBI	BB	SO	PO	A
MORENO, Sandy	CF	5	1	2	0	0	1	3	0
AVELLAN, Jorge Luis	2B	5	2	3	3	0	0	2	4
PORRAS, Nemesio	1B	5	0	1	0	0	0	11	0
ROA, Henry	3B	3	1	1	0	2	0	0	1
BACA, Erasmo	DH	5	0	1	1	0	0	0	0
VEGA, Anibal	LF	1	1	0	0	1	0	0	0
ZAMORA, Fredy	PH	1	1	1	0	0	0	0	0
PADILLA, Jose Ramon	RF	4	2	2	2	0	2	1	0
DAVILA MONTIEL, Bayardo	SS	3	1	1	2	0	0	0	5
OSEJO, Julio Cesar	C	3	1	1	1	0	1	7	0
QUIROZ, Jose Luis	P	0	0	0	0	0	0	0	2
MAIRENA, Oswaldo	P	0	0	0	0	0	0	0	0
Totals		35	10	13	9	3	4	24	12

Pitchers	W/L/S	IP	H	R	ER	BB	SO
QUIROZ, Jose Luis	W	7	3	0	0	3	6
MAIRENA, Oswaldo		1	2	0	0	0	1
Totals		8	5	0	0	3	7

UMPIRES
HP	HERNANDEZ, Robert	USA
1B	ALEXANDER, Richard	USA
2B	LIM, Kyung-Ko	KOR
3B	van GRONINGEN SCHINKEL, Fred	NED

PRELIMINARIES — NED 8 ITA 7

Team	1	2	3	4	5	6	7	8	9	R	H	E
NED	3	0	0	0	0	1	1	0	3	8	13	1
ITA	0	0	0	3	0	1	0	0	3	7	9	1

TEAM: NED Netherlands
Coach: LEURS, Jan Dick   Asst. Coach: MAAT, Boudewijn

Batters	POS	AB	R	H	RBI	BB	SO	PO	A
DIX, Eddie	2B	5	0	1	0	0	1	4	2
NANNE, Paul	DH	4	1	1	0	0	1	0	0
	P	0	0	0	0	0	0	0	0
ten BOSCH, Giel	3B	4	2	2	1	1	0	1	2
JOOST, Marcel	RF	5	1	2	1	0	0	1	0
KRUYT, Marcel	LF	5	1	2	2	0	1	0	0
KEMP, Adonis	CF	5	0	2	1	0	2	2	0
de BRUIN, Eric	1B	3	1	2	1	1	0	10	1
't HOEN, Evert-Jan	SS	4	2	1	1	0	0	0	3
CORDEMANS, Rob	P	0	0	0	0	0	0	0	1
KOHL, Geoffry	P	0	0	0	0	0	0	0	1
Totals		39	8	13	7	2	6	27	10

Pitchers	W/L/S	IP	H	R	ER	BB	SO
CORDEMANS, Rob	W	6 1/3	7	4	4	2	7
KOHL, Geoffry		2	2	3	3	1	1
NANNE, Paul	S	2/3	0	0	0	1	0
Totals		9	9	7	7	4	8

TEAM: ITA Italy
Coach: AMBROSIONI, Silvano   Asst. Coach: VARRIALE, Salvatore

Batters	POS	AB	R	H	RBI	BB	SO	PO	A
RIGOLI, David	SS	3	1	0	0	2	1	2	1
UBANI, Marco	LF	5	1	1	3	0	0	3	0
LIVERZIANI, Claudio	RF	4	1	1	0	1	1	3	0
CASOLARI, Francesco	DH	5	1	2	2	0	1	0	0
	1B	0	0	0	0	0	0	0	0
CARROZZA, Luigi	C	2	1	2	0	0	0	5	0
ILLUMINATI, Pier Paolo	C	1	0	0	0	0	0	2	0
FOCHI, Massimo	2B	4	1	2	1	0	1	0	1
CECCAROLI, Paolo	1B	4	0	0	0	0	2	5	2
	P	0	0	0	0	0	0	0	0
BAGIALEMANI, Ruggero	3B	3	0	1	0	1	0	1	2
VECCHI, Enrico	CF	3	0	0	0	0	2	3	0
de FRANCESCHI, Roberto	PH	0	0	0	0	0	0	0	0
d'AURIA, Alberto	PR	0	1	0	0	0	0	0	0
CABALISTI, Roberto	P	0	0	0	0	0	0	2	2
CRETIS, Rolando	P	0	0	0	0	0	0	0	0
Totals		34	7	9	6	4	8	27	8

Pitchers	W/L/S	IP	H	R	ER	BB	SO
CABALISTI, Roberto	L	6	8	5	5	1	5
CRETIS, Rolando		2 1/3	4	3	0	1	0
CECCAROLI, Paolo		2/3	1	0	0	0	1
Totals		9	13	8	5	2	6

UMPIRES
HP	HERNANDEZ REYES, Jose	MEX
1B	ROSARIO, Anibal	PUR
2B	BENITO, Hensley	AHO
3B	JACQUES, Leon	USA

PRELIMINARIES — NCA 7 CUB 8

Team	1	2	3	4	5	6	7	8	9	R	H	E
NCA	1	0	3	1	2	0	0	0	0	7	13	1
CUB	0	2	2	1	2	0	0	1	-	8	12	1

TEAM: NCA Nicaragua
Coach: SANCHEZ REYNOSA, Julio   Asst. Coach: TORRES, Alejandro

Batters	POS	AB	R	H	RBI	BB	SO	PO	A
MORENO, Sandy	CF	3	1	1	0	2	1	6	0
AVELLAN, Jorge Luis	2B	4	1	1	0	0	0	1	0
	SS	0	0	0	0	0	0	0	1
PORRAS, Nemesio	1B	5	1	3	1	0	2	7	0
ROA, Henry	3B	5	1	3	1	0	1	0	1
BACA, Erasmo	DH	5	1	1	2	0	1	0	0
VEGA, Anibal	LF	4	0	0	0	1	1	0	0
PADILLA, Jose Ramon	RF	4	1	3	1	1	1	4	0
DAVILA MONTIEL, Bayardo	SS	2	0	0	0	0	2	2	0
CARDOZE, Norman	2B	1	0	0	0	1	1	1	2
OSEJO, Julio Cesar	C	4	1	1	2	0	1	5	1
FLORES, Asdrudes	P	0	0	0	0	0	0	0	0
OBANDO VARELA, Omar	P	0	0	0	0	0	0	0	1
COREA, Fredy	P	0	0	0	0	0	0	0	0
Totals		37	7	13	7	5	11	24	6

Pitchers	W/L/S	IP	H	R	ER	BB	SO
FLORES, Asdrudes		2	2	2	2	2	2
OBANDO VARELA, Omar		2	4	3	3	1	0
COREA, Fredy	L	4	6	3	3	1	3
Totals		8	12	8	8	4	5

TEAM: CUB Cuba
Coach: FUENTES FLEITAS, Jorge   Asst. Coach: GONZALEZ ALMO, Luis

Batters	POS	AB	R	H	RBI	BB	SO	PO	A
ESTRADA, Jose	CF	5	0	2	1	0	1	3	0
ULACIA, Luis	RF	5	2	4	1	0	0	0	0
LINARES, Omar	3B	5	2	3	3	0	2	1	1
KINDELAN, Orestes	DH	4	2	1	1	1	0	0	0
PACHECO, Antonio	2B	4	1	1	2	0	1	3	3
VARGAS, Lazaro	1B	4	0	0	0	0	0	7	0
MANRIQUE, Juan	C	2	1	1	0	2	0	11	1
CALDES, Miguel	LF	4	0	0	0	0	0	2	1
PARET, Eduardo	SS	3	0	0	0	1	0	0	3
MONTES de OCA, Eliecer	P	0	0	0	0	0	0	0	0
CONTRERAS, Jose Ariel	P	0	0	0	0	0	0	0	0
LAZO, Pedro Luis	P	0	0	0	0	0	0	0	0
Totals		36	8	12	8	4	5	27	11

Pitchers	W/L/S	IP	H	R	ER	BB	SO
MONTES de OCA, Eliecer		2	7	4	3	2	2
CONTRERAS, Jose Ariel		4 2/3	6	3	3	2	6
LAZO, Pedro Luis	W	2 1/3	0	0	0	1	3
Totals		9	13	7	6	5	11

UMPIRES
HP	JOHNSON, Glen	CAN
1B	YEAST, Davis	USA
2B	LIM, Kyung-Ko	KOR
3B	TANAKA, Yoshikazu	JPN

Men / *Messieurs*

PRELIMINARIES — KOR 4, JPN 14

Team	1	2	3	4	5	6	7	8	9	R	H	E
KOR	1	0	0	0	0	3	0			4	8	2
JPN	0	0	2	3	5	3	1			14	19	0

TEAM: KOR Korea
Coach: KIM, Choong-Nam   Asst. Coach: CHO, Doo-Bok

Batters	POS	AB	R	H	RBI	BB	SO	PO	A
CHOI, Man-Ho	CF	4	1	2	0	0	0	1	0
LEE, Byoung-Kyu	LF	4	0	0	0	0	2	2	0
KANG, Hyuk	RF	2	1	2	1	0	0	1	0
AN, Hee-Bong	1B	3	0	1	0	0	0	5	1
JIN, Kab-Yong	C	3	1	1	1	0	0	6	0
CHO, In-Sung	DH	3	1	1	2	0	0	0	0
BACK, Jae-Ho	SS	3	0	0	0	0	3	0	3
KIM, Soo-Kwan	2B	2	0	0	0	0	0	3	0
KANG, Pil-Sun	2B	1	0	0	0	0	1	0	1
	3B	0	0	0	0	0	0	1	0
LEE, Dong	3B	3	0	1	0	0	0	0	1
	2B	0	0	0	0	0	0	1	0
OH, Chul-Min	P	0	0	0	0	0	0	0	0
SON, Min-Han	P	0	0	0	0	0	0	0	0
KIM, Sun-Woo	P	0	0	0	0	0	0	0	0
MUN, Dong-Hwan	P	0	0	0	0	0	0	0	1
Totals		28	4	8	4	0	6	20	7

Pitchers	W/L/S	IP	H	R	ER	BB	SO
OH, Chul-Min	L	3	4	3	3	2	6
SON, Min-Han		1 1/3	5	4	4	0	0
KIM, Sun-Woo		1	5	6	4	0	0
MUN, Dong-Hwan		1 1/3	5	1	1	0	0
Totals		6 2/3	19	14	12	2	6

TEAM: JPN Japan
Coach: KAWASHIMA, Katsuji   Asst. Coach: OTAGAKI, Kozo

Batters	POS	AB	R	H	RBI	BB	SO	PO	A
TAKABAYASHI, Takayuki	RF	5	1	1	1	0	2	3	0
SAIGO, Yasuyuki	LF	4	1	2	2	0	0	1	0
TANI, Yoshitomo	CF	5	1	2	2	0	0	1	0
MATSUNAKA, Nobuhiko	1B	5	2	3	1	0	1	7	1
OKUBO, Hideaki	C	4	2	0	0	0	1	7	0
SATO, Tomoaki	DH	4	2	2	0	1	1	0	0
IGUCHI, Tadahito	SS	5	3	5	3	0	0	0	2
IMAOKA, Makoto	2B	2	0	1	1	1	0	1	1
FUKUDOME, Kosuke	3B	4	2	3	3	0	1	1	2
SUGIURA, Masanori	P	0	0	0	0	0	0	0	2
KAWAMURA, Takeo	P	0	0	0	0	0	0	0	0
Totals		38	14	19	13	2	6	21	8

Pitchers	W/L/S	IP	H	R	ER	BB	SO
SUGIURA, Masanori	W	5 2/3	7	4	4	0	3
KAWAMURA, Takeo		1 1/3	1	0	0	0	3
Totals		7	8	4	4	0	6

UMPIRES
HP	HODGDON, Michael	USA
1B	DIAZ BLANCO, Nelson	CUB
2B	MARCHI, Roberto	ITA
3B	HERNANDEZ, Robert	USA

PRELIMINARIES — USA 17, NED 1

Team	1	2	3	4	5	6	7	8	9	R	H	E
USA	5	0	2	2	1	4	3			17	18	1
NED	0	0	0	1	0	0	0			1	3	3

TEAM: USA United States of America
Coach: BERTMAN, J.   Asst. Coach: POLK, Ronald

Batters	POS	AB	R	H	RBI	BB	SO	PO	A
WILLIAMS, Jason	SS	1	1	1	0	0	0	0	0
OJEDA, Augie	SS	2	1	0	0	1	1	0	1
KOTSAY, Mark	LF	4	2	1	1	1	1	2	0
JONES, Jacque	CF	5	4	4	2	0	0	1	0
LEE, Travis	1B	5	4	4	3	0	0	5	0
LeCROY, Matt	DH	1	2	1	2	1	0	0	0
GREEN, Chad	PH	1	1	1	1	1	0	0	0
	DH	0	0	0	0	0	0	0	0
ALLEN, Chad	RF	5	1	2	4	0	0	2	0
GLAUS, Troy	3B	5	0	2	0	0	2	0	1
LOYD, Brian	C	5	1	2	3	0	1	9	1
MORRIS, Warren	2B	2	0	0	0	0	1	0	2
HARKRIDER, Kip	2B	2	0	0	0	0	0	1	0
DICKEY, R. A.	P	0	0	0	0	0	0	1	0
Totals		38	17	18	16	4	6	21	5

Pitcher	W/L/S	IP	H	R	ER	BB	SO
DICKEY, R. A.	W	7	3	1	1	1	9
Totals		7	3	1	1	1	9

TEAM: NED Netherlands
Coach: LEURS, Jan Dick   Asst. Coach: MAAT, Boudewijn

Batters	POS	AB	R	H	RBI	BB	SO	PO	A
ten BOSCH, Giel	2B	3	0	0	0	0	2	3	1
't HOEN, Evert-Jan	SS	3	0	0	0	0	2	1	1
de BRUIN, Eric	1B	0	0	0	0	0	0	0	0
NANNE, Paul	PH	2	0	0	0	0	0	0	0
	1B	0	0	0	0	0	0	3	1
JOOST, Marcel	RF	2	0	1	0	0	0	1	0
CRANSTON, Jeffrey	CF	1	0	0	0	0	0	0	0
MARTIS, Edsel	DH	3	1	1	1	0	1	0	0
KRUYT, Marcel	LF	3	0	0	0	0	2	2	1
	RF	0	0	0	0	0	0	0	0
KEMP, Adonis	CF	3	0	1	0	0	1	4	0
	LF	0	0	0	0	0	0	0	0
FLUONIA, Marlon	C	3	0	0	0	0	0	6	0
WARD, Ruben	3B	2	0	0	0	1	1	0	1
WOUT, Daniel	P	0	0	0	0	0	0	0	0
van MARIS, Andreas	P	0	0	0	0	0	0	1	0
NANNE, Tom	P	0	0	0	0	0	0	0	0
CALLENBACH, Peter	P	0	0	0	0	0	0	0	0
Totals		25	1	3	1	1	9	21	5

Pitchers	W/L/S	IP	H	R	ER	BB	SO
WOUT, Daniel	L	2 1/3	8	7	7	1	4
van MARIS, Andreas		3	6	7	5	1	0
NANNE, Tom		1	3	3	3	2	1
CALLENBACH, Peter		2/3	1	0	0	0	1
Totals		7	18	17	15	4	6

UMPIRES
HP	BONILLA BARBERENA, Alberto Jose	NCA
1B	LIM, Kyung-Ko	KOR
2B	TANAKA, Yoshikazu	JPN
3B	ROSARIO, Anibal	PUR

PRELIMINARIES — ITA 1, JPN 12

Team	1	2	3	4	5	6	7	8	9	R	H	E
ITA	0	0	0	1	0	0	0	0		1	6	1
JPN	1	2	0	1	3	2	1	2		12	13	0

TEAM: ITA Italy
Coach: AMBROSIONI, Silvano   Asst. Coach: VARRIALE, Salvatore

Batters	POS	AB	R	H	RBI	BB	SO	PO	A
RIGOLI, David	CF	4	0	0	0	0	1	1	0
UBANI, Marco	LF	3	0	0	0	1	1	2	0
LIVERZIANI, Claudio	RF	3	0	0	0	0	0	3	0
VECCHI, Enrico	PH	1	0	0	0	0	0	0	0
	RF	0	0	0	0	0	0	0	0
CASOLARI, Francesco	1B	3	0	0	0	1	1	4	0
CARROZZA, Luigi	DH	4	1	3	0	0	1	0	0
FOCHI, Massimo	2B	3	0	0	0	1	1	1	4
BAGIALEMANI, Ruggero	3B	3	0	1	1	0	1	1	0
ILLUMINATI, Pier Paolo	C	3	0	1	0	0	1	8	0
EVANGELISTI, Andrea	SS	3	0	1	0	0	2	2	1
MASIN, Massimiliano	P	0	0	0	0	0	0	0	0
BETTO, Fabio	P	0	0	0	0	0	0	0	0
CRETIS, Rolando	P	0	0	0	0	0	0	0	0
CECCAROLI, Paolo	P	0	0	0	0	0	0	0	0
CARBINI, Dante	P	0	0	0	0	0	0	0	0
Totals		30	1	6	1	2	9	22	5

Pitchers	W/L/S	IP	H	R	ER	BB	SO
MASIN, Massimiliano	L	1 1/3	2	3	2	3	0
BETTO, Fabio		2 2/3	4	3	3	0	4
CRETIS, Rolando		1	2	1	1	0	3
CECCAROLI, Paolo		2	4	3	3	1	1
CARBINI, Dante		1/3	1	2	2	0	0
Totals		7 1/3	13	12	11	4	8

TEAM: JPN Japan
Coach: KAWASHIMA, Katsuji   Asst. Coach: OTAGAKI, Kozo

Batters	POS	AB	R	H	RBI	BB	SO	PO	A
TAKABAYASHI, Takayuki	RF	5	0	0	0	0	1	1	0
SAIGO, Yasuyuki	LF	3	2	2	0	2	1	0	0
	1B	0	0	0	0	0	0	1	1
TANI, Yoshitomo	CF	4	0	2	2	0	1	3	0
	LF	0	0	0	0	0	0	0	0
MATSUNAKA, Nobuhiko	1B	3	0	0	1	0	1	8	0
NAKAMURA, Daishin	PR	1	1	0	0	0	0	0	0
	CF	0	0	0	0	0	0	1	0
OKUBO, Hideaki	C	4	1	1	1	0	0	8	0
KUROSU, Takashi	PH	1	0	0	0	0	0	0	0
	C	0	0	0	0	0	0	1	0
SATO, Tomoaki	DH	4	3	2	1	1	0	0	0
IGUCHI, Tadahito	SS	3	1	1	1	1	2	0	2
NOJIMA, Masahiro	SS	0	1	0	0	0	0	0	1
IMAOKA, Makoto	2B	5	2	3	4	0	2	0	4
	3B	0	0	0	0	0	0	0	0
FUKUDOME, Kosuke	3B	3	0	1	1	0	0	0	0
KUWAMOTO, Takao	PH	1	1	1	0	0	0	0	0
	2B	0	0	0	0	0	0	0	0
MISAWA, Koichi	P	0	0	0	0	0	0	0	0
KIMURA, Jutaro	P	0	0	0	0	0	0	0	0
MORI, Masahiko	P	0	0	0	0	0	0	1	0
Totals		37	12	13	11	4	8	24	8

Pitchers	W/L/S	IP	H	R	ER	BB	SO
MISAWA, Koichi		3 2/3	4	1	1	1	3
KIMURA, Jutaro	W	2 1/3	1	0	0	0	3
MORI, Masahiko		2	1	0	0	1	3
Totals		8	6	1	1	2	9

UMPIRES
HP	DIAZ BLANCO, Nelson	CUB
1B	van GRONINGEN SCHINKEL, Fred	NED
2B	YEAST, Davis	USA
3B	ALEXANDER, Richard	USA

Men / Messieurs

PRELIMINARIES — AUS 11 KOR 8

Team	1	2	3	4	5	6	7	8	9	R	H	E
AUS	0	0	0	8	0	0	1	2	0	11	14	2
KOR	2	2	3	0	0	0	1	0	0	8	10	3

TEAM: AUS Australia
Coach: KNAPP, Donald Asst. Coach: DERKSEN, Robert

Batters	POS	AB	R	H	RBI	BB	SO	PO	A
HEWITT, Jason	3B	5	1	1	2	0	3	0	3
	2B	0	0	0	0	0	0	1	2
HINTON, Steven	SS	4	2	2	2	0	0	2	4
THOMPSON, Stuart	DH	5	0	1	0	0	3	0	0
SCOTT, Andrew	1B	5	2	2	2	0	0	12	0
HYNES, David	LF	4	2	2	0	1	0	1	0
MOORE, John	LF	0	0	0	0	0	0	0	0
TUNKIN, Scott	2B	3	0	0	1	0	0	0	3
DOUBLEDAY, Mark	3B	1	0	1	0	0	0	0	0
McDONALD, Grant	CF	5	1	2	1	0	1	3	0
DAWES, Scott	C	4	1	1	0	1	1	6	0
VOGLER, Peter	RF	3	2	2	2	1	0	2	0
NAKAMURA, Michael	P	0	0	0	0	0	0	0	0
LINDBERG, Sten	P	0	0	0	0	0	0	0	0
TONKIN, Shane	P	0	0	0	0	0	0	0	1
Totals		39	11	14	10	3	8	27	13

Pitchers	W/L/S	IP	H	R	ER	BB	SO
NAKAMURA, Michael		1 1/3	4	4	4	0	1
LINDBERG, Sten		1 2/3	2	3	0	0	0
TONKIN, Shane	W	6	4	1	1	0	5
Totals		9	10	8	5	0	6

TEAM: KOR Korea
Coach: KIM, Choong-Nam Asst. Coach: CHO, Doo-Bok

Batters	POS	AB	R	H	RBI	BB	SO	PO	A
CHOI, Man-Ho	CF	5	1	2	1	0	1	2	0
LEE, Byoung-Kyu	LF	4	1	1	0	0	0	2	0
KANG, Hyuk	RF	4	0	0	0	0	0	2	0
AN, Hee-Bong	1B	4	2	2	2	0	0	7	1
JIN, Kab-Yong	C	4	1	1	2	0	1	7	2
CHO, In-Sung	DH	4	1	2	1	0	1	0	0
KIM, Soo-Kwan	PR	0	0	0	0	0	0	0	0
	DH	0	0	0	0	0	0	0	0
LEE, Dong	2B	4	1	1	0	0	1	3	3
KANG, Pil-Sun	3B	4	1	1	2	0	0	0	3
BACK, Jae-Ho	SS	3	0	0	0	0	1	4	3
CHO, Kyung-Hwam	PH	1	0	0	0	0	1	0	0
LIM, Sun-Dong	P	0	0	0	0	0	0	0	0
JEON, Seung-Nam	P	0	0	0	0	0	0	0	0
MUN, Dong-Hwan	P	0	0	0	0	0	0	0	0
Totals		37	8	10	8	0	6	27	12

Pitchers	W/L/S	IP	H	R	ER	BB	SO
LIM, Sun-Dong		3 1/3	8	6	6	2	2
JEON, Seung-Nam	L	3	4	3	3	0	2
MUN, Dong-Hwan		2 2/3	2	2	1	1	4
Totals		9	14	11	10	3	8

UMPIRES
HP	HERNANDEZ, Robert	USA
1B	HODGDON, Michael	USA
2B	JACQUES, Leon	USA
3B	MARCHI, Roberto	ITA

SEMIFINALS — NCA 1 CUB 8

Team	1	2	3	4	5	6	7	8	9	R	H	E
NCA	0	1	0	0	0	0	0	0	0	1	6	2
CUB	0	0	0	3	0	3	0	2	-	8	14	2

TEAM: NCA Nicaragua
Coach: SANCHEZ REYNOSA, Julio Asst. Coach: TORRES, Alejandro

Batters	POS	AB	R	H	RBI	BB	SO	PO	A
MORENO, Sandy	CF	4	0	2	0	0	0	4	0
AVELLAN, Jorge Luis	2B	3	0	0	0	1	0	3	1
	3B	0	0	0	0	0	0	1	1
PORRAS, Nemesio	1B	4	0	0	0	0	0	5	0
ROA, Henry	3B	2	1	1	0	0	0	2	1
CARDOZE, Norman	2B	1	0	0	0	0	0	0	0
BACA, Erasmo	DH	4	0	2	0	0	1	0	0
VEGA, Anibal	LF	2	0	0	1	0	0	1	0
BERRIOS, Carlos Alberto	PH	2	0	0	0	0	1	0	0
	LF	0	0	0	0	0	0	0	0
PADILLA, Jose Ramon	RF	3	0	0	0	0	1	2	1
DAVILA MONTIEL, Bayardo	SS	3	0	1	0	0	0	2	5
OSEJO, Julio Cesar	C	2	0	0	0	0	0	3	2
ALEMAN, Martin	PH	1	0	0	0	0	0	0	0
	C	0	0	0	0	0	0	1	0
FLORES, Asdrudes	P	0	0	0	0	0	0	0	0
MIRANDA, Luis Daniel	P	0	0	0	0	0	0	0	0
Totals		31	1	6	1	1	3	24	11

Pitchers	W/L/S	IP	H	R	ER	BB	SO
FLORES, Asdrudes	L	5 2/3	7	6	5	4	2
MIRANDA, Luis Daniel		2 1/3	7	2	2	0	1
Totals		8	14	8	7	4	3

TEAM: CUB Cuba
Coach: FUENTES FLEITAS, Jorge Asst. Coach: GONZALEZ ALMO, Luis

Batters	POS	AB	R	H	RBI	BB	SO	PO	A
ESTRADA, Jose	CF	2	1	1	1	2	0	1	0
ULACIA, Luis	RF	5	1	2	0	0	0	0	0
LINARES, Omar	3B	5	1	1	0	0	1	2	5
KINDELAN, Orestes	DH	4	2	2	3	1	1	0	0
PACHECO, Antonio	2B	3	0	1	0	1	1	2	5
PADILLA, Juan	2B	0	0	0	0	0	0	0	0
VARGAS, Lazaro	1B	4	1	1	0	0	0	14	2
CALDES, Miguel	LF	4	0	1	0	0	0	1	0
MANRIQUE, Juan	C	4	1	2	3	0	0	2	0
PARET, Eduardo	SS	4	1	3	0	0	0	4	4
ROMERO, Osmany	P	0	0	0	0	0	0	1	2
AJETE, Omar	P	0	0	0	0	0	0	0	1
Totals		35	8	14	7	4	3	27	19

Pitchers	W/L/S	IP	H	R	ER	BB	SO
ROMERO, Osmany	W	5 2/3	5	1	1	1	0
AJETE, Omar	S	3 1/3	1	0	0	0	3
Totals		9	6	1	1	1	3

UMPIRES
HP	YEAST, Davis	USA
1B	BENITO, Hensley	AHO
2B	LIM, Kyung-Ko	KOR
3B	TANAKA, Yoshikazu	JPN

SEMIFINALS — JPN 11 USA 2

Team	1	2	3	4	5	6	7	8	9	R	H	E
JPN	0	3	0	0	3	0	2	2	1	11	15	0
USA	0	0	0	0	0	2	0	0	0	2	6	1

TEAM: JPN Japan
Coach: KAWASHIMA, Katsuji Asst. Coach: OTAGAKI, Kozo

Batters	POS	AB	R	H	RBI	BB	SO	PO	A
TAKABAYASHI, Takayuki	RF	5	1	1	2	0	0	1	0
SAIGO, Yasuyuki	LF	5	1	3	0	0	1	3	0
	1B	0	0	0	0	0	0	0	1
TANI, Yoshitomo	CF	4	1	1	0	0	1	2	0
	LF	0	0	0	0	0	0	0	0
MATSUNAKA, Nobuhiko	1B	3	1	1	2	2	1	8	1
NAKAMURA, Daishin	PR	0	1	0	0	0	0	0	0
	CF	0	0	0	0	0	0	0	0
OKUBO, Hideaki	C	5	2	2	2	0	2	10	0
SATO, Tomoaki	DH	5	0	2	2	0	2	0	0
IGUCHI, Tadahito	SS	4	2	2	1	0	0	1	1
IMAOKA, Makoto	2B	5	1	2	2	0	3	0	5
FUKUDOME, Kosuke	3B	4	1	1	0	0	1	0	2
SUGIURA, Masanori	P	0	0	0	0	0	0	1	0
KAWAMURA, Takeo	P	0	0	0	0	0	0	1	0
Totals		40	11	15	11	2	11	27	10

Pitchers	W/L/S	IP	H	R	ER	BB	SO
SUGIURA, Masanori	W	5 2/3	6	2	2	1	6
KAWAMURA, Takeo	S	3 1/3	0	0	0	2	4
Totals		9	6	2	2	3	10

TEAM: USA United States of America
Coach: BERTMAN, J. Asst. Coach: POLK, Ronald

Batters	POS	AB	R	H	RBI	BB	SO	PO	A
WILLIAMS, Jason	SS	4	0	0	0	0	0	1	5
KOTSAY, Mark	LF	4	0	0	0	0	4	2	0
	RF	0	0	0	0	0	0	0	0
JONES, Jacque	CF	4	1	2	0	0	0	1	0
LEE, Travis	1B	4	0	2	0	0	1	10	0
LeCROY, Matt	DH	4	1	1	2	0	1	0	0
ALLEN, Chad	RF	2	0	1	0	1	0	0	0
GREEN, Chad	PH	1	0	0	0	0	0	0	0
	LF	0	0	0	0	0	0	0	0
GLAUS, Troy	3B	2	0	0	0	1	1	1	2
HARKRIDER, Kip	3B	1	0	0	0	0	1	0	0
HINCH, A. J.	C	3	0	0	0	0	0	11	2
LOYD, Brian	PH	1	0	0	0	0	0	0	0
MORRIS, Warren	2B	3	0	0	1	1	1	1	3
BENSON, Kris	P	0	0	0	0	0	0	0	0
WEAVER, Jeff	P	0	0	0	0	0	0	0	0
PARQUE, Jim	P	0	0	0	0	0	0	0	0
KOCH, Billy	P	0	0	0	0	0	0	0	0
Totals		33	2	6	3		10	27	12

Pitchers	W/L/S	IP	H	R	ER	BB	SO
BENSON, Kris	L	4	8	5	5	1	5
WEAVER, Jeff		2 1/3	5	3	3	0	2
PARQUE, Jim		1	2	2	2	0	3
KOCH, Billy		1 2/3	0	1	0	1	1
Totals		9	15	11	10	2	11

UMPIRES
HP	JOHNSON, Glen	CAN
1B	MARCHI, Roberto	ITA
2B	HERNANDEZ REYES, Jose	MEX
3B	van GRONINGEN SCHINKEL, Fred	NED

FINAL - BRONZE MATCH   USA 10   NCA 3

Team	1	2	3	4	5	6	7	8	9	R	H	E
USA	4	0	0	1	0	1	1	3	0	10	12	1
NCA	3	0	0	0	0	0	0	0	0	3	3	2

TEAM: USA United States of America

Coach: BERTMAN, J.   Asst. Coach: POLK, Ronald

Batters	POS	AB	R	H	RBI	BB	SO	PO	A
WILLIAMS, Jason	SS	4	1	2	3	1	2	0	6
OJEDA, Augie	SS	0	0	0	0	1	0	0	3
KOTSAY, Mark	LF	2	1	0	0	2	0	1	0
GREEN, Chad	PR	1	1	0	0	0	0	0	0
	LF	0	0	0	0	0	0	0	0
JONES, Jacque	CF	4	1	0	0	0	1	3	0
LEE, Travis	1B	4	1	1	3	1	2	13	0
LeCROY, Matt	DH	5	1	3	2	0	0	0	0
ALLEN, Chad	RF	5	0	0	0	0	1	4	0
GLAUS, Troy	3B	5	1	1	1	0	0	0	2
HINCH, A. J.	C	4	2	2	0	0	0	4	0
LOYD, Brian	C	1	0	0	0	0	1	1	0
MORRIS, Warren	2B	2	1	2	1	1	0	1	3
HARKRIDER, Kip	2B	1	0	1	0	0	0	0	0
GREISINGER, Seth	P	0	0	0	0	0	0	0	0
LOOPER, Braden	P	0	0	0	0	0	0	0	0
Totals		38	10	12	10	6	7	27	14

Pitchers	W/L/S	IP	H	R	ER	BB	SO
GREISINGER, Seth	W	7	2	3	3	1	5
LOOPER, Braden		2	1	0	0	1	1
Totals		9	3	3	3	2	6

TEAM: NCA Nicaragua

Coach: SANCHEZ REYNOSA, Julio   Asst. Coach: TORRES, Alejandro

Batters	POS	AB	R	H	RBI	BB	SO	PO	A
MORENO, Sandy	CF	2	1	0	0	1	0	2	0
ZAMORA, Fredy	PH	1	0	0	0	0	1	0	0
	CF	0	0	0	0	0	0	0	0
AVELLAN, Jorge Luis	SS	4	1	1	0	0	0	2	6
PORRAS, Nemesio	1B	3	0	0	1	0	1	11	1
ROA, Henry	3B	4	1	1	1	0	0	0	0
BACA, Erasmo	DH	4	0	1	1	0	1	0	0
VEGA, Anibal	LF	4	0	0	0	0	1	1	0
PADILLA, Jose Ramon	RF	3	0	0	0	0	2	2	0
CARDOZE, Norman	2B	3	0	0	0	0	0	2	6
OSEJO, Julio Cesar	C	2	0	0	0	0	0	5	0
ALEMAN, Martin	C	0	0	0	0	1	0	2	0
QUIROZ, Jose Luis	P	0	0	0	0	0	0	0	0
MAIRENA, Oswaldo	P	0	0	0	0	0	0	0	1
OBANDO VARELA, Omar	P	0	0	0	0	0	0	0	0
Totals		30	3	3	3	2	6	27	14

Pitchers	W/L/S	IP	H	R	ER	BB	SO
QUIROZ, Jose Luis	L	1	2	4	4	3	2
MAIRENA, Oswaldo		6	9	6	5	1	3
OBANDO VARELA, Omar		2	1	0	0	2	2
Totals		9	12	10	9	6	7

UMPIRES

HP	DIAZ BLANCO, Nelson	CUB
1B	TANAKA, Yoshikazu	JPN
2B	JOHNSON, Glen	CAN
3B	LIM, Kyung-Ko	KOR

FINAL - GOLD MATCH   JPN 9   CUB 13

Team	1	2	3	4	5	6	7	8	9	R	H	E
JPN	0	0	0	1	5	0	1	0	2	9	9	1
CUB	3	3	0	0	0	4	1	2	-	13	14	0

TEAM: JPN Japan

Coach: KAWASHIMA, Katsuji   Asst. Coach: OTAGAKI, Kozo

Batters	POS	AB	R	H	RBI	BB	SO	PO	A
TAKABAYASHI, Takayuki	RF	3	1	0	0	1	2	1	1
NAKAMURA, Daishin	CF	1	1	1	0	0	0	0	0
SAIGO, Yasuyuki	LF	3	2	1	1	1	0	0	0
	RF	0	0	0	0	0	0	0	0
KUROSU, Takashi	PH	1	0	0	0	0	1	0	0
TANI, Yoshitomo	CF	5	3	3	3	0	0	1	0
	LF	0	0	0	0	0	0	1	0
MATSUNAKA, Nobuhiko	1B	5	1	2	5	0	1	6	0
OKUBO, Hideaki	C	5	0	1	0	0	2	13	0
SATO, Tomoaki	DH	3	0	0	0	1	1	0	0
KUWAMOTO, Takao	PH	1	0	0	0	0	0	0	0
IGUCHI, Tadahito	SS	4	0	1	0	0	2	1	0
IMAOKA, Makoto	2B	3	0	0	0	1	1	0	2
FUKUDOME, Kosuke	3B	2	1	0	0	1	1	1	2
SUGIURA, Masanori	P	0	0	0	0	0	0	0	0
KIMURA, Jutaro	P	0	0	0	0	0	0	0	0
KAWAMURA, Takeo	P	0	0	0	0	0	0	0	0
MORINAKA, Masao	P	0	0	0	0	0	0	0	0
MORI, Masahiko	P	0	0	0	0	0	0	0	0
MISAWA, Koichi	P	0	0	0	0	0	0	0	0
Totals		36	9	9	9	5	11	24	5

Pitchers	W/L/S	IP	H	R	ER	BB	SO
SUGIURA, Masanori		1 2/3	5	5	5	0	1
KIMURA, Jutaro	L	3 1/3	3	2	2	2	7
KAWAMURA, Takeo		2/3	3	3	3	0	1
MORINAKA, Masao		1	2	1	1	0	1
MORI, Masahiko		1	1	2	2	1	2
MISAWA, Koichi		1/3	0	0	0	0	1
Totals		8	14	13	13	3	13

TEAM: CUB Cuba

Coach: FUENTES FLEITAS, Jorge   Asst. Coach: GONZALEZ ALMO, Luis

Batters	POS	AB	R	H	RBI	BB	SO	PO	A
ESTRADA, Jose	CF	5	1	1	1	0	3	2	0
ULACIA, Luis	RF	5	3	4	2	0	0	0	0
LINARES, Omar	3B	4	3	3	6	1	1	1	2
KINDELAN, Orestes	DH	5	1	1	1	0	4	0	0
PACHECO, Antonio	2B	4	1	1	1	0	2	1	6
VARGAS, Lazaro	1B	4	0	0	0	0	0	11	0
CALDES, Miguel	LF	4	2	3	1	0	1	0	0
MANRIQUE, Juan	C	3	0	0	0	1	2	11	0
PARET, Eduardo	SS	3	2	1	1	1	0	1	1
LUIS, Omar	P	0	0	0	0	0	0	0	0
LAZO, Pedro Luis	P	0	0	0	0	0	0	0	0
Totals		37	13	14	13	3	13	27	9

Pitchers	W/L/S	IP	H	R	ER	BB	SO
LUIS, Omar		4 2/3	5	6	6	2	4
LAZO, Pedro Luis	W	4 1/3	4	3	3	3	7
Totals		9	9	9	9	5	11

UMPIRES

HP	ROSARIO, Anibal	PUR
1B	BENITO, Hensley	AHO
2B	HODGDON, Michael	USA
3B	BONILLA BARBERENA, Alberto Jose	NCA

TEAM STANDINGS - PRELIMINARIES

Rnk	Team	Games Played	Won	Lost	Runs For	Against	W/L Avg	G behind
1	CUB	7	7	0	97	49	1.000	0
2	USA	7	6	1	81	27	0.857	1
3	JPN	7	4	3	69	45	0.571	3
4	NCA	7	4	3	44	30	0.571	3
5	NED	7	2	5	32	76	0.285	5
6	ITA	7	2	5	33	71	0.285	5
7	AUS	7	2	5	47	86	0.285	5
8	KOR	7	1	6	40	59	0.142	6

FINAL SUMMARY

Phase	Teams	Score
Semifinals	CUB - NCA	8 - 1
Semifinals	USA - JPN	2 - 11
Final - Bronze	NCA - USA	3 - 10
Final - Gold	CUB - JPN	13 - 9

FINAL TEAM STANDINGS

Rnk	Team	Games	Wins	Losses	
1	CUB	9	9	0	Gold
2	JPN	9	5	4	Silver
3	USA	9	7	2	Bronze
4	NCA	9	4	5	
5	NED	7	2	5	
6	ITA	7	2	5	
7	AUS	7	2	5	
8	KOR	7	1	6	

BASKETBALL
BASKETBALL

Abbreviations and terms used in Basketball results tables
Abréviations et termes employés dans les tableaux de résultats de basketball

Term	English	Français
2 Pts	Two Point Field Goals	Panier à deux points
3 Pts	Three Point Field Goals	Panier à trois points
A	Assists	Passes décisives
Against	Against	Contre
Assistant Coach	Assistant Coach	Entraîneur adjoint
Bronze	Bronze Medal	Médaille de bronze
Classification	Classification	Classement
Coach	Coach	Entraîneur
Ctry	Country	Pays
F	Fouls	Fautes
FT	Free Throws	Lancers francs
Final-Bronze	Final-Bronze	Finale-Bronze
Final Classification	Final Classification	Classement final
Final-Gold	Final-Gold	Finale-Or
Final Score	Final Score	Score final
Finals	Finals	Finales
For	For	Pour
Gold	Gold Medal	Médaille d'or
Group	Group	Groupe
Halftime Score	Halftime Score	Score à mi-temps
Lost	Lost	Perdu
Matches	Matches	Matchs
Mins	Minutes	Minutes
Names	Names	Noms
Played	Played	Joué
Points	Points	Points
Preliminaries	Preliminaries	Eliminatoires
Pts	Points	Points
Quarterfinals	Quarterfinals	Quarts de finale
Reb	Rebounds	Rebonds
Referees	Referees	Arbitres
Rnk	Rank	Classement
S	Starting Lineup	Liste de départ
Semifinals	Semifinals	Demi-finales
Silver	Silver Medal	Médaille d'argent
Stl	Steals	Interceptions
Team	Team	Equipe
To	Turnovers	Pertes de possession de la balle
Totals	Totals	Totaux
Won	Won	Gagné

International Basketball Federation (FIBA)
Fédération Internationale de Basketball
Boschetsriederstrasse 67
D-81379 Munich
Germany

Basketball / *Basketball*

Men / *Messieurs*

Team: CHN People's Republic of China
Coach: GONG, Lu-ming   Assistant Coach: CHEN, De-Chun

Names	Pts	2 Pts	3 Pts	FT	A	Stl	To	Reb	F	Mins	
LI, Xiao-yong	0	0/0	0/1	0/0	0	0	2	1	1	11:52	S
ZHENG, Wu	3	0/1	1/1	0/2	0	0	0	3	3	11:53	S
SUN, Jun	14	3/6	2/4	2/2	1	0	8	4	2	36:35	S
LIU, Yu-dong	10	2/8	0/0	6/8	1	1	3	7	2	19:32	S
BA, Tere	0	0/0	0/0	0/0	0	0	1	1	2	05:36	S
WANG, Zhi-zhi	17	6/10	0/0	5/5	1	0	2	11	1	32:00	
HU, Wei-dong	15	1/2	2/4	7/8	3	1	2	5	4	31:32	
WU, Nai-qin	0	0/0	0/0	0/0	0	0	0	0	0	00:00	
WU, Qing-long	4	1/1	0/3	2/4	2	2	6	1	3	28:08	
LI, Nan	0	0/0	0/0	0/0	0	0	0	0	0	00:00	
SHAN, Tao	0	0/0	0/0	0/0	0	0	0	0	0	00:00	
GONG, Xiao-bin	7	1/5	0/0	5/5	2	0	3	4	3	22:52	
Totals	70	14/33	5/13	27/34	10	4	27	37	21		

Team: ANG Angola
Coach: ROMERO, Vladimiro   Assistant Coach: TAVARES, Nelson

Names	Pts	2 Pts	3 Pts	FT	A	Stl	To	Reb	F	Mins	
MOREIRA, Anibal	4	2/5	0/2	0/0	2	2	2	2	5	24:36	S
VICTORIANO, Angelo	13	2/4	3/5	0/0	1	3	3	6	3	31:56	S
UCUAHAMBA, Benjamin	6	1/5	1/1	5	4	5	5	3	2	31:08	S
COIMBRA, Herlander	10	0/0	2/10	4/5	1	0	2	3	4	26:10	S
DIAS, David	11	4/7	0/0	3/5	2	0	4	3	5	27:39	S
VICTORIANO, Edmar	0	0/0	0/0	0/0	0	0	0	0	0	00:00	
TROSO, Honorato	5	1/1	1/3	0/0	0	1	0	0	0	06:20	
CARVALHO, Antonio	13	2/2	2/7	3/6	1	0	0	3	3	17:23	
VICTORIANO, Justino	4	2/5	0/1	0/2	0	2	2	3	5	20:16	
ROMANO, Benjamin	1	0/0	0/1	1/2	1	0	1	1	0	04:13	
GUIMARAES, Jose	0	0/1	0/2	0/0	2	1	1	3	1	10:19	
CONCEICAO, Jean-Jacques	0	0/0	0/0	0/0	0	0	0	0	0	00:00	
Totals	67	14/30	9/32	12/21	15	11	21	27	28		

Referees: PIOVESAN NETO, Jose   BRA   BREA DIAZ, Juan   CUB

Team: LTU Lithuania
Coach: GARASTAS, Vladas   Assistant Coaches: KAZLAUSKAS, Jonas   NELSON, Donn

Names	Pts	2 Pts	3 Pts	FT	A	Stl	To	Reb	F	Mins	
KURTINAITIS, Rimas	12	0/3	3/7	3/5	1	1	3	4	3	36:57	S
SABONIS, Arvydas	20	7/9	0/2	6/9	3	2	2	14	5	47:44	S
KARNISOVAS, Arturas	16	3/4	0/2	10/15	4	1	1	6	4	41:29	S
MARCIULIONIS, Sarunas	14	4/8	0/5	6/8	1	1	5	1	5	33:10	S
EINIKIS, Gintaras	9	4/8	0/0	1/1	0	0	0	2	4	21:08	S
VAISVILA, Rytis	4	2/2	0/1	0/0	6	1	2	1	1	31:37	
ZUKAUSKAS, Mindaugas	0	0/2	0/1	0/0	1	2	0	1	5	14:01	
ZUKAUSKAS, Eurelijus	0	0/0	0/0	0/0	0	0	0	0	1	02:16	
PACESAS, Tomas	0	0/0	0/0	0/0	0	0	0	0	0	00:00	
STOMBERGAS, Saulius	8	1/1	1/2	3/4	0	0	0	2	5	11:33	
LUKMINAS, Darius	0	0/1	0/1	0/0	0	1	1	0	1	10:05	
Totals	83	21/38	4/21	29/42	16	9	14	31	34		

Team: CRO Croatia
Coach: SKANSI, Petar   Assistant Coaches: REPESA, Jasmin   KROLO, Mirko

Names	Pts	2 Pts	3 Pts	FT	A	Stl	To	Reb	F	Mins	
KOMAZEC, Arijan	4	2/3	0/1	0/0	0	0	1	1	5	25:16	S
ALANOVIC, Vladan	4	1/1	0/2	2/2	0	0	3	1	4	23:02	S
VRANKOVIC, Stojan	8	3/4	0/0	2/2	0	0	3	4	5	15:55	S
RADJA, Dino	12	2/9	0/0	8/10	2	2	0	12	3	40:19	S
MARCELIC, Davor	0	0/3	0/2	0/0	0	0	1	3	2	22:38	S
VRANKOVIC, Josip	0	0/0	0/0	0/0	0	0	0	0	0	00:00	
PERASOVIC, Velimir	8	1/2	1/1	3/4	0	1	2	1	5	26:12	
KUKOC, Toni	33	3/9	3/7	18/22	6	1	4	11	3	44:51	
RIMAC, Slaven	9	1/1	1/2	4/6	0	1	5	1	0	19:07	
TABAK, Zan	3	1/3	0/0	1/3	0	0	3	3	5	19:49	
MULAOMEROVIC, Damir	0	0/1	0/2	0/0	1	0	0	1	5	07:51	
MRSIC, Veljko	0	0/2	0/0	0/0	0	0	0	0	0	05:00	
Totals	81	14/38	5/17	38/49	9	5	22	38	37		

Referees: BETANCOR LEON, Miguel   ESP   LAPAIX GUANCE, Jose   DOM

Team: USA United States of America
Coach: WILKENS, Lenny   Assistant Coaches: CREMINS, Bobby   SLOAN, Jerry

Names	Pts	2 Pts	3 Pts	FT	A	Stl	To	Reb	F	Mins	
BARKLEY, Charles	9	4/5	0/0	1/1	0	0	1	4	2	14:39	S
ROBINSON, David	18	5/7	0/0	8/10	0	1	3	7	2	17:19	S
PIPPEN, Scottie	8	3/7	0/0	2/2	2	3	2	4	2	22:31	S
MILLER, Reggie	6	2/2	0/3	2/2	2	0	1	2	3	22:04	S
STOCKTON, John	6	2/2	0/1	2/2	3	1	4	0	2	12:01	S
HILL, Grant	10	5/7	0/0	0/0	5	1	2	4	1	25:22	
HARDAWAY, Anfernee	4	1/3	0/0	2/2	5	2	2	5	1	22:47	
RICHMOND, Mitch	9	1/3	1/1	4/4	1	1	3	1	2	23:12	
MALONE, Karl	5	2/4	0/0	1/2	0	0	1	2	2	09:43	
O'NEAL, Shaquille	13	6/8	0/0	1/3	0	1	0	4	0	12:57	
PAYTON, Gary	2	1/3	0/1	0/2	2	0	1	3	4	10:22	
OLAJUWON, Hakeem	6	3/5	0/0	0/0	0	1	0	1	4	07:03	
Totals	96	35/56	1/6	23/30	20	11	20	37	25		

Team: ARG Argentina
Coach: VECCHIO, Guillermo   Assistant Coaches: MAGNANO, Ruben   DURO, Fernando

Names	Pts	2 Pts	3 Pts	FT	A	Stl	To	Reb	F	Mins	
NICOLA, Marcelo	13	2/3	2/6	3/4	2	3	4	4	4	30:16	S
MILANESIO, Marcelo	8	1/3	1/2	3/3	7	1	3	2	2	35:46	S
ESPIL, Juan	27	4/8	3/7	10/11	0	2	3	2	2	32:30	S
OSELLA, Diego	1	0/1	0/0	1/4	1	0	1	0	3	15:19	S
WOLKOWISKY, Ruben	9	2/5	0/1	5/10	1	1	4	2	3	27:44	S
FARABELLO, Daniel	0	0/0	0/0	0/0	0	1	2	0	0	04:45	
VILLAR, Luis	0	0/0	0/0	0/0	0	0	0	0	3	03:51	
de la FUENTE, Esteban	0	0/0	0/0	0/0	0	0	0	0	0	00:00	
MICHEL, Ernesto	2	1/1	0/0	0/0	0	1	1	1	1	02:30	
OBERTO, Fabricio	0	0/1	0/0	0/0	0	1	4	3	1	09:37	
RACCA, Jorge	6	1/2	1/2	1/2	2	1	3	3	3	27:23	
PEREZ, Esteban	2	1/1	0/2	0/0	0	0	0	0	1	10:19	
Totals	68	12/25	7/20	23/34	14	10	25	17	23		

Referees: COLUCCI, Gennaro   ITA   KOUKOULEKIDIS, Stylianos   GRE

Team: CRO Croatia
Coach: SKANSI, Petar   Assistant Coaches: REPESA, Jasmin   KROLO, Mirko

Names	Pts	2 Pts	3 Pts	FT	A	Stl	To	Reb	F	Mins	
KOMAZEC, Arijan	36	5/8	6/7	8/9	6	3	0	5	4	34:25	S
KUKOC, Toni	9	1/4	2/4	1/2	12	1	4	2	1	32:41	S
ALANOVIC, Vladan	2	1/1	0/0	0/0	1	0	0	0	1	10:17	S
VRANKOVIC, Stojan	2	0/2	0/1	2/4	2	1	2	9	3	23:11	S
RADJA, Dino	21	7/10	0/0	7/9	3	2	4	7	4	34:25	S
VRANKOVIC, Josip	0	0/0	0/0	0/0	0	0	0	0	0	00:00	
PERASOVIC, Velimir	0	0/0	0/0	0/0	0	0	0	0	0	00:00	
RIMAC, Slaven	2	1/2	0/1	0/0	1	0	1	0	1	09:43	
TABAK, Zan	24	10/13	0/0	4/4	1	0	2	8	1	22:24	
MULAOMEROVIC, Damir	7	2/2	1/2	0/0	4	3	0	2	2	20:00	
MRSIC, Veljko	0	0/0	0/0	0/0	0	0	0	0	0	00:00	
MARCELIC, Davor	6	0/0	2/4	0/0	1	0	1	1	1	12:54	
Totals	109	27/42	11/19	22/28	31	10	14	34	18		

Team: CHN People's Republic of China
Coach: GONG, Lu-ming   Assistant Coach: CHEN, De-Chun

Names	Pts	2 Pts	3 Pts	FT	A	Stl	To	Reb	F	Mins	
LI, Xiao-yong	14	3/4	2/4	2/2	4	0	3	2	4	32:41	S
ZHENG, Wu	15	5/8	1/1	2/2	0	1	4	2	1	21:59	S
SUN, Jun	8	1/3	2/5	0/0	6	0	2	1	1	28:18	S
LIU, Yu-dong	2	1/3	0/0	0/0	1	0	0	0	0	06:41	S
BA, Tere	4	2/4	0/0	0/0	1	1	0	3	5	16:07	S
WANG, Zhi-zhi	15	2/9	0/0	11/12	0	1	2	7	4	29:43	
HU, Wei-dong	7	1/2	1/7	2/2	3	3	1	1	2	29:43	
WU, Nai-qin	0	0/0	0/0	0/0	0	0	0	0	0	00:00	
WU, Qing-long	0	0/0	0/0	0/0	0	0	0	0	0	00:00	
LI, Nan	1	0/1	0/0	1/2	0	0	2	2	1	07:19	
SHAN, Tao	0	0/0	0/0	0/0	0	0	0	0	0	00:00	
GONG, Xiao-bin	12	3/9	1/1	3/4	1	2	1	8	1	27:29	
Totals	78	18/43	7/19	21/24	16	8	15	26	19		

Referees: PELISSARI, Jose   BRA   KIM, Chul-Hwan   KOR

Men / *Messieurs*

PRELIMINARIES - GROUP A — FINAL SCORE: ARG 65 LTU 61 / HALFTIME SCORE: ARG 31 LTU 25

Team: ARG Argentina
Coach: VECCHIO, Guillermo Assistant Coaches: MAGNANO, Ruben DURO, Fernando

Names	Pts	2 Pts	3 Pts	FT	A	Stl	To	Reb	F	Mins	
NICOLA, Marcelo	6	2/2	0/2	2/2	0	1	3	2	0	15:11	S
MILANESIO, Marcelo	15	1/3	4/6	1/2	6	1	1	3	1	39:06	S
ESPIL, Juan	25	3/7	4/11	7/8	2	2	4	6	2	35:42	S
RACCA, Jorge	0	0/2	0/1	0/0	2	4	0	0	1	19:18	S
WOLKOWISKY, Ruben	2	1/3	0/0	0/0	0	0	1	4	4	21:24	S
FARABELLO, Daniel	0	0/0	0/0	0/0	0	0	0	0	0	00:46	
VILLAR, Luis	8	1/2	1/1	3/3	0	0	0	2	5	17:36	
de la FUENTE, Esteban	4	2/3	0/2	0/1	0	0	2	1	1	15:52	
MICHEL, Ernesto	0	0/0	0/0	0/0	0	0	0	0	0	00:00	
OSELLA, Diego	2	0/2	0/0	2/4	0	2	2	1	0	21:19	
OBERTO, Fabricio	0	0/0	0/0	0/0	0	1	0	0	2	04:30	
PEREZ, Esteban	3	0/0	1/2	0/0	1	0	0	0	0	09:16	
Totals	65	10/24	10/25	15/20	11	11	13	19	16		

Team: LTU Lithuania
Coach: GARASTAS, Vladas Assistant Coaches: KAZLAUSKAS, Jonas NELSON, Donn

Names	Pts	2 Pts	3 Pts	FT	A	Stl	To	Reb	F	Mins	
STOMBERGAS, Saulius	6	3/4	0/2	0/1	2	0	1	2	3	32:09	S
KURTINAITIS, Rimas	5	1/3	1/6	0/0	2	2	3	4	3	23:43	S
SABONIS, Arvydas	30	11/14	0/1	8/8	2	4	3	11	4	40:00	S
MARCIULIONIS, Sarunas	6	2/6	0/2	2/4	8	1	2	2	3	33:48	S
EINIKIS, Gintaras	12	6/12	0/0	0/0	0	2	0	4	3	35:07	S
VAISVILA, Rytis	0	0/0	0/1	0/0	2	0	3	3	4	19:32	
ZUKAUSKAS, Mindaugas	0	0/0	0/0	0/0	0	0	0	1	0	04:11	
ZUKAUSKAS, Eurelijus	0	0/0	0/0	0/0	0	0	0	0	0	00:00	
PACESAS, Tomas	0	0/0	0/0	0/0	0	0	0	0	0	00:00	
LUKMINAS, Darius	2	1/1	0/1	0/0	2	0	2	1	2	11:30	
KARNISOVAS, Arturas	0	0/0	0/0	0/0	0	0	0	0	0	00:00	
Totals	61	24/40	1/13	10/13	18	9	14	28	22		

Referees: JUNGEBRAND, Carl FIN FIGUEROA, Juan PUR

PRELIMINARIES - GROUP A — FINAL SCORE: ANG 54 USA 87 / HALFTIME SCORE: ANG 31 USA 44

Team: ANG Angola
Coach: ROMERO, Vladimiro Assistant Coach: TAVARES, Nelson

Names	Pts	2 Pts	3 Pts	FT	A	Stl	To	Reb	F	Mins	
MOREIRA, Anibal	2	0/2	0/2	2/2	3	0	1	1	4	24:44	S
VICTORIANO, Angelo	8	1/5	2/4	0/0	1	1	4	2	3	22:17	S
UCUAHAMBA, Benjamin	2	1/3	0/2	0/0	5	1	1	1	4	27:09	S
CARVALHO, Antonio	16	2/2	4/9	0/0	1	1	2	4	1	28:45	S
DIAS, David	10	1/4	2/6	2/2	0	0	2	5	2	30:58	S
VICTORIANO, Edmar	4	0/1	0/1	4/4	2	1	1	0	4	15:16	
TROSO, Honorato	0	0/0	0/0	0/0	0	0	0	0	0	00:00	
COIMBRA, Herlander	0	0/0	0/1	0/0	0	0	0	1	0	07:33	
VICTORIANO, Justino	6	3/5	0/0	0/0	0	0	6	1	4	26:45	
ROMANO, Benjamin	6	0/1	2/3	0/0	0	0	0	1	0	11:15	
GUIMARAES, Jose	0	0/1	0/0	0/0	0	0	1	1	0	05:18	
CONCEICAO, Jean-Jacques	0	0/0	0/0	0/0	0	0	0	0	0	00:00	
Totals	54	8/24	10/28	8/8	12	4	18	17	22		

Team: USA United States of America
Coach: WILKENS, Lenny Assistant Coaches: CREMINS, Bobby SLOAN, Jerry

Names	Pts	2 Pts	3 Pts	FT	A	Stl	To	Reb	F	Mins	
HILL, Grant	7	2/3	0/0	3/3	3	1	0	6	2	19:33	S
HARDAWAY, Anfernee	2	1/1	0/2	0/1	2	0	2	2	2	16:50	S
RICHMOND, Mitch	10	2/4	2/4	0/0	2	1	1	1	2	19:18	S
MALONE, Karl	12	6/11	0/0	0/0	0	2	0	6	0	21:59	S
O'NEAL, Shaquille	7	3/7	0/0	1/3	1	1	1	3	1	19:50	S
BARKLEY, Charles	7	3/3	0/0	1/2	7	0	1	9	2	18:01	
ROBINSON, David	4	2/4	0/0	0/0	0	0	0	1	0	10:03	
PIPPEN, Scottie	11	5/9	0/0	1/2	3	2	0	2	2	20:27	
MILLER, Reggie	10	2/3	2/3	0/0	0	0	0	2	0	20:42	
STOCKTON, John	7	1/1	1/1	2/2	2	1	2	1	1	09:23	
PAYTON, Gary	8	3/4	0/1	2/3	3	1	2	2	2	13:47	
OLAJUWON, Hakeem	2	0/0	0/0	2/2	1	0	2	2	1	10:07	
Totals	87	30/50	5/11	12/18	24	9	11	37	15		

Referees: BUTLER, Michael AUS JOVANCIC, Tomislav YUG

PRELIMINARIES - GROUP A — FINAL SCORE: CHN 87 ARG 77 / HALFTIME SCORE: CHN 51 ARG 38

Team: CHN People's Republic of China
Coach: GONG, Lu-ming Assistant Coach: CHEN, De-Chun

Names	Pts	2 Pts	3 Pts	FT	A	Stl	To	Reb	F	Mins	
LI, Xiao-yong	17	3/5	1/4	8/8	5	0	1	8	2	40:00	S
ZHENG, Wu	22	7/11	0/2	8/8	0	0	2	9	1	40:00	S
SUN, Jun	0	0/1	0/0	0/0	3	0	1	1	1	06:21	S
LIU, Yu-dong	10	4/10	0/0	2/2	2	3	3	3	3	16:26	S
BA, Tere	4	1/1	0/0	2/2	0	0	1	2	4	10:26	S
WANG, Zhi-zhi	4	1/8	0/0	2/3	0	1	2	6	5	23:34	
HU, Wei-dong	22	5/6	2/4	6/9	4	4	3	1	2	33:39	
WU, Nai-qin	0	0/0	0/0	0/0	0	0	0	0	0	00:00	
WU, Qing-long	0	0/0	0/0	0/0	0	0	0	0	0	00:00	
LI, Nan	0	0/0	0/0	0/0	0	0	0	0	1	00:00	
SHAN, Tao	0	0/0	0/0	0/0	0	0	0	0	0	00:00	
GONG, Xiao-bin	8	2/7	0/0	4/6	4	2	2	4	2	29:34	
Totals	87	23/49	3/10	32/38	18	10	15	34	20		

Team: ARG Argentina
Coach: VECCHIO, Guillermo Assistant Coach: MAGNANO, Ruben DURO, Fernando

Names	Pts	2 Pts	3 Pts	FT	A	Stl	To	Reb	F	Mins	
VILLAR, Luis	5	2/6	0/0	1/2	0	0	1	2	4	22:28	S
MILANESIO, Marcelo	9	0/0	3/5	0/0	8	1	3	4	2	36:22	S
ESPIL, Juan	25	3/5	6/10	1/1	2	1	5	1	4	31:52	S
OSELLA, Diego	4	0/3	0/0	4/4	1	0	1	5	5	31:01	S
RACCA, Jorge	12	1/1	2/9	4/4	0	1	0	2	2	13:19	S
NICOLA, Marcelo	0	0/0	0/0	0/0	0	0	0	0	0	00:00	
FARABELLO, Daniel	0	0/0	0/0	0/0	0	0	0	0	1	03:38	
de la FUENTE, Esteban	2	1/7	0/2	0/0	4	1	3	5	3	20:16	
MICHEL, Ernesto	2	1/1	0/0	0/2	0	0	0	1	2	03:11	
OBERTO, Fabricio	8	3/8	0/0	2/2	1	1	1	2	3	20:31	
PEREZ, Esteban	10	5/6	0/7	0/0	2	3	3	7	1	17:22	
WOLKOWISKY, Ruben	0	0/0	0/0	0/0	0	0	0	0	0	00:00	
Totals	77	16/37	11/33	12/15	18	8	17	29	27		

Referees: BARNETT, Robert AUS RYZHYK, Roman UKR

PRELIMINARIES - GROUP A — FINAL SCORE CRO 71 ANG 48 / HALFTIME SCORE: CRO 26 ANG 23

Team: CRO Croatia
Coach: SKANSI, Petar Assistant Coaches: REPESA, Jasmin KROLO, Mirko

Names	Pts	2 Pts	3 Pts	FT	A	Stl	To	Reb	F	Mins	
KOMAZEC, Arijan	11	2/6	2/8	1/3	1	2	4	8	2	40:00	S
KUKOC, Toni	16	2/5	0/6	12/16	6	2	4	8	1	40:00	S
ALANOVIC, Vladan	0	0/1	0/1	0/0	0	2	0	3	2	20:00	S
TABAK, Zan	3	1/3	0/0	1/2	0	0	3	6	4	13:49	S
RADJA, Dino	20	8/18	0/0	4/6	2	0	2	9	2	40:00	S
VRANKOVIC, Josip	0	0/0	0/0	0/0	0	0	0	0	0	00:00	
PERASOVIC, Velimir	0	0/0	0/0	0/0	0	0	0	0	0	00:00	
RIMAC, Slaven	0	0/0	0/0	0/0	0	0	0	0	0	00:00	
VRANKOVIC, Stojan	13	5/7	0/0	3/5	0	0	1	8	2	26:11	
MULAOMEROVIC, Damir	8	2/3	0/0	4/4	0	0	0	3	1	20:00	
MRSIC, Veljko	0	0/0	0/0	0/0	0	0	0	0	0	00:00	
MARCELIC, Davor	0	0/0	0/0	0/0	0	0	0	0	0	00:00	
Totals	71	20/43	2/15	25/36	9	6	14	45	14		

Team: ANG Angola
Coach: ROMERO, Vladimiro Assistant Coach: TAVARES, Nelson

Names	Pts	2 Pts	3 Pts	FT	A	Stl	To	Reb	F	Mins	
MOREIRA, Anibal	9	2/6	1/1	2/3	1	2	3	5	4	20:08	S
UCUAHAMBA, Benjamin	2	1/3	0/1	0/0	2	0	4	4	2	28:23	S
CARVALHO, Antonio	2	1/3	0/3	0/0	1	0	1	2	6	24:56	S
VICTORIANO, Justino	5	2/5	0/0	1/1	0	0	1	2	2	18:21	S
DIAS, David	10	4/15	0/2	2/4	1	2	4	12	4	36:32	S
VICTORIANO, Edmar	4	2/6	0/0	0/0	0	2	4	6	5	23:03	
VICTORIANO, Angelo	10	0/4	3/6	1/1	0	2	0	5	4	25:07	
TROSO, Honorato	0	0/0	0/0	0/0	0	0	0	0	0	00:00	
COIMBRA, Herlander	6	0/1	2/5	0/0	0	0	0	1	4	11:53	
ROMANO, Benjamin	0	0/2	0/0	0/0	0	0	0	1	0	11:37	
GUIMARAES, Jose	0	0/0	0/0	0/0	0	0	0	0	0	00:00	
CONCEICAO, Jean-Jacques	0	0/0	0/0	0/0	0	0	0	0	0	00:00	
Totals	48	12/45	6/18	6/9	5	8	17	38	31		

Referees: ISHIDA, Hidetoshi JPN BOULANOV, Serguei RUS

PRELIMINARIES - GROUP A   FINAL SCORE: LTU 82   USA 104   HALFTIME SCORE: LTU 42   USA 50

Team: LTU Lithuania

Coach: GARASTAS, Vladas   Assistant Coach: KAZLAUSKAS, Jonas   NELSON, Donn

Names	Pts	2 Pts	3 Pts	FT	A	Stl	To	Reb	F	Mins	
VAISVILA, Rytis	7	2/2	1/3	0/0	1	0	2	1	1	25:13	S
STOMBERGAS, Saulius	5	0/1	1/3	2/2	1	1	2	1	3	21:31	S
KURTINAITIS, Rimas	8	1/1	1/4	3/3	1	1	0	1	2	14:17	S
SABONIS, Arvydas	6	0/4	2/2	0/0	1	0	2	2	2	12:14	S
EINIKIS, Gintaras	21	8/14	0/1	5/5	2	0	4	7	3	36:03	S
ZUKAUSKAS, Mindaugas	0	0/2	0/0	0/0	0	0	1	0	4	08:01	
ZUKAUSKAS, Eurelijus	0	0/1	0/1	0/0	0	0	1	6	5	16:45	
PACESAS, Tomas	5	1/2	1/1	0/0	5	0	4	3	2	18:42	
LUKMINAS, Darius	15	3/4	3/4	0/0	1	0	4	0	2	21:48	
KARNISOVAS, Arturas	15	3/5	1/2	6/8	4	1	2	7	4	25:26	
MARCIULIONIS, Sarunas	0	0/0	0/0	0/0	0	0	0	0	0	00:00	
Totals	82	18/36	10/21	16/18	16	3	22	28	28		

Team: USA United States of America

Coach: WILKENS, Lenny   Assistant Coach: CREMINS, Bobby   SLOAN, Jerry

Names	Pts	2 Pts	3 Pts	FT	A	Stl	To	Reb	F	Mins	
BARKLEY, Charles	16	4/5	0/1	8/12	3	1	1	5	1	18:34	S
PIPPEN, Scottie	13	6/7	0/2	1/5	1	1	1	4	3	20:52	S
MILLER, Reggie	14	2/5	3/6	1/1	2	3	0	1	1	22:44	S
PAYTON, Gary	8	0/0	2/2	2/2	4	1	3	2	2	19:05	S
OLAJUWON, Hakeem	2	1/4	0/0	0/0	3	2	1	3	3	13:17	S
HILL, Grant	9	2/2	1/3	2/4	3	5	0	2	2	22:53	
HARDAWAY, Anfernee	6	1/1	1/2	1/2	3	2	1	2	0	11:06	
ROBINSON, David	6	2/5	0/0	2/3	0	0	0	2	2	09:18	
RICHMOND, Mitch	7	0/2	2/4	1/4	1	1	0	3	1	17:16	
MALONE, Karl	14	5/7	0/0	4/4	2	0	0	3	3	18:41	
STOCKTON, John	3	1/2	0/0	1/2	4	2	1	2	1	12:25	
O'NEAL, Shaquille	6	3/6	0/0	0/1	2	0	1	3	1	13:49	
Totals	104	27/46	9/20	23/40	28	18	9	33	20		

Referees: ZYCH, Wieslaw POL   REYES RONFINI, Jose   MEX

PRELIMINARIES - GROUP A   FINAL SCORE: ANG 49   LTU 85   HALFTIME SCORE: ANG 21   LTU 37

Team: ANG Angola

Coach: ROMERO, Vladimiro   Assistant Coach: TAVARES, Nelson

Names	Pts	2 Pts	3 Pts	FT	A	Stl	To	Reb	F	Mins	
MOREIRA, Anibal	5	0/8	0/5	5/6	3	0	0	6	4	31:54	S
VICTORIANO, Angelo	18	4/5	3/6	1/2	1	0	0	1	4	22:07	S
UCUAHAMBA, Benjamin	7	1/2	1/1	2/2	1	0	0	0	4	21:53	S
CARVALHO, Antonio	1	0/5	0/2	1/2	4	2	1	3	1	24:27	S
DIAS, David	9	4/8	0/3	1/2	1	1	2	6	1	31:16	S
VICTORIANO, Edmar	0	0/1	0/1	0/0	0	0	0	4	0	09:15	
TROSO, Honorato	0	0/0	0/0	0/0	0	0	0	0	0	00:00	
COIMBRA, Herlander	0	0/0	0/5	0/0	0	1	0	0	0	07:36	
VICTORIANO, Justino	9	4/8	0/0	1/2	0	2	1	2	1	33:25	
ROMANO, Benjamin	0	0/1	0/0	0/2	0	0	0	0	0	05:01	
GUIMARAES, Jose	0	0/2	0/2	0/0	0	1	2	3	2	13:06	
CONCEICAO, Jean-Jacques	0	0/0	0/0	0/0	0	0	0	0	0	00:00	
Totals	49	13/40	4/25	11/18	10	7	7	25	17		

Team: LTU Lithuania

Coach: GARASTAS, Vladas   Assistant Coaches: KAZLAUSKAS, Jonas   NELSON, Donn

Names	Pts	2 Pts	3 Pts	FT	A	Stl	To	Reb	F	Mins	
VAISVILA, Rytis	4	0/0	1/2	1/2	6	0	3	5	1	15:37	S
STOMBERGAS, Saulius	9	3/5	1/1	0/0	1	0	1	4	3	27:26	S
KURTINAITIS, Rimas	9	0/0	3/9	0/0	2	0	2	2	2	25:59	S
SABONIS, Arvydas	12	2/7	1/1	5/5	8	0	0	10	3	22:48	S
KARNISOVAS, Arturas	20	8/9	1/3	1/2	2	1	0	5	2	27:32	S
ZUKAUSKAS, Mindaugas	6	3/4	0/1	0/0	2	1	1	2	2	12:11	
ZUKAUSKAS, Eurelijus	1	0/0	0/0	1/2	2	0	1	3	1	09:42	
PACESAS, Tomas	2	1/1	0/1	0/0	1	0	4	3	2	14:01	
LUKMINAS, Darius	15	0/2	4/5	3/3	0	1	1	4	2	27:29	
MARCIULIONIS, Sarunas	0	0/0	0/0	0/0	0	0	0	0	0	00:00	
EINIKIS, Gintaras	7	2/3	0/0	3/4	1	0	0	6	0	17:15	
Totals	85	19/32	11/23	14/18	25	3	13	44	18		

Referees: PELISSARI, Jose BRA   BARNETT, Robert AUS

PRELIMINARIES - GROUP A   FINAL SCORE: ARG 75   CRO 90   HALFTIME SCORE: ARG 29   CRO 43

Team: ARG Argentina

Coach: VECCHIO, Guillermo   Assistant Coaches: MAGNANO, Ruben   DURO, Fernando

Names	Pts	2 Pts	3 Pts	FT	A	Stl	To	Reb	F	Mins	
VILLAR, Luis	14	6/9	0/2	2/2	0	0	2	3	4	21:58	S
MILANESIO, Marcelo	8	3/4	0/4	2/2	5	0	0	2	3	33:28	S
ESPIL, Juan	17	3/10	1/5	8/8	3	2	1	4	4	35:46	S
OSELLA, Diego	8	4/5	0/1	0/0	0	0	1	6	4	28:51	S
PEREZ, Esteban	5	1/3	1/3	0/0	0	1	0	3	4	23:19	S
NICOLA, Marcelo	0	0/0	0/0	0/0	0	0	0	0	0	00:00	
FARABELLO, Daniel	0	0/1	0/1	0/0	2	1	3	0	2	08:32	
de la FUENTE, Esteban	0	0/0	0/0	0/0	0	0	0	0	0	00:00	
MICHEL, Ernesto	0	0/0	0/0	0/0	0	0	0	0	0	00:00	
OBERTO, Fabricio	8	2/5	0/0	4/6	1	0	1	4	5	20:45	
RACCA, Jorge	15	6/8	0/3	3/6	2	1	2	4	2	27:21	
WOLKOWISKY, Ruben	0	0/0	0/0	0/0	0	0	0	0	0	00:00	
Totals	75	25/45	2/19	19/24	13	5	10	26	28		

Team: CRO Croatia

Coach: SKANSI, Petar   Assistant Coaches: REPESA, Jasmin   KROLO, Mirko

Names	Pts	2 Pts	3 Pts	FT	A	Stl	To	Reb	F	Mins	
KOMAZEC, Arijan	28	5/8	3/3	9/9	3	1	3	7	5	38:58	S
KUKOC, Toni	12	5/9	0/4	2/3	7	0	3	8	1	33:20	S
ALANOVIC, Vladan	14	3/4	2/4	2/5	2	0	1	3	5	33:21	S
RADJA, Dino	3	1/5	0/0	1/2	0	0	0	6	4	13:16	S
MARCELIC, Davor	4	2/2	0/1	0/0	0	0	0	4	3	25:57	S
VRANKOVIC, Josip	10	3/3	1/2	1/4	2	1	2	5	3	15:05	
PERASOVIC, Velimir	0	0/0	0/0	0/0	0	0	0	0	0	00:00	
RIMAC, Slaven	0	0/0	0/0	0/0	0	0	0	0	0	00:51	
TABAK, Zan	18	6/10	0/0	6/6	0	0	2	5	5	30:31	
VRANKOVIC, Stojan	0	0/0	0/0	0/0	0	0	0	0	0	00:00	
MULAOMEROVIC, Damir	1	0/0	0/1	1/4	3	0	1	0	0	08:41	
MRSIC, Veljko	0	0/0	0/0	0/0	0	0	0	0	0	00:00	
Totals	90	25/41	6/15	22/33	17	2	12	38	26		

Referees: PIOVESAN NETO, Jose BRA   DORIZON, Pascal Noel FRA

PRELIMINARIES - GROUP A   FINAL SCORE: USA 133   CHN 70   HALFTIME SCORE: USA 65   CHN 28

Team: USA United States of America

Coach: WILKENS, Lenny   Assistant Coaches: CREMINS, Bobby   SLOAN, Jerry

Names	Pts	2 Pts	3 Pts	FT	A	Stl	To	Reb	F	Mins	
PIPPEN, Scottie	24	6/9	4/5	0/0	4	0	0	2	0	17:20	S
MILLER, Reggie	17	1/1	5/8	0/0	1	1	0	1	1	18:08	S
MALONE, Karl	11	5/7	0/0	1/2	3	2	3	6	2	22:41	S
O'NEAL, Shaquille	13	5/8	0/0	3/3	3	1	1	10	2	20:57	S
PAYTON, Gary	0	0/0	0/0	0/0	9	1	1	2	0	14:11	S
BARKLEY, Charles	0	0/0	0/0	0/0	0	0	0	0	0	00:00	
HILL, Grant	19	5/7	1/2	6/7	5	5	0	4	0	22:40	
HARDAWAY, Anfernee	15	6/6	0/2	3/3	10	4	3	1	0	21:16	
ROBINSON, David	8	4/4	0/0	0/0	0	0	1	3	0	06:32	
RICHMOND, Mitch	14	3/5	2/7	2/2	2	3	0	0	0	21:52	
STOCKTON, John	5	2/4	0/0	1/1	2	4	1	1	1	15:20	
OLAJUWON, Hakeem	7	3/6	0/0	1/2	2	0	2	5	0	19:03	
Totals	133	40/57	12/24	17/20	41	21	12	35	6		

Team: CHN People's Republic of China

Coach: GONG, Lu-ming   Assistant Coach: CHEN, De-Chun

Names	Pts	2 Pts	3 Pts	FT	A	Stl	To	Reb	F	Mins	
LI, Xiao-yong	2	1/2	0/2	0/0	5	1	3	3	1	30:47	S
ZHENG, Wu	5	1/2	1/3	0/0	1	1	2	1	1	20:00	S
SUN, Jun	7	2/2	1/3	0/0	4	1	9	3	2	25:56	S
LIU, Yu-dong	18	7/13	0/1	4/7	2	1	4	5	1	26:36	S
BA, Tere	6	3/6	0/0	0/0	1	2	2	6	5	22:29	S
WANG, Zhi-zhi	6	3/6	0/1	0/0	1	1	5	3	4	24:46	
HU, Wei-dong	15	3/3	3/6	0/0	3	1	2	3	0	20:00	
WU, Nai-qin	0	0/0	0/0	0/0	0	0	0	0	0	06:09	
WU, Qing-long	7	0/0	2/4	1/2	0	0	2	0	2	09:13	
LI, Nan	4	2/3	0/3	0/0	1	1	4	3	2	14:04	
SHAN, Tao	0	0/0	0/0	0/0	0	0	0	0	0	00:00	
GONG, Xiao-bin	0	0/0	0/0	0/0	0	0	0	0	0	00:00	
Totals	70	22/37	7/23	5/9	18	9	33	27	18		

Referees: CLINE, Donald CAN   ISHIDA, Hidetoshi JPN

Men / Messieurs

PRELIMINARIES - GROUP A — FINAL SCORE: CHN 55 LTU 116 — HALFTIME SCORE: CHN 23 LTU 53

Team: CHN People's Republic of China
Coach: GONG, Lu-ming — Assistant Coach: CHEN, De-Chun

Names	Pts	2 Pts	3 Pts	FT	A	Stl	To	Reb	F	Mins	
LI, Xiao-yong	9	0/3	3/7	0/0	4	1	5	2	2	40:00	S
ZHENG, Wu	0	0/1	0/1	0/0	0	0	1	0	0	13:03	S
SUN, Jun	2	1/1	0/2	0/0	0	0	0	0	2	20:00	S
WU, Nai-qin	0	0/1	0/0	0/0	0	0	0	1	0	03:18	S
BA, Tere	0	0/2	0/0	0/0	2	0	2	2	5	13:39	S
WANG, Zhi-zhi	18	7/15	0/0	4/4	0	0	3	5	1	28:23	
HU, Wei-dong	8	1/2	2/5	0/0	1	0	2	2	3	20:00	
WU, Qing-long	0	0/0	0/0	0/0	0	0	0	0	0	00:00	
LIU, Yu-dong	6	3/7	0/1	0/0	0	0	0	3	3	14:40	
LI, Nan	12	4/7	1/2	1/2	1	0	1	4	2	26:57	
SHAN, Tao	0	0/0	0/0	0/0	0	0	0	0	0	00:00	
GONG, Xiao-bin	0	0/4	0/0	0/0	0	0	2	0	2	20:00	
Totals	55	16/43	6/18	5/6	8	1	17	19	20		

Team: LTU Lithuania
Coach: GARASTAS, Vladas — Assistant Coaches: KAZLAUSKAS, Jonas   NELSON, Donn

Names	Pts	2 Pts	3 Pts	FT	A	Stl	To	Reb	F	Mins	
KURTINAITIS, Rimas	17	1/2	5/7	0/0	2	0	1	4	1	22:14	S
SABONIS, Arvydas	13	6/9	0/1	1/1	3	3	1	7	0	20:28	S
KARNISOVAS, Arturas	12	2/6	0/1	8/9	5	0	1	7	2	26:03	S
MARCIULIONIS, Sarunas	10	2/3	2/2	0/0	7	1	1	3	0	21:59	S
EINIKIS, Gintaras	14	5/7	0/0	4/5	0	2	2	9	2	22:45	S
VAISVILA, Rytis	0	0/0	0/0	0/0	3	1	0	0	0	11:20	
ZUKAUSKAS, Mindaugas	10	4/8	0/0	2/2	1	0	0	4	1	14:18	
ZUKAUSKAS, Eurelijus	6	3/6	0/0	0/2	0	0	0	5	2	13:08	
PACESAS, Tomas	0	0/1	0/0	0/0	4	0	0	2	0	10:45	
STOMBERGAS, Saulius	19	6/8	2/3	1/1	1	1	1	2	2	19:14	
LUKMINAS, Darius	15	3/3	3/4	0/0	1	0	0	0	1	17:46	
Totals	116	32/53	12/18	16/20	27	8	7	43	11		

Referees: REYES RONFINI, Jose MEX — FIGUEROA, Juan PUR

PRELIMINARIES - GROUP A — FINAL SCORE: CRO 71 USA 102 — HALFTIME SCORE: CRO 38 USA 57

Team: CRO Croatia
Coach: SKANSI, Petar — Assistant Coaches: REPESA, Jasmin   KROLO, Mirko

Names	Pts	2 Pts	3 Pts	FT	A	Stl	To	Reb	F	Mins	
KUKOC, Toni	10	2/5	2/6	0/0	10	0	3	3	1	32:41	S
ALANOVIC, Vladan	2	1/3	0/2	0/0	2	2	2	2	1	27:18	S
RIMAC, Slaven	14	1/2	3/3	3/4	0	0	4	1	1	18:50	S
VRANKOVIC, Stojan	2	1/2	0/0	0/0	1	0	0	2	5	11:47	S
RADJA, Dino	9	4/11	0/0	1/2	0	0	3	4	3	34:57	S
VRANKOVIC, Josip	6	0/0	2/3	0/0	1	1	1	1	0	11:31	
PERASOVIC, Velimir	0	0/2	0/0	0/0	0	0	2	1	3	14:01	
KOMAZEC, Arijan	0	0/0	0/0	0/0	0	0	0	0	0	00:00	
TABAK, Zan	19	8/13	0/0	3/4	0	1	3	7	1	22:32	
MULAOMEROVIC, Damir	7	1/2	1/2	2/4	3	1	1	2	2	12:42	
MRSIC, Veljko	0	0/0	0/0	0/0	0	0	0	0	0	00:00	
MARCELIC, Davor	2	1/1	0/1	0/0	1	1	1	0	1	13:41	
Totals	71	19/41	8/17	9/14	18	6	21	23	18		

Team: USA United States of America
Coach: WILKENS, Lenny — Assistant Coaches: CREMINS, Bobby   SLOAN, Jerry

Names	Pts	2 Pts	3 Pts	FT	A	Stl	To	Reb	F	Mins	
BARKLEY, Charles	14	7/9	0/0	0/0	1	2	3	12	1	24:21	S
ROBINSON, David	13	4/5	0/0	5/9	0	1	0	3	2	15:21	S
PIPPEN, Scottie	9	0/2	3/7	0/0	3	2	0	1	1	19:00	S
RICHMOND, Mitch	16	4/5	1/3	5/5	3	1	0	5	0	24:39	S
PAYTON, Gary	8	1/3	1/2	3/4	7	1	0	4	1	21:52	S
HILL, Grant	9	4/6	0/0	1/2	2	3	2	0	3	21:00	
HARDAWAY, Anfernee	0	0/4	0/1	0/0	6	0	2	4	1	12:48	
MILLER, Reggie	7	2/4	1/3	0/0	3	1	1	0	0	15:21	
MALONE, Karl	10	4/5	0/0	2/4	1	2	2	3	3	15:39	
STOCKTON, John	2	1/2	0/0	0/0	2	1	0	2	1	05:20	
O'NEAL, Shaquille	8	3/5	0/0	2/4	0	1	0	3	2	12:09	
OLAJUWON, Hakeem	6	3/6	0/0	0/0	1	0	1	4	0	12:30	
Totals	102	33/56	6/16	18/28	29	15	11	41	15		

Referees: BARNETT, Robert AUS — JUNGEBRAND, Carl FIN

PRELIMINARIES - GROUP A — FINAL SCORE: ARG 66 ANG 62 — HALFTIME SCORE: ARG 27 ANG 32

Team: ARG Argentina
Coach: VECCHIO, Guillermo — Assistant Coaches: MAGNANO, Ruben   DURO, Fernando

Names	Pts	2 Pts	3 Pts	FT	A	Stl	To	Reb	F	Mins	
VILLAR, Luis	14	5/8	0/0	4/4	0	0	1	6	4	27:43	S
MILANESIO, Marcelo	2	1/1	0/1	0/0	3	2	2	3	1	28:15	S
ESPIL, Juan	21	3/8	4/6	3/4	4	0	1	2	0	35:51	S
OSELLA, Diego	4	2/5	0/0	0/0	5	1	1	2	3	28:35	S
RACCA, Jorge	10	2/5	1/2	3/3	2	0	1	4	1	38:57	S
NICOLA, Marcelo	0	0/0	0/0	0/0	0	0	0	0	0	00:00	
FARABELLO, Daniel	4	2/2	0/1	0/0	0	1	1	0	1	10:46	
de la FUENTE, Esteban	0	0/0	0/0	0/0	0	0	0	0	0	00:00	
MICHEL, Ernesto	0	0/1	0/0	0/0	0	1	0	1	1	06:58	
OBERTO, Fabricio	11	5/6	0/1	1/2	0	1	1	4	3	17:58	
PEREZ, Esteban	0	0/1	0/1	0/2	0	0	0	0	0	04:57	
WOLKOWISKY, Ruben	0	0/0	0/0	0/0	0	0	0	0	0	00:00	
Totals	66	20/37	5/12	11/15	14	6	9	22	14		

Team: ANG Angola
Coach: ROMERO, Vladimiro — Assistant Coach: TAVARES, Nelson

Names	Pts	2 Pts	3 Pts	FT	A	Stl	To	Reb	F	Mins	
MOREIRA, Anibal	14	4/7	2/3	0/1	3	0	2	7	5	33:11	S
VICTORIANO, Angelo	10	3/6	0/3	4/4	0	0	2	3	2	37:45	S
UCUAHAMBA, Benjamin	2	1/5	0/0	0/0	4	2	3	3	2	35:03	S
CARVALHO, Antonio	7	2/4	1/6	0/0	0	1	0	5	0	32:54	S
DIAS, David	17	6/14	0/0	5/6	2	1	0	7	3	34:38	S
VICTORIANO, Edmar	0	0/1	0/0	0/0	0	0	1	1	1	05:22	
TROSO, Honorato	0	0/0	0/0	0/0	0	0	0	0	0	01:39	
COIMBRA, Herlander	2	0/0	0/0	2/2	0	0	1	0	1	04:42	
VICTORIANO, Justino	8	3/4	0/0	2/2	0	0	0	4	2	07:37	
ROMANO, Benjamin	2	1/1	0/1	0/0	0	1	1	0	0	03:18	
GUIMARAES, Jose	0	0/0	0/0	0/0	2	1	0	0	1	03:51	
CONCEICAO, Jean-Jacques	0	0/0	0/0	0/0	0	0	0	0	0	00:00	
Totals	62	20/42	3/13	13/15	11	5	11	30	17		

Referees: ZYCH, Wieslaw POL — CHONG, Kyoung KOR

PRELIMINARIES - GROUP B — FINAL SCORE: AUS 111 KOR 88 — HALFTIME SCORE: AUS 64 KOR 37

Team: AUS Australia
Coach: BARNES, Barry — Assistant Coach: BLACK, Allan   BROWN, Brett

Names	Pts	2 Pts	3 Pts	FT	A	Stl	To	Reb	F	Mins	
RONALDSON, Tony	10	2/3	2/4	0/0	2	1	1	3	1	28:29	S
GAZE, Andrew	26	10/13	1/4	3/4	2	1	2	2	4	37:11	S
HEAL, Shane	23	2/2	5/12	4/5	11	1	6	3	3	33:45	S
BRADTKE, Mark	15	7/8	0/0	1/2	4	2	3	9	1	25:44	S
VLAHOV, Andrew	15	5/9	0/1	5/6	4	1	1	7	2	22:15	S
MAHER, Brett	0	0/3	0/0	0/0	1	0	0	1	0	09:04	
FISHER, Scott	14	5/6	0/1	4/4	1	0	2	4	1	17:37	
REIDY, Pat	0	0/0	0/0	0/0	0	0	1	0	1	02:26	
MacKINNON, Sam	7	3/6	0/0	1/2	0	2	0	5	1	15:19	
JENSEN, Tonny	0	0/0	0/0	0/0	0	0	0	0	0	00:00	
DORGE, John	1	0/5	0/0	1/2	0	0	2	10	0	08:10	
BORNER, Ray	0	0/0	0/0	0/0	0	0	0	0	0	00:00	
Totals	111	34/52	8/25	19/25	25	8	18	44	14		

Team: KOR Korea
Coach: CHOI, In-Chul — Assistant Coach: KIM, Nam-Ki

Names	Pts	2 Pts	3 Pts	FT	A	Stl	To	Reb	F	Mins	
KANG, Dong-Hee	11	1/3	3/4	0/0	8	0	3	1	1	23:37	S
HUR, Jae	9	0/1	3/6	0/0	4	1	8	2	4	22:30	S
CHUN, Hee-Chul	4	2/4	0/1	0/0	1	0	3	3	2	19:20	S
JUNG, Jae-Kun	23	10/13	0/2	3/5	1	2	4	8	2	32:24	S
CHUNG, Kyung-Ho	6	3/5	0/0	0/0	1	0	0	3	4	15:15	S
LEE, Sang-Min	2	1/4	0/2	0/0	2	1	0	0	1	10:46	
YANG, Hee-Seung	6	0/0	2/3	0/0	4	1	2	3	1	12:18	
WOO, Ji-Won	0	0/0	0/0	0/0	0	0	0	0	0	00:00	
HYUN, Joo-Yeop	8	3/3	0/0	2/2	4	1	2	1	3	22:03	
MOON, Kyung-Eun	17	1/2	5/12	0/0	3	1	1	1	3	23:38	
OH, Sung-Sik	2	1/3	0/3	0/0	2	0	0	0	1	18:09	
GI, Dong-Kee	0	0/0	0/0	0/0	0	0	0	0	0	00:00	
Totals	88	22/38	13/33	5/7	30	7	23	22	22		

Referees: NAKIC, Davorin CRO — ISHIDA, Hidetoshi JPN

Men / Messieurs

PRELIMINARIES - GROUP B FINAL SCORE: GRE 63 YUG 71 | HALFTIME SCORE: GRE 30 YUG 30

Team: GRE Greece
Coach: DEDRINOS, Makis — Assistant Coaches: TSAVAS, Lakis FILIPPOU, Nikos

Names	Pts	2 Pts	3 Pts	FT	A	Stl	To	Reb	F	Mins	
BAKATSIAS, Efthimios	2	1/2	0/1	0/0	3	1	1	2	3	15:36	S
SIGALAS, Giorgos	6	0/3	2/4	0/0	4	0	3	5	2	31:04	S
ECONOMOU, Nikos	15	3/6	1/6	6/6	1	3	2	1	1	35:55	S
FASSOULAS, Panayotis	21	9/14	0/0	3/8	2	1	2	10	3	40:00	S
CHRISTODOULOU, Theofanis	7	2/5	1/4	0/0	0	3	1	0	5	22:52	S
PATAVOUKAS, Costas	5	1/1	1/2	0/0	1	0	0	1	3	15:03	
GIANNAKIS, Panayotis	6	1/3	1/1	1/2	2	0	1	2	1	22:36	
PAPANIKOLAOU, Dimitris	0	0/0	0/0	0/0	0	0	0	0	0	00:00	
KAKIOUSIS, Eleftherios	0	0/0	0/0	0/0	0	0	0	0	0	00:00	
ALVERTIS, Fragiskos	1	0/2	0/1	1/2	2	0	0	1	1	16:54	
AGELIDIS, Dinos	0	0/0	0/0	0/0	0	0	0	0	0	00:00	
RENTZIAS, Efthimis	0	0/0	0/0	0/0	0	0	0	0	0	00:00	
Totals	63	17/36	6/19	11/18	15	8	10	22	19		

Team: YUG Yugoslavia
Coach: OBRADOVIC, Zelimir — Assistant Coaches: DARKO, Russo NIKOLIC, Miroslav

Names	Pts	2 Pts	3 Pts	FT	A	Stl	To	Reb	F	Mins	
DANILOVIC, Predrag	16	2/4	3/8	3/4	1	1	3	1	1	35:37	S
PASPALJ, Zarko	0	0/1	0/0	0/0	2	1	0	1	0	12:37	S
DJORDJEVIC, Aleksandar	14	3/6	2/2	2/2	6	1	3	5	3	26:43	S
DIVAC, Vlade	6	3/5	0/0	0/0	3	3	6	8	4	22:40	S
SAVIC, Zoran	21	9/11	0/1	3/6	1	1	1	7	4	31:59	S
BODIROGA, Dejan	3	0/4	1/1	0/0	1	0	1	5	1	27:23	
OBRADOVIC, Sasa	3	0/2	1/2	0/0	0	1	0	0	1	17:40	
LONCAR, Nikola	0	0/0	0/0	0/0	0	0	0	0	0	00:00	
BERIC, Miroslav	0	0/0	0/0	0/0	0	0	0	0	0	00:00	
REBRACA, Zeljko	8	4/4	0/0	0/0	3	0	0	2	4	25:21	
TOMASEVIC, Dejan	0	0/0	0/0	0/0	0	0	0	0	0	00:00	
TOPIC, Milenko	0	0/0	0/0	0/0	0	0	0	0	0	00:00	
Totals	71	21/37	7/14	8/14	16	7	15	28	19		

Referees: CLINE, Donald CAN   JUNGEBRAND, Carl FIN

PRELIMINARIES - GROUP B FINAL SCORE: PUR 98 BRA 101 | HALFTIME SCORE: PUR 54 BRA 58

Team: PUR Puerto Rico
Coach: MORALES, Carlos — Assistant Coaches: LOPEZ, Angel CALCANO, Carlos

Names	Pts	2 Pts	3 Pts	FT	A	Stl	To	Reb	F	Mins	
ORTIZ, Jose Piculin	35	13/19	1/2	6/11	3	0	5	11	3	37:21	S
ALICEA, Pablo	0	0/1	0/2	0/0	3	0	1	2	3	15:24	S
MINCY, Jerome	13	1/3	2/4	5/6	7	1	1	4	3	33:19	S
RIVAS, Ramon	16	6/8	0/0	4/4	1	0	4	4	5	28:30	S
TORRES, Georgie	11	1/3	3/4	0/0	0	1	1	0	3	23:24	S
CURBELO, Joel	2	1/2	0/1	0/0	2	0	0	1	1	05:20	
SOTO, Richard	7	1/1	1/1	2/2	0	1	1	1	4	09:59	
RIVERA, Eddie	0	0/0	0/0	0/0	2	0	1	3	2	14:38	
TRAVIESO, Carmelo	3	0/0	1/2	0/0	4	0	0	1	0	11:33	
PADILLA, Edgar	5	1/2	1/2	0/3	3	1	3	2	3	12:33	
SOTO, Eugenio	0	0/0	0/0	0/0	0	0	0	0	0	00:00	
SANTIAGO, Daniel	6	2/5	0/0	2/4	0	0	0	3	1	10:34	
Totals	98	26/44	9/18	19/30	25	4	17	32	28		

Team: BRA Brazil
Coach: VIDAL, Ary — Assistant Coaches: RODRIGUES, Carlos SILVA, Joao

Names	Pts	2 Pts	3 Pts	FT	A	Stl	To	Reb	F	Mins	
FONSECA, Andre	8	2/6	0/2	4/5	10	3	3	3	3	30:49	S
VIANNA, Joao Jose	10	3/5	0/0	4/4	1	1	0	8	4	25:00	S
MINUCI, Wilson Fernando	6	2/5	0/0	2/2	3	0	0	5	0	21:21	S
dos SANTOS, Aristides Josuel	14	5/9	0/0	4/4	1	1	4	7	3	26:55	S
SCHMIDT, Oscar	45	4/8	10/22	7/7	0	1	3	0	4	39:43	S
FERRACIU, Demetrius	2	0/0	0/2	2/4	3	2	2	2	0	09:31	
CASSIOLATO, Caio	0	0/0	0/0	0/0	0	0	0	0	0	00:00	
do NASCIMENTO, Carlos Olivia	0	0/2	0/0	0/0	0	0	0	3	2	05:48	
SILVEIRA, Caio Franco	0	0/2	0/0	0/0	0	0	0	2	3	06:55	
SANTANA, Antonio Jose	2	0/0	0/0	2/2	0	0	0	0	3	06:44	
KLAFKE, Rogerio	10	1/1	1/5	5/6	1	1	0	3	1	18:56	
JOERKE, Joelcio	4	1/1	0/0	2/2	0	0	0	0	2	08:18	
Totals	101	18/39	11/31	32/36	19	9	12	33	25		

Referees: DORIZON, Pascal Noel FRA   BRAZAUSKAS, Romualdas LTU

PRELIMINARIES - GROUP B FINAL SCORE: BRA 87 GRE 89 | HALFTIME SCORE: BRA 54 GRE 54

Team: BRA Brazil
Coach: VIDAL, Ary — Assistant Coaches: RODRIGUES, Carlos SILVA, Joao

Names	Pts	2 Pts	3 Pts	FT	A	Stl	To	Reb	F	Mins	
FONSECA, Andre	0	0/1	0/1	0/0	3	0	3	1	1	17:43	S
VIANNA, Joao Jose	4	2/5	0/0	0/0	1	0	3	3	5	18:47	S
MINUCI, Wilson Fernando	2	1/5	0/0	0/0	6	1	2	4	3	22:47	S
dos SANTOS, Aristides Josuel	11	3/8	1/1	2/2	1	1	1	10	3	27:16	S
SCHMIDT, Oscar	32	1/5	7/16	9/11	0	1	3	3	5	32:53	S
FERRACIU, Demetrius	8	1/2	2/2	0/0	5	1	1	0	4	22:38	
CASSIOLATO, Caio	0	0/0	0/0	0/0	0	0	0	0	0	00:00	
do NASCIMENTO, Carlos Olivia	14	3/5	0/2	8/8	1	1	1	7	5	22:25	
SILVEIRA, Caio Franco	0	0/0	0/0	0/0	0	0	0	0	0	00:00	
SANTANA, Antonio Jose	0	0/0	0/0	0/0	0	0	0	0	0	00:00	
KLAFKE, Rogerio	14	3/4	2/6	2/2	0	1	2	2	1	24:20	
JOERKE, Joelcio	2	1/1	0/0	0/2	0	0	0	2	2	11:11	
Totals	87	15/36	12/28	21/25	17	6	17	32	29		

Team: GRE Greece
Coach: DEDRINOS, Makis — Assistant Coach: TSAVAS, Lakis FILIPPOU, Nikos

Names	Pts	2 Pts	3 Pts	FT	A	Stl	To	Reb	F	Mins	
BAKATSIAS, Efthimios	8	1/1	0/0	6/6	5	0	2	3	3	27:20	S
SIGALAS, Giorgos	13	2/2	3/6	0/0	2	1	0	1	4	19:15	S
ECONOMOU, Nikos	36	6/9	3/3	15/20	1	0	2	5	3	35:33	S
FASSOULAS, Panayotis	16	6/12	0/0	4/8	0	0	4	6	2	32:05	S
CHRISTODOULOU, Theofanis	0	0/1	0/4	0/0	3	1	0	2	4	20:36	S
PATAVOUKAS, Costas	0	0/0	0/0	0/0	0	0	0	0	0	00:00	
GIANNAKIS, Panayotis	5	1/1	1/1	0/0	2	0	2	0	1	12:40	
PAPANIKOLAOU, Dimitris	4	1/2	0/0	2/4	1	1	1	3	4	17:59	
KAKIOUSIS, Eleftherios	0	0/0	0/0	0/0	0	0	0	0	0	00:00	
ALVERTIS, Fragiskos	3	0/0	1/2	0/0	1	0	1	0	2	22:10	
AGELIDIS, Dinos	2	1/1	0/0	0/0	0	0	0	0	1	03:49	
RENTZIAS, Efthimis	2	0/1	0/0	2/2	1	0	0	2	1	08:33	
Totals	89	18/30	8/16	29/40	16	3	12	22	25		

Referees: DEROSA, Joseph USA   BETANCOR LEON, Miguel ESP

PRELIMINARIES - GROUP B FINAL SCORE: KOR 86 PUR 98 | HALFTIME SCORE: KOR 52 PUR 51

Team: KOR Korea
Coach: CHOI, In-Chul — Assistant Coach: KIM, Nam-Ki

Names	Pts	2 Pts	3 Pts	FT	A	Stl	To	Reb	F	Mins	
KANG, Dong-Hee	13	1/4	3/5	2/2	1	1	1	3	1	33:32	S
HYUN, Joo-Yeop	16	5/8	0/0	6/7	3	1	0	11	4	40:00	S
HUR, Jae	16	3/7	3/12	1/2	12	1	4	3	1	40:00	S
MOON, Kyung-Eun	20	1/1	5/10	3/3	0	1	0	0	5	23:38	S
JUNG, Jae-Kun	9	2/6	1/2	2/2	1	1	0	3	5	13:52	S
LEE, Sang-Min	0	0/0	0/0	0/0	0	0	0	0	0	00:00	
YANG, Hee-Seung	0	0/0	0/0	0/0	0	0	0	0	0	00:00	
WOO, Ji-Won	0	0/0	0/0	0/0	0	0	0	0	0	00:00	
OH, Sung-Sik	0	0/2	0/2	0/0	0	0	0	1	1	12:43	
GI, Dong-Kee	0	0/0	0/0	0/0	0	0	0	0	0	00:00	
CHUN, Hee-Chul	12	6/11	0/0	0/0	2	1	0	3	3	28:10	
CHUNG, Kyung-Ho	0	0/2	0/0	0/0	1	0	0	1	0	08:05	
Totals	86	18/41	12/31	14/16	20	6	5	22	20		

Team: PUR Puerto Rico
Coach: MORALES, Carlos — Assistant Coaches: LOPEZ, Angel CALCANO, Carlos

Names	Pts	2 Pts	3 Pts	FT	A	Stl	To	Reb	F	Mins	
ORTIZ, Jose Piculin	37	16/22	0/1	5/7	4	1	1	14	0	35:01	S
ALICEA, Pablo	3	0/0	1/4	0/0	9	2	4	3	2	21:57	S
MINCY, Jerome	6	0/0	2/5	0/0	0	0	0	3	3	24:51	S
RIVAS, Ramon	18	9/10	0/1	0/1	3	1	0	7	3	31:10	S
TORRES, Georgie	16	3/5	2/8	4/4	6	0	2	8	4	36:38	S
CURBELO, Joel	0	0/0	0/1	0/0	0	0	1	0	2	01:51	
SOTO, Richard	4	1/2	0/0	2/2	2	0	1	1	0	14:13	
RIVERA, Eddie	3	0/0	0/0	3/4	3	0	0	2	0	08:52	
TRAVIESO, Carmelo	2	1/1	0/1	0/0	1	0	0	1	3	06:26	
PADILLA, Edgar	2	0/1	0/1	2/2	1	0	0	0	2	10:11	
SOTO, Eugenio	2	1/1	0/0	0/0	0	0	2	1	0	03:51	
SANTIAGO, Daniel	5	2/5	0/0	1/2	0	0	1	1	0	04:59	
Totals	98	33/44	5/22	17/22	29	4	12	41	19		

Referees: RYZHYK, Roman UKR   SOARES de CAMPOS, Antonio ANG

Men / Messieurs

PRELIMINARIES - GROUP B FINAL SCORE: YUG 91 AUS 68 | HALFTIME SCORE: YUG 54 AUS 28

Team: YUG Yugoslavia
Coach: OBRADOVIC, Zelimir Assistant Coaches: DARKO, Russo NIKOLIC, Miroslav

Names	Pts	2 Pts	3 Pts	FT	A	Stl	To	Reb	F	Mins	
DANILOVIC, Predrag	16	7/8	0/2	2/2	6	2	0	4	3	25:27	S
PASPALJ, Zarko	11	4/6	1/1	0/1	2	2	1	2	2	15:25	S
DJORDJEVIC, Aleksandar	0	0/2	0/1	0/0	4	0	1	1	0	05:55	S
DIVAC, Vlade	4	2/5	0/0	0/0	0	0	1	3	2	17:28	S
SAVIC, Zoran	8	3/4	0/0	2/2	2	1	0	5	1	17:57	S
BODIROGA, Dejan	12	5/6	0/1	2/2	3	0	2	2	4	23:40	
OBRADOVIC, Sasa	18	2/4	3/6	5/5	2	2	1	3	3	28:58	
LONCAR, Nikola	8	1/3	2/2	0/0	3	1	1	0	1	11:50	
BERIC, Miroslav	2	1/2	0/0	0/0	1	0	0	0	1	08:45	
REBRACA, Zeljko	12	6/8	0/0	0/0	1	0	2	5	2	23:41	
TOMASEVIC, Dejan	0	0/3	0/0	0/0	0	0	1	2	3	07:37	
TOPIC, Milenko	0	0/1	0/1	0/0	1	1	0	3	1	13:17	
Totals	91	31/52	6/14	11/12	25	9	10	30	23		

Team: AUS Australia
Coach: BARNES, Barry Assistant Coaches: BLACK, Allan BROWN, Brett

Names	Pts	2 Pts	3 Pts	FT	A	Stl	To	Reb	F	Mins	
RONALDSON, Tony	3	0/0	1/4	0/0	3	0	0	1	2	24:37	S
GAZE, Andrew	14	3/6	2/4	2/4	8	1	2	7	2	35:22	S
HEAL, Shane	2	1/1	0/6	0/0	1	0	3	1	3	30:19	S
BRADTKE, Mark	18	8/12	0/0	2/3	1	0	4	3	2	29:58	S
VLAHOV, Andrew	8	3/6	0/2	2/7	0	0	2	4	2	23:22	S
MAHER, Brett	2	1/3	0/0	0/0	1	1	1	3	0	07:37	
FISHER, Scott	7	2/4	1/1	0/0	0	0	1	2	3	13:25	
REIDY, Pat	2	0/0	0/1	2/2	1	0	0	0	1	07:30	
MacKINNON, Sam	4	2/4	0/0	0/0	2	2	3	6	1	17:48	
JENSEN, Tonny	0	0/0	0/0	0/0	0	0	0	0	0	00:00	
DORGE, John	8	3/4	0/0	2/4	0	1	1	6	2	10:02	
BORNER, Ray	0	0/0	0/0	0/0	0	0	0	0	0	00:00	
Totals	68	23/40	4/18	10/20	17	5	18	33	18		

Referees: ZYCH, Wieslaw POL REYES RONFINI, Jose MEX

PRELIMINARIES - GROUP B FINAL SCORE: YUG 118 KOR 65 | HALFTIME SCORE: YUG 57 KOR 28

Team: YUG Yugoslavia
Coach: OBRADOVIC, Zelimir Assistant Coaches: DARKO, Russo NIKOLIC, Miroslav

Names	Pts	2 Pts	3 Pts	FT	A	Stl	To	Reb	F	Mins	
DANILOVIC, Predrag	19	8/8	1/3	0/1	5	0	1	3	2	25:43	S
PASPALJ, Zarko	8	4/6	0/0	0/0	1	1	2	1	2	18:35	S
DJORDJEVIC, Aleksandar	9	3/5	1/3	0/0	10	2	3	4	0	23:04	S
DIVAC, Vlade	5	2/2	0/0	1/1	3	1	1	8	0	11:53	S
SAVIC, Zoran	12	6/7	0/0	0/0	1	1	2	6	1	18:28	S
BODIROGA, Dejan	16	8/8	0/1	0/0	1	0	0	1	1	17:55	
OBRADOVIC, Sasa	4	2/4	0/2	0/0	2	3	0	1	0	11:47	
LONCAR, Nikola	5	1/2	1/2	0/0	4	0	2	0	1	14:12	
BERIC, Miroslav	11	1/2	3/3	0/0	1	0	4	1	3	14:17	
REBRACA, Zeljko	11	5/5	0/0	1/1	0	1	0	4	0	12:37	
TOMASEVIC, Dejan	15	6/7	0/1	3/4	5	3	0	7	4	15:30	
TOPIC, Milenko	3	1/1	0/1	1/2	3	0	0	4	1	15:59	
Totals	118	47/57	6/16	6/9	36	12	15	40	15		

Team: KOR Korea
Coach: CHOI, In-Chul Assistant Coach: KIM, Nam-Ki

Names	Pts	2 Pts	3 Pts	FT	A	Stl	To	Reb	F	Mins	
KANG, Dong-Hee	8	1/6	2/6	0/0	4	5	2	4	1	27:42	S
HYUN, Joo-Yeop	20	9/14	0/0	2/2	1	0	1	3	2	36:13	S
HUR, Jae	7	2/5	1/5	0/0	5	3	4	0	1	26:10	S
MOON, Kyung-Eun	6	0/2	2/5	0/0	0	0	1	1	0	22:14	S
JUNG, Jae-Kun	6	2/7	0/1	2/2	2	0	2	2	3	26:59	S
LEE, Sang-Min	0	0/0	0/0	0/0	1	0	1	0	1	06:30	
YANG, Hee-Seung	0	0/0	0/0	0/0	0	0	0	0	0	00:00	
WOO, Ji-Won	0	0/0	0/0	0/0	0	0	0	0	0	00:00	
OH, Sung-Sik	0	0/0	0/0	0/0	1	0	1	1	2	13:33	
GI, Dong-Kee	0	0/0	0/0	0/0	0	0	0	0	0	00:00	
CHUN, Hee-Chul	12	6/8	0/1	0/0	2	1	2	1	2	26:03	
CHUNG, Kyung-Ho	6	2/2	0/0	2/4	1	1	0	1	3	14:36	
Totals	65	22/44	5/18	6/8	17	10	14	13	15		

Referees: DEROSA, Joseph USA THONGPILA, Virun THA

PRELIMINARIES - GROUP B FINAL SCORE: AUS 109 BRA 101 | HALFTIME SCORE: AUS 41 BRA 46

Team: AUS Australia
Coach: BARNES, Barry Assistant Coaches: BLACK, Allan BROWN, Brett

Names	Pts	2 Pts	3 Pts	FT	A	Stl	To	Reb	F	Mins	
RONALDSON, Tony	12	3/7	1/5	3/6	2	0	1	3	2	44:43	S
GAZE, Andrew	28	4/7	3/12	11/13	2	1	2	5	4	50:00	S
HEAL, Shane	35	2/3	8/15	7/7	6	0	1	2	0	50:00	S
BRADTKE, Mark	10	4/9	0/0	2/2	4	0	4	15	4	38:02	S
VLAHOV, Andrew	9	2/7	1/1	2/4	3	1	4	10	2	29:07	S
MAHER, Brett	0	0/0	0/0	0/0	0	0	0	0	0	00:00	
FISHER, Scott	8	3/6	0/0	2/2	1	2	0	2	2	26:10	
REIDY, Pat	0	0/0	0/0	0/0	0	0	0	0	0	00:00	
MacKINNON, Sam	0	0/0	0/0	0/0	0	0	0	0	0	00:00	
JENSEN, Tonny	0	0/0	0/0	0/0	0	0	0	0	0	00:00	
DORGE, John	7	2/4	0/0	3/4	0	0	0	8	3	11:58	
BORNER, Ray	0	0/0	0/0	0/0	0	0	0	0	0	00:00	
Totals	109	20/43	13/33	30/38	18	4	12	45	17		

Team: BRA Brazil
Coach: VIDAL, Ary Assistant Coaches: RODRIGUES, Carlos SILVA, Joao

Names	Pts	2 Pts	3 Pts	FT	A	Stl	To	Reb	F	Mins	
FONSECA, Andre	5	1/4	1/4	0/0	5	2	1	4	5	37:19	S
VIANNA, Joao Jose	13	6/10	0/1	1/2	0	1	0	5	5	28:16	S
MINUCI, Wilson Fernando	8	4/7	0/0	0/0	6	0	2	4	5	25:53	S
dos SANTOS, Aristides Josuel	20	8/13	0/0	4/4	2	1	1	13	3	43:22	S
SCHMIDT, Oscar	24	6/11	4/16	0/0	3	1	4	4	2	50:00	S
FERRACIU, Demetrius	0	0/0	0/0	0/0	1	0	0	1	2	13:08	
CASSIOLATO, Caio	2	1/2	0/0	0/0	0	0	0	0	1	04:41	
do NASCIMENTO, Carlos Olivia	3	0/0	1/1	0/0	0	0	0	1	2	09:20	
SILVEIRA, Caio Franco	0	0/0	0/0	0/0	0	0	0	0	0	00:00	
SANTANA, Antonio Jose	3	0/0	0/0	3/4	0	0	1	2	2	05:06	
KLAFKE, Rogerio	21	5/10	2/3	5/8	1	2	1	6	2	26:31	
JOERKE, Joelcio	2	1/1	0/0	0/0	0	0	1	3	1	06:24	
Totals	101	32/60	8/25	13/18	19	7	11	43	30		

Referees: CLINE, Donald CAN JUNGEBRAND, Carl FIN

PRELIMINARIES - GROUP B FINAL SCORE: GRE 80 PUR 69 | HALFTIME SCORE: GRE 51 PUR 33

Team: GRE Greece
Coach: DEDRINOS, Makis Assistant Coaches: TSAVAS, Lakis FILIPPOU, Nikos

Names	Pts	2 Pts	3 Pts	FT	A	Stl	To	Reb	F	Mins	
BAKATSIAS, Efthimios	6	3/3	0/0	0/0	1	1	1	4	3	23:55	S
SIGALAS, Giorgos	10	2/3	2/7	0/0	0	1	1	0	3	24:08	S
ECONOMOU, Nikos	19	6/13	1/3	4/5	3	1	3	8	1	31:33	S
FASSOULAS, Panayotis	14	4/10	0/0	6/14	0	1	0	5	3	32:14	S
CHRISTODOULOU, Theofanis	11	1/2	2/5	3/4	5	0	0	3	1	17:57	S
PATAVOUKAS, Costas	3	0/0	1/2	0/0	1	1	1	1	1	15:14	
GIANNAKIS, Panayotis	6	2/2	0/1	2/2	2	1	3	4	2	22:48	
PAPANIKOLAOU, Dimitris	0	0/0	0/0	0/0	0	0	1	0	1	03:53	
KAKIOUSIS, Eleftherios	0	0/0	0/0	0/0	2	0	0	0	5	10:51	
ALVERTIS, Fragiskos	7	3/4	0/1	1/2	0	0	0	3	0	10:41	
AGELIDIS, Dinos	0	0/0	0/0	0/0	0	0	0	0	0	00:00	
RENTZIAS, Efthimis	4	2/2	0/0	0/2	1	0	2	5	4	06:46	
Totals	80	23/39	6/19	16/29	13	6	12	33	24		

Team: PUR Puerto Rico
Coach: MORALES, Carlos Assistant Coaches: LOPEZ, Angel CALCANO, Carlos

Names	Pts	2 Pts	3 Pts	FT	A	Stl	To	Reb	F	Mins	
ORTIZ, Jose Piculin	13	4/7	0/1	5/7	5	1	4	7	5	25:40	S
ALICEA, Pablo	4	0/2	1/4	1/2	2	0	1	2	0	23:24	S
MINCY, Jerome	20	2/4	4/7	4/7	1	2	2	8	4	40:00	S
RIVAS, Ramon	17	7/9	0/2	3/3	3	0	1	6	5	25:20	S
TORRES, Georgie	8	1/5	1/2	3/5	2	3	2	5	2	33:14	S
CURBELO, Joel	0	0/1	0/0	0/0	0	0	0	0	0	00:00	
SOTO, Richard	0	0/0	0/0	0/0	0	0	0	0	0	04:01	
RIVERA, Eddie	2	1/4	0/1	0/0	1	1	1	1	1	15:48	
TRAVIESO, Carmelo	3	0/2	1/3	0/0	1	0	1	0	2	09:11	
PADILLA, Edgar	0	0/1	0/0	0/0	0	0	0	0	1	02:00	
SOTO, Eugenio	2	1/2	0/1	0/4	0	0	2	4	4	12:22	
SANTIAGO, Daniel	0	0/0	0/0	0/2	0	0	3	0	1	09:00	
Totals	69	16/37	7/21	16/30	14	8	16	34	25		

Referees: COLUCCI, Gennaro ITA CHAVES SAGEL, Raul ARG

Basketball / Basketball **133**

Men / *Messieurs*

PRELIMINARIES - GROUP B — FINAL SCORE: PUR 96 AUS 101 — HALFTIME SCORE: PUR 53 AUS 51

Team: PUR Puerto Rico
Coach: MORALES, Carlos   Assistant Coaches: LOPEZ, Angel   CALCANO, Carlos

Names	Pts	2 Pts	3 Pts	FT	A	Stl	To	Reb	F	Mins	
ORTIZ, Jose Piculin	30	8/12	2/3	8/10	6	1	7	11	4	38:03	S
ALICEA, Pablo	6	0/1	2/3	0/0	4	1	3	0	2	15:30	S
MINCY, Jerome	15	1/2	3/8	4/5	2	2	4	7	2	39:42	S
RIVAS, Ramon	5	2/5	0/0	1/2	0	0	2	2	5	23:04	S
TORRES, Georgie	10	2/3	1/2	3/4	1	0	0	2	1	18:13	S
CURBELO, Joel	0	0/0	0/0	0/0	0	0	0	0	0	00:00	
SOTO, Richard	2	1/2	0/0	0/0	0	0	2	1	1	05:48	
RIVERA, Eddie	0	0/0	0/1	0/0	1	0	0	0	0	08:12	
TRAVIESO, Carmelo	16	2/3	4/5	0/0	1	0	0	2	2	23:05	
PADILLA, Edgar	4	1/3	0/2	2/2	7	1	1	2	2	16:36	
SOTO, Eugenio	1	0/0	0/0	1/2	0	0	0	0	0	01:43	
SANTIAGO, Daniel	7	3/3	0/0	1/3	0	0	0	1	4	10:04	
Totals	96	20/34	12/24	20/28	22	5	19	28	23		

Team: AUS Australia
Coach: BARNES, Barry   Assistant Coaches: BLACK, Allan   BROWN, Brett

Names	Pts	2 Pts	3 Pts	FT	A	Stl	To	Reb	F	Mins	
RONALDSON, Tony	17	3/11	3/4	2/2	5	3	1	1	5	27:13	S
GAZE, Andrew	29	5/9	3/7	10/10	5	0	3	4	3	40:00	S
HEAL, Shane	28	4/6	6/12	2/2	7	1	1	1	1	40:00	S
BRADTKE, Mark	14	7/9	0/0	0/2	1	1	1	6	4	23:26	S
VLAHOV, Andrew	2	0/1	0/0	2/2	4	2	1	4	4	33:38	S
MAHER, Brett	0	0/0	0/0	0/0	0	0	0	0	0	00:00	
FISHER, Scott	5	1/4	0/0	3/4	0	0	2	6	2	19:09	
REIDY, Pat	0	0/0	0/0	0/0	0	0	0	0	0	00:00	
MacKINNON, Sam	0	0/0	0/0	0/0	0	0	0	0	0	00:00	
JENSEN, Tonny	0	0/0	0/0	0/0	0	0	0	0	0	00:00	
DORGE, John	6	1/1	0/0	4/4	1	4	0	4	4	16:34	
BORNER, Ray	0	0/0	0/0	0/0	0	0	0	0	0	00:00	
Totals	101	21/41	12/23	23/26	23	11	9	26	23		

Referees: BETANCOR LEON, Miguel ESP   LAPAIX GUANCE, Jose DOM

PRELIMINARIES - GROUP B — FINAL SCORE: KOR 86 GRE 108 — HALFTIME SCORE: KOR 44 GRE 56

Team: KOR Korea
Coach: CHOI, In-Chul   Assistant Coach: KIM, Nam-Ki

Names	Pts	2 Pts	3 Pts	FT	A	Stl	To	Reb	F	Mins	
KANG, Dong-Hee	2	1/3	0/5	0/0	10	3	2	4	1	27:10	S
HYUN, Joo-Yeop	24	10/14	0/0	4/6	2	0	3	6	4	40:00	S
HUR, Jae	10	0/0	1/6	7/8	3	0	4	0	2	17:59	S
CHUN, Hee-Chul	6	3/12	0/0	0/0	4	2	2	4	2	32:51	S
JUNG, Jae-Kun	20	5/7	3/5	1/1	0	1	2	3	5	20:58	S
LEE, Sang-Min	5	1/2	1/3	0/0	3	0	1	2	0	21:31	
YANG, Hee-Seung	0	0/0	0/0	0/0	0	0	0	0	0	00:00	
WOO, Ji-Won	0	0/0	0/0	0/0	0	0	0	0	0	00:00	
MOON, Kyung-Eun	19	2/3	4/10	3/3	2	1	0	3	4	34:06	
OH, Sung-Sik	0	0/0	0/0	0/0	1	0	2	1	1	05:25	
GI, Dong-Kee	0	0/0	0/0	0/0	0	0	0	0	0	00:00	
CHUNG, Kyung-Ho	0	0/0	0/0	0/0	0	0	0	0	0	00:00	
Totals	86	22/41	9/29	15/18	25	7	16	23	19		

Team: GRE Greece
Coach: DEDRINOS, Makis   Assistant Coaches: TSAVAS, Lakis   FILIPPOU, Nikos

Names	Pts	2 Pts	3 Pts	FT	A	Stl	To	Reb	F	Mins	
BAKATSIAS, Efthimios	4	2/3	0/1	0/0	6	0	3	3	2	22:09	S
SIGALAS, Giorgos	22	6/7	3/6	1/2	6	1	3	6	2	23:45	S
ALVERTIS, Fragiskos	19	4/7	3/4	2/3	4	1	1	5	1	25:16	S
ECONOMOU, Nikos	13	6/10	0/1	1/1	4	0	1	3	3	24:35	S
FASSOULAS, Panayotis	10	5/10	0/0	0/1	0	0	2	6	3	19:10	S
PATAVOUKAS, Costas	5	1/2	1/2	0/0	3	0	1	1	0	17:36	
GIANNAKIS, Panayotis	2	1/1	0/0	0/0	3	1	0	1	1	11:05	
PAPANIKOLAOU, Dimitris	14	7/9	0/0	0/0	1	2	2	7	5	10:49	
KAKIOUSIS, Eleftherios	1	0/0	0/0	1/4	2	1	2	0	1	14:03	
AGELIDIS, Dinos	10	4/7	0/0	2/3	0	0	0	5	2	15:25	
RENTZIAS, Efthimis	8	4/7	0/0	0/0	1	1	1	8	1	16:07	
CHRISTODOULOU, Theofanis	0	0/0	0/0	0/0	0	0	0	0	0	00:00	
Totals	108	40/63	7/14	7/14	30	7	16	45	21		

Referees: BRAZAUSKAS, Romualdas LTU   CUI, Yi CHN

PRELIMINARIES - GROUP B — FINAL SCORE: BRA 82 YUG 101 — HALFTIME SCORE: BRA 31 YUG 55

Team: BRA Brazil
Coach: VIDAL, Ary   Assistant Coaches: RODRIGUES, Carlos   SILVA, Joao

Names	Pts	2 Pts	3 Pts	FT	A	Stl	To	Reb	F	Mins	
FONSECA, Andre	4	1/2	0/1	2/2	4	3	1	2	4	16:15	S
VIANNA, Joao Jose	2	1/3	0/0	0/0	1	0	2	1	3	12:55	S
MINUCI, Wilson Fernando	8	2/5	0/1	4/5	1	1	0	2	3	19:36	S
dos SANTOS, Aristides Josuel	4	2/3	0/0	0/1	0	0	2	2	1	15:24	S
SCHMIDT, Oscar	14	3/5	0/2	8/8	0	0	3	2	1	20:48	S
FERRACIU, Demetrius	2	1/5	0/0	0/2	0	0	1	3	3	17:55	
CASSIOLATO, Caio	19	7/11	1/1	2/2	3	1	3	3	3	24:17	
do NASCIMENTO, Carlos Olivia	0	0/0	0/0	0/0	0	0	0	0	0	00:00	
SILVEIRA, Caio Franco	1	0/3	0/0	1/2	0	1	1	1	3	14:51	
SANTANA, Antonio Jose	11	5/7	0/0	1/1	1	0	0	5	4	17:19	
KLAFKE, Rogerio	6	3/10	0/3	0/0	4	1	0	3	0	21:09	
JOERKE, Joelcio	11	3/7	0/0	5/9	1	0	0	6	3	19:31	
Totals	82	28/61	1/8	23/32	15	7	13	30	28		

Team: YUG Yugoslavia
Coach: OBRADOVIC, Zelimir   Assistant Coaches: DARKO, Russo   NIKOLIC, Miroslav

Names	Pts	2 Pts	3 Pts	FT	A	Stl	To	Reb	F	Mins	
DANILOVIC, Predrag	21	9/9	0/2	3/4	3	2	1	3	1	27:43	S
PASPALJ, Zarko	7	2/6	0/0	3/4	0	0	0	1	3	14:04	S
DJORDJEVIC, Aleksandar	13	5/6	1/2	0/0	5	1	4	3	1	23:55	S
DIVAC, Vlade	10	1/2	1/1	5/8	3	0	0	6	1	17:26	S
SAVIC, Zoran	5	2/4	0/0	1/3	5	2	4	2	2	23:33	S
BODIROGA, Dejan	14	5/5	1/1	1/2	4	1	1	4	2	19:31	
OBRADOVIC, Sasa	1	0/2	0/2	1/2	6	0	0	2	2	16:05	
LONCAR, Nikola	0	0/1	0/2	0/0	0	0	1	0	1	06:54	
BERIC, Miroslav	7	1/1	1/2	2/4	1	1	1	1	3	11:48	
REBRACA, Zeljko	12	5/7	0/0	2/3	0	1	2	4	1	17:43	
TOMASEVIC, Dejan	9	4/5	0/0	1/1	1	0	3	6	4	13:47	
TOPIC, Milenko	2	1/1	0/0	0/2	0	1	0	3	2	07:31	
Totals	101	35/49	4/12	19/33	28	8	15	35	23		

Referees: COLUCCI, Gennaro ITA   CHAVES SAGEL, Raul ARG

PRELIMINARIES - GROUP B — FINAL SCROE: AUS 103 GRE 62 — HALFTIME SCORE: AUS 52 GRE 30

Team: AUS Australia
Coach: BARNES, Barry   Assistant Coaches: BLACK, Allan   BROWN, Brett

Names	Pts	2 Pts	3 Pts	FT	A	Stl	To	Reb	F	Mins	
RONALDSON, Tony	11	2/3	1/3	4/4	0	0	0	5	1	18:01	S
GAZE, Andrew	17	2/2	2/4	7/10	4	1	2	2	2	29:20	S
HEAL, Shane	13	2/3	3/6	0/0	5	0	1	0	1	25:27	S
BRADTKE, Mark	7	3/10	0/0	1/2	2	0	1	8	4	17:32	S
VLAHOV, Andrew	8	4/8	0/0	0/0	1	0	2	5	2	23:48	S
MAHER, Brett	1	0/3	0/1	1/2	3	1	3	1	0	11:17	
FISHER, Scott	9	3/5	1/1	0/0	3	1	1	4	3	17:01	
REIDY, Pat	12	1/1	3/3	1/2	0	1	0	2	3	18:23	
MacKINNON, Sam	11	3/4	1/2	2/3	1	0	0	2	2	11:45	
JENSEN, Tonny	6	3/3	0/1	0/0	1	1	0	2	0	04:58	
DORGE, John	6	3/6	0/0	0/0	1	0	0	5	1	16:49	
BORNER, Ray	2	1/2	0/0	0/0	0	0	0	2	0	05:39	
Totals	103	27/50	11/21	16/23	21	5	10	38	19		

Team: GRE Greece
Coach: DEDRINOS, Makis   Assistant Coaches: TSAVAS, Lakis   FILIPPOU, Nikos

Names	Pts	2 Pts	3 Pts	FT	A	Stl	To	Reb	F	Mins	
BAKATSIAS, Efthimios	0	0/1	0/0	0/0	0	0	3	3	0	14:57	S
SIGALAS, Giorgos	0	0/1	0/0	0/0	1	1	2	0	5	06:48	S
ECONOMOU, Nikos	22	4/9	4/4	2/3	0	0	3	1	2	27:28	S
FASSOULAS, Panayotis	6	3/7	0/0	0/0	0	0	2	1	3	17:57	S
CHRISTODOULOU, Theofanis	0	0/0	0/2	0/0	1	0	0	1	0	05:55	S
PATAVOUKAS, Costas	2	1/1	0/0	0/0	0	1	0	3	1	16:15	
GIANNAKIS, Panayotis	6	1/4	1/2	1/2	4	2	0	1	1	26:04	
PAPANIKOLAOU, Dimitris	0	0/5	0/1	0/0	3	2	1	6	3	18:14	
KAKIOUSIS, Eleftherios	0	0/1	0/1	0/0	2	1	1	0	0	10:05	
ALVERTIS, Fragiskos	12	4/9	0/1	4/5	2	0	3	4	2	21:42	
AGELIDIS, Dinos	7	1/6	1/1	2/2	0	0	2	1	1	12:32	
RENTZIAS, Efthimis	7	3/3	0/0	1/4	1	0	0	4	3	22:03	
Totals	62	17/47	6/14	10/16	14	7	18	25	21		

Referees: DORIZON, Pascal Noel FRA   LAPAIX GUANCE, Jose DOM

Men / *Messieurs*

PRELIMINARIES - GROUP B FINAL SCORE: YUG 97 PUR 86 | HALFTIME SCORE: YUG 45 PUR 34

Team: YUG Yugoslavia
Coach: OBRADOVIC, Zelimir   Assistant Coaches: DARKO, Russo   NIKOLIC, Miroslav

Names	Pts	2 Pts	3 Pts	FT	A	Stl	To	Reb	F	Mins	
DANILOVIC, Predrag	22	5/9	2/3	6/7	4	0	2	3	0	33:53	S
PASPALJ, Zarko	4	1/4	0/1	2/2	1	0	0	2	1	15:49	S
DJORDJEVIC, Aleksandar	21	5/6	1/4	8/10	7	2	3	3	2	27:57	S
DIVAC, Vlade	10	3/8	0/1	4/4	4	2	2	10	3	32:11	S
SAVIC, Zoran	18	7/9	0/1	4/10	0	1	1	6	4	21:15	S
BODIROGA, Dejan	8	3/5	0/2	2/5	2	2	2	4	1	06:01	
OBRADOVIC, Sasa	2	1/2	0/4	0/0	3	0	2	2	1	14:09	
LONCAR, Nikola	0	0/0	0/0	0/0	0	0	0	0	0	00:00	
BERIC, Miroslav	0	0/0	0/3	0/0	0	0	0	0	0	04:03	
REBRACA, Zeljko	12	5/5	0/0	2/3	0	1	0	5	3	22:49	
TOMASEVIC, Dejan	0	0/1	0/0	0/0	0	0	1	1	0	04:03	
TOPIC, Milenko	0	0/0	0/0	0/0	0	0	0	0	0	00:00	
Totals	97	30/49	3/19	28/41	21	8	13	36	15		

Team: PUR Puerto Rico
Coach: MORALES, Carlos   Assistant Coaches: LOPEZ, Angel   CALCANO, Carlos

Names	Pts	2 Pts	3 Pts	FT	A	Stl	To	Reb	F	Mins	
ORTIZ, Jose Piculin	20	9/15	0/2	2/4	1	0	4	11	5	36:04	S
ALICEA, Pablo	0	0/1	0/3	0/0	3	0	1	2	1	13:36	S
MINCY, Jerome	9	0/0	3/8	0/0	1	1	3	7	5	31:23	S
RIVAS, Ramon	8	3/8	0/1	2/4	3	1	3	7	4	28:23	S
TORRES, Georgie	16	2/4	4/8	0/0	2	1	2	1	4	26:36	S
CURBELO, Joel	3	0/0	1/1	0/0	0	0	0	0	0	00:36	
SOTO, Richard	0	0/0	0/0	0/0	0	0	0	0	0	02:54	
RIVERA, Eddie	2	1/1	0/0	0/0	0	0	0	1	0	05:16	
TRAVIESO, Carmelo	17	5/6	1/2	4/6	1	1	2	3	3	25:24	
PADILLA, Edgar	9	3/3	1/3	0/0	9	2	2	1	3	21:08	
SOTO, Eugenio	2	1/1	0/0	0/2	1	0	0	1	1	06:23	
SANTIAGO, Daniel	0	0/0	0/0	0/0	0	0	0	0	3	02:17	
Totals	86	24/39	10/28	8/16	21	6	17	34	29		

Referees: CLINE, Donald CAN   BOULANOV, Serguei RUS

PRELIMINARIES - GROUP B FINAL SCORE: BRA 127 KOR 97 | HALFTIME SCORE: BRA 66 KOR 49

Team: BRA Brazil
Coach: VIDAL, Ary   Assistant Coaches: RODRIGUES, Carlos   SILVA, Joao

Names	Pts	2 Pts	3 Pts	FT	A	Stl	To	Reb	F	Mins	
FONSECA, Andre	13	5/6	1/2	0/0	8	1	2	5	4	18:34	S
VIANNA, Joao Jose	8	4/7	0/0	0/0	1	2	0	5	3	23:47	S
MINUCI, Wilson Fernando	12	5/9	0/1	2/2	9	2	0	6	2	29:33	S
dos SANTOS, Aristides Josuel	17	8/11	0/0	1/1	3	4	1	8	1	26:35	S
SCHMIDT, Oscar	25	4/7	5/11	2/2	2	0	1	5	0	22:12	S
FERRACIU, Demetrius	6	1/6	1/2	1/2	4	0	1	4	3	16:42	
CASSIOLATO, Caio	6	2/5	0/0	2/2	3	2	1	4	3	11:16	
do NASCIMENTO, Carlos Olivia	6	2/2	0/0	2/2	0	0	2	2	4	06:23	
SILVEIRA, Caio Franco	0	0/0	0/0	0/0	1	0	0	2	1	04:02	
SANTANA, Antonio Jose	7	3/5	0/0	1/2	0	0	2	4	1	09:50	
KLAFKE, Rogerio	11	2/3	2/4	1/2	1	0	3	0	1	21:09	
JOERKE, Joelcio	16	5/7	0/0	6/7	0	0	1	5	3	09:57	
Totals	127	41/68	9/20	18/22	32	11	14	50	26		

Team: KOR Korea
Coach: CHOI, In-Chul   Assistant Coach: KIM, Nam-Ki

Names	Pts	2 Pts	3 Pts	FT	A	Stl	To	Reb	F	Mins	
KANG, Dong-Hee	24	8/10	2/5	2/4	7	3	4	5	2	32:10	S
HYUN, Joo-Yeop	23	6/15	0/0	11/14	0	1	1	6	2	40:00	S
MOON, Kyung-Eun	16	1/1	4/8	2/2	2	0	1	5	2	24:52	S
CHUN, Hee-Chul	4	2/6	0/0	0/4	1	1	1	3	3	36:34	S
JUNG, Jae-Kun	10	2/3	2/5	0/0	3	0	4	1	0	27:43	S
LEE, Sang-Min	12	2/3	1/1	5/5	2	2	2	0	2	15:48	
YANG, Hee-Seung	6	0/0	2/3	0/0	1	0	1	1	3	11:10	
WOO, Ji-Won	0	0/0	0/0	0/0	0	0	0	0	0	00:00	
HUR, Jae	0	0/0	0/0	0/0	0	0	0	0	0	00:00	
OH, Sung-Sik	0	0/0	0/0	0/0	1	0	0	0	0	03:44	
GI, Dong-Kee	2	0/1	0/0	2/2	2	0	2	1	5	07:59	
CHUNG, Kyung-Ho	0	0/0	0/0	0/0	0	0	0	0	0	00:00	
Totals	97	21/39	11/22	22/31	19	7	17	22	19		

Referees: ZHU, Jiazhong CHN   JOVANCIC, Tomislav YUG

FINAL CLASSIFICATION - GROUP A

		Matches			Points		
Rnk	Team	Played	Won	Lost	For	Against	Points
1	USA	5	5	0	522	345	10
2	LTU	5	3	2	427	354	8
3	CRO	5	3	2	422	386	8
4	CHN	5	2	3	360	502	7
5	ARG	5	2	3	351	396	7
6	ANG	5	0	5	280	379	5

FINAL CLASSIFICATION - GROUP B

		Matches			Points		
Rnk	Team	Played	Won	Lost	For	Against	Points
1	YUG	5	5	0	478	364	10
2	AUS	5	4	1	492	438	9
3	GRE	5	3	2	402	416	8
4	BRA	5	2	3	498	494	7
5	PUR	5	1	4	447	465	6
6	KOR	5	0	5	422	562	5

CLASSIFICATION 9 - 12 FINAL SCORE: ARG 97 KOR 79 | HALFTIME SCORE: ARG 44 KOR 41

Team: ARG Argentina
Coach: VECCHIO, Guillermo   Assistant Coaches: MAGNANO, Ruben   DURO, Fernando

Names	Pts	2 Pts	3 Pts	FT	A	Stl	To	Reb	F	Mins	
VILLAR, Luis	8	4/7	0/1	0/1	0	0	2	2	4	21:49	S
MILANESIO, Marcelo	16	4/4	2/6	2/2	6	2	1	4	3	34:13	S
ESPIL, Juan	26	1/3	8/12	0/0	8	1	2	6	2	33:52	S
OSELLA, Diego	8	4/8	0/0	0/0	3	0	1	6	0	25:35	S
PEREZ, Esteban	18	6/9	2/6	0/0	4	3	5	9	2	40:00	S
NICOLA, Marcelo	0	0/0	0/0	0/0	0	0	0	0	0	00:00	
FARABELLO, Daniel	4	2/2	0/0	0/0	2	0	2	1	0	11:55	
de la FUENTE, Esteban	0	0/0	0/0	0/0	0	0	0	0	0	00:00	
MICHEL, Ernesto	0	0/0	0/0	0/0	1	0	0	0	2	06:41	
OBERTO, Fabricio	17	8/10	0/0	1/1	5	1	1	5	2	25:55	
RACCA, Jorge	0	0/0	0/0	0/0	0	0	0	0	0	00:00	
WOLKOWISKY, Ruben	0	0/0	0/0	0/0	0	0	0	0	0	00:00	
Totals	97	29/43	12/25	3/4	29	7	14	33	15		

Team: KOR Korea
Coach: CHOI, In-Chul   Assistant Coach: KIM, Nam-Ki

Names	Pts	2 Pts	3 Pts	FT	A	Stl	To	Reb	F	Mins	
KANG, Dong-Hee	14	4/4	2/8	0/0	8	2	4	5	2	37:01	S
HYUN, Joo-Yeop	16	7/14	0/1	2/2	4	1	1	6	1	40:00	S
MOON, Kyung-Eun	10	2/4	2/9	0/0	4	1	0	1	1	28:21	S
GI, Dong-Kee	2	1/1	0/0	0/0	1	0	1	0	1	13:59	S
JUNG, Jae-Kun	17	4/6	2/6	3/5	2	0	3	4	2	26:44	S
LEE, Sang-Min	0	0/1	0/0	0/0	0	0	0	1	1	02:59	
YANG, Hee-Seung	6	1/2	1/2	1/1	1	0	0	1	1	18:44	
WOO, Ji-Won	0	0/0	0/0	0/0	0	0	0	0	0	00:00	
HUR, Jae	0	0/0	0/0	0/0	0	0	0	0	0	00:00	
OH, Sung-Sik	0	0/0	0/0	0/0	0	0	0	0	0	00:00	
CHUN, Hee-Chul	14	4/9	1/1	3/5	1	1	3	8	4	32:12	
CHUNG, Kyung-Ho	0	0/0	0/0	0/0	0	0	0	0	0	00:00	
Totals	79	23/41	8/27	9/13	21	5	12	26	13		

Referees: DEROSA, Joseph USA   ZHU, Jiazhong CHN

Basketball / *Basketball*   **135**

Men / *Messieurs*

CLASSIFICATION 9 - 12 — FINAL SCORE: PUR 76 ANG 67 — HALFTIME SCORE: PUR 38 ANG 36

Team: PUR Puerto Rico

Coach: MORALES, Carlos   Assistant Coaches: LOPEZ, Angel   CALCANO, Carlos

Names	Pts	2 Pts	3 Pts	FT	A	Stl	To	Reb	F	Mins	
ORTIZ, Jose Piculin	19	7/12	0/0	5/7	3	1	4	6	1	36:35	S
ALICEA, Pablo	8	0/1	2/3	2/2	5	0	3	3	4	21:26	S
MINCY, Jerome	10	0/1	1/5	7/7	0	0	2	6	1	30:41	S
RIVAS, Ramon	10	3/6	0/1	4/4	3	1	2	7	2	33:07	S
TORRES, Georgie	12	1/3	3/6	1/1	2	2	0	3	1	29:34	S
CURBELO, Joel	2	1/2	0/0	0/0	0	0	0	0	0	01:43	
SOTO, Richard	0	0/2	0/0	0/0	0	0	0	3	0	05:41	
RIVERA, Eddie	0	0/0	0/0	0/0	1	0	1	0	1	01:43	
TRAVIESO, Carmelo	6	2/7	0/2	2/4	1	2	0	4	0	18:15	
PADILLA, Edgar	9	2/2	1/3	2/4	3	1	1	2	2	16:51	
SOTO, Eugenio	0	0/0	0/0	0/0	0	0	0	1	0	01:02	
SANTIAGO, Daniel	0	0/1	0/0	0/0	0	0	0	1	0	03:22	
Totals	76	16/37	7/20	23/29	18	7	13	36	12		

Team: ANG Angola

Coach: ROMERO, Vladimiro   Assistant Coach: TAVARES, Nelson

Names	Pts	2 Pts	3 Pts	FT	A	Stl	To	Reb	F	Mins	
MOREIRA, Anibal	15	3/6	3/5	0/0	6	0	1	5	5	31:37	S
VICTORIANO, Angelo	6	0/2	2/8	0/0	0	0	2	5	3	31:36	S
UCUAHAMBA, Benjamin	9	3/4	1/1	0/0	3	0	1	3	1	17:09	S
CARVALHO, Antonio	9	3/7	1/7	0/0	0	0	2	4	1	25:31	S
DIAS, David	12	6/9	0/1	0/0	2	0	2	11	4	36:06	S
VICTORIANO, Edmar	0	0/0	0/0	0/0	0	0	0	0	0	00:00	
TROSO, Honorato	10	3/4	1/3	1/2	5	1	2	2	2	22:27	
COIMBRA, Herlander	6	0/0	2/8	0/0	0	1	1	4	0	15:57	
VICTORIANO, Justino	0	0/0	0/0	0/0	0	0	2	0	4	12:18	
ROMANO, Benjamin	0	0/0	0/0	0/0	0	0	0	0	0	00:00	
GUIMARAES, Jose	0	0/0	0/1	0/0	0	0	0	2	0	07:19	
CONCEICAO, Jean-Jacques	0	0/0	0/0	0/0	0	0	0	0	0	00:00	
Totals	67	18/32	10/34	1/2	16	2	13	36	20		

Referees: RYZHYK, Roman   UKR   REYES RONFINI, Jose   MEX

CLASSIFICATION 5 - 8 — FINAL SCORE: BRA 80 CRO 74 — HALFTIME SCORE: BRA 39 CRO 27

Team: BRA Brazil

Coach: VIDAL, Ary   Assistant Coaches: RODRIGUES, Carlos   SILVA, Joao

Names	Pts	2 Pts	3 Pts	FT	A	Stl	To	Reb	F	Mins	
FONSECA, Andre	4	1/2	0/2	2/2	7	1	1	3	2	27:55	S
VIANNA, Joao Jose	6	3/7	0/0	0/0	5	4	0	4	3	36:16	S
MINUCI, Wilson Fernando	3	1/4	0/1	1/2	1	0	1	1	4	25:00	S
dos SANTOS, Aristides Josuel	8	3/8	0/0	2/4	2	2	0	7	2	21:25	S
SCHMIDT, Oscar	32	5/9	5/11	7/7	0	0	3	2	4	30:50	S
FERRACIU, Demetrius	6	1/2	0/0	4/6	2	1	2	4	1	09:47	
CASSIOLATO, Caio	0	0/0	0/0	0/0	0	0	1	0	1	04:23	
do NASCIMENTO, Carlos Olivia	3	0/0	0/0	3/4	0	0	0	0	1	03:28	
SILVEIRA, Caio Franco	0	0/0	0/0	0/0	0	0	0	0	0	00:00	
SANTANA, Antonio Jose	0	0/0	0/0	0/0	0	0	0	0	0	00:00	
KLAFKE, Rogerio	14	4/8	1/1	3/4	2	0	1	2	3	22:21	
JOERKE, Joelcio	4	1/5	0/0	2/4	0	0	0	7	4	18:35	
Totals	80	19/45	6/15	24/33	19	8	9	30	25		

Team: CRO Croatia

Coach: SKANSI, Peter   Assistant Coaches: REPESA, Jasmin   TRNINIC, Slavko

Names	Pts	2 Pts	3 Pts	FT	A	Stl	To	Reb	F	Mins	
KUKOC, Toni	10	2/4	1/3	3/5	5	1	6	7	3	35:36	S
ALANOVIC, Vladan	7	1/2	1/3	2/2	0	0	1	2	5	25:37	S
RIMAC, Slaven	7	2/4	1/2	0/0	0	0	2	1	5	24:29	S
TABAK, Zan	18	7/11	0/0	4/9	1	1	1	8	3	29:57	S
VRANKOVIC, Stojan	4	2/2	0/0	0/0	0	0	1	2	3	12:20	S
VRANKOVIC, Josip	0	0/1	0/2	0/0	0	0	0	1	1	07:05	
PERASOVIC, Velimir	0	0/0	0/0	0/0	0	0	0	0	0	00:00	
KOMAZEC, Arijan	0	0/0	0/0	0/0	0	0	0	0	0	00:00	
MULAOMEROVIC, Damir	13	4/4	0/2	5/8	4	0	2	4	5	25:31	
MRSIC, Veljko	0	0/0	0/0	0/0	0	0	0	0	0	00:00	
RADJA, Dino	13	6/11	0/0	1/3	1	3	1	5	2	31:00	
MARCELIC, Davor	2	1/1	0/3	0/0	0	0	0	1	0	08:25	
Totals	74	25/40	3/15	15/27	11	5	14	31	27		

Referees: BRAZAUSKAS, Romualdas   LTU   REYES RONFINI, Jose   MEX

CLASSIFICATION 5 - 8 — FINAL SCORE: CHN 75 GRE 115 — HALFTIME SCORE: CHN 24 GRE 50

Team: CHN People's Republic of China

Coach: GONG, Lu-ming   Assistant Coach: CHEN, De-Chun

Names	Pts	2 Pts	3 Pts	FT	A	Stl	To	Reb	F	Mins	
LI, Xiao-yong	2	1/2	0/7	0/0	7	0	0	2	1	35:57	S
ZHENG, Wu	9	2/5	1/1	2/2	2	0	4	3	3	25:35	S
SUN, Jun	10	3/3	1/7	1/1	5	0	2	2	1	24:03	S
LIU, Yu-dong	12	4/16	0/0	4/6	2	0	0	8	2	31:13	S
BA, Tere	12	4/9	0/0	4/6	0	1	1	6	2	24:04	S
WANG, Zhi-zhi	8	4/8	0/0	0/0	0	0	2	4	5	15:56	
HU, Wei-dong	2	1/2	0/3	0/0	3	0	0	2	3	22:55	
WU, Nai-qin	0	0/0	0/0	0/0	0	0	2	1	0	04:21	
WU, Qing-long	20	0/2	5/6	5/5	1	0	0	0	1	11:30	
LI, Nan	0	0/0	0/0	0/0	0	0	0	0	0	00:00	
SHAN, Tao	0	0/0	0/0	0/0	0	0	0	0	0	00:00	
GONG, Xiao-bin	0	0/2	0/0	0/0	0	0	0	1	0	04:26	
Totals	75	19/49	7/24	16/20	20	1	11	29	18		

Team: GRE Greece

Coach: DEDRINOS, Makis   Assistant Coaches: TSAVAS, Lakis   FILIPPOU, Nikos

Names	Pts	2 Pts	3 Pts	FT	A	Stl	To	Reb	F	Mins	
BAKATSIAS, Efthimios	16	6/8	0/1	4/5	6	0	1	5	1	21:25	S
SIGALAS, Giorgos	14	5/9	1/1	1/3	6	0	0	6	3	22:43	S
ECONOMOU, Nikos	6	3/7	0/0	0/0	2	1	0	1	0	09:30	S
FASSOULAS, Panayotis	20	8/11	0/0	4/6	0	1	1	8	2	27:09	S
CHRISTODOULOU, Theofanis	11	1/2	3/6	0/0	8	3	1	12	1	31:24	S
PATAVOUKAS, Costas	12	1/2	3/6	1/2	2	1	0	6	1	19:51	
GIANNAKIS, Panayotis	2	1/3	0/0	0/0	5	0	1	2	0	11:55	
PAPANIKOLAOU, Dimitris	14	7/13	0/0	0/0	2	2	0	4	0	14:39	
KAKIOUSIS, Eleftherios	0	0/0	0/0	0/0	3	0	1	0	0	05:35	
ALVERTIS, Fragiskos	6	0/3	2/3	0/0	0	1	1	2	2	14:22	
AGELIDIS, Dinos	6	3/4	0/0	0/0	0	0	0	1	1	08:36	
RENTZIAS, Efthimis	8	4/7	0/0	0/0	0	0	0	6	4	12:51	
Totals	115	39/69	9/17	10/16	34	9	6	53	15		

Referees: DEROSA, Joseph   USA   JOVANCIC, Tomislav   YUG

QUARTERFINALS — FINAL SCORE: USA 98 BRA 75 — HALFTIME SCORE: USA 52 BRA 36

Team: USA United States of America

Coach: WILKENS, Lenny   Assistant Coaches: CREMINS, Bobby   SLOAN, Jerry

Names	Pts	2 Pts	3 Pts	FT	A	Stl	To	Reb	F	Mins	
PIPPEN, Scottie	13	5/6	1/3	0/0	6	3	3	4	1	23:27	S
MILLER, Reggie	12	3/3	2/6	0/0	2	0	2	1	0	21:48	S
MALONE, Karl	9	4/7	0/0	1/3	2	1	0	5	2	21:21	S
O'NEAL, Shaquille	11	5/8	0/0	1/1	0	0	0	11	4	20:57	S
PAYTON, Gary	7	3/6	0/0	1/4	7	1	3	5	2	22:36	S
BARKLEY, Charles	9	3/4	1/2	0/0	2	0	1	2	3	15:20	
HILL, Grant	4	2/5	0/1	0/0	3	3	2	1	4	16:33	
HARDAWAY, Anfernee	14	4/4	0/0	6/9	4	1	0	2	0	17:24	
ROBINSON, David	5	1/3	0/0	3/4	0	0	0	5	1	09:26	
RICHMOND, Mitch	7	0/1	2/2	1/1	1	1	3	0	0	09:37	
STOCKTON, John	0	0/1	0/0	0/0	2	1	0	0	0	08:35	
OLAJUWON, Hakeem	7	2/2	0/0	3/5	1	0	0	2	0	12:56	
Totals	98	32/50	6/14	16/27	28	12	15	38	17		

Team: BRA Brazil

Coach: VIDAL, Ary   Assistant Coaches: RODRIGUES, Carlos   SILVA, Joao

Names	Pts	2 Pts	3 Pts	FT	A	Stl	To	Reb	F	Mins	
FONSECA, Andre	2	1/2	0/2	0/0	3	3	1	3	2	17:18	S
VIANNA, Joao Jose	6	2/5	0/1	2/2	0	1	0	4	0	26:31	S
MINUCI, Wilson Fernando	11	5/8	0/0	1/2	5	2	0	4	2	30:18	S
SCHMIDT, Oscar	26	4/10	4/10	6/6	2	0	7	5	3	30:46	S
JOERKE, Joelcio	5	2/8	0/0	1/8	1	1	2	10	4	30:37	S
FERRACIU, Demetrius	0	0/3	0/0	0/0	0	0	0	1	0	02:44	
CASSIOLATO, Caio	14	4/8	2/4	0/0	3	1	1	0	2	19:58	
do NASCIMENTO, Carlos Olivia	5	1/3	1/4	0/0	1	0	2	5	3	10:48	
SILVEIRA, Caio Franco	3	1/4	0/0	1/2	1	1	1	2	2	07:19	
SANTANA, Antonio Jose	0	0/0	0/0	0/0	0	0	0	1	1	04:02	
dos SANTOS, Aristides Josuel	0	0/0	0/0	0/0	0	0	0	0	0	00:00	
KLAFKE, Rogerio	3	0/0	1/3	0/0	1	1	3	0	2	19:39	
Totals	75	20/49	8/24	11/20	17	10	18	35	21		

Referees: DORIZON, Pascal Noel   FRA   LAPAIX GUANCE, Jose   DOM

Men / *Messieurs*

QUARTERFINALS FINAL SCORE: YUG 128 CHN 61   HALFTIME SCORE: YUG 63 CHN 29

Team: YUG Yugoslavia

Coach: OBRADOVIC, Zelimir   Assistant Coaches: DARKO, Russo   NIKOLIC, Miroslav

Names	Pts	2 Pts	3 Pts	FT	A	Stl	To	Reb	F	Mins	
DANILOVIC, Predrag	12	5/7	0/1	2/3	2	1	1	2	2	20:00	S
PASPALJ, Zarko	15	7/10	0/0	1/2	0	4	0	4	3	16:33	S
DJORDJEVIC, Aleksandar	4	2/3	0/2	0/0	6	1	3	2	0	16:15	S
DIVAC, Vlade	5	2/5	0/0	1/1	5	1	2	4	1	17:59	S
SAVIC, Zoran	9	3/5	0/0	3/3	3	0	1	4	1	11:46	S
BODIROGA, Dejan	7	3/3	0/0	1/1	2	0	1	1	0	14:50	
OBRADOVIC, Sasa	16	3/5	2/8	4/5	2	3	2	1	1	25:32	
LONCAR, Nikola	6	0/0	2/3	0/0	1	0	0	1	1	06:50	
BERIC, Miroslav	14	3/3	1/3	5/7	6	4	3	1	4	20:00	
REBRACA, Zeljko	22	9/10	0/0	4/4	0	4	0	1	3	16:51	
TOMASEVIC, Dejan	12	6/7	0/0	0/0	1	1	3	7	0	12:56	
TOPIC, Milenko	6	1/2	1/1	1/2	1	2	0	8	1	20:28	
Totals	128	44/60	6/18	22/28	31	18	16	36	14		

Team: CHN People's Republic of China

Coach: GONG, Lu-ming   Assistant Coach: CHEN, De-Chun

Names	Pts	2 Pts	3 Pts	FT	A	Stl	To	Reb	F	Mins	
LI, Xiao-yong	2	1/3	0/2	0/0	3	1	2	1	3	34:47	S
ZHENG, Wu	6	3/4	0/1	0/0	0	0	1	1	2	16:38	S
SUN, Jun	10	1/7	2/6	2/2	2	1	3	1	3	34:29	S
WU, Nai-qin	12	6/8	0/0	0/0	2	1	7	4	1	24:39	S
BA, Tere	4	2/3	0/0	0/0	0	0	2	1	4	09:42	S
WANG, Zhi-zhi	13	3/8	0/0	7/8	2	1	2	4	2	30:32	
HU, Wei-dong	7	2/2	1/5	0/0	1	1	4	1	3	20:00	
WU, Qing-long	3	0/0	1/2	0/0	1	0	2	1	1	05:13	
LIU, Yu-dong	2	0/1	0/0	2/2	0	1	1	2	3	08:23	
LI, Nan	2	0/0	0/0	2/2	1	0	3	0	0	08:53	
SHAN, Tao	0	0/1	0/0	0/0	1	1	0	0	0	03:22	
GONG, Xiao-bin	0	0/1	0/0	0/0	0	0	2	0	2	03:22	
Totals	61	18/38	4/16	13/14	13	7	30	16	24		

Referees: ISHIDA, Hidetoshi JPN   COLUCCI, Gennaro ITA

QUARTERFINALS FINAL SCORE: LTU 99 GRE 66   HALFTIME SCORE: LTU 45 GRE 19

Team: LTU Lithuania

Coach: GARASTAS, Vladas   Assistant Coaches: KAZLAUSKAS, Jonas   NELSON, Donn

Names	Pts	2 Pts	3 Pts	FT	A	Stl	To	Reb	F	Mins	
ZUKAUSKAS, Mindaugas	8	4/5	0/0	0/0	0	1	1	1	4	12:51	S
KURTINAITIS, Rimas	15	0/1	5/8	0/0	1	1	3	5	1	23:46	S
SABONIS, Arvydas	10	4/7	0/0	2/2	4	1	1	11	3	25:08	S
KARNISOVAS, Arturas	15	3/4	0/1	9/10	1	1	1	6	1	29:12	S
MARCIULIONIS, Sarunas	16	4/5	2/3	2/2	7	1	2	5	2	26:00	S
VAISVILA, Rytis	0	0/0	0/0	0/0	1	1	2	1	1	07:59	
ZUKAUSKAS, Eurelijus	2	0/0	0/0	2/2	1	0	0	1	4	08:46	
PACESAS, Tomas	4	0/0	0/1	4/4	1	0	1	1	0	06:18	
STOMBERGAS, Saulius	9	1/1	0/1	7/8	1	0	1	2	4	17:12	
LUKMINAS, Darius	8	0/1	2/5	2/2	3	0	2	2	2	17:08	
EINIKIS, Gintaras	12	3/6	0/0	6/8	1	1	0	3	5	25:40	
Totals	99	19/30	9/19	34/38	21	7	14	38	27		

Team: GRE Greece

Coach: DEDRINOS, Makis   Assistant Coaches: TSAVAS, Lakis   FILIPPOU, Nikos

Names	Pts	2 Pts	3 Pts	FT	A	Stl	To	Reb	F	Mins	
BAKATSIAS, Efthimios	2	1/1	0/0	0/2	1	1	1	2	1	11:19	S
SIGALAS, Giorgos	18	4/10	1/5	7/10	5	2	0	3	4	31:53	S
ECONOMOU, Nikos	1	0/0	0/1	1/2	0	4	0	4		18:11	S
FASSOULAS, Panayotis	7	3/7	0/0	1/4	0	1	0	1	2	24:47	S
CHRISTODOULOU, Theofanis	0	0/1	0/2	0/0	0	0	2	1	4	18:12	S
PATAVOUKAS, Costas	0	0/0	0/0	0/0	2	1	0	1	1	13:46	
GIANNAKIS, Panayotis	2	1/2	0/1	0/0	0	2	1	3	1	11:27	
PAPANIKOLAOU, Dimitris	6	2/5	0/2	2/4	2	0	0	3	2	17:00	
KAKIOUSIS, Eleftherios	7	2/6	0/1	3/4	1	0	2	1	2	10:44	
ALVERTIS, Fragiskos	7	1/5	1/2	2/2	1	1	0	3	3	13:29	
AGELIDIS, Dinos	8	2/2	1/1	1/1	0	1	0	2	2	13:59	
RENTZIAS, Efthimis	8	0/2	0/0	8/10	0	0	1	4	4	15:13	
Totals	66	16/41	3/15	25/39	12	9	11	24	30		

Referees: BETANCOR LEON, Miguel ESP   CHAVES SAGEL, Raul ARG

QUARTERFINALS FINAL SCORE: AUS 73 CRO 71   HALFTIME SCORE: AUS 41 CRO 33

Team: AUS Australia

Coach: BARNES, Barry   Assistant Coaches: BLACK, Allan   BROWN, Brett

Names	Pts	2 Pts	3 Pts	FT	A	Stl	To	Reb	F	Mins	
RONALDSON, Tony	17	2/9	3/4	4/5	1	1	1	2	1	34:08	S
GAZE, Andrew	26	3/4	5/9	5/6	3	1	2	2	3	37:48	S
HEAL, Shane	11	0/3	2/9	5/7	7	2	0	5	1	40:00	S
BRADTKE, Mark	8	3/6	0/0	2/2	1	2	2	5	4	24:45	S
VLAHOV, Andrew	2	1/2	0/1	0/0	1	2	1	3	1	22:01	S
MAHER, Brett	0	0/0	0/0	0/0	0	0	0	0	0	00:00	
FISHER, Scott	7	1/3	1/1	2/2	3	1	1	3	0	26:03	
REIDY, Pat	0	0/0	0/0	0/0	0	0	0	0	0	00:00	
MacKINNON, Sam	0	0/0	0/1	0/0	0	0	0	0	0	00:00	
JENSEN, Tonny	0	0/0	0/0	0/0	0	0	0	0	0	00:00	
DORGE, John	2	1/2	0/0	0/0	0	0	1	4	1	15:15	
BORNER, Ray	0	0/0	0/0	0/0	0	0	0	0	0	00:00	
Totals	73	11/29	11/24	18/22	16	9	8	24	11		

Team: CRO Croatia

Coach: SKANSI, Peter   Assistant Coaches: REPESA, Jasmin   TRNINIC, Slavko

Names	Pts	2 Pts	3 Pts	FT	A	Stl	To	Reb	F	Mins	
KUKOC, Toni	13	5/8	1/7	0/0	8	3	4	9	2	38:02	S
ALANOVIC, Vladan	18	3/5	4/6	0/0	2	0	2	2	2	37:06	S
VRANKOVIC, Stojan	16	7/9	0/0	2/2	1	0	1	11	3	40:00	S
RADJA, Dino	0	0/5	0/0	0/0	0	0	0	2	2	15:21	S
MARCELIC, Davor	2	1/1	0/0	0/0	0	1	1	1	0	06:26	S
VRANKOVIC, Josip	12	3/3	2/4	0/1	1	0	0	3	3	23:29	
PERASOVIC, Velimir	0	0/2	0/0	0/0	0	0	2	1	0	07:57	
KOMAZEC, Arijan	0	0/0	0/0	0/0	0	0	0	0	0	00:00	
RIMAC, Slaven	2	1/1	0/1	0/0	0	0	0	0	0	00:34	
TABAK, Zan	6	3/7	0/0	0/0	2	1	1	3	2	24:05	
MULAOMEROVIC, Damir	2	1/2	0/1	0/0	1	0	0	0	0	07:00	
MRSIC, Veljko	0	0/0	0/0	0/0	0	0	0	0	0	00:00	
Totals	71	24/43	7/19	2/3	15	5	11	32	14		

Referees: ZYCH, Wieslaw POL   FIGUEROA, Juan PUR

SEMIFINALS FINAL SCORE: USA 101 AUS 73   HALFTIME SCORE: USA 51 AUS 41

Team: USA United States of America

Coach: WILKENS, Lenny   Assistant Coaches: CREMINS, Bobby   SLOAN, Jerry

Names	Pts	2 Pts	3 Pts	FT	A	Stl	To	Reb	F	Mins	
BARKLEY, Charles	24	6/6	1/1	9/11	2	1	1	11	1	24:03	S
ROBINSON, David	14	7/11	0/0	0/0	0	0	2	9	3	21:57	S
PIPPEN, Scottie	6	2/5	0/5	2/2	5	2	0	10	3	29:28	S
RICHMOND, Mitch	9	3/6	0/2	3/3	0	1	0	2	3	13:02	S
PAYTON, Gary	6	2/10	0/0	2/4	2	0	1	4	4	19:10	S
HILL, Grant	0	0/0	0/0	0/0	0	0	0	0	0	00:00	
HARDAWAY, Anfernee	14	4/5	2/5	0/1	1	0	2	3	1	18:38	
MILLER, Reggie	5	1/1	1/5	0/0	3	1	0	0	3	21:39	
MALONE, Karl	6	3/7	0/0	0/0	3	1	3	6	4	18:40	
STOCKTON, John	3	1/4	0/0	1/2	2	2	1	0	2	15:20	
O'NEAL, Shaquille	14	5/7	0/0	4/8	1	0	2	8	2	18:03	
OLAJUWON, Hakeem	0	0/0	0/0	0/0	0	0	0	0	0	00:00	
Totals	101	34/62	4/19	21/31	19	8	12	53	26		

Team: AUS Australia

Coach: BARNES, Barry   Assistant Coaches: BLACK, Allan   BROWN, Brett

Names	Pts	2 Pts	3 Pts	FT	A	Stl	To	Reb	F	Mins	
RONALDSON, Tony	4	1/3	0/3	2/2	2	0	0	1	4	27:53	S
GAZE, Andrew	25	3/7	3/5	10/11	3	1	3	4	2	37:40	S
HEAL, Shane	19	1/3	4/8	5/7	5	0	4	4	1	34:56	S
BRADTKE, Mark	9	3/15	0/0	3/4	0	1	3	11	2	29:16	S
VLAHOV, Andrew	9	2/7	1/1	2/2	2	2	2	3	3	23:25	S
MAHER, Brett	0	0/0	0/0	0/0	0	0	0	0	0	02:20	
FISHER, Scott	1	0/2	0/0	1/2	0	0	1	3	4	10:27	
REIDY, Pat	2	1/2	0/2	0/0	1	0	1	0	2	11:31	
MacKINNON, Sam	2	1/1	0/0	0/0	0	0	0	2	1	05:55	
JENSEN, Tonny	0	0/0	0/0	0/0	0	0	0	0	0	01:29	
DORGE, John	0	0/0	0/0	0/0	0	0	1	1	5	11:06	
BORNER, Ray	2	0/2	0/0	2/2	0	0	3	2	1	04:02	
Totals	73	12/42	8/19	25/30	14	4	19	31	25		

Referees: CHAVES SAGEL, Raul ARG   KOUKOULEKIDIS, Stylianos GRE

Basketball / *Basketball* 137

Men / *Messieurs*

SEMIFINALS — FINAL SCORE: YUG 66 LTU 58 | HALFTIME SCORE: YUG 35 LTU 31

Team: YUG Yugoslavia
Coach: OBRADOVIC, Zelimir Assistant Coaches: DARKO, Russo NIKOLIC, Miroslav

Names	Pts	2 Pts	3 Pts	FT	A	Stl	To	Reb	F	Mins	
DANILOVIC, Predrag	19	4/6	1/5	8/8	2	1	1	3	4	36:10	S
PASPALJ, Zarko	3	1/5	0/0	1/2	0	1	0	0	0	08:59	S
DJORDJEVIC, Aleksandar	16	2/5	3/6	3/3	1	1	2	3	0	37:16	S
DIVAC, Vlade	9	3/8	1/1	0/0	1	3	0	8	2	37:59	S
SAVIC, Zoran	8	3/4	0/0	2/2	2	0	1	4	3	18:51	S
BODIROGA, Dejan	7	2/6	0/1	3/4	4	0	2	3	2	29:00	
OBRADOVIC, Sasa	0	0/0	0/0	0/0	0	0	0	1	3	08:35	
LONCAR, Nikola	0	0/0	0/0	0/0	0	0	0	0	0	00:00	
BERIC, Miroslav	0	0/0	0/0	0/0	0	0	0	0	0	00:00	
REBRACA, Zeljko	4	2/3	0/0	0/0	0	0	2	6	4	23:10	
TOMASEVIC, Dejan	0	0/0	0/0	0/0	0	0	0	0	0	00:00	
TOPIC, Milenko	0	0/0	0/0	0/0	0	0	0	0	0	00:00	
Totals	66	17/37	5/13	17/19	10	6	8	28	18		

Team: LTU Lithuania
Coach: GARASTAS, Vladas Assistant Coaches: KAZLAUSKAS Jonas, NELSON, Donn

Names	Pts	2 Pts	3 Pts	FT	A	Stl	To	Reb	F	Mins	
KURTINAITIS, Rimas	22	1/3	5/7	5/7	1	1	1	1	4	36:42	S
SABONIS, Arvydas	14	6/14	0/1	2/2	3	1	5	13	4	40:00	S
KARNISOVAS, Arturas	8	0/2	2/5	2/2	1	0	3	0	4	26:09	S
MARCIULIONIS, Sarunas	5	1/3	1/6	0/0	6	0	2	4	3	34:28	S
EINIKIS, Gintaras	6	3/7	0/0	0/0	0	0	0	3	2	35:55	S
VAISVILA, Rytis	0	0/0	0/0	0/0	0	0	0	0	0	00:00	
ZUKAUSKAS, Mindaugas	0	0/0	0/0	0/0	0	0	0	0	0	00:00	
ZUKAUSKAS, Eurelijus	0	0/0	0/0	0/0	0	0	0	0	0	00:00	
PACESAS, Tomas	0	0/0	0/0	0/0	0	0	0	0	0	00:00	
STOMBERGAS, Saulius	0	0/0	0/0	0/0	3	0	0	0	1	14:16	
LUKMINAS, Darius	3	0/2	1/3	0/0	0	0	0	1	2	12:30	
Totals	58	11/31	9/22	9/11	14	2	11	22	20		

Referees: ZYCH, Wieslaw POL LAPAIX GUANCE, Jose DOM

FINAL 11 - 12 — FINAL SCORE: KOR 61 ANG 99 | HALFTIME SCORE: KOR 33 ANG 48

Team: KOR Korea
Coach: CHOI, In-Chul Assistant Coach: KIM, Nam-Ki

Names	Pts	2 Pts	3 Pts	FT	A	Stl	To	Reb	F	Mins	
KANG, Dong-Hee	17	7/10	1/4	0/0	6	1	3	0	1	34:05	S
HYUN, Joo-Yeop	9	2/5	0/0	5/6	1	1	4	4	4	30:13	S
HUR, Jae	2	1/3	0/4	0/0	2	1	2	0	0	21:52	S
MOON, Kyung-Eun	11	1/3	3/6	0/0	1	0	2	4	2	24:50	S
JUNG, Jae-Kun	4	2/7	0/0	0/0	1	2	4	3	3	27:45	S
LEE, Sang-Min	4	0/1	0/3	4/4	6	0	2	3	3	19:33	
YANG, Hee-Seung	8	4/4	0/1	0/0	0	0	0	0	0	08:31	
WOO, Ji-Won	0	0/0	0/0	0/0	0	0	0	0	0	00:00	
OH, Sung-Sik	0	0/0	0/0	0/0	0	0	0	0	0	00:00	
GI, Dong-Kee	0	0/0	0/0	0/0	0	0	0	0	1	03:34	
CHUN, Hee-Chul	4	2/5	0/0	0/0	0	0	0	5	4	15:41	
CHUNG, Kyung-Ho	2	1/3	0/0	0/2	1	0	1	1	5	13:56	
Totals	61	20/41	4/18	9/12	18	5	18	20	23		

Team: ANG Angola
Coach: ROMERO, Vladimiro Assistant Coach: TAVARES, Nelson

Names	Pts	2 Pts	3 Pts	FT	A	Stl	To	Reb	F	Mins	
MOREIRA, Anibal	5	1/4	1/3	0/0	5	1	2	4	5	19:40	S
VICTORIANO, Angelo	11	5/9	0/3	1/1	2	0	0	5	2	28:37	S
TROSO, Honorato	2	1/3	0/1	0/0	3	1	2	3	0	27:23	S
CARVALHO, Antonio	18	3/4	4/7	0/0	1	0	1	1	3	24:26	S
DIAS, David	27	9/15	0/0	9/11	2	1	1	11	1	30:41	S
VICTORIANO, Edmar	7	2/3	0/0	3/5	0	0	1	3	0	06:59	
UCUAHAMBA, Benjamin	0	0/0	0/0	0/0	0	0	0	0	0	00:00	
COIMBRA, Herlander	5	0/0	1/3	2/2	2	1	1	2	1	15:26	
VICTORIANO, Justino	9	3/5	0/0	3/4	0	4	7	3		17:33	
ROMANO, Benjamin	7	3/5	0/0	1/2	2	0	1	3	3	18:20	
GUIMARAES, Jose	8	3/3	0/1	2/2	2	2	0	2	0	10:55	
CONCEICAO, Jean-Jacques	0	0/0	0/0	0/0	0	0	0	0	0	00:00	
Totals	99	30/51	6/18	21/27	19	6	13	41	18		

Referees: REYES RONFINI, Jose MEX BREADIAZ, Juan CUB

FINAL 9 - 10 — FINAL SCORE: ARG 87 PUR 77 | HALFTIME SCORE: ARG 43 PUR 38

Team: ARG Argentina
Coach: VECCHIO, Guillermo Assistant Coaches: MAGNANO, Ruben DURO, Fernando

Names	Pts	2 Pts	3 Pts	FT	A	Stl	To	Reb	F	Mins	
MILANESIO, Marcelo	11	2/3	1/3	4/4	7	1	2	7	4	35:09	S
ESPIL, Juan	17	2/3	1/5	10/12	7	0	2	5	0	37:44	S
OSELLA, Diego	17	7/13	0/0	3/3	0	0	0	5	4	24:57	S
OBERTO, Fabricio	14	5/11	0/0	4/6	2	1	1	7	3	33:46	S
PEREZ, Esteban	16	4/7	2/6	2/2	0	2	1	4	4	37:19	S
NICOLA, Marcelo	0	0/0	0/0	0/0	0	0	0	0	0	00:00	
FARABELLO, Daniel	4	0/0	1/1	1/2	0	0	0	0	0	07:13	
VILLAR, Luis	8	2/6	1/2	1/2	0	0	3	2	2	18:15	
de la FUENTE, Esteban	0	0/0	0/0	0/0	0	0	0	0	0	00:00	
MICHEL, Ernesto	0	0/0	0/0	0/0	0	0	0	1	1	03:02	
RACCA, Jorge	0	0/0	0/0	0/0	1	0	0	0	1	02:35	
WOLKOWISKY, Ruben	0	0/0	0/0	0/0	0	0	0	0	0	00:00	
Totals	87	22/43	6/17	25/31	17	4	9	31	19		

Team: PUR Puerto Rico
Coach: MORALES, Carlos Assistant Coaches: LOPEZ, Angel CALCANO, Carlos

Names	Pts	2 Pts	3 Pts	FT	A	Stl	To	Reb	F	Mins	
ORTIZ, Jose Piculin	21	8/12	0/1	5/8	1	0	1	11	4	28:27	S
ALICEA, Pablo	0	0/0	0/1	0/0	2	0	2	1	0	07:36	S
MINCY, Jerome	11	3/4	1/5	2/4	1	0	2	9	3	32:57	S
RIVAS, Ramon	16	6/11	0/1	4/8	0	1	3	8	3	32:34	S
TORRES, Georgie	1	0/4	0/1	1/4	2	1	0	2	0	25:06	S
CURBELO, Joel	0	0/0	0/0	0/0	0	0	0	0	0	01:51	
SOTO, Richard	0	0/2	0/0	0/0	2	1	1	2	3	05:06	
RIVERA, Eddie	8	4/7	0/1	0/0	4	1	0	1	3	22:16	
TRAVIESO, Carmelo	9	3/4	1/3	0/0	5	1	1	3	3	21:30	
PADILLA, Edgar	2	1/4	0/0	0/0	1	1	2	1	3	10:35	
SOTO, Eugenio	0	0/0	0/0	0/0	0	0	1	1	0	03:07	
SANTIAGO, Daniel	9	4/4	0/0	1/2	0	0	1	2	2	08:55	
Totals	77	29/52	2/14	13/26	18	6	14	41	24		

Referees: NAKIC, Davorin CRO SOARES de CAMPOS, Antonio ANG

FINAL 7 - 8 — FINAL SCORE: CHN 85 CRO 99 | HALFTIME SCORE: CHN 39 CRO 49

Team: CHN People's Republic of China
Coach: GONG, Lu-ming Assistant Coach: CHEN, De-Chun

Names	Pts	2 Pts	3 Pts	FT	A	Stl	To	Reb	F	Mins	
LI, Xiao-yong	11	0/1	2/3	5/6	5	0	3	4	0	40:00	S
ZHENG, Wu	1	0/1	0/0	1/2	0	0	0	1	2	05:15	S
SUN, Jun	12	1/3	3/8	1/1	5	1	1	2	4	24:20	S
WU, Nai-qin	0	0/0	0/0	0/0	1	0	0	0	1	06:33	S
BA, Tere	11	3/10	1/1	2/2	0	0	1	5	5	13:08	S
WANG, Zhi-zhi	8	4/9	0/0	0/0	3	1	5	5	0	36:15	
HU, Wei-dong	22	0/1	7/9	1/2	2	2	3	0	0	20:00	
WU, Qing-long	0	0/0	0/0	0/0	0	0	0	0	0	00:00	
LIU, Yu-dong	0	0/0	0/0	0/0	0	0	0	0	0	00:00	
LI, Nan	8	4/7	0/1	0/0	3	2	1	5	5	30:55	
SHAN, Tao	0	0/0	0/0	0/0	0	0	0	0	0	00:00	
GONG, Xiao-bin	12	5/7	0/0	2/2	1	0	2	9	5	23:34	
Totals	85	17/40	13/22	12/15	20	6	16	31	22		

Team: CRO Croatia
Coach: SKANSI, Peter Assistant Coaches: REPESA, Jasmin TRNINIC, Slavko

Names	Pts	2 Pts	3 Pts	FT	A	Stl	To	Reb	F	Mins	
PERASOVIC, Velimir	0	0/2	0/1	0/0	1	0	0	0	0	12:40	S
KUKOC, Toni	26	6/11	2/4	8/10	8	1	0	10	0	32:36	S
ALANOVIC, Vladan	9	0/3	3/4	0/0	4	2	0	3	2	20:00	S
VRANKOVIC, Stojan	2	1/3	0/0	0/0	2	1	1	5	1	12:40	S
RADJA, Dino	14	6/7	0/0	2/5	1	0	0	6	0	20:00	S
VRANKOVIC, Josip	3	0/0	1/3	0/0	3	0	1	1	0	07:24	
KOMAZEC, Arijan	0	0/0	0/0	0/0	0	0	0	0	0	00:00	
RIMAC, Slaven	11	3/4	1/5	2/2	2	3	0	0	2	27:20	
TABAK, Zan	21	9/12	0/0	3/6	0	0	2	8	2	27:20	
MULAOMEROVIC, Damir	8	0/1	2/4	2/2	5	1	2	1	3	20:00	
MRSIC, Veljko	0	0/0	0/0	0/0	0	0	0	0	0	00:00	
MARCELIC, Davor	5	1/2	1/3	0/0	3	4	2	1	4	20:00	
Totals	99	26/45	10/24	17/25	29	12	8	35	14		

Referees: BARNETT, Robert AUS CHAVES SAGEL, Raul ARG

FINAL 5 - 6   FINAL SCORE: GRE 91   BRA 72   HALFTIME SCORE: GRE 45   BRA 49

Team: GRE Greece

Coach: DEDRINOS, Makis   Assistant Coaches: TSAVAS, Lakis   FILIPPOU, Nikos

Names	Pts	2 Pts	3 Pts	FT	A	Stl	To	Reb	F	Mins	
GIANNAKIS, Panayotis	3	1/2	0/0	1/2	3	2	0	4	1	18:32	S
SIGALAS, Giorgos	35	5/9	8/10	1/2	2	0	5	4	3	39:35	S
ECONOMOU, Nikos	9	1/5	1/2	4/4	2	0	2	2	3	21:33	S
FASSOULAS, Panayotis	10	4/10	0/0	2/5	2	0	2	7	4	35:34	S
CHRISTODOULOU, Theofanis	10	2/4	2/7	0/0	6	2	3	7	3	32:57	S
BAKATSIAS, Efthimios	0	0/0	0/0	0/0	0	0	1	0	0	01:23	
PATAVOUKAS, Costas	8	0/0	1/2	5/6	7	2	0	5	1	27:43	
PAPANIKOLAOU, Dimitris	2	1/1	0/0	0/0	0	0	0	0	0	00:25	
KAKIOUSIS, Eleftherios	0	0/0	0/0	0/0	1	0	0	1	0	02:03	
ALVERTIS, Fragiskos	14	2/5	3/5	1/2	0	1	1	4	2	19:25	
AGELIDIS, Dinos	0	0/0	0/0	0/0	0	0	0	0	0	00:25	
RENTZIAS, Efthimis	0	0/0	0/0	0/0	0	0	1	0	0	00:25	
Totals	91	16/36	15/26	14/21	23	7	15	34	17		

Team: BRA Brazil

Coach: VIDAL, Ary   Assistant Coaches: RODRIGUES, Carlos   SILVA, Joao

Names	Pts	2 Pts	3 Pts	FT	A	Stl	To	Reb	F	Mins	
FONSECA, Andre	7	2/4	1/2	0/0	7	3	1	1	3	30:19	S
VIANNA, Joao Jose	2	1/5	0/0	0/0	5	1	1	11	3	37:52	S
MINUCI, Wilson Fernando	23	10/12	0/0	3/4	1	0	1	4	2	31:26	S
dos SANTOS, Aristides Josuel	9	4/9	0/0	1/2	1	1	2	3	2	15:01	S
SCHMIDT, Oscar	21	2/6	5/17	2/2	1	1	5	4	3	34:18	S
FERRACIU, Demetrius	0	0/1	0/0	0/0	2	2	0	1	2	09:41	
CASSIOLATO, Caio	0	0/0	0/0	0/0	0	0	0	0	0	00:00	
do NASCIMENTO, Carlos Olivia	0	0/1	0/0	0/0	0	0	1	1	1	02:08	
SILVEIRA, Caio Franco	0	0/0	0/0	0/0	0	0	0	0	0	00:00	
SANTANA, Antonio Jose	0	0/0	0/0	0/0	0	0	0	0	0	00:00	
KLAFKE, Rogerio	4	2/4	0/3	0/0	1	1	1	3	0	14:16	
JOERKE, Joelcio	6	2/5	0/0	2/4	0	2	2	4	2	24:59	
Totals	72	23/47	6/22	8/12	18	11	14	32	18		

Referees: RYZHYK, Roman UKR   FIGUEROA, Juan PUR

FINAL - BRONZE MATCH   FINAL SCORE: LTU 80   AUS 74   HALFTIME SCORE: LTU 36   AUS 34

Team: LTU Lithuania

Coach: GARASTAS, Vladas   Assistant Coaches: KAZLAUSKAS, Jonas   NELSON, Donn

Names	Pts	2 Pts	3 Pts	FT	A	Stl	To	Reb	F	Mins	
ZUKAUSKAS, Mindaugas	4	2/2	0/0	0/0	0	0	1	1	2	24:30	S
KURTINAITIS, Rimas	9	3/8	1/2	0/0	3	0	2	3	2	34:08	S
SABONIS, Arvydas	30	9/15	3/4	3/3	2	0	0	13	3	40:00	S
KARNISOVAS, Arturas	21	4/6	3/6	4/5	2	3	5	5	2	38:46	S
MARCIULIONIS, Sarunas	16	2/5	2/5	6/8	9	1	0	4	2	32:36	S
VAISVILA, Rytis	0	0/0	0/0	0/0	0	0	0	0	0	00:00	
ZUKAUSKAS, Eurelijus	0	0/0	0/0	0/0	0	0	0	0	0	00:00	
PACESAS, Tomas	0	0/0	0/0	0/0	0	0	0	0	0	00:00	
STOMBERGAS, Saulius	0	0/0	0/0	0/0	2	0	0	1	3	03:58	
LUKMINAS, Darius	0	0/1	0/1	0/0	0	0	0	1	0	13:16	
EINIKIS, Gintaras	0	0/0	0/0	0/0	0	0	0	0	2	12:46	
Totals	80	20/37	9/18	13/16	18	4	8	28	16		

Team: AUS Australia

Coach: BARNES, Barry   Assistant Coaches: BLACK, Allan   BROWN, Brett

Names	Pts	2 Pts	3 Pts	FT	A	Stl	To	Reb	F	Mins	
RONALDSON, Tony	7	2/5	1/2	0/0	1	1	0	3	0	26:07	S
GAZE, Andrew	25	3/7	5/9	4/4	4	2	1	2	4	40:00	S
HEAL, Shane	11	1/3	3/9	0/0	5	0	3	3	0	40:00	S
BRADTKE, Mark	13	4/7	0/0	5/7	2	1	1	5	4	30:04	S
VLAHOV, Andrew	4	2/4	0/0	0/0	2	1	1	4	4	28:33	S
MAHER, Brett	0	0/0	0/0	0/0	0	0	0	0	0	00:00	
FISHER, Scott	13	4/6	1/1	2/2	3	0	1	1	5	25:20	
REIDY, Pat	0	0/0	0/0	0/0	0	0	0	0	0	00:00	
MacKINNON, Sam	0	0/0	0/0	0/0	0	0	0	0	0	00:00	
JENSEN, Tonny	0	0/0	0/0	0/0	0	0	0	0	0	00:00	
DORGE, John	1	0/2	0/0	1/2	0	0	0	4	2	09:56	
BORNER, Ray	0	0/0	0/0	0/0	0	0	0	0	0	00:00	
Totals	74	16/34	10/21	12/15	17	5	6	22	19		

Referees: DEROSA, Joseph USA   FIGUEROA, Juan PUR

FINAL - GOLD MATCH   FINAL SCORE: YUG 69   USA 95   HALFTIME SCORE: YUG 38   USA 43

Team: YUG Yugoslavia

Coach: OBRADOVIC, Zelimir   Assistant Coaches: DARKO, Russo   NIKOLIC, Miroslav

Names	Pts	2 Pts	3 Pts	FT	A	Stl	To	Reb	F	Mins	
BODIROGA, Dejan	13	4/6	0/1	5/7	1	0	1	5	2	30:22	S
DANILOVIC, Predrag	9	2/3	0/3	5/10	0	1	4	2	2	40:00	S
PASPALJ, Zarko	19	7/10	1/1	2/4	0	2	4	2	4	31:49	S
DJORDJEVIC, Aleksandar	13	3/7	1/1	4/5	6	1	5	5	4	35:31	S
DIVAC, Vlade	4	0/5	0/1	4/6	0	1	1	3	5	24:40	S
OBRADOVIC, Sasa	6	0/0	1/2	3/5	0	0	0	2	2	15:06	
LONCAR, Nikola	0	0/0	0/0	0/0	0	0	0	0	0	01:59	
BERIC, Miroslav	0	0/0	0/0	0/0	0	0	0	0	0	00:00	
REBRACA, Zeljko	4	2/6	0/0	0/2	3	0	2	3	5	18:04	
SAVIC, Zoran	0	0/0	0/0	0/0	0	0	0	0	0	00:00	
TOMASEVIC, Dejan	1	0/0	0/0	1/2	0	0	1	1	1	01:21	
TOPIC, Milenko	0	0/0	0/0	0/0	0	0	0	0	0	01:08	
Totals	69	18/37	3/9	24/41	10	5	18	23	25		

Team: USA United States of America

Coach: WILKENS, Lenny   Assistant Coaches: CREMINS, Bobby   SLOAN, Jerry

Names	Pts	2 Pts	3 Pts	FT	A	Stl	To	Reb	F	Mins	
PIPPEN, Scottie	4	2/3	0/1	0/0	2	0	2	4	4	18:38	S
MILLER, Reggie	20	3/4	3/7	5/6	4	2	1	1	3	30:14	S
MALONE, Karl	0	0/3	0/0	0/2	0	0	1	5	3	10:28	S
PAYTON, Gary	2	1/4	0/0	0/0	2	1	2	2	2	16:12	S
OLAJUWON, Hakeem	5	1/6	0/0	3/4	0	1	0	5	1	12:39	S
BARKLEY, Charles	8	2/2	0/0	4/6	2	2	2	3	5	13:52	
HILL, Grant	0	0/0	0/0	0/0	0	0	0	0	0	00:00	
HARDAWAY, Anfernee	17	4/7	1/1	6/7	4	2	1	3	3	23:48	
ROBINSON, David	28	9/11	0/0	10/14	0	2	1	7	1	26:13	
RICHMOND, Mitch	5	1/2	1/3	0/0	0	1	0	1	3	23:32	
STOCKTON, John	4	1/1	0/0	2/2	7	0	2	0	3	19:10	
O'NEAL, Shaquille	2	1/1	0/0	0/0	0	1	0	0	1	05:14	
Total	95	25/44	5/12	30/41	21	12	12	31	29		

Referees: BETANCOR LEON, Miguel ESP   REYES RONFINI, Jose MEX

FINAL CLASSIFICATION

Rnk	Ctry	
1	United States of America	**Gold**
2	Yugoslavia	**Silver**
3	Lithuania	**Bronze**
4	Australia	
5	Greece	
6	Brazil	
7	Croatia	
8	People's Republic of China	
9	Argentina	
10	Puerto Rico	
11	Angola	
12	Korea	

Basketball / *Basketball*

Women / *Dames*

PRELIMINARIES - GROUP A **FINAL SCORE:** **BRA 69** **CAN 56** **HALFTIME SCORE:** **BRA 38** **CAN 27**

Team: BRA Brazil

Coach: ANGELO, Miguel   Assistant Coaches: DUARTE, Sergio   BALBINO, Hermes

Names	Pts	2 Pts	3 Pts	FT	A	Stl	To	Reb	F	Mins	
OLIVA, Hortencia de Fatima Marcari	10	5/8	0/1	0/2	2	1	1	1	2	29:58	S
SILVA, Maria Paula Goncalves da	17	4/10	2/4	3/4	3	2	8	4	1	33:27	S
ARCAIN, Janeth dos Santos	17	8/14	0/0	1/3	4	1	3	8	3	39:27	S
SOBRAL, Marta de Souza	14	1/6	2/2	6/8	1	2	4	5	3	32:46	S
OLIVEIRA, Alessandra Santos de	3	1/2	0/0	1/2	0	0	0	5	4	18:50	S
SILVA, Maria Angelica G. da	2	0/2	0/0	2/2	2	0	0	0	3	18:37	
SANTOS, Ariana Aparecida dos	0	0/0	0/0	0/0	0	0	0	0	0	00:00	
SOBRAL, Leila de Souza	6	2/6	0/0	2/4	3	4	0	7	2	19:12	
GUSTAVO, Roseli do Carmo	0	0/0	0/0	0/0	0	0	0	0	0	00:00	
LUZ, Silvia Andrea Santos	0	0/0	0/0	0/0	0	0	0	0	0	00:00	
SANTOS, Cintia Silva dos	0	0/1	0/0	0/0	0	0	0	1	0	07:43	
PASTOR, Claudia Maria	0	0/0	0/0	0/0	0	0	0	0	0	00:00	
Totals	69	21/49	4/7	15/25	15	10	16	31	18		

Team: CAN Canada

Coach: ENNIS, Peter   Assistant Coaches: HARLE, Shawnee   LORDON, Pauline

Names	Pts	2 Pts	3 Pts	FT	A	Stl	To	Reb	F	Mins	
SMITH, Beverly	8	1/7	2/6	0/0	2	2	2	7	1	30:54	S
GAILUS, Karla Karch	2	1/3	0/1	0/0	0	1	3	2	1	14:40	S
MOLCAK, Shawna	8	3/9	0/1	2/2	3	1	2	4	2	27:58	S
JOHNSTON, Cynthia	8	3/6	0/0	2/2	0	1	2	5	2	26:31	S
NORMAN, Diane	7	1/5	0/0	5/7	2	1	2	4	5	20:56	S
THOMPSON, Camille	0	0/4	0/0	0/0	1	0	1	3	0	06:55	
STEWART, Susan	0	0/1	0/3	0/0	0	0	1	0	2	13:28	
EVANS, Jodi	8	2/4	0/0	4/4	4	1	1	6	2	26:16	
JERANT, Martina	0	0/0	0/0	0/0	0	0	0	0	0	00:00	
BOUCHER, Kelly	0	0/1	0/0	0/0	1	0	3	1	1	09:41	
BLACKWELL, Andrea	11	5/5	0/0	1/2	0	1	2	3	2	16:00	
LANGE-HARRIS, Marlelynn	4	2/3	0/0	0/1	0	0	1	1	2	06:41	
Totals	56	18/48	2/11	14/18	13	8	20	36	20		

Referees: BARNETT, Robert AUS   JOVANCIC, Tomislav YUG

PRELIMINARIES - GROUP A **FINAL SCORE:** **JPN 63** **RUS 73** **HALFTIME SCORE:** **JPN 37** **RUS 45**

Team: JPN Japan

Coach: NAKAGAWA, Fumikazu   Assistant Coaches: NAGAI, Yoshitake   KOMURE, Ikuo

Names	Pts	2 Pts	3 Pts	FT	A	Stl	To	Reb	F	Mins	
ICHIJO, Aki	7	2/4	1/2	0/0	1	2	1	4	2	19:17	S
MURAKAMI, Chikako	3	0/5	1/3	0/0	6	2	3	7	2	31:44	S
HAGIWARA, Mikiko	14	4/11	2/6	0/2	1	0	1	2	2	29:43	S
KATO, Takako	15	5/13	1/2	2/3	1	1	3	9	3	27:31	S
HAMAGUCHI, Noriko	7	1/6	0/0	5/7	2	2	4	3	3	33:34	S
OYAMA, Taeko	6	0/1	2/2	0/0	0	1	1	1	0	11:45	
MIKAWA, Kikuko	0	0/0	0/0	0/0	0	0	0	0	0	00:00	
YAMADA, Kagari	4	1/2	0/0	2/3	0	0	0	1	1	06:26	
HARADA, Yuka	0	0/0	0/1	0/0	2	0	0	0	1	08:16	
OKAZATO, Akemi	3	0/0	1/6	0/0	0	1	1	1	0	12:49	
KAWASAKI, Mayumi	0	0/0	0/0	0/0	0	0	0	1	1	06:26	
NAGATA, Mutsuko	4	1/4	0/0	2/3	0	2	1	2	2	12:29	
Totals	63	14/46	8/22	11/18	13	11	15	31	17		

Team: RUS Russian Federation

Coach: KAPRANOV, Vadim   Assistant Coaches: KOVALEV, Valeri   GROUDINE, Igor

Names	Pts	2 Pts	3 Pts	FT	A	Stl	To	Reb	F	Mins	
BARANOVA, Yelena	21	8/17	1/2	2/2	3	1	5	13	2	30:18	S
KOUZNETSOVA, Svetlana	0	0/4	0/1	0/0	0	0	1	2	3	13:08	S
SUMNIKOVA, Irina	3	0/2	1/1	0/0	5	3	3	4	5	25:32	S
SHAKIROVA, Elen	4	2/7	0/0	0/2	1	1	1	4	0	20:12	S
ANTIPOVA, Svetlana	2	1/5	0/2	0/0	2	1	0	2	2	21:50	S
NIKONOVA, Yevgeniya	14	5/11	1/1	1/2	2	2	1	0	1	22:10	
KONOVALOVA, Lyudmila	0	0/0	0/0	0/0	1	1	0	1	0	09:43	
RUTKOVSKAYA, Irina	13	3/4	0/0	7/8	0	1	3	8	4	27:37	
STEPANOVA, Mariya	0	0/0	0/0	0/0	0	0	0	0	0	00:23	
SVINOUKHOVA, Natalia	8	2/5	0/0	4/5	0	0	1	6	1	15:34	
ZAKAULYUZHANAYA, Oksana	0	0/0	0/0	0/0	0	0	0	0	0	00:00	
PSHIKOVA, Yelena	8	3/7	0/1	2/2	0	0	1	5	1	13:33	
Totals	73	24/62	3/8	16/21	14	10	17	45	19		

Referees: BELL, Sally USA   THONGPILA, Virun THA

PRELIMINARIES - GROUP A **FINAL SCORE:** **ITA 62** **CHN 53** **HALFTIME SCORE:** **ITA 27** **CHN 36**

Team: ITA Italy

Coach: SALES, Riccaro   Assistant Coaches: NANI, Renato   CARZANIGA, Dante

Names	Pts	2 Pts	3 Pts	FT	A	Stl	To	Reb	F	Mins	
ZANUSSI, Stefania	4	2/4	0/2	0/0	2	2	2	3	1	16:11	S
FULLIN, Mara	2	1/5	0/2	0/1	2	1	1	1	2	25:07	S
CASELIN, Nicoletta	16	5/9	1/1	3/3	3	1	2	0	3	23:56	S
POLLINI, Catarina	5	2/6	0/0	1/2	2	2	0	0	3	23:29	S
TUFANO, Giuseppina	5	2/4	0/0	1/4	1	2	3	4	3	23:12	S
BONFIGLIO, Susanna	6	2/3	0/1	2/2	0	3	0	2	4	22:09	
PAPARAZZO, Elena	0	0/2	0/0	0/0	0	0	1	3	0	04:32	
GARDELLIN, Valentina	10	1/1	2/4	2/3	1	0	0	1	0	16:04	
BALLABIO, Viviana	2	0/2	0/1	2/2	3	1	1	4	1	16:33	
REZOAGLI, Marta	0	0/0	0/0	0/0	0	0	0	0	0	00:00	
ARNETOLI, Lorenza	6	3/5	0/0	0/0	0	0	1	3	2	12:16	
SCHIESARO, Novella	6	3/6	0/0	0/0	2	0	0	5	4	16:31	
Totals	62	21/47	3/11	11/17	16	12	11	26	19		

Team: CHN People's Republic of China

Coach: CHEN, Daohong   Assistant Coaches: MA, Lianbao   HU, Hilin

Names	Pts	2 Pts	3 Pts	FT	A	Stl	To	Reb	F	Mins	
LI, Xin	15	5/8	1/1	2/4	4	2	6	2	1	33:22	S
ZHENG, Dongmei	8	0/1	2/6	2/2	2	2	5	5	1	40:00	S
LIANG, Xin	0	0/3	0/0	0/0	1	0	1	5	0	17:05	S
ZHENG, Haixia	8	3/9	0/1	2/4	0	4	5	3	3	34:41	S
MA, Zongqing	1	0/0	0/0	1/2	0	0	1	0	2	04:59	S
MIAO, Bo	0	0/0	0/0	0/0	0	1	2	2	1	08:48	
LIU, Jun	15	4/7	1/2	4/4	1	0	1	3	4	32:51	
SHEN, Li	0	0/0	0/0	0/0	0	0	0	0	0	00:00	
CHU, Hui	0	0/0	0/0	0/0	0	0	0	0	0	00:00	
HE, Jun	0	0/0	0/0	0/0	0	0	0	0	0	00:00	
LI, Dongmei	6	3/5	0/0	0/1	4	1	1	4	4	28:14	
MA, Chengqing	0	0/0	0/0	0/0	0	0	0	0	0	00:00	
Totals	53	15/34	4/10	11/17	13	7	21	26	16		

Referees: REYES RONFINI, Jose MEX   SOARES DE CAMPOS, Antonio ANG

PRELIMINARIES - GROUP A **FINAL SCORE:** **CHN 72** **JPN 75** **HALFTIME SCORE:** **CHN 42** **JPN 35**

Team: CHN People's Republic of China

Coach: CHEN, Daohong   Assistant Coaches: MA, Lianbao   HU, Hilin

Names	Pts	2 Pts	3 Pts	FT	A	Stl	To	Reb	F	Mins	
LI, Xin	13	3/6	1/2	4/6	6	1	2	2	0	26:03	S
ZHENG, Dongmei	10	2/2	2/3	0/0	1	1	1	1	4	24:03	S
LIANG, Xin	5	2/5	0/0	1/1	5	0	0	7	1	32:51	S
LI, Dongmei	4	1/5	0/0	2/2	1	0	2	2	2	15:22	S
MA, Zongqing	2	1/1	0/0	0/0	0	0	1	0	0	09:22	S
MIAO, Bo	0	0/0	0/0	0/0	1	0	1	0	1	02:25	
LIU, Jun	4	2/3	0/4	0/1	2	1	4	3	2	21:05	
SHEN, Li	0	0/0	0/1	0/0	1	0	3	3	4	15:57	
CHU, Hui	0	0/0	0/0	0/0	0	0	0	0	0	00:00	
ZHENG, Haixia	31	15/23	0/0	1/5	0	0	3	16	3	31:34	
HE, Jun	3	0/0	1/1	0/0	1	0	1	0	2	21:18	
MA, Chengqing	0	0/0	0/0	0/0	0	0	0	0	0	00:00	
Totals	72	26/46	4/11	8/15	19	3	18	36	21		

Team: JPN Japan

Coach: NAKAGAWA, Fumikazu   Assistant Coaches: NAGAI, Yoshitake   KOMURE, Ikuo

Names	Pts	2 Pts	3 Pts	FT	A	Stl	To	Reb	F	Mins	
MURAKAMI, Chikako	12	2/2	2/3	2/2	4	3	0	2	1	35:32	S
OYAMA, Taeko	6	3/8	0/4	0/0	1	1	0	4	3	31:35	S
HAGIWARA, Mikiko	23	8/10	1/3	4/4	0	1	0	3	1	31:59	S
KATO, Takako	8	2/11	0/1	4/4	2	0	3	10	4	32:13	S
HAMAGUCHI, Noriko	12	6/8	0/0	0/0	3	2	0	4	5	21:35	S
ICHIJO, Aki	3	0/2	0/1	3/4	1	0	1	0	0	08:38	
MIKAWA, Kikuko	0	0/0	0/0	0/0	0	0	0	0	0	00:00	
YAMADA, Kagari	1	0/4	0/0	1/2	1	0	2	2	0	08:01	
HARADA, Yuka	0	0/1	0/1	0/0	0	0	0	0	1	04:28	
OKAZATO, Akemi	0	0/0	0/0	0/0	0	0	0	0	0	00:00	
KAWASAKI, Mayumi	6	3/7	0/0	0/0	2	1	1	4	1	18:12	
NAGATA, Mutsuko	4	2/3	0/0	0/0	1	0	0	2	1	07:47	
Totals	75	26/56	3/13	14/16	13	9	5	32	17		

Referees: DORIZON, Pascal Noel FRA   KABASELE, Chikala ZAI

Women / *Dames*

PRELIMINARIES - GROUP A   FINAL SCORE: CAN 54   ITA 59   HAFLTIME SCORE: CAN 34   ITA 24

Team: CAN Canada

Coach: ENNIS, Peter   Assistant Coaches: HARLE, Shawnee   LORDON, Pauline

Names	Pts	2 Pts	3 Pts	FT	A	Stl	To	Reb	F	Mins	
SMITH, Beverly	13	5/5	0/3	3/4	3	1	1	7	2	32:27	S
MOLCAK, Shawna	12	5/9	0/0	2/2	1	0	0	5	2	32:11	S
EVANS, Jodi	0	0/3	0/1	0/0	5	2	0	6	1	26:39	S
NORMAN, Diane	4	2/5	0/0	0/0	2	3	3	6	4	28:27	S
BLACKWELL, Andrea	4	2/4	0/0	0/0	0	0	4	1	1	11:25	S
GAILUS, Karla Karch	2	1/2	0/1	0/0	1	0	3	1	2	12:59	
THOMPSON, Camille	2	1/1	0/0	0/0	0	0	0	2	0	02:50	
STEWART, Susan	0	0/1	0/1	0/0	0	0	0	0	0	04:27	
JOHNSTON, Cynthia	7	2/5	0/0	3/3	2	0	10	5	2	32:01	
JERANT, Martina	0	0/0	0/0	0/0	0	0	0	0	0	00:00	
BOUCHER, Kelly	10	2/3	0/0	6/6	1	0	3	0	5	14:52	
LANGE-HARRIS, Marlelynn	0	0/1	0/1	0/0	0	0	1	0	2	01:42	
Totals	54	20/39	0/7	14/15	15	6	25	33	21		

Team: ITA Italy

Coach: SALES, Riccaro   Assistant Coaches: NANI, Renato   CARZANIGA, Dante

Names	Pts	2 Pts	3 Pts	FT	A	Stl	To	Reb	F	Mins	
ZANUSSI, Stefania	0	0/2	0/0	0/0	1	1	1	1	1	15:41	S
FULLIN, Mara	15	1/3	2/4	7/8	1	1	3	1	1	25:22	S
CASELIN, Nicoletta	5	1/3	1/2	0/0	0	0	2	0	4	14:18	S
POLLINI, Catarina	4	2/6	0/0	0/0	0	0	5	4	4	24:25	S
ARNETOLI, Lorenza	6	3/3	0/0	0/0	0	0	1	0	1	18:54	S
BONFIGLIO, Susanna	4	1/6	0/0	2/2	2	1	2	3	3	18:25	
PAPARAZZO, Elena	0	0/2	0/0	0/0	0	0	0	0	1	06:31	
GARDELLIN, Valentina	8	1/2	2/3	0/2	3	2	1	0	1	25:42	
BALLABIO, Viviana	15	2/2	3/4	2/2	1	1	1	1	3	20:32	
REZOAGLI, Marta	0	0/0	0/0	0/0	0	0	0	0	0	00:00	
TUFANO, Giuseppina	1	0/3	0/0	1/2	0	0	0	4	2	11:40	
SCHIESARO, Novella	1	0/1	0/0	1/2	2	0	0	1	1	18:30	
Totals	59	11/33	8/13	13/18	10	6	16	15	22		

Referees: LAPAIX GUANCE, Jose   DOM   BRAZAUSKAS, Romualdas   LTU

PRELIMINARIES - GROUP A   FINAL SCORE: RUS 68   BRA 82   HALFTIME SCORE: RUS 36   BRA 41

Team: RUS Russian Federation

Coach: KAPRANOV, Vadim   Assistant Coaches: KOVALEV, Valeri   GROUDINE, Igor

Names	Pts	2 Pts	3 Pts	FT	A	Stl	To	Reb	F	Mins	
RUTKOVSKAYA, Irina	18	3/7	1/1	9/10	1	2	1	2	3	31:57	S
BARANOVA, Yelena	15	6/14	0/2	3/4	0	2	1	9	3	37:38	S
SUMNIKOVA, Irina	4	2/5	0/0	0/0	0	1	4	2	2	22:08	S
SHAKIROVA, Elen	11	3/5	0/0	5/6	2	0	1	5	2	23:38	S
PSHIKOVA, Yelena	5	1/1	1/3	0/0	0	0	3	3	3	17:14	S
NIKONOVA, Yevgeniya	2	1/3	0/1	0/0	1	1	0	0	1	11:02	
KONOVALOVA, Lyudmila	0	0/0	0/0	0/0	0	0	0	0	0	00:00	
STEPANOVA, Mariya	0	0/0	0/0	0/0	0	0	0	0	0	00:59	
SVINOUKHOVA, Natalia	2	0/4	0/0	2/2	1	0	1	3	1	12:36	
KOUZNETSOVA, Svetlana	11	4/5	0/1	3/4	0	0	2	1	3	27:25	
ZAKAULYUZHANAYA, Oksana	0	0/0	0/0	0/0	0	0	0	0	0	00:00	
ANTIPOVA, Svetlana	0	0/1	0/3	0/0	3	0	3	1	1	15:23	
Totals	68	20/45	2/11	22/26	8	6	16	26	18		

Team: BRA Brazil

Coach: ANGELO, Miguel   Assistant Coaches: DUATE, Sergio   BALBINO, Hermes

Names	Pts	2 Pts	3 Pts	FT	A	Stl	To	Reb	F	Mins	
OLIVA, Hortencia de Fatima Marcari	20	7/12	0/0	6/6	4	0	1	6	3	37:03	S
SILVA, Maria Paula Goncalves da	11	2/10	2/4	1/2	4	1	2	2	3	29:34	S
ARCAIN, Janeth dos Santos	11	4/12	0/0	3/4	4	3	3	2	2	35:06	S
SOBRAL, Marta de Souza	17	6/9	1/1	2/2	2	2	6	9	5	30:50	S
OLIVEIRA, Alessandra Santos de	8	3/5	0/0	2/5	0	1	1	5	3	27:04	S
SILVA, Maria Angelica G. da	5	1/3	1/2	0/0	3	0	0	0	0	18:17	
SANTOS, Ariana Aparecida dos	0	0/0	0/0	0/0	0	0	0	0	0	00:00	
SOBRAL, Leila de Souza	10	4/4	0/0	2/2	2	3	0	3	4	20:49	
GUSTAVO, Roseli do Carmo	0	0/0	0/0	0/0	0	0	0	0	0	00:00	
LUZ, Silvia Andrea Santos	0	0/0	0/0	0/0	0	0	0	1	0	00:00	
SANTOS, Cintia Silva dos	0	0/0	0/0	0/0	0	0	0	0	0	01:04	
PASTOR, Claudia Maria	0	0/0	0/0	0/0	0	0	0	1	0	00:13	
Totals	82	27/55	4/7	16/21	19	10	14	28	20		

Referees: FIGUEROA, Juan   PUR   KOUKOULEKIDIS, Stylianos   GRE

PRELIMINARIES - GROUP A   FINAL SCORE: ITA 70   RUS 75   HALFTIME SCORE: ITA 37   RUS 41

Team: ITA Italy

Coach: SALES, Riccaro   Assistant Coaches: NANI, Renato   CARZANIGA, Dante

Names	Pts	2 Pts	3 Pts	FT	A	Stl	To	Reb	F	Mins	
FULLIN, Mara	12	2/4	2/5	2/2	5	1	3	1	1	31:20	S
CASELIN, Nicoletta	4	2/6	0/0	0/0	4	0	2	1	2	19:29	S
BALLABIO, Viviana	5	0/7	1/2	2/2	2	4	1	3	5	26:02	S
POLLINI, Catarina	22	9/15	0/0	4/6	0	2	2	8	4	35:24	S
TUFANO, Giuseppina	12	4/6	0/0	4/5	0	0	0	7	4	20:45	S
ZANUSSI, Stefania	0	0/0	0/1	0/0	1	0	0	0	3	03:24	
BONFIGLIO, Susanna	1	0/6	0/0	1/2	1	0	1	1	2	13:12	
PAPARAZZO, Elena	6	2/6	0/0	2/4	0	0	2	3	2	16:55	
GARDELLIN, Valentina	6	0/2	2/4	0/0	2	2	0	0	0	21:33	
REZOAGLI, Marta	0	0/0	0/0	0/0	0	0	0	1	0	05:16	
ARNETOLI, Lorenza	0	0/0	0/0	0/0	0	0	1	0	0	02:04	
SCHIESARO, Novella	2	1/1	0/0	0/0	0	0	0	0	1	04:36	
Totals	70	20/53	5/12	15/21	15	9	12	25	24		

Team: RUS Russian Federation

Coach: KAPRANOV, Vadim   Assistant Coaches: KOVALEV, Valeri   GROUDINE, Igor

Names	Pts	2 Pts	3 Pts	FT	A	Stl	To	Reb	F	Mins	
RUTKOVSKAYA, Irina	6	1/6	0/2	4/4	3	1	2	2	4	25:40	S
BARANOVA, Yelena	14	7/10	0/0	0/0	0	1	3	12	5	26:34	S
SUMNIKOVA, Irina	4	2/2	0/1	0/2	9	0	7	3	3	40:00	S
SHAKIROVA, Elen	24	7/11	0/0	10/14	4	1	2	12	3	36:19	S
PSHIKOVA, Yelena	4	1/5	0/3	2/2	0	4	2	3	3	29:04	S
NIKONOVA, Yevgeniya	14	3/5	2/3	2/2	0	2	1	4	1	24:31	
KONOVALOVA, Lyudmila	0	0/0	0/0	0/0	0	0	0	0	0	00:00	
STEPANOVA, Mariya	0	0/0	0/0	0/0	0	0	0	0	0	00:00	
SVINOUKHOVA, Natalia	7	1/1	0/0	5/5	0	0	1	2	4	08:41	
KOUZNETSOVA, Svetlana	2	0/0	0/0	2/2	0	0	1	1	1	09:11	
ZAKAULYUZHANAYA, Oksana	0	0/0	0/0	0/0	0	0	0	0	0	00:00	
ANTIPOVA, Svetlana	0	0/0	0/0	0/0	0	0	0	0	0	00:00	
Totals	75	22/40	2/9	25/31	16	9	19	39	24		

Referees: NAKIC, Davorin   CRO   CHAVES SAGEL, Raul   ARG

PRELIMINARIES - GROUP A   FINAL SCORE: BRA 100   JPN 80   HALFTIME SCORE: BRA 57   JPN 46

Team: BRA Brazil

Coach: ANGELO, Miguel   Assistant Coaches: DUARTE, Sergio   BALBINO, Hermes

Names	Pts	2 Pts	3 Pts	FT	A	Stl	To	Reb	F	Mins	
OLIVA, Hortencia de Fatima Marcari	2	1/3	0/0	0/0	1	0	0	2	1	06:44	S
SILVA, Maria Paula Goncalves da	25	5/10	5/9	0/1	10	0	5	3	1	32:28	S
ARCAIN, Janeth dos Santos	17	8/18	0/1	1/1	7	2	1	7	1	36:57	S
SOBRAL, Marta de Souza	21	7/13	1/2	4/4	3	2	2	12	3	35:09	S
OLIVEIRA, Alessandra Santos de	20	9/13	0/0	2/6	0	0	3	9	4	29:41	S
SILVA, Maria Angelica G. da	0	0/0	0/0	0/0	2	3	1	1	0	04:26	
SANTOS, Ariana Aparecida dos	2	1/1	0/1	0/0	0	0	0	0	0	03:08	
SOBRAL, Leila de Souza	9	4/8	0/0	1/2	5	6	2	14	3	30:47	
GUSTAVO, Roseli do Carmo	0	0/1	0/0	0/2	0	0	0	0	0	03:03	
LUZ, Silvia Andrea Santos	0	0/0	0/0	0/0	2	0	2	1	1	05:05	
SANTOS, Cintia Silva dos	4	1/4	0/0	2/2	0	1	1	4	2	10:03	
PASTOR, Claudia Maria	0	0/0	0/0	0/0	0	0	0	1	0	02:29	
Totals	100	36/71	6/13	10/18	30	13	17	54	16		

Team: JPN Japan

Coach: NAKAGAWA, Fumikazu   Assistant Coaches: NAGAI, Yoshitake   KOMURE, Ikuo

Names	Pts	2 Pts	3 Pts	FT	A	Stl	To	Reb	F	Mins	
ICHIJO, Aki	16	3/5	3/8	1/2	2	0	2	4	3	28:02	S
MURAKAMI, Chikako	6	1/2	1/3	1/2	4	2	3	5	1	30:21	S
HAGIWARA, Mikiko	12	3/8	2/3	0/0	3	0	2	2	1	29:28	S
KATO, Takako	7	1/6	1/1	2/2	1	0	4	4	4	18:09	S
HAMAGUCHI, Noriko	9	2/6	0/0	5/5	3	2	3	2	4	26:24	S
OYAMA, Taeko	0	0/1	0/0	0/0	0	0	0	0	2	03:04	
MIKAWA, Kikuko	3	0/0	1/2	0/0	1	0	0	1	0	03:03	
YAMADA, Kagari	9	2/3	1/3	2/2	1	0	1	2	4	08:51	
HARADA, Yuka	4	1/2	0/1	2/2	1	0	1	1	0	09:39	
OKAZATO, Akemi	3	0/0	1/4	0/0	1	0	0	0	0	08:43	
KAWASAKI, Mayumi	2	1/3	0/0	0/0	0	0	1	1	0	13:36	
NAGATA, Mutsuko	9	4/8	0/0	1/2	2	0	3	5	0	20:40	
Totals	80	18/44	10/25	14/17	19	4	16	27	19		

Referees: BUTLER, Michael   AUS   BETANCOR LEON, Miguel   ESP

Basketball / *Basketball*   **141**

VARSHA M PISE • LEO PISKIC • JULIE R PISKUR • ROSANNA PISTILLI FALOCCO • JOE R PITARD • MERRY JO J PITASI • LORRI A PITCHELL • KIMBERLY A PITCHER • BARBARA PITKIN • JU-DITH A PITLOCK • MARY T PITMAN • PAUL PITNEY • TOM PITNEY JR • PATRICIA A PITOSCIA • DEBRA J PITT • DIANE S PITT • JEANETTE C PITT • NATALIE D PITT • ROBERT PITT • SUSAN L PITT • TREVOR S PITT • BETTY T PITTARD • TOMMY H PITTARD • MICHAEL C PITTARI • CAROL J PITTILLO • ANDREW LEROY PITTMAN • ARLO C PITTMAN • BILLY R PITTMAN • BOBBY PITTMAN

Women / *Dames*

PRELIMINARIES - GROUP A   FINAL SCORE: CAN 49   CHN 61   HALFTIME SCORE: CAN 25   CHN 28

Team: CAN Canada
Coach: ENNIS, Peter   Assistant Coaches: HARLE, Shawnee   LORDON, Pauline

Names	Pts	2 Pts	3 Pts	FT	A	Stl	To	Reb	F	Mins	
SMITH, Beverly	8	4/8	0/5	0/0	2	2	2	6	3	32:07	S
MOLCAK, Shawna	8	4/11	0/0	0/0	3	1	3	3	1	27:08	S
EVANS, Jodi	2	1/2	0/0	0/0	5	3	2	3	2	19:42	S
JOHNSTON, Cynthia	4	1/4	0/0	2/2	3	0	1	8	3	26:57	S
NORMAN, Diane	8	3/7	0/0	2/4	1	0	2	9	5	25:01	S
GAILUS, Karla Karch	4	0/1	1/3	1/2	1	0	1	2	1	13:11	
THOMPSON, Camille	2	1/1	0/0	0/0	0	1	0	0	1	01:36	
STEWART, Susan	3	1/2	0/3	1/3	0	0	0	1	0	07:11	
JERANT, Martina	0	0/0	0/0	0/0	0	0	0	0	0	00:00	
BOUCHER, Kelly	4	2/7	0/1	0/0	3	1	0	5	0	21:45	
BLACKWELL, Andrea	6	3/11	0/0	0/2	2	1	1	0	0	22:26	
LANGE-HARRIS, Marlelynn	0	0/0	0/0	0/0	0	0	0	0	1	02:56	
Totals	49	20/54	1/12	6/13	20	9	12	37	17		

Team: CHN People's Republic of China
Coach: CHEN, Daohong   Assistant Coaches: MA, Lianbao   HU, Hilin

Names	Pts	2 Pts	3 Pts	FT	A	Stl	To	Reb	F	Mins	
LI, Xin	9	3/4	0/2	3/4	1	1	1	2	0	19:45	S
ZHENG, Dongmei	3	0/2	1/3	0/0	4	1	0	1	1	22:40	S
LIANG, Xin	4	2/2	0/0	0/0	2	0	0	3	2	17:20	S
ZHENG, Haixia	19	7/13	0/0	5/8	2	0	3	16	2	34:12	S
MA, Zongqing	3	1/3	0/0	1/2	1	1	0	0	0	11:21	S
MIAO, Bo	0	0/1	0/0	0/0	0	0	1	1	0	01:18	
LIU, Jun	12	4/8	1/2	1/2	3	1	3	2	2	27:13	
SHEN, Li	3	0/0	1/1	0/0	1	1	2	3	2	17:20	
CHU, Hui	0	0/0	0/0	0/0	0	0	0	0	0	00:00	
HE, Jun	2	1/2	0/3	0/0	2	2	2	2	0	20:23	
LI, Dongmei	6	3/6	0/0	0/0	0	1	1	4	4	28:28	
MA, Chengqing	0	0/0	0/0	0/0	0	0	0	0	0	00:00	
Totals	61	21/41	3/11	10/16	16	8	13	34	13		

Referees: BELL, Sally   USA   KOUKOULEKIDIS, Stylianos   GRE

PRELIMINARIES - GROUP A   FINAL SCORE: JPN 52   ITA 66   HALFTIME SCORE: JPN 30   ITA 27

Team: JPN Japan
Coach: NAKAGAWA, Fumikazu   Assistant Coaches: NAGAI, Yoshitake   KOMURE, Ikuo

Names	Pts	2 Pts	3 Pts	FT	A	Stl	To	Reb	F	Mins	
ICHIJO, Aki	11	1/3	3/9	0/1	1	0	1	9	4	28:50	S
MURAKAMI, Chikako	13	1/2	3/4	2/2	5	1	2	6	2	27:56	S
HAGIWARA, Mikiko	8	4/6	0/3	0/0	2	0	3	3	2	25:33	S
KATO, Takako	8	3/13	0/0	2/2	1	1	6	3	3	30:57	S
HAMAGUCHI, Noriko	2	1/1	0/0	0/0	0	0	0	3	3	28:45	S
OYAMA, Taeko	2	1/2	0/4	0/0	1	0	0	2	1	13:25	
MIKAWA, Kikuko	0	0/0	0/0	0/0	0	0	0	0	0	00:00	
YAMADA, Kagari	3	0/0	0/0	3/4	1	0	1	1	3	14:46	
HARADA, Yuka	0	0/2	0/1	0/0	1	1	1	1	0	12:04	
OKAZATO, Akemi	0	0/0	0/1	0/0	0	0	0	0	1	02:15	
KAWASAKI, Mayumi	4	2/3	0/0	0/0	0	0	0	0	0	11:15	
NAGATA, Mutsuko	1	0/0	0/0	1/2	0	0	0	4	0	04:14	
Totals	52	13/32	6/22	8/11	12	3	14	32	19		

Team: ITA Italy
Coach: SALES, Riccaro   Assistant Coaches: NANI, Renato   CARZANIGA, Dante

Names	Pts	2 Pts	3 Pts	FT	A	Stl	To	Reb	F	Mins	
BONFIGLIO, Susanna	4	2/7	0/0	0/0	1	1	0	1	2	15:07	S
FULLIN, Mara	11	3/7	1/6	2/2	2	2	3	11	2	40:00	S
GARDELLIN, Valentina	5	2/3	0/2	1/2	1	0	1	2	1	23:46	S
POLLINI, Catarina	13	6/12	0/0	1/2	3	0	0	6	2	30:54	S
ARNETOLI, Lorenza	13	4/6	0/1	5/6	1	2	1	3	3	32:51	S
ZANUSSI, Stefania	2	1/2	0/0	0/0	1	1	0	0	0	08:02	
PAPARAZZO, Elena	0	0/0	0/0	0/0	0	0	0	0	0	00:00	
CASELIN, Nicoletta	8	3/7	0/0	2/2	2	1	1	2	1	16:14	
BALLABIO, Viviana	8	1/1	1/1	3/4	3	1	0	3	3	16:51	
REZOAGLI, Marta	0	0/1	0/0	0/0	0	0	0	1	2	09:06	
TUFANO, Giuseppina	0	0/0	0/0	0/0	0	0	0	0	0	00:00	
SCHIESARO, Novella	2	1/2	0/0	0/0	0	0	0	3	1	07:09	
Totals	66	23/48	2/10	14/18	14	8	6	32	17		

Referees: BARNETT, Robert   AUS   FIGUEROA, Juan   PUR

PRELIMINARIES - GROUP A   FINAL SCORE: CHN 83   BRA 98   HALFTIME SCORE: CHN 38   BRA 51

Team: CHN People's Republic of China
Coach: CHEN, Daohong   Assistant Coaches: MA, Lianbao   HU, Hilin

Names	Pts	2 Pts	3 Pts	FT	A	Stl	To	Reb	F	Mins	
ZHENG, Dongmei	11	3/3	1/7	2/2	6	1	6	2	1	28:21	S
LIANG, Xin	16	7/11	0/0	2/3	0	2	0	5	3	30:30	S
ZHENG, Haixia	3	1/3	0/0	1/2	0	1	1	2	5	13:49	S
HE, Jun	22	1/3	6/9	2/2	4	1	3	4	2	33:11	S
MA, Zongqing	6	1/1	0/0	4/6	3	0	3	1	4	16:34	S
MIAO, Bo	0	0/0	0/1	0/0	1	0	0	0	1	05:06	
LI, Xin	0	0/0	0/0	0/0	0	0	0	0	0	00:00	
LIU, Jun	7	2/3	0/4	3/5	6	0	1	4	2	25:09	
SHEN, Li	0	0/0	0/2	0/0	2	0	0	1	4	11:39	
CHU, Hui	0	0/0	0/0	0/0	0	0	0	0	0	00:00	
LI, Dongmei	6	3/3	0/0	0/0	0	0	0	1	1	12:51	
MA, Chengqing	12	6/9	0/0	0/0	0	0	0	4	2	22:50	
Totals	83	24/36	7/23	14/20	22	5	14	24	25		

Team: BRA Brazil
Coach: ANGELO, Miguel   Assistant Coach: DUARTE, Sergio   BALBINO, Hermes

Names	Pts	2 Pts	3 Pts	FT	A	Stl	To	Reb	F	Mins	
SILVA, Maria Angelica G. da	0	0/1	0/1	0/0	1	0	0	3	1	14:55	S
SILVA, Maria Paula Goncalves da	12	3/5	1/4	3/3	8	0	3	1	1	32:16	S
ARCAIN, Janeth dos Santos	26	8/15	1/5	7/7	3	2	1	9	4	39:31	S
SOBRAL, Marta de Souza	22	6/10	1/4	7/8	4	3	2	6	3	26:04	S
OLIVEIRA, Alessandra Santos de	9	3/5	0/0	3/6	0	2	2	9	2	26:43	S
OLIVA, Hortencia de Fatima Marcari	0	0/0	0/0	0/0	0	0	0	0	0	00:00	
SANTOS, Ariana Aparecida dos	0	0/0	0/0	0/0	1	0	0	0	0	04:55	
SOBRAL, Leila de Souza	17	5/10	0/0	7/9	0	3	0	9	0	20:36	
GUSTAVO, Roseli do Carmo	0	0/0	0/0	0/0	0	1	0	1	0	00:29	
LUZ, Silvia Andrea Santos	8	1/1	2/3	0/0	4	1	1	0	2	22:19	
SANTOS, Cintia Silva dos	4	2/3	0/0	0/0	1	0	0	1	2	12:12	
PASTOR, Claudia Maria	0	0/0	0/0	0/0	0	0	0	0	0	00:00	
Totals	98	28/50	5/17	27/33	22	12	9	39	15		

Referees: DEROSA, Joseph   USA   RYZHYK, Roman   UKR

PRELIMINARIES - GROUP A   FINAL SCORE: RUS 68   CAN 49   HALFTIME SCORE: RUS 35   CAN 29

Team: RUS Russian Federation
Coach: KAPRANOV, Vadim   Assistant Coaches: KOVALEV, Valeri   GROUDINE, Igor

Names	Pts	2 Pts	3 Pts	FT	A	Stl	To	Reb	F	Mins	
RUTKOVSKAYA, Irina	1	0/3	0/1	1/2	2	1	2	4	2	19:40	S
BARANOVA, Yelena	16	5/9	0/2	6/10	1	2	4	11	4	38:20	S
SUMNIKOVA, Irina	4	2/3	0/1	0/0	5	1	3	4	3	31:45	S
SHAKIROVA, Elen	14	3/9	0/0	8/10	3	2	2	9	3	31:05	S
PSHIKOVA, Yelena	10	2/8	1/6	3/5	1	0	2	7	3	34:56	S
NIKONOVA, Yevgeniya	18	4/8	2/3	4/6	1	3	2	0	1	29:10	
KONOVALOVA, Lyudmila	0	0/0	0/0	0/0	0	0	0	0	0	00:00	
STEPANOVA, Mariya	0	0/0	0/0	0/0	0	0	0	0	0	00:00	
SVINOUKHOVA, Natalia	5	2/6	0/0	1/3	0	1	0	3	2	14:14	
KOUZNETSOVA, Svetlana	0	0/0	0/0	0/0	0	0	0	0	0	00:50	
ZAKAULYUZHANAYA, Oksana	0	0/0	0/0	0/0	0	0	0	0	0	00:00	
ANTIPOVA, Svetlana	0	0/0	0/0	0/0	0	0	0	0	0	00:00	
Totals	68	18/46	3/13	23/36	13	10	15	38	18		

Team: CAN Canada
Coach: ENNIS, Peter   Assistant Coaches: HARLE, Shawnee   LORDON, Pauline

Names	Pts	2 Pts	3 Pts	FT	A	Stl	To	Reb	F	Mins	
SMITH, Beverly	2	1/5	0/2	0/0	2	1	3	6	5	25:00	S
MOLCAK, Shawna	4	2/5	0/2	0/0	0	0	3	1	2	28:53	S
EVANS, Jodi	6	2/4	0/0	2/2	2	3	1	4	1	21:21	S
JOHNSTON, Cynthia	7	3/6	0/0	1/2	2	2	2	7	3	23:44	S
NORMAN, Diane	15	5/14	0/0	5/7	1	2	5	8	4	30:44	S
GAILUS, Karla Karch	3	0/0	0/1	3/3	1	0	2	1	4	15:28	
THOMPSON, Camille	0	0/0	0/0	0/0	0	0	0	0	0	00:00	
STEWART, Susan	2	0/0	0/1	2/2	0	0	1	0	2	10:46	
JERANT, Martina	2	1/1	0/0	0/0	0	0	1	0	1	03:00	
BOUCHER, Kelly	4	1/0	0/2	2/2	1	0	1	4	2	24:04	
BLACKWELL, Andrea	4	2/7	0/0	0/0	0	0	3	2	1	12:35	
LANGE-HARRIS, Marlelynn	0	0/0	0/0	0/0	0	0	1	0	2	04:25	
Totals	49	17/49	0/8	15/18	9	8	23	33	27		

Referees: BUTLER, Michael   AUS   JUNGEBRAND, Carl   FIN

Women / *Dames*

PRELIMINARIES - GROUP A FINAL SCORE: RUS 94 CHN 78 | HAFLTIME SCORE: RUS 44 CHN 43

Team: RUS Russian Federation

Coach: KAPRANOV, Vadim Assistant Coaches: KOVALEV, Valeri GROUDINE, Igor

Names	Pts	2 Pts	3 Pts	FT	A	Stl	To	Reb	F	Mins	
NIKONOVA, Yevgeniya	16	4/6	2/6	2/3	0	0	0	1	1	29:05	S
RUTKOVSKAYA, Irina	6	1/2	1/2	1/2	0	3	2	3	1	14:13	S
BARANOVA, Yelena	26	9/17	0/1	8/8	1	4	2	18	2	34:58	S
SUMNIKOVA, Irina	10	3/4	1/3	1/2	10	3	4	2	3	39:12	S
SHAKIROVA, Elen	9	4/10	0/0	1/2	2	0	0	7	2	28:39	S
KONOVALOVA, Lyudmila	0	0/0	0/0	0/0	0	0	0	0	0	00:00	
STEPANOVA, Mariya	0	0/0	0/0	0/0	0	0	0	0	1	01:03	
SVINOUKHOVA, Natalia	1	0/3	0/0	1/2	0	0	1	3	0	10:12	
KOUZNETSOVA, Svetlana	15	3/6	1/3	6/8	4	0	2	6	0	32:34	
ZAKAULYUZHANAYA, Oksana	0	0/0	0/0	0/0	0	0	0	0	0	00:00	
PSHIKOVA, Yelena	11	3/4	0/0	5/6	1	1	1	3	4	10:04	
ANTIPOVA, Svetlana	0	0/0	0/0	0/0	0	0	0	0	0	00:00	
Totals	94	27/52	5/15	25/33	18	11	12	43	14		

Team: CHN People's Republic of China

Coach: CHEN, Daohong Assistant Coaches: MA, Lianbao HU, Hilin

Names	Pts	2 Pts	3 Pts	FT	A	Stl	To	Reb	F	Mins	
ZHENG, Dongmei	14	4/8	2/3	0/0	5	1	1	2	5	38:03	S
LIANG, Xin	12	6/10	0/0	0/0	3	2	2	6	3	35:40	S
ZHENG, Haixia	11	4/7	0/0	3/5	1	0	2	4	2	31:08	S
HE, Jun	10	2/4	2/4	0/0	3	2	0	5	5	23:12	S
MA, Zongqing	14	6/9	0/0	2/2	3	0	2	1	3	28:05	S
MIAO, Bo	2	0/2	0/0	2/2	0	0	1	0	1	05:19	
LI, Xin	0	0/0	0/0	0/0	0	0	0	0	0	00:00	
LIU, Jun	11	3/6	0/2	5/6	2	0	3	1	1	23:24	
SHEN, Li	0	0/0	0/0	0/0	0	0	1	1	1	01:57	
CHU, Hui	0	0/0	0/0	0/0	0	0	0	0	0	00:00	
LI, Dongmei	4	2/5	0/0	0/0	0	0	0	2	1	09:24	
MA, Chengqing	0	0/2	0/0	0/0	0	0	0	1	1	03:48	
Totals	78	27/53	4/9	12/15	17	5	12	23	23		

Referees: ZYCH, Wieslaw POL   SOARES de CAMPOS, Antonio ANG

PRELIMINARIES - GROUP A FINAL SCORE: ITA 73 BRA 75 | HALFTIME SCORE: ITA 37 BRA 38

Team: ITA Italy

Coach: SALES, Riccaro Assistant Coaches: NANI, Renato CARZANIGA, Dante

Names	Pts	2 Pts	3 Pts	FT	A	Stl	To	Reb	F	Mins	
BONFIGLIO, Susanna	15	6/11	0/0	3/4	1	0	1	4	4	23:55	S
FULLIN, Mara	2	1/1	0/1	0/0	1	2	0	0	2	11:04	S
PAPARAZZO, Elena	4	2/2	0/0	0/0	0	0	0	0	0	10:06	S
CASELIN, Nicoletta	11	4/10	1/1	0/0	3	1	1	3	3	21:45	S
POLLINI, Catarina	9	4/9	0/0	1/2	4	1	0	5	5	24:08	S
ZANUSSI, Stefania	4	0/4	1/2	1/2	2	0	1	0	2	11:06	
GARDELLIN, Valentina	4	1/3	0/0	2/2	2	1	1	0	1	18:54	
BALLABIO, Viviana	8	3/4	0/1	2/3	2	1	2	3	2	27:15	
REZOAGLI, Marta	3	1/2	0/0	1/2	0	1	0	0	0	06:01	
TUFANO, Giuseppina	11	5/7	0/0	1/1	1	3	0	4	3	26:21	
ARNETOLI, Lorenza	0	0/1	0/0	0/0	0	0	1	0	1	04:16	
SCHIESARO, Novella	2	0/3	0/0	2/2	0	0	2	2	1	15:09	
Totals	73	27/57	2/5	13/18	16	10	9	21	24		

Team: BRA Brazil

Coach: ANGELO, Miguel Assistant Coaches: DUARTE, Sergio BALBINO, Hermes

Names	Pts	2 Pts	3 Pts	FT	A	Stl	To	Reb	F	Mins	
SILVA, Maria Angelica G. da	5	1/1	1/2	0/0	4	0	0	0	1	20:29	S
SILVA, Maria Paula Goncalves da	15	2/5	3/6	2/3	2	1	5	2	2	34:36	S
ARCAIN, Janeth dos Santos	17	7/14	0/0	3/3	5	0	3	6	3	34:41	S
SOBRAL, Marta de Souza	12	3/5	1/5	3/7	2	0	2	8	3	35:28	S
OLIVEIRA, Alessandra Santos de	6	2/5	0/0	2/2	0	1	2	7	3	23:28	S
OLIVA, Hortencia de Fatima Marcari	0	0/0	0/0	0/0	0	0	0	0	0	00:00	
SANTOS, Ariana Aparecida dos	0	0/0	0/1	0/0	0	0	0	0	1	02:43	
SOBRAL, Leila de Souza	11	4/7	0/0	3/3	0	3	3	6	3	24:35	
GUSTAVO, Roseli do Carmo	0	0/0	0/0	0/0	0	0	0	0	0	00:00	
LUZ, Silvia Andrea Santos	9	3/3	0/1	3/4	1	1	0	1	3	19:28	
SANTOS, Cintia Silva dos	0	0/0	0/0	0/0	0	0	1	1	0	04:32	
PASTOR, Claudia Maria	0	0/0	0/0	0/0	0	0	0	0	0	00:00	
Totals	75	22/40	5/15	16/22	14	6	16	31	19		

Referees: BELL, Sally USA   BRAZAUSKAS, Romualdas LTU

PRELIMINARIES - GROUP A FINAL SCORE: CAN 85 JPN 95 | HALFTIME SCORE: CAN 45 JPN 41

Team: CAN Canada

Coach: ENNIS, Peter Assistant Coaches: HARLE, Shawnee LORDON, Pauline

Names	Pts	2 Pts	3 Pts	FT	A	Stl	To	Reb	F	Mins	
SMITH, Beverly	14	3/5	2/4	2/2	2	2	5	7	5	28:51	S
MOLCAK, Shawna	4	2/5	0/2	0/0	1	3	0	2	3	34:36	S
EVANS, Jodi	7	3/7	0/0	1/1	4	2	2	7	4	30:45	S
JOHNSTON, Cynthia	8	1/3	0/0	6/11	0	0	0	2	2	18:00	S
NORMAN, Diane	13	5/7	1/1	0/2	2	0	5	10	5	26:39	S
GAILUS, Karla Karch	4	2/3	0/2	0/0	2	1	1	0	0	21:32	
THOMPSON, Camille	0	0/0	0/0	0/0	0	0	0	0	0	00:00	
STEWART, Susan	0	0/1	0/0	0/0	1	0	0	1	1	04:14	
JERANT, Martina	15	6/11	0/0	3/8	2	1	4	3	1	19:50	
BOUCHER, Kelly	4	1/2	0/0	2/2	1	1	1	3	3	12:28	
BLACKWELL, Andrea	2	1/2	0/0	0/0	1	0	1	2	0	09:38	
LANGE-HARRIS, Marlelynn	14	5/7	0/0	4/4	2	0	3	2	3	18:27	
Totals	85	29/53	3/9	18/30	18	10	22	39	27		

Team: JPN Japan

Coach: NAKAGAWA, Fumikazu Assistant Coaches: NAGAI, Yoshitake KOMURE, Ikuo

Names	Pts	2 Pts	3 Pts	FT	A	Stl	To	Reb	F	Mins	
ICHIJO, Aki	16	1/4	4/9	2/2	2	1	1	5	4	24:32	S
MURAKAMI, Chikako	20	4/9	0/2	12/12	5	2	2	5	2	40:00	S
HAGIWARA, Mikiko	26	4/9	4/7	6/7	1	3	2	4	3	43:02	S
KATO, Takako	14	5/10	0/1	4/4	5	2	5	4	5	37:29	S
HAMAGUCHI, Noriko	1	0/3	0/0	1/2	1	0	1	2	5	15:10	S
OYAMA, Taeko	13	0/1	4/5	1/2	3	0	1	3	1	21:31	
MIKAWA, Kikuko	0	0/0	0/0	0/0	0	0	0	0	0	00:07	
YAMADA, Kagari	0	0/0	0/0	0/0	0	0	1	1	2	06:03	
HARADA, Yuka	0	0/0	0/0	0/0	3	0	0	0	0	05:39	
OKAZATO, Akemi	0	0/0	0/0	0/0	0	0	0	0	0	00:00	
KAWASAKI, Mayumi	5	2/3	0/0	1/2	2	0	1	2	4	29:11	
NAGATA, Mutsuko	0	0/1	0/0	0/0	1	0	1	0	1	02:16	
Totals	95	16/40	12/24	27/31	23	8	15	26	27		

Referees: NAKIC, Davorin CRO   CHAVES SAGEL, Raul ARG

PRELIMINARIES - GROUP B FINAL SCORE: ZAI 65 UKR 81 | HALFTIME SCORE: ZAI 65 UKR 81

Team: ZAI Zaire

Coach: MOZINGO, Mongamaluku Assistant Coach: MBUYI, Kadima

Names	Pts	2 Pts	3 Pts	FT	A	Stl	To	Reb	F	Mins	
MWADI, Mabika	14	3/13	2/4	2/2	1	0	5	4	4	27:57	S
NGALULA, Lukengu	7	2/9	0/2	3/4	1	3	4	7	3	34:22	S
AMBA, Kongolo	9	3/6	0/0	3/3	0	0	0	4	1	21:54	S
KAMANGA, Kasala	10	1/2	2/7	2/3	4	1	5	4	0	26:24	S
TSHIJUKA, Muene	7	2/4	0/0	3/6	1	1	1	7	2	32:58	S
PIKININI, Kakengwa	0	0/1	0/0	0/0	0	0	0	1	0	03:08	
KAPEPULA, Zaina	6	2/3	0/0	2/2	0	1	0	1	0	07:27	
NGOYI, Nsunda	7	3/4	0/2	1/2	1	1	2	4	4	20:34	
BONZALI, Lileko	0	0/0	0/0	0/0	0	0	0	0	0	00:00	
MBAMBI, Kaninga	0	0/0	0/0	0/0	0	0	0	0	0	00:00	
LOBELA, Daunai	3	0/2	0/0	3/6	0	1	2	1	1	09:04	
MBUYI, Mukendi	2	1/4	0/0	0/0	1	0	1	5	2	16:12	
Totals	65	17/48	4/15	19/28	9	8	20	38	17		

Team: UKR Ukraine

Coach: RYZHOV, Volodymyr

Names	Pts	2 Pts	3 Pts	FT	A	Stl	To	Reb	F	Mins	
ZHIRKO, Yelena	12	3/9	1/5	3/3	5	2	3	4	4	28:41	S
TKACHENKO, Marina	27	8/13	1/2	8/10	5	4	3	3	1	32:08	S
SILYANOVA, Natalya	6	0/0	2/2	0/0	4	0	1	3	2	22:50	S
SHYLAKOVA, Olga	6	3/4	0/0	0/2	0	0	0	4	0	19:02	S
NAZARENKO, Lyudmila	8	3/8	0/0	2/4	0	1	1	9	2	26:59	S
KYRYTCHENKO, Ruslana	5	1/1	1/2	0/0	0	0	1	1	3	08:53	
BURENOK, Viktorya	2	1/2	0/1	0/0	2	0	0	2	3	12:13	
OBEREMKO, Yelena	2	1/2	0/0	0/0	2	0	0	2	0	05:49	
PARADIZ, Viktorya	0	0/1	0/1	0/0	1	1	0	2	1	04:23	
LELEKA, Viktoria	0	0/0	0/0	0/0	0	0	0	0	0	03:46	
DOVGALYUK, Oksana	3	1/1	0/0	1/2	2	0	1	3	5	17:53	
SADOVNIKOVA, Diana	10	5/12	0/0	0/0	0	1	4	6	2	17:23	
Totals	81	26/53	5/15	14/21	21	10	14	39	25		

Referees: CUI, Yi CHN   DEAKIN, Janice CAN

Women / *Dames*

PRELIMINARIES - GROUP B   FINAL SCORE: USA 101   CUB 84

Team: USA United States of America

Coach: VanDERVEER, Tara   Assistant Coaches: WASHINGTON, Marian   BARRY, Ceal

Names	Pts	2 Pts	3 Pts	FT	A	Stl	To	Reb	F	Mins	
EDWARDS, Teresa	6	3/3	0/1	0/2	9	2	4	5	1	24:18	S
BOLTON, Ruthie	8	2/4	1/3	1/2	1	4	1	4	3	24:15	S
SWOOPES, Sheryl	12	6/11	0/2	0/0	2	2	3	3	2	20:19	S
LESLIE, Lisa	24	8/11	0/0	8/11	3	2	3	7	3	23:28	S
McCLAIN, Katrina	9	3/5	0/0	3/6	1	0	2	5	4	21:53	S
STALEY, Dawn	4	1/1	0/0	2/2	7	2	2	1	2	17:39	
AZZI, Jennifer	3	0/0	1/1	0/0	1	0	0	0	4	08:18	
McGHEE, Carla	2	0/5	0/0	2/2	0	0	0	4	0	08:01	
STEDING, Katy	11	3/6	1/6	2/4	0	1	1	6	1	17:31	
LOBO, Rebecca	8	3/3	0/1	2/2	1	2	1	6	2	13:55	
LACEY, Venus	8	3/3	0/0	2/4	0	0	0	5	2	12:43	
McCRAY, Nikki	6	3/5	0/0	0/0	0	0	0	1	1	07:40	
Totals	101	35/57	3/14	22/35	25	15	17	47	25		

HALFTIME SCORE: USA 54   CUB 44

Team: CUB Cuba

Coach: del RIO LOPEZ, Miguel   Assistant Coaches: DIAZ CABRERA, Ernesto   MEDINA PLACENCIA, Jose

Names	Pts	2 Pts	3 Pts	FT	A	Stl	To	Reb	F	Mins	
SEINO, Tania	11	3/8	1/2	2/2	1	0	3	5	2	23:23	S
LEON, Maria	9	3/7	0/0	3/6	1	2	1	6	1	20:43	S
MARTINEZ, Yamilet	21	8/24	0/0	5/8	2	0	1	7	4	34:51	S
HENRY, Delia Hernandez	7	3/10	0/0	1/2	5	0	2	4	1	29:36	S
ENRIQUEZ, Milayda	8	4/7	0/0	0/0	0	0	2	1	5	11:12	S
VICTORES, Lisdeivis	7	2/9	0/0	3/3	2	2	1	8	1	20:52	
VIGIL, Olga	2	0/0	0/0	2/2	0	1	0	0	0	04:27	
HERRERA, Grisel	3	0/0	1/4	0/0	0	1	1	0	2	15:35	
LAGNO, Biosotis	4	0/1	1/4	1/2	6	3	5	2	4	21:10	
AQUILA, Judith	11	5/5	0/0	1/3	1	0	0	3	2	12:03	
HECHEVARRIA, Cariola	0	0/0	0/0	0/0	2	0	1	0	0	05:13	
GOMEZ, Gertrudis	1	0/0	0/0	1/2	0	0	0	1	0	00:55	
Totals	84	28/71	3/10	19/30	20	8	18	37	22		

Referees: ZYCH, Wieslaw   POL   ZHU, Jiazhong   CHN

PRELIMINARIES - GROUP B   FINAL SCORE: KOR 61   AUS 76

Team: KOR Korea

Coach: LEE, Syung-Kook   Assistant Coach: LEE, Moon-Kyu

Names	Pts	2 Pts	3 Pts	FT	A	Stl	To	Reb	F	Mins	
CHUN, Joo-Weon	12	3/5	1/2	3/5	5	2	3	4	4	40:00	S
YOO, Young-Joo	16	5/7	1/7	3/3	1	1	3	9	3	38:53	S
CHUN, Eun-Sook	13	1/1	3/5	2/2	4	1	2	1	5	23:53	S
JUNG, Sun-Min	2	1/3	0/0	0/0	1	1	2	3	4	17:31	S
CHUNG, Eun-Soon	13	6/16	0/0	1/2	2	0	4	4	4	40:00	S
KIM, Ji-Yoon	0	0/0	0/0	0/0	0	0	0	0	0	00:00	
KWUN, Eun-Jeong	3	0/0	1/3	0/0	0	0	1	1	3	17:14	
HAN, Hyun-Sun	2	0/2	0/0	2/2	3	1	2	2	3	22:29	
PARK, Jung-Eun	0	0/0	0/0	0/0	0	0	0	0	0	00:00	
KIM, Jung-Min	0	0/0	0/0	0/0	0	0	0	0	0	00:00	
AN, Sun-Mi	0	0/0	0/0	0/0	0	0	0	0	0	00:00	
LEE, Jong-Ae	0	0/0	0/0	0/0	0	0	0	0	0	00:00	
Totals	61	16/34	6/17	11/14	16	6	17	24	26		

HALFTIME SCORE: KOR 37   AUS 34

Team: AUS Australia

Coach: MAHER, Thomas   Assistant Coaches: CHEESMAN, Jennifer   GRAF, Carrie

Names	Pts	2 Pts	3 Pts	FT	A	Stl	To	Reb	F	Mins	
MAHER, Robyn	1	0/1	0/0	1/2	1	1	5	5	2	24:46	S
TIMMS, Michele	11	2/4	0/3	7/8	5	2	2	1	3	32:08	S
SANDIE, Shelley	8	4/6	0/3	0/0	1	1	1	10	2	28:19	S
SPORN, Rachael	21	10/16	0/0	1/2	0	1	0	10	3	28:06	S
BROGAN, Michelle	2	1/5	0/0	0/0	1	1	1	2	1	14:11	S
COOK, Allison	5	1/3	1/3	0/0	1	2	0	3	2	17:08	
BRONDELLO, Sandy	2	0/4	0/0	2/2	2	0	3	3	1	16:55	
FALLON, Trisha	18	6/9	0/0	6/11	0	1	7	2	2	21:39	
CHANDLER, Michelle	0	0/0	0/0	0/0	0	0	0	0	0	00:00	
ROBINSON, Fiona	0	0/0	0/0	0/0	0	0	0	0	0	00:00	
BOYD, Carla	0	0/0	0/0	0/0	0	0	0	0	0	00:00	
WHITTLE, Jennifer	8	2/3	1/1	1/2	2	0	0	1	0	16:48	
Totals	76	26/51	2/10	18/27	14	8	13	42	16		

Referees: BOULANOV, Serguei   RUS   CHAVES SAGEL, Raul   ARG

PRELIMINARIES - GROUP B   FINAL SCORE: USA 98   UKR 65

Team: USA United States of America

Coach: VanDERVEER, Tara   Assistant Coaches: WASHINGTON, Marian   BARRY, Ceal

Names	Pts	2 Pts	3 Pts	FT	A	Stl	To	Reb	F	Mins	
EDWARDS, Teresa	10	5/5	0/0	0/0	2	0	1	1	0	18:25	S
BOLTON, Ruthie	21	5/6	2/4	5/5	2	3	3	4	1	20:32	S
SWOOPES, Sheryl	11	4/8	1/3	0/0	7	2	2	6	3	27:39	S
LESLIE, Lisa	12	4/10	0/0	4/8	1	1	1	9	2	20:26	S
McCLAIN, Katrina	17	8/9	0/0	1/2	5	1	2	6	2	26:39	S
STALEY, Dawn	6	0/1	0/0	6/8	2	2	4	0	0	17:28	
AZZI, Jennifer	0	0/3	0/0	0/0	2	0	1	1	3	11:40	
McGHEE, Carla	2	1/2	0/0	0/0	0	1	1	3	3	12:01	
STEDING, Katy	0	0/0	0/0	0/2	0	0	1	1	3	10:18	
LOBO, Rebecca	7	2/3	1/1	0/0	1	0	1	1	1	11:42	
LACEY, Venus	4	1/4	0/0	2/3	0	0	3	5	3	09:12	
McCRAY, Nikki	8	2/4	0/0	4/4	1	1	3	2	1	13:58	
Totals	98	32/55	4/8	22/32	23	11	23	38	22		

HALFTIME SCORE: USA 52   UKR 34

Team: UKR Ukraine

Coach: RYZHOV, Volodymyr

Names	Pts	2 Pts	3 Pts	FT	A	Stl	To	Reb	F	Mins	
ZHIRKO, Yelena	11	4/9	0/5	3/4	2	2	3	3	5	25:03	S
TKACHENKO, Marina	13	2/8	3/3	0/0	2	2	2	0	3	20:17	S
DOVGALYUK, Oksana	0	0/2	0/0	0/0	1	1	0	1	1	24:02	S
SADOVNIKOVA, Diana	4	2/3	0/0	0/0	2	1	3	4	5	18:03	S
NAZARENKO, Lyudmila	14	5/11	0/0	4/8	1	0	6	4	4	32:12	S
KYRYTCHENKO, Ruslana	6	1/1	1/1	1/2	0	2	0	3	2	22:26	
BURENOK, Viktorya	13	3/5	1/1	4/7	1	1	2	4	3	19:40	
OBEREMKO, Yelena	0	0/0	0/0	0/0	0	0	0	0	0	00:00	
PARADIZ, Viktorya	0	0/0	0/0	0/0	0	0	0	0	0	00:00	
LELEKA, Viktoria	2	0/1	0/0	2/2	0	0	1	0	1	07:51	
SILYANOVA, Natalya	0	0/1	0/1	0/0	1	1	4	0	1	16:20	
SHYLAKOVA, Olga	2	1/5	0/0	0/0	0	1	3	5	2	14:06	
Totals	65	18/46	5/13	14/23	12	9	27	23	26		

Referees: ISHIDA, Hidetoshi   JPN   COLUCCI, Gennaro   ITA

PRELIMINARIES - GROUP B   FINAL SCORE: AUS 91   ZAI 45

Team: AUS Australia

Coach: MAHER, Thomas   Assistant Coaches: CHEESMAN, Jennifer   GRAF, Carrie

Names	Pts	2 Pts	3 Pts	FT	A	Stl	To	Reb	F	Mins	
MAHER, Robyn	3	1/5	0/0	1/2	2	2	0	4	1	18:44	S
TIMMS, Michele	12	0/1	4/8	0/0	4	3	1	5	1	16:41	S
SANDIE, Shelley	18	8/13	0/1	2/2	1	1	0	8	0	21:15	S
SPORN, Rachael	4	2/7	0/0	0/0	2	1	0	6	0	13:00	S
BROGAN, Michelle	10	1/5	1/1	5/8	3	0	1	5	2	22:56	S
COOK, Allison	2	1/5	0/3	0/0	2	0	1	3	0	17:43	
BRONDELLO, Sandy	17	7/10	0/0	3/3	3	2	1	2	1	18:17	
FALLON, Trisha	10	4/6	0/0	2/2	4	1	1	4	1	14:39	
CHANDLER, Michelle	0	0/1	0/0	0/0	1	0	1	5	0	13:49	
ROBINSON, Fiona	6	1/2	0/0	4/6	0	0	2	4	0	08:15	
BOYD, Carla	2	1/5	0/0	0/0	2	2	1	2	1	18:22	
WHITTLE, Jennifer	7	2/7	0/1	3/5	0	0	1	5	1	16:19	
Totals	91	28/67	5/14	20/28	24	12	10	53	8		

HALFTIME SCORE: AUS 55   ZAI 22

Team: ZAI Zaire

Coach: MOZINGO, Mongamaluku   Assistant Coach: MBUYI, Kadima

Names	Pts	2 Pts	3 Pts	FT	A	Stl	To	Reb	F	Mins	
MWADI, Mabika	9	3/15	1/3	0/0	3	0	3	3	4	32:40	S
NGALULA, Lukengu	12	6/15	0/1	0/0	1	3	5	3	4	32:28	S
KAMANGA, Kasala	3	0/1	1/2	0/0	5	0	3	1	2	25:11	S
TSHIJUKA, Muene	15	6/15	0/0	3/4	0	0	2	10	2	37:21	S
MBUYI, Mukendi	0	0/3	0/0	0/0	1	0	1	4	5	20:18	S
PIKININI, Kakengwa	0	0/0	0/1	0/0	1	1	1	0	1	14:49	
KAPEPULA, Zaina	0	0/2	0/0	0/0	0	0	0	0	0	02:41	
NGOYI, Nsunda	0	0/1	0/0	0/0	0	0	1	1	2	12:11	
AMBA, Kongolo	2	1/2	0/0	0/0	0	0	3	3	3	13:12	
BONZALI, Lileko	0	0/0	0/0	0/0	0	0	0	0	0	00:00	
MBAMBI, Kaninga	0	0/0	0/0	0/0	0	0	0	0	0	00:00	
LOBELA, Daunai	4	1/6	0/0	2/2	0	1	2	3	3	09:09	
Totals	45	17/60	2/7	5/6	11	5	22	28	26		

Referees: CLINE, Donald   CAN   CHONG, Kyoung   KOR

Women / *Dames*

Team: CUB Cuba

Coach: del RIO LOPEZ, Miguel   Assistant Coaches: DIAZ CABRERA, Ernesto   MEDINA PLACENCIA, Jose

Names	Pts	2 Pts	3 Pts	FT	A	Stl	To	Reb	F	Mins	
VICTORES, Lisdeivis	4	2/6	0/0	0/1	1	1	1	13	4	25:16	S
SEINO, Tania	2	1/4	0/1	0/0	2	0	1	1	3	18:20	S
LEON, Maria	20	6/8	0/2	8/9	4	4	5	1	4	32:03	S
MARTINEZ, Yamilet	19	7/16	0/0	5/8	0	0	5	14	3	30:35	S
HENRY, Delia Hernandez	5	2/7	0/0	1/4	4	0	4	11	2	37:56	S
VIGIL, Olga	0	0/0	0/0	0/0	0	0	0	0	1	02:04	
HERRERA, Grisel	3	0/1	1/4	0/0	0	0	2	3	0	14:47	
LAGNO, Biosotis	0	0/0	0/1	0/0	2	0	0	0	1	08:17	
AQUILA, Judith	5	2/3	0/0	1/1	0	0	0	2	2	07:00	
HECHEVARRIA, Cariola	6	0/0	0/0	6/6	2	0	1	0	0	06:44	
GOMEZ, Gertrudis	0	0/0	0/0	0/0	0	0	0	0	0	00:00	
ENRIQUEZ, Milayda	6	3/4	0/0	0/0	0	1	1	4	2	16:58	
Totals	70	23/49	1/8	21/29	15	6	22	49	22		

Team: KOR Korea

Coach: LEE, Syung-Kook   Assistant Coach: LEE, Moon-Kyu

Names	Pts	2 Pts	3 Pts	FT	A	Stl	To	Reb	F	Mins	
CHUN, Joo-Weon	11	1/3	2/7	3/6	1	3	3	9	3	39:19	S
YOO, Young-Joo	12	2/10	2/9	2/4	1	0	3	6	3	34:43	S
CHUN, Eun-Sook	10	3/3	1/5	1/2	3	2	5	1	5	32:19	S
JUNG, Sun-Min	16	5/15	0/0	6/6	2	0	2	5	3	40:00	S
CHUNG, Eun-Soon	0	0/8	0/0	0/2	2	4	1	4	4	34:52	S
KIM, Ji-Yoon	2	1/2	0/0	0/1	0	0	0	0	1	02:30	
KWUN, Eun-Jeong	1	0/0	0/4	1/2	0	0	0	0	4	05:49	
HAN, Hyun-Sun	3	0/1	1/2	0/0	2	0	1	1	1	10:10	
PARK, Jung-Eun	0	0/0	0/0	0/0	0	0	0	0	0	00:00	
KIM, Jung-Min	0	0/0	0/0	0/0	0	0	0	0	0	00:00	
AN, Sun-Mi	0	0/0	0/0	0/0	0	0	0	0	0	00:18	
LEE, Jong-Ae	0	0/0	0/0	0/0	0	0	0	0	0	00:00	
Totals	55	12/42	6/27	13/23	11	9	14	26	24		

Referees: NAKIC, Davorin CRO   DEAKIN, Janice CAN

Team: USA United States of America

Coach: VanDERVEER, Tara   Assistant Coaches: WASHINGTON, Marian   BARRY, Ceal

Names	Pts	2 Pts	3 Pts	FT	A	Stl	To	Reb	F	Mins	
EDWARDS, Teresa	2	1/3	0/0	0/0	5	0	2	5	1	15:21	S
BOLTON, Ruthie	15	2/6	3/4	2/2	1	3	1	4	2	14:34	S
SWOOPES, Sheryl	11	5/6	0/2	1/2	2	1	1	3	2	20:50	S
LESLIE, Lisa	4	1/2	0/0	2/4	1	0	0	1	4	09:36	S
McCLAIN, Katrina	11	5/7	0/0	1/1	3	1	0	6	1	15:26	S
STALEY, Dawn	0	0/2	0/0	0/0	3	1	1	0	3	14:25	
AZZI, Jennifer	18	5/7	1/1	5/7	3	3	0	2	1	25:26	
McGHEE, Carla	10	4/9	0/0	2/5	1	0	3	4	2	19:53	
STEDING, Katy	7	2/3	1/2	0/0	2	4	0	4	0	18:50	
LOBO, Rebecca	5	1/3	0/0	3/4	2	1	0	2	0	15:52	
LACEY, Venus	13	4/5	0/0	5/6	0	1	0	7	1	13:56	
McCRAY, Nikki	11	2/6	1/1	4/7	1	0	2	8	2	15:51	
Totals	107	32/59	6/10	25/38	24	15	10	46	19		

Team: ZAI Zaire

Coach: MOZINGO, Mongamaluku   Assistant Coach: MBUYI, Kadima

Names	Pts	2 Pts	3 Pts	FT	A	Stl	To	Reb	F	Mins	
MWADI, Mabika	9	4/12	0/4	1/2	3	0	5	0	3	31:05	S
NGALULA, Lukengu	17	7/13	0/2	3/3	2	2	8	4	4	36:07	S
KAMANGA, Kasala	0	0/0	0/2	0/0	1	0	3	1	2	14:02	S
TSHIJUKA, Muene	6	2/9	0/0	2/4	0	0	4	5	2	31:28	S
MBUYI, Mukendi	2	1/5	0/0	0/0	1	2	0	2	5	17:34	S
PIKININI, Kakengwa	2	1/1	0/1	0/0	0	1	0	1	2	19:35	
KAPEPULA, Zaina	0	0/0	0/0	0/0	0	0	0	0	0	00:00	
NGOYI, Nsunda	2	1/4	0/2	0/0	0	0	2	3	4	17:56	
AMBA, Kongolo	4	2/6	0/0	0/0	1	0	0	2	3	10:59	
BONZALI, Lileko	0	0/0	0/0	0/0	0	0	0	0	0	01:15	
MBAMBI, Kaninga	0	0/0	0/0	0/0	0	0	0	0	0	00:00	
LOBELA, Daunai	5	1/4	0/0	3/4	1	0	1	5	4	19:59	
Totals	47	19/54	0/11	9/13	9	5	24	23	29		

Referees: BREADIAZ, Juan CUB   SOARES de CAMPOS, Antonio ANG

Team: KOR Korea

Coach: LEE, Syung-Kook   Assistant Coach: LEE, Moon-Kyu

Names	Pts	2 Pts	3 Pts	FT	A	Stl	To	Reb	F	Mins	
CHUN, Joo-Weon	11	2/4	1/3	4/6	5	2	3	3	4	37:41	S
YOO, Young-Joo	14	1/4	2/6	6/8	1	1	4	4	5	28:08	S
CHUN, Eun-Sook	14	1/3	3/4	3/3	5	3	3	1	1	17:02	S
JUNG, Sun-Min	11	3/8	0/0	5/6	0	3	3	7	3	20:00	S
CHUNG, Eun-Soon	13	5/14	0/0	3/5	4	3	2	6	3	20:00	S
KIM, Ji-Yoon	0	0/0	0/0	0/0	0	0	0	0	0	00:00	
KWUN, Eun-Jeong	3	0/0	1/1	0/0	0	0	0	1	0	05:17	
HAN, Hyun-Sun	6	1/1	1/1	1/2	1	0	0	0	0	11:52	
PARK, Jung-Eun	0	0/0	0/0	0/0	0	0	0	0	0	00:00	
KIM, Jung-Min	0	0/0	0/0	0/0	0	0	0	0	0	00:00	
AN, Sun-Mi	0	0/0	0/0	0/0	0	0	0	0	0	00:00	
LEE, Jong-Ae	0	0/0	0/0	0/0	0	0	0	0	0	00:00	
Totals	72	13/34	8/15	22/30	16	12	15	22	16		

Team: UKR Ukraine

Coach: RYZHOV, Volodymyr

Names	Pts	2 Pts	3 Pts	FT	A	Stl	To	Reb	F	Mins	
KYRYTCHENKO, Ruslana	5	1/1	1/2	0/0	2	1	2	2	5	17:40	S
ZHIRKO, Yelena	17	5/20	0/2	7/7	8	3	2	5	3	17:50	S
DOVGALYUK, Oksana	0	0/0	0/0	0/0	0	0	4	2	1	13:00	S
SHYLAKOVA, Olga	6	3/6	0/0	0/0	1	0	2	7	2	12:47	S
NAZARENKO, Lyudmila	10	5/7	0/0	0/0	0	0	4	7	5	20:00	S
BURENOK, Viktorya	4	1/2	0/0	2/2	1	0	2	1	4	03:20	
OBEREMKO, Yelena	0	0/0	0/0	0/0	0	0	0	0	0	00:00	
PARADIZ, Viktorya	0	0/0	0/0	0/0	0	0	0	0	0	00:00	
TKACHENKO, Marina	21	4/12	3/6	4/6	3	5	4	11	3	15:23	
LELEKA, Viktoria	0	0/0	0/0	0/0	0	0	0	0	0	00:00	
SADOVNIKOVA, Diana	0	0/0	0/0	0/0	0	0	0	0	0	00:00	
SILYANOVA, Natalya	4	2/3	0/0	0/0	2	1	1	2	3	00:00	
Totals	67	21/51	4/10	13/15	17	10	21	35	26		

Referees: LAPAIX GUANCE, Jose DOM   JOVANCIC, Tomislav YUG

Team: CUB Cuba

Coach: del RIO LOPEZ, Miguel   Assistant Coaches: DIAZ CABRERA, Ernesto   MEDINA PLACENCIA, Jose

Names	Pts	2 Pts	3 Pts	FT	A	Stl	To	Reb	F	Mins	
VICTORES, Lisdeivis	6	1/6	0/0	4/6	1	1	1	7	2	27:57	S
SEINO, Tania	0	0/5	0/2	0/0	4	1	1	3	0	13:05	S
LEON, Maria	6	1/2	1/1	1/2	1	0	4	3	2	24:27	S
MARTINEZ, Yamilet	19	7/19	0/0	5/7	0	0	0	11	5	31:26	S
HENRY, Delia Hernandez	4	2/8	0/0	0/0	0	0	1	3	1	25:19	S
VIGIL, Olga	6	3/4	0/0	0/0	1	1	1	0	2	09:35	
HERRERA, Grisel	6	0/1	2/4	0/0	0	0	0	1	0	14:06	
LAGNO, Biosotis	6	1/3	1/3	1/2	1	0	3	2	3	12:49	
AQUILA, Judith	2	1/2	0/0	0/0	0	0	0	0	0	02:42	
HECHEVARRIA, Cariola	2	1/2	0/1	0/0	0	1	2	3	2	20:03	
GOMEZ, Gertrudis	0	0/0	0/0	0/0	0	0	0	0	0	00:00	
ENRIQUEZ, Milayda	6	3/5	0/0	0/0	2	1	2	4	3	18:31	
Totals	63	20/57	4/11	11/17	20	5	15	37	20		

Team: AUS Australia

Coach: MAHER, Thomas   Assistant Coaches: CHEESMAN, Jennifer   GRAF, Carrie

Names	Pts	2 Pts	3 Pts	FT	A	Stl	To	Reb	F	Mins	
MAHER, Robyn	2	1/6	0/1	0/0	1	1	2	6	3	29:28	S
TIMMS, Michele	19	3/12	3/7	4/4	3	0	3	5	3	29:24	S
SANDIE, Shelley	18	6/13	1/2	3/4	3	2	1	7	1	31:23	S
SPORN, Rachael	12	5/11	0/0	2/4	1	0	0	12	2	29:38	S
BROGAN, Michelle	1	0/1	0/0	1/2	4	1	3	4	5	21:24	S
COOK, Allison	0	0/2	0/0	0/0	3	0	1	0	0	07:50	
BRONDELLO, Sandy	10	3/10	0/0	4/4	1	0	0	3	0	18:17	
FALLON, Trisha	11	5/11	0/0	1/1	2	0	1	10	0	26:56	
CHANDLER, Michelle	0	0/0	0/0	0/0	0	0	0	0	0	00:00	
ROBINSON, Fiona	0	0/0	0/0	0/0	0	0	0	0	0	00:00	
BOYD, Carla	0	0/0	0/0	0/0	0	0	0	0	0	00:00	
WHITTLE, Jennifer	2	1/1	0/0	0/0	0	1	0	0	1	05:40	
Totals	75	24/67	4/10	15/19	18	5	11	47	15		

Referees: PELISSARI, Jose BRA   DORIZON, Pascal Noel FRA

Women / Dames

PRELIMINARIES - GROUP B   FINAL SCORE: ZAI 71   KOR 95   HALFTIME SCORE: ZAI 36   KOR 49

Team: ZAI Zaire

Coach: MOZINGO, Mongamaluku   Assistant Coach: MBUYI, Kadima

Names	Pts	2 Pts	3 Pts	FT	A	Stl	To	Reb	F	Mins	
MWADI, Mabika	30	10/19	2/5	4/6	2	2	6	4	3	40:00	S
PIKININI, Kakengwa	0	0/0	0/0	0/0	0	0	0	0	3	04:59	S
NGALULA, Lukengu	9	4/8	0/2	1/2	3	2	5	7	2	40:00	S
LOBELA, Daunai	7	3/7	0/0	1/2	1	0	3	8	5	20:33	S
TSHIJUKA, Muene	14	7/12	0/0	0/3	0	1	0	7	3	32:17	S
KAPEPULA, Zaina	0	0/0	0/0	0/0	0	0	0	0	0	00:00	
NGOYI, Nsunda	0	0/0	0/0	0/0	0	0	0	0	0	00:00	
AMBA, Kongolo	8	2/9	0/0	4/4	0	1	2	6	4	19:34	
BONZALI, Lileko	0	0/0	0/0	0/0	0	0	0	0	0	00:00	
MBAMBI, Kaninga	0	0/0	0/0	0/0	0	0	0	0	0	00:00	
KAMANGA, Kasala	3	0/0	1/4	0/0	5	1	3	2	1	35:01	
MBUYI, Mukendi	0	0/2	0/0	0/0	1	0	0	1	2	07:36	
Totals	71	26/57	3/11	10/17	12	7	19	35	23		

Team: KOR Korea

Coach: LEE, Syung-Kook   Assistant Coach: LEE, Moon-Kyu

Names	Pts	2 Pts	3 Pts	FT	A	Stl	To	Reb	F	Mins	
CHUN, Joo-Weon	16	4/5	2/9	2/4	3	4	1	6	5	34:21	S
YOO, Young-Joo	18	4/5	3/6	1/2	2	0	1	2	3	30:47	S
CHUN, Eun-Sook	29	3/5	6/10	5/5	14	2	4	3	1	36:40	S
JUNG, Sun-Min	11	3/4	0/0	5/6	1	2	2	5	5	26:15	S
CHUNG, Eun-Soon	10	3/4	0/0	4/6	0	1	1	5	4	33:37	S
KIM, Ji-Yoon	2	1/3	0/0	0/0	1	0	0	0	0	03:20	
KWUN, Eun-Jeong	0	0/0	0/0	0/0	0	0	0	0	0	00:00	
HAN, Hyun-Sun	0	0/3	0/0	0/0	3	0	0	0	2	15:39	
PARK, Jung-Eun	0	0/0	0/1	0/0	2	1	1	0	0	03:20	
KIM, Jung-Min	0	0/0	0/0	0/0	0	0	0	0	0	01:17	
AN, Sun-Mi	7	2/2	1/3	0/0	0	0	1	1	0	11:24	
LEE, Jong-Ae	2	1/1	0/0	0/0	0	0	0	0	0	03:20	
Totals	95	21/32	12/29	17/23	26	10	10	23	20		

Referees: PIOVESAN NETO, Jose BRA   ZHU, Jiazhong CHN

PRELIMINARIES - GROUP B   FINAL SCORE: UKR 87   CUB 75   HALFTIME SCORE: UKR 43   CUB 43

Team: UKR Ukraine

Coach: RYZHOV, Volodymyr

Names	Pts	2 Pts	3 Pts	FT	A	Stl	To	Reb	F	Mins	
KYRYTCHENKO, Ruslana	3	0/2	1/1	0/0	2	0	0	3	1	27:07	S
ZHIRKO, Yelena	22	8/13	2/6	0/1	5	2	4	6	5	28:27	S
TKACHENKO, Marina	19	4/9	1/4	8/13	6	1	0	7	4	36:40	S
SADOVNIKOVA, Diana	6	3/6	0/0	0/0	1	0	1	3	5	13:12	S
NAZARENKO, Lyudmila	19	5/10	0/0	9/12	4	0	1	8	1	37:35	S
BURENOK, Viktorya	0	0/0	0/0	0/0	0	0	0	0	0	00:00	
OBEREMKO, Yelena	2	1/3	0/1	0/2	2	0	2	3	3	14:53	
PARADIZ, Viktorya	0	0/0	0/0	0/0	0	0	0	0	0	00:00	
LELEKA, Viktoria	0	0/0	0/0	0/0	0	0	0	0	0	00:00	
DOVGALYUK, Oksana	0	0/0	0/0	0/0	0	0	0	0	0	00:00	
SILYANOVA, Natalya	4	2/3	0/0	0/0	1	0	0	2	1	12:53	
SHYLAKOVA, Olga	12	5/6	0/0	2/2	1	2	0	4	2	29:13	
Totals	87	28/52	4/12	19/30	22	5	8	36	22		

Team: CUB Cuba

Coach: del RIO LOPEZ, Miguel   Assistant Coaches: DIAZ CABRERA, Ernesto MEDINA PLACENCIA, Jose

Names	Pts	2 Pts	3 Pts	FT	A	Stl	To	Reb	F	Mins	
HERRERA, Grisel	17	0/1	5/9	2/2	3	0	1	3	4	22:36	S
AQUILA, Judith	0	0/3	0/0	0/0	0	1	0	5	4	08:33	S
LEON, Maria	2	1/8	0/1	0/0	3	0	2	0	1	21:02	S
MARTINEZ, Yamilet	20	9/25	0/1	2/7	0	0	3	12	4	38:51	S
HENRY, Delia Hernandez	11	3/10	0/0	5/6	3	1	3	9	3	40:00	S
VICTORES, Lisdeivis	0	0/0	0/0	0/2	0	0	1	4	2	07:06	
SEINO, Tania	8	1/3	1/3	3/4	2	1	2	1	4	24:23	
VIGIL, Olga	0	0/0	0/0	0/0	0	0	0	0	0	00:00	
LAGNO, Biosotis	0	0/4	0/0	0/0	1	0	2	2	0	11:59	
HECHEVARRIA, Cariola	0	0/0	0/0	0/0	0	0	0	0	0	00:00	
GOMEZ, Gertrudis	0	0/0	0/0	0/0	0	0	0	0	0	00:00	
ENRIQUEZ, Milayda	17	6/10	0/0	5/8	1	1	1	9	3	25:30	
Totals	75	20/64	6/14	17/29	13	4	15	45	25		

Referees: BELL, Sally USA   KOUKOULEKIDIS, Stylianos GRE

PRELIMINARIES - GROUP B   FINAL SCORE: AUS 79   USA 96   HALFTIME SCORE: AUS 43   USA 46

Team: AUS Australia

Coach: MAHER, Thomas   Assistant Coaches: CHEESMAN, Jennifer   GRAF, Carrie

Names	Pts	2 Pts	3 Pts	FT	A	Stl	To	Reb	F	Mins	
MAHER, Robyn	6	3/7	0/1	0/0	3	1	2	3	4	29:56	S
TIMMS, Michele	26	3/8	4/11	8/8	2	1	2	5	3	33:42	S
SANDIE, Shelley	11	5/10	0/2	1/2	2	1	1	2	3	25:55	S
SPORN, Rachael	9	4/7	0/0	1/2	1	3	5	7	4	29:13	S
BROGAN, Michelle	2	1/2	0/2	0/0	1	0	1	2	2	17:58	S
COOK, Allison	0	0/0	0/1	0/0	0	0	0	1	1	05:20	
BRONDELLO, Sandy	6	3/6	0/0	0/0	1	0	1	1	1	14:57	
FALLON, Trisha	13	3/11	0/0	7/9	1	2	2	4	3	22:31	
CHANDLER, Michelle	0	0/0	0/0	0/0	0	0	0	0	0	00:00	
ROBINSON, Fiona	0	0/0	0/0	0/0	0	0	0	0	0	00:00	
BOYD, Carla	2	0/0	0/0	2/2	1	1	0	1	0	07:36	
WHITTLE, Jennifer	4	2/4	0/1	0/0	0	0	1	2	2	12:52	
Totals	79	24/55	4/18	19/23	12	9	15	28	23		

Team: USA United States of America

Coach: VanDERVEER, Tara   Assistant Coaches: WASHINGTON, Marian   BARRY, Ceal

Names	Pts	2 Pts	3 Pts	FT	A	Stl	To	Reb	F	Mins	
EDWARDS, Teresa	20	7/8	0/0	6/11	15	1	5	7	3	33:40	S
BOLTON, Ruthie	7	2/5	1/6	0/3	1	0	2	5	1	25:06	S
SWOOPES, Sheryl	17	6/9	1/2	2/2	3	4	2	5	2	23:18	S
LESLIE, Lisa	16	7/17	0/1	2/3	4	2	4	6	4	22:54	S
McCLAIN, Katrina	24	12/14	0/0	0/0	1	1	3	11	3	27:44	S
STALEY, Dawn	0	0/1	0/0	0/0	1	0	0	0	2	07:58	
AZZI, Jennifer	0	0/0	0/0	0/0	2	0	0	3	1	11:22	
McGHEE, Carla	0	0/1	0/0	0/0	0	0	0	0	1	07:57	
STEDING, Katy	0	0/1	0/0	0/0	0	2	2	2	1	09:33	
LOBO, Rebecca	0	0/1	0/0	0/0	1	0	1	1	0	05:22	
LACEY, Venus	8	2/5	0/0	4/4	0	0	1	5	0	11:44	
McCRAY, Nikki	4	1/3	0/0	2/2	0	1	1	2	3	13:22	
Totals	96	37/66	2/9	16/25	28	11	21	47	21		

Referees: BRAZAUSKAS, Romualdas LTU   DEAKIN, Janice CAN

PRELIMINARIES - GROUP B   FINAL SCORE: UKR 54   AUS 48   HALFTIME SCORE: UKR 29   AUS 29

Team: UKR Ukraine

Coach: RYZHOV, Volodymyr

Names	Pts	2 Pts	3 Pts	FT	A	Stl	To	Reb	F	Mins	
KYRYTCHENKO, Ruslana	2	1/2	0/1	0/1	0	0	0	2	1	16:48	S
BURENOK, Viktorya	4	2/4	0/0	0/0	3	0	2	3	4	22:28	S
ZHIRKO, Yelena	4	2/8	0/4	0/0	2	2	4	3	4	32:53	S
TKACHENKO, Marina	10	2/9	0/0	6/9	3	2	1	7	2	35:41	S
NAZARENKO, Lyudmila	13	5/13	0/0	3/3	0	0	0	15	2	37:05	S
OBEREMKO, Yelena	6	3/6	0/1	0/0	2	0	1	2	3	17:16	
PARADIZ, Viktorya	0	0/0	0/0	0/0	0	0	0	0	0	00:00	
LELEKA, Viktoria	0	0/0	0/0	0/0	0	0	0	0	0	00:00	
DOVGALYUK, Oksana	15	4/8	1/1	4/7	0	2	2	2	3	19:21	
SADOVNIKOVA, Diana	0	0/2	0/0	0/0	0	0	2	2	3	02:55	
SILYANOVA, Natalya	0	0/0	0/0	0/0	0	0	0	0	0	13:40	
SHYLAKOVA, Olga	0	0/0	0/0	0/0	0	0	0	1	0	01:53	
Totals	54	19/52	1/7	13/20	10	6	12	37	22		

Team: AUS Australia

Coach: MAHER, Thomas   Assistant Coaches: CHEESMAN, Jennifer   GRAF, Carrie

Names	Pts	2 Pts	3 Pts	FT	A	Stl	To	Reb	F	Mins	
MAHER, Robyn	1	0/4	0/0	1/2	0	0	2	7	4	29:06	S
TIMMS, Michele	13	2/6	2/8	3/4	3	3	3	4	3	37:02	S
SANDIE, Shelley	10	4/12	0/3	2/2	1	1	1	9	2	28:07	S
SPORN, Rachael	6	2/6	0/0	2/2	0	0	2	10	4	26:40	S
BROGAN, Michelle	7	2/6	0/0	3/4	0	2	1	5	2	20:07	S
COOK, Allison	0	0/2	0/0	0/0	0	0	0	0	0	02:06	
BRONDELLO, Sandy	1	0/7	0/0	1/2	0	0	1	2	2	15:30	
FALLON, Trisha	9	3/10	0/0	3/4	1	2	1	5	4	22:52	
CHANDLER, Michelle	0	0/0	0/0	0/0	0	0	0	0	0	00:00	
ROBINSON, Fiona	0	0/0	0/0	0/0	0	0	0	0	0	00:00	
BOYD, Carla	0	0/1	0/0	0/0	0	0	0	1	1	06:41	
WHITTLE, Jennifer	1	0/2	0/1	1/2	1	0	0	5	1	11:49	
Totals	48	13/56	2/12	16/22	6	8	11	48	23		

Referees: FIGUEROA, Juan PUR   THONGPILA, Virun THA

Women / *Dames*

PRELIMINARIES - GROUP B   FINAL SCORE: KOR 64   USA 105   HALFTIME SCORE: KOR 50   USA 60

Team: KOR Korea

Coach: LEE, Syung-Kook   Assistant Coach: LEE, Moon-Kyu

Names	Pts	2 Pts	3 Pts	FT	A	Stl	To	Reb	F	Mins	
CHUN, Joo-Weon	7	1/2	1/6	2/2	7	1	2	4	5	26:50	S
YOO, Young-Joo	12	0/1	4/12	0/0	5	2	1	2	4	31:49	S
CHUN, Eun-Sook	9	3/4	1/4	0/0	3	2	3	0	1	28:13	S
JUNG, Sun-Min	17	8/11	0/0	1/2	3	3	3	6	3	38:06	S
CHUNG, Eun-Soon	12	5/8	0/0	2/5	4	1	4	4	4	29:34	S
KIM, Ji-Yoon	2	1/2	0/0	0/0	1	0	2	0	1	06:17	
KWUN, Eun-Jeong	3	0/1	1/9	0/0	0	0	1	5	1	13:40	
HAN, Hyun-Sun	0	0/1	0/2	0/0	0	0	0	1	2	18:16	
PARK, Jung-Eun	2	1/1	0/2	0/0	1	0	1	2	0	05:47	
KIM, Jung-Min	0	0/0	0/0	0/0	0	0	0	0	0	00:00	
AN, Sun-Mi	0	0/0	0/3	0/0	0	0	1	0	0	01:28	
LEE, Jong-Ae	0	0/0	0/0	0/0	0	0	0	0	0	00:00	
Totals	64	19/31	7/38	5/9	24	9	18	24	21		

Team: USA United States of America

Coach: VanDERVEER, Tara   Assistant Coaches: WASHINGTON, Marian   BARRY, Ceal

Names	Pts	2 Pts	3 Pts	FT	A	Stl	To	Reb	F	Mins	
EDWARDS, Teresa	4	2/3	0/0	0/0	3	2	2	0	1	12:39	S
BOLTON, Ruthie	15	4/8	2/5	1/2	2	2	0	5	0	16:41	S
SWOOPES, Sheryl	12	3/6	2/3	0/0	4	0	0	2	1	18:00	S
LESLIE, Lisa	14	6/6	0/0	2/4	2	2	1	8	2	16:18	S
McCLAIN, Katrina	4	2/3	0/0	0/0	0	1	0	2	1	11:02	S
STALEY, Dawn	11	2/4	2/2	1/2	2	1	1	2	2	24:28	
AZZI, Jennifer	8	4/8	0/2	0/0	3	0	2	2	3	23:19	
McGHEE, Carla	7	3/4	0/0	1/2	0	1	2	2	2	12:37	
STEDING, Katy	3	1/2	0/2	1/2	0	0	2	5	0	19:14	
LOBO, Rebecca	7	2/3	0/1	3/5	0	2	2	2	0	12:31	
LACEY, Venus	4	1/4	0/0	2/4	0	1	2	6	0	11:11	
McCRAY, Nikki	16	7/8	0/1	2/2	2	1	1	9	0	22:00	
Totals	105	37/59	6/16	13/23	19	13	15	45	12		

Referees: CUI, Yi   CHN   DEAKIN, Janice   CAN

PRELIMINARIES - GROUP B   FINAL SCORE: CUB 73   ZAI 59   HALFTIME SCORE: CUB 36   ZAI 36

Team: CUB Cuba

Coach: del RIO LOPEZ, Miguel   Assistant Coaches: DIAZ CABRERA, Ernesto   MEDINA PLACENCIA, Jose

Names	Pts	2 Pts	3 Pts	FT	A	Stl	To	Reb	F	Mins	
HERRERA, Grisel	5	1/2	1/5	0/0	2	1	1	10	1	24:33	S
LEON, Maria	20	6/13	0/2	8/10	2	2	1	4	1	26:43	S
MARTINEZ, Yamilet	18	8/19	0/0	2/6	0	0	2	12	3	32:38	S
HENRY, Delia Hernandez	4	1/7	0/0	2/2	7	2	4	8	1	35:28	S
ENRIQUEZ, Milayda	6	3/7	0/0	0/2	1	2	1	5	1	22:42	S
VICTORES, Lisdeivis	2	1/3	0/0	0/0	1	0	0	4	4	15:24	
SEINO, Tania	6	2/5	0/1	2/3	2	0	4	4	1	15:33	
VIGIL, Olga	0	0/1	0/0	0/0	0	0	2	2	1	04:32	
LAGNO, Biosotis	0	0/0	0/0	0/0	0	0	1	0	0	02:30	
AQUILA, Judith	0	0/1	0/0	0/0	0	0	0	0	0	01:54	
HECHEVARRIA, Cariola	8	4/5	0/1	0/0	0	0	1	1	0	10:52	
GOMEZ, Gertrudis	4	1/3	0/0	2/2	0	0	0	1	0	07:11	
Totals	73	27/66	1/9	16/25	15	7	17	51	13		

Team: ZAI Zaire

Coach: MOZINGO, Mongamaluku   Assistant Coach: MBUYI, Kadima

Names	Pts	2 Pts	3 Pts	FT	A	Stl	To	Reb	F	Mins	
MWADI, Mabika	27	10/23	2/5	1/2	3	4	0	2	0	38:33	S
NGALULA, Lukengu	10	4/15	0/1	2/2	2	1	7	9	3	35:59	S
KAMANGA, Kasala	3	0/0	1/6	0/0	3	2	3	1	0	20:45	S
TSHIJUKA, Muene	7	3/8	0/0	1/1	1	0	3	5	2	31:45	S
MBUYI, Mukendi	0	0/0	0/0	0/0	1	0	1	2	5	09:48	S
PIKININI, Kakengwa	0	0/1	0/3	0/0	3	1	1	1	2	16:50	
KAPEPULA, Zaina	0	0/0	0/0	0/0	0	0	0	0	0	00:00	
NGOYI, Nsunda	0	0/1	0/0	0/0	0	0	0	0	1	02:25	
AMBA, Kongolo	0	0/0	0/0	0/0	0	0	0	0	0	00:00	
BONZALI, Lileko	2	1/2	0/0	0/0	0	0	0	1	1	05:28	
MBAMBI, Kaninga	4	1/3	0/0	2/2	1	1	1	3	1	09:01	
LOBELA, Daunai	6	3/8	0/0	0/0	1	0	0	6	4	29:26	
Totals	59	22/61	3/15	6/7	15	9	16	30	19		

Referees: BUTLER, Michael   AUS   BOULANOV, Serguei   RUS

FINAL CLASSIFICATION - GROUP A

Rnk	Team	Matches Played	Won	Lost	Points For	Against	Points
1	BRA	5	5	0	424	360	10
2	RUS	5	4	1	378	342	9
3	ITA	5	3	2	330	309	8
4	JPN	5	2	3	365	396	7
5	CHN	5	1	4	347	378	6
6	CAN	5	0	5	293	352	5

FINAL CLASSIFICATION - GROUP B

Rnk	Team	Matches Played	Won	Lost	Points For	Against	Points
1	USA	5	5	0	507	339	10
2	UKR	5	3	2	354	358	8
3	AUS	5	3	2	369	319	8
4	CUB	5	2	3	365	377	7
5	KOR	5	2	3	347	389	7
6	ZAI	5	0	5	287	447	5

CLASSIFICATION 9 - 12   FINAL SCORE: CHN 91   ZAI 67   HALFTIME SCORE: CHN 47   ZAI 36

Team: CHN People's Republic of China

Coach: CHEN, Daohong   Assistant Coaches: MA, Lianbao   HU, Hilin

Names	Pts	2 Pts	3 Pts	FT	A	Stl	To	Reb	F	Mins	
ZHENG, Dongmei	16	2/4	3/9	3/4	3	0	1	5	1	33:54	S
LIANG, Xin	8	4/12	0/0	0/0	4	2	2	4	3	28:26	S
ZHENG, Haixia	26	11/16	0/0	4/6	2	3	2	10	3	31:44	S
HE, Jun	12	1/1	3/7	1/1	4	0	1	4	1	32:17	S
MA, Zongqing	6	3/4	0/1	0/0	6	1	0	2	1	17:06	S
MIAO, Bo	0	0/1	0/1	0/0	0	0	1	1	1	06:27	
LI, Xin	0	0/0	0/0	0/0	0	0	0	0	0	00:00	
LIU, Jun	16	1/3	3/5	5/6	3	2	2	6	2	24:10	
SHEN, Li	2	1/1	0/1	0/0	1	0	0	1	1	06:06	
CHU, Hui	3	1/2	0/0	1/1	0	0	1	0	2	04:35	
LI, Dongmei	0	0/1	0/0	0/0	2	1	2	1	0	06:59	
MA, Chengqing	2	1/1	0/0	0/0	0	0	0	0	1	08:16	
Totals	91	25/46	9/24	14/18	25	9	12	34	16		

Team: ZAI Zaire

Coach: MOZINGO, Mongamaluku   Assistant Coach: MBUYI, Kadima

Names	Pts	2 Pts	3 Pts	FT	A	Stl	To	Reb	F	Mins	
MWADI, Mabika	30	10/20	3/5	1/2	0	2	4	4	4	40:00	S
NGALULA, Lukengu	2	1/5	0/1	0/0	3	2	7	6	4	29:45	S
KAMANGA, Kasala	2	1/1	0/1	0/0	0	0	1	0	0	12:57	S
TSHIJUKA, Muene	12	4/9	0/0	4/4	2	1	2	7	0	28:39	S
MBUYI, Mukendi	6	2/7	0/0	2/3	0	1	1	3	0	15:38	S
PIKININI, Kakengwa	2	0/3	0/3	2/2	1	2	1	0	5	2	31:14
KAPEPULA, Zaina	0	0/2	0/0	0/0	0	0	1	1	1	03:43	
NGOYI, Nsunda	0	0/0	0/0	0/0	0	0	0	0	0	00:00	
AMBA, Kongolo	0	0/0	0/0	0/0	0	0	0	0	0	00:00	
BONZALI, Lileko	0	0/0	0/0	0/0	0	0	1	1	1	02:39	
MBAMBI, Kaninga	0	0/0	0/0	0/0	0	0	0	0	0	00:00	
LOBELA, Daunai	13	5/10	0/0	3/5	2	4	1	9	3	35:25	
Totals	67	23/57	3/10	12/16	9	11	18	36	15		

Referees: PELISSARI, Jose   BRA   KIM, Chul-Hwan   KOR

Women / *Dames*

CLASSIFICATION 9 - 12 — FINAL SCORE: KOR 88 CAN 79 | HALFTIME SCORE: KOR 37 CAN 41

Team: KOR Korea
Coach: LEE, Byung-Kuk   Assistant Coach: LEE, Moon-Kyu

Names	Pts	2 Pts	3 Pts	FT	A	Stl	To	Reb	F	Mins	
CHUN, Joo-Weon	31	7/8	3/8	8/9	9	3	5	3	4	40:00	S
YOO, Young-Joo	12	3/3	1/9	3/4	2	1	0	4	5	36:02	S
CHUN, Eun-Sook	7	1/1	1/1	2/4	2	2	2	2	4	26:00	S
JUNG, Sun-Min	22	9/14	0/0	4/4	4	3	1	4	4	36:04	S
CHUNG, Eun-Soon	2	1/5	0/0	0/0	0	1	1	3	3	13:26	S
KIM, Ji-Yoon	5	2/2	0/0	1/1	0	0	1	0	1	05:41	
KWAN, Eun-Jeong	2	1/3	0/2	0/0	1	0	1	1	1	12:25	
HAN, Hyun-Sun	7	2/2	0/0	3/4	2	3	1	3	4	30:22	
PARK, Jung-Eun	0	0/0	0/0	0/0	0	0	0	0	0	00:00	
KIM, Jung-Min	0	0/0	0/0	0/0	0	0	0	0	0	00:00	
AN, Sun-Mi	0	0/0	0/0	0/0	0	0	0	0	0	00:00	
LEE, Jong-Ae	0	0/0	0/0	0/0	0	0	0	0	0	00:00	
Totals	88	26/38	5/20	21/26	20	13	12	20	26		

Team: CAN Canada
Coach: ENNIS, Peter   Assistant Coaches: HARLE, Shawnee   LORDON, Pauline

Names	Pts	2 Pts	3 Pts	FT	A	Stl	To	Reb	F	Mins	
SMITH, Beverly	8	2/6	0/4	4/4	3	3	2	5	3	33:10	S
MOLCAK, Shawna	7	2/5	1/1	0/0	4	1	3	2	2	32:01	S
EVANS, Jodi	6	2/7	0/0	2/2	3	0	3	6	4	27:10	S
JOHNSTON, Cynthia	4	1/2	0/0	2/4	0	1	3	1	2	11:38	S
NORMAN, Diane	17	6/10	0/1	5/7	0	0	1	8	2	27:21	S
GAILUS, Karla Karch	5	0/1	1/1	2/2	8	0	4	5	3	18:39	
THOMPSON, Camille	2	1/4	0/0	0/0	0	0	0	0	2	03:07	
STEWART, Susan	4	0/0	1/2	1/2	1	0	1	0	0	09:00	
JERANT, Martina	14	5/9	0/0	4/4	0	0	1	4	2	18:55	
BOUCHER, Kelly	0	0/0	0/0	0/0	0	0	0	0	0	00:00	
BLACKWELL, Andrea	10	4/8	0/0	2/2	1	0	2	5	0	15:21	
LANGE-HARRIS, Marlelynn	2	1/1	0/0	0/0	0	0	0	0	2	03:38	
Totals	79	24/53	3/9	22/27	20	5	20	36	22		

Referees: BARNETT, Robert AUS   PIOVESAN NETO, Jose BRA

CLASSIFICATION 5 - 8 — FINAL SCORE: CUB 78 ITA 70 | HALFTIME SCORE: CUB 37 ITA 40

Team: CUB Cuba
Coach: del RIO LOPEZ, Miguel   Assistant Coaches: DIAZ CABRERA, Ernesto   MEDINA PLACENCIA, Jose

Names	Pts	2 Pts	3 Pts	FT	A	Stl	To	Reb	F	Mins	
SEINO, Tania	10	4/8	0/0	2/2	3	1	1	2	4	28:01	S
VIGIL, Olga	0	0/1	0/0	0/0	1	0	1	1	2	07:12	S
MARTINEZ, Yamilet	23	9/20	0/0	5/9	1	0	1	9	3	40:00	S
HENRY, Delia Hernandez	6	2/7	0/0	2/2	5	0	3	5	3	33:46	S
ENRIQUEZ, Milayda	8	3/8	0/0	2/4	0	0	4	17	2	28:32	S
VICTORES, Lisdeivis	4	2/3	0/0	0/0	0	0	1	1	2	07:54	
HERRERA, Grisel	18	2/2	4/9	2/2	0	3	0	3	3	23:51	
LAGNO, Biosotis	0	0/0	0/0	0/0	0	0	0	0	0	00:00	
AQUILA, Judith	0	0/1	0/0	0/0	0	0	1	1	1	03:34	
LEON, Maria	4	2/2	0/0	0/1	1	0	0	1	1	07:56	
HECHEVARRIA, Cariola	5	1/3	1/3	0/0	3	2	1	1	0	19:14	
GOMEZ, Gertrudis	0	0/0	0/0	0/0	0	0	0	0	0	00:00	
Totals	78	25/55	5/12	13/20	14	6	13	41	21		

Team: ITA Italy
Coach: SALES, Riccaro   Assistant Coaches: NANI, Renato   CARZANIGA, Dante

Names	Pts	2 Pts	3 Pts	FT	A	Stl	To	Reb	F	Mins	
BONFIGLIO, Susanna	4	1/1	0/0	2/2	2	1	0	0	0	11:51	S
FULLIN, Mara	2	1/5	0/2	0/0	3	1	0	1	0	22:18	S
PAPARAZZO, Elena	4	2/4	0/0	0/0	0	0	0	1	1	07:12	S
CASELIN, Nicoletta	12	2/7	1/1	5/6	3	1	2	2	1	24:21	S
POLLINI, Catarina	15	6/11	0/0	3/3	1	0	3	7	4	29:50	S
ZANUSSI, Stefania	0	0/1	0/0	0/0	0	0	0	0	0	06:54	
GARDELLIN, Valentina	4	1/6	0/4	2/2	1	1	3	2	0	15:39	
BALLABIO, Viviana	14	2/5	1/3	7/9	3	1	2	8	4	26:24	
REZOAGLI, Marta	2	1/2	0/0	0/0	1	0	1	2	2	13:47	
TUFANO, Giuseppina	8	2/6	0/0	4/4	0	0	0	8	1	24:26	
ARNETOLI, Lorenza	3	0/1	1/1	0/0	0	0	0	1	3	07:08	
SCHIESARO, Novella	2	1/3	0/0	0/0	0	0	0	1	1	10:10	
Totals	70	19/52	3/11	23/26	14	6	10	32	17		

Referees: DORIZON, Pascal Noel FRA   BELL, Sally USA

CLASSIFICATION 5 - 8 — FINAL SCORE: JPN 69 RUS 80 | HALFTIME SCORE: JPN 34 RUS 39

Team: JPN Japan
Coach: NAKAGAWA, Fumikazu   Assistant Coaches: NAGAI, Yoshitake   KOMURE, Ikuo

Names	Pts	2 Pts	3 Pts	FT	A	Stl	To	Reb	F	Mins	
ICHIJO, Aki	10	2/8	1/7	3/5	1	2	2	12	4	33:14	S
MURAKAMI, Chikako	14	2/2	0/1	10/11	7	0	0	2	2	40:00	S
HAGIWARA, Mikiko	16	5/8	2/9	0/2	1	1	1	2	2	32:31	S
KATO, Takako	19	7/11	0/3	5/8	0	0	4	5	4	36:50	S
HAMAGUCHI, Noriko	2	1/6	0/0	0/0	0	2	4	4	2	18:56	S
OYAMA, Taeko	6	0/1	1/4	3/3	0	2	1	3	2	24:12	
MIKAWA, Kikuko	0	0/0	0/0	0/0	0	0	0	0	0	00:00	
YAMADA, Kagari	0	0/0	0/0	0/0	0	0	1	1	1	05:38	
HARADA, Yuka	0	0/0	0/0	0/0	0	0	0	0	0	00:00	
OKAZATO, Akemi	0	0/0	0/0	0/0	0	1	0	1	0	02:34	
KAWASAKI, Mayumi	2	1/4	0/0	0/0	1	0	1	3	1	06:05	
NAGATA, Mutsuko	0	0/0	0/0	0/0	0	0	0	0	0	00:00	
Totals	69	18/40	4/24	21/29	10	8	14	33	18		

Team: RUS Russian Federation
Coach: KAPRANOV, Vadim   Assistant Coaches: KOVALEV, Valeri   GROUDINE, Igor

Names	Pts	2 Pts	3 Pts	FT	A	Stl	To	Reb	F	Mins	
NIKONOVA, Yevgeniya	6	2/6	0/1	2/4	2	2	2	2	3	34:22	S
RUTKOVSKAYA, Irina	8	1/1	1/1	3/4	2	0	1	2	4	18:20	S
BARANOVA, Yelena	37	14/19	0/2	9/10	1	4	4	13	2	36:23	S
SUMNIKOVA, Irina	4	2/2	0/0	0/0	14	1	3	5	4	40:00	S
PSHIKOVA, Yelena	5	2/9	0/2	1/2	3	1	1	3	4	24:22	S
KONOVALOVA, Lyudmila	0	0/0	0/0	0/0	0	0	0	0	0	00:00	
STEPANOVA, Mariya	11	5/10	0/0	1/1	0	1	0	5	1	14:26	
SVINOUKHOVA, Natalia	0	0/0	0/0	0/0	0	0	0	0	0	00:00	
KOUZNETSOVA, Svetlana	5	1/4	0/2	3/4	1	0	3	2	2	21:40	
ZAKAULYUZHANAYA, Oksana	0	0/0	0/0	0/0	0	0	0	0	0	00:00	
SHAKIROVA, Elen	4	2/3	0/0	0/0	0	0	0	1	1	04:49	
ANTIPOVA, Svetlana	0	0/1	0/1	0/0	1	0	0	0	0	05:38	
Totals	80	29/55	1/9	19/25	24	9	14	33	21		

Referees: DEAKIN, Janice CAN   CUI, Yi CHN

QUARTERFINALS — FINAL SCORE: BRA 101 CUB 69 | HALFTIME SCORE: BRA 50 CUB 33

Team: BRA Brazil
Coach: ANGELO, Miguel   Assistant Coaches: DUARTE, Sergio BALBINO, Hermes

Names	Pts	2 Pts	3 Pts	FT	A	Stl	To	Reb	F	Mins	
OLIVA, Hortencia de Fatima Marcari	17	5/8	0/3	7/8	3	0	1	2	3	29:48	S
SILVA, Maria Paula Goncalves da	19	1/2	4/11	5/6	4	1	3	2	2	32:48	S
ARCAIN, Janeth dos Santos	19	6/14	0/0	7/7	6	1	2	10	2	35:28	S
SOBRAL, Marta de Souza	18	6/8	1/5	3/4	1	1	1	10	2	32:28	S
OLIVEIRA, Alessandra Santos de	10	4/5	0/0	2/0	1	2	9	2	2	24:43	S
SILVA, Maria Angelica G. da	3	0/1	1/1	0/0	1	1	0	2	0	06:21	
SANTOS, Ariana Aparecida dos	3	1/1	0/1	1/2	0	1	0	0	1	03:58	
SOBRAL, Leila de Souza	2	0/0	0/0	2/2	1	0	3	1	5	07:21	
GUSTAVO, Roseli do Carmo	2	0/0	0/0	2/2	0	0	1	2	1	04:32	
LUZ, Silvia Andrea Santos	6	1/1	1/1	1/2	0	0	0	0	2	07:05	
SANTOS, Cintia Silva dos	0	0/1	0/0	0/0	0	0	0	1	2	12:10	
PASTOR, Claudia Maria	2	0/0	0/0	2/2	0	0	0	2	1	03:18	
Totals	101	24/41	7/22	32/40	16	6	13	41	23		

Team: CUB Cuba
Coach: del RIO LOPEZ, Miguel   Assistant Coaches: DIAZ CABRERA, Ernesto   MEDINA PLACENCIA, Jose

Names	Pts	2 Pts	3 Pts	FT	A	Stl	To	Reb	F	Mins	
SEINO, Tania	2	1/6	0/1	0/0	1	2	0	0	3	16:36	S
LEON, Maria	8	3/8	0/3	2/5	1	1	1	3	4	22:42	S
MARTINEZ, Yamilet	25	11/19	0/0	3/6	2	0	2	9	4	32:55	S
HENRY, Delia Hernandez	6	3/8	0/0	0/0	1	0	3	2	3	26:54	S
ENRIQUEZ, Milayda	5	2/8	0/0	1/2	2	1	1	8	2	27:29	S
VICTORES, Lisdeivis	5	1/2	0/0	3/4	0	0	2	7	0	15:39	
VIGIL, Olga	6	2/2	0/0	2/6	2	3	1	1	3	21:14	
HERRERA, Grisel	3	0/0	1/2	0/0	1	0	0	0	3	07:17	
LAGNO, Biosotis	3	0/1	0/2	3/4	2	1	0	2	2	12:05	
AQUILA, Judith	0	0/0	0/0	0/0	0	0	0	0	0	00:00	
HECHEVARRIA, Cariola	4	2/4	0/0	0/1	0	0	4	3	3	13:12	
GOMEZ, Gertrudis	2	0/0	0/0	2/2	0	1	1	0	3	03:57	
Totals	69	25/58	1/8	16/30	12	8	15	35	30		

Referees: JOVANCIC, Tomislav YUG   SOARES de CAMPOS, Antonio ANG

Women / *Dames*

QUARTERFINALS — FINAL SCORE: USA 108 JPN 93 — HALFTIME SCORE: USA 59 JPN 44

Team: USA United States of America

Coach: VanDERVEER, Tara   Assistant Coach: BARRY, Ceal   DARSCH, Nancy

Names	Pts	2 Pts	3 Pts	FT	A	Stl	To	Reb	F	Mins	
EDWARDS, Teresa	4	2/5	0/0	0/0	12	1	1	3	0	27:35	S
BOLTON, Ruthie	9	3/9	1/5	0/0	1	4	1	4	3	26:25	S
SWOOPES, Sheryl	9	3/5	1/2	0/0	5	0	1	2	4	20:40	S
LESLIE, Lisa	35	16/21	0/0	3/5	4	1	2	8	2	26:30	S
McCLAIN, Katrina	18	8/14	0/0	2/2	2	1	1	16	2	25:19	S
STALEY, Dawn	0	0/2	0/1	0/0	3	0	1	0	1	11:13	
AZZI, Jennifer	7	1/1	1/1	2/2	1	0	1	1	1	09:11	
McGHEE, Carla	2	1/3	0/0	0/0	0	0	0	0	1	09:02	
STEDING, Katy	0	0/1	0/0	0/0	0	0	0	1	1	05:02	
LOBO, Rebecca	2	1/2	0/0	0/0	0	0	1	2	0	03:40	
LACEY, Venus	10	4/4	0/0	2/2	1	0	1	1	2	11:39	
McCRAY, Nikki	12	5/5	0/0	2/6	2	0	0	2	0	23:44	
Totals	108	44/72	3/9	11/17	31	7	10	40	17		

Team: JPN Japan

Coach: NAKAGAWA, Fumikazu   Assistant Coaches: NAGAI, Yoshitake   KOMURE, Ikuo

Names	Pts	2 Pts	3 Pts	FT	A	Stl	To	Reb	F	Mins	
ICHIJO, Aki	22	3/6	4/9	4/5	2	0	2	2	3	24:26	S
MURAKAMI, Chikako	4	1/4	0/3	2/2	10	0	3	2	1	27:24	S
HAGIWARA, Mikiko	22	4/8	4/5	2/2	1	0	2	3	2	34:36	S
KATO, Takako	14	6/13	0/1	2/2	2	1	1	8	5	31:29	S
HAMAGUCHI, Noriko	8	4/4	0/0	0/0	3	1	1	4	4	23:17	S
OYAMA, Taeko	15	3/4	3/9	0/0	2	0	1	2	1	22:48	
MIKAWA, Kikuko	0	0/0	0/1	0/0	0	0	0	0	0	00:41	
YAMADA, Kagari	2	1/1	0/0	0/1	1	0	1	1	0	08:34	
HARADA, Yuka	3	0/3	1/2	0/0	2	0	1	1	1	12:36	
OKAZATO, Akemi	3	0/0	1/1	0/0	0	0	0	1	1	09:37	
KAWASAKI, Mayumi	0	0/0	0/1	0/0	0	0	0	0	0	04:32	
NAGATA, Mutsuko	0	0/0	0/0	0/0	0	0	0	0	0	00:00	
Totals	93	22/43	13/32	10/12	23	2	12	24	18		

Referees: KOUKOULEKIDIS, Stylianos GRE   THONGPILA, Virun THA

QUARTERFINALS — FINAL SCORE: RUS 70 AUS 74 — HALFTIME SCORE: RUS 38 AUS 38

Team: RUS Russian Federation

Coach: KAPRANOV, Vadim   Assistant Coaches: KOVALEV, Valeri   GROUDINE, Igor

Names	Pts	2 Pts	3 Pts	FT	A	Stl	To	Reb	F	Mins	
NIKONOVA, Yevgeniya	16	3/9	2/4	4/4	2	3	3	6	1	33:41	S
BARANOVA, Yelena	13	5/11	0/0	3/4	4	1	4	21	3	40:15	S
SUMNIKOVA, Irina	10	3/7	1/1	1/1	5	0	4	5	2	42:08	S
SHAKIROVA, Elen	9	4/11	0/0	1/2	1	0	1	5	3	41:41	S
PSHIKOVA, Yelena	9	2/5	1/3	2/2	0	2	4	1	5	18:31	S
KONOVALOVA, Lyudmila	0	0/0	0/0	0/0	0	0	0	0	0	00:00	
RUTKOVSKAYA, Irina	3	1/3	0/0	1/2	0	1	2	2	2	15:54	
STEPANOVA, Mariya	0	0/0	0/0	0/0	0	0	0	0	0	00:00	
SVINOUKHOVA, Natalia	4	2/5	0/0	0/0	0	0	2	1	3	12:42	
KOUZNETSOVA, Svetlana	6	3/6	0/1	0/0	2	1	2	0	4	20:08	
ZAKAULYUZHANAYA, Oksana	0	0/0	0/0	0/0	0	0	0	0	0	00:00	
ANTIPOVA, Svetlana	0	0/0	0/0	0/0	0	0	0	0	0	00:00	
Totals	70	23/57	4/9	12/15	14	8	22	41	23		

Team: AUS Australia

Coach: MAHER, Thomas   Assistant Coaches: CHEESMAN, Jennifer   GRAF, Carrie

Names	Pts	2 Pts	3 Pts	FT	A	Stl	To	Reb	F	Mins	
MAHER, Robyn	2	1/5	0/1	0/0	2	2	1	3	2	21:41	S
TIMMS, Michele	10	5/10	0/5	0/0	3	2	3	7	4	37:28	S
SANDIE, Shelley	0	0/3	0/0	0/0	1	1	0	3	1	13:24	S
SPORN, Rachael	9	4/10	0/0	1/1	0	1	1	6	2	33:10	S
BROGAN, Michelle	17	5/7	0/1	7/10	3	2	2	8	3	30:00	S
COOK, Allison	0	0/2	0/1	0/0	1	0	0	1	0	06:43	
BRONDELLO, Sandy	13	4/11	0/0	5/6	0	2	0	1	1	26:38	
FALLON, Trisha	12	4/11	0/0	4/6	0	1	6	6	0	32:14	
CHANDLER, Michelle	0	0/0	0/0	0/0	0	0	0	0	0	00:00	
ROBINSON, Fiona	0	0/0	0/0	0/0	0	0	0	0	0	00:00	
BOYD, Carla	0	0/0	0/0	0/0	0	0	0	0	0	00:00	
WHITTLE, Jennifer	11	5/11	0/1	1/1	0	0	1	8	0	23:42	
Totals	74	28/70	0/9	18/24	11	9	14	43	13		

Referees: CLINE, Donald CAN   JUNGEBRAND, Carl FIN

QUARTERFINALS — FINAL SCORE: UKR 59 ITA 50 — HALFTIME SCORE: UKR 25 ITA 22

Team: UKR Ukraine

Coach: RYZHOV, Volodymyr

Names	Pts	2 Pts	3 Pts	FT	A	Stl	To	Reb	F	Mins	
KYRYTCHENKO, Ruslana	4	2/5	0/0	0/0	0	1	1	5	0	27:34	S
BURENOK, Viktorya	4	2/3	0/0	0/2	1	0	0	2	3	20:45	S
ZHIRKO, Yelena	15	4/11	2/4	1/2	4	4	2	15	3	37:31	S
TKACHENKO, Marina	9	3/8	1/5	0/1	6	4	4	4	0	37:48	S
NAZARENKO, Lyudmila	16	7/12	0/0	2/2	0	2	1	4	4	35:09	S
OBEREMKO, Yelena	0	0/0	0/0	0/0	0	0	0	0	0	00:00	
PARADIZ, Viktorya	0	0/0	0/0	0/0	0	0	0	0	0	00:00	
LELEKA, Viktoria	0	0/0	0/0	0/0	0	0	0	0	0	00:00	
DOVGALYUK, Oksana	5	1/4	0/0	3/4	4	0	2	2	0	15:19	
SADOVNIKOVA, Diana	2	1/2	0/0	0/0	0	0	2	2	2	13:01	
SILYANOVA, Natalya	4	2/2	0/0	0/0	2	0	2	1	3	12:53	
SHYLAKOVA, Olga	0	0/0	0/0	0/0	0	0	0	0	0	00:00	
Totals	59	22/47	3/9	6/11	17	11	14	35	15		

Team: ITA Italy

Coach: SALES, Riccaro   Assistant Coaches: NANI, Renato   CARZANIGA, Dante

Names	Pts	2 Pts	3 Pts	FT	A	Stl	To	Reb	F	Mins	
BONFIGLIO, Susanna	8	2/8	0/1	4/5	0	1	2	4	0	21:39	S
FULLIN, Mara	10	3/7	1/5	1/2	3	3	3	5	1	29:29	S
CASELIN, Nicoletta	0	0/3	0/0	0/0	2	1	2	0	1	17:05	S
POLLINI, Catarina	13	6/11	0/0	1/1	3	2	2	8	4	32:32	S
TUFANO, Giuseppina	2	1/1	0/0	0/0	0	0	0	2	3	10:33	S
ZANUSSI, Stefania	2	0/2	0/1	2/2	1	0	2	1	0	19:18	
PAPARAZZO, Elena	9	3/8	0/0	3/7	1	0	1	5	0	21:37	
GARDELLIN, Valentina	0	0/2	0/1	0/0	0	1	1	1	1	15:45	
BALLABIO, Viviana	6	0/1	1/3	3/3	0	1	0	4	4	16:44	
REZOAGLI, Marta	0	0/0	0/0	0/0	0	0	0	0	0	00:00	
ARNETOLI, Lorenza	0	0/2	0/0	0/0	1	1	1	6	3	15:18	
SCHIESARO, Novella	0	0/0	0/0	0/0	0	0	0	0	0	00:00	
Totals	50	15/45	2/11	14/20	11	9	15	32	17		

Referees: BETANCOR LEON, Miguel ESP   DEAKIN, Janice CAN

SEMIFINALS — FINAL SCORE: UKR 60 BRA 81 — HALFTIME SCORE: UKR 36 BRA 48

Team: UKR Ukraine

Coach: RYZHOV, Volodymyr

Names	Pts	2 Pts	3 Pts	FT	A	Stl	To	Reb	F	Mins	
BURENOK, Viktorya	10	3/7	1/2	1/2	0	1	2	0	3	19:45	S
ZHIRKO, Yelena	15	6/10	1/5	0/0	4	3	1	3	0	30:10	S
TKACHENKO, Marina	3	0/5	1/5	0/0	5	2	2	2	1	23:05	S
DOVGALYUK, Oksana	4	2/5	0/0	0/0	1	0	1	5	4	20:12	S
NAZARENKO, Lyudmila	4	2/5	0/0	0/0	1	0	1	0	1	24:09	S
KYRYTCHENKO, Ruslana	0	0/0	0/0	0/0	0	1	0	0	0	08:25	
OBEREMKO, Yelena	2	1/3	0/1	0/0	2	0	1	3	3	15:32	
PARADIZ, Viktorya	0	0/0	0/0	0/0	1	0	0	2	1	06:45	
LELEKA, Viktoria	8	2/4	1/2	1/2	0	0	1	4	1	09:19	
SADOVNIKOVA, Diana	6	2/3	0/0	2/4	1	0	4	6	2	20:23	
SILYANOVA, Natalya	0	0/0	0/1	0/0	0	0	0	0	0	06:32	
SHYLAKOVA, Olga	8	3/7	0/0	2/2	1	0	1	4	1	15:43	
Totals	60	21/49	4/16	6/10	16	7	15	29	19		

Team: BRA Brazil

Coach: ANGELO, Miguel   Assistant Coaches: DUARTE, Sergio   BALBINO, Hermes

Names	Pts	2 Pts	3 Pts	FT	A	Stl	To	Reb	F	Mins	
OLIVA, Hortencia de Fatima Marcari	20	7/12	1/1	3/3	3	1	3	0	1	30:05	S
SILVA, Maria Paula Goncalves da	24	4/7	5/9	1/1	6	0	3	4	2	36:37	S
ARCAIN, Janeth dos Santos	11	4/11	0/0	3/4	3	0	3	6	3	38:00	S
SOBRAL, Marta de Souza	13	2/2	2/3	3/4	0	0	3	4	3	21:12	S
OLIVEIRA, Alessandra Santos de	8	2/4	0/0	4/6	1	1	2	13	3	31:56	S
SILVA, Maria Angelica G. da	1	0/0	0/1	1/2	0	0	0	0	0	02:53	
SANTOS, Ariana Aparecida dos	0	0/0	0/1	0/0	0	1	0	0	0	02:00	
SOBRAL, Leila de Souza	2	1/5	0/0	0/0	1	1	0	3	3	21:13	
GUSTAVO, Roseli do Carmo	0	0/2	0/0	0/0	0	0	0	1	1	02:00	
LUZ, Silvia Andrea Santos	2	1/1	0/0	0/0	3	0	0	2	0	10:25	
SANTOS, Cintia Silva dos	0	0/1	0/0	0/0	1	0	0	0	0	03:18	
PASTOR, Claudia Maria	0	0/0	0/0	0/0	0	0	0	0	0	00:21	
Totals	81	21/45	8/15	15/20	18	4	14	33	16		

Referees: DORIZON, Pascal Noel FRA   LAPAIX GUANCE, Jose DOM

Basketball / *Basketball* 149

Women / Dames

SEMIFINALS — FINAL SCORE: AUS 71 USA 93 — HALFTIME SCORE: AUS 32 USA 47

Team: AUS Australia

Coach: MAHER, Thomas Assistant Coaches: CHEESMAN, Jennifer GRAF, Carrie

Names	Pts	2 Pts	3 Pts	FT	A	Stl	To	Reb	F	Mins	
MAHER, Robyn	1	0/2	0/0	1/2	2	0	2	6	4	20:43	S
TIMMS, Michele	27	6/10	5/10	0/3	4	2	3	3	4	32:36	S
SANDIE, Shelley	7	2/9	0/2	3/4	1	0	4	3	3	26:33	S
SPORN, Rachael	2	1/8	0/0	0/0	0	1	1	2	3	19:04	S
BROGAN, Michelle	9	3/3	1/4	0/0	1	2	1	3	1	23:41	S
COOK, Allison	8	4/5	0/4	0/0	1	2	0	0	2	13:14	
BRONDELLO, Sandy	7	1/9	1/2	2/2	2	2	1	2	1	17:30	
FALLON, Trisha	6	3/9	0/1	0/0	1	1	2	3	1	24:34	
CHANDLER, Michelle	0	0/0	0/0	0/0	0	0	1	0	0	00:00	
ROBINSON, Fiona	2	1/1	0/0	0/0	0	0	1	0	0	02:58	
BOYD, Carla	2	1/1	0/0	0/2	0	1	0	2	0	09:06	
WHITTLE, Jennifer	0	0/2	0/1	0/0	0	0	0	1	0	10:01	
Totals	71	22/59	7/24	6/13	12	12	15	25	19		

Team: USA United States of America

Coach: VanDERVEER, Tara Assistant Coaches: WASHINGTON, Marian BARRY, Ceal

Names	Pts	2 Pts	3 Pts	FT	A	Stl	To	Reb	F	Mins	
EDWARDS, Teresa	0	0/2	0/2	0/0	8	0	3	5	2	26:25	S
BOLTON, Ruthie	12	1/4	2/5	4/5	2	2	2	3	3	24:27	S
SWOOPES, Sheryl	16	8/13	0/2	0/0	3	2	2	4	1	30:52	S
LESLIE, Lisa	22	10/16	0/0	2/4	3	1	5	13	3	32:58	S
McCLAIN, Katrina	18	7/9	0/0	4/6	2	3	2	15	2	29:40	S
STALEY, Dawn	3	1/2	0/1	1/1	7	2	5	2	2	13:35	
AZZI, Jennifer	7	2/2	1/1	0/0	1	0	2	0	1	05:54	
McGHEE, Carla	0	0/1	0/0	0/0	0	0	3	1	2	09:20	
STEDING, Katy	2	1/1	0/0	0/0	0	0	1	1	0	01:44	
LOBO, Rebecca	0	0/0	0/0	0/0	0	0	0	0	0	01:44	
LACEY, Venus	2	1/1	0/0	0/0	0	0	0	1	0	04:34	
McCRAY, Nikki	11	4/5	0/0	3/4	1	0	2	3	2	18:47	
Totals	93	35/56	3/8	14/20	27	10	27	48	20		

Referees: COLUCCI, Gennaro ITA JOVANCIC, Tomislav YUG

FINAL 11 - 12 — FINAL SCORE: ZAI 46 CAN 88 — HALFTIME SCORE: ZAI 20 CAN 52

Team: ZAI Zaire

Coach: MOZINGO, Mongamaluku Assistant Coach: MBUYI, Kadima

Names	Pts	2 Pts	3 Pts	FT	A	Stl	To	Reb	F	Mins	
MWADI, Mabika	2	1/11	0/3	0/1	1	0	4	5	4	23:21	S
NGALULA, Lukengu	12	3/10	1/2	3/4	2	0	6	4	5	26:19	S
KAMANGA, Kasala	5	1/4	1/4	0/0	0	0	5	3	3	15:52	S
TSHIJUKA, Muene	11	4/9	0/0	3/5	0	0	2	9	1	36:02	S
MBUYI, Mukendi	2	0/4	0/1	2/2	0	2	3	7	4	22:31	S
PIKININI, Kakengwa	2	1/3	0/3	0/0	2	1	1	4	3	35:24	
KAPEPULA, Zaina	2	1/5	0/0	0/0	0	1	0	0	2	08:41	
NGOYI, Nsunda	0	0/0	0/0	0/0	0	0	0	0	0	00:00	
AMBA, Kongolo	0	0/0	0/0	0/0	0	0	0	0	0	00:00	
BONZALI, Lileko	0	0/0	0/0	0/0	0	0	0	0	0	00:00	
MBAMBI, Kaninga	0	0/0	0/0	0/0	0	0	0	0	0	00:00	
LOBELA, Daunai	10	4/9	0/0	2/12	0	3	4	8	2	31:50	
Totals	46	15/55	2/13	10/24	5	7	26	40	24		

Team: CAN Canada

Coach: ENNIS, Peter Assistant Coaches: HARLE, Shawnee LORDON, Pauline

Names	Pts	2 Pts	3 Pts	FT	A	Stl	To	Reb	F	Mins	
SMITH, Beverly	21	7/10	1/3	4/4	3	0	1	4	4	26:12	S
GAILUS, Karla Karch	6	3/5	0/2	0/0	6	3	0	1	5	18:59	S
EVANS, Jodi	7	3/5	0/0	1/2	3	1	6	8	2	25:54	S
NORMAN, Diane	20	10/12	0/0	0/0	3	2	1	10	2	24:31	S
BLACKWELL, Andrea	11	3/8	0/0	5/6	3	0	1	4	1	19:11	S
THOMPSON, Camille	4	1/2	0/0	2/2	0	0	0	0	0	08:56	
STEWART, Susan	7	2/4	0/4	3/6	1	2	3	3	0	22:13	
MOLCAK, Shawna	1	0/2	0/0	1/2	4	2	3	5	1	23:29	
JOHNSTON, Cynthia	6	1/1	0/0	4/4	0	2	3	2	5	11:28	
JERANT, Martina	3	1/2	0/0	1/2	0	0	1	3	0	12:05	
BOUCHER, Kelly	0	0/0	0/0	0/0	0	0	0	0	0	00:00	
LANGE-HARRIS, Marlelynn	2	1/1	0/0	0/0	0	1	0	0	3	07:02	
Totals	88	32/52	1/9	21/28	22	14	16	40	23		

Referees: BUTLER, Michael USA BOULANOV, Serguei RUS

FINAL 9 - 10 — FINAL SCORE: CHN 85 KOR 71 — HALFTIME SCORE: CHN 48 KOR 39

Team: CHN People's Republic of China

Coach: CHEN, Daohong Assistant Coaches: MA, Lianbao HU, Hilin

Names	Pts	2 Pts	3 Pts	FT	A	Stl	To	Reb	F	Mins	
ZHENG, Dongmei	3	0/1	1/4	0/0	10	0	3	3	1	32:24	S
LIANG, Xin	13	6/10	0/0	1/1	1	2	1	4	3	25:44	S
ZHENG, Haixia	29	13/21	0/0	3/4	1	1	3	10	1	33:51	S
HE, Jun	8	1/1	2/4	0/0	8	0	0	3	5	24:54	S
MA, Zongqing	12	5/6	0/0	2/3	3	0	3	4	4	28:07	S
MIAO, Bo	0	0/0	0/0	0/0	0	0	0	0	0	00:00	
LI, Xin	0	0/0	0/0	0/0	0	0	0	0	0	00:00	
LIU, Jun	12	0/3	4/7	0/0	8	2	2	2	0	26:59	
SHEN, Li	0	0/0	0/0	0/0	2	0	0	0	1	07:36	
CHU, Hui	0	0/0	0/0	0/0	0	0	0	0	0	00:00	
LI, Dongmei	8	4/7	0/0	0/0	1	1	2	8	2	20:25	
MA, Chengqing	0	0/0	0/0	0/0	0	0	0	0	0	00:00	
Totals	85	29/49	7/15	6/8	34	6	15	34	17		

Team: KOR Korea

Coach: LEE, Syung-Kook Assistant Coach: LEE, Moon-Kyu

Names	Pts	2 Pts	3 Pts	FT	A	Stl	To	Reb	F	Mins	
CHUN, Joo-Weon	20	3/6	3/4	5/8	4	3	1	1	4	40:00	S
HAN, Hyun-Sun	9	3/7	0/7	3/4	5	2	0	4	2	35:22	S
YOO, Young-Joo	11	1/3	3/6	0/0	3	1	2	6	3	37:40	S
AN, Sun-Mi	7	1/1	1/2	2/2	1	0	1	0	0	11:05	S
JUNG, Sun-Min	18	7/15	0/0	4/4	2	1	2	3	4	40:00	S
KIM, Ji-Yoon	4	2/4	0/0	0/0	1	0	0	0	0	08:08	
KWAN, Eun-Jeong	2	1/1	0/1	0/0	4	1	1	1	1	26:27	
PARK, Jung-Eun	0	0/0	0/2	0/0	0	0	0	0	0	01:18	
KIM, Jung-Min	0	0/0	0/0	0/0	0	0	0	0	0	00:00	
CHUN, Eun-Sook	0	0/0	0/0	0/0	0	0	0	0	0	00:00	
LEE, Jong-Ae	0	0/0	0/0	0/0	0	0	0	0	0	00:00	
CHUNG, Eun-Soon	0	0/0	0/0	0/0	0	0	0	0	0	00:00	
Totals	71	18/37	7/22	14/18	20	8	7	15	14		

Referees: BELL, Sally USA ISHIDA, Hidetoshi JPN

FINAL 7 - 8 — FINAL SCORE: JPN 81 ITA 69 — HALFTIME SCORE: JPN 41 ITA 32

Team: JPN Japan

Coach: NAKAGAWA, Fumikazu Assistant Coaches: NAGAI, Yoshitake KOMURE, Ikuo

Names	Pts	2 Pts	3 Pts	FT	A	Stl	To	Reb	F	Mins	
ICHIJO, Aki	14	1/3	4/9	0/0	3	2	3	4	3	33:35	S
MURAKAMI, Chikako	14	3/5	2/4	2/2	1	1	0	4	4	24:46	S
HAGIWARA, Mikiko	21	3/6	4/7	3/4	3	0	2	9	1	32:54	S
KATO, Takako	16	6/11	0/0	4/5	1	1	6	7	2	31:44	S
HAMAGUCHI, Noriko	9	3/6	0/1	3/4	3	0	2	9	3	22:01	S
OYAMA, Taeko	3	1/2	0/1	1/2	0	0	1	0	0	07:54	
MIKAWA, Kikuko	0	0/0	0/1	0/0	0	0	0	0	0	01:23	
YAMADA, Kagari	0	0/1	0/0	0/0	2	1	1	2	4	09:04	
HARADA, Yuka	2	1/1	0/1	0/0	5	1	4	2	1	15:14	
OKAZATO, Akemi	0	0/0	0/0	0/0	0	0	0	1	0	00:46	
KAWASAKI, Mayumi	2	1/2	0/0	0/0	2	1	2	2	0	17:59	
NAGATA, Mutsuko	0	0/2	0/0	0/0	0	0	1	0	1	02:40	
Totals	81	19/39	10/24	13/17	20	7	22	40	20		

Team: ITA Italy

Coach: SALES, Riccaro Assistant Coaches: NANI, Renato CARZANIGA, Dante

Names	Pts	2 Pts	3 Pts	FT	A	Stl	To	Reb	F	Mins	
BONFIGLIO, Susanna	2	1/2	0/0	0/0	2	0	0	2	0	11:58	S
FULLIN, Mara	2	1/6	0/0	0/0	2	2	3	0	1	14:28	S
GARDELLIN, Valentina	5	1/4	1/4	0/0	2	1	2	2	3	27:55	S
POLLINI, Catarina	15	7/14	0/0	1/4	1	3	3	6	3	32:59	S
ARNETOLI, Lorenza	4	2/2	0/0	0/0	0	0	2	1	2	06:01	S
ZANUSSI, Stefania	5	1/2	0/3	3/4	1	0	0	3	2	18:43	
PAPARAZZO, Elena	19	8/13	0/0	3/5	1	0	2	5	2	33:59	
CASELIN, Nicoletta	6	2/6	0/1	2/2	5	3	3	2	2	21:18	
BALLABIO, Viviana	9	0/2	2/2	3/4	3	3	2	1	3	25:38	
REZOAGLI, Marta	2	1/1	0/0	0/0	0	1	1	2	0	07:01	
TUFANO, Giuseppina	0	0/0	0/0	0/0	0	0	0	0	0	00:00	
SCHIESARO, Novella	0	0/0	0/0	0/0	0	0	0	0	0	00:00	
Totals	69	24/52	3/10	12/19	17	13	16	25	17		

Referees: CUI, Yi CHN PELISSARI, Jose BRA

Women / Dames

FINAL 5 - 6   FINAL SCORE: RUS 91 CUB 74   HALFTIME SCORE: RUS 44 CUB 41

Team: RUS Russian Federation

Coach: KAPRANOV, Vadim   Assistant Coaches: KOVALEV, Valeri   GROUDINE, Igor

Names	Pts	2 Pts	3 Pts	FT	A	Stl	To	Reb	F	Mins	
NIKONOVA, Yevgeniya	14	3/6	0/3	8/9	3	2	1	2	4	26:35	S
BARANOVA, Yelena	20	7/9	0/2	6/6	0	4	4	8	3	34:16	S
SUMNIKOVA, Irina	4	2/5	0/0	0/0	8	0	1	3	2	21:22	S
SHAKIROVA, Elen	9	4/8	0/0	1/2	2	1	0	5	3	31:45	S
PSHIKOVA, Yelena	7	3/5	0/0	1/2	0	0	1	2	0	09:19	S
KONOVALOVA, Lyudmila	0	0/0	0/0	0/0	0	0	0	0	0	00:00	
RUTKOVSKAYA, Irina	17	1/4	3/5	6/8	2	2	2	6	1	22:03	
STEPANOVA, Mariya	0	0/0	0/0	0/0	0	0	0	0	0	00:00	
SVINOUKHOVA, Natalia	10	3/6	0/0	4/5	1	0	0	3	1	13:59	
KOUZNETSOVA, Svetlana	10	3/6	0/1	4/6	0	2	2	4	2	30:41	
ZAKAULYUZHANAYA, Oksana	0	0/0	0/0	0/0	0	0	0	0	0	00:00	
ANTIPOVA, Svetlana	0	0/0	0/0	0/0	0	0	0	0	0	00:00	
Totals	91	26/49	3/11	30/38	16	11	11	33	16		

Team: CUB Cuba

Coach: del RIO LOPEZ, Miguel   Assistant Coaches: DIAZ CABRERA, Ernesto   MEDINA PLACENCIA, Jose

Names	Pts	2 Pts	3 Pts	FT	A	Stl	To	Reb	F	Mins	
SEINO, Tania	7	1/4	1/1	2/2	4	0	2	8	5	25:15	S
LEON, Maria	6	2/5	0/1	2/2	2	1	2	1	3	20:47	S
MARTINEZ, Yamilet	19	8/23	0/0	3/4	1	0	4	11	5	36:59	S
HENRY, Delia Hernandez	4	2/7	0/0	0/0	3	0	3	3	4	28:51	S
ENRIQUEZ, Milayda	8	3/9	0/0	2/4	2	0	0	3	4	16:27	S
VICTORES, Lisdeivis	10	3/7	0/0	4/4	0	2	1	7	5	21:14	
VIGIL, Olga	4	1/4	0/1	2/2	0	2	0	3	4	09:53	
HERRERA, Grisel	16	2/4	4/7	0/1	3	0	1	6	3	29:40	
LAGNO, Biosotis	0	0/0	0/0	0/0	0	0	0	0	0	00:00	
AQUILA, Judith	0	0/1	0/0	0/0	0	1	0	0	1	05:20	
HECHEVARRIA, Cariola	0	0/1	0/0	0/0	0	0	1	1	0	05:24	
GOMEZ, Gertrudis	0	0/0	0/0	0/0	0	0	0	0	0	00:00	
Totals	74	22/65	5/10	15/19	15	6	14	43	34		

Referees: BARNETT, Robert USA   THONGPILA, Virun THA

FINAL - BRONZE MATCH   FINAL SCORE: UKR 56 AUS 66   HALFTIME SCORE: UKR 24 AUS 33

Team: UKR Ukraine

Coach: RYZHOV, Volodymyr

Names	Pts	2 Pts	3 Pts	FT	A	Stl	To	Reb	F	Mins	
KYRYTCHENKO, Ruslana	0	0/2	0/1	0/0	1	0	1	3	3	15:57	S
BURENOK, Viktorya	0	0/1	0/0	0/0	0	1	2	1	5	14:19	S
ZHIRKO, Yelena	16	4/12	2/6	2/2	3	1	4	9	2	35:08	S
TKACHENKO, Marina	7	2/8	0/2	3/4	2	1	3	5	1	33:50	S
NAZARENKO, Lyudmila	9	3/8	0/0	3/6	3	0	1	5	2	37:00	S
OBEREMKO, Yelena	0	0/1	0/0	0/0	1	0	2	0	0	04:08	
PARADIZ, Viktorya	0	0/0	0/0	0/0	0	0	0	0	0	00:00	
LELEKA, Viktoria	2	1/1	0/1	0/0	0	0	0	2	0	02:48	
DOVGALYUK, Oksana	4	1/1	0/1	2/2	0	0	0	4	3	17:53	
SADOVNIKOVA, Diana	4	2/2	0/0	0/0	1	0	3	3	1	16:02	
SILYANOVA, Natalya	14	4/4	2/2	0/0	1	0	1	2	1	22:55	
SHYLAKOVA, Olga	0	0/0	0/0	0/0	0	0	0	0	0	00:00	
Totals	56	17/40	4/13	10/14	12	3	17	32	20		

Team: AUS Australia

Coach: MAHER, Thomas   Assistant Coaches: CHEESMAN, Jennifer   GRAF, Carrie

Names	Pts	2 Pts	3 Pts	FT	A	Stl	To	Reb	F	Mins	
MAHER, Robyn	2	1/4	0/1	0/0	2	1	0	4	3	25:46	S
TIMMS, Michele	2	1/7	0/1	0/2	4	4	2	3	4	29:50	S
SANDIE, Shelley	11	5/8	0/0	1/2	1	0	4	5	2	26:11	S
SPORN, Rachael	4	1/4	0/0	2/2	1	0	2	6	3	26:23	S
BROGAN, Michelle	19	6/9	0/1	7/10	2	3	2	12	2	32:56	S
COOK, Allison	0	0/3	0/1	0/0	0	1	0	0	0	08:19	
BRONDELLO, Sandy	13	4/9	0/0	5/6	3	0	1	1	0	21:05	
FALLON, Trisha	8	2/7	0/0	4/4	1	0	0	2	2	12:45	
CHANDLER, Michelle	0	0/0	0/0	0/0	0	0	0	0	0	00:00	
ROBINSON, Fiona	0	0/0	0/0	0/0	0	0	0	0	0	00:00	
BOYD, Carla	0	0/1	0/0	0/0	0	0	0	0	0	05:38	
WHITTLE, Jennifer	7	2/4	1/1	0/0	0	1	1	4	0	11:07	
Totals	66	22/56	1/5	19/26	14	10	12	37	16		

Referees: SOARES de CAMPOS, Antonio ANG   DEAKIN, Janice CAN

FINAL - GOLD MATCH   FINAL SCORE: BRA 87 USA 111   HALFTIME SCORE: BRA 46 USA 57

Team: BRA Brazil

Coach: ANGELO, Miguel   Assistant Coaches: DUARTE, Sergio   BALBINO, Hermes

Names	Pts	2 Pts	3 Pts	FT	A	Stl	To	Reb	F	Mins	
OLIVA, Hortencia de Fatima Marcari	11	4/7	1/4	0/1	3	0	4	4	1	27:56	S
SILVA, Maria Paula Goncalves da	7	0/4	1/4	4/4	10	1	3	2	1	38:03	S
ARCAIN, Janeth dos Santos	24	10/17	0/1	4/8	3	1	1	4	4	37:16	S
SOBRAL, Marta de Souza	19	6/10	0/4	7/10	0	0	4	4	4	25:12	S
OLIVEIRA, Alessandra Santos de	10	5/10	0/0	0/0	0	3	1	9	3	34:43	S
SILVA, Maria Angelica G. da	0	0/0	0/0	0/0	1	0	0	0	1	04:41	
SANTOS, Ariana Aparecida dos	0	0/0	0/0	0/0	0	0	0	0	0	00:00	
SOBRAL, Leila de Souza	7	2/3	1/1	0/1	0	1	2	2	2	16:31	
GUSTAVO, Roseli do Carmo	0	0/0	0/0	0/0	0	0	0	0	0	00:00	
LUZ, Silvia Andrea Santos	9	0/1	3/4	0/0	1	0	1	1	2	12:04	
SANTOS, Cintia Silva dos	0	0/0	0/0	0/0	0	0	0	1	1	03:34	
PASTOR, Claudia Maria	0	0/0	0/0	0/0	0	0	0	0	0	00:00	
Totals	87	27/52	6/18	15/24	18	6	16	27	19		

Team: USA United States of America

Coach: VanDERVEER, Tara   Assistant Coach: BARRY, Ceal   DARSCH, Nancy

Names	Pts	2 Pts	3 Pts	FT	A	Stl	To	Reb	F	Mins	
EDWARDS, Teresa	9	3/7	1/1	0/0	10	2	2	4	1	24:28	S
BOLTON, Ruthie	15	2/5	3/5	2/2	5	5	0	5	1	29:09	S
SWOOPES, Sheryl	16	5/8	2/4	0/0	5	1	0	3	4	23:53	S
LESLIE, Lisa	29	12/14	0/0	5/5	1	0	4	6	4	31:21	S
McCLAIN, Katrina	12	6/8	0/0	0/0	1	0	2	5	5	19:55	S
STALEY, Dawn	9	0/0	0/1	9/10	3	1	1	0	2	14:25	
AZZI, Jennifer	4	1/2	0/0	2/2	2	1	1	1	1	08:16	
McGHEE, Carla	2	1/1	0/0	0/0	1	0	0	0	1	02:50	
STEDING, Katy	2	1/1	0/0	0/0	0	0	0	0	0	05:11	
LOBO, Rebecca	2	1/1	0/0	0/0	0	0	1	2	1	05:51	
LACEY, Venus	4	2/2	0/0	0/2	0	1	1	5	2	20:03	
McCRAY, Nikki	7	3/4	0/1	1/1	2	1	3	1	0	14:38	
Totals	111	37/53	6/12	19/22	30	12	15	32	22		

Referees: ZYCH, Wieslaw POL   BRAZAUSKAS, Romualdas LTU

FINAL CLASSIFICATION

Rnk	Ctry	
1	United States of America	Gold
2	Brazil	Silver
3	Australia	Bronze
4	Ukraine	
5	Russian Federation	
6	Cuba	
7	Japan	
8	Italy	
9	People's Republic of China	
10	Korea	
11	Canada	
12	Zaire	

PHILIP G PORCHER • PETER L PORLING •
MARCELA M PORPORATO • CLAUDIA PORSCHE •
ANNA C PORSO • DAVIS M PORT • SANDRA A POR-
TANOVA • CHARLENE D PORTEE • JACQUELINE E
PORTEOUS • ALAN W PORTER • BEVERLY A
PORTER • BONNIE A PORTER • BRENDA D PORTER
• CARLIN M PORTER • CAROLYN E PORTER •
CASANDRA D PORTER • DANIELLE L PORTER •
DEBORAH E PORTER • DEXTER V PORTER •
DOROTHY J PORTER • GEORGE A PORTER • JAN
PORTER • JIM PORTER • JOHN L PORTER • KAREN
E PORTER • KATHLEEN D PORTER • MARGARET M
PORTER • MICHAEL W PORTER • MIMI M PORTER •
NONA P PORTER • PAUL R PORTER • RAMONA
PORTER • ROBERT L PORTER • ROBIN D PORTER •
RUTH B PORTER • SATIMA A PORTER • VICKIE V
PORTER • DEBORAH A PORTER-GLENN • JAMES
L PORTER ATC • POLLY A PORTER ATC • JOEY
PORTERFIELD • DAVID B PORTILLO • JORUE
PORTILLO • ANTOINETTE PORTIS • ROBERT L
PORTIS • AMY SUSANNE PORTMANN • KATH-
LEEN A PORTO • ANNA KATHARYN PORTWOOD •
FRANCIS K PORTWOOD • MITCHELL G PORT-
WOOD • LILLIAN L POSADA • RYAN M POSENER •
ARV`OREAL POSEY • BETTY P POSEY • DORIS J
POSEY • MARILYN G POSKITT • CRISTIAN L POSS
• JOHN C POSS • MARY LEE L POSS • SUSAN A
POSS • ANN O POST • JASON W POST • JENNIFER
A POST • JEREMY S POST • MARK D POST •
MICHAEL J POST • RACHEL C POST • SHEA K
POST • SHEILA M POST • BARBARA J POSTELL •
CAROL POSTELL • JOHN H POSTELL • LAVERNE
POSTELL • PAMELA H POSTELL • R. ELAINE
POSTLETHWAIT • BRIAN C POSTLEWAITE •
JACQUELYN L POSTMA • HELEN N POSTON •
MARTHA A POSTON • RACHEL S POSTON • CATALI-
NA POTDEVIN • ERNESTO POTDEVIN • MARIA POT-
DEVIN • JENNIFER W POTEET • JAMES D POTEETE
• MARTY J POTEETE • RONALD L POTEETE •
PIERRE POTIE • EDWARD S POTKANOWICZ • NAN-
CY A POTOSKY • SUSAN M POTREPKA • TIMOTHY
M POTTEN • ANDREW W POTTER • BENTON H
POTTER • JANICE K POTTER • JEAN K POTTER •
JEFFERY L POTTER • JUDY D POTTER • LLOYD B
POTTER • MARK M POTTER • MARY POTTER •
ROBERT J POTTER • ROBIN K POTTER • SADYE W
POTTER • SADYE WATSON POTTER • STACIA M
POTTER • WILLIAM O POTTER • LORI A POTTER
ATC • CAROL POTTINGER • RAQUEL S POT-
TINGER • BARBARA J POTTS • BONNIE H POTTS •
DONALD S POTTS • JILL F POTTS • KELLY A
POTTS • SHARON M POTTS • SHERRY S POTTS •
STEVEN A POTTS • SUSAN B POTTS • WANDA G
POTTS • COLLEEN J POTTS RN • CLAIRE POTVIN
• JAMES A POTVIN • LAURA POU • LEO H POU •
JENNIFER T POULAKIDAS • BETHANY M POULIN
• SHARIE A POULIN • CARLTON J POULNOT • DI-
ANNE L POULOS • SAM POULOS • AARON S
POULSEN • MICHAEL POULTON • THERESA K
POULTON • FOSTER E POUND • JAMES K POUND
• LINDA M POUND • MELISSA R POUND • NELLIE
L POUND • ROBERT E POUND • ROBERT E POUND
• JULIE M POUNDERS • LAURA H POUNDERS •
EDITH A POUNDS • JAMES E POUNDS • JEFFREY
L POUNDS • MARIAN S POUNDS • ALEXANDRE
JUSTIN POUPAULT • HENGAMEH POURFAKHR •
MICHAEL POURREAU • MAX L POUX • ANTHONY J
POVILAITIS • MARGARET A POVOLNY • JAMES
POWE • ALAN W POWELL • ALLISON POWELL •
ARTHUR E POWELL • BENJETT A POWELL •
BONI Z POWELL • CARL L POWELL • CARLA M
POWELL • CASSANDRA POWELL • CHERYL B
POWELL • COY W POWELL • CRYSTAL D POWELL
• CYNTHIA A POWELL • CYNTHIA D POWELL •
DANIELLE POWELL • DAVID M POWELL • DONNA
H POWELL • DONNA K POWELL • DUNCAN M
POWELL • ELLA M POWELL • EVANGELIA L POW-
ELL • FRED L POWELL • FREDERICK G POWELL •
FRITH J POWELL • HOWARD C POWELL • JACK H
POWELL • JENNIFER J POWELL • JOAN R POW-
ELL • JOANNA M POWELL • JOHN J POWELL •
JOHN R POWELL • KATHERINE R POWELL • KEN-
NETH L POWELL • LARA K. POWELL • LAWRENCE
D POWELL • LISA MARIE POWELL • MARGIE POW-
ELL • MOZELL POWELL • NANCY A POWELL •
NANCY H POWELL • NORMA JEAN POWELL •
PRISCILLA G POWELL • RANDALL W POWELL •
REBECCA POWELL • RENEE POWELL • RICK D
POWELL • ROMETTA E POWELL • RONALD C
POWELL • SHEILA N POWELL • SUSAN E POWELL
• THOMAS D POWELL • WILLIAM G POWELL •
WILLIAM R POWELL • DARIN S POWELL ATC •
HENRY M POWELL JR • NORMAN E POWELL JR •
AMY POWER • CHERYL MARIE POWER • TAMMY L
POWER • THOMAS A POWER • ASHLEY E POW-
ERS • BARBARA A POWERS • CATHARINE B POW-
ERS • DONALD R POWERS • E RENEE POWERS •
JIMMY D POWERS • JUDY K POWERS • KATIE
POWERS • KELLY D POWERS • LAURA L POWERS
• MARY BETH POWERS • MAUREEN T POWERS •
MICHAEL J POWERS • RUSSELL G POWERS •
SAMUEL W POWERS • THEODORE R POWERS •
THOMAS W POWERS • WILLIAM S POWERS •
MICHAEL E POWERS ATC • ROBERT J POWERS JR
• SCOTT POYTHRESS • ROGER POZEZNIK L MT •
BRIAN POZGAY • JERZY F POZIOMBKO • CATHER-
INE R POZNIAK • CATHERINE M PRABHU • NANCY
L PRADO • CATHERINE D PRAEGER • SANDY D
PRAILLEAU • DUANE E PRAMBERG • MARILYN J
PRAMBERG • ANJALI PRASAD • CHRISTOPHER P
PRASAD • ANGILEENE PRATER • POLLY S PRATER •
STEVE M PRATER • BELINDA D PRATHER • DAVID
LEE PRATHER • JANET PRATHER • JULIE PRATHER
• KENNETH ALLEN PRATHER • LAYNE L PRATHER •
PATRICIA P PRATHER • RITA L PRATHER • SHEL-
BY R PRATHER • IRVINE D PRATHER DO • ALMA B
PRATOR • JOHN A.C. PRATT • LILAS K PRATT •
LILLIAN A PRATT • MONA J PRATT • PETER F
PRATT • TOBY E PRATT • ALBERTA A PRATT-SEN-
SIE • JOHN M PRATTE • PATRICIA A PRATTE • ANI-
TA PRATTO • BILL C PRAY • GREGORY T PRAY •
JASNA PRCIC • BARBARA G PREBBLE • PAUL C
PREBBLE • ADAM S PREBLE • DANIEL A PREBLE
• DARRELL W PREBLE • DENISE E PREBLE • JODY
R PREISCHE ATC • MARVIN W PRELLBERG • JANE
M PRENDERGAST • SHARON A PRENDERGAST •
ANTHONY J PRENNI • BENJAMIN M PRENTISS •
JOSEPH PRESBERRY • BETTYE M PRESCOTT •
JOYCE L PRESCOTT • LOUISE H PRESCOTT • MICK-
IE E PRESCOTT • ROY H PRESCOTT • MARK PRES-
GROVE • BIRDIE M PRESLEY • CAROL E PRESLEY •
DARNELL R PRESLEY • EDWARD PRESLEY JR •
TUNSTILL O PRESLEY JR • KATHRYN L PRESNAL •
WILLIAM H PRESNELL • CHARLES R PRESSEL •
MARILYN G PRESSER • KELLI A PRESTIDGE •
JUDY L PRESTIGIACOMO • KARA L PRESTIGIACO-
MO • KELLI N PRESTIGIACOMO • KRISTA L PRES-
TIGIACOMO • GERRI V PRESTON • JUDY ANN
PRESTON • KAMERON D PRESTON • LISA PRE-
STON • LISA M PRESTON • MARCELINE O PRE-
STON • PATRICK W PRESTON • PETER J PRE-
STON • ROBERT M PRESTON • ROY E PRESTON •
THOMAS JR M PRESTON • TODD M PRESTON • VI-
VIAN L PRESTON • WENDY M PRESTON • WILLIAM
PRESTON • JAMES N PRESTON JR • KAREN R
PRESTWOOD • ADRIANO PRETO • NOEL PRETO-
RIUS • JUDITH PRETTY • STEVE PRETTYMAN •
MARIANNE PREUDHOMME • HOLGER PREUSS •
CAROLE PREVOST • JOE C PREVOST • JOHN P
PREVOST • MARJORIE L PREVOST • SHARI A
PREVOST • ALLEN PREWETT • COURTNEY P
PREWETT • GAY S PREWETT • SHARON PREWETT
• PATSY PREWIT • PHYLLIS C PREWITT • AMY K
PREZBINDOWSKI • JEAN C PREZEL • NIKSA
PREZZI • DOUG PRIAR • MICHAEL PRIBYL ATC •
ALAN W PRICE • ANDREA M PRICE • ANNA J
PRICE • ANNA J PRICE • AVOLINE EILAND PRICE
• CALVIN L PRICE • CAMPBELL J PRICE • CAROL
A PRICE • CHRISTINA PRICE • CINDY A PRICE •
DANIEL G PRICE • DENISE R PRICE • DOROTHY H
PRICE • DOUGLAS C PRICE • GEROME PRICE •
HELEN MICHELE PRICE • JAMES E PRICE •
JAMES P PRICE • JANET L PRICE • JANINE Y
PRICE • JEAN W PRICE • JEFFREY R PRICE • JOAN
M PRICE • JOEL G PRICE • JOHN PRICE • JUDITH
A PRICE • KIMBERLY D PRICE • KRISTIE L PRICE •
LAWRANCE E PRICE • LAWRENCE W PRICE • LYN-
DA G PRICE • LYNDA R PRICE • MARILYNN H
PRICE • MARY K PRICE • MICHELLE PRICE • PA-
TRICIA PRICE • PAULETTE PRICE • POLLY J
PRICE • PRISCILLA S PRICE • REGENIA W PRICE
• RICHARD PRICE • ROSALYNNE V PRICE • RUTH
U PRICE • SABRINA L PRICE • SUSAN E PRICE •
TERRILYN PRICE • THELMA M PRICE • THOMAS L
PRICE • VIRGINIA PRICE • WALTER H PRICE •
WILLIAM L PRICE • WILLIE A PRICE • YVONNE
PRICE • ZOANA PRICE • ELIZABETH A PRICHARD
• THOMAS K PRICHARD • MELLISSA P PRICHER •
WILLLAM D PRICKETT • ELIZABETH S PRIDDY •
NICOLAS D PRIDDY • BOBBIE M PRIDE • DIANE
PRIDEMORE • DANIEL C PRIDGEN • GREGORY G
PRIDGEON • JONATHAN M PRIDMORE • GAVIN A
PRIEBE • KIRSTEN M PRIEBE • ALAN J PRIEST •
ANTHONY J PRIEST • JAMES L PRIEST • THOMAS
J PRIEST • NEAL A PRIEST MD • STANLEY V
PRIESTER • ELENA PRIETO CABRERA • NAN
SOOKYONG PRIKRYL • JOHNIE L PRIMAS • LINDA
M PRIME • MARY L PRIMEL • HILLARY PRIMIANI •
EDITH B PRIMM • SUSAN A PRIMO • STACIE T
PRIMROSE • SUSAN A PRIMROSE • MARTIN A
PRIMUS • COREY A PRINCE • DEBORAH E
PRINCE • FRANCES MARY PRINCE • JANE R
PRINCE • LEEDEL M PRINCE • MARK PRINCE •
NICK PRINCE • ROBYN E PRINCE • SYLVIA R
PRINCE • THOMAS G PRINCE • TRACEY L PRINCE
• WILLIE G PRINCE • BOBBY D PRINCE MD • REX
A PRINGLE • SAMONICA R PRINGLE • CHERYL H
PRINSTER • MARY A PRIOR • ROBERT M PRIOR •
DANIEL PRITCHARD • HELENE M PRITCHARD •
JACQUELINE L PRITCHARD • JANIS J PRITCHARD •
KAREN F PRITCHARD • KENNY R PRITCHARD •
RUTH E PRITCHARD • BECKY PRITCHETT • ELGIN J
PRITCHETT • GLORIA C PRITCHETT • JAMES D
PRITCHETT • JIMMY PRITCHETT • JOHN CHU
PRITCHETT • TAMMY T PRITCHETT • TERESA M
PRITCHETT • JOAN K PRITZKER • BETH PRIVEN •
MARTIN A PRIVETTE • LYNNE F PRIZZI • DAWN L
PROBST • GALE B PROBST • KENNETH X PROBST •
WILLIAM R PROBST • KORNELIA PROBST-MACK-
OWIAK • LISA V PROCHNOW • KENNETH R PROCK •
BETTY B PROCTOR • EMMA PROCTOR • ERIC D
PROCTOR • GEORGE PROCTOR • JOHN C PROC-
TOR • LINDA M PROCTOR • SARAH E PROCTOR •
SHERRENISE ROSE PROCTOR • TERESA D
PROCTOR • TREVA D PROCTOR • WALTER B
PROCTOR • KATHRYN A PROFFITT • RICHARD E
PROFFITT • JOHN L PROGELHOF • JACK PROKES
• PETER PRONK • BETTY H PROPES • RANDOLPH
R PROPHATER • STEPHEN G. PROPST • GRADY L
PROSSER JR • HELEN D PROTHO • JAMES W
PROTHO • VENESSA D PROTHRO • DANNY S
PROUDFOOT • KATHRYN A PROUGH • FABIEN P
PROUVOST • CAROLYN D PROVENCHER •
CHARLES D PROVITT • TOM PROVOST • KAY H
PRUDENTE • DANIEL C PRUDHOMME • MARY
ANN PRUDNER • CHRISTY L PRUEITT • ALISON L
PRUETT • BRIAN S PRUETT • MARY E PRUETT •
MOLLY R PRUETT • BRENDA B PRUITT • BRYAN J
PRUITT • CARLAS M PRUITT • DIANE B PRUITT •
DON L PRUITT • KYMY H PRUITT • LAURA L PRUITT
• LOIS W PRUITT • MELISSA SARA PRUITT •
SHIRLEY A PRUITT • SHYRA S PRUITT • STEPHEN L
PRUITT • THOMAS A PRUITT • ANDREW L PRUITT
ATC • MARTA L PRUPAS • DOUGLAS J PRUSS •
SANDRA M PRUSS • BERTRAND J PRUVOST •
CHRISTOPHER S PRYBYLO • KEITH PRYBYLSKI •
JULIE A PRYDE ATC • MARY V PRYLES • MILLIE F
PRYLES • DAVID L PRYOR • GREGORY R PRYOR •
LEAH Y PRYOR • LEO K PRYOR • PENNY L PRYOR
• SHARON J PRYOR • TODD F PRYOR • EDMUND
PRYTHERCH • JOAN C PRZYSTASZ • MARY C
PSAILA • DARIA E PSILOPOULOS • ANDRE M
PTAK • BONNIE I PTAK • MALAGAMATUMUA
PUAILOA • JOHN PUAKEA • FRANK J PUCCIANO •
JEANNE F PUCHALA • BETTY A PUCKETT • BEV-
ERLY N PUCKETT • DEBRA J PUCKETT • IAN G
PUCKETT • JAMES B PUCKETT • JAMES R PUCK-
ETT • JANE PUCKETT • JANE G PUCKETT • JOAN C
PUCKETT • KIMERON D PUCKETT • RENAE B PUCK-
ETT • KATARZYNA W PUCKHABER • CASE PUDIK •
STEPHEN YVES PUECHBERTY • CINDY D PUETT •
MARGARET L PUETZ • FORSTER D PUFFE • JAMES C
PUFFER • JON T PUFFER • AGNES E PUGH • D
ANN M PUGH • DAMITA A PUGH • FRANCES PUGH
• JOHN C PUGH • MABEL G PUGH • MELVIN A
PUGH • MICHAEL L PUGH • GLENN W PUGH ATC •
NANCY J PUHR • RITA A PUIG • PEDRO PUJOL •
WILLIAM L PULGRAM • DARYL L PULIS • PATRICIA
L PULLAR SCOTT • DIANE C PULLEN • JAMES S
PULLEN • PAULA R PULLEN • RICHARD A PULLEN
• SUSAN D PULLEN • EMILY B PULLIAM • PAMELA
C PULLIE • CAROL L PULLIEN • PRESTON A PULL-
MAN • ANDREW B PULSIFER • MATTHEW V PUL-
STS • ANN W PULVER • ROBERT T PULVER • SUN-
NIE L PULVERS • CONNIE S PUMPELLY ATC • KIRK
L PUMPHREY • INNOCENT S PUNNOOSE • ALAN
F PURCELL • ANDREW J PURCELL • CARYN R
PURCELL • KAREN E PURCELL • KRISTAN L PUR-
CELL • MELANIE D PURCELL • SEAN C PURCELL
• WANDA M PURCELL • TIMOTHY PURDON • AN-
DREW W PURDY • JUDY B PURDY • JYL M PURDY •
LINDA S PURDY • ROBERT B PURDY • TISHA PURI
• MANDELL D PURKETT • RAYMOND M PURPUR •
JAN M PURSER • KATHLEEN M PURSER • CAROL
L PURSLEY • NANCY N PURSLEY • DAVID G PURS-
LEY MD • ADRIENNE K PURVES • DONALD E PUR-
VIANCE • JAMIE W PURVIS • MARIA L PURWIN •
SUSAN PURZNER • VINCE F PUSATERI •
CHARLES S PUTNAM • DONALD G PUTNAM • JU-
DITH PUTNAM • PHILIP PUTNAM • ROBERT PUT-
NAM • HOWARD N PUTTER • JACK H PYBURN •
LACEY R PYBURN • LILLIAN P PYBURN • DAVID K
PYE • KAREN B PYE • LEON G. PYE • MILLY C PYE •
KRZYSTOF PYKA • BRENDA J PYLE • GAIL C PYLE
• SARAH PYLE • VICKI PYLES-HUTCHINSON •
HANK K QADIR • LIN QIU • YEN L QUACH • CINDY
L QUAIFE • RANDALL J QUALITZA • AARON P
QUALLS • FERRIS R QUALLS • VNITA S QUALLS •
RICHARD F QUALTER ATC • ELAINE C QUAN • PE-
TER C QUAN • RONALD L QUARANTINO • COR-
NELIA S QUARLES • ELLEN M QUARLES • JILL R
QUARLES • MARY P QUARLES • SABRINA D
QUARLES • TOMMY JAY QUARLES • ZENJA R
QUARLES • JOSEPH V QUARLES III • CYNTHIA F
QUARTERMAN • G. WILLIAM QUARTERMAN •
RON QUARTERMAN • MARIA QUATRARO • CARL E
QUATTLEBAUM • AMANDA B QUEEN • LISA S
QUEEN • MARION L QUEEN • REBECCA B QUEEN
• SUSAN E QUEEN • THOMAS C QUEEN • TRACEY
QUEEN • ALBERT QUEEN JR • WADE A QUEEN JR
• PATRICIA G QUEENEY • ALVARO G QUESADA •
RODOLFO QUESADA • RICHARD B QUESENBER-
RY • RICHARD P QUESNELL • JENNY QUESTELL •
JULIAN QUEZADA • DANTE R QUICK • JUDY G
QUICK • MARTHA L QUICK • SUSAN B QUICK •
CEEON D QUIETT • GLORIA B. QUILL • JUDY S
QUILLEN • MARY B QUILLIAN • ROBERT A QUIN •
KATHLEEN W QUINBY • DIANA N QUINCY • JEN-
NIFER A QUINLAN • LORI H QUINLAN • JAMES C
QUINLIVAN • CHRIS QUINN • JERRY B QUINN •
JOYE L QUINN • KATHY E QUINN • NANCY P
QUINN • PAUL QUINN • RON G QUINN • THOMAS
J QUINN • THOMAS W QUINN • JEFFREY M QUINN
ATC • MARK E QUINN ATC • MARGARITA
QUINONES • MICHAEL A QUINONES • NORMA
QUINTANA • PABLO QUINTANILLA • PETRA QUIN-
TERO • AUGUSTINE C QUINTERO JR • ANNETTE
M QUINTING • AMY M QUIRK • MICHELLE QUIRKE
• JORGE H QUIROZ • FLORENCE L QUON • MARI-
LYN E QUOSS • URSULA A QUOYESER • AZHAR A
QURESHI • MOHAMMED N QURESHI • TSVI K
RAAB • PETER J RAACK • PAUL V RAAKE • ALLI-
SON C RAASCH • HEIDI RAASS • MONIKA RAB •
MARIA ISABEL RABASA • KELLY R RABB • MO-
HAMMAD F RABBI • SONIA A RABBOW • JUDITH V
RABEL • SCOTT A RABENOLD • TAMMY T RABERN
• ANDREW B RABHAN • NANCY P RABHAN • BAR-
BARA L RABIN • ROBERT E RABIN • BETH C RABI-
NOWITZ • RUTH R RABON • SOLEDAD P RABORN
• WILLIAM K RABREN • VIRGIL O RABUN • AN-
DREW MICHAEL RABY • LANCE JASON
RACHELEFSKY • MARVIN A RACHELEFSKY •
PAULA M RACHELEFSKY • YVONNE M RACHOU •
APRIL M RACKARD • LISA D RACKARD • JEFFREY
C RACKLIFFE • BARNABAS RACKS • ROBERT
RACZ • THERESA A RADACK • BRAD E RADAKER •
MILOS RADAN • DANNY P RADCLIFF • GORDON
RADDER • DALE A RADECKI • MATTHEW J
RADELET ATC • MARK A RADELL • SARA J
RADEMACHER • FRANKLIN E RADER • CHAVDAR
A RADEV • LISA A RADFORD • NEAL T RADFORD •
PRENTICE L RADFORD ATC • PRIYA RADHAKR-
ISHNAN • RAJ RADHAKRISHNAN • MARY ELLEN
RADICS • JAMES A RADLOFF • JON S RADLOFF •
DONALD RADMAN • JANE B RADMAN • ERIKA L
RADTKE • ADRIANA M RADY • ALE RADY • JERZY
W RADZ • LOUISE M RAEL • JENNIFER M RAFA •
RAFAEL RAFAEL RIVERA-MENDEZ • DEBORAH
RAFE • JANICE L RAFFA • JEAN FRANCOIS
RAFFALLI-EBEZANT • CHRISTINA S RAFFERTY •
LISA R RAFFERTY • PATRICK A RAFFERTY •

BOXING
BOXE

Abbreviations and terms used in Boxing results tables
Abréviations et termes employés dans les tableaux de résultats de boxe

Term	English	Français
1/16 Elimination	1/16 Elimination	1/16 de finale
1/8 Elimination	1/8 Elimination	1/8 de finale
Bronze	Bronze Medal	Médaille de bronze
Bronze Medal	Bronze Medal	Médaille de bronze
BYE	Bye	Exemption
Ctry	Country	Pays
Final Classification	Final Classification	Classement final
Gold	Gold Medal	Médaille d'or
Gold Medal	Gold Medal	Médaille d'or
KO	Knockout	Mise hors de combat
Medal Round	Medal Round	Tour pour les médailles
Name	Name	Nom
No	Number	Numéro
PTS	Points	Points
Quarterfinals	Quarterfinals	Quarts de finale
RSC	Referee Stops Contest	Arrêt de l'arbitre
RSCH	Referee Stops Contest— Head Blows	Arrêt de l'arbitre — Coups à la tête
RSCI	Referee Stops Contest— Injury	Arrêt de l'arbitre — Blessure
Rnk	Rank	Classement
Semifinals	Semifinals	Demi-finales
Silver	Silver Medal	Médaille d'argent
Silver Medal	Silver Medal	Médaille d'argent
TB	Tiebreak	Jugement décisif

International Amateur Boxing Association (AIBA)
Association Internationale de Boxe Amateur
P.O. Box 0141
10321 Berlin
Germany

Boxing / *Boxe*

Light Flyweight, 48 kg (106 lb), Men / *Mi-mouche, 48 kg, Messieurs*

1/16 ELIMINATION			1/8 ELIMINATION	QUARTERFINALS	SEMIFINALS	MEDAL ROUND
No	Name	Ctry				
1	MUNCHYAN, Nshan	ARM	MUNCHYAN, N.			
2	BYE			BOJILOV, D. P.		
3	BOJILOV, Daniel Petrov	BUL		PTS 11:5		
4	BYE		BOJILOV, D. P.		BOJILOV, D. P.	
5	GIRITIL, Yasar	TUR			PTS 18:6	
6	KAMSING, Somrot	THA	KAMSING, S.			
7	BORNEI, Sabin Marius	ROM	PTS 19:4	KAMSING, S.		
8	PEREZ, Jose	DOM	BORNEI, S. M.	PTS 18:7		BOJILOV, D. P.
			PTS 16:10			PTS 17:8
9	MENDOZA, Beibis	COL				
10	FILIANI, Domenic	CAN	MENDOZA, B.			
11	QAMBRANI, Abdul Rashid	PAK	PTS 12:1	KIRYUKHIN, O.		
12	KIRYUKHIN, Oleg	UKR	KIRYUKHIN, O.	PTS 18:6		
13	RASOANAIVO, Anicet	MAD	PTS 17:3		KIRYUKHIN, O.	
14	BACA, Geovany	HON	RASOANAIVO, A.		PTS 19:14	
15	HEALER, Modiradilo	BOT	PTS 12:0	GUARDADO, A.		
16	GUARDADO, Albert	USA	GUARDADO, A.	PTS 9:4		
			PTS 11:9			
17	AGUILERA, Yosvani	CUB				
18	STROM, Stefan	SWE	AGUILERA, Y.			
19	TSAI, Chih-Hsiu	TPE	RSC 2 2:26	VELASCO, M.		
20	VELASCO, Mansueto	PHI	VELASCO, M.	PTS 14:5		
21	BERHILI, Hamid	MAR	RSCH 1 2:27		VELASCO, M.	
22	TETTEH, Alfred	GHA	BERHILI, H.		PTS 20:10	
23	ROSSELL, Alberto	PER	PTS 10:5	BERHILI, H.		
24	YANG, Xiangzhong	CHN	YANG, X.	PTS 14:9		VELASCO, M.
			PTS 16:7			PTS 22:10
25	BENHARD, Joseph	NAM				
26	LOZANO, Rafael	ESP	LOZANO, R.			
27	DEBENDRA, Thapa	IND	PTS 10:2	LOZANO, R.		
28	MAKEPULA, Masibulele	RSA	MAKEPULA, M.	PTS 14:3		
29	SAPOK, Biki	MAS	RSCH 1 1:41		LOZANO, R.	
30	MARTINEZ, Jesus	MEX	MARTINEZ, J.		PTS 10:9	
31	LAPAINI, Lamasara	INA	PTS 15:4	LAPAINI, L.		
32	BALAZ, Peter	SVK	LAPAINI, L.	PTS 8:1		
			PTS 13:3			

FINAL CLASSIFICATION

Rnk	Name	Ctry	
1	BOJILOV, Daniel Petrov	BUL	Gold
2	VELASCO, Mansueto	PHI	Silver
3	KIRYUKHIN, Oleg	UKR	Bronze
3	LOZANO, Rafael	ESP	Bronze
4	KAMSING, Somrot	THA	
5	GUARDADO, Albert	USA	
6	BERHILI, Hamid	MAR	
7	LAPAINI, Lamasara	INA	

GOLD MEDAL

BOJILOV, D. P.   BUL
PTS 19:6

SILVER MEDAL

VELASCO, M.   PHI

BRONZE MEDAL

KIRYUKHIN, O.   UKR

LOZANO, R.   ESP

Flyweight, 51 kg (112 lb), Men / *Mouche, 51 kg, Messieurs*

No.	Name	Ctry	1/8 ELIMINATION	QUARTERFINALS	SEMIFINALS	MEDAL ROUND
1	MUKUKA, Borniface	ZAM	MUKUKA, B.			
2	ZBIR, Mohamad	MAR	PTS 11:4	PAKEEV, A.		
3	SUNEE, Richard	MRI	PAKEEV, A.	PTS 13:4		
4	PAKEEV, Albert	RUS	PTS 8:1		PAKEEV, A.	
5	PHOSUVAN, Parmuansak	THA			TB 13:13	
6	FALAH, Khaled	SYR	FALAH, K.			
7	BEHONEBN, Tebebu	ETH	PTS 11:9	REYES, D.		
8	REYES, Daniel	COL	REYES, D.	PTS 15:13		ROMERO, M.
			PTS 16:2			PTS 12:6
9	MOREL, Eric	USA				
10	ROMERO, Maikro	CUB	ROMERO, M.			
11	TSUJIMOTO, Kazumasa	JPN	PTS 24:12	ROMERO, M.		
12	PAPIAN, Lernik	ARM	PAPIAN, L.	PTS 22:6		
13	ADORNO, Omar	PUR	PTS 10:5		ROMERO, M.	
14	SAMOILENKO, Igor	MDA	SAMOILENKO, I.		PTS 18:3	
15	RECAIDO, Elias	PHI	PTS 20:8	RECAIDO, E.		
16	MAPFUMO, Arson	ZIM	RECAIDO, E.	PTS 12:8		
			PTS 13:2			
17	DJOUMADILOV, Boulat	KAZ				
18	NEYMAN, Vladislav	ISR	DJOUMADILOV, B.			
19	KOVGANKO, Sergei	UKR	PTS 18:7	DJOUMADILOV, B.		
20	ANGELES, Darwin	HON	KOVGANKO, S.	PTS 21:4		
21	MOLARO, Carmine	ITA	PTS 12:6		DJOUMADILOV, B.	
22	HUSSEIN, Hussein	AUS	HUSSEIN, H.		PTS 13:6	
23	STROGOV, Julian	BUL	PTS 11:8	KELLY, D.		
24	KELLY, Damaen	IRL	KELLY, D.	PTS 27:20		DJOUMADILOV, B.
			PTS 12:11			PTS 23:18
25	NARVAEZ, Omar	ARG				
26	GUZMAN, Joan	DOM	NARVAEZ, O.			
27	ASSOUS, Mahdi	ALG	PTS 9:4	ASSOUS, M.		
28	GEREO, Howard	PNG	ASSOUS, M.	PTS 20:4		
29	LUNKA, Zoltan	GER	PTS 11:4		LUNKA, Z.	
30	CASTILLO, Martin	MEX	LUNKA, Z.		PTS 19:6	
31	BOULINGUI, Guy-Elie	GAB	PTS 13:7	LUNKA, Z.		
32	HERMENSEN, Ballo	INA	HERMENSEN, B.	PTS 18:12		
			PTS 6:2			

FINAL CLASSIFICATION

Rnk	Name	Ctry	
1	ROMERO, Maikro	CUB	Gold
2	DJOUMADILOV, Boulat	KAZ	Silver
3	PAKEEV, Albert	RUS	Bronze
3	LUNKA, Zoltan	GER	Bronze
4	REYES, Daniel	COL	
5	RECAIDO, Elias	PHI	
6	KELLY, Damaen	IRL	
7	ASSOUS, Mahdi	ALG	

GOLD MEDAL

ROMERO, M.   CUB
PTS 12:11

SILVER MEDAL

DJOUMADILOV, B.   KAZ

BRONZE MEDAL

PAKEEV, A.   RUS

LUNKA, Z.   GER

Boxing / *Boxe*

Bantamweight, 54 kg (119 lb), Men / *Coq, 54 kg, Messieurs*

1/16 ELIMINATION

No	Name	Ctry
1	KRIZAN, Gabriel	SVK
2	BYE	
3	BOUAITA, Rachid	FRA
4	ABUBAKIROV, Bektas	KAZ
5	HOE, Jong Gil	PRK
6	RAHEEM, Zahir	USA
7	MESA, Arnaldo	CUB
8	LARBI, John H.	SWE
9	VICERA, Virgilio	PHI
10	BAE, Ki-Woong	KOR
11	CHONGO, Oscar	ZAM
12	TSEYEN-OIDOV, Davaatseren	MGL
13	MALAKHBEKOV, Raimkul	RUS
14	COTTO, Jose M.	PUR
15	BOULEHIA, Abdelaziz	ALG
16	TSIRIPIDIS, Agathagelos	GRE
17	NOLASCO, Johnny	DOM
18	NARAINA, Steve	MRI
19	VERBAL, Marcos	COL
20	NAFIL, Hicham	MAR
21	KHADPO, Vichairachanon	THA
22	LAMBERT, Claude	CAN
23	BARRETO, Carlos	VEN
24	HRISTOV, Alexander	BUL
25	ALVAREZ, Samuel	MEX
26	OLTEANU, Crinu	ROM
27	SWAN, James	AUS
28	RIADH, Kalai	TUN
29	AWEDA, Kehinde	NGR
30	KHASANOV, Khurshed	TJK
31	KOVACS, Istvan	HUN
32	KARAOZ, Soner	TUR

1/8 ELIMINATION

- KRIZAN, G.
- BOUAITA, R. — PTS 10:4
- RAHEEM, Z. — PTS 19:4
- MESA, A. — PTS 19:5
- BAE, K.-W. — PTS 8:4
- TSEYEN-OIDOV, D. — PTS 13:7
- MALAKHBEKOV, R. — PTS 16:6
- BOULEHIA, A. — PTS 10:6
- NOLASCO, J. — PTS 18:14
- NAFIL, H. — PTS 16:3
- KHADPO, V. — PTS 12:2
- BARRETO, C. — PTS 9:3
- OLTEANU, C. — RSC 3 2:23
- RIADH, K. — PTS 14:4
- KHASANOV, K. — PTS 20:10
- KOVACS, I. — PTS 15:3

QUARTERFINALS

- BOUAITA, R. — PTS 13:6
- MESA, A. — RSC 1 2:15
- TSEYEN-OIDOV, D. — PTS 11:10
- MALAKHBEKOV, R. — RSC 3 2:52
- NAFIL, H. — PTS 18:6
- KHADPO, V. — PTS 14:6
- OLTEANU, C. — PTS 16:3
- KOVACS, I. — PTS 17:3

SEMIFINALS

- MESA, A. — PTS 15:8
- MALAKHBEKOV, R. — PTS 21:9
- KHADPO, V. — PTS 13:4
- KOVACS, I. — PTS 24:2

MEDAL ROUND

- MESA, A. — TB 14:14
- KOVACS, I. — PTS 12:7

FINAL CLASSIFICATION

Rnk	Name	Ctry	
1	KOVACS, Istvan	HUN	Gold
2	MESA, Arnaldo	CUB	Silver
3	MALAKHBEKOV, Raimkul	RUS	Bronze
3	KHADPO, Vichairachanon	THA	Bronze
4	BOUAITA, Rachid	FRA	
5	TSEYEN-OIDOV, Davaatseren	MGL	
6	NAFIL, Hicham	MAR	
7	OLTEANU, Crinu	ROM	

GOLD MEDAL

KOVACS, I. — HUN — PTS 14:7

SILVER MEDAL

MESA, A. — CUB

BRONZE MEDAL

MALAKHBEKOV, R. — RUS
KHADPO, V. — THA

Featherweight, 57 kg (125 lb), Men / *Plume, 57 kg, Messieurs*

No	Name	Ctry
1	OUZLIAN, Tigran	GRE
2	BYE	
3	PALIANI, Ramaz	RUS
4	SHIN, Soo Young	KOR
5	NDOU, Phillip	RSA
6	PATTON, Casey	CAN
7	KAMSING, Somrot	THA
8	SEDA, Daniel	PUR
9	ATTAH, Daniel	NGR
10	IPERA, Lynch	PNG
11	KELMAN, John	BAR
12	NAGY, Janos	HUN
13	GRAY, Tyson	JAM
14	CHACON, Pablo Julio	ARG
15	LEBON, Josian	MRI
16	YAGLI, Serdar	TUR
17	HUSTE, Falk	GER
18	BURKE, David	GBR
19	IBRAGIMOV, Ulugbek	UZB
20	JAMGAN, Naramchogt	MGL
21	PEDEN, Robert	AUS
22	ACHIK, Mohamed	MAR
23	TODOROV, Serafim	BUL
24	SHESTAKOV, Evgenii	UKR
25	de BRITO, Rogelio	BRA
26	BAHARI, Nemo	INA
27	ARAGON, Lorenzo	CUB
28	MADJHOUND, Noureddine	ALG
29	TILEGANOV, Bakhtiyar	KAZ
30	MAYWEATHER, Floyd	USA
31	KONAMEGUI, Elvis	CMR
32	GEVORGYAN, Artur	ARM

1/8 ELIMINATION

- OUZLIAN, T.
- PALIANI, R. — PTS 10:7
- NDOU, P. — RSC 2 2:55
- KAMSING, S. — PTS 13:2
- ATTAH, D. — PTS 14:2
- NAGY, J. — RSCH 3 1:36
- CHACON, P. J. — PTS 6:5
- LEBON, J. — PTS 9:8
- HUSTE, F. — PTS 13:9
- IBRAGIMOV, U. — RSCI 2 0:44
- PEDEN, R. — PTS 15:7
- TODOROV, S. — PTS 11:4
- de BRITO, R. — PTS 12:3
- ARAGON, L. — PTS 9:6
- MAYWEATHER, F. — RSCI 2 0:57
- GEVORGYAN, A. — PTS 10:3

QUARTERFINALS

- PALIANI, R. — PTS 27:2
- KAMSING, S. — PTS 12:7
- NAGY, J. — PTS 14:12
- CHACON, P. J. — PTS 14:7
- HUSTE, F. — PTS 8:4
- TODOROV, S. — PTS 20:8
- ARAGON, L. — PTS 16:6
- MAYWEATHER, F. — PTS 16:3

SEMIFINALS

- KAMSING, S. — PTS 13:4
- CHACON, P. J. — PTS 18:7
- TODOROV, S. — PTS 14:6
- MAYWEATHER, F. — PTS 12:11

MEDAL ROUND

- KAMSING, S. — PTS 20:8
- TODOROV, S. — PTS 10:9

FINAL CLASSIFICATION

Rnk	Name	Ctry	
1	KAMSING, Somrot	THA	Gold
2	TODOROV, Serafim	BUL	Silver
3	CHACON, Pablo Julio	ARG	Bronze
3	MAYWEATHER, Floyd	USA	Bronze
4	PALIANI, Ramaz	RUS	
5	NAGY, Janos	HUN	
6	HUSTE, Falk	GER	
7	ARAGON, Lorenzo	CUB	

GOLD MEDAL

KAMSING, S. — THA — PTS 8:5

SILVER MEDAL

TODOROV, S. — BUL

BRONZE MEDAL

CHACON, P. J. — ARG
MAYWEATHER, F. — USA

Boxing / *Boxe*

Lightweight, 60 kg (132 lb), Men / *Léger, 60 kg, Messieurs*

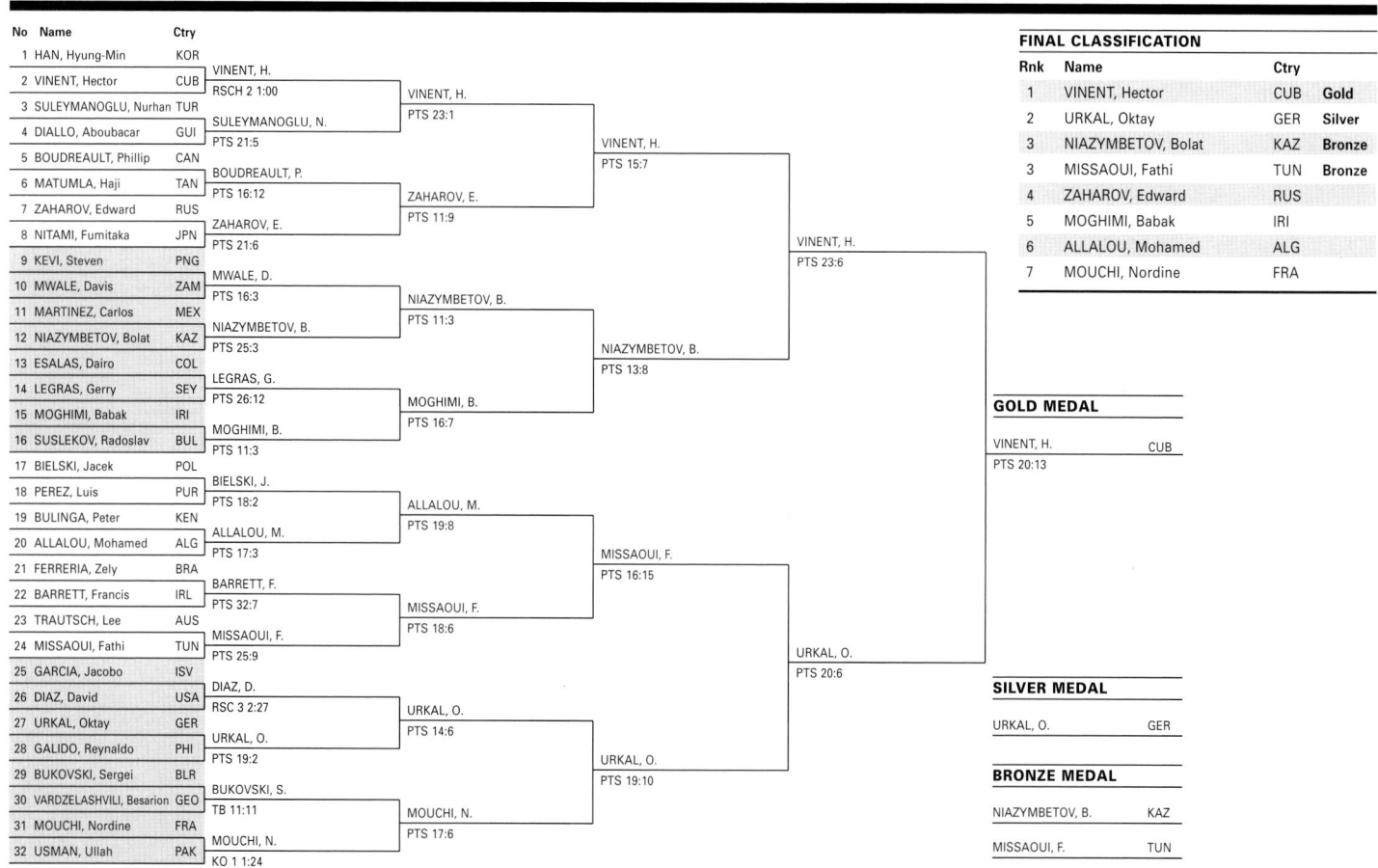

1/16 ELIMINATION	1/8 ELIMINATION	QUARTERFINALS	SEMIFINALS	MEDAL ROUND

No	Name	Ctry
1	GHAZARYAN, Mikhak	ARM
2	BYE	
3	MARTINEZ, Francisco	MEX
4	STRANGE, Michael	CAN
5	ZIMBA, Dennis	ZAM
6	OSTROCHAPKINE, Serguei	BLR
7	TAYKOU, Oktavian	MDA
8	TONTCHEV, Tontcho	BUL
9	KABORE, Irissa	BUR
10	KONECNY, Jaroslav	CZE
11	BUHLALU, Irvin	RSA
12	PHONGSIT, Veongviact	THA
13	UITUMEN, Tumentsetseg	MGL
14	MOJICA, Miguel	DOM
15	ABDULLAEV, Mahamatkodir	UZB
16	CAUTHEN, Terrance	USA
17	MAINA, George	KEN
18	SHIN, Eun-Chui	KOR
19	AGENTHO, Franco	UGA
20	NIEVAS, Fabrizio	ARG
21	SOLTANI, Hocine	ALG
22	IASEVER, Vahdettin	TUR
23	KUNSI, Henry	PNG
24	NUNEZ, Agnaldo	BRA
25	GIANTOMASSI, Cristian	ITA
26	KOPENKIN, Sergey	KGZ
27	MBOUMBA, Julio	GAB
28	DOROFTEI, Leonard	ROM
29	BRIN, Romeo	PHI
30	GONZALEZ VALLADARES, J.	CUB
31	GOGOLADZE, Koba	GEO
32	CHOL, Ri	PRK

FINAL CLASSIFICATION

Rnk	Name	Ctry	
1	SOLTANI, Hocine	ALG	Gold
2	TONTCHEV, Tontcho	BUL	Silver
3	CAUTHEN, Terrance	USA	Bronze
3	DOROFTEI, Leonard	ROM	Bronze
4	STRANGE, Michael	CAN	
5	PHONGSIT, Veongviact	THA	
6	SHIN, Eun-Chui	KOR	
7	GOGOLADZE, Koba	GEO	

GOLD MEDAL

SOLTANI, H. — ALG
TB 3:3

SILVER MEDAL

TONTCHEV, T. — BUL

BRONZE MEDAL

CAUTHEN, T. — USA

DOROFTEI, L. — ROM

Light Welterweight, 63.5 kg (139 lb), Men / *Mi-welter, 63,5 kg, Messieurs*

No	Name	Ctry
1	HAN, Hyung-Min	KOR
2	VINENT, Hector	CUB
3	SULEYMANOGLU, Nurhan	TUR
4	DIALLO, Aboubacar	GUI
5	BOUDREAULT, Phillip	CAN
6	MATUMLA, Haji	TAN
7	ZAHAROV, Edward	RUS
8	NITAMI, Fumitaka	JPN
9	KEVI, Steven	PNG
10	MWALE, Davis	ZAM
11	MARTINEZ, Carlos	MEX
12	NIAZYMBETOV, Bolat	KAZ
13	ESALAS, Dairo	COL
14	LEGRAS, Gerry	SEY
15	MOGHIMI, Babak	IRI
16	SUSLEKOV, Radoslav	BUL
17	BIELSKI, Jacek	POL
18	PEREZ, Luis	PUR
19	BULINGA, Peter	KEN
20	ALLALOU, Mohamed	ALG
21	FERRERIA, Zely	BRA
22	BARRETT, Francis	IRL
23	TRAUTSCH, Lee	AUS
24	MISSAOUI, Fathi	TUN
25	GARCIA, Jacobo	ISV
26	DIAZ, David	USA
27	URKAL, Oktay	GER
28	GALIDO, Reynaldo	PHI
29	BUKOVSKI, Sergei	BLR
30	VARDZELASHVILI, Besarion	GEO
31	MOUCHI, Nordine	FRA
32	USMAN, Ullah	PAK

FINAL CLASSIFICATION

Rnk	Name	Ctry	
1	VINENT, Hector	CUB	Gold
2	URKAL, Oktay	GER	Silver
3	NIAZYMBETOV, Bolat	KAZ	Bronze
3	MISSAOUI, Fathi	TUN	Bronze
4	ZAHAROV, Edward	RUS	
5	MOGHIMI, Babak	IRI	
6	ALLALOU, Mohamed	ALG	
7	MOUCHI, Nordine	FRA	

GOLD MEDAL

VINENT, H. — CUB
PTS 20:13

SILVER MEDAL

URKAL, O. — GER

BRONZE MEDAL

NIAZYMBETOV, B. — KAZ

MISSAOUI, F. — TUN

Boxing / *Boxe*

Welterweight, 67 kg (147 lb), Men / *Welter, 67 kg, Messieurs*

1/16 ELIMINATION

No	Name	Ctry
1	MARTINEZ, Rogelio	DOM
2	AL, Hasan	DEN
3	PARKPOOM, Jangphonak	THA
4	DZINZIRUK, Sergiy	UKR
5	MESKHADZE, Tengiz	GEO
6	VARGAS, Fernando	USA
7	BAYRAM, Hussein	FRA
8	SIMION, Marian	ROM
9	SINOIA, Lucas	MOZ
10	MEZGA, Vadim	BLR
11	NAGY, Jazcef	HUN
12	HERNANDEZ, Juan	CUB
13	SMANOV, Nurzhan	KAZ
14	HOSKING, Lynden	AUS
15	RASHEED, Abdul	PAK
16	FLORES, Jesus	MEX
17	SUME, Cahit	TUR
18	SAITOV, Oleg	RUS
19	SAPUTO, Guillermo	ARG
20	BAE, Ho-Jo	KOR
21	MZONGE, Hassan	TAN
22	KARPACIAUSKAS, Vitalijus	LTU
23	CHATER, Kamel	TUN
24	KYVELOS, Hercules	CAN
25	ATAYEV, Nariman	UZB
26	EVANS, Ashira	KEN
27	HEAPS, Shane	TGA
28	KASSENOV, Nourbek	KGZ
29	HERNANDEZ, Luis	ECU
30	LAHSEN, Kabil	MAR
31	SANTOS, Daniel	PUR
32	ATANGANA MBOA, Ernest	CMR

1/8 ELIMINATION

AL, H. — RSCI 3 2:35
DZINZIRUK, S. — PTS 20:10
VARGAS, F. — PTS 10:4
SIMION, M. — PTS 13:6
MEZGA, V. — PTS 11:6
HERNANDEZ, J. — RSC 2 1:48
SMANOV, N. — RSCI 2 1:42
RASHEED, A. — PTS 12:7
SAITOV, O. — PTS 11:1
BAE, H.-J. — PTS 11:7
KARPACIAUSKAS, V. — PTS 9:1
CHATER, K. — TB 4:4
ATAYEV, N. — PTS 15:10
KASSENOV, N. — PTS 11:2
LAHSEN, K. — PTS 18:9
SANTOS, D. — RSC 1 2:54

QUARTERFINALS

AL, H. — PTS 10:4
SIMION, M. — PTS 8:7
HERNANDEZ, J. — PTS 12:2
SMANOV, N. — PTS 13:9
SAITOV, O. — PTS 9:5
CHATER, K. — RSC 1 1:16
ATAYEV, N. — PTS 11:7
SANTOS, D. — PTS 16:4

SEMIFINALS

SIMION, M. — PTS 16:8
HERNANDEZ, J. — PTS 16:8
SAITOV, O. — PTS 9:3
SANTOS, D. — PTS 28:15

MEDAL ROUND

HERNANDEZ, J. — PTS 20:7
SAITOV, O. — PTS 13:11

FINAL CLASSIFICATION

Rnk	Name	Ctry	
1	SAITOV, Oleg	RUS	Gold
2	HERNANDEZ, Juan	CUB	Silver
3	SIMION, Marian	ROM	Bronze
3	SANTOS, Daniel	PUR	Bronze
4	AL, Hasan	DEN	
5	SMANOV, Nurzhan	KAZ	
6	CHATER, Kamel	TUN	
7	ATAYEV, Nariman	UZB	

GOLD MEDAL

SAITOV, O. — RUS
PTS 14:9

SILVER MEDAL

HERNANDEZ, J. — CUB

BRONZE MEDAL

SIMION, M. — ROM
SANTOS, D. — PUR

Light Middleweight, 71 kg (156 lb), Men / *Mi-moyen, 71 kg, Messieurs*

No	Name	Ctry
1	ARYEE, Ashiakwei	GHA
2	BYE	
3	SILVA, Jorge	BRA
4	CADEAU, Rival	SEY
5	GOMEZ, Oscar	ARG
6	TULAGANOV, Karim	UZB
7	SINNETT, Kirt	TRI
8	WOLDE, Yared	ETH
9	REID, David	USA
10	LEE, Wan-Kyun	KOR
11	POLAKOVIC, Pavol	CZE
12	KUNENE, Victor	RSA
13	MARMOURI, Mohamed Salah	TUN
14	MASOE, Maselino	ASA
15	BLACK, Sean	JAM
16	JOHNSON, Jorn	NOR
17	MIZSEI, Gyorgy	HUN
18	ROWLES, Richard	AUS
19	BEYER, Markus	GER
20	VASTAG, Francisc	ROM
21	MANGUNSONG, Hendrik	INA
22	KWANGWALD, Alexander	ZIM
23	FARRELL, Nick	CAN
24	IBRAIMOV, Ermakhan	KAZ
25	EROMOSELE, Albert	NGR
26	GORODNITCHEV, Serguei	UKR
27	DUVERGEL, Alfredo	CUB
28	GILEWSKI, Jozef	POL
29	QUINONES, Jose	PUR
30	PERUGINO, Antonio	ITA
31	PETTERSSON, Roger	SWE
32	KOURBANOV, Shokhrat	TKM

1/8 ELIMINATION

ARYEE, A.
CADEAU, R. — PTS 22:7
TULAGANOV, K. — RSC 3 2:50
WOLDE, Y. — PTS 11:10
REID, D. — PTS 20:4
POLAKOVIC, P. — PTS 8:1
MARMOURI, M. S. — PTS 11:8
JOHNSON, J. — PTS 13:7
MIZSEI, G. — PTS 10:2
BEYER, M. — PTS 17:12
MANGUNSONG, H. — PTS 12:1
IBRAIMOV, E. — PTS 15:4
GORODNITCHEV, S. — PTS 18:4
DUVERGEL, A. — PTS 10:2
PERUGINO, A. — PTS 10:8
PETTERSSON, R. — PTS 7:2

QUARTERFINALS

CADEAU, R. — PTS 18:6
TULAGANOV, K. — PTS 13:9
REID, D. — PTS 12:5
MARMOURI, M. S. — PTS 17:4
BEYER, M. — PTS 14:6
IBRAIMOV, E. — RSCH 1 2:14
DUVERGEL, A. — PTS 15:2
PERUGINO, A. — PTS 18:4

SEMIFINALS

TULAGANOV, K. — RSCH 1 1:24
REID, D. — PTS 13:8
IBRAIMOV, E. — PTS 19:9
DUVERGEL, A. — PTS 15:8

MEDAL ROUND

REID, D. — PTS 12:4
DUVERGEL, A. — PTS 28:19

FINAL CLASSIFICATION

Rnk	Name	Ctry	
1	REID, David	USA	Gold
2	DUVERGEL, Alfredo	CUB	Silver
3	TULAGANOV, Karim	UZB	Bronze
3	IBRAIMOV, Ermakhan	KAZ	Bronze
4	CADEAU, Rival	SEY	
5	MARMOURI, Mohamed Salah	TUN	
6	BEYER, Markus	GER	
7	PERUGINO, Antonio	ITA	

GOLD MEDAL

REID, D. — USA
KO 3 0:36

SILVER MEDAL

DUVERGEL, A. — CUB

BRONZE MEDAL

TULAGANOV, K. — UZB
IBRAIMOV, E. — KAZ

Boxing / *Boxe*   **157**

Boxing / *Boxe*

Middleweight, 75 kg (165 lb), Men / *Moyen, 75 kg, Messieurs*

1/16 ELIMINATION

No	Name	Ctry
1	BEYLEROGLU, Malik	TUR
2	BYE	
3	ERDEL, Zsolt	HUN
4	LOPEZ, Juan Pablo	MEX
5	MOSBAHI, Mohamed	MAR
6	BOROWSKI, Tomasz	POL
7	CHEN, Tao	CHN
8	MOTO, Hirokuni	JPN
9	ARANEDA, Ricardo	CHI
10	KAKAURIDZE, Akaki	GEO
11	THOMAS, Marcus	BAR
12	BAHARI, Mohamed	ALG
13	THOMPSON, Randall	CAN
14	MAGEE, Brian	IRL
15	TETSIA, Bertrand	CMR
16	MOON, Lim-Chul	KOR
17	GASIO, Bob	SAM
18	RODRIGUEZ, Ricardo	BRA
19	MOLLAL, Sefid Dashti K.	IRI
20	WELLS, Rhoshii	USA
21	JOHANSEN, Brian	DEN
22	YARBEKOV, Dilshood	UZB
23	PLACHETKA, Lukovik	CZE
24	MATHUNJAWA, Dan	SWZ
25	KBARY, Salim	EGY
26	HERNANDEZ, Ariel	CUB
27	OTTKE, Sven	GER
28	MENDY, Jean-Paul	FRA
29	LEBZIAK, Alexander	RUS
30	DONALDSON, Rowan	JAM
31	SHIVUTE, Sackey	NAM
32	CRAWFORD, Justann	AUS

1/8 ELIMINATION

BEYLEROGLU, M.

ERDEL, Z.
RSC 3 1:38

BOROWSKI, T.
PTS 9:6

MOTO, H.
PTS 15:10

KAKAURIDZE, A.
PTS 10:3

BAHARI, M.
RSCH 2 2:20

MAGEE, B.
PTS 13:5

TETSIA, B.
PTS 12:2

RODRIGUEZ, R.
PTS 11:4

WELLS, R.
PTS 24:7

YARBEKOV, D.
RSCI 3 2:47

PLACHETKA, L.
PTS 20:4

HERNANDEZ, A.
PTS 11:2

OTTKE, S.
PTS 11:4

LEBZIAK, A.
PTS 20:4

CRAWFORD, J.
PTS 12:3

QUARTERFINALS

BEYLEROGLU, M.
PTS 9:8

BOROWSKI, T.
PTS 11:6

BAHARI, M.
PTS 8:5

MAGEE, B.
PTS 11:6

WELLS, R.
PTS 16:2

YARBEKOV, D.
TB 4:4

HERNANDEZ, A.
PTS 5:0

LEBZIAK, A.
RSCH 3 0:34

SEMIFINALS

BEYLEROGLU, M.
PTS 16:12

BAHARI, M.
PTS 15:9

WELLS, R.
TB 8:8

HERNANDEZ, A.
PTS 15:8

MEDAL ROUND

BEYLEROGLU, M.
TB 11:11

HERNANDEZ, A.
PTS 17:8

FINAL CLASSIFICATION

Rnk	Name	Ctry	
1	HERNANDEZ, Ariel	CUB	Gold
2	BEYLEROGLU, Malik	TUR	Silver
3	BAHARI, Mohamed	ALG	Bronze
3	WELLS, Rhoshii	USA	Bronze
4	BOROWSKI, Tomasz	POL	
5	MAGEE, Brian	IRL	
6	YARBEKOV, Dilshood	UZB	
7	LEBZIAK, Alexander	RUS	

GOLD MEDAL

HERNANDEZ, A.   CUB
PTS 11:3

SILVER MEDAL

BEYLEROGLU, M.   TUR

BRONZE MEDAL

BAHARI, M.   ALG

WELLS, R.   USA

Light Heavyweight, 81 kg (178 lb), Men / *Mi-lourd, 81 kg, Messieurs*

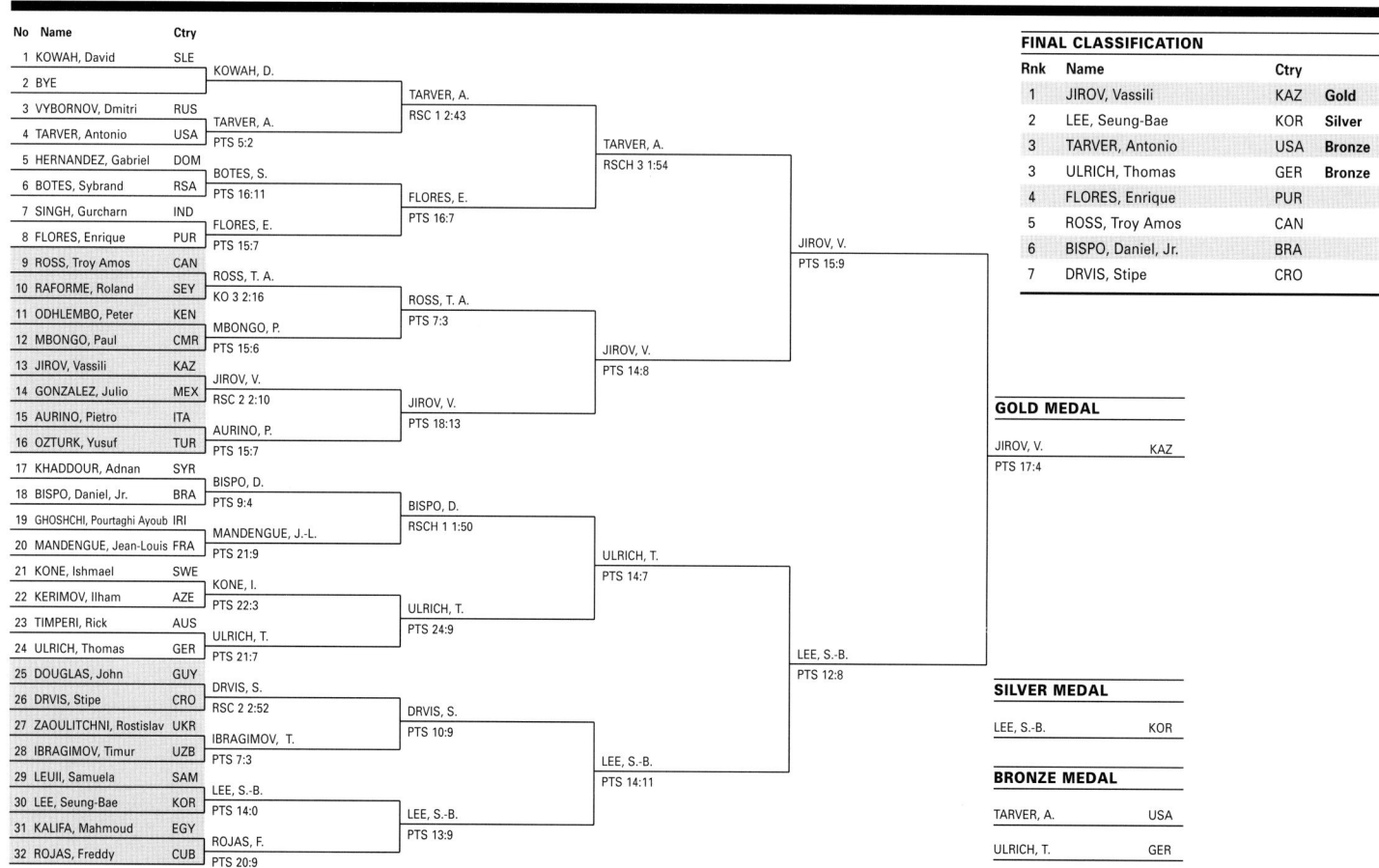

No	Name	Ctry
1	KOWAH, David	SLE
2	BYE	
3	VYBORNOV, Dmitri	RUS
4	TARVER, Antonio	USA
5	HERNANDEZ, Gabriel	DOM
6	BOTES, Sybrand	RSA
7	SINGH, Gurcharn	IND
8	FLORES, Enrique	PUR
9	ROSS, Troy Amos	CAN
10	RAFORME, Roland	SEY
11	ODHLEMBO, Peter	KEN
12	MBONGO, Paul	CMR
13	JIROV, Vassili	KAZ
14	GONZALEZ, Julio	MEX
15	AURINO, Pietro	ITA
16	OZTURK, Yusuf	TUR
17	KHADDOUR, Adnan	SYR
18	BISPO, Daniel, Jr.	BRA
19	GHOSHCHI, Pourtaghi Ayoub	IRI
20	MANDENGUE, Jean-Louis	FRA
21	KONE, Ishmael	SWE
22	KERIMOV, Ilham	AZE
23	TIMPERI, Rick	AUS
24	ULRICH, Thomas	GER
25	DOUGLAS, John	GUY
26	DRVIS, Stipe	CRO
27	ZAOULITCHNI, Rostislav	UKR
28	IBRAGIMOV, Timur	UZB
29	LEUII, Samuela	SAM
30	LEE, Seung-Bae	KOR
31	KALIFA, Mahmoud	EGY
32	ROJAS, Freddy	CUB

KOWAH, D.

TARVER, A.
PTS 5:2

BOTES, S.
PTS 16:11

FLORES, E.
PTS 15:7

ROSS, T. A.
KO 3 2:16

MBONGO, P.
PTS 15:6

JIROV, V.
RSC 2 2:10

AURINO, P.
PTS 15:7

BISPO, D.
PTS 9:4

MANDENGUE, J.-L.
PTS 21:9

KONE, I.
PTS 22:3

ULRICH, T.
PTS 21:7

DRVIS, S.
RSC 2 2:52

IBRAGIMOV, T.
PTS 7:3

LEE, S.-B.
PTS 14:0

ROJAS, F.
PTS 20:9

TARVER, A.
RSC 1 2:43

FLORES, E.
PTS 16:7

ROSS, T. A.
PTS 7:3

JIROV, V.
PTS 18:13

BISPO, D.
RSCH 1 1:50

ULRICH, T.
PTS 24:9

DRVIS, S.
PTS 10:9

LEE, S.-B.
PTS 13:9

TARVER, A.
RSCH 3 1:54

JIROV, V.
PTS 14:8

ULRICH, T.
PTS 14:7

LEE, S.-B.
PTS 14:11

JIROV, V.
PTS 15:9

LEE, S.-B.
PTS 12:8

FINAL CLASSIFICATION

Rnk	Name	Ctry	
1	JIROV, Vassili	KAZ	Gold
2	LEE, Seung-Bae	KOR	Silver
3	TARVER, Antonio	USA	Bronze
3	ULRICH, Thomas	GER	Bronze
4	FLORES, Enrique	PUR	
5	ROSS, Troy Amos	CAN	
6	BISPO, Daniel, Jr.	BRA	
7	DRVIS, Stipe	CRO	

GOLD MEDAL

JIROV, V.   KAZ
PTS 17:4

SILVER MEDAL

LEE, S.-B.   KOR

BRONZE MEDAL

TARVER, A.   USA

ULRICH, T.   GER

Boxing / *Boxe*

Heavyweight, 91 kg (201 lb), Men / *Lourd, 91 kg, Messieurs*

1/16 ELIMINATION	1/8 ELIMINATION	QUARTERFINALS	SEMIFINALS	MEDAL ROUND

No	Name	Ctry
1	JONES, Nate	USA
2	BYE	
3	OKESOLA, Fola	GBR
4	BYE	
5	KIZZA, Charles	UGA
6	BYE	
7	JIANG, Tao	CHN
8	BYE	
9	MENDY, Christophe	FRA
10	BYE	
11	BALI, Ovidiu	ROM
12	BYE	
13	DEFIAGBON, David	CAN
14	BYE	
15	OMAR, Ahmed	KEN
16	BYE	
17	KSHININ, Igor	RUS
18	AMROU, Mustapha	EGY
19	KRASNIQI, Luan	GER
20	CHAGAYEV, Ruslan	UZB
21	O'GRADY, Cathal	IRL
22	DA SILVA, Garth	NZL
23	DYCHKOV, Serguei	BLR
24	KUKLINS, Romans	LAT
25	BARTNIK, Woiciech	POL
26	SINGH, Lakha	IND
27	KANDELAKI, Giorgi	GEO
28	GARCIA, Thompson	ECU
29	KO, Young-Sam	KOR
30	TURKSON, Kwamena	SWE
31	KUMYAVKA, Andrei	KGZ
32	SAVON, Felix	CUB

1/8 ELIMINATION

- JONES, N.
- OKESOLA, F.
- KIZZA, C.
- JIANG, T.
- MENDY, C.
- BALI, O.
- DEFIAGBON, D.
- OMAR, A.
- KSHININ, I. — PTS 17:4
- KRASNIQI, L. — PTS 12:4
- DA SILVA, G. — RSC 1 1:40
- DYCHKOV, S. — PTS 16:6
- BARTNIK, W. — PTS 14:2
- KANDELAKI, G. — RET 3 0:00
- TURKSON, K. — PTS 12:8
- SAVON, F. — PTS 9:3

QUARTERFINALS

- JONES, N. — RSCI 3 2:53
- JIANG, T. — PTS 10:7
- MENDY, C. — RSCH 2 0:44
- DEFIAGBON, D. — PTS 15:4
- KRASNIQI, L. — PTS 10:2
- DYCHKOV, S. — PTS 12:8
- KANDELAKI, G. — PTS 6:1
- SAVON, F. — KO 1 2:29

SEMIFINALS

- JONES, N. — PTS 21:4
- DEFIAGBON, D. — DQ 3 1:01
- KRASNIQI, L. — PTS 10:5
- SAVON, F. — PTS 20:4

MEDAL ROUND

- DEFIAGBON, D. — PTS 16:10
- SAVON, F. — WO 1 0:00

FINAL CLASSIFICATION

Rnk	Name	Ctry	
1	SAVON, Felix	CUB	Gold
2	DEFIAGBON, David	CAN	Silver
3	JONES, Nate	USA	Bronze
3	KRASNIQI, Luan	GER	Bronze
4	JIANG, Tao	CHN	
5	MENDY, Christophe	FRA	
6	DYCHKOV, Serguei	BLR	
7	KANDELAKI, Giorgi	GEO	

GOLD MEDAL

SAVON, F. — CUB — PTS 20:2

SILVER MEDAL

DEFIAGBON, D. — CAN

BRONZE MEDAL

JONES, N. — USA

KRASNIQI, L. — GER

Super Heavyweight, +91 kg (+201 lb), Men / *Super-lourd, +91 kg, Messieurs*

No	Name	Ctry
1	BERGERON, Jean-Francois	CAN
2	BYE	
3	LEVIN, Attila	SWE
4	BYE	
5	KLYCHKO, Volodymyr	UKR
6	BYE	
7	CLAY-BEY, Lawrence	USA
8	BYE	
9	LEZIN, Alexei	RUS
10	BYE	
11	JOURCHENKO, Mikhail	KAZ
12	BYE	
13	AHMED, Said Ahmed	EGY
14	BYE	
15	MONSE, Rene	GER
16	BYE	
17	WOLFGRAM, Paea	TGA
18	BYE	
19	DAHOVITCH, Serguei	BLR
20	BYE	
21	RUBALCABA, Alexis	CUB
22	BYE	
23	VIDOZ, Paolo	ITA
24	BYE	
25	KHAN, Sifarish	PAK
26	BYE	
27	SAMADI, Mohamed Reza	IRI
28	DOKIWARI, Duncan	NGR
29	BLOCUS, Josue	FRA
30	GUEVARA, Jesus	VEN
31	MAMEDOV, Adaliat	AZE
32	HORACEK, Petr	CZE

1/8 ELIMINATION

- BERGERON, J.-F.
- LEVIN, A.
- KLYCHKO, V.
- CLAY-BEY, L.
- LEZIN, A.
- JOURCHENKO, M.
- AHMED, S. A.
- MONSE, R.
- WOLFGRAM, P.
- DAHOVITCH, S.
- RUBALCABA, A.
- VIDOZ, P.
- KHAN, S.
- DOKIWARI, D. — RSCI 2 0:39
- BLOCUS, J. — RSC 2 2:13
- MAMEDOV, A. — RSCI 2 1:50

QUARTERFINALS

- LEVIN, A. — RSCH 1 0:59
- KLYCHKO, V. — PTS 10:8
- LEZIN, A. — RSCI 1 2:42
- MONSE, R. — PTS 12:9
- WOLFGRAM, P. — PTS 10:9
- RUBALCABA, A. — RSCH 1 2:39
- DOKIWARI, D. — RSCH 2 1:25
- MAMEDOV, A. — RSC 1 2:11

SEMIFINALS

- KLYCHKO, V. — RSC 1 1:43
- LEZIN, A. — PTS 9:5
- WOLFGRAM, P. — PTS 17:12
- DOKIWARI, D. — RSCH 3 0:23

MEDAL ROUND

- KLYCHKO, V. — PTS 4:1
- WOLFGRAM, P. — PTS 7:6

FINAL CLASSIFICATION

Rnk	Name	Ctry	
1	KLYCHKO, Volodymyr	UKR	Gold
2	WOLFGRAM, Paea	TGA	Silver
3	LEZIN, Alexei	RUS	Bronze
3	DOKIWARI, Duncan	NGR	Bronze
4	LEVIN, Attila	SWE	
5	MONSE, Rene	GER	
6	RUBALCABA, Alexis	CUB	
7	MAMEDOV, Adaliat	AZE	

GOLD MEDAL

KLYCHKO, V. — UKR — PTS 7:3

SILVER MEDAL

WOLFGRAM, P. — TGA

BRONZE MEDAL

LEZIN, A. — RUS

DOKIWARI, D. — NGR

ROBERT L RANDOLPH JR. • LAURA A
RANDQUIST • KAREN Y RANDS • MELINDA
RANERE-LOTERO • CATHERINE P RANEY •
PENELOPE S RANEY • ROMAYNE N RANFORD •
JUDITH A RANGEL • MARTHA P RANGEL •
JOSHUA P RANGSIKITPHO • DAVID R RANKIN •
JENNIFER E RANKIN • JERRY L RANKIN • KRISTI
RANKIN • WILLIAM H RANKIN • ROGER A
RANKIN-WATSON • SUE RANKIN-WHITE •
WAYNE RANKINS • LEE A RANSAW • BLAIR B
RANSOM • DOROTHY R RANSOM • DOUGLAS W
RANSOM • JEFF RANSOM • ROBERT L RANSOM •
VERONICA L RANSOM • DANIEL E RANTA • BABU
RAO • SHEILA Y RAO • SUDARSHAN RAO • GARY
D RAPER • HAL S RAPER • JESSICA G RAPER •
STEPHEN C RAPER EMT • CORY P RAPHAELSON
• JENNIFER M RAPIER • LAURA RAPINCHUK •
MANLANYO RAPLEY • LIESE S RAPOZO • WAL-
LACE G RAPOZO • CARL S RAPP • CURT W RAPP •
WILLETT M RAPP • GUY E RAPPAPORT • SUSAN
RAPPAPORT • STEPHEN A RAPPENECKER JR •
MARYANN F RAPPOSELLI • RUBEN JESUS RAR-
RICK • PATRICK C RARY • JEFFREY S RASBURY •
CAROLYN B RASCHE • CELINE C RASCHE-SCHU-
MANN • CLARE G RASE • STEPHEN H RASE •
AMIR R RASHID-FAROKHI • ROBERT RASILE •
SUZANNE RASK • GRADY G RASKIN • JED RASKIN
• RICK RASMUSSEN • SUSAN M RASMUSSEN •
VERENA B RASMUSSEN • ADAM B RASNER •
JOANNE RASSIE • ALVA G RAST • KOYS RASTISLAV
• LAROSE L. RASTON • ALEX H RATCLIFF • GLEN
RATCLIFF • REGINALD A RATCLIFF • CAL RAT-
CLIFF JR • CHRIS T RATCLIFFE • KAREN A RAT-
CLIFFE • LINDA L RATCLIFFE • PEGGY W RAT-
CLIFFE • SHARI L RATES • DARLENE W RATH •
JOHN A RATH • STEVEN E RATHBONE • JOANN
RATHBUN • JODY L RATHBUN • WILLIAM M
RATHBURN • KARL E RATHVON • HEATHER L
RATLIFF • MASILU J RATOPOLA • SUZANNE L
RATTAZZI • STEPHEN E RATTERMAN • RYBURN C
RATTERREE • DENNIS I RATTHAUS • SUZANNE D
RATTHAUS • RENA E RATTRAY • RONDA A RAT-
TRAY • JOE C RATTZ • ALEXANDER RAU • DEAN D
RAU • MARY C RAU • MARY E RAU • JAAK M RAUD-
SEPP • FRANK P RAULS • JAMIE A RAUSCH •
JANET S RAUSCHER • AVANI I RAVAL • ROBERTA
S RAVAN • BLANCHE A RAVENEL • CATRINA L
RAVENEL • ALICE W RAVER • JAMES L RAVER •
CHRISTOPHER J RAWDING • FREDERICK W
RAWE • BARBARA J RAWLINGS • LAURE OH
RAWLINGS • KARLENE RAWLINS • HOLLY M
RAWLINSON • KIM RAWLINSON • WILLIAM E
RAWLINSON • DELTA D RAWLS • DONNEL R
RAWLS • LISA KENYADA RAWLS • RENARD A
RAWLS • SUSAN E RAWLS • SCOTT S RAWSON •
AMY N RAY • ANTHONY D RAY • AUSTIN T RAY •
BERNICE RAY • BETTYE J RAY • BRENDA L RAY •
BRIAN O RAY • CARLA R RAY • CHARLES B RAY •
CHRISTOPHER J RAY • DAVID A RAY • DENISE J
RAY • EILEEN F RAY • ELOISE RAY • FAY C RAY •
FRED W RAY • GERALDINE A RAY • GLORIA
LAWANNA RAY • JACK B RAY • JASON RAY • JOHN
M RAY • JOYCE A RAY • KHRISTOPHER E RAY •
KRISHNA RAY • LARRY A RAY • LINDA M RAY •
MICHAEL JAMES RAY • SUSAN D RAY • VERRILL G
RAY • VICKI A RAY • WILFORD R RAY • YVETTE H
RAY • REBEKAH R RAY ATC • BARRY L RAY EMT •
CLAUDE E RAY III • LOUIS RAY JR • WILLIAM S
RAY JR • VIKRAM RAYA • ROBERT L RAYBON •
SHARON B RAYBON • JUDY RAYBORN • SUSAN
AMANDA TRUE RAYBORN • EUGENE G RAYBUCK
• ERIC T RAYBURN • CHARLES H RAYE MD • TAM-
MY L RAYEVICH • VICTORIA D RAYLE • STEPHEN
J RAYMOND • BRENT R RAYMOND • CARLOS A
RAYMOND • CLAUDE M RAYMOND • JEFFREY A
RAYMOND • JEFFREY A RAYMOND • JOHN M RAY-
MOND • JUSTIN M RAYMOND • KATHRYN E RAY-
MOND • PHILIP C RAYMOND • ELIZABETH S
RAYNOR • JAMES E RAYNOR JR PHD • GOGINENI
N RAYUDU • EHSAN RAZAVI • HOSEIN ALI RAZA-
VI • ANDREW RAZMADZE • HADI RAZZAQ •
JAMES C REA • RICHARD A REA • BARBARA R
READ • DENNIS S READ • PATRICIA READ •
PHILLIP A READ • SALLIE PAIGE READER •
MICHAEL J READY • BERNARD REAGAN • CARL
W REAGAN • DARLENE L REAGAN • MARY C REA-
GAN • PEGGY L REAGAN • SAM W REAGAN •
SYLVIA J REAGAN • HARVEY F REAGIN • HARVEY
F REAGIN • D ENDSLEY REAL • ELIZABETH A
REALE • MARK B REALE • MILDRED REAMS •
CAROL R REAP • JAMES K REAP • ELIZABETH F
REARDON • J BRIAN REARDON • LISA D REAR-
DON • MICHELE E REARDON • THOMAS REARDON
• EDWARD L REASE • DAVID C REASER • NORMA S
REASER • BETTY M REAVES • BILLIE J REAVES •
CATHY E REAVES • DEBORAH B REAVES • GEORGE
C REAVES • HAROLD K REAVES • MABEL A REAVES
• MATTHEW D REAVES • OSADEL REAVES •
CHRISTOPHER K REAVIS • CHRISTINE H REAY MT
• RICHARD D REBIDUE • RAYMOND J REBOULET •
NANCY E RECCHIA • CHRISTINA J RECCORD •
LYNN R RECHTMAN • LISA S RECHTZIGEL • JEN-
NIFER L RECK • RUSSELL K RECKA • TAMMY T
RECKA • PAUL A RECKAMP • MICHAEL E RECKLEY
• MARY D RECKNAGEL • JOSEPH F RECKNAGEL
ATC • CAROL A RECTOR • DEBBIE RED • DIANNE
L RED • ROBIN L REDD • MICHAEL D REDD ATC •
SUSAN L REDDAWAY • GENE T REDDEN •
THOMAS J REDDEN • DEWEY REDDICK • JOANNA
J REDDICK • OLSON D REDDICK • CHATEUBRIAND
REDDING • DARLYN M REDDING • JEFFREY J RED-
DING • PETER M REDDING • GREGORY W REDDISH
• ASHOK S REDDY • KAVITHA P REDDY • VASUDHA
REDDY • RITA V REDEAU • TAMARA REDFERN •
MERLE C REDFIELD • RUTHANNE REDFIELD •
DANA Y REDFORD • TRUDI REDIVINE • CINDY L
REDKO • JOAN L REDLEAF • DARA REDLER •

EDDIE R REDMAN • ERIC T REDMAN • BRENT E
REDMON • DAVID REDMOND • GRAHAM RED-
MOND • JAMES W REDMOND • JOSEPH T RED-
MOND • KAY B REDMOND • PATRICIA S RED-
MOND • JOAN A REDMOND LEONARD • SANDRA
REDOCK • SANFORD A REDOCK • LUIS J REDON-
DO • DAVID J REDUS • BOB KIE REDWINE • JACK
REDWINE • PHYLLIS J REDWINE • THOMAS RED-
WINE • ANNIE REECE • DUANE H REECE • FRANK
S REECE • HEATH R REECE • ANGELA M REED •
BARNEY D REED • BARNEY J REED • BELINDA J
REED • BERNARD REED • BETTY J REED • BRIAN
K REED • CAROL J REED • CAROLYN REED •
CORAL M REED • CYNTHIA A REED • DANIEL R
REED • DANIEL S REED • DE ANA P REED • DEN-
NIS E REED • DIANE G REED • ED REED • FAY M
REED • FRANCES REED • GREGORY S REED •
JAMES REED • JAMES REED • JAMES B REED •
JAMIE L REED • JANICE M REED • JEFFREY H
REED • JENNIFER E REED • JENNIFER T REED •
JOAN C REED • JOHN REED • KANCHAN REED •
KAREN L REED • KATHERYN J REED • KEVIN R
REED • KIMBERLY J REED • LAVERNA J REED •
LENORE REED • LESA G REED • LOUIS G REED •
MADELYNE REED • MARY E REED • MICHAEL A
REED • MICHAEL P REED • MICK REED • NANCY
M REED • QUAYE C REED • RONALD E REED •
SAMUEL REED • SONRISA D REED • SONUIA O
REED • STEPHANIE REED • SUSAN REED • TIMO-
THY R REED • TRACI L REED • TRAVIS J REED •
VERONA REED • DEBORAH D REED-WILLS • BJ J
REED DAVIS • WILLIAM M REED II • ROBERT E
REED III • CINDY M REEDER • LINDA H REEDER •
SUSAN REEDER • TAMARA L REEDER • SUSAN E
REEF • CONNIS J REEL • MARTIN J REEL • NAN-
CY C REEL • JAMES K REES • JENNIFER R REES •
CAROLE E REESE • CHRISTOPHER D REESE •
DOUGLAS C REESE • ELVERIA REESE • FREDER-
ICK D REESE • GEORGE M REESE • GRETCHEN F
REESE • HERMAN L REESE • JOHN F REESE •
JOHNNY REESE • KAREN L REESE • KATHLEEN R
REESE • KATHRYN W REESE • KAY N REESE •
KENNETH H REESE • MARY L REESE • MELISSA K
REESE • MYRA F REESE • ROGER L REESE •
RUBENIA V REESE • THADDEUS REESE •
WILLIAM H REESE • TROY V REESE PHARM D •
ALLIE M REEVES • ANN D REEVES • CAMERON
LAFAYETTE REEVES • CAROLYN Y REEVES •
DEAN REEVES • DEAN G REEVES • DIAN Q
REEVES • GLENNA P REEVES • JAMES H REEVES
• JEFFREY C REEVES • JOEL F REEVES • LAV-
ERNE F REEVES • LISA A REEVES • MAEMELLE J
REEVES • ROB S REEVES • ROSEMARIE REEVES
• TEXANNA M REEVES • RICHARD B REFF •
WILLIAM L REFFITT • GREEN MCCARTHY REGAN
• JANE M REGAN • JUNE REGAN • ESTHER REGE
• MEGAN J REGIER ATC • MARK D REGISTER • DI-
ANE C REGITZ • JOHN A REGITZ • LORRAINE M
REGITZ • SARAH E REGITZ • GUNDI REH • ROBB
S REHBERG ATC • ROLF B REHDER • FRANKIE E
REHG • TOM L REHG • MATTHEW J REHM • TANYA
M REHRMANN • JONATHAN B REICH •
JONATHAN D REICH • LEONARD J REICH •
PATRICK F REICH • ANN M REICHE • CARSTEN M
REICHEL • CHARLES E REICHEL • TODD H RE-
ICHELT • TEDDIE M REICHENBACH • JENNIFER E
REICHER • EVA C REICHERT • JASON C RE-
ICHERT • JULIA P REICHERT • SANDRA B RE-
ICHERT • WAUNELL NELSON REICHERT •
WILLIAM W REICHERT • OWEN S REICHMAN •
CAROLYN R REICHNER • GRETCHEN H REI-
CHOW • ALLAN F REID • ANDREA D REID • BREN-
DA T REID • CAMERON W REID • DANIEL L REID •
DARLENE J REID • DIANA REID • DONNA V REID •
ERIC G REID • EVA REID • FITZGERALD D REID •
GAIL P REID • JEFFREY A REID • JELANI O REID •
JOLANCKE REID • KELLY Q REID • KELVIN L REID
• LADANA A REID • LAURA D REID • LENNOX
DWAYNE A REID • LESLIE O REID • LINDEN REID
• MALCOLM K REID • MARTHA W REID • PAULA E
REID • ROBERT K REID • ROBIN REID • SANDRA L
REID • SUSAN L REID • TIM A REID • TONYA Y
REID • TRACI M REID • VERDELL S REID • WAL-
TER H REID • WILLIE REID • WILLIE L REID • AN-
THONY T REID JR • DEBORAH A REIDMILLER •
VICKI R REIDY • BRENDA S REIFF • MARK A REIFF
• RALPH V REIFF ATC • JERRY D REIGHARD •
BARBARA A REILLY • KAREN REILLY • PATRICIA
M REILLY • SUSAN M REILLY • VIRGINIA M
REIMANN • MARK A REIN • JAMES REINDEL •
DELLA K REINEKE • TONI N REINER • JOHN J
REINER JR • JOHN R REINERS • TINA REINERS •
DAVID REINES • JOEL R REINFORD • CATHY
REINHARDT • SUSAN J REINHART • DONNA R
REINIG • PETE REINIGER • RICHARD REINKE •
JEFFREY W REINKE CATC • MARIE S REINKE-
MEYER • DIETER REINMUTH • CATHRYN L REI-
NOEHL • STEPHEN E REINSCH • AMY E REIS •
SHANNON M REIS • KYU H REISCH • MONIKA
REISCH • DAVID E REISCHMAN • ELEANORE
REISS • JESSICA E REISSIG • KATJA REISSWE-
BER • MARY C REISWEBER • BRUCE E REITER •
CARL REITER • DAVID J REITER • DEBRA REITER
• ERICH C REITER • JOCELYN S REITER •
WILLIAM E REITH • CARL A REITINGER • BRENT
A REITZ • JOYCE E REJBA • EUGENE RELEFORD
• SHENETHA L RELEFORD • MARY A RELLIHAN •
SANDRA M RELLINGER • BRENDA O REMBERT •
ROBERT L REMBERT • DANNA L REMENSNYDER
• STERLING H REMER • DAVID J REMICK • JAMES
D REMICK • ALICE D REMIGAILO • DAMON REMIGAI-
LO • RICHARD V REMIGAILO • JUDY REMISZEWSKI •
MARTY P REMMELL • ANNA P REMPE • PEGGY J
REMPENAULT • ELISABETH M REMY • SHERI L RE-
NAUD • JONI D RENBARGER • RITA Y RENCHER •
SUSAN E RENDEIRO • JAMES C RENDEIRO JR •
MATTHEW S RENDLE • JOEY RENERT •

CHARLES C RENFRO • INGE B RENFROE • KAY
RENFROE • LINDA W RENFROE • TONY REN-
FROE • CHRISTY E RENFROE SAT • GLORIA J
RENKERT • DAVID H RENN • BENJAMIN L REN-
NARD • KIMBERLY L RENNER • LAURA L RENNER
• SCOTT J RENNER • THOMAS L RENNER •
ROBERT S RENNICKS • BRENDA F RENNOLDS •
DENIS L RENO • GLENDA J RENSI • LEANNA D
RENSI • SANDRA RENTSCHLER • BARBARA A
RENTZELL • DENNIS J RENYI • DOUG P RENZ •
MICHELLE L RENZ • RAY A REPIC • MARY B RE-
PINE • ROBERT T REPINE JR • STEPHANIE R
REPP • JANET M RERECICH • TERESA A RESCH •
ZOYA RESENER • TIM A RESER • DEBORAH M RE-
SETAR • ROXANNE V RESLIER • RUTH A RESNI-
COW • DOROTHY M RESPRESS • SETH A RESSL •
LARRY A RESTLE • KEVIN RESTLER • DONALD E
RESZEL • GREGORY E RESZUTEK • MARGARET V
RESZUTEK • ALICIA O RETENELLER • DANIEL P
RETENELLER • KAREN D RETENELLER •
STEPHEN RETENELLER • THOMAS J RETTBERG •
JACK L RETTIG • JOSEPH REUBEN • KATHERINE A
REULAND • DAGMAR M REUTER • JASON E REUT-
TER • MICHAEL J REUTTER • FRANCES B REVEL
• DENNIS G REVELL • CAROLINE M REVOLON • R
KEVIN REW • R. KEVIN REW • LOUIS J REWALT •
KEITH A REXROTH • CHARLES-HENRY REY •
MATHILDE REY • SEVERINE REY • TOBY T
REYELTS • ALBERT V REYES • ALICIA G REYES •
GISELA REYES • HILKA X REYES • PEDRO V REYES
• RON J REYES • MARY M REYES-MUNGO • AR-
TURO C REYES JR • SYLVIA A REYNA • CHRISTIAN
M REYNARD • CECILE C REYNAUD • VELOY C
REYNDERS • BETTIE J REYNOLDS • BEVERLY R
REYNOLDS • BILLY T REYNOLDS • BLANE L REYNOLDS
• BOB REYNOLDS • BRENDA J REYNOLDS • CAR-
OL B REYNOLDS • CATHY W REYNOLDS • DAVID
A REYNOLDS • DAVID A REYNOLDS • DEBBIE A.
REYNOLDS • DIONNE REYNOLDS • DUANE
REYNOLDS • EARLETTA A REYNOLDS •
ELLEN F REYNOLDS • FARAH G REYNOLDS •
GARETH W REYNOLDS • HARRY R REYNOLDS •
JACQUELYN P REYNOLDS • JAMES A REYNOLDS •
JAMES R REYNOLDS • JAMES W REYNOLDS • JAMES W
REYNOLDS • JEAN M REYNOLDS • JIM REYNOLDS •
JOHN A REYNOLDS • JOHN P REYNOLDS •
JOSEPH M REYNOLDS • KATHLEEN M REYNOLDS •
KENT B REYNOLDS • MATTHEW D REYNOLDS •
NEISHA B REYNOLDS • PAMELA R REYNOLDS • PAUL
REYNOLDS • SHEKINIA M REYNOLDS • SHIRLEY B
REYNOLDS • STEVEN L REYNOLDS • SUE H
REYNOLDS • SUSAN D REYNOLDS • SUSAN J
REYNOLDS • TERESE L REYNOLDS • VANESSA M
REYNOLDS • WILLIAM F REYNOLDS • SUSAN REZAI •
ANNA REZNIK • JOHN S RHAMSTINE • BEVERLY A
RHEA • DIANE K RHEA • JAMES W RHEA • JERRY C
RHEA • JOHN D RHEA • WILLIAM B RHEA • MELLONEE
RHEAMS • KYU S RHEE • ROXANE D RHEINHEIMER •
MICHAEL A RHETT • TRACY RHEUDASIL • FLORENCE
RHINARD • CECIL RHINE • JEANNINE RHINE • DAVID
RHINES • KAREN RHINO • SHAWN B RHOADES • GRE-
GORY P RHOADS • ROBERT J RHOADS • GEORGE
L RHODE • BONNIE F RHODEN • ABBY RHODES •
AMANDA K RHODES • ANNIE L RHODES • ATHA M
RHODES • AUDREY M RHODES • CAROLYN H
RHODES • COURTNEY L RHODES • DEBORAH A
RHODES • DOROTHY H RHODES • ELGIN L
RHODES • HENRY J RHODES • JEFFREY PHILLIP
RHODES • JOANIA C RHODES • JOANIE J RHODES
• LORINN C RHODES • MARGARET RHODES •
MARSHA K RHODES • MARY A RHODES • MONTY C
RHODES • PAMELA J RHODES • PATRICIA E
RHODES • ROBERT RHODES • ROBERT A RHODES
• ROBERT S RHODES • RONALD E RHODES •
SHERI L RHODES • TARA L RHODES • THOMAS R
RHODES • URSULA RHODES • SEIYEON RHOE •
JEFFREY T RHULE • DONALD W RHYMER • PA-
TRICIA RHYMER • MAGD RIAD • ANDREA M RIBA
• JOANNE M RIBBLE • JOAQUIM P RIBEIRO •
SYLVIA RIBEIRO-LOPES • MELISSA D RICARD •
DONALD F RICCARDI • JAMES A RICCI • MAX A
RICCI • AARON C RICE • BARBARA L RICE • BET-
TY G RICE • CLAIR T RICE • CLINTON V RICE • DI-
ANNE H RICE • DORSEY E RICE • FRANK RICE •
GAYLE R RICE • HEATHER A RICE • JAN O RICE •
JEANA M RICE • JOSEPH A RICE • JUDY A RICE •
KAMI RICE • KAREN M RICE • KEITH E RICE • KEL-
LY S RICE • KIRK A RICE • MARTHA S RICE •
MICHAL P RICE • PARKS E RICE • RAISHAUN A
RICE • RENE R RICE • SALLY A RICE • SANDRA G
RICE • SHANNON RICE • SHIRLEY L RICE •
WILLIAM M RICE • YVORNNIE A RICE • CHELCIE
RICE III • ARNOLD M RICH • JORDANA E RICH •
KENNETH G RICH • LEA E RICH • MARK RICH •
MICKI RICH • SYMMA K RICH • YVONNE RICH •
DALE J RICHARD • MARIA T RICHARD • MELISSA
S RICHARD • PASCAL RICHARD • AMBYR E
RICHARDS • ANNE S RICHARDS • BARBARA E
RICHARDS • BRENDA J RICHARDS • CARRIE C
RICHARDS • CHRISTOPHER A RICHARDS •
DAVID C RICHARDS • DONALD J RICHARDS •
ELIZABETH R RICHARDS • JOHN RICHARDS •
JON M RICHARDS • PATRICK G RICHARDS • PEN-
INA S RICHARDS • SHANE D RICHARDS •
STEPHANIE L RICHARDS • STEVEN A RICHARDS
• SUZANNE RICHARDS • THOMAS P RICHARDS •
WILLIAM S RICHARDS • AMANDA RICHARDSON •
ANDREW B RICHARDSON • ANNIE W RICHARD-
SON • BETTY C RICHARDSON • CARRIE RICHARD-
SON • CASANDRA W RICHARDSON • CHRISTINE
RICHARDSON • COBY G RICHARDSON • CON-
STANCE J RICHARDSON • DAVID A RICHARDSON •
DAVID GUY RICHARDSON • DEBRA S RICHARD-
SON • DENNIS A RICHARDSON • DERRICK A
RICHARDSON • DOUG M RICHARDSON • DYAN S
RICHARDSON • EARNESTINE J RICHARDSON • GRE-
GORY G RICHARDSON • HELEN L RICHARDSON •

CANOE / KAYAK—SLALOM
CANOË / KAYAK—SLALOM

Abbreviations and terms used in Canoe/Kayak—Slalom results tables
Abréviations et mots employés dans les tableaux de résultats de Canoë /Kayak — Slalom

Term	English	Français
B	Bronze Medal	Médaille de bronze
Continued	Continued	Continué
Ctry	Country	Pays
DNF	Did Not Finish	Abandon
Final	Final	Finale
G	Gold Medal	Médaille d'or
Penalty	Penalty	Pénalité
Rnk	Rank	Classement
Run	Run	Manche
S	Silver Medal	Médaille d'argent
Time Behind	Time Behind	Temps en arrière
Total	Total	Total

International Canoeing Federation (FIC)
Fédération Internationale de Canoë
H-1143 Budapest
Dózsa Gyorgy ut 1-3
Hungary

Canoe/Kayak—Slalom / *Canoë/Kayak—Slalom*

Kayak Single, Men / *Kayak simple, Messieurs*

FINAL

Rnk	Name	Ctry	Run 1	Penalty	Total	Run 2	Penalty	Total	Time behind
1	FIX, Oliver	GER	141.22	0	141.22	154.75	55	209.75	0.00 G
2	VEHOVAR, Andraz	SLO	145.38	0	145.38	141.65	0	141.65	0.43 S
3	BECKER, Thomas	GER	144.48	0	144.48	142.79	0	142.79	1.57 B
4	BURTZ, Laurent	FRA	154.18	5	159.18	144.33	0	144.33	3.11
5	WILEY, Ian	IRL	145.21	0	145.21	147.26	60	207.26	3.99
6	WEISS, Rich	USA	144.45	5	149.45	145.78	0	145.78	4.56
7	ABRAMIC, Jernej	SLO	151.59	0	151.59	145.81	0	145.81	4.59
8	LETTMANN, Jochen	GER	145.99	0	145.99	140.97	10	150.97	4.77
9	RASPIN, Ian	GBR	146.15	0	146.15	149.11	60	209.11	4.93
10	STANOVSKY, Miroslav	SVK	155.17	10	165.17	146.59	0	146.59	5.37
11	REYS, Michael	NED	146.79	0	146.79	150.49	60	210.49	5.57
12	SHIPLEY, Scott	USA	143.31	5	148.31	144.34	5	149.34	7.09
13	NAGY, Peter	SVK	151.54	60	211.54	148.35	0	148.35	7.13
14	RATCLIFFE, Paul	GBR	148.49	5	153.49	143.37	5	148.37	7.15
15	FORD, David	CAN	149.23	0	149.23	145.83	50	195.83	8.01
16	GLUCKS, Andrej	CRO	155.75	0	155.75	150.12	0	150.12	8.90
17	FERRAZZI, Pierpaolo	ITA	146.10	50	196.10	145.76	5	150.76	9.54
18	HILGERT, Lubos	CZE	146.10	5	151.10	146.99	50	196.99	9.88
19	PRSKAVEC, Jiri	CZE	182.29	115	297.29	151.15	0	151.15	9.93
20	GIDDENS, Eric	USA	151.15	50	201.15	146.65	5	151.65	10.43
21	KLAVINS, Aldis	LAT	156.08	10	166.08	152.67	0	152.67	11.45
22	ETXANIZ, Xabier	ESP	160.81	60	220.81	148.77	5	153.77	12.55

FINAL - continued

Rnk	Name	Ctry	Run 1	Penalty	Total	Run 2	Penalty	Total	Time behind
23	CHEUTIN, Jean-Yves	FRA	160.13	60	220.13	148.95	5	153.95	12.73
24	MacQUIRE, Richard	AUS	148.97	5	153.97	153.07	65	218.07	12.75
25	PEARCE, Shaun	GBR	154.76	0	154.76	152.94	15	167.94	13.54
26	MARUSIC, Fedja	SLO	145.70	10	155.70	153.24	5	158.24	14.48
27	SANDERA, Jerzy	POL	152.78	20	172.78	155.79	0	155.79	14.57
28	OBLINGER, Helmut	AUT	154.22	5	159.22	157.06	0	157.06	15.84
29	POPOVSKI, Lazar	MKD	159.53	0	159.53	158.30	0	158.30	17.08
30	FERREIRA FERNANDES, A.	POR	158.72	0	158.72	160.00	10	170.00	17.50
31	HUGHES, Owen	NZL	154.79	10	164.79	155.28	5	160.28	19.06
32	SELBACH, Gustavo	BRA	153.33	15	168.33	162.48	0	162.48	21.26
33	KVANLI, Benjamin	GUA	162.28	20	182.28	159.34	5	164.34	23.12
34	ARACAMA, Esteban	ESP	149.66	15	164.66	155.17	110	265.17	23.44
35	LAZKO, Anton	RUS	161.11	5	166.11	155.56	135	290.56	24.89
36	FUJINO, Tsuyoshi	JPN	162.26	5	167.26	157.94	10	167.94	26.04
37	SINS, Fritz	NED	154.42	55	209.42	149.33	20	169.33	28.11
38	PALLISTER, Matthew	AUS	161.88	75	236.88	159.19	20	179.19	37.97
39	MADRIGAL, Roger	CRC	175.34	5	180.34	164.97	55	219.97	39.12
40	BOLAND, Andrew	IRL	191.92	10	201.92	174.51	10	184.51	43.29
41	KARABASIC, Samir	BIH	213.01	35	248.01	191.85	5	196.85	55.63
42	KOEHLER, Manuel	AUT	156.01	105	261.01	144.54	65	209.54	68.32
43	AYOB, Sal	MAS	189.15	70	259.15	174.54	55	229.54	88.32
44	MULLER, Scott	PAN	232.24	10	242.24	207.89	35	242.89	101.02

Canoe/Kayak—Slalom / *Canoë/Kayak—Slalom*

Kayak Single, Women / *Kayak simple, Dames*

FINAL

Rnk	Name	Ctry	Run 1	Penalty	Total	Run 2	Penalty	Total	Time behind
1	HILGERTOVA, Stepanka	CZE	164.49	5	169.49	166.97	5	171.97	0.00 G
2	CHLADEK, Dana	USA	181.60	205	386.60	164.49	5	169.49	0.00 S
3	FOX-JERUSALMI, Myriam	FRA	170.22	5	175.22	166.00	5	171.00	1.51 B
4	GIAI PRON, Cristina	ITA	171.86	155	326.86	166.84	5	171.84	2.35
5	BROSKOVA, Gabriela	SVK	170.67	60	230.67	167.57	5	172.57	3.08
6	BOIXEL, Anne	FRA	162.79	10	172.79	162.88	105	267.88	3.30
7	HEARN, Cathy	USA	173.03	0	173.03	169.93	60	229.93	3.54
8	LANGFORD, Margaret	CAN	178.49	15	193.49	168.59	5	173.59	4.10
9	SADILOVA, Marcela	CZE	181.22	55	236.22	174.47	0	174.47	4.98
10	MICHELER-JONES, E.	GER	171.56	5	176.56	156.73	305	461.73	7.07
11	STRIEPECKE, Kordula	GER	171.63	155	326.63	176.98	0	176.98	7.49
12	WOODWARD, Danielle	AUS	181.05	105	286.05	177.60	0	177.60	8.11
13	FRIEDLI, Sandra	SUI	172.90	5	177.90	221.01	10	231.01	8.41
14	FARRANCE, Mia	AUS	192.58	0	192.58	180.30	0	180.30	10.81
15	NADALIN, Barbara	ITA	201.04	105	306.04	171.14	10	181.14	11.65

FINAL - continued

Rnk	Name	Ctry	Run 1	Penalty	Total	Run 2	Penalty	Total	Time behind
16	PAVELKOVA, Irena	CZE	184.45	55	239.45	166.89	15	181.89	12.40
17	KOBAYASHI, Hiroko	JPN	178.66	5	183.66	186.01	5	191.01	14.17
18	CROSBEE, Rachel	GBR	165.24	25	190.24	168.94	25	193.94	20.75
19	KALISKA, Elena	SVK	174.85	55	229.85	170.45	20	190.45	20.96
20	EIZMENDI, Maria	ESP	186.49	5	191.49	184.83	20	204.83	22.00
21	KNAPCZYK, Boguslawa	POL	185.20	15	200.20	194.45	15	209.45	30.71
22	FERREIRA FERNANDES, F.	POR	192.19	20	212.19	203.20	5	208.20	38.71
23	SIMPSON, Lynn	GBR	177.07	160	337.07	161.71	50	211.71	42.22
24	MARTINEZ, Cristina	ESP	204.09	20	224.09	215.91	65	280.91	54.60
25	KURZINA, Elena	BLR	210.14	15	225.14	214.37	70	284.37	55.65
26	EL-DESOUKI, Nagwa	SUI	185.39	55	240.39	220.68	15	235.68	66.19
27	BOYLE, Sheryl	CAN	227.89	15	242.89	194.41	50	244.41	73.40
28	MONTENEGRO, Gilda	CRC	236.97	135	371.97	240.93	25	265.93	96.44
29	UGRINOVSKA, Ana	MKD	261.93	85	346.93	218.17	265	483.17	177.44
30	BLUMA, Dzintra	LAT			DNF	267.81	105	372.81	203.32

Canoe/Kayak—Slalom / *Canoë/Kayak — Slalom*

Canoe Single, Men / *Canoë simple, Messieurs*

FINAL

Rnk	Name	Ctry	Run 1	Penalty	Total	Run 2	Penalty	Total	Time behind
1	MARTIKAN, Michal	SVK	160.88	0	160.88	151.03	0	151.03	0.00 G
2	POLLERT, Lukas	CZE	151.17	0	151.17	158.25	20	178.25	0.14 S
3	ESTANGUET, Patrice	FRA	152.84	0	152.84	150.89	10	160.89	1.81 B
4	MARRIOTT, Gareth	GBR	155.83	0	155.83	154.14	5	159.14	4.80
5	DELAMARRE, Herve	FRA	155.98	0	155.98	168.77	10	178.77	4.95
6	BRUGVIN, Emmanuel	FRA	158.28	5	163.28	151.71	5	156.71	5.68
7	LANG, Martin	GER	154.91	5	159.91	157.24	10	167.24	8.88
8	MORDARSKI, Ryszard	POL	156.00	5	161.00	156.86	5	161.86	9.97
9	HEARN, David	USA	159.07	5	164.07	157.51	5	162.51	11.48
10	CORCORAN, Mike	IRL	162.90	0	162.90	163.61	10	173.61	11.87
11	WIECZOREK, Mariusz	POL	159.21	5	164.21	176.17	5	181.17	13.18
12	HUSEK, Vitus	GER	162.48	5	167.48	159.29	5	164.29	13.26
13	de MONTI, Renato	ITA	168.75	50	218.75	160.03	5	165.03	14.00
14	DELANEY, Mark	GBR	161.52	5	166.52	155.67	10	165.67	14.64
15	MINCIK, Juraj	SVK	182.60	0	182.60	161.45	5	166.45	15.42

FINAL - *continued*

Rnk	Name	Ctry	Run 1	Penalty	Total	Run 2	Penalty	Total	Time behind
16	BOOCOCK, Justin	AUS	161.96	5	166.96	170.08	5	175.08	15.93
17	KAUFMANN, Soeren	GER	158.43	10	168.43	162.25	15	177.25	17.40
18	NORMAN, Larry	CAN	176.57	10	186.57	170.12	0	170.12	19.09
19	CLAWSON, Adam	USA	157.53	15	172.53	165.74	100	265.74	21.50
20	JANDA, Pavel	CZE	167.71	10	177.71	185.87	55	240.87	26.68
21	HERREROS, Toni	ESP	174.38	5	179.38	183.83	115	298.83	28.35
22	MOCHIDA, Masanari	JPN	175.45	5	180.45	205.69	10	215.69	29.42
23	SELBACH, Leonardo	BRA	206.51	10	216.51	179.54	5	184.54	33.51
24	TERDIC, Gregor	SLO	182.79	5	187.79	194.08	5	199.08	36.76
25	O'FLAHERTY, Stephen	IRL	178.65	10	188.65	195.73	25	220.73	37.62
26	STEFANI, Francesco	ITA	162.63	300	462.63	169.60	20	189.60	38.57
27	KUZNETSOV, Danila	RUS	213.36	60	273.36	176.06	50	226.06	75.03
28	HOCEVAR, Simon	SLO	197.90	55	252.90	166.00	65	231.00	79.97
29	HERCEG, Danko	CRO	163.07	305	468.07	165.94	110	275.94	124.91
30	TRPOVSKI, Nenad	MKD	191.19	125	316.19			DNF	165.16

Canoe/Kayak—Slalom / *Canoë/Kayak — Slalom*

Canoe Double, Men / *Canoë double, Messieurs*

FINAL

Rnk	Names	Ctry	Run 1	Penalty	Total	Run 2	Penalty	Total	Time behind
1	ADISSON, Frank / FORGUES, Wilfrid	FRA	182.85	10	192.85	158.82	0	158.82	0.00 G
2	SIMEK, Miroslav / ROHAN, Jiri	CZE	161.77	70	231.77	160.16	0	160.16	1.34 S
3	EHRENBERG, Andre / SENFT, Michael	GER	162.33	5	167.33	158.72	5	163.72	4.90 B
4	BERRO, Manfred / TRUMMER, Michael	GER	165.55	15	180.55	163.72	0	163.72	4.90
5	del REY, Emmanuel / SAIDI, Thierry	FRA	168.43	5	173.43	160.47	5	165.47	6.65
6	STERCL, Pavel / STERCL, Petr	CZE	163.45	5	168.45	179.53	160	339.53	9.63
7	KOLOMANSKI, Krzysztof / STANISZEWSKI, Michal	POL	163.78	10	173.78	164.95	5	169.95	11.13
8	GAUTHIER, Benoit / LETOURNEAU, Francois	CAN	164.83	15	179.83	167.67	5	172.67	13.85
9	MATTI, Peter / MATTI, Ueli	SUI	181.31	5	186.31	168.67	5	173.67	14.85
10	SOSKA, Lubos / SOSKA, Peter	SVK	179.90	5	184.90	170.38	5	175.38	16.56
11	HOLDEN, Horace / DICKERT, Wayne	USA	174.69	50	224.69	175.90	5	180.90	22.08
12	BROWN, Craig / PITT, Stewart	GBR	179.81	10	189.81	170.96	10	180.96	22.14
13	STRBA, Roman / VAJS, Roman	SVK	174.40	20	194.40	175.67	25	200.67	35.58
14	WILSON, Andrew / FELTON, John	AUS	184.48	70	254.48	184.06	15	199.06	40.24
15	WOJS, Andrzej / MORDARSKI, Slawomir	POL	201.51	25	226.51	193.07	20	213.07	54.25

Venue Map
Plan du site

Canoe / Kayak—Slalom
Canoë / Kayak — Slalom
Ocoee Whitewater Center
Centre des épreuves en eaux vives de l'Ocoee, Tennessee

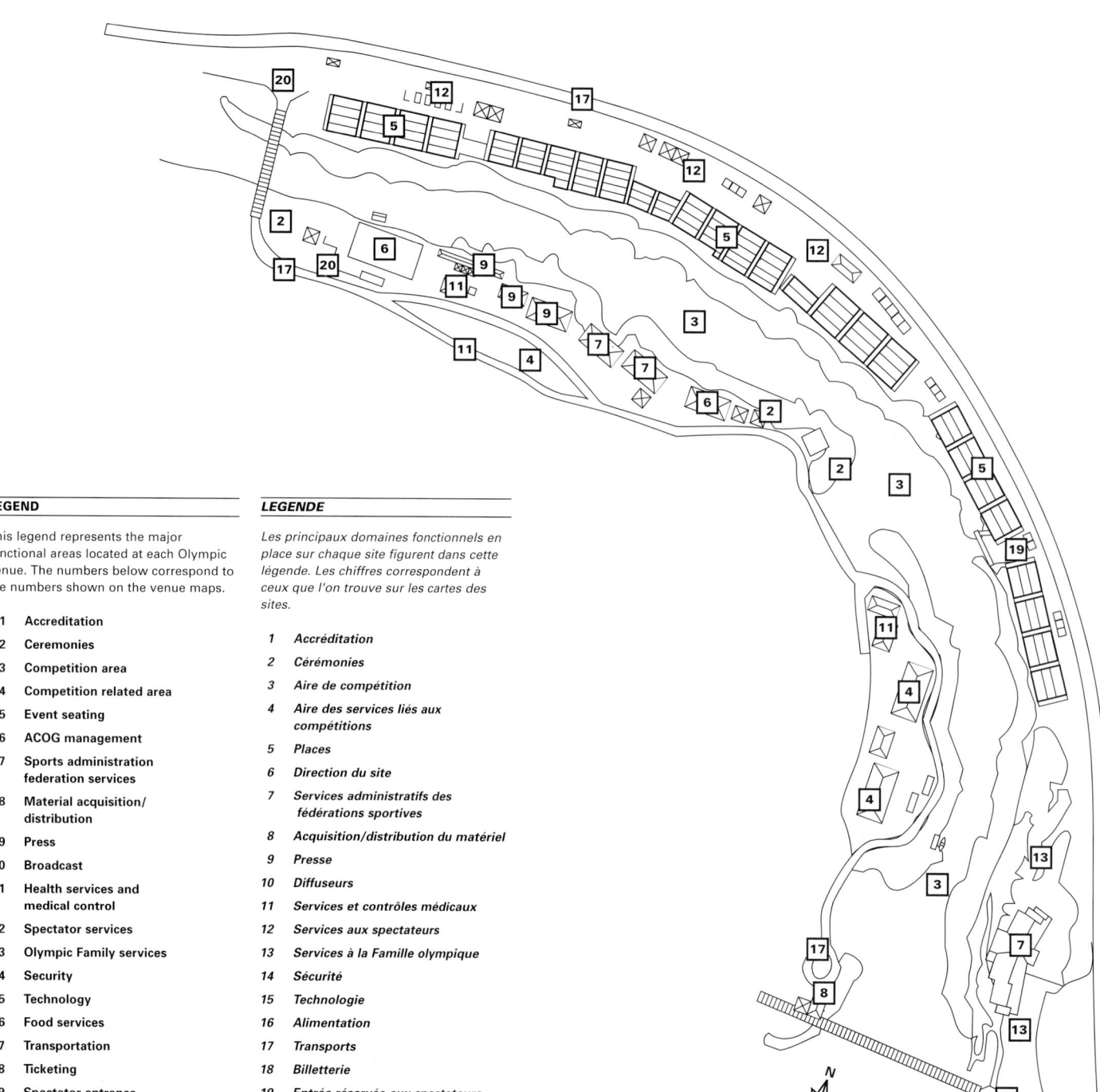

<table>
<tr><td>

LEGEND

This legend represents the major
functional areas located at each Olympic
venue. The numbers below correspond to
the numbers shown on the venue maps.

1	Accreditation
2	Ceremonies
3	Competition area
4	Competition related area
5	Event seating
6	ACOG management
7	Sports administration federation services
8	Material acquisition/ distribution
9	Press
10	Broadcast
11	Health services and medical control
12	Spectator services
13	Olympic Family services
14	Security
15	Technology
16	Food services
17	Transportation
18	Ticketing
19	Spectator entrance
20	Athlete entrance

</td><td>

LEGENDE

*Les principaux domaines fonctionnels en
place sur chaque site figurent dans cette
légende. Les chiffres correspondent à
ceux que l'on trouve sur les cartes des
sites.*

1	*Accréditation*
2	*Cérémonies*
3	*Aire de compétition*
4	*Aire des services liés aux compétitions*
5	*Places*
6	*Direction du site*
7	*Services administratifs des fédérations sportives*
8	*Acquisition/distribution du matériel*
9	*Presse*
10	*Diffuseurs*
11	*Services et contrôles médicaux*
12	*Services aux spectateurs*
13	*Services à la Famille olympique*
14	*Sécurité*
15	*Technologie*
16	*Alimentation*
17	*Transports*
18	*Billetterie*
19	*Entrée réservée aux spectateurs*
20	*Entrée réservée aux athlètes*

</td></tr>
</table>

CANOE / KAYAK—SPRINT
CANOË / KAYAK—SPRINT

Abbreviations and terms used in Canoe / Kayak—Sprint results tables
Abréviations et mots employés dans les tableaux de résultats de Canoë / Kayak—Sprint

Term	English	Français
B	Bronze Medal	Médaille de bronze
Continued	Continued	Continué
Ctry	Country	Pays
DQ	Disqualified	Disqualifié
Final	Final	Finale
G	Gold Medal	Médaille d'or
Heat	Heat	Série
Ln	Lane	Couloir
Name	Name	Nom
Repechage	Repechage	Repêchage
Rnk	Rank	Classement
S	Silver Medal	Médaille d'argent
Semifinal	Semifinal	Demi-finale
Time	Time	Temps
Time Behind	Time Behind	Temps en arrière

International Canoeing Federation (FIC)
Fédération Internationale de Canoë
H-1143 Budapest
Dózsa Gyorgy ut 1-3
Hungary

Canoe/Kayak—Sprint / *Canoë/Kayak—Sprint*

500 m Kayak Single, Men / *500 m kayak simple, Messieurs*

HEAT 1

Rnk	Ln	Name	Ctry	Time	Time behind
1	5	MAGYAR, Geza	ROM	1:42.391	0
2	1	MARKIEWICZ, Piotr	POL	1:42.731	0.340
3	9	KALESNIK, Sergey	BLR	1:43.279	0.888
4	8	ANTAL, Zoltan	HUN	1:43.343	0.952
5	7	ERBAN, Robert	SVK	1:43.563	1.172
6	2	YEGOROV, Yevgeniy	KAZ	1:47.823	5.432
7	6	LAWLER, Ivan	GBR	1:48.991	6.600
8	3	KRANTZ, Tom	SWE	1:49.695	7.304

HEAT 2

Rnk	Ln	Name	Ctry	Time	Time behind
1	4	HOLMANN, Knut	NOR	1:41.524	0
2	8	McFADZEAN, Cameron	AUS	1:42.160	0.636
3	1	GARCIA, Miguel	ESP	1:42.180	0.656
4	6	CRICHLOW, Renn	CAN	1:42.652	1.128
5	7	CUATTRIN, Sebastian	BRA	1:44.328	2.804
6	2	VERLIN, Sergey	RUS	1:45.228	3.704
7	3	HELDE, Hain	EST	1:47.316	5.792
8	9	GARCIA, Jose	POR	1:52.760	11.236
9	5	ABIA, Koutoua	CIV	1:55.208	13.684

HEAT 3

Rnk	Ln	Name	Ctry	Time	Time behind
1	8	ROSSI, Antonio	ITA	1:40.411	0
2	5	LIWOWSKI, Lutz	GER	1:41.079	0.668
3	1	KOLEHMAINEN, Mikko	FIN	1:41.171	0.760
4	2	CORREA, Javier	ARG	1:42.691	2.280
5	3	MERKOV, Petar	BUL	1:43.815	3.404
6	7	HERBERT, Mike	USA	1:44.763	4.352
7	4	TERESHCHENKO, Vladyslav	UKR	1:45.523	5.112
8	9	SIBINKIC, Petar	YUG	1:45.799	5.388
9	6	POPOV, Aleksandr	UZB	1:56.827	16.416

REPECHAGE 1

Rnk	Ln	Name	Ctry	Time	Time behind
1	4	ERBAN, Robert	SVK	1:43.184	0
2	3	HERBERT, Mike	USA	1:43.384	0.200
3	5	CORREA, Javier	ARG	1:44.076	0.892
4	6	CUATTRIN, Sebastian	BRA	1:44.204	1.020
5	2	HELDE, Hain	EST	1:44.340	1.156
6	7	LAWLER, Ivan	GBR	1:45.220	2.036
7	8	SIBINKIC, Petar	YUG	1:46.532	3.348
8	1	ABIA, Koutoua	CIV	1:53.432	10.248

REPECHAGE 2

Rnk	Ln	Name	Ctry	Time	Time behind
1	6	MERKOV, Petar	BUL	1:42.851	0
2	4	CRICHLOW, Renn	CAN	1:43.055	0.204
3	5	ANTAL, Zoltan	HUN	1:43.343	0.492
4	7	VERLIN, Sergey	RUS	1:43.359	0.508
5	2	TERESHCHENKO, Vladyslav	UKR	1:44.143	1.292
6	3	YEGOROV, Yevgeniy	KAZ	1:47.035	4.184
7	8	KRANTZ, Tom	SWE	1:47.815	4.964
8	9	POPOV, Aleksandr	UZB	1:51.623	8.772
9	1	GARCIA, Jose	POR	1:56.103	13.252

SEMIFINAL 1

Rnk	Ln	Name	Ctry	Time	Time behind
1	4	ROSSI, Antonio	ITA	1:39.185	0
2	5	HOLMANN, Knut	NOR	1:39.929	0.744
3	7	KOLEHMAINEN, Mikko	FIN	1:40.765	1.580
4	8	ERBAN, Robert	SVK	1:41.425	2.240
5	6	MARKIEWICZ, Piotr	POL	1:41.565	2.380
6	2	CRICHLOW, Renn	CAN	1:41.749	2.564
7	9	ANTAL, Zoltan	HUN	1:41.873	2.688
8	3	KALESNIK, Sergey	BLR	1:42.505	3.320
9	1	CUATTRIN, Sebastian	BRA	1:43.045	3.860

SEMIFINAL 2

Rnk	Ln	Name	Ctry	Time	Time behind
1	6	LIWOWSKI, Lutz	GER	1:40.319	0
2	5	MAGYAR, Geza	ROM	1:40.615	0.296
3	7	GARCIA, Miguel	ESP	1:40.687	0.368
4	4	McFADZEAN, Cameron	AUS	1:41.083	0.764
5	1	VERLIN, Sergey	RUS	1:41.791	1.472
6	9	TERESHCHENKO, Vladyslav	UKR	1:41.883	1.564
7	2	CORREA, Javier	ARG	1:42.071	1.752
8	8	HERBERT, Mike	USA	1:42.335	2.016
9	3	MERKOV, Petar	BUL	1:42.379	2.060

FINAL

Rnk	Ln	Name	Ctry	Time	Time behind	
1	5	ROSSI, Antonio	ITA	1:37.423	0	G
2	6	HOLMANN, Knut	NOR	1:38.339	0.916	S
3	9	MARKIEWICZ, Piotr	POL	1:38.615	1.192	B
4	3	MAGYAR, Geza	ROM	1:38.975	1.552	
5	4	LIWOWSKI, Lutz	GER	1:39.307	1.884	
6	2	GARCIA, Miguel	ESP	1:40.047	2.624	
7	7	KOLEHMAINEN, Mikko	FIN	1:40.331	2.908	
8	8	ERBAN, Robert	SVK	1:40.407	2.984	
9	1	McFADZEAN, Cameron	AUS	1:41.023	3.600	

Canoe/Kayak—Sprint / *Canoë/Kayak—Sprint*

500 m Kayak Single, Women / *500 m kayak simple, Dames*

HEAT 1

Rnk	Ln	Name	Ctry	Time	Time behind
1	7	IDEM, Josefa	ITA	1:50.303	0
2	8	KOBAN, Rita	HUN	1:50.423	0.120
3	1	GUNNARSSON, Susanne	SWE	1:52.943	2.640
4	4	PASTUSZKA, Aneta	POL	1:54.015	3.712
5	5	MICHAUT, Anne	FRA	1:57.263	6.960
6	6	CARMI, Lior	ISR	1:57.675	7.372
7	2	GAO, Beibei	CHN	1:59.543	9.240
8	3	PHILLIPS, Traci	USA	2:02.847	12.544

HEAT 2

Rnk	Ln	Name	Ctry	Time	Time behind
1	5	PROFANTER, Ursula	AUT	1:51.440	0
2	2	BRUNET, Caroline	CAN	1:53.024	1.584
3	3	FISCHER, Birgit	GER	1:54.880	3.440
4	1	MARUYAMA, Sayuri	JPN	1:58.160	6.720
5	8	HARALAMOW, Ingrid	SUI	1:58.520	7.080
6	6	DURON, Erika	MEX	1:58.884	7.444
7	4	LYALINA, Irina	UZB	1:59.996	8.556
8	7	LEHRER, Heidi	ANT	3:00.672	1:09.232

HEAT 3

Rnk	Ln	Name	Ctry	Time	Time behind
1	6	BORCHERT, Katrin	AUS	1:53.767	0
2	5	NORTJE, Ruth	RSA	1:54.695	0.928
3	7	SANCHEZ, Belen	ESP	1:55.043	1.276
4	3	VAN de VENNE, Delphine	BEL	1:57.363	3.596
5	8	DALLAWAY, Andrea	GBR	1:58.531	4.764
6	1	IONITA, Raluca	ROM	2:00.059	6.292
7	4	JOBANKOVA, Pavlina	CZE	2:07.811	14.044

REPECHAGE 1

Rnk	Ln	Name	Ctry	Time	Time behind
1	6	HARALAMOW, Ingrid	SUI	1:57.891	0
2	5	PASTUSZKA, Aneta	POL	1:58.359	0.468
3	4	VAN de VENNE, Delphine	BEL	1:59.027	1.136
4	7	GAO, Beibei	CHN	1:59.095	1.204
5	8	PHILLIPS, Traci	USA	2:00.371	2.480
6	3	DURON, Erika	MEX	2:02.847	4.956
7	2	JOBANKOVA, Pavlina	CZE	2:12.219	14.328

REPECHAGE 2

Rnk	Ln	Name	Ctry	Time	Time behind
1	5	MARUYAMA, Sayuri	JPN	2:04.829	0
2	6	DALLAWAY, Andrea	GBR	2:04.885	0.056
3	4	MICHAUT, Anne	FRA	2:05.477	0.648
4	3	CARMI, Lior	ISR	2:05.737	0.908
5	8	LYALINA, Irina	UZB	2:08.017	3.188
6	7	IONITA, Raluca	ROM	2:11.941	7.112

500 m Kayak Single, Women / *500 m kayak simple, Dames*

SEMIFINAL 1

Rnk	Ln	Name	Ctry	Time	Time behind
1	6	KOBAN, Rita	HUN	1:48.842	0
2	3	GUNNARSSON, Susanne	SWE	1:49.886	1.044
3	5	PROFANTER, Ursula	AUT	1:50.066	1.224
4	8	HARALAMOW, Ingrid	SUI	1:50.830	1.988
5	4	BORCHERT, Katrin	AUS	1:51.142	2.300
6	7	SANCHEZ, Belen	ESP	1:52.322	3.480
7	2	DALLAWAY, Andrea	GBR	1:55.842	7.000
8	9	MICHAUT, Anne	FRA	1:55.930	7.088
9	1	GAO, Beibei	CHN	1:57.498	8.656

SEMIFINAL 2

Rnk	Ln	Name	Ctry	Time	Time behind
1	5	IDEM, Josefa	ITA	1:49.079	0
2	4	BRUNET, Caroline	CAN	1:49.575	0.496
3	7	FISCHER, Birgit	GER	1:51.863	2.784
4	8	PASTUSZKA, Aneta	POL	1:53.255	4.176
5	6	NORTJE, Ruth	RSA	1:53.611	4.532
6	2	VAN de VENNE, Delphine	BEL	1:54.687	5.608
7	1	CARMI, Lior	ISR	1:54.899	5.820
8	3	MARUYAMA, Sayuri	JPN	1:54.943	5.864
9	9	PHILLIPS, Traci	USA	1:55.339	6.260

FINAL

Rnk	Ln	Name	Ctry	Time	Time behind	
1	5	KOBAN, Rita	HUN	1:47.655	0	G
2	3	BRUNET, Caroline	CAN	1:47.891	0.236	S
3	4	IDEM, Josefa	ITA	1:48.731	1.076	B
4	2	FISCHER, Birgit	GER	1:49.383	1.728	
5	6	GUNNARSSON, Susanne	SWE	1:49.591	1.936	
6	7	PROFANTER, Ursula	AUT	1:50.271	2.616	
7	9	BORCHERT, Katrin	AUS	1:50.811	3.156	
8	8	HARALAMOW, Ingrid	SUI	1:50.875	3.220	
9	1	PASTUSZKA, Aneta	POL	1:52.451	4.796	

Canoe/Kayak—Sprint / *Canoë/Kayak—Sprint*

500 m Kayak Double, Men / *500 m kayak double, Messieurs*

HEAT 1

Rnk	Ln	Ctry	Names	Time	Time behind
1	4	ITA	BONOMI, Beniamino / SCARPA, Daniele	1:31.491	0
2	1	POL	FREIMUT, Maciej / WYSOCKI, Adam	1:32.463	0.972
3	6	ESP	GONZALEZ, Jovino / VICENTE, Gregorio	1:32.791	1.300
4	3	SWE	OSCARSSON, Markus / MALMSTEN, Staffan	1:33.411	1.920
5	5	POR	QUEIROS, Joaquim / FERNANDES, Rui	1:33.859	2.368
6	7	CZE	LESTINA, Karel / POLIVKA, Jiri	1:34.107	2.616
7	8	UZB	ANOSOV, Vitaliy / YURABAYEV, Akram	1:39.291	7.800

HEAT 2

Rnk	Ln	Ctry	Names	Time	Time behind
1	8	GER	BLUHM, Kay / GUTSCHE, Torsten	1:31.361	0
2	2	AUS	TRIM, Andrew / COLLINS, Daniel	1:31.433	0.072
3	3	RUS	TISHCHENKO, Anatoliy / GOROBIY, Oleg	1:31.589	0.228
4	4	DEN	NIELSEN, Thor / STAAL, Jesper	1:32.641	1.280
5	1	LTU	KUPCINSKAS, Vidas / MIZERAS, Vaidas	1:36.685	5.324
6	6	BUL	DUSHEV, Andrian / KAZANOV, Milko	1:36.801	5.440
7	7	CHN	XU, Haifeng / WU, Yubiao	1:37.677	6.316
8	5	KAZ	TORLOPOV, Dmitriy / GATIYATULLIN, Ilfat	1:37.833	6.472

HEAT 3

Rnk	Ln	Ctry	Names	Time	Time behind
1	2	HUN	GYULAY, Zsolt / BARTFAI, Krisztian	1:32.030	0
2	5	ROM	STOIAN, Daniel / SERBAN, Romica	1:32.926	0.896
3	7	USA	MOONEY, John / JORGENSEN, Stein	1:33.642	1.612
4	1	MEX	HEINZE, Roberto / HEINZE, Ralph	1:36.918	4.888
5	4	BEL	TABOUREAU, David / VENDEWEYER, Mark	1:37.118	5.088
6	3	ARG	MANGIN, Sergio / CANEPA, Diego	1:38.594	6.564
7	8	IRL	MAWER, Gary / MALONEY, Conor	1:43.074	11.044
8	6	KGZ	MITKOVETS, Andrey / ULIACHENKO, Yury	1:43.722	11.692

REPECHAGE 1

Rnk	Ln	Ctry	Names	Time	Time behind
1	3	BUL	DUSHEV, Andrian / KAZANOV, Milko	1:37.928	0
2	5	SWE	OSCARSSON, Markus / MALMSTEN, Staffan	1:39.176	1.248
3	6	LTU	KUPCINSKAS, Vidas / MIZERAS, Vaidas	1:40.500	2.572
4	7	UZB	ANOSOV, Vitaliy / YURABAYEV, Akram	1:42.524	4.596
5	4	MEX	HEINZE, Roberto / HEINZE, Ralph	1:42.848	4.920
6	1	KGZ	MITKOVETS, Andrey / ULIACHENKO, Yury	1:44.324	6.396
7	2	IRL	MAWER, Gary / MALONEY, Conor	1:44.376	6.448

REPECHAGE 2

Rnk	Ln	Ctry	Names	Time	Time behind
1	5	DEN	NIELSEN, Thor / STAAL, Jesper	1:36.419	0
2	3	CZE	LESTINA, Karel / POLIVKA, Jiri	1:37.119	0.700
3	4	POR	QUEIROS, Joaquim / FERNANDES, Rui	1:37.499	1.080
4	7	ARG	MANGIN, Sergio / CANEPA, Diego	1:39.535	3.116
5	6	BEL	TABOUREAU, David / VENDEWEYER, Mark	1:39.619	3.200
6	2	KAZ	TORLOPOV, Dmitriy / GATIYATULLIN, Ilfat	1:40.215	3.796
7	8	CHN	XU, Haifeng / WU, Yubiao	1:41.035	4.616

SEMIFINAL 1

Rnk	Ln	Ctry	Names	Time	Time behind
1	5	ITA	BONOMI, Beniamino / SCARPA, Daniele	1:29.661	0
2	6	AUS	TRIM, Andrew / COLLINS, Daniel	1:29.937	0.276
3	8	BUL	DUSHEV, Andrian / KAZANOV, Milko	1:30.641	0.980
4	4	HUN	GYULAY, Zsolt / BARTFAI, Krisztian	1:30.725	1.064
5	3	ESP	GONZALEZ, Jovino / VICENTE, Gregorio	1:31.137	1.476
6	7	USA	MOONEY, John / JORGENSEN, Stein	1:32.253	2.592
7	2	CZE	LESTINA, Karel / POLIVKA, Jiri	1:32.517	2.856
8	9	LTU	KUPCINSKAS, Vidas / MIZERAS, Vaidas	1:32.693	3.032
9	1	ARG	MANGIN, Sergio / CANEPA, Diego	1:37.177	7.516

SEMIFINAL 2

Rnk	Ln	Ctry	Names	Time	Time behind
1	5	GER	BLUHM, Kay / GUTSCHE, Torsten	1:29.883	0
2	7	RUS	TISHCHENKO, Anatoliy / GOROBIY, Oleg	1:30.031	0.148
3	4	POL	FREIMUT, Maciej / WYSOCKI, Adam	1:30.243	0.360
4	6	ROM	STOIAN, Daniel / SERBAN, Romica	1:30.611	0.728
5	3	DEN	NIELSEN, Thor / STAAL, Jesper	1:30.659	0.776
6	2	POR	QUEIROS, Joaquim / FERNANDES, Rui	1:31.559	1.676
7	8	SWE	OSCARSSON, Markus / MALMSTEN, Staffan	1:31.811	1.928
8	9	BEL	TABOUREAU, David / VENDEWEYER, Mark	1:34.807	4.924
9	1	UZB	ANOSOV, Vitaliy / YURABAYEV, Akram	1:35.543	5.660

FINAL

Rnk	Ln	Ctry	Names	Time	Time behind	
1	4	GER	BLUHM, Kay / GUTSCHE, Torsten	1:28.697	0	G
2	5	ITA	BONOMI, Beniamino / SCARPA, Daniele	1:28.729	0.032	S
3	6	AUS	TRIM, Andrew / COLLINS, Daniel	1:29.409	0.712	B
4	3	RUS	TISHCHENKO, Anatoliy / GOROBIY, Oleg	1:29.677	0.980	
5	2	POL	FREIMUT, Maciej / WYSOCKI, Adam	1:29.937	1.240	
6	8	HUN	GYULAY, Zsolt / BARTFAI, Krisztian	1:30.001	1.304	
7	1	ROM	STOIAN, Daniel / SERBAN, Romica	1:30.053	1.356	
8	7	BUL	DUSHEV, Andrian / KAZANOV, Milko	1:30.513	1.816	
9	9	DEN	NIELSEN, Thor / STAAL, Jesper	1:30.753	2.056	

Canoe/Kayak—Sprint / *Canoë/Kayak—Sprint*

500 m Kayak Double, Women / *500 m kayak double, Dames*

HEAT 1

Rnk	Ln	Ctry	Names	Time	Time behind
1	6	GER	FISCHER, Birgit / PORTWICH, Ramona	1:45.504	0
2	4	SUI	HARALAMOW, Ingrid / BAUMER, Daniela	1:45.764	0.260
3	2	ROM	TOMA, Sanda / IORDACHE, Viorica	1:47.200	1.696
4	7	UKR	BALABANOVA, Anya / YURCHENKO, Kateryna	1:48.436	2.932
5	1	BUL	PINDZHEVA, Bonka / ZAFIROVA, Neli	1:48.652	3.148
6	5	UZB	LEVINA, Tatyana / ISAKOVA, Inna	1:50.544	5.040
7	3	MEX	ROJAS, Sandra / HERNANDEZ, Renata	1:51.252	5.748

HEAT 2

Rnk	Ln	Ctry	Names	Time	Time behind
1	3	SWE	ANDERSSON, Agneta / GUNNARSSON, Susanne	1:43.022	0
2	4	ESP	ARAMBURU, Izaskun / MANCHON, Beatriz	1:44.038	1.016
3	5	POL	DYLEWSKA-SWIATOWIAK, Izabela / URBANCZYK, Elzbieta	1:44.906	1.884
4	6	RUS	GULIY, Natalya / KOSORUKOVA, Larisa	1:47.186	4.164
5	1	USA	HEMMENS, Deanne / ROUSSET, Lia	1:47.914	4.892
6	2	CZE	JOBANKOVA, Pavlina / JANACKOVA, Jitka	1:51.346	8.324
7	7	GBR	GILBY, Helen / THOROGOOD, Alison	1:51.386	8.364

HEAT 3

Rnk	Ln	Ctry	Names	Time	Time behind
1	2	HUN	KOBAN, Rita / MEDNYANSZKI, Szilvia	1:43.313	0
2	6	AUS	WOOD, Anna / BORCHERT, Katrin	1:43.633	0.320
3	3	CAN	GIBEAU, Marie-Josee / KENNEDY, Corrina	1:44.685	1.372
4	4	FRA	KLEINHENZ, Sabine / LOYAU, Severine	1:46.989	3.676
5	1	CHN	NING, Menghua / HU, Dongmei	1:50.721	7.408
6	5	JPN	AKAGI, Chieko / WATANABE, Asako	1:52.109	8.796

REPECHAGE 1

Rnk	Ln	Ctry	Names	Time	Time behind
1	4	FRA	KLEINHENZ, Sabine / LOYAU, Severine	1:51.417	0
2	6	USA	HEMMENS, Deanne / ROUSSET, Lia	1:52.669	1.252
3	5	UKR	BALABANOVA, Anya / YURCHENKO, Kateryna	1:54.373	2.956
4	3	CZE	JOBANKOVA, Pavlina / JANACKOVA, Jitka	1:55.377	3.960
5	7	MEX	ROJAS, Sandra / HERNANDEZ, Renata	1:55.801	4.384

REPECHAGE 2

Rnk	Ln	Ctry	Names	Time	Time behind
1	5	RUS	GULIY, Natalya / KOSORUKOVA, Larisa	1:52.520	0
2	6	CHN	NING, Menghua / HU, Dongmei	1:53.544	1.024
3	4	BUL	PINDZHEVA, Bonka / ZAFIROVA, Neli	1:53.644	1.124
4	8	GBR	GILBY, Helen / THOROGOOD, Alison	1:55.088	2.568
5	3	UZB	LEVINA, Tatyana / ISAKOVA, Inna	1:56.896	4.376
6	7	JPN	AKAGI, Chieko / WATANABE, Asako	1:57.944	5.424

SEMIFINAL 1

Rnk	Ln	Ctry	Names	Time	Time behind
1	4	HUN	KOBAN, Rita / MEDNYANSZKI, Szilvia	1:42.789	0
2	5	GER	FISCHER, Birgit / PORTWICH, Ramona	1:43.069	0.280
3	6	ESP	ARAMBURU, Izaskun / MANCHON, Beatriz	1:44.433	1.644
4	7	CAN	GIBEAU, Marie-Josee / KENNEDY, Corrina	1:44.461	1.672
5	8	FRA	KLEINHENZ, Sabine / LOYAU, Severine	1:46.589	3.800
6	3	ROM	TOMA, Sanda / IORDACHE, Viorica	1:47.061	4.272
7	9	UKR	BALABANOVA, Anya / YURCHENKO, Kateryna	1:48.857	6.068
8	2	CHN	NING, Menghua / HU, Dongmei	1:49.189	6.400
9	1	GBR	GILBY, Helen / THOROGOOD, Alison	1:49.849	7.060

SEMIFINAL 2

Rnk	Ln	Ctry	Names	Time	Time behind
1	5	SWE	ANDERSSON, Agneta / GUNNARSSON, Susanne	1:43.521	0
2	6	AUS	WOOD, Anna / BORCHERT, Katrin	1:43.729	0.208
3	7	POL	DYLEWSKA-SWIATOWIAK, Izabela / URBANCZYK, Elzbieta	1:45.190	1.669
4	3	RUS	GULIY, Natalya / KOSORUKOVA, Larisa	1:45.505	1.984
5	4	SUI	HARALAMOW, Ingrid / BAUMER, Daniela	1:46.629	3.108
6	2	BUL	PINDZHEVA, Bonka / ZAFIROVA, Neli	1:48.313	4.792
7	1	CZE	JOBANKOVA, Pavlina / JANACKOVA, Jitka	1:49.125	5.604
8	8	USA	HEMMENS, Deanne / ROUSSET, Lia	1:49.465	5.944
9	9	MEX	ROJAS, Sandra / HERNANDEZ, Renata	1:52.053	8.532

FINAL

Rnk	Ln	Ctry	Names	Time	Time behind	
1	4	SWE	ANDERSSON, Agneta / GUNNARSSON, Susanne	1:39.329	0	G
2	6	GER	FISCHER, Birgit / PORTWICH, Ramona	1:39.689	0.360	S
3	3	AUS	WOOD, Anna / BORCHERT, Katrin	1:40.641	1.312	B
4	5	HUN	KOBAN, Rita / MEDNYANSZKI, Szilvia	1:40.893	1.564	
5	8	CAN	GIBEAU, Marie-Josee / KENNEDY, Corrina	1:41.313	1.984	
6	7	ESP	ARAMBURU, Izaskun / MANCHON, Beatriz	1:42.621	3.292	
7	2	POL	DYLEWSKA-SWIATOWIAK, Izabela / URBANCZYK, Elzbieta	1:42.753	3.424	
8	1	RUS	GULIY, Natalya / KOSORUKOVA, Larisa	1:43.237	3.908	
9	9	FRA	KLEINHENZ, Sabine / LOYAU, Severine	1:43.449	4.120	

Canoe/Kayak—Sprint / *Canoë/Kayak—Sprint*

500 m Kayak Fours, Women / *500 m kayak à quatre, Dames*

HEAT 1

Rnk	Ln	Ctry	Names	Time	Time behind
1	6	CHN	XIAN, Bangdi / GAO, Beibei / DONG, Ying / ZHANG, Qin	1:40.045	0
2	1	SUI	HARALAMOW, Ingrid / BAUMER, Daniela / EICHENBERGER, Sabine / MUELLER, Garbiela	1:40.197	0.152
3	3	AUS	OATES, Shelley / NOSSITER, Yanda / LEHMANN, Lynda / HUNTER, Natalie	1:41.185	1.140
4	5	ROM	IORDACHE, Viorica / BENE, Mihaela / TOMA, Sanda / IONITA, Raluca	1:41.685	1.640

HEAT 1 - *continued*

Rnk	Ln	Ctry	Names	Time	Time behind
5	7	HUN	MEDNYANSZKI, Szilvia / DONUSZ, Eva / MESZAROS, Erika / CZIGANY, Kinga	1:42.821	2.776
6	2	UKR	BALABANOVA, Anya / FIKLISOVA, Natalya / TEKLYAN, Tetyana / YURCHENKO, Kateryna	1:43.381	3.336
7	4	UZB	LEVINA, Tatyana / LEBEDYEVA, Yelena / ISAKOVA, Inna / LYALINA, Irina	1:45.905	5.860
8	8	JPN	MARUYAMA, Sayuri / MUTO, Keiko / WATANABE, Asako / NISHI, Natsuki	1:49.505	9.460

500 m Kayak Fours, Women / *500 m kayak à quatre, Dames*

HEAT 2

Rnk	Ln	Ctry	Names	Time	Time behind
1	6	GER	FISCHER, Birgit / SCHUCK, Anett / PORTWICH, Ramona / MUCKE, Manuela	1:37.895	0
2	8	SWE	ROSENQVIST, Susanne / OLSSON, Anna / ANDERSSON, Agneta / ERICSSON, Ingela	1:39.363	1.468
3	7	CAN	GIBEAU, Marie-Josee / HERST, Alison / KENNEDY, Corrina / MacASKILL, Klari	1:39.691	1.796
4	2	ESP	ARAMBURU, Izaskun / MANCHON, Beatriz / PENAS, Ana Maria / SANCHEZ, Belen	1:39.863	1.968

HEAT 2 - continued

Rnk	Ln	Ctry	Names	Time	Time behind
5	1	RUS	TISHCHENKO, Olga / KOSORUKOVA, Larisa / GULIY, Natalya / TISHCHENKO, Tatyana	1:41.695	3.800
6	5	USA	HEMMENS, Deanne / ROUSSET, Lia / HARBOLD, Alexandra / VAN HENGEL, Drusilla	1:43.311	5.416
7	3	CZE	HLUCHA, Katerina / JANACKOVA, Jitka / PERGNEROVA, Milena / HEKOVA, Katerina	1:44.707	6.812
8	4	MEX	DURON, Erika / HERNANDEZ, Renata / ROJAS, Sandra / REZA, Itzel	1:45.215	7.320

SEMIFINAL 1

Rnk	Ln	Ctry	Names	Time	Time behind
1	4	CAN	GIBEAU, Marie-Josee / HERST, Alison / KENNEDY, Corrina / MacASKILL, Klari	1:38.712	0
2	5	RUS	TISHCHENKO, Olga / KOSORUKOVA, Larisa / GULIY, Natalya / TISHCHENKO, Tatyana	1:39.764	1.052
3	3	ROM	IORDACHE, Viorica / BENE, Mihaela / TOMA, Sanda / IONITA, Raluca	1:40.088	1.376

SEMIFINAL 1 - continued

Rnk	Ln	Ctry	Names	Time	Time behind
4	2	UKR	BALABANOVA, Anya / FIKLISOVA, Natalya / TEKLYAN, Tetyana / YURCHENKO, Kateryna	1:40.092	1.380
5	6	CZE	HLUCHA, Katerina / JANACKOVA, Jitka / PERGNEROVA, Milena / HEKOVA, Katerina	1:42.216	3.504
6	1	JPN	MARUYAMA, Sayuri / MUTO, Keiko / WATANABE, Asako / NISHI, Natsuki	1:45.996	7.284

SEMIFINAL 2

Rnk	Ln	Ctry	Names	Time	Time behind
1	5	HUN	MEDNYANSZKI, Szilvia / DONUSZ, Eva / MESZAROS, Erika / CZIGANY, Kinga	1:37.145	0
2	3	ESP	ARAMBURU, Izaskun / MANCHON, Beatriz / PENAS, Ana Maria / SANCHEZ, Belen	1:37.365	0.220
3	4	AUS	OATES, Shelley / NOSSITER, Yanda / LEHMANN, Lynda / HUNTER, Natalie	1:37.905	0.760

SEMIFINAL 2 - continued

Rnk	Ln	Ctry	Names	Time	Time behind
4	2	USA	HEMMENS, Deanne / ROUSSET, Lia / HARBOLD, Alexandra / VAN HENGEL, Drusilla	1:40.045	2.900
5	6	UZB	LEVINA, Tatyana / LEBEDYEVA, Yelena / ISAKOVA, Inna / LYALINA, Irina	1:40.893	3.748
6	1	MEX	DURON, Erika / HERNANDEZ, Renata / ROJAS, Sandra / REZA, Itzel	1:42.157	5.012

FINAL

Rnk	Ln	Ctry	Names	Time	Time behind	
1	4	GER	FISCHER, Birgit / SCHUCK, Anett / PORTWICH, Ramona / MUCKE, Manuela	1:31.077	0	G
2	6	SUI	HARALAMOW, Ingrid / BAUMER, Daniela / EICHENBERGER, Sabine / MUELLER, Garbiela	1:32.701	1.624	S
3	3	SWE	ROSENQVIST, Susanne / OLSSON, Anna / ANDERSSON, Agneta / ERICSSON, Ingela	1:32.917	1.840	B
4	5	CHN	XIAN, Bangdi / GAO, Beibei / DONG, Ying / ZHANG, Qin	1:33.089	2.012	
5	7	CAN	GIBEAU, Marie-Josee / HERST, Alison / KENNEDY, Corrina / MacASKILL, Klari	1:33.093	2.016	

FINAL - continued

Rnk	Ln	Ctry	Names	Time	Time behind
6	1	ESP	ARAMBURU, Izaskun / MANCHON, Beatriz / PENAS, Ana Maria / SANCHEZ, Belen	1:33.577	2.500
7	8	RUS	TISHCHENKO, Olga / KOSORUKOVA, Larisa / GULIY, Natalya / TISHCHENKO, Tatyana	1:34.345	3.268
8	9	AUS	OATES, Shelley / NOSSITER, Yanda / LEHMANN, Lynda / HUNTER, Natalie	1:34.673	3.596
9	2	HUN	MEDNYANSZKI, Szilvia / DONUSZ, Eva / MESZAROS, Erika / CZIGANY, Kinga	1:34.693	3.616

Canoe/Kayak—Sprint / *Canoë/Kayak—Sprint*
1,000 m Kayak Single, Men / *1 000 m kayak simple, Messieurs*

HEAT 1

Rnk	Ln	Name	Ctry	Time	Time behind
1	8	KOLEHMAINEN, Mikko	FIN	3:48.075	0
2	4	GAJEWSKI, Andrzej	POL	3:49.507	1.432
3	7	SZTRUM, Abelardo	ARG	3:50.547	2.472
4	1	GARCIA, Jose	POR	3:56.059	7.984
5	5	OLLA, Vincent	FRA	3:58.075	10.000
6	2	SAFARYAN, Andrey	KAZ	4:00.599	12.524
7	9	GERVAIS, Erik	CAN	4:01.707	13.632
8	3	KIREYEV, Ivan	UZB	4:05.299	17.224

HEAT 2

Rnk	Ln	Name	Ctry	Time	Time behind
1	2	HOLMANN, Knut	NOR	3:45.192	0
2	1	CALDERON, Agustin	ESP	3:45.484	0.292
3	3	POPESCU, Marin	ROM	3:47.968	2.776
4	5	ERBAN, Robert	SVK	3:48.956	3.764
5	6	CUATTRIN, Sebastian	BRA	3:49.308	4.116
6	4	HARBOLD, Mike	USA	3:58.760	13.568
7	8	HELDE, Hain	EST	3:59.136	13.944

HEAT 3

Rnk	Ln	Name	Ctry	Time	Time behind
1	1	BONOMI, Beniamino	ITA	3:43.520	0
2	4	ROBINSON, Clint	AUS	3:44.768	1.248
3	5	LIWOWSKI, Lutz	GER	3:44.776	1.256
4	6	LAWLER, Ivan	GBR	3:51.580	8.060
5	3	TERESHCHENKO, Vladyslav	UKR	3:51.772	8.252
6	8	KAMMERER, Zoltan	HUN	4:02.724	19.204
7	2	KRANTZ, Tom	SWE	4:03.324	19.804
8	7	EDOUKOU, Miezan	CIV	4:31.680	48.160

1,000 m Kayak Single, Men / *1 000 m kayak simple, Messieurs*

REPECHAGE 1					
Rnk	Ln	Name	Ctry	Time	Time behind
1	6	CUATTRIN, Sebastian	BRA	4:02.527	0
2	4	OLLA, Vincent	FRA	4:04.147	1.620
3	3	KAMMERER, Zoltan	HUN	4:05.859	3.332
4	5	LAWLER, Ivan	GBR	4:06.555	4.028
5	2	HELDE, Hain	EST	4:08.375	5.848
6	7	GERVAIS, Erik	CAN	4:08.743	6.216
7	8	EDOUKOU, Miezan	CIV	4:44.155	41.628

REPECHAGE 2					
Rnk	Ln	Name	Ctry	Time	Time behind
1	4	ERBAN, Robert	SVK	4:01.917	0
2	7	HARBOLD, Mike	USA	4:05.225	3.308
3	5	GARCIA, Jose	POR	4:05.677	3.760
4	6	TERESHCHENKO, Vladyslav	UKR	4:08.681	6.764
5	2	KRANTZ, Tom	SWE	4:10.057	8.140
6	3	SAFARYAN, Andrey	KAZ	4:10.633	8.716
7	8	KIREYEV, Ivan	UZB	4:12.105	10.188

SEMIFINAL 1					
Rnk	Ln	Name	Ctry	Time	Time behind
1	4	BONOMI, Beniamino	ITA	3:40.831	0
2	5	HOLMANN, Knut	NOR	3:41.635	0.804
3	7	LIWOWSKI, Lutz	GER	3:42.567	1.736
4	6	GAJEWSKI, Andrzej	POL	3:43.399	2.568
5	8	CUATTRIN, Sebastian	BRA	3:44.443	3.612
6	3	SZTRUM, Abelardo	ARG	3:44.587	3.756
7	2	HARBOLD, Mike	USA	3:44.663	3.832
8	9	GARCIA, Jose	POR	3:48.859	8.028
9	1	LAWLER, Ivan	GBR	3:55.583	14.752

SEMIFINAL 2					
Rnk	Ln	Name	Ctry	Time	Time behind
1	6	ROBINSON, Clint	AUS	3:43.657	0
2	7	POPESCU, Marin	ROM	3:44.249	0.592
3	4	CALDERON, Agustin	ESP	3:44.777	1.120
4	5	KOLEHMAINEN, Mikko	FIN	3:45.613	1.956
5	3	ERBAN, Robert	SVK	3:46.633	2.976
6	9	HELDE, Hain	EST	3:47.237	3.580
7	2	KAMMERER, Zoltan	HUN	3:49.589	5.932
8	8	OLLA, Vincent	FRA	3:51.537	7.880
9	1	TERESHCHENKO, Vladyslav	UKR	3:56.649	12.992

FINAL						
Rnk	Ln	Name	Ctry	Time	Time behind	
1	6	HOLMANN, Knut	NOR	3:25.785	0	G
2	5	BONOMI, Beniamino	ITA	3:27.073	1.288	S
3	4	ROBINSON, Clint	AUS	3:29.713	3.928	B
4	7	LIWOWSKI, Lutz	GER	3:30.025	4.240	
5	2	CALDERON, Agustin	ESP	3:31.397	5.612	
6	8	GAJEWSKI, Andrzej	POL	3:32.521	6.736	
7	3	POPESCU, Marin	ROM	3:34.549	8.764	
8	9	CUATTRIN, Sebastian	BRA	3:34.669	8.884	
9	1	KOLEHMAINEN, Mikko	FIN	3:35.841	10.056	

Canoe/Kayak—Sprint / *Canoë/Kayak — Sprint*

1,000 m Kayak Double, Men / *1 000 m kayak double, Messieurs*

HEAT 1					
Rnk	Ln	Ctry	Names	Time	Time behind
1	6	ITA	ROSSI, Antonio / SCARPA, Daniele	3:33.786	0
2	8	POL	KOTOWICZ, Grzegorz / BIALKOWSKI, Dariusz	3:37.986	4.200
3	9	BUL	DUSHEV, Andrian / KAZANOV, Milko	3:39.914	6.128
4	7	CZE	KUCERA, Rene / HRUSKA, Petr	3:42.882	9.096
5	2	ESP	ROMAN, Juan / SANCHEZ, Juan Manuel	3:43.970	10.184
6	1	SVK	KADNAR, Juraj / SZABO, Attila	3:49.026	15.240
7	3	KAZ	YEGOROV, Yevgeniy / SKRYPNIK, Sergey	3:50.394	16.608
8	5	CHN	XU, Haifeng / WU, Yubiao	3:50.978	17.192
9	4	POR	QUEIROS, Joaquim / FERNANDES, Rui	3:59.390	25.604

HEAT 2					
Rnk	Ln	Ctry	Names	Time	Time behind
1	5	GER	BLUHM, Kay / GUTSCHE, Torsten	3:39.388	0
2	8	DEN	NIELSEN, Thor / STAAL, Jesper	3:41.640	2.252
3	6	GBR	BOURNE, Grayson / DARBY-DOWMAN, Paul	3:43.384	3.996
4	4	USA	NEWTON, Peter / MOONEY, John	3:46.852	7.464
5	7	ARG	CORREA, Javier / SZTRUM, Abelardo	3:49.864	10.476
6	3	IRL	MAWER, Gary / MALONEY, Conor	4:03.432	24.044
7	1	KGZ	MITKOVETS, Andrey / ULIACHENKO, Yury	4:08.916	29.528

HEAT 3					
Rnk	Ln	Ctry	Names	Time	Time behind
1	5	AUS	SCOTT, Peter / LEURY, Grant	3:40.114	0
2	4	FRA	LUBAC, Pierre / LANCEREAU, Patrick	3:40.198	0.084
3	7	HUN	HEGEDUS, Robert / ALMASI, Peter	3:40.754	0.640
4	3	SWE	MALMSTEN, Staffan / OSCARSSON, Markus	3:44.174	4.060
5	6	BEL	TABOUREAU, David / VENDEWEYER, Mark	3:44.778	4.664
6	2	RUS	IVANIK, Aleksandr / TISIN, Andrey	3:46.558	6.444
7	8	LTU	KUPCINSKAS, Vidas / MIZERAS, Vaidas	3:51.842	11.728
8	1	UZB	ALIMDYANOV, Vladimir / ISLAMOV, Rafael	4:01.522	21.408

REPECHAGE 1					
Rnk	Ln	Ctry	Names	Time	Time behind
1	6	ARG	CORREA, Javier / SZTRUM, Abelardo	3:34.244	0
2	4	SWE	MALMSTEN, Staffan / OSCARSSON, Markus	3:34.480	0.236
3	5	CZE	KUCERA, Rene / HRUSKA, Petr	3:35.216	0.972
4	2	LTU	KUPCINSKAS, Vidas / MIZERAS, Vaidas	3:38.428	4.184
5	7	KAZ	YEGOROV, Yevgeniy / SKRYPNIK, Sergey	3:40.040	5.796
6	3	IRL	MAWER, Gary / MALONEY, Conor	3:40.656	6.412
7	8	CHN	XU, Haifeng / WU, Yubiao	3:41.196	6.952
8	1	UZB	ALIMDYANOV, Vladimir / ISLAMOV, Rafael	3:43.320	9.076

REPECHAGE 2					
Rnk	Ln	Ctry	Names	Time	Time behind
1	5	USA	NEWTON, Peter / MOONEY, John	3:34.424	0
2	3	SVK	KADNAR, Juraj / SZABO, Attila	3:34.436	0.012
3	7	RUS	IVANIK, Aleksandr / TISIN, Andrey	3:35.200	0.776
4	4	ESP	ROMAN, Juan / SANCHEZ, Juan Manuel	3:36.264	1.840
5	9	POR	QUEIROS, Joaquim / FERNANDES, Rui	3:36.488	2.064
6	6	BEL	TABOUREAU, David / VENDEWEYER, Mark	3:36.976	2.552
7	8	KGZ	MITKOVETS, Andrey / ULIACHENKO, Yury	3:44.200	9.776

SEMIFINAL 1					
Rnk	Ln	Ctry	Names	Time	Time behind
1	5	ITA	ROSSI, Antonio / SCARPA, Daniele	3:16.848	0
2	6	DEN	NIELSEN, Thor / STAAL, Jesper	3:17.420	0.572
3	3	BUL	DUSHEV, Andrian / KAZANOV, Milko	3:18.480	1.632
4	7	HUN	HEGEDUS, Robert / ALMASI, Peter	3:18.524	1.676
5	4	AUS	SCOTT, Peter / LEURY, Grant	3:19.056	2.208
6	2	SVK	KADNAR, Juraj / SZABO, Attila	3:20.904	4.056
7	9	CZE	KUCERA, Rene / HRUSKA, Petr	3:21.384	4.536
8	1	ESP	ROMAN, Juan / SANCHEZ, Juan Manuel	3:24.032	7.184
9	8	ARG	CORREA, Javier / SZTRUM, Abelardo	3:28.128	11.280

1,000 m Kayak Double, Men / *1 000 m kayak double, Messieurs*

SEMIFINAL 2						
Rnk	Ln	Ctry	Names	Time	Time behind	
1	4	POL	KOTOWICZ, Grzegorz / BIALKOWSKI, Dariusz	3:18.026	0	
2	6	FRA	LUBAC, Pierre / LANCEREAU, Patrick	3:18.722	0.696	
3	5	GER	BLUHM, Kay / GUTSCHE, Torsten	3:19.394	1.368	
4	8	SWE	MALMSTEN, Staffan / OSCARSSON, Markus	3:19.606	1.580	
5	3	USA	NEWTON, Peter / MOONEY, John	3:19.834	1.808	
6	9	POR	QUEIROS, Joaquim / FERNANDES, Rui	3:22.270	4.244	
7	2	RUS	IVANIK, Aleksandr / TISIN, Andrey	3:22.306	4.280	
8	1	LTU	KUPCINSKAS, Vidas / MIZERAS, Vaidas	3:24.462	6.436	
9	7	GBR	BOURNE, Grayson / DARBY-DOWMAN, Paul	3:25.346	7.320	

FINAL						
Rnk	Ln	Ctry	Names	Time	Time behind	
1	5	ITA	ROSSI, Antonio / SCARPA, Daniele	3:09.190	0	G
2	2	GER	BLUHM, Kay / GUTSCHE, Torsten	3:10.518	1.328	S
3	7	BUL	DUSHEV, Andrian / KAZANOV, Milko	3:11.206	2.016	B
4	4	POL	KOTOWICZ, Grzegorz / BIALKOWSKI, Dariusz	3:11.262	2.072	
5	3	FRA	LUBAC, Pierre / LANCEREAU, Patrick	3:11.402	2.212	
6	6	DEN	NIELSEN, Thor / STAAL, Jesper	3:12.054	2.864	
7	9	AUS	SCOTT, Peter / LEURY, Grant	3:13.054	3.864	
8	1	SWE	MALMSTEN, Staffan / OSCARSSON, Markus	3:14.182	4.992	
9	8	HUN	HEGEDUS, Robert / ALMASI, Peter	3:14.282	5.092	

Canoe/Kayak—Sprint / *Canoë/Kayak—Sprint*
1,000 m Kayak Fours, Men / *1 000 m kayak à quatre, Messieurs*

HEAT 1						
Rnk	Ln	Ctry	Names	Time	Time behind	
1	1	GER	REINECK, Thomas / ZABEL, Mark / HOFMAN, Detlef / WINTER, Olaf	3:07.908	0	
2	5	RUS	TISHCHENKO, Anatoliy / GOROBIY, Oleg / VERLIN, Sergey / TSYBULNIKOV, Georgiy	3:11.128	3.220	
3	8	AUS	WALKER, Jim / MORTON, Brian / LYNCH, Paul / ANDERSSON, Ramon	3:11.752	3.844	
4	6	ESP	VICENTE, Gregorio / GARCIA, Miguel / GONZALEZ, Jovino / MERCHAN, Emilio	3:14.224	6.316	

HEAT 1 - *continued*						
Rnk	Ln	Ctry	Names	Time	Time behind	
5	7	CAN	APOSTOL, Mihai / CRICHLOW, Renn / GILES, Peter / JEWELL, Liam	3:15.208	7.300	
6	2	ITA	LUPETTI, Enrico / COVI, Andrea / LUSSIGNOLI, Ivano / NEGRI, Luca	3:17.144	9.236	
7	3	CZE	LESTINA, Karel / MRAZ, Pavel / POLIVKA, Jiri / OTAHAL, Martin	3:19.868	11.960	
8	4	USA	HAMILTON, Mark / BADER, Curt / BOCCARA, Philippe / MEIDL, Cliff	3:23.352	15.444	

HEAT 2						
Rnk	Ln	Ctry	Names	Time	Time behind	
1	8	HUN	CSIPES, Ferenc / HORVATH, Gabor / ADROVICZ, Attila / RAJNA, Andras	3:07.517	0	
2	5	POL	MARKIEWICZ, Piotr / KALETA, Grzegorz / WITKOWSKI, Marek / WYSOCKI, Adam	3:10.625	3.108	
3	2	BUL	YORDANOV, Nikolay / KARADZHOV, Petar / MERKOV, Petar / CHOYKOV, Georgi	3:13.165	5.648	
4	3	SWE	OSCARSSON, Mattias / NILSSON, Henrik / MADSEN, Paw / FAGER, Jonas	3:13.809	6.292	

HEAT 2 - *continued*						
Rnk	Ln	Ctry	Names	Time	Time behind	
5	4	KAZ	TORLOPOV, Dmitriy / SAFARYAN, Andrey / SKRYPNIK, Sergey / GATIYATULLIN, Ilfat	3:15.493	7.976	
6	7	UKR	SLIVINSKIYY, Oleksey / KULIDA, Vyacheslav / PETROV, Andriy / BORZUKOV, Andriy	3:16.297	8.780	
7	1	NOR	IVARSEN, Morten / NAESS, Mattis / SELVIK, Tom / ROANDER, Thomas	3:17.021	9.504	
8	6	UZB	YASHIN, Konstantin / TYURIN, Anatoliy / KAZANTSEV, Vladimir / SHILIN, Andrey	3:27.133	19.616	

SEMIFINAL 1						
Rnk	Ln	Ctry	Names	Time	Time behind	
1	3	ESP	VICENTE, Gregorio / GARCIA, Miguel / GONZALEZ, Jovino / MERCHAN, Emilio	3:00.799	0	
2	5	CAN	APOSTOL, Mihai / CRICHLOW, Renn / GILES, Peter / JEWELL, Liam	3:01.307	0.508	
3	4	BUL	YORDANOV, Nikolay / KARADZHOV, Petar / MERKOV, Petar / CHOYKOV, Georgi	3:01.427	0.628	

SEMIFINAL 1 - *continued*						
Rnk	Ln	Ctry	Names	Time	Time behind	
4	2	UKR	SLIVINSKIYY, Oleksey / KULIDA, Vyacheslav / PETROV, Andriy / BORZUKOV, Andriy	3:05.643	4.844	
5	6	CZE	LESTINA, Karel / MRAZ, Pavel / POLIVKA, Jiri / OTAHAL, Martin	3:06.611	5.812	
6	1	USA	HAMILTON, Mark / BADER, Curt / BOCCARA, Philippe / MEIDL, Cliff	3:06.855	6.056	

SEMIFINAL 2						
Rnk	Ln	Ctry	Names	Time	Time behind	
1	4	AUS	WALKER, Jim / MORTON, Brian / LYNCH, Paul / ANDERSSON, Ramon	3:01.806	0	
2	3	SWE	OSCARSSON, Mattias / NILSSON, Henrik / MADSEN, Paw / FAGER, Jonas	3:02.202	0.396	
3	2	ITA	LUPETTI, Enrico / COVI, Andrea / LUSSIGNOLI, Ivano / NEGRI, Luca	3:03.218	1.412	

SEMIFINAL 2 - *continued*						
Rnk	Ln	Ctry	Names	Time	Time behind	
4	6	NOR	IVARSEN, Morten / NAESS, Mattis / SELVIK, Tom / ROANDER, Thomas	3:03.870	2.064	
5	5	KAZ	TORLOPOV, Dmitriy / SAFARYAN, Andrey / SKRYPNIK, Sergey / GATIYATULLIN, Ilfat	3:06.850	5.044	
6	1	UZB	YASHIN, Konstantin / TYURIN, Anatoliy / KAZANTSEV, Vladimir / SHILIN, Andrey	3:11.146	9.340	

FINAL						
Rnk	Ln	Ctry	Names	Time	Time behind	
1	5	GER	REINECK, Thomas / ZABEL, Mark / HOFMAN, Detlef / WINTER, Olaf	2:51.528	0	G
2	4	HUN	CSIPES, Ferenc / HORVATH, Gabor / ADROVICZ, Attila / RAJNA, Andras	2:53.184	1.656	S
3	6	RUS	TISHCHENKO, Anatoliy / GOROBIY, Oleg / VERLIN, Sergey / TSYBULNIKOV, Georgiy	2:53.996	2.468	B
4	3	POL	MARKIEWICZ, Piotr / KALETA, Grzegorz / WITKOWSKI, Marek / WYSOCKI, Adam	2:54.772	3.244	
5	7	ESP	VICENTE, Gregorio / GARCIA, Miguel / GONZALEZ, Jovino / MERCHAN, Emilio	2:55.884	4.356	

FINAL - *continued*						
Rnk	Ln	Ctry	Names	Time	Time behind	
6	1	SWE	OSCARSSON, Mattias / NILSSON, Henrik / MADSEN, Paw / FAGER, Jonas	2:55.908	4.380	
7	8	CAN	APOSTOL, Mihai / CRICHLOW, Renn / GILES, Peter / JEWELL, Liam	2:56.664	5.136	
8	9	BUL	YORDANOV, Nikolay / KARADZHOV, Petar / MERKOV, Petar / CHOYKOV, Georgi	2:56.696	5.168	
9	2	AUS	WALKER, Jim / MORTON, Brian / LYNCH, Paul / ANDERSSON, Ramon	2:57.560	6.032	

Canoe/Kayak—Sprint / Canoë/Kayak—Sprint
500 m Canoe Single, Men / 500 m canoë simple, Messieurs

HEAT 1

Rnk	Ln	Name	Ctry	Time	Time behind
1	2	DOKTOR, Martin	CZE	1:52.907	0
2	8	KNAZOVICKY, Slavomir	SVK	1:52.971	0.064
3	9	GILES, Steve	CAN	1:53.803	0.896
4	3	SLIVINSKIYY, Mykhaylo	UKR	1:54.283	1.376
5	6	BUKHALOV, Nikolay	BUL	1:54.727	1.820
6	5	NEGODYAYEV, Konstantin	KAZ	1:55.859	2.952
7	7	TERRELL, Jim	USA	1:57.295	4.388
8	4	CRESPO, Jose Manuel	ESP	1:57.915	5.008
9	1	PLATCHINTA, Andrei	MDA	1:59.423	6.516

HEAT 2

Rnk	Ln	Name	Ctry	Time	Time behind
1	1	ZERESKE, Thomas	GER	1:53.840	0
2	3	PULAI, Imre	HUN	1:54.244	0.404
3	2	LE LEUCH, Eric	FRA	1:54.544	0.704
4	4	FREDERIKSEN, Christian	DEN	1:55.056	1.216
5	6	HUIDU, Florin	ROM	1:58.140	4.300
6	7	FUNTAK, Drazen	CRO	2:00.076	6.236
7	8	PEREIRA, Silvestre	POR	2:01.576	7.736
8	5	ASTANIN, Yevgeniy	UZB	2:02.532	8.692

SEMIFINAL 1

Rnk	Ln		Name	Ctry	Time	Time behind
1	3	UKR	SLIVINSKIYY, Mykhaylo		1:52.093	0
2	2	KAZ	NEGODYAYEV, Konstantin		1:52.421	0.328
3	4	FRA	LE LEUCH, Eric		1:53.305	1.212
4	1	ESP	CRESPO, Jose Manuel		1:54.121	2.028
5	5	ROM	HUIDU, Florin		1:56.733	4.640
6	7	MDA	PLATCHINTA, Andrei		1:57.457	5.364
7	6	POR	PEREIRA, Silvestre		1:57.949	5.856

SEMIFINAL 2

Rnk	Ln	Name	Ctry	Time	Time behind
1	4	GILES, Steve	CAN	1:51.614	0
2	5	BUKHALOV, Nikolay	BUL	1:51.914	0.300
3	3	FREDERIKSEN, Christian	DEN	1:52.174	0.560
4	6	TERRELL, Jim	USA	1:54.086	2.472
5	2	FUNTAK, Drazen	CRO	1:58.570	6.956
6	1	ASTANIN, Yevgeniy	UZB	1:59.042	7.428

FINAL

Rnk	Ln	Name	Ctry	Time	Time behind	
1	5	DOKTOR, Martin	CZE	1:49.934	0	G
2	6	KNAZOVICKY, Slavomir	SVK	1:50.510	0.576	S
3	3	PULAI, Imre	HUN	1:50.758	0.824	B
4	7	SLIVINSKIYY, Mykhaylo	UKR	1:51.714	1.780	
5	4	ZERESKE, Thomas	GER	1:52.358	2.424	
6	9	FREDERIKSEN, Christian	DEN	1:52.846	2.912	
7	8	NEGODYAYEV, Konstantin	KAZ	1:53.158	3.224	
8	2	GILES, Steve	CAN	1:53.326	3.392	
	1	BUKHALOV, Nikolay	BUL	DQ		

Canoe/Kayak—Sprint / Canoë/Kayak—Sprint
500 m Canoe Double, Men / 500 m canoë double, Messieurs

HEAT 1

Rnk	Ln	Ctry	Names	Time	Time behind
1	6	HUN	KOLONICS, Gyorgy / HORVATH, Csaba	1:43.907	0
2	1	ESP	BEA, Jose Alfredo / SHELESTENKO, Oleg	1:45.635	1.728
3	4	RUS	KABANOV, Andrey / KONOVALOV, Pavel	1:46.307	2.400
4	7	CRO	FUNTAK, Drazen / SABJAN, Ivan	1:47.235	3.328
5	2	CAN	BUDAY, Attila / BUDAY, Tamas, Jr.	1:47.551	3.644
6	3	BLR	MASEYKOV, Aleksandr / DOVGALYONOK, Dmitriy	1:47.923	4.016
7	5	CZE	FUKSA, Petr / BEDNAR, Pavel	1:47.955	4.048

HEAT 2

Rnk	Ln	Ctry	Names	Time	Time behind
1	4	MDA	JURAVSCHI, Nikolai / RENEISCHI, Victor	1:44.477	0
2	2	GER	DITTMER, Andreas / KIRCHBACH, Gunar	1:45.145	0.668
3	6	BUL	MARINOV, Martin / STOYANOV, Blagovest	1:45.545	1.068
4	3	SVK	PALES, Peter / OROSZ, Csaba	1:45.893	1.416
5	1	KOR	JUN, Kwang-Rak / PARK, Chang-Kyu	1:47.453	2.976
6	7	POL	BARASZKIEWICZ, Pawel / KOBIERSKI, Marcin	1:48.357	3.880
7	5	UZB	SHAYSLAMOV, Vladimir / SHAYSLAMOV, Sergey	1:51.929	7.452

HEAT 3

Rnk	Ln	Ctry	Names	Time	Time behind
1	6	ROM	ANDRIEV, Gheorghe / OBREJA, Grigore	1:43.548	0
2	2	UKR	LYTVYNENKO, Oleksandr / IHRAYEV, Oleksiy	1:46.652	3.104
3	5	ITA	CANNONE, Domenico / MARMORINO, Antonio	1:46.996	3.448
4	3	GBR	TRAIN, Andrew / TRAIN, Stephen	1:47.892	4.344
5	4	KAZ	NURMAGANBETOV, Kaysar / SERGEYEV, Sergey	1:49.252	5.704

REPECHAGE 1

Rnk	Ln	Ctry	Names	Time	Time behind
1	4	CAN	BUDAY, Attila / BUDAY, Tamas, Jr.	1:49.820	0
2	5	GBR	TRAIN, Andrew / TRAIN, Stephen	1:50.476	0.656
3	7	CZE	FUKSA, Petr / BEDNAR, Pavel	1:50.480	0.660
4	6	KOR	JUN, Kwang-Rak / PARK, Chang-Kyu	1:50.776	0.956
5	3	UZB	SHAYSLAMOV, Vladimir / SHAYSLAMOV, Sergey	1:52.768	2.948

REPECHAGE 2

Rnk	Ln	Ctry	Names	Time	Time behind
1	3	BLR	MASEYKOV, Aleksandr / DOVGALYONOK, Dmitriy	1:47.837	0
2	4	SVK	PALES, Peter / OROSZ, Csaba	1:47.965	0.128
3	7	POL	BARASZKIEWICZ, Pawel / KOBIERSKI, Marcin	1:48.093	0.256
4	5	CRO	FUNTAK, Drazen / SABJAN, Ivan	1:50.473	2.636
5	6	KAZ	NURMAGANBETOV, Kaysar / SERGEYEV, Sergey	1:51.533	3.696

SEMIFINAL 1

Rnk	Ln	Ctry	Names	Time	Time behind
1	4	ROM	ANDRIEV, Gheorghe / OBREJA, Grigore	1:41.653	0
2	5	MDA	JURAVSCHI, Nikolai / RENEISCHI, Victor	1:42.029	0.376
3	6	ESP	BEA, Jose Alfredo / SHELESTENKO, Oleg	1:42.397	0.744
4	3	RUS	KABANOV, Andrey / KONOVALOV, Pavel	1:43.141	1.488
5	2	SVK	PALES, Peter / OROSZ, Csaba	1:43.757	2.104
6	8	CAN	BUDAY, Attila / BUDAY, Tamas, Jr.	1:44.213	2.560
7	1	KOR	JUN, Kwang-Rak / PARK, Chang-Kyu	1:44.453	2.800
8	9	POL	BARASZKIEWICZ, Pawel / KOBIERSKI, Marcin	1:44.793	3.140
9	7	ITA	CANNONE, Domenico / MARMORINO, Antonio	1:47.557	5.904

500 m Canoe Double, Men   /   *500 m canoë double, Messieurs*

<table>
<tr><td colspan="6">SEMIFINAL 2</td></tr>
<tr><td>Rnk</td><td>Ln</td><td>Ctry</td><td>Names</td><td>Time</td><td>Time behind</td></tr>
<tr><td>1</td><td>5</td><td>HUN</td><td>KOLONICS, Gyorgy / HORVATH, Csaba</td><td>1:42.186</td><td>0</td></tr>
<tr><td>2</td><td>4</td><td>GER</td><td>DITTMER, Andreas / KIRCHBACH, Gunar</td><td>1:43.650</td><td>1.464</td></tr>
<tr><td>3</td><td>3</td><td>BLR</td><td>MASEYKOV, Aleksandr / DOVGALYONOK, Dmitriy</td><td>1:43.938</td><td>1.752</td></tr>
<tr><td>4</td><td>7</td><td>BUL</td><td>MARINOV, Martin / STOYANOV, Blagovest</td><td>1:44.130</td><td>1.944</td></tr>
<tr><td>5</td><td>1</td><td>CRO</td><td>FUNTAK, Drazen / SABJAN, Ivan</td><td>1:44.770</td><td>2.584</td></tr>
<tr><td>6</td><td>2</td><td>CZE</td><td>FUKSA, Petr / BEDNAR, Pavel</td><td>1:44.902</td><td>2.716</td></tr>
<tr><td>7</td><td>8</td><td>GBR</td><td>TRAIN, Andrew / TRAIN, Stephen</td><td>1:45.638</td><td>3.452</td></tr>
<tr><td>8</td><td>9</td><td>KAZ</td><td>NURMAGANBETOV, Kaysar / SERGEYEV, Sergey</td><td>1:45.998</td><td>3.812</td></tr>
<tr><td>9</td><td>6</td><td>UKR</td><td>LYTVYNENKO, Oleksandr / IHRAYEV, Oleksiy</td><td>1:51.010</td><td>8.824</td></tr>
</table>

<table>
<tr><td colspan="7">FINAL</td></tr>
<tr><td>Rnk</td><td>Ln</td><td>Ctry</td><td>Names</td><td>Time</td><td>Time behind</td><td></td></tr>
<tr><td>1</td><td>4</td><td>HUN</td><td>KOLONICS, Gyorgy / HORVATH, Csaba</td><td>1:40.420</td><td>0</td><td>G</td></tr>
<tr><td>2</td><td>6</td><td>MDA</td><td>JURAVSCHI, Nikolai / RENEISCHI, Victor</td><td>1:40.456</td><td>0.036</td><td>S</td></tr>
<tr><td>3</td><td>5</td><td>ROM</td><td>ANDRIEV, Gheorghe / OBREJA, Grigore</td><td>1:41.336</td><td>0.916</td><td>B</td></tr>
<tr><td>4</td><td>3</td><td>GER</td><td>DITTMER, Andreas / KIRCHBACH, Gunar</td><td>1:41.760</td><td>1.340</td><td></td></tr>
<tr><td>5</td><td>1</td><td>BUL</td><td>MARINOV, Martin / STOYANOV, Blagovest</td><td>1:42.208</td><td>1.788</td><td></td></tr>
<tr><td>6</td><td>8</td><td>RUS</td><td>KABANOV, Andrey / KONOVALOV, Pavel</td><td>1:42.496</td><td>2.076</td><td></td></tr>
<tr><td>7</td><td>7</td><td>ESP</td><td>BEA, Jose Alfredo / SHELESTENKO, Oleg</td><td>1:43.572</td><td>3.152</td><td></td></tr>
<tr><td>8</td><td>9</td><td>SVK</td><td>PALES, Peter / OROSZ, Csaba</td><td>1:44.116</td><td>3.696</td><td></td></tr>
<tr><td>9</td><td>2</td><td>BLR</td><td>MASEYKOV, Aleksandr / DOVGALYONOK, Dmitriy</td><td>1:46.840</td><td>6.420</td><td></td></tr>
</table>

Canoe/Kayak—Sprint / *Canoë/Kayak—Sprint*
1,000 m Canoe Single, Men   /   *1 000 m canoë simple, Messieurs*

<table>
<tr><td colspan="6">HEAT 1</td></tr>
<tr><td>Rnk</td><td>Ln</td><td>Name</td><td>Ctry</td><td>Time</td><td>Time behind</td></tr>
<tr><td>1</td><td>8</td><td>DOKTOR, Martin</td><td>CZE</td><td>4:19.918</td><td>0</td></tr>
<tr><td>2</td><td>5</td><td>SCHULZE, Patrick</td><td>GER</td><td>4:21.114</td><td>1.196</td></tr>
<tr><td>3</td><td>6</td><td>KLEMENTJEVS, Ivan</td><td>LAT</td><td>4:24.678</td><td>4.760</td></tr>
<tr><td>4</td><td>4</td><td>PARTNOI, Victor</td><td>ROM</td><td>4:25.894</td><td>5.976</td></tr>
<tr><td>5</td><td>3</td><td>NIELSSON, Arne</td><td>DEN</td><td>4:30.258</td><td>10.340</td></tr>
<tr><td>6</td><td>7</td><td>SYLVOZ, Pascal</td><td>FRA</td><td>4:33.618</td><td>13.700</td></tr>
<tr><td>7</td><td>9</td><td>KUBICA, Jan</td><td>SVK</td><td>4:33.810</td><td>13.892</td></tr>
<tr><td>8</td><td>1</td><td>NEGODYAYEV, Konstantin</td><td>KAZ</td><td>4:40.842</td><td>20.924</td></tr>
<tr><td>9</td><td>2</td><td>BUKHALOV, Nikolay</td><td>BUL</td><td>4:43.562</td><td>23.644</td></tr>
</table>

<table>
<tr><td colspan="6">HEAT 2</td></tr>
<tr><td>Rnk</td><td>Ln</td><td>Name</td><td>Ctry</td><td>Time</td><td>Time behind</td></tr>
<tr><td>1</td><td>3</td><td>ZALA, Gyorgy</td><td>HUN</td><td>4:23.399</td><td>0</td></tr>
<tr><td>2</td><td>1</td><td>BUNDZ, Roman</td><td>UKR</td><td>4:26.555</td><td>3.156</td></tr>
<tr><td>3</td><td>9</td><td>SABJAN, Ivan</td><td>CRO</td><td>4:28.375</td><td>4.976</td></tr>
<tr><td>4</td><td>2</td><td>SALCUTAN, Vadim</td><td>MDA</td><td>4:32.095</td><td>8.696</td></tr>
<tr><td>5</td><td>4</td><td>CRESPO, Jose Manuel</td><td>ESP</td><td>4:34.071</td><td>10.672</td></tr>
<tr><td>6</td><td>8</td><td>MAXWELL, Gavin</td><td>CAN</td><td>4:36.971</td><td>13.572</td></tr>
<tr><td>7</td><td>5</td><td>ASTANIN, Yevgeniy</td><td>UZB</td><td>4:39.839</td><td>16.440</td></tr>
<tr><td>8</td><td>6</td><td>PEREIRA, Silvestre</td><td>POR</td><td>4:42.715</td><td>19.316</td></tr>
<tr><td>9</td><td>7</td><td>HARPER, Joseph</td><td>USA</td><td>4:45.467</td><td>22.068</td></tr>
</table>

<table>
<tr><td colspan="6">SEMIFINAL 1</td></tr>
<tr><td>Rnk</td><td>Ln</td><td>Name</td><td>Ctry</td><td>Time</td><td>Time behind</td></tr>
<tr><td>1</td><td>4</td><td>SABJAN, Ivan</td><td>CRO</td><td>4:13.901</td><td>0</td></tr>
<tr><td>2</td><td>3</td><td>PARTNOI, Victor</td><td>ROM</td><td>4:14.333</td><td>0.432</td></tr>
<tr><td>3</td><td>5</td><td>NIELSSON, Arne</td><td>DEN</td><td>4:14.573</td><td>0.672</td></tr>
<tr><td>4</td><td>6</td><td>KUBICA, Jan</td><td>SVK</td><td>4:22.773</td><td>8.872</td></tr>
<tr><td>5</td><td>1</td><td>NEGODYAYEV, Konstantin</td><td>KAZ</td><td>4:26.261</td><td>12.360</td></tr>
<tr><td>6</td><td>2</td><td>MAXWELL, Gavin</td><td>CAN</td><td>4:27.721</td><td>13.820</td></tr>
<tr><td>7</td><td>7</td><td>HARPER, Joseph</td><td>USA</td><td>4:39.949</td><td>26.048</td></tr>
</table>

<table>
<tr><td colspan="6">SEMIFINAL 2</td></tr>
<tr><td>Rnk</td><td>Ln</td><td>Name</td><td>Ctry</td><td>Time</td><td>Time behind</td></tr>
<tr><td>1</td><td>4</td><td>KLEMENTJEVS, Ivan</td><td>LAT</td><td>4:10.455</td><td>0</td></tr>
<tr><td>2</td><td>2</td><td>SYLVOZ, Pascal</td><td>FRA</td><td>4:11.483</td><td>1.028</td></tr>
<tr><td>3</td><td>7</td><td>BUKHALOV, Nikolay</td><td>BUL</td><td>4:14.415</td><td>3.960</td></tr>
<tr><td>4</td><td>5</td><td>CRESPO, Jose Manuel</td><td>ESP</td><td>4:15.939</td><td>5.484</td></tr>
<tr><td>5</td><td>3</td><td>SALCUTAN, Vadim</td><td>MDA</td><td>4:16.639</td><td>6.184</td></tr>
<tr><td>6</td><td>6</td><td>ASTANIN, Yevgeniy</td><td>UZB</td><td>4:19.151</td><td>8.696</td></tr>
<tr><td>7</td><td>1</td><td>PEREIRA, Silvestre</td><td>POR</td><td>4:31.199</td><td>20.744</td></tr>
</table>

<table>
<tr><td colspan="7">FINAL</td></tr>
<tr><td>Rnk</td><td>Ln</td><td>Name</td><td>Ctry</td><td>Time</td><td>Time behind</td><td></td></tr>
<tr><td>1</td><td>5</td><td>DOKTOR, Martin</td><td>CZE</td><td>3:54.418</td><td>0</td><td>G</td></tr>
<tr><td>2</td><td>2</td><td>KLEMENTJEVS, Ivan</td><td>LAT</td><td>3:54.954</td><td>0.536</td><td>S</td></tr>
<tr><td>3</td><td>4</td><td>ZALA, Gyorgy</td><td>HUN</td><td>3:56.366</td><td>1.948</td><td>B</td></tr>
<tr><td>4</td><td>6</td><td>SCHULZE, Patrickv</td><td>GER</td><td>3:57.778</td><td>3.360</td><td></td></tr>
<tr><td>5</td><td>1</td><td>SYLVOZ, Pascal</td><td>FRA</td><td>3:59.014</td><td>4.596</td><td></td></tr>
<tr><td>6</td><td>8</td><td>PARTNOI, Victor</td><td>ROM</td><td>3:59.858</td><td>5.440</td><td></td></tr>
<tr><td>7</td><td>3</td><td>BUNDZ, Roman</td><td>UKR</td><td>4:02.078</td><td>7.660</td><td></td></tr>
<tr><td>8</td><td>7</td><td>SABJAN, Ivan</td><td>CRO</td><td>4:04.066</td><td>9.648</td><td></td></tr>
<tr><td>9</td><td>9</td><td>BUKHALOV, Nikolay</td><td>BUL</td><td>4:13.034</td><td>18.616</td><td></td></tr>
</table>

Canoe/Kayak—Sprint / *Canoë/Kayak—Sprint*
1,000 m Canoe Double, Men   /   *1 000 m canoë double, Messieurs*

<table>
<tr><td colspan="6">HEAT 1</td></tr>
<tr><td>Rnk</td><td>Ln</td><td>Ctry</td><td>Names</td><td>Time</td><td>Time behind</td></tr>
<tr><td>1</td><td>3</td><td>ROM</td><td>GLAVAN, Marcel / BORSAN, Antonel</td><td>4:06.481</td><td>0</td></tr>
<tr><td>2</td><td>2</td><td>HUN</td><td>KOLONICS, Gyorgy / HORVATH, Csaba</td><td>4:08.709</td><td>2.228</td></tr>
<tr><td>3</td><td>9</td><td>SVK</td><td>PALES, Peter / OROSZ, Csaba</td><td>4:12.789</td><td>6.308</td></tr>
<tr><td>4</td><td>1</td><td>BUL</td><td>MARINOV, Martin / STOYANOV, Blagovest</td><td>4:15.529</td><td>9.048</td></tr>
<tr><td>5</td><td>4</td><td>POL</td><td>KOSZYKOWSKI, Dariusz / GOLIASZ, Tomasz</td><td>4:22.181</td><td>15.700</td></tr>
<tr><td>6</td><td>7</td><td>KOR</td><td>JUN, Kwang-Rak / PARK, Chang-Kyu</td><td>4:23.961</td><td>17.480</td></tr>
<tr><td>7</td><td>5</td><td>CAN</td><td>GILES, Steve / HOWE, Dan</td><td>4:33.613</td><td>27.132</td></tr>
<tr><td>8</td><td>6</td><td>UZB</td><td>SHAYSLAMOV, Vladimir / SHAYSLAMOV, Sergey</td><td>4:43.221</td><td>36.740</td></tr>
<tr><td>9</td><td>8</td><td>ANT</td><td>LEHRER, Jacob / LEHRER, Pieter</td><td>5:20.421</td><td>1:13.940</td></tr>
</table>

<table>
<tr><td colspan="6">HEAT 2</td></tr>
<tr><td>Rnk</td><td>Ln</td><td>Ctry</td><td>Names</td><td>Time</td><td>Time behind</td></tr>
<tr><td>1</td><td>2</td><td>GER</td><td>DITTMER, Andreas / KIRCHBACH, Gunar</td><td>4:00.851</td><td>0</td></tr>
<tr><td>2</td><td>7</td><td>GBR</td><td>TRAIN, Andrew / TRAIN, Stephen</td><td>4:01.263</td><td>0.412</td></tr>
<tr><td>3</td><td>5</td><td>CRO</td><td>FUNTAK, Drazen / SABJAN, Ivan</td><td>4:02.831</td><td>1.980</td></tr>
<tr><td>4</td><td>3</td><td>ESP</td><td>BEA, Jose Alfredo / SHELESTENKO, Oleg</td><td>4:05.203</td><td>4.352</td></tr>
<tr><td>5</td><td>8</td><td>KAZ</td><td>NURMAGANBETOV, Kaysar / SERGEYEV, Sergey</td><td>4:10.399</td><td>9.548</td></tr>
<tr><td>6</td><td>6</td><td>UKR</td><td>LYTVYNENKO, Oleksandr / IHRAYEV, Oleksiy</td><td>4:13.683</td><td>12.832</td></tr>
<tr><td>7</td><td>1</td><td>MDA</td><td>JURAVSCHI, Nikolai / RENEISCHI, Victor</td><td>4:25.183</td><td>24.332</td></tr>
<tr><td>8</td><td>4</td><td>CZE</td><td>FUKSA, Petr / BEDNAR, Pavel</td><td>4:25.295</td><td>24.444</td></tr>
</table>

1,000 m Canoe Double, Men / *1 000 m canoë double, Messieurs*

SEMIFINAL 1

Rnk	Ln	Ctry	Names	Time	Time behind
1	6	CAN	GILES, Steve / HOWE, Dan	3:45.077	0
2	3	BUL	MARINOV, Martin / STOYANOV, Blagovest	3:45.129	0.052
3	2	UKR	LYTVYNENKO, Oleksandr / IHRAYEV, Oleksiy	3:46.845	1.768
4	4	CRO	FUNTAK, Drazen / SABJAN, Ivan	3:48.677	3.600
5	5	POL	KOSZYKOWSKI, Dariusz / GOLIASZ, Tomasz	3:48.721	3.644
6	1	UZB	SHAYSLAMOV, Vladimir / SHAYSLAMOV, Sergey	3:57.037	11.960

SEMIFINAL 2

Rnk	Ln	Ctry	Names	Time	Time behind
1	6	MDA	JURAVSCHI, Nikolai / RENEISCHI, Victor	3:44.008	0
2	4	SVK	PALES, Peter / OROSZ, Csaba	3:44.628	0.620
3	3	ESP	BEA, Jose Alfredo / SHELESTENKO, Oleg	3:45.616	1.608
4	5	KAZ	NURMAGANBETOV, Kaysar / SERGEYEV, Sergey	3:51.360	7.352
5	1	CZE	FUKSA, Petr / BEDNAR, Pavel	3:51.576	7.568
6	2	KOR	JUN, Kwang-Rak / PARK, Chang-Kyu	3:52.044	8.036

FINAL

Rnk	Ln	Ctry	Names	Time	Time behind	
1	4	GER	DITTMER, Andreas / KIRCHBACH, Gunar	3:31.870	0	G
2	5	ROM	GLAVAN, Marcel / BORSAN, Antonel	3:32.294	0.424	S
3	6	HUN	KOLONICS, Gyorgy / HORVATH, Csaba	3:32.514	0.644	B
4	8	BUL	MARINOV, Martin / STOYANOV, Blagovest	3:34.382	2.512	
5	2	MDA	JURAVSCHI, Nikolai / RENEISCHI, Victor	3:35.198	3.328	
6	3	GBR	TRAIN, Andrew / TRAIN, Stephen	3:36.694	4.824	
7	1	SVK	PALES, Peter / OROSZ, Csaba	3:36.938	5.068	
8	9	ESP	BEA, Jose Alfredo / SHELESTENKO, Oleg	3:37.154	5.284	
9	7	CAN	GILES, Steve / HOWE, Dan	3:46.102	14.232	

CYCLING
CYCLISME

Abbreviations and terms used in Cycling results tables
Abréviations et termes employés dans les tableaux de résultats de cyclisme

Term	English	Français
@	About	A peu près
1/8 Finals	1/8 Finals	1/8 de finale
1/8 Finals Repechage	1/8 Finals Repechage	Repêchage de 1/8 de finale
B	Bronze Medal	Médaille de bronze
Behind	Time Behind	Temps en arrière
Best Time	Best Time	Meilleur temps
Bronze	Bronze Medal	Médaille de bronze
Continued	Continued	Continué
Ctry	Country	Pays
DNF	Did Not Finish	Abandon
DNS	Did Not Start	Absent au départ
Final	Final	Finale
Final Classification	Final Classification	Classement final
Final Time	Final Time	Temps final
First Round	First Round	Premier tour
First Round Repechage	First Round Repechage	Repêchage du premier tour
Flying Time Trial	Flying Time Trial	Epreuve contre la montre lancée
G	Gold Medal	Médaille d'or
Gold	Gold Medal	Médaille d'or
Heat	Heat	Série
km/h	Kilometers Per Hour	Kilomètres par heure
Lap	Lap	Tour
Lap 1 Time	Lap 1 Time	Temps Tour 1
Lap 2 time	Lap 2 Time	Temps Tour 2
Lap 3 time	Lap 3 Time	Temps Tour 3
Lapped	Lapped	Doublé
Laps down	Laps Down	Tours en arrière
Name	Name	Nom
O	Olympic Record	Record olympique
OVT	Overtaken	Doublé
Points	Points	Points
Qualification Round	Qualification Round	Tour de qualification
Quarterfinals	Quarterfinals	Quarts de finale
REL	Relegated	Relégué
Rnk	Rank	Classement
S	Silver Medal	Médaille d'argent
Second Round	Second Round	Deuxième tour
Second Round Repechage	Second Round Repechage	Repêchage du deuxième tour
Semifinals	Semifinals	Demi-finales
Silver	Silver Medal	Médaille d'argent
Speed	Speed	Vitesse
Start Order	Start Order	Ordre de départ
Time	Time	Temps
Total Laps	Total Laps	Total des tours
W	World Record	Record du monde

International Cycling Union (UCI)
Union Cycliste Internationale
37, route de Chavannes
1007 Lausanne
Switzerland

Cycling—Mountain Bike / *Cyclisme — VTT*

Cross Country, Men / *Cross-country, Messieurs*

FINAL

Rnk	Name	Ctry	Start Order	Total Laps	Time	km/h	Behind	Lapped
1	BRENTJENS, Bart	NED	7	5	2:17:38	21.2		G
2	FRISCHKNECHT, Thomas	SUI	4	5	2:20:14	20.8	@02:36	S
3	MARTINEZ, Miguel	FRA	22	5	2:20:36	20.8	@02:58	B
4	DUPOUEY, Christophe	FRA	40	5	2:25:03	20.2	@07:25	
5	PONTONI, Daniele	ITA	41	5	2:25:08	20.1	@07:30	
6	BRENES, Jose Andres	CRC	10	5	2:25:51	20.0	@08:13	
7	KRISTENSEN, Lennie	DEN	5	5	2:26:02	20.0	@08:24	
8	BRAMATI, Luca	ITA	23	5	2:26:05	20.0	@08:27	
9	EVANS, Cadel	AUS	26	5	2:26:15	20.0	@08:37	
10	BERNER, Ralph	GER	34	5	2:27:45	19.8	@10:07	
11	HOYDAHL, Rune	NOR	3	5	2:28:16	19.7	@10:38	
12	FOORD, Gary	GBR	37	5	2:29:10	19.6	@11:32	
13	SALLENBACK, Warren	CAN	17	5	2:29:57	19.5	@12:19	
14	WABEL, Beat	SUI	29	5	2:32:17	19.2	@14:39	
15	BAKER, David	GBR	19	5	2:32:30	19.2	@14:52	
16	WOODS, Robert	AUS	43	5	2:33:14	19.1	@15:36	
17	PAULISSEN, Roel	BEL	15	5	2:33:53	19.0	@16:15	
18	OESTERGAARD, Jan Erik	DEN	30	5	2:34:30	18.9	@16:52	
19	JUAREZ, David	USA	2	5	2:35:15	18.8	@17:37	
20	MYRAH, Don	USA	28	5	2:35:50	18.8	@18:12	
21	PERSSON, Roger	SWE	9	5	2:37:17	18.6	@19:39	
22	MUJIKA, Jokin	ESP	42	5	2:41:15	18.1	@23:37	

FINAL - *continued*

Rnk	Name	Ctry	Start Order	Total Laps	Time	km/h	Behind	Lapped
23	ARIAS SANCHEZ, Jhon	COL	44	5	2:42:04	18.0	@24:26	
24	FORT, Radovan	CZE	12	5	2:42:43	18.0	@25:05	
25	EARLEY, Martin	IRL	6	5	2:43:56	17.8	@26:18	
26	MIURA, Kyoshi	JPN	18	5	2:45:03	17.7	@27:25	
27	RAVELLI, Marcio	BRA	20	5	2:45:16	17.7	@27:38	
28	DENIFL, Ernst	AUT	16	5	2:45:34	17.7	@27:56	
29	GALINSKI, Marek	POL	21	5	2:45:54	17.6	@28:16	
30	HRIC, Peter	SVK	13	5	2:46:22	17.6	@28:44	
31	HESTLER, Andreas	CAN	36	5	2:46:45	17.5	@29:07	
32	MARTIN, Alastair	IRL	31	5	2:47:46	17.4	@30:08	
33	CAMRDA, Pavel	CZE	33	5	2:49:09	17.3	@31:31	
34	ARIAS ACOSTA, Juan	COL	27	5	2:50:44	17.1	@33:06	
35	LOPES, Ivanir	BRA	38	5	2:53:29	16.9	@35:51	
36	BARUL, Slawomir	POL	39	5	2:53:56	16.8	@36:18	
37	CHAVEZ, Lautaro	ARG	25	4	DNF			
38	GONSALVES, Rory	ANT	11	4	DNF			
	MAASIKMETS, Alges	EST	1	3	DNF			
	KLUGE, Mike	GER	14	3	DNF			
	LEZAUN, Roberto	ESP	24	2	DNF			
	ARNTZ, Marcel	NED	32	2	DNF			
	VAN den ABEELE, Peter	BEL	35	1	DNF			
	LEE, Jin-Ok	KOR	8		DNS			

Cycling—Mountain Bike / *Cyclisme — VTT*

Cross Country, Women / *Cross-country, Dames*

FINAL

Rnk	Name	Ctry	Start Order	Total Laps	Time	km/h	Behind	Lapped
1	PEZZO, Paola	ITA	4	3	1:50:51	17.3		G
2	SYDOR, Alison	CAN	13	3	1:51:58	17.1	@01:07	S
3	DeMATTEI, Susan	USA	29	3	1:52:36	17.0	@01:45	B
4	DAHLE, Gunn-Rita	NOR	19	3	1:53:50	16.8	@02:59	
5	VINK, Elsbeth	NED	16	3	1:54:38	16.7	@03:47	
6	STROPPARO, Annabella	ITA	21	3	1:55:56	16.5	@05:05	
7	MARUNDE, Regina	GER	12	3	1:57:21	16.3	@06:30	
8	LYNCH, Kathy	NZL	15	3	1:57:40	16.3	@06:49	
9	ORVOSOVA-LOWE, Eva	SVK	6	3	1:57:56	16.2	@07:05	
10	FURTADO, Juliana	USA	18	3	1:58:32	16.1	@07:41	
11	LEBOUCHER, Laurence	FRA	5	3	1:59:00	16.1	@08:09	
12	GASSMANN, Daniela	SUI	20	3	1:59:11	16.1	@08:20	
13	TOMLINSON, Lesley	CAN	27	3	2:01:04	15.8	@10:13	
14	YEPIFANOVA, Alla	RUS	8	3	2:01:35	15.7	@10:44	
15	GRIGSON, Mary	AUS	2	3	2:02:38	15.6	@11:47	

FINAL - *continued*

Rnk	Name	Ctry	Start Order	Total Laps	Time	km/h	Behind	Lapped
16	FURST, Silvia	SUI	3	3	2:03:04	15.5	@12:13	
17	GREEN, Erica	RSA	11	3	2:03:06	15.5	@12:15	
18	NEUMANNOVA, Katerina	CZE	9	3	2:04:03	15.4	@13:12	
19	HANUSOVA, Katerina	CZE	26	3	2:04:05	15.4	@13:14	
20	BLANCO, Laura	ESP	7	3	2:04:20	15.4	@13:29	
21	ILAVSKA, Lenka	SVK	23	3	2:04:43	15.3	@13:52	
22	MURRELL, Deb	GBR	28	3	2:04:44	15.3	@13:53	
23	TANIKAWA, Kanako	JPN	14	3	2:05:44	15.2	@14:53	
24	TEMPORELLI, Sandra	FRA	22	3	2:06:57	15.1	@16:06	
25	GAO, Hongying	CHN	10	3	2:09:08	14.8	@18:17	
26	ROVIRA, Silvia	ESP	24	3	2:09:17	14.8	@18:26	
27	PASHKOVA, Nadezhda	RUS	25	3	2:16:36	14.0	@25:45	
	ALEXANDER, Caroline	GBR	17	1	DNF			
	AMBROSIO, Sandra	ARG	1		DNF			

Cycling—Road / *Cyclisme — Route*
Road Race, Men / *Course sur route, Messieurs*

Rnk	Name	Ctry	Time	km/h	Behind
1	RICHARD, Pascal	SUI	4:53:56	45.29	G
2	SORENSEN, Rolf	DEN	4:53:56	"	S
3	SCJANDRI, Maximilian	GBR	4:53:58	45.28	@00:02 B
4	ANDREU, Francisco	USA	4:55:10	45.10	@01:14
5	VIRENQUE, Richard	FRA	4:55:10	"	"
6	MAURI, Melchor	ESP	4:55:11	45.09	@01:15
7	BALDATO, Fabio	ITA	4:55:24	45.06	@01:28
8	BARTOLI, Michele	ITA	4:55:24	"	"
9	SPRUCH, Zbigniew	POL	4:55:25	45.06	@01:29
10	MUSEEUW, Johan	BEL	4:55:25	"	"
11	SKIBBY, Jesper	DEN	4:55:25	"	"
12	ARMSTRONG, Lance	USA	4:55:25	"	"
13	KONYSHEV, Dmitriy	RUS	4:56:25	44.91	@02:29
14	USHAKOV, Serhiy	UKR	4:56:25	"	"
15	PEETERS, Wilfried	BEL	4:56:28	44.90	@02:32
16	LUDWIG, Olaf	GER	4:56:32	44.89	@02:36
17	BROCHARD, Laurent	FRA	4:56:33	44.89	@02:37
18	PIZIKS, Arvis	LAT	4:56:33	"	"
19	STEPHENS, Neil	AUS	4:56:34	44.88	@02:38
20	ZABEL, Erik	GER	4:56:43	44.86	@02:47
21	JALABERT, Laurent	FRA	4:56:43	"	"
22	OZERS, Kaspars	LAT	4:56:43	"	"
23	McEWEN, Robert	AUS	4:56:44	44.86	@02:48
24	KIRSIPUU, Jaan	EST	4:56:44	"	"
25	van den BROUCKE, Frank	BEL	4:56:44	"	"
26	INDURAIN, Miguel	ESP	4:56:44	"	"
27	DAVIDENKO, Vasiliy	RUS	4:56:44	"	"
28	ALDAG, Rolf	GER	4:56:44	"	"
29	KIVILEV, Andrey	KAZ	4:56:44	"	"
30	SVORADA, Jan	CZE	4:56:44	"	"
31	SILOVS, Juris	LAT	4:56:44	"	"
32	CASAGRANDE, Francesco	ITA	4:56:44	44.86	@02:48
33	CHMIL, Andriy	UKR	4:56:44	"	"
34	LAFIS, Michel	SWE	4:56:44	"	"
35	MAGNUSSON, Glenn	SWE	4:56:45	44.86	@02:49
36	AUS, Lauri	EST	4:56:45	"	"
37	FONDRIEST, Maurizio	ITA	4:56:45	"	"
38	DEKKER, Hendrik	NED	4:56:45	"	"
39	RODRIGUES, Orlando	POR	4:56:45	"	"
40	HOLM, Brian	DEN	4:56:45	"	"
41	BAUER, Steven	CAN	4:56:45	"	"
42	MICHAELSEN, Lars	DEN	4:56:45	"	"
43	PANKOV, Oleh	UKR	4:56:45	"	"
44	RIEBENBAUER, Werner	AUT	4:56:45	"	"
45	BREUKINK, Erik	NED	4:56:45	"	"
46	MORSCHER, Harald	AUT	4:56:45	"	"
47	MARIN VALENCIA, Ruber	COL	4:56:45	"	"
48	LOPES, Pedro	POR	4:56:45	"	"
49	LAUK, Andres	EST	4:56:46	44.85	@02:50
50	CHRZANOWSKI, Slawomir	POL	4:56:46	"	"
51	TONKOV, Pavel	RUS	4:56:46	"	"
52	ZBERG, Beat	SUI	4:56:46	"	"
53	VINOKUROV, Aleksandr	KAZ	4:56:46	"	"
54	WROLICH, Peter	AUT	4:56:46	"	"
55	ANDERSSON, Markus	SWE	4:56:46	"	"
56	VIERHOUTEN, Aart	NED	4:56:46	"	"
57	LAUKKA, Joona	FIN	4:56:46	"	"
58	UGRYUMOV, Pyotr	RUS	4:56:46	"	"
59	DVORSCIK, Milan	SVK	4:56:46	"	"
60	BRUYNEEL, Johan	BEL	4:56:47	44.85	@02:51
61	RYDER, Douglas	RSA	4:56:47	"	"
62	TOTSCHNIG, Georg	AUT	4:56:47	"	"

Rnk	Name	Ctry	Time	km/h	Behind
63	MIIRYLAINEN, Kari	FIN	4:56:47	44.85	@02:51
64	BARRY, Michael	CAN	4:56:47	"	"
65	McDONALD, Damian	AUS	4:56:47	"	"
66	REID, Richard	NZL	4:56:47	"	"
67	OLANO, Abraham	ESP	4:56:48	44.85	@02:52
68	VALACH, Jan	SVK	4:56:48	"	"
69	KAVETSKIY, Pavel	BLR	4:56:48	"	"
70	PINTARIC, Robert	SLO	4:56:48	"	"
71	GRACIANO, Eduardo	MEX	4:56:49	44.85	@02:53
72	McCANN, David	IRL	4:56:49	"	"
73	ORIOL, Veceslav	MDA	4:56:49	"	"
74	RANDOLPH, Gregory	USA	4:56:49	"	"
75	FRASER, Gord	CAN	4:56:49	"	"
76	HINCAPIE, George	USA	4:56:49	"	"
77	FERNANDEZ, Manuel	ESP	4:56:49	"	"
78	MARTA, Nuno	POR	4:56:49	"	"
79	ELLIOT, Malcolm	GBR	4:56:49	"	"
80	WOHLBERG, Eric	CAN	4:56:50	44.84	@02:54
81	LUTTENBERGER, Peter	AUT	4:56:50	"	"
82	CIPOLLINI, Mario	ITA	4:56:50	"	"
83	ROUS, Didier	FRA	4:56:50	"	"
84	ZAPATA VILLADA, Javier	COL	4:56:50	"	"
85	SHEFER, Aleksandr	KAZ	4:56:50	"	"
86	GIRALDO HERNANDEZ, Oscar	COL	4:56:50	"	"
87	RIIS, Bjarne	DEN	4:56:51	44.84	@02:55
88	LANDRY, Jacques	CAN	4:56:51	"	"
89	TETERYUK, Andrey	KAZ	4:56:51	"	"
90	URIBE, Eduardo	MEX	4:56:51	"	"
91	RIBEIRO, Mauro	BRA	4:56:51	"	"
92	OZOLS, Dainis	LAT	4:56:51	"	"
93	HEGG, Steve	USA	4:56:51	"	"
94	BROZYNA, Tomasz	POL	4:56:52	44.84	@02:56
95	LUPEIKIS, Remigijus	LTU	4:56:52	"	"
96	KODANIPORK, Raido	EST	4:56:52	"	"
97	WIKNER, Blayne	RSA	4:56:52	"	"
98	HODGE, Stephen	AUS	4:56:53	44.84	@02:57
99	TANNER, John	GBR	4:56:53	"	"
100	ABDUZHAPAROV, Dzhamolidin	UZB	4:56:53	"	"
101	ALONSO, Marino	ESP	4:56:53	"	"
102	JONKER, Patrick	AUS	4:56:53	"	"
103	BERZIN, Yevgeniy	RUS	4:56:53	"	"
104	ZULLE, Alex	SUI	4:56:54	44.83	@02:58
105	JAERMANN, Rolf	SUI	4:56:54	"	"
106	VAINSTEINS, Romans	LAT	4:56:54	"	"
107	MONCASSIN, Frederic	FRA	4:56:55	44.83	@02:59
108	HOFFMAN, Tristan Henri	NED	4:56:55	"	"
109	STEELS, Tom	BEL	4:56:56	44.83	@03:00
110	FRISCHKNECHT, Thomas	SUI	4:57:04	44.81	@03:08
111	NELISSEN, Daniel	NED	4:57:10	44.79	@03:14
112	BARBOSA, Candido	POR	5:01:29	44.15	@07:33
113	GOLOVANOV, Yevgeniy	BLR	5:05:38	43.55	@11:42
114	ZAUBAN, Pavol	SVK	5:05:39	43.55	@11:43
115	MONSALVE, Hussein	VEN	5:05:39	"	"
116	AGUILAR, Irving	MEX	5:05:39	"	"
	GUEVARA REIDTLER, Manuel	VEN	DNF		
	PULNIKOV, Volodymyr	UKR	DNF		
	ALI, Darwish	UAE	DNF		
	AZEVEDO, Jose	POR	DNF		
	SUMIDA, Osamu	JPN	DNF		
	HOLESTOL, Svein-Gaute	NOR	DNF		
	RAMIREZ RODRIGUEZ, Duban	COL	DNF		

Rnk	Name	Ctry	Time	km/h	Behind
	VILLATORO, Anthon	GUA	DNF		
	MONTANA HERRERA, Raul	COL	DNF		
	CAICEDO, Paulo	ECU	DNF		
	RODRIGUEZ, Pedro	ECU	DNF		
	PUGACH, Igor	MDA	DNF		
	OCHOA, Omar	GUA	DNF		
	PANIAGUA GARCIA, Marlon	GUA	DNF		
	LOPEZ CABRERA, Felipe	GUA	DNF		
	SANTOS GARCIA, Edvin	GUA	DNF		
	BONDARIK, Oleg	BLR	DNF		
	GERMAN, Vyacheslav	BLR	DNF		
	RUMSAS, Raimondas	LTU	DNF		
	GARRIDO ZENTENO, Victor	CHI	DNF		
	GHAZARYAN, Arsen	ARM	DNF		
	WONG, Kam Po	HKG	DNF		
	PARK, Min-Soo	KOR	DNF		
	TUMUR-OCHIR, Dashnyam	MGL	DNF		
	CHEN, Chih-Hao	TPE	DNF		
	JONES, Timothy	ZIM	DNF		
	KHALILOV, Mykhaylo	UKR	DNF		
	RICH, Michael	GER	DNF		
	BODROGI, Laszlo	HUN	DNF		
	IVANOV, Ruslan	MDA	DNF		
	VILCINSKAS, Raimondas	LTU	DNF		
	ABREU RIVERO, Ruben	VEN	DNF		
	MAYA, Carlos	VEN	DNF		
	BONCIUKOV, Igor	MDA	DNF		
	TANOVITCH, Oleg	MDA	DNF		
	PESCHEL, Uwe	GER	DNF		
	BARANOWSKI, Dariusz	POL	DNF		
	SMITH, Brian	GBR	DNF		
	CHILES, Hector	ECU	DNF		
	ANDERSSON, Michael	SWE	DNF		
	LIPTAK, Miroslav	SVK	DNF		
	NAGY, Robert	SVK	DNF		
	BALCIUNAS, Linas	LTU	DNF		
	ROMANOVAS, Ivanas	LTU	DNF		
	BARE ROSSARIO, Gregorio	URU	DNF		
	RESIK, Lauri	EST	DNF		
	FOWLER, Brian	NZL	DNF		
	GUYTON, Scott	NZL	DNF		
	MUSAI, Besnik	ALB	DNF		
	ARTACHO, Gustavo	ARG	DNF		
	GERER, Ricardo	URU	DNF		
	QUADRI, Hernandes	BRA	DNF		
	PEGORIN, Ruben	ARG	DNF		
	JUAREZ, Adan	MEX	DNF		
	MITCHELL, Glen	NZL	DNF		
	HUBBARD, Elliot	BER	DNF		
	BALAUSTRE, Jose	VEN	DNF		
	SUAIDEN, Jamil	BRA	DNF		
	MAY, Marcio	BRA	DNF		
	ROGELIN, Daniel	BRA	DNF		
	MANABE, Kazuyuki	JPN	DNF		
	DIRKSZ, Lucien	ARU	DNF		
	al SHAKAILI, Yousuf Khanfar	OMA	DNF		
	SHARAPOV, Aleksandr	BLR	DNF		
	GONZALEZ, Domingo	MEX	DNF		
	SHADI, Yousef	LBA	DNF		
	BARAUD, Stefan	CAY	DNF		
	KARLSSON, Jan	SWE	DNF		

Cycling—Road / *Cyclisme — Route*

Road Race, Women / *Course sur route, Dames*

FINAL

Rnk	Name	Ctry	Time	km/h	Behind
1	LONGO-CIPRELLI, Jeannie	FRA	2:36:13	40.10	G
2	CHIAPPA, Imelda	ITA	2:36:38	39.99	@00:25 S
3	HUGHES, Clara	CAN	2:36:44	39.97	@00:31 B
4	HOHLFELD, Vera	GER	2:37:06	39.87	@00:53
5	POLIKEVICIUTE, Jolanta	LTU	2:37:06	"	"
6	ZABIROVA, Zulfiya	RUS	2:37:06	"	"
7	CAPPELLOTTO, Alessandra	ITA	2:37:06	"	"
8	HEEB, Barbara	SUI	2:37:06	"	"
9	WATT, Kathryn	AUS	2:37:06	"	"
10	PALMER, Susan	CAN	2:37:06	"	"
11	PURVIS, Marie	GBR	2:37:06	"	"
12	POLIKEVICIUTE, Rasa	LTU	2:37:06	"	"
13	SCHNORF, Yvonne	SUI	2:37:06	"	"
14	STAGURSKAYA, Zinaida	BLR	2:37:06	"	"
15	RAST, Diana	SUI	2:37:06	"	"
16	MARSAL, Catherine	FRA	2:37:06	"	"
17	WILSON, Anna	AUS	2:37:06	"	"
18	KOSTOLL, Ragnhild	NOR	2:37:06	"	"
19	PHILLIPS, Sarah	GBR	2:37:06	"	"
20	van de VIJVER, Heidi	BEL	2:37:06	"	"

FINAL - *continued*

Rnk	Name	Ctry	Time	km/h	Behind
21	SOMARRIBA, Joane	ESP	2:37:06	39.87	@00:53
22	KLEIN, Tanja	AUT	2:37:06	"	"
23	BARROS, Ana	POR	2:37:06	"	"
24	ILAVSKA, Lenka	SVK	2:37:06	"	"
25	LJUNGSKOG, Susanne	SWE	2:37:06	"	"
26	BRUNEN, Yvonne Anna	NED	2:37:06	"	"
27	ORVOSOVA-LOWE, Eva	SVK	2:37:06	"	"
28	VINK, Elsbeth	NED	2:37:06	"	"
29	GOLAY, Jeanne	USA	2:37:06	"	"
30	KISHCHUK, Natalya	UKR	2:37:06	"	"
31	PRYDE, Susannah	NZL	2:37:06	"	"
32	BONANOMI, Roberta	ITA	2:37:06	"	"
33	BAILEY, Rebecca	NZL	2:37:06	"	"
34	VIKSTEDT-NYMAN, Tea Riitta	FIN	2:37:06	"	"
35	GREEN, Erica	RSA	2:37:21	39.81	@01:08
36	BRENNEMAN, Linda	USA	2:40:27	39.04	@04:14
37	DUNLAP, Allison	USA	2:41:21	38.82	@05:08
38	CLIGNET, Marion	FRA	2:41:50	38.71	@05:37
39	WATSON, Tracey	AUS	2:42:35	38.53	@06:22

FINAL - *continued*

Rnk	Name	Ctry	Time	km/h	Behind
40	BLAZQUEZ, Fatima	ESP	2:46:27	37.63	@10:14
41	GUO, Xinghong	CHN	2:49:47	36.89	@13:34
42	MARTIN, Jacqueline	RSA	2:53:12	36.17	@16:59
43	ALEXANDER, Caroline	GBR	2:53:47	36.04	@17:34
	JACKSON, Linda	CAN	DNF		
	ZHAO, Haijuan	CHN	DNF		
	PEREZ, Dania	CUB	DNF		
	SOLIS, Camille	BIZ	DNF		
	SAMOKHVALOVA, Svetlana	RUS	DNF		
	BOLLERUD, Ingunn	NOR	DNF		
	VASILENKO, Alla	KAZ	DNF		
	ZILIUTE, Diana	LTU	DNF		
	NELSON, Jacqueline	NZL	DNF		
	KAILA, Maureen	ESA	DNF		
	CARREDOR ALVAREZ, Maritza	COL	DNF		
	HARINGA, Ingrid	NED	DNF		
	KIM, Yong-Mi	KOR	DNF		
	BUBNENKOVA, Svetlana	RUS	DNF		
	BENGOA, Izaskun	ESP	DNF		

Cycling—Road / *Cyclisme — Route*

Individual Time Trial, Men / *Course individuelle contre la montre, Messieurs*

FINAL

Rnk	Name	Ctry	Lap 1 time	Lap 2 time	Lap 3 time	Final time	Behind	km/h
1	INDURAIN, Miguel	ESP	16:09	32:14	48:15	1:04:05		48.87 G
2	OLANO, Abraham	ESP	16:08	32:26	48:35	1:04:17	@00:12	48.72 S
3	BOARDMAN, Chris	GBR	15:51	32:11	48:27	1:04:36	@00:31	48.48 B
4	FONDRIEST, Maurizio	ITA	16:12	32:43	48:55	1:05:01	@00:56	48.17
5	ROMINGER, Tony	SUI	16:35	33:12	49:45	1:06:00	@02:00	47.39
6	ARMSTRONG, Lance	USA	16:15	32:49	49:30	1:06:28	@02:23	47.12
7	ZULLE, Alex	SUI	16:21	33:08	49:59	1:06:33	@02:28	47.06
8	JONKER, Patrick	AUS	16:22	33:07	49:54	1:06:54	@02:49	46.82
9	BARANOWSKI, Dariusz	POL	16:29	33:22	50:16	1:07:08	@03:03	46.65
10	RICH, Michael	GER	16:38	33:26	50:24	1:07:08	@03:03	46.65
11	DEKKER, Hendrik	NED	16:25	33:22	50:18	1:07:08	@03:03	46.65
12	PESCHEL, Uwe	GER	16:28	33:27	50:24	1:07:33	@03:28	46.37
13	JALABERT, Laurent	FRA	16:46	33:55	50:57	1:07:34	@03:29	46.35
14	RIIS, Bjarne	DEN	16:52	33:46	50:34	1:07:47	@03:42	46.21
15	BERZIN, Yevgeniy	RUS	16:37	33:39	50:43	1:07:53	@03:48	46.14
16	HEGG, Steve	USA	16:49	33:58	51:05	1:08:29	@04:24	45.73
17	BREUKINK, Erik	NED	16:57	34:10	51:15	1:08:33	@04:28	45.69
18	KARLSSON, Jan	SWE	17:01	34:19	51:34	1:08:52	@04:47	45.48
19	CASAGRANDE, Francesco	ITA	16:49	34:20	51:48	1:09:18	@05:13	45.19
20	BROCHARD, Laurent	FRA	16:43	34:04	51:40	1:09:22	@05:17	45.15

FINAL - *continued*

Rnk	Name	Ctry	Lap 1 time	Lap 2 time	Lap 3 time	Final time	Behind	km/h
21	KASPUTIS, Arturas	LTU	16:47	34:20	51:44	1:09:39	@05:34	44.97
22	BROZYNA, Tomasz	POL	16:55	34:37	52:18	1:09:48	@05:43	44.87
23	HODGE, Stephen	AUS	17:24	35:12	52:36	1:09:59	@05:54	44.75
24	BRUYNEEL, Johan	BEL	17:07	34:58	52:33	1:10:12	@06:07	44.62
25	VILLATORO, Anthon	GUA	17:36	35:23	53:05	1:10:34	@06:29	44.38
26	WOHLBERG, Eric	CAN	16:57	34:42	52:46	1:10:36	@06:31	44.36
27	IVANOV, Ruslan	MDA	17:05	35:02	52:58	1:10:55	@06:50	44.16
28	LUPEIKIS, Remigijus	LTU	17:19	34:52	52:53	1:11:03	@06:58	44.08
29	RAMIREZ RODIRIGUEZ, Duban	COL	17:30	35:17	53:11	1:11:18	@07:13	43.93
30	ZARATE, Jesus	MEX	17:53	35:48	53:46	1:11:42	@07:37	43.68
31	LIPTAK, Miroslav	SVK	17:59	36:01	54:00	1:12:28	@08:23	43.22
32	PINTARIC, Robert	SLO	17:32	35:30	53:30	1:12:35	@08:30	43.15
33	BONCIUKOV, Igor	MDA	17:36	36:01	54:13	1:12:48	@08:43	43.02
34	DVORSCIK, Milan	SVK	17:50	36:24	54:33	1:12:54	@08:49	42.96
35	QUADRI, Hernandes	BRA	17:48	36:32	55:19	1:14:12	@10:07	42.21
36	LERMEN, Valdir	BRA	18:09	36:51	55:40	1:14:48	@10:43	41.87
37	ZAPATA VILLADA, Javier	COL	18:40	37:35	56:10	1:15:09	@11:04	41.68
	ANDERSSON, Michael	SWE				DNF		
	TONKOV, Pavel	RUS				DNS		
	SORENSEN, Rolf	DEN				DNS		

Cycling—Road / *Cyclisme — Route*

Individual Time Trial, Women / *Course individuelle contre la montre, Dames*

FINAL

Rnk	Name	Ctry	Lap 1 time	Final time	Time behind	km/h
1	ZABIROVA, Zulfiya	RUS	18:21	36:40		42.71 G
2	LONGO-CIPRELLI, Jeannie	FRA	18:13	37:00	@00:20	42.32 S
3	HUGHES, Clara	CAN	18:16	37:13	@00:33	42.08 B
4	WATT, Kathryn	AUS	18:52	37:53	@01:13	41.34
5	CLIGNET, Marion	FRA	18:37	38:14	@01:34	40.96
6	VIKSTEDT-NYMAN, Tea	FIN	18:56	38:24	@01:44	40.78
7	POLIKEVICIUTE, Jolanta	LTU	18:55	38:27	@01:47	40.73
8	CHIAPPA, Imelda	ITA	19:15	38:47	@02:07	40.38
9	JACKSON, Linda	CAN	19:10	38:50	@02:10	40.33
10	WILSON, Anna	AUS	18:58	38:50	@02:10	40.33
11	BRENNEMAN, Linda	USA	19:01	38:52	@02:12	40.29
12	POLIKEVICIUTE, Rasa	LTU	19:16	38:53	@02:13	40.27
13	SOMARRIBA, Joane	ESP	19:12	38:55	@02:15	40.24

FINAL - *continued*

Rnk	Name	Ctry	Lap 1 time	Final time	Time behind	km/h
14	McGREGOR, Yvonne	GBR	19:14	39:09	@02:29	40.00
15	RAST, Diana	SUI	19:31	39:28	@02:48	39.68
16	GOLAY, Jeanne	USA	19:30	39:36	@02:56	39.55
17	ILAVSKA, Lenka	SVK	19:43	39:57	@03:17	39.20
18	BUBNENKOVA, Svetlana	RUS	19:51	40:16	@03:36	38.89
19	BRUNEN, Yvonne Anna	NED	19:48	40:39	@03:59	38.52
20	NELSON, Jacqueline	NZL	20:11	40:58	@04:18	38.23
21	PHILLIPS, Sarah	GBR	20:14	41:16	@04:36	37.95
22	BAILEY, Rebecca	NZL	20:29	41:45	@05:05	37.51
23	KLEIN, Tanja	AUT	20:28	42:03	@05:23	37.24
24	CORREDOR ALVAREZ, Maritza	COL	20:47	42:06	@05:26	37.20
	HARTWELL, May	NOR		DNS		

VENUE MAP
PLAN DU SITE

Road Cycling Course
Parcours de cyclisme sur route
Atlanta / *Atlanta*

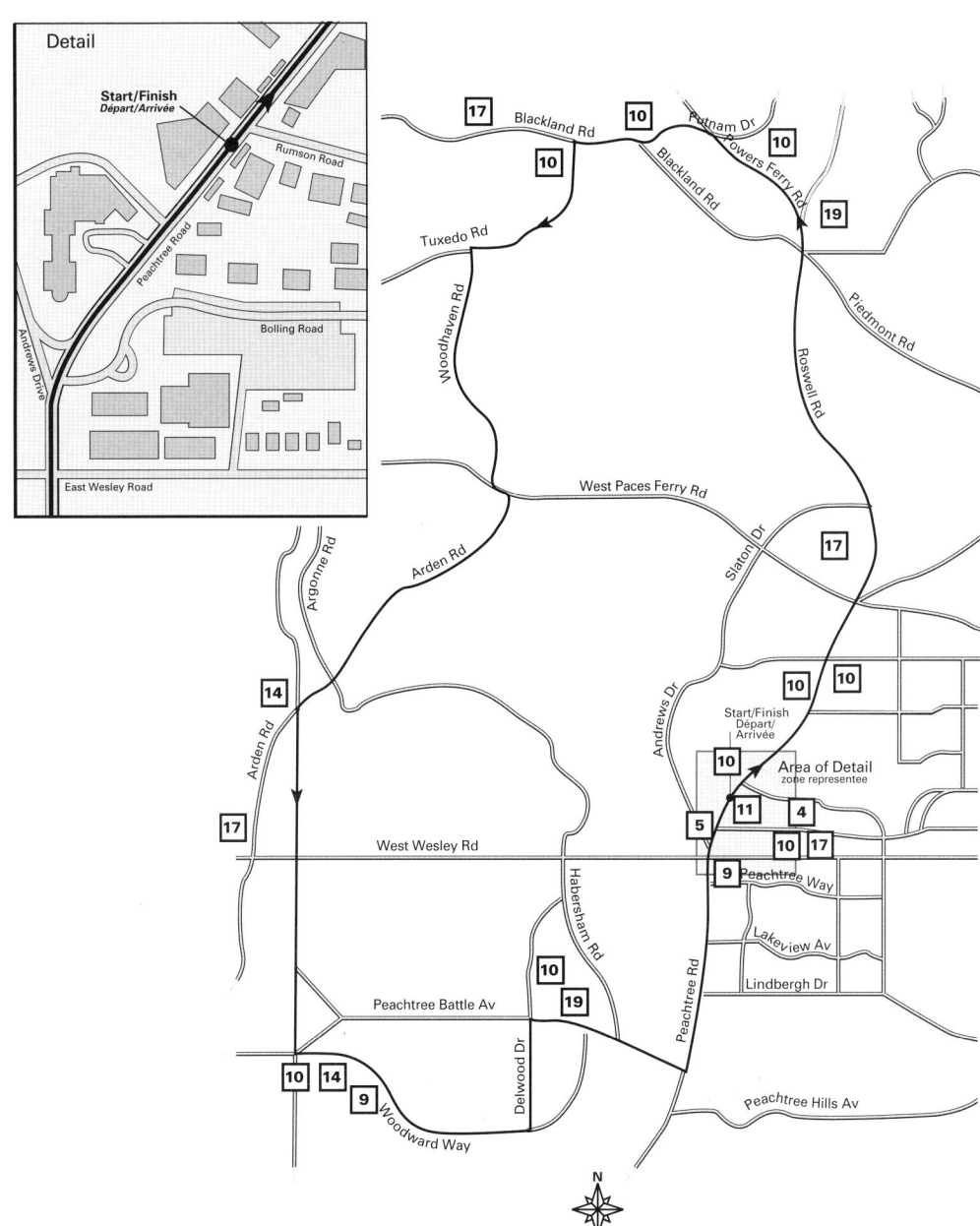

LEGEND / *LEGENDE*

This legend represents the major functional areas located at each Olympic venue. The numbers below correspond to the numbers shown on the venue maps.

Les principaux domaines fonctionnels en place sur chaque site figurent dans cette légende. Les chiffres correspondent à ceux que l'on trouve sur les cartes des sites.

1　Accreditation / *Accréditation*
2　Ceremonies / *Cérémonies*
3　Competition area / *Aire de compétition*
4　Competition related area / *Aire des services liés aux compétitions*
5　Event seating / *Places*
6　ACOG management / *Direction du site*
7　Sports administration federation services / *Services administratifs des fédérations sportives*
8　Material acquisition /distribution / *Acquisition/distribution du matériel*
9　Press / *Presse*
10　Broadcasters / *Diffuseurs*
11　Health services and medical control / *Services et contrôles médicaux*
12　Spectator services / *Services aux spectateurs*
13　Olympic Family services / *Services à la Famille olympique*
14　Security / *Sécurité*
15　Technology / *Technologie*
16　Food services / *Alimentation*
17　Transportation / *Transports*
18　Ticketing / *Billetterie*
19　Spectator entrance / *Entrée réservée aux spectateurs*
20　Athlete entrance / *Entrée réservée aux athlètes*

Cycling—Track / *Cyclisme — Piste*
1 km Time Trial, Men / *Course de 1 km contre la montre, Messieurs*

FINAL

Rnk	Name	Ctry	250 m	500 m	750 m	1 km	km/h	
1	ROUSSEAU, Florian	FRA	18.709	32.549	47.014	1:02.712	57.40	O G
2	HARTWELL, Erin	USA	18.892	33.059	47.616	1:02.940	57.19	S
3	JUMONJI, Takanobu	JPN	18.725	32.632	47.315	1:03.261	56.90	B
4	LAUSBERG, Soren	GER	19.403	33.208	47.743	1:03.514	56.68	
5	van ZYL, Jean-Pierre	RSA	18.975	33.049	47.959	1:04.214	56.06	
6	KREJNER, Grzegorz	POL	19.472	33.482	48.481	1:04.697	55.64	
7	GEORGALIS, Dimitrios	GRE	19.654	33.877	48.876	1:04.995	55.38	
8	KIKSIS, Ainars	LAT	19.341	33.510	48.902	1:05.457	54.99	
9	MEIDLINGER, Christian	AUT	19.453	34.256	49.424	1:05.530	54.93	
10	SAMUEL, Gene	TRI	19.277	33.644	49.082	1:05.533	54.93	

FINAL - *continued*

Rnk	Name	Ctry	250 m	500 m	750 m	1 km	km/h
11	BONDARYEV, Bohdan	UKR	20.771	35.230	50.002	1:05.658	54.82
12	van HAMEREN, Theodorus	NED	19.401	33.709	49.061	1:05.886	54.63
13	ESCUREDO, Jose	ESP	19.828	34.078	49.339	1:05.944	54.59
14	McKENZIE POTTER, Darren	NZL	19.568	34.311	49.870	1:06.311	54.28
15	CAPITANO, Gianluca	ITA	19.878	34.179	49.538	1:06.408	54.21
16	WALLACE, Shaun	GBR	19.767	34.590	50.068	1:06.456	54.17
17	COLLA, Angel	ARG	19.774	34.417	49.897	1:06.619	54.03
18	KIRICHENKO, Aleksandr	RUS	19.446	34.218	49.987	1:07.013	53.72
19	HONG, Suk	KOR	19.591	34.367	50.118	1:07.099	53.65
	KELLY, Shane	AUS				DNF	

Cycling—Track / *Cyclisme — Piste*
Sprint, Men / *Sprint, Messieurs*

200 m FLYING TIME TRIAL

Rnk	Name	Ctry	200 m	km/h	
1	NEIWAND, Gary	AUS	10.129	71.08	O
2	HARNETT, Curt	CAN	10.175	70.76	
3	NOTHSTEIN, Marty	USA	10.176	70.75	
4	FIEDLER, Jens	GER	10.232	70.36	
5	POKORNY, Eyk	GER	10.233	70.36	
6	HILL, Darryn	AUS	10.329	69.70	
7	BURAN, Pavel	CZE	10.389	69.30	
8	ROUSSEAU, Florian	FRA	10.397	69.25	

200 m FLYING TIME TRIAL - *continued*

Rnk	Name	Ctry	200 m	km/h
9	BERZINS, Viesturs	LAT	10.463	68.81
10	CHIAPPA, Roberto	ITA	10.473	68.74
11	MORENO, Jose	ESP	10.492	68.62
12	CLAY, William	USA	10.543	68.29
13	HIMONETOS, George	GRE	10.559	68.18
14	MAGNE, Frederic	FRA	10.602	67.91
15	ESCUREDO, Jose	ESP	10.630	67.73
16	HRBACEK, Martin	SVK	10.693	67.33

200 m FLYING TIME TRIAL - *continued*

Rnk	Name	Ctry	200 m	km/h
17	van ZYL, Jean-Pierre	RSA	10.695	67.32
18	VASSILOPOULOS, Labros	GRE	10.726	67.12
19	KAMIYAMA, Yuichiro	JPN	10.772	66.83
20	BAZALIK, Peter	SVK	10.837	66.43
21	CAPITANO, Gianluca	ITA	10.895	66.08
22	HYUN, Byung	KOR	11.001	65.44
23	McKENZIE POTTER, Darren	NZL	11.211	64.22
24	MARTINEZ ARROYO, Claus	BOL	12.341	58.34

FIRST ROUND

Heat	Rnk	Name	Ctry	200 m
1	1	NEIWAND, Gary	AUS	14.373
	2	MARTINEZ ARROYO, Claus	BOL	
2	1	HARNETT, Curt	CAN	11.380
	2	McKENZIE POTTER, Darren	NZL	
3	1	NOTHSTEIN, Marty	USA	11.415
	2	HYUN, Byung	KOR	
4	1	FIEDLER, Jens	GER	11.722
	2	CAPITANO, Gianluca	ITA	

FIRST ROUND - *continued*

Heat	Rnk	Name	Ctry	200 m
5	1	POKORNY, Eyk	GER	10.995
	2	BAZALIK, Peter	SVK	
6	1	HILL, Darryn	AUS	11.192
	2	KAMIYAMA, Yuichiro	JPN	
7	1	BURAN, Pavel	CZE	11.700
	2	VASSILOPOULOS, Labros	GRE	
8	1	ROUSSEAU, Florian	FRA	11.296
	2	van ZYL, Jean-Pierre	RSA	

FIRST ROUND - *continued*

Heat	Rnk	Name	Ctry	200 m
9	1	BERZINS, Viesturs	LAT	11.008
	2	HRBACEK, Martin	SVK	
10	1	CHIAPPA, Roberto	ITA	10.896
	2	ESCUREDO, Jose	ESP	
11	1	MAGNE, Frederic	FRA	10.740
	2	MORENO, Jose	ESP	
12	1	HIMONETOS, George	GRE	11.182
	2	CLAY, William	USA	

FIRST ROUND REPECHAGE

Heat	Rnk	Name	Ctry	200 m
1	1	CLAY, William	USA	11.191
	2	MARTINEZ ARROYO, Claus	BOL	
2	1	MORENO, Jose	ESP	11.017
	2	McKENZIE POTTER, Darren	NZL	
3	1	ESCUREDO, Jose	ESP	11.257
	2	HYUN, Byung	KOR	
4	1	HRBACEK, Martin	SVK	11.076
	2	CAPITANO, Gianluca	ITA	
5	1	BAZALIK, Peter	SVK	11.222
	2	van ZYL, Jean-Pierre	RSA	
6	1	VASSILOPOULOS, Labros	GRE	11.060
	2	KAMIYAMA, Yuichiro	JPN	

SECOND ROUND

Heat	Rnk	Name	Ctry	200 m
1	1	NEIWAND, Gary	AUS	11.249
	2	VASSILOPOULOS, Labros	GRE	
2	1	HARNETT, Curt	CAN	11.058
	2	BAZALIK, Peter	SVK	
3	1	NOTHSTEIN, Marty	USA	10.899
	2	HRBACEK, Martin	SVK	
4	1	FIEDLER, Jens	GER	10.597
	2	ESCUREDO, Jose	ESP	
5	1	POKORNY, Eyk	GER	10.966
	2	MORENO, Jose	ESP	

SECOND ROUND - *continued*

Heat	Rnk	Name	Ctry	200 m
6	1	HILL, Darryn	AUS	10.811
	2	CLAY, William	USA	
7	1	BURAN, Pavel	CZE	11.272
	2	HIMONETOS, George	GRE	
8	1	ROUSSEAU, Florian	FRA	10.745
	2	MAGNE, Frederic	FRA	
9	1	BERZINS, Viesturs	LAT	11.044
	2	CHIAPPA, Roberto	ITA	

Sprint, Men / *Sprint, Messieurs*

SECOND ROUND REPECHAGE

Heat	Rnk	Name	Ctry	200 m
1	1	CHIAPPA, Roberto	ITA	11.378
	2	VASSILOPOULOS, Labros	GRE	
	3	CLAY, William	USA	REL
2	1	MORENO, Jose	ESP	11.089
	2	HIMONETOS, George	GRE	
	3	BAZALIK, Peter	SVK	
3	1	MAGNE, Frederic	FRA	11.035
	2	HRBACEK, Martin	SVK	
	3	ESCUREDO, Jose	ESP	

1/8 FINALS

Heat	Rnk	Name	Ctry	200 m
1	1	NEIWAND, Gary	AUS	11.625
	2	MAGNE, Frederic	FRA	
2	1	HARNETT, Curt	CAN	10.793
	2	MORENO, Jose	ESP	
3	1	NOTHSTEIN, Marty	USA	11.047
	2	CHIAPPA, Roberto	ITA	
4	1	FIEDLER, Jens	GER	10.808
	2	BERZINS, Viesturs	LAT	
5	1	ROUSSEAU, Florian	FRA	10.828
	2	POKORNY, Eyk	GER	
6	1	HILL, Darryn	AUS	11.008
	2	BURAN, Pavel	CZE	

1/8 FINALS REPECHAGE

Heat	Rnk	Name	Ctry	200 m
1	1	MAGNE, Frederic	FRA	10.975
	2	BURAN, Pavel	CZE	
	3	BERZINS, Viesturs	LAT	
2	1	POKORNY, Eyk	GER	10.982
	2	CHIAPPA, Roberto	ITA	
	3	MORENO, Jose	ESP	

QUARTERFINALS

Heat	Rnk	Name	Ctry	1	2	3
1	1	NEIWAND, Gary	AUS	10.794	11.091	
	2	POKORNY, Eyk	GER			
2	1	HARNETT, Curt	CAN	11.127	REL	10.712
	2	MAGNE, Frederic	FRA		11.022	
3	1	NOTHSTEIN, Marty	USA	10.950	10.650	
	2	HILL, Darryn	AUS			
4	1	FIEDLER, Jens	GER	10.752	10.957	
	2	ROUSSEAU, Florian	FRA			

FINAL 5 - 8

Rnk	Name	Ctry	200 m
5	HILL, Darryn	AUS	11.072
6	MAGNE, Frederic	FRA	
7	POKORNY, Eyk	GER	
8	ROUSSEAU, Florian	FRA	

SEMIFINALS

Heat	Rnk	Name	Ctry	1	2	3
1	1	FIEDLER, Jens	GER	10.618	10.974	
	2	NEIWAND, Gary	AUS			
2	1	NOTHSTEIN, Marty	USA	10.731	10.905	
	2	HARNETT, Curt	CAN			

FINAL

Heat	Rnk	Name	Ctry	1	2	3
Gold	1	FIEDLER, Jens	GER	10.664	11.074	
	2	NOTHSTEIN, Marty	USA			
Bronze	1	HARNETT, Curt	CAN	10.947	10.949	
	2	NEIWAND, Gary	AUS			

FINAL CLASSIFICATION

Rnk	Name	Ctry	
1	FIEDLER, Jens	GER	**Gold**
2	NOTHSTEIN, Marty	USA	**Silver**
3	HARNETT, Curt	CAN	**Bronze**
4	NEIWAND, Gary	AUS	

FINAL CLASSIFICATION - *continued*

Rnk	Name	Ctry
5	HILL, Darryn	AUS
6	MAGNE, Frederic	FRA
7	POKORNY, Eyk	GER
8	ROUSSEAU, Florian	FRA

Cycling—Track / *Cyclisme — Piste*
Sprint, Women / *Sprint, Dames*

200 m FLYING TIME TRIAL

Rnk	Name	Ctry	200 m	km/h
1	FERRIS, Michelle	AUS	11.212	64.21 O
2	BALLANGER, Felicia	FRA	11.277	63.84
3	GRISHINA, Oksana	RUS	11.298	63.72
4	HARINGA, Ingrid	NED	11.456	62.84
5	WANG, Yan	CHN	11.519	62.50
6	NEUMANN, Annett	GER	11.536	62.41
7	PARASKEVIN-YOUNG, Connie	USA	11.545	62.36
8	DUBNICOFF, Tanya	CAN	11.566	62.25
9	SALUMAE, Erika	EST	11.566	62.25
10	LARREAL, Daniela	VEN	11.878	60.61
11	KASSLIN, Mira	FIN	11.924	60.38
12	WYND, Donna	NZL	11.961	60.19
13	RAZMAITE, Rita	LTU	11.971	60.14
14	CONTRERAS, Nancy	MEX	11.992	60.04

1/8 FINALS

Heat	Rnk	Name	Ctry	200 m
1	1	FERRIS, Michelle	AUS	11.932
	2	WYND, Donna	NZL	
2	1	BALLANGER, Felicia	FRA	11.901
	2	KASSLIN, Mira	FIN	
3	1	GRISHINA, Oksana	RUS	12.209
	2	LARREAL, Daniela	VEN	
4	1	HARINGA, Ingrid	NED	12.164
	2	SALUMAE, Erika	EST	
5	1	DUBNICOFF, Tanya	CAN	12.002
	2	WANG, Yan	CHN	
6	1	NEUMANN, Annett	GER	12.078
	2	PARASKEVIN-YOUNG, Connie	USA	

1/8 FINALS REPECHAGE

Heat	Rnk	Name	Ctry	200 m
1	1	SALUMAE, Erika	EST	12.018
	2	PARASKEVIN-YOUNG, Connie	USA	
	3	WYND, Donna	NZL	
2	1	WANG, Yan	CHN	12.067
	2	LARREAL, Daniela	VEN	
	3	KASSLIN, Mira	FIN	

QUARTERFINALS

Heat	Rnk	Name	Ctry	1	2	3
1	1	FERRIS, Michelle	AUS	11.825	11.932	
	2	WANG, Yan	CHN			
2	1	BALLANGER, Felicia	FRA	11.831	12.082	
	2	SALUMAE, Erika	EST			
3	1	NEUMANN, Annett	GER		11.864	12.060
	2	GRISHINA, Oksana	RUS	12.119		
4	1	HARINGA, Ingrid	NED			12.049
	2	DUBNICOFF, Tanya	CAN	12.020	REL	

FINAL 5 - 8

Rnk	Name	Ctry	200 m
5	GRISHINA, Oksana	RUS	12.416
6	SALUMAE, Erika	EST	
7	WANG, Yan	CHN	
8	DUBNICOFF, Tanya	CAN	

SEMIFINALS

Heat	Rnk	Name	Ctry	1	2	3
1	1	FERRIS, Michelle	AUS	12.080	12.078	
	2	HARINGA, Ingrid	NED			
2	1	BALLANGER, Felicia	FRA	12.022	12.046	
	2	NEUMANN, Annett	GER			

Sprint, Women / *Sprint, Dames*

FINALS

Heat	Rnk	Name	Ctry	1	2	3
Gold	1	BALLANGER, Felicia	FRA	11.903	12.096	
	2	FERRIS, Michelle	AUS			
Bronze	1	HARINGA, Ingrid	NED		12.074	11.782
	2	NEUMANN, Annett	GER	12.620		

FINAL CLASSIFICATION

Rnk	Name	Ctry	
1	BALLANGER, Felicia	FRA	Gold
2	FERRIS, Michelle	AUS	Silver
3	HARINGA, Ingrid	NED	Bronze
4	NEUMANN, Annett	GER	

FINAL CLASSIFICATION - *continued*

Rnk	Name	Ctry
5	GRISHINA, Oksana	RUS
6	SALUMAE, Erika	EST
7	WANG, Yan	CHN
8	DUBNICOFF, Tanya	CAN

Cycling—Track / *Cyclisme — Piste*
Individual Pursuit, Men / *Poursuite individuelle, Messieurs*

QUALIFICATION ROUND

Rnk	Heat	Name	Ctry	1 km	2 km	3 km	4 km	km/h
1	8	COLLINELLI, Andrea	ITA	1:09.221	2:12.654	3:16.346	4:19.699	55.44 W
2	7	ERMENAULT, Philippe	FRA	1:09.297	2:13.507	3:17.481	4:21.295	55.11 O
3	6	MARKOV, Aleksey	RUS	1:10.152	2:15.368	3:21.007	4:27.074	53.91
4	8	MARTINEZ, Juan	ESP	1:08.871	2:14.227	3:20.836	4:27.909	53.74
5	9	McGEE, Bradley	AUS	1:07.470	2:12.027	3:19.211	4:27.954	53.74
6	6	SZONN, Heiko	GER	1:09.916	2:15.208	3:21.844	4:29.931	53.34
7	4	PEREZ, Walter	ARG	1:11.010	2:16.976	3:23.101	4:30.715	53.19
8	3	YATSENKO, Andriy	UKR	1:11.025	2:16.795	3:23.310	4:30.751	53.18
9	5	BOSTICK, Kent	USA	1:09.500	2:15.407	3:23.081	4:33.008	52.74

QUALIFICATION ROUND - *continued*

Rnk	Heat	Name	Ctry	1 km	2 km	3 km	4 km	km/h
10	3	KASPUTIS, Arturas	LTU	1:12.161	2:18.551	3:25.279	4:33.748	52.60
11	9	OBREE, Graeme	GBR	1:10.839	2:17.447	3:25.569	4:34.297	52.49
12	2	KARSNICKI, Robert	POL	1:11.492	2:18.117	3:25.938	4:35.193	52.32
13	2	ANDERSON, Gary	NZL	1:11.639	2:19.209	3:28.379	4:36.918	52.00
14	5	KRAVCHENKO, Vadim	KAZ	1:10.355	2:17.258	3:26.612	4:37.212	51.94
15	1	GEORGE, David	RSA	1:10.538	2:19.620	3:29.650	4:39.531	51.51
16	1	COLLINS, Phillip	IRL	1:13.291	2:21.833	3:30.987	4:41.207	51.20
	4	HEINIKAINEN, Jukka	FIN	1:14.199	2:22.857		OVT	Lap 11
	7	PIETERS, Peter	NED	1:13.084			OVT	Lap 8

QUARTERFINALS

Rnk	Heat	Name	Ctry	1 km	2 km	3 km	4 km	km/h
1	4	COLLINELLI, Andrea	ITA	1:09.727	2:13.406	3:16.218	4:19.153	55.56 W
2	3	ERMENAULT, Philippe	FRA	1:09.609	2:14.914	3:19.078	4:22.826	54.78
3	2	MARKOV, Aleksey	RUS	1:09.351	2:13.719	3:18.962	4:24.863	54.36
4	1	McGEE, Bradley	AUS	1:09.573	2:14.097	3:19.391	4:24.943	54.35

QUARTERFINALS - *continued*

Rnk	Heat	Name	Ctry	1 km	2 km	3 km	4 km	km/h
5	1	MARTINEZ, Juan	ESP	1:09.926	2:14.862	3:21.537	4:28.310	53.66
6	2	SZONN, Heiko	GER	1:09.159	2:14.706	3:22.041	4:31.583	53.02
7	4	YATSENKO, Andriy	UKR	1:11.307	2:16.526	3:22.005	OVT	Lap 15
8	3	PEREZ, Walter	ARG	1:10.909	2:17.749		OVT	Lap 12

SEMIFINALS

Rnk	Heat	Name	Ctry	1 km	2 km	3 km	4 km	km/h
1	2	COLLINELLI, Andrea	ITA	1:07.821	2:11.992	3:17.454	4:22.775	54.79
2	1	ERMENAULT, Philippe	FRA	1:08.402	2:12.672	3:17.614	4:24.082	54.52
3	2	McGEE, Bradley	AUS	1:10.294	2:14.953	3:20.862	4:26.121	54.11
4	1	MARKOV, Aleksey	RUS	1:09.404	2:14.450	3:20.623	4:26.828	53.96

FINAL

Rnk	Name	Ctry	1 km	2 km	3 km	4 km	km/h
1	COLLINELLI, Andrea	ITA	1:07.854	2:11.160	3:15.749	4:20.893	55.19
2	ERMENAULT, Philippe	FRA	1:07.852	2:12.130	3:17.966	4:22.714	54.81

FINAL CLASSIFICATION

Rnk	Name	Ctry	Best time	Speed	Round	
1	COLLINELLI, Andrea	ITA	4:19.153	55.56	Quarterfinals	Gold
2	ERMENAULT, Philippe	FRA	4:21.295	55.11	Qualification	Silver
3	McGEE, Bradley	AUS	4:24.943	54.35	Quarterfinals	Bronze
4	MARKOV, Aleksey	RUS	4:24.863	54.36	Quarterfinals	
5	MARTINEZ, Juan	ESP	4:27.909	53.74	Qualification	
6	SZONN, Heiko	GER	4:29.931	53.34	Qualification	
7	YATSENKO, Andriy	UKR	4:30.751	53.18	Qualification	
8	PEREZ, Walter	ARG	4:30.715	53.19	Qualification	
9	BOSTICK, Kent	USA	4:33.008	52.74	Qualification	
10	KASPUTIS, Arturas	LTU	4:33.748	52.60	Qualification	
11	OBREE, Graeme	GBR	4:34.297	52.49	Qualification	
12	KARSNICKI, Robert	POL	4:35.193	52.32	Qualification	
13	ANDERSON, Gary	NZL	4:36.918	52.00	Qualification	
14	KRAVCHENKO, Vadim	KAZ	4:37.212	51.94	Qualification	
15	GEORGE, David	RSA	4:39.531	51.51	Qualification	
16	COLLINS, Phillip	IRL	4:41.207	51.20	Qualification	

Cycling—Track / *Cyclisme — Piste*
Individual Pursuit, Women / *Poursuite individuelle, Dames*

QUALIFICATION ROUND

Rnk	Heat	Name	Ctry	1 km	2 km	3 km	km/h
1	5	BELLUTTI, Antonella	ITA	1:16.782	2:24.967	3:34.130	50.43 O
2	4	CLIGNET, Marion	FRA	1:14.910	2:25.165	3:35.774	50.05 O
3	5	McGREGOR, Yvonne	GBR	1:16.314	2:26.655	3:39.545	49.19
4	6	TWIGG, Rebecca	USA	1:15.608	2:26.229	3:39.849	49.12
5	3	ARNDT, Judith	GER	1:14.282	2:26.087	3:40.335	49.01 O
6	1	ULMER, Sarah	NZL	1:17.059	2:26.723	3:43.176	48.39
7	3	MAZEIKYTE, Rasa	LTU	1:16.452	2:28.532	3:43.590	48.30
8	6	WATT, Kathryn	AUS	1:16.631	2:28.812	3:43.658	48.28
9	2	HARTWELL, May	NOR	1:16.579	2:29.270	3:43.824	48.25
10	4	KARIMOVA, Natalya	RUS	1:16.067	2:30.969	3:45.246	47.94
11	1	WANG, Qingzhi	CHN	1:18.741	2:33.189	3:49.823	46.99
12	2	HASHIMOTO, Seiko	JPN	1:17.536	2:33.783	3:52.745	46.40

QUARTERFINALS

Rnk	Heat	Name	Ctry	1 km	2 km	3 km	km/h
1	4	BELLUTTI, Antonella	ITA	1:14.134	2:22.108	3:32.371	50.85 O
2	3	CLIGNET, Marion	FRA	1:13.677	2:23.627	3:36.446	49.89
3	1	ARNDT, Judith	GER	1:13.381	2:25.285	3:38.898	49.33
4	2	McGREGOR, Yvonne	GBR	1:17.367	2:28.593	3:41.287	48.80
5	1	TWIGG, Rebecca	USA	1:16.452	2:28.492	3:41.611	48.73
6	3	MAZEIKYTE, Rasa	LTU	1:14.530	2:27.952	3:42.129	48.62
7	2	ULMER, Sarah	NZL	1:17.835	2:29.807	3:45.761	47.83
8	4	WATT, Kathryn	AUS	1:16.566	2:28.922	OVT	Lap 10

SEMIFINALS

Rnk	Heat	Name	Ctry	1 km	2 km	3 km	km/h
1	2	BELLUTTI, Antonella	ITA	1:14.481	2:23.855	3:34.404	50.37
2	1	CLIGNET, Marion	FRA	1:14.495	2:23.989	3:35.412	50.13
3	1	ARNDT, Judith	GER	1:14.476	2:26.399	3:38.744	49.37
4	2	McGREGOR, Yvonne	GBR	1:15.697	2:27.218	3:40.885	48.89

FINAL

Rnk	Name	Ctry	1 km	2 km	3 km	km/h
1	BELLUTTI, Antonella	ITA	1:13.302	2:22.567	3:33.595	50.56
2	CLIGNET, Marion	FRA	1:14.239	2:24.593	3:38.571	49.41

FINAL CLASSIFICATION

Rnk	Name	Ctry	Best time	Speed	Round	
1	BELLUTTI, Antonella	ITA	3:32.371	50.85	Quarterfinals	Gold
2	CLIGNET, Marion	FRA	3:35.412	50.13	Semifinals	Silver
3	ARNDT, Judith	GER	3:38.744	49.37	Semifinals	Bronze
4	McGREGOR, Yvonne	GBR	3:39.545	49.19	Qualification	
5	TWIGG, Rebecca	USA	3:39.849	49.12	Qualification	
6	MAZEIKYTE, Rasa	LTU	3:42.129	48.62	Quarterfinals	
7	ULMER, Sarah	NZL	3:43.176	48.39	Qualification	
8	WATT, Kathryn	AUS	3:43.658	48.28	Qualification	
9	HARTWELL, May	NOR	3:43.824	48.25	Qualification	
10	KARIMOVA, Natalya	RUS	3:45.246	47.94	Qualification	
11	WANG, Qingzhi	CHN	3:49.823	46.99	Qualification	
12	HASHIMOTO, Seiko	JPN	3:52.745	46.40	Qualification	

Cycling—Track / *Cyclisme — Piste*
Team Pursuit, Men / *Poursuite par équipes, Messieurs*

QUALIFICATION ROUND

Rnk	Ctry	Names	1 km	2 km	3 km	4 km	km/h
1	FRA	CAPELLE, Christophe / ERMENAULT, Philippe / MONIN, Jean-Michel / MOREAU, Francis	1:05.929	2:07.180	3:08.367	4:09.570	57.69
2	ITA	CAPELLI, Adler / TRENTINI, Mauro / COLLINELLI, Andrea / CITTON, Cristiano	1:06.805	2:07.722	3:08.881	4:09.695	57.67
3	AUS	AITKEN, Brett / O'GRADY, Stuart / O'SHANNESSEY, Timothy / WOODS, Dean	1:04.772	2:05.160	3:07.101	4:09.750	57.65
4	UKR	BONDARYEV, Bohdan / FEDENKO, Oleksandr / YATSENKO, Andriy / SIMONENKO, Alexander	1:06.948	2:07.969	3:09.575	4:11.545	57.24
5	RUS	GRITSUN, Eduard / KUZNETSOV, Nikolay / MARKOV, Aleksey / CHANTYR, Anton	1:06.826	2:07.994	3:09.785	4:11.665	57.21
6	USA	COPELAND, Dirk / FRIEDICK, Mariano / LAURENT, Adam / McCARTHY, Michael	1:05.897	2:06.577	3:08.297	4:11.950	57.15
7	ESP	MARTINEZ, Juan / LLANERAS, Juan / GONZALEZ, Santos / ALPERI, Adolfo	1:08.258	2:09.588	3:10.994	4:12.780	56.96
8	NZL	HENDERSON, Gregory / CAMERON, Brendon / CARSWELL, Timothy / DEAN, Julian	1:07.127	2:10.007	3:12.569	4:14.990	56.47
9	GER	BARTKO, Robert / FULST, Guido / HONDO, Danilo / SZONN, Heiko	1:06.107	2:08.283	3:11.415	4:15.140	56.43
10	GBR	HAYLES, Robert / ILLINGWORTH, Matthew / STEEL, Bryan / NEWTON, Chris	1:07.311	2:09.592	3:12.751	4:15.510	56.35
11	LTU	KASPUTIS, Arturas / LUPEIKIS, Remigijus / UMARAS, Mindaugas / TRUMPAUSKAS, Arturas	1:08.012	2:09.806	3:12.461	4:16.050	56.23
12	NED	BAKKER, Jarich / SLIPPENS, Robertus Michie / ROZENDAAL, Richard / SCHEP, Peter	1:07.437	2:09.942	3:12.786	4:16.175	56.21
13	DEN	BERTELSEN, Frederik / MADSEN, Jimmi / NIELSEN, Michael / PIIL, Jakob	1:07.892	2:11.530	3:15.002	4:18.000	55.81
14	ARG	PEREZ, Walter / SIMON, Edgardo / GARCIA, Gonzalo / CURUTCHET, Gabriel	1:07.819	2:11.461	3:16.251	4:20.840	55.20
15	KOR	CHUN, Dae-Hong / CHUNG, Young / KIM, Jong-Mo / NOH, Young-Sik	1:09.896	2:14.579	3:19.610	4:25.215	54.29
16	CHI	MEDINA, Jose / SEPULVEDA, Luis / ARRIAGADA, Marco / ARRIAGADA, Marcelo	1:08.660	2:13.569	3:19.841	4:25.960	54.14
17	COL	GARCIA, John / PEREZ, Marlon / LOPEZ, Yovani / VELASQUEZ de la CUESTA, Jos	1:08.731	2:13.652	3:18.998	4:26.400	54.05

Team Pursuit, Men / *Poursuite par équipes, Messieurs*

QUARTERFINALS

Rnk	Heat	Ctry	Names	1 km	2 km	3 km	4 km	km/h
1	1	RUS	GRITSUN, Eduard / KUZNETSOV, Nikolay / MARKOV, Aleksey / CHANTYR, Anton	1:06.597	2:06.919	3:07.585	4:08.785	57.88 O
2	4	FRA	CAPELLE, Christophe / ERMENAULT, Philippe / MONIN, Jean-Michel / MOREAU, Francis	1:05.811	2:06.919	3:08.482	4:08.965	57.83
3	3	ITA	CAPELLI, Adler / TRENTINI, Mauro / COLLINELLI, Andrea / CITTON, Cristiano	1:06.699	2:07.470	3:07.933	4:09.215	57.78
4	2	AUS	AITKEN, Brett / McGEE, Bradley / O'GRADY, Stuart / WOODS, Dean	1:04.987	2:05.160	3:06.506	4:09.650	57.68
5	3	ESP	MARTINEZ, Juan / LLANERAS, Juan / GONZALEZ, Santos / ALPERI, Adolfo	1:07.967	2:08.834	3:09.970	4:11.310	57.29
6	2	USA	COPELAND, Dirk / FRIEDICK, Mariano / LAURENT, Adam / McCARTHY, Michael	1:06.052	2:06.763	3:08.224	4:12.470	57.03
7	1	UKR	FEDENKO, Oleksandr / YATSENKO, Andriy / MATVEYEV, Serhiy / SIMONENKO, Alexander	1:06.124	2:07.142	3:09.008	4:12.794	56.96
8	4	NZL	HENDERSON, Gregory / CAMERON, Brendon / CARSWELL, Timothy / DEAN, Julian	1:06.558	2:09.170	3:12.799	4:15.610	56.33

SEMIFINALS

Rnk	Heat	Ctry	Names	1 km	2 km	3 km	4 km	km/h
1	1	FRA	CAPELLE, Christophe / ERMENAULT, Philippe / MONIN, Jean-Michel / MOREAU, Francis	1:05.460	2:05.496	3:06.070	4:06.880	58.32 O
2	2	RUS	GRITSUN, Eduard / KUZNETSOV, Nikolay / MARKOV, Aleksey / CHANTYR, Anton	1:05.337	2:05.005	3:05.873	4:06.885	58.32
3	2	AUS	McGEE, Bradley / O'GRADY, Stuart / O'SHANNESSEY, Timothy / WOODS, Dean	1:05.053	2:04.657	3:05.302	4:07.570	58.16
4	1	ITA	CAPELLI, Adler / TRENTINI, Mauro / COLLINELLI, Andrea / CITTON, Cristiano	1:05.623	2:06.250	3:07.294	4:08.460	57.95

FINAL

Rnk	Ctry	Names	1 km	2 km	3 km	4 km	km/h
1	FRA	CAPELLE, Christophe / ERMENAULT, Philippe / MONIN, Jean-Michel / MOREAU, Francis	1:04.812	2:04.565	3:05.120	4:05.930	58.55 O
2	RUS	GRITSUN, Eduard / KUZNETSOV, Nikolay / MARKOV, Aleksey / CHANTYR, Anton	1:05.568	2:05.591	3:06.497	4:07.730	58.12

FINAL CLASSIFICATION

Rnk	Ctry	Best time	Speed	
1	France	4:05.930	58.55	Gold
2	Russian Federation	4:06.885	58.32	Silver
3	Australia	4:07.570	58.16	Bronze
4	Italy	4:08.460	57.95	
5	Spain	4:11.310	57.29	
6	United States of America	4:12.470	57.03	
7	Ukraine	4:12.794	56.96	
8	New Zealand	4:15.610	56.33	

Cycling—Track / *Cyclisme — Piste*
Point Race, Men / *Course aux points, Messieurs*

FINAL

Rnk	Name	Ctry	Laps down	Points	
1	MARTINELLO, Silvio	ITA		37	G
2	WALTON, Brian	CAN		29	S
3	O'GRADY, Stuart	AUS		25	B
4	YAKOVLEV, Vasyl	UKR		24	
5	MOREAU, Francis	FRA		21	
6	LLANERAS, Juan	ESP		17	
7	WYNANTS, Milton	URU		6	
8	CHO, Ho-Sung	KOR	-1	14	
9	McLEAY, Glenn	NZL	-1	8	
10	FULST, Guido	GER	-1	7	
11	LAVRENENKO, Sergey	KAZ	-1	6	
12	STOCHER, Franz	AUT	-1	5	
13	LUPEIKIS, Remigijus	LTU	-1	4	
14	KHAMIDULIN, Pavel	RUS	-1	4	
15	YASUHARA, Masahiro	JPN	-1	2	
16	VAKKER, Yevgeniy	KGZ	-1	1	
17	RISI, Bruno	SUI	-2	8	
18	PETERSEN, Jan	DEN	-2	7	
19	McDONOUGH, Brian	USA	-2	5	
20	GODOY FRANKE, Sergio	GUA	-2	0	
21	PIETERS, Peter	NED	-2	0	
22	LONERGAN, Declan	IRL	-2	0	
23	CURUCHET, Juan	ARG	-2	0	
24	de WILDE, Etienne	BEL	-2	0	
	PEREZ, Marion	COL		DNF	
	ZARAGOZA, Marco	MEX		DNF	
	MERHEB, Juan	PUR		DNF	
	GEORGE, David	RSA		DNF	

Cycling—Track / *Cyclisme — Piste*
Point Race, Women / *Course aux points, Dames*

FINAL

Rnk	Name	Ctry	Laps down	Points	
1	LANCIEN, Nathalie	FRA		24	G
2	HARINGA, Ingrid	NED		23	S
3	TYLER-SHARMAN, Lucy	AUS		17	B
4	SAMOKHVALOVA, Svetlana	RUS		14	
5	KAILA VERGARA, Maureen	ESA		11	
6	GOROZHANSKAYA, Lyudmila	BLR		11	
7	VIKSTEDT-NYMAN, Tea	FIN		9	
8	NELSON, Jacqueline	NZL		8	
9	HASHIMOTO, Seiko	JPN		7	
10	CRISTOFOLI, Nada	ITA		6	
11	GUERRERO, Belem	MEX		4	
12	VASILENKO, Alla	KAZ		2	
13	ARNDT, Judith	GER		2	
14	LAWRENCE, Maria	GBR		1	
15	LARREAL, Daniela	VEN		0	
16	KLEIN, Tanja	AUT		0	
17	GOLAY, Jeanne	USA		0	
18	PEREZ, Dania	CUB		0	
	WANG, Yan	CHN		DNF	
	KIM, Yong-Mi	KOR		DNF	
	HARTWELL, May	NOR		DNF	
	BENGOA, Izaskun	ESP		DNF	
	RAZMAITE, Rita	LTU		DNF	

EQUESTRIAN
SPORTS ÉQUESTRES

Abbreviations and terms used in Equestrian results tables
Abréviations et termes employés dans les tableaux de résultats des sports équestres

Term	English	Français
% GP Score	% Grand Prix Score	% Score du Grand Prix
% GP + %GPS	% Grand Prix + % Grand Prix Special	% Grand Prix + % Grand Prix spécial
% GPS Score	% Grand Prix Special Score	% Score du Grand Prix spécial
% Score	% Score	% Score
1st Qualifier	First Qualifier	Première manche
B	Bronze Medal	Médaille de bronze
Continued	Continued	Continué
Ctry	Country	Pays
Dressage	Dressage	Dressage
EL	Eliminated	Eliminé
Endurance	Endurance	Endurance
Error	Error	Erreur
Final	Final	Finale
Final Results Summary	Final Results Summary	Sommaire des résultats finaux
Freestyle	Freestyle	Reprise libre
G	Gold Medal	Médaille d'or
GP Score	Grand Prix Score	Score du Grand Prix
Grand Prix	Grand Prix	Grand Prix
Grand Prix Freestyle	Grand Prix Freestyle	Grand Prix reprise libre
Grand Prix Special	Grand Prix Special	Grand Prix spécial
Ground Jury	Ground Jury	Jury de terrain
Horse	Horse	Cheval
Judges' Marks	Judges' Marks	Scores des juges
Jump Off	Jump Off	Barrage
Jump Penalty	Jump Penalty	Pénalité de saut
Jumping	Jumping	Saut
Name	Name	Nom
Penalties	Penalties	Pénalités
Q	Qualified	Qualifié
RT	Retired	Abandon
Rnk	Rank	Classement
Round	Round	Tour
S	Silver Medal	Médaille d'argent
Time Penalty	Time Penalty	Pénalité de temps
Time Taken	Time Taken	Temps pris
Total	Total	Total
WD	Withdrawn	Absent au départ

International Equestrian Federation (FEI)
Fédération Equestre Internationale
Mon-Repos 24
Boite Postale 157
CH-1000, Lausanne 5
Switzerland

TONY J ROBINSON • TRACI E ROBINSON • TYRONE J ROBINSON • VICKIE L ROBINSON • VIRGINIA S ROBINSON • WALTER G ROBINSON • WALTER K ROBINSON • WALTER S ROBINSON • WARREN L ROBINSON • WILFRED K ROBINSON • WILLIAM P ROBINSON • DOROTHY ROBINSON-COLEMAN • TERRY M ROBINSON ATC • DURAND ROBINSON III • DOUGLAS ROBINSON IV • WALTER L ROBINSON JR • WILLIAM M ROBINSON JR • TODD H ROBINSON MD • CHRISTINE F ROBINSON MT • GEENA ROBINSON MT • ALICE S ROBISON • ANN S ROBISON • CARYLE A ROBISON • MAC M ROBISON •

185

Equestrian / *Sports équestres*
Individual 3-Day Event / *Concours complet individuel*

DRESSAGE

Rnk	Name	Horse	Ctry	Judges' Marks* H	C	M	Penalties Error	Total
1	KING, Mary	KING WILLIAM	GBR	191	189	182		31.60
2	O'CONNOR, David	CUSTOM MADE	USA	176	178	178		37.60
3	BISHOP, Nikki	WISHFUL THINKING	AUS	169	173	178		40.00
4	DEPUY, Mara	HOPPER	USA	163	182	174		40.20
5	TEULERE, Jean	RODOSTO	FRA	163	173	178		41.20
6	BLOCKER, Herbert	KIWI DREAM	GER	169	167	172		42.40
7	WILLEFERT, Didier	SEDUCTEUR BIOLAY	FRA	170	167	170		42.60
8	GREEN, David	CHATSBY	AUS	169	166	156		45.80
9	MILLIKIN, Kerry	OUT AND ABOUT	USA	167	156	159		47.60
10	DUROY, Marie-Christine	UT DU PLACINEAU	FRA	162	156	163		47.80
11	NICHOLSON, Andrew	BUCKLEY PROVINCE	NZL	158	162	158		48.40
12	HUNNABLE, Chris	MR. BOOTSIE	GBR	158	157	158		49.40
13	BATHE, Charlotte	THE COOL CUSTOMER	GBR	166	161	144		49.80
14	CLARK, Sally	SQUIRREL HILL	NZL	164	150	160	2	51.20
15	TAIT, Blyth	READY TEDDY	NZL	162	147	153		51.60
15	de ALMEIDA, Artemus	BURYAND	BRA	153	153	156		51.60
17	CAPPAI, Marco	NIGHT COURT	ITA	154	153	152		52.20
18	THOMSEN, Peter	WHITE GIRL 3	GER	158	153	141		53.60
19	HAAGENSEN, Nils	TROUPIER	DEN	154	151	142		54.60
20	FOSTER, David	TILT 'N' TURN	IRL	158	141	147		54.80
21	McMULLEN TEMPLE, Kelli	AMSTERDAM	CAN	158	141	145		55.20
22	VAN RIJCKEVORSEL, Constantin	OTIS	BEL	156	136	149		55.80
23	von PAEPCKE, Hendrik	AMADEUS 188	GER	156	128	155		56.20
24	HOSONO, Shigeyuki	AS DU PERCHE	JPN	141	139	143		59.40
25	GENTINI, Roberta	ZIGOLO di SAN CALOGERO	ITA	143	138	140		59.80
26	REVUELTA, Javier	HOOCHI KOOCHI	ESP	140	139	139		60.40
27	CANDISANO, Juan	REMONTA OFRECIDO	ARG	141	128	145		61.20
28	PIASECKI, Piotr	LADY NALECZOWIANKA	POL	147	130	129		62.80
29	HOY, Andrew	GERSHWIN	AUS	138	138	137	2	63.40
30	NEMTIN, Anita	KAESAR	HUN	136	128	129		65.40
31	BECA, Ramon	PERSEUS II	ESP	130	118	127		69.00
32	SARASOLA, Enrique	REBABY	ESP	132	117	120		70.20
33	JONSSON, Fredrik	ULFUNG	SWE	132	120	124	2	70.80
34	KOWATA, Yoshihiko	STARS DE RIOLS	JPN	123	117	124		71.20
35	LAMBA, Indrajit	KARISHMA	IND	108	100	115		79.40
	KOZAK, Chelan	SOWETO	CAN					WD

ENDURANCE

Rnk	Name	Horse	Ctry	Penalties Dressage	Endurance	Total
1	TAIT, Blyth	READY TEDDY	NZL	51.60	5.20	56.80
2	CLARK, Sally	SQUIRREL HILL	NZL	51.20	9.20	60.40
3	MILLIKIN, Kerry	OUT AND ABOUT	USA	47.60	19.60	67.20
4	TEULERE, Jean	RODOSTO	FRA	41.20	26.00	67.20
5	O'CONNOR, David	CUSTOM MADE	USA	37.60	30.80	68.40
6	VAN RIJCKEVORSEL, Constantin	OTIS	BEL	55.80	21.60	77.40
7	KING, Mary	KING WILLIAM	GBR	31.60	46.40	78.00
8	BATHE, Charlotte	THE COOL CUSTOMER	GBR	49.80	28.80	78.60
9	HUNNABLE, Chris	MR. BOOTSIE	GBR	49.40	32.00	81.40
10	von PAEPCKE, Hendrik	AMADEUS 188	GER	56.20	26.00	82.20
11	WILLEFERT, Didier	SEDUCTEUR BIOLAY	FRA	42.60	41.60	84.20
12	DEPUY, Mara	HOPPER	USA	40.20	44.80	85.00
13	CAPPAI, Marco	NIGHT COURT	ITA	52.20	50.80	103.00
14	JONSSON, Fredrik	ULFUNG	SWE	70.80	39.60	110.40
15	HOY, Andrew	GERSHWIN	AUS	63.40	49.20	112.60
16	GENTINI, Roberta	ZIGOLO di SAN CALOGERO	ITA	59.80	79.20	139.00
17	BECA, Ramon	PERSEUS II	ESP	69.00	72.00	141.00
18	BLOCKER, Herbert	KIWI DREAM	GER	42.40	111.20	153.60
19	McMULLEN TEMPLE, Kelli	AMSTERDAM	CAN	55.20	101.60	156.80
20	NEMTIN, Anita	KAESAR	HUN	65.40	139.20	204.60
	BISHOP, Nikki	WISHFUL THINKING	AUS	40.00	EL	EL
	de ALMEIDA, Artemus	BURYAND	BRA	51.60	EL	EL
	LAMBA, Indrajit	KARISHMA	IND	79.40	EL	EL
	HOSONO, Shigeyuki	AS DU PERCHE	JPN	59.40	EL	EL
	KOWATA, Yoshihiko	STARS DE RIOLS	JPN	71.20	EL	EL
	PIASECKI, Piotr	LADY NALECZOWIANKA	POL	62.80	EL	EL
	SARASOLA, Enrique	REBABY	ESP	70.20	EL	EL
	GREEN, David	CHATSBY	AUS	45.80	RT	RT
	HAAGENSEN, Nils	TROUPIER	DEN	54.60	RT	RT
	DUROY, Marie-Christine	UT DU PLACINEAU	FRA	47.80	RT	RT
	FOSTER, David	TILT 'N' TURN	IRL	54.80	RT	RT
	NICHOLSON, Andrew	BUCKLEY PROVINCE	NZL	48.40	RT	RT
	REVUELTA, Javier	HOOCHI KOOCHI	ESP	60.40	RT	RT
	THOMSEN, Peter	WHITE GIRL 3	GER	53.60	WD	WD
	KOZAK, Chelan	SOWETO	CAN	WD		WD

* GROUND JURY - TEAM 3-DAY EVENT

Judge's Mark	Ctry	Judge
H	USA	LeGOFF, Jack
C	ITA	GRIGNOLO, Giovanni
M	GER	SPRINGORUM, Bernd

JUMPING

Rnk	Name	Horse	Ctry	Penalties Dressage	Endurance	Jumping	Total
1	TAIT, Blyth	READY TEDDY	NZL	51.60	5.20	0.00	56.80 G
2	CLARK, Sally	SQUIRREL HILL	NZL	51.20	9.20	0.00	60.40 S
3	MILLIKIN, Kerry	OUT AND ABOUT	USA	47.60	19.60	6.50	73.70 B
4	TEULERE, Jean	RODOSTO	FRA	41.20	26.00	10.00	77.20
5	O'CONNOR, David	CUSTOM MADE	USA	37.60	30.80	11.75	80.15
6	DEPUY, Mara	HOPPER	USA	40.20	44.80	0.00	85.00
7	von PAEPCKE, Hendrik	AMADEUS 188	GER	56.20	26.00	5.00	87.20
8	VAN RIJCKEVORSEL, C.	OTIS	BEL	55.80	21.60	10.00	87.40
9	WILLEFERT, Didier	SEDUCTEUR BIOLAY	FRA	42.60	41.60	5.00	89.20
10	HUNNABLE, Chris	MR. BOOTSIE	GBR	49.40	32.00	30.00	111.40
11	HOY, Andrew	GERSHWIN	AUS	63.40	49.20	0.00	112.60
12	KING, Mary	KING WILLIAM	GBR	31.60	46.40	40.00	118.00
13	JONSSON, Fredrik	ULFUNG	SWE	70.80	39.60	16.75	127.15
14	CAPPAI, Marco	NIGHT COURT	ITA	52.20	50.80	35.00	138.00
15	GENTINI, Roberta	ZIGOLO di SAN CALOGERO	ITA	59.80	79.20	7.75	146.75
16	BLOCKER, Herbert	KIWI DREAM	GER	42.40	111.20	6.50	160.10
17	BECA, Ramon	PERSEUS II	ESP	69.00	72.00	23.75	164.75
18	McMULLEN TEMPLE, K.	AMSTERDAM	CAN	55.20	101.60	15.00	171.80

JUMPING - *continued*

Rnk	Name	Horse	Ctry	Penalties Dressage	Endurance	Jumping	Total
19	NEMTIN, Anita	KAESAR	HUN	65.40	139.20	5.25	209.85
	BATHE, Charlotte	THE COOL CUSTOMER	GBR	49.80	28.80	WD	WD
	BISHOP, Nikki	WISHFUL THINKING	AUS	40.00	EL		EL
	de ALMEIDA, Artemus	BURYAND	BRA	51.60	EL		EL
	LAMBA, Indrajit	KARISHMA	IND	79.40	EL		EL
	HOSONO, Shigeyuki	AS DU PERCHE	JPN	59.40	EL		EL
	KOWATA, Yoshihiko	STARS DE RIOLS	JPN	71.20	EL		EL
	SARASOLA, Enrique	REBABY	ESP	70.20	EL		EL
	GREEN, David	CHATSBY	AUS	45.80	RT		RT
	HAAGENSEN, Nils	TROUPIER	DEN	54.60	RT		RT
	DUROY, Marie-Christine	UT DU PLACINEAU	FRA	47.80	RT		RT
	FOSTER, David	TILT 'N' TURN	IRL	54.80	RT		RT
	NICHOLSON, Andrew	BUCKLEY PROVINCE	NZL	48.40	RT		RT
	PIASECKI, Piotr	LADY NALECZOWIANKA	POL	62.80	RT		RT
	REVUELTA, Javier	HOOCHI KOOCHI	ESP	60.40	RT		RT
	THOMSEN, Peter	WHITE GIRL 3	GER	53.60	RT		WD
	KOZAK, Chelan	SOWETO	CAN	WD			WD

Equestrian / *Sports équestres*
Team 3-Day Event / *Concours complet par équipes*

FINAL

Rnk	Ctry	Names	Horse	Penalties Dressage	Penalties Endurance	Penalties Jumping	Total
1	AUS	Australia		156.40	27.29	20.25	203.85 G
		SCHAEFFER, Wendy	SUNBURST	49.40	11.60	0.00	61.00 *
		DUTTON, Phillip	TRUE BLUE GIRDWOOD	50.60	8.80	10.00	69.40 *
		ROLTON, Gillian	PEPPERMINT GROVE	57.00	WD		WD
		HOY, Andrew	DARIEN POWERS	56.40	6.80	10.25	73.45 *
2	USA	United States of America		123.00	121.60	16.50	261.10 S
		O'CONNOR, Karen	BIKO	39.60	66.00	0.00	105.60 *
		O'CONNOR, David	GILTEDGE	40.80	35.20	0.00	76.00 *
		DAVIDSON, Bruce	HEYDAY	42.60	20.40	16.50	79.50 *
		HENNEBERG, Jill	NIRVANA	57.00	RT		RT
3	NZL	New Zealand		135.60	120.20	12.75	268.55 B
		TAIT, Blyth	CHESTERFIELD	48.80	20.80	0.50	70.10 *
		NICHOLSON, Andrew	JAGERMEISTER II	47.20	51.20	2.25	100.65 *
		LATTA, Victoria	BROADCAST NEWS	41.00	RT		RT
		JEFFERIS, Vaughn	BOUNCE	47.40	40.40	10.00	97.80 *
4	FRA	France		162.40	106.00	39.25	307.65
		DUROY, Marie-Christine	YARLANDS SUMMER SONG	44.40	RT		RT
		SCHERER, Rodolphe	URANE DES PINS	50.60	40.80	17.75	109.15 *
		VIEULES, Koris	TANDRESSE de CANTA	81.60	28.00	10.00	119.60 *
		DULCY, Jacques	UPONT	67.40	0.00	11.50	78.90 *
5	GBR	Great Britain		127.80	170.60	14.50	312.90
		STARK, Ian	STANWICK GHOST	35.20	121.20	15.25	171.65
		FOX-PITT, William	COSMOPOLITAN II	49.00	62.80	5.75	117.55 *
		PARSONAGE, Gary	MAGIC ROGUE	62.60	37.20	7.00	106.80 *
		DIXON, Karen	TOO SMART	43.60	43.20	1.75	88.55 *
6	JPN	Japan		161.60	147.80	16.75	326.15
		IWATANI, Kazuhiro	SEJANE DE VOZERIER	48.40	47.60	5.00	101.00 *
		FUSE, Masaru	TALISMAN DE JARRY	53.40	94.40	6.25	154.05
		KOWATA, Yoshihiko	HELL AT DAWN	59.80	57.20	5.50	122.50 *
		TSUCHIYA, Takeaki	RIGHT ON TIME	61.60	34.80	6.25	102.65 *
7	SWE	Sweden		166.80	163.20	15.25	345.25
		TORNQVIST, Paula	MONAGHAN	58.80	35.20	5.00	99.00 *
		ALGOTSSON, Linda	LAFAYETTE	51.80	16.40	10.25	78.45 *
		OLAVSSON, Therese	HECTOR T	61.40	106.40	0.00	167.80 *
		ALBERT, Dag	NICE 'N' EASY	56.20	RT		RT
8	ESP	Spain		172.60	395.80	53.25	621.65
		ALVAREZ-CERVERA, Luis	PICO'S NIPPUR	77.60	184.80	11.00	273.40 *
		CENTENERA, Santiago	JUST DIXON	47.80	73.20	40.00	161.00 *
		REVUELTA, Javier	TOBY	61.00	124.00	2.25	187.25 *
		SARASOLA, Enrique	NEW VENTURE	63.80	EL		EL

FINAL - *continued*

Rnk	Ctry	Names	Horse	Penalties Dressage	Penalties Endurance	Penalties Jumping	Total
9	GER	Germany		145.00	1047.40	11.75	1204.15
		BATTENBERG, Bodo	SAM THE MAN	52.00	32.40	5.00	89.40 *
		BLUM, Juergen	BROWNIE MCGEE	61.60	RT		RT *
		EHRENBRINK, Ralf	CONNECTION L	44.20	EL		EL
		OVERESCH-BOEKER, B.	WATERMILL STREAM	48.80	59.20	6.75	114.75 *
10	SUI	Switzerland		190.60	1121.40	5.50	1317.50
		MEIER, Christoph	HUNTER V	56.80	122.00	0.00	178.80 *
		MARRO, Marius	GAI JEANNOT CH	65.00	EL		EL *
		WEHRLI, Heinz	PING PONG	68.80	64.40	5.50	138.70 *
11	IRL	Ireland		167.60	1162.80	54.00	1384.40
		FOSTER, David	DUNEIGHT CARNIVAL	52.20	36.00	5.00	93.20 *
		McGRATH, Virginia	THE YELLOW EARL	61.20	181.00	49.00	291.20 *
		BULLER, Alfie	SIR KNIGHT	74.60	WD		WD *
		SMILEY, Eric	ENTERPRISE	54.20	WD		WD
12	ITA	Italy		166.40	1193.80	34.25	1394.45
		CAMPELLO, Ranieri	MILL BANK	64.20	RT		RT *
		della CHIESA, Giacomo	DIVER DAN	61.80	WD		WD
		VILLATA, Lara	NIKKI DOW	50.60	124.80	18.75	194.15 *
		delli SANTI, Nicola	DONNIZETTI	54.00	130.80	15.50	200.30 *
13	HUN	Hungary		195.60	1220.00	18.50	1434.10
		SCHALLER, Gabor	ALBATTROSZ	60.80	RT		RT *
		SOS, Attila	ZSIZSIK	63.00	158.80	11.50	233.30 *
		TUSKA, Pal	ZATONY	71.80	122.00	7.00	200.80 *
		HERCZEGFALVI, Tibor	LUMP	72.40	RT		RT
14	CAN	Canada		139.20	1935.20	0.00	2074.40
		WASHTOCK, Therese	ARISTOTLE	40.00	EL		EL *
		McMULLEN TEMPLE, Kelli	KILKENNY	47.20	27.20	0.00	74.40 *
		SMITH, Claire	GORDON GIBBONS	53.00	RT		RT *
		YOUNG-BLACK, Stuart	MARKET VENTURE	52.00	WD		WD
15	BRA	Brazil		208.60	1959.60	6.25	2174.45
		FOFANOFF, Serguei	KAISER EDEN	73.40	94.80	6.25	174.45 *
		de SOUZA, Sidney	AVALON da MATA	68.00	WD		WD *
		GIOVANINI, Andre	AL do BETO	67.20	EL		EL *
		MIRANDA, Luciano	XILENA	74.40	RT		RT
16	POL	Poland		182.80	2005.40	9.75	2197.95
		CHOYNOWSKI, Rafal	VIVA 5	67.20	EL		EL *
		JARECKI, Boguslaw	POLISA	61.00	127.20	9.75	197.95 *
		SPOLOWICZ, Artur	HAZARD	63.00	EL		EL *
		OWCZAREK, Boguslaw	ASKAR	58.80	EL		EL

* Score counts for team total.

* Score compté pour le total de l'équipe.

GROUND JURY - TEAM 3-DAY EVENT

Judge's Mark	Ctry	Judge
H	USA	LeGOFF, Jack
C	ITA	GRIGNOLO, Giovanni
M	GER	SPRINGORUM, Bernd

Equestrian / *Sports équestres*

Individual Dressage / *Dressage individuel*

GRAND PRIX

Rnk	Ctry	Name	Horse	GP Score	%GP Score
1	GER	WERTH, Isabell	GIGOLO	1915	76.60
2	NED	van GRUNSVEN, Anky	BONFIRE	1893	75.72
3	USA	GIBSON, Michelle	PERON	1880	75.20
4	NED	ROTHENBERGER, Sven	WEYDEN	1854	74.16
5	GER	THEODORESCU, Monica	GRUNOX	1845	73.80
6	GER	BALKENHOL, Klaus	GOLDSTERN	1793	71.72
7	FRA	OTTO-CREPIN, Margit	LUCKY LORD	1783	71.32
8	GER	UPHOFF-BECKER, Nicole	REMBRANDT	1751	70.04
9	ESP	RAMBLA, Ignacio	EVENTO	1744	69.76
10	USA	SEIDEL, Guenter	GRAF GEORGE	1734	69.36
11	DEN	PETERSEN, Lars	UFFE KORSHOJGAARD	1705	68.20
12	USA	PETERS, Steffen	UDON	1695	67.80
13	NED	BARTELS-de VRIES, Tineke	OLYMPIC BARBRIA	1690	67.60
14	SWE	SOLMELL, Annette	STRAUSS	1673	66.92
15	GBR	DAVISON, Richard	ASKARI	1668	66.72
16	SWE	HAKANSSON, Ulla	BOBBY	1666	66.64
17	SUI	STUECKELBERGER, Christine	AQUAMARIN	1662	66.48
18	BEL	HOLSTERS, Arlette	FAIBLE	1658	66.32
19	FRA	BRIEUSSEL, Dominique	AKAZIE	1650	66.00
20	USA	DOVER, Robert	METALLIC	1649	65.96
21	AUS	HANNA, Mary	MOSAIC	1644	65.76
22	IRL	HOLSTEIN, Heike	BALLASEYR DEVEREAUX	1631	65.24

GRAND PRIX - *continued*

Rnk	Ctry	Name	Horse	GP Score	%GP Score
23	SUI	STAUB, Hans	DUKAAT	1628	65.12
24	FIN	KYRKLUND, Kyra	AMIRAL	1620	64.80
25	CAN	BRAMALL, Leonie	GILBONA	1613	64.52
26	FRA	d'ESME, Dominique	ARNOLDO	1612	64.48
27	AUT	HATLAPA, Caroline	MERLIN	1609	64.36
28	ESP	FERRER SALAT, Beatriz	BRILLANT	1604	64.16
29	SUI	SENN, Eva	RENZO	1603	64.12
30	ITA	LAUS, Pia	LIEBENBERG	1600	64.00
31	ITA	GIANI MARGI, Paolo	DESTINO di ACCIARELLA	1595	63.80
32	GBR	JACKSON, Joanna	MESTER MOUSE	1577	63.08
33	SWE	WILHELMSSON, Tinne	CAPRICE	1542	61.68
34	ESP	SOTO, Rafael	INVASOR	1527	61.08
35	GBR	THOMPSON, Vicky	ENFANT	1516	60.64
36	BER	DUNKLEY, Suzanne	ELLIOT	1502	60.08
37	ITA	FANTONI, Daria	SONNY BOY	1496	59.84
38	GBR	BREDIN, Jane	CUPIDO	1468	58.72
39	CAN	STRASSER, Evi	LAVINIA	1462	58.48
40	CAN	SMITH, Gina	FAUST	1434	57.36
41	ITA	PUCCINI, Fausto	FIFFIKUS	1418	56.72
42	ESP	MATUTE, Juan	HERMES	1416	56.64
43	SUI	von GREBEL SCHIENDORFER, Barbara	RAMAR	1324	52.96
44	CAN	DVORAK, Thomas	WORLD CUP	WD	WD

GRAND PRIX SPECIAL

Rnk	Ctry	Name	Horse	%GP score	E	H	C	M	B	Total	%GPS score	%GP+ %GPS
1	NED	van GRUNSVEN, Anky	BONFIRE	75.72	346 (1)	325 (1)	330 (1)	330 (1)	340 (1)	1671	77.72	153.44
2	GER	WERTH, Isabell	GIGOLO	76.60	323 (2)	315 (2)	323 (5)	324 (3)	338 (2)	1623	75.49	152.09
3	USA	GIBSON, Michelle	PERON	75.20	320 (5)	308 (8)	324 (4)	320 (4)	325 (5)	1597	74.28	149.48
4	NED	ROTHENBERGER, Sven	WEYDEN	74.16	318 (6)	310 (6)	321 (6)	327 (2)	315 (9)	1591	74.00	148.16
5	GER	THEODORESCU, Monica	GRUNOX	73.80	322 (3)	311 (4)	314 (8)	315 (7)	327 (4)	1589	73.91	147.71
6	GER	BALKENHOL, Klaus	GOLDSTERN	71.72	315 (8)	311 (4)	325 (2)	315 (7)	321 (7)	1587	73.81	145.53
7	FRA	OTTO-CREPIN, Margit	LUCKY LORD	71.32	322 (3)	309 (7)	310 (10)	316 (5)	311 (11)	1568	72.93	144.25
8	GER	UPHOFF-BECKER, Nicole	REMBRANDT	70.04	318 (6)	312 (3)	315 (7)	300 (11)	325 (5)	1570	73.02	143.06
9	GER	SCHAUDT, Martin	DURGO	71.24	296 (17)	301 (9)	312 (9)	301 (10)	316 (8)	1526	70.98	142.22
10	USA	SEIDEL, Guenter	GRAF GEORGE	69.36	315 (8)	301 (9)	307 (11)	308 (9)	313 (10)	1544	71.81	141.17
11	ESP	RAMBLA, Ignacio	EVENTO	69.76	303 (11)	299 (12)	304 (13)	298 (12)	305 (12)	1509	70.19	139.95
12	SWE	NATHHORST, Louise	WALK ON TOP	66.28	312 (10)	300 (11)	325 (2)	316 (5)	328 (3)	1581	73.53	139.81
13	DEN	PETERSEN, Lars	UFFE KORSHOJGAARD	68.20	297 (16)	297 (13)	300 (14)	292 (14)	292 (15)	1478	68.74	136.94
14	NED	BARTELS-de VRIES, Tineke	OLYMPIC BARBRIA	67.60	300 (14)	291 (14)	293 (17)	294 (13)	290 (19)	1468	68.28	135.88
15	USA	PETERS, Steffen	UDON	67.80	301 (12)	286 (18)	291 (20)	285 (17)	291 (16)	1454	67.63	135.43
16	NED	ROTHENBERGER, Gonnelien	OLYMPIC DONDOLO	66.92	300 (14)	290 (15)	307 (11)	283 (19)	291 (16)	1471	68.42	135.34
17	SUI	STUECKELBERGER, Christine	AQUAMARIN	66.48	301 (12)	290 (15)	292 (19)	284 (18)	297 (14)	1464	68.09	134.57
18	BEL	HOLSTERS, Arlette	FAIBLE	66.32	290 (18)	288 (17)	298 (15)	290 (15)	299 (13)	1465	68.14	134.46
19	SWE	SOLMELL, Annette	STRAUSS	66.92	281 (22)	286 (18)	293 (17)	281 (20)	288 (20)	1429	66.47	133.39
20	SWE	HAKANSSON, Ulla	BOBBY	66.64	281 (22)	282 (20)	290 (21)	289 (16)	288 (20)	1430	66.51	133.15
21	GBR	DAVISON, Richard	ASKARI	66.72	287 (19)	274 (23)	278 (23)	267 (24)	291 (16)	1397	64.98	131.70
22	DEN	HANSEN, Finn	BERGERAC	65.44	282 (21)	280 (21)	295 (16)	275 (21)	279 (23)	1411	65.63	131.07
23	FRA	BRIEUSSEL, Dominique	AKAZIE	66.00	278 (24)	276 (22)	283 (22)	270 (23)	272 (24)	1379	64.14	130.14
24	AUS	HANNA, Mary	MOSAIC	65.76	283 (20)	271 (24)	276 (24)	271 (22)	282 (22)	1383	64.33	130.09
25	USA	DOVER, Robert	METALLIC	65.96	264 (25)	248 (25)	250 (25)	252 (25)	250 (25)	1264	58.79	124.75

Judges' Marks*

* GROUND JURY - GRAND PRIX SPECIAL

Judge's Mark	Ctry	Judge
E	NED	PEETERS, Jan
H	FRA	MAUREL, Bernd
C	SWE	LETTE, Eric
M	USA	ZANG, Linda
B	GER	MECHLEM, Uwe

Individual Dressage / *Dressage individuel*

FREESTYLE

| Rnk | Ctry | Name | Horse | Judges' Marks* | | | | | Total | % score |
				E	H	C	M	B		
1	GER	WERTH, Isabell	GIGOLO	16.63 (1)	16.60 (2)	16.80 (1)	16.73 (1)	16.25 (1)	83.00	83.00
2	NED	van GRUNSVEN, Anky	BONFIRE	15.68 (2)	16.68 (1)	15.82 (2)	15.78 (3)	15.63 (2)	79.58	79.58
3	GER	THEODORESCU, Monica	GRUNOX	15.07 (5)	15.35 (4)	15.25 (4)	15.75 (4)	15.43 (3)	76.85	76.85
4	NED	ROTHENBERGER, Sven	WEYDEN	14.73 (7)	15.57 (3)	15.48 (3)	15.80 (2)	15.20 (5)	76.78	76.78
5	GER	BALKENHOL, Klaus	GOLDSTERN	15.30 (4)	15.10 (5)	15.03 (6)	15.43 (6)	15.43 (4)	76.28	76.28
6	FRA	OTTO-CREPIN, Margit	LUCKY LORD	15.40 (3)	14.70 (6)	15.18 (5)	15.40 (7)	14.88 (7)	75.55	75.55
7	USA	SEIDEL, Guenter	GRAF GEORGE	14.48 (8)	14.63 (7)	14.68 (9)	15.20 (9)	14.88 (7)	73.85	73.85
8	USA	GIBSON, Michelle	PERON	14.80 (6)	14.38 (9)	14.05 (11)	15.23 (8)	14.90 (6)	73.35	73.35
9	SWE	NATHHORST, Louise	WALK ON TOP	13.65 (10)	14.53 (8)	14.70 (8)	15.55 (5)	14.30 (11)	72.73	72.73
10	ESP	RAMBLA, Ignacio	EVENTO	13.90 (9)	14.30 (10)	14.73 (7)	14.82 (10)	14.43 (10)	72.18	72.18
11	DEN	PETERSEN, Lars	UFFE KORSHOJGAARD	13.55 (12)	14.30 (10)	14.53 (10)	14.57 (12)	13.93 (12)	70.88	70.88
12	GER	SCHAUDT, Martin	DURGO	13.60 (11)	13.75 (13)	13.85 (13)	14.78 (11)	14.55 (9)	70.53	70.53
13	NED	BARTELS-de VRIES, Tineke	OLYMPIC BARBRIA	13.40 (13)	14.23 (12)	14.00 (12)	14.30 (13)	13.73 (13)	69.66	69.66

* GROUND JURY - FREESTYLE

Judge's Mark	Ctry	Judge
E	FRA	MAUREL, Bernd
H	NED	PEETERS, Jan
C	SWE	LETTE, Eric
M	GER	MECHLEM, Uwe
B	USA	ZANG, Linda

FINAL RESULTS SUMMARY

Rnk	Ctry	Name	Horse	Grand Prix	Grand Prix Special	Grand Prix Freestyle	Total	
1	GER	WERTH, Isabell	GIGOLO	76.60	75.49	83.00	235.09	G
2	NED	van GRUNSVEN, Anky	BONFIRE	75.72	77.72	79.58	233.02	S
3	NED	ROTHENBERGER, Sven	WEYDEN	74.16	74.00	76.78	224.94	B
4	GER	THEODORESCU, Monica	GRUNOX	73.80	73.91	76.85	224.56	
5	USA	GIBSON, Michelle	PERON	75.20	74.28	73.35	222.83	
6	GER	BALKENHOL, Klaus	GOLDSTERN	71.72	73.81	76.28	221.81	
7	FRA	OTTO-CREPIN, Margit	LUCKY LORD	71.32	72.93	75.55	219.80	
8	USA	SEIDEL, Guenter	GRAF GEORGE	69.36	71.81	73.85	215.02	
9	GER	SCHAUDT, Martin	DURGO	71.24	70.98	70.53	212.75	
10	SWE	NATHHORST, Louise	WALK ON TOP	66.28	73.53	72.73	212.54	
11	ESP	RAMBLA, Ignacio	EVENTO	69.76	70.19	72.18	212.13	
12	DEN	PETERSEN, Lars	UFFE KORSHOJGAARD	68.20	68.74	70.88	207.82	
13	NED	BARTELS-de VRIES, Tineke	OLYMPIC BARBRIA	67.60	68.28	69.66	205.54	

Equestrian / *Sports équestres*
Team Dressage / *Dressage par équipes*

Rnk	Ctry	Names	Horse	Judges' Marks†					Total	
				E	H	C	M	B		
1	GER	Germany							5553	G
		WERTH, Isabell	GIGOLO	386	390	387	378	374	1915 *	
		BALKENHOL, Klaus	GOLDSTERN	358	363	366	359	347	1793 *	
		THEODORESCU, Monica	GRUNOX	365	370	376	368	366	1845 *	
		SCHAUDT, Martin	DURGO	365	347	360	355	354	1781	
2	NED	Netherlands							5437	S
		BARTELS-de VRIES, Tineke	OLYMPIC BARBRIA	330	340	335	346	339	1690 *	
		ROTHENBERGER, Sven	WEYDEN	380	367	373	377	357	1854 *	
		van GRUNSVEN, Anky	BONFIRE	382	382	383	378	368	1893 *	
		ROTHENBERGER, Gonnelien	OLYMPIC DONDOLO	339	340	332	341	321	1673	
3	USA	United States of America							5309	B
		DOVER, Robert	METALLIC	315	336	326	339	333	1649	
		GIBSON, Michelle	PERON	393	378	377	370	362	1880 *	
		PETERS, Steffen	UDON	351	342	342	332	328	1695 *	
		SEIDEL, Guenter	GRAF GEORGE	355	354	341	355	329	1734 *	
4	FRA	France							5045	
		d'ESME, Dominique	ARNOLDO	313	325	326	320	328	1612 *	
		OTTO-CREPIN, Margit	LUCKY LORD	351	365	355	353	359	1783 *	
		BRIEUSSEL, Dominique	AKAZIE	324	335	328	328	335	1650 *	
		SYRE, Marie-Helene	MARLON	305	307	295	308	301	1516	
5	SWE	Sweden							4996	
		WILHELMSSON, Tinne	CAPRICE	312	329	318	308	275	1542	
		SOLMELL, Annette	STRAUSS	330	335	346	336	326	1673 *	
		HAKANSSON, Ulla	BOBBY	338	336	337	329	326	1666 *	
		NATHHORST, Louise	WALK ON TOP	328	344	320	328	337	1657 *	
6	SUI	Switzerland							4893	
		SENN, Eva	RENZO	321	325	320	322	315	1603 *	
		STAUB, Hans	DUKAAT	324	321	338	322	323	1628 *	
		STUECKELBERGER, Christine	AQUAMARIN	328	330	337	325	342	1662 *	
		von GREBEL SCHIENDORFER, Barbara	RAMAR	273	262	257	263	269	1324	
7	ESP	Spain							4875	
		SOTO, Rafael	INVASOR	311	309	296	299	312	1527 *	
		FERRER SALAT, Beatriz	BRILLANT	323	318	326	323	314	1604 *	
		MATUTE, Juan	HERMES	292	300	286	280	258	1416	
		RAMBLA, Ignacio	EVENTO	347	344	355	349	349	1744 *	
8	GBR	Great Britain							4761	
		JACKSON, Joanna	MESTER MOUSE	320	319	316	321	301	1577 *	
		BREDIN, Jane	CUPIDO	286	304	306	288	284	1468	
		THOMPSON, Vicky	ENFANT	301	310	300	301	304	1516 *	
		DAVISON, Richard	ASKARI	335	341	330	332	330	1668 *	
9	ITA	Italy							4691	
		GIANI MARGI, Paolo	DESTINO di ACCIARELLA	304	334	320	320	317	1595 *	
		PUCCINI, Fausto	FIFFIKUS	272	289	290	282	285	1418	
		FANTONI, Daria	SONNY BOY	313	295	297	301	290	1496 *	
		LAUS, Pia	LIEBENBERG	321	325	320	329	305	1600 *	
10	CAN	Canada							4509	
		DVORAK, Thomas	WORLD CUP						WD	
		STRASSER, Evi	LAVINIA	294	301	290	291	286	1462 *	
		BRAMALL, Leonie	GILBONA	320	322	328	332	311	1613 *	
		SMITH, Gina	FAUST	295	297	288	280	274	1434 *	

* Score counts for team total.

* *Score compté pour le total de l'équipe.*

† **GROUND JURY - TEAM DRESSAGE**

Judge's Mark	Ctry	Judge
E	USA	ZANG, Linda
H	GER	MECHLEM, Uwe
C	SWE	LETTE, Eric
M	NED	PEETERS, Jan
B	FRA	MAUREL, Bernd

Equestrian / *Sports équestres*
Individual Jumping / *Saut d'obstacles individuel*

Rnk	Ctry	Name	Horse	Time taken	Time penalty	Jump penalty	Total
1	AUT	MORBITZER, Helmut	RACAL	98.02	0.00	0	0.00
1	BEL	PHILIPPAERTS, Ludo	KING DARCO	101.10	0.00	0	0.00
1	GER	BEERBAUM, Ludger	RATINA	103.35	0.00	0	0.00
1	ITA	SOZZI, Valerio	GASTON M	101.05	0.00	0	0.00
1	NED	TOPS, Jan	TOP GUN	100.28	0.00	0	0.00
1	USA	KURSINSKI, Anne	EROS	99.23	0.00	0	0.00
1	USA	BURR-HOWARD, Leslie	EXTREME	102.04	0.00	0	0.00
8	GBR	BILLINGTON, Geoff	IT'S OTTO	105.62	0.25	0	0.25
9	FRA	DELAVEAU, Patrice	ROXANE DE GRUCHY	106.02	0.50	0	0.50
9	MEX	MADARIAGA, Jose	GENIUS	106.16	0.50	0	0.50
11	BRA	PESSOA, Rodrigo de Paula	TOMBOY	109.96	1.25	0	1.25
12	KSA	al-DUHAMI, Ramzy	LET'S TALK ABOUT	110.42	1.50	0	1.50
13	JPN	SHIRAI, Takeshi	VICOMTE DU MESNIL	112.70	2.00	0	2.00
14	AUT	SIMON, Hugo	ET	94.62	0.00	4	4.00
14	AUT	BAUER, Martin	REMUS	101.76	0.00	4	4.00
14	BEL	WAUTERS, Eric	BON AMI	103.26	0.00	4	4.00
14	ESP	SANCHEZ, Pedro	RICCARDA	102.80	0.00	4	4.00
14	GBR	WHITAKER, John	WELHAM	100.41	0.00	4	4.00
14	GER	SLOOTHAAK, Franke	JOLY	101.05	0.00	4	4.00
14	GER	KIRCHHOFF, Ulrich	JUS DE POMMES	104.04	0.00	4	4.00
14	IRL	MACKEN, Eddie	SCHALKHAAR	99.61	0.00	4	4.00
14	ITA	CHIAUDANI, Natale	RHEINGOLD DE LUYNE	101.61	0.00	4	4.00
14	MEX	CHEDRAUI, Antonio	ELASTIQUE	98.82	0.00	4	4.00
14	MEX	GUERRA, Jaime	RISUENO	103.00	0.00	4	4.00
14	NED	LANSINK, Jozef	CARTHAGO	101.86	0.00	4	4.00
14	NED	HENDRIX, Emile	FINESSE	98.92	0.00	4	4.00
14	NED	ROMP, Bert	SAMANTHA	100.70	0.00	4	4.00
14	SUI	MELLIGER, Willi	CALVARO	100.57	0.00	4	4.00
14	SUI	MANDLI, Beat	CITY BANKING	103.93	0.00	4	4.00
14	SUI	FAH, Urs	JEREMIA	101.91	0.00	4	4.00
14	SWE	BENGTSSON, Rolf-Goran	PARADISO	103.02	0.00	4	4.00
14	SWE	ERIKSSON, Peter	ROBIN	100.67	0.00	4	4.00
14	USA	MATZ, Michael	RHUM	97.22	0.00	4	4.00
34	FRA	GODIGNON, Herve	VIKING DU TILLARD	105.41	0.25	4	4.25
35	ARG	KIERKEGAARD, Ricardo	RENOMME	106.79	0.50	4	4.50
36	FRA	BOST, Roger-Yves	SOUVIENS TOI	107.29	0.75	4	4.75
37	ESP	LATHAM, Rutherford	SOURIRE d'AZE	108.26	1.00	4	5.00
37	ESP	JORDA, Alenjandro	HERNANDO DU SABLON	108.90	1.00	4	5.00
37	JPN	MORIMOTO, Kenji	ALCAZAR	108.53	1.00	4	5.00
40	AUS	PARLEVLIET, Jennifer	ANOTHER FLOOD	111.72	1.75	4	5.75
41	AUS	ROYCROFT, Vicki	COALMINER	96.77	0.00	8	8.00

Rnk	Ctry	Name	Horse	Time taken	Time penalty	Jump penalty	Total
41	BRA	MIRANDA NETO, Alvaro A. de	ASPEN	101.08	0.00	8	8.00
41	CAN	MILLAR, Ian	PLAY IT AGAIN	104.48	0.00	8	8.00
41	CAN	DELIA, Christopher	SILENT SAM	97.70	0.00	8	8.00
41	FRA	LEDERMANN, Alexandra	ROCHET M	103.36	0.00	8	8.00
41	GER	NIEBERG, Lars	FOR PLEASURE	99.84	0.00	8	8.00
41	IRL	GARDINER, Damian	ARTHOS	101.82	0.00	8	8.00
41	IRL	CHESNEY, Jessica	DIAMOND EXCHANGE	101.54	0.00	8	8.00
41	ITA	BOLOGNI, Arnaldo	EILLEEN	104.13	0.00	8	8.00
41	KSA	BAHAMDAN, Kamal	MISSOURI	100.21	0.00	8	8.00
51	BRA	JOHANNPETER, Andre Bier	CALEI	105.91	0.25	8	8.25
51	CAN	CONE, Malcolm	ELUTE	105.08	0.25	8	8.25
51	ITA	SMIT, Jerry	CONSTANTIJN	105.54	0.25	8	8.25
51	KSA	al-EID, Khaled	EASTERN KNIGHT	105.51	0.25	8	8.25
55	BEL	BLATON, Michel	REVOULINO	108.12	1.00	8	9.00
55	SWE	GRETZER, Maria	MARCOVILLE	108.81	1.00	8	9.00
57	PHI	COJUANGCO, Denise	CHOUMAN	111.09	1.75	8	9.75
58	ESP	SARASOLA, Fernando	ENNIO	112.91	2.00	8	10.00
59	ARG	ALBARRACIN, Justo	DINASTIA PAMPERO	97.67	0.00	12	12.00
59	AUS	JOHNSTONE, Russell	SOUTHERN CONTRAST	101.88	0.00	12	12.00
59	BEL	VAN PAESSCHEN, Stanny	MULGA BILL	99.27	0.00	12	12.00
59	COL	TORRES, Manuel	CARTAGENA	101.39	0.00	12	12.00
59	GBR	SKELTON, Nick	SHOW TIME	100.87	0.00	12	12.00
59	POR	LEAL, Miguel	SURCOUF DE REVEL	102.37	0.00	12	12.00
59	USA	LEONE, Peter	LEGATO	101.83	0.00	12	12.00
66	SWE	BARYARD, Malin	CORRMINT	106.49	0.50	12	12.50
67	ARG	FUENTES, Oscar	HENRY J. SPEED	107.90	0.75	12	12.75
67	CAN	SOUTHERN-HEATHCOTT, Linda	ADVANTAGE	107.58	0.75	12	12.75
69	IRL	CHARLES, Peter	BENETON	111.53	1.75	12	13.75
69	POR	VOZONE, Antonio	MR. CER	111.50	1.75	12	13.75
71	COL	DAVILA, Alejandro	EJEMPLO	103.22	0.00	16	16.00
72	JPN	NAKANO, Yoshihiro	SISAL DE JALESNES	106.37	0.50	16	16.50
72	PUR	EARLE, Alexander	SAME OLD SONG	106.98	0.50	16	16.50
74	JPN	SUGITANI, Taizo	COUNTRYMAN	107.82	0.75	16	16.75
75	BRA	AZEVEDO, Luiz Felipe de	CASSIANA	108.63	1.00	16	17.00
76	GBR	WHITAKER, Michael	TWO STEP	117.36	3.25	19	22.25
77	AUS	COOPER, David	RED SAILS	102.90	0.00	24	24.00
78	MEX	ROMO, Alfonso	FLASH	123.11	4.75	23	27.75
79	ARG	CASTAING, Federico	LANDLORD	124.99	5.00	23	28.00
80	SUI	FUCHS, Markus	ADELFOS	129.44	6.25	25	31.25
81	NZL	MEECH, Daniel	FUTURE VISION	125.35	5.25	35	40.25
82	AUT	METZGER, Thomas	ROYAL FLASH			RT	60.25

FINAL

Rnk	Ctry	Name	Horse	Round A	Round B	Total	Jump off
1	GER	KIRCHHOFF, Ulrich	JUS de POMMES	0.00	1.00	1.00	G
2	SUI	MELLIGER, Willi	CALVARO	0.00	4.00	4.00	0.00 S
3	FRA	LEDERMANN, Alexandra	ROCHET M	4.00	0.00	4.00	0.00 B
4	AUT	SIMON, Hugo	ET	4.00	0.00	4.00	4.00
5	SUI	FAH, Urs	JEREMIA	0.00	4.00	4.00	4.00
6	GBR	BILLINGTON, Geoff	IT'S OTTO	4.00	0.00	4.00	4.00
7	NED	TOPS, Jan	TOP GUN	0.00	4.00	4.00	8.00
8	BRA	MIRANDA NETO, Alvaro A. de	ASPEN	0.00	4.00	4.00	16.00
9	BRA	PESSOA, Rodrigo de Paula	TOMBOY	4.00	0.25	4.25	
9	GBR	WHITAKER, John	WELHAM	4.00	0.25	4.25	
11	AUT	BAUER, Martin	REMUS	0.00	8.00	8.00	
11	ESP	SARASOLA, Fernando	ENNIO	0.00	8.00	8.00	
11	IRL	CHARLES, Peter	BENETON	0.00	8.00	8.00	

FINAL - *continued*

Rnk	Ctry	Name	Horse	Round A	Round B	Total	Jump off
11	NED	LANSINK, Jozef	CARTHAGO	4.00	4.00	8.00	
11	SUI	MANDLI, Beat	CITY BANKING	4.00	4.00	8.00	
11	USA	BURR-HOWARD, Leslie	EXTREME	4.00	4.00	8.00	
17	FRA	GODIGNON, Herve	VIKING DU TILLARD	0.00	9.00	9.00	
18	BRA	JOHANNPETER, Andre Bier	CALEI	4.00	8.00	12.00	
19	ITA	SMIT, Jerry	CONSTANTIJN	4.00	8.25	12.25	
20	BEL	PHILIPPAERTS, Ludo	KING DARCO	4.00	12.00	16.00	
20	GER	NIEBERG, Lars	FOR PLEASURE	0.00	16.00	16.00	
20	USA	KURSINSKI, Anne	EROS	4.00	12.00	16.00	
23	GBR	SKELTON, Nick	SHOW TIME	4.00	12.25	16.25	
24	ESP	LATHAM, Rutherford	SOURIRE d'AZE	4.00	12.50	16.50	
25	AUT	MORBITZER, Helmut	RACAL	4.00	25.00	29.00	

Equestrian / *Sports équestres*
Team Jumping / *Saut d'obstacles par équipes*

FINAL

Rnk	Ctry	Names	Horse	Round 1	Round 2	Total
1	GER	Germany		0.75	1.00	1.75 **G**
		NIEBERG, Lars	FOR PLEASURE	0.00 *	12.00	
		SLOOTHAAK, Franke	JOLY	60.25	0.00 *	
		KIRCHHOFF, Ulrich	JUS de POMMES	0.75 *	0.75 *	
		BEERBAUM, Ludger	RATINA	0.00 *	0.25 *	
2	USA	United States of America		8.00	4.00	12.00 **S**
		KURSINSKI, Anne	EROS	0.00 *	8.00	
		BURR-HOWARD, Leslie	EXTREME	14.00	0.00 *	
		LEONE, Peter	LEGATO	4.00 *	0.00 *	
		MATZ, Michael	RHUM	4.00 *	4.00 *	
3	BRA	Brazil		4.50	12.75	17.25 **B**
		MIRANDA NETO, Alvaro A. de	ASPEN	0.25 *	8.00	
		JOHANNPETER, Andre Bier	CALEI	4.25 *	8.00	
		AZEVEDO, Luiz Felipe de	CASSIANA	8.00	4.00 *	
		PESSOA, Rodrigo de Paula	TOMBOY	0.00 *	0.75 *	
4	FRA	France		16.25	4.00	20.25
		LEDERMANN, Alexandra	ROCHET M	4.00 *	4.00 *	
		DELAVEAU, Patrice	ROXANE de GRUCHY	8.00	8.00	
		BOST, Roger-Yves	SOUVIENS TOI	8.00 *	0.00 *	
		GODIGNON, Herve	VIKING DU TILLARD	4.25 *	0.00 *	
5	ESP	Spain		13.00	16.75	29.75
		SARASOLA, Fernando	ENNIO	0.00 *	0.25 *	
		LATHAM, Rutherford	SOURIRE d'AZE	8.00	8.00 *	
		JORDA, Alenjandro	HERNANDO DU SABLON	5.00 *	8.50 *	
		SANCHEZ, Pedro	RICCARDA	8.00 *	12.00	
6	SUI	Switzerland		20.00	12.00	32.00
		MELLIGER, Willi	CALVARO	12.00	0.00 *	
		MANDLI, Beat	CITY BANKING	8.00 *	4.00 *	
		FUCHS, Markus	ADELFOS	8.00 *	16.00	
		FAH, Urs	JEREMIA	4.00 *	8.00 *	
6	NED	Netherlands		16.00	16.25	32.25
		LANSINK, Jozef	CARTHAGO	8.00 *	8.00 *	
		HENDRIX, Emile	FINESSE	12.00	4.00 *	
		ROMP, Bert	SAMANTHA	8.00 *	12.00	
		TOPS, Jan	TOP GUN	0.00 *	4.25 *	
8	IRL	Ireland		12.50	22.00	34.50
		GARDINER, Damian	ARTHOS	28.50	16.00	
		CHARLES, Peter	BENETON	0.00 *	4.00 *	
		CHESNEY, Jessica	DIAMOND EXCHANGE	8.50 *	4.00 *	
		MACKEN, Eddie	SCHALKHAAR	4.00 *	14.00 *	
9	ITA	Italy		28.00	8.00	36.00
		BOLOGNI, Arnaldo	EILLEEN	12.00 *	24.00	
		CHIAUDANI, Natale	RHEINGOLD DE LUYNE	12.00	4.00 *	
		SMIT, Jerry	CONSTANTIJN	4.00 *	4.00 *	
		SOZZI, Valerio	GASTON M	12.00 *	0.00 *	
10	SWE	Sweden		16.00	20.75	36.75
		BARYARD, Malin	CORRMINT	12.25	4.25 *	
		GRETZER, Maria	MARCOVILLE	4.00 *	12.50 *	
		BENGTSSON, Rolf-Goran	PARADISO	4.00 *	20.00	
		ERIKSSON, Peter	ROBIN	8.00 *	4.00 *	

FINALS - *continued*

Rnk	Ctry	Names	Horse	Round 1	Round 2	Total
11	AUT	Austria		20.00	20.00	40.00
		SIMON, Hugo	ET	4.00 *	8.00 *	
		MORBITZER, Helmut	RACAL	16.00 *	4.00 *	
		BAUER, Martin	REMUS	0.00 *	8.00 *	
		METZGER, Thomas	ROYAL FLASH	60.25	57.50	
11	GBR	Great Britain		24.00	16.00	40.00
		BILLINGTON, Geoff	IT'S OTTO	12.00 *	0.00 *	
		SKELTON, Nick	SHOW TIME	8.00 *	4.00 *	
		WHITAKER, Michael	TWO STEP	16.00	12.00 *	
		WHITAKER, John	WELHAM	4.00 *	14.50	
13	BEL	Belgium		32.00	16.50	48.50
		WAUTERS, Eric	BON AMI	16.00 *	37.50	
		VAN PAESSCHEN, Stanny	MULGA BILL	12.00 *	8.00 *	
		BLATON, Michel	REVOULINO	17.75	8.50 *	
		PHILIPPAERTS, Ludo	KING DARCO	4.00 *	0.00 *	
14	MEX	Mexico		41.50	20.00	61.50
		CHEDRAUI, Antonio	ELASTIQUE	20.00 *	8.00 *	
		ROMO, Alfonso	FLASH	12.00 *	8.00 *	
		MADARIAGA, Jose	GENIUS	20.00	16.25	
		GUERRA, Jaime	RISUENO	9.50 *	4.00 *	
15	JPN	Japan		32.25	40.50	72.75
		MORIMOTO, Kenji	ALCAZAR	60.25	57.50	
		SUGITANI, Taizo	COUNTRYMAN	16.00 *	16.00 *	
		NAKANO, Yoshihiro	SISAL de JALESNES	8.00 *	20.00 *	
		SHIRAI, Takeshi	VICOMTE DU MESNIL	8.25 *	4.50 *	
16	CAN	Canada		36.00	40.75	76.75
		SOUTHERN-HEATHCOTT, Linda	ADVANTAGE	12.00 *	20.75 *	
		CONE, Malcolm	ELUTE	12.00 *	12.00 *	
		MILLAR, Ian	PLAY IT AGAIN	12.00 *	8.00 *	
		DELIA, Christopher	SILENT SAM	16.00	32.00	
17	ARG	Argentina		44.00	33.25	77.25
		ALBARRACIN, Justo	DINASTIA PAMPERO	8.00 *	4.00 *	
		FUENTES, Oscar	HENRY J. SPEED	60.25	57.50	
		CASTAING, Federico	LANDLORD	16.00 *	24.00 *	
		KIERKEGAARD, Ricardo	RENOMME	20.00 *	5.25 *	
18	KSA	Saudi Arabia		37.75	82.25	120.00
		al-EID, Khaled	EASTERN KNIGHT	8.50 *	8.00 *	
		al-DUHAMI, Ramzy	LET'S TALK ABOUT	5.00 *	16.75 *	
		BAHAMDAN, Kamal	MISSOURI	24.25 *	57.50 *	
19	AUS	Australia		77.00	52.00	129.00
		PARLEVLIET, Jennifer	ANOTHER FLOOD	37.00 *	57.50	
		ROYCROFT, Vicki	COALMINER	16.00 *	16.00 *	
		COOPER, David	RED SAILS	40.25	24.00 *	
		JOHNSTONE, Russell	SOUTHERN CONTRAST	24.00 *	12.00 *	

* Score counts for team total.

* Score compté pour le total de l'équipe.

Equestrian / *Sports équestres*

FENCING
ESCRIME

Abbreviations and terms used in Fencing results tables
Abréviations et termes employés dans les tableaux de résultats d'escrime

Term	English	Français
5th-6th Place	5th-6th Place	5e-6e place
7th-8th Place	7th-8th Place	7e-8e place
9th-10th Place	9th-10th Place	9e-10e place
11th Place	11th Place	11e place
Bronze	Bronze Medal	Médaille de bronze
Bronze Medal	Bronze Medal	Médaille de bronze
BYE	Bye	Exemption
Continued	Continued	Continué
Ctry	Country	Pays
Final	Final	Finale
Gold	Gold Medal	Médaille d'or
Gold Medal	Gold Medal	Médaille d'or
Name	Name	Nom
Round	Round	Tour
Rnk	Rank	Classement
Seed	Seed	Tête de série
Semifinals	Semifinals	Demi-finales
Silver	Silver Medal	Médaille d'argent
Silver Medal	Silver Medal	Médaille d'argent

International Fencing Federation (FIE)
Fédération Internationale d'Escrime
32, rue de la Boétie
75008 Paris
France

Fencing / *Escrime*

Individual Epée, Men / *Epée individuelle, Messieurs*

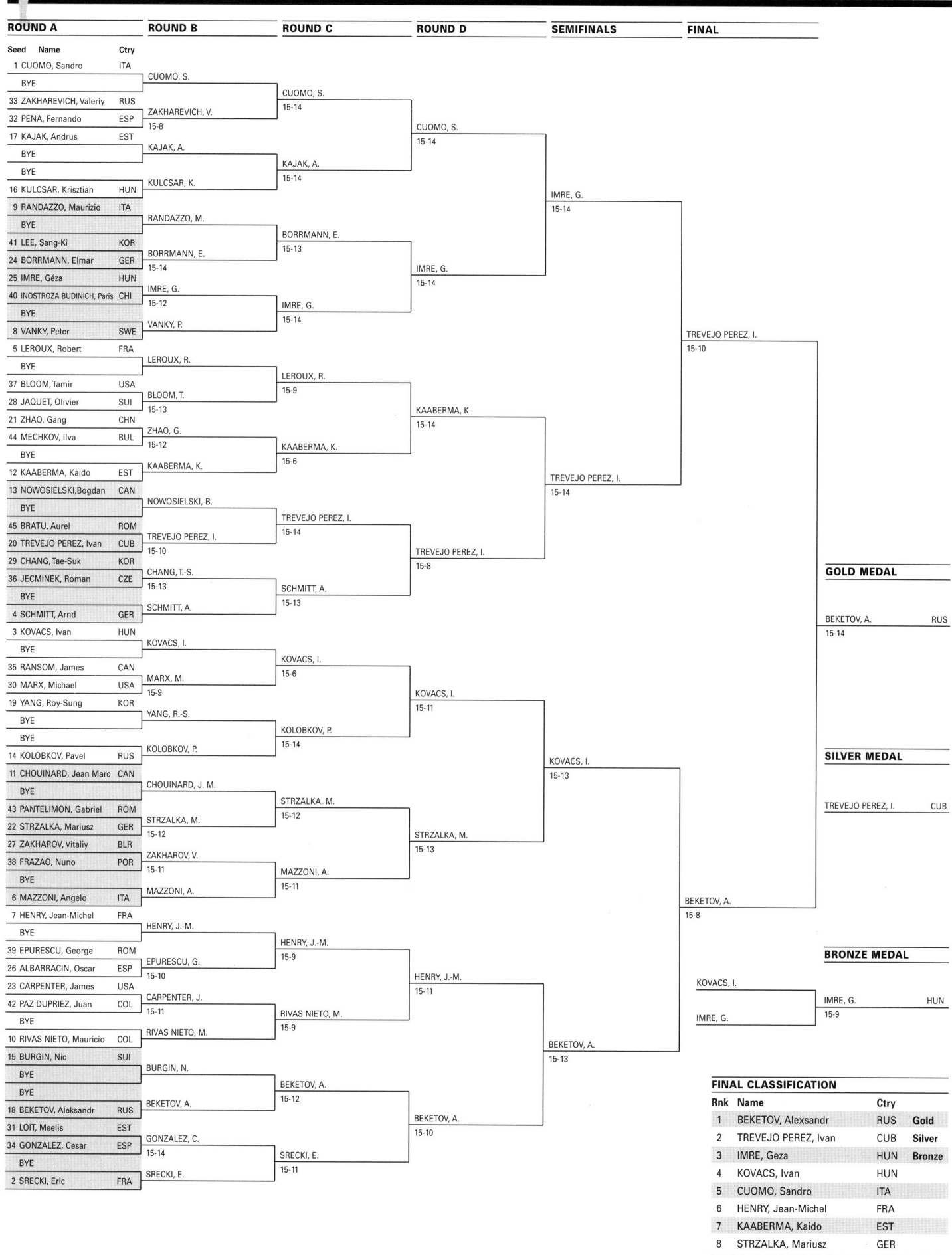

ROUND A	ROUND B	ROUND C	ROUND D	SEMIFINALS	FINAL

Seed	Name	Ctry

1 CUOMO, Sandro ITA
BYE
— CUOMO, S.
33 ZAKHAREVICH, Valeriy RUS
— ZAKHAREVICH, V. 15-8
32 PENA, Fernando ESP
17 KAJAK, Andrus EST
BYE
— KAJAK, A.
BYE
16 KULCSAR, Krisztian HUN
— KULCSAR, K.

CUOMO, S. 15-14

9 RANDAZZO, Maurizio ITA
BYE
— RANDAZZO, M.
41 LEE, Sang-Ki KOR
24 BORRMANN, Elmar GER
— BORRMANN, E. 15-14
25 IMRE, Géza HUN
40 INOSTROZA BUDINICH, Paris CHI
— IMRE, G. 15-12
BYE
8 VANKY, Peter SWE
— VANKY, P.

CUOMO, S. 15-14
CUOMO, S. 15-14
KAJAK, A. 15-14

BORRMANN, E. 15-13
IMRE, G. 15-14

IMRE, G. 15-14

5 LEROUX, Robert FRA
BYE
— LEROUX, R.
37 BLOOM, Tamir USA
28 JAQUET, Olivier SUI
— BLOOM, T. 15-13
21 ZHAO, Gang CHN
44 MECHKOV, Ilva BUL
— ZHAO, G. 15-12
BYE
12 KAABERMA, Kaido EST
— KAABERMA, K.

LEROUX, R. 15-9
KAABERMA, K. 15-14

13 NOWOSIELSKI, Bogdan CAN
BYE
— NOWOSIELSKI, B.
45 BRATU, Aurel ROM
20 TREVEJO PEREZ, Ivan CUB
— TREVEJO PEREZ, I. 15-10
29 CHANG, Tae-Suk KOR
36 JECMINEK, Roman CZE
— CHANG, T.-S. 15-13
BYE
4 SCHMITT, Arnd GER
— SCHMITT, A.

KAABERMA, K. 15-6

TREVEJO PEREZ, I. 15-14
SCHMITT, A. 15-13

TREVEJO PEREZ, I. 15-8

IMRE, G. 15-14
TREVEJO PEREZ, I. 15-10

TREVEJO PEREZ, I. 15-14

3 KOVACS, Ivan HUN
BYE
— KOVACS, I.
35 RANSOM, James CAN
30 MARX, Michael USA
— MARX, M. 15-9
19 YANG, Roy-Sung KOR
BYE
— YANG, R.-S.
BYE
14 KOLOBKOV, Pavel RUS
— KOLOBKOV, P.

KOVACS, I. 15-6
KOLOBKOV, P. 15-14

11 CHOUINARD, Jean Marc CAN
BYE
— CHOUINARD, J. M.
43 PANTELIMON, Gabriel ROM
22 STRZALKA, Mariusz GER
— STRZALKA, M. 15-12
27 ZAKHAROV, Vitaliy BLR
38 FRAZAO, Nuno POR
— ZAKHAROV, V. 15-11
BYE
6 MAZZONI, Angelo ITA
— MAZZONI, A.

KOVACS, I. 15-11

STRZALKA, M. 15-12
MAZZONI, A. 15-11

STRZALKA, M. 15-13

KOVACS, I. 15-13

7 HENRY, Jean-Michel FRA
BYE
— HENRY, J.-M.
39 EPURESCU, George ROM
26 ALBARRACIN, Oscar ESP
— EPURESCU, G. 15-10
23 CARPENTER, James USA
42 PAZ DUPRIEZ, Juan COL
— CARPENTER, J. 15-11
BYE
10 RIVAS NIETO, Mauricio COL
— RIVAS NIETO, M.

HENRY, J.-M. 15-9
RIVAS NIETO, M. 15-9

15 BURGIN, Nic SUI
BYE
— BURGIN, N.
BYE
18 BEKETOV, Aleksandr RUS
— BEKETOV, A. 15-12
31 LOIT, Meelis EST
34 GONZALEZ, Cesar ESP
— GONZALEZ, C. 15-14
BYE
2 SRECKI, Eric FRA
— SRECKI, E.

HENRY, J.-M. 15-11

BEKETOV, A. 15-12
SRECKI, E. 15-11

BEKETOV, A. 15-10

BEKETOV, A. 15-13

BEKETOV, A. 15-8

GOLD MEDAL

BEKETOV, A. RUS
15-14

SILVER MEDAL

TREVEJO PEREZ, I. CUB

BRONZE MEDAL

KOVACS, I.

IMRE, G.

IMRE, G. HUN
15-9

FINAL CLASSIFICATION

Rnk	Name	Ctry	
1	BEKETOV, Alexsandr	RUS	Gold
2	TREVEJO PEREZ, Ivan	CUB	Silver
3	IMRE, Geza	HUN	Bronze
4	KOVACS, Ivan	HUN	
5	CUOMO, Sandro	ITA	
6	HENRY, Jean-Michel	FRA	
7	KAABERMA, Kaido	EST	
8	STRZALKA, Mariusz	GER	

Fencing / *Escrime*

Individual Epée, Women / *Epée individuelle, Dames*

ROUND A		
Seed	Name	Ctry
1	NAGY, Timea	HUN
	BYE	
33	LE, Nhi Lan	USA
32	KIM, Hee-Jeong	KOR
17	MAZINA, Mariya	RUS
48	ESCANELLAS, Mitch	PUR
	BYE	
16	UGA, Elisa	ITA
9	BARLOIS, Valerie	FRA
	BYE	
41	ELINDER, Helena	SWE
24	LEHTOLA, Minna	FIN
25	GARCIA, Mirayda	CUB
40	ARAI, Yuko	JPN
	BYE	
8	BUERKI, Gianna	SUI
5	MORESEE-PICHOT, Sophie	FRA
	BYE	
37	KUBO, Noriko	JPN
28	YAN, Jing	CHN
21	VYBORNOVA, Yeva	UKR
44	SCHMIT, Mariette	LUX
	BYE	
12	ITTNER, Eva-Maria	GER
13	ZALAFFI, Margherita	ITA
	BYE	
45	TANAKA, Nanae	JPN
20	AZNAVURYAN, Karina	RUS
29	SIDIROPOULOU, Niki	GRE
36	OSVATH, Sarah	AUS
	BYE	
4	BOKEL, Claudia	GER
3	FLESSEL, Laura	FRA
	BYE	
35	CHERIS, Elaine	USA
30	CHIESA, Laura	ITA
19	JAKIMIUK, Joanna	POL
46	ZAOUALI, Henda	TUN
	BYE	
14	TITOVA, Victorya	UKR
11	NASS, Katja	GER
	BYE	
43	KENEL, Sandra	SUI
22	ROHI, Heidi	EST
27	PALMA GONZALES, Milagros	CUB
38	LEE, Keun-Nam	KOR
	BYE	
6	HORMAY, Adrienn	HUN
7	CHAPPE, Taymi	ESP
	BYE	
39	ESTERI ALMEIDA, Tamara	CUB
26	KO, Jung-Sun	KOR
23	MARX, Leslie	USA
42	WOLF, Michele	SUI
	BYE	
10	VOSU, Maarika	EST
15	JERMAKOVA, Oksana	EST
	BYE	
47	FJELLERUP BECK, Eva	DEN
18	CASTILLEJO, Rosa Maria	ESP
31	SOTRA, Tamara	YUG
34	GARAYEVA, Yuliya	RUS
	BYE	
2	SZALAY, Gyongyi	HUN

ROUND B

NAGY, T.
KIM, H.-J. 15-13
MAZINA, M. 15-11
UGA, E.
BARLOIS, V.
ELINDER, H. 15-8
GARCIA, M. 15-13
BUERKI, G.
MORESEE-PICHOT, S.
YAN, J. 15-10
VYBORNOVA, Y. 15-8
ITTNER, E.-M.
ZALAFFI, M.
AZNAVURYAN, K. 15-5
SIDIROPOULOU, N. 15-8
BOKEL, C.
FLESSEL, L.
CHIESA, L. 15-13
JAKIMIUK, J. 15-7
TITOVA, V.
NASS, K.
ROHI, H. 15-14
LEE, K.-N. 15-12
HORMAY, A.
CHAPPE, T.
KO, J.-S. 15-12
MARX, L. 15-14
VOSU, M.
JERMAKOVA, O.
FJELLERUP BECK, E. 15-13
GARAYEVA, Y. 15-7
SZALAY, G.

ROUND C

NAGY, T. 15-5
UGA, E. 15-9
BARLOIS, V. 15-3
BUERKI, G. 15-11
MORESEE-PICHOT, S. 15-14
ITTNER, E.-M. 15-7
ZALAFFI, M. 15-12
BOKEL, C. 15-10
FLESSEL, L. 15-10
TITOVA, V. 15-4
NASS, K. 15-12
HORMAY, A. 15-9
KO, J.-S. 15-12
MARX, L. 15-13
JERMAKOVA, O. 15-14
SZALAY, G. 15-14

ROUND D

NAGY, T. 15-9
BARLOIS, V. 15-14
ITTNER, E.-M. 15-10
ZALAFFI, M. 15-8
FLESSEL, L. 15-11
HORMAY, A. 15-9
KO, J.-S. 15-12
SZALAY, G. 15-6

SEMIFINALS

BARLOIS, V. 15-9
ZALAFFI, M. 15-10
FLESSEL, L. 15-12
SZALAY, G. 15-5

FINAL

BARLOIS, V. 15-6
FLESSEL, L. 15-10

GOLD MEDAL

FLESSEL, L.   FRA
15-12

SILVER MEDAL

BARLOIS, V.   FRA

BRONZE MEDAL

ZALAFFI, M.
SZALAY, G.   HUN
15-13

FINAL CLASSIFICATION

Rnk	Name	Ctry	
1	FLESSEL, Laura	FRA	**Gold**
2	BARLOIS, Valerie	FRA	**Silver**
3	SZALAY, Gyongyi	HUN	**Bronze**
4	ZALAFFI, Margherita	ITA	
5	NAGY, Timea	HUN	
6	HORMAY, Adrienn	HUN	
7	ITTNER, Eva-Maria	GER	
8	KO, Jung-Sun	KOR	

Fencing / *Escrime*

Team Epée, Men / *Epée par équipes, Messieurs*

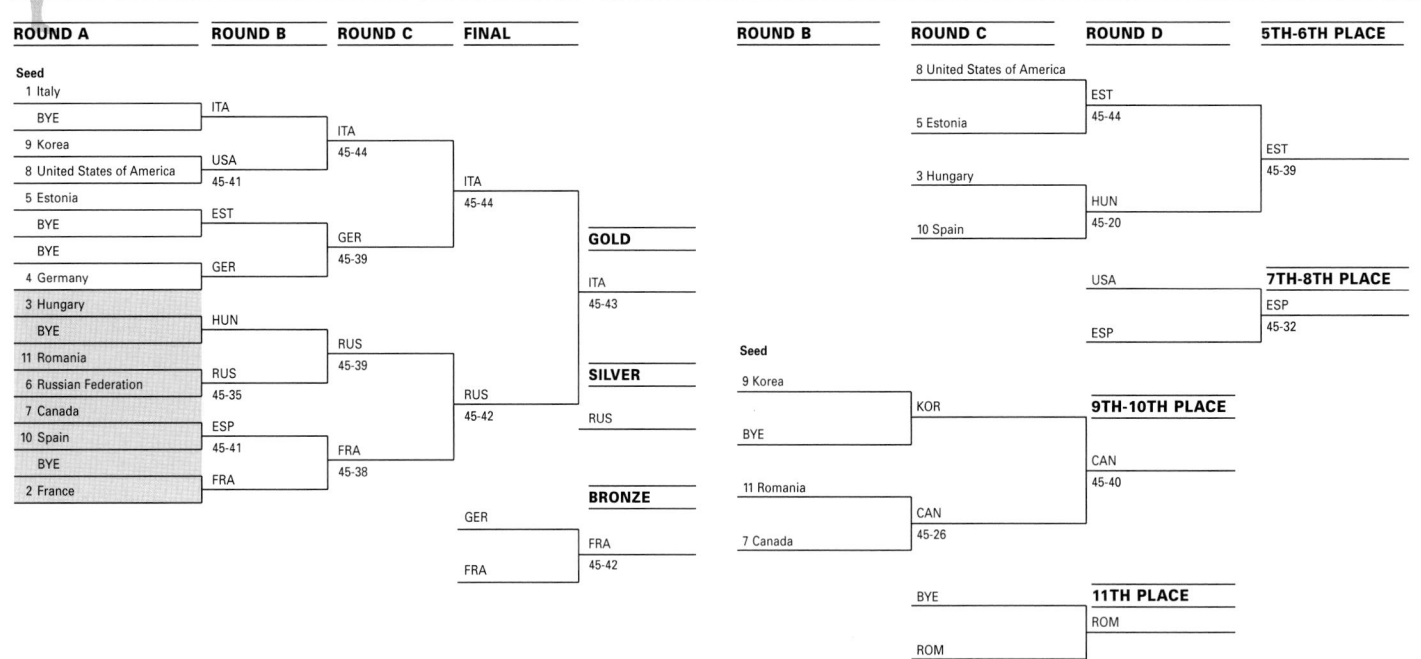

FINAL CLASSIFICATION

Rnk	Ctry	Names	
1	ITA	CUOMO, Sandro / MAZZONI, Angelo / RANDAZZO, Maurizio	Gold
2	RUS	BEKETOV, Aleksandr / KOLOBKOV, Pavel / ZAKHAREVICH, Valeriy	Silver
3	FRA	HENRY, Jean-Michel / LEROUX, Robert / SRECKI, Eric	Bronze
4	GER	BORRMANN, Elmar / SCHMITT, Arnd / STRZALKA, Mariusz	

FINAL CLASSIFICATION - *continued*

Rnk	Ctry	Names
5	EST	KAABERMA, Kaido / KAJAK, Andrus / LOIT, Meelis
6	HUN	IMRE, Geza / KOVACS, Ivan / KULCSAR, Krisztian
7	ESP	ALBARRACIN, Oscar / GONZALEZ, Cesar / MAROTO, Raul
8	USA	BLOOM, Tamir / CARPENTER, James / MARX, Michael

Fencing / *Escrime*

Team Epée, Women   / *Epée par équipes, Dames*

FINAL CLASSIFICATION

Rnk	Ctry	Names	
1	FRA	BARLOIS, Valerie / FLESSEL, Laura / MORESEE-PICHOT, Sophie	Gold
2	ITA	CHIESA, Laura / UGA, Elisa / ZALAFFI, Margherita	Silver
3	RUS	AZNAVURYAN, Karina / GARAYEVA, Yuliya / MAZINA, Mariya	Bronze
4	HUN	HORMAY, Adrienn / NAGY, Timea / SZALAY, Gyongyi	

FINAL CLASSIFICATION - *continued*

Rnk	Ctry	Names
5	EST	JERMAKOVA, Oksana / ROHI, Heidi / VOSU, Maarika
6	CUB	ESTERI ALMEIDA, Tamara / GARCIA, Mirayda / PALMA GONZALES, Milagros
7	GER	BOKEL, Claudia / ITTNER, Eva-Maria / NASS, Katja
8	USA	CHERIS, Elaine / LE, Nhi Lan / MARX, Leslie

Fencing / *Escrime*

Individual Foil, Men / *Fleuret individuel, Messieurs*

ROUND A			ROUND B	ROUND C	ROUND D	SEMIFINALS	FINAL

Seed · Name · Ctry

1 TUCKER LEON, Rolando Samuel · CUB
BYE
TUCKER LEON, R. S.
33 WANG, Haibin · CHN
32 DEVINE, Peter · USA
WANG, H. · 15-12
TUCKER LEON, R. S. · 15-11
17 MARSI, Mark · HUN
BYE
MARSI, M.
BYE
16 ERSEK, Zsolt · HUN
ERSEK, Z.
ERSEK, Z. · 15-10
TUCKER LEON, R. S. · 15-4

9 WIENAND, Wolfgang · GER
BYE
WIENAND, W.
41 MARCHETTI, Leandro · ARG
24 FALCHETTO, Marco · AUT
MARCHETTI, L. · 15-13
WIENAND, W. · 15-1
25 KIELPIKOWSKI, Piotr · POL
40 ICHIGATANI, Hiroki · JPN
KIELPIKOWSKI, P. · 15-13
BYE
8 CERIONI, Stefano · ITA
CERIONI, S.
KIELPIKOWSKI, P. · 15-7
WIENAND, W. · 15-11

WIENAND, W. · 15-12

5 PLUMENAIL, Lionel · FRA
BYE
PLUMENAIL, L.
37 RODRIGUEZ VARGAS, Carlos · VEN
28 LUDWIG, Michael · AUT
LUDWIG, M. · 15-11
PLUMENAIL, L. · 15-12
21 PAVLOVICH, Vladislav · RUS
44 PEREZ ARAQUE, Alfredo · VEN
PAVLOVICH, V. · 15-2
BYE
12 GUERRA, Jose · ESP
GUERRA, J.
PAVLOVICH, V. · 15-11
PLUMENAIL, L. · 15-12

13 KOCH, Alexander · GER
BYE
KOCH, A.
45 RUZIYEV, Rafkat · UZB
20 CHONG, Ye · CHN
CHONG, Y. · 15-4
CHONG, Y. · 15-13
29 KISS, Robert · HUN
36 KIM, Yong-Kook · KOR
KIM, Y.-K. · 15-11
BYE
4 GOLUBYTSKY, Serhiy · UKR
GOLUBYTSKY, S.
GOLUBYTSKY, S. · 15-4
GOLUBYTSKY, S. · 15-14

PLUMENAIL, L. · 15-13

PLUMENAIL, L. · 15-9

3 GREGORY, Elvis · CUB
BYE
GREGORY, E.
35 BRAVIN, Eric · USA
30 KRZESINSKI, Adam · POL
KRZESINSKI, A. · 15-14
GREGORY, E. · 15-10
19 GRIGORYEV, Vyacheslav · KAZ
BYE
GRIGORYEV, V.
BYE
14 OMNES, Philippe · FRA
OMNES, P.
OMNES, P. · 15-4
OMNES, P. · 15-14

11 GARCIA PEREZ, Oscar Manuel · CUB
BYE
GARCIA PEREZ, O. M.
43 SUAREZ, Rafael · VEN
22 GARCIA, Javier · ESP
GARCIA, J. · 15-10
GARCIA, J. · 15-11
27 MAMEDOV, Ilgar · RUS
38 CHUNG, Soo-Ki · KOR
CHUNG, S.-K. · 15-8
BYE
6 BOIDIN, Franck · FRA
BOIDIN, F.
BOIDIN, F. · 15-14
BOIDIN, F. · 15-12

BOIDIN, F. · 15-11

PUCCINI, A. · 15-13

7 PUCCINI, Alessandro · ITA
BYE
PUCCINI, A.
39 BRYZGALOV, Oleksiy · UKR
26 BAYER, Cliff · USA
BRYZGALOV, O. · 15-11
PUCCINI, A. · 15-12
23 SOBCZAK, Ryszard · POL
42 ALI, Abdulmuhsen · KUW
SOBCZAK, R. · 15-7
BYE
10 ARPINO, Marco · ITA
ARPINO, M.
SOBCZAK, R. · 15-14
PUCCINI, A. · 15-4

15 ROMER, Uwe · GER
BYE
ROMER, U.
BYE
18 WENDT, Joachim · AUT
WENDT, J.
ROMER, U. · 15-7
31 KIM, Young-Ho · KOR
34 DONG, Zhaozhi · CHN
KIM, Y.-H. · 15-12
KIM, Y.-H. · 15-13
BYE
2 SHEVCHENKO, Dmitriy · RUS
SHEVCHENKO, D.
KIM, Y.-H. · 15-13

PUCCINI, A. · 15-14

GOLD MEDAL

PUCCINI, A. · ITA · 15-12

SILVER MEDAL

PLUMENAIL, L. · FRA

BRONZE MEDAL

WIENAND, W.

BOIDIN, F.

BOIDIN, F. · FRA · 15-11

FINAL CLASSIFICATION

Rnk	Name	Ctry	
1	PUCCINI, Alessandro	ITA	**Gold**
2	PLUMENAIL, Lionel	FRA	**Silver**
3	BOIDIN, Franck	FRA	**Bronze**
4	WIENAND, Wolfgang	GER	
5	TUCKER LEON, Rolando Samuel	CUB	
6	GOLUBYTSKY, Serhiy	UKR	
7	OMNES, Philippe	FRA	
8	KIM, Young-Ho	KOR	

Fencing / *Escrime*
Individual Foil, Women / *Fleuret individuel, Dames*

ROUND A	ROUND B	ROUND C	ROUND D	SEMIFINALS	FINAL

Seed Name Ctry

1 VEZZALI, Valentina ITA
BYE
VEZZALI, V.
33 CHUN, Mi-Kyung KOR
CHUN, M.-K.
15-14
VEZZALI, V.
15-12
32 PAXTON, Margaret USA
17 VELITCHKO, Olga RUS
BYE
VELITCHKO, O.
BYE
VELITCHKO, O.
15-14
16 ROMACZNE LANTOS, Gabriella HUN
ROMACZNE LANTOS, G.
VEZZALI, V.
15-13

9 MARSH, Ann USA
BYE
MARSH, A.
BYE
MARSH, A.
15-9
24 MAGNAN, Clothilde FRA
MAGNAN, C.
25 OHAYON, Ayelet ISR
40 RODRIGUEZ OLIVA, Carmen GUA
OHAYON, A.
15-2
BAU, S.
15-10
BYE
8 BAU, Sabine GER
BAU, S.
MARSH, A.
15-8

VEZZALI, V.
15-10

5 WEBER-KOSZTO, Monika GER
BYE
WEBER-KOSZTO, M.
37 ZAOUALI, Henda TUN
WEBER-KOSZTO, M.
15-14
28 FELUSIAK, Katarzyna POL
FELUSIAK, K.
15-9
21 ZIMMERMAN, Felicia USA
BYE
ZIMMERMAN, F.
BYE
CZUCKERMANN-HATUEL, L.
15-12
12 CZUCKERMANN-HATUEL, Lydia ISR
CZUCKERMANN-HATUEL, L.
WEBER-KOSZTO, M.
15-13

13 MODAINE-CESSAC, Laurence FRA
BYE
MODAINE-CESSAC, L.
BYE
MODAINE-CESSAC, L.
15-14
20 SHARKOVA, Olga RUS
SHARKOVA, O.
29 WANG, Huifeng CHN
36 CARBONE, Alejandra ARG
WANG, H.
15-4
BIANCHEDI, D.
15-10
BYE
4 BIANCHEDI, Diana ITA
BIANCHEDI, D.
MODAINE-CESSAC, L.
15-0

MODAINE-CESSAC, L.
15-14

VEZZALI, V.
15-7

3 BADEA, Laura ROM
BYE
BADEA, L.
35 IANNUZZI, Yanina ARG
BADEA, L.
15-5
30 PARISKY, Lilach ISR
PARISKY, L.
15-7
19 SZABO-LAZAR, Reka ROM
BYE
SZABO-LAZAR, R.
BYE
WUILLEME, A.
15-12
14 WUILLEME, Adeline FRA
WUILLEME, A.
BADEA, L.
15-6

11 MOHAMED, Aida HUN
BYE
MOHAMED, A.
BYE
MOHAMED, A.
15-8
22 RYBICKA, Anna POL
RYBICKA, A.
27 LIANG, Jun CHN
38 SALHI, Ferial ALG
LIANG, J.
15-7
FICHTEL NAURITZ, A.
15-10
BYE
6 FICHTEL NAURITZ, Anja GER
FICHTEL NAURITZ, A.
MOHAMED, A.
15-14

BADEA, L.
15-8

7 NEMETHNE JANOSI, Zsuzsa HUN
BYE
NEMETHNE JANOSI, Z.
39 PAMPIN, Dolores ARG
NEMETHNE JANOSI, Z.
15-11
26 SZEWCZYK, Barbara POL
SZEWCZYK, B.
15-8
23 ANGELOVA, Anna BUL
BYE
ANGELOVA, A.
BYE
XIAO, A.
15-4
10 XIAO, Aihua CHN
XIAO, A.
XIAO, A.
15-7

15 BOYKO, Svetlana RUS
BYE
BOYKO, S.
BYE
SCARLAT, R.
15-10
18 SCARLAT, Roxana ROM
SCARLAT, R.
31 GEORGIEVA, Ivana BUL
34 McINTOSH, Fiona GBR
GEORGIEVA, I.
15-4
TRILLINI, G.
15-8
BYE
2 TRILLINI, Giovanna ITA
TRILLINI, G.
TRILLINI, G.
15-11

BADEA, L.
15-14

GOLD MEDAL

BADEA, L. ROM
15-10

SILVER MEDAL

VEZZALI, V. ITA

BRONZE MEDAL

MODAINE-CESSAC, L.
TRILLINI, G. ITA
TRILLINI, G.
15-9

FINAL CLASSIFICATION

Rnk	Name	Ctry	
1	BADEA, Laura	ROM	Gold
2	VEZZALI, Valentina	ITA	Silver
3	TRILLINI, Giovanna	ITA	Bronze
4	MODAINE-CESSAC, Laurence	FRA	
5	WEBER-KOSZTO, Monika	GER	
6	XIAO, Aihua	CHN	
7	MARSH, Ann	USA	
8	MOHAMED, Aida	HUN	

Fencing / *Escrime*

Team Foil, Men / *Fleuret par équipes, Messieurs*

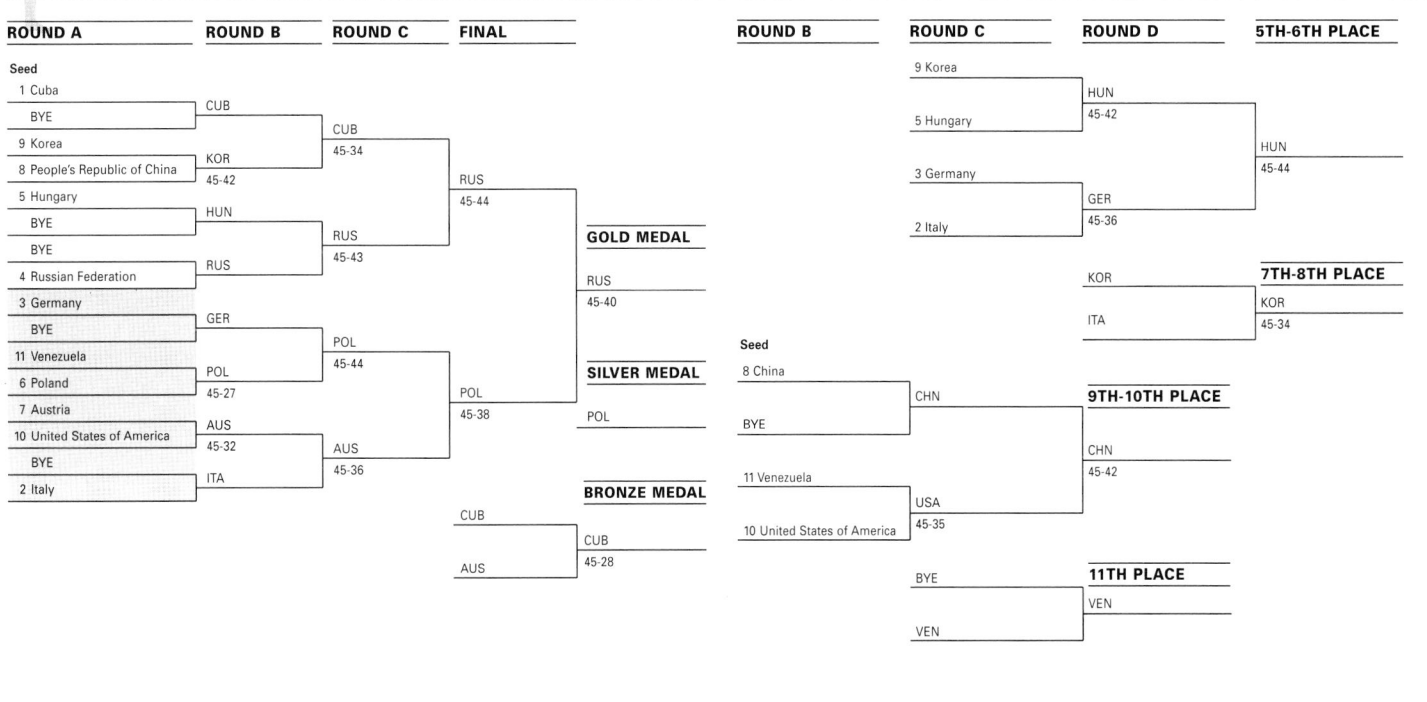

FINAL CLASSIFICATION

Rnk	Ctry	Names	
1	RUS	MAMEDOV, Ilgar / PAVLOVICH, Vladislav / SHEVCHENKO, Dmitriy	Gold
2	POL	RODZEWICZ, Jaroslaw / KRZESINSKI, Adam / SOBCZAK, Ryszard	Silver
3	CUB	GARCIA PEREZ, Oscar Manuel / GREGORY, Elvis / TUCKER LEON, Rolando Samuel	Bronze
4	AUT	FALCHETTO, Marco / LUDWIG, Michael / WENDT, Joachim	

FINAL CLASSIFICATION - *continued*

Rnk	Ctry	Names
5	HUN	ERSEK, Zsolt / KISS, Robert / MARSI, Mark
6	GER	KOCH, Alexander / ROMER, Uwe / WIENAND, Wolfgang
7	KOR	CHUNG, Soo-Ki / KIM, Yong-Kook / KIM, Young-Ho
8	ITA	ARPINO, Marco / CERIONI, Stefano / PUCCINI, Alessandro

Fencing / *Escrime*

Team Foil, Women / *Fleuret par équipes, Dames*

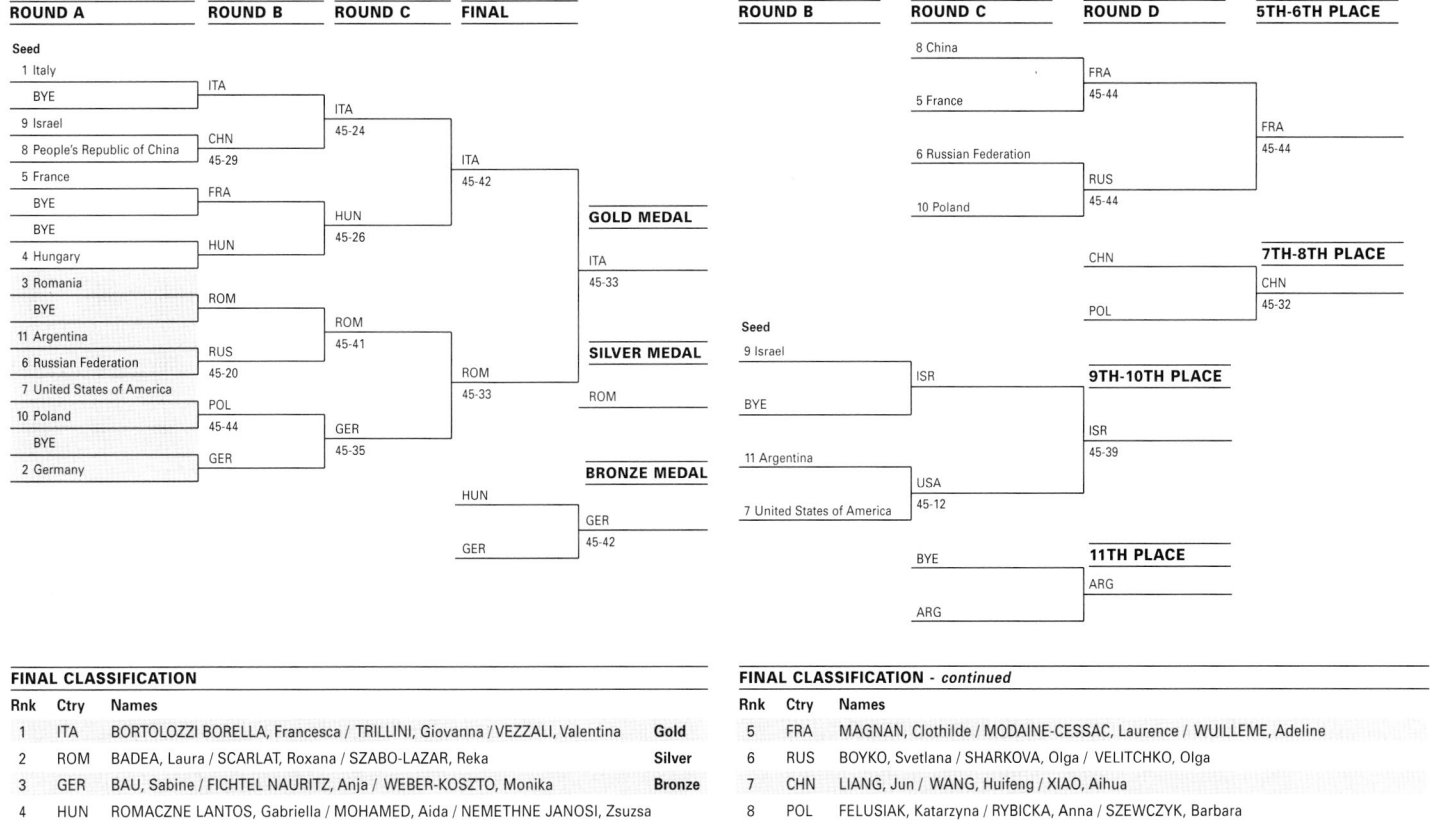

FINAL CLASSIFICATION

Rnk	Ctry	Names	
1	ITA	BORTOLOZZI BORELLA, Francesca / TRILLINI, Giovanna / VEZZALI, Valentina	Gold
2	ROM	BADEA, Laura / SCARLAT, Roxana / SZABO-LAZAR, Reka	Silver
3	GER	BAU, Sabine / FICHTEL NAURITZ, Anja / WEBER-KOSZTO, Monika	Bronze
4	HUN	ROMACZNE LANTOS, Gabriella / MOHAMED, Aida / NEMETHNE JANOSI, Zsuzsa	

FINAL CLASSIFICATION - *continued*

Rnk	Ctry	Names
5	FRA	MAGNAN, Clothilde / MODAINE-CESSAC, Laurence / WUILLEME, Adeline
6	RUS	BOYKO, Svetlana / SHARKOVA, Olga / VELITCHKO, Olga
7	CHN	LIANG, Jun / WANG, Huifeng / XIAO, Aihua
8	POL	FELUSIAK, Katarzyna / RYBICKA, Anna / SZEWCZYK, Barbara

Fencing / *Escrime*

Individual Sabre, Men / *Sabre individuel, Messieurs*

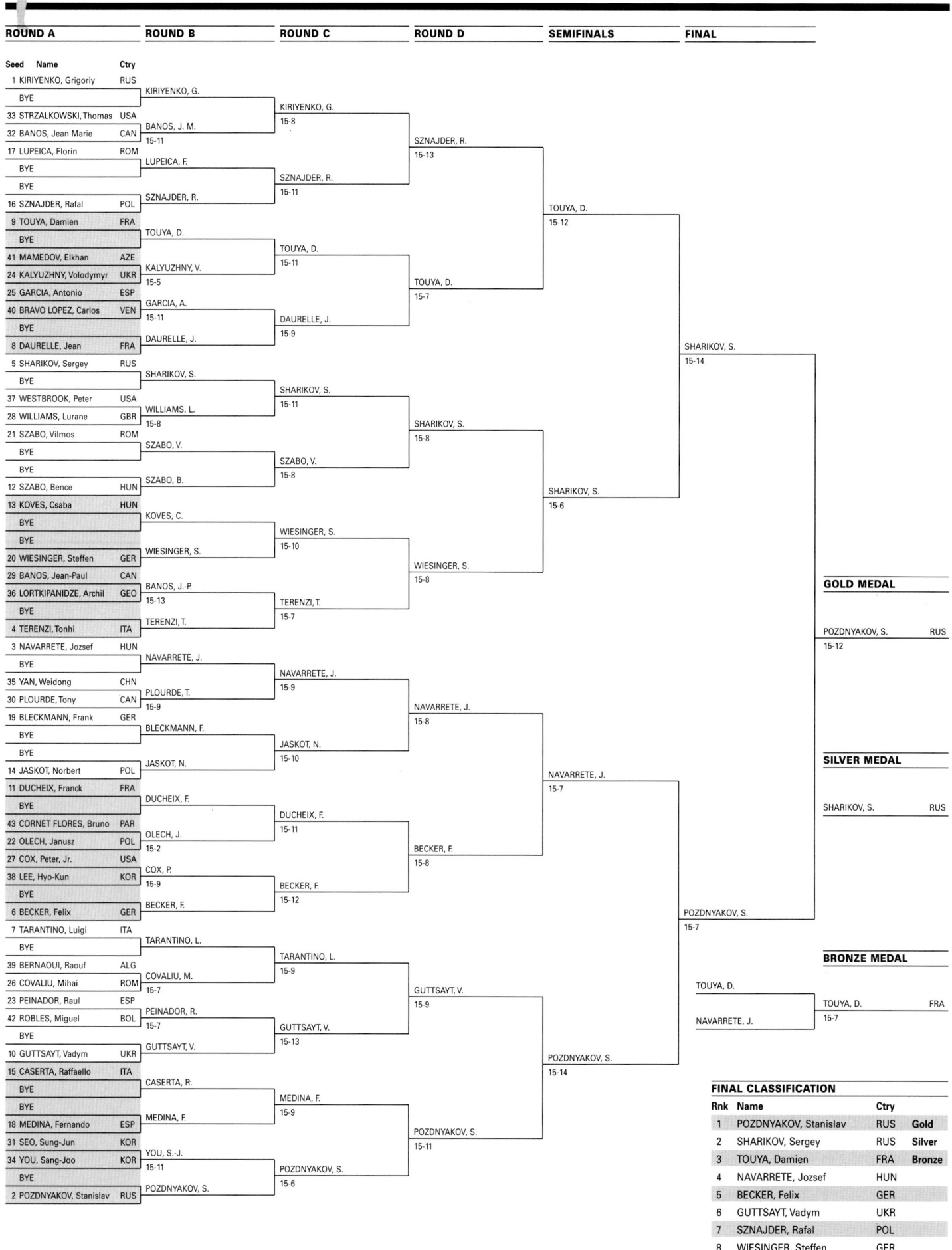

ROUND A	ROUND B	ROUND C	ROUND D	SEMIFINALS	FINAL

Seed	Name	Ctry
1	KIRIYENKO, Grigoriy	RUS
	BYE	
33	STRZALKOWSKI, Thomas	USA
32	BANOS, Jean Marie	CAN
17	LUPEICA, Florin	ROM
	BYE	
	BYE	
16	SZNAJDER, Rafal	POL
9	TOUYA, Damien	FRA
	BYE	
41	MAMEDOV, Elkhan	AZE
24	KALYUZHNY, Volodymyr	UKR
25	GARCIA, Antonio	ESP
40	BRAVO LOPEZ, Carlos	VEN
	BYE	
8	DAURELLE, Jean	FRA
5	SHARIKOV, Sergey	RUS
	BYE	
37	WESTBROOK, Peter	USA
28	WILLIAMS, Lurane	GBR
21	SZABO, Vilmos	ROM
	BYE	
	BYE	
12	SZABO, Bence	HUN
13	KOVES, Csaba	HUN
	BYE	
	BYE	
20	WIESINGER, Steffen	GER
29	BANOS, Jean-Paul	CAN
36	LORTKIPANIDZE, Archil	GEO
	BYE	
4	TERENZI, Tonhi	ITA
3	NAVARRETE, Jozsef	HUN
	BYE	
35	YAN, Weidong	CHN
30	PLOURDE, Tony	CAN
19	BLECKMANN, Frank	GER
	BYE	
	BYE	
14	JASKOT, Norbert	POL
11	DUCHEIX, Franck	FRA
	BYE	
43	CORNET FLORES, Bruno	PAR
22	OLECH, Janusz	POL
27	COX, Peter, Jr.	USA
38	LEE, Hyo-Kun	KOR
	BYE	
6	BECKER, Felix	GER
7	TARANTINO, Luigi	ITA
	BYE	
39	BERNAOUI, Raouf	ALG
26	COVALIU, Mihai	ROM
23	PEINADOR, Raul	ESP
42	ROBLES, Miguel	BOL
	BYE	
10	GUTTSAYT, Vadym	UKR
15	CASERTA, Raffaello	ITA
	BYE	
	BYE	
18	MEDINA, Fernando	ESP
31	SEO, Sung-Jun	KOR
34	YOU, Sang-Joo	KOR
	BYE	
2	POZDNYAKOV, Stanislav	RUS

ROUND B
KIRIYENKO, G.
BANOS, J. M. — 15-11
LUPEICA, F.
SZNAJDER, R.
TOUYA, D.
KALYUZHNY, V. — 15-5
GARCIA, A. — 15-11
DAURELLE, J.
SHARIKOV, S.
WILLIAMS, L. — 15-8
SZABO, V.
SZABO, B.
KOVES, C.
WIESINGER, S.
BANOS, J.-P. — 15-13
TERENZI, T.
NAVARRETE, J.
PLOURDE, T. — 15-9
BLECKMANN, F.
JASKOT, N.
DUCHEIX, F.
OLECH, J. — 15-2
COX, P. — 15-9
BECKER, F.
TARANTINO, L.
COVALIU, M. — 15-7
PEINADOR, R. — 15-7
GUTTSAYT, V.
CASERTA, R.
MEDINA, F.
YOU, S.-J. — 15-11
POZDNYAKOV, S.

ROUND C
KIRIYENKO, G. — 15-8
SZNAJDER, R. — 15-11
TOUYA, D. — 15-11
DAURELLE, J. — 15-9
SHARIKOV, S. — 15-11
SZABO, V. — 15-8
WIESINGER, S. — 15-10
TERENZI, T. — 15-7
NAVARRETE, J. — 15-9
JASKOT, N. — 15-10
DUCHEIX, F. — 15-11
BECKER, F. — 15-12
TARANTINO, L. — 15-9
GUTTSAYT, V. — 15-13
MEDINA, F. — 15-9
POZDNYAKOV, S. — 15-6

ROUND D
SZNAJDER, R. — 15-13
TOUYA, D. — 15-7
SHARIKOV, S. — 15-8
WIESINGER, S. — 15-8
NAVARRETE, J. — 15-8
BECKER, F. — 15-8
GUTTSAYT, V. — 15-9
POZDNYAKOV, S. — 15-11

SEMIFINALS
TOUYA, D. — 15-12
SHARIKOV, S. — 15-6
NAVARRETE, J. — 15-7
POZDNYAKOV, S. — 15-14

FINAL
SHARIKOV, S. — 15-14
POZDNYAKOV, S. — 15-7

GOLD MEDAL
POZDNYAKOV, S.   RUS
15-12

SILVER MEDAL
SHARIKOV, S.   RUS

BRONZE MEDAL
TOUYA, D.
NAVARRETE, J.
TOUYA, D.   FRA
15-7

FINAL CLASSIFICATION

Rnk	Name	Ctry	
1	POZDNYAKOV, Stanislav	RUS	Gold
2	SHARIKOV, Sergey	RUS	Silver
3	TOUYA, Damien	FRA	Bronze
4	NAVARRETE, Jozsef	HUN	
5	BECKER, Felix	GER	
6	GUTTSAYT, Vadym	UKR	
7	SZNAJDER, Rafal	POL	
8	WIESINGER, Steffen	GER	

Fencing / *Escrime*

Team Sabre, Men / *Sabre par équipes, Messieurs*

Rnk	Ctry	Names	
1	RUS	KIRIYENKO, Grigoriy / POZDNYAKOV, Stanislav / SHARIKOV, Sergey	Gold
2	HUN	KOVES, Csaba / NAVARRETE, József / SZABO, Bence	Silver
3	ITA	CASERTA, Raffaello / TARANTINO, Luigi / TERENZI, Tonhi	Bronze
4	POL	JASKOT, Norbert / OLECH, Janusz / SZNAJDER, Rafal	
5	FRA	DAURELLE, Jean / DUCHEIX, Franck / TOUYA, Damien	
6	ESP	GARCIA, Antonio / MEDINA, Fernando / PEINADOR, Raul	
7	ROM	COVALIU, Mihai / LUPEICA, Florin / SZABO, Vilmos	
8	GER	BECKER, Felix / BLECKMANN, Frank / WIESINGER, Steffen	

FINAL CLASSIFICATION

• CHRISTINE A ROSENBLOOM • ROBERT H
ROSENBLOOM • DEBORAH ANN ROSENBLUM •
STEVEN A ROSENBURG • ROBERT C ROSENE •
LISA M ROSENFIELD • MARK ROSENFIELD • RE-
NEE D ROSENHECK • KIMBERLY L ROSENKOET-
TER • MARC D ROSENKOETTER • BERNADETTE
A ROSENKRANZ • ERIK D ROSENLUND • MARTIN
F ROSENMANN • JULIA A ROSENQUIST • DALE
ROSENSTEIN • EILEEN B ROSENSTEIN • AN-
DREA E ROSENTHAL • DAVID ROSENTHAL •
DAVID S ROSENTHAL • JENNIFER L ROSENTHAL
• MARTIN D ROSENTHAL • MATTHEW S ROSEN-
THAL • MICHAEL L ROSENTHAL • MILTON F
ROSENTHAL • ARLENE S ROSENTHAL-GILL •
TEGRA A ROSERA • EVELYN M ROSETTE • KRIS-
TEN B ROSEVALLY • CHRISTINE L ROSHEIM •
MARK ROSING • STEPHEN ROSKO III • CURT E
ROSMAIER • SCOTT T ROSMAIER • PAULA D ROS-
NER • SUSAN MARIE ROSOVSKY • ALBAELYIN D
ROSS • ALONZO B ROSS • ANNETTE J ROSS •
BARBARA L ROSS • BILLIE D ROSS • CASSAN-
DRA R ROSS • CHAP ROSS • DAVID S ROSS •
DENISE ROSS • DORIS E ROSS • EARLINE ROSS
• EDWARD J ROSS • EMILY B ROSS • EMMETT B
ROSS • ETHAN K ROSS • FLAVIA R ROSS • FRANK
J ROSS • FREDERICK B ROSS • GEORGE H ROSS
• GLENWOOD ROSS • JAMES P ROSS • JASON F
ROSS • JEAN M ROSS • JENNIFER A ROSS • JOAN
B ROSS • JOSEPH E ROSS • KAREN C ROSS •
KAREN G ROSS • KAREN M ROSS • KIM W ROSS •
KRISTIN ROSS • LAWRENCE A ROSS • MAR-
GARET H ROSS • MARY E ROSS • MEGAN I ROSS •
MICHAEL H ROSS • MIRAY L ROSS • PATRICIA D
ROSS • PATRICK E ROSS • QUENTIN D ROSS •
SARAH K ROSS • SCOTT R ROSS • SEDRIC D ROSS
• SETH O ROSS • SHARON C ROSS • STEVEN P
ROSS • SUSAN J ROSS • WILLIAM ROSS •
WILLIAM B ROSS • WILLIAM C ROSS • STACY D
ROSS-MALONE • CHARLES B ROSS JR. • DAVE J
ROSSELLE • BRENDA L ROSSER • EDITH M ROSS-
ER • MARGARET S ROSSER • SHARRA M ROSSER
• WILLIAM T ROSSER • LENITA D ROSSER-IVER-
SON • KAREN Y ROSSER-NEWBOLD • CHRISTO-
PHER D ROSSI • TERRANCE S ROSSI • VERNON E
ROSSIN • JOHN W ROSSINO • LINDA S ROSSLER
• CARA E ROSSON • JAN N ROSSON • EILEEN C
ROSSOW • GWENDOLYN A ROSTICK • KIMBERLY
T. ROSTICK • CATHY A ROSZELL • LAUREN E
ROTCHFORD • CINDY H ROTE • DANIEL S ROTE •
JACQUES L ROTH • ANDREA L ROTH • BRUNO G
ROTH • CONSTANCE L ROTH • DAN M ROTH • JEN-
NIFER T ROTH • JOHN T ROTH • JULIANA M ROTH
• MARGARET A ROTH • SUSAN ROTH • EDWARD H
ROTHBERGER • KAREN L ROTHERMEL • JEFFREY
ROTHFUS • SHANNON K ROTHGEB • ALEX ROTH-
MAN • MICHAEL H ROTHMAN • RICHARD I ROTH-
MAN • RODNEY J ROTHOFF • LINDA G ROTH-
SCHILD • ADAM ROTHSTEIN • ALAN S
ROTHSTEIN • BRENDA L ROTHSTEIN • DONNA A
ROTHSTEIN • GABRIEL ROTHSTEIN • NEIL M
ROTHSTEIN • PAUL ROTHWEILER • STEPHANIE R
ROTKOW • THOMAS M ROTROFF • UWE ROTSCH •
PETER C ROTTER • VALENTINA G ROTUNDO •
FLORITA B ROUAT • ALAIN ROULEAU • WILLIAM
E ROUNDTREE MD • CHARLOTTE W ROUNTREE
• GEORGIA A ROUNTREE • JAMES M ROUNTREE
• KENNETH B ROUNTREE • RHETT M ROUNTREE
• HAROLD E ROUPE • JEANETTE E ROUPE • LYN
M ROURKE • MICHAEL P ROURKE • ROBERT D
ROURKE • JENNIFER ROUSE • MERIEN M ROUSE
• SHONDA E ROUSE • DONALD J ROUSH •
MICHAEL ROUSH • STEVEN M ROUSH •
MATTHEW B ROUSH MD • WILLIAM P ROUSMAN-
IERE • JOSEPH ROUSSEAU • JERRY J ROUS-
SELLE • GEOFFREY L ROUTSON • MARY A ROUT-
SON • BRETT C ROVER • ANDREA P ROWAN •
JEAN T ROWAN • CATHERINE L ROWAN PT • RE-
BECCA A ROWDEN • ALISON ROWE • CARRIE S.
ROWE • EDITH ROWE • GLEN S ROWE • JASON M
ROWE • JULIANA Y ROWE • KRISTIN L ROWE •
KYSHA D ROWE • MATTHEW B ROWE • MELINDA
K ROWE • MICHAEL ROWE • ROSALIND D ROWE
• SHERMAN ROWE • STEPHEN H ROWE • SUSAN
L ROWE • TRACEY BIBI Z ROWEDDER • ANDREW
S ROWELL • JIM L ROWELL • JUDY C ROWELL •
MARK A ROWELL • DEXTER O ROWLAND •
DOROTHY C ROWLAND • JACK M ROWLAND •
JOHN ROWLAND • JOHN D ROWLAND • MARK D
ROWLAND • MARY K ROWLAND • NANCY E ROW-
LAND • CHAD M ROWLEE • JAMES B ROWLETT •
CHERYL L ROWLEY • JOHN ROX • BETTY L ROY •
DIANE R ROY • JENNIFER R ROY • LEONARD L
ROY • NAGESH ROY • WILLIAM J ROYAL • IDA B
ROYALL • MICHELLE L ROYALL • DEANDRE ROY-
ALS • ERNEST E ROYALS • GEORGETTA D ROY-
ALS • GAIL R ROYCE • JENNIFER L ROYCE • JIM A
ROYCE • IGNACIA ROYER • JAMES H ROYER •
MARCIE ROYER • JIM J ROYETON • MARVIN R
ROYSTER • DEBORAH B ROYSTON • WILLIAM W
ROYSTON • MARY K ROZDAY • CHRISTINA A
ROZEK • GERALDINE A ROZEK • ERIC I ROZEN
ATC • DAVID R ROZIER • JAMES M RUANE • AN-
DREA M RUARK • CELESTE RUBANICK • LISA D
RUBARTH • MARYVAL C RUBEL • DAVE P RUBEN-
STEIN • GEORGE RUBENSTEIN • DONALD A RU-
BERTI • MICHAEL A RUBESCH • JOSEP RUBIES •
ALFRED RUBIN • BARRY S RUBIN • ELLYN J RU-
BIN • LAURENCE J RUBIN • LILLIAN B RUBIN •
LISA BETH RUBIN • SAUL J RUBIN • EDWARD J
RUBINSTEIN • CYNTHIA F RUBIO • GUILLERMO
RUBIO • YVONNE M RUBIO • DARLENE L RUBLE
• COLLEEN M RUBSAM • KENT H RUBY • MATH-
EW J RUCK • NANCY J RUCK • BETTINA G RUCK-
ELSHAUS • CHRISTOPHER A RUCKER • DIXIE B
RUCKER • JOEL H RUCKER • RONALD RUCKER •
WILMA L RUCKER • ROSA RUCKERDEWITT •
SUZANNE K RUCKERT • PHILLIP E RUCKS JR •

LILIAS R RUD • KIMBERLY RUDA • MATTHEW G
RUDA • ROSEMARY RUDASILL • KIM S RUDDELL
• TOM H RUDDY • JOHN J RUDDY JR • JUSTIN J
RUDELSON • JACKIE M RUDER • CAROL L RUDIN
• CYNTHIA R RUDIN • REBECCA S RUDISILL •
MICHAEL BENNETT RUDNICK • ANGELA L
RUDOLPH • BETTY C RUDOLPH • ERIC B RUDOLPH
• GREGORY B RUDOLPH • GREGORY T RUDOLPH •
INGRID RUDOLPH • NANCY D RUDOLPH • PAMELA
A RUDOLPH • RICHARD D RUDOLPH • SONJA M
RUDOLPH • VALERIE L RUDOLPH • DAVID W
RUDRUD • KRISTINA LEE RUDRUD • GREGORY B
RUDY • NANCY L RUDY • KRISTEN E RUE • SHERYL
A RUEDEBUSCH • MELANIE RUEFLI • ROBIN P
RUEGG • JEFFREY A RUEPPEL • MANFRED R
RUESS • ANDREE RUEST • MARK A RUETTIGER •
DONNA RUFA • J MIKE RUFF • PAUL RUFFENACH
• DARLENE M RUFFIN • DEBRA RUFFIN • JEF-
FREY Q RUFFIN • ROBERT D RUGER • BRUCE A
RUGG • NICOLE A RUGG • VERONICA J RUGGLES
• DORIS A RUHL • ROBERT J RUHL • MELISSA A
RUIC • EULOGIO RUIZ • FRANCISCO RUIZ • JA-
NIS L RUIZ • JOAQUIN RUIZ • JUAN M RUIZ •
TERESA M RUIZ • BARRIE H RULAND • CAROL A
RULE • REBECCA A RULE • WENDY G RUMARY •
ROBERT F RUMBLE • ROBERT J RUMLEY •
GEORGINA B RUMSEY • JOHN L RUMSEY • CAROL
J RUNDLE • TRACY L RUNDSTROM • CHARLES H
RUNGE • NANCY U RUNION • JILL A RUNKEL •
RUSSELL G RUNNION • DAVID RUNYAN • JANE A
RUNYAN • RAMESH R RUPARELIA • JEFF L RUPE
• EDWARD J RUPERT • GENEVIEVE B RUPLEY •
DAN F RUPNOW • ROGER F RUPNOW • COREY
MICHAEL RUPP • DEBORAH B RUPP • WENDY L
RUPP • JOHN T RUPPERT • MARTHA L RUPPERT
• TOM O RUPPERT • GREGORY M RUPRECHT •
JILL D RUSCHEINSKI • KARA J RUSCHEINSKI •
BOB RUSH • DEBBY H RUSH • ELOISE D RUSH •
JACKIE S RUSH • JOHN W RUSH • LEMUEL J
RUSH • RHUDINE L RUSH • WOODY RUSH •
JULIE M RUSHIN • MARILYN RUSHIN • PATRICE A
RUSHIN • GREG RUSHING • JOLEEN C RUSHING
• IAN K RUSHTON • ROBERT A RUSHTON • BAR-
BARA S RUSIECKI • CAROL E RUSK • SYLVIA K
RUSKIN • SHERRILL Y RUSS • PAULA M RUS-
SELL • BARKLEY M RUSSELL • CAROL G RUS-
SELL • CAROLYN J RUSSELL • CHRISTINE RUS-
SELL • CYNTHIA L RUSSELL • DAVID L RUSSELL
• DEBRA C RUSSELL • EILEEN K RUSSELL •
JAMES E RUSSELL • JAMES T RUSSELL • JEN-
NIFER L RUSSELL • JEROME H RUSSELL • JILL M
RUSSELL • JIM W RUSSELL • JOHN W RUSSELL •
KAREN W RUSSELL • KARL E RUSSELL •
KATHERINE B RUSSELL • KATHY A RUSSELL •
KAY J RUSSELL • LAWRENCE RUSSELL • LEIGH
ANNE RUSSELL • LILTRA K RUSSELL • LINDA
L RUSSELL • LINDA W RUSSELL • LLOYD
E RUSSELL • LOWELL R RUSSELL • MARGARET
M RUSSELL • MARIANNE D RUSSELL • MARLENE
N RUSSELL • MARTHA A RUSSELL • MELISSA
J RUSSELL • MICHAEL A RUSSELL • MILDRED
B RUSSELL • MILES BRANDON RUSSELL
• MITCHELL A RUSSELL • NADINE A RUSSELL •
PHYLLIS RUSSELL • REVA RUSSELL • RICHARD C
RUSSELL • ROBERT J RUSSELL • SARAH H RUS-
SELL • SHARON E RUSSELL • SHERONDA N RUS-
SELL • STACY RUSSELL • STEPHEN F RUSSELL •
WILDA R RUSSELL • WILLIAM P RUSSELL •
MICHAEL RUSSELLE • SANDRA L RUSSMAN • DE-
BRA S RUSSO • DIANE M RUSSO • FRANCES R
RUSSO • GARTH S RUSSO • JOSEPH M RUSSO •
LISA M RUSSO • NATALIE D RUSSO • ROBERT G
RUSSO • WILLIAM F RUSSO • TERRY L RUSSOM •
WENDY E RUST • STACIA D RUSTAD • EILEEN S
RUSTIN • LINDA A RUSTIN • MARY M RUSZNAK •
JO RUTA • CHARLES M RUTER • BRIAN RUTH •
JANET F RUTH • JOHN I RUTH • NADJA E RUTH •
SHIRLEY M RUTH • DONNA RUTHERFORD •
DORIS S RUTHERFORD • DOUGLAS K RUTHER-
FORD • ILONA M RUTHERFORD • THOMAS R
RUTHERFORD • STEVEN P RUTHSATZ • CRYSTAL
J RUTLAND • HEATHER J RUTLAND • JOHN R
RUTLEDGE • JOHN W RUTLEDGE • KATHLEEN
RUTLEDGE • SHARRON A RUTLEDGE • TODD C
RUTLEDGE • WALTER C RUTLEDGE • MARK J RUT-
LEDGE PT • MARY F RUTTE • CECILIA E RUTTKAY
• THOMAS W RUTTKAY • KENNETH J RUTZ • NAN-
CY E RUZSA • PAWEL RUZYLLO • ALICE N RYAN •
ANGELA I RYAN • ANN E RYAN • ARLENE RYAN •
BARBARA J RYAN • CAROLINE RYAN • CARRIE
RYAN • GEORGE RYAN • JAMES J RYAN • JAMES T
RYAN • JOHN B RYAN • KELLY E RYAN • KIMBERLY
D RYAN • LAUREL N RYAN • MARK P RYAN • MARY
KATE RYAN • MATTHEW D RYAN • MICHAEL S
RYAN • NANCY S RYAN • NELL P RYAN • ROBERT
E RYAN • SCOTT RYAN • SHEILA P RYAN • THERE-
SA L RYAN • WILLAM P RYAN • WILLIAM J RYAN •
HARVEY VINCENT RYAN PM • JUDEAN B RYANS •
PEGGY A RYDBERG • BARBARA L RYDER • SEAN E
RYDER • JOHN S RYDESKI • MELANIE M RYER •
KATHERINE D RYLE • LYN S RYMAN • CHRISTINA
L RYMER • FRANK A RYMER • IWONA RYNIAK •
ARDATH C RYNNING • SUNG-BOK RYU • JACEK
RZUCIDLO • DANIEL N SAADE • THOMAS J SAAM
• JOHN C SAARI • LINDA E SAARINEN • SCOTT
SAARLAS • JOHN A SAAVEDRA • MICHAEL J
SABATELLE • JASON P SABATINO • ROBERT L
SABIN • KELLI B SABISTON ATC • RUDOLPH
SABLO • CARA SABO • JOHN D SABO • CATHER-
INE SABONIS-CHAFEE • ABDUL-JALEEL SABREE
• SARAH A SABREE • ADAM JASON SABRIN • GRE-
GORY D SACCO • CHERYL J SACHEN • JOSEPH S
SACHNO • NICHOLAS M SACHON • CHARLES B
SACHS • MICHAEL P SACHS • SYLVIA M SACIA •
BARBARA M. SACK • JONATHAN D SACK •
THOMAS J SACKMASTER • ARIA J SACKREITER •
RALPH SACKS • DONNA R SADAKA • ROGER W

SADECKI • CHARLES R SADEN • GARY M SADEN •
THELMA R SADEN • CHARLES D SADLER • COLIN
SADLER • FRANCES E SADLER • MYRON D
SADLER • SCOTT W SADLER • SETH BRIAN
SADLER • CHARLES W SADOWSKI • DANIEL A
SADOWSKY • AMY L SAEGER • JUAN C SAENZ •
PAUL S SAENZ • TERESITA B SAETHANG •
HAROLD E SAETHER • SCOTT D SAFER • JANNA L
SAFFER • LONEL N SAFFO • MAHAMMAD DAOUD
SAFI • GLORIA SAGAR • DALE L SAGE • DONNA L
SAGE • CAROLA SAGEBARTH • SUSAN M SAGEL
MT • PENNY L SAGGUS • MERCEDES E SAGHINI •
LYNN M SAGINAR • IGNACIO SAGNIER • THOMAS
S SAHARA • STAFFAN LR SAHLISTROM • DONNA
B SAHLMAN • VIVEK SAHNEY • ANITA SAHNI •
SIMRAN K SAHNI • TEJINDER S SAHNI • ROXANA
N SAHORA • SUE L SAIAH • AMEL SAIED • JOAN M
SAIEVA • MAKI SAIKAWA • ALEXANDRA SAILE •
SHELBRA F SAILORS • JERMAINE SAILSMAN •
KAREN G SAINT AMAND • MICHAEL D SAINT
AMAND • PIERRE SAINT MARTIN • BRIGITTE F
SAIPP • JUNICHI SAITO • MARIANNE SAITZ •
RICHARD P SAIZAN • TAKAKI SAKAI • TOLLY P
SAKATSIE • ZISIS SAKELLARIOU • KEIKO SAKIYA-
MA • RUTHY F. SAKNINI • KHALED A SAKR • VIN-
CENT A SAKRAIDA • RACHEL L SAKS • DOLORS
SALA BATLLE • CYNTHIA A SALAAM • THERESA A
SALADINO • JAHEZ A SALAHUDDIN SAT • REBEC-
CA R SALAKORY • MARIELLA SALAMANCA • ZIAD
Y SALAMEH • MELANIE L SALAS • SARA SALAS •
TIFFANI L SALAS • PETER C. SALAVERRY •
RAFAEL A SALAZAR • CECILIA M SALAZAR •
LORETTA R SALAZAR • STELLA SALAZAR •
MELISSA H SALDERFER • CAROL SALE • SUSAN
G SALE • RAYMER SALE JR • FUAD B SALEH •
CHRISTINA SALEM • MARWAN B SALEM • KIRBY
SALERNO • SHAWN A SALES • ELVIN Z SALGADO
• MIGUEL SALGADO • MIGUEL ANGEL SALGADO •
IRA SALIGMAN • WILLIAM P SALINA • EMILY C
SALINAS • GEORGE SALINAS • VICKY D SALINAS
• GREG M SALISBURY • JULIE D SALISBURY •
JEANNE M SALITURI • REBECCA W SALIU •
JONATHAN L SALKOFF • GLORIA D SALLEE •
MARK K SALLETTE • RIKU M SALMENKYLA • JEF-
FREY J SALMON • JONI K SALMON • SHAYLA E
SALMONS • ALLICIA J SALOMON • JOAN E SA-
LOMONE • BARBARA A SALOTTO • YEKATERINA
VALERIYERNA SALOVA • KEVIN W SALT • RITA D
SALTEN • ADRIAN L SALTER • CASSANDRA
SALTER • JACKSON SALTER • JAMES SALTER •
JOHN A SALTER • LISA J SALTER • LOUISE
SALTER • NED W SALTER • PATRICIA A SALTER •
REBA C SALTER • SARAH W SALTER • WALLACE B
SALTER • TWILA D SALTHOUSE • AMANDA E
SALTIN • DENISE M SALTSMAN • EDWARD M
SALTZMAN • STEVEN L SALTZMAN • XAVIER SAL-
VAT • KARLA A SALVATORE • RONALD S SALVEMI-
NI • DAVID G SALYERS • DOUGLAS D SALYERS •
LYNN S SALYERS • LON E SALZMAN • TEREZA
SAMARKOVA • MAMADOU M SAMBA • MARIETOU
SAMBA • NDEYE A SAMBA • RAMESH SAMBASI-
VAN • DORA P SAMBDMAN • RITA L SAMBER •
CANDACE M SAMBROOK • CHERYL J SAMET •
DARLENE D SAMFORD • TOM A SAMFORD • TOM A
SAMFORD • SUSAN G SAMMON • JANET P SAM-
MONS • JULIE ANNE SAMMONS • SARA E SAM-
MONS • TONY SAMMONS • SHEREEN M SA-
MONDS • EMILY C SAMOSE • REKESH N SAMPAT •
ERIC M SAMPLE • GIOVANNAH SAMPLE • R H
BARRY SAMPLE • R H BARRY SAMPLE • TAMARA
L SAMPLER • ELAINE L SAMPSON • HELEN R
SAMPSON • ROSANDRA S SAMPSON • JO ANN
SAMPSON ATC • GERALD N SAMS • MARIAN H
SAMS • NICOLE E SAMS • RISA R SAMS • ROBERT
G SAMS • SHARON O SAMS • LANA SAMSKY • PE-
TER D SAMUEL • SYLVIA SAMUEL • CHARLES
SAMUEL JR • ANGELIQUE M SAMUELS • GLENN F
SAMUELS • JASON F SAMUELS • JONATHAN
SAMUELS • MICHAEL SAMUELS • NORA P
SAMUELS • YVONNE SAMUELS • CHRIS J SAMUEL-
SON • CHERYL F SAMULSKI • RAFAEL I SAN
MIGUEL • MARSHA SANABRIA • NICOLE F
SANABRIA • GUY R SANAN • AJIT J SANARAS-
INGHE • ALISON B SANBORN • JENNIFER A SAN-
BORN • KRISTIN L SANBORN • OLIVIER F SANCHE
• CHARLES R SANCHES • CYNTHIA L SANCHES •
AZALEA B SANCHEZ • BENJAMIN SANCHEZ •
ELOISA E SANCHEZ • EVA MARIE SANCHEZ • JULIE
E SANCHEZ • MISSY A SANCHEZ • PACO SANCHEZ
• YAMILE-EUGENIA S SANCHEZ • ALVARO
SANCHEZ-CIFUENTES • CATARINA R SANCHEZ-
PHILLIPS • ELAINE C SANCHEZ-TOKUCHI • DIANE
L SAND • FRANCIS M SANDA • CAROL L SANDAHL-
MURRAY • MARCI SANDBERG • DEB SANDEN •
RICHARD A SANDER • ALLEN SANDERS • AMY D
SANDERS • AMY J SANDERS • ANDREW C SANDERS
• ANGELA D SANDERS • APRIL M SANDERS • BAR-
BARA K SANDERS • BETTY W SANDERS • BETTYE G
SANDERS • CRISCHANDRA D SANDERS • DARRYL J
SANDERS • DAVID W SANDERS • DEWEY K
SANDERS • DIANE M SANDERS • DON H SANDERS
• DONNA SANDERS • ELLEN P SANDERS • EMILY R
SANDERS • ENA L SANDERS • EUGENE C SANDERS
• FRANCES W SANDERS • GLORIA H SANDERS •
HERBERT SANDERS • HOLLY A SANDERS •
JACQUELINE L SANDERS • JASON S SANDERS •
JEWELL J SANDERS • JOANNA O SANDERS •
JOHN E SANDERS • KAREN B SANDERS • KIM M
SANDERS • KIMBERLY A SANDERS • KIRBY L
SANDERS • LARRY E SANDERS • LARRY L
SANDERS • LELA R SANDERS • LESHE M SANDERS
• LISA-MARIE B SANDERS • LORETTA SANDERS •
LYNNE B SANDERS • MATTHEW R SANDERS •
MEREDITH C SANDERS • NANCY SANDERS •
NANCY J SANDERS • NANCY L SANDERS •
NEHEMIAH SANDERS • OPHELIA D SANDERS •
PATRICK R SANDERS • PATTI H SANDERS •

FOOTBALL
FOOTBALL

Abbreviations and terms used in Football results tables
Abréviations et termes employés dans les tableaux de résultats de football

Term	English	Français
Assistant Coach	Assistant Coach	Entraîneur adjoint
Bronze	Bronze Medal	Médaille de bronze
CK	Corner Kicks	Corner
Coach	Coach	Entraîneur
Continued	Continued	Continué
D	Defender	Défenseur
Diff	Difference	Différence
F	Forward	Avant
FK	Free Kicks	Coups francs
Final	Final	Finale
Final Score	Final Score	Score final
G	Goalkeeper	Gardien de but
G/A	Goals/Attempts	Buts/Tentés
Games	Games	Matchs
Goals Against	Goals Against	Buts contre
Goals For	Goals For	Buts pour
Gold	Gold Medal	Médaille d'or
Group	Group	Groupe
Hdr	Header	Coup de tête
Halftime Score	Halftime Score	Score à mi-temps
IA	Inside Area	Zone de réparation
Intermediate Rounds	Intermediate Rounds	Tours intermédiaires
Linesmen	Linesmen	Juge de touche
Losses	Losses	Pertes
M	Midfielder	Demi
Min	Minutes Played	Minutes jouées
Name	Name	Nom
OA	Outside Area	Ailier
Off	Offsides	Hors-jeu
Own goals by opponent	Own Goals by Opponent	Buts contre sa propre équipe
PK	Penalty Kicks	Coups de réparation
Phase	Phase	Phase
Pos	Position	Position
Preliminaries	Preliminaries	Eliminatoires
Pts	Points	Points
Quarterfinals	Quarterfinals	Quarts de finale
RC	Red Card	Carton rouge
Referees	Referees	Arbitres
Rnk	Rank	Classement
Score	Score	Score
Semifinals	Semifinals	Demi-finales
Silver	Silver Medal	Médaille d'argent
Summary	Summary	Sommaire
Team	Team	Equipe
Ties	Ties	Egalités
Totals	Totals	Totaux
Wins	Wins	Victoires
YC	Yellow Card	Carton jaune

International Association Football Federation (FIFA)
Fédération Internationale de Football Association
P.O. Box 85
Hitzigweg 11
8030 Zurich
Switzerland

Football / Football

Men / Messieurs

PRELIMINARIES - GROUP A **FINAL SCORE:** ARG 3 USA 1 **HALFTIME SCORE:** ARG 1 USA 1

Team: USA United States of America

Coach: ARENA, Bruce   Assistant Coach: MYERNICK, Glenn

Name	Pos	Min	FK	PK	Hdr	IA	OA	G/A	CK	Off	YC	RC
KELLER, Kasey	G	90										
McKEON, Matthew	D	20								1		
WALSH, Billy	M	0										
POPE, Eddie	D	90			0/1			0/1			1	
PEAY, Clint	D	85										
LALAS, Alexi	D	90									1	
BABA, Imad	M	90					0/1	0/1	1			
KIROVSKI, Jovan	F	90					0/1	0/1				
WOOD, A. J.	F	46					0/1	0/1				
REYNA, Claudio	M	90	0/2			1/2	0/2	1/6	4			
JOSEPH, Miles	F	45										
POLLARD, Brandon	D	0										
HEJDUK, Frankie	D	90										
MAISONNEUVE, Brian	M	90										
VARGAS, Nelson	M	6										
SMITH, Rob	M	0										
SILVERA, Damian	M	71									1	
SNITKO, Chris	G	0										
Own goals by opponent												
Totals			0/2		0/1	1/2	0/5	1/10	5	1	3	

Referees: BOUCHARDEAU, Lucian NIG   DALLAS, Hugh GBR

Team: ARG Argentina

Coach: PASSARELLA, Daniel   Assistant Coach: GALLEGO, Americo

Name	Pos	Min	FK	PK	Hdr	IA	OA	G/A	CK	Off	YC	RC
BOSSIO, Carlos Gustavo	G	90										
AYALA, Roberto Fabian	D	84			0/1			0/1				
CHAMOT, Jose Antonio	D	90										
ZANETTI, Javier Adelmar	D	90				0/1		0/1		1		
ALMEYDA, Matias Jesus	M	90				0/1		0/1				
SENSINI, Roberto Nestor	D	90			0/2			0/2				
LOPEZ, Claudio Javier	F	21								1		
SIMEONE, Diego Pablo	M	90				1/3		1/3				
CRESPO, Hernan Jorge	F	90				1/2		1/2		3	1	
ORTEGA, Arnaldo Ariel	F	70					0/1	0/1	5	3		
MORALES, Hugo Alberto	M	0										
CAVALLERO, Pablo Oscar	G	0										
PINEDA, Hector Mauricio	D	0										
PAZ, Pablo Ariel	D	7										
BASSEDAS, Christian Gustavo	M	0										
LOPEZ, Gustavo Adrian	M	90	0/1			1/1	0/1	1/3				
DELGADO, Marcelo Alejandro	F	65					0/1	0/1		1	1	
GALLARDO, Marcelo Daniel	M	26			0/1		0/1	0/2	4			
Own goals by opponent												
Totals			0/1		0/4	3/8	0/4	3/17	9	9	2	

Linesmen: NEUENSTEIN, Heiner GER   UGURDUR, Akif TUR

PRELIMINARIES - GROUP A **FINAL SCORE:** POR 2 TUN 0 **HALFTIME SCORE:** POR 1 TUN 0

Team: POR Portugal

Coach: VINGADA, Eduardo   Assistant Coach: OLIVEIRA, Agostinho

Name	Pos	Min	FK	PK	Hdr	IA	OA	G/A	CK	Off	YC	RC
COSTINHA, Paulo	G	95										
SANTOS, Daniel	F	16			0/1		0/2	0/3				
BENTO, Rui	D	95										
PEIXE, Emilio	D	95	0/1			0/1		0/2		1		
SEVERO, Roberto	F	0										
OLIVEIRA, Luis	D	82									2	
DOMINGUEZ, Jose	F	38							2	1		
ROCHA, Nuno	D	58									2	
ALVES, Paulo	F	71			0/1		0/1					
AGRA, Afonso	M	95	0/1			1/1	1/1	2/3	4			
OLIVEIRA, Rui	D	95										
SANTO, Nuno	G	0										
VIDIGAL, Jose	M	95										
SILVA, Jose	M	0										
RIBEIRO, Nuno	F	24					0/1	0/1				
PORFIRIO, Hugo	F	0										
MAGALHAES, Carlos	D	95								1		
CARVALHO, Daniel	F	80				0/1	0/3	0/4		1		
Own goals by opponent												
Totals			0/2		0/2	1/3	1/7	2/14	6	4	4	

Referees: LENNIE, Edward AUS   PEREIRA da SILVA, Antonio BRA

Team: TUN Tunisia

Coach: KASPERCZAK, Henri   Assistant Coach: SELMI, Ali

Name	Pos	Min	FK	PK	Hdr	IA	OA	G/A	CK	Off	YC	RC
el OUAER, Chokri	G	95										
BEN YOUNES, Imed	F	60					0/1	0/1				
BACCOUCHE, Lotfi	D	48										
BADRA, Khaled	M	84					0/1	0/1				
MKACHER, Mohamed	F	47									1	
CHOUCHANE, Ferid	D	95										
KANZARI, Maher	M	0										
BEYA, Zoubeir	F	95							1			
GABSI, Hassan	F	12										
GHODHBANE, Kaies	M	95					0/2	0/2				
SELLIM, Adel	F	95		0/1			0/1	0/2		3		
BOKRI, Marouane	D	0										
BOUAZIZI, Riadh	F	74				0/1		0/1			2	
JABALLAH, Sabri	D	0										
JAIDI, Radhi	D	95									1	
BABA, Hamdi	F	0										
BEN CHROUDA, Tarek	D	95			0/1			0/1				
BEN SLIMANE, Mehdi	F	35										
Own goals by opponent												
Totals				0/1	0/1	0/1	0/5	0/8	1	3	4	

Linesmen: al MOSSAWI, Mohammed Ahmed OMA   FRED, Lencie VAN

Men / *Messieurs*

PRELIMINARIES - GROUP A   FINAL SCORE: ARG 1 POR 1   HALFTIME SCORE: ARG 1 POR 0

Team: ARG Argentina
Coach: PASSARELLA, Daniel   Assistant Coach: GALLEGO, Americo

Name	Pos	Min	FK	PK	Hdr	IA	OA	G/A	CK	Off	YC	RC
BOSSIO, Carlos Gustavo	G	90										1
AYALA, Roberto Fabian	D	90		0/1				0/1				
CHAMOT, Jose Antonio	D	90										1
ZANETTI, Javier Adelmar	D	90										
ALMEYDA, Matias Jesus	M	90					0/2	0/2				
SENSINI, Roberto Nestor	D	90										
LOPEZ, Claudio Javier	F	90				0/6	0/2	0/8			2	
SIMEONE, Diego Pablo	M	90										1
CRESPO, Hernan Jorge	F	90			0/1	0/2	0/1	0/4			2	
ORTEGA, Arnaldo Ariel	F	90	0/1			1/1	0/1	1/3	8			
MORALES, Hugo Alberto	M	77				0/3	0/1	0/4				
CAVALLERO, Pablo Oscar	G	0										
PINEDA, Hector Mauricio	D	0										
PAZ, Pablo Ariel	D	0										
BASSEDAS, Christian Gustavo	M	0										
LOPEZ, Gustavo Adrian	M	14							1			
DELGADO, Marcelo Alejandro	F	0										
GALLARDO, Marcelo Daniel	M	0										
Own goals by opponent												
Totals			0/1	0/1	0/1	1/12	0/7	1/22	9		4	3

Referees: al-MUHANNA, Omar Seleh Saad KSA   GARCIA-ARANDA ENCINAR, Jose ESP

Team: POR Portugal
Coach: VINGADA, Eduardo   Assistant Coach: OLIVEIRA, Agostinho

Name	Pos	Min	FK	PK	Hdr	IA	OA	G/A	CK	Off	YC	RC
COSTINHA, Paulo	G	40										
SANTOS, Daniel	F	0										
BENTO, Rui	D	90										
PEIXE, Emilio	D	12					0/1	0/1				
SEVERO, Roberto	F	0										
OLIVEIRA, Luis	D	0										
DOMINGUEZ, Jose	F	0										
ROCHA, Nuno	D	90					0/2	0/2				1
ALVES, Paulo	F	79										
AGRA, Afonso	M	90	0/1					0/1	1			
OLIVEIRA, Rui	D	90										
SANTO, Nuno	G	51										
VIDIGAL, Jose	M	90					0/1	0/1				
SILVA, Jose	M	90					0/1	0/1				
RIBEIRO, Nuno	F	90				1/1		1/1			2	
PORFIRIO, Hugo	F	45				0/1	0/1	0/2				
MAGALHAES, Carlos	D	90										
CARVALHO, Daniel	F	45										
Own goals by opponent												
Totals			0/1			1/3	0/5	1/9	1		2	1

Linesmen: ARANGO CARDONA, Jorge Luis COL   DUPANOV, Yuri BLR

PRELIMINARIES - GROUP A   FINAL SCORE: USA 2 TUN 0   HALFTIME SCORE: USA 1 TUN 0

Team: USA United States of America
Coach: ARENA, Bruce   Assistant Coach: MYERNICK, Glenn

Name	Pos	Min	FK	PK	Hdr	IA	OA	G/A	CK	Off	YC	RC
KELLER, Kasey	G	91										
McKEON, Matthew	D	0										
WALSH, Billy	M	0										
POPE, Eddie	D	91										
PEAY, Clint	D	91										
LALAS, Alexi	D	91					0/1	0/1				
BABA, Imad	M	91				0/3	0/2	0/5	3	1		
KIROVSKI, Jovan	F	90	1/1			0/2	0/1	1/4		2		
WOOD, A. J.	F	1										
REYNA, Claudio	M	91					0/1	0/1	4	1		
JOSEPH, Miles	F	91				0/2	0/1	0/3				1
POLLARD, Brandon	D	0										
HEJDUK, Frankie	D	91					0/2	0/2				
MAISONNEUVE, Brian	M	91				1/1	0/1	1/2				
VARGAS, Nelson	M	0										
SMITH, Rob	M	0										
SILVERA, Damian	M	91					0/2	0/2	1			
SNITKO, Chris	G	0										
Own goals by opponent												
Totals			1/1			1/8	0/11	2/20	8	4		1

Referees: BOUCHARDEAU, Lucian NIG   DALLAS, Hugh GBR

Team: TUN Tunisia
Coach: KASPERCZAK, Henri   Assistant Coach: SELMI, Ali

Name	Pos	Min	FK	PK	Hdr	IA	OA	G/A	CK	Off	YC	RC
el OUAER, Chokri	G	91										
BEN YOUNES, Imed	F	0										
BACCOUCHE, Lotfi	D	57										
BADRA, Khaled	M	91					0/2	0/2			1	
MKACHER, Mohamed	F	0										
CHOUCHANE, Ferid	D	67									2	
KANZARI, Maher	M	28										
BEYA, Zoubeir	F	45					0/1	0/1	2			
GABSI, Hassan	F	45										
GHODHBANE, Kaies	M	18					0/1	0/1				
SELLIM, Adel	F	45	0/1		0/3	0/1	0/1	0/6			2	
BOKRI, Marouane	D	34										
BOUAZIZI, Riadh	F	0										
JABALLAH, Sabri	D	91										
JAIDI, Radhi	D	45										
BABA, Hamdi	F	0										
BEN CHROUDA, Tarek	D	87					0/1	0/1			2	
Own goals by opponent												
Totals			0/1		0/3	0/1	0/6	0/11	2		2	5

Linesmen: HOLM, Gitte DEN   NEUENSTEIN, Heiner GER

Men / *Messieurs*

PRELIMINARIES - GROUP A   **FINAL SCORE:** ARG 1 TUN 1   **HALFTIME SCORE:** ARG 1 TUN 0

Team: ARG Argentina
Coach: PASSARELLA, Daniel   Assistant Coach: GALLEGO, Americo

Name	Pos	Min	FK	PK	Hdr	IA	OA	G/A	CK	Off	YC	RC
BOSSIO, Carlos Gustavo	G	0										
AYALA, Roberto Fabian	D	90			0/1			0/1				
CHAMOT, Jose Antonio	D	90									1	
ZANETTI, Javier Adelmar	D	90					0/1	0/1				
ALMEYDA, Matias Jesus	M	90									1	
SENSINI, Roberto Nestor	D	0										
LOPEZ, Claudio Javier	F	67					0/2	0/2		2		
SIMEONE, Diego Pablo	M	78			0/1			0/1				
CRESPO, Hernan Jorge	F	45				0/3		0/3				
ORTEGA, Arnaldo Ariel	F	90				1/4	0/1	1/5	7			
MORALES, Hugo Alberto	M	0										
CAVALLERO, Pablo Oscar	G	90										
PINEDA, Hector Mauricio	D	0										
PAZ, Pablo Ariel	D	90			0/2			0/2			1	
BASSEDAS, Christian Gustavo	M	13			0/1			0/1				
LOPEZ, Gustavo Adrian	M	90					0/3	0/3	1			
DELGADO, Marcelo Alejandro	F	45					0/1	0/1				
GALLARDO, Marcelo Daniel	M	24				0/1	0/1	0/2	5			
Own goals by opponent												
Totals					0/5	1/8	0/9	1/22	13	2	3	

Referees: JONSSON, Ingrid SWE   UN-PRASERT, Pirom THA

Team: TUN Tunisia
Coach: KASPERCZAK, Henri   Assistant Coach: SELMI, Ali

Name	Pos	Min	FK	PK	Hdr	IA	OA	G/A	CK	Off	YC	RC
el OUAER, Chokri	G	90										
BEN YOUNES, Imed	F	87				0/1	0/1	0/2	4		1	
CHOUCHANE, Ferid	D	0										
GHODHBANE, Kaies	M	45					0/1	0/1				
KANZARI, Maher	M	13									1	
BACCOUCHE, Lotfi	D	45									2	
GABSI, Hassan	F	4										
BEYA, Zoubeir	F	45					0/1	0/1				
BOKRI, Marouane	D	33				0/1		0/1				
JABALLAH, Sabri	D	0										
MKACHER, Mohamed	F	45										
JAIDI, Radhi	D	45										
BEN CHROUDA, Tarek	D	0										
SELLIM, Adel	F	45					0/1	0/1		1		
BADRA, Khaled	M	45										
BABA, Hamdi	F	0										
BOUAZIZI, Riadh	F	45				0/1		0/1				
Own goals by opponent												
Totals					1/2	0/4	0/8	1/14	8	2	4	

Linesmen: NEUENSTEIN, Heiner GER   UGURDUR, Akif TUR

PRELIMINARIES - GROUP A   **FINAL SCORE:** USA 1 POR 1   **HALFTIME SCORE:** POR 1 USA 0

Team: USA United States of America
Coach: ARENA, Bruce   Assistant Coach: MYERNICK, Glenn

Name	Pos	Min	FK	PK	Hdr	IA	OA	G/A	CK	Off	YC	RC
KELLER, Kasey	G	90										
McKEON, Matthew	D	8										
WALSH, Billy	M	0										
POPE, Eddie	D	90					0/1	0/1			1	
PEAY, Clint	D	67										
LALAS, Alexi	D	90			0/1			0/1				
BABA, Imad	M	90				0/1		0/1	2			
KIROVSKI, Jovan	F	90			0/1		0/2	0/3		2		
WOOD, A. J.	F	38			0/1	0/1		0/2			1	
REYNA, Claudio	M	90	0/1			0/2	0/2	0/5	14			
JOSEPH, Miles	F	90			0/1	0/1		0/2				
POLLARD, Brandon	D	24										
HEJDUK, Frankie	D	90				0/2	0/1	0/3				
MAISONNEUVE, Brian	M	83				1/2	0/1	1/3				
VARGAS, Nelson	M	0										
SMITH, Rob	M	0										
SILVERA, Damian	M	53										
SNITKO, Chris	G	0										
Own goals by opponent												
Totals			0/1		0/4	1/9	0/7	1/21	16	2	2	

Referees: GARCIA-ARANDA ENCINAR, Jose ESP   LENNIE, Edward AUS

Team: POR Portugal
Coach: VINGADA, Eduardo   Assistant Coach: OLIVEIRA, Agostinho

Name	Pos	Min	FK	PK	Hdr	IA	OA	G/A	CK	Off	YC	RC
COSTINHA, Paulo	G	0										
SANTOS, Daniel	F	90					0/1	0/1	1			
BENTO, Rui	D	90										
PEIXE, Emilio	D	0										
SEVERO, Roberto	F	6										
OLIVEIRA, Luis	D	90										
DOMINGUEZ, Jose	F	61					0/1	0/1	1	2		
ROCHA, Nuno	D	36									1	
ALVES, Paulo	F	90				1/1		1/1	1			
AGRA, Afonso	M	0										
OLIVEIRA, Rui	D	90									1	
SANTO, Nuno	G	90										
VIDIGAL, Jose	M	90				0/1		0/1			1	
SILVA, Jose	M	90				0/2		0/2	4			
RIBEIRO, Nuno	F	0										
PORFIRIO, Hugo	F	55										
MAGALHAES, Carlos	D	90										
CARVALHO, Daniel	F	25					0/4	0/4	1			
Own goals by opponent												
Totals						1/4	0/6	1/10	6	5	2	

Linesmen: al MOSSAWI, Mohamed Ahmed OMA   FRED, Lencie VAN

Football / *Football*

Men / *Messieurs*

PRELIMINARIES GROUP B FINAL SCORE: **FRA 2 AUS 0** HALFTIME SCORE: **FRA 1 AUS 0**

Team: FRA France
Coach: DOMENECH, Raymond Assistant Coach: THIEBAUT, Jacky

Name	Pos	Min	FK	PK	Hdr	IA	OA	G/A	CK	Off	YC	RC
LETIZI, Lionel	G	89									1	
DJETOU, Martin	D	89										
BONNISSEL, Jerome	D	89										
LAVILLE, Florent	D	0										
MOREAU, Patrick	D	89										
MAKELELE, Claude	M	89				0/1		0/1	2	1	1	
DHORASOO, Vikash	M	89									1	
MAURICE, Florian	F	78				1/1	0/1	1/2		4		
SIBIERSKI, Antoine	F	47					0/1	0/1				
PIRES, Robert	F	87				1/1	0/1	1/2	2		1	
TOYES, Geoffray	D	0										
CANDELA, Vincent	D	89										
DACOURT, Olivier	M	43					0/1	0/1				
VAIRELLES, Tony	F	12				0/2	0/1	0/3			1	
FERNANDEZ, Vincent	G	0										
WILTORD, Sylvain	F	2										
LEGWINSKY, Sylvain	F	89										
DIENG, Oumar	F	0										
Own goals by opponent												
Totals						2/5	0/5	2/10	4	5	5	

Referees: ARCHUNDIA TELLEZ, Benito MEX RUSCIO, Roberto Ruben ARG

Team: AUS Australia
Coach: THOMSON, Edward Assistant Coach: SCHEINFLUG, Leslie

Name	Pos	Min	FK	PK	Hdr	IA	OA	G/A	CK	Off	YC	RC
JURIC, Frank	G	89										
LOZANOVSKI, Goran	M	0										
MORIC, Ante	M	89							2			
BABIC, Mark	D	89										
MUSCAT, Kevin	D	89									1	
HORVAT, Steven	D	78									1	
TSEKENIS, Peter	M	0										
CORICA, Steve	M	89							1	1		
VIDUKA, Mark	F	67					0/1	0/1		4		
VIDMAR, Aurelio	F	89									1	
TIATTO, Daniel	F	21										1
SPITERI, Jospeh	F	23										
FOXE, Hayden	D	0										
AGOSTINO, Paul	F	89	0/1		0/1			0/2		1		
CASSERLY, Luke	D	89										
ENES, Roberto	M	0										
ALOISI, Ross	M	11										
PETKOVIC, Michael	G	0										
Own goals by opponent												
Totals			0/1		0/1		0/1	0/3	3	6	3	1

Linesmen: JEON, Young Hyun KOR VELAZQUEZ PINTOS, Carlos Adan URU

PRELIMINARIES - GROUP B FINAL SCORE: **ESP 1 KSA 0** HALFTIME SCORE: **ESP 0 KSA 0**

Team: ESP Spain
Coach: CLEMENTE, Javier Assistant Coach: SAEZ, Ignacio

Name	Pos	Min	FK	PK	Hdr	IA	OA	G/A	CK	Off	YC	RC
MORA, Juan L.	G	92										
MENDIETA, Gaizka	D	92									1	
ARANZABAL, Augustin	D	92										
VICENTE, Francisco	D	0										
DENIA, Santiago	D	92									1	
GARCIA, Oscar	M	29			1/1			1/1				
GONZALEZ, Raul	F	92			0/1			0/1	2	1		
FRESNEDOSO, Roberto	M	29				0/1	0/1	0/2				
CORINO, Sergio	D	92										
SAENZ, Jose	M	92										
INDIAKEZ, Inigo	M	63			0/1			0/1	1			
KARANKA, Aitor	D	20										
AIZKORRETA, Jorge	G	0										
MORIENTES, Fernando	F	63			0/2		0/1	0/3		1		
de la PENA, Ivan	M	72	0/1					0/1	7			
LARDIN, Jordi	F	92	0/1				0/2	0/3	1			
SUAREZ, Jose	D	0										
GARCIA, Daniel	F	0										
Own goals by opponent												
Totals			0/2		1/5	0/1	0/4	1/12	11	2	2	

Referees: COLLINA, Pierluigi ITA UN-PRASERT, Pirom THA

Team: KSA Saudi Arabia
Coach: WORTMANN, Ivo

Name	Pos	Min	FK	PK	Hdr	IA	OA	G/A	CK	Off	YC	RC
al-SADIG, Hussain	G	92										
al-JAHANI, Mohammed	D	92					0/1	0/1				
al-SHAHRANI, Abdullah	D	0										
al-KHILAIWI, Mohammed	D	92										
ZUBROMAWI, Abdullah S.	D	92										
AMIN, Fuad Anwar	M	92				0/1	0/3	0/4		1		
al-ZAHRANI, Khamees	M	0										
SULIMANI, Hussain	D	84										1
FALATAH, Hamzah	F	92			0/2		0/2	0/4		2		
al-HARBI, Ibrahim	M	92										
al-DOSSARY, Obied	F	92				0/2	0/1	0/3		3		
al-MASAARI, Hussain	M	0										
al-RASHAID, Khalid	M	92							1			
al-GARNI, Abdulla	M	0										
al-MARZOUG, Abdulaziz	D	0										
al-DOSSARI, Khamis	M	92										
SIFEEN, Rahman Abdul	F	8										
al-MEGRIN, Rashid	G	0										
Own goals by opponent												
Totals					0/2	0/3	0/7	0/12	1	6		1

Linesmen: DANTE, Dramane MLI TORRES ZUNIGA, Luis Fernando CRC

PRELIMINARIES - GROUP B — FINAL SCORE: KSA 1 AUS 2 — HALFTIME SCORE: KSA 1 AUS 1

Team: KSA Saudi Arabia
Coach: WORTMANN, Ivo

Name	Pos	Min	FK	PK	Hdr	IA	OA	G/A	CK	Off	YC	RC
al-SADIG, Hussain	G	94										
al-JAHANI, Mohammed	D	94				0/1	0/1				1	
al-SHAHRANI, Abdullah	D	0										
al-KHILAIWI, Mohammed	D	94			1/1		1/1					
ZUBROMAWI, Abdullah S.	D	94										1
AMIN, Fuad Anwar	M	94	0/1		0/2	0/1	0/2	0/6		3		
al-ZAHRANI, Khamees	M	0										
SULIMANI, Hussain	D	26										
FALATAH, Hamzah	F	94				0/2		0/2				
al-HARBI, Ibrahim	M	94										
al-DOSSARY, Obied	F	94	0/1					0/1	5	2		
al-MASAARI, Hussain	M	0										
al-RASHAID, Khalid	M	94								2		
al-GARNI, Abdulla	M	26										
al-MARZOUG, Abdulaziz	D	45										
al-DOSSARI, Khamis	M	68										
SIFEEN, Rahman Abdul	F	23									1	1
al-MEGRIN, Rashid	G	0										
Own goals by opponent												
Totals			0/1	0/1	1/3	0/3	0/3	1/11	8	6	2	

Referees: BAHARMAST, Esfandiar USA   el-GHANDOUR, Gamal Mahmoud EGY

Team: AUS Australia
Coach: THOMSON, Edward   Assistant Coach: SCHEINFLUG, Leslie

Name	Pos	Min	FK	PK	Hdr	IA	OA	G/A	CK	Off	YC	RC
JURIC, Frank	G	94										
LOZANOVSKI, Goran	M	0										
MORIC, Ante	M	94				0/2	0/2		3		1	
BABIC, Mark	D	94										
MUSCAT, Kevin	D	94			0/1	0/1		0/2				
HORVAT, Steven	D	0										
TSEKENIS, Peter	M	94			1/2			1/2				
CORICA, Steve	M	94							2		1	
VIDUKA, Mark	F	80			0/2	1/3	0/1	1/6				
VIDMAR, Aurelio	F	94			0/1		0/1	0/2				
TIATTO, Daniel	F	0										
SPITERI, Jospeh	F	94				0/5	0/2	0/7		3		1
FOXE, Hayden	D	0										
AGOSTINO, Paul	F	0										
CASSERLY, Luke	D	94										
ENES, Roberto	M	14										
ALOISI, Ross	M	94										
PETKOVIC, Michael	G	0										
Own goals by opponent												
Totals			0/4		2/11	0/6		2/21	5	4	2	

Linesmen: KELLY, Peter TRI   OSMAN MOHAMED, Amir SUD

PRELIMINARIES - GROUP B — FINAL SCORE: ESP 1 FRA 1 — HALFTIME SCORE: ESP 0 FRA 1

Team: ESP Spain
Coach: CLEMENTE, Javier   Assistant Coach: SAEZ, Ignacio

Name	Pos	Min	FK	PK	Hdr	IA	OA	G/A	CK	Off	YC	RC
MORA, Juan L.	G	90										
MENDIETA, Gaizka	D	0										
ARANZABAL, Augustin	D	26										
VICENTE, Francisco	D	90			0/1			0/1				
DENIA, Santiago	D	90										
GARCIA, Oscar	M	90	0/1			1/1		1/2			1	
GONZALEZ, Raul	F	90							1	1		
FRESNEDOSO, Roberto	M	65								2		
CORINO, Sergio	D	57										
SAENZ, Jose	M	90					0/1	0/1				
INDIAKEZ, Inigo	M	0										
KARANKA, Aitor	D	90										
AIZKORRETA, Jorge	G	0										
MORIENTES, Fernando	F	0										
de la PENA, Ivan	M	25	0/1					0/1	1		1	
LARDIN, Jordi	F	34								1		
SUAREZ, Jose	D	65									1	
GARCIA, Daniel	F	90							1	3		
Own goals by opponent												
Totals			0/1	0/1	0/1	1/1	0/1	1/5	3	7	3	

Referees: COLLINA, Pierluigi ITA   UN-PRASERT, Pirom THA

Team: FRA France
Coach: DOMENECH, Raymond   Assistant Coach: THIEBAUT, Jacky

Name	Pos	Min	FK	PK	Hdr	IA	OA	G/A	CK	Off	YC	RC
LETIZI, Lionel	G	90										
DJETOU, Martin	D	90	0/1					0/1			1	
BONNISSEL, Jerome	D	0										
LAVILLE, Florent	D	0										
MOREAU, Patrick	D	90								1		
MAKELELE, Claude	M	90				0/1	0/1	0/2	5	1		
DHORASOO, Vikash	M	90								1		
MAURICE, Florian	F	0										
SIBIERSKI, Antoine	F	0										
PIRES, Robert	F	11				0/1		0/1		1		
TOYES, Geoffray	D	90										
CANDELA, Vincent	D	90										
DACOURT, Olivier	M	0										
VAIRELLES, Tony	F	90				0/1		0/1		1	1	
FERNANDEZ, Vincent	G	0										
WILTORD, Sylvain	F	80				0/1		0/1		1	1	
LEGWINSKY, Sylvain	F	90			1/1			1/1				
DIENG, Oumar	F	90										
Own goals by opponent												
Totals			0/1		1/2	0/4		1/7	5	6	3	

Linesmen: RODRIGUEZ ROMAN, Maria del Socorro MEX   DANTE, Dramane MLI

Men / *Messieurs*

PRELIMINARIES - GROUP B | FINAL SCORE: KSA 1 FRA 2 | HALFTIME SCORE: KSA 1 FRA 1

Team: KSA Saudi Arabia
Coach: WORTMANN, Ivo

Name	Pos	Min	FK	PK	Hdr	IA	OA	G/A	CK	Off	YC	RC
al-SADIG, Hussain	G	90										
al-JAHANI, Mohammed	D	75										
al-SHAHRANI, Abdullah	D	15										
al-KHILAIWI, Mohammed	D	90										
ZUBROMAWI, Abdullah S.	D	90										
AMIN, Fuad Anwar	M	90					1/4	1/4		6		
al-ZAHRANI, Khamees	M	0										
SULIMANI, Hussain	D	90					0/1	0/1		1		
FALATAH, Hamzah	F	45										
al-HARBI, Ibrahim	M	90										
al-DOSSARY, Obied	F	90							2	2		
al-MASAARI, Hussain	M	0										
al-RASHAID, Khalid	M	90					0/1	0/1		1		
al-GARNI, Abdulla	M	45										
al-MARZOUG, Abdulaziz	D	0										
al-DOSSARI, Khamis	M	90										
SIFEEN, Rahman Abdul	F	0										
al-MEGRIN, Rashid	G	0										
Own goals by opponent												
Totals							1/6	1/6	2	10		

Referees: ARCHUNDIA TELLEZ, Benito MEX — el-GHANDOUR, Gamal Mahmoud EGY

Team: FRA France
Coach: DOMENECH, Raymond   Assistant Coach: THIEBAUT, Jacky

Name	Pos	Min	FK	PK	Hdr	IA	OA	G/A	CK	Off	YC	RC
LETIZI, Lionel	G	90										
DJETOU, Martin	D	85		0/1			0/1	0/2				
BONNISSEL, Jerome	D	90			0/1			0/1				
LAVILLE, Florent	D	90			0/1			0/1				
MOREAU, Patrick	D	6										
MAKELELE, Claude	M	0										
DHORASOO, Vikash	M	90			0/1		0/1	0/2				
MAURICE, Florian	F	90	1/1	0/1			0/2	1/4			1	
SIBIERSKI, Antoine	F	62			1/2		0/1	1/3			1	
PIRES, Robert	F	73			0/1			0/1		9		
TOYES, Geoffray	D	0										
CANDELA, Vincent	D	90										
DACOURT, Olivier	M	90										
VAIRELLES, Tony	F	0										
FERNANDEZ, Vincent	G	0										
WILTORD, Sylvain	F	29								1	2	
LEGWINSKY, Sylvain	F	18										
DIENG, Oumar	F	90					0/1	0/1	0/2			
Own goals by opponent												
Totals			1/1	0/4	1/6		0/5	2/16		10	4	

Linesmen: JEON, Young Hyun KOR — VELAZQUEZ PINTOS, Carlos Adan URU

PRELIMINARIES - GROUP B | FINAL SCORE: ESP 3 AUS 2 | HALFTIME SCORE: AUS 2 ESP 1

Team: ESP Spain
Coach: CLEMENTE, Javier   Assistant Coach: SAEZ, Ignacio

Name	Pos	Min	FK	PK	Hdr	IA	OA	G/A	CK	Off	YC	RC
MORA, Juan L.	G	90										
MENDIETA, Gaizka	D	33					0/1	0/1				
ARANZABAL, Augustin	D	90										1
NAVARRO, Javier	D	90										1
DENIA, Santiago	D	90				1/1		1/1			1	1
GARCIA, Oscar	M	90				0/1	0/1	0/2				
GONZALEZ, Raul	F	90	1/1		1/1		0/1	2/3				
FRESNEDOSO, Roberto	M	0										
CORINO, Sergio	D	0										
SAENZ, Jose	M	60					0/1	0/1				
INDIAKEZ, Inigo	M	21				0/1		0/1			1	
KARANKA, Aitor	D	90										
AIZKORRETA, Jorge	G	0										
MORIENTES, Fernando	F	70			0/2			0/2			2	1
de la PENA, Ivan	M	31								1		
LARDIN, Jordi	F	58				0/1		0/1		2		
SUAREZ, Jose	D	0										
GARCIA, Daniel	F	90					0/1	0/1		4	1	
Own goals by opponent												
Totals			1/1		1/4	1/4	0/4	3/13		7	5	4

Referees: BOUCHARDEAU, Lucian NIG — DALLAS, Hugh GBR

Team: AUS Australia
Coach: THOMSON, Edward   Assistant Coach: SCHEINFLUG, Leslie

Name	Pos	Min	FK	PK	Hdr	IA	OA	G/A	CK	Off	YC	RC
JURIC, Frank	G	90										
LOZANOVSKI, Goran	M	19	0/1					0/1	1		1	
MORIC, Ante	M	57										1
BABIC, Mark	D	90										
MUSCAT, Kevin	D	90										
HORVAT, Steven	D	90										
TSEKENIS, Peter	M	90			0/1			0/1				
CORICA, Steve	M	90										
VIDUKA, Mark	F	90			0/1			0/1				
VIDMAR, Aurelio	F	72				2/4		2/4			1	1
TIATTO, Daniel	F	54										
SPITERI, Jospeh	F	37										1
FOXE, Hayden	D	0										
AGOSTINO, Paul	F	0										
CASSERLY, Luke	D	90			0/1			0/1				
ENES, Roberto	M	0										
ALOISI, Ross	M	34										
PETKOVIC, Michael	G	0										
Own goals by opponent												
Totals			0/1		0/3	2/4		2/8	1		2	3

Linesmen: DANTE, Dramane MLI — TORRES ZUNIGA, Luis Fernando CRC

Men / Messieurs

PRELIMINARIES - GROUP C | **FINAL SCORE:** ITA 0 MEX 1 | **HALFTIME SCORE:** ITA 0 MEX 0

Team: ITA Italy

Coach: MALDINI, Cesare   Assistant Coach: NICCOLAI, Comunardo

Name	Pos	Min	FK	PK	Hdr	IA	OA	G/A	CK	Off	YC	RC
PAGLIUCA, Gianluca	G	91										
NESTA, Alessandro	D	91									1	
CANNAVARO, Fabio	D	91				0/1	0/1					
GALANTE, Fabio	D	91										
FRESI, Salvatore	D	91	0/1				0/1					
AMETRANO, Raffaele	M	0										
CRIPPA, Massimo	M	91				0/2	0/2				1	
BRANCA, Marco	F	91									1	
BRAMBILLA, Massimo	M	64										
del VECCHIO, Marco	F	13				0/1	0/1					
BUFFON, Gianluigi	G	0										
PISTONE, Alessandro	D	0										
TOMMASI, Damiano	M	91				0/1	0/1	1				
PECCHIA, Fabio	M	91										
MORFEO, Domenico	F	5										
LUCARELLI, Cristiano	F	78				0/1	0/1	0/2				
BERNARDINI, Antonino	M	0										
SARTOR, Luigi	D	0										
Own goals by opponent												
Totals			0/1			0/2	0/5	0/8	1	1	2	

Referees: BOUCHARDEAU, Lucian NIG   DALLAS, Hugh GBR

PRELIMINARIES - GROUP C | **FINAL SCORE:** GHA 0 KOR 1 | **HALFTIME SCORE:** GHA 0 KOR 1

Team: MEX Mexico

Coach: de los COBOS, Carlos   Assistant Coach: MILUTINOVIC, Velibor

Name	Pos	Min	FK	PK	Hdr	IA	OA	G/A	CK	Off	YC	RC
SANCHEZ, Oswaldo	G	0										
SUAREZ, Claudio	D	91			0/1		0/1					
OTEO, David	D	0										
VILLA, German	M	91				0/1	0/1					
DAVINO, Duilio	D	91			0/1		0/1					
LARA, Rodrigo	M	91				0/1	0/1				1	
GARCIA, Jose	M	91	0/1			0/1	0/1	0/3	3			
SOL, Manuel	M	91	0/1				0/1	1				
CAMPOS, Jorge	F	91										
GARCIA POSTIGO, Luis	F	91			0/4	0/1	0/5	2	1			
BLANCO, Cuauhtemoc	M	21										
SANCHEZ, Javier	D	0										
PARDO, Pavel	D	91			0/1	0/1	0/2					
ALVARADO, Edson	F	0										
ARELLANO, Jesus	M	0										
ALFARO, Enrique	F	91				0/1	0/1					
PALENCIA, Francisco	F	25				1/1	1/1	2				
ABUNDIS, Jose	F	66				0/2	0/2	2				
Own goals by opponent												
Totals			0/2			0/2	0/9	1/6	1/19	6	5	1

Linesmen: NEUENSTEIN, Heiner GER   UGURDUR, Akif TUR

Team: GHA Ghana

Coach: ARDAY, Samuel   Assistant Coach: PAHA, Isaac

Name	Pos	Min	FK	PK	Hdr	IA	OA	G/A	CK	Off	YC	RC
KINGSTON, Richard	G	0										
NETTEY, Jacob	D	0										
WELBECK, Nii Aryee	F	85				0/1	0/1	1			1	
BAIDOO, Stephen	M	0										
ADDO, Joseph	D	90				0/2	0/2					
DOUDU, Afo	M	90			0/1		0/1					
KUFFOUR, Osei S.	D	90			0/2	0/1	0/3					
YAHAYA, Mallam	M	0										
ARHINFUL, Augustine	F	90				0/2	0/2	0/4				
AKUNNOR, Charles	F	90	0/1		0/1		0/2					
DUAH, Emmanuel	F	90				0/1	0/1	4				
ABOAGYE, Felix	F	34			0/1	0/3	0/4					
OHENE, Kennedy	F	57			0/1	0/1	0/2	1				
HAGAN, Ebenezer	M	90			0/1	0/2	0/3					
SABAH, Christian	D	90				0/2	0/2	1				
ADDO, Simon	G	90										
KUFFOUR, Osei E.	D	0										
KORANTENG, Prince	F	6										
Own goals by opponent												
Totals			0/1		0/7	0/5	0/12	0/25	5	2	1	

Referees: LENNIE, Edward AUS   PEREIRA da SILVA, Antonio BRA

Team: KOR Korea

Coach: BYCHOVETS, Anatoli   Assistant Coach: CHO, Byung-Deuk

Name	Pos	Min	FK	PK	Hdr	IA	OA	G/A	CK	Off	YC	RC
SEO, Dong-Myung	G	90										
PARK, Choong-Kyoon	D	0										
CHOI, Sung-Yong	D	90										
LEE, Sang-Hun	D	90										
LEE, Kyung-Soo	M	0										
LEE, Ki-Hyung	M	90				0/1	0/1	2				
LEE, Woo-Young	F	0										
YOON, Jong-Hwan	M	78	1/1		0/1	0/1	1/3	3				
CHUNG, Sang-Nam	F	13			0/1		0/1					
CHOI, Yong-Su	F	12										
LEE, Won-Shik	F	0										
LEE, Dae-Hee	G	0										
KIM, Hyun-Su	D	90									1	
KIM, Sang-Hoon	D	90										
LEE, Lim-Saeng	D	90										
CHOI, Yoon-Yeol	M	90										
HA, Seok-Ju	F	90				0/1	0/1					
HWANG, Sun-Hong	F	79	0/1		0/1		0/2	1				
Own goals by opponent												
Totals			1/1		0/1	0/4	0/2	1/8	5	1	1	

Linesmen: ARANGO CARDONA, Jorge Luis COL   DUPANOV, Yuri BLR

Men / *Messieurs*

PRELIMINARIES - GROUP C   **FINAL SCORE:**   KOR 0   MEX 0   **HALFTIME SCORE:**   KOR 0   MEX 0

Team: KOR Korea
Coach: BYCHOVETS, Anatoli   Assistant Coach: CHO, Byung-Deuk

Name	Pos	Min	FK	PK	Hdr	IA	OA	G/A	CK	Off	YC	RC
SEO, Dong-Myung	G	90										
PARK, Choong-Kyoon	D	0										
CHOI, Sung-Yong	D	90										
LEE, Sang-Hun	D	90										
LEE, Kyung-Soo	M	74									1	
LEE, Ki-Hyung	M	90	0/1					0/1				
LEE, Woo-Young	F	0										
YOON, Jong-Hwan	M	90					0/1	0/1	1		1	
CHUNG, Sang-Nam	F	1										
CHOI, Yong-Su	F	90			0/1	0/1		0/2		1		
LEE, Won-Shik	F	55				0/1		0/1		1		
LEE, Dae-Hee	G	0										
KIM, Hyun-Su	D	90										
KIM, Sang-Hoon	D	0										
LEE, Lim-Saeng	D	16										
CHOI, Yoon-Yeol	M	90										
HA, Seok-Ju	F	90	0/1		0/1	0/1		0/3				
HWANG, Sun-Hong	F	35				0/1		0/1				
Own goals by opponent												
Totals			0/2		0/2	0/4	0/1	0/9	1	2	2	

Referee: BOUCHARDEAU, Lucian NIG

Team: MEX Mexico
Coach: de los COBOS, Carlos   Assistant Coach: MILUTINOVIC, Velibor

Name	Pos	Min	FK	PK	Hdr	IA	OA	G/A	CK	Off	YC	RC
SANCHEZ, Oswaldo	G	0										
SUAREZ, Claudio	D	90					0/2	0/2				
OTEO, David	D	0										
VILLA, German	M	90					0/4	0/4				
DAVINO, Duilio	D	90									1	
LARA, Rodrigo	M	90										
GARCIA, Jose	M	90					0/3	0/3	2	1		
SOL, Manuel	M	90	0/1				0/1	0/2				
CAMPOS, Jorge	F	90										
GARCIA POSTIGO, Luis	F	90					0/1	0/1	3	2	1	
BLANCO, Cuauhtemoc	M	62										
SANCHEZ, Javier	D	0										
PARDO, Pavel	D	90					0/3	0/3			1	
ALVARADO, Edson	F	0										
ARELLANO, Jesus	M	0										
ALFARO, Enrique	F	29										
PALENCIA, Francisco	F	24			0/1		0/1	0/2				
ABUNDIS, Jose	F	22				0/1	0/2	0/3				
Own goals by opponent												
Totals			0/1		0/1	0/1	0/17	0/20	5	3	3	

Linesmen: NEUENSTEIN, Heiner GER   UGURDUR, Akif TUR

PRELIMINARIES - GROUP C   **FINAL SCORE:**   GHA 3   ITA 2   **HALFTIME SCORE:**   GHA 1   ITA 2

Team: GHA Ghana
Coach: ARDAY, Samuel   Assistant Coach: PAHA, Isaac

Name	Pos	Min	FK	PK	Hdr	IA	OA	G/A	CK	Off	YC	RC
KINGSTON, Richard	G	0										
NETTEY, Jacob	D	0										
WELBECK, Nii Aryee	F	0										
BAIDOO, Stephen	M	0										
ADDO, Joseph	D	90	0/1					0/1			1	
DOUDU, Afo	M	90									1	
KUFFOUR, Osei S.	D	90				0/1		0/1				
YAHAYA, Mallam	M	60	0/1				0/1	0/2			1	
ARHINFUL, Augustine	F	90		1/1	0/1			1/2	1			
AKUNNOR, Charles	F	31										
DUAH, Emmanuel	F	90				0/4	0/2	0/6	7		1	
ABOAGYE, Felix	F	90				0/2		0/2		4		
OHENE, Kennedy	F	0										
HAGAN, Ebenezer	M	90									1	
SABAH, Christian	D	90	0/1			1/1	1/1	2/3			1	
ADDO, Simon	G	90										
KUFFOUR, Osei E.	D	0										
KORANTENG, Prince	F	90					0/1	0/1				
Own goals by opponent												
Totals			0/3	1/1	0/1	1/8	1/5	3/18	8	4	6	

Referees: GARCIA-ARANDA ENCINAR, Jose ESP   al-MUHANNA, Omar Seleh Saad KSA

Team: ITA Italy
Coach: MALDINI, Cesare   Assistant Coach: NICCOLAI, Comunardo

Name	Pos	Min	FK	PK	Hdr	IA	OA	G/A	CK	Off	YC	RC
PAGLIUCA, Gianluca	G	90									1	
NESTA, Alessandro	D	90										
CANNAVARO, Fabio	D	90									1	
GALANTE, Fabio	D	62									1	1
FRESI, Salvatore	D	90									1	
AMETRANO, Raffaele	M	0										
CRIPPA, Massimo	M	90					0/1	0/1	1			
BRANCA, Marco	F	90	0/2	1/1		1/1		2/4			1	
BRAMBILLA, Massimo	M	0										
del VECCHIO, Marco	F	45					0/2	0/2				
BUFFON, Gianluigi	G	0										
PISTONE, Alessandro	D	13										
TOMMASI, Damiano	M	90					0/1	0/1				
PECCHIA, Fabio	M	22										
MORFEO, Domenico	F	0										
LUCARELLI, Cristiano	F	45										
BERNARDINI, Antonino	M	69										
SARTOR, Luigi	D	78					0/1	0/1				
Own goals by opponent												
Totals			0/2	1/1		1/1	0/5	2/9	1		5	1

Linesmen: al MOSSAWI, Mohamed Ahmed OMA   FRED, Lencie VAN

Men / *Messieurs*

PRELIMINARIES - GROUP C **FINAL SCORE:** KOR 1 ITA 2 | **HALFTIME SCORE:** KOR 0 ITA 1

Team: KOR Korea
Coach: BYCHOVETS, Anatoli   Assistant Coach: CHO, Byung-Deuk

Name	Pos	Min	FK	PK	Hdr	IA	OA	G/A	CK	Off	YC	RC
SEO, Dong-Myung	G	90										
PARK, Choong-Kyoon	D	0										
CHOI, Sung-Yong	D	90									1	
LEE, Sang-Hun	D	90				0/1		0/1				
LEE, Kyung-Soo	M	81					0/1	0/1				
LEE, Ki-Hyung	M	90				0/1	1/3	1/4				
LEE, Woo-Young	F	0										
YOON, Jong-Hwan	M	90	0/1			0/2		0/3	6			
CHUNG, Sang-Nam	F	10					0/1	0/1				
CHOI, Yong-Su	F	90				0/1	0/1	0/2				
LEE, Won-Shik	F	0										
LEE, Dae-Hee	G	0										
KIM, Hyun-Su	D	90										
KIM, Sang-Hoon	D	0										
CHOI, Yoon-Yeol	M	90					0/1	0/1				
HA, Seok-Ju	F	90	0/1					0/1				
HWANG, Sun-Hong	F	0										
LEE, Kyung-Chun	D	90										
Own goals by opponent												
Totals			0/1		0/1	0/5	1/7	1/14	6		1	

Referees: RUSCIO, Robert Ruben ARG   UN-PRASERT, Pirom THA

Team: ITA Italy
Coach: MALDINI, Cesare   Assistant Coach: NICCOLAI, Comunardo

Name	Pos	Min	FK	PK	Hdr	IA	OA	G/A	CK	Off	YC	RC
PAGLIUCA, Gianluca	G	90										
NESTA, Alessandro	D	90									1	
CANNAVARO, Fabio	D	90									2	
GALANTE, Fabio	D	0										
FRESI, Salvatore	D	90										
AMETRANO, Raffaele	M	90								2	1	
CRIPPA, Massimo	M	90					0/1	0/1				
BRANCA, Marco	F	90	1/1			0/1	1/1	0/1	2/4		2	
BRAMBILLA, Massimo	M	75								4		
del VECCHIO, Marco	F	52				0/1		0/1				
BUFFON, Gianluigi	G	0										
PISTONE, Alessandro	D	90				0/1		0/1				
TOMMASI, Damiano	M	90					0/3	0/3				
PECCHIA, Fabio	M	16										
MORFEO, Domenico	F	39				0/1		0/1				
LUCARELLI, Cristiano	F	0										
BERNARDINI, Antonino	M	0										
SARTOR, Luigi	D	0										
Own goals by opponent												
Totals			1/1		0/1	1/3	0/6	2/11	6	2	4	

Linesmen: NEUENSTEIN, Heiner GER   UGURDUR, Akif TUR

PRELIMINARIES - GROUP C **FINAL SCORE:** GHA 1 MEX 1 | **HALFTIME SCORE:** GHA 1 MEX 0

Team: GHA
Coach: ARDAY, Samuel   Assistant Coach: PAHA, Isaac

Name	Pos	Min	FK	PK	Hdr	IA	OA	G/A	CK	Off	YC	RC
KINGSTON, Richard	G	0										
NETTEY, Jacob	D	0										
WELBECK, Nii Aryee	F	16										
BAIDOO, Stephen	M	12									1	
ADDO, Joseph	D	90										
DUODU, Afo	M	45										
KUFFOUR, Osei S.	D	90				0/2		0/2				
YAHAYA, Mallam	M	90										
ARHINFUL, Augustine	F	90				0/1		0/1	2			
AKUNNOR, Charles	F	0										
DUAH, Emmanuel	F	90				0/1		0/1	4			
ABOAGYE, Felix	F	90							1			
OHENE, Kennedy	F	0										
HAGAN, Ebenezer	M	75				1/1	0/1	1/2				
SABAH, Christian	D	90				0/2		0/2	1			
ADDO, Simon	G	90										
KUFFOUR, Osei E.	D	0										
KORANTENG, Prince	F	90					0/1	0/1				
Own goals by opponent												
Totals					0/2	1/2	0/5	1/9	4	4	1	

Referees: PEREIRA da SILVA, Antonio BRA   GARCIA-ARANDA ENCINAR, Jose ESP

Team: MEX Mexico
Coach: de los COBOS, Carlos   Assistant Coach: MILUTINOVIC, Velibor

Name	Pos	Min	FK	PK	Hdr	IA	OA	G/A	CK	Off	YC	RC
SANCHEZ, Oswaldo	G	0										
SUAREZ, Claudio	D	90									1	
OTEO, David	D	0										
VILLA, German	M	90								1		
DAVINO, Duilio	D	90										
LARA, Rodrigo	M	90										
GARCIA, Jose	M	62	0/1			0/1	0/2		1			
SOL, Manuel	M	52				0/1	0/1					
CAMPOS, Jorge	G	90										
GARCIA POSTIGO, Luis	F	90				0/2	0/2	1	1			
BLANCO, Cuauhtemoc	M	29										
SANCHEZ, Javier	D	0										
PARDO, Pavel	D	90										
ALVARADO, Edson	F	0										
ARELLANO, Jesus	M	39										
ALFARO, Enrique	F	90				0/1	0/1	0/2	0/4			
PALENCIA, Francisco	F	23				0/1		0/1		2	1	
ABUNDIS, Jose	F	68				1/1	0/1	1/2				
Own goals by opponent												
Totals			0/1		1/2	0/3	0/6	1/12	1	5	2	

Linesmen: ARANGO CARDONA, Jorge Luis COL   DUPANOV, Yuri BLR

Football / *Football*

SHARIQ SAYEED • JENNIFER SAYLER • ANNE L SAYLES • WILLIAM A SAYLES • WILLIAM J SAYLES • DAVID N SAYLOR • RICHARD A SAYLOR • JANICE D SAYLORS • KEVIN K SAYLORS • STEPHANIE R SAYRES • JACKIE SAYRING • TERRY E SAYRING • MICHAEL P SBROCCHI • JAMES M SCAGGS • VIRGINIA M SCAHILL • MATTHEW P SCALABRINO • ROBERT B SCALDINO • GLORIA A SCALES • JOYCE A SCALES • LINDA D SCALES • TANICA SCALES • YVONNE SCALES • ALAN T SCALLY • JACQUELINE E SCALLY • SUSAN A SCALLY • BILL SCANDRETT EMT •

Men / Messieurs

PRELIMINARIES - GROUP D — FINAL SCORE: HUN 0 NGR 1 — HALFTIME SCORE: HUN 0 NGR 0

Team: HUN Hungary
Coach: DUNAI, Antal Assistant Coach: BENE, Ferenc

Name	Pos	Min	FK	PK	Hdr	IA	OA	G/A	CK	Off	YC	RC
SZUCS, Lajos	G	0										
SEBOK, Vilmos	D	90										
PETO, Zoltan	D	90										
LENDVAI, Miklos	D	90							1			
DOMBI, Tibor	F	90										
SANDOR, Tamas	F	83					0/1	0/1				
SZANYO, Karoly	M	0										
LISZTES, Krisztian	M	90					0/1	0/1	1			
EGRESSY, Gabor	F	75					0/2	0/2	5			
MOLNAR, Zoltan	D	90										
MADAR, Csaba	M	0										
ZAVADSZKY, Gabor	F	0										
PREISINGER, Sandor	F	8										
SZATMARI, Csaba	M	90									1	
DRAGONER, Attila	D	90									1	
SAFAR, Szabolcs	G	90										
HERCZEG, Miklos	D	15					0/1	0/1				
BUKSZEGI, Zoltan	D	0										
Own goals by opponent												
Totals							0/5	0/5	7		2	

Referees: COLLINA, Pierluigi ITA — UN-PRASERT, Pirom THA

Team: NGR
Coach: BAZUAYE, Willy Assistant Coach: ABDULLAHI, Musa

Name	Pos	Min	FK	PK	Hdr	IA	OA	G/A	CK	Off	YC	RC
BABAYARO, Emmanuel	F	0										
BABAYARO, Celestine	F	90									1	
WEST, Taribo	F	90									1	
KANU, Nwankwo	F	81				1/2		1/2		2		
UCHE, Okechukwu	F	90			0/1			0/1				
AMUNIKE, Emmanuel	F	76					0/2	0/2	4			
BABANGIDA, Tijani	F	90				0/1		0/1	4	1		
ORUMA, Wilson	F	0										
FATUSI, Teslim	F	0										
OKOCHA, Augustine	F	90					0/6	0/6	1			
IKPEBA, Victor	F	10				0/1		0/1				
OBAFEMI, Abiodon	F	0										
LAWAL, Garba	F	15										
AMOKACHI, Daniel	F	90									1	
OLISEH, Sunday	F	90							1			
OBIEKWU, Kingsley	F	0										
OBARAKU, Mobi	F	90										
DOSU, Joseph	F	90										
Own goals by opponent												
Totals					0/1	1/4	0/8	1/13	8	5	3	

Linesmen: DANTE, Dramane MLI — TORRES ZUNIGA, Luis Fernando CRC

PRELIMINARIES - GROUP D — FINAL SCORE: BRA 0 JPN 1 — HALFTIME SCORE: BRA 0 JPN 1

Team: BRA Brazil
Coach: ZAGALLO, Mario Assistant Coach: da COSTA, Americo

Name	Pos	Min	FK	PK	Hdr	IA	OA	G/A	CK	Off	YC	RC
SILVA, Nelson de Jesus	G	90										
FERREIRA, Jose Marcelo	D	47									1	1
SANTOS, Aldair Nascimento	D	47			0/2		0/1	0/3				
GUIARO, Ronaldo	D	47										
CONCEICAO, Flavio da	M	47					0/3	0/3	4			
SILVA, Roberto Carlos	D	47	0/2		0/1		0/2	0/5	1	2		
OLIVEIRA, Jose Roberto Gama	F	47	0/1		0/1	0/2	0/1	0/5	1			
MARIANO, Alexandre da Silva	M	47										
GIROLDO JUNIOR, Oswaldo	M	47	0/1			0/3	0/3	0/7	3	1		
FERREIRA, Rivaldo Victor Borba	F	47	0/1		0/2			0/3	2			
PIMENTEL, Savio Bortolini	F	65			0/1			0/1	3	2		
HINTERHLOZ, Danrlei de Deus	G	0										
SANTOS, Narciso dos	D	0										
MOREIRA, Andre Luiz	D	0										
MOEDIM JUNIOR, Jose Elias	M	0										
SOUZA, Marcelo Jose de	M	0										
GOULART, Luiz Carlos	F	0										
LIMA, Ronaldo Luis Nazario	F	25				0/1		0/1				
Own goals by opponent												
Totals			0/5		0/7	0/6	0/10	0/28	13	8		

Referees: ARCHUNDIA TELLEZ, Benito MEX — BAHARMAST, Esfandiar USA

Team: JPN Japan
Coach: NISHINO, Akira Assistant Coach: YAMAMOTO, Masakuni

Name	Pos	Min	FK	PK	Hdr	IA	OA	G/A	CK	Off	YC	RC
KAWAGUCHI, Yoshikatsu	G	90										
SHIRAI, Hiroyuki	D	0										
SUZUKI, Hideto	D	47									1	
HIRONAGA, Yuji	M	0										
TANAKA, Makoto	D	47										
HATTORI, Toshihiro	M	47									1	
MAEZONO, Masakiyo	M	47					0/1		4			
ITO, Teruyoshi	M	47				1/1		1/1				
JO, Shoji	F	88								2		
ENDO, Akihiro	M	76										
MORIOKA, Shigeru	F	0										
UEMURA, Kenichi	D	0									1	
MATSUDA, Naoki	D	47										
NAKATA, Hidetoshi	M	83			0/1		0/1	0/2	1			
AKIBA, Tadahiro	M	0										
MATSUBARA, Yoshika	F	0									1	
MICHIKI, Ryuji	M	47										
SHIMODA, Takashi	G	0										
Own goals by opponent												
Totals					0/1	1/1	0/2	1/4	4	5	2	

Linesmen: KELLY, Peter TRI — OSMAN MOHAMED, Amir SUD

Men / *Messieurs*

Team: JPN Japan

Coach: NISHINO, Akira   Assistant Coach: YAMAMOTO, Masakuni

Name	Pos	Min	FK	PK	Hdr	IA	OA	G/A	CK	Off	YC	RC
KAWAGUCHI, Yoshikatsu	G	90										
SHIRAI, Hiroyuki	D	90								1		
SUZUKI, Hideto	D	90										
HIRONAGA, Yuji	M	4										
TANAKA, Makoto	D	72										
HATTORI, Toshihiro	M	87										
MAEZONO, Masakiyo	M	90							3		1	
ITO, Teruyoshi	M	90										
JO, Shoji	F	90				0/1	0/1	0/2			1	
ENDO, Akihiro	M	0										
MORIOKA, Shigeru	F	0										
UEMURA, Kenichi	D	0										
MATSUDA, Naoki	D	90										
NAKATA, Hidetoshi	M	90				0/1	0/1		1			
AKIBA, Tadahiro	M	19										
MATSUBARA, Yoshika	F	0										
MICHIKI, Ryuji	M	90									1	
SHIMODA, Takashi	G	0										
Own goals by opponent												
Totals						0/1	0/2	0/3	3	2	3	

Referee: COLLINA, Pierluigi ITA

Team: NGR Nigeria

Coach: BAZUAYE, Willy   Assistant Coach: ABDULLAHI, Musa

Name	Pos	Min	FK	PK	Hdr	IA	OA	G/A	CK	Off	YC	RC
BABAYARO, Emmanuel	F	0										
BABAYARO, Celestine	F	90									1	
WEST, Taribo	F	90										
KANU, Nwankwo	F	87					0/1	0/1				
UCHE, Okechukwu	F	90			0/1			0/1				
AMUNIKE, Emmanuel	F	73				0/2		0/2	4			
BABANGIDA, Tijani	F	90			0/1	0/1		0/2	1			
ORUMA, Wilson	F	0										
FATUSI, Teslim	F	0										
OKOCHA, Augustine	F	90	1/1				0/1	1/2		1		
IKPEBA, Victor	F	3										
OBAFEMI, Abiodon	F	0										
LAWAL, Garba	F	18							1	2		
AMOKACHI, Daniel	F	90				0/1		0/1	3			
OLISEH, Sunday	F	90										
OBIEKWU, Kingsley	F	0										
OBARAKU, Mobi	F	90									1	
DOSU, Joseph	F	90										
Own goals by opponent								1				
Totals				1/1	0/2	0/4	0/2	2/9	6	6	2	

Linesmen: VIENNOT, Nelly FRA   TORRES ZUNIGA, Luis Fernando CRC

Team: BRA Brazil

Coach: ZAGALLO, Mario   Assistant Coach: da COSTA, Americo

Name	Pos	Min	FK	PK	Hdr	IA	OA	G/A	CK	Off	YC	RC
SILVA, Nelson de Jesus	G	90										
FERREIRA, Jose Marcelo	D	90								2		
SANTOS, Aldair Nascimento	D	90										
GUIARO, Ronaldo	D	90										
CONCEICAO, Flavio da	M	90				0/3	0/3					
SILVA, Roberto Carlos	D	90				0/2	0/2		5		1	
OLIVEIRA, Jose Roberto Gama	F	90	0/3			0/2	1/2	1/7		2		
MARIANO, Alexandre da Silva	M	16										
GIROLDO JUNIOR, Oswaldo	M	90	0/1			1/1		1/4	6			
FERREIRA, Rivaldo Victor Borba	F	75	0/1			0/1		0/2				
PIMENTEL, Savio Bortolini	F	16				0/1		0/1	2			
HINTERHLOZ, Danrlei de Deus	G	0										
SANTOS, Narciso dos	D	0										
MOREIRA, Andre Luiz	D	0										
MOEDIM JUNIOR, Jose Elias	M	90				0/1	0/1				1	
SOUZA, Marcelo Jose de	M	0										
GOULART, Luiz Carlos	F	0										
LIMA, Ronaldo Luiz Nazario	F	74			0/1	1/3		1/4	1	2		
Own goals by opponent												
Totals			0/5		0/1	2/8	1/8	3/24	14	6	2	

Referees: BAHARMAST, Esfandiar USA   el-GHANDOUR, Gamal Mahmoud EGY

Team: HUN Hungary

Coach: DUNAI, Antal   Assistant Coach: BENE, Ferenc

Name	Pos	Min	FK	PK	Hdr	IA	OA	G/A	CK	Off	YC	RC
SZUCS, Lajos	G	0										
SEBOK, Vilmos	D	90								2		
PETO, Zoltan	D	90	0/1					0/1				
LENDVAI, Miklos	D	90				0/1		0/1		1		
DOMBI, Tibor	F	90				0/1		0/1	3			
SANDOR, Tamas	F	0										
SZANYO, Karoly	M	25							1			
LISZTES, Krisztian	M	65	0/1					0/1	4			
EGRESSY, Gabor	F	0										
MOLNAR, Zoltan	D	90										
MADAR, Csaba	M	45			1/1			1/1	1			
ZAVADSZKY, Gabor	F	0										
PREISINGER, Sandor	F	0										
SZATMARI, Csaba	M	90									1	
DRAGONER, Attila	D	45										
SAFAR, Szabolcs	G	90										
HERCZEG, Miklos	D	90									1	
BUKSZEGI, Zoltan	D	90				0/1		0/1	1			
Own goals by opponent												
Totals			0/2		1/1	0/2	0/1	1/6	7	4	4	

Linesmen: JEON, Young Hyun KOR   VELAZQUEZ PINTOS, Carlos Adan URU

Men / Messieurs

PRELIMINARIES - GROUP D FINAL SCORE: JPN 3 HUN 2 HALFTIME SCORE: JPN 1 HUN 1

Team: JPN Japan
Coach: NISHINO, Akria Assistant Coach: YAMAMOTO, Masakuni

Name	Pos	Min	FK	PK	Hdr	IA	OA	G/A	CK	Off	YC	RC
KAWAGUCHI, Yoshikatsu	G	90										
SHIRAI, Hiroyuki	D	0										
SUZUKI, Hideto	D	90									1	
HIRONAGA, Yuji	M	55	0/1					0/1				
TANAKA, Makoto	D	90				0/1		0/1				
HATTORI, Toshihiro	M	90	0/2				0/1	0/3			1	
MAEZONO, Masakiyo	M	90	0/2	1/1		1/1	0/1	2/5	5			
ITO, Teruyoshi	M	90										
JO, Shoji	F	90			0/3		0/2	0/1	0/6			
ENDO, Akihiro	M	0										
MORIOKA, Shigeru	F	36										
UEMURA, Kenichi	D	1				1/1		1/1				
MATSUDA, Naoki	D	90										
NAKATA, Hidetoshi	M	0										
AKIBA, Tadahiro	M	0										
MATSUBARA, Yoshika	F	90			0/1	0/1	0/1	0/3		1		
MICHIKI, Ryuji	M	90										
SHIMODA, Takashi	G	0										
Own goals by opponent												
Totals			0/5	1/1	1/5	1/5	0/4	3/20	5	1	2	

Referees: BOUCHARDEAU, Lucian NIG   DALLAS, Hugh GBR

Team: HUN Hungary
Coach: DUNAI, Antal Assistant Coach: BENE, Ferenc

Name	Pos	Min	FK	PK	Hdr	IA	OA	G/A	CK	Off	YC	RC
SZUCS, Lajos	G	0										
SEBOK, Vilmos	D	0										
PETO, Zoltan	D	90										
LENDVAI, Miklos	D	90										
DOMBI, Tibor	F	90					0/1	0/1			2	
SANDOR, Tamas	F	90				1/1		1/1				1
SZANYO, Karoly	M	14	0/1					0/1		1		
LISZTES, Krisztian	M	77										
EGRESSY, Gabor	F	90					0/1	0/1				
MOLNAR, Zoltan	D	90										1
MADAR, Csaba	M	90					1/1	1/1			1	1
ZAVADSZKY, Gabor	F	17										
PREISINGER, Sandor	F	74			0/1	0/1		0/2			1	
SZATMARI, Csaba	M	0										
DRAGONER, Attila	D	0										
SAFAR, Szabolcs	G	90										
HERCZEG, Miklos	D	0										
BUKSZEGI, Zoltan	D	90										
Own goals by opponent												
Totals			0/1		0/1	1/2	1/3	2/7		1	4	3

Linesmen: TORRES ZUNIGA, Luis Fernando CRC   DANTE, Dramane MLI

PRELIMINARIES - GROUP D FINAL SCORE: BRA 1 NGR 0 HALFTIME SCORE: BRA 1 NGR 0

Team: BRA Brazil
Coach: ZAGALLO, Mario Assistant Coach: da COSTA, Americo

Name	Pos	Min	FK	PK	Hdr	IA	OA	G/A	CK	Off	YC	RC
SILVA, Nelson de Jesus	G	90										
FERREIRA, Jose Marcelo	D	90								1		
SANTOS, Aldair Nascimento	D	90										
GUIARO, Ronaldo	D	90										
CONCEICAO, Flavio da	M	90					0/4	0/4				
SILVA, Roberto Carlos	D	90							3			
OLIVEIRA, Jose Roberto Gama	F	90				0/1	0/1	0/2				
MARIANO, Alexandre da Silva	M	19										
GIROLDO JUNIOR, Oswaldo	M	90							2			.
FERREIRA, Rivaldo Victor Borba	F	71				0/1	0/2	0/3				
PIMENTEL, Savio Bortolini	F	8								1		
HINTERHLOZ, Danrlei de Deus	G	0										
SANTOS, Narciso dos	D	0										
MOREIRA, Andre Luiz	D	0										
MOEDIM JUNIOR, Jose Elias	M	90										
SOUZA, Marcelo Jose de	M	0										
GOULART, Luiz Carlos	F	0										
LIMA, Ronaldo Luiz Nazario	F	83				0/1	1/2	1/3		3		
Own goals by opponent												
Totals						0/3	1/9	1/12	5	5		

Referees: BAHARMAST, Esfandiar USA   ARCHUNDIA TELLEZ, Benito MEX

Team: NGR Nigeria
Coach: BONFRERE, Johannes Assistant Coach: ABDULLAHI, Musa

Name	Pos	Min	FK	PK	Hdr	IA	OA	G/A	CK	Off	YC	RC
BABAYARO, Emmanuel	G	0										
BABAYARO, Celestine	D	0										
WEST, Taribo	D	90					0/1	0/1				
KANU, Nwankwo	F	90			0/1		0/1	0/2		1		
UCHE, Okechukwu	D	90										
AMUNIKE, Emmanuel	M	63				0/2	0/1	0/3	1	2		
BABANGDIA, Tijani	F	81							1	3		
ORUMA, Wilson	M	0										
FATUSI, Teslim	M	10								1		
OKOCHA, Augustine	M	90				0/1	0/4	0/5	1			
IKPEBA, Victor	F	28					0/1	0/1	1			
OBAFEMI, Abiodon	D	47										
LAWAL, Garba	M	44					0/1	0/1		1		
AMOKACHI, Daniel	M	90			0/1		0/2	0/3				
OLISEH, Sunday	M	90										
OBIEKWU, Kingsley	D	0										
OBARAKU, Mobi	D	90					0/1	0/1				
DOSU, Joseph	G	90										
Own goals by opponent												
Totals					0/2	0/6	0/9	0/17	4	8		

Linesmen: KELLY, Peter TRI   JEON, Young Hyun KOR

SUMMARY: PRELIMINARIES - GROUP A

Rnk	Team	ARG	POR	USA	TUN	Games	Wins	Losses	Ties	Goals For	Goals Against	Diff
1	ARG		1-1	3-1	1-1	3	1	0	2	5	3	2
2	POR	1-1		1-1	2-0	3	1	0	2	4	2	2
3	USA	1-3	1-1		2-0	3	1	1	1	4	4	0
4	TUN	1-1	0-2	0-2		3	0	2	1	1	5	-4

SUMMARY: PRELIMINARIES - GROUP B

Rnk	Team	FRA	ESP	AUS	KSA	Games	Wins	Losses	Ties	Goals For	Goals Against	Diff
1	FRA		1-1	2-0	2-1	3	2	0	1	5	2	3
2	ESP	1-1		3-2	1-0	3	2	0	1	5	3	2
3	AUS	0-2	2-3		2-1	3	1	2	0	4	6	-2
4	KSA	1-2	0-1	1-2		3	0	3	0	2	5	-3

SUMMARY: PRELIMINARIES - GROUP C

Rnk	Team	MEX	GHA	KOR	ITA	Games	Wins	Losses	Ties	Goals For	Goals Against	Diff
1	MEX		1-1	0-0	1-0	3	1	0	2	2	1	1
2	GHA	1-1		0-1	3-2	3	1	1	1	4	4	0
3	KOR	0-0	1-0		1-2	3	1	1	1	2	2	0
4	ITA	0-1	2-3	2-1		3	1	2	0	4	5	-1

SUMMARY: PRELIMINARIES - GROUP D

Rnk	Team	BRA	NGR	JPN	HUN	Games	Wins	Losses	Ties	Goals For	Goals Against	Diff
1	BRA		1-0	0-1	3-1	3	2	1	0	4	2	2
2	NGR	0-1		2-0	1-0	3	2	1	0	3	1	2
3	JPN	1-0	0-2		3-2	3	2	1	0	4	4	0
4	HUN	1-3	0-1	2-3		3	0	3	0	3	7	-4

Men / Messieurs

QUARTERFINALS	FINAL SCORE:	ARG 4 ESP 0	HALFTIME SCORE:	ARG 0 ESP 0

Team: ARG Argentina

Coach: PASSARELLA, Daniel   Assistant Coach: GALLEGO, Americo

Name	Pos	Min	FK	PK	Hdr	IA	OA	G/A	CK	Off	YC	RC
BOSSIO, Carlos Gustavo	G	0										
AYALA, Roberto Fabian	D	90										
CHAMOT, Jose Antonio	D	0										
ZANETTI, Javier Adelmar	D	90										
ALMEYDA, Matias Jesus	M	90				0/1		0/1				
SENSINI, Roberto Nestor	D	90										
LOPEZ, Claudio Javier	F	90	0/1		0/1	1/4		1/6			3	
SIMEONE, Diego Pablo	M	13		0/1				0/1			1	
CRESPO, Hernan Jorge	F	90		1/1	1/1	0/1	0/2	2/5			1	
ORTEGA, Arnaldo Ariel	F	75							3			1
MORALES, Hugo Alberto	M	80				0/1		0/1				
CAVALLERO, Pablo Oscar	G	90										
PINEDA, Hector Mauricio	D	90										
PAZ, Pablo Ariel	D	0										
BASSEDAS, Christian Gustavo	M	78				0/1		0/1				
LOPEZ, Gustavo Adrian	M	11				0/1		0/1				
DELGADO, Marcelo Alejandro	F	0										
GALLARDO, Marcelo Daniel	M	16							2			
Own goals by opponent								1				
Totals			0/1	1/1	1/3	1/9	0/2	4/16	5		5	1

Referees: el-GHANDOUR, Gamal Mahmoud EGY   LENNIE, Edward AUS

Team: ESP Spain

Coach: CLEMENTE, Javier   Assistant Coach: SAEZ, Ignacio

Name	Pos	Min	FK	PK	Hdr	IA	OA	G/A	CK	Off	YC	RC
MORA, Juan L.	G	90										
MENDIETA, Gaizka	D	0										
ARANZABAL, Augustine	D	90										
NAVARRO, Javier	D	90			0/1		0/1	0/2				
DENIA, Santiago	D	0										
GARCIA, Oscar	M	90				0/1		0/1				
GONZALEZ, Raul	F	90				0/1	0/3	0/4	1		1	
FRESNEDOSO, Roberto	M	56										
CORINO, Sergio	D	90			0/1		0/1	0/2				
SAENZ, Jose	M	90					0/2	0/2			1	
INDIAKEZ, Inigo	M	56				0/1	0/1	0/1	1		1	
KARANKA, Aitor	D	90										
AIZKORRETA, Jorge	G	0										
MORIENTES, Fernando	F	0										
de la PENA, Ivan	M	35						1				
LARDIN, Jordi	F	35									1	
SUAREZ, Jose	D	0										
GARCIA, Daniel	F	90							6			
Own goals by opponent												
Totals					0/2	0/2	0/8	0/12	9		4	

Linesmen: FRED, Lencie VAN   KELLY, Peter TRI

QUARTERFINALS	FINAL SCORE:	FRA 1 POR 2	HALFTIME SCORE:	FRA 0 POR 1

Team: FRA France

Coach: DOMENECH, Raymond   Assistant Coach: THIEBAUT, Jacky

Name	Pos	Min	FK	PK	Hdr	IA	OA	G/A	CK	Off	YC	RC
LETIZI, Lionel	G	105										
DJETTOU, Martin	D	105	0/3					0/3				
BONNISSEL, Jerome	D	105									1	1
LAVILLE, Florent	D	0										
MOREAU, Patrick	D	105										
MAKELELE, Claude	M	105				0/2		0/2	4	2		
DHORASOO, Vikash	M	105					0/2	0/2				
MAURICE, Florian	F	90	0/1	1/1	0/1	0/2	0/1	1/6		1	1	
SIBIERSKI, Antoine	F	0										
PIRES, Robert	F	105				0/4	0/2	0/6	4	1		
TOYES, Geoffray	D	0										
CANDELA, Vincent	D	0										
DACOURT, Olivier	M	60					0/2	0/2				
VAIRELLES, Tony	F	45					0/1	0/1			1	
FERNANDEZ, Vincent	G	0										
WILTORD, Sylvain	F	15										
LEGWINSKY, Sylvain	F	105									1	1
DIENG, Oumar	D	105									1	
Own goals by opponent												
Totals			0/4	1/1	0/1	0/8	0/8	1/22	8	5	5	1

Referees: COLLINA, Pierluigi ITA   BOUCHARDEAU, Lucian NIG

Team: POR Portugal

Coach: VINGADA, Eduardo   Assistant Coach: OLIVEIRA, Agostinho

Name	Pos	Min	FK	PK	Hdr	IA	OA	G/A	CK	Off	YC	RC
COSTINHA, Paulo	G	0										
SANTOS, Daniel	F	105									1	
BENTO, Rui	D	105										
PEIXE, Emilio	D	105				0/1	0/1	0/2			1	
SEVERO, Roberto	F	92										
OLIVEIRA, Luis	D	105									1	
DOMINGUEZ, Jose	F	0										
ROCHA, Nuno	D	51				1/1		1/1		6	1	
ALVES, Paulo	F	105				0/2	0/1	0/3				
AGRA, Afonso	M	44							1		1	
OLIVEIRA, Rui	D	62										
SANTO, Nuno	G	105										
VIDIGAL, Jose	M	105			0/1			0/1			1	
SILVA, Jose	M	105	1/1					1/1	2			
RIBEIRO, Nuno	F	0										
PORFIRIO, Hugo	F	0										
MAGALHAES, Carlos	D	13										
CARVALHO, Daniel	F	55				0/2		0/2				
Own goals by opponent												
Totals			1/1		0/1	1/4	0/4	2/10	3	6	6	

Linesmen: URURDUR, Akif TUR   NEUENSTEIN, Heiner GER

Men / *Messieurs*

QUARTERFINALS   FINAL SCORE: MEX 0   NGR 2   HALFTIME SCORE: MEX 0   NGR 1

Team: MEX Mexico
Coach: de los COBOS, Carlos   Assistant Coach: MILUTINOVIC, Velibor

Name	Pos	Min	FK	PK	Hdr	IA	OA	G/A	CK	Off	YC	RC
SANCHEZ, Oswaldo	G	0										
SUAREZ, Claudio	D	90				0/1		0/1			1	
OTEO, David	D	0										
VILLA, German	M	90					0/1	0/1				
DAVINO, Duilio	D	45										1
LARA, Rodrigo	M	90										
GARCIA, Jose	M	45				0/2		0/2	2			
SOL, Manuel	M	24				0/1		0/1				
CAMPOS, Jorge	G	90										
GARCIA POSTIGO, Luis	F	90			0/1	0/2	0/2	0/5				
BLANCO, Cuauhtemoc	M	45			0/1			0/1				
SANCHEZ, Francisco	D	0										
PARDO, Pavel	D	90			0/1		0/2	0/3	3			
ALVARADO, Edson	F	0										
ARELLANO, Jesus	M	67					0/2	0/2	3		1	
ALFARO, Enrique	F	66				0/1		0/1				
PALENCIA, Francisco	F	25			0/1		0/1	0/2				
ABUNDIS, Jose	F	90			0/1		0/2	0/3		2		
Own goals by opponent												
Totals			0/4		0/8	0/10	0/22	8		3	1	1

Referees: al-MUHANNA, Omar Seleh Saad   KSA   LENNIE, Edward   AUS

Team: NGR Nigeria
Coach: BONFRERE, Johannes   Assistant Coach: ABDULLAHI, Musa

Name	Pos	Min	FK	PK	Hdr	IA	OA	G/A	CK	Off	YC	RC
BABAYARO, Emmanuel	G	0										
BABAYARO, Celestine	D	90					1/1	1/1				
WEST, Taribo	D	90										
KANU, Nwankwo	F	67				0/1		0/1		1		
UCHE, Okechukwu	D	90							1		1	
AMUNIKE, Emmanuel	M	86					0/2	0/2	2	3		
BABANGIDA, Tijani	F	56				0/1		0/1	2			
ORUMA, Wilson	M	0										
FATUSI, Teslim	M	24									1	
OKOCHA, Augustine	M	90					1/6	1/6				
IKPEBA, Victor	F	35			0/1	0/1		0/2		1		
OBAFEMI, Abiodon	D	0										
LAWAL, Garba	M	4							1			
AMOKACHI, Daniel	M	90					0/3	0/3	2	1		
OLISEH, Sunday	M	90										2
OBIEKWU, Kingsley	D	0										
OBARAKU, Mobi	D	90					0/1	0/1				
DOSU, Joseph	G	90										
Own goals by opponent												
Totals			0/1		1/7	1/9	2/17	8		6	4	

Linesmen: al MOSSAWI, Mohamed Ahmed   OMA   VELAZQUEZ PINTOS, Carlos Adan   URU

QUARTERFINALS   FINAL SCORE: BRA 4   GHA 2   HALFTIME SCORE: BRA 1   GHA 1

Team: BRA Brazil
Coach: ZAGALLO, Mario   Assistant Coach: da COSTA, Americo

Name	Pos	Min	FK	PK	Hdr	IA	OA	G/A	CK	Off	YC	RC
SILVA, Nelson de Jesus	G	90										
FERREIRA, Jose Marcelo	D	90									1	
SANTOS, Aldair Nascimento	D	90										
GUIARO, Ronaldo	D	90										
CONCEICAO, Flavio da	M	90					0/1	0/1				
SILVA, Roberto Carlos	D	86	0/1				0/1	0/1	1			
OLIVEIRA, Jose Roberto Gama	F	90	0/1			1/3		1/4	1	1		
MARIANO, Alexandre da Silva	M	26										
GIROLDO JUNIOR, Oswaldo	M	90				0/3		0/3	7		1	
FERREIRA, Rivaldo Victor Borba	F	65										
PIMENTEL, Savio Bortolini	F	0										
HINTERHLOZ, Danrlei de Deus	G	0										
SANTOS, Narciso dos	D	0										
MOREIRA, Andre Luiz	D	5										
MOEDIM JUNIOR, Jose Elias	M	90					0/1	0/1				
SOUZA, Marcelo Jose de	M	0										
GOULART, Luiz Carlos	F	0										
LIMA, Ronaldo Luiz Nazario	F	90			0/1	2/7	0/2	2/10		1		
Own goals by opponent							1					
Totals			0/2		0/1	3/13	0/4	4/20	9	3	1	

Referees: UN-PRASERT, Pirom   THA   BAHARMAST, Esfandiar   USA

Team: GHA Ghana
Coach: ARDAY, Samuel   Assistant Coach: PAHA, Isaac

Name	Pos	Min	FK	PK	Hdr	IA	OA	G/A	CK	Off	YC	RC
KINGSTON, Richard	G	0										
NETTEY, Jacob	D	0										
WELBECK, Nii Aryee	F	0										
BAIDOO, Stephen	M	0										
ADDO, Jospeh	D	90										
DUODO, Afo	M	90										
KUFFOUR, Osei S.	D	90										
YAHAYA, Mallam	M	90					0/3	0/3			1	
ARHINFUL, Augustine	F	90				0/1		0/1		2		
AKUNNOR, Charles	F	90				1/2		1/2	1	2		
DUAH, Emmanuel	F	88							3	2	1	
ABOAGYE, Felix	F	90	1/2			0/1		1/3	8	1		
OHENE, Kennedy	F	0										
HAGAN, Ebenezer	M	56										
SABAH, Christian	D	90				0/1	0/1	0/2			2	
ADDO, Simon	G	90										
KUFFOUR, Osei E.	D	3										
AMOAKO, Prince	F	35					0/1	0/1				
Own goals by opponent												
Totals			1/2		0/2	1/8	2/12	4		14	5	

Linesmen: DUPANOV, Yuri   BLR   TORRES ZUNIGA, Luis Fernando   CRC

Men / *Messieurs*

SEMIFINALS — FINAL SCORE: ARG 2 POR 0 — HALFTIME SCORE: ARG 0 POR 0

Team: ARG Argentina
Coach: PASSARELLA, Daniel — Assistant Coach: GALLEGO, Americo

Name	Pos	Min	FK	PK	Hdr	IA	OA	G/A	CK	Off	YC	RC
BOSSIO, Carlos Gustavo	G	0										
AYALA, Roberto Fabian	D	90			0/2			0/2				
CHAMOT, Jose Antonio	D	90			0/1			0/1				
ZANETTI, Javier Adelmar	D	90										
ALMEYDA, Matias Jesus	M	90				0/2	0/1	0/3				
SENSINI, Roberto Nestor	D	90										
LOPEZ, Claudio Javier	F	90				0/4	0/2	0/6				
SIMEONE, Diego Pablo	M	16				0/1		0/1				
CRESPO, Hernan Jorge	F	79			1/3	0/1	1/2	2/6	2			
ORTEGA, Arnaldo Ariel	F	90				0/2	0/1	0/3	11			
MORALLES, Hugo Alberto	M	67				0/1	0/2	0/3			1	
CAVALLERO, Pablo Oscar	G	90										
PINEDA, Hector Mauricio	D	0										
PAZ, Pablo Ariel	D	0										
BASSEDAS, Christian Gustavo	M	75									1	
LOPEZ, Gustavo Adrian	M	24										
DELGADO, Marcelo Alejandro	F	0										
GALLARDO, Marcelo Daniel	M	12				0/1	0/1					
Own goals by opponent												
Totals					1/6	0/11	1/9	2/26	13	2	2	

Referees: BAHARMAST, Esfandiar USA — al-MUHANNA, Omar Seleh Saad KSA

Team: POR Portugal
Coach: VINGADA, Eduardo — Assistant Coach: OLIVEIRA, Agostinho

Name	Pos	Min	FK	PK	Hdr	IA	OA	G/A	CK	Off	YC	RC
COSTINHA, Paulo	G	0										
SANTOS, Daniel	F	0										
BENTO, Rui	D	90										
PEIXE, Emilio	D	90										
SEVERO, Roberto	F	8										
OLIVEIRA, Luis	D	65									1	
DOMINGUEZ, Jose	F	90				0/1		0/1				
ROCHA, Nuno	D	0										
ALVES, Paulo	F	26										
AGRA, Afonso	M	58									1	
OLIVEIRA, Rui	D	90					0/2	0/2				
SANTO, Nuno	G	90										
VIDIGAL, Jose	M	90				0/1		0/1				
SILVA, Jose	M	90				0/1	0/3	0/4	1			
RIBEIRO, Nuno	F	90				0/2		0/2				
PORFIRIO, Hugo	F	33				0/1	0/1	0/2	1			
CARVALHO, Daniel	F	0										
AFONSO, Nuno	D	45				0/1		0/1				
Own goals by opponent												
Totals						0/6	0/7	0/13	3		1	

Linesmen: DANTE, Dramane MLI — TORRES ZUNIGA, Luis Fernando CRC

SEMIFINALS — FINAL SCORE: NGR 4 BRA 3 — HALFTIME SCORE: NGR 1 BRA 3

Team: NGR Nigeria
Coach: BONFRERE, Johannes — Assistant Coach: ABDULLAHI, Musa

Name	Pos	Min	FK	PK	Hdr	IA	OA	G/A	CK	Off	YC	RC
BABAYARO, Emmanuel	G	0										
BABAYARO, Celestine	D	105				0/1		0/1			1	
WEST, Taribo	D	105			0/1			0/1				
KANU, Nwankwo	F	105			2/2			2/2			1	
UCHE, Okechukwu	D	105			0/1			0/1				
AMUNIKE, Emmanuel	M	45							4	2		
BABANGIDA, Tijani	F	68					0/2	0/2	3		1	
ORUMA, Wilson	M	23										
FATUSI, Teslim	M	38										
OKOCHA, Augustine	M	105			0/1		0/5	0/6				
IKPEBA, Victor	F	60					1/1	1/1	1		1	
OBAFEMI, Abiodon	D	0										
LAWAL, Garba	M	105					0/3	0/3			1	
AMOKACHI, Daniel	M	105								3	1	
OLISEH, Sunday	M	0										
OBIEKWU, Kingsley	D	0										
OBARAKU, Mobi	D	83				0/1		0/1			1	
DOSU, Joseph	G	105										
Own goals by opponent								1				
Totals			0/1	0/2	2/5	1/10		4/18	8	8	4	

Referees: GARCIA-ARANDA ENCINAR, Jose ESP — COLLINA, Pierluigi ITA

Team: BRA Brazil
Coach: ZAGALLO, Mario — Assistant Coach: da COSTA, Americo

Name	Pos	Min	FK	PK	Hdr	IA	OA	G/A	CK	Off	YC	RC
SILVA, Nelson de Jesus	G	105										
FERREIRA, Jose Marcelo	D	105					0/1	0/1	3	1		
SANTOS, Aldair Nascimento	D	105										
GUIARO, Ronaldo	D	105									1	
CONCEICAO, Flavio da	M	105				1/1	1/3	2/4				
SILVA, Roberto Carlos	D	105									1	
OLIVEIRA, Jose Roberto Gama	F	105				0/1	1/1	1/2	1			
MARIANO, Alexandre da Silva	M	105										
GIROLDO JUNIOR, Oswaldo	M	67							2	1		
FERREIRA, Rivaldo Victor Borba	F	39				0/1		0/1			1	
PIMENTEL, Savio Bortolini	F	21										
HINTERHLOZ, Danrlei de Deus	G	0										
SANTOS, Narciso dos	D	0										
MOREIRA, Andre Luiz	D	0										
MOEDIM JUNIOR, Jose Elias	M	105										
SOUZA, Marcelo Jose de	M	0										
GOULART, Luiz Carlos	F	0										
LIMA, Ronaldo Luiz Nazario	F	85				0/3	0/2	0/5				
Own goals by opponent												
Totals					0/2	2/5	1/6	3/13	5	3	3	

Linesmen: NEUENSTEIN, Heiner GER — UGURDUR, Akif TUR

SUMMARY: INTERMEDIATE ROUNDS

Phase	Teams	Score
Quarterfinal	FRA - POR	1-2
Quarterfinal	ARG - ESP	4-0
Quarterfinal	MEX - NGR	0-2
Quarterfinal	BRA - GHA	4-2
Semifinal	ARG - POR	2-0
Semifinal	NGR - BRA	4-3

Men / Messieurs

FINAL - BRONZE MATCH FINAL SCORE: POR 0 BRA 5 HALFTIME SCORE: POR 0 BRA 2

Team: POR Portugal
Coach: VINGADA, Eduardo   Assistant Coach: OLIVEIRA, Agostinho

Name	Pos	Min	FK	PK	Hdr	IA	OA	G/A	CK	Off	YC	RC
COSTINHA, Paulo	G	90										
SANTOS, Daniel	F	90				0/2	0/2	0/4			1	
BENTO, Rui	D	90										
PEIXE, Emilio	D	57										
SEVERO, Roberto	F	0										
OLIVEIRA, Luis	D	0										
DOMINGUEZ, Jose	F	90										
ROCHA, Nuno	D	45			0/2			0/2				
ALVES, Paulo	F	46										1
AGRA, Afonso	M	45									2	1
OLIVEIRA, Rui	D	34										
SANTO, Nuno	G	0										
VIDIGAL, Jose	M	90					0/1	0/1				
SILVA, Jose	M	90	0/1				0/1	0/2	5			
RIBEIRO, Nuno	F	45			0/1		0/1		5			
PORFIRIO, Hugo	F	0										
CARVALHO, Daniel	F	90							2			
AFONSO, Nuno	D	90					0/1	0/1				
Own goals by opponent												
Totals			0/1		0/3	0/3	0/4	0/11	9	7	1	

Referees: el-GHANDOUR, Gamal Mahmoud EGY   BOUCHARDEAU, Lucian NIG

Team: BRA Brazil
Coach: ZAGALLO, Mario   Assistant Coach: da COSTA, Americo

Name	Pos	Min	FK	PK	Hdr	IA	OA	G/A	CK	Off	YC	RC
SILVA, Nelson de Jesus	G	90										
FERREIRA, Jose Marcelo	D	90					0/2	0/2				
SANTOS, Aldair Nascimento	D	81				0/1		0/1	1			
GUIARO, Ronaldo	D	90				0/1		0/1			1	
CONCEICAO, Flavio da	M	90				1/2		1/2	1			
SILVA, Roberto Carlos	D	90					0/1	0/1	1			
OLIVEIRA, Jose Roberto Gama	F	90		1/1		2/3	0/1	3/5	1			
MARIANO, Alexandre da Silva	M	85										
GIROLDO JUNIOR, Oswaldo	M	90				0/1	0/1	0/2	4	1	1	
FERREIRA, Rivaldo Victor Borba	F	0										
PIMENTEL, Savio Bortolini	F	0										
HINTERHLOZ, Danrlei de Deus	G	0										
SANTOS, Narciso dos	D	10										
MOREIRA, Andre Luiz	D	0										
MOEDIM JUNIOR, Jose Elias	M	90					0/1	0/1			1	
SOUZA, Marcelo Jose de	M	6										
GOULART, Luiz Carlos	F	13				0/2		0/2				
LIMA, Ronaldo Luiz Nazario	F	78				1/3	0/4	1/7	1			
Own goals by opponent												
Totals				1/1		4/13	0/10	5/24	4	6	3	

Linesmen: al MOSSAWI, Mohamed Ahmed OMA   DANTE, Dramane MLI

FINAL - GOLD MATCH FINAL SCORE: ARG 2 NGR 3 HALFTIME SCORE: ARG 1 NGR 1

Team: ARG Argentina
Coach: PASSARELLA, Daniel   Assistant Coach: GALLEGO, Americo

Name	Pos	Min	FK	PK	Hdr	IA	OA	G/A	CK	Off	YC	RC
BOSSIO, Carlos Gustavo	G	0										
AYALA, Roberto Fabian	D	90										
CHAMOT, Jose Antonio	D	90					0/1	0/1				
ZANETTI, Javier Adelmar	D	90										
ALMEYDA, Matias Jesus	M	90										
SENSINI, Roberto Nestor	D	90										1
LOPEZ, Claudio Javier	F	90			1/1	0/2	0/1	1/4			1	
SIMEONE, Diego Pablo	M	33										
CRESPO, Hernan Jorge	F	90		1/1	0/2	0/4	0/2	1/9			1	
ORTEGA, Arnaldo Ariel	F	90				0/2	0/1	0/3	2			
MORALES, Hugo Alberto	M	58										
CAVALLERO, Pablo Oscar	G	90										
PINEDA, Hector Mauricio	D	0										
PAZ, Pablo Ariel	D	0										
BASSEDAS, Christian Gustavo	M	90										
LOPEZ, Gustavo Adrian	M	0										
DELGADO, Marcelo Alejandro	F	0										
GALLARDO, Marcelo Daniel	M	0										
Own goals by opponent												
Totals				1/1	1/3	0/9	0/4	2/17	3		1	1

Referees: COLLINA, Pierluigi ITA   UN-PRASERT, Pirom THA

Team: NGR Nigeria
Coach: BONFRERE, Johannes   Assistant Coach: ABDULLAHI, Musa

Name	Pos	Min	FK	PK	Hdr	IA	OA	G/A	CK	Off	YC	RC
BABAYARO, Emmanuel	G	0										
BABAYARO, Celestine	D	90			1/1			1/1				
WEST, Taribo	D	90										
KANU, Nwankwo	F	90					0/1	0/1	2			
UCHE, Okechukwu	D	90		0/1		0/1		0/2			1	
AMUNIKE, Emmanuel	M	19			1/1	0/1		1/2	1			
BABANGIDA, Tijani	F	90				0/3	0/2	0/5	6			
ORUMA, Wilson	M	30							1			1
FATUSI, Teslim	M	0										
OKOCHA, Augustine	M	59					0/4	0/4				
IKPEBA, Victor	F	72				0/2	0/3	0/5	2			
OBAFEMI, Abiodon	D	0										
LAWAL, Garba	M	32										
AMOKACHI, Daniel	M	90				1/2		1/2	1			
OLISEH, Sunday	M	90					0/5	0/5			1	
OBIEKWU, Kingsley	D	0										
OBARAKU, Mobi	D	61										
DOSU, Joseph	G	90										
Own goals by opponent												
Totals				1/2		2/9	0/16	3/27	11		2	3

Linesmen: FRED, Lencie VAN   KELLY, Peter TRI

FINAL CLASSIFICATION

Rnk	Team	Games	Wins	Losses	Ties	Goals For	Goals Against	Diff	Pts	
1	Nigeria	6	5	1	0	12	6	6	15	Gold
2	Argentina	6	3	1	2	13	6	7	11	Silver
3	Brazil	6	4	2	0	16	8	8	12	Bronze
4	Portugal	6	2	2	2	6	10	-4	8	
5	France	4	2	1	1	6	4	2	7	
6	Spain	4	2	1	1	5	7	-2	7	
7	Mexico	4	1	1	2	2	3	-1	5	
8	Ghana	4	1	2	1	6	8	-2	4	

FINAL CLASSIFICATION - *continued*

Rnk	Team	Games	Wins	Losses	Ties	Goals For	Goals Against	Diff	Pts
9	Japan	3	2	1	0	4	4	0	6
10	United States of America	3	1	1	1	4	4	0	4
11	Korea	3	1	1	1	2	2	0	4
12	Italy	3	1	2	0	4	5	-1	3
13	Australia	3	1	2	0	4	6	-2	3
14	Tunisia	3	0	2	1	1	5	-4	1
15	Saudi Arabia	3	0	3	0	2	5	-3	0
16	Hungary	3	0	3	0	3	7	-4	0

Football / *Football*
Women / *Dames*

PRELIMINARIES - GROUP E **FINAL SCORE:** SWE 0 CHN 2 **HALFTIME SCORE:** SWE 0 CHN 2

Team: SWE Sweden
Coach: SIMONSSON, Bengt Assistant Coach: DOMANSKI LYFORS, Marika

Name	Pos	Min	FK	PK	Hdr	IA	OA	G/A	CK	Off	YC	RC
NILSSON, Annelie	G	96										
SANDELL, Cecilia	D	96										
JAKOBSSON, Asa	D	47										
NESSVOLD, Annika	D	96							1			
BENGTSSON, Kristin	D	96							2	1		
POHJANEN, Anna	M	60									1	1
SUNDHAGE, Pia	M	96	0/1			0/1		0/2				
SWEDBERG, Malin	M	96									1	1
ANDERSSON, Malin	M	31					0/2	0/2				
KALTE, Ulrika	M	72										
VIDEKULL, Lena	F	96					0/3	0/3	2			
KARLSSON, Ulrika	G	0										
SVENSSON, Camilla	D	50										
KUN, Maria	F	65										
CARLSSON, Julia	F	0										
LJUNGBERG, Hanna	F	24							1			
Own goals by opponent												
Totals			0/1			0/3	0/3	0/7	3	5	2	1

Referees: el-GHANDOUR, Gamal Mahmound EGY   RUSCIO, Roberto Ruben ARG

Team: CHN People's Republic of China
Coach: MA, Yuanan Assistant Coach: LI, Bi

Name	Pos	Min	FK	PK	Hdr	IA	OA	G/A	CK	Off	YC	RC
ZHONG, Honglian	G	0										
WANG, Liping	D	96								1		
FAN, Yunjie	D	96										
YU, Hongqi	F	35									1	
XIE, Huilin	D	96										
ZHAO, Lihong	M	96				0/1	1/2	1/3	1	1		
WEI, Haiying	F	35							1	1		
SHUI, Qingxia	F	61								2		
SUN, Wen	M	96					0/2	0/2	1			
LIU, Ailing	M	96				0/1	0/3	0/4				
SUN, Qingmei	M	96										
WEN, Lirong	D	96					0/1	0/1				
LIU, Ying	M	30					0/1	0/1				
CHEN, Yufeng	M	0										
SHI, Guihong	M	62				1/2	0/1	1/3	2			
GAO, Hong	G	96										
Own goals by opponent												
Totals						1/7	1/7	2/14	5	5	1	

Linesmen: VELAZQUEZ PINTOS, Carlos Adan URU   JEON, Young Hyun KOR

PRELIMINARIES - GROUP E **FINAL SCORE:** USA 3 DEN 0 **HALFTIME SCORE:** USA 2 DEN 0

Team: USA United States of America
Coach: DICICCO, Anthony Assistant Coach: GREGG, Lauren

Name	Pos	Min	FK	PK	Hdr	IA	OA	G/A	CK	Off	YC	RC
SCURRY, Briana	G	91										
HARVEY, Mary	G	0										
PARLOW, Cindy	M	29										
OVERBECK, Carla	D	91										
ROBERTS, Tiffany	M	25										1
CHASTAIN, Brandi	D	91										
WILSON, Staci	D	0										
MacMILLAN, Shannon	M	91				0/2	0/1	0/3	2			
HAMM, Mia	F	76	0/1			1/2	0/3	1/6	1			
AKERS, Michelle	F	62				0/1	0/2	0/3				
FOUDY, Julie	M	91					0/2	0/2				
GABARRA, Carin	F	16							1			
LILLY, Kristine	F	91	0/1			0/1	0/1	0/3				
FAWCETT, Joy	D	91										
VENTURINI, Tisha	M	91				1/2	0/2	1/4				
MILBRETT, Tiffeny	F	67				1/2	0/1	1/3				
Own goals by opponent												
Totals			0/2			3/10	0/12	3/24	4			1

Referees: VASCONCELOS GUEDES, Claudia BRA   SKOGVANG, Bente NOR

Team: DEN Denmark
Coach: GANTZHORN, Keld

Name	Pos	Min	FK	PK	Hdr	IA	OA	G/A	CK	Off	YC	RC
LARSEN, Doerthe	G	91										
LAURSEN, Annette	D	23										
MADSEN, Bonny	D	91										
FLAENG, Kamma Bodil	D	91									1	
HOLM, Rikke	D	91									1	
PETERSEN, Christina	M	91										
CHRISTENSEN, Birgit	M	91										
KOLDING, Lisbet	M	68										
JENSEN, Helle	F	0										
KROGH, Gitte	F	80							2			
MADSEN, Lene	F	91										
TERP, Lene	D	91										
NIELSEN, Anne	M	91										
PEDERSEN, Merete	M	0										
BONDE, Christina	F	11										
BJERREGAARD, Helle	G	0										
Own goals by opponent												
Totals									2		2	

Linesmen: VIENNOT, Nelly FRA   RODRIGUEZ ROMAN, Maria Del Socorro MEX

Football / *Football*

Women / *Dames*

PRELIMINARIES - GROUP E FINAL SCORE: DEN 1 CHN 5 | HALFTIME SCORE: DEN 0 CHN 4

Team: DEN Denmark
Coach: GANTZHORN, Keid

Name	Pos	Min	FK	PK	Hdr	IA	OA	G/A	CK	Off	YC	RC
LARSEN, Doerthe	G	90										
LAURSEN, Annette	D	7										
MADSEN, Bonny	D	90										
FLAENG, Kamma Bodil	D	90					0/1	0/1				
HOLM, Rikke	D	90				0/1		0/1				
PETERSEN, Christina	M	84										
CHRISTENSEN, Birgit	M	90					0/1	0/1				
KOLDING, Lisbet	M	90				0/1		0/1	1		1	
JENSEN, Helle	F	45									1	
KROGH, Gitte	F	90	0/-1		0/3			0/2			1	
MADSEN, Lene	F	50	1/1					1/1				
TERP, Lene	D	90										
NIELSEN, Anne	M	45										
PEDERSEN, Merete	M	0										
BONDE, Christina	F	45										
BJERREGAARD, Helle	G	0										
Own goals by opponent												
Totals			1/0		0/3	0/2	0/2	1/7	1		3	

Referee: ARCHUNDIA TELLEZ, Benito MEX

Team: CHN People's Republic of China
Coach: MA, Yuanan Assistant Coach: LI, Bi

Name	Pos	Min	FK	PK	Hdr	IA	OA	G/A	CK	Off	YC	RC
ZHONG, Honglian	G	0										
WANG, Liping	D	90								1		
FAN, Yunjie	D	90				1/1	0/1	1/2				
YU, Hongqi	F	0					0/1	0/1				
XIE, Huilin	D	90										
ZHAO, Lihong	M	90					0/1	0/1	2			
WEI, Haiying	F	0										
SHUI, Qingxia	F	90							2			
SUN, Wen	M	42				0/1		0/1				
LIU, Ailing	M	84	0/1			1/1	0/1	1/3				
SUN, Qingmei	M	61			1/1	1/2		2/3				
WEN, Lirong	D	90										
LIU, Ying	M	0					0/1	0/1	2			
CHEN, Yufeng	M	48										
SHI, Guihong	M	90				1/7		1/7		3		
GAO, Hong	G	90										
Own goals by opponent												
Totals			0/1		1/1	4/12	0/5	5/19	6	4		

Linesmen: KELLY, Peter TRI   OSMAN MOHAMED, Amir SUD

PRELIMINARIES - GROUP E FINAL SCORE: USA 2 SWE 1 | HALFTIME SCORE: USA 1 SWE 0

Team: USA United States of America
Coach: DICICCO, Anthony Assistant Coach: GREGG, Lauren

Name	Pos	Min	FK	PK	Hdr	IA	OA	G/A	CK	Off	YC	RC
SCURRY, Briana	G	90										
HARVEY, Mary	G	0										
PARLOW, Cindy	M	0										
OVERBECK, Carla	D	90										
ROBERTS, Tiffany	M	33										
CHASTAIN, Brandi	D	90										
WILSON, Staci	D	0										
MacMILLAN, Shannon	M	90	0/1			1/2	0/1	1/4	2			
HAMM, Mia	F	85	0/1		0/1	0/1		0/4	6			
AKERS, Michelle	F	90			0/1		0/1	0/2				
FOUDY, Julie	M	90					0/1	0/1				
GABARRA, Carin	F	6										
LILLY, Kristine	F	90			0/2		0/2	0/4	1	2		
FAWCETT, Joy	D	90										
VENTURINI, Tisha	M	90			1/4	0/1	0/1	1/6				
MILBRETT, Tiffeny	F	58			0/1			0/1				
Own goals by opponent												
Totals			0/2		1/9	1/4	0/6	2/22	9	2		

Referee: SKOGVANG, Bente NOR

Team: SWE Sweden
Coach: SIMONSON, Bengt Assistant Coach: DOMANSKI LYFORS, Marika

Name	Pos	Min	FK	PK	Hdr	IA	OA	G/A	CK	Off	YC	RC
NILSSON, Anneile	G	90										
SANDELL, Cecilia	D	67										1
JAKOBSSON, Asa	D	24										
NESSVOLD, Annika	D	90									1	1
BENGTSSON, Kristin	D	90									1	
POHJANEN, Anna	M	0										
SUNDHAGE, Pia	M	90										
SWEDBERG, Malin	M	90										
ANDERSSON, Malin	M	90	0/1				0/1	0/2				
KALTE, Ulrika	M	85										
VIDEKULL, Lena	F	90				0/1	0/1	0/2				
KARLSSON, Ulrika	G	0										
SVENSSON, Camilla	D	90										
KUN, Maria	F	6										
CARLSSON, Julia	F	56										
LJUNGBERG, Hanna	F	35										
Own goals by opponent								1				
Totals			0/1			0/1	0/2	1/4			2	2

Linesmen: DANTE, Dramane MLI   RODRIGUEZ ROMAN, Maria Del Socorro MEX

Women / Dames

PRELIMINARIES - GROUP E **FINAL SCORE:** DEN 1 SWE 3 **HALFTIME SCORE:** DEN 0 SWE 0

Team: DEN Denmark
Coach: GANTZHORN, Keld

Name	Pos	Min	FK	PK	Hdr	IA	OA	G/A	CK	Off	YC	RC
LARSEN, Doerthe	G	90										
LAURSEN, Annette	D	45										
MADSEN, Bonny	D	90										
FLAENG, Kamma Bodil	D	90	0/1					0/1				
HOLM, Rikke	D	90										
PETERSEN, Christina	M	70				0/1		0/1	1			
CHRISTENSEN, Birgit	M	90			0/1		0/1	0/2				
KOLDING, Lisbet	M	0										
JENSEN, Helle	F	45				1/2		1/2				
KROGH, Gitte	F	90				0/1		0/1			1	1
MADSEN, Lene	F	90				0/1		0/1				
TERP, Lene	D	90										
NIELSEN, Anne	M	90				0/1		0/1	2			
PEDERSEN, Merete	M	21					0/1	0/1				
BONDE, Christina	F	0										
BJERREGAARD, Helle	G	0										
Own goals by opponent												
Totals			0/1		0/1	1/6	0/2	1/10	3		1	1

Referees: VASCONCELOS GUEDES, Claudia BRA   SKOGVANG, Bente NOR

Team: SWE Sweden
Coach: SIMONSON, Bengt   Assistant Coach: DOMANSKI LYFORS, Marika

Name	Pos	Min	FK	PK	Hdr	IA	OA	G/A	CK	Off	YC	RC
NILSSON, Annelie	G	32										
SANDELL, Cecilia	D	28										
JAKOBSSON, Asa	D	63										
NESSVOLD, Annika	D	90								1		
BENGTSSON, Kristin	D	90								3		
POHJANEN, Anna	M	90					0/1	0/1				
SUNDHAGE, Pia	M	90				0/2	0/3	0/5				
SWEDBERG, Malin	M	90			1/1	1/2	0/1	2/4				
ANDERSSON, Malin	M	90				0/1	0/1	0/2				
KALTE, Ulrika	M	84				0/1	0/1	0/2			1	
VIDEKULL, Lena	F	90				1/2	0/1	1/3				
KARLSSON, Ulrika	G	59										
SVENSSON, Camilla	D	90										
KUN, Maria	F	7										
CARLSSON, Julia	F	0										
LJUNGBERG, Hanna	F	0										
Own goals by opponent												
Totals					1/2	2/8	0/7	3/17		4	1	

Linesmen: RODRIGUEZ ROMAN, Maria Del Socorro MEX   VIENNOT, Nelly FRA

PRELIMINARIES - GROUP E **FINAL SCORE:** USA 0 CHN 0 **HALFTIME SCORE:** USA 0 CHN 0

Team: USA United States of America
Coach: DICICCO, Anthony   Assistant Coach: GREGG, Lauren

Name	Pos	Min	FK	PK	Hdr	IA	OA	G/A	CK	Off	YC	RC
SCURRY, Briana	G	90										
HARVEY, Mary	G	0										
PARLOW, Cindy	M	29			0/1			0/1	0/2			
OVERBECK, Carla	D	90			0/1			0/1				
ROBERTS, Tiffany	M	90										
CHASTAIN, Brandi	D	90				0/1	0/1	0/1	0/3		1	
WILSON, Staci	D	0										
MacMILLAN, Shannon	M	90					0/1	0/1	0/2	8		
HAMM, Mia	F	0										
AKERS, Michelle	F	90						0/1	0/1		1	
FOUDY, Julie	M	90					0/1	0/2	0/3		1	
GABARRA, Carin	F	62									1	
LILLY, Kristine	F	90				0/2	0/3	0/5				1
FAWCETT, Joy	D	90									1	
VENTURINI, Tisha	M	62						0/1	0/1			
MILBRETT, Tiffeny	F	29						0/1	0/1			
Own goals by opponent												
Totals						0/3	0/5	0/11	0/19	8	5	1

Referees: COLLINA, Pierluigi ITA   el-GHANDOUR, Gamal Mahmoud EGY

Team: CHN People's Republic of China
Coach: MA , Yuanan   Assistant Coach: LI, Bi

Name	Pos	Min	FK	PK	Hdr	IA	OA	G/A	CK	Off	YC	RC
ZHONG, Honglian	G	0										
WANG, Liping	D	90					0/1	0/2	0/3			
FAN, Yunjie	D	90										
YU, Hongqui	F	0										
XIE, Huilin	D	90						0/1	0/1			
ZHAO, Lihong	M	90					0/1	0/1		4	1	
WEI, Haiying	F	4										
SHUI, Qingxia	F	90								2		
SUN, Wen	M	90						0/1	0/1			
LIU, Ailing	M	90						0/1	0/1		1	
SUN, Qingmei	M	90										
WEN, Lirong	D	90										
LIU, Ying	M	0										
CHEN, Yufeng	M	38										
SHI, Guihong	M	87										2
GAO, Hong	G	90										1
Own goals by opponent												
Totals							0/2	0/5	0/7	6	2	3

Linesmen: VELAZQUEZ PINTOS, Carlos Adan URU   OSMAN MOHAMED, Amir SUD

Women / *Dames*

PRELIMINARIES - GROUP F **FINAL SCORE:** GER 3 JPN 2 **HALFTIME SCORE:** GER 2 JPN 2

Team: GER Germany
Coach: THEUNE MEYER, Christina Assistant Coach: BISANZ, Gero

Name	Pos	Min	FK	PK	Hdr	IA	OA	G/A	CK	Off	YC	RC
GOLLER, Manuela	G	90										
NARDENBACH, Jutta	D	52				0/1	0/1	0/2				
AUSTERMUHL, Birgitt	D	52										
STEGEMANN, Kerstin	D	0				0/2		0/2				
FITSCHEN, Doris	D	52										
POHLMANN, Dagmar	M	0										
VOSS, Martina	M	97				0/1		0/1	4			
WIEGMANN, Bettina	M	97				1/1	0/3	1/4				
MOHR, Heidi	F	52				0/3	1/2	1/5				
NEID, Silvia	M	52				0/1		0/1				
BROCKER, Patrizia	F	61					0/1	0/1	2		1	
KRAUS, Katja	G	0										
MINNERT, Sandra	D	52										
WUNDERLICH, Pia	M	73	0/1				0/1	0/2				
PRINZ, Birgit	F	36				0/2		0/2	1			1
LINGOR, Renate	M	0										
Own goals by opponent								1				
Totals			0/1			1/11	1/8	3/20	7		1	1

Referees: DENONCOURT, Sonia CAN JONSSON, Ingrid SWE

Team: JPN Japan
Coach: SAITO, Makoto Assistant Coach: YAMAMOTO, Hiroyasu

Name	Pos	Min	FK	PK	Hdr	IA	OA	G/A	CK	Off	YC	RC
OZAWA, Junko	G	97										
TOMEI, Yumi	D	97										
YAMAKI, Rie	D	97										
HANETA, Maki	D	97										1
OBE, Yumi	D	97				0/1	0/1	0/2				1
NISHINA, Kae	D	97										
SAWA, Homare	M	97									1	
TAKAKURA, Asako	M	97										
KIOKA, Futaba	M	97				1/1	0/1	1/2	1			
NODA, Akemi	F	97	0/1			1/1	0/1	1/3				
HANDA, Etsuko	M	0					0/1	0/1				
UCHIYAMA, Tamaki	F	52										
OTAKE, Nami	M	0										
KADOHARA, Kaoru	M	0										
IZUMI, Miyuki	F	0										
ONODERA, Shiho	G	0										
Own goals by opponent												
Totals			0/1			2/3	0/4	2/8	1		1	2

Linesmen: GETTEMEYER, Janice USA HOLM, Gitte DEN

PRELIMINARIES - GROUP F **FINAL SCORE:** NOR 2 BRA 2 **HALFTIME SCORE:** NOR 1 BRA 0

Team: NOR Norway
Coach: PELLERUD, Even Assistant Coach: KNUTSEN, Hans

Name	Pos	Min	FK	PK	Hdr	IA	OA	G/A	CK	Off	YC	RC
NORDBY, Bente	G	90										1
CARLSEN, Agnete	D	90										
ESPESETH, Gro	D	90				0/1	0/1	0/2	7			1
NYMARK ANDERSEN, Nina	D	90										
MYKLEBUST, Merete	D	90										
RIISE, Hege	M	90				0/3	0/2	0/5	6			
NYMARK ANDERSEN, Anne	M	90										
STOERE, Heidi	M	31										
PETTERSEN, Marianne	F	0										
MEDALEN, Linda	F	90				0/2	1/3	1/5				1
SANDAUNE, Brit	F	59				0/1	0/1	0/2				
THUN, Kjersti	F	0										
SVENSSON, Tina	D	14										
HAUGEN, Tone	M	76				0/1	0/2	0/3				
TANGERAAS, Trine	M	0										
AARONES, Ann Kristin	M	90				1/1	0/1	1/2				
Own goals by opponent												
Totals			1/4			0/7	1/8	2/19	13			3

Referees: GARCIA-ARANDA ENCINAR, Jose ESP al-MUHANNA, Omar Seleh Saad KSA

Team: BRA Brazil
Coach: DUARTE, Jose

Name	Pos	Min	FK	PK	Hdr	IA	OA	G/A	CK	Off	YC	RC
PIORESAN, Margarete Maria	G	90										
CAVALCANTE, Alissandra Regina	D	85										
OLIVEIRA, Suzy Bitencourt de	D	0										
MOTTA, Roselane Camargo	D	90							3			
TAFAREL, Marcia	M	90										
REGO, Elane dos Santos	D	90										
GONCALVES, Delma	F	86				2/2		2/2		2		
MOTA, Miraildes Maciel	M	90										
SANTOS, Marileia dos	F	4										
AMOR, Sisleide Lima do	M	90				0/1	0/1	0/2				
BELO, Roseli de	F	90				0/1		0/1		4		
BARRETO, Diedja Roque	G	0										
NOGUEIRA, Marisa Pires	D	7										
RIBEIRO, Tania Maria Pereira	D	90										
SILVA, Katia Cilene Teixeira da	D	7										
COSTA, Sonia Maria Roque da	M	83										
Own goals by opponent												
Totals						2/4	0/1	2/5	3	6		

Linesmen: al MOSSAWI, Mohamed Ahmed OMA FRED, Lencie VAN

PRELIMINARIES - GROUP F   FINAL SCORE: BRA 2 JPN 0   HALFTIME SCORE: BRA 0 JPN 0

Team: BRA Brazil
Coach: DUARTE, Jose

Name	Pos	Min	FK	PK	Hdr	IA	OA	G/A	CK	Off	YC	RC
PIORESAN, Margarete Maria	G	0										
CAVALCANTE, Alissandra Regina	D	90					0/3	0/3				
OLIVEIRA, Suzy Bitencourt de	D	0										
MOTTA, Roselane Camargo	D	90				0/1		0/1	4			
TAFAREL, Marcia	M	90					0/4	0/4				
REGO, Elane dos Santos	D	90	0/2					0/2				
GONCALVES, Delma	F	90			1/1		0/2	1/3		2		
MOTA, Miiraildes Maciel	M	90					0/2	0/2				
SANTOS, Marileia dos	F	0										
AMOR, Sisleide Lima do	M	90	0/1			0/3	0/2	0/6				
BELO, Roseli de	F	90				0/3	0/2	0/5		1		
BARRETO, Diedja Roque	G	90										
NOGUEIRA, Marisa Pires	D	0										
RIBEIRO, Tania Maria Pereira	D	90										
COSTA, Sonia Maria Roque da	M	37									1	
SILVA, Katia Cilene Teixeira da	D	54				1/1	0/1	1/2		1		
Own goals by opponent												
Totals			0/3		1/1	1/10	0/14	2/28	4	4	1	

Referee: JONSSON, Ingrid SWE

Team: JPN Japan
Coach: SAITO, Makoto   Assistant Coach: YAMAMOTO, Hiroyasu

Name	Pos	Min	FK	PK	Hdr	IA	OA	G/A	CK	Off	YC	RC
OZAWA, Junko	G	90										
TOMEI, Yumi	D	90										
YAMAKI, Rie	D	90										
HANETA, Maki	D	90										
OBE, Yumi	D	90	0/1					0/1				
NISHINA, Kae	D	90										
SAWA, Homare	M	90					0/1	0/1				
TAKAKURA, Asako	M	72				0/1		0/1				
KIOKA, Futaba	M	90					0/1	0/1	4			
NODA, Akemi	F	90				0/1	0/1	0/2		1		
HANDA, Etsuko	M	0										
UCHIYAMA, Tamaki	F	90								1		
OTAKE, Nami	M	19										
KADOHARA, Kaoru	M	0										
IZUMI, Miyuki	F	0										
ONODERA, Shiho	G	0										
Own goals by opponent												
Totals			0/1			0/1	0/2	0/6	4	2		

Linesman: GETTEMEYER, Janice USA   HOLM, Gitte DEN

PRELIMINARIES - GROUP F   FINAL SCORE: NOR 3 GER 2   HALFTIME SCORE: NOR 2 GER 1

Team: NOR Norway
Coach: PELLERUD, Even   Assistant Coach: KNUTSEN, Hans

Name	Pos	Min	FK	PK	Hdr	IA	OA	G/A	CK	Off	YC	RC
NORDBY, Bente	G	90										
CARLSEN, Agnete	D	90					0/1	0/1				
ESPESETH, Gro	D	90									1	
NYMARK ANDERSEN, Nina	D	90										
MYKLEBUST, Merete	D	90										
RIISE, Hege	M	90	1/1			0/1		1/2	1			
NYMARK ANDERSEN, Anne	M	90					0/1	0/1				
PETTERSEN, Marianne	F	66										
MEDALEN, Linda	F	90			1/1	0/1		1/2				
SANDAUNE, Brit	F	0										
THUN, Kjersti	F	0										
SVENSSON, Tina	D	77										
HAUGEN, Tone	M	14										
TANGERAAS, Trine	M	25										
AARONES, Ann Kristin	M	90			1/1	0/2		1/3	1			
FRUSTOL, Tone Gunn	M	0										
Own goals by opponent												
Totals			1/1		2/2	0/4	0/2	3/9	2		1	

Referee: LENNIE, Edward AUS

Team: GER Germany
Coach: BISANZ, Gero   Assistant Coach: THEUNE MEYER, Christina

Name	Pos	Min	FK	PK	Hdr	IA	OA	G/A	CK	Off	YC	RC
GOLLER, Manuela	G	90										
NARDENBACH, Jutta	D	90										
AUSTERMUHL, Birgitt	D	90										
STEGEMANN, Kerstin	D	36							1			
FITSCHEN, Doris	D	90					0/1	0/1				
POHLMANN, Dagmar	M	0										
VOSS, Martina	M	90					0/1	0/1				
WIEGMANN, Bettina	M	90				1/1		1/1		1		
MOHR, Heidi	F	90				0/1	0/1	0/2		1		
NEID, Silvia	M	77										
BROCKER, Patrizia	F	53							1			
KRAUS, Katja	G	0										
MINNERT, Sandra	D	90					0/1	0/1				
WUNDERLICH, Pia	M	55				0/1		0/1		1		
PRINZ, Birgit	F	38				1/1		1/1				
LINGOR, Renate	M	14										
Own goals by opponent												
Totals			0/1			2/4	0/3	2/8	2	3		

Linesman: ARANGO CARDONA, Jorge Luis COL   DUPANOV, Yuri BLR

Women / *Dames*

PRELIMINARIES - GROUP F   FINAL SCORE: BRA 1   GER 1   HALFTIME SCORE: BRA 0   GER 1

Team: BRA Brazil
Coach: DUARTE, Jose

Name	Pos	Min	FK	PK	Hdr	IA	OA	G/A	CK	Off	YC	RC
PIORESAN, Margarete Maria	G	90										
CAVALCANTE, Alissandra Regina	D	90				0/1		0/1				
OLIVEIRA, Suzy Bitencourt de	D	0										
MOTTA, Roselane Camargo	D	90										1
TAFAREL, Marcia	M	90										
REGO, Elane dos Santos	D	90					0/1	0/1				
GONCALVES, Delma	F	90				0/1		0/1				
MOTA, Miraildes Maciel	M	90				0/1		0/1				
SANTOS, Marileia dos	F	0										
AMOR, Sisleide Lima do	M	90				1/3	0/1	1/4	1			
BELO, Roseli de	F	90				0/3	0/3	0/6		1		
BARRETO, Diedja Roque	G	0										
NOGUEIRA, Marisa Pires	D	0										
RIBEIRO, Tania Maria Pereira	D	90										1
COSTA, Sonia Maria Roque da	M	6										
SILVA, Katia Cilene Teixeira da	D	85	0/1					0/1				
Own goals by opponent												
Totals			0/1			1/9	0/5	1/15	1	1		2

Referees: DENONCOURT, Sonia CAN   UN-PRASERT, Pirom THA

PRELIMINARIES - GROUP F   (GER)

Team: GER Germany
Coach: BISANZ, Gero   Assistant Coach: THEUNE MEYER, Christina

Name	Pos	Min	FK	PK	Hdr	IA	OA	G/A	CK	Off	YC	RC
GOLLER, Manuela	G	90										
NARDENBACH, Jutta	D	45										
AUSTERMUHL, Birgitt	D	90					0/1	0/1			1	
STEGEMANN, Kerstin	D	46				0/2		0/2	2			
FITSCHEN, Doris	D	90			0/2	0/2		0/4				
POHLMANN, Dagmar	M	23					0/1	0/1	2			
VOSS, Martina	M	90							5			
WIEGMANN, Bettina	M	90				0/1	0/6	0/7				
MOHR, Heid	F	90					0/1	0/1				
NEID, Silva	M	68					0/1	0/1				
BROCKER, Patrizia	F	42			0/1	0/1	0/1	0/3	2	2		
KRAUS, Katja	G	0										
MINNERT, Sandra	D	90					0/1	0/1				
WUNDERLICH, Pia	M	90				1/3	0/5	1/8				
PRINZ, Birgit	F	48				0/2		0/2				
LINGOR, Renate	M	0										
Own goals by opponent												
Totals					0/3	1/11	0/17	1/31	11	2	1	

Linesmen: GETTEMEYER, Janice USA   HOLM, Gitte DEN

PRELIMINARIES - GROUP F   FINAL SCORE: NOR 4   JPN 0   HALFTIME SCORE: NOR 1   JPN 0

Team: NOR Norway
Coach: PELLERUD, Even   Assistant Coach: KNUTSEN, Hans

Name	Pos	Min	FK	PK	Hdr	IA	OA	G/A	CK	Off	YC	RC
NORDBY, Bente	G	90										
CARLSEN, Agnete	D	90				0/1	0/2	0/3				
ESPESETH, Gro	D	77	0/1			0/1		0/2	7			
NYMARK ANDERSEN, Nina	D	90										
MYKLEBUST, Merete	D	90										
RIISE, Hege	M	70					0/2	0/2	4			
NYMARK ANDERSEN, Anne	M	90					0/2	0/2	2			
PETTERSEN, Marianne	F	90				1/4	1/2	2/6				
MEDALEN, Linda	F	61				1/2		1/2				
SANDAUNE, Brit	F	21				0/1		0/1				
THUN, Kjersti	F	0										
SVENSSON, Tina	D	90										
HAUGEN, Tone	M	14										
TANGERAAS, Trine	M	30				1/1		1/1				
AARONES, Ann Kristin	M	90				0/2	0/1	0/3				
FRUSTOL, Tone Gunn	M	0										
Own goals by opponent												
Totals			0/1			2/13	2/4	4/22	13			

Referees: al-MUHANNA, Omar Seleh Saad KSA   LENNIE, Edward AUS

Team: JPN Japan
Coach: SUZUKI, Tamotsu   Assistant Coach: YAMAMOTO, Hiroyasu

Name	Pos	Min	FK	PK	Hdr	IA	OA	G/A	CK	Off	YC	RC
OZAWA, Junko	G	0										
TOMEI, Yumi	D	90										
YAMAKI, Rie	D	90										
HANETA, Maki	D	90										
OBE, Yumi	D	78										
NISHINA, Kae	D	90										
SAWA, Homare	M	90										
TAKAKURA, Asako	M	90										
KIOKA, Futaba	M	90									1	1
NODA, Akemi	F	90					0/1	0/1	4			
HANDA, Etsuko	M	0										
UCHIYAMA, Tamaki	F	81									1	
OTAKE, Nami	M	0										
KADOHARA, Kaoru	M	13										
IZUMI, Miyuki	F	10										
ONODERA, Shiho	G	90										
Own goals by opponent												
Totals							0/1	0/1	1	6		

Linesmen: al MOSSAWI, Mohamed Ahmed OMA   FRED, Lencie VAN

SUMMARY: PRELIMINARIES - GROUP E

Rnk	Team	CHN	USA	SWE	DEN	Games	Wins	Losses	Ties	Goals For	Goals Against	Diff
1	CHN		0-0	2-0	5-1	3	2	0	1	7	1	6
2	USA	0-0		2-1	3-0	3	2	0	1	5	1	4
3	SWE	0-2	1-2		3-1	3	1	2	0	4	5	-1
4	DEN	1-5	0-3	1-3		3	0	3	0	2	11	-9

SUMMARY: PRELIMINARIES - GROUP F

Rnk	Team	NOR	BRA	GER	JPN	Games	Wins	Losses	Ties	Goals For	Goals Against	Diff
1	NOR		2-2	3-2	4-0	3	2	0	1	9	4	5
2	BRA	2-2		1-1	2-0	3	1	0	2	5	3	2
3	GER	2-3	1-1		3-2	3	1	1	1	6	6	0
4	JPN	0-4	0-2	2-3		3	0	3	0	2	9	-7

Women / Dames

SEMIFINALS   FINAL SCORE: CHN 3 BRA 2   HALFTIME SCORE: CHN 1 BRA 0

Team: CHN People's Republic of China

Coach: MA, Yuanan   Assistant Coach: LI, Bi

Name	Pos	Min	FK	PK	Hdr	IA	OA	G/A	CK	Off	YC	RC
ZHONG, Honglian	G	0										
WANG, Liping	D	90										
FAN, Yunjie	D	90					0/1	0/1				
YU, Hongqi	F	21										
XIE, Huilin	D	90										
ZHAO, Lihong	M	90							1			
WEI, Haiying	F	36				2/3		2/3	1			
SHUI, Qingxia	F	70							2			
SUN, Wen	M	90				0/1	0/1	0/2				
LIU, Ailing	M	90					0/2	0/2				
SUN, Qingmei	M	90				0/1	1/3	1/4		2		
WEN, Lirong	D	61										1
LIU, Ying	M	0										
CHEN, Yufeng	M	0										
SHI, Guihong	M	55				0/2	0/1	0/3				
GAO, Hong	G	90										
Own goals by opponent												
Totals						2/7	1/8	3/15	4	2		1

Referees: JONSSON, Ingrid SWE   SKOGVANG, Bente NOR

Team: BRA Brazil

Coach: DUARTE, Jose

Name	Pos	Min	FK	PK	Hdr	IA	OA	G/A	CK	Off	YC	RC
PIORESAN, Margarete Maria	G	90										
CAVALCANTE, Alissandra Regina	D	90										
OLIVEIRA, Suzy Bitencourt de	D	45										
MOTTA, Roselane Camargo	D	90					0/1	0/1				
TAFAREL, Marcia	M	90										
REGO, Elane dos Santos	D	90										
GONCALVES, Delma	F	90				1/2	0/1	1/3	1			
MOTA, Miraildes Maciel	M	90										
SANTOS, Marileia dos	F	0										
AMOR, Sisleide Lima do	M	90					0/3	0/3				
BELO, Roseli de	F	90				1/2		1/2	1			
BARRETO, Diedja Roque	G	0										
NOGUEIRA, Marisa Pires	D	0										
RIBEIRO, Tania Maria Pereira	D	43									2	1
COSTA, Sonia Maria Roque da	M	0										
SILVA, Katia Cilene Teixeira da	D	45										
Own goals by opponent												
Totals						2/4	0/5	2/9	2		2	1

Linesmen: RODRIGUEZ ROMAN, Maria Del Socorro MEX   VIENNOT, Nelly FRA

SEMIFINALS   FINAL SCORE: NOR 1 USA 2   HALFTIME SCORE: NOR 1 USA 0

Team: NOR Norway

Coach: PELLERUD, Even   Assistant Coach: KNUTSEN, Hans

Name	Pos	Min	FK	PK	Hdr	IA	OA	G/A	CK	Off	YC	RC
NORDBY, Bente	G	105										
CARLSEN, Agnete	D	86					0/1	0/1			1	1
ESPESETH, Gro	D	105									1	
NYMARK ANDERSEN, Nina	D	105										
MYKLEBUST, Merete	D	105										
RIISE, Hege	M	105										
NYMARK ANDERSEN, Anne	M	105				0/1	0/1	0/2	1			
PETTERSEN, Marianne	F	105								2		
MEDALEN, Linda	F	105				1/1	0/3	1/4				
SANDAUNE, Brit	F	0										
SETH, Reidun	F	0										
SVENSSON, Tina	D	71										
HAUGEN, Tone	M	0										
TANGERAAS, Trine	M	35										
AARONES, Ann Kristin	M	105					0/1	0/1				
FRUSTOL, Tone Gunn	M	0										
Own goals by opponent												
Totals						1/2	0/6	1/8	1	2	2	1

Referees: DENONCOURT, Sonia CAN   GARCIA-ARANDA ENCINAR, Jose ESP

Team: USA United States of America

Coach: DICICCO, Anthony   Assistant Coach: GREGG, Lauren

Name	Pos	Min	FK	PK	Hdr	IA	OA	G/A	CK	Off	YC	RC
SCURRY, Briana	G	105										
HARVEY, Mary	G	0										
PARLOW, Cindy	M	0										
OVERBECK, Carla	D	105										
ROBERTS, Tiffany	M	105										
CHASTAIN, Brandi	D	105										
WILSON, Staci	D	0										
MacMILLIAN, Shannon	M	10				1/1		1/1				
HAMM, Mia	F	105		0/1		0/2	0/3	0/6	6	5		
AKERS, Michelle	F	105	1/1	0/2		0/3	0/4	1/10				
FOUDY, Julie	M	105				0/1	0/1	0/2				
GABARRA, Carin	F	0										
LILLY, Kristine	F	105				0/1	0/2	0/3	3			
FAWCETT, Joy	D	105								1		
VENTURINI, Tisha	M	105				0/1	0/1	0/2				
MLBRETT, Tiffeny	F	96		0/2		0/1	0/1	0/4				
Own goals by opponent												
Totals			1/1	0/5		1/10	0/12	2/28	9	6		

Linesmen: HOLM, Gitte DEN   ARANGO CARDONA, Jorge Luis COL

SUMMARY: INTERMEDIATE ROUNDS

Phase	Teams	Score
Semifinal	CHN - BRA	3-2
Semifinal	NOR - USA	1-2

Women / Dames

FINAL - BRONZE MATCH

FINAL SCORE: BRA 0 NOR 2 **HALFTIME SCORE:** BRA 0 NOR 2

Team: BRA Brazil
Coach: DUARTE, Jose

Name	Pos	Min	FK	PK	Hdr	IA	OA	G/A	CK	Off	YC	RC
PIORESAN, Margarete Maria	G	90										
CAVALCANTE, Alissandra Regina	D	5										
OLIVEIRA, Suzy Bitencourt de	D	90										
MOTTA, Roselane Camargo	D	90							1	1		
TAFAREL, Marcia	M	45					0/2	0/2				
REGO, Elane dos Santos	D	90										
GONCALVES, Delma	F	90				0/2		0/2		3		
MOTA, Miraildes Maciel	M	90								1		
SANTOS, Marileia dos	F	20										
AMOR, Sisleide Lima do	M	86				0/1		0/1	2			
BELO, Roseli de	F	90				0/1	0/2	0/3		4		
BARRETO, Diedja Roque	G	0										
NOGUEIRA, Maria Pires	D	90										
RIBEIRO, Tania Maria Pereira	D	0										
COSTA, Sonia Maria Roque da	M	71				0/1		0/1				
SILVA, Katia Cilene Teixeira da	D	45										
Own goals by opponent												
Totals						0/5	0/4	0/9	3	9		

Referees: JONSSON, Ingrid SWE   UN-PRASERT, Pirom THA

Team: NOR Norway
Coach: PELLERUD, Even   Assistant Coach: KNUTSEN, Hans

Name	Pos	Min	FK	PK	Hdr	IA	OA	G/A	CK	Off	YC	RC
NORDBY, Bente	G	90										
CARLSEN, Agnete	D	0										
ESPESETH, Gro	D	90									1	
NYMARK ANDERSEN, Nina	D	45										
MYKLEBUST, Merete	D	90										
RIISE, Hege	M	90				0/2	0/4	0/6	7			
NYMARK ANDERSEN, Anne	M	90							6			
PETTERSEN, Marianne	F	90				0/4	0/2	0/6				
MEDALEN, Linda	F	90			0/5	0/1	0/1	0/7		1		
SANDAUNE, Brit	F	90					0/1	0/1				
SETH, Reidun	F	0										
SVENSSON, Tina	D	45										
HAUGEN, Tone	M	1										
TANGERAAS, Trine	M	90				0/2	0/1	0/3				
AARONES, Ann Kristin	M	90				2/3		2/3				
FRUSTOL, Tone Gunn	M	0										
Own goals by opponent												
Totals					0/5	2/12	0/9	2/26	13	1	1	

Linesmen: VELAZQUEZ PINTOS, Carlos Adan URU   HOLM, Gitte DEN

FINAL - GOLD MATCH

FINAL SCORE: CHN 1 USA 2 **HALFTIME SCORE:** CHN 1 USA 1

Team: CHN People's Repbulic of China
Coach: MA, Yuanan   Assistant Coach: LI, Bi

Name	Pos	Min	FK	PK	Hdr	IA	OA	G/A	CK	Off	YC	RC
ZHONG, Honglian	G	0										
WANG, Liping	D	87										
FAN, Yunjie	D	90										
YU, Hongqi	F	4					0/1	0/1				
XIE, Huilin	D	90										1
ZHAO, Lihong	M	90							2			
WEI, Haiying	F	21										
SHUI, Qingxia	F	90							1			
SUN, Wen	M	90				1/2		1/2				
LIU, Ailing	M	90					0/3	0/3				
SUN, Qingmei	M	90										
WEN, Lirong	D	0										
LIU, Ying	M	90					0/1	0/1	1			
CHEN, Yufeng	M	0										
SHI, Guihong	M	70									1	
GAO, Hong	G	90										
Own goals by opponent												
Totals						1/2	0/5	1/7	4		1	1

Referees: SKOGVANG, Bente NOR   DENONCOURT, Sonia CAN

Team: USA United States of America
Coach: DICICCO, Anthony   Assistant Coach: GREGG, Lauren

Name	Pos	Min	FK	PK	Hdr	IA	OA	G/A	CK	Off	YC	RC
SCURRY, Briana	G	90									1	
HARVEY, Mary	G	0										
PARLOW, Cindy	M	0										
OVERBECK, Carla	D	90										
ROBERTS, Tiffany	M	20								1		
CHASTAIN, Brandi	D	90										
WILSON, Staci	D	0										
MacMILLIAN, Shannon	M	90				1/1	0/2	1/3	7			
HAMM, Mia	F	90				0/3		0/3	3	2		
AKERS, Michelle	F	90										
FOUDY, Julie	M	90										
GABARRA, Carin	F	0										
LILLY, Kristine	F	90					0/1	0/1			1	
FAWCETT, Joy	D	90										
VENTURINI, Tisha	M	90			0/1		0/1	0/2				
MILBRETT, Tiffeny	F	71				1/2		1/2			1	
Own goals by opponent												
Totals					0/1	2/6	0/4	2/11	10	3	3	

Linesmen: RODRIGUEZ ROMAN, Maria Del Socorro MEX   VIENNOT, Nelly FRA

FINAL CLASSIFICATION

Rnk	Team	Games	Wins	Losses	Ties	Goals For	Goals Against	Diff	Pts	
1	United States of America	5	4	0	1	9	3	6	13	Gold
2	People's Republic of China	5	3	1	1	11	5	6	10	Silver
3	Norway	5	3	1	1	12	6	6	10	Bronze
4	Brazil	5	1	2	2	7	8	-1	5	
5	Germany	3	1	1	1	6	6	0	4	
6	Sweden	3	1	2	0	4	5	-1	3	
7	Japan	3	0	3	0	2	9	-7	0	
8	Denmark	3	0	3	0	2	11	-9	0	

COREY SCHULTZ • DARLENE K SCHULTZ • DI-
ANNE M SCHULTZ • FRANCES M SCHULTZ • J
RANDALL SCHULTZ • JENNIFER A SCHULTZ •
JENNY SCHULTZ • JOHN C SCHULTZ • JOHN P
SCHULTZ • KATHLEEN M SCHULTZ • LYNNE G
SCHULTZ • PETER J SCHULTZ • REBECCA C
SCHULTZ • ROBERT SCHULTZ • TERRY L SCHULTZ
• GREGORY M SCHULZ • CHRISTINA M SCHU-
MACHER • CYNTHIA LEE SCHUMACHER •
RICHARD T SCHUMACHER • SANDEE LG SCHU-
MACHER • MARY V SCHUMAN • GABRIELA
A SCHUMANN • MARY L SCHUMANN • VINCENT
SCHUMUCKER • JULIE A SCHUNEMAN • MARY T
SCHUPETA • CHRISTIAN SCHUSTER • STEFFI E
SCHUSTER • THOMAS E SCHUTTE • BARBARA
R SCHUYLER • JAMES E SCHUYLER • MARI P
SCHUYLER • PAT M SCHUYLER • SALLY
H SCHUYLER • JULIETTE L SCHWAB • JAMES E
SCHWABEROW • ALISON M SCHWABROW • LORI K
SCHWACOFER • KATHRYN J SCHWALB •
M D SCHWALB • EMILY A SCHWALM • RICK H
SCHWAMB • GARY J SCHWANDER MT • BARBARA
A SCHWARTZ • CHARLES N SCHWARTZ • CHAR-
LY V SCHWARTZ • CINDY R SCHWARTZ • DIANA G
SCHWARTZ • ELISE A SCHWARTZ • ELIZABETH
A SCHWARTZ • ELLEN R SCHWARTZ • FRED
SCHWARTZ • JAMES J SCHWARTZ • KARI L
SCHWARTZ • LARRY S SCHWARTZ • LEWIS H
SCHWARTZ • MARC J SCHWARTZ • MARTHA
M SCHWARTZ • MICHAEL G SCHWARTZ •
MICHAEL R SCHWARTZ • PATRICIA W
SCHWARTZ • PAUL SCHWARTZ • PHILLIPS H
SCHWARTZ • ROBERT I SCHWARTZ • WILLIAM
SCHWARTZ • KEVIN R SCHWARTZ CATC • STEVE
SCHWEERS • HENRY JOSEPH SCHWEINBOLD •
RHONDA L SCHWEINBOLD • BOB SCHWEITZER
• ANTHONY W SCHWEIZEK • JEANNE N
SCHWENK • SIGRID SCHYDLOWSKI-SCHEFFER
• JOSHUA P SCIAME • JO-ANN P SCIARRONE •
PAUL SCIBONA • JULIE SCILLIERI • CHERLYN A
SCIRO • JOSEPH J SCITURRO • ANTHONY D SCI-
ULLI • KAREN A SCIULLI • LINDA M SCIULLO •
MATTHEW P SCIULLO • DENISE L SCOBEE •
ELIZABETH A SCOFIELD • THOMAS SCOFIELD •
KAREN L SCOGGINS • KENNETH R. SCOGGINS •
RANDALL B SCOGGINS • LINDA L SCOLES •
KEVIN P SCOLLARD • EDA L SCOPEL • PAUL A
SCOPEL • LISA M SCORSOLINI • DENISE R
SCOTCH ATC • AMMA T SCOTT • ANN-MARIE F
SCOTT • AUDRA R SCOTT • BARRY E SCOTT •
BERTRAM SCOTT • BILLY D SCOTT • BONNIE
SCOTT • CANDICE C SCOTT • CARRIE L SCOTT •
CHARLES L SCOTT • CLARA M SCOTT • CLIVE G
SCOTT • DANA M SCOTT • DANA S SCOTT • DAVID
C. SCOTT • DAVID W SCOTT • DEBORAH K SCOTT
• DON E SCOTT • ELIZABETH B SCOTT • EVAN A
SCOTT • FARRELL L SCOTT • FRANCOISE M
SCOTT • GAIL D SCOTT • GAIL E SCOTT • GERALD
D SCOTT • GLENN W SCOTT • HARRELL D SCOTT
• HELEN R SCOTT • JANE SCOTT • JANET C
SCOTT • JOHN R. SCOTT • JOSEPH P SCOTT • JU-
LIAN H SCOTT • KATHERINE M SCOTT • KELLI R
SCOTT • KEVIN L SCOTT • KEVIN M SCOTT •
KRISTIN V SCOTT • LAMAR SCOTT • LAURA M
SCOTT • LINDA S SCOTT • MARK A SCOTT • MARY
L SCOTT • MAUREEN S SCOTT • MEG SCOTT •
MELANIE A SCOTT • MICHAEL A SCOTT • MIGUEL
SCOTT • MONA L SCOTT • OPAL W SCOTT • PAT
SCOTT • PEGGY SCOTT • PERRY L SCOTT • RICKY
E SCOTT • RITA A SCOTT • ROBERTA Z SCOTT •
ROBIN SCOTT • RODNEY R SCOTT • RONALD D
SCOTT • RUSSELL W SCOTT • SHARON D SCOTT
• SHELBY SCOTT • STEWART SCOTT • SUSANNE
SCOTT • THOMAS SCOTT • THOMAS N SCOTT •
TIMOTHY SCOTT • TREASURE W SCOTT • VIRGIL
M SCOTT • WILLIE F SCOTT • MARY I SCOTT-
BRADFORD • CAROLINE S SCOTT-LEE • JOANN
SCOTT-PETTY • VAN C SCOTT JR • MICHAEL J
SCOTT DO • MARY C SCOTT EMT • ORVILLE V
SCOTT JR • GERALD A SCOTT MT • MICHAEL D
SCOTT PM • ELBERT L SCOTTI • VINCENT SCOT-
TON • OLIVIA A SCRIVEN • BOBBIE SCROGGINS
• LANA W SCROGGINS • ANNETTE C SCROGGS •
JANE SCROGGS • JOHN E SCROGGS • MARCIA E
SCROGGS • LINDA G SCROGGY • JEFFREY K
SCRUGGS • RICHARD P SCRUGGS • TRACY A
SCRUGGS • ANNE L SCUDDER • PAMELA L SCUL-
LY • DELORIS J SCURLOCK • EARL SCURLOCK •
KENNETH E SCURLOCK • ARCH C SCURLOCK JR
• VALENCIA M SCURRY • STANLEY J SCZECIENS-
KI • THOMAS L SCZEPANSKI PT • FRANCES H
SEABOLT • CLAUDIA E SEABORN-COLLINS •
CHERROLD W SEABROOK • FREDERICK
SEABROOK • PHYLLIS T SEABROOK-YOUNG •
CAYMAN SEACREST • ANNETTE E SEAGO • CYN-
THIA A SEAGO • DAVID M SEAGO • JESSE L. SEA-
GO • PAMELIA J SEAGO • DAVID H SEAGRAVES •
JO ANN SEAGRAVES • LINDA K SEAGRAVES •
MICHAEL S SEAL • RICARDO F SEALE • BONNIE
D SEALEY • CLARA P SEALS • NICOLE J SEALS •
VICKIE D SEALS • CARLISLE SEALY • JAMES T
SEALY PM • CATHERINE SEAMAN • GORDON
SEAMAN • LINDA K SEAMAN • JACQUELINE D
SEAMANS • KATHERINE L SEAMON • CAMILLE H
SEARCY • COURTNEY E SEARCY • DARRELL B
SEARCY • KATHLEEN W SEARCY • LETTY R
SEARCY • MARY E SEARCY • VALERIE SEARCY •
DANIEL D SEARL • CLAYTON E SEARLE • KAREN
C SEARLE • WILLIAM C SEARLE JR • DIANE M
SEARLES • SEAN P SEARLES • ILSE N SEARS •
MARY PATRICIA B SEARS • SUSAN R SEARS •
GEORGE R SEASTROM • HAL W SEATON • JANE B
SEATON • SUSAN SEATON • BILLIE L SEATZ •
CARLA F SEAY • HEATHER M SEAY • MICHELE L
SEAY • REBECCA A SEAY • ROBERT A SEAY • VA-
LENCIA M SEAY • EUGENE A SEBASTIAN •
CHARLES M SEBER • JOSEPH R SEBESTYEN •

NANCY C SEBREN • KEVIN L SEBRING • MPHO
SECHOARO • MAMADOU L SECK • DORIS B SEC-
KA • ISABELLA L. SECKINGTON • MACK D SEC-
ORD • DAWN SECRIST • CHARLOTTE A SECTOR •
JONATHAN K SECUNDA • EUGENIO E SEDA •
FERNANDO A SEDA • JORGE F SEDA • STEPHEN
O SEDA • WILLIAM D SEDDON • KELLEY B SEDG-
LEY • KIMBERLY M SEDGLEY • RONALD M SEDG-
LEY • GENE SEDLACKO • CATHLEEN A SEDLAK •
JESSICA R SEDNEY • CINDY L SEDRAN • BRUCE
H SEE • ANNA M SEEGER • KEITH E SEELEY • LEE
M SEELIG • BARBARA S SEELINGER • DONNA E
SEEMAN • ZUBEIDAH SEERS • JOHATHAN
SEEYAVE • CAROLE S SEFFRIN • CHRIS C SEGAL
• GEORGIA SEGAL • GRANT E SEGAL • GREGORY
E SEGAL • WILLIAM C SEGAL • BERNARD M
SEGER • FERN A SEGERLIND • ADELINA J SEGIS-
MUNDO • ROBERTO M SEGISMUNDO • DARRELL
D SEGRAVES • BERTA SEGURA • MIREIA SEGURA
• ELSA SEGURON • CHHAYA SEI • LYDIA R
SEIBER • NANCY K SEIBERT • PATRICIA SEIBERT
• REBECCA L SEIBERT • LISA A SEIDEL • MARCIA
L SEIDEL • RONA L SEIDEL • RALPH M SEIDEN-
SPINNER • DEBRA J SEIDL • MICHAEL SEIDMAN
• MICHAEL SEIDMAN • JANET C SEIGLER • JUNE
B SEILER • KATHLEEN A SEILS • PETER D SEIPEL
• LINDA J SEITZ • TIMOTHY L SEITZ • JOHN SEKE-
TA • CHIE SEKINE • SHARON L SELADI • MAR-
GARET M SELASKY • EDGAR R SELAYA • CATHY M
SELBY • KIMBERLY A SELBY • SHARON S SELBY
• TONI P SELBY • JRNE E SELDOMRIDGE •
MELANIE R SELESNICK • CAROL S SELF • DI-
ANNE W SELF • FLOYD J SELF • GAIL M SELF •
KEVIN K SELF • PATRICK C SELF • JOHN K SELFE
• MELANIE A SELFE • STANLEY HARRIS SELIG •
ANDREW J SELIN • GEORGE J SELL • HARVEY E
SELL • KAREN J SELL • PAMELA L SELL • TERESA
E SELL • LESLIE R SELLE • JOHN SELLER JR •
CATHERINE L SELLERS • CHRISTOPHER J SELL-
ERS • DONALD B SELLERS • FREDERICK B SELL-
ERS • GORDON E SELLERS • JAMES L SELLERS •
JOANNA C SELLERS • NANCY L SELLERS •
PAMELA S SELLERS • PAULA S SELLERS • REED
M SELLERS • SONJA A SELLERS • THOMAS W
SELLERS • GEORGE E SELLERS III • RACHEL
SELLERS WILLIAMS • CHARLES SELLNER • JUDI
E SELLS • LINNETTE J SELLS • RICHARD A
SELLS • JULIE R SELMAN • BILL E SELMON •
CLAYTON C SELPH • MARYLOU SELTZER • BAL-
APPA SELVARAJ • MARIA SEMECO • CARYN B
SEMELKA • KAREN L SEMENIUK • EMILY SEMIEN
• AUDREY SEMMELMAN • MARK SEMPLE •
STEVEN SEMPLE • GABRIELA C SENATORE • AN-
DREA P SENDOBRY • JAIME SENDRA • MICHAEL
A SENG • SHARON A SENG • ARUN SENGPUTA •
NICOLE R SENGSTOCK • WAYNE L SENGSTOCK •
BHASWATI SENGUPTA • INU I SENGUPTA • PRA-
TIMA SENGUPTA • STEPHEN S SENGUPTA • MAG-
DA J SENIOR • THELMA L SENIOR • TERRY A
SENNE • IDA SENTINELLI • MI JEONG SEO • AN-
NETTE N SEOANES • HYUK K SEOH • ROBERT J
SEPPALA • STEPHANIE L SERABIN • AIMEE SER-
AFIN • CHRISTINE B SERAFIN • HEATHER M
SERALE • NEAL SERBA • SAL SERBIN • JOHN R
SERDAR • BRADLEY P SERFF • DONNA M SER-
GENT • WILLIAM SERGENT • MICHAEL T SERI-
JAN • MARGARET B SERINA • BENOIT SERINGE •
TODD I SERINSKY • MICHAEL G SERKEDAKIS •
SHARON L SERKEDAKIS • KATHLYN E SERMER-
SHEIM • BARRY C SERMONS • ELIZABETH M
SERODINO • DESIREE A SERPAS • CHRIS SERRA
• DAVID P SERRA • KAREN L SERRA • NICOLE M
SERRAO • ALANA F SERRETTE • ALVA F SER-
RETTE • AMY SERRITELLA • I. EREM SERTKAYA •
DANIELLE C SERVICE • JUDITH A SERVICE •
PENNY L SERVIES • KAREN D SERVISS •
MATTHEW R SERVISS • GLYNN M SERVY •
PAMELA SERY • SAHID A SESAY • EMMA W SES-
SION • TANA M SESSION-THOMPSON •
MATTHEW C SESSIONS • LEE S SESSOMS • SAN-
DRA R SESSOMS • STELLA A SESSUM • RAY E
SETA • ASHA SETHI • KAMAL K SETHI • MADHAVI
B SETHNA • CRAIG K SETO • SCOTT S SETO •
CHRISTOPHER M SETTEL • APRIL M SETTLE •
DENISE E SETTLE • DONNA C SETTLES • MA-
HESH A SETTY • ADRIANNE L SETZER •
MATTHEW SEVEL • ANTHONY D SEVER • DEAN M
SEVER • F DOUG SEVERANCE • LINDA L SEVERO
• BARRY SEVERSON • MICHAEL SEVIGNY • DU-
ANE C SEVILLIAN • MARIE C SEVIN • CAROLE M
SEWARD • DARRELL L SEWARD • JOELLYN M SE-
WARD • MELISA L SEWARD • MICHEAL S SE-
WARD • CATHY A SEWELL • CLARISSA A SEWELL
• DAVID SEWELL • FRANCES B SEWELL • KAR-
LETTA D SEWELL • PATRICIA O SEWELL •
ROBERT A SEWELL • SHELLEY E SEWELL •
DEMETRA SEWELL-STANFORD • ALBERT C
SEWELL III • EILEEN T SEXTON • LEAH M SEX-
TON • ROBERT B SEXTON • SUSAN T SEXTON •
SUZANNE SEXTON • WILLIAM H SEXTON •
FARAH SEYED • AMY SEYMOUR • ANNE K SEY-
MOUR • GEORGE F SEYMOUR • GUY O SEYMOUR
• JOHN E SEYMOUR • ROBERT W SEYMOUR •
RONALD J SEYMOUR PT • MARIA D SFERRAZZA •
EDWARD M SFIDA • ROCCO A SGRIGNOLI • LISA
M SHABALA • GWENDOLYN SHACK THOMAS •
ALAN SHACKELFORD • ELIZABETH V SHACK-
ELFORD • LANA L SHACKELFORD • LISA A
SHACKELFORD • LOUISE S SHACKELFORD •
MARIE SHACKELFORD • PETER SHACKELFORD
• SANDRA K SHACKELFORD • YVONNE M SHACK-
ELFORD • MARTHA SHACKLEFORD • WILLIAM M
SHADDEN • BERTHA T SHADE • LYN C SHADE •
JEAN SHADOMY • KATHERINE L SHADRICK •
JOHN R SHAF • DANIEL R SHAFER • JOSEPH E
SHAFER • RANDALL L SHAFER • ROBERT P
SHAFER • STEVEN R SHAFF • CAROLINE W

SHAFFER • DIAN SHAFFER • DOROTHY B SHAF-
FER • DOUGLAS J SHAFFER • FREIDA SHAFFER •
JAMES M SHAFFER • JANECE A SHAFFER • KAR-
LA L SHAFFER • KELLY N SHAFFER • KRISTAN L
SHAFFER • NANCY E SHAFFER • SCOTT S SHAF-
FER • AALIYAH Q SHAFIQ • FLORENCE B SHAFIQ
• BINDI A SHAH • DJPAK SHAH • MANISH D SHAH
• NAIMISHKU SHAH • NEETU ANIL SHAH • NINA
N SHAH • NITA SHAH • PRATHMESH S SHAH •
RAJ M SHAH • RAJESH R SHAH • REENA P SHAH
• SACHIN N SHAH • SEEMA SHAH • SHALIN N
SHAH • SIMIT SHAH • ANDREW D SHAHAN •
JENOHN M SHAHAN • ROBERTA A SHAHDA • FA-
TIMAH A SHAHEED • NAIM G SHAHEED • CHRIS-
TINE M SHAHEEN • CYNTHIA A SHAHEEN • ADI-
LAH H SHAHID • KHURRAM SHAHZAD • NANCY J
SHAIDNAGLE • BERNICE I SHAINKER • ALI M
SHAIRI • SHANNON P SHAKKOUR • MARC J SHA-
LAM • YURIY G SHALANSKY • KAREN M SHAM-
BURG • REX A SHAMBURGER • ANDREI V
SHAMENKO • BETSY L SHAMHART • IVAN E
SHAMMAS • SANDY F SHAMROCK • GOVIND
SHANADI • KEVIN M SHANAHAN • JONATHAN
SHAND • JIM SHANDALOV • J PAT SHANE •
MELINDA A SHANE • PAUL SHANE • KENNETH D
SHANG • YANCONG SHANGGUAN • HARRIETTE L
SHANK • LARRY R SHANK • NANCY A SHANK • JY-
OTI SHANKAR • SATHY SHANKAR • MONICA N
SHANKS • JENNIFER Y SHANKWEILER • JOSEPH
E SHANLEY • CAROLYN K SHANNON • CHAR-
LOTTE D SHANNON • DAWN W SHANNON • ER-
ICKA L SHANNON • ERIN A SHANNON • GEORGE
W SHANNON • JOE S SHANNON • KEVIN M
SHANNON • LAURIE J SHANNON • MICHAEL P
SHANNON • NED B SHANNON • ROBERT L SHAN-
NON • SUSAN B SHANNON • GEORGE SHANTZEK •
ANN SHAO • YONG SHAO • DAVID L SHAPIRA • JEN-
NIFER F SHAPIRA • ANDREW B SHAPIRO • HARVEY
M SHAPIRO • JIMMY B SHAPIRO • LOUIS L
SHAPIRO • PAMELA S SHAPIRO • REBECCA R
SHAPIRO • RICK SHAPIRO • ROBERT SHAPIRO •
SANDRA H SHAPIRO • CALVIN H SHAPLEY • JU-
LIANNA SHAPPY • GAIL A SHARBER • ROBERT E
SHARBER • MUATTAZ M SHARKASI • KIM E
SHARKEY • ANISH M. SHARMA • JAYA SHARMA •
MUKUT B SHARMA • NEELU SHARMA • PRIYA D
SHARMA • PURNIMA SHARMA • RENU SHARMA •
SUCHETA SHARMA • TUSHAR SHARMA • A.
THOMAS SHARP • ALEXANDER A SHARP • AMY M
SHARP • BOB A SHARP • BRETT A SHARP • DI-
ANA M SHARP • ERIC SHARP • KAREN L SHARP •
MARCY L SHARP • MARY ANNE SHARP • PAMELA
L SHARP • PATRICIA J SHARP • REUBEN B
SHARP • SELINA A SHARP • TRICIA E SHARP •
WILLIAM T SHARP • WILLIE D SHARP • BRENDA L
SHARPE • CATRIA M SHARPE • LUCY M SHARPE •
SHERI S SHARPE • TALITHA A SHARPE •
THOMAS B SHARPE • VICKIE S SHARPE • ZAKIYA
SHARPE • MELISSA L SHARPLES • CAROLYN J
SHARPLESS • JOSEPH B SHARPLESS • RONALD
C SHARPLESS • JUDITH DURRANCE SHARRETT
• SUSAN SHARROW • SHERRILYN Y SHATTEEN •
DEBRA B SHAUGER • JOHN C SHAUGER •
KATHRYN SHAUGER • DORIS A SHAUGHNESSY •
MARY R SHAUGHNESSY • MARGARITA SHAULO-
VA • JIMMIE E SHAVER • ROSEMARY G SHAVER •
EVETT SHAVIES • TOSHIA SHAVIES • ABBY T
SHAW • ALAN M SHAW • BARRY E SHAW • BECKY
J SHAW • BETTY L SHAW • BURT W SHAW •
CATHY R SHAW • CHRISTINE M SHAW •
CHRISTOPHER H SHAW • CONNIE F SHAW •
COREY D SHAW • CYNTHIA A SHAW • DANNY
SHAW • DAVID I SHAW • DAVID L SHAW • DAVID M
SHAW • DIANE H SHAW • DONNA H SHAW • DON-
NA R SHAW • EARNESTINE G SHAW • EILEEN R
SHAW • GEORGE T SHAW • GORDON D SHAW •
JANE D SHAW • JENNY M SHAW • JOANNE M
SHAW • KENNY SHAW • KIMBERLYN D SHAW •
LA'KEABIAN D SHAW • LULA M SHAW • MAR-
GARET H SHAW • MARILYN V SHAW • MARY. J
SHAW • MERCHELLE K SHAW • RANDY P SHAW •
REDALIA SHAW • RICHARD J SHAW • STEVEN J
SHAW • YVONNE SHAW • TAREK M SHAWKY •
DUSTIN P SHAWNEGO • CATHERINE J SHAY •
HAROLD J SHAY • KIMBERLY ANN SHAY • BEVER-
LY B SHEA • COURTNEY E SHEA • DONALD P
SHEA • GREGORY F SHEA • KATHRYN J SHEA • PA-
TRICIA J SHEA • THOMAS O SHEA • DEBRA E
SHEAFFER • JOHN J SHEAFFER • LAUREN M
SHEAFFER • MICHAEL L SHEAFFER • CHRIS A
SHEAGREN • MARGARET SHEAHAN • HALLIE S
SHEALY • MELTON D SHEALY • NANCY F SHEALY •
JAY A SHEAR • ROBERT D SHEAR • BOB J SHEAR-
ER • CATHERINE E SHEARER • CURTIS J SHEAR-
ER • SCOTT R SHEARER • NESBIT B SHEAROUSE
• HELEN SHEARS • CINDY A SHEASBY • BUDDY
SHEATS • RUDOLPH SHEATS • ANNE SHECUT •
CHERYL E SHEDD • CANDACE M SHEDDEN •
CHRISTEEN K SHEEHAN • WILLIAM J SHEEHAN •
DIANE E SHEELER • KIMBERLY E SHEERIN •
ELAINE F SHEETS • JOHN R SHEETS • MICHELLE
MARIE SHEETS • STEPHANIE L SHEETS • ABIGAIL
M SHEFER • ANDREW P SHEFF • JO A SHEFF •
ANNA C SHEFFIELD • CAREY E SHEFFIELD • CARL
W SHEFFIELD • CATHY A SHEFFIELD • CHARLES
R SHEFFIELD • CORLISS R SHEFFIELD • EDNA L
SHEFFIELD • JOHN B SHEFFIELD • JOHN C
SHEFFIELD • KENNETH L SHEFFIELD • M TRACEY
SHEFFIELD • MICHAEL S SHEFFIELD • MEHDI
SHEIBANI • NAZIR A SHEIKH • ABBAS
SHEIKHZEINEDDIN • JEAN M SHEKTER • SCOTT N
SHELAR • NEILESH G SHELAT • CASSANDRA
SHELDON • GARY C SHELDON • ROBERT N SHEL-
DON • STUART H SHELDON • JEANNE M SHEL-
HIMER • JOHN B SHELL • VINCENT L SHELL •
DONALD SHELL MD • ELISABETH SHELLEN-
BERGER • HELEN J SHELLEY • LAURA L SHELLEY

GYMNASTICS—ARTISTIC
GYMNASTIQUE — ARTISTIQUE

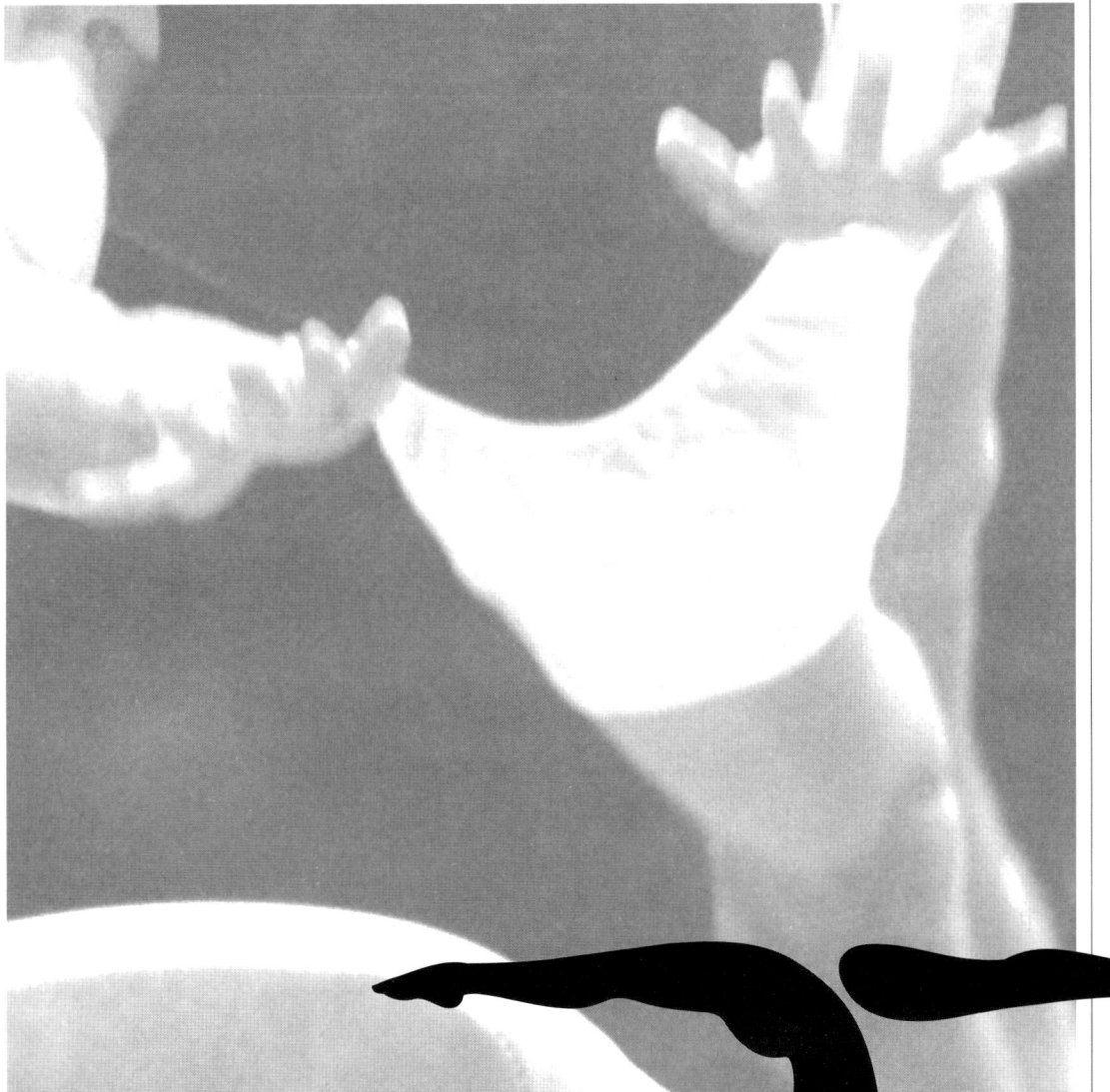

Abbreviations and terms used in Artistic Gymnastics results tables
Abréviations et termes employés dans les tableaux de résultats de gymnastique artistique

Term	English	Français
1a	First Attempt	Premier essai
1b	Second Attempt	Deuxième essai
B	Bronze Medal	Médaille de bronze
Balance Beam	Balance Beam	Poutre
Classification	Classification	Classement
Continued	Continued	Continué
Ctry	Country	Pays
Final	Final	Finale
Final Team Classification	Final Team Classification	Classement final par équipes
Floor	Floor	Sol
G	Gold Medal	Médaille d'or
H Bar	Horizontal Bar	Barre fixe
Horizontal Bar	Horizontal Bar	Barre fixe
Individual Results	Individual Results	Résultats individuels
Name	Name	Nom
P Bars	Parallel Bars	Barres parallèles
P Horse	Pommel Horse	Cheval d'arçons
Parallel Bars	Parallel Bars	Barres parralèles
Pommel Horse	Pommel Horse	Cheval d'arçons
Result	Result	Résultat
Rings	Rings	Anneaux
Rnk	Rank	Classement
S	Silver Medal	Médaille d'argent
Team Competition	Team Competition	Concours par équipes
Total	Total	Total
Uneven Bars	Uneven Bars	Barres asymétriques
Vault	Vault	Saut de cheval

International Gymnastics Federation (FIG)
Fédération Internationale de Gymnastique
**Rue des Oeches 10
Case postale 359
2740 Moutier 1
Switzerland**

CLASSIFICATION FLOOR

Rnk	Name	Ctry	Ia	Ib	Total
1	PODGORNI, Eugeni	RUS	9.737	9.812	19.549
2	SCHERBO, Vitaly	BLR	9.687	9.775	19.462
3	NEMOV, Alexei	RUS	9.700	9.750	19.450
4	MELISSANIDIS, Ioannis	GRE	9.575	9.800	19.375
5	MISUTIN, Grigory	UKR	9.625	9.737	19.362
6	LI, Xiaoshuang	CHN	9.575	9.775	19.350
7	VASILENKO, Dmitri	RUS	9.662	9.687	19.349
8	IVANOV, Ivan	BUL	9.612	9.712	19.324
8	AYMES, Thierry	FRA	9.587	9.737	19.324
10	ROETHLISBERGER, John	USA	9.587	9.725	19.312
11	YEO, Hong-Chul	KOR	9.575	9.725	19.300
12	VOROPAEV, Alexei	RUS	9.587	9.662	19.249
13	JOVTCHEV, Jordan	BUL	9.525	9.712	19.237
14	KAN, Andrei	BLR	9.525	9.700	19.225
14	TSUKAHARA, Naoya	JPN	9.600	9.625	19.225
14	SVETLICHNYI, Alexandre	UKR	9.575	9.650	19.225
14	LYNCH, Jair	USA	9.500	9.725	19.225
18	IANCULESCU, Adrian	ROM	9.537	9.687	19.224
19	JUNG, Jin-Soo	KOR	9.512	9.687	19.199
20	FAN, Hongbin	CHN	9.562	9.625	19.187
21	BELENKI, Valeri	GER	9.450	9.700	19.150
22	LEE, Joo-Hyung	KOR	9.587	9.550	19.137
23	RUDNITSKI, Vitaly	BLR	9.425	9.700	19.125
24	PAVLOVSKI, Ivan	BLR	9.562	9.562	19.124
25	NIKIFEROW, Jan-Peter	GER	9.475	9.637	19.112
26	GALLI, Roberto	ITA	9.487	9.612	19.099
27	TAYAC, Sebastien	FRA	9.500	9.587	19.087
28	GIORGADZE, Ilia	GEO	9.512	9.550	19.062
29	FEDORCHENKO, Sergei	KAZ	9.475	9.575	19.050
30	TRUSH, Dmitriy	RUS	9.500	9.512	19.012
31	CHO, Seong-Min	KOR	9.375	9.625	19.000
32	WECKER, Andreas	GER	9.600	9.375	18.975
33	HUANG, Huadong	CHN	9.487	9.475	18.962
34	MACREADY, John	USA	9.475	9.450	18.925
34	SINKEVICH, Aleksey	BLR	9.500	9.425	18.925
36	HATAKEDA, Yoshiaki	JPN	9.537	9.375	18.912

CLASSIFICATION FLOOR - *continued*

Rnk	Name	Ctry	Ia	Ib	Total
37	KURIHARA, Shigeru	JPN	9.475	9.425	18.900
38	SHARIPOV, Rustam	UKR	9.450	9.425	18.875
38	STROIA, Nicu	ROM	9.450	9.425	18.875
40	TANAKA, Hikaru	JPN	9.425	9.425	18.850
41	ZHANG, Jinjing	CHN	9.387	9.462	18.849
42	HAN, Yoon-Soo	KOR	9.425	9.400	18.825
43	LERIC, Cristian	ROM	9.275	9.525	18.800
44	SHEN, Jian	CHN	9.575	9.200	18.775
44	UCHIYAMA, Takashi	JPN	9.450	9.325	18.775
46	SHAMENKO, Vladimir	UKR	9.325	9.437	18.762
47	CHECHI, Yuri	ITA	9.275	9.450	18.725
47	DOUNEV, Krasimir	BUL	9.425	9.300	18.725
49	SARGYSIAN, Norayr	ARM	9.175	9.537	18.712
50	WILSON, Blaine	USA	9.500	9.200	18.700
50	DEMIANOV, Aleksei	CRO	9.375	9.325	18.700
50	SANDRO, Nistor	ROM	9.425	9.275	18.700
50	JORDANOV, Krisztian	HUN	9.250	9.450	18.700
54	WALTHER, Oliver	GER	9.325	9.350	18.675
54	KOROBCHINSKI, Igor	UKR	9.325	9.350	18.675
54	SATO, Toshiharu	JPN	9.500	9.175	18.675
57	BILLERBECK, Uwe	GER	9.462	9.200	18.662
58	SUPOLA, Zoltan	HUN	9.375	9.275	18.650
58	LEMOINE, Frederic	FRA	9.475	9.175	18.650
60	SIMONS, Kip	USA	9.300	9.325	18.625
61	WANNER, Erich	SUI	9.150	9.462	18.612
62	PRETI, Boris	ITA	9.400	9.200	18.600
63	CASIMIR, Patrice	FRA	9.275	9.300	18.575
64	LUNCHEV, Dimitar	BUL	9.250	9.300	18.550
64	UMPHREY, Chainey	USA	9.300	9.250	18.550
66	HRISTOZOV, Kalofer	BUL	9.300	9.225	18.525
67	LIZARDI, Diego	PUR	9.025	9.475	18.500
68	DIMITRIENKO, Alexei	KAZ	9.225	9.250	18.475
68	LUINI, Sergio	ITA	9.250	9.225	18.475
70	BARBIERI, Marcello	ITA	9.200	9.250	18.450
71	KIM, Dong-Hwa	KOR	9.425	9.000	18.425
72	NICOLAS, Frederick	FRA	9.075	9.325	18.400

CLASSIFICATION FLOOR - *continued*

Rnk	Name	Ctry	Ia	Ib	Total
72	McDERMOTT, Lee	GBR	9.350	9.050	18.400
72	NOLET, Alan	CAN	9.250	9.150	18.400
75	HUDSON, Bret	AUS	8.900	9.412	18.312
76	LI, Donghua	SUI	9.275	9.025	18.300
77	CSOLLANY, Szilveszter	HUN	9.275	9.000	18.275
78	TORDANOV, Deyan	BUL	9.075	9.175	18.250
79	ALEXANDERSSON, Runar	ISL	8.900	9.300	18.200
80	IKEDA, Richard	CAN	9.375	8.675	18.050
81	BURLEY, Kristan	CAN	9.250	8.775	18.025
82	BUCCI, Paolo	ITA	9.250	8.750	18.000
83	DOWRICK, Brennon	AUS	9.200	8.750	17.950
84	TACIULET, Robert	ROM	9.250	8.675	17.925
85	BRINDLE, Dominic	GBR	9.225	8.575	17.800
86	CARBALLO, Jesus	ESP	9.075	8.675	17.750
87	FIRT, Jiri	CZE	8.875	8.825	17.700
88	ENGELER, Michael	SUI	8.500	9.000	17.500
89	PALACIO, Marcelo	ARG	9.025	8.425	17.450
90	de FREITAS, Shane	BAR	8.600	8.675	17.275
91	McDONALD, Barry	IRL	9.000	8.200	17.200
92	SOLBERG, Flemming	NOR	8.375	8.675	17.050
93	PAE, Gil Su	PRK	9.025	7.725	16.750
94	CHARKOV, Sergei	RUS	0.000	9.662	9.662
95	FAN, Bin	CHN	0.000	9.625	9.625
96	KRUKOV, Nikolay	RUS	9.525	0.000	9.525
97	YERMAKOV, Yuri	UKR	9.475	0.000	9.475
98	KOSIAK, Oleg	UKR	0.000	9.450	9.450
99	HUANG, Liping	CHN	9.400	0.000	9.400
99	BURINCA, Dan	ROM	9.400	0.000	9.400
101	SHOSTAK, Alexander	BLR	0.000	9.375	9.375
102	POUJADE, Eric	FRA	0.000	9.350	9.350
103	DARRIGADE, Sebastien	FRA	9.300	0.000	9.300
104	OELSCH, Karsten	GER	0.000	9.275	9.275
104	URZICA, Marius	ROM	0.000	9.275	9.275
106	BELANOVSKI, Alexander	BLR	9.250	0.000	9.250
107	TOBA, Marius	GER	9.225	0.000	9.225

CLASSIFICATION POMMEL HORSE

Rnk	Name	Ctry	Ia	Ib	Total
1	FAN, Bin	CHN	9.762	9.787	19.549
1	URZICA, Marius	ROM	9.712	9.837	19.549
3	LI, Donghua	SUI	9.675	9.812	19.487
4	POUJADE, Eric	FRA	9.700	9.737	19.437
5	CASIMIR, Patrice	FRA	9.625	9.800	19.425
5	HUANG, Huadong	CHN	9.700	9.725	19.425
7	NEMOV, Alexei	RUS	9.662	9.750	19.412
8	LI, Xiaoshuang	CHN	9.700	9.700	19.400
9	HATAKEDA, Yoshiaki	JPN	9.700	9.662	19.362
10	HAN, Yoon-Soo	KOR	9.675	9.662	19.337
11	IANCULESCU, Adrian	ROM	9.575	9.725	19.300
12	SINKEVICH, Aleksey	BLR	9.625	9.625	19.250
13	PAE, Gil Su	PRK	9.462	9.775	19.237
13	KRUKOV, Nikolay	RUS	9.675	9.562	19.237
15	SHEN, Jian	CHN	9.737	9.450	19.187
16	COLOMBO, Francesco	ITA	9.475	9.637	19.112
17	ZHANG, Jinjing	CHN	9.462	9.637	19.099
18	KAN, Andrei	BLR	9.375	9.712	19.087
18	SHOSTAK, Alexander	BLR	9.425	9.662	19.087
20	SUPOLA, Zoltan	HUN	9.450	9.625	19.075
21	LEE, Joo-Hyung	KOR	9.612	9.462	19.074
22	LYNCH, Jair	USA	9.475	9.587	19.062
23	SHARIPOV, Rustam	UKR	9.450	9.562	19.012
24	TANAKA, Hikaru	JPN	9.575	9.412	18.987
25	WILSON, Blaine	USA	9.350	9.625	18.975
25	BELANOVSKI, Alexander	BLR	9.525	9.450	18.975
25	VETZEV, Vassil	BUL	9.575	9.400	18.975
28	TSUKAHARA, Naoya	JPN	9.425	9.537	18.962

CLASSIFICATION POMMEL HORSE - *continued*

Rnk	Name	Ctry	Ia	Ib	Total
29	JOVTCHEV, Jordon	BUL	9.575	9.375	18.950
29	SVETLICHNYI, Alexandre	UKR	9.650	9.300	18.950
29	SATO, Toshiharu	JPN	9.625	9.325	18.950
32	STROIA, Nicu	ROM	9.425	9.500	18.925
33	VASILENKO, Dmitri	RUS	9.375	9.512	18.887
34	HUANG, Liping	CHN	9.400	9.475	18.875
34	YERMAKOV, Yuri	UKR	9.725	9.150	18.875
36	NIKIFEROW, Jan-Peter	GER	9.175	9.662	18.837
36	TAYAC, Sebastien	FRA	9.275	9.562	18.837
36	LUINI, Sergio	ITA	9.325	9.512	18.837
39	VOROPAEV, Alexei	RUS	9.325	9.500	18.825
39	CHECHI, Yuri	ITA	9.300	9.525	18.825
39	TRUSH, Dmitriy	RUS	9.575	9.250	18.825
42	GIORGADZE, Ilia	GEO	9.487	9.325	18.812
42	LUNCHEV, Dimitar	BUL	9.325	9.487	18.812
42	KIM, Bong-Hyun	KOR	9.512	9.300	18.812
45	ROETHLISBERGER, John	USA	9.700	9.100	18.800
45	DOWRICK, Brennon	AUS	9.350	9.450	18.800
45	IKEDA, Richard	CAN	9.475	9.325	18.800
48	SHAMENKO, Vladimir	UKR	9.350	9.425	18.775
49	WALTHER, Oliver	GER	9.175	9.575	18.750
50	LERIC, Cristian	ROM	9.125	9.600	18.725
50	MACREADY, John	USA	9.350	9.375	18.725
50	HRISTOZOV, Kalofer	BUL	9.275	9.450	18.725
53	TORDANOV, Deyan	BUL	9.175	9.512	18.687
54	WECKER, Andreas	GER	9.450	9.200	18.650
54	DOUNEV, Krasimir	BUL	9.375	9.275	18.650
56	BAGIU, Mihai	USA	9.637	9.000	18.637

CLASSIFICATION POMMEL HORSE - *continued*

Rnk	Name	Ctry	Ia	Ib	Total
57	PODGORNI, Eugeni	RUS	9.275	9.350	18.625
58	SCHERBO, Vitaly	BLR	9.612	9.000	18.612
59	RUDNITSKI, Vitaly	BLR	9.150	9.450	18.600
60	CSOLLANY, Szilveszter	HUN	9.350	9.175	18.525
61	NICOLAS, Frederick	FRA	9.150	9.350	18.500
62	UMPHREY, Chainey	USA	9.225	9.250	18.475
63	KOROBCHINSKI, Igor	UKR	9.712	8.750	18.462
64	CARBALLO, Jesus	ESP	9.175	9.275	18.450
64	FEDORCHENKO, Sergei	KAZ	9.475	8.975	18.450
66	BELENKI, Valeri	GER	8.700	9.725	18.425
66	LEMOINE, Frederic	FRA	9.300	9.125	18.425
68	SOLBERG, Flemming	NOR	9.025	9.375	18.400
69	DARRIGADE, Sebastien	FRA	8.800	9.500	18.300
70	FIRT, Jiri	CZE	9.300	8.925	18.225
71	PRETI, Boris	ITA	9.000	9.200	18.200
71	DIMITRIENKO, Alexei	KAZ	9.200	9.000	18.200
73	HUDSON, Bret	AUS	9.175	8.975	18.150
74	ENGELER, Michael	SUI	9.000	9.125	18.125
75	ALEXANDERSSON, Runar	ISL	8.500	9.537	18.037
76	GALLI, Roberto	ITA	9.075	8.925	18.000
76	SARGYSIAN, Norayr	ARM	9.175	8.825	18.000
78	NOLET, Alan	CAN	9.025	8.925	17.950
78	TACIULET, Robert	ROM	8.800	9.150	17.950
80	SANDRO, Nistor	ROM	9.425	8.475	17.900
81	KURIHARA, Shigeru	JPN	9.175	8.550	17.725
82	MELISSANIDIS, Ioannis	GRE	8.800	8.900	17.700
83	UCHIYAMA, Takashi	JPN	8.800	8.775	17.575

continued on next page / suite à la page suivante

CLASSIFICATION POMMEL HORSE - *continued*

Rnk	Name	Ctry	Ia	Ib	Total
84	OELSCH, Karsten	GER	8.450	8.775	17.225
85	KIM, Dong-Hwa	KOR	8.350	8.550	16.900
86	PALACIO, Marcelo	ARG	8.625	8.250	16.875
87	McDONALD, Barry	IRL	8.475	8.300	16.775
88	BRINDLE, Dominic	GBR	7.550	9.200	16.750
89	McDERMOTT, Lee	GBR	7.450	9.175	16.625
90	CHO, Seong-Min	KOR	9.250	7.350	16.600

CLASSIFICATION POMMEL HORSE - *continued*

Rnk	Name	Ctry	Ia	Ib	Total
91	DEMIANOV, Aleksei	CRO	7.500	9.050	16.550
92	TOBA, Marius	GER	7.200	9.325	16.525
93	LIZARDI, Diego	PUR	8.350	8.125	16.475
94	WANNER, Erich	SUI	7.350	8.575	15.925
95	JORDANOV, Krisztian	HUN	6.875	8.975	15.850
96	BURLEY, Kristan	CAN	7.275	8.325	15.600

CLASSIFICATION POMMEL HORSE - *continued*

Rnk	Name	Ctry	Ia	Ib	Total
97	de FREITAS, Shane	BAR	7.325	7.950	15.275
98	BUCCI, Paolo	ITA	3.000	9.150	12.150
99	MISUTIN, Grigory	UKR	0.000	9.625	9.625
100	JUNG, Jin-Soo	KOR	9.450	0.000	9.450
101	KOSIAK, Oleg	UKR	9.375	0.000	9.375
102	YEO, Hong-Chul	KOR	0.000	8.375	8.375

CLASSIFICATION RINGS

Rnk	Name	Ctry	Ia	Ib	Total
1	CHECHI, Yuri	ITA	9.675	9.837	19.512
2	JOVTCHEV, Jordan	BUL	9.612	9.762	19.374
3	WECKER, Andreas	GER	9.575	9.775	19.350
3	TOBA, Marius	GER	9.650	9.700	19.350
5	WILSON, Blaine	USA	9.612	9.725	19.337
6	CSOLLANY, Szilveszter	HUN	9.600	9.712	19.312
7	BURINCA, Dan	ROM	9.475	9.825	19.300
8	FAN, Hongbin	CHN	9.537	9.750	19.287
9	VOROPAEV, Alexei	RUS	9.525	9.725	19.250
10	SVETLICHNYI, Alexandre	UKR	9.537	9.687	19.224
11	ROETHLISBERGER, John	USA	9.600	9.600	19.200
12	SHEN, Jian	CHN	9.500	9.662	19.162
12	CHARKOV, Sergei	RUS	9.450	9.712	19.162
14	NEMOV, Alexei	RUS	9.500	9.650	19.150
15	BELENKI, Valeri	GER	9.450	9.687	19.137
16	SHARIPOV, Rustam	UKR	9.487	9.637	19.124
17	KURIHARA, Shigeru	JPN	9.425	9.687	19.112
17	SIMONS, Kip	USA	9.462	9.650	19.112
19	BUCCI, Paolo	ITA	9.512	9.575	19.087
20	DEMIANOV, Aleksei	CRO	9.450	9.625	19.075
20	SANDRO, Nistor	ROM	9.375	9.700	19.075
22	DOUNEV, Krasimir	BUL	9.437	9.612	19.049
23	IVANOV, Ivan	BUL	9.437	9.600	19.037
24	WALTHER, Oliver	GER	9.350	9.675	19.025
25	SHAMENKO, Vladimir	UKR	9.425	9.575	19.000
25	UMPHREY, Chainey	USA	9.375	9.625	19.000
25	TRUSH, Dmitriy	RUS	9.400	9.600	19.000
28	FAN, Bin	CHN	9.425	9.562	18.987
29	VASILENKO, Dmitri	RUS	9.400	9.575	18.975
30	KAN, Andrei	BLR	9.400	9.550	18.950
30	SCHERBO, Vitaly	BLR	9.425	9.525	18.950
32	KIM, Dong-Hwa	KOR	9.225	9.712	18.937
33	RUDNITSKI, Vitaly	BLR	9.250	9.675	18.925
33	BELANOVSKI, Alexander	BLR	9.350	9.575	18.925

CLASSIFICATION RINGS - *continued*

Rnk	Name	Ctry	Ia	Ib	Total
35	ZHANG, Jinjing	CHN	9.375	9.525	18.900
35	LEE, Joo-Hyung	KOR	9.250	9.650	18.900
35	CASIMIR, Patrice	FRA	9.350	9.550	18.900
38	JUNG, Jin-Soo	KOR	9.325	9.550	18.875
39	PRETI, Boris	ITA	9.350	9.512	18.862
39	GALLI, Roberto	ITA	9.250	9.612	18.862
41	NIKIFEROW, Jan-Peter	GER	9.275	9.575	18.850
41	HRISTOZOV, Kalofer	BUL	9.325	9.525	18.850
43	PODGORNI, Eugeni	RUS	9.325	9.512	18.837
44	MACREADY, John	USA	9.325	9.487	18.812
45	PAVLOVSKI, Ivan	BLR	9.200	9.600	18.800
46	LEMOINE, Frederic	FRA	9.250	9.537	18.787
47	KOSIAK, Oleg	UKR	9.275	9.500	18.775
48	TSUKAHARA, Naoya	JPN	9.225	9.537	18.762
49	STROIA, Nicu	ROM	9.125	9.625	18.750
49	KOROBCHINSKI, Igor	UKR	9.275	9.475	18.750
49	SHOSTAK, Alexander	BLR	9.250	9.500	18.750
52	CARBALLO, Jesus	ESP	9.225	9.500	18.725
52	McDERMOTT, Lee	GBR	9.300	9.425	18.725
54	YEO, Hong-Chul	KOR	9.200	9.512	18.712
54	BARBIERI, Marcello	ITA	9.175	9.537	18.712
56	TAYAC, Sebastien	FRA	9.325	9.350	18.675
57	OELSCH, Karsten	GER	9.150	9.512	18.662
58	TANAKA, Hikaru	JPN	9.025	9.625	18.650
59	SATO, Toshiharu	JPN	9.275	9.350	18.625
60	NICOLAS, Frederick	FRA	9.200	9.375	18.575
60	TACIULET, Robert	ROM	9.150	9.425	18.575
60	COLOMBO, Francesco	ITA	9.175	9.400	18.575
60	DARRIGADE, Sebastien	FRA	9.275	9.300	18.575
64	LYNCH, Jair	USA	9.250	9.300	18.550
65	GIORGADZE, Ilia	GEO	9.325	9.200	18.525
66	SUPOLA, Zoltan	HUN	9.275	9.225	18.500
66	HUANG, Huadong	CHN	9.200	9.300	18.500
68	FIRT, Jiri	CZE	9.325	9.150	18.475

CLASSIFICATION RINGS - *continued*

Rnk	Name	Ctry	Ia	Ib	Total
69	UCHIYAMA, Takashi	JPN	9.050	9.400	18.450
69	DOWRICK, Brennon	AUS	9.300	9.150	18.450
71	HAN, Yoon-Soo	KOR	8.975	9.425	18.400
71	SARGYSIAN, Norayr	ARM	9.100	9.300	18.400
73	FEDORCHENKO, Sergei	KAZ	9.150	9.200	18.350
74	LUNCHEV, Dimitar	BUL	9.075	9.250	18.325
74	WANNER, Erich	SUI	9.075	9.250	18.325
76	HATAKEDA, Yoshiaki	JPN	8.875	9.425	18.300
76	DIMITRIENKO, Alexei	KAZ	9.175	9.125	18.300
78	HUDSON, Bret	AUS	9.075	9.200	18.275
78	AYMES, Thierry	FRA	9.150	9.125	18.275
80	IANCULESCU, Adrian	ROM	9.175	9.050	18.225
81	LI, Xiaoshuang	CHN	8.350	9.800	18.150
81	ENGELER, Michael	SUI	9.225	8.925	18.150
81	NOLET, Alan	CAN	8.900	9.250	18.150
84	BRINDLE, Dominic	GBR	9.025	9.025	18.050
85	TORDANOV, Deyan	BUL	9.200	8.800	18.000
86	LERIC, Cristian	ROM	8.950	8.950	17.900
86	MELISSANIDIS, Ioannis	GRE	9.175	8.725	17.900
88	ALEXANDERSSON, Runar	ISL	8.825	8.750	17.575
88	LIZARDI, Diego	PUR	8.250	9.325	17.575
90	PALACIO, Marcello	ARG	8.400	8.925	17.325
91	SOLBERG, Flemming	NOR	8.300	9.000	17.300
92	LI, Donghua	SUI	8.525	8.750	17.275
93	JORDANOV, Krisztian	HUN	8.575	8.250	16.825
94	de FREITAS, Shane	BAR	8.150	8.500	16.650
95	McDONALD, Barry	IRL	8.225	8.150	16.375
96	IKEDA, Richard	CAN	7.175	9.075	16.250
97	BURLEY, Kristan	CAN	8.450	7.575	16.025
98	MISUTIN, Grigory	UKR	0.000	9.700	9.700
99	YERMAKOV, Yuri	UKR	9.400	0.000	9.400
100	CHO, Seong-Min	KOR	0.000	9.375	9.375
101	KIM, Bong-Hyun	KOR	9.200	0.000	9.200
102	PAE, Gil Su	PRK	8.125	0.000	8.125

CLASSIFICATION VAULT

Rnk	Name	Ctry	Ia	Ib	Total
1	VOROPAEV, Alexei	RUS	9.750	9.700	19.450
2	NEMOV, Alexei	RUS	9.600	9.825	19.425
3	YEO, Hong-Chul	KOR	9.587	9.812	19.399
4	SCHERBO, Vitaly	BLR	9.725	9.650	19.375
5	KOROBCHINSKI, Igor	UKR	9.750	9.600	19.350
6	LI, Xiaoshuang	CHN	9.575	9.762	19.337
7	IVANOV, Ivan	BUL	9.687	9.637	19.324
8	PAVLOVSKI, Ivan	BLR	9.675	9.612	19.287
9	SHARIPOV, Rustam	UKR	9.687	9.587	19.274
10	CHARKOV, Sergei	RUS	9.625	9.637	19.262
10	VASILENKO, Dmitri	RUS	9.562	9.700	19.262
12	DOUNEV, Krasimir	BUL	9.675	9.575	19.250
12	FEDORCHENKO, Sergei	KAZ	9.675	9.575	19.250
12	HUANG, Liping	CHN	9.625	9.625	19.250
15	SHEN, Jian	CHN	9.587	9.662	19.249
15	SUPOLA, Zoltan	HUN	9.687	9.562	19.249
17	ZHANG, Jinjing	CHN	9.600	9.612	19.212
17	PODGORNI, Eugeni	RUS	9.650	9.562	19.212
17	KRUKOV, Nikolay	RUS	9.512	9.700	19.212

CLASSIFICATION VAULT - *continued*

Rnk	Name	Ctry	Ia	Ib	Total
20	WILSON, Blaine	USA	9.575	9.625	19.200
20	CHECHI, Yuri	ITA	9.600	9.600	19.200
20	JOVTCHEV, Jordon	BUL	9.625	9.575	19.200
23	TSUKAHARA, Naoya	JPN	9.637	9.537	19.174
23	LERIC, Cristian	ROM	9.562	9.612	19.174
25	WECKER, Andreas	GER	9.575	9.587	19.162
25	LYNCH, Jair	USA	9.587	9.575	19.162
27	RUDNITSKI, Vitaly	BLR	9.650	9.500	19.150
28	BELENKI, Valeri	GER	9.562	9.587	19.149
29	ROETHLISBERGER, John	USA	9.562	9.575	19.137
30	SHOSTAK, Alexander	BLR	9.650	9.475	19.125
30	MISUTIN, Grigory	UKR	9.425	9.700	19.125
32	SATO, Toshiharu	JPN	9.537	9.575	19.112
33	MELISSANIDIS, Ioannis	GRE	9.550	9.550	19.100
34	SARGYSIAN, Norayr	ARM	9.487	9.612	19.099
35	IANCULESCU, Adrian	ROM	9.550	9.537	19.087
36	LEE, Joo-Hyung	KOR	9.575	9.500	19.075
37	SVETLICHNYI, Alexandre	UKR	9.637	9.425	19.062
38	KAN, Andrei	BLR	9.500	9.537	19.037

CLASSIFICATION VAULT - *continued*

Rnk	Name	Ctry	Ia	Ib	Total
39	BUCCI, Paolo	ITA	9.512	9.512	19.024
40	TANAKA, Hikaru	JPN	9.525	9.475	19.000
40	BURLEY, Kristan	CAN	9.525	9.475	19.000
42	GALLI, Roberto	ITA	9.550	9.400	18.950
42	LUNCHEV, Dimitar	BUL	9.550	9.400	18.950
42	CHO, Seong-Min	KOR	9.525	9.425	18.950
42	SIMONS, Kip	USA	9.525	9.425	18.950
46	CASIMIR, Patrice	FRA	9.562	9.375	18.937
46	BILLERBECK, Uwe	GER	9.537	9.400	18.937
48	NIKIFEROW, Jan-Peter	GER	9.462	9.450	18.912
49	SHAMENKO, Vladimir	UKR	9.587	9.300	18.887
50	PRETI, Boris	ITA	9.600	9.275	18.875
51	LIZARDI, Diego	PUR	9.562	9.275	18.837
51	POUJADE, Eric	FRA	9.587	9.250	18.837
53	HATAKEDA, Yoshiaki	JPN	9.475	9.350	18.825
53	TORDANOV, Deyan	BUL	9.525	9.300	18.825
55	TAYAC, Sebastien	FRA	9.425	9.375	18.800
55	HUDSON, Bret	AUS	9.525	9.275	18.800

continued on next page / suite à la page suivante

CLASSIFICATION VAULT - *continued*

Rnk	Name	Ctry	Ia	Ib	Total
55	TACIULET, Robert	ROM	9.275	9.525	18.800
58	KURIHARA, Shigeru	JPN	9.525	9.250	18.775
59	STROIA, Nicu	ROM	9.512	9.200	18.712
60	WALTHER, Oliver	GER	9.525	9.175	18.700
60	LUINI, Sergio	ITA	9.450	9.250	18.700
62	BELANOVSKI, Alexander	BLR	9.587	9.100	18.687
63	FAN, Bin	CHN	9.575	9.100	18.675
63	HAN, Yoon-Soo	KOR	9.350	9.325	18.675
63	DEMIANOV, Aleksei	CRO	9.425	9.250	18.675
63	HRISTOZOV, Kalofer	BUL	9.450	9.225	18.675
63	FIRT, Jiri	CZE	9.425	9.250	18.675
63	CSOLLANY, Szilveszter	HUN	9.525	9.150	18.675
69	CARBALLO, Jesus	ESP	9.462	9.200	18.662
69	ENGELER, Michael	SUI	9.537	9.125	18.662
69	WANNER, Erich	SUI	9.512	9.150	18.662
72	SANDRO, Nistor	ROM	9.350	9.300	18.650
72	de FREITAS, Shane	BAR	9.375	9.275	18.650

CLASSIFICATION VAULT - *continued*

Rnk	Name	Ctry	Ia	Ib	Total
74	BARBIERI, Marcello	ITA	9.475	9.125	18.600
75	OELSCH, Karsten	GER	9.537	9.050	18.587
76	NICOLAS, Frederick	FRA	9.400	9.175	18.575
76	MACREADY, John	USA	9.425	9.150	18.575
76	McDERMOTT, Lee	GBR	9.325	9.250	18.575
76	NOLET, Alan	CAN	9.350	9.225	18.575
76	AYMES, Thierry	FRA	9.400	9.175	18.575
81	GIORGADZE, Ilia	GEO	9.075	9.400	18.475
82	BRINDLE, Dominic	GBR	9.375	9.075	18.450
83	LI, Donghua	SUI	9.475	8.950	18.425
84	JORDANOV, Krisztian	HUN	9.662	8.675	18.337
85	SOLBERG, Flemming	NOR	9.250	9.025	18.275
86	KIM, Dong-Hwa	KOR	9.250	9.000	18.250
87	DIMITRIENKO, Alexei	KAZ	9.125	9.100	18.225
87	KOSIAK, Oleg	UKR	8.650	9.575	18.225
89	ALEXANDERSSON, Runar	ISL	9.275	8.925	18.200

CLASSIFICATION VAULT - *continued*

Rnk	Name	Ctry	Ia	Ib	Total
90	UCHIYAMA, Takashi	JPN	9.450	8.725	18.175
90	IKEDA, Richard	CAN	9.275	8.900	18.175
92	DOWRICK, Brennon	AUS	9.350	8.800	18.150
93	PAE, Gil Su	PRK	9.100	8.900	18.000
94	PALACIO, Marcelo	ARG	8.825	9.050	17.875
95	McDONALD, Barry	IRL	9.250	8.600	17.850
96	FAN, Hongbin	CHN	0.000	9.650	9.650
97	BAGIU, Mihai	USA	9.587	0.000	9.587
98	HUANG, Huadong	CHN	9.537	0.000	9.537
99	DARRIGADE, Sebastien	FRA	9.450	0.000	9.450
99	KIM, Bong-Hyun	KOR	9.450	0.000	9.450
101	JUNG, Jin-Soo	KOR	0.000	9.400	9.400
102	URZICA, Marius	ROM	9.375	0.000	9.375
103	UMPHREY, Chainey	USA	0.000	9.300	9.300
104	LEMOINE, Frederic	FRA	0.000	9.200	9.200
104	BURINCA, Dan	ROM	0.000	9.200	9.200

CLASSIFICATION PARALLEL BARS

Rnk	Name	Ctry	Ia	Ib	Total
1	NEMOV, Alexei	RUS	9.650	9.737	19.387
1	HUANG, Liping	CHN	9.650	9.737	19.387
3	LYNCH, Jair	USA	9.650	9.725	19.375
4	SCHERBO, Vitaly	BLR	9.687	9.687	19.374
5	CHARKOV, Sergei	RUS	9.637	9.675	19.312
6	ZHANG, Jinjing	CHN	9.587	9.712	19.299
7	LI, Xiaoshuang	CHN	9.637	9.625	19.262
8	KRUKOV, Nikolay	RUS	9.562	9.675	19.237
9	SHARIPOV, Rustam	UKR	9.575	9.625	19.200
9	SHEN, Jian	CHN	9.475	9.725	19.200
11	LEE, Joo-Hyung	KOR	9.575	9.587	19.162
11	JUNG, Jin-Soo	KOR	9.500	9.662	19.162
13	ROETHLISBERGER, John	USA	9.575	9.575	19.150
13	HATAKEDA, Yoshiaki	JPN	9.500	9.650	19.150
15	KAN, Andrei	BLR	9.625	9.512	19.137
15	KOROBCHINSKI, Igor	UKR	9.500	9.637	19.137
17	TANAKA, Hikaru	JPN	9.400	9.650	19.050
17	URZICA, Marius	ROM	9.500	9.550	19.050
19	TSUKAHARA, Naoya	JPN	9.450	9.587	19.037
20	SHAMENKO, Vladimir	UKR	9.550	9.475	19.025
20	DARRIGADE, Sebastien	FRA	9.500	9.525	19.025
22	FAN, Bin	CHN	9.350	9.662	19.012
22	YERMAKOV, Yuri	UKR	9.500	9.512	19.012
24	VOROPAEV, Alexi	RUS	9.475	9.525	19.000
24	HAN, Yoon-Soo	KOR	9.475	9.525	19.000
26	PRETI, Boris	ITA	9.425	9.537	18.962
27	WECKER, Andreas	GER	9.500	9.450	18.950
27	VASILENKO, Dmitri	RUS	9.350	9.600	18.950
29	JOVTCHEV, Jordon	BUL	9.525	9.400	18.925
29	WILSON, Blaine	USA	9.500	9.425	18.925
29	DOUNEV, Krasimir	BUL	9.450	9.475	18.925
29	SVETLICHNYI, Alexandre	UKR	9.400	9.525	18.925
33	HUANG, Huadong	CHN	9.400	9.512	18.912
34	BELENKI, Valeri	GER	9.612	9.250	18.862
35	SATO, Toshiharu	JPN	9.300	9.550	18.850
35	IVANOV, Ivan	BUL	9.425	9.425	18.850

CLASSIFICATION PARALLEL BARS - *continued*

Rnk	Name	Ctry	Ia	Ib	Total
35	SHOSTAK, Alexander	BLR	9.375	9.475	18.850
35	BILLERBECK, Uwe	GER	9.375	9.475	18.850
39	SIMONS, Kip	USA	9.300	9.537	18.837
40	CARBALLO, Jesus	ESP	9.250	9.550	18.800
40	POUJADE, Eric	FRA	9.400	9.400	18.800
42	BELANOVSKI, Alexander	BLR	9.350	9.425	18.775
43	SUPOLA, Zoltan	HUN	9.475	9.275	18.750
44	LERIC, Cristian	ROM	9.125	9.537	18.662
45	BUCCI, Paolo	ITA	9.300	9.350	18.650
46	CASIMIR, Patrice	FRA	9.575	9.050	18.625
46	RUDNITSKI, Vitaly	BLR	9.350	9.275	18.625
46	ENGELER, Michael	SUI	9.375	9.250	18.625
49	GALLI, Roberto	ITA	9.400	9.200	18.600
50	TAYAC, Sebastien	FRA	9.175	9.400	18.575
50	DIMITRIENKO, Alexei	KAZ	9.450	9.125	18.575
50	LUINI, Sergio	ITA	9.175	9.400	18.575
53	IANCLUESCU, Adrian	ROM	9.350	9.200	18.550
53	NICOLAS, Frederick	FRA	9.175	9.375	18.550
55	HUDSON, Bret	AUS	9.225	9.275	18.500
56	DOWRICK, Brennon	AUS	9.325	9.150	18.475
57	WALTHER, Oliver	GER	9.200	9.250	18.450
57	GIORGADZE, Ilia	GEO	9.150	9.300	18.450
57	KOSIAK, Oleg	UKR	9.050	9.400	18.450
60	DEMIANOV, Aleksei	CRO	8.975	9.462	18.437
61	STROIA, Nicu	ROM	9.175	9.225	18.400
61	KURIHARA, Shigeru	JPN	9.150	9.250	18.400
61	YEO, Hong-Chul	KOR	9.225	9.175	18.400
64	NIKIFEROW, Jan-Peter	GER	9.050	9.325	18.375
64	LUNCHEV, Dimitar	BUL	9.375	9.000	18.375
64	McDERMOTT, Lee	GBR	9.350	9.025	18.375
64	BURLEY, Kristan	CAN	9.200	9.175	18.375
68	FEDORCHENKO, Sergei	KAZ	9.300	9.050	18.350
68	TORDANOV, Deyan	BUL	9.350	9.000	18.350
68	LI, Donghua	SUI	9.400	8.950	18.350
68	JORDANOV, Krisztian	HUN	8.950	9.400	18.350

CLASSIFICATION PARALLEL BARS - *continued*

Rnk	Name	Ctry	Ia	Ib	Total
72	UCHIYAMA, Takashi	JPN	8.875	9.450	18.325
73	MACREADY, John	USA	9.450	8.850	18.300
73	HRISTOZOV, Kalofer	BUL	9.000	9.300	18.300
75	MELISSANIDIS, Ioannis	GRE	9.050	9.200	18.250
76	CHO, Seong-Min	KOR	9.275	8.875	18.150
77	BRINDLE, Dominic	GBR	9.275	8.825	18.100
78	CSOLLANY, Szilveszter	HUN	9.150	8.850	18.000
79	SANDRO, Nistor	ROM	9.350	8.575	17.925
80	NOLET, Alan	CAN	9.350	8.525	17.875
80	BARBIERI, Marcello	ITA	8.650	9.225	17.875
82	McDONALD, Barry	IRL	8.725	8.950	17.675
83	FIRT, Jiri	CZE	8.450	9.100	17.550
83	OELSCH, Karsten	GER	9.425	8.125	17.550
85	de FREITAS, Shane	BAR	8.800	8.725	17.525
86	SARGYSIAN, Norayr	ARM	8.975	8.475	17.450
87	CHECHI, Yuri	ITA	7.800	9.637	17.437
88	SOLBERG, Flemming	NOR	9.025	8.350	17.375
89	WANNER, Erich	SUI	9.275	8.075	17.350
90	PALACIO, Marcelo	ARG	8.775	8.325	17.100
91	IKEDA, Richard	CAN	9.300	7.775	17.075
92	ALEXANDERSSON, Runar	ISL	7.800	8.300	16.100
93	LIZARDI, Diego	PUR	8.350	7.500	15.850
94	PAE, Gil Su	PRK	5.450	8.875	14.325
95	TRUSH, Dmitriy	RUS	9.637	0.000	9.637
96	SINKEVICH, Aleksey	BLR	0.000	9.625	9.625
97	AYMES, Thierry	FRA	0.000	9.537	9.537
98	KIM, Dong-Hwa	KOR	9.400	0.000	9.400
99	BURINCA, Dan	ROM	9.375	0.000	9.375
100	KIM, Bong-Hyun	KOR	0.000	9.350	9.350
101	TACIULET, Robert	ROM	0.000	9.325	9.325
102	BAGIU, Mihai	USA	0.000	9.300	9.300
103	PODGORNI, Eugeni	RUS	0.000	9.225	9.225
104	UMPHREY, Chainey	USA	9.200	0.000	9.200
105	LEMOINE, Frederic	FRA	8.500	0.000	8.500
106	PAVLOVSKI, Ivan	BLR	0.000	8.025	8.025

CLASSIFICATION HORIZONTAL BAR

Rnk	Name	Ctry	Ia	Ib	Total
1	NEMOV, Alexei	RUS	9.750	9.787	19.537
2	SCHERBO, Vitaly	BLR	9.687	9.750	19.437
3	WECKER, Andreas	GER	9.600	9.787	19.387
4	FAN, Bin	CHN	9.650	9.725	19.375
5	CARBALLO, Jesus	ESP	9.612	9.762	19.374
6	VOROPAEV, Alexei	RUS	9.612	9.750	19.362
7	LEE, Joo-Hyung	KOR	9.612	9.687	19.299

CLASSIFICATION HORIZONTAL BAR - *continued*

Rnk	Name	Ctry	Ia	Ib	Total
7	DOUNEV, Krasimir	BUL	9.587	9.712	19.299
9	LI, Xiaoshuang	CHN	9.550	9.737	19.287
9	ROETHLISBERGER, John	USA	9.500	9.787	19.287
11	SUPOLA, Zoltan	HUN	9.587	9.687	19.274
12	HAN, Yoon-Soo	KOR	9.637	9.625	19.262
12	PRETI, Boris	ITA	9.587	9.675	19.262
14	CHARKOV, Sergei	RUS	9.600	9.650	19.250

CLASSIFICATION HORIZONTAL BAR - *continued*

Rnk	Name	Ctry	Ia	Ib	Total
15	ZHANG, Jinjing	CHN	9.475	9.762	19.237
16	STROIA, Nicu	ROM	9.550	9.662	19.212
16	JOVTCHEV, Jordon	BUL	9.512	9.700	19.212
18	WILSON, Blaine	USA	9.475	9.725	19.200
19	BELENKI, Valeri	GER	9.612	9.575	19.187
20	OELSCH, Karsten	GER	9.575	9.587	19.162

continued on next page / suite à la page suivante

CLASSIFICATION HORIZONTAL BAR - *continued*

Rnk	Name	Ctry	Ia	Ib	Total
21	LUNCHEV, Dimitar	BUL	9.475	9.675	19.150
22	KRUKOV, Nikolay	RUS	9.600	9.525	19.125
23	NIKIFEROW, Jan-Peter	GER	9.525	9.587	19.112
23	TANAKA, Hikaru	JPN	9.587	9.525	19.112
23	TAYAC, Sebastien	FRA	9.400	9.712	19.112
26	KOROBCHINSKI, Igor	UKR	9.487	9.612	19.099
27	SHAMENKO, Vladimir	UKR	9.500	9.537	19.037
27	MACREADY, John	USA	9.500	9.537	19.037
29	JUNG, Jin-Soo	KOR	9.500	9.500	19.000
30	TSUKAHARA, Naoya	JPN	9.450	9.537	18.987
31	PODGORNI, Eugeni	RUS	9.450	9.525	18.975
31	KOSIAK, Oleg	UKR	9.375	9.600	18.975
31	TRUSH, Dmitriy	RUS	9.450	9.525	18.975
34	WALTHER, Oliver	GER	9.425	9.537	18.962
34	CASIMIR, Patrice	FRA	9.537	9.425	18.962
36	LUINI, Sergio	ITA	9.400	9.550	18.950
36	BILLERBECK, Uwe	GER	9.425	9.525	18.950
38	SIMONS, Kip	USA	9.400	9.537	18.937
39	KAN, Andrei	BLR	9.525	9.400	18.925
39	LERIC, Cristian	ROM	9.250	9.675	18.925
39	HUANG, Liping	CHN	9.550	9.375	18.925
42	NICOLAS, Frederick	FRA	9.400	9.500	18.900
42	BELANOVSKI, Alexander	BLR	9.500	9.400	18.900
44	SHARIPOV, Rustam	UKR	9.350	9.537	18.887
45	DIMITRIENKO, Alexi	KAZ	9.450	9.425	18.875
46	URZICA, Marius	ROM	9.475	9.375	18.850
46	YERMAKOV, Yuri	UKR	9.475	9.375	18.850
48	GALLI, Roberto	ITA	9.350	9.475	18.825
49	SANDRO, Nistor	ROM	9.175	9.637	18.812
50	IANCULESCU, Adrian	ROM	9.350	9.400	18.750
51	BRINDLE, Dominic	GBR	9.275	9.450	18.725
51	LEMOINE, Frederic	FRA	9.400	9.325	18.725
53	DOWRICK, Brennan	AUS	9.350	9.325	18.675
54	SHEN, Jian	CHN	9.350	9.300	18.650
55	HATAKEDA, Yoshiaki	JPN	9.500	9.125	18.625
55	ENGELER, Michael	SUI	9.225	9.400	18.625
57	McDERMOTT, Lee	GBR	9.275	9.325	18.600
57	SINKEVICH, Aleksey	BLR	9.225	9.375	18.600
57	COLOMBO, Francesco	ITA	9.225	9.375	18.600
60	SATO, Toshiharu	JPN	9.400	9.175	18.575
61	SARGYSIAN, Norayr	ARM	9.300	9.250	18.550
62	KIM, Dong-Hwa	KOR	9.400	9.125	18.525
62	BURINCA, Dan	ROM	9.500	9.025	18.525
64	SVETLICHNYI, Alexandre	UKR	9.425	9.075	18.500
65	CHECHI, Yuri	ITA	9.512	8.975	18.487
66	POUJADE, Eric	FRA	9.512	8.900	18.412
67	LI, Donghua	SUI	9.225	9.150	18.375
68	BAGIU, Mihai	USA	8.550	9.787	18.337
69	UCHIYAMA, Takashi	JPN	9.325	8.975	18.300
70	TORDANOV, Deyan	BUL	9.300	8.975	18.275
71	HRISTOZOV, Kalofer	BUL	9.200	9.025	18.225
72	RUDNITSKI, Vitaly	BLR	9.400	8.800	18.200
72	HUANG, Huadong	CHN	9.200	9.000	18.200
74	NOLET, Alan	CAN	9.350	8.800	18.150
75	HUDSON, Bret	AUS	8.900	9.225	18.125
76	de FREITAS, Shane	BAR	9.100	8.900	18.000
77	FIRT, Jiri	CZE	8.425	9.462	17.887
78	GIORGADZE, Ilia	GEO	8.475	9.400	17.875
79	PAVLOVSKI, Ivan	BLR	8.750	9.100	17.850
80	JORDANOV, Krisztian	HUN	8.550	9.175	17.725
81	MELISSANIDIS, Ioannis	GRE	8.825	8.825	17.650
82	KURIHARA, Shigeru	JPN	8.400	9.200	17.600
83	WANNER, Erich	SUI	9.050	8.525	17.575
84	SOLBERG, Flemming	NOR	8.075	9.425	17.500
85	CSOLLANY, Szilveszter	HUN	9.175	8.250	17.425
86	PALACIO, Marcelo	ARG	8.750	8.650	17.400
87	DEMIANOV, Aleksei	CRO	7.975	9.350	17.325
88	BURLEY, Kristan	CAN	9.300	7.975	17.275
89	LIZARDI, Diego	PUR	8.675	8.500	17.175
90	KIM, Bong-Hyun	KOR	7.825	9.300	17.125
91	IKEDA, Richard	CAN	9.575	7.475	17.050
92	FEDORCHENKO, Sergei	KAZ	7.675	9.350	17.025
93	McDONALD, Barry	IRL	8.200	8.775	16.975
94	PAE, Gil Su	PRK	7.675	8.625	16.300
95	ALEXANDERSSON, Runar	ISL	7.025	9.200	16.225
96	AYMES, Thierry	FRA	0.000	9.650	9.650
97	CHO, Seong-Min	KOR	0.000	9.612	9.612
97	IVANOV, Ivan	BUL	0.000	9.612	9.612
99	UMPHREY, Chainey	USA	0.000	9.587	9.587
100	DARRIGADE, Sebastien	FRA	9.512	0.000	9.512
101	BUCCI, Paolo	ITA	0.000	9.487	9.487
102	YEO, Hong-Chul	KOR	9.300	0.000	9.300
103	VETZEV, Vassil	BUL	9.225	0.000	9.225
104	LYNCH, Jair	USA	9.200	0.000	9.200
105	BARBIERI, Marcello	ITA	9.150	0.000	9.150

TEAM COMPETITION - INDIVIDUAL RESULTS

Rnk	Name	Ctry	Floor	P Horse	Rings	Vault	P Bars	H Bar	Total
1	NEMOV, Alexei	RUS	19.450	19.412	19.150	19.425	19.387	19.537	116.361
2	SCHERBO, Vitaly	BLR	19.462	18.612	18.950	19.375	19.374	19.437	115.210
3	VOROPAEV, Alexei	RUS	19.249	18.825	19.250	19.450	19.000	19.362	115.136
4	JOVTCHEV, Jordon	BUL	19.237	18.950	19.374	19.200	18.925	19.212	114.898
5	ROETHLISBERGER, John	USA	19.312	18.800	19.200	19.137	19.150	19.287	114.886
6	LI, Xiaoshuang	CHN	19.350	19.400	18.150	19.337	19.262	19.287	114.786
7	LEE, Joo-Hyung	KOR	19.137	19.074	18.900	19.075	19.162	19.299	114.647
8	ZHANG, Jinjing	CHN	18.849	19.099	18.900	18.212	19.299	19.237	114.596
9	WECKER, Andreas	GER	18.975	18.650	19.350	19.162	18.950	19.387	114.474
10	SHARIPOV, Rustam	UKR	18.875	19.012	19.124	19.274	19.200	18.887	114.372
11	KAN, Andrei	BLR	19.225	19.087	18.950	19.037	19.137	18.925	114.361
12	WILSON, Blaine	USA	18.700	18.975	19.337	19.200	18.925	19.200	114.337
13	SHEN, Jian	CHN	18.775	19.187	19.162	19.249	19.200	18.650	114.223
14	TSUKAHARA, Naoya	JPN	19.225	18.962	18.762	19.174	19.037	18.987	114.147
15	BELENKI, Valeri	GER	19.150	18.425	19.137	19.149	18.862	19.187	113.910
16	DOUNEV, Krasimir	BUL	18.725	18.650	19.049	19.250	18.925	19.299	113.898
17	SVETLICHNYI, Alexandre	UKR	19.225	18.950	19.224	19.062	18.925	18.500	113.886
18	TANAKA, Hikaru	JPN	18.850	18.987	18.650	19.000	19.050	19.112	113.649
19	HAN, Yoon-Soo	KOR	18.825	19.337	18.400	18.675	19.000	19.262	113.499
20	SUPOLA, Zoltan	HUN	18.650	19.075	18.500	19.249	18.750	19.274	113.498
21	SHAMENKO, Vladimir	UKR	18.762	18.775	19.000	18.887	19.025	19.037	113.486
22	KOROBCHINSKI, Igor	UKR	18.675	18.462	18.750	19.350	19.137	19.099	113.473
23	CASIMIR, Patrice	FRA	18.575	19.425	18.900	18.937	18.625	18.962	113.424
24	NIKIFEROW, Jan-Peter	GER	19.112	18.837	18.850	18.912	18.375	19.112	113.198
25	HATAKEDA, Yoshiaki	JPN	18.912	19.362	18.300	18.825	19.150	18.625	113.174
26	IANCULESCU, Adrian	ROM	19.224	19.300	18.225	19.087	18.550	18.750	113.136
27	TAYAC, Sebastien	FRA	19.087	18.837	18.675	18.800	18.575	19.112	113.086
28	STROIA, Nicu	ROM	18.875	18.925	18.750	18.712	18.400	19.212	112.874
29	SATO, Toshiharu	JPN	18.675	18.950	18.625	19.112	18.850	18.575	112.787
30	PRETI, Boris	ITA	18.600	18.800	18.862	18.962	18.962	19.262	112.761
31	RUDNITSKI, Vitaly	BLR	19.125	18.600	18.925	19.150	18.625	18.200	112.625
32	WALTHER, Oliver	GER	18.675	18.750	19.025	18.700	18.450	18.962	112.562
33	MACREADY, John	USA	18.925	18.725	18.812	18.575	18.300	19.037	112.374
34	GALLI, Roberto	ITA	19.099	18.000	18.862	18.950	18.600	18.825	112.336
35	CHECHI, Yuri	ITA	18.725	18.825	19.512	19.200	17.437	18.487	112.186
35	LERIC, Cristian	ROM	18.800	18.725	17.900	19.174	18.662	18.925	112.186
37	LUNCHEV, Dimitar	BUL	18.550	18.812	18.325	18.950	18.375	19.150	112.162
38	CARBALLO, Jesus	ESP	17.750	18.450	18.725	18.662	18.800	19.374	111.761
39	NICOLAS, Frederick	FRA	18.400	18.500	18.575	18.575	18.550	18.900	111.500
40	HRISTOZOV, Kalofer	BUL	18.525	18.725	18.850	18.675	18.300	18.225	111.300
41	GIORGADZE, Ilia	GEO	19.062	18.812	18.525	18.475	18.450	17.875	111.199
42	SANDRO, Nistor	ROM	18.700	17.900	19.075	18.650	17.925	18.812	111.062
43	DIMITRIENKO, Alexi	KAZ	18.475	18.200	18.300	18.225	18.575	18.875	110.650
44	KURIHARA, Shigeru	JPN	18.900	17.725	19.112	18.775	18.400	17.600	110.512
45	DOWRICK, Brennan	AUS	17.950	18.800	18.450	18.150	18.475	18.675	110.500
46	FEDORCHENKO, Sergei	KAZ	19.050	18.450	18.350	19.250	18.350	17.025	110.475
47	TORDANOV, Deyan	BUL	18.250	18.687	18.000	18.825	18.350	18.275	110.387
48	LI, Donghua	SUI	18.300	19.487	17.275	18.425	18.350	18.375	110.212
48	CSOLLANY, Szilveszter	HUN	18.275	18.525	19.312	18.675	18.000	17.425	110.212
50	SARGYSIAN, Norayr	ARM	18.712	18.000	18.400	19.099	17.450	18.550	110.211
51	HUDSON, Bret	AUS	18.312	18.150	18.275	18.800	18.500	18.125	110.162
52	MELISSANIDIS, Ioannis	GRE	19.375	17.700	17.900	19.100	18.250	17.650	109.975
53	ENGELER, Michael	SUI	17.500	18.125	18.150	18.662	18.625	18.625	109.687
54	UCHIYAMA, Takashi	JPN	18.775	17.575	18.450	18.175	18.325	18.300	109.600
55	McDERMOTT, Lee	GBR	18.400	16.625	18.725	18.575	18.375	18.600	109.300
56	NOLET, Alan	CAN	18.400	17.950	18.150	18.575	17.875	18.150	109.100
57	DEMIANOV, Aleksei	CRO	18.700	16.550	19.075	18.675	18.437	17.325	108.762
58	FIRT, Jiri	CZE	17.700	18.225	18.475	18.675	17.550	17.887	108.512
59	BRINDLE, Dominic	GBR	17.800	16.750	18.050	18.450	18.100	18.725	107.875
60	WANNER, Erich	SUI	18.612	15.925	18.325	18.662	17.350	17.575	106.449
61	SOLBERG, Flemming	NOR	17.050	18.400	17.300	18.275	17.375	17.500	105.900
62	JORDANOV, Krisztian	HUN	18.700	15.850	18.825	18.337	18.350	17.725	105.787
63	IKEDA, Richard	CAN	18.050	18.800	16.250	18.175	17.075	17.050	105.400
64	FAN, Bin	CHN	9.625	19.549	18.987	18.175	19.012	19.375	105.223
65	LYNCH, Jair	USA	19.225	19.062	18.550	19.162	19.375	9.200	104.574
66	PODGORNI, Eugeni	RUS	19.549	18.625	18.837	19.212	9.225	18.975	104.423
67	LIZARDI, Diego	PUR	18.500	16.475	17.575	18.837	15.850	17.175	104.412
68	ALEXANDERSSON, Runar	ISL	18.200	18.037	17.575	18.200	16.100	16.225	104.337
69	BURLEY, Kristan	CAN	18.025	15.600	16.025	19.000	18.375	17.275	104.300

continued on next page / suite à la page suivante

Team, Men / *Concours général par équipes, Messieurs*

TEAM COMPETITION - INDIVIDUAL RESULTS - *continued*

Rnk	Name	Ctry	Floor	P Horse	Rings	Vault	P Bars	H Bar	Total
70	PALACIO, Marcelo	ARG	17.450	16.875	17.325	17.875	17.100	17.400	104.025
71	HUANG, Huadong	CHN	18.962	19.425	18.500	9.537	18.912	18.200	103.536
72	BELANOVSKI, Alesander	BLR	9.250	18.975	18.925	18.687	18.775	18.900	103.512
73	de FREITAS, Shane	BAR	17.275	15.275	16.650	18.650	17.525	18.000	103.375
74	McDONALD, Barry	IRL	17.200	16.775	16.375	17.850	17.675	16.975	102.850
75	OELSCH, Karsten	GER	9.275	17.225	18.662	18.587	17.550	19.162	100.461
76	KIM, Dong-Hwa	KOR	18.425	16.900	18.937	18.250	9.400	18.525	100.437
77	BUCCI, Paolo	ITA	18.000	12.150	19.087	19.024	18.650	9.487	96.398
78	VASILENKO, Dmitri	RUS	19.349	18.887	18.975	19.262	18.950	0.000	95.423
79	JUNG, Jin-Soo	KOR	19.199	9.450	18.875	9.400	19.162	19.000	95.086
80	SIMONS, Kip	USA	18.625	0.000	19.112	18.950	18.837	18.937	94.461
81	LUINI, Sergio	ITA	18.475	18.837	0.000	18.700	18.575	18.950	93.537
82	YEO, Hong-Chul	KOR	19.300	8.375	18.712	19.399	18.400	9.300	93.486
83	KOSIAK, Oleg	UKR	9.450	9.375	18.775	18.225	18.450	18.975	93.250
84	PAE, Gil Su	PRK	16.750	19.237	8.125	18.000	14.325	16.300	92.737
85	LEMOINE, Frederic	FRA	18.650	18.425	18.787	9.200	8.500	18.725	92.287
86	CHO, Seong-Min	KOR	19.000	16.600	9.375	18.950	18.150	9.612	91.687
87	CHARKOV, Sergei	RUS	9.662	0.000	19.162	19.262	19.312	19.250	86.648
88	KRUKOV, Nikolay	RUS	9.525	19.237	0.000	19.212	19.237	19.125	86.336
89	IVANOV, Ivan	BUL	19.324	0.000	19.037	19.324	18.850	9.612	86.147
90	HUANG, Liping	CHN	9.400	18.875	0.000	19.250	19.387	18.925	85.837
91	TRUSH, Dmitriy	RUS	19.012	18.825	19.000	0.000	9.637	18.975	85.449
92	SHOSTAK, Alexander	BLR	9.375	19.087	18.750	19.125	18.850	0.000	85.187
93	POUJADE, Eric	FRA	9.350	19.437	0.000	18.837	18.800	18.412	84.836
94	DARRIGADE, Sebastien	FRA	9.300	18.300	18.575	9.450	19.025	9.512	84.162
95	UMPHREY, Chainey	USA	18.550	18.475	19.000	9.300	9.200	9.587	84.112
96	PAVLOVSKI, Ivan	BLR	19.124	0.000	18.800	19.287	8.025	17.850	83.086
97	BARBIERI, Marcello	ITA	18.450	0.000	18.712	18.600	17.875	9.150	82.787
98	TACIULET, Robert	ROM	17.925	17.950	18.575	18.800	9.325	0.000	82.575
99	URZICA, Marius	ROM	9.275	19.549	0.000	9.375	19.050	18.850	76.099
100	YERMAKOV, Yuri	UKR	9.475	18.875	9.400	0.000	19.012	18.850	75.612
101	BILLERBECK, Uwe	GER	18.662	0.000	0.000	18.937	18.850	18.950	75.399
102	AYMES, Thierry	FRA	19.324	0.000	18.275	18.575	9.537	9.650	75.361
103	SINKEVICH, Aleksey	BLR	18.925	19.250	0.000	9.625	18.600		66.400
104	BURINCA, Dan	ROM	9.400	0.000	19.300	9.200	9.375	18.525	65.800
105	KIM, Bong-Hyun	KOR	0.000	18.812	9.200	9.450	9.350	17.125	63.937
106	MISUTIN, Grigory	UKR	19.362	9.625	9.700	19.125	0.000	0.000	57.812
107	COLOMBO, Francesco	ITA	0.000	19.112	18.575	0.000	0.000	18.600	56.287
108	BAGIU, Mihai	USA	0.000	18.637	0.000	9.587	9.300	18.337	55.861
109	FAN, Hongbin	CHN	19.187	0.000	19.287	9.650	0.000	0.000	48.124
110	TOBA, Marius	GER	9.225	16.525	19.350	0.000	0.000	0.000	45.100
111	VETZEV, Vassil	BUL	0.000	18.975	0.000	0.000	0.000	9.225	28.200

FINAL TEAM CLASSIFICATION

Rnk	Ctry	Floor	P Horse	Rings	Vault	P Bars	H Bar	Total
1	Russian Federation	96.784	95.286	95.537	96.749	96.173	96.249	576.778 G
2	People's Republic of China	95.561	96.685	95.336	96.273	96.210	95.474	575.539 S
3	Ukraine	95.149	94.974	95.223	95.973	95.299	94.923	571.541 B
4	Belarus	95.861	95.461	94.600	96.061	95.036	94.362	571.381
5	United States of America	94.837	94.449	95.461	95.336	95.037	95.498	570.618
6	Bulgaria	94.361	94.349	94.760	95.549	93.725	94.823	567.567
7	Germany	94.649	92.437	95.712	94.935	93.862	95.810	567.405
8	Korea	95.511	92.848	94.049	94.949	94.524	95.173	567.054
9	Romania	94.274	95.074	93.925	94.523	93.587	94.874	566.257
10	Japan	94.737	94.211	93.674	94.886	94.687	93.824	566.019
11	France	94.436	94.999	93.512	93.799	94.062	94.973	565.781
12	Italy	93.399	93.199	95.035	94.774	93.099	94.636	564.142

Gymnastics—Artistic / *Gymnastique — Artistique*

Team, Women / *Concours général par équipes, Dames*

CLASSIFICATION BALANCE BEAM

Rnk	Name	Ctry	Ia	Ib	Total
1	MILLER, Shannon	USA	9.737	9.862	19.599
2	MOCEANU, Dominique	USA	9.687	9.850	19.537
3	KOCHETKOVA, Dina	RUS	9.675	9.825	19.500
3	PODKOPAYEVA, Lilia	UKR	9.700	9.800	19.500
5	GALIYEVA, Rozalia	RUS	9.600	9.862	19.462
6	CHORKINA, Svetlana	RUS	9.512	9.800	19.312
7	GOGEAN, Gina	ROM	9.437	9.825	19.262
8	MILOSOVICI, Lavinia	ROM	9.400	9.825	19.225
9	MARINESCU, Alexandra	ROM	9.600	9.600	19.200
10	TESLENKO, Olga	UKR	9.475	9.700	19.175
11	DAWES, Dominique	USA	9.425	9.725	19.150
11	MAO, Yanling	CHN	9.475	9.675	19.150
13	POLOZKOVA, Alena	BLR	9.550	9.587	19.137
14	KUZNETSOVA, Eugenia	RUS	9.400	9.712	19.112
15	STRUG, Kerri	USA	9.350	9.737	19.087
16	ZELEPOUKINA, Svetlana	UKR	9.387	9.675	19.062
16	LOAIES, Ionela	ROM	9.387	9.675	19.062
18	QIAO, Ya	CHN	9.312	9.737	19.049
19	BORDEN, Amanda	USA	9.312	9.725	19.037
20	SHEREMETA, Lioubov	UKR	9.312	9.700	19.012
21	GROSHEVA, Elena	RUS	9.550	9.437	18.987
22	MO, Huilan	CHN	9.650	9.312	18.962
23	TUGURLAN, Mirela	ROM	9.287	9.650	18.937
23	KNIJNIK, Oksana	UKR	9.350	9.587	18.937
25	BI, Wenjing	CHN	9.262	9.650	18.912
26	VITIUKOVA, Ludmila	BLR	9.462	9.412	18.874
27	BOGUINSKAIA, Svetlana	BLR	9.425	9.425	18.850
28	LIU, Xuan	CHN	9.550	9.275	18.825

CLASSIFICATION BALANCE BEAM - *continued*

Rnk	Name	Ctry	Ia	Ib	Total
29	KUI, Yuanyuan	CHN	8.925	9.875	18.800
30	MONIZ, Ruth	AUS	9.275	9.512	18.787
30	TOUSEK, Yvonne	CAN	9.212	9.575	18.787
32	PISKUN, Yelena	BLR	9.187	9.587	18.774
33	MIRGORODSKAIA, Anna	UKR	9.475	9.287	18.762
34	LIAPINA, Oksana	RUS	9.500	9.225	18.725
35	YURKINA, Olga	BLR	9.362	9.362	18.724
36	ONODI, Henrietta	HUN	9.262	9.437	18.699
37	PACHECO, Mercedes	ESP	9.262	9.375	18.637
38	PHELPS, Jaycie	USA	9.012	9.600	18.612
38	MARTIN, Monica	ESP	9.187	9.425	18.612
40	VOLLE, Emilie	FRA	9.050	9.550	18.600
41	JUAREZ, Joana	ESP	9.350	9.225	18.575
42	VARGA, Adrienn	HUN	9.162	9.412	18.574
42	SKINNER, Lisa	AUS	9.287	9.287	18.574
44	SEVERINO, Isabelle	FRA	9.037	9.500	18.537
45	AMANAR, Simona	ROM	8.687	9.800	18.487
46	TSAVDARIDOU, Vasiliki	GRE	9.375	9.100	18.475
47	MORO, Lisa	AUS	9.312	9.162	18.474
47	EXALTACION, Jennifer	CAN	9.237	9.237	18.474
49	TEZA, Elvire	FRA	8.750	9.662	18.412
50	ROCCHI, Giordana	ITA	9.212	9.187	18.399
51	NYESTE, Adrienn	HUN	9.175	9.212	18.387
52	FIRINIDOU, Kyriaki	GRE	9.000	9.350	18.350
53	OBATA, Satsuki	JPN	9.162	9.162	18.324
54	PLAZA, Diana	ESP	9.237	9.062	18.299
55	CASTRO, Veronica	ESP	9.075	9.200	18.275
56	DZYUNDZYAK, Anastasia	UZB	9.025	9.225	18.250

CLASSIFICATION BALANCE BEAM - *continued*

Rnk	Name	Ctry	Ia	Ib	Total
57	HOSHIYAMA, Naho	JPN	8.912	9.337	18.249
58	SMITH, Jennyfer	AUS	9.012	9.187	18.199
59	KARENTZOU, Virginia	GRE	8.887	9.300	18.187
60	SUGAWARA, Risa	JPN	8.762	9.400	18.162
61	CHOUSOVITINA, Oksana	UZB	9.300	8.837	18.137
62	HUGHES, Joanna	AUS	8.950	9.175	18.125
63	MOROTTI, Francesca	ITA	9.037	9.087	18.124
64	KONG, Yoon-Jin	KOR	8.825	9.275	18.100
65	MARGARITI, Constantina	GRE	9.312	8.737	18.049
66	CANQUETEAU, Cecile	FRA	8.700	9.337	18.037
67	MOLNAR, Andrea	HUN	8.787	9.237	18.024
68	BALOG, Ildiko	HUN	8.812	9.037	17.849
69	FURNON, Ludivine	FRA	8.750	9.075	17.825
70	GROSSENBACHER, Pascale	SUI	8.637	9.162	17.799
71	GELY, Laure	FRA	8.550	9.200	17.750
72	VALLE, Elisabeth	ESP	8.425	9.212	17.637
73	REEDER, Annika	GBR	8.825	8.800	17.625
74	KOZEVNIKOVA, Olga	KAZ	9.212	8.387	17.599
74	TEMPOU, Georgia	GRE	8.687	8.912	17.599
76	ZHARGANOVA, Tatiana	BLR	9.150	8.387	17.537
77	MIURA, Hanako	JPN	8.875	8.637	17.512
78	STARK, Kathleen	GER	8.887	8.600	17.487
79	HASHIGUCHI, Miho	JPN	9.000	8.475	17.475
80	SEKINE, Aya	JPN	9.012	8.425	17.437
81	TEXEIRA, Diana	POR	8.812	8.437	17.249
82	PRINCE, Ludmila	LAT	8.412	8.700	17.112
83	DIAZ, Eileen	PUR	8.687	8.412	17.099

continued on next page / suite à la page suivante

Team, Women / *Concours général par équipes, Dames*

CLASSIFICATION BALANCE BEAM - *continued*

Rnk	Name	Ctry	Ia	Ib	Total
84	KRCMAROVA, Gabriela	CZE	8.162	8.912	17.074
85	KINSKA, Klaudia	SVK	7.800	9.125	16.925
86	DESTEFANO, Ana	ARG	8.012	8.762	16.774
87	MACEACHERN, Shanyn	CAN	8.087	8.600	16.687
88	KRAUSZ, Nikolett	HUN	9.250	7.362	16.612
89	PIOCH, Yvonne	GER	8.000	8.475	16.475
90	GENTCHEVA, Veselina	BUL	8.300	7.400	15.700
91	LAWRENCE, Sonia	GBR	7.375	8.037	15.412
92	el RHOUATI, Naima	MAR	6.881	7.800	14.681
93	KANTEK, Nicole	AUS	0.000	9.400	9.400
94	PAPANIKOLAOU, Kyriaki	GRE	0.000	9.212	9.212
95	MAMOUTI, Ekaterini	GRE	8.837	0.000	8.837

CLASSIFICATION VAULT

Rnk	Name	Ctry	Ia	Ib	Total
1	AMANAR, Simona	ROM	9.800	9.875	19.675
2	GOGEAN, Gina	ROM	9.837	9.800	19.637
3	MILOSOVICI, Lavinia	ROM	9.837	9.737	19.574
4	MO, Huilan	CHN	9.737	9.800	19.537
5	STRUG, Kerri	USA	9.812	9.712	19.524
6	GALIYEVA, Rozalia	RUS	9.837	9.675	19.512
7	GROSHEVA, Elena	RUS	9.800	9.700	19.500
8	DAWES, Dominique	USA	9.725	9.762	19.487
9	BOGUINSKAIA, Svetlana	BLR	9.737	9.737	19.474
10	MILLER, Shannon	USA	9.762	9.700	19.462
11	CHOW, Amy	USA	9.700	9.712	19.412
12	JI, Liya	CHN	9.675	9.725	19.400
13	KOCHETKOVA, Dina	RUS	9.737	9.662	19.399
14	DOLGOPOLOVA, Elena	RUS	9.650	9.737	19.387
15	MARINESCU, Alexandra	ROM	9.675	9.687	19.362
16	CHORKINA, Svetlana	RUS	9.650	9.700	19.350
16	PISKUN, Yelena	BLR	9.700	9.650	19.350
18	KNIJNIK, Oksana	UKR	9.675	9.650	19.325
19	PODKOPAYEVA, Lilia	UKR	9.762	9.525	19.287
20	CHOUSOVITINA, Oksana	UZB	9.637	9.637	19.274
21	PHELPS, Jaycie	USA	9.587	9.662	19.249
22	TUGURLAN, Mirela	ROM	9.650	9.587	19.237
22	VALLE, Elisabeth	ESP	9.587	9.650	19.237
24	MIRGORODSKAIA, Anna	UKR	9.637	9.587	19.224
25	TSAVDARIDOU, Vasiliki	GRE	9.662	9.550	19.212
26	POLOZKOVA, Alena	BLR	9.637	9.562	19.199
26	TARASEVICH, Svetlana	BLR	9.562	9.637	19.199
28	ZELEPOUKINA, Svetlana	UKR	9.550	9.612	19.162
29	NYESTE, Adrienn	HUN	9.675	9.475	19.150
29	KUI, Yuanyuan	CHN	9.525	9.625	19.150
31	FURNON, Ludivine	FRA	9.537	9.600	19.137
31	SHAPARNA, Olena	UKR	9.525	9.612	19.137
33	QIAO, Ya	CHN	9.487	9.625	19.112

CLASSIFICATION VAULT - *continued*

Rnk	Name	Ctry	Ia	Ib	Total
34	KRAUSZ, Nikolett	HUN	9.525	9.575	19.100
35	LOAIES, Ionela	ROM	9.587	9.512	19.099
36	VARGA, Adrienn	HUN	9.612	9.475	19.087
36	VITIUKOVA, Ludmila	BLR	9.612	9.475	19.087
38	JUAREZ, Joana	ESP	9.525	9.550	19.075
39	MARTIN, Monica	ESP	9.450	9.600	19.050
40	ONODI, Henrietta	HUN	9.512	9.525	19.037
41	HUGHES, Joanna	AUS	9.525	9.500	19.025
42	PRINCE, Ludmila	LAT	9.475	9.537	19.012
43	MAO, Yanling	CHN	9.387	9.587	18.974
44	SEVERINO, Isabelle	FRA	9.425	9.487	18.912
45	STARK, Kathleen	GER	9.375	9.525	18.900
46	SHEREMETA, Lioubov	UKR	9.350	9.537	18.887
47	DZYUNDZYAK, Anastasia	UZB	9.400	9.475	18.875
48	MOCEANU, Dominique	USA	9.662	9.200	18.862
48	MIURA, Hanako	JPN	9.462	9.400	18.862
50	ROCCHI, Giordana	ITA	9.387	9.450	18.837
51	MOLNAR, Andrea	HUN	9.425	9.387	18.812
52	MACEACHERN, Shanyn	CAN	9.275	9.525	18.800
53	SMITH, Jennyfer	AUS	9.362	9.437	18.799
54	FIRINIDOU, Kyriaki	GRE	9.437	9.337	18.774
55	TEZA, Elvire	FRA	9.362	9.400	18.762
55	YURKINA, Olga	BLR	9.325	9.437	18.762
55	TEXEIRA, Diana	POR	9.425	9.337	18.762
58	TOUSEK, Yvonne	CAN	9.250	9.500	18.750
59	SUGAWARA, Risa	JPN	9.362	9.375	18.737
60	GENTCHEVA, Veselina	BUL	9.275	9.450	18.725
61	DESTEFANO, Ana	ARG	9.337	9.387	18.724
62	KONG, Yoon-Jin	KOR	9.375	9.337	18.712
62	KOZEVNIKOVA, Olga	KAZ	9.375	9.337	18.712
62	OVARY, Eszter	HUN	9.312	9.400	18.712
65	VOLLE, Emilie	FRA	9.287	9.387	18.674

CLASSIFICATION VAULT - *continued*

Rnk	Name	Ctry	Ia	Ib	Total
66	PLAZA, Diana	ESP	9.325	9.337	18.662
66	REEDER, Annika	GBR	9.337	9.325	18.662
68	KARENTZOU, Virginia	GRE	9.262	9.375	18.637
69	PACHECO, Mercedes	ESP	9.300	9.325	18.625
70	KANTEK, Nicole	AUS	9.212	9.412	18.624
71	MAMOUTI, Ekaterini	GRE	9.175	9.437	18.612
72	SKINNER, Lisa	AUS	9.200	9.400	18.600
73	KRCMAROVA, Gabriela	CZE	9.325	9.262	18.587
74	CANQUETEAU, Cecile	FRA	9.150	9.425	18.575
75	MARGARITI, Constantina	GRE	9.362	9.212	18.574
75	HASHIGUCHI, Miho	JPN	9.287	9.287	18.574
77	CASTRO, Veronica	ESP	9.262	9.287	18.549
78	LAWRENCE, Sonia	GBR	9.137	9.350	18.487
79	TROSCOMPT, Orelie	FRA	9.125	9.350	18.475
80	EXALTACION, Jennifer	CAN	9.200	9.262	18.462
81	el RHOUATI, Naima	MAR	9.087	9.250	18.337
82	MOROTTI, Francesca	ITA	9.225	9.087	18.312
82	OKAWA, Masumi	JPN	9.075	9.237	18.312
84	MONIZ, Ruth	AUS	8.950	9.325	18.275
85	GROSSENBACHER, Pascale	SUI	8.987	9.275	18.262
85	SEKINE, Aya	JPN	9.137	9.125	18.262
87	TEMPOU, Georgia	GRE	8.887	9.300	18.187
88	HOSHIYAMA, Naho	JPN	9.000	9.175	18.175
89	KINSKA, Klaudia	SVK	9.075	8.987	18.062
90	PIOCH, Yvonne	GER	8.600	9.325	17.925
91	DIAZ, Eileen	PUR	8.700	7.925	16.625
92	LIU, Xuan	CHN	0.000	9.650	9.650
93	KUZNETSOVA, Eugenia	RUS	0.000	9.637	9.637
94	BI, Wenjing	CHN	9.625	0.000	9.625
95	LIAPINA, Oksana	RUS	9.575	0.000	9.575
96	MORO, Lisa	AUS	0.000	9.300	9.300
97	PAZ, Gemma	ESP	0.000	0.000	0.000

CLASSIFICATION UNEVEN BARS

Rnk	Name	Ctry	Ia	Ib	Total
1	AMANAR, Simona	ROM	9.850	9.825	19.675
2	CHORKINA, Svetlana	RUS	9.812	9.850	19.662
2	PODKOPAYEVA, Lilia	UKR	9.837	9.825	19.662
4	KOCHETKOVA, Dina	RUS	9.825	9.800	19.625
5	DAWES, Dominique	USA	9.762	9.850	19.612
6	CHOW, Amy	USA	9.762	9.837	19.599
7	MILOSOVICI, Lavinia	ROM	9.850	9.737	19.587
8	BI, Wenjing	CHN	9.750	9.825	19.575
9	MILLER, Shannon	USA	9.775	9.787	19.562
9	MARINESCU, Alexandra	ROM	9.787	9.775	19.562
11	MOCEANU, Dominique	USA	9.725	9.812	19.537
12	GALIYEVA, Rozalia	RUS	9.750	9.762	19.512
13	PHELPS, Jaycie	USA	9.712	9.787	19.499
14	STRUG, Kerri	USA	9.675	9.787	19.462
15	TEZA, Elvire	FRA	9.737	9.712	19.449
16	PACHECO, Mercedes	ESP	9.750	9.687	19.437
16	TESLENKO, Olga	UKR	9.687	9.750	19.437
18	KUZNETSOVA, Eugenia	RUS	9.675	9.725	19.400
19	PISKUN, Yelena	BLR	9.812	9.575	19.387
19	SEVERINO, Isabelle	FRA	9.687	9.700	19.387
21	TSAVDARIDOU, Vasiliki	GRE	9.675	9.700	19.375
22	GOGEAN, Gina	ROM	9.737	9.625	19.362
23	TUGURLAN, Mirela	ROM	9.687	9.662	19.349

CLASSIFICATION UNEVEN BARS - *continued*

Rnk	Name	Ctry	Ia	Ib	Total
24	POLOZKOVA, Alena	BLR	9.750	9.562	19.312
25	ZELEPOUKINA, Svetlana	UKR	9.650	9.650	19.300
26	JI, Liya	CHN	9.687	9.612	19.299
27	MAO, Yanling	CHN	9.650	9.637	19.287
27	KRAUSZ, Nikolett	HUN	9.700	9.587	19.287
29	SHEREMETA, Lioubov	UKR	9.525	9.712	19.237
29	MO, Huilan	CHN	9.437	9.800	19.237
29	CHOUSOVITINA, Oksana	UZB	9.625	9.612	19.237
32	NYESTE, Adrienn	HUN	9.537	9.687	19.224
32	JUAREZ, Joana	ESP	9.712	9.512	19.224
34	MARTIN, Monica	ESP	9.650	9.550	19.200
35	MORO, Lisa	AUS	9.675	9.475	19.150
36	LOAIES, Ionela	ROM	9.537	9.612	19.149
36	TARASEVICH, Svetlana	BLR	9.662	9.487	19.149
38	MIRGORODSKAIA, Anna	UKR	9.400	9.725	19.125
38	VARGA, Adrienn	HUN	9.750	9.375	19.125
40	VOLLE, Emilie	FRA	9.612	9.500	19.112
40	FURNON, Ludivine	FRA	9.587	9.525	19.112
40	MONIZ, Ruth	AUS	9.487	9.625	19.112
43	PLAZA, Diana	ESP	9.587	9.500	19.087
44	SHAPARNA, Olena	UKR	9.612	9.462	19.074
45	VALLE, Elisabeth	ESP	9.537	9.500	19.037
46	MOROTTI, Francesca	ITA	9.550	9.475	19.025

CLASSIFICATION UNEVEN BARS - *continued*

Rnk	Name	Ctry	Ia	Ib	Total
47	GROSHEVA, Elena	RUS	9.275	9.737	19.012
48	LIU, Xuan	CHN	9.250	9.737	18.987
48	SUGAWARA, Risa	JPN	9.512	9.475	18.987
50	SKINNER, Lisa	AUS	9.550	9.412	18.962
51	GENTCHEVA, Veselina	BUL	9.412	9.500	18.912
52	DZYUNDZYAK, Anastasia	UZB	9.475	9.425	18.900
53	MOLNAR, Andrea	HUN	9.437	9.450	18.887
54	DOLGOPOLOVA, Elena	RUS	9.662	9.212	18.874
55	MACEACHERN, Shanyn	CAN	9.362	9.462	18.824
56	GELY, Laure	FRA	9.537	9.275	18.812
57	DESTEFANO, Ana	ARG	9.462	9.275	18.737
58	KARENTZOU, Virginia	GRE	9.262	9.450	18.712
59	CANQUETEAU, Cecile	FRA	9.187	9.475	18.662
59	BALOG, Ildiko	HUN	9.137	9.525	18.662
61	MARGARITI, Constantina	GRE	9.475	9.137	18.612
62	GROSSENBACHER, Pascale	SUI	9.325	9.275	18.600
62	ZHARGANOVA, Tatiana	BLR	9.675	8.925	18.600
64	BOGUINSKAIA, Svetlana	BLR	9.412	9.175	18.587
65	QIAO, Ya	CHN	9.650	8.900	18.550
66	TEXEIRA, Diana	POR	9.112	9.437	18.549
67	STARK, Kathleen	GER	9.625	8.900	18.525
68	EXALTACION, Jennifer	CAN	9.337	9.187	18.524

continued on next page / suite à la page suivante

CLASSIFICATION UNEVEN BARS - *continued*

Rnk	Name	Ctry	Ia	Ib	Total
69	YURKINA, Olga	BLR	9.475	9.012	18.487
70	KOZEVNIKOVA, Olga	KAZ	9.562	8.900	18.462
71	ROCCHI, Giordana	ITA	9.175	9.275	18.450
71	TOUSEK, Yvonne	CAN	9.450	9.000	18.450
73	DIAZ, Eileen	PUR	9.187	9.237	18.424
74	HOSHIYAMA, Naho	JPN	9.487	8.825	18.312
75	LAWRENCE, Sonia	GBR	9.475	8.812	18.287
76	HUGHES, Joanna	AUS	8.962	9.287	18.249
77	HASHIGUCHI, Miho	JPN	9.087	9.112	18.199
78	PIOCH, Yvonne	GER	9.275	8.912	18.187

CLASSIFICATION UNEVEN BARS - *continued*

Rnk	Name	Ctry	Ia	Ib	Total
79	TEMPOU, Georgia	GRE	8.775	9.400	18.175
80	PRINCE, Ludmila	LAT	9.000	9.150	18.150
81	SMITH, Jennyfer	AUS	8.687	9.462	18.149
82	OBATA, Satsuki	JPN	8.825	9.237	18.062
83	REEDER, Annika	GBR	8.818	9.212	18.030
84	KRCMAROVA, Gabriela	CZE	8.987	8.975	17.962
85	KINSKA, Klaudia	SVK	8.850	8.837	17.687
86	KONG, Yoon-Jin	KOR	9.168	8.412	17.580
87	FIRINIDOU, Kyriaki	GRE	8.725	8.750	17.475
88	el RHOUATI, Naima	MAR	8.562	8.887	17.449

CLASSIFICATION UNEVEN BARS - *continued*

Rnk	Name	Ctry	Ia	Ib	Total
89	MIURA, Hanako	JPN	8.512	8.475	16.987
90	CASTRO, Veronica	ESP	9.487	0.000	9.487
91	PAZ, Gemma	ESP	0.000	9.425	9.425
92	ONODI, Henrietta	HUN	0.000	9.412	9.412
93	PAPANIKOLAOU, Kyriaki	GRE	0.000	9.387	9.387
93	OVARY, Eszter	HUN	9.387	0.000	9.387
95	KANTEK, Nicole	AUS	0.000	9.312	9.312
96	SEKINE, Aya	JPN	0.000	8.762	8.762
97	OKAWA, Masumi	JPN	8.425	0.000	8.425
98	MAMOUTI, Ekaterini	GRE	8.050	0.000	8.050

CLASSIFICATION FLOOR

Rnk	Name	Ctry	Ia	Ib	Result
1	STRUG, Kerri	USA	9.825	9.837	19.662
2	PODKOPAYEVA, Lilia	UKR	9.850	9.762	19.612
3	AMANAR, Simona	ROM	9.712	9.887	19.599
4	MOCEANU, Dominique	USA	9.750	9.837	19.587
4	JI, Liya	CHN	9.762	9.825	19.587
6	GOGEAN, Gina	ROM	9.712	9.850	19.562
7	DAWES, Dominique	USA	9.687	9.850	19.537
8	MO, Huilan	CHN	9.750	9.775	19.525
8	GROSHEVA, Elena	RUS	9.750	9.775	19.525
10	BORDEN, Amanda	USA	9.712	9.762	19.474
11	KOCHETKOVA, Dina	RUS	9.737	9.725	19.462
12	MILOSOVICI, Lavinia	ROM	9.643	9.812	19.455
13	KUI, Yuanyuan	CHN	9.687	9.762	19.449
14	DOLGOPOLOVA, Elena	RUS	9.675	9.750	19.425
15	MARINESCU, Alexandra	ROM	9.650	9.762	19.412
15	PHELPS, Jaycie	USA	9.662	9.750	19.412
15	MIRGORODSKAIA, Anna	UKR	9.700	9.712	19.412
18	MILLER, Shannon	USA	9.787	9.618	19.405
19	FURNON, Ludivine	FRA	9.750	9.650	19.400
20	SHEREMETA, Lioubov	UKR	9.637	9.750	19.387
21	SEVERINO, Isabelle	FRA	9.650	9.687	19.337
21	LIAPINA, Oksana	RUS	9.625	9.712	19.337
23	CHORKINA, Svetlana	RUS	9.662	9.662	19.324
24	TUGURLAN, Mirela	ROM	9.600	9.712	19.312
24	BOGUINSKAIA, Svetlana	BLR	9.737	9.575	19.312
26	MAO, Yanling	CHN	9.600	9.687	19.287
27	PISKUN, Yelena	BLR	9.700	9.575	19.275
28	KNIJNIK, Oksana	UKR	9.687	9.575	19.262
29	GALIYEVA, Rozalia	RUS	9.737	9.500	19.237
30	MARTIN, Monica	ESP	9.650	9.550	19.200
31	LOAIES, Ionela	ROM	9.525	9.662	19.187
31	TSAVDARIDOU, Vasiliki	GRE	9.512	9.675	19.187
31	CANQUETEAU, Cecile	FRA	9.487	9.700	19.187

CLASSIFICATION FLOOR - *continued*

Rnk	Name	Ctry	Ia	Ib	Result
34	ZELEPOUKINA, Svetlana	UKR	9.587	9.587	19.174
34	TEZA, Elvire	FRA	9.587	9.587	19.174
34	CHOUSOVITINA, Oksana	UZB	9.612	9.562	19.174
34	KRAUSZ, Nikolett	HUN	9.587	9.587	19.174
38	VARGA, Adrienn	HUN	9.525	9.612	19.137
38	HUGHES, Joanna	AUS	9.537	9.600	19.137
40	LIU, Xuan	CHN	9.525	9.600	19.125
40	SHAPARNA, Olena	UKR	9.525	9.600	19.125
42	QIAO, Ya	CHN	9.662	9.462	19.124
42	VITIUKOVA, Ludmila	BLR	9.512	9.612	19.124
44	NYESTE, Adrienn	HUN	9.512	9.537	19.049
45	PACHECO, Mercedes	ESP	9.462	9.575	19.037
46	MORO, Lisa	AUS	9.437	9.587	19.024
47	POLOZKOVA, Alena	BLR	9.637	9.362	18.999
48	ONODI, Henrietta	HUN	9.500	9.462	18.962
49	SKINNER, Lisa	AUS	9.500	9.450	18.950
50	VOLLE, Emilie	FRA	9.412	9.537	18.949
50	DZYUNDZYAK, Anastasia	UZB	9.512	9.437	18.949
52	JUAREZ, Joana	ESP	9.737	9.200	18.937
53	PRINCE, Ludmila	LAT	9.362	9.550	18.912
54	HASHIGUCHI, Miho	JPN	9.425	9.450	18.875
55	SUGAWARA, Risa	JPN	9.362	9.512	18.874
56	TOUSEK, Yvonne	CAN	9.600	9.187	18.787
57	VALLE, Elisabeth	ESP	9.500	9.275	18.775
57	MARGARITI, Constantina	GRE	9.150	9.625	18.775
59	SMITH, Jennyfer	AUS	9.212	9.562	18.774
60	CASTRO, Veronica	ESP	9.375	9.375	18.750
61	PLAZA, Diana	ESP	9.575	9.150	18.725
61	KOZEVNIKOVA, Olga	KAZ	9.375	9.350	18.725
63	MIURA, Hanako	JPN	9.312	9.412	18.724
64	ROCCHI, Giordana	ITA	9.162	9.525	18.687
65	STARK, Kathleen	GER	9.275	9.350	18.625

CLASSIFICATION FLOOR - *continued*

Rnk	Name	Ctry	Ia	Ib	Result
65	TARASEVICH, Svetlana	BLR	9.300	9.325	18.625
67	MACEACHERN, Shanyn	CAN	9.175	9.437	18.612
68	TROSCOMPT, Orelie	FRA	9.275	9.312	18.587
69	MOROTTI, Francesca	ITA	9.237	9.337	18.574
69	HOSHIYAMA, Naho	JPN	9.337	9.237	18.574
71	DESTEFANO, Ana	ARG	9.150	9.387	18.537
72	KONG, Yoon-Jin	KOR	9.262	9.250	18.512
73	FIRINIDOU, Kyriaki	GRE	8.925	9.575	18.500
74	KARENTZOU, Virginia	GRE	8.987	9.500	18.487
74	GROSSENBACHER, Pascale	SUI	9.087	9.400	18.487
74	KRCMAROVA, Gabriela	CZE	9.050	9.437	18.487
77	KANTEK, Nicole	AUS	9.012	9.450	18.462
77	REEDER, Annika	GBR	9.462	9.000	18.462
79	OKAWA, Masumi	JPN	9.275	9.075	18.350
80	MONIZ, Ruth	AUS	9.400	8.925	18.325
81	YURKINA, Olga	BLR	9.375	8.937	18.312
82	EXALTACION, Jennifer	CAN	9.337	8.925	18.262
83	SEKINE, Aya	JPN	9.112	9.137	18.249
84	MOLNAR, Andrea	HUN	9.000	9.237	18.237
85	MAMOUTI, Ekaterini	GRE	8.737	9.425	18.162
86	TEXEIRA, Diana	POR	9.187	8.862	18.049
87	GENTCHEVA, Veselina	BUL	8.718	9.312	18.030
88	KINSKA, Klaudia	SVK	8.937	8.937	17.874
89	LAWRENCE, Sonia	GBR	9.175	8.537	17.712
90	DIAZ, Eileen	PUR	8.400	9.000	17.400
91	el RHOUATI, Naima	MAR	8.612	8.775	17.387
92	PIOCH, Yvonne	GER	8.950	8.150	17.100
93	PAPANIKOLAOU, Kyriaki	GRE	0.000	9.437	9.437
94	OVARY, Eszter	HUN	0.000	9.300	9.300
95	BALOG, Ildiko	HUN	9.175	0.000	9.175
96	TEMPOU, Georgia	GRE	8.512	0.000	8.512
97	PAZ, Gemma	ESP	0.000	0.000	0.000

TEAM COMPETITION - INDIVIDUAL RESULTS

Rnk	Name	Ctry	Vault	U Bars	Beam	Floor	Total
1	PODKOPAYEVA, Lilia	UKR	19.287	19.662	19.500	19.612	78.061
2	MILLER, Shannon	USA	19.462	19.562	19.599	19.405	78.028
3	KOCHETKOVA, Dina	RUS	19.399	19.625	19.500	19.462	77.986
4	MILOSOVICI, Lavinia	ROM	19.574	19.587	19.225	19.455	77.841
5	GOGEAN, Gina	ROM	19.637	19.362	19.262	19.562	77.823
6	DAWES, Dominique	USA	19.487	19.612	19.150	19.537	77.786
7	STRUG, Kerri	USA	19.524	19.462	19.087	19.662	77.735
8	GALIYEVA, Rozalia	RUS	19.512	19.512	19.462	19.237	77.723
9	CHORKINA, Svetlana	RUS	19.350	19.662	19.312	19.324	77.648
10	MARINESCU, Alexandra	ROM	19.362	19.562	19.200	19.412	77.536
11	MOCEANU, Dominique	USA	18.862	19.537	19.537	19.587	77.523
12	AMANAR, Simona	ROM	19.675	19.675	18.487	19.599	77.436
13	MO, Huilan	CHN	19.537	19.237	18.962	19.525	77.261
14	GROSHEVA, Elena	RUS	19.500	19.012	18.987	19.525	77.024
15	TUGURLAN, Mirela	ROM	19.237	19.349	18.937	19.312	76.835
16	PISKUN, Yelena	BLR	19.350	19.387	18.774	19.275	76.786
17	PHELPS, Jaycie	USA	19.249	19.499	18.612	19.412	76.772

TEAM COMPETITION - INDIVIDUAL RESULTS - *continued*

Rnk	Name	Ctry	Vault	U Bars	Beam	Floor	Total
18	MAO, Yanling	CHN	18.974	19.287	19.150	19.287	76.698
18	ZELEPOUKINA, Svetlana	UKR	19.162	19.300	19.062	19.174	76.698
20	POLOZKOVA, Alena	BLR	19.199	19.312	19.137	18.999	76.647
21	SHEREMETA, Lioubov	UKR	18.887	19.237	19.012	19.387	76.523
21	MIRGORODSKAIA, Anna	UKR	19.224	19.125	18.762	19.412	76.523
23	LOAIES, Ionela	ROM	19.099	19.149	19.062	19.187	76.497
24	TSAVDARIDOU, Vasiliki	GRE	19.212	19.375	18.475	19.187	76.249
25	BOGUINSKAIA, Svetlana	BLR	19.474	18.587	18.850	19.312	76.223
26	SEVERINO, Isabelle	FRA	18.912	19.387	18.537	19.337	76.173
27	MARTIN, Monica	ESP	19.050	19.200	18.612	19.200	76.062
28	VARGA, Adrienn	HUN	19.087	19.125	18.574	19.137	75.923
29	QIAO, Ya	CHN	19.112	18.550	19.049	19.124	75.835
30	CHOUSOVITINA, Oksana	UZB	19.274	19.237	18.137	19.174	75.822
31	JUAREZ, Joana	ESP	19.075	19.224	18.575	18.937	75.811
32	NYESTE, Adrienn	HUN	19.150	19.224	18.387	19.049	75.810
33	TEZA, Elvire	FRA	18.762	19.449	18.412	19.174	75.797

continued on next page / suite à la page suivante

Team, Women / *Concours général par équipes, Dames*

Rnk	Name	Ctry	Vault	U Bars	Beam	Floor	Total
34	PACHECO, Mercedes	ESP	18.625	19.437	18.637	19.037	75.736
35	FURNON, Ludivine	FRA	19.137	19.112	17.825	19.400	75.474
36	VOLLE, Emilie	FRA	18.674	19.112	18.600	18.949	75.335
37	SKINNER, Lisa	AUS	18.600	18.962	18.574	18.950	75.086
38	DZYUNDZYAK, Anastasia	UZB	18.875	18.900	18.250	18.949	74.974
39	TOUSEK, Yvonne	CAN	18.750	18.450	18.787	18.787	74.774
40	PLAZA, Diana	ESP	18.662	19.087	18.299	18.725	74.773
41	SUGAWARA, Risa	JPN	18.737	18.987	18.162	18.874	74.760
42	VALLE, Elisabeth	ESP	19.237	19.037	17.637	18.775	74.686
43	HUGHES, Joanna	AUS	19.025	18.249	18.125	19.137	74.536
44	MONIZ, Ruth	AUS	18.275	19.112	18.787	18.325	74.499
45	CANQUETEAU, Cecile	FRA	18.575	18.662	18.037	19.187	74.461
46	ROCCHI, Giordana	ITA	18.837	18.450	18.399	18.687	74.373
47	YURKINA, Olga	BLR	18.762	18.487	18.724	18.312	74.285
48	KRAUSZ, Nikolett	HUN	19.100	19.287	16.612	19.174	74.173
49	MOROTTI, Francesca	ITA	18.312	19.025	18.124	18.574	74.035
50	KARENTZOU, Virginia	GRE	18.637	18.712	18.187	18.487	74.023
51	MARGARITI, Constantina	GRE	18.574	18.612	18.049	18.775	74.010
52	MOLNAR, Andrea	HUN	18.812	18.887	18.024	18.237	73.960
53	SMITH, Jennyfer	AUS	18.799	18.149	18.199	18.774	73.921
54	EXALTACION, Jennifer	CAN	18.462	18.524	18.474	18.262	73.722
55	STARK, Kathleen	GER	18.900	18.525	17.487	18.625	73.537
56	KOZEVNIKOVA, Olga	KAZ	18.712	18.462	17.599	18.725	73.498
57	HOSHIYAMA, Naho	JPN	18.175	18.312	18.249	18.574	73.310
58	PRINCE, Ludmila	LAT	19.012	18.150	17.112	18.912	73.186
59	GROSSENBACHER, Pascale	SUI	18.262	18.600	17.799	18.487	73.148
60	HASHIGUCHI, Miho	JPN	18.574	18.199	17.475	18.875	73.123
61	FIRINIDOU, Kyriaki	GRE	17.774	17.475	18.350	18.500	73.099
62	MACEACHERN, Shanyn	CAN	18.800	18.824	16.687	18.612	72.923
63	KONG, Yoon-Jin	KOR	18.712	17.580	18.100	18.512	72.904
64	REEDER, Annika	GBR	18.662	18.030	17.625	18.462	72.779
65	DESTEFANO, Ana	ARG	18.724	18.737	16.774	18.537	72.772
66	TEXEIRA, Diana	POR	18.762	18.549	17.249	18.049	72.609
67	KRCMAROVA, Gabriela	CZE	18.587	17.962	17.074	18.487	72.110
68	MIURA, Hanako	JPN	18.862	16.987	17.512	18.724	72.085
69	GENTCHEVA, Veselina	BUL	18.725	18.912	15.700	18.030	71.367

Rnk	Name	Ctry	Vault	U Bars	Beam	Floor	Total
70	KINSKA, Klaudia	SVK	18.062	17.687	16.925	17.874	70.548
71	LAWRENCE, Sonia	GBR	18.487	18.287	15.412	17.712	69.898
72	PIOCH, Yvonne	GER	17.925	18.187	16.475	17.100	69.687
73	DIAZ, Eileen	PUR	16.625	18.424	17.099	17.400	69.548
74	el RHOUATI, Naima	MAR	18.337	17.449	14.681	17.387	67.854
75	LIU, Xuan	CHN	9.650	18.987	18.825	19.125	66.587
76	ONODI, Henrietta	HUN	19.037	9.412	18.699	18.962	66.110
77	MORO, Lisa	AUS	9.300	19.150	18.474	19.024	65.948
78	CASTRO, Veronica	ESP	18.549	9.487	18.275	18.750	65.061
79	SEKINE, Aya	JPN	18.262	8.762	17.437	18.249	62.710
80	TEMPOU, Georgia	GRE	18.187	18.175	17.599	8.512	62.473
81	JI, Liya	CHN	19.400	19.299	0.000	19.587	58.286
82	DOLGOPOLOVA, Elena	RUS	19.387	18.874	0.000	19.425	57.686
83	KNIJNIK, Oksana	UKR	19.325	0.000	18.937	19.262	57.524
84	KUI, Yuanyuan	CHN	19.150	0.000	18.800	19.449	57.399
85	SHAPARNA, Olena	UKR	19.137	19.074	0.000	19.125	57.336
86	VITIUKOVA, Ludmila	BLR	19.087	0.000	18.874	19.124	57.085
87	TARASEVICH, Svetlana	BLR	19.199	19.149	0.000	18.625	56.973
88	KANTEK, Nicole	AUS	18.624	9.312	9.400	18.462	55.798
89	MAMOUTI, Ekaterini	GRE	18.612	8.050	8.837	18.162	53.661
90	KUZNETSOVA, Eugenia	RUS	9.637	19.400	19.112	0.000	48.149
91	BI, Wenjing	CHN	9.625	19.575	18.912	0.000	48.112
92	LIAPINA, Oksana	RUS	9.575	0.000	18.725	19.337	47.637
93	BALOG, Ildiko	HUN	0.000	18.662	17.849	9.175	45.686
94	OKAWA, Masumi	JPN	18.312	8.425	0.000	18.350	45.087
95	CHOW, Amy	USA	19.412	19.599	0.000	0.000	39.011
96	TESLENKO, Olga	UKR	0.000	19.437	19.175	0.000	38.612
97	BORDEN, Amanda	USA	0.000	0.000	19.037	19.474	38.511
98	OVARY, Eszter	HUN	18.712	9.387	0.000	9.300	37.399
99	TROSCOMPT, Orelie	FRA	18.475	0.000	0.000	18.587	37.062
100	GELY, Laure	FRA	0.000	18.812	17.750	0.000	36.562
101	OBATA, Satsuki	JPN	0.000	18.062	18.324	0.000	36.386
102	ZHARGOANOVA, Tatiana	BLR	0.000	18.600	17.537	0.000	36.137
103	PAPANIKOLAOU, Kyriaki	GRE	0.000	9.387	9.212	9.437	28.036
104	PAZ, Gemma	ESP	0.000	9.425	0.000	0.000	9.425

FINAL TEAM CLASSIFICATION

Rnk	Ctry	Vault	U Bars	Beam	Floor	Total	
1	United States of America	97.209	97.809	96.410	97.797	389.225	G
2	Russian Federation	97.148	97.598	96.473	97.185	388.404	S
3	Romania	97.485	97.535	95.886	97.340	388.246	B
4	People's Republic of China	96.474	96.785	95.498	97.110	385.867	
5	Ukraine	96.147	96.973	95.849	96.872	385.841	
6	Belarus	96.309	95.185	94.359	95.410	381.263	

FINAL TEAM CLASSIFICATION - *continued*

Rnk	Ctry	Vault	U Bars	Beam	Floor	Total
7	Spain	94.649	95.985	92.548	94.899	378.081
8	France	94.060	96.072	91.536	96.047	377.715
9	Hungary	95.199	95.472	91.996	94.797	377.464
10	Australia	93.648	94.385	92.647	94.735	375.415
11	Greece	93.897	92.986	91.285	93.123	371.291
12	Japan	92.797	90.834	89.972	93.459	367.062

Gymnastics—Artistic / *Gymnastique — Artistique*

Individual All-Around, Men / *Concours général individuel, Messieurs*

FINAL

Rnk	Name	Ctry	Floor	P Horse	Rings	Vault	P Bars	Horiz Bar	Total	
1	LI, Xiaoshuang	CHN	9.687	9.712	9.775	9.812	9.650	9.787	58.423	G
2	NEMOV, Alexei	RUS	9.700	9.800	9.612	9.700	9.762	9.800	58.374	S
3	SCHERBO, Vitaly	BLR	9.762	9.662	9.587	9.687	9.712	9.787	58.197	B
4	ZHANG, Jinjing	CHN	9.637	9.750	9.562	9.650	9.762	9.787	58.148	
5	SHEN, Jian	CHN	9.537	9.650	9.637	9.662	9.700	9.675	57.861	
6	BELENKI, Valeri	GER	9.612	9.762	9.612	9.600	9.625	9.637	57.848	
7	ROETHLISBERGER, John	USA	9.675	9.662	9.650	9.575	9.475	9.725	57.762	
8	SHARIPOV, Rustam	UKR	9.625	9.637	9.650	9.400	9.750	9.650	57.712	
9	SVETLICHNYI, Alexandre	UKR	9.650	9.587	9.662	9.537	9.625	9.637	57.698	
10	WILSON, Blaine	USA	9.600	9.637	9.737	9.600	9.450	9.662	57.686	
11	LERIC, Cristian	ROM	9.625	9.562	9.412	9.700	9.600	9.675	57.574	
12	TSUKAHARA, Naoya	JPN	9.612	9.612	9.650	9.512	9.625	9.550	57.561	
13	WECKER, Andreas	GER	9.600	9.025	9.750	9.662	9.600	9.775	57.412	
13	CARBALLO, Jesus	ESP	9.400	9.675	9.512	9.450	9.625	9.750	57.412	
15	HATAKEDA, Yoshiaki	JPN	9.425	9.637	9.487	9.350	9.612	9.700	57.211	
15	KOROBCHINSKI, Igor	UKR	9.450	9.625	9.462	9.512	9.675	9.487	57.211	
17	JOVTCHEV, Jordan	BUL	9.650	9.600	9.737	9.375	9.050	9.712	57.124	
17	CHECHI, Yuri	ITA	9.450	9.587	9.800	9.050	9.550	9.687	57.124	

FINAL - *continued*

Rnk	Name	Ctry	Floor	P Horse	Rings	Vault	P Bars	Horiz Bar	Total
19	TANAKA, Hikaru	JPN	9.562	9.450	9.637	9.425	9.550	9.375	56.999
20	LEE, Joo-Hyung	KOR	9.375	9.612	9.712	9.637	9.600	9.050	56.986
21	DOUNEV, Krasimir	BUL	9.125	9.500	9.575	9.587	9.475	9.712	56.974
22	SUPOLA, Zoltan	HUN	8.875	9.712	9.575	9.525	9.550	9.725	56.962
23	NIKIFEROW, Jan-Peter	GER	9.587	9.450	9.575	9.400	9.437	9.375	56.824
24	VOROPAEV, Alexei	RUS	9.687	8.400	9.737	9.662	9.625	9.712	56.823
25	GIORGADZE, Ilia	GEO	9.525	9.512	9.325	9.375	9.450	9.612	56.799
26	TAYAC, Sebastien	FRA	9.562	9.512	9.425	9.525	9.200	9.475	56.699
27	PRETI, Boris	ITA	9.350	9.350	9.512	9.250	9.512	9.687	56.661
28	GALLI, Roberto	ITA	9.625	8.950	9.562	9.350	9.425	9.537	56.449
29	MACREADY, John	USA	8.525	9.537	9.537	9.562	9.487	9.562	56.210
30	KAN, Andrei	BLR	9.600	9.675	9.562	9.525	8.600	9.000	55.962
30	RUDNITSKI, Vitaly	BLR	9.675	9.700	9.600	9.512	9.350	8.125	55.962
32	LUNCHEV, Dimitar	BUL	9.200	9.662	9.275	9.300	9.462	9.000	55.899
33	NICOLAS, Frederick	FRA	9.350	8.750	9.500	9.225	9.500	9.537	55.862
34	HAN, Yoon-Soo	KOR	9.300	9.737	9.512	9.300	9.612	8.375	55.836
35	DOWRICK, Brennon	AUS	9.200	9.600	9.400	0.000	9.250	9.450	46.900

Gymnastics—Artistic / *Gymnastique — Artistique*

Individual All-Around, Women / *Concours général individuel, Dames*

FINAL

Rnk	Name	Ctry	Vault	U Bar	Beam	Floor	Total	
1	PODKOPAYEVA, Lilia	UKR	9.781	9.800	9.787	9.887	39.255	G
2	GOGEAN, Gina	ROM	9.775	9.700	9.800	9.800	39.075	S
3	AMANAR, Simona	ROM	9.843	9.762	9.725	9.737	39.067	B
3	MILOSOVICI, Lavinia	ROM	9.743	9.737	9.775	9.812	39.067	B
5	MO, Huilan	CHN	9.799	9.800	9.800	9.650	39.049	
6	KOCHETKOVA, Dina	RUS	9.581	9.787	9.825	9.787	38.980	
7	GALIYEVA, Rozalia	RUS	9.681	9.762	9.825	9.637	38.905	
8	MILLER, Shannon	USA	9.724	9.750	9.862	9.475	38.811	
9	MOCEANU, Dominique	USA	9.706	9.762	9.600	9.687	38.755	
10	CHOUSOVITINA, Oksana	UZB	9.631	9.687	9.675	9.750	38.743	
11	QIAO, Ya	CHN	9.718	9.600	9.725	9.675	38.718	
12	PISKUN, Yelena	BLR	9.687	9.712	9.675	9.575	38.649	
13	SEVERINO, Isabelle	FRA	9.562	9.675	9.587	9.700	38.524	
14	BOGUINSKAIA, Svetlana	BLR	9.687	9.675	9.537	9.600	38.499	
15	CHORKINA, Svetlana	RUS	9.706	9.262	9.787	9.700	38.455	
16	TEZA, Elvire	FRA	9.493	9.687	9.687	9.587	38.454	
17	MARTIN, Monica	ESP	9.556	9.475	9.625	9.662	38.318	
17	DAWES, Dominique	USA	9.681	9.812	9.825	9.000	38.318	

FINAL - *continued*

Rnk	Name	Ctry	Vault	U Bar	Beam	Floor	Total
19	FURNON, Ludivine	FRA	9.606	9.425	9.462	9.750	38.243
19	MAO, Yanling	CHN	9.693	9.700	9.200	9.650	38.243
21	TSAVDARIDOU, Vasiliki	GRE	9.518	9.562	9.687	9.450	38.217
22	SHEREMETA, Lioubov	UKR	9.468	9.637	9.587	9.512	38.204
23	ZELEPOUKINA, Svetlana	UKR	9.512	9.650	9.325	9.537	38.024
24	JUAREZ, Joana	ESP	9.568	9.575	9.300	9.512	37.955
25	POLOZKOVA, Alena	BLR	9.587	9.162	9.450	9.600	37.799
26	TOUSEK, Yvonne	CAN	9.493	9.100	9.575	9.625	37.793
27	PACHECO, Mercedes	ESP	9.462	9.625	9.137	9.562	37.786
28	VARGA, Adrienn	HUN	9.606	9.187	9.312	9.487	37.592
29	SUGAWARA, Risa	JPN	9.412	9.475	8.950	9.562	37.399
30	NYESTE, Adrienn	HUN	9.575	9.462	8.925	9.275	37.237
31	DZYUNDZYAK, Anastasia	UZB	9.512	9.275	9.125	9.312	37.224
32	KRAUSZ, Nikolett	HUN	9.612	8.837	8.912	9.575	36.936
33	ROCCHI, Giordana	ITA	9.418	9.075	9.337	8.987	36.817
34	HUGHES, Joanna	AUS	9.456	8.350	9.162	9.600	36.568
35	MONIZ, Ruth	AUS	9.256	9.525	8.937	8.700	36.418
36	SKINNER, Lisa	AUS	9.375	9.412	8.475	8.937	36.199

Gymnastics—Artistic / *Gymnastique — Artistique*
Individual Apparatus, Men / *Par engin, Messieurs*

FLOOR - FINAL

Rnk	Name	Ctry	Result
1	MELISSANIDIS, Ioannis	GRE	9.850 **G**
2	LI, Xiaoshuang	CHN	9.837 **S**
3	NEMOV, Alexei	RUS	9.800 **B**
4	IVANOV, Ivan	BUL	9.750
4	AYMES, Thierry	FRA	9.750
6	PODGORNI, Eugeni	RUS	9.550
7	SCHERBO, Vitaly	BLR	9.275
8	MISUTIN, Grigory	UKR	9.100

POMMEL HORSE - FINAL

Rnk	Name	Ctry	Result
1	LI, Donghua	SUI	9.875 **G**
2	URZICA, Marius	ROM	9.825 **S**
3	NEMOV, Alexei	RUS	9.787 **B**
4	CASIMIR, Patrice	FRA	9.762
5	HATAKEDA, Yoshiaki	JPN	9.712
5	HUANG, Huadong	CHN	9.712
7	POUJADE, Eric	FRA	9.350
8	FAN, Bin	CHN	9.300

RINGS - FINAL

Rnk	Name	Ctry	Result
1	CHECHI, Yuri	ITA	9.887 **G**
2	CSOLLANY, Szilveszter	HUN	9.812 **S**
2	BURINCA, Dan	ROM	9.812 **S**
4	JOVTCHEV, Jordan	BUL	9.800
5	WECKER, Andreas	GER	9.762
5	FAN, Hongbin	CHN	9.762
7	TOBA, Marius	GER	9.737
7	WILSON, Blaine	USA	9.737

VAULT - FINAL

Rnk	Name	Ctry	Ia	Ib	Result
1	NEMOV, Alexei	RUS	9.762	9.812	9.787 **G**
2	YEO, Hong-Chul	KOR	9.837	9.675	9.756 **S**
3	SCHERBO, Vitaly	BLR	9.712	9.737	9.724 **B**
4	IVANOV, Ivan	BUL	9.687	9.600	9.643
4	LI, Xiaoshuang	CHN	9.500	9.787	9.643
6	VOROPAEV, Alexei	RUS	9.637	9.600	9.618
7	KOROBCHINSKI, Igor	UKR	9.637	9.500	9.568
8	PAVLOVSKI, Ivan	BLR	9.612	9.375	9.493

PARALLEL BARS - FINAL

Rnk	Name	Ctry	Result
1	SHARIPOV, Rustam	UKR	9.837 **G**
2	LYNCH, Jair	USA	9.825 **S**
3	SCHERBO, Vitaly	BLR	9.800 **B**
4	ZHANG, Jinjing	CHN	9.750
4	NEMOV, Alexei	RUS	9.750
6	HUANG, Liping	CHN	9.737
7	LEE, Joo-Hyung	KOR	9.687
8	CHARKOV, Sergei	RUS	9.650

HORIZONTAL BAR - FINAL

Rnk	Name	Ctry	Result
1	WECKER, Andreas	GER	9.850 **G**
2	DOUNEV, Krasimir	BUL	9.825 **S**
3	SCHERBO, Vitaly	BLR	9.800 **B**
3	FAN, Bin	CHN	9.800 **B**
3	NEMOV, Alexei	RUS	9.800 **B**
6	VOROPAEV, Alexei	RUS	9.712
7	CARBALLO, Jesus	ESP	9.350
8	LEE, Joo-Hyung	KOR	8.525

Gymnastics—Artistic / *Gymnastique — Artistique*
Individual Apparatus, Women / *Par engin, Dames*

FLOOR - FINAL

Rnk	Name	Ctry	Result
1	PODKOPAYEVA, Lilia	UKR	9.887 **G**
2	AMANAR, Simona	ROM	9.850 **S**
3	DAWES, Dominique	USA	9.837 **B**
4	MOCEANU, Dominique	USA	9.825
5	KOCHETKOVA, Dina	RUS	9.800
6	MO, Huilan	CHN	9.700
7	GOGEAN, Gina	ROM	9.662
8	JI, Liya	CHN	9.637

BALANCE BEAM - FINAL

Rnk	Name	Ctry	Result
1	MILLER, Shannon	USA	9.862 **G**
2	PODKOPAYEVA, Lilia	UKR	9.825 **S**
3	GOGEAN, Gina	ROM	9.787 **B**
4	KOCHETKOVA, Dina	RUS	9.737
5	TESLENKO, Olga	UKR	9.625
6	MOCEANU, Dominique	USA	9.125
7	GALIYEVA, Rozalia	RUS	9.112
8	MARINESCU, Alexandra	ROM	8.462

VAULT - FINAL

Rnk	Name	Ctry	Ia	Ib	Result
1	AMANAR, Simona	ROM	9.875	9.775	9.825 **G**
2	MO, Huilan	CHN	9.825	9.712	9.768 **S**
3	GOGEAN, Gina	ROM	9.800	9.700	9.750 **B**
4	GALIYEVA, Rozalia	RUS	9.787	9.700	9.743
5	BOGUINSKAIA, Svetlana	BLR	9.800	9.625	9.712
6	DAWES, Dominique	USA	9.662	9.637	9.649
7	GROSHEVA, Elena	RUS	9.737	9.537	9.637
8	MILLER, Shannon	USA	9.650	9050	9.350

UNEVEN BARS - FINAL

Rnk	Name	Ctry	Result
1	CHORKINA, Svetlana	RUS	9.850 **G**
2	BI, Wenjing	CHN	9.837 **S**
2	CHOW, Amy	USA	9.837 **S**
4	DAWES, Dominique	USA	9.800
5	AMANAR, Simona	ROM	9.787
5	KOCHETKOVA, Dina	RUS	9.787
5	PODKOPAYEVA, Lilia	UKR	9.787
8	MILOSOVICI, Lavinia	ROM	9.750

• LYLA N SHUMATE • MARY K SHUMATE • RICHARD C SHUMATE • AMY R SHUMP • VENESSA SHUMPERT • MARY P SHUMWAY • CHU SHUNCHIA • LOUIS S SHURINA • SONDRA D SHURLING • SANDRA K SHUSTER • SHARI B SHUTT • ELIZABETH SHY • YLADIMIR SHYAHOV • CHRISTINE E SIBENAC • BARRY L SIBLEY • HELEN K SIBLEY • MICHAEL C SIBLEY • SASHA SIBREE • ANNA M SICAM • MATTHEW A SICIGNANO • CAROL J SICILIANO MT • JENNIFER A SICKELS • CRYSTAL L SIDBERRY • CARLA D SIDDALL • SHAHAB SIDDIQUI • SHAHID A SIDDIQUI • PATRICIA L SIDEBOTHAM • GAIL A SIDEMAN • MARTIN A SIDMAN • DONALD R SIDNEY • KATHRYN MAUREEN SIDORIK • KIMBERLY A SIDORIK • ANN B SIEBERT • RICHARD H SIEBERT • SHERRI A SIEBERT • RALPH D SIEBOLDT • ZBIGNIEW SIECZKA • KEITH W SIEDENTOP • AMANDA L SIEGEL • ANDREW H SIEGEL • BOOTSIE SIEGEL • DAVID F SIEGEL • HELEN R SIEGEL • KAREN S SIEGEL • MARC L SIEGEL • MARGARET L SIEGEL • MARY ANN G SIEGEL • MARY F SIEGEL • PHILIP J SIEGEL • SHARON B SIEGEL • SHERYL L SIEGEL • DAN E SIEGLER • CAROLINE A SIERRA • LAURA M SIERRA • RICARDO SIERRA • RIGOBERTO L SIERRA-ANDERSON • JAMES P SIEVE • JOERG SIEVERDING • RONALD A SIEVERS • JASON SIEVERT • JASON SIEVERT • SHERRY SIEVERT • DEBRA A SIEVERT-METZGER • CONNIE R SIEWERT • CORINNE B SIGAFOOS • CAREY N SIGAFOOSE • SHANNON C SIGL • BRIAN S SIGLER • CATHARINE C SIGMAN • MICHAEL B SIGMAN • CLAY S SIGMON • CRAIG E SIGMON • ELIZABETH K SIGMON • REBECCA L SIGMUND • CHARLES R SIKES • DIANE R SIKES • HOLLY A SIKES • IRENE S SIKES • MARGARET L SIKES • MATTHEW M SIKES • PEGGY F SIKES • SUSAN L SIKES • TONYA L SIKES • WILBUR N SIKES • JENNIFER E SIKKELEE • PATRICIA M SIKKELEE • LAURENNE SIKLOSSY • ARKADIUSZ A SIKORA • GREG SILACCI • PHILIPPE SILACCI • JACQUELINE LEE SILANSKAS • STEVEN W SILAS • TORANDA SILAS • ANDREW F SILBERNAGEL • JOHN A SILBERNAGEL • SANDRA E SILBERNAGEL • DIANE T. SILBERSTEIN • DANA M SILBIGER • DANIEL H SILCOX • CATHERINE E SILER • CINDY M SILER • DIANE T SILER • TEMESHA SILER • LINDA M SILFIES MT • SUSAN G SILHAVY • JO S SILKEN • GLORIA A SILL • KARL P SILLAY • CAROL F SILVA • EDSON SILVA • EUGENE F SILVA • JAMES R SILVA • JOHN SILVA • GARY R SILVER • WILLIAM E SILVER MD • BIBIANNA SILVERA • BENJAMIN P SILVERBERG • WILLIAM L SILVERBERG • MINDY I SILVERBOARD • AARON SILVERMAN • FAYE J SILVERMAN • HARRIET K SILVERMAN • LAURA A SILVERMAN • LEONARD J SILVERMAN • MARK E SILVERMAN • NAN SILVERMAN • LAURA A SILVERNAIL • PATRICIA SILVERS • ANDREW M SILVERSTONE • KAREN D SILVESTROS • GEORGE A SILVEY • JOHN C SILVEY • KATHERINE W SILVEY • RENEE SILVEY • SUSAN K SILVEY • HEIDI M SILVIA • STEVEN T SILVIO • SIMONE SIMBURG • KENDALL L SIMCOX • ROBERTA C SIMERLY • MILAN SIMIC • DOROTHY E SIMISTER • DENIS J SIMKO • NEAL SIMKOWITZ • SOMCHAY N SIMMAVANH • SHANNON A SIMMERS • GLEN SIMMONDS • MONICA SIMMONDS • ADEREMI O SIMMONS • AKITA M SIMMONS • ANDREW P SIMMONS • ANGELA DIANE SIMMONS • ARNEE D. SIMMONS • BARBARA Q SIMMONS • BELINDA M SIMMONS • BEVERLY A SIMMONS • BRAD SIMMONS • BRENT C SIMMONS • BRIGHAM R SIMMONS • CARMEL SIMMONS • CAROL M SIMMONS • CAROLYN S SIMMONS • CHARLOTTE M SIMMONS • DASHUN SIMMONS • DEANNA B SIMMONS • DIANA J SIMMONS • DONZALIA A SIMMONS • DORETHA E SIMMONS • ELENORA A SIMMONS • ELIZABETH D SIMMONS • FAYE E SIMMONS • GLENDA Y SIMMONS • HERBIE L SIMMONS • HOWARD D SIMMONS • JERRY E SIMMONS • JIMMIE SIMMONS • KATE SIMMONS • KATHRYN T SIMMONS • KATHY T SIMMONS • KATRINA SIMMONS • KENT F SIMMONS • LAURA B SIMMONS • LINDA F SIMMONS • LINDA K SIMMONS • LYNN A SIMMONS • MARGOES A SIMMONS • MARGUERITE S SIMMONS • MARTHA E SIMMONS • MERI G SIMMONS • NATHAN SIMMONS • NIA T SIMMONS • OPAL T SIMMONS • PETER R SIMMONS • RICHARD SIMMONS • ROBERT O SIMMONS • ROY L SIMMONS • SCOTT A SIMMONS • SHARON SIMMONS • STEVAN M SIMMONS • SYNETHIA L SIMMONS • TASHIA SIMMONS • TIMOTHY H SIMMONS • WARREN D SIMMONS • MILTON SIMMONS JR • THOMAS G SIMMONS CATC • ANDERSON SIMMONS JR • BARBARA J SIMMONS MD • SAVARIA E SIMMS • CYREN SIMMS • DARLENE S SIMMS • RANONA R SIMMS • CANDICE S SIMON • CAROL J SIMON • CLARK G SIMON • ELEANOR G SIMON • ERNESTINE SIMON • ESAN O SIMON • JAYNE A SIMON • JONATHAN SIMON • KENT SIMON • LAWRENCE H SIMON • MIGUEL SIMON • PRISCILLA P SIMON • RACHEL LOUISE SIMON • SABU SIMON • STEVEN P SIMON • THERESA A SIMON • GARY S SIMON MD • ANNETTE G SIMONDS • BILLIE G SIMONDS • HEATHER SIMONE • JOSEPH K SIMONET • PATRICIA E SIMONI • ALAN D SIMONS • BETTY L SIMONS • CARMEN D SIMONS • DEBRA B SIMONS • JANE V SIMONS • JASON D SIMONS • JULIE A SIMONS • AIMEE C SIMONTON • JAY C SIMONTON • LESLIE SIMONTON • REBECCA A SIMONTON • LARKYN M SIMONY • DAVID C SIMPKINS • HENRIET SIMPKINS • ALYSON CLAIRE SIMPSON • BEATRICE M SIMPSON • BENJAMIN O SIMPSON • BETSY E SIMPSON • BRYAN E SIMPSON • CASEY L SIMPSON • CHERYL B SIMPSON • CLYDIE SIMPSON • DEBBIE E SIMPSON • DOUGLAS H SIMPSON • GREGORY F SIMPSON • HAYWOOD SIMPSON • JANET E SIMPSON • JANET L SIMPSON • JANZETTER SIMPSON • JENNIFER L SIMPSON • JOHN E SIMPSON • KATIE SIMPSON • KEITH SIMPSON • L. ELAINE SIMPSON • LAVITA C SIMPSON • LETRELL E SIMPSON • LOREN A SIMPSON • LUCINDA G SIMPSON • MARY C SIMPSON • ONDREA H SIMPSON • PEGGY M SIMPSON • PHILLISSA KAY SIMPSON • RICHARD K SIMPSON • RICHARD R SIMPSON • RONALD J SIMPSON • SILVEY J SIMPSON • STACY E SIMPSON • STEPHANIE E SIMPSON • WILL A SIMPSON • WILLIE M SIMPSON • JAMES B SIMPSON II • AMY C SIMS • BETTY C SIMS • BRAD J. SIMS • CARLETTA E SIMS • CURTIS E SIMS • EDWARD D SIMS • FELESSA R SIMS • FRANK S SIMS • GEOFF B SIMS • GLENDORA SIMS • HAROLD L SIMS • HELEN M SIMS • JACQUELYN SIMS • JEAN T SIMS • JENNIFER M SIMS • JOSEPH D SIMS • JUANITA E SIMS • KATIE O SIMS • KEEBLER T SIMS • KEITH L SIMS • LISA L. SIMS • MAC M SIMS • MARCO SIMS • MARIE W SIMS • MARVIN SIMS • MARY H SIMS • MELISSA C SIMS • MICHAEL SIMS • MICHELE L SIMS • PARIS G SIMS • PATRICIA J SIMS • ROBERTINE R SIMS • SYLVIA E SIMS • TRINETTE SIMS • WILLIE V SIMS • DAVID SIMS JR • CHRISTOPHER A SIMSER • DARLENE Y SIMUEL • HYUN SIN • JOYCE A SINCAVAGE • CAROL R SINCLAIR • JULIE G SINCLAIR • REGINA M SINCLAIR • RUFFIN M SINCLAIR • MICHAEL D SINCO • STACY M SINDELL • CATHERINE A. SINDOS • TRICIA SINEATH • RICHARD R SINES • SIMA SINGADIA KULKARNI • BALAJI SINGARACHARU • BERT SINGER • ERIC SINGER • HAROLD R SINGER • IRVING A SINGER • LINDA G SINGER • MICHAEL R SINGER • ROBERT R SINGER • THOMAS R SINGERS • ANJULA SINGH • ARCHANA SINGH • ERIC SINGH • SURINDERPAL SINGH • AMAN SINGLA • LAURA C SINGLETARY • LILLIAN M SINGLETARY • MARGIE SINGLETARY • MARSHA K SINGLETARY • SHARRON K SINGLETARY • WILLIAM R. SINGLETARY • ANDREW W SINGLETON • ARTHUR W SINGLETON • CANDACE SINGLETON • CHARLENE H SINGLETON • GAY W SINGLETON • GINGER J SINGLETON • KRYSTAL SINGLETON • LAMAR J SINGLETON • LINDA P SINGLETON • MARTHA M SINGLETON • MARY K SINGLETON • PAMELA L SINGLETON • SHELBY S SINGLETON • TIMOTHY O SINGLETON • FREDERIC W SINGTON III • SANJAY SINHA • HUGH C SINIARD • THEO W SINKLER • ELISABETH E SINNIGER • CLAIRE R SINNOTT • LISA L SINON • RAFFAELA M SINOPOLI • KEITH R SINOR • BARBARA A SINSHEIMER • ROBIN S SINTON • REBECCA SIPES • GIANINA SIPITCA • STEFANIE L SIRC • ANDREW J SIRK • ADRIANE M SIRKUS • ROBERT SIRKUS • CARLA J SISK • JACQUELYN H SISK • KAREN L SISK • PAUL P SISK • LAMAY SISONGKHAM • MICHAEL V SISSINE • BRENDA E SISSON • REID B SISSON • RAMANI V SISTA • JEUNE F SISTRUNK • FRANK D SISYA • AMY I SITTON • JOE H SITZ III • GUSTAV R SIVAK • NARAYANAN SIVANESAN • MORRIS M SIYMAN • CHONGAE SIZEMORE • CHRISTINE C SIZEMORE • GEORGIA E SIZEMORE • MARKLI JAYNE M SIZER • GERALD P SJOGREN • JEFFREY S SJOGREN • LYNNETTE E SJOQUIST • NATHAN M SKACEL • DAVID A SKADELAND • ANGELA SKAGGS • DANIEL Z SKALICKY • LORRAINE E SKALKO • CYNTHIA SKARBEK • JOSEPH D SKARBEK • STACIE SKARBEK • CAROLYN L SKEEAN • ELIZABETH A SKEEN • MERVYN O SKEETE • GREGORY T SKEETER • NORMAN M SKEIRIK • LAWRENCE J SKELLEY • DAVID B SKELLY • JACK E SKELLY • JAMES F SKELLY • BERRY T SKELTON • KIM D SKELTON • JANE A SKELTON CRNA • KATONYA SKERRETT ATC • ROSEANN G SKETEL • ANN SKIBA • BEATRICE M SKIBA • LEONARD R SKIBA • JOHN E SKIBBE • MARY JANE SKIDMORE • THOMAS H SKIDMORE • ALECIA N SKIFF • BRADFORD C SKIFF • MARK E SKILLAN • CHARLES W SKILLAS • MATTHEW B SKILLMAN • ANDREW F SKINNER • CAREY M SKINNER • CHARLES W SKINNER • CHARLOTTE E SKINNER • CHRISTINA A SKINNER • DAVE SKINNER • KELLY M SKINNER • LEIGH A SKINNER • LUCILLE S SKINNER • SYLVIA A SKINNER • WILLIAM H SKINNER • ANDREW W SKIPPER • CYNTHIA A SKIPPER • LINDA J SKIPPER • STEPHANIE A SKIPPER • VALORI L SKIPPER • KEVIN E SKIRDE • RICHARD L SKIRVIN • DAVID G SKITT • SHIRLEY T SKLAR • ANDREW J SKLARZ • CAROLYN J SKOK • CECILIA I SKOLD • ROBERT M SKOPINSKI • PATRYK A SKOPLAK • EDMUND H SKORUPSKI • VLADISLAV A SKOTAR • GEORGE E SKOUFIS • IOANNIS P SKOURAS ATC • RICHARD D SKOW • JENNIFER A SKRIBA • JENNY A SKRIDULIS • DAVID P SKRINNIKOFF • ANATOLI G SKRIPNIKOV • TIMOTHY C SKRMETTI • ELIZABETH K SKRYNECKI • MARK W SKUTLE • SANDRA L SLABIK • FRANNIE I SLABONIK • KYRA FELECIA SLACK • VIRGINIA R SLACK • DONNA M SLACK-MCNEELY • DAVID F SLADE • DAVID P SLADE • GREGORY S SLADE • JOHN SLADE • RALPH J SLADE • AUGUSTIN SLADEK • CYNTHIA J SLADEK • DANIELA SLADKOVA • GARY S SLAGLE • ALEX J SLAKIE • ELYSIA F SLAKIE • NANCY W SLANEY • ALICE SLAPE • KELLEY C SLAPPEY • PHYLLIS A SLATE • CYNTHIA B SLATER • DICKSON W SLATER • EDWARD SLATER • EDWIN D SLATER • GRACIA W SLATER • JANET A SLATER • JOHN W SLATER • LISA D SLATER • WANDA J SLATER • DON SLATON • MARIE D SLATON • SHERRY H SLATTERY • EDWIN SLAUGHTER • GLORIA M SLAUGHTER • JAN C SLAUGHTER • JERILENE S SLAUGHTER • KIP C SLAUGHTER • REGINALD A SLAUGHTER • THOMAS M SLAUGHTER • TODD R SLAUGHTER • JILL A SLAVIN • CODY M SLAY • GAIL D SLAY • HEATHER A SLAY • MARCUS E SLAY • EDWARD W SLAYTON • JOHN R SLAYTON • ELIZABETH J SLEDGE • LAURA M SLEDGE • VIVIAN D SLEDGE • DONALD D SLEEMAN • JOANIE M SLEISTER • SHELIA R SLEMP • CAMILLA SLETTEN • CATHERINE T SLICHENMYER • KEISHA D SLIDE • ROBERTA SLIGER • LISA L SLITER ATC • KUBA K SLIWINSKI • CLAUDE F SLOAN • DEBRA A SLOAN • JAMES K SLOAN • JAMES M SLOAN • JUSTIN D SLOAN • ROGER W SLOAN • ROY F SLOAN • SARAH R SLOAN • SCOTT E SLOAN • STEPHANIE SLOAN • WILEY G SLOAN • WYMAN P SLOAN III MD • BRIAN SLOCUM • LINDA S SLOCUM • BELINDA G SLOCUMB • WILLIAM R SLOGER • ANNE SLUHAN • KAREN M SLUPECKI • PATRICIA A SLUSS • MARTIN SLUTSKY • KENNETH M SLYE • LINDA T SLYE • AMIR SMAILBEGOVIC • SYLVIA C SMALBERGER • PIRITTA E SMALDON • DAVID D SMALE • BRYANT D SMALL • DAVID G SMALL • JOHN F SMALL • MICHAEL S SMALL • NETARCIA L SMALL • PEGGY A SMALL • SHAWN A SMALL • SHIRLEY S SMALL • MARY B SMALLEY • GERI SMALLIE • SHANNA M SMALLING • ERNEST SMALLMAN III • JARIAN K SMALLS • MARIAM E SMALLS • MICHAEL J SMALLS • PEGGY L SMALLS • RHONDA L SMALLS • JERRY STANLEY SMALLWOOD • JOE T SMALLWOOD • ROY T SMALLWOOD • BARBARA J SMARR • KAYE K SMARSLIK • AMANDA M SMART • JONATHAN S SMART • PHILIP S SMART • SHERRY L SMART • JEANNE M SMART RN • KATHLEEN N SMATHERS • LESLIE N SMEE • BONNIE M SMELLEY • DEBRA J SMELLEY • JACK R SMELSER • CAREY M SMELTZER • TERESITA C SMETS • HARRISON T SMIDDY • CHAD R SMIDT ATC • JOYCE H SMILACK • SUSAN M SMILACK • BIANCA L SMILEY • CAROLE J SMILEY • DEBBY D SMILEY • JACQUELYN M SMILEY • LARRY A SMILEY • CHARLIE W SMILEY III • RHONDA K SMILEY MT • STEPHEN D SMILIE • LARISSA A SMIRNOVA • ABBY L SMITH • ADELE EA SMITH • AIMEE C SMITH • AIMEE E SMITH • AIMEE M SMITH • ALICE V SMITH • ALICE W SMITH • ALISON A SMITH • ALLEN D SMITH • ALLEN L SMITH • ALLISON J SMITH • ALLISON L SMITH • AMBER D SMITH • AMEEA SMITH • AMY A SMITH • AMY R SMITH • ANDREA B SMITH • ANDREW A SMITH • ANGELA R SMITH • ANGELYN L SMITH • ANGIE SMITH • ANITA C SMITH • ANITA K SMITH • ANNALEE S SMITH • ANNE C SMITH • ANNIE V SMITH • ANSLEY N SMITH • ANTHONY B SMITH • ANTHONY S SMITH • ANTHONY T SMITH • ANTONIO SMITH • ANWAR SMITH • ANWAR SMITH • ARNITA H SMITH • ARTHUR SMITH • ASHLEY M SMITH • AUDREY M SMITH • B SHARRON SMITH • BARNETT F SMITH • BEDFORD H SMITH • BELINDA L SMITH • BELINDA S SMITH • BELITA T SMITH • BEN W SMITH • BENNIE R SMITH • BETSY M SMITH • BETSY P SMITH • BETTY SMITH • BETTY J SMITH • BETTY J SMITH • BETTY L SMITH • BILLY B SMITH • BOISE B SMITH • BOYD T SMITH • BRADLEY A SMITH • BRANDON A SMITH • BRENDA B SMITH • BRENDA D SMITH • BRENDA K SMITH • BRENDA L SMITH • BRENDA P SMITH • BRIAN A SMITH • BRIAN E SMITH • BRIAN W SMITH • BROCK H SMITH • BRYAN B SMITH • CALLIE L SMITH • CALVIN L SMITH • CANDACE A SMITH • CANDACE M SMITH • CAROL A SMITH • CAROL H SMITH • CAROL J SMITH • CAROL R SMITH • CAROLE M SMITH • CARY R SMITH • CASANDRA T SMITH • CASEY T SMITH • CASS SMITH • CATHERINE R SMITH • CATHERINE S SMITH • CATHY G SMITH • CECILIA K SMITH • CHARLES C SMITH • CHARLES H SMITH • CHARLES L SMITH • CHARLES L SMITH • CHERYL M SMITH • CHERYL D SMITH • CHIP E SMITH • CHRISTIE A SMITH • CHRISTINA R SMITH • CHRISTINE L SMITH • CHRISTOPHER R SMITH • CINDY E SMITH • CLARA M SMITH • CLARK W SMITH • CLARKE C SMITH • CLAUDIA SMITH • CLAUDINE B SMITH • COLLEEN M SMITH • COREY SMITH • CURTIS H SMITH • CYNDI D SMITH • CYNTHIA A SMITH • D. MARSHALL SMITH • DANIEL G SMITH • DANIEL M SMITH • DANIEL P SMITH • DANIELLE M SMITH • DAVID SMITH • DAVID A SMITH • DAVID J SMITH • DAVID L SMITH • DAVID W SMITH • DAVID W SMITH • DAWN A SMITH • DAWN N SMITH • DEBORAH SMITH • DEBORAH H SMITH • DEBORAH H SMITH • DEBORAH H. SMITH • DEBORAH M SMITH • DEBORAH T SMITH • DEBRA K SMITH • DELBERT E SMITH • DELORES R SMITH • DEMICA SMITH • DENISE M SMITH • DEREK L SMITH • DIANE I SMITH • DINAH L SMITH • DONALD E SMITH • DONALD G SMITH • DONALD J SMITH • DONNA M SMITH • DORETTE C SMITH • DOROTHY G SMITH • DOROTHY J SMITH • DOROTHY VICTORIA SMITH • DOUGLAS A SMITH • DOUGLAS A SMITH • DOUGLAS H SMITH • DOUGLAS H SMITH • DOUGLAS J SMITH • DOUGLAS J SMITH • DUNCAN SMITH • EARLE W SMITH • EDWARD A SMITH • EDWARD T SMITH • ELEANOR W SMITH • ELIZABETH B SMITH • ELIZABETH B SMITH • ELIZABETH E SMITH • ELIZABETH L SMITH • ELLEN W SMITH • ELLIS B SMITH • ELVA S SMITH • EMMETT SMITH • ERIC B SMITH • ERIC G SMITH • ERICA F SMITH • ERICK A SMITH • ESTELLE F SMITH • ETHEL E SMITH • EUGENE S SMITH • EVELYN SMITH • EVELYN W SMITH • EVELYNLYNN R SMITH • FELICIA O SMITH • FELICIA S SMITH • FIONA M SMITH • FLORENCE Q SMITH • FRANK D SMITH • GAIL A SMITH • GARY A SMITH • GAYE M SMITH • GEOFFREY K SMITH • GEORGE SMITH • GEORGE L SMITH • GEORGIANNA B SMITH • GERALD J SMITH • GILL J SMITH • GORDON A SMITH • GREGG SMITH • GREGG L SMITH • GREGORY L SMITH • GREGORY P SMITH • GREGORY S SMITH • GREGORY W SMITH •

GYMNASTICS—RHYTHMIC
GYMNASTIQUE — RYTHMIQUE

Abbreviations and terms used in Rhythmic Gymnastics results tables
Abréviations et termes employés dans les tableaux de résultats de gymnastique rythmique

Term	English	Français
3b2r	Three balls, two ribbons	Trois ballons, deux rubans
5h	Five Hoops	Cinq cerceaux
B	Bronze Medal	Médaille de bronze
Ball	Ball	Ballon
Clubs	Clubs	Massues
Ctry	Country	Pays
Final	Final	Finale
G	Gold Medal	Médaille d'or
Preliminaries	Preliminaries	Eliminatoires
Q	Qualified	Qualifiée
Ribbon	Ribbon	Ruban
Rope	Rope	Corde
Roster	Team Roster	Liste des participants par équipes
Rnk	Rank	Classement
S	Silver Medal	Médaille d'argent
Summary Chart	Summary Chart	Tableau récapitulatif
Semifinals	Semifinals	Demi-finales
Total	Total	Total

International Gymnastics Federation (FIG)
Fédération Internationale de Gymnastique
Rue des Oeches 10
Case postale 359
2740 Moutier 1
Switzerland

Gymnastics—Rhythmic / *Gymnastique — Rythmique*
Individual All-Around, Women / *Concours général individuel, Dames*

Rnk	Name	Ctry	Rope	Ball	Clubs	Ribbon	Total	
1	VITRICHENKO, Olena	UKR	9.800	9.800	9.800	9.800	39.200	Q
2	SEREBRYANSKA, Kateryna	UKR	9.799	9.783	9.832	9.699	39.113	Q
3	ZARIPOVA, Amina	RUS	9.716	9.699	9.583	9.750	38.748	Q
4	LOUKIANENKO, Larisa	BLR	9.699	9.366	9.716	9.700	38.481	Q
5	CID TOSTADO, Almudena	ESP	9.600	9.600	9.600	9.600	38.400	Q
6	PETROVA, Maria	BUL	9.666	9.183	9.800	9.733	38.382	Q
7	SERRANO, Eva	FRA	9.516	9.600	9.466	9.566	38.148	Q
8	PANGALOU, Maria	GRE	9.500	9.500	9.533	9.450	37.983	Q
9	OGRYZKO, Tatiana	BLR	8.766	9.750	9.750	9.633	37.899	Q
10	POPOVA, Diana	BUL	9.550	9.500	9.516	9.283	37.849	Q
11	CARIDE COSTAS, Alba	ESP	9.416	9.433	9.532	9.400	37.781	Q
12	STOICA, Alina	ROM	9.316	9.499	9.500	9.466	37.781	Q
13	BATRYCHINKO, Ianina	RUS	9.816	9.266	9.350	9.316	37.748	Q
14	SROKA, Kristin	GER	9.432	9.450	9.399	9.416	37.697	Q
15	BRZESKA, Magdalena	GER	9.566	8.933	9.533	9.583	37.615	Q
16	GERMINI, Irene	ITA	9.466	9.466	9.216	9.400	37.548	Q
17	ZHOU, Xiao Jing	CHN	9.333	9.416	9.416	9.383	37.548	Q
18	YAMADA, Miho	JPN	9.350	9.350	9.249	9.182	37.131	Q
19	YAMAO, Akane	JPN	9.183	9.366	9.283	9.283	37.115	Q
20	PIETROSANTI, Katia	ITA	8.983	9.400	9.366	9.350	37.099	Q
21	LESKIEWICZ, Krystyna	POL	9.250	9.232	9.250	9.250	36.982	
22	OULEHLOVA, Lenka	CZE	9.232	9.266	9.266	9.199	36.963	
23	FRATER, Viktoria	HUN	9.233	9.116	9.333	9.249	36.931	
24	SCHIELIN, Birgit	AUT	9.200	9.166	9.266	9.249	36.881	
25	ABRAMIA, Akaterina	GEO	9.200	9.250	9.183	9.200	36.833	
26	SOTIRIOU, Evagelia	GRE	9.233	9.183	9.299	8.983	36.698	
27	KWITNIEWSKA, Anna	POL	9.233	8.932	9.349	9.166	36.680	
28	SEBESTOVA, Andrea	CZE	9.366	8.783	9.249	9.200	36.598	
29	TABORSKY, Nina	AUT	9.133	9.183	9.083	9.166	36.565	
30	DAVIS, Jessica	USA	9.166	9.200	9.216	8.982	36.564	
31	STOLLENBERG, Cindy	BEL	9.033	9.166	9.149	9.116	36.464	
32	CARTELEANU, Dana	ROM	9.150	9.166	9.050	9.016	36.382	
33	MARTENS, Camille	CAN	9.333	8.599	9.316	9.116	36.364	
34	KALPALA, Katri	FIN	9.182	8.800	9.166	9.200	36.348	
35	WU, Bei	CHN	9.216	9.249	8.933	8.899	36.297	
36	SZALAY, Andrea	HUN	9.000	9.033	8.883	8.982	35.898	
37	KLIUKEVICIUTE, Kristina	LTU	9.199	8.966	8.499	9.083	35.747	

Rnk	Name	Ctry	Rope	Ball	Clubs	Ribbon	Total	
1	SEREBRYANSKA, Kateryna	UKR	9.916	9.933	9.583	9.900	39.332	Q
2	VITRICHENKO, Olena	UKR	9.750	9.900	9.750	9.866	39.266	Q
3	BATRYCHINKO, Ianina	RUS	9.850	9.866	9.733	9.783	39.232	Q
4	PETROVA, Maria	BUL	9.716	9.750	9.733	9.700	38.899	Q
5	LOUKIANENKO, Larisa	BLR	9.700	9.750	9.616	9.683	38.749	Q
6	OGRYZKO, Tatiana	BLR	9.633	9.682	9.700	9.666	38.681	Q
7	ZARIPOVA, Amina	RUS	9.716	9.850	9.782	9.316	38.664	Q
8	SERRANO, Eva	FRA	9.666	9.700	9.566	9.683	38.615	Q
9	CID TOSTADO, Almudena	ESP	9.583	9.700	9.616	9.549	38.448	Q
10	BRZESKA, Magdalena	GER	9.550	9.583	9.516	9.583	38.232	Q
11	POPOVA, Diana	BUL	9.449	9.466	9.466	9.449	37.830	
12	PANGALOU, Maria	GRE	9.516	9.500	9.333	9.466	37.815	
13	GERMINI, Irene	ITA	9.266	9.500	9.250	9.500	37.516	
14	PIETROSANTI, Katia	ITA	9.366	9.366	9.250	9.333	37.315	
15	STOICA, Alina	ROM	9.483	9.533	8.766	9.466	37.248	
16	SROKA, Kristin	GER	9.283	9.550	8.900	9.400	37.133	
17	ZHOU, Xiao Jing	CHN	9.200	9.266	9.250	9.400	37.116	
18	YAMAO, Akane	JPN	9.233	8.966	9.216	9.383	36.798	
19	CARIDE COSTAS, Alba	ESP	9.049	9.449	8.933	9.266	36.697	
20	YAMADA, Miho	JPN	9.316	9.133	9.200	8.616	36.265	

Rnk	Name	Ctry	Rope	Ball	Clubs	Ribbon	Total	
1	SEREBRYANSKA, Kateryna	UKR	9.950	9.950	9.950	9.833	39.683	G
2	BATRYCHINKO, Ianina	RUS	9.850	9.916	9.933	9.683	39.382	S
3	VITRICHENKO, Olena	UKR	9.866	9.800	9.849	9.816	39.331	B
4	ZARIPOVA, Amina	RUS	9.783	9.866	9.832	9.783	39.264	
5	PETROVA, Maria	BUL	9.733	9.783	9.733	9.750	38.999	
6	SERRANO, Eva	FRA	9.683	9.700	9.700	9.733	38.816	
7	LOUKIANENKO, Larisa	BLR	9.466	9.750	9.700	9.750	38.666	
8	OGRYZKO, Tatiana	BLR	9.583	9.682	9.599	9.666	38.530	
9	CID TOSTADO, Almudena	ESP	9.700	9.566	9.683	9.566	38.515	
10	BRZESKA, Magdalena	GER	9.516	9.600	9.566	9.633	38.315	

Gymnastics—Rhythmic / *Gymnastique — Rythmique*
Team, Women / *Concours d'ensemble, Dames*

Rnk	Ctry	5h	3b2r	Total	
1	Bulgaria	19.466	19.550	39.016	
2	Spain	19.500	19.466	38.966	
3	Russian Federation	19.516	19.366	38.882	
4	Belarus	19.300	19.133	38.433	
5	France	19.200	19.033	38.233	
6	People's Republic of China	19.133	18.999	38.132	
7	Italy	19.283	18.733	38.016	
8	Germany	19.050	18.832	37.882	
9	United States of America	18.400	18.233	36.633	

Rnk	Ctry	5h	3b2r	Total	
1	Spain	19.483	19.450	38.933	G
2	Bulgaria	19.416	19.450	38.866	S
3	Russian Federation	19.466	18.899	38.365	B
4	France	19.149	19.050	38.199	
5	People's Republic of China	19.199	18.800	37.999	
6	Belarus	19.266	18.716	37.982	

BLR Belarus
BOUDILO, Natalla
JDANOVITCH, Oxana
POHODINA, Alesija
LOUZANOVA, Svetlana
DEMSKAIA, Olga
MALACHENKO, Galina

BUL Bulgaria
TALEVA, Ivelina
KEVLIAN, Valentina
VATACHKA, Vjara
KOLEVA, Maria
TABAKOVA, Maja
DELTCHEVA, Ina

CHN People's Republic of China
ZHENG, Ni
ZHONG, Li
CAI, Yingying
HUANG, Ting
HUANG, Ying

ESP Spain
CABANILLAS, Nuria
GIMENEZ, Estela
MARTINEZ, Estibaliz
LAMARCA, Tania
GURENDEZ, Lorena
BALDO, Marta

FRA France
CAMBOULIVES, Charlotte
DIDONE, Sylvie
CHIMOT, Caroline
LEHON, Frederique
GROSCLAUDE, Audrey
MIMOUN, Nadia

GER Germany
STABLEIN, Luise
WILDERMUTH, Katharina
BITTNER, Nicole
HOFFMANN, Katrin
JUNG, Anne
SCHILTZ, Dorte

ITA Italy
BOCCHINI, Manuela
MARINO, Valentina
TINTI, Nicoletta
PINCIROLI, Sara
PAPI, Sara
ROVETTA, Valentina

RUS Russian Federation
BOTCHKAREVA, Evguenia
CHTYRENKO, Olga
IVANOVA, Ioulia
KRIVOCHEI, Elena
IOUCHKOVA, Angelina
DZIOUBA, Irina

USA United States of America
SIEVERS, Challen
SIEGEL, Brandi
NELSON, Kate
JAMES, Mandy
TURNER, Becky
MATA-BAQUEROT, Alaine

HANDBALL
HANDBALL

Abbreviations and terms used in Handball results tables
Abréviations et termes employés dans les tableaux de résultats de handball

Term	English	Français
% Eff	% Efficency	% d'efficacité
1st Referee	1st Referee	Premier arbitre
2nd Referee	2nd Referee	Deuxième arbitre
6-Meter shots	6-Meter shots	Jet de 6 m
9-Meter shots	9-Meter shots	Jet de 9 m
A	Assists	Passes décisives
Against	Against	Contre
Assists	Assists	Passes décisives
Assistant Coach	Assistant Coach	Entraîneur adjoint
Attempted	Attempted	Tenté
Bl	Blocked Shots	Lancers bloqués
Blocks	Blocks	Bloqués
Breakthroughs	Breakthroughs	Pénétrations
Bronze	Bronze Medal	Médaille de bronze
CB	Center Back	Arrière-centre
Classification	Classification	Classement
Coach	Coach	Entraîneur
Diff pts	Difference in Points	Ecart en points
Drawn	Drawn	Egalités
End of Playing Time	End of Playing Time	Fin du temps de jeu
Fast breaks	Fast breaks	Contre-attaques éclairs
Final	Final	Finale
Final Classification	Final Classification	Classement final
For	For	Pour
Fouls	Fouls	Fautes
GK	Goalkeeper	Gardien de but
Games	Games	Matchs
Goals	Goals	Buts
Goalkeeper	Goalkeeper	Gardien de but
Gold	Gold Medal	Médaille d'or
Group	Group	Groupe
Halftime Score	Halftime Score	Score à mi-temps
LB	Left Back	Arrière gauche
LW	Left Wing	Aile gauche
Lost	Lost	Perdu
M/A	Goals Made / Attempts	Buts marqués / tentés
Name	Name	Nom
P	Pivot	Avant-centre
Phase	Phase	Phase
Played	Played	Joué
Pos	Position	Position
Preliminaries	Preliminaries	Eliminatoires
RB	Right Back	Arrière droit
RW	Right Wing	Aile droite
Rnk	Rank	Classement
Score	Score	Score
Semifinals	Semifinals	Demi-finales
Shots Saved	Shots Saved	Tirs bloqués
Steals	Steals	Interceptions
Stl	Steals	Interceptions
Summary	Summary	Sommaire
Team	Team	Equipe
To	Turnovers	Pertes de possession de la balle
Total shots	Total shots	Total des tirs
Turnovers	Turnovers	Pertes de possession de la balle
Wing shots	Wing shots	Tirs d'aile
Won	Won	Gagné

International Handball Federation (IHF)
Fédération Internationale de Handball
Postfach 312
Ch-4020 Basel
Switzerland

KAREN R SMITH • KAREN T SMITH • KARYN N SMITH • KATHY ANN SMITH • KATHY L SMITH • KAY FRANCES SMITH • KEITH A SMITH • KEITH W SMITH • KEITH W SMITH • KELLIE W SMITH • KELLY A SMITH • KELLY J SMITH • KEN E SMITH • KENAN SMITH • KENNETH R SMITH • KENNY R SMITH • KENT S SMITH • KENYA A SMITH • KERRIE D SMITH • KERRY O SMITH • KEVIN B SMITH • KEVIN M SMITH • KEVIN R SMITH • KIA Q SMITH • KIMBERLEY A SMITH • KIMBERLY L SMITH • KISHA ANN SMITH • KLYNE L SMITH • KRISTA M SMITH • KRISTAL K SMITH • KYLE A SMITH • L ROSLYN SMITH

243

Handball / *Handball*
Men / *Messieurs*

PRELIMINARIES - GROUP A

RUS 32 - 20 KUW
Halftime Score: 18 - 10

Russian Federation			Kuwait	
5/7	71.4%	**6-Meter shots**	4/6	66.7%
2/6	33.3%	**Wing shots**	1/4	25.0%
5/9	55.6%	**9-Meter shots**	7/14	50.0%
4/4	100.0%	**7-Meter shots**	1/2	50.0%
13/14	92.9%	**Fast breaks**	3/3	100.0%
3/3	100.0%	**Breakthroughs**	4/4	100.0%
32/43	74.4%	**Total shots**	20/33	60.6%
14		**Assists**	5	
8		**Turnovers**	19	
6		**Steals**	1	
3		**Blocks**	1	
5		**Fouls**	5	

1st Referee:	GER	THOMAS, Hans
2nd Referee:	GER	THOMAS, Jurgen

TEAM: RUS Russian Federation

Coach: MAXIMOV, Vladimir   Assistant Coach: KOROSTOCHEVITCH, Leonid

Names	Pos	M/A	% Eff	A	To	Stl	Bl
LAVROV, Andrei	GK	0/0	0.0%				
LAVROV, Igor	CB	3/4	75.0%	1			
FRANTSUZOV, Aleksey	P	0/0	0.0%				
KOULECHOV, Oleg	CB	7/7	100.0%	1	2	1	
KRIVOSHLYKOV, Denis	RW	0/0	0.0%				
VORONIN, Lev	RW	4/7	57.1%				
GOPIN, Valeri	LW	5/8	62.5%	1	1		
KOUDINOV, Vassili	LB	2/3	66.7%	1	2		
TORGOVANOV, Dmitri	P	3/3	100.0%	4	2	1	
SUKOSSIAN, Pavel	GK	0/0	0.0%			1	
GREBNEV, Oleg	P	2/3	66.7%				2
KISSELEV, Oleg	RB	1/1	100.0%	5		2	1
GORPICHIN, Viatcheslav	LB	1/2	50.0%	1	1	1	
POGORELOV, Serguei	RB	4/5	80.0%				
FILIPPOV, Dmitriy	LW	0/0	0.0%				

Goalkeepers	Shots Saved	Attempted	% Eff
LAVROV, Andrei	7	20	35.0%
SUKOSSIAN, Pavel	2	13	15.4%

TEAM: KUW Kuwait

Coach: PULJEVIC, Ilija   Assistant Coach: ALRANDI, Musaed

Names	Pos	M/A	% Eff	A	To	Stl	Bl
ALBLOUSHI, Abdulrazak	GK	0/0	0.0%				
al-HARBI, Abbas	CB	3/7	42.9%	1	3		
ALKHASHTI, Khaldoun	P	3/4	75.0%	2			
al-MARZOUQ, Salem	CB	0/0	0.0%	2			
ALOTAIBI, Ibrahim	RW	0/0	0.0%				
ALSHEMRI, Bandar	RW	0/1	0.0%	1			
ALKAHAM, Adel	LW	2/2	100.0%			1	
ALALI, Mishal	RB	1/1	100.0%	1			
SH ZADAH, Ismaeel	P	0/0	0.0%				
al-MARZOUQ, Khaled	GK	0/0	0.0%				
ALMARZOUQ, Salah	LB	6/13	46.2%	2	5	1	
ALMULLAH, Khaled	LW	3/3	100.0%				
ALMULLAH, Salah	LW	0/0	0.0%				
ALADWANI, Qaied	RB	0/0	0.0%				
ALOTAIBI, Naser	GK	2/2	100.0%	2	4		
ALMULLAH, Tareq	P	0/0	0.0%				

Goalkeeper	Shots Saved	Attempted	% Eff
ALBLOUSHI, Abdulrazak	8	43	18.6%

PRELIMINARIES - GROUP A

CRO 23 - 22 SUI
Halftime Score: 12 - 14

Croatia			Switzerland	
5/8	62.5%	**6-Meter shots**	5/8	62.5%
5/7	71.4%	**Wing shots**	6/8	75.0%
5/16	31.3%	**9-Meter shots**	5/22	22.7%
2/4	50.0%	**7-Meter shots**	1/1	100.0%
1/1	100.0%	**Fast breaks**	1/1	100.0%
5/6	83.3%	**Breakthroughs**	4/4	100.0%
23/42	54.8%	**Total shots**	22/44	50.0%
10		**Assists**	11	
5		**Turnovers**	6	
1		**Steals**	1	
1		**Blocks**	3	
6		**Fouls**	3	

1st Referee:	ROM	DANCESCU, Valter
2nd Referee:	ROM	MATEESCU, Ion

TEAM: CRO Croatia

Coach: KLJAIC, Velimir

Names	Pos	M/A	% Eff	A	To	Stl	Bl
JELCIC, Vladimir	LW	2/4	50.0%				
PERKOVAC, Goran	LW	1/3	33.3%				
SMAJLAGIC, Irfan	LW	6/8	75.0%				
JOVIC, Bozidar	P	0/0	0.0%				
NACINOVIC, Alvaro	P	1/2	50.0%				1
SUJSTER, Vladimir	RW	0/0	0.0%				
GUDELJ, Bruno	LW	0/0	0.0%				
KLJAIC, Nenad	P	0/1	0.0%	3	1		
PUC, Iztok	CB	1/5	20.0%	4	1		
MIKULIC, Zoran	CB	0/1	0.0%				
LOSERT, Venio	GK	0/0	0.0%				
CAVAR, Patrik	CB	8/10	80.0%	1	2		
FRANKOVIC, Valner	P	0/0	0.0%				
GOLUZA, Slavko	CB	1/2	50.0%	1	1	1	
MATOSEVIC, Valter	GK	0/0	0.0%				
SARACEVIC, Zlatko	LB	3/6	50.0%	1			

Goalkeepers	Shots Saved	Attempted	% Eff
LOSERT, Venio	8	19	42.1%
MATOSEVIC, Valter	8	25	32.0%

TEAM: SUI Switzerland

Coach: EMRICH, Armin   Assistant Coach: DEMIROVIC, Halid

Names	Pos	M/A	% Eff	A	To	Stl	Bl
DOBLER, Rolf	GK	0/0	0.0%				
VASILAKIS, Alex	LW	0/0	0.0%				
SPENGLER, Daniel	LW	4/6	66.7%				
CHRISTEN, Nicolas	CB	3/5	60.0%	2	2		
SCHARER, Urs	CB	0/0	0.0%				
BRUNNER, Roman	CB	4/12	33.3%	3	4		2
ZUMSTEIN, Matthias	P	0/0	0.0%				
SCHARER, Stefan	LW	3/3	100.0%	2		1	1
SUTER, Michael	LW	0/0	0.0%				
BRANDENBERGER, Michael	P	0/0	0.0%				
HEIMANN, Urs	GK	0/0	0.0%				
BAUMGARTNER, Marc	CB	5/13	38.5%	4			
KOSTADINOVICH, Robbie	CB	0/0	0.0%				
BARTH, Rene	P	2/4	50.0%				
MEISTERHANS, Christian	GK	0/0	0.0%				
LIMA, Carlos	RW	1/1	100.0%				

Goalkeepers	Shots Saved	Attempted	% Eff
ZUMSTEIN, Matthias	0	0	0.0%
MEISTERHANS, Christian	12	42	28.6%

PRELIMINARIES - GROUP A

SWE 23 - 19 USA
Halftime Score: 11 - 9

Sweden			United States of America	
4/5	80.0%	**6-Meter shots**	5/6	83.3%
3/5	60.0%	**Wing shots**	3/8	37.5%
7/21	33.3%	**9-Meter shots**	6/23	26.1%
2/2	100.0%	**7-Meter shots**	2/4	50.0%
5/7	71.4%	**Fast breaks**	2/2	100.0%
2/3	66.7%	**Breakthroughs**	1/1	100.0%
23/43	53.5%	**Total shots**	19/44	43.2%
10		**Assists**	8	
9		**Turnovers**	10	
6		**Steals**	4	
3		**Blocks**	3	
5		**Fouls**	7	

1st Referee:	LTU	GEDVILAS, Feliksas
2nd Referee:	LTU	GUTERMAN, Grigorij

TEAM: SWE Sweden

Coach: JOHANSSON, Bengt

Names	Pos	M/A	% Eff	A	To	Stl	Bl
OLSSON, Mats	GK	0/0	0.0%				
HEDIN, Robert	CB	4/4	100.0%				
WISLANDER, Magnus	CB	5/6	83.3%		2	1	2
SIVERTSSON, Thomas	P	0/0	0.0%				
LINDGREN, Ola	CB	0/1	0.0%	1	1	2	
CARLEN, Per	P	2/2	100.0%		1		1
HAJAS, Erik	LW	4/7	57.1%	2	1	1	
PETERSON, Johan	RW	3/7	42.9%	2		2	
LOVGREN, Stefan	CB	3/7	42.9%	2			
ANDERSSON, Robert	CB	0/4	0.0%	3	1		
THORSSON, Pierre	RW	0/0	0.0%				
OLSSON, Staffan	CB	0/0	0.0%				
ANDERSSON, Magnus	CB	2/5	40.0%	2	1		
LARSSON, Andreas	CB	0/0	0.0%				
SVENSSON, Thomas	GK	0/0	0.0%				
FRANDESJO, Martin	LW	0/0	0.0%				

Goalkeepers	Shots Saved	Attempted	% Eff
OLSSON, Mats	10	21	47.6%
SVENSSON, Thomas	8	23	34.8%

TEAM: USA United States of America

Coach: OLEKSYK, Richard   Assistant Coach: NICHOL, Rhett

Name	Pos	M/A	% Eff	A	To	Stl	Bl
MANNON, Cliff	GK	0/1	0.0%				
FERCHO, Denny	P	0/0	0.0%				
FITZGERALD, Thomas	LW	3/5	60.0%	1	1		
FITZGERALD, Joseph	CB	1/2	50.0%		2		
PENN, Steven	CB	2/6	33.3%	1	2		
BROWN, Derek	RW	1/1	100.0%				
RYAN, Matt	P	3/5	60.0%	3		2	
DUNN, Robert	LW	0/0	0.0%				
KELLER, John	RB	2/4	50.0%	1			
HEATH, Darrick	LB	4/15	26.7%	6	3	1	
DACHNIWSKY, Yaro	GK	0/0	0.0%				
CACCIA, Greg	RB	0/0	0.0%				
SCHMOCKER, Mark	GK	0/0	0.0%				
DeGRAAF, Dave	P	1/1	100.0%				
THORNBERRY, Michael	P	2/4	50.0%				1
VAN OS, Chip, Jr.	LB	0/0	0.0%	1			

Goalkeepers	Shots Saved	Attempted	% Eff
MANNON, Cliff	11	34	32.4%
SCHMOCKER, Mark	1	9	11.1%

PRELIMINARIES - GROUP A

KUW 22 - 31 CRO
Halftime Score: 11 - 16

Kuwait			Croatia	
4/8	50.0%	6-Meter shots	7/11	63.6%
2/6	33.3%	Wing shots	7/12	58.3%
8/15	53.3%	9-Meter shots	3/8	37.5%
3/5	60.0%	7-Meter shots	5/5	100.0%
3/3	100.0%	Fast breaks	7/8	87.5%
2/3	66.7%	Breakthroughs	2/2	100.0%
22/40	55.0%	Total shots	31/46	67.4%
	5	Assists	22	
	19	Turnovers	10	
	2	Steals	9	
	0	Blocks	3	
	5	Fouls	8	

1st Referee: ESP GALLEGO SANTOS, Silvino
2nd Referee: ESP LAMAS PEREZ, Victor

PRELIMINARIES - GROUP A

SUI 19 - 26 SWE
Halftime Score: 8 - 14

Switzerland			Sweden	
3/3	100.0%	6-Meter shots	7/8	87.5%
6/10	60.0%	Wing shots	6/8	75.0%
6/26	23.1%	9-Meter shots	2/16	12.5%
3/3	100.0%	7-Meter shots	1/2	50.0%
1/1	100.0%	Fast breaks	7/9	77.8%
0/3	0.0%	Breakthroughs	3/4	75.0%
19/46	41.3%	Total shots	26/47	55.3%
	7	Assists	17	
	19	Turnovers	17	
	4	Steals	7	
	2	Blocks	6	
	6	Fouls	10	

1st Referee: FRA GARCIA, Francois
2nd Referee: FRA MORENO, Jean Pierre

PRELIMINARIES - GROUP A

RUS 31 - 16 USA
Halftime Score: 16 - 9

Russian Federation			United States of America	
4/7	57.1%	6-Meter shots	2/8	25.0%
6/8	75.0%	Wing shots	1/3	33.3%
10/15	66.7%	9-Meter shots	6/22	27.3%
1/2	50.0%	7-Meter shots	2/2	100.0%
8/11	72.7%	Fast breaks	1/2	50.0%
2/3	66.7%	Breakthroughs	4/4	100.0%
31/46	67.4%	Total shots	16/41	39.0%
	16	Assists	6	
	10	Turnovers	17	
	5	Steals	5	
	6	Blocks	2	
	6	Fouls	8	

1st Referee: CGO MOELLE MABOUNDA, Michel
2nd Referee: CGO MVOULA, Daniel

TEAM: KUW Kuwait
Coach: PULJEVIC, Ilija   Assistant Coach: ALRANDI, Musaed

Names	Pos	M/A	% Eff	A	To	Stl	Bl
ALBLOUSHI, Abdulrazak	GK	0/0	0.0%	1		1	
al-HARBI, Abbas	CB	4/5	80.0%	1	5		
ALKHASHTI, Khaldoun	P	2/2	100.0%		1		
al-MARZOUQ, Salem	CB	1/4	25.0%	1	2		
ALOTAIBI, Ibrahim	RW	0/0	0.0%				
ALSHEMRI, Bandar	RW	0/1	0.0%		1		
ALKAHAM, Adel	LW	2/3	66.7%				
ALALI, Mishal	RB	2/4	50.0%		2		
SH ZADAH, Ismaeel	P	0/0	0.0%		1		
al-MARZOUQ, Khaled	GK	0/0	0.0%				
ALMARZOUQ, Salah	LB	6/12	50.0%	1	4	1	
ALMULLAH, Khaled	LW	3/5	60.0%	1			
ALADWANI, Qaied	RB	2/4	50.0%		3		
ALOTAIBI, Naser	GK	0/0	0.0%				
ALMULLAH, Tareq	P	0/0	0.0%				
ALMULLAH, Salah	LW	0/0	0.0%				

Goalkeepers	Shots Saved	Attempted	% Eff
ALBLOUSHI, Abdulrazak	11	45	24.4%
ALOTAIBI, Naser	0	1	0.0%

TEAM: SUI Switzerland
Coach: EMRICH, Armin   Assistant Coach: DEMIROVIC, Halid

Names	Pos	M/A	% Eff	A	To	Stl	Bl
DOBLER, Rolf	GK	0/0	0.0%	1	1		
VASILAKIS, Alex	LW	0/0	0.0%				
SPENGLER, Daniel	LW	3/6	50.0%		1		
CHRISTEN, Nicolas	CB	2/5	40.0%		3		
SCHARER, Urs	CB	1/3	33.3%	2	3		
BRUNNER, Roman	CB	3/13	23.1%	1	2		2
ZUMSTEIN, Matthias	P	2/2	100.0%		3		
SCHARER, Stefan	LW	0/2	0.0%		2		
SUTER, Michael	LW	0/0	0.0%				
BRANDENBERGER, Michael	P	0/0	0.0%				
HEIMANN, Urs	GK	0/0	0.0%				
BAUMGARTNER, Marc	CB	5/10	50.0%	2	1		
KOSTADINOVICH, Robbie	CB	1/3	33.3%	1	1	2	
BARTH, Rene	P	0/0	0.0%		1		
MEISTERHANS, Christian	GK	0/0	0.0%			1	
LIMA, Carlos	RW	2/2	100.0%		1	1	

Goalkeepers	Shots Saved	Attempted	% Eff
DOBLER, Rolf	6	15	40.0%
MEISTERHANS, Christian	6	32	18.8%

TEAM: RUS Russian Federation
Coach: MAXIMOV, Vladimir   Assistant Coach: KOROSTOCHEVITCH, Leonid

Names	Pos	M/A	% Eff	A	To	Stl	Bl
LAVROV, Andrei	GK	0/0	0.0%				
LAVROV, Igor	CB	4/7	57.1%	1			
FRANTSUZOV, Aleksey	P	0/0	0.0%				
KOULECHOV, Oleg	CB	1/6	16.7%	3			
KRIVOSHLYKOV, Denis	RW	0/0	0.0%				
VORONIN, Lev	RW	5/6	83.3%		1	1	
GOPIN, Valeri	LW	4/5	80.0%	5	2	2	
KOUDINOV, Vassili	LB	10/12	83.3%	3			
TORGOVANOV, Dmitri	P	2/4	50.0%	1	1		
SUKOSSIAN, Pavel	GK	0/0	0.0%				
GREBNEV, Oleg	P	1/1	100.0%	2		2	
KISSELEV, Oleg	RB	2/3	66.7%	2		1	
GORPICHIN, Viatcheslav	LB	0/0	0.0%	2		2	
POGORELOV, Serguei	RB	2/2	100.0%	2	2	1	1
FILIPPOV, Dmitriy	LW	0/0	0.0%				

Goalkeepers	Shots Saved	Attempted	% Eff
LAVROV, Andrei	7	22	31.8%
SUKOSSIAN, Pavel	6	19	31.6%

TEAM: CRO Croatia
Coach: KLJAIC, Velimir

Names	Pos	M/A	% Eff	A	To	Stl	Bl
JELCIC, Vladimir	LW	2/5	40.0%	2			
PERKOVAC, Goran	LW	1/1	100.0%	1	1	1	
SMAJLAGIC, Irfan	LW	4/9	44.4%		2	2	
JOVIC, Bozidar	P	7/7	100.0%	3	3	4	1
NACINOVIC, Alvaro	P	1/1	100.0%				
SUJSTER, Vladimir	RW	0/0	0.0%				
GUDELJ, Bruno	LW	1/2	50.0%	3	1		
KLJAIC, Nenad	P	0/0	0.0%				
PUC, Iztok	CB	0/0	0.0%				
MIKULIC, Zoran	CB	0/0	0.0%				
LOSERT, Venio	GK	0/0	0.0%				
CAVAR, Patrik	CB	10/11	90.9%	4	2		
FRANKOVIC, Valner	P	0/0	0.0%				
GOLUZA, Slavko	CB	2/3	66.7%	5	2		2
MATOSEVIC, Valter	GK	0/0	0.0%				
SARACEVIC, Zlatko	LB	3/7	42.9%	4	1		

Goalkeepers	Shots Saved	Attempted	% Eff
JELCIC, Vladimir	2	8	25.0%
MATOSEVIC, Valter	11	32	34.4%

TEAM: SWE Sweden
Coach: JOHANSSON, Bengt

Names	Pos	M/A	% Eff	A	To	Stl	Bl
OLSSON, Mats	GK	0/1	0.0%	2	2		
HEDIN, Robert	CB	3/5	60.0%		1		
WISLANDER, Magnus	CB	0/1	0.0%	5	5	1	1
SIVERTSSON, Thomas	P	5/5	100.0%	1			1
LINDGREN, Ola	CB	0/1	0.0%		1		1
CARLEN, Per	P	2/2	100.0%		1		1
HAJAS, Erik	LW	6/8	75.0%	3	2		
PETERSON, Johan	RW	0/0	0.0%				
LOVGREN, Stefan	CB	0/1	0.0%	1	1		
ANDERSSON, Robert	CB	0/0	0.0%				
THORSSON, Pierre	RW	5/9	55.6%	1		2	
OLSSON, Staffan	CB	2/9	22.2%	5	3	1	2
ANDERSSON, Magnus	CB	3/5	60.0%	2		1	
LARSSON, Andreas	CB	0/0	0.0%				
SVENSSON, Thomas	GK	0/0	0.0%				
FRANDESJO, Martin	LW	0/0	0.0%				

Goalkeeper	Shots Saved	Attempted	% Eff
OLSSON, Mats	12	46	26.1%

TEAM: USA United States of America
Coach: OLEKSYK, Richard   Assistant Coach: NICHOL, Rhett

Names	Pos	M/A	% Eff	A	To	Stl	Bl
MANNON, Cliff	GK	0/0	0.0%				
FERCHO, Denny	P	0/1	0.0%	1	1	1	
FITZGERALD, Thomas	LW	2/3	66.7%	1	3	1	
FITZGERALD, Joseph	CB	2/3	66.7%	1	3		
PENN, Steven	CB	4/9	44.4%	2			
BROWN, Derek	RW	0/0	0.0%				
RYAN, Matt	P	1/2	50.0%	1		1	
DUNN, Robert	LW	0/0	0.0%				
KELLER, John	RB	3/4	75.0%	1		1	
HEATH, Darrick	LB	3/11	27.3%	1	4	1	1
DACHNIWSKY, Yaro	GK	0/0	0.0%				
CACCIA, Greg	RB	1/2	50.0%	1			
SCHMOCKER, Mark	GK	0/0	0.0%				
DeGRAAF, Dave	P	0/1	0.0%		2	1	
THORNBERRY, Michael	P	0/5	0.0%	1			
VAN OS, Chip, Jr.	LB	0/0	0.0%				

Goalkeepers	Shots Saved	Attempted	% Eff
MANNON, Cliff	7	27	25.9%
SCHMOCKER, Mark	3	19	15.8%

PRELIMINARIES - GROUP A

SUI 33 - 16 KUW
Halftime Score: 18 - 8

Switzerland			Kuwait	
7/8	87.5%	6-Meter shots	2/6	33.3%
6/13	46.2%	Wing shots	1/5	20.0%
6/10	60.0%	9-Meter shots	6/24	25.0%
3/5	60.0%	7-Meter shots	4/6	66.7%
11/13	84.6%	Fast breaks	1/5	20.0%
0/4	0.0%	Breakthroughs	2/3	66.7%
33/53	62.3%	Total shots	16/49	32.7%
14		Assists	2	
11		Turnovers	18	
3		Steals	4	
5		Blocks	1	
6		Fouls	9	

1st Referee:	LTU	GEDVILAS, Feliksas
2nd Referee:	LTU	GUTERMAN, Grigorij

PRELIMINARIES - GROUP A

SWE 22 - 20 RUS
Halftime Score: 11 - 11

Sweden			Russian Federation	
3/6	50.0%	6-Meter shots	3/4	75.0%
2/4	50.0%	Wing shots	5/5	100.0%
7/15	46.7%	9-Meter shots	5/17	29.4%
2/2	100.0%	7-Meter shots	3/6	50.0%
2/3	66.7%	Fast breaks	3/4	75.0%
6/6	100.0%	Breakthroughs	1/1	100.0%
22/36	61.1%	Total shots	20/37	54.1%
9		Assists	7	
8		Turnovers	7	
0		Steals	2	
5		Blocks	3	
7		Fouls	8	

1st Referee:	ESP	GALLEGO SANTOS, Silvino
2nd Referee:	ESP	LAMAS PEREZ, Victor

PRELIMINARIES - GROUP A

CRO 35 - 27 USA
Halftime Score: 20 - 9

Croatia			United States of America	
1/2	50.0%	6-Meter shots	6/8	75.0%
8/14	57.1%	Wing shots	6/7	85.7%
11/15	73.3%	9-Meter shots	4/15	26.7%
5/6	83.3%	7-Meter shots	3/4	75.0%
8/12	66.7%	Fast breaks	6/8	75.0%
2/5	40.0%	Breakthroughs	2/3	66.7%
35/54	64.8%	Total shots	27/45	60.0%
15		Assists	16	
11		Turnovers	20	
5		Steals	2	
3		Blocks	1	
9		Fouls	8	

1st Referee:	FRA	GARCIA, Francois
2nd Referee:	FRA	MORENO, Jean Pierre

TEAM: SUI Switzerland
Coach: EMRICH, Armin   Assistant Coach: DEMIROVIC, Halid

Names	Pos	M/A	% Eff	A	To	Stl	Bl
DOBLER, Rolf	GK	1/2	50.0%		1		
VASILAKIS, Alex	LW	0/0	0.0%				
SPENGLER, Daniel	LW	6/9	66.7%	1			
CHRISTEN, Nicolas	CB	2/4	50.0%	1	1		
SCHARER, Urs	CB	1/2	50.0%	1			
BRUNNER, Roman	CB	4/4	100.0%	2	1		3
ZUMSTEIN, Matthias	P	1/3	33.3%				1
SCHARER, Stefan	LW	5/7	71.4%	1	1	1	
SUTER, Michael	LW	0/0	0.0%				
BRANDENBERGER, Michael	P	0/0	0.0%				
HEIMANN, Urs	GK	0/0	0.0%				
BAUMGARTNER, Marc	CB	3/7	42.9%	4	5	1	
KOSTADINOVICH, Robbie	CB	1/2	50.0%	3	1		
BARTH, Rene	P	6/7	85.7%	1		1	
MEISTERHANS, Christian	GK	0/0	0.0%	1			
LIMA, Carlos	RW	3/6	50.0%			1	

Goalkeepers	Shots Saved	Attempted	% Eff
DOBLER, Rolf	15	27	55.6%
MEISTERHANS, Christian	6	22	27.3%

TEAM: SWE Sweden
Coach: JOHANSSON, Bengt

Names	Pos	M/A	% Eff	A	To	Stl	Bl
OLSSON, Mats	GK	0/0	0.0%				
HEDIN, Robert	CB	2/2	100.0%				
WISLANDER, Magnus	CB	3/3	100.0%	1	1		1
SIVERTSSON, Thomas	P	2/2	100.0%				
LINDGREN, Ola	CB	1/3	33.3%				1
CARLEN, Per	P	1/3	33.3%		1		1
HAJAS, Erik	LW	1/3	33.3%	1	3		
PETERSON, Johan	RW	0/0	0.0%				
LOVGREN, Stefan	CB	4/6	66.7%	1			
ANDERSSON, Robert	CB	0/0	0.0%				
THORSSON, Pierre	RW	3/4	75.0%				
OLSSON, Staffan	CB	0/1	0.0%	4	1		2
ANDERSSON, Magnus	CB	5/9	55.6%	2	2		
LARSSON, Andreas	CB	0/0	0.0%				
SVENSSON, Thomas	GK	0/0	0.0%				
FRANDESJO, Martin	LW	0/0	0.0%				

Goalkeepers	Shots Saved	Attempted	% Eff
OLSSON, Mats	6	26	23.1%
SVENSSON, Thomas	3	11	27.3%

TEAM: CRO Croatia
Coach: KLJAIC, Velimir

Names	Pos	M/A	% Eff	A	To	Stl	Bl
JELCIC, Vladimir	LW	2/2	100.0%	2	1	1	
PERKOVAC, Goran	LW	3/4	75.0%	2	3	1	
SMAJLAGIC, Irfan	LW	11/14	78.6%			1	
JOVIC, Bozidar	P	2/5	40.0%	1			1
NACINOVIC, Alvaro	P	0/0	0.0%				
SUJSTER, Vladimir	RW	0/0	0.0%				
GUDELJ, Bruno	LW	0/0	0.0%				
KLJAIC, Nenad	P	0/1	0.0%		1		
PUC, Iztok	CB	0/0	0.0%				
MIKULIC, Zoran	CB	1/1	100.0%				
LOSERT, Venio	GK	0/0	0.0%				
CAVAR, Patrik	CB	10/16	62.5%	2	4	1	2
FRANKOVIC, Valner	P	0/0	0.0%				
GOLUZA, Slavko	CB	3/5	60.0%	5	1	1	
MATOSEVIC, Valter	GK	0/0	0.0%	1			
SARACEVIC, Zlatko	LB	3/6	50.0%	3			

Goalkeepers	Shots Saved	Attempted	% Eff
LOSERT, Venio	5	26	19.2%
MATOSEVIC, Valter	6	19	31.6%

TEAM: KUW Kuwait
Coach: PULJEVIC, Ilija   Assistant Coach: ALRANDI, Musaed

Names	Pos	M/A	% Eff	A	To	Stl	Bl
ALBLOUSHI, Abdulrazak	GK	1/1	100.0%	1	2		
al-HARBI, Abbas	CB	2/8	25.0%	2			
ALKHASHTI, Khaldoun	P	1/6	16.7%	1	5		
al-MARZOUQ, Salem	CB	2/4	50.0%	1	1		
ALOTAIBI, Ibrahim	RW	0/0	0.0%				
ALSHEMRI, Bandar	RW	1/3	33.3%	3			
ALKAHAM, Adel	LW	1/3	33.3%				
ALALI, Mishal	RB	4/8	50.0%				1
SH ZADAH, Ismaeel	P	0/0	0.0%				
al-MARZOUQ, Khaled	GK	0/0	0.0%				
ALMARZOUQ, Salah	LB	1/7	14.3%	4			
ALMULLAH, Khaled	LW	0/2	0.0%				
ALADWANI, Qaied	RB	3/7	42.9%	4			
ALOTAIBI, Naser	GK	0/0	0.0%				
ALMULLAH, Tareq	P	0/0	0.0%				
ALMULLAH, Salah	LW	0/0	0.0%				

Goalkeeper	Shots Saved	Attempted	% Eff
ALBLOUSHI, Abdulrazak	13	53	24.5%

TEAM: RUS Russian Federation
Coach: MAXIMOV, Vladimir   Assistant Coach: KOROSTOCHEVITCH, Leonid

Names	Pos	M/A	% Eff	A	To	Stl	Bl
LAVROV, Andrei	GK	0/0	0.0%				
LAVROV, Igor	CB	0/1	0.0%	3			
FRANTSUZOV, Aleksey	P	0/0	0.0%				1
KOULECHOV, Oleg	CB	2/6	33.3%				
KRIVOSHLYKOV, Denis	RW	0/0	0.0%				
VORONIN, Lev	RW	3/4	75.0%	1			
GOPIN, Valeri	LW	5/7	71.4%	1			
KOUDINOV, Vassili	LB	3/6	50.0%	5	3		
TORGOVANOV, Dmitri	P	5/7	71.4%				
SUKOSSIAN, Pavel	GK	0/0	0.0%				
GREBNEV, Oleg	P	0/0	0.0%			1	1
KISSELEV, Oleg	RB	0/0	0.0%				1
GORPICHIN, Viatcheslav	LB	1/1	100.0%	1			
POGORELOV, Serguei	RB	1/5	20.0%	1			
FILIPPOV, Dmitriy	LW	0/0	0.0%				

Goalkeeper	Shots Saved	Attempted	% Eff
LAVROV, Andrei	11	36	30.6%

TEAM: USA United States of America
Coach: OLEKSYK, Richard   Assistant Coach: NICHOL, Rhett

Names	Pos	M/A	% Eff	A	To	Stl	Bl
MANNON, Cliff	GK	0/0	0.0%				
FERCHO, Denny	P	0/0	0.0%				
FITZGERALD, Thomas	LW	1/1	100.0%				
FITZGERALD, Joseph	CB	3/5	60.0%	2	1		
PENN, Steven	CB	1/3	33.3%	1	1		
BROWN, Derek	RW	8/9	88.9%	3			
RYAN, Matt	P	1/2	50.0%	5	3		
DUNN, Robert	LW	5/6	83.3%	1	1		
KELLER, John	RB	2/3	66.7%	2	2		
HEATH, Darrick	LB	3/11	27.3%	5	8	1	
DACHNIWSKY, Yaro	GK	0/0	0.0%				
CACCIA, Greg	RB	0/0	0.0%				
SCHMOCKER, Mark	GK	0/0	0.0%				
DeGRAAF, Dave	P	2/3	66.7%	1	1		
THORNBERRY, Michael	P	1/2	50.0%				1
VAN OS, Chip, Jr.	LB	0/0	0.0%				

Goalkeepers	Shots Saved	Attempted	% Eff
MANNON, Cliff	14	38	36.8%
SCHMOCKER, Mark	3	16	18.8%

Men / *Messieurs*

PRELIMINARIES - GROUP A

SWE 33 - 18 KUW
Halftime Score: 16 - 7

Sweden		6-Meter shots	Kuwait	
4/9	44.4%	6-Meter shots	7/12	58.3%
4/7	57.1%	Wing shots	2/5	40.0%
10/16	62.5%	9-Meter shots	2/16	12.5%
2/3	66.7%	7-Meter shots	4/4	100.0%
11/18	61.1%	Fast breaks	1/2	50.0%
2/2	100.0%	Breakthroughs	2/2	100.0%
33/55	60.0%	Total shots	18/41	43.9%
	14	Assists	8	
	7	Turnovers	23	
	10	Steals	3	
	5	Blocks	0	
	5	Fouls	4	

1st Referee:	NED	BRUSSEL, Peter
2nd Referee:	NED	van DONGEN, Anton

PRELIMINARIES - GROUP A

RUS 24 - 25 CRO
Halftime Score: 13 - 11

Russian Federation		6-Meter shots	Croatia	
1/5	20.0%	6-Meter shots	7/7	100.0%
6/8	75.0%	Wing shots	2/7	28.6%
7/11	63.6%	9-Meter shots	7/14	50.0%
4/6	66.7%	7-Meter shots	1/1	100.0%
4/5	80.0%	Fast breaks	6/8	75.0%
2/3	66.7%	Breakthroughs	2/4	50.0%
24/38	63.2%	Total shots	25/41	61.0%
	11	Assists	8	
	13	Turnovers	8	
	0	Steals	6	
	0	Blocks	0	
	5	Fouls	5	

1st Referee:	DEN	ELBROND, Per
2nd Referee:	DEN	LOVQVIST, Kjeld

PRELIMINARIES - GROUP A

USA 20 - 29 SUI
Halftime Score: 9 - 12

United States		6-Meter shots	Switzerland	
4/6	66.7%	6-Meter shots	8/8	100.0%
3/4	75.0%	Wing shots	3/5	60.0%
7/19	36.8%	9-Meter shots	7/17	41.2%
2/3	66.7%	7-Meter shots	7/8	87.5%
3/5	60.0%	Fast breaks	3/4	75.0%
1/4	25.0%	Breakthroughs	1/1	100.0%
20/41	48.8%	Total shots	29/43	67.4%
	9	Assists	8	
	15	Turnovers	8	
	1	Steals	2	
	1	Blocks	4	
	12	Fouls	8	

1st Referee:	GER	THOMAS, Hans
2nd Referee:	GER	THOMAS, Jurgen

TEAM: SWE Sweden
Coach: JOHANSSON, Bengt

Names	Pos	M/A	% Eff	A	To	Stl	Bl
OLSSON, Mats	GK	0/0	0.0%				
HEDIN, Robert	CB	6/8	75.0%		1		3
WISLANDER, Magnus	CB	1/2	50.0%	1			1
SIVERTSSON, Thomas	P	1/4	25.0%		1	1	2
LINDGREN, Ola	CB	0/0	0.0%				
CARLEN, Per	P	0/2	0.0%	1			3
HAJAS, Erik	LW	0/0	0.0%				
PETERSON, Johan	RW	10/14	71.4%	1	1		
LOVGREN, Stefan	CB	2/5	40.0%	1			
ANDERSSON, Robert	CB	1/1	100.0%	2	2		1
THORSSON, Pierre	RW	0/0	0.0%			1	
OLSSON, Staffan	CB	0/0	0.0%				
ANDERSSON, Magnus	CB	1/2	50.0%	3		1	
LARSSON, Andreas	CB	5/6	83.3%	1	2		1
SVENSSON, Thomas	GK	0/0	0.0%	3		1	
FRANDESJO, Martin	LW	6/11	54.5%	1			

Goalkeeper	Shots Saved	Attempted	% Eff
SVENSSON, Thomas	12	41	29.3%

TEAM: RUS Russian Federation
Coach: MAXIMOV, Vladimir   Assistant Coach: KOROSTOCHEVITCH, Leonid

Names	Pos	M/A	% Eff	A	To	Stl	Bl
LAVROV, Andrei	GK	0/0	0.0%				
LAVROV, Igor	CB	1/2	50.0%	1	1		
FRANTSUZOV, Aleksey	P	0/0	0.0%				
KOULECHOV, Oleg	CB	2/3	66.7%				
KRIVOSHLYKOV, Denis	RW	0/0	0.0%				
VORONIN, Lev	RW	2/3	66.7%		1		
GOPIN, Valeri	LW	7/10	70.0%	1	1		
KOUDINOV, Vassili	LB	4/7	57.1%	4	2		
TORGOVANOV, Dmitri	P	5/9	55.6%	2	1		
SUKOSSIAN, Pavel	GK	0/0	0.0%				
GREBNEV, Oleg	P	0/0	0.0%				
KISSELEV, Oleg	RB	1/1	100.0%	1	2		
GORPICHIN, Viatcheslav	LB	0/0	0.0%				
POGORELOV, Serguei	RB	2/3	66.7%	2	5		
FILIPPOV, Dmitriy	LW	0/0	0.0%				

Goalkeepers	Shots Saved	Attempted	% Eff
LAVROV, Andrei	5	25	20.0%
SUKOSSIAN, Pavel	5	16	31.3%

TEAM: USA United States of America
Coach: OLEKSYK, Richard   Assistant Coach: NICHOL, Rhett

Names	Pos	M/A	% Eff	A	To	Stl	Bl
MANNON, Cliff	GK	0/0	0.0%	2			
FERCHO, Denny	P	0/0	0.0%				
FITZGERALD, Thomas	LW	0/0	0.0%				
FITZGERALD, Joseph	CB	1/1	100.0%	1			
PENN, Steven	CB	3/9	33.3%	2	1		
BROWN, Derek	RW	4/7	57.1%		2		
RYAN, Matt	P	0/2	0.0%	1	1		1
DUNN, Robert	LW	3/4	75.0%		5		
KELLER, John	RB	0/0	0.0%	1	2		
HEATH, Darrick	LB	7/14	50.0%	2	4	1	
DACHNIWSKY, Yaro	GK	0/0	0.0%				
CACCIA, Greg	RB	0/0	0.0%				
SCHMOCKER, Mark	GK	0/0	0.0%				
DeGRAAF, Dave	P	0/0	0.0%				
THORNBERRY, Michael	P	2/3	66.7%				
VAN OS, Chip, Jr.	LB	0/1	0.0%				

Goalkeepers	Shots Saved	Attempted	% Eff
MANNON, Cliff	4	27	14.8%
SCHMOCKER, Mark	4	16	25.0%

TEAM: KUW Kuwait
Coach: PULJEVIC, Ilija   Assistant Coach: ALRANDI, Musaed

Names	Pos	M/A	% Eff	A	To	Stl	Bl
ALBLOUSHI, Abdulrazak	GK	0/0	0.0%		1		
al-HARBI, Abbas	CB	1/2	50.0%	2	6		
ALKHASHTI, Khaldoun	P	3/5	60.0%				
al-MARZOUQ, Salem	CB	2/5	40.0%	3	4	2	
ALOTAIBI, Ibrahim	RW	0/0	0.0%				
ALSHEMRI, Bandar	RW	0/0	0.0%	2			
ALKAHAM, Adel	LW	0/1	0.0%				
ALALI, Mishal	RB	4/5	80.0%	1			
SH ZADAH, Ismaeel	P	3/4	75.0%	1			
al-MARZOUQ, Khaled	GK	0/0	0.0%				
ALMARZOUQ, Salah	LB	3/12	25.0%	3	4		
ALMULLAH, Khaled	LW	2/5	40.0%			1	
ALADWANI, Qaied	RB	0/2	0.0%	4			
ALOTAIBI, Naser	GK	0/0	0.0%				
ALMULLAH, Tareq	P	0/0	0.0%				
ALMULLAH, Salah	LW	0/0	0.0%				

Goalkeepers	Shots Saved	Attempted	% Eff
ALBLOUSHI, Abdulrazak	13	48	27.1%
ALOTAIBI, Naser	2	7	28.6%

TEAM: CRO Croatia
Coach: KLJAIC, Velimir

Names	Pos	M/A	% Eff	A	To	Stl	Bl
JELCIC, Vladimir	LW	2/3	66.7%		2		
PERKOVAC, Goran	LW	1/4	25.0%	1	1		
SMAJLAGIC, Irfan	LW	2/3	66.7%		2	1	
JOVIC, Bozidar	P	7/8	87.5%	1	1	1	
NACINOVIC, Alvaro	P	0/0	0.0%				
SUJSTER, Vladimir	RW	0/0	0.0%				
GUDELJ, Bruno	LW	0/0	0.0%				
KLJAIC, Nenad	P	0/0	0.0%				
PUC, Iztok	CB	3/4	75.0%	2	2		
MIKULIC, Zoran	CB	0/0	0.0%				
LOSERT, Venio	GK	0/0	0.0%				
CAVAR, Patrik	CB	4/5	80.0%	2		2	
FRANKOVIC, Valner	P	0/0	0.0%				
GOLUZA, Slavko	CB	1/3	33.3%	1	1		
MATOSEVIC, Valter	GK	0/0	0.0%				
SARACEVIC, Zlatko	LB	5/11	45.5%	1	1		

Goalkeepers	Shots Saved	Attempted	% Eff
LOSERT, Venio	3	8	37.5%
MATOSEVIC, Valter	9	30	30.0%

TEAM: SUI Switzerland
Coach: EMRICH, Armin   Assistant Coach: DEMIROVIC, Halid

Names	Pos	M/A	% Eff	A	To	Stl	Bl
DOBLER, Rolf	GK	0/0	0.0%				
VASILAKIS, Alex	LW	0/0	0.0%				
SPENGLER, Daniel	LW	4/4	100.0%	1	3		1
CHRISTEN, Nicolas	CB	2/3	66.7%	1	2		
SCHARER, Urs	CB	0/0	0.0%				
BRUNNER, Roman	CB	3/7	42.9%	1			
ZUMSTEIN, Matthias	P	0/0	0.0%				
SCHARER, Stefan	LW	5/8	62.5%	2	1	1	
SUTER, Michael	LW	0/0	0.0%				
BRANDENBERGER, Michael	P	0/0	0.0%				
HEIMANN, Urs	GK	0/0	0.0%				
BAUMGARTNER, Marc	CB	13/17	76.5%	4	1	1	1
KOSTADINOVICH, Robbie	CB	0/0	0.0%				
BARTH, Rene	P	2/4	50.0%				1
MEISTERHANS, Christian	GK	0/0	0.0%				
LIMA, Carlos	RW	0/0	0.0%				1

Goalkeeper	Shots Saved	Attempted	% Eff
MEISTERHANS, Christian	13	41	31.7%

Men / *Messieurs*

PRELIMINARIES - GROUP A

RUS 30 - 23 SUI
Halftime Score: 14 - 11

Russian Federatiom			Switzerland	
8/11	72.7%	6-Meter shots	0/1	0.0%
2/5	40.0%	Wing shots	7/7	100.0%
10/17	58.8%	9-Meter shots	8/19	42.1%
4/5	80.0%	7-Meter shots	3/4	75.0%
5/7	71.4%	Fast breaks	2/3	66.7%
1/1	100.0%	Breakthroughs	3/4	75.0%
30/46	65.2%	Total shots	23/38	60.5%
13		Assists	8	
8		Turnovers	17	
5		Steals	0	
5		Blocks	2	
10		Fouls	11	

1st Referee: FRA   GARCIA, Francois
2nd Referee: FRA   MORENO, Jean Pierre

PRELIMINARIES - GROUP A

CRO 18 - 27 SWE
Halftime Score: 7 - 10

Croatia			Sweden	
5/15	33.3%	6-Meter shots	6/9	66.7%
2/9	22.2%	Wing shots	6/9	66.7%
8/18	44.4%	9-Meter shots	4/11	36.4%
1/4	25.0%	7-Meter shots	3/3	100.0%
1/3	33.3%	Fast breaks	7/8	87.5%
1/2	50.0%	Breakthroughs	1/1	100.0%
18/51	35.3%	Total shots	27/41	65.8%
6		Assists	16	
11		Turnovers	16	
5		Steals	3	
1		Blocks	3	
6		Fouls	8	

1st Referee: GER   THOMAS, Hans
2nd Referee: GER   THOMAS, Jurgen

PRELIMINARIES - GROUP A

KUW 24 - 29 USA
Halftime Score: 10 - 13

Kuwait			United States of America	
5/12	41.7%	6-Meter shots	16/20	80.0%
3/3	100.0%	Wing shots	2/5	40.0%
9/26	34.6%	9-Meter shots	2/7	28.6%
3/5	60.0%	7-Meter shots	1/4	25.0%
1/3	33.3%	Fast breaks	6/7	85.7%
3/4	75.0%	Breakthroughs	2/5	40.0%
24/53	45.3%	Total shots	29/48	60.4%
9		Assists	21	
15		Turnovers	17	
4		Steals	8	
1		Blocks	13	
5		Fouls	4	

1st Referee: ROM   DANCESCU, Valter
2nd Referee: ROM   MATEESCU, Ion

TEAM: RUS Russian Federation
Coach: MAXIMOV, Vladimir   Assistant Coach: KOROSTOCHEVITCH, Leonid

Names	Pos	M/A	% Eff	A	To	Stl	Bl
LAVROV, Andrei	GK	0/0	0.0%	1			
LAVROV, Igor	CB	0/0	0.0%				
FRANTSUZOV, Aleksey	P	0/0	0.0%				
KOULECHOV, Oleg	CB	9/12	75.0%		3		
KRIVOSHLYKOV, Denis	RW	0/0	0.0%				
VORONIN, Lev	RW	2/5	40.0%	1	1	1	1
GOPIN, Valeri	LW	3/5	60.0%	5	1		
KOUDINOV, Vassili	LB	4/9	44.4%	3	1		
TORGOVANOV, Dmitri	P	5/6	83.3%	1		2	1
SUKOSSIAN, Pavel	GK	0/0	0.0%				
GREBNEV, Oleg	P	1/1	100.0%			1	3
KISSELEV, Oleg	RB	0/0	0.0%	1	1		
GORPICHIN, Viatcheslav	LB	0/0	0.0%	1		1	
POGORELOV, Serguei	RB	4/6	66.7%	1			
FILIPPOV, Dmitriy	LW	2/2	100.0%				

Goalkeepers	Shots Saved	Attempted	% Eff
LAVROV, Andrei	4	19	21.1%
SUKOSSIAN, Pavel	2	19	10.5%

TEAM: CRO Croatia
Coach: KLJAIC, Velimir

Names	Pos	M/A	% Eff	A	To	Stl	Bl
JELCIC, Vladimir	LW	3/12	25.0%		1	2	
PERKOVAC, Goran	LW	1/7	14.3%		1	1	
SMAJLAGIC, Irfan	LW	0/0	0.0%				
JOVIC, Bozidar	P	1/2	50.0%				
NACINOVIC, Alvaro	P	1/2	50.0%				
SUJSTER, Vladimir	RW	2/5	40.0%				
GUDELJ, Bruno	LW	1/2	50.0%	2	1	1	
KLJAIC, Nenad	P	2/3	66.7%		1	1	
PUC, Iztok	CB	0/0	0.0%				
MIKULIC, Zoran	CB	6/11	54.5%	2	3		
LOSERT, Venio	GK	0/0	0.0%				
CAVAR, Patrik	CB	0/0	0.0%				
FRANKOVIC, Valner	P	0/2	0.0%		1		
GOLUZA, Slavko	CB	1/4	25.0%	2	3		1
MATOSEVIC, Valter	GK	0/1	0.0%				
SARACEVIC, Zlatko	LB	0/0	0.0%				

Goalkeepers	Shots Saved	Attempted	% Eff
LOSERT, Venio	2	15	13.3%
MATOSEVIC, Valter	7	26	26.9%

TEAM: KUW Kuwait
Coach: PULJEVIC, Ilija   Assistant Coach: ALRANDI, Musaed

Names	Pos	M/A	% Eff	A	To	Stl	Bl
ALBLOUSHI, Abdulrazak	GK	0/0	0.0%	1			
al-HARBI, Abbas	CB	2/8	25.0%	4	2		
ALKHASHTI, Khaldoun	P	2/6	33.3%				
al-MARZOUQ, Salem	CB	1/3	33.3%	2	3	1	
ALOTAIBI, Ibrahim	RW	0/0	0.0%				
ALSHEMRI, Bandar	RW	2/2	100.0%		1	1	
ALKAHAM, Adel	LW	1/1	100.0%	1			
ALALI, Mishal	RB	2/4	50.0%				
SH ZADAH, Ismaeel	P	3/8	37.5%				
al-MARZOUQ, Khaled	GK	0/0	0.0%				
ALMARZOUQ, Salah	LB	9/17	52.9%		4	2	1
ALMULLAH, Khaled	LW	0/0	0.0%	1	3		
ALADWANI, Qaied	RB	2/4	50.0%	1	1		
ALOTAIBI, Naser	GK	0/0	0.0%				
ALMULLAH, Tareq	P	0/0	0.0%				
ALMULLAH, Salah	LW	0/0	0.0%				

Goalkeeper	Shots Saved	Attempted	% Eff
ALBLOUSHI, Abdulrazak	12	48	25.0%

TEAM: SUI Switzerland
Coach: EMRICH, Armin   Assistant Coach: DEMIROVIC, Halid

Names	Pos	M/A	% Eff	A	To	Stl	Bl
DOBLER, Rolf	GK	0/0	0.0%				
VASILAKIS, Alex	LW	0/0	0.0%				
SPENGLER, Daniel	LW	8/9	88.9%		2		
CHRISTEN, Nicolas	CB	0/1	0.0%	1	2		
SCHARER, Urs	CB	0/0	0.0%				
BRUNNER, Roman	CB	6/13	46.2%	1	1		1
ZUMSTEIN, Matthias	P	0/0	0.0%		1		
SCHARER, Stefan	LW	2/2	100.0%		1		
SUTER, Michael	LW	0/0	0.0%				
BRANDENBERGER, Michael	P	0/0	0.0%				
HEIMANN, Urs	GK	0/0	0.0%				
BAUMGARTNER, Marc	CB	5/10	50.0%	2	2		
KOSTADINOVICH, Robbie	CB	1/1	100.0%	2	5		
BARTH, Rene	P	0/1	0.0%		1		1
MEISTERHANS, Christian	GK	0/0	0.0%	1	1		
LIMA, Carlos	RW	1/1	100.0%	1	1		

Goalkeepers	Shots Saved	Attempted	% Eff
DOBLER, Rolf	4	16	25.0%
MEISTERHANS, Christian	5	30	16.7%

TEAM: SWE Sweden
Coach: JOHANSSON, Bengt

Names	Pos	M/A	% Eff	A	To	Stl	Bl
OLSSON, Mats	GK	0/0	0.0%	1			
HEDIN, Robert	CB	1/1	100.0%	1			
WISLANDER, Magnus	CB	2/5	40.0%	2	1	1	1
SIVERTSSON, Thomas	P	2/3	66.7%		1		
LINDGREN, Ola	CB	1/1	100.0%	1	1	1	1
CARLEN, Per	P	1/3	33.3%	1	2		1
HAJAS, Erik	LW	7/9	77.8%				
PETERSON, Johan	RW	0/0	0.0%				
LOVGREN, Stefan	CB	4/5	80.0%	2	2		
ANDERSSON, Robert	CB	0/0	0.0%				
THORSSON, Pierre	RW	7/8	87.5%		2	1	
OLSSON, Staffan	CB	1/4	25.0%	7	5		
ANDERSSON, Magnus	CB	0/0	0.0%				
LARSSON, Andreas	CB	1/2	50.0%	2	1		
SVENSSON, Thomas	GK	0/0	0.0%				
FRANDESJO, Martin	LW	0/0	0.0%				

Goalkeeper	Shots Saved	Attempted	% Eff
OLSSON, Mats	24	51	47.1%

TEAM: USA United States of America
Coach: OLEKSYK, Richard   Assistant Coach: NICHOL, Rhett

Names	Pos	M/A	% Eff	A	To	Stl	Bl
MANNON, Cliff	GK	0/1	0.0%	1			
FERCHO, Denny	P	0/0	0.0%				
FITZGERALD, Thomas	LW	0/0	0.0%				
FITZGERALD, Joseph	CB	2/4	50.0%	3			1
PENN, Steven	CB	0/1	0.0%				
BROWN, Derek	RW	6/9	66.7%	3	5	1	
RYAN, Matt	P	3/3	100.0%	3		3	4
DUNN, Robert	LW	3/7	42.9%	1	1	1	1
KELLER, John	RB	0/0	0.0%				
HEATH, Darrick	LB	2/5	40.0%	7	4	1	
DACHNIWSKY, Yaro	GK	0/0	0.0%				
CACCIA, Greg	RB	0/1	0.0%	1	3		
SCHMOCKER, Mark	GK	0/0	0.0%	1	1		
DeGRAAF, Dave	P	13/17	76.5%	2	2	2	7
THORNBERRY, Michael	P	0/0	0.0%				
VAN OS, Chip, Jr.	LB	0/0	0.0%				

Goalkeepers	Shots Saved	Attempted	% Eff
MANNON, Cliff	2	14	14.3%
SCHMOCKER, Mark	8	39	20.5%

Men / *Messieurs*

PRELIMINARIES - GROUP B

FRA 27 - 25 ESP
Halftime Score: 10 - 9

France				Spain
6/8	75.0%	**6-Meter shots**	3/6	50.0%
3/7	42.9%	**Wing shots**	5/8	62.5%
9/20	45.0%	**9-Meter shots**	9/21	42.9%
3/3	100.0%	**7-Meter shots**	5/5	100.0%
4/5	80.0%	**Fast breaks**	2/3	66.7%
2/3	66.7%	**Breakthroughs**	1/1	100.0%
27/46	58.7%	**Total shots**	25/44	56.8%
8		**Assists**	4	
7		**Turnovers**	11	
4		**Steals**	2	
5		**Blocks**	1	
8		**Fouls**	10	

1st Referee: CRO VUJNOVIC, Vladimir
2nd Referee: CRO MLADINIC, Petar

PRELIMINARIES - GROUP B

EGY 19 - 16 ALG
Halftime Score: 7 - 9

Egypt				Algeria
3/4	75.0%	**6-Meter shots**	5/8	62.5%
3/11	27.3%	**Wing shots**	2/5	40.0%
8/15	53.3%	**9-Meter shots**	4/20	20.0%
2/4	50.0%	**7-Meter shots**	1/3	33.3%
1/1	100.0%	**Fast breaks**	2/3	66.7%
2/5	40.0%	**Breakthroughs**	2/4	50.0%
19/40	47.5%	**Total shots**	16/43	37.2%
4		**Assists**	2	
13		**Turnovers**	13	
4		**Steals**	6	
8		**Blocks**	0	
7		**Fouls**	10	

1st Referee: DEN ELBROND, Per
2nd Referee: DEN LOVQVIST, Kjeld

PRELIMINARIES - GROUP B

GER 30 - 20 BRA
Halftime Score: 12 - 7

Germany				Brazil
7/11	63.6%	**6-Meter shots**	4/7	57.1%
8/9	88.9%	**Wing shots**	3/5	60.0%
6/8	75.0%	**9-Meter shots**	8/24	33.3%
3/4	75.0%	**7-Meter shots**	2/4	50.0%
5/6	83.3%	**Fast breaks**	3/4	75.0%
1/1	100.0%	**Breakthroughs**	0/1	0.0%
30/39	76.9%	**Total shots**	20/45	44.4%
19		**Assists**	5	
15		**Turnovers**	15	
6		**Steals**	9	
5		**Blocks**	1	
5		**Fouls**	9	

1st Referee: USA BOJSEN, Thomas
2nd Referee: USA BOEHNE, Bruce

TEAM: FRA France
Coach: COSTANTINI, Daniel   Assistant Coach: LEPOINTE, Jean-Pierre

Names	Pos	M/A	% Eff	A	To	Stl	Bl
GAUDIN, Christian	GK	0/0	0.0%				
MAHE, Pascal	LB	0/0	0.0%	1	1	1	1
SCHAAF, Philippe	LB	0/0	0.0%				
VOLLE, Frederic	P	3/9	33.3%	2	1		3
LATHOUD, Denis	CB	1/2	50.0%	3	1		
KERVADEC, Gueric	P	6/8	75.0%		1		
CORDINIER, Stephane	LW	0/0	0.0%				
MONTHUREL, Gael	RB	1/1	100.0%				
ANQUETIL, Gregory	RW	5/8	62.5%		2	1	
AMALOU, Eric	LW	2/3	66.7%		1		
MARTINI, Bruno	GK	0/0	0.0%				
JOULIN, Stephane	RW	0/0	0.0%				
PRANDI, Raoul	LW	2/3	66.7%				
DELATTRE, Yohan	GK	0/0	0.0%				
RICHARDSON, Jackson	CB	3/4	75.0%		1	1	1
STOECKLIN, Stephane	CB	4/8	50.0%	2			

Goalkeepers	Shots Saved	Attempted	% Eff
GAUDIN, Christian	0	1	0.0%
MARTINI, Bruno	12	43	27.9%

TEAM: EGY Egypt
Coach: GARCIA CUESTA, Javier   Assistant Coach: el SADANY, Asem

Names	Pos	M/A	% Eff	A	To	Stl	Bl
el AWADY, Ahmed	GK	0/0	0.0%				
el ATTAR, Ahmed	LB	0/0	0.0%				
ALI, Ahmed	CB	0/0	0.0%	1		2	5
ABD ALLA, Hossam	RB	1/4	25.0%				
SOLIMAN, Mahmoud	RW	1/5	20.0%		1		
GOHAR, Gohar	P	2/3	66.7%	3			1
MAHMOUD, Yaser	CB	0/0	0.0%				
MAHMOUD, Khaled	LW	0/0	0.0%				
el ALFY, Ayman	RW	0/0	0.0%	1	2	1	
BAKIR, Mohamed	GK	0/0	0.0%				
el GEIOUSHY, Amero	P	8/12	66.7%	1	1	1	2
MABROUK, Ashraf	CB	4/8	50.0%				
SOLIMAN, Ayman	GK	0/0	0.0%				
BELAL, Ahmed	CB	2/4	50.0%	1	3		
BELAL, Saber	RB	0/0	0.0%				
ABD ELWARESS, Sameh	LW	1/4	25.0%	3			

Goalkeepers	Shots Saved	Attempted	% Eff
BAKIR, Mohamed	1	3	33.3%
SOLIMAN, Ayman	12	40	30.0%

TEAM: GER Germany
Coach: EHRET, Arno

Names	Pos	M/A	% Eff	A	To	Stl	Bl
FRITZ, Henning	GK	0/0	0.0%				
BAUR, Markus	CB	1/1	100.0%	1	1		
KRETZSCHMAR, Stefan	LW	0/0	0.0%				
FEGTER, Jan	LB	1/1	100.0%	2	1		
SCHWARZER, Christian	P	2/4	50.0%	2	1		
PETERSEN, Klaus-Dieter	P	5/5	100.0%			1	2
KNORR, Thomas	LB	2/6	33.3%	4	2	2	
ZERBE, Volker	RB	1/1	100.0%	1	3	1	2
THIEL, Andreas	GK	0/0	0.0%	1			
SCHEFFLER, Christian	LW	6/8	75.0%	1	1	2	
SCHWALB, Martin	RB	4/4	100.0%	3	2		
KOHLHAAS, Karsten	LB	0/0	0.0%				
HOLPERT, Jan	GK	0/0	0.0%				
SCHMIDT, Martin	RW	0/0	0.0%				
STEPHAN, Daniel	CB	1/2	50.0%	3	1		1
LOHR, Holger	RW	7/7	100.0%	2	2		

Goalkeepers	Shots Saved	Attempted	% Eff
THIEL, Andreas	10	26	38.5%
HOLPERT, Jan	8	19	42.1%

TEAM: ESP Spain
Coach: ROMAN, Jvande   Assistant Coach: HERNANDEZ, Juan

Names	Pos	M/A	% Eff	A	To	Stl	Bl
FORT, Jaume	GK	0/0	0.0%		1		
LOZANO, Demetrio	RB	1/5	20.0%	1			
ESQUER, Salvador	LW	1/2	50.0%				
GUIJOSA, Rafael	LW	1/2	50.0%				
HERNANDEZ, Fernando	RW	0/0	0.0%				
GONZALEZ, Raul	RW	0/1	0.0%		1		
URDANGARIN, Inaki	LB	4/5	80.0%		1	1	
OLALLA, Jesus	RB	2/6	33.3%		1		1
GARRALDA, Mateo	LB	1/2	50.0%	1	6		
DUJSHEBAEV, Talant	CB	6/9	66.7%	1			
FERNANDEZ, Jesus	CB	0/0	0.0%				
NUNEZ, Jordi	GK	0/0	0.0%			1	
URDIALES, Alberto	RW	8/10	80.0%				
PEREZ, Juan	P	0/0	0.0%				
HOMBRADOS, Jose	GK	0/0	0.0%				
ETXABURU, Aitor	P	1/2	50.0%	1	1		

Goalkeepers	Shots Saved	Attempted	% Eff
FORT, Jaume	12	41	29.3%
NUNEZ, Jordi	0	5	0.0%

TEAM: ALG Algeria
Coach: MACHOU, Mohammed   Assistant Coach: BOUCHEKRIOU, Salah

Names	Pos	M/A	% Eff	A	To	Stl	Bl
DAOUD, Amar	GK	0/0	0.0%				
LOUKIL, Abdelghani	LW	1/3	33.3%		1		
AOUACHRIA, Redouane	CB	2/3	66.7%		3	1	
NEDJEL-HAMMOU, Salim	CB	1/9	11.1%		1		
ROUABHI, Nabil	CB	0/0	0.0%				
SAIDI, Redouane	RW	5/7	71.4%		2	1	
BEGHOUACH, Benali	P	2/2	100.0%	1	1		
LAMALI, Sofiane	CB	0/0	0.0%				
BOUANANI, AbedIdjalil	P	0/0	0.0%				
BOUANIK, Mahmoud	CB	3/10	30.0%	1	3		
GHERBI, Rabah	CB	1/6	16.7%				4
HASNI, Achour	CB	1/1	100.0%				
KHALFALLAH, Sofiane	LW	0/0	0.0%				
BOUZIANE, Mohamed	CB	0/0	0.0%				
ABES, Salim	CB	0/2	0.0%				
el MAOUHAB, Karim	GK	0/0	0.0%		1		

Goalkeepers	Shots Saved	Attempted	% Eff
DAOUD, Amar	0	2	0.0%
el MAOUHAB, Karim	15	38	39.5%

TEAM: BRA Brazil
Coach: RIGOLO, Alberto   Assistant Coach: SILVA JUNIOR, Washington

Names	Pos	M/A	% Eff	A	To	Stl	Bl
LIMA, Cesar	GK	0/0	0.0%				
FRIERE, Edison Alves	GK	0/0	0.0%				
PINHEIRO, Ivan	LB	3/8	37.5%	1	6	1	
CEZAR, Marcos	CB	0/1	0.0%	1	1	1	
NASCIMENTO, Jose	RW	1/3	33.3%		1		
STEINWANDTER, Fausto	CB	3/4	75.0%			2	1
MORATORE, Paulo	RB	0/1	0.0%				
PELISSARI, Milton	P	2/4	50.0%				
ANDRADE, Daniel	RW	0/0	0.0%				
MATOS, Agberto	LB	2/8	25.0%		4	2	
SAMPAIO, Marcelo	GK	0/0	0.0%				
BARROS, Winglitton	LW	4/6	66.7%	1		2	
MAZIERO, Ivan	LW	2/3	66.7%				
HOFFELDER, Rodrigo	CB	3/7	42.9%	2	3	1	
INOCENTE FILHO, Osvaldo	GK	0/0	0.0%				
ERTEL, Carlos	P	0/0	0.0%				

Goalkeeper	Shots Saved	Attempted	% Eff
SAMPAIO, Marcelo	4	39	10.3%

Handball / *Handball*   **249**

• ROCKWELL T SMITH • RODNEY SMITH • ROMAYLIA A SMITH • RONALD M SMITH • RONNETTE V SMITH • ROSELYN G SMITH • ROY SMITH • RUBY E SMITH • RUSSELL B SMITH • RYAN SMITH • RYAN C SMITH • SALLY M SMITH • SAMUEL D SMITH • SANDRA SMITH • SANDRA D SMITH • SANDRA M SMITH • SANDRA P SMITH • SANDRA R SMITH • SARA M SMITH • SARAH SMITH • SARAH H SMITH • SAVANNAH L SMITH • SCOTT C SMITH • SCOTT S SMITH • SCOTTIE H. SMITH • SEAN D SMITH • SHANNON SMITH • SHANNON C SMITH • SHARON L SMITH •

Men / *Messieurs*

PRELIMINARIES - GROUP B

ALG 22 - 33 FRA
Halftime Score: 10 - 13

Algeria		6-Meter shots	France	
5/6	83.3%	6-Meter shots	7/8	87.5%
1/2	50.0%	Wing shots	2/4	50.0%
10/31	32.3%	9-Meter shots	6/10	60.0%
2/3	66.7%	7-Meter shots	2/3	66.7%
4/5	80.0%	Fast breaks	5/7	71.4%
0/0	0.0%	Breakthroughs	11/12	91.7%
22/47	46.8%	Total shots	33/44	75.0%
	4	Assists	14	
	22	Turnovers	17	
	4	Steals	6	
	1	Blocks	4	
	4	Fouls	7	

1st Referee: NOR OEIE, Svein
2nd Referee: NOR HOGSNES, Bjorn

PRELIMINARIES - GROUP B

ESP 22 - 20 GER
Halftime Score: 11 - 10

Spain			Germany	
2/2	100.0%	6-Meter shots	0/5	0.0%
2/5	40.0%	Wing shots	2/7	28.6%
10/18	55.6%	9-Meter shots	11/25	44.0%
2/3	66.7%	7-Meter shots	2/2	100.0%
3/5	60.0%	Fast breaks	3/5	60.0%
3/3	100.0%	Breakthroughs	2/2	100.0%
22/36	61.1%	Total shots	20/46	43.5%
	8	Assists	4	
	16	Turnovers	8	
	4	Steals	4	
	7	Blocks	2	
	7	Fouls	5	

1st Referee: NED BRUSSEL, Peter
2nd Referee: NED van DONGEN, Anton

PRELIMINARIES - GROUP B

BRA 20 - 31 EGY
Halftime Score: 10 - 15

Brazil			Egypt	
7/9	77.8%	6-Meter shots	2/4	50.0%
2/3	66.7%	Wing shots	3/7	42.9%
0/19	0.0%	9-Meter shots	9/15	60.0%
6/7	85.7%	7-Meter shots	1/3	33.3%
2/2	100.0%	Fast breaks	9/12	75.0%
3/5	60.0%	Breakthroughs	7/10	70.0%
20/45	44.4%	Total shots	31/51	60.8%
	9	Assists	6	
	17	Turnovers	10	
	1	Steals	2	
	1	Blocks	8	
	5	Fouls	6	

1st Referee: KUW al HOULI, Mohammad
2nd Referee: KUW ALENEZI, Khalaf

TEAM: ALG Algeria
Coach: MACHOU, Mohammed Assistant Coach: BOUCHEKRIOU, Salah

Names	Pos	M/A	% Eff	A	To	Stl	Bl
DAOUD, Amar	GK	0/0	0.0%				
LOUKIL, Abdelghani	LW	0/0	0.0%				
AOUACHRIA, Redouane	CB	2/2	100.0%	2	4	1	
NEDJEL-HAMMOU, Salim	CB	4/10	40.0%		2		
ROUABHI, Nabil	CB	0/3	0.0%		1		
SAIDI, Redouane	RW	4/6	66.7%	1	2		
BEGHOUACH, Benali	P	2/2	100.0%		1		
LAMALI, Sofiane	CB	5/14	35.7%		7		
BOUANANI, Abedldjalil	P	0/0	0.0%				
BOUANIK, Mahmoud	CB	0/0	0.0%				
GHERBI, Rabah	CB	2/6	33.3%		2		
HASNI, Achour	CB	1/1	100.0%			1	
KHALFALLAH, Sofiane	LW	0/0	0.0%				
BOUZIANE, Mohamed	CB	1/1	100.0%			1	
ABES, Salim	CB	1/2	50.0%	1	2	1	1
el MAOUHAB, Karim	GK	0/0	0.0%		1		

Goalkeepers	Shots Saved	Attempted	% Eff
DAOUD, Amar	3	20	15.0%
el MAOUHAB, Karim	6	24	25.0%

TEAM: ESP Spain
Coach: ROMAN, Jvande Assistant Coach: HERNANDEZ, Juan

Names	Pos	M/A	% Eff	A	To	Stl	Bl
FORT, Jaume	GK	0/0	0.0%				
LOZANO, Demetrio	RB	0/0	0.0%				
ESQUER, Salvador	LW	2/4	50.0%			2	
GUIJOSA, Rafael	LW	3/3	100.0%	1			
HERNANDEZ, Fernando	RW	0/0	0.0%				
GONZALEZ, Raul	RW	1/1	100.0%				
URDANGARIN, Inaki	LB	2/3	66.7%		2	1	1
OLALLA, Jesus	RB	4/5	80.0%	3	4		1
GARRALDA, Mateo	LB	4/7	57.1%	1	4		5
DUJSHEBAEV, Talant	CB	3/8	37.5%	2	5		
FERNANDEZ, Jesus	CB	0/0	0.0%				
NUNEZ, Jordi	GK	0/0	0.0%				
URDIALES, Alberto	RW	1/3	33.3%	2		1	
PEREZ, Juan	P	0/0	0.0%				
HOMBRADOS, Jose	GK	0/0	0.0%				
ETXABURU, Aitor	P	2/2	100.0%				

Goalkeepers	Shots Saved	Attempted	% Eff
FORT, Jaume	15	45	33.3%
NUNEZ, Jordi	0	1	0.0%

TEAM: BRA Brazil
Coach: RIGOLO, Alberto Assistant Coach: SILVA JUNIOR, Washington

Names	Pos	M/A	% Eff	A	To	Stl	Bl
LIMA, Cesar	GK	0/0	0.0%				
FRIERE, Edison Alves	GK	0/0	0.0%				
PINHEIRO, Ivan	LB	0/10	0.0%	2	3	1	1
CEZAR, Marcos	CB	0/0	0.0%				
NASCIMENTO, Jose	RW	3/4	75.0%	3	2		
STEINWANDTER, Fausto	CB	3/6	50.0%	2			
MORATORE, Paulo	RB	0/1	0.0%		2		
PELISSARI, Milton	P	2/4	50.0%		1		
ANDRADE, Daniel	RW	1/1	100.0%	1			
MATOS, Agberto	LB	0/0	0.0%				
SAMPAIO, Marcelo	GK	0/0	0.0%				
BARROS, Winglitton	LW	5/8	62.5%	3			
MAZIERO, Ivan	LW	1/1	100.0%				
HOFFELDER, Rodrigo	CB	3/8	37.5%	2	5		
INOCENTE FILHO, Osvaldo	GK	0/0	0.0%				
ERTEL, Carlos	P	2/2	100.0%				

Goalkeepers	Shots Saved	Attempted	% Eff
LIMA, Cesar	9	39	23.1%
SAMPAIO, Marcelo	1	12	8.3%

TEAM: FRA France
Coach: COSTANTINI, Daniel Assistant Coach: LEPOINTE, Jean-Pierre

Names	Pos	M/A	% Eff	A	To	Stl	Bl
GAUDIN, Christian	GK	0/0	0.0%	1	1		
MAHE, Pascal	LB	1/2	50.0%				3
SCHAAF, Philippe	LB	0/1	0.0%	1	1		
VOLLE, Frederic	P	4/5	80.0%	2	1	1	1
LATHOUD, Denis	CB	0/0	0.0%				
KERVADEC, Gueric	P	3/3	100.0%		1		
CORDINIER, Stephane	LW	1/2	50.0%				
MONTHUREL, Gael	RB	0/0	0.0%	2	2		
ANQUETIL, Gregory	RW	0/0	0.0%				
AMALOU, Eric	LW	0/0	0.0%				
MARTINI, Bruno	GK	0/0	0.0%				
JOULIN, Stephane	RW	5/6	83.3%	3		1	
PRANDI, Raoul	LW	6/7	85.7%	2			
DELATTRE, Yohan	GK	0/0	0.0%				
RICHARDSON, Jackson	CB	4/5	80.0%	3	1	3	
STOECKLIN, Stephane	CB	9/13	69.2%	2	8	1	

Goalkeeper	Shots Saved	Attempted	% Eff
GAUDIN, Christian	13	47	27.7%

TEAM: GER Germany
Coach: EHRET, Arno

Names	Pos	M/A	% Eff	A	To	Stl	Bl
FRITZ, Henning	GK	0/0	0.0%				
BAUR, Markus	CB	1/2	50.0%	1			
KRETZSCHMAR, Stefan	LW	0/0	0.0%				
FEGTER, Jan	LB	0/0	0.0%				
SCHWARZER, Christian	P	1/3	33.3%		1	1	1
PETERSEN, Klaus-Dieter	P	0/0	0.0%			1	1
KNORR, Thomas	LB	4/10	40.0%	1	3	1	
ZERBE, Volker	RB	6/7	85.7%	2			
THIEL, Andreas	GK	0/0	0.0%				
SCHEFFLER, Christian	LW	2/6	33.3%	1			
SCHWALB, Martin	RB	2/3	66.7%	1			
KOHLHAAS, Karsten	LB	3/7	42.9%	1	1		
HOLPERT, Jan	GK	0/0	0.0%				
SCHMIDT, Martin	RW	0/0	0.0%				
STEPHAN, Daniel	CB	0/3	0.0%				
LOHR, Holger	RW	1/5	20.0%			1	

Goalkeepers	Shots Saved	Attempted	% Eff
PETERSEN, Klaus-Dieter	0	0	0.0%
THIEL, Andreas	6	18	33.3%
HOLPERT, Jan	2	18	11.1%

TEAM: EGY Egypt
Coach: GARCIA CUESTA, Javier Assistant Coach: el SADANY, Asem

Names	Pos	M/A	% Eff	A	To	Stl	Bl
el AWADY, Ahmed	GK	0/0	0.0%				
el ATTAR, Ahmed	LB	5/9	55.6%	1			
ALI, Ahmed	CB	1/2	50.0%				3
ABD ALLA, Hossam	RB	2/3	66.7%	1			1
SOLIMAN, Mahmoud	RW	2/4	50.0%				
GOHAR, Gohar	P	4/5	80.0%	1	2	1	
MAHMOUD, Yaser	CB	0/4	0.0%	2	2	1	1
MAHMOUD, Khaled	LW	0/0	0.0%				
el ALFY, Ayman	RW	2/3	66.7%	2			
BAKIR, Mohamed	GK	0/0	0.0%				
el GEIOUSHY, Amero	P	5/7	71.4%	1	3		2
MABROUK, Ashraf	CB	4/5	80.0%				
SOLIMAN, Ayman	GK	0/0	0.0%				
BELAL, Ahmed	CB	0/0	0.0%				
BELAL, Saber	RB	0/0	0.0%				
ABD ELWARESS, Sameh	LW	6/9	66.7%	1			1

Goalkeepers	Shots Saved	Attempted	% Eff
el AWADY, Ahmed	5	22	22.7%
BAKIR, Mohamed	8	23	34.8%

Men / *Messieurs*

PRÉLIMINARIES - GROUP B

ESP 20 - 14 ALG
Halftime Score: 12 - 5

Spain				Algeria	
2/4	50.0%	6-Meter shots	2/4	50.0%	
5/8	62.5%	Wing shots	2/6	33.3%	
4/7	57.1%	9-Meter shots	2/22	9.1%	
3/3	100.0%	7-Meter shots	0/0	0.0%	
5/5	100.0%	Fast breaks	4/5	80.0%	
1/1	100.0%	Breakthroughs	4/7	57.1%	
20/28	71.4%	Total shots	14/44	31.8%	
	4	Assists	7		
	13	Turnovers	11		
	5	Steals	4		
	5	Blocks	1		
	8	Fouls	6		

1st Referee: KUW al HOULI, Mohammad
2nd Referee: KUW ALENEZI, Khalaf

PRELIMINARIES - GROUP B

GER 22 - 24 EGY
Halftime Score: 9 - 11

Germany				Egypt	
4/5	80.0%	6-Meter shots	5/9	55.6%	
1/5	20.0%	Wing shots	1/1	100.0%	
8/17	47.1%	9-Meter shots	6/21	28.6%	
1/2	50.0%	7-Meter shots	4/6	66.7%	
3/4	75.0%	Fast breaks	5/7	71.4%	
5/7	71.4%	Breakthroughs	3/4	75.0%	
22/40	55.0%	Total shots	24/48	50.0%	
	5	Assists	10		
	10	Turnovers	6		
	3	Steals	3		
	6	Blocks	0		
	5	Fouls	8		

1st Referee: ROM DANCESCU, Valter
2nd Referee: ROM MATEESCU, Ion

PRELIMINARIES - GROUP B

FRA 37 - 23 BRA
Halftime Score: 16 - 10

France				Brazil	
8/9	88.9%	6-Meter shots	6/7	85.7%	
8/13	61.5%	Wing shots	2/4	50.0%	
7/12	58.3%	9-Meter shots	7/29	24.1%	
0/0	0.0%	7-Meter shots	0/1	0.0%	
10/12	83.3%	Fast breaks	5/9	55.6%	
4/5	80.0%	Breakthroughs	3/4	75.0%	
37/51	72.5%	Total shots	23/54	42.6%	
	20	Assists	9		
	12	Turnovers	15		
	9	Steals	6		
	7	Blocks	0		
	6	Fouls	5		

1st Referee: CGO MOELLE MABOUNDA, Michel
2nd Referee: CGO MVOULA, Daniel

TEAM: ESP Spain
Coach: ROMAN, Jvande   Assistant Coach: HERNANDEZ, Juan

Names	Pos	M/A	% Eff	A	To	Stl	Bl
FORT, Jaume	GK	0/0	0.0%				
LOZANO, Demetrio	RB	0/0	0.0%				
ESQUER, Salvador	LW	3/3	100.0%			1	
GUIJOSA, Rafael	LW	5/6	83.3%	1			
HERNANDEZ, Fernando	RW	0/0	0.0%				
GONZALEZ, Raul	RW	1/1	100.0%	3			
URDANGARIN, Inaki	LB	3/3	100.0%		2	1	3
OLALLA, Jesus	RB	0/0	0.0%	1	1	1	
GARRALDA, Mateo	LB	0/1	0.0%	2	2		2
DUJSHEBAEV, Talant	CB	3/5	60.0%	1	2	1	
FERNANDEZ, Jesus	CB	0/0	0.0%				
NUNEZ, Jordi	GK	0/0	0.0%				
URDIALES, Alberto	RW	5/7	71.4%			1	
PEREZ, Juan	P	0/0	0.0%				
HOMBRADOS, Jose	GK	0/0	0.0%				
ETXABURU, Aitor	P	0/2	0.0%		2		

Goalkeeper	Shots Saved	Attempted	% Eff
FORT, Jaume	17	44	38.6%

TEAM: GER Germany
Coach: EHRET, Arno

Names	Pos	M/A	% Eff	A	To	Stl	Bl
FRITZ, Henning	GK	0/0	0.0%				
BAUR, Markus	CB	2/4	50.0%	2	1		
KRETZSCHMAR, Stefan	LW	2/4	50.0%	1			
FEGTER, Jan	LB	2/6	33.3%	1			
SCHWARZER, Christian	P	4/6	66.7%	1			2
PETERSEN, Klaus-Dieter	P	0/1	0.0%	1		2	4
KNORR, Thomas	LB	3/5	60.0%	1	2	1	
ZERBE, Volker	RB	2/4	50.0%	1			
THIEL, Andreas	GK	0/0	0.0%				
SCHEFFLER, Christian	LW	0/0	0.0%				
SCHWALB, Martin	RB	6/7	85.7%	4			
KOHLHAAS, Karsten	LB	0/0	0.0%				
HOLPERT, Jan	GK	0/0	0.0%				
SCHMIDT, Martin	RW	1/2	50.0%				
STEPHAN, Daniel	CB	0/1	0.0%				
LOHR, Holger	RW	0/0	0.0%				

Goalkeepers	Shots Saved	Attempted	% Eff
THIEL, Andreas	0	1	0.0%
HOLPERT, Jan	12	47	25.5%
SCHMIDT, Martin	0	0	0.0%

TEAM: FRA France
Coach: COSTANTINI, Daniel   Assistant Coach: LEPOINTE, Jean-Pierre

Names	Pos	M/A	% Eff	A	To	Stl	Bl
GAUDIN, Christian	GK	0/0	0.0%				
MAHE, Pascal	LB	0/0	0.0%				
SCHAAF, Philippe	LB	0/1	0.0%	2			2
VOLLE, Frederic	P	14/18	77.8%	2	1	2	2
LATHOUD, Denis	CB	4/5	80.0%	2	4		1
KERVADEC, Gueric	P	3/3	100.0%	1	1		2
CORDINIER, Stephane	LW	0/0	0.0%				
MONTHUREL, Gael	RB	0/0	0.0%		2	1	
ANQUETIL, Gregory	RW	4/5	80.0%	5			
AMALOU, Eric	LW	1/4	25.0%	2	1	1	
MARTINI, Bruno	GK	0/0	0.0%	1	1		
JOULIN, Stephane	RW	5/8	62.5%				
PRANDI, Raoul	LW	4/4	100.0%	2	1		
DELATTRE, Yohan	GK	0/0	0.0%				
RICHARDSON, Jackson	CB	2/3	66.7%	3	1		5
STOECKLIN, Stephane	CB	0/0	0.0%				

Goalkeepers	Shots Saved	Attempted	% Eff
MARTINI, Bruno	10	31	32.3%
DELATTRE, Yohan	8	23	34.8%

TEAM: ALG Algeria
Coach: MACHOU, Mohammed   Assistant Coach: BOUCHEKRIOU, Salah

Names	Pos	M/A	% Eff	A	To	Stl	Bl
DAOUD, Amar	GK	0/0	0.0%				
LOUKIL, Abdelghani	LW	1/6	16.7%	1			
AOUACHRIA, Redouane	CB	0/0	0.0%	1	1		
NEDJEL-HAMMOU, Salim	CB	2/11	18.2%	1	1		
ROUABHI, Nabil	CB	0/0	0.0%				
SAIDI, Redouane	RW	0/0	0.0%				
BEGHOUACH, Benali	P	2/3	66.7%				
LAMALI, Sofiane	CB	2/8	25.0%	1	3		
BOUANANI, AbedIdjalil	P	0/0	0.0%				
BOUANIK, Mahmoud	CB	0/0	0.0%				
GHERBI, Rabah	CB	1/2	50.0%	1			
HASNI, Achour	CB	0/2	0.0%	1	1	1	
KHALFALLAH, Sofiane	LW	3/4	75.0%	1	1		
BOUZIANE, Mohamed	CB	2/6	33.3%	1	2	1	1
ABES, Salim	CB	1/2	50.0%	1			
el MAOUHAB, Karim	GK	0/0	0.0%	1	1		

Goalkeepers	Shots Saved	Attempted	% Eff
DAOUD, Amar	0	5	0.0%
el MAOUHAB, Karim	6	23	26.1%

TEAM: EGY Egypt
Coach: GARCIA CUESTA, Javier   Assistant Coach: el SADANY, Asem

Names	Pos	M/A	% Eff	A	To	Stl	Bl
el AWADY, Ahmed	GK	0/0	0.0%				
el ATTAR, Ahmed	LB	5/10	50.0%	1			
ALI, Ahmed	CB	0/0	0.0%				
ABD ALLA, Hossam	RB	1/1	100.0%				
SOLIMAN, Mahmoud	RW	3/5	60.0%	1			
GOHAR, Gohar	P	3/4	75.0%	4		1	
MAHMOUD, Yaser	CB	0/0	0.0%				
MAHMOUD, Khaled	LW	0/0	0.0%				
el ALFY, Ayman	RW	0/1	0.0%	1			
BAKIR, Mohamed	GK	0/0	0.0%				
el GEIOUSHY, Amero	P	3/6	50.0%	1	1		
MABROUK, Ashraf	CB	4/8	50.0%	2			
SOLIMAN, Ayman	GK	0/0	0.0%	1			
BELAL, Ahmed	CB	2/6	33.3%	1	2		
BELAL, Saber	RB	0/0	0.0%				
ABD ELWARESS, Sameh	LW	3/7	42.9%	1	1	1	

Goalkeepers	Shots Saved	Attempted	% Eff
BAKIR, Mohamed	11	25	44.0%
SOLIMAN, Ayman	5	15	33.3%

TEAM: BRA Brazil
Coach: RIGOLO, Alberto   Assistant Coach: SILVA JUNIOR, Washington

Names	Pos	M/A	% Eff	A	To	Stl	Bl
LIMA, Cesar	GK	0/0	0.0%				
FRIERE, Edison Alves	GK	2/2	100.0%	2			
PINHEIRO, Ivan	LB	4/14	28.6%	3	3		
CEZAR, Marcos	CB	0/0	0.0%	1			
NASCIMENTO, Jose	RW	3/5	60.0%	2	2	1	
STEINWANDTER, Fausto	CB	0/1	0.0%				
MORATORE, Paulo	RB	0/2	0.0%	2			
PELISSARI, Milton	P	7/13	53.8%	1	1		
ANDRADE, Daniel	RW	0/0	0.0%				
MATOS, Agberto	LB	0/0	0.0%				
SAMPAIO, Marcelo	GK	0/0	0.0%				
BARROS, Winglitton	LW	2/5	40.0%	1		1	
MAZIERO, Ivan	LW	1/1	100.0%			1	2
HOFFELDER, Rodrigo	CB	4/11	36.4%	1	3		
INOCENTE FILHO, Osvaldo	GK	0/0	0.0%	2		1	
ERTEL, Carlos	P	0/0	0.0%				

Goalkeepers	Shots Saved	Attempted	% Eff
SAMPAIO, Marcelo	5	25	20.0%
INOCENTE FILHO, Osvaldo	3	26	11.5%

Men / *Messieurs*

PRELIMINARIES - GROUP B

EGY 20 - 25 FRA
Halftime Score: 9 - 12

Egypt			France	
3/4	75.0%	6-Meter shots	5/12	41.7%
4/8	50.0%	Wing shots	2/2	100.0%
11/27	40.7%	9-Meter shots	6/12	50.0%
0/0	0.0%	7-Meter shots	1/2	50.0%
1/2	50.0%	Fast breaks	4/5	80.0%
1/1	100.0%	Breakthroughs	7/8	87.5%
20/42	47.6%	Total shots	25/41	61.0%
7		Assists	8	
13		Turnovers	13	
3		Steals	4	
0		Blocks	6	
6		Fouls	6	

1st Referee: NOR HOGSNES, Bjorn
2nd Referee: NOR OEIE, Svein

PRELIMINARIES - GROUP B

GER 25 - 23 ALG
Halftime Score: 13 - 12

Germany			Algeria	
5/7	71.4%	6-Meter shots	6/10	60.0%
6/8	75.0%	Wing shots	2/5	40.0%
5/9	55.6%	9-Meter shots	1/8	12.5%
5/8	62.5%	7-Meter shots	5/6	83.3%
2/3	66.7%	Fast breaks	7/8	87.5%
2/5	40.0%	Breakthroughs	2/2	100.0%
25/40	62.5%	Total shots	23/39	59.0%
11		Assists	8	
15		Turnovers	14	
3		Steals	7	
2		Blocks	1	
7		Fouls	6	

1st Referee: CRO VUJNOVIC, Vladimir
2nd Referee: CRO MLADINIC, Petar

PRELIMINARIES - GROUP B

BRA 17 - 27 ESP
Halftime Score: 10 - 12

Brazil			Spain	
5/7	71.4%	6-Meter shots	3/5	60.0%
2/5	40.0%	Wing shots	2/5	40.0%
5/17	29.4%	9-Meter shots	9/12	75.0%
1/1	100.0%	7-Meter shots	6/8	75.0%
1/2	50.0%	Fast breaks	3/4	75.0%
3/3	100.0%	Breakthroughs	4/6	66.7%
17/35	48.6%	Total shots	27/40	67.5%
8		Assists	12	
16		Turnovers	8	
2		Steals	6	
1		Blocks	2	
7		Fouls	5	

1st Referee: USA BOEHNE, Bruce
2nd Referee: USA BOJSEN, Thomas

TEAM: EGY Egypt
Coach: GARCIA CUESTA, Javier   Assistant Coach: el SADANY, Asem

Names	Pos	M/A	% Eff	A	To	Stl	Bl
el AWADY, Ahmed	GK	0/0	0.0%				
el ATTAR, Ahmed	LB	2/6	33.3%	1			
ALI, Ahmed	CB	0/1	0.0%				
ABD ALLA, Hossam	RB	0/1	0.0%				
SOLIMAN, Mahmoud	RW	5/8	62.5%	2	1		
GOHAR, Gohar	P	2/4	50.0%	1	2	1	
MAHMOUD, Yaser	CB	0/0	0.0%				
MAHMOUD, Khaled	LW	0/0	0.0%				
el ALFY, Ayman	RW	1/1	100.0%		3		
BAKIR, Mohamed	GK	0/0	0.0%		1		
el GEIOUSHY, Amero	P	3/4	75.0%		3	1	
MABROUK, Ashraf	CB	2/5	40.0%	1			
SOLIMAN, Ayman	GK	0/0	0.0%				
BELAL, Ahmed	CB	2/3	66.7%	3	1	1	
BELAL, Saber	RB	0/0	0.0%				
ABD ELWARESS, Sameh	LW	3/9	33.3%	1			

Goalkeeper	Shots Saved	Attempted	% Eff
BAKIR, Mohamed	8	41	19.5%

TEAM: GER Germany
Coach: EHRET, Arno

Names	Pos	M/A	% Eff	A	To	Stl	Bl
FRITZ, Henning	GK	0/0	0.0%				
BAUR, Markus	CB	3/9	33.3%	1	2		
KRETZSCHMAR, Stefan	LW	5/8	62.5%		1		
FEGTER, Jan	LB	2/3	66.7%	1			1
SCHWARZER, Christian	P	3/3	100.0%	2	1	2	
PETERSEN, Klaus-Dieter	P	1/1	100.0%				1
KNORR, Thomas	LB	4/6	66.7%	1	3		
ZERBE, Volker	RB	0/0	0.0%				
THIEL, Andreas	GK	0/0	0.0%				
SCHEFFLER, Christian	LW	0/0	0.0%				
SCHWALB, Martin	RB	4/7	57.1%	6	4		
KOHLHAAS, Karsten	LB	0/0	0.0%				
HOLPERT, Jan	GK	0/0	0.0%				
SCHMIDT, Martin	RW	3/3	100.0%		4	1	
STEPHAN, Daniel	CB	0/0	0.0%				
LOHR, Holger	RW	0/0	0.0%				

Goalkeepers	Shots Saved	Attempted	% Eff
THIEL, Andreas	5	23	21.7%
HOLPERT, Jan	4	16	25.0%

TEAM: BRA Brazil
Coach: RIGOLO, Alberto   Assistant Coach: SILVA JUNIOR, Washington

Names	Pos	M/A	% Eff	A	To	Stl	Bl
LIMA, Cesar	GK	0/0	0.0%				
FRIERE, Edison Alves	GK	0/0	0.0%		1		
PINHEIRO, Ivan	LB	2/10	20.0%	4	1	2	1
CEZAR, Marcos	CB	0/0	0.0%		2		
NASCIMENTO, Jose	RW	3/6	50.0%	2	1		
STEINWANDTER, Fausto	CB	1/1	100.0%		1		
MORATORE, Paulo	RB	1/2	50.0%	1			
PELISSARI, Milton	P	1/1	100.0%		4		
ANDRADE, Daniel	RW	1/3	33.3%	1	3		
MATOS, Agberto	LB	0/0	0.0%				
SAMPAIO, Marcelo	GK	0/0	0.0%				
BARROS, Winglitton	LW	0/0	0.0%				
MAZIERO, Ivan	LW	1/3	33.3%		1		
HOFFELDER, Rodrigo	CB	7/9	77.8%	2			
INOCENTE FILHO, Osvaldo	GK	0/0	0.0%				
ERTEL, Carlos	P	0/0	0.0%				

Goalkeepers	Shots Saved	Attempted	% Eff
LIMA, Cesar	1	9	11.1%
SAMPAIO, Marcelo	6	31	19.4%

TEAM: FRA France
Coach: COSTANTINI, Daniel   Assistant Coach: LEPOINTE, Jean-Pierre

Names	Pos	M/A	% Eff	A	To	Stl	Bl
GAUDIN, Christian	GK	0/1	0.0%				
MAHE, Pascal	LB	0/0	0.0%		1		2
SCHAAF, Philippe	LB	0/0	0.0%				
VOLLE, Frederic	P	7/8	87.5%	1	1		
LATHOUD, Denis	CB	8/12	66.7%	2	1		
KERVADEC, Gueric	P	1/4	25.0%		2		3
CORDINIER, Stephane	LW	0/0	0.0%				
MONTHUREL, Gael	RB	2/2	100.0%				
ANQUETIL, Gregory	RW	2/4	50.0%	3	2		
AMALOU, Eric	LW	1/1	100.0%		1		1
MARTINI, Bruno	GK	0/0	0.0%				
JOULIN, Stephane	RW	0/0	0.0%				
PRANDI, Raoul	LW	0/1	0.0%	1	2	1	
DELATTRE, Yohan	GK	0/0	0.0%				
RICHARDSON, Jackson	CB	1/1	100.0%			2	
STOECKLIN, Stephane	CB	3/7	42.9%	1	3	1	

Goalkeepers	Shots Saved	Attempted	% Eff
GAUDIN, Christian	7	30	23.3%
MARTINI, Bruno	2	12	16.7%

TEAM: ALG Algeria
Coach: MACHOU, Mohammed   Assistant Coach: BOUCHEKRIOU, Salah

Names	Pos	M/A	% Eff	A	To	Stl	Bl
DAOUD, Amar	GK	0/0	0.0%	1			
LOUKIL, Abdelghani	LW	4/5	80.0%	1	1	1	
AOUACHRIA, Redouane	CB	4/6	66.7%	1	3	3	
NEDJEL-HAMMOU, Salim	CB	3/7	42.9%	2	2		
ROUABHI, Nabil	CB	0/0	0.0%				
SAIDI, Redouane	RW	6/10	60.0%	1	4	1	
BEGHOUACH, Benali	P	4/5	80.0%				
LAMALI, Sofiane	CB	1/4	25.0%		2		
BOUANANI, AbedIdjalil	P	0/0	0.0%				
BOUANIK, Mahmoud	CB	0/0	0.0%				
GHERBI, Rabah	CB	0/0	0.0%				
HASNI, Achour	CB	0/0	0.0%				1
KHALFALLAH, Sofiane	LW	0/0	0.0%				
BOUZIANE, Mohamed	CB	1/2	50.0%	1	1	1	
ABES, Salim	CB	0/0	0.0%	1	1	1	
el MAOUHAB, Karim	GK	0/0	0.0%				

Goalkeepers	Shots Saved	Attempted	% Eff
DAOUD, Amar	7	20	35.0%
el MAOUHAB, Karim	3	20	15.0%

TEAM: ESP Spain
Coach: ROMAN, Jvande   Assistant Coach: HERNANDEZ, Juan

Names	Pos	M/A	% Eff	A	To	Stl	Bl
FORT, Jaume	GK	0/0	0.0%				
LOZANO, Demetrio	RB	0/1	0.0%				
ESQUER, Salvador	LW	5/6	83.3%	1	1	1	
GUIJOSA, Rafael	LW	3/5	60.0%	2			
HERNANDEZ, Fernando	RW	3/5	60.0%			2	
GONZALEZ, Raul	RW	0/0	0.0%				
URDANGARIN, Inaki	LB	6/8	75.0%	3	4		
OLALLA, Jesus	RB	3/3	100.0%	1	2	1	
GARRALDA, Mateo	LB	0/0	0.0%				
DUJSHEBAEV, Talant	CB	4/7	57.1%	4			
FERNANDEZ, Jesus	CB	0/0	0.0%			1	1
NUNEZ, Jordi	GK	0/0	0.0%				
URDIALES, Alberto	RW	2/4	50.0%	1		1	
PEREZ, Juan	P	1/1	100.0%		1		1
HOMBRADOS, Jose	GK	0/0	0.0%				
ETXABURU, Aitor	P	0/0	0.0%				

Goalkeeper	Shots Saved	Attempted	% Eff
NUNEZ, Jordi	10	35	28.6%

Men / *Messieurs*

PRELIMINARIES - GROUP B

EGY 19 - 20 ESP
Halftime Score: 8 - 11

Egypt	%		Spain	%
4/6	66.7%	6-Meter shots	1/3	33.3%
2/6	33.3%	Wing shots	2/5	40.0%
11/29	37.9%	9-Meter shots	3/9	33.3%
0/0	0.0%	7-Meter shots	5/7	71.4%
1/1	100.0%	Fast breaks	5/6	83.3%
1/1	100.0%	Breakthroughs	4/8	50.0%
19/43	44.2%	Total shots	20/38	52.6%
3		Assists	5	
11		Turnovers	8	
3		Steals	5	
1		Blocks	6	
8		Fouls	9	

1st Referee: LTU GUTERMAN, Grigorij
2nd Referee: LTU GEDVILAS, Feliksas

PRELIMINARIES - GROUP B

FRA 23 - 24 GER
Halftime Score: 10 - 12

France	%		Germany	%
3/4	75.0%	6-Meter shots	0/3	0.0%
0/2	0.0%	Wing shots	2/3	66.7%
9/24	37.5%	9-Meter shots	8/18	44.4%
3/3	100.0%	7-Meter shots	4/5	80.0%
6/8	75.0%	Fast breaks	6/10	60.0%
2/4	50.0%	Breakthroughs	4/5	80.0%
23/45	51.1%	Total shots	24/44	54.5%
9		Assists	8	
13		Turnovers	10	
2		Steals	5	
2		Blocks	2	
6		Fouls	7	

1st Referee: NED BRUSSEL, Peter
2nd Referee: NED van DONGEN, Anton

PRELIMINARIES - GROUP B

ALG 20 - 20 BRA
Halftime Score: 9 - 11

Algeria	%		Brazil	%
2/5	40.0%	6-Meter shots	7/10	70.0%
5/10	50.0%	Wing shots	5/7	71.4%
7/18	38.9%	9-Meter shots	6/13	46.2%
1/3	33.3%	7-Meter shots	1/2	50.0%
3/3	100.0%	Fast breaks	1/4	25.0%
2/5	40.0%	Breakthroughs	0/1	0.0%
20/44	45.5%	Total shots	20/37	54.1%
5		Assists	12	
20		Turnovers	21	
2		Steals	5	
0		Blocks	1	
9		Fouls	7	

1st Referee: CGO MOELLE MABOUNDA, Michel
2nd Referee: CGO MVOULA, Daniel

TEAM: EGY Egypt
Coach: GARCIA CUESTA, Javier   Assistant Coach: el SADANY, Asem

Names	Pos	M/A	% Eff	A	To	Stl	Bl
el AWADY, Ahmed	GK	0/0	0.0%				
el ATTAR, Ahmed	LB	3/10	30.0%		4		
ALI, Ahmed	CB	0/0	0.0%				
ABD ALLA, Hossam	RB	0/0	0.0%				
SOLIMAN, Mahmoud	RW	6/8	75.0%	1			
GOHAR, Gohar	P	1/2	50.0%	1	1		1
MAHMOUD, Yaser	CB	0/0	0.0%				
MAHMOUD, Khaled	LW	0/0	0.0%				
el ALFY, Ayman	RW	1/2	50.0%				
BAKIR, Mohamed	GK	0/0	0.0%				
el GEIOUSHY, Amero	P	1/4	25.0%		2		
MABROUK, Ashraf	CB	3/8	37.5%	1	2	1	
SOLIMAN, Ayman	GK	0/0	0.0%				
BELAL, Ahmed	CB	1/1	100.0%	1	2		
BELAL, Saber	RB	0/0	0.0%				
ABD ELWARESS, Sameh	LW	3/8	37.5%	1			

Goalkeepers	Shots Saved	Attempted	% Eff
BAKIR, Mohamed	1	3	33.3%
SOLIMAN, Ayman	14	35	40.0%

TEAM: FRA France
Coach: COSTANTINI, Daniel   Assistant Coach: LEPOINTE, Jean-Pierre

Names	Pos	M/A	% Eff	A	To	Stl	Bl
GAUDIN, Christian	GK	0/0	0.0%	.			
MAHE, Pascal	LB	0/0	0.0%				
SCHAAF, Philippe	LB	0/3	0.0%		2		
VOLLE, Frederic	P	2/4	50.0%				
LATHOUD, Denis	CB	0/0	0.0%				
KERVADEC, Gueric	P	2/2	100.0%	1	3		1
CORDINIER, Stephane	LW	3/3	100.0%	2		1	
MONTHUREL, Gael	RB	0/0	0.0%				
ANQUETIL, Gregory	RW	0/0	0.0%				
AMALOU, Eric	LW	0/0	0.0%				
MARTINI, Bruno	GK	0/0	0.0%				
JOULIN, Stephane	RW	0/3	0.0%		1	1	
PRANDI, Raoul	LW	6/11	54.5%	4	3		1
DELATTRE, Yohan	GK	0/0	0.0%				
RICHARDSON, Jackson	CB	4/7	57.1%	2	2		
STOECKLIN, Stephane	CB	6/12	50.0%	2			

Goalkeepers	Shots Saved	Attempted	% Eff
MARTINI, Bruno	8	26	30.8%
DELATTRE, Yohan	5	18	27.8%

TEAM: ALG Algeria
Coach: MACHOU, Mohammed   Assistant Coach: BOUCHEKRIOU, Salah

Names	Pos	M/A	% Eff	A	To	Stl	Bl
DAOUD, Amar	GK	0/0	0.0%				
LOUKIL, Abdelghani	LW	5/6	83.3%	1	1		
AOUACHRIA, Redouane	CB	0/0	0.0%				
NEDJEL-HAMMOU, Salim	CB	5/10	50.0%	1	5		
ROUABHI, Nabil	CB	0/3	0.0%				
SAIDI, Redouane	RW	2/5	40.0%	1	1		
BEGHOUACH, Benali	P	0/1	0.0%		2		
LAMALI, Sofiane	CB	1/5	20.0%		2		
BOUANANI, Abedldjalil	P	0/0	0.0%				
BOUANIK, Mahmoud	CB	0/0	0.0%				
GHERBI, Rabah	CB	0/0	0.0%				
HASNI, Achour	CB	1/1	100.0%				1
KHALFALLAH, Sofiane	LW	1/5	20.0%	1			
BOUZIANE, Mohamed	CB	4/7	57.1%	1	2	1	
ABES, Salim	CB	1/1	100.0%	1	6		
el MAOUHAB, Karim	GK	0/0	0.0%				

Goalkeepers	Shots Saved	Attempted	% Eff
DAOUD, Amar	4	18	22.2%
el MAOUHAB, Karim	8	19	42.1%

TEAM: ESP Spain
Coach: ROMAN, Jvande   Assistant Coach: HERNANDEZ, Juan

Names	Pos	M/A	% Eff	A	To	Stl	Bl
FORT, Jaume	GK	0/0	0.0%				
LOZANO, Demetrio	RB	0/0	0.0%				
ESQUER, Salvador	LW	2/2	100.0%			2	1
GUIJOSA, Rafael	LW	0/1	0.0%				
HERNANDEZ, Fernando	RW	0/0	0.0%				
GONZALEZ, Raul	RW	1/1	100.0%	1			
URDANGARIN, Inaki	LB	1/1	100.0%	1			
OLALLA, Jesus	RB	2/3	66.7%	2		2	
GARRALDA, Mateo	LB	2/8	25.0%	1	3	2	3
DUJSHEBAEV, Talant	CB	4/8	50.0%	3		1	
FERNANDEZ, Jesus	CB	0/0	0.0%				
NUNEZ, Jordi	GK	0/0	0.0%				
URDIALES, Alberto	RW	8/12	66.7%	1	1		
PEREZ, Juan	P	0/0	0.0%				
HOMBRADOS, Jose	GK	0/0	0.0%				
ETXABURU, Aitor	P	0/2	0.0%				

Goalkeeper	Shots Saved	Attempted	% Eff
FORT, Jaume	11	43	25.6%

TEAM: GER Germany
Coach: EHRET, Arno

Names	Pos	M/A	% Eff	A	To	Stl	Bl
FRITZ, Henning	GK	0/0	0.0%				
BAUR, Markus	CB	0/0	0.0%				
KRETZSCHMAR, Stefan	LW	0/0	0.0%				
FEGTER, Jan	LB	7/14	50.0%	1	1	1	
SCHWARZER, Christian	P	1/2	50.0%	1	2	2	
PETERSEN, Klaus-Dieter	P	0/1	0.0%	1		1	2
KNORR, Thomas	LB	0/0	0.0%				
ZERBE, Volker	RB	2/2	100.0%	2	1		
THIEL, Andreas	GK	0/0	0.0%				
SCHEFFLER, Christian	LW	4/8	50.0%		2		
SCHWALB, Martin	RB	5/8	62.5%	1	1	1	
KOHLHAAS, Karsten	LB	2/3	66.7%				
HOLPERT, Jan	GK	0/0	0.0%				
SCHMIDT, Martin	RW	0/0	0.0%	1	2		
STEPHAN, Daniel	CB	3/6	50.0%	1	1		
LOHR, Holger	RW	0/0	0.0%				

Goalkeepers	Shots Saved	Attempted	% Eff
THIEL, Andreas	17	44	38.6%
HOLPERT, Jan	0	1	0.0%

TEAM: BRA Brazil
Coach: RIGOLO, Alberto   Assistant Coach: SILVA JUNIOR, Washington

Names	Pos	M/A	% Eff	A	To	Stl	Bl
LIMA, Cesar	GK	0/0	0.0%				
FRIERE, Edison Alves	GK	0/0	0.0%				
PINHEIRO, Ivan	LB	2/4	50.0%	4	3	2	
CEZAR, Marcos	CB	0/0	0.0%	1	1		
NASCIMENTO, Jose	RW	4/6	66.7%	4	1	1	
STEINWANDTER, Fausto	CB	2/4	50.0%	3			1
MORATORE, Paulo	RB	0/0	0.0%				
PELISSARI, Milton	P	3/6	50.0%	1	4		
ANDRADE, Daniel	RW	5/7	71.4%	1		1	
MATOS, Agberto	LB	0/0	0.0%				
SAMPAIO, Marcelo	GK	0/1	0.0%				
BARROS, Winglitton	LW	2/2	100.0%	2			
MAZIERO, Ivan	LW	1/3	33.3%	2	1		
HOFFELDER, Rodrigo	CB	1/4	25.0%	1	5		
INOCENTE FILHO, Osvaldo	GK	0/0	0.0%				
ERTEL, Carlos	P	0/0	0.0%				

Goalkeepers	Shots Saved	Attempted	% Eff
SAMPAIO, Marcelo	17	43	39.5%
INOCENTE FILHO, Osvaldo	0	1	0.0%

Men / *Messieurs*

CLASSIFICATION

KUW 25 - 31 BRA
Halftime Score: 13 - 16

Kuwait				Brazil
3/6	50.0%	6-Meter shots	4/8	50.0%
7/7	100.0%	Wing shots	3/8	37.5%
2/11	18.2%	9-Meter shots	6/18	33.3%
1/1	100.0%	7-Meter shots	0/0	0.0%
7/10	70.0%	Fast breaks	11/15	73.3%
5/8	62.5%	Breakthroughs	7/10	70.0%
25/43	58.1%	Total shots	31/59	52.5%
	15	Assists	13	
	25	Turnovers	11	
	4	Steals	3	
	0	Blocks	2	
	4	Fouls	4	

1st Referee: USA BOEHNE, Bruce
2nd Referee: USA BOJSEN, Thomas

CLASSIFICATION

ALG 26 - 27 USA
Halftime Score: 12 - 10
End of Playing Time: 22 - 22

Algeria				United States of America
2/3	66.7%	6-Meter shots	9/13	69.2%
2/6	33.3%	Wing shots	5/9	55.6%
5/23	21.7%	9-Meter shots	5/12	41.7%
3/3	100.0%	7-Meter shots	2/2	100.0%
5/7	71.4%	Fast breaks	5/5	100.0%
9/9	100.0%	Breakthroughs	1/2	50.0%
26/51	51.0%	Total shots	27/43	62.8%
	8	Assists	12	
	14	Turnovers	20	
	4	Steals	3	
	0	Blocks	5	
	9	Fouls	11	

1st Referee: KUW al HOULI, Mohammad
2nd Referee: KUW ALENEZI, Khalaf

CLASSIFICATION

SUI 16 - 23 GER
Halftime Score: 10 - 12

Switzerland				Germany
5/8	62.5%	6-Meter shots	5/7	71.4%
3/4	75.0%	Wing shots	7/7	100.0%
0/13	0.0%	9-Meter shots	5/16	31.3%
2/4	50.0%	7-Meter shots	2/2	100.0%
5/6	83.3%	Fast breaks	4/5	80.0%
1/1	100.0%	Breakthroughs	0/1	0.0%
16/36	44.4%	Total shots	23/38	60.5%
	10	Assists	12	
	13	Turnovers	10	
	4	Steals	2	
	0	Blocks	3	
	4	Fouls	5	

1st Referee: DEN ELBROND, Per
2nd Referee: DEN LOVQVIST, Kjeld

TEAM: KUW Kuwait
Coach: PULJEVIC, Ilija   Assistant Coach: ALRANDI, Musaed

Names	Pos	M/A	% Eff	A	To	Stl	Bl
ALBLOUSHI, Abdulrazak	GK	0/0	0.0%		1		
al-HARBI, Abbas	CB	5/8	62.5%	1	2	1	
ALKHASHTI, Khaldoun	P	4/7	57.1%		2		
al-MARZOUQ, Salem	CB	1/3	33.3%		6		
ALOTAIBI, Ibrahim	RW	0/0	0.0%				
ALSHEMRI, Bandar	RW	4/5	80.0%		2		
ALKAHAM, Adel	LW	3/3	100.0%	2	1		
ALALI, Mishal	RB	0/0	0.0%	2	2		
SH ZADAH, Ismaeel	P	5/6	83.3%	4		2	
al-MARZOUQ, Khaled	GK	0/0	0.0%				
ALMARZOUQ, Salah	LB	1/6	16.7%	2	3	1	
ALMULLAH, Khaled	LW	1/1	100.0%		3		
ALADWANI, Qaied	RB	1/4	25.0%	4	3		
ALOTAIBI, Naser	GK	0/0	0.0%				
ALMULLAH, Tareq	P	0/0	0.0%				
ALMULLAH, Salah	LW	0/0	0.0%				

Goalkeepers	Shots Saved	Attempted	% Eff
ALBLOUSHI, Abdulrazak	22	51	43.1%
ALOTAIBI, Naser	1	8	12.5%

TEAM: ALG Algeria
Coach: MACHOU, Mohammed   Assistant Coach: BOUCHEKRIOU, Salah

Names	Pos	M/A	% Eff	A	To	Stl	Bl
DAOUD, Amar	GK	0/0	0.0%	1			
LOUKIL, Abdelghani	LW	4/12	33.3%		2		
AOUACHRIA, Redouane	CB	2/3	66.7%	1	3	1	
NEDJEL-HAMMOU, Salim	CB	5/14	35.7%		2		
ROUABHI, Nabil	CB	0/0	0.0%				
SAIDI, Redouane	RW	6/7	85.7%	3	2	1	
BEGHOUACH, Benali	P	1/2	50.0%		2		
LAMALI, Sofiane	CB	3/6	50.0%	1	2		
BOUANANI, Abedldjalil	P	0/0	0.0%				
BOUANIK, Mahmoud	CB	0/0	0.0%				
GHERBI, Rabah	CB	0/0	0.0%				
HASNI, Achour	CB	0/0	0.0%				
KHALFALLAH, Sofiane	LW	0/0	0.0%				
BOUZIANE, Mohamed	CB	5/7	71.4%	2	1	1	
ABES, Salim	CB	0/0	0.0%			1	
el MAOUHAB, Karim	GK	0/0	0.0%				

Goalkeepers	Shots Saved	Attempted	% Eff
DAOUD, Amar	9	31	29.0%
el MAOUHAB, Karim	1	12	8.3%

TEAM: SUI Switzerland
Coach: EMRICH, Armin   Assistant Coach: DEMIROVIC, Halid

Names	Pos	M/A	% Eff	A	To	Stl	Bl
DOBLER, Rolf	GK	0/0	0.0%				
VASILAKIS, Alex	LW	0/0	0.0%				
SPENGLER, Daniel	LW	3/5	60.0%	2		1	
CHRISTEN, Nicolas	CB	1/3	33.3%	1	2	1	
SCHARER, Urs	CB	0/2	0.0%		1		
BRUNNER, Roman	CB	0/3	0.0%		1		
ZUMSTEIN, Matthias	P	0/0	0.0%	1		1	
SCHARER, Stefan	LW	6/7	85.7%	1	1		
SUTER, Michael	LW	0/0	0.0%				
BRANDENBERGER, Michael	P	0/0	0.0%				
HEIMANN, Urs	GK	0/0	0.0%				
BAUMGARTNER, Marc	CB	4/14	28.6%	3	5		
KOSTADINOVICH, Robbie	CB	0/0	0.0%	1	1		
BARTH, Rene	P	2/2	100.0%	1	1		
MEISTERHANS, Christian	GK	0/0	0.0%				
LIMA, Carlos	RW	0/0	0.0%		1	1	

Goalkeepers	Shots Saved	Attempted	% Eff
DOBLER, Rolf	6	18	33.3%
MEISTERHANS, Christian	4	20	20.0%

TEAM: BRA Brazil
Coach: RIGOLO, Alberto   Assistant Coach: SILVA JUNIOR, Washington

Names	Pos	M/A	% Eff	A	To	Stl	Bl
LIMA, Cesar	GK	0/0	0.0%				
FRIERE, Edison Alves	GK	0/0	0.0%				
PINHEIRO, Ivan	LB	2/6	33.3%	1	1		
CEZAR, Marcos	CB	1/3	33.3%	4			
NASCIMENTO, Jose	RW	7/10	70.0%	3	1	2	
STEINWANDTER, Fausto	CB	1/1	100.0%		1		2
MORATORE, Paulo	RB	2/4	50.0%	1			
PELISSARI, Milton	P	4/7	57.1%	3	1		
ANDRADE, Daniel	RW	6/10	60.0%	1			
MATOS, Agberto	LB	0/0	0.0%				
SAMPAIO, Marcelo	GK	0/0	0.0%	2			
BARROS, Winglitton	LW	4/6	66.7%	1			
MAZIERO, Ivan	LW	2/5	40.0%	1			
HOFFELDER, Rodrigo	CB	2/7	28.6%	1	3		
INOCENTE FILHO, Osvaldo	GK	0/0	0.0%				
ERTEL, Carlos	P	0/0	0.0%				

Goalkeepers	Shots Saved	Attempted	% Eff
LIMA, Cesar	3	10	30.0%
SAMPAIO, Marcelo	8	33	24.2%

TEAM: USA United States of America
Coach: OLEKSYK, Richard   Assistant Coach: NICHOL, Rhett

Names	Pos	M/A	% Eff	A	To	Stl	Bl
MANNON, Cliff	GK	0/0	0.0%		1		
FERCHO, Denny	P	0/0	0.0%				
FITZGERALD, Thomas	LW	0/0	0.0%				
FITZGERALD, Joseph	CB	3/6	50.0%	4	6		
PENN, Steven	CB	2/4	50.0%		1		
BROWN, Derek	RW	7/11	63.6%		5		
RYAN, Matt	P	4/5	80.0%	4			1
DUNN, Robert	LW	2/2	100.0%	2	2		
KELLER, John	RB	1/1	100.0%	1		1	2
HEATH, Darrick	LB	4/8	50.0%	1	2		
DACHNIWSKY, Yaro	GK	0/0	0.0%				
CACCIA, Greg	RB	0/0	0.0%				
SCHMOCKER, Mark	GK	0/0	0.0%				
DeGRAAF, Dave	P	3/4	75.0%	3		1	
THORNBERRY, Michael	P	1/2	50.0%	2			
VAN OS, Chip, Jr.	LB	0/0	0.0%				

Goalkeepers	Shots Saved	Attempted	% Eff
MANNON, Cliff	14	50	28.0%
DACHNIWSKY, Yaro	0	1	0.0%

TEAM: GER Germany
Coach: EHRET, Arno

Names	Pos	M/A	% Eff	A	To	Stl	Bl
FRITZ, Henning	GK	0/0	0.0%				
BAUR, Markus	CB	0/1	0.0%				
KRETZSCHMAR, Stefan	LW	0/0	0.0%				
FEGTER, Jan	LB	2/6	33.3%	1	2		
SCHWARZER, Christian	P	4/6	66.7%	1	2		1
PETERSEN, Klaus-Dieter	P	0/0	0.0%		1		
KNORR, Thomas	LB	0/0	0.0%				
ZERBE, Volker	RB	0/2	0.0%	2	1		
THIEL, Andreas	GK	0/1	0.0%	1			
SCHEFFLER, Christian	LW	5/5	100.0%	1			
SCHWALB, Martin	RB	2/2	100.0%	1			1
KOHLHAAS, Karsten	LB	2/3	66.7%	1	1		
HOLPERT, Jan	GK	0/0	0.0%				
SCHMIDT, Martin	RW	0/0	0.0%				
STEPHAN, Daniel	CB	5/7	71.4%	3	2		1
LOHR, Holger	RW	3/5	60.0%	1	1	2	

Goalkeeper	Shots Saved	Attempted	% Eff
THIEL, Andreas	15	36	41.7%

Handball / *Handball*

BARRY R SMOUSE • JANET A SMUCKER • TROY M SMURAWA MD • DAVID SMYTH • DONNA D SMYTHE • PHILIP J SMYTHE • TERRY ANN SMYTHE • CHARLENE SNAIR • KELLY L SNAJKOWSKI • HARRY SNAPPERMAN • HYACINTH L SNEAD • WALTER S SNEAD III • JAMES A SNEDDON • JAMES R SNEED • RICHARD L SNEED • SUSAN H SNEED • TOBIAS S SNEED • EILEEN M SNELL • EMILY S SNELL • JAMES L SNELL • LAURIE SNELL • VIRGINIA SNELL • CAROL A SNELLEN • EDWARD W SNELLING • SANDRA U SNELLING • TERESA SNELLINGS • ROBERT L SNELSON

Men / *Messieurs*

CLASSIFICATION

EGY 26 - 29 RUS
Halftime Score: 11 - 15

Egypt			Russian Federation	
4/5	80.0%	6-Meter shots	7/12	58.3%
1/2	50.0%	Wing shots	2/5	40.0%
13/33	39.4%	9-Meter shots	9/13	69.2%
2/2	100.0%	7-Meter shots	1/2	50.0%
5/7	71.4%	Fast breaks	8/10	80.0%
1/2	50.0%	Breakthroughs	2/2	100.0%
26/51	51.0%	Total shots	29/44	65.9%
7		Assists	12	
6		Turnovers	14	
3		Steals	0	
1		Blocks	5	
6		Fouls	7	

1st Referee: ESP   GALLEGO SANTOS, Silvino
2nd Referee: ESP   LAMAS PEREZ, Victor

SEMIFINALS

SWE 25 - 20 ESP
Halftime Score: 11 - 12

Sweden			Spain	
5/7	71.4%	6-Meter shots	3/5	60.0%
8/9	88.9%	Wing shots	1/4	25.0%
7/17	41.2%	9-Meter shots	4/22	18.2%
2/2	100.0%	7-Meter shots	5/6	83.3%
1/5	20.0%	Fast breaks	4/4	100.0%
2/3	66.7%	Breakthroughs	3/4	75.0%
25/43	58.1%	Total shots	20/45	44.4%
13		Assists	7	
14		Turnovers	11	
1		Steals	2	
3		Blocks	3	
9		Fouls	7	

1st Referee: NED   BRUSSEL, Peter
2nd Referee: NED   van DONGEN, Anton

SEMIFINALS

FRA 20 - 24 CRO
Halftime Score: 8 - 12

France			Croatia	
2/3	66.7%	6-Meter shots	2/4	50.0%
2/9	22.2%	Wing shots	2/8	25.0%
9/17	52.9%	9-Meter shots	8/21	38.1%
1/2	50.0%	7-Meter shots	6/7	85.7%
5/7	71.4%	Fast breaks	3/3	100.0%
1/2	50.0%	Breakthroughs	3/4	75.0%
20/40	50.0%	Total shots	24/47	51.1%
6		Assists	6	
14		Turnovers	7	
3		Steals	4	
4		Blocks	0	
4		Fouls	8	

1st Referee: NOR   HOGSNES, Bjorn
2nd Referee: NOR   OEIE, Svein

TEAM: EGY Egypt
Coach: GARCIA CUESTA, Javier   Assistant Coach: el SADANY, Asem

Names	Pos	M/A	% Eff	A	To	Stl	Bl
el AWADY, Ahmed	GK	0/0	0.0%				
el ATTAR, Ahmed	LB	10/17	58.8%	1			
ALI, Ahmed	CB	1/1	100.0%				
ABD ALLA, Hossam	RB	0/0	0.0%				
SOLIMAN, Mahmoud	RW	4/8	50.0%	1	1		
GOHAR, Gohar	P	0/0	0.0%				
MAHMOUD, Yaser	CB	0/0	0.0%				
MAHMOUD, Khaled	LW	3/3	100.0%				
el ALFY, Ayman	RW	1/2	50.0%				
BAKIR, Mohamed	GK	0/0	0.0%				
el GEIOUSHY, Amero	P	2/4	50.0%	1			
MABROUK, Ashraf	CB	1/4	25.0%	2			
SOLIMAN, Ayman	GK	0/0	0.0%				
BELAL, Ahmed	CB	1/3	33.3%	4	2	3	1
BELAL, Saber	RB	0/1	0.0%				
ABD ELWARESS, Sameh	LW	3/8	37.5%	1			

Goalkeepers	Shots Saved	Attempted	% Eff
BAKIR, Mohamed	10	43	23.3%
SOLIMAN, Ayman	0	1	0.0%

TEAM: SWE Sweden
Coach: JOHANSSON, Bengt

Names	Pos	M/A	% Eff	A	To	Stl	Bl
OLSSON, Mats	GK	0/0	0.0%	1			
HEDIN, Robert	CB	0/0	0.0%				
WISLANDER, Magnus	CB	2/5	40.0%	1	1		1
SIVERTSSON, Thomas	P	0/0	0.0%				
LINDGREN, Ola	CB	1/2	50.0%			1	2
CARLEN, Per	P	3/3	100.0%				
HAJAS, Erik	LW	5/8	62.5%	1	1		
PETERSON, Johan	RW	0/0	0.0%				
LOVGREN, Stefan	CB	2/4	50.0%	4	2		
ANDERSSON, Robert	CB	0/0	0.0%				
THORSSON, Pierre	RW	7/8	87.5%				
OLSSON, Staffan	CB	1/4	25.0%	5	7		
ANDERSSON, Magnus	CB	4/9	44.4%	1	3		
LARSSON, Andreas	CB	0/0	0.0%				
SVENSSON, Thomas	GK	0/0	0.0%				
FRANDESJO, Martin	LW	0/0	0.0%				

Goalkeepers	Shots Saved	Attempted	% Eff
OLSSON, Mats	16	44	36.4%
SVENSSON, Thomas	0	1	0.0%

TEAM: FRA France
Coach: COSTANTINI, Daniel   Assistant Coach: LEPOINTE, Jean-Pierre

Names	Pos	M/A	% Eff	A	To	Stl	Bl
GAUDIN, Christian	GK	0/0	0.0%				
MAHE, Pascal	LB	0/0	0.0%				
SCHAAF, Philippe	LB	0/0	0.0%				
VOLLE, Frederic	P	3/6	50.0%		2	1	1
LATHOUD, Denis	CB	2/4	50.0%	3			
KERVADEC, Gueric	P	3/3	100.0%		2		2
CORDINIER, Stephane	LW	0/0	0.0%				
MONTHUREL, Gael	RB	0/0	0.0%				
ANQUETIL, Gregory	RW	1/6	16.7%	1			
AMALOU, Eric	LW	1/4	25.0%	2	1		1
MARTINI, Bruno	GK	0/0	0.0%				
JOULIN, Stephane	RW	0/0	0.0%				
PRANDI, Raoul	LW	0/0	0.0%				
DELATTRE, Yohan	GK	0/0	0.0%				
RICHARDSON, Jackson	CB	2/4	50.0%	2	2	2	
STOECKLIN, Stephane	CB	8/13	61.5%	2	3		

Goalkeepers	Shots Saved	Attempted	% Eff
GAUDIN, Christian	15	46	32.6%
MARTINI, Bruno	0	1	0.0%

TEAM: RUS Russian Federation
Coach: MAXIMOV, Vladimir   Assistant Coach: KOROSTOCHEVITCH, Leonid

Names	Pos	M/A	% Eff	A	To	Stl	Bl
LAVROV, Andrei	GK	0/0	0.0%				
LAVROV, Igor	CB	2/3	66.7%	3			
FRANTSUZOV, Aleksey	P	0/0	0.0%				
KOULECHOV, Oleg	CB	2/3	66.7%				
KRIVOSHLYKOV, Denis	RW	0/0	0.0%				
VORONIN, Lev	RW	5/6	83.3%	4			
GOPIN, Valeri	LW	6/7	85.7%	5			
KOUDINOV, Vassili	LB	5/6	83.3%	3			
TORGOVANOV, Dmitri	P	4/7	57.1%	1			
SUKOSSIAN, Pavel	GK	0/0	0.0%				
GREBNEV, Oleg	P	0/0	0.0%	1	1		1
KISSELEV, Oleg	RB	1/3	33.3%	3			2
GORPICHIN, Viatcheslav	LB	3/4	75.0%	1			2
POGORELOV, Serguei	RB	1/5	20.0%	2	2		
FILIPPOV, Dmitriy	LW	0/0	0.0%				

Goalkeepers	Shots Saved	Attempted	% Eff
LAVROV, Andrei	4	19	21.1%
SUKOSSIAN, Pavel	6	32	18.8%

TEAM: ESP Spain
Coach: ROMAN, Jvande   Assistant Coach: HERNANDEZ, Juan

Names	Pos	M/A	% Eff	A	To	Stl	Bl
FORT, Jaume	GK	0/0	0.0%				
LOZANO, Demetrio	RB	0/0	0.0%				
ESQUER, Salvador	LW	3/4	75.0%				
GUIJOSA, Rafael	LW	5/6	83.3%				
HERNANDEZ, Fernando	RW	0/0	0.0%				
GONZALEZ, Raul	RW	2/3	66.7%	2	3		
URDANGARIN, Inaki	LB	0/2	0.0%				1
OLALLA, Jesus	RB	0/2	0.0%	3			
GARRALDA, Mateo	LB	1/7	14.3%	1			1
DUJSHEBAEV, Talant	CB	3/11	27.3%	2	2		
FERNANDEZ, Jesus	CB	0/0	0.0%				
NUNEZ, Jordi	GK	0/0	0.0%				
URDIALES, Alberto	RW	2/4	50.0%	2		1	
PEREZ, Juan	P	1/3	33.3%				
HOMBRADOS, Jose	GK	0/0	0.0%				
ETXABURU, Aitor	P	3/3	100.0%		3	1	1

Goalkeepers	Shots Saved	Attempted	% Eff
FORT, Jaume	7	32	21.9%
NUNEZ, Jordi	4	11	36.4%

TEAM: CRO Croatia
Coach: KLJAIC, Velimir

Names	Pos	M/A	% Eff	A	To	Stl	Bl
JELCIC, Vladimir	LW	0/0	0.0%				
PERKOVAC, Goran	LW	4/8	50.0%	2	1	1	
SMAJLAGIC, Irfan	LW	2/6	33.3%	1			
JOVIC, Bozidar	P	3/4	75.0%				
NACINOVIC, Alvaro	P	0/0	0.0%				
SUJSTER, Vladimir	RW	0/0	0.0%				
GUDELJ, Bruno	LW	0/0	0.0%				
KLJAIC, Nenad	P	1/1	100.0%				
PUC, Iztok	CB	2/3	66.7%	1	1		
MIKULIC, Zoran	CB	0/2	0.0%				
LOSERT, Venio	GK	0/0	0.0%				
CAVAR, Patrik	CB	8/12	66.7%	1	1	2	
FRANKOVIC, Valner	P	0/0	0.0%				
GOLUZA, Slavko	CB	2/5	40.0%	1			
MATOSEVIC, Valter	GK	0/0	0.0%	1			
SARACEVIC, Zlatko	LB	2/6	33.3%	1	2	1	

Goalkeeper	Shots Saved	Attempted	% Eff
MATOSEVIC, Valter	12	40	30.0%

Handball / *Handball*   **255**

FINAL - BRONZE MATCH

ESP 27 - 25 FRA
Halftime Score: 13 -12

	Spain		France	
5/7	71.4%	6-Meter shots	8/10	80.0%
3/6	50.0%	Wing shots	2/4	50.0%
7/25	28.0%	9-Meter shots	5/22	22.7%
3/5	60.0%	7-Meter shots	1/2	50.0%
5/6	83.3%	Fast breaks	5/5	100.0%
4/6	66.7%	Breakthroughs	4/4	100.0%
27/55	49.1%	Total shots	25/47	53.2%
	14	Assists	12	
	9	Turnovers	15	
	5	Steals	5	
	5	Blocks	7	
	6	Fouls	7	

1st Referee: DEN ELBROND, Per
2nd Referee: DEN LOVQVIST, Kjeld

FINAL - GOLD MATCH

SWE 26 - 27 CRO
Halftime Score: 11 - 16

	Sweden		Croatia	
5/7	71.4%	6-Meter shots	10/10	100.0%
10/14	71.4%	Wing shots	2/7	28.6%
4/11	36.4%	9-Meter shots	7/19	36.8%
1/3	33.3%	7-Meter shots	0/0	0.0%
5/6	83.3%	Fast breaks	4/4	100.0%
1/1	100.0%	Breakthroughs	4/4	100.0%
26/42	61.9%	Total shots	27/44	61.4%
	16	Assists	13	
	10	Turnovers	10	
	1	Steals	3	
	2	Blocks	3	
	6	Fouls	7	

1st Referee: ESP GALLEGO SANTOS, Silvino
2nd Referee: ESP LAMAS PEREZ, Victor

TEAM: ESP Spain
Coach: ROMAN, Jvande   Assistant Coach: HERNANDEZ, Juan

Names	Pos	M/A	% Eff	A	To	Stl	Bl
FORT, Jaume	GK	0/0	0.0%				
LOZANO, Demetrio	RB	5/6	83.3%	1			
ESQUER, Salvador	LW	5/6	83.3%	1			
GUIJOSA, Rafael	LW	2/4	50.0%				
HERNANDEZ, Fernando	RW	0/0	0.0%				
GONZALEZ, Raul	RW	0/1	0.0%	3	1		
URDANGARIN, Inaki	LB	2/9	22.2%	3	2	3	1
OLALLA, Jesus	RB	3/8	37.5%	4	1	1	2
GARRALDA, Mateo	LB	0/0	0.0%				
DUJSHEBAEV, Talant	CB	3/12	25.0%	2	1	1	
FERNANDEZ, Jesus	CB	0/0	0.0%				
NUNEZ, Jordi	GK	0/0	0.0%				
URDIALES, Alberto	RW	5/7	71.4%	1	1		
PEREZ, Juan	P	0/0	0.0%				1
HOMBRADOS, Jose	GK	0/0	0.0%				
ETXABURU, Aitor	P	2/2	100.0%		2		1

Goalkeepers	Shots Saved	Attempted	% Eff
FORT, Jaume	12	45	26.7%
NUNEZ, Jordi	0	2	0.0%
HOMBRADOS, Jose	0	0	0.0%

TEAM: FRA France
Coach: COSTANTINI, Daniel   Assistant Coach: LEPOINTE, Jean-Pierre

Names	Pos	M/A	% Eff	A	To	Stl	Bl
GAUDIN, Christian	GK	0/0	0.0%				
MAHE, Pascal	LB	1/1	100.0%	1	2		3
SCHAAF, Philippe	LB	0/0	0.0%				
VOLLE, Frederic	P	2/8	25.0%	1	1		4
LATHOUD, Denis	CB	0/1	0.0%	2	3		
KERVADEC, Gueric	P	3/3	100.0%	1	1	1	
CORDINIER, Stephane	LW	7/9	77.8%	1			
MONTHUREL, Gael	RB	0/0	0.0%				
ANQUETIL, Gregory	RW	0/0	0.0%				
AMALOU, Eric	LW	0/0	0.0%				
MARTINI, Bruno	GK	0/0	0.0%				
JOULIN, Stephane	RW	1/2	50.0%	1		1	
PRANDI, Raoul	LW	2/4	50.0%	3	2		
DELATTRE, Yohan	GK	0/0	0.0%				
RICHARDSON, Jackson	CB	3/4	75.0%	2	2	3	
STOECKLIN, Stephane	CB	6/15	40.0%	1	3		

Goalkeepers	Shots Saved	Attempted	% Eff
GAUDIN, Christian	0	0	0.0%
MARTINI, Bruno	9	26	34.6%
DELATTRE, Yohan	8	29	27.6%

TEAM: SWE Sweden
Coach: JOHANSSON, Bengt

Names	Pos	M/A	% Eff	A	To	Stl	Bl
OLSSON, Mats	GK	0/0	0.0%				
HEDIN, Robert	CB	0/1	0.0%				
WISLANDER, Magnus	CB	3/5	60.0%	1	3		1
SIVERTSSON, Thomas	P	2/2	100.0%		1		1
LINDGREN, Ola	CB	0/0	0.0%	1	1		
CARLEN, Per	P	0/1	0.0%	2	1		
HAJAS, Erik	LW	7/7	100.0%	1			
PETERSON, Johan	RW	0/0	0.0%				
LOVGREN, Stefan	CB	2/4	50.0%	2			
ANDERSSON, Robert	CB	0/0	0.0%				
THORSSON, Pierre	RW	8/13	61.5%	1			
OLSSON, Staffan	CB	3/7	42.9%	6	1		
ANDERSSON, Magnus	CB	1/2	50.0%	2	3		
LARSSON, Andreas	CB	0/0	0.0%				
SVENSSON, Thomas	GK	0/0	0.0%	1			
FRANDESJO, Martin	LW	0/0	0.0%				

Goalkeepers	Shots Saved	Attempted	% Eff
OLSSON, Mats	1	6	16.7%
SVENSSON, Thomas	11	38	28.9%

TEAM: CRO Croatia
Coach: KLJAIC, Velimir

Names	Pos	M/A	% Eff	A	To	Stl	Bl
JELCIC, Vladimir	LW	0/1	0.0%	1	1		
PERKOVAC, Goran	LW	6/10	60.0%	1			
SMAJLAGIC, Irfan	LW	6/8	75.0%	4	4		
JOVIC, Bozidar	P	6/6	100.0%	2		1	
NACINOVIC, Alvaro	P	0/0	0.0%				
SUJSTER, Vladimir	RW	0/0	0.0%				
GUDELJ, Bruno	LW	0/0	0.0%				
KLJAIC, Nenad	P	2/2	100.0%	2		1	1
PUC, Iztok	CB	0/0	0.0%				
MIKULIC, Zoran	CB	2/2	100.0%	1			
LOSERT, Venio	GK	0/0	0.0%				
CAVAR, Patrik	CB	3/6	50.0%			1	1
FRANKOVIC, Valner	P	0/0	0.0%				
GOLUZA, Slavko	CB	2/7	28.6%	2	3		1
MATOSEVIC, Valter	GK	0/0	0.0%				
SARACEVIC, Zlatko	LB	0/2	0.0%	1	1		

Goalkeepers	Shots Saved	Attempted	% Eff
LOSERT, Venio	0	2	0.0%
MATOSEVIC, Valter	8	40	20.0%

SUMMARY: PRELIMINARIES - GROUP A

		Games			Goals			
Rnk	Team	Played	Won	Drawn	Lost	For	Against	Diff pts
1	SWE	5	5	0	0	131	94	37
2	CRO	5	4	0	1	132	122	10
3	RUS	5	3	0	2	137	106	31
4	SUI	5	2	0	3	126	115	11
5	USA	5	1	0	4	111	142	-31
6	KUW	5	0	0	5	100	158	-58

SUMMARY: PRELIMINARIES - GROUP B

		Games			Goals			
Rnk	Team	Played	Won	Drawn	Lost	For	Against	Diff pts
1	FRA	5	4	0	1	145	114	31
2	ESP	5	4	0	1	114	97	17
3	EGY	5	3	0	2	113	103	10
4	GER	5	3	0	2	121	112	09
5	ALG	5	0	1	4	95	117	-22
6	BRA	5	0	1	4	100	145	-45

FINAL MATCH SUMMARY

Phase	Teams	Score
Classification	KUW - BRA	25 - 31
Classification	ALG - USA	26 - 27
Classification	SUI - GER	16 - 23
Classification	EGY - RUS	26 - 29
Semifinal	SWE - ESP	25 - 20
Semifinal	FRA - CRO	20 - 24
Final - Bronze	ESP - FRA	27 - 25
Final - Gold	SWE - CRO	26 - 27

FINAL CLASSIFICATION

Rnk	Ctry	
1	Croatia	Gold
2	Sweden	Silver
3	Spain	Bronze
4	France	
5	Russian Federation	
6	Egypt	
7	Germany	
8	Switzerland	

Handball / *Handball*
Women / *Dames*

PRELIMINARIES - GROUP A

HUN 29 - 19 CHN
Halftime Score: 14 - 11

Hungary			People's Rep. of China	
6/7	85.7%	6-Meter shots	3/4	75.0%
2/5	40.0%	Wing shots	0/5	0.0%
4/14	28.6%	9-Meter shots	6/23	26.1%
7/11	63.6%	7-Meter shots	1/1	100.0%
4/4	100.0%	Fast breaks	6/6	100.0%
6/6	100.0%	Breakthroughs	3/4	75.0%
29/47	61.7%	Total shots	19/43	44.2%
	10	Assists	7	
	22	Turnovers	23	
	5	Steals	2	
	5	Blocks	0	
	5	Fouls	6	

1st Referee: NOR OEIE, Svein
2nd Referee: NOR HOGSNES, Bjorn

PRELIMINARIES - GROUP A

DEN 29 - 19 USA
Halftime Score: 13 - 9

Denmark			United States of America	
4/5	80.0%	6-Meter shots	3/4	75.0%
6/13	46.2%	Wing shots	2/7	28.6%
2/8	25.0%	9-Meter shots	4/23	17.4%
5/8	62.5%	7-Meter shots	5/5	100.0%
6/6	100.0%	Fast breaks	4/5	80.0%
6/8	75.0%	Breakthroughs	1/1	100.0%
29/48	60.4%	Total shots	19/45	42.2%
	14	Assists	7	
	15	Turnovers	17	
	2	Steals	4	
	4	Blocks	0	
	3	Fouls	6	

1st Referee: NED BRUSSEL, Peter
2nd Referee: NED van DONGEN, Anton

PRELIMINARIES - GROUP A

CHN 21 - 33 DEN
Halftime Score: 9 - 19

People's Rep. of China			Denmark	
3/9	33.3%	6-Meter shots	5/7	71.4%
2/6	33.3%	Wing shots	3/13	23.1%
4/17	23.5%	9-Meter shots	4/10	40.0%
1/2	50.0%	7-Meter shots	4/5	80.0%
6/10	60.0%	Fast breaks	11/15	73.3%
5/7	71.4%	Breakthroughs	6/6	100.0%
21/51	41.2%	Total shots	33/56	58.9%
	9	Assists	18	
	20	Turnovers	19	
	4	Steals	11	
	0	Blocks	1	
	8	Fouls	5	

1st Referee: CGO MOELLE MABOUNDA, Michel
2nd Referee: CGO MVOULA, Daniel

TEAM: HUN Hungary
Coach: LAURENCZ, Laszlo

Names	Pos	M/A	% Eff	A	To	Stl	Bl
MEKSZ, Aniko	GK	0/0	0.0%			1	
MATFEI, Eszter	LB	11/18	61.1%	1	3		
MATYAS, Auguszta	LB	0/0	0.0%				
TOTH, Beatrix	RB	0/0	0.0%				
PADAR, Ildiko	P	0/0	0.0%		1		
KOCSIS, Erzsebet	P	5/5	100.0%		1		
NEMETH, Helga	RB	4/8	50.0%	1	5		1
SITI, Beata	CB	0/0	0.0%	2	1		
ERDOS, Eva	LW	0/0	0.0%				
HOFFMANN, Beata	GK	0/0	0.0%				
KANTOR, Aniko	LW	0/0	0.0%			1	
NAGY, Aniko	CB	3/4	75.0%	1	3		1
KOKENY, Beatrix	RB	1/3	33.3%	4	2	1	3
FARKAS, Andrea	GK	0/0	0.0%		1		
SZILAGYI, Katalin	RW	4/6	66.7%	4			
SZANTO, Anna	RW	1/3	33.3%	1	1	2	

Goalkeepers	Shots Saved	Attempted	% Eff
MEKSZ, Aniko	3	19	15.8%
FARKAS, Andrea	10	24	41.7%

TEAM: DEN Denmark
Coach: WILBEK, Ulrik Assistant Coach: BASTRUP JORGENSEN, Henrik

Names	Pos	M/A	% Eff	A	To	Stl	Bl
RANTALA, Lene	GK	0/0	0.0%				
TANDERUP, Anne	LB	0/1	0.0%	2	1	1	
ANDERSEN, Camilla	RB	1/5	20.0%	3			
BOTTZAU, Tina	RB	3/5	60.0%	2			
HOFFMAN, Anette	LW	5/7	71.4%	2			
HANSEN, Anja	P	2/2	100.0%				1
FLORMAN, Marianne	LW	3/5	60.0%	3			
KOLLING, Janne	RW	2/6	33.3%	2			
HAMANN, Conny	P	0/0	0.0%				
ANDERSEN, Anja Jul	LB	8/11	72.7%	7	4	1	2
SUNESEN, Gitte	GK	0/0	0.0%				
MADSEN, Gitte	RW	0/0	0.0%				
ASTRUP, Heidi	CB	2/3	66.7%	1			1
KJAERGAARD, Tonje	P	3/3	100.0%	1			
LAURITSEN, Susanne	GK	0/0	0.0%		1		
ANDERSEN, Kristine	LB	0/0	0.0%				

Goalkeepers	Shots Saved	Attempted	% Eff
RANTALA, Lene	0	1	0.0%
LAURITSEN, Susanne	17	44	38.6%

TEAM: CHN People's Republic of China
Coach: HAN, Naiguo Assistant Coach: WANG, Yaoting

Names	Pos	M/A	% Eff	A	To	Stl	Bl
WANG, Xiaojiong	GK	0/0	0.0%				
YUE, Liane	RB	0/0	0.0%				
ZHANG, Li	LW	1/2	50.0%				
CHE, Zhihong	LW	0/0	0.0%				
CONG, Yanxia	CB	3/8	37.5%	4			
ZHAI, Chao	P	5/11	45.5%	4	7	2	
CHEN, Bangping	RB	1/3	33.3%				
JIA, Shujun	LB	0/0	0.0%				
CHEN, Haiyun	CB	0/1	0.0%				
ZHAO, Ying	LW	2/5	40.0%				
WANG, Tao	GK	0/0	0.0%		1		
ZHANG, Limei	P	3/6	50.0%	1	4		
LI, Jianfang	RW	0/0	0.0%		1		
YU, Geli	GK	0/0	0.0%				
SHI, Wei	LB	6/12	50.0%	4	3	2	
WU, Li	CB	0/0	0.0%				

Goalkeepers	Shots Saved	Attempted	% Eff
WANG, Tao	15	41	36.6%
YU, Geli	1	15	6.7%

TEAM: CHN People's Republic of China
Coach: HAN, Naiguo Assistant Coach: WANG, Yaoting

Names	Pos	M/A	% Eff	A	To	Stl	Bl
WANG, Xiaojiong	GK	0/0	0.0%				
YUE, Liane	RB	0/0	0.0%				
ZHANG, Li	LW	2/4	50.0%	3			
CHE, Zhihong	LW	0/0	0.0%			1	
CONG, Yanxia	CB	3/3	100.0%	2			
ZHAI, Chao	P	3/7	42.9%	1	7		
CHEN, Bangping	RB	1/3	33.3%	2	1		
JIA, Shujun	LB	0/0	0.0%				
CHEN, Haiyun	CB	1/1	100.0%				
ZHAO, Ying	LW	0/1	0.0%				
WANG, Tao	GK	0/0	0.0%				
ZHANG, Limei	P	1/3	33.3%	1	5		
LI, Jianfang	RW	3/6	50.0%				1
YU, Geli	GK	0/0	0.0%	1			
SHI, Wei	LB	5/15	33.3%	2	5		
WU, Li	CB	0/0	0.0%				

Goalkeepers	Shots Saved	Attempted	% Eff
WANG, Tao	2	14	14.3%
YU, Geli	5	33	15.2%

TEAM: USA United States of America
Coach: HELLGREN, Claes Assistant Coach: CLANTON, Reita

Names	Pos	M/A	% Eff	A	To	Stl	Bl
FELLNER, Laurie	GK	0/0	0.0%	1			
JAMESON, Toni	P	1/1	100.0%		1		
MARPLE, Dawn	RW	0/0	0.0%				
COENEN, Laura	P	1/2	50.0%		2	1	
EAGEN, Lisa	LW	0/0	0.0%				
CAIN, Sharon	CB	5/11	45.5%	2	4	2	
CLARKE, Kim	RB	0/1	0.0%	1	1		
LEININGER, Dannette	CB	2/7	28.6%	4			
HIRES, Chryssandra	LW	8/12	66.7%	2			
ALLINGER, Dawn	CB	0/0	0.0%				
HORTON, Jennifer	GK	0/0	0.0%				
DANIHY, Kristen	P	0/0	0.0%				
PETERKA, Carol	LB	1/8	12.5%	1	1		
NEDER, Pat	RW	1/3	33.3%	2	2	1	
JAMESON, Tami	GK	0/0	0.0%				
ABPLANALP, Cheryl	RW	0/0	0.0%				

Goalkeepers	Shots Saved	Attempted	% Eff
FELLNER, Laurie	0	4	0.0%
JAMESON, Tami	10	44	22.7%

TEAM: DEN Denmark
Coach: WILBEK, Ulrik Assistant Coach: BASTRUP JORGENSEN, Henrik

Names	Pos	M/A	% Eff	A	To	Stl	Bl
RANTALA, Lene	GK	0/0	0.0%				
TANDERUP, Anne	LB	2/3	66.7%	3	3	1	
ANDERSEN, Camilla	RB	1/4	25.0%	3	1		1
BOTTZAU, Tina	RB	0/0	0.0%				
HOFFMAN, Anette	LW	4/7	57.1%	1			
HANSEN, Anja	P	0/0	0.0%				
FLORMAN, Marianne	LW	1/7	14.3%	1	2		
KOLLING, Janne	RW	2/6	33.3%	1	2		
HAMANN, Conny	P	4/4	100.0%	1	3		
ANDERSEN, Anja Jul	LB	3/5	60.0%	3	6	3	
SUNESEN, Gitte	GK	0/0	0.0%				
MADSEN, Gitte	RW	7/8	87.5%	4	1	2	
ASTRUP, Heidi	CB	4/5	80.0%		1		3
KJAERGAARD, Tonje	P	5/7	71.4%	1			2
LAURITSEN, Susanne	GK	0/0	0.0%				
ANDERSEN, Kristine	LB	0/0	0.0%				

Goalkeepers	Shots Saved	Attempted	% Eff
SUNESEN, Gitte	9	27	33.3%
LAURITSEN, Susanne	12	24	50.0%

Women / *Dames*

PRELIMINARIES - GROUP A

USA 24 - 30 HUN
Halftime Score: 8 - 19

United States of America			Hungary	
5/5	100.0%	6-Meter shots	5/7	71.4%
3/5	60.0%	Wing shots	5/8	62.5%
7/26	26.9%	9-Meter shots	8/13	61.5%
5/6	83.3%	7-Meter shots	4/4	100.0%
4/5	80.0%	Fast breaks	3/5	60.0%
0/0	0.0%	Breakthroughs	5/5	100.0%
24/47	51.1%	Total shots	30/42	71.4%
10		Assists	8	
18		Turnovers	19	
9		Steals	7	
0		Blocks	5	
9		Fouls	7	

1st Referee: GER THOMAS, Jurgen
2nd Referee: GER THOMAS, Hans

PRELIMINARIES - GROUP A

HUN 22 - 27 DEN
Halftime Score: 12 - 14

Hungary			Denmark	
4/5	80.0%	6-Meter shots	2/3	66.7%
4/8	50.0%	Wing shots	6/9	66.7%
7/21	33.3%	9-Meter shots	7/20	35.0%
2/4	50.0%	7-Meter shots	5/5	100.0%
2/4	50.0%	Fast breaks	4/6	66.7%
3/3	100.0%	Breakthroughs	3/5	60.0%
22/45	48.9%	Total shots	27/48	56.3%
6		Assists	11	
16		Turnovers	8	
2		Steals	6	
3		Blocks	5	
6		Fouls	7	

1st Referee: ESP GALLEGO SANTOS, Silvino
2nd Referee: ESP LAMAS PEREZ, Victor

PRELIMINARIES - GROUP A

CHN 31 - 21 USA
Halftime Score: 16 - 11

People's Republic of China			United States of America	
7/8	87.5%	6-Meter shots	5/8	62.5%
5/12	41.7%	Wing shots	5/11	45.5%
4/9	44.4%	9-Meter shots	5/22	22.7%
5/6	83.3%	7-Meter shots	3/4	75.0%
2/2	100.0%	Fast breaks	2/2	100.0%
8/8	100.0%	Breakthroughs	1/3	33.3%
31/45	68.9%	Total shots	21/50	42.0%
8		Assists	10	
15		Turnovers	16	
5		Steals	4	
1		Blocks	0	
9		Fouls	7	

1st Referee: LTU GUTERMAN, Grigorij
2nd Referee: LTU GEDVILAS, Feliksas

TEAM: USA United States of America
Coach: HELLGREN, Claes   Assistant Coach: CLANTON, Reita

Names	Pos	M/A	% Eff	A	To	Stl	Bl
FELLNER, Laurie	GK	0/0	0.0%		1		
JAMESON, Toni	P	4/4	100.0%		1	1	
MARPLE, Dawn	RW	0/0	0.0%				
COENEN, Laura	P	2/2	100.0%	2	2		
EAGEN, Lisa	LW	0/0	0.0%				
CAIN, Sharon	CB	7/15	46.7%	1	6	2	
CLARKE, Kim	RB	2/4	50.0%	3			
LEININGER, Dannette	CB	1/2	50.0%	1	1		
HIRES, Chryssandra	LW	8/17	47.1%	1	2	1	
ALLINGER, Dawn	CB	0/0	0.0%	1		1	
HORTON, Jennifer	GK	0/0	0.0%				
DANIHY, Kristen	P	0/0	0.0%				
PETERKA, Carol	LB	0/3	0.0%		4	1	
NEDER, Pat	RW	0/0	0.0%	1	1	3	
JAMESON, Tami	GK	0/0	0.0%				
ABPLANALP, Cheryl	RW	0/0	0.0%				

Goalkeepers	Shots Saved	Attempted	% Eff
FELLNER, Laurie	6	32	18.8%
COENEN, Laura	0	2	0.0%
JAMESON, Tami	0	8	0.0%

TEAM: HUN Hungary
Coach: LAURENCZ, Laszlo

Names	Pos	M/A	% Eff	A	To	Stl	Bl
MEKSZ, Aniko	GK	0/0	0.0%				
MATEFI, Eszter	LB	7/14	50.0%	2	2		
MATYAS, Auguszta	LB	0/0	0.0%				
TOTH, Beatrix	RB	0/0	0.0%				
PADAR, Ildiko	P	0/1	0.0%				
KOCSIS, Erzsebet	P	4/5	80.0%		1	1	
NEMETH, Helga	RB	4/8	50.0%		2	1	
SITI, Beata	CB	0/0	0.0%		1		
ERDOS, Eva	LW	4/4	100.0%	2			
HOFFMANN, Beata	GK	0/0	0.0%				
KANTOR, Aniko	LW	0/0	0.0%				
NAGY, Aniko	CB	0/1	0.0%		1		2
KOKENY, Beatrix	RB	2/8	25.0%	2	8		1
FARKAS, Andrea	GK	0/0	0.0%		1		
SZILAGYI, Katalin	RW	1/4	25.0%				
SZANTO, Anna	RW	0/0	0.0%				

Goalkeepers	Shots Saved	Attempted	% Eff
MEKSZ, Aniko	8	25	32.0%
FARKAS, Andrea	6	23	26.1%

TEAM: CHN People's Republic of China
Coach: HAN, Naiguo   Assistant Coach: WANG, Yaoting

Names	Pos	M/A	% Eff	A	To	Stl	Bl
WANG, Xiaojiong	GK	0/0	0.0%				
YUE, Liane	RB	0/0	0.0%				
ZHANG, Li	LW	2/5	40.0%			1	
CHE, Zhihong	LW	0/0	0.0%	1			
CONG, Yanxia	CB	2/2	100.0%		2		
ZHAI, Chao	P	11/15	73.3%	4	3	2	1
CHEN, Bangping	RB	0/0	0.0%				
JIA, Shujun	LB	0/0	0.0%				
CHEN, Haiyun	CB	1/1	100.0%				
ZHAO, Ying	LW	0/0	0.0%				
WANG, Tao	GK	0/0	0.0%				
ZHANG, Limei	P	3/4	75.0%	3	1		
LI, Jianfang	RW	4/4	100.0%				
YU, Geli	GK	0/0	0.0%	1			
SHI, Wei	LB	8/14	57.1%	8	2		
WU, Li	CB	0/0	0.0%				

Goalkeepers	Shots Saved	Attempted	% Eff
WANG, Tao	3	15	20.0%
YU, Geli	14	35	40.0%

TEAM: HUN Hungary
Coach: LAURENCZ, Laszlo

Names	Pos	M/A	% Eff	A	To	Stl	Bl
MEKSZ, Aniko	GK	0/0	0.0%				
MATFEI, Eszter	LB	9/11	81.8%	1	2		
MATYAS, Auguszta	LB	0/0	0.0%				
TOTH, Beatrix	RB	0/1	0.0%				
PADAR, Ildiko	P	0/0	0.0%				
KOCSIS, Erzsebet	P	5/5	100.0%		1		
NEMETH, Helga	RB	6/9	66.7%	2	7	1	2
SITI, Beata	CB	0/0	0.0%		1	2	
ERDOS, Eva	LW	2/4	50.0%	2	2	2	
HOFFMANN, Beata	GK	0/1	0.0%				
KANTOR, Aniko	LW	0/0	0.0%				
NAGY, Aniko	CB	0/1	0.0%				3
KOKENY, Beatrix	RB	4/5	80.0%	3	6	2	
FARKAS, Andrea	GK	0/0	0.0%				
SZILAGYI, Katalin	RW	4/5	80.0%				
SZANTO, Anna	RW	0/0	0.0%				

Goalkeepers	Shots Saved	Attempted	% Eff
HOFFMANN, Beata	0	11	0.0%
FARKAS, Andrea	7	36	19.4%

TEAM: DEN Denmark
Coach: WILBEK, Ulrik   Assistant Coach: BASTRUP JORGENSEN, Henrik

Names	Pos	M/A	% Eff	A	To	Stl	Bl
RANTALA, Lene	GK	0/0	0.0%				
TANDERUP, Anne	LB	1/4	25.0%	2	1		2
ANDERSEN, Camilla	RB	7/12	58.3%	3	2	1	
BOTTZAU, Tina	RB	4/10	40.0%		1	1	
HOFFMAN, Anette	LW	4/6	66.7%	3	1		
HANSEN, Anja	P	3/3	100.0%				2
FLORMAN, Marianne	LW	0/0	0.0%				
KOLLING, Janne	RW	3/4	75.0%		1		
HAMANN, Conny	P	0/1	0.0%				
ANDERSEN, Anja Jul	LB	2/5	40.0%	5	1		
SUNESEN, Gitte	GK	0/0	0.0%				
MADSEN, Gitte	RW	3/3	100.0%	1		1	1
ASTRUP, Heidi	CB	0/0	0.0%				
KJAERGAARD, Tonje	P	0/0	0.0%		1		
LAURITSEN, Susanne	GK	0/0	0.0%				
ANDERSEN, Kristine	LB	0/0	0.0%				

Goalkeepers	Shots Saved	Attempted	% Eff
RANTALA, Lene	1	15	6.7%
LAURITSEN, Susanne	10	30	33.3%

TEAM: USA United States of America
Coach: HELLGREN, Claes   Assistant Coach: CLANTON, Reita

Names	Pos	M/A	% Eff	A	To	Stl	Bl
FELLNER, Laurie	GK	0/0	0.0%				
JAMESON, Toni	P	5/6	83.3%	2	2		
MARPLE, Dawn	RW	2/2	100.0%	1			
COENEN, Laura	P	0/2	0.0%				
EAGEN, Lisa	LW	0/0	0.0%				
CAIN, Sharon	CB	2/10	20.0%	2	4	1	
CLARKE, Kim	RB	0/5	0.0%	1	1	1	
LEININGER, Dannette	CB	1/4	25.0%	1	1		
HIRES, Chryssandra	LW	6/15	40.0%	1	1	1	
ALLINGER, Dawn	CB	0/0	0.0%	1			
HORTON, Jennifer	GK	0/0	0.0%				
DANIHY, Kristen	P	0/0	0.0%				
PETERKA, Carol	LB	1/1	100.0%	3	2		
NEDER, Pat	RW	4/5	80.0%	2	1		
JAMESON, Tami	GK	0/0	0.0%	1			
ABPLANALP, Cheryl	RW	0/0	0.0%				

Goalkeepers	Shots Saved	Attempted	% Eff
COENEN, Laura	0	1	0.0%
HORTON, Jennifer	2	13	15.4%
JAMESON, Tami	5	31	16.1%

258   Handball / *Handball*

KRISTINE M SOGGE RN • MYEONG-SOO SOHN • BEATRIZ SOHNI • JOY L SOILEAU • PEGGY-ANN P SOILEAU • VERNAL J SOILEAU • FRED L SOKOL • JOHN F SOKOL • MORENE J SOKOL • ANNE H SOKOLOWSKI • SHIRLEY S SOKOLOWSKI • DOROTHY A SOKOWSKI • GREGG A SOLAZO • JOANNA R SOLAZO • HOLLY A SOLBERG • HOWARD S SOLBERG • SARAH H SOLBERG • LYNDA J SOLDER • CYNTHIA L SOLESBEE • BRIAN D SOLIGON • LAURA S SOLMAZ • ROMAN T SOLOHUB • ALEXANDER P SOLOMON • BRENDA W SOLOMON • DAVID SOLOMON •

Women / *Dames*

PRELIMINARIES - GROUP B

NOR 30 - 18 ANG
Halftime Score: 15 - 7

Norway			Angola	
1/3	33.3%	6-Meter shots	4/5	80.0%
3/5	60.0%	Wing shots	1/1	100.0%
6/20	30.0%	9-Meter shots	5/10	50.0%
7/8	87.5%	7-Meter shots	4/7	57.1%
7/8	87.5%	Fast breaks	2/4	50.0%
6/6	100.0%	Breakthroughs	2/3	66.7%
30/50	60.0%	Total shots	18/30	60.0%
9		Assists	6	
10		Turnovers	25	
7		Steals	1	
0		Blocks	3	
7		Fouls	6	

1st Referee: USA BOEHNE, Bruce
2nd Referee: USA BOJSEN, Thomas

PRELIMINARIES - GROUP B

KOR 33 - 20 GER
Halftime Score: 17 - 12

Korea			Germany	
5/7	71.4%	6-Meter shots	5/8	62.5%
2/5	40.0%	Wing shots	1/5	20.0%
4/16	25.0%	9-Meter shots	3/15	20.0%
7/7	100.0%	7-Meter shots	3/4	75.0%
13/15	86.7%	Fast breaks	4/5	80.0%
2/2	100.0%	Breakthroughs	4/4	100.0%
33/52	63.5%	Total shots	20/41	48.8%
13		Assists	10	
11		Turnovers	23	
3		Steals	4	
2		Blocks	2	
3		Fouls	2	

1st Referee: DEN ELBROND, Per
2nd Referee: DEN LOVQVIST, Kjeld

PRELIMINARIES - GROUP B

ANG 19 - 25 KOR
Halftime Score: 8 - 15

Angola			Korea	
4/9	44.4%	6-Meter shots	0/2	0.0%
0/1	0.0%	Wing shots	0/1	0.0%
1/3	33.3%	9-Meter shots	9/24	37.5%
3/3	100.0%	7-Meter shots	3/7	42.9%
1/3	33.3%	Fast breaks	11/11	100.0%
10/12	83.3%	Breakthroughs	2/2	100.0%
19/31	61.3%	Total shots	25/47	53.2%
6		Assists	9	
26		Turnovers	14	
8		Steals	8	
4		Blocks	0	
2		Fouls	3	

1st Referee: ROM DANCESCU, Valter
2nd Referee: ROM MATEESCU, Ion

TEAM: NOR Norway
Coach: BREIVIK, Marit   Assistant Coach: ROGNLAND, Lars

Names	Pos	M/A	% Eff	A	To	Stl	Bl
TJUGUM, Heidi	GK	0/0	0.0%	3			
LARSEN, Tonje	LB	0/1	0.0%	1	2	1	
GRINI, Kjersti	LB	10/19	52.6%		2	3	
DUVHOLT, Kristine	RW	2/2	100.0%			1	
GOKSOR, Susann	CB	5/7	71.4%	3	1		
SOLEM, Kari	P	1/1	100.0%				
DAHLE, Mona	LW	3/4	75.0%				
ERIKSEN, Ann	RW	1/1	100.0%		2		
KVITSAND, Hege	P	0/1	0.0%		1		
HALTVIK, Trine	RB	7/13	53.8%	2	2	2	
MOLDESTAD, Kristine	RW	0/0	0.0%				
SKOTVOLL, Annette	GK	0/0	0.0%				
DAVIDSEN, Mette	LW	1/1	100.0%				
HAUSMANN, Sahra	LW	0/0	0.0%				
BOLSET, Silje	RB	0/0	0.0%				
OSTBO, Hilde	GK	0/0	0.0%				

Goalkeepers	Shots Saved	Attempted	% Eff
TJUGUM, Heidi	8	25	32.0%
SKOTVOLL, Annette	3	5	60.0%
OSTBO, Hilde	0	0	0.0%

TEAM: KOR Korea
Coach: CHUNG, Hyung-Kyun

Names	Pos	M/A	% Eff	A	To	Stl	Bl
MOON, Hyang-Ja	GK	0/0	0.0%				
HUH, Soon-Young	P	0/0	0.0%				
KIM, Mi-Sim	LW	1/3	33.3%		1		
HAN, Sun-Hee	LW	0/0	0.0%				
KWAG, Hye-Jeong	RW	0/0	0.0%				
LIM, O-Kyeong	CB	7/10	70.0%	1	2	1	1
KIM, Rang	P	4/6	66.7%	1	3		
KIM, Jeong-Mi	CB	0/0	0.0%				
OH, Seong-Ok	LB	5/9	55.6%	5	3	1	1
HONG, Jeong-Ho	RB	2/6	33.3%	4	1		
OH, Yong-Ran	GK	0/0	0.0%				
PARK, Jeong-Rim	RB	5/5	100.0%				
KIM, Eun-Mi	RW	5/6	83.3%	1		1	
LEE, Sang-Eun	CB	4/7	57.1%	1	1		
CHO, Eun-Hee	GK	0/0	0.0%				
KIM, Cheong-Shim	LB	0/0	0.0%				

Goalkeepers	Shots Saved	Attempted	% Eff
MOON, Hyang-Ja	2	16	12.5%
OH, Yong-Ran	13	25	52.0%

TEAM: ANG Angola
Coach: JUNIOR, Alberto   Assistant Coach: JUNIOR, Velasco

Names	Pos	M/A	% Eff	A	To	Stl	Bl
TORRES, Rosa	GK	0/0	0.0%				
NETO, Anica	P	1/1	100.0%				
GONCALVES, Maria	CB	0/1	0.0%	1	2		
FRANCISCO, Conceicao	CB	0/0	0.0%				
TRINDADE, Filomena	CB	3/4	75.0%			1	
CORDEIRO, Domingas	CB	0/0	0.0%				
FAIAL, Maura	CB	0/0	0.0%	1	1		1
JOAQUIM, Ana Bela	CB	0/2	0.0%		3	3	
WEBBA, Elisa	P	7/10	70.0%		2		
de ALMEIDA, Palmira	CB	0/2	0.0%	1	8	1	1
BEZERRA, Luzia Maria	CB	4/4	100.0%		8	2	1
PRACA, Justina	GK	0/0	0.0%				
PAULO, Lia	CB	0/0	0.0%				
RAPOSO, Fabia	CB	0/0	0.0%				
JOAQUIM, Maria	CB	4/7	57.1%	3	2	1	1
PERES, Elisa	GK	0/0	0.0%				

Goalkeepers	Shots Saved	Attempted	% Eff
PRACA, Justina	9	35	25.7%
PERES, Elisa	0	12	0.0%

TEAM: ANG Angola
Coach: JUNIOR, Alberto   Assistant Coach: JUNIOR, Velasco

Names	Pos	M/A	% Eff	A	To	Stl	Bl
TORRES, Rosa	GK	0/0	0.0%				
NETO, Anica	P	0/0	0.0%				
GONCALVES, Maria	CB	0/0	0.0%				
FRANCISCO, Conceicao	CB	0/0	0.0%				
TRINDADE, Filomena	CB	3/6	50.0%	4			
CORDEIRO, Domingas	CB	3/4	75.0%				
FAIAL, Maura	CB	3/4	75.0%	1	4		
JOAQUIM, Ana Bela	CB	1/2	50.0%	1			
WEBBA, Elisa	P	2/2	100.0%	4		3	
de ALMEIDA, Palmira	CB	4/6	66.7%	3	7	1	
BEZERRA, Luzia Maria	CB	0/1	0.0%	2	2		
PRACA, Justina	GK	0/0	0.0%				
PAULO, Lia	CB	0/0	0.0%				
RAPOSO, Fabia	CB	0/0	0.0%				
JOAQUIM, Maria	CB	2/5	40.0%	3			
PERES, Elisa	GK	0/0	0.0%				

Goalkeepers	Shots Saved	Attempted	% Eff
PRACA, Justina	7	26	26.9%
PERES, Elisa	4	24	16.7%

TEAM: GER Germany
Coach: HOFFMANN, Ekke   Assistant Coach: FLECK, Ottone

Names	Pos	M/A	% Eff	A	To	Stl	Bl
SCHANZE, Michaela	GK	0/0	0.0%				
RITSKIAVITCHIUS, Miroslava	CB	3/6	50.0%	3	4		
LUCA, Emilia	LW	4/8	50.0%		3		
JURACK, Grit	CB	2/4	50.0%	1	2		
MURRWEISS, Heike	P	0/0	0.0%				
ELEKES, Csilla	P	1/2	50.0%				
URBANKE, Bianca	RW	0/0	0.0%				
BOLK, Andrea	RB	3/4	75.0%	4	7		
ERLER, Michaela	P	4/6	66.7%	1	2	3	
LINDEMANN, Christine	GK	0/0	0.0%				
BLACHA, Kathrin	P	0/0	0.0%				
HEINZ, Franziska	LB	0/2	0.0%		2	1	
BRAM, Eike	GK	0/0	0.0%				
WAELZER, Marlies	P	0/1	0.0%		2		
KISS-GYORI, Eva	CB	3/8	37.5%	1	1		2
SCHLIECKER, Melanie	P	0/0	0.0%				

Goalkeepers	Shots Saved	Attempted	% Eff
LINDEMANN, Christine	5	22	22.7%
BRAM, Eike	7	30	23.3%

TEAM: KOR Korea
Coach: CHUNG, Hyung-Kyun

Names	Pos	M/A	% Eff	A	To	Stl	Bl
MOON, Hyang-Ja	GK	0/0	0.0%	2			
HUH, Soon-Young	P	0/0	0.0%				
KIM, Mi-Sim	LW	2/2	100.0%		1		
HAN, Sun-Hee	LW	0/0	0.0%				
KWAG, Hye-Jeong	RW	0/0	0.0%				
LIM, O-Kyeong	CB	5/8	62.5%	1	3	1	
KIM, Rang	P	0/2	0.0%		2		
KIM, Jeong-Mi	CB	0/0	0.0%				
OH, Seong-Ok	LB	5/9	55.6%	2	4	2	
HONG, Jeong-Ho	RB	5/14	35.7%		2	2	
OH, Yong-Ran	GK	0/0	0.0%				
PARK, Jeong-Rim	RB	1/2	50.0%		1	1	
KIM, Eun-Mi	RW	3/5	60.0%	3	2		
LEE, Sang-Eun	CB	4/5	80.0%	1	1		
CHO, Eun-Hee	GK	0/0	0.0%				
KIM, Cheong-Shim	LB	0/0	0.0%				

Goalkeepers	Shots Saved	Attempted	% Eff
MOON, Hyang-Ja	7	26	26.9%
CHO, Eun-Hee	0	5	0.0%

Women / Dames

PRELIMINARIES - GROUP B

GER 23 - 28 NOR
Halftime Score: 11 - 15

Germany			Norway	
4/6	66.7%	6-Meter shots	4/5	80.0%
4/5	80.0%	Wing shots	5/6	83.3%
5/17	29.4%	9-Meter shots	7/14	50.0%
5/5	100.0%	7-Meter shots	5/6	83.3%
2/2	100.0%	Fast breaks	2/3	66.7%
3/5	60.0%	Breakthroughs	5/6	83.3%
23/40	57.5%	Total shots	28/40	70.0%
	11	Assists	11	
	11	Turnovers	13	
	2	Steals	2	
	1	Blocks	2	
	8	Fouls	9	

1st Referee: FRA GARCIA, Francois
2nd Referee: FRA MORENO, Jean Pierre

TEAM: GER Germany
Coach: HOFFMANN, Ekke   Assistant Coach: FLECK, Ottone

Names	Pos	M/A	% Eff	A	To	Stl	Bl
SCHANZE, Michaela	GK	0/0	0.0%				
RITSKIAVITCHIUS, Miroslava	CB	8/10	80.0%	5	1	2	1
LUCA, Emilia	LW	7/9	77.8%		2		
JURACK, Grit	CB	0/2	0.0%				
MURRWEISS, Heike	P	2/4	50.0%	1	1		
ELEKES, Csilla	P	0/0	0.0%				
URBANKE, Bianca	RW	2/6	33.3%		1		
BOLK, Andrea	RB	1/3	33.3%	3	1		
ERLER, Michaela	P	1/2	50.0%		4		
LINDEMANN, Christine	GK	0/0	0.0%				
BLACHA, Kathrin	P	0/0	0.0%				
HEINZ, Franziska	LB	0/0	0.0%	1			
BRAM, Eike	GK	0/0	0.0%	1			
WAELZER, Marlies	P	0/0	0.0%				
KISS-GYORI, Eva	CB	2/4	50.0%	1			
SCHLIECKER, Melanie	P	0/0	0.0%				

Goalkeepers	Shots Saved	Attempted	% Eff
SCHANZE, Michaela	0	2	0.0%
BRAM, Eike	8	38	21.1%

TEAM: NOR Norway
Coach: BREIVIK, Marit   Assistant Coach: ROGNLAND, Lars

Names	Pos	M/A	% Eff	A	To	Stl	Bl
TJUGUM, Heidi	GK	0/0	0.0%				
LARSEN, Tonje	LB	2/4	50.0%				
GRINI, Kjersti	LB	10/17	58.8%	3	2		1
DUVHOLT, Kristine	RW	4/5	80.0%		2	2	
GOKSOR, Susann	CB	1/2	50.0%	4	3		
SOLEM, Kari	P	0/0	0.0%		1		
DAHLE, Mona	LW	1/2	50.0%	2			
ERIKSEN, Ann	RW	0/0	0.0%				
KVITSAND, Hege	P	4/4	100.0%		1		
HALTVIK, Trine	RB	5/5	100.0%	1	2		
MOLDESTAD, Kristine	RW	1/1	100.0%	3			1
SKOTVOLL, Annette	GK	0/0	0.0%				
DAVIDSEN, Mette	LW	0/0	0.0%				
HAUSMANN, Sahra	LW	0/0	0.0%				
BOLSET, Silje	RB	0/0	0.0%				
OSTBO, Hilde	GK	0/0	0.0%				

Goalkeepers	Shots Saved	Attempted	% Eff
TJUGUM, Heidi	11	34	32.4%
SKOTVOLL, Annette	0	6	0.0%

PRELIMINARIES - GROUP B

GER 27 - 12 ANG
Halftime Score: 10 - 6

Germany			Angola	
5/8	62.5%	6-Meter shots	3/4	75.0%
5/7	71.4%	Wing shots	3/7	42.9%
5/19	26.3%	9-Meter shots	3/18	16.7%
2/3	66.7%	7-Meter shots	2/5	40.0%
10/13	76.9%	Fast breaks	0/1	0.0%
0/0	0.0%	Breakthroughs	1/4	25.0%
27/50	54.0%	Total shots	12/39	30.8%
	17	Assists	3	
	12	Turnovers	27	
	6	Steals	2	
	1	Blocks	4	
	5	Fouls	5	

1st Referee: KUW al HOULI, Mohammad
2nd Referee: KUW ALENEZI, Khalaf

TEAM: GER Germany
Coach: HOFFMANN, Ekke   Assistant Coach: FLECK, Ottone

Names	Pos	M/A	% Eff	A	To	Stl	Bl
SCHANZE, Michaela	GK	0/0	0.0%				
RITSKIAVITCHIUS, Miroslava	CB	1/6	16.7%	1	2	2	
LUCA, Emilia	LW	3/4	75.0%	1	1		
JURACK, Grit	CB	5/11	45.5%	2	2		1
MURRWEISS, Heike	P	0/0	0.0%				
ELEKES, Csilla	P	3/3	100.0%	1			
URBANKE, Bianca	RW	2/5	40.0%		1		
BOLK, Andrea	RB	3/5	60.0%	4	1	1	
ERLER, Michaela	P	3/5	60.0%	1	1	1	
LINDEMANN, Christine	GK	0/0	0.0%		1		
BLACHA, Kathrin	P	0/0	0.0%				
HEINZ, Franziska	LB	1/2	50.0%	1			
BRAM, Eike	GK	0/0	0.0%				
WAELZER, Marlies	P	5/7	71.4%	4	2	2	
KISS-GYORI, Eva	CB	0/0	0.0%				
SCHLIECKER, Melanie	P	1/2	50.0%	2	1		

Goalkeeper	Shots Saved	Attempted	% Eff
LINDEMANN, Christine	14	39	35.9%

TEAM: ANG Angola
Coach: JUNIOR, Alberto   Assistant Coach: JUNIOR, Velasco

Names	Pos	M/A	% Eff	A	To	Stl	Bl
TORRES, Rosa	GK	0/0	0.0%				
NETO, Anica	P	0/0	0.0%				
GONCALVES, Maria	CB	0/3	0.0%		1		
FRANCISCO, Conceicao	CB	0/0	0.0%				
TRINDADE, Filomena	CB	3/7	42.9%		6		
CORDEIRO, Domingas	CB	0/1	0.0%				
FAIAL, Maura	CB	0/0	0.0%				
JOAQUIM, Ana Bela	CB	0/3	0.0%		2		
WEBBA, Elisa	P	5/7	71.4%		4		2
de ALMEIDA, Palmira	CB	1/8	12.5%		5		
BEZERRA, Luzia Maria	CB	2/6	33.3%	1	3		1
PRACA, Justina	GK	0/0	0.0%			1	
PAULO, Lia	CB	0/0	0.0%	1	1		
RAPOSO, Fabia	CB	0/0	0.0%				
JOAQUIM, Maria	CB	1/4	25.0%	1	5	1	1
PERES, Elisa	GK	0/0	0.0%				

Goalkeepers	Shots Saved	Attempted	% Eff
PRACA, Justina	3	22	13.6%
PERES, Elisa	10	28	35.7%

PRELIMINARIES - GROUP B

KOR 25 - 21 NOR
Halftime Score: 12 - 10

Korea			Norway	
7/8	87.5%	6-Meter shots	5/7	71.4%
1/4	25.0%	Wing shots	1/3	33.3%
3/14	21.4%	9-Meter shots	7/14	50.0%
7/8	87.5%	7-Meter shots	1/1	100.0%
1/2	50.0%	Fast breaks	1/2	50.0%
6/7	85.7%	Breakthroughs	6/9	66.7%
25/43	58.1%	Total shots	21/36	58.3%
	9	Assists	4	
	10	Turnovers	15	
	0	Steals	9	
	1	Blocks	1	
	5	Fouls	3	

1st Referee: CRO VUJNOVIC, Vladimir
2nd Referee: CRO MLADINIC, Petar

TEAM: KOR Korea
Coach: CHUNG, Hyung-Kyun

Names	Pos	M/A	% Eff	A	To	Stl	Bl
MOON, Hyang-Ja	GK	0/0	0.0%				
HUH, Soon-Young	P	0/0	0.0%				
KIM, Mi-Sim	LW	1/3	33.3%				
HAN, Sun-Hee	LW	0/0	0.0%				
KWAG, Hye-Jeong	RW	0/0	0.0%				
LIM, O-Kyeong	CB	9/12	75.0%	2	4		1
KIM, Rang	P	6/6	100.0%				
KIM, Jeong-Mi	CB	0/0	0.0%				
OH, Seong-Ok	LB	3/7	42.9%	5	3		
HONG, Jeong-Ho	RB	4/10	40.0%	1	2		
OH, Yong-Ran	GK	0/0	0.0%				
PARK, Jeong-Rim	RB	0/1	0.0%		1		
KIM, Eun-Mi	RW	2/4	50.0%	1			
LEE, Sang-Eun	CB	0/0	0.0%				
CHO, Eun-Hee	GK	0/0	0.0%				
KIM, Cheong-Shim	LB	0/0	0.0%				

Goalkeeper	Shots Saved	Attempted	% Eff
MOON, Hyang-Ja	11	36	30.6%

TEAM: NOR Norway
Coach: BREIVIK, Marit   Assistant Coach: ROGNLAND, Lars

Names	Pos	M/A	% Eff	A	To	Stl	Bl
TJUGUM, Heidi	GK	0/0	0.0%				
LARSEN, Tonje	LB	0/1	0.0%		5		
GRINI, Kjersti	LB	7/12	58.3%	2	3	3	
DUVHOLT, Kristine	RW	1/1	100.0%		1	1	
GOKSOR, Susann	CB	5/6	83.3%		3	1	1
SOLEM, Kari	P	0/0	0.0%				
DAHLE, Mona	LW	0/0	0.0%	1			
ERIKSEN, Ann	RW	0/0	0.0%				
KVITSAND, Hege	P	1/4	25.0%	1	1	3	
HALTVIK, Trine	RB	4/8	50.0%		1	1	
MOLDESTAD, Kristine	RW	3/4	75.0%				
SKOTVOLL, Annette	GK	0/0	0.0%				
DAVIDSEN, Mette	LW	0/0	0.0%				
HAUSMANN, Sahra	LW	0/0	0.0%	1			
BOLSET, Silje	RB	0/0	0.0%				
OSTBO, Hilde	GK	0/0	0.0%				

Goalkeepers	Shots Saved	Attempted	% Eff
TJUGUM, Heidi	11	42	26.2%
OSTBO, Hilde	0	1	0.0%

Women / *Dames*

USA 23 - 24 ANG

Halftime Score: 11 - 11

United States of America				Angola	
4/4	100.0%	6-Meter shots	6/9	66.7%	
4/6	66.7%	Wing shots	5/12	41.7%	
7/21	33.3%	9-Meter shots	4/10	40.0%	
2/6	33.3%	7-Meter shots	4/6	66.7%	
4/6	66.7%	Fast breaks	2/3	66.7%	
2/2	100.0%	Breakthroughs	3/5	60.0%	
23/45	51.1%	Total shots	24/45	53.3%	
	9	Assists	9		
	15	Turnovers	18		
	5	Steals	2		
	3	Blocks	4		
	5	Fouls	7		

1st Referee: CGO   MVOULA, Daniel
2nd Referee: CGO   MOELLE MAGOUNDA, Michel

CLASSIFICATION

GER 26 - 28 CHN

Halftime Score: 12 - 16

Germany			People's Rep. of China		
8/12	66.7%	6-Meter shots	1/1	100.0%	
4/6	66.7%	Wing shots	3/4	75.0%	
4/16	25.0%	9-Meter shots	6/21	28.6%	
3/3	100.0%	7-Meter shots	10/12	83.3%	
3/3	100.0%	Fast breaks	2/4	50.0%	
4/5	80.0%	Breakthroughs	6/7	85.7%	
26/45	57.8%	Total shots	28/49	57.1%	
	15	Assists	5		
	16	Turnovers	12		
	4	Steals	3		
	4	Blocks	1		
	3	Fouls	8		

1st Referee: CRO   VUJNOVIC, Vladimir
2nd Referee: CRO   MLADINIC, Petar

SEMIFINALS

DEN 23 - 19 NOR

Halftime Score: 12 - 6

Denmark			Norway		
1/3	33.3%	6-Meter shots	5/8	62.5%	
1/3	33.3%	Wing shots	2/4	50.0%	
5/15	33.3%	9-Meter shots	5/25	20.0%	
9/11	81.8%	7-Meter shots	4/5	80.0%	
0/2	0.0%	Fast breaks	1/3	33.3%	
7/7	100.0%	Breakthroughs	2/3	66.7%	
23/41	56.1%	Total shots	19/48	39.6%	
	4	Assists	5		
	14	Turnovers	13		
	2	Steals	5		
	6	Blocks	1		
	12	Fouls	10		

1st Referee: GER   THOMAS, Hans
2nd Referee: GER   THOMAS, Jurgen

TEAM: USA United States of America

Coach: HELLGREN, Claes   Assistant Coach: CLANTON, Reita

Names	Pos	M/A	% Eff	A	To	Stl	Bl
FELLNER, Laurie	GK	0/0	0.0%		1		
JAMESON, Toni	P	0/1	0.0%		2		
MARPLE, Dawn	RW	0/0	0.0%				
COENEN, Laura	P	3/4	75.0%		1		2
EAGEN, Lisa	LW	1/1	100.0%				
CAIN, Sharon	CB	8/16	50.0%	3	3	2	
CLARKE, Kim	RB	0/0	0.0%				
LEININGER, Dannette	CB	4/8	50.0%	1			
HIRES, Chryssandra	LW	4/11	36.4%	1	6		1
ALLINGER, Dawn	CB	0/0	0.0%				
HORTON, Jennifer	GK	0/0	0.0%				
DANIHY, Kristen	P	1/1	100.0%	1		1	
PETERKA, Carol	LB	0/0	0.0%				
NEDER, Pat	RW	2/3	66.7%	3	2	2	
JAMESON, Tami	GK	0/0	0.0%				
ABPLANALP, Cheryl	RW	0/0	0.0%				

Goalkeepers	Shots Saved	Attempted	% Eff
FELLNER, Laurie	13	42	30.9%
COENEN, Laura	1	1	100.0%
HORTON, Jennifer	1	2	50.0%

TEAM: GER Germany

Coach: HOFFMANN, Ekke   Assistant Coach: FLECK, Ottone

Names	Pos	M/A	% Eff	A	To	Stl	Bl
SCHANZE, Michaela	GK	0/0	0.0%				
RITSKIAVITCHIUS, Miroslava	CB	5/9	55.6%	4	2		2
LUCA, Emilia	LW	2/4	50.0%	1	2		
JURACK, Grit	CB	1/6	16.7%	3			
MURRWEISS, Heike	P	3/5	60.0%		1		
ELEKES, Csilla	P	1/1	100.0%	1	1	1	
URBANKE, Bianca	RW	0/0	0.0%				1
BOLK, Andrea	RB	0/3	0.0%	2	3		1
ERLER, Michaela	P	4/4	100.0%	2	4	2	
LINDEMANN, Christine	GK	0/0	0.0%				
BLACHA, Kathrin	P	0/0	0.0%				
HEINZ, Franziska	LB	7/8	87.5%	1	2	1	
BRAM, Eike	GK	0/0	0.0%				
WAELZER, Marlies	P	3/5	60.0%	1	1		
KISS-GYORI, Eva	CB	0/0	0.0%				
SCHLIECKER, Melanie	P	0/0	0.0%				

Goalkeepers	Shots Saved	Attempted	% Eff
SCHANZE, Michaela	8	37	21.6%
BRAM, Eike	2	12	16.7%

TEAM: DEN Denmark

Coach: WILBEK, Ulirk   Assistant Coach: BASTRUP JORGENSEN, Henrik

Names	Pos	M/A	% Eff	A	To	Stl	Bl
RANTALA, Lene	GK	0/0	0.0%				
TANDERUP, Anne	LB	0/0	0.0%		1		
ANDERSEN, Camilla	RB	7/11	63.6%	2	3		
BOTTZAU, Tina	RB	0/1	0.0%				
HOFFMAN, Anette	LW	0/1	0.0%		1		
HANSEN, Anja	P	0/2	0.0%				2
FLORMAN, Marianne	LW	0/0	0.0%				
KOLLING, Janne	RW	2/3	66.7%	3			
HAMANN, Conny	P	0/0	0.0%				
ANDERSEN, Anja Jul	LB	9/16	56.3%	1	4	1	3
SUNESEN, Gitte	GK	0/0	0.0%				
MADSEN, Gitte	RW	2/4	50.0%	1			1
ASTRUP, Heidi	CB	3/3	100.0%	1			
KJAERGAARD, Tonje	P	0/0	0.0%	2			
LAURITSEN, Susanne	GK	0/0	0.0%				
ANDERSEN, Kristine	LB	0/0	0.0%				

Goalkeepers	Shots Saved	Attempted	% Eff
RANTALA, Lene	0	1	0.0%
LAURITSEN, Susanne	19	47	40.4%

TEAM: ANG Angola

Coach: JUNIOR, Alberto   Assistant Coach: JUNIOR, Velasco

Names	Pos	M/A	% Eff	A	To	Stl	Bl
TORRES, Rosa	GK	0/0	0.0%				
NETO, Anica	P	3/4	75.0%	2	1	1	1
GONCALVES, Maria	CB	0/1	0.0%		1		
FRANCISCO, Conceicao	CB	0/0	0.0%				
TRINDADE, Filomena	CB	4/6	66.7%	1	1		
CORDEIRO, Domingas	CB	0/0	0.0%				
FAIAL, Maura	CB	0/0	0.0%				
JOAQUIM, Ana Bela	CB	3/6	50.0%		2		
WEBBA, Elisa	P	0/6	0.0%		1	1	3
de ALMEIDA, Palmira	CB	6/10	60.0%	4	2		
BEZERRA, Luzia Maria	CB	5/7	71.4%	1	4		
PRACA, Justina	GK	0/0	0.0%		1		
PAULO, Lia	CB	0/0	0.0%				
RAPOSO, Fabia	CB	0/0	0.0%				
JOAQUIM, Maria	CB	3/5	60.0%	1	5		
PERES, Elisa	GK	0/0	0.0%				

Goalkeepers	Shots Saved	Attempted	% Eff
PRACA, Justina	10	35	28.6%
PERES, Elisa	1	10	10.0%

TEAM: CHN People's Republic of China

Coach: HAN, Naiguo   Assistant Coach: WANG, Yaoting

Names	Pos	M/A	% Eff	A	To	Stl	Bl
WANG, Xiaojiong	GK	0/0	0.0%				
YUE, Liane	RB	0/0	0.0%				
ZHANG, Li	LW	4/5	80.0%	2	1		
CHE, Zhihong	LW	0/0	0.0%				
CONG, Yanxia	CB	1/1	100.0%	1			
ZHAI, Chao	P	10/19	52.6%	1	1		
CHEN, Bangping	RB	0/0	0.0%	1			
JIA, Shujun	LB	0/0	0.0%				
CHEN, Haiyun	CB	0/0	0.0%				
ZHAO, Ying	LW	0/0	0.0%	3			
WANG, Tao	GK	0/0	0.0%				
ZHANG, Limei	P	1/2	50.0%	2	3		
LI, Jianfang	RW	0/0	0.0%				
YU, Geli	GK	0/0	0.0%				
SHI, Wei	LB	12/22	54.5%	2	2	1	1
WU, Li	CB	0/0	0.0%				

Goalkeepers	Shots Saved	Attempted	% Eff
WANG, Tao	11	29	37.9%
YU, Geli	3	16	18.8%

TEAM: NOR Norway

Coach: BREIVIK, Marit   Assistant Coach: ROGNLAND, Lars

Names	Pos	M/A	% Eff	A	To	Stl	Bl
TJUGUM, Heidi	GK	0/0	0.0%				
LARSEN, Tonje	LB	4/8	50.0%	2	2	2	
GRINI, Kjersti	LB	4/13	30.8%	2	3		
DUVHOLT, Kristine	RW	0/0	0.0%				
GOKSOR, Susann	CB	3/11	27.3%	3	2		
SOLEM, Kari	P	1/1	100.0%				1
DAHLE, Mona	LW	1/3	33.3%	1	1		
ERIKSEN, Ann	RW	1/1	100.0%	1			
KVITSAND, Hege	P	1/3	33.3%				
HALTVIK, Trine	RB	1/3	33.3%	2			
MOLDESTAD, Kristine	RW	3/5	60.0%	1	1		
SKOTVOLL, Annette	GK	0/0	0.0%				
DAVIDSEN, Mette	LW	0/0	0.0%				
HAUSMANN, Sahra	LW	0/0	0.0%				
BOLSET, Silje	RB	0/0	0.0%				
OSTBO, Hilde	GK	0/0	0.0%				

Goalkeepers	Shots Saved	Attempted	% Eff
TJUGUM, Heidi	13	39	33.3%
OSTBO, Hilde	0	2	0.0%

Women / *Dames*

SEMIFINALS

KOR 39 - 25 HUN
Halftime Score: 19 - 10

Korea			Hungary	
6/6	100.0%	6-Meter shots	5/6	83.3%
2/4	50.0%	Wing shots	3/7	42.9%
8/17	47.1%	9-Meter shots	3/11	27.3%
8/10	80.0%	7-Meter shots	5/6	83.3%
8/9	88.9%	Fast breaks	3/6	50.0%
7/8	87.5%	Breakthroughs	6/9	66.7%
39/54	72.2%	Total shots	25/45	55.6%
15		Assists	11	
12		Turnovers	19	
4		Steals	2	
3		Blocks	4	
9		Fouls	7	

1st Referee: NED BRUSSEL, Peter
2nd Referee: NED van DONGEN, Anton

FINAL - BRONZE MATCH

NOR 18 - 20 HUN
Halftime Score: 9 - 7

Norway			Hungary	
2/2	100.0%	6-Meter shots	2/6	33.3%
3/4	75.0%	Wing shots	2/4	50.0%
4/15	26.7%	9-Meter shots	0/8	0.0%
5/7	71.4%	7-Meter shots	3/3	100.0%
3/3	100.0%	Fast breaks	6/6	100.0%
1/1	100.0%	Breakthroughs	7/8	87.5%
18/32	56.3%	Total shots	20/35	57.1%
5		Assists	10	
16		Turnovers	14	
1		Steals	4	
1		Blocks	1	
10		Fouls	9	

1st Referee: NED BRUSSEL, Peter
2nd Referee: NED van DONGEN, Anton

FINAL - GOLD MATCH

DEN 37 - 33 KOR
Halftime Score: 13 - 17
End of Playing Time: 29 - 29

Denmark			Korea	
6/9	66.7%	6-Meter shots	3/5	60.0%
6/9	66.7%	Wing shots	6/14	42.9%
8/14	57.1%	9-Meter shots	6/15	40.0%
3/5	60.0%	7-Meter shots	9/10	90.0%
5/9	55.6%	Fast breaks	5/9	55.6%
9/12	75.0%	Breakthroughs	4/7	57.1%
37/58	63.8%	Total shots	33/60	55.0%
14		Assists	11	
15		Turnovers	17	
5		Steals	5	
3		Blocks	0	
4		Fouls	11	

1st Referee: GER THOMAS, Jurgen
2nd Referee: GER THOMAS, Hans

TEAM: KOR Korea
Coach: CHUNG, Hyung-Kyun

Names	Pos	M/A	% Eff	A	To	Stl	Bl
MOON, Hyang-Ja	GK	0/0	0.0%	1			
HUH, Soon-Young	P	0/0	0.0%				
KIM, Mi-Sim	LW	4/4	100.0%			1	1
HAN, Sun-Hee	LW	2/2	100.0%			1	1
KWAG, Hye-Jeong	RW	0/0	0.0%				
LIM, O-Kyeong	CB	5/8	62.5%	3	2		
KIM, Rang	P	1/1	100.0%	1	1		1
KIM, Jeong-Mi	CB	0/0	0.0%				
OH, Seong-Ok	LB	8/13	61.5%	4	2	1	
HONG, Jeong-Ho	RB	9/12	75.0%	3	4		
OH, Yong-Ran	GK	0/0	0.0%				
PARK, Jeong-Rim	RB	2/3	66.7%	1	1		
KIM, Eun-Mi	RW	4/6	66.7%				
LEE, Sang-Eun	CB	4/4	100.0%	2	1	1	1
CHO, Eun-Hee	GK	0/0	0.0%				
KIM, Cheong-Shim	LB	0/1	0.0%				

Goalkeepers	Shots Saved	Attempted	% Eff
MOON, Hyang-Ja	10	36	27.8%
OH, Yong-Ran	0	9	0.0%

TEAM: NOR Norway
Coach: BREIVIK, Marit   Assistant Coach: ROGNLAND, Lars

Names	Pos	M/A	% Eff	A	To	Stl	Bl
TJUGUM, Heidi	GK	0/0	0.0%				
LARSEN, Tonje	LB	2/3	66.7%	2	2	1	1
GRINI, Kjersti	LB	8/13	61.5%	1	2		
DUVHOLT, Kristine	RW	1/1	100.0%		1		
GOKSOR, Susann	CB	4/6	66.7%	2	2		
SOLEM, Kari	P	1/1	100.0%				
DAHLE, Mona	LW	2/3	66.7%				
ERIKSEN, Ann	RW	0/0	0.0%				
KVITSAND, Hege	P	0/0	0.0%			1	
HALTVIK, Trine	RB	0/2	0.0%		5		
MOLDESTAD, Kristine	RW	0/0	0.0%			1	
SKOTVOLL, Annette	GK	0/0	0.0%				
DAVIDSEN, Mette	LW	0/3	0.0%		2		
HAUSMANN, Sahra	LW	0/0	0.0%				
BOLSET, Silje	RB	0/0	0.0%				
OSTBO, Hilde	GK	0/0	0.0%				

Goalkeepers	Shots Saved	Attempted	% Eff
TJUGUM, Heidi	7	31	22.6%
SKOTVOLL, Annette	1	4	25.0%

TEAM: DEN Denmark
Coach: WILBEK, Ulirk   Assistant Coach: BASTRUP JORGENSEN, Henrik

Names	Pos	M/A	% Eff	A	To	Stl	Bl
RANTALA, Lene	GK	0/0	0.0%				
TANDERUP, Anne	LB	0/1	0.0%	1	2		
ANDERSEN, Camilla	RB	4/5	80.0%	6	3		
BOTTZAU, Tina	RB	0/0	0.0%				
HOFFMAN, Anette	LW	6/9	66.7%	1	1	2	
HANSEN, Anja	P	4/5	80.0%				
FLORMAN, Marianne	LW	0/0	0.0%				
KOLLING, Janne	RW	3/6	50.0%	4			
HAMANN, Conny	P	0/0	0.0%				
ANDERSEN, Anja Jul	LB	11/18	61.1%	6	2	1	
SUNESEN, Gitte	GK	0/0	0.0%				
MADSEN, Gitte	RW	3/4	75.0%			1	2
ASTRUP, Heidi	CB	5/7	71.4%	2	1	1	
KJAERGAARD, Tonje	P	1/2	50.0%	1			
LAURITSEN, Susanne	GK	0/1	0.0%				
ANDERSEN, Kristine	LB	0/0	0.0%				

Goalkeepers	Shots Saved	Attempted	% Eff
SUNESEN, Gitte	8	22	36.4%
LAURITSEN, Susanne	14	38	36.8%

TEAM: HUN Hungary
Coach: LAURENCZ, Laszlo

Names	Pos	M/A	% Eff	A	To	Stl	Bl
MEKSZ, Aniko	GK	0/0	0.0%	1			
MATFEI, Eszter	LB	5/9	55.6%	3	1		1
MATYAS, Auguszta	LB	0/0	0.0%				
TOTH, Beatrix	RB	0/0	0.0%				
PADAR, Ildiko	P	0/0	0.0%				
KOCSIS, Erzsebet	P	3/5	60.0%		1		1
NEMETH, Helga	RB	2/7	28.6%	1	6	1	
SITI, Beata	CB	1/1	100.0%	2	2		
ERDOS, Eva	LW	0/1	0.0%				
HOFFMANN, Beata	GK	0/0	0.0%				
KANTOR, Aniko	LW	1/1	100.0%				
NAGY, Aniko	CB	4/6	66.7%	1	5		1
KOKENY, Beatrix	RB	2/4	50.0%	1	1		1
FARKAS, Andrea	GK	0/0	0.0%				
SZILAGYI, Katalin	RW	3/6	50.0%	1			
SZANTO, Anna	RW	4/5	80.0%	1	3	1	

Goalkeepers	Shots Saved	Attempted	% Eff
MEKSZ, Aniko	3	26	11.5%
FARKAS, Andrea	3	28	10.7%

TEAM: HUN Hungary
Coach: LAURENCZ, Laszlo

Names	Pos	M/A	% Eff	A	To	Stl	Bl
MEKSZ, Aniko	GK	0/0	0.0%				
MATFEI, Eszter	LB	3/6	50.0%	1	2		
MATYAS, Auguszta	LB	0/0	0.0%				
TOTH, Beatrix	RB	0/0	0.0%				
PADAR, Ildiko	P	0/0	0.0%				
KOCSIS, Erzsebet	P	3/4	75.0%		2		
NEMETH, Helga	RB	2/2	100.0%		3	1	
SITI, Beata	CB	3/4	75.0%				
ERDOS, Eva	LW	0/0	0.0%	1			
HOFFMANN, Beata	GK	0/0	0.0%				
KANTOR, Aniko	LW	2/3	66.7%	1	2		
NAGY, Aniko	CB	1/5	20.0%	1	2	1	
KOKENY, Beatrix	RB	3/5	60.0%	7		2	1
FARKAS, Andrea	GK	0/0	0.0%				
SZILAGYI, Katalin	RW	1/3	33.3%				
SZANTO, Anna	RW	2/3	66.7%	2			

Goalkeepers	Shots Saved	Attempted	% Eff
MEKSZ, Aniko	8	31	25.8%
FARKAS, Andrea	0	1	0.0%

TEAM: KOR Korea
Coach: CHUNG, Hyung-Kyun

Names	Pos	M/A	% Eff	A	To	Stl	Bl
MOON, Hyang-Ja	GK	0/0	0.0%				
HUH, Soon-Young	P	0/0	0.0%				
KIM, Mi-Sim	LW	5/10	50.0%	1	2	1	
HAN, Sun-Hee	LW	0/0	0.0%				
KWAG, Hye-Jeong	RW	0/0	0.0%				
LIM, O-Kyeong	CB	15/20	75.0%	1	5		
KIM, Rang	P	3/4	75.0%				
KIM, Jeong-Mi	CB	0/0	0.0%				
OH, Seong-Ok	LB	3/9	33.3%	7	6	3	
HONG, Jeong-Ho	RB	3/8	37.5%	2			
OH, Yong-Ran	GK	0/0	0.0%				
PARK, Jeong-Rim	RB	0/1	0.0%	1			
KIM, Eun-Mi	RW	2/5	40.0%	1		1	
LEE, Sang-Eun	CB	2/3	66.7%	2			
CHO, Eun-Hee	GK	0/0	0.0%				
KIM, Cheong-Shim	LB	0/0	0.0%				

Goalkeepers	Shots Saved	Attempted	% Eff
MOON, Hyang-Ja	13	44	29.5%
OH, Yong-Ran	3	14	21.4%

Women / *Dames*

SUMMARY: PRELIMINARIES - GROUP A

			Games			Goals		
Rnk	Team	Played	Won	Drawn	Lost	For	Against	Diff pts
1	DEN	3	3	0	0	89	62	27
2	HUN	3	2	0	1	81	70	11
3	CHN	3	1	0	2	71	83	-12
4	USA	3	0	0	3	64	90	-26

SUMMARY: PRELIMINARIES - GROUP B

			Games			Goals		
Rnk	Team	Played	Won	Drawn	Lost	For	Against	Diff pts
1	KOR	3	3	0	0	83	60	23
2	NOR	3	2	0	1	79	66	13
3	GER	3	1	0	2	70	73	-03
4	ANG	3	0	0	3	49	82	-33

FINAL MATCH SUMMARY

Phase	Teams	Score
Classification	USA - ANG	23 - 24
Classification	GER - CHN	26 - 28
Semifinal	DEN - NOR	23 - 19
Semifinal	KOR - HUN	39 - 25
Final - Bronze	NOR - HUN	18 - 20
Final - Gold	DEN - KOR	37 - 33

FINAL CLASSIFICATION

Rnk	Ctry	
1	Denmark	**Gold**
2	Korea	**Silver**
3	Hungary	**Bronze**
4	Norway	
5	People's Republic of China	
6	Germany	
7	Angola	
8	United States of America	

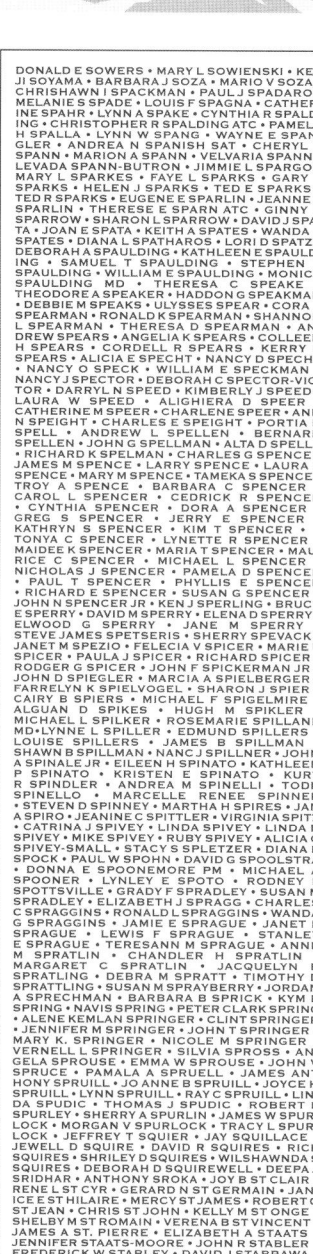

DONALD E SOWERS • MARY L SOWIENSKI • KEIJI SOYAMA • BARBARA J SOZA • MARIO V SOZA • CHRISHAWN I SPACKMAN • PAUL J SPADARO • MELANIE S SPADE • LOUIS F SPAGNA • CATHERINE SPAHR • LYNN A SPAKE • CYNTHIA R SPALDING • CHRISTOPHER R SPALDING ATC • PAMELA H SPALLA • LYNN W SPANG • WAYNE E SPANGLER • ANDREA N SPANISH SAT • CHERYL D SPANN • MARION A SPANN • VELVARIA SPANN • LEVADA SPANN-BUTRON • JIMMIE L SPARGO • MARY L SPARKES • FAYE L SPARKS • GARY V SPARKS • HELEN J SPARKS • TED E SPARKS • TED R SPARKS • EUGENE E SPARLIN • JEANNE K SPARLIN • THERESE E SPARN ATC • GINNY D SPARROW • SHARON L SPARROW • DAVID J SPATA • JOAN E SPATA • KEITH A SPATES • WANDA R SPATES • DIANA L SPATHAROS • LORI D SPATZ • DEBORAH A SPAULDING • KATHLEEN E SPAULDING • SAMUEL T SPAULDING • STEPHEN S SPAULDING • WILLIAM E SPAULDING • MONICA SPAULDING MD • THERESA C SPEAKE • THEODORE A SPEAKER • HADDON G SPEAKMAN • DEBBIE M SPEAKS • ULYSSES SPEAR • CORA R SPEARMAN • RONALD K SPEARMAN • SHANNON L SPEARMAN • THERESA D SPEARMAN • ANDREW SPEARS • ANGELIA K SPEARS • COLLEEN H SPEARS • CORDELL R SPEARS • KERRY D SPEARS • ALICIA E SPECHT • NANCY D SPECHT • NANCY O SPECK • WILLIAM E SPECKMAN • NANCY J SPECTOR • DEBORAH C SPECTOR-VICTOR • DARRYL N SPEED • KIMBERLY J SPEED • LAURA W SPEED • ALIGHIERA D SPEER • CATHERINE M SPEER • CHARLENE SPEER • ANN N SPEIGHT • CHARLES E SPEIGHT • PORTIA R SPELL • ANDREW L SPELLEN • BERNARD SPELLEN • JOHN G SPELLMAN • ALTA D SPELLS • RICHARD K SPELMAN • CHARLES G SPENCE • JAMES M SPENCE • LARRY SPENCE • LAURA K SPENCE • MARY M SPENCE • TAMEKA S SPENCE • TROY A SPENCE • BARBARA C SPENCER • CAROL L SPENCER • CEDRICK R SPENCER • CYNTHIA SPENCER • DORA A SPENCER • GREG S SPENCER • JERRY E SPENCER • KATHRYN S SPENCER • KIM T SPENCER • L TONYA C SPENCER • LYNETTE R SPENCER • MAIDEE K SPENCER • MARIA T SPENCER • MAURICE C SPENCER • MICHAEL L SPENCER • NICHOLAS J SPENCER • PAMELA D SPENCER • PAUL T SPENCER • PHYLLIS E SPENCER • RICHARD E SPENCER • SUSAN G SPENCER • JOHN N SPENCER JR • KEN J SPERLING • BRUCE E SPERRY • DAVID M SPERRY • ELENA D SPERRY • ELWOOD G SPERRY • JANE M SPERRY • STEVE JAMES SPETSERIS • SHERRY SPEVACK • JANET M SPEZIO • FELECIA V SPICER • MARIE U SPICER • PAULA J SPICER • RICHARD SPICER • RODGER G SPICER • JOHN F SPICKERMAN JR • JOHN D SPIEGLER • MARCIA A SPIELBERGER • FARRELYN K SPIELVOGEL • SHARON J SPIER • CAIRY B SPIERS • MICHAEL F SPIGELMIRE • ALGUAN D SPIKES • HUGH M SPIKLER • MICHAEL L SPILKER • ROSEMARIE SPILLANE MD•LYNNE L SPILLER • EDMUND SPILLERS • LOUISE SPILLERS • JAMES B SPILLMAN • SHAWN B SPILLMAN • NANC J SPILLNER • JOHN A SPINALE JR • EILEEN H SPINATO • KATHLEEN P SPINATO • KRISTEN E SPINATO • KURT R SPINDLER • ANDREA M SPINELLI • TODD SPINELLO • MARCELLE RENEE SPINNER • STEVEN D SPINNEY • MARTHA H SPIRES • JAN A SPIRO • JEANINE C SPITTLER • VIRGINIA SPITZ • CATRINA J SPIVEY • LINDA SPIVEY • LINDA D SPIVEY • MIKE SPIVEY • RUBY SPIVEY • ALICIA G SPIVEY-SMALL • STACY S SPLETZER • DIANA E SPOCK • PAUL W SPOHN • DAVID G SPOOLSTRA • DONNA E SPOONEMORE PM • MICHAEL A SPOONER • LYNLEY E SPOTO • RODNEY L SPOTTSVILLE • GRADY F SPRADLEY • SUSAN M SPRADLEY • ELIZABETH J SPRAGG • CHARLES C SPRAGGINS • RONALD L SPRAGGINS • WANDA G SPRAGGINS • JAMIE E SPRAGUE • JANET L SPRAGUE • LEWIS F SPRAGUE • STANLEY E SPRAGUE • TERESANN M SPRAGUE • ANNE M SPRATLIN • CHANDLER H SPRATLIN • MARGARET C SPRATLIN • JACQUELYN B SPRATLING • DEBRA M SPRATT • TIMOTHY D SPRATTLING • SUSAN M SPRAYBERRY • JORDAN A SPRECHMAN • BARBARA B SPRICK • KYM E SPRING • NAVIS SPRING • PETER CLARK SPRING • ALENE KEMLAN SPRINGER • CLINT SPRINGER • JENNIFER M SPRINGER • JOHN T SPRINGER • MARY K. SPRINGER • NICOLE M SPRINGER • VERNELL L SPRINGER • SILVIA SPROSS • ANGELA SPROUSE • EMMA W SPROUSE • JOHN V SPRUCE • PAMALA A SPRUELL • JAMES ANTHONY SPRUILL • JO ANNE B SPRUILL • JOYCE H SPRUILL • LYNN SPRUILL • RAY C SPRUILL • LINDA SPUDIC • THOMAS J SPUDIC • ROBERT L SPURLEY • SHERRY A SPURLIN • JAMES W SPURLOCK • MORGAN V SPURLOCK • TRACY L SPURLOCK • JEFFREY T SQUIER • JAY SQUILLACE • JEWELL D SQUIRE • DAVID R SQUIRES • RICK SQUIRES • SHRILEY D SQUIRES • WILSHAWNDA S SQUIRES • DEBORAH D SQUIREWELL • DEEPA J SRIDHAR • ANTHONY SROKA • JOY B ST CLAIR • RENE L ST CYR • GERARD N ST GERMAIN • JANICE E ST HILAIRE • MERCY ST JAMES • ROBERT G ST JEAN • CHRIS ST JOHN • KELLY M ST ONGE • SHELBY M ST ROMAIN • VERENA B ST VINCENT • JAMES A ST. PIERRE • ELIZABETH A STAATS • JENNIFER STAATS-MOORE • JOHN R STABLER • FREDERICK W STABLEY • DAVID J STABRAWA • ALPHA O STACER • CHALESE MARIE STACHOWIAK • ANN R STACK • CHELLE STACK • PAUL S STACK • WALTER F STACK • CATHERINE STACKPOLE • ALAN STACY • BEVERLY L STACY • HOWARD A STACY • LINDA T STACY • LUTHER D STACY • SHIERLEY ROSS STACY • LEO M STADTMILLER • BETSY D STAFFORD • BRANDON RS STAFFORD • DARREN P STAFFORD • JEANNINE D STAFFORD • JOHN G STAFFORD • MARION W STAFFORD • RICHARD W STAFFORD • WAYNE W STAFFORD • JOHN H STAGMEIER • SUE D STAHL • DONALD W STAHLE • STEVE W STAHLMAN • SUSAN R STAHLMAN • MICHAEL K STAHLSCHMIDT • KRISTI M STAHNKE • JOSEPH V STAIANO • WILLIAM E STAIGER • JAMES R STAINBROOK • MICHELE A STAINES • YADWIGA P STAINES • BRIAN M STALEY • CORA A STALEY • EILEEN STALEY • JOSEPH C STALEY • LINDA M STALEY • MIKE M STALEY • OLIVER N STALEY • TODD A STALEY • MICHELE STALLING • RICKY O STALLING • ALISHA H STALLINGS • CLAIRE W STALLINGS • DAWN S STALLINGS • TAMMY R STALLINGS • EMMETT J STALLINGS III • CHARLES G STALLWORTH • FANNIE C STALLWORTH • LINDA STALLWORTH • JOSEPH D STALNAKER • CAROLYN S STALTER • BENJAMIN F STAMEY • MARIYANA L STAMEY • TERRIE C STAMEY • BETTY L STAMM • GAYNELLE N STAMM • MICHAEL J STAMM • BECKY STAMPER • NANETTE STAMPER • PATRICIA H STAMPER • SANDRA R STAMPS • STEPHEN W STANA • MARY T STANBRA ATC • ALLAN P STANBRIDGE • ANGELA R STANCIL • CINDY C STANCIL • SAMUEL J STANCIL • SUSAN ANNETTE STANCLIFF • ROBERT L STANDBACK • SHEILA STANDEN • WILLIAM W STANDEN • WAYNE H STANDIFER • JOHN M STANFIELD • MARIA L STANFIELD • MARIAN A STANFIELD • MARY SUE STANFIELD • SHELBY I STANFIELD • WILLIAM G STANFIELD • BOBBY A STANFORD • DAVID S STANFORD • DEENIE M STANFORD • JAMES H STANFORD • JOHN O STANFORD • MELBA J STANFORD • ROGER D STANFORD • TAMMY R STANFORD • TAMMY R STANFORD • THEODORE A STANFORD • RICHARD F STANG • RYAN P STANGER • KARIN D STANGLAND • PATRICIA L STANHOPE • WAYNE R STANHOUSE • JACOB N STANIFER • CYNTHIA L STANKIEWICZ • NIKOLA STANKOVIC • OLIVER STANKOVIC • ALICE W STANLEY • BRADLEY G STANLEY • CHARLIE STANLEY • DEANDRA STANLEY • DON STANLEY • EMILY C STANLEY • EMMA L STANLEY • FRANK D STANLEY • JOAN F STANLEY • JOE STANLEY • LARUE A STANLEY • LISA M STANLEY • LORI A STANLEY • MEGAN STANLEY • PATRICIA STANLEY • THERESA L STANLEY • THOMAS M STANLEY • VANESSA A STANLEY • WILLIAM E STANLEY • ELLIS STANLEY JR • JOANNE M STANOSKI • SONJA L STANSBERRY • WALTER W STANSBERRY • LAROYE L STANSBERRY BRUSNAHAN • FIBBI E STANSELL • GAIL W STANSELL • JANET S STANSELL • MICHEAL STANSKY • BRIAN P STANTON • BROCK STANTON • CAROL F STANTON • FRANK C STANTON • MARK M STANTON • ROBERT E STANTON • SUSAN L STANTON • WILLIAM J STANTON • FRANK C STANTON JR • VITO STANZIOLA • ROSE E STAPFER • DONNA A STAPLETON • P P STAPLETON • PATRICK S STAPLETON • SCOT E STAPLETON • VANESSA D STAPLETON • JAMES B STAPLETON JR • GERALD M STAPLETON MD • TIMOTHY R STAPLETON MD • ELLEN C STARA • WILLIAM L STARA • EDGAR R STARBIRD • RAY H STARBIRD • ANA STARCEVIC • HANNAH E STARCHER • VICTOR M STARCHEVSKIY • JON W STARCHICH • DANIEL W STARCK • LYNDA K STARGEL • JEFFREY D STARGELL • RANDY V STARITA • BARBARA H STARK • CHARLES F STARK • DAWN M STARK • ERIK S STARK • TONY STARK • GREGORY L STARKE • KARA J STARKE • ROBERT M STARKELL • JIM L STARKOVICH • BENJAMIN K STARKS • CAROLE B STARKS • FREDERICK M STARKS • OLGA R STARKS • RONALD L STARKS • SHERRI A STARKS • SONJA R STARKS • ROBERT E STARLEY • STEPHEN P STARLEY • AMANDA J STARLING • BRANDON STARLING • HAROLD N STARLING • PATRICK L STARLING • RICHARD H STARLING • ROD L STARLING • CAROLYN V STARNES • CONNIE F STARNES • JANET M STARNES • PATRICIA A STARNES • SCOTT B STARNES • JOSEPH S STARON • LANCE A STARON • SHARON K STARON • STEPHANIE K STARON • CHRISCHAEL M STARR • COLLEEN R STARR • GRETA M STARR • GWENDOLYN D STARR • JOHN P STARR • ROGER S STARR • SHANDRA L STARR • SONDRA A STARR • STACEY L STARR • TERESA J STARR • KRISTEN A STARY • MARK D STASINOS • TERRI B STATEN • MICKEY R STATHAM • NANCY A STATHAM • MARC G STATHOS • LOREN I STATIA • WALTER E STATKUM • DONNA E STATON • GLORIA C STATON • LEE A STATON • MARGARET A STATON • EDDIE J STAUB • KARI E STAUDER • SARAH H STAUGLER • ANDREA G STAUNCH • AMY E STAUROVSKY • HARRIET L STAVRO • MELISSA J STAWICK • CLAUDIA G STAYTON • JEFFREY T STAYTON • REBECCA S STCLAIR • MARY B STEADMAN • RICHARD T STEADMAN • SANDRA S STEADMAN • CHARLES L STEARNS • CHARLES R STEARNS • JOHN F STEARNS • KIT D STEBBINS • PETER D STECKL • ERICA L STECKLER • DAVID A STEDALL • BEVERLY A STEED • PAULA W STEED • ROSE STEED • SANDRA STEED • DANA L STEELE • DAVID A STEELE • ERIC D STEELE • FRANK A STEELE • HERMAN W STEELE • JACKIE STEELE • JASON D STEELE • KATHRYN A STEELE • KRISTI L STEELE • LESLIE R STEELE • LISA A STEELE • LULA H STEELE • MEREDITH L STEELE • MICHAEL J STEELE • MYRA B STEELE • PATRICIA B STEELE • RICHARD S STEELE • RONALD B STEELE • RUSS STEELE • RYAN D STEELE • THOMAS D STEELE • VANESSA D STEELE • URLINE STEELE RN • JANICE E STEELE SAT • DAN STEELY • KERRY L STEEN • KIMBERLY LYNN STEEN • ELMIEN E STEENKAMP • AVA H STEENSTRUP • KARLA H STEFANI • SANDRA S STEFANI • MAUREEN E STEFANINI • NICOLE A STEFANINI • STUART A STEFANINI • ALLISON M STEFANOV • THOMAS G STEFANOV • ROBERT A STEFANOWSKI • SUSANNE A STEFANOWSKI • JANET M STEFFEN • STELLA P STEFFEN • PRENTICE D STEFFEN MD • BETH L STEFFES • FRANKLIN J STEFFES • JON S STEFFEY ATC • PAVLINA STEFKOVA • CAROL J STEGALL • JOHN R STEGALL • JULIEANN STEGALL • NICOLE STEGALL • ELIZABETH A STEGE • ROBERT J STEGEMEIER • ROBERT J STEHLIK • DANIEL A STEHR • DAVID S STEIGERWALD • PAUL J STEIGERWALD • AARON J STEIN • ADAM STEIN • AMY L STEIN • GLENN S STEIN • JACQUELINE G STEIN • JOAN STEIN • JON A STEIN • MICHAEL STEIN • ROBIN M STEIN • RONALD B STEIN • SANDRA S STEIN • JAMES J STEINBACH • JAMES P STEINBERG • JONATHAN A STEINBERG • LAUREN C STEINBERG • RON STEINBERG • JOMARIE STEINBRENNER • MARY R STEINBRENNER • KATHRYN R STEINEMANN • AGNES T STEINER • BIANCA S STEINER • JOHN W STEINER • SCOTT A STEINGARD DO • STAN STEINGOLD • SHELBY A STEINHAUER • MARY JO STEINHAUSEN • TED STEINHAUSEN • KIMBERLY J STEINKE • BARBARA K STEINLAGE • REBECCA R STEINMANN • ERIC A STEINNAGEL • HELEN B STELL • MONTSERRAT H STELLJES • GENE L STELTEN • WILLIAM W STELTEN • LEEANN STELZENMULLER • ERIC H STELZER • KRIS L STELZIG ATC • MERRITT A STEMBLER • PHYLLIS STEMEN • CATHERINE L STEMMANS ATC • LARRY C STEMMLER • EDWARD K STENDER • HELGE STENERSEN • WHITNEY R STENGEL • RANDALL S STENGER • SALLY S STENGER • JAMES A STENNETT • ALAN G STENSLAND • JESSICA L STENSLAND • BRENDA STENSON-FULLER • CIA M STENSTROM • BETH S STENZ • ELISE STEPHAN • JAMES R STEPHAN • KATHERINE C STEPHAN • PETER S STEPHAN • GROSS D STEPHANIE • BRENT T STEPHEN • KATHLEEN H STEPHEN • ALAN C STEPHENS • ALBERT L STEPHENS • ALLAN STEPHENS • ALLISON C STEPHENS • ALRIANNA K STEPHENS • ALT HEA L STEPHENS • ANNETTE STEPHENS • ANTHONY D STEPHENS • ANTONIO STEPHENS • BARBARA G STEPHENS • BILLIE L STEPHENS • CANDIS K STEPHENS • CAROL L STEPHENS • CATHERINE J STEPHENS • CYNTHIA E STEPHENS • DANIEL J STEPHENS • DEBORAH A STEPHENS • DONALD K STEPHENS • DOUGLAS H STEPHENS • ELIZABETH C STEPHENS • ELIZABETH J STEPHENS • GLENDA R STEPHENS • JACQUELINE STEPHENS • JAMES H STEPHENS • JANNA M STEPHENS • JEANNE C STEPHENS • JEFFREY STEPHENS • JOHN W STEPHENS • JOSEPH A STEPHENS • JULIE D STEPHENS • KAREN A STEPHENS • KATHY A STEPHENS • LATONYA D STEPHENS • LAURA A STEPHENS • LAVERN R STEPHENS • LOMORAH L STEPHENS • MARJORIE M STEPHENS • MARY A STEPHENS • MAXINE B STEPHENS • MELANIE L STEPHENS • MICHAEL L STEPHENS • MIKE STEPHENS • MYRON N STEPHENS • PENNYE D STEPHENS • RICHARD BURL STEPHENS • ROBERT L STEPHENS • ROBERT W STEPHENS • RONALD T STEPHENS • SAMUEL A STEPHENS • SARAH L STEPHENS • SHANE G STEPHENS • SYNELLA J STEPHENS • TABATHA L STEPHENS • TOISAUN L STEPHENS • VIRGINIA A STEPHENS • CHERYL STEPHENSON • DAVID E STEPHENSON • DOUGLAS M STEPHENSON • JUDY A STEPHENSON • LINDA STEPHENSON • MATTIE B STEPHENSON • MYRON JH STEPHENSON • SUSAN T STEPHENSON • PAUL S STEPKOSKI • JOHN STEPP • STEPHANIE STEPP • STEVEN L STEPP ATC • DAVID M STERBENZ • JO STERINO • DEBRA R STERLING • DIXIE L STERLING • ELNORIA G STERLING • SHERYL J STERLING • CHARLES STERLING JR • STACIE P STERMOLE • ANDREW L STERN • CLIFFORD H STERN • DANNY STERN • DARRIN STERN • JUDY K STERN • KARIN H STERN • LESTER M STERN • STEVEN J STERN • ANNA A STERNE • MARCUS STERNE • TRUDI GERTRUDE M STERNE • ROY A STERNES CATC • MARCUS R STETSON • BRUCE H STEVENS • CAMERON B STEVENS • CATHERINE W STEVENS • CHANDRA T STEVENS • CHRISTOPHER STEVENS • GARY M STEVENS • GERALD K STEVENS • GERALD R STEVENS • GREG MICHAEL STEVENS • JAMES A STEVENS • JESSE H STEVENS • JORDAN E STEVENS • MARTIN M STEVENS • MARY F STEVENS • MARY LEE D STEVENS • MARYLU STEVENS • MICHAEL J STEVENS • PAMELA M STEVENS • PATRICIA B. STEVENS • PATRICK STEVENS • RON M STEVENS • SANDRA J STEVENS • SCOTT R STEVENS • SHANE M STEVENS • SUSAN STEVENS • SYLVIA STEVENS • THOMAS J STEVENS • TOM B STEVENS • W E STEVENS • WANDA L STEVENS • ELOISE STEVENS-JONES • HARRY B STEVENS JR • AUTUMN E STEVENSON • DAVID STEVENSON • DONALD STEVENSON • DONNA VIRGINIA STEVENSON • DWANA M STEVENSON • ELIZABETH A STEVENSON • FRANCES L STEVENSON • GREGORY M STEVENSON • JANET L STEVENSON • JOHN M STEVENSON • MARTHA R STEVENSON • MARY J STEVENSON • MATTHEW S STEVENSON • PATRICE J STEVENSON • SHEADRICK D STEVENSON • SUSAN C STEVENSON • TINA L STEVENSON • TOMME R STEVENSON • MARTHA A STEVENSON MT • JANE H STEWARD • JACK L STEWARD • NANCY B STEWARD • ALICIA L STEWART • AMELIA L STEWART • ANNETTE R STEWART • BETTY K STEWART • BRETT S STEWART • CARL G STEWART • CINDY J STEWART • CLARA E STEWART • CLAY STEWART

HOCKEY
HOCKEY

Abbreviations and terms used in Hockey results tables
Abréviations et termes employés dans les tableaux de résultats de hockey

Term	English	Français
25Y	Possessions Inside 25Y Area	Possession de la balle dans les 22,90 m
Against	Against	Contre
Bronze	Bronze Medal	Médaille de bronze
Classification	Classification	Classement
Coach	Coach	Entraîneur
Continued	Continued	Continué
Diff	Difference	Différence
Drawn	Drawn	Egalité
FG	Field Goals	Buts sur actions
Final Classification	Final Classification	Classement final
Final	Final	Finale
Final Score	Final Score	Score final
Final Summary	Final Summary	Récapitulatif final
For	For	Pour
Gold	Gold Medal	Médaille d'or
Group	Group	Groupe
Halftime Score	Halftime Score	Score à mi-temps
Int	Interceptions	Interceptions
Lost	Lost	Perdu
Matches	Matches	Matchs
Medal	Medal	Médaille
Names	Names	Noms
Off	Offsides	Hors-jeu
PC	Penalty Corner	Coup de coin de pénalité
PIC	Possessions Inside Circle	Possessions de la balle dans le cercle
PS	Penalty Stroke	Coup de pénalité
Phase	Phase	Phase
Played	Played	Joué
Points	Points	Points
Preliminaries	Preliminaries	Eliminatoires
Score	Score	Score
Semifinals	Semifinals	Demi-finales
Rnk	Rank	Classement
Silver	Silver Medal	Médaille d'argent
Stl	Steals	Subtilisations
To	Turnovers	Pertes de possession de la balle
Team	Team	Equipe
Time Played	Time Played	Temps joué
Total	Total	Total
Umpires	Umpires	Arbitres
Won	Won	Gagné

International Hockey Federation (FIH)
Fédération Internationale de Hockey
1, Box 5 Avenue des Arts
1040 Brussels
Belgium

• CYNTHIA D STEWART • DAVID M STEWART • DICK STEWART • ELIZABETH W STEWART • ERIC M STEWART • FREDERICK R STEWART • GLENN D STEWART • HELEN B STEWART • JAMES STEWART • JAMES A STEWART • JAMES W STEWART • JEFFREY M STEWART • JIM A STEWART • JIM W STEWART • JOANNE E STEWART • JUDY K STEWART • JULIA F STEWART • KATHY A STEWART • KEN R STEWART • KEVIN D. STEWART • LARRY E STEWART • LARRY J STEWART • LEAH C STEWART • LINDA D STEWART • MARGO STEWART • MARTHA T STEWART • MARY M STEWART • MAX E STEWART •

265

PRELIMINARIES - GROUP A **FINAL SCORE:** ESP 1 GER 0 **HALFTIME SCORE:** ESP 0 GER 0

Team: ESP Spain Coach: FORRELLAT, Antonio

Names	Time played	FG	PS	PC	Total	Off	To	Int	Stl	PIC	25Y
JUFRESA, Ramon	1:10										
BARRENA, Oscar	0:00										
MALGOSA, Joaquin	1:10						11				
ARNAU, Jordi	0:59						5	1			
GARCIA-MAURINO, Juantxo	0:57						4	1	1		
AMAT, Jaime	1:10						6				
ESCARRE, Juan	0:59	0/1		0/1			6		3		
PUJOL, Victor	0:43						5				
COBOS, Ignacio	0:25						3				
ESCUDE, Xavier	0:47						8				
ARNAU, Javier	0:38	0/1		1/1	1/2		5				
SALA, Ramon	1:08						2				
DINARES, Juan	1:06						10	1	1		
AMAT, Pablo	0:28					1	3		1		
USOZ, Pablo	0:53						8	1	1		
GONZALEZ, Antonio	0:10										
Totals		0/2	0/0	1/1	1/3	1	76	3	8	5	17

Umpires: PRIOR, Don AUS   MADDEN, Craig GBR

Team: GER Germany Coach: LISSEK, Paul

Names	Time played	FG	PS	PC	Total	Off	To	Int	Stl	PIC	25Y
REITZ, Christopher	1:10										
TEWES, Jan Peter	1:10						2				
FISCHER, Carsten	1:10	0/1		0/2	0/3		2				
BLUNCK, Christian	1:07	0/1			0/1		4				
EMMERLING, Bjorn	0:00										
BELLENBAUM, Patrick	1:05						2				
MEINHARDT, Sven	1:04						7		1		
BECHMANN, Christoph	0:53						2				
DOMKE, Oliver	0:10										
BECKER, Andreas	1:02						1				
GREEN, Michael	0:19						1		1		
MICHLER, Klaus	1:10						2	1	2		
FRIED, Volker	1:09						6				
MAYERHOEFER, Christian	0:42						2				
SALIGER, Stefan	0:35						7				
KNAUTH, Michael	0:00										
Totals		0/2	0/0	0/2	0/4	0	38	1	4	6	31

PRELIMINARIES - GROUP A **FINAL SCORE:** PAK 4 USA 0 **HALFTIME SCORE:** PAK 3 USA 0

Team: PAK Pakistan Coach: BUTT, Jahangir

Names	Time played	FG	PS	PC	Total	Off	To	Int	Stl	PIC	25Y
AHMED, Mansoor	0:35										
KALEEM, Mohammad	0:19			0/2	0/2		1		1		
ALAM, Naveed	1:03			0/2	0/2		1		1		
USMAN, Muhammad	1:10						9		1		
KHALID, Muhammad	0:40						4		1		
SHAFQAT, Mohammad	0:06										
SARWAR, Muhammad	1:02						4				
TAHIR, Zaman	1:10	1/2		0/1	1/3		9		1		
ASHRAF, Kamran	1:10	2/5			2/5		10		1		
SHAHBAZ, Muhammad	1:10	1/2			1/2	1	9				
SHAHBAZ, Ahmed	0:55	0/1			0/1		11				
MEHMOOD, Khalid	0:27										
ALI, Rana	0:50										
MAHMOOD, Irfan	1:04	0/1			0/1		3		1		
RAZA, Aleem	0:08					1	2				
KAHN, Rahim	0:00										
Totals		4/11	0/0	0/5	4/16	2	63	0	7	24	41

Umpires: VASUTHEVEN, Sasidharan MAS   VAN BENEDEN, Patrick BEL

Team: USA United States of America Coach: CLARK, Jonathan

Names	Time played	FG	PS	PC	Total	Off	To	Int	Stl	PIC	25Y
VANO, Tom	0:00										
DANIELSON, Steve	0:42						4				
AMAR, Larry	1:10						9	1			
MELLOR, Marq	0:14	0/2		0/1	0/3		6	1			
WILLIAMS, Scott	0:50						2		1		
JENNINGS, Steve	0:49						6				
VAN RANDWYCK, Steven	1:05						7				
WENTGES, Mark	0:04						3				
O'NEILL, John	0:25						1				
WASSENAAR, Eelco	1:01						3				
BUTCHER, Nick	1:00						13	1			
ELMAGHRABY, Ahmed	0:56						5		1		
SYKES, Phil	1:00						3		1		
STEFFERS, Otto	1:08						6	1			
MARUQUIN, Ben	0:55			0/2	0/2		3	2			
WAGNER, Steve	1:10										
Totals		0/2	0/0	0/3	0/5	0	71	6	3	11	24

PRELIMINARIES - GROUP A **FINAL SCORE:** IND 0 ARG 1 **HALFTIME SCORE:** IND 0 ARG 0

Team: IND India Coach: D'SOUZA, Cedric

Names	Time played	FG	PS	PC	Total	Off	To	Int	Stl	PIC	25Y
ANJAPARAVANDA, Subbaiah	1:10										
SINGH, Harpreet	1:01						3	1	2		
RIAZ, Mohamed	1:03						3	2			
KUMAR, Sanjeev	0:56						6	2			
SINGH, Baljeet	0:43						8	2	3		
VARKEY, Sabu	0:42						5	1			
NANDONOORI, Mukesh Kumar	0:54						6				
SINGH, Rahul	0:12										
PILLAY, Dhanraj	0:59	0/1			0/1	1	9		1		
POWAR, Pargat Singh	1:06			0/2	0/2		7	4	2		
DHILLON, Baljit Singh	0:31						7				
EDWARDS, Alloysuis	0:00										
ALEXANDER, Anil	1:09			0/1	0/1		1	1	1		
FERREIRA, Gavin	1:00					1	3	1	1		
SINGH, Ramandeep	1:04						5	2			
TIRKEY, Dilip	0:01										
Totals		0/1	0/0	0/3	0/4	2	63	16	10	8	33

Umpires: AYMAN, Amin EGY   von RETH, Peter NED

Team: ARG Argentina Coach: MacCORMIK, Miguel

Names	Time played	FG	PS	PC	Total	Off	To	Int	Stl	PIC	25Y
MOREIRA, Pablo	1:10										
QUEREJETA, Jorge	0:00										
PAILOS, Edgardo	1:07								2		
CHIODO, Diego	0:14										
DOHERTY, Alejandro	1:07						4	2			
MORESI, Fernando	1:07						4		1		
PEREZ, Rodolfo	1:07					1	9	1	2		
RETEGUI, Carlos	0:58			0/1	0/1		11	3	2		
LOMBI, Jorge	1:01	0/1		0/1	0/2		4	2			
MINADEO, Gabriel	0:27						2	1			
FERRARA, Fernando	1:05	0/1			0/1	1	6	1			
BACCARO, Leandro	0:27										
SCHMITT, Rodolfo	0:00										
CAPURRO, Santiago	0:23						2	1			
CALDAS, Maximiliano	1:07						2	1			
LOMBI, Pablo	1:05	1/1			1/1		8	1	2		
Totals		1/3	0/0	0/2	1/5	2	52	11	11	5	35

Men / *Messieurs*

PRELIMINARIES - GROUP A FINAL SCORE: PAK 0 ESP 3 HALFTIME SCORE: PAK 0 ESP 2

Team: PAK Pakistan Coach: BUTT, Jahangir

Names	Time played	FG	PS	PC	Total	Off	To	Int	Stl	PIC	25Y
AHMED, Mansoor	1:10										
KALEEM, Mohammad	1:09						2	1	2		
ALAM, Naveed	1:10		0/1	0/1			5		2		
USMAN, Muhammad	0:35						5	5	2		
KHALID, Muhammad	0:35						4	2	2		
SHAFQAT, Mohammad	0:00						1	1	1		
SARWAR, Muhammad	0:31						5	1	1		
TAHIR, Zaman	1:04	0/1		0/1			5	1	1		
ASHRAF, Kamran	1:10		0/1	0/1			3	1			
SHAHBAZ, Muhammad	1:10					1	7		1		
SHAHBAZ, Ahmed	1:03	0/1		0/1	0/2		4		1		
MEHMOOD, Khalid	0:00										
ALI, Rana	0:00						2	5	1		
MAHMOOD, Irfan	1:10						4	3			
RAZA, Aleem	0:06										
KAHN, Rahim	0:44	0/1			0/1		6	1	2		
Totals		0/3	0/0	0/3	0/6	1	48	26	16	8	41

Umpires: AYMAN, Amin EGY von RETH, Peter NED

Team: ESP Spain Coach: FORRELLAT, Antonio

Names	Time played	FG	PS	PC	Total	Off	To	Int	Stl	PIC	25Y
JUFRESA, Ramon	1:07										
BARRENA, Oscar	0:37										
MALGOSA, Joaquin	1:10						4	3	2		
ARNAU, Jordi	1:10						3	2	3		
GARCIA-MAURINO, Juantxo	0:26						4	4	3		
AMAT, Jaime	1:10						3	3	2		
ESCARRE, Juan	0:54		1/1	1/1			7	2	1		
PUJOL, Victor	0:53						6	4			
COBOS, Ignacio	0:20						3				
ESCUDE, Xavier	0:24	0/2			0/2		3				
ARNAU, Javier	0:18	1/2	0/1	1/3	2/6		9	1			
SALA, Ramon	1:08						3	2			
DINARES, Juan	0:53						3	4	1		
AMAT, Pablo	1:17	0/1			0/1	1	3				
USOZ, Pablo	0:25						2	8	3		
GONZALEZ, Antonio	0:02										
Totals		1/5	0/1	2/4	3/10	1	53	33	15	14	36

PRELIMINARIES - GROUP A FINAL SCORE: GER 1 IND 1 HALFTIME SCORE: GER 0 IND 0

Team: GER Germany Coach: LISSEK, Paul

Names	Time played	FG	PS	PC	Total	Off	To	Int	Stl	PIC	25Y
REITZ, Christopher	1:10										
KNAUTH, Michael	0:00										
TEWES, Jan Peter	1:10						5	1	1		
FISCHER, Carsten	1:10		0/3	0/3			5	5			
BLUNCK, Christian	1:07						7	1	1		
SALIGER, Stefan	0:37	1/1			1/1		2				
EMMERLING, Bjorn	0:00										
BELLENBAUM, Patrick	0:48						3	3			
MEINHARDT, Sven	0:57	0/1			0/1		3		2		
BECHMANN, Christoph	0:37	0/1			0/1		1		1		
DOMKE, Oliver	0:29		0/1	0/1			1	1			
BECKER, Andreas	0:49	0/1		0/1	0/2		5	1			
GREEN, Michael	0:40						1	2			
MICHLER, Klaus	1:10		0/2	0/2			3	5			
FRIED, Volker	1:09						3	1			
MAYERHOEFER, Christian	0:52	0/1			0/1		3	1			
Totals		1/5	0/0	0/7	1/12	0	39	23	6	6	42

Umpires: IDENBURG, Floris NED ST ROSE, Roger TRI

Team: IND India Coach: D'SOUZA, Cedric

Names	Time played	FG	PS	PC	Total	Off	To	Int	Stl	PIC	25Y
ANJAPARAVANDA, Subbaiah	1:10										
SINGH, Harpreet	1:10							3			
RIAZ, Mohamed	1:10						3	3			
KUMAR, Sanjeev	0:57						4	3			
SINGH, Baljeet	1:05						8	1	3		
VARKEY, Sabu	0:19	0/1		0/1			1				
NANDONOORI, Mukesh Kumar	1:10	1/1		1/1		2	8	3			
SINGH, Rahul	0:00										
PILLAY, Dhanraj	1:07					1	10		1		
POWAR, Pargat Singh	1:10						9	4	1		
DHILLON, Baljit Singh	0:06						1				
EDWARDS, Alloysuis	0:00										
ALEXANDER, Anil	1:10						1	3	3		
FERREIRA, Gavin	1:03						4	1			
SINGH, Ramandeep	1:10						3	9			
TIRKEY, Dilip	0:00										
Totals		1/2	0/0	0/0	1/2	3	52	30	8	8	21

PRELIMINARIES - GROUP A FINAL SCORE: USA 2 ARG 5 HALFTIME SCORE: USA 0 ARG 5

Team: USA United States of America Coach: CLARK, Jonathan

Names	Time played	FG	PS	PC	Total	Off	To	Int	Stl	PIC	25Y
VANO, Tom	0:00										
DANIELSON, Steve	0:26						3				
AMAR, Larry	1:10						5	4			
MELLOR, Marq	0:48	0/1		1/2	1/3		2	1			
WILLIAMS, Scott	0:44						5	1			
JENNINGS, Steve	1:10		1/1	1/1			2	2			
VAN RANDWYCK, Steven	0:54	0/1			0/1		6	4			
WENTGES, Mark	0:27						3				
O'NEILL, John	0:25								1		
WASSENAAR, Eelco	0:56						2	3	2		
BUTCHER, Nick	0:35						7	1	1		
ELMAGHRABY, Ahmed	0:14	0/1			0/1				1		
SYKES, Phil	0:24							5			
STEFFERS, Otto	0:35						1	3			
MARUQUIN, Ben	0:35		0/1	0/1			2	3			
WAGNER, Steve	0:35							1			
Totals		0/3	0/0	2/4	2/7	0	38	28	5	6	27

Umpires: PLATONOV, Yuri RUS PRIOR, Don AUS

Team: ARG Argentina Coach: MacCORMIK, Miguel

Names	Time played	FG	PS	PC	Total	Off	To	Int	Stl	PIC	25Y
MOREIRA, Pablo	0:35										
QUEREJETA, Jorge	0:35								1		
PAILOS, Edgardo	0:35						4	8	3		
CHIODO, Diego	0:00							3	3		
DOHERTY, Alejandro	0:35						1	5			
MORESI, Fernando	0:35	0/1			0/1		8	2	3		
PEREZ, Rodolfo	0:25						7				
RETEGUI, Carlos	0:35	0/1			0/1		5	1	1		
LOMBI, Jorge	0:35	2/4		0/1	2/5		7	2	3		
MINADEO, Gabriel	0:14							2	1		
FERRARA, Fernando	0:33	1/1		1/2	2/3		6				
BACCARO, Leandro	0:01						2				
SCHMITT, Rodolfo	0:00										
CAPURRO, Santiago	0:09	1/1			1/1		2				
CALDAS, Maximiliano	0:35						1	2	1		
LOMBI, Pablo	0:20						6	2			
Totals		4/8	0/0	1/3	5/11	0	49	27	16	11	31

PRELIMINARIES - GROUP A FINAL SCORE: USA 0 IND 4

Team: USA United States of America — Coach: CLARK, Jonathan

Names	Time played	FG	PS	PC	Total	Off	To	Int	Stl	PIC	25Y
VANO, Tom	0:00										
DANIELSON, Steve	0:10			0/1	0/1						
AMAR, Larry	1:10						3	3			
MELLOR, Marq	0:42						1				
WILLIAMS, Scott	1:08						1	1	1		
JENNINGS, Steve	1:09						1	2	3		
VAN RANDWYCK, Steven	0:34						4		1		
WENTGES, Mark	0:39							2			
O'NEILL, John	0:42						2	4			
WASSENAAR, Eelco	1:10						1	1	1		
BUTCHER, Nick	1:10						5	1	1		
ELMAGHRABY, Ahmed	0:47						1				
SYKES, Phil	0:21						1	2	1		
STEFFERS, Otto	1:08						4	7	1		
MARUQUIN, Ben	1:06						5	2			
WAGNER, Steve	1:10								1		
Totals		0/0	0/0	0/1	0/1	0	29	26	9	7	28

Umpires: LANGLE, Guillaume FRA MADDEN, Craig GBR

HALFTIME SCORE: USA 0 IND 2

Team: IND India — Coach: D'SOUZA, Cedric

Names	Time played	FG	PS	PC	Total	Off	To	Int	Stl	PIC	25Y
ANJAPARAVANDA, Subbaiah	1:10							1			
SINGH, Harpreet	0:57							5	2		
RIAZ, Mohamed	1:10							4	8	7	
KUMAR, Sanjeev	1:05	1/3		0/1	1/4		6	3	3		
SINGH, Baljeet	0:50							3	1	1	
VARKEY, Sabu	0:27	0/1			0/1		1	2	2		
NANDONOORI, Mukesh Kumar	0:56	0/1			0/1	0	4				
SINGH, Rahul	0:00										
PILLAY, Dhanraj	1:10	2/4			2/4		6				
POWAR, Pargat Singh	0:12			0/2	0/2						
DHILLON, Baljit Singh	0:21	0/1			0/1		2		1		
EDWARDS, Alloysuis	0:00										
ALEXANDER, Anil	1:06							1	2		
FERREIRA, Gavin	1:00	0/2			0/2	1	6	2			
SINGH, Ramandeep	1:10		1/1		1/1		6	8	4		
TIRKEY, Dilip	1:10			0/2	0/2		7	2			
Totals		3/12	1/1	0/5	4/18	1	43	35	22	26	53

PRELIMINARIES - GROUP A FINAL SCORE: ESP 2 ARG 1

Team: ESP Spain — Coach: FORRELLAT, Antonio

Names	Time played	FG	PS	PC	Total	Off	To	Int	Stl	PIC	25Y
JUFRESA, Ramon	1:10										
BARRENA, Oscar	0:07						1				
MALGOSA, Joaquin	1:10						3	7			
ARNAU, Jordi	1:02						2	3			
GARCIA-MAURINO, Juantxo	0:56						2	1			
AMAT, Jaime	1:10						9	1			
ESCARRE, Juan	1:01	0/2		1/1	1/3	1	6	2			
PUJOL, Victor	0:47						8		1		
COBOS, Ignacio	0:24						2	1	1		
ESCUDE, Xavier	0:44						1	4	1		
ARNAU, Javier	0:56	1/2		0/2	1/4		3	1	1		
SALA, Ramon	1:08						3	4	5		
DINARES, Juan	0:55			0/1	0/1		4	2			
AMAT, Pablo	0:21						2	1			
USOZ, Pablo	0:53						5	2	1		
GONZALEZ, Antonio	0:00										
Totals		1/4	0/0	1/4	2/8	1	51	29	10	12	46

Umpires: IDENBURG, Floris NED von RETH, Peter NED

HALFTIME SCORE: ESP 0 ARG 1

Team: ARG Argentina — Coach: MacCORMIK, Miguel

Names	Time played	FG	PS	PC	Total	Off	To	Int	Stl	PIC	25Y
MOREIRA, Pablo	1:10						1	2			
QUEREJETA, Jorge	0:11						1				
PAILOS, Edgardo	1:10						2	3			
CHIODO, Diego	0:40						2	1			
DOHERTY, Alejandro	1:10						2	3	1		
MORESI, Fernando	0:58						6	1	1		
PEREZ, Rodolfo	1:10						4	3	1		
RETEGUI, Carlos	0:47	0/1			0/1		2	2			
LOMBI, Jorge	1:06	0/1		1/3	1/4	1	7				
MINADEO, Gabriel	0:37						2	2	2		
FERRARA, Fernando	1:10			0/2	0/2		6	1	1		
BACCARO, Leandro	0:17							1			
SCHMITT, Rodolfo	0:00										
CAPURRO, Santiago	0:00										
CALDAS, Maximiliano	1:10						5	7	3		
LOMBI, Pablo	1:10	0/1			0/1		7	1			
Totals		0/3	0/0	1/5	1/8	1	47	27	9	6	19

PRELIMINARIES - GROUP A FINAL SCORE: GER 3 PAK 1

Team: GER Germany — Coach: LISSEK, Paul

Names	Time played	FG	PS	PC	Total	Off	To	Int	Stl	PIC	25Y
REITZ, Christopher	1:10										
KNAUTH, Michael	0:00										
TEWES, Jan Peter	1:08						5	1			
FISCHER, Carsten	1:10			0/1	0/1		8	6	1		
BLUNCK, Christian	0:34	0/2			0/2		5	7	2		
EMMERLING, Bjorn	0:49						4	1			
BELLENBAUM, Patrick	0:40						3				
MEINHARDT, Sven	0:39	1/1			1/1		5	2			
BECHMANN, Christoph	0:29						2	1			
DOMKE, Oliver	1:01	0/1			0/1		1				
BECKER, Andreas	0:21	0/1	2/2	0/1	2/4		1	1	1		
GREEN, Michael	1:01						4				
MICHLER, Klaus	1:10						1	2	1		
FRIED, Volker	1:10						5	4	3		
SALIGER, Stefan	0:29						3	2	1		
MAYERHOEFER, Christian	1:06						3	2			
Totals		1/5	2/2	0/2	3/9	0	41	37	10	9	33

Umpires: PRIOR, Don AUS VAN BENEDEN, Patrick BEL

HALFTIME SCORE: GER 1 PAK 0

Team: PAK Pakistan — Coach: BUTT, Jahangir

Names	Time played	FG	PS	PC	Total	Off	To	Int	Stl	PIC	25Y
AHMED, Mansoor	1:10						1	3			
KALEEM, Mohammad	1:10							4			
ALAM, Naveed	1:10						1	5			
USMAN, Muhammad	1:10						2	6	2		
KHALID, Muhammad	1:10	0/1		1/2	1/3		4	1			
SHAFQAT, Mohammad	0:03										
SARWAR, Muhammad	0:59						7		2		
TAHIR, Zaman	1:10		0/1	0/1	0/2		5	1			
ASHRAF, Kamran	0:51						2				
SHAHBAZ, Muhammad	1:10						1	4	1		
SHAHBAZ, Ahmed	1:10							4	1		
MEHMOOD, Khalid	0:00										
ALI, Rana	0:03										
MAHMOOD, Irfan	1:06						4	4	2		
RAZA, Aleem	0:18										
KAHN, Rahim	0:06							1			
Totals		0/1	0/1	1/3	1/5	1	31	29	7	9	28

Men / Messieurs

PRELIMINARIES - GROUP A | FINAL SCORE: GER 3 ARG 0 | HALFTIME SCORE: GER 2 ARG 0

Team: GER Germany — Coach: LISSEK, Paul

Names	Time played	FG	PS	PC	Total	Off	To	Int	Stl	PIC	25Y
REITZ, Christopher	1:10										
KNAUTH, Michael	0:02										
TEWES, Jan Peter	1:07							11	1		
FISCHER, Carsten	1:10			0/2	0/2		2	3			
BLUNCK, Christian	1:09	0/1			0/1		2	6	1		
SALIGER, Stefan	0:33	1/1			1/1		2		1		
EMMERLING, Bjorn	0:00										
BELLENBAUM, Patrick	0:41	1/1			1/1		5	1			
MEINHARDT, Sven	0:49			0/1	0/1		4	1	1		
BECHMANN, Christoph	0:40			0/1	0/1		3	1	1		
DOMKE, Oliver	0:21	0/2			0/2		1				
BECKER, Andreas	0:42	1/1	0/1		1/2	1	5				
GREEN, Michael	0:56						4	3			
MICHLER, Klaus	1:10						2	8	1		
FRIED, Volker	1:04						6	3	1		
MAYERHOEFER, Christian	1:09						3	4			
Totals		3/6	0/1	0/4	3/11	1	39	41	7	17	48

Umpires: IDENBURG, Floris NED   PRIOR, Don AUS

Team: ARG Argentina — Coach: MacCORMIK, Miguel

Names	Time played	FG	PS	PC	Total	Off	To	Int	Stl	PIC	25Y
MOREIRA, Pablo	1:10							1	2		
QUEREJETA, Jorge	1:10							3	11		
PAILOS, Edgardo	1:10							8	6	2	
CHIODO, Diego	0:00										
DOHERTY, Alejandro	1:02							2	3		
MORESI, Fernando	1:05							1			
PEREZ, Rodolfo	1:03							5		1	
RETEGUI, Carlos	1:01							5	2		
LOMBI, Jorge	1:03			0/2	0/2			6			
MINADEO, Gabriel	0:13							1	2		
FERRARA, Fernando	1:08			0/2	0/2			6	1		
BACCARO, Leandro	0:16							1		1	
SCHMITT, Rodolfo	0:02										
CAPURRO, Santiago	0:14									1	
CALDAS, Maximiliano	1:07							2	12		
LOMBI, Pablo	1:00							2	1	1	
Totals		0/0	0/0	0/4	0/4	0	43	40	6	2	27

PRELIMINARIES - GROUP A | FINAL SCORE: PAK 0 IND 0 | HALFTIME SCORE: PAK 0 IND 0

Team: PAK Pakistan — Coach: BUTT, Jahangir

Names	Time played	FG	PS	PC	Total	Off	To	Int	Stl	PIC	25Y
AHMED, Mansoor	1:10							1			
KALEEM, Mohammad	1:10			0/1	0/1		5	6	1		
ALAM, Naveed	0:06							1	1		
USMAN, Muhammad	1:09						8	2	1		
KHALID, Muhammad	1:10						1	10	4		
SHAFQAT, Mohammad	0:03							1			
SARWAR, Muhammad	0:30							1	1		
TAHIR, Zaman	1:04			0/1	0/1		5	2	5		
ASHRAF, Kamran	0:50	0/1			0/1	3	8				
SHAHBAZ, Muhammad	1:05	0/3			0/3		3	4			
SHAHBAZ, Ahmed	1:10	0/1			0/1		2	1			
MEHMOOD, Khalid	0:00										
ALI, Rana	1:10						2	5	2		
MAHMOOD, Irfan	1:06						2	4	1		
RAZA, Aleem	0:18							1	1		
KAHN, Rahim	0:45	0/1			0/1		2				
Totals		0/6	0/0	0/2	0/8	3	37	40	17	11	42

Umpires: von RETH, Peter NED   MADDEN, Craig GBR

Team: IND India — Coach: D'SOUZA, Cedric

Names	Time played	FG	PS	PC	Total	Off	To	Int	Stl	PIC	25Y
ANJAPARAVANDA, Subbaiah	1:10							1	1		
SINGH, Harpreet	1:10						4	3	1		
RIAZ, Mohamed	1:10						4	3	3		
KUMAR, Sanjeev	0:48							3			
SINGH, Baljeet	0:58						10		3		
VARKEY, Sabu	0:16								4		
NANDONOORI, Mukesh Kumar	0:51					1	6	1	1		
SINGH, Rahul	0:09						1	1	1		
PILLAY, Dhanraj	1:05	0/1			0/1	1	10		1		
POWAR, Pargat Singh	1:10			0/1	0/1		1	9			
DHILLON, Baljit Singh	0:29						1		1		
EDWARDS, Alloysuis	0:00										
ALEXANDER, Anil	1:10						2	1	3		
FERREIRA, Gavin	1:10						3	3	1		
SINGH, Ramandeep	1:10						1	9	6		
TIRKEY, Dilip	0:00										
Totals		0/1	0/0	0/1	0/2	2	44	38	21	11	45

PRELIMINARIES - GROUP A | FINAL SCORE: ESP 7 USA 1 | HALFTIME SCORE: ESP 3 USA 0

Team: ESP Spain — Coach: FORRELLAT, Antonio

Names	Time played	FG	PS	PC	Total	Off	To	Int	Stl	PIC	25Y
JUFRESA, Ramon	1:03							2			
BARRENA, Oscar	0:15							2			
MALGOSA, Joaquin	1:10						2	5	1		
ARNAU, Jordi	1:10						2	3			
GARCIA-MAURINO, Juantxo	0:51	0/1			0/1		2	1	1		
AMAT, Jaime	1:03						5	3			
ESCARRE, Juan	0:54	1/1	1/1		2/2		4	3	3		
PUJOL, Victor	0:53	1/2			1/2		7	1			
COBOS, Ignacio	0:36	1/3			1/3	1	3	1	2		
ESCUDE, Xavier	0:36						5	2	1		
ARNAU, Javier	0:49	0/2	1/1	0/1	1/4		2		1		
SALA, Ramon	1:00						5		1		
DINARES, Juan	0:53						3	2			
AMAT, Pablo	0:34	2/4			2/4		2		4		
USOZ, Pablo	0:51						3	1	2		
GONZALEZ, Antonio	0:06										
Totals		5/13	2/2	0/1	7/16	1	38	30	19	22	37

Umpires: PLATONOV, Yuri RUS   ST ROSE, Roger TRI

Team: USA United States of America — Coach: CLARK, Jonathan

Names	Time played	FG	PS	PC	Total	Off	To	Int	Stl	PIC	25Y
VANO, Tom	0:15							1	2		
DANIELSON, Steve	1:06			0/1	0/1		7	6	2		
AMAR, Larry	0:59	0/1			0/1		2	2	1		
MELLOR, Marq	0:46	0/1		0/2	0/3						
WILLIAMS, Scott	0:57						1	2			
JENNINGS, Steve	1:10						6	2	1		
VAN RANDWYCK, Steven	1:02						5		1		
WENTGES, Mark	0:24										
O'NEILL, John	0:22						3	1	1		
WASSENAAR, Eelco	1:10						2	5	1		
BUTCHER, Nick	1:09		1/2		1/2		4	3			
ELMAGHRABY, Ahmed	0:07										
SYKES, Phil	0:48						5		1		
STEFFERS, Otto	0:24						4	2			
MARUQUIN, Ben	1:10			0/2	0/2		7	5	1		
WAGNER, Steve	0:54						1	6			
Totals		0/2	0/0	1/7	1/9	0	43	41	9	6	24

Men / *Messieurs*

Team: PAK Pakistan   Coach: BUTT, Jahangir

Names	Time played	FG	PS	PC	Total	Off	To	Int	Stl	PIC	25Y
AHMED, Mansoor	0:35										
KALEEM, Mohammad	0:35		0/1	0/1			3	4		5	
ALAM, Naveed	0:00										
USMAN, Muhammad	0:35						6	4		1	
KHALID, Muhammad	0:35						3	4		3	
SHAFQAT, Mohammad	0:00										
SARWAR, Muhammad	0:35	2/4			2/4	1	5	1			
TAHIR, Zaman	0:23	1/2	0/1		1/3		8	2			
ASHRAF, Kamran	0:35	0/1			0/1		5				
SHAHBAZ, Muhammad	0:35	0/2			0/2	3	10	1		1	
SHAHBAZ, Ahmed	0:35	3/3			3/3	2	7			1	
MEHMOOD, Khalid	0:00										
ALI, Rana	0:35						2	4			
MAHMOOD, Irfan	0:35					1	4	4		1	
RAZA, Aleem	0:00										
KAHN, Rahim	0:11						2				
Totals		6/12	0/0	0/2	6/14	7	55	24	12	18	49

Umpires: AYMAN, Amin EGY   MADDEN, Craig GBR

Team: ARG Argentina   Coach: MacCORMIK, Miguel

Names	Time played	FG	PS	PC	Total	Off	To	Int	Stl	PIC	25Y
MOREIRA, Pablo	0:35							1			
QUEREJETA, Jorge	0:00							2			
PAILOS, Edgardo	0:35						2	6			
CHIODO, Diego	0:35						1	·	2		
DOHERTY, Alejandro	0:35						2	2			
MORESI, Fernando	0:35		0/1		0/1		4	3			
PEREZ, Rodolfo	0:35	1/2			1/2		7	1			
RETEGUI, Carlos	0:35						5	4	2		
LOMBI, Jorge	0:35	0/1	1/1		1/2		7				
MINADEO, Gabriel	0:00						1	2	1		
FERRARA, Fernando	0:35	0/1		0/1	0/2		12				
BACCARO, Leandro	0:00						1				
SCHMITT, Rodolfo	0:00										
CAPURRO, Santiago	0:00						1				
CALDAS, Maximiliano	0:35						1	3	1		
LOMBI, Pablo	0:35						9		2		
Totals		1/4	1/1	0/2	2/7	0	53	24	8	9	40

Team: GER Germany   Coach: LISSEK, Paul

Names	Time played	FG	PS	PC	Total	Off	To	Int	Stl	PIC	25Y
REITZ, Christopher	0:00										
KNAUTH, Michael	1:10							1			
TEWES, Jan Peter	1:10		0/1		0/1		1	2		5	
FISCHER, Carsten	1:10		2/3		2/3		4	7	1		
BLUNCK, Christian	0:57	0/1		1/1	1/2		5	2		1	
SALIGER, Stefan	0:50	0/1			0/1		4	1	2		
EMMERLING, Bjorn	0:12						2	1			
BELLENBAUM, Patrick	0:52						5	2			
MEINHARDT, Sven	0:36						4				
BECHMANN, Christoph	0:21	0/1			0/1		2				
DOMKE, Oliver	0:57	0/1			0/1		5	1	4		
BECKER, Andreas	0:45	0/3			0/3		6				
GREEN, Michael	0:43	0/2			0/2		4		3		
MICHLER, Klaus	1:10	0/1			0/1		1		3		
FRIED, Volker	1:09						1	3	3		
MAYERHOEFER, Christian	0:43	0/1			0/1		2		2		
Totals		0/11	0/0	3/5	3/16	0	45	21	24	18	53

Umpires: VASUTHEVEN, Sasidharan MAS   von RETH, Peter NED

Team: USA United States of America   Coach: CLARK, Jonathan

Names	Time played	FG	PS	PC	Total	Off	To	Int	Stl	PIC	25Y
VANO, Tom	1:10							2			
DANIELSON, Steve	1:10		0/1		0/1		3	5			
AMAR, Larry	1:10						3	2	2		
MELLOR, Marq	0:40	0/1		0/1	0/2		2				
WILLIAMS, Scott	0:43						4				
JENNINGS, Steve	1:06						3	1	1		
VAN RANDWYCK, Steven	0:54	0/1			0/1		10	2	2		
WENTGES, Mark	0:31						7		1		
O'NEILL, John	0:12						1				
WASSENAAR, Eelco	0:17						1	1			
BUTCHER, Nick	1:10						5				
ELMAGHRABY, Ahmed	0:15						2		1		
SYKES, Phil	1:08							4	4		
STEFFERS, Otto	1:10						3	7			
MARUQUIN, Ben	1:10						4	4	1		
WAGNER, Steve	0:00										
Totals		0/2	0/0	0/2	0/4	0	48	28	12	7	27

Team: ESP Spain   Coach: FORRELLAT, Antonio

Names	Time played	FG	PS	PC	Total	Off	To	Int	Stl	PIC	25Y
JUFRESA, Ramon	1:05						2				
BARRENA, Oscar	0:09										
MALGOSA, Joaquin	1:05						1	1			
ARNAU, Jordi	1:10						2	1			
GARCIA-MAURINO, Juantxo	0:51						3		1		
AMAT, Jaime	1:00						1	3	1		
ESCARRE, Juan	0:52						2	2	3		
PUJOL, Victor	0:52						3				
COBOS, Ignacio	0:32					1	3				
ESCUDE, Xavier	0:40		1/1		1/1		3	2	1		
ARNAU, Javier	0:52	0/1			0/1		3	2			
SALA, Ramon	1:09						3	2	5		
DINARES, Juan	0:50						2	4	1		
AMAT, Pablo	0:32						3				
USOZ, Pablo	1:01						2	3			
GONZALEZ, Antonio	0:04										
Totals		0/1	0/0	1/1	1/2	1	28	23	14	4	27

Umpires: O'CONNOR, Ray IRL   SANA, Kiyoshi JPN

Team: IND India   Coach: D'SOUZA, Cedric

Names	Time played	FG	PS	PC	Total	Off	To	Int	Stl	PIC	25Y
ANJAPARAVANDA, Subbaiah	1:10							3			
SINGH, Harpreet	1:09						5	3	1		
RIAZ, Mohamed	0:51						2	2	3		
KUMAR, Sanjeev	1:04						2	6	3		
SINGH, Baljeet	0:57						3	4	2		
VARKEY, Sabu	0:17	1/1			1/1						
NANDONOORI, Mukesh Kumar	0:55	0/3			0/3		9	1	1		
SINGH, Rahul	0:20						1	3			
PILLAY, Dhanraj	1:01	0/1			0/1	1	9		2		
POWAR, Pargat Singh	1:10						6	6	4		
DHILLON, Baljit Singh	0:22			0/1	0/1		1	2			
EDWARDS, Alloysuis	0:00										
ALEXANDER, Anil	1:10						5	9	2		
FERREIRA, Gavin	1:05	2/2			2/2	1	6	2	2		
SINGH, Ramandeep	1:10	0/1			0/1		1	2			
TIRKEY, Dilip	0:03		0/1		0/1						
Totals		3/8	0/0	0/2	3/10	2	50	43	20	12	40

Men / *Messieurs*

FINAL CLASSIFICATION - GROUP A

		Matches			Goals			
Rnk	Team	Played	Won	Drawn	Lost	For	Against	Diff	Points
1	ESP	5	4	0	1	14	5	9	8
2	GER	5	3	1	1	10	3	7	7
3	IND	5	2	2	1	8	3	5	6
4	PAK	5	2	1	2	11	8	3	5
5	ARG	5	2	0	3	9	13	-4	4
6	USA	5	0	0	5	3	23	-20	0

PRELIMINARIES - GROUP B   **FINAL SCORE:**   NED 2   MAS 0   **HALFTIME SCORE:**   NED 2   MAS 0

Team: NED Netherlands   Coach: OLTMANS, Roelant

Names	Time played	FG	PS	PC	Total	Off	To	Int	Stl	PIC	25Y
JANSEN, Ronald	1:10						1	1			
LOMANS, Bram	0:02										
KLEIN GEBBINK, Leo	1:10	1/2			1/2		4	6			
JAZET, Erik	1:10						3	6			
van MEER, Tycho	0:00										
van PELT, Wouter	1:07						5	7			
DELISSEN, Marcus	1:10	1/3			1/3		6				
BRINKMAN, Jacques	1:10						5	2			
CRUCQ, Maurits	0:56						1	3	1		
VEEN, Stephan	1:10						4	2			
BOVELANDER, Floris Jan	1:10			0/2	0/2		7	4			
DELMEE, Jeroen	0:00										
VOGELS, Guus	0:00										
de NOOIJER, Teun	0:57						3	1	1		
van WIJK, Remco	0:26	0/1			0/1	1	5	1			
van den HONERT, Taco	1:10			0/2	0/2		7				
Totals		2/6	0/0	0/4	2/10	1	51	33	2	14	40

Umpires: O'CONNOR, Ray IRL   RUIZ, Eduardo ARG

Team: MAS Malaysia   Coach: KNAPP, Volker

Names	Time played	FG	PS	PC	Total	Off	To	Int	Stl	PIC	25Y
IBRAHIM, Mohd Nasihin	1:10										
MAGMAR SINGH, Maninderjit	1:10						12	7	1		
ABU HASSAN, Lailin	0:00										
SIVA, Brian Jayhan	0:54	0/1			0/1		3	1			
LIM, Chiow Chuan	1:10						4	4	1		
DAVID, Charles	1:09						1				
ABDUL AZIZ, Chairil Anwar	0:58						6	2			
LAM, Mun Fatt	0:11						1				
RAMU, Shankar	1:10						2	4			
NASIRUDDIN, Nor Saiful Za	0:58	0/1		0/1	0/2		3	2			
PATHAM, Vickneswaran	0:11						1				
SINGH, Aphthar	0:36						2				
NAWAWI, Mirnawan	1:07	0/2			0/2		4				
FERNANDEZ, Calvin	1:10						1	3			
SHANMUGANATHAN, Kuhan	0:53	0/1			0/1		4	1			
HAMZAH, Hamdan	0:00										
Totals		0/5	0/0	0/1	0/6	0	44	24	2	8	25

PRELIMINARIES - GROUP B   **FINAL SCORE:**   GBR 2   KOR 2   **HALFTIME SCORE:**   GBR 1   KOR 1

Team: GBR Great Britain   Coach: COPP, Jonathan

Names	Time played	FG	PS	PC	Total	Off	To	Int	Stl	PIC	25Y
MASON, Simon	1:10										
LUCKES, David	0:00						1				
WYATT, Jon	1:10						2	2	2		
HALLS, Julian	1:07						5	4	1		
SINGH, Soma	1:10						9	1	2		
HAZLITT, Simon	0:21						2		1		
LASLETT, Jason	1:07						1	1			
TAKHER, Kalbir	1:06						2	1	3		
THOMPSON, Nicky	1:10	0/1			0/1		6	3	2		
MAYER, Chris	0:47						7				
McGUIRE, Phillip	0:51						3	1	1		
GARCIA, Russell	1:10						5	1	3		
SHAW, John	0:22						3	1	1		
GILES, Calum	0:05			2/3	2/3						
HALL, Daniel	0:32						2		1		
LEE, Jason	0:37	0/1			0/1				1		
Totals		0/2	0/0	2/3	2/5	0	47	16	18	8	23

Umpires: EHLERS, Henrik DEN   SANA, Kiyoshi JPN

Team: KOR Korea   Coach: JEON, Jae-Hong

Names	Time played	FG	PS	PC	Total	Off	To	Int	Stl	PIC	25Y
KOO, Jin-Soo	1:10						1				
SHIN, Seok-Kyo	1:10						4	1			
HAN, Beung-Kook	0:51						5	1			
YOU, Myung-Keun	0:14						1				
CHO, Myung-Jun	1:10						4	1			
JEON, Jong-Ha	0:55						1	1			
YOU, Seung-Jin	1:10						3	4	5		
PARK, Shin-Heum	1:10		1/1		1/1		10	4			
KANG, Keon-Wook	1:02	1/2			1/2		2	1			
KIM, Jong-Yi	0:13										
JEONG, Yong-Kyun	1:03						10	2	2		
SONG, Seung-Tae	0:46	0/1			0/1	2	6	1	1		
KIM, Yong-Bae	0:18										
HONG, Kyung-Suep	0:20						1				
KIM, Young-Kyu	1:10	0/3			0/3		2				
KIM, Yoon	0:02						1				
Totals		1/6	1/1	0/0	2/7	2	43	22	10	15	38

Men / Messieurs

PRELIMINARIES - GROUP B

FINAL SCORE: RSA 1 AUS 1 **HALFTIME SCORE:** RSA 0 AUS 0

Team: RSA Republic of South Africa — Coach: FEATHERSTONE, Gavin

Names	Time played	FG	PS	PC	Total	Off	To	Int	Stl	PIC	25Y
MYBURGH, Brian	1:10							1	1		
MILNE, Brad	0:00										
COOKE, Shaun	1:05						11	7	4		
JACKSON, Craig	1:00						5	2	1		
FULTON, Craig	0:49						1	1			
MICHALARO, Bradley	0:48						1		1		
CLARK, Gregg	0:36	0/2			0/2		2	1	3		
BODDINGTON, Gary	1:09						3	1			
FREDERICKS, Allistar	0:35						2		1		
GRAHAM, Wayne	1:10						2	2	5		
CHREE, Kevin	1:09						3	1	1		
TEVERSHAM, Charles	1:04							2	2		
NICOL, Gregory	1:01	1/2			1/2		2	1			
HALLOWES, Matthew	0:49								1		
FULTON, William	0:06							1			
ANDERSON, Murray	0:13										
Totals		1/4	0/0	0/0	1/4	0	33	20	19	6	23

Umpires: LANGLE, Guillaume FRA   HORGAN, Steve USA

Team: AUS Australia — Coach: MURRAY, Frank

Names	Time played	FG	PS	PC	Total	Off	To	Int	Stl	PIC	25Y
HAGER, Mark	1:03	1/3			1/3		2				
DAVIES, Stephen	1:02	0/1			0/1	1	4	1	2		
CHOPPY, Baeden	0:32					1	4	2			
ELMER, Lachlan	0:46						2	6	1		
CARRUTHERS, Stuart	0:03										
SMITH, Grant	0:31	0/1			0/1		5	1			
DILETTI, Damon	0:11										
DREHER, Lachlan	1:10							1			
GARARD, Brendan	0:20							1	1		
GAUDOIN, Paul	1:10	0/2		0/4	0/6		5	1	1		
LEWIS, Paul	0:43	0/1			0/1		3		1		
SMITH, Matthew	0:55	0/2			0/2	1	4	3			
STACY, Jason	1:01	0/1		0/2	0/3		7	2	2		
SPROULE, Daniel	0:58						5	6	1		
WARK, Kenneth	1:10						1	6	4		
YORK, Michael	1:08							3			
Totals		1/11	0/0	0/6	1/17	3	43	32	13	20	41

PRELIMINARIES - GROUP B

FINAL SCORE: NED 2 GBR 2 **HALFTIME SCORE:** NED 1 GBR 1

Team: NED Netherlands — Coach: OLTMANS, Roelant

Names	Time played	FG	PS	PC	Total	Off	To	Int	Stl	PIC	25Y
JANSEN, Ronald	1:10										
LOMANS, Bram	0:05										
KLEIN GEBBINK, Leo	0:35						5	4	1		
JAZET, Erik	0:35						3	5	2		
van MEER, Tycho	0:00										
van PELT, Wouter	0:34						1	3	2		
DELISSEN, Marc	0:35	0/2	1/1		1/3	1	3		1		
BRINKMAN, Jacques	0:34						7	4	1		
CRUCQ, Maurits	0:04						2				
VEEN, Stephan	0:35						1	4	1		
BOVELANDER, Floris Jan	0:35			1/3	1/3		9	1			
DELMEE, Jeroen	1:32						1	2			
VOGELS, Guus	0:00										
de NOOIJER, Teun	0:56						4	1	2		
van WIJK, Remco	0:48						3	1			
van den HONERT, Taco	1:23			0/1	0/1		5		1		
Totals		0/2	1/1	1/4	2/7	1	44	25	11	13	37

Umpires: MORALES LOPEZ, Antonio ESP   WOLTER, Richard GER

Team: GBR Great Britain — Coach: COPP, Jonathan

Names	Time played	FG	PS	PC	Total	Off	To	Int	Stl	PIC	25Y
MASON, Simon	1:10								1		
LUCKES, David	0:00										
WYATT, Jon	1:10						5	8	2		
HALLS, Julian	0:59						2	1	1		
SINGH, Soma	1:09						3	5			
HAZLITT, Simon	0:24						1	2	1		
LASLETT, Jason	1:10						3	1			
TAKHER, Kalbir	1:08	0/1			0/1		2	8	2		
LEE, Jason	0:19						2				
THOMPSON, Nicky	1:10						4	3	3		
MAYER, Chris	0:26	0/1			0/1		6				
McGUIRE, Phillip	1:10						5				
GARCIA, Russell	1:10		1/1		1/1		7		1		
SHAW, John	0:42	0/1			0/1	1	4				
GILES, Calum	0:01			1/2	1/2						
HALL, Daniel	0:37						3				
Totals		0/3	1/1	1/2	2/6	1	47	29	10	8	26

PRELIMINARIES - GROUP B

FINAL SCORE: MAS 2 RSA 2 **HALFTIME SCORE:** MAS 0 RSA 1

Team: MAS Malaysia — Coach: KNAPP, Volker

Names	Time played	FG	PS	PC	Total	Off	To	Int	Stl	PIC	25Y
IBRAHIM, Mohd Nasihin	1:10										
MAGMAR SINGH, Maninderjit	1:10			0/3	0/3		5	3			
ABU HASSAN, Lailin	0:00						1				
SIVA, Brian Jayhan	0:42					1	2		1		
LIM, Chiow Chuan	1:10			0/1	0/1		8	1			
DAVID, Charles	1:10						1	1	3		
ABDUL AZIZ, Chairil Anwar	0:29	0/1			0/1	1	3	3			
LAM, Mun Fatt	0:11					1	1				
RAMU, Shankar	1:10						5	4			
NASIRUDDIN, Nor Saiful Za	0:58			0/1	0/1		5	1	2		
MUNIANDY, Kaliswaran	0:20						3		1		
SINGH, Aphthar	0:35								1		
NAWAWI, Mirnawan	1:06	1/2		1/1	2/3		9	4	2		
FERNANDEZ, Calvin	1:10					1	6	2	1		
SHANMUGANATHAN, Kuhan	0:56						7		1		
HAMZAH, Hamdan	0:00										
Totals		1/3	0/0	1/6	2/9	4	56	19	12	13	27

Umpires: EHLERS, Henrik DEN   SANA, Kiyoshi JPN

Team: RSA Republic of South Africa — Coach: FEATHERSTONE, Gavin

Names	Time played	FG	PS	PC	Total	Off	To	Int	Stl	PIC	25Y
MYBURGH, Brian	1:10										
MILNE, Brad	0:00										
COOKE, Shaun	1:03						12	1	3		
JACKSON, Craig	1:10						5				
FULTON, Craig	0:39						5	5	2		
MICHALARO, Bradley	0:55						4	2	1		
CLARK, Gregg	0:49						2				
BODDINGTON, Gary	1:03						4	1	2		
FREDERICKS, Allistar	0:32						3	1			
GRAHAM, Wayne	1:10						3	1			
CHREE, Kevin	1:02	0/1			0/1	1	1	1	3		
TEVERSHAM, Charles	0:36						6	1			
NICOL, Gregory	0:56			1/1	1/1	2	5				
HALLOWES, Matthew	1:01						1	1	1		
FULTON, William	0:21			1/2	1/2		1				
ANDERSON, Murray	0:18						1				
Totals		0/1	0/0	2/3	2/4	3	53	14	12	10	31

Men / Messieurs

PRELIMINARIES - GROUP B FINAL SCORE: AUS 3 KOR 2 | HALFTIME SCORE: AUS 2 KOR 2

Team: AUS Australia — Coach: MURRAY, Frank

Names	Time played	FG	PS	PC	Total	Off	To	Int	Stl	PIC	25Y
HAGER, Mark	0:55					1	2	2	1		
DAVIES, Stephen	1:10	1/2			1/2		5		2		
CHOPPY, Baeden	0:31					1	3		1		
ELMER, Lachlan	1:10						10	4	2		
CARRUTHERS, Stuart	0:00										
SMITH, Grant	0:05										
DILETTI, Damon	0:00										
DREHER, Lachlan	1:10										
GARARD, Brendan	0:00										
GAUDOIN, Paul	1:10	0/1		1/3	1/4		5	4	1		
LEWIS, Paul	1:10	0/2			0/2	1	7	7	1		
SMITH, Matthew	0:23	0/1			0/1		2	1			
STACY, Jason	1:10	1/1			1/1		10	3	1		
SPROULE, Daniel	1:10						2	3			
WARK, Kenneth	1:10						4	5	3		
YORK, Michael	1:10						4	1			
Totals		2/7	0/0	1/3	3/10	3	50	34	12	10	38

Team: KOR Korea — Coach: JEON, Jae-Hong

Names	Time played	FG	PS	PC	Total	Off	To	Int	Stl	PIC	25Y
KOO, Jin-Soo	1:10						1				
SHIN, Seok-Kyo	1:09			1/3	1/3		13	5	1		
HAN, Beung-Kook	0:52						3	2			
YOU, Myung-Keun	0:35						2				
CHO, Myung-Jun	1:10	0/1			0/1		2	2	3		
JEON, Jong-Ha	0:29		0/1		0/1		2	4			
YOU, Seung-Jin	1:10						3	1	2		
PARK, Shin-Heum	1:10		1/1		1/1		5	3	2		
KANG, Keon-Wook	1:10	0/1			0/1		1	2	2		
KIM, Jong-Yi	0:19						2		1		
JEONG, Yong-Kyun	0:25						3		2		
SONG, Seung-Tae	1:04						4	2			
KIM, Yong-Bae	0:17						2	1			
HONG, Kyung-Suep	0:05										
KIM, Young-Kyu	1:03	0/1			0/1		3				
KIM, Yoon	0:00										
Totals		0/3	1/1	1/4	2/8	0	46	22	13	11	28

Umpires: O'CONNOR, Ray IRL   RUIZ, Eduardo ARG

PRELIMINARIES - GROUP B FINAL SCORE: KOR 3 RSA 3 | HALFTIME SCORE: KOR 1 RSA 0

Team: KOR Korea — Coach: JEON, Jae-Hong

Names	Time played	FG	PS	PC	Total	Off	To	Int	Stl	PIC	25Y
KOO, Jin-Soo	1:10										
SHIN, Seok-Kyo	1:09			1/5	1/5		3	4	1		
HAN, Beung-Kook	0:00										
YOU, Myung-Keun	0:03										
CHO, Myung-Jun	1:09						2	2			
JEON, Jong-Ha	1:05						1	5	1		
YOU, Seung-Jin	0:53						5		2		
PARK, Shin-Heum	1:10	0/2		1/1	1/3		6	1	5		
KANG, Keon-Wook	1:05	0/1			0/1		4	1	1		
KIM, Jong-Yi	0:08						1				
JEONG, Yong-Kyun	1:07						7	3	2		
SONG, Seung-Tae	0:53	0/3			0/3		3				
KIM, Yong-Bae	1:10						5	3	2		
HONG, Kyung-Suep	0:41						3	3			
KIM, Young-Kyu	1:03	1/1			1/1		5	2			
KIM, Yoon	0:00										
Totals		1/7	0/0	2/6	3/13	0	44	25	14	15	38

Team: RSA Republic of South Africa — Coach: FEATHERSTONE, Gavin

Names	Time played	FG	PS	PC	Total	Off	To	Int	Stl	PIC	25Y
MYBURGH, Brian	1:10										
MILNE, Brad	0:00										
COOKE, Shaun	0:51						9	8	1		
JACKSON, Craig	1:09	0/1		0/2	0/3		1	6			
FULTON, Craig	0:28						1				
MICHALARO, Bradley	1:10						2	2	1		
CLARK, Gregg	0:49						4				
BODDINGTON, Gary	1:08						7				
FREDERICKS, Allistar	0:31						1				
GRAHAM, Wayne	1:10						2	5	1		
CHREE, Kevin	1:07						4	4	1		
TEVERSHAM, Charles	0:37						5	5	1		
NICOL, Gregory	1:08			2/3	2/3	1	3	1			
HALLOWES, Matthew	1:08						4	2			
FULTON, William	0:08		1/1		1/1						
ANDERSON, Murray	0:11						1				
Totals		0/1	1/1	2/5	3/7	1	44	33	5	13	39

Umpires: EHLERS, Henrik DEN   WOLTER, Richard GER

PRELIMINARIES - GROUP B FINAL SCORE: MAS 2 GBR 2 | HALFTIME SCORE: MAS 1 GBR 0

Team: MAS Malaysia — Coach: KNAPP, Volker

Names	Time played	FG	PS	PC	Total	Off	To	Int	Stl	PIC	25Y
IBRAHIM, Mohd Nasihin	1:10										
MAGMAR SINGH, Maninderjit	1:10						4	1	1		
ABU HASSAN, Lailin	0:21										
SIVA, Brian Jayhan	0:58						2	3	1		
LIM, Chiow Chuan	0:55						4	1			
DAVID, Charles	0:53						1	1			
ABDUL AZIZ, Chairil Anwar	1:02			1/2	1/2		7	2			
LAM, Mun Fatt	0:13										
RAMU, Shankar	1:10						9	2	3		
NASIRUDDIN, Nor Saiful Za	0:56			1/2	1/2		5				
MUNIANDY, Kaliswaran	0:10						1				
SINGH, Aphthar	0:39						3	1			
NAWAWI, Mirnawan	1:05						2	1			
FERNANDEZ, Calvin	1:10						1	3	2		
SHANMUGANATHAN, Kuhan	0:56					1	3	1	2		
HAMZAH, Hamdan	0:00										
Totals		0/0	0/0	2/4	2/4	1	42	16	9	0	21

Team: GBR Great Britain — Coach: COPP, Jonathan

Names	Time played	FG	PS	PC	Total	Off	To	Int	Stl	PIC	25Y
MASON, Simon	1:10										
LUCKES, David	0:00										
WYATT, Jon	1:10			0/1	0/1		5	3	1		
HALLS, Julian	1:08						4		1		
SINGH, Soma	1:10						5	3	1		
HAZLITT, Simon	0:13			0/1	0/1		2	1	1		
LASLETT, Jason	1:10	0/1			0/1		6	2	1		
TAKHER, Kalbir	1:06						3	2			
LEE, Jason	0:26	0/1			0/1		3		1		
THOMPSON, Nicky	1:10	0/1			0/1		4		1		
MAYER, Chris	0:42	0/1			0/1		5				
McGUIRE, Phillip	1:00						5	5			
GARCIA, Russell	1:10						6	1	1		
SHAW, John	0:45	1/1			1/1		3				
GILES, Calum	0:05			1/2	1/2						
HALL, Daniel	0:20	0/1			0/1		2				
Totals		1/6	0/0	1/4	2/10	0	49	21	8	13	43

Umpires: AYMAN, Mostafa EGY   MORALES LOPEZ, Antonio ESP

Hockey / Hockey   273

Men / *Messieurs*

Team: NED Netherlands   Coach: OLTMANS, Roelant

Names	Time played	FG	PS	PC	Total	Off	To	Int	Stl	PIC	25Y
JANSEN, Ronald	0:43										
LOMANS, Bram	0:02										
KLEIN GEBBINK, Leo	1:10						6	3			
JAZET, Erik	1:10						5	3			
van MEER, Tycho	0:01										
van PELT, Wouter	1:08						4	1	1		
DELISSEN, Marc	1:10					1	7		2		
BRINKMAN, Jacques	1:10						4	3	2		
CRUCQ, Maurits	0:03						1	1			
VEEN, Stephan	1:10	0/1			0/1		3	4	1		
BOVELANDER, Floris Jan	1:02			1/3	1/3		8	2	1		
DELMEE, Jeroen	1:08						4	2	1		
VOGELS, Guus	0:00										
de NOOIJER, Teun	0:51	0/1		1/1	1/2		1	1	1		
van WIJK, Remco	1:07					1	3				
van den HONERT, Taco	0:21	1/1		0/1	1/2	1	3	1			
Totals		1/3	0/0	2/5	3/8	3	48	21	10	4	27

Umpires: O'CONNOR, Ray IRL   HORGAN, Steve USA

Team: AUS Australia   Coach: MURRAY, Frank

Names	Time played	FG	PS	PC	Total	Off	To	Int	Stl	PIC	25Y
HAGER, Mark	1:00	1/3			1/3	1	7				
DAVIES, Stephen	1:02	0/2			0/2	2	9	1			
CHOPPY, Baeden	0:56	0/1			0/1		3	1			
ELMER, Lachlan	1:05						4	2	1		
CARRUTHERS, Stuart	0:18						1				
SMITH, Grant	0:11						2				
DILETTI, Damon	0:00										
DREHER, Lachlan	1:10						1		1		
GARARD, Brendan	0:07						1	1			
GAUDOIN, Paul	1:10			0/2	0/2		4	1	1		
LEWIS, Paul	1:10	0/1			0/1		9	2	1		
SMITH, Matthew	0:02										
STACY, Jason	1:10	0/2		0/1	0/3		5	2	2		
SPROULE, Daniel	1:08			1/1	1/1		4	7	2		
WARK, Kenneth	0:54						2	4	1		
YORK, Michael	1:10						1	1	1		
Totals		1/9	0/0	1/4	2/13	3	52	23	10	10	34

Team: MAS Malaysia   Coach: KNAPP, Volker

Names	Time played	FG	PS	PC	Total	Off	To	Int	Stl	PIC	25Y
IBRAHIM, Mohd Nasihin	0:11										
MAGMAR SINGH, Maninderjit	1:08						2	3			
ABU HASSAN, Lailin	0:56						1	2	1		
SIVA, Brian Jayhan	0:58						4	1	3		
LIM, Chiow Chuan	0:43			0/4	0/4		8	3			
DAVID, Charles	0:13										
ABDUL AZIZ, Chairil Anwar	1:10	0/1			0/1		2	5			
LAM, Mun Fatt	0:25						1	1			
RAMU, Shankar	1:10						3	3	3		
NASIRUDDIN, Nor Saiful Za	0:43	1/1			1/1		3	3			
MUNIANDY, Kaliswaran	0:23						1				
SINGH, Aphthar	0:37						1				
NAWAWI, Mirnawan	1:04	0/1			0/1		9	1			
FERNANDEZ, Calvin	1:05						4	1			
SHANMUGANATHAN, Kuhan	0:59						2	4	1		
HAMZAH, Hamdan	0:58										
Totals		1/3	0/0	0/4	1/7	0	37	30	9	7	36

Umpires: VAN BENEDEN, Patrick BEL   WOLTER, Richard GER

Team: AUS Australia   Coach: MURRAY, Frank

Names	Time played	FG	PS	PC	Total	Off	To	Int	Stl	PIC	25Y
HAGER, Mark	0:51						3	2			
DAVIES, Stephen	0:55		1/1		1/1	1	7	3			
CHOPPY, Baeden	0:56	3/6			3/6	1	9	3			
ELMER, Lachlan	0:50						3	3	2		
CARRUTHERS, Stuart	0:11										
SMITH, Grant	0:31						6	1			
DILETTI, Damon	0:09										
DREHER, Lachlan	1:00										
GARARD, Brendan	0:33						1	5	3		
GAUDOIN, Paul	0:55						8	1			
LEWIS, Paul	0:55	1/3			1/3			3			
SMITH, Matthew	0:22	0/1			0/1	1	7	3	1		
STACY, Jason	0:24	0/1			0/1	1	6	7			
SPROULE, Daniel	0:35						4				
WARK, Kenneth	0:35						1	4	1		
YORK, Michael	0:35						1	2			
Totals		4/11	1/1	0/0	5/12	4	48	44	8	18	42

Team: RSA Republic of South Africa   Coach: FEATHERSTONE, Gavin

Names	Time played	FG	PS	PC	Total	Off	To	Int	Stl	PIC	25Y
MYBURGH, Brian	1:10						1	1			
MILNE, Brad	0:00										
COOKE, Shaun	1:10						5		1		
JACKSON, Craig	1:10						3	3			
FULTON, Craig	0:30						2	1			
MICHALARO, Bradley	1:10						5	2	1		
CLARK, Gregg	0:33						1				
BODDINGTON, Gary	1:10						2	3	2		
FREDERICKS, Allistar	0:41	0/1			0/1		2		1		
GRAHAM, Wayne	0:33						3		1		
CHREE, Kevin	1:08						3	1	1		
TEVERSHAM, Charles	1:01						3	3	2		
NICOL, Gregory	0:59	0/3		0/1	0/4		5		1		
HALLOWES, Matthew	1:02	0/1			0/1		2	1			
FULTON, William	0:03						1				
ANDERSON, Murray	0:24						1				
Totals		0/5	0/0	0/1	0/6	0	39	15	10	4	39

Umpires: RUIZ, Eduardo ARG   HORGAN, Steve USA

Team: GBR Great Britain   Coach: COPP, Jonathan

Names	Time played	FG	PS	PC	Total	Off	To	Int	Stl	PIC	25Y
MASON, Simon	1:09										
LUCKES, David	0:00										
WYATT, Jon	0:52			1/1	1/1		1	2			
HALLS, Julian	1:05						1	5	1		
SINGH, Soma	1:10						7	3	6		
HAZLITT, Simon	0:41						3		1		
LASLETT, Jason	1:10	0/1			0/1		5	5	1		
TAKHER, Kalbir	1:05						3	1	1		
LEE, Jason	0:54	0/2			0/2		2	1	1		
THOMPSON, Nicky	0:57						6	1	1		
MAYER, Chris	0:32										
McGUIRE, Phillip	0:36						3	1	1		
GARCIA, Russell	1:10						9	1	2		
SHAW, John	0:39	0/1			0/1		5				
GILES, Calum	0:07			1/5	1/5		1				
HALL, Daniel	0:35						1				
Totals		0/4	0/0	2/6	2/10	0	47	20	15	14	37

Men / Messieurs

PRELIMINARIES - GROUP B FINAL SCORE: NED 3 KOR 1 HALFTIME SCORE: NED 0 KOR 1

Team: NED Netherlands Coach: OLTMANS, Roelant

Names	Time played	FG	PS	PC	Total	Off	To	Int	Stl	PIC	25Y
JANSEN, Ronald	1:10						1				
LOMANS, Bram	0:03							1			
KLEIN GEBBINK, Leo	1:10					1	5	1			
JAZET, Erik	1:09						1	1	2		
van MEER, Tycho	0:07										
van PELT, Wouter	1:07						3	3	1		
DELISSEN, Marc	1:05	0/1			0/1	1	7		2		
BRINKMAN, Jacques	1:10	0/1			0/1		3	6	2		
CRUCQ, Maurits	0:04										
VEEN, Stephan	1:10						1	5			
BOVELANDER, Floris Jan	0:53			0/1	0/1		6	3	3		
DELMEE, Jeroen	1:06	0/1			0/1			8	1		
VOGELS, Guus	0:02										
de NOOIJER, Teun	0:51	1/1			1/1		2	2			
van WIJK, Remco	0:28					1	9	1	1		
van den HONERT, Taco	1:10	0/1		2/3	2/4	1	4	1	2		
Totals		1/5	0/0	2/4	3/9	4	42	32	14	13	43

Umpires: EHLERS, Henrik DEN   ST ROSE, Roger TRI

Team: KOR Korea Coach: JEON, Jae-Hong

Names	Time played	FG	PS	PC	Total	Off	To	Int	Stl	PIC	25Y
KOO, Jin-Soo	1:10						1	2			
SHIN, Seok-Kyo	0:59					1	7	10	1		
HAN, Beung-Kook	1:00						2	2			
YOU, Myung-Keun	0:15							1			
CHO, Myung-Jun	1:09						1	3	1		
JEON, Jong-Ha	1:10						2	1	1		
YOU, Seung-Jin	1:08						2	3	3		
PARK, Shin-Heum	1:10						6	3			
KANG, Keon-Wook	1:10						4	1			
KIM, Jong-Yi	0:00										
JEONG, Yong-Kyun	1:08						3	3	1		
SONG, Seung-Tae	0:54	0/2		0/1	0/3		6	2			
KIM, Yong-Bae	0:06										
HONG, Kyung-Suep	0:14								1		
KIM, Young-Kyu	1:10	0/1		1/1	1/2	1	4		2		
KIM, Yoon	0:00										
Totals		0/3	0/0	1/2	1/5	2	38	31	10	7	28

PRELIMINARIES - GROUP B FINAL SCORE: GBR 0 AUS 2 HALFTIME SCORE: GBR 0 AUS 2

Team: GBR Great Britain Coach: COPP, Jonathan

Names	Time played	FG	PS	PC	Total	Off	To	Int	Stl	PIC	25Y
MASON, Simon	1:10										
LUCKES, David	0:00										
WYATT, Jon	1:10						6	2	4		
HALLS, Julian	1:10							4	2		
SINGH, Soma	1:10	0/1			0/1		2	3	2		
HAZLITT, Simon	0:18						2	2			
LASLETT, Jason	1:10						5	3	1		
TAKHER, Kalbir	1:09						3	1			
LEE, Jason	0:36	0/1			0/1		3				
THOMPSON, Nicky	1:10						2	3	3		
MAYER, Chris	0:39						3	2			
McGUIRE, Phillip	0:52						4	4	1		
GARCIA, Russell	1:02			0/1	0/1		6	2			
SHAW, John	0:41						1				
GILES, Calum	0:01			0/1	0/1						
HALL, Daniel	0:29						2				
Totals		0/2	0/0	0/2	0/4	0	39	26	13	6	32

Umpires: EHLERS, Henrik DEN   WOLTER, Richard GER

Team: AUS Australia Coach: MURRAY, Frank

Names	Time played	FG	PS	PC	Total	Off	To	Int	Stl	PIC	25Y
HAGER, Mark	0:57	1/1			1/1	1	4		1		
DAVIES, Stephen	0:58	0/2			0/2	1	8	2	1		
CHOPPY, Baeden	0:53	0/1			0/1		1		2		
ELMER, Lachlan	1:10						4	4	1		
CARRUTHERS, Stuart	0:11										
SMITH, Grant	0:10						1		1		
DILETTI, Damon	0:00										
DREHER, Lachlan	1:10										
GARARD, Brendan	0:09										
GAUDOIN, Paul	1:10			0/1	0/1		4	3	2		
LEWIS, Paul	1:03	0/1			0/1		2	2	4		
SMITH, Matthew	0:19					1	5	3			
STACY, Jason	1:05	1/1		0/3	1/4		8	4	3		
SPROULE, Daniel	1:10	0/1			0/1		2	1	1		
WARK, Kenneth	1:10						4	3	5		
YORK, Michael	1:10						1	3	3		
Totals		2/7	0/0	0/4	2/11	3	44	25	24	9	31

PRELIMINARIES - GROUP B FINAL SCORE: MAS 2 KOR 4 HALFTIME SCORE: MAS 0 KOR 1

Team: MAS Malaysia Coach: KNAPP, Volker

Names	Time played	FG	PS	PC	Total	Off	To	Int	Stl	PIC	25Y
IBRAHIM, Mohd Nasihin	0:00										
MAGMAR SINGH, Maninderjit	1:10			0/2	0/2		3	9	1		
ABU HASSAN, Lailin	0:35						1	10			
SIVA, Brian Jayhan	1:04						1	1	1		
LIM, Chiow Chuan	1:09						4	8	2		
DAVID, Charles	0:21							2			
ABDUL AZIZ, Chairil Anwar	1:00	0/1			0/1		2	2			
LAM, Mun Fatt	0:37						1				
RAMU, Shankar	1:07						1	2	3		
NASIRUDDIN, Nor Saiful Za	0:02			1/1	1/1		1				
MUNIANDY, Kaliswaran	0:24						2				
SINGH, Aphthar	0:44						6	2			
NAWAWI, Mirnawan	1:06	1/1			1/1		7	4			
FERNANDEZ, Calvin	1:06						1	1			
SHANMUGANATHAN, Kuhan	0:39						3	2			
HAMZAH, Hamdan	1:10										
Totals		1/2	0/0	1/3	2/5	0	33	43	7	7	32

Umpires: RUIZ, Eduardo ARG   HORGAN, Steve USA

Team: KOR Korea Coach: JEON, Jae-Hong

Names	Time played	FG	PS	PC	Total	Off	To	Int	Stl	PIC	25Y
KOO, Jin-Soo	1:10										
SHIN, Seok-Kyo	1:08						2	4	2		
HAN, Beung-Kook	0:27						1	3			
YOU, Myung-Keun	0:15						1				
CHO, Myung-Jun	1:06						2	5	1		
JEON, Jong-Ha	1:06							5			
YOU, Seung-Jin	0:55	0/2			0/2		3	6	1		
PARK, Shin-Heum	1:10		1/1		1/1		6	6	1		
KANG, Keon-Wook	0:40	2/4			2/4		3				
KIM, Jong-Yi	0:45	1/1			1/1		2	3			
JEONG, Yong-Kyun	0:50	0/1			0/1		2	3			
SONG, Seung-Tae	0:41						1	2			
KIM, Yong-Bae	0:47						1	5			
HONG, Kyung-Suep	0:54					1	3	2			
KIM, Young-Kyu	0:50	0/3			0/3		1		2		
KIM, Yoon	0:00										
Totals		3/11	1/1	0/0	4/12	1	28	44	7	20	48

Men / *Messieurs*

PRELIMINARIES - GROUP B   FINAL SCORE: NED 4   RSA 1   HALFTIME SCORE: NED 3   RSA 0

Team: NED Netherlands   Coach: OLTMANS, Roelant

Names	Time played	FG	PS	PC	Total	Off	To	Int	Stl	PIC	25Y
JANSEN, Ronald	0:35						2				
LOMANS, Bram	0:36	1/1		1/2	2/3		1	1	1		
KLEIN GEBBINK, Leo	1:10						6	2	3		
JAZET, Erik	1:10						3	1			
van MEER, Tycho	0:27						2	1			
van PELT, Wouter	1:10	0/1		0/1			7	3	1		
DELISSEN, Marc	0:56	1/5			1/5	3	6		1		
BRINKMAN, Jacques	1:10						5		1		
CRUCQ, Maurits	1:10	0/1		0/1	0/2		4	8			
VEEN, Stephan	1:04						9	3	1		
BOVELANDER, Floris Jan	0:01										
DELMEE, Jeroen	0:33							3			
VOGELS, Guus	0:33										
de NOOIJER, Teun	0:29					1	5	1	1		
van WIJK, Remco	0:38						2				
van den HONERT, Taco	1:02	1/1		0/1	1/2		6	1	1		
Totals		3/9	0/0	1/4	4/13	4	53	28	11	14	37

Umpires: AYMAN, Amin EGY   O'CONNOR, Ray IRL

Team: RSA Republic of South Africa   Coach: FEATHERSTONE, Gavin

Names	Time played	FG	PS	PC	Total	Off	To	Int	Stl	PIC	25Y
MYBURGH, Brian	1:05							1	1		
MILNE, Brad	0:03										
COOKE, Shaun	1:01						4	2			
JACKSON, Craig	1:10						2	4	1		
FULTON, Craig	0:24						1	2			
MICHALARO, Bradley	0:42						3	2			
CLARK, Gregg	0:54						3				
BODDINGTON, Gary	1:03			0/1	0/1		2	3	2		
FREDERICKS, Allistar	0:41	0/1			0/1		1		1		
GRAHAM, Wayne	1:10					1	3	2			
CHREE, Kevin	1:00						4		2		
TEVERSHAM, Charles	0:50						7	2	2		
NICOL, Gregory	0:46	0/1		1/1	1/2	2	4				
HALLOWES, Matthew	0:50	0/1			0/1		3				
FULTON, William	0:37			0/1	0/1		1				
ANDERSON, Murray	0:26						1	4			
Totals		0/3	0/0	1/3	1/6	4	43	18	8	7	30

FINAL CLASSIFICATION - GROUP B

Rnk	Team	Played	Won	Drawn	Lost	For	Against	Diff	Points
1	NED	5	4	1	0	14	6	8	9
2	AUS	5	3	1	1	13	7	6	7
3	GBR	5	1	3	1	8	8	0	5
4	KOR	5	1	2	2	12	13	-1	4
5	RSA	5	0	3	2	7	12	-5	3
6	MAS	5	0	2	3	7	15	-8	2

CLASSIFICATION   FINAL SCORE: ARG 4   MAS 4   HALFTIME SCORE: ARG 1   MAS 1

Team: ARG Argentina   Coach: MacCORMIK, Miguel

Names	Time played	FG	PS	PC	Total	Off	To	Int	Stl	PIC	25Y
MOREIRA, Pablo	1:10							1			
QUEREJETA, Jorge	0:54						1	2			
PAILOS, Edgardo	1:10						2	6	2		
CHIODO, Diego	0:20						2	2	1		
DOHERTY, Alejandro	1:10	0/1			0/1		2	4	1		
MORESI, Fernando	0:39						3		2		
PEREZ, Rodolfo	0:55					1	5	1			
RETEGUI, Carlos	1:10	1/3	1/1		2/4		3	9	2		
LOMBI, Jorge	1:10	1/3		0/1	1/4	1	7	3			
MINADEO, Gabriel	0:41	0/1			0/1		5	1			
FERRARA, Fernando	1:10	1/7		0/1	1/8		6	1			
BACCARO, Leandro	0:21	0/1			0/1						
SCHMITT, Rodolfo	0:00										
CAPURRO, Santiago	0:14										
CALDAS, Maximiliano	1:10						4	10			
LOMBI, Pablo	0:32						4		1		
Totals		3/16	1/1	0/2	4/19	2	44	40	9	16	43

Umpires: SANA, Kiyoshi JPN   VAN BENEDEN, Patrick BEL

Team: MAS Malaysia   Coach: KNAPP, Volker

Names	Time played	FG	PS	PC	Total	Off	To	Int	Stl	PIC	25Y
IBRAHIM, Mohd Nasihin	0:00										
MAGMAR SINGH, Maninderjit	1:10						1	2	3		
ABU HASSAN, Lailin	0:39	0/1			0/1		1	2			
SIVA, Brian Jayhan	1:03	1/1			1/1		2	4	2		
LIM, Chiow Chuan	1:01						5	5	1		
DAVID, Charles	1:10							4			
ABDUL AZIZ, Chairil Anwar	0:45	0/1			0/1		6	2			
LAM, Mun Fatt	0:33						4		1		
RAMU, Shankar	1:10						2	2	1		
NASIRUDDIN, Nor Saiful Za	0:01										
MUNIANDY, Kaliswaran	0:00										
SINGH, Aphthar	0:53	1/1			1/1		2				
NAWAWI, Mirnawan	1:06	1/4			1/4		5		1		
FERNANDEZ, Calvin	1:05	0/1			0/1		1	2	1		
SHANMUGANATHAN, Kuhan	0:59	0/1		1/1	1/2		2	1	2		
HAMZAH, Hamdan	1:10							1			
Totals		3/10	0/0	1/1	4/11	0	31	25	12	20	38

Men / *Messieurs*

CLASSIFICATION   FINAL SCORE: RSA 3   USA 0   HALFTIME SCORE: RSA 1   USA 0

Team: RSA Republic of South Africa   Coach: FEATHERSTONE, Gavin

Names	Time played	FG	PS	PC	Total	Off	To	Int	Stl	PIC	25Y
MYBURGH, Brian	1:10						1	1			
MILNE, Brad	0:00										
COOKE, Shaun	1:01						7	6	1		
JACKSON, Craig	1:10						2	8	2		
FULTON, Craig	0:25	1/1		1/1			5	1			
MICHALARO, Bradley	1:06						5	4			
CLARK, Gregg	0:56	0/2		0/2			2	2	1		
BODDINGTON, Gary	0:59	0/1		0/1			4	5	1		
FREDERICKS, Allistar	0:13						1		1		
GRAHAM, Wayne	1:04						2	2	2		
CHREE, Kevin	1:01	0/1		0/1			5	9			
TEVERSHAM, Charles	0:51						2	6			
NICOL, Gregory	1:01	1/2		0/1	1/3	1	5	2			
HALLOWES, Matthew	0:54						5	5	1		
FULTON, William	0:25			1/1	1/1		1	1			
ANDERSON, Murray	0:27						2	2			
Totals		2/7	0/0	1/2	3/9	1	49	54	9	14	42

Umpires: AYMAN, Amin EGY   IDENBURG, Floris NED

Team: USA United States of America   Coach: CLARK, Jonathan

Names	Time played	FG	PS	PC	Total	Off	To	Int	Stl	PIC	25Y
VANO, Tom	0:00										
DANIELSON, Steve	1:10						2	3	1		
AMAR, Larry	1:10	0/1		0/1			4	3			
MELLOR, Marq	0:35					1	3	1			
WILLIAMS, Scott	0:00										
JENNINGS, Steve	1:10						3	3			
VAN RANDWYCK, Steven	0:35	0/1		0/1	2	5	2	2			
WENTGES, Mark	0:35						1	1			
O'NEILL, John	0:18						1		1		
WASSENAAR, Eelco	1:10						3	5			
BUTCHER, Nick	1:10					1	4	5			
ELMAGHRABY, Ahmed	0:35						2				
SYKES, Phil	1:10						2	10	2		
STEFFERS, Otto	0:51						6	3			
MARUQUIN, Ben	1:10		0/1	0/1			4	4			
WAGNER, Steve	1:10						1	2			
Totals		0/2	0/0	0/1	0/3	4	41	42	6	7	31

CLASSIFICATION   FINAL SCORE: IND 3   KOR 3   HALFTIME SCORE: IND 1   KOR 1

Team: IND India   Coach: D'SOUZA, Cedric

Names	Time played	FG	PS	PC	Total	Off	To	Int	Stl	PIC	25Y
ANJAPARAVANDA, Subbaiah	1:10										
SINGH, Harpreet	1:10						3	5	1		
RIAZ, Mohamed	0:52			0/1	0/1		2	2	1		
KUMAR, Sanjeev	1:02						2	4	3		
SINGH, Baljeet	1:03	0/2		0/2	1	7	5				
VARKEY, Sabu	0:20						1				
NANDONOORI, Mukesh Kumar	1:10	0/1		1/1	1/2		5		1		
SINGH, Rahul	0:17						1				
PILLAY, Dhanraj	0:32						5				
POWAR, Pargat Singh	0:35	0/1		0/1			1	2	1		
DHILLON, Baljit Singh	0:31	0/2		0/1	0/3		4				
EDWARDS, Alloysuis	0:00										
ALEXANDER, Anil	1:09						2	2	1		
FERREIRA, Gavin	1:10	1/3			1/3		2	3			
SINGH, Ramandeep	1:10		1/1		1/1		4	5	1		
TIRKEY, Dilip	0:35						1	3	2		
Totals		1/9	1/1	1/3	3/13	1	39	32	11	9	29

Umpires: LANGLE, Guillaume FRA   HORGAN, Steve USA

Team: KOR Korea   Coach: JEON, Jae-Hong

Names	Time played	FG	PS	PC	Total	Off	To	Int	Stl	PIC	25Y
KOO, Jin-Soo	1:10										
SHIN, Seok-Kyo	1:10		2/2	2/2			3	4	3		
HAN, Beung-Kook	1:07						2				
YOU, Myung-Keun	0:03										
CHO, Myung-Jun	1:09						3				
JEON, Jong-Ha	1:10						2	5			
YOU, Seung-Jin	1:09							2			
PARK, Shin-Heum	1:10	0/1		1/1	1/2		4	2			
KANG, Keon-Wook	1:10	0/1		0/1			5	1			
KIM, Jong-Yi	0:31							1			
JEONG, Yong-Kyun	0:36						1	2	1		
SONG, Seung-Tae	0:22						2				
KIM, Yong-Bae	0:03										
HONG, Kyung-Suep	0:32	0/1		0/1			1				
KIM, Young-Kyu	1:10						4				
KIM, Yoon	0:00										
Totals		0/3	0/0	3/3	3/6	0	23	19	6	6	29

CLASSIFICATION   FINAL SCORE: GBR 1   PAK 2   HALFTIME SCORE: GBR 1   PAK 1

Team: GBR Great Britain   Coach: COPP, Jonathan

Names	Time played	FG	PS	PC	Total	Off	To	Int	Stl	PIC	25Y
MASON, Simon	0:35						1				
LUCKES, David	0:00										
WYATT, Jon	0:35						4	4	1		
HALLS, Julian	0:35						2	8	1		
SINGH, Soma	0:35						6	1			
HAZLITT, Simon	0:01						3				
LASLETT, Jason	0:35	0/1		0/1			3	5	1		
TAKHER, Kalbir	0:33	0/1		0/1			3	3	1		
LEE, Jason	0:35	0/1		0/1			3	1			
THOMPSON, Nicky	0:35	0/2		0/2	1	3	3	1			
MAYER, Chris	0:31	0/2		0/2			5	1			
McGUIRE, Phillip	0:35						6	4			
GARCIA, Russell	0:35						3	4	2		
SHAW, John	0:02						2	1			
GILES, Calum	0:01			1/4	1/4						
HALL, Daniel	0:00						3				
Totals		0/7	0/0	1/4	1/11	1	40	41	8	21	42

Umpires: EHLERS, Henrik DEN   ST ROSE, Roger TRI

Team: PAK Pakistan   Coach: BUTT, Jahangir

Names	Time played	FG	PS	PC	Total	Off	To	Int	Stl	PIC	25Y
AHMED, Mansoor	0:35						1				
KALEEM, Mohammad	0:20						1	1			
ALAM, Naveed	0:14			0/1	0/1		1	2	1		
USMAN, Muhammad	0:35						2	4			
KHALID, Muhammad	0:35						2	5	2		
SHAFQAT, Mohammad	0:00	0/1		0/1							
SARWAR, Muhammad	0:35	1/3		1/3			1	3	1		
TAHIR, Zaman	0:35	0/2		0/2	1	4	7				
ASHRAF, Kamran	0:35	0/1		0/1	2	4					
SHAHBAZ, Muhammad	0:28	0/1		0/1	1	5	3				
SHAHBAZ, Ahmed	0:35						4	1			
MEHMOOD, Khalid	0:00										
ALI, Rana	0:35			0/1	0/1		1	2	1		
MAHMOOD, Irfan	0:35						5	4	2		
RAZA, Aleem	0:06	0/1		0/1			3				
KAHN, Rahim	0:00	1/1		1/1			1	1	2		
Totals		2/10	0/0	0/2	2/12	4	34	34	9	16	46

Men / *Messieurs*

SEMIFINALS — FINAL SCORE: ESP 2 AUS 1 — HALFTIME SCORE: ESP 0 AUS 0

Team: ESP Spain — Coach: FORRELLAT, Antonio

Names	Time played	FG	PS	PC	Total	Off	To	Int	Stl	PIC	25Y
JUFRESA, Ramon	1:10										
BARRENA, Oscar	0:00										
MALGOSA, Joaquin	1:10						5	5			
ARNAU, Jordi	1:10						2	1	3		
GARCIA-MAURINO, Juantxo	1:02						3	5	1		
AMAT, Jaime	1:10	1/1			1/1		2	2	1		
ESCARRE, Juan	1:06	0/1	1/1	0/1	1/3		8		1		
PUJOL, Victor	0:56	0/1			0/1		1	1	2		
COBOS, Ignacio	0:25	0/1			0/1		1				
ESCUDE, Xavier	0:39	0/1			0/1		2	1			
ARNAU, Javier	0:48			0/2	0/2		4	1			
SALA, Ramon	1:10						2	2	3		
DINARES, Juan	0:59			0/1	0/1		1	2			
AMAT, Pablo	0:25	0/1			0/1						
USOZ, Pablo	0:37						3	2	1		
GONZALEZ, Antonio	0:00										
Totals		1/6	1/1	0/4	2/11	0	34	22	12	13	33

Umpires: von RETH, Peter NED — WOLTER, Richard GER

Team: AUS Australia — Coach: MURRAY, Frank

Names	Time played	FG	PS	PC	Total	Off	To	Int	Stl	PIC	25Y
HAGER, Mark	1:10	0/2			0/2	1	8	1	1		
DAVIES, Stephen	1:06	0/1			0/1	1	8	1	3		
CHOPPY, Baeden	0:52	0/1			0/1		11				
ELMER, Lachlan	1:10						3	6	1		
CARRUTHERS, Stuart	0:05						1				
SMITH, Grant	0:00										
DILETTI, Damon	0:00										
DREHER, Lachlan	1:10										
GARARD, Brendan	0:07						1	1			
GAUDOIN, Paul	1:02			1/2	1/2		2	6	1		
LEWIS, Paul	1:10	0/1			0/1		8	3	3		
SMITH, Matthew	0:17						2				
STACY, Jason	1:09	0/2		0/2	0/4		2	2	2		
SPROULE, Daniel	1:10					1	4	5	2		
WARK, Kenneth	1:08						4	5	4		
YORK, Michael	1:10						1	9	1		
Totals		0/7	0/0	1/4	1/11	3	55	39	18	17	42

SEMIFINALS — FINAL SCORE: GER 1 NED 3 — HALFTIME SCORE: GER 0 NED 1

Team: GER Germany — Coach: LISSEK, Paul

Names	Time played	FG	PS	PC	Total	Off	To	Int	Stl	PIC	25Y
REITZ, Christopher	1:10							1			
KNAUTH, Michael	0:00										
TEWES, Jan Peter	1:10						5	2	1		
FISCHER, Carsten	1:10			0/1	0/1		6	7	1		
BLUNCK, Christian	1:10	0/1			0/1		9	1	1		
SALIGER, Stefan	0:30						4				
EMMERLING, Bjorn	0:00										
BELLENBAUM, Patrick	0:40	0/1			0/1		1				
MEINHARDT, Sven	0:49		1/1		1/1		6				
BECHMANN, Christoph	0:40	0/1			0/1		2	1			
DOMKE, Oliver	0:32						2	1			
BECKER, Andreas	0:31						2				
GREEN, Michael	1:04	0/1			0/1		2	3	2		
MICHLER, Klaus	1:10	0/1			0/1		4	2	1		
FRIED, Volker	1:02						3	6			
MAYERHOEFER, Christian	1:10						8	4	1		
Totals		0/5	0/0	1/2	1/7	0	54	28	7	8	37

Umpires: O'CONNOR, Ray IRL — PRIOR, Don AUS

Team: NED Netherlands — Coach: OLTMANS, Roelant

Names	Time played	FG	PS	PC	Total	Off	To	Int	Stl	PIC	25Y
JANSEN, Ronald	1:10							1			
LOMANS, Bram	0:01										
KLEIN GEBBINK, Leo	1:10						3	1	1		
JAZET, Erik	1:10						5	3	1		
van MEER, Tycho	0:00										
van PELT, Wouter	1:10						8	7	1		
DELISSEN, Marc	1:07					1	7	1	1		
BRINKMAN, Jacques	1:10	0/1			0/1		1	5			
CRUCQ, Maurits	0:03										
VEEN, Stephan	1:10						5	3	1		
BOVELANDER, Floris Jan	0:35						8	1	2		
DELMEE, Jeroen	0:35						1	1	1		
VOGELS, Guus	0:00										
de NOOIJER, Teun	0:22	0/1			0/1		3	2	1		
van WIJK, Remco	0:12						5	2			
van den HONERT, Taco	0:35	1/1		2/2	3/3		9	4	2		
Totals		1/3	0/0	2/2	3/5	1	55	31	11	8	28

FINAL 11-12 — FINAL SCORE: MAS 4 USA 1 — HALFTIME SCORE: MAS 1 USA 0

Team: MAS Malaysia — Coach: KNAPP, Volker

Names	Time played	FG	PS	PC	Total	Off	To	Int	Stl	PIC	25Y
IBRAHIM, Mohd Nasihin	0:00										
MAGMAR SINGH, Maninderjit	1:10			0/1	0/1		7	11	4		
ABU HASSAN, Lailin	0:18										
SIVA, Brian Jayhan	1:10	0/1			0/1		1	1	1		
LIM, Chiow Chuan	0:53		2/2		2/2		1	3			
DAVID, Charles	1:08							7			
ABDUL AZIZ, Chairil Anwar	0:25	0/1			0/1		1				
LAM, Mun Fatt	0:36						1	1	1		
RAMU, Shankar	1:06						2	1	5		
NASIRUDDIN, Nor Saiful Za	0:03										
MUNIANDY, Kaliswaran	0:26										
SINGH, Aphthar	0:57					1	6	1	1		
NAWAWI, Mirnawan	1:07	0/1		1/1	1/2		8	5	1		
FERNANDEZ, Calvin	1:10						2	4	1		
SHANMUGANATHAN, Kuhan	1:04	1/3		0/1	1/4		6	1	1		
HAMZAH, Hamdan	1:10						1	1			
Totals		1/6	2/2	1/3	4/11	1	36	36	15	17	36

Umpires: EHLERS, Henrik DEN — MORALES LOPEZ, Antonio ESP

Team: USA United States of America — Coach: CLARK, Jonathan

Names	Time played	FG	PS	PC	Total	Off	To	Int	Stl	PIC	25Y
VANO, Tom	1:10						2	2			
DANIELSON, Steve	1:10						3	4	1		
AMAR, Larry	1:10	0/1			0/1		3	2			
MELLOR, Marq	0:57	0/1		0/2	0/3		2				
WILLIAMS, Scott	0:33						1	2	1		
JENNINGS, Steve	1:09			0/1	0/1		5	4			
VAN RANDWYCK, Steven	0:55						3	1			
WENTGES, Mark	0:18	0/1			0/1		2				
O'NEILL, John	0:57						1				
WASSENAAR, Eelco	0:45							6	1		
BUTCHER, Nick	1:10	1/3			1/3		4	1			
ELMAGHRABY, Ahmed	0:20	0/1			0/1		2	1			
SYKES, Phil	0:50						2	5	1		
STEFFERS, Otto	0:12										
MARUQUIN, Ben	1:10	0/1		0/3	0/4		5	6	1		
WAGNER, Steve	0:00										
Totals		1/8	0/0	0/6	1/14	0	33	35	7	16	33

Men / *Messieurs*

FINAL 9 - 10   FINAL SCORE: ARG 3   RSA 2   HALFTIME SCORE: ARG 1   RSA 1

Team: ARG Argentina   Coach: MacCORMIK, Miguel

Names	Time played	FG	PS	PC	Total	Off	To	Int	Stl	PIC	25Y
MOREIRA, Pablo	1:10										
QUEREJETA, Jorge	1:10						1	6	1		
PAILOS, Edgardo	1:10						3	7			
CHIODO, Diego	0:18						1				
DOHERTY, Alejandro	1:10						3	4			
MORESI, Fernando	0:44		0/1	0/1			3	3	1		
PEREZ, Rodolfo	0:00										
RETEGUI, Carlos	1:10	0/2		0/1	0/3	2	10	6	1		
LOMBI, Jorge	1:05	0/2		1/3	1/5	2	6				
MINADEO, Gabriel	0:25							1	1		
FERRARA, Fernando	1:05	1/3		0/1	1/4	1	7	1			
BACCARO, Leandro	0:52						6	1	1		
SCHMITT, Rodolfo	0:00										
CAPURRO, Santiago	0:27	1/4			1/4		1	2			
CALDAS, Maximiliano	1:10			0/1	0/1		3	4			
LOMBI, Pablo	0:51						2	1			
Totals		2/11	0/0	1/7	3/18	5	46	36	5	14	45

Umpires: LANGLE, Guillaume FRA   MADDEN, Craig GBR

Team: RSA Republic of South Africa   Coach: FEATHERSTONE, Gavin

Names	Time played	FG	PS	PC	Total	Off	To	Int	Stl	PIC	25Y
MYBURGH, Brian	1:10							1	1		
MILNE, Brad	0:00										
COOKE, Shaun	1:00	0/1			0/1		6	2	1		
JACKSON, Craig	1:10						5	6	1		
FULTON, Craig	0:46						6	3			
MICHALARO, Bradley	0:00										
CLARK, Gregg	0:53	0/1			0/1		2	1			
BODDINGTON, Gary	1:03	0/2			0/2		1	3			
FREDERICKS, Allistar	0:09										
GRAHAM, Wayne	1:10						1	1			
CHREE, Kevin	0:47						2	2	1		
TEVERSHAM, Charles	1:10						5	2			
NICOL, Gregory	1:00	0/2		1/4	1/6	1	5	2			
HALLOWES, Matthew	0:42	1/1			1/1		3	1			
FULTON, William	1:02						1	1			
ANDERSON, Murray	0:43						1	3			
Totals		1/7	0/0	1/4	2/11	1	39	28	3	13	32

FINAL 7 - 8   FINAL SCORE: IND 3   GBR 4   HALFTIME SCORE: IND 2   GBR 1

Team: IND India   Coach: D'SOUZA, Cedric

Names	Time played	FG	PS	PC	Total	Off	To	Int	Stl	PIC	25Y
ANJAPARAVANDA, Subbaiah	0:04										
SINGH, Harpreet	1:10						4	2	1		
RIAZ, Mohamed	1:01						1	3	2		
KUMAR, Sanjeev	0:45	0/1			0/1		2	1	1		
SINGH, Baljeet	1:02	0/1			0/1		4		1		
VARKEY, Sabu	0:28	0/1			0/1		1		1		
NANDONOORI, Mukesh Kumar	0:45						7				
SINGH, Rahul	0:14								1		
PILLAY, Dhanraj	0:22										
POWAR, Pargat Singh	1:07			1/2	1/2	1	4	5	3		
DHILLON, Baljit Singh	1:01	1/3		0/1	1/4		3	2	1		
EDWARDS, Alloysuis	1:05										
ALEXANDER, Anil	1:04							1			
FERREIRA, Gavin	1:02	0/1			0/1		2	2			
SINGH, Ramandeep	1:08		1/1		1/1		1	6	3		
TIRKEY, Dilip	0:25						1	1			
Totals		1/7	1/1	1/3	3/11	1	29	23	15	18	36

Umpires: RUIZ, Eduardo ARG   ST ROSE, Roger TRI

Team: GBR Great Britain   Coach: COPP, Jonathan

Names	Time played	FG	PS	PC	Total	Off	To	Int	Stl	PIC	25Y
MASON, Simon	0:00										
LUCKES, David	1:10										
WYATT, Jon	1:10			1/1	1/1		1	6	3		
HALLS, Julian	1:06							2			
SINGH, Soma	1:10						1	1	2		
HAZLITT, Simon	0:46			0/1	0/1		4	2	2		
LASLETT, Jason	1:10	1/2			1/2		3	2			
TAKHER, Kalbir	0:54	0/1			0/1			2	3		
LEE, Jason	0:26						2				
THOMPSON, Nicky	1:03	0/2			0/2		2	2	2		
MAYER, Chris	1:03	1/1			1/1		2	1			
McGUIRE, Phillip	1:02	0/1			0/1		4	4			
GARCIA, Russell	0:54						3				
SHAW, John	0:34	1/1			1/1		3	1	1		
GILES, Calum	0:03			0/4	0/4						
HALL, Daniel	0:15						1				
Totals		3/8	0/0	1/6	4/14	0	26	23	13	10	36

FINAL 5 - 6   FINAL SCORE: KOR 3   PAK 1   HALFTIME SCORE: KOR 2   PAK 1

Team: KOR Korea   Coach: JEON, Jae-Hong

Names	Time played	FG	PS	PC	Total	Off	To	Int	Stl	PIC	25Y
KOO, Jin-Soo	0:27										
SHIN, Seok-Kyo	0:35			1/3	1/3		6	3			
HAN, Beung-Kook	0:33						3	3			
YOU, Myung-Keun	0:35						1	5	1		
CHO, Myung-Jun	0:35							2	1		
JEON, Jong-Ha	0:01			1/2	1/2		1				
YOU, Seung-Jin	0:35						2	2	1		
PARK, Shin-Heum	0:35						4	1	2		
KANG, Keon-Wook	0:30						7				
KIM, Jong-Yi	0:04	0/1			0/1		2				
JEONG, Yong-Kyun	0:33						1	2	1		
SONG, Seung-Tae	0:14	1/1			1/1		3	2			
KIM, Yong-Bae	0:00			0/1	0/1						
HONG, Kyung-Suep	0:21					1	5	1			
KIM, Young-Kyu	0:35	0/1			0/1		6	2			
KIM, Yoon	0:07										
Totals		1/3	0/0	2/6	3/9	1	41	23	6	6	32

Umpires: WOLTER, Richard GER   MADDEN, Craig GBR

Team: PAK Pakistan   Coach: BUTT, Jahangir

Names	Time played	FG	PS	PC	Total	Off	To	Int	Stl	PIC	25Y
AHMED, Mansoor	0:35										
KALEEM, Mohammad	0:00		0/1	0/1			1				
ALAM, Naveed	0:35						1	4	1		
USMAN, Muhammad	0:35						2	3	1		
KHALID, Muhammad	0:35						3	6	2		
SHAFQAT, Mohammad	0:00										
SARWAR, Muhammad	0:21						5		1		
TAHIR, Zaman	0:35	0/1		0/1	0/2		8	5	1		
ASHRAF, Kamran	0:35	1/2			1/2	1	7	1			
SHAHBAZ, Muhammad	0:35	0/1			0/1		6	1	1		
SHAHBAZ, Ahmed	0:35			0/1	0/1		4	1			
MEHMOOD, Khalid	0:00										
ALI, Rana	0:35			0/2	0/2				1		
MAHMOOD, Irfan	0:35						2	1			
RAZA, Aleem	0:00										
KAHN, Rahim	0:13						3				
Totals		1/4	0/0	0/5	1/9	1	42	22	8	11	38

Men / *Messieurs*

FINAL - BRONZE MATCH FINAL SCORE: AUS 3 GER 2 HALFTIME SCORE: AUS 1 GER 0

Team: AUS Australia Coach: MURRAY, Frank

Names	Time played	FG	PS	PC	Total	Off	To	Int	Stl	PIC	25Y
HAGER, Mark	1:01						2				
DAVIES, Stephen	1:00	0/1			0/1		7	1			
CHOPPY, Baeden	0:41			1/1	1/1		5	1			
ELMER, Lachlan	1:09						5	8	2		
CARRUTHERS, Stuart	0:03						1				
SMITH, Grant	0:11						2				
DILETTI, Damon	0:00										
DREHER, Lachlan	1:10										
GARARD, Brendan	0:27						2	1	1		
GAUDOIN, Paul	0:44			0/1	0/1						
LEWIS, Paul	1:03	0/1			0/1		2	3	2		
SMITH, Matthew	0:41						3		2		
STACY, Jason	1:05			2/2	2/2		6	1			
SPROULE, Daniel	1:10						4	7	2		
WARK, Kenneth	1:09						3	7	6		
YORK, Michael	1:10						2	4			
Totals		0/2	0/0	3/4	3/6	0	44	33	15	11	31

Umpires: RUIZ, Eduardo ARG von RETH, Peter NED

Team: GER Germany Coach: LISSEK, Paul

Names	Time played	FG	PS	PC	Total	Off	To	Int	Stl	PIC	25Y
REITZ, Christopher	1:10										
KNAUTH, Michael	0:07										
TEWES, Jan Peter	1:08						3	3	2		
FISCHER, Carsten	1:10			0/4	0/4		3	6	1		
BLUNCK, Christian	1:09						3	4	3		
SALIGER, Stefan	0:41	0/1			0/1	1	2	1	1		
EMMERLING, Bjorn	0:00										
BELLENBAUM, Patrick	0:57						4	5			
MEINHARDT, Sven	0:37			1/1	1/1		4	1			
BECHMANN, Christoph	0:39						1	4	1		
DOMKE, Oliver	0:37	1/1			1/1			1	2		
BECKER, Andreas	0:33	0/1		0/2	0/3		1				
GREEN, Michael	0:37						1	1			
MICHLER, Klaus	1:10	0/1			0/1		2	3	4		
FRIED, Volker	1:07						3	4			
MAYERHOEFER, Christian	1:02						5	2	1		
Totals		1/4	0/0	1/7	2/11	2	35	32	14	7	33

FINAL - GOLD MATCH FINAL SCORE: ESP 1 NED 3 HALFTIME SCORE: ESP 0 NED 0

Team: ESP Spain Coach: FORRELLAT, Antonio

Names	Time played	FG	PS	PC	Total	Off	To	Int	Stl	PIC	25Y
JUFRESA, Ramon	1:08										
BARRENA, Oscar	0:01										
MALGOSA, Joaquin	1:10						9	7	2		
ARNAU, Jordi	1:10						1	4			
GARCIA-MAURINO, Juantxo	1:02						6	3			
AMAT, Jaime	1:08						3	1	2		
ESCARRE, Juan	1:00	0/1			0/1		6		1		
PUJOL, Victor	0:50	1/1			1/1			2			
COBOS, Ignacio	0:33	0/2			0/2		3				
ESCUDE, Xavier	0:36						3	1			
ARNAU, Javier	0:48	0/1		0/1	0/2		3				
SALA, Ramon	1:08						4	5	2		
DINARES, Juan	0:54	0/1			0/1		2	1			
AMAT, Pablo	0:30	0/1			0/1		2	2			
USOZ, Pablo	0:43	0/1			0/1		2	1	2		
GONZALEZ, Antonio	0:01										
Totals		1/8	0/0	0/1	1/9	0	44	27	9	9	25

Umpires: O'CONNOR, Ray IRL PRIOR, Don AUS

Team: NED Netherlands Coach: OLTMANS, Roelant

Names	Time played	FG	PS	PC	Total	Off	To	Int	Stl	PIC	25Y
JANSEN, Ronald	1:10							2			
LOMANS, Bram	0:21			1/1	1/1		1				
KLEIN GEBBINK, Leo	1:10						6	4	1		
JAZET, Erik	1:10						1	6			
van MEER, Tycho	0:00										
van PELT, Wouter	0:51	0/1			0/1		2	3	1		
DELISSEN, Marc	1:06					1	7	1	1		
BRINKMAN, Jacques	1:10	0/1			0/1		3	3	2		
CRUCQ, Maurits	0:00										
VEEN, Stephan	1:10					1	8	2			
BOVELANDER, Floris Jan	1:04			2/3	2/3		7	2	1		
DELMEE, Jeroen	0:32						8	1			
VOGELS, Guus	0:00										
de NOOIJER, Teun	0:21						6	4	1		
van WIJK, Remco	0:15	0/1			0/1		5		1		
van den HONERT, Taco	0:35	0/1			0/1		5	1			
Totals		0/4	0/0	3/4	3/8	2	51	36	9	14	31

CLASSIFICATION - FINAL SUMMARY

Phase	Teams	Score
A5 - B6	ARG - MAS	4 - 4
A3 - B4	IND - KOR	3 - 3
B5 - A6	RSA - USA	3 - 0
B3 - A4	GBR - PAK	1 - 2

SEMIFINALS - FINAL SUMMARY

Phase	Teams	Score
A1 - B2	ESP - AUS	2 - 1
A2 - B1	GER - NED	1 - 3

FINAL SUMMARY

Phase	Teams	Score
Final - Gold	ESP - NED	1 - 3
Final - Bronze	AUS - GER	3 - 2
Final 5 - 6	KOR - PAK	3 - 1

FINAL SUMMARY - *continued*

Phase	Teams	Score
Final 7 - 8	IND - GBR	3 - 4
Final 9 - 10	ARG - RSA	3 - 2
Final 11 - 12	MAS - USA	4 - 1

FINAL CLASSIFICATION

Rnk	Team	Matches Played	Won	Drawn	Lost	Goals For	Against	Diff	Points	
1	NED	5	4	1	0	14	6	8	9	Gold
2	ESP	5	4	0	0	14	5	9	8	Silver
3	AUS	5	3	1	1	13	7	6	7	Bronze
4	GER	5	3	1	1	10	3	7	7	
5	KOR	5	1	2	2	12	13	-1	4	
6	PAK	5	4	1	2	11	8	3	5	
7	GBR	5	1	3	2	8	8	0	5	
8	IND	5	2	2	1	8	3	5	6	
9	ARG	5	2	0	3	9	13	-4	4	
10	RSA	5	5	2	2	7	12	-5	3	
11	MAS	5	0	2	3	7	15	-8	2	
12	USA	5	0	0	5	3	23	-20	0	

Hockey / *Hockey*

Hockey / *Hockey*
Women / *Dames*

Team: USA United States of America Coach: HIXON, Pamela

Names	Time played	FG	PS	PC	Total	Off	To	Int	Stl	PIC	25Y
SHEA, Patty	1:10										
MARTIN, Laurel	0:07						1				
TCHOU, Liz	0:01										
PANKRATZ, Marcia	0:51			1/1	1/1		6		1		
WERLEY, Cindy	1:01	0/1			0/1	1	3				
MADL, Diane	0:18						1				
FILLAT, Kris	1:05						4	4			
JAMES, Kelli	1:10	0/2			0/2		11				
FUCHS, Tracey	1:10						10	2	3		
LUCAS, Antoinette	1:10						10	1	1		
KAUFFMAN, Katie	0:04						1				
WIELAND, Andrea	0:00										
LYNESS, Leslie	1:10						15	5	2		
MAROIS, Barb	1:10						11	8	2		
REEVE, Jill	1:10						7		2		
BUSTIN, Pamela	1:10						4	1	1		
Totals		0/3	0/0	1/1	1/4	1	84	21	12	6	31

Umpires: KATO, Naomi JPN   SPITALERI, Gina ITA

Team: NED Netherlands Coach: van `T HEK, Thomas

Names	Time played	FG	PS	PC	Total	Off	To	Int	Stl	PIC	25Y
TOXOPEUS, Jacqueline	1:10										
de HEIJ, Stella	0:13										
van de KIEFT, Fleur	0:10										
THATE, Carole	1:10						5	4	3		
KUIPERS, Ellen	0:51	1/4			1/4	1	11				
LEWIN, Jeannette	1:02						10	2			
KOOLEN, Nicky	0:11	0/1			0/1		3				
van den BOOGAARD, Dilliane	1:05					1	8	1	1		
TEEUWEN, Margje	1:09						2				
DONNERS, Myntje	0:59	0/1			0/1		7		1		
DUYSTER, Willemijn	1:07						7		3		
PLESMAN, Suzanne	0:00										
HOLSBOER, Noor	1:10						4	3	1		
STEENBERGHE, Florentine	1:10						2				
de RUITER, Wietske	0:47			0/5	0/5		6		1		
van der WIELEN, Suzan	0:31	0/1			0/1		2				
Totals		1/7	0/0	0/5	1/12	2	67	10	10	12	35

Team: AUS Australia Coach: CHARLESWORTH, Richard

Names	Time played	FG	PS	PC	Total	Off	To	Int	Stl	PIC	25Y
MAITLAND, Clover	0:31										
ROCHE, Danielle	0:31	0/1			0/1		2				
TOOTH, Liane	1:04							1			
ANNAN, Alyson	0:54	1/1			1/1	1	5	1	1		
HASLAM, Juliet	1:03	0/1			0/1	1	4	2			
MORRIS, Jennifer	1:06		0/1		0/1		4	5			
DOBSON, Louise	0:44						3	2	1		
POWELL, Lisa	0:43	1/2			1/2		4	2	2		
MARSDEN, Karen	0:38										
STARRE, Kate	0:57						4	3	4		
FARRELL, Renita	0:50			0/1	0/1		2	2			
PEREIRA, Jacqueline	0:55	0/1			0/1	1	5		1		
PERIS-KNEEBONE, Nova	0:32						4	8			
HAWKES, Rechelle	0:55	1/1			1/1		4	2			
POWELL, Katrina	0:38	0/2			0/2		2		2		
ANDREWS, Michelle	0:40	1/2		0/1	1/3		4	1			
Totals		4/11	0/0	0/3	4/14	2	42	33	13	18	38

Umpires: van GEMERT, Miriam NED   YASUEDA, Kazuko JPN

Team: ESP Spain Coach: BRASSA, José

Names	Time played	FG	PS	PC	Total	Off	To	Int	Stl	PIC	25Y
CARRION, Elena	0:00										
DORADO, Natalia	1:02			0/1	0/1		8	2	2		
GONZALEZ, Maria Cruz	0:52						5	6	4		
BAREA, Carmen	1:10						1	2	2		
MANRIQUE, Silvia	0:29						4	1			
GABELLANES, Nagore	0:53	0/1			0/1		1	3			
MOTOS, Teresa	0:57						5				
BARRIO, Sonia	0:58						5				
RUEDA, Monica	0:19						1		1		
LOPEZ, Luci	0:20										
FEITO, Mar	0:28						1		1		
TELLERIA, Maider	1:02						2	1	2		
URQUIZU, Elena	1:09						3	2			
LARZABAL, Bego	1:06						2	2	1		
de IGNACIO-SIMO, Sonia	0:49						1	1	2		
GONZALEZ, Maria Victoria	1:10										
Totals		0/1	0/0	0/1	0/2	0	39	20	15	3	16

Team: ARG Argentina Coach: MENDOZA, Roldolfo

Names	Time played	FG	PS	PC	Total	Off	To	Int	Stl	PIC	25Y
ARNAL, Mariana	1:10										
MACKENZIE, Sofia	1:10			0/3	0/3		10	8	1		
AICEGA, Magdalena	1:10						2	7	1		
CORVALAN, Silvina	1:10						1	6			
GAMBERO, Ana	1:10						2	5	1		
CASTELLAN, Julieta	0:40						1				
PANDO, Danelotti	0:54						4	1			
SANCHEZ, Gabriela	1:08						3	3	1		
ONETO, Vanina	1:02		0/1		0/1		7	1	1		
RIMOLDI PUIG, Jorgelina	1:10	0/1			0/1		7	3	1		
MASOTTA, Karina	1:04						5		1		
CASTELLI, Maria Paula	0:25	0/2			0/2		4	1			
ARTICA, Veronica	0:00										
ROGNONI, Cecilia	0:32			0/2	0/2		4	3			
STEPNIK, Ayelen	0:00										
GONZALEZ, Mariana	0:00										
Totals		0/3	0/1	0/5	0/9	0	50	37	8	15	26

Umpires: CHATAS, Renee USA   McDONALD, Janice GBR

Team: GER Germany Coach: RAUTH, Berthold

Names	Time played	FG	PS	PC	Total	Off	To	Int	Stl	PIC	25Y
WOLLSCHLAGER, Susanne	1:10										
BEYER, Birgit	0:00										
SCHMORANZER van KOOPEREN	0:23	1/1			1/1		3		1		
DICKENSCHEID, Tanja	0:34								1		
ERNSTING-KRIENKE, Nadine	0:58	0/1			0/1	1	5		1		
THOMASCHINSKI, Simone	1:10						4	4	1		
KUHNT, Irina	0:24						1	1			
CREMER, Melanie	0:58					1	5	3			
HENTSCHEL, Franziska	0:32	0/1		0/3	0/4		5	2			
PETERS, Kristina	1:10						7	5	3		
HAGENBAEUMER, Eva	1:10						2	4			
BECKER, Britta	1:01			0/1	0/1		5	5	2		
KELLER, Natascha	0:28						2		1		
SUXDORF, Philippa	1:09						1	5			
LAETZSCH, Heike	0:41	1/1			1/1		4	1			
KAUSCHKE, Katrin	0:58	0/1			0/1		5	5			
Totals		2/5	0/0	0/4	2/9	3	49	35	9	10	26

Women / *Dames*

PRELIMINARIES   FINAL SCORE: KOR 5   GBR 0   HALFTIME SCORE: KOR 1   GBR 0

Team: KOR Korea   Coach: CHOI, Song-Ryul

Names	Time played	FG	PS	PC	Total	Off	To	Int	Stl	PIC	25Y
YOU, Jae-Sook	1:10										
CHOI, Eun-Kyung	1:10						5	3			
CHO, Eun-Jung	1:10			2/5	2/5		4	7	1		
OH, Seung-Shin	0:07						1	1			
LIM, Jeong-Sook	0:38						1	1			
KIM, Myung-Ok	1:10						5	6			
CHANG, Eun-Jung	1:10	0/1		0/2	0/3		2	7			
LEE, Ji-Young	1:01	0/1			0/1		6				
LEE, Eun-Kyung	0:48	0/1			0/1		7	3			
KOWN, Soo-Hyun	1:03	0/1		1/1	1/2		7	7			
WOO, Hyun-Jung	0:06										
CHOI, Mi-Soon	0:29	1/2			1/2	1	2				
LEE, Eun-Young	1:01						2	3			
JEON, Young-Sun	0:32							3			
KWON, Chang-Sook	1:10			1/1	1/1		5	1	2		
JIN, Deok-San	0:00										
Totals		1/6	0/0	4/9	5/15	1	42	44	6	16	43

Umpires: LANNING, Margaret CAN   LARIO RUIZ, Angela ESP

Team: GBR Great Britain   Coach: SLOCOMBE, Susan

Names	Time played	FG	PS	PC	Total	Off	To	Int	Stl	PIC	25Y
THOMPSON, Joanne	0:00										
ROSE, Hilary	1:10						1	3			
COOK, Christine	0:24										
CULLEN, Tina	0:09										
BROWN, Karen	1:10						2	11	1		
ATKINS, Jill	1:10						3	8			
FRASER, Sue	1:10						4	6	1		
SIMPSON, Rhona	0:57						6	1			
NICHOLLS, Mandy	0:38						5	2			
SIXSMITH, Jane	0:53	0/1			0/1		6	2			
ROBERTSON, Pauline	0:47						5	1	1		
MOULD, Jo	0:27						3				
MILLER, Tammy	1:04						4	4	1		
BENNETT, Anna	0:44						2				
DAVIES, Mandy	0:53						4	3	1		
JOHNSON, Kathryn	1:10						6	10	2		
Totals		0/1	0/0	0/0	0/1	0	51	51	7	2	14

PRELIMINARIES   FINAL SCORE: ESP 1   GER 2   HALFTIME SCORE: ESP 1   GER 1

Team: ESP Spain   Coach: BRASSA, José

Names	Time played	FG	PS	PC	Total	Off	To	Int	Stl	PIC	25Y
CARRION, Elena	0:00										
DORADO, Natalia	1:02	0/1		0/1	0/2		3	3	1		
GONZALEZ, Maria Cruz	1:03						4	2	2		
BAREA, Carmen	1:10						6	5			
MANRIQUE, Silvia	0:08						1				
GABELLANES, Nagore	0:43	0/1		0/1	0/2		4		1		
MOTOS, Teresa	0:46						5	2			
BARRIO, Sonia	0:56	0/3			0/3		10	2	1		
RUEDA, Monica	0:10						1	1			
LOPEZ, Luci	0:24						2	3			
FEITO, Mar	0:40	0/1			0/1		2	2			
TELLERIA, Maider	1:04		1/1		1/1		5	5			
URQUIZU, Elena	1:09						2	3			
LARZABAL, Bego	1:10						4	5			
de IGNACIO-SIMO, Sonia	1:10	0/1			0/1		2	7	1		
GONZALEZ, Maria Victoria	1:10										
Totals		0/7	1/1	0/2	1/10	0	50	40	7	6	29

Umpires: CLARKE, Gillian GBR   CRESPO, Laura ARG

Team: GER Germany   Coach: RAUTH, Berthold

Names	Time played	FG	PS	PC	Total	Off	To	Int	Stl	PIC	25Y
WOLLSCHLAGER, Susanne	1:10										
BEYER, Birgit	0:00										
SCHMORANZER van KOOPEREN	0:26	1/1			1/1		2				
DICKENSCHEID, Tanja	0:40						2	3	1		
ERNSTING-KRIENKE, Nadine	0:57	0/1			0/1		5	1			
THOMASCHINSKI, Simone	1:10						6	9			
KUHNT, Irina	0:24						3	2			
CREMER, Melanie	0:59						3	3	1		
HENTSCHEL, Franziska	0:30	0/1		1/2	1/3		3	3	1		
PETERS, Kristina	1:10						4	5			
HAGENBAEUMER, Eva	1:10						2	4	2		
BECKER, Britta	0:55			0/1	0/1		6	3	1		
KELLER, Natascha	0:12										
SUXDORF, Philippa	1:10						2	8	1		
LAETZSCH, Heike	0:48	0/1			0/1		8		1		
KAUSCHKE, Katrin	1:04						3	1			
Totals		1/4	0/0	1/3	2/7	0	49	42	8	12	25

PRELIMINARIES   FINAL SCORE: NED 1   GBR 1   HALFTIME SCORE: NED 1   GBR 0

Team: NED Netherlands   Coach: van 'T HEK, Thomas

Names	Time played	FG	PS	PC	Total	Off	To	Int	Stl	PIC	25Y
TOXOPEUS, Jacqueline	1:10							1			
de HEIJ, Stella	0:00										
van de KIEFT, Fleur	0:19						1				
THATE, Carole	1:01						6	4	1		
KUIPERS, Ellen	0:53	0/1			0/1		6				
LEWIN, Jeannette	1:10	1/1			1/1		10	10	1		
KOOLEN, Nicky	0:41						3	5	1		
van den BOOGAARD, Dilliane	0:48						5	9			
TEEUWEN, Margje	0:49						1	5			
DONNERS, Myntje	0:55						8		1		
DUYSTER, Willemijn	1:10						2	1			
PLESMAN, Suzanne	0:24						2	1			
HOLSBOER, Noor	1:10						2	5	3		
STEENBERGHE, Florentine	0:54							3			
de RUITER, Wietske	0:40			0/3	0/3		1	1			
van der WIELEN, Suzan	0:41			0/1	0/1		2	1			
Totals		1/2	0/0	0/4	1/6	0	49	46	7	4	22

Umpires: BUCKLEY, Peri AUS   LEE, Mi KOR

Team: GBR Great Britain   Coach: SLOCOMBE, Susan

Names	Time played	FG	PS	PC	Total	Off	To	Int	Stl	PIC	25Y
THOMPSON, Joanne	0:00										
ROSE, Hilary	1:10								1		
COOK, Christine	1:12		1/1		1/1		2	1			
CULLEN, Tina	0:00										
BROWN, Karen	1:09						8	16	1		
ATKINS, Jill	1:10		0/1		0/1		4	11	3		
FRASER, Sue	1:03		0/1		0/1		7	5	1		
SIMPSON, Rhona	0:58	0/1			0/1		6				
NICHOLLS, Mandy	1:12						1	1			
SIXSMITH, Jane	0:29						8				
ROBERTSON, Pauline	0:56						9	8			
MOULD, Jo	0:00										
MILLER, Tammy	0:32						3				
BENNETT, Anna	0:55						1				
DAVIES, Mandy	1:10						1	6			
JOHNSON, Kathryn	1:10						6	7			
Totals		0/1	1/1	0/2	1/4	0	56	56	5	3	23

Women / *Dames*

PRELIMINARIES		FINAL SCORE:	AUS 7	ARG 1		HALFTIME SCORE:	AUS 3	ARG 0

Team: AUS Australia   Coach: CHARLESWORTH, Richard

Names	Time played	FG	PS	PC	Total	Off	To	Int	Stl	PIC	25Y
MAITLAND, Clover	0:05										
ROCHE, Danielle	0:19	1/1			1/1		6	3			
TOOTH, Liane	0:35						2				
ANNAN, Alyson	0:29	1/1	2/2		3/3		12	4			
HASLAM, Juliet	0:28						9	2	2		
MORRIS, Jennifer	0:35			0/1	0/1		7	1			
DOBSON, Louise	0:21						3	1	1		
POWELL, Lisa	0:20	1/2			1/2		5	1	1		
MARSDEN, Karen	0:00										
STARRE, Kate	0:18	0/1			0/1		3	2			
FARRELL, Renita	0:25	1/2			1/2		4	2	2		
PEREIRA, Jacqueline	0:00										
PERIS-KNEEBONE, Nova	0:35						3	3	3		
HAWKES, Rechelle	0:28	0/1			0/1		11	2	1		
POWELL, Katrina	0:25	1/4			1/4		5	1			
ANDREWS, Michelle	0:26	0/1			0/1		12				
Totals		5/13	2/2	0/1	7/16	0	80	24	10	20	50

Umpires: HEINRICHS, Carola GER   LARIO RUIZ, Angela ESP

Team: ARG Argentina   Coach: MENDOZA, Roldolfo

Names	Time played	FG	PS	PC	Total	Off	To	Int	Stl	PIC	25Y
ARNAL, Mariana	0:05										
MACKENZIE, Sofia	0:35		0/2		0/2		17	4	1		
AICEGA, Magdalena	0:35						11	6	1		
CORVALAN, Silvina	0:35						5	3	2		
GAMBERO, Ana	0:29	0/1			0/1		6	6			
CASTELLAN, Julieta	0:35						3	1	1		
PANDO, Danelotti	0:22						1				
SANCHEZ, Gabriela	0:35						9	1			
ONETO, Vanina	0:28						11	2	1		
RIMOLDI PUIG, Jorgelina	0:30	1/2			1/2		8	2			
MASOTTA, Karina	0:35						4				
CASTELLI, Maria Paula	0:24						2				
ARTICA, Veronica	0:00										
ROGNONI, Cecilia	0:00						8	2			
STEPNIK, Ayelen	0:00										
GONZALEZ, Mariana	0:04						3	2	2		
Totals		1/3	0/0	0/2	1/5	0	88	29	8	8	27

PRELIMINARIES		FINAL SCORE:	USA 3	KOR 2		HALFTIME SCORE:	USA 2	KOR 0

Team: USA United States of America   Coach: HIXON, Pamela

Names	Time played	FG	PS	PC	Total	Off	To	Int	Stl	PIC	25Y
SHEA, Patty	1:10						1				
MARTIN, Laurel	0:08						3	1			
TCHOU, Liz	0:57						5	5	1		
PANKRATZ, Marcia	0:46	1/1			1/1		2	3			
WERLEY, Cindy	0:49						5	1			
MADL, Diane	0:27	0/1			0/1	1	5	1			
FILLAT, Kris	1:10						4	4			
JAMES, Kelli	1:10	0/1			0/1	1	9	2			
FUCHS, Tracey	1:10	1/1	0/1		1/2		7	5			
LUCAS, Antoinette	0:01						2				
KAUFFMAN, Katie	0:18						1				
WIELAND, Andrea	0:00										
LYNESS, Leslie	1:10						8	5			
MAROIS, Barb	1:10			1/4	1/4		11	13	1		
REEVE, Jill	1:10						8	6			
BUSTIN, Pamela	1:10						3	5	2		
Totals		2/4	0/1	1/4	3/9	2	71	54	4	8	19

Umpires: KATO, Naomi JPN   LANNING, Maragret CAN

Team: KOR Korea   Coach: CHOI, Song-Ryul

Names	Time played	FG	PS	PC	Total	Off	To	Int	Stl	PIC	25Y
YOU, Jae-Sook	1:10										
CHOI, Eun-Kyung	1:10						3	1			
CHO, Eun-Jung	1:10			0/5	0/5		8	5	1		
OH, Seung-Shin	0:09			0/1	0/1		1	1			
LIM, Jeong-Sook	0:51						3	1	2		
KIM, Myung-Ok	1:10						1	3	1		
CHANG, Eun-Jung	1:02	1/1		0/3	1/4		10	4	1		
LEE, Ji-Young	1:08						6	1			
LEE, Eun-Kyung	1:04	1/2		0/1	1/3		2		1		
KOWN, Soo-Hyun	1:04	0/2			0/2	1	5	1	1		
WOO, Hyun-Jung	0:00										
CHOI, Mi-Soon	0:17	0/1			0/1				1		
LEE, Eun-Young	0:42						2	3	1		
JEON, Young-Sun	0:43						2	4	1		
KWON, Chang-Sook	1:05			0/1	0/1		5	2			
JIN, Deok-San	0:00										
Totals		2/6	0/0	0/11	2/17	1	48	26	10	17	38

PRELIMINARIES		FINAL SCORE:	AUS 1	GER 0		HALFTIME SCORE:	AUS 1	GER 0

Team: AUS Australia   Coach: CHARLESWORTH, Richard

Names	Time played	FG	PS	PC	Total	Off	To	Int	Stl	PIC	25Y
MAITLAND, Clover	0:00										
ROCHE, Danielle	0:40	1/1			1/1		2	2			
TOOTH, Liane	1:10						7	1			
ANNAN, Alyson	0:53			0/1	0/1	1	5	2			
HASLAM, Juliet	0:52						2	3			
MORRIS, Jennifer	1:10			0/4	0/4		10	3	1		
DOBSON, Louise	0:34						2	1			
POWELL, Lisa	0:50						8				
MARSDEN, Karen	1:10						1				
STARRE, Kate	0:52						5	3			
FARRELL, Renita	0:54						5	2	1		
PEREIRA, Jacqueline	0:00										
PERIS-KNEEBONE, Nova	1:01						3	3			
HAWKES, Rechelle	0:59	0/2			0/2		5				
POWELL, Katrina	0:57	0/1			0/1		9	4			
ANDREWS, Michelle	0:41			0/1	0/1		4	1			
Totals		1/4	0/0	0/6	1/10	1	68	25	2	12	40

Umpires: LEE, Mi KOR   SPITALERI, Gina ITA

Team: GER Germany   Coach: RAUTH, Berthold

Names	Time played	FG	PS	PC	Total	Off	To	Int	Stl	PIC	25Y
WOLLSCHLAGER, Susanne	1:10										
BEYER, Birgit	0:00										
SCHMORANZER van KOOPEREN	0:39						2	1			
DICKENSCHEID, Tanja	0:45					1	5	1	1		
ERNSTING-KRIENKE, Nadine	0:56	0/1			0/1		5	2	1		
THOMASCHINSKI, Simone	1:09						7	3	1		
KUHNT, Irina	0:19						3	2			
CREMER, Melanie	0:59			0/1	0/1		4				
HENTSCHEL, Franziska	0:47			0/1	0/1		4	2			
PETERS, Kristina	1:10						11	7			
HAGENBAEUMER, Eva	1:10						8	2			
BECKER, Britta	0:59						4	1	1		
KELLER, Natascha	0:17							1			
SUXDORF, Philippa	1:10						6	1	1		
LAETZSCH, Heike	0:51						4				
KAUSCHKE, Katrin	0:25						1				
Totals		0/1	0/0	0/2	0/3	1	64	23	5	6	18

Women / *Dames*

PRELIMINARIES — FINAL SCORE: ESP 0 ARG 1 — HALFTIME SCORE: ESP 0 ARG 0

Team: ESP Spain — Coach: BRASSA, José

Names	Time played	FG	PS	PC	Total	Off	To	Int	Stl	PIC	25Y
CARRION, Elena	0:00										
DORADO, Natalia	1:07		0/3		0/3		4	2	2		
GONZALEZ, Maria Cruz	1:05						4	5	2		
BAREA, Carmen	1:10						11	6	4		
MANRIQUE, Silvia	0:22						1	1	1		
GABELLANES, Nagore	0:49						2				
MOTOS, Teresa	0:46						6				
BARRIO, Sonia	1:04		0/1		0/1		5	1	1		
RUEDA, Monica	0:10						1	1			
LOPEZ, Luci	0:22						2				
FEITO, Mar	0:29						2				
TELLERIA, Maider	1:10						8	6	2		
URQUIZU, Elena	1:00						3	1	1		
LARZABAL, Bego	1:04						3	1	1		
de IGNACIO-SIMO, Sonia	0:56	0/1		0/1			5	2			
GONZALEZ, Maria Victoria	1:10										
Totals		0/1	0/0	0/4	0/5	0	55	28	14	8	26

Umpires: van GEMERT, Miriam NED   McDONALD, Janice GBR

Team: ARG Argentina — Coach: MENDOZA, Roldolfo

Names	Time played	FG	PS	PC	Total	Off	To	Int	Stl	PIC	25Y
ARNAL, Mariana	0:00										
MACKENZIE, Sofia	1:09		0/1		0/1		10	3	3		
AICEGA, Magdalena	1:10						5	2	2		
CORVALAN, Silvia	1:10						4	1	1		
GAMBERO, Ana	1:04						3	4	1		
CASTELLAN, Julieta	1:10						5	4			
PANDO, Danelotti	0:58						3	1	1		
SANCHEZ, Gabriela	1:08	0/2			0/2		3	7	4		
ONETO, Vanina	0:54	0/4			0/4		5				
RIMOLDI PUIG, Jorgelina	0:56	1/1			1/1	1	9	6			
MASOTTA, Karina	1:09	0/2			0/2		5		2		
CASTELLI, Maria Paula	0:24	0/1			0/1		5		2		
ARTICA, Veronica	1:10							1			
ROGNONI, Cecilia	0:11		0/1		0/1						
STEPNIK, Ayelen	0:09										
GONZALEZ, Mariana	0:03										
Totals		1/10	0/0	0/2	1/12	1	57	29	16	14	36

PRELIMINARIES — FINAL SCORE: NED 1 KOR 3 — HALFTIME SCORE: NED 0 KOR 0

Team: NED Netherlands — Coach: van `T HEK, Thomas

Names	Time played	FG	PS	PC	Total	Off	To	Int	Stl	PIC	25Y
TOXOPEUS, Jacqueline	1:10										
de HEIJ, Stella	0:00										
van de KIEFT, Fleur	0:49						1	3			
THATE, Carole	0:36						4	1	1		
KUIPERS, Ellen	1:10						1	6		1	
LEWIN, Jeannette	1:00	0/1		0/1	0/2		5	4	1		
KOOLEN, Nicky	0:46						1	1			
van den BOOGAARD, Dilliane	1:10						3	7	1		
TEEUWEN, Margje	0:26						2	4			
DONNERS, Myntje	0:52	0/1			0/1		11	1			
DUYSTER, Willemijn	1:10						2		1		
PLESMAN, Suzanne	0:56						1				
HOLSBOER, Noor	1:10						4	12	4		
STEENBERGHE, Florentine	0:46							3			
de RUITER, Wietske	0:28			1/3	1/3		4		1		
van der WIELEN, Suzan	0:15						2	5			
Totals		0/2	0/0	1/4	1/6	2	45	41	10	5	26

Umpires: CHATAS, Renee USA   CLARKE, Gillian GBR

Team: KOR Korea — Coach: CHOI, Song-Ryul

Names	Time played	FG	PS	PC	Total	Off	To	Int	Stl	PIC	25Y
YOU, Jae-Sook	1:10							3			
CHOI, Eun-Kyung	1:10						3	5			
CHO, Eun-Jung	1:10			1/2	1/2		7	15			
OH, Seung-Shin	0:00										
LIM, Jeong-Sook	0:19						1	5	1		
KIM, Myung-Ok	1:10						4	6	2		
CHANG, Eun-Jung	1:10	1/3		1/1	2/4		7				
LEE, Ji-Young	0:58						7				
LEE, Eun-Kyung	1:09						6				
KOWN, Soo-Hyun	1:10						6	2			
WOO, Hyun-Jung	0:00										
CHOI, Mi-Soon	0:11						1				
LEE, Eun-Young	1:02						3	1			
JEON, Young-Sun	0:57						3	1			
KWON, Chang-Sook	1:10						2	14	3		
JIN, Deok-San	0:00										
Totals		1/3	0/0	2/3	3/6	0	50	52	6	16	31

PRELIMINARIES — FINAL SCORE: USA 0 GBR 1 — HALFTIME SCORE: USA 0 GBR 0

Team: USA United States of America — Coach: HIXON, Pamela

Names	Time played	FG	PS	PC	Total	Off	To	Int	Stl	PIC	25Y
SHEA, Patty	1:10							1			
MARTIN, Laurel	0:00	0/1			0/1						
TCHOU, Liz	0:02										
PANKRATZ, Marcia	1:10						5	2	2		
WERLEY, Cindy	0:54						1				
MADL, Diane	0:10						1				
FILLAT, Kris	1:08						7	3			
JAMES, Kelli	1:10	0/2			0/2		6				
FUCHS, Tracey	1:10			0/1	0/1		9	2			
LUCAS, Antoinette	1:10			0/2	0/2		3	7			
KAUFFMAN, Katie	0:00										
WIELAND, Andrea	0:00										
LYNESS, Leslie	1:10						4				
MAROIS, Barb	1:10			0/2	0/2		5	17			
REEVE, Jill	1:10						4	4			
BUSTIN, Pamela	1:10						4	8	2		
Totals		0/3	0/0	0/5	0/8	0	49	44	4	4	20

Umpires: CRESPO, Laura ARG   YASUEDA, Kazuko JPN

Team: GBR Great Britain — Coach: SLOCOMBE, Susan

Names	Time played	FG	PS	PC	Total	Off	To	Int	Stl	PIC	25Y
THOMPSON, Joanne	0:00										
ROSE, Hilary	1:10							1			
COOK, Christine	0:28						6				
CULLEN, Tina	0:14					1	5	2	1		
BROWN, Karen	0:48						2	9			
ATKINS, Jill	1:10						1	3			
FRASER, Sue	1:10			0/1	0/1		3	7			
SIMPSON, Rhona	0:44	1/2			1/2		4				
NICHOLLS, Mandy	0:40	0/1			0/1		6	1			
SIXSMITH, Jane	0:44	0/2			0/2		5	2			
ROBERTSON, Pauline	0:56						8	4			
MOULD, Jo	0:00										
MILLER, Tammy	0:56						2	5	1		
BENNETT, Anna	0:48	0/1			0/1		5	1	1		
DAVIES, Mandy	1:10	0/1			0/1		9				
JOHNSON, Kathryn	1:10						4	5	1		
Totals		1/7	0/0	0/1	1/8	1	51	49	4	12	34

Women / *Dames*

| PRELIMINARIES | FINAL SCORE: | ESP 2 | GBR 2 | | HALFTIME SCORE: | ESP 1 | GBR 1 |

Team: ESP Spain — Coach: BRASSA, José

Names	Time played	FG	PS	PC	Total	Off	To	Int	Stl	PIC	25Y
CARRION, Elena	0:00										
DORADO, Natalia	1:06		1/3	1/3			4	6	1		
GONZALEZ, Maria Cruz	1:07						11	5	2		
BAREA, Carmen	1:10						13	4			
MANRIQUE, Silvia	0:03										
GABELLANES, Nagore	0:37		1/1	1/1			1		1		
MOTOS, Teresa	0:21						1		1		
BARRIO, Sonia	1:04		0/2	0/2			3		1		
RUEDA, Monica	0:10										
LOPEZ, Luci	1:07						2	2			
FEITO, Mar	0:31						3				
TELLERIA, Maider	0:59	0/1		0/1			2	5	1		
URQUIZU, Elena	1:07						3		3		
LARZABAL, Bego	1:10	0/1		0/1			5	3	2		
de IGNACIO-SIMO, Sonia	1:10						6	3	3		
GONZALEZ, Maria Victoria	1:10										
Totals		0/2	0/0	2/6	2/8	0	54	28	15	5	20

Umpires: CHATAS, Renee USA   LEE, Mi KOR

Team: GBR Great Britain — Coach: SLOCOMBE, Susan

Names	Time played	FG	PS	PC	Total	Off	To	Int	Stl	PIC	25Y
THOMPSON, Joanne	0:00										
ROSE, Hilary	1:10										
COOK, Christine	0:42						3	3	1		
CULLEN, Tina	0:39	0/1		0/1			2	1	1		
BROWN, Karen	1:08						12	6			
ATKINS, Jill	1:10						3	3	2		
FRASER, Sue	1:10		1/4	1/4			5	4			
SIMPSON, Rhona	0:39						3		1		
NICHOLLS, Mandy	0:43	0/1		0/1			4	1			
SIXSMITH, Jane	0:49						3	8	1		
ROBERTSON, Pauline	0:52						5	2	1		
MOULD, Jo	0:05						1		1		
MILLER, Tammy	0:56						1	1	1		
BENNETT, Anna	0:35						1	8	2		
DAVIES, Mandy	1:01						2	4	1		
JOHNSON, Kathryn	1:04	1/1	0/2	1/3			5	7	3		
Totals		1/3	0/0	1/6	2/9	4	62	34	14	10	33

| PRELIMINARIES | FINAL SCORE: | NED 4 | GER 3 | | HALFTIME SCORE: | NED 2 | GER 1 |

Team: NED Netherlands — Coach: van 'T HEK, Thomas

Names	Time played	FG	PS	PC	Total	Off	To	Int	Stl	PIC	25Y
TOXOPEUS, Jacqueline	1:10							1			
de HEIJ, Stella	0:00										
van de KIEFT, Fleur	0:22						3				
THATE, Carole	1:10						3	6	1		
KUIPERS, Ellen	0:55	1/2		1/2			1	1			
LEWIN, Jeannette	0:51						5	6			
KOOLEN, Nicky	0:22						3				
van den BOOGAARD, Dilliane	1:10						8	8			
TEEUWEN, Margje	1:07	0/1		0/1			3	8	1		
DONNERS, Myntje	0:44	1/1	1/1	2/2			5				
DUYSTER, Willemijn	0:54						1	2	1		
PLESMAN, Suzanne	0:07						1				
HOLSBOER, Noor	1:09						2	12	2		
STEENBERGHE, Florentine	1:10						2	4			
de RUITER, Wietske	0:43		1/3	1/3			3	1			
van der WIELEN, Suzan	0:46						3	3			
Totals		2/4	1/1	1/3	4/8	0	43	52	5	12	34

Umpires: CRESPO, Laura ARG   LANNING, Margaret CAN

Team: GER Germany — Coach: RAUTH, Berthold

Names	Time played	FG	PS	PC	Total	Off	To	Int	Stl	PIC	25Y
WOLLSCHLAGER, Susanne	1:10										
BEYER, Birgit	0:00										
SCHMORANZER van KOOPEREN	0:07										
DICKENSCHEID, Tanja	1:00		0/1	0/1			3				
ERNSTING-KRIENKE, Nadine	0:57						2	2	1		
THOMASCHINSKI, Simone	1:10						2	8	2		
KUHNT, Irina	0:17										
CREMER, Melanie	0:49		1/1	1/1			7	3			
HENTSCHEL, Franziska	0:33		0/2	0/2			2	4	1		
PETERS, Kristina	1:09						9	9	1		
HAGENBAEUMER, Eva	1:10						2	5			
BECKER, Britta	1:03		2/2	2/2			1	4			
KELLER, Natascha	0:17						4				
SUXDORF, Philippa	1:10						5	9			
LAETZSCH, Heike	0:52						4	2			
KAUSCHKE, Katrin	0:59						1	2			
Totals		0/0	2/2	1/4	3/6	0	42	48	5	4	27

| PRELIMINARIES | FINAL SCORE: | AUS 3 | KOR 3 | | HALFTIME SCORE: | AUS 2 | KOR 0 |

Team: AUS Australia — Coach: CHARLESWORTH, Richard

Names	Time played	FG	PS	PC	Total	Off	To	Int	Stl	PIC	25Y
MAITLAND, Clover	0:35										
ROCHE, Danielle	0:26						4	1			
TOOTH, Liane	1:10						4	6	1		
ANNAN, Alyson	0:56	1/2		1/2			2	1	3		
HASLAM, Juliet	0:47										
MORRIS, Jennifer	1:10		1/5	1/5			2	7			
DOBSON, Louise	0:38						2	4	1		
POWELL, Lisa	0:34						1		3		
MARSDEN, Karen	0:35										
STARRE, Kate	0:56							3			
FARRELL, Renita	0:55						2	3	2		
PEREIRA, Jacqueline	0:31	0/1		0/1			2		2		
PERIS-KNEEBONE, Nova	0:55						4	6	3		
HAWKES, Rechelle	1:04	0/1		0/1			4	1	2		
POWELL, Katrina	0:45	1/3		1/3			4	2	3		
ANDREWS, Michelle	0:47	0/2	0/1	0/3			2		1		
Totals		2/9	0/0	1/6	3/15	0	33	34	21	20	45

Umpires: CLARKE, Gillian GBR   LARIO RUIZ, Angela ESP

Team: KOR Korea — Coach: CHOI, Song-Ryul

Names	Time played	FG	PS	PC	Total	Off	To	Int	Stl	PIC	25Y
YOU, Jae-Sook	1:10										
CHOI, Eun-Kyung	1:10						5	9	2		
CHO, Eun-Jung	1:10		1/2	1/2			5	8			
OH, Seung-Shin	0:04										
LIM, Jeong-Sook	0:57						1	3	1		
KIM, Myung-Ok	1:10						5	7			
CHANG, Eun-Jung	1:10	1/2	1/3	2/5			6	1	2		
LEE, Ji-Young	1:09	0/1		0/1			8	2			
LEE, Eun-Kyung	0:55		0/1	0/1			4				
KOWN, Soo-Hyun	1:08						2	2	1		
WOO, Hyun-Jung	0:00										
CHOI, Mi-Soon	0:12						1	2			
LEE, Eun-Young	0:48						3	5	1		
JEON, Young-Sun	0:34						1	1	1		
KWON, Chang-Sook	1:10		0/1	0/1			1	13	3		
JIN, Deok-San	0:00										
Totals		1/3	0/0	2/7	3/10	0	42	53	11	12	34

Women / Dames

PRELIMINARIES — FINAL SCORE: USA 1 ARG 2 — HALFTIME SCORE: USA 1 ARG 1

Team: USA United States of America — Coach: HIXON, Pamela

Names	Time played	FG	PS	PC	Total	Off	To	Int	Stl	PIC	25Y
SHEA, Patty	1:10							1			
MARTIN, Laurel	0:21	0/1			0/1		2				
TCHOU, Liz	0:06			0/1	0/1						
PANKRATZ, Marcia	0:57						4				
WERLEY, Cindy	0:46	0/1			0/1		2				
MADL, Diane	0:30						2				
FILLAT, Kris	1:09						7	5	1		
JAMES, Kelli	0:59						4				
FUCHS, Tracey	1:10						4	2	2		
LUCAS, Antoinette	1:10						5	6	1		
KAUFFMAN, Katie	0:00										
WIELAND, Andrea	0:00										
LYNESS, Leslie	1:10						3	4	4		
MAROIS, Barb	1:10			1/8	1/8		5	9	1		
REEVE, Jill	1:05						5	7	2		
BUSTIN, Pamela	1:03						1	2	2		
Totals		0/2	0/0	1/9	1/11	0	44	36	13	8	34

Umpires: BUCKLEY, Peri AUS — HEINRICHS, Carola GER

Team: ARG Argentina — Coach: MENDOZA, Roldolfo

Names	Time played	FG	PS	PC	Total	Off	To	Int	Stl	PIC	25Y
ARNAL, Mariana	0:00										
MACKENZIE, Sofia	1:10			1/2	1/2		11	11	1		
AICEGA, Magdalena	1:10						2	4			
CORVALAN, Silvina	0:39						4	1			
GAMBERO, Ana	1:10						1	6	2		
CASTELLAN, Julieta	1:09						5	1	3		
PANDO, Danelotti	0:51							2			
SANCHEZ, Gabriela	1:07						2	4			
ONETO, Vanina	0:48						4	1			
RIMOLDI PUIG, Jorgelina	0:56	0/2			0/2		3	3	4		
MASOTTA, Karina	1:10	0/2		1/1	1/3		5	2	1		
CASTELLI, Maria Paula	0:20						2		1		
ARTICA, Veronica	1:10										
ROGNONI, Cecilia	0:34	0/1		0/1	0/2		3	2	3		
STEPNIK, Ayelen	0:03	0/1			0/1						
GONZALEZ, Mariana	0:28						2	1			
Totals		0/6	0/0	2/4	2/10	0	44	38	15	9	18

PRELIMINARIES — FINAL SCORE: USA 1 GER 1 — HALFTIME SCORE: USA 0 GER 1

Team: USA United States of America — Coach: HIXON, Pamela

Names	Time played	FG	PS	PC	Total	Off	To	Int	Stl	PIC	25Y
SHEA, Patty	1:10							1			
MARTIN, Laurel	0:10						2	1			
TCHOU, Liz	0:11						2				
PANKRATZ, Marcia	1:00						2	1	1		
WERLEY, Cindy	0:50	1/1			1/1	1	5	3	1		
MADL, Diane	0:18						1		1		
FILLAT, Kris	1:09	0/1			0/1		6	5	2		
JAMES, Kelli	1:01						8	1			
FUCHS, Tracey	1:08						7	3	2		
LUCAS, Antoinette	1:09						6	1	1		
KAUFFMAN, Katie	0:20										
WIELAND, Andrea	0:00										
LYNESS, Leslie	1:01						7	3			
MAROIS, Barb	1:10			0/1	0/1		9	7	1		
REEVE, Jill	1:10						7	6	3		
BUSTIN, Pamela	0:56						3	4	2		
Totals		1/2	0/0	0/1	1/3	1	63	38	14	6	37

Umpires: YASUEDA, Kazuko JPN — McDONALD, Janice GBR

Team: GER Germany — Coach: RAUTH, Berthold

Names	Time played	FG	PS	PC	Total	Off	To	Int	Stl	PIC	25Y
WOLLSCHLAGER, Susanne	1:10										
BEYER, Birgit	0:00										
SCHMORANZER van KOOPEREN	1:06						1	4	2		
DICKENSCHEID, Tanja	0:44	0/1			0/1	1	6	1			
ERNSTING-KRIENKE, Nadine	0:22						5	4			
THOMASCHINSKI, Simone	0:35						3	7			
KUHNT, Irina	0:10						2				
CREMER, Melanie	0:35	1/2			1/2		4	3	1		
HENTSCHEL, Franziska	0:12	0/1		0/5	0/6		4	2	1		
PETERS, Kristina	0:35						8	4			
HAGENBAEUMER, Eva	0:35						2	1			
BECKER, Britta	0:29						4	2			
KELLER, Natascha	0:10	0/1			0/1		1	1			
SUXDORF, Philippa	0:35						3	3			
LAETZSCH, Heike	0:21	0/1			0/1		2	6			
KAUSCHKE, Katrin	0:31						5	2			
Totals		1/6	0/0	0/5	1/11	2	52	38	3	12	26

PRELIMINARIES — FINAL SCORE: AUS 1 GBR 0 — HALFTIME SCORE: AUS 1 GBR 0

Team: AUS Australia — Coach: CHARLESWORTH, Richard

Names	Time played	FG	PS	PC	Total	Off	To	Int	Stl	PIC	25Y
MAITLAND, Clover	0:34										
ROCHE, Danielle	0:34					2	4	2			
TOOTH, Liane	1:10						7	1			
ANNAN, Alyson	0:48	0/2		0/1	0/3		4	4			
HASLAM, Juliet	0:35					1	3	1	1		
MORRIS, Jennifer	1:10		0/4		0/4		2	9			
DOBSON, Louise	0:37						7	3	2		
POWELL, Lisa	0:38					1	3	1	1		
MARSDEN, Karen	0:35						1	2			
STARRE, Kate	0:45						2	6			
FARRELL, Renita	0:59			0/1	0/1		2	5			
PEREIRA, Jacqueline	0:49					1	6	1			
PERIS-KNEEBONE, Nova	1:08						5	2	4		
HAWKES, Rechelle	0:51						5	1			
POWELL, Katrina	0:51	0/1			0/1		6	2	1		
ANDREWS, Michelle	0:40	1/1		0/2	1/3		2				
Totals		1/4	0/0	0/8	1/12	5	52	46	10	15	46

Umpires: KATO, Naomi JPN — van GEMERT, Miriam NED

Team: GBR Great Britain — Coach: SLOCOMBE, Susan

Names	Time played	FG	PS	PC	Total	Off	To	Int	Stl	PIC	25Y
THOMPSON, Joanne	0:00										
ROSE, Hilary	1:10										
COOK, Christine	0:35						1				
CULLEN, Tina	0:46						3	2			
BROWN, Karen	0:58						3	8	1		
ATKINS, Jill	1:10						1	10	2		
FRASER, Sue	1:10						15	6	2		
SIMPSON, Rhona	0:37						3	1			
NICHOLLS, Mandy	0:39	0/1			0/1		1		1		
SIXSMITH, Jane	0:45						4	2			
ROBERTSON, Pauline	0:57						5	1			
MOULD, Jo	0:11						1				
MILLER, Tammy	0:48						2				
BENNETT, Anna	0:39						3		1		
DAVIES, Mandy	1:09						2	7			
JOHNSON, Kathryn	1:10						4	5			
Totals		0/1	0/0	0/0	0/1	0	46	44	7	8	23

Hockey / Hockey

Women / Dames

PRELIMINARIES

FINAL SCORE: ESP 0 KOR 2   **HALFTIME SCORE: ESP 0 KOR 1**

Team: ESP Spain — Coach: BRASSA, José

Names	Time played	FG	PS	PC	Total	Off	To	Int	Stl	PIC	25Y
CARRION, Elena	0:00										
DORADO, Natalia	1:05		0/2	0/2			2	5			
GONZALEZ, Maria Cruz	1:09						3	3	1		
BAREA, Carmen	1:10						6	11			
MANRIQUE, Silvia	0:51						3	1	1		
GABELLANES, Nagore	0:29						2	3			
MOTOS, Teresa	0:59	0/1		0/1			7		2		
BARRIO, Sonia	0:54	0/2	0/2	0/4				1			
RUEDA, Monica	0:19										
LOPEZ, Luci	0:06										
FEITO, Mar	0:23						2				
TELLERIA, Maider	0:49						3	5	1		
URQUIZU, Elena	1:01						5	1			
LARZABAL, Bego	1:10	0/1		0/1			2	6			
de IGNACIO-SIMO, Sonia	1:06						7	8	1		
GONZALEZ, Maria Victoria	1:10						1				
Totals		0/4	0/0	0/4	0/8	0	42	45	6	5	32

Umpires: BUCKLEY, Peri AUS   HEINRICHS, Carola GER

Team: KOR Korea — Coach: CHOI, Song-Ryul

Names	Time played	FG	PS	PC	Total	Off	To	Int	Stl	PIC	25Y
YOU, Jae-Sook	1:10						1	1			
CHOI, Eun-Kyung	0:55						6		2		
CHO, Eun-Jung	1:10		0/2	0/2			3	12			
OH, Seung-Shin	0:15						2				
LIM, Jeong-Sook	1:10						4	5			
KIM, Myung-Ok	1:10						9	5			
CHANG, Eun-Jung	1:10		1/3	1/3			3	4	1		
LEE, Ji-Young	1:05	0/2		0/2	1		5	1			
LEE, Eun-Kyung	0:37		0/1	0/1			4	1			
KOWN, Soo-Hyun	0:52						8	1	1		
WOO, Hyun-Jung	0:05	0/1		0/1			2	1			
CHOI, Mi-Soon	0:37	0/3		0/3			1	1	1		
LEE, Eun-Young	0:55	1/1		1/1				1			
JEON, Young-Sun	0:26						3	2			
KWON, Chang-Sook	1:10						1	3	1		
JIN, Deok-San	0:00										
Totals		1/7	0/0	1/3	2/13	1	44	46	6	16	46

PRELIMINARIES

FINAL SCORE: NED 4 ARG 1   **HALFTIME SCORE: NED 2 ARG 0**

Team: NED Netherlands — Coach: van `T HEK, Thomas

Names	Time played	FG	PS	PC	Total	Off	To	Int	Stl	PIC	25Y
TOXOPEUS, Jacqueline	1:10										
de HEIJ, Stella	0:00										
van de KIEFT, Fleur	0:24	0/1		0/1			3				
THATE, Carole	1:10	0/1		0/1			6	1	3		
KUIPERS, Ellen	0:47						6				
LEWIN, Jeannette	1:10						8	8	2		
KOOLEN, Nicky	0:49						2	2			
van den BOOGAARD, Dilliane	1:10						1	5	2		
TEEUWEN, Margje	1:02	0/2		0/2			7	9			
DONNERS, Myntje	0:46		1/1	1/1			11	1			
DUYSTER, Willemijn	0:20										
PLESMAN, Suzanne	0:06						1		2		
HOLSBOER, Noor	1:10						3	7			
STEENBERGHE, Florentine	1:10						4	1			
de RUITER, Wietske	0:55	3/4		0/1	3/5	1	7	1	1		
van der WIELEN, Suzan	0:37						1	1			
Totals		3/8	1/1	0/1	4/10	1	58	36	12	13	36

Umpires: LARIO RUIZ, Angela ESP   SPITARELI, Gina ITA

Team: ARG Argentina — Coach: MENDOZA, Roldolfo

Names	Time played	FG	PS	PC	Total	Off	To	Int	Stl	PIC	25Y
ARNAL, Mariana	0:00										
MACKENZIE, Sofia	1:10		0/5	0/5			5	6			
AICEGA, Magdalena	1:10						6	2			
CORVALAN, Silvina	0:49						2	5			
GAMBERO, Ana	1:10								2		
CASTELLAN, Julieta	1:10						2	2			
PANDO, Danelotti	0:50						2				
SANCHEZ, Gabriela	1:10						3	2			
ONETO, Vanina	1:06		0/1	0/1			10	1	2		
RIMOLDI PUIG, Jorgelina	1:05						5	2			
MASOTTA, Karina	1:10		1/1	1/1			2		1		
CASTELLI, Maria Paula	0:23								1		
ARTICA, Veronica	1:10							1			
ROGNONI, Cecilia	0:20						4	1	2		
STEPNIK, Ayelen	0:00										
GONZALEZ, Mariana	0:04										
Totals		0/0	1/1	0/6	1/7	0	41	22	8	8	34

PRELIMINARIES

FINAL SCORE: GER 2 GBR 3   **HALFTIME SCORE: GER 1 GBR 0**

Team: GER Germany — Coach: RAUTH, Berthold

Names	Time played	FG	PS	PC	Total	Off	To	Int	Stl	PIC	25Y
WOLLSCHLAGER, Susanne	1:10						2	1			
BEYER, Birgit	0:00										
SCHMORANZER van KOOPEREN	0:31						5				
DICKENSCHEID, Tanja	0:39	0/1		0/1	0/2	1	4				
ERNSTING-KRIENKE, Nadine	0:44	0/1		0/1			9				
THOMASCHINSKI, Simone	1:10						4	4			
KUHNT, Irina	0:21					1	1				
CREMER, Melanie	0:54		0/1	0/1			3	1			
HENTSCHEL, Franziska	0:30		1/2	1/2			1	4	1		
PETERS, Kristina	1:10						3				
HAGENBAEUMER, Eva	1:09						3	2	2		
BECKER, Britta	0:58		1/1	1/1			5	1	2		
KELLER, Natascha	0:24	0/1		0/1			2	1			
SUXDORF, Philippa	1:10						2	5			
LAETZSCH, Heike	0:49						2	3	2		
KAUSCHKE, Katrin	1:07	0/1		0/1			3	2			
Totals		0/4	1/1	1/4	2/9	2	49	24	7	8	27

Umpires: CRESPO, Laura ARG   van GEMERT, Miriam NED

Team: GBR Great Britain — Coach: SLOCOMBE, Susan

Names	Time played	FG	PS	PC	Total	Off	To	Int	Stl	PIC	25Y
THOMPSON, Joanne	0:00										
ROSE, Hilary	1:10							1			
COOK, Christine	0:36						1				
CULLEN, Tina	0:32						7	1			
BROWN, Karen	1:08						2	3	1		
ATKINS, Jill	1:10		2/3	2/3			1	1			
FRASER, Sue	0:41		0/2	0/2			1				
SIMPSON, Rhona	0:32	0/2		0/2			6				
NICHOLLS, Mandy	0:52	0/1		0/1	0/2			7	2		
SIXSMITH, Jane	0:55	1/1		1/1	1/1	1	11				
ROBERTSON, Pauline	1:02						2	5			
MOULD, Jo	0:16										
MILLER, Tammy	0:57						3	2	1		
BENNETT, Anna	0:37						5		1		
DAVIES, Mandy	1:07						3	7	2		
JOHNSON, Kathryn	1:10						6	9			
Totals		1/4	0/0	2/6	3/10	1	54	31	6	9	33

Women / Dames

PRELIMINARIES FINAL SCORE: AUS 4 USA 0

Team: AUS Australia — Coach: CHARLESWORTH, Richard

Names	Time played	FG	PS	PC	Total	Off	To	Int	Stl	PIC	25Y
MAITLAND, Clover	1:01										
ROCHE, Danielle	0:43	0/1			0/1			5			
TOOTH, Liane	0:59						1	5			
ANNAN, Alyson	0:51	0/1		0/2	0/3		4	3	3		
HASLAM, Juliet	0:56	0/1			0/1		5	2	1		
MORRIS, Jennifer	1:10			1/2	1/2		2	5	3		
DOBSON, Louise	0:46			0/1	0/1		5	4			
POWELL, Lisa	0:46	1/1			1/1	1	2	2			
MARSDEN, Karen	0:08										
STARRE, Kate	0:46	1/1			1/1		3	2	2		
FARRELL, Renita	0:51			0/2	0/2		2	8			
PEREIRA, Jacqueline	0:46	0/3			0/3	1	1	2	1		
PERIS-KNEEBONE, Nova	0:47						4	5	2		
HAWKES, Rechelle	0:40						4	2	1		
POWELL, Katrina	0:40	1/1			1/1		3	2	2		
ANDREWS, Michelle	0:53	0/1		0/1	0/2	1	5	3			
Totals		3/10	0/0	1/8	4/18	3	41	50	15	26	51

Umpires: CLARKE, Gillian GBR   YASUEDA, Kazuko JPN

HALFTIME SCORE: AUS 4 USA 0

Team: USA United States of America — Coach: HIXON, Pamela

Names	Time played	FG	PS	PC	Total	Off	To	Int	Stl	PIC	25Y
SHEA, Patty	0:35						1				
MARTIN, Laurel	0:04							2			
TCHOU, Liz	0:01										
PANKRATZ, Marcia	0:49						2				
WERLEY, Cindy	0:44						1	1			
MADL, Diane	0:21						1	1	2		
FILLAT, Kris	0:41						4	3	1		
JAMES, Kelli	1:02						2	1			
FUCHS, Tracey	1:10						3	4			
LUCAS, Antoinette	1:10						4	2			
KAUFFMAN, Katie	1:04						4	5	5		
WIELAND, Andrea	0:35							1			
LYNESS, Leslie	1:10			0/1	0/1		6	4	2		
MAROIS, Barb	1:10						12	14	2		
REEVE, Jill	1:10						4	5	1		
BUSTIN, Pamela	1:00						2	3	1		
Totals		0/0	0/0	0/1	0/1	0	46	46	14	5	16

PRELIMINARIES FINAL SCORE: ESP 2 NED 4

Team: ESP Spain — Coach: BRASSA, José

Names	Time played	FG	PS	PC	Total	Off	To	Int	Stl	PIC	25Y
CARRION, Elena	1:10						1	1			
DORADO, Natalia	1:10			0/4	0/4		4	3	1		
GONZALEZ, Maria Cruz	0:45						4	1	1		
BAREA, Carmen	1:10						9	6			
MANRIQUE, Silvia	0:21						1				
GABELLANES, Nagore	0:46	0/2			0/2						
MOTOS, Teresa	0:27						1	1			
BARRIO, Sonia	1:03	0/1		1/1	1/2		4	1	1		
RUEDA, Monica	0:10										
LOPEZ, Luci	0:42	1/1			1/1		4	1	1		
FEITO, Mar	0:33						2				
TELLERIA, Maider	1:00						1	2	1		
URQUIZU, Elena	1:08						1	4			
LARZABAL, Bego	1:10						5	1			
de IGNACIO-SIMO, Sonia	1:10						8	3	1		
GONZALEZ, Maria Victoria	0:00										
Totals		1/4	0/0	1/5	2/9	0	45	24	6	8	27

Umpires: KATO, Naomi JPN   LEE, Mi KOR

HALFTIME SCORE: ESP 1 NED 3

Team: NED Netherlands — Coach: van 'T HEK, Thomas

Names	Time played	FG	PS	PC	Total	Off	To	Int	Stl	PIC	25Y
TOXOPEUS, Jacqueline	1:10										
de HEIJ, Stella	0:02										
van de KIEFT, Fleur	0:20						1		1		
THATE, Carole	1:00	1/1			1/1		7	4			
KUIPERS, Ellen	0:52					1	6	1			
LEWIN, Jeannette	1:03					1	7	7	1		
KOOLEN, Nicky	1:10						2	4			
van den BOOGAARD, Dilliane	1:07						3	7			
TEEUWEN, Margje	1:10						10	10			
DONNERS, Myntje	0:48	1/1			1/1		9	3			
DUYSTER, Willemijn	0:00										
PLESMAN, Suzanne	0:16						1		1		
HOLSBOER, Noor	1:10						5	8			
STEENBERGHE, Florentine	1:10						1	1			
de RUITER, Wietske	0:42	1/1		1/2	2/3		10	4			
van der WIELEN, Suzan	0:46						3	2			
Totals		3/3	0/0	1/2	4/5	2	65	51	3	16	33

PRELIMINARIES FINAL SCORE: ARG 2 KOR 2

Team: ARG Argentina — Coach: MENDOZA, Roldolfo

Names	Time played	FG	PS	PC	Total	Off	To	Int	Stl	PIC	25Y
ARNAL, Mariana	1:10							1			
MACKENZIE, Sofia	1:10			1/2	1/2		13	8			
AICEGA, Magdalena	1:10	0/1			0/1		1	6			
CORVALAN, Silvina	1:10						2	2	1		
GAMBERO, Ana	1:06						1	5	1		
CASTELLAN, Julieta	1:10						4	1	2		
PANDO, Danelotti	0:06										
SANCHEZ, Gabriela	1:10						6	5	1		
ONETO, Vanina	1:03						3	1	2		
RIMOLDI PUIG, Jorgelina	1:04	0/1			0/1		7	3			
MASOTTA, Karina	1:10						3	1			
CASTELLI, Maria Paula	0:07			1/2	1/2						
ARTICA, Veronica	0:00										
ROGNONI, Cecilia	0:03										
STEPNIK, Ayelen	0:00										
GONZALEZ, Mariana	1:07						1	2			
Totals		0/2	0/0	2/4	2/6	0	41	35	7	9	20

Umpires: CHATAS, Renee USA   LANNING, Margaret CAN

HALFTIME SCORE: ARG 2 KOR 1

Team: KOR Korea — Coach: CHOI, Song-Ryul

Names	Time played	FG	PS	PC	Total	Off	To	Int	Stl	PIC	25Y
YOU, Jae-Sook	1:10							1			
CHOI, Eun-Kyung	1:05						3	5	3		
CHO, Eun-Jung	1:10			1/3	1/3		3	10			
OH, Seung-Shin	0:05										
LIM, Jeong-Sook	0:48						1	3			
KIM, Myung-Ok	1:10						3	4	1		
CHANG, Eun-Jung	1:07	0/4		1/2	1/6		6	4	2		
LEE, Ji-Sook	1:03						11	1	1		
LEE, Eun-Kyung	0:51	0/1			0/1		5				
KOWN, Soo-Hyun	1:06	0/2			0/2	3	5	3			
WOO, Hyun-Jung	0:02										
CHOI, Mi-Soon	0:25						4				
LEE, Eun-Young	1:09	0/1			0/1		7	4	1		
JEON, Young-Sun	0:21						2	3			
KWON, Chang-Sook	1:07						4	8	1		
JIN, Deok-San	0:03										
Totals		0/8	0/0	2/5	2/13	3	54	46	9	26	55

Hockey / *Hockey*

Women / *Dames*

PRELIMINARIES	FINAL SCORE:	ARG 0	GBR 5

HALFTIME SCORE:	ARG 0	GBR 2

Team: ARG Argentina Coach: MENDOZA, Roldolfo

Names	Time played	FG	PS	PC	Total	Off	To	Int	Stl	PIC	25Y
ARNAL, Mariana	1:10										
MACKENZIE, Sofia	1:10		0/2		0/2		10	14	1		
AICEGA, Magdalena	1:10						3	2	2		
CORVALAN, Silvina	1:10						1	3	2		
GAMBERO, Ana	1:10						3	8	3		
CASTELLAN, Julieta	1:10						2	4	2		
PANDO, Danelotti	0:00										
SANCHEZ, Gabriela	1:10						9	4	5		
ONETO, Vanina	1:07	0/3			0/3		10	3	3		
RIMOLDI PUIG, Jorgelina	1:10						10	5	4		
MASOTTA, Karina	1:10						3	2	1		
CASTELLI, Maria Paula	0:04	0/1			0/1		1				
ARTICA, Veronica	0:00										
ROGNONI, Cecilia	0:00										
STEPNIK, Ayelen	0:00										
GONZALEZ, Mariana	1:08						5	1			
Totals		0/4	0/0	0/2	0/6	0	52	50	24	16	42

Umpires: BUCKLEY, Peri AUS   CHATAS, Renee USA

Team: GBR Great Britain Coach: SLOCOMBE, Susan

Names	Time played	FG	PS	PC	Total	Off	To	Int	Stl	PIC	25Y
THOMPSON, Joanne	0:32										
ROSE, Hilary	0:37										
COOK, Christine	0:37						1	8	3		
CULLEN, Tina	0:39		0/1		0/1		3	1	1		
BROWN, Karen	1:10						5	10	6		
ATKINS, Jill	1:10		0/4		0/4		1	4	1		
FRASER, Sue	0:50		0/1		0/1		4	6	3		
SIMPSON, Rhona	0:32	0/1			0/1		4	1			
NICHOLLS, Mandy	0:40	2/2			2/2		4				
SIXSMITH, Jane	0:52	1/1		2/2	3/3		4	2	1		
ROBERTSON, Pauline	0:51						8	2			
MOULD, Jo	0:19						5	3	2		
MILLER, Tammy	0:50						1	2	2		
BENNETT, Anna	0:44	0/1			0/1	1	3	1	1		
DAVIES, Mandy	1:10						4	7	5		
JOHNSON, Kathryn	1:10						9	6	4		
Totals		3/5	0/0	2/8	5/13	1	56	53	29	10	31

PRELIMINARIES	FINAL SCORE:	GER 0	KOR 1

HALFTIME SCORE:	GER 0	KOR 1

Team: GER Germany Coach: RAUTH, Berthold

Names	Time played	FG	PS	PC	Total	Off	To	Int	Stl	PIC	25Y
WOLLSCHLAGER, Susanne	0:00										
BEYER, Birgit	1:10						5				
SCHMORANZER van KOOPEREN	0:39	0/1			0/1		2				
DICKENSCHEID, Tanja	0:37						2				
ERNSTING-KRIENKE, Nadine	0:36	0/1			0/1	1	5	3	1		
THOMASCHINSKI, Simone	1:08						7	4			
KUHNT, Irina	0:13										
CREMER, Melanie	0:57						1	1	1		
HENTSCHEL, Franziska	0:32	0/1		0/4	0/5		5	7	1		
PETERS, Kristina	1:10	0/1			0/1		3	6	2		
HAGENBAEUMER, Eva	1:10						1	4	2		
BECKER, Britta	0:58		0/2		0/2		3	3	1		
KELLER, Natascha	0:38						2	2			
SUXDORF, Philippa	1:10						1	3	2		
LAETZSCH, Heike	0:47						8	1			
KAUSCHKE, Katrin	0:59						4	1			
Totals		0/4	0/0	0/6	0/10	1	37	43	14	14	34

Umpires: KATO, Naomi JPN   SPITALERI, Gina ITA

Team: KOR Korea Coach: CHOI, Song-Ryul

Names	Time played	FG	PS	PC	Total	Off	To	Int	Stl	PIC	25Y
YOU, Jae-Sook	1:10							1			
CHOI, Eun-Kyung	0:55							6			
CHO, Eun-Jung	1:10	0/2		0/2	0/4		6	7	2		
OH, Seung-Shin	0:32							2			
LIM, Jeong-Sook	0:56						1	3			
KIM, Myung-Ok	1:10						3	6			
CHANG, Eun-Jung	1:10	0/2		1/3	1/5		3	3	1		
LEE, Ji-Young	1:07	0/1			0/1		5	1			
LEE, Eun-Kyung	0:32	0/3			0/3		1		1		
KOWN, Soo-Hyun	1:02	0/1			0/1		6	2	1		
WOO, Hyun-Jung	0:00										
CHOI, Mi-Soon	0:35						1	2			
LEE, Eun-Young	1:03						2	3	2		
JEON, Young-Sun	0:12						2	1	1		
KWON, Chang-Sook	1:10						3	6	2		
JIN, Deok-San	0:00										
Totals		0/9	0/0	1/5	1/14	0	33	43	10	22	50

PRELIMINARIES	FINAL SCORE:	ESP 0	USA 2

HALFTIME SCORE:	ESP 0	USA 1

Team: ESP Spain Coach: BRASSA, José

Names	Time played	FG	PS	PC	Total	Off	To	Int	Stl	PIC	25Y
CARRION, Elena	1:10										
DORADO, Natalia	1:10		0/5		0/5		3		3		
GONZALEZ, Maria Cruz	1:04						6	5	2		
BAREA, Carmen	1:10						5	8			
MANRIQUE, Silvia	0:13							1			
GABELLANES, Nagore	0:33						2				
MOTOS, Teresa	0:50	0/1			0/1	1	7	3	1		
BARRIO, Sonia	1:07	0/3		0/4	0/7		6	1	3		
RUEDA, Monica	0:07							1			
LOPEZ, Luci	0:40					1	3	2			
FEITO, Mar	0:22	0/1			0/1		3				
TELLERIA, Maider	1:02						8	4	2		
URQUIZU, Elena	1:00						3	6	1		
LARZABAL, Bego	1:10						2	1			
de IGNACIO-SIMO, Sonia	1:06	0/1			0/1		6	2	2		
GONZALEZ, Maria Victoria	0:00										
Totals		0/6	0/0	0/9	0/15	2	52	35	15	15	44

Umpires: HERNANDEZ, Carlos MEX   McDONALD, Janice GBR

Team: USA Unites States of America Coach: HIXON, Pamela

Names	Time played	FG	PS	PC	Total	Off	To	Int	Stl	PIC	25Y
SHEA, Patty	1:10						1	4			
MARTIN, Laurel	0:24						3	1			
TCHOU, Liz	0:02	1/1			1/1				1		
PANKRATZ, Marcia	1:10	1/2			1/2	1	5		2		
WERLEY, Cindy	0:59	0/3			0/3		2	2	2		
MADL, Diane	0:18						3		1		
FILLAT, Kris	1:09						1	2	2		
JAMES, Kelli	0:35					1	4		1		
FUCHS, Tracey	1:10	0/1		0/1	0/2		4	6			
LUCAS, Antoinette	1:10		0/2		0/2		12	3	1		
KAUFFMAN, Katie	0:00										
WIELAND, Andrea	0:00										
LYNESS, Leslie	1:10						6	7	2		
MAROIS, Barb	1:10		0/1		0/1		7	8	2		
REEVE, Jill	1:10						4	7			
BUSTIN, Pamela	1:09						2	1	1		
Totals		2/7	0/0	0/4	2/11	2	54	41	15	10	25

Hockey / *Hockey*   **289**

Women / Dames

PRELIMINARIES — FINAL SCORE: AUS 4 NED 0 — HALFTIME SCORE: AUS 0 NED 0

Team: AUS Australia Coach: CHARLESWORTH, Richard

Names	Time played	FG	PS	PC	Total	Off	To	Int	Stl	PIC	25Y
MAITLAND, Clover	0:34							1			
ROCHE, Danielle	0:45	1/1			1/1		4	2			
TOOTH, Liane	0:48						6				
ANNAN, Alyson	0:42	0/1		1/1	1/2		5	3	1		
HASLAM, Juliet	0:59	0/2			0/2		4	1	1		
MORRIS, Jennifer	0:54			1/2	1/2		4	4			
DOBSON, Louise	0:59			0/1	0/1		4	7	3		
POWELL, Lisa	0:52						5		3		
MARSDEN, Karen	0:35							1			
STARRE, Kate	0:49						5	7	1		
FARRELL, Renita	0:43						2	1	1		
PEREIRA, Jacqueline	0:49						2		1		
PERIS-KNEEBONE, Nova	0:58						4	5			
HAWKES, Rechelle	0:45						6	2	2		
POWELL, Katrina	0:46	0/1			0/1		2	2	1		
ANDREWS, Michelle	0:43	1/1			1/1		8				
Totals		2/6	0/0	2/4	4/10	0	51	41	19	8	41

Team: NED Netherlands Coach: van `T HEK, Thomas

Names	Time played	FG	PS	PC	Total	Off	To	Int	Stl	PIC	25Y
TOXOPEUS, Jacqueline	1:10							1	1		
de HEIJ, Stella	0:00										
van de KIEFT, Fleur	0:24						3		1		
THATE, Carole	1:10						5	2	2		
KUIPERS, Ellen	0:45						3	1			
LEWIN, Jeannette	1:10						6	5	3		
KOOLEN, Nicky	1:08						4	4	2		
van den BOOGAARD, Dilliane	0:57						3	3	2		
TEEUWEN, Margje	1:10						2	2	2		
DONNERS, Myntje	0:49						6	1	2		
DUYSTER, Willemijn	0:01										
PLESMAN, Suzanne	0:12							1	1		
HOLSBOER, Noor	1:10						1	4	3		
STEENBERGHE, Florentine	1:10						1	1			
de RUITER, Wietske	0:48			0/3	0/3		4	5			
van der WIELEN, Suzan	0:42	0/1			0/1		2	2			
Totals		0/1	0/0	0/3	0/4	0	42	31	18	8	24

Umpires: CRESPO, Laura ARG   LARIO RUIZ, Angela ESP

FINAL - BRONZE MATCH — FINAL SCORE: GBR 0 NED 0 — HALFTIME SCORE: GBR 0 NED 0

Team: GBR Great Britain Coach: SLOCOMBE, Susan

Names	Time played	FG	PS	PC	Total	Off	To	Int	Stl	PIC	25Y
THOMPSON, Joanne	1:10										
ROSE, Hilary	0:00										
COOK, Christine	0:41						3	4			
CULLEN, Tina	0:35						5				
BROWN, Karen	1:09						10	19	3		
ATKINS, Jill	1:10						1	11			
FRASER, Sue	1:10						13	12	2		
SIMPSON, Rhona	0:35	0/1			0/1		4	1			
NICHOLLS, Mandy	0:43						4				
SIXSMITH, Jane	0:55	0/1			0/1		5	3			
ROBERTSON, Pauline	0:49						3	1			
MOULD, Jo	0:00										
MILLER, Tammy	0:50						5	1	1		
BENNETT, Anna	0:38						1		1		
DAVIES, Mandy	1:10						1	4	2		
JOHNSON, Kathryn	1:10						1	7	2		
Totals		0/2	0/0	0/0	0/2	0	56	63	11	11	28

Team: NED Netherlands Coach: van `T HEK, Thomas

Names	Time played	FG	PS	PC	Total	Off	To	Int	Stl	PIC	25Y
TOXOPEUS, Jacqueline	1:10							1			
de HEIJ, Stella	0:00										
van de KIEFT, Fleur	0:14						1	3			
THATE, Carole	1:10						4	4	4		
KUIPERS, Ellen	0:26			0/1	0/1		3		1		
LEWIN, Jeannette	1:10			0/1	0/1		10	6	1		
KOOLEN, Nicky	1:10						10	8			
van den BOOGAARD, Dilliane	1:10			0/2	0/2		7	10	2		
TEEUWEN, Margje	1:10						3	11	2		
DONNERS, Myntje	1:10	0/1		0/1	0/2		7				
DUYSTER, Willemijn	0:00										
PLESMAN, Suzanne	0:00										
HOLSBOER, Noor	1:10						2	17	4		
STEENBERGHE, Florentine	1:10						5	2	1		
de RUITER, Wietske	0:50			0/2	0/2		3	1	1		
van der WIELEN, Suzan	0:48	0/1			0/1		4	1	1		
Totals		0/2	0/0	0/7	0/9	0	59	64	17	11	37

Umpires: LARIO RUIZ, Angela ESP   YASUEDA, Kazuko JPN

FINAL - GOLD MATCH — FINAL SCORE: AUS 3 KOR 1 — HALFTIME SCORE: AUS 1 KOR 1

Team: AUS Australia Coach: CHARLESWORTH, Richard

Names	Time played	FG	PS	PC	Total	Off	To	Int	Stl	PIC	25Y
MAITLAND, Clover	1:10										
ROCHE, Danielle	0:29						3				
TOOTH, Liane	1:10						1	11	1		
ANNAN, Alyson	0:57	0/2	1/1	1/2	2/5	1	13	4	1		
HASLAM, Juliet	0:58						2	4			
MORRIS, Jennifer	1:10						5	6	1		
DOBSON, Louise	0:12						3				
POWELL, Lisa	0:31	0/1			0/1	1	5	1			
MARSDEN, Karen	0:00										
STARRE, Kate	0:52						5	6	3		
FARRELL, Renita	0:58						2	5			
PEREIRA, Jacqueline	0:38	0/2			0/2		6				
PERIS-KNEEBONE, Nova	1:08						7	4			
HAWKES, Rechelle	0:59	0/1			0/1		6	1			
POWELL, Katrina	0:45	1/4			1/4		2		1		
ANDREWS, Michelle	0:46	0/2			0/2		8				
Totals		1/12	1/1	1/2	3/15	2	58	48	11	15	42

Team: KOR Korea Coach: CHOI, Song-Ryul

Names	Time played	FG	PS	PC	Total	Off	To	Int	Stl	PIC	25Y
YOU, Jae-Sook	1:10										
CHOI, Eun-Kyung	0:19						1	1			
CHO, Eun-Jung	1:10			1/1	1/1		10	9	1		
OH, Seung-Shin	0:50						1	2	1		
LIM, Jeong-Sook	0:51						2	5			
KIM, Myung-Ok	1:10						5	4			
CHANG, Eun-Jung	1:06	0/1		0/1	0/2		3	2			
LEE, Ji-Young	1:04					1	5				
LEE, Eun-Kyung	0:37						2				
KOWN, Soo-Hyun	1:10					3	6	2	1		
WOO, Hyun-Jung	0:00										
CHOI, Mi-Soon	0:37	0/1			0/1	1	3				
LEE, Eun-Young	0:58						3	7	1		
JEON, Young-Sun	0:38						6	6			
KWON, Chang-Sook	1:05						2	6			
JIN, Deok-San	0:00										
Totals		0/2	0/0	1/2	1/4	5	49	44	4	4	33

Umpires: CLARKE, Gillian GBR   van GEMERT, Miriam NED

Hockey / Hockey

Women / *Dames*

FINAL SUMMARY

Phase	Teams	Score
Final - Gold	AUS - KOR	3-1
Final - Bronze	GBR - NED	0-0
Final 5 - 6	USA - GER	1-1
Final 7 - 8	ARG - ESP	1-0

FINAL CLASSIFICATION

Rnk	Team	Played	Matches Won	Drawn	Lost	Goals For	Against	Diff	Points	
1	AUS	7	6	1	0	24	4	20	13	Gold
2	KOR	7	4	2	1	18	9	9	10	Silver
3	NED	7	3	2	2	15	15	0	8	Bronze
4	GBR	7	3	2	2	12	11	1	8	
5	USA	7	2	2	3	8	11	-3	6	
6	GER	7	2	1	4	10	11	-1	5	
7	ARG	7	2	1	4	7	21	-14	5	
8	ESP	7	0	1	6	5	17	-12	1	

GREGORY A SUTHERLAND • HOLLY M SUTHERLAND • NEIL A SUTHERLAND • STUART A SUTLIFF • WILLIAM G. SUTLIVE • CHARLES SUTTEN • BRIAN D SUTTIE • LULA P SUTTLE • CHIP SUTTLES • EDDIE SUTTLES • TERRY A SUTTLES • ANDREA C SUTTON • CHERYL M SUTTON • EDYE L SUTTON • GARY S SUTTON • GEOFFREY C SUTTON • GLORIA T SUTTON • JAMIE S SUTTON • JEFFREY A SUTTON • KAY W SUTTON • KYRA L SUTTON • LOIS L SUTTON • MARYLN M SUTTON • NEDRA M SUTTON • ROBERT G SUTTON • STACIE D SUTTON • STARK A SUTTON • TIMOTHY L SUTTON • ANTHONY F SUTTON ATC • ANGELA M SUTYLO • LINDA SUTYLO • KUMIKO SUZUKI • YUICHI SUZUKI • DAINA SVEICA • GUNILLA SVENSSON • MALIN A SVENSSON • MARIA E SVENSSON • LINDA M SVOBODA • DENISE S SWABY • ASHLEY C SWADEL • MARY A SWADER • BEN W SWAFFORD • DOROTHY J SWAFFORD • JOSHUA N SWAFFORD • JUDITH A SWAFFORD • RONALD E SWAFFORD • WALTER L SWAFFORD • THOMAS J SWAFFORD JR • AMANDA N SWAIM • CAROL R SWAIM • HELEN W SWAIM • LARRY M SWAIM • RAY D SWAIM • RUTH SWAIM • WILLIAM F SWAIM JR • ELAINE L SWAIN • MICHELLE R SWAIN • JULIE M SWAIN ATC • PAIGE L SWAINE • KRISTINA L. SWALANDER • BALA SWAMINATHAN • BRIAN A SWAN • CATHERINE D SWAN • CLYDE E SWAN • JACQUELYN G SWAN • JULIE A SWAN • KIMBERLY L SWAN • MICHAEL L SWAN • NANCY SWAN • PAMELA I SWAN • RANDALL SWAN • SUSAN K SWAN • SUSAN K SWAN • PATRICIA B SWAN-BARBOZA • VIRGINIA N SWANCEY • BARBARA B SWANN • CYNTHIA P SWANN • DOROTHY T SWANN • ELEANOR S SWANN • GREGORY B SWANN • JULIE L. SWANN • MARSHA J SWANN • SCOTT C SWANN • BETTY M SWANSON • CHERYL C SWANSON • DAVID J SWANSON • HEATHER D SWANSON • HOWARD C SWANSON • JOEL D SWANSON • LYNNETTE S. SWANSON • MARGO A SWANSON • MARY F. SWANSON • MYLES E SWANSON ATC • REGG E SWANSON CATC • DAVID G SWANZ • ANNE H SWARTZ • DAVID SWARTZ • JULIE L SWARTZ • RON SWARTZ • TRENTON G SWARTZ • WENDY E SWARTZELL • LAUREN D SWARTZENTRUBER • WENDYL R SWARTZENTRUBER • SANDRA L SWARY • TOM W SWAYER • ANNE L SWEANEY • JENNIFER SWEARINGER • AMY D SWEAT • STEVE R SWEAT • CARL SWEATMAN • MARGARET H SWEATT • LAURA SWEDLOW • GERAHINE G SWEENEY • JOHN L SWEENEY • JOYCE K SWEENEY • KASINA J SWEENEY • LAERNE J SWEENEY • LEONARD W SWEENEY • EVELYN R SWEENEY MT • JAMES G SWEENY • SUSAN S SWEENY • DOROTHY S SWEEPER • JULIE C SWEET • SHANE T SWEET • BRENDA I SWEETING • JOHN H SWEITZER • LETITIA D SWEITZER • STEPHEN S SWENEY • ERIK J SWENSEN • SAMANTHA J SWENSEN • JULIE Y SWENSON • BETTY J SWIATOWSKI • VINCENT W SWIATOWSKI • CHRISTINE A SWIENTEK • JOHN M SWIERZ • AMANDA L SWIFT • CHRISTINA E SWIFT • DON L SWIFT • DONALD R SWIFT • KAREN A SWIFT • LEE A SWIFT • LINDSAY SWIFT • LLOYD S SWIFT • PATRICIA G SWIFT • ANNA K SWIGART • BOBBIE D SWIGER • GWENDA S SWIGER • STEVEN M SWIGER • ANDREA SWILLEY • GEORGE S SWILLEY • TONYA J SWILLEY • GREGORY N SWINDELL • ERIC L SWINEBROAD • SHARON J SWINEHAMER • THOMAS R SWINFORD • THOMAS R SWINFORD • JACQUELINE C SWINGER • JOHN A SWINNEA • IRENE J SWINNEA RN • BARBARA L SWINT • BENNIE SWINT • QUILLA R SWINT • ERNESTINE SWINTON • VERNITA K SWINTON • KIMBERLY A SWIRBUL • CAROL I SWISHER • PETER J SWISHER PM • STEVEN SWISTAK • STEVE E SWIT • DONNA J SWITTENBURG • JOE SWITZ • ANN M SWITZER • BRAD A SWITZER • CLIFFORD W SWITZER • DEBRA J SWITZER • PAULETTE SWOFFORD • JANICE F SWOOPE • MARY ALICE SWOPE • TAMMIE L SWOPES • DONNA R SWORDS • LORI A SWORDS • JEREMY J SWYGARD • MOUSSA D SY • HENDRIK SYBERDEN • MICHEAL L SYBRANDT • KIMBERLY C SYDNOR • MICHAEL S SYDNOR • STEVE J SYFAN • EDWARD P SYGUDA • ALYSE SYKES • BRIDGET L SYKES • DOROTHY D SYKES • GAIL R SYKES • JACQUELINE E SYKES • JOAN J SYKES • LEIGH C SYKES • LEIGH C SYKES • LORETTA SYKES • MARY BETH SYKES • MICHAEL SYKES • VLADIMIR A SYKORA • RHONDA A SYLER • VALERIA F SYLVAIN • NEIL SYLVERSTON • JENNIFER L SYLVESTER • KRISTINA L SYLVESTER • RICHARD J SYLVIA JR • HYTHO B SYMBAS • JOHN D SYMBAS • WILLIAM H SYMINGTON • DAVE B SYMOLON • ALICE R SYMONDS • AMY H SYMONS • DONNA L SYRJA • NATALYA SYTINA • KATHLEEN L SZEGDA • JOELLE M SZENDEL • TOMASZ SZEWCZYK • ROMAN SZLAM • JOSEPH SZMYD • JUANITA SZOKE • JENNIFER SZOKODY • BARBARA L SZOPA • GARY W SZWAST • ERIKA E SZYCHOWSKI • MARYSE L SZYDLOWSKI • CAROLYN C SZYMCZYK • RAYMOND SZYNAL •MIKE A TABAKA • MANUEL F TABARES • LOUIS A TABAT • SALLY T TABB • MARVIN L TABLE • DIANE F TABOR • ESTELL M TABOR • JANET J TABOR • MICHAEL J TABOR • NATHAN A TABOR • KIM R TABORN • AGNES V TABOURNE • HIROSHI TACHIKAWA • CAROL S TACKETT • JOHN R TACKETT • KARIN TACKETT • GARY M TACKLING • JOSEPH W TACTO • BARBARA A TADDEO • LISA M TADDIA • ABDELNOUR A TADROS • RANDY TADROS • WADIE I TADROS • JOHN R TAFF • PAMELA R TAFF • JEAN SANDRA S TAFFEL • MYLES T TAFFEL • NANCY M TAFFEL • AMANDA L TAFT • JENNIFER E TAFT • VONDA A TAFT • WANDA M TAFT • TIMOTHY N TAFT MD • HEMANT R TAGGARSI • DENISE Y TAGGART • MARSHALL TAGGART • FRANCINE TAGUE • AARON S TAHAN •

STEVEN P TAHSLER • LUCA TAIDELLI • BARBARA D TAKACS • DAVID J TAKACS • ROBERT K TAKANO • KUMI TAKASUMI • KIKUKA TAKATSUKI • NOBUKO TAKAYAMA • TSUYOSHI TAKEHANA • MEGUMI TAKEI • DANNY K TALATI • RASHMIKANT TALATI • EDMOND P TALBOT • KATHRYN R TALBOT • BARBARA J TALBOTT • JOEL D. TALCOTT • JOHN E. TALIPSKY • ERNEST J TALL • CHRISTINE D TALLENT • JOSEPH P TALLENT • BARBARA D TALLEY • JUDY W TALLEY • PAMELA J TALLEY • PHYLLIS H TALLEY • USTAINE TALLEY • JIM B TALLEY III • JOHN W TALLEY JR • NICHOLAS D TALLINGTON • CAROL TALLMAN • DUANE K TALLMAN • TROY W TALLY • PATRICK J TALMA • KATHY B TALMAN • PAMELA I TALUYO • PEDRO L TAMAYO MD • PATRICIA J TAMBURINI • SANDRA WOJTECKI TAMEL • ARATA TAMURA • KATSUYUKI TAMURA • KAZUMI TAMURA • AUDREY L TAN • JOSEPHINE K TAN • KAI-JIAW TAN • MAKBULE TAN • SHUEN HWEE R TAN • WENXIAO TAN • XIAOLEI TAN • ANTHONY J TANACSOS • AKIHIKO TANAKA • DEDY TANDO • KAWALJIT S TANDON • DANIELLE K TANEFO • TARA A TANESKI • DON TANG • JEANNE TANG • YINGYING TANG • SUSAN L TANGCO • KERRY G TANIS • GAIL A TANKERSLEY • BRUCE A TANKLEFF • STEVEN J TANKS • SABRINA TANN • ELLIOTT G TANNENBAUM • BETTY J TANNER • DAVID A TANNER • DEBORAH L TANNER • JANA P TANNER • JOHN E TANNER • KRISTINA TANNER • LARRY L TANNER • LISA M TANNER • PATRICIA A TANNER • ROBIN E TANNER • RUSSELL H TANNER • SARAH TANNER • SUE S TANNER • TERESA T TANNER • STEPHANIE S TANSEY • HAROLD T TANT • MARY TANTILLO • KWANCHANOK TANTIVEJKUL • AYESHA TANZEEM • FELICIA M TANZOSCH • LORI A TANZOSCH • ISRAEL TAPIA • BENJAMIN L TAPLEY • JOHN H TAPLEY • JON E TAPLEY • SOPHIA B TAPLEY • BETHANY M TAPP • LYNNE R TAPPER • BARBARA ANN TARANTINE • KARA L TARANTINO • THOMAS R TARANTINO • DAVID A TARASAVAGE • TITKI D TARASSOUM • JOHN F TARBERT • RICHARD TARDITS • SONER TARI • FRED N TARKENTON • JACKIE W TARKENTON • NICHOLAS D TARLTON • ALBON TARNEAUD • BRUCE TARNOPOLSKI • CRYSTAL M TARPKINS • ALACIA J TARPLEY • LEONARD C TARPLIN • OLGA TARPOFF • ALLAN F TARR • LISA M TARR • RACHEL TARR • HEATHER E TARRANT • KATHLEEN C TARRANT • KATHRYN D TARRANT • JENNEFER L TARRER • JOSEPH C TARTAGLIONE • MOLLY W. TARTT • BESSIE L TARVER • MARY B TARVER • OLLIE W TARVER • LUCILLE TARVIN • MASAHIKO TASAKI • MAIJA-LIISA TASANEN • DEBRA I TASIOUDIS • DONNA P TASSA • MARTINA N TASSIUS • PAUL J TASTENHOYE • MARY E TATE • CHINITA A TATE • CHRIS J TATE • CRAIG S TATE • DALE W TATE • ELAINE H TATE • ELVIRA M TATE • GAYLE V TATE • GLORIA L TATE • ILLANA T TATE • JAMES A TATE • JEANNETTE TATE • KIMMERLY W TATE • MARSHA R TATE • RAWLIN L TATE • RICKY W TATE • SHIRLEY A TATE • TOMEKIA TATE • VALERIE Y TATE • CHARLES D TATHAM • CARLA E TATUM • CATHY D TATUM • JAMES A TATUM • LEDA L TATUM • LINDA F TATUM • MICHAEL L TATUM • RUDOLPH R TATUM • SHARON B TATUM • SUE C TATUM • VANESSA L TATUM • LARRY R TAUB • KIMBERLY L TAUBE • BRIAN D TAUBERT • KRISTI M TAUBERT • CAROLYN J TAUER • MARK H TAUPEKA • THEODORE J TAUTGES • RICHARD E TAVERNARO • FRANCES M TAWES • AMANDA J TAYLOR • AMY E TAYLOR • ANGELA Y TAYLOR • BARBARA A TAYLOR • BARRY E TAYLOR • BRENDA A TAYLOR • BRIAN S TAYLOR • BRIDGET E TAYLOR • BRINDA D TAYLOR • BRUCE K TAYLOR • CAROL P TAYLOR • CAROLYN C TAYLOR • CHARLES E TAYLOR • CHARLES P TAYLOR • CLAIRE B TAYLOR • COLETTE A TAYLOR • CYNTHIA A TAYLOR • CYNTHIA K TAYLOR • DAN C TAYLOR • DARRELL TAYLOR • DARRELL C TAYLOR • DAVID R TAYLOR • DEBBY R TAYLOR • DEBRA A TAYLOR • DEBRA D TAYLOR • DEBRA J TAYLOR • DEBRA V TAYLOR • DENNIS W TAYLOR • DONNETHER J TAYLOR • EDNA CAROL TAYLOR • ELIZABETH A TAYLOR • ELIZABETH C TAYLOR • ELVIS G TAYLOR • ERIC H TAYLOR • ERIC M TAYLOR • EVA M TAYLOR • FRANK A TAYLOR • FRANK A TAYLOR • GAIL TAYLOR • GERI TAYLOR • GLORIA W TAYLOR • GREGORY TAYLOR • GWENDOLYN A TAYLOR • GWYNLYN J TAYLOR • HARRY TAYLOR • HELEN TAYLOR • HELEN T TAYLOR • HENRY L TAYLOR • HERBERT E TAYLOR • HORACENA J TAYLOR • JACK P TAYLOR • JACQUELINE TAYLOR • JAMES M TAYLOR • JAMES R TAYLOR • JANET M TAYLOR • JEAN C TAYLOR • JEANNE D TAYLOR • JEFF TAYLOR • JEFF M TAYLOR • JENELLE B TAYLOR • JENNIFER L TAYLOR • JOAN E TAYLOR • JOANN J TAYLOR • JOHN B TAYLOR • JOHN L TAYLOR • JOIE C TAYLOR • JULIA A TAYLOR • JULIE TAYLOR • JULIE M TAYLOR • KARLA O TAYLOR • KATE V TAYLOR • KAVIN C TAYLOR • KENNETH M TAYLOR • KIMILEE D TAYLOR • KIRSTEN J TAYLOR • LARRY B TAYLOR • LAUREN M TAYLOR • LEAH R TAYLOR • LEE A TAYLOR • LEIGH A TAYLOR • LENORD L TAYLOR • LESLIE M TAYLOR • LINDA TAYLOR • LINDA A TAYLOR • LINDA B TAYLOR • LISA A TAYLOR • LISA I TAYLOR • LOIS R TAYLOR • LONNIE A TAYLOR • LOUISE TAYLOR • LYNN E. TAYLOR • MARIA TAYLOR • MARIA TAYLOR • MARILYN A TAYLOR • MARK WILLIAM TAYLOR • MARSHA D TAYLOR • MARTHA W TAYLOR • MARY E TAYLOR • MARY H TAYLOR • MATTHEW TAYLOR • MATTHEW P TAYLOR • MEREDITH D TAYLOR • MICKI TAYLOR • MILLICENT TAYLOR • MITZI Y TAYLOR • MONICA M TAYLOR • NANCY B TAYLOR • NATALIE M TAYLOR • PAMELA TAYLOR • PAMELA D TAYLOR • PAMELLA TAYLOR • PAMELLA P TAYLOR • PATRICIA A TAYLOR • PAUL E TAYLOR • PAULA TAYLOR •

PEGGY T TAYLOR • PHILIP R TAYLOR • RANDALL L TAYLOR • RANDY TAYLOR • REBECCA S TAYLOR • RICHARD V TAYLOR • RITA TAYLOR • ROBERT TAYLOR • ROBERTA W TAYLOR • ROBIN TAYLOR • SAM R TAYLOR • SAMANTHA N TAYLOR • SANDY A TAYLOR • SARAH TAYLOR • SCOTT E TAYLOR • SEAN L TAYLOR • SHARON H TAYLOR • SHELLY J TAYLOR • STELLA H TAYLOR • STEPHEN A TAYLOR • STUART TAYLOR • SUSAN H TAYLOR • SUSAN M TAYLOR • TERESA C TAYLOR • TIMOTHY D TAYLOR • TYRONE J TAYLOR • VICKY H TAYLOR • VIVIAN TAYLOR • WESLEY R TAYLOR • WILLIAM H TAYLOR • WILLIE J TAYLOR • YUMI TAYLOR • MOLLY M TAYLOR-MADDALENA • DENNIS TAYLOR III • JAMES E TAYLOR III • ANSON W TAYLOR JR • FRANK P TAYLOR JR • THOMAS TAYLOR JR • JUDY A TAYLOR PENDLETON • T'CHALLA • GEORGE R TEACHEY • PATRICIA H TEAGLE • ANDRE J TEAGUE • CATI TEAGUE • DAVID L TEAGUE • HELEN B TEAGUE • JACK S TEAGUE • JANE T TEAGUE • JERALDINE T TEAGUE • JIM R TEAGUE • JOHNIE L TEAGUE • JOSEPH W TEAGUE • MARILYN W TEAGUE • RICHARD H TEAGUE • RITA L TEAGUE • TERRI L TEAGUE • THERESA L TEAGUE • TIFFANY C TEAGUE • JULIE L TEAHAN • DANIEL B TEAHAN ATC • JANET MARGARET TEAL • JOE C TEAL • JUDY V TEAL • ROY J TEAL • SHARYN E TEAL • DALORES A TEAMER • ARLENE F TEARE • KELLY L TEASLEY • EDWARD K TEATE • JENNIFER P TEATES • DIANNE TEDDER • SHERRI B TEDDER • FRANK M TEDESCHI • KATHLEEN ANN TEDESCHI • PEGGY C TEDESCO RN • CHERYL L TEDFORD • GENEVIEVE J TEDJAMULIA • MONICA M TEDJARAHARDJA • CAROL G TEDOFF • IRA L TEDOFF • TRUMAN H TEED • AMANDA L TEEL • DELCINA Y TEEL • JENNIFER L TEEL • JENNIFER O TEEL • ROBERT L TEEL • LISA M TEER • KEVIN J TEETS • LINDA L TEETZ • MENELIK TEFERA • SARA A TEGETHOFF • ARVID Y TEGNER • SAM A TEHRANI • EUGENE TEIGLAND • DEBORAH A TEITSMAN • MARIANE C TEIXEIRA • JUDI L TEKAUTZ • GEORGE A TEKMITCHOV • ANDY J TELATOVICH • BARBARA E TELFORD • JAMES R TELFORD • ELIZABETH J TELGENHOFF • ANTONIO L TELLA • LOURDES O TELLEZ • DEIRDRE D TELLIGMAN • CLAUDIA TELLIHO • MARK STEWART TELLING • GAIL M TELLO • JOSE A TELLO • JAYVIN B TEMONEY • KAREN D TEMPEL • DIANNE R TEMPLETON • GAIL MARIE TEMPLETON • NANCY L TEMPLETON • VICKI L TEN KATE • JAMES E TENDER • JAMIE TENNESSEE • ANGELA M TENNEY • JENNIFER TENNEY • JENIFER A TENTLER • TOD A TENTLER • TOD A TENTLER • RHODA S TEPLOW • DALE A TEPP • KRISTEN TEPPER • NEIL TEPPER • EIJI TERAGOUCHI • ALEXIS J TERESZCUK • JOAN H TERHUNE • RAMON T TERLAJE • CLAUDE C TERLIZZI • GWEN M TERPAK • CAROLYN M TERRANCE • BETTY TERRANO • ALISA R TERRELL • ANITA COLLINS TERRELL • CHRISTY R TERRELL • ELIZABETH A TERRELL • JOYCE G TERRELL • KELLY C TERRELL • THOMAS R TERRELL • TODD A TERRELL • WILLIE G TERRELL • OTHEL TERRELL JR • GILLIAN D TERRELONGE • BRADLEY R TERRIS • ALISON G. TERRY • ANETRICE D TERRY • AVA M TERRY • BARBARA G TERRY • BETTY J TERRY • CARLISS A TERRY • ELAINE M TERRY • GLENN C TERRY • JANE B TERRY • JIM A TERRY • JIMMY TERRY • LARRY C TERRY • MICHAEL M TERRY • OCTAVIUS M TERRY • RANDY B TERRY • SCOTT S TERRY • STEVEN P TERRY • YVETTE TERRY • YVONNE TERRY • RITVA-LIISA TERVO • RUTH A TESANOVICH • ALLAN A TESKE • KAREN K TESKE • MERI LEE K TESTA • RICHARD M TESTA MT • IWONA T TESTANI • SUDIE A TESZLER • MICHAEL TETALMAN • TAMARA A TETRADZE • ASHLEY TETTERTON • DARRELL R TEUBNER • DINO A TEVES JR. • DARLENE C TEW • MARY S TEWELL • JAMES D TEWS • MURILO TEXEIRA • GARY L THACKER • GARY S THACKER • LYNNETTE THACKER • TRENT D THACKER • KENT D THACKREY • MICHAEL P THACKREY • VIDWAT V THAKAR • VINCENT V THAKORE • CHETAN S THALESHWAR • LUCY C THALIATH • EDWARD T THAM • IRENE M THAM • IRIS THAM • TOM THAM • BETH THAMES • JOHN A THAMES • PATRICIA A THAMES • TODD D THAMES • STANLEY I THANGARAJ • STEVEN T THANNISCH • MARLENE C THANOS • CHRISTY L THARENOS • LANE R THARP • JANICE W THARPE • KEVIN J THARPE • MARION E THARPE • BRIGITTE H THAYER • DONNA J THAYER • FRED J THAYER • KENDRA J THAYER • SUSANNAH L THAYER • NANCY M THEALL • ALICE T. THEBO • EDWARD L THEBO • WILLIAM F THEE • CYNTHIA S THEILER • DAVID P THEILER • ALEXIS L THEIS • MARY E THEIS • KELLY J THELEN • ERIC THEODOROPOULOS • JOHN C THEOFILOS • LUDIWINE THERIOT • PATRICIA A THERNELL • MICHAEL A THERRIEN • ANDREW R THEUERLING • BABACAR THIAM • CAROLYN A THIBADEAU • LEONARD W THIBADEAU • MATHIEU THIBAULT • DANIEL P THIEL • TERENCE R THIEL • EVELYN C THIELE • JOHN M THIELE • STEPHEN T THIELE • DONALD J THIELKE • EARL S THIELKE • KATHRYN B THIELKE • KEN E THIERY • SUSAN M THIGPEN • OUDONE THIRAKOUNE • KATHY M THOLEN • TRICIA THOLEN • THERESA A THOM • LARRY M THOMAN • LANDON M THOMAS • ADDIE J THOMAS • AL L THOMAS • ALEXANDER J THOMAS • ALI M THOMAS • ALLISON P THOMAS • ALVIN R THOMAS • AMANDA E THOMAS • AMY M THOMAS • ANDREA THOMAS • ANGIE M THOMAS • ANNIE D THOMAS • ANTHONY W THOMAS • ARLENE THOMAS • AUSTIN THOMAS • BARBARA THOMAS • BARBARA A THOMAS • BELINDA THOMAS • BERTHA L THOMAS • BETTYE W THOMAS • BOB R THOMAS • BORIS CHUCKA THOMAS • BRECK A THOMAS

JUDO
JUDO

Abbreviations and terms used in Judo results tables
Abréviations et termes employés dans les tableaux de résultats de judo

Term	English	Français
1st Round	First Round	Premier tour
2nd Round	Second Round	Deuxième tour
3rd Round	Third Round	Troisième tour
Bronze	Bronze Medal	Médaille de bronze
BYE	Bye	Exemption
CHU (Chui)	Caution	Remarque
Final	Final	Finale
FUS (Fusen-gachi)	Win by Default	Victoire par défaut
Gold	Gold Medal	Médaille d'or
HAN (Hansoku-make)	Disqualification	Disqualification
IPO (Ippon)	Full Point	Point
KEI (keikoku)	Warning	Avertissement
KIK (Kiken-gachi)	Win by Withdrawal	Victoire par abandon
KOK (Koka)	Almost Yuko	Presque yuko
Pool	Pool	Poule
Preliminaries	Preliminaries	Eliminatoires
Quarterfinals	Quarterfinals	Quarts de finale
Repechage and Summary	Repechage and Summary	Repêchage et sommaire
Round	Round	Tour
SHI (Shido)	Note	Attention
SOG (Sogo-gachi)	Compound Win	Victoire par combinaison
Semifinals	Semifinals	Demi-finales
Silver	Silver Medal	Médaille d'argent
WAZ (Waza-ari)	Almost a Point	Presque un point
WIP (Wazaari-awesete-ippon)	Two waza-aris score point	Deux waza ari valant ippon
YUK (Yuko)	Almost Waza-uri	Presque waza-uri
YUS (Yusei-gachi)	Superiority Win	Victoire par supériorité

Techniques	Techniques
AGJ	Ashi-gatame-jime
AGU	Ashi-guruma
DAB	De-ashi-barai
HIG	Hiza-gatame
HKG	Hon-kesa-gatame
HRG	Harai-goshi
JG	Juji-gatame
KEG	Kesa-gatame
KGU	Kata-guruma
KKE	Kuzure-kesa-gatame
KKS	Kuzure-kami-shiho-gatame
KOG	Koshi-guruma
KSA	Kami-sanakaku-gatame
KSH	Kami-shiho-gatame
KSK	Ko-soto-gake
KTA	Kosiki-taoshi
KUG	Ko-uchi-gari
KUM	Ko-uchi-makikomi
KYS	Kuzure-yoko-shiho-gatame
MGA	Morote-gari
MSN	Morote-seoi-nage
OAB	Okuri-ashi-barai
OEJ	Okuri-eri-jime
OGA	O-soto-gaeshi
OGO	O-goshi
OS1	O-soto-otoshi
OSG	O-soto-gari
OUC	O-uchi-gaeshi
OUG	O-uchi-gari
SAJ	Sankaku-jime
SMK	Soto-makikomi
SN	Seoi-nage
SOT	Sumi-otoshi
STA	Sasae-tsuri-komi-ashe
SUG	Sumi-gaeshi
SUK	Sukui-nage
TGO	Tsuri-goshi
TGU	Te-guruma
TKG	Tsuri-komi-goshi
TN	Tomoe-nage
TNO	Tani-otoshi
TO	Tai-otoshi
TSG	Tate-shiho-gatame
UKG	Ushiro-kesa-gatame
UM	Uchi-mata
UMS	Uchi-mata-sukashi
UNA	Ura-nage
YOT	Yoko-otoshi
YSG	Yoko-shio-gatame
YTN	Yoko-tomoe-nage

International Judo Federation (IJF)
Fédération Internationale de Judo
Ferraz, 16
Madrid 28008
Spain

BRENDA A THOMAS • BRIAN G THOMAS • BRIAN J THOMAS • CAMERON B THOMAS • CARMEN M THOMAS • CAROLE P THOMAS • CASSANDRA L THOMAS • CATHERINE A THOMAS • CEDRIC THOMAS • CHAD THOMAS • CHARLES R THOMAS • CHARLIE O THOMAS • CHRISTOPHER S THOMAS • CHRISTY THOMAS • CLAUDIA D THOMAS • CLIFFORD THOMAS • COLIN J THOMAS • CYNTHIA A THOMAS • DAMON THOMAS • DANIEL W THOMAS • DANIEL W THOMAS • DARRIAN T THOMAS • DAVID J THOMAS • DAVID M THOMAS • DAVID R THOMAS • DAWN THOMAS • DENNIS J THOMAS •

293

Judo / *Judo*

Extra Lightweight, 60 kg, Men / *Super-léger, 60 kg, Messieurs*

Preliminaries

1ST ROUND	2ND ROUND	3RD ROUND	QUARTERFINALS	SEMIFINALS	FINAL

Pool A

MERIDJA, Amar — ALG	
BYE	MERIDJA, A.
NOVACEK, Roman — CZE	
BYE	NOVACEK, R.

MERIDJA, A.
4:02 / IPO / TOS

MERIDJA, A.
0:00 / WAZ / TWG

NAVEIRA, Roberto — ESP	
BYE	NAVEIRA, R.
LIAO, Chun Chian — TPE	
BYE	LIAO, C. C.

NAVEIRA, R.
0:00 / KOK / TNO

NOMURA, T.
0:39 / IPO / SON

OYEGIN, Nikolay — RUS	
BYE	OYEGIN, N.
AYED, Makrem — TUN	
BYE	AYED, M.

OYEGIN, N.
0:00 / YUK / SON

NOMURA, T.
0:00 / WAZ / TKG

NOMURA, Tadahiro — JPN	
BYE	NOMURA, T.
CARCAMO GUTIERREZ, Leonardo — HON	
BYE	CARCAMO GUTIERREZ, L.

NOMURA, T.
4:22 / IPO / HRM

NOMURA, T. — JPN
1:54 / IPO / UMG

MENDEZ, Melvin — PUR	
BYE	MENDEZ, M.
NARMANDAKH, Dorjpalam — MGL	
BYE	NARMANDAKH, D.

NARMANDAKH, D.
3:49 / IPO / KGU

NARMANDAKH, D.
0:00 / KOK / KTA

BEATON, Ewan — CAN	
CARAVANA, Pedro — POR	CARAVANA, P. 0:00 / WAZ / SON
DONOHUE, Nigel — GBR	
BYE	DONOHUE, N.

DONOHUE, N.
2:52 / IPO / SON

NARMANDAKH, D.
1:12 / IPO / UMA

IDRISSI CHORFI, Abdelouahed — MAR	
BYE	IDRISSI CHORFI, A.
BOKIYEV, Rustam — TJK	
BYE	BOKIYEV, R.

IDRISSI CHORFI, A.
0:00 / WAZ / TOS

MUKHTAROV, A.
1:39 / IPO / UMA

MUKHTAROV, Alisher — UZB	
BYE	MUKHTAROV, A.
GARCIA, Alexandre — BRA	
BYE	GARCIA, A.

MUKHTAROV, A.
0:00 / YUK / STG

Pool B

MATUSZEK, Marek — SVK	
BYE	MATUSZEK, M.
CHAMBILY, Franck — FRA	
BYE	CHAMBILY, F.

CHAMBILY, F.
0:00 / YUS

GIOVINAZZO, G.
1:21 / IPO / ISN

VAZAGASHVILI, Giorgi — GEO	
BYE	VAZAGASHVILI, G.
GIOVINAZZO, Girolamo — ITA	
BYE	GIOVINAZZO, G.

GIOVINAZZO, G.
0:00 / WAZ / TNG

GIOVINAZZO, G.
4:36 / IPO / SON

LENCINA, Jorge — ARG	
BYE	LENCINA, J.
GUSEYNOV, Nazim — AZE	
BYE	GUSEYNOV, N.

GUSEYNOV, N.
2:04 / IPO / KSH

ACUNA, R.
0:00 / CHU / P12

ACUNA, Ricardo — MEX	
BYE	ACUNA, R.
POWER, Brian — AUS	
BYE	POWER, B.

ACUNA, R.
3:03 / IPO / TSG

GIOVINAZZO, G. — ITA
2:35 / IPO / SON

SUNADA, Clifton — USA	
BYE	SUNADA, C.
TRAUTMANN, Richard — GER	
BYE	TRAUTMANN, R.

TRAUTMANN, R.
4:05 / IPO / JG

TRAUTMANN, R.
0:00 / SHI / P29

BAGIROV, Natik — BLR	
BYE	BAGIROV, N.
SULLIVAN, Sean — IRL	
SINGH, Narender — IND	SINGH, N. 0:08 / IPO / SUK

BAGIROV, N.
0:00 / YUK / KSG

TRAUTMANN, R.
1:17 / IPO / YSG

POULOT RAMOS, Manolo — CUB	
BYE	POULOT RAMOS, M.
KIM, Jong-Won — KOR	
BYE	KIM, J.-W.

KIM, J.
3:15 / IPO / UMA

KIM, J.
0:00 / WAZ / OSG

KAMROWSKI, Piotr — POL	
BYE	KAMROWSKI, P.
KUNYIK, Zsolt — HUN	
BYE	KUNYIK, Z.

KAMROWSKI, P.
1:07 / IPO / JG

continued on next page / continué à la page suivante

Extra Lightweight, 60 kg, Men / *Super-léger, 60 kg, Messieurs*

continued from previous page / suite de la page précédente

FINAL		GOLD	
NOMURA, Tadahiro	JPN		
		NOMURA, T.	JPN
GIOVINAZZO, Girolamo	ITA	0:27 / IPO / SON	

SILVER	
GIOVINAZZO, G	ITA

Repechage and Summary

Pool A

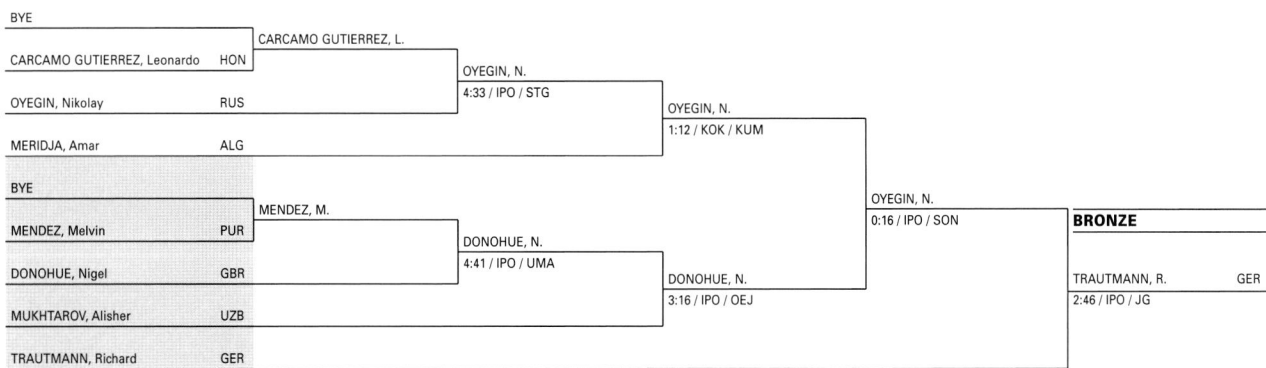

```
BYE
                              CARCAMO GUTIERREZ, L.
CARCAMO GUTIERREZ, Leonardo  HON
                                        OYEGIN, N.
OYEGIN, Nikolay              RUS        4:33 / IPO / STG
                                                          OYEGIN, N.
MERIDJA, Amar                ALG                          1:12 / KOK / KUM
                                                                             OYEGIN, N.
BYE                                                                          0:16 / IPO / SON      BRONZE
                              MENDEZ, M.
MENDEZ, Melvin               PUR
                                        DONOHUE, N.                                                TRAUTMANN, R.    GER
DONOHUE, Nigel               GBR        4:41 / IPO / UMA                                            2:46 / IPO / JG
                                                          DONOHUE, N.
MUKHTAROV, Alisher           UZB                          3:16 / IPO / OEJ

TRAUTMANN, Richard           GER
```

Pool B

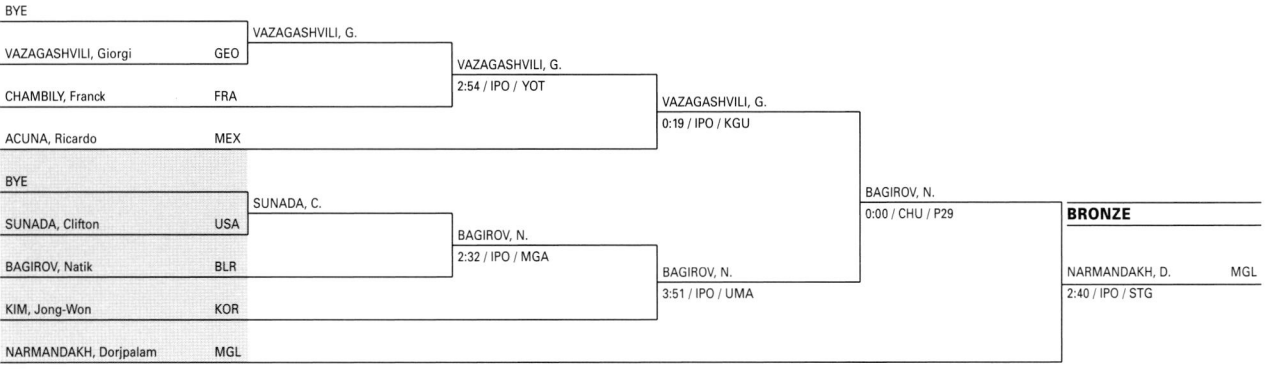

```
BYE
                              VAZAGASHVILI, G.
VAZAGASHVILI, Giorgi         GEO
                                        VAZAGASHVILI, G.
CHAMBILY, Franck             FRA        2:54 / IPO / YOT
                                                          VAZAGASHVILI, G.
ACUNA, Ricardo               MEX                          0:19 / IPO / KGU
                                                                             BAGIROV, N.
BYE                                                                          0:00 / CHU / P29      BRONZE
                              SUNADA, C.
SUNADA, Clifton              USA
                                        BAGIROV, N.                                                NARMANDAKH, D.   MGL
BAGIROV, Natik               BLR        2:32 / IPO / MGA                                            2:40 / IPO / STG
                                                          BAGIROV, N.
KIM, Jong-Won                KOR                          3:51 / IPO / UMA

NARMANDAKH, Dorjpalam        MGL
```

FINAL CLASSIFICATION

Rnk	Name	Ctry	
1	NOMURA, Tadahiro	JPN	**Gold**
2	GIOVINAZZO, Girolamo	ITA	**Silver**
3	NARMANDAKH, Dorjpalam	MGL	**Bronze**
	TRAUTMANN, Richard	GER	**Bronze**
5	BAGIROV, Natik	BLR	
	OYEGIN, Nikolay	RUS	
7	DONOHUE, Nigel	GBR	
	VAZAGASHVILI, Giorgi	GEO	

Judo / *Judo*
Extra Lightweight, 48 kg, Women / *Super-léger, 48 kg, Dames*

Preliminaries

FIRST ROUND	SECOND ROUND	QUARTERFINALS	SEMIFINALS	FINAL

Pool A

KIRKMAN, Tina — AUS
YU, Shu-Chen — TPE
WOLF, Hillary — USA
BYE

YU, S.-C.
0:00 / YUK / KTA

WOLF, H.

WOLF, H.
2:12 / IPO / JG

SENYURT, Hulya — TUR
SOUAKRI, Salima — ALG
SAVON, Amarilis — CUB
BYE

SOUAKRI, S.
2:04 / IPO / KKS

SAVON, A.

SAVON, A.
0:00 / KOK / KUG

SAVON, A.
2:12 / IPO / JG

TORTORA, Giovanna — ITA
BERTI, Andrea — BRA
ATAYEVA, Galina — TKM
BYE

TORTORA, G.
0:00 / YUS

ATAYEVA, G.

TORTORA, G.
0:00 / YUK / OUC

MALDONADO, Dora — HON
BYE
TAMURA, Ryoko — JPN
MOSKVINA, Tatyana — BLR

MALDONADO, D.

TAMURA, R.
2:03 / IPO / TOS

TAMURA, R.
2:57 / IPO / SON

TAMURA, R.
0:00 / WAZ / SON

TAMURA, R.
1:40 / IPO / SON

Pool B

CAO NGOC, Phoung Trinh — VIE
BYE
LI, Aiyue — CHN
NICHILO, Sarah — FRA

CAO NGOX, P. T.

NICHILO, S.
0:00 / SHI / P29

NICHILO, S.
3:46 / IPO / HRM

MEIJER, Tamara — NED
KULIGINA, Natalya — KGZ
KYE, Sun Hui — PRK
BYE

MEIJER, T.
0:00 / WAZ / OSG

KYE, S. H.

KYE, S. H.
0:00 / YUK / MGA

KYE, S. H.
0:00 / YUK / MGA

PERLBERG, Jana — GER
BYE
ROSZKOWSKA, Malgorzata — POL
BYE

PERLBERG, J.

ROSZKOWSKA, M.

ROSZKOWSKA, M.
0:00 / KOK / UMA

HERON, Joyce — GBR
BYE
LEPAGE, Carolyne — CAN
SOLER, Yolanda — ESP

HERON, J.

SOLER, Y.
1:46 / IPO / SON

SOLER, Y.
2:03 / IPO / OUG

SOLER, Y.
0:00 / WAZ / SON

KYE, S. H.
3:04 / IPO / OGO

GOLD

KYE, S. H. — PRK
0:00 / KOK / HRA

SILVER

TAMURA, R. — JPN

FINAL CLASSIFICATION

Rnk	Name	Ctry	
1	KYE, Sun Hui	PRK	Gold
2	TAMURA, Ryoko	JPN	Silver
3	SAVON, Amarilis	CUB	Bronze
	SOLER, Yolanda	ESP	Bronze
5	NICHILO, Sarah	FRA	
	SOUAKRI, Salima	ALG	
7	MOSKVINA, Tatyana	BLR	
	ROSZKOWSKA, Malgorzata	POL	

Repechage and Summary

Pool A

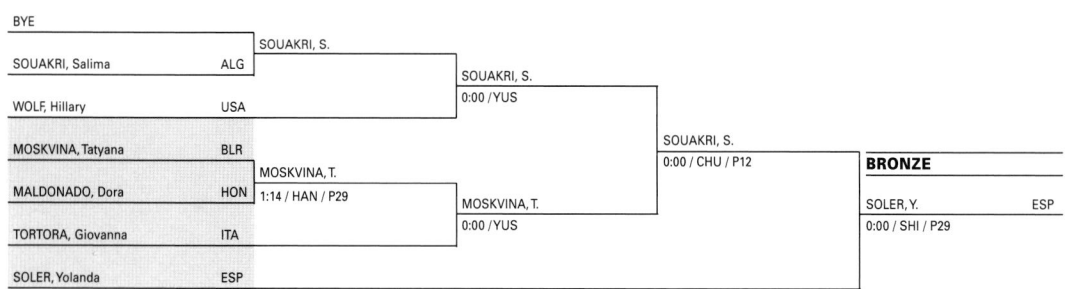

BYE
SOUAKRI, Salima — ALG
WOLF, Hillary — USA

SOUAKRI, S.

SOUAKRI, S.
0:00 / YUS

MOSKVINA, Tatyana — BLR
MALDONADO, Dora — HON
TORTORA, Giovanna — ITA
SOLER, Yolanda — ESP

MOSKVINA, T.
1:14 / HAN / P29

MOSKVINA, T.
0:00 / YUS

SOUAKRI, S.
0:00 / CHU / P12

BRONZE

SOLER, Y. — ESP
0:00 / SHI / P29

Pool B

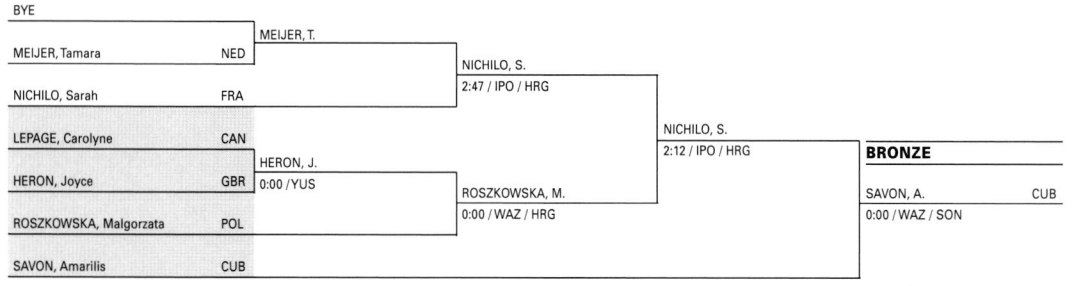

BYE
MEIJER, Tamara — NED
NICHILO, Sarah — FRA

MEIJER, T.

NICHILO, S.
2:47 / IPO / HRG

LEPAGE, Carolyne — CAN
HERON, Joyce — GBR
ROSZKOWSKA, Malgorzata — POL
SAVON, Amarilis — CUB

HERON, J.
0:00 / YUS

ROSZKOWSKA, M.
0:00 / WAZ / HRG

NICHILO, S.
2:12 / IPO / HRG

BRONZE

SAVON, A. — CUB
0:00 / WAZ / SON

Judo / *Judo*
Half-Lightweight, 65 kg, Men / *Mi-léger, 65 kg, Messieurs*

Preliminaries

1ST ROUND	2ND ROUND	3RD ROUND	QUARTERFINALS	SEMIFINALS	FINAL

Pool A

DAVIES, Julian — GBR
BYE
→ DAVIES, J.
→ DAVIES, J. 2:45 / IPO / JG

SECK, Abdou Karim — SEN
BYE
→ SECK, A. K.

TORO, Jose — ESP
BYE
→ TORO, J.
→ LEWAK, J. 3:59 / IPO / KTA

LEWAK, Jaroslaw — POL
BYE
→ LEWAK, J.

→ LEWAK, J. 0:00 / YUK / TNO

ACHIROV, Sergei — KAZ
BYE
→ ACHIROV, S.
→ FUENTES, O. 0:00 / SHI / P12

FUENTES, Orlando — USA
BYE
→ FUENTES, O.

MORALES, Francisco — ARG
REVAZISHVILI, Giorgi — GEO
→ REVAZISHVILI, G. 0:00 / WAZ / UMA
→ LAATS, P. 4:24 / IPO / TNG

LAATS, Philip — BEL
BYE
→ LAATS, P.

→ LAATS, P. 3:59 / IPO / HRG

→ LAATS, P. 0:00 / KOK / KGU

ZHANG, Guangjun — CHN
BYE
→ ZHANG, G.
→ TAN, T. 0:00 / KOK / KUG

TAN, Taro — CAN
BYE
→ TAN, T.

ALMEIDA, Michel — POR
PEREZ, Jose — PUR
→ ALMEIDA, M. 4:54 / IPO / KGU
→ ALMEIDA, M. 0:00 / KOK / SUG

GIORGI, Francesco — ITA
BYE
→ GIORGI, F.

→ ALMEIDA, M. 0:00 / YUK / STA

HERNANDEZ PLANA, Israel — CUB
BYE
→ HERNANDEZ PLANA, I.
→ HERNANDEZ PLANA, I. 1:27 / IPO / OUG

FAGAN, Darren — AUS
BYE
→ FAGAN, D.

→ QUELLMALZ, U. 3:57 / IPO / STA

QUELLMALZ, Udo — GER
BYE
→ QUELLMALZ, U.
→ QUELLMALZ, U. 4:34 / IPO / OUG

FIGUEREO, Francis — DOM
BYE
→ FIGUEREO, F.

→ QUELLMALZ, U. 2:22 / IPO / JG

QUELLMALZ, U. — GER, 3:31 / IPO / TOS

Pool B

NYAMLHAGVA, Purevdorj — MGL
BYE
→ NYAMLHAGVA, P.
→ NYAMLHAGVA, P. 4:24 / IPO / STG

LAUREN, Pasi — FIN
RAMIREZ, Carlos — ESA
→ LAUREN, P. 0:23 / IPO / UMA

NAKAMURA, Yukimasa — JPN
BYE
→ NAKAMURA, Y.
→ NAKAMURA, Y. 0:22 / SOG / P12

MATSIEV, Islam — RUS
BYE
→ MATSIEV, I.

→ NAKAMURA, Y. 0:00 / CHU / P12

MUKHAMEDKHANOV, Timur — UZB
BYE
→ MUKHAMEDKHANOV, T.
→ MUKHAMEDKHANOV, T. 4:34 / IPO / JG

MOLNE, Tony — AND
BYE
→ MOLNE, T.

→ NETOV, I. 0:00 / SHI / P12

NETOV, Ivan — BUL
BYE
→ NETOV, I.
→ NETOV, I. 2:07 / IPO / HTA

WARD, Ciaran — IRL
BYE
→ WARD, C.

→ NAKAMURA, Y. 1:32 / IPO / STG

CSAK, Jozsef — HUN
BYE
→ CSAK, J.
→ CSAK, J. 2:59 / IPO / TNG

AGA, Najib — IND
BYE
→ AGA, N.

→ CSAK, J. 2:25 / IPO / JG

STEFFANO, Leonardo — URU
BYE
→ STEFFANO, L.
→ MacKINNON, D. 3:47 / IPO / SON

MacKINNON, Duncan — RSA
BYE
→ MacKINNON, D.

→ CSAK, J. 0:00 / YUK / OUG

GUIMARAES, Henrique Carlos — BRA
BYE
→ GUIMARAES, H. C.
→ GUIMARAES, H. C. 0:00 / KOK / KSG

BENBOUDAOUD, Larbi — FRA
BYE
→ BENBOUDAOUD, L.

→ GUIMARAES, H. C. 0:00 / YUS

DEMIREL, Bektas — TUR
BYE
→ DEMIREL, B.
→ LEE, S. 0:00 / KEI / P21

LEE, Sung-Hoon — KOR
BYE
→ LEE, S.

NAKAMURA, Y. — JPN, 0:00 / YUK / KUG

continued on next page / continué à la page suivante

Half-Lightweight, 65 kg, Men / *Mi-léger, 65 kg, Messieurs*

continued from previous page / suite de la page précédente

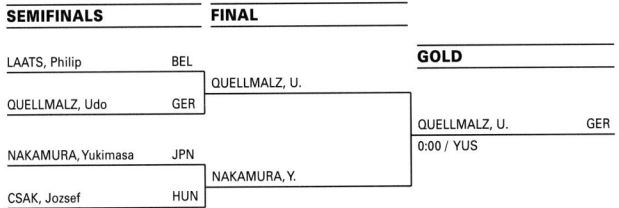

SEMIFINALS

LAATS, Philip — BEL

QUELLMALZ, Udo — GER

QUELLMALZ, U.

NAKAMURA, Yukimasa — JPN

NAKAMURA, Y.

CSAK, Jozsef — HUN

FINAL

GOLD

QUELLMALZ, U. — GER
0:00 / YUS

SILVER

NAKAMURA, Y. — JPN

Repechage and Summary

Pool A

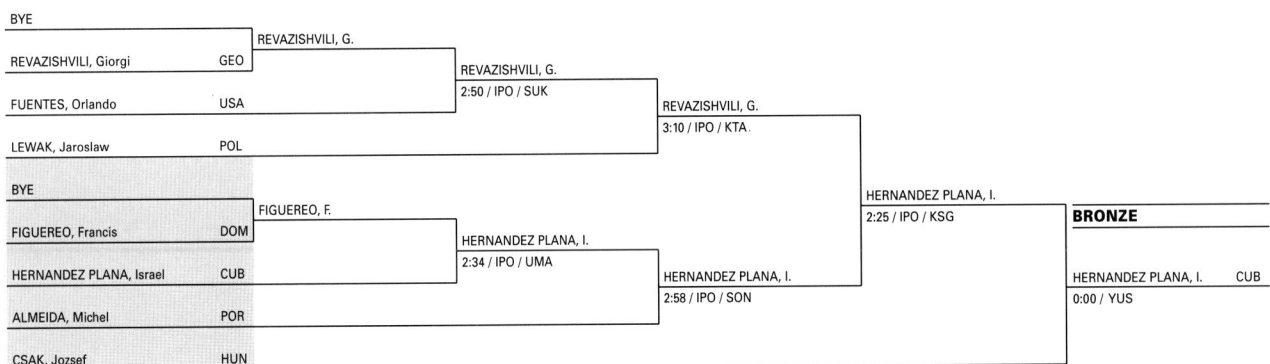

BYE

REVAZISHVILI, Giorgi — GEO

REVAZISHVILI, G.

FUENTES, Orlando — USA

REVAZISHVILI, G.
2:50 / IPO / SUK

LEWAK, Jaroslaw — POL

REVAZISHVILI, G.
3:10 / IPO / KTA.

BYE

FIGUEREO, Francis — DOM

FIGUEREO, F.

HERNANDEZ PLANA, Israel — CUB

HERNANDEZ PLANA, I.
2:34 / IPO / UMA

ALMEIDA, Michel — POR

HERNANDEZ PLANA, I.
2:58 / IPO / SON

CSAK, Jozsef — HUN

HERNANDEZ PLANA, I.
2:25 / IPO / KSG

BRONZE

HERNANDEZ PLANA, I. — CUB
0:00 / YUS

Pool B

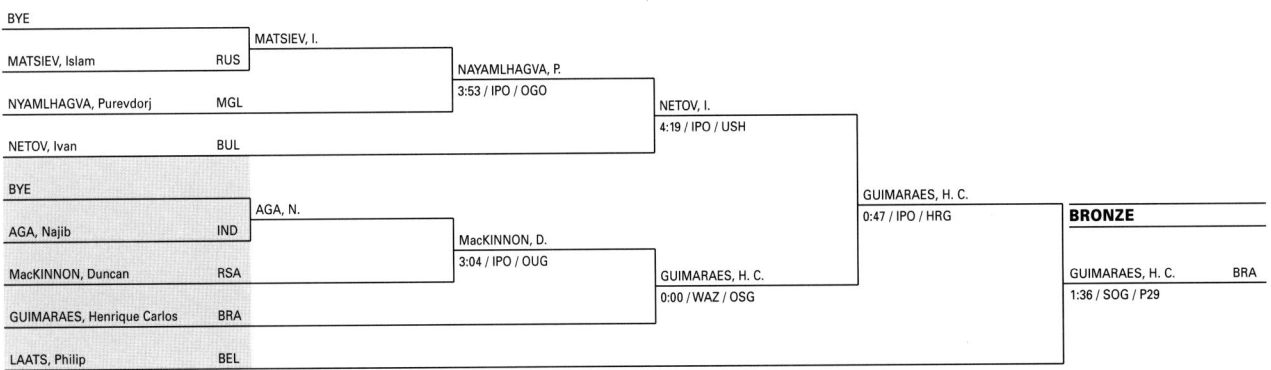

BYE

MATSIEV, Islam — RUS

MATSIEV, I.

NYAMLHAGVA, Purevdorj — MGL

NAYAMLHAGVA, P.
3:53 / IPO / OGO

NETOV, Ivan — BUL

NETOV, I.
4:19 / IPO / USH

BYE

AGA, Najib — IND

AGA, N.

MacKINNON, Duncan — RSA

MacKINNON, D.
3:04 / IPO / OUG

GUIMARAES, Henrique Carlos — BRA

GUIMARAES, H. C.
0:00 / WAZ / OSG

LAATS, Philip — BEL

GUIMARAES, H. C.
0:47 / IPO / HRG

BRONZE

GUIMARAES, H. C. — BRA
1:36 / SOG / P29

FINAL CLASSIFICATION

Rnk	Name	Ctry	
1	QUELLMALZ, Udo	GER	Gold
2	NAKAMURA, Yukimasa	JPN	Silver
3	GUIMARAES, Henrique Carlos	BRA	Bronze
	HERNANDEZ PLANA, Israel	CUB	Bronze
5	CSAK, Jozsef	HUN	
	LAATS, Philip	BEL	
7	NETOV, Ivan	BUL	
	REVAZISHVILI, Giorgi	GEO	

Judo / *Judo*
Half-Lightweight, 52 kg, Women / *Mi-léger, 52 kg, Dames*

Preliminaries

FIRST ROUND	SECOND ROUND	QUARTERFINALS	SEMIFINALS	FINAL

Pool A

- KRAUSE, Larysa — POL
- BYE
  - KRAUSE, L.
- RENDLE, Sharon — GBR
- MEKZINE, Lynda — ALG
  - MEKZINE, L. — 1:23 / IPO / KSK
    - KRAUSE, L. — 2:34 / IPO / SON
- MUNOZ, Almudena — ESP
- BYE
  - MUNOZ, A.
    - MUNOZ, A. — 0:00 / CHU / P29
      - KRAUSE, L. — 0:00 / YUS
- SCHMUTZ, Isabelle — SUI
- KOVRIGINA, Marina — RUS
  - KOVRIGINA, M. — 0:00 / YUK / HKG
- SANTAELLA, Katty — VEN
- BYE
  - SANTAELLA, K.
    - PEDULLA, M. — 1:26 / IPO / SUK
- GOOSSENS, Heidi — BEL
- PEDULLA, Marisa — USA
  - PEDULLA, M. — 0:00 / WAZ / OUG
    - RESTOUX, M.-C. — 0:00 / WAZ / TNO
- BRAIN, Catherine — AUS
- BYE
  - BRAIN, C.
    - RESTOUX, M.-C. — 3:09 / IPO / OSG
- RESTOUX, Marie-Claire — FRA
- BYE
  - RESTOUX, M.-C.

RESTOUX, M.-C. — FRA — 0:00 / YUS

Pool B

- MARIANI, Carolina — ARG
- BYE
  - MARIANI, C.
- GOSSELIN, Nathalie — CAN
- BYE
  - GOSSELIN, N.
    - MARIANI, C. — 0:00 / WAZ / STG
- TSENG, Hsiao-Fen — TPE
- BYE
  - TSENG, H.-F.
    - HYUN, S.-H. — 1:31 / WIP / OUG
      - HYUN, S.-H. — 2:40 / IPO / TNO
- HYUN, Sook-Hee — KOR
- GIUNGI, Alessandra — ITA
  - HYUN, S.-H. — 0:00 / WAZ / UMA
- von SCHWICHOW, Alexa — GER
- BYE
  - von SCHWICHOW, A.
    - VERDECIA, L. — 3:41 / IPO / STG
- VERDECIA, Legna — CUB
- BYE
  - VERDECIA, L.
    - VERDECIA, L. — 0:00 / YUS
- SUGAWARA, Noriko — JPN
- WANG, Jin — CHN
  - SUGAWARA, N. — 1:42 / IPO / YSG
- THAKUR, Sunith — IND
- BYE
  - THAKUR, S.
    - SUGAWARA, N. — 3:28 / IPO / KSG

HYUN, S.-H. — KOR — 0:00 / CHU / P29

GOLD

RESTOUX, M.-C. — FRA — 0:00 / YUK / USH

SILVER

HYUN, S.-H. — KOR

FINAL CLASSIFICATION

Rnk	Name	Ctry	
1	RESTOUX, Marie-Claire	FRA	Gold
2	HYUN, Sook-Hee	KOR	Silver
3	SUGAWARA, Noriko	JPN	Bronze
	VERDECIA, Legna	CUB	Bronze
5	KRAUSE, Larysa	POL	
	MUNOZ, Almudena	ESP	
7	MARIANI, Carolina	ARG	
	PEDULLA, Marisa	USA	

Repechage and Summary

Pool A

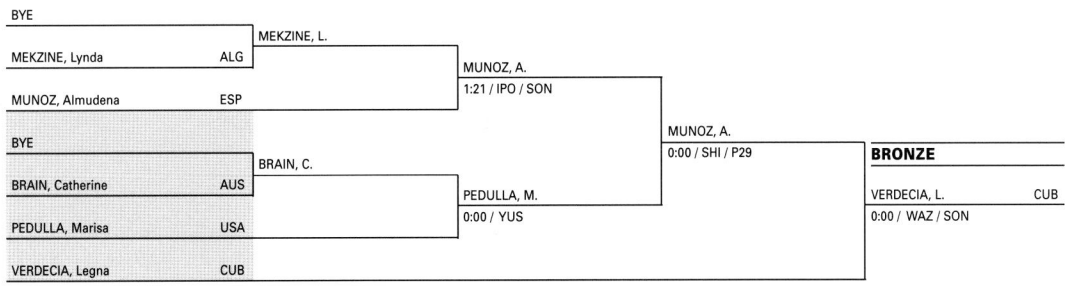

- BYE
- MEKZINE, Lynda — ALG
  - MEKZINE, L.
- MUNOZ, Almudena — ESP
    - MUNOZ, A. — 1:21 / IPO / SON
- BYE
- BRAIN, Catherine — AUS
  - BRAIN, C.
      - MUNOZ, A. — 0:00 / SHI / P29
- PEDULLA, Marisa — USA
- VERDECIA, Legna — CUB
    - PEDULLA, M. — 0:00 / YUS

BRONZE

VERDECIA, L. — CUB — 0:00 / WAZ / SON

Pool B

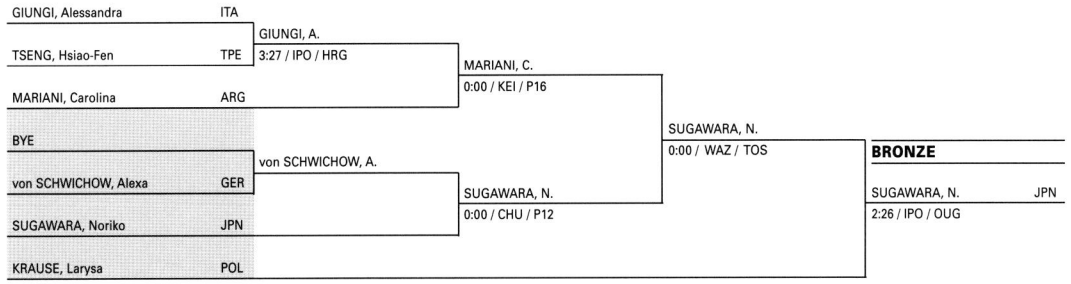

- GIUNGI, Alessandra — ITA
- TSENG, Hsiao-Fen — TPE
  - GIUNGI, A. — 3:27 / IPO / HRG
- MARIANI, Carolina — ARG
    - MARIANI, C. — 0:00 / KEI / P16
- BYE
- von SCHWICHOW, Alexa — GER
  - von SCHWICHOW, A.
      - SUGAWARA, N. — 0:00 / WAZ / TOS
- SUGAWARA, Noriko — JPN
- KRAUSE, Larysa — POL
    - SUGAWARA, N. — 0:00 / CHU / P12

BRONZE

SUGAWARA, N. — JPN — 2:26 / IPO / OUG

Judo / *Judo*

Lightweight, 71 kg, Men / *Léger, 71 kg, Messieurs*

Preliminaries

1ST ROUND	2ND ROUND	3RD ROUND	QUARTERFINALS	SEMIFINALS	FINAL

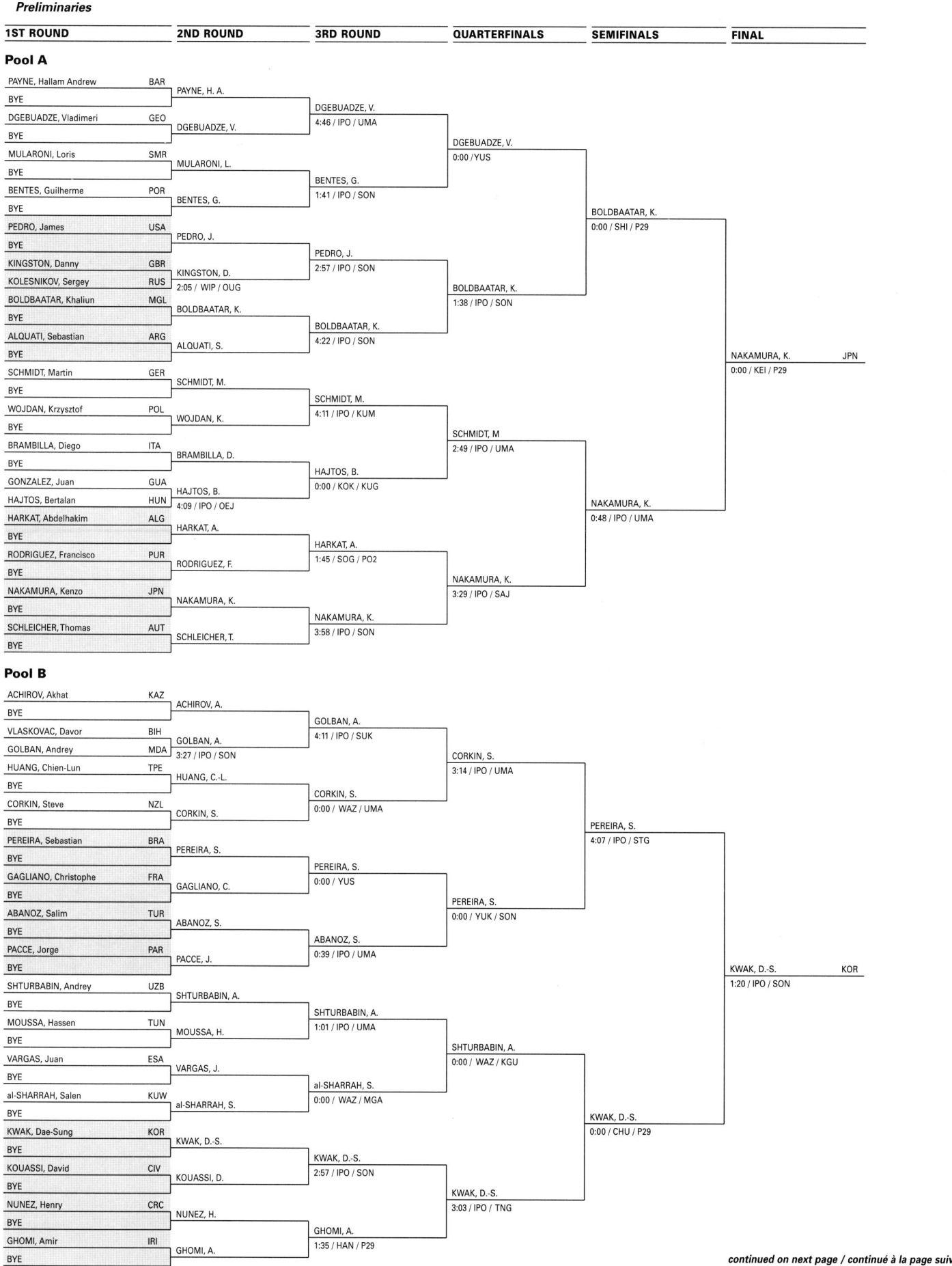

Pool A

PAYNE, Hallam Andrew — BAR
BYE
→ PAYNE, H. A.

DGEBUADZE, Vladimeri — GEO
BYE
→ DGEBUADZE, V.
→ DGEBUADZE, V. — 4:46 / IPO / UMA

MULARONI, Loris — SMR
BYE
→ MULARONI, L.

BENTES, Guilherme — POR
BYE
→ BENTES, G.
→ BENTES, G. — 1:41 / IPO / SON

→ DGEBUADZE, V. — 0:00 / YUS

PEDRO, James — USA
BYE
→ PEDRO, J.

KINGSTON, Danny — GBR
KOLESNIKOV, Sergey — RUS
→ KINGSTON, D. — 2:05 / WIP / OUG
→ PEDRO, J. — 2:57 / IPO / SON

BOLDBAATAR, Khaliun — MGL
BYE
→ BOLDBAATAR, K.

ALQUATI, Sebastian — ARG
BYE
→ ALQUATI, S.
→ BOLDBAATAR, K. — 4:22 / IPO / SON

→ BOLDBAATAR, K. — 1:38 / IPO / SON

→ BOLDBAATAR, K. — 0:00 / SHI / P29

SCHMIDT, Martin — GER
BYE
→ SCHMIDT, M.

WOJDAN, Krzysztof — POL
BYE
→ WOJDAN, K.
→ SCHMIDT, M. — 4:11 / IPO / KUM

BRAMBILLA, Diego — ITA
BYE
→ BRAMBILLA, D.

GONZALEZ, Juan — GUA
HAJTOS, Bertalan — HUN
→ HAJTOS, B. — 4:09 / IPO / OEJ
→ HAJTOS, B. — 0:00 / KOK / KUG

→ SCHMIDT, M — 2:49 / IPO / UMA

HARKAT, Abdelhakim — ALG
BYE
→ HARKAT, A.

RODRIGUEZ, Francisco — PUR
BYE
→ RODRIGUEZ, F.
→ HARKAT, A. — 1:45 / SOG / PO2

NAKAMURA, Kenzo — JPN
BYE
→ NAKAMURA, K.

SCHLEICHER, Thomas — AUT
BYE
→ SCHLEICHER, T.
→ NAKAMURA, K. — 3:58 / IPO / SON

→ NAKAMURA, K. — 3:29 / IPO / SAJ

→ NAKAMURA, K. — 0:48 / IPO / UMA

→ NAKAMURA, K. — JPN — 0:00 / KEI / P29

Pool B

ACHIROV, Akhat — KAZ
BYE
→ ACHIROV, A.

VLASKOVAC, Davor — BIH
GOLBAN, Andrey — MDA
→ GOLBAN, A. — 3:27 / IPO / SON
→ GOLBAN, A. — 4:11 / IPO / SUK

HUANG, Chien-Lun — TPE
BYE
→ HUANG, C.-L.

CORKIN, Steve — NZL
BYE
→ CORKIN, S.
→ CORKIN, S. — 0:00 / WAZ / UMA

→ CORKIN, S. — 3:14 / IPO / UMA

PEREIRA, Sebastian — BRA
BYE
→ PEREIRA, S.

GAGLIANO, Christophe — FRA
BYE
→ GAGLIANO, C.
→ PEREIRA, S. — 0:00 / YUS

→ PEREIRA, S. — 0:00 / YUK / SON

ABANOZ, Salim — TUR
BYE
→ ABANOZ, S.

PACCE, Jorge — PAR
BYE
→ PACCE, J.
→ ABANOZ, S. — 0:39 / IPO / UMA

→ PEREIRA, S. — 4:07 / IPO / STG

SHTURBABIN, Andrey — UZB
BYE
→ SHTURBABIN, A.

MOUSSA, Hassen — TUN
BYE
→ MOUSSA, H.
→ SHTURBABIN, A. — 1:01 / IPO / UMA

VARGAS, Juan — ESA
BYE
→ VARGAS, J.

al-SHARRAH, Salen — KUW
BYE
→ al-SHARRAH, S.
→ al-SHARRAH, S. — 0:00 / WAZ / MGA

→ SHTURBABIN, A. — 0:00 / WAZ / KGU

KWAK, Dae-Sung — KOR
BYE
→ KWAK, D.-S.

KOUASSI, David — CIV
BYE
→ KOUASSI, D.
→ KWAK, D.-S. — 2:57 / IPO / SON

NUNEZ, Henry — CRC
BYE
→ NUNEZ, H.

GHOMI, Amir — IRI
BYE
→ GHOMI, A.
→ GHOMI, A. — 1:35 / HAN / P29

→ KWAK, D.-S. — 3:03 / IPO / TNG

→ KWAK, D.-S. — 0:00 / CHU / P29

→ KWAK, D.-S. — KOR — 1:20 / IPO / SON

continued on next page / continué à la page suivante

Lightweight, 71 kg, Men / *Léger, 71 kg, Messieurs*

continued from previous page / suite de la page précédente

FINAL		GOLD	
NAKAMURA, Kenzo	JPN		
		NAKAMURA, K.	JPN
KWAK, Dae-Sung	KOR	0:00 / YUS	

SILVER

KWAK, Dae-Sung   KOR

Repechage and Summary

Pool A

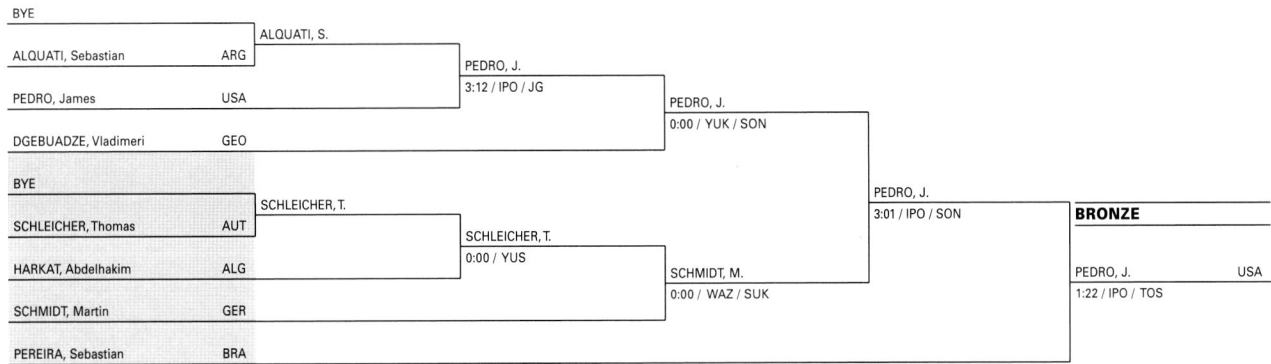

Pool B

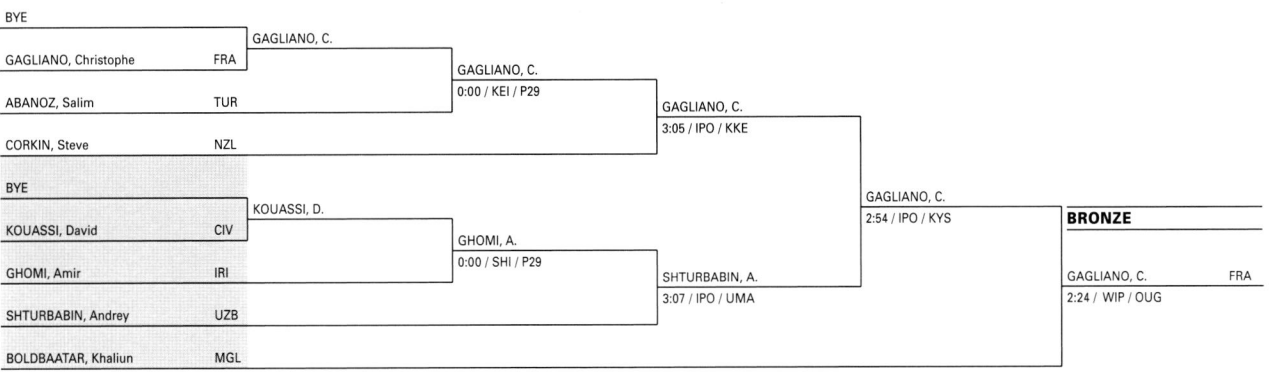

FINAL CLASSIFICATION		
Rnk Name	Ctry	
1 NAKAMURA, Kenzo	JPN	**Gold**
2 KWAK, Dae-Sung	KOR	**Silver**
3 GAGLIANO, Christophe	FRA	**Bronze**
PEDRO, James	USA	**Bronze**
5 BOLDBAATAR, Khaliun	MGL	
PEREIRA, Sebastian	BRA	
7 SCHMIDT, Martin	GER	
SHTURBABIN, Andrey	UZB	

Judo / *Judo*

Lightweight, 56 kg, Women / *Léger, 56 kg, Dames*

Preliminaries

FIRST ROUND	SECOND ROUND	QUARTERFINALS	SEMIFINALS	FINAL

Pool A

MIZOGUCHI, Noriko — JPN
MYREN, Ursula — SWE
   MIZOGUCHI, N.
   3:09 / IPO / KUG
MORNEAU, Marie Josee — CAN
BYE
   MORNEAU, M. J.
      MIZOGUCHI, N.
      2:05 / IPO / TSG

JUNG, Sun-Yong — KOR
BYE
   JUNG, S.-Y.
      JUNG, S.-Y.
      0:00 / KOK / KSK
LOMBA, Marisabel — BEL
BYE
   LOMBA, M.
      JUNG, S.-Y.
      0:00 / WAZ / UMA

RODRIGUEZ, Jeny — HON
PEKLI, Maria — HUN
   PEKLI, M.
   3:21 / IPO / TKG
ZANGRANDO, Danielle — BRA
BYE
   ZANGRANDO, D.
      PEKLI, M.
      0:00 / YUS

GUSEYNOVA, Zulfiya — AZE
BYE
   GUSEYNOVA, Z.
      FERNANDEZ, I.
      0:00 / KOK / KSK
HILL, Narelle — AUS
FERNANDEZ, Isabel — ESP
   FERNANDEZ, I.
   0:00 / WAZ / UMA
      FERNANDEZ, I.
      0:00 / CHU / P16

Pool B

GAL, Jessica — NED
BYE
   GAL, J.
GONZALEZ, Driulis — CUB
BATON, Magali — FRA
   GONZALEZ, D.
   0:00 / YUS
      GONZALEZ, D.
      0:00 / SHI / P29

FAIRBROTHER, Nicola — GBR
CHAARI, Raoudha — TUN
   FAIRBROTHER, N.
   1:17 / IPO / UNS
KUCHARZEWSKA, Beata — POL
BYE
   KUCHARZEWSKA, B.
      FAIRBROTHER, N.
      0:00 / YUS

GARIPOVA, Zulfiya — RUS
LIU, Chuang — CHN
   LIU, C.
   1:59 / IPO / SON
WEST, Corinna — USA
BYE
   WEST, C.
      LIU, C.
      0:40 / IPO / OSG

HUANG, Ai-Chun — TPE
BYE
   HUANG, A.-C.
      HUANG, A.-C.
      0:00 / YUS
CAVALLERI, Filipa — POR
BYE
   CAVALLERI, F.

Semifinals/Final bracket:

JUNG, S.-Y. — KOR
0:00 / YUK / OSG

GONZALEZ, D. — CUB
0:00 / YUS

GONZALEZ, D. — CUB
3:39 / IPO / OUG

LIU, C.
2:30 / IPO / KYS

GOLD

GONZALEZ, D. — CUB
0:00 / YUK / SON

SILVER

JUNG, S.-Y. — KOR

FINAL CLASSIFICATION

Rnk	Name	Ctry	
1	GONZALEZ, Driulis	CUB	**Gold**
2	JUNG, Sun-Yong	KOR	**Silver**
3	FERNANDEZ, Isabel	ESP	**Bronze**
	LOMBA, Marisabel	BEL	**Bronze**
5	FAIRBROTHER, Nicola	GBR	
	LIU, Chuang	CHN	
7	GARIPOVA, Zulfiya	RUS	
	GUSEYNOVA, Zulfiya	AZE	

Repechage and Summary

Pool A

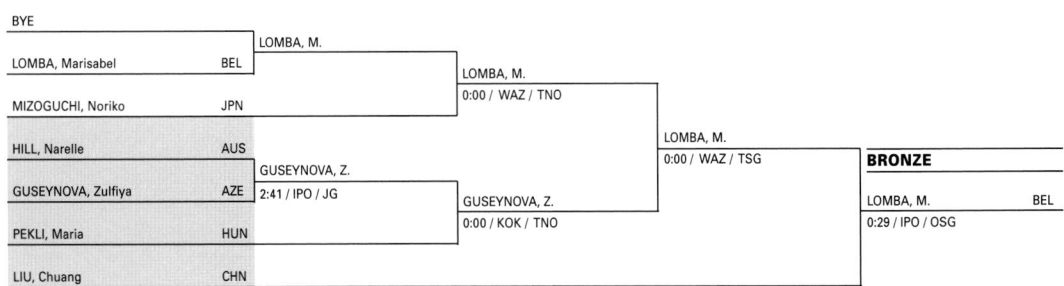

BYE
LOMBA, Marisabel — BEL
   LOMBA, M.
MIZOGUCHI, Noriko — JPN
      LOMBA, M.
      0:00 / WAZ / TNO

HILL, Narelle — AUS
GUSEYNOVA, Zulfiya — AZE
   GUSEYNOVA, Z.
   2:41 / IPO / JG
PEKLI, Maria — HUN
LIU, Chuang — CHN
      GUSEYNOVA, Z.
      0:00 / KOK / TNO

LOMBA, M.
0:00 / WAZ / TSG

BRONZE

LOMBA, M. — BEL
0:29 / IPO / OSG

Pool B

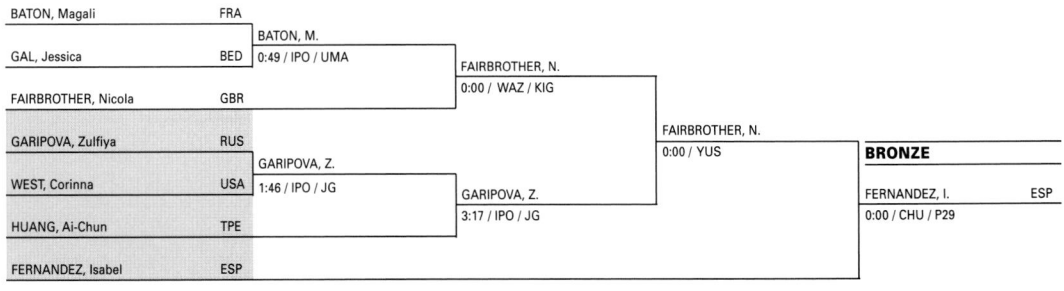

BATON, Magali — FRA
GAL, Jessica — BED
   BATON, M.
   0:49 / IPO / UMA
FAIRBROTHER, Nicola — GBR
      FAIRBROTHER, N.
      0:00 / WAZ / KIG

GARIPOVA, Zulfiya — RUS
WEST, Corinna — USA
   GARIPOVA, Z.
   1:46 / IPO / JG
HUANG, Ai-Chun — TPE
FERNANDEZ, Isabel — ESP
      GARIPOVA, Z.
      3:17 / IPO / JG

FAIRBROTHER, N.
0:00 / YUS

BRONZE

FERNANDEZ, I. — ESP
0:00 / CHU / P29

Judo / *Judo*
Half-Middleweight, 78 kg, Men / *Mi-moyen, 78 kg, Messieurs*

Preliminaries

1ST ROUND	2ND ROUND	3RD ROUND	QUARTERFINALS	SEMIFINALS	FINAL

Pool A

- CHO, In-Chul — KOR
- BYE
  - CHO, I.-C.
- CRETUL, Oleg — MDA
- BYE
  - CRETUL, O.
    - CHO, I.-C.
    - 1:05 / IPO / UKG
- MORGAN, Colin — CAN
- BYE
  - MORGAN, C.
- LIPARTELIANI, Soso — GEO
- BYE
  - LIPARTELIANI, S.
    - LIPARTELIANI, S.
    - 1:57 / IPO / KSK
      - CHO, I.-C.
      - 0:58 / IPO / OGO
- REITER, Patrick — AUT
- SHMAKOV, Vladimir — UZB
  - SHMAKOV, V.
  - 3:29 / IPO / OSG
- CIUPE, Alexandru — ROM
- BYE
  - CIUPE, A.
    - SHMAKOV, V.
    - 4:11 / IPO / TOS
- CHERIFI, Lyes — ALG
- BYE
  - CHERIFI, L.
- MUSA, Seleman — NGR
- BYE
  - MUSA, S.
    - CHERIFI, L.
    - 2:48 / IPO / KAG
      - SHMAKOV, V.
      - 4:35 / IPO / OSG
        - CHO, I.-C.
        - 2:33 / IPO / HRG

- VOLMAR, Adler — HAI
- BYE
  - VOLMAR, A.
- CANTO, Flavio — BRA
- BYE
  - CANTO, F.
    - CANTO, F.
    - 3:21 / IPO / JG
- SEYLKHANOV, Ruslan — KAZ
- BYE
  - SEYLKHANOV, R.
- VATRICAN, Thierry — MON
- BYE
  - VATRICAN, T.
    - VATRICAN, T.
    - 1:19 / WIP / KYS
      - CANTO, F.
      - 3:49 / IPO / JG
- WOLKOWICZ, Bronislaw — POL
- BYE
  - WOLKOWICZ, B.
- SZABO, Gabor — AUS
- BYE
  - SZABO, G.
    - WOLKOWICZ, B.
    - 0:00 / IPO / KYS
      - KOGA, T.
      - 0:00 / WAZ / KSG
- KOGA, Toshihiko — JPN
- BYE
  - KOGA, T.
- LO, Yu-Wei — TPE
- BYE
  - LO, Y.-W.
    - KOGA, T.
    - 0:00 / WAZ / UNA
      - KOGA, T.
      - 0:58 / IPO / TKG

- KOGA, T. — JPN
- 0:00 / KEI / P16

Pool B

- BOURAS, Djamel — FRA
- BYE
  - BOURAS, D.
- SAVCHISHKIN, Konstantin — RUS
- BYE
  - SAVCHISHKIN, K.
    - BOURAS, D.
    - 0:00 / SHI / P12
- YUAN, Chao — CHN
- BYE
  - YUAN, C.
- GEVORKIN, Arsen — ARM
- BYE
  - GEVORKIN, A.
    - YUAN, C.
    - 1:58 / IPO / OSG
      - BOURAS, D.
      - 0:00 / CHU / P29
- FIGUEROA, Jose — PUR
- BYE
  - FIGUEROA, J.
- KLAS, Patrick — NED
- BYE
  - KLAS, P.
    - KLAS, P.
    - 0:00 / YUK / OAB
- BELGAID, Adil — MAR
- BYE
  - BELGAID, A.
- GARCIA, Dario — ARG
- BYE
  - GARCIA, D.
    - GARCIA, D.
    - 3:02 / IPO / UNA
      - GARCIA, D.
      - 2:01 / IPO / YGU
        - BOURAS, D.
        - 3:54 / IPO / OSG

- MORRIS, Jason — USA
- BYE
  - MORRIS, J.
- BALAYAN, Karen — UKR
- BYE
  - BALAYAN, K.
    - MORRIS, J.
    - 0:00 / KOK / OSO
- SMADJA, Shay-Oren — ISR
- RANDALL, Graeme — GBR
  - SMADJA, S.-O.
  - 1:47 / IPO / KSK
- UZNADZE, Irakli — TUR
- BYE
  - UZNADZE, I.
    - UZNADZE, I.
    - 0:00 / KOK / OUG
      - UZNADZE, I.
      - 0:00 / WAZ / HRG
- DOTT, Stefan — GER
- BYE
  - DOTT, S.
- DIXON, Ricky — NCA
- BYE
  - DIXON, R.
    - DOTT, S.
    - 3:57 / IPO / JG
- LAATS, Johan — BEL
- BYE
  - LAATS, J.
- RADULOVIC, Dragoljub — YUG
- BYE
  - RADULOVIC, D.
    - LAATS, J.
    - 4:16 / IPO / TNG
      - DOTT, S.
      - 2:34 / IPO / STG
        - DOTT, S.
        - 3:43 / IPO / KUG

- BOURAS, D. — FRA
- 0:00 / KEI / P29

continued on next page / continué à la page suivante

Judo / *Judo* **303**

Half-Middleweight, 78 kg, Men / *Mi-moyen, 78 kg, Messieurs*

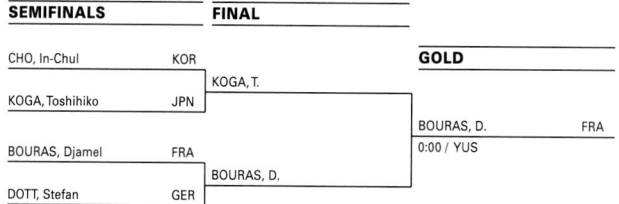

continued from previous page / suite de la page précédente

SEMIFINALS		FINAL

CHO, In-Chul — KOR

KOGA, Toshihiko — JPN

KOGA, T.

BOURAS, Djamel — FRA

DOTT, Stefan — GER

BOURAS, D.

GOLD

BOURAS, D. — FRA
0:00 / YUS

SILVER

KOGA, T. — JPN

Repechage and Summary

Pool A

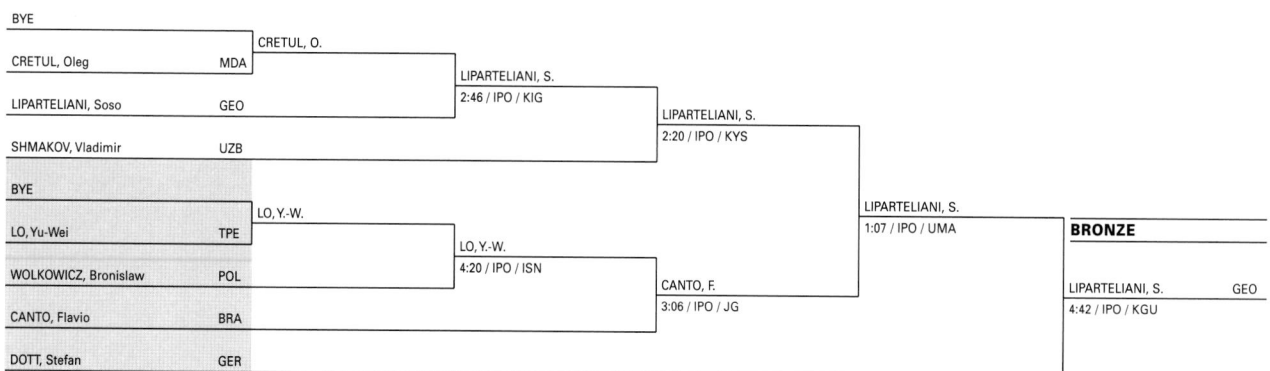

BYE
CRETUL, Oleg — MDA
CRETUL, O.
LIPARTELIANI, Soso — GEO
LIPARTELIANI, S.
2:46 / IPO / KIG
SHMAKOV, Vladimir — UZB
LIPARTELIANI, S.
2:20 / IPO / KYS
BYE
LO, Yu-Wei — TPE
LO, Y.-W.
WOLKOWICZ, Bronislaw — POL
LO, Y.-W.
4:20 / IPO / ISN
CANTO, Flavio — BRA
CANTO, F.
3:06 / IPO / JG
DOTT, Stefan — GER
LIPARTELIANI, S.
1:07 / IPO / UMA

BRONZE

LIPARTELIANI, S. — GEO
4:42 / IPO / KGU

Pool B

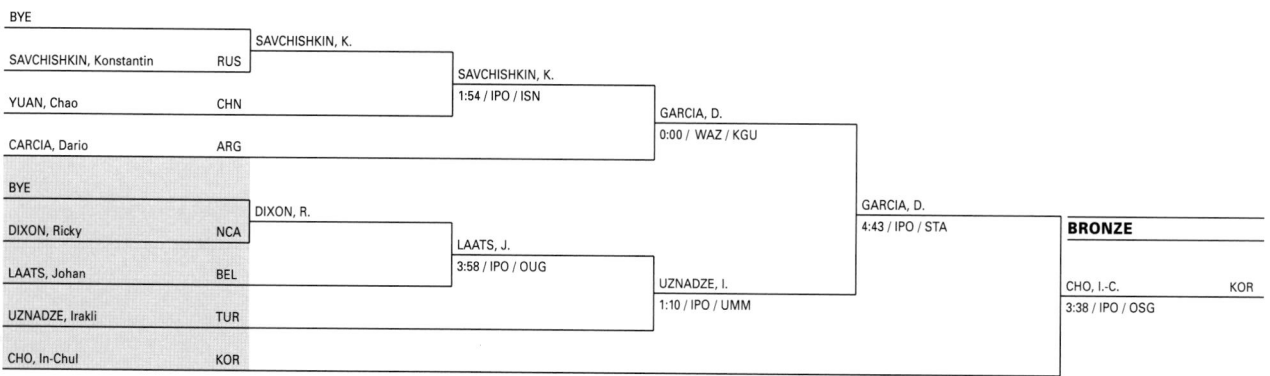

BYE
SAVCHISHKIN, Konstantin — RUS
SAVCHISHKIN, K.
YUAN, Chao — CHN
SAVCHISHKIN, K.
1:54 / IPO / ISN
CARCIA, Dario — ARG
GARCIA, D.
0:00 / WAZ / KGU
BYE
DIXON, Ricky — NCA
DIXON, R.
LAATS, Johan — BEL
LAATS, J.
3:58 / IPO / OUG
UZNADZE, Irakli — TUR
UZNADZE, I.
1:10 / IPO / UMM
CHO, In-Chul — KOR
GARCIA, D.
4:43 / IPO / STA

BRONZE

CHO, I.-C. — KOR
3:38 / IPO / OSG

FINAL CLASSIFICATION			
Rnk	Name	Ctry	
1	BOURAS, Djamel	FRA	Gold
2	KOGA, Toshihiko	JPN	Silver
3	CHO, In-Chul	KOR	Bronze
	LIPARTELIANI, Soso	GEO	Bronze
5	DOTT, Stefan	GER	
	GARCIA, Dario	ARG	
7	CANTO, Flavio	BRA	
	UZNADZE, Irakli	TUR	

Judo / *Judo*
Half-Middleweight, 61 kg, Women / *Mi-moyen, 61 kg, Dames*

Preliminaries

FIRST ROUND	SECOND ROUND	QUARTERFINALS	SEMIFINALS	FINAL

Pool A

- SCHUTZ, Celita — USA
- GRIFFITH, Xiomara — VEN → GRIFFITH, X. 0:56 / IPO / HRG
- VERNEROVA, Michaela — CZE → VERNEROVA, M. → GRIFFITH, X. 1:43 / IPO / HRM
- BYE
- VANDECAVEYE, Gella — BEL → VANDECAVEYE, G. → VANDECAVEYE, G. 3:34 / IPO / UMA → VANDECAVEYE, G. 2:34 / IPO / JG
- BYE
- WU, Ching — HKG → TBESSI, H. 0:55 / IPO / UMA
- TBESSI, Hajar — TUN
- JUNG, Sung-Sook — KOR → JUNG, S.-S. 0:00 / YUK / UMA → JUNG, S.-S. 3:00 / IPO / SAJ → JUNG, S.-S. 2:29 / IPO / SAJ
- SINGER, Susann — GER
- PACE, Laurie — MLT → PACE, L.
- BYE
- LIU, Lizhe — CHN → LIU, L.
- BYE → KOBAS, I. 0:00 / WAZ / KUG
- KOBAS, Ilknur — TUR → KOBAS, I. 0:52 / IPO / KKE
- PARMIGIANO, Cristiane — BRA

Pool B

- EMOTO, Yuko — JPN → EMOTO, Y. 0:00 / WAZ / OSG → EMOTO, Y. 0:00 / YUS → EMOTO, Y. 0:00 / WAZ / UMA
- BOGOMYAGKOVA, Tatyana — RUS
- FLEURY-VACHON, Catherine — FRA → FLEURY-VACHON, C.
- BYE
- KAMSULEVA, Valentina — KAZ → KAMSULEVA, V.
- BYE → ARAD, Y. 3:05 / IPO / OSG
- BLUM, Birgit — LIE → ARAD, Y. 0:00 / YUK / SON
- ARAD, Yael — ISR
- ALVAREZ, Sara — ESP → ALVAREZ, S.
- BYE → ALVAREZ, S. 0:00 / WAZ / TNO
- BELL, Diane — GBR → BELL, D. 0:00 / YUS
- SULLIVAN, Lara — AUS
- BELTRAN, Ileana — CUB → BELTRAN, I.
- BYE → GAL, J. 0:00 / KOK / KEG → GAL, J. 2:46 / WIP / KKE
- GAL, Jenny — NED → GAL, J. 1:16 / WIP / KYS
- BUCKINGHAM, Michelle — CAN

FINAL
- VANDECAVEYE, G. — BEL 0:00 / YUK / HRG
- EMOTO, Y. — JPN 0:00 / KOK / OUG

GOLD
- EMOTO, Y. — JPN 3:05 / IPO / UMA

SILVER
- VANDECAVEYE, G. — BEL

FINAL CLASSIFICATION

Rnk	Name	Ctry	
1	EMOTO, Yuko	JPN	Gold
2	VANDECAVEYE, Gella	BEL	Silver
3	GAL, Jenny	NED	Bronze
	JUNG, Sung-Sook	KOR	Bronze
5	ARAD, Yael	ISR	
	KOBAS, Ilknur	TUR	
7	ALVAREZ, Sara	ESP	
	GRIFFITH, Xiomara	VEN	

Repechage and Summary

Pool A

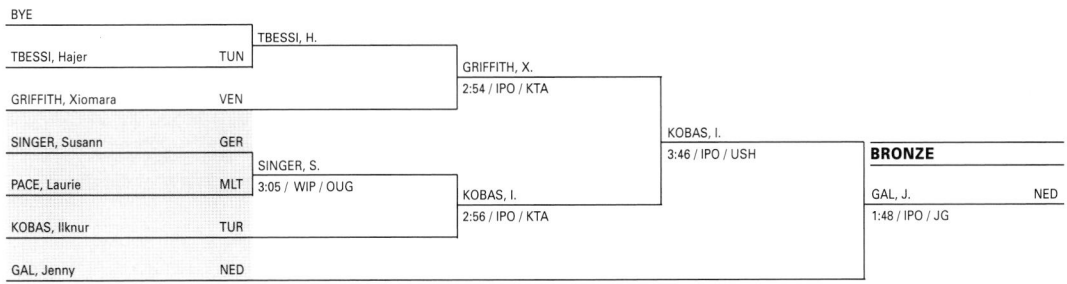

- BYE → TBESSI, H.
- TBESSI, Hajer — TUN
- GRIFFITH, Xiomara — VEN → GRIFFITH, X. 2:54 / IPO / KTA
- SINGER, Susann — GER → SINGER, S. 3:05 / WIP / OUG
- PACE, Laurie — MLT → KOBAS, I. 2:56 / IPO / KTA → KOBAS, I. 3:46 / IPO / USH
- KOBAS, Ilknur — TUR
- GAL, Jenny — NED

BRONZE
- GAL, J. — NED 1:48 / IPO / JG

Pool B

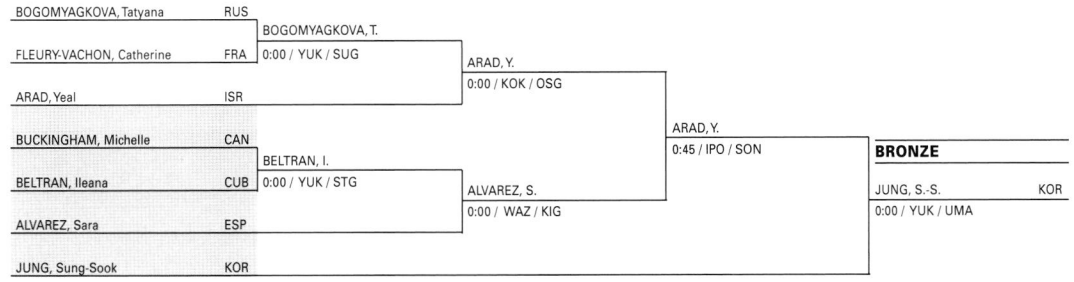

- BOGOMYAGKOVA, Tatyana — RUS → BOGOMYAGKOVA, T. 0:00 / YUK / SUG → ARAD, Y. 0:00 / KOK / OSG
- FLEURY-VACHON, Catherine — FRA
- ARAD, Yeal — ISR → ARAD, Y. 0:45 / IPO / SON
- BUCKINGHAM, Michelle — CAN
- BELTRAN, Ileana — CUB → BELTRAN, I. 0:00 / YUK / STG → ALVAREZ, S. 0:00 / WAZ / KIG
- ALVAREZ, Sara — ESP
- JUNG, Sung-Sook — KOR

BRONZE
- JUNG, S.-S. — KOR 0:00 / YUK / UMA

Preliminaries

1ST ROUND	2ND ROUND	3RD ROUND	QUARTERFINALS	SEMIFINALS	FINAL

Pool A

MALTSEV, Oleg — RUS
BYE
→ MALTSEV, O.

PISULA, Marek — POL
AO, Tegan — CHN
→ AO, T. — 3:35 / IPO / SON

→ MALTSEV, O. — 2:00 / IPO / KKS

CELESTIN, Somoza — HAI
BYE
→ CELESTIN, S.

BAGDASAROV, Armen — UZB
BYE
→ BAGDASAROV, A.

→ BAGDASAROV, A. — 4:14 / IPO / HRG

→ BAGDASAROV, A. — 2:26 / IPO / UNA

OLSON, Brian — USA
BYE
→ OLSON, B.

WU, Kuo-Hui — TPE
BYE
→ WU, K.-H.

→ OLSON, B. — 0:00 / YUK / KSK

MERKEVICIUS, Algimantas — LTU
BYE
→ MERKEVICIUS, A.

LACINA, Petr — CZE
BYE
→ LACINA, P.

→ MERKEVICIUS, A. — 2:25 / IPO / UNA

→ MERKEVICIUS, A. — 0:00 / WAZ / SUK

→ BADGASAROV, A. — 2:10 / WIP / TNO

YOSHIDA, Hidehiko — JPN
BYE
→ YOSHIDA, H.

CROITORU, Adrian — ROM
BYE
→ CROITORU, A.

→ CROITORU, A. — 2:58 / IPO / KSK

MASHURENKO, Ruslan — UKR
BYE
→ MASHURENKO, R.

MURRAY, Sergio — AHO
BYE
→ MURRAY, S.

→ MASHURENKO, R. — 4:34 / IPO / UMA

→ CROITORU, A. — 0:00 / CHU / P29

KLISCHIN, Sergej — AUT
BYE
→ KLISCHIN, S.

WILKINSON, David — AUS
BYE
→ WILKINSON, D.

→ WILKINSON, D. — 3:36 / IPO / TKG

BIRCH, Ryan — GBR
BYE
→ BIRCH, R.

YANDZI, Darcel — FRA
BYE
→ YANDZI, D.

→ YANDZI, D. — 0:00 / WAZ / STA

→ YANDZI, D. — 0:00 / WAZ / KSG

→ CROITORU, A. — 4:36 / IPO / OGA

BAGDASAROV, A. — UZB — 0:00 / YUK / KSK

Pool B

ALIMZHANOV, Sergey — KAZ
BYE
→ ALIMZHANOV, S.

SPITTKA, Marko — GER
BYE
→ SPITTKA, M.

→ SPITTKA, M. — 4:40 / IPO / STG

TSMINDASHVILI, Giorgi — GEO
BYE
→ TSMINDASHVILI, G.

ZANOL, Edelmar — BRA
BYE
→ ZANOL, E.

→ ZANOL, E. — 0:00 / YUK / TOS

→ SPITTKA, M. — 0:00 / KEI / P29

GILL, Nicholas — CAN
CANO, Rodolfo — GUA
→ GILL, N. — 3:18 / WIP / YOT

NDENGUET, Abel — CGO
BYE
→ NDENGUET, A.

→ GILL, N. — 3:45 / IPO / OSG

BAYU, Krisno — INA
BYE
→ BAYU, K.

VILLAR, Leon — ESP
BYE
→ VILLAR, L.

→ VILLAR, L. — 3:14 / IPO / KYS

→ GILL, N. — 0:40 / IPO / JG

→ SPITTKA, M. — 3:55 / IPO / YGU

ELISII, Pablo — ARG
BYE
→ ELISII, P.

KAABA, Adil — MAR
BYE
→ KAABA, A.

→ ELISII, P. — 1:15 / HAN / P29

HACHICHA, Skandar — TUN
BYE
→ HACHICHA, S.

DESPAIGNE, Yosvanne — CUB
BYE
→ DESPAIGNE, Y.

→ DESPAIGNE, Y. — 0:00 / SHI / P29

→ DESPAIGNE, Y. — 0:00 / YUS

JEON, Ki-Young — KOR
BYE
→ JEON, K.-Y.

HUIZINGA, Mark — NED
BYE
→ HUIZINGA, M.

→ JEON, K.-Y. — 0:00 / YUS

BIWOLE ABOLO, Serge — CMR
BYE
→ BIWOLE ABOLO, S.

RAPHAEL, Jean Claude — MRI
BYE
→ RAPHAEL, J. C.

→ BIWOLE ABOLO, S. — 5:00 / FUS

→ JEON, K.-Y. — 4:30 / IPO / UMA

→ JEON, K.-Y. — 3:21 / IPO / SON

JEON, K.-Y. — KOR — 1:05 / IPO / UMA

continued on next page / continué à la page suivante

Middleweight, 86 kg, Men / *Moyen, 86 kg, Messieurs*

continued from previous page / suite de la page précédente

FINAL	GOLD

BAGDASAROV, Armen   UZB

JEON, Ki-Young   KOR

JEON, K.-Y.   KOR
0:49 / IPO / SON

SILVER

BAGDASAROV, Armen   UZB

Repechage and Summary

Pool A

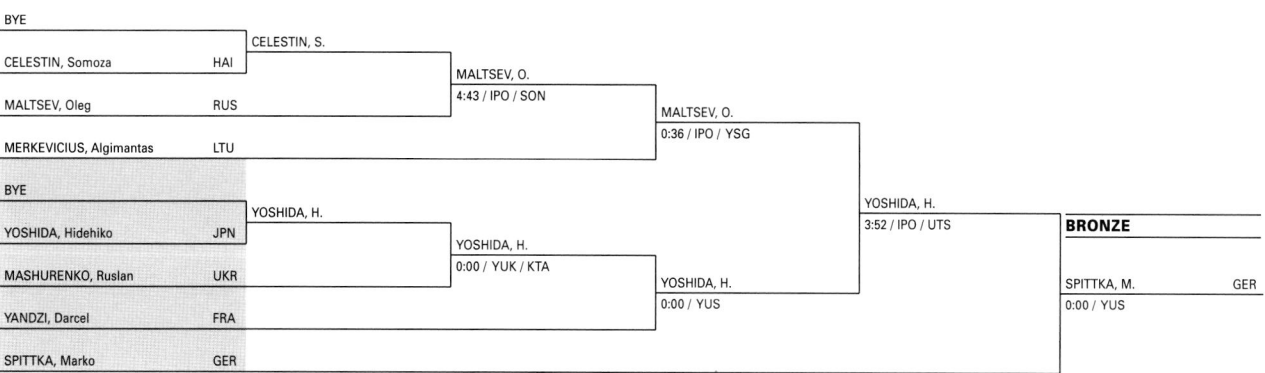

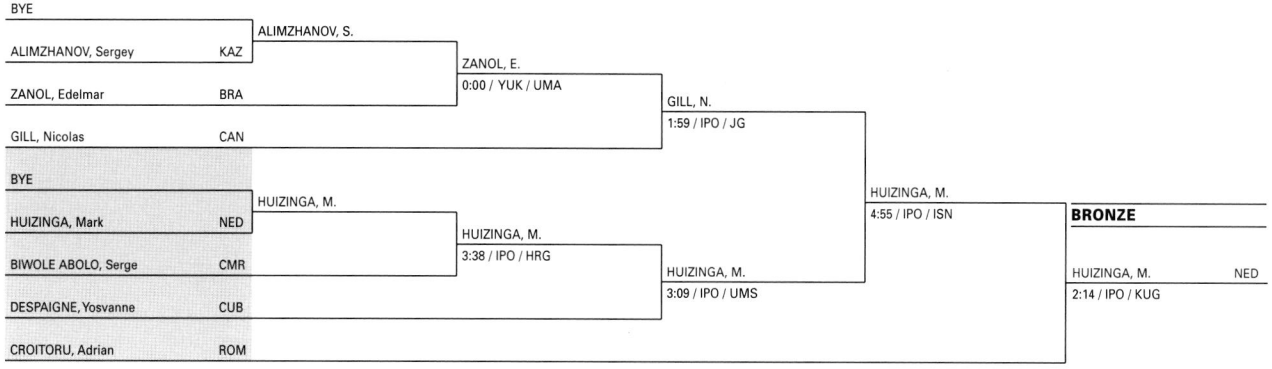

FINAL CLASSIFICATION		
Rnk **Name**	**Ctry**	
1 JEON, Ki-Young	KOR	Gold
2 BAGDASAROV, Armen	UZB	Silver
3 HUIZINGA, Mark	NED	Bronze
SPITTKA, Marko	GER	Bronze
5 CROITORU, Adrian	ROM	
YOSHIDA, Hidehiko	JPN	
7 GILL, Nicolas	CAN	
MALTSEV, Oleg	RUS	

Judo / *Judo*
Middleweight, 66 kg, Women / *Moyen, 66 kg, Dames*

Preliminaries

FIRST ROUND	SECOND ROUND	QUARTERFINALS	SEMIFINALS	FINAL

Pool A

OGASAWARA, Liliko — USA
BYE
→ OGASAWARA, L.

ZWIERS, Claudia — NED
BYE
→ ZWIERS, C.
→ ZWIERS, C. — 0:00 / YUK / KSK

STUSAKOVA, Radka — CZE
KAZUMI, Risa — JPN
→ KAZUMI, R. — 0:02 / IPO / YSG
→ WU, M.-L. — 3:50 / IPO / ISN

WU, Mei-Ling — TPE
BYE
→ WU, M.-L.

→ ZWIERS, C. — 0:00 / KEI / P29

CHERRY, Priscilla — MRI
BYE
→ CHERRY, P.
→ PINA, D. — 0:00 / KEI / P29

PINA, Dulce — DOM
BYE
→ PINA, D.

→ CHO, M.-S. — 3:52 / IPO / OUG

WANG, Xianbo — CHN
BYE
→ WANG, X.
→ CHO, M.-S. — 2:38 / IPO / YSG

CHO, Min-Sun — KOR
CAMPOS, Rosicleia — BRA
→ CHO, M.-S. — 2:25 / IPO / TSG

→ CHO, M.-S. — KOR — 3:03 / IPO / OUG

Pool B

KOTELNIKOVA, Yelena — RUS
BYE
→ KOTELNIKOVA, E.
→ SPACEK, M. — 0:00 / YUS

SPACEK, Mariela — AUT
BYE
→ SPACEK, M.

→ DUBOIS, A. — 0:00 / WAZ / STG

DUBOIS, Alice — FRA
BYE
→ DUBOIS, A.
→ DUBOIS, A. — 0:00 / YUS

REVE, Odalis — CUB
DIXON, Carly — AUS
→ REVE, O. — 1:09 / IPO / JG

NGUEMA, Melanie — GAB
BYE
→ NGUEMA, M.
→ SZCZEPANSKA, A. — 2:47 / IPO / TOS

SZCZEPANSKA, Aneta — POL
BYE
→ SZCZEPANSKA, A.

→ SZCZEPANSKA, A. — 3:24 / IPO / UMA

VON REKOWSKI, Anja — GER
PIERANTOZZI, Emanuela — ITA
→ VON REKOWSKI, A. — 2:41 / IPO / JG
→ SWEATMAN, R. — 0:00 / KOK / KUG

SWEATMAN, Rowena — GBR
BYE
→ SWEATMAN, R.

→ SZCZEPANSKA, A. — POL — 0:04 / IPO / KSG

GOLD

CHO, M.-S. — KOR — 0:18 / WIP / YSG

SILVER

SZCZEPANSKA, A. — POL

FINAL CLASSIFICATION

Rnk	Name	Ctry	
1	CHO, Min-Sun	KOR	Gold
2	SZCZEPANSKA, Aneta	POL	Silver
3	WANG, Xianbo	CHN	Bronze
	ZWIERS, Claudia	NED	Bronze
5	DUBOIS, Alice	FRA	
	REVE, Odalis	CUB	
7	OGASAWARA, Liliko	USA	
	SWEATMAN, Rowena	GBR	

Repechage and Summary

Pool A

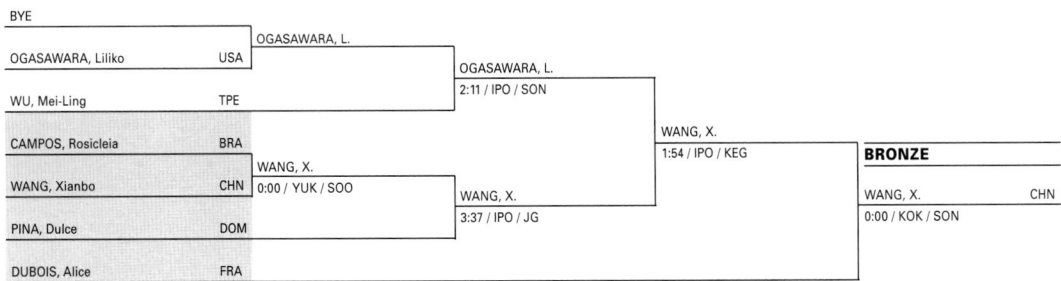

BYE
OGASAWARA, Liliko — USA
→ OGASAWARA, L.

WU, Mei-Ling — TPE
→ OGASAWARA, L. — 2:11 / IPO / SON

CAMPOS, Rosicleia — BRA
WANG, Xianbo — CHN
→ WANG, X. — 0:00 / YUK / SOO

PINA, Dulce — DOM
DUBOIS, Alice — FRA
→ WANG, X. — 3:37 / IPO / JG

→ WANG, X. — 1:54 / IPO / KEG

BRONZE

WANG, X. — CHN — 0:00 / KOK / SON

Pool B

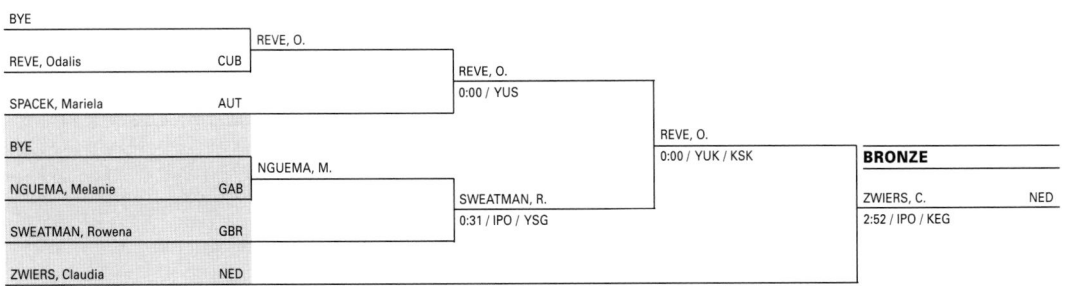

BYE
REVE, Odalis — CUB
→ REVE, O.

SPACEK, Mariela — AUT
→ REVE, O. — 0:00 / YUS

BYE
NGUEMA, Melanie — GAB
→ NGUEMA, M.

SWEATMAN, Rowena — GBR
→ SWEATMAN, R. — 0:31 / IPO / YSG

ZWIERS, Claudia — NED

→ REVE, O. — 0:00 / YUK / KSK

BRONZE

ZWIERS, C. — NED — 2:52 / IPO / KEG

Judo / *Judo*

Half-Heavyweight, 95 kg, Men / *Mi-lourd, 95 kg, Messieurs*

Preliminaries

1ST ROUND	2ND ROUND	3RD ROUND	QUARTERFINALS	SEMIFINALS	FINAL

Pool A

BENDER, Alejandro ARG	BENDER, A.				
BYE		MIGUEL, A. F.			
MIGUEL, Aurelio Fernandes BRA	MIGUEL, A. F.	0:02 / IPO / SOO			
BYE			MIGUEL, A. F.		
CHAKIMOV, Sergey KAZ	CHAKIMOV, S.		1:47 / HAN / P29		
BYE		CHAKIMOV, S.			
QEREWAQA, Nacanieli FIJ	QEREWAQA, N.	1:32 / WIP / KSG		MIGUEL, A. F.	
BYE				3:00 / IPO / UMA	
BOUZA, William URU	BOUZA, W.				
BYE		FELICITE, A.			
FELICITE, Antonio MRI	FELICITE, A.	0:00 / WAZ / OUG			
BYE			FELICITE, A.		
GUTIERREZ, Arturo MEX	GUTIERREZ, A.		2:03 / IPO / TNO		
BYE		MORGAN, K.			
MORGAN, Keith CAN	MORGAN, K.	0:00 / CHU / P29			NASTULA, P. POL
BYE					0:00 / CHU / PO5
NASTULA, Pawel POL	NASTULA, P.				
BYE		NASTULA, P.			
KOVACS, Antal HUN	KOVACS, A.	4:01 / IPO / JG			
BYE			NASTULA, P.		
GUIDO, Luigi ITA	GUIDO, L.		1:01 / WIP / OUC		
BYE		GUIDO, L.			
KHAIROULLO, Nazriev TJK	KHAIROULLO, N.	0:00 / CHU / P13		NASTULA, P.	
GOMEZ, Ronny CRC	4:14 / IPO / SON			2:43 / IPO / ISN	
SANCHEZ ARMENTERO, A. CUB	SANCHEZ ARMENTERO, A.				
BYE		SANCHEZ ARMENTERO, A.			
RADU, Yvan ROM	RADU, Y.	4:37 / IPO / KSK			
BYE			SOARES, P.		
KNORREK, Detlef GER	KNORREK, D.		1:16 / IPO / OSG		
BYE		SOARES, P.			
SOARES, Pedro POR	SOARES, P.	2:14 / IPO / OUG			
BYE					

Pool B

SONNEMANS, Benardus NED	SONNEMANS, B.				
BYE		SONNEMANS, B.			
BYE	BYE				
BYE			SONNEMANS, B.		
el GHARABAWI, Bassel EGY	el GHARABAWI, B.		0:00 / CHU / P29		
BYE		STEVENS, R.			
STEVENS, Raymond GBR	STEVENS, R.	0:00 / YUS		KIM, M.-S.	
BYE				0:00 / WAZ / KSK	
THORLEIFSSON, Vernhard ISL	THORLEIFSSON, V.				
BYE		KIM, M.-S.			
KIM, Min-Soo KOR	KIM, M.-S.	0:02 / HAN / P29			
BYE			KIM, M.-S.		
SERGUEEV, Dmitri RUS	SERGUEEV, D.		0:00 / WAZ / KSK		
BYE		SERBYEEV, D.			
SOLOVYOV, Dmitriy UZB	SOLOVYOV, D.	2:12 / IPO / OUG			KIM, M.-S. KOR
BYE					1:54 / IPO / ISN
BYE	BYE				
BYE		NAKAMURA, Y.			
NAKAMURA, Yoshio JPN	NAKAMURA, Y.				
BYE			NAKAMURA, Y.		
CAPO, Rene USA	CAPO, R.		4:37 / IPO / TKG		
BYE		LOBJANIDZE, M.			
LOBJANIDZE, Mevlud GEO	LOBJANIDZE, M.	1:33 / IPO / HRM			
BYE				TRAINEAU, S.	
TRAINEAU, Stephane FRA	TRAINEAU, S.			4:51 / IPO / KTA	
BYE		TRAINEAU, S.			
SVIRID, Leonid BLR	SVIRID, L.	0:00 / KEI / P29			
BYE			TRAINEAU, S.		
GOWING, Daniel NZL	GOWING, D.		2:04 / IPO / JG		
BYE		GOWING, D.			
PEPIC, Semir SVK	PEPIC, S.	1:09 / IPO / KYS			
bu-SAKHER, Mohamed KUW	4:35 / IPO / OUG				

continued on next page / continué à la page suivante

Half-Heavyweight, 95 kg, Men / *Mi-lourd, 95 kg, Messieurs*

continued from previous page / suite de la page précédente

SEMIFINALS	FINAL		GOLD	
MIGUEL, Aurelio Fernandes BRA	NASTULA, P.			
NASTULA, Pawel POL			NASTULA, P. POL	
			3:27 / IPO / KKE	
KIM, Min-Soo KOR	KIM, M.-S.			
TRAINEAU, Stephane FRA				

SILVER

KIM, M.-S. KOR

Repechage and Summary

Pool A

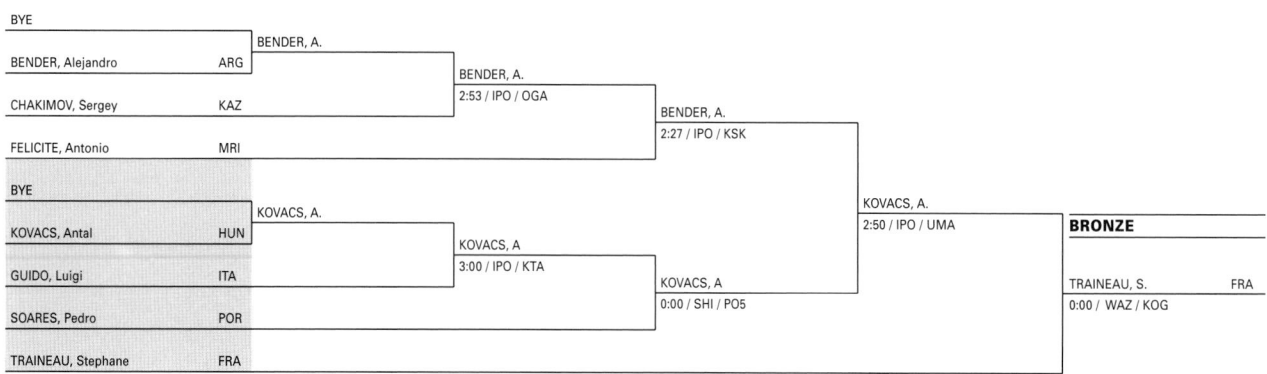

BYE	BENDER, A.		
BENDER, Alejandro ARG		BENDER, A.	
CHAKIMOV, Sergey KAZ		2:53 / IPO / OGA	BENDER, A.
FELICITE, Antonio MRI			2:27 / IPO / KSK
BYE	KOVACS, A.		
KOVACS, Antal HUN		KOVACS, A	KOVACS, A.
GUIDO, Luigi ITA		3:00 / IPO / KTA	2:50 / IPO / UMA
SOARES, Pedro POR		KOVACS, A	
TRAINEAU, Stephane FRA		0:00 / SHI / PO5	

BRONZE

TRAINEAU, S. FRA
0:00 / WAZ / KOG

Pool B

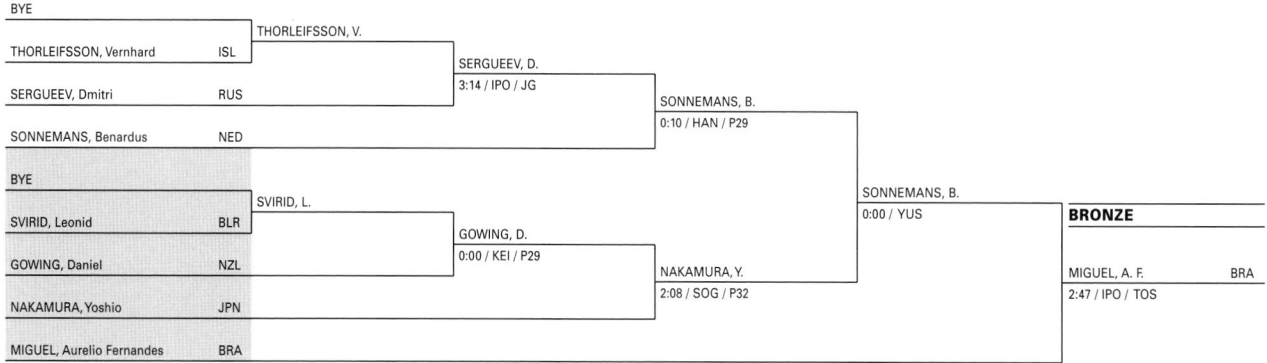

BYE	THORLEIFSSON, V.		
THORLEIFSSON, Vernhard ISL		SERGUEEV, D.	
SERGUEEV, Dmitri RUS		3:14 / IPO / JG	SONNEMANS, B.
SONNEMANS, Benardus NED			0:10 / HAN / P29
BYE	SVIRID, L.		
SVIRID, Leonid BLR		GOWING, D.	SONNEMANS, B.
GOWING, Daniel NZL		0:00 / KEI / P29	0:00 / YUS
NAKAMURA, Yoshio JPN		NAKAMURA, Y.	
MIGUEL, Aurelio Fernandes BRA		2:08 / SOG / P32	

BRONZE

MIGUEL, A. F. BRA
2:47 / IPO / TOS

FINAL CLASSIFICATION

Rnk	Name	Ctry	
1	NASTULA, Pawel	POL	Gold
2	KIM, Min-Soo	KOR	Silver
3	MIGUEL, Aurelio Fernandes	BRA	Bronze
	TRAINEAU, Stephane	FRA	Bronze
5	KOVACS, Antal	HUN	
	SONNEMANS, Benardus	NED	
7	BENDER, Alejandro	ARG	
	NAKAMURA, Yoshio	JPN	

Judo / *Judo*
Half-Heavyweight, 72 kg, Women / *Mi-lourd, 72 kg, Dames*

Preliminaries

FIRST ROUND	SECOND ROUND	QUARTERFINALS	SEMIFINALS	FINAL

Pool A

- SCAPIN, Ylenia — ITA
- BYE
  - SCAPIN, Y.
- LENG, Chunhui — CHN
- CHEN, Chiu-Ping — TPE
  - LENG, C.-P. — 0:00 / WIP / YSG
    - SCAPIN, Y. — 0:00 / YUK / OUC
- BELYAYEVA, Tetyana — UKR
- ST LOUIS, Marie Michelle — MRI
  - BELIAEVA, T. — 3:31 / IPO / SMK
- RICHTER, Simona — ROM
- BYE
  - RICHTER, S.
    - BELIAEVA, T. — 0:00 / SHI / PO5
      - BELIAEVA, T. — 0:00 / CHU / P16
- GALYANT, Svetlana — RUS
- BYE
  - GALANTE, S.
- WERBROUCK, Ulla — BEL
- BYE
  - WERBROUCK, U.
    - WERBROUCK, U. — 0:00 / SHI / PO5
- NAZARENKO, Olessia — TKM
- BE
  - NAZARENKO, O.
- BOGUNOVA, Yevgeniya — KAZ
- CURTO, Cristina — ESP
  - CURTO, C. — 0:00 / YUK / UMG
    - CURTO, C. — 0:00 / YUK / AUG
      - WERBROUCK, U. — 0:53 / IPO / KYS
        - WERBROUCK, U. — BEL — 3:34 / IPO / UMA

Pool B

- HOWEY, Kate — GBR
- BYE
  - HOWEY, K.
- KIENHUIS, Karin — NED
- BYE
  - KIENHUIS, K.
    - HOWEY, K. — 0:00 / YUK / KGU
- BACHER, Sandra — USA
- ERTEL, Hannah — GER
  - ERTEL, H. — 0:21 / IPO / JG
- TANABE, Yoko — JPN
- BYE
  - TANABE, Y.
    - TANABE, Y. — 2:32 / IPO / UMA
      - TANABE, Y. — 1:33 / IPO / UMA
- LUNA CASTELLANO, Diadenis — CUB
- BYE
  - LUNA CASTELLANO, D.
- ESSOMBE, Estha — FRA
- JENKINS, Niki — CAN
  - ESSOMBE, E. — 0:44 / WIP / OUG
    - ESSOMBE, E. — 0:00 / SHI / P12
- GALEA, Natalie — AUS
- BYE
  - GALEA, N.
- GOMEZ, Francis — VEN
- BYE
  - GOMEZ, F.
    - GOMEZ, F. — 0:00 / YUS
      - ESSOMBE, E. — 3:05 / WIP / HRG
        - TANABE, Y. — JPN — 0:00 / CHU / P29

FINAL CLASSIFICATION

Rnk	Name	Ctry	
1	WERBROUCK, Ulla	BEL	Gold
2	TANABE, Yoko	JPN	Silver
3	LUNA CASTELLANO, Diadenis	CUB	Bronze
	SCAPIN, Ylenia	ITA	Bronze
5	BELYAYEVA, Tatyana	UKR	
	ESSOMBE, Estha	FRA	
7	ERTEL, Hannah	GER	
	GALYANTE, Svetlana	RUS	

GOLD

WERBROUCK, U. — BEL — 0:02 / IPO / UMS

SILVER

TANABE, Y. — JPN

Repechage and Summary

Pool A

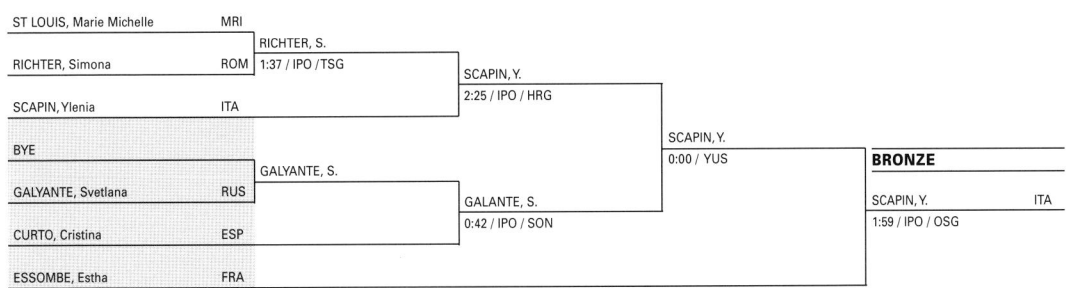

- ST LOUIS, Marie Michelle — MRI
- RICHTER, Simona — ROM
  - RICHTER, S. — 1:37 / IPO / TSG
- SCAPIN, Ylenia — ITA
- BYE
    - SCAPIN, Y. — 2:25 / IPO / HRG
- GALYANTE, Svetlana — RUS
- CURTO, Cristina — ESP
  - GALYANTE, S.
- ESSOMBE, Estha — FRA
    - GALANTE, S. — 0:42 / IPO / SON
      - SCAPIN, Y. — 0:00 / YUS
        - **BRONZE**
        - SCAPIN, Y. — ITA — 1:59 / IPO / OSG

Pool B

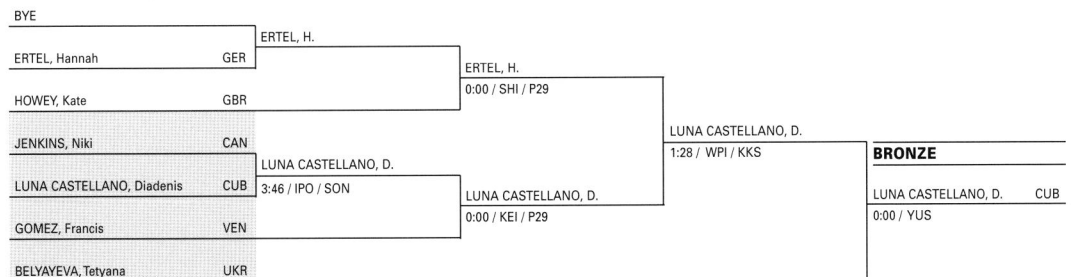

- BYE
- ERTEL, Hannah — GER
  - ERTEL, H.
- HOWEY, Kate — GBR
    - ERTEL, H. — 0:00 / SHI / P29
- JENKINS, Niki — CAN
- LUNA CASTELLANO, Diadenis — CUB
  - LUNA CASTELLANO, D. — 3:46 / IPO / SON
- GOMEZ, Francis — VEN
- BELYAYEVA, Tetyana — UKR
    - LUNA CASTELLANO, D. — 0:00 / KEI / P29
      - LUNA CASTELLANO, D. — 1:28 / WPI / KKS
        - **BRONZE**
        - LUNA CASTELLANO, D. — CUB — 0:00 / YUS

Judo / *Judo*

Heavyweight, +95 kg, Men / *Lourd, plus de 95 kg, Messieurs*

Preliminaries

1ST ROUND	2ND ROUND	3RD ROUND	QUARTERFINALS	SEMIFINALS	FINAL

Pool A

KEEVE, Damon — USA		
BYE	KEEVE, D.	
CHARAPOV, Rouslan — BLR		CHARAPOV, R.
BYE	CHARAPOV, R.	3:02 / IPO / HRM
KUBACKI, Rafal — POL		
BYE	KUBACKI, R.	
PERTELSON, Indrek — EST		KUBACKI, R.
BYE	PERTELSON, I.	0:27 / SOG / UMA

KUBACKI, R.
0:00 / CHU / P29

OGAWA, Naoya — JPN		
BYE	OGAWA, N.	
BETANCO GALEANO, Arnulfo — NCA		OGAWA, N.
BYE	BETANCO GALEANO, A.	4:43 / IPO / KSK
PAPAIOANNOU, Harris — GRE		
BYE	PAPAIOANNOU, H.	
SZABO, Miklos — AUS		PAPAIOANNOU, H.
BYE	SZABO, M.	4:27 / IPO / UNA

OGAWA, N.
4:30 / IPO / UNK

OGAWA, N.
0:00 / YUS

MURADOV, Kamol — UZB		
BYE	MURADOV, K.	
MUELLER, Igor — LUX		MUELLER, I.
BYE	MUELLER, I.	3:00 / IPO / YSG
DOUILLET, David — FRA		
BYE	DOUILLET, D.	
MORENO GARCIA, Frank Estaban — CUB		DOUILLET, D.
VAN BARNEVELD, Harry — BEL	VAN BARNEVELD, H.	0:00 / KEI / P29
	0:00 / CHU / P29	

DOUILLET, D.
0:50 / SOG / SMK

RAKHIMOV, Saidakhtam — TJK		
BYE	RAKHIMOV, S.	
BACCION, Orlando — ARG		RAKHIMOV, S.
BYE	BACCION, O.	0:22 / IPO / KEG
KRIEGER, Eric — AUT		
BYE	KRIEGER, E.	
LARBI, Kamel — ALG		KRIEGER, E.
BYE	LARBI, K.	1:43 / IPO / KYS

KRIEGER, E.
0:00 / KOK / OUG

DOUILLET, D.
3:45 / KIK

DOUILLET, D. — FRA
0:00 / SHI / PO5

Pool B

PEREZ, Ernesto — ESP		
BYE	PEREZ, E.	
TATAROGLU, Selim — TUR		PEREZ, E.
BYE	TATAROGLU, S.	0:00 / YUK / HRG
MOELLER, Frank — GER		
BYE	MOELLER, F.	
EBBERS, Danny — NED		MOELLER, F.
BYE	EBBERS, D.	4:27 / IPO / YGA

PEREZ, E.
0:00 / YUS

AGREGI, Slim — TUN		
BYE	AGREBI, S.	
PESHKOV, Igor — KAZ		PESHKOV, I.
BYE	PESHKOV, I.	3:09 / WIP / KKS
MILINKOVIC, Mitar — YUG		
BYE	MILINKOVIC, M.	
CSOSZ, Imre — HUN		CSOSZ, I.
BYE	CSOSZ, I.	0:29 / HAN / P29

CSOSZ, I.
0:00 / WAZ / OUG

PEREZ, E.
3:04 / IPO / UMA

KAMPITA, Pitak — THA		
BYE	KAMPITA, P.	
FLEXA, Frederico Kuntze — BRA		FLEXA, F. K.
BYE	FLEXA, F. K.	2:10 / IPO / HRM
GERALDINO, Jose — DOM		
BYE	GERALDINO, J.	
KOSOROTOV, Sergey — RUS		KOSOROTOV, S.
BYE	KOSOROTOV, S.	4:43 / IPO / KSK

KOSOROTOV, S.
4:19 / IPO / JG

KHALIFA, Diouf — SEN		
BYE	KHALIFA, D.	
SERGEYEV, Vadim — KGZ		SERGEYEV, V.
BYE	SERGEYEV, V.	0:00 / KEI / P29
KHAKHALEISHVILI, David — GEO		
LUNGU, Alexandru — ROM	LUNGU, A.	
	5:00 / FUS	LIU, S.
LIU, Shenggang — CHN	LIU, S.	0:39 / HAN / P12
BYE		

LIU, S.
0:00 / CHU / P12

LIU, S.
4:50 / IPO / UMA

PEREZ, E. — ESP
0:00 / WAZ / OS

continued on next page / continué à la page suivante

Heavyweight, +95 kg, Men   /   *Lourd, plus de 95 kg, Messieurs*

continued from previous page / suite de la page précédente

FINAL		**GOLD**	
DOUILLET, David	FRA		
		DOUILLET, D.	FRA
PEREZ, Ernesto	ESP	2:57 / IPO / UMA	

SILVER	
PEREZ, Ernesto	ESP

Repechage and Summary

Pool A

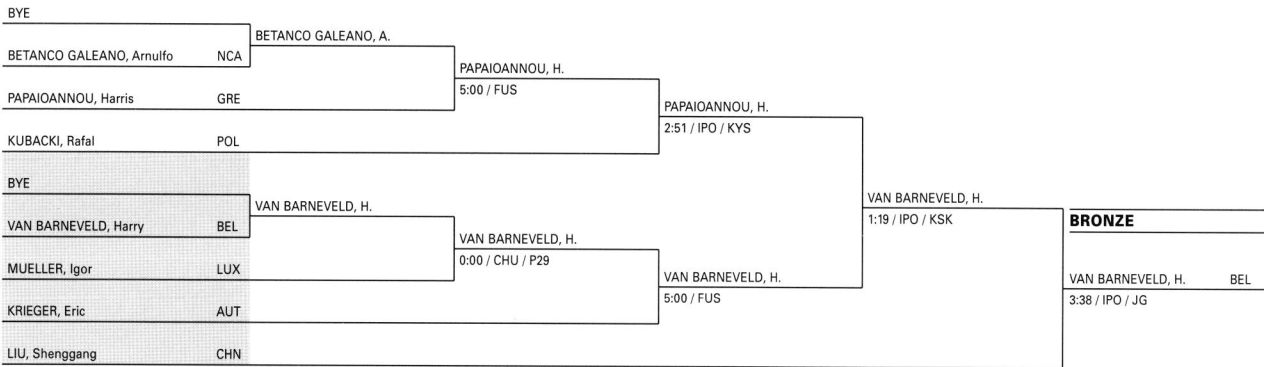

Pool B

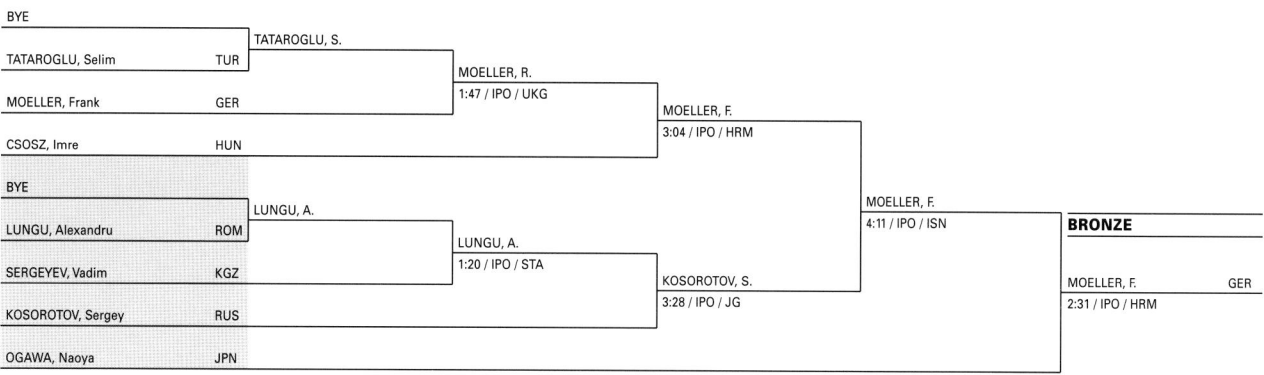

FINAL CLASSIFICATION		
Rnk Name	**Ctry**	
1 DOUILLET, David	FRA	**Gold**
2 PEREZ, Ernesto	ESP	**Silver**
3 MOELLER, Frank	GER	**Bronze**
VAN BARNEVELD, Harry	BEL	**Bronze**
5 LIU, Shenggang	CHN	
OGAWA, Naoya	JPN	
7 KOSOROTOV, Sergey	RUS	
PAPAIOANNOU, Harris	GRE	

Judo / *Judo*
Heavyweight, +72 kg, Women / *Lourd, plus de 72 kg, Dames*

Preliminaries

FIRST ROUND	SECOND ROUND	QUARTERFINALS	SEMIFINALS	FINAL

Pool A

GOUALOU, Marguerita — CIV	GOUALOU, M.
BYE	
GRANICZ, Eva — HUN	GRANICZ, E.
BYE	
ANNO, Noriko — JPN	da SILVA, E.
da SILVA, Edinanci — BRA	3:25 / IPO / UMA
GUNDARENKO, Svetlana — RUS	GUNDARENKO, S.
BYE	
SUN, Fuming — CHN	SUN, F.
BYE	
ROGERS, Michelle — GBR	ROGERS, M.
BYE	
SERIESE, Angelique — NED	HAGN, J.
HAGN, Johanna — GER	0:00 / CHU / P29
BURGATTA, Donata — ITA	BURGATTA, D.
BYE	

Quarterfinals (Pool A):
- GRANICZ, E. — 0:03 / IPO / UKG
- GUNDARENKO, S. — 0:00 / YUK / HRG
- SUN, F. — 0:00 / SHI / PO5
- HAGN, J. — 0:00 / YUS

Semifinals (Pool A):
- GUNDARENKO, S. — 0:00 / YUS
- SUN, F. — 0:00 / YUK / SON

Pool B

FILTEAU, Nancy — CAN	FILTEAU, N.
BYE	
YEH, Wen-Hua — TPE	YEH, W.-H.
BYE	
KOHLI, Shah — IND	RODRIGUEZ, E.
RODRIGUEZ, Estela — CUB	3:30 / IPO / HRG
SHON, Hyun-Me — KOR	SHON, H.-M.
BYE	
BURNETT, Heidi — AUS	BURNETT, H.
ROSENSTEEL, Colleen — USA	3:45 / IPO / UNA
HEFNY, Heba — EGY	HEFNY, H.
BYE	
MAKSYMOWA, Beata — POL	MAKSYMOWA, B.
BYE	
CICOT, Christine — FRA	CICOT, C.
BYE	

Quarterfinals (Pool B):
- FILTEAU, N. — 1:17 / IPO / TSG
- RODRIGUEZ, E. — 0:00 / WAZ / OUG
- HEFNY, H. — 3:47 / IPO / HNM
- MAKSYMOWA, B. — 3:17 / IPO / OUG

Semifinals (Pool B):
- RODRIGUEZ, E. — 3:48 / IPO / HRG
- MAKSYMOWA, B. — 2:03 / IPO / UMA

FINAL:
- SUN, F. — CHN — 0:00 / WAZ / SON
- RODRIGUEZ, E. — CUB — 3:06 / IPO / KEG

GOLD
SUN, F. — CHN — 0:00 / YUK / ISN

SILVER
RODRIGUEZ, E. — CUB

FINAL CLASSIFICATION

Rnk	Name	Ctry	
1	SUN, Fuming	CHN	Gold
2	RODRIGUEZ, Estela	CUB	Silver
3	CICOT, Christine	FRA	Bronze
	HAGN, Johanna	GER	Bronze
5	GUNDARENKO, Svetlana	RUS	
	MAKSYMOWA, Beata	POL	
7	da SILVA, Edinanci	BRA	
	SHON, Hyun-Me	KOR	

Repechage and Summary

Pool A

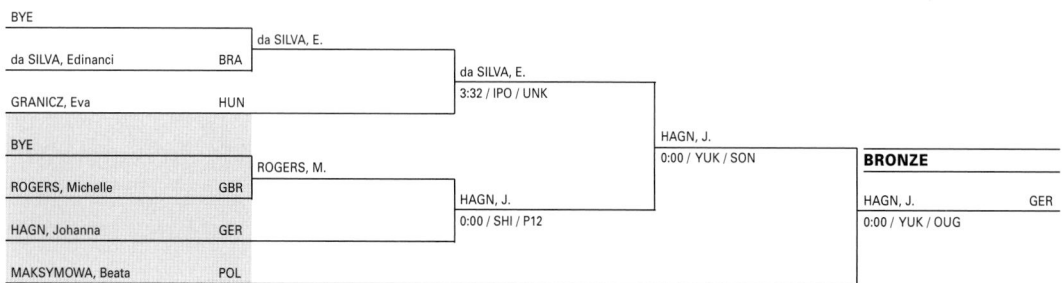

BYE	da SILVA, E.
da SILVA, Edinanci — BRA	
GRANICZ, Eva — HUN	
BYE	ROGERS, M.
ROGERS, Michelle — GBR	
HAGN, Johanna — GER	HAGN, J.
MAKSYMOWA, Beata — POL	

- da SILVA, E. — 3:32 / IPO / UNK
- HAGN, J. — 0:00 / SHI / P12
- HAGN, J. — 0:00 / YUK / SON

BRONZE
HAGN, J. — GER — 0:00 / YUK / OUG

Pool B

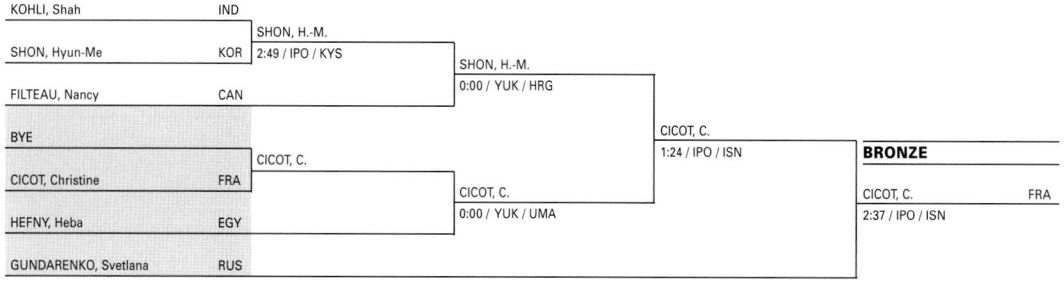

KOHLI, Shah — IND	SHON, H.-M.
SHON, Hyun-Me — KOR	2:49 / IPO / KYS
FILTEAU, Nancy — CAN	
BYE	CICOT, C.
CICOT, Christine — FRA	
HEFNY, Heba — EGY	
GUNDARENKO, Svetlana — RUS	

- SHON, H.-M. — 0:00 / YUK / HRG
- CICOT, C. — 0:00 / YUK / UMA
- CICOT, C. — 1:24 / IPO / ISN

BRONZE
CICOT, C. — FRA — 2:37 / IPO / ISN

MODERN PENTATHLON
PENTATHLON MODERNE

Term	English	Français
Actual Time	Actual Time	Temps à l'arrivée
B	Bronze Medal	Médaille de bronze
Continued	Continued	Continué
Ctry	Country	Pays
Def	Defeats	Pertes
FEN	Fencing	Escrime
Fencing	Fencing	Escrime
Final Classification	Final Classification	Classement final
G	Gold Medal	Médaille d'or
Handicap Time	Handicap Time	Temps de handicap
Horse	Horse	Cheval
Name	Name	Nom
P-obs	Penalties-Obstacles	Pénalités-obstacles
P-time	Penalties-Time	Pénalités-temps
P-warm	Penalties - Warm-up	Pénalités à l'échauffement
Pen	Penalties	Pénalités
Pts	Points	Points
RIDE	Riding	Equitation
Riding	Riding	Equitation
Recorded Time	Recorded Time	Temps enregistré
Rnk	Rank	Classement
RUN	Running	Course à pied
Running	Running	Course à pied
Score	Score	Marque
SH	Shooting	Tir
Shooting	Shooting	Tir
S	Silver Medal	Médaille d'argent
SWIM	Swimming	Natation
Swimming	Swimming	Natation
Time	Time	Temps
Total	Total	Total
Vict	Victories	Victoires

International Modern Pentathlon and Biathlon Union (UIPMB)
Union Internationale de Pentathlon Moderne et Biathlon
Ekeby House
Luiksestraat 23
NL-2587 AL The Hague
Netherlands

Modern Pentathlon / *Pentathlon moderne*
Men / *Messieurs*

SHOOTING

Rnk	Name	Ctry	Score	Pen	Pts
1	WAEFFLER, Philipp	SUI	185	0	1156
2	TIIDEMANN, Imre	EST	184	0	1144
3	JOHNSON, Alexander	AUS	184	0	1144
4	CLOETE, Claud	RSA	183	0	1132
5	TOADER, Adrian	ROM	183	0	1132
6	CONFORTO, Alessandro	ITA	182	0	1120
7	TORALDO, Cesare	ITA	181	0	1108
8	NEBULONI, Fabio	ITA	180	0	1096
9	ZENOVKA, Eduard	RUS	179	0	1084
10	HANZELY, Akos	HUN	179	0	1084
11	PARYGUIN, Alexandre	KAZ	178	0	1072

SHOOTING - *continued*

Rnk	Name	Ctry	Score	Pen	Pts
12	WARABIDA, Igor	POL	178	0	1072
13	DELEIGNE, Sebastien	FRA	178	0	1072
14	de la VEGA, Horacio	MEX	177	0	1060
15	RUER, Christophe	FRA	177	0	1060
16	CZYZOWICZ, Maciej	POL	176	0	1048
17	DANIELSSON, Per-Olov	SWE	176	0	1048
18	TYURIN, Dmitriy	KAZ	176	0	1048
19	SARFALVI, Peter	HUN	175	0	1036
20	DUHANOVS, Vjacheslavs	LAT	173	0	1012
21	SVATKOVSKIY, Dmitriy	RUS	173	0	1012
22	CHYMERYS, Heorhiy	UKR	173	0	1012

SHOOTING - *continued*

Rnk	Name	Ctry	Score	Pen	Pts
23	MARTINEK, Janos	HUN	172	0	1000
24	BARROSO, Manuel	POR	171	0	988
25	FELDMAN, Igor	KGZ	170	0	976
26	KIM, Mi-Sub	KOR	170	0	976
27	GOSTIGIAN, Michael	USA	170	0	976
28	SALAZAR, Sergio	MEX	170	0	976
29	YAGORASHVILI, Vakhtang	GEO	168	0	952
30	BREMEL, Grigoriy	RUS	167	0	940
31	PHELPS, Richard	GBR	166	0	928
32	ZADNEPROVSKIS, Andriejus	LTU	163	0	892

FENCING

Rnk	Name	Ctry	Vict	Def	Pen	Pts
1	CHYMERYS, Heorhiy	UKR	21	10	0	970
2	PARYGUIN, Alexandre	KAZ	21	10	0	970
3	YAGORASHVILI, Vakhtang	GEO	20	11	0	940
4	HANZELY, Akos	HUN	20	11	0	940
5	MARTINEK, Janos	HUN	19	12	0	910
6	KIM, Mi-Sub	KOR	19	12	0	910
7	SVATKOVSKIY, Dmitriy	RUS	18	13	0	880
8	SALAZAR, Sergio	MEX	18	13	0	880
9	CONFORTO, Alessandro	ITA	18	13	0	880
10	TORALDO, Cesare	ITA	18	13	0	880
11	DANIELSSON, Per-Olov	SWE	17	14	0	850

FENCING - *continued*

Rnk	Name	Ctry	Vict	Def	Pen	Pts
12	BREMEL, Grigoriy	RUS	17	14	0	850
13	ZADNEPROVSKIS, Andriejus	LTU	17	14	10	840
14	SARFALVI, Peter	HUN	16	15	0	820
15	NEBULONI, Fabio	ITA	16	15	0	820
16	TIIDEMANN, Imre	EST	16	15	0	820
17	ZENOVKA, Eduard	RUS	16	15	0	820
18	WARABIDA, Igor	POL	15	16	0	790
19	RUER, Christophe	FRA	15	16	0	790
20	GOSTIGIAN, Michael	USA	15	16	0	790
21	DUHANOVS, Vjacheslavs	LAT	15	16	0	790
22	CLOETE, Claud	RSA	15	16	10	780

FENCING - *continued*

Rnk	Name	Ctry	Vict	Def	Pen	Pts
23	PHELPS, Richard	GBR	14	17	0	760
24	DELEIGNE, Sebastien	FRA	13	18	0	730
25	de la VEGA, Horacio	MEX	12	19	0	700
26	CZYZOWICZ, Maciej	POL	12	19	0	700
27	TOADER, Adrian	ROM	12	19	0	700
28	BARROSO, Manuel	POR	11	20	0	670
29	TYURIN, Dmitriy	KAZ	10	21	0	640
30	FELDMAN, Igor	KGZ	10	21	0	640
31	JOHNSON, Alexander	AUS	10	21	0	640
32	WAEFFLER, Philipp	SUI	8	23	10	570

SWIMMING

Rnk	Name	Ctry	Time	Pen	Pts
1	YAGORASHVILI, Vakhtang	GEO	3:15.04	0	1312
2	KIM, Mi-Sub	KOR	3:15.08	0	1312
3	TOADER, Adrian	ROM	3:16.09	0	1304
4	RUER, Christophe	FRA	3:16.26	0	1304
5	GOSTIGIAN, Michael	USA	3:16.38	0	1304
6	JOHNSON, Alexander	AUS	3:16.91	0	1300
7	TORALDO, Cesare	ITA	3:17.16	0	1296
8	de la VEGA, Horacio	MEX	3:17.92	0	1292
9	SARFALVI, Peter	HUN	3:18.27	0	1288
10	PHELPS, Richard	GBR	3:19.42	0	1280
11	CHYMERYS, Heorhiy	UKR	3:19.60	0	1276

SWIMMING - *continued*

Rnk	Name	Ctry	Time	Pen	Pts
12	ZADNEPROVSKIS, Andriejus	LTU	3:19.69	0	1276
13	SALAZAR, Sergio	MEX	3:20.04	0	1272
14	ZENOVKA, Eduard	RUS	3:20.50	0	1268
15	CZYZOWICZ, Maciej	POL	3:21.58	0	1260
16	MARTINEK, Janos	HUN	3:23.16	0	1248
17	DUHANOVS, Vjacheslavs	LAT	3:23.29	0	1248
18	SVATKOVSKIY, Dmitriy	RUS	3:23.33	0	1248
19	BARROSO, Manuel	POR	3:23.35	0	1248
20	DANIELSSON, Per-Olov	SWE	3:24.81	0	1236
21	HANZELY, Akos	HUN	3:24.90	0	1236
22	TYURIN, Dmitriy	KAZ	3:25.27	0	1232

SWIMMING - *continued*

Rnk	Name	Ctry	Time	Pen	Pts
23	TIIDEMANN, Imre	EST	3:27.86	0	1212
24	WARABIDA, Igor	POL	3:28.42	0	1208
25	WAEFFLER, Philipp	SUI	3:29.44	0	1200
26	DELEIGNE, Sebastien	FRA	3:29.52	0	1196
27	PARYGUIN, Alexandre	KAZ	3:29.86	0	1196
28	NEBULONI, Fabio	ITA	3:33.62	0	1164
29	CLOETE, Claud	RSA	3:35.25	0	1152
30	BREMEL, Grigoriy	RUS	3:36.96	0	1140
31	CONFORTO, Alessandro	ITA	3:37.38	0	1136
32	FELDMAN, Igor	KGZ	3:44.17	0	1080

RIDING

Rnk	Name	Horse	Ctry	Time	P-time	P-obs	P-warm	Pts
1	MARTINEK, Janos	Mike	HUN	65.65	0	0	0	1100
2	PHELPS, Richard	Medicine Man	GBR	71.41	0	0	0	1100
3	WARABIDA, Igor	Longknife	POL	74.84	0	0	0	1100
4	ZADNEPROVSKIS, Andriejus	Mike	LTU	69.85	0	30	0	1070
5	BARROSO, Manuel	The Invader	POR	75.07	0	30	0	1070
6	CLOETE, Claud	Charlie	RSA	76.04	0	30	0	1070
7	GOSTIGIAN, Michael	Warren	USA	85.55	27	30	0	1043
8	PARYGUIN, Alexandre	Longknife	KAZ	68.22	0	60	0	1040
9	TORALDO, Cesare	Kirby	ITA	75.22	0	60	0	1040
10	DANIELSSON, Per-Olov	The Invader	SWE	77.57	3	60	0	1037
11	ZENOVKA, Eduard	Jazz	RUS	84.78	24	60	0	1016
12	SVATKOVSKIY, Dmitriy	Perry	RUS	68.42	0	90	0	1010
13	KIM, Mi-Sub	Czar	KOR	73.67	0	90	0	1010
14	NEBULONI, Fabio	Dutch Biko	ITA	74.68	0	90	0	1010
15	SALAZAR, Sergio	Brilliant Spectical	MEX	82.96	18	90	0	992
16	RUER, Christophe	Jumping Doctor	FRA	81.85	15	120	0	965

RIDING - *continued*

Rnk	Name	Horse	Ctry	Time	P-time	P-obs	P-warm	Pts
17	BREMEL, Grigoriy	Perry	RUS	67.77	0	150	0	950
18	DUHANOVS, Vjacheslavs	Leroy	LAT	69.02	0	150	0	950
19	TOADER, Adrian	Roanoke	ROM	70.70	0	150	0	950
20	TIIDEMANN, Imre	Leroy	EST	71.46	0	150	0	950
21	HANZELY, Akos	Dutch Biko	HUN	77.32	3	150	0	947
22	SARFALVI, Peter	Medicine Man	HUN	80.24	12	150	0	938
23	DELEIGNE, Sebastien	Jumping Doctor	FRA	84.73	24	150	0	926
24	de la VEGA, Horacio	Czar	MEX	66.07	0	180	0	920
25	CZYZOWICZ, Maciej	Jazz	POL	91.78	45	150	0	905
26	CHYMERYS, Heorhiy	Warren	UKR	65.53	0	210	0	890
27	YAGORASHVILI, Vakhtang	Charlie	GEO	66.85	0	210	0	890
28	FELDMAN, Igor	Brilliant Spectical	KGZ	73.65	0	210	0	890
29	CONFORTO, Alessandro	Sleeper	ITA	78.29	6	210	0	884
30	WAEFFLER, Philipp	Roanoke	SUI	66.72	0	240	0	860
31	JOHNSON, Alexander	Kirby	AUS	140.69	192	295	0	613
32	TYURIN, Dmitriy	Sleeper	KAZ	ELI	0	0	0	0

Men / *Messieurs*

RUNNING

Rnk	Name	Ctry	Actual Time	Handicap Time	Recorded Time	Pen	Pts
1	ZENOVKA, Eduard	RUS	13:06.820	00:45.33	12:21.487	0	1342
2	SVATKOVSKIY, Dmitriy	RUS	13:20.930	00:58.00	12:22.930	0	1339
3	TIIDEMANN, Imre	EST	13:45.040	01:06.00	12:39.040	0	1288
4	ZADNEPROVSKIS, Andriejus	LTU	14:02.730	01:22.00	12:40.730	0	1285
5	WARABIDA, Igor	POL	13:32.910	00:51.33	12:41.577	0	1282
6	PARYGUIN, Alexandre	KAZ	12:59.700	00:15.33	12:44.367	0	1273
7	BARROSO, Manuel	POR	14:41.690	01:56.00	12:45.690	0	1270
8	SALAZAR, Sergio	MEX	13:54.940	01:08.00	12:46.940	0	1267
9	TOADER, Adrian	ROM	14:11.770	01:19.33	12:52.437	0	1249
10	RUER, Christophe	FRA	14:02.470	01:08.33	12:54.137	0	1244
11	MARTINEK, Janos	HUN	13:16.380	00:22.00	12:54.380	0	1243
12	HANZELY, Akos	HUN	13:38.430	00:39.00	12:59.430	0	1228
13	de la VEGA, Horacio	MEX	15:02.660	01:57.33	13:05.327	0	1210
14	DANIELSSON, Per-Olov	SWE	13:58.560	00:51.00	13:07.560	0	1204
15	NEBULONI, Fabio	ITA	14:28.790	01:18.00	13:10.790	0	1195
16	GOSTIGIAN, Michael	USA	14:21.660	01:10.33	13:11.327	0	1192

RUNNING - *continued*

Rnk	Name	Ctry	Actual Time	Handicap Time	Recorded Time	Pen	Pts
17	DUHANOVS, Vjacheslavs	LAT	15:01.380	01:48.00	13:13.380	0	1186
18	PHELPS, Richard	GBR	14:38.970	01:25.33	13:13.637	0	1186
19	CLOETE, Claud	RSA	14:20.690	01:03.33	13:17.357	0	1174
20	KIM, Mi-Sub	KOR	14:01.010	00:38.66	13:22.344	0	1159
21	DELEIGNE, Sebastien	FRA	15:39.940	02:13.33	13:26.607	0	1147
22	YAGORASHVILI, Vakhtang	GEO	14:48.580	01:16.66	13:31.914	0	1132
23	SARFALVI, Peter	HUN	14:58.250	01:20.66	13:37.584	0	1114
24	CONFORTO, Alessandro	ITA	15:20.340	01:41.33	13:39.007	0	1108
25	CZYZOWICZ, Maciej	POL	15:56.450	02:17.00	13:39.450	0	1108
26	TORALDO, Cesare	ITA	13:49.330	00:00.00	13:49.330	0	1078
27	CHYMERYS, Heorhiy	UKR	15:11.710	00:58.66	14:13.044	0	1006
28	WAEFFLER, Philipp	SUI	17:19.050	02:59.33	14:19.717	0	988
29	FELDMAN, Igor	KGZ	18:28.870	04:00.00	14:28.870	0	961
30	TYURIN, Dmitriy	KAZ	18:29.160	04:00.00	14:29.160	0	958
31	BREMEL, Grigoriy	RUS	17:07.330	02:28.00	14:39.330	0	928
32	JOHNSON, Alexander	AUS	DNS	03:29.00	00:00.000	0	0

FINAL CLASSIFICATION

Rnk	Name	Ctry	SH	FEN	SWIM	RIDE	RUN	Total	
1	PARYGUIN, Alexandre	KAZ	1072	970	1196	1040	1273	5551	G
2	ZENOVKA, Eduard	RUS	1084	820	1268	1016	1342	5530	S
3	MARTINEK, Janos	HUN	1000	910	1248	1100	1243	5501	B
4	SVATKOVSKIY, Dmitriy	RUS	1012	880	1248	1010	1339	5489	
5	WARABIDA, Igor	POL	1072	790	1208	1100	1282	5452	
6	HANZELY, Akos	HUN	1084	940	1236	947	1228	5435	
7	TIIDEMANN, Imre	EST	1144	820	1212	950	1288	5414	
8	TORALDO, Cesare	ITA	1108	880	1296	1040	1078	5402	
9	SALAZAR, Sergio	MEX	976	880	1272	992	1267	5387	
10	DANIELSSON, Per-Olov	SWE	1048	850	1236	1037	1204	5375	
11	KIM, Mi-Sub	KOR	976	910	1312	1010	1159	5367	
12	RUER, Christophe	FRA	1060	790	1304	965	1244	5363	
13	ZADNEPROVSKIS, Andriejus	LTU	892	840	1276	1070	1285	5363	
14	TOADER, Adrian	ROM	1132	700	1304	950	1249	5335	
15	CLOETE, Claud	RSA	1132	780	1152	1070	1174	5308	
16	GOSTIGIAN, Michael	USA	976	790	1304	1043	1192	5305	

FINAL CLASSIFICATION - *continued*

Rnk	Name	Ctry	SH	FEN	SWIM	RIDE	RUN	Total
17	NEBULONI, Fabio	ITA	1096	820	1164	1010	1195	5285
18	PHELPS, Richard	GBR	928	760	1280	1100	1186	5254
19	BARROSO, Manuel	POR	988	670	1248	1070	1270	5246
20	YAGORASHVILI, Vakhtang	GEO	952	940	1312	890	1132	5226
21	SARFALVI, Peter	HUN	1036	820	1288	938	1114	5196
22	DUHANOVS, Vjacheslavs	LAT	1012	790	1248	950	1186	5186
23	de la VEGA, Horacio	MEX	1060	700	1292	920	1210	5182
24	CHYMERYS, Heorhiy	UKR	1012	970	1276	890	1006	5154
25	CONFORTO, Alessandro	ITA	1120	880	1136	884	1108	5128
26	DELEIGNE, Sebastien	FRA	1072	730	1196	926	1147	5071
27	CZYZOWICZ, Maciej	POL	1048	700	1260	905	1108	5021
28	BREMEL, Grigoriy	RUS	940	850	1140	950	928	4808
29	WAEFFLER, Philipp	SUI	1156	570	1200	860	988	4774
30	FELDMAN, Igor	KGZ	976	640	1080	890	961	4547
31	TYURIN, Dmitriy	KAZ	1048	640	1232	ELI	958	3878
32	JOHNSON, Alexander	AUS	1144	640	1300	613	DNS	3697

JULIE TOLLMAN • ERNEST W TOLLNER • LYNNE A TOLMAN • ALISON N TOLSON • DONNA M TOLSON • RICHARD I TOLSON • SANDRA G TOLSON • TRUNNELL A TOLSON • KATHY G TOMAJKO • RONALD J TOMAJKO • HOLLY A TOMAL • MICHAEL TOMASELLO • NEAL J. TOMASIN • EVELYN J TOMASINO • GLENN A TOMCHIK • KATE TOMCHIK • KATHLEEN T TOMCZAK • KENNETH C TOMCZAK • RONALD D TOMCZYK • DEBORAH J TOMECEK • MILAGROS TOMEI • BARBARA A TOMES • LESLIE L TOMICH • GARY E TOMICK • ELAINE TOMKINSON • MARIETTA J TOMLIN • MELANLE S TOMLIN • ANNE TOMLINSON • BARBARA TOMLINSON • EARLENE W TOMLINSON • JAMES E TOMLINSON • KAZUHIKO TOMOOKA • OLUMNATOSIN O TOMORI • ELAINE TOMPKINS • ELLEN J TOMPKINS • EMILY D TOMPKINS • JEANNE S TOMPKINS • ROBERTA TOMPKINS • SAM R TOMPKINS • TEDMON D TOMPKINS • BRIAN A TOMS • ATC TONDA M SEALS • BARBARA A TONEY • DWAIN A TONEY • LINDA C TONEY • SAUNDRA TONGPITUK • DAVID TONINI • JEANNE M TONKIN • SHARI M TONKS MD • JUDITH L TONNESON • BARBARA D TONTIC • STEVAN TONTIC • KATRI P TONTTI • SHIRLEY A TOOGOOD • EILEEN N TOOHER • JAMES M TOOHER • KENNETH P TOOK • CYNTHIA D TOOKES • CYRUS TOOKES • PATRICIA A. TOOLE • SYLVIA A TOOLE • IRA M TOOMER • THERESA L TOOMER • BRIDGET A TOOMEY • KATHLEEN E TOOMEY • DEBRA A TOON • MARILYNN M TOON • MICHAEL A TOONE • THEO TOOTLE • MARGARET B TOPKEN • DAVID A TOPPER • JENNIFER M TOPPER • BETHANY TOPPERT • IAN N TOPPIN • WILLIAM J TOPPIN • SHARON A TOPPING • BRENDA L TOPPINS • TONY TOPPS • ABBAS TORABI • WALTER R TORBERT • LIBBY M TORBUSH • BRETT T TORGRIMSON • RENEE C TORINA • HIROSHI TORIUMI • STACEY E TORMAN • MIRTHA TORO • JANET C TORRANCE • DONNAMARIE A TORRE • JACQUELINE A TORRE • MARYANNE TORRELLAS • CAROL L TORRENCE • ALEX E TORRES • AMARILIS TORRES • DAVID TORRES • JORGE L TORRES • MARJORIE TORRES • JORGE R TORRES-NADAL • DAVID A TORREY • MARGARET A TOSDAL • ANN TOTH • ANNA TOTH • PAUL A TOTH • PAUL A TOTH • TAMARA L TOTH • THEO L TOTH • ROCCO TOTINO • GARY A TOTTEN • PATRICIA K TOTTEN • LORRAINE T TOUCHSTONE • RANDALL E TOUCHSTONE • JENNIFER I TOUGAS • JOHN A TOUGAS • DAVID P TOUHEY • STACY TOULUCH • DARRYL E TOUPKIN • NICK TOURAS • VILIA TOURKOVA • ATHARA V TOUSSAINT • NICOLAS TOUVET • CORY B TOVIN • IAN H TOVIN • ROBERT D TOWE • LARRY D TOWERS • MATTHEW J TOWEY • GREG W TOWLE • CATHERINE W TOWLES • DUANE TOWLES • LAURA C TOWLES • STEPHEN G TOWLES • GARY TOWN • DARLENE J TOWNE • ASHLIE A TOWNES • CALVIN L TOWNS • DAVID C TOWNS • FORREST C TOWNS • ROBERT D TOWNS • KENNETH A TOWNSEL • CRISTEN P TOWNSEND • DAMEAN TOWNSEND • DEBRA A TOWNSEND • GREGORY A TOWNSEND • HULDIE L TOWNSEND • LUCILLE S TOWNSEND • MASSIMILLA A TOWNSEND • MICHELLE J TOWNSEND • ROBERT C TOWNSEND • TERYL A TOWNSEND • CHRISTINE E TOWNSEND ATC • MICHAEL A TOWNSEND ATC • EDGAR G TOWNSLEY • ALICIA G TOWNSON • BRYCE TOWSLEY • TOBY W TOWSON • YUKI TOYOTA • HILARY TOYRYLA • BENTZ P TOZER • STEVEN T TOZER • MICHAEL J TRACEY • KENNETH W TRACEY CATC • ALBERT H TRACY • COLLEEN E TRACY • FRANK P TRACY • MICHAEL N TRADER • DENISE M TRAHAN • JOSEPH V TRAHAN • DENISE A TRAICOFF • JACQUELINE A TRAIL • GERALDINE TRAINA • ALICE L TRAINER • KEVIN J TRAINOR • ANITA S TRAMMELL • DANA M TRAMMELL • KERRY TRAMMELL • STACEY L TRAMMELL • STEPHEN M TRAMMELL • CARLO D TRAMONTOZZI • ADRIAN T TRAMUTOLA • BINH T TRAN • CHUONG TRAN • LISA N TRAN • NGOC L TRAN • SANDRA M TRANI • DONALD J TRANTOW • MICHAEL R TRANTUM • DARCIE J TRAPASSO • JOSEPH A TRAPASSO • KATHLEEN C TRAPP • JOSEPH R TRAVER • NANCY S TRAVER • PENNEL A TRAVER • JEROME M TRAVERS • JEROME M TRAVERS • KATHY TRAVERS • ANDREW S TRAVIS • JOSEPH V TRAVIS • LINDA W TRAVIS • PATRICIA L TRAVIS • R MARK TRAVIS • TINA D TRAVIS • WILLIAM K TRAVIS • KATHLEEN D TRAVITZ • WILLIAM A TRAVITZ JR • PETER A TRAVNICEK • JOHNNY D TRAWICK • DIANE E TRAWICKY • BOBBY A TRAYLOR • PHILLIP TRAYNOR • PATRICK S TREADAWAY • BRYAN K TREADWAY • RICK TREADWELL • TERESA D TREADWELL • BRIAN P TREAT • JOHN LEONARD TREBINO • KAREN I TREBITZ • JIM TRECKER • TRENT B TREES • JOE TREESE • BURTON G TREGER • DARRYL A TRELL • HEATHER J TRELL • JULIE A TRELL • KATHLEEN M TRELLA • GUSTAVO A TRELLES • CHRISTOPHER E TREMANN • WILBERT TREMBLE • DARLENE G TREMBULAK • SCOTT D TREMLETT • JEANNE P TREMONTI • HENRY S TREMPER • REBECCA TRENARY • MELISSA P TRENT • TOM V TRENT • NICOLE TREPES • ADAM S TRESS • PAMELA K TRETTEL • PEGGY F TRETTEL • MARY LEE B TREVETT TRAPP • KEITH TREVINO • ANDREA M TREVISAN • JOHN K TREXEL • CHRISTOPHER D TREXLER • RUSSELL D TRIAGA • MAUREEN E TRIAL • SANDRA J TRIANA • AMY K TRIANDIFLOU • KATHERINE H TRIBBLE • LYNNE L TRIBBLE • MARY KATE TRIBBLE • NANCY F TRIBBLE • PAMELA R TRIBBLE • SONIA E TRIBBLE • DAVID TRICE • SUSAN E TRICE • WALTER P TRICE • DARROLL K TRICHE • MATTHEW TRICHE • ARTHUR TRICHE JR • JONATHON D TRICK •

TERI K TRICK • BRUCE B TRICKEL • HELEN L TRICKEL • ANDREW R. TRICKEY • JEREMY K TRICKIE • DEANA J TRIEMER • RUSSELL S TRIER • DONNA V TRIESCHMANN • LEA TRIFANOFF • SERENA K TRIGG • ANGELA B TRILLHAASE • NOELA TRIM • CHARNETTE TRIMBLE • ROBERT W TRIMBLE • YVONNE R TRIMBLE • JOSEPH E TRIMYER • PHUONG K TRINH • SARAH E TRINITE • MARVIN D TRINKAUS ATC • PENNY C TRINKER • MARY A TRIPPE • ALLEN R TRIPPEER • MARTHA B TRISLER • WILLIAM TRISLER • JEANIE E TRITSCHLER • IVANA TRITTO • COLLEEN E TRIUMPH • INGRID M TRIVINO • WILSON LUBIN TRIVINO • LESLEY P TROBAUGH • JEANNE M TROCHECK • ANN TRODELLO • STEPHANIE TRODELLO • JENNY TROEDSSON • KONSTANTIN A TROFIMOV • BRAD TROGDON • SHAYE M TROHA • SUSAN K TROIANO • ASTRID K TROLLE • JOHN B TROLLINGER • MARION J TROLLOPE • ANN-CHRISTIN TROMM • DANIEL L TROMPETER • JOSEPH M TRONCALE • JUDITH D TRONCALE • LILLAGENE U TRONCALLI • KATHERINE H TROOBOFF • ILENE S TROSSMAN • MICHAEL J TROTH • ZANE R TROTT • DONALD G. TROTTER • FRANCES P TROTTER • INA M TROTTER • PAMELA D TROTTER • STACY W TROTTER • INGE TROTTER MT • PETER W TROTTIER • MICHELLE K TROUGHT • DIANE L TROUT • BRUCE H TROUTMAN • CHRISTOPHER P TROUTMAN • GENE TROUTMAN • JANET S TROUTMAN • LINDA R TROUTMAN • MATTHEW TROUTMAN • WILLIAM H TROUTMAN • MARK A TROWBRIDGE • BRADLEY R TROWER • TEVIS R. TROWER • BRADLEY C TROXEL • ERIC J TROY • PRISCILLA L TROY • RYAN D TROY • CHRISTOPHER S TROYANOS • DONALD L TROYER • LORETTA A TROYER • ROBERT R TROYER • AMY C TRUDEAU • CORINNE E TRUELL • LIANE J TRUELL • MOLLIE B TRUELL • ELAINE M TRUESDALE • GLENDA TRUESDALE • WANDA W TRUESDALE • SETH TRUGMAN • CHRISTINE N TRUITT • RENNIE J TRUITT • EDUARDO E. TRUJILLO • MARTHA A TRULL • JERRIE TRUMAN • PAULA S TRUMBLE • DOMINIQUE TRUMMER • OLENNA TRUSKETT • JAMESON D TRUSS • BRANDON TRUSSELL • R E TRUSSELL • SANDRA TRUSSELL • JEANNE M TRUST • LEANN TRUSTY • STEVEN A TRYPUC • BEATRICE R TSAI • ILING TSAI • STEPHEN TSAI • ANDREA G TSCHERTER • MARY H TSCHOPP • YI C TSE • YUH TSENG • ELANA TSIALAS • DIANA TSIANG • MELINA TSIGARIDOU • RODOULA TSIOTSOU • TRACY T TSUBOKAWA • ROGER C TSUI • WEN TSUI • YURI TSUKADA • RICHARD I TSUKUSHI MT • TOSHIO R TSURUNAGA • CHEN HSUN TU • RENJIN TU • BRIAN D TUBIAK • TONY TUCCI • HOLLEY A TUCCILLO • M RONALD-KEITH TUCK • ALAN J TUCKER • AMY TUCKER • ANTHONY L TUCKER • BILLY R TUCKER • CALOISE R TUCKER • CHARLES TUCKER • CLIFF TUCKER • D J TUCKER • DEBORAH K TUCKER • DELLA L TUCKER • ELISE A TUCKER • ESTELLA W TUCKER • FELICIA M TUCKER • FREDERICK L TUCKER • GLORIA B TUCKER • GWEN R TUCKER • JACK D TUCKER • LAURA E TUCKER • LYNELLE D TUCKER • MATTHEW A TUCKER • MILLIE B TUCKER • MORGAN S TUCKER • NORMA M TUCKER • SUSAN L TUCKER • WILLIAM N TUCKER • WILMA D TUCKER • AMELIA TUCKER-SHAW • RENEE E TUCKER-WILLIAMS • CHRISTOPHER S TUCKER ATC • GEORGE E TUCKER JR • SHARON L TUCKERMAN • STEPHEN D TUDAY • JAMES E TUDOR • GORDON TUENGE • LAURA A TUERS • DAVID F TUFTS • LOURAINE R TUGENDHAFT • ANTHONY E. TUGGLE • BARBARA Y TUGGLE • LEAH J TUGGLE • RONALD M TUGGLE • STEPHANIE M TUGGLE • JEAN C TUGMAN • ELINA M TUHKANEN • DONNA M TUITE • GLENN D TUITT • BRANDIE K TULLER • DANIEL R TULLER • MICHAEL M TULLER • ALYCIA A TULLOCH • KIM TULLY • PETER TULLY • DANIEL J TULMAN • DAMETA J TUMLIN • JENNIFER J TUMLIN • LINDA S TUMLIN • MALONE TUMLIN • RODNEY M TUMLIN • RAYMOND S TUMLIN JR. • BARBARA K TUMPERI • LINDA B TUMPERI • SUSANNE TUNNO • EVELYN H TUNSTALL • ROBERT W TUNSTALL • CATHIE M TUOHY WATTLES • DONALD E TUPPER • RICHARD A TURBE • JANET G TURBYVILLE • ANNE K TURCHI • SHARRON E TURCOTTE • DIANE E TURGEON ATC • AUDE TURIER • CARMEN M TURK • GEOFFREY S TURK • GREGOR R TURK • KATHLEEN K TURK • JOANNE C TURK ATC • IRV T TURKFELD • BETTY H TURLEY • LYNDA C TURLEY • STEPHEN J TURLEY • MABLE L TURMAN • SIMONE L TURMAN • JIMMIE L TURNAGE • ALAN R TURNER • ALICE M TURNER • BARBARA L TURNER • BARZELLA TURNER • BETTY K TURNER • BETTY Y TURNER • BEVERLY D TURNER • BOB B TURNER • BRIAN TURNER • BRUCE E TURNER • BYRON J TURNER • CAROL J TURNER • CATHERINE M TURNER • CHENOA A TURNER • CHRISTOPHER J TURNER • CINDY F TURNER • CORBETT H TURNER • CRAIG M TURNER • DANA L TURNER • DAVID J TURNER • DEBRA J TURNER • DELORES TURNER • DENNIS S TURNER • DONNA J TURNER • DONNA M TURNER • DWAYNE E TURNER • ED TURNER • ELEASE TURNER • ELIZABETH E TURNER • ELIZABETH H TURNER • ESTELLE M TURNER • GAYLE D TURNER • GLENDA F TURNER • GLORIA F TURNER • HELENA H TURNER • IMOGENE K TURNER • JAN TURNER • JASON A TURNER • JENNIFER D TURNER • JERE TURNER • JILL F TURNER • JULIUS D TURNER • KATHERINE E TURNER • KATHLEEN C TURNER • KATHLEEN J TURNER • KENNETH L TURNER • KIMBERLY M TURNER • LARRY TURNER • LAURA T TURNER • LAURIE B TURNER • LESTER T TURNER • LUCY B TURNER • MARCUS D TURNER

• MARGARET S TURNER • MARTHA W TURNER • MARY M TURNER • MAUREEN A TURNER • MICHAEL F TURNER • MIKE J TURNER • MIKOEL TURNER • PAM TURNER • PAMELA TURNER • PAMELA K TURNER • PATRICIA M TURNER • PATRICK TURNER • PAUL E TURNER • PAULA V TURNER • RHONDA L TURNER • RITA V TURNER • ROBERT L TURNER • ROSEATTA TURNER • SANDI L TURNER • SHELIA D TURNER • SHERRELL TURNER • SHIRLEY E TURNER • STEVEN TURNER • SYNJA L TURNER • THUR B TURNER • TIMOTHY A TURNER • TRACEY T TURNER • VANESSA C TURNER • WENDY L TURNER • WILLIAM L TURNER • AZELL TURNER III • IRA TURNER JR • JAMES E TURNER JR • KELLY D TURNEY • DENNIS E TURNHAM • STEFANI K TURNIPSEED • FREDERICK R TUROFF • AARON G TURPIN • ELEANOR I TURPIN • FRANK L TURPIN • KEN N TURPIN • RICHARD L TURPIN • SUZANNE L TUSCHER • SHOSHANA JENET TUSSING • TIMOTHY C TUSSING • BARBARA A TUTELIAN • THOMAS W TUTEN • TIPPI P TUTEN • MOLLY M TUTER • CAROL L TUTOR • GREGORY H TUTTLE • RONALD F TUTTLE • ANNELIESE TUYMER • EARL T TVEIT • LINDA L TWADDELL • ROBERT L TWADDELL • MICHELLE J TWAROG • RONALD J TWAROG • CHARLES TWEED • TIMOTHY E TWEEDLE • WILLIAM D TWEHUES ATC • JOHN TWINE • JACQUELIN O TWISS • JASON TWISS • KRISTINA G TWITTY • JEFFREY M TYACK • KENNETH C TYBURSKI • EUGENE TYCHANSKI • CLARE E TYERS • RONA L TYGER • ATHLYNNE TYLER • DAVID TYLER • EVA DIANE TYLER • GREGORY TYLER • GWENDOLYN R TYLER • J. L. TYLER • JONATHAN B TYLER • KAREN M TYLER • LYNSLEY A TYLER • RICHARD T TYLER • WAYNE C TYLER • WILLIAM J TYLER • LISA R TYLOR • ANDREW D TYMCHUK • ELLA Z TYMCHUK • CRAIG S TYMESON • DAVID H TYNER • NANCY J TYNER • KEVIN S TYO • CHARLOTTE C TYRE • ALISON J TYRER • LILLIAN TYRRELL • ANN D TYSON • JACK TYSON • JOHN B TYSON • L BARRETT TYSON • PATRICIA A TYSON • MARIA A TZAGOURNIS • GAYLE TZEMACH • JOHN A TZIKAS • CHRISTOPHER J UBERTO • PETER B UBERTO • MELISA M UCHIDA • SUNDAY UDEH • THOMAS G UDELL • RONNI C UDOFF • USEN E UDOH • AUDREY M UEBERSCHAER • SVEN U UENTZELMANN • JOHN T UETSUKI • ITORO E UFOT • MARIA A UGARTE • NICOLE S UGEL • LESTER Y UGGERUD • CHRISTOPHER UHER • JOSEPH K UHER • DOROTHY M UHL MT • TIMOTHY L UHL PT • BRENDA A UHLER • KAREN E UHLER • LINDA BALDREE UHLER • MARK S UHLES • ALICE J UHLIR • URSULA UHLIR • DONALD R UHLS • BEVERLEY UIPI • JANET R UISCHNER • BARBARA J ULANOWSKA • SHARON C ULIANA • ALBERT J ULLMAN • JENNIFER S ULLMAN • KENDI S. ULLMAN • DIANNE J ULM • CHRISTIAN H ULRICH • ROBERT ULZHEIMER • SUSAN M UMANSKY • SHAWNA R UMBARGER • KEITH A UMBERGER • SALLY L UMBERGER • MARYANN UMSCHEID • KARL R UMSTADTER • CYNTHIA K UNDERSET • AL L UNDERWOOD • BARBARA UNDERWOOD • BOBBYE S UNDERWOOD • CATHERINE A UNDERWOOD • CHRISTINE S UNDERWOOD • CYNTHIA K UNDERWOOD • JILL UNDERWOOD • LINDA M UNDERWOOD • MARJORIE Y UNDERWOOD • NORMAN L UNDERWOOD • PHILLIP A UNDERWOOD • TERRY L UNDERWOOD • TRACEY C UNDERWOOD • WALLACE W UNDERWOOD • WALTER L UNDERWOOD • LEE UNDERWOOD JR • RONALD L UNDERWOOD JR • DEBORAH JOSEPHINE UNDSETH • PETER M UNGER • TED H UNGER • ELIZABETH UNISLAWSKI • ERIC A UNOLD • EDWARD W UNSER • GAIL UNSWORTH • NELLIE JOY UNTALAN • DEBRA M UNTERMAN • BEVERLEY D UPCHURCH • FRANK H UPCHURCH • JENNIFER E UPCHURCH • KENNETH T UPCHURCH • KIMBERLY M UPCHURCH • MELANIE L UPCHURCH • LARRY L UPDIKE • SANDRA N UPDIKE • AMANDA G UPSHAW • COLETTE M UPSHAW • JAMES A UPSHAW • MARY L UPSHAW • SARAH E UPSHAW • ASHFAQ URAIZEE • KEIKO URAKAMI • CATHERINE H URBAN • KATHRYN A URBAN • PAMELA L URBAN • ZUZANA URBANEK • JOHN S URBANIA • GUSTAVO A URIBE • JOHN THOMAS URIBE • HOLLY R URICK • MADELINE P URKEN • MARYON L URQUHART • LUZ L URRUTIA • ROXANA URRUTIA SILVER • AMELIA M URSO • JEFFREY URSTADT • GERALD O URSULET • LUIS C URTEAGA • CATHERINE E URWIN • YOLANDA-IVONNE N USECHE • MICHIKO Y USELTON • PEGGY J USELTON • CHARLES H USHER • DAVID M USHER • FRANCES USHER • MYRON M USHER • TYRONE USHER • WALTON O USHER • STAN USHRY • GRAST K USRY • RONALD S USRY • CLAIRE P USSERY • JANET P USSERY • JOHN R USSERY • KIM R USSERY • ROBERT C USSERY • ROHN O USSERY • ROBERT A USZYNSKI • BRIAN S UTHLAUT • TERESA J UTLEY • KYLE S UTSUMI • DONNA A UTT • BRIAN L UTTER • KAREN UTTERBACK • BARBARA L UTZ • JOHN M UTZ • JOSEF K UTZ • TARU T UUSITALO • RUFUS C UWAJE • KENNETH G UYL • IDORENYIN UYOE • CHINYERE UZOUKWU • HUSEYIN UZUNALIOGLU • DANIEL J VACALA CATC • MARY R VACALA CATC • MARY K VACCARINO • LAURA A VACCARO • RALPH R VACCARO • R. VAN VACHON • RITA G VADEN • DAVID S VADNAIS • GINA VADNAIS • THOMAS A VADNAIS • MARK E VAHUE • ISAM G VAID • HELEN M VAIL • JOHN S VAIL • JUDITH M VAIL • LORETTA L VAIL • MIJA J VAIL • WILLIAM J VAIL JR • NELSON B VAILS • RUPAL D VAISHNAV • CARMEN I VAISKAUSKAS • LAURENT A VAJDA • NIKOLA VAJDA • DAVID A VALACHOVIC • THAMBAN VALAPPIL • TOMAS VALASEK •

ROWING
AVIRON

Abbreviations and terms used in Rowing results tables
Abréviations et termes employés dans les tableaux de résultats d'aviron

Term	English	Français
*	False Start	Faux départ
2	Second Position	Deuxième position
3	Third Position	Troisième position
4	Fourth Position	Quatrième position
5	Fifth Position	Cinquième position
6	Sixth Position	Sixième position
7	Seventh Position	Septième position
b	Bow	Proue
Bronze	Bronze Medal	Médaille de bronze
Ctry	Country	Pays
D	Semifinal	Demi-finale
FA	Final 1-6	Finale 1-6
FB	Final 7-12	Finale 7-12
FC	Final 13-18	Finale 13-18
FD	Final 19-24	Finale 19-24
Final	Final	Finale
Gold	Gold Medal	Médaille d'or
Heat	Heat	Série
Ln	Lane	Couloir
Name	Name	Nom
Pos	Position	Position
Q	Qualified	Qualifié
R	Repechage	Repêchage
Repechage	Repechage	Repêchage
Rerace	Rerace	Course répétée
Rnk	Rank	Classement
s	Stern	Arrière
Silver	Silver Medal	Médaille d'argent
Semifinal	Semifinal	Demi-finale
Time	Time	Temps
Time Behind	Time Behind	Temps en arrière

Internaltional Rowing Federation (FISA)
Fédération Internationale des Sociétés d'Aviron
Blochstrasse 2
CH-3653 Oberhofen amThunersee
Switzerland

HEAT 1

Rnk	Ln	Pos	Name	Ctry	Time	Time Behind	Q
1	4	b	MULLER, Xeno	SUI	7:26.75	0	D
2	3	b	COP, Iztok	SLO	7:32.69	5.94	R
3	5	b	NUSSBAUMER, Horst	AUT	7:36.15	9.40	R
4	1	b	CALABRESE, Giovanni	ITA	7:39.90	13.15	R
5	6	b	SEMA, Anton	RUS	7:49.44	22.69	R
6	2*	b	TAKEDA, Daisaku	JPN	7:56.93	30.18	R

HEAT 2

Rnk	Ln	Pos	Name	Ctry	Time	Time Behind	Q
1	3	b	PORTER, Derek	CAN	7:31.75	0	D
2	4	b	SZOGI, Laszlo	HUN	7:38.31	6.56	R
3	2	b	CAMERON, David	AUS	7:53.55	21.80	R
4	1	b	KHIMICH, Oleksandr	UKR	7:57.05	25.30	R
5	5*	b	TSE, Michael	HKG	8:11.51	39.76	R

HEAT 3

Rnk	Ln	Pos	Name	Ctry	Time	Time Behind	Q
1	4	b	LANGE, Thomas	GER	7:34.52	0	D
2	5	b	FERNANDEZ, Sergio	ARG	7:37.53	3.01	R
3	2	b	IBRAHIM, Aly	EGY	7:41.17	6.65	R
4	1	b	HAINING, Peter	GBR	7:42.55	8.03	R
5	3	b	JAANSON, Juri	EST	8:10.01	35.49	R

HEAT 4

Rnk	Ln	Pos	Name	Ctry	Time	Time Behind	Q
1	4	b	CHALUPA, Vaclav	CZE	7:35.48	0	D
2	5	b	BEKKEN, Fredrik	NOR	7:39.36	3.88	R
3	3	b	BEASLEY, Cyrus	USA	7:44.79	9.31	R
4	2	b	WADDELL, Robert	NZL	7:48.69	13.21	R
5	1	b	SODERBLOM, Tomas	FIN	7:53.46	17.98	R

REPECHAGE 1

Rnk	Ln	Pos	Name	Ctry	Time	Time Behind	Q
1	3	b	COP, Iztok	SLO	7:41.83	0	D
2	2	b	HAINING, Peter	GBR	7:45.95	4.12	D
3	4	b	CAMERON, David	AUS	7:49.24	7.41	D
4	1	b	SODERBLOM, Tomas	FIN	7:52.52	10.69	D
5	5	b	TAKEDA, Daisaku	JPN	7:59.77	17.94	D

REPECHAGE 2

Rnk	Ln	Pos	Name	Ctry	Time	Time Behind	Q
1	1	b	WADDELL, Robert	NZL	7:42.87	0	D
2	2	b	IBRAHIM, Aly	EGY	7:45.64	2.77	D
3	3	b	SZOGI, Laszlo	HUN	7:53.04	10.17	D
4	4	b	SEMA, Anton	RUS	8:46.71	1:03.84	D

REPECHAGE 3

Rnk	Ln	Pos	Name	Ctry	Time	Time Behind	Q
1	3	b	FERNANDEZ, Sergio	ARG	7:42.63	0	D
2	2	b	BEASLEY, Cyrus	USA	7:44.36	1.73	D
3	1	b	CALABRESE, Giovanni	ITA	7:45.53	2.90	D
4	4	b	TSE, Michael	HKG	8:31.41	48.78	D

REPECHAGE 4

Rnk	Ln	Pos	Name	Ctry	Time	Time Behind	Q
1	3	b	BEKKEN, Fredrik	NOR	7:47.31	0	D
2	2	b	NUSSBAUMER, Horst	AUT	7:49.79	2.48	D
3	4	b	KHIMICH, Oleksandr	UKR	7:56.15	8.84	D
4	1	b	JAANSON, Juri	EST	8:15.25	27.94	D

SEMIFINAL 1

Rnk	Ln	Pos	Name	Ctry	Time	Time Behind	Q
1	3	b	MULLER, Xeno	SUI	7:10.07	0	FA
2	4	b	PORTER, Derek	CAN	7:14.91	4.84	FA
3	2	b	BEKKEN, Fredrik	NOR	7:19.82	9.75	FA
4	6	b	IBRAHIM, Aly	EGY	7:22.43	12.36	FB
5	5	b	FERNANDEZ, Sergio	ARG	7:23.70	13.63	FB
6	1	b	HAINING, Peter	GBR	7:30.47	20.40	FB

SEMIFINAL 2

Rnk	Ln	Pos	Name	Ctry	Time	Time Behind	Q
1	4	b	LANGE, Thomas	GER	7:12.30	0	FA
2	2	b	COP, Iztok	SLO	7:15.07	2.77	FA
3	3	b	CHALUPA, Vaclav	CZE	7:16.97	4.67	FA
4	5	b	WADDELL, Robert	NZL	7:18.52	6.22	FB
5	6	b	BEASLEY, Cyrus	USA	7:31.49	19.19	FB
6	1	b	NUSSBAUMER, Horst	AUT	7:35.52	23.22	FB

SEMIFINAL 3

Rnk	Ln	Pos	Name	Ctry	Time	Time Behind	Q
1	3	b	CAMERON, David	AUS	7:25.38	0	FC
2	4	b	SZOGI, Laszlo	HUN	7:27.92	2.54	FC
3	2	b	JAANSON, Juri	EST	7:28.89	3.51	FC
4	5	b	TAKEDA, Daisaku	JPN	7:32.63	7.25	FD
5	1	b	TSE, Michael	HKG	7:51.15	25.77	FD

SEMIFINAL 4

Rnk	Ln	Pos	Name	Ctry	Time	Time Behind	Q
1	2	b	CALABRESE, Giovanni	ITA	7:23.59	0	FC
2	4	b	SODERBLOM, Tomas	FIN	7:23.88	0.29	FC
3	1	b	SEMA, Anton	RUS	7:28.44	4.85	FC
4	3	b	KHIMICH, Oleksandr	UKR	7:31.24	7.65	FD

FINAL D

Rnk	Ln	Pos	Name	Ctry	Time	Time Behind
1	3	b	KHIMICH, Oleksandr	UKR	7:40.54	0
2	2	b	TAKEDA, Daisaku	JPN	7:45.23	4.69
3	1	b	TSE, Michael	HKG	8:06.43	25.89

FINAL C

Rnk	Ln	Pos	Name	Ctry	Time	Time Behind
1	4	b	CAMERON, David	AUS	7:30.55	0
2	2	b	SODERBLOM, Tomas	FIN	7:32.86	2.31
3	5	b	SZOGI, Laszlo	HUN	7:34.23	3.68
4	6	b	SEMA, Anton	RUS	7:44.93	14.38
5	3	b	CALABRESE, Giovanni	ITA	7:48.63	18.08
6	1	b	JAANSON, Juri	EST	8:33.53	1:02.98

FINAL B

Rnk	Ln	Pos	Name	Ctry	Time	Time Behind
1	4	b	WADDELL, Robert	NZL	6:49.55	0
2	3	b	IBRAHIM, Aly	EGY	6:52.11	2.56
3	6	b	NUSSBAUMER, Horst	AUT	6:53.20	3.65
4	5	b	BEASLEY, Cyrus	USA	6:54.17	4.62
5	1	b	HAINING, Peter	GBR	6:55.06	5.51
6	2	b	FERNANDEZ, Sergio	ARG	6:56.97	7.42

FINAL A

Rnk	Ln	Pos	Name	Ctry	Time	Time Behind	
1	4	b	MULLER, Xeno	SUI	6:44.85	0	Gold
2	2	b	PORTER, Derek	CAN	6:47.45	2.60	Silver
3	3	b	LANGE, Thomas	GER	6:47.72	2.87	Bronze
4	5	b	COP, Iztok	SLO	6:51.71	6.86	
5	1	b	CHALUPA, Vaclav	CZE	6:55.65	10.80	
6	6	b	BEKKEN, Fredrik	NOR	6:59.51	14.66	

Rowing / *Aviron*

Single Sculls, Women / *Skiff, Dames*

HEAT 1

Rnk	Ln	Pos	Name	Ctry	Time	Time Behind	Q
1	4	b	BRANDIN, Maria	SWE	8:00.70	0	D
2	3	b	NEYKOVA, Rumyana	BUL	8:12.85	12.15	R
3	5	b	SVAIER, Tonia	GRE	8:17.49	16.79	R
4	1	b	SAKICKIENE, Birute	LTU	8:21.78	21.08	R
5	2	b	EVERS, Meike	GER	8:24.14	23.44	R
6	6	b	URBANO, Elina	ARG	8:42.59	41.89	R

HEAT 2

Rnk	Ln	Pos	Name	Ctry	Time	Time Behind	Q
1	3	b	KHODOTOVICH, Ekaterina	BLR	8:03.73	0	D
2	4	b	BREDAEL, Annelies	BEL	8:08.40	4.67	R
3	2	b	DAVIDON, Ruth	USA	8:09.78	6.05	R
4	5	s	GARCIA, Celine	FRA	8:10.22	6.49	R
5	6	s	LIPA, Elisabeta	ROM	8:22.92	19.19	R
6	1	b	HIRECHE, Samia	ALG	9:08.31	1:04.58	R

HEAT 3

Rnk	Ln	Pos	Name	Ctry	Time	Time Behind	Q
1	4	b	HANSEN, Trine	DEN	8:02.06	0	D
2	3	b	LAUMANN, Silken	CAN	8:10.57	8.51	R
3	5	b	LIU, Xiaochun	CHN	8:12.82	10.76	R
4	1	b	BATTEN, Guin	GBR	8:16.75	14.69	R
5	2	b	FINSKA-BEZERRA, Laila	FIN	8:31.56	29.50	R

REPECHAGE 1

Rnk	Ln	Pos	Name	Ctry	Time	Time Behind	Q
1	4	b	DAVIDON, Ruth	USA	8:33.73	0	D
2	3	b	NEYKOVA, Rumyana	BUL	8:41.37	7.64	D
3	2	b	BATTEN, Guin	GBR	8:44.73	11.00	D
4	1	b	EVERS, Meike	GER	8:54.05	20.32	FC
5	5	b	HIRECHE, Samia	ALG	9:28.41	54.68	FC

REPECHAGE 2

Rnk	Ln	Pos	Name	Ctry	Time	Time Behind	Q
1	4	s	LIPA, Elisabeta	ROM	8:30.97	0	D
2	3	b	BREDAEL, Annelies	BEL	8:33.72	2.75	D
3	2	b	LIU, Xiaochun	CHN	8:37.01	6.04	D
4	1	b	SAKICKIENE, Birute	LTU	8:41.08	10.11	FC

REPECHAGE 3

Rnk	Ln	Pos	Name	Ctry	Time	Time Behind	Q
1	3	b	LAUMANN, Silken	CAN	8:28.88	0	D
2	2	s	GARCIA, Celine	FRA	8:32.58	3.70	D
3	1	b	FINSKA-BEZERRA, Laila	FIN	8:35.72	6.84	D
4	4	b	SVAIER, Tonia	GRE	8:49.44	20.56	FC
5	5	b	URBANO, Elina	ARG	9:04.66	35.78	FC

SEMIFINAL 1

Rnk	Ln	Pos	Name	Ctry	Time	Time Behind	Q
1	2	b	LAUMANN, Silken	CAN	7:57.68	0	FA
2	4	b	KHODOTOVICH, Ekaterina	BLR	8:00.02	2.34	FA
3	3	b	BRANDIN, Maria	SWE	8:01.55	3.87	FA
4	5	b	BREDAEL, Annelies	BEL	8:05.78	8.10	FB
5	6	b	NEYKOVA, Rumyana	BUL	8:15.63	17.95	FB
6	1	b	FINSKA-BEZERRA, Laila	FIN	8:25.00	27.32	FB

SEMIFINAL 2

Rnk	Ln	Pos	Name	Ctry	Time	Time Behind	Q
1	3	b	HANSEN, Trine	DEN	7:53.45	0	FA
2	4	b	DAVIDON, Ruth	USA	7:54.97	1.52	FA
3	1	b	BATTEN, Guin	GBR	7:56.61	3.16	FA
4	5	s	LIPA, Elisabeta	ROM	8:01.84	8.39	FB
5	2	s	GARCIA, Celine	FRA	8:13.37	19.92	FB
6	6	b	LIU, Xiaochun	CHN	8:15.83	22.38	FB

FINAL C

Rnk	Ln	Pos	Name	Ctry	Time	Time Behind
1	2	b	EVERS, Meike	GER	8:16.51	0
2	3	b	SAKICKIENE, Birute	LTU	8:17.80	1.29
3	4	b	SVAIER, Tonia	GRE	8:25.83	9.32
4	5	b	URBANO, Elina	ARG	8:41.51	25.00
5	1	b	HIRECHE, Samia	ALG	9:09.92	53.41

FINAL B

Rnk	Ln	Pos	Name	Ctry	Time	Time Behind
1	3	b	BREDAEL, Annelies	BEL	7:25.83	0
2	2	b	NEYKOVA, Rumyana	BUL	7:27.77	1.94
3	4	b	LIPA, Elisabeta	ROM	7:28.79	2.96
4	5	s	GARCIA, Celine	FRA	7:33.30	7.47
5	1	b	LIU, Xiaochun	CHN	7:33.67	7.84
6	6	b	FINSKA-BEZERRA, Laila	FIN	7:34.85	9.02

FINAL A

Rnk	Ln	Pos	Name	Ctry	Time	Time Behind	
1	5	b	KHODOTOVICH, Ekaterina	BLR	7:32.21	0	Gold
2	3	b	LAUMANN, Silken	CAN	7:35.15	2.94	Silver
3	4	b	HANSEN, Trine	DEN	7:37.20	4.99	Bronze
4	1	b	BRANDIN, Maria	SWE	7:42.58	10.37	
5	6	b	BATTEN, Guin	GBR	7:45.08	12.87	
6	2	b	DAVIDON, Ruth	USA	7:46.47	14.26	

Rowing / *Aviron*
Double Sculls, Men / *Deux rameurs en couple, Messieurs*

HEAT 1

Rnk	Ln	Pos	Names	Ctry	Time	Time Behind	Q
1	3	b	UNDSET, Kjetil	NOR	6:43.35	0	D
		s	STORSETH, Steffen				
2	2	b	BRONIEWSKI, Kajetan	POL	6:48.13	4.78	R
		s	KOROL, Adam				
3	4	b	ANTONIE, Peter	AUS	6:50.15	6.80	R
		s	DAY, Jason				
4	5	b	HAMBALEK, Ondrej	SVK	6:55.87	12.52	R
		s	ZISKA, Jan				
5	1	b	LEE, In-Soo	KOR	7:11.56	28.21	R
		s	LEE, Ho				

HEAT 2

Rnk	Ln	Pos	Names	Ctry	Time	Time Behind	Q
1	3	b	CHRISTENSEN, Lars	DEN	6:48.75	0	D
		s	HALDBO HANSEN, Martin				
2	4	b	MAYER, Sebastian	GER	6:51.41	2.66	R
		s	OPFER, Roland				
3	1	b	SYMOENS, Tom	BEL	6:54.80	6.05	R
		s	HENDRICKX, Bjorn				
4	5	b	TUL, Erik	SLO	7:02.48	13.73	R
		s	SPIK, Luka				
5	2	b	VERDURAS, Melquiades	ESP	7:13.99	25.24	R
		s	MERIN, Jose Antonio				

HEAT 3

Rnk	Ln	Pos	Names	Ctry	Time	Time Behind	Q
1	3	b	TIZZANO, Davide	ITA	6:48.22	0	D
		s	ABBAGNALE, Agostino				
2	5	b	LASMANIS, Ugis	LAT	6:52.80	4.58	R
		s	REINHOLDS, Andris				
3	1	b	TELISMAN, Hrvoje	CRO	6:55.40	7.18	R
		s	BAJLO, Danijel				
4	4	b	JONKE, Arnold	AUT	6:56.55	8.33	R
		s	ZERBST, Christoph				
5	2	b	POOLEY, Guy	GBR	7:00.74	12.52	R
		s	THATCHER, Robert				

HEAT 4

Rnk	Ln	Pos	Names	Ctry	Time	Time Behind	Q
1	2	b	KOWAL, Frederic	FRA	6:44.01	0	D
		s	BARATHAY, Samuel				
2	3	b	FORGERON, Michael	CAN	6:48.03	4.02	R
		s	HALLETT, Todd				
3	4	b	SILVA, Marcelus	BRA	6:49.92	5.91	R
		s	MARINHO, Dirceu				
4	1	b	DANI, Zsolt	HUN	6:57.63	13.62	R
		s	MITRING, Gabor				

REPECHAGE 1

Rnk	Ln	Pos	Names	Ctry	Time	Time Behind	Q
1	1	b	JONKE, Arnold	AUT	6:43.52	0	D
		s	ZERBST, Christoph				
2	3	b	SYMOENS, Tom	BEL	6:48.45	4.93	D
		s	HENDRICKX, Bjorn				
3	2	b	BRONIEWSKI, Kajetan	POL	6:53.21	9.69	D
		s	KOROL, Adam				

REPECHAGE 2

Rnk	Ln	Pos	Names	Ctry	Time	Time Behind	Q
1	3	b	MAYER, Sebastian	GER	6:47.52	0	D
		s	OPFER, Roland				
2	2	b	TELISMAN, Hrvoje	CRO	6:48.02	0.50	D
		s	BAJLO, Danijel				
3	4	b	DANI, Zsolt	HUN	6:50.02	2.50	D
		s	MITRING, Gabor				
4	1	b	LEE, In-Soo	KOR	7:09.71	22.19	D
		s	LEE, Ho				

REPECHAGE 3

Rnk	Ln	Pos	Names	Ctry	Time	Time Behind	Q
1	2	b	LASMANIS, Ugis	LAT	6:51.19	0	D
		s	REINHOLDS, Andris				
2	4	b	HAMBALEK, Ondrej	SVK	6:53.64	2.45	D
		s	ZISKA, Jan				
3	3	b	SILVA, Marcelus	BRA	6:56.93	5.74	D
		s	MARINHO, Dirceu				
4	1	b	VERDURAS, Melquiades	ESP	6:59.57	8.38	D
		s	MERIN, Jose Antonio				

REPECHAGE 4

Rnk	Ln	Pos	Names	Ctry	Time	Time Behind	Q
1	3	b	FORGERON, Michael	CAN	6:51.93	0	D
		s	HALLETT, Todd				
2	2	b	ANTONIE, Peter	AUS	6:51.98	0.05	D
		s	DAY, Jason				
3	1	b	POOLEY, Guy	GBR	7:00.81	8.88	D
		s	THATCHER, Robert				
4	4	b	TUL, Erik	SLO	7:06.06	14.13	D
		s	SPIK, Luka				

RERACE 1

Rnk	Ln	Pos	Names	Ctry	Time	Time Behind	Q
1	2	b	DANI, Zsolt	HUN	6:47.77	0	FC
		s	MITRING, Gabor				
2	1	b	CRACKNELL, James	GBR	6:51.22	3.45	FC
		s	THATCHER, Robert				
3	3	b	VERDURAS, Melquiades	ESP	6:55.00	7.23	
		s	MERIN, Jose Antonio				

RERACE 2

Rnk	Ln	Pos	Names	Ctry	Time	Time Behind	Q
1	2	b	BRONIEWSKI, Kajetan	POL	6:48.53	0	FC
		s	KOROL, Adam				
2	3	b	SILVA, Marcelus	BRA	6:52.73	4.20	FC
		s	MARINHO, Dirceu				
3	4	b	TUL, Erik	SLO	6:56.43	7.90	FC
		s	SPIK, Luka				
4	1	b	LEE, In-Soo	KOR	7:05.08	16.55	
		s	LEE, Ho				

Double Sculls, Men / *Deux rameurs en couple, Messieurs*

SEMIFINAL 1

Rnk	Ln	Pos	Names	Ctry	Time	Time Behind	Q
1	4	b	TIZZANO, Davide	ITA	6:37.49	0	FA
		s	ABBAGNALE, Agostino				
2	3	b	UNDSET, Kjetil	NOR	6:40.15	2.66	FA
		s	STORSETH, Steffen				
3	5	b	MAYER, Sebastian	GER	6:42.57	5.08	FA
		s	OPFER, Roland				
4	2	b	FORGERON, Michael	CAN	6:46.35	8.86	FB
		s	HALLETT, Todd				
5	1	b	SYMOENS, Tom	BEL	6:48.13	10.64	FB
		s	HENDRICKX, Bjorn				
6	6	b	HAMBALEK, Ondrej	SVK	6:55.73	18.24	FB
		s	ZISKA, Jan				

SEMIFINAL 2

Rnk	Ln	Pos	Names	Ctry	Time	Time Behind	Q
1	3	b	KOWAL, Frederic	FRA	6:32.86	0	FA
		s	BARATHAY, Samuel				
2	2	b	JONKE, Arnold	AUT	6:35.76	2.90	FA
		s	ZERBST, Christoph				
3	4	b	CHRISTENSEN, Lars	DEN	6:37.10	4.24	FA
		s	HALDBO HANSEN, Martin				
4	1	b	ANTONIE, Peter	AUS	6:39.49	6.63	FB
		s	DAY, Jason				
5	5	b	LASMANIS, Ugis	LAT	6:40.38	7.52	FB
		s	REINHOLDS, Andris				
6	6	b	TELISMAN, Hrvoje	CRO	7:03.53	30.67	FB
		s	BAJLO, Danijel				

FINAL C

Rnk	Ln	Pos	Name	Ctry	Time	Time Behind
1	4	b	BRONIEWSKI, Kajetan	POL	6:40.62	0
		s	KOROL, Adam			
2	1	b	TUL, Erik	SLO	6:43.55	2.93
		s	SPIK, Luka			
3	2	b	SILVA, Marcelus	BRA	6:47.12	6.50
		s	MARINHO, Dirceu			
4	3	b	DANI, Zsolt	HUN	6:50.90	10.28
		s	MITRING, Gabor			
5	5	b	CRACKNELL, James	GBR	6:51.41	10.79
		s	THATCHER, Robert			

FINAL B

Rnk	Ln	Pos	Names	Ctry	Time	Time Behind
1	4	b	FORGERON, Michael	CAN	6:18.37	0
		s	HALLETT, Todd			
2	3	b	ANTONIE, Peter	AUS	6:19.25	0.88
		s	DAY, Jason			
3	5	b	LASMANIS, Ugis	LAT	6:20.82	2.45
		s	REINHOLDS, Andris			
4	2	b	SYMOENS, Tom	BEL	6:21.89	3.52
		s	HENDRICKX, Bjorn			
5	1	b	HAMBALEK, Ondrej	SVK	6:26.51	8.14
		s	ZISKA, Jan			
6	6	b	TELISMAN, Hrvoje	CRO	6:26.84	8.47
		s	BAJLO, Danijel			

FINAL A

Rnk	Ln	Pos	Names	Ctry	Time	Time Behind	
1	4	b	TIZZANO, Davide	ITA	6:16.98	0	**Gold**
		s	ABBAGNALE, Agostino				
2	2	b	UNDSET, Kjetil	NOR	6:18.42	1.44	**Silver**
		s	STORSETH, Steffen				
3	3	b	KOWAL, Frederic	FRA	6:19.85	2.87	**Bronze**
		s	BARATHAY, Samuel				
4	1	b	CHRISTENSEN, Lars	DEN	6:24.77	7.79	
		s	HALDBO HANSEN, Martin				
5	5	b	JONKE, Arnold	AUT	6:25.17	8.19	
		s	ZERBST, Christoph				
6	6	b	MAYER, Sebastian	GER	6:29.32	12.34	
		s	OPFER, Roland				

Rowing / *Aviron*

Double Sculls, Women / *Deux rameuses en couple, Dames*

HEAT 1

Rnk	Ln	Pos	Names	Ctry	Time	Time Behind	Q
1	3	b	McBEAN, Marnie	CAN	7:23.07	0	D
		s	HEDDLE, Kathleen				
2	4	b	CAO, Mianying	CHN	7:26.47	3.40	D
		s	ZHANG, Xiuyun				
3	5	b	DEVINE, Jennifer	USA	7:31.98	8.91	D
		s	KNOX ZALOOM, Michelle				
4	2	b	OZOLINA, Sanita	LAT	7:36.18	13.11	R
		s	LUTERE, Liene				
5	1	b	BELLO, Erika	ITA	7:47.07	24.00	R
		s	BARELLI, Marianna				

HEAT 2

Rnk	Ln	Pos	Names	Ctry	Time	Time Behind	Q
1	4	b	HATZAKIS, Marina	AUS	7:20.10	0	D
		s	ROYE, Bronwyn				
2	3	b	THIEME, Jana	GER	7:21.13	1.03	D
		s	LUTZE, Manuela				
3	2	b	ORONOVA, Daniela	BUL	7:36.48	16.38	D
		s	KAMENOVA, Galina				
4	1	b	AMAYA, Dolores	ARG	7:57.05	36.95	R
		s	GARISOAIN, Maria Julia				
5	5	b	MIN, Byung-Soon	KOR	8:34.55	1:14.45	R
		s	PARK, Young-Ja				

Double Sculls, Women / *Deux rameuses en couple, Dames*

HEAT 3

Rnk	Ln	Pos	Names	Ctry	Time	Time Behind	Q
1	3	b	EIJS, Irene	NED	7:23.12	0	D
		s	van NES, Eeke				
2	2	b	BAKER, Philippa	NZL	7:26.83	3.71	D
		s	LAWSON, Brenda				
3	1	b	USTYUZHANINA, Tetyana	UKR	7:27.12	4.00	D
		s	REUTOVA, Olena				
4	4	b	BJERKNES, Kristine	NOR	7:30.32	7.20	R
		s	KLAVENESS, Kristine				

REPECHAGE 1

Rnk	Ln	Pos	Names	Ctry	Time	Time Behind	Q
1	3	b	BJERKNES, Kristine	NOR	7:43.75	0	D
		s	KLAVENESS, Kristine				
2	2	b	OZOLINA, Sanita	LAT	7:48.02	4.27	D
		s	LUTERE, Liene				
3	1	b	BELLO, Erika	ITA	7:52.07	8.32	D
		s	BARELLI, Marianna				
4	4	b	AMAYA, Dolores	ARG	8:09.24	25.49	
		s	GARISOAIN, Maria Julia				
5	5	b	MIN, Byung-Soon	KOR	8:44.34	1:00.59	
		s	PARK, Young-Ja				

SEMIFINAL 1

Rnk	Ln	Pos	Names	Ctry	Time	Time Behind	Q
1	4	b	McBEAN, Marnie	CAN	7:11.21	0	FA
		s	HEDDLE, Kathleen				
2	2	b	BAKER, Philippa	NZL	7:15.57	4.36	FA
		s	LAWSON, Brenda				
3	3	b	HATZAKIS, Marina	AUS	7:15.58	4.37	FA
		s	ROYE, Bronwyn				
4	6	b	ORONOVA, Daniela	BUL	7:18.33	7.12	FB
		s	KAMENOVA, Galina				
5	5	b	KNOX ZALOOM, Michelle	USA	7:21.97	10.76	FB
		s	DEVINE, Jennifer				
6	1	b	BELLO, Erika	ITA	7:38.85	27.64	FB
		s	BARELLI, Marianna				

SEMIFINAL 2

Rnk	Ln	Pos	Names	Ctry	Time	Time Behind	Q
1	4	b	CAO, Mianying	CHN	7:15.47	0	FA
		s	ZHANG, Xiuyun				
2	3	b	EIJS, Irene	NED	7:16.39	0.92	FA
		s	van NES, Eeke				
3	2	b	THIEME, Jana	GER	7:19.62	4.15	FA
		s	LUTZE, Manuela				
4	6	b	BJERKNES, Kristine	NOR	7:26.24	10.77	FB
		s	KLAVENESS, Kristine				
5	5	b	USTYUZHANINA, Tetyana	UKR	7:28.53	13.06	FB
		s	REUTOVA, Olena				
6	1	b	OZOLINA, Sanita	LAT	7:32.00	16.53	FB
		s	LUTERE, Liene				

FINAL B

Rnk	Ln	Pos	Names	Ctry	Time	Time Behind
1	4	b	BJERKNESS, Kristine	NOR	6:53.31	0
		s	KLAVENESS, Kristine			
2	2	b	USTYUZHANINA, Tetyana	UKR	6:53.96	0.65
		s	REUTOVA, Olena			
3	5	b	KNOX ZALOOM, Michelle	USA	6:58.78	5.47
		s	DEVINE, Jennifer			
4	3	b	ORONOVA, Daniela	BUL	7:00.14	6.83
		s	KAMENOVA, Galina			
5	1	b	OZOLINA, Sanita	LAT	7:06.47	13.16
		s	LUTERE, Liene			
6	6	b	BELLO, Erika	ITA	7:16.54	23.23
		s	BARELLI, Marianna			

FINAL A

Rnk	Ln	Pos	Names	Ctry	Time	Time Behind	
1	4	b	McBEAN, Marnie	CAN	6:56.84	0	Gold
		s	HEDDLE, Kathleen				
2	3	b	CAO, Mianying	CHN	6:58.35	1.51	Silver
		s	ZHANG, Xiuyun				
3	5	b	EIJS, Irene	NED	6:58.72	1.88	Bronze
		s	van NES, Eeke				
4	1	b	HATZAKIS, Marina	AUS	7:01.26	4.42	
		s	ROYE, Bronwyn				
5	6	b	THIEME, Jana	GER	7:04.14	7.30	
		s	LUTZE, Manuela				
6	2	b	BAKER, Philippa	NZL	7:09.92	13.08	
		s	LAWSON, Brenda				

Rowing / *Aviron*
Lightweight Double Sculls, Men / *Deux rameurs en couple poids léger, Messieurs*

HEAT 1

Rnk	Ln	Pos	Names	Ctry	Time	Time Behind	Q
1	4	b	van der LINDEN, Maarten	NED	6:49.93	0	D
		s	AARDEWIJN, Pepijn				
2	1	b	AUTH, Thomas	USA	6:50.55	0.62	R
		s	PETERSON, Stephen				
3	2	b	POLYMEROS, Vasileios	GRE	6:50.57	0.64	R
		s	KOURKOURIKIS, Ioannis				
4	5	b	ZAPATA, Fernando	ARG	7:07.50	17.57	R
		s	ROCHA, Agustin				
5	3	b	TICHY, Mattias	SWE	7:18.87	28.94	R
		s	CHRISTENSSON, Anders				

HEAT 2

Rnk	Ln	Pos	Names	Ctry	Time	Time Behind	Q
1	5	b	de MARCO, Jose Maria	ESP	6:46.66	0	D
		s	SAEZ, Juan Carlos				
2	4	b	AUDISIO, Marco	ITA	6:47.26	0.60	R
		s	CRISPI, Michelangelo				
3	3	b	SYCZ, Robert	POL	6:54.68	8.02	R
		s	WDOWIAK, Grzegorz				
4	2	b	DOLAN, Brendan	IRL	6:56.28	9.62	R
		s	O'TOOLE, Niall				
5	1	b	STRANGE, Nick	GBR	6:56.86	10.20	R
		s	SINTON, Andrew				

HEAT 3

Rnk	Ln	Pos	Names	Ctry	Time	Time Behind	Q
1	4	b	GIER, Markus	SUI	6:47.28	0	D
		s	GIER, Michael				
2	3	b	SIGL, Wolfgang	AUT	6:54.36	7.08	R
		s	RANTASA, Walter				
3	2	b	KVALVIK, Magne	NOR	6:57.37	10.09	R
		s	ERDSAL, Tor-Albert				
4	5	b	LEON, Raul	CUB	7:01.13	13.85	R
		s	ARIAS, Alexis				
5	1	b	MICHALEK, Adam	CZE	7:16.07	28.79	R
		s	VABROUSEK, Michal				

HEAT 4

Rnk	Ln	Pos	Names	Ctry	Time	Time Behind	Q
1	3	b	EDWARDS, Anthony	AUS	6:49.95	0	D
		s	HICK, Bruce				
2	2	b	UHRIG, Peter	GER	6:54.82	4.87	R
		s	EULER, Ingo				
3	4	b	OBINATA, Kenichi	JPN	6:56.17	6.22	R
		s	HASE, Hitoshi				
4	1	b	HAMILL, Rob	NZL	7:09.61	19.66	R
		s	RODGER, Mike				

REPECHAGE 1

Rnk	Ln	Pos	Names	Ctry	Time	Time Behind	Q
1	4	b	TICHY, Mattias	SWE	6:17.84	0	D
		s	CHRISTENSSON, Anders				
2	2	b	UHRIG, Peter	GER	6:18.11	0.27	D
		s	EULER, Ingo				
3	1	b	DOLAN, Brendan	IRL	6:18.38	0.54	D
		s	O'TOOLE, Niall				
4	3	b	KVALVIK, Magne	NOR	6:25.68	7.84	D
		s	ERDSAL, Tor-Albert				

REPECHAGE 2

Rnk	Ln	Pos	Names	Ctry	Time	Time Behind	Q
1	2	b	SIGL, Wolfgang	AUT	6:21.10	0	D
		s	RANTASA, Walter				
2	3	b	SYCZ, Robert	POL	6:24.19	3.09	D
		s	WDOWIAK, Grzegorz				
3	1	b	ZAPATA, Fernando	ARG	6:28.08	6.98	D
		s	ROCHA, Agustin				

REPECHAGE 3

Rnk	Ln	Pos	Names	Ctry	Time	Time Behind	Q
1	3	b	AUDISIO, Marco	ITA	6:19.95	0	D
		s	CRISPI, Michelangelo				
2	2	b	POLYMEROS, Vasileios	GRE	6:24.40	4.45	D
		s	KOURKOURIKIS, Ioannis				
3	4	b	MICHALEK, Adam	CZE	6:30.34	10.39	D
		s	VABROUSEK, Michal				
4	1	b	HAMILL, Rob	NZL	6:34.78	14.83	D
		s	RODGER, Mike				

REPECHAGE 4

Rnk	Ln	Pos	Names	Ctry	Time	Time Behind	Q
1	2	b	AUTH, Thomas	USA	6:20.93	0	D
		s	PETERSON, Stephen				
2	1	b	STRANGE, Nick	GBR	6:22.27	1.34	D
		s	SINTON, Andrew				
3	4	b	LEON, Raul	CUB	6:23.52	2.59	D
		s	ARIAS, Alexis				
4	3	b	OBINATA, Kenichi	JPN	6:24.68	3.75	D
		s	HASE, Hitoshi				

SEMIFINAL 1

Rnk	Ln	Pos	Names	Ctry	Time	Time Behind	Q
1	4	b	GIER, Michael	SUI	6:25.37	0	FA
		s	GIER, Markus				
2	3	b	van der LINDEN, Maarten	NED	6:27.07	1.70	FA
		s	AARDEWIJN, Pepijn				
3	2	b	SIGL, Wolfgang	AUT	6:28.06	2.69	FA
		s	RANTASA, Walter				
4	5	b	AUTH, Thomas	USA	6:29.80	4.43	FB
		s	PETERSON, Stephen				
5	1	b	POLYMEROS, Vasilios	GRE	6:34.84	9.47	FB
		s	KOURKOURIKIS, Ioannis				
6	6	b	UHRIG, Peter	GER	6:40.14	14.77	FB
		s	EULER, Ingo				

SEMIFINAL 2

Rnk	Ln	Pos	Names	Ctry	Time	Time Behind	Q
1	2	b	TICHY, Mattias	SWE	6:29.17	0	FA
		s	CHRISTENSSON, Anders				
2	3	b	EDWARDS, Anthony	AUS	6:29.27	0.10	FA
		s	HICK, Bruce				
3	4	b	de MARCO, Jose Maria	ESP	6:29.37	0.20	FA
		s	SAEZ, Juan Carlos				
4	5	b	AUDISIO, Marco	ITA	6:30.46	1.29	FB
		s	CRISPI, Michelangelo				
5	6	b	STRANGE, Nicholas	GBR	6:39.20	10.03	FB
		s	SINTON, Andrew				
6	1	b	SYCZ, Robert	POL	6:39.56	10.39	FB
		s	WDOWIAK, Grzegorz				

Lightweight Double Sculls, Men / *Deux rameurs en couple poids léger, Messieurs*

SEMIFINAL 3

Rnk	Ln	Pos	Names	Ctry	Time	Time Behind	Q
1	1	b	MICHALEK, Adam	CZE	6:41.41	0	FC
		s	VABROUSEK, Michal				
2	3	b	OBINATA, Kenichi	JPN	6:45.08	3.67	FC
		s	HASE, Hitoshi				
3	2	b	DOLAN, Brendan	IRL	8:14.64	1:33.23	
		s	O'TOOLE, Niall				

SEMIFINAL 4

Rnk	Ln	Pos	Names	Ctry	Time	Time Behind	Q
1	4	b	KVALVIK, Magne	NOR	6:36.30	0	FC
		s	ERSDAL, Tor-Albert				
2	2	b	LEON, Raul	CUB	6:37.40	1.10	FC
		s	ARIAS, Alexis				
3	3	b	ZAPATA, Fernando	ARG	6:38.55	2.25	FC
		s	ROCHA, Agustin				
4	1	b	HAMILL, Rob	NZL	6:41.39	5.09	
		s	RODGER, Mike				

FINAL C

Rnk	Ln	Pos	Names	Ctry	Time	Time Behind
1	4	b	MICHALEK, Adam	CZE	6:53.14	0
		s	VABROUSEK, Michal			
2	3	b	KVALVIK, Magne	NOR	6:55.35	2.21
		s	ERSDAL, Tor-Albert			
3	2	b	OBINATA, Kenichi	JPN	6:56.13	2.99
		s	HASE, Hitoshi			
4	5	b	LEON, Raul	CUB	6:58.63	5.49
		s	ARIAS, Alexis			
5	1	b	ZAPATA, Fernando	ARG	7:04.67	11.53
		s	ROCHA, Agustin			

FINAL B

Rnk	Ln	Pos	Names	Ctry	Time	Time Behind
1	1	b	SYCZ, Robert	POL	6:24.95	0
		s	WDOWIAK, Grzegorz			
2	4	b	AUDISIO, Marco	ITA	6:25.04	0.09
		s	CRISPI, Michelangelo			
3	3	b	AUTH, Thomas	USA	6:25.89	0.94
		s	PETERSON, Stephen			
4	5	b	POLYMEROS, Vasilios	GRE	6:27.94	2.99
		s	KOURKOURIKIS, Ioannis			
5	6	b	UHRIG, Peter	GER	6:30.43	5.48
		s	EULER, Ingo			
6	2	b	STRANGE, Nicholas	GBR	6:31.15	6.20
		s	SINTON, Andrew			

FINAL A

Rnk	Ln	Pos	Names	Ctry	Time	Time Behind	
1	3	b	GIER, Markus	SUI	6:23.47	0	Gold
		s	GIER, Michael				
2	5	b	van der LINDEN, Maarten	NED	6:26.48	3.01	Silver
		s	AARDEWIJN, Pepijn				
3	2	b	EDWARDS, Anthony	AUS	6:26.69	3.22	Bronze
		s	HICK, Bruce				
4	1	b	de MARCO, Jose Maria	ESP	6:28.09	4.62	
		b	SAEZ, Juan Carlos				
5	6	b	SIGL, Wolfgang	AUT	6:30.85	7.38	
		s	RANTASA, Walter				
6	4	b	TICHY, Mattias	SWE	6:34.78	11.31	
		s	CHRISTENSSON, Anders				

Rowing / *Aviron*

Lightweight Double Sculls, Women / *Deux rameuses en couple poids léger, Dames*

HEAT 1

Rnk	Ln	Pos	Names	Ctry	Time	Time Behind	Q
1	3	b	BURNS, Lindsay	USA	7:28.28	0	D
		s	BELL, Teresa Z.				
2	2	b	BERTINI, Lisa	ITA	7:31.58	3.30	R
		s	ORZAN, Martina				
3	4	b	VERMULST, Laurien	NED	7:32.30	4.02	R
		s	MELIESIE, Ellen				
4	5	b	LI, Fei	CHN	7:36.71	8.43	R
		s	OU, Shaoyan				
5	1	b	LAMOLLE, Myriam	FRA	7:36.75	8.47	R
		s	MULLER, Catherine				
6	6	b	GREMOU, Aggeliki	GRE	8:01.60	33.32	R
		s	BISKITZI, Chrissa				

HEAT 2

Rnk	Ln	Pos	Names	Ctry	Time	Time Behind	Q
1	2	b	LEE, Virginia	AUS	7:33.16	0	D
		s	JOYCE, Rebecca				
2	4	b	DARVILL, Michelle	GER	7:45.52	12.36	R
		s	KAPS, Ruth				
3	3	b	KNEJP, Monika	SWE	7:48.13	14.97	R
		s	KNEJP, Kristina				
4	5	b	MARQUEZ, Esperanza	ESP	7:51.05	17.89	R
		s	DOMINGUEZ, Nuria				
5	1	b	YOSHIDA, Ayako	JPN	7:55.99	22.83	R
		s	SHIBUTA, Noriko				

Lightweight Double Sculls, Women / *Deux rameuses en couple poids léger, Dames*

HEAT 3

Rnk	Ln	Pos	Names	Ctry	Time	Time Behind	Q
1	5	b	BURCICA, Constanta	ROM	7:33.61	0	D
		s	MACOVICIUC, Camelia				
2	4	b	CHRISTOFFERSEN, Berit	DEN	7:36.47	2.86	R
		s	ANDERSSON, Lene				
3	3	b	MILLER, Colleen	CAN	7:41.20	7.59	R
		s	WIEBE, Wendy				
4	2	b	SCHUSTEREDER, Carola	AUT	7:45.45	11.84	R
		s	FELIZETER, Monika				
5	1	b	SOBERANES, Ana Sofi	MEX	8:00.92	27.31	R
		s	BOLTZ, Andrea				

REPECHAGE 1

Rnk	Ln	Pos	Names	Ctry	Time	Time Behind	Q
1	2	b	VERMULST, Laurien	NED	7:00.17	0	D
		s	MELIESIE, Ellen				
2	3	b	DARVILL, Michelle	GER	7:05.29	5.12	D
		s	KAPS, Ruth				
3	4	b	SCHUSTEREDER, Carola	AUT	7:07.34	7.17	D
		s	FELIZETER, Monika				
4	1	b	YOSHIDA, Ayako	JPN	7:15.61	15.44	FC
		s	SHIBUTA, Noriko				
5	5	b	GREMOU, Aggeliki	GRE	7:21.39	21.22	FC
		s	BISKITZI, Chrissa				

REPECHAGE 2

Rnk	Ln	Pos	Names	Ctry	Time	Time Behind	Q
1	2	b	BERTINI, Lisa	ITA	6:59.06	0	D
		s	ORZAN, Martina				
2	3	b	MILLER, Colleen	CAN	7:02.54	3.48	D
		s	WIEBE, Wendy				
3	1	b	LAMOLLE, Myriam	FRA	7:03.27	4.21	D
		s	MULLER, Catherine				
4	4	b	MARQUEZ, Esperanza	ESP	7:12.96	13.90	FC
		s	DOMINGUEZ, Nuria				

REPECHAGE 3

Rnk	Ln	Pos	Names	Ctry	Time	Time Behind	Q
1	3	b	CHRISTOFFERSEN, Berit	DEN	7:03.80	0	D
		s	ANDERSSON, Lene				
2	2	b	KNEJP, Monika	SWE	7:08.68	4.88	D
		s	KNEJP, Kristina				
3	4	b	LI, Fei	CHN	7:10.96	7.16	D
		s	OU, Shaoyan				
4	1	b	SOBERANES, Ana Sofi	MEX	7:18.31	14.51	FC
		s	BOLTZ, Andrea				

SEMIFINAL 1

Rnk	Ln	Pos	Names	Ctry	Time	Time Behind	Q
1	4	b	BELL, Teresa Z.	USA	7:09.47	0	FA
		s	BURNS, Lindsay				
2	3	b	BURCICA, Constanta	ROM	7:11.13	1.66	FA
		s	MACOVICIUC, Camelia				
3	2	b	BERTINI, Lisa	ITA	7:15.29	5.82	FA
		s	ORZAN, Martina				
4	5	b	DARVILL, Michelle	GER	7:19.69	10.22	FB
		s	KAPS, Ruth				
5	6	b	LAMOLLE, Myriam	FRA	7:20.11	10.64	FB
		s	MULLER, Catherine				
6	1	b	KNEJP, Monika	SWE	7:27.01	17.54	FB
		s	KNEJP, Kristina				

SEMIFINAL 2

Rnk	Ln	Pos	Names	Ctry	Time	Time Behind	Q
1	3	b	JOYCE, Rebecca	AUS	7:17.67	0	FA
		s	LEE, Virginia				
2	4	b	VERMULST, Laurien	NED	7:19.02	1.35	FA
		s	MELIESIE, Ellen				
3	5	b	CHRISTOFFERSEN, Berit	DEN	7:19.79	2.12	FA
		s	ANDERSSON, Lene				
4	6	b	LI, Fei	CHN	7:23.46	5.79	FB
		s	OU, Shaoyan				
5	2	b	MILLER, Colleen	CAN	7:27.19	9.52	FB
		s	WIEBE, Wendy				
6	1	b	SCHUSTEREDER, Carola	AUT	7:32.07	14.40	FB
		s	FELIZETER, Monika				

FINAL C

Rnk	Ln	Pos	Names	Ctry	Time	Time Behind
1	2	b	YOSHIDA, Ayako	JPN	7:44.81	0
		s	SHIBUTA, Noriko			
2	1	b	SOBERANES, Ana Sofi	MEX	7:46.57	1.76
		s	BOLTZ, Andrea			
3	4	b	GREMOU, Aggeliki	GRE	7:51.80	6.99
		s	BISKITZI, Chrissa			
4	3	b	MARQUEZ, Esperanza	ESP	7:55.84	11.03
		s	ACCENSI, Anna			

FINAL B

Rnk	Ln	Pos	Names	Ctry	Time	Time Behind
1	2*	b	MILLER, Colleen	CAN	7:03.87	0
		s	WIEBE, Wendy			
2	3*	b	DARVILL, Michelle	GER	7:04.31	0.44
		s	KAPS, Ruth			
3	4	b	LI, Fei	CHN	7:07.81	3.94
		s	OU, Shaoyan			
4	5	b	LAMOLLE, Myriam	FRA	7:09.95	6.08
		s	MULLER, Catherine			
5	6	b	SCHUSTEREDER, Carola	AUT	7:11.22	7.35
		s	FELIZETER, Monika			
6	1	b	KNEJP, Monika	SWE	7:12.03	8.16
		s	KNEJP, Kristina			

FINAL A

Rnk	Ln	Pos	Names	Ctry	Time	Time Behind	
1	2	b	BURCICA, Constanta	ROM	7:12.78	0	Gold
		s	MACOVICIUC, Camelia				
2	4	b	BELL, Teresa Z.	USA	7:14.65	1.87	Silver
		s	BURNS, Lindsay				
3	3	b	JOYCE, Rebecca	AUS	7:16.56	3.78	Bronze
		s	LEE, Virginia				
4	1	b	BERTINI, Lisa	ITA	7:16.83	4.05	
		s	ORZAN, Martina				
5	6	b	CHRISTOFFERSEN, Berit	DEN	7:18.20	5.42	
		s	ANDERSSON, Lene				
6	5	b	VERMULST, Laurien	NED	7:21.92	9.14	
		s	MELIESIE, Ellen				

Rowing / *Aviron*

Quadruple Sculls, Men / *Quatre rameurs en couple sans barreur, Messieurs*

HEAT 1

Rnk	Ln	Pos	Names	Ctry	Time	Time Behind	Q
1	3	b	HOOKER, Janusz	AUS	6:05.60	0	D
		2	FREE, Duncan				
		3	SNOOK, Ronald				
		s	HANSON, Boden				
2	1	b	van der MARCK, Sander	NED	6:06.98	1.38	D
		2	MIDDAG, Adri				
		3	LOEFS, Joris				
		s	van ANDEL, Pieter				
3	2	b	BELEVICH, Konstantin	BLR	6:08.38	2.78	D
		2	TARASEVICH, Sergey				
		3	SOLOMAKHIN, Oleg				
		s	TABAKO, Denis				
4	5	b	LAMARQUE, Yves	FRA	6:12.69	7.09	R
		2	LEPVRAUD, Vincent				
		3	VIEILLEDENT, Sebastien				
		s	LECLERC, Fabrice				
5	4	b	NOWICKI, Jaroslaw	POL	6:52.62	47.02	R
		2	LEWANDOWSKI, Przemyslaw				
		3	KOLBOWICZ, Marek				
		s	BUJNAROWSKI, Piotr				

HEAT 2

Rnk	Ln	Pos	Names	Ctry	Time	Time Behind	Q
1	3	b	PARADISO, Massimo	ITA	6:05.75	0	D
		2	CORONA, Alessandro				
		3	GALTAROSSA, Rossano				
		s	SARTORI, Alessio				
2	4	b	YOUNG, Tim	USA	6:06.95	1.20	D
		2	JAMIESON, Brian				
		3	MUELLER, Eric				
		s	GAILES, Jason				
3	2	b	KRAVTSOV, Igor	RUS	6:10.62	4.87	D
		2	SPINEV, Nikolay				
		3	NIKITIN, Georgiy				
		s	SOKOLOV, Vladimir				
4	5	b	PAGES, Carlos	ARG	6:16.16	10.41	R
		2	FERNANDEZ, Santiago				
		3	KNULST, Ruben				
		s	PFAAB, Guillermo				
5	1	b	COSTA, Andre	BRA	6:36.60	30.85	R
		2	VALENTINA, Giovani				
		3	KUSTER, Oswaldo				
		s	SOARES, Alexandre				

HEAT 3

Rnk	Ln	Pos	Names	Ctry	Time	Time Behind	Q
1	2	b	STEINER, Andre	GER	6:06.33	0	D
		2	VOLKERT, Stephan				
		3	HAJEK, Andreas				
		s	WILLMS, Andre				
2	3	b	BENGUEREL, Rene	SUI	6:08.37	2.04	D
		2	ERDLEN, Michael				
		3	BODENMANN, Ulrich				
		s	STURM, Simon				
3	4	b	FLODIN, Johan	SWE	6:10.39	4.06	D
		2	EK, Pontus				
		3	HULTEN, Fredrik				
		s	NILSSON, Henrik				
4	1	b	MARCHENKO, Oleksandr	UKR	6:13.04	6.71	R
		2	ZASKALKO, Oleksandr				
		3	CHUPRYNA, Mykola				
		s	SHAPOSHNIKOV, Leonid				

REPECHAGE 1

Rnk	Ln	Pos	Names	Ctry	Time	Time Behind	Q
1	1	b	NOWICKI, Jaroslaw	POL	5:51.15	0	D
		2	LEWANDOWSKI, Przemyslaw				
		3	KOLBOWICZ, Marek				
		s	BUJNAROWSKI, Piotr				
2	2	b	MARCHENKO, Oleksandr	UKR	5:51.51	0.36	D
		2	ZASKALKO, Oleksandr				
		3	CHUPRYNA, Mykola				
		s	SHAPOSHNIKOV, Leonid				
3	3	b	LAMARQUE, Yves	FRA	5:51.82	0.67	D
		2	LEPVRAUD, Vincent				
		3	VIEILLEDENT, Sebastien				
		s	LECLERC, Fabrice				
4	4	b	PAGES, Carlos	ARG	5:52.89	1.74	
		2	FERNANDEZ, Santiago				
		3	KNULST, Ruben				
		s	PFAAB, Guillermo				
5	5	b	COSTA, Andre	BRA	6:12.86	21.71	
		2	VALENTINA, Giovani				
		3	KUSTER, Oswaldo				
		s	SOARES, Alexandre				

Quadruple Sculls, Men / *Quatre rameurs en couple sans barreur, Messieurs*

SEMIFINAL 1

Rnk	Ln	Pos	Names	Ctry	Time	Time Behind	Q
1	4	b	PARADISO, Massimo	ITA	5:57.10	0	FA
		2	SARTORI, Alessio				
		3	GALTAROSSA, Rossano				
		s	CORONA, Alessandro				
2	3	b	HOOKER, Janusz	AUS	5:58.41	1.31	FA
		2	FREE, Duncan				
		3	SNOOK, Ronald				
		s	HANSON, Boden				
3	2	b	STUERM, Simon	SUI	5:59.63	2.53	FA
		2	BODENMANN, Ueli				
		3	ERDLEN, Michael				
		s	BENGUEREL, Rene				
4	5	b	SPINEV, Nikolay	RUS	5:59.91	2.81	FB
		2	KRAVTSOV, Igor				
		3	NIKITIN, Georgiy				
		s	SOKOLOV, Vladimir				
5	6	b	LAMARQUE, Yves	FRA	6:03.74	6.64	FB
		2	LEPVRAUD, Vincent				
		3	VIEILLEDENT, Sebastien				
		s	LECLERC, Fabrice				
6	1	b	BELEVICH, Konstantin	BLR	6:15.07	17.97	FB
		2	TARASEVICH, Sergey				
		3	SOLOMAKHIN, Oleg				
		s	TABAKO, Denis				

SEMIFINAL 2

Rnk	Ln	Pos	Names	Ctry	Time	Time Behind	Q
1	3	b	STEINER, Andre	GER	5:55.10	0	FA
		2	VOLKERT, Stephan				
		3	HAJEK, Andreas				
		s	WILLMS, Andre				
2	4	b	YOUNG, Tim	USA	5:57.97	2.87	FA
		2	JAMIESON, Brian				
		3	MUELLER, Eric				
		s	GAILES, Jason				
3	5	b	FLODIN, Johan	SWE	6:00.09	4.99	FA
		2	EK, Pontus				
		3	HULTEN, Fredrik				
		s	NILSSON, Henrik				
4	2	b	van der MARCK, Sander	NED	6:03.72	8.62	FB
		2	MIDDAG, Adri				
		3	LOEFS, Joris				
		s	van ANDEL, Pieter				
5	1	b	MARCHENKO, Oleksandr	UKR	6:05.65	10.55	FB
		2	ZASKALKO, Oleksandr				
		3	CHUPRYNA, Mykola				
		s	SHAPOSHNIKOV, Leonid				
6	6	b	NOWICKI, Jaroslaw	POL	6:11.62	16.52	FB
		2	LEWANDOWSKI, Przemyslaw				
		3	KOLBOWICZ, Marek				
		s	BUJNAROWSKI, Piotr				

FINAL B

Rnk	Ln	Pos	Names	Ctry	Time	Time Behind
1	2	b	MARCHENKO, Oleksandr	UKR	5:53.46	0
		2	ZASKALKO, Oleksandr			
		3	CHUPRYNA, Mykola			
		s	SHAPOSHNIKOV, Leonid			
2	4	b	SPINEV, Nikolay	RUS	5:54.98	1.52
		2	KRAVTSOV, Igor			
		3	NIKITIN, Georgiy			
		s	SOKOLOV, Vladimir			
3	6	b	NOWICKI, Jaroslaw	POL	5:55.10	1.64
		2	LEWANDOWSKI, Przemyslaw			
		3	KOLBOWICZ, Marek			
		s	BUJNAROWSKI, Piotr			
4	3	b	van der MARCK, Sander	NED	5:55.15	1.69
		2	MIDDAG, Adri			
		3	LOEFS, Joris			
		s	van ANDEL, Pieter			
5	1	b	TABAKO, Denis	BLR	5:55.52	2.06
		2	BELEVICH, Konstantin			
		3	KINYAKIN, Sergey			
		s	SOLOMAKHIN, Oleg			
6	5	b	LAMARQUE, Yves	FRA	6:00.48	7.02
		2	LEPVRAUD, Vincent			
		3	VIEILLEDENT, Sebastien			
		s	LECLERC, Fabrice			

FINAL A

Rnk	Ln	Pos	Names	Ctry	Time	Time Behind	
1	4	b	STEINER, Andre	GER	5:56.93	0	Gold
		2	HAJEK, Andreas				
		3	VOLKERT, Stephan				
		s	WILLMS, Andre				
2	2	b	YOUNG, Tim	USA	5:59.10	2.17	Silver
		2	JAMIESON, Brian				
		3	MUELLER, Eric				
		s	GAILES, Jason				
3	5	b	HOOKER, Janusz	AUS	6:01.65	4.72	Bronze
		2	FREE, Duncan				
		3	SNOOK, Ronald				
		s	HANSON, Boden				
4	3	b	PARADISO, Massimo	ITA	6:02.12	5.19	
		2	SARTORI, Alessio				
		3	GALTAROSSA, Rossano				
		s	CORONA, Alessandro				
5	1	b	BENGUEREL, Rene	SUI	6:04.52	7.59	
		2	ERDLEN, Michael				
		3	BODENMANN, Ueli				
		s	STUERM, Simon				
6	6	b	FLODIN, Johan	SWE	6:07.75	10.82	
		2	EK, Pontus				
		3	HULTEN, Fredrik				
		s	NILSSON, Henrik				

Rowing / *Aviron*

Quadruple Sculls, Women / *Quatre rameuses en couple sans barreuse, Dames*

HEAT 1

Rnk	Ln	Pos	Names	Ctry	Time	Time Behind	Q
1	3	b	BIESENTHAL, Laryssa	CAN	6:39.32	0	FA
		2	McBEAN, Marnie				
		3	O'GRADY, Diane				
		s	HEDDLE, Kathleen				
2	4	b	EIJS, Irene	NED	6:43.76	4.44	R
		2	van DRIEL, Meike				
		3	PENNINX, Nelleke				
		s	van NES, Eeke				
3	5	b	CAO, Mianying	CHN	6:46.00	6.68	R
		2	ZHANG, Xiuyun				
		3	LIU, Xirong				
		s	GU, Xiaoli				
4	1	b	ROBINSON, Jane	AUS	6:48.58	9.26	R
		2	NEWMARCH, Sally				
		3	HATZAKIS, Marina				
		s	ROYE, Bronwyn				
5	2	b	TAMAS, Angela	ROM	6:50.93	11.61	R
		2	SUSANU, Viorica				
		3	BULIE, Iulia				
		s	ROBU, Doina				

HEAT 2

Rnk	Ln	Pos	Names	Ctry	Time	Time Behind	Q
1	4	b	SORGERS, Jana	GER	6:36.00	0	FA
		2	RUTSCHOW, Katrin				
		3	BORON, Kathrin				
		s	KOEPPEN, Kerstin				
2	2	b	BOGDANOVA, Margarita	RUS	6:37.59	1.59	R
		2	FEDOTOVA, Irina				
		3	MERK, Larisa				
		s	DORODNOVA, Oksana				
3	1	b	PORS, Inger	DEN	6:38.25	2.25	R
		2	HANSEN, Ulla				
		3	LAURITZEN, Sarah				
		s	PEDERSEN, Dorthe				
4	3	b	RONZHINA, Olena	UKR	6:46.17	10.17	R
		2	FROLOVA, Inna				
		3	MAZIY, Svitlana				
		s	MIFTAKHUTDINOVA, Diana				
5	5	b	THIES, Andrea	USA	6:54.73	18.73	R
		2	CHILICKI, Julia				
		3	SYMON, Catherine				
		s	TUCKER, Cecile				

REPECHAGE 1

Rnk	Ln	Pos	Names	Ctry	Time	Time Behind	Q
1	3	b	PORS, Inger	DEN	6:15.45	0	FA
		2	HANSEN, Ulla				
		3	LAURITZEN, Sarah				
		s	PEDERSEN, Dorthe				
2	2	b	EIJS, Irene	NED	6:15.92	0.47	FA
		2	van DRIEL, Meike				
		3	PENNINX, Nelleke				
		s	van NES, Eeke				
3	1	b	ROBINSON, Jane	AUS	6:16.85	1.40	FB
		2	NEWMARCH, Sally				
		3	HATZAKIS, Marina				
		s	ROYE, Bronwyn				
4	4	b	THIES, Andrea	USA	6:25.54	10.09	FB
		2	TUCKER, Cecile				
		3	SYMON, Catherine				
		s	CHILICKI, Julia				

REPECHAGE 2

Rnk	Ln	Pos	Names	Ctry	Time	Time Behind	Q
1	1	b	RONZHINA, Olena	UKR	6:19.11	0	FA
		2	FROLOVA, Inna				
		3	MAZIY, Svitlana				
		s	MYFTAKHUTDOVINA, Dina				
2	2	b	CAO, Mianying	CHN	6:21.23	2.12	FA
		2	ZHANG, Xiuyun				
		3	LIU, Xirong				
		s	GU, Xiaoli				
3	4	b	TAMAS, Angela	ROM	6:26.27	7.16	FB
		2	SUSANU, Viorica				
		3	BULIE, Iulia				
		s	ROBU, Doina				
4	3	b	BOGDANOVA, Margarita	RUS	0:00.00		FB
		2	FEDOTOVA, Irina				
		3	MERK, Larisa				
		s	DORODNOVA, Oksana				

FINAL B

Rnk	Ln	Pos	Names	Ctry	Time	Time Behind	
1	1*	b	FEDOTOVA, Irina	RUS	6:24.10	0	
		2	DORODNOVA, Oksana				
		3	MERK, Larisa				
		s	BOGDANOVA, Margarita				
2	4	b	THIES, Andrea	USA	6:24.49	0.39	
		2	TUCKER, Cecile				
		3	SYMON, Catherine				
		s	CHILICKI, Julia				
3	2	b	NEWMARCH, Sally	AUS	6:25.73	1.63	
		2	ROBINSON, Jane				
		3	HATZAKIS, Marina				
		s	ROYE, Bronwyn				
4	3	b	TAMAS, Angela	ROM	6:31.35	7.25	
		2	SUSANU, Viorica				
		3	BULIE, Iulia				
		s	ROBU, Doina				

FINAL A

Rnk	Ln	Pos	Names	Ctry	Time	Time Behind	
1	4	b	SORGERS, Jana	GER	6:27.44	0	Gold
		2	RUTSCHOW, Katrin				
		3	BORON, Kathrin				
		s	KOEPPEN, Kerstin				
2	2	b	RONZHINA, Olena	UKR	6:30.36	2.92	Silver
		2	FROLOVA, Inna				
		3	MAZIY, Svitlana				
		s	MYFTAKHUTDOVINA, Dina				
3	3	b	BIESENTHAL, Laryssa	CAN	6:30.38	2.94	Bronze
		2	McBEAN, Marnie				
		3	O'GRADY, Diane				
		s	HEDDLE, Kathleen				
4	5	b	PORS, Inger	DEN	6:30.92	3.48	
		2	HANSEN, Ulla				
		3	LAURITZEN, Sarah				
		s	PEDERSEN, Dorthe				
5	1	b	CAO, Mianying	CHN	6:31.10	3.66	
		2	ZHANG, Xiuyun				
		3	LIU, Xirong				
		s	GU, Xiaoli				
6	6	b	EIJS, Irene	NED	6:35.54	8.10	
		2	van DRIEL, Meike				
		3	PENNINX, Nelleke				
		s	van NES, Eeke				

HEAT 1

Rnk	Ln	Pos	Names	Ctry	Time	Time Behind	Q
1	4	b	ANDRIEUX, Michel	FRA	6:35.75	0	D
		s	ROLLAND, Jean-Christophe				
2	3	b	PENNA, Marco	ITA	6:39.34	3.59	R
		s	BOTTEGA, Walter				
3	6	b	SCHAPER, David	NZL	6:42.15	6.40	R
		s	DUNLOP, Toni				
4	5	b	GOIRIS, Luc	BEL	6:43.83	8.08	R
		s	van DRIESSCHE, Jaak				
5	2	b	BAGDONAS, Juozas	LTU	6:45.92	10.17	R
		s	PETKUS, Einius				
6	1	b	NADER, Andreas	AUT	6:46.18	10.43	R
		s	BAUER, Hermann				

HEAT 2

Rnk	Ln	Pos	Names	Ctry	Time	Time Behind	Q
1	3	b	REDGRAVE, Steven	GBR	6:50.04	0	D
		s	PINSENT, Matthew				
2	4	b	BANOVIC, Marko	CRO	6:54.05	4.01	R
		s	SARAGA, Ninoslav				
3	2	b	PALAVECINO, Carlos	ARG	6:56.03	5.99	R
		s	BALUNEK, Walter				
4	5	b	UNGEMACH, Matthias	GER	6:57.78	7.74	R
		s	ETTINGSHAUSEN, Colin				
5	6	b	van IWAARDEN, George	NED	7:00.45	10.41	R
		s	COMPAGNER, Kai				
6	1	b	BAYNE, Gregory	RSA	7:01.05	11.01	R
		s	CALLIE, John				

HEAT 3

Rnk	Ln	Pos	Names	Ctry	Time	Time Behind	Q
1	3	b	WEIGHTMAN, David	AUS	6:46.12	0	D
		s	SCOTT, Robert				
2	4	b	PETERSON, Michael	USA	6:53.95	7.83	R
		s	HOLLAND, Jonathan				
3	2	b	NINOV, Orlin	BUL	6:56.09	9.97	R
		s	KOLEV, Nikolay				
4	6	b	PLECHISTIK, Dmitriy	BLR	6:57.57	11.45	R
		s	MIRONCHIK, Dmitriy				
5	5	b	RACZ, Attila	ROM	6:57.77	11.65	R
		s	SPIRCU, Nicolae				
6	1	b	KODAMA, Takeshi	JPN	7:06.56	20.44	R
		s	KURATA, Kazuhiko				

REPECHAGE 1

Rnk	Ln	Pos	Names	Ctry	Time	Time Behind	Q
1	3	b	PENNA, Marco	ITA	7:10.25	0	D
		s	BOTTEGA, Walter				
2	5	b	BAGDONAS, Juozas	LTU	7:10.47	0.22	D
		s	PETKUS, Einius				
3	2	b	PALAVECINO, Carlos	ARG	7:10.57	0.32	D
		s	BALUNEK, Walter				
4	1	b	BAYNE, Gregory	RSA	7:11.14	0.89	FC
		s	CALLIE, John				
5	4	b	PLECHISTIK, Dmitriy	BLR	7:12.14	1.89	FC
		s	MIRONCHIK, Dmitriy				

REPECHAGE 2

Rnk	Ln	Pos	Names	Ctry	Time	Time Behind	Q
1	3	b	BANOVIC, Marko	CRO	7:05.81	0	D
		s	SARAGA, Ninoslav				
2	2	b	GOIRIS, Luc	BEL	7:06.76	0.95	D
		s	van DRIESSCHE, Jaak				
3	4	b	NINOV, Orlin	BUL	7:13.48	7.67	D
		s	KOLEV, Nikolay				
4	1	b	van IWAARDEN, George	NED	7:24.17	18.36	FC
		s	COMPAGNER, Kai				
5	5	b	KODAMA, Takeshi	JPN	7:36.68	30.87	FC
		s	KURATA, Kazuhiko				

REPECHAGE 3

Rnk	Ln	Pos	Names	Ctry	Time	Time Behind	Q
1	3	b	PETERSON, Michael	USA	7:02.13	0	D
		s	HOLLAND, Jonathan				
2	1	b	NADER, Andreas	AUT	7:03.86	1.73	D
		s	BAUER, Hermann				
3	4	b	SCHAPER, David	NZL	7:04.40	2.27	D
		s	DUNLOP, Toni				
4	5	b	RACZ, Attila	ROM	7:07.96	5.83	FC
		s	SPIRCU, Nicolae				
5	2	b	UNGEMACH, Matthias	GER	7:11.67	9.54	FC
		s	ETTINGSHAUSEN, Colin				

SEMIFINAL 1

Rnk	Ln	Pos	Names	Ctry	Time	Time Behind	Q
1	4	b	WEIGHTMAN, David	AUS	6:46.43	0	FA
		s	SCOTT, Robert				
2	3	b	ANDRIEUX, Michel	FRA	6:49.15	2.72	FA
		s	ROLLAND, Jean-Christophe				
3	2	b	BANOVIC, Marko	CRO	6:55.89	9.46	FA
		s	SARAGA, Ninoslav				
4	6	b	NADER, Andreas	AUT	6:57.44	11.01	FB
		s	BAUER, Hermann				
5	5	b	BAGDONAS, Juozas	LTU	6:57.75	11.32	FB
		s	PETKUS, Einius				
6	1	b	NINOV, Orlin	BUL	7:00.12	13.69	FB
		s	KOLEV, Nikolay				

SEMIFINAL 2

Rnk	Ln	Pos	Names	Ctry	Time	Time Behind	Q
1	4	b	REDGRAVE, Steven	GBR	6:50.30	0	FA
		s	PINSENT, Matthew				
2	1	b	DUNLOP, Toni	NZL	6:51.64	1.34	FA
		s	SCHAPER, David				
3	3	b	PENNA, Marco	ITA	6:52.32	2.02	FA
		s	BOTTEGA, Walter				
4	2	b	PETERSON, Michael	USA	6:52.92	2.62	FB
		s	HOLLAND, Jonathan				
5	5	b	GOIRIS, Luc	BEL	6:55.84	5.54	FB
		s	van DRIESSCHE, Jaak				
6	6	b	PALAVECINO, Carlos	ARG	7:14.59	24.29	FB
		s	BALUNEK, Walter				

Coxless Pair, Men / *Deux rameurs en pointe sans barreur, Messieurs*

FINAL C

Rnk	Ln	Pos	Names	Ctry	Time	Time Behind
1	4	b	RACZ, Attila	ROM	7:01.94	0
		s	SPIRCU, Nicolae			
2	6	b	PLECHISTIK, Dmitriy	BLR	7:03.31	1.37
		s	MIRONCHIK, Dmitriy			
3	1	b	UNGEMACH, Matthias	GER	7:06.88	4.94
		s	ETTINGSHAUSEN, Colin			
4	3	b	BAYNE, Gregory	RSA	7:09.91	7.97
		s	CALLIE, John			
5	2	b	van IWAARDEN, George	NED	7:10.43	8.49
		s	COMPAGNER, Kai			
6	5	b	KODAMA, Takeshi	JPN	7:21.31	19.37
		s	KURATA, Kazuhiko			

FINAL B

Rnk	Ln	Pos	Names	Ctry	Time	Time Behind
1	4	b	PETERSON, Michael	USA	6:33.81	0
		s	HOLLAND, Jonathan			
2	2	b	GOIRIS, Luc	BEL	6:34.46	0.65
		s	van DRIESSCHE, Jaak			
3	6	b	NINOV, Orlin	BUL	6:35.71	1.90
		s	KOLEV, Nikolay			
4	5	b	BAGDONAS, Juozas	LTU	6:38.12	4.31
		s	PETKUS, Einius			
5	3	b	NADER, Andreas	AUT	6:38.60	4.79
		s	BAUER, Hermann			
6	1	b	PALAVECINO, Carlos	ARG	6:49.34	15.53
		s	BALUNEK, Walter			

FINAL A

Rnk	Ln	Pos	Names	Ctry	Time	Time Behind	
1	4	b	REDGRAVE, Steven	GBR	6:20.09	0	**Gold**
		s	PINSENT, Matthew				
2	3	b	WEIGHTMAN, David	AUS	6:21.02	0.93	**Silver**
		s	SCOTT, Robert				
3	2	b	ANDRIEUX, Michel	FRA	6:22.15	2.06	**Bronze**
		s	ROLLAND, Jean-Christophe				
4	1	b	PENNA, Marco	ITA	6:28.61	8.52	
		s	BOTTEGA, Walter				
5	5	b	DUNLOP, Toni	NZL	6:29.24	9.15	
		s	SCHAPER, David				
6	6	b	BANOVIC, Marko	CRO	6:30.48	10.39	
		s	SARAGA, Ninoslav				

Rowing / *Aviron*

Coxless Pair, Women / *Deux rameuses en pointe sans barreuse, Dames*

HEAT 1

Rnk	Ln	Pos	Names	Ctry	Time	Time Behind	Q
1	4	b	STILL, Megan	AUS	7:26.92	0	D
		s	SLATTER, Kate				
2	3	b	HAACKER, Katherin	GER	7:28.65	1.73	D
		s	WERREMEIER, Stefani				
3	2	b	MEIJER, Elien	NED	7:43.58	16.66	D
		s	VENEMA, Anneke				
4	5	b	FLEMING, Helen	RSA	7:48.69	21.77	R
		s	ORSMOND, Colleen				
5	1	b	CORENGIA, Lorena	ARG	8:12.58	45.66	R
		s	RAMIREZ, Julieta				

HEAT 2

Rnk	Ln	Pos	Names	Ctry	Time	Time Behind	Q
1	3	b	GOSSE, Christine	FRA	7:31.91	0	D
		s	CORTIN, Helene				
2	2	b	LIGACHOVA, Albina	RUS	7:42.76	10.85	D
		s	POCHITAYEVA, Vera				
3	1	b	CAZAC, Liliana	ROM	7:49.94	18.03	D
		s	CAZAC, Angela				
4	4	b	MACKENZIE, Kate	GBR	8:03.53	31.62	R
		s	CROSS, Philippa				

HEAT 3

Rnk	Ln	Pos	Names	Ctry	Time	Time Behind	Q
1	2	b	KRAFT, Karen	USA	7:34.29	0	D
		s	SCHWEN, Missy				
2	3	b	ROBINSON, Emma	CAN	7:38.98	4.69	D
		s	van der KAMP, Anna				
3	4	b	LIANG, Xiling	CHN	7:46.80	12.51	D
		s	JING, Yanhua				
4	1	b	TELENSKA, Sabina	CZE	7:54.72	20.43	R
		s	DARIUSOVA, Hana				

REPECHAGE 1

Rnk	Ln	Pos	Names	Ctry	Time	Time Behind	Q
1	2	b	TELENSKA, Sabina	CZE	8:01.50	0	D
		s	DARIUSOVA, Hana				
2	3	b	FLEMING, Helen	RSA	8:11.90	10.40	D
		s	ORSMOND, Colleen				
3	1	b	MACKENZIE, Kate	GBR	8:15.26	13.76	D
		s	CROSS, Philippa				
4	4	b	CORENGIA, Lorena	ARG	8:35.53	34.03	
		s	RAMIREZ, Julieta				

Coxless Pair, Women / *Deux rameuses en pointe sans barreuse, Dames*

SEMIFINAL 1

Rnk	Ln	Pos	Names	Ctry	Time	Time Behind	Q
1	4	b	SCHWEN, Missy	USA	7:29.31	0	FA
		s	KRAFT, Karen				
2	3	b	STILL, Megan	AUS	7:32.47	3.16	FA
		s	SLATTER, Kate				
3	5	b	LIGACHOVA, Albina	RUS	7:36.37	7.06	FA
		s	POCHITAYEVA, Vera				
4	6	b	LIANG, Xiling	CHN	7:36.40	7.09	FB
		s	JING, Yanhua				
5	2	b	MEIJER, Elien	NED	7:48.40	19.09	FB
		s	VENEMA, Anneke				
6	1	b	FLEMING, Helen	RSA	7:56.41	27.10	FB
		s	ORSMOND, Colleen				

SEMIFINAL 2

Rnk	Ln	Pos	Names	Ctry	Time	Time Behind	Q
1	4	b	GOSSE, Christine	FRA	7:30.21	0	FA
		s	CORTIN, Helene				
2	2	b	ROBINSON, Emma	CAN	7:32.02	1.81	FA
		s	van der KAMP, Anna				
3	3	b	HAACKER, Katherin	GER	7:34.80	4.59	FA
		s	WERREMEIER, Stefani				
4	5	b	CAZAC, Liliana	ROM	7:44.47	14.26	FB
		s	CAZAC, Angela				
5	6	b	TELENSKA, Sabina	CZE	7:48.40	18.19	FB
		s	DARIUSOVA, Hana				
6	1	b	MACKENZIE, Kate	GBR	7:59.57	29.36	FB
		s	CROSS, Philippa				

FINAL B

Rnk	Ln	Pos	Names	Ctry	Time	Time Behind
1	4	b	LIANG, Xiling	CHN	7:15.41	0
		s	JING, Yanhua			
2	2	b	MEIJER, Elien	NED	7:17.26	1.85
		s	VENEMA, Anneke			
3	5	b	TELENSKA, Sabina	CZE	7:20.24	4.83
		s	DARIUSOVA, Hana			
4	3	b	CAZAC, Liliana	ROM	7:20.60	5.19
		s	CAZAC, Angela			
5	6	b	FLEMING, Helen	RSA	7:28.30	12.89
		s	ORSMOND, Colleen			
6	1	b	MACKENZIE, Kate	GBR	7:34.68	19.27
		s	CROSS, Philippa			

FINAL A

Rnk	Ln	Pos	Names	Ctry	Time	Time Behind	
1	2	b	STILL, Megan	AUS	7:01.39	0	**Gold**
		s	SLATTER, Kate				
2	4	b	SCHWEN, Missy	USA	7:01.78	0.39	**Silver**
		s	KRAFT, Karen				
3	3	b	GOSSE, Christine	FRA	7:03.82	2.43	**Bronze**
		s	CORTIN, Helene				
4	1	b	HAACKER, Katherin	GER	7:08.49	7.10	
		s	WERREMEIER, Stefani				
5	5	b	ROBINSON, Emma	CAN	7:12.27	10.88	
		s	van der KAMP, Anna				
	6	b	LIGACHOVA, Albina	RUS	DQ		
		s	POCHITAYEVA, Vera				

Rowing / *Aviron*
Coxless Four, Men / *Quatre rameurs en pointe sans barreur, Messieurs*

HEAT 1

Rnk	Ln	Pos	Names	Ctry	Time	Time Behind	Q
1	4	b	MOLEA, Valter	ITA	6:14.25	0	D
		2	dei ROSSI, Riccardo				
		3	LEONARDO, Raffaello				
		s	MORNATI, Carlo				
2	3	b	MARIN, Claudiu	ROM	6:18.03	3.78	D
		2	ALUPEI, Dorin				
		3	POPESCU, Dimitrie				
		s	MASTACAN, Vasile				
3	5	b	SANNES LANDE, Halvor	NOR	6:19.79	5.54	D
		2	BUSTNES, Odd-Even				
		3	TUFTE, Olaf				
		s	BERGESEN, Morten				
4	1	b	FORSTER, Stefan	GER	6:21.98	7.73	R
		2	LANDVOIGT, Ike				
		3	FISCHER, Claas				
		s	SCHOLZ, Stefan				
5	2	b	SCURI, Daniel	ARG	6:33.29	19.04	R
		2	SICILIA, Horacio				
		3	SOSA, Mariano				
		s	KOWALCZYK, Mariano				

HEAT 2

Rnk	Ln	Pos	Names	Ctry	Time	Time Behind	Q
1	4	b	OBHOLZER, Rupert	GBR	6:14.74	0	D
		2	SEARLE, Jonny				
		3	SEARLE, Greg				
		s	FOSTER, Timothy				
2	3	b	SKELIN, Sinisa	CRO	6:17.42	2.68	D
		2	MARUSIC, Sead				
		3	BORASKA, Igor				
		s	FRANKOVIC, Tihomir				
3	1	b	STREICH, Jacek	POL	6:19.15	4.41	D
		2	JANKOWSKI, Wojciech				
		3	OLSZWESKI, Piotr				
		s	BASTA, Piotr				
4	2	b	HALL, M. Sean	USA	6:20.72	5.98	R
		2	SCOTT, Jason				
		3	MURRAY, Tom				
		s	KLEPACKI, Jeff				
5	5	b	HUANG, Xiaoping	CHN	6:30.16	15.42	R
		2	SUN, Jun				
		3	LIANG, Hongming				
		s	LIU, Xianbin				

Coxless Four, Men / *Quatre rameurs en pointe sans barreur, Messieurs*

HEAT 3

Rnk	Ln	Pos	Names	Ctry	Time	Time Behind	Q
1	3	b	GINN, Drew	AUS	6:15.05	0	D
		2	TOMKINS, James				
		3	GREEN, Nicholas				
		s	McKAY, Michael				
2	4	b	ZVEGELJ, Denis	SLO	6:15.86	0.81	D
		2	KLEMENCIC, Jani				
		3	JANSA, Milan				
		s	MUJKIC, Sadik				
3	2	b	BOSQUET, Gilles	FRA	6:18.70	3.65	D
		2	FAUCHE, Daniel				
		3	VECTEN, Bertrand				
		s	MONCELET, Olivier				
4	1	b	MACKINTOSH, Alastair	NZL	6:30.03	14.98	R
		2	WRIGHT, Ian				
		3	WHITE, Christopher				
		s	BROWNLEE, Scott				

REPECHAGE 1

Rnk	Ln	Pos	Names	Ctry	Time	Time Behind	Q
1	3*	b	FORSTER, Stefan	GER	6:29.10	0	D
		2	LANDVOIGT, Ike				
		3	FISCHER, Claas				
		s	SCHOLZ, Stefan				
2	5	b	HUANG, Xiaoping	CHN	6:29.95	0.85	D
		2	SUN, Jun				
		3	LIANG, Hongming				
		s	LIU, Xianbin				
3	4	b	SCOTT, Jason	USA	6:30.95	1.85	D
		2	HALL, M. Sean				
		3	KLEPACKI, Jeff				
		s	MURRAY, Tom				
4	2	b	MACKINTOSH, Alastair	NZL	6:35.58	6.48	
		2	WRIGHT, Ian				
		3	WHITE, Christopher				
		s	BROWNLEE, Scott				
5	1	b	SCURI, Daniel	ARG	6:37.85	8.75	
		2	SICILIA, Horacio				
		3	SOSA, Mariano				
		s	KOWALCZYK, Mariano				

SEMIFINAL 1

Rnk	Ln	Pos	Names	Ctry	Time	Time Behind	Q
1	5	b	BOSQUET, Gilles	FRA	6:09.58	0	FA
		2	FAUCHE, Daniel				
		3	VECTEN, Bertrand				
		s	MONCELET, Olivier				
2	3	b	MOLEA, Valter	ITA	6:09.62	0.04	FA
		2	dei ROSSI, Riccardo				
		3	LEONARDO, Raffaello				
		s	MORNATI, Carlo				
3	4	b	GINN, Drew	AUS	6:09.95	0.37	FA
		2	TOMKINS, James				
		3	GREEN, Nicholas				
		s	McKAY, Michael				
4	2	b	SKELIN, Sinisa	CRO	6:12.40	2.82	FB
		2	MARUSIC, Sead				
		3	BORASKA, Igor				
		s	FRANKOVIC, Tihomir				
5	1	b	SANNES LANDE, Halvor	NOR	6:15.17	5.59	FB
		2	BUSTNES, Odd-Even				
		3	TUFTE, Olaf				
		s	BERGESEN, Morten				
6	6	b	HUANG, Xiaoping	CHN	6:25.79	16.21	FB
		2	SUN, Jun				
		3	LIANG, Hongming				
		s	LIU, Xianbin				

SEMIFINAL 2

Rnk	Ln	Pos	Names	Ctry	Time	Time Behind	Q
1	4	b	OBHOLZER, Rupert	GBR	6:10.78	0	FA
		2	SEARLE, Jonny				
		3	SEARLE, Greg				
		s	FOSTER, Timothy				
2	3	b	MARIN, Claudiu	ROM	6:11.84	1.06	FA
		2	ALUPEI, Dorin				
		3	POPESCU, Dimitrie				
		s	MASTACAN, Vasile				
3	2	b	ZVEGELJ, Denis	SLO	6:13.14	2.36	FA
		2	KLEMENCIC, Jani				
		3	JANSA, Milan				
		s	MUJKIC, Sadik				
4	5	b	OLSZEWSKI, Piotr	POL	6:16.65	5.87	FB
		2	STREICH, Jacek				
		3	JANKOWSKI, Wojciech				
		s	BASTA, Piotr				
5	6	b	SCOTT, Jason	USA	6:18.68	7.90	FB
		2	HALL, M. Sean				
		3	KLEPACKI, Jeff				
		s	MURRAY, Tom				
6	1	b	FORSTER, Stefan	GER	6:19.06	8.28	FB
		2	LANDVOIGT, Ike				
		3	FISCHER, Claas				
		s	SCHOLZ, Stefan				

Coxless Four, Men / *Quatre rameurs en pointe sans barreur, Messieurs*

<table>
<tr><td colspan="7">FINAL B</td><td colspan="8">FINAL A</td></tr>
<tr><th>Rnk</th><th>Ln</th><th>Pos</th><th>Names</th><th>Ctry</th><th>Time</th><th>Time Behind</th><th>Rnk</th><th>Ln</th><th>Pos</th><th>Names</th><th>Ctry</th><th>Time</th><th>Time Behind</th><th></th></tr>
<tr><td>1</td><td>3</td><td>b</td><td>SKELIN, Sinisa</td><td>CRO</td><td>5:54.58</td><td>0</td><td>1</td><td>6</td><td>b</td><td>GINN, Drew</td><td>AUS</td><td>6:06.37</td><td>0</td><td>Gold</td></tr>
<tr><td></td><td></td><td>2</td><td>MARUSIC, Sead</td><td></td><td></td><td></td><td></td><td></td><td>2</td><td>TOMKINS, James</td><td></td><td></td><td></td><td></td></tr>
<tr><td></td><td></td><td>3</td><td>BORASKA, Igor</td><td></td><td></td><td></td><td></td><td></td><td>3</td><td>GREEN, Nicholas</td><td></td><td></td><td></td><td></td></tr>
<tr><td></td><td></td><td>s</td><td>FRANKOVIC, Tihomir</td><td></td><td></td><td></td><td></td><td></td><td>s</td><td>McKAY, Michael</td><td></td><td></td><td></td><td></td></tr>
<tr><td>2</td><td>2</td><td>b</td><td>SANNES LANDE, Halvor</td><td>NOR</td><td>5:55.19</td><td>0.61</td><td>2</td><td>4</td><td>b</td><td>BOSQUET, Gilles</td><td>FRA</td><td>6:07.03</td><td>0.66</td><td>Silver</td></tr>
<tr><td></td><td></td><td>2</td><td>BUSTNES, Odd-Even</td><td></td><td></td><td></td><td></td><td></td><td>2</td><td>FAUCHE, Daniel</td><td></td><td></td><td></td><td></td></tr>
<tr><td></td><td></td><td>3</td><td>TUFTE, Olaf</td><td></td><td></td><td></td><td></td><td></td><td>3</td><td>VECTEN, Bertrand</td><td></td><td></td><td></td><td></td></tr>
<tr><td></td><td></td><td>s</td><td>BERGESEN, Morten</td><td></td><td></td><td></td><td></td><td></td><td>s</td><td>MONCELET, Olivier</td><td></td><td></td><td></td><td></td></tr>
<tr><td>3</td><td>6</td><td>b</td><td>FORSTER, Stefan</td><td>GER</td><td>5:57.77</td><td>3.19</td><td>3</td><td>3</td><td>b</td><td>OBHOLZER, Rupert</td><td>GBR</td><td>6:07.28</td><td>0.91</td><td>Bronze</td></tr>
<tr><td></td><td></td><td>2</td><td>LANDVOIGT, Ike</td><td></td><td></td><td></td><td></td><td></td><td>2</td><td>SEARLE, Jonny</td><td></td><td></td><td></td><td></td></tr>
<tr><td></td><td></td><td>3</td><td>FISCHER, Claas</td><td></td><td></td><td></td><td></td><td></td><td>3</td><td>SEARLE, Greg</td><td></td><td></td><td></td><td></td></tr>
<tr><td></td><td></td><td>s</td><td>SCHOLZ, Stefan</td><td></td><td></td><td></td><td></td><td></td><td>s</td><td>FOSTER, Timothy</td><td></td><td></td><td></td><td></td></tr>
<tr><td>4</td><td>1</td><td>b</td><td>HUANG, Xiaoping</td><td>CHN</td><td>5:58.22</td><td>3.64</td><td>4</td><td>1</td><td>b</td><td>ZVEGELJ, Denis</td><td>SLO</td><td>6:07.87</td><td>1.50</td><td></td></tr>
<tr><td></td><td></td><td>2</td><td>SUN, Jun</td><td></td><td></td><td></td><td></td><td></td><td>2</td><td>KLEMENCIC, Jani</td><td></td><td></td><td></td><td></td></tr>
<tr><td></td><td></td><td>3</td><td>LIANG, Hongming</td><td></td><td></td><td></td><td></td><td></td><td>3</td><td>JANSA, Milan</td><td></td><td></td><td></td><td></td></tr>
<tr><td></td><td></td><td>s</td><td>LIU, Xianbin</td><td></td><td></td><td></td><td></td><td></td><td>s</td><td>MUJKIC, Sadik</td><td></td><td></td><td></td><td></td></tr>
<tr><td>5</td><td>5</td><td>b</td><td>SCOTT, Jason</td><td>USA</td><td>5:59.91</td><td>5.33</td><td>5</td><td>5</td><td>b</td><td>MARIN, Claudiu</td><td>ROM</td><td>6:08.97</td><td>2.60</td><td></td></tr>
<tr><td></td><td></td><td>2</td><td>HALL, M. Sean</td><td></td><td></td><td></td><td></td><td></td><td>2</td><td>ALUPEI, Dorin</td><td></td><td></td><td></td><td></td></tr>
<tr><td></td><td></td><td>3</td><td>KLEPACKI, Jeff</td><td></td><td></td><td></td><td></td><td></td><td>3</td><td>POPESCU, Dimitrie</td><td></td><td></td><td></td><td></td></tr>
<tr><td></td><td></td><td>s</td><td>MURRAY, Tom</td><td></td><td></td><td></td><td></td><td></td><td>s</td><td>MASTACAN, Vasile</td><td></td><td></td><td></td><td></td></tr>
<tr><td>6</td><td>4</td><td>b</td><td>OLSZEWSKI, Piotr</td><td>POL</td><td>6:00.57</td><td>5.99</td><td>6</td><td>2</td><td>b</td><td>MOLEA, Valter</td><td>ITA</td><td>6:10.60</td><td>4.23</td><td></td></tr>
<tr><td></td><td></td><td>2</td><td>STREICH, Jacek</td><td></td><td></td><td></td><td></td><td></td><td>2</td><td>dei ROSSI, Riccardo</td><td></td><td></td><td></td><td></td></tr>
<tr><td></td><td></td><td>3</td><td>JANKOWSKI, Wojciech</td><td></td><td></td><td></td><td></td><td></td><td>3</td><td>LEONARDO, Raffaello</td><td></td><td></td><td></td><td></td></tr>
<tr><td></td><td></td><td>s</td><td>BASTA, Piotr</td><td></td><td></td><td></td><td></td><td></td><td>s</td><td>MORNATI, Carlo</td><td></td><td></td><td></td><td></td></tr>
</table>

Rowing / *Aviron*

Lightweight Coxless Four, Men / *Quatre rameurs en pointe sans barreur poids léger, Messieurs*

<table>
<tr><td colspan="8">HEAT 1</td><td colspan="8">HEAT 2</td></tr>
<tr><th>Rnk</th><th>Ln</th><th>Pos</th><th>Names</th><th>Ctry</th><th>Time</th><th>Time Behind</th><th>Q</th><th>Rnk</th><th>Ln</th><th>Pos</th><th>Names</th><th>Ctry</th><th>Time</th><th>Time Behind</th><th>Q</th></tr>
<tr><td>1</td><td>3</td><td>b</td><td>HENRIKSEN, Niels</td><td>DEN</td><td>6:20.13</td><td>0</td><td>D</td><td>1</td><td>4</td><td>b</td><td>LAY, Jeffrey</td><td>CAN</td><td>6:18.55</td><td>0</td><td>D</td></tr>
<tr><td></td><td></td><td>2</td><td>POULSEN, Thomas</td><td></td><td></td><td></td><td></td><td></td><td></td><td>2</td><td>BOYES, David</td><td></td><td></td><td></td><td></td></tr>
<tr><td></td><td></td><td>3</td><td>EBBESEN, Eskild</td><td></td><td></td><td></td><td></td><td></td><td></td><td>3</td><td>HASSETT, Gavin</td><td></td><td></td><td></td><td></td></tr>
<tr><td></td><td></td><td>s</td><td>FEDDERSEN, Victor</td><td></td><td></td><td></td><td></td><td></td><td></td><td>s</td><td>PEAKER, Brian</td><td></td><td></td><td></td><td></td></tr>
<tr><td>2</td><td>4</td><td>b</td><td>HOLLAND, Derek</td><td>IRL</td><td>6:23.82</td><td>3.69</td><td>R</td><td>2</td><td>2</td><td>b</td><td>PFAENDTNER, Jeff</td><td>USA</td><td>6:21.85</td><td>3.30</td><td>R</td></tr>
<tr><td></td><td></td><td>2</td><td>LYNCH, Samuel</td><td></td><td></td><td></td><td></td><td></td><td></td><td>2</td><td>COLLINS, David</td><td></td><td></td><td></td><td></td></tr>
<tr><td></td><td></td><td>3</td><td>MAXWELL, Neville</td><td></td><td></td><td></td><td></td><td></td><td></td><td>3</td><td>SCHNEIDER, Marc</td><td></td><td></td><td></td><td></td></tr>
<tr><td></td><td></td><td>s</td><td>O'CONNOR, Anthony</td><td></td><td></td><td></td><td></td><td></td><td></td><td>s</td><td>CARLUCCI, William</td><td></td><td></td><td></td><td></td></tr>
<tr><td>3</td><td>6</td><td>b</td><td>KARRASCH, Haimish</td><td>AUS</td><td>6:25.87</td><td>5.74</td><td>R</td><td>3</td><td>3</td><td>b</td><td>MITYUSHEV, Vladimir</td><td>RUS</td><td>6:26.39</td><td>7.84</td><td>R</td></tr>
<tr><td></td><td></td><td>2</td><td>BELCHER, David</td><td></td><td></td><td></td><td></td><td></td><td></td><td>2</td><td>USTINOV, Aleksandr</td><td></td><td></td><td></td><td></td></tr>
<tr><td></td><td></td><td>3</td><td>LYNAGH, Gary</td><td></td><td></td><td></td><td></td><td></td><td></td><td>3</td><td>CHEVEL, Andrey</td><td></td><td></td><td></td><td></td></tr>
<tr><td></td><td></td><td>s</td><td>BURGESS, Simon</td><td></td><td></td><td></td><td></td><td></td><td></td><td>s</td><td>KARTASHOV, Dmitriy</td><td></td><td></td><td></td><td></td></tr>
<tr><td>4</td><td>5</td><td>b</td><td>PETTINARI, Leonardo</td><td>ITA</td><td>6:26.80</td><td>6.67</td><td>R</td><td>4</td><td>6</td><td>b</td><td>CLIMENT, Fernando</td><td>ESP</td><td>6:28.05</td><td>9.50</td><td>R</td></tr>
<tr><td></td><td></td><td>2</td><td>ZASIO, Ivano</td><td></td><td></td><td></td><td></td><td></td><td></td><td>2</td><td>MORALES, David</td><td></td><td></td><td></td><td></td></tr>
<tr><td></td><td></td><td>3</td><td>GADDI, Carlo</td><td></td><td></td><td></td><td></td><td></td><td></td><td>3</td><td>FLORIDO, Juan Manuel</td><td></td><td></td><td></td><td></td></tr>
<tr><td></td><td></td><td>s</td><td>RE, Andrea</td><td></td><td></td><td></td><td></td><td></td><td></td><td>s</td><td>GIRON, Alfredo</td><td></td><td></td><td></td><td></td></tr>
<tr><td>5</td><td>1</td><td>b</td><td>LEMON, David</td><td>GBR</td><td>6:35.95</td><td>15.82</td><td>R</td><td>5</td><td>1</td><td>b</td><td>NAKAMIZO, Katsuhiko</td><td>JPN</td><td>6:30.16</td><td>11.61</td><td>R</td></tr>
<tr><td></td><td></td><td>2</td><td>McNIVEN, James</td><td></td><td></td><td></td><td></td><td></td><td></td><td>2</td><td>TANABE, Yasunori</td><td></td><td></td><td></td><td></td></tr>
<tr><td></td><td></td><td>3</td><td>KAY, Thomas</td><td></td><td></td><td></td><td></td><td></td><td></td><td>3</td><td>IWAGURO, Michinori</td><td></td><td></td><td></td><td></td></tr>
<tr><td></td><td></td><td>s</td><td>HELM, Benjamin</td><td></td><td></td><td></td><td></td><td></td><td></td><td>s</td><td>MIMOTO, Kazuaki</td><td></td><td></td><td></td><td></td></tr>
<tr><td>6</td><td>2</td><td>b</td><td>LEGUIZAMON, Hernan</td><td>ARG</td><td>6:43.58</td><td>23.45</td><td>R</td><td>6</td><td>5</td><td>b</td><td>AGUIAR, Samuel</td><td>POR</td><td>7:37.13</td><td>1:18.58</td><td>R</td></tr>
<tr><td></td><td></td><td>2</td><td>ENRIQUEZ, Jorge</td><td></td><td></td><td></td><td></td><td></td><td></td><td>2</td><td>FERNANDES, Joao</td><td></td><td></td><td></td><td></td></tr>
<tr><td></td><td></td><td>3</td><td>QUERIN, Federico</td><td></td><td></td><td></td><td></td><td></td><td></td><td>3</td><td>BAIXINHO, Henrique</td><td></td><td></td><td></td><td></td></tr>
<tr><td></td><td></td><td>s</td><td>SCORTIQUINI, Gabriel</td><td></td><td></td><td></td><td></td><td></td><td></td><td>s</td><td>FERNANDES, Manuel</td><td></td><td></td><td></td><td></td></tr>
</table>

Lightweight Coxless Four, Men / *Quatre rameurs en pointe sans barreur poids léger, Messieurs*

HEAT 3

Rnk	Ln	Pos	Names	Ctry	Time	Time Behind	Q
1	5	b	COSTA, Gareth	RSA	6:19.98	0	D
		2	ROWAND, Mark				
		3	TOBLER, Roger				
		s	HASSELBACH, Michael				
2	3	b	ROSE, Tobias	GER	6:22.97	2.99	R
		2	WEIS, Martin				
		3	BUCHHEIT, Michael				
		s	STOMPOROWSKI, Bernhard				
3	4	b	KOBAU, Martin	AUT	6:24.59	4.61	R
		2	HOFMANN, Harald				
		3	SCHMOELZER, Christoph				
		s	FAEDERBAUER, Gernot				
4	1	b	KERN, Nicolai	SUI	6:26.50	6.52	R
		2	FEUSI, Markus				
		3	BINDER, Mathias				
		s	BANNINGER, Michael				
5	2	b	BARRE, Stephane	FRA	6:26.84	6.86	R
		2	DORFMANN, Xavier				
		3	GUERINOT, Stephane				
		s	DALL'ACQUA, Henri-Pierre				

REPECHAGE 1

Rnk	Ln	Pos	Names	Ctry	Time	Time Behind	Q
1	3	b	COLLINS, David	USA	5:58.58	0	D
		2	PFAENDTNER, Jeff				
		3	SCHNEIDER, Marc				
		s	CARLUCCI, William				
2	4	b	KARRASCH, Haimish	AUS	6:02.04	3.46	D
		2	LYNAGH, Gary				
		3	BELCHER, David				
		s	BURGESS, Simon				
3	2	b	KERN, Nicolai	SUI	6:04.38	5.80	D
		2	FEUSI, Markus				
		3	BINDER, Mathias				
		s	BANNINGER, Michael				
4	1	b	NAKAMIZO, Katsuhiko	JPN	6:06.77	8.19	FC
		2	TANABE, Yasunori				
		3	IWAGURO, Michinori				
		s	MIMOTO, Kazuaki				
5	5*	b	LEGUIZAMON, Hernan	ARG	6:09.86	11.28	FC
		2	ENRIQUEZ, Jorge				
		3	QUERIN, Federico				
		s	SCORTIQUINI, Gabriel				

REPECHAGE 2

Rnk	Ln	Pos	Names	Ctry	Time	Time Behind	Q
1	2	b	HOLLAND, Derek	IRL	6:00.99	0	D
		2	LYNCH, Samuel				
		3	MAXWELL, Neville				
		s	O'CONNOR, Anthony				
2	1	b	LEMON, David	GBR	6:02.65	1.66	D
		2	McNIVEN, James				
		3	KAY, Thomas				
		s	HELM, Benjaman				
3	3	b	KOBAU, Martin	AUT	6:02.76	1.77	D
		2	HOFMANN, Harald				
		3	SCHMOELZER, Christoph				
		s	FAEDERBAUER, Gernot				
4	4	b	CLIMENT, Fernando	ESP	6:03.33	2.34	FC
		2	MORALES, David				
		3	FLORIDO, Juan Manuel				
		s	GIRON, Alfredo				

REPECHAGE 3

Rnk	Ln	Pos	Names	Ctry	Time	Time Behind	Q
1	3	b	ROSE, Tobias	GER	5:58.90	0	D
		2	WEIS, Martin				
		3	BUCHHEIT, Michael				
		s	STOMPOROWSKI, Bernhard				
2	4	b	PETTINARI, Leonardo	ITA	5:59.67	0.77	D
		2	ZASIO, Ivano				
		3	GADDI, Carlo				
		s	RE, Andrea				
3	1	b	BARRE, Stephane	FRA	5:59.95	1.05	D
		2	DORFMANN, Xavier				
		3	GUERINOT, Stephane				
		s	DALL'ACQUA, Henri-Pierre				
4	2	b	MITYUSHEV, Vladimir	RUS	6:00.03	1.13	FC
		2	USTINOV, Aleksandr				
		3	CHEVEL, Andrey				
		s	KARTASHOV, Dmitriy				
5	5	b	AGUIAR, Samuel	POR	6:15.82	16.92	FC
		2	FERNANDES, Joao				
		3	BAIXINHO, Henrique				
		s	FERNANDES, Manuel				

Lightweight Coxless Four, Men / *Quatre rameurs en pointe sans barreur poids léger, Messieurs*

SEMIFINAL 1

Rnk	Ln	Pos	Names	Ctry	Time	Time Behind	Q
1	4	b	HENRIKSEN, Niels	DEN	6:13.21	0	FA
		2	POULSEN, Thomas				
		3	EBBESEN, Eskild				
		s	FEDDERSEN, Victor				
2	1	b	KARRASCH, Haimish	AUS	6:15.47	2.26	FA
		2	LYNAGH, Gary				
		3	BELCHER, David				
		s	BURGESS, Simon				
3	5	b	HOLLAND, Derek	IRL	6:15.66	2.45	FA
		2	LYNCH, Samuel				
		3	MAXWELL, Neville				
		s	O'CONNOR, Anthony				
4	3	b	TOBLER, Roger	RSA	6:16.65	3.44	FB
		2	ROWAND, Mark				
		3	COSTA, Gareth				
		s	HASSELBACH, Michael				
5	2	b	RE, Andrea	ITA	6:17.84	4.63	FB
		2	PETTINARI, Leonardo				
		3	ZASIO, Ivano				
		s	GADDI, Carlo				
6	6	b	KOBAU, Martin	AUT	6:22.60	9.39	FB
		2	HOFMANN, Harald				
		3	SCHMOELZER, Christoph				
		s	FAEDERBAUER, Gernot				

SEMIFINAL 2

Rnk	Ln	Pos	Names	Ctry	Time	Time Behind	Q
1	4	b	COLLINS, David	USA	6:09.89	0	FA
		2	PFAENDTNER, Jeff				
		3	SCHNEIDER, Marc				
		s	CARLUCCI, William				
2	3	b	LAY, Jeffrey	CAN	6:10.38	0.49	FA
		2	BOYES, David				
		3	HASSETT, Gavin				
		s	PEAKER, Brian				
3	2	b	ROSE, Tobias	GER	6:12.73	2.84	FA
		2	WEIS, Martin				
		3	BUCHHEIT, Michael				
		s	STOMPOROWSKI, Bernhard				
4	6	b	BARRE, Stephane	FRA	6:15.75	5.86	FB
		2	DORFMANN, Xavier				
		3	GUERINOT, Stephane				
		s	DALL'ACQUA, Henri-Pierre				
5	5	b	LEMON, David	GBR	6:19.07	9.18	FB
		2	McNIVEN, James				
		3	KAY, Thomas				
		s	HELM, Benjaman				
6	1	b	BAENNINGER, Michael	SUI	6:20.98	11.09	FB
		2	BINDER, Mathias				
		3	FEUSI, Markus				
		s	KERN, Nicolai				

FINAL C

Rnk	Ln	Pos	Names	Ctry	Time	Time Behind
1	4	b	USTINOV, Aleksandr	RUS	6:23.59	0
		2	KARTASHOV, Dmitriy			
		3	CHEVEL, Andrey			
		s	MITYUSHEV, Vladimir			
2	2	b	CLIMENT, Fernando	ESP	6:25.81	2.22
		2	MORALES, David			
		3	FLORIDO, Juan Manuel			
		s	GIRON, Alfredo			
3	1	b	AGUIAR, Samuel	POR	6:27.07	3.48
		2	FERNANDES, Joao			
		3	BAIXINHO, Henrique			
		s	FERNANDES, Manuel			
4	3	b	NAKAMIZO, Katsuhiko	JPN	6:28.60	5.01
		2	TANABE, Yasunori			
		3	IWAGURO, Michinori			
		s	MIMOTO, Kazuaki			
5	5	b	LEGUIZAMON, Hernan	ARG	6:30.64	7.05
		2	ENRIQUEZ, Jorge			
		3	QUERIN, Federico			
		s	SCORTIQUINI, Gabriel			

FINAL B

Rnk	Ln	Pos	Names	Ctry	Time	Time Behind
1	4	b	BARRE, Stephane	FRA	6:02.39	0
		2	DORFMANN, Xavier			
		3	GUERINOT, Stephane			
		s	DALL'ACQUA, Henri-Pierre			
2	5	b	RE, Andrea	ITA	6:03.25	0.86
		2	PETTINARI, Leonardo			
		3	ZASIO, Ivano			
		s	GADDI, Carlo			
3	3	b	TOBLER, Roger	RSA	6:04.13	1.74
		2	ROWAND, Mark			
		3	COSTA, Gareth			
		s	HASSELBACH, Michael			
4	2	b	LEMON, David	GBR	6:05.13	2.74
		2	McNIVEN, James			
		3	KAY, Thomas			
		s	HELM, Benjaman			
5	6	b	BAENNINGER, Michael	SUI	6:05.92	3.53
		2	BINDER, Mathias			
		3	FEUSI, Markus			
		s	KERN, Nicolai			
6	1	b	KOBAU, Martin	AUT	6:06.09	3.70
		2	HOFMANN, Harald			
		3	SCHMOELZER, Christoph			
		s	FAEDERBAUER, Gernot			

Lightweight Coxless Four, Men   /   *Quatre rameurs en pointe sans barreur poids léger, Messieurs*

FINAL A

Rnk	Ln	Pos	Names	Ctry	Time	Time Behind	
1	3	b	HENRIKSEN, Niels	DEN	6:09.58	0	Gold
		2	POULSEN, Thomas				
		3	EBBESEN, Eskild				
		s	FEDDERSEN, Victor				
2	5	b	LAY, Jeffrey	CAN	6:10.13	0.55	Silver
		2	BOYES, David				
		3	HASSETT, Gavin				
		s	PEAKER, Brian				
3	4	b	COLLINS, David	USA	6:12.29	2.71	Bronze
		2	PFAENDTNER, Jeff				
		3	SCHNEIDER, Marc				
		s	CARLUCCI, William				

FINAL A - *continued*

Rnk	Ln	Pos	Names	Ctry	Time	Time Behind
4	6	b	HOLLAND, Derek	IRL	6:13.51	3.93
		2	LYNCH, Samuel			
		3	MAXWELL, Neville			
		s	O'CONNOR, Anthony			
5	1	b	ROSE, Tobias	GER	6:14.79	5.21
		2	WEIS, Martin			
		3	BUCHHEIT, Michael			
		s	STOMPOROWSKI, Bernhard			
6	2	b	KARRASCH, Haimish	AUS	6:18.16	8.58
		2	LYNAGH, Gary			
		3	BELCHER, David			
		s	BURGESS, Simon			

Rowing / *Aviron*

Eight, Men   /   *Huit, Messieurs*

HEAT 1

Rnk	Ln	Pos	Names	Ctry	Time	Time Behind	Q
1	3	b	ZWOLLE, Henk-Jan	NED	5:41.41	0	FA
		2	SIMON, Diederik				
		3	BARTMAN, Michiel				
		4	MAASDIJK, Koos				
		5	van der ZWAN, Niels				
		6	van STEENIS, Niels				
		7	FLORIJN, Ronald				
		s	RIENKS, Nico				
		c	DUYSTER, Jeroen				
2	4	b	STEVENSON, Gregory	CAN	5:44.00	2.59	R
		2	GRAHAM, Philip				
		3	HERING, Henry				
		4	PLATT, Mark				
		5	BARBER, Darren				
		6	CROSBY, Andrew				
		7	BRODIE, Scott				
		s	PARFITT, Adam				
		c	NEWMAN, Patrick				
3	5	b	STEWART, James	AUS	5:46.83	5.42	R
		2	STEWART, Geoffrey				
		3	JAHRLING, Robert				
		4	PORZIG, Nicholas				
		5	FERNANDEZ, Jaime				
		6	DODWELL, Benjamin				
		7	WALKER, Robert				
		s	WEARNE, Richard				
		c	HAYMAN, Brett				
4	1	b	PARISH, Matthew	GBR	5:49.37	7.96	R
		2	WALKER, James				
		3	STORY, Alex				
		4	HAMILTON, Richard				
		5	BROWN, Roger				
		6	BRIDGE, Peter				
		7	HUNT-DAVIS, Benjaman				
		s	SMITH, Graham				
		c	HERBERT, Garry				
5	2	b	SHARONIN, Yevhen	UKR	5:55.32	13.91	R
		2	GRYNEVYCH, Roman				
		3	RAYEVSKYY, Vitaliy				
		4	SAMARA, Valeriy				
		5	LYKOV, Oleh				
		6	MARTYNENKO, Ihor				
		7	MOHYLNYY, Ihor				
		s	KAPUSTIN, Oleksandr				
		c	DMYTRENKO, Hryhoriy				

HEAT 2

Rnk	Ln	Pos	Names	Ctry	Time	Time Behind	Q
1	3	b	BURDEN, Doug	USA	5:44.87	0	FA
		2	KAEHLER, Bob				
		3	COLLINS, Porter				
		4	MURPHY, Edward				
		5	KOVEN, Jamie				
		6	BROWN, Jonathan				
		7	SMITH, Donald				
		s	HONEBEIN, Fred				
		c	SEGALOFF, Steven				
2	5	b	HUHN, Wolfram	GER	5:46.04	1.17	R
		2	KLEINSCHMIDT, Mark				
		3	KIRCHHOFF, Detlef				
		4	WEBER, Marc				
		5	RICHTER, Frank				
		6	STREPPELHOFF, Thorsten				
		7	VIEFERS, Ulrich				
		s	BAAR, Roland				
		c	THIEDE, Peter				
3	1	b	MATVEYEV, Sergey	RUS	5:48.63	3.76	R
		2	GLUKHOV, Andrey				
		3	ROZINKEVICH, Dmitriy				
		4	SOKOLOV, Vladimir				
		5	AKSYONOV, Nikolay				
		6	MONCHENKO, Roman				
		7	MELNIKOV, Pavel				
		s	CHERMASHENTSEV, Anton				
		c	LUKYANOV, Aleksandr				
4	4	b	MARIN, Claudiu	ROM	5:54.34	9.47	R
		2	BANICA, Andrei				
		3	NEMTOC, Cornel				
		4	ALUPEI, Dorin				
		5	TALAPAN, Viorel				
		6	TAGA, Neculai				
		7	ROBU, Valentin				
		s	RUICAN, Iulica				
		c	GHEORGHE, Marin				
5	2	b	ABBAGNALE, Carmine	ITA	5:54.59	9.72	R
		2	CASANOVA, Patrick				
		3	MATTEI, Francesco				
		4	BLANDA, Roberto				
		5	CARBONCINI, Lorenzo				
		6	TROMBETTA, Mattia				
		7	LA MURA, Roby				
		s	ZUCCHI, Franco				
		c	di PALMA, Vincenzo				

Eight, Men / *Huit, Messieurs*

REPECHAGE 1

Rnk	Ln	Pos	Names	Ctry	Time	Time Behind	Q
1	3	b	STEVENSON, Gregory	CAN	5:30.76	0	FA
		2	GRAHAM, Philip				
		3	HERING, Henry				
		4	PLATT, Mark				
		5	BARBER, Darren				
		6	CROSBY, Andrew				
		7	BRODIE, Scott				
		s	PARFITT, Adam				
		c	NEWMAN, Patrick				
2	2	b	MATVEYEV, Sergey	RUS	5:32.98	2.22	FA
		2	GLUKHOV, Andrey				
		3	ROZINKEVICH, Dmitriy				
		4	AKSYONOV, Nikolay				
		5	MONCHENKO, Roman				
		6	MELNIKOV, Pavel				
		7	CHERMASHENTSEV, Anton				
		s	VOLODENKOV, Vladimir				
		c	LUKYANOV, Aleksandr				
3	1	b	PARISH, Matthew	GBR	5:33.22	2.46	FB
		2	SMITH, Graham				
		3	STORY, Alex				
		4	BRIDGE, Peter				
		5	HUNT-DAVIS, Benjaman				
		6	WALKER, James				
		7	BROWN, Roger				
		s	HAMILTON, Richard				
		c	HERBERT, Garry				
4	4	b	ABBAGNALE, Carmine	ITA	5:34.40	3.64	FB
		2	CASANOVA, Patrick				
		3	MATTEI, Francesco				
		4	BLANDA, Roberto				
		5	CARBONCINI, Lorenzo				
		6	TROMBETTA, Mattia				
		7	LA MURA, Roby				
		s	ZUCCHI, Franco				
		c	di PALMA, Vincenzo				

REPECHAGE 2

Rnk	Ln	Pos	Names	Ctry	Time	Time Behind	Q
1	2	b	HUHN, Wolfram	GER	5:30.61	0	FA
		2	KLEINSCHMIDT, Mark				
		3	KIRCHHOFF, Detlef				
		4	WEBER, Marc				
		5	RICHTER, Frank				
		6	STREPPELHOFF, Thorsten				
		7	VIEFERS, Ulrich				
		s	BAAR, Roland				
		c	THIEDE, Peter				
2	3	b	STEWART, James	AUS	5:31.33	0.72	FA
		2	STEWART, Geoffrey				
		3	JAHRLING, Robert				
		4	PORZIG, Nicholas				
		5	FERNANDEZ, Jaime				
		6	DODWELL, Benjamin				
		7	WALKER, Robert				
		s	WEARNE, Richard				
		c	HAYMAN, Brett				
3	1	b	MARIN, Claudiu	ROM	5:31.88	1.27	FB
		2	BANICA, Andrei				
		3	NEMTOC, Cornel				
		4	ALUPEI, Dorin				
		5	TALAPAN, Viorel				
		6	TAGA, Neculai				
		7	ROBU, Valentin				
		s	RUICAN, Iulica				
		c	GHEORGHE, Marin				
4	4	b	SHARONIN, Yevhen	UKR	5:42.43	11.82	FB
		2	KAPUSTIN, Oleksandr				
		3	RAYEVSKYY, Vitaliy				
		4	SAMARA, Valeriy				
		5	LYKOV, Oleh				
		6	MARTYNENKO, Ihor				
		7	MOHYLNYY, Ihor				
		s	GRYNEVYCH, Roman				
		c	DMYTRENKO, Hryhoriy				

FINAL B

Rnk	Ln	Pos	Names	Ctry	Time	Time Behind
1	2	b	MARIN, Claudiu	ROM	5:37.65	0
		2	BANICA, Andrei			
		3	NEMTOC, Cornel			
		4	ALUPEI, Dorin			
		5	TALAPAN, Viorel			
		6	TAGA, Neculai			
		7	ROBU, Valentin			
		s	RUICAN, Iulica			
		c	GHEORGHE, Marin			
2	3	b	PARISH, Matthew	GBR	5:40.23	2.58
		2	SMITH, Graham			
		3	STORY, Alexander			
		4	BRIDGE, Peter			
		5	HUNT-DAVIS, Benjaman			
		6	WALKER, James			
		7	BROWN, Roger			
		s	HAMILTON, Richard			
		c	HERBERT, Garry			

FINAL B - *continued*

Rnk	Ln	Pos	Names	Ctry	Time	Time Behind
3	4	b	ABBAGNALE, Carmine	ITA	5:41.95	4.30
		2	CASANOVA, Patrick			
		3	MATTEI, Francesco			
		4	BLANDA, Roberto			
		5	CARBONCINI, Lorenzo			
		6	TROMBETTA, Mattia			
		7	LA MURA, Roby			
		s	ZUCCHI, Franco			
		c	di PALMA, Vincenzo			
4	1	b	SHARONIN, Yevhen	UKR	5:44.89	7.24
		2	KAPUSTIN, Oleksandr			
		3	RAYEVSKYY, Vitaliy			
		4	SAMARA, Valeriy			
		5	LYKOV, Oleh			
		6	MARTYNENKO, Ihor			
		7	MOHYLNYY, Ihor			
		s	GRYNEVYCH, Roman			
		c	DMYTRENKO, Hryhoriy			

Eight, Men / *Huit, Messieurs*

Rnk	Ln	Pos	Names	Ctry	Time	Time Behind	
1	3	b	ZWOLLE, Henk-Jan	NED	5:42.74	0	Gold
		2	SIMON, Diederik				
		3	BARTMAN, Michiel				
		4	MAASDIJK, Koos				
		5	van der ZWAN, Niels				
		6	van STEENIS, Niels				
		7	FLORIJN, Ronald				
		s	RIENKS, Nico				
		c	DUYSTER, Jeroen				
2	2	b	RICHTER, Frank	GER	5:44.58	1.84	Silver
		2	KLEINSCHMIDT, Mark				
		3	HUHN, Wolfram				
		4	WEBER, Marc				
		5	KIRCHHOFF, Detlef				
		6	STREPPELHOFF, Thorsten				
		7	VIEFERS, Ulrich				
		s	BAAR, Roland				
		c	THIEDE, Peter				
3	1	b	CHERMASHENTSEV, Anton	RUS	5:45.77	3.03	Bronze
		2	GLUKHOV, Andrey				
		3	ROZINKEVICH, Dmitriy				
		4	VOLODENKOV, Vladimir				
		5	AKSYONOV, Nikolay				
		6	MONCHENKO, Roman				
		7	MELNIKOV, Pavel				
		s	MATVEYEV, Sergey				
		c	LUKYANOV, Aleksandr				

Rnk	Ln	Pos	Names	Ctry	Time	Time Behind
4	5	b	STEVENSON, Gregory	CAN	5:46.54	3.80
		2	GRAHAM, Philip			
		3	HERING, Henry			
		4	PLATT, Mark			
		5	BARBER, Darren			
		6	CROSBY, Andrew			
		7	BRODIE, Scott			
		s	PARFITT, Adam			
		c	NEWMAN, Patrick			
5	4	b	BURDEN, Doug	USA	5:48.45	5.71
		2	KAEHLER, Bob			
		3	COLLINS, Porter			
		4	MURPHY, Edward			
		5	KOVEN, Jamie			
		6	BROWN, Jonathan			
		7	SMITH, Donald			
		s	HONEBEIN, Fred			
		c	SEGALOFF, Steven			
6	6	b	STEWART, James	AUS	5:58.82	16.08
		2	STEWART, Geoffrey			
		3	JAHRLING, Robert			
		4	PORZIG, Nicholas			
		5	FERNANDEZ, Jaime			
		6	DODWELL, Benjamin			
		7	WALKER, Robert			
		s	WEARNE, Richard			
		c	HAYMAN, Brett			

Rowing / *Aviron*

Eight, Women / *Huit, Dames*

Rnk	Ln	Pos	Names	Ctry	Time	Time Behind	Q
1	1	b	LAVRINENKO, Natalya	BLR	6:24.61	0	FA
		2	PANKINA, Aleksandra				
		3	VOLCHEK, Natalya				
		4	DAVYDENKO, Tamara				
		5	SKRABATUN, Valentina				
		6	MIKULICH, Yelena				
		7	STASYUK, Natalya				
		s	ZNAK, Marina				
		c	PAVLOVICH, Yaroslava				
2	3	b	KAKELA, Anne	USA	6:28.45	3.84	R
		2	McCAGG, Mary				
		3	KORHOLZ, Laurel				
		4	FALLON, Catriona				
		5	McCAGG, Betsy				
		6	TRANEL MICHINI, Monica				
		7	FULLER, Amy				
		s	DORE, Jennifer				
		c	FAROOQ, Yasmin				

Rnk	Ln	Pos	Names	Ctry	Time	Time Behind	Q
3	2	b	BOELEN, Femke	NED	6:32.71	8.10	R
		2	van der VELDEN, Marleen				
		3	van KOERT, Astrid				
		4	WESTERHOF, Marieke				
		5	de JONG, Rita				
		6	KNAVEN, Tessa				
		7	APPELDOORN, Tessa				
		s	van SCHILFGAARDE, Muriel				
		c	de WOLF, Jissy				
4	4	b	LUFF, Jennifer	AUS	6:35.69	11.08	R
		2	DOUGLAS, Georgina				
		3	SAFE, Amy				
		4	OZOLINS, Anna				
		5	WIELAND, Karina				
		6	DAVIES, Alison				
		7	KLOMP, Carmen				
		s	THOMPSON, Bronwyn				
		c	HICK, Kaylynn				

Eight, Women / *Huit, Dames*

HEAT 2

Rnk	Ln	Pos	Names	Ctry	Time	Time Behind	Q
1	2	b	TANASE, Anca	ROM	6:23.94	0	FA
		2	COCHELEA, Vera				
		3	GAFENCU, Liliana				
		4	SPIRCU, Doina				
		5	OLTEANU, Ioana				
		6	LIPA, Elisabeta				
		7	POPESCU, Marioara				
		s	IGNAT, Doina				
		c	GEORGESCU, Elena				
2	3	b	McDERMID, Heather	CAN	6:29.08	5.14	R
		2	TSANG, Tosha				
		3	MAUNDER, Maria				
		4	KORN, Alison				
		5	ROBINSON, Emma				
		6	van der KAMP, Anna				
		7	MONROE, Jessica				
		s	LUKE, Theresa				
		c	THOMPSON, Lesley				

HEAT 2 - *continued*

Rnk	Ln	Pos	Names	Ctry	Time	Time Behind	Q
3	1	b	JUSTH, Ina	GER	6:33.90	9.96	R
		2	REHAAG, Antje				
		3	NASER, Kathleen				
		4	GESCH, Andrea				
		5	PYRITZ, Dana				
		6	SCHMIDT, Micaela				
		7	PYRITZ, Anja				
		s	SCHELL, Ute				
		c	NEUNAST, Daniela				
4	4	b	STAPLETON, Annamarie	GBR	6:39.34	15.40	R
		2	EYRE, Lisa				
		3	BLACKIE, Dot				
		4	POLLITT, Kate				
		5	BATTEN, Miriam				
		6	BISHOP, Catherine				
		7	TURVEY, Jo				
		s	GILL, Alison				
		c	ELLIS, Suzie				

REPECHAGE 1

Rnk	Ln	Pos	Names	Ctry	Time	Time Behind	Q
1	3	b	KAKELA, Anne	USA	6:06.17	0	FA
		2	McCAGG, Mary				
		3	KORHOLZ, Laurel				
		4	FALLON, Catriona				
		5	McCAGG, Betsy				
		6	TRANEL MICHINI, Monica				
		7	FULLER, Amy				
		s	DORE, Jennifer				
		c	FAROOQ, Yasmin				
2	4	b	McDERMID, Heather	CAN	6:06.49	0.32	FA
		2	TSANG, Tosha				
		3	MAUNDER, Maria				
		4	KORN, Alison				
		5	ROBINSON, Emma				
		6	van der KAMP, Anna				
		7	MONROE, Jessica				
		s	LUKE, Theresa				
		c	THOMPSON, Lesley				
3	5	b	van KOERT, Astrid	NED	6:08.85	2.68	FA
		2	BOELEN, Femke				
		3	van der VELDEN, Marleen				
		4	WESTERHOF, Marieke				
		5	de JONG, Rita				
		6	KNAVEN, Tessa				
		7	APPELDOORN, Tessa				
		s	van SCHILFGAARDE, Muriel				
		c	de WOLF, Jissy				

REPECHAGE 1 - *continued*

Rnk	Ln	Pos	Names	Ctry	Time	Time Behind	Q
4	1	b	LUFF, Jennifer	AUS	6:08.92	2.75	FA
		2	DOUGLAS, Georgina				
		3	SAFE, Amy				
		4	OZOLINS, Anna				
		5	WIELAND, Karina				
		6	DAVIES, Alison				
		7	KLOMP, Carmen				
		s	THOMPSON, Bronwyn				
		c	HICK, Kaylynn				
5	2	b	JUSTH, Ina	GER	6:09.43	3.26	FB
		2	REHAAG, Antje				
		3	NASER, Kathleen				
		4	GESCH, Andrea				
		5	PYRITZ, Dana				
		6	SCHMIDT, Micaela				
		7	PYRITZ, Anja				
		s	SCHELL, Ute				
		c	NEUNAST, Daniela				
6	6	b	STAPLETON, Annamarie	GBR	6:12.28	6.11	FB
		2	EYRE, Lisa				
		3	BLACKIE, Dot				
		4	POLLITT, Kate				
		5	BATTEN, Miriam				
		6	BISHOP, Catherine				
		7	TURVEY, Jo				
		s	GILL, Alison				
		c	ELLIS, Suzie				

FINAL B

Rnk	Ln	Pos	Names	Ctry	Time	Time Behind
1	1	b	STAPLETON, Annamarie	GBR	6:15.21	0
		2	EYRE, Lisa			
		3	BLACKIE, Dorothy			
		4	POLLITT, Katerine			
		5	BATTEN, Miriam			
		6	BISHOP, Catherine			
		7	TURVEY, Joanne			
		s	GILL, Alison			
		c	ELLIS, Suzie			

FINAL B - *continued*

Rnk	Ln	Pos	Names	Ctry	Time	Time Behind
2	2	b	JUSTH, Ina	GER	6:17.73	2.52
		2	REHAAG, Antje			
		3	NASER, Kathleen			
		4	GESCH, Andrea			
		5	PYRITZ, Dana			
		6	SCHMIDT, Micaela			
		7	PYRITZ, Anja			
		s	SCHELL, Ute			
		c	NEUNAST, Daniela			

Eight, Women / *Huit, Dames*

FINAL A

Rnk	Ln	Pos	Names	Ctry	Time	Time Behind	
1	3	b	TANASE, Anca	ROM	6:19.73	0	Gold
		2	COCHELEA, Vera				
		3	GAFENCU, Liliana				
		4	SPIRCU, Doina				
		5	OLTEANU, Ioana				
		6	LIPA, Elisabeta				
		7	POPESCU, Marioara				
		s	IGNAT, Doina				
		c	GEORGESCU, Elena				
2	2	b	McDERMID, Heather	CAN	6:24.05	4.32	Silver
		2	TSANG, Tosha				
		3	MAUNDER, Maria				
		4	KORN, Alison				
		5	ROBINSON, Emma				
		6	van der KAMP, Anna				
		7	MONROE, Jessica				
		s	LUKE, Theresa				
		c	THOMPSON, Lesley				
3	4	b	LAVRINENKO, Natalya	BLR	6:24.44	4.71	Bronze
		2	PANKINA, Aleksandra				
		3	VOLCHEK, Natalya				
		4	DAVYDENKO, Tamara				
		5	SKRABATUN, Valentina				
		6	MIKULICH, Yelena				
		7	STASYUK, Natalya				
		s	ZNAK, Marina				
		c	PAVLOVICH, Yaroslava				

FINAL A - *continued*

Rnk	Ln	Pos	Names	Ctry	Time	Time Behind
4	5	b	KAKELA, Anne	USA	6:26.19	6.46
		2	McCAGG, Mary			
		3	KORHOLZ, Laurel			
		4	FALLON, Catriona			
		5	McCAGG, Betsy			
		6	TRANEL MICHINI, Monica			
		7	FULLER, Amy			
		s	DORE, Jennifer			
		c	FAROOQ, Yasmin			
5	1	b	LUFF, Jennifer	AUS	6:30.10	10.37
		2	DOUGLAS, Georgina			
		3	SAFE, Amy			
		4	OZOLINS, Anna			
		5	WIELAND, Karina			
		6	DAVIES, Alison			
		7	KLOMP, Carmen			
		s	THOMPSON, Bronwyn			
		c	HICK, Kaylynn			
6	6	b	BOELEN, Femke	NED	6:31.11	11.38
		2	van der VELDEN, Marleen			
		3	van KOERT, Astrid			
		4	WESTERHOF, Marieke			
		5	de JONG, Rita			
		6	KNAVEN, Tessa			
		7	APPELDOORN, Tessa			
		s	van SCHILFGAARDE, Muriel			
		c	de WOLF, Jissy			

SHOOTING
TIR

Abbreviations and terms used in Shooting results tables
Abréviations et termes employés dans les tableaux de résultats de tir

Term	English	Français
1st day	First Day	Premier jour
2nd day	Second Day	Deuxième jour
Bronze	Bronze Medal	Médaille de bronze
Ctry	Country	Pays
f1	Fast 1	Vite 1
f2	Fast 2	Vite 2
f3	Fast 3	Vite 3
Final	Final	Finale
Final Pts	Final Points	Points finaux
Gold	Gold Medal	Médaille d'or
Kneeling	Kneeling	A genou
Name	Name	Nom
O	Olympic Record	Record olympique
p1	Precision 1	Précision 1
p2	Precision 2	Précision 2
p3	Precision 3	Précision 3
Preliminaries	Preliminaries	Eliminatoires
Prone	Prone	Couché
Qual Pts	Qualification Points	Points de qualification
r1	Rapid 1	Rapide 1
r2	Rapid 2	Rapide 2
r3	Rapid 3	Rapide 3
Rnk	Rank	Classement
s1	Slow 1	Lent 1
s2	Slow 2	Lent 2
s3	Slow 3	Lent 3
Silver	Silver Medal	Médaille d'argent
Standing	Standing	Debout
Total	Total	Total
W	World Record	Record du monde

International Shooting Union (UIT)
Union Internationale de Tir
Bavariaring 21
D-80336 Munich
Germany

Shooting / *Tir*

50 m Free Pistol, Men / *Pistolet libre à 50 m, Messieurs*

PRELIMINARIES

Rnk	Name	Ctry	1	2	3	4	5	6	Total
1	KOKOREV, Boris	RUS	97	94	97	96	94	92	570
2	di DONNA, Roberto	ITA	93	93	90	97	98	98	569
2	FAIT, Vigilio	ITA	94	92	94	98	96	95	569
4	BASINSKI, Igor	BLR	94	94	96	94	95	92	565
5	LOUKACHIK, Konstantin	BLR	96	94	95	93	90	96	564
5	TENK, Martin	CZE	95	94	95	94	91	95	564
5	WANG, Yifu	CHN	96	95	94	95	91	93	564
8	AKHMEDOV, Shukhrat	UZB	94	92	94	95	94	94	563
8	PIETRZAK, Jerzy	POL	95	92	92	95	95	94	563
8	SANCHEZ, Sergio	GUA	92	95	89	98	94	95	563
11	DUMOULIN, Franck	FRA	93	91	93	92	94	97	560
11	KIM, Sung-Joon	KOR	94	94	95	91	94	92	560
11	NAKASHIGE, Masaru	JPN	95	95	94	93	91	92	560
11	NOWAK, Marek	POL	92	95	94	92	93	94	560
15	JIRKAL, Stanislav	CZE	93	95	94	95	96	86	559
16	DANILOV, Alexander	RUS	94	96	90	91	91	96	558
16	TOBAR, Bernardo	COL	89	95	87	95	96	96	558
16	TRIPOLSKI, Alex	ISR	89	96	95	94	94	90	558
19	ZAKHARIEV, Kolio	BUL	92	91	94	94	96	90	557
20	BABII, Sorin	ROM	95	90	93	92	94	92	556
20	FABO, Jan	SVK	89	93	94	99	91	90	556
20	KIRIAKOV, Tanu	BUL	99	93	89	92	94	89	556
20	MAKAROV, Viktor	UKR	90	94	92	91	93	96	556
20	MELENTIEV, Yuriy	KGZ	96	94	90	89	92	95	556
25	AMONETTE, Ben	USA	91	95	90	93	95	91	555
25	BLIZNYUCHENKO, Oleksandr	UKR	90	92	93	91	97	92	555
25	SKANAKER, Ragnar	SWE	94	91	94	93	88	95	555
28	FERNANDEZ, Gerard	FRA	95	88	94	90	92	94	553

PRELIMINARIES - continued

Rnk	Name	Ctry	1	2	3	4	5	6	Total
28	PAPANITZ, Zoltan	HUN	95	96	89	91	88	94	553
30	ADAMS, Phillip	AUS	90	90	90	95	94	93	552
30	TARLOIU, Constantin	ROM	90	89	95	91	95	92	552
30	XU, Dan	CHN	91	93	92	89	92	95	552
33	KARACS, Zsolt	HUN	91	92	97	90	90	91	551
34	TU, Tai-Hsing	TPE	91	89	95	93	89	93	550
35	NEUMAIER, Hans-Juergen	GER	96	89	88	92	92	92	549
35	SANDSTROM, Bengt	AUS	94	91	94	91	95	84	549
37	GEVORGIAN, Arthur	GER	93	95	93	88	90	89	548
37	KIM, Sung-Jun	KOR	91	86	91	93	97	90	548
39	CALOIA, Neal	USA	85	93	90	93	92	91	544
40	HEMBRE, Pal	NOR	95	85	95	88	88	91	542
40	KLOMJAI, Surin	THA	94	88	86	92	89	93	542
42	ANDERSSON, Lennart	SWE	92	85	90	90	90	91	538
43	PANICHPATIKUM, Jakkrit	THA	86	87	90	92	90	91	536
44	TRINH QUOC, Viet	VIE	89	85	92	86	92	91	535
45	RANA, Jaspal	IND	93	89	92	88	79	93	534

FINAL

Rnk	Name	Ctry	Qual pts	Final pts	Total		
1	KOKOREV, Boris	RUS	570	96.4	666.4	O	**Gold**
2	BASINSKI, Igor	BLR	565	97.0	662.0		**Silver**
3	di DONNA, Roberto	ITA	569	92.8	661.8		**Bronze**
4	LOUKACHIK, Konstantin	BLR	564	96.1	660.1		
5	FAIT, Vigilio	ITA	569	90.8	659.8		
6	WANG, Yifu	CHN	564	95.3	659.3		
7	TENK, Martin	CZE	564	93.7	657.7		
8	SANCHEZ, Sergio	GUA	563	94.1	657.1		

Shooting / *Tir*

25 m Rapid Fire Pistol, Men / *Pistolet de tir rapide à 25 m, Messieurs*

PRELIMINARIES

Rnk	Name	Ctry	1st day	2nd day	Total	
1	SCHUMANN, Ralf	GER	298	298	596	O
2	MILEV, Emil	BUL	294	296	590	
3	KUCHARCZYK, Krzysztof	POL	292	297	589	
3	VOKHMYANIN, Vladimir	KAZ	293	296	589	
5	MENG, Gang	CHN	291	296	587	
6	IHNATYUK, Myroslav	UKR	295	291	586	
6	LEONHARD, Daniel	GER	293	293	586	
6	LISOCONI, Ghenadie	MDA	295	291	586	
6	PALINKAS, Lajos	HUN	290	296	586	
10	KUZMINS, Afanasijs	LAT	290	295	585	
11	RAICEA, Iulian	ROM	292	292	584	
12	ANSERMET, Michel	SUI	293	290	583	
12	KIDA, Tomohiro	JPN	290	293	583	
12	McNALLY, John	USA	288	295	583	
12	TOBLER, Urs	SUI	290	293	583	
16	CHAUSHEV, Sabin	BUL	286	296	582	
16	SPIRELJA, Roman	CRO	291	291	582	
18	MAR, Roger	USA	292	289	581	
19	ETELANIEMI, Petri	FIN	290	289	579	
20	LAU, Anders	DEN	292	286	578	
21	DUMOULIN, Franck	FRA	285	290	575	
21	MURRAY, Patrick	AUS	285	290	575	
23	TOBAR, Bernardo	COL	279	286	565	

FINAL

Rnk	Name	Ctry	Qual pts	Final pts	Total		
1	SCHUMANN, Ralf	GER	596	102.0	698.0	O	**Gold**
2	MILEV, Emil	BUL	590	102.1	692.1		**Silver**
3	VOKHMYANIN, Vladimir	KAZ	589	102.5	691.5		**Bronze**
4	KUCHARCZYK, Krzysztof	POL	589	101.5	690.5		
5	MENG, Gang	CHN	587	100.1	687.1		
6	LISOCONI, Ghenadie	MDA	586	101.0	687.0		
7	PALINKAS, Lajos	HUN	586	99.9	685.9		
8	LEONHARD, Daniel	GER	586	97.6	683.6		

Shooting / *Tir*

25 m Sport Pistol, Women / *Pistolet sport à 25 m, Dames*

PRELIMINARIES

Rnk	Name	Ctry	p1	p2	p3	r1	r2	r3	Total
1	LI, Duihong	CHN	99	98	99	98	98	97	589 O
2	SALUKVADZE, Nino	GEO	98	98	99	96	97	98	586
3	JORGOVA, Diana	BUL	98	95	99	96	98	99	585
4	BOO, Soon-Hee	KOR	96	96	98	99	98	96	583
4	LOGVINENKO, Marina	RUS	97	97	99	96	96	98	583
6	MACUR, Julita	POL	96	96	97	98	95	98	580
6	OTRYAD, Gundegmaa	MGL	95	98	96	98	97	96	580
6	SEKARIC, Jasna	YUG	97	98	96	99	98	92	580
9	BONDAREVA, Yuliya	KAZ	96	98	95	96	95	98	578
9	FERNANDEZ, Maria	ESP	97	92	96	98	99	96	578
9	MA, Ge	CHN	96	93	95	98	96	98	578
9	PETRACEK, Connie	USA	96	95	97	98	95	97	578
9	SINIAK, Iouliia	BLR	92	96	97	97	99	97	578
14	CHITIK, Ianna	BLR	96	97	94	96	98	96	577
15	ASHUMOVA, Irada	AZE	98	96	96	97	94	95	576
15	DORJSUREN, Munkhbayar	MGL	94	96	95	97	96	98	576
15	KASSOUMI, Agathi	GRE	94	99	95	95	97	96	576
15	SHEHU, Enkelejda	ALB	95	95	98	95	98	95	576
15	SMIRNOVA, Svetlana	RUS	93	97	95	97	97	97	576
20	MATA, Diana	ALB	94	95	97	98	95	96	575
21	GROZDEVA, Mariya	BUL	95	96	96	98	93	96	574
21	PARK, Jung-Hee	KOR	98	95	95	93	95	98	574
23	CALLAHAN, Libby	USA	94	96	94	99	97	93	573
23	STIZZOLI, Barbara	ITA	95	96	93	98	96	95	573

PRELIMINARIES - *continued*

Rnk	Name	Ctry	p1	p2	p3	r1	r2	r3	Total
23	VOELKER, Anke	GER	96	100	97	89	96	95	573
23	WOODWARD, Annette	AUS	94	95	95	96	94	99	573
27	JIRKALOVA, Regina	CZE	95	90	96	98	97	96	572
27	UCHADZE, Nino	GEO	95	95	91	97	96	98	572
29	GUADO, Lorena	ARG	92	94	94	96	97	96	569
30	BELIAEVA, Galina	KAZ	97	94	95	96	87	98	567
30	PAGE, Carol	GBR	94	93	98	94	92	96	567
30	SUPPO, Michela	ITA	95	96	95	90	94	97	567
33	GALLO, Cristina	ARG	94	93	96	94	93	95	565
34	MEYERHOFF, Susanne	DEN	96	94	94	94	95	91	564
35	INADA, Yoko	JPN	94	96	97	86	94	96	563
36	SKOKO-KOVACEVIC, Mirela	CRO	97	96	96	88	87	97	561
37	TOMCALA, Carol	AUS	91	96	92	97	91	91	558

FINAL

Rnk	Name	Ctry	Qual pts	Final pts	Total	
1	LI, Duihong	CHN	589	98.9	687.9 O	Gold
2	JORGOVA, Diana	BUL	585	99.8	684.8	Silver
3	LOGVINENKO, Marina	RUS	583	101.2	684.2	Bronze
4	BOO, Soon-Hee	KOR	583	100.9	683.9	
5	OTRYAD, Gundegmaa	MGL	580	101.3	681.3	
6	SEKARIC, Jasna	YUG	580	100.4	680.4	
7	SALUKVADZE, Nino	GEO	586	91.6	677.6	
8	MACUR, Julita	POL	580	97.4	677.4	

Shooting / *Tir*

10 m Air Pistol, Men / *Pistolet à air comprimé à 10 m, Messieurs*

PRELIMINARIES

Rnk	Name	Ctry	1	2	3	4	5	6	Total
1	WANG, Yifu	CHN	99	96	99	97	98	98	587 O
2	di DONNA, Roberto	ITA	98	100	98	97	98	94	585
2	PIETRZAK, Jerzy	POL	97	97	97	99	98	97	585
4	KIRIAKOV, Tanu	BUL	96	98	96	99	98	97	584
5	PYZHYANOV, Sergey	RUS	97	96	98	99	96	97	583
5	SACK, Friedhelm	NAM	98	95	96	99	98	97	583
7	BASINSKI, Igor	BLR	96	98	99	96	97	96	582
8	TAN, Zongliang	CHN	95	98	97	96	97	98	581
9	GEVORGIAN, Arthur	GER	98	94	94	99	98	97	580
9	LOUKACHIK, Konstantin	BLR	98	99	96	97	94	96	580
9	NEUMAIER, Hans-Juergen	GER	98	97	96	96	95	98	580
12	FERNANDEZ, Gerard	FRA	94	95	95	100	98	97	579
12	ISAKOV, Vladimir	RUS	99	98	95	93	96	98	579
12	KIM, Sung-Jun	KOR	96	98	96	96	97	96	579
12	MAKAROV, Viktor	UKR	95	95	97	96	98	98	579
12	MELENTIEV, Yuriy	KGZ	98	95	96	97	98	95	579
17	FAIT, Vigilio	ITA	97	96	98	95	96	96	578
17	TARLOIU, Constantin	ROM	94	96	97	95	99	97	578
19	AKHMEDOV, Shukhrat	UZB	97	97	98	97	91	97	577
19	BLIZNYUCHENKO, Oleksandr	UKR	94	96	99	96	97	95	577
19	PAPANITZ, Zoltan	HUN	95	98	97	96	95	96	577
19	TOBAR, Bernardo	COL	95	93	97	98	96	98	577
23	ANDERSSON, Lennart	SWE	94	97	94	98	96	97	576
23	KARACS, Zsolt	HUN	95	97	96	96	98	94	576
23	TENK, Martin	CZE	94	97	97	95	98	95	576
26	BABII, Sorin	ROM	92	98	96	97	96	96	575
26	HEMBRE, Pal	NOR	96	94	97	96	95	97	575
26	SKANAKER, Ragnar	SWE	96	97	93	98	96	95	575
29	ADAMS, Phillip	AUS	93	94	95	99	97	96	574
29	KIDA, Tomohiro	JPN	96	93	98	96	97	94	574
29	KUZMINS, Afanasijs	LAT	96	91	96	98	96	97	574
29	NOWAK, Marek	POL	97	93	96	96	96	96	574
29	PANICHPATIKUM, Jakkrit	THA	96	94	97	95	98	94	574

PRELIMINARIES - *continued*

Rnk	Name	Ctry	1	2	3	4	5	6	Total
29	RANA, Jaspal	IND	99	97	95	97	93	93	574
29	SANDSTROM, Bengt	AUS	95	96	96	95	95	97	574
36	DUMOULIN, Franck	FRA	95	99	98	94	94	93	573
36	KIM, Sung-Joon	KOR	97	92	93	95	99	97	573
36	SANCHEZ, Sergio	GUA	98	95	93	98	95	94	573
39	JIRKAL, Stanislav	CZE	94	97	96	96	93	96	572
39	TRIPOLSKI, Alex	ISR	97	97	95	96	95	92	572
41	CALOIA, Neal	USA	94	95	96	96	95	95	571
41	TU, Tai-Hsing	TPE	97	92	97	96	95	94	571
43	SPIRELJA, Roman	CRO	94	94	96	99	93	94	570
44	AMONETTE, Ben	USA	90	93	96	98	95	97	569
44	FABO, Jan	SVK	91	95	95	93	98	97	569
44	HASSAN, Hassan	IRQ	93	97	93	96	96	94	569
47	ZAKHARIEV, Kolio	BUL	92	95	93	97	98	93	568
48	NAKASHIGE, Masaru	JPN	95	95	94	91	93	99	567
49	SOE, Myint	MYA	94	94	90	93	93	91	555
50	KLOMJAI, Surin	THA	91	93	89	92	91	91	547

FINAL

Rnk	Name	Ctry	Qual pts	Final pts	Total	
1	di DONNA, Roberto	ITA	585	99.2	684.2	Gold
2	WANG, Yifu	CHN	587	97.1	684.1	Silver
3	KIRIAKOV, Tanu	BUL	584	99.8	683.8	Bronze
4	PYZHYANOV, Sergey	RUS	583	100.5	683.5	
5	PIETRZAK, Jerzy	POL	585	97.7	682.7	
6	TAN, Zongliang	CHN	581	101.0	682.0	
7	BASINSKI, Igor	BLR	582	99.8	681.8	
8	SACK, Friedhelm	NAM	583	97.2	680.2	

Shooting / *Tir*

10 m Air Pistol, Women / *Pistolet à air comprimé à 10 m, Dames*

PRELIMINARIES

Rnk	Name	Ctry	1	2	3	4	Total
1	LOGVINENKO, Marina	RUS	99	99	95	97	390 O
2	GROZDEVA, Mariya	BUL	96	100	97	96	389
2	KLOCHNEVA, Olga	RUS	97	97	99	96	389
4	SALUKVADZE, Nino	GEO	96	95	98	96	385
5	BELIAEVA, Galina	KAZ	97	95	97	95	384
5	SEKARIC, Jasna	YUG	92	98	98	96	384
7	BONDAREVA, Yuliya	KAZ	100	94	93	96	383
8	LEE, Ho-Sook	KOR	95	95	96	96	382
8	MILCHINA, Lolita	BLR	92	98	96	96	382
10	ASHUMOVA, Irada	AZE	95	95	94	97	381
10	SINIAK, Iouliia	BLR	96	96	95	94	381
10	SKOKO-KOVACEVIC, Mirela	CRO	97	96	95	93	381
10	JORGOVA, Diana	BUL	97	98	91	95	381
14	LU, Fang	CHN	97	96	95	92	380
15	BOO, Soon-Hee	KOR	95	94	94	96	379
15	INADA, Yoko	JPN	97	95	94	93	379
15	LI, Duihong	CHN	98	95	95	91	379
15	MEYERHOFF, Susanne	DEN	98	95	93	93	379
19	FERNANDEZ, Maria	ESP	95	95	93	95	378
19	SUPPO, Michela	ITA	94	95	97	92	378
21	DORJSUREN, Munkhbayar	MGL	93	96	93	95	377
21	SHEHU, Enkelejda	ALB	95	96	96	90	377
23	FORDER, Annemarie	AUS	92	95	94	95	376
23	HJORTSHOJ, Majbritt	DEN	96	91	94	95	376
23	PAGE, Carol	GBR	97	92	90	97	376
23	STIZZOLI, Barbara	ITA	93	95	94	94	376

PRELIMINARIES - *continued*

Rnk	Name	Ctry	1	2	3	4	Total
27	MACUR, Julita	POL	92	96	94	93	375
27	VOELKER, Anke	GER	95	93	95	92	375
29	GALLO, Cristina	ARG	91	94	94	95	374
30	OTRYAD, Gundegmaa	MGL	91	91	94	96	372
30	SNYDER, Rebecca	USA	90	94	93	95	372
32	GUADO, Lorena	ARG	92	96	90	93	371
32	SEVIN, Jo Ann	USA	93	92	92	94	371
34	MLADENOVIC, Marija	YUG	94	90	95	91	370
34	TOMCALA, Carol	AUS	94	89	93	94	370
36	UCHADZE, Nino	GEO	94	92	89	94	369
37	JIRKALOVA, Regina	CZE	91	93	91	89	364
38	MATA, Diana	ALB	90	91	90	92	363
39	de FALCONI, Blanca	ECU	89	91	89	92	361
39	MARCHI, Nadia	SMR	94	91	86	90	361
41	SCHUVERER, Jenny	PAN	88	87	87	92	354

FINAL

Rnk	Name	Ctry	Qual pts	Final pts	Total	
1	KLOCHNEVA, Olga	RUS	389	101.1	490.1 O	**Gold**
2	LOGVINENKO, Marina	RUS	390	98.5	488.5	**Silver**
3	GROZDEVA, Mariya	BUL	389	99.5	488.5	**Bronze**
4	SEKARIC, Jasna	YUG	384	103.1	487.1	
5	SALUKVADZE, Nino	GEO	385	99.0	484.0	
6	BELIAEVA, Galina	KAZ	384	97.7	481.7	
7	BONDAREVA, Yuliya	KAZ	383	96.3	479.3	
8	MILCHINA, Lolita	BLR	382	97.1	479.1	

Shooting / *Tir*

10 m Air Rifle, Men / *Carabine à air comprimé à 10 m, Messieurs*

PRELIMINARIES

Rnk	Name	Ctry	1	2	3	4	5	6	Total
1	WAIBEL, Wolfram, Jr.	AUT	97	99	100	100	100	100	596 O
2	HARBISON, Rob	USA	99	100	100	97	99	99	594
2	KHADZHIBEKOV, Artem	RUS	99	100	98	100	100	97	594
4	ALEINIKOV, Evgeni	RUS	98	98	99	98	98	100	591
4	AMAT, Jean-Pierre	FRA	99	98	97	99	99	99	591
4	BAKES, Milan	CZE	96	100	98	99	100	98	591
4	DEBEVEC, Rajmond	SLO	98	98	98	98	99	100	591
4	ECKHARDT, Maik	GER	99	100	99	100	98	95	591
4	HAAKEDAL, Nils Petter	NOR	99	99	100	98	98	97	591
4	ROLLAND, Leif Steinar	NOR	98	98	100	99	97	99	591
11	KLIMENKO, Anatoli	BLR	95	97	100	99	99	100	590
11	KURKA, Petr	CZE	96	99	98	98	100	99	590
11	LEE, Eun-Chul	KOR	97	99	96	99	99	100	590
11	LIM, Young-Sueb	KOR	100	97	99	97	99	98	590
15	HIRVI, Juha	FIN	98	99	96	99	98	99	589
15	MAKSIMOVIC, Goran	YUG	98	98	100	99	98	96	589
15	MIROSAVLJEV, Nemanja	YUG	99	99	98	99	95	99	589
18	BADIOU, Franck	FRA	97	99	97	99	98	98	588
18	GRABNER, Dieter	AUT	97	98	99	100	98	96	588
18	NING, Li Jia	CHN	98	100	97	98	97	98	588
18	RIEDERER, Johann	GER	95	98	99	97	99	100	588
22	LI, Haicong	CHN	95	99	96	100	100	97	587
22	LOMOV, Yuriy	KGZ	99	97	99	98	97	97	587
22	YANAGIDA, Masaru	JPN	98	98	99	97	97	98	587
25	FAZLIJA, Nedzad	BIH	95	98	98	98	98	99	586
26	NEKHAEV, Gueorgi	BLR	98	97	98	99	98	95	585
26	RUSTICUCCI, Ricardo	ARG	96	99	97	100	97	96	585
28	GONCI, Jozef	SVK	95	98	99	99	96	97	584
28	ZUMBACH, Andreas	SUI	95	99	98	98	97	97	584
30	KRASKOWSKI, Robert	POL	96	96	99	97	97	98	583

PRELIMINARIES - *continued*

Rnk	Name	Ctry	1	2	3	4	5	6	Total
30	SENECAL, Jean-Francois	CAN	98	98	98	98	96	95	583
32	MYKHAYLOV, Oleh	UKR	99	98	97	95	98	95	582
33	POLAK, Boris	ISR	95	96	98	99	98	95	581
33	SAIFUL ALAM, Saiful	BAN	96	97	96	97	98	97	581
33	VARI, Zsolt	HUN	99	95	96	96	98	97	581
36	NASESKI, Darko	MKD	99	95	95	97	97	97	580
37	al-KHATRI, Khalaf	OMA	99	95	93	95	98	98	578
38	BELIAEV, Sergey	KAZ	96	95	97	97	96	96	577
38	KURITA, Naoki	JPN	97	94	96	97	97	96	577
38	VELARTE, Angel	ARG	95	95	96	97	96	98	577
41	DUBIS, Glenn	USA	97	95	99	95	96	94	576
42	GONZALEZ, Jorge	ESP	91	94	98	98	98	96	575
43	TAHLAK, Nabil	UAE	96	97	95	91	96	94	569
44	MARTINEZ, Walter	NCA	97	94	94	94	93	94	566

FINAL

Rnk	Name	Ctry	Qual pts	Final pts	Total	
1	KHADZHIBEKOV, Artem	RUS	594	101.7	695.7 O	**Gold**
2	WAIBEL, Wolfram, Jr.	AUT	596	99.2	695.2	**Silver**
3	AMAT, Jean-Pierre	FRA	591	102.1	693.1	**Bronze**
4	ALEINIKOV, Evgeni	RUS	591	101.9	692.9	
5	ROLLAND, Leif Steinar	NOR	591	101.5	692.5	
6	DEBEVEC, Rajmond	SLO	591	101.1	692.1	
7	HARBISON, Rob	USA	594	97.8	691.8	
8	BAKES, Milan	CZE	591	99.5	690.5	

Shooting / *Tir*
10 m Air Rifle, Women / *Carabine à air comprimé à 10 m, Dames*

PRELIMINARIES

Rnk	Name	Ctry	1	2	3	4	Total
1	HORNEBER, Petra	GER	100	100	98	99	397 O
2	BELLENOUE, Valerie	FRA	99	99	98	99	395
2	IVOSEV, Aleksandra	YUG	100	98	99	98	395
2	MAUER, Renata	POL	99	98	99	99	395
2	NEDVEDOVA, Marta	CZE	98	99	100	98	395
6	LESKIV, Lesya	UKR	100	97	99	98	394
6	POGREBNIAK, Olga	BLR	99	99	97	99	394
8	BINDER, Aranka	YUG	97	98	98	100	393
8	CHILOVA, Irina	BLR	98	100	96	99	393
8	JIN, Soon-Young	KOR	99	99	97	98	393
8	JOO, Eva	HUN	97	96	100	100	393
8	XU, Yanhua	CHN	97	100	98	98	393
13	BOURLAND, Elizabeth	USA	98	98	98	98	392
13	BUEHLMANN, Gaby	SUI	97	97	98	100	392
13	FOURNEL, Amelia	ARG	97	100	99	96	392
13	FUCHS, Sabina	SUI	99	98	99	96	392
13	GRIGORIEVA, Marina	RUS	99	100	96	97	392
13	LETCHEVA, Vessela	BUL	96	100	98	98	392
19	KIM, Jung-Mi	KOR	96	98	99	98	391
20	BILKOVA, Dagmar	CZE	96	99	98	97	390
20	CHEN, Muhua	CHN	98	96	98	98	390
20	MALENICA, Mladenka	CRO	98	96	100	96	390
20	MALOUKHINA, Anna	RUS	95	97	100	98	390
20	MATOVA, Nonka	BUL	100	97	95	98	390
25	BOUQUE, Cindy	BEL	96	98	97	98	389
25	HANSEN, Lindy	NOR	100	96	95	98	389
25	RAMANAYAKE, Pushpamali	SRI	96	98	98	97	389
25	SKOKO, Suzana	CRO	95	96	100	98	389
29	DANGPIAM, Jarintorn	THA	96	96	98	98	388
29	NESTEROVA, Tetyana	UKR	94	96	98	100	388

PRELIMINARIES - *continued*

Rnk	Name	Ctry	1	2	3	4	Total
31	BANKS, Sue	AUS	99	95	97	96	387
31	BISSO, Anni	DEN	96	96	98	97	387
31	FORIAN, Eva	HUN	99	97	94	97	387
31	IWAKI, Masami	JPN	94	97	97	99	387
31	KREMER-ROSENECK, Iris	LUX	95	97	98	97	387
36	ANTOLIN, Cristina	ESP	94	96	98	98	386
36	KNELLS, Bettina	GER	94	98	96	98	386
36	NAPOLSKI, Nancy	USA	95	97	98	96	386
39	MINAMOTO, Yoko	JPN	96	97	95	97	385
39	PASETTI, Fabienne	MON	99	98	95	93	385
41	COUESNON, Carole	FRA	99	96	94	95	384
41	KSIAZKIEWICZ, Malgorzata	POL	96	97	97	94	384
43	BARRY, Rhona	IRL	94	95	96	97	382
44	VATAKER, Hanne	NOR	93	94	98	96	381
44	WICKRAMASINGHE, Malini	SRI	92	95	97	97	381
46	FARIMAN, Lida	IRI	96	93	94	96	379
47	ANTUNES, Sara	POR	91	94	93	99	377
48	RIBEIRO, Carla	POR	95	93	91	96	375
49	RAI, Bivaswari	NEP	87	91	89	92	359

FINAL

Rnk	Name	Ctry	Qual pts	Final pts	Total	
1	MAUER, Renata	POL	395	102.6	497.6	**Gold**
2	HORNEBER, Petra	GER	397	100.4	497.4	**Silver**
3	IVOSEV, Aleksandra	YUG	395	102.2	497.2	**Bronze**
4	BELLENOUE, Valerie	FRA	395	101.6	496.6	
5	POGREBNIAK, Olga	BLR	394	102.4	496.4	
6	NEDVEDOVA, Marta	CZE	395	100.1	495.1	
7	JOO, Eva	HUN	393	101.5	494.5	
8	LESKIV, Lesya	UKR	394	100.2	494.2	

Shooting / *Tir*
50 m Free Rifle 3 Position, Men / *Carabine libre 3 positions à 50 m, Messieurs*

PRELIMINARIES

Rnk	Name	Ctry	Prone	Standing	Kneeling	Total
1	AMAT, Jean-Pierre	FRA	396	387	392	1175 O
1	BELYAYEV, Sergey	KAZ	399	382	394	1175 O
3	MAKSIMOVIC, Goran	YUG	394	387	392	1173
4	HARBISON, Rob	USA	394	388	388	1170
4	WAIBEL, Wolfram, Jr.	AUT	394	389	387	1170
6	BECVAR, Vaclav	CZE	398	381	389	1168
7	DEBEVEC, Rajmond	SLO	397	381	388	1166
7	GONCI, Jozef	SVK	393	382	391	1166
7	MARTYNOV, Serguei	BLR	397	377	392	1166
10	DUBIS, Glenn	USA	398	379	388	1165
10	ECKHARDT, Maik	GER	397	382	386	1165
10	NING, Li Jia	CHN	397	377	391	1165
13	FARNIK, Thomas	AUT	393	382	389	1164
13	HIRVI, Juha	FIN	397	379	388	1164
13	KHADZHIBEKOV, Artem	RUS	393	384	387	1164
13	PETIKYAN, Hrachya	ARM	396	379	389	1164
13	STARIK, Guy	ISR	396	379	389	1164
18	BAKES, Milan	CZE	395	378	390	1163
18	BOCHKAREV, Vjatcheslav	RUS	398	380	385	1163
18	FAZLIJA, Nedzad	BIH	395	377	391	1163
18	LEE, Eun-Chul	KOR	395	377	391	1163
22	GABRIELSSON, Peter	SWE	387	385	390	1162
22	HENN, Jaco	RSA	397	382	383	1162
22	KRASKOWSKI, Robert	POL	394	375	393	1162
22	POLAK, Boris	ISR	398	379	385	1162
26	MYKHAYLOV, Oleh	UKR	396	382	383	1161
27	VARI, Zsolt	HUN	393	374	393	1160
28	HAAKEDAL, Nils Petter	NOR	398	377	383	1158

PRELIMINARIES - *continued*

Rnk	Name	Ctry	Prone	Standing	Kneeling	Total
28	HARSKOV, Jens	DEN	399	368	391	1158
28	KLIMENKO, Anatoli	BLR	391	380	387	1158
28	YANAGIDA, Masaru	JPN	395	383	380	1158
32	CZERWINSKI, Tadeusz	POL	396	375	386	1157
32	LOMOV, Yuriy	KGZ	396	377	384	1157
32	ZUMBACH, Andreas	SUI	392	377	388	1157
35	CHASSAT, Roger	FRA	392	385	379	1156
35	PLETIKOSIC, Stevan	YUG	398	369	389	1156
37	GONZALEZ, Jorge	ESP	399	368	388	1155
37	KLEES, Christian	GER	397	376	382	1155
37	KURITA, Naoki	JPN	400	374	381	1155
40	CHA, Young-Chul	KOR	393	375	386	1154
41	STENVAAG, Harald	NOR	395	380	378	1153
42	CHEN, Xianjun	CHN	399	369	380	1148
43	DION, Michel	CAN	396	365	384	1145
44	VELARTE, Angel	ARG	392	363	387	1142
45	RUSTICUCCI, Ricardo	ARG	392	364	383	1139

FINAL

Rnk	Name	Ctry	Qual pts	Final pts	Total	
1	AMAT, Jean-Pierre	FRA	1175	98.9	1273.9 O	**Gold**
2	BELYAYEV, Sergey	KAZ	1175	97.3	1272.3	**Silver**
3	WAIBEL, Wolfram, Jr.	AUT	1170	99.6	1269.6	**Bronze**
4	MAKSIMOVIC, Goran	YUG	1173	95.8	1268.8	
5	GONCI, Jozef	SVK	1166	101.7	1267.7	
6	HARBISON, Rob	USA	1170	97.7	1267.7	
7	BECVAR, Vaclav	CZE	1168	96.0	1264.0	
8	MARTYNOV, Serguei	BLR	1166	97.9	1263.9	

Shooting / *Tir*

50 m Standard Rifle 3 Position, Women / *Carabine standard 3 positions à 50 m, Dames*

PRELIMINARIES

Rnk	Name	Ctry	Prone	Standing	Kneeling	Total
1	MAUER, Renata	POL	200	192	197	589 O
2	IVOSEV, Aleksandra	YUG	199	193	195	587
3	GERASIMENOK, Irina	RUS	196	194	195	585
4	MATOVA, Nonka	BUL	197	191	196	584
4	OBEL, Kirsten	GER	200	194	190	584
6	BOURLAND, Elizabeth	USA	195	194	194	583
6	KONG, Hyun-Ah	KOR	198	191	194	583
8	NESTEROVA, Tetyana	UKR	197	191	193	581
9	BUEHLMANN, Gaby	SUI	199	192	188	579
9	HORNEBER, Petra	GER	197	189	193	579
9	LESKIV, Lesya	UKR	199	185	195	579
12	FOSTER, Jean	USA	197	187	194	578
12	HANSEN, Lindy	NOR	197	191	190	578
12	LETCHEVA, Vessela	BUL	195	188	195	578
12	NEDVEDOVA, Marta	CZE	197	190	191	578
12	SKOKO, Suzana	CRO	192	194	192	578
17	CHILOVA, Irina	BLR	197	188	192	577
17	POGREBNIAK, Olga	BLR	197	186	194	577
17	ZHANG, Qiuping	CHN	197	188	192	577
20	CHEN, Muhua	CHN	197	188	191	576
20	JOO, Eva	HUN	197	190	189	576
22	BILKOVA, Dagmar	CZE	198	187	189	574
22	BINDER, Aranka	YUG	197	189	188	574
22	BISSO, Anni	DEN	194	190	190	574
22	FUCHS, Sabina	SUI	196	186	192	574

PRELIMINARIES - *continued*

Rnk	Name	Ctry	Prone	Standing	Kneeling	Total
26	MALOUKHINA, Anna	RUS	193	186	194	573
26	MINAMOTO, Yoko	JPN	196	183	194	573
28	MALENICA, Mladenka	CRO	196	190	186	572
29	ANTUNES, Sara	POR	195	185	191	571
30	DANGPIAM, Jarintorn	THA	193	183	194	570
30	FORIAN, Eva	HUN	191	188	191	570
32	RIBEIRO, Carla	POR	197	180	191	568
32	WEON, Gyung-Sook	KOR	194	185	189	568
34	VATAKER, Hanne	NOR	195	185	186	566
35	WICKRAMASINGHE, Malini	SRI	195	193	177	565
36	RAMANAYAKE, Pushpamali	SRI	194	188	182	564
37	KSIAZKIEWICZ, Malgorzata	POL	194	181	188	563
38	ANTOLIN, Cristina	ESP	189	186	182	557

FINAL

Rnk	Name	Ctry	Qual pts	Final pts	Total	
1	IVOSEV, Aleksandra	YUG	587	99.1	686.1 O	Gold
2	GERASIMENOK, Irina	RUS	585	95.1	680.1	Silver
3	MAUER, Renata	POL	589	90.8	679.8	Bronze
4	OBEL, Kirsten	GER	584	95.2	679.2	
5	MATOVA, Nonka	BUL	584	94.8	678.8	
6	KONG, Hyun-Ah	KOR	583	92.8	675.8	
7	BOURLAND, Elizabeth	USA	583	91.0	674.0	
8	NESTEROVA, Tetyana	UKR	581	92.3	673.3	

Shooting / *Tir*

50 m Free Rifle Prone, Men / *Carabine libre position couchée à 50 m, Messieurs*

PRELIMINARIES

Rnk	Name	Ctry	1	2	3	4	5	6	Total
1	KLEES, Christian	GER	100	100	100	100	100	100	600 O
2	GONCI, Jozef	SVK	99	100	100	100	100	100	599
3	BELYAYEV, Sergey	KAZ	99	100	100	100	99	100	598
3	MARTYNOV, Serguei	BLR	100	100	98	100	100	100	598
5	GONZALEZ, Jorge	ESP	100	100	100	100	97	100	597
5	MEEK, Bill	USA	100	99	100	100	98	100	597
7	DEBEVEC, Rajmond	SLO	100	100	99	100	99	98	596
7	KOVALENKO, Serguei	RUS	99	100	100	99	100	98	596
7	LEE, Eun-Chul	KOR	100	99	99	99	99	100	596
7	MACH, Milan	CZE	99	100	100	99	99	99	596
11	BECVAR, Vaclav	CZE	98	100	99	99	100	99	595
11	KRASKOWSKI, Robert	POL	100	99	98	99	99	100	595
11	LI, Wenjie	CHN	98	99	99	100	99	100	595
11	LOMOV, Yuriy	KGZ	100	98	99	99	99	100	595
11	MYKHAYLOV, Oleh	UKR	98	99	100	100	99	99	595
11	PIREKEEV, Igor	TKM	99	99	99	99	100	99	595
11	PLETIKOSIC, Stevan	YUG	100	100	99	99	99	98	595
11	RUECKER, Bernd	GER	99	100	98	99	100	99	595
11	VARI, Zsolt	HUN	99	100	99	99	100	98	595
20	CHEN, Xianjun	CHN	98	100	100	98	98	100	594
20	CZERWINSKI, Tadeusz	POL	98	98	100	100	99	99	594
20	KHADZHIBEKOV, Artem	RUS	99	99	100	100	99	97	594
20	KOCH, Kurt	SUI	100	98	99	100	97	100	594
20	MAKSIMOVIC, Goran	YUG	98	99	100	99	100	98	594
20	POLAK, Boris	ISR	100	98	98	99	99	100	594
26	HARSKOV, Jens	DEN	99	95	100	99	100	100	593
26	HENN, Jaco	RSA	99	98	100	100	99	97	593
26	STARIK, Guy	ISR	98	99	98	99	100	99	593
26	ZUMBACH, Andreas	SUI	99	98	99	97	100	100	593
30	BURY, Michel	FRA	99	98	100	99	97	99	592
30	DION, Michel	CAN	99	99	99	99	99	97	592
30	KURITA, Naoki	JPN	99	99	98	100	97	99	592
30	NEKHAEV, Gueorgi	BLR	99	98	99	99	97	100	592

PRELIMINARIES - *continued*

Rnk	Name	Ctry	1	2	3	4	5	6	Total
30	STENVAAG, Harald	NOR	100	99	98	99	98	98	592
30	UPTAGRAFFT, Eric	USA	99	100	97	99	99	98	592
36	CHA, Young-Chul	KOR	98	98	100	98	98	99	591
36	HAAKEDAL, Nils Petter	NOR	97	98	98	99	99	99	591
36	PETTERSON, Stephen	NZL	99	98	98	100	97	99	591
39	CHASSAT, Roger	FRA	99	99	97	99	96	100	590
39	GRIMMEL, Torben	DEN	97	100	98	99	99	97	590
39	WAIBEL, Wolfram, Jr.	AUT	97	98	98	99	100	98	590
42	FARNIK, Thomas	AUT	97	97	100	99	98	98	589
42	GABRIELSSON, Peter	SWE	100	98	97	97	98	99	589
42	HIRVI, Juha	FIN	98	99	99	98	98	97	589
42	MEREDITH, Bruce	ISV	99	99	95	100	98	98	589
42	YANAGIDA, Masaru	JPN	99	99	99	97	96	99	589
47	RODRIGUEZ, Ralph	PUR	98	99	97	98	98	98	588
48	STERN, Jonathan	GBR	97	98	99	97	99	97	587
49	DESAI, Anuj	KEN	99	96	100	97	98	96	586
50	al-KHATRI, Khalaf	OMA	96	98	99	95	98	98	584
51	FAZLIJA, Nedzad	BIH	97	100	96	96	99	95	583
52	DUFF, Gary	IRL	98	99	95	96	96	96	580

FINAL

Rnk	Name	Ctry	Qual pts	Final pts	Total	
1	KLEES, Christian	GER	600	104.8	704.8 W	Gold
2	BELYAYEV, Sergey	KAZ	598	105.3	703.3	Silver
3	GONCI, Jozef	SVK	599	102.9	701.9	Bronze
4	GONZALEZ, Jorge	ESP	597	104.7	701.7	
5	MACH, Milan	CZE	596	104.9	700.9	
6	MARTYNOV, Serguei	BLR	598	101.6	699.6	
7	LEE, Eun-Chul	KOR	596	103.1	699.1	
8	MEEK, Bill	USA	597	101.9	698.9	

Shooting / *Tir*

Trap, Men / *Fosse olympique, Messieurs*

PRELIMINARIES

Rnk	Name	Ctry	1	2	3	4	5	Total
1	DIAMOND, Michael	AUS	25	24	25	25	25	124 O
2	BADE, Lance	USA	24	24	25	25	25	123
2	LAKATOS, Josh	USA	25	24	25	25	24	123
2	MAXWELL, John	AUS	25	25	25	24	24	123
5	SLAMKA, Vladimir	SVK	24	25	25	24	24	122
5	VIEIRA, Manuel	POR	24	23	25	25	25	122
5	ZHANG, Bing	CHN	25	24	25	24	24	122
8	BINDRICH, Karsten	GER	25	25	25	23	23	121
8	BODEN, Peter	GBR	25	25	24	24	23	121
8	GACH, Jiri	CZE	25	23	24	24	25	121
8	LEARY, George	CAN	23	25	25	23	25	121
8	ZHANG, Yongjie	CHN	24	25	23	24	25	121
13	BODO, Zoltan	HUN	23	25	24	24	24	120
13	KUBEC, Pavel	CZE	24	24	25	24	23	120
13	MARK, Russell	AUS	23	24	25	24	24	120
13	PARK, Chul-Sung	KOR	25	25	25	23	22	120
13	PELLIELO, Giovanni	ITA	24	24	24	24	24	120
13	PEREZ, Jose	ESP	25	24	25	24	22	120
13	REBELO, Joao	POR	25	23	22	25	25	120
20	al-DEEHANI, Fehaid	KUW	22	24	25	24	24	119
20	BOUVIER, Xavier	SUI	24	25	25	23	22	119
20	DAMME, Joerg	GER	24	24	24	22	25	119
20	DUPONT, Philippe	BEL	23	24	24	25	23	119
20	ERICKSON, Bret	USA	23	25	24	23	24	119
20	GOMBOS, Karoly	HUN	22	24	25	24	24	119
20	LABATUT, Jean	BRA	23	23	25	24	24	119
20	LEE, Wung Yew	SIN	24	24	25	24	22	119
20	PACE, Frans	MLT	24	24	24	25	22	119
20	TITTARELLI, Marcello	ITA	22	25	24	23	25	119
20	VENTURINI, Marco	ITA	22	23	25	25	24	119
31	AMICI, Francesco	SMR	23	24	23	24	24	118
31	CARO, Danilo	COL	25	24	23	22	24	118
31	FERNANDEZ, Alejandro	MEX	24	23	25	23	23	118
31	KOSTELECKY, David	CZE	22	23	25	25	23	118

PRELIMINARIES - *continued*

Rnk	Name	Ctry	1	2	3	4	5	Total
31	SINGH, Mansher	IND	22	24	23	25	24	118
31	ZHAO, Guisheng	CHN	24	22	24	23	25	118
37	BARCIA, Gerard	AND	22	23	23	24	25	117
37	GILL, Kevin	GBR	23	25	23	22	24	117
37	GULEV, Ivan	BUL	25	21	23	23	25	117
37	HANSEN, Keld	DEN	23	24	23	23	24	117
37	VICARD, Christophe	FRA	23	24	23	24	23	117
42	ALLEN, Thomas	IRL	23	23	24	22	24	116
42	DOUSEMONT, Armand	LUX	24	22	23	24	23	116
42	WOODWARD, Brant	NZL	24	25	22	24	21	116
45	FRANCA, Paulo	ANG	23	25	22	23	22	115
45	JAANSALU, Heikki	EST	23	20	25	23	24	115
45	MONAKOV, Dmytro	UKR	22	22	23	24	24	115
45	SHAW, Ian	CAN	23	22	23	24	23	115
49	ARTECONA, Jose	PUR	23	25	22	21	23	114
49	BOZA, Francisco	PER	24	19	25	22	24	114
49	CHENG, Shu Ming	HKG	23	23	21	24	23	114
49	DAOU, Michel	AHO	22	24	22	24	22	114
49	KIZILSU, Alp	TUR	23	22	24	23	22	114
49	MOELLER, Uwe	GER	21	23	24	23	23	114
49	PEETERS, Frans	BEL	22	24	23	23	22	114
56	EARNSHAW, George	PHI	22	22	25	21	23	113
57	ELPIKIDIS, Michail	GRE	20	22	22	22	25	111
57	HUANG, I-Chien	TPE	23	21	21	22	24	111

FINAL

Rnk	Name	Ctry	Qual pts	Final pts	Total	
1	DIAMOND, Michael	AUS	124	25	149 O	Gold
2	LAKATOS, Josh	USA	123	24	147	Silver
3	BADE, Lance	USA	123	24	147	Bronze
4	MAXWELL, John	AUS	123	23	146	
5	ZHANG, Bing	CHN	122	24	146	
6	SLAMKA, Vladimir	SVK	122	23	145	

Shooting / *Tir*

Double Trap, Men / *Double trap, Messieurs*

PRELIMINARIES

Rnk	Name	Ctry	1	2	3	Total
1	HUANG, I-Chien	TPE	49	46	46	141 O
1	MARK, Russell	AUS	47	46	48	141 O
3	ZHANG, Bing	CHN	49	45	46	140
4	FAULDS, Richard	GBR	47	46	46	139
4	PERA, Albano	ITA	45	50	44	139
6	ALCORIZA, David	USA	46	45	47	138
6	LI, Bo	CHN	47	47	44	138
6	PARK, Chul-Sung	KOR	47	43	48	138
9	CENCI, Mirco	ITA	46	47	44	137
10	al-DEEHANI, Fehaid	KUW	48	47	41	136
10	BADE, Lance	USA	43	45	48	136
12	BOZA, Francisco	PER	45	48	42	135
12	GROS, Jean-Paul	FRA	47	43	45	135
12	REYNOLDS, Kirk	CAN	43	45	47	135
15	BINDRICH, Karsten	GER	46	45	42	133
15	KAUPPILA, Raimo	FIN	42	44	47	133
17	HABERMAN, Steve	AUS	45	41	45	131
17	MENNESSIER, Marc	FRA	42	47	42	131
19	BOLL, Rod	CAN	40	45	45	130
19	DUPONT, Philippe	BEL	47	43	40	130
19	GACH, Jiri	CZE	42	47	41	130
22	PEETERS, Frans	BEL	41	42	45	128
22	SCHANZ, Waldemar	GER	42	42	44	128

PRELIMINARIES - *continued*

Rnk	Name	Ctry	1	2	3	Total
24	GOMBOS, Karoly	HUN	40	44	43	127
25	ALLEN, Thomas	IRL	41	44	41	126
25	SLAMKA, Vladimir	SVK	41	44	41	126
27	BODO, Zoltan	HUN	42	41	42	125
27	EARNSHAW, George	PHI	44	41	40	125
27	GILL, Kevin	GBR	43	45	37	125
30	SOTIROPOULOS, Christos	GRE	40	45	39	124
31	KIZILSU, Alp	TUR	37	46	40	123
32	PACE, Frans	MLT	37	41	43	121
33	ARTECONA, Jose	PUR	43	40	37	120
33	DOUSEMONT, Armand	LUX	42	37	41	120
35	DAOU, Michel	AHO	42	34	37	113

FINAL

Rnk	Name	Ctry	Qual pts	Final pts	Total	
1	MARK, Russell	AUS	141	48	189 O	Gold
2	PERA, Albano	ITA	139	44	183	Silver
3	ZHANG, Bing	CHN	140	43	183	Bronze
4	PARK, Chul-Sung	KOR	138	45	183	
5	FAULDS, Richard	GBR	139	41	180	
6	HUANG, I-Chien	TPE	141	37	178	

Shooting / *Tir*

Double Trap, Women / *Double trap, Dames*

PRELIMINARIES

Rnk	Name	Ctry	1	2	3	Total
1	RHODE, Kim	USA	36	37	35	108 O
2	MURTONIEMI, Riitta-Mari	FIN	35	38	34	107
3	DEWITT, Terry	USA	34	37	34	105
3	KIERMAYER, Susanne	GER	37	36	32	105
3	KIRA, Yoshiko	JPN	33	35	37	105
6	GAO, E	CHN	32	35	36	103
6	HUDDLESTON, Deserie	AUS	34	34	35	103
6	PASELLO, Giovanna	ITA	36	33	34	103
6	ROBERTS, Annmaree	AUS	35	36	32	103
10	GUDZINEVICIUTE, Daina	LTU	32	35	34	101
11	PUSILA, Satu	FIN	34	34	32	100

PRELIMINARIES - *continued*

Rnk	Name	Ctry	1	2	3	Total
11	QUINTANAL, Maria	ESP	29	37	34	100
11	XU, Xiang	CHN	32	33	35	100
14	BERNARD, Muriel	FRA	34	35	29	98
15	GELISIO, Deborah	ITA	37	34	26	97
15	MEYER, Cynthia	CAN	31	38	28	97
17	DEMINA, Svetlana	RUS	32	30	33	95
17	LEE, Sang-Hee	KOR	31	35	29	95
19	RABAIA, Elena	RUS	35	31	27	93
20	FOCAN, Anne	BEL	35	27	29	91
21	USIETO, Gemma	ESP	32	30	28	90

FINAL

Rnk	Name	Ctry	Qual pts	Final pts	Total	
1	RHODE, Kim	USA	108	33	141 O	Gold
2	KIERMAYER, Susanne	GER	105	34	139	Silver
3	HUDDLESTON, D.	AUS	103	36	139	Bronze
4	DEWITT, Terry	USA	105	32	137	
5	MURTONIEMI, R.-M.	FIN	107	26	133	
6	KIRA, Yoshiko	JPN	105	27	132	

Shooting / *Tir*

Skeet, Men / *Skeet, Messieurs*

PRELIMINARIES

Rnk	Name	Ctry	1	2	3	4	5	Total
1	FALCO, Ennio	ITA	25	25	25	25	25	125 O
2	BENELLI, Andrea	ITA	24	25	25	24	25	123
2	RZEPKOWSKI, Miroslaw	POL	25	25	25	24	24	123
4	RASMUSSEN, Ole	DEN	24	24	25	24	25	122
4	TIMOFEJEVS, Boriss	LAT	25	25	24	24	24	122
4	TIOPLIY, Nikolai	RUS	25	24	24	24	25	122
7	ANDREOU, Antonis	CYP	24	24	24	25	24	121
7	CHEN, Dongjie	CHN	24	24	24	24	25	121
7	DURBESSON, Franck	FRA	25	24	24	23	25	121
7	IMNAISHVILI, Tamaz	GEO	25	23	24	25	24	121
7	INESHIN, Andrey	EST	25	23	25	24	24	121
7	RODRIGUEZ, Juan	CUB	24	25	23	25	24	121
7	ROY, Bill	USA	25	24	23	24	25	121
7	ZHANG, Xindong	CHN	25	25	23	24	24	121
15	al-ATTIYA, Nasser	QAT	25	22	24	25	24	120
15	DOMPELING, Hennie	NED	22	25	25	25	23	120
15	GRAVES, Todd	USA	25	24	24	25	22	120
15	ITO, Soichiro	JPN	24	24	24	25	23	120
15	SYCHRA, Jan	CZE	24	23	25	23	25	120
20	CUNNINGHAM, David	AUS	23	25	25	23	23	119
20	HOCHWALD, Bernhard	GER	25	22	25	25	22	119
20	MEULEMAN, Craig	AUS	23	23	23	25	25	119
20	MILLER, Clayton	CAN	25	24	24	24	22	119
20	ROSSETTI, Bruno	ITA	25	24	22	24	24	119
20	TORRES, Alfredo	CUB	24	24	23	24	24	119
26	HEINRICH, Jan-Henrik	GER	23	24	23	24	24	118
26	JENSEN, Harald	NOR	24	24	24	23	23	118
26	NICOLAIDES, Antonis	CYP	21	24	24	25	24	118
26	QUIGLEY, George	USA	24	24	22	24	24	118
26	ROMERO, Juan	GUA	25	25	25	22	21	118
26	WEGNER, Axel	GER	22	25	24	24	23	118
32	al-MOTERY, Saaid	KSA	23	23	23	24	24	117

PRELIMINARIES - *continued*

Rnk	Name	Ctry	1	2	3	4	5	Total
32	BECHYNSKY, Bronislav	CZE	23	22	24	24	24	117
32	HLAVACEK, Leos	CZE	23	24	23	22	25	117
32	KOURTELLAS, Christos	CYP	22	24	23	24	24	117
32	SWINKELS, Eric	NED	24	24	23	22	24	117
32	TOMAN, Ion	ROM	24	23	24	22	24	117
38	BOZA, Esteban	PER	25	23	23	22	23	116
38	PULDON, Servando	CUB	24	23	24	23	22	116
38	SZAMREJ, Tadeusz	POL	22	25	23	22	24	116
38	TIMOKHIN, Valeri	AZE	21	24	23	25	23	116
42	al-RASHIDI, Abdullah	KUW	22	23	23	23	24	115
42	COLOMER, Pascal	CHI	25	22	20	24	24	115
42	GIHA, Juan	PER	24	24	24	21	22	115
45	GIL, Marcelo	ARG	20	23	22	24	24	113
45	HAINS, Mel	RSA	23	22	23	22	23	113
45	KHORSHED, Mohamed	EGY	22	23	22	22	24	113
45	ROMERO, Francisco	GUA	21	25	22	23	22	113
49	al-QASEM, Mohammad	JOR	25	22	23	24	18	112
49	HAKEEM, Prince Abdul	BRU	23	21	23	24	21	112
49	HAMDY, Moustafa	EGY	20	22	24	22	24	112
49	MASKELL, Michael	BAR	22	22	23	22	23	112
53	CASWELL, Jason	CAN	23	19	24	22	23	111
54	KAW, Fun Ying	MAS	20	24	23	21	22	110

FINAL

Rnk	Name	Ctry	Qual pts	Final pts	Total	
1	FALCO, Ennio	ITA	125	24	149 O	Gold
2	RZEPKOWSKI, Miroslaw	POL	123	25	148	Silver
3	BENELLI, Andrea	ITA	123	24	147	Bronze
4	RASMUSSEN, Ole	DEN	122	25	147	
5	TIOPLIY, Nikolai	RUS	122	24	146	
6	TIMOFEJEVS, Boriss	LAT	122	23	145	

Shooting / *Tir*

10 m Running Target, Men / *Cible mobile à 10 m, Messieurs*

PRELIMINARIES

Rnk	Name	Ctry	s1	s2	s3	f1	f2	f3	Total
1	YANG, Ling	CHN	99	97	98	97	98	96	585 O
2	LYKINE, Dmitri	RUS	99	100	99	96	95	92	581
3	JANUS, Miroslav	CZE	97	99	96	95	95	98	580
4	SIKE, Jozsef	HUN	96	99	98	95	95	96	579
5	HOLMBERG, Krister	FIN	98	98	98	96	96	92	578
6	XIAO, Jun	CHN	95	99	95	93	98	97	577
7	ZIMMERMANN, Jens	GER	94	99	97	97	94	93	574
8	SOLTI, Attila	GUA	90	98	98	93	94	97	570
9	ERMOLENKO, Iouri	RUS	92	99	96	90	96	96	569
9	MOLDOVAN, Oleg	MDA	94	94	96	92	98	95	569
11	JAKOSITS, Michael	GER	89	98	99	95	91	96	568
12	RODNOV, Yuriy	KAZ	97	94	99	95	92	90	567
13	RACANSKY, Lubos	CZE	96	95	96	93	95	90	565
14	BURKUS, Tamas	HUN	91	96	98	87	95	97	564
15	AVRAMENKO, Hennadiy	UKR	96	98	93	90	92	94	563
15	HEKHT, Yevhen	UKR	92	91	99	95	96	90	563
17	COLOMBO, Carlo	ITA	95	93	100	88	90	96	562
18	KIM, Man-Chol	PRK	93	98	95	91	89	94	560
18	WILSON, Bryan	AUS	91	94	98	95	93	89	560
20	SAATHOFF, Adam	USA	89	96	91	93	90	96	555

FINAL

Rnk	Name	Ctry	Qual pts	Final pts	Total		
1	YANG, Ling	CHN	585	100.8	685.8 O	**Gold**
2	XIAO, Jun	CHN	577	102.8	679.8	**Silver**
3	JANUS, Miroslav	CZE	580	98.4	678.4	**Bronze**
4	SIKE, Jozsef	HUN	579	98.1	677.1	
5	LYKINE, Dmitri	RUS	581	95.7	676.7	
6	HOLMBERG, Krister	FIN	578	94.4	672.4	
7	ZIMMERMANN, Jens	GER	574	98.2	672.2	
8	SOLTI, Attila	GUA	570	97.0	667.0	

LENNY T WALKER • LINDA A WALKER • LINDA S WALKER • LISA C WALKER • LORENZA P WALKER • LORI R WALKER • LORI S WALKER • LUCILLE WALKER • LUCINDA WALKER • MALCOLM WALKER • MANDY WALKER • MARY J WALKER • MELANIE K WALKER • MICHAEL WALKER • MICHAEL L WALKER • MICHELE WALKER • MYRON C WALKER • NATHANIEL WALKER • PATRICIA WALKER • RANDALL W WALKER • RANDOLPH WALKER • RICHARD P WALKER • RICK F WALKER • ROBERT G WALKER • ROBIN M WALKER • SANDRA G WALKER • SANDRA L WALKER • SCOTT ANDREW WALKER • SHARON N WALKER • SHEILA I WALKER • SONDRA J WALKER • STEPHANIE C WALKER • STEPHEN M WALKER • STEVE WALKER • STEVEN H WALKER • SYLVIA E WALKER • TERRY R WALKER • THOMAS L WALKER • THOMAS W WALKER • TIMOTHY A WALKER • TIMOTHY M WALKER • VAN D WALKER • VAN DYKE A WALKER • VERNEST J WALKER • VICKI E WALKER • VIVIAN C WALKER • WILLARD L WALKER • WILLIAM B WALKER • WILLIAM D WALKER • WONDA J WALKER • ANNIE L WALKER-BRYANT • GUY O WALKER ATC • CURTIS WALKER JR • EARL M WALKER JR • ELVEN WALKER JR • MELFORD W WALKER JR • LEROY WALKER JR. • MICHAEL CHAZ WALKES • JOYCE A WALKO • MICHAEL C WALKO • BRENDA E WALL • DANA S WALL • DAPHNE D WALL • DEBORAH B WALL • DENNIS A WALL • DUSTIN Q WALL • KAREN K WALL • LOCHRAINE WALL • SANDRA P WALL • THERESE L WALL • TILDA P WALL • TIMOTHY E WALL ATC • DAVID M WALL PM • AKOLI M WALLACE • ALEX G WALLACE • ALICIA M WALLACE • BARBARA A WALLACE • BETH A WALLACE • BETTY J WALLACE • CARLETTA B WALLACE • CAROLE E WALLACE • CHARLES F WALLACE • CHRISTOPHER B WALLACE • CHRISTOPHER W WALLACE • DAVID L WALLACE • DIANA J WALLACE • DONALD L WALLACE • DOUGLAS W WALLACE • ELIZABETH H WALLACE • ERIC R WALLACE • GEORGE J WALLACE • GREGORY H WALLACE • JAMES H WALLACE • JANICE P WALLACE • JENNIFER C WALLACE • JOHN LEE WALLACE • JOHN M WALLACE • JON C WALLACE • KATHERINE M WALLACE • KAY Y WALLACE • KENNETH W WALLACE • KERI LEIGH WALLACE • LAURA S WALLACE • MARION E WALLACE • MARVIN E WALLACE • MATTHEW D WALLACE • MAXWELL C WALLACE • MICHELE A WALLACE • NANCY K WALLACE • PAIGE W WALLACE • PAMELA A WALLACE • RODERICK R WALLACE • ROSALIND W WALLACE • RUTHIE M WALLACE • SALLY A WALLACE • SANDRA G WALLACE • SHARON M WALLACE • SHERRY J WALLACE • SUZETTE M WALLACE • THOMAS H WALLACE • TIFFANY M WALLACE • VERIA D WALLACE • VICKI M WALLACE • SCOTT M WALLACH • KELLY MARIE WALLDEN • CAROL F WALLEN • DANIEL J WALLENBERG • ULLA B WALLENGREN • ERIC W WALLENS • BENNY E WALLER • DONNICE S WALLER • GAYNELLE S WALLER • JACK WALLER • JACK WALLER • JAMES K WALLER • JOHN W WALLER • KEITH E WALLER • KENNETH P WALLER • MARY A WALLER • MICHAEL N WALLER • TERESA A WALLER • TERRA M WALLER • VALORIE M WALLER • WILLIAM G WALLER JR • MAUREEN M WALLIN • SHERYL J WALLIN • JOHN WALLIS • LARRY O WALLIS • PILLIP WALLIS • MELISSA S WALLIS PT • ROBIN WALLNER • ARTHUR J WALLS • CARL M WALLS • CATHY A WALLS • CHUCK WALLS • DRUSILLA WALLS • KELLY K WALLS • LAURA D WALLS • LAURI L WALLS • STACEY A WALLS • GEORGE F WALRAVEN • ELIZABETH A WALSER • ANDREW J WALSH • BILLY J WALSH • DENISE C WALSH • DONAL WALSH • GERALDINE D WALSH • JANET L WALSH • JANET L WALSH • JEANETTE M WALSH • JOHN WALSH • JOHN P WALSH • JOHN P WALSH • JOSEPH M WALSH • KARYN M WALSH • KATHLEEN A WALSH • KELLY D WALSH • MAUREEN A WALSH • MEGHAN A. WALSH • MICHAEL T WALSH • SHAWN WALSH • TERRENCE W WALSH • THERESE E WALSH • THOMAS D WALSH • TIM WALSH • TIMOTHY M WALSH • DAVID A WALSH ATC • KATIE WALSH ATC • THOMAS F WALSH ATC • LEON G WALSH III • RICHARD L WALSMAN • VIRGINIA M WALSMAN • JAMES R WALSTON • SUZETTE WALSTON • BECKEY A WALTER • BRYANT WALTER • FRANCES C WALTER • JAMES N WALTER • LAMAR C WALTER • MARK A WALTER • MARY M WALTER • PAUL E WALTER • SARA E WALTER • WAYNE B WALTER • AMANDA E WALTERS • AMYE J WALTERS • BARBARA C WALTERS • BETTY S WALTERS • DELORES A WALTERS • DONALD H WALTERS • DOUGLAS WALTERS • FRANCES Y WALTERS • HOWARD W WALTERS • JAMES F WALTERS • JAMES M WALTERS • JOHN WALTERS • JOYCE A WALTERS • KAREN M WALTERS • KEVIN L WALTERS • LINDA M WALTERS • MARK H WALTERS • MERRILL D WALTERS • ROBERT C WALTERS • THOMAS A WALTERS • THOMAS A WALTERS • TIM WALTERS • CRAIG C WALTERS JR • CHARRHONDA P WALTHOUR • BARBARA D WALTON • CYNTHIA C WALTON • DORIS P WALTON • DWIGHT WALTON • FRANK G WALTON • GAIL M WALTON • GARY P WALTON • KATRINA L WALTON • KEITH D WALTON • KRISTEN W WALTON • MICHAEL A WALTON • PATRICIA R WALTON • STEPHFON J WALTON • TONI M WALTON • WILLIAM G WALTON • YVONNE WALTON • JENNIFER WALTON-DOBBINS • MERCER D WALTON III • OZANNA B WALTZ-ALLEN • GREGORY J WALZ • TAMMY WALZ • QUINCY W WALZER • ANDREW J WAMBERG • MEGAN M WAMBERG • PAMELA D WAMBERG • SUZANNE WAMBLE • MARCELLA WAMBOLD • CHARLIE WAMPLER • JUDY WAMPLER • PEI-CHUN T. WAN • FRANCES WAND •

CHUN C WANG • EDDIE S WANG • EUNHEE WANG • FEILING WANG • FRANK T WANG • HSIN-YU P WANG • HUI WANG • JENNY WANG • JIANGYAN WANG • LIH-JEN C WANG • LINBING WANG • LISA S WANG • MIAN WANG • RICHARD S WANG • ROMY H WANG • WENDY W WANG • XIAOYUN WANG • YI WANG • EMANUEL L WANI • RUAN E WANNENBURG • RICHARD S WANNINGER • GERALD S WANSLEY • JEFF T WANSLEY • ISAAC A WANTLAND • ROBERT G WANYANGE • MARY E WANYO • BERNICE L WARBINGTON • RONNIE R WARBINGTON • JAMES M WARBURTON • JOHN M WARBURTON • ADELE M WARD • ANDY P WARD • BENJAMIN N WARD • BRADLEY J WARD • BROOK S WARD • CHRYSTINE M WARD • CLEO B WARD • DEBORAH M WARD • DORIS M WARD • GAIL H WARD • GERALD P WARD • GREGORY A WARD • GREGORY M WARD • HARRIET A WARD • HASKELL G. WARD • JAMES L WARD • JASON S WARD • JOHN P WARD • JOSEPH T WARD • K. MARIE WARD • KENNETH A WARD • KURT WARD • LAREE WARD • LARRY W WARD • MARCI A WARD • MARCIA W WARD • MARLA E WARD • MARNIE L WARD • MELVIN L WARD • MIRIAM L. WARD • NANC A WARD • NAOMI K WARD • ORLANDO A WARD • PATRICIA A WARD • PATRICIA K WARD • PATTI S WARD • RAYMOND C WARD • RICHARD C WARD • RICK O WARD • ROGER WARD • SHIRLEY C WARD • TERRI M WARD • THERESA C WARD • THOMAS H WARD • TODD L WARD • TWELA E WARD • WARREN J WARD • WILLIAM WARD • KELLY P WARD ATC • JOHN A WARD III • DAVID E WARDELL • CALVIN A WARDLAW • DAVID E WARDLAW • DOUGLAS WARDLEY • ALICE LEE WARDREP • BRUCE N WARDREP • CHRISTOPHER B WARDROP • DIANE R WARDROP • A NELSON WARE • CAROL T WARE • CAROLE M WARE • CHARLES H WARE • DOROTHY J WARE • FRED JR WARE • GWENDOLYN WARE • JEAN C WARE • KELLY DEAN WARE • KIRK D WARE • KRISTINE L WARE • LILLIAN J WARE • LINDA P WARE • MARIE WARE • MARK W WARE • MICHAEL K WARE • MORRIS T WARE • SARAH L WARE • SHERRY R WARE • TODD D WARE • WENDY L WARE • WILLLAM J WARE • WYATT J WARE • PER-OLOF P WARENDH • CATHERINE A WARFIELD • GARY W WARFIELD • HEATHER A WARFIELD • RAJA D WARFIELD • DARRELL A WARGO • DARREN WARGO • JOANNE WARGO • ROBERT M WARGO • DORIAN S WARING • GEORGE O WARING • TERESA D WARLEY • FRANKLIN R WARLICK • NATHAN B WARMBROD • KARIN WARNECHE • SARAH H WARNECKE • ALAN D WARNER • AMANDA H WARNER • ANITA K WARNER • CATHERINE A WARNER • CPT. RANDY WARNER • DERRICK L WARNER • GREG WARNER • GREG WARNER • HOWARD D WARNER • JANICE M WARNER • JOANN J WARNER • JOSEPH R WARNER • LINDA L WARNER • MELVA B WARNER • PAMELA J WARNER • STEPHANIE M WARNER • STEPHEN G WARNER • V.FREESTON WARNER • VALENCIA J WARNER • VIRGINIA WARNER • WENDY L WARNER • WILLIAM M WARNER • ROBERT WARNOCK • WIMBERLY WARNOCK • WILLIAM L WARONKER • DORIS V WARPOLE • INELL P WARR • LINDA S WARR • JA NETTE L WARRELL PM • BRANDY L WARREN • BUCKY B WARREN • CATHY WARREN • CHARLOTTE WARREN • DAVID W WARREN • DAYN A WARREN • DONNA G WARREN • DOUGLAS E WARREN • ELLEN WARREN • FUQUAN G WARREN • GERALDINE WARREN • HELEN S WARREN • JAMES F WARREN • JAMES R WARREN • JEAN W WARREN • JEFFREY S WARREN • JOCELYN W WARREN • KERRY L WARREN • LAWANDA WARREN • LEE L WARREN • LILLIAN G WARREN • PATRICIA T WARREN • POLLY P WARREN • RAMONA G WARREN • RAYMOND C WARREN • ROSE M WARREN • SANDRA L. WARREN • SCOTT E WARREN • SHAYLA L WARREN • TAMMARA LYNN WARREN • TOMISHA C WARREN • VALERIE J WARREN • JAMES A WARREN JR • PATRICIA L WARRER • DOUGLAS R. WARRICK • ABDIGAFAR S. WARSAME • WARREN M WARSAW • JEFF D WARSHAW • AILA I WARTELL • ELIZABETH C WARWICK • DIANE WARYOLD • THOMAS WARYOLD • MARY ANN WARZECHA • DANIEL L WASH • ALICE B WASHBURN • SALLY O WASHBURN • WILLIAM WASHBURN • ALMA A WASHINGTON • ANGELO WASHINGTON • CAREY A WASHINGTON • CARMELITA Y WASHINGTON • CASSANDRA WASHINGTON • CHARLES L WASHINGTON • CHERYL Y WASHINGTON • DAVID WASHINGTON • DAVID C WASHINGTON • EDWARD WASHINGTON • EDWARD WASHINGTON • ELLA M WASHINGTON • EMMA L WASHINGTON • ERNESTINE G WASHINGTON • GREGORY J WASHINGTON • IRENE K WASHINGTON • JACQUELINE M WASHINGTON • JAMES H WASHINGTON • KATHLEEN L WASHINGTON • KOREY M WASHINGTON • LEE B WASHINGTON • LISA WASHINGTON • LISA F WASHINGTON • MARC A WASHINGTON • MARILYN D WASHINGTON • NATALIE WASHINGTON • NELLIE M WASHINGTON • NICOLE R WASHINGTON • PATRICIA A WASHINGTON • QUEEN S WASHINGTON • RELLAMICHELLE E WASHINGTON • RHODA K WASHINGTON • ROLAND WASHINGTON • SANDRA WASHINGTON • TERI WASHINGTON • TOMMY WASHINGTON • TRACEY C WASHINGTON • TROYE L WASHINGTON • WYATT WASHINGTON • YVONNE Y WASHINGTON • ODESSA WASHINGTON-WILLIAMS • CURTIS C WASHINGTON JR • CARL V WASHINGTON JR MD • MATTHEW D WASHLICK • TODD C WASHOWICH • MARK T WASIK • SHERYL A WASILEWSKI • ANDREW J WASKEY • MARTHA G WASKEY • JAMES E WASLASKI MT • LISA M WASLIS • MELISSA K WASOWSKI •

STEPHEN L WASSELL • JOSEPH WASSER • KATHLEEN G WASSERMAN • NEIL S WASSERMAN • KRIS A WASSERMANN • DEANA M WASSON • LISA WATANABE • STEPHANIE J WATCHORN • RICHARD WATERHOUSE • BRETT A WATERS • CARLA M WATERS • CARRIE P WATERS • CHRISTOPHER WATERS • DEBORAH L WATERS • DONNA M WATERS • EVA E WATERS • GEORGE C WATERS • JAMES J WATERS • JENNY P WATERS • JOE WATERS • JUDY A WATERS • JULE G WATERS • KAREN H WATERS • KATHLEEN R WATERS • LAKEISHA WATERS • LEE W WATERS • MARCUS L WATERS • MELANIE J WATERS • MELISSA C WATERS • MICHAEL WATERS • PHYLLIS E WATERS • RANDALL WATERS • RICHARD B WATERS • RITA B WATERS • ROBERTA WATERS • SHARON WATERS • SHARON A WATERS • SUSAN P WATERS • THOMAS J WATERS • ROBERT L WATERS III • RICKY R WATFORD • CHAD E WATKINS • ANDERSON WATKINS • ANDRETTA WATKINS • ANNA E WATKINS • ANNA S WATKINS • BARBARA J WATKINS • BRADFORD L WATKINS • CAROL A WATKINS • CASSANDRA N WATKINS • CECILIA M WATKINS • CHARLES H WATKINS • COLIN A WATKINS • COURTNEY A WATKINS • CURTIS WATKINS • CYNTHIA WATKINS • DAN L WATKINS • DEREK J WATKINS • DESMOND J WATKINS • DION J WATKINS • DORETTA H WATKINS • DORIS H WATKINS • EDWARD A WATKINS • ERIC H WATKINS • EVANGELINE O WATKINS • FRED WATKINS • GAYLE J WATKINS • GINGER WATKINS • HARRIETTE D WATKINS • HEATHER M WATKINS • JOHN M WATKINS • JOHNATHAN H WATKINS • JOSEPH R WATKINS • JUDITH A WATKINS • KEITH L WATKINS • KEN R WATKINS • LATRICE D WATKINS • MARCELLE COX WATKINS • MARGARET M WATKINS • MARIE G WATKINS • MARK E WATKINS • MICHAEL R WATKINS • MONA K WATKINS • MYRA ANN WATKINS • NANCY B WATKINS • NANCY L WATKINS • RAEANNE M WATKINS • SALLY R WATKINS • SUSAN G WATKINS • SUZANNE R WATKINS • VERA WATKINS • WALKER L WATKINS • WALTER WATKINS • WANDA L WATKINS • WILLIE M WATKINS • ZARA K WATKINS • GEORGE S WATKINS JR • SAMUEL S WATKINS JR • WILLIAM A WATKINS MD • JULIE A WATKINSON • RHONDA A WATLINGTON • MELVYN F WATMAN • ALAN K WATSON • BARBARA G WATSON • BENJAMIN A WATSON • BETH A WATSON • BETTY A WATSON • BONNIE J WATSON • BRANDI WATSON • BRIANNA M WATSON • BYRN A WATSON • CARLOS W WATSON • CONSTANCE W WATSON • DAVID L WATSON • DAWN A WATSON • DIANA B WATSON • DOROTHY A WATSON • DOUGLAS C WATSON • DUSTEANA S WATSON • ED WATSON • ELIJAH WATSON • FOY W WATSON • GLORIA B WATSON • GRETCHEN B WATSON • GWEN WATSON • JAY B WATSON • JOAN S WATSON • JOANNA M WATSON • JODY WATSON • JULIE A WATSON • KENNETH J WATSON • LEE A WATSON • LYDIA H WATSON • MADONNA A WATSON • MARY ANN H WATSON • MARY D. WATSON • MELISSA L WATSON • MICHAEL E WATSON • MICHELE A WATSON • NANCY H WATSON • NORMAN E WATSON • PATRICIA M WATSON • ROBERT C WATSON • ROBERT L WATSON • RUTH P WATSON • SANDRA J WATSON • SHERRIE M WATSON • SUSAN H WATSON • TAYLOR M WATSON • THOMAS C WATSON • TONY C WATSON • WADE W. WATSON • ROBERT W WATSON JR • THEODIS WATSON JR • DAVID T. WATSON M.D. • ADAM B WATTERS • BARBARA W WATTERS • CATHY A WATTERSON • ANNETTE WATTS • BUD WATTS • CHRISTINA P WATTS • FELICIA C WATTS • HEIDEMARIE C WATTS • INDI D WATTS • JAMES E WATTS • JOY P WATTS • KAREN M WATTS • LAURA A WATTS • LAWANDA WATTS • LENNY F WATTS • MARY D WATTS • MARY H WATTS • MICHAEL D WATTS • MITCHELL H WATTS • NATALIE A WATTS • POLLY B WATTS • REGGIE B WATTS • SUSAN T WATTS • TIM WATTS • KATHLENE M WATZ ATC • SARAH B WAUER • JEAN P WAUGAMAN • ROBERT T WAUGAMAN • LINDA L WAWRA • ALAN WAXMAN • LAUREN J WAY • BETH R WAYMAN • GERALD WAYMER • DAVID A WAYNE • JOAN WAYNE • VALETTA R WAYNE • ADILAH S WAZEERUDDIN • SULIEMAN A WAZEERUDDIN • ARDUINNE B WAZELLE • ANGELINE C WEAD • LAINIE WEADE • SONYA F WEAKLEY • TERRENCE D WEAKLEY • LISA A WEARING • CASSANDRA B WEATHERFORD • DONNA L WEATHERFORD • MELONIE L WEATHERFORD • RICHARD K WEATHERFORD • THERESA C WEATHERFORD • MARY E WEATHERLY • TARA M WEATHERLY • ALVIS M WEATHERLY JR • ANDREA D WEATHERS • BETTY F WEATHERS • CHARLES K WEATHERS • JAMES WEATHERS • MARK T WEATHERS • PATRICK WEATHERS • SIMON N WEATHERS • KIMBERLY J WEATHERSPOON • MICHELE C WEATHINGTON • SUSAN W WEATLEY • ALVIN X WEAVER • CATHERINE A WEAVER • CHERYL M WEAVER • CLARK E WEAVER • CONNIE R WEAVER • DAVID D WEAVER • DEBORAH B WEAVER • DENISE M WEAVER • DONALD C WEAVER • ELIZABETH M WEAVER • FRANCINE A WEAVER • FRED R WEAVER • GENEVA L WEAVER • GREG WEAVER • HOUSTON T WEAVER • HUGH W WEAVER • JACK M WEAVER • JAMES L WEAVER • JEAN C WEAVER • JEFFREY E WEAVER • JO BETH WEAVER • JOHN S WEAVER • JULIE M WEAVER • KAREN WEAVER • KENNETH G WEAVER • KRISTY L WEAVER • LETITIA N WEAVER • MARIDELL H WEAVER • MARK H WEAVER • MARY A WEAVER • PATRICK R WEAVER • PAUL R WEAVER • PHIL G WEAVER • RICHARD A WEAVER • SHANNON G WEAVER • SONYA A WEAVER • TERESA S WEAVER • THERESA M WEAVER • TIFFANY L WEAVER

SOFTBALL
SOFTBALL

Abbreviations and terms used in Softball results tables
Abréviations et termes employés dans les tableaux de résultats de softball

Term	English	Français
1B	First Base	Première base
2B	Second Base	Deuxième base
3B	Third Base	Troisième base
A	Assists	Assistances
AB	At Bats	A la batte
Asst. Coach	Asst. Coach	Entraîneur adjoint
BB	Bases On Balls	Bases sur balles
Bronze	Bronze Medal	Médaille de bronze
C	Catcher	Receveur
CF	Center Field	Champ centre
Coach	Coach	Entraîneur
DH	Designated Hitter	Frappeur désigné
E	Errors	Erreurs
ER	Earned Runs	Points mérités
Final	Final	Finale
Final Team Standings	Final Team Standings	Classement final par équipes
Games	Games	Matchs
Gold	Gold Medal	Médaille d'or
Grand Final	Grand Final	Grande finale
H	Hits	Coups sûrs
HP	Home Plate	Marbre
IP	Innings Pitched	Manches lancées
L	Losses	Pertes
LF	Left Field	Champ gauche
Losses	Losses	Pertes
P	Pitcher	Lanceur
PH	Pinch Hitter	Frappeur d'urgence
PO	Put Outs	Retraits
POS	Position	Position
PR	Pinch Runner	Coureur d'urgence
Pitcher	Pitcher	Lanceur
Preliminaries	Preliminaries	Eliminatoires
RF	Right Field	Champ droite
R	Runs	Points
RBI	Runs Batted In	Points produits
RF	Right Field	Champ droit
Runs Against	Runs Against	Points contre
Runs For	Runs For	Points pour
S	Saves	Sauvetages
SO	Strike Outs	Retraits sur 3 prises
SS	Short Stop	Arrêt-court
Semifinals	Semifinals	Demi-finales
Silver	Silver Medal	Médaille d'argent
Team	Team	Equipe
Team Standings— Preliminaries	Team Standings— Preliminaries	Classement par équipes — Eliminatoires
UMPIRES	Umpires	Arbitres
W/L/S	Wins/Losses/ Saves	Victoires/Pertes/ Sauvetages
W/L Avg	Win/Loss Average	Moyenne victoire/perte
W	Wins	Victoires
Wins	Wins	Victoires

International Softball Federation (ISF)
Fédération Internationale de Softball
2801 N.E. 50th Street
Oklahoma City, OK 73111-7203
USA

JAMES M WEAVER JR • BILLY E WEAVER MT • VICTORIA L WEBB • AMANDA A WEBB • AMANDA J WEBB • ANDREW J WEBB • ANNETTE F WEBB • BENJAMIN T WEBB • BOBBY WEBB • BRUCE A WEBB • CARMEN R WEBB • CHARLES L WEBB • CLAUDIA J WEBB • EMILY W WEBB • FRAN L WEBB • GILBERT S WEBB • HERSHEL D WEBB • HORACE P WEBB • JACQUELYN WEBB • JAMES V WEBB • JENNIFER G WEBB • JERRY W WEBB • JILLIAN WEBB • JUDITH B WEBB • JUDITH L WEBB • KIMBERLY L WEBB • LATISHA WEBB • MARGARET SUSAN WEBB • MARY C WEBB • MARY N WEBB •

353

Softball / *Softball*
Women / *Dames*

PRELIMINARIES   PUR 0   USA 10

Team	1	2	3	4	5	6	7	8	9	R	H	E
PUR	0	0	0	0	0	0				0	2	3
USA	2	0	3	0	0	5				10	13	0

TEAM: PUR Puerto Rico
Coach: AGOSTO, Jose   Asst. Coach: NIEVES, Jacinto

Batters	POS	AB	R	H	RBI	BB	SO	PO	A
BAEZ, Lourdes	2B	2	0	0	0	1	1	3	4
VAZQUEZ, Clara	LF	3	0	2	0	0	0	3	0
PARKS, Janice	DH	3	0	0	0	0	2	0	0
ORTIZ, Jaqueline	RF	2	0	0	0	0	1	1	0
GONZALEZ, Maria	CF	2	0	0	0	0	1	1	1
SEGARRA, Myriam	1B	2	0	0	0	0	1	8	0
ROSARIO, Sandra	C	2	0	0	0	0	0	0	2
SOTO, Eve	3B	2	0	0	0	0	2	1	1
MARTINEZ, Lisa	P	1	0	0	0	0	1	0	0
MIZE, Lisa	P	1	0	0	0	0	1	0	0
MIRANDA, Aida	SS	0	0	0	0	0	0	0	4
Totals		20	0	2	0	1	10	17	12

Pitchers	W/L/S	IP	H	R	ER	BB	SO
MARTINEZ, Lisa	L	2 1/3	7	5	4	1	0
MIZE, Lisa		3 1/3	6	5	2	2	0
Totals		5 2/3	13	10	6	3	0

TEAM: USA United States of America
Coach: RAYMOND, Ralph   Asst. Coach: WRIGHT, Marjorie

Batters	POS	AB	R	H	RBI	BB	SO	PO	A
RICHARDSON, Dorothy	SS	4	2	2	1	0	0	0	2
SMITH, Julie	2B	3	0	0	0	0	0	1	0
FERNANDEZ, Lisa	3B	3	3	2	1	1	0	0	1
MAHER, Kim Ly	LF	4	1	2	0	0	0	0	0
CORNELL, Sheila	1B	4	1	2	1	0	0	5	0
HARRIS, Dionna	PR	0	1	0	0	0	0	0	0
SMITH, Michele	DH	3	1	1	1	1	0	0	0
BOXX, Gillian	C	4	1	2	2	0	0	10	0
O'BRIEN, Leah	RF	3	0	2	0	1	0	1	1
BERG, Laura	CF	2	0	0	0	0	0	1	0
GRANGER, Michele	P	0	0	0	0	0	0	0	0
Totals		30	10	13	6	3	0	18	4

Pitcher	W/L/S	IP	H	R	ER	BB	SO
GRANGER, Michele	W	6	2	0	0	1	10
Totals		6	2	0	0	1	10

UMPIRES

HP	STERKENBURG, Rene	NED
1B	LINDBERG, Geralyn	SWE
2B	STAUBLE, Clifford	CAN
3B	PERALTA, Roberto	PAN

PRELIMINARIES   TPE 1   CAN 2

Team	1	2	3	4	5	6	7	8	9	10	R	H	E
TPE	0	1	0	0	0	0	0	0	0	0	1	5	1
CAN	0	0	0	0	0	0	1	0	0	1	2	8	3

TEAM: TPE Chinese Taipei
Coach: WANG, Cheng-Fu   Asst. Coach: CHANG CHIEN, Chin-Ling

Batters	POS	AB	R	H	RBI	BB	SO	PO	A
CHIEN, Chen Ju	LF	3	0	0	0	1	0	1	0
YEN, Show-Tzu	3B	3	0	0	0	0	0	4	1
CHUNG, Chiung Yao	DH	4	0	0	0	0	2	0	0
WANG, Ya-Fen	SS	3	1	2	0	0	0	3	1
YANG, Hui-Chun	C	4	0	1	0	0	0	9	0
LEE, Ming-Chieh	2B	3	0	1	0	0	0	1	1
LIU, Tzu Hsin	CF	4	0	1	0	0	1	4	0
CHIEN, Pei-Chi	1B	3	0	0	0	0	0	4	0
CHANG, Nsiao-Chi	PH	1	0	0	0	0	0	0	0
LIU, Chia Chi	RF	3	0	0	0	0	1	3	0
OU, Ching Chieh	PH	1	0	0	0	0	0	0	0
TU, Hui-Mei	P	0	0	0	0	0	0	0	0
TU, Hui-Ping	P	0	0	0	0	0	0	0	0
Totals		32	1	5	0	1	4	29	3

Pitchers	W/L/S	IP	H	R	ER	BB	SO
TU, Hui-Mei		2	3	0	0	1	1
TU, Hui-Ping	L	7 2/3	5	2	0	0	8
Totals		9 2/3	8	2	0	1	9

TEAM: CAN Canada
Coach: KENNEDY, Lesle   Asst. Coach: STANIFORTH, Brenda

Batters	POS	AB	R	H	RBI	BB	SO	PO	A
MAURICE, Pauline	CF	5	0	3	1	0	0	3	0
VAIRO, Carmelina	2B	4	0	2	0	0	2	3	2
PARRIS-WASHINGTON, Christine	3B	5	0	1	1	0	0	2	3
DOELL, Karen	DH	3	0	0	0	1	0	0	0
STEPHENSON, Alecia	SS	4	0	0	0	0	3	2	3
CLAYTON, Juanita	C	4	0	0	0	0	1	5	2
KELLAND, Kelly	1B	4	0	1	0	0	1	11	0
MURRAY, Candace	PR	0	1	0	0	0	0	0	0
THORBURN, Colleen	LF	4	1	1	0	0	1	1	1
McGAW, Kara	RF	3	0	0	0	0	0	3	0
BEASLEY, Sandra	PH	1	0	0	0	0	1	0	0
SONNENBERG, Debbie	P	0	0	0	0	0	0	0	1
SIPPEL, Lori	P	0	0	0	0	0	0	0	0
Totals		37	2	8	2	1	9	30	13

Pitchers	W/L/S	IP	H	R	ER	BB	SO
SONNENBERG, Debbie		5	4	1	0	1	2
SIPPEL, Lori	W	5	1	0	0	0	2
Totals		10	5	1	0	1	4

UMPIRES

HP	JOHNSON, Julie	USA
1B	McAULIFFE, Alan	AUS
2B	KATO, Kenzo	JPN
3B	STRAHM, Kathy	USA

PRELIMINARIES   CHN 6   AUS 0

Team	1	2	3	4	5	6	7	8	9	R	H	E
CHN	2	0	0	1	0	0	3			6	6	0
AUS	0	0	0	0	0	0	0			0	2	0

TEAM: CHN People's Republic of China
Coach: LI, Minkuan   Asst. Coach: LIU, Yaming

Batters	POS	AB	R	H	RBI	BB	SO	PO	A
ZHANG, Chunfang	CF	3	1	1	0	0	1	1	0
YAN, Fang	2B	2	0	1	0	0	1	0	4
LIU, Xuqing	SS	2	1	0	0	1	2	1	2
WANG, Ying	1B	2	1	1	2	0	0	7	0
TAO, Hua	3B	2	1	1	1	1	1	1	0
AN, Zhongxin	C	3	1	1	0	0	1	10	0
OU, Jingbai	DH	2	0	0	0	0	2	0	0
XU, Jian	PH	1	0	0	0	0	0	0	0
	DH	0	0	0	0	0	0	0	0
CHEN, Hong	LF	3	0	0	0	1	1	0	0
WEI, Qiang	RF	3	1	1	3	0	2	2	0
WANG, Lihong	P	0	0	0	0	0	0	0	1
Totals		23	6	6	6	3	11	21	7

Pitcher	W/L/S	IP	H	R	ER	BB	SO
WANG, Lihong	W	7	2	0	0	1	10
Totals		7	2	0	0	1	10

TEAM: AUS Australia
Coach: CRUDGINGTON, Robert   Asst. Coach: PEEL, Carole

Batters	POS	AB	R	H	RBI	BB	SO	PO	A
McRAE, Francine	RF	3	0	0	0	0	1	0	0
LESTER, Jocelyn	C	1	0	0	0	0	1	6	0
DIENELT, Kerry	C	1	0	0	0	1	0	4	3
McDERMID, Sally	3B	3	0	0	0	0	0	0	0
HARDING, Tanya	DH	3	0	1	0	0	1	0	0
WARD, Natalie	2B	3	0	0	0	0	2	4	2
PETRIE, Haylea	CF	2	0	0	0	0	2	1	1
BROWN, Joanne	1B	2	0	1	0	0	1	5	0
RICHARDSON, Nicole	LF	2	0	0	0	0	1	0	0
COOPER, Kim	SS	2	0	0	0	0	1	1	0
ROCHE, Melanie	P	0	0	0	0	0	0	0	1
WILKINS, Brooke	P	0	0	0	0	0	0	0	1
CRUDGINGTON, Carolyn	P	0	0	0	0	0	0	0	0
Totals		22	0	2	0	1	10	21	8

Pitchers	W/L/S	IP	H	R	ER	BB	SO
ROCHE, Melanie	L	3	2	2	2	0	6
WILKINS, Brooke		3	2	1	1	2	3
CRUDGINGTON, Carolyn		1	2	3	3	1	2
Totals		7	6	6	6	3	11

UMPIRES

HP	ALEXANDER, Emily	USA
1B	CARMICHAEL, Lucie	CAN
2B	STERKENBURG, Rene	NED
3B	HANSEN, Jeffrey	USA

Women / *Dames*

PRELIMINARIES — JPN 3 NED 0

Team	1	2	3	4	5	6	7	8	9	R	H	E
JPN	0	0	0	0	0	0	3			3	7	0
NED	0	0	0	0	0	0	0			0	2	0

TEAM: JPN Japan
Coach: SUZUMURA, Mitsutoshi   Asst. Coach: NAGASAWA, Hiroyuki

Batters	POS	AB	R	H	RBI	BB	SO	PO	A
INOUE, Mayumi	LF	3	0	0	0	0	0	0	0
HARADA, Noriko	2B	3	0	1	0	0	0	3	2
FUKITA, Ikuko	PH	1	0	0	0	0	0	0	0
ANDO, Misako	SS	2	0	0	0	1	0	1	2
SAITO, Haruka	1B	3	0	0	0	0	0	8	0
FUJIMOTO, Yoshiko	DH	3	1	2	1	0	0	0	0
YAMAJI, Noriko	C	3	1	1	1	0	0	8	0
KODAMA, Chika	3B	3	0	0	0	0	0	1	2
MATSUMOTO, Naomi	RF	2	0	0	0	0	1	0	0
MOCHIDA, Kyoko	PH	1	1	1	1	0	0	0	0
TSUKADA, Emi	CF	3	0	2	0	0	1	0	0
TAKAYAMA, Juri	P	0	0	0	0	0	0	0	3
Totals		27	3	7	3	1	2	21	9

Pitcher	W/L/S	IP	H	R	ER	BB	SO
TAKAYAMA, Juri	W	7	2	0	0	1	7
Totals		7	2	0	0	1	7

TEAM: NED Netherlands
Coach: ELFERS, Rudolf   Asst. Coach: WEDMAN, Donald

Batters	POS	AB	R	H	RBI	BB	SO	PO	A
BEEK, Madelon	RF	3	0	0	0	0	1	1	0
REIJNEN, Gerardina	2B	3	0	0	0	0	0	1	0
van der PUTTEN, Maria	DH	3	0	0	0	0	2	0	0
BEEK, Petra	SS	2	0	1	0	1	0	2	3
de HEER, Jacqueline	3B	3	0	0	0	0	2	0	3
GEELS, Luciene	1B	2	0	1	0	0	0	12	0
STIEMER, Martine	CF	2	0	0	0	0	0	1	0
NIEUWVEEN, Sandra	C	2	0	0	0	0	0	2	0
de JONG, Marjolein	LF	2	0	0	0	0	2	2	0
MELS, Anouk	P	0	0	0	0	0	0	0	2
PANNEN, Sonja	P	0	0	0	0	0	0	0	1
Totals		22	0	2	0	1	7	21	9

Pitchers	W/L/S	IP	H	R	ER	BB	SO
MELS, Anouk	L	6	5	2	2	1	2
PANNEN, Sonja		1	2	1	1	0	0
Totals		7	7	3	3	1	2

UMPIRES
HP	HORNAK, Michael	CAN
1B	PERALTA, Roberto	PAN
2B	STAUBLE, Clifford	CAN
3B	JOHNSON, Julie	USA

PRELIMINARIES — AUS 4 TPE 0

Team	1	2	3	4	5	6	7	8	9	R	H	E
AUS	0	1	2	1	0	0	0			4	7	0
TPE	0	0	0	0	0	0	0			0	4	0

TEAM: AUS Australia
Coach: CRUDGINGTON, Robert   Asst. Coach: PEEL, Carole

Batters	POS	AB	R	H	RBI	BB	SO	PO	A
COOPER, Kim	SS	3	0	0	0	1	0	1	2
LESTER, Jocelyn	DH	2	1	1	0	0	0	0	0
McRAE, Francine	RF	3	0	0	0	0	0	0	0
McDERMID, Sally	3B	3	1	1	2	0	0	0	0
WARD, Natalie	2B	3	0	0	0	0	0	2	4
BROWN, Joanne	1B	3	1	1	1	0	1	5	0
	C	0	0	0	0	0	0	4	0
DIENELT, Kerry	C	1	1	1	1	0	0	2	0
CRUDGINGTON, Carolyn	PR	1	0	0	0	0	0	0	0
	1B	0	0	0	0	0	0	6	0
RICHARDSON, Nicole	LF	3	0	1	0	0	0	0	0
PETRIE, Haylea	CF	3	0	2	0	0	0	2	0
HOLLIDAY, Jennifer	P	0	0	0	0	0	0	0	1
HARDING, Tanya	P	0	0	0	0	0	0	0	1
Totals		25	4	7	4	1	1	22	8

Pitchers	W/L/S	IP	H	R	ER	BB	SO
HOLLIDAY, Jennifer		1 1/3	2	0	0	2	0
HARDING, Tanya	W	5 2/3	2	0	0	0	6
Totals		7	4	0	0	2	6

TEAM: TPE Chinese Taipei
Coach: WANG, Cheng-Fu   Asst. Coach: CHANG CHIEN, Chin-Ling

Batters	POS	AB	R	H	RBI	BB	SO	PO	A
CHIEN, Chen Ju	LF	4	0	0	0	0	1	1	0
LEE, Ming-Chieh	2B	3	0	0	0	0	0	4	3
YANG, Hui-Chun	C	2	0	1	0	1	1	1	0
WANG, Ya-Fen	SS	3	0	2	0	0	0	3	4
OU, Ching Chieh	RF	3	0	1	0	0	2	0	0
CHUNG, Chiung Yao	DH	4	0	0	0	0	0	0	0
YEN, Show-Tzu	3B	2	0	0	0	1	0	1	2
CHIEN, Pei-Chi	1B	3	0	0	0	0	2	9	0
LIU, Tzu Hsin	CF	2	0	0	0	0	0	1	0
HAN, Hsin Lin	P	0	0	0	0	0	0	0	1
CHIU, Chen Ting	P	0	0	0	0	0	0	0	0
TU, Hui-Mei	P	0	0	0	0	0	0	0	2
Totals		26	0	4	0	2	6	20	12

Pitchers	W/L/S	IP	H	R	ER	BB	SO
HAN, Hsin Lin	L	2	3	2	2	1	1
CHIU, Chen Ting		1	2	2	2	0	0
TU Hui-Mei		4	2	0	0	0	0
Totals		7	7	4	4	1	1

UMPIRES
HP	STRAHM, Kathy	USA
1B	STERKENBURG, Rene	NED
2B	CARMICHAEL, Lucie	CAN
3B	HORNAK, Michael	CAN

PRELIMINARIES — CHN 0 JPN 3

Team	1	2	3	4	5	6	7	8	9	R	H	E
CHN	0	0	0	0	0	0	0			0	6	0
JPN	0	0	0	0	0	3	–			3	5	1

TEAM: CHN People's Republic of China
Coach: LI, Minkuan   Asst. Coach: LIU, Yaming

Batters	POS	AB	R	H	RBI	BB	SO	PO	A
ZHANG, Chunfang	CF	3	0	1	0	1	0	0	0
YAN, Fang	2B	4	0	0	0	0	1	1	0
LIU, Xuqing	SS	3	0	0	0	0	0	0	0
WANG, Ying	1B	3	0	1	0	0	1	3	0
TAO, Hua	3B	3	0	0	0	0	0	1	2
AN, Zhongxin	C	3	0	0	0	0	1	12	2
OU, Jingbai	DH	3	0	2	0	0	0	0	0
CHEN, Hong	LF	3	0	2	0	0	0	1	0
LEI, Li	PR	0	0	0	0	0	0	0	0
WEI, Qiang	RF	1	0	0	0	0	0	0	0
	PR	0	0	0	0	0	0	0	0
XU, Jian	PH	1	0	0	0	0	0	0	0
WANG, Lihong	P	0	0	0	0	0	0	0	0
LIU, Yaju	P	0	0	0	0	0	0	0	0
Totals		27	0	6	0	1	3	18	4

Pitchers	W/L/S	IP	H	R	ER	BB	SO
WANG, Lihong	L	5 2/3	5	3	3	2	12
LIU, Yaju		1/3	0	0	0	0	0
Totals		6	5	3	3	2	12

TEAM: JPN Japan
Coach: SUZUMURA, Mitsutoshi   Asst. Coach: NAGASAWA, Hiroyuki

Batters	POS	AB	R	H	RBI	BB	SO	PO	A
ANDO, Misako	SS	3	0	0	0	0	2	1	5
INOUE, Mayumi	LF	3	1	1	0	0	1	4	0
FUJIMOTO, Yoshiko	DH	2	1	1	0	1	1	0	0
YAMAJI, Noriko	C	2	0	1	2	1	1	3	0
FUKITA, Ikuko	PR	0	0	0	0	0	0	0	0
TSUKADA, Emi	CF	2	0	0	0	0	2	0	0
MOCHIDA, Kyoko	PH	1	0	0	0	0	1	0	0
SAITO, Haruka	1B	3	0	1	1	0	1	7	0
KODAMA, Chika	3B	2	0	0	0	0	2	2	2
MATSUMOTO, Naomi	RF	2	0	0	0	1	1	1	0
HARADA, Noriko	2B	2	1	1	0	0	0	3	0
WATANABE, Tomoko	P	0	0	0	0	0	0	0	0
Totals		22	3	5	3	2	12	21	7

Pitcher	W/L/S	IP	H	R	ER	BB	SO
WATANABE, Tomoko	W	7	6	0	0	1	3
Totals		7	6	0	0	1	3

UMPIRES
HP	McAULIFFE, Alan	AUS
1B	ALEXANDER, Emily	USA
2B	JOHNSON, Julie	USA
3B	LINDBERG, Geralyn	SWE

PRELIMINARIES PUR 0 CAN 4

Team	1	2	3	4	5	6	7	8	9	R	H	E
PUR	0	0	0	0	0	0	0			0	2	1
CAN	0	0	0	0	0	4	–			4	4	0

TEAM: PUR Puerto Rico

Coach: AGOSTO, Jose   Asst. Coach: NIEVES, Jacinto

Batters	POS	AB	R	H	RBI	BB	SO	PO	A
BAEZ, Lourdes	2B	3	0	0	0	0	2	2	0
VAZQUEZ, Clara	LF	2	0	1	0	0	0	3	0
PARKS, Janice	SS	3	0	0	0	0	2	1	2
ORTIZ, Jaqueline	RF	3	0	0	0	0	2	0	0
GONZALEZ, Maria	CF	2	0	0	0	0	2	2	0
SEGARRA, Myriam	1B	2	0	0	0	0	2	8	0
ROSARIO, Sandra	C	3	0	1	0	0	0	2	0
LEBRON, Elba	PR	0	0	0	0	0	0	0	0
CORNIEL, Sheree	DH	2	0	0	0	1	1	0	0
SOTO, Eve	3B	2	0	0	0	0	2	0	3
ECHEVARRIA, Ivelisse	P	0	0	0	0	0	0	0	4
Totals		22	0	2	0	1	13	18	9

Pitcher	W/L/S	IP	H	R	ER	BB	SO
ECHEVARRIA, Ivelisse	L	6	4	4	0	3	1
Totals		6	4	4	0	3	1

TEAM: CAN Canada

Coach: KENNEDY, Lesle   Asst. Coach: STANIFORTH, Brenda

Batters	POS	AB	R	H	RBI	BB	SO	PO	A
MAURICE, Pauline	CF	3	0	1	0	0	0	0	0
THORBURN, Colleen	LF	3	1	1	0	0	0	0	0
PARRIS-WASHINGTON, Christine	3B	2	1	0	0	1	0	0	1
DOELL, Karen	DH	3	0	1	0	0	0	0	0
STEPHENSON, Alecia	SS	2	1	0	1	1	0	4	1
MURRAY, Candace	2B	3	0	1	2	0	1	1	0
KELLAND, Kelly	1B	2	0	0	0	1	0	4	1
FLEMMER, Carrie	C	3	0	0	0	0	0	12	2
McGAW, Kara	RF	2	1	0	0	0	0	0	0
SNELGROVE, Karen	P	0	0	0	0	0	0	0	0
SONNENBERG, Debbie	P	0	0	0	0	0	0	0	0
Totals		23	4	4	3	3	1	21	5

Pitchers	W/L/S	IP	H	R	ER	BB	SO
SNELGROVE, Karen	W	6	2	0	0	1	12
SONNENBERG, Debbie		1	0	0	0	0	1
Totals		7	2	0	0	1	13

UMPIRES

HP	PERALTA, Roberto	PAN
1B	HANSEN, Jeffrey	USA
2B	HORNAK, Michael	CAN
3B	CARMICHAEL, Lucie	CAN

PRELIMINARIES NED 0 USA 9

Team	1	2	3	4	5	6	7	8	9	R	H	E
NED	0	0	0	0	0	0	0			0	2	3
USA	0	5	0	3	1	0	–			9	10	1

TEAM: NED Netherlands

Coach: ELFERS, Rudolf   Asst. Coach WEDMAN, Donald

Batters	POS	AB	R	H	RBI	BB	SO	PO	A
BEEK, Madelon	LF	3	0	0	0	0	3	1	0
REIJNEN, Gerardina	2B	3	0	0	0	0	0	4	3
van der PUTTEN, Maria	DH	3	0	0	0	0	1	0	0
BEEK, Petra	SS	3	0	0	0	0	1	2	1
de HEER, Jacqueline	3B	3	0	0	0	0	1	0	0
GEELS, Luciene	1B	2	0	0	0	1	0	5	0
STIEMER, Martine	RF	2	0	0	0	1	2	1	0
NIEUWVEEN, Sandra	C	3	0	1	0	0	1	3	0
KOSSEN, Anita	CF	2	0	1	0	0	1	2	0
KNOL, Jacqueline	P	0	0	0	0	0	0	0	1
PANNEN, Sonja	P	0	0	0	0	0	0	0	0
Totals		24	0	2	0	2	10	18	5

Pitchers	W/L/S	IP	H	R	ER	BB	SO
KNOL, Jacqueline	L	1 1/3	4	5	5	1	0
PANNEN, Sonja		4 2/3	6	4	3	1	3
Totals		6	10	9	8	2	3

TEAM: USA United States of America

Coach: RAYMOND, Ralph   Asst. Coach: WRIGHT, Marjorie

Batters	POS	AB	R	H	RBI	BB	SO	PO	A
RICHARDSON, Dorothy	SS	4	1	1	3	0	1	0	2
TYLER, Danielle	2B	4	1	2	0	0	1	0	2
FERNANDEZ, Lisa	3B	4	0	1	0	0	0	1	2
MAHER, Kim Ly	LF	3	1	0	0	1	0	1	0
CORNELL, Sheila	1B	3	2	2	3	0	0	7	0
SMITH, Michele	DH	3	1	1	1	0	0	0	0
HARRIS, Dionna	RF	3	2	3	1	0	0	0	0
BERG, Laura	CF	2	0	0	0	0	0	2	0
STOKES, Shelly	C	2	1	0	0	1	1	10	0
WILLIAMS, Christa Lee	P	0	0	0	0	0	0	0	1
Totals		28	9	10	8	2	3	21	7

Pitcher	W/L/S	IP	H	R	ER	BB	SO
WILLIAMS, Christa Lee	W	7	2	0	0	2	10
Totals		7	2	0	0	2	10

UMPIRES

HP	STAUBLE, Clifford	CAN
1B	KATO, Kenzo	JPN
2B	STRAHM, Kathy	USA
3B	McAULIFFE, Alan	AUS

PRELIMINARIES CHN 2 CAN 1

Team	1	2	3	4	5	6	7	8	9	R	H	E
CHN	2	0	0	0	0	0	0			2	5	1
CAN	0	0	1	0	0	0	0			1	5	2

TEAM: CHN People's Republic of China

Coach: LI, Minkuan   Asst. Coach: LIU, Yaming

Batters	POS	AB	R	H	RBI	BB	SO	PO	A
ZHANG, Chunfang	CF	3	1	1	0	0	0	0	0
YAN, Fang	2B	2	1	0	0	0	0	0	2
LIU, Xuqing	SS	3	0	0	0	0	1	1	3
WANG, Ying	1B	3	0	1	0	0	0	7	0
TAO, Hua	3B	3	0	0	0	0	0	0	0
CHEN, Hong	LF	2	0	0	0	1	1	0	0
AN, Zhongxin	C	3	0	2	0	0	0	13	0
WEI, Qiang	RF	3	0	0	0	0	2	0	0
LEI, Li	DH	2	0	1	0	0	1	0	0
XU, Jian	PH	1	0	0	0	0	0	0	0
	DH	0	0	0	0	0	0	0	0
LIU, Yaju	P	0	0	0	0	0	0	0	1
WANG, Lihong	P	0	0	0	0	0	0	0	1
Totals		25	2	5	0	1	5	21	7

Pitchers	W/L/S	IP	H	R	ER	BB	SO
LIU, Yaju		2	3	1	0	0	4
WANG, Lihong	W	5	2	0	0	2	9
Totals		7	5	1	0	2	13

TEAM: CAN Canada

Coach: KENNEDY, Lesle   Asst. Coach: STANIFORTH, Brenda

Batters	POS	AB	R	H	RBI	BB	SO	PO	A
MAURICE, Pauline	CF	3	0	0	0	1	1	1	1
VAIRO, Carmelina	2B	4	0	0	0	0	3	3	2
PARRIS-WASHINGTON, Christine	3B	3	0	0	0	0	2	1	1
DOELL, Karen	DH	3	0	1	0	0	0	0	0
CLAYTON, Juanita	C	3	0	0	0	0	2	5	0
STEPHENSON, Alecia	SS	2	0	0	0	0	2	1	2
BEASLEY, Sandra	PH	1	0	0	0	0	0	0	0
KELLAND, Kelly	1B	2	1	1	0	1	0	7	0
MURRAY, Candace	PR	0	0	0	0	0	0	0	0
THORBURN, Colleen	LF	3	0	2	0	0	1	0	0
McGAW, Kara	RF	3	0	1	0	0	2	3	0
SIPPEL, Lori	P	0	0	0	0	0	0	0	1
Totals		27	1	5	0	2	13	21	7

Pitcher	W/L/S	IP	H	R	ER	BB	SO
SIPPEL, Lori	L	7	5	2	1	1	5
Totals		7	5	2	1	1	5

UMPIRES

HP	HANSEN, Jeffrey	USA
1B	STRAHM, Kathy	USA
2B	STERKENBURG, Rene	NED
3B	KATO, Kenzo	JPN

Women / *Dames*

PRELIMINARIES — TPE 7 NED 1

Team	1	2	3	4	5	6	7	8	9	R	H	E
TPE	0	0	0	0	0	5	2			7	12	0
NED	0	0	0	0	1	0	0			1	6	1

TEAM: TPE Chinese Taipei
Coach: WANG, Cheng-Fu   Asst. Coach: CHANG CHIEN, Chin-Ling

Batters	POS	AB	R	H	RBI	BB	SO	PO	A
CHIEN, Chen Ju	LF	4	0	1	1	0	0	1	0
LEE, Ming-Chieh	2B	3	1	1	0	0	0	1	4
YANG, Hui-Chun	C	3	2	2	0	1	1	7	0
WANG, Ya-Fen	SS	3	0	2	0	0	0	4	2
CHUNG, Chiung Yao	DH	2	2	0	0	1	0	0	0
LIU, Chia Chi	RF	0	0	0	1	0	0	0	0
OU, Ching Chieh	PH	3	1	1	4	0	1	0	0
	RF	0	0	0	0	0	0	0	1
LIU, Tzu Hsin	CF	3	1	2	1	1	0	1	0
CHIEN, Pei-Chi	1B	4	0	2	0	0	1	7	0
CHANG, Nsiao-Ching	3B	1	0	0	0	0	0	0	1
YEN, Show-Tzu	PH	3	0	1	0	0	0	0	0
	3B	3	0	0	0	0	0	0	1
TU, Hui-Mei	P	0	0	0	0	0	0	0	1
TU, Hui-Ping	P	0	0	0	0	0	0	0	0
Totals		29	7	12	7	3	3	21	10

Pitchers	W/L/S	IP	H	R	ER	BB	SO
TU, Hui-Mei	W	5 1/3	5	1	1	1	5
TU, Hui-Ping		1 2/3	1	0	0	1	0
Totals		7	6	1	1	2	5

TEAM: NED Netherlands
Coach: ELFERS, Rudolf   Asst. Coach: WEDMAN, Donald

Batters	POS	AB	R	H	RBI	BB	SO	PO	A
BEEK, Madelon	RF	2	0	0	0	0	1	2	0
	PH	0	0	0	0	0	0	0	0
KOSSEN, Anita	PH	2	0	0	0	0	1	0	0
	CF	0	0	0	0	0	0	0	0
REIJNEN, Gerardina	2B	3	0	1	0	0	0	1	6
OCKHUYSEN, Corrine	PH	1	0	0	0	0	0	0	0
van der PUTTEN, Maria	DH	2	0	1	0	1	1	0	0
BEEK, Petra	SS	3	0	1	0	0	1	2	2
de HEER, Jacqueline	3B	3	0	0	0	0	0	1	0
GEELS, Luciene	1B	3	1	1	0	0	0	8	0
STIEMER, Martine	CF	3	0	1	0	0	1	0	0
	RF	0	0	0	0	0	0	0	1
NIEUWVEEN, Sandra	C	2	0	1	1	1	0	5	1
de JONG, Marjolein	LF	1	0	0	0	0	0	2	1
le NOBLE, Penny	PH	1	0	0	0	0	0	0	0
MELS, Anouk	P	0	0	0	0	0	0	0	2
PANNEN, Sonja	P	0	0	0	0	0	0	0	0
KNOL, Jacqueline	P	0	0	0	0	0	0	0	0
Totals		26	1	6	1	2	5	21	13

Pitchers	W/L/S	IP	H	R	ER	BB	SO
MELS, Anouk	L	6	8	5	4	2	3
PANNEN, Sonja		0	2	2	2	1	0
KNOL, Jacqueline		1	2	0	0	0	0
Totals		7	12	7	6	3	3

UMPIRES
HP	LINDBERG, Geralyn	SWE
1B	JOHNSON, Julie	USA
2B	ALEXANDER, Emily	USA
3B	STAUBLE, Clifford	CAN

PRELIMINARIES — JPN 1 USA 6

Team	1	2	3	4	5	6	7	8	9	R	H	E
JPN	0	0	0	0	1	0	0			1	3	1
USA	3	0	0	0	0	3	–			6	10	0

TEAM: JPN Japan
Coach: SUZUMURA, Mitsutoshi   Asst. Coach: NAGASAWA, Hiroyuki

Batters	POS	AB	R	H	RBI	BB	SO	PO	A
ANDO, Misako	SS	2	0	1	0	1	0	2	2
INOUE, Mayumi	LF	2	0	0	0	0	0	1	0
MOCHIDA, Kyoko	PH	1	0	0	0	0	1	0	0
FUJIMOTO, Yoshiko	DH	3	0	0	0	0	3	0	0
YAMAJI, Noriko	C	2	0	0	0	0	1	4	2
TSUKADA, Emi	CF	2	0	0	0	0	1	2	0
SAITO, Haruka	1B	3	1	1	1	0	0	4	1
KODAMA, Chika	3B	2	0	0	0	0	0	1	2
FUKITA, Ikuko	PH	1	0	0	0	0	1	0	0
MATSUMOTO, Naomi	RF	3	0	1	0	0	2	3	0
HARADA, Noriko	2B	1	0	0	0	1	1	3	0
KOBAYASHI, Kyoko	P	0	0	0	0	0	0	0	0
WATANABE, Masako	P	0	0	0	0	0	0	0	0
Totals		22	1	3	1	3	11	18	7

Pitchers	W/L/S	IP	H	R	ER	BB	SO
KOBAYASHI, Kyoko	L	1	3	3	3	0	1
WATANABE, Masako		5	7	3	3	3	3
Totals		6	10	6	6	3	4

TEAM: USA United States of America
Coach: RAYMOND, Ralph   Asst. Coach: WRIGHT, Marjorie

Batters	POS	AB	R	H	RBI	BB	SO	PO	A
RICHARDSON, Dorothy	SS	3	0	0	0	0	1	1	1
SMITH, Julie	2B	3	2	3	0	1	0	1	2
FERNANDEZ, Lisa	3B	4	2	2	3	0	2	0	3
MAHER, Kim Ly	LF	4	1	1	3	0	0	0	0
CORNELL, Sheila	1B	3	0	1	0	1	1	7	0
HARRIS, Dionna	DH	1	0	1	0	1	0	0	0
BOXX, Gillian	C	2	0	0	0	0	0	11	0
O'BRIEN, Leah	RF	3	0	0	0	0	0	1	0
BERG, Laura	CF	2	1	2	0	0	0	0	0
SMITH, Michele	P	0	0	0	0	0	0	0	0
Totals		25	6	10	6	3	4	21	6

Pitcher	W/L/S	IP	H	R	ER	BB	SO
SMITH, Michele	W	7	3	1	1	3	11
Totals		7	3	1	1	3	11

UMPIRES
HP	CARMICHAEL, Lucie	CAN
1B	HANSEN, Jeffrey	USA
2B	McAULIFFE, Alan	AUS
3B	STERKENBURG, Rene	NED

PRELIMINARIES — AUS 0 PUR 2

Team	1	2	3	4	5	6	7	8	9	R	H	E
AUS	0	0	0	0	0	0	0			0	2	1
PUR	0	2	0	0	0	–				2	2	1

TEAM: AUS Australia
Coach: CRUDGINGTON, Robert   Asst. Coach: PEEL, Carole

Batters	POS	AB	R	H	RBI	BB	SO	PO	A
COOPER, Kim	SS	3	0	0	0	0	0	0	1
LESTER, Jocelyn	C	3	0	0	0	0	0	9	1
McRAE, Francine	RF	3	0	0	0	0	0	1	0
HARDING, Tanya	DH	3	0	0	0	0	0	0	0
McDERMID, Sally	3B	3	0	1	0	0	0	0	0
BROWN, Joanne	1B	3	0	0	0	0	0	4	1
WARD, Natalie	2B	2	0	1	0	0	0	2	0
RICHARDSON, Nicole	LF	1	0	0	0	0	0	0	0
EDEBONE, Peta	PH	2	0	0	0	0	0	0	0
PETRIE, Haylea	CF	2	0	0	0	0	0	1	0
WILKINS, Brooke	P	0	0	0	0	0	0	1	0
ROCHE, Melanie	P	0	0	0	0	0	0	0	3
Totals		24	0	2	0	0	0	18	6

Pitchers	W/L/S	IP	H	R	ER	BB	SO
WILKINS, Brooke	L	2	2	2	2	2	1
ROCHE, Melanie		4	0	0	0	0	6
Totals		6	2	2	2	2	7

TEAM: PUR Puerto Rico
Coach: AGOSTO, Jose   Asst. Coach: NIEVES, Jacinto

Batters	POS	AB	R	H	RBI	BB	SO	PO	A
BAEZ, Lourdes	2B	2	0	0	0	1	1	3	0
VAZQUEZ, Clara	LF	2	0	0	0	0	0	1	0
ROSARIO, Sandra	C	3	0	0	0	0	0	0	0
ORTIZ, Jaqueline	RF	2	0	0	0	0	1	1	0
CORNIEL, Sheree	DH	2	0	0	0	0	2	0	0
SEGARRA, Myriam	1B	2	0	1	0	0	1	10	0
PARKS, Janice	SS	1	1	0	0	1	0	3	5
GONZALEZ, Maria	CF	2	1	1	1	0	1	2	0
SOTO, Eve	3B	2	0	0	0	0	1	1	3
ECHEVARRIA, Ivelisse	P	0	0	0	0	0	0	0	3
Totals		18	2	2	1	2	7	21	11

Pitcher	W/L/S	IP	H	R	ER	BB	SO
ECHEVARRIA, Ivelisse	W	7	2	0	0	0	0
Totals		7	2	0	0	0	0

UMPIRES
HP	KATO, Kenzo	JPN
1B	HORNAK, Michael	CAN
2B	PERALTA, Roberto	PAN
3B	ALEXANDER, Emily	USA

Game 1 — TPE 0 / USA 4

PRELIMINARIES TPE 0 USA 4

Team	1	2	3	4	5	6	7	8	9	R	H	E
TPE	0	0	0	0	0	0	0			0	2	4
USA	1	1	2	0	0	-				4	5	1

TEAM: TPE Chinese Taipei
Coach: WANG, Cheng-Fu   Asst. Coach: CHANG CHIEN, Chin-Ling

Batters	POS	AB	R	H	RBI	BB	SO	PO	A
CHIEN, Chen Ju	LF	3	0	0	0	0	2	2	0
LEE, Ming-Chieh	2B	3	0	0	0	0	0	5	2
YANG, Hui-Chun	C	3	0	0	0	0	1	1	0
WANG, Ya-Fen	SS	3	0	0	0	0	0	1	4
OU, Ching Chieh	RF	2	0	1	0	0	1	0	0
	PH	0	0	0	0	0	0	0	0
LIU, Chia Chi	RF	1	0	0	0	0	0	1	0
YEN, Show-Tzu	3B	2	0	0	0	0	0	1	2
CHUNG, Chiung Yao	DH	2	0	0	0	0	0	0	0
CHIEN, Pei-Chi	1B	2	0	0	0	0	0	6	0
LIU, Tzu Hsin	CF	2	0	1	0	0	1	1	0
TU, Hui-Mei	P	0	0	0	0	0	0	0	1
TU, Hui-Ping	P	0	0	0	0	0	0	0	0
Totals		23	0	2	0	0	5	18	9

Pitchers	W/L/S	IP	H	R	ER	BB	SO
TU, Hui-Mei	L	2	3	2	1	3	1
TU, Hui-Ping		4	2	2	2	2	0
Totals		6	5	4	3	5	1

TEAM: USA United States of America
Coach: RAYMOND, Ralph   Asst. Coach: WRIGHT, Marjorie

Batters	POS	AB	R	H	RBI	BB	SO	PO	A
RICHARDSON, Dorothy	SS	2	1	0	0	2	0	4	1
TYLER, Danielle	2B	3	0	0	0	0	0	1	1
	3B	0	0	0	0	0	0	0	0
FERNANDEZ, Lisa	3B	1	0	1	1	1	0	0	1
SMITH, Julie	PR	1	0	0	0	0	0	0	0
	2B	0	0	0	0	0	0	2	1
MAHER, Kim Ly	LF	3	1	0	0	0	1	2	0
CORNELL, Sheila	1B	2	1	1	2	1	0	4	0
SMITH, Michele	DH	3	1	2	0	0	0	0	0
HARRIS, Dionna	RF	3	0	0	0	0	0	1	0
BERG, Laura	CF	3	0	1	0	0	0	2	0
STOKES, Shelly	C	1	0	0	1	1	0	5	1
HARRIGAN, Lori	P	0	0	0	0	0	0	0	1
Totals		22	4	5	4	5	1	21	6

Pitcher	W/L/S	IP	H	R	ER	BB	SO
HARRIGAN, Lori	W	7	2	0	0	0	5
Totals		7	2	0	0	0	5

UMPIRES

HP	HORNAK, Michael	CAN
1B	McAULIFFE, Alan	AUS
2B	CARMICHAEL, Lucie	CAN
3B	LINDBERG, Geralyn	SWE

Game 2 — CHN 10 / PUR 0

PRELIMINARIES CHN 10 PUR 0

Team	1	2	3	4	5	6	7	8	9	R	H	E
CHN	0	5	1	4	0					10	11	0
PUR	0	0	0	0	0					0	1	5

TEAM: CHN People's Republic of China
Coach: LI, Minkuan   Asst. Coach: LIU, Yaming

Batters	POS	AB	R	H	RBI	BB	SO	PO	A
ZHANG, Chunfang	CF	4	2	3	1	0	0	0	0
YAN, Fang	2B	4	1	1	1	0	0	2	2
LIU, Xuqing	SS	4	0	2	2	0	0	0	1
WANG, Ying	1B	2	1	0	0	0	1	3	0
TAO, Hua	3B	3	3	3	3	0	0	0	0
CHEN, Hong	LF	2	1	1	1	1	0	0	0
AN, Zhongxin	C	2	0	0	0	1	0	10	1
WEI, Qiang	RF	1	1	0	0	0	0	0	0
OU, Jingbai	PH	1	0	0	0	0	0	0	0
LEI, Li	DH	2	1	1	0	1	0	0	0
MA, Ying	P	0	0	0	0	0	0	0	1
Totals		25	10	11	8	3	1	15	5

Pitcher	W/L/S	IP	H	R	ER	BB	SO
MA, Ying	W	5	1	0	0	0	10
Totals		5	1	0	0	0	10

TEAM: PUR Puerto Rico
Coach: AGOSTO, Jose   Asst. Coach: NIEVES, Jacinto

Batters	POS	AB	R	H	RBI	BB	SO	PO	A
BAEZ, Lourdes	2B	2	0	0	0	0	2	1	2
VAZQUEZ, Clara	LF	2	0	0	0	0	1	1	0
ROSARIO, Sandra	DH	1	0	0	0	0	1	0	0
ROSARIO, Penelope	PH	1	0	0	0	0	0	0	0
	DH	0	0	0	0	0	0	0	0
ORTIZ, Jaqueline	RF	2	0	1	0	0	1	0	0
CORNIEL, Sheree	C	2	0	0	0	0	0	2	1
SEGARRA, Myriam	1B	2	0	0	0	0	2	5	0
PARKS, Janice	SS	2	0	0	0	0	1	3	1
GONZALEZ, Maria	CF	1	0	0	0	0	1	1	0
SOTO, Eve	3B	1	0	0	0	0	1	0	1
MIZE, Lisa	P	0	0	0	0	0	0	0	0
MARTINEZ, Lisa	P	0	0	0	0	0	0	2	3
Totals		16	0	1	0	0	10	15	8

Pitchers	W/L/S	IP	H	R	ER	BB	SO
MIZE, Lisa	L	2 2/3	6	5	5	2	1
MARTINEZ, Lisa		2 1/3	5	5	2	1	0
Totals		5	11	10	7	3	1

UMPIRES

HP	STAUBLE, Clifford	CAN
1B	KATO, Kenzo	JPN
2B	HANSEN, Jeffrey	USA
3B	PERALTA, Roberto	PAN

Game 3 — AUS 1 / NED 0

PRELIMINARIES AUS 1 NED 0

Team	1	2	3	4	5	6	7	8	9	R	H	E
AUS	0	0	0	0	0	0	0	1		1	5	0
NED	0	0	0	0	0	0	0	0		0	2	0

TEAM: AUS Australia
Coach: CRUDGINGTON, Robert   Asst. Coach: PEEL, Carole

Batters	POS	AB	R	H	RBI	BB	SO	PO	A
COOPER, Kim	SS	3	1	1	0	0	0	0	2
	PR	0	0	0	0	0	0	0	0
McRAE, Francine	PH	1	0	1	0	0	0	0	0
LESTER, Jocelyn	C	3	0	3	1	0	0	10	0
McDERMID, Sally	3B	3	0	0	0	0	2	0	3
HARDING, Tanya	DH	3	0	0	0	0	2	0	0
PETRIE, Haylea	CF	3	0	0	0	0	0	1	0
WARD, Natalie	2B	3	0	0	0	0	0	6	2
BROWN, Joanne	LF	1	0	0	0	2	0	0	1
DIENELT, Kerry	1B	3	0	0	0	0	0	6	2
EDEBONE, Peta	RF	3	0	0	0	0	0	0	0
HOLLIDAY, Jennifer	P	0	0	0	0	0	0	1	1
Totals		26	1	5	1	2	10	24	11

Pitcher	W/L/S	IP	H	R	ER	BB	SO
HOLLIDAY, Jennifer	W	8	2	0	0	2	10
Totals		8	2	0	0	2	10

TEAM: NED Netherlands
Coach: ELFERS, Rudolf   Asst. Coach: WEDMAN, Donald

Batters	POS	AB	R	H	RBI	BB	SO	PO	A
STIEMER, Martine	RF	1	0	0	0	2	1	1	0
REIJNEN, Gerardina	2B	3	0	0	0	0	2	4	0
GEELS, Luciene	1B	3	0	0	0	0	1	8	0
BEEK, Petra	SS	3	0	1	0	0	0	1	2
van der PUTTEN, Maria	DH	3	0	0	0	0	1	0	0
NIEUWVEEN, Sandra	C	3	0	0	0	0	2	6	0
KOSSEN, Anita	CF	2	0	0	0	0	1	4	0
BEEK, Madelon	PH	1	0	0	0	0	1	0	0
de HEER, Jacqueline	3B	2	0	0	0	0	0	0	3
OCKHUYSEN, Corrine	PH	1	0	0	0	0	1	0	0
de JONG, Marjolein	LF	3	0	1	0	0	0	0	0
MELS, Anouk	P	0	0	0	0	0	0	0	4
Totals		25	0	2	0	2	4	24	9

Pitcher	W/L/S	IP	H	R	ER	BB	SO
MELS, Anouk	L	8	5	1	1	2	4
Totals		8	5	1	1	2	4

UMPIRES

HP	STRAHM, Kathy	USA
1B	CARMICHAEL, Lucie	CAN
2B	LINDBERG, Geralyn	SWE
3B	JOHNSON, Julie	USA

Women / *Dames*

PRELIMINARIES — CAN 0   JPN 4

Team	1	2	3	4	5	6	7	8	9	R	H	E
CAN	0	0	0	0	0	0	0			0	5	0
JPN	1	0	0	3	0	0	–			4	9	1

TEAM: CAN Canada
Coach: KENNEDY, Lesle   Asst. Coach: STANIFORTH, Brenda

Batters	POS	AB	R	H	RBI	BB	SO	PO	A
MAURICE, Pauline	CF	3	0	1	0	0	0	1	0
THORBURN, Colleen	LF	4	0	0	0	0	0	0	0
PARRIS-WASHINGTON, Christine	3B	3	0	2	0	0	0	1	2
DOELL, Karen	DH	2	0	1	0	1	0	0	0
CLAYTON, Juanita	C	3	0	0	0	0	0	6	1
STEPHENSON, Alecia	SS	2	0	0	0	0	1	3	0
BEASLEY, Sandra	PH	1	0	0	0	0	1	0	0
KELLAND, Kelly	1B	3	0	1	0	0	0	3	0
VAIRO, Carmelina	PR	0	0	0	0	0	0	0	0
MURRAY, Candace	2B	3	0	0	0	0	1	2	0
McGAW, Kara	RF	2	0	0	0	0	1	2	0
SONNENBERG, Debbie	P	0	0	0	0	0	0	0	0
SNELGROVE, Karen	P	0	0	0	0	0	0	0	0
Totals		26	0	5	0	1	6	18	3

Pitchers	W/L/S	IP	H	R	ER	BB	SO
SONNENBERG, Debbie	L	3 1/3	5	4	4	1	3
SNELGROVE, Karen		2 2/3	4	0	0	0	3
Totals		6	9	4	4	1	6

TEAM: JPN Japan
Coach: SUZUMURA, Mitsutoshi   Asst. Coach: NAGASAWA, Hiroyuki

Batters	POS	AB	R	H	RBI	BB	SO	PO	A
SAITO, Haruka	1B	3	1	1	0	0	0	6	0
INOUE, Mayumi	LF	2	0	0	0	0	1	3	0
MOCHIDA, Kyoko	C	3	0	0	0	0	1	6	1
FUJIMOTO, Yoshiko	DH	2	1	1	1	1	1	0	0
ANDO, Misako	SS	3	0	0	0	0	1	0	1
TSUKADA, Emi	CF	3	1	2	2	0	0	1	0
KODAMA, Chika	3B	3	1	3	0	0	0	1	0
MATSUMOTO, Naomi	RF	3	0	1	1	0	1	0	0
HARADA, Noriko	2B	2	0	1	0	0	1	3	2
FUKITA, Ikuko	PH	1	0	0	0	0	0	0	0
TAKAYAMA, Juri	P	0	0	0	0	0	0	1	2
Totals		25	4	9	4	1	4	21	6

Pitcher	W/L/S	IP	H	R	ER	BB	SO
TAKAYAMA, Juri	W	7	5	0	0	1	4
Totals		7	5	0	0	1	4

UMPIRES
HP	HANSEN, Jeffrey	USA
1B	ALEXANDER, Emily	USA
2B	KATO, Kenzo	JPN
3B	STERKENBURG, Rene	NED

PRELIMINARIES — NED 0   CHN 8

Team	1	2	3	4	5	6	7	8	9	R	H	E
NED	0	0	0	0	0	0	0			0	0	3
CHN	2	0	0	3	2	1	–			8	13	1

TEAM: NED Netherlands
Coach: ELFERS, Rudolf   Asst. Coach: WEDMAN, Donald

Batters	POS	AB	R	H	RBI	BB	SO	PO	A
STIEMER, Martine	RF	2	0	0	0	0	1	0	0
	LF	0	0	0	0	0	0	0	0
REIJNEN, Gerardina	2B	3	0	0	0	0	0	2	2
GEELS, Luciene	1B	3	0	0	0	0	2	3	0
BEEK, Petra	SS	3	0	0	0	0	1	4	1
OCKHUYSEN, Corrine	DH	3	0	0	0	0	2	0	0
NIEUWVEEN, Sandra	C	3	0	0	0	0	0	6	3
KOSSEN, Anita	CF	2	0	0	0	0	1	1	0
de HEER, Jacqueline	3B	1	0	0	0	0	1	0	0
BEEK, Madelon	3B	0	0	0	0	0	0	0	0
de JONG, Marjolein	LF	1	0	0	0	0	0	1	0
le NOBLE, Penny	LF	1	0	0	0	0	1	0	0
	RF	0	0	0	0	0	0	1	0
PANNEN, Sonja	P	0	0	0	0	0	0	0	1
KNOL, Jacqueline	P	0	0	0	0	0	0	0	0
Totals		22	0	0	0	0	9	18	7

Pitchers	W/L/S	IP	H	R	ER	BB	SO
PANNEN, Sonja	L	4	8	5	4	0	5
KNOL, Jacqueline		2	5	3	3	1	1
Totals		6	13	8	7	1	6

TEAM: CHN People's Republic of China
Coach: LI, Minkuan   Asst. Coach: LIU, Yaming

Batters	POS	AB	R	H	RBI	BB	SO	PO	A
ZHANG, Chunfang	CF	3	0	1	1	1	2	0	0
YAN, Fang	2B	4	1	3	0	0	0	2	1
LIU, Xuqing	SS	4	1	1	3	0	0	1	4
WANG, Ying	1B	3	1	1	0	0	2	8	0
TAO, Hua	3B	4	1	1	2	0	1	0	3
CHEN, Hong	LF	3	1	1	0	0	0	0	0
AN, Zhongxin	C	2	0	1	0	0	0	8	0
WEI, Qiang	RF	3	1	1	0	0	1	2	0
LEI, Li	DH	3	2	3	0	0	0	0	0
HE, Liping	P	0	0	0	0	0	0	0	2
LIU, Yaju	P	0	0	0	0	0	0	0	0
Totals		29	8	13	6	1	6	21	10

Pitchers	W/L/S	IP	H	R	ER	BB	SO
HE, Liping	W	4	0	0	0	0	5
LIU, Yaju		3	0	0	0	0	4
Totals		7	0	0	0	0	9

UMPIRES
HP	McAULIFFE, Alan	AUS
1B	LINDBERG, Geralyn	SWE
2B	STRAHM, Kathy	USA
3B	CARMICHAEL, Lucie	CAN

PRELIMINARIES — AUS 10   JPN 0

Team	1	2	3	4	5	6	7	8	9	R	H	E
AUS	0	0	0	0	4	0	6			10	11	0
JPN	0	0	0	0	0	0	0			0	4	2

TEAM: AUS Australia
Coach: CRUDGINGTON, Robert   Asst. Coach: PEEL, Carole

Batters	POS	AB	R	H	RBI	BB	SO	PO	A
COOPER, Kim	SS	3	1	1	0	1	1	3	2
LESTER, Jocelyn	C	3	0	0	0	0	0	6	1
RICHARDSON, Nicole	PH	1	1	1	2	0	0	0	0
McRAE, Francine	DH	4	0	0	0	0	1	0	0
DIENELT, Kerry	1B	4	1	1	1	0	2	5	2
McDERMID, Sally	3B	4	2	3	2	0	0	0	1
BROWN, Joanne	LF	4	1	1	0	0	0	1	0
WARD, Natalie	2B	3	2	2	2	0	0	3	1
PETRIE, Haylea	CF	3	1	1	0	0	1	1	0
EDEBONE, Peta	RF	2	1	1	3	0	0	1	0
ROCHE, Melanie	P	0	0	0	0	0	0	1	0
Totals		31	10	11	10	1	5	21	7

Pitcher	W/L/S	IP	H	R	ER	BB	SO
ROCHE, Melanie	W	7	4	0	0	1	7
Totals		7	4	0	0	1	7

TEAM: JPN Japan
Coach: SUZUMURA, Mitsutoshi   Asst. Coach: NAGASAWA, Hiroyuki

Batters	POS	AB	R	H	RBI	BB	SO	PO	A
SAITO, Haruka	1B	3	0	1	0	0	0	8	1
INOUE, Mayumi	LF	3	0	0	0	0	2	0	0
FUJIMOTO, Yoshiko	DH	2	0	0	0	1	1	0	0
YAMAJI, Noriko	C	3	0	0	0	0	1	5	1
TSUKADA, Emi	CF	3	0	0	0	0	2	1	0
ANDO, Misako	SS	3	0	1	0	0	0	3	4
KODAMA, Chika	3B	1	0	1	0	0	0	1	3
MATSUMOTO, Naomi	RF	2	0	0	0	0	1	0	0
HARADA, Noriko	2B	2	0	1	0	0	0	3	1
WATANABE, Tomoko	P	0	0	0	0	0	0	0	0
WATANABE, Masako	P	0	0	0	0	0	0	0	2
Totals		22	0	4	0	1	7	21	12

Pitchers	W/L/S	IP	H	R	ER	BB	SO
WATANABE, Tomoko	L	4 1/3	5	4	4	0	3
WATANABE, Masako		2 2/3	6	6	6	1	2
Totals		7	11	10	10	1	5

UMPIRES
HP	ALEXANDER, Emily	USA
1B	JOHNSON, Julie	USA
2B	HORNAK, Michael	CAN
3B	HANSEN, Jeffrey	USA

Women / *Dames*

PRELIMINARIES — PUR 2 — TPE 10

Team	1	2	3	4	5	6	7	8	9	R	H	E
PUR	1	1	0	0	0	0	0			2	6	0
TPE	0	1	0	0	9	0	–			10	11	1

TEAM: PUR Puerto Rico
Coach: AGOSTO, Jose   Asst. Coach: NIEVES, Jacinto

Batters	POS	AB	R	H	RBI	BB	SO	PO	A
BAEZ, Lourdes	2B	3	1	1	0	1	0	1	4
VAZQUEZ, Clara	LF	3	0	1	1	1	0	3	1
ROSARIO, Sandra	C	3	0	1	0	0	0	3	0
LEBRON, Elba	PR	0	0	0	0	0	0	0	0
ORTIZ, Jaqueline	RF	3	0	1	0	0	1	1	0
PARKS, Janice	SS	3	0	0	0	0	2	1	1
SEGARRA, Myriam	1B	2	0	0	0	1	2	8	0
GONZALEZ, Maria	CF	3	0	0	0	0	1	0	0
ROSARIO, Penelope	DH	3	1	1	0	0	0	0	0
SOTO, Eve	3B	3	0	1	0	0	1	0	3
ECHEVARRIA, Ivelisse	P	0	0	0	0	0	0	0	1
MIZE, Lisa	P	0	0	0	0	0	0	0	0
MARTINEZ, Lisa	P	0	0	0	0	0	0	0	1
Totals		26	2	6	1	3	5	18	11

Pitchers	W/L/S	IP	H	R	ER	BB	SO
ECHEVARRIA, Ivelisse	L	4	6	7	7	3	2
MIZE, Lisa		2/3	5	3	3	0	0
MARTINEZ, Lisa		1 1/3	0	0	0	0	0
Totals		6	11	10	10	3	2

TEAM: TPE Chinese Taipei
Coach: WANG, Cheng-Fu   Asst. Coach: CHANG CHIEN, Chin-Ling

Batters	POS	AB	R	H	RBI	BB	SO	PO	A
LIU, Tzu Hsin	CF	2	0	0	0	0	1	1	0
OU, Ching Chieh	PH	2	1	2	2	0	0	0	0
LEE, Ming-Chieh	2B	3	1	0	1	1	0	2	1
YANG, Hui-Chun	C	3	1	0	1	1	0	6	0
WANG, Ya-Fen	SS	4	2	2	3	0	0	5	3
CHUNG, Chiung Yao	DH	4	1	1	1	0	0	0	0
LIU, Chia Chi	RF	3	0	0	0	0	1	0	1
CHIEN, Chen Ju	LF	2	2	1	1	1	0	1	0
CHIEN, Pei-Chi	1B	2	0	1	1	0	0	5	0
	PH	0	0	0	0	0	0	0	0
CHANG, Nsiao-Chi	PH	1	1	1	0	0	0	0	0
YEN, Show-Tzu	3B	3	1	3	0	0	0	1	1
TU, Hui-Ping	P	0	0	0	0	0	0	0	0
TU, Hui-Mei	P	0	0	0	0	0	0	0	1
HAN, Hsin Lin	P	0	0	0	0	0	0	0	1
Totals		29	10	11	10	3	2	21	8

Pitchers	W/L/S	IP	H	R	ER	BB	SO
TU, Hui-Ping		1 2/3	5	1	1	0	2
TU, Hui-Mei	W	4 1/3	1	0	0	3	3
HAN, Hsin Lin		1	0	0	0	0	0
Totals		7	7	2	2	3	5

UMPIRES

HP	CARMICHAEL, Lucie	CAN
1B	STRAHM, Kathy	USA
2B	PERALTA, Roberto	PAN
3B	LINDBERG, Geralyn	SWE

PRELIMINARIES — USA 4 — CAN 2

Team	1	2	3	4	5	6	7	8	9	R	H	E
USA	0	0	0	1	1	0	2			4	4	1
CAN	0	0	0	0	2	0	0			2	6	5

TEAM: USA United States of America
Coach: RAYMOND, Ralph   Asst. Coach: WRIGHT, Marjorie

Batters	POS	AB	R	H	RBI	BB	SO	PO	A
RICHARDSON, Dorothy	SS	4	1	2	1	0	0	2	1
SMITH, Julie	2B	3	0	1	1	0	1	1	0
FERNANDEZ, Lisa	3B	3	0	0	0	1	0	1	0
TYLER, Danielle	PR	0	0	0	0	0	0	0	0
MAHER, Kim Ly	LF	4	0	0	0	0	0	2	0
CORNELL, Sheila	1B	3	0	0	0	0	2	3	2
SMITH, Michele	DH	3	0	0	0	0	1	0	0
BOXX, Gillian	C	2	1	1	0	0	0	11	2
HARRIS, Dionna	PR	0	1	0	0	0	0	0	0
O'BRIEN, Leah	RF	1	1	0	0	1	0	0	0
BERG, Laura	CF	3	0	0	0	0	0	1	0
GRANGER, Michele	P	0	0	0	0	0	0	0	0
WILLIAMS, Christa Lee	P	0	0	0	0	0	0	0	1
Totals		26	4	4	2	2	4	21	6

Pitchers	W/L/S	IP	H	R	ER	BB	SO
GRANGER, Michele		4 1/3	5	2	2	3	7
WILLIAMS, Christa Lee	W	2 2/3	1	0	0	0	5
Totals		7	6	2	2	3	12

TEAM: CAN Canada
Coach: KENNEDY, Lesle   Asst. Coach: STANIFORTH, Brenda

Batters	POS	AB	R	H	RBI	BB	SO	PO	A
MAURICE, Pauline	CF	4	1	1	1	0	2	2	0
VAIRO, Carmelina	1B	4	0	1	1	0	1	8	0
PARRIS-WASHINGTON, Christine	3B	3	0	1	0	1	1	1	4
DOELL, Karen	DH	4	0	0	0	0	3	0	0
STEPHENSON, Alecia	SS	2	0	0	0	1	2	0	0
MURRAY, Candace	2B	2	0	0	0	1	1	2	3
FLEMMER, Carrie	C	3	0	0	0	0	1	5	0
THORBURN, Colleen	LF	3	0	0	0	0	1	1	0
McGAW, Kara	RF	3	1	3	0	0	0	2	0
SNELGROVE, Karen	P	0	0	0	0	0	0	0	1
SIPPEL, Lori	P	0	0	0	0	0	0	0	0
Totals		28	2	6	2	3	12	21	8

Pitchers	W/L/S	IP	H	R	ER	BB	SO
SNELGROVE, Karen	L	6	3	4	2	1	4
SIPPEL, Lori		1	1	0	0	1	0
Totals		7	4	4	2	2	4

UMPIRES

HP	STERKENBURG, Rene	NED
1B	STAUBLE, Clifford	CAN
2B	KATO, Kenzo	JPN
3B	JOHNSON, Julie	USA

PRELIMINARIES — JPN 8 — PUR 1

Team	1	2	3	4	5	6	7	8	9	R	H	E
JPN	0	0	1	4	0	2	1			8	12	1
PUR	0	0	0	0	0	1	0			1	3	0

TEAM: JPN Japan
Coach: SUZUMURA, Mitsutoshi   Asst. Coach: NAGASAWA, Hiroyuki

Batters	POS	AB	R	H	RBI	BB	SO	PO	A
SAITO, Haruka	1B	5	3	3	7	0	0	8	1
KODAMA, Chika	3B	4	1	3	0	1	0	1	2
ANDO, Misako	SS	5	0	0	0	0	1	1	3
FUJIMOTO, Yoshiko	RF	3	0	1	1	1	1	0	0
MATSUMOTO, Naomi	RF	0	0	0	0	0	0	0	0
MOCHIDA, Kyoko	C	4	0	1	0	0	0	4	2
YAMAJI, Noriko	C	0	0	0	0	0	0	0	0
FUKITA, Ikuko	DH	4	0	1	0	0	0	0	0
TSUKADA, Emi	CF	2	1	1	0	2	1	2	0
HARADA, Noriko	2B	2	1	0	0	1	1	5	2
INOUE, Mayumi	LF	4	2	2	0	0	0	0	0
TAKAYAMA, Juri	P	0	0	0	0	0	0	0	0
KOBAYASHI, Kyoko	P	0	0	0	0	0	0	0	0
Totals		33	8	12	8	5	4	21	10

Pitchers	W/L/S	IP	H	R	ER	BB	SO
TAKAYAMA, Juri	W	5	2	0	0	2	4
KOBAYASHI, Kyoko		2	1	1	1	0	0
Totals		7	3	1	1	2	4

TEAM: PUR Puerto Rico
Coach: AGOSTO, Jose   Asst. Coach: NIEVES, Jacinto

Batters	POS	AB	R	H	RBI	BB	SO	PO	A
BAEZ, Lourdes	2B	3	0	0	0	0	0	3	1
ROSARIO, Penelope	LF	3	0	0	0	0	1	3	0
ROSARIO, Sandra	DH	3	0	0	0	0	1	0	0
ORTIZ, Jaqueline	RF	3	1	1	1	0	0	3	0
PARKS, Janice	SS	3	0	1	0	0	0	0	3
LEBRON, Elba	PR	0	0	0	0	0	0	0	0
CORNIEL, Sheree	C	2	0	0	0	0	1	4	0
GONZALEZ, Maria	CF	2	0	0	0	1	1	2	0
SEGARRA, Myriam	1B	1	0	0	0	1	0	6	0
SOTO, Eve	3B	2	0	1	0	0	0	0	2
MARTINEZ, Lisa	P	0	0	0	0	0	0	0	1
ECHEVARRIA, Ivelisse	P	0	0	0	0	0	0	0	0
Totals		22	1	3	1	2	4	21	7

Pitchers	W/L/S	IP	H	R	ER	BB	SO
MARTINEZ, Lisa	L	5	7	3	3	5	4
ECHEVARRIA, Ivelisse		2	5	5	5	0	0
Totals		7	12	8	8	5	4

UMPIRES

HP	STAUBLE, Clifford	CAN
1B	STRAHM, Kathy	USA
2B	PERALTA, Roberto	PAN
3B	KATO, Kenzo	JPN

Women / *Dames*

PRELIMINARIES — USA 1 · AUS 2

Team	1	2	3	4	5	6	7	8	9	10	R	H	E
USA	0	0	0	0	0	0	0	0	0	1	1	6	0
AUS	0	0	0	0	0	0	0	0	0	2	2	1	2

TEAM: USA United States of America
Coach: RAYMOND, Ralph   Asst. Coach: WRIGHT, Marjorie

Batters	POS	AB	R	H	RBI	BB	SO	PO	A
RICHARDSON, Dorothy	SS	4	0	1	0	0	0	0	0
SMITH, Julie	2B	4	0	0	0	0	0	3	2
HARRIS, Dionna	RF	4	1	1	0	0	1	0	0
MAHER, Kim Ly	LF	4	0	0	0	0	2	0	0
CORNELL, Sheila	1B	4	0	2	0	0	0	8	0
O'BRIEN, Leah	PR	0	0	0	0	0	0	0	0
SMITH, Michele	DH	4	0	0	0	0	0	0	0
TYLER, Danielle	3B	4	0	1	0	0	1	1	5
BERG, Laura	CF	3	0	0	0	0	0	0	0
STOKES, Shelly	C	3	0	1	0	0	0	16	0
FERNANDEZ, Lisa	P	0	0	0	0	0	0	1	0
Totals		34	1	6	0	0	4	29	7

Pitcher	W/L/S	IP	H	R	ER	BB	SO
FERNANDEZ, Lisa	L	9 2/3	1	2	1	0	15
Totals		9 2/3	1	2	1	0	15

TEAM: AUS Australia
Coach: CRUDGINGTON, Robert   Asst. Coach: PEEL, Carole

Batters	POS	AB	R	H	RBI	BB	SO	PO	A
COOPER, Kim	SS	3	0	0	0	0	3	0	5
McRAE, Francine	PH	1	0	0	0	0	1	0	0
LESTER, Jocelyn	C	4	0	0	0	0	0	4	1
BROWN, Joanne	LF	4	1	1	2	0	1	1	0
DIENELT, Kerry	1B	3	0	0	0	0	1	17	0
McDERMID, Sally	3B	3	0	0	0	0	0	0	3
HARDING, Tanya	P	3	0	0	0	0	2	1	3
PETRIE, Haylea	CF	3	0	0	0	0	2	1	0
WARD, Natalie	2B	3	0	0	0	0	2	5	5
EDEBONE, Peta	RF	3	0	0	0	0	3	1	0
RICHARDSON, Nicole	PR	0	1	0	0	0	0	0	0
Totals		30	2	1	2	0	15	30	17

Pitcher	W/L/S	IP	H	R	ER	BB	SO
HARDING, Tanya	W	10	6	1	0	0	4
Totals		10	6	1	0	0	4

UMPIRES
HP	CARMICHAEL, Lucie	CAN
1B	HORNAK, Michael	CAN
2B	LINDBERG, Geralyn	SWE
3B	McAULIFFE, Alan	AUS

PRELIMINARIES — NED 1 · CAN 4

Team	1	2	3	4	5	6	7	8	9	R	H	E
NED	0	1	0	0	0	0	0			1	2	4
CAN	0	0	2	1	0	1	–			4	5	1

TEAM: NED Netherlands
Coach: ELFERS, Rudolf   Asst. Coach: WEDMAN, Donald

Batters	POS	AB	R	H	RBI	BB	SO	PO	A
STIEMER, Martine	RF	1	0	0	0	1	1	0	0
REIJNEN, Gerardina	2B	3	0	0	0	0	0	3	2
GEELS, Luciene	1B	3	0	0	0	0	0	5	0
BEEK, Petra	SS	3	1	1	1	0	0	2	0
BEEK, Madelon	DH	3	0	0	0	0	1	0	0
NIEUWVEEN, Sandra	C	3	0	0	0	0	0	3	1
de HEER, Jacqueline	3B	2	0	0	0	0	1	1	1
van der PUTTEN, Maria	PH	0	0	0	0	1	0	0	0
KOSSEN, Anita	CF	2	0	0	0	0	0	0	0
OCKHUYSEN, Corrine	PH	1	0	0	0	0	1	0	0
de JONG, Marjolein	LF	2	0	1	0	0	0	4	1
MELS, Anouk	P	0	0	0	0	0	0	0	2
PANNEN, Sonja	P	0	0	0	0	0	0	0	1
Totals		23	1	2	1	2	4	18	8

Pitchers	W/L/S	IP	H	R	ER	BB	SO
MELS, Anouk	L	3 2/3	2	3	0	1	2
PANNEN, Sonja		2 1/3	3	1	0	0	0
Totals		6	5	4	0	1	2

TEAM: CAN Canada
Coach: KENNEDY, Lesle   Asst. Coach: STANIFORTH, Brenda

Batters	POS	AB	R	H	RBI	BB	SO	PO	A
MAURICE, Pauline	CF	4	0	1	1	0	1	0	0
VAIRO, Carmelina	2B	4	0	1	1	0	0	1	5
PARRIS-WASHINGTON, Christine	3B	3	0	1	0	1	0	0	7
DOELL, Karen	DH	3	0	0	0	0	0	0	0
CLAYTON, Juanita	C	3	0	0	0	0	1	4	0
KELLAND, Kelly	1B	3	1	1	0	0	0	13	1
STEPHENSON, Alecia	SS	2	2	1	0	0	0	2	2
THORBURN, Colleen	LF	1	1	0	0	0	0	0	0
McGAW, Kara	RF	1	0	0	0	0	0	1	0
BEASLEY, Sandra	PH	1	0	0	0	0	0	0	0
SIPPEL, Lori	P	0	0	0	0	0	0	0	1
SONNENBERG, Debbie	P	0	0	0	0	0	0	0	0
Totals		25	4	5	2	1	2	21	16

Pitchers	W/L/S	IP	H	R	ER	BB	SO
SIPPEL, Lori	W	6	2	1	1	1	3
SONNENBERG, Debbie	S	1	0	0	0	1	1
Totals		7	2	1	1	2	4

UMPIRES
HP	JOHNSON, Julie	USA
1B	STERKENBURG, Rene	NED
2B	HORNAK, Michael	CAN
3B	PERALTA, Roberto	PAN

PRELIMINARIES — CHN 1 · TPE 0

Team	1	2	3	4	5	6	7	8	9	R	H	E
CHN	0	0	1	0	0	0	0			1	5	2
TPE	0	0	0	0	0	0	0			0	1	0

TEAM: CHN People's Republic of China
Coach: LI, Minkuan   Asst. Coach: LIU, Yaming

Batters	POS	AB	R	H	RBI	BB	SO	PO	A
ZHANG, Chunfang	CF	3	1	1	1	1	1	0	0
YAN, Fang	2B	2	0	0	0	0	0	3	1
LIU, Xuqing	SS	3	0	2	0	0	0	1	3
WANG, Ying	1B	3	0	0	0	0	1	6	2
TAO, Hua	3B	2	0	1	0	1	1	1	0
CHEN, Hong	LF	3	0	0	0	0	0	0	0
AN, Zhongxin	C	2	0	0	0	0	2	10	1
XU, Jian	PH	1	0	1	0	0	0	0	0
WEI, Qiang	RF	3	0	0	0	0	0	0	0
LEI, Li	DH	2	0	0	0	0	0	0	0
OU, Jingbai	PH	0	0	0	0	1	0	0	0
	DH	0	0	0	0	0	0	0	0
LIU, Yaju	P	0	0	0	0	0	0	0	1
WANG, Lihong	P	0	0	0	0	0	0	0	1
Totals		24	1	5	1	3	5	21	9

Pitchers	W/L/S	IP	H	R	ER	BB	SO
LIU, Yaju		2	1	0	0	0	0
WANG, Lihong	W	5	0	0	0	0	10
Totals		7	1	0	0	0	10

TEAM: TPE Chinese Taipei
Coach: WANG, Cheng-Fu   Asst. Coach: CHANG CHIEN, Chin-Ling

Batters	POS	AB	R	H	RBI	BB	SO	PO	A
YANG, Hui-Chun	C	3	0	0	0	0	1	6	0
YEN, Show-Tzu	3B	2	0	0	0	0	1	0	4
OU, Ching Chieh	PH	1	0	0	0	0	1	0	0
CHUNG, Chiung Yao	DH	3	0	0	0	0	2	0	0
WANG, Ya-Fen	SS	3	0	1	0	0	2	3	1
CHIEN, Chen Ju	LF	1	0	0	0	0	1	2	0
LEE, Ming-Chieh	2B	2	0	0	0	0	1	1	1
LIU, Tzu Hsin	CF	2	0	0	0	0	1	1	0
CHIEN, Pei-Chi	1B	2	0	0	0	0	0	7	0
LIU, Chia Chi	RF	2	0	0	0	0	0	1	0
TU, Hui-Mei	P	0	0	0	0	0	0	0	0
CHIU, Chen Ting	P	0	0	0	0	0	0	0	1
Totals		21	0	1	0	0	10	21	7

Pitchers	W/L/S	IP	H	R	ER	BB	SO
TU, Hui-Mei	L	3	2	1	1	1	3
CHIU, Chen Ting		4	3	0	0	2	2
Totals		7	5	1	1	3	5

UMPIRES
HP	HANSEN, Jeffrey	USA
1B	STAUBLE, Clifford	CAN
2B	McAULIFFE, Alan	AUS
3B	ALEXANDER, Emily	USA

Women / *Dames*

CAN vs AUS

Team	1	2	3	4	5	6	7	8	9	R	H	E
CAN	0	0	0	2	0	0	0			2	4	0
AUS	2	0	0	0	3	0	–			5	9	3

TEAM: CAN Canada

Coach: KENNEDY, Lesle   Asst. Coach: STANIFORTH, Brenda

Batters	POS	AB	R	H	RBI	BB	SO	PO	A
MAURICE, Pauline	CF	3	1	1	0	0	0	0	0
VAIRO, Carmelina	2B	3	1	0	0	0	1	5	2
PARRIS-WASHINGTON, Christine	3B	3	0	1	0	0	0	1	4
DOELL, Karen	DH	3	0	0	0	0	1	0	0
KELLAND, Kelly	1B	3	0	2	1	0	0	6	1
MURRAY, Candace	PR	0	0	0	0	0	0	0	0
STEPHENSON, Alecia	SS	2	0	0	0	0	2	0	0
BEASLEY, Sandra	PH	1	0	0	0	0	0	0	0
THORBURN, Colleen	LF	3	0	0	0	0	2	1	0
FLEMMER, Carrie	C	2	0	0	0	0	2	3	1
CLAYTON, Juanita	C	1	0	0	0	0	0	2	0
McGAW, Kara	RF	2	0	0	0	0	1	0	0
SNELGROVE, Karen	P	0	0	0	0	0	0	0	0
SONNENBERG, Debbie	P	0	0	0	0	0	0	0	0
SIPPEL, Lori	P	0	0	0	0	0	0	0	0
Totals		26	2	4	1	0	9	18	8

Pitchers	W/L/S	IP	H	R	ER	BB	SO
SNELGROVE, Karen	L	4 1/3	6	4	4	1	2
SONNENBERG, Debbie		2/3	3	1	1	1	1
SIPPEL, Lori		1	0	0	0	0	0
Totals		6	9	5	5	2	3

TEAM: AUS Australia

Coach: CRUDGINGTON, Robert   Asst. Coach: PEEL, Carole

Batters	POS	AB	R	H	RBI	BB	SO	PO	A
COOPER, Kim	SS	1	1	0	0	1	0	1	4
RICHARDSON, Nicole	PH	1	0	0	0	0	0	0	0
LESTER, Jocelyn	C	3	0	0	0	0	1	8	1
HARDING, Tanya	PH	1	1	1	1	0	0	0	0
BROWN, Joanne	LF	3	1	1	2	0	1	0	0
DIENELT, Kerry	1B	3	1	2	2	0	0	7	0
McDERMID, Sally	3B	3	0	1	0	0	0	0	1
McRAE, Francine	DH	2	0	0	0	1	0	0	0
PETRIE, Haylea	CF	3	0	1	0	0	1	1	0
WARD, Natalie	2B	3	0	1	0	0	0	3	0
EDEBONE, Peta	RF	2	1	2	0	0	0	0	0
ROCHE, Melanie	P	0	0	0	0	0	0	1	2
Totals		25	5	9	5	2	3	21	8

Pitcher	W/L/S	IP	H	R	ER	BB	SO
ROCHE, Melanie	W	7	4	2	0	0	9
Totals		7	4	2	0	0	9

UMPIRES

HP	ALEXANDER, Emily	USA
1B	HANSEN, Jeffrey	USA
2B	STRAHM, Kathy	USA
3B	JOHNSON, Julie	USA

NED vs PUR

Team	1	2	3	4	5	6	7	8	9	R	H	E
NED	0	0	0	2	0	0	0			2	8	1
PUR	0	0	0	0	0	0	0			0	3	3

TEAM: NED Netherlands

Coach: ELFERS, Rudolf   Asst. Coach: WEDMAN, Donald

Batters	POS	AB	R	H	RBI	BB	SO	PO	A
STIEMER, Martine	RF	3	0	2	0	1	0	0	0
van der PUTTEN, Maria	DH	3	0	2	0	0	1	0	0
GEELS, Luciene	1B	2	0	0	0	0	0	13	0
BEEK, Petra	SS	3	0	0	0	0	0	1	7
BEEK, Madelon	3B	3	1	1	0	0	0	0	3
NIEUWVEEN, Sandra	C	3	0	0	0	0	1	5	0
LE NOBLE, Penny	2B	2	1	1	0	1	0	2	0
KOSSEN, Anita	CF	3	0	1	0	0	0	0	0
de JONG, Marjolein	LF	2	0	1	0	0	0	0	0
OCKHUYSEN, Corrine	PH	1	0	0	0	0	0	0	0
MELS, Anouk	P	0	0	0	0	0	0	0	5
Totals		25	2	8	0	2	2	21	15

Pitcher	W/L/S	IP	H	R	ER	BB	SO
MELS, Anouk	W	7	3	0	0	1	5
Totals		7	3	0	0	1	5

TEAM: PUR Puerto Rico

Coach: AGOSTO, Jose   Asst. Coach: NIEVES, Jacinto

Batters	POS	AB	R	H	RBI	BB	SO	PO	A
BAEZ, Lourdes	2B	3	0	0	0	0	0	3	4
ROSARIO, Penelope	LF	2	0	0	0	0	0	1	0
ROSARIO, Sandra	C	3	0	2	0	0	0	2	0
LEBRON, Elba	PR	0	0	0	0	0	0	0	0
ORTIZ, Jaqueline	RF	3	0	0	0	0	2	2	0
PARKS, Janice	SS	3	0	0	0	0	0	1	4
GONZALEZ, Maria	CF	2	0	0	0	0	1	1	1
MARTINEZ, Lisa	PH	1	0	0	0	0	1	0	0
SEGARRA, Myriam	1B	2	0	0	0	0	0	8	1
VAZQUEZ, Clara	PH	1	0	0	0	0	0	0	0
CORNIEL, Sheree	DH	3	0	1	0	0	1	0	0
SOTO, Eve	3B	2	0	0	0	1	0	2	1
ECHEVARRIA, Ivelisse	P	0	0	0	0	0	0	1	0
Totals		25	0	3	0	1	5	21	11

Pitcher	W/L/S	IP	H	R	ER	BB	SO
ECHEVARRIA, Ivelisse	L	7	8	2	2	2	2
Totals		7	8	2	2	2	2

UMPIRES

HP	STAUBLE, Clifford	CAN
1B	STERKENBURG, Rene	NED
2B	LINDBERG, Geralyn	SWE
3B	PERALTA, Roberto	PAN

CHN vs USA

Team	1	2	3	4	5	6	7	8	9	R	H	E
CHN	0	0	0	0	0	2	0			2	5	0
USA	0	1	0	0	0	2	–			3	8	1

TEAM: CHN People's Republic of China

Coach: LI, Minkuan   Asst. Coach: LIU, Yaming

Batters	POS	AB	R	H	RBI	BB	SO	PO	A
ZHANG, Chunfang	CF	3	1	0	0	0	1	0	0
YAN, Fang	2B	3	0	0	0	0	1	2	1
LIU, Xuqing	SS	3	1	2	2	0	0	1	1
WANG, Ying	1B	2	0	1	0	0	1	6	1
TAO, Hua	3B	3	0	1	0	0	1	0	2
CHEN, Hong	LF	2	0	0	0	0	2	2	0
XU, Jian	PH	1	0	0	0	0	1	0	0
AN, Zhongxin	C	3	0	0	0	0	2	5	0
WEI, Qiang	RF	2	0	0	0	0	1	2	0
OU, Jingbai	PH	1	0	0	0	0	1	0	0
LEI, Li	DH	3	0	1	0	0	1	0	0
MA, Ying	P	0	0	0	0	0	0	0	0
LIU, Yaju	P	0	0	0	0	0	0	0	2
WANG, Lihong	P	0	0	0	0	0	0	0	1
Totals		26	2	5	2	0	12	18	8

Pitchers	W/L/S	IP	H	R	ER	BB	SO
MA, Ying		1	3	1	1	0	0
LIU, Yaju		4	3	1	1	1	3
WANG, Lihong	L	1	2	1	1	0	1
Totals		6	8	3	3	1	4

TEAM: USA United States of America

Coach: RAYMOND, Ralph   Asst. Coach: WRIGHT, Marjorie

Batters	POS	AB	R	H	RBI	BB	SO	PO	A
RICHARDSON, Dorothy	SS	4	0	0	0	0	2	2	1
TYLER, Danielle	2B	3	0	0	0	0	0	0	0
FERNANDEZ, Lisa	3B	3	0	0	0	0	0	1	1
MAHER, Kim Ly	LF	2	2	2	0	1	0	0	0
CORNELL, Sheila	1B	3	1	2	2	0	0	4	0
HARRIS, Dionna	DH	3	0	2	0	0	0	0	0
BOXX, Gillian	C	1	0	0	1	0	1	12	0
O'BRIEN, Leah	RF	3	0	1	0	0	1	0	0
BERG, Laura	CF	2	0	1	0	0	0	2	0
SMITH, Michele	P	0	0	0	0	0	0	0	1
Totals		24	3	8	3	1	4	21	3

Pitcher	W/L/S	IP	H	R	ER	BB	SO
SMITH, Michele	W	7	5	2	2	0	12
Totals		7	5	2	2	0	12

UMPIRES

HP	HORNAK, Michael	CAN
1B	CARMICHAEL, Lucie	CAN
2B	McAULIFFE, Alan	AUS
3B	STAUBLE, Clifford	CAN

Women / *Dames*

PRELIMINARIES — JPN 5   TPE 1

Team	1	2	3	4	5	6	7	8	9	R	H	E
JPN	0	0	1	0	2	2	0			5	10	0
TPE	0	1	0	0	0	0	0			1	6	0

TEAM: JPN Japan
Coach: SUZUMURA, Mitsutoshi   Asst. Coach: NAGASAWA, Hiroyuki

Batters	POS	AB	R	H	RBI	BB	SO	PO	A
SAITO, Haruka	1B	3	0	0	0	0	0	7	0
KODAMA, Chika	3B	4	2	4	1	0	0	2	1
ANDO, Misako	SS	3	0	0	1	0	1	1	3
FUJIMOTO, Yoshiko	DH	4	0	1	1	0	1	0	0
YAMAJI, Noriko	C	4	1	2	1	0	0	5	0
TSUKADA, Emi	CF	1	0	1	0	2	0	3	0
MATSUMOTO, Naomi	RF	3	0	0	0	0	0	1	0
HARADA, Noriko	2B	2	0	0	0	0	1	0	1
FUKITA, Ikuko	PH	1	1	1	1	0	0	0	0
INOUE, Mayumi	LF	1	1	1	0	0	0	2	0
MOCHIDA, Kyoko	PH	1	0	0	0	0	1	0	0
WATANABE, Masako	P	0	0	0	0	0	0	0	0
KOBAYASHI, Kyoko	P	0	0	0	0	0	0	0	2
TAKAYAMA, Juri	P	0	0	0	0	0	0	0	0
Totals		27	5	10	5	2	4	21	7

Pitchers	W/L/S	IP	H	R	ER	BB	SO
WATANABE, Masako		2 1/3	5	1	1	0	3
KOBAYASHI, Kyoko	W	2 2/3	1	0	0	1	0
TAKAYAMA, Juri		2	0	0	0	0	2
Totals		7	6	1	1	1	5

TEAM: TPE Chinese Taipei
Coach: WANG, Cheng-Fu   Asst. Coach: CHANG CHIEN, Chin-Ling

Batters	POS	AB	R	H	RBI	BB	SO	PO	A
CHIEN, Chen Ju	DH	4	0	1	0	0	1	0	0
YEN, Show-Tzu	3B	2	0	1	0	0	0	0	1
CHANG, Nsiao-Ching	3B	1	0	0	0	0	0	1	0
CHUNG, Chiug Yao	LF	2	0	1	0	1	0	2	0
WANG, Ya-Fen	SS	3	1	1	1	0	0	3	1
YANG, Hui-Chun	C	3	0	0	0	0	1	5	1
OU, Ching Chieh	RF	3	0	0	0	0	0	0	0
LEE, Ming-Chieh	2B	3	0	1	0	0	0	3	5
CHIEN, Pei-Chi	1B	3	0	1	0	0	1	7	0
LIU, Tzu Hsin	CF	1	0	0	0	0	1	1	0
LIU, Chia Chi	PH	2	0	0	0	0	0	0	0
	CF	0	0	0	0	0	0	0	0
HAN, Hsin Lin	P	0	0	0	0	0	0	0	3
CHIU, Chen Ting	P	0	0	0	0	0	0	0	0
TU, Hui-Ping	P	0	0	0	0	0	0	0	0
Totals		27	1	6	1	1	5	21	11

Pitchers	W/L/S	IP	H	R	ER	BB	SO
HAN, Hsin Lin	L	4 2/3	8	3	3	0	2
CHIU, Chen Ting		1 1/3	2	2	2	1	1
TU, Hui-Ping		1	0	0	0	1	1
Totals		7	10	5	5	2	4

UMPIRES

HP	JOHNSON, Julie	USA
1B	ALEXANDER, Emily	USA
2B	KATO, Kenzo	JPN
3B	STERKENBURG, Rene	NED

SEMIFINALS — CHN 0   USA 1

Team	1	2	3	4	5	6	7	8	9	10	R	H	E
CHN	0	0	0	0	0	0	0	0	0	0	0	3	2
USA	0	0	0	0	0	0	0	0	0	1	1	10	0

TEAM: CHN People's Republic of China
Coach: LI, Minkuan   Asst. Coach: LIU, Yaming

Batters	POS	AB	R	H	RBI	BB	SO	PO	A
ZHANG, Chunfang	CF	4	0	1	0	0	1	1	0
YAN, Fang	2B	3	0	0	0	0	0	1	4
LIU, Xuqing	SS	4	0	1	0	0	3	2	3
WANG, Ying	1B	4	0	0	0	0	1	8	1
TAO, Hua	3B	4	0	0	0	0	1	1	2
CHEN, Hong	LF	3	0	1	0	0	1	3	0
XU, Jian	PH	1	0	0	0	0	1	0	0
AN, Zhongxin	C	3	0	0	0	0	2	8	1
WEI, Qiang	RF	3	0	0	0	0	1	4	2
LEI, Li	DH	3	0	0	0	0	2	0	0
LIU, Yaju	P	0	0	0	0	0	0	0	3
WANG, Lihong	P	0	0	0	0	0	0	0	0
Totals		32	0	3	0	0	13	28	16

Pitchers	W/L/S	IP	H	R	ER	BB	SO
LIU, Yaju		6	8	0	0	1	2
WANG, Lihong	L	3 1/3	2	1	0	1	5
Totals		9 1/3	10	1	0	2	7

TEAM: USA United States of America
Coach: RAYMOND, Ralph   Asst. Coach: WRIGHT, Marjorie

Batters	POS	AB	R	H	RBI	BB	SO	PO	A
RICHARDSON, Dorothy	SS	5	1	1	0	0	2	1	2
SMITH, Julie	2B	4	0	1	0	0	3	3	2
HARRIS, Dionna	RF	5	0	1	0	0	0	0	0
MAHER, Kim Ly	LF	5	0	2	0	0	1	0	0
CORNELL, Sheila	1B	4	0	1	1	1	0	8	0
O'BRIEN, Leah	PR	0	0	0	0	0	0	0	0
BOXX, Gillian	C	4	0	1	0	0	2	15	0
TYLER, Danielle	3B	4	0	0	0	0	2	2	2
BERG, Laura	CF	3	0	1	0	0	0	1	0
FERNANDEZ, Lisa	P	3	0	2	0	1	0	0	3
SMITH, Michele	PR	0	0	0	0	0	0	0	0
Totals		37	1	10	1	2	7	30	9

Pitcher	W/L/S	IP	H	R	ER	BB	SO
FERNANDEZ, Lisa	W	10	3	0	0	0	13
Totals		10	3	0	0	0	13

UMPIRES

HP	STAUBLE, Clifford	CAN
1B	STERKENBURG, Rene	NED
2B	McAULIFFE, Alan	AUS
3B	CARMICHAEL, Lucie	CAN

SEMIFINALS — AUS 3   JPN 0

Team	1	2	3	4	5	6	7	8	9	R	H	E
AUS	0	0	0	0	1	0	2			3	9	0
JPN	0	0	0	0	0	0	0			0	2	1

TEAM: AUS Australia
Coach: CRUDGINGTON, Robert   Asst. Coach: PEEL, Carole

Batters	POS	AB	R	H	RBI	BB	SO	PO	A
COOPER, Kim	SS	3	0	2	0	1	0	3	3
LESTER, Jocelyn	C	3	0	1	0	0	1	8	1
McRAE, Francine	PH	1	0	0	0	0	0	0	0
BROWN, Joanne	LF	4	1	1	0	0	1	2	0
DIENELT, Kerry	1B	4	1	3	2	0	1	4	0
RICHARDSON, Nicole	PR	0	0	0	0	0	0	0	0
McDERMID, Sally	3B	1	0	0	0	2	0	2	0
WARD, Natalie	2B	3	0	0	0	0	1	2	1
HARDING, Tanya	P	3	0	0	0	0	1	0	1
PETRIE, Haylea	CF	2	1	1	1	1	1	0	0
EDEBONE, Peta	RF	3	0	1	0	0	0	0	0
Totals		27	3	9	3	4	6	21	6

Pitcher	W/L/S	IP	H	R	ER	BB	SO
HARDING, Tanya	W	7	2	0	0	0	9
Totals		7	2	0	0	0	9

TEAM: JPN Japan
Coach: SUZUMURA, Mitsutoshi   Asst. Coach: NAGASAWA, Hiroyuki

Batters	POS	AB	R	H	RBI	BB	SO	PO	A
SAITO, Haruka	1B	3	0	0	0	0	2	2	1
KODAMA, Chika	3B	2	0	0	0	0	1	0	1
ANDO, Misako	SS	2	0	0	0	0	0	4	2
FUJIMOTO, Yoshiko	DH	3	0	1	0	0	1	0	0
YAMAJI, Noriko	C	3	0	0	0	0	1	7	2
TSUKADA, Emi	CF	2	0	1	0	0	1	1	1
MOCHIDA, Kyoko	PH	1	0	0	0	0	0	0	0
MATSUMOTO, Naomi	RF	1	0	0	0	0	1	0	0
FUKITA, Ikuko	PH	1	0	0	0	0	0	0	0
HARADA, Noriko	2B	2	0	0	0	0	2	6	1
INOUE, Mayumi	LF	2	0	0	0	0	0	1	0
TAKAYAME, Juri	P	0	0	0	0	0	0	0	0
Totals		22	0	2	0	0	9	21	8

Pitcher	W/L/S	IP	H	R	ER	BB	SO
TAKAYAMA, Juri	L	7	9	3	1	4	6
Totals		7	9	3	1	4	6

UMPIRES

HP	HANSEN, Jeffrey	USA
1B	ALEXANDER, Emily	USA
2B	HORNAK, Michael	CAN
3B	STRAHM, Kathy	USA

Women / *Dames*

FINAL - BRONZE MATCH CHN 4 AUS 2

Team	1	2	3	4	5	6	7	8	9	R	H	E
CHN	0	1	0	1	1	0	1			4	5	2
AUS	0	2	0	0	0	0	0			2	2	2

TEAM: CHN People's Republic of China
Coach: LI, Minkuan   Asst. Coach: LIU, Yaming

Batters	POS	AB	R	H	RBI	BB	SO	PO	A
ZHANG, Chunfang	CF	4	2	2	0	0	1	2	0
YAN, Fang	2B	4	0	0	0	0	3	0	2
LIU, Xuqing	SS	3	1	1	0	0	1	2	2
WANG, Ying	1B	3	1	1	1	1	0	5	0
TAO, Hua	3B	3	0	0	0	0	0	0	0
CHEN, Hong	LF	3	0	1	1	0	1	1	0
AN, Zhongxin	C	2	0	0	0	1	0	11	2
WEI, Qiang	RF	2	0	0	0	0	2	0	0
XU, Jian	PH	1	0	0	0	0	1	0	0
LEI, Li	DH	2	0	0	0	0	1	0	0
OU, Jingbai	PH	1	0	0	0	0	1	0	0
	DH	0	0	0	0	0	0	0	0
WANG, Lihong	P	0	0	0	0	0	0	0	1
Totals		28	4	5	2	2	11	21	7

Pitcher	W/L/S	IP	H	R	ER	BB	SO
WANG, Lihong	W	7	2	2	0	2	10
Totals		7	2	2	0	2	10

TEAM: AUS Australia
Coach: CRUDGINGTON, Robert Asst. Coach: PEEL, Carole

Batters	POS	AB	R	H	RBI	BB	SO	PO	A
COOPER, Kim	SS	3	0	0	0	0	2	0	3
LESTER, Jocelyn	C	3	0	0	0	0	1	11	0
BROWN, Joanne	LF	3	0	0	0	0	2	1	0
DIENELT, Kerry	1B	3	1	1	0	0	0	4	1
McDERMID, Sally	3B	1	0	0	0	2	1	2	0
HARDING, Tanya	DH	3	1	1	0	0	1	0	0
WARD, Natalie	2B	1	0	0	0	0	0	2	0
McRAE, Francine	PH	1	0	0	0	0	1	0	0
PETRIE, Haylea	CF	2	0	0	0	0	2	0	0
EDEBONE, Peta	RF	2	0	0	0	0	0	1	0
ROCHE, Melanie	P	0	0	0	0	0	0	0	1
HOLLIDAY, Jennifer	P	0	0	0	0	0	0	0	0
Totals		22	2	2	0	2	10	21	5

Pitchers	W/L/S	IP	H	R	ER	BB	SO
ROCHE, Melanie	L	4 1/3	4	3	1	1	8
HOLLIDAY, Jennifer		2 2/3	1	1	0	1	3
Totals		7	5	4	1	2	11

UMPIRES

HP	JOHNSON, Julie	USA
1B	HANSEN, Jeffrey	USA
2B	ALEXANDER, Emily	USA
3B	KATO, Kenzo	JPN

GRAND FINAL - GOLD MATCH CHN 1 USA 3

Team	1	2	3	4	5	6	7	8	9	R	H	E
CHN	0	0	0	0	0	1	0			1	4	2
USA	0	0	3	0	0	0	–			3	4	0

TEAM: CHN People's Republic of China
Coach: LI, Minkuan   Asst. Coach: LIU, Yaming

Batters	POS	AB	R	H	RBI	BB	SO	PO	A
ZHANG, Chunfang	CF	3	1	2	0	0	1	1	0
YAN, Fang	2B	3	0	1	0	0	0	3	3
LIU, Xuqing	SS	2	0	1	0	1	1	3	3
WANG, Ying	1B	3	0	0	0	0	2	7	0
TAO, Hua	3B	3	0	0	0	0	1	0	1
CHEN, Hong	LF	3	0	0	0	0	3	2	0
AN, Zhongxin	C	2	0	0	0	0	1	2	1
XU, Jian	PH	1	0	0	0	0	1	0	0
WEI, Qiang	RF	2	0	0	0	0	1	0	0
LEI, Li	DH	2	0	0	0	0	0	0	0
LIU, Yaju	P	0	0	0	0	0	0	0	1
Totals		24	1	4	0	1	11	18	9

Pitcher	W/L/S	IP	H	R	ER	BB	SO
LIU, Yaju	L	6	4	3	2	2	2
Totals		6	4	3	2	2	2

TEAM: USA United States of America
Coach: RAYMOND, Ralph   Asst. Coach: WRIGHT, Marjorie

Batters	POS	AB	R	H	RBI	BB	SO	PO	A
RICHARDSON, Dorothy	SS	3	1	2	2	0	0	2	3
SMITH, Julie	2B	3	0	0	0	0	0	0	0
FERNANDEZ, Lisa	3B	2	0	0	0	1	0	0	1
	P	0	0	0	0	0	0	0	0
MAHER, Kim Ly	LF	3	1	0	0	0	1	0	0
CORNELL, Sheila	1B	2	0	0	0	1	1	5	0
O'BRIEN, Leah	PR	0	0	0	0	0	0	0	0
SMITH, Michele	DH	3	0	0	0	0	0	0	0
HARRIS, Dionna	RF	3	0	1	0	0	0	0	0
BOXX, Gillian	C	3	0	0	0	0	0	14	1
BERG, Laura	CF	2	1	1	0	0	0	0	0
GRANGER, Michele	P	0	0	0	0	0	0	0	0
TYLER, Danielle	3B	0	0	0	0	0	0	0	0
Totals		24	3	4	2	2	2	21	5

Pitchers	W/L/S	IP	H	R	ER	BB	SO
GRANGER, Michele	W	5 2/3	4	1	0	1	8
FERNANDEZ, Lisa	S	1 1/3	0	0	0	0	3
Totals		7	4	1	0	1	11

UMPIRES

HP	CARMICHAEL, Lucie	CAN
1B	STAUBLE, Clifford	CAN
2B	STERKENBURG, Rene	NED
3B	HORNAK, Michael	CAN

TEAM STANDINGS - PRELIMINARIES

Team	Games	Wins	Losses	Runs For	Runs Against	W/L Avg
USA	7	6	1	37	7	.857
CHN	7	5	2	29	7	.714
AUS	7	5	2	22	11	.714
JPN	6	4	2	19	17	.666
CAN	7	3	4	15	18	.428
TPE	6	2	4	18	14	.333
NED	7	1	6	4	32	.142
PUR	7	1	6	5	44	.142

FINAL TEAM STANDINGS

Rnk	Team	Games	Wins	Losses	
1	USA	9	8	1	Gold
2	CHN	10	6	4	Silver
3	AUS	9	6	3	Bronze
4	JPN	8	5	3	
5	CAN	7	3	4	
6	TPE	7	2	5	
7	NED	7	1	6	
8	PUR	7	1	6	

TABLE TENNIS
TENNIS DE TABLE

Abbreviations and terms used in Table Tennis results tables
Abréviations et termes employés dans les tableaux de résultats de tennis de table

Term	English	Français
1/8 Elimination	1/8 Elimination	1/8 de finale
Bronze Medal	Bronze Medal	Médaille de bronze
Ctry	Country	Pays
Games	Games	Manches
Gold Medal	Gold Medal	Médaille d'or
Group	Group	Groupe
L	Lost	Perdu
Matches	Matches	Matchs
Medal Round	Medal Round	Tour pour les médailles
Name	Name	Nom
P	Played	Joué
Points	Points	Points
Quarterfinals	Quarterfinals	Quarts de finale
Rnk	Rank	Classement
Semifinals	Semifinals	Demi-finales
Silver Medal	Silver Medal	Médaille d'argent
W	Won	Gagné

International Table Tennis Federation (ITTF)
Fédération Internationale de Tennis de Table
53 London Road, St. Leonards-on-Sea, East Sussez TN 37 6AY, England

• JONATHAN I WELLS • KAREN S WELLS • KENNETH L WELLS • LANDON WELLS • LINDA WELLS • LINDA F WELLS • MARY E WELLS • MERIAM JILL WELLS • NANCI L WELLS • PAMELA D WELLS • PATRICIA A WELLS • PENN WELLS • PHYLLIS A WELLS • RICK A WELLS • ROBERT E WELLS • ROBERT F WELLS • ROBERT L WELLS • ROSEMARIE G WELLS • SCOTT L WELLS • STACEY L WELLS • STEPHANIE J WELLS • SUZANNE E WELLS • MARCIA I WELLS-LAWSON • RICHARD WELLS JR • JADE L WELLS SAT • ROLAND B. WELMAKER • RYAN B WELMAKER • ROLAND B WELMAKER JR •

365

Table Tennis / *Tennis de table*
Singles, Men / *Simples, Messieurs*

GROUP A

Rnk	Name	Ctry	Matches P	Matches W	Matches L	Games W	Games L	Points W	Points L
1	KONG, Linghui	CHN	3	3	0	6	0	126	75
2	CHIANG, Peng-Lung	TPE	3	2	1	4	2	118	89
3	TASAKI, Toshio	JPN	3	1	2	2	4	96	107
4	OSAMA, Ahmed	SUD	3	0	3	0	6	57	126

GROUP B

Rnk	Name	Ctry	Matches P	Matches W	Matches L	Games W	Games L	Points W	Points L
1	WANG, Tao	CHN	3	3	0	6	1	148	111
2	TSIOKAS, Dany	GRE	3	2	1	4	2	114	98
3	HEISTER, Danny	NED	3	1	2	3	4	129	120
4	MUTAMBUZE, Paul	UGA	3	0	3	0	6	64	126

GROUP C

Rnk	Name	Ctry	Matches P	Matches W	Matches L	Games W	Games L	Points W	Points L
1	SAIVE, Jean-Michel	BEL	3	3	0	6	0	126	94
2	FLOREA, Vasile	ROM	3	2	1	4	2	121	93
3	FRANZ, Peter	GER	3	1	2	2	4	107	102
4	ALHABASHI, Dukhail	KUW	3	0	3	0	6	61	126

GROUP D

Rnk	Name	Ctry	Matches P	Matches W	Matches L	Games W	Games L	Points W	Points L
1	WALDNER, Jan-Ove	SWE	3	3	0	6	0	126	85
2	LEE, Chul-Seung	KOR	3	2	1	4	4	148	145
3	LUPULESKU, Ilija	YUG	3	1	2	3	4	132	123
4	OPOKU, Isaac	GHA	3	0	3	1	6	88	141

GROUP E

Rnk	Name	Ctry	Matches P	Matches W	Matches L	Games W	Games L	Points W	Points L
1	ROSSKOPF, Joerg	GER	3	3	0	6	0	126	81
2	SHIBUTANI, Hiroshi	JPN	3	2	1	4	2	111	98
3	LO, Chuen Tsung	HKG	3	1	2	2	4	99	112
4	MUNOZ, Guillermo	MEX	3	0	3	0	6	81	126

GROUP F

Rnk	Name	Ctry	Matches P	Matches W	Matches L	Games W	Games L	Points W	Points L
1	LIU, Guoliang	CHN	3	3	0	6	1	147	100
2	GRUJIC, Slobodan	YUG	3	2	1	5	4	162	163
3	SAIVE, Philippe	BEL	3	1	2	3	4	133	125
4	SMYTHE, Mark	AUS	3	0	3	1	6	88	142

GROUP G

Rnk	Name	Ctry	Matches P	Matches W	Matches L	Games W	Games L	Points W	Points L
1	KORBEL, Petr	CZE	3	3	0	6	1	141	102
2	GATIEN, Jean-Philippe	FRA	3	2	1	4	2	116	75
3	CHOE, Kyong	PRK	3	1	2	3	4	115	131
4	MORALES MARENGO, Augusto	CHI	3	0	3	0	6	62	126

GROUP H

Rnk	Name	Ctry	Matches P	Matches W	Matches L	Games W	Games L	Points W	Points L
1	SAMSONOV, Vladimir	BLR	3	3	0	6	1	143	74
2	MAZUNOV, Andrey	RUS	3	2	1	5	3	147	143
3	PREAN, Carl	GBR	3	1	2	3	4	110	117
4	HYLTON, Stephen	JAM	3	0	3	0	6	60	126

GROUP I

Rnk	Name	Ctry	Matches P	Matches W	Matches L	Games W	Games L	Points W	Points L
1	KIM, Taek-Soo	KOR	3	3	0	6	0	127	80
2	NEMET, Karoly	HUN	3	2	1	4	3	123	122
3	DING, Yi	AUT	3	1	2	3	5	148	147
4	LANGLEY, Paul	AUS	3	0	3	1	6	93	142

GROUP J

Rnk	Name	Ctry	Matches P	Matches W	Matches L	Games W	Games L	Points W	Points L
1	PRIMORAC, Zoran	CRO	3	3	0	6	1	143	95
2	SCHLAGER, Werner	AUT	3	2	1	4	2	118	99
3	BATORFI, Zoltan	HUN	3	1	2	3	4	122	123
4	al-HAMMADI, Hamad	QAT	3	0	3	0	6	60	126

GROUP K

Rnk	Name	Ctry	Matches P	Matches W	Matches L	Games W	Games L	Points W	Points L
1	HOYAMA, Hugo	BRA	3	3	0	6	1	151	131
2	PERSSON, Jorgen	SWE	3	2	1	5	2	135	115
3	KIM, Song	PRK	3	1	2	2	4	121	116
4	ST. LOUIS, Dexter	TRI	3	0	3	0	6	82	127

GROUP L

Rnk	Name	Ctry	Matches P	Matches W	Matches L	Games W	Games L	Points W	Points L
1	MAZUNOV, Dmitriy	RUS	3	3	0	6	0	128	95
2	KARLSSON, Peter	SWE	3	2	1	4	3	123	124
3	BUTLER, Jim	USA	3	1	2	3	4	133	136
4	HODZIC, Tarik	BIH	3	0	3	0	6	97	126

GROUP M

Rnk	Name	Ctry	Matches P	Matches W	Matches L	Games W	Games L	Points W	Points L
1	HUANG, Wen	CAN	3	3	0	6	0	126	76
2	CHEN, Xinhua	GBR	3	2	1	4	4	142	145
3	ZHUANG, David	USA	3	1	2	3	4	122	126
4	OLALEYE, Sule	NGR	3	0	3	1	6	102	145

GROUP N

Rnk	Name	Ctry	Matches P	Matches W	Matches L	Games W	Games L	Points W	Points L
1	YOO, Nam-Kyu	KOR	3	3	0	6	0	126	85
2	LI, Gun Sang	PRK	3	2	1	4	3	134	116
3	KARAKASEVIC, Aleksandar	YUG	3	1	2	3	4	120	128
4	HYATT, Michael	JAM	3	0	3	0	6	75	126

GROUP O

Rnk	Name	Ctry	Matches P	Matches W	Matches L	Games W	Games L	Points W	Points L
1	MATSUSHITA, Koji	JPN	3	3	0	6	1	143	124
2	GRUBBA, Andrzej	POL	3	2	1	5	2	146	116
3	SUSENO, Anton	INA	3	1	2	2	4	100	105
4	NG, Gideon	CAN	3	0	3	0	6	82	126

GROUP P

Rnk	Name	Ctry	Matches P	Matches W	Matches L	Games W	Games L	Points W	Points L
1	CHILA, Patrick	FRA	3	3	0	6	2	158	120
2	KREANGA, Kalin	GRE	3	2	1	5	2	133	114
3	TORIOLA, Segun	NGR	3	1	2	2	5	98	133
4	BABOOR, Chetan	IND	3	0	3	2	6	132	154

Singles, Men / *Simples, Messieurs*

1/8 ELIMINATION		
Name	Ctry	
KONG, Linghui	CHN	
KIM, Taek-Soo	KOR	
CHILA, Patrick	FRA	
ROSSKOPF, Joerg	GER	
LIU, Guoliang	CHN	
MATSUSHITA, Koji	JPN	
HUANG, Wen	CAN	
WALDNER, Jan-Ove	SWE	
SAIVE, Jean-Michel	BEL	
PRIMORAC, Zoran	CRO	
HOYAMA, Hugo	BRA	
KORBEL, Petr	CZE	
SAMSONOV, Vladimir	BLR	
MAZUNOV, Dmitriy	RUS	
YOO, Nam-Kyu	KOR	
WANG, Tao	CHN	

QUARTERFINALS

KIM, T.-S. (3)-(1) — 21:17, 21:18, 20:22 21:12
ROSSKOPF, J. (3)-(0) — 21:16, 21:16, 23:21
LIU, G. (3)-(0) — 21:18, 21:10, 21:17
HUANG, W. (3)-(1) — 21:15, 17:21, 21:16 21:15
SAIVE, J.-M. (3)-(0) — 21:13, 21:16, 21:8
KORBEL, P. (3)-(2) — 17:21, 19:21, 21:17 21:14, 21:13
SAMSONOV, V. (3)-(0) — 21:14, 21:15, 21:13
WANG, T. (3)-(0) — 21:15, 21:16, 21:9

SEMIFINALS

ROSSKOPF, J. (3)-(2) — 12:21, 26:24, 21:12 16:21, 26:24
LIU, G. (3)-(1) — 9:21, 21:19, 21:16 21:16
KORBEL, P. (3)-(0) — 21:10, 21:13, 21:19
WANG, T. (3)-(2) — 16:21, 16:21, 21:10 21:15, 21:15

MEDAL ROUND

LIU, G. (3)-(1) — 21:17, 18:21, 21:18 21:18
WANG, T. (3)-(0) — 23:21, 21:7, 21:16

GOLD MEDAL

LIU, G. (3)-(2) CHN — 21:12, 22:24, 21:19 15:21, 21:6

SILVER MEDAL

WANG, T. CHN

BRONZE MEDAL

ROSSKOPF, J.
ROSSKOPF, J. (3)-(1) GER — 21:17, 19:21, 21:18 21:19
KORBEL, P.

FINAL CLASSIFICATION		
Rnk	Name	Ctry
1	LIU, Guoliang	CHN
2	WANG, Tao	CHN
3	ROSSKOPF, Joerg	GER
4	KORBEL, Petr	CZE

Table Tennis / *Tennis de table*
Singles, Women / *Simples, Dames*

GROUP A

Rnk	Name	Ctry	Matches P	W	L	Games W	L	Points W	L
1	DENG, Yaping	CHN	3	3	0	6	0	126	53
2	SVENSSON, Marie	SWE	3	2	1	4	2	103	81
3	LOMAS, Lisa	GBR	3	1	2	2	4	90	101
4	KYAKOBYE, Nadunga	UGA	3	0	3	0	6	42	126

GROUP B

Rnk	Name	Ctry	Matches P	W	L	Games W	L	Points W	L
1	QIAO, Hong	CHN	3	3	0	6	0	126	71
2	SATO, Rika	JPN	3	2	1	4	2	118	89
3	WANG-DRECHOU, Xiao Ming	FRA	3	1	2	2	4	103	97
4	MUSOKE, Mary	UGA	3	0	3	0	6	36	126

GROUP C

Rnk	Name	Ctry	Matches P	W	L	Games W	L	Points W	L
1	CHEN, Jing	TPE	3	3	0	6	1	145	88
2	LI, Chunli	NZL	3	2	1	4	2	109	76
3	ARISI, Alessia	ITA	3	1	2	3	4	116	120
4	CHOUAIB, Larissa	LIB	3	0	3	0	6	40	126

GROUP D

Rnk	Name	Ctry	Matches P	W	L	Games W	L	Points W	L
1	LIU, Wei	CHN	3	3	0	6	2	161	112
2	FENG, Amy	USA	3	2	1	5	2	129	112
3	POPOVA, Valentina	SVK	3	1	2	3	4	126	119
4	RODRIGUEZ OLATE, Berta	CHI	3	0	3	0	6	53	126

GROUP E

Rnk	Name	Ctry	Matches P	W	L	Games W	L	Points W	L
1	CHAI, Po Wa	HKG	3	3	0	6	1	144	78
2	SIMION, Adriana	ROM	3	2	1	5	2	126	106
3	HOOMAN-KLOPPENBURG, Mirjam	NED	3	1	2	2	4	100	114
4	RAMOS, Fabi	VEN	3	0	3	0	6	54	126

GROUP F

Rnk	Name	Ctry	Matches P	W	L	Games W	L	Points W	L
1	GENG, Lijuan	CAN	3	3	0	4	0	84	58
2	PARK, Kyoung-Ae	KOR	3	2	1	2	2	71	74
3	KEEN, Geertje	NED	3	1	2	0	4	61	84

GROUP G

Rnk	Name	Ctry	Matches P	W	L	Games W	L	Points W	L
1	STRUSE, Nicole	GER	3	3	0	6	1	144	80
2	TODO, Taeko	JPN	3	2	1	5	2	135	95
3	BOROS, Tamara	CRO	3	1	2	2	4	92	110
4	TOUATI, Sonia	TUN	3	0	3	0	6	40	126

GROUP H

Rnk	Name	Ctry	Matches P	W	L	Games W	L	Points W	L
1	KOYAMA, Chire	JPN	3	3	0	6	1	141	110
2	PALINA, Irina	RUS	3	2	1	5	2	134	104
3	DOBESOVA, Jana	CZE	3	1	2	2	4	108	102
4	ALEJO, Blanca	DOM	3	0	3	0	6	59	126

Singles, Women / *Simples, Dames*

GROUP I

Rnk	Name	Ctry	Matches P	Matches W	Matches L	Games W	Games L	Points W	Points L
1	KIM, Hyon	PRK	3	3	0	6	0	128	100
2	SCHOPP, Jie	GER	3	2	1	4	2	120	88
3	TIMINA, Yelena	RUS	3	1	2	2	4	108	113
4	OSHONAIKE, Olufunke	NGR	3	0	3	0	6	71	126

GROUP J

Rnk	Name	Ctry	Matches P	Matches W	Matches L	Games W	Games L	Points W	Points L
1	JING, Jun Hong	SIN	3	3	0	6	1	146	105
2	KIM, Hyang	PRK	3	2	1	5	3	159	135
3	XU, Jing	TPE	3	1	2	3	4	120	123
4	CADA, Petra	CAN	3	0	3	0	6	64	126

GROUP K

Rnk	Name	Ctry	Matches P	Matches W	Matches L	Games W	Games L	Points W	Points L
1	PARK, Hae-Jung	KOR	3	3	0	6	0	128	86
2	NEMES, Olga	GER	3	2	1	4	2	120	100
3	CHEN, Chiu-Tan	TPE	3	1	2	2	4	104	103
4	STESHENKO, Aida	TKM	3	0	3	0	6	63	126

GROUP L

Rnk	Name	Ctry	Matches P	Matches W	Matches L	Games W	Games L	Points W	Points L
1	TU, Jong-Sil	PRK	3	3	0	6	0	126	78
2	RYU, Ji-Hae	KOR	3	2	1	4	3	135	105
3	SVENSSON, Asa	SWE	3	1	2	3	4	116	131
4	GONZALEZ, Eliana	PER	3	0	3	0	6	63	126

GROUP M

Rnk	Name	Ctry	Matches P	Matches W	Matches L	Games W	Games L	Points W	Points L
1	BATORFI, Csilla	HUN	3	3	0	6	0	126	95
2	BULATOVA-ABBATE, Fliura	ITA	3	2	1	4	2	119	97
3	ZHOU, Shirley	AUS	3	1	2	2	4	106	97
4	PRATIWI DIPOYANTI, Rossy	INA	3	0	3	0	6	64	126

GROUP N

Rnk	Name	Ctry	Matches P	Matches W	Matches L	Games W	Games L	Points W	Points L
1	BADESCU, Otilia	ROM	3	3	0	6	1	144	82
2	GARKAUSKAITE, Ruta	LTU	3	2	1	5	3	132	136
3	VRIESEKOOP, Huberta	NED	3	1	2	3	4	124	116
4	RADHIKA, Ambika	IND	3	0	3	0	6	60	126

GROUP O

Rnk	Name	Ctry	Matches P	Matches W	Matches L	Games W	Games L	Points W	Points L
1	CHAN, Tan Lui	HKG	3	3	0	6	1	144	108
2	YIP, Lily	USA	3	2	1	4	2	106	97
3	TOTH, Krisztina	HUN	3	1	2	3	4	134	121
4	DOTI, Monica	BRA	3	0	3	0	6	68	126

GROUP P

Rnk	Name	Ctry	Matches P	Matches W	Matches L	Games W	Games L	Points W	Points L
1	TU, Yong	SUI	3	3	0	6	1	148	95
2	KOSAKA, Lyanne	BRA	3	2	1	4	2	99	105
3	CIOSU, Emilia Elena	ROM	3	1	2	3	5	151	157
4	KAFFO, Bose	NGR	3	0	3	1	6	103	144

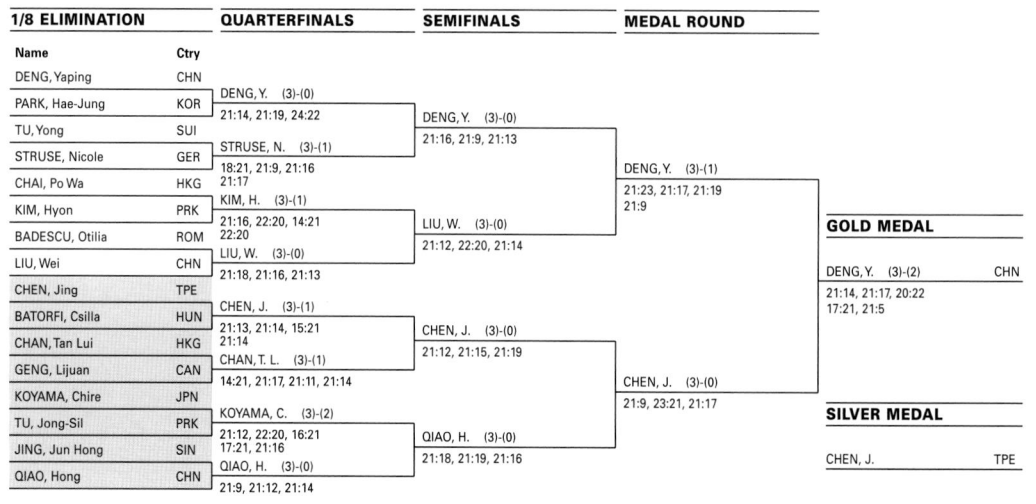

1/8 ELIMINATION	
Name	Ctry
DENG, Yaping	CHN
PARK, Hae-Jung	KOR
TU, Yong	SUI
STRUSE, Nicole	GER
CHAI, Po Wa	HKG
KIM, Hyon	PRK
BADESCU, Otilia	ROM
LIU, Wei	CHN
CHEN, Jing	TPE
BATORFI, Csilla	HUN
CHAN, Tan Lui	HKG
GENG, Lijuan	CAN
KOYAMA, Chire	JPN
TU, Jong-Sil	PRK
JING, Jun Hong	SIN
QIAO, Hong	CHN

QUARTERFINALS

DENG, Y.   (3)-(0)
21:14, 21:19, 24:22

STRUSE, N.   (3)-(1)
18:21, 21:9, 21:16
21:17

KIM, H.   (3)-(1)
21:16, 22:20, 14:21
22:20

LIU, W.   (3)-(0)
21:18, 21:16, 21:13

CHEN, J.   (3)-(1)
21:13, 21:14, 15:21
21:14

CHAN, T. L.   (3)-(1)
14:21, 21:17, 21:11, 21:14

KOYAMA, C.   (3)-(2)
21:12, 22:20, 16:21
17:21, 21:16

QIAO, H.   (3)-(0)
21:9, 21:12, 21:14

SEMIFINALS

DENG, Y.   (3)-(0)
21:16, 21:9, 21:13

LIU, W.   (3)-(0)
21:12, 22:20, 21:14

CHEN, J.   (3)-(0)
21:12, 21:15, 21:19

QIAO, H.   (3)-(0)
21:18, 21:19, 21:16

MEDAL ROUND

DENG, Y.   (3)-(1)
21:23, 21:17, 21:19
21:9

CHEN, J.   (3)-(0)
21:9, 23:21, 21:17

GOLD MEDAL

DENG, Y.   (3)-(2)   CHN
21:14, 21:17, 20:22
17:21, 21:5

SILVER MEDAL

CHEN, J.   TPE

LIU, W.

QIAO, H.

BRONZE MEDAL

QIAO, H.   (3)-(1)   CHN
21:17, 15:21, 21:19
21:11

FINAL CLASSIFICATION

Rnk	Name	Ctry
1	DENG, Yaping	CHN
2	CHEN, Jing	TPE
3	Qiao, Hong	CHN
4	LIU, Wei	CHN

Table Tennis / *Tennis de table*
Doubles, Men / *Doubles, Messieurs*

GROUP A

Rnk	Names	Ctry	Matches P	Matches W	Matches L	Games W	Games L	Points W	Points L
1	LU, Lin / WANG, Tao	CHN	3	3	0	6	0	126	74
2	DING, Yi / QIAN, Qian Li	AUT	3	2	1	4	3	123	119
3	ATIKOVIC, Damir / PRIMORAC, Zoran	CRO	3	1	2	3	5	131	144
4	LANGLEY, Paul / LAVALE, Russell	AUS	3	0	3	1	6	95	138

GROUP B

Rnk	Names	Ctry	Matches P	Matches W	Matches L	Games W	Games L	Points W	Points L
1	PERSSON, Jorgen / WALDNER, Jan-Ove	SWE	3	3	0	6	2	160	139
2	HEISTER, Danny / KEEN, Trienko	NED	3	2	1	5	3	157	140
3	TASAKI, Toshio / YUZAWA, Ryo	JPN	3	1	2	4	4	152	144
4	MORALES MARENGO, Augusto / SALAMANCA GONZALEZ, Juan	CHI	3	0	3	0	6	80	126

GROUP C

Rnk	Names	Ctry	Matches P	Matches W	Matches L	Games W	Games L	Points W	Points L
1	KONG, Linghui / LIU, Guoliang	CHN	3	3	0	6	0	126	77
2	CHILA, Patrick / LEGOUT, Christopher	FRA	3	2	1	4	3	133	102
3	KARLSSON, Peter / von SCHEELE, Thomas	SWE	3	1	2	3	4	116	120
4	ADDY, Winfred / OPOKU, Isaac	GHA	3	0	3	0	6	50	126

GROUP D

Rnk	Names	Ctry	Matches P	Matches W	Matches L	Games W	Games L	Points W	Points L
1	ELOI, Damien / GATIEN, Jean-Philippe	FRA	3	3	0	6	0	126	74
2	CHAN, Kong Wah / LO, Chuen Tsung	HKG	3	2	1	4	3	126	129
3	CHOE, Kyong / LI, Gun Sang	PRK	3	1	2	3	4	116	128
4	HYATT, Michael / HYLTON, Stephen	JAM	3	0	3	0	6	89	126

GROUP E

Rnk	Names	Ctry	Matches P	Matches W	Matches L	Games W	Games L	Points W	Points L
1	FETZNER, Steffen / ROSSKOPF, Joerg	GER	3	3	0	6	0	127	81
2	JINDRAK, Karl / SCHLAGER, Werner	AUT	3	2	1	4	3	144	125
3	HUANG, Wen / NG, Gideon	CAN	3	1	2	2	4	97	106
4	HOYAMA, Hugo / PEIXOTO, Giuliano	BRA	3	0	3	1	6	93	149

GROUP F

Rnk	Names	Ctry	Matches P	Matches W	Matches L	Games W	Games L	Points W	Points L
1	KANG, Hee-Chan / KIM, Taek-Soo	KOR	3	3	0	4	0	84	62
2	BLASZCZYK, Lucjan / GRUBBA, Andrzej	POL	3	2	1	2	3	100	97
3	CHIANG, Peng-Lung / WU, Wen-Chia	TPE	3	1	2	1	4	82	107

GROUP G

Rnk	Names	Ctry	Matches P	Matches W	Matches L	Games W	Games L	Points W	Points L
1	LEE, Chul-Seung / YOO, Nam-Kyu	KOR	3	3	0	6	0	126	89
2	MAZUNOV, Andrey / MAZUNOV, Dmitriy	RUS	3	2	1	4	2	120	104
3	SAMSONOV, Vladimir / SHCHETININ, Yegveniy	BLR	3	1	2	2	4	103	113
4	BUTLER, Jim / SWEERIS, Todd	USA	3	0	3	0	6	83	126

GROUP H

Rnk	Names	Ctry	Matches P	Matches W	Matches L	Games W	Games L	Points W	Points L
1	MATSUSHITA, Koji / SHIBUTANI, Hiroshi	JPN	3	3	0	6	0	129	95
2	GRUJIC, Slobodan / LUPULESKU, Ilija	YUG	3	2	1	4	2	117	115
3	OLALEYE, Sule / TORIOLA, Segun	NGR	3	1	2	2	4	114	115
4	KORBEL, Petr / PLACHY, Josef	CZE	3	0	3	0	6	94	129

QUARTERFINALS

Name	Ctry
LU, Lin / WANG, Tao	CHN
KANG, Hee-Chan / KIM, Taek-Soo	KOR
FETZNER, Steffen / ROSSKOPF, Joerg	GER
ELOI, Damien / GATIEN, Jean-Philippe	FRA
KONG, Linghui / LIU, Guoliang	CHN
MATSUSHITA, Koji / SHIBUTANI, Hiroshi	JPN
LEE, Chul-Seung / YOO, Nam-Kyu	KOR
PERSSON, Jorgen / WALDNER, Jan-Ove	SWE

SEMIFINALS

LU, L. / WANG, T.   (3)-(2)
21:12, 18:21, 18:21
21:12, 21:12

FETZNER, S. / ROSSKOPF, J. (3)-(0)
21:12, 21:17, 21:10

KONG, L. / LIU, G.   (3)-(0)
21:15, 21:19, 21:15

LEE, C.-S. / YOO, N.-K.   (3)-(0)
21:18, 21:16, 21:17

MEDAL ROUND

LU, L. / WANG, T.   (3)-(0)
21:19, 21:17, 21:7

KONG, L. / LIU, G.   (3)-(0)
21:17, 21:16, 21:19

GOLD MEDAL

KONG, L. / LIU, G.   (3)-(1)   CHN
21:8, 13:21, 21:19
21:11

SILVER MEDAL

LU, L. / WANG, T.   CHN

BRONZE MEDAL

FETZNER, S. / ROSSKOPF, J.

LEE, C.-S. / YOO, N.-K.

LEE, C.-S. / YOO, N.-K.   (3)-(0) KOR
21:18, 21:13, 22:20

FINAL CLASSIFICATION

Rnk	Ctry
1	People's Republic of China
2	People's Republic of China
3	Korea
4	Germany

Table Tennis / *Tennis de table*
Doubles, Women / *Doubles, Dames*

GROUP A

Rnk	Names	Ctry	Matches			Games		Points	
			P	W	L	W	L	W	L
1	DENG, Yaping / QIAO, Hong	CHN	3	3	0	4	0	86	39
2	COUBAT, Emmanuelle / WANG-DRECHOU, Xiao Ming	FRA	3	2	1	2	2	53	71
3	CHIU, Barbara / GENG, Lijuan	CAN	3	1	2	0	4	57	86

GROUP B

Rnk	Names	Ctry	Matches			Games		Points	
			P	W	L	W	L	W	L
1	LIU, Wei / QIAO, Yunping	CHN	3	3	0	6	1	146	65
2	NEMES, Olga / SCHOPP, Jie	GER	3	2	1	5	2	128	120
3	HOLT, Andrea / LOMAS, Lisa	GBR	3	1	2	2	4	96	119
4	RODRIGUEZ OLATE, Berta / TEPES CANCINO, Sofija	CHI	3	0	3	0	6	60	126

GROUP C

Rnk	Names	Ctry	Matches			Games		Points	
			P	W	L	W	L	W	L
1	CHAI, Po Wa / CHAN, Tan Lui	HKG	3	2	1	4	2	122	91
2	KIM, Hyon / TU, Jong-Sil	PRK	3	2	1	4	2	122	92
3	PETTERSSON, Pernilla / SVENSSON, Asa	SWE	3	2	1	4	2	120	108
4	GONZALEZ, Eliana / GORRITI, Milagritos	PER	3	0	3	0	6	53	126

GROUP D

Rnk	Names	Ctry	Matches			Games		Points	
			P	W	L	W	L	W	L
1	PARK, Hae-Jung / RYU, Ji-Hae	KOR	3	3	0	6	0	126	82
2	BAI, Hui-Yin / XU, Jing	TPE	3	2	1	4	3	130	118
3	CIOSU, Emilia Elena / COJOCARU, Georgeta	ROM	3	1	2	3	4	132	118
4	KYAKOBYE, Nadunga / MUSOKE, Mary	UGA	3	0	3	0	6	56	126

GROUP E

Rnk	Names	Ctry	Matches			Games		Points	
			P	W	L	W	L	W	L
1	CHEN, Chiu-Tan / CHEN, Jing	TPE	3	2	1	5	3	159	138
2	BATORFI, Csilla / TOTH, Krisztina	HUN	3	2	1	4	2	119	100
3	KIM, Hyang / SON, Mi	PRK	3	2	1	4	4	141	149
4	ZHOU, Shirley / ZHOU, Stella	AUS	3	0	3	2	6	123	155

GROUP F

Rnk	Names	Ctry	Matches			Games		Points	
			P	W	L	W	L	W	L
1	PALINA, Irina / TIMINA, Yelena	RUS	3	3	0	6	0	126	76
2	WANG, Wei / YIP, Lily	USA	3	2	1	4	4	130	137
3	NOOR, Emily / VRIESEKOOP, Huberta	NED	3	1	2	3	4	122	131
4	KAFFO, Bose / OSHONAIKE, Olufunke	NGR	3	0	3	1	6	102	136

GROUP G

Rnk	Names	Ctry	Matches			Games		Points	
			P	W	L	W	L	W	L
1	KOYAMA, Chire / TODO, Taeko	JPN	3	3	0	6	2	148	123
2	SCHALL, Elke / STRUSE, Nicole	GER	3	2	1	5	3	160	124
3	KEEN, Geertje / HOOMAN-KLOPPENBURG, Mirjam	NED	3	1	2	3	5	126	161
4	ARISI, Alessia / NEGRISOLI, Laura	ITA	3	0	3	2	6	129	155

GROUP H

Rnk	Names	Ctry	Matches			Games		Points	
			P	W	L	W	L	W	L
1	KIM, Moo-Kyo / PARK, Kyoung-Ae	KOR	3	3	0	6	0	126	79
2	KAIZU, Fumiyo / SATO, Rika	JPN	3	2	1	4	2	113	89
3	AGANOVIC, Eldijana / BOROS, Tamara	CRO	3	1	2	2	4	101	117
4	DOTI, Monica / KOSAKA, Lyanne	BRA	3	0	3	0	6	71	126

QUARTERFINALS

Name	Ctry
DENG, Yaping / QIAO, Hong	CHN
CHEN, Chiu-Tan / CHEN, Jing	TPE
KIM, Moo-Kyo / PARK, Kyoung-Ae	KOR
CHAI, Po Wa / CHAN, Tan Lui	HKG
PARK, Hae-Jung / RYU, Ji-Hae	KOR
PALINA, Irina / TIMINA, Yelena	RUS
KOYAMA, Chire / TODO, Taeko	JPN
LIU, Wei / QIAO, Yunping	CHN

SEMIFINALS

DENG, Y. / QIAO, H.   (3)-(2)
18:21, 21:16, 21:19
22:24, 23:21

KIM, M.-K. / PARK, K.-A.   (3)-(0)
21:18, 21:13, 21:13

PARK, H.-J. / RYU, J.-H.   (3)-(1)
23:21, 21:18, 20:22
21:15

LIU, W. / QIAO, Y.   (3)-(0)
21:9, 21:15, 21:15

MEDAL ROUND

DENG, Y. / QIAO, H.   (3)-(1)
21:15, 19:21, 21:15
21:19

LIU, W. / QIAO, Y.   (3)-(1)
21:13, 16:21, 22:20
21:11

KIM, M.-K. / PARK, K.-A.

PARK, H.-J. / RYU, J.-H.

GOLD MEDAL

DENG, Y. / QIAO, H.   (3)-(1)   CHN
18:21, 25:23, 22:20
21:14

SILVER MEDAL

LIU, W. / QIAO, Y.   CHN

BRONZE MEDAL

PARK, H.-J. / RYU, J.-H.   (3)-(1)   KOR
21:16, 21:8, 14:21
21:13

FINAL CLASSIFICATION

Rnk	Ctry
1	People's Republic of China
2	People's Republic of China
3	Korea
4	Korea

TENNIS
TENNIS

Abbreviations and terms used in Tennis results tables
Abréviations et termes employés dans les tableaux de résultats de tennis

Term	English	Français
1st Round	First Round	Premier tour
2nd Round	Second Round	Deuxième tour
3rd Round	Third Round	Troisième tour
Bronze Medal	Bronze Medal	Médaille de bronze
Ctry	Country	Pays
Final Classification	Final Classification	Classement final
Gold Medal	Gold Medal	Médaille d'or
Medal Round	Medal Round	Tour pour les médailles
Name	Name	Nom
Quarterfinals	Quarterfinals	Quarts de finale
Rnk	Rank	Classement
Semifinals	Semifinals	Demi-finales
Silver Medal	Silver Medal	Médaille d'argent

International Tennis Federation (ITF)
Fédération Internationale de Tennis
**Palliser Road, Barons Court
London W14 9EN
Great Britain**

Tennis / *Tennis*
Singles, Men / *Simples, Messieurs*

1ST ROUND		2ND ROUND	3RD ROUND	QUARTERFINALS	SEMIFINALS	MEDAL ROUND

Name	Ctry
AGASSI, Andre (1)*	USA
BJORKMAN, Jonas	SWE
KUCERA, Karol	SVK
TOMASHEVICH, Dmitriy	UZB
PESCARIU, Dinu	ROM
ORTIZ, Oscar	MEX
GAUDENZI, Andrea	ITA
COSTA, Carlos (15)*	ESP
SIEMERINK, Jan (9)*	NED
WOODBRIDGE, Todd	AUS
MATSUOKA, Shuzo	JPN
HENMAN, Tim	GBR
BLACK, Byron	ZIM
RAOUX, Guillaume	FRA
ETLIS, Gaston	ARG
FERREIRA, Wayne (5)*	RSA
ENQVIST, Thomas (3)*	SWE
GOELLNER, Marc-Kevin	GER
SARGSIAN, Sargis	ARM
NESTOR, Daniel	CAN
PEREIRA, Nicolas	VEN
GUMY, Hernan	ARG
PAES, Leander	IND
RENEBERG, Richey (11)*	USA
FURLAN, Renzo (14)*	ITA
NOVAK, Jiri	CZE
MOREJON, Luis	ECU
FILIPPINI, Marcelo	URU
FETTERLEIN, Frederik	DEN
ELTINGH, Jacco	NED
ARAZI, Hicham	MAR
ROSSET, Marc (8)*	SUI
BOETSCH, Arnaud (7)*	FRA
STEVEN, Brett	NZL
PAVEL, Andrei	ROM
BRUGUERA, Sergi	ESP
FRANA, Javier	ARG
RUSEDSKI, Greg	GBR
AGENOR, Ronald	HAI
GUSTAFSSON, Magnus (13)*	SWE
STOLTENBERG, Jason (10)*	AUS
LADIPO, Sule	NGR
CARLSEN, Kenneth	DEN
KNOWLES, Mark	BAH
NOSZALY, Sandor	HUN
OGORODOV, Oleg	UZB
KROSLAK, Jan	SVK
WASHINGTON, MaliVai (4)*	USA
COSTA, Alberto (6)*	ESP
LAREAU, Sebastien	CAN
MELIGENI, Fernando	BRA
PESCOSOLIDO, Stefano	ITA
BLACK, Wayne	ZIM
SZYMANSKI, Jimy	VEN
PHILIPPOUSSIS, Mark	AUS
HAARHUIS, Paul (12*)	NED
VACEK, Daniel (16)*	CZE
PRINOSIL, David	GER
LAPENTTI, Nicolas	ECU
OLHOVSKIY, Andrei	RUS
HERNANDEZ, Alejandro	MEX
RUUD, Christian	NOR
ONDRUSKA, Marcos	RSA
IVANISEVIC, Goran (2)*	CRO

2ND ROUND

- AGASSI, A. (1) — 7-6(-6), 7-6(-5)
- KUCERA, K. — 6-3, 2-6, 6-0
- ORTIZ, O. — 6-2, 6-2
- GAUDENZI, A. — 6-3, 6-2
- WOODBRIDGE, T. — 6-2, 6-4
- HENMAN, T. — 7-6(-4), 6-3
- BLACK, B. — 6-3, 3-6, 6-2
- FERREIRA, W. (5) — 6-4, 6-3
- ENQVIST, T. (3) — 7-6(-4), 4-6, 6-4
- SARGSIAN, S. — 6-4, 6-4
- PEREIRA, N. — 6-4, 6-0
- PAES, L. — 6-7(-2), 7-6(-7), 1-0 (Retired)
- FURLAN, R. (14) — 4-6, 6-4, 6-3
- FILIPPINI, M. — 6-7(-3), 7-5, 6-1
- FETTERLEIN, F. — 6-4, 4-6, 8-6
- ROSSET, M. (8) — 6-2, 6-3
- BOETSCH, A. (7) — 6-2, 7-6(-2)
- BRUGUERA, S. — 2-6, 6-1, 8-6
- RUSEDSKI, G. — 4-6, 7-5, 6-3
- GUSTAFSSON, M. (13) — 6-2, 6-4
- STOLTENBERG, J. (10) — 7-6(-4), 6-3
- CARLSEN, K. — 7-5, 6-3
- OGORODOV, O. — 7-5, 7-6(-6)
- WASHINGTON, M. (4) — 6-3, 7-6(-3)
- COSTA, A. (6) — 7-6(-11), 6-4
- MELIGENI, F. — 6-4, 6-2
- BLACK, W. — 6-7(-4), 6-4, 6-3
- PHILIPPOUSSIS, M. — 7-6(-4), 7-6(-2)
- VACEK, D. (16) — 6-4, 2-6, 6-4
- OLHOVSKIY, A. — 6-1, 3-6, 8-6
- RUUD, C. — 6-3, 2-6, 8-6
- ONDRUSKA, M. — 6-2, 6-4

3RD ROUND

- AGASSI, A. (1) — 6-4, 6-4
- GAUDENZI, A. — 6-1, 7-6(-5)
- WOODBRIDGE, T. — 7-6(-6), 7-6(-5)
- FERREIRA, W. (5) — 6-2, 7-5
- ENQVIST, T. (3) — 4-6, 7-6(-2), 6-4
- PAES, L. — 6-2, 6-3
- FURLAN, R. (14) — 7-5, 6-2
- ROSSET, M. (8) — 7-6(-5), 7-5
- BRUGUERA, S. — 7-6(-7), 4-6, 6-2
- RUSEDSKI, G. — 6-7(-4), 7-6(-3), 6-3
- CARLSEN, K. — 6-2, 3-6, 6-3
- WASHINGTON, M. (4) — 6-3, 6-4
- MELIGENI, F. — 7-6(-5), 6-4
- PHILIPPOUSSIS, M. — 6-4, 6-2
- OLHOVSKIY, A. — 6-3, 7-6(-1)
- RUUD, C. — 7-6(-6), 7-6(-1)

QUARTERFINALS

- AGASSI, A. (1) — 2-6, 6-4, 6-2
- FERREIRA, W. (5) — 7-6(-3), 7-6(-5)
- PAES, L. — 7-5, 7-6(-3)
- FURLAN, R. (14) — 6-0, 4-2 (Retired)
- BRUGUERA, S. — 7-6(-7), 6-3
- WASHINGTON, M. (4) — 6-7(-8), 6-0, 6-2
- MELIGENI, F. — 7-6(-7), 4-6, 8-6
- OLHOVSKIY, A. — 6-4, 6-3

SEMIFINALS

- AGASSI, A. (1) — 7-5, 4-6, 7-5
- PAES, L. — 6-1, 7-5
- BRUGUERA, S. — 7-6(-8), 4-6, 7-5
- MELIGENI, F. — 6-7(-5), 7-5, 6-3

MEDAL ROUND

- AGASSI, A. (1) — 7-6(-5), 6-3
- BRUGUERA, S. — 7-6(-9), 6-2
- PAES, L. — (left) / MELIGENI, F.

FINAL CLASSIFICATION

Rnk	Name	Ctry
1	AGASSI, Andre (1)	USA
2	BRUGUERA, Sergi	ESP
3	PAES, Leander	IND
4	MELIGENI, Fernando	BRA
5	FERREIRA, Wayne (5)	RSA
5	FURLAN, Renzo (14)	ITA
5	WASHINGTON, MaliVai (4)	USA
5	OLHOVSKIY, Andrei	RUS

GOLD MEDAL

AGASSI, A. (1) — USA
6-2, 6-3, 6-1

SILVER MEDAL

BRUGUERA, S. — ESP

BRONZE MEDAL

PAES, L. — IND
3-6, 6-2, 6-4
MELIGENI, F.

*Player's seed is indicated by the number in parentheses after name.

La tête de série est indiquée par le chiffre entre parenthèses après le nom.

BART L WHALEY • BART L WHALEY • DAVID N WHALEY • SHELBA D WHALEY • WILLIAM WHALEY • WALTER J WHARTON • WALTER J WHARTON • JANELLE E WHATELEY • ANN S WHATLEY • CLEMMIE B WHATLEY • CORLISS Y WHATLEY • STEVE D WHATMORE • DALE WHEALTON • JAMIE L WHEAT • MYRA E WHEAT • LORETTA E WHEATLEY • JUDITH L WHEATON • ELIZABETH A WHEELAN • AARON K WHEELER • ADRIENNE WHEELER • CHRISSY WHEELER • CHRISTOPHER D WHEELER • COURTNEY E WHEELER • CYNTHIA M WHEELER

Tennis / *Tennis*

Singles, Women / *Simples, Dames*

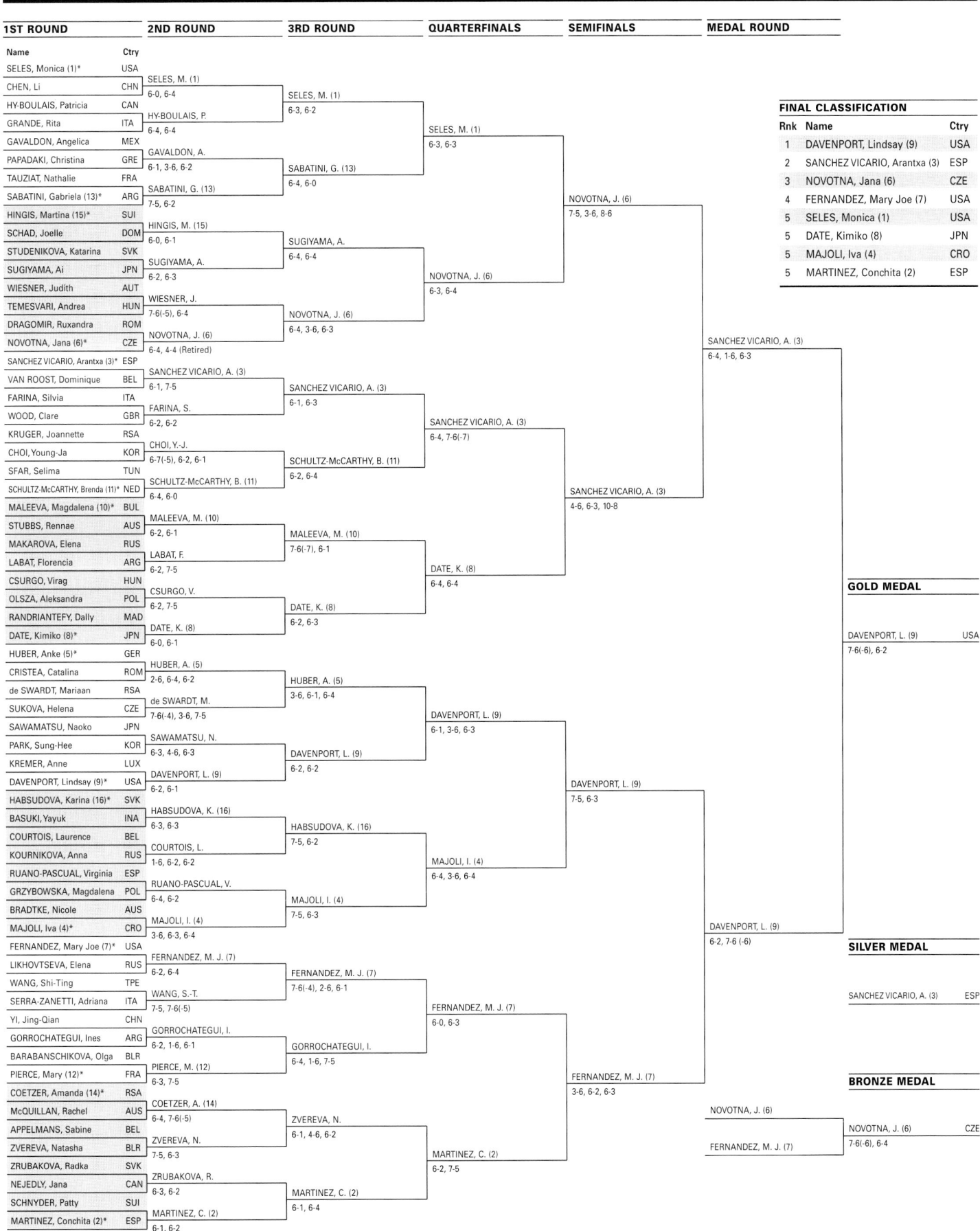

1ST ROUND

Name	Ctry
SELES, Monica (1)*	USA
CHEN, Li	CHN
HY-BOULAIS, Patricia	CAN
GRANDE, Rita	ITA
GAVALDON, Angelica	MEX
PAPADAKI, Christina	GRE
TAUZIAT, Nathalie	FRA
SABATINI, Gabriela (13)*	ARG
HINGIS, Martina (15)*	SUI
SCHAD, Joelle	DOM
STUDENIKOVA, Katarina	SVK
SUGIYAMA, Ai	JPN
WIESNER, Judith	AUT
TEMESVARI, Andrea	HUN
DRAGOMIR, Ruxandra	ROM
NOVOTNA, Jana (6)*	CZE
SANCHEZ VICARIO, Arantxa (3)*	ESP
VAN ROOST, Dominique	BEL
FARINA, Silvia	ITA
WOOD, Clare	GBR
KRUGER, Joannette	RSA
CHOI, Young-Ja	KOR
SFAR, Selima	TUN
SCHULTZ-McCARTHY, Brenda (11)*	NED
MALEEVA, Magdalena (10)*	BUL
STUBBS, Rennae	AUS
MAKAROVA, Elena	RUS
LABAT, Florencia	ARG
CSURGO, Virag	HUN
OLSZA, Aleksandra	POL
RANDRIANTEFY, Dally	MAD
DATE, Kimiko (8)*	JPN
HUBER, Anke (5)*	GER
CRISTEA, Catalina	ROM
de SWARDT, Mariaan	RSA
SUKOVA, Helena	CZE
SAWAMATSU, Naoko	JPN
PARK, Sung-Hee	KOR
KREMER, Anne	LUX
DAVENPORT, Lindsay (9)*	USA
HABSUDOVA, Karina (16)*	SVK
BASUKI, Yayuk	INA
COURTOIS, Laurence	BEL
KOURNIKOVA, Anna	RUS
RUANO-PASCUAL, Virginia	ESP
GRZYBOWSKA, Magdalena	POL
BRADTKE, Nicole	AUS
MAJOLI, Iva (4)*	CRO
FERNANDEZ, Mary Joe (7)*	USA
LIKHOVTSEVA, Elena	RUS
WANG, Shi-Ting	TPE
SERRA-ZANETTI, Adriana	ITA
YI, Jing-Qian	CHN
GORROCHATEGUI, Ines	ARG
BARABANSCHIKOVA, Olga	BLR
PIERCE, Mary (12)*	FRA
COETZER, Amanda (14)*	RSA
McQUILLAN, Rachel	AUS
APPELMANS, Sabine	BEL
ZVEREVA, Natasha	BLR
ZRUBAKOVA, Radka	SVK
NEJEDLY, Jana	CAN
SCHNYDER, Patty	SUI
MARTINEZ, Conchita (2)*	ESP

2ND ROUND

SELES, M. (1)
6-0, 6-4

HY-BOULAIS, P.
6-4, 6-4

GAVALDON, A.
6-1, 3-6, 6-2

SABATINI, G. (13)
7-5, 6-2

HINGIS, M. (15)
6-0, 6-1

SUGIYAMA, A.
6-2, 6-3

WIESNER, J.
7-6(-5), 6-4

NOVOTNA, J. (6)
6-4, 4-4 (Retired)

SANCHEZ VICARIO, A. (3)
6-1, 7-5

FARINA, S.
6-2, 6-2

CHOI, Y.-J.
6-7(-5), 6-2, 6-1

SCHULTZ-McCARTHY, B. (11)
6-4, 6-0

MALEEVA, M. (10)
6-2, 6-1

LABAT, F.
6-2, 7-5

CSURGO, V.
6-2, 7-5

DATE, K. (8)
6-0, 6-1

HUBER, A. (5)
2-6, 6-4, 6-2

de SWARDT, M.
7-6(-4), 3-6, 7-5

SAWAMATSU, N.
6-3, 4-6, 6-3

DAVENPORT, L. (9)
6-2, 6-1

HABSUDOVA, K. (16)
6-3, 6-3

COURTOIS, L.
1-6, 6-2, 6-2

RUANO-PASCUAL, V.
6-4, 6-2

MAJOLI, I. (4)
3-6, 6-3, 6-4

FERNANDEZ, M. J. (7)
6-2, 6-4

WANG, S.-T.
7-5, 7-6(-5)

GORROCHATEGUI, I.
6-2, 1-6, 6-1

PIERCE, M. (12)
6-3, 7-5

COETZER, A. (14)
6-4, 7-6(-5)

ZVEREVA, N.
7-5, 6-3

ZRUBAKOVA, R.
6-3, 6-2

MARTINEZ, C. (2)
6-1, 6-2

3RD ROUND

SELES, M. (1)
6-3, 6-2

SABATINI, G. (13)
6-4, 6-0

SUGIYAMA, A.
6-4, 6-4

NOVOTNA, J. (6)
6-4, 3-6, 6-3

SANCHEZ VICARIO, A. (3)
6-1, 6-3

SCHULTZ-McCARTHY, B. (11)
6-2, 6-4

MALEEVA, M. (10)
7-6(-7), 6-1

DATE, K. (8)
6-2, 6-3

HUBER, A. (5)
3-6, 6-1, 6-4

DAVENPORT, L. (9)
6-2, 6-2

HABSUDOVA, K. (16)
7-5, 6-2

MAJOLI, I. (4)
7-5, 6-3

FERNANDEZ, M. J. (7)
7-6(-4), 2-6, 6-1

GORROCHATEGUI, I.
6-4, 1-6, 7-5

ZVEREVA, N.
6-1, 4-6, 6-2

MARTINEZ, C. (2)
6-1, 6-4

QUARTERFINALS

SELES, M. (1)
6-3, 6-3

NOVOTNA, J. (6)
6-3, 6-4

SANCHEZ VICARIO, A. (3)
6-4, 7-6(-7)

DATE, K. (8)
6-4, 6-4

DAVENPORT, L. (9)
6-1, 3-6, 6-3

MAJOLI, I. (4)
6-4, 3-6, 6-4

FERNANDEZ, M. J. (7)
6-0, 6-3

MARTINEZ, C. (2)
6-2, 7-5

SEMIFINALS

NOVOTNA, J. (6)
7-5, 3-6, 8-6

SANCHEZ VICARIO, A. (3)
4-6, 6-3, 10-8

DAVENPORT, L. (9)
7-5, 6-3

FERNANDEZ, M. J. (7)
3-6, 6-2, 6-3

MEDAL ROUND

SANCHEZ VICARIO, A. (3)
6-4, 1-6, 6-3

DAVENPORT, L. (9)
6-2, 7-6 (-6)

NOVOTNA, J. (6)

FERNANDEZ, M. J. (7)

FINAL CLASSIFICATION

Rnk	Name	Ctry
1	DAVENPORT, Lindsay (9)	USA
2	SANCHEZ VICARIO, Arantxa (3)	ESP
3	NOVOTNA, Jana (6)	CZE
4	FERNANDEZ, Mary Joe (7)	USA
5	SELES, Monica (1)	USA
5	DATE, Kimiko (8)	JPN
5	MAJOLI, Iva (4)	CRO
5	MARTINEZ, Conchita (2)	ESP

GOLD MEDAL

DAVENPORT, L. (9)   USA
7-6(-6), 6-2

SILVER MEDAL

SANCHEZ VICARIO, A. (3)   ESP

BRONZE MEDAL

NOVOTNA, J. (6)   CZE
7-6(-6), 6-4

Player's seed is indicated by the number in parentheses after name.

La tête de série est indiquée par le chiffre entre parenthèses après le nom.

Tennis / *Tennis*

Doubles, Men / *Doubles, Messieurs*

1ST ROUND		2ND ROUND	QUARTERFINALS	SEMIFINALS	MEDAL ROUND
Name	**Ctry**				
WOODBRIDGE, Todd / WOODFORDE, Mark (1)*	AUS	WOODBRIDGE, T. / WOODFORDE, M. (1)			
BOETSCH, Arnaud / RAOUX, Guillaume	FRA	6-2, 3-6, 6-3	WOODBRIDGE, T. / WOODFORDE, M. (1)		
BHUPATHI, Mahesh / PAES, Leander	IND	BHUPATHI, M. / PAES, L.	4-6, 6-2, 6-2		
PAN, Bing / XIA, Jia-Ping	CHN	4-6, 6-4, 6-4		WOODBRIDGE, T. / WOODFORDE, M. (1)	
IWABUCHI, Satoshi / SUZUKI, Takao	JPN	IWABUCHI, S. / SUZUKI, T.		6-4, 6-1	
BIANCHI, Juan Carlos / PEREIRA, Nicolas	VEN	4-6, 7-6(-5), 8-6	BRUGUERA, S. / CARBONELL, T.		
BRUGUERA, Sergi / CARBONELL, Tomas	ESP	BRUGUERA, S. / CARBONELL, T.	6-7(-1), 6-2, 7-5		WOODBRIDGE, T. / WOODFORDE, M. (1)
FRANA, Javier / LOBO, Luis (7)*	ARG	6-3, 7-6(-6)			6-2, 5-7, 18-16
ELTINGH, Jacco / HAARHUIS, Paul (3)*	NED	ELTINGH, J. / HAARHUIS, P. (3)			
PAVEL, Andrei / PESCARIU, Dinu	ROM	6-2, 6-7(-1), 6-4	ELTINGH, J. / HAARHUIS, P. (3)		
N'GORAN, Claude / N'GORAN, Clement	CIV	N'GORAN, C. / N'GORAN, C.	6-4, 6-4		
CHEN, Chih-Jung / LIEN, Yu-Hui	TPE	6-2, 6-2		ELTINGH, J. / HAARHUIS, P. (3)	
AGASSI, Andre / WASHINGTON, MaliVai	USA	AGASSI, A. / WASHINGTON, M.		7-6(-4), 7-6(-4)	
HERNANDEZ, Alejandro / ORTIZ, Oscar	MEX	6-3, 4-6, 6-4	FERREIRA, E. / FERREIRA, W. (6)		GOLD MEDAL
KOVES, Gabor / MARKOVITS, Laszlo	HUN	FERREIRA, E. / FERREIRA, W. (6)	7-5, 6-7(-2), 6-0		
FERREIRA, Ellis / FERREIRA, Wayne (6)*	RSA	6-4, 6-1			WOODBRIDGE, T. / WOODFORDE, M. (1) AUS
BLACK, Byron / BLACK, Wayne (8)*	ZIM	BLACK, B. / BLACK, W. (8)			6-4, 6-4, 6-2
LEE, Hyung-Taik / YOON, Yong-Il	KOR	6-4, 6-2	GOELLNER, M.-K. / PRINOSIL, D.		
GOELLNER, Marc-Kevin / PRINOSIL, David	GER	GOELLNER, M.-K. / PRINOSIL, D.	6-4, 7-6(-6)		
GAUDENZI, Andrea / NARGISO, Diego	ITA	4-6, 6-1, 7-5		GOELLNER, M.-K. / PRINOSIL, D.	
KNOWLES, Mark / SMITH, Roger	BAH	KNOWLES, M. / SMITH, R.		6-2, 6-3	
COUTO, Emanuel / MOTA, Bernardo	POR	7-6(-6), 7-6(-4)	HIRSZON, S. / IVANISEVIC, G.		
HIRSZON, Sasa / IVANISEVIC, Goran	CRO	HIRSZON, S. / IVANISEVIC, G.	7-6(-4), 6-3		
BJORKMAN, Jonas / KULTI, Nicklas (4)*	SWE	7-6(-4), 7-6(-4)			BROAD, N. / HENMAN, T.
NOVAK, Jiri / VACEK, Daniel (5)*	CZE	NOVAK, J. / VACEK, D. (5)			4-6, 6-3, 10-8
OGORODOV, Oleg / TOMASHEVICH, Dmitri	UZB	(Walkover)	NOVAK, J. / VACEK, D. (5)		
CARLSEN, Kenneth / FETTERLEIN, Frederik	DEN	CAMPANA, P. / LAPENTTI, N.	7-5, 6-4		
CAMPANA, Pablo / LAPENTTI, Nicolas	ECU	6-4, 3-6, 6-3		BROAD, N. / HENMAN, T.	
BROAD, Neil / HENMAN, Tim	GBR	BROAD, N. / HENMAN, T.		7-6(-4), 6-4	
KROSLAK, Jan / KUCERA, Karol	SVK	6-3, 6-3	BROAD, N. / HENMAN, T.		SILVER MEDAL
BARRON, Scott / CASEY, Owen	IRL	CONNELL, G. / NESTOR, D. (2)	7-6(-5), 4-6, 6-4		
CONNELL, Grant / NESTOR, Daniel (2)*	CAN	6-4, 6-4			BROAD, N. / HENMAN, T. GBR

*Player's seed is indicated by the number in parentheses after name.

La tête de série est indiquée par le chiffre entre parenthèses après le nom.

BRONZE MEDAL

ELTINGH, J. / HAARHUIS, P. (3)		GOELLNER, M.-K. / PRINOSIL, D. GER
	GOELLNER, M.-K. / PRINOSIL, D.	6-2, 7-5

FINAL CLASSIFICATION

Rnk	Name	Ctry
1	WOODBRIDGE, Todd / WOODFORDE, Mark (1)	AUS
2	BROAD, Neil / HENMAN, Tim	GBR
3	GOELLNER, Marc-Kevin / PRINOSIL, David	GER
4	ELTINGH, Jacco / HAARHUIS, Paul (3)	NED
5	BRUGUERA, Sergi / CARBONELL, Tomas	ESP
5	FERREIRA, Ellis / FERREIRA, Wayne (6)	RSA
5	HIRSZON, Sasa / IVANISEVIC, Goran	CRO
5	NOVAK, Jiri / VACEK, Daniel (5)	CZE

Tennis / *Tennis*

Doubles, Women / *Doubles, Dames*

1ST ROUND		2ND ROUND	QUARTERFINALS	SEMIFINALS	MEDAL ROUND

Name / **Ctry**

Name	Ctry
FERNANDEZ, Gigi / FERNANDEZ, Mary Joe (1)*	USA
BYE	
PIERCE, Mary / TAUZIET, Nathalie	FRA
GRYZYBOWSKA, Magdalena / OLSZA, Aleksandra	POL
LAKE, Valda / WOOD, Clare	GBR
MALEEVA, Katerina / MALEEVA, Magdalena	BUL
KIM, Eun-Ha / PARK, Sung-Hee	KOR
COETZER, Amanda / de SWARDT, Mariaan (7)*	RSA
BOLLEGRAF, Manon / SCHULTZ-McCARTHY, Brenda (3)*	NED
LUGINA, Olga / MEDVEDEVA, Natalia	UKR
CSURGO, Virag / TEMESVARI, Andrea	HUN
CABEZAS, Paula / CASTRO, Barbara	CHI
HINGIS, Martina / SCHNYDER, Patty	SUI
HABSUDOVA, Karina / ZRUBAKOVA, Radka	SVK
APPELMANS, Sabine / COURTOIS, Laurence	BEL
SABATINI, Gabriela / TARABINI, Patricia (6)*	ARG
BRADTKE, Nicole / STUBBS, Rennae (5)*	AUS
CHEN, Li / YI, Jing-Qian	CHN
SANGARAM, Benjamas / TANASUGARN, Tamarine	THA
PAPADAKI, Christina / ZACHARIADOU, Christina	GRE
MAJOLI, Iva / MURIC, Maja	CRO
FARINA, Silvia / GOLARSA, Laura	ITA
RANDRIANTEFY, Dally / RANDRIANTEFY, Natacha	MAD
MARTINEZ, Conchita / SANCHEZ VICARIO, Arantxa (4)*	ESP
NAGATSUKA, Kyoko / SUGIYAMA, Ai (8)*	JPN
HETHERINGTON, Jill / HY-BOULAIS, Patricia	CAN
BARABANSCHIKOVA, Olga / ZVEREVA, Natasha	BLR
d'AGOSTINI, Miriam / MENGA, Vanessa	BRA
BASUKI, Yayuk / TEDJAKUSUMA, Romana	INA
CRISTEA, Catalina / DRAGOMIR, Ruxandra	ROM
KOURNIKOVA, Anna / MAKAROVA, Elena	RUS
NOVOTNA, Jana / SUKOVA, Helena (2)	CZE

2ND ROUND

FERNANDEZ, G. / FERNANDEZ, M. J. (1)

PIERCE, M. / TAUZIET, N.
6-2, 3-6, 6-0

LAKE, V. / WOOD, C.
3-6, 7-6(-8), 6-3

COETZER, A. / de SWARDT (7)
6-1, 6-3

BOLLEGRAF, M. / SCHULTZ-McCARTHY, B. (3)
(Walkover)

CSURGO, V. / TEMESVARI, A.
6-4, 1-6, 6-3

HINGIS, M. / SCHNYDER, P.
3-6, 6-4, 6-2

APPELMANS, S. / COURTOIS, L.
5-7, 6-3, 6-4

CHEN, L. / YI, J.-Q.
(Walkover)

SANGARAM, B. / TANASUGARN, T.
6-2, 6-7(-3), 6-2

MAJOLI, I. / MURIC, M.
7-6(-2), 4-6, 9-7

MARTINEZ, C. / SANCHEZ VICARIO, A. (4)
6-1, 6-3

HETHERINGTON, J. / HY-BOULAIS, P.
7-6(-2), 6-1

BARABANSCHIKOVA, O. / ZVEREVA, N.
6-2, 6-3

BASUKI, Y. / TEDJAKUSUMA, R.
(Walkover)

NOVOTNA, J. / SUKOVA, H. (2)
6-2, 6-2

QUARTERFINALS

FERNANDEZ, G. / FERNANDEZ, M. J. (1)
6-4, 6-3

LAKE, V. / WOOD, C.
7-5, 7-5

BOLLEGRAF, M. / SCHULTZ-McCARTHY, B. (3)
7-6(-5), 7-6(-5)

HINGIS, M. / SCHNYDER, P.
2-6, 6-1, 7-5

SANGARAM, B. / TANASUGARN, T.
2-6, 6-4, 6-4

MARTINEZ, C. / SANCHEZ VICARIO, A. (4)
6-2, 6-1

HETHERINGTON, J. / HY-BOULAIS, P.
2-6, 6-4, 6-1

NOVOTNA, J. / SUKOVA , H. (2)
6-2, 6-3

SEMIFINALS

FERNANDEZ, G. / FERNANDEZ, M. J. (1)
6-2, 6-1

BOLLEGRAF, M. / SCHULTZ-McCARTHY, B. (3)
6-4, 6-3

MARTINEZ, C. / SANCHEZ VICARIO, A. (4)
6-2, 6-1

NOVOTNA, J. / SUKOVA, H. (2)
6-2. 6-4

MEDAL ROUND

FERNANDEZ, G. / FERNANDEZ, M. J. (1)
7-5, 7-6(-3)

NOVOTNA, J. / SUKOVA, H. (2)
6-2. 7-6(-1)

GOLD MEDAL

FERNANDEZ, G. / FERNANDEZ, M. J. (1) USA
7-6(-6), 6-4

SILVER MEDAL

NOVOTNA, J. / SUKOVA, H. (2)   CZE

BRONZE MEDAL

BOLLEGRAF, M. / SCHULTZ-McCARTHY, B. (3)

MARTINEZ, C. / SANCHEZ VICARIO, A. (4) ESP
6-1, 6-3

MARTINEZ, C. / SANCHEZ VICARIO, A. (4)

*Player's seed is indicated by the number in parentheses after name.

La tête de série est indiquée par le chiffre entre parenthèses après le nom.

FINAL CLASSIFICATION

Rnk	Name	Ctry
1	FERNANDEZ, Gigi / FERNANDEZ, Mary Joe (1)	USA
2	NOVOTNA, Jana / SUKOVA, Helena (2)	CZE
3	MARTINEZ, Conchita / SANCHEZ VICARIO, Arantxa (4)	ESP
4	BOLLEGRAF, Manon / SCHULTZ-McCARTHY, Brenda (3)	NED
5	HETHERINGTON, Jill / HY-BOULAIS, Patricia	CAN
5	HINGIS, Martina / SCHNYDER, Patty	SUI
5	LAKE, Valda / WOOD, Clare	GBR
5	SANGARAM, Benjamas / TANASUGARN, Tamarine	THA

Abbreviations and terms used in Volleyball results tables
Abréviations et termes employés dans les tableaux de résultats de volleyball

Term	English	Français
*	Substitute	Remplaçant
(-/Total)	Errors/Total Opportunities	Erreurs/occas-ions totales
(+/Total)	Successes/ Total Opportunities	Succès/ Occasions totales
1st Referee	First Referee	Premier arbitre
1st Set	First Set	Première manche
2nd Referee	Second Referee	Deuxième arbitre
2nd Set	Second Set	Deuxième manche
5th Place	Fifth Place	Cinquième place
7th Place	Seventh Place	Septième place
9th Place	Ninth Place	Neuvième place
13th Place	Thirteenth Place	Treizième place
17th Place	Seventeenth Place	Dix-septième place
Against	Against	Contre
Assistant Coach	Assistant Coach	Entraîneur adjoint
Att	Attempts	Essais
Attack S/O	Attack Side Out	Attaque changement de service
Attack Total	Attack Total	Total d'attaques
Attacks	Attacks	Attaques
Block	Block	Bloc
Bronze	Bronze Medal	Médaille de bronze
Bronze Match	Bronze Match	Match pour le médaille de bronze
Classifications	Classifications	Classement
Coach	Coach	Entraîneur
Continued	Continued	Continué
Dig	Dig	Passe basse
Duration	Duration	Durée
Errors	Errors	Erreurs
F/A	For/Against	Pour/Contre
Final Classification	Final Classification	Classement final
Final	Final	Finale
For	For	Pour
Games	Games	Matchs
General Summary	General Summary	Récapitulatif général
Gold	Gold Medal	Médaille d'or
Gold Match	Gold Match	Match pour la médaille d'or
Group	Group	Groupe
Lost	Lost	Perdu
Medal	Medal	Médaille
Names	Names	Noms
Non-Scoring Skills	Non-Scoring Skills	Autres techniques
Opp. Error	Opponent Error	Erreur de l'adversaire
Phase	Phase	Phase
Played	Played	Joué
Points	Points	Points
Positive	Positive	Positif
Preliminaries	Preliminaries	Eliminatoires
Pts	Points	Points
Pts + S/O	Points + Side Out	Points + hors jeu
Pts Won	Points Won	Points gagnés service
Quarterfinals	Quarterfinals	Quarts de finale
Reception	Reception	Réception
Result	Result	Résultat
Rnk	Rank	Classement
Round	Round	Tour
S	Starting Lineup	Liste de départ
S/O	Side Outs	Hors jeu
Score	Score	Score
Scoring Skills	Scoring Skills	Techniques de points/marques
Semifinals	Semifinals	Demi-finales
Serve	Serve	Service
Set	Set	Manche
Silver	Silver Medal	Médaille d'argent
Team	Team	Equipe
Total	Total	Total
Total Pts	Total Points	Total des points
Won	Won	Gagné
W/L	Wins/Losses	Victoires/pertes

International Volleyball Federation (FIVB)
Fédération Internationale de Volleyball
Avenue de la Gare 12
1003 Lausanne, Switzerland

VOLLEYBALL
VOLLEYBALL

Volleyball—Beach / *Volleyball — De plage*
Men / *Messieurs*

ROUND 1 — ESP 11 CZE 15 — Duration: 00:25 — 1st Referee: JPN KONNO, Masaaki — 2nd Referee: USA SALVATORE, Patty

ESP Spain

Names	\[Scoring Skills (Pts + S/O)\] Serve	Attack	Block	Opp Error	Total	\[Non-Scoring Skills (+ / Total)\] Reception	Dig	\[Positive (+ / Total)\] Attack S/O	Attack Total	\[Errors (– / Total)\] Attack Total	Serve
YUSTE MUNIZ, Javier	1	1 + 5	0 + 0		2 + 5	6 / 7	5	3 / 7	6 / 15	2 / 15	2 / 13
MARTIN PRIETO, Miguel Angel	1	1 + 3	2 + 0		4 + 3	12 / 13	2	3 / 13	4 / 18	3 / 18	2 / 11
Totals	2	2 + 8	2 + 0	5 + 3	11 + 11	18 / 20	7	6 / 20	10 / 33	5 / 33	4 / 24

CZE Czech Republic

Names	Serve	Attack	Block	Opp Error	Total	Reception	Dig	Attack S/O	Attack Total	Attack Total	Serve
PALINEK, Michal	0	5 + 2	0 + 0		5 + 2	4 / 5	4	2 / 15	7 / 15	2 / 15	0 / 11
PAKOSTA, Marek	2	1 + 5	2 + 0		5 + 5	8 / 8	5	5 / 16	6 / 16	3 / 16	1 / 13
Totals	2	6 + 7	2 + 0	5 + 5	15 + 12	12 / 13	9	7 / 31	13 / 31	5 / 31	1 / 24

ROUND 1 — ESP 15 INA 7 — Duration: 00:41 — 1st Referee: FRA BIAU, Patrick — 2nd Referee: AUS HRESZCZUK, Peter

ESP Spain

Names	\[Scoring Skills (Pts + S/O)\] Serve	Attack	Block	Opp. Error	Total	\[Non-Scoring Skills (+ / Total)\] Reception	Dig	\[Positive (+ / Total)\] Attack S/O	Attack Total	\[Errors (– / Total)\] Attack Total	Serve
JIMENEZ GALAN, Sixto	0	6 + 10	0 + 0		6 + 10	14 / 16	9	10 / 16	16 / 27	0 / 27	0 / 18
BOSMA MINGUEZ, Javier	0	3 + 11	2 + 0		5 + 11	9 / 11	6	9 / 11	14 / 20	2 / 20	6 / 24
Totals	0	9 + 21	2 + 0	4 + 6	15 + 27	23 / 27	15	19 / 27	30 / 47	2 / 47	6 / 42

INA Indonesia

Names	Serve	Attack	Block	Opp. Error	Total	Reception	Dig	Attack S/O	Attack Total	Attack Total	Serve
NURMUFID, Mochamad	1	2 + 8	0 + 0		3 + 8	16 / 18	3	7 / 24	10 / 24	2 / 24	2 / 16
MARKOJI, Markoji	2	1 + 12	0 + 0		3 + 12	16 / 18	9	8 / 26	13 / 26	3 / 26	2 / 18
Totals	3	3 + 20	0 + 0	1 + 7	7 + 27	32 / 36	12	15 / 50	23 / 50	5 / 50	4 / 34

ROUND 1 — EST 8 FRA 15 — Duration: 00:48 — 1st Referee: PUR MENDOZA BAS, Aurelio — 2nd Referee: ESP CARRENO, Mirela

EST Estonia

Names	\[Scoring Skills (Pts + S/O)\] Serve	Attack	Block	Opp. Error	Total	\[Non-Scoring Skills (+ / Total)\] Reception	Dig	\[Positive (+ / Total)\] Attack S/O	Attack Total	\[Errors (– / Total)\] Attack Total	Serve
KEEL, Avo	0	1 + 12	1 + 0		2 + 12	19 / 20	3	12 / 20	13 / 28	1 / 28	4 / 23
KREEN, Kaido	1	2 + 19	0 + 0		3 + 19	28 / 29	8	19 / 29	21 / 33	3 / 33	2 / 22
Totals	1	3 + 31	1 + 0	3 + 5	8 + 36	47 / 49	11	31 / 49	34 / 61	4 / 61	6 / 45

FRA France

Names	Serve	Attack	Block	Opp. Error	Total	Reception	Dig	Attack S/O	Attack Total	Attack Total	Serve
JODARD, Jean-Philippe	0	4 + 20	0 + 0		4 + 20	27 / 28	10	19 / 39	24 / 39	4 / 39	1 / 24
PENIGAUD, Christian	0	1 + 9	5 + 1		6 + 10	7 / 10	2	7 / 16	10 / 16	0 / 16	1 / 27
Totals	0	5 + 29	5 + 1	5 + 7	15 + 37	34 / 38	12	26 / 55	34 / 55	4 / 55	2 / 51

ROUND 1 — AUS 15 CAN 6 — Duration: 00:35 — 1st Referee: USA LEMAIRE, Sue — 2nd Referee: GBR BREHAUT, Jeff

AUS Australia

Names	\[Scoring Skills (Pts + S/O)\] Serve	Attack	Block	Opp. Error	Total	\[Non-Scoring Skills (+ / Total)\] Reception	Dig	\[Positive (+ / Total)\] Attack S/O	Attack Total	\[Errors (– / Total)\] Attack Total	Serve
ZAHNER, Lee	0	1 + 11	2 + 0		3 + 11	15 / 16	4	11 / 16	12 / 21	4 / 21	1 / 19
PROSSER, Julien	0	3 + 7	2 + 0		5 + 7	5 / 6	6	6 / 6	10 / 15	1 / 15	1 / 20
Totals	0	4 + 18	4 + 0	7 + 6	15 + 24	20 / 22	10	17 / 22	22 / 36	5 / 36	2 / 39

CAN Canada

Names	Serve	Attack	Block	Opp. Error	Total	Reception	Dig	Attack S/O	Attack Total	Attack Total	Serve
DUNN, Marc	2	0 + 6	0 + 0		2 + 6	12 / 14	1	6 / 18	6 / 18	6 / 18	4 / 17
DRAKICH, Edward Raymond	0	0 + 13	2 + 0		2 + 13	20 / 23	2	11 / 24	13 / 24	0 / 24	2 / 13
Totals	2	0 + 19	2 + 0	2 + 5	6 + 24	32 / 37	3	17 / 42	19 / 42	6 / 42	6 / 30

ROUND 1 — NZL 8 ITA 15 — Duration: 00:39 — 1st Referee: MEX RAMIREZ RIVERA, Miguel — 2nd Referee: FRA BIAU, Patrick

NZL New Zealand

Names	\[Scoring Skills (Pts + S/O)\] Serve	Attack	Block	Opp. Error	Total	\[Non-Scoring Skills (+ / Total)\] Reception	Dig	\[Positive (+ / Total)\] Attack S/O	Attack Total	\[Errors (– /Total)\] Attack Total	Serve
HAMILTON, Reid	1	0 + 6	1 + 0		2 + 6	13 / 13	6	4 / 13	6 / 18	1 / 18	2 / 19
HAMILTON, Glenn	0	1 + 12	3 + 1		4 + 13	22 / 23	5	11 / 23	13 / 28	3 / 28	4 / 16
Totals	1	1 + 18	4 + 1	2 + 6	8 + 25	35 / 36	11	15 / 36	19 / 46	4 / 46	6 / 35

ITA Italy

Names	Serve	Attack	Block	Opp. Error	Total	Reception	Dig	Attack S/O	Attack Total	Attack Total	Serve
GRIGOLO, Nicola	0	4 + 10	1 + 0		5 + 10	17 / 18	7	9 / 23	14 / 23	1 / 23	2 / 23
GHIURGHI, Andrea	0	3 + 10	3 + 0		6 + 10	9 / 10	8	10 / 23	13 / 23	2 / 23	3 / 18
Totals	0	7 + 20	4 + 0	4 + 7	15 + 27	26 / 28	15	19 / 46	27 / 46	3 / 46	5 / 41

Men / Messieurs

ROUND 1 GER 15 JPN 8 Duration: 00:51 1st Referee: POR CORBAL S. AZEVEDO, Avelino 2nd Referee: PUR MENDOZA BAS, Aurelio

GER Germany

Names	Serve	Attack	Block	Opp. Error	Total	Reception	Dig	Attack S/O	Attack Total	Attack Total	Serve
		Scoring Skills (Pts + S/O)				Non-Scoring Skills (+ / Total)		Positive (+ / Total)		Errors (− / Total)	
AHMANN, Jorg	1	8 + 14	0 + 0		9 + 14	21 / 23	15	14 / 23	22 / 36	3 / 36	7 / 26
HAGER, Axel	0	0 + 12	3 + 2		3 + 14	12 / 12	5	8 / 12	12 / 16	1 / 16	4 / 29
Totals	1	8 + 26	3 + 2	3 + 12	15 + 40	33 / 35	20	22 / 35	34 / 52	4 / 52	11 / 55

JPN Japan

Names	Serve	Attack	Block	Opp. Error	Total	Reception	Dig	Attack S/O	Attack Total	Attack Total	Serve
SETOYAMA, Shoji	2	0 + 8	1 + 0		3 + 8	11 / 13	6	7 / 20	8 / 20	2 / 20	6 / 25
TAKAO, Kazuyuki	0	2 + 18	1 + 0		3 + 18	29 / 30	10	16 / 40	20 / 40	1 / 40	6 / 24
Totals	2	2 + 26	2 + 0	2 + 14	8 + 40	40 / 43	16	23 / 60	28 / 60	3 / 60	12 / 49

ROUND 1 SWE 3 CUB 15 Duration: 00:27 1st Referee: USA ROBB, Steve 2nd Referee: USA LEMAIRE, Sue

SWE Sweden

Names	Serve	Attack	Block	Opp. Error	Total	Reception	Dig	Attack S/O	Attack Total	Attack Total	Serve
ENGLEN, Tom	0	0 + 10	0 + 0		0 + 10	19 / 21	1	10 / 21	10 / 25	4 / 25	1 / 12
PETERSSON, Fredrik	0	2 + 3	0 + 0		2 + 3	6 / 7	8	2 / 7	5 / 13	2 / 13	2 / 12
Totals	0	2 + 13	0 + 0	1 + 7	3 + 20	25 / 28	9	12 / 28	15 / 38	6 / 38	3 / 24

CUB Cuba

Names	Serve	Attack	Block	Opp. Error	Total	Reception	Dig	Attack S/O	Attack Total	Attack Total	Serve
ALVAREZ, Francisco	0	6 + 8	0 + 0		6 + 8	13 / 13	7	7 / 19	14 / 19	0 / 19	1 / 17
ROSELL MILANES, Juan Miguel	1	1 + 9	2 + 0		4 + 9	8 / 8	4	8 / 13	10 / 13	0 / 13	5 / 18
Totals	1	7 + 17	2 + 0	5 + 4	15 + 21	21 / 21	11	15 / 32	24 / 32	0 / 32	6 / 35

ROUND 1 NED 8 POR 15 Duration: 00:51 1st Referee: USA OWEN, Steve 2nd Referee: JPN KONNO, Masaaki

NED Netherlands

Names	Serve	Attack	Block	Opp. Error	Total	Reception	Dig	Attack S/O	Attack Total	Attack Total	Serve
EVERAERT, Michel	0	0 + 13	0 + 0		0 + 13	27 / 28	8	12 / 28	13 / 36	2 / 36	3 / 21
MULDER, Sander	0	3 + 11	2 + 1		5 + 12	11 / 11	8	8 / 11	14 / 22	3 / 22	4 / 21
Totals	0	3 + 24	2 + 1	3 + 8	8 + 33	38 / 39	16	20 / 39	27 / 58	5 / 58	7 / 42

POR Portugal

Names	Serve	Attack	Block	Opp. Error	Total	Reception	Dig	Attack S/O	Attack Total	Attack Total	Serve
BARBOSA MAIA, Luis Miguel	1	4 + 16	0 + 0		5 + 16	21 / 21	9	14 / 33	20 / 33	3 / 33	3 / 25
PEREIRA BRENHA ALVES, Joao Carlos	0	2 + 10	2 + 1		4 + 11	13 / 14	6	9 / 25	12 / 25	1 / 25	4 / 22
Totals	1	6 + 26	2 + 1	6 + 7	15 + 34	34 / 35	15	23 / 58	32 / 58	4 / 58	7 / 47

ROUND 2 BRA 15 CZE 5 Duration: 00:34 1st Referee: ESP CARRENO, Mirelo 2nd Referee: GBR BREHAUT, Jeff

BRA Brazil

Names	Serve	Attack	Block	Opp Error	Total	Reception	Dig	Attack S/O	Attack Total	Attack Total	Serve
da COSTA LOPES, Roberto	2	1 + 5	0 + 0		3 + 5	7 / 7	5	5 / 7	6 / 10	0 / 10	2 / 20
VIEIRA NETO, Franco Jos	2	4 + 14	3 + 0		9 + 14	18 / 19	2	14 / 19	18 / 25	1 / 25	2 / 20
Totals	4	5 + 19	3 + 0	3 + 7	15 + 26	25 / 26	7	19 / 26	24 / 35	1 / 35	4 / 40

CZE Czech Republic

Names	Serve	Attack	Block	Opp Error	Total	Reception	Dig	Attack S/O	Attack Total	Attack Total	Serve
PALINEK, Michal	0	3 + 16	0 + 0		3 + 16	24 / 26	5	14 / 32	19 / 32	5 / 32	1 / 16
PAKOSTA, Marek	0	0 + 5	1 + 0		1 + 5	6 / 6	3	4 / 9	5 / 9	0 / 9	4 / 15
Totals	0	3 + 21	1 + 0	1 + 4	5 + 25	30 / 32	8	18 / 41	24 / 41	5 / 41	5 / 31

ROUND 2 CAN 1 ESP 15 Duration: 00:31 1st Referee: USA LEMAIRE, Sue 2nd Referee: AUS HRESZCZUK, Peter

CAN Canada

Names	Serve	Attack	Block	Opp Error	Total	Reception	Dig	Attack S/O	Attack Total	Attack Total	Serve
CHILD, John	0	0 + 7	0 + 0		0 + 7	9 / 10	6	2 / 10	7 / 18	3 / 18	3 / 10
HEESE, Mark	0	0 + 9	0 + 1		0 + 10	21 / 23	7	7 / 23	9 / 29	7 / 29	0 / 12
Totals	0	0 + 16	0 + 1	1 + 3	1 + 20	30 / 33	13	9 / 33	16 / 47	10 / 47	3 / 22

ESP Spain

Names	Serve	Attack	Block	Opp Error	Total	Reception	Dig	Attack S/O	Attack Total	Attack Total	Serve
JIMENEZ GALAN, Sixto	0	5 + 8	0 + 0		5 + 8	10 / 10	9	7 / 22	13 / 22	0 / 22	0 / 15
BOSMA MINGUEZ, Javier	0	0 + 8	2 + 0		2 + 8	8 / 9	3	6 / 13	8 / 13	1 / 13	3 / 20
Totals	0	5 + 16	2 + 0	8 + 5	15 + 21	18 / 19	12	13 / 35	21 / 35	1 / 35	3 / 35

Men / *Messieurs*

ROUND 2   BRA 15 FRA 1   Duration: 00:27   1st Referee: ITA BORGATO, Maurizio   2nd Referee: USA ROBB, Steve

BRA Brazil

Names	Serve	Attack	Block	Opp Error	Total	Reception	Dig	Attack S/O	Attack Total	Attack Total	Serve
		Scoring Skills (Pts + S/O)				Non-Scoring Skills (+ / Total)		Positive (+ / Total)		Errors (– / Total)	
de MELO FERREIRA N., Jose Marco	0	5 + 8	0 + 0		5 + 8	9 / 9	9	8 / 9	13 / 20	0 / 20	0 / 16
REGO, Emanuel	0	3 + 8	1 + 0		4 + 8	8 / 8	2	7 / 8	11 / 12	0 / 12	2 / 17
Totals	0	8 + 16	1 + 0	6 + 2	15 + 18	17 / 17	11	15 / 17	24 / 32	0 / 32	2 / 33

FRA France

Names	Serve	Attack	Block	Opp Error	Total	Reception	Dig	Attack S/O	Attack Total	Attack Total	Serve
		Scoring Skills (Pts + S/O)				Non-Scoring Skills (+ / Total)		Positive (+ / Total)		Errors (– / Total)	
JODARD, Jean-Philippe	0	0 + 6	0 + 0		0 + 6	5 / 5	4	5 / 12	6 / 12	2 / 12	1 / 10
PENIGAUD, Christian	0	0 + 10	1 + 0		1 + 10	25 / 26	2	8 / 25	10 / 25	4 / 25	1 / 9
Totals	0	0 + 16	1 + 0	0 + 2	1 + 18	30 / 31	6	13 / 37	16 / 37	6 / 37	2 / 19

ROUND 2   USA 15 AUS 10   Duration: 00:49   1st Referee: FRA BIAU, Patrick   2nd Referee: BRA VILLA BOAS, Maria Amelia

USA United States of America

Names	Serve	Attack	Block	Opp Error	Total	Reception	Dig	Attack S/O	Attack Total	Attack Total	Serve
		Scoring Skills (Pts + S/O)				Non-Scoring Skills (+ / Total)		Positive (+ / Total)		Errors (– / Total)	
WHITMARSH, Mike	2	3 + 16	5 + 0		10 + 16	24 / 24	1	13 / 24	19 / 32	1 / 32	0 / 29
DODD, Michael	0	1 + 18	0 + 0		1 + 18	20 / 21	15	14 / 21	19 / 30	3 / 30	0 / 26
Totals	2	4 + 34	5 + 0	4 + 5	15 + 39	44 / 45	16	27 / 45	38 / 62	4 / 62	0 / 55

AUS Australia

Names	Serve	Attack	Block	Opp Error	Total	Reception	Dig	Attack S/O	Attack Total	Attack Total	Serve
		Scoring Skills (Pts + S/O)				Non-Scoring Skills (+ / Total)		Positive (+ / Total)		Errors (– / Total)	
ZAHNER, Lee	0	3 + 18	1 + 1		4 + 19	33 / 33	8	17 / 40	21 / 40	4 / 40	1 / 25
PROSSER, Julien	0	4 + 17	1 + 0		5 + 17	20 / 20	5	18 / 30	21 / 30	1 / 30	3 / 24
Totals	0	7 + 35	2 + 1	1 + 3	10 + 39	53 / 53	13	35 / 70	42 / 70	5 / 70	4 / 49

ROUND 2   USA 15 ITA 7   Duration: 00:36   1st Referee: JPN KONNO, Masaaki   2nd Referee: ESP CARRENO, Mirela

USA United States of America

Names	Serve	Attack	Block	Opp Error	Total	Reception	Dig	Attack S/O	Attack Total	Attack Total	Serve
		Scoring Skills (Pts + S/O)				Non-Scoring Skills (+ / Total)		Positive (+ / Total)		Errors (– / Total)	
STEFFES, Kent	0	4 + 4	1 + 0		5 + 4	8 / 8	7	3 / 8	8 / 15	2 / 15	2 / 20
KIRALY, Karch	1	3 + 9	2 + 0		6 + 9	10 / 11	8	8 / 11	12 / 20	0 / 20	1 / 18
Totals	1	7 + 13	3 + 0	4 + 10	15 + 23	18 / 19	15	11 / 19	20 / 35	2 / 35	3 / 38

ITA Italy

Names	Serve	Attack	Block	Opp Error	Total	Reception	Dig	Attack S/O	Attack Total	Attack Total	Serve
		Scoring Skills (Pts + S/O)				Non-Scoring Skills (+ / Total)		Positive (+ / Total)		Errors (– / Total)	
GRIGOLO, Nicola	1	1 + 11	0 + 0		2 + 11	21 / 22	3	11 / 28	12 / 28	1 / 28	1 / 16
GHIURGHI, Andrea	3	0 + 7	0 + 1		3 + 8	11 / 12	4	6 / 15	7 / 15	4 / 15	6 / 14
Totals	4	1 + 18	0 + 1	2 + 4	7 + 23	32 / 34	7	17 / 43	19 / 43	5 / 43	7 / 30

ROUND 2   NOR 16 GER 17   Duration: 01:08   1st Referee: USA OWEN, Steve   2nd Referee: USA LEMAIRE, Sue

NOR Norway

Names	Serve	Attack	Block	Opp Error	Total	Reception	Dig	Attack S/O	Attack Total	Attack Total	Serve
		Scoring Skills (Pts + S/O)				Non-Scoring Skills (+ / Total)		Positive (+ / Total)		Errors (– / Total)	
KVALHEIM, Jan	2	5 + 13	0 + 0		7 + 13	18 / 18	6	13 / 18	18 / 25	0 / 25	8 / 36
MAASEIDE, Bjorn	0	2 + 23	0 + 1		2 + 24	32 / 33	7	22 / 33	25 / 39	4 / 39	2 / 27
Totals	2	7 + 36	0 + 1	7 + 9	16 + 46	50 / 51	13	35 / 51	43 / 64	4 / 64	10 / 63

GER Germany

Names	Serve	Attack	Block	Opp Error	Total	Reception	Dig	Attack S/O	Attack Total	Attack Total	Serve
		Scoring Skills (Pts + S/O)				Non-Scoring Skills (+ / Total)		Positive (+ / Total)		Errors (– / Total)	
AHMANN, Jorg	0	3 + 21	0 + 0		3 + 21	30 / 32	8	18 / 39	24 / 39	2 / 39	2 / 28
HADER, Axel	4	2 + 14	3 + 0		9 + 14	19 / 19	5	11 / 30	16 / 30	4 / 30	6 / 35
Totals	4	5 + 35	3 + 0	5 + 12	17 + 47	49 / 51	13	29 / 69	40 / 69	6 / 69	8 / 63

ROUND 2   ARG 11 CUB 15   Duration: 00:41   1st Referee: USA SALVATORE, Patty   2nd Referee: ITA BORGATO, Maurizio

ARG Argentina

Names	Serve	Attack	Block	Opp Error	Total	Reception	Dig	Attack S/O	Attack Total	Attack Total	Serve
		Scoring Skills (Pts + S/O)				Non-Scoring Skills (+ / Total)		Positive (+ / Total)		Errors (– / Total)	
MARTINEZ, Eduardo Esteban	0	1 + 16	1 + 0		2 + 16	24 / 28	3	16 / 28	17 / 31	1 / 31	2 / 20
CONDE, Martin Alejo	0	5 + 6	1 + 0		6 + 6	7 / 8	6	5 / 8	11 / 17	2 / 17	4 / 15
Totals	0	6 + 22	2 + 0	3 + 2	11 + 24	31 / 36	9	21 / 36	28 / 48	3 / 48	6 / 35

CUB Cuba

Names	Serve	Attack	Block	Opp Error	Total	Reception	Dig	Attack S/O	Attack Total	Attack Total	Serve
		Scoring Skills (Pts + S/O)				Non-Scoring Skills (+ / Total)		Positive (+ / Total)		Errors (– / Total)	
ALVAREZ, Francisco	0	4 + 14	0 + 0		4 + 14	18 / 18	10	12 / 28	18 / 28	2 / 28	1 / 18
ROSELL MILANES, Juan Miguel	2	4 + 5	2 + 0		8 + 5	7 / 7	2	5 / 18	9 / 18	1 / 18	0 / 21
Totals	2	8 + 19	2 + 0	3 + 6	15 + 25	25 / 25	12	17 / 46	27 / 46	3 / 46	1 / 39

ROUND 2   USA 15 POR 7   Duration: 00:36   1st Referee: PUR MENDOZA BAS, Aurelio   2nd Referee: FRA BIAU, Patrick

USA United States of America

Names	Scoring Skills (Pts + S/O)					Non-Scoring Skills (+ / Total)		Positive (+ / Total)		Errors (– / Total)	
	Serve	Attack	Block	Opp Error	Total	Reception	Dig	Attack S/O	Attack Total	Attack Total	Serve
SMITH, Christopher St. John	0	4 + 5	0 + 0		4 + 5	11 / 13	8	5 / 13	9 / 19	3 / 19	1 / 16
HENKEL, Carl	2	1 + 8	6 + 0		9 + 8	6 / 6	1	6 / 6	9 / 14	3 / 14	2 / 16
Totals	2	5 + 13	6 + 0	2 + 4	15 + 17	17 / 19	9	11 / 19	18 / 33	6 / 33	3 / 32

POR Portugal

Names	Scoring Skills (Pts + S/O)					Non-Scoring Skills (+ / Total)		Positive (+ / Total)		Errors (– / Total)	
	Serve	Attack	Block	Opp Error	Total	Reception	Dig	Attack S/O	Attack Total	Attack Total	Serve
BARBOSA MAIA, Luis Miguel	0	2 + 5	0 + 0		2 + 5	13 / 13	6	4 / 17	7 / 17	1 / 17	1 / 11
PEREIRA BRENHA ALVES, Joao Carlos	1	0 + 7	0 + 0		1 + 7	14 / 14	2	6 / 19	7 / 19	1 / 19	3 / 13
Totals	1	2 + 12	0 + 0	4 + 5	7 + 17	27 / 27	8	10 / 36	14 / 36	2 / 36	4 / 24

17TH PLACE   NED 6 CZE 15   Duration: 00:35   1st Referee: USA SALVATORE, Patty   2nd Referee: FRA BIAU, Patrick

NED Netherlands

Names	Scoring Skills (Pts + S/O)					Non-Scoring Skills (+ / Total)		Positive (+ / Total)		Errors (– / Total)	
	Serve	Attack	Block	Opp Error	Total	Reception	Dig	Attack S/O	Attack Total	Attack Total	Serve
EVERAERT, Michel	1	2 + 9	0 + 0		3 + 9	19 / 21	4	9 / 21	11 / 23	0 / 23	3 / 12
MULDER, Sander	0	2 + 4	0 + 0		2 + 4	4 / 4	7	2 / 4	6 / 14	2 / 14	2 / 12
Totals	1	4 + 13	0 + 0	1 + 4	6 + 17	23 / 25	11	11 / 25	17 / 37	2 / 37	5 / 24

CZE Czech Republic

Names	Scoring Skills (Pts + S/O)					Non-Scoring Skills (+ / Total)		Positive (+ / Total)		Errors (– / Total)	
	Serve	Attack	Block	Opp Error	Total	Reception	Dig	Attack S/O	Attack Total	Attack Total	Serve
PALINEK, Michal	1	4 + 9	0 + 0		5 + 9	12 / 13	6	8 / 18	13 / 18	0 / 18	1 / 16
PAKOSTA, Marek	2	4 + 4	1 + 0		7 + 4	4 / 5	5	4 / 14	8 / 14	0 / 14	3 / 16
Totals	3	8 + 13	1 + 0	3 + 5	15 + 18	16 / 18	11	12 / 32	21 / 32	0 / 32	4 / 32

17TH PLACE   SWE 2 CAN 15   Duration: 00:28   1st Referee: USA LEMAIRE, Sue   2nd Referee: PUR MENDOZA BAS, Aurelio

SWE Sweden

Names	Scoring Skills (Pts + S/O)					Non-Scoring Skills (+ / Total)		Positive (+ / Total)		Errors (– / Total)	
	Serve	Attack	Block	Opp Error	Total	Reception	Dig	Attack S/O	Attack Total	Attack Total	Serve
ENGLEN, Tom	0	0 + 10	0 + 0		0 + 10	20 / 20	5	9 / 20	10 / 28	1 / 28	1 / 11
PETERSSON, Fredrik	0	1 + 5	0 + 0		1 + 5	10 / 12	12	3 / 12	6 / 20	2 / 20	0 / 10
Totals	0	1 + 15	0 + 0	1 + 4	2 + 19	30 / 32	17	12 / 32	16 / 48	3 / 48	1 / 21

CAN Canada

Names	Scoring Skills (Pts + S/O)					Non-Scoring Skills (+ / Total)		Positive (+ / Total)		Errors (– / Total)	
	Serve	Attack	Block	Opp Error	Total	Reception	Dig	Attack S/O	Attack Total	Attack Total	Serve
CHILD, John	0	6 + 5	0 + 1		6 + 6	9 / 9	11	5 / 20	11 / 20	2 / 20	0 / 18
HEESE, Mark	0	5 + 6	3 + 0		8 + 6	9 / 10	9	4 / 21	11 / 21	1 / 21	2 / 16
Totals	0	11 + 11	3 + 1	1 + 5	15 + 17	18 / 19	20	9 / 41	22 / 41	3 / 41	2 / 34

17TH PLACE   JPN 12 FRA 15   Duration: 00:47   1st Referee: BRA VILLAS BOAS, Maria Amelia   2nd Referee: GBR BREHAUT, Jeff

JPN Japan

Names	Scoring Skills (Pts + S/O)					Non-Scoring Skills (+ / Total)		Positive (+ / Total)		Errors (– / Total)	
	Serve	Attack	Block	Opp Error	Total	Reception	Dig	Attack S/O	Attack Total	Attack Total	Serve
SETOYAMA, Shoji	0	1 + 20	0 + 0		1 + 20	32 / 34	7	18 / 34	21 / 42	5 / 42	3 / 21
TAKAO, Kazuyuki	0	2 + 6	3 + 0		5 + 6	8 / 8	9	4 / 8	8 / 18	1 / 18	3 / 20
Totals	0	3 + 26	3 + 0	6 + 2	12 + 28	40 / 42	16	22 / 42	29 / 60	6 / 60	6 / 41

FRA France

Names	Scoring Skills (Pts + S/O)					Non-Scoring Skills (+ / Total)		Positive (+ / Total)		Errors (– / Total)	
	Serve	Attack	Block	Opp Error	Total	Reception	Dig	Attack S/O	Attack Total	Attack Total	Serve
JODARD, Jean-Philippe	0	2 + 9	0 + 0		2 + 9	14 / 16	6	9 / 25	11 / 25	1 / 25	1 / 21
PENIGAUD, Christian	0	0 + 11	8 + 0		8 + 11	17 / 19	6	9 / 23	11 / 23	4 / 23	0 / 22
Totals	0	2 + 20	8 + 0	5 + 9	15 + 29	31 / 35	12	18 / 48	22 / 48	5 / 48	1 / 43

17TH PLACE   NZL 8 AUS 15   Duration: 00:38   1st Referee: JPN KONNO, Masaaki   2nd Referee: ESP CARRENO, Mirela

NZL New Zealand

Names	Scoring Skills (Pts + S/O)					Non-Scoring Skills (+ / Total)		Positive (+ / Total)		Errors (– / Total)	
	Serve	Attack	Block	Opp Error	Total	Reception	Dig	Attack S/O	Attack Total	Attack Total	Serve
HAMILTON, Reid	0	1 + 11	0 + 0		1 + 11	14 / 16	4	11 / 16	12 / 22	1 / 22	3 / 15
HAMILTON, Glenn	1	1 + 11	1 + 0		3 + 11	19 / 19	5	9 / 19	12 / 24	4 / 24	1 / 19
Totals	1	2 + 22	1 + 0	4 + 4	8 + 26	33 / 35	9	20 / 35	24 / 46	5 / 46	4 / 34

AUS Australia

Names	Scoring Skills (Pts + S/O)					Non-Scoring Skills (+ / Total)		Positive (+ / Total)		Errors (– / Total)	
	Serve	Attack	Block	Opp Error	Total	Reception	Dig	Attack S/O	Attack Total	Attack Total	Serve
ZAHNER, Lee	1	0 + 9	0 + 0		1 + 9	15 / 15	6	7 / 20	9 / 20	2 / 20	2 / 16
PROSSER, Julien	1	9 + 12	0 + 0		10 + 12	13 / 14	8	12 / 23	21 / 23	1 / 23	2 / 25
Totals	2	9 + 21	0 + 0	4 + 5	15 + 26	28 / 29	14	19 / 43	30 / 43	3 / 43	4 / 41

Men / *Messieurs*

17TH PLACE — CAN 8 ITA 15

Duration: 00:45 | **1st Referee: AUS HRESZCZUK, Peter** | **2nd Referee: MEX RAMIREZ RIVERA, Miguel**

CAN Canada

Names	Serve	Attack	Block	Opp Error	Total	Reception	Dig	Attack S/O	Attack Total	Attack Total	Serve
		Scoring Skills (Pts + S/O)				Non-Scoring Skills (+ / Total)		Positive (+ / Total)		Errors (– / Total)	
DUNN, Mark	0	2 + 9	1 + 0		3 + 9	10 / 10	9	6 / 10	11 / 22	4 / 22	6 / 20
DRAKICH, Edward Raymond	0	0 + 15	2 + 0		2 + 15	30 / 32	4	15 / 32	15 / 34	3 / 34	4 / 22
Totals	0	2 + 24	3 + 0	3 + 9	8 + 33	40 / 42	13	21 / 42	26 / 56	7 / 56	10 / 42

ITA Italy

Names	Serve	Attack	Block	Opp Error	Total	Reception	Dig	Attack S/O	Attack Total	Attack Total	Serve
		Scoring Skills (Pts + S/O)				Non-Scoring Skills (+ / Total)		Positive (+ / Total)		Errors (– / Total)	
GRIGOLO, Nicola	0	1 + 14	0 + 0		1 + 14	20 / 21	8	14 / 26	15 / 26	2 / 26	2 / 25
GHIURGHI, Andrea	0	5 + 8	1 + 1		6 + 9	11 / 11	8	7 / 22	13 / 22	2 / 22	4 / 23
Totals	0	6 + 22	1 + 1	8 + 11	15 + 34	31 / 32	16	21 / 48	28 / 48	4 / 48	6 / 48

17TH PLACE — EST 2 NOR 15

Duration: 00:31 | **1st Referee: FRA BIAU, Patrick** | **2nd Referee: USA ROBB, Steve**

EST Estonia

Names	Serve	Attack	Block	Opp Error	Total	Reception	Dig	Attack S/O	Attack Total	Attack Total	Serve
		Scoring Skills (Pts + S/O)				Non-Scoring Skills (+ / Total)		Positive (+ / Total)		Errors (– / Total)	
KEEL, Avo	0	0 + 9	0 + 1		0 + 10	15 / 18	1	9 / 18	9 / 19	0 / 19	2 / 16
KREEN, Kaido	0	0 + 11	0 + 0		0 + 11	14 / 14	4	10 / 14	11 / 20	3 / 20	4 / 14
Totals	0	0 + 20	0 + 1	2 + 6	2 + 27	29 / 32	5	19 / 32	20 / 39	3 / 39	6 / 30

NOR Norway

Names	Serve	Attack	Block	Opp Error	Total	Reception	Dig	Attack S/O	Attack Total	Attack Total	Serve
		Scoring Skills (Pts + S/O)				Non-Scoring Skills (+ / Total)		Positive (+ / Total)		Errors (– / Total)	
KVALHEIM, Jan	1	3 + 8	1 + 1		5 + 9	14 / 14	4	8 / 17	11 / 17	2 / 17	4 / 20
MAASEIDE, Bjorn	4	3 + 9	1 + 0		8 + 9	10 / 10	5	9 / 18	12 / 18	1 / 18	1 / 21
Totals	5	6 + 17	2 + 1	2 + 9	15 + 27	24 / 24	9	17 / 35	23 / 35	3 / 35	5 / 41

17TH PLACE — INA 5 ARG 15

Duration: 00:45 | **1st Referee: PUR MENDOZA BAS, Aurelio** | **2nd Referee: USA OWEN, Steve**

INA Indonesia

Names	Serve	Attack	Block	Opp Error	Total	Reception	Dig	Attack S/O	Attack Total	Attack Total	Serve
		Scoring Skills (Pts + S/O)				Non-Scoring Skills (+ / Total)		Positive (+ / Total)		Errors (– / Total)	
NURMUFID, Mochamad	1	1 + 13	0 + 1		2 + 14	30 / 30	9	13 / 30	14 / 38	4 / 38	2 / 16
MARKOJI, Markoji	1	0 + 5	1 + 0		2 + 5	6 / 6	10	3 / 6	5 / 15	2 / 15	1 / 13
Totals	2	1 + 18	1 + 1	1 + 4	5 + 23	36 / 36	19	16 / 36	19 / 53	6 / 53	3 / 29

ARG Argentina

Names	Serve	Attack	Block	Opp Error	Total	Reception	Dig	Attack S/O	Attack Total	Attack Total	Serve
		Scoring Skills (Pts + S/O)				Non-Scoring Skills (+ / Total)		Positive (+ / Total)		Errors (– / Total)	
MARTINEZ, Eduardo Esteban	0	4 + 14	1 + 0		5 + 14	17 / 17	6	13 / 25	18 / 25	1 / 25	1 / 14
CONDE, Martin Alejo	0	4 + 4	0 + 0		4 + 4	6 / 7	15	4 / 20	8 / 20	1 / 20	1 / 23
Totals	0	8 + 18	1 + 0	6 + 6	15 + 24	23 / 24	21	17 / 45	26 / 45	2 / 45	2 / 37

17TH PLACE — ESP 8 POR 15

Duration: 00:49 | **1st Referee: ITA BORGATO, Maurizio** | **2nd Referee: JPN KONNO, Masaaki**

ESP Spain

Names	Serve	Attack	Block	Opp Error	Total	Reception	Dig	Attack S/O	Attack Total	Attack Total	Serve
		Scoring Skills (Pts + S/O)				Non-Scoring Skills (+ / Total)		Positive (+ / Total)		Errors (– / Total)	
YUSTE MUNIZ, Javier	0	3 + 20	0 + 0		3 + 20	31 / 32	10	19 / 32	23 / 43	2 / 43	4 / 20
MARTIN PRIETO, Miguel Angel	0	0 + 8	1 + 0		1 + 8	7 / 10	6	4 / 10	8 / 17	1 / 17	2 / 23
Totals	0	3 + 28	1 + 0	4 + 5	8 + 33	38 / 42	16	23 / 42	31 / 60	3 / 60	6 / 43

POR Portugal

Names	Serve	Attack	Block	Opp Error	Total	Reception	Dig	Attack S/O	Attack Total	Attack Total	Serve
		Scoring Skills (Pts + S/O)				Non-Scoring Skills (+ / Total)		Positive (+ / Total)		Errors (– / Total)	
BARBOSA MAIA, Luis Miguel	0	5 + 13	0 + 0		5 + 13	14 / 16	13	11 / 27	18 / 27	3 / 27	2 / 25
PEREIRA BRENHA ALVES, Joao Carlos	1	4 + 14	4 + 0		9 + 14	21 / 21	6	13 / 30	18 / 30	0 / 30	3 / 25
Totals	1	9 + 27	4 + 0	1 + 8	15 + 35	35 / 37	19	24 / 57	36 / 57	3 / 57	5 / 50

ROUND 3 — BRA 9 ESP 15

Duration: 01:11 | **1st Referee: JPN KONNO, Masaaki** | **2nd Referee: USA LEMAIRE, Sue**

BRA Brazil

Names	Serve	Attack	Block	Opp Error	Total	Reception	Dig	Attack S/O	Attack Total	Attack Total	Serve
		Scoring Skills (Pts + S/O)				Non-Scoring Skills (+ / Total)		Positive (+ / Total)		Errors (– / Total)	
da COSTA LOPES, Roberto	0	4 + 18	0 + 0		4 + 18	24 / 27	14	17 / 27	22 / 39	2 / 39	5 / 35
VIEIRA NETO, Franco Jos	0	2 + 23	1 + 1		3 + 24	34 / 35	6	21 / 35	25 / 45	2 / 45	3 / 33
Totals	0	6 + 41	1 + 1	2 + 17	9 + 59	58 / 62	20	38 / 62	47 / 84	4 / 84	8 / 68

ESP Spain

Names	Serve	Attack	Block	Opp Error	Total	Reception	Dig	Attack S/O	Attack Total	Attack Total	Serve
		Scoring Skills (Pts + S/O)				Non-Scoring Skills (+ / Total)		Positive (+ / Total)		Errors (– / Total)	
JIMENEZ GALAN, Sixto	0	6 + 31	0 + 0		6 + 31	40 / 40	16	30 / 55	37 / 55	1 / 55	3 / 34
BOSMA MINGUEZ, Javier	1	1 + 17	3 + 1		5 + 18	19 / 19	9	14 / 30	18 / 30	5 / 30	8 / 40
Totals	1	7 + 48	3 + 1	4 + 9	15 + 58	59 / 59	25	44 / 85	55 / 85	6 / 85	11 / 74

Men / Messieurs

ROUND 3 **BRA 9 USA 15** Duration: 00:44 1st Referee: GBR BREHAUT, Jeff 2nd Referee: ESP CARRENO, Mirela

BRA Brazil

Names		Scoring Skills (Pts + S/O)				Non-Scoring Skills (+ / Total)		Positive (+ / Total)		Errors (– / Total)	
	Serve	Attack	Block	Opp Error	Total	Reception	Dig	Attack S/O	Attack Total	Attack Total	Serve
de MELO FERREIRA N., Jose Marco	0	4 + 22	0 + 0		4 + 22	38 / 39	10	22 / 39	26 / 52	4 / 52	3 / 20
REGO, Emanuel	0	1 + 9	1 + 0		2 + 9	7 / 7	8	6 / 7	10 / 13	0 / 13	1 / 23
Totals	0	5 + 31	1 + 0	3 + 2	9 + 33	45 / 46	18	28 / 46	36 / 65	4 / 65	4 / 43

USA United States of America

Names		Scoring Skills (Pts + S/O)				Non-Scoring Skills (+ / Total)		Positive (+ / Total)		Errors (– / Total)	
	Serve	Attack	Block	Opp Error	Total	Reception	Dig	Attack S/O	Attack Total	Attack Total	Serve
WHITMARSH, Mike	0	1 + 17	6 + 1		7 + 18	22 / 24	4	14 / 28	18 / 28	2 / 28	1 / 22
DODD, Michael	0	4 + 10	0 + 0		4 + 10	13 / 14	10	8 / 24	14 / 24	0 / 24	1 / 26
Totals	0	5 + 27	6 + 1	4 + 6	15 + 34	35 / 38	14	22 / 52	32 / 52	2 / 52	2 / 48

ROUND 3 **USA 15 GER 5** Duration: 00:32 1st Referee: BRA VILLAS BOAS, Maria Amelia 2nd Referee: PUR MENDOZA BAS, Aurelio

USA United States of America

Names		Scoring Skills (Pts + S/O)				Non-Scoring Skills (+ / Total)		Positive (+ / Total)		Errors (– / Total)	
	Serve	Attack	Block	Opp Error	Total	Reception	Dig	Attack S/O	Attack Total	Attack Total	Serve
STEFFES, Kent	2	1 + 11	0 + 0		3 + 11	12 / 16	3	10 / 16	12 / 21	4 / 21	2 / 21
KIRALY, Karch	2	3 + 9	2 + 0		7 + 9	9 / 9	4	9 / 9	12 / 13	0 / 13	4 / 15
Totals	4	4 + 20	2 + 0	5 + 3	15 + 23	21 / 25	7	19 / 25	24 / 34	4 / 34	6 / 36

GER Germany

Names		Scoring Skills (Pts + S/O)				Non-Scoring Skills (+ / Total)		Positive (+ / Total)		Errors (– / Total)	
	Serve	Attack	Block	Opp Error	Total	Reception	Dig	Attack S/O	Attack Total	Attack Total	Serve
AHMANN, Jorg	0	1 + 5	0 + 0		1 + 5	13 / 14	2	5 / 15	6 / 15	3 / 15	2 / 15
HAGER, Axel	0	1 + 8	0 + 0		1 + 8	9 / 12	4	6 / 16	9 / 16	1 / 16	1 / 13
Totals	0	2 + 13	0 + 0	3 + 8	5 + 21	22 / 26	6	11 / 31	15 / 31	4 / 31	3 / 28

ROUND 3 **CUB 13 USA 15** Duration: 00:52 1st Referee: AUS HRESZCZUK, Peter 2nd Referee: FRA BIAU, Patrick

CUB Cuba

Names		Scoring Skills (Pts + S/O)				Non-Scoring Skills (+ / Total)		Positive (+ / Total)		Errors (– / Total)	
	Serve	Attack	Block	Opp Error	Total	Reception	Dig	Attack S/O	Attack Total	Attack Total	Serve
ALVAREZ, Francisco	0	4 + 15	0 + 0		4 + 15	23 / 26	12	12 / 26	19 / 34	4 / 34	1 / 23
ROSELL MILANES, Juan Miguel	1	2 + 11	2 + 0		5 + 11	14 / 17	3	10 / 17	13 / 22	2 / 22	3 / 23
Totals	1	6 + 26	2 + 0	4 + 7	13 + 33	37 / 43	15	22 / 43	32 / 56	6 / 56	4 / 46

USA United States of America

Names		Scoring Skills (Pts + S/O)				Non-Scoring Skills (+ / Total)		Positive (+ / Total)		Errors (– / Total)	
	Serve	Attack	Block	Opp Error	Total	Reception	Dig	Attack S/O	Attack Total	Attack Total	Serve
SMITH, Christopher St. John	0	1 + 17	0 + 0		1 + 17	32 / 35	9	17 / 42	18 / 42	3 / 42	2 / 24
HENKEL, Carl	0	5 + 7	1 + 0		6 + 7	6 / 6	1	7 / 13	12 / 13	0 / 13	4 / 25
Totals	0	6 + 24	1 + 0	8 + 9	15 + 33	38 / 41	10	24 / 55	30 / 55	3 / 55	6 / 49

13TH PLACE **POR 15 ARG 5** Duration: 00:35 1st Referee: USA ROBB, Steve 2nd Referee: ITA BORGATO, Maurizio

POR Portugal

Names		Scoring Skills (Pts + S/O)				Non-Scoring Skills (+ / Total)		Positive (+ / Total)		Errors (– / Total)	
	Serve	Attack	Block	Opp Error	Total	Reception	Dig	Attack S/O	Attack Total	Attack Total	Serve
BARBOSA MAIA, Luis Miguel	1	3 + 9	0 + 1		4 + 10	16 / 16	8	9 / 16	12 / 25	1 / 25	1 / 17
PEREIRA BRENHA ALVES, Joao Carlos	1	2 + 8	4 + 1		7 + 9	6 / 7	2	6 / 7	10 / 12	2 / 12	1 / 21
Totals	2	5 + 17	4 + 2	4 + 4	15 + 23	22 / 23	10	15 / 23	22 / 37	3 / 37	2 / 38

ARG Argentina

Names		Scoring Skills (Pts + S/O)				Non-Scoring Skills (+ / Total)		Positive (+ / Total)		Errors (– / Total)	
	Serve	Attack	Block	Opp Error	Total	Reception	Dig	Attack S/O	Attack Total	Attack Total	Serve
MARTINEZ, Eduardo Esteban	0	0 + 15	1 + 0		1 + 15	29 / 29	0	15 / 29	15 / 29	3 / 29	0 / 16
CONDE, Martin Alejo	0	1 + 4	1 + 0		2 + 4	5 / 5	7	4 / 13	5 / 13	0 / 13	4 / 12
Totals	0	1 + 19	2 + 0	2 + 4	5 + 23	34 / 34	7	19 / 42	20 / 42	3 / 42	4 / 28

13TH PLACE **NOR 15 ITA 11** Duration: 00:43 1st Referee: USA LEMAIRE, Sue 2nd Referee: USA SALVATORE, Patty

NOR Norway

Names		Scoring Skills (Pts + S/O)				Non-Scoring Skills (+ / Total)		Positive (+ / Total)		Errors (– / Total)	
	Serve	Attack	Block	Opp Error	Total	Reception	Dig	Attack S/O	Attack Total	Attack Total	Serve
KVALHEIM, Jan	3	1 + 16	3 + 0		7 + 16	28 / 29	4	15 / 29	17 / 32	4 / 32	6 / 22
MAASEIDE, Bjorn	0	2 + 9	1 + 0		3 + 9	7 / 7	7	7 / 7	11 / 14	0 / 14	3 / 22
Totals	3	3 + 25	4 + 0	5 + 8	15 + 33	35 / 36	11	22 / 36	28 / 46	4 / 46	9 / 44

ITA Italy

Names		Scoring Skills (Pts + S/O)				Non-Scoring Skills (+ / Total)		Positive (+ / Total)		Errors (– / Total)	
	Serve	Attack	Block	Opp Error	Total	Reception	Dig	Attack S/O	Attack Total	Attack Total	Serve
GRIGOLO, Nicola	1	2 + 6	0 + 1		3 + 7	16 / 17	6	6 / 23	8 / 23	5 / 23	1 / 21
GHIURGHI, Andrea	0	1 + 10	2 + 0		3 + 10	14 / 16	2	9 / 19	11 / 19	3 / 19	3 / 22
Totals	1	3 + 16	2 + 1	5 + 10	11 + 27	30 / 33	8	15 / 42	19 / 42	8 / 42	4 / 43

Men / Messieurs

13TH PLACE — AUS 15 FRA 13

Duration: 00:52 — 1st Referee: USA OWEN, Steve — 2nd Referee: GBR BREHAUT, Jeff

AUS Australia

Names	Scoring Skills (Pts + S/O)					Non-Scoring Skills (+ / Total)		Positive (+ / Total)		Errors (– / Total)	
	Serve	Attack	Block	Opp Error	Total	Reception	Dig	Attack S/O	Attack Total	Attack Total	Serve
ZAHNER, Lee	1	3 + 18	1 + 1		5 + 19	31 / 31	8	17 / 31	21 / 40	3 / 40	1 / 28
PROSSER, Julien	0	2 + 13	2 + 0		4 + 13	15 / 15	6	12 / 15	15 / 25	3 / 25	4 / 25
Totals	1	5 + 31	3 + 1	6 + 6	15 + 38	46 / 46	14	29 / 46	36 / 65	6 / 65	5 / 53

FRA France

Names	Scoring Skills (Pts + S/O)					Non-Scoring Skills (+ / Total)		Positive (+ / Total)		Errors (– / Total)	
	Serve	Attack	Block	Opp Error	Total	Reception	Dig	Attack S/O	Attack Total	Attack Total	Serve
JODARD, Jean-Philippe	1	6 + 22	0 + 0		7 + 22	35 / 35	13	19 / 49	28 / 49	7 / 49	2 / 27
PENIGAUD, Christian	0	0 + 8	3 + 1		3 + 9	12 / 12	3	7 / 15	8 / 15	0 / 15	2 / 24
Totals	1	6 + 30	3 + 1	3 + 8	13 + 39	47 / 47	16	26 / 64	36 / 64	7 / 64	4 / 51

13TH PLACE — CAN 15 CZE 9

Duration: 00:46 — 1st Referee: ESP CARRENO, Mirela — 2nd Referee: AUS HRESZCZUK, Peter

CAN Canada

Names	Scoring Skills (Pts + S/O)					Non-Scoring Skills (+ / Total)		Positive (+ / Total)		Errors (– / Total)	
	Serve	Attack	Block	Opp Error	Total	Reception	Dig	Attack S/O	Attack Total	Attack Total	Serve
CHILD, John	0	4 + 9	1 + 0		5 + 9	8 / 9	6	9 / 9	13 / 18	0 / 18	3 / 23
HEESE, Mark	1	4 + 22	1 + 0		6 + 22	25 / 26	7	21 / 26	26 / 36	4 / 36	4 / 29
Totals	1	8 + 31	2 + 0	4 + 7	15 + 38	33 / 35	13	30 / 35	39 / 54	4 / 54	7 / 52

CZE Czech Republic

Names	Scoring Skills (Pts + S/O)					Non-Scoring Skills (+ / Total)		Positive (+ / Total)		Errors (– / Total)	
	Serve	Attack	Block	Opp Error	Total	Reception	Dig	Attack S/O	Attack Total	Attack Total	Serve
PALINEK, Michal	0	0 + 18	0 + 0		0 + 18	28 / 28	2	18 / 27	18 / 27	1 / 27	1 / 22
PAKOSTA, Marek	2	0 + 10	3 + 0		5 + 10	13 / 13	6	6 / 23	10 / 23	2 / 23	5 / 25
Totals	2	0 + 28	3 + 0	4 + 8	9 + 36	41 / 41	8	24 / 50	28 / 50	3 / 50	6 / 47

9TH PLACE — POR 15 BRA 12

Duration: 00:54 — 1st Referee: MENDOZA BAS, Aurelio — 2nd Referee: GBR BREHAUT, Jeff

POR Portugal

Names	Scoring Skills (Pts + S/O)					Non-Scoring Skills (+ / Total)		Positive (+ / Total)		Errors (– / Total)	
	Serve	Attack	Block	Opp Error	Total	Reception	Dig	Attack S/O	Attack Total	Attack Total	Serve
BARBOSA MAIA, Luis Miguel	2	4 + 14	0 + 0		6 + 14	22 / 23	10	11 / 23	18 / 38	5 / 38	4 / 27
PEREIRA BRENHA ALVES, Joao Carlos	0	2 + 20	1 + 0		3 + 20	25 / 25	14	17 / 25	22 / 37	3 / 37	2 / 27
Totals	2	6 + 34	1 + 0	6 + 6	15 + 40	47 / 48	24	28 / 48	40 / 75	8 / 75	6 / 54

BRA Brazil

Names	Scoring Skills (Pts + S/O)					Non-Scoring Skills (+ / Total)		Positive (+ / Total)		Errors (– / Total)	
	Serve	Attack	Block	Opp Error	Total	Reception	Dig	Attack S/O	Attack Total	Attack Total	Serve
de MELO FERREIRA N., Jose Marco	0	2 + 20	0 + 0		2 + 20	35 / 35	13	16 / 51	22 / 51	4 / 51	1 / 26
REGO, Emanuel	0	3 + 10	2 + 0		5 + 10	10 / 11	7	6 / 22	13 / 22	4 / 22	3 / 25
Totals	0	5 + 30	2 + 0	5 + 9	12 + 39	45 / 46	20	22 / 73	35 / 73	8 / 73	4 / 51

9TH PLACE — NOR 15 BRA 10

Duration: 00:51 — 1st Referee: FRA BIAU, Patrick — 2nd Referee: AUS HRESZCAUK, Peter

NOR Norway

Names	Scoring Skills (Pts + S/O)					Non-Scoring Skills (+ / Total)		Positive (+ / Total)		Errors (– / Total)	
	Serve	Attack	Block	Opp Error	Total	Reception	Dig	Attack S/O	Attack Total	Attack Total	Serve
KVALHEIM, Jan	1	1 + 23	5 + 0		7 + 23	27 / 28	4	20 / 28	24 / 32	0 / 32	5 / 28
MAASEIDE, Bjorn	1	4 + 14	0 + 0		5 + 14	16 / 16	8	14 / 16	18 / 28	0 / 28	1 / 28
Totals	2	5 + 37	5 + 0	3 + 5	15 + 42	43 / 44	12	34 / 44	42 / 60	0 / 60	6 / 56

BRA Brazil

Names	Scoring Skills (Pts + S/O)					Non-Scoring Skills (+ / Total)		Positive (+ / Total)		Errors (– / Total)	
	Serve	Attack	Block	Opp Error	Total	Reception	Dig	Attack S/O	Attack Total	Attack Total	Serve
da COSTO LOPES, Roberto	0	4 + 12	0 + 0		4 + 12	18 / 18	6	11 / 27	16 / 27	1 / 27	3 / 26
VIEIRA NETO, Franco Jos	3	1 + 22	2 + 0		6 + 22	28 / 30	4	20 / 36	23 / 36	2 / 36	2 / 26
Totals	3	5 + 34	2 + 0	0 + 7	10 + 41	46 / 48	10	31 / 63	39 / 63	3 / 63	5 / 52

9TH PLACE — AUS 6 CUB 15

Duration: 00:35 — 1st Referee: JPN KONNO, Masaaki — 2nd Referee: BRA VILLAS BOAS, Maria Amelia

AUS Australia

Names	Scoring Skills (Pts + S/O)					Non-Scoring Skills (+ / Total)		Positive (+ / Total)		Errors (– / Total)	
	Serve	Attack	Block	Opp Error	Total	Reception	Dig	Attack S/O	Attack Total	Attack Total	Serve
ZAHNER, Lee	0	0 + 6	0 + 0		0 + 6	6 / 7	7	3 / 7	6 / 16	4 / 16	1 / 14
PROSSER, Julien	3	0 + 14	0 + 0		3 + 14	21 / 27	3	13 / 27	14 / 30	5 / 30	1 / 16
Totals	3	0 + 20	0 + 0	3 + 4	6 + 24	27 / 34	10	16 / 34	20 / 46	9 / 46	2 / 30

CUB Cuba

Names	Scoring Skills (Pts + S/O)					Non-Scoring Skills (+ / Total)		Positive (+ / Total)		Errors (– / Total)	
	Serve	Attack	Block	Opp Error	Total	Reception	Dig	Attack S/O	Attack Total	Attack Total	Serve
ALVAREZ, Francisco	0	3 + 12	0 + 0		3 + 12	13 / 14	8	9 / 21	15 / 21	1 / 21	2 / 21
ROSELL MILANES, Juan Miguel	1	2 + 9	1 + 0		4 + 9	11 / 11	4	8 / 17	11 / 17	1 / 17	2 / 18
Totals	1	5 + 21	1 + 0	8 + 3	15 + 24	24 / 25	12	17 / 38	26 / 38	2 / 38	4 / 39

Men / Messieurs

9TH PLACE — CAN 15 GER 7
Duration: 00:42 | 1st Referee: MEX RAMIREZ RIVERA, Miguel | 2nd Referee: USA ROBB, Steve

CAN Canada

Names	Serve	Attack	Block	Opp Error	Total	Reception	Dig	Attack S/O	Attack Total	Attack Total	Serve
		Scoring Skills (Pts + S/O)				Non-Scoring Skills (+ / Total)		Positive (+ / Total)		Errors (– / Total)	
CHILD, John	0	5 + 9	2 + 2		7 + 11	5 / 5	8	6 / 5	14 / 17	0 / 17	3 / 23
HEESE, Mark	1	2 + 17	0 + 0		3 + 17	27 / 30	6	17 / 30	19 / 33	1 / 33	3 / 24
Totals	1	7 + 26	2 + 2	5 + 4	15 + 32	32 / 35	14	23 / 35	33 / 50	1 / 50	6 / 47

GER Germany

Names	Serve	Attack	Block	Opp Error	Total	Reception	Dig	Attack S/O	Attack Total	Attack Total	Serve
		Scoring Skills (Pts + S/O)				Non-Scoring Skills (+ / Total)		Positive (+ / Total)		Errors (– / Total)	
AHMANN, Jorg	0	3 + 6	0 + 0		3 + 6	7 / 7	8	5 / 19	9 / 19	2 / 19	1 / 19
HAGER, Axel	0	2 + 20	1 + 0		3 + 20	32 / 33	3	18 / 37	22 / 37	3 / 37	3 / 20
Totals	0	5 + 26	1 + 0	1 + 6	7 + 32	39 / 40	11	23 / 56	31 / 56	5 / 56	4 / 39

ROUND 4 — ESP 6 USA 15
Duration: 00:30 | 1st Referee: ITA BORGATO, Maurizio | 2nd Referee: BRA VILLAS BOAS, Maria Amelia

ESP Spain

Names	Serve	Attack	Block	Opp Error	Total	Reception	Dig	Attack S/O	Attack Total	Attack Total	Serve
		Scoring Skills (Pts + S/O)				Non-Scoring Skills (+ / Total)		Positive (+ / Total)		Errors (– / Total)	
JIMENEZ GALAN, Sixto	0	2 + 14	0 + 0		2 + 14	32 / 32	10	13 / 32	16 / 39	4 / 39	0 / 11
BOSMA MINGUEZ, Javier	1	2 + 1	0 + 0		3 + 1	0 / 0	1	0 / 0	3 / 5	0 / 5	1 / 12
Totals	1	4 + 15	0 + 0	1 + 2	6 + 17	32 / 32	11	13 / 32	19 / 44	4 / 44	1 / 23

USA United States of America

Names	Serve	Attack	Block	Opp Error	Total	Reception	Dig	Attack S/O	Attack Total	Attack Total	Serve
		Scoring Skills (Pts + S/O)				Non-Scoring Skills (+ / Total)		Positive (+ / Total)		Errors (– / Total)	
WHITMARSH, Mike	0	1 + 12	7 + 0		8 + 12	15 / 15	3	11 / 20	13 / 20	2 / 20	0 / 16
DODD, Michael	0	4 + 3	0 + 0		4 + 3	6 / 6	13	2 / 17	7 / 17	1 / 17	0 / 16
Totals	0	5 + 15	7 + 0	3 + 2	15 + 17	21 / 21	16	13 / 37	20 / 37	3 / 37	0 / 32

ROUND 4 — USA 17 USA 15
Duration: 00:54 | 1st Referee: GBR BREHAUT, Jeff | 2nd Referee: JPN KONNO, Masaaki

USA United States of America

Names	Serve	Attack	Block	Opp Error	Total	Reception	Dig	Attack S/O	Attack Total	Attack Total	Serve
		Scoring Skills (Pts + S/O)				Non-Scoring Skills (+ / Total)		Positive (+ / Total)		Errors (– / Total)	
STEFFES, Kent	1	5 + 9	3 + 0		9 + 9	13 / 13	6	9 / 13	14 / 23	1 / 23	3 / 24
KIRALY, Karch	0	4 + 19	3 + 0		7 + 19	28 / 28	6	17 / 28	23 / 37	2 / 37	2 / 26
Totals	1	9 + 28	6 + 0	1 + 6	17 + 34	41 / 41	12	26 / 41	37 / 60	3 / 60	5 / 50

USA United States of America

Names	Serve	Attack	Block	Opp Error	Total	Reception	Dig	Attack S/O	Attack Total	Attack Total	Serve
		Scoring Skills (Pts + S/O)				Non-Scoring Skills (+ / Total)		Positive (+ / Total)		Errors (– / Total)	
SMITH, Christopher St. John	0	3 + 14	0 + 0		3 + 14	23 / 23	5	13 / 29	17 / 29	0 / 29	0 / 25
HENKEL, Carl	1	2 + 14	5 + 1		8 + 15	20 / 20	4	14 / 28	16 / 28	1 / 28	6 / 24
Totals	1	5 + 28	5 + 1	4 + 5	15 + 34	43 / 43	9	27 / 57	33 / 57	1 / 57	6 / 49

7TH PLACE — POR 15 NOR 3
Duration: 00:28 | 1st Referee: USA LEMAIRE, Sue | 2nd Referee: USA OWEN, Steve

POR Portugal

Names	Serve	Attack	Block	Opp Error	Total	Reception	Dig	Attack S/O	Attack Total	Attack Total	Serve
		Scoring Skills (Pts + S/O)				Non-Scoring Skills (+ / Total)		Positive (+ / Total)		Errors (– / Total)	
BARBOSA MAIA, Luis Miguel	1	5 + 6	0 + 0		6 + 6	6 / 6	8	4 / 6	11 / 14	1 / 14	2 / 13
PEREIRA BRENHA ALVES, Joao Carlos	2	2 + 7	3 + 0		7 + 7	10 / 10	4	6 / 10	9 / 17	0 / 17	1 / 16
Totals	3	7 + 13	3 + 0	2 + 3	15 + 16	16 / 16	12	10 / 16	20 / 31	1 / 31	3 / 29

NOR Norway

Names	Serve	Attack	Block	Opp Error	Total	Reception	Dig	Attack S/O	Attack Total	Attack Total	Serve
		Scoring Skills (Pts + S/O)				Non-Scoring Skills (+ / Total)		Positive (+ / Total)		Errors (– / Total)	
KVALHEIM, Jan	0	0 + 3	1 + 0		1 + 3	7 / 8	2	3 / 11	3 / 11	1 / 11	2 / 8
MAASEIDE, Bjorn	0	2 + 6	0 + 0		2 + 6	14 / 15	4	5 / 20	8 / 20	1 / 20	1 / 11
Totals	0	2 + 9	1 + 0	0 + 5	3 + 14	21 / 23	6	8 / 31	11 / 31	2 / 31	3 / 19

7TH PLACE — CUB 4 CAN 15
Duration: 00:30 | 1st Referee: USA SALVATORE, Patty | 2nd Referee: USA ROBB, Steve

CUB Cuba

Names	Serve	Attack	Block	Opp Error	Total	Reception	Dig	Attack S/O	Attack Total	Attack Total	Serve
		Scoring Skills (Pts + S/O)				Non-Scoring Skills (+ / Total)		Positive (+ / Total)		Errors (– / Total)	
ALVAREZ, Francisco	0	3 + 11	0 + 0		3 + 11	22 / 24	5	9 / 24	14 / 27	5 / 27	0 / 12
ROSELL MILANES, Juan Miguel	0	0 + 6	0 + 0		0 + 6	7 / 7	3	5 / 7	6 / 11	1 / 11	1 / 12
Totals	0	3 + 17	0 + 0	1 + 2	4 + 19	29 / 31	8	14 / 31	20 / 38	6 / 38	1 / 24

CAN Canada

Names	Serve	Attack	Block	Opp Error	Total	Reception	Dig	Attack S/O	Attack Total	Attack Total	Serve
		Scoring Skills (Pts + S/O)				Non-Scoring Skills (+ / Total)		Positive (+ / Total)		Errors (– / Total)	
CHILD, John	0	3 + 15	2 + 0		5 + 15	17 / 17	5	15 / 22	18 / 22	0 / 22	0 / 16
HEESE, Mark	1	1 + 3	1 + 0		3 + 3	6 / 6	2	3 / 9	4 / 9	1 / 9	2 / 18
Totals	1	4 + 18	3 + 0	7 + 2	15 + 20	23 / 23	7	18 / 31	22 / 31	1 / 31	2 / 34

Volleyball—Beach / Volleyball — De plage

Men / Messieurs

5TH PLACE — POR 15 USA 13 — Duration: 01:10 — 1st Referee: BRA VILLAS BOAS, Maria Amelia — 2nd Referee: GBR BREHAUT, Jeff

POR Portugal

Names	Serve	Attack	Block	Opp Error	Total	Reception	Dig	Attack S/O	Attack Total	Attack Total	Serve
		Scoring Skills (Pts + S/O)				Non-Scoring Skills (+ / Total)		Positive (+ / Total)		Errors (– / Total)	
BARBOSA MAIA, Luis Miguel	1	6 + 17	0 + 0		7 + 17	29 / 29	11	15 / 29	23 / 40	1 / 40	2 / 33
PEREIRA BRENHA ALVES, Joao Carlos	2	3 + 16	1 + 0		6 + 16	19 / 20	6	12 / 20	19 / 35	2 / 35	3 / 26
Totals	3	9 + 33	1 + 0	2 + 11	15 + 44	48 / 49	17	27 / 49	42 / 75	3 / 75	5 / 59

USA United States of America

Names	Serve	Attack	Block	Opp Error	Total	Reception	Dig	Attack S/O	Attack Total	Attack Total	Serve
		Scoring Skills (Pts + S/O)				Non-Scoring Skills (+ / Total)		Positive (+ / Total)		Errors (– / Total)	
SMITH, Christopher St. John	0	2 + 24	0 + 0		2 + 24	34 / 37	11	21 / 45	26 / 45	1 / 45	1 / 29
HENKEL, Carl	1	3 + 14	5 + 0		9 + 14	12 / 14	4	13 / 25	17 / 25	1 / 25	6 / 28
Totals	1	5 + 38	5 + 0	2 + 6	13 + 44	46 / 51	15	34 / 70	43 / 70	2 / 70	7 / 57

5TH PLACE — CAN 15 ESP 4 — Duration: 00:32 — 1st Referee: USA OWEN, Steve — 2nd Referee: JPN KONNO, Masaaki

CAN Canada

Names	Serve	Attack	Block	Opp Error	Total	Reception	Dig	Attack S/O	Attack Total	Attack Total	Serve
		Scoring Skills (Pts + S/O)				Non-Scoring Skills (+ / Total)		Positive (+ / Total)		Errors (– / Total)	
CHILD, John	1	6 + 5	0 + 0		7 + 5	9 / 9	5	6 / 9	11 / 14	0 / 14	1 / 22
HEESE, Mark	3	3 + 11	0 + 0		6 + 11	12 / 13	7	9 / 13	14 / 18	0 / 18	2 / 17
Totals	4	9 + 16	0 + 0	2 + 8	15 + 24	21 / 22	12	15 / 22	25 / 32	0 / 32	3 / 39

ESP Spain

Names	Serve	Attack	Block	Opp Error	Total	Reception	Dig	Attack S/O	Attack Total	Attack Total	Serve
		Scoring Skills (Pts + S/O)				Non-Scoring Skills (+ / Total)		Positive (+ / Total)		Errors (– / Total)	
JIMENEZ GALAN, Sixto	1	1 + 12	0 + 0		2 + 12	26 / 27	3	12 / 29	13 / 29	2 / 29	2 / 16
BOSMA MINGUEZ, Javier	0	0 + 7	0 + 0		0 + 7	4 / 5	2	5 / 10	7 / 10	2 / 10	3 / 12
Totals	1	1 + 19	0 + 0	2 + 4	4 + 23	30 / 32	5	17 / 39	20 / 39	4 / 39	5 / 28

SEMIFINALS — USA 15 POR 13 — Duration: 01:05 — 1st Referee: JPN KONNO, Masaaki — 2nd Referee: AUS HRESZCZUK, Peter

USA United States of America

Names	Serve	Attack	Block	Opp Error	Total	Reception	Dig	Attack S/O	Attack Total	Attack Total	Serve
		Scoring Skills (Pts + S/O)				Non-Scoring Skills (+ / Total)		Positive (+ / Total)		Errors (– / Total)	
WHITMARSH, Mike	0	1 + 18	0 + 0		1 + 18	26 / 29	5	13 / 29	19 / 36	4 / 36	1 / 30
DODD, Michael	0	7 + 16	0 + 0		7 + 16	20 / 21	15	15 / 21	23 / 35	1 / 35	0 / 26
Totals	0	8 + 34	0 + 0	7 + 9	15 + 43	46 / 50	20	28 / 50	42 / 71	5 / 71	1 / 56

POR Portugal

Names	Serve	Attack	Block	Opp Error	Total	Reception	Dig	Attack S/O	Attack Total	Attack Total	Serve
		Scoring Skills (Pts + S/O)				Non-Scoring Skills (+ / Total)		Positive (+ / Total)		Errors (– / Total)	
BARBOSA MAIA, Luis Miguel	1	1 + 12	0 + 0		2 + 12	14 / 14	8	11 / 26	13 / 26	4 / 26	4 / 29
PEREIRA BRENHA ALVES, Joao Carlos	0	4 + 28	1 + 1		5 + 29	42 / 42	4	27 / 51	32 / 51	5 / 51	1 / 27
Totals	1	5 + 40	1 + 1	6 + 1	13 + 42	56 / 56	12	38 / 77	45 / 77	9 / 77	5 / 56

SEMIFINALS — USA 15 CAN 11 — Duration: 00:40 — 1st Referee: GBR BREHAUT, Jeff — 2nd Referee: ESP CARRENO, Mirela

USA United States of America

Names	Serve	Attack	Block	Opp Error	Total	Reception	Dig	Attack S/O	Attack Total	Attack Total	Serve
		Scoring Skills (Pts + S/O)				Non-Scoring Skills (+ / Total)		Positive (+ / Total)		Errors (– / Total)	
STEFFES, Kent	2	6 + 6	1 + 0		9 + 6	11 / 11	7	6 / 11	12 / 19	1 / 19	3 / 22
KIRALY, Karch	0	2 + 12	1 + 0		3 + 12	17 / 18	3	11 / 18	14 / 21	1 / 21	3 / 19
Totals	2	8 + 18	2 + 0	3 + 7	15 + 25	28 / 29	10	17 / 29	26 / 40	2 / 40	6 / 41

CAN Canada

Names	Serve	Attack	Block	Opp Error	Total	Reception	Dig	Attack S/O	Attack Total	Attack Total	Serve
		Scoring Skills (Pts + S/O)				Non-Scoring Skills (+ / Total)		Positive (+ / Total)		Errors (– / Total)	
CHILD, John	0	2 + 10	0 + 0		2 + 10	17 / 20	4	10 / 20	12 / 25	1 / 25	4 / 20
HEESE, Mark	1	2 + 7	4 + 1		7 + 8	13 / 13	4	7 / 13	9 / 17	2 / 17	3 / 17
Totals	1	4 + 17	4 + 1	2 + 8	11 + 26	30 / 33	8	17 / 33	21 / 42	3 / 42	7 / 37

FINAL - BRONZE MATCH — 1st Set: POR 5 CAN 12 — Duration: 00:37 — 1st Referee: AUS HRESZCZUK, Peter — 2nd Referee: JPN KONNO, Masaaki
2nd Set: POR 8 CAN 12 — Duration: 00:40

POR Portugal

Names	Serve	Attack	Block	Opp Error	Total	Reception	Dig	Attack S/O	Attack Total	Attack Total	Serve
		Scoring Skills (Pts + S/O)				Non-Scoring Skills (+ / Total)		Positive (+ / Total)		Errors (– / Total)	
BARBOSA MAIA, Luis Miguel	0	5 + 16	1 + 0		6 + 16	23 / 30	16	12 / 30	21 / 39	2 / 39	4 / 37
PEREIRA BRENHA ALVES, Joao Carlos	0	3 + 25	3 + 0		6 + 25	36 / 39	2	21 / 39	28 / 48	2 / 48	3 / 28
Totals	0	8 + 41	4 + 0	1 + 10	13 + 51	59 / 69	18	33 / 69	49 / 87	4 / 87	7 / 65

CAN Canada

Names	Serve	Attack	Block	Opp Error	Total	Reception	Dig	Attack S/O	Attack Total	Attack Total	Serve
		Scoring Skills (Pts + S/O)				Non-Scoring Skills (+ / Total)		Positive (+ / Total)		Errors (– / Total)	
CHILD, John	3	5 + 19	3 + 2		11 + 21	18 / 24	8	15 / 24	24 / 35	1 / 35	2 / 39
HEESE, Mark	1	5 + 22	1 + 1		7 + 23	33 / 34	16	17 / 34	27 / 52	3 / 52	5 / 37
Totals	4	10 + 41	4 + 3	6 + 7	24 + 51	51 / 58	24	32 / 58	51 / 87	4 / 87	7 / 76

Men / *Messieurs*

FINAL - GOLD MATCH			
1st Set: USA 5 USA 12	Duration: 00:24	1st Referee: GBR BREHAUT, Jeff	2nd Referee: ESP CARRENO, Mirela
2nd Set: USA 8 USA 12	Duration: 00:38		

USA United States of America

Names	Serve	Attack	Block	Opp Error	Total	Reception	Dig	Attack S/O	Attack Total	Attack Total	Serve
		Scoring Skills (Pts + S/O)				Non-Scoring Skills (+ / Total)		Positive (+ / Total)		Errors (– / Total)	
WHITMARSH, Mike	0	2 + 15	3 + 0		5 + 15	26 / 27	2	13 / 27	17 / 35	3 / 35	0 / 25
DODD, Michael	0	4 + 13	0 + 0		4 + 13	22 / 23	16	9 / 23	17 / 40	3 / 40	2 / 27
Totals	0	6 + 28	3 + 0	4 + 10	13 + 28	48 / 50	18	22 / 50	34 / 75	6 / 75	2 / 52

USA United States of America

Names	Serve	Attack	Block	Opp Error	Total	Reception	Dig	Attack S/O	Attack Total	Attack Total	Serve
		Scoring Skills (Pts + S/O)				Non-Scoring Skills (+ / Total)		Positive (+ / Total)		Errors (– / Total)	
STEFFES, Kent	3	5 + 9	2 + 1		10 + 10	12 / 12	14	7 / 12	14 / 32	3 / 32	5 / 32
KIRALY, Karch	0	6 + 25	1 + 0		7 + 25	37 / 38	16	20 / 38	31 / 54	2 / 54	4 / 30
Totals	3	11 + 34	3 + 1	7 + 4	24 + 39	49 / 50	30	27 / 50	45 / 86	5 / 86	9 / 62

FINAL CLASSIFICATION

Rnk	Team	Names	
1	USA	KIRALY / STEFFES	Gold
2	USA	DODD / WHITMARSH	Silver
3	CAN	CHILD / HEESE	Bronze
4	POR	MAIA / BRENHA	
5	ESP	BOSMA / JIMENEZ	
5	USA	SMITH / HENKEL	
7	CUB	ALVAREZ / ROSELL	
7	NOR	KVALHEIM / MAASEIDE	

Volleyball—Beach / *Volleyball — De plage*

Women / *Dames*

ROUND 1	CAN 10 INA 15	Duration: 00:43	1st Referee: MEX RAMIREZ RIVERA, Miguel	2nd Referee: FRA BIAU, Patrick

CAN Canada

Names	Serve	Attack	Block	Opp Error	Total	Reception	Dig	Attack S/O	Attack Total	Attack Total	Serve
		Scoring Skills (Pts + S/O)				Non-Scoring Skills (+ / Total)		Positive (+ / Total)		Errors (– / Total)	
BROEN OUELLETTE, Barb	0	3 + 13	0 + 0		3 + 13	13 / 14	12	11 / 14	16 / 26	2 / 26	3 / 19
MALOWNEY, Margo	0	1 + 10	0 + 0		1 + 10	19 / 21	6	9 / 21	11 / 26	2 / 26	5 / 17
Totals	0	4 + 23	0 + 0	6 + 5	10 + 28	32 / 35	18	20 / 35	27 / 52	4 / 52	8 / 36

INA Indonesia

Names	Serve	Attack	Block	Opp Error	Total	Reception	Dig	Attack S/O	Attack Total	Attack Total	Serve
		Scoring Skills (Pts + S/O)				Non-Scoring Skills (+ / Total)		Positive (+ / Total)		Errors (– / Total)	
KAIZE, Engel Berta	3	6 + 12	0 + 0		9 + 12	14 / 14	8	11 / 30	18 / 30	3 / 30	3 / 24
YUDHANI RAHAYU, Ni Putu Timy	0	4 + 3	0 + 0		4 + 3	12 / 14	9	3 / 17	7 / 17	1 / 17	2 / 19
Totals	3	10 + 15	0 + 0	2 + 11	15 + 26	26 / 28	17	14 / 47	25 / 47	4 / 47	5 / 43

ROUND 1	MEX 11 FRA 15	Duration: 00:28	1st Referee: POR CORBAL SIMOES AZEVEDO, Avelino	2nd Referee: JPN KONNO, Masaaki

MEX Mexico

Names	Serve	Attack	Block	Opp Error	Total	Reception	Dig	Attack S/O	Attack Total	Attack Total	Serve
		Scoring Skills (Pts + S/O)				Non-Scoring Skills (+ / Total)		Positive (+ / Total)		Errors (– / Total)	
EGUILUZ SOTO, Velia	0	1 + 5	0 + 0		1 + 5	11 / 13	5	3 / 13	6 / 18	5 / 18	2 / 11
HUERTA HERNADEZ, Mayra Yaratzeth	0	1 + 4	2 + 1		3 + 5	7 / 9	4	2 / 9	5 / 13	3 / 13	2 / 12
Totals	0	2 + 9	2 + 1	7 + 2	11 + 12	18 / 22	9	5 / 22	11 / 31	8 / 31	4 / 23

FRA France

Names	Serve	Attack	Block	Opp Error	Total	Reception	Dig	Attack S/O	Attack Total	Attack Total	Serve
		Scoring Skills (Pts + S/O)				Non-Scoring Skills (+ / Total)		Positive (+ / Total)		Errors (– / Total)	
LESAGE, Brigitte	0	0 + 3	1 + 0		1 + 3	2 / 4	1	2 / 8	3 / 8	2 / 8	2 / 11
PRAWERMAN, Anabelle	3	1 + 5	0 + 0		4 + 5	13 / 15	6	5 / 17	6 / 17	2 / 17	0 / 16
Totals	3	1 + 8	1 + 0	10 + 4	15 + 12	15 / 19	7	7 / 25	9 / 25	4 / 25	2 / 27

Women / *Dames*

ROUND 2 — JPN 10 AUS 15 | Duration: 00:23 | 1st Referee: USA ROBB, Steve | 2nd Referee: USA LEMAIRE, Sue

JPN Japan

Names	Serve	Attack	Block	Opp Error	Total	Reception	Dig	Attack S/O	Attack Total	Attack Total	Serve
		Scoring Skills (Pts + S/O)				Non-Scoring Skills (+ / Total)		Positive (+ / Total)		Errors (– / Total)	
TAKAHASHI, Yukiko	1	4 + 3	0 + 0		5 + 3	8 / 8	4	2 / 8	7 / 17	3 / 17	0 / 14
FUJITA, Sachiko	0	1 + 4	0 + 0		1 + 4	14 / 15	7	4 / 15	5 / 18	2 / 18	0 / 8
Totals	1	5 + 7	0 + 0	4 + 5	10 + 12	22 / 23	11	6 / 23	12 / 35	5 / 35	0 / 22

AUS Australia

Names	Serve	Attack	Block	Opp Error	Total	Reception	Dig	Attack S/O	Attack Total	Attack Total	Serve
		Scoring Skills (Pts + S/O)				Non-Scoring Skills (+ / Total)		Positive (+ / Total)		Errors (– / Total)	
FENWICK, Liane	1	3 + 4	2 + 0		6 + 4	4 / 5	4	3 / 16	7 / 16	4 / 16	2 / 9
SPRING, Anita	0	4 + 7	1 + 0		5 + 7	14 / 16	7	5 / 19	11 / 19	1 / 19	1 / 18
Totals	1	7 + 11	3 + 0	4 + 1	15 + 12	18 / 21	11	8 / 35	18 / 35	5 / 35	3 / 27

ROUND 2 — BRA 17 ITA 15 | Duration: 00:57 | 1st Referee: USA OWEN, Steve | 2nd Referee: PUR MENDOZA BAS, Aurelio

BRA Brazil

Names	Serve	Attack	Block	Opp Error	Total	Reception	Dig	Attack S/O	Attack Total	Attack Total	Serve
		Scoring Skills (Pts + S/O)				Non-Scoring Skills (+ / Total)		Positive (+ / Total)		Errors (– / Total)	
SAMUEL, Adriana Ramos	3	2 + 8	0 + 0		5 + 8	9 / 10	10	7 / 10	10 / 20	0 / 20	2 / 24
RODRIGUES, Monica	0	4 + 18	1 + 0		5 + 18	24 / 30	11	15 / 30	22 / 44	9 / 44	3 / 24
Totals	3	6 + 26	1 + 0	7 + 6	17 + 32	33 / 40	21	22 / 40	32 / 64	9 / 64	5 / 48

ITA Italy

Names	Serve	Attack	Block	Opp Error	Total	Reception	Dig	Attack S/O	Attack Total	Attack Total	Serve
		Scoring Skills (Pts + S/O)				Non-Scoring Skills (+ / Total)		Positive (+ / Total)		Errors (– / Total)	
TURETTA, Consuelo	1	2 + 11	1 + 2		4 + 13	24 / 29	8	9 / 35	13 / 35	2 / 35	2 / 20
SOLAZZI, Anna Maria	0	2 + 10	0 + 0		2 + 10	9 / 11	12	8 / 24	12 / 24	4 / 24	4 / 27
Totals	1	4 + 21	1 + 2	9 + 9	15 + 32	33 / 40	20	17 / 59	25 / 59	6 / 59	6 / 47

ROUND 2 — USA 15 NOR 8 | Duration: 00:41 | 1st Referee: BRA VILLAS BOAS, Maria Amelia | 2nd Referee: POR CORBAL SIMOES AZEVEDO, A.

USA United States of America

Names	Serve	Attack	Block	Opp Error	Total	Reception	Dig	Attack S/O	Attack Total	Attack Total	Serve
		Scoring Skills (Pts + S/O)				Non-Scoring Skills (+ / Total)		Positive (+ / Total)		Errors (– / Total)	
HANLEY, Linda	0	4 + 7	1 + 0		5 + 7	7 / 7	10	4 / 7	11 / 21	1 / 21	2 / 19
FONTANA HARRIS, Barbra	2	3 + 10	0 + 0		5 + 10	18 / 20	9	10 / 20	13 / 30	4 / 30	4 / 23
Totals	2	7 + 17	1 + 0	5 + 10	15 + 27	25 / 27	19	14 / 27	24 / 51	5 / 51	6 / 42

NOR Norway

Names	Serve	Attack	Block	Opp Error	Total	Reception	Dig	Attack S/O	Attack Total	Attack Total	Serve
		Scoring Skills (Pts + S/O)				Non-Scoring Skills (+ / Total)		Positive (+ / Total)		Errors (– / Total)	
BERNTSEN, Merita	2	0 + 9	0 + 1		2 + 10	22 / 24	8	8 / 31	9 / 31	5 / 31	2 / 19
HESTAD, Ragni	0	1 + 8	0 + 1		1 + 9	8 / 10	7	6 / 21	9 / 21	3 / 21	4 / 16
Totals	2	1 + 17	0 + 2	5 + 8	8 + 27	30 / 34	15	14 / 52	18 / 52	8 / 52	6 / 35

ROUND 2 — USA 15 NED 4 | Duration: 00:34 | 1st Referee: ITA BORGATO, Maurizio | 2nd Referee: MEX RAMIREZ RIVERA, Miguel

USA United States of America

Names	Serve	Attack	Block	Opp Error	Total	Reception	Dig	Attack S/O	Attack Total	Attack Total	Serve
		Scoring Skills (Pts + S/O)				Non-Scoring Skills (+ / Total)		Positive (+ / Total)		Errors (– / Total)	
RICHARDSON, Debra	2	3 + 9	0 + 0		5 + 9	8 / 10	7	6 / 10	12 / 21	1 / 21	2 / 17
CASTRO, Gail	0	4 + 6	0 + 0		4 + 6	7 / 9	11	6 / 9	10 / 22	0 / 22	1 / 19
Totals	2	7 + 15	0 + 0	6 + 7	15 + 22	15 / 19	18	12 / 19	22 / 43	1 / 43	3 / 36

NED Netherlands

Names	Serve	Attack	Block	Opp Error	Total	Reception	Dig	Attack S/O	Attack Total	Attack Total	Serve
		Scoring Skills (Pts + S/O)				Non-Scoring Skills (+ / Total)		Positive (+ / Total)		Errors (– / Total)	
SCHOON KADIJK, Debora	1	1 + 5	0 + 0		2 + 5	14 / 17	7	4 / 22	6 / 22	3 / 22	3 / 14
van de VEN, Lisette	0	0 + 12	0 + 1		0 + 13	12 / 14	7	8 / 26	12 / 26	3 / 26	3 / 12
Totals	1	1 + 17	0 + 1	2 + 3	4 + 21	26 / 31	14	12 / 48	18 / 48	6 / 48	6 / 26

ROUND 2 — AUS 15 GBR 4 | Duration: 00:35 | 1st Referee: USA SALVATORE, Patty | 2nd Referee: USA OWEN, Steve

AUS Australia

Names	Serve	Attack	Block	Opp Error	Total	Reception	Dig	Attack S/O	Attack Total	Attack Total	Serve
		Scoring Skills (Pts + S/O)				Non-Scoring Skills (+ / Total)		Positive (+ / Total)		Errors (– / Total)	
COOK, Natalie	0	8 + 7	1 + 0		9 + 7	8 / 11	6	7 / 11	15 / 20	0 / 20	2 / 15
POTTHARST, Kerri Ann	2	1 + 10	0 + 0		3 + 10	7 / 11	7	7 / 11	11 / 17	2 / 17	4 / 24
Totals	2	9 + 17	1 + 0	3 + 8	15 + 25	15 / 22	13	14 / 22	26 / 37	2 / 37	6 / 39

GBR Great Britain

Names	Serve	Attack	Block	Opp Error	Total	Reception	Dig	Attack S/O	Attack Total	Attack Total	Serve
		Scoring Skills (Pts + S/O)				Non-Scoring Skills (+ / Total)		Positive (+ / Total)		Errors (– / Total)	
GLOVER, Amanda	0	1 + 5	0 + 0		1 + 5	8 / 11	4	4 / 17	6 / 17	1 / 17	5 / 13
COOPER, Audrey	0	0 + 12	0 + 0		0 + 12	17 / 20	5	11 / 23	12 / 23	2 / 23	2 / 16
Totals	0	1 + 17	0 + 0	3 + 7	4 + 24	25 / 31	9	15 / 40	18 / 40	3 / 40	7 / 29

Women / Dames

ROUND 2 GER 15 JPN 8 Duration: 00:36 1st Referee: AUS HRESZCZUK, Peter 2nd Referee: USA ROBB, Steve

GER Germany

Names	Serve	Attack	Block	Opp Error	Total	Reception	Dig	Attack S/O	Attack Total	Attack Total	Serve
		Scoring Skills (Pts + S/O)				Non-Scoring Skills (+ / Total)		Positive (+ / Total)		Errors (− / Total)	
BUHLER, Beate	2	1 + 9	1 + 1		4 + 10	21 / 23	6	9 / 23	10 / 24	3 / 24	3 / 21
MUSCH, Danja	0	4 + 6	3 + 0		7 + 6	5 / 6	5	5 / 6	10 / 18	3 / 18	3 / 17
Totals	2	5 + 15	4 + 1	4 + 8	15 + 24	26 / 29	11	14 / 29	20 / 42	6 / 42	6 / 38

JPN Japan

Names	Serve	Attack	Block	Opp Error	Total	Reception	Dig	Attack S/O	Attack Total	Attack Total	Serve
ISHIZAKA, Yukiko	1	0 + 6	0 + 0		1 + 6	18 / 23	8	5 / 21	6 / 21	4 / 21	1 / 17
NAKANO, Teruko	0	1 + 6	0 + 0		1 + 6	7 / 7	5	6 / 20	7 / 20	2 / 20	1 / 15
Totals	1	1 + 12	0 + 0	6 + 11	8 + 23	25 / 30	13	11 / 41	13 / 41	6 / 41	2 / 32

ROUND 2 BRA 15 INA 2 Duration: 00:25 1st Referee: GBR BREHAUT, Jeff 2nd Referee: ITA BORGATO, Maurizio

BRA Brazil

Names	Serve	Attack	Block	Opp Error	Total	Reception	Dig	Attack S/O	Attack Total	Attack Total	Serve
SILVA, Jacqueline Louise Cruz	1	1 + 7	1 + 0		3 + 7	7 / 7	4	6 / 7	8 / 10	1 / 10	2 / 11
PIRES, Sandra Tavares	1	5 + 5	0 + 0		6 + 5	7 / 8	9	5 / 8	10 / 18	2 / 18	1 / 19
Totals	2	6 + 12	1 + 0	6 + 4	15 + 16	14 / 15	13	11 / 15	18 / 28	3 / 28	3 / 30

INA Indonesia

Names	Serve	Attack	Block	Opp Error	Total	Reception	Dig	Attack S/O	Attack Total	Attack Total	Serve
KAIZE, Engle Berta	1	1 + 8	0 + 0		2 + 8	8 / 12	2	7 / 19	9 / 19	2 / 19	2 / 9
YUDHANI RAHAYU, Ni Putu Timy	0	0 + 1	0 + 0		0 + 1	12 / 13	3	1 / 11	1 / 11	4 / 11	0 / 9
Totals	1	1 + 9	0 + 0	0 + 6	2 + 15	20 / 25	5	8 / 30	10 / 30	6 / 30	2 / 18

ROUND 2 USA 15 FRA 4 Duration: 00:33 1st Referee: ESP CARRENO, Mirela 2nd Referee: BRA VILLAS BOAS, Maria Amelia

USA United States of America

Names	Serve	Attack	Block	Opp Error	Total	Reception	Dig	Attack S/O	Attack Total	Attack Total	Serve
McPEAK, Holly	1	4 + 6	0 + 0		5 + 6	10 / 10	9	6 / 10	10 / 16	2 / 16	2 / 20
RENO, Nancy	0	4 + 12	1 + 0		5 + 12	11 / 11	6	10 / 11	16 / 20	0 / 20	5 / 15
Totals	1	8 + 18	1 + 0	5 + 3	15 + 21	21 / 21	15	16 / 21	26 / 36	2 / 36	7 / 35

FRA France

Names	Serve	Attack	Block	Opp Error	Total	Reception	Dig	Attack S/O	Attack Total	Attack Total	Serve
LESAGE, Brigitte	0	1 + 2	0 + 0		1 + 2	6 / 6	3	1 / 10	3 / 10	0 / 10	3 / 11
PRAWERMAN, Anabelle	1	0 + 10	0 + 0		1 + 10	18 / 21	3	8 / 23	10 / 23	3 / 23	0 / 14
Totals	1	1 + 12	0 + 0	2 + 8	4 + 20	24 / 27	6	9 / 33	13 / 33	3 / 33	3 / 25

17TH PLACE CAN 13 FRA 15 Duration: 01:08 1st Referee: BRA VILLAS BOAS, Maria Amelia 2nd Referee: POR CORBAL SIMOES AZEVEDO, A.

CAN Canada

Names	Serve	Attack	Block	Opp Error	Total	Reception	Dig	Attack S/O	Attack Total	Attack Total	Serve
BROEN OUELLETTE, Barb	1	3 + 17	0 + 0		4 + 17	25 / 27	7	15 / 27	20 / 33	4 / 33	8 / 32
MALOWNEY, Margo	3	2 + 26	0 + 0		5 + 26	26 / 30	6	24 / 30	28 / 38	2 / 38	12 / 33
Totals	4	5 + 43	0 + 0	4 + 7	13 + 50	51 / 57	13	39 / 57	48 / 71	6 / 71	20 / 65

FRA France

Names	Serve	Attack	Block	Opp Error	Total	Reception	Dig	Attack S/O	Attack Total	Attack Total	Serve
LESAGE, Brigitte	1	0 + 10	2 + 0		3 + 10	14 / 16	4	10 / 17	10 / 17	2 / 17	2 / 33
PRAWERMAN, Anabelle	3	5 + 18	0 + 0		8 + 18	21 / 24	9	17 / 36	23 / 36	1 / 36	3 / 33
Totals	4	5 + 28	2 + 0	4 + 24	15 + 52	35 / 40	13	27 / 53	33 / 53	3 / 53	5 / 66

17TH PLACE MEX 5 INA 15 Duration: 00:29 1st Referee: ITA BORGATO, Maurizio 2nd Referee: USA ROBB, Steve

MEX Mexico

Names	Serve	Attack	Block	Opp Error	Total	Reception	Dig	Attack S/O	Attack Total	Attack Total	Serve
EGUILUZ SOTO, Velia	0	0 + 5	0 + 0		0 + 5	12 / 14	5	4 / 14	5 / 19	5 / 19	3 / 11
HUERTA HERNANDEZ, Mayra Yaratzeth	0	1 + 4	1 + 1		2 + 5	7 / 11	3	4 / 11	5 / 13	2 / 13	0 / 11
Totals	0	1 + 9	1 + 1	3 + 17	5 + 17	19 / 25	8	8 / 25	10 / 32	7 / 32	3 / 22

INA Indonesia

Names	Serve	Attack	Block	Opp Error	Total	Reception	Dig	Attack S/O	Attack Total	Attack Total	Serve
KAIZE, Engel Berta	0	2 + 8	0 + 0		2 + 8	5 / 5	7	7 / 20	10 / 20	2 / 20	3 / 17
YUDHANI RAHAYU, Ni Putu Timy	1	3 + 5	0 + 0		4 + 5	13 / 14	7	5 / 13	8 / 13	1 / 13	2 / 15
Totals	1	5 + 13	0 + 0	9 + 4	15 + 17	18 / 19	14	12 / 33	18 / 33	3 / 33	5 / 32

Women / Dames

13TH PLACE — GBR 15 NED 12 — Duration: 00:50 — 1st Referee: USA SALVATORE, Patty — 2nd Referee: USA OWEN, Steve

GBR Great Britain

Names	Serve	Attack	Block	Opp Error	Total	Reception	Dig	Attack S/O	Attack Total	Attack Total	Serve
		Scoring Skills (Pts + S/O)				Non-Scoring Skills (+ / Total)		Positive (+ / Total)		Errors (– / Total)	
GLOVER, Amanda	1	2 + 12	1 + 0		4 + 12	22 / 25	6	12 / 25	14 / 32	4 / 32	2 / 19
COOPER, Audrey	2	4 + 5	0 + 0		6 + 5	8 / 8	16	3 / 8	9 / 25	2 / 25	2 / 27
Totals	3	6 + 17	1 + 0	5 + 13	15 + 30	30 / 33	22	15 / 33	23 / 57	6 / 57	4 / 46

NED Netherlands

Names	Serve	Attack	Block	Opp Error	Total	Reception	Dig	Attack S/O	Attack Total	Attack Total	Serve
		Scoring Skills (Pts + S/O)				Non-Scoring Skills (+ / Total)		Positive (+ / Total)		Errors (– / Total)	
SCHOON KADIJK, Debora	2	2 + 12	0 + 0		4 + 12	26 / 27	9	12 / 38	14 / 38	6 / 38	3 / 21
van de VEN, Lisette	0	3 + 9	0 + 0		3 + 9	11 / 12	17	7 / 26	12 / 26	3 / 26	4 / 21
Totals	2	5 + 21	0 + 0	5 + 9	12 + 30	37 / 39	26	19 / 64	26 / 64	9 / 64	7 / 42

13TH PLACE — NOR 15 ITA 11 — Duration: 00:42 — 1st Referee: AUS HRESZCZUK, Peter — 2nd Referee: MEX RAMIREZ RIVERA, Miguel

NOR Norway

Names	Serve	Attack	Block	Opp Error	Total	Reception	Dig	Attack S/O	Attack Total	Attack Total	Serve
		Scoring Skills (Pts + S/O)				Non-Scoring Skills (+ / Total)		Positive (+ / Total)		Errors (– / Total)	
BERNTSEN, Merita	1	4 + 6	0 + 0		5 + 6	10 / 14	10	6 / 14	10 / 20	2 / 20	2 / 21
HESTAD, Ragni	0	4 + 10	0 + 0		4 + 10	11 / 13	12	9 / 13	14 / 32	2 / 32	2 / 16
Totals	1	8 + 16	0 + 0	6 + 7	15 + 23	21 / 27	22	15 / 27	24 / 52	4 / 52	4 / 37

ITA Italy

Names	Serve	Attack	Block	Opp Error	Total	Reception	Dig	Attack S/O	Attack Total	Attack Total	Serve
		Scoring Skills (Pts + S/O)				Non-Scoring Skills (+ / Total)		Positive (+ / Total)		Errors (– / Total)	
TURETTA, Consuelo	2	2 + 11	0 + 0		4 + 11	12 / 17	8	7 / 25	13 / 25	3 / 25	1 / 20
SOLAZZI, Anna Maria	0	4 + 4	0 + 0		4 + 4	14 / 15	11	4 / 29	8 / 29	4 / 29	4 / 14
Totals	2	6 + 15	0 + 0	3 + 7	11 + 22	26 / 32	19	11 / 54	21 / 54	7 / 54	5 / 34

13TH PLACE — FRA 8 JPN 15 — Duration: 00:26 — 1st Referee: ESP CARRENO, Mirela — 2nd Referee: PUR MENDOZA BAS, Aurelio

FRA France

Names	Serve	Attack	Block	Opp Error	Total	Reception	Dig	Attack S/O	Attack Total	Attack Total	Serve
		Scoring Skills (Pts + S/O)				Non-Scoring Skills (+ / Total)		Positive (+ / Total)		Errors (– / Total)	
LESAGE, Brigitte	0	1 + 2	1 + 0		2 + 2	5 / 7	3	2 / 7	3 / 17	0 / 17	1 / 12
PRAWERMAN, Anabelle	0	4 + 7	0 + 0		4 + 7	16 / 16	12	7 / 16	11 / 23	1 / 23	1 / 8
Totals	0	5 + 9	1 + 0	2 + 3	8 + 12	21 / 23	15	9 / 23	14 / 40	1 / 40	2 / 20

JPN Japan

Names	Serve	Attack	Block	Opp Error	Total	Reception	Dig	Attack S/O	Attack Total	Attack Total	Serve
		Scoring Skills (Pts + S/O)				Non-Scoring Skills (+ / Total)		Positive (+ / Total)		Errors (– / Total)	
ISHIZAKA, Yukiko	1	4 + 3	0 + 0		5 + 3	12 / 12	11	3 / 21	7 / 21	2 / 21	0 / 15
NAKANO, Teruko	2	4 + 6	1 + 0		7 + 6	6 / 6	9	2 / 19	10 / 19	0 / 19	1 / 12
Totals	3	8 + 9	1 + 0	3 + 3	15 + 12	18 / 18	20	5 / 40	17 / 40	2 / 40	1 / 27

13TH PLACE — JPN 15 INA 0 — Duration: 00:18 — 1st Referee: GBR BREHAUT, Jeff — 2nd Referee: ITA BORGATO, Maurizio

JPN Japan

Names	Serve	Attack	Block	Opp Error	Total	Reception	Dig	Attack S/O	Attack Total	Attack Total	Serve
		Scoring Skills (Pts + S/O)				Non-Scoring Skills (+ / Total)		Positive (+ / Total)		Errors (– / Total)	
TAKAHASHI, Yukiko	0	7 + 4	0 + 0		7 + 4	4 / 4	11	3 / 4	11 / 18	0 / 18	1 / 10
FUJITA, Sachiko	0	1 + 6	0 + 0		1 + 6	4 / 6	6	4 / 6	7 / 9	0 / 9	1 / 16
Totals	0	8 + 10	0 + 0	7 + 2	15 + 12	8 / 10	17	7 / 10	18 / 27	0 / 27	2 / 26

INA Indonesia

Names	Serve	Attack	Block	Opp Error	Total	Reception	Dig	Attack S/O	Attack Total	Attack Total	Serve
		Scoring Skills (Pts + S/O)				Non-Scoring Skills (+ / Total)		Positive (+ / Total)		Errors (– / Total)	
KAIZE, Engel Berta	0	0 + 2	0 + 0		0 + 2	1 / 2	3	2 / 11	2 / 11	3 / 11	2 / 6
YUDHANI RAHAYU, Ni Putu Timy	0	0 + 7	0 + 0		0 + 7	17 / 21	6	5 / 19	7 / 19	1 / 19	0 / 6
Totals	0	0 + 9	0 + 0	0 + 2	0 + 11	18 / 23	9	7 / 30	9 / 30	4 / 30	2 / 12

ROUND 3 — BRA 15 AUS 13 — Duration: 00:45 — 1st Referee: POR CORBAL SIMOES AZEVEDO, Avelino — 2nd Referee: USA OWEN, Steve

BRA Brazil

Names	Serve	Attack	Block	Opp Error	Total	Reception	Dig	Attack S/O	Attack Total	Attack Total	Serve
		Scoring Skills (Pts + S/O)				Non-Scoring Skills (+ / Total)		Positive (+ / Total)		Errors (– / Total)	
SILVA, Jacqueline Louise Cruz	0	3 + 9	2 + 0		5 + 9	16 / 20	13	9 / 20	12 / 29	3 / 29	3 / 19
PIRES, Sandra Tavares	0	3 + 9	0 + 0		3 + 9	11 / 14	7	6 / 14	12 / 26	4 / 26	1 / 21
Totals	0	6 + 18	2 + 0	7 + 7	15 + 25	27 / 34	20	15 / 34	24 / 55	7 / 55	4 / 40

AUS Australia

Names	Serve	Attack	Block	Opp Error	Total	Reception	Dig	Attack S/O	Attack Total	Attack Total	Serve
		Scoring Skills (Pts + S/O)				Non-Scoring Skills (+ / Total)		Positive (+ / Total)		Errors (– / Total)	
FENWICK, Liane	0	3 + 8	1 + 0		4 + 8	6 / 7	3	6 / 22	11 / 22	3 / 22	4 / 19
SPRING, Anita	0	0 + 12	0 + 0		0 + 12	26 / 29	17	11 / 32	12 / 32	4 / 32	0 / 19
Totals	0	3 + 20	1 + 0	9 + 5	13 + 25	32 / 36	20	17 / 54	23 / 54	7 / 54	4 / 38

Women / Dames

ROUND 3 — BRA 15 USA 10

Duration: 00:55 1st Referee: MEX RAMIREZ RIVERA, Miguel 2nd Referee: JPN KONNO, Masaaki

BRA Brazil

Names	Serve	Attack	Block	Opp Error	Total	Reception	Dig	Attack S/O	Attack Total	Attack Total (err)	Serve (err)
SAMUEL, Adriana Ramos	2	4 + 8	0 + 0		6 + 8	8 / 9	10	7 / 9	12 / 18	0 / 18	2 / 27
RODRIGUES, Monica	0	7 + 23	0 + 0		7 + 23	28 / 30	6	22 / 30	30 / 39	5 / 39	3 / 24
Totals	2	11 + 31	0 + 0	2 + 5	15 + 36	36 / 39	16	29 / 39	42 / 57	5 / 57	5 / 51

USA United States of America

Names	Serve	Attack	Block	Opp Error	Total	Reception	Dig	Attack S/O	Attack Total	Attack Total (err)	Serve (err)
HANLEY, Linda	1	0 + 3	1 + 0		2 + 3	3 / 4	1	3 / 8	3 / 8	1 / 8	2 / 22
FONTANA HARRIS, Barbra	2	2 + 27	0 + 0		4 + 27	35 / 40	6	26 / 44	29 / 44	2 / 44	2 / 24
Totals	3	2 + 30	1 + 0	4 + 6	10 + 36	38 / 44	7	29 / 52	32 / 52	3 / 52	4 / 46

ROUND 3 — USA 7 AUS 15

Duration: 00:38 1st Referee: GBR BREHAUT, Jeff 2nd Referee: ITA BORGATO, Maurizio

USA United States of America

Names	Serve	Attack	Block	Opp Error	Total	Reception	Dig	Attack S/O	Attack Total	Attack Total (err)	Serve (err)
RICHARDSON, Debra	1	0 + 5	0 + 0		1 + 5	1 / 2	5	0 / 2	5 / 9	1 / 9	2 / 14
CASTRO, Gail	1	1 + 10	0 + 0		2 + 10	25 / 25	5	9 / 25	11 / 29	3 / 29	2 / 17
Totals	2	1 + 15	0 + 0	4 + 8	7 + 23	26 / 27	10	9 / 27	16 / 38	4 / 38	4 / 31

AUS Australia

Names	Serve	Attack	Block	Opp Error	Total	Reception	Dig	Attack S/O	Attack Total	Attack Total (err)	Serve (err)
COOK, Natalie	0	3 + 8	0 + 0		3 + 8	13 / 13	8	7 / 19	11 / 19	2 / 19	2 / 17
POTTHARST, Kerri Ann	4	4 + 11	0 + 0		8 + 11	11 / 12	5	11 / 23	15 / 23	3 / 23	5 / 21
Totals	4	7 + 19	0 + 0	4 + 4	15 + 23	24 / 25	13	18 / 42	26 / 42	5 / 42	7 / 38

ROUND 3 — GER 6 USA 15

Duration: 00:36 1st Referee: POR CORBAL S. AZEVEDO, Avelino 2nd Referee: AUS HRESZCZUK, Peter

GER Germany

Names	Serve	Attack	Block	Opp Error	Total	Reception	Dig	Attack S/O	Attack Total	Attack Total (err)	Serve (err)
BUHLER, Beate	0	0 + 11	0 + 0		0 + 11	13 / 15	1	10 / 15	11 / 15	0 / 15	1 / 14
MUSCH, Danja	1	2 + 4	0 + 0		3 + 4	9 / 12	0	4 / 12	6 / 14	4 / 14	1 / 12
Totals	1	2 + 15	0 + 0	3 + 4	6 + 19	22 / 27	1	14 / 27	17 / 29	4 / 29	2 / 26

POR Portugal

Names	Serve	Attack	Block	Opp Error	Total	Reception	Dig	Attack S/O	Attack Total	Attack Total (err)	Serve (err)
McPEAK, Holly	4	1 + 8	0 + 0		5 + 8	11 / 13	4	8 / 12	9 / 12	0 / 12	1 / 21
RENO, Nancy	0	4 + 9	1 + 0		5 + 9	10 / 10	3	9 / 16	13 / 16	2 / 16	2 / 13
Totals	4	5 + 17	1 + 0	5 + 3	15 + 20	21 / 23	7	17 / 28	22 / 28	2 / 28	3 / 34

9TH PLACE — JPN 6 USA 15

Duration: 00:36 1st Referee: FRA BIAU, Patrick 2nd Referee: POR CORBAL S. AZEVEDO, Avelino

JPN Japan

Names	Serve	Attack	Block	Opp Error	Total	Reception	Dig	Attack S/O	Attack Total	Attack Total (err)	Serve (err)
ISHIZAKA, Yukiko	0	0 + 6	0 + 0		0 + 6	20 / 22	6	5 / 22	6 / 37	2 / 37	0 / 14
NAKANO, Teruko	0	2 + 9	0 + 0		2 + 9	8 / 9	8	8 / 9	11 / 51	2 / 51	1 / 14
Totals	0	2 + 15	0 + 0	4 + 5	6 + 20	28 / 31	14	13 / 31	17 / 88	4 / 88	1 / 28

USA United States of America

Names	Serve	Attack	Block	Opp Error	Total	Reception	Dig	Attack S/O	Attack Total	Attack Total (err)	Serve (err)
HANLEY, Linda	0	6 + 8	1 + 0		7 + 8	5 / 5	10	6 / 46	14 / 46	0 / 46	3 / 22
FONTANA HARRIS, Barbra	1	3 + 11	0 + 0		4 + 11	16 / 24	6	10 / 56	14 / 56	2 / 56	0 / 21
Totals	1	9 + 19	1 + 0	4 + 2	15 + 21	21 / 29	16	16 / 102	28 / 102	2 / 102	3 / 43

9TH PLACE — GBR 12 AUS 15

Duration: 00:38 1st Referee: USA ROBB, Steve 2nd Referee: USA SALVATORE, Patty

GBR Great Britain

Names	Serve	Attack	Block	Opp Error	Total	Reception	Dig	Attack S/O	Attack Total	Attack Total (err)	Serve (err)
GLOVER, Amanda	0	2 + 6	0 + 0		2 + 6	16 / 16	2	6 / 16	8 / 19	1 / 19	2 / 19
COOPER, Audrey	0	5 + 9	0 + 0		5 + 9	11 / 11	9	8 / 11	14 / 20	1 / 20	2 / 14
Totals	0	7 + 15	0 + 0	5 + 6	12 + 21	27 / 27	11	14 / 27	22 / 39	2 / 39	4 / 33

AUS Australia

Names	Serve	Attack	Block	Opp Error	Total	Reception	Dig	Attack S/O	Attack Total	Attack Total (err)	Serve (err)
FENWICK, Liane	3	3 + 11	0 + 0		6 + 11	13 / 15	4	9 / 23	14 / 23	2 / 23	4 / 21
SPRING, Anita	0	6 + 6	0 + 0		6 + 6	14 / 14	9	6 / 20	12 / 20	2 / 20	2 / 15
Totals	3	9 + 17	0 + 0	3 + 4	15 + 21	27 / 29	13	15 / 43	26 / 43	4 / 43	6 / 36

Women / *Dames*

9TH PLACE — NOR 9 GER 15 — Duration: 00:45 — 1st Referee: USA LEMAIRE, Sue — 2nd Referee: BRA VILLAS BOAS, Maria Amelia

NOR Norway

Names	Serve	Attack	Block	Opp Error	Total	Reception	Dig	Attack S/O	Attack Total	Attack Total	Serve
		Scoring Skills (Pts + S/O)				Non-Scoring Skills (+ / Total)		Positive (+ / Total)		Errors (– / Total)	
BERNTSEN, Merita	3	0 + 11	0 + 0		3 + 11	22 / 25	11	10 / 25	11 / 37	7 / 37	2 / 21
HESTAD, Ragni	2	0 + 11	0 + 0		2 + 11	11 / 12	5	10 / 12	11 / 18	1 / 18	6 / 21
Totals	5	0 + 22	0 + 0	4 + 12	9 + 34	33 / 37	16	20 / 37	22 / 55	8 / 55	8 / 42

GER Germany

Names	Serve	Attack	Block	Opp Error	Total	Reception	Dig	Attack S/O	Attack Total	Attack Total	Serve
BUHLER, Beate	1	2 + 10	1 + 0		4 + 10	12 / 13	5	8 / 20	12 / 20	2 / 20	4 / 23
MUSCH, Danja	1	3 + 12	0 + 0		4 + 12	14 / 15	17	9 / 30	15 / 30	5 / 30	4 / 26
Totals	2	5 + 22	1 + 0	7 + 11	15 + 33	26 / 28	22	17 / 50	27 / 50	7 / 50	8 / 49

9TH PLACE — JPN 15 USA 11 — Duration: 00:49 — 1st Referee: GBR BREHAUT, Jeff — 2nd Referee: ESP CARRENO, Mirela

JPN Japan

Names	Serve	Attack	Block	Opp Error	Total	Reception	Dig	Attack S/O	Attack Total	Attack Total	Serve
TAKAHASHI, Yukiko	1	7 + 10	0 + 0		8 + 10	11 / 11	10	6 / 11	17 / 27	1 / 27	0 / 26
FUJITA, Sachiko	0	1 + 20	0 + 0		1 + 20	32 / 32	5	20 / 32	21 / 33	5 / 33	1 / 25
Totals	1	8 + 30	0 + 0	6 + 7	15 + 37	43 / 43	15	26 / 43	38 / 60	6 / 60	1 / 51

USA United States of America

Names	Serve	Attack	Block	Opp Error	Total	Reception	Dig	Attack S/O	Attack Total	Attack Total	Serve
RICHARDSON, Debra	0	1 + 3	1 + 0		2 + 3	1 / 2	6	3 / 11	4 / 11	2 / 11	3 / 23
CASTRO, Gail	1	2 + 32	0 + 0		3 + 32	46 / 47	5	30 / 53	34 / 53	5 / 53	1 / 25
Totals	1	3 + 35	1 + 0	6 + 1	11 + 36	47 / 49	11	33 / 64	38 / 64	7 / 64	4 / 48

ROUND 4 — BRA 15 BRA 4 — Duration: 00:33 — 1st Referee: USA SALVATORE, Patty — 2nd Referee: MEX RAMIREZ RIVERA, Miguel

BRA Brazil

Names	Serve	Attack	Block	Opp Error	Total	Reception	Dig	Attack S/O	Attack Total	Attack Total	Serve
SILVA, Jacqueline Louise Cruz	2	5 + 13	0 + 0		7 + 13	15 / 16	3	12 / 16	18 / 23	1 / 23	2 / 20
PIRES, Sandra Tavares	3	0 + 3	0 + 0		3 + 3	4 / 4	3	2 / 4	3 / 5	1 / 5	2 / 13
Totals	5	5 + 16	0 + 0	5 + 2	15 + 18	19 / 20	6	14 / 20	21 / 28	2 / 28	4 / 33

BRA Brazil

Names	Serve	Attack	Block	Opp Error	Total	Reception	Dig	Attack S/O	Attack Total	Attack Total	Serve
SAMUEL, Adriana Ramos	0	1 + 10	0 + 0		1 + 10	18 / 21	3	10 / 22	11 / 22	2 / 22	1 / 13
RODRIGUES, Monica	0	1 + 2	0 + 0		1 + 2	3 / 3	2	2 / 6	3 / 6	2 / 6	1 / 9
Totals	0	2 + 12	0 + 0	2 + 6	4 + 18	21 / 24	5	12 / 28	14 / 28	4 / 28	2 / 22

ROUND 4 — AUS 15 USA 13 — Duration: 01:05 — 1st Referee: ITA BORGATO, Maurizio — 2nd Referee: POR CORBAL SIMOES AZEVEDO, A.

AUS Australia

Names	Serve	Attack	Block	Opp Error	Total	Reception	Dig	Attack S/O	Attack Total	Attack Total	Serve
COOK, Natalie	0	6 + 14	0 + 0		6 + 14	24 / 28	12	13 / 28	20 / 42	2 / 42	1 / 24
POTTHARST, Kerri Ann	2	1 + 8	1 + 0		4 + 8	7 / 10	11	4 / 10	9 / 19	1 / 19	4 / 25
Totals	2	7 + 22	1 + 0	5 + 13	15 + 35	31 / 38	23	17 / 38	29 / 61	3 / 61	5 / 49

USA United States of America

Names	Serve	Attack	Block	Opp Error	Total	Reception	Dig	Attack S/O	Attack Total	Attack Total	Serve
McPEAK, Holly	1	2 + 16	1 + 0		4 + 16	30 / 31	17	15 / 39	18 / 39	5 / 39	4 / 26
RENO, Nancy	0	7 + 11	1 + 0		8 + 11	9 / 10	4	10 / 27	18 / 27	2 / 27	5 / 23
Totals	1	9 + 27	2 + 0	1 + 7	13 + 34	39 / 41	21	25 / 66	36 / 66	7 / 66	9 / 49

7TH PLACE — USA 15 AUS 6 — Duration: 00:37 — 1st Referee: POR CORBAL SIMOES AZEVEDO, Avelino — 2nd Referee: JPN KONNO, Masaaki

USA United States of America

Names	Serve	Attack	Block	Opp Error	Total	Reception	Dig	Attack S/O	Attack Total	Attack Total	Serve
HANLEY, Linda	0	4 + 10	0 + 0		4 + 10	10 / 12	4	9 / 12	14 / 21	0 / 21	3 / 15
FONTANA HARRIS, Barbra	1	2 + 9	0 + 0		3 + 9	13 / 13	7	8 / 13	11 / 17	1 / 17	2 / 23
Totals	1	6 + 19	0 + 0	8 + 6	15 + 25	23 / 25	11	17 / 25	25 / 38	1 / 38	5 / 38

AUS Australia

Names	Serve	Attack	Block	Opp Error	Total	Reception	Dig	Attack S/O	Attack Total	Attack Total	Serve
FENWICK, Liane	0	4 + 12	1 + 0		5 + 12	5 / 5	5	10 / 24	16 / 24	3 / 24	3 / 13
SPRING, Anita	0	0 + 5	0 + 0		0 + 5	22 / 26	8	5 / 19	5 / 19	4 / 19	2 / 16
Totals	0	4 + 17	1 + 0	1 + 5	6 + 22	27 / 31	13	15 / 43	21 / 43	7 / 43	5 / 29

Women / *Dames*

7TH PLACE — GER 4, JPN 15
Duration: 00:32 1st Referee: MEX RAMIREZ RIVERA, Miguel 2nd Referee: USA ROBB, Steve

GER Germany

Names	Serve	Attack	Block	Opp Error	Total	Reception	Dig	Attack S/O	Attack Total	Attack Total	Serve
		Scoring Skills (Pts + S/O)				Non-Scoring Skills (+ / Total)		Positive (+ / Total)		Errors (– / Total)	
BUHLER, Beate	1	1 + 19	1 + 0		3 + 19	27 / 30	7	17 / 30	20 / 34	2 / 34	3 / 13
MUSCH, Danja	0	1 + 2	0 + 0		1 + 2	5 / 5	4	1 / 5	3 / 10	4 / 10	1 / 13
Totals	1	2 + 21	1 + 0	0 + 0	4 + 21	32 / 35	11	18 / 35	23 / 44	6 / 44	4 / 26

JPN Japan

Names	Serve	Attack	Block	Opp Error	Total	Reception	Dig	Attack S/O	Attack Total	Attack Total	Serve
		Scoring Skills (Pts + S/O)				Non-Scoring Skills (+ / Total)		Positive (+ / Total)		Errors (– / Total)	
TAKAHASHI, Yukiko	1	7 + 13	0 + 0		8 + 13	16 / 17	7	12 / 33	20 / 33	0 / 33	0 / 18
FUJITA, Sachiko	0	0 + 3	0 + 0		0 + 3	4 / 4	7	3 / 5	3 / 5	0 / 5	0 / 18
Totals	1	7 + 16	0 + 0	7 + 6	15 + 22	20 / 21	14	15 / 38	23 / 38	0 / 38	0 / 36

5TH PLACE — USA 15, USA 10
Duration: 00:49 1st Referee: FRA BIAU, Patrick 2nd Referee: AUS HRESZCZUK, Peter

USA United States of America

Names	Serve	Attack	Block	Opp Error	Total	Reception	Dig	Attack S/O	Attack Total	Attack Total	Serve
		Scoring Skills (Pts + S/O)				Non-Scoring Skills (+ / Total)		Positive (+ / Total)		Errors (– / Total)	
HANLEY, Linda	2	6 + 15	0 + 0		8 + 15	19 / 21	11	13 / 21	21 / 35	0 / 35	0 / 23
FONTANA HARRIS, Barbra	0	4 + 5	0 + 1		4 + 6	8 / 10	9	5 / 10	9 / 17	1 / 17	1 / 21
Totals	2	10 + 20	0 + 1	3 + 7	15 + 28	27 / 31	20	18 / 31	30 / 52	1 / 52	1 / 44

USA United States of America

Names	Serve	Attack	Block	Opp Error	Total	Reception	Dig	Attack S/O	Attack Total	Attack Total	Serve
		Scoring Skills (Pts + S/O)				Non-Scoring Skills (+ / Total)		Positive (+ / Total)		Errors (– / Total)	
McPEAK, Holly	3	3 + 15	0 + 0		6 + 15	24 / 25	10	14 / 31	18 / 31	2 / 31	3 / 22
RENO, Nancy	0	1 + 12	1 + 0		2 + 12	14 / 16	5	11 / 27	13 / 27	3 / 27	1 / 16
Totals	3	4 + 27	1 + 0	2 + 1	10 + 28	38 / 41	15	25 / 58	31 / 58	5 / 58	4 / 38

5TH PLACE — JPN 6, BRA 15
Duration: 00:45 1st Referee: USA ROBB, Steve 2nd Referee: ESP CARRENO, Mirela

JPN Japan

Names	Serve	Attack	Block	Opp Error	Total	Reception	Dig	Attack S/O	Attack Total	Attack Total	Serve
		Scoring Skills (Pts + S/O)				Non-Scoring Skills (+ / Total)		Positive (+ / Total)		Errors (– / Total)	
TAKAHASHI, Yukiko	1	0 + 11	0 + 0		1 + 11	10 / 10	11	6 / 10	11 / 27	2 / 27	0 / 20
FUJITA, Sachiko	0	2 + 14	0 + 0		2 + 14	27 / 31	10	13 / 31	16 / 34	5 / 34	2 / 19
Totals	1	2 + 25	0 + 0	3 + 7	6 + 32	37 / 41	21	19 / 41	27 / 61	7 / 61	2 / 39

BRA Brazil

Names	Serve	Attack	Block	Opp Error	Total	Reception	Dig	Attack S/O	Attack Total	Attack Total	Serve
		Scoring Skills (Pts + S/O)				Non-Scoring Skills (+ / Total)		Positive (+ / Total)		Errors (– / Total)	
SAMUEL, Adriana Ramos	1	2 + 7	0 + 0		3 + 7	5 / 6	14	6 / 20	9 / 20	0 / 20	2 / 28
RODRIGUES, Monica	0	4 + 21	1 + 0		5 + 21	28 / 30	10	17 / 41	25 / 41	4 / 41	3 / 19
Totals	1	6 + 28	1 + 0	7 + 5	15 + 33	33 / 36	24	23 / 61	34 / 61	4 / 61	5 / 47

SEMIFINALS — BRA 15, USA 8
Duration: 00:39 1st Referee: FRA BIAU, Patrick 2nd Referee: ITA BORGATO, Maurizio

BRA Brazil

Names	Serve	Attack	Block	Opp Error	Total	Reception	Dig	Attack S/O	Attack Total	Attack Total	Serve
		Scoring Skills (Pts + S/O)				Non-Scoring Skills (+ / Total)		Positive (+ / Total)		Errors (– / Total)	
SILVA, Jacqueline Louise Cruz	0	4 + 8	1 + 0		5 + 8	12 / 12	4	8 / 12	12 / 17	1 / 17	1 / 16
PIRES, Sandra Tavares	1	5 + 13	1 + 0		7 + 13	14 / 15	9	12 / 15	18 / 24	1 / 24	1 / 21
Totals	1	9 + 21	2 + 0	3 + 1	15 + 22	26 / 27	13	20 / 27	30 / 41	2 / 41	2 / 37

USA United States of America

Names	Serve	Attack	Block	Opp Error	Total	Reception	Dig	Attack S/O	Attack Total	Attack Total	Serve
		Scoring Skills (Pts + S/O)				Non-Scoring Skills (+ / Total)		Positive (+ / Total)		Errors (– / Total)	
HANLEY, Linda	2	1 + 6	0 + 0		3 + 6	8 / 8	4	5 / 15	7 / 15	2 / 15	0 / 17
FONTANA HARRIS, Barbra	0	3 + 13	1 + 0		4 + 13	23 / 26	6	13 / 29	16 / 29	1 / 29	1 / 13
Totals	2	4 + 19	1 + 0	1 + 3	8 + 22	31 / 34	10	18 / 44	23 / 44	3 / 44	1 / 30

SEMIFINALS — AUS 3, BRA 15
Duration: 00:27 1st Referee: PUR MENDOZA BAS, Aurelio 2nd Referee: MEX RAMIREZ RIVERA, Miguel

AUS Australia

Names	Serve	Attack	Block	Opp Error	Total	Reception	Dig	Attack S/O	Attack Total	Attack Total	Serve
		Scoring Skills (Pts + S/O)				Non-Scoring Skills (+ / Total)		Positive (+ / Total)		Errors (– / Total)	
COOK, Natalie	0	2 + 6	0 + 0		2 + 6	19 / 22	5	5 / 22	8 / 26	2 / 26	1 / 7
POTTHARST, Kerri Ann	1	0 + 4	0 + 0		1 + 4	2 / 3	5	3 / 3	4 / 7	1 / 7	2 / 10
Totals	1	2 + 10	0 + 0	0 + 3	3 + 13	21 / 25	10	8 / 25	12 / 33	3 / 33	3 / 17

BRA Brazil

Names	Serve	Attack	Block	Opp Error	Total	Reception	Dig	Attack S/O	Attack Total	Attack Total	Serve
		Scoring Skills (Pts + S/O)				Non-Scoring Skills (+ / Total)		Positive (+ / Total)		Errors (– / Total)	
SAMUEL, Adriana Ramos	0	4 + 5	1 + 0		5 + 5	4 / 5	10	4 / 15	9 / 15	0 / 15	0 / 16
RODRIGUES, Monica	0	4 + 6	0 + 0		4 + 6	8 / 8	6	5 / 15	10 / 15	0 / 15	3 / 12
Totals	0	8 + 11	1 + 0	6 + 3	15 + 14	12 / 13	16	9 / 30	19 / 30	0 / 30	3 / 28

Women / *Dames*

FINAL -	Set 1: USA 11	AUS 12	Duration: 01:04	1st Referee: FRA BIAU, Patrick	2nd Referee: ITA BORGATO, Maurizio
BRONZE MATCH	Set 2: USA 7	AUS 12	Duration: 00:47		

USA United States of America

Names	Serve	Scoring Skills (Pts + S/O)				Non-Scoring Skills (+ / Total)		Positive (+ / Total)		Errors (– / Total)	
		Attack	Block	Opp Error	Total	Reception	Dig	Attack S/O	Attack Total	Attack Total	Serve
HANLEY, Linda	1	7 + 22	1 + 0		9 + 22	23 / 23	23	19 / 23	29 / 48	2 / 48	8 / 50
FONTANA HARRIS, Barbra	1	3 + 41	0 + 0		4 + 41	65 / 66	6	41 / 66	44 / 75	3 / 75	5 / 49
Totals	2	10 + 63	1 + 0	5 + 15	18 + 78	88 / 89	29	60 / 89	73 / 123	5 / 123	13 / 99

AUS Australia

Names	Serve	Scoring Skills (Pts + S/O)				Non-Scoring Skills (+ / Total)		Positive (+ / Total)		Errors (– / Total)	
		Attack	Block	Opp Error	Total	Reception	Dig	Attack S/O	Attack Total	Attack Total	Serve
COOK, Natalie	0	8 + 42	2 + 1		10 + 43	57 / 60	19	37 / 77	50 / 77	3 / 77	5 / 49
POTTHARST, Kerri Ann	2	9 + 22	0 + 0		11 + 22	21 / 24	22	19 / 46	31 / 46	2 / 46	8 / 56
Totals	2	17 + 64	2 + 1	3 + 16	24 + 81	78 / 84	41	56 / 123	81 / 123	5 / 123	13 / 105

FINAL -	Set 1: BRA 12	BRA 11	Duration: 00:38	1st Referee: JPN KONNO, Masaaki	2nd Referee: FRA BIAU, Patrick
GOLD MATCH	Set 2: BRA 12	BRA 6	Duration: 00:31		

BRA Brazil

Names	Serve	Scoring Skills (Pts + S/O)				Non-Scoring Skills (+ / Total)		Positive (+ / Total)		Errors (– / Total)	
		Attack	Block	Opp Error	Total	Reception	Dig	Attack S/O	Attack Total	Attack Total	Serve
SILVA, Jacqueline Louise Cruz	1	9 + 11	2 + 1		12 + 12	12 / 13	13	7 / 13	20 / 30	1 / 30	0 / 34
PIRES, Sandra Tavares	3	1 + 24	0 + 0		4 + 24	33 / 37	7	22 / 37	25 / 42	3 / 42	3 / 31
Totals	4	10 + 35	2 + 1	8 + 6	24 + 42	45 / 50	20	29 / 50	45 / 72	4 / 72	3 / 65

BRA Brazil

Names	Serve	Scoring Skills (Pts + S/O)				Non-Scoring Skills (+ / Total)		Positive (+ / Total)		Errors (– / Total)	
		Attack	Block	Opp Error	Total	Reception	Dig	Attack S/O	Attack Total	Attack Total	Serve
SAMUEL, Adriana Ramos	1	4 + 19	0 + 0		5 + 19	36 / 41	8	19 / 41	23 / 52	5 / 52	0 / 26
RODRIGUES, Monica	3	4 + 17	0 + 0		7 + 17	14 / 17	11	14 / 17	21 / 27	3 / 27	5 / 33
Totals	4	8 + 36	0 + 0	5 + 4	17 + 40	50 / 58	19	33 / 58	44 / 79	8 / 79	5 / 59

FINAL CLASSIFICATION

Rnk	Team	Names	
1	BRA	SILVA / PIRES	Gold
2	BRA	SAMUEL / RODRIGUES	Silver
3	AUS	COOK / POTTHARST	Bronze
4	USA	FONTANA / HANLEY	
5	JPN	FUJITA / TAKAHASHI	
5	USA	McPEAK / RENO	
7	GER	BUHLER / MUSCH	
7	AUS	FENWICK / SPRING	

PRELIMINARIES - GROUP A

BUL 0 - 3 CUB

Set	1	2	3	4	5	Total pts
Result	9 - 15	7 - 15	7 - 15			23 - 45
Duration	0:30	0:32	0:28			1:30

	Bulgaria				Cuba	
Att	Pts won	S/O		Att	Pts won	S/O
147	8	64	Attacks	119	9	57
54	5	3	Blocks	72	14	1
115	1		Serves	136	9	

1st Referee: CHN QU, Zheng Zhong
2nd Referee: ARG PAREDES, Guillermo

PRELIMINARIES - GROUP A

POL 0 - 3 USA

Set	1	2	3	4	5	Total pts
Result	13 - 15	6 - 15	8 - 15			27 - 45
Duration	0:30	0:22	0:32			1:24

	Poland				United States of America	
Att	Pts won	S/O		Att	Pts won	S/O
131	4	41	Attacks	137	14	52
58	6	5	Blocks	67	12	1
101	2		Serves	117	7	

1st Referee: KOR CHO, Young-Ho
2nd Referee: AUS TURNER, Dean

PRELIMINARIES - GROUP A

BRA 1 - 3 ARG

Set	1	2	3	4	5	Total pts
Result	15 - 9	8 - 15	14 - 16	6 - 15		43 - 55
Duration	0:29	0:33	0:43	0:34		2:19

	Brazil				Argentina	
Att	Pts won	S/O		Att	Pts won	S/O
181	17	76	Attacks	210	29	87
116	12	5	Blocks	87	4	4
164	4		Serves	175	6	

1st Referee: FIN SALONEN, Jarmo
2nd Referee: CAN HENRY, Peter

PRELIMINARIES - GROUP A

BRA 0 - 3 BUL

Set	1	2	3	4	5	Total pts
Result	11 - 15	13 - 15	8 - 15			32 - 45
Duration	0:34	0:35	0:27			1:36

	Brazil				Bulgaria	
Att	Pts won	S/O		Att	Pts won	S/O
137	18	57	Attacks	123	9	56
61	10	2	Blocks	67	12	2
120	0		Serves	131	8	

1st Referee: CAN HENRY, Peter
2nd Referee: KOR CHO, Young-Ho

Team: BUL Bulgaria
Coach: KJUTCHOUKOV, Bogdan
Assistant Coach: GENTCHEV, Eugeni

Names	Pts + S/O	1	2	3	4	5
STOEV, Martin	1 + 3	S		*		
NAIDENOV, Ludmil	0 + 0		*			
GANEV, Lubomir	4 + 20	*	S	S		
TONEV, Dimo	1 + 3	S	S	S		
JELIAZKOV, Nikolay	4 + 12	S	S	S		
HRISTOV, Plamen	0 + 0			*		
OUZOUNOV, Petar	0 + 5	*				
NAYDENOV, Nayden	2 + 11	S	S	S		
IVANOV, Nikolay	0 + 1	S	S	S		
GAVRILOV, Ivaylo	0 + 0	S				
IVANOV, Evgeni	0 + 0			*		
KONSTANTINOV, Plamen	2 + 12	*	S	S		

Team: POL Poland
Coach: KREBOK, Wiktor
Assistant Coach: RYS, Grzegorz

Names	Pts + S/O	1	2	3	4	5
STELMACH, Andrzej	1 + 1	S	S			
DACEWICZ, Damian	0 + 5	S	S	*		
STELMACH, Krzysztof	4 + 7	S	S	S		
SZYSZKO, Mariusz	0 + 0		*	S		
NOWAK, Marcin	3 + 7	S	S	S		
GRUSZKA, Piotr	0 + 10	S	S	S		
PRYGIEL, Robert	0 + 0					
SMIGIEL, Krzysztof	1 + 2	*	S			
URBANOWICZ, Leszek	1 + 3	S		S		
JANCZAK, Krzysztof	1 + 2		*			
ROMAN, Witold	1 + 9		*	S		
ZAGUMNY, Pawel	0 + 0					

Team: BRA Brazil
Coach: GUIMARAES, Jose
Assistant Coach: MIRANDA, Marcos

Names	Pts + S/O	1	2	3	4	5
NEGRAO, Marcelo	4 + 10	S	S	S	*	
PEREIRA, Cassio Leandro	0 + 0				*	
GAVIO, Giovane	16 + 17	S	S	S	S	
SILVA, Paulo "Paulao"	2 + 1	S	S	*	S	
LIMA, Mauricio	0 + 1	S	S	S	S	
MARCELINO, Fabio "Pinha"	0 + 5	*	*			
GOUVEIA, Antonio "Carlao"	0 + 0					
PEREIRA, Max	0 + 0					
BITENCOURT, Nalbert	0 + 12	S	S	S		
SAMUEL, Alexandre "Tande"	8 + 16	S	S	S	S	
BERNARDO, Gilson	1 + 10	*	*	*	S	
SCHWANKE, Carlos	2 + 9			S	S	

Team: BRA Brazil
Coach: GUIMARAES, Jose
Assistant Coach: MIRANDA, Marcos

Names	Pts + S/O	1	2	3	4	5
NEGRAO, Marcelo	4 + 8	S	S			
PEREIRA, Cassio Leandro	0 + 0					
GAVIO, Giovane	4 + 9	S	S	S		
SILVA, Paulo "Paulao"	1 + 8	S	S			
LIMA, Mauricio	0 + 0	S	S	S		
MARCELINO, Fabio "Pinha"	0 + 0			*	*	
GOUVEIA, Antonio "Carlao"	0 + 0					
PEREIRA, Max	3 + 3	*	*	S		
BITENCOURT, Nalbert	0 + 0	*	*			
SAMUEL, Alexandre "Tande"	10 + 13	S	S	S		
BERNARDO, Gilson	3 + 14		*	S		
SCHWANKE, Carlos	3 + 4	S	S	S		

Team: CUB Cuba
Coach: DIAZ MARINO, Juan Jesus
Assistant Coach: MORALES GONZALES, Justo L.

Names	Pts + S/O	1	2	3	4	5
BROOKS, Freddy	12 + 12	S	S	S		
VIVES, Nicolas	0 + 0					
VANTES, Ricardo	0 + 0	*		*		
DESPAIGNE, Joel	3 + 17	S	S	S		
SANCHEZ, Rodolfo	0 + 0					
DIAGO, Raul	3 + 0	S	S	S		
HERNANDEZ, Osvaldo	10 + 11	S	S	S		
ROCA, Alain	2 + 7	S	S	S		
HERNANDEZ, Ihosvany	1 + 11	S	S	S		
BELTRAN, Angel	1 + 0	*	*	*		
BATLE, Alexis	0 + 0					
MARIN, Lazaro	0 + 0					

Team: USA United States of America
Coach: STURM, Frederick
Assistant Coach: SUWARA, Rudy

Names	Pts + S/O	1	2	3	4	5
BALL, Lloy	0 + 2	S	S	S		
HYDEN, John	0 + 0					
CTVRTLIK, Bob	7 + 4	S	S	S		
IVIE, Bryan	5 + 13	S	S	S		
SORENSEN, Tom	0 + 0					
FORTUNE, Scott	0 + 0					
STORK, Jeff	0 + 0					
NYGAARD, Jeff	9 + 6	S	S	S		
LAMBERT, Mike	10 + 21	S	S	S		
WATTS, Ethan	0 + 0					
LANDRY, Dan	2 + 7	S	S	S		
WINSLOW, Brett	0 + 0					

Team: ARG Argentina
Coach: CASTELLANI, Daniel Jorge
Assistant Coach: GETZELEVICH, Carlos Alberto

Names	Pts + S/O	1	2	3	4	5
MILINKOVIC, Marcos	13 + 28	S	S	S	S	
ELGUETA, Jorge	0 + 0			*	*	
JABIF, Sebastian	3 + 8		*	S	S	
MALY, Leonardo	1 + 1		*	*	*	
QUAINI, Guillermo	15 + 21	S	S	S	S	
WEBER, Javier	0 + 0	S	S	S		
BORRERO, Fernando	4 + 13	S	S	S		
ROMANO, Alejandro	1 + 12	S	S	*	S	
FIRPO, Sebastian	0 + 0					
PEREIRA, Pablo	2 + 8	S	S	S		
MARTINEZ, Guillermo	0 + 0					
RODRIGUEZ, Eduardo	0 + 0					

Team: BUL Bulgaria
Coach: KJUTCHOUKOV, Bogdan
Assistant Coach: GENTCHEV, Eugeni

Names	Pts + S/O	1	2	3	4	5
STOEV, Martin	9+ 18	S	S	S		
NAIDENOV, Ludmil	0 + 0			*		
GANEV, Lubomir	7 + 15	S	S	S		
TONEV, Dimo	2 + 2	S	S			
JELIAZKOV, Nikolay	8 + 6	S	S	S		
HRISTOV, Plamen	0 + 2	S	S	S		
OUZOUNOV, Petar	0 + 0	*	*	*		
NAYDENOV, Nayden	2 + 14	S	S	S		
IVANOV, Nikolay	0 + 0					
GAVRILOV, Ivaylo	1 + 1	*	*			
IVANOV, Evgeni	0 + 0					
KONSTANTINOV, Plamen	0 + 0					

Men / *Messieurs*

PRELIMINARIES - GROUP A

ARG 0 - 3 USA

Set	1	2	3	4	5	Total pts
Result	7 - 15	8 - 15	11 - 15			26 - 45
Duration	0:31	0:28	0:35			1:34

	Argentina				United States of America	
Att	Pts won	S/O		Att	Pts won	S/O
155	4	52	Attacks	154	19	57
69	13	3	Blocks	89	12	4
116	1		Serves	134	4	

1st Referee: FRA   RACHARD, Patrick
2nd Referee: RUS   ZHARIKOV, Guennadi

PRELIMINARIES - GROUP A

CUB 3 - 0 POL

Set	1	2	3	4	5	Total pts
Result	15 - 13	15 - 2	15 - 3			45 - 28
Duration	0:28	0:23	0:42			1:33

	Cuba				Poland	
Att	Pts won	S/O		Att	Pts won	S/O
149	17	59	Attacks	163	14	60
75	9	4	Blocks	61	3	6
130	5		Serves	114	2	

1st Referee: JPN   SHIMOYAMA, Takashi
2nd Referee: CHN   QU, Zheng Zhong

PRELIMINARIES - GROUP A

BUL 1 - 3 ARG

Set	1	2	3	4	5	Total pts
Result	10 - 15	8 - 15	15 - 11	10 - 15		43 - 56
Duration	0:30	0:29	0:28	0:31		1:58

	Bulgaria				Argentina	
Att	Pts won	S/O		Att	Pts won	S/O
206	15	75	Attacks	202	20	73
96	13	6	Blocks	102	12	6
152	2		Serves	164	5	

1st Referee: AUS   TURNER, Dean
2nd Referee: NED   SCHEFFER, Petrus Carolus

PRELIMINARIES - GROUP A

POL 0 - 3 BRA

Set	1	2	3	4	5	Total pts
Result	7 - 15	11 - 15	8 - 15			26 - 45
Duration	0:28	0:36	0:46			1:50

	Poland				Brazil	
Att	Pts won	S/O		Att	Pts won	S/O
149	10	45	Attacks	147	19	58
61	3	5	Blocks	78	13	3
101	5		Serves	117	5	

1st Referee: CHN   QU, Zheng Zhong
2nd Referee: ITA   TROIA, Pasquale

Team: ARG Argentina

Coach: CASTELLANI, Daniel Jorge
Assistant Coach: GETZELEVICH, Carlos Alberto

Names	Pts + S/O	1	2	3	4	5
MILINKOVIC, Marcos	2 + 8	S	S	S		
ELGUETA, Jorge	3 + 6		*	*		
JABIF, Sebastian	3 + 6	*	S	S		
MALY, Leonardo	0 + 0		*			
QUAINI, Guillermo	1 + 7	S	S	S		
WEBER, Javier	1 + 3	S	S	S		
BORRERO, Fernando	0 + 4	S	S			
ROMANO, Alejandro	4 + 11	S	S	S		
FIRPO, Sebastian	0 + 0					
PEREIRA, Pablo	1 + 7	S		*		
MARTINEZ, Guillermo	0 + 0			*		
RODRIGUEZ, Eduardo	3 + 3			S		

Team: CUB Cuba

Coach: DIAZ MARINO, Juan Jesus
Assistant Coach: MORALES GONZALES, Justo L.

Names	Pts + S/O	1	2	3	4	5
BROOKS, Freddy	9 + 13	S	S	S		
VIVES, Nicolas	0 + 0					
VANTES, Ricardo	0 + 0	*	*	*		
DESPAIGNE, Joel	2 + 19	S	S	S		
SANCHEZ, Rodolfo	0 + 0					
DIAGO, Raul	6 + 0	S	S	S		
HERNANDEZ, Osvaldo	6 + 15	S	S	S		
ROCA, Alain	5 + 8	S	S	S		
HERNANDEZ, Ihosvany	3 + 8	S	S	S		
BELTRAN, Angel	0 + 0	*		*		
BATLE, Alexis	0 + 0					
MARIN, Lazaro	0 + 0					

Team: BUL Bulgaria

Coach: KJUTCHOUKOV, Bogdan
Assistant Coach: GENTCHEV, Eugeni

Names	Pts + S/O	1	2	3	4	5
STOEV, Martin	2 + 5	S	S			
NAIDENOV, Ludmil	0 + 0				*	
GANEV, Lubomir	2 + 7	S	S			
TONEV, Dimo	4 + 9	S	S		*	
JELIAZKOV, Nikolay	3 + 16	S	S	S	S	
HRISTOV, Plamen	1 + 1	S				
OUZOUNOV, Petar	4 + 4			S	S	
NAYDENOV, Nayden	4 + 9	S	S	S	S	
IVANOV, Nikolay	1 + 1	*	S	S	S	
GAVRILOV, Ivaylo	6 + 22	*	*	S	S	
IVANOV, Evgeni	0 + 0					
KONSTANTINOV, Plamen	3 + 7		*	S	S	

Team: POL Poland

Coach: KREBOK, Wiktor
Assistant Coach: RYS, Grzegorz

Names	Pts + S/O	1	2	3	4	5
STELMACH, Andrzej	1 + 0	S				
DACEWICZ, Damian	0 + 6	S	*	S		
STELMACH, Krzysztof	5 + 4	S	S	S		
SZYSZKO, Mariusz	0 + 0	*				
NOWAK, Marcin	4 + 7			S	S	
GRUSZKA, Piotr	1 + 18	S	S	S		
PRYGIEL, Robert	0 + 0					
SMIGIEL, Krzysztof	5 + 4	S	S	S		
URBANOWICZ, Leszek	0 + 0			*		
JANCZAK, Krzysztof	0 + 0			*		
ROMAN, Witold	1 + 7	S	S			
ZAGUMNY, Pawel	1 + 4	*	S	S		

Team: USA United States of America

Coach: STURM, Frederick
Assistant Coach: SUWARA, Rudy

Names	Pts + S/O	1	2	3	4	5
BALL, Lloy	7 + 1	S	S	S		
HYDEN, John	0 + 0					
CTVRTLIK, Bob	2 + 10	S	S	S		
IVIE, Bryan	9 + 13	S	S	S		
SORENSEN, Tom	0 + 0					
FORTUNE, Scott	0 + 0					
STORK, Jeff	0 + 0					
NYGAARD, Jeff	7 + 6	S	S	S		
LAMBERT, Mike	6 + 20	S	S	S		
WATTS, Ethan	0 + 0					
LANDRY, Dan	4 + 11	S	S	S		
WINSLOW, Brett	0 + 0					

Team: POL Poland

Coach: KREBOK, Wiktor
Assistant Coach: RYS, Grzegorz

Names	Pts + S/O	1	2	3	4	5
STELMACH, Andrzej	0 + 2			S		
DACEWICZ, Damian	3 + 6		*	S		
STELMACH, Krzysztof	4 + 14	S	S	S		
SZYSZKO, Mariusz	1 + 1	S	S	*		
NOWAK, Marcin	0 + 6	S	S			
GRUSZKA, Piotr	6 + 14	S	S	S		
PRYGIEL, Robert	0 + 0					
SMIGIEL, Krzysztof	3 + 9	*		S		
URBANOWICZ, Leszek	1 + 4	S	S			
JANCZAK, Krzysztof	0 + 0					
ROMAN, Witold	1 + 10	S	S	S		
ZAGUMNY, Pawel	0 + 0	*				

Team: ARG Argentina

Coach: CASTELLANI, Daniel Jorge
Assistant Coach: GETZELEVICH, Carlos Alberto

Names	Pts + S/O	1	2	3	4	5
MILINKOVIC, Marcos	10 + 12	S	S	S	*	
ELGUETA, Jorge	13 + 17	S	S	S	S	
JABIF, Sebastian	6 + 15	S	S	S	S	
MALY, Leonardo	0 + 0			*		
QUAINI, Guillermo	1 + 6			*	S	
WEBER, Javier	1 + 4	S	S	S	S	
BORRERO, Fernando	2 + 9	S	S	S	S	
ROMANO, Alejandro	2 + 12	S	S	S	S	
FIRPO, Sebastian	0 + 0				*	
PEREIRA, Pablo	2 + 4				*	
MARTINEZ, Guillermo	0 + 0			*		
RODRIGUEZ, Eduardo	0 + 0	*				

Team: BRA Brazil

Coach: GUIMARAES, Jose
Assistant Coach: MIRANDA, Marcos

Names	Pts + S/O	1	2	3	4	5
NEGRAO, Marcelo	6 + 13	S	S	S		
PEREIRA, Cassio Leandro	0 + 0					
GAVIO, Giovane	16 + 15	S	S	S		
SILVA, Paulo "Paulao"	0 + 0					
LIMA, Mauricio	1 + 2	S	S	S		
MARCELINO, Fabio "Pinha"	0 + 0			*		
GOUVEIA, Antonio "Carlao"	0 + 0					
PEREIRA, Max	6 + 15	S	S	S		
BITENCOURT, Nalbert	0 + 0					
SAMUEL, Alexandre "Tande"	5 + 13	S	S	S		
BERNARDO, Gilson	0 + 0					
SCHWANKE, Carlos	3 + 3	S	S	S		

Men / Messieurs

PRELIMINARIES - GROUP A

USA 2 - 3 CUB

Set	1	2	3	4	5	Total pts
Result	15 - 4	9 - 15	16 - 14	8 - 15	16 - 18	64 - 66
Duration	0:23	0:31	0:37	0:29	0:19	2:19

	United States of America			Cuba	
Att	Pts won	S/O		Att	Pts won	S/O
209	28	70	Attacks	196	27	72
99	11	5	Blocks	103	14	2
164	8		Serves	166	2	

1st Referee: THA CHAREONPONG, Songsak
2nd Referee: RUS ZHARIKOV, Guennadi

PRELIMINARIES - GROUP A

ARG 0 - 3 CUB

Set	1	2	3	4	5	Total pts
Result	10 - 15	12 - 15	9 - 15			31 - 45
Duration	0:34	0:36	0:24			1:34

	Argentina			Cuba	
Att	Pts won	S/O		Att	Pts won	S/O
145	11	63	Attacks	135	23	54
60	7	1	Blocks	77	8	3
116	6		Serves	129	5	

1st Referee: RUS ZHARIKOV, Guennadi
2nd Referee: FRA RACHARD, Patrick

PRELIMINARIES - GROUP A

BUL 3 - 0 POL

Set	1	2	3	4	5	Total pts
Result	15 - 4	15 - 10	15 - 7			45 - 21
Duration	0:26	0:31	0:21			1:18

	Bulgaria			Poland	
Att	Pts won	S/O		Att	Pts won	S/O
120	17	57	Attacks	121	3	52
66	11	3	Blocks	63	6	1
115	5		Serves	92	1	

1st Referee: NED SCHEFFER, Petrus Carolus
2nd Referee: ITA TROIA, Pasquale

PRELIMINARIES - GROUP A

BRA 3 - 0 USA

Set	1	2	3	4	5	Total pts
Result	15 - 11	15 - 11	15 - 7			45 - 29
Duration	0:48	0:33	0:30			1:51

	Brazil			United States of America	
Att	Pts won	S/O		Att	Pts won	S/O
168	21	66	Attacks	182	12	67
75	8	10	Blocks	82	3	4
144	1		Serves	129	5	

1st Referee: JPN SHIMOYAMA, Takashi
2nd Referee: FIN SALONEN, Jarmo

Team: USA United States of America

Coach: STURM, Frederick
Assistant Coach: SUWARA, Rudy

Names	Pts + S/O	1	2	3	4	5
BALL, Lloy	4 + 3	S	S	S	S	S
HYDEN, John	0 + 0		*			
CTVRTLIK, Bob	6 + 9	S	S	S	S	S
IVIE, Bryan	9 + 22	S	S	S	S	S
SORENSEN, Tom	3 + 7			*	S	
FORTUNE, Scott	2 + 3	*	*	S		
STORK, Jeff	0 + 0					
NYGAARD, Jeff	8 + 9	S	S	S	S	S
LAMBERT, Mike	10 + 16	S	S	S	*	S
WATTS, Ethan	0 + 0					
LANDRY, Dan	5 + 6	S	S	*	S	S
WINSLOW, Brett	0 + 0					

Team: ARG Argentina

Coach: CASTELLANI, Daniel Jorge
Assistant Coach: GETZELEVICH, Carlos Alberto

Names	Pts + S/O	1	2	3	4	5
MILINKOVIC, Marcos	4 + 15	*	S	S		
ELGUETA, Jorge	4 + 8	S	S			
JABIF, Sebastian	2 + 3	S				
MALY, Leonardo	2 + 1		*	S		
QUAINI, Guillermo	2 + 3	S				
WEBER, Javier	1 + 0	S	S	S		
BORRERO, Fernando	1 + 8	S	S	*		
ROMANO, Alejandro	3 + 18	S	S	S		
FIRPO, Sebastian	0 + 0					
PEREIRA, Pablo	5 + 6	*	S	S		
MARTINEZ, Guillermo	0 + 0			*		
RODRIGUEZ, Eduardo	0 + 2		*	S		

Team: BUL Bulgaria

Coach: KJUTCHOUKOV, Bogdan
Assistant Coach: GENTCHEV, Eugeni

Names	Pts + S/O	1	2	3	4	5
STOEV, Martin	11 + 19	S	S	S		
NAIDENOV, Ludmil	0 + 0		*			
GANEV, Lubomir	0 + 7	*	S			
TONEV, Dimo	7 + 5	S	S	S		
JELIAZKOV, Nikolay	3 + 8	S	S	S		
HRISTOV, Plamen	0 + 0	S	S	S		
OUZOUNOV, Petar	0 + 0		*			
NAYDENOV, Nayden	9 + 12	S	S	S		
IVANOV, Nikolay	0 + 0					
GAVRILOV, Ivaylo	3 + 9	S	*	S		
IVANOV, Evgeni	0 + 0			*		
KONSTANTINOV, Plamen	0 + 0					

Team: BRA Brazil

Coach: GUIMARAES, Jose
Assistant Coach: MIRANDA, Marcos

Names	Pts + S/O	1	2	3	4	5
NEGRAO, Marcelo	5 + 18	S	S	S		
PEREIRA, Cassio Leandro	0 + 0					
GAVIO, Giovane	5 + 16	S	S	S		
SILVA, Paulo "Paulao"	0 + 0			*		
LIMA, Mauricio	1 + 3	S	S	S		
MARCELINO, Fabio "Pinha"	1 + 7	*		*		
GOUVEIA, Antonio "Carlao"	0 + 0					
PEREIRA, Max	4 + 11	S	S	S		
BITENCOURT, Nalbert	0 + 0	*	*			
SAMUEL, Alexandre "Tande"	13 + 14	S	S	S		
BERNARDO, Gilson	0 + 0					
SCHWANKE, Carlos	1 + 7	S	S	S		

Team: CUB Cuba

Coach: DIAZ MARINO, Juan Jesus
Assistant Coach: MORALES GONZALES, Justo L.

Names	Pts + S/O	1	2	3	4	5
BROOKS, Freddy	5 + 12	S	S	S	S	S
VIVES, Nicolas	0 + 0			*		
VANTES, Ricardo	0 + 0		*	*	*	S
DESPAIGNE, Joel	10 + 19	S	S	S	S	S
SANCHEZ, Rodolfo	8 + 8	*	*	S	S	S
DIAGO, Raul	5 + 3	S	S	S	S	S
HERNANDEZ, Osvaldo	9 + 15	S	S	S	S	S
ROCA, Alain	0 + 4	S	S		*	*
HERNANDEZ, Ihosvany	6 + 13	S	S	S	S	S
BELTRAN, Angel	0 + 0					*
BATLE, Alexis	0 + 0	*		*		
MARIN, Lazaro	0 + 0			*		

Team: CUB Cuba

Coach: DIAZ MARINO, Juan Jesus
Assistant Coach: MORALES GONZALES, Justo L.

Names	Pts + S/O	1	2	3	4	5
BROOKS, Freddy	8 + 11	S	S	S		
VIVES, Nicolas	0 + 0		*			
VANTES, Ricardo	0 + 0	*	*	*		
DESPAIGNE, Joel	6 + 12	S	S	S		
SANCHEZ, Rodolfo	0 + 0					
DIAGO, Raul	2 + 1	S	S	S		
HERNANDEZ, Osvaldo	3 + 16	S	S	S		
ROCA, Alain	13 + 5	S	S	S		
HERNANDEZ, Ihosvany	4 + 12	S	S	S		
BELTRAN, Angel	0 + 0		*			
BATLE, Alexis	0 + 0					
MARIN, Lazaro	0 + 0					

Team: POL Poland

Coach: KREBOK, Wiktor
Assistant Coach: RYS, Grzegorz

Names	Pts + S/O	1	2	3	4	5
STELMACH, Andrzej	0 + 0	S				
DACEWICZ, Damian	0 + 8	*	S	S		
STELMACH, Krzysztof	4 + 13	S	S	S		
SZYSZKO, Mariusz	0 + 0	*	S			
NOWAK, Marcin	2 + 3	S	S	S		
GRUSZKA, Piotr	0 + 5	S	S	S		
PRYGIEL, Robert	0 + 0					
SMIGIEL, Krzysztof	0 + 0	*	*	*		
URBANOWICZ, Leszek	2 + 8	S	S	*		
JANCZAK, Krzysztof	2 + 14		*	S		
ROMAN, Witold	0 + 2	S		*		
ZAGUMNY, Pawel	0 + 0		*	S		

Team: USA United States of America

Coach: STURM, Frederick
Assistant Coach: SUWARA, Rudy

Names	Pts + S/O	1	2	3	4	5
BALL, Lloy	1 + 0	S	S	*		
HYDEN, John	0 + 0					
CTVRTLIK, Bob	3 + 12	S	S	S		
IVIE, Bryan	0 + 17	S	S	S		
SORENSEN, Tom	1 + 4		*			
FORTUNE, Scott	2 + 2			*		
STORK, Jeff	1 + 2		*	S		
NYGAARD, Jeff	3 + 9	S	S	*		
LAMBERT, Mike	6 + 10	S	S	S		
WATTS, Ethan	0 + 0					
LANDRY, Dan	3 + 14	S	S	S		
WINSLOW, Brett	0 + 1		*	S		

Volleyball—Indoor / Volleyball — En salle

Men / *Messieurs*

PRELIMINARIES - GROUP A

POL 1 - 3 ARG

Set	1	2	3	4	5	Total pts
Result	15 - 7	15 - 17	10 - 15	9 - 15		49 - 54
Duration	0:28	0:34	0:37	0:36		2:15

	Poland				Argentina	
Att	Pts won	S/O		Att	Pts won	S/O
216	19	88	Attacks	233	23	95
118	11	3	Blocks	110	12	2
174	3		Serves	178	7	

1st Referee: KSA al-KHLAIFI, Abdullah
2nd Referee: NED SCHEFFER, Petrus Carolus

PRELIMINARIES - GROUP A

USA 2 - 3 BUL

Set	1	2	3	4	5	Total pts
Result	11 - 15	15 - 13	15 - 11	5 - 15	12 - 15	58 - 69
Duration	0:30	0:39	0:38	0:28	0:13	2:28

	United States of America				Bulgaria	
Att	Pts won	S/O		Att	Pts won	S/O
228	34	80	Attacks	228	34	91
109	6	4	Blocks	107	17	4
182	7		Serves	191	5	

1st Referee: CHN QU, Zheng Zhong
2nd Referee: AUS TURNER, Dean

PRELIMINARIES - GROUP A

CUB 0 - 3 BRA

Set	1	2	3	4	5	Total pts
Result	11 - 15	10 - 15	11 - 15			32 - 45
Duration	0:33	0:31	0:35			1:39

	Cuba				Brazil	
Att	Pts won	S/O		Att	Pts won	S/O
151	12	65	Attacks	140	21	54
62	10	3	Blocks	65	5	2
118	2		Serves	129	4	

1st Referee: FRA RACHARD, Patrick
2nd Referee: GRE MARGARITIS, Konstantinos

Team: POL Poland
Coach: KREBOK, Wiktor
Assistant Coach: RYS, Grzegorz

Names	Pts + S/O	1	2	3	4	5
STELMACH, Andrzej	1 + 2				*	*
DACEWICZ, Damian	3 + 12	S	S	S	S	
STELMACH, Krzysztof	10 + 23	S	S	S	S	
SZYSZKO, Mariusz	0 + 0		*		*	
NOWAK, Marcin	3 + 5	S	S	S	*	
GRUSZKA, Piotr	8 + 23	S	S	S	S	
PRYGIEL, Robert	0 + 0					
SMIGIEL, Krzysztof	7 + 12	S	S	S	S	
URBANOWICZ, Leszek	0 + 2				*	
JANCZAK, Krzysztof	0 + 7				*	
ROMAN, Witold	0 + 4			*	*	S
ZAGUMNY, Pawel	1 + 1	S	S	S	S	

Team: USA United States of America
Coach: STURM, Frederick
Assistant Coach: SUWARA, Rudy

Names	Pts + S/O	1	2	3	4	5
BALL, Lloy	1 + 2	S	S	S	S	S
HYDEN, John	13 + 14	S	S	S	S	S
CTVRTLIK, Bob	3 + 12	S	S	S	S	S
IVIE, Bryan	6 + 12	S	S	S	S	S
SORENSEN, Tom	13 + 18	*	S	S	S	S
FORTUNE, Scott	0 + 0					
STORK, Jeff	0 + 0				*	
NYGAARD, Jeff	6 + 21	S	S	S	S	S
LAMBERT, Mike	4 + 1	S				*
WATTS, Ethan	0 + 0					
LANDRY, Dan	1 + 3	S	*	*	*	
WINSLOW, Brett	0 + 1				*	

Team: CUB Cuba
Coach: DIAZ MARINO, Juan Jesus
Assistant Coach: MORALES GONZALES, Justo L.

Names	Pts + S/O	1	2	3	4	5
BROOKS, Freddy	0 + 0					
VIVES, Nicolas	3 + 1	*	*	S		
VANTES, Ricardo	1 + 3	*	*	S		
DESPAIGNE, Joel	1 + 0	*				
SANCHEZ, Rodolfo	6 + 14	S	S	S		
DIAGO, Raul	1 + 1	S	S			
HERNANDEZ, Osvaldo	0 + 8	S	S			
ROCA, Alain	0 + 4	S	S			
HERNANDEZ, Ihosvany	3 + 16	S	S	S		
BELTRAN, Angel	0 + 0					
BATLE, Alexis	6 + 14	S	S	S		
MARIN, Lazaro	3 + 7		*	S		

Team: ARG Argentina
Coach: CASTELLANI, Daniel Jorge
Assistant Coach: GETZELEVICH, Carlos Alberto

Names	Pts + S/O	1	2	3	4	5
MILINKOVIC, Marcos	10 + 27	S	S	S	S	
ELGUETA, Jorge	4 + 12	S	S	S	S	
JABIF, Sebastian	11 + 21	S	S	S	S	
MALY, Leonardo	4 + 6			*	S	S
QUAINI, Guillermo	1 + 2		S		·	
WEBER, Javier	0 + 2	S	S	S	S	
BORRERO, Fernando	1 + 0	S				
ROMANO, Alejandro	0 + 3	S				
FIRPO, Sebastian	0 + 0				*	
PEREIRA, Pablo	11 + 20	*	S	S	S	
MARTINEZ, Guillermo	0 + 3				*	
RODRIGUEZ, Eduardo	0 + 1	*				

Team: BUL Bulgaria
Coach: KJUTCHOUKOV, Bogdan
Assistant Coach: GENTCHEV, Eugeni

Names	Pts + S/O	1	2	3	4	5
STOEV, Martin	11 + 18	S	S	S	S	S
NAIDENOV, Ludmil	0 + 0		*	*	*	*
GANEV, Lubomir	14 + 23	S	S	*	S	S
TONEV, Dimo	9 + 12	S	S	S	S	S
JELIAZKOV, Nikolay	12 + 14	S	S	S	S	S
HRISTOV, Plamen	1 + 2	S	S	S		
OUZOUNOV, Petar	0 + 2	*	*	*	*	*
NAYDENOV, Nayden	7 + 19	S	S	S	S	S
IVANOV, Nikolay	0 + 1				S	S
GAVRILOV, Ivaylo	2 + 4	*	*	S		*
IVANOV, Evgeni	0 + 0				*	
KONSTANTINOV, Plamen	0 + 0					

Team: BRA Brazil
Coach: GUIMARAES, Jose
Assistant Coach: MIRANDA, Marcos

Names	Pts + S/O	1	2	3	4	5
NEGRAO, Marcelo	2 + 12	S	S	S		
PEREIRA, Cassio Leandro	0 + 0					
GAVIO, Giovane	5 + 22	S	S	S		
SILVA, Paulo "Paulao"	0 + 0	*				
LIMA, Mauricio	0 + 0	S	S	S		
MARCELINO, Fabio "Pinha"	0 + 5			*	*	
GOUVEIA, Antonio "Carlao"	0 + 0					
PEREIRA, Max	2 + 2	S	S	S		
BITENCOURT, Nalbert	0 + 0	*	*			
SAMUEL, Alexandre "Tande"	15 + 13	S	S	S		
BERNARDO, Gilson	0 + 0					
SCHWANKE, Carlos	6 + 2	S	S	S		

FINAL CLASSIFICATION - GROUP A

Rnk	Team	Pts	Games			Sets			Points		
			Played	Won	Lost	Won	Lost	W/L	For	Against	F/A
1	CUB	9	5	4	1	12	5	2.40	233	191	1.21
2	BRA	8	5	3	2	10	6	1.66	210	187	1.12
3	BUL	8	5	3	2	10	8	1.25	225	212	1.06
4	ARG	8	5	3	2	9	9	1.00	222	225	0.98
5	USA	7	5	2	3	10	9	1.11	241	233	1.03
6	POL	5	5	0	5	1	15	0.06	151	234	0.64

Men / *Messieurs*

TUN 0 - 3 NED

Set	1	2	3	4	5	Total pts
Result	4 - 15	4 - 15	2 - 15			10 - 45
Duration	0:20	0:24	0:24			1:08

	Tunisia				Netherlands	
Att	Pts won	S/O		Att	Pts won	S/O
121	4	44	Attacks	109	24	40
34	5	2	Blocks	70	7	1
67	0		Serves	101	2	

1st Referee: KSA al-KHLAIFI, Abdullah
2nd Referee: USA BLUE, Thomas

Team: TUN Tunisia
Coach: M'KAOUAR, Fathi
Assistant Coach: BELKHODJA, Hassine

Names	Pts + S/O	1	2	3	4	5
KOUBAA, Ghazi	1 + 4	*	S	S		
HEDHILI, Riadh	0 + 4	S	S	S		
BAGHDADI, Mohamed	4 + 18	S	S	S		
GHANDRI, Riadh	3 + 6	S	S	S		
LOUKIL, Atef	0 + 0	S				
BELAID, Khaled	0 + 0	*	*	*		
BEN ROMDHANE, Hichem	0 + 0		*			
AOUNI, Tarak	0 + 0			*		
BEN AMARA, Faycal	1 + 3	S	S	S		
HFAIEDH, Nouredding	0 + 10	S	S	S		
GUIDARA, Ghazi	0 + 1			*		
TOUMI, Majdi	0 + 0					

Team: NED Netherlands
Coach: ALBERDA, Joop
Assistant Coach: V. D. BURGT, Toon

Names	Pts + S/O	1	2	3	4	5
LATUHIHIN, Misha	0 + 0					
HELD, Henk-Jan	5 + 5	S	S	S		
RODENBURG, Brecht	0 + 0					
GORTZEN, Guido	6 + 4	S	S	S		
SCHUIL, Richard	0 + 0		*	*		
ZWERVER, Ron	8 + 6	S	S	S		
van de GOOR, Bas	2 + 13	S	S	S		
POSTHUMA, Jan	0 + 2		*			
van der MEULEN, Olof	7 + 7	S	S	S		
BLANGE, Peter	4 + 4	S	S	S		
GRABERT, Rob	1 + 0		*			
van de GOOR, Mike	0 + 0					

KOR 0 - 3 ITA

Set	1	2	3	4	5	Total pts
Result	13 - 15	12 - 15	8 - 15			33 - 45
Duration	0:39	0:30	0:27			1:36

	Korea				Italy	
Att	Pts won	S/O		Att	Pts won	S/O
158	18	62	Attacks	155	16	74
56	6	3	Blocks	87	9	4
126	1		Serves	136	8	

1st Referee: CUB SANLER DIAZ, Jose
2nd Referee: GRE MARGARITIS, Konstantinos

Team: KOR Korea
Coach: SONG, Man-Duck
Assistant Coach: HAN, Jang-Suk

Names	Pts + S/O	1	2	3	4	5
IM, Do-Hun	0 + 0	*	*	*		
KIM, Se-Jin	6 + 12	S	S	S		
SHIN, Young-Chul	1 + 1	S	S	S		
BANG, Sin-Bong	0 + 0	*	*	*		
KIM, Sang-Woo	6 + 9	S	S	S		
HA, Jong-Hwa	0 + 0					
CHOI, Cheon-Sik	1 + 9	S	S	S		
PARK, Hee-Sang	1 + 19	S	S	S		
LEE, Sung-Hee	0 + 0					
SHIN, Jung-Sub	0 + 0					
SHIN, Jin-Sik	10 + 15	S	S	S		
PARK, Sun-Chool	0 + 0					

Team: ITA Italy
Coach: VELASCO, Julio
Assistant Coach: FRIGONI, Angiolino

Names	Pts + S/O	1	2	3	4	5
GARDINI, Andrea	9 + 13	S	S	S		
MEONI, Marco	1 + 1		*	S		
GRAVINA, Pasquale	2 + 11	S	S	S		
TOFOLI, Paolo	0 + 0	S	S			
PAPI, Samuele	0 + 0		*			
SARTORETTI, Andrea	1 + 0	*	*	*		
BRACCI, Marco	1 + 5	S	S			
BERNARDI, Lorenzo	8 + 21	S	S	S		
CANTAGALLI, Luca	1 + 11	*	*	S		
ZORZI, Andrea	0 + 0					
GIANI, Andrea	9 + 14	S	S	S		
BOVOLENTA, Vigor	1 + 2			*		

YUG 3 - 1 RUS

Set	1	2	3	4	5	Total pts
Result	10 - 15	15 - 13	15 - 10	15 - 11		55 - 49
Duration	0:33	0:36	0:31	0:41		2:21

	Yugoslavia				Russian Federation	
Att	Pts won	S/O		Att	Pts won	S/O
232	26	105	Attacks	225	17	88
121	17	3	Blocks	104	16	2
182	6		Serves	177	2	

1st Referee: JPN SHIMOYAMA, Takashi
2nd Referee: USA DRAGON, Barry

Team: YUG Yugoslavia
Coach: GAJIC, Zoran
Assistant Coach: CVETKOVIC, Jovica

Names	Pts + S/O	1	2	3	4	5
DJURIC, Djorde	0 + 0					
PETROVIC, Zarko	1 + 6	S	S		*	
BATEZ, Vladimir	9 + 23	*	*	S	S	
TANASKOVIC, Zeljko	11 + 8	S	S	S	S	
BRDJOVIC, Dejan	3 + 7	S	S		*	
MESTER, Djula	3 + 11		*	S	S	
KOVAC, Slobodan	3 + 5	S	S		*	
GRBIC, Nikola	4 + 2	S	S	S	S	
GRBIC, Vladimir	3 + 27	S	S	S	S	
JOKANOVIC, Rajko	0 + 0					
GERIC, Andrija	0 + 0					
VUJEVIC, Goran	12 + 19	*	*	S	S	

Team: RUS Russian Federation
Coach: PLATONOV, Viatcheslav
Assistant Coach: MOLIBOGA, Oleg

Names	Pts + S/O	1	2	3	4	5
CHATOUNOV, Oleg	6 + 9	S	S	S	S	
KHAMOUTSKICH, Vadim	3 + 1	S	S	S	S	
ORLENKO, Serguei	0 + 0					
OLIKHVER, Rouslan	0 + 0					
KAZAKOV, Alexei	1 + 0	*	*	*	*	
FOMIN, Dmitri	8 + 23	S	S	S	S	
TETIOUKHIN, Serguei	0 + 0		*	*		
CHICHKIN, Pavel	5 + 13		*	S	*	
OUCHAKOV, Konstantin	0 + 0					
DINEIKIN, Stanislav	6 + 27	S	S	S	S	
CHOULEPOV, Igor	3 + 6	S	S	*	S	
GORIOUCHEV, Valeri	3 + 11	S	S	S	S	

RUS 0 - 3 NED

Set	1	2	3	4	5	Total pts
Result	9 - 15	9 - 15	9 - 15			27 - 45
Duration	0:42	0:38	0:28			1:48

	Russian Federation				Netherlands	
Att	Pts won	S/O		Att	Pts won	S/O
165	11	80	Attacks	178	21	83
92	8	4	Blocks	76	13	1
135	2		Serves	151	3	

1st Referee: FIN SALONEN, Jarmo
2nd Referee: GER LEUTHAEUSSER, Frank

Team: RUS Russian Federation
Coach: PLATONOV, Viatcheslav
Assistant Coach: MOLIBOGA, Oleg

Names	Pts + S/O	1	2	3	4	5
CHATOUNOV, Oleg	2 + 13	S	S	S		
KHAMOUTSKICH, Vadim	0 + 1	S	S	*		
ORLENKO, Serguei	0 + 0					
OLIKHVER, Rouslan	0 + 0					
KAZAKOV, Alexei	0 + 0			*		
FOMIN, Dmitri	6 + 25	S	S	S		
TETIOUKHIN, Serguei	2 + 4			S		
CHICHKIN, Pavel	4 + 9	S	S	S		
OUCHAKOV, Konstantin	1 + 2		*	S		
DINEIKIN, Stanislav	1 + 8	S	*	*		
CHOULEPOV, Igor	2 + 7	*	S	S		
GORIOUCHEV, Valeri	3 + 15	S	S	*		

Team: NED Netherlands
Coach: ALBERDA, Joop
Assistant Coach: V. D. BURGT, Toon

Names	Pts + S/O	1	2	3	4	5
LATUHIHIN, Misha	0 + 0					
HELD, Henk-Jan	1 + 12	S	S	S		
RODENBURG, Brecht	0 + 0					
GORTZEN, Guido	9 + 20	S	S	S		
SCHUIL, Richard	0 + 0					
ZWERVER, Ron	10 + 12	S	S	S		
van de GOOR, Bas	8 + 13	S	S	S		
POSTHUMA, Jan	0 + 0			*		
van der MEULEN, Olof	9 + 23	S	S	S		
BLANGE, Peter	0 + 4	S	S	S		
GRABERT, Rob	0 + 0					
van de GOOR, Mike	0 + 0					

Men / *Messieurs*

PRELIMINARIES - GROUP B

ITA 3 - 0 TUN

Set	1	2	3	4	5	Total pts
Result	15 - 9	15 - 5	15 - 1			45 - 15
Duration	0:21	0:23	0:17			1:01

	Italy				Tunisia	
Att	Pts won	S/O		Att	Pts won	S/O
104	19	46	Attacks	110	6	31
53	10	0	Blocks	36	1	2
99	3		Serves	68	2	

1st Referee: MEX NAVA ABARCA, Fernando
2nd Referee: USA LUEBKE, Neill

PRELIMINARIES - GROUP B

YUG 3 - 0 KOR

Set	1	2	3	4	5	Total pts
Result	15 - 5	15 - 6	16 - 14			46 - 25
Duration	0:30	0:34	0:.35			1:39

	Yugoslavia				Korea	
Att	Pts won	S/O		Att	Pts won	S/O
158	15	70	Attacks	178	10	65
105	16	7	Blocks	58	5	2
143	5		Serves	122	2	

1st Referee: USA DRAGON, Barry
2nd Referee: CUB SANLER DIAZ, Jose

PRELIMINARIES - GROUP B

NED 0 - 3 ITA

Set	1	2	3	4	5	Total pts
Result	8 - 15	8 - 15	13 - 15			29 - 45
Duration	0:34	0:37	0:43			1:54

	Netherlands				Italy	
Att	Pts won	S/O		Att	Pts won	S/O
186	12	79	Attacks	178	21	78
85	5	3	Blocks	88	6	6
137	4		Serves	151	8	

1st Referee: FIN SALONEN, Jarmo
2nd Referee: ARG PAREDES, Guillermo

PRELIMINARIES - GROUP B

TUN 1 - 3 YUG

Set	1	2	3	4	5	Total pts
Result	4 - 15	17 - 15	3 - 15	3 - 15		27 - 60
Duration	0:23	0:41	0:18	0:19		1:41

	Tunisia				Yugoslavia	
Att	Pts won	S/O		Att	Pts won	S/O
178	9	63	Attacks	174	25	73
87	10	7	Blocks	109	13	4
122	3		Serves	154	8	

1st Referee: USA LUEBKE, Neill
2nd Referee: JPN SHIMOYAMA, Takashi

Team: ITA Italy

Coach: VELASCO, Julio
Assistant Coach: FRIGONI, Angiolino

Names	Pts + S/O	1	2	3	4	5
GARDINI, Andrea	1 + 9	S	S	S		
MEONI, Marco	1 + 0	S	S	S		
GRAVINA, Pasquale	3 + 2	S	S			
TOFOLI, Paolo	0 + 0					
PAPI, Samuele	6 + 5		S	S		
SARTORETTI, Andrea	0 + 0	*				
BRACCI, Marco	0 + 0					
BERNARDI, Lorenzo	2 + 3	S				
CANTAGALLI, Luca	7 + 8	S	S	S		
ZORZI, Andrea	0 + 0					
GIANI, Andrea	10 + 15	S	S	S		
BOVOLENTA, Vigor	2 + 4		*	S		

Team: YUG Yugoslavia

Coach: GAJIC, Zoran
Assistant Coach: CVETKOVIC, Jovica

Names	Pts + S/O	1	2	3	4	5
DJURIC, Djorde	0 + 0					
PETROVIC, Zarko	0 + 2			*		
BATEZ, Vladimir	8 + 18	S	S	S		
TANASKOVIC, Zeljko	4 + 11	S	S	S		
BRDJOVIC, Dejan	0 + 0					
MESTER, Djula	1 + 9	S	S	S		
KOVAC, Slobodan	0 + 0		*	*		
GRBIC, Nikola	9 + 0	S	S	S		
GRBIC, Vladimir	8 + 16	S	S	S		
JOKANOVIC, Rajko	0 + 0					
GERIC, Andrija	0 + 0			*		
VUJEVIC, Goran	6 + 21	S	S	S		

Team: NED Netherlands

Coach: ALBERDA, Joop
Assistant Coach: V. D. BURGT, Toon

Names	Pts + S/O	1	2	3	4	5
LATUHIHIN, Misha	1 + 1		*	*		
HELD, Henk-Jan	3 + 12	S	*	S		
RODENBURG, Brecht	0 + 0					
GORTZEN, Guido	3 + 16	S	S	S		
SCHUIL, Richard	0 + 1	*	*			
ZWERVER, Ron	6 + 14	S	S	S		
van de GOOR, Bas	2 + 9	S	S	S		
POSTHUMA, Jan	1 + 4	*	S	*		
van der MEULEN, Olof	5 + 24	S	S	S		
BLANGE, Peter	0 + 1	S	S	S		
GRABERT, Rob	0 + 0	*				
van de GOOR, Mike	0 + 0					

Team: TUN Tunisia

Coach: M'KAOUAR, Fathi
Assistant Coach: BELKHODJA, Hassine

Names	Pts + S/O	1	2	3	4	5
KOUBAA, Ghazi	4 + 4	S	S	S	S	
HEDHILI, Riadh	4 + 8	S	S	S	S	
BAGHDADI, Mohamed	3 + 18	S	S	S	S	
GHANDRI, Riadh	3 + 19	S	S	S	S	
LOUKIL, Atef	0 + 0					
BELAID, Khaled	6 + 7	S	S	S	S	
BEN ROMDHANE, Hichem	0 + 0	*	*	*	*	
AOUNI, Tarak	0 + 0					
BEN AMARA, Faycal	0 + 0					
HFAIEDH, Nouredding	0 + 0					
GUIDARA, Ghazi	0 + 0					
TOUMI, Majdi	2 + 14	S	S	S	S	

Team: TUN Tunisia

Coach: M'KAOUAR, Fathi
Assistant Coach: BELKHODJA, Hassine

Names	Pts + S/O	1	2	3	4	5
KOUBAA, Ghazi	1 + 2	S	S	S		
HEDHILI, Riadh	0 + 1	S	S	S		
BAGHDADI, Mohamed	4 + 10	S	S	S		
GHANDRI, Riadh	0 + 7	S	S	S		
LOUKIL, Atef	0 + 0					
BELAID, Khaled	2 + 7	S	S	S		
BEN ROMDHANE, Hichem	0 + 0		*	*		
AOUNI, Tarak	0 + 0			*		
BEN AMARA, Faycal	2 + 6	S	S	S		
HFAIEDH, Nouredding	0 + 0					
GUIDARA, Ghazi	0 + 0					
TOUMI, Majdi	0 + 0					

Team: KOR Korea

Coach: SONG, Man-Duck
Assistant Coach: HAN, Jang-Suk

Names	Pts + S/O	1	2	3	4	5
IM, Do-Hun	5 + 12	S	*	S		
KIM, Se-Jin	1 + 9	S	S	*		
SHIN, Young-Chul	0 + 0					
BANG, Sin-Bong	1 + 0		*	S		
KIM, Sang-Woo	4 + 15	S	S	S		
HA, Jong-Hwa	2 + 1			S		
CHOI, Cheon-Sik	0 + 1	S				
PARK, Hee-Sang	1 + 13	S	S	S		
LEE, Sung-Hee	1 + 0	*	S	S		
SHIN, Jung-Sub	0 + 0					
SHIN, Jin-Sik	1 + 13	S	S			
PARK, Sun-Chool	1 + 3	*	S			

Team: ITA Italy

Coach: VELASCO, Julio
Assistant Coach: FRIGONI, Angiolino

Names	Pts + S/O	1	2	3	4	5
GARDINI, Andrea	5 + 15	S	S	S		
MEONI, Marco	1 + 1	S	S	S		
GRAVINA, Pasquale	0 + 0			*		
TOFOLI, Paolo	0 + 0					
PAPI, Samuele	2 + 5	*	*	*		
SARTORETTI, Andrea	0 + 0	*	*	*		
BRACCI, Marco	0 + 0					
BERNARDI, Lorenzo	10 + 15	S	S	S		
CANTAGALLI, Luca	3 + 12	S	S	S		
ZORZI, Andrea	0 + 0					
GIANI, Andrea	10 + 26	S	S	S		
BOVOLENTA, Vigor	4 + 10	S	S	S		

Team: YUG Yugoslavia

Coach: GAJIC, Zoran
Assistant Coach: CVETKOVIC, Jovica

Names	Pts + S/O	1	2	3	4	5
DURIC, Dorde	3 + 9				S	
PETROVIC, Zarko	6 + 8	S	S	S		
BATEZ, Vladimir	0 + 0		*			
TANASKOVIC, Zeljko	5 + 2		*	S	S	
BRDOVIC, Dejan	7 + 21	S	S	S		
MESTER, Dula	0 + 1		*		S	
KOVAC, Slobodan	10 + 8	S	S	S	S	
GRBIC, Nikola	0 + 0					
GRBIC, Vladimir	0 + 0					
JOKANOVIC, Rajko	0 + 10	S	S	S		
GERIC, Andrija	5 + 3	S	S			
VUJEVIC, Goran	10 + 15	S	S	S	S	

Men / *Messieurs*

PRELIMINARIES - GROUP B

KOR 0 - 3 RUS

Set	1	2	3	4	5	Total pts
Result	8 - 15	4 - 15	14 - 16			26 - 46
Duration	0:32	0:25	0:37			1:34

	Korea				Russian Federation	
Att	Pts won	S/O		Att	Pts won	S/O
171	13	58	Attacks	149	15	69
66	3	2	Blocks	102	20	4
116	3		Serves	134	1	

1st Referee: CAN HENRY, Peter
2nd Referee: GRE MARGARITIS, Konstantinos

PRELIMINARIES - GROUP B

RUS 0 - 3 ITA

Set	1	2	3	4	5	Total pts
Result	11 - 15	6 - 15	12 - 15			29 - 45
Duration	0:41	0:28	0:39			1:48

	Russian Federation				Italy	
Att	Pts won	S/O		Att	Pts won	S/O
176	16	71	Attacks	194	21	86
92	4	5	Blocks	72	7	3
137	3		Serves	152	4	

1st Referee: GER LEUTHAEUSSER, Frank
2nd Referee: CHN QU, Zheng Zhong

PRELIMINARIES - GROUP B

YUG 0 - 3 NED

Set	1	2	3	4	5	Total pts
Result	7 - 15	6 - 15	9 - 15			22 - 45
Duration	0:34	0:30	0:29			1:33

	Yugoslavia				Netherlands	
Att	Pts won	S/O		Att	Pts won	S/O
164	12	66	Attacks	132	21	58
59	4	1	Blocks	81	9	0
107	5		Serves	129	0	

1st Referee: GRE MARGARITIS, Konstantinos
2nd Referee: ESP GIMENEZ, Gabriel

PRELIMINARIES - GROUP B

KOR 3 - 0 TUN

Set	1	2	3	4	5	Total pts
Result	15 - 4	15 - 6	15 - 6			45 - 16
Duration	0:22	0:18	0:24			1:04

	Korea				Tunisia	
Att	Pts won	S/O		Att	Pts won	S/O
101	16	43	Attacks	123	4	46
52	12	0	Blocks	47	5	1
103	3		Serves	77	3	

1st Referee: USA DRAGON, Barry
2nd Referee: BRA PALMEIRIM, Josebel

Team: KOR Korea
Coach: SONG, Man-Duck
Assistant Coach: HAN, Jang-Suk

Names	Pts + S/O	1	2	3	4	5
IM, Do-Hun	4 + 18	*	S	S		
KIM, Se-Jin	4 + 14	S	S	S		
SHIN, Young-Chul	0 + 0	S	*	S		
BANG, Sin-Bong	1 + 3	*	S	S		
KIM, Sang-Woo	1 + 4	S	S			
HA, Jong-Hwa	4 + 2			*		
CHOI, Cheon-Sik	0 + 1	S		*		
PARK, Hee-Sang	1 + 17	S	S	S		
LEE, Sung-Hee	0 + 0	*	S			
SHIN, Jung-Sub	0 + 0					
SHIN, Jin-Sik	4 + 1	S		S		
PARK, Sun-Chool	0 + 0					

Team: RUS Russian Federation
Coach: PLATONOV, Viatcheslav
Assistant Coach: MOLIBOGA, Oleg

Names	Pts + S/O	1	2	3	4	5
CHATOUNOV, Oleg	1 + 3	S				
KHAMOUTSKICH, Vadim	0 + 0	S	S			
ORLENKO, Serguei	0 + 5			S		
OLIKHVER, Rouslan	2 + 6	S	S			
KAZAKOV, Alexei	0 + 2	*	*			
FOMIN, Dmitri	0 + 0					
TETIOUKHIN, Serguei	2 + 14	*	S	S		
CHICHKIN, Pavel	3 + 8	S	S			
OUCHAKOV, Konstantin	2 + 1	*	*	S		
DINEIKIN, Stanislav	5 + 18	S	S			
CHOULEPOV, Igor	5 + 13	S	S	S		
GORIOUCHEV, Valeri	3 + 6		*	S		

Team: YUG Yugoslavia
Coach: GAJIC, Zoran
Assistant Coach: CVETKOVIC, Jovica

Names	Pts + S/O	1	2	3	4	5
DJURIC, Djorde	1 + 4		S			
PETROVIC, Zarko	2 + 8	S	S	S		
BATEZ, Vladimir	2 + 14	S	*	S		
TANASKOVIC, Zeljko	0 + 2	S				
BRDJOVIC, Dejan	0 + 0					
MESTER, Djula	1 + 4		S	S		
KOVAC, Slobodan	5 + 8	*	*	S		
GRBIC, Nikola	2 + 3	S	S			
GRBIC, Vladimir	6 + 13	S	S	S		
JOKANOVIC, Rajko	0 + 0		*			
GERIC, Andrija	0 + 0					
VUJEVIC, Goran	2 + 11	S	S			

Team: KOR Korea
Coach: SONG, Man-Duck
Assistant Coach: HAN, Jang-Suk

Names	Pts + S/O	1	2	3	4	5
IM, Do-Hun	2 + 2			*		
KIM, Se-Jin	9 + 10	S	S	S		
SHIN, Young-Chul	1 + 1	S	S	S		
BANG, Sin-Bong	3 + 1		*	S		
KIM, Sang-Woo	6 + 12	S	S	S		
HA, Jong-Hwa	0 + 0					
CHOI, Cheon-Sik	2 + 2	S	S			
PARK, Hee-Sang	6 + 8	S	S	S		
LEE, Sung-Hee	0 + 0					
SHIN, Jung-Sub	0 + 0			*		
SHIN, Jin-Sik	2 + 7	S	S	S		
PARK, Sun-Chool	0 + 0					

Team: RUS Russian Federation
Coach: PLATONOV, Viatcheslav
Assistant Coach: MOLIBOGA, Oleg

Names	Pts + S/O	1	2	3	4	5
CHATOUNOV, Oleg	6 + 11	S	S	S		
KHAMOUTSKICH, Vadim	2 + 2	S	S	S		
ORLENKO, Serguei	0 + 0					
OLIKHVER, Rouslan	0 + 0					
KAZAKOV, Alexei	0 + 0	*	*			
FOMIN, Dmitri	6 + 5	S	S	*		
TETIOUKHIN, Serguei	0 + 0					
CHICHKIN, Pavel	4 + 10	S	S	S		
OUCHAKOV, Konstantin	0 + 0	*	*	*		
DINEIKIN, Stanislav	8 + 21	S	S	S		
CHOULEPOV, Igor	7 + 15	S	S	S		
GORIOUCHEV, Valeri	3 + 9		*	S		

Team: ITA Italy
Coach: VELASCO, Julio
Assistant Coach: FRIGONI, Angiolino

Names	Pts + S/O	1	2	3	4	5
GARDINI, Andrea	1 + 14	S	S	S		
MEONI, Marco	2 + 0	S	S	S		
GRAVINA, Pasquale	0 + 0			*		
TOFOLI, Paolo	0 + 0					
PAPI, Samuele	5 + 7	*	S	S		
SARTORETTI, Andrea	0 + 0		*			
BRACCI, Marco	0 + 1			*		
BERNARDI, Lorenzo	5 + 14	S	S	S		
CANTAGALLI, Luca	5 + 7	S		*		
ZORZI, Andrea	0 + 0					
GIANI, Andrea	10 + 32	S	S	S		
BOVOLENTA, Vigor	4 + 14	S	S	S		

Team: NED Netherlands
Coach: ALBERDA, Joop
Assistant Coach: V. D. BURGT, Toon

Names	Pts + S/O	1	2	3	4	5
LATUHIHIN, Misha	0 + 0					
HELD, Henk-Jan	5 + 9	S	S	S		
RODENBURG, Brecht	0 + 0					
GORTZEN, Guido	5 + 13	S	S	S		
SCHUIL, Richard	0 + 0	*	*	*		
ZWERVER, Ron	7 + 6	S	S	S		
van de GOOR, Bas	4 + 9	S	S	S		
POSTHUMA, Jan	0 + 0	*	*	*		
van der MEULEN, Olof	7 + 20	S	S	S		
BLANGE, Peter	2 + 1	S	S	S		
GRABERT, Rob	0 + 0		*	*		
van de GOOR, Mike	0 + 0					

Team: TUN Tunisia
Coach: M'KAOUAR, Fathi
Assistant Coach: BELKHODJA, Hassine

Names	Pts + S/O	1	2	3	4	5
KOUBAA, Ghazi	3 + 2	S	S			
HEDHILI, Riadh	0 + 1	S	S			
BAGHDADI, Mohamed	0 + 16	S	S	S		
GHANDRI, Riadh	3 + 6	S	S	S		
LOUKIL, Atef	1 + 14	S	S	S		
BELAID, Khaled	1 + 5	S	S	S		
BEN ROMDHANE, Hichem	0 + 0		*	*		
AOUNI, Tarak	1 + 2			S		
BEN AMARA, Faycal	0 + 0					
HFAIEDH, Nouredding	0 + 0					
GUIDARA, Ghazi	3 + 1		.	*	S	
TOUMI, Majdi	0 + 0					

Volleyball—Indoor / *Volleyball — En salle*

Men / *Messieurs*

PRELIMINARIES - GROUP B

ITA 3 - 0 YUG

Set	1	2	3	4	5	Total pts
Result	15 - 12	15 - 8	15 - 12			45 - 32
Duration	0:32	0:26	0:30			1:28

Italy				Yugoslavia		
Att	Pts won	S/O		Att	Pts won	S/O
153	19	59	Attacks	156	13	60
73	7	3	Blocks	65	4	0
122	4		Serves	110	3	

1st Referee: ARG PAREDES, Guillermo
2nd Referee: FIN SALONEN, Jarmo

PRELIMINARIES - GROUP B

TUN 0 - 3 RUS

Set	1	2	3	4	5	Total pts
Result	9 - 15	10 - 15	11 - 15			30 - 45
Duration	0:34	0:24	0:28			1:26

Tunisia				Russian Federation		
Att	Pts won	S/O		Att	Pts won	S/O
163	15	63	Attacks	144	18	58
60	2	1	Blocks	94	18	8
110	4		Serves	123	2	

1st Referee: USA BLUE, Thomas
2nd Referee: BRA PALMEIRIM, Josebel

PRELIMINARIES - GROUP B

NED 3 - 0 KOR

Set	1	2	3	4	5	Total pts
Result	15 - 4	15 - 11	15- 12			45 - 27
Duration	0:21	0:50	0:35			1:46

Netherlands				Korea		
Att	Pts won	S/O		Att	Pts won	S/O
159	15	87	Attacks	182	10	82
113	14	3	Blocks	76	7	6
156	7		Serves	139	2	

1st Referee: CAN HENRY, Peter
2nd Referee: MEX NAVA ABARCA, Fernando

Team: ITA Italy

Coach: VELASCO, Julio
Assistant Coach: FRIGONI, Angiolino

Names	Pts + S/O	1	2	3	4	5
GARDINI, Andrea	1 + 10	S	S	S		
MEONI, Marco	2 + 0		*	*		
GRAVINA, Pasquale	5 + 10	S	S	S		
TOFOLI, Paolo	1 + 1	S	S	S		
PAPI, Samuele	8 + 11	S	S	S		
SARTORETTI, Andrea	3 + 2		*	*		
BRACCI, Marco	5 + 9	S	S	S		
BERNARDI, Lorenzo	2 + 0	*				
CANTAGALLI, Luca	1 + 0			*		
ZORZI, Andrea	0 + 0					
GIANI, Andrea	2 + 19	S	S	S		
BOVOLENTA, Vigor	0 + 0					

Team: TUN Tunisia

Coach: M'KAOUAR, Fathi
Assistant Coach: BELKHODJA, Hassine

Names	Pts + S/O	1	2	3	4	5
KOUBAA, Ghazi	1 + 7	S	S	S		
HEDHILI, Riadh	3 + 3	S	S	S		
BAGHDADI, Mohamed	6 + 24	S	S	S		
GHANDRI, Riadh	4 + 9	S	S	S		
LOUKIL, Atef	6 + 14	S	S	S		
BELAID, Khaled	0 + 7	S	S	S		
BEN ROMDHANE, Hichem	0 + 0		*			
AOUNI, Tarak	1 + 0			*		
BEN AMARA, Faycal	0 + 0					
HFAIEDH, Nouredding	0 + 0					
GUIDARA, Ghazi	0 + 0					
TOUMI, Majdi	0 + 0					

Team: NED Netherlands

Coach: ALBERDA, Joop
Assistant Coach: V. D. BURGT, Toon

Names	Pts + S/O	1	2	3	4	5
LATUHIHIN, Misha	0 + 0					
HELD, Henk-Jan	3 + 19	S	S	S		
RODENBURG, Brecht	1 + 5	*	*	*		
GORTZEN, Guido	1 + 13	S	S	S		
SCHUIL, Richard	2 + 1			*		
ZWERVER, Ron	4 + 5	S	S	S		
van de GOOR, Bas	7 + 28	S	S	S		
POSTHUMA, Jan	0 + 0					
van der MEULEN, Olof	15 + 14	S	S	S		
BLANGE, Peter	3 + 5	S	S	S		
GRABERT, Rob	0 + 0					
van de GOOR, Mike	0 + 0					

Team: YUG Yugoslavia

Coach: GAJIC, Zoran
Assistant Coach: CVETKOVIC, Jovica

Names	Pts + S/O	1	2	3	4	5
DJURIC, Djorde	2 + 17	S	S			
PETROVIC, Zarko	1 + 3	S	S			
BATEZ, Vladimir	1 + 4	*	*	S		
TANASKOVIC, Zeljko	5 + 5	S	S	S		
BRDJOVIC, Dejan	0 + 0					
MESTER, Djula	1 + 3		*	S		
KOVAC, Slobodan	1 + 9	S	S			
GRBIC, Nikola	4 + 1	S	S	S		
GRBIC, Vladimir	5 + 13	S	S	S		
JOKANOVIC, Rajko	0 + 0					
GERIC, Andrija	0 + 0					
VUJEVIC, Goran	0 + 5		S			

Team: RUS Russian Federation

Coach: PLATONOV, Viatcheslav
Assistant Coach: MOLIBOGA, Oleg

Names	Pts + S/O	1	2	3	4	5
CHATOUNOV, Oleg	5 + 3	S	S			
KHAMOUTSKICH, Vadim	1 + 1	S	S			
ORLENKO, Serguei	0 + 1			*		
OLIKHVER, Rouslan	0 + 9	S	S	S		
KAZAKOV, Alexei	6 + 2	*	*	S		
FOMIN, Dmitri	0 + 0					
TETIOUKHIN, Serguei	1 + 6	*	*	S		
CHICHKIN, Pavel	3 + 5	S	S			
OUCHAKOV, Konstantin	2 + 0	*		S		
DINEIKIN, Stanislav	11 + 20	S	S	S		
CHOULEPOV, Igor	9 + 18	S	S	S		
GORIOUCHEV, Valeri	0 + 1			*		

Team: KOR Korea

Coach: SONG, Man-Duck
Assistant Coach: HAN, Jang-Suk

Names	Pts + S/O	1	2	3	4	5
IM, Do-Hun	3 + 10	*	S	S		
KIM, Se-Jin	5 + 34	S	S	S		
SHIN, Young-Chul	0 + 0					
BANG, Sin-Bong	2 + 12	S	S	S		
KIM, Sang-Woo	3 + 18	S	S	S		
HA, Jong-Hwa	0 + 0					
CHOI, Cheon-Sik	0 + 0					
PARK, Hee-Sang	0 + 0	S		*		
LEE, Sung-Hee	2 + 1	S	S	S		
SHIN, Jung-Sub	0 + 0					
SHIN, Jin-Sik	4 + 13	S	S	S		
PARK, Sun-Chool	0 + 0					

FINAL CLASSIFICATION - GROUP B

Rnk	Team	Pts	Games			Sets			Points		
			Played	Won	Lost	Won	Lost	W/L	For	Against	F/A
1	ITA	10	5	5	0	15	0	MAX	225	138	1.63
2	NED	9	5	4	1	12	3	4.00	209	131	1.59
3	YUG	8	5	3	2	9	8	1.12	215	191	1.12
4	RUS	7	5	2	3	7	9	0.77	196	201	0.97
5	KOR	6	5	1	4	3	12	0.25	156	198	0.78
6	TUN	5	5	0	5	1	15	0.06	98	240	0.40

QUARTERFINALS

CUB 0 - 3 RUS

Set	1	2	3	4	5	Total pts
Result	13 - 15	15 - 17	11 - 15			39 - 47
Duration	0:40	0:37	0:38			1:55

	Cuba				Russian Federation	
Att	Pts won	S/O		Att	Pts won	S/O
183	14	81	Attacks	168	18	77
81	12	1	Blocks	90	11	3
142	6		Serves	148	6	

1st Referee: JPN SHIMOYAMA, Takashi
2nd Referee: THA CHAREONPONG, Songsak

QUARTERFINALS

BUL 1 - 3 NED

Set	1	2	3	4	5	Total pts
Result	14 - 16	15 - 9	3 - 15	13 - 15		45 - 55
Duration	0:32	0:22	0:22	0:36		1:52

	Bulgaria				Netherlands	
Att	Pts won	S/O		Att	Pts won	S/O
168	14	77	Attacks	159	18	76
83	16	3	Blocks	86	16	1
140	5		Serves	149	4	

1st Referee: GER LEUTHAEUSSER, Frank
2nd Referee: USA BLUE, Thomas

QUARTERFINALS

BRA 2 - 3 YUG

Set	1	2	3	4	5	Total pts
Result	6 - 15	5 - 15	15 - 8	16 - 14	10 - 15	52 - 67
Duration	0:30	0:28	0:35	0:41	0:14	2:28

	Brazil				Yugoslavia	
Att	Pts won	S/O		Att	Pts won	S/O
212	22	83	Attacks	216	30	87
119	17	3	Blocks	97	19	2
159	3		Serves	170	2	

1st Referee: CHN QU, Zheng Zhong
2nd Referee: KOR CHO, Young-Ho

QUARTERFINALS

ARG 1 - 3 ITA

Set	1	2	3	4	5	Total pts
Result	15 - 12	9 - 15	7 - 15	4 - 15		35 - 57
Duration	0:31	0:35	0:24	0:23		1:53

	Argentina				Italy	
Att	Pts won	S/O		Att	Pts won	S/O
187	15	68	Attacks	182	26	62
76	5	3	Blocks	96	17	3
133	8		Serves	152	4	

1st Referee: USA DRAGON, Barry
2nd Referee: FRA RACHARD, Patrick

Team: CUB Cuba

Coach: DIAZ MARINO, Juan Jesus
Assistant Coach: MORALES GONZALES, Justo L.

Names	Pts + S/O	1	2	3	4	5
BROOKS, Freddy	3 + 15	S	S	S		
VIVES, Nicolas	0 + 0					
VANTES, Ricardo	0 + 0	*	*	*		
DESPAIGNE, Joel	5 + 18	S	S	S		
SANCHEZ, Rodolfo	1 + 5	*	S	*		
DIAGO, Raul	7 + 1	S	S	S		
HERNANDEZ, Osvaldo	5 + 23	S	S	S		
ROCA, Alain	3 + 3	S	*	S		
HERNANDEZ, Ihosvany	8 + 17	S	S	S		
BELTRAN, Angel	0 + 0					
BATLE, Alexis	0 + 0					
MARIN, Lazaro	0 + 0					

Team: BUL Bulgaria

Coach: KJUTCHOUKOV, Bogdan
Assistant Coach: GENTCHEV, Eugeni

Names	Pts + S/O	1	2	3	4	5
STOEV, Martin	6 + 13	S	S	S	S	
NAIDENOV, Ludmil	0 + 1	*		*	*	
GANEV, Lubomir	5 + 17	S	S	S	S	
TONEV, Dimo	6 + 10	S	S	S	S	
JELIAZKOV, Nikolay	7 + 17	S	S	S	S	
HRISTOV, Plamen	0 + 0			*		
OUZOUNOV, Petar	2 + 0	*	*	*	*	
NAYDENOV, Nayden	3 + 8	S	S	S	S	
IVANOV, Nikolay	5 + 3	S	S	S	S	
GAVRILOV, Ivaylo	1 + 11	*	*	*	*	
IVANOV, Evgeni	0 + 0					
KONSTANTINOV, Plamen	0 + 0			*		

Team: BRA Brazil

Coach: GUIMARAES, Jose
Assistant Coach: MIRANDA, Marcos

Names	Pts + S/O	1	2	3	4	5
NEGRAO, Marcelo	3 + 9	S	S		*	S
PEREIRA, Cassio Leandro	0 + 0	*	*		*	*
GAVIO, Giovane	8 + 31	S	S	S	S	S
SILVA, Paulo "Paulao"	1 + 0		*			*
LIMA, Mauricio	2 + 3	S	S	S	S	S
MARCELINO, Fabio "Pinha"	0 + 1	*		*	*	
GOUVEIA, Antonio "Carlao"	0 + 0					
PEREIRA, Max	6 + 2	S	S	S		
BITENCOURT, Nalbert	6 + 4		S	S	S	
SAMUEL, Alexandre "Tande"	12 + 30	S	S	S	S	S
BERNARDO, Gilson	1 + 5	*	*			
SCHWANKE, Carlos	3 + 1	S	S	S	S	

Team: ARG Argentina

Coach: CASTELLANI, Daniel Jorge
Assistant Coach: GETZELEVICH, Carlos Alberto

Names	Pts + S/O	1	2	3	4	5
MILINKOVIC, Marcos	9 + 22	S	S	S	S	
ELGUETA, Jorge	7 + 12	S	S	S	S	
JABIF, Sebastian	1 + 6	S	S	S		
MALY, Leonardo	3 + 13	S	S	S	S	
QUAINI, Guillermo	2 + 5		*	*	*	
WEBER, Javier	0 + 1	S	S	S	S	
BORRERO, Fernando	0 + 0					
ROMANO, Alejandro	4 + 3	S	S		*	
FIRPO, Sebastian	0 + 0				*	
PEREIRA, Pablo	1 + 7		*	S	S	
MARTINEZ, Guillermo	1 + 2	*	*	*	S	
RODRIGUEZ, Eduardo	0 + 0	*				

Team: RUS Russian Federation

Coach: PLATONOV, Viatcheslav
Assistant Coach: MOLIBOGA, Oleg

Names	Pts + S/O	1	2	3	4	5
CHATOUNOV, Oleg	7 + 5	S	S	S		
KHAMOUTSKICH, Vadim	5 + 2	S	S	S		
ORLENKO, Serguei	0 + 0					
OLIKHVER, Rouslan	0 + 0		*			
KAZAKOV, Alexei	0 + 0	*	*	*		
FOMIN, Dmitri	8 + 24	S	S	S		
TETIOUKHIN, Serguei	2 + 1	*	*	*		
CHICHKIN, Pavel	6 + 12	S	S	S		
OUCHAKOV, Konstantin	0 + 0					
DINEIKIN, Stanislav	5 + 24	S	S	S		
CHOULEPOV, Igor	2 + 12	S	S	S		
GORIOUCHEV, Valeri	0 + 0					

Team: NED Netherlands

Coach: ALBERDA, Joop
Assistant Coach: V. D. BURGT, Toon

Names	Pts + S/O	1	2	3	4	5
LATUHIHIN, Misha	1 + 0		*			
HELD, Henk-Jan	2 + 7	S	S			
RODENBURG, Brecht	0 + 0				*	
GORTZEN, Guido	3 + 7	S	S	S	S	
SCHUIL, Richard	1 + 2	*	S			
ZWERVER, Ron	13 + 14	S	S	S	S	
van de GOOR, Bas	5 + 19	S	S	S	S	
POSTHUMA, Jan	2 + 6		*	S	*	
van der MEULEN, Olof	6 + 21	S	*	S	S	
BLANGE, Peter	5 + 1	S	S	S		
GRABERT, Rob	0 + 0	*	*			
van de GOOR, Mike	0 + 0			*		

Team: YUG Yugoslavia

Coach: GAJIC, Zoran
Assistant Coach: CVETKOVIC, Jovica

Names	Pts + S/O	1	2	3	4	5
DJURIC, Djorde	0 + 0					
PETROVIC, Zarko	0 + 1			*	*	
BATEZ, Vladimir	10 + 27	S	S	S	S	S
TANASKOVIC, Zeljko	8 + 8	S	S	S	S	S
BRDJOVIC, Dejan	0 + 0					
MESTER, Djula	8 + 6	S	S	S	S	S
KOVAC, Slobodan	1 + 4	S	S	S	S	S
GRBIC, Nikola	3 + 2	S	S	S	S	S
GRBIC, Vladimir	14 + 20	S	S	S	S	S
JOKANOVIC, Rajko	0 + 0					
GERIC, Andrija	0 + 0				*	*
VUJEVIC, Goran	7 + 21	S	S	S	S	S

Team: ITA Italy

Coach: VELASCO, Julio
Assistant Coach: FRIGONI, Angiolino

Names	Pts + S/O	1	2	3	4	5
GARDINI, Andrea	7 + 14	S	S	S	S	
MEONI, Marco	1 + 0	S	S	S	S	
GRAVINA, Pasquale	9 + 5	*	S	S	S	
TOFOLI, Paolo	0 + 0		*	*	*	
PAPI, Samuele	7 + 16	*	S	S	S	
SARTORETTI, Andrea	8 + 15	S	S	S	S	
BRACCI, Marco	0 + 0	*				
BERNARDI, Lorenzo	10 + 13	S	S	S	S	
CANTAGALLI, Luca	0 + 0	S	*	*		
ZORZI, Andrea	3 + 1		*	*	*	
GIANI, Andrea	0 + 0					
BOVOLENTA, Vigor	2 + 1	S			*	

Men / *Messieurs*

CLASSIFICATION 5 - 8

BRA 3 - 1 ARG

Set	1	2	3	4	5	Total pts
Result	15 - 10	15 - 3	13 - 15	15 - 9		58 - 37
Duration	0:32	0:29	0:33	0:37		2:11

	Brazil				Argentina	
Att	Pts won	S/O		Att	Pts won	S/O
213	25	98	**Attacks**	226	15	100
133	17	3	**Blocks**	108	10	4
187	5		**Serves**	167	4	

1st Referee: GRE MARGARITIS, Konstantinos
2nd Referee: FIN SALONEN, Jarmo

CLASSIFICATION 5 - 8

CUB 3 - 1 BUL

Set	1	2	3	4	5	Total pts
Result	15 - 4	15 - 12	16 - 17	15 - 12		61 - 45
Duration	0:18	0:33	0:43	0:43		2:17

	Cuba				Bulgaria	
Att	Pts won	S/O		Att	Pts won	S/O
203	18	91	**Attacks**	220	15	95
120	20	5	**Blocks**	102	15	6
194	14		**Serves**	179	6	

1st Referee: CHN QU, Zheng Zhong
2nd Referee: KOR CHO, Young-Ho

FINAL 7 - 8

BUL 3 - 2 ARG

Set	1	2	3	4	5	Total pts
Result	15 - 10	15 - 10	7 - 15	7 - 15	20 - 18	64 - 68
Duration	0:34	0:25	0:23	0:22	0:18	2:02

	Bulgaria				Argentina	
Att	Pts won	S/O		Att	Pts won	S/O
176	23	67	**Attacks**	175	22	66
87	19	4	**Blocks**	71	10	3
160	8		**Serves**	164	13	

1st Referee: USA LUEBKE, Neill
2nd Referee: CAN HENRY, Peter

FINAL 5 - 6

CUB 0 - 3 BRA

Set	1	2	3	4	5	Total pts
Result	12 - 15	14 - 16	14 - 16			40 - 47
Duration	0:35	0:32	0:40			1:47

	Cuba				Brazil	
Att	Pts won	S/O		Att	Pts won	S/O
162	13	75	**Attacks**	156	20	79
76	13	2	**Blocks**	65	6	0
143	7		**Serves**	148	7	

1st Referee: FIN SALONEN, Jarmo
2nd Referee: NED SCHEFFER, Petrus Carolus

Team: BRA Brazil

Coach: GUIMARAES, Jose
Assistant Coach: MIRANDA, Marcos

Names	Pts + S/O	1	2	3	4	5
NEGRAO, Marcelo	0 + 0					
PEREIRA, Cassio Leandro	1 + 0			*	S	
GAVIO, Giovane	8 + 25	S	S	S	S	
SILVA, Paulo "Paulao"	5 + 11	S	S	S		
LIMA, Mauricio	4 + 3	S	S	S		
MARCELINO, Fabio "Pinha"	13 + 45	S	S	S	S	
GOUVEIA, Antonio "Carlao"	0 + 0					
PEREIRA, Max	0 + 0					
BITENCOURT, Nalbert	0 + 0			*		
SAMUEL, Alexandre "Tande"	10 + 9	S	S	S	S	
BERNARDO, Gilson	0 + 0					
SCHWANKE, Carlos	6 + 8	S	S	S	S	

Team: CUB Cuba

Coach: DIAZ MARINO, Juan Jesus
Assistant Coach: MORALES GONZALES, Justo L.

Names	Pts + S/O	1	2	3	4	5
BROOKS, Freddy	6 + 11	S	S	S		
VIVES, Nicolas	0 + 0			*		
VANTES, Ricardo	0 + 0	*	*	*		
DESPAIGNE, Joel	6 + 22	S	S	S	S	
SANCHEZ, Rodolfo	4 + 5				S	
DIAGO, Raul	6 + 3	S	S	S	S	
HERNANDEZ, Osvaldo	7 + 19	S	S	S	S	
ROCA, Alain	13 + 15	S	S	S	S	
HERNANDEZ, Ihosvany	9 + 18	S	S	S	S	
BELTRAN, Angel	0 + 0			*	*	
BATLE, Alexis	0 + 0					
MARIN, Lazaro	1 + 3			*		*

Team: BUL Bulgaria

Coach: KJUTCHOUKOV, Bogdan
Assistant Coach: GENTCHEV, Eugeni

Names	Pts + S/O	1	2	3	4	5
STOEV, Martin	0 + 0					
NAIDENOV, Ludmil	9 + 13	S	S	S	S	
GANEV, Lubomir	8 + 18	S	S	S	S	
TONEV, Dimo	0 + 0					
JELIAZKOV, Nikolay	10 + 11	S	S	S	S	S
HRISTOV, Plamen	1 + 0				*	
OUZOUNOV, Petar	0 + 0	*		*	*	*
NAYDENOV, Nayden	0 + 0					
IVANOV, Nikolay	4 + 2	S	S	S	S	S
GAVRILOV, Ivaylo	6 + 2				*	S
IVANOV, Evgeni	7 + 18	S	S	S	S	S
KONSTANTINOV, Plamen	5 + 7	S	S	S	S	S

Team: CUB Cuba

Coach: DIAZ MARINO, Juan Jesus
Assistant Coach: MORALES GONZALES, Justo L.

Names	Pts + S/O	1	2	3	4	5
BROOKS, Freddy	8 + 20	S	S	S		
VIVES, Nicolas	0 + 0					
VANTES, Ricardo	0 + 0	*	*	*		
DESPAIGNE, Joel	3 + 11	S	S			
SANCHEZ, Rodolfo	1 + 2			*		
DIAGO, Raul	4 + 0	S	S	S		
HERNANDEZ, Osvaldo	1 + 16	S	S	S		
ROCA, Alain	5 + 9	S	S	S		
HERNANDEZ, Ihosvany	7 + 9	S	S	S		
BELTRAN, Angel	0 + 0			*		
BATLE, Alexis	3 + 8			S		
MARIN, Lazaro	1 + 2			*		

Team: ARG Argentina

Coach: CASTELLANI, Daniel Jorge
Assistant Coach: GETZELEVICH, Carlos Alberto

Names	Pts + S/O	1	2	3	4	5
MILINKOVIC, Marcos	12 + 28	S	S	S	S	
ELGUETA, Jorge	5 + 8	S	S	S	*	
JABIF, Sebastian	2 + 13		*	S	S	
MALY, Leonardo	1 + 7	S	*	S		
QUAINI, Guillermo	0 + 14	*	S			
WEBER, Javier	2 + 2	S	S	S	S	
BORRERO, Fernando	1 + 8			*	S	
ROMANO, Alejandro	0 + 1	S				
FIRPO, Sebastian	0 + 0		*			
PEREIRA, Pablo	2 + 11	S	S		*	
MARTINEZ, Guillermo	3 + 5			S	S	S
RODRIGUEZ, Eduardo	1 + 7			*	*	S

Team: BUL Bulgaria

Coach: KJUTCHOUKOV, Bogdan
Assistant Coach: GENTCHEV, Eugeni

Names	Pts + S/O	1	2	3	4	5
STOEV, Martin	1 + 6	S	S	*	*	
NAIDENOV, Ludmil	0 + 1			*	*	*
GANEV, Lubomir	7 + 29			S	S	S
TONEV, Dimo	0 + 8	S	S		*	
JELIAZKOV, Nikolay	13 + 24	S	S	S	S	
HRISTOV, Plamen	0 + 0					
OUZOUNOV, Petar	1 + 16	*	*	S	S	
NAYDENOV, Nayden	4 + 7	S	S	S	S	
IVANOV, Nikolay	3 + 2	S	S	S	S	
GAVRILOV, Ivaylo	1 + 2	S		*		
IVANOV, Evgeni	0 + 0					
KONSTANTINOV, Plamen	6 + 6				S	S

Team: ARG Argentina

Coach: CASTELLANI, Daniel Jorge
Assistant Coach: GETZELEVICH, Carlos Alberto

Names	Pts + S/O	1	2	3	4	5
MILINKOVIC, Marcos	15 + 16	S	S	S	S	S
ELGUETA, Jorge	5 + 9	S	*	S	S	S
JABIF, Sebastian	3 + 13	S	S	S	S	S
MALY, Leonardo	7 + 7			S	S	S
QUAINI, Guillermo	3 + 2			S		
WEBER, Javier	2 + 3	S	S			
BORRERO, Fernando	0 + 4	*	S			
ROMANO, Alejandro	1 + 11	S	S			
FIRPO, Sebastian	2 + 0				*	*
PEREIRA, Pablo	7 + 4		*	S	S	S
MARTINEZ, Guillermo	0 + 0				*	*
RODRIGUEZ, Eduardo	0 + 0	*			*	*

Team: BRA Brazil

Coach: GUIMARAES, Jose
Assistant Coach: MIRANDA, Marcos

Names	Pts + S/O	1	2	3	4	5
NEGRAO, Marcelo	0 + 0					
PEREIRA, Cassio Leandro	0 + 0			*		
GAVIO, Giovane	10 + 20	S	S	S		
SILVA, Paulo "Paulao"	2 + 10	S	S	S		
LIMA, Mauricio	0 + 0	S	S	S		
MARCELINO, Fabio "Pinha"	6 + 30	S	S	S		
GOUVEIA, Antonio "Carlao"	0 + 0					
PEREIRA, Max	0 + 0	*	*	*		
BITENCOURT, Nalbert	0 + 0	*	*	*		
SAMUEL, Alexandre "Tande"	13 + 14	S	S	S		
BERNARDO, Gilson	0 + 0					
SCHWANKE, Carlos	2 + 5	S	S	S		

Men / *Messieurs*

SEMIFINALS

RUS 0 - 3 NED

Set	1	2	3	4	5	Total pts
Result	6 - 15	6 - 15	10 - 15			22 - 45
Duration	0:28	0:25	0:33			1:26

Russian Federation				Netherlands		
Att	Pts won	S/O		Att	Pts won	S/O
139	5	64	Attacks	136	19	63
59	6	2	Blocks	79	13	1
100	2		Serves	121	6	

1st Referee: CUB SANLER DIAZ, Jose
2nd Referee: GER LEUTHAEUSSER, Frank

SEMIFINALS

YUG 1 - 3 ITA

Set	1	2	3	4	5	Total pts
Result	12 - 15	15 - 8	6 - 15	7 - 15		40 - 53
Duration	0:34	0:37	0:32	0:37		2:20

Yugoslavia				Italy		
Att	Pts won	S/O		Att	Pts won	S/O
236	17	87	Attacks	215	16	82
108	11	7	Blocks	125	13	1
161	3		Serves	173	4	

1st Referee: BRA PALMEIRIM, Josebel
2nd Referee: FRA RACHARD, Patrick

FINAL - BRONZE MATCH

RUS 1 - 3 YUG

Set	1	2	3	4	5	Total pts
Result	8 - 15	15 - 7	8 - 15	9 - 15		40 - 52
Duration	0:34	0:26	0:26	0:31		1:57

Russian Federation				Yugoslavia		
Att	Pts won	S/O		Att	Pts won	S/O
185	14	71	Attacks	201	27	77
105	16	2	Blocks	80	9	4
132	2		Serves	143	4	

1st Referee: JPN SHIMOYAMA, Takashi
2nd Referee: GRE MARGARITIS, Konstantinos

FINAL - GOLD MATCH

NED 3 - 2 ITA

Set	1	2	3	4	5	Total pts
Result	15 - 12	9 - 15	16 - 14	9 - 15	17 - 15	66 - 71
Duration	0:39	0:35	0:34	0:27	0:16	2:31

Netherlands				Italy		
Att	Pts won	S/O		Att	Pts won	S/O
245	39	84	Attacks	257	41	90
128	12	8	Blocks	108	9	5
183	5		Serves	190	6	

1st Referee: CUB SANLER DIAZ, Jose
2nd Referee: ARG PAREDES, Guillermo

Team: RUS Russian Federation
Coach: PLATONOV, Viatcheslav
Assistant Coach: MOLIBOGA, Oleg

Names	Pts + S/O	1	2	3	4	5
CHATOUNOV, Oleg	1 + 2	S		*		
KHAMOUTSKICH, Vadim	1 + 1	S	S			
ORLENKO, Serguei	0 + 0					
OLIKHVER, Rouslan	2 + 7	*	S	S		
KAZAKOV, Alexei	0 + 0		*			
FOMIN, Dmitri	4 + 23	S	S	S		
TETIOUKHIN, Serguei	0 + 0		*	*		
CHICHKIN, Pavel	1 + 5	S	S	S		
OUCHAKOV, Konstantin	1 + 1	*	*	S		
DINEIKIN, Stanislav	2 + 13	S	S	S		
CHOULEPOV, Igor	0 + 10	S	S	S		
GORIOUCHEV, Valeri	1 + 4			*		

Team: NED Netherlands
Coach: ALBERDA, Joop
Assistant Coach: V. D. BURGT, Toon

Names	Pts + S/O	1	2	3	4	5
LATUHIHIN, Misha	0 + 0					
HELD, Henk-Jan	9 + 15	S	S	S		
RODENBURG, Brecht	0 + 0					
GORTZEN, Guido	6 + 9	S	S	S		
SCHUIL, Richard	0 + 0			*		
ZWERVER, Ron	1 + 9	S	S	S		
van de GOOR, Bas	5 + 17	S	S	S		
POSTHUMA, Jan	0 + 0	*		*		
van der MEULEN, Olof	15 + 12	S	S	S		
BLANGE, Peter	2 + 2	S	S	S		
GRABERT, Rob	0 + 0					
van de GOOR, Mike	0 + 0					

Team: YUG Yugoslavia
Coach: GAJIC, Zoran
Assistant Coach: CVETKOVIC, Jovica

Names	Pts + S/O	1	2	3	4	5
DURIC, Dorde	1 + 7				*	
PETROVIC, Zarko	1 + 8			*	S	
BATEZ, Vladimir	2 + 21	S	S	S	S	
TANASKOVIC, Zeljko	3 + 7	S	S	S		
BRDOVIC, Dejan	0 + 0					
MESTER, Dula	2 + 12	S	S	S	*	
KOVAC, Slobodan	6 + 13	*	S	S		
GRBIC, Nikola	4 + 2	S	S	S	S	
GRBIC, Vladimir	9 + 16	S	S	S	S	
JOKANOVIC, Rajko	0 + 1			*	*	
GERIC, Andrija	0 + 0					
VUJEVIC, Goran	3 + 7	S		*	S	

Team: ITA Italy
Coach: VELASCO, Julio
Assistant Coach: FRIGONI, Angiolino

Names	Pts + S/O	1	2	3	4	5
GARDINI, Andrea	2 + 11	S	S	S	S	
MEONI, Marco	2 + 0	S	S	S		
GRAVINA, Pasquale	2 + 2			*	S	
TOFOLI, Paolo	0 + 0	*	*			
PAPI, Samuele	2 + 3				*	
SARTORETTI, Andrea	0 + 0				*	*
BRACCI, Marco	2 + 0			*		
BERNARDI, Lorenzo	14 + 21	S	S	S	S	
CANTAGALLI, Luca	4 + 17	S	S	S	S	
ZORZI, Andrea	0 + 3	*	*		*	
GIANI, Andrea	3 + 19	S	S	S	S	
BOVOLENTA, Vigor	2 + 7	S	S	S		

Team: RUS Russian Federation
Coach: PLATONOV, Viatcheslav
Assistant Coach: MOLIBOGA, Oleg

Names	Pts + S/O	1	2	3	4	5
CHATOUNOV, Oleg	3 + 4	S	S	S	S	
KHAMOUTSKICH, Vadim	2 + 0	S	S			
ORLENKO, Serguei	0 + 0					
OLIKHVER, Rouslan	3 + 8	*	S	S	S	
KAZAKOV, Alexei	0 + 0	*				
FOMIN, Dmitri	13 + 26	S	S	S	S	
TETIOUKHIN, Serguei	2 + 3		*		*	
CHICHKIN, Pavel	4 + 10	S	S	S		
OUCHAKOV, Konstantin	0 + 0			*	*	
DINEIKIN, Stanislav	1 + 7	S			*	
CHOULEPOV, Igor	0 + 2	S				
GORIOUCHEV, Valeri	4 + 13	*	S	S	S	

Team: YUG Yugoslavia
Coach: GAJIC, Zoran
Assistant Coach: CVETKOVIC, Jovica

Names	Pts + S/O	1	2	3	4	5
DJURIC, Djorde	9 + 23	S	S	S	S	
PETROVIC, Zarko	3 + 11	S	S	S	*	
BATEZ, Vladimir	0 + 1			*	*	
TANASKOVIC, Zeljko	7 + 3			*	S	
BRDJOVIC, Dejan	0 + 0					
MESTER, Djula	2 + 1			*	*	S
KOVAC, Slobodan	4 + 9	S	S			
GRBIC, Nikola	3 + 4	S	S	S		
GRBIC, Vladimir	9 + 20	S	S	S	S	
JOKANOVIC, Rajko	0 + 0					
GERIC, Andrija	0 + 0					
VUJEVIC, Goran	3 + 9			*	S	S

Team: NED Netherlands
Coach: ALBERDA, Joop
Assistant Coach: V. D. BURGT, Toon

Names	Pts + S/O	1	2	3	4	5
LATUHIHIN, Misha	0 + 0					
HELD, Henk-Jan	9 + 18	S	S	S	S	S
RODENBURG, Brecht	0 + 0	*	*	*	*	
GORTZEN, Guido	4 + 11	S	S	S	S	
SCHUIL, Richard	2 + 6	*	*	*	*	*
ZWERVER, Ron	14 + 9	S	S	S	S	S
van de GOOR, Bas	13 + 23	S	S	S	S	S
POSTHUMA, Jan	0 + 0	*		*		*
van der MEULEN, Olof	13 + 23	S	S	S	S	S
BLANGE, Peter	1 + 2	S	S	S	S	S
GRABERT, Rob	0 + 0			*		
van de GOOR, Mike	0 + 0					*

Team: ITA Italy
Coach: VELASCO, Julio
Assistant Coach: FRIGONI, Angiolino

Names	Pts + S/O	1	2	3	4	5
GARDINI, Andrea	8 + 20	S	S	S	S	S
MEONI, Marco	0 + 0	S	S	*		*
GRAVINA, Pasquale	1 + 13	S	S	S	S	
TOFOLI, Paolo	1 + 0			*	S	S
PAPI, Samuele	12 + 15	*	S	S	S	S
SARTORETTI, Andrea	0 + 0	*	*			
BRACCI, Marco	0 + 0				*	
BERNARDI, Lorenzo	12 + 18	S	S	S	S	S
CANTAGALLI, Luca	0 + 3	S				*
ZORZI, Andrea	0 + 2	*			*	*
GIANI, Andrea	21 + 20	S	S	S	S	S
BOVOLENTA, Vigor	1 + 4			*		S

Men / *Messieurs*

GENERAL SUMMARY

Phase	Teams	Score
Quarterfinals	CUB - RUS	0 - 3
Quarterfinals	BUL - NED	1 - 3
Quarterfinals	BRA - YUG	2 - 3
Quarterfinals	ARG - ITA	1 - 3
Classification 5 - 8	BRA - ARG	3 - 1
Classification 5 - 8	CUB - BUL	3 - 1

GENERAL SUMMARY - *continued*

Phase	Teams	Score
Final 7 - 8	BUL - ARG	3 - 2
Final 5 - 6	CUB - BRA	0 - 3
Semifinals	RUS - NED	0 - 3
Semifinals	YUG - ITA	1 - 3
Final - Bronze	RUS - YUG	1 - 3
Final - Gold	NED - ITA	3 - 2

FINAL CLASSIFICATION

Rnk	Team	
1	Netherlands	**Gold**
2	Italy	**Silver**
3	Yugoslavia	**Bronze**
4	Russian Federation	
5	Brazil	
6	Cuba	
7	Bulgaria	
8	Argentina	

Volleyball—Indoor / *Volleyball — En salle*
Women / *Dames*

PRELIMINARIES - GROUP A

NED 0 - 3 CHN

Set	1	2	3	4	5	Total pts
Result	10 - 15	5 - 15	7 - 15			22 - 45
Duration	0:24	0:20	0:29			1:13

	Netherlands				People's Republic of China	
Att	Pts won	S/O		Att	Pts won	S/O
141	10	37	**Attacks**	130	22	40
50	4	2	**Blocks**	48	8	2
73	1		**Serves**	95	1	

1st Referee: BRA PALMEIRIM, Josebel
2nd Referee: RUS ZHARIKOV, Guennadi

PRELIMINARIES - GROUP A

JPN 0 - 3 KOR

Set	1	2	3	4	5	Total pts
Result	10 - 15	12 - 15	10 - 15			32 - 45
Duration	0:30	0:36	0:31			1:37

	Japan				Korea	
Att	Pts won	S/O		Att	Pts won	S/O
189	16	44	**Attacks**	198	25	45
79	5	2	**Blocks**	98	8	4
97	1		**Serves**	108	0	

1st Referee: ARG PAREDES, Guillermo
2nd Referee: ITA TROIA, Pasquale

PRELIMINARIES - GROUP A

USA 3 - 0 UKR

Set	1	2	3	4	5	Total pts
Result	15 - 8	15 - 5	15 - 11			45 - 24
Duration	0:17	0:24	0:32			1:13

	United States of America				Ukraine	
Att	Pts won	S/O		Att	Pts won	S/O
127	22	35	**Attacks**	127	10	31
67	10	4	**Blocks**	67	7	3
97	5		**Serves**	77	1	

1st Referee: AUS TURNER, Dean
2nd Referee: THA CHAREONPONG, Songsak

Team: NED Netherlands
Coach: GOEDKOOP, Bert
Assistant Coach: VERMEULEN, Gido

Names	Pts + S/O	1	2	3	4	5
FLEURKE, Jerine	0 + 0					
van HINTUM, Saskia	0 + 0					
BRINKMAN, Erna	4 + 7	S	S	S		
BOERSMA, Cintha	2 + 3	S	S	S		
MACHOVCAK, Irena	2 + 4	S	S	S		
de JONG, Marjolein	0 + 0			*		
WEERSING, Henriette	4 + 17	S	S	S		
LEENSTRA, Marrit	0 + 0					
LEFERINK, Elles	0 + 0	*		*		
van THIEL, Claudia	0 + 0					
FLEDDERUS, Riette	2 + 1	S	S	S		
VISSER, Ingrid	1 + 7	S	S	S		

Team: JPN Japan
Coach: YOSHIDA, Kuniaki
Assistant Coach: YOSHIKAWA, Masahiro

Names	Pts + S/O	1	2	3	4	5
NAKANISHI, Chieko	0 + 3	S	S	S		
OBAYASHI, Motoko	7 + 19	S	S	S		
NAGATOMI, Aki	0 + 0					
YAMAUCHI, Mika	0 + 0	S				
YOSHIHARA, Tomoko	6 + 6	S	S	S		
TORII, Chiho	0 + 0					
NAKAMURA, Kazumi	1 + 0	*	*	*		
SAKAMOTO, Kiyomi	0 + 0	*	*			
SAIKI, Mika	3 + 4	*	S	S		
TAJIMI, Asako	3 + 4	S	S	S		
HOSHINO, Kayo	0 + 0					
OGAKE, Ikumi	2 + 10	S	S	S		

Team: USA United States of America
Coach: LISKEVYCH, Taras
Assistant Coach: BERZINS, Aldis

Names	Pts + S/O	1	2	3	4	5
WILLIAMS, Tonya	1 + 5	S	S	S		
ZETTERLUND, Yoko	0 + 0		*			
WEISHOFF, Paula	6 + 3		*	S		
KEMNER, Caren	1 + 2		*	*		
ENDICOTT, Lori	1 + 0	S	S	S		
KLEIN, Kristin	0 + 0	*				
ODEN, Beverly	9 + 3	S	S	S		
LILEY, Tammy	5 + 4	S	S			
ODEN, Elaina	3 + 6	S	S	*		
SCOTT, Danielle	2 + 5			S		
CROSS-BATTLE, Tara	9 + 8	S	S	S		
YOUNGS, Elaine	0 + 3			*		

Team: CHN People's Republic of China
Coach: LANG, Ping
Assistant Coach: CHEN, Zhong He

Names	Pts + S/O	1	2	3	4	5
LAI, Yawen	10 + 3	S	S	S		
LI, Yan	6 + 9	S	S	S		
CUI, Yongmei	4 + 6	S	S	S		
ZHU, Yunying	0 + 0					
WU, Yongmei	0 + 0					
WANG, Yi	5 + 11	S	S	S		
HE, Qi	1 + 0	S	S	S		
PAN, Wenli	0 + 0					
LIU, Xiaoning	0 + 0					
WANG, Ziling	0 + 0					
SUN, Yue	5 + 13	S	S	S		
WANG, Lina	0 + 0					

Team: KOR Korea
Coach: KIM, Cheol-Yong
Assistant Coach: SHIN, Il-Kyoun

Names	Pts + S/O	1	2	3	4	5
YOO, Yon-Kyung	0 + 0					
CHANG, Yoon-Hee	7 + 8	S	S	S		
LEE, Soo-Jung	2 + 1	S	S	S		
KANG, Hye-Mi	0 + 0	*	*	*		
CHUNG, Sun-Hye	5 + 14	S	S	S		
KIM, Nam-Soon	7 + 6	S	S	S		
PARK, Soo-Jeong	7 + 6	S	S	S		
HONG, Ji-Yeon	4 + 12	S	S	S		
LEE, In-Sook	0 + 0					
EOH, Yeon-Soon	0 + 0					
CHANG, So-Yun	1 + 2	*	*	*		
CHOI, Kwang-Hee	0 + 0	*				

Team: UKR Ukraine
Coach: YEGIAZAROV, Gariy
Assistant Coach: FILICHTINSKI, Igor

Names	Pts + S/O	1	2	3	4	5
KOLOMIYETS, Olga	0 + 0			*		
MATESHIK, Vita	1 + 1		*	S		
POLYAKOVA, Mariya	1 + 8	S	S	S		
SYDORENKO, Olena	4 + 10	S	S	S		
IVANYUSHKYNA, Tetyana	3 + 6	S	S	S		
MYLOSSERDOVA, Regina	0 + 0		*			
KRAVETS, Alla	0 + 0					
PAVLOVA, Olga	2 + 0	S	S	S		
BOZHENOVA, Nataliya	4 + 9	S	S	S		
FOMINA, Olexandra	3 + 0	S	S	*		
BUYEVA, Yuliya	0 + 0					
KRYVONOSSOVA, Olena	0 + 0					

Women / *Dames*

PRELIMINARIES - GROUP A

CHN 3 - 2 KOR

Set	1	2	3	4	5	Total pts
Result	17 - 16	16 - 14	2 - 15	13 - 15	15 - 13	63 - 73
Duration	0:40	0:40	0:23	0:44	0:15	2:42

People's Republic of China				Korea		
Att	Pts won	S/O		Att	Pts won	S/O
314	30	93	Attacks	342	45	87
160	17	6	Blocks	133	7	3
168	2		Serves	181	5	

1st Referee: GER LEUTHAEUSSER, Frank
2nd Referee: ESP GIMENEZ, Gabriel

PRELIMINARIES - GROUP A

UKR 0 - 3 JPN

Set	1	2	3	4	5	Total pts
Result	9 - 15	5 - 15	4 - 15			18 - 45
Duration	0:33	0:21	0:18			1:12

Ukraine				Japan		
Att	Pts won	S/O		Att	Pts won	S/O
132	5	42	Attacks	131	19	48
67	5	7	Blocks	50	7	0
78	2		Serves	104	7	

1st Referee: CAN HENRY, Peter
2nd Referee: BRA PALMEIRIM, Josebel

PRELIMINARIES - GROUP A

NED 1 - 3 USA

Set	1	2	3	4	5	Total pts
Result	15 - 12	10 - 15	15 - 17	7 - 15		47 - 59
Duration	0:25	0:27	0:35	0:31		1:58

Netherlands				United States of America		
Att	Pts won	S/O		Att	Pts won	S/O
206	16	53	Attacks	218	30	52
95	12	5	Blocks	89	10	3
127	6		Serves	138	3	

1st Referee: ARG PAREDES, Guillermo
2nd Referee: ITA TRIOA, Pasquale

PRELIMINARIES - GROUP A

JPN 0 - 3 NED

Set	1	2	3	4	5	Total pts
Result	3 - 15	10 - 15	3 - 15			16 - 45
Duration	0:23	0:31	0:23			1:17

Japan				Netherlands		
Att	Pts won	S/O		Att	Pts won	S/O
151	6	45	Attacks	139	21	52
53	1	1	Blocks	66	11	3
82	3		Serves	109	4	

1st Referee: BRA PALMEIRIM, Josebel
2nd Referee: CAN HENRY, Peter

Team: CHN People's Republic of China
Coach: LANG, Ping
Assistant Coach: CHEN, Zhong He

Names	Pts + S/O	1	2	3	4	5
LAI, Yawen	6 + 12	S	S	S	S	S
LI, Yan	13 + 21	S	S	S	S	S
CUI, Yongmei	6 + 14	S	S	S	S	S
ZHU, Yunying	0 + 0					
WU, Yongmei	3 + 4			*	*	S
WANG, Yi	4 + 21	S	S	S	S	
HE, Qi	2 + 1	S	S	S	S	
PAN, Wenli	0 + 0					
LIU, Xiaoning	0 + 0					
WANG, Ziling	2 + 5		*		*	
SUN, Yue	13 + 21	S	S	S	S	
WANG, Lina	0 + 0			*		

Team: UKR Ukraine
Coach: YEGIAZAROV, Gariy
Assistant Coach: FILICHTINSKI, Igor

Names	Pts + S/O	1	2	3	4	5
KOLOMIYETS, Olga	0 + 0					
MATESHIK, Vita	0 + 0	*	*	S		
POLYAKOVA, Mariya	2 + 2	S	S			
SYDORENKO, Olena	4 + 16	S	S	S		
IVANYUSHKYNA, Tetyana	0 + 8	S	S	S		
MYLOSSERDOVA, Regina	1 + 5		*	S		
KRAVETS, Alla	0 + 0					
PAVLOVA, Olga	0 + 2	S	S	S		
BOZHENOVA, Nataliya	2 + 5	S	S			
FOMINA, Olexandra	3 + 11	S	S	S		
BUYEVA, Yuliya	0 + 0					
KRYVONOSSOVA, Olena	0 + 0					

Team: NED Netherlands
Coach: GOEDKOOP, Bert
Assistant Coach: VERMEULEN, Gido

Names	Pts + S/O	1	2	3	4	5
FLEURKE, Jerine	0 + 0					
van HINTUM, Saskia	0 + 0	*			*	
BRINKMAN, Erna	5 + 11	S	S	S	S	
BOERSMA, Cintha	9 + 7	S	S	S	S	
MACHOVCAK, Irena	3 + 6	S	S	S	S	
de JONG, Marjolein	0 + 0	*		*		
WEERSING, Henriette	6 + 20	S	S	S	S	
LEENSTRA, Marrit	0 + 1				*	
LEFERINK, Elles	0 + 2	*	*	*	*	
van THIEL, Claudia	0 + 0			*		
FLEDDERUS, Riette	2 + 2	S	S	S	S	
VISSER, Ingrid	9 + 9	S	S	S	S	

Team: JPN Japan
Coach: YOSHIDA, Kuniaki
Assistant Coach: YOSHIKAWA, Masahiro

Names	Pts + S/O	1	2	3	4	5
NAKANISHI, Chieko	1 + 2	S	S	S		
OBAYASHI, Motoko	2 + 12	S	S	S		
NAGATOMI, Aki	0 + 0	*		*		
YAMAUCHI, Mika	0 + 0					
YOSHIHARA, Tomoko	4 + 12	S	S	S		
TORII, Chiho	0 + 0					
NAKAMURA, Kazumi	0 + 1	S	*	*		
SAKAMOTO, Kiyomi	0 + 0	*	*	*		
SAIKI, Mika	2 + 6	*	S	S		
TAJIMI, Asako	0 + 11	S	S	S		
HOSHINO, Kayo	0 + 0					
OGAKE, Ikumi	1 + 2	S	S	S		

Team: KOR Korea
Coach: KIM, Cheol-Yong
Assistant Coach: SHIN, Il-Kyoun

Names	Pts + S/O	1	2	3	4	5
YOO, Yon-Kyung	0 + 0					
CHANG, Yoon-Hee	13 + 24	S	S	S	S	S
LEE, Soo-Jung	1 + 1	S	S	S	S	S
KANG, Hye-Mi	0 + 0	*	*	*	*	*
CHUNG, Sun-Hye	12 + 17	S	S	S	S	S
KIM, Nam-Soon	13 + 12	S	S	S	S	S
PARK, Soo-Jeong	12 + 17	S	S	S	S	S
HONG, Ji-Yeon	6 + 16	S	S	S	S	S
LEE, In-Sook	0 + 0					
EOH, Yeon-Soon	0 + 0					
CHANG, So-Yun	0 + 3	*	*	*	*	*
CHOI, Kwang-Hee	0 + 0		*	*	*	

Team: USA United States of America
Coach: LISKEVYCH, Taras
Assistant Coach: BERZINS, Aldis

Names	Pts + S/O	1	2	3	4	5
WILLIAMS, Tonya	1 + 3	S	S		*	
ZETTERLUND, Yoko	0 + 0	*		*		
WEISHOFF, Paula	3 + 2	*	*	*	*	
KEMNER, Caren	0 + 0	*		*	*	
ENDICOTT, Lori	1 + 3	S	S	S	S	
KLEIN, Kristin	0 + 0	*				
ODEN, Beverly	1 + 7	S	S	S	S	
LILEY, Tammy	7 + 11	S	S	S	S	
ODEN, Elaina	11 + 10	S	S	S	S	
SCOTT, Danielle	0 + 0					
CROSS-BATTLE, Tara	14 + 15	S	S	S	S	
YOUNGS, Elaine	5 + 4		*	S	S	

Team: NED Netherlands
Coach: GOEDKOOP, Bert
Assistant Coach: VERMEULEN, Gido

Names	Pts + S/O	1	2	3	4	5
FLEURKE, Jerine	0 + 0					
van HINTUM, Saskia	0 + 0					
BRINKMAN, Erna	8 + 10	S	S	S		
BOERSMA, Cintha	4 + 12	S	S	S		
MACHOVCAK, Irena	6 + 6	S	S	S		
de JONG, Marjolein	1 + 0	*	*	*		
WEERSING, Henriette	10 + 18	S	S	S		
LEENSTRA, Marrit	0 + 0					
LEFERINK, Elles	0 + 0	*	*	*		
van THIEL, Claudia	0 + 0					
FLEDDERUS, Riette	4 + 1	S	S	S		
VISSER, Ingrid	3 + 8	S	S	S		

Volleyball—Indoor / *Volleyball — En salle*

LINDA J WILLIAMS • LINDA M WILLIAMS • LINDA M WILLIAMS • LINDA S WILLIAMS • LLOYD D WILLIAMS • LOREEN P WILLIAMS • LORI A. WILLIAMS • LORRAINE WILLIAMS • LYDIA WILLIAMS • LYN A WILLIAMS • LYNETTE WILLIAMS • M SCOT WILLIAMS • MACEO C WILLIAMS • MANUEL A WILLIAMS • MAPLE R WILLIAMS • MARCIA V WILLIAMS • MARGARET K WILLIAMS • MARGARET M WILLIAMS • MARGARET M WILLIAMS • MARIAN A WILLIAMS • MARIE WILLIAMS • MARIE WILLIAMS • MARILYN D WILLIAMS •

Women / *Dames*

PRELIMINARIES - GROUP A

USA 1 - 3 CHN

Set	1	2	3	4	5	Total pts
Result	8 - 15	2 - 15	15 - 12	12 - 15		37 - 57
Duration	0:25	0:21	0:31	0:36		1:53

United States of America				People's Republic of China		
Att	Pts won	S/O		Att	Pts won	S/O
224	19	63	Attacks	204	23	53
104	8	1	Blocks	94	13	4
115	0		Serves	134	7	

1st Referee: ESP GIMENEZ, Gabriel
2nd Referee: FRA RACHARD, Patrick

PRELIMINARIES - GROUP A

KOR 3 - 0 UKR

Set	1	2	3	4	5	Total pts
Result	15 - 3	15 - 10	15 - 7			45 - 20
Duration	0:15	0:31	0:23			1:09

Korea				Ukraine		
Att	Pts won	S/O		Att	Pts won	S/O
132	22	34	Attacks	143	8	44
57	5	5	Blocks	47	1	2
96	10		Serves	72	4	

1st Referee: CUB SANLER DIAZ, Jose
2nd Referee: GER LEUTHAEUSSER, Frank

PRELIMINARIES - GROUP A

NED 3 - 1 KOR

Set	1	2	3	4	5	Total pts
Result	15 - 11	15 - 12	7 - 15	15 - 8		52 - 46
Duration	0:32	0:37	0:21	0:30		2:00

Netherlands				Korea		
Att	Pts won	S/O		Att	Pts won	S/O
264	24	75	Attacks	270	21	68
124	15	6	Blocks	105	7	4
146	6		Serves	141	2	

1st Referee: ARG PAREDES, Guillermo
2nd Referee: CUB SANLER DIAZ, Jose

PRELIMINARIES - GROUP A

CHN 3 - 0 UKR

Set	1	2	3	4	5	Total pts
Result	15 - 4	15 - 4	15 - 6			45 - 14
Duration	0:19	0:22	0:22			1:03

People's Republic of China				Ukraine		
Att	Pts won	S/O		Att	Pts won	S/O
108	20	35	Attacks	129	2	42
58	9	0	Blocks	49	2	2
95	5		Serves	65	6	

1st Referee: KSA al-KHLAIFI, Abdullah
2nd Referee: MEX NAVA ABARCA, Fernando

Team: USA United States of America
Coach: LISKEVYCH, Taras
Assistant Coach: BERZINS, Aldis

Names	Pts + S/O	1	2	3	4	5
WILLIAMS, Tonya	6 + 7	S	S	S	S	
ZETTERLUND, Yoko	1 + 1	*	*	S	S	
WEISHOFF, Paula	1 + 5		*	*	*	
KEMNER, Caren	2 + 1	*			*	
ENDICOTT, Lori	0 + 0	S	S			
KLEIN, Kristin	0 + 0			*	*	
ODEN, Beverly	0 + 1	S	S			
LILEY, Tammy	2 + 15	S	S	S	S	
ODEN, Elaina	6 + 17	S	S	S	S	
SCOTT, Danielle	2 + 12		*	S	S	
CROSS-BATTLE, Tara	7 + 5	S	S	S	S	
YOUNGS, Elaine	0 + 0		*			

Team: KOR Korea
Coach: KIM, Cheol-Yong
Assistant Coach: SHIN, Il-Kyoun

Names	Pts + S/O	1	2	3	4	5
YOO, Yon-Kyung	0 + 0					
CHANG, Yoon-Hee	5 + 7	S	S	S		
LEE, Soo-Jung	3 + 0	S	S	S		
KANG, Hye-Mi	0 + 0	*	*	*		
CHUNG, Sun-Hye	7 + 9	S	S	S		
KIM, Nam-Soon	6 + 9	S	S	S		
PARK, Soo-Jeong	9 + 7	S	S	S		
HONG, Ji-Yeon	6 + 7	S	S	S		
LEE, In-Sook	0 + 0					
EOH, Yeon-Soon	0 + 0					
CHANG, So-Yun	1 + 3	*	*	*		
CHOI, Kwang-Hee	0 + 0		*	*		

Team: NED Netherlands
Coach: GOEDKOOP, Bert
Assistant Coach: VERMEULEN, Gido

Names	Pts + S/O	1	2	3	4	5
FLEURKE, Jerine	0 + 0					
van HINTUM, Saskia	0 + 0					
BRINKMAN, Erna	7 + 13	S	S	S	S	
BOERSMA, Cintha	4 + 15	S	S	S	S	
MACHOVCAK, Irena	1 + 7	S	S	S	S	
de JONG, Marjolein	0 + 1	*	*		*	
WEERSING, Henriette	19 + 35	S	S	S	S	
LEENSTRA, Marrit	0 + 0					
LEFERINK, Elles	0 + 0	*	*	*	*	
van THIEL, Claudia	0 + 0					
FLEDDERUS, Riette	7 + 3	S	S	S	S	
VISSER, Ingrid	7 + 7	S	S	S	S	

Team: CHN People's Republic of China
Coach: LANG, Ping
Assistant Coach: CHEN, Zhong He

Names	Pts + S/O	1	2	3	4	5
LAI, Yawen	5 + 4	S	S	S		
LI, Yan	9 + 9	S	S	S		
CUI, Yongmei	9 + 5	S	S	S		
ZHU, Yunying	0 + 0					
WU, Yongmei	3 + 6		*	S		
WANG, Yi	4 + 1	S	S			
HE, Qi	0 + 0	S	S	S		
PAN, Wenli	0 + 0					
LIU, Xiaoning	0 + 0					
WANG, Ziling	0 + 0					
SUN, Yue	4 + 10	S	S	S		
WANG, Lina	0 + 0					

Team: CHN People's Republic of China
Coach: LANG, Ping
Assistant Coach: CHEN, Zhong He

Names	Pts + S/O	1	2	3	4	5
LAI, Yawen	4 + 10	S	S	S	S	
LI, Yan	6 + 16	S	S	S	S	
CUI, Yongmei	10 + 6	S	S	S	S	
ZHU, Yunying	0 + 0					
WU, Yongmei	0 + 0					
WANG, Yi	8 + 5	S	S	S	S	
HE, Qi	1 + 2	S	S	S	S	
PAN, Wenli	0 + 0					
LIU, Xiaoning	0 + 0					
WANG, Ziling	0 + 0			*	*	
SUN, Yue	14 + 16	S	S	S	S	
WANG, Lina	0 + 2				*	

Team: UKR Ukraine
Coach: YEGIAZAROV, Gariy
Assistant Coach: FILICHTINSKI, Igor

Names	Pts + S/O	1	2	3	4	5
KOLOMIYETS, Olga	2 + 9	*	S	S		
MATESHIK, Vita	0 + 0	S				
POLYAKOVA, Mariya	1 + 9	S	S	S		
SYDORENKO, Olena	7 + 5	S	S	S		
IVANYUSHKYNA, Tetyana	0 + 13	S	S	S		
MYLOSSERDOVA, Regina	3 + 10	S	S	S		
KRAVETS, Alla	0 + 0					
PAVLOVA, Olga	0 + 0	S	S	S		
BOZHENOVA, Nataliya	0 + 0					
FOMINA, Olexandra	0 + 0					
BUYEVA, Yuliya	0 + 0					
KRYVONOSSOVA, Olena	0 + 0					

Team: KOR Korea
Coach: KIM, Cheol-Yong
Assistant Coach: SHIN, Il-Kyoun

Names	Pts + S/O	1	2	3	4	5
YOO, Yon-Kyung	0 + 0					
CHANG, Yoon-Hee	7 + 18	S	S	S	S	
LEE, Soo-Jung	1 + 2	S	S			
KANG, Hye-Mi	0 + 1	*	*	S	S	
CHUNG, Sun-Hye	4 + 17	S	S	S	S	
KIM, Nam-Soon	6 + 6	S	S	S	S	
PARK, Soo-Jeong	6 + 15	S	S	S	S	
HONG, Ji-Yeon	4 + 8	S	S	S	S	
LEE, In-Sook	0 + 0					
EOH, Yeon-Soon	0 + 0					
CHANG, So-Yun	2 + 5	*	*		*	
CHOI, Kwang-Hee	0 + 0	*	*	*	*	

Team: UKR Ukraine
Coach: YEGIAZAROV, Gariy
Assistant Coach: FILICHTINSKI, Igor

Names	Pts + S/O	1	2	3	4	5
KOLOMIYETS, Olga	0 + 13	S	S	S		
MATESHIK, Vita	0 + 0			*		
POLYAKOVA, Mariya	2 + 6	S	S	S		
SYDORENKO, Olena	2 + 5	S	S	S		
IVANYUSHKYNA, Tetyana	2 + 12	S	S	S		
MYLOSSERDOVA, Regina	0 + 0					
KRAVETS, Alla	0 + 0					
PAVLOVA, Olga	2 + 4	S	S	S		
BOZHENOVA, Nataliya	0 + 0					
FOMINA, Olexandra	0 + 0					
BUYEVA, Yuliya	0 + 0					
KRYVONOSSOVA, Olena	2 + 4	S	S	S		

Women / *Dames*

PRELIMINARIES - GROUP A

USA 3 - 0 JPN

Set	1	2	3	4	5	Total pts
Result	15 - 11	15 - 7	15 - 12			45 - 30
Duration	0:32	0:32	0:34			1:38

United States of America				Japan		
Att	Pts won	S/O		Att	Pts won	S/O
195	19	53	**Attacks**	216	11	50
113	12	3	**Blocks**	69	6	5
113	3		**Serves**	100	5	

1st Referee: RUS ZHARIKOV, Guennadi
2nd Referee: GER LEUTHAEUSSER, Frank

PRELIMINARIES - GROUP A

JPN 0 - 3 CHN

Set	1	2	3	4	5	Total pts
Result	14 - 16	11 - 15	10 - 15			35 - 46
Duration	0:45	0:28	0:28			1:41

Japan				People's Republic of China		
Att	Pts won	S/O		Att	Pts won	S/O
207	23	66	**Attacks**	188	25	66
65	4	1	**Blocks**	99	12	2
116	3		**Serves**	124	1	

1st Referee: GER LEUTHAEUSSER, Frank
2nd Referee: KSA al-KHLAIFI, Abdullah

PRELIMINARIES - GROUP A

KOR 1 - 3 USA

Set	1	2	3	4	5	Total pts
Result	15 - 10	13 - 15	9 - 15	3 - 15		40 - 55
Duration	0:35	0:33	0:25	0:21		1:54

Korea				United States of America		
Att	Pts won	S/O		Att	Pts won	S/O
228	17	67	**Attacks**	230	31	68
89	9	3	**Blocks**	129	16	4
121	1		**Serves**	135	3	

1st Referee: GRE MARGARITIS, Konstantinos
2nd Referee: ARG PAREDES, Guillermo

PRELIMINARIES - GROUP A

UKR 0 - 3 NED

Set	1	2	3	4	5	Total pts
Result	3 - 15	5 - 15	5 - 15			13 - 45
Duration	0:17	0:24	0:20			1:01

Ukraine				Netherlands		
Att	Pts won	S/O		Att	Pts won	S/O
108	5	32	**Attacks**	104	20	36
43	2	3	**Blocks**	56	11	2
64	1		**Serves**	95	5	

1st Referee: ITA TROIA, Pasquale
2nd Referee: FRA RACHARD, Patrick

Team: USA United States of America
Coach: LISKEVYCH, Taras
Assistant Coach: BERZINS, Aldis

Names	Pts + S/O	1	2	3	4	5
WILLIAMS, Tonya	0 + 0	S				
ZETTERLUND, Yoko	3 + 1	*	S	S		
WEISHOFF, Paula	2 + 3	*	*	*		
KEMNER, Caren	6 + 4	*	*	*		
ENDICOTT, Lori	0 + 0	S				
KLEIN, Kristin	0 + 0		*			
ODEN, Beverly	3 + 9	S	S	S		
LILEY, Tammy	4 + 9	S	S	S		
ODEN, Elaina	6 + 10	S	S	*		
SCOTT, Danielle	4 + 5			S		
CROSS-BATTLE, Tara	4 + 9	S	S	S		
YOUNGS, Elaine	2+ 6	*	S	S		

Team: JPN Japan
Coach: YOSHIDA, Kuniaki
Assistant Coach: YOSHIKAWA, Masahiro

Names	Pts + S/O	1	2	3	4	5
NAKANISHI, Chieko	2 + 3	S	S	S		
OBAYASHI, Motoko	9 + 17	S	S	S		
NAGATOMI, Aki	1 + 0			*		
YAMAUCHI, Mika	3 + 6	*		S		
YOSHIHARA, Tomoko	2 + 9	S	S	S		
TORII, Chiho	1 + 2		*	*		
NAKAMURA, Kazumi	0 + 0	*		*		
SAKAMOTO, Kiyomi	0 + 0			*		
SAIKI, Mika	4 + 10	S	S			
TAJIMI, Asako	6 + 13,	S	S	S		
HOSHINO, Kayo	0 + 0					
OGAKE, Ikumi	2 + 7	S	S	S		

Team: KOR Korea
Coach: KIM, C heol-Yong
Assistant Coach: SHIN, Il-Kyoun

Names	Pts + S/O	1	2	3	4	5
YOO, Yon-Kyung	0 + 0					
CHANG, Yoon-Hee	5 + 3	S		*		
LEE, Soo-Jung	3 + 3	S	S	S	S	
KANG, Hye-Mi	0 + 0	*	*	*	*	
CHUNG, Sun-Hye	5 + 18	S	S	S	S	
KIM, Nam-Soon	5 + 14	S	S	S	S	
PARK, Soo-Jeong	3 + 9	S	S	S	S	
HONG, Ji-Yeon	4 + 13	S	S	S	S	
LEE, In-Sook	0 + 0					
EOH, Yeon-Soon	0 + 0					
CHANG, So-Yun	0 + 3	*	*	*	*	
CHOI, Kwang-Hee	2 + 7 ,	*	S	S	S	

Team: UKR Ukraine
Coach: YEGIAZAROV, Gariy
Assistant Coach: FILICHTINSKI, Igor

Names	Pts + S/O	1	2	3	4	5
KOLOMIYETS, Olga	3 + 3	S	S			
MATESHIK, Vita	0 + 4		*	S		
POLYAKOVA, Mariya	1 + 1	S				
SYDORENKO, Olena	2 + 18	S	S	S		
IVANYUSHKYNA, Tetyana	0 + 6	S	S	S		
MYLOSSERDOVA, Regina	0 + 0					
KRAVETS, Alla	1 + 0			S		
PAVLOVA, Olga	0 + 0	S	S			
BOZHENOVA, Nataliya	0 + 0					
FOMINA, Olexandra	0 + 0					
BUYEVA, Yuliya	0 + 0		S	S		
KRYVONOSSOVA, Olena	1 + 3	S	S	S		

Team: JPN Japan
Coach: YOSHIDA, Kuniaki
Assistant Coach: YOSHIKAWA, Masahiro

Names	Pts + S/O	1	2	3	4	5
NAKANISHI, Chieko	1 + 1	S	S	S		
OBAYASHI, Motoko	5 + 12	S	S	S		
NAGATOMI, Aki	1 + 3		*			
YAMAUCHI, Mika	0 + 0			*		
YOSHIHARA, Tomoko	2 + 9	S	S	S		
TORII, Chiho	0 + 0					
NAKAMURA, Kazumi	0 + 0	*	*	*		
SAKAMOTO, Kiyomi	0 + 0	*		*		
SAIKI, Mika	4 + 11	S	S	S		
TAJIMI, Asako	4 + 8	S	S	S		
HOSHINO, Kayo	0 + 0	*				
OGAKE, Ikumi	5 + 11	S	S	S		

Team: CHN People's Republic of China
Coach: LANG, Ping
Assistant Coach: CHEN, Zhong He

Names	Pts + S/O	1	2	3	4	5
LAI, Yawen	8 + 10	S	S	S		
LI, Yan	10 + 15	S	S	S		
CUI, Yongmei	6 + 13	S	S	S		
ZHU, Yunying	0 + 0					
WU, Yongmei	4 + 10	*	*	S		
WANG, Yi	0 + 2	S	S			
HE, Qi	3 + 0	S	S	S		
PAN, Wenli	0 + 0					
LIU, Xiaoning	0 + 0					
WANG, Ziling	0 + 1			*		
SUN, Yue	1 + 12	S	S	*		
WANG, Lina	6 + 5		*	S		

Team: USA United States of America
Coach: LISKEVYCH, Taras
Assistant Coach: BERZINS, Aldis

Names	Pts + S/O	1	2	3	4	5
WILLIAMS, Tonya	6 + 5	*	S	S	S	
ZETTERLUND, Yoko	3 + 2	S	S	S		
WEISHOFF, Paula	1 + 2	*	*	*	*	
KEMNER, Caren	0 + 0	*				
ENDICOTT, Lori	1 + 0			*	S	
KLEIN, Kristin	0 + 0				*	
ODEN, Beverly	2 + 2	S	S			
LILEY, Tammy	7 + 15	S	S	S		
ODEN, Elaina	7 + 15	S	S	S		
SCOTT, Danielle	5 + 12		*	S	S	
CROSS-BATTLE, Tara	16 + 19	S	S	S		
YOUNGS, Elaine	2 + 0	S				

Team: NED Netherlands
Coach: GOEDKOOP, Bert
Assistant Coach: VERMEULEN, Gido

Names	Pts + S/O	1	2	3	4	5
FLEURKE, Jerine	2 + 3			S		
van HINTUM, Saskia	0 + 0					
BRINKMAN, Erna	10 + 8	S	S	S		
BOERSMA, Cintha	7 + 6	S	S	S		
MACHOVCAK, Irena	3 + 4	S	S			
de JONG, Marjolein	0 + 0					
WEERSING, Henriette	4 + 10	S	S	S		
LEENSTRA, Marrit	1 + 1			*		
LEFERINK, Elles	1 + 2		*	*		
van THIEL, Claudia	0 + 0			*		
FLEDDERUS, Riette	1 + 0	S	S	S		
VISSER, Ingrid	7 + 4	S	S	S		

Women / *Dames*

FINAL CLASSIFICATION - GROUP A

Rnk	Team	Pts	Games			Sets			Points		
			Played	Won	Lost	Won	Lost	W/L	For	Against	F/A
1	CHN	10	5	5	0	15	3	5.00	256	181	1.41
2	USA	9	5	4	1	13	5	2.60	241	198	1.21
3	NED	8	5	3	2	10	7	1.42	211	179	1.17
4	KOR	7	5	2	3	10	9	1.11	249	222	1.12
5	JPN	6	5	1	4	3	12	0.25	158	199	0.79
6	UKR	5	5	0	5	0	15	0.00	89	225	0.39

PRELIMINARIES - GROUP B

RUS 3 - 0 GER

Set	1	2	3	4	5	Total pts
Result	15 - 5	15 - 10	15 - 7			45 - 22
Duration	0:20	0:27	0:21			1:08

Russian Federation				Germany		
Att	Pts won	S/O		Att	Pts won	S/O
133	22	44	Attacks	125	7	40
55	11	1	Blocks	43	7	1
102	4		Serves	80	0	

1st Referee: GRE MARGARITIS, Konstantinos
2nd Referee: JPN SHIMOYAMA, Takashi

PRELIMINARIES - GROUP B

CAN 0 - 3 CUB

Set	1	2	3	4	5	Total pts
Result	8 - 15	8 - 15	5 - 15			21 - 45
Duration	0:20	0:23	0:21			1:04

Canada				Cuba		
Att	Pts won	S/O		Att	Pts won	S/O
107	5	22	Attacks	95	18	28
41	3	2	Blocks	47	10	0
65	4		Serves	87	2	

1st Referee: MEX NAVA ABARCA, Fernando
2nd Referee: ESP GIMENEZ, Gabriel

PRELIMINARIES - GROUP B

BRA 3 - 0 PER

Set	1	2	3	4	5	Total pts
Result	15 - 7	15 - 1	15 - 5			45 - 13
Duration	0:21	0:15	0:24			1:00

Brazil				Peru		
Att	Pts won	S/O		Att	Pts won	S/O
99	18	31	Attacks	100	6	28
46	10	3	Blocks	28	2	1
88	5		Serves	59	0	

1st Referee: FRA RACHARD, Patrick
2nd Referee: NED SCHEFFER, Petrus Carolus

Team: RUS Russian Federation

Coach: KARPOL, Nikolai
Assistant Coach: OMELTCHENKO, Mikhail

Names	Pts + S/O	1	2	3	4	5
OGIENKO, Valentina	0 + 0	*		*		
MOROZOVA, Natalia	3 + 4	S	S	S		
NIKOULINA, Marina	1 + 1	S	S	S		
BATOUKHTINA, Elena	1 + 7	S	S	S		
ILCHENKO, Irina	13 + 14	S	S	S		
GODINA, Elena	0 + 0			*		
MENCHOVA, Tatiana	0 + 0					
ARTAMONOVA, Evguenia	13 + 11	S	S	S		
TICHTCHENKO, Elizaveta	6 + 8	S	S	S		
TIMONOVA, Ioulia	0 + 0					
GRATCHEVA, Tatiana	0 + 0		*	*		
SOKOLOVA, Liubov	0 + 0					

Team: CAN Canada

Coach: BURCHUK, Mike
Assistant Coach: ST JEAN, R.

Names	Pts + S/O	1	2	3	4	5
RATNIK, Diane	0 + 1	S	S	S		
CORBEIL, Josee	0 + 0	*	*	*		
VON SASS, Katrina	1 + 3	S	S	S		
SOUCY, Brigitte	5 + 10	S	S	S		
RUSSO, Erminia	0 + 0	*				
SAWATZKY, Michelle	0 + 0					
KELLY, Janis	4 + 5	S	S	S		
MUNDT, Lori Ann	0 + 0		*	*		
TOUGH, Kathy	0 + 0	S	S	S		
GUENETTE, Wanda	2 + 2	*	*	*		
STARK, Christine	0 + 0					
BUCHBERGER, Kerri	0 + 3	S	S	S		

Team: BRA Brazil

Coach: REZENDE, Bernardo
Assistant Coach: TABACH, Ricardo

Names	Pts + S/O	1	2	3	4	5
MOSER, Ana Beatriz	6 + 7	S	S	S		
ALVARES, Ana Margarida Vieira	1 + 1			*		
CONNELLY, Ana Paula Rodrigues	3 + 5	S	S	S		
BARROS, Leila Gomes de	0 + 0					
CALDEIRAS, Hilma Aparecida	10 + 7	S	S	S		
DIAS, Virna Cristine Dantas	0 + 0			*		
CUNHA, Marcia Regina	7 + 4	S	S	S		
BODZICK, Ericleia	0 + 1			*		
SANGLARD, Ana Flavia Chritaro	4 + 7	S	S	S		
VENTURINI, Fernanda Porto	2 + 2	S	S	S		
SOUZA, Helia Rogerio de	0 + 0					
SURUAGY, Sandra Maria Lima	0 + 0					

Team: GER Germany

Coach: KOEHLER, Siegfried
Assistant Coach: LEE, Hee-Wan

Names	Pts + S/O	1	2	3	4	5
LAHME, Susanne	4 + 11	S	S	S		
HART, Tanja	0 + 0			*		
RADFAN, Constance	0 + 0					
ROLL, Sylvia	0 + 4		S	S		
STEPPIN, Ute	0 + 3	S				
HORNINGER, Karin	0 + 0					
PIANKA, Ines	1 + 2	S	S	S		
SCHULTZ, Christina	0 + 1	S				
WILKE, Claudia	0 + 0					
CELIS, Nancy	4 + 13	S	S	S		
NAUMANN, Grit	3 + 4	S	S	S		
PACHALE, Hanka	2 + 3	*	S	S		

Team: CUB Cuba

Coach: GEORGE LAFITA, Eugenio R.
Assistant Coach: PERDOMO ESTRELLA, Antonio

Names	Pts + S/O	1	2	3	4	5
RUIZ, Yumilka	0 + 0					
COSTA, Marleny	2 + 3	S	S	S		
LUIS, Mireya	2 + 2	S	S	S		
IZQUIERDO, Lilia	0 + 0					
GATO, Idalmis	0 + 0					
O'FARRILL, Raiza	5 + 2	S	S	S		
BELL, Regla	7 + 4	S	S	S		
TORRES, Regla	1 + 0			*		
AGUERO, Taismari	0 + 0					
FERNANDEZ, Ana Ibis	4 + 11	S	S	S		
CARVAJAL, Magalys	9 + 6	S	S	S		
FRANCIA, Mirka	0 + 0					

Team: PER Peru

Coach: PARK, Jong Dug
Assistant Coach: APARICIO SALDANA, Carlos Efrain

Names	Pts + S/O	1	2	3	4	5
JOYA LOBATON, Sara	0 + 1	S	S			
FALCON DORITA, Iris	1 + 7	S	S	*		
CONTRERAS FLORES, Milagros	0 + 0	S	S	S		
RAMOS YDORA, Paola	1 + 0			*		
CAMERE PUGA, Milagros	3 + 10	S	S	S		
MOY ALVARADO, Milagros	2 + 8	S	S	S		
RODRIGUEZ VILLANEUVA, S.	0 + 0					
BAYLON FRANCIS, Luren	0 + 2	*	*	S		
VILCHEZ SOJO, Marjorie	0 + 0					
CHIHUAN RAMOS, Leyla	0 + 0					
ZAMUDIO ORL, Yulissa	0 + 0		*	S		
DELGADO PRADA, Yolanda	1 + 1	S	S	S		

Women / *Dames*

PRELIMINARIES - GROUP B

RUS 3 - 0 CAN

Set	1	2	3	4	5	Total pts
Result	15 - 1	15 - 7	15 - 9			45 - 17
Duration	0:20	0:22	0:28			1:10

Russian Federation				Canada		
Att	Pts won	S/O		Att	Pts won	S/O
101	23	31	Attacks	123	4	45
55	8	2	Blocks	53	5	0
96	2		Serves	69	3	

1st Referee: THA CHAREONPONG, Songsak
2nd Referee: MEX NAVA ABARCA, Fernando

PRELIMINARIES - GROUP B

GER 3 - 0 PER

Set	1	2	3	4	5	Total pts
Result	15 - 11	15 - 6	15 - 3			45 - 20
Duration	0:31	0:17	0:15			1:03

Germany				Peru		
Att	Pts won	S/O		Att	Pts won	S/O
121	18	27	Attacks	138	7	28
63	9	4	Blocks	39	5	2
83	2		Serves	61	3	

1st Referee: USA LUEBKE, Neill
2nd Referee: KSA al-KHLAIFI, Abdullah

PRELIMINARIES - GROUP B

CUB 0 - 3 BRA

Set	1	2	3	4	5	Total pts
Result	11 - 15	10 - 15	4 - 15			25 - 45
Duration	0:27	0:28	0:20			1:15

Cuba				Brazil		
Att	Pts won	S/O		Att	Pts won	S/O
134	13	40	Attacks	107	14	36
50	3	0	Blocks	74	16	3
82	4		Serves	101	5	

1st Referee: NED SCHEFFER, Petrus Carolus
2nd Referee: FIN SALONEN, Jarmo

PRELIMINARIES - GROUP B

CAN 0 - 3 GER

Set	1	2	3	4	5	Total pts
Result	5 - 15	12 - 15	6 - 15			23 - 45
Duration	0:21	0:36	0:22			1:19

Canada				Germany		
Att	Pts won	S/O		Att	Pts won	S/O
152	8	35	Attacks	144	21	37
54	4	5	Blocks	57	8	0
77	3		Serves	97	2	

1st Referee: KSA al-KHLAIFI, Abdullah
2nd Referee: ARG PAREDES, Guillermo

Team: RUS Russian Federation
Coach: KARPOL, Nikolai
Assistant Coach: OMELTCHENKO, Mikhail

Names	Pts + S/O	1	2	3	4	5
OGIENKO, Valentina	1 + 0		*	*		
MOROZOVA, Natalia	1 + 2	S	S	S		
NIKOULINA, Marina	0 + 1	S	S	S		
BATOUKHTINA, Elena	10 + 2	S	S	S		
ILCHENKO, Irina	8 + 14	S	S	S		
GODINA, Elena	0 + 0					
MENCHOVA, Tatiana	0 + 0					
ARTAMONOVA, Evguenia	12 + 9	S	S	S		
TICHTCHENKO, Elizaveta	1 + 4	S	S	S		
TIMONOVA, Ioulia	0 + 0					
GRATCHEVA, Tatiana	0 + 1		*	*		
SOKOLOVA, Liubov	0 + 0			*		

Team: GER Germany
Coach: KOEHLER, Siegfried
Assistant Coach: LEE, Hee-Wan

Names	Pts + S/O	1	2	3	4	5
LAHME, Susanne	8 + 7	S	S	S		
HART, Tanja	0 + 0					
RADFAN, Constance	0 + 0					
ROLL, Sylvia	3 + 1	S	S			
STEPPIN, Ute	4 + 2	*				
HORNINGER, Karin	0 + 0					
PIANKA, Ines	0 + 4	S	S	S		
SCHULTZ, Christina	5 + 5	S	S	S		
WILKE, Claudia	0 + 0					
CELIS, Nancy	5 + 10	S	S	S		
NAUMANN, Grit	3 + 2	S	S	S		
PACHALE, Hanka	1 + 0			*		

Team: CUB Cuba
Coach: GEORGE LAFITA, Eugenio R.
Assistant Coach: PERDOMO ESTRELLA, Antonio

Names	Pts + S/O	1	2	3	4	5
RUIZ, Yumilka	0 + 0					
COSTA, Marleny	0 + 2	S	S	S		
LUIS, Mireya	6 + 11	S	S	S		
IZQUIERDO, Lilia	0 + 0		*	S		
GATO, Idalmis	0 + 1			*		
O'FARRILL, Raiza	1 + 1	S	S			
BELL, Regla	3 + 10	S	S	S		
TORRES, Regla	2 + 4		S	S		
AGUERO, Taismari	0 + 0					
FERNANDEZ, Ana Ibis	0 + 4	S		*		
CARVAJAL, Magalys	8 + 7	S	S	S		
FRANCIA, Mirka	0 + 0					

Team: CAN Canada
Coach: BURCHUK, Mike
Assistant Coach: ST JEAN, R.

Names	Pts + S/O	1	2	3	4	5
RATNIK, Diane	0 + 0	S				
CORBEIL, Josee	0 + 0	*	*	*		
VON SASS, Katrina	4 + 8	S	S	S		
SOUCY, Brigitte	2 + 8	S	S	S		
RUSSO, Erminia	0 + 0		*			
SAWATZKY, Michelle	0 + 1	*	S	S		
KELLY, Janis	6 + 17	S	S	S		
MUNDT, Lori Ann	0 + 0			*		
TOUGH, Kathy	0 + 1	S	S	*		
GUENETTE, Wanda	2 + 3	*	*	S		
STARK, Christine	0 + 0					
BUCHBERGER, Kerri	1 + 2	S	S	S		

Team: CAN Canada
Coach: BURCHUK, Mike
Assistant Coach: ST JEAN, R.

Names	Pts + S/O	1	2	3	4	5
RATNIK, Diane	0 + 2	S	S			
CORBEIL, Josee	0 + 0	*	*			
VON SASS, Katrina	4 + 7	S	S	S		
SOUCY, Brigitte	1 + 8	S	S	S		
RUSSO, Erminia	0 + 0		*	*		
SAWATZKY, Michelle	0 + 1			S		
KELLY, Janis	3 + 14	S	S	S		
MUNDT, Lori Ann	0 + 0					
TOUGH, Kathy	2 + 7	S	S	S		
GUENETTE, Wanda	0 + 4	*	*	*		
STARK, Christine	0 + 0			*		
BUCHBERGER, Kerri	2 + 2	S	S	S		

Team: PER Peru
Coach: PARK, Jong Dug
Assistant Coach: APARICIO SALDANA, Carlos Efrain

Names	Pts + S/O	1	2	3	4	5
JOYA LOBATON, Sara	2 + 1	S	S	S		
FALCON DORITA, Iris	2 + 4	S	S	*		
CONTRERAS FLORES, Milagros	0 + 1	S	S	S		
RAMOS YDORA, Paola	0 + 1		*	S		
CAMERE PUGA, Milagros	2 + 7	S	S	S		
MOY ALVARADO, Milagros	2 + 11	S	S	S		
RODRIGUEZ VILLANEUVA, S.	0 + 0	*				
BAYLON FRANCIS, Luren	1 + 0	*	*	*		
VILCHEZ SOJO, Marjorie	0 + 0					
CHIHUAN RAMOS, Leyla	0 + 0					
ZAMUDIO ORL, Yulissa	0 + 0			*		
DELGADO PRADA, Yolanda	6 + 5	S	S	S		

Team: BRA Brazil
Coach: REZENDE, Bernardo
Assistant Coach: TABACH, Ricardo

Names	Pts + S/O	1	2	3	4	5
MOSER, Ana Beatriz	10 + 7	S	S	S		
ALVARES, Ana Margarida Vieira	0 + 0					
CONNELLY, Ana Paula Rodrigues	6 + 2	S	S	S		
BARROS, Leila Gomes de	0 + 0					
CALDEIRAS, Hilma Aparecida	7 + 15	S	S	S		
DIAS, Virna Cristine Dantas	0 + 0	*				
CUNHA, Marcia Regina	9 + 11	S	S	S		
BODZICK, Ericleia	0 + 0	*	*	*		
SANGLARD, Ana Flavia Chritaro	2 + 3	S	S	S		
VENTURINI, Fernanda Porto	1 + 1	S	S	S		
SOUZA, Helia Rogerio de	0 + 0					
SURUAGY, Sandra Maria Lima	0 + 0					

Team: GER Germany
Coach: KOEHLER, Siegfried
Assistant Coach: LEE, Hee-Wan

Names	Pts + S/O	1	2	3	4	5
LAHME, Susanne	2 + 7	S	S	S		
HART, Tanja	0 + 0					
RADFAN, Constance	0 + 0					
ROLL, Sylvia	10 + 12	S	S	S		
STEPPIN, Ute	0 + 0					
HORNINGER, Karin	0 + 0					
PIANKA, Ines	4 + 1	S	S	S		
SCHULTZ, Christina	2 + 2	S	S	S		
WILKE, Claudia	0 + 0					
CELIS, Nancy	10 + 8	S	S	S		
NAUMANN, Grit	3 + 7	S	S	S		
PACHALE, Hanka	0 + 0		*			

Women / *Dames*

PRELIMINARIES - GROUP B

BRA 3 - 0 RUS

Set	1	2	3	4	5	Total pts
Result	15 - 3	15 - 11	15 - 13			45 - 27
Duration	0:16	0:28	0:28			1:12

	Brazil				Russian Federation	
Att	Pts won	S/O		Att	Pts won	S/O
126	16	44	**Attacks**	133	9	46
57	10	3	**Blocks**	61	8	0
101	7		**Serves**	85	3	

1st Referee: THA   CHAREONPONG, Songsak
2nd Referee: KOR   CHO, Young-Ho

PRELIMINARIES - GROUP B

PER 0 - 3 CUB

Set	1	2	3	4	5	Total pts
Result	2 - 15	5 - 15	10 - 15			17 - 45
Duration	0:24	0:17	0:20			1:01

	Peru				Cuba	
Att	Pts won	S/O		Att	Pts won	S/O
94	4	24	**Attacks**	106	20	44
31	0	3	**Blocks**	48	7	0
67	1		**Serves**	97	7	

1st Referee: ITA   TROIA, Pasquale
2nd Referee: AUS   TURNER, Dean

PRELIMINARIES - GROUP B

RUS 3 - 0 PER

Set	1	2	3	4	5	Total pts
Result	15 - 11	15 - 8	15 - 1			45 - 20
Duration	0:26	0:25	0:16			1:07

	Russian Federation				Peru	
Att	Pts won	S/O		Att	Pts won	S/O
101	9	40	**Attacks**	121	8	34
51	14	3	**Blocks**	37	2	0
95	6		**Serves**	72	4	

1st Referee: USA   BLUE, Thomas
2nd Referee: CHN   QU, Zheng Zhong

PRELIMINARIES - GROUP B

GER 0 - 3 CUB

Set	1	2	3	4	5	Total pts
Result	6 - 15	8 - 15	4 - 15			18 - 45
Duration	0:18	0:21	0:24			1:03

	Germany				Cuba	
Att	Pts won	S/O		Att	Pts won	S/O
125	9	33	**Attacks**	112	18	42
55	3	5	**Blocks**	65	11	2
70	2		**Serves**	96	8	

1st Referee: AUS   TURNER, Dean
2nd Referee: JPN   SHIMOYAMA, Takashi

Team: BRA Brazil

Coach: REZENDE, Bernardo
Assistant Coach: TABACH, Ricardo

Names	Pts + S/O	1	2	3	4	5
MOSER, Ana Beatriz	9 + 7	S	S	S		
ALVARES, Ana Margarida Vieira	0 + 0					
CONNELLY, Ana Paula Rodrigues	4 + 4	S	S	S		
BARROS, Leila Gomes de	0 + 0					
CALDEIRAS, Hilma Aparecida	0 + 0					
DIAS, Virna Cristine Dantas	4 + 16	S	S	S		
CUNHA, Marcia Regina	9 + 14	S	S	S		
BODZICK, Ericleia	0 + 0		*	*		
SANGLARD, Ana Flavia Chritaro	3 + 3	S	S	S		
VENTURINI, Fernanda Porto	4 + 3	S	S	S		
SOUZA, Helia Rogerio de	0 + 0					
SURUAGY, Sandra Maria Lima	0 + 0					

Team: PER Peru

Coach: PARK, Jong Dug
Assistant Coach: APARICIO SALDANA, Carlos Efrain

Names	Pts + S/O	1	2	3	4	5
JOYA LOBATON, Sara	1 + 2	S	S	S		
FALCON DORITA, Iris	0 + 8	S	S	S		
CONTRERAS FLORES, Milagros	0 + 0	S	S	S		
RAMOS YDORA, Paola	1 + 2	*	S	S		
CAMERE PUGA, Milagros	1 + 9	S	S	S		
MOY ALVARADO, Milagros	0 + 0					
RODRIGUEZ VILLANEUVA, S.	0 + 0			*		
BAYLON FRANCIS, Luren	1 + 0			*		
VILCHEZ SOJO, Marjorie	0 + 0					
CHIHUAN RAMOS, Leyla	0 + 0					
ZAMUDIO ORL, Yulissa	0 + 0	S				
DELGADO PRADA, Yolanda	1 + 6	S	S	S		

Team: RUS Russian Federation

Coach: KARPOL, Nikolai
Assistant Coach: OMELTCHENKO, Mikhail

Names	Pts + S/O	1	2	3	4	5
OGIENKO, Valentina	0 + 0					
MOROZOVA, Natalia	3 + 6	S	S			
NIKOULINA, Marina	0 + 0	S	S			
BATOUKHTINA, Elena	4 + 2	S	S			
ILCHENKO, Irina	1 + 7	S	*			
GODINA, Elena	5 + 4		*	S		
MENCHOVA, Tatiana	5 + 4	*	S	S		
ARTAMONOVA, Evguenia	3 + 6	S	S	*		
TICHTCHENKO, Elizaveta	3 + 9	S	S	S		
TIMONOVA, Ioulia	0 + 1		*	S		
GRATCHEVA, Tatiana	0 + 2	*	*	S		
SOKOLOVA, Liubov	5 + 2		*	S		

Team: GER Germany

Coach: KOEHLER, Siegfried
Assistant Coach: LEE, Hee-Wan

Names	Pts + S/O	1	2	3	4	5
LAHME, Susanne	0 + 8	S	S	S		
HART, Tanja	0 + 1			*		
RADFAN, Constance	1 + 3	*	S	S		
ROLL, Sylvia	4 + 6	S	S	S		
STEPPIN, Ute	0 + 2			*		
HORNINGER, Karin	0 + 0			*		
PIANKA, Ines	3 + 2	S	S	S		
SCHULTZ, Christina	0 + 2	S				
WILKE, Claudia	0 + 2			*		
CELIS, Nancy	3 + 8	S	S	S		
NAUMANN, Grit	2 + 1	S	S	S		
PACHALE, Hanka	1 + 3			*		

Team: RUS Russian Federation

Coach: KARPOL, Nikolai
Assistant Coach: OMELTCHENKO, Mikhail

Names	Pts + S/O	1	2	3	4	5
OGIENKO, Valentina	1 + 5	*	*	*		
MOROZOVA, Natalia	1 + 2	S	S	S		
NIKOULINA, Marina	1 + 0	S	S	S		
BATOUKHTINA, Elena	4 + 9	S	S	S		
ILCHENKO, Irina	4 + 9	S	S	S		
GODINA, Elena	0 + 1		*			
MENCHOVA, Tatiana	1 + 1			*		
ARTAMONOVA, Evguenia	6 + 12	S	S	S		
TICHTCHENKO, Elizaveta	2 + 7	S	S	S		
TIMONOVA, Ioulia	0 + 0					
GRATCHEVA, Tatiana	0 + 0					
SOKOLOVA, Liubov	0 + 0					

Team: CUB Cuba

Coach: GEORGE LAFITA, Eugenio R.
Assistant Coach: PERDOMO ESTRELLA, Antonio

Names	Pts + S/O	1	2	3	4	5
RUIZ, Yumilka	1 + 4			*		
COSTA, Marleny	0 + 4	S	S	S		
LUIS, Mireya	5 + 7	S	S	S		
IZQUIERDO, Lilia	4 + 3	S	S	S		
GATO, Idalmis	2 + 0			S		
O'FARRILL, Raiza	0 + 0					
BELL, Regla	3 + 6	S	S			
TORRES, Regla	14 + 10	S	S	S		
AGUERO, Taismari	0 + 0					
FERNANDEZ, Ana Ibis	5 + 10	S	S	S		
CARVAJAL, Magalys	0 + 0					
FRANCIA, Mirka	0 + 0					

Team: PER Peru

Coach: PARK, Jong Dug
Assistant Coach: APARICIO SALDANA, Carlos Efrain

Names	Pts + S/O	1	2	3	4	5
JOYA LOBATON, Sara	0 + 4	S	S	S		
FALCON DORITA, Iris	1 + 8	S	S	S		
CONTRERAS FLORES, Milagros	0 + 1	S	S	S		
RAMOS YDORA, Paola	1 + 1	*				
CAMERE PUGA, Milagros	4 + 9	S	S	S		
MOY ALVARADO, Milagros	2 + 5	S	S	S		
RODRIGUEZ VILLANEUVA, S.	1 + 0		*			
BAYLON FRANCIS, Luren	0 + 0	*	*	*		
VILCHEZ SOJO, Marjorie	0 + 0					
CHIHUAN RAMOS, Leyla	0 + 0					
ZAMUDIO ORL, Yulissa	0 + 0			*		
DELGADO PRADA, Yolanda	5 + 6	S	S	S		

Team: CUB Cuba

Coach: GEORGE LAFITA, Eugenio R.
Assistant Coach: PERDOMO ESTRELLA, Antonio

Names	Pts + S/O	1	2	3	4	5
RUIZ, Yumilka	0 + 0					
COSTA, Marleny	2 + 2	S	S	S		
LUIS, Mireya	11 + 11	S	S	S		
IZQUIERDO, Lilia	0 + 0					
GATO, Idalmis	0 + 0					
O'FARRILL, Raiza	8 + 2	S	S	S		
BELL, Regla	4 + 14	S	S	S		
TORRES, Regla	0 + 0					
AGUERO, Taismari	0 + 0					
FERNANDEZ, Ana Ibis	4 + 7	S	S	S		
CARVAJAL, Magalys	8 + 8	S	S	S		
FRANCIA, Mirka	0 + 0					

PRELIMINARIES - GROUP B

CAN 0 - 3 BRA

Set	1	2	3	4	5	Total pts
Result	6 - 15	6 - 15	11 - 15			23 - 45
Duration	0:22	0:22	0:30			1:14

	Canada				Brazil	
Att	Pts won	S/O		Att	Pts won	S/O
146	10	25	Attacks	153	21	32
64	3	3	Blocks	59	6	1
70	2		Serves	90	2	

1st Referee: ITA TROIA, Pasquale
2nd Referee: THA CHAREONPONG, Songsak

PRELIMINARIES - GROUP B

BRA 3 - 1 GER

Set	1	2	3	4	5	Total pts
Result	15 - 4	13 - 15	15 - 6	15 - 8		58 - 33
Duration	0:19	0:38	0:18	0:33		1:48

	Brazil				Germany	
Att	Pts won	S/O		Att	Pts won	S/O
212	28	67	Attacks	197	12	55
86	12	4	Blocks	93	9	7
141	6		Serves	117	2	

1st Referee: THA CHAREONPONG, Songsak
2nd Referee: MEX NAVA ABARCA, Fernando

PRELIMINARIES - GROUP B

CUB 1 - 3 RUS

Set	1	2	3	4	5	Total pts
Result	15 - 10	6 - 15	7 - 15	8 - 15		36 - 55
Duration	0:22	0:19	0:22	0:28		1:31

	Cuba				Russian Federation	
Att	Pts won	S/O		Att	Pts won	S/O
160	12	56	Attacks	146	16	57
90	14	2	Blocks	90	15	4
117	5		Serves	134	6	

1st Referee: JPN SHIMOYAMA, Takashi
2nd Referee: AUS TURNER, Dean

PRELIMINARIES - GROUP B

PER 2 - 3 CAN

Set	1	2	3	4	5	Total pts
Result	17 - 16	6 - 15	15 - 11	9 - 15	12 - 15	59 - 72
Duration	0:31	0:15	0:27	0:27	0:13	1:53

	Peru				Canada	
Att	Pts won	S/O		Att	Pts won	S/O
217	28	50	Attacks	192	33	45
67	9	0	Blocks	105	14	4
126	3		Serves	138	8	

1st Referee: KOR CHO, Young-Ho
2nd Referee: FIN SALONEN, Jarmo

Team: CAN Canada
Coach: BURCHUK, Mike
Assistant Coach: ST JEAN, R.

Names	Pts + S/O	1	2	3	4	5
RATNIK, Diane	0 + 0					
CORBEIL, Josee	1 + 0	S	*			
VON SASS, Katrina	0 + 0					
SOUCY, Brigitte	6 + 4	*	*	*		
RUSSO, Erminia	0 + 1	S	S	S		
SAWATZKY, Michelle	1 + 0	S				
KELLY, Janis	3 + 10	S	S	S		
MUNDT, Lori Ann	0 + 0			*		
TOUGH, Kathy	1 + 4	*	S	S		
GUENETTE, Wanda	1 + 3	S	S	S		
STARK, Christine	2 + 4	S	S	S		
BUCHBERGER, Kerri	0 + 2	*	*	*		

Team: BRA Brazil
Coach: REZENDE, Bernardo
Assistant Coach: TABACH, Ricardo

Names	Pts + S/O	1	2	3	4	5
MOSER, Ana Beatriz	10 + 11	S	S	S	S	
ALVARES, Ana Margarida Vieira	1 + 2				*	
CONNELLY, Ana Paula Rodrigues	6 + 8	S	S	S	S	
BARROS, Leila Gomes de	3 + 2				*	
CALDEIRAS, Hilma Aparecida	0 + 0					
DIAS, Virna Cristine Dantas	11 + 23	S	S	S	S	
CUNHA, Marcia Regina	5 + 12	S	S	S	S	
BODZICK, Ericleia	0 + 0		*			
SANGLARD, Ana Flavia Chritaro	7 + 7	S	S	S	S	
VENTURINI, Fernanda Porto	3 + 6	S	S	S	S	
SOUZA, Helia Rogerio de	0 + 0					
SURUAGY, Sandra Maria Lima	0 + 0					

Team: CUB Cuba
Coach: GEORGE LAFITA, Eugenio R.
Assistant Coach: PERDOMO ESTRELLA, Antonio

Names	Pts + S/O	1	2	3	4	5
RUIZ, Yumilka	0 + 0					
COSTA, Marleny	0 + 7	S	S	S	S	
LUIS, Mireya	5 + 7	S	S	S	S	
IZQUIERDO, Lilia	0 + 0				*	
GATO, Idalmis	1 + 4			*	S	
O'FARRILL, Raiza	4 + 8	S	S	S	S	
BELL, Regla	4 + 4	S	S	S	*	
TORRES, Regla	2 + 3				*	
AGUERO, Taismari	0 + 0					
FERNANDEZ, Ana Ibis	4 + 9	S	S	S	S	
CARVAJAL, Magalys	11 + 16	S	S	S	S	
FRANCIA, Mirka	0 + 0					

Team: PER Peru
Coach: PARK, Jong Dug
Assistant Coach: APARICIO SALDANA, Carlos Efrain

Names	Pts + S/O	1	2	3	4	5
JOYA LOBATON, Sara	7 + 7	S	S	S	S	S
FALCON DORITA, Iris	5 + 11	S	S	S	S	S
CONTRERAS FLORES, Milagros	1 + 3	S	S	S	S	S
RAMOS YDORA, Paola	0 + 0			*		*
CAMERE PUGA, Milagros	12 + 15	S	S	S	S	S
MOY ALVARADO, Milagros	14 + 13	S	S	S	S	S
RODRIGUEZ VILLANEUVA, S.	0 + 0	*			*	
BAYLON FRANCIS, Luren	0 + 0	*		*	*	
VILCHEZ SOJO, Marjorie	0 + 0					
CHIHUAN RAMOS, Leyla	0 + 0					
ZAMUDIO ORL, Yulissa	0 + 0					
DELGADO PRADA, Yolanda	1 + 1	·S	S	S	S	S

Team: BRA Brazil
Coach: REZENDE, Bernardo
Assistant Coach: TABACH, Ricardo

Names	Pts + S/O	1	2	3	4	5
MOSER, Ana Beatriz	3 + 3	S	S			
ALVARES, Ana Margarida Vieira	3 + 3		S	S		
CONNELLY, Ana Paula Rodrigues	3 + 5	S	*	S		
BARROS, Leila Gomes de	3 + 7		*	S		
CALDEIRAS, Hilma Aparecida	0 + 0					
DIAS, Virna Cristine Dantas	5 + 8	S	S	S		
CUNHA, Marcia Regina	8 + 3	S	S	S		
BODZICK, Ericleia	1 + 2			*		
SANGLARD, Ana Flavia Chritaro	1 + 2		S			
VENTURINI, Fernanda Porto	2 + 0	S	S	S		
SOUZA, Heila Rogerio de	0 + 0			*		
SURUAGY, Sandra Maria Lima	0 + 0			*	*	

Team: GER Germany
Coach: KOEHLER, Siegfried
Assistant Coach: LEE, Hee-Wan

Names	Pts + S/O	1	2	3	4	5
LAHME, Susanne	2 + 8	S	S	S	S	
HART, Tanja	0 + 3	*		*	S	
RADFAN, Constance	0 + 1				S	
ROLL, Sylvia	5 + 14	S	S	S		
STEPPIN, Ute	0 + 5		*	*	S	
HORNINGER, Karin	0 + 0				*	
PIANKA, Ines	0 + 1	S	S	S		
SCHULTZ, Christina	1 + 0	S				
WILKE, Claudia	2 + 1			*		
CELIS, Nancy	6 + 13	S	S	S	S	
NAUMANN, Grit	5 + 5	S	S	S		
PACHALE, Hanka	2 + 11	*	S	S	S	

Team: RUS Russian Federation
Coach: KARPOL, Nikolai
Assistant Coach: OMELTCHENKO, Mikhail

Names	Pts + S/O	1	2	3	4	5
OGIENKO, Valentina	0 + 0		*	*	*	
MOROZOVA, Natalia	5 + 8	S	S	S	S	
NIKOULINA, Marina	1 + 2	S	S	S	S	
BATOUKHTINA, Elena	6 + 10	S	S	S	S	
ILCHENKO, Irina	8 + 10	S	S	S	S	
GODINA, Elena	0 + 0					
MENCHOVA, Tatiana	0 + 3			*		
ARTAMONOVA, Evguenia	8 + 23	S	S	S	S	
TICHTCHENKO, Elizaveta	8 + 5	S	S	S	S	
TIMONOVA, Ioulia	0 + 0					
GRATCHEVA, Tatiana	1 + 0				*	
SOKOLOVA, Liubov	0 + 0					

Team: CAN Canada
Coach: BURCHUK, Mike
Assistant Coach: ST JEAN, R.

Names	Pts + S/O	1	2	3	4	5
RATNIK, Diane	0 + 0					
CORBEIL, Josee	1 + 2	*		*	*	*
VON SASS, Katrina	12 + 12	S	S	S	S	S
SOUCY, Brigitte	12 + 9	S	S	S	S	S
RUSSO, Erminia	1 + 0	*	*	*	*	*
SAWATZKY, Michelle	3 + 0	S	S	S	S	S
KELLY, Janis	11 + 12	S	S	S	S	S
MUNDT, Lori Ann	0 + 0					
TOUGH, Kathy	4 + 3	S	S	S	S	S
GUENETTE, Wanda	6 + 7	*		*	*	*
STARK, Christine	0 + 0					
BUCHBERGER, Kerri	5 + 4	S	S	S	S	S

Women / Dames

FINAL CLASSIFICATION - GROUP B

Rnk	Team	Pts	Games			Sets			Points		
			Played	Won	Lost	Won	Lost	W/L	For	Against	F/A
1	BRA	10	5	5	0	15	1	15.00	238	121	1.96
2	RUS	9	5	4	1	12	4	3.00	217	140	1.55
3	CUB	8	5	3	2	10	6	1.66	196	156	1.25
4	GER	7	5	2	3	7	9	0.77	163	191	0.85
5	CAN	6	5	1	4	3	14	0.21	156	239	0.65
6	PER	5	5	0	5	2	15	0.13	129	252	0.51

QUARTERFINALS

CHN 3 - 0 GER

Set	1	2	3	4	5	Total pts
Result	15 - 12	15 - 8	15 - 8			45 - 28
Duration	0:31	0:25	0:25			1:21

People's Republic of China				Germany		
Att	Pts won	S/O		Att	Pts won	S/O
159	21	47	Attacks	163	17	43
66	11	4	Blocks	72	5	3
101	3		Serves	86	3	

1st Referee: ARG PAREDES, Guillermo
2nd Referee: MEX NAVA ABARCA, Fernando

QUARTERFINALS

NED 1 - 3 RUS

Set	1	2	3	4	5	Total pts
Result	15 - 10	7 - 15	9 - 15	10 - 15		41 - 55
Duration	0:29	0:24	0:25	0:28		1:46

Netherlands				Russian Federation		
Att	Pts won	S/O		Att	Pts won	S/O
186	16	63	Attacks	180	25	69
93	10	5	Blocks	96	12	1
130	6		Serves	143	4	

1st Referee: GRE MARGARITIS, Konstantinos
2nd Referee: KSA al-KHLAIFI, Abdullah

QUARTERFINALS

USA 0 - 3 CUB

Set	1	2	3	4	5	Total pts
Result	1 - 15	10 - 15	12 - 15			23 - 45
Duration	0:16	0:30	0:30			1:16

United States of America				Cuba		
Att	Pts won	S/O		Att	Pts won	S/O
121	8	45	Attacks	124	17	51
62	6	1	Blocks	64	19	1
87	3		Serves	108	2	

1st Referee: FIN SALONEN, Jarmo
2nd Referee: AUS TURNER, Dean

Team: CHN People's Republic of China
Coach: LANG, Ping
Assistant Coach: CHEN, Zhong He

Names	Pts + S/O	1	2	3	4	5
LAI, Yawen	9 + 9	S	S	S		
LI, Yan	5 + 11	S	S	S		
CUI, Yongmei	5 + 5	S	S	S		
ZHU, Yunying	0 + 0					
WU, Yongmei	3 + 8	*	S	S		
WANG, Yi	2 + 2	S				
HE, Qi	5 + 1	S	S	S		
PAN, Wenli	0 + 0					
LIU, Xiaoning	0 + 0					
WANG, Ziling	0 + 0	*	*			
SUN, Yue	6 + 15	S	S	S		
WANG, Lina	0 + 0					

Team: NED Netherlands
Coach: GOEDKOOP, Bert
Assistant Coach: VERMEULEN, Gido

Names	Pts + S/O	1	2	3	4	5
FLEURKE, Jerine	6 + 11		*	S	S	
van HINTUM, Saskia	0 + 0					
BRINKMAN, Erna	5 + 14	S	S	S	S	
BOERSMA, Cintha	3 + 12	S	S	S	S	
MACHOVCAK, Irena	0 + 3	S	S		*	
de JONG, Marjolein	0 + 0	*		*	*	
WEERSING, Henriette	3 + 10	S	S	S		
LEENSTRA, Marrit	0 + 0					
LEFERINK, Elles	3 + 13	*	*	*	S	
van THIEL, Claudia	0 + 0					
FLEDDERUS, Riette	7 + 2	S	S	S	S	
VISSER, Ingrid	5 + 3	S	S	S	S	

Team: USA United States of America
Coach: LISKEVYCH, Taras
Assistant Coach: BERZINS, Aldis

Names	Pts + S/O	1	2	3	4	5
WILLIAMS, Tonya	0 + 0	S				
ZETTERLUND, Yoko	0 + 0	*		*		
WEISHOFF, Paula	0 + 2	*	*	*		
KEMNER, Caren	3 + 5	*	*	*		
ENDICOTT, Lori	0 + 2	S	S	S		
KLEIN, Kristin	0 + 0			*		
ODEN, Beverly	0 + 1	S				
LILEY, Tammy	0 + 10	S	S	S		
ODEN, Elaina	3 + 6	S	S	S		
SCOTT, Danielle	4 + 8		S	S		
CROSS-BATTLE, Tara	5 + 9	S	S	S		
YOUNGS, Elaine	2 + 3		S	S		

Team: GER Germany
Coach: KOEHLER, Siegfried
Assistant Coach: LEE, Hee-Wan

Names	Pts + S/O	1	2	3	4	5
LAHME, Susanne	4 + 10	S	S	S		
HART, Tanja	0 + 0		*	*		
RADFAN, Constance	0 + 0					
ROLL, Sylvia	6 + 9	S	S	S		
STEPPIN, Ute	0 + 0					
HORNINGER, Karin	0 + 0					
PIANKA, Ines	1 + 1	S	S	S		
SCHULTZ, Christina	6 + 6	S	S	S		
WILKE, Claudia	0 + 0					
CELIS, Nancy	5 + 11	S	S	S		
NAUMANN, Grit	3 + 8	S	S	S		
PACHALE, Hanka	0 + 1			*		

Team: RUS Russian Federation
Coach: KARPOL, Nikolai
Assistant Coach: OMELTCHENKO, Mikhail

Names	Pts + S/O	1	2	3	4	5
OGIENKO, Valentina	0 + 2	S		*	*	
MOROZOVA, Natalia	6 + 2	*	S	S	S	
NIKOULINA, Marina	3 + 2	*	S	S	S	
BATOUKHTINA, Elena	8 + 15	S	S	S	S	
ILCHENKO, Irina	1 + 0	S				
GODINA, Elena	10 + 16	*	S	S	S	
MENCHOVA, Tatiana	0 + 0			*	*	
ARTAMONOVA, Evguenia	10 + 20	S	S	S	S	
TICHTCHENKO, Elizaveta	3 + 12	S	S	S	S	
TIMONOVA, Ioulia	0 + 0					
GRATCHEVA, Tatiana	0 + 1	S			*	
SOKOLOVA, Liubov	0 + 0					

Team: CUB Cuba
Coach: GEORGE LAFITA, Eugenio R.
Assistant Coach: PERDOMO ESTRELLA, Antonio

Names	Pts + S/O	1	2	3	4	5
RUIZ, Yumilka	0 + 0					
COSTA, Marleny	3 + 5	S	S	S		
LUIS, Mireya	11 + 10	S	S	S		
IZQUIERDO, Lilia	0 + 0					
GATO, Idalmis	0 + 0					
O'FARRILL, Raiza	4 + 2	S	S	S		
BELL, Regla	5 + 11	S	S	S		
TORRES, Regla	0 + 1			*		
AGUERO, Taismari	0 + 0					
FERNANDEZ, Ana Ibis	3 + 9	S	S	S		
CARVAJAL, Magalys	12 + 14	S	S	S		
FRANCIA, Mirka	0 + 0					

Women / *Dames*

QUARTERFINALS

KOR 0 - 3 BRA

Set	1	2	3	4	5	Total pts
Result	4 - 15	2 - 15	10 - 15			16 - 45
Duration	0:22	0:17	0:26			1:05

	Korea				Brazil	
Att	Pts won	S/O		Att	Pts won	S/O
138	5	28	Attacks	123	20	38
49	1	1	Blocks	71	8	4
60	2		Serves	87	3	

1st Referee: ITA TROIA, Pasquale
2nd Referee: FRA RACHARD, Patrick

CLASSIFICATION 5 - 8

GER 2 - 3 NED

Set	1	2	3	4	5	Total pts
Result	12 - 15	15 - 9	15 - 13	9 - 15	10 - 15	61 - 67
Duration	0:43	0:26	0:28	0:29	0:11	2:17

	Germany				Netherlands	
Att	Pts won	S/O		Att	Pts won	S/O
240	26	64	Attacks	256	36	78
106	13	3	Blocks	94	9	3
158	7		Serves	162	7	

1st Referee: USA LUEBKE, Neill
2nd Referee: BRA PALMEIRIM, Josebel

CLASSIFICATION 5 - 8

USA 0 - 3 KOR

Set	1	2	3	4	5	Total pts
Result	12 - 15	5 - 15	11 - 15			28 - 45
Duration	0:30	0:24	0:37			1:31

	United States of America				Korea	
Att	Pts won	S/O		Att	Pts won	S/O
192	16	56	Attacks	179	26	47
83	6	1	Blocks	82	9	2
93	2		Serves	108	4	

1st Referee: ESP GIMENEZ, Gabriel
2nd Referee: RUS ZHARIKOV, Guennadi

FINAL 7 - 8

GER 1 - 3 USA

Set	1	2	3	4	5	Total pts
Result	16 - 17	6 - 15	15 - 5	6 - 15		43 - 52
Duration	0:36	0:33	0:19	0:20		1:48

	Germany				United States of America	
Att	Pts won	S/O		Att	Pts won	S/O
202	17	51	Attacks	208	25	65
93	9	12	Blocks	88	11	4
125	3		Serves	133	4	

1st Referee: THA CHAREONPONG, Songsak
2nd Referee: MEX NAVA ABARCA, Fernando

Team: KOR Korea
Coach: KIM, Cheol-Yong
Assistant Coach: SHIN, Il-Kyoun

Names	Pts + S/O	1	2	3	4	5
YOO, Yon-Kyung	0 + 0					
CHANG, Yoon-Hee	2 + 10	S	S	S		
LEE, Soo-Jung	1 + 2	S	S	S		
KANG, Hye-Mi	0 + 0	*		*		
CHUNG, Sun-Hye	2 + 6	S	S	S		
KIM, Nam-Soon	0 + 5	S	S	S		
PARK, Soo-Jeong	1 + 3	S	S	S		
HONG, Ji-Yeon	1 + 1	S	S	S		
LEE, In-Sook	0 + 0					
EOH, Yeon-Soon	0 + 0					
CHANG, So-Yun	1 + 2	*		*		
CHOI, Kwang-Hee	0 + 0	*	*	*		

Team: GER Germany
Coach: KOEHLER, Siegfried
Assistant Coach: LEE, Hee-Wan

Names	Pts + S/O	1	2	3	4	5
LAHME, Susanne	12 + 11	S	S	S	S	S
HART, Tanja	0 + 0				*	*
RADFAN, Constance	0 + 0					
ROLL, Sylvia	12 + 25	S	S	S	S	S
STEPPIN, Ute	1 + 0				*	
HORNINGER, Karin	0 + 0					
PIANKA, Ines	1 + 3	S	S	S	S	S
SCHULTZ, Christina	4 + 9	S	S	S	S	S
WILKE, Claudia	0 + 0					
CELIS, Nancy	12 + 13	S	S	S	S	S
NAUMANN, Grit	1 + 6	S	S	S	S	S
PACHALE, Hanka	3 + 0			*		*

Team: USA United States of America
Coach: LISKEVYCH, Taras
Assistant Coach: BERZINS, Aldis

Names	Pts + S/O	1	2	3	4	5
WILLIAMS, Tonya	0 + 0	*	*			
ZETTERLUND, Yoko	1 + 1		*	*		
WEISHOFF, Paula	0 + 5	*	*	*		
KEMNER, Caren	1 + 2	*		*		
ENDICOTT, Lori	0 + 2	S	S	S		
KLEIN, Kristin	0 + 0			*		
ODEN, Beverly	0 + 0		*			
LILEY, Tammy	2 + 10	S	S	S		
ODEN, Elaina	6 + 11	S	S	S		
SCOTT, Danielle	2 + 7	S	S	S		
CROSS-BATTLE, Tara	8 + 13	S	S	S		
YOUNGS, Elaine	4 + 6	S	S	S		

Team: GER Germany
Coach: KOEHLER, Siegfried
Assistant Coach: LEE, Hee-Wan

Names	Pts + S/O	1	2	3	4	5
LAHME, Susanne	7 + 17	S	S	S	S	
HART, Tanja	0 + 2	*	S	S	S	
RADFAN, Constance	3 + 0		*	S	S	
ROLL, Sylvia	8 + 16	S	S	S	S	
STEPPIN, Ute	3 + 7		*	S	S	
HORNINGER, Karin	1 + 4		*	S	S	
PIANKA, Ines	1 + 0	S				
SCHULTZ, Christina	2 + 8	S	S			
WILKE, Claudia	0 + 0				*	
CELIS, Nancy	1 + 3	S				
NAUMANN, Grit	1 + 4	S	S			
PACHALE, Hanka	2 + 2	*	S			

Team: BRA Brazil
Coach: REZENDE, Bernardo
Assistant Coach: TABACH, Ricardo

Names	Pts + S/O	1	2	3	4	5
MOSER, Ana Beatriz	9 + 13	S	S	S		
ALVARES, Ana Margarida Vieira	0 + 0					
CONNELLY, Ana Paula Rodrigues	8 + 5	S	S	S		
BARROS, Leila Gomes de	0 + 0					
CALDEIRAS, Hilma Aparecida	0 + 0					
DIAS, Virna Cristine Dantas	4 + 8	S	S	S		
CUNHA, Marcia Regina	5 + 11	S	S	S		
BODZICK, Ericleia	0 + 0					
SANGLARD, Ana Flavia Chritaro	3 + 3	S	S	S		
VENTURINI, Fernanda Porto	2 + 2	S	S	S		
SOUZA, Helia Rogerio de	0 + 0					
SURUAGY, Sandra Maria Lima	0 + 0					

Team: NED Netherlands
Coach: GOEDKOOP, Bert
Assistant Coach: VERMEULEN, Gido

Names	Pts + S/O	1	2	3	4	5
FLEURKE, Jerine	0 + 0					
van HINTUM, Saskia	0 + 0					
BRINKMAN, Erna	6 + 15	S	S	S	*	S
BOERSMA, Cintha	7 + 12	S	S	S	S	S
MACHOVCAK, Irena	2 + 5	S	S	S	S	S
de JONG, Marjolein	0 + 0					
WEERSING, Henriette	11 + 21	S	S	S	*	
LEENSTRA, Marrit	4 + 3				*	S
LEFERINK, Elles	14 + 15	*	*	*	S	S
van THIEL, Claudia	0 + 0	*				
FLEDDERUS, Riette	3 + 1	S	S	S	S	S
VISSER, Ingrid	5 + 9	S	S	S	S	S

Team: KOR Korea
Coach: KIM, Cheol-Yong
Assistant Coach: SHIN, Il-Kyoun

Names	Pts + S/O	1	2	3	4	5
YOO, Yon-Kyung	0 + 0					
CHANG, Yoon-Hee	8 + 11	S	S	S		
LEE, Soo-Jung	4 + 2	S	S	S		
KANG, Hye-Mi	0 + 0	*	*	*		
CHUNG, Sun-Hye	11 + 11	S	S	S		
KIM, Nam-Soon	10 + 10	S	S	S		
PARK, Soo-Jeong	3 + 7	S	S	S		
HONG, Ji-Yeon	2 + 7	S	S	S		
LEE, In-Sook	0 + 0					
EOH, Yeon-Soon	0 + 0					
CHANG, So-Yun	1 + 1	*	*	*		
CHOI, Kwang-Hee	0 + 0	*	*	*		

Team: USA United States of America
Coach: LISKEVYCH, Taras
Assistant Coach: BERZINS, Aldis

Names	Pts + S/O	1	2	3	4	5
WILLIAMS, Tonya	0 + 1				*	
ZETTERLUND, Yoko	3 + 2	S	S	S	S	
WEISHOFF, Paula	5 + 9	*	S	S	S	
KEMNER, Caren	6 + 9	*	S	S	S	
ENDICOTT, Lori	0 + 0			*		
KLEIN, Kristin	0 + 0	*	*	*	*	
ODEN, Beverly	0 + 1			*		
LILEY, Tammy	0 + 3	S		*		
ODEN, Elaina	6 + 7	S	S	S	S	
SCOTT, Danielle	10 + 19	S	S	S	S	
CROSS-BATTLE, Tara	8 + 17	S	S	S	S	
YOUNGS, Elaine	2 + 1	S		*		

Volleyball—Indoor / *Volleyball — En salle*

Women / *Dames*

FINAL 5 - 6

NED 3 - 0 KOR

Set	1	2	3	4	5	Total pts
Result	15 - 9	15 - 9	15 - 13			45 - 31
Duration	0:29	0:28	0:29			1:26

Netherlands				Korea		
Att	Pts won	S/O		Att	Pts won	S/O
174	18	57	Attacks	166	16	44
72	7	2	Blocks	72	6	2
111	7		Serves	99	0	

1st Referee: BRA PALMEIRIM, Josebel
2nd Referee: ESP GIMENEZ, Gabriel

SEMIFINALS

CHN 3 - 1 RUS

Set	1	2	3	4	5	Total pts
Result	12 - 15	15 - 5	15 - 8	15 - 12		57 - 40
Duration	0:31	0:25	0:31	0:22		1:49

People's Republic of China				Russian Federation		
Att	Pts won	S/O		Att	Pts won	S/O
203	24	61	Attacks	208	15	68
88	15	4	Blocks	99	14	5
144	4		Serves	128	1	

1st Referee: CAN HENRY, Peter
2nd Referee: USA BLUE, Thomas

SEMIFINALS

CUB 3 - 2 BRA

Set	1	2	3	4	5	Total pts
Result	5 - 15	15 - 8	10 - 15	15 - 13	15 - 12	60 - 63
Duration	0:22	0:26	0:30	0:27	0:13	1:58

Cuba				Brazil		
Att	Pts won	S/O		Att	Pts won	S/O
199	32	62	Attacks	198	25	60
102	17	2	Blocks	107	11	6
146	2		Serves	148	8	

1st Referee: NED SCHEFFER, Petrus Carolus
2nd Referee: GER LEUTHAEUSSER, Frank

FINAL - BRONZE MATCH

RUS 2 - 3 BRA

Set	1	2	3	4	5	Total pts
Result	13 - 15	15 - 4	14 - 16	15 - 8	13 - 15	70 - 58
Duration	0:22	0:16	0:35	0:26	0:13	1:52

Russian Federation				Brazil		
Att	Pts won	S/O		Att	Pts won	S/O
186	22	56	Attacks	207	30	62
92	22	1	Blocks	88	16	1
144	7		Serves	130	2	

1st Referee: USA DRAGON, Barry
2nd Referee: CHN QU, Zheng Zhong

Team: NED Netherlands
Coach: GOEDKOOP, Bert
Assistant Coach: VERMEULEN, Gido

Names	Pts + S/O	1	2	3	4	5
FLEURKE, Jerine	0 + 0			*		
van HINTUM, Saskia	0 + 0					
BRINKMAN, Erna	3 + 8	S	S	S		
BOERSMA, Cintha	5 + 10	S	S	S		
MACHOVCAK, Irena	5 + 9	S	S	S		
de JONG, Marjolein	0 + 0	*	*			
WEERSING, Henriette	12 + 19	S	S	S		
LEENSTRA, Marrit	0 + 0					
LEFERINK, Elles	0 + 0	*	*	*		
van THIEL, Claudia	0 + 0					
FLEDDERUS, Riette	6 + 4	S	S	S		
VISSER, Ingrid	1 + 9	S	S	S		

Team: KOR Korea
Coach: KIM, Cheol-Yong
Assistant Coach: SHIN, Il-Kyoun

Names	Pts + S/O	1	2	3	4	5
YOO, Yon-Kyung	0 + 0					
CHANG, Yoon-Hee	5 + 13	S	S	S		
LEE, Soo-Jung	1 + 1	S	S	*		
KANG, Hye-Mi	0 + 0	*	*	S		
CHUNG, Sun-Hye	4 + 7	S	S	S		
KIM, Nam-Soon	1 + 4	S	S	*		
PARK, Soo-Jeong	4 + 8	S	S	S		
HONG, Ji-Yeon	2 + 8	S	S	S		
LEE, In-Sook	0 + 0					
EOH, Yeon-Soon	0 + 0					
CHANG, So-Yun	5 + 5	*	*	*		
CHOI, Kwang-Hee	0 + 0	*	*	*		

Team: CHN People's Republic of China
Coach: LANG, Ping
Assistant Coach: CHEN, Zhong He

Names	Pts + S/O	1	2	3	4	5
LAI, Yawen	8 + 14	S	S	S	S	
LI, Yan	7 + 13	S	S	S	S	
CUI, Yongmei	6 + 9	S	S	S	S	
ZHU, Yunying	0 + 0					
WU, Yongmei	13 + 12	*	S	S	S	
WANG, Yi	1 + 1	S				
HE, Qi	1 + 2	S	S	S	S	
PAN, Wenli	0 + 0					
LIU, Xiaoning	0 + 0					
WANG, Ziling	0 + 0	*	*			
SUN, Yue	7 + 14	S	S	S	S	
WANG, Lina	0 + 0	*				

Team: RUS Russian Federation
Coach: KARPOL, Nikolai
Assistant Coach: OMELTCHENKO, Mikhail

Names	Pts + S/O	1	2	3	4	5
OGIENKO, Valentina	0 + 2	*	*	*	*	
MOROZOVA, Natalia	5 + 4	S	S	S	S	
NIKOULINA, Marina	1 + 1	S	S	S	S	
BATOUKHTINA, Elena	2 + 6	S	S	S	S	
ILCHENKO, Irina	5 + 13	S	S	S		
GODINA, ELena	1 + 1	*				
MENCHOVA, Tatiana	2 + 9			*	S	
ARTAMONOVA, Evguenia	10 + 25	S	S	S	S	
TICHTCHENKO, Elizaveta	4 + 14	S	S	S	S	
TIMONOVA, Ioulia	0 + 0					
GRATCHEVA, Tatiana	0 + 0			*	*	
SOKOLOVA, Liubov	0 + 0					

Team: CUB Cuba
Coach: GEORGE LAFITA, Eugenio R.
Assistant Coach: PERDOMO ESTRELLA, Antonio

Names	Pts + S/O	1	2	3	4	5
RUIZ, Yumilka	0 + 0					
COSTA, Marleny	3 + 7	S	S	S	S	S
LUIS, Mireya	13 + 15	S	S	S	S	S
IZQUIERDO, Lilia	3 + 3	*	S			
GATO, Idalmis	0 + 0				*	
O'FARRILL, Raiza	1 + 3	S	S	*	S	S
BELL, Regla	8 + 15	S	S	S	S	S
TORRES, Regla	9 + 9	*	S	S	S	S
AGUERO, Taismari	0 + 0					
FERNANDEZ, Ana Ibis	0 + 2	S				
CARVAJAL, Magalys	14 + 10	S	S	S	S	S
FRANCIA, Mirka	0 + 0					

Team: BRA Brazil
Coach: REZENDE, Bernardo
Assistant Coach: TABACH, Ricardo

Names	Pts + S/O	1	2	3	4	5
MOSER, Ana Beatriz	7 + 11	S	S	S	S	S
ALVARES, Ana Margarida Vieira	0 + 0				*	
CONNELLY, Ana Paula Rodrigues	6 + 4	S	S	S	S	S
BARROS, Leila Gomes de	0 + 0					
CALDEIRAS, Hilma Aparecida	0 + 0					
DIAS, Virna Cristine Dantas	10 + 30	S	S	S	S	S
CUNHA, Marcia Regina	14 + 16	S	S	S	S	S
BODZICK, Ericleia	0 + 0				*	*
SANGLARD, Ana Flavia Chritaro	4 + 1	S	S	S		
VENTURINI, Fernanda Porto	2 + 4	S	S	S		
SOUZA, Helia Rogerio de	1 + 0			*	*	*
SURUAGY, Sandra Maria Lima	0 + 0					

Team: RUS Russian Federation
Coach: KARPOL, Nikolai
Assistant Coach: OMELTCHENKO, Mikhail

Names	Pts + S/O	1	2	3	4	5
OGIENKO, Valentina	0 + 0	*		*		*
MOROZOVA, Natalia	12 + 1	S	S	S	S	S
NIKOULINA, Marina	2 + 0	S	S	S	S	S
BATOUKHTINA, Elena	5 + 9	S	S	S	S	S
ILCHENKO, Irina	2 + 1	S				
GODINA, ELena	4 + 18	*	S	S	S	S
MENCHOVA, Tatiana	6 + 5			*	*	S
ARTAMONOVA, Evguenia	7 + 9	S	S	S	S	S
TICHTCHENKO, Elizaveta	13 + 14	S	S	S	S	S
TIMONOVA, Ioulia	0 + 0					
GRATCHEVA, Tatiana	0 + 0				*	
SOKOLOVA, Liubov	0 + 0					

Team: BRA Brazil
Coach: REZENDE, Bernardo
Assistant Coach: TABACH, Ricardo

Names	Pts + S/O	1	2	3	4	5
MOSER, Ana Beatriz	13 + 11	S	S	S	S	S
ALVARES, Ana Margarida Vieira	2 + 10		*	*	S	S
CONNELLY, Ana Paula Rodrigues	7 + 10	S	S	S	S	S
BARROS, Leila Gomes de	6 + 4			*	S	S
CALDEIRAS, Hilma Aparecida	0 + 0					
DIAS, Virna Cristine Dantas	4 + 5	S	S	S	*	
CUNHA, Marcia Regina	4 + 7	S	S	S		
BODZICK, Ericleia	10 + 8		*	*	S	S
SANGLARD, Ana Flavia Chritaro	0 + 6	S	S	S		*
VENTURINI, Fernanda Porto	2 + 2	S	S	S	S	
SOUZA, Helia Rogerio de	0 + 0		*	*		*
SURUAGY, Sandra Maria Lima	0 + 0					

Women / *Dames*

FINAL - GOLD MATCH

CHN 1 - 3 CUB

Set	1	2	3	4	5	Total pts
Result	16 - 14	12 - 15	16 - 17	6 - 15		50 - 61
Duration	0:28	0:32	0:37	0:26		2:03

People's Republic of China				Cuba		
Att	Pts won	S/O		Att	Pts won	S/O
228	19	73	**Attacks**	216	30	83
87	9	2	**Blocks**	126	17	3
147	7		**Serves**	157	6	

1st Referee:	FIN	SALONEN, Jarmo
2nd Referee:	FRA	RACHARD, Patrick

Team: CHN People's Republic of China
Coach: LANG, Ping
Assistant Coach: CHEN, Zhong He

Names	Pts + S/O	1	2	3	4	5
LAI, Yawen	4 + 10	S	S	S	S	
LI, Yan	7 + 13	S	S	S	S	
CUI, Yongmei	6 + 8	S	S	S	S	
ZHU, Yunying	0 + 0					
WU, Yongmei	1 + 2			*	S	
WANG, Yi	5 + 11	S	S	S	*	
HE, Qi	4 + 3	S	S	S	S	
PAN, Wenli	0 + 0					
LIU, Xiaoning	0 + 0					
WANG, Ziling	0 + 0					
SUN, Yue	8 + 26	S	S	S	S	
WANG, Lina	0 + 2			*	*	

Team: CUB Cuba
Coach: GEORGE LAFITA, Eugenio R.
Assistant Coach: PERDOMO ESTRELLA, Antonio

Names	Pts + S/O	1	2	3	4	5
RUIZ, Yumilka	0 + 0					
COSTA, Marleny	8 + 6	S	S	S	S	
LUIS, Mireya	9 + 25	S	S	S	S	
IZQUIERDO, Lilia	0 + 1			*	S	
GATO, Idalmis	0 + 0					
O'FARRILL, Raiza	3 + 4	S	S	S		
BELL, Regla	15 + 20	S	S	S	S	
TORRES, Regla	7 + 17	S	S	S	S	
AGUERO, Taismari	0 + 0					
FERNANDEZ, Ana Ibis	3 + 1			*		
CARVAJAL, Magalys	8 + 12	S		S	S	
FRANCIA, Mirka	0 + 0					

GENERAL SUMMARY

Phase	Teams	Score
Quarterfinals	CHN - GER	3 - 0
Quarterfinals	NED - RUS	1 - 3
Quarterfinals	USA - CUB	0 - 3
Quarterfinals	KOR - BRA	0 - 3
Classification 5 - 8	GER - NED	2 - 3
Classification 5 - 8	USA - KOR	0 - 3

GENERAL SUMMARY - *continued*

Phase	Teams	Score
Final 7 - 8	GER - USA	1 - 3
Final 5 - 6	NED - KOR	3 - 0
Semifinals	CHN - RUS	3 - 1
Semifinals	CUB - BRA	3 - 2
Final - Bronze	RUS - BRA	2 - 3
Final - Gold	CHN - CUB	1 - 3

FINAL CLASSIFICATION

Rnk	Team	
1	Cuba	**Gold**
2	People's Republic of China	**Silver**
3	Brazil	**Bronze**
4	Russian Federation	
5	Netherlands	
6	Korea	
7	United States of America	
8	Germany	

WEIGHTLIFTING
HALTÉROPHILIE

Abbreviations and terms used in Weightlifting results tables
Abréviations et termes employés dans les tableaux de résultats d'haltérophilie

Term	English	Français
B	Bronze Medal	Médaille de bronze
Bodyweight Category	Bodyweight Category	Catégorie de poids
C. and Jerk	Clean and Jerk Weight	Poids épaulé-jeté
Clean/jerk wt	Clean and Jerk Weight	Poids épaulé-jeté
Ctry	Country	Pays
Final	Final	Finale
G	Gold Medal	Médaille d'or
Group	Group	Groupe
Name	Name	Nom
Lift	Lift	Lever
Olympic Records	Olympic Records	Records olympiques
Result	Result	Résultat
Rnk	Rank	Classement
Snatch wt	Snatch Weight	Poids arraché
S	Silver Medal	Médaille d'argent
Total	Total	Total
WD	Withdrawn	Abandon
Weight	Weight	Poids
World Records	World Records	Records du monde

International Weightlifting Federation (IWF)
Fédération Internationale d'Haltérophilie
1054 Budapest
Hold U 1
Hungary

Weightlifting / *Haltérophilie*
54 kg, Men / *54 kg, Messieurs*

FINAL

Rnk	Name	Ctry	Weight	Group	Snatch wt	Clean/jerk wt	Total	
1	MUTLU, Halil	TUR	53.91	A	132.5	155.0	287.5	G
2	ZHANG, Xiangsen	CHN	53.39	A	130.0	150.0	280.0	S
3	MINCHEV, Sevdalin	BUL	54.00	A	125.0	152.5	277.5	B
4	LAN, Shizhang	CHN	53.61	A	125.0	150.0	275.0	
5	CIHAREAN, Traian	ROM	53.90	A	120.0	145.0	265.0	
6	IVANOV, Ivan	BUL	53.90	A	112.5	145.0	257.5	
7	KO, Kwang-Ku	KOR	53.89	A	115.0	140.0	255.0	
8	FERNANDEZ, Juan	COL	53.94	B	110.0	145.0	255.0	
9	WANG, Shin-Yuan	TPE	53.56	B	105.0	145.0	250.0	
10	NOTOMI, Toshiyuki	JPN	53.60	A	110.0	140.0	250.0	
11	BONNEL, Eric	FRA	53.68	B	115.0	135.0	250.0	

FINAL - *continued*

Rnk	Name	Ctry	Weight	Group	Snatch wt	Clean/jerk wt	Total
12	SETIAWAN, Hari	INA	53.90	B	105.0	145.0	250.0
13	GORZELNIAK, Marek	POL	53.85	A	107.5	137.5	245.0
14	YANSKY, Viktor	UZB	53.94	B	107.5	135.0	242.5
15	SCARANTINO, Giovanni	ITA	53.89	B	110.0	130.0	240.0
16	CASTRO VELASQUEZ, Nelson	COL	53.05	B	105.0	130.0	235.0
17	NGUYEN, John	AUS	54.00	B	100.0	132.5	232.5
18	ADISEKHAR, Badathala	IND	53.93	B	105.0	125.0	230.0
19	MOROZOVS, Vladimirs	LAT	53.81	B	100.0	122.5	222.5
20	MEDRANO, Luis	GUA	53.41	B	100.0	120.0	220.0
21	SOUPPRAYEN PADIATTY, Gino	MRI	53.43	B	95.0	105.0	200.0
	KARCZAG, Tibor	HUN	53.96	B	0.0	0.0	0.0

Weightlifting / *Haltérophilie*
59 kg, Men / *59 kg, Messieurs*

FINAL

Rnk	Name	Ctry	Weight	Group	Snatch wt	Clean/jerk wt	Total	
1	TANG, Lingsheng	CHN	58.61	A	137.5	170.0	307.5	G
2	SABANIS, Leonidas	GRE	58.53	A	137.5	167.5	305.0	S
3	PECHALOV, Nikolai	BUL	58.88	A	137.5	165.0	302.5	B
4	IKEHATA, Hiroshi	JPN	58.66	B	132.5	165.0	297.5	
5	VARGAS, William	CUB	58.73	A	135.0	162.5	297.5	
6	XU, Dong	CHN	58.60	A	132.5	162.5	295.0	
7	SARKISIAN, Yurik	AUS	58.60	A	125.0	155.0	280.0	
8	FARKAS, Zoltan	HUN	58.90	B	130.0	150.0	280.0	
9	JACOB, Bryan	USA	58.82	B	122.5	150.0	272.5	
10	STANISLAV, Petr	CZE	58.70	B	112.5	142.5	255.0	

FINAL - *continued*

Rnk	Name	Ctry	Weight	Group	Snatch wt	Clean/jerk wt	Total
11	CHANDRASEKHARAN, Raghavan	IND	58.89	B	112.5	140.0	252.5
12	SINYAK, Viktor	BLR	58.70	B	112.5	137.5	250.0
13	RODRIGUEZ, Cesar	PUR	58.21	B	110.0	132.5	242.5
14	ALVES, Nuno	POR	58.28	B	102.5	135.0	237.5
15	al-DAWSARI, Bonayan	KSA	58.89	B	102.5	125.0	227.5
16	BUIHAMGHET, Mostapha	MAR	56.62	B	90.0	120.0	210.0
	CHUN, Byung-Kwan	KOR	58.95	A	135.0	0.0	0.0
	MELIKOV, Assif	AZE	58.74	A	0.0	0.0	0.0
	STEPHEN, Marcus	NRU	58.88	A	0.0	0.0	0.0
	SULEYMANOGLU, Hafiz	TUR	58.90	A	135.0	0.0	0.0

Weightlifting / *Haltérophilie*
64 kg, Men / *64 kg, Messieurs*

FINAL

Rnk	Name	Ctry	Weight	Group	Snatch wt	Clean/jerk wt	Total	
1	SULEYMANOGLU, Naim	TUR	63.90	A	147.5	187.5	335.0	G
2	LEONIDIS, Valerios	GRE	63.22	A	145.0	187.5	332.5	S
3	XIAO, Jiangang	CHN	63.15	A	145.0	177.5	322.5	B
4	TZELILIS, Yorgos	GRE	63.50	A	145.0	177.5	322.5	
5	POPA, Adrian	HUN	63.93	A	135.0	172.5	307.5	
6	ILIEV, Ilian	BUL	63.90	A	142.5	162.5	305.0	
7	YAGCI, Mucahit	TUR	63.46	B	135.0	167.5	302.5	
8	KECSKES, Zoltan	HUN	63.60	A	135.0	167.5	302.5	
9	PETROV, Petar	BUL	63.68	A	140.0	160.0	300.0	
10	MIYAJI, Yoshihisa	JPN	63.63	B	140.0	157.5	297.5	
11	EDELKHANOV, Umar	RUS	63.90	B	132.5	162.5	295.0	
12	DARBINIAN, Eduard	ARM	63.61	A	132.5	160.0	292.5	
13	HWANG, Eui-Youl	KOR	63.88	A	132.5	160.0	292.5	
14	LIAO, Hsing-Chou	TPE	63.74	B	125.0	165.0	290.0	
15	TACHIBANA, Masato	JPN	63.63	B	125.0	162.5	287.5	
16	OKHRAMENKO, Aleksandr	KAZ	63.65	C	127.5	160.0	287.5	
17	POPOV, Vladimir	MDA	63.74	B	130.0	157.5	287.5	
18	CIHAREAN, Marius	ROM	62.90	B	130.0	155.0	285.0	

FINAL - *continued*

Rnk	Name	Ctry	Weight	Group	Snatch wt	Clean/jerk wt	Total
19	MAXINIANU, Lucian	ROM	63.74	B	130.0	155.0	285.0
20	MAJAUSKAS, Gustavo	ARG	63.99	C	125.0	160.0	285.0
21	NATUSIEWICZ, Wojciech	POL	63.62	B	122.5	160.0	282.5
22	PATAO, Vernon	USA	64.00	C	122.5	160.0	282.5
23	EM, Oleg	KAZ	63.59	C	130.0	150.0	280.0
24	BASBAS, Azzedine	ALG	63.76	B	120.0	160.0	280.0
25	NDICKA MATAM, Samson	CMR	63.95	B	125.0	155.0	280.0
26	BERRIO, Roger	COL	63.63	C	122.5	155.0	277.5
27	BATISTA, Alexi	PAN	63.87	B	122.5	150.0	272.5
28	LAVERTUE, Jean	CAN	63.92	C	125.0	145.0	270.0
29	BOUZENADA, Fouad	ALG	63.98	C	115.0	152.5	267.5
30	GRULLART, Alfonso	DOM	63.79	C	115.0	145.0	260.0
31	CACERES, Francisco	ESA	64.00	C	115.0	145.0	260.0
32	NGUYEN, Than	USA	63.93	C	112.5	145.0	257.5
33	KUMAR, Sandeep	IND	63.57	C	110.0	142.5	252.5
34	KOVACIC, Miodrag	YUG	63.90	C	110.0	137.5	247.5
	ANALAU, Tony	SOL	61.87	C	0.0	0.0	0.0
	WANG, Guohua	CHN	63.45	A	0.0	0.0	0.0

Weightlifting / *Haltérophilie*
70 kg, Men / *70 kg, Messieurs*

FINAL

Rnk	Name	Ctry	Weight	Group	Snatch wt	Clean/jerk wt	Total	
1	ZHAN, Xugang	CHN	69.98	A	162.5	195.0	357.5	G
2	KIM, Myong Nam	PRK	69.79	A	160.0	185.0	345.0	S
3	FERI, Attila	HUN	69.20	A	152.5	187.5	340.0	B
4	ZHELYAZKOV, Plamen	BUL	69.61	A	155.0	180.0	335.0	
5	YAHIAOUI, Abdelmanaame	ALG	69.62	B	150.0	185.0	335.0	
6	MILITOSIAN, Israyel	ARM	69.88	A	152.5	182.5	335.0	
7	WAN, Jianhui	CHN	69.50	A	152.5	180.0	332.5	
8	ARANDA, Idalberto	CUB	69.84	A	145.0	187.5	332.5	
9	VASILEV, Zlatan	BUL	69.31	A	150.0	180.0	330.0	
10	BEHM, Andreas	GER	69.39	A	147.5	180.0	327.5	
11	BATMAZ, Ergun	TUR	69.55	A	150.0	175.0	325.0	
12	EGIAZARIAN, Haik	ARM	69.86	A	145.0	180.0	325.0	
13	SPYROU, Hristos	GRE	69.51	B	145.0	177.5	322.5	
14	McRAE, Tim	USA	69.86	B	145.0	177.5	322.5	

FINAL - *continued*

Rnk	Name	Ctry	Weight	Group	Snatch wt	Clean/jerk wt	Total
15	KHIZHNIAK, Oleksiy	UKR	69.94	B	142.5	177.5	320.0
16	KRETSOU, Serguei	MDA	69.68	B	142.5	172.5	315.0
17	GRONMAN, Jouni	FIN	69.56	B	142.5	170.0	312.5
18	OLUWA, Mojisola	NGR	68.84	C	140.0	170.0	310.0
19	HORIKOSHI, Noriaki	JPN	69.22	B	137.5	170.0	307.5
20	LUKAC, Rudolf	SVK	69.38	C	135.0	167.5	302.5
21	ALDENHOV, Andre	SWE	69.83	B	135.0	165.0	300.0
22	al SEBAEI, Abdalla	SYR	69.89	C	130.0	160.0	290.0
23	KABEER, Samsudeen	IND	69.75	C	125.0	150.0	275.0
24	GANDOLFO, Marcelo	ARG	69.05	C	120.0	140.0	260.0
	GULER, Fedail	TUR	69.96	A	WD	0.0	0.0
	KILAPA, Peter	PNG	69.22	C	120.0	0.0	0.0
	LEMME, Gabriel	ARG	69.39	B	0.0	0.0	0.0
	MOLNAR, Gabor	HUN	69.44	B	0.0	0.0	0.0

Weightlifting / *Haltérophilie*
76 kg, Men / *76 kg, Messieurs*

76 KG FINAL

Rnk	Name	Ctry	Weight	Group	Snatch wt	Clean/jerk wt	Total	
1	LARA, Pablo	CUB	75.91	A	162.5	205.0	367.5	G
2	YOTOV, Yoto	BUL	75.91	A	160.0	200.0	360.0	S
3	JON, Chol Ho	PRK	75.62	A	162.5	195.0	357.5	B
4	MITROU, Viktor	GRE	75.82	A	162.5	195.0	357.5	
5	LIN, Shoufeng	CHN	75.91	A	157.5	195.0	352.5	
6	STEINHOEFEL, Ingo	GER	75.77	A	160.0	187.5	347.5	
7	FILIMONOV, Sergey	RUS	75.96	B	160.0	185.0	345.0	
8	BARSEGIAN, Hovhannes	ARM	75.97	A	155.0	190.0	345.0	
9	LOBACHOV, Leonid	BLR	75.65	A	160.0	182.5	342.5	
10	POITSCHKE, Andrey	GER	75.41	B	155.0	180.0	335.0	
11	KECHKO, Oleg	BLR	75.79	A	155.0	180.0	335.0	
12	VELASCO, Alvaro	COL	75.92	B	145.0	180.0	325.0	

FINAL - *continued*

Rnk	Name	Ctry	Weight	Group	Snatch wt	Clean/jerk wt	Total
13	BIRSA, Vladimir	MDA	75.55	B	147.5	175.0	322.5
14	SULI, Ilirjan	ALB	75.93	B	147.5	175.0	322.5
15	RAI, Satheesha	IND	75.53	C	140.0	177.5	317.5
16	FATU, Ilie	ROM	75.09	B	135.0	180.0	315.0
17	BROWN, Damian	AUS	75.91	C	140.0	175.0	315.0
18	OFISA, Ofisa	SAM	75.87	C	127.5	160.0	287.5
19	SILVA, Edward	URU	74.43	C	120.0	147.5	267.5
20	DETENAMO, Quincy	NRU	75.97	C	110.0	142.5	252.5
21	FARO, Junior	ARU	75.95	C	112.5	137.5	250.0
	KYAPANAKSIAN, Khachatur	ARM	75.53	A	165.0	0.0	0.0
	NURULLAEV, Bakhtiyar	UZB	74.58	C	0.0	0.0	0.0
	YILMAZ, Mehmet	TUR	75.86	B	157.5	0.0	0.0

Weightlifting / *Haltérophilie*
83 kg, Men / *83 kg, Messieurs*

83 KG FINAL

Rnk	Name	Ctry	Weight	Group	Snatch wt	Clean/jerk wt	Total	
1	DIMAS, Pyrros	GRE	82.06	A	180.0	212.5	392.5	G
2	HUSTER, Marc	GER	82.36	A	170.0	213.5	383.5	S
3	COFALIK, Andrzej	POL	82.44	A	170.0	202.5	372.5	B
4	KOUNEV, Kiril	AUS	82.73	A	170.0	200.0	370.0	
5	VACARCIUC, Vadim	MDA	82.63	A	165.0	202.5	367.5	
6	CHAKHOIAN, Sergo	ARM	80.87	A	170.0	195.0	365.0	
7	SEVINC, Dursun	TUR	82.80	A	165.0	197.5	362.5	
8	MILEV, Krastu	BUL	82.71	B	160.0	200.0	360.0	
9	MIKIASHVILI, Bidzina	GEO	82.97	A	160.0	200.0	360.0	
10	MANSUROV, Rishat	KAZ	82.72	B	155.0	182.5	337.5	

FINAL - *continued*

Rnk	Name	Ctry	Weight	Group	Snatch wt	Clean/jerk wt	Total
11	GEYDAROV, Tofik	AZE	82.83	B	150.0	180.0	330.0
12	ARTHUR, Anthony	GBR	81.99	B	147.5	180.0	327.5
13	TREMBLAY, Serge	CAN	82.44	B	150.0	177.5	327.5
14	WU, Tsai-Fu	TPE	77.89	B	137.5	175.0	312.5
15	ZILITIS, Dainis	LAT	82.53	B	145.0	167.5	312.5
16	KUO, Tai-Chih	TPE	81.86	B	125.0	165.0	290.0
17	VAREA, Rupeni	FIJ	81.01	B	115.0	150.0	265.0
18	BACCUS, Steven	SEY	81.11	B	115.0	145.0	260.0
	BLYSHCHYK, Oleksandr	UKR	82.56	A	167.5	0.0	0.0
	RYMKULOV, Kuanysh	KAZ	82.82	B	0.0	0.0	0.0

Weightlifting / *Haltérophilie*
91 kg, Men / *91 kg, Messieurs*

FINAL

Rnk	Name	Ctry	Weight	Group	Snatch wt	Clean/jerk wt	Total	
1	PETROV, Aleksey	RUS	90.89	A	187.5	215.0	402.5	G
2	KOKAS, Leonidas	GRE	89.28	A	175.0	215.0	390.0	S
3	CARUSO, Oliver	GER	90.65	A	175.0	215.0	390.0	B
4	BULUT, Sunay	TUR	90.82	A	177.5	212.5	390.0	
5	ALEKSEEV, Igor	RUS	90.50	A	182.5	205.0	387.5	
6	HERNANDEZ, Carlos Alexis	CUB	90.87	A	175.0	207.5	382.5	
7	CHUMAK, Oleh	UKR	89.46	A	167.5	212.5	380.0	
8	BRATOYCHEV, Plamen	BUL	90.93	A	175.0	205.0	380.0	
9	LUNA, Julio	VEN	90.28	B	165.0	210.0	375.0	
10	TESOVIC, Martin	SVK	90.39	B	162.5	210.0	372.5	
11	MASLANY, Marek	POL	90.63	B	165.0	205.0	370.0	
12	SABARI, Enrique	CUB	90.72	A	165.0	205.0	370.0	
13	KARAPETIAN, Aleksan	ARM	90.25	A	167.5	200.0	367.5	

FINAL - *continued*

Rnk	Name	Ctry	Weight	Group	Snatch wt	Clean/jerk wt	Total
14	GOUGH, Tom	USA	90.92	B	167.5	200.0	367.5
15	KHLUD, Vladimir	BLR	90.05	B	165.0	195.0	360.0
16	GOODMAN, Harvey	AUS	89.94	B	157.5	200.0	357.5
17	BELYATSKIY, Viktor	BLR	90.56	A	167.5	190.0	357.5
18	MAKAROV, Andrey	KAZ	86.58	A	165.0	190.0	355.0
19	PLANCON, Cedric	FRA	87.56	B	155.0	190.0	345.0
20	IM, Dong-Ki	KOR	89.82	B	155.0	190.0	345.0
21	MANCINO, Raffaele	ITA	90.21	B	160.0	180.0	340.0
22	BROWN, Eric	ASA	90.05	B	150.0	180.0	330.0
23	VYSNIAUSKAS, Ramunas	LTU	90.35	B	140.0	175.0	315.0
24	GARABWAN, Gerard	NRU	90.87	B	115.0	150.0	265.0
	TAPAATOUTAI, Viliami	TGA	88.67	B	105.0	0.0	0.0

Weightlifting / *Haltérophilie*
99 kg, Men / *99 kg, Messieurs*

FINAL

Rnk	Name	Ctry	Weight	Group	Snatch wt	Clean/jerk wt	Total	
1	KAKIASVILIS, Akakios	GRE	96.78	A	185.0	235.0	420.0	G
2	KHRAPATUY, Anatoliy	KAZ	98.40	A	187.5	222.5	410.0	S
3	GOTFRID, Denis	UKR	97.17	A	187.5	215.0	402.5	B
4	RYBALCHENKO, Stanislav	UKR	98.55	A	182.5	212.5	395.0	
5	RUBIN, Vyacheslav	RUS	98.83	A	175.0	215.0	390.0	
6	SMIRNOV, Dmitry	RUS	98.86	A	175.0	215.0	390.0	
7	SADYKOV, Igor	GER	98.34	A	177.5	207.5	385.0	
8	GRIGORIAN, Aghvan	ARM	98.33	A	175.0	205.0	380.0	
9	CHIRITSO, Oleg	BLR	98.63	A	172.5	207.5	380.0	
10	CHOI, Dong-Kil	KOR	97.23	B	165.0	207.5	372.5	
11	BENDARY, Tharwat	EGY	97.81	B	167.5	205.0	372.5	
12	CARRIO, Lorenzo	ESP	98.60	B	167.5	200.0	367.5	
13	URINOV, Aleksandr	UZB	97.72	B	172.5	192.5	365.0	
14	KELLEY, Pete	USA	98.96	B	160.0	197.5	357.5	

FINAL - *continued*

Rnk	Name	Ctry	Weight	Group	Snatch wt	Clean/jerk wt	Total
15	NISHIMOTO, Yoshimitsu	JPN	98.07	B	155.0	200.0	355.0
16	JOKEL, Jaroslav	SVK	98.35	B	160.0	192.5	352.5
17	VIHODET, Mihail	MDA	98.20	B	162.5	185.0	347.5
18	VALENCIA HERNANDEZ, Deivan J.	COL	98.31	B	152.5	195.0	347.5
19	POLOM, Roman	CZE	98.53	B	160.0	187.5	347.5
20	ZDANOVSKIS, Ivars	LAT	98.79	B	150.0	187.5	337.5
21	DANTAS, Edmilson	BRA	98.81	C	152.5	182.5	335.0
22	ESCALANTE, Cristian	CHI	98.46	C	142.5	172.5	315.0
23	AHMED, Raed	IRQ	97.80	C	137.5	165.0	302.5
24	NUNUKU PERA, Samuel	COK	98.11	C	120.0	165.0	285.0
25	OKOTHNYAWALLO, Collins	KEN	98.14	C	125.0	150.0	275.0
26	SHAABAN, Redha	KUW	97.83	C	115.0	140.0	255.0
	IVANOVSKI, Viaceslav	ISR	98.50	B	0.0	0.0	0.0
	KOPYTOV, Sergey	KAZ	98.93	A	170.0	0.0	0.0

Weightlifting / *Haltérophilie*
108 kg, Men / *108 kg, Messieurs*

FINAL

Rnk	Name	Ctry	Weight	Group	Snatch wt	Clean/jerk wt	Total	
1	TAYMAZOV, Timur	UKR	107.32	A	195.0	235.0	430.0	G
2	SYRTSOV, Sergey	RUS	107.22	A	195.0	225.0	420.0	S
3	VLAD, Nicu	ROM	107.70	A	197.5	222.5	420.0	B
4	EMELYANOV, Vladimir	BLR	107.41	A	187.5	220.0	407.5	
5	CUI, Wenhua	CHN	102.52	A	190.0	215.0	405.0	
6	BARNETT, Wes	USA	107.88	A	175.0	220.0	395.0	
7	VARDANIAN, Ara	ARM	107.93	A	180.0	215.0	395.0	
8	OSUCH, Dariusz	POL	105.70	A	177.5	215.0	392.5	
9	KALINKE, Mario	GER	102.30	B	177.5	212.5	390.0	
10	SCERBATIHS, Viktors	LAT	107.17	B	177.5	212.5	390.0	
11	PROCHOROW, Dimitri	GER	107.32	B	175.0	215.0	390.0	
12	STARIKOVITCH, Konstantine	USA	106.90	A	177.5	210.0	387.5	

FINAL - *continued*

Rnk	Name	Ctry	Weight	Group	Snatch wt	Clean/jerk wt	Total
13	CHUN, Sang-Suk	KOR	107.93	B	170.0	210.0	380.0
14	KANERVA, Janne	FIN	107.44	B	160.0	200.0	360.0
15	YOSHIMOTO, Hisaya	JPN	107.92	B	170.0	190.0	360.0
16	MANUSHEV, Valentin	UZB	107.81	B	160.0	190.0	350.0
17	WANWANG, Nopadol	THA	107.33	B	140.0	177.5	317.5
18	RUMMUN, Shirish	MRI	107.89	B	132.5	155.0	287.5
19	KAVUMA, Ali	UGA	106.95	B	110.0	150.0	260.0
	FLERKO, Sergey	RUS	107.90	A	185.0	0.0	0.0
	GOGIA, Mukhran	GEO	106.16	A	WD	0.0	0.0
	PANATIDIS, Alexandros	GRE	107.88	B	0.0	0.0	0.0
	RAZORENOV, Ihor	UKR	106.90	A	0.0	WD	0.0
	SHCHEKALO, Gennadiy	BLR	107.27	A	175.0	0.0	0.0

Weightlifting / *Haltérophilie*
108+ kg, Men / *Plus de 108 kg, Messieurs*

FINAL

Rnk	Name	Ctry	Weight	Group	Snatch wt	Clean/jerk wt	Total	
1	CHEMERKIN, Andrey	RUS	165.47	A	197.5	260.0	457.5	G
2	WELLER, Ronny	GER	138.09	A	200.0	255.0	455.0	S
3	BOTEV, Stefan	AUS	123.96	A	200.0	250.0	450.0	B
4	KIM, Tae-Hyun	KOR	133.30	A	190.0	247.5	437.5	
5	KURLOVICH, Aleksandr	BLR	133.74	A	195.0	230.0	425.0	
6	NERLINGER, Manfred	GER	164.42	A	185.0	237.5	422.5	
7	SALTSIDIS, Pavlos	GRE	132.79	A	185.0	235.0	420.0	
8	STARK, Tibor	HUN	128.78	A	187.5	227.5	415.0	
9	BERGMANIS, Raimonds	LAT	131.85	B	177.5	225.0	402.5	

FINAL - *continued*

Rnk	Name	Ctry	Weight	Group	Snatch wt	Clean/jerk wt	Total
10	GRIMSETH, Stian	NOR	141.96	A	180.0	220.0	400.0
11	ASLAN, Erdinc	TUR	138.08	B	170.0	227.5	397.5
12	BERGSTROM, Anders	SWE	131.21	B	175.0	220.0	395.0
13	DANIELIAN, Ashot	ARM	148.53	B	177.5	217.5	395.0
14	HENRY, Mark	USA	184.92	A	175.0	202.5	377.5
15	KETTNER, Steven	AUS	136.38	B	170.0	205.0	375.0
16	INGALSBE, Thomas	USA	151.22	B	165.0	200.0	365.0
17	JOSHI, Sunil	NEP	115.61	B	120.0	162.5	282.5
	HALILOV, Igor	UZB	131.73	A	177.5	WD	0.0
	TARANENKO, Leonid	BLR	150.55	A	WD	0.0	0.0

WEIGHTLIFTING RECORDS OF THE 1996 CENTENNIAL OLYMPIC GAMES / *Records d'haltérophilie aux Jeux Olympiques du Centenaire de 1996*

World Records

Bodyweight Category	Lift	Result	Name	Ctry
54 kg	Snatch	132.5 kg	MUTLU, Halil	TUR
59 kg	Total	307.5 kg	TANG, Lingsheng	CHN
64 kg	Clean and Jerk	185.0 kg	SULEYMANOGLU, Naim	TUR
	Clean and Jerk	187.5 kg	LEONIDIS, Valerios	GRE
	Total	332.5 kg	SULEYMANOGLU, Naim	TUR
	Total	335.0 kg	SULEYMANOGLU, Naim	TUR
70 kg	Snatch	162.5 kg	ZHAN, Xugang	CHN
	Clean and Jerk	195.0 kg	ZHAN, Xugang	CHN
	Total	357.5 kg	ZHAN, Xugang	CHN
83 kg	Snatch	180.0 kg	DIMAS, Pyrros	GRE
	Clean and Jerk	213.0 kg	DIMAS, Pyrros	GRE
	Clean and Jerk	213.5 kg	HUSTER, Marc	GER
	Total	392.5 kg	DIMAS, Pyrros	GRE
91 kg	Snatch	187.5 kg	PETROV, Aleksey	RUS
99 kg	Clean and Jerk	235.0 kg	KAKIASVILIS, Akakios	GRE
	Total	420.0 kg	KAKIASVILIS, Akakios	GRE
108 kg	Clean and Jerk	236.0 kg	TAYMAZOV, Timur	UKR
+108 kg	Clean and Jerk	255.0 kg	WELLER, Ronny	GER
	Clean and Jerk	260.0 kg	CHEMERKIN, Andrey	RUS

Olympic Records

Bodyweight Category	Lift	Result	Name	Ctry
54 kg	Snatch	130.0 kg	MUTLU, Halil	TUR
	Snatch	132.5 kg	MUTLU, Halil	TUR
	Total	287.5 kg	MUTLU, Halil	TUR
59 kg	Clean and Jerk	170.0 kg	TANG, Lingsheng	CHN
	Total	305.0 kg	TANG, Lingsheng	CHN
	Total	307.5 kg	TANG, Lingsheng	CHN
64 kg	Clean and Jerk	185.0 kg	SULEYMANOGLU, Naim	TUR
	Clean and Jerk	187.5 kg	LEONIDIS, Valerios	GRE
	Total	332.5 kg	SULEYMANOGLU, Naim	TUR
	Total	335.0 kg	SULEYMANOGLU, Naim	TUR
70 kg	Snatch	162.5 kg	ZHAN, Xugang	CHN
	Clean and Jerk	195.0 kg	ZHAN, Xugang	CHN
	Total	352.5 kg	ZHAN, Xugang	CHN
	Total	357.5 kg	ZHAN, Xugang	CHN
83 kg	Snatch	180.0 kg	DIMAS, Pyrros	GRE
	Clean and Jerk	212.5 kg	DIMAS, Pyrros	GRE
	Total	387.5 kg	DIMAS, Pyrros	GRE
	Total	392.5 kg	DIMAS, Pyrros	GRE
91 kg	Snatch	187.5 kg	PETROV, Aleksey	RUS
99 kg	Clean and Jerk	235.0 kg	KAKIASVILIS, Akakios	GRE
	Total	420.0 kg	KAKIASVILIS, Akakios	GRE
108 kg	Clean and Jerk	235.0 kg	TAYMAZOV, Timur	UKR
+108 kg	Clean and Jerk	255.0 kg	WELLER, Ronny	GER
	Clean and Jerk	260.0 kg	CHEMERKIN, Andrey	RUS
	Total	457.5 kg	CHEMERKIN, Andrey	RUS

Note: These records were established in the A groups of the corresponding competitions.

Remarque : Ces records ont été établis dans les groupes A des compétitions correspondantes.

JOYCELYN N WILSON • JULIE C WILSON • JULIE C WILSON • KAREN J WILSON • KAREN L WILSON • KATHERINE E WILSON • KATHERINE S WILSON • KATHLEEN A WILSON • KELLIE WILSON • KIKI WILSON • KIMBERLEY E WILSON • KRISTINA E WILSON • LARNELLE R WILSON • LAWRENCE G WILSON • LESLIE E WILSON • LINDA Y WILSON • LORI A WILSON • LUCILE M WILSON • MARGARET E WILSON • MARGARET L WILSON • MARGO WILSON • MARIE H WILSON • MARK WILSON • MARK A WILSON • MARSHALL D WILSON • MARTHA F WILSON • MARY WILSON • MARY-MARTHA WILSON • MARY W WILSON • MARYANN B WILSON • MATTHEW B WILSON • MATTHEW J WILSON • MICHAEL E WILSON • MICHAEL E WILSON • MICHAEL K WILSON • MICHELLE A WILSON • MICHELLE B WILSON • MICHELLE L WILSON • MIKE WILSON • MIKEL F WILSON • NITIKA A WILSON • PALMER WILSON • PAMELA WILSON • PAMELA R WILSON • PATRICIA WILSON • PATRICIA A WILSON • PATRICIA G WILSON • PHILIP J WILSON • RALEIGH R WILSON • RANDAL J WILSON • RHONDA M WILSON • RICHARD WILSON • RICHARD G WILSON • RICHARD J WILSON • RICHARD M WILSON • RITA A WILSON • ROBERT C WILSON • ROBERT L WILSON • RODERICK G WILSON • RONNIE D WILSON • RUTH A WILSON • SANDRA L WILSON • SAUNDRA J WILSON • SCOTT K WILSON • SHARON H WILSON • SHAWN-TA S WILSON • SHEILA M WILSON • SHELLY L WILSON • SHERRIE L WILSON • SHERRY L WILSON • SKIPPER C WILSON • SOPHIA Y WILSON • STEPHANIA L WILSON • STEPHEN L WILSON • STEVEN D WILSON • SUE W WILSON • SUSAN D WILSON • TANIA D WILSON • TANYA G WILSON • TERESA C WILSON • THERESA E WILSON • THERESA HUTCHINS WILSON • THERESA M WILSON • THOMAS A WILSON • THOMAS W WILSON • TINY B WILSON • TRACEY E WILSON • TWAN L WILSON • VALARIE WILSON • VIVIAN B WILSON • WENDY S WILSON • WHITNEY L WILSON • WILLIAM C WILSON • WILLIAM F WILSON • WILLIAM H WILSON • WILLIAM L WILSON • WINONA L WILSON • KATHLEEN M WILSON-CHU • CHARLETTA WILSON JACKS • HAROLD E WILSON JR • HAROLD H WILSON JR • REUBEN WILSON JR • FRANCIS E WILSON JR. • JOSEPH S WILSON JR. • ROBYN W WILSON MT • KIRA E WILSTERMAN • BOB WILT • LAURA E WILT • WILLIAM L WILTBANK • MARY I WILTON • CECILIA M WILTZ • AUDREY M WIMBERLY • RHEBA R WIMBERLY • WILLIAM NICK WIMBERLY • SHON L WIMBISH • TAWANA WIMBISH • WILLIE BILL WIMBUSH • BRANDY L WIMMER • KATRINA M WINBERG • JOHN M WINBORN • JOHN G WINBURN • CHARLES J WINCHELL • JUDY A WINCHELL • SARAH M WINCHESTER • EVERT WIND • GERHARD A WIND • PAUL E WINDERS • SUSAN E WINDERWEEDLE • LAURA A WINDHAM • DEBORAH B WINDHORST • MARLENE WINDLE • KEITH A WINDMILLER ATC • LORI B WINDMILLER CATC • SAUNDRA H WINDOM • JUDITH B WINDSOR • MATTHEW P WINDSOR • DONNA H WINEBARGER • LAUREN F WINEBURGH • DARIN S WINEGAR • RONALD D WINEGAR • RICHARD S WINER • WENDY KAPLAN WINER • EMERSON J WINFIELD • NICOLE M WINFIELD • RENEE A WINFREY • ROY W WINFREY • ANNE L WINGATE • DEBORAH L WINGATE • GAIL G WINGATE • MICHAEL A WINGATE • BARBARA A WINGEL • JODI M WINGFIELD • L'INDA M WINGFIELD • MARYANN E WINGFIELD • MILTON W WINGFIELD • THOMAS K WINGFIELD • JEFFERSON D WINGFIELD JR • HENRY D WINGFIELD MT • JEAN S WINGIS • GRACE E WINGO • MARVIN R WINGO • PHYLLIS A WINGO • MARJORIE ALWES WINHAM • PETER G WINHAM • LISA WINIKOR • ALLEN B WINISKI • CATHERINE WINKERT • JOHN T WINKERT • JEAN E WINKLE • TARYN WINKLEMAN • ELAINE B WINKLER • KEVIN P WINKLER • MATT V WINKLER • WILLIAM G WINKLER • ALAN R WINN • MATTHEW B WINN • PATSY M WINN • TERRY A WINN • JAYME L WINNICK • LINELL L WINNICKI • STEVEN J WINOKUR • SARA S WINSHIP • GERRY L WINSLETTE • ANITA L WINSLOW • DONNA WINSLOW • HENNY H WINSLOW • JON J WINSLOW • KATHLEEN Y WINSLOW • KENNETH WINSLOW • MARCUS B WINSLOW • DEREK S WINSOR • DEREK S WINSOR • BETH WINSTEAD • CATHY L WINSTEAD • CHRIS L WINSTEAD • JESSICA F WINSTEAD • MYRA B WINSTEAD • PATRICIA G WINSTEAD • SUE E WINSTEAD • ARTHUR WINSTEAD III MD • CHAUNCEY C WINSTON • DENISE M WINSTON • KHALILAH J WINSTON • PAUL L WINSTON • ROBERT J WINSTON • STACEY A WINSTON • PAMELA SUE S WINTEMUTE • DANA F.D. WINTER • ELIZABETH J WINTER • GERI WINTER • MARIETTA S WINTER • WILLIAM O WINTER • ANN D WINTERS • BRENDAN WINTERS • DEBORAH L WINTERS • GENE W WINTERS • GREGG WINTERS • JOHN A WINTERS • KIRBY J WINTERS • LEONARD A WINTERS • LORI S WINTERS • SARAH C WINTERSTEIN • EVA WINTHER • CYNTHIA Y WINTHROP • EDWARD F WINTHROP • DENISE WINTON • KENT A WIPF • JERRE L WIPPERMANN • SARAH BETH WIPPERMANN • ALVA T WIRTH • CAROL A WISE • DAVID A WISE • DEBORAH A WISE • DENISE F WISE • JOEL A WISE • JOHN L WISE • KATHERINE T WISE • KHALID W WISE • LAURIE K WISE • MARYJANE WISE • MICHAEL J WISE • OMAR M WISE • ROBERT DOUGLAS WISE • SHIRLEY L WISE • EDDIE M WISE JR • MARIA C WISE MILLER • KAY L WISE MT • MILLA S WISECARVER • DONNA T WISELY ATC • CHERYL M WISEMAN • LUCI A WISEMAN • JACOB H WISENALL JR • KAREN F WISER • MICHAEL R WISER • MICHELLE L WISER • ROBERT K WISER • TRAVIS S WISER • BOBBY E WISHAM • CHAD E WISHAM • LEE ANN WISHAM • ALICIA D WISHARD • WILLIAM R WISHARD • ALBERT F WISIALKO • DIANNE C WISNER • HENRY WISNIEWSKI • MIKE WISOTZKE • GABI WISST • LISA R WISTROM • MELVIN T WITCHER • KIMBERLY D WITCHET • SHAREN WITCHEY • DEAN A WITHAM • ALAN K WITHEROW • CAROLEN C WITHEROW • RACHEL P WITHERS • ELLIE D WITHERSPOON • MARY T WITHERSPOON • RHONDA WITHERSPOON • SIMONA WITHERSPOON • KEVIN C WITHROW • ROGER K. WITHROW • JESSE R WITKOWSKI • KATARZYNA A WITKOWSKI • LEE J WITKOWSKI • LARRY R WITLEN • JON S WITSCHY • GILBERT P WITSELL • AUTUMN J WITT • CAROLE J WITT • EILEEN M WITT • ELLEN P WITT • PAMELA E WITT • REGINA B WITT • SUSAN M WITT • MICHAEL J WITTE • SUSAN S WITTE • JANE T WITTEN • JOHN M WITTEN • MARY HELEN WITTEN • VALERIE I WITTENBERG • PATRICIA A WITTENMYER • GENE WITTENSTROM • KATIE S WITTLING • LYNN M WITTSTOCK • EVAN E WIX • SHAREN L WIXOM • ANNA WLASIUK • LOUISE WLLLINGHAM • AMY C WOEBKENBERG • KELLY M WOEBKENBERG • RICHARD A WOEHNKER • JANEEN WOELFER • JUDITH L WOELLNER • DORI S WOFFORD • ELAINE S WOFFORD • ROGER L WOFFORD • SUE B WOFFORD • DAVID P WOHLHUETER • HEIKO C WOHNSDORF • AMY R WOITKOVICH • FREDERIC WOJCIECHOWSKI • CHESTER J WOJNA • SHIFI B WOJNOWICH • KATHLEEN H WOKEN ATC • SCOTT WOKEN ATC • LORRAINE L WOLAVER • NICHOLAS E WOLAVER • JIM F WOLBRINK • HOWARD NATHAN WOLCHANSKY • GIL M WOLCHOCK • MICHAEL A WOLD • URSULA D WOLD • KASAHUM WOLDERMARIAM • CELIA B WOLDRIDGE • ADAM E WOLF • BO WOLF • BONNIE WOLF • JULIAN WOLF • KEVIN S WOLF • KRISTEN A WOLF • MICHELE S WOLF • NIKKI WOLF • PHILIP S WOLF • RICHARD L WOLF • TOM R WOLF • WAYNE WOLF • KEVIN M WOLF ATC • STEVEN C WOLF CATC • ROBERT WOLFARTH • AMY M WOLFE • ANTHONY C WOLFE • BRENDA G WOLFE • CHARLES R WOLFE • CONSTANCE J WOLFE • DALE A WOLFE • DAVID WOLFE • DEANNA P WOLFE • ELIZABETH R WOLFE • GWEN E WOLFE • JAMES D WOLFE • JULIE M WOLFE • MARILYN W WOLFE • MELISSA K WOLFE • MICHAEL K WOLFE • NORA WOLFE • R WARREN WOLFE • ROBERTA E WOLFE • ROYCE D WOLFE • STEPHANIE J WOLFE • SUE P WOLFE • TAMMI E WOLFE • THOMAS E WOLFE • TREVOR G WOLFE • WILLIAM M WOLFE • CHARLES A WOLFE III • LEE S WOLFE JR • GAYLE L WOLFENSON • KIM M WOLFF • SCOTT W WOLFF ATC • MARY E WOLFORD • MELANIE WOLFORD • JOY M WOLFRAM • PEARL B WOLFSON • DENNIS WOLKIN • DARREN M WOLKOW • JANA E WOLKOW • MICHAEL J WOLKOW • TERRI B WOLKOW • ROBERT J WOLKOWITZ • JEAN WOLLAM • KERSTIN WOLNY • WALTER WOLOS • MARK W WOLOZIN • DIANE A WOLPERT • LORELLEE W WOLTERS • RICHARD F WOLTERS • ERIC S WOLTHUIS • CONNIE J WOLTZ • JOHNNIE WOLUEWICH • MARILYN L WOLVEN • MELINDA K WOLZ • MICHAEL E WOMAC • BRADLEY D WOMACK • CLAUDIA S WOMACK • DENNIS R WOMACK • MAGDALENE D WOMACK • MARY A WOMACK • MARY E WOMACK • YTASHA WOMACK • WAYNE L WOMACK JR • MICHAEL S WOMACK MD • DEBBIE S WOMBLE • FREDERICK A WOMBLE • JOSEPH WOMBLE • JA-YOUNG WON • CAROL C WONG • ERIC H WONG • GEORGE Y WONG • JENNIFER T WONG • JUE R WONG • LISA A WONG • SANDRA Y WONG • SHARLEEN L WONG • STEPHEN WONG • VERA W WONG-GONG • AMIE E WOO • BESS G WOO • HONG JOON WOO • LYNNE C WOO • MARILYN L WOO • SHERRON L WOO • ANGELA K WOOD • ARANYA WOOD • BARBARA L WOOD • BETTY A WOOD • CAROL M WOOD • CARRIE A WOOD • CARTER J WOOD • CECILE A WOOD • CHRISTINE WOOD • CLARENCE E WOOD • DANNIELLE R WOOD • DAVID G WOOD • DAVID L WOOD • DAVID L WOOD • DEBBIE WOOD • DEWEY B WOOD • DONICE E WOOD • ELAINE R WOOD • EMILY H WOOD • FRANCES S WOOD • GEORGE K WOOD • GRAHAME WOOD • HEATHER R WOOD • HOLLY WOOD • JAMES R WOOD • JANE M WOOD • JEANNE M WOOD • JIM M WOOD • JOANN WOOD • JOEL K WOOD • JOHN E WOOD • JOHN M WOOD • JUDY WOOD • KENNETH W WOOD • KRISTIN G WOOD • LARRY C WOOD • LARRY M WOOD • LARRY O WOOD • LAWRENCE K WOOD • LINDA L WOOD • LINDA P WOOD • LINDA S WOOD • MARGARET P WOOD • MICHAEL F WOOD • MICHAEL J WOOD • MICHAEL R WOOD • MONICA WOOD • PATRICK E WOOD • RICKEY L WOOD • SARAH A WOOD • SARAH C WOOD • SEAN WOOD • SIDNEY M WOOD • STEVEN B WOOD • SUSAN K WOOD • SUSAN L WOOD • SUSANNE M WOOD • TERRY R WOOD • THOMAS M WOOD • WHITNEY R WOOD • WILLIAM A WOOD • WILLIAM T WOOD • YVONNE C WOOD • JUDI S WOOD-CARTER • MARGARET A WOOD-TAYLOR • SHARON R WOOD ATC • CONSTANCE WOODALL • FRANKLIN D WOODALL • HEATHER L WOODALL • KATHY M WOODALL • LINDA WOODALL • PAGE WOODALL • RHONDA K WOODALL • SUE C WOODALL • THOMAS E WOODALL • WILLIAM R WOODALL • OSCAR C WOODALL JR • BENNIE M WOODARD • DIANE E WOODARD • GEORGE WOODARD • LONZELL WOODARD • LUTRICIA A WOODARD • MARIA T WOODARD • MARSHA L WOODARD • MARY WOODARD • MICHAL S WOODARD • RYAN WOODARD • TIMOTHY W WOODARD • TRACEY WOODARD • WILLIAM T WOODARD • KAREN J WOODBECK ATC • JULIA T WOODBURY • BRIAN WOODCOCK • CARRIE M WOODCOCK • RICHARD H WOODCOCK • NORMA D WOODCOME • SUSAN F WOODELL • DALLAS W WOODEN • MARY LEE WOODEN • BLANE A WOODFIN • MICHELE L WOODFORD • RICHARD G WOODFORD • ROSEMARY E WOODFORD • DANA WOODHALL • ETHLYN C WOODHAM • MARTHA A WOODHAM • ROBERTA K WOODHOUSE • KIMBERLY R WOODIN • DALE E WOODLAND • RICHARD H WOODLEE • JOSEPH D WOODMAN • KELLI R WOODMAN • AMY N WOODRICK • ED WOODRICK • STEPHENS B WOODROUGH JR • THOMAS R WOODROW • CECIL C WOODRUFF • DALE K WOODRUFF • DIANA L WOODRUFF • ELIZABETH W WOODRUFF • JOANN WOODRUFF • MARANDA J WOODRUFF • MELVIN D WOODRUFF • MEREDITH WOODRUFF • NATHAN WOODRUFF • STEPHANIE L WOODRUFF • AMI E WOODS • CAMERON M WOODS • CHRISTOPHER A WOODS • DARCEY D WOODS • ELIZABETH L WOODS • GERALD W WOODS • INEZ WOODS • JAMES B WOODS • MARY E WOODS • NANCY R WOODS • NICOLE Y WOODS • PEGGY D WOODS • PHILLIP WOODS • RAMONA T WOODS • RANDALL O WOODS • RASHAAD WOODS • SYLVIA J WOODS • TAMMY D WOODS • TIMOTHY WOODS • TONI W WOODS • YVONNE S WOODS • LAWRENCE WOODS JR • JERRY WOODSON • KRISTA M WOODSON • TAMMY WOODSON • THOMAS C WOODSON • ALAN T WOODWARD • CHARLES RAY WOODWARD • DANA W WOODWARD • JULIA L WOODWARD • KAREN E WOODWARD • KELLY A WOODWARD • MICHELLE A WOODWARD • PAMELA T WOODWARD • RANDOLPH C WOODWARD • RONNA G WOODWARD • STEPHEN L WOODWARD • JC WOODWARD JR • SCOTT A WOODWORTH • THOMAS E WOODWORTH • BIVIAN M WOODY • CLAUDIA L WOODY • ELIZABETH C WOODY • JACKLYN WOODY • JANEY P WOODY • JEAN C WOODY • JOHN B WOODY • JULIE A WOODY • KEVIN R WOODY • N REES WOODY • N REES WOODY • PATRICIA A WOODY • NORRIS R WOODY JR • JOHN C WOODYARD • HANK WOOLARD • JACK C WOOLARD • VIRGINIA B WOOLBRIGHT • CAMILLE WOOLCOCK • ANITA B WOOLDRIDGE • MARY M WOOLDRIDGE • TAYLOR WOOLERY • WILLIAM A WOOLERY • E. WARREN WOOLF • EDWARD P WOOLF • SUE B WOOLF • RALPH WOOLFOLK • TIMOTHY R WOOLHEATER • PHILIP A WOOSNAM • AIMEE C WOOSTER • DEBORAH L WOOSTER • JANICE WOOSTER • ROY III D WOOSTER • ROY JR D WOOSTER • KRIS S WOOTEN • LEAH M WOOTEN • LOIS C WOOTEN • MICHAEL H WOOTEN • ROGER S WOOTEN • TERRELL G WOOTEN • THOMAS W WOOTEN JR • CHARLES D WOOTERS • CASSANDRA B WOOTTEN • THOMAS D WOOTTEN • SUSAN H. WOOTTON • MARIJAN E WORD • SYLVIA WORD • WESLEY B WORD • PAUL T WORDEN • REEDA A WORDEN • SHAURA L WORKMAN • CHARITY WORKS • ROBERT D WORKS • TAHIRAH WORKS • DAVID D WORLEY • GREGG M WORLEY • JENNIFER D WORLEY • KRISTIN WORLEY • LYNWOOD P WORLEY • MARY M WORLEY • MICHAEL G WORLEY • SARA J WORLEY • TED S WORLEY • JULIE A WORNER • ANN MICHELE WORRALL • DEBORAH H WORRELL • JENNIFER L WORRELL • PAT ANN WORRELL • SONDRA L WORRELL • EMORY L WORSHAM • SUZANNE JANIE WORSHAM • HUGH S WORSHAM DVM • ROGER W WORSLEY • TAINA M WORSTER • JAY D WORTH • RITA N WORTH • STEPHEN WORTH • ROBERT D WORTH JR • DIANE WORTHAM • DWARTNEY WORTHAM • NANCY S WORTHEN • WILLIAM M WORTHINGTON • GREGORY C WORTHY • JERRY L. WORTHY • SANDRA D WORTHY • VANN WORTHY • VERNON WORTHY • WILLIAM J WORTMAN • TORI A WOSKOSKI • JASON WOULLARD • ANNE MARIE WOZNIAK • JASON A WOZNIAK • PAUL D WOZNIAK • MARISIN D WRAY • TERIA A WRAY • CARLA L WREN • KATHLEEN P WRENN • MARGARET W WRENN • ELIZABETH S WRENN-ESTES • ALISON S WRIGHT • AMY D WRIGHT • ANITA W WRIGHT • ANNA H WRIGHT • ANNE M WRIGHT • ANTHONY P WRIGHT • ARCHER S WRIGHT • ARETHA N WRIGHT • ARLEEN B WRIGHT • AUDREY T WRIGHT • BARRY WRIGHT • BRENT S WRIGHT • CANDY L WRIGHT • CARLOS A WRIGHT • CAROLE M WRIGHT • CARY WRIGHT

WRESTLING
LUTTE

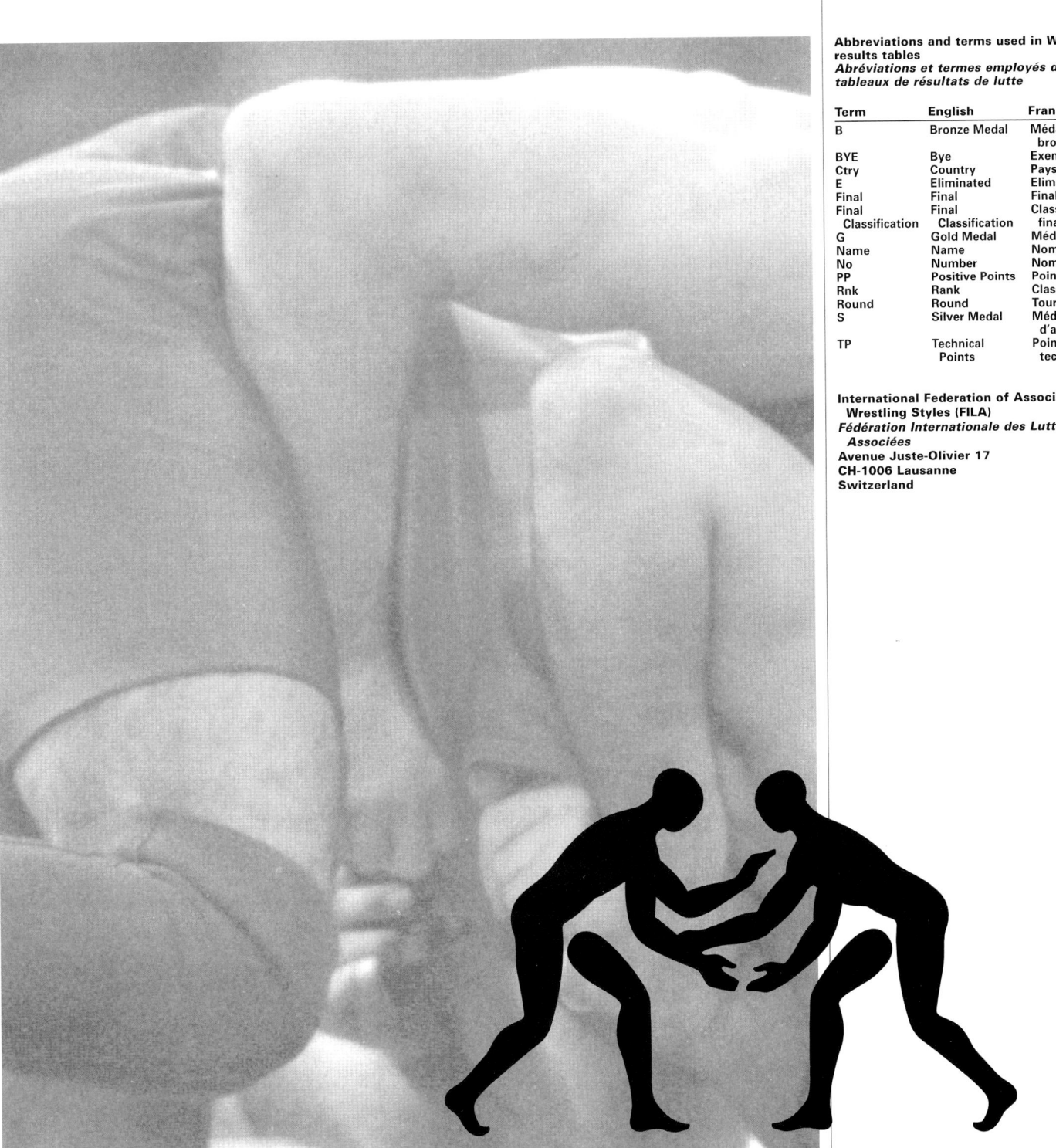

Abbreviations and terms used in Wrestling results tables
Abréviations et termes employés dans les tableaux de résultats de lutte

Term	English	Français
B	Bronze Medal	Médaille de bronze
BYE	Bye	Exemption
Ctry	Country	Pays
E	Eliminated	Eliminé
Final	Final	Finale
Final Classification	Final Classification	Classement final
G	Gold Medal	Médaille d'or
Name	Name	Nom
No	Number	Nombre
PP	Positive Points	Points positifs
Rnk	Rank	Classement
Round	Round	Tour
S	Silver Medal	Médaille d'argent
TP	Technical Points	Points techniques

International Federation of Associated Wrestling Styles (FILA)
Fédération Internationale des Luttes Associées
Avenue Juste-Olivier 17
CH-1006 Lausanne
Switzerland

Wrestling / *Lutte*

Freestyle, 48 kg (105.5 lb), Men / *Libre, 48 kg, Messieurs*

3RD - 4TH	ROUND 6	ROUND 5	ROUND 4	ROUND 3	ROUND 2
CUB 5	MDA 0	ROM 0	NGR 6	KGZ 0	NGR 3
RUS 2	CUB 10	RUS 10	ROM 7	NGR 0	GUA 0
	RUS 5	CUB	RUS 10	MKD 3	COL 4
	KOR 1	BYE	USA 4	ROM 7	MKD 15
			UKR 0	RUS 10	ROM 6
			CUB 8	MEX 0	SWE 3
				USA 11	RUS 12
				GRE 2	CAN 0
				UKR 5	KGZ
				MGL 1	BYE

5TH - 6TH

MDA 0
KOR 4

7TH - 8TH

ROM 3
USA 1

ROUND 1

No	Name	Ctry	TP
1	JACOB, Isaac	NGR	0
2	VILA PERDOMO, Alexis	CUB	4
3	RAMIREZ FUENTES, Mynor	GUA	0
4	EITER, Rob	USA	12
5	MKRCHYAN, Armen	ARM	10
6	RESTREPO GONZALEZ, Jose Manuel	COL	0
7	RAILEAN, Vitalii	MDA	10
8	SOKOLOV, Vlado	MKD	0
9	CORDUNEANU, Gheorghe	ROM	2
10	TSKOUASSELI, Nougzar	GRE	3
11	KIM, Il	PRK	12
12	MOSTAGHIM BESARATI, Jafar	SWE	2
13	ORUDZHOV, Vugar	RUS	4
14	YEFTENI, Viktor	UKR	6
15	RAGUSA, Paul	CAN	1
16	SERGELENBAATAR, Luvsan-Ish	MGL	7
17	TORGOVKIN, Vladimir	KGZ	0
18	JUNG, Soon-Won	KOR	11
19	FERNANDEZ, Filiberto	MEX	
	BYE		

1/8	1/4	1/2	FINAL
MEX 0	CUB 2	ARM 7	ARM 4
CUB 11	ARM 4	MDA 2	PRK 5
USA 2	MDA	PRK 3	
ARM 9	BYE	KOR 1	
MDA 10	PRK		
GRE 1	BYE		
PRK 3	KOR		
UKR 0	BYE		
MGL 1			
KOR 3			

FINAL CLASSIFICATION

Rnk	Name	Ctry	PP	TP	
1	KIM, Il	PRK	13	23	G
2	MKRCHYAN, Armen	ARM	14	34	S
3	VILA PERDOMO, Alexis	CUB	18	40	B
4	ORUDZHOV, Vugar	RUS	20	53	
5	JUNG, Soon-Won	KOR	12	20	
6	RAILEAN, Vitalii	MDA	8	22	
7	CORDUNEANU, Gheorghe	ROM	13	25	
8	EITER, Rob	USA	10	30	

Wrestling / *Lutte*

Freestyle, 52 kg (114.5 lb), Men / *Libre, 52 kg, Messieurs*

3RD - 4TH	ROUND 6	ROUND 5	ROUND 4	ROUND 3	ROUND 2
RUS 2	IRI 1	CAN 1	USA 0	ROM 2	GRE 1
KAZ 3	RUS 3	TUR 13	CAN 0	USA 4	USA 3
	TUR 5	RUS	TUR 5	SVK 3	SVK 3
	KAZ 11	BYE	JPN 1	CAN 6	CUB 2
			RUS 4	ALG 0	AUS 0
			UZB 0	TUR 3	CAN 6
				JPN 12	ALG 2
				FRA 5	MEX 0
				UKR 1	ROM
				RUS 2	Bye

5TH - 6TH

IRI 4
TUR 2

7TH - 8TH

CAN 0
UZB 11

ROUND 1

No	Name	Ctry	TP
1	KARDANOV, Amiran	GRE	1
2	ACHILOV, Adkhamjon	UZB	11
3	ABDULLAYEV, Namik	AZE	7
4	ROSSELLI, Lou	USA	0
5	SASAYAMA, Hideo	JPN	6
6	KOLLAR, Roman	SVK	0
7	VARELA GONZALEZ, Carlos	CUB	0
8	MOHAMMADI, Gholamreza	IRI	4
9	FITZGERALD, Gregory	AUS	0
10	LEGRAND, David	FRA	10
11	MAMYROV, Maulen	KAZ	10
12	WOODCROFT, Gregory	CAN	0
13	KEDJAOUER, Omar	ALG	0
14	TOHUZOV, Volodymyr	UKR	10
15	RODRIGUEZ, Victor	MEX	0
16	DIMITROV JORDANOV, Valentin	BUL	10
17	MONGUSH, Chechenol	RUS	11
18	CORDUNEANU, Constantin	ROM	4
19	TOPAKTAS, Metin	TUR	
	BYE		

1/8	1/4	1/2	FINAL
TUR 5	UZB 0	AZE 10	AZE 3
UZB 7	AZE 11	IRI 0	BUL 4
AZE 11	IRI	KAZ 3	
JPN 0	BYE	BUL 7	
IRI 5	KAZ		
FRA 0	BYE		
KAZ 3	BUL		
UKR 1	BYE		
BUL 4			
RUS 2			

FINAL CLASSIFICATION

Rnk	Name	Ctry	PP	TP	
1	DIMITROV JORDANOV, Valentin	BUL	13	25	G
2	ABDULLAYEV, Namik	AZE	16	42	S
3	MAMYROV, Maulen	KAZ	14	30	B
4	MONGUSH, Chechenol	RUS	15	24	
5	MOHAMMADI, Gholamreza	IRI	10	14	
6	TOPAKTAS, Metin	TUR	15	33	
7	ACHILOV, Adkhamjon	UZB	11	29	
8	WOODCROFT, Gregory	CAN	12	13	

Wrestling / *Lutte*

Freestyle, 57 kg (125.5 lb), Men / *Libre, 57 kg, Messieurs*

ROUND 1

No	Name	Ctry	TP
1	TALAEI, Mohammad	IRI	4
2	ABDULLAYEV, Arif	AZE	1
3	ZAKHARTDINOV, Damir	UZB	5
4	FIDAROV, Aslanbek	UKR	3
5	ALIDZHANOV, Nazim	MDA	8
6	FYODOROV, Artur	KAZ	10
7	TSOGTBAYAR, Tserenbaatar	MGL	3
8	SISSAOURI, Giuvi	CAN	8
9	UMAKHANOV, Bagavden	RUS	4
10	LIUZZI, Michele	ITA	0
11	CIUFULESCU, Bogdan	ROM	0
12	ABE, Sanshiro	JPN	10
13	CROSS, Kendall	USA	10
14	EMBALO, Talata	GBS	0
15	RI, Yong Sam	PRK	3
16	DOGAN, Harun	TUR	0
17	O'BRIEN, Cory	AUS	0
18	BARZAKOV, Serafim	BUL	10
19	PUERTO DIAZ, Alejandro	CUB	3
20	TRSTENA, Saban	MKD	4
21	GUZOV, Aleksandr	BLR	
	BYE		

Championship bracket (right side):

1/8	1/4	1/2	FINAL
BLR 5 / IRI 3	MKD 7 / BLR 3	MKD 1 / CAN 4	CAN 3 / USA 5
UZB 3 / KAZ 1	UZB 0 / CAN 8	USA 12 / PRK 2	
CAN 1 / RUS 1	USA / BYE		
JPN 2 / USA 4	PRK / BYE		
PRK 5 / BUL 1			
MKD / BYE			

Repechage / placement bracket (left side):

3RD - 4TH	ROUND 6	ROUND 5	ROUND 4	ROUND 3	ROUND 2
TUR 0 / PRK 3	MKD 2 / TUR 3	UZB 2 / IRI 4	AZE 1 / TUR 3	AZE 4 / MDA 3	AZE 11 / UKR 0
	IRI 0 / PRK 4	TUR 3 / BLR 0	IRI 1 / RUS 0	ITA 0 / TUR 4	MDA 7 / MGL 6
			JPN 5 / BLR 6	CUB 0 / IRI 5	ITA 5 / ROM 1
			UZB / BYE	KAZ 2 / RUS 5	GBS 0 / TUR 3
				JPN 5 / BUL 3	AUS 1 / CUB 9

5TH - 6TH: MKD 4 / IRI 3

7TH - 8TH: UZB 2 / BLR 3

FINAL CLASSIFICATION

Rnk	Name	Ctry	PP	TP	
1	CROSS, Kendall	USA	14	31	G
2	SISSAOURI, Giuvi	CAN	13	24	S
3	RI, Yong Sam	PRK	14	17	B
4	DOGAN, Harun	TUR	16	16	
5	TRSTENA, Saban	MKD	12	18	
6	TALAEI, Mohammad	IRI	13	20	
7	GUZOV, Aleksandr	BLR	10	17	
8	ZAKHARTDINOV, Damir	UZB	8	12	

Wrestling / *Lutte*

Freestyle, 62 kg (136.5 lb), Men / *Libre, 62 kg, Messieurs*

ROUND 1

No	Name	Ctry	TP
1	WADA, Takahiro	JPN	11
2	MUMJIEV, Serban	ROM	0
3	CUBAS, Enrique	PER	7
4	KRZESIAK, Jan	POL	7
5	BARSEGUIAN, Aroutioun	CYP	2
6	JANG, Jae-Sung	KOR	5
7	du PLESSIS, Tjaart	RSA	1
8	TEDEYEV, Elbrus	UKR	5
9	DEMETER, Istvan	HUN	3
10	NIEVES, Anibal	PUR	0
11	HAJI KENARI, Abbas	IRI	0
12	BRANDS, Tom	USA	3
13	MULLER, Martin	SUI	0
14	SMAL, Sergey	BLR	6
15	CALDER, Marty	CAN	2
16	SCHEIBE, Juergen	GER	4
17	AZIZOV, Magomed	RUS	10
18	VATH, Chamroeun	CAM	0
19	SCHILLACI, Giovanni	ITA	10
20	ZASLAVSKY, Leonid	AUS	0
21	ISLAMOV, Ramil	UZB	
	BYE		

Championship bracket (right side):

1/8	1/4	1/2	FINAL
UZB 2 / JPN 3	ITA 4 / JPN 3	ITA 1 / KOR 1	KOR 0 / USA 7
PER 0 / KOR 3	KOR 3 / UKR 1	USA 4 / RUS 1	
UKR 11 / HUN 1	USA / BYE		
USA 5 / BLR 0	RUS / BYE		
GER 2 / RUS 8			
ITA / BYE			

Repechage / placement bracket (left side):

3RD - 4TH	ROUND 6	ROUND 5	ROUND 4	ROUND 3	ROUND 2
UKR 3 / JPN 1	ITA 3 / UKR 10	UKR 5 / UZB 4	CYP 4 / CAN 10	ROM 2 / CYP 7	ROM 12 / POL 1
	JPN 10 / RUS 0	CAN 3 / JPN 7	UZB 6 / HUN 1	PUR 0 / CAN 3	CYP 3 / RSA 1
			BLR 0 / JPN 3	AUS 0 / UZB 10	PUR 8 / IRI 3
			UKR / BYE	PER 1 / HUN 11	SUI 0 / CAN 6
				BLR 8 / GER 1	CAM 0 / AUS 9

5TH - 6TH: ITA 0 / RUS 0

7TH - 8TH: UZB 1 / CAN 9

FINAL CLASSIFICATION

Rnk	Name	Ctry	PP	TP	
1	BRANDS, Tom	USA	12	19	G
2	JANG, Jae-Sung	KOR	12	12	S
3	TEDEYEV, Elbrus	UKR	17	35	B
4	WADA, Takahiro	JPN	19	38	
5	AZIZOV, Magomed	RUS	12	19	
6	SCHILLACI, Giovanni	ITA	9	18	
7	CALDER, Marty	CAN	14	33	
8	ISLAMOV, Ramil	UZB	10	23	

Wrestling / *Lutte*

Freestyle, 68 kg (149.5 lb), Men / *Libre, 68 kg, Messieurs*

3RD - 4TH	ROUND 6	ROUND 5	ROUND 4	ROUND 3	ROUND 2
UKR 8	KOR 0	CUB 6	IRI 1	AUS 0	IRI 1
CUB 6	UKR 7	EST 0	CUB 3	IRI 5	NGR 0
	CUB 8	UKR	SYR 1	HUN 2	SEN 1
	ARM 4	BYE	EST 4	CUB 6	HUN 13
5TH - 6TH					
KOR 0			BLR 1	SYR 11	ARG 0
ARM 0			UKR 6	UZB 9	CUB 10
				EST 5	SYR 4
				AZE 1	TUR 1
7TH - 8TH					
EST 7				BLR 4	AUS
SYR 2				CAN 0	BYE

ROUND 1

No	Name	Ctry	TP
1	FADZAEV, Arsen	UZB	2
2	FALLAH, Akbar	IRI	2
3	ZAZIROV, Zaza	UKR	10
4	IBO, Oziti	NGR	0
5	DIEDHIOU, Felix	SEN	0
6	KOIV, Kullo	EST	12
7	FORIZS, Janos	HUN	0
8	ALLAKHVERDIEV, Elshad	AZE	3
9	HWANG, Sang-Ho	KOR	7
10	IBIRE, Paulo	ARG	0
11	SANCHEZ LARRUDE, Yosvany	CUB	1
12	GOGOL, Oleg	BLR	3
13	GEVORGYAN, Arayik	ARM	9
14	ALAOSTA, Ahmad	SYR	1
15	SANLI, Yuksel	TUR	1
16	SAUNDERS, Townsend	USA	3
17	ROBERTS, Craig	CAN	12
18	WEISS, Richard	AUS	2
19	BOGIYEV, Vadim	RUS	
	BYE		

1/8	1/4	1/2	FINAL
RUS 3	RUS 6	RUS 3	RUS 1
UZB 1	UKR 4	KOR 2	USA 1
UKR 5	KOR	ARM 0	
EST 0	BYE	USA 4	
AZE 3	ARM		
KOR 5	BYE		
BLR 2	USA		
ARM 3	BYE		
USA 3			
CAN 1			

FINAL CLASSIFICATION

Rnk	Name	Ctry	PP	TP	
1	BOGIYEV, Vadim	RUS	12	13	G
2	SAUNDERS, Townsend	USA	10	11	S
3	ZAZIROV, Zaza	UKR	18	40	B
4	SANCHEZ LARRUDE, Yosvany	CUB	18	40	
5	GEVORGYAN, Arayik	ARM	10	16	
6	HWANG, Sang-Ho	KOR	7	14	
7	KOIV, Kullo	EST	13	28	
8	ALAOSTA, Ahmad	SYR	9	19	

Wrestling / *Lutte*

Freestyle, 74 kg (163 lb), Men / *Libre, 74 kg, Messieurs*

3RD - 4TH	ROUND 6	ROUND 5	ROUND 4	ROUND 3	ROUND 2
BUL 3	BUL 8	GER 3	GER 10	CMR 0	CAN 11
JPN 5	GER 4	AZE 0	CAN 2	CAN 10	AUS 5
	JPN 4	MDA 4	AZE 6	HUN 2	MEX 0
	USA 2	JPN 5	CUB 2	AZE 3	HUN 12
5TH - 6TH					
GER 0			UZB 3	CUB 4	AZE 4
USA 0			MDA 5	IRI 1	KAZ 0
			MKD 0	UZB 4	TUR 0
			JPN 7	BLR 2	CUB 7
7TH - 8TH					
AZE 0				MDA 5	IRI 3
MDA 0				SVK 0	GRE 0
				GER	CMR
				BYE	BYE

ROUND 1

No	Name	Ctry	TP
1	HOHL, David	CAN	3
2	BUDAYEV, Boris	UZB	4
3	OZOLINE, Rein	AUS	7
4	VERHUSIN, Valerij	MKD	15
5	OTA, Takuya	JPN	11
6	GUZMAN, Felipe	MEX	0
7	RITTER, Arpad	HUN	3
8	KOZYR, Igor	BLR	5
9	PARK, Jang-Soon	KOR	4
10	GADZHIYEV, Mahomed Salam	AZE	1
11	KURUGLIYEV, Magomed	KAZ	1
12	PEICOV, Victor	MDA	7
13	KERTANTI, Radion	SVK	4
14	CEYLAN, Turan	TUR	3
15	RODRIGUEZ HERNANDEZ, Alberto	CUB	1
16	MONDAY, Kenny	USA	1
17	SAYTYEV, Buvaysa	RUS	8
18	MOMENI, Eisa	IRI	0
19	LEIPOLD, Alexander	GER	6
20	LOIZIDIS, Lazaros	GRE	0
21	AVOM BUME, Anthony	CMR	0
22	PASKALEV, Plamen	BUL	10

1/8	1/4	1/2	FINAL
UZB 0	BUL 12	BUL 3	KOR 0
MKD 8	MKD 0	KOR 5	RUS 5
JPN 4	JPN 0	USA 1	
BLR 1	KOR 5	RUS 6	
KOR 3	USA		
MDA 0	BYE		
SVK 1	RUS		
USA 5	BYE		
RUS 3			
GER 1			
BUL			
BYE			

FINAL CLASSIFICATION

Rnk	Name	Ctry	PP	TP	
1	SAYTYEV, Buvaysa	RUS	12	22	G
2	PARK, Jang-Soon	KOR	12	17	S
3	OTA, Takuya	JPN	19	36	B
4	PASKALEV, Plamen	BUL	13	36	
5	LEIPOLD, Alexander	GER	15	24	
6	MONDAY, Kenny	USA	8	9	
7	PEICOV, Victor	MDA	14	21	
8	GADZHIYEV, Mahomed Salam	AZE	10	14	

Wrestling / *Lutte*

Freestyle, 82 kg (180.5 lb), Men / *Libre, 82 kg, Messieurs*

3RD - 4TH	ROUND 6	ROUND 5	ROUND 4	ROUND 3	ROUND 2
TUR 0	KAZ 0	USA 2	AZE 6	ROM 3	ROM 4
IRI 0	TUR 0	AZE 3	GEO 4	AZE 5	PUR 3
	AZE 0	TUR 5	TUR 5	BUL 1	BLR 0
	IRI 3	CUB 4	MDA 1	GEO 4	AZE 5
			CUB 3	TUR 7	AUS 2
			HUN 1	JPN 1	BUL 8
			USA	UKR 0	SEN 2
			BYE	MDA 3	GEO 6
				CUB 3	TUR 5
				UZB 2	VEN 2

ROUND 1

No	Name	Ctry	TP
1	YOKOYAMA, Hidekazu	JPN	9
2	GHITA, Nicolae	ROM	1
3	ROSA, Orlando	PUR	1
4	GUBRYNYUK, Sergey	UKR	3
5	SAVKO, Aleksandr	BLR	2
6	GUTCHES, Les	USA	3
7	JABRAILOV, Elmadi	KAZ	4
8	IBRAGIMOV, Magomed	AZE	1
9	JABRAILOV, Lucman	MDA	10
10	BROWN, Cris	AUS	0
11	PENEV, Plamen	BUL	1
12	RAMOS WILSON, Ariel	CUB	3
13	DIOUF, Alioune	SEN	0
14	MAGOMEDOV, Khadzhimurad	RUS	3
15	KHADEM AZGHADI, Amir Reza	IRI	3
16	GOGOLISHVILI, Avtandil	GEO	0
17	OZTURK, Sebahattin	TUR	2
18	KHINCHAGOV, Ruslan	UZB	3
19	DVORAK, Laszlo	HUN	6
20	VARELA, Luis	VEN	2
21	YANG, Hyun-Mo	KOR	
	BYE		

1/8	1/4	1/2	FINAL
KOR 4	HUN 0	KOR 3	KOR 1
JPN 2	KOR 2	KAZ 2	RUS 2
UKR 0	USA 1	RUS 4	
USA 4	KAZ 2	IRI 0	
KAZ 10	RUS		
MDA 8	BYE		
CUB 4	IRI		
RUS 7	BYE		
IRI 1			
UZB 0			
HUN			
BYE			

5TH - 6TH	7TH - 8TH
KAZ 0	USA 3
AZE 0	CUB 0

FINAL CLASSIFICATION

Rnk	Name	Ctry	PP	TP	
1	MAGOMEDOV, Khadzhimurad	RUS	12	16	G
2	YANG, Hyun-Mo	KOR	10	10	S
3	KHADEM AZGHADI, Amir Reza	IRI	12	7	B
4	OZTURK, Sebahattin	TUR	17	24	
5	IBRAGIMOV, Magomed	AZE	17	20	
6	JABRAILOV, Elmadi	KAZ	10	18	
7	GUTCHES, Les	USA	11	13	
8	RAMOS WILSON, Ariel	CUB	11	17	

Wrestling / *Lutte*

Freestyle, 90 kg (198 lb), Men / *Libre, 90 kg, Messieurs*

3RD - 4TH	ROUND 6	ROUND 5	ROUND 4	ROUND 3	ROUND 2
SVK 0	SVK 10	KOR 0	HUN 4	BUL 5	ASA 0
GEO 5	NGR 0	NGR 7	NGR 7	HUN 7	BUL 4
	GEO 10	GEO 1	LTU 1	NGR 7	HUN 5
	UKR 4	USA 0	GEO 5	CAN 0	JPN 2
			KAZ 0	PAK 0	PUR 0
			USA 3	LTU 12	NGR 10
			KOR	GEO 6	CAN 3
			BYE	MGL 1	POL 2
				KAZ 3	AUS 3
				GER 0	PAK 7

ROUND 1

No	Name	Ctry	TP
1	PAULIUKONIS, Ricardas	LTU	11
2	PURCELL, Louis	ASA	0
3	KURTANIDZE, Eldari	GEO	11
4	BAEV, Kaloyan	BUL	0
5	KIM, Ik-Hee	KOR	2
6	BACSA, Peter	HUN	1
7	LOHYNA, Jozef	SVK	5
8	KAWAI, Tatsuo	JPN	0
9	GANTOGTOKH, Bayanmunkh	MGL	5
10	BETANCOURT, Jose E.	PUR	0
11	KODEI, Victor	NGR	1
12	KHADEM AZGHADI, Rasull	IRI	6
13	BIANCO, Scott	CAN	2
14	BAYRAMUKOV, Islam	KAZ	5
15	KOSTECKI, Robert	POL	4
16	TYEDYEYEV, Dzambolat	UKR	5
17	RENNEY, Bob	AUS	1
18	BALZ, Heiko	GER	11
19	MUHAMMAD, Bashir	PAK	0
20	KHADARTSEV, Makharbek	RUS	10
21	DOUGLAS, Melvin	USA	
	BYE		

1/8	1/4	1/2	FINAL
USA 5	RUS 4	RUS 7	RUS 0
LTU 0	USA 1	SVK 1	IRI 3
GEO 2	KOR 0	IRI 3	
KOR 3	SVK 3	UKR 0	
SVK 5	IRI		
MGL 3	BYE		
IRI 4	UKR		
KAZ 3	BYE		
UKR 4			
GER 1			
RUS			
BYE			

5TH - 6TH	7TH - 8TH
NGR 0	KOR 0
UKR 12	USA 6

FINAL CLASSIFICATION

Rnk	Name	Ctry	PP	TP	
1	KHADEM AZGHADI, Rasull	IRI	12	16	G
2	KHADARTSEV, Makharbek	RUS	10	21	S
3	KURTANIDZE, Eldari	GEO	20	40	B
4	LOHYNA, Jozef	SVK	14	24	
5	TYEDYEYEV, Dzambolat	UKR	11	25	
6	KODEI, Victor	NGR	14	32	
7	DOUGLAS, Melvin	USA	10	15	
8	KIM, Ik-Hee	KOR	6	5	

Wrestling / *Lutte*

Freestyle, 100 kg (220 lb), Men / *Libre, 100 kg, Messieurs*

ROUND 1

No	Name	Ctry	TP
1	KOVALEVSKIY, Sergey	BLR	0
2	SABEJEW, Arawat	GER	3
3	KIM, Tae-Woo	KOR	0
4	MORALES SUAREZ, Wilfredo	CUB	6
5	SUMIYABAZAR, Dolgorsuren	MGL	0
6	ANGLE, Kurt	USA	4
7	ALEKSANDROV, Konstantin	KGZ	2
8	MAZAC, Milan	SVK	1
9	SANCHEZ, Daniel	PUR	0
10	AAVIK, Arvi	EST	8
11	KHABELOV, Leri	RUS	2
12	TKHESKELASHVILI, Zaza	GEO	0
13	MAGOMEDOV, Davoud	AZE	0
14	JADIDI, Abbas	IRI	4
15	TROPLINI, Shkelqim	ALB	0
16	LADIK, Oleg	CAN	7
17	VINCENT, Benjamin	AUS	0
18	GARMULEWICZ, Marek	POL	11
19	MURTAZALIYEV, Sahid	UKR	BYE

Bracket

ROUND 2: BLR 3 / KOR 1 · MGL 4 / SVK 2 · PUR 2 / GEO 3 · AZE 10 / ALB 0 · AUS / BYE

ROUND 3: AUS 0 / BLR 10 · MGL 6 / GEO 2 · AZE 1 / GER 3 · CUB 3 / EST 1 · RUS 0 / CAN 0

ROUND 4: BLR 3 / MGL 0 · GER 3 / CUB 2 · CAN 1 / UKR 4

ROUND 5: BLR 8 / UKR 4 · GER / BYE

ROUND 6: KGZ 0 / GER 10 · BLR 4 / POL 0

3RD - 4TH: GER 7 / BLR 4

5TH - 6TH: KGZ 0 / POL 0

7TH - 8TH: UKR 3 / CAN 1

1/8: UKR 13 / GER 3 · CUB 0 / USA 2 · KGZ 1 / EST 0 · RUS 0 / IRI 4 · CAN 0 / POL 3

1/4: UKR 3 / USA 4 · KGZ / BYE · IRI / BYE · POL / BYE

1/2: USA 4 / KGZ 1 · IRI 4 / POL 1

FINAL: USA 1 / IRI 1

FINAL CLASSIFICATION

Rnk	Name	Ctry	PP	TP	
1	ANGLE, Kurt	USA	15	15	G
2	JADIDI, Abbas	IRI	10	13	S
3	SABEJEW, Arawat	GER	17	29	B
4	KOVALEVSKIY, Sergey	BLR	18	32	
5	GARMULEWICZ, Marek	POL	12	15	
6	ALEKSANDROV, Konstantin	KGZ	7	4	
7	MURTAZALIYEV, Sahid	UKR	12	27	
8	LADIK, Oleg	CAN	10	09	

Wrestling / *Lutte*

Freestyle, 130 kg (286 lb), Men / *Libre, 130 kg, Messieurs*

ROUND 1

No	Name	Ctry	TP
1	SINGH, Amarjit	GBR	2
2	MEHRABAN ROUDBANEH, Ebrahim	IRI	6
3	GOMBOS, Zsolt	HUN	7
4	KRANZ, Robert	GUM	0
5	BAUMGARTNER, Bruce	USA	10
6	BORODOW, Andy	CAN	0
7	KLIMOV, Igor	KAZ	1
8	SHUMILIN, Andrey	RUS	4
9	TURMANIDZE, Zaza	GEO	8
10	PIKOS, Mick	AUS	0
11	MEDVEDEV, Aleksey	BLR	7
12	BOURDOULIS, Petros	GRE	1
13	FAR GIANOPULOS, Alfredo	PAN	0
14	FENG, Aigang	CHN	11
15	THIELE, Sven	GER	1
16	KOVALEVSKIY, Aleksandr	KGZ	0
17	VALIYEV, Merabi	UKR	1
18	DEMIR, Mahmut	TUR	1

Bracket

ROUND 2: GBR 3 / GUM 0 · CAN 5 / KAZ 3 · AUS 0 / GRE 6 · PAN 0 / KGZ 4 · UKR / BYE

ROUND 3: UKR 4 / GBR 0 · CAN 0 / GRE 1 · KGZ 3 / IRI 2 · USA 14 / GEO 2 · CHN / BYE

ROUND 4: CHN 1 / UKR 3 · GRE 1 / KGZ 7 · USA 11 / HUN 0

ROUND 5: UKR 1 / KGZ 3 · USA / BYE

ROUND 6: RUS 3 / KGZ 0 · USA 3 / GER 0

3RD - 4TH: RUS 1 / USA 1

5TH - 6TH: KGZ 3 / GER 1

7TH - 8TH: UKR 5 / GRE 1

1/8: IRI 0 / HUN 3 · USA 1 / RUS 6 · GEO 1 / BLR 3 · CHN 1 / GER 1 · TUR / BYE

1/4: TUR 4 / HUN 0 · RUS / BYE · BLR / BYE · GER / BYE

1/2: TUR 1 / RUS 0 · BLR 0 / GER 0

FINAL: TUR 3 / BLR 0

FINAL CLASSIFICATION

Rnk	Name	Ctry	PP	TP	
1	DEMIR, Mahmut	TUR	12	9	G
2	MEDVEDEV, Aleksey	BLR	9	10	S
3	BAUMGARTNER, Bruce	USA	19	40	B
4	SHUMILIN, Andrey	RUS	11	14	
5	KOVALEVSKIY, Aleksandr	KGZ	16	20	
6	THIELE, Sven	GER	7	3	
7	VALIYEV, Merabi	UKR	11	14	
8	BOURDOULIS, Petros	GRE	10	10	

Wrestling / *Lutte*

Greco-Roman, 48 kg (105.5 lb), Men / *Gréco-romaine, 48 kg, Messieurs*

ROUND 1

No	Name	Ctry	TP
1	GULYOV, Zafar	RUS	3
2	KADO, Hiroshi	JPN	2
3	OZDEMIR, Bayram	TUR	11
4	AGUILAR, Enrique	MEX	0
5	YLLESCAS, Jorge	PER	0
6	AGAKATZANIAN, Varntan Ioann	GRE	10
7	COSTANTINO, Francesco	ITA	6
8	PAPASHVILI, Gela	GEO	8
9	TSENOV, Bratan	BUL	10
10	AL EZANI, Abdullah	YEM	0
11	KOUTCHERENKO, Oleg	GER	10
12	ZAHIDOV, Tahir	AZE	0
13	SANCHEZ AMITA, Wilber	CUB	12
14	MAYNARD, Mujaahid	USA	3
15	PAVLOV, Aleksandr	BLR	11
16	OCHOA, Jose	VEN	0
17	KANG, Yong	PRK	9
18	JABLONSKI, Piotr	POL	3
19	SIM, Kwon-Ho	KOR	
	BYE		

Championship bracket

1/8	1/4	1/2	FINAL
KOR 2	KOR 4	KOR 11	KOR 4
RUS 1	GRE 1	GEO 0	BLR 0
TUR 2	GEO	CUB 0	
GRE 3	BYE	BLR 5	
GEO 7	CUB		
BUL 4	BYE		
GER 1	BLR		
CUB 1	BYE		
BLR 3			
PRK 2			

Repechage / Classification rounds

(Class.)	ROUND 6	ROUND 5	ROUND 4	ROUND 3	ROUND 2
3RD - 4TH RUS 4	GEO 0	JPN 0	JPN 4	POL 1	JPN 10
PRK 0	RUS 6	PRK 11	ITA 0	JPN 9	MEX 0
	PRK 7	RUS	RUS 7	ITA 5	PER 0
	CUB 0	BYE	TUR 0	AZE 0	ITA 10
5TH - 6TH GEO 0			PRK 10	USA 0	YEM 0
CUB 4			GRE 0	RUS 6	AZE 11
				TUR 4	USA 4
				BUL 0	VEN 2
7TH - 8TH JPN 1				GER 0	POL
GRE 0				PRK 3	BYE

FINAL CLASSIFICATION

Rnk	Name	Ctry	PP	TP	
1	SIM, Kwon-Ho	KOR	13	21	G
2	PAVLOV, Aleksandr	BLR	10	19	S
3	GULYOV, Zafar	RUS	16	27	B
4	KANG, Yong	PRK	18	42	
5	SANCHEZ AMITA, Wilber	CUB	9	17	
6	PAPASHVILI, Gela	GEO	6	15	
7	KADO, Hiroshi	JPN	15	26	
8	AGAKATZANIAN, Varntan Ioann	GRE	9	14	

Wrestling / *Lutte*

Greco-Roman, 52 kg (114.5 lb), Men / *Gréco-romaine, 52 kg, Messieurs*

ROUND 1

No	Name	Ctry	TP
1	REBEGEA, Valentin	ROM	0
2	JABLONSKI, Dariusz	POL	6
3	DANIELYAN, Samvel	RUS	11
4	KHUDAYBERDYEV, Shamsatdin	UZB	4
5	YADAV, Pappu	IND	0
6	HA, Tae-Yeon	KOR	10
7	KALASHNIKOV, Andriy	UKR	0
8	NAZARYAN, Armen	ARM	10
9	RONNINGEN, Jon	NOR	0
10	RIVAS SCULL, Lazaro	CUB	5
11	TER-MKRTCHYAN, Alfred	GER	1
12	FARAJ, Khaled	SYR	3
13	ANEV, Yordan	BUL	11
14	GODSWILL, Tiebiri	NGR	0
15	VARTANOV, Ruslan	LTU	1
16	DYUSENOV, Nurym	KAZ	4
17	AKHMEDOV, Ibad	BLR	11
18	VALENTIN, Ulises	DOM	0
19	BASALDUA, Joel	PER	0
20	PAULSON, Brandon	USA	6

Championship bracket

1/8	1/4	1/2	FINAL
POL 0	RUS 0	ARM 7	ARM 5
RUS 8	ARM 3	CUB 1	USA 1
KOR 2	CUB	BUL 2	
ARM 12	BYE	USA 6	
CUB 5	BUL		
SYR 0	BYE		
BUL 9	USA		
KAZ 6	BYE		
BLR 1			
USA 6			

Repechage / Classification rounds

(Class.)	ROUND 6	ROUND 5	ROUND 4	ROUND 3	ROUND 2
3RD - 4TH RUS 1	CUB 8	UKR 8	UKR 3	ROM 1	ROM 12
UKR 4	RUS 9	POL 5	GER 0	UKR 3	UZB 0
	UKR 5	RUS	POL 3	GER 8	IND 0
	BUL 0	BYE	KOR 2	LTU 0	UKR 11
5TH - 6TH CUB 5			KAZ 0	DOM 0	NOR 0
BUL 0			RUS 11	POL 3	GER 9
				KOR 10	NGR 0
				SYR 0	LTU 4
7TH - 8TH POL 2				KAZ 5	DOM 14
KOR 3				BLR 4	PER 1

FINAL CLASSIFICATION

Rnk	Name	Ctry	PP	TP	
1	NAZARYAN, Armen	ARM	17	37	G
2	PAULSON, Brandon	USA	11	19	S
3	KALASHNIKOV, Andriy	UKR	20	34	B
4	DANIELYAN, Samvel	RUS	14	40	
5	RIVAS SCULL, Lazaro	CUB	11	24	
6	ANEV, Yordan	BUL	8	22	
7	HA, Tae-Yeon	KOR	13	27	
8	JABLONSKI, Dariusz	POL	13	19	

Wrestling / *Lutte*

Greco-Roman, 57 kg (125.5 lb), Men / *Gréco-romaine, 57 kg, Messieurs*

ROUND 1

No	Name	Ctry	TP
1	SALHI, Nabil	TUN	0
2	MANUKYAN, Aghasi	ARM	4
3	KHAKYMOV, Ruslan	UKR	5
4	SUKEVICIUS, Remigijus	LTU	1
5	IGNATENKO, Aleksandr	RUS	0
6	MELNICHENKO, Yuriy	KAZ	11
7	SANDU, Marian	ROM	3
8	ELGKIAN, Sarkis	GRE	2
9	FERNANDEZ, Armando	MEX	0
10	YILDIZ, Rifat	GER	12
11	SARMIENTO HERNANDEZ, Luis	CUB	5
12	MAIA, David	POR	0
13	NISHIMI, Kenkichi	JPN	6
14	PARK, Chi-Ho	KOR	17
15	EROGLU, Seref	TUR	0
16	HALL, Dennis	USA	3
17	JANSONS, Aigars	LAT	4
18	PAWLOSKI, Stanislaw	POL	3
19	AGAYEV, Vilayat	AZE	4
20	SHENG, Zetian	CHN	5

Championship bracket

1/8		1/4		1/2		FINAL	
ARM	0	UKR	1	KAZ	3	KAZ	4
UKR	11	KAZ	8	GER	0	USA	1
KAZ	4	GER		USA	1		
ROM	0	BYE		CHN	0		
GER	4	USA					
CUB	1	BYE					
KOR	2	CHN					
USA	3	BYE					
LAT	1						
CHN	7						

Repechage / placement

ROUND 2		ROUND 3		ROUND 4		ROUND 5		ROUND 6	
TUN	0	LTU	5	GRE	4	GRE	2	GER	2
LTU	11	GRE	6	JPN	2	CUB	4	UKR	3
RUS	2	MEX	0	AZE	0	UKR		CUB	2
GRE	3	JPN	12	CUB	1	BYE		CHN	8
MEX	7	AZE	7	LAT	4				
POR	3	ARM	2	UKR	9				
JPN	8	ROM	0						
TUR	7	CUB	7						
POL	3	KOR	2						
AZE	4	LAT	9						

3RD - 4TH		5TH - 6TH		7TH - 8TH	
UKR	0	GER	0	GRE	5
CHN	4	CUB	0	JPN	4

FINAL CLASSIFICATION

Rnk	Name	Ctry	PP	TP	
1	MELNICHENKO, Yuriy	KAZ	16	30	G
2	HALL, Dennis	USA	10	8	S
3	SHENG, Zetian	CHN	12	24	B
4	KHAKYMOV, Ruslan	UKR	14	29	
5	YILDIZ, Rifat	GER	12	18	
6	SARMIENTO HERNANDEZ, Luis	CUB	14	20	
7	ELGKIAN, Sarkis	GRE	14	22	
8	NISHIMI, Kenkichi	JPN	10	32	

Wrestling / *Lutte*

Greco-Roman, 62 kg (136.5 lb), Men / *Gréco-romaine, 62 kg, Messieurs*

ROUND 1

No	Name	Ctry	TP
1	ROUMPENIAN, Aroutic	GRE	1
2	GULIASHVILI, Koba	GEO	4
3	ZAWADZKI, Wlodzimierz	POL	4
4	PETRENKO, Igor	BLR	3
5	SANCHEZ, Marco	PUR	5
6	AZIZ, Usama	SWE	6
7	MANUKYAN, Mkhitar	ARM	11
8	HU, Guohong	CHN	0
9	KAMYSHENKO, Hryhoriy	UKR	10
10	SANTOS FUENTES, Winston	VEN	0
11	IVANOV, Ivan	BUL	1
12	PIRIM, Mehmet	TUR	1
13	ZUNIGA, David	USA	3
14	ROBINSON, Ainsley	CAN	2
15	CHOI, Sang-Sun	KOR	0
16	MARTYNOV, Sergey	RUS	3
17	MAREN DELIS, Juan Luis	CUB	5
18	PAZAJ, Ahad	IRI	2
19	KURBANOV, Bakhodir	UZB	
	BYE		

Championship bracket

1/8		1/4		1/2		FINAL	
UZB	3	GEO	1	POL	8	POL	3
GEO	10	POL	3	UKR	2	CUB	1
POL	3	UKR		BUL	1		
SWE	1	BYE		CUB	4		
ARM	2	BUL					
UKR	3	BYE					
BUL	3	CUB					
USA	1	BYE					
RUS	4						
CUB	5						

Repechage / placement

ROUND 2		ROUND 3		ROUND 4		ROUND 5		ROUND 6	
GRE	1	IRI	6	IRI	0	TUR	9	UKR	1
BLR	3	BLR	2	TUR	4	ARM	4	TUR	2
PUR	3	CHN	1	KOR	0	GEO		GEO	3
CHN	8	TUR	3	ARM	5	BYE		BUL	1
VEN	0	KOR	11	RUS	2				
TUR	5	UZB	1	GEO	7				
CAN	0	SWE	0						
KOR	7	ARM	4						
IRI		USA	6						
BYE		RUS	6						

3RD - 4TH		5TH - 6TH		7TH - 8TH	
TUR	9	UKR	0	ARM	0
GEO	0	BUL	3	RUS	0

FINAL CLASSIFICATION

Rnk	Name	Ctry	PP	TP	
1	ZAWADZKI, Wlodzimierz	POL	15	21	G
2	MAREN DELIS, Juan Luis	CUB	10	15	S
3	PIRIM, Mehmet	TUR	19	33	B
4	GULIASHVILI, Koba	GEO	13	25	
5	IVANOV, Ivan	BUL	11	9	
6	KAMYSHENKO, Hryhoriy	UKR	9	16	
7	MANUKYAN, Mkhitar	ARM	17	26	
8	MARTYNOV, Sergey	RUS	8	15	

Wrestling / *Lutte*

Greco-Roman, 68 kg (149.5 lb), Men / *Gréco-romaine, 68 kg, Messieurs*

3RD - 4TH	ROUND 6	ROUND 5	ROUND 4	ROUND 3	ROUND 2	1/8	1/4	1/2	FINAL
RUS 4	UZB 0	EST 0	JPN 0	HUN 0	GEO 0	CUB 3	POL 6	POL 3	POL 7
BLR 0	RUS 6	RUS 4	EST 6	EST 2	EST 6	ROM 0	CUB 0	UZB 0	FRA 0
	BUL 1	BUL 4	ARM 0	ARM 9	ARM 12	TUR 1	USA 0	BLR 1	
	BLR 3	CUB 0	RUS 5	CAN 3	COL 0	USA 12	UZB 4	FRA 4	
5TH - 6TH UZB 1			TUR 0	UKR 1	CAN 5	UZB 2	BLR		
BUL 2			BUL 5	RUS 3	MAR 4	BUL 0	BYE		
			CUB 3	ROM 4	KOR 1	BLR 5	FRA		
			USA 2	TUR 9	UKR 2	FIN 0	BYE		
7TH - 8TH EST 1				BUL 1	SWE 2	JPN 0			
CUB 6				FIN 1	RUS 9	FRA 10			
				JPN	HUN	POL			
				BYE	BYE	BYE			

ROUND 1

No	Name	Ctry	TP
1	MELELASHVILI, Tarieli	GEO	2
2	COLAS ORIS, Liubal	CUB	4
3	MEMET, Ender	ROM	3
4	NIKITIN, Valeri	EST	0
5	KARAPINAR, Yalcin	TUR	3
6	MANUKYAN, Samvel	ARM	0
7	SMITH, Rodney	USA	6
8	ESCOBAR, Jose	COL	1
9	PULYAYEV, Grigoriy	UZB	12
10	DAYNES, Colin	CAN	0
11	KANDAFIL, Anwar	MAR	0
12	GEORGIEV, Biser	BUL	10
13	MADZHIDOV, Kamandar	BLR	3
14	KIM, Young-Il	KOR	1
15	YLI-HANNUKSELA, Marko	FIN	6
16	ADZHY, Rustam	UKR	2
17	MIYAKE, Yasushi	JPN	4
18	MAGNUSSON, Anders	SWE	2
19	TRETYAKOV, Aleksandr	RUS	0
20	YOLOUZ, Ghani	FRA	8
21	WOLNY, Ryszard	POL	6
22	REPKA, Attila	HUN	1

FINAL CLASSIFICATION

Rnk	Name	Ctry	PP	TP	
1	WOLNY, Ryszard	POL	12	22	G
2	YOLOUZ, Ghani	FRA	10	22	S
3	TRETYAKOV, Aleksandr	RUS	18	31	B
4	MADZHIDOV, Kamandar	BLR	10	12	
5	GEORGIEV, Biser	BUL	17	23	
6	PULYAYEV, Grigoriy	UZB	11	19	
7	COLAS ORIS, Liubal	CUB	12	16	
8	NIKITIN, Valeri	EST	11	15	

Wrestling / *Lutte*

Greco-Roman, 74 kg (163 lb), Men / *Gréco-romaine, 74 kg, Messieurs*

3RD - 4TH	ROUND 6	ROUND 5	ROUND 4	ROUND 3	ROUND 2	1/8	1/4	1/2	FINAL
GER 2	RUS 5	POL 4	POL 6	POL 2	MAR 2	CZE 1	HUN 2	CUB 5	CUB 8
POL 4	GER 8	BUL 2	SWE 0	KAZ 1	POL 9	HUN 5	CUB 6	RUS 4	FIN 2
	POL 3	GER	BUL 5	SWE 2	MEX 0	USA 1	RUS	UKR 0	
	UKR 1	BYE	KOR 0	TUR 0	KAZ 6	CUB 10	BYE	FIN 10	
5TH - 6TH RUS 0			GER 3	BUL 5	VEN 1	RUS 4	UKR		
UKR 0			HUN 1	CZE 0	SWE 9	KOR 0	BYE		
				USA 2	TUR 3	UKR 2	FIN		
				KOR 3	BLR 2	GER 1	BYE		
7TH - 8TH BUL 0				GER 5	ALG 0	JPN 2			
HUN 0				JPN 2	BUL 5	FIN 4			

ROUND 1

No	Name	Ctry	TP
1	KHALFI, Aziz	MAR	0
2	ZEMAN, Jaroslav	CZE	7
3	TRACZ, Jozef	POL	0
4	BERZICZA, Tamas	HUN	1
5	MORGAN, Gordy	USA	10
6	HERNANDEZ, Rodolfo	MEX	0
7	ASCUY AGUILERA, Feliberto	CUB	9
8	BAYSEYTOV, Bakhtiar	KAZ	1
9	ISKANDARYAN, Mnatsakan	RUS	10
10	GARCIA, Nestor	VEN	0
11	KIM, Jin-Soo	KOR	11
12	KORNBAKK, Torbjorn	SWE	0
13	DZIHASOV, Artur	UKR	3
14	AVLUCA, Nazmi	TUR	0
15	KOPYTOV, Vladimir	BLR	2
16	HAHN, Erik	GER	4
17	KATAYAMA, Takamitsu	JPN	13
18	BOUGUERRA, Youcef	ALG	2
19	STOYANOV, Stoyan	BUL	2
20	ASELL, Marko	FIN	4

FINAL CLASSIFICATION

Rnk	Name	Ctry	PP	TP	
1	ASCUY AGUILERA, Feliberto	CUB	15	33	G
2	ASELL, Marko	FIN	11	20	S
3	TRACZ, Jozef	POL	18	28	B
4	HAHN, Erik	GER	14	23	
5	ISKANDARYAN, Mnatsakan	RUS	13	23	
6	BERZICZA, Tamas	HUN	12	9	
7	KIM, Jin-Soo	KOR	7	14	
8	KATAYAMA, Takamitsu	JPN	6	17	

Wrestling / *Lutte*

Greco-Roman, 82 kg (180.5 lb), Men / *Gréco-romaine, 82 kg, Messieurs*

3RD - 4TH	ROUND 6	ROUND 5	ROUND 4	ROUND 3	ROUND 2	ROUND 1			1/8	1/4	1/2	FINAL
						No	**Name**	**Ctry TP**				
BLR 4	SWE 1	ARM 1	YUG 0	ROM 0	VEN 1	1	TURLYKHANOV, Daulet	KAZ 10	TUR 7	TUR 5	TUR 1	TUR 3
KAZ 0	BLR 4	KAZ 3	ARM 2	YUG 5	YUG 11	2	MARCANO, Elias	VEN 0	KAZ 0	BLR 0	SWE 0	GER 0
	KAZ 4	BLR	KAZ 4	CZE 2	BEL 0	3	SANATBAYEV, Raatbek	KGZ 3	KGZ 1	SWE	GER 3	
	ISR 0	BYE	KGZ 3	ARM 3	CZE 2	4	JOVANCEVIC, Aleksandar	YUG 0	BLR 7	BYE	ISR 1	
5TH - 6TH						5	TSILENT, Valeriy	BLR 10	USA 1	GER		
SWE 0			RUS 0	FIN 3	ARM 4	6	WAFFLARD, Jean Pierre	BEL 0	SWE 3	BYE		
ISR 0			BLR 10	KAZ 7	HUN 0	7	HENDERSON, Daniel	USA 3	RUS 0	ISR		
				KGZ 3	PER 0	8	FRINTA, Pavel	CZE 1	GER 4	BYE		
7TH - 8TH				USA 2	FIN 11	9	LIDBERG, Martin	SWE 2	ISR 4			
ARM 0				RUS 11	ROM	10	GEGHAMYAN, Levon	ARM 0	KOR 1			
KGZ 0				KOR 0	BYE	11	TSVIR, Sergey	RUS 3				
						12	FARKAS, Peter	HUN 0				
						13	ISISOLA, Felix	PER 0				
						14	ZANDER, Thomas	GER 10				
						15	KARILA, Tuomo	FIN 0				
						16	TZITZUASHVILY, Gotcha	ISR 2				
						17	PARK, Myung-Suk	KOR 5				
						18	ARGHIRA, Anton	ROM 3				
						19	YERLIKAYA, Hamza BYE	TUR				

FINAL CLASSIFICATION

Rnk	Name	Ctry	PP	TP	
1	YERLIKAYA, Hamza	TUR	12	16	G
2	ZANDER, Thomas	GER	11	17	S
3	TSILENT, Valeriy	BLR	17	35	B
4	TURLYKHANOV, Daulet	KAZ	16	28	
5	TZITZUASHVILY, Gotcha	ISR	11	7	
6	LIDBERG, Martin	SWE	7	6	
7	GEGHAMYAN, Levon	ARM	14	10	
8	SANATBAYEV, Raatbek	KGZ	8	10	

Wrestling / *Lutte*

Greco-Roman, 90 kg (198 lb), Men / *Gréco-romaine, 90 kg, Messieurs*

3RD - 4TH	ROUND 6	ROUND 5	ROUND 4	ROUND 3	ROUND 2	ROUND 1			1/8	1/4	1/2	FINAL
						No	**Name**	**Ctry TP**				
GER 2	TUR 0	USA 0	HUN 0	HUN 2	KOR 4	1	UEON, Jin-Han	KOR 1	BUL 3	BUL 3	TUR 0	UKR 6
BLR 0	GER 4	GER 4	USA 6	RUS 1	RUS 4	2	PENA BORROTO, Reynaldo	CUB 2	CUB 0	TUR 5	UKR 3	POL 0
	BLR 5	CZE 1	CZE 4	BIH 0	CAN 2	3	BASAR, Hakki	TUR 6	TUR 3	UKR 4	POL 6	
	GRE 0	BLR 3	CUB 2	USA 12	BIH 5	4	KOGUASHVILI, Gogi	RUS 1	YUG 0	GER 2	GRE 0	
5TH-6TH						5	KASUM, Goran	YUG 3	UKR 4	POL		
TUR 4			BLR 3	EGY 4	FIN 1	6	COX, Doug	CAN 0	KAZ 1	BYE		
GRE 1			ARM 1	CZE 8	USA 11	7	OLIYNYK, Vyacheslav	UKR 12	BLR 0	GRE		
			BUL 0	CUB 3	EGY 4	8	HODZIC, Fahrudin	BIH 0	GER 1	BYE		
			GER 11	YUG 0	MAR 0	9	KOSKELA, Harri	FIN 0	POL 12			
7TH-8TH				KAZ 1	CZE 10	10	MATVIYENKO, Sergey	KAZ 7	TKM 2			
USA 10				BLR 1	PER 0	11	SIDORENKO, Aleksandr	BLR 3	GRE 12			
CZE 2				TKM 2	HUN	12	WALDROUP, Derrick	USA 0	ARM 0			
				ARM 5	BYE	13	BULLMANN, Maik	GER 3				
						14	HUSSEIN, Mostafa	EGY 0				
						15	FAFINSKI, Jacek	POL 4				
						16	ESSAFOUI, Abdelaziz	MAR 0				
						17	SVEC, Marek	CZE 1				
						18	REDZHEPOV, Rozy	TKM 3				
						19	VASQUEZ, Lucio	PER 0				
						20	KONSTANTINIDIS, Iordanis	GRE 10				
						21	YEGHISHYAN, Tsolak	ARM 5				
						22	GELENESI, Nandor	HUN 1				
						23	DIMITROV, Khristo BYE	BUL				

FINAL CLASSIFICATION

Rnk	Name	Ctry	PP	TP	
1	OLIYNYK, Vyacheslav	UKR	16	29	G
2	FAFINSKI, Jacek	POL	11	22	S
3	BULLMANN, Maik	GER	21	27	B
4	SIDORENKO, Aleksandr	BLR	15	15	
5	BASAR, Hakki	TUR	13	18	
6	KONSTANTINIDIS, Iordanis	GRE	8	23	
7	WALDROUP, Derrick	USA	14	39	
8	SVEC, Marek	CZE	13	26	

Wrestling / *Lutte*

Greco-Roman, 100 kg (220 lb), Men / *Gréco-romaine, 100 kg, Messieurs*

3RD - 4TH	ROUND 6	ROUND 5	ROUND 4	ROUND 3	ROUND 2	ROUND 1	1/8	1/4	1/2	FINAL
SWE 3	SWE 5	BUL 1	JPN 0	JPN 3	JPN 10		SWE 5	SWE 5	SWE 1	BLR 0
RUS 0	MDA 0	RUS 3	BUL 2	VEN 0	MAR 0		CRO 0	UKR 0	BLR 2	POL 0
	RUS 1	MDA 0	CRO 0	BUL 3	VEN 3		RUS 3	BLR	CUB 0	
	CUB 0	BYE	RUS 5	GEO 0	COL 0		UKR 6	BYE	POL 2	
5TH - 6TH			MDA 2	SUI 3	BUL 4		BLR 3	CUB		
MDA 0			UKR 2	CRO 6	CHN 0		USA 0	BYE		
CUB 0				RUS 4	CAN 0		CUB 3	POL		
				USA 1	GEO 3		ITA 0	BYE		
7TH - 8TH				ITA 2	SUI 11		MDA 0			
BUL 0				MDA 3	TUN 0		POL 0			
UKR 0										

ROUND 1

No	Name	Ctry	TP
1	NONOMURA, Takashi	JPN	0
2	LJUNGBERG, Mikael	SWE	10
3	DAMJANOVIC, Stipe	CRO	6
4	BASRI, Mohamed	MAR	0
5	EDISHERASHVILI, Teymuraz	RUS	6
6	SUAREZ, Emilio	VEN	0
7	GIRALDO COBALEDA, Juan Diego	COL	0
8	SOLDADZE, Heorhiy	UKR	4
9	LISHTVAN, Sergey	BLR	2
10	MANOV, Todor	BUL	0
11	GLEASMAN, Jason	USA	15
12	BA, Yanchuan	CHN	2
13	MILIAN PEREZ, Hector	CUB	12
14	BELL, Colbie	CAN	0
15	GIUNTA, Giuseppe	ITA	1
16	GOGITIDZE, Bakur	GEO	1
17	GRABOVETSKI, Igor	MDA	4
18	BURGLER, Urs	SUI	1
19	WRONSKI, Andrzej	POL	10
20	NAOUAR, Mohamed	TUN	0

FINAL CLASSIFICATION

Rnk	Name	Ctry	PP	TP	
1	WRONSKI, Andrzej	POL	13	12	G
2	LISHTVAN, Sergey	BLR	9	7	S
3	LJUNGBERG, Mikael	SWE	20	29	B
4	EDISHERASHVILI, Teymuraz	RUS	16	22	
5	MILIAN PEREZ, Hector	CUB	11	15	
6	GRABOVETSKI, Igor	MDA	9	9	
7	SOLDADZE, Heorhiy	UKR	12	12	
8	MANOV, Todor	BUL	10	10	

Wrestling / *Lutte*

Greco-Roman, 130 kg (286 lb), Men / *Gréco-romaine, 130 kg, Messieurs*

3RD - 4TH	ROUND 6	ROUND 5	ROUND 4	ROUND 3	ROUND 2	ROUND 1	1/8	1/4	1/2	FINAL
UKR 0	GRE 1	JPN 0	JPN 8	JPN 4	MAR 2		FIN 2	FIN 0	RUS 8	RUS 1
MDA 1	UKR 3	MDA 11	TJK 0	TUN 3	TUN 4		SWE 0	RUS 4	GRE 0	USA 0
	MDA 5	UKR	SWE 0	CAN 0	ROM 1		RUS 2	GRE	USA 4	
	GER 0	BYE	MDA 3	TJK 2	CAN 3		MDA 0	BYE	GER 0	
5TH - 6TH			UKR 2	UZB 1	MEX 2		EST 0	USA		
GRE 3			FIN 0	SWE 1	TJK 4		GRE 3	BYE		
GER 0				MDA 4	UZB 6		UKR 0	GER		
				EST 0	CHN 1		USA 3	BYE		
7TH - 8TH				UKR 4	JPN		GER 2			
JPN 0				HUN 0	BYE		HUN 0			
SWE 8										

ROUND 1

No	Name	Ctry	TP
1	BELAZIZ, Rachid	MAR	0
2	JOHANSSON, Tomas	SWE	8
3	KARELIN, Aleksandr	RUS	10
4	AYARI, Omrane	TUN	0
5	MOUREIKO, Serguei	MDA	12
6	AMARIEI, Laurentiu	ROM	1
7	JOHL, Yogi	CAN	0
8	HALLIK, Helger	EST	0
9	DIAZ, Guillermo	MEX	0
10	POIKILIDIS, Panayiotis	GRE	10
11	KOTOK, Petro	UKR	5
12	DGVARELI, Raoul	TJK	0
13	GHAFFARI, Matt	USA	7
14	KUZIYEV, Shermukhammad	UZB	1
15	LIU, Guoke	CHN	0
16	SCHIEKEL, Rene	GER	3
17	SUZUKI, Kenichi	JPN	0
18	KEKES, Gyorgy	HUN	3
19	AHOKAS, Juha	FIN	
	BYE		

FINAL CLASSIFICATION

Rnk	Name	Ctry	PP	TP	
1	KARELIN, Aleksandr	RUS	18	25	G
2	GHAFFARI, Matt	USA	9	14	S
3	MOUREIKO, Serguei	MDA	20	36	B
4	KOTOK, Petro	UKR	12	14	
5	POIKILIDIS, Panayiotis	GRE	11	17	
6	SCHIEKEL, Rene	GER	6	5	
7	JOHANSSON, Tomas	SWE	10	17	
8	SUZUKI, Kenichi	JPN	6	12	

CHARLES H YATMAN • FION F YAU • JEAN C YAU • PETER Y YAU • CHERYL K YAWATA • CHESTER H YAWN • LARRY M YAWN • PAMELA K YAWN • MARJA L YAZBAK • WALLY M YAZBAK • CHRIS A YEAGER • DAVID A YEAGER • JACK E YEAGER • SHARON M YEAGER • PAUL F YEAKLE • JENNIE S YEARWOOD • JOHN H YEARWOOD • BRADLEY L YEATES • TRACY L YEATES • ERICA L YEATON • JANETTE S YEATTS • STAN K YEATTS • ADRIENNE K YEE • ANGELA YEE • BRENDA K YEE • ERIN K YEE • HENRY J YEE • MAURINE A YEE • TIMOTHY W YEE • ALLISON G YEH • CHRISTINE YEH • YANG JEN YEH • SALLY L YEISER • GARY B YELLIN • JASON K YELTON • KEN E YELTON • LOUISE B YELTON • STEVEN F YELTON • SAMUEL H YEN • ERNEST YEO • MATTHEW T YEOH • OON OON YEOH • ALLISON J YEOMANS • KATHLEEN M YERDON • YUKSEL YESILTEPE • CAROL YETZER • BARBARA L YEUNG • PETER S YEUNG • HYUK YI • JOO HI YI • KEUN SOO YI • SU HYI • YUNG YI • MAN YICK • BRENDA L YIKE • MARILYN M YIKE • ROGER M YIKE • STACY L YIKE • AZIZ YILMAZ • TOLBERT H YILMAZ • EYRUSALEM YIMTATU • RASAMY B YIN • JUN YING • MICHELLE S YING • MISCHELLETTE D YISRAEL • YAACOV B YISRAEL • CORI A YOCHIM • TARA C YOCUM • ALEXANDRA G YODER • CHAD L YODER • CONNIE D YODER • KAREN J YODER • AJIT P. YOGANATHAN • ROBBIN L YOHE • TOMOKO YOKOI • YUKA YOKOYAMA • MELINDA A YON • MASAYOSHI YONEZAWA • DAVID L YONG • ROBERT E YONGUE • FATHIA YONIS • DOJOO YOO • SUNG-JIN YOON • JIM YORG • LARRY A YORI • CURTIS YORK • DARRYL R YORK • DAVID E YORK • JON YORK • KELLY R YORK • MARGUERITE B YORK • MATTHEW E YORK • MIKE YORK • VICKI L YORK • WILLIAM E YORK • WILLIAM J YORK • YASMIN Z YORKER • NOBORU YOSHIFUJI • PATSY Y YOSHIHARA • ERIKO YOSHIOKA • TAKAKO YOSHITANI • ANDREW M YOUHAS • BRIAN C YOUMANS • WILLIAM R YOUNCE • ADDIE P YOUNG • ALLAN E YOUNG • AMY L YOUNG • ANDREA L YOUNG • ANDREA R YOUNG • ANDREW YOUNG • ANNA L YOUNG • ANNA M YOUNG • ANNE M YOUNG • BARBARA A YOUNG • BILL R YOUNG • BONNIE W YOUNG • BRENDA K YOUNG • BRENDA W YOUNG • C L V YOUNG • CAROL E YOUNG • CAROLYN E YOUNG • CATHERINE L. YOUNG • CATHERINE S YOUNG • CHARLES L YOUNG • CHERYL F YOUNG • CHRISTEL D YOUNG • CRAIG E YOUNG • CRAIG R YOUNG • CYNTHIA A YOUNG • DANNY YOUNG • DANNY YOUNG • DANTON L YOUNG • DARREN J YOUNG • DAVID J YOUNG • DAVID L YOUNG • DEBORAH A YOUNG • DEBORAH W YOUNG • DIANA L YOUNG • DONALD H YOUNG • DOROTHY YOUNG • ELMA B YOUNG • FRANK P YOUNG • FRED YOUNG • GAIL YOUNG • GARY YOUNG • GLENN E YOUNG • GLORIA S YOUNG • GRACE B YOUNG • JAMES C YOUNG • JAMILLE YOUNG • JASON YOUNG • JEFFREY J YOUNG • JENNIFER L YOUNG • JULIA V YOUNG • KEVIN YOUNG • KIMBERLY D YOUNG • KIMBERLY V YOUNG • KRISTI J YOUNG • LATANYA J YOUNG • LAUREN L YOUNG • LINDA YOUNG •

LINDA M YOUNG • LISA N YOUNG • LUANA E YOUNG • LUCILLE B YOUNG • LUCY B YOUNG • LYDIA D YOUNG • MARA B YOUNG • MARK YOUNG • MARK J YOUNG • MARY ELIZABETH YOUNG • MARY L YOUNG • MEL-CHRISTOPHER L YOUNG • MELANIE A YOUNG • MELANIE K YOUNG • MELANIE M YOUNG • NESTOR J YOUNG • NICOLAS B YOUNG • NIKKI T YOUNG • NOEL E YOUNG • PATRICIA YOUNG • PATRICK YOUNG • PATTI V YOUNG • RANDY D YOUNG • RAYMOND W YOUNG • RONNIE R YOUNG • ROSEMARY A YOUNG • SANDRA R YOUNG • SHAUN YOUNG • SHAWN YOUNG • SHIRLEY I YOUNG • STEPHEN R YOUNG • STEPHIE YOUNG • STEVE H YOUNG • TAWANAH YOUNG • TIMOTHY K YOUNG • TRACY B YOUNG • VIRGINIA B YOUNG • WILLIAM M YOUNG • JAMES L YOUNG III • ALVIN B YOUNG JR • JAMES C YOUNG JR • LESTER YOUNG JR • JOSEPH A YOUNG MT • LORA A YOUNG WALKER • CYNTHIA YOUNGBLOOD • JANET L YOUNGBLOOD • PAUL A YOUNGBLOOD • SUE YOUNGBLOOD • JOHN L YOUNGER • MARY SUE YOUNGER • JAN M YOUNGERS • MARGARET D YOUNGGREN • GARY S YOUNGLING • JOAN O YOUNGMAN • ROBIN L YOUNGS • PAMELA G YOUNKER • RONALD J YOUNKER • LESLIE P YOUNKINS • JUDITH W YOUNTS • RANDALL W YOUSE • JOSEPH H YOUSSEF • JAN L YOUTIE • WILLIAM S YOUTIE • CAMILE W YOW • GRACE A YU • HUN CHO YU • JEN J YU • JOSH Z YU • MARIA C YU • MI AE YU • SARAH JANE W YU • WEILI YU • YANG YU • TING SU YUAN • SATOSHI YUASA • ALFRED YUE • CHRISTOPHER L YUEH • SHANNON JARRED YUM • KAZUMI YUMOTO • CHUN SOO YUN • SON AH YUN • TRACY YUNKER • FELICIA E YURGALAVAGE • CAROL D YURICK • RUSSELL H YURK • FERIDOON YUSEFZADEH • R. DON YUSZKIEWCZ • HELENE YVER • KATHRYN ZACCARI • MARIE ZACHAR • MARY EVELYN ZACHAR • ZDENEK ZACHAR • DANIEL A ZACHARIAS • CHERRIE A ZACHARY • CHERYL A ZACHARY • DRAMANE R ZACHARY • MARCUS D ZACHARY • LOYDEAN B ZACHERY • SELINA ZACHERY • STEVEN ZACHOK III • LURENA ZACKERY • SHIRLEY ZACKERYSMITH • WHITNEY ZAEH • CHRISTINE F ZAEHNER • CAROL L ZAESKE RN • LIZ ZAHAROPOULOS • STEVEN J ZAHN • WINNIE ZAHN • LARRY G ZAHRADKA ATC • AKBAR A ZAIDI • PATTI ZAINO • GREGORY O ZAKERS • KIRTHNEY ZAKERS • INGRID L ZAMECNIK • OMAR R ZAMORA • MICHAEL F ZAMPINO • LAURA E ZAMPROGNA • CHARLES ZANDAZA • DUTCH ZANDBERGEN • MAURICE D ZANDERS • HANS R ZANDSTRA • JEEPJE J ZANDSTRA • ROBERTO C ZANDUETA • JOHN ZANENGO • KIMBERLY A ZANIBONI • FABIO ZANNI • SANDRA E ZANNI • PAUL T ZANTZINGER • AMY ZANUZOSKI • MONICA B ZAPATA • KAREN A ZAPKO • ELIZABETH M ZARAGOZA • JOSEPH F ZARCONE • DAVID J ZAREMBA • JILL A ZAREMBA • LEIGH B ZAREMBA • SHERRY A ZAREMBA • MILES J ZAREMSKI • JILL ZARENSKY • HELEN ZARVAS • JOHN T ZARZYCKI • JEREMIAH A ZASTROW • CHARLES H ZATSICK • ANGELO P

ZATZOS • CLAUDETTE B ZAUCHE • JEREMY S ZAUDER • BALTAZAR ZAVALA • JOSE D ZAVALETA • ROBERT E ZAWORSKI • FRANK A ZAYAS • JOSE A ZAYAS • VLADIMIR ZAYCHIK • STEPHANIE ZAZA • CAROL L ZBOREAK • ERICKA N ZDENEK • JEFFERSON G ZEANAH • ANN L ZEBERLEIN • GLORIA J ZEBNY • NORBERT J ZEBNY • JANINE C ZEBROWSKI • WENDY S ZECH • BARBARA ZECHES • JOHNNY ZECOPOULOS • MICHAEL ZEE • KAREN M ZEEDYK • LINDA E ZEEMAN • AZIZ ZEERAK • JENNIFER ZEH • THOMAS P ZEHAS • LAURA E ZEHE • PAUL A ZEHE • SANDRA V ZEHNDER • SHARON G ZEHNER • MICHELLE S. ZEHR • MARJE M ZEICHERT • JOSH P ZEIDE • JEANETTE R ZEIDLER • KURT W ZEIGER • ALBERT B ZEIGLER • ANDREW B ZEIGLER • CLARE D ZEIGLER • PHILIP J ZEIGLER • JONATHAN ZEILLER • HEIDE M ZEISER • BARRY I ZEITMAN • JOHN R ZEITZ • STRATTON M ZELACK • TWYLA E ZELACK • RAMONA J ZELASKO • JAMES E ZELICHOWSKI • MIKE ZELKIND • EVA L ZELL • NANCY J ZELL • RICHARD W ZELLER • CHARLOTTE D ZELLNER • MERRILEE ZELLNER • PAULA L ZELNER • STEPHEN B ZELNAK • LAURIE J ZELNICK • ALLISON L ZELSKI • RUDOLPH L ZEMAN • MARTHA T ZEMANEK • JERI E ZEMKE • PAUL R ZEMLIN • INGRIDA M ZEMZARS • ERICA L ZENDEL • PETER K ZENDT • QIANDONG ZENG • ANNE C ZENGERLE • ELEONORA L ZENINA-NIKULINA • CURTIS J ZENO • SUE M ZENTNER • ADAM JR ZEPEDA • RAYMOND J ZEPP • DANIEL R ZEROSKI • KIMBERLY A ZESKE • KIM ZETTERBERG • SELAMAWIT A ZEWDE • GALE A ZGRAGGEN • DIANE ZHANG • FUQING ZHANG • HAO ZHANG • HONG ZHANG • HUAYING ZHANG • HUI ZHANG • LILI ZHANG • LING Y ZHANG • LIPING ZHANG • PING ZHANG • QIXIA ZHANG • YOULIN ZHANG • YUANLIN ZHANG • ZEEMAN ZHANG • SIXUAN ZHONG • TING ZHOU • ZHONGHUA ZHOU • BEATRIZ ANNE B ZIALCITA • MARIE CHRISTINE B ZIALCITA • BERNARD L ZIDAR • MICHELLE L ZIDE • LINDA E ZIDER • JULIE DAWN ZIEGELMAN • BLANCHE C ZIEGLER • KIMBERLY L ZIEGLER • MICHAEL E ZIELASKIEWICZ • JEANNIE M ZIELINSKI • MARSHA M ZIEMBA • LARRY B ZIESEL • DANIEL G ZILBER • EILEEN R ZILINSKAS • AYN ZILLMAN • PHILIP ZILLMANN • DIANNA H ZIMA • DONALD P ZIMA • ALFRED E ZIMMERMAN • MARK T ZIMMER • MARTHA F ZIMMER • MARTHA P ZIMMER • KAREN J ZIMMERLY • ADAM F ZIMMERMAN • GREGORY B ZIMMERMAN • JILL ZIMMERMAN • JO L ZIMMERMAN • JULIE R ZIMMERMAN • KIMBERLY S ZIMMERMAN • MATTHEW ZIMMERMAN • PATRICK ZIMMERMAN • ROBERT ZIMMERMAN • SCOTT D ZIMMERMAN • SUE B ZIMMERMAN • TED D ZIMMERMAN • TERRY L ZIMMERMAN • TRE C ZIMMERMAN • WENDY S ZIMMERMAN • GILBERT G ZIMMERMANN • FREDERK W ZIMNY • PAMELA M ZIMPFER • VICKI L ZINGG • DUSTIN L ZINK • EDWIN A ZINK • DEBORAH J ZINN • SHARI D ZINSENHEIM • MONIQUE M ZINSER • NOMA J ZINSMASTER • DOROTHY D ZINSMEISTER • ANSELME ZINSOU • JESSICA R ZIPF • LEIGH B ZIPPERER •

YACHTING
YACHTING

Abbreviations and terms used in Yachting results tables
Abréviations et termes employés dans les tableaux de résultats de yachting

Term	English	Français
B	Bronze Medal	Médaille de bronze
C	Crew	Equipage
Ctry	Country	Pays
DNC	Did Not Compete	N'a pas concouru
DNF	Did Not Finish	Abandon
DNS	Did Not Start	Absent au départ
DSQ	Disqualified	Disqualifié
Final	Final	Finale
G	Gold Medal	Médaille d'or
Net pts	Net Points	Points nets
PMS	Premature Start	Départ prématuré
Points	Points	Points
Pos	Position	Position
Race	Race	Course
Rank	Rank	Classement
Rnk	Rank	Classement
S	Silver Medal	Médaille d'argent
S (Pos)	Skipper	Skipper
Total Points	Total Points	Total des points
YMP	Yacht Materially Prejudiced	Voilier notablement lésé

International Yacht Racing Union (IYRU)
Union Internationale de Yachting
27 Broadwall, Waterloo
London SEI 9PL
England

Yachting / *Yachting*
Board (IMCO One-Design: Mistral), Men / *Planche à voile (IMCO/Mistral), Messieurs*

FINAL

				RANK POINTS												
Rnk	Name	Ctry	Pos	Race 1	Race 2	Race 3	Race 4	Race 5	Race 6	Race 7	Race 8	Race 9	Race 10	Race 11	Total pts	Net pts
1	KAKLAMANAKIS, Nikolaos	GRE	S	5	1	2	6	1	9	1	1	DNF			73.00	17.00 G
				5.00	1.00	2.00	6.00	1.00	9.00	1.00	1.00	47.00				
2	ESPINOLA, Carlos Mauricio	ARG	S	2	4	4	2	3	6	PMS	2	2			72.00	19.00 S
				2.00	4.00	4.00	2.00	3.00	6.00	47.00	2.00	2.00				
3	FRIDMAN, Gal	ISR	S	1	6	5	3	10	1	9	4	1			40.00	21.00 B
				1.00	6.00	5.00	3.00	10.00	1.00	9.00	4.00	1.00				
4	McINTOSH, Aaron	NZL	S	4	3	1	18	15	2	5	3	9			60.00	27.00
				4.00	3.00	1.00	18.00	15.00	2.00	5.00	3.00	9.00				
5	de CHAVIGNY, Jean-Max	FRA	S	7	5	10	1	14	5	2	7	10			61.00	37.00
				7.00	5.00	10.00	1.00	14.00	5.00	2.00	7.00	10.00				
6	GEBHARDT, Mike	USA	S	10	16	3	4	5	23	4	11	4			80.00	41.00
				10.00	16.00	3.00	4.00	5.00	23.00	4.00	11.00	4.00				
7	RODRIGUES, Joao	POR	S	14	8	9	5	2	4	6	12	8			68.00	42.00
				14.00	8.00	9.00	5.00	2.00	4.00	6.00	12.00	8.00				
8	TODD, Brendan	AUS	S	11	2	8	7	9	10	3	9	20			79.00	48.00
				11.00	2.00	8.00	7.00	9.00	10.00	3.00	9.00	20.00				
9	HUANG, Wei	TPE	S	6	15	16	8	4	12	13	10	6			90.00	59.00
				6.00	15.00	16.00	8.00	4.00	12.00	13.00	10.00	6.00				
10	BORNHAEUSER, Matthias	GER	S	3	11	13	27	PMS	15	7	8	3			134.00	60.00
				3.00	11.00	13.00	27.00	47.00	15.00	7.00	8.00	3.00				
11	MALEK, Miroslaw	POL	S	8	14	6	DSQ	8	7	11	PMS	17			165.00	71.00
				8.00	14.00	6.00	47.00	8.00	7.00	11.00	47.00	17.00				
12	QIAN, Hong	CHN	S	27	12	19	10	11	13	10	6	12			120.00	74.00
				27.00	12.00	19.00	10.00	11.00	13.00	10.00	6.00	12.00				
13	SULAKSANA I GUSTI, Made Oka	INA	S	21	7	15	9	13	18	PMS	14	5			149.00	81.00
				21.00	7.00	15.00	9.00	13.00	18.00	47.00	14.00	5.00				
14	PHILP, Tony	FIJ	S	9	13	7	11	PMS	14	25	16	15			157.00	85.00
				9.00	13.00	7.00	11.00	47.00	14.00	25.00	16.00	15.00				
15	MACIEL, Jorge	ESP	S	31	9	23	14	7	3	18	22	14			141.00	87.00
				31.00	9.00	23.00	14.00	7.00	3.00	18.00	22.00	14.00				
16	BOLDUC, Alain	CAN	S	38	10	18	13	22	17	8	18	11			155.00	95.00
				38.00	10.00	18.00	13.00	22.00	17.00	8.00	18.00	11.00				
17	CHRISTOFFERSEN, Morten Egebald	DEN	S	22	20	17	15	PMS	8	15	19	7			170.00	101.00
				22.00	20.00	17.00	15.00	47.00	8.00	15.00	19.00	7.00				
18	van GEEMEN, Martjin	NED	S	15	17	12	23	12	29	PMS	20	19			194.00	118.00
				15.00	17.00	12.00	23.00	12.00	29.00	47.00	20.00	19.00				
19	PALM, Fredrik	SWE	S	34	19	11	22	16	31	PMS	13	16			209.00	128.00
				34.00	19.00	11.00	22.00	16.00	31.00	47.00	13.00	16.00				
20	DALE, Ansis	LAT	S	24	25	29	20	6	22	24	29	13			192.00	134.00
				24.00	25.00	29.00	20.00	6.00	22.00	24.00	29.00	13.00				
21	HOMRARUEN, Arun	THA	S	13	27	14	DNC	31	28	17	5	34			216.00	135.00
				13.00	27.00	14.00	47.00	31.00	28.00	17.00	5.00	34.00				
22	TORUNLAR, Kutlu	TUR	S	17	18	22	26	20	19	27	17	29			195.00	139.00
				17.00	18.00	22.00	26.00	20.00	19.00	27.00	17.00	29.00				
23	STOEKEN, Paul	ISV	S	28	21	30	21	17	21	19	32	18			207.00	145.00
				28.00	21.00	30.00	21.00	17.00	21.00	19.00	32.00	18.00				
24	PLUMB, Howard	GBR	S	35	PMS	24	12	25	11	22	21	32			229.00	147.00
				35.00	47.00	24.00	12.00	25.00	11.00	22.00	21.00	32.00				
25	OBEREMKO, Maksym	UKR	S	20	31	21	17	26	38	12	30	24			219.00	150.00
				20.00	31.00	21.00	17.00	26.00	38.00	12.00	30.00	24.00				
26	MILOSEVIC, Roland	VEN	S	12	30	28	DSQ	18	26	20	33	21			235.00	155.00
				12.00	30.00	28.00	47.00	18.00	26.00	20.00	33.00	21.00				
27	POLLAK, Patrik	SVK	S	19	23	25	19	29	16	35	25	28			219.00	155.00
				19.00	23.00	25.00	19.00	29.00	16.00	35.00	25.00	28.00				
28	WONG, Tak Sum	HKG	S	18	39	26	30	21	PMS	16	23	22			242.00	156.00
				18.00	39.00	26.00	30.00	21.00	47.00	16.00	23.00	22.00				
29	TAGUTI, Yuri	BRA	S	37	24	20	16	32	20	29	37	33			248.00	174.00
				37.00	24.00	20.00	16.00	32.00	20.00	29.00	37.00	33.00				
30	HRDINA, Patrik	CZE	S	32	26	32	31	35	24	14	24	42			260.00	183.00
				32.00	26.00	32.00	31.00	35.00	24.00	14.00	24.00	42.00				
31	MOYSEYEV, Vladimir	RUS	S	36	29	27	33	36	34	21	26	25			267.00	195.00
				36.00	29.00	27.00	33.00	36.00	34.00	21.00	26.00	25.00				
32	LAPPAS, Demetris	CYP	S	26	22	39	25	27	36	33	27	35			269.00	195.00
				26.00	22.00	39.00	25.00	27.00	36.00	33.00	27.00	35.00				

Table continued on next page / Tableau continué à la page suivante

Board (IMCO One-Design: Mistral), Men / *Planche à voile (IMCO/Mistral), Messieurs*

FINAL - *continued from previous page / suite de la page précédente*

Rnk	Name	Ctry	Pos	Race 1	Race 2	Race 3	Race 4	Race 5	Race 6	Race 7	Race 8	Race 9	Race 10	Race 11	Total pts	Net pts
33	OK, Duck-Pil	KOR	S	23	40	36	24	PMS	25	PMS	28	26			296.00	202.00
				23.00	40.00	36.00	24.00	47.00	25.00	47.00	28.00	26.00				
34	SILVEIRA, Pedro	MEX	S	33	35	35	28	19	32	31	31	30			274.00	204.00
				33.00	35.00	35.00	28.00	19.00	32.00	31.00	31.00	30.00				
35	ANDERSON, Matt	PUR	S	39	32	37	35	24	PMS	26	34	23			297.00	211.00
				39.00	32.00	37.00	35.00	24.00	47.00	26.00	34.00	23.00				
36	ZINALI, Andrea	ITA	S	29	28	33	29	23	35	PMS	41	41			306.00	218.00
				29.00	28.00	33.00	29.00	23.00	35.00	47.00	41.00	41.00				
37	SARAGOSA, Constantino	AHO	S	41	34	39	DNC	28	39	28	15	40			311.00	223.00
				41.00	34.00	39.00	47.00	28.00	39.00	28.00	15.00	40.00				
38	WILSON, Andrew	MLT	S	40	37	31	32	30	27	32	36	39			304.00	225.00
				40.00	37.00	31.00	32.00	30.00	27.00	32.00	36.00	39.00				
39	ISOLA, Andres	URU	S	16	38	40	DSQ	38	30	30	39	37			314.00	227.00
				16.00	38.00	40.00	47.00	38.00	30.00	30.00	39.00	37.00				
40	GADORFALVI, Aron	HUN	S	25	33	34	DSQ	34	33	37	39	31			313.00	227.00
				25.00	33.00	34.00	47.00	34.00	33.00	37.00	39.00	31.00				
41	MARSHALL, Oneal	BAR	S	45	41	44	37	37	40	23	35	27			329.00	240.00
				45.00	41.00	44.00	37.00	37.00	40.00	23.00	35.00	27.00				
42	IRIARTE, Jan	GUM	S	30	36	DNF	38	33	42	PMS	43	36			352.00	258.00
				30.00	36.00	47.00	38.00	33.00	42.00	47.00	43.00	36.00				
43	GROGONO, David	CAY	S	42	43	42	34	39	37	34	40	38			349.00	264.00
				42.00	43.00	42.00	34.00	39.00	37.00	34.00	40.00	38.00				
44	BARBE, Jonathan	SEY	S	43	42	41	36	40	41	36	42	44			365.00	278.00
				43.00	42.00	41.00	36.00	40.00	41.00	36.00	42.00	44.00				
45	RUATA, Cristian	GUA	S	44	44	43	DSQ	41	43	38	45	43			388.00	269.00
				44.00	44.00	43.00	47.00	41.00	43.00	38.00	45.00	43.00				
46	ALI ADOU, Roble	DJI	S	DNF	45	45	39	DNF	DNS	PMS	44	45			406.00	312.00
				47.00	45.00	45.00	39.00	47.00	47.00	47.00	44.00	45.00				

Yachting / *Yachting*
Board (IMCO One-Design: Mistral), Women / *Planche à voile (IMCO/Mistral), Dames*

FINAL

Rnk	Name	Ctry	Pos	Race 1	Race 2	Race 3	Race 4	Race 5	Race 6	Race 7	Race 8	Race 9	Race 10	Race 11	Total pts	Net pts	
1	LEE, Lai Shan	HKG	S	3	2	2	2	4	2	7	1	DNC			51.00	16.00	G
				3.00	2.00	2.00	2.00	4.00	2.00	7.00	1.00	28.00					
2	KENDALL, Barbara	NZL	S	2	3	6	1	10	5	5	6	2			40.00	24.00	S
				2.00	3.00	6.00	1.00	10.00	5.00	5.00	6.00	2.00					
3	SENSINI, Alessandra	ITA	S	1	8	1	6	7	15	14	5	1			57.00	28.00	B
				1.00	8.00	1.00	6.00	7.00	15.00	14.00	5.00	1.00					
4	LI, Ke	CHN	S	4	14	5	9	2	7	6	2	3			51.00	29.00	
				4.00	14.00	5.00	9.00	2.00	7.00	6.00	2.00	3.00					
5	HORGEN, Jorunn	NOR	S	7	9	4	4	3	1	8	4	PMS			67.00	31.00	
				7.00	9.00	4.00	4.00	3.00	1.00	8.00	4.00	28.00					
6	STASZEWSKA, Dorota	POL	S	6	4	8	12	13	3	9	3	5			63.00	38.00	
				6.00	4.00	8.00	12.00	13.00	3.00	9.00	3.00	5.00					
7	WILSON, Penny	GBR	S	5	YMP	14	5	5	6	4	20	PMS			92.00	44.00	
				5.00	5.00	14.00	5.00	5.00	6.00	4.00	20.00	28.00					
8	HERBERT, Maud	FRA	S	8	1	17	8	1	9	11	10	9			74.00	46.00	
				8.00	1.00	17.00	8.00	1.00	9.00	11.00	10.00	9.00					
9	STURGES, Natasha	AUS	S	12	10	3	3	12	4	10	11	7			71.00	47.00	
				12.00	10.00	3.00	3.00	12.00	4.00	10.00	11.00	7.00					
10	de VRIES, Dorien	NED	S	13	5	DSQ	10	8	8	3	12	6			93.00	52.00	
				13.00	5.00	28.00	10.00	8.00	8.00	3.00	12.00	6.00					
11	BUTLER, Lanee	USA	S	9	15	18	7	11	13	1	8	4			85.00	53.00	
				9.00	15.00	18.00	7.00	11.00	13.00	1.00	8.00	4.00					
12	ALIE, Carroll-Ann	CAN	S	11	7	7	16	6	10	2	14	PMS			100.00	56.00	
				11.00	7.00	7.00	16.00	6.00	10.00	2.00	14.00	28.00					

Table continued on next page / Tableau continué à la page suivante

Board (IMCO One-Design: Mistral), Women / *Planche à voile (IMCO/Mistral), Dames*

FINAL - *continued from previous page* / *suite de la page précédente*

Rnk	Name	Ctry	Pos	Race 1	Race 2	Race 3	Race 4	Race 5	Race 6	Race 7	Race 8	Race 9	Race 10	Race 11	Total pts	Net pts
13	CASAS, Mireia	ESP	S	14	13	11	11	23	11	15	7	12			116.00	78.00
				14.00	13.00	11.00	11.00	23.00	11.00	15.00	7.00	12.00				
14	NEUBURGER, Lisa	ISV	S	10	12	15	13	9	12	12	13	11			106.00	78.00
				10.00	12.00	15.00	13.00	9.00	12.00	12.00	13.00	11.00				
15	IMAI, Masako	JPN	S	18	11	16	17	16	17	18	9	10			131.00	95.00
				18.00	11.00	16.00	17.00	16.00	17.00	18.00	9.00	10.00				
16	JOO, Soon-Ahn	KOR	S	15	20	9	14	14	14	13	16	16			131.00	95.00
				15.00	20.00	9.00	14.00	14.00	14.00	13.00	16.00	16.00				
17	FECHINO, Monica	ARG	S	17	18	10	18	25	16	20	15	14			153.00	108.00
				17.00	18.00	10.00	18.00	25.00	16.00	20.00	15.00	14.00				
18	DZELME, Ilona	LAT	S	20	19	20	15	17	25	17	17	8			158.00	113.00
				20.00	19.00	20.00	15.00	17.00	25.00	17.00	17.00	8.00				
19	MARTINEZ, Lucia	PUR	S	16	17	12	20	19	18	PMS	23	15			168.00	117.00
				16.00	17.00	12.00	20.00	19.00	18.00	28.00	23.00	15.00				
20	AALTO, Minna	FIN	S	21	22	13	19	18	20	16	18	13			160.00	117.00
				21.00	22.00	13.00	19.00	18.00	20.00	16.00	18.00	13.00				
21	FAGUNDES, Catarina	POR	S	PMS	16	19	21	15	23	23	19	20			184.00	133.00
				28.00	16.00	19.00	21.00	15.00	23.00	23.00	19.00	20.00				
22	VOGEL, Turia	COK	S	24	26	21	27	24	19	19	22	17			199.00	146.00
				24.00	26.00	21.00	27.00	24.00	19.00	19.00	22.00	17.00				
23	SKARLATOU, Angeliki	GRE	S	23	21	24	22	22	24	21	21	19			197.00	149.00
				23.00	21.00	24.00	22.00	22.00	24.00	21.00	21.00	19.00				
24	MORRISON, Fiona	AND	S	PMS	23	25	24	20	22	22	24	18			206.00	153.00
				28.00	23.00	25.00	24.00	20.00	22.00	22.00	24.00	18.00				
25	SOZERI, Ayse	TUR	S	22	25	22	25	21	21	24	25	21			206.00	156.00
				22.00	25.00	22.00	25.00	21.00	21.00	24.00	25.00	21.00				
26	MATTOSO, Christina	BRA	S	19	24	23	23	DNC	DNC	DNC	DNC	DNC			229.00	173.00
				19.00	24.00	23.00	23.00	28.00	28.00	28.00	28.00	28.00				
27	MOORE-LINN, Cathleen	GUM	S	25	27	26	26	26	26	25	26	22			229.00	176.00
				25.00	27.00	26.00	26.00	26.00	26.00	25.00	26.00	22.00				

Yachting / *Yachting*

Single-Handed Dinghy (Finn), Men / *Dériveur solitaire (Finn), Messieurs*

FINAL

Rnk	Name	Ctry	Pos	Race 1	Race 2	Race 3	Race 4	Race 5	Race 6	Race 7	Race 8	Race 9	Race 10	Race 11	Total pts	Net pts	
1	KUSZNIEREWICZ, Mateusz	POL	S	10	4	20	4	9	1	2	1	1	10		62.00	32.00	G
				10.00	4.00	20.00	4.00	9.00	1.00	2.00	1.00	1.00	10.00				
2	GODEFROID, Sebastien	BEL	S	13	24	5	5	4	3	16	7	2	6		85.00	45.00	S
				13.00	24.00	5.00	5.00	4.00	3.00	16.00	7.00	2.00	6.00				
3	HEINER, Roy	NED	S	21	7	6	11	6	11	1	12	6	2		83.00	50.00	B
				21.00	7.00	6.00	11.00	6.00	11.00	1.00	12.00	6.00	2.00				
4	SPITZAUER, Hans	AUT	S	4	1	10	7	11	4	5	PMS	12	12		98.00	54.00	
				4.00	1.00	10.00	7.00	11.00	4.00	5.00	32.00	12.00	12.00				
5	LOOF, Fredrik	SWE	S	8	3	1	6	14	19	11	11	15	3		91.00	57.00	
				8.00	3.00	1.00	6.00	14.00	19.00	11.00	11.00	15.00	3.00				
6	McKENZIE, Paul	AUS	S	9	28	14	20	1	17	13	3	3	7		115.00	67.00	
				9.00	28.00	14.00	20.00	1.00	17.00	13.00	3.00	3.00	7.00				
7	van der PLOEG, Jose Maria	ESP	S	1	8	15	DNS	17	8	15	6	11	5		118.00	69.00	
				1.00	8.00	15.00	32.00	17.00	8.00	15.00	6.00	11.00	5.00				
8	AINSLIE, Ian	RSA	S	25	10	7	2	10	10	14	2	26	17		123.00	72.00	
				25.00	10.00	7.00	2.00	10.00	10.00	14.00	2.00	26.00	17.00				
9	CLARKE, Richard	CAN	S	14	6	3	10	PMS	28	3	17	21	1		135.00	75.00	
				14.00	6.00	3.00	10.00	32.00	28.00	3.00	17.00	21.00	1.00				
10	BERGMANN, Christoph	BRA	S	19	2	9	1	5	20	8	21	19	16		120.00	79.00	
				19.00	2.00	9.00	1.00	5.00	20.00	8.00	21.00	19.00	16.00				
11	MAKILA, Jali	FIN	S	17	5	12	9	3	22	7	16	13	21		125.00	82.00	
				17.00	5.00	12.00	9.00	3.00	22.00	7.00	16.00	13.00	21.00				

Table continued on next page / *Tableau continué à la page suivante*

Single-Handed Dinghy (Finn), Men / *Dériveur solitaire (Finn), Messieurs*

FINAL - *continued from previous page / suite de la page précédente*

Rnk	Name	Ctry	Pos	Race 1	Race 2	Race 3	Race 4	Race 5	Race 6	Race 7	Race 8	Race 9	Race 10	Race 11	Total pts	Net pts
12	STENHOUSE, Richard	GBR	S	18	14	8	21	8	12	20	4	8	11		124.00	83.00
				18.00	14.00	8.00	21.00	8.00	12.00	20.00	4.00	8.00	11.00			
13	MONK, Craig	NZL	S	22	9	4	13	2	13	18	5	28	25		139.00	86.00
				22.00	9.00	4.00	13.00	2.00	13.00	18.00	5.00	28.00	25.00			
14	MAIER, Michael	CZE	S	3	15	17	18	19	29	12	8	5	8		134.00	86.00
				3.00	15.00	17.00	18.00	19.00	29.00	12.00	8.00	5.00	8.00			
15	PRESTI, Philippe	FRA	S	6	13	19	3	13	15	6	19	18	13		125.00	87.00
				6.00	13.00	19.00	3.00	13.00	15.00	6.00	19.00	18.00	13.00			
16	DEVOTI, Luca	ITA	S	7	25	21	15	18	9	9	PMS	7	4		147.00	90.00
				7.00	25.00	21.00	15.00	18.00	9.00	9.00	32.00	7.00	4.00			
17	TOKOVYY, Yuriy	UKR	S	2	20	22	14	16	5	17	9	10	18		133.00	91.00
				2.00	20.00	22.00	14.00	16.00	5.00	17.00	9.00	10.00	18.00			
18	KHOPERSKIY, Oleg	RUS	S	27	18	13	16	7	27	25	10	4	14		161.00	107.00
				27.00	18.00	13.00	16.00	7.00	27.00	25.00	10.00	4.00	14.00			
19	KURET, Karlo	CRO	S	DSQ	11	2	19	12	23	24	18	9	15		165.00	109.00
				32.00	11.00	2.00	19.00	12.00	23.00	24.00	18.00	9.00	15.00			
20	FELLMANN, Michael	GER	S	15	12	11	17	15	26	26	15	14	22		173.00	121.00
				15.00	12.00	11.00	17.00	15.00	26.00	26.00	15.00	14.00	22.00			
21	WESTERGAARD, Bjoern	DEN	S	12	16	25	8	23	14	4	PMS	22	23		179.00	122.00
				12.00	16.00	25.00	8.00	23.00	14.00	4.00	32.00	22.00	23.00			
22	BATISTA, Vasco	POR	S	16	23	23	22	26	7	22	14	16	9		178.00	129.00
				16.00	23.00	23.00	22.00	26.00	7.00	22.00	14.00	16.00	9.00			
23	MARTIN, Will	USA	S	PMS	22	18	12	21	2	PMS	25	17	19		200.00	136.00
				32.00	22.00	18.00	12.00	21.00	2.00	32.00	25.00	17.00	19.00			
24	DRISCOLL, John	IRL	S	23	19	16	24	20	21	10	13	24	20		190.00	142.00
				23.00	19.00	16.00	24.00	20.00	21.00	10.00	13.00	24.00	20.00			
25	VALASEK, Marek	SVK	S	5	17	26	28	27	6	23	20	25	26		203.00	148.00
				5.00	17.00	26.00	28.00	27.00	6.00	23.00	20.00	25.00	26.00			
26	LITKEY, Farkas	HUN	S	11	29	24	23	22	25	19	22	20	24		219.00	165.00
				11.00	29.00	24.00	23.00	22.00	25.00	19.00	22.00	20.00	24.00			
27	PAPATHANASIOU, Amilios	GRE	S	26	21	DNF	27	PMS	16	21	23	29	DNF		259.00	195.00
				26.00	21.00	32.00	27.00	32.00	16.00	21.00	23.00	29.00	32.00			
28	FRATILA, Dumitru	ROM	S	20	26	27	25	24	24	27	26	27	28		254.00	199.00
				20.00	26.00	27.00	25.00	24.00	24.00	27.00	26.00	27.00	28.00			
29	CLARKE, Mark	CAY	S	28	27	28	26	25	18	28	PMS	23	27		262.00	202.00
				28.00	27.00	28.00	26.00	25.00	18.00	28.00	32.00	23.00	27.00			
30	MENDEZ, Manuel	PUR	S	24	30	30	29	28	30	29	DSQ	31	29		292.00	229.00
				24.00	30.00	30.00	29.00	28.00	30.00	29.00	32.00	31.00	29.00			
31	TAYLOR, Geoffrey	FIJ	S	29	31	29	30	DNF	31	30	24	30	30		296.00	233.00
				29.00	31.00	29.00	30.00	32.00	31.00	30.00	24.00	30.00	30.00			

Yachting / *Yachting*

Single-Handed Dinghy (Europe), Women / *Dériveur solitaire (Europe), Dames*

FINAL

Rnk	Name	Ctry	Pos	Race 1	Race 2	Race 3	Race 4	Race 5	Race 6	Race 7	Race 8	Race 9	Race 10	Race 11	Total pts	Net pts	
1	ROUG, Kristine	DEN	S	2	1	3	2	1	2	8	1	8	7	5	40.00	24.00	G
				2.00	1.00	3.00	2.00	1.00	2.00	8.00	1.00	8.00	7.00	5.00			
2	MATTHIJSSE, Margriet	NED	S	PMS	2	1	10	2	1	1	4	12	15	4	71.00	30.00	S
				29.00	2.00	1.00	10.00	2.00	1.00	1.00	4.00	12.00	15.00	4.00			
3	BECKER-DEY, Courtenay	USA	S	1	8	2	4	7	6	3	14	9	2	6	62.00	39.00	B
				1.00	8.00	2.00	4.00	7.00	6.00	3.00	14.00	9.00	2.00	6.00			
4	ROBERTSON, Shirley	GBR	S	3	7	18	1	6	3	22	2	4	12	3	81.00	41.00	
				3.00	7.00	18.00	1.00	6.00	3.00	22.00	2.00	4.00	12.00	3.00			
5	FERRIS, Sharon	NZL	S	7	16	5	5	11	18	19	3	2	6	18	110.00	73.00	
				7.00	16.00	5.00	5.00	11.00	18.00	19.00	3.00	2.00	6.00	18.00			
6	POWARZYNSKI, Sibylle	GER	S	18	3	4	7	10	10	25	18	21	4	1	121.00	75.00	
				18.00	3.00	4.00	7.00	10.00	10.00	25.00	18.00	21.00	4.00	1.00			

Table continued on next page / Tableau continué à la page suivante

Single-Handed Dinghy (Europe), Women / *Dériveur solitaire (Europe), Dames*

FINAL - *continued from previous page* / *suite de la page précédente*

Rnk	Name	Ctry	Pos	Race 1	Race 2	Race 3	Race 4	Race 5	Race 6	Race 7	Race 8	Race 9	Race 10	Race 11	Total pts	Net pts
								RANK								
								POINTS								
7	KONTTORP, Linda	NOR	S	9	4	15	20	3	19	12	21	16	1	2	122.00	81.00
				9.00	4.00	15.00	20.00	3.00	19.00	12.00	21.00	16.00	1.00	2.00		
8	AMATO, Serena	ARG	S	8	17	8	8	16	15	6	5	1	16	14	114.00	81.00
				8.00	17.00	8.00	8.00	16.00	15.00	6.00	5.00	1.00	16.00	14.00		
9	MILLBOURN, Malin	SWE	S	5	19	13	13	14	4	10	9	3	11	16	117.00	82.00
				5.00	19.00	13.00	13.00	14.00	4.00	10.00	9.00	3.00	11.00	16.00		
10	BOWMAN, Aisling	IRL	S	10	6	14	6	5	7	21	15	10	20	9	123.00	82.00
				10.00	6.00	14.00	6.00	5.00	7.00	21.00	15.00	10.00	20.00	9.00		
11	BRIDGE, Christine	AUS	S	16	10	22	12	4	5	13	6	15	10	11	124.00	86.00
				16.00	10.00	22.00	12.00	4.00	5.00	13.00	6.00	15.00	10.00	11.00		
12	BOGATEC, Arianna	ITA	S	15	14	7	9	8	12	2	17	20	9	17	130.00	93.00
				15.00	14.00	7.00	9.00	8.00	12.00	2.00	17.00	20.00	9.00	17.00		
13	MOBERG-PARKER, Tine	CAN	S	4	15	9	3	12	DSQ	17	19	22	8	7	145.00	94.00
				4.00	15.00	9.00	3.00	12.00	29.00	17.00	19.00	22.00	8.00	7.00		
14	LEWIN, Paula	BER	S	20	9	6	15	15	14	14	8	5	17	8	131.00	94.00
				20.00	9.00	6.00	15.00	15.00	14.00	14.00	8.00	5.00	17.00	8.00		
15	MEYLAN, Nicole	SUI	S	14	5	21	11	13	11	9	25	DNF	3	13	154.00	100.00
				14.00	5.00	21.00	11.00	13.00	11.00	9.00	25.00	29.00	3.00	13.00		
16	PELLICANO, Marcia	BRA	S	19	20	17	16	9	8	7	16	11	13	10	146.00	107.00
				19.00	20.00	17.00	16.00	9.00	8.00	7.00	16.00	11.00	13.00	10.00		
17	MONTILLA, Helena	ESP	S	6	18	12	17	21	PMS	4	7	7	19	21	161.00	111.00
				6.00	18.00	12.00	17.00	21.00	29.00	4.00	7.00	7.00	19.00	21.00		
18	DEKLEVA, Vesna	SLO	S	17	21	11	21	17	21	5	10	6	15	12	156.00	114.00
				17.00	21.00	11.00	21.00	17.00	21.00	5.00	10.00	6.00	15.00	12.00		
19	SMEDBERG, Chita	FIN	S	12	13	10	14	19	9	15	22	18	18	23	173.00	128.00
				12.00	13.00	10.00	14.00	19.00	9.00	15.00	22.00	18.00	18.00	23.00		
20	GLINKIEWICZ, Weronika	POL	S	11	11	16	DNF	20	24	20	13	14	14	19	191.00	138.00
				11.00	11.00	16.00	29.00	20.00	24.00	20.00	13.00	14.00	14.00	19.00		
21	BELLEMANS, Ingrid	BEL	S	21	12	19	19	18	17	18	12	13	27	20	196.00	148.00
				21.00	12.00	19.00	19.00	18.00	17.00	18.00	12.00	13.00	27.00	20.00		
22	MYLONA, Maria	GRE	S	13	22	20	22	24	13	11	11	19	21	24	200.00	152.00
				13.00	22.00	20.00	22.00	24.00	13.00	11.00	11.00	19.00	21.00	24.00		
23	SAITO, Aiko	JPN	S	23	23	25	24	22	16	26	20	26	23	15	243.00	191.00
				23.00	23.00	25.00	24.00	22.00	16.00	26.00	20.00	26.00	23.00	15.00		
24	KRUUV, Krista	EST	S	22	25	26	23	23	20	23	26	17	22	22	249.00	197.00
				22.00	25.00	26.00	23.00	23.00	20.00	23.00	26.00	17.00	22.00	22.00		
25	PRATAS, Joana	POR	S	25	24	23	27	25	23	16	24	24	25	26	262.00	209.00
				25.00	24.00	23.00	27.00	25.00	23.00	16.00	24.00	24.00	25.00	26.00		
26	PODOBED, Anastasia	BLR	S	24	26	24	26	27	26	24	23	23	24	25	272.00	219.00
				24.00	26.00	24.00	26.00	27.00	26.00	24.00	23.00	23.00	24.00	25.00		
27	TAN, Tracey	SIN	S	26	27	27	18	26	22	27	27	25	26	27	278.00	224.00
				26.00	27.00	27.00	18.00	26.00	22.00	27.00	27.00	25.00	26.00	27.00		
28	LEPPER, Roberta	FIJ	S	27	28	28	25	28	25	28	28	27	28	DNC	301.00	244.00
				27.00	28.00	28.00	25.00	28.00	25.00	28.00	28.00	27.00	28.00	29.00		

Yachting / *Yachting*

Double-Handed Dinghy (470), Men / *Dériveur à deux places (470), Messieurs*

FINAL

Rnk	Name	Ctry	Pos	Race 1	Race 2	Race 3	Race 4	Race 5	Race 6	Race 7	Race 8	Race 9	Race 10	Race 11	Total pts	Net pts
								RANK								
								POINTS								
1	BRASLAVETS, Yevhen	UKR	S	2	2	3	1	16	5	1	9	10	7	DNC	93.00	40.00 **G**
	MATVIYENKO, Ihor		C	2.00	2.00	3.00	1.00	16.00	5.00	1.00	9.00	10.00	7.00	37.00		
2	MERRICKS, John	GBR	S	15	1	4	27	DSQ	4	2	6	15	2	11	124.00	60.00 **S**
	WALKER, Ian		C	15.00	1.00	4.00	27.00	37.00	4.00	2.00	6.00	15.00	2.00	11.00		
3	ROCHA, Hugo	POR	S	5	10	17	7	4	8	9	5	2	12	15	94.00	62.00 **B**
	BARRETO, Nuno		C	5.00	10.00	17.00	7.00	4.00	8.00	9.00	5.00	2.00	12.00	15.00		
4	LESKINEN, Petri	FIN	S	PMS	14	19	4	7	6	8	1	16	6	3	121.00	65.00
	AARNIKKA, Mika		C	37.00	14.00	19.00	4.00	7.00	6.00	8.00	1.00	16.00	6.00	3.00		
5	BERYOZKIN, Dmitriy	RUS	S	13	25	5	2	3	1	11	20	19	4	8	111.00	66.00
	BURMATNOV, Yevgeniy		C	13.00	25.00	5.00	2.00	3.00	1.00	11.00	20.00	19.00	4.00	8.00		

Table continued on next page / *Tableau continué à la page suivante*

Double-Handed Dinghy (470), Men / *Dériveur à deux places (470), Messieurs*

FINAL - *continued from previous page / suite de la page précédente*

Rnk	Name	Ctry	Pos	Race 1	Race 2	Race 3	Race 4	Race 5	Race 6	Race 7	Race 8	Race 9	Race 10	Race 11	Total pts	Net pts
6	BERTHET, Jean-Francois	FRA	S	16	6	9	28	15	23	3	2	17	3	1	123.00	72.00
	BERTHET, Gwenael		C	16.00	6.00	9.00	28.00	15.00	23.00	3.00	2.00	17.00	3.00	1.00		
7	BILLOCH, Martin	ARG	S	12	23	1	22	20	3	4	12	1	8	12	118.00	73.00
	RODRIGUEZ, Martin		C	12.00	23.00	1.00	22.00	20.00	3.00	4.00	12.00	1.00	8.00	12.00		
8	REESER, Morgan	USA	S	20	9	6	9	1	11	DSQ	4	PMS	1	13	148.00	74.00
	BURNHAM, Kevin		C	20.00	9.00	6.00	9.00	1.00	11.00	37.00	4.00	37.00	1.00	13.00		
9	CALAFAT, Jordi	ESP	S	1	17	14	20	2	19	5	PMS	3	13	2	133.00	76.00
	SANCHEZ, Francisco		C	1.00	17.00	14.00	20.00	2.00	19.00	5.00	37.00	3.00	13.00	2.00		
10	TONISTE, Tonu	EST	S	7	16	8	3	19	PMS	30	3	6	15	18	162.00	95.00
	TONISTE, Toomas		C	7.00	16.00	8.00	3.00	19.00	37.00	30.00	3.00	6.00	15.00	18.00		
11	KOSMATOPOULOS, Andreas	GRE	S	11	19	18	13	5	2	15	18	5	10	24	140.00	97.00
	TRIGONIS, Konstantinos		C	11.00	19.00	18.00	13.00	5.00	2.00	15.00	18.00	5.00	10.00	24.00		
12	RENSCH, Ronald	GER	S	PMS	8	2	10	22	9	22	11	14	29	6	170.00	104.00
	HAVERLAND, Torsten		C	37.00	8.00	2.00	10.00	22.00	9.00	22.00	11.00	14.00	29.00	6.00		
13	KURET, Ivan	CRO	S	3	15	15	21	11	12	31	22	9	14	16	169.00	116.00
	MISURA, Marko		C	3.00	15.00	15.00	21.00	11.00	12.00	31.00	22.00	9.00	14.00	16.00		
14	COPI, Tomaz	SLO	S	14	20	13	11	8	PMS	16	17	7	25	10	178.00	116.00
	MARGON, Mitja		C	14.00	20.00	13.00	11.00	8.00	37.00	16.00	17.00	7.00	25.00	10.00		
15	IVALDI, Matteo	ITA	S	9	4	25	8	14	PMS	17	7	31	DSQ	5	194.00	120.00
	IVALDI, Michele		C	9.00	4.00	25.00	8.00	14.00	37.00	17.00	7.00	31.00	37.00	5.00		
16	CHOCIAN, Marek	POL	S	PMS	18	22	19	17	7	21	13	8	5	17	184.00	125.00
	STANIUL, Zdzislaw		C	37.00	18.00	22.00	19.00	17.00	7.00	21.00	13.00	8.00	5.00	17.00		
17	NAKAMURA, Kenji	JPN	S	PMS	3	16	25	10	13	28	14	21	16	9	192.00	127.00
	TAKAKI, Masato		C	37.00	3.00	16.00	25.00	10.00	13.00	28.00	14.00	21.00	16.00	9.00		
18	WESTERLAND, Marcus	SWE	S	6	7	21	5	13	PMS	6	PMS	24	24	23	203.00	129.00
	WALLIN, Henrik		C	6.00	7.00	21.00	5.00	13.00	37.00	6.00	37.00	24.00	24.00	23.00		
19	SHENTAL, Nir	ISR	S	17	13	29	6	6	26	19	PMS	22	9	14	198.00	132.00
	SHENTAL, Ran		C	17.00	13.00	29.00	6.00	6.00	26.00	19.00	37.00	22.00	9.00	14.00		
20	HANNAM, Paul	CAN	S	10	21	12	23	21	29	20	PMS	13	11	4	201.00	135.00
	STOREY, Brian		C	10.00	21.00	12.00	23.00	21.00	29.00	20.00	37.00	13.00	11.00	4.00		
21	LITKEY, Botond	HUN	S	4	26	30	16	12	14	10	15	18	22	DSQ	204.00	137.00
	NYARI, Zoltan		C	4.00	26.00	30.00	16.00	12.00	14.00	10.00	15.00	18.00	22.00	37.00		
22	COOKE, Rohan	NZL	S	8	11	10	14	25	22	18	10	27	27	21	193.00	139.00
	STONE, Andrew		C	8.00	11.00	10.00	14.00	25.00	22.00	18.00	10.00	27.00	27.00	21.00		
23	KING, Tom	AUS	S	19	12	20	26	27	16	7	PMS	25	17	7	213.00	149.00
	McMAHON, Owen		C	19.00	12.00	20.00	26.00	27.00	16.00	7.00	37.00	25.00	17.00	7.00		
24	KOUWENHOVEN, Ben	NED	S	DNS	5	11	32	24	10	24	8	30	20	DSQ	238.00	164.00
	KOUWENHOVEN, Jan		C	37.00	5.00	11.00	32.00	24.00	10.00	24.00	8.00	30.00	20.00	37.00		
25	SIH, Brady	TPE	S	24	27	28	12	35	15	14	24	4	26	26	235.00	172.00
	SIH, Bryant		C	24.00	27.00	28.00	12.00	35.00	15.00	14.00	24.00	4.00	26.00	26.00		
26	FERNANDEZ, Pedro	CUB	S	22	29	26	17	9	27	13	19	PMS	21	DSQ	257.00	183.00
	JIMENEZ, Angel Alfredo		C	22.00	29.00	26.00	17.00	9.00	27.00	13.00	19.00	37.00	21.00	37.00		
27	RAMON, David	AND	S	23	31	24	35	23	17	12	26	11	28	19	249.00	183.00
	RAMON, Oscar		C	23.00	31.00	24.00	35.00	23.00	17.00	12.00	26.00	11.00	28.00	19.00		
28	KIM, Dae-Young	KOR	S	18	28	7	29	31	28	26	16	26	23	28	260.00	201.00
	JUNG, Sung-Ahn		C	18.00	28.00	7.00	29.00	31.00	28.00	26.00	16.00	26.00	23.00	28.00		
29	AMADO, Rodrigo	BRA	S	26	32	23	24	18	PMS	25	25	12	18	29	269.00	200.00
	SANTOS, Leonardo		C	26.00	32.00	23.00	24.00	18.00	37.00	25.00	25.00	12.00	18.00	29.00		
30	RAST, Christopher	SUI	S	21	22	27	18	26	30	27	21	29	19	20	260.00	200.00
	ZIEGERT, Jean-Pierre		C	21.00	22.00	27.00	18.00	26.00	30.00	27.00	21.00	29.00	19.00	20.00		
31	EPIPHANIOU, Nicolas	CYP	S	25	24	33	15	32	24	23	23	20	32	25	276.00	211.00
	ELTON, Peter		C	25.00	24.00	33.00	15.00	32.00	24.00	23.00	23.00	20.00	32.00	25.00		
32	KARVAS, Igor	SVK	S	28	36	31	31	29	20	34	29	23	31	32	324.00	254.00
	FERIANEC, Jaroslav		C	28.00	36.00	31.00	31.00	29.00	20.00	34.00	29.00	23.00	31.00	32.00		
33	GOODING, Andrew	JAM	S	27	33	34	34	33	18	33	30	32	34	27	335.00	267.00
	STOCKHAUSEN, Joseph		C	27.00	33.00	34.00	34.00	33.00	18.00	33.00	30.00	32.00	34.00	27.00		
34	SANUS, Sukru	TUR	S	29	30	36	DNF	34	21	29	28	33	33	30	340.00	267.00
	OZKAN, B. Kerem		C	29.00	30.00	36.00	37.00	34.00	21.00	29.00	28.00	33.00	33.00	30.00		
35	SIEW, Shaw Her	SIN	S	PMS	35	32	33	28	31	32	27	28	30	31	344.00	272.00
	LIM, Yi Yong		C	37.00	35.00	32.00	33.00	28.00	31.00	32.00	27.00	28.00	30.00	31.00		
36	CHAN, Yuk Wah	HKG	S	PMS	34	35	30	30	25	35	31	34	35	22	348.00	276.00
	SERVICE, Andrew		C	37.00	34.00	35.00	30.00	30.00	25.00	35.00	31.00	34.00	35.00	22.00		

Yachting / *Yachting*

Double-Handed Dinghy (470), Women / *Dériveur à deux places (470), Dames*

FINAL

Rnk	Name	Ctry	Pos	Race 1	Race 2	Race 3	Race 4	Race 5	Race 6	Race 7	Race 8	Race 9	Race 10	Race 11	Total pts	Net pts	
1	ZABELL, Theresa	ESP	S	4	2	11	8	2	1	3	10	3	1	1	46.00	25.00	G
	VIA DUFRESNE, Begona		C	4.00	2.00	11.00	8.00	2.00	1.00	3.00	10.00	3.00	1.00	1.00			
2	SHIGE, Yumiko	JPN	S	3	7	13	6	1	3	2	11	1	6	7	60.00	36.00	S
	KINOSHITA, Alicia		C	3.00	7.00	13.00	6.00	1.00	3.00	2.00	11.00	1.00	6.00	7.00			
3	TARAN, Ruslana	UKR	S	1	5	4	9	12	8	18	1	4	4	2	68.00	38.00	B
	PAKHOLCHIK, Olena		C	1.00	5.00	4.00	9.00	12.00	8.00	18.00	1.00	4.00	4.00	2.00			
4	STOOKEY, Kris	USA	S	2	8	2	1	4	12	14	2	14	5	11	75.00	47.00	
	VAN VOORHIS, Louise		C	2.00	8.00	2.00	1.00	4.00	12.00	14.00	2.00	14.00	5.00	11.00			
5	BAUCKHOLT, Susanne	GER	S	16	6	5	5	3	4	6	7	11	2	12	77.00	49.00	
	ADLKOFER, Kathrin		C	16.00	6.00	5.00	5.00	3.00	4.00	6.00	7.00	11.00	2.00	12.00			
6	WARD, Susanne	DEN	S	6	3	15	2	14	2	4	12	18	7	6	89.00	56.00	
	WARD, Lise Michaela		C	6.00	3.00	15.00	2.00	14.00	2.00	4.00	12.00	18.00	7.00	6.00			
7	SALVA, Federica	ITA	S	11	4	9	15	15	13	9	9	2	3	4	94.00	64.00	
	SOSSI, Emanuela		C	11.00	4.00	9.00	15.00	15.00	13.00	9.00	9.00	2.00	3.00	4.00			
8	LIDGETT, Jennifer	AUS	S	7	9	7	4	19	16	15	3	5	9	5	99.00	64.00	
	BUCEK, Addy		C	7.00	9.00	7.00	4.00	19.00	16.00	15.00	3.00	5.00	9.00	5.00			
9	DAVIS, Penny	CAN	S	PMS	1	3	20	6	10	5	8	19	8	16	119.00	76.00	
	PEARSON, Leigh		C	23.00	1.00	3.00	20.00	6.00	10.00	5.00	8.00	19.00	8.00	16.00			
10	ANDERSEN, Ida	NOR	S	12	11	8	16	5	9	12	6	9	14	9	111.00	81.00	
	ANDERSEN, Linda		C	12.00	11.00	8.00	16.00	5.00	9.00	12.00	6.00	9.00	14.00	9.00			
11	RAGGATT, Bethan	GBR	S	5	12	10	3	9	15	11	18	12	12	15	122.00	89.00	
	CARR, Susan		C	5.00	12.00	10.00	3.00	9.00	15.00	11.00	18.00	12.00	12.00	15.00			
12	KEDMY, Shany	ISR	S	8	15	DSQ	7	10	14	DSQ	13	10	13	3	139.00	93.00	
	FABRIKANT, Anat		C	8.00	15.00	23.00	7.00	10.00	14.00	23.00	13.00	10.00	13.00	3.00			
13	LYTTLE, Denise	IRL	S	10	10	14	13	11	17	8	5	8	16	19	131.00	95.00	
	COLE, Louise		C	10.00	10.00	14.00	13.00	11.00	17.00	8.00	5.00	8.00	16.00	19.00			
14	CARLSSON, Lena	SWE	S	18	17	12	11	16	7	1	19	6	20	8	135.00	96.00	
	BENGTSSON, Boel		C	18.00	17.00	12.00	11.00	16.00	7.00	1.00	19.00	6.00	20.00	8.00			
15	LE BRUN, Florence	FRA	S	13	13	PMS	12	7	5	19	14	13	11	10	140.00	98.00	
	CHAULVIN, Annabel		C	13.00	13.00	23.00	12.00	7.00	5.00	19.00	14.00	13.00	11.00	10.00			
16	EGNOT, Leslie	NZL	S	14	18	1	17	8	11	7	4	21	PMS	PMS	147.00	101.00	
	SHEARER, Janet		C	14.00	18.00	1.00	17.00	8.00	11.00	7.00	4.00	21.00	23.00	23.00			
17	KALOUDI, Katerina	GRE	S	9	20	6	19	18	6	16	17	17	18	13	159.00	120.00	
	TSOULFA, Emilia		C	9.00	20.00	6.00	19.00	18.00	6.00	16.00	17.00	17.00	18.00	13.00			
18	BACSICS, Katalin	HUN	S	17	19	PMS	10	17	18	10	16	16	10	14	170.00	128.00	
	NEMETH, Eniko		C	17.00	19.00	23.00	10.00	17.00	18.00	10.00	16.00	16.00	10.00	14.00			
19	OREL, Janja	SLO	S	20	21	17	14	20	19	13	21	7	15	18	185.00	143.00	
	OREL, Alenka		C	20.00	21.00	17.00	14.00	20.00	19.00	13.00	21.00	7.00	15.00	18.00			
20	CHEUNG, Mei Han	HKG	S	19	22	PMS	18	13	21	20	22	15	19	17	209.00	164.00	
	TUNG, Chun Mei		C	19.00	22.00	23.00	18.00	13.00	21.00	20.00	22.00	15.00	19.00	17.00			
21	LIU, Haimei	CHN	S	15	14	PMS	21	21	22	21	15	20	PMS	20	215.50	169.50	
	JI, Fengqim		C	15.00	14.00	23.00	21.00	21.00	22.00	21.00	15.00	20.00	23.00	20.50			
22	REINOSO, Paula	ARG	S	PMS	16	16	22	22	20	17	20	22	17	20	215.50	170.50	
	USANDIZAGA, Sofia		C	23.00	16.00	16.00	22.00	22.00	20.00	17.00	20.00	22.00	17.00	20.50			

Yachting / *Yachting*

Dinghy (Laser), Mixed / *Dériveur (Laser), Mixte*

FINAL

Rnk	Name	Ctry	Pos	Race 1	Race 2	Race 3	Race 4	Race 5	Race 6	Race 7	Race 8	Race 9	Race 10	Race 11	Total pts	Net pts	
1	SCHEIDT, Robert	BRA	S	2	9	3	6	1	3	7	2	1	1	DSQ	92.00	26.00	G
				2.00	9.00	3.00	6.00	1.00	3.00	7.00	2.00	1.00	1.00	57.00			
2	AINSLIE, Ben	GBR	S	28	4	7	2	2	1	2	1	16	2	DSQ	121.00	37.00	S
				28.00	4.00	7.00	2.00	2.00	1.00	2.00	1.00	16.00	2.00	57.00			
3	MOBERG, Peer	NOR	S	1	7	9	1	9	10	1	21	3	5	11	78.00	46.00	B
				1.00	7.00	9.00	1.00	9.00	10.00	1.00	21.00	3.00	5.00	11.00			
4	BLACKBURN, Michael	AUS	S	5	6	6	22	10	22	5	4	7	4	1	92.00	48.00	
				5.00	6.00	6.00	22.00	10.00	22.00	5.00	4.00	7.00	4.00	1.00			

Table continued on next page / Tableau continué à la page suivante

FINAL - *continued from previous page / suite de la page précédente*

Rnk	Name	Ctry	Pos	Race 1	Race 2	Race 3	Race 4	Race 5	Race 6	Race 7	Race 8	Race 9	Race 10	Race 11	Total pts	Net pts
				RANK / POINTS												
5	WARKALLA, Stefan	GER	S	13	2	2	3	12	4	15	6	5	7	DSQ	126.00	54.00
				13.00	2.00	2.00	3.00	12.00	4.00	15.00	6.00	5.00	7.00	57.00		
6	HARRYSSON, John	SWE	S	3	8	8	33	4	6	20	7	9	8	2	108.00	55.00
				3.00	8.00	8.00	33.00	4.00	6.00	20.00	7.00	9.00	8.00	2.00		
7	SERPA, Vasco	POR	S	8	3	10	PMS	3	9	11	11	12	16	7	147.00	74.00
				8.00	3.00	10.00	57.00	3.00	9.00	11.00	11.00	12.00	16.00	7.00		
8	JOHANSON, Thomas	FIN	S	18	14	4	8	11	13	6	15	4	13	5	111.00	78.00
				18.00	14.00	4.00	8.00	11.00	13.00	6.00	15.00	4.00	13.00	5.00		
9	LANGE, Santiago	ARG	S	4	1	5	14	23	11	19	DSQ	2	19	4	159.00	79.00
				4.00	1.00	5.00	14.00	23.00	11.00	19.00	57.00	2.00	19.00	4.00		
10	PEPPER, Hamish	NZL	S	15	PMS	19	19	6	2	4	3	21	6	10	162.00	84.00
				15.00	57.00	19.00	19.00	6.00	2.00	4.00	3.00	21.00	6.00	10.00		
11	LYTTLE, Mark	IRL	S	DSQ	13	1	9	14	5	8	DSQ	10	10	18	202.00	88.00
				57.00	13.00	1.00	9.00	14.00	5.00	8.00	57.00	10.00	10.00	18.00		
12	BRUNI, Francesco	ITA	S	12	5	11	4	24	20	PMS	10	8	3	17	171.00	90.00
				12.00	5.00	11.00	4.00	24.00	20.00	57.00	10.00	8.00	3.00	17.00		
13	KATS, Serge	NED	S	6	PMS	12	13	5	7	22	DSQ	19	11	3	212.00	98.00
				6.00	57.00	12.00	13.00	5.00	7.00	22.00	57.00	19.00	11.00	3.00		
14	URLESBERGER, Franz	AUT	S	19	30	15	16	16	23	14	12	6	9	15	175.00	122.00
				19.00	30.00	15.00	16.00	16.00	23.00	14.00	12.00	6.00	9.00	15.00		
15	FLORENT, Guillaume	FRA	S	7	17	14	12	25	21	21	8	14	22	DSQ	218.00	136.00
				7.00	17.00	14.00	12.00	25.00	21.00	21.00	8.00	14.00	22.00	57.00		
16	HIBBERD, David	RSA	S	10	10	20	20	8	17	31	13	29	18	22	198.00	138.00
				10.00	10.00	20.00	20.00	8.00	17.00	31.00	13.00	29.00	18.00	22.00		
17	ECKARDT, Jens	DEN	S	31	16	17	11	7	8	26	17	13	27	DNF	230.00	142.00
				31.00	16.00	17.00	11.00	7.00	8.00	26.00	17.00	13.00	27.00	57.00		
18	BERGMANS, Philippe	BEL	S	11	11	25	10	20	15	25	22	28	24	6	197.00	144.00
				11.00	11.00	25.00	10.00	20.00	15.00	25.00	22.00	28.00	24.00	6.00		
19	ECHENIQUE, Luis Felipe	CHI	S	20	PMS	31	15	18	16	9	26	31	15	8	246.00	158.00
				20.00	57.00	31.00	15.00	18.00	16.00	9.00	26.00	31.00	15.00	8.00		
20	ZELENOVSKIY, Aleksandr	BLR	S	38	23	28	26	21	18	13	16	15	17	14	229.00	163.00
				38.00	23.00	28.00	26.00	21.00	18.00	13.00	16.00	15.00	17.00	14.00		
21	ADAMSON, Nick	USA	S	9	DSQ	13	7	13	14	10	DSQ	27	14	DSQ	278.00	164.00
				9.00	57.00	13.00	7.00	13.00	14.00	10.00	57.00	27.00	14.00	57.00		
22	GARROTE, Anton	ESP	S	17	15	18	36	26	31	18	18	17	12	DSQ	265.00	172.00
				17.00	15.00	18.00	36.00	26.00	31.00	18.00	18.00	17.00	12.00	57.00		
23	KIM, Ho-Kon	KOR	S	16	18	30	5	15	12	35	28	32	26	23	240.00	173.00
				16.00	18.00	30.00	5.00	15.00	12.00	35.00	28.00	32.00	26.00	23.00		
24	SARASKIN, Peter	EST	S	14	27	21	29	30	33	12	14	18	21	20	239.00	176.00
				14.00	27.00	21.00	29.00	30.00	33.00	12.00	14.00	18.00	21.00	20.00		
25	HIRST, Robert	IVB	S	39	19	29	17	31	25	32	9	20	30	12	263.00	192.00
				39.00	19.00	29.00	17.00	31.00	25.00	32.00	9.00	20.00	30.00	12.00		
26	DAVIES, Rod	CAN	S	22	PMS	24	25	17	28	23	25	26	23	9	279.00	194.00
				22.00	57.00	24.00	25.00	17.00	28.00	23.00	25.00	26.00	23.00	9.00		
27	THEODORAKIS, Dimitrios	GRE	S	21	28	16	18	33	26	28	20	25	25	24	264.00	203.00
				21.00	28.00	16.00	18.00	33.00	26.00	28.00	20.00	25.00	25.00	24.00		
28	SASAKI, Tomoyuki	JPN	S	24	22	22	21	19	19	42	31	30	29	26	284.00	211.00
				24.00	22.00	22.00	21.00	19.00	19.00	42.00	31.00	30.00	29.00	26.00		
29	KIRILYUK, Andrey	RUS	S	36	25	26	31	32	24	29	19	22	20	16	280.00	212.00
				36.00	25.00	26.00	31.00	32.00	24.00	29.00	19.00	22.00	20.00	16.00		
30	FABINI, Ricardo	URU	S	25	12	38	23	22	32	16	30	35	DSQ	21	310.00	215.00
				25.00	12.00	38.00	23.00	22.00	32.00	16.00	30.00	35.00	57.00	21.00		
31	ESZES, Tamas	HUN	S	DSQ	20	33	43	37	30	27	5	11	28	DSQ	348.00	234.00
				57.00	20.00	33.00	43.00	37.00	30.00	27.00	5.00	11.00	28.00	57.00		
32	CAO, Xiaobo	CHN	S	30	24	32	28	28	29	30	27	38	32	13	311.00	241.00
				30.00	24.00	32.00	28.00	28.00	29.00	30.00	27.00	38.00	32.00	13.00		
33	GOETERS, Antonio	MEX	S	34	38	42	30	43	36	17	24	23	33	30	350.00	265.00
				34.00	38.00	42.00	30.00	43.00	36.00	17.00	24.00	23.00	33.00	30.00		
34	DIELEMANS, Paul	AHO	S	33	21	23	42	29	27	39	35	24	36	DSQ	366.00	267.00
				33.00	21.00	23.00	42.00	29.00	27.00	39.00	35.00	24.00	36.00	57.00		
35	LUKA, Rodion	UKR	S	27	34	43	37	44	34	3	23	36	37	DSQ	374.00	273.00
				27.00	34.00	43.00	37.00	44.00	34.00	3.00	23.00	36.00	37.00	57.00		
36	TAN, Chi	SIN	S	41	PMS	34	24	27	35	38	37	39	31	19	382.00	284.00
				41.00	57.00	34.00	24.00	27.00	35.00	38.00	37.00	39.00	31.00	19.00		

Table continued on next page / Tableau continué à la page suivante

Dinghy (Laser), Mixed / *Dériveur (Laser), Mixte*

FINAL - *continued from previous page* / *suite de la page précédente*

Rnk	Name	Ctry	Pos	Race 1	Race 2	Race 3	Race 4	Race 5	Race 6	Race 7	Race 8	Race 9	Race 10	Race 11	Total pts	Net pts
								RANK POINTS								
37	LIM, Kevin	MAS	S	32	26	36	34	35	39	48	33	40	41	25	389.00	300.00
				32.00	26.00	36.00	34.00	35.00	39.00	48.00	33.00	40.00	41.00	25.00		
38	JULIE, Allen	SEY	S	YMP	36	27	DNF	38	44	47	42	34	35	27	409.00	305.00
				22.00	36.00	27.00	57.00	38.00	44.00	47.00	42.00	34.00	35.00	27.00		
39	van BATENBURG STAFFORD, John	CAY	S	37	29	44	27	34	38	41	36	52	45	32	415.00	318.00
				37.00	29.00	44.00	27.00	34.00	38.00	41.00	36.00	52.00	45.00	32.00		
40	ALPAGUT, V. Alp	TUR	S	35	32	37	40	40	40	40	41	33	38	33	409.00	328.00
				35.00	32.00	37.00	40.00	40.00	40.00	40.00	41.00	33.00	38.00	33.00		
41	TABONE, John	MLT	S	26	39	35	44	49	42	33	38	46	46	34	431.00	336.00
				26.00	39.00	35.00	44.00	49.00	42.00	33.00	38.00	46.00	46.00	34.00		
42	SMITH, Malcolm	BER	S	40	31	41	32	42	45	46	40	43	34	35	429.00	338.00
				40.00	31.00	41.00	32.00	42.00	45.00	46.00	40.00	43.00	34.00	35.00		
43	JAMES, Karl	ANT	S	45	35	39	35	39	DNF	34	45	49	40	28	446.00	340.00
				45.00	35.00	39.00	35.00	39.00	57.00	34.00	45.00	49.00	40.00	28.00		
44	CHIVERS, Brett	GUM	S	29	37	50	45	36	37	45	44	44	39	29	435.00	340.00
				29.00	37.00	50.00	45.00	36.00	37.00	45.00	44.00	44.00	39.00	29.00		
45	GREEN, Michael	LCA	S	42	40	40	38	41	41	37	32	42	44	31	428.00	342.00
				42.00	40.00	40.00	38.00	41.00	41.00	37.00	32.00	42.00	44.00	31.00		
46	YANG, Fung	HKG	S	44	33	47	39	46	43	44	29	47	43	36	451.00	357.00
				44.00	33.00	47.00	39.00	46.00	43.00	44.00	29.00	47.00	43.00	36.00		
47	DUNKLEY, Robert	BAH	S	48	41	46	41	45	46	43	43	41	42	37	473.00	379.00
				48.00	41.00	46.00	41.00	45.00	46.00	43.00	43.00	41.00	42.00	37.00		
48	ISPAS, Horia	ROM	S	43	43	49	DNF	47	DNF	24	DSQ	45	48	38	508.00	394.00
				43.00	43.00	49.00	57.00	47.00	57.00	24.00	57.00	45.00	48.00	38.00		
49	al-HITMI, Khalifa	QAT	S	46	42	45	DNF	48	DNF	DSQ	34	37	47	41	511.00	397.00
				46.00	42.00	45.00	57.00	48.00	57.00	57.00	34.00	37.00	47.00	41.00		
50	VEDANI, Gaston	ECU	S	47	44	48	48	50	DNF	36	39	48	50	39	506.00	399.00
				47.00	44.00	48.00	48.00	50.00	57.00	36.00	39.00	48.00	50.00	39.00		
51	al-SADA, Mohamed	BRN	S	50	45	51	47	DNF	DNS	50	47	50	49	40	542.00	428.00
				50.00	45.00	51.00	47.00	57.00	57.00	50.00	47.00	50.00	49.00	40.00		
52	READER, Rodney	BAR	S	52	47	52	46	52	DNF	PMS	48	54	51	42	557.00	443.00
				52.00	47.00	52.00	46.00	52.00	57.00	57.00	48.00	54.00	51.00	42.00		
53	SCARPETTA, Constantino	PAR	S	51	46	53	DNF	51	DNF	DSQ	46	51	52	43	563.00	449.00
				51.00	46.00	53.00	57.00	51.00	57.00	57.00	46.00	51.00	52.00	43.00		
54	CROFOOT, Tiko	FIJ	S	YMP	49	54	DNF	53	DNF	PMS	51	53	54	44	577.00	463.00
				48.00	49.00	54.00	57.00	53.00	57.00	57.00	51.00	53.00	54.00	44.00		
55	YOUSSOUF, Mohamed	DJI	S	53	48	56	DNF	DNF	DNS	51	50	56	53	45	582.00	468.00
				53.00	48.00	56.00	57.00	57.00	57.00	51.00	50.00	56.00	53.00	45.00		
56	BELLUZZI, Luca	SMR	S	54	DNF	55	DNF	DNC	DNC	49	49	55	55	46	590.00	476.00
				54.00	57.00	55.00	57.00	57.00	57.00	49.00	49.00	55.00	55.00	46.00		

Yachting / *Yachting*

Multihull (Tornado), Mixed / *Multicoque (Tornado), Mixte*

FINAL

Rnk	Name	Ctry	Pos	Race 1	Race 2	Race 3	Race 4	Race 5	Race 6	Race 7	Race 8	Race 9	Race 10	Race 11	Total pts	Net pts
								RANK POINTS								
1	LEON, Fernando	ESP	S	2	2	4	5	5	2	4	3	PMS	3	DNC	70.00	30.00 G
	BALLESTER, Jose Luis		C	2.00	2.00	4.00	5.00	5.00	2.00	4.00	3.00	20.00	3.00	20.00		
2	BOOTH, Mitchell	AUS	S	1	5	6	2	14	17	1	1	PMS	2	10	79.00	42.00 S
	LANDENBERGER, Andrew		C	1.00	5.00	6.00	2.00	14.00	17.00	1.00	1.00	20.00	2.00	10.00		
3	GRAEL, Lars Schmidt	BRA	S	12	16	1	8	6	8	2	5	3	7	3	71.00	43.00 B
	PELLICANO, Henrique		C	12.00	16.00	1.00	8.00	6.00	8.00	2.00	5.00	3.00	7.00	3.00		
4	HAGARA, Andreas	AUT	S	4	3	5	6	1	7	10	13	7	13	1	70.00	44.00
	SCHNEEBERGER, Florian		C	4.00	3.00	5.00	6.00	1.00	7.00	10.00	13.00	7.00	13.00	1.00		
5	PIRINOLI, Walter	ITA	S	16	12	PMS	3	3	5	6	4	5	4	2	80.00	44.00
	PIRINOLI, Marco		C	16.00	12.00	20.00	3.00	3.00	5.00	6.00	4.00	5.00	4.00	2.00		
6	LE PEUTREC, Frederic	FRA	S	8	1	3	7	8	4	5	11	4	6	9	66.00	46.00
	CITEAU, Franck		C	8.00	1.00	3.00	7.00	8.00	4.00	5.00	11.00	4.00	6.00	9.00		

Table continued on next page / *Tableau continué à la page suivante*

Multihull (Tornado), Mixed / *Multicoque (Tornado), Mixte*

FINAL - *continued from previous page* / *suite de la page précédente*

Rnk	Name	Ctry	Pos	Race 1	Race 2	Race 3	Race 4	Race 5	Race 6	Race 7	Race 8	Race 9	Race 10	Race 11	Total pts	Net pts
								RANK POINTS								
7	GABLER, Roland	GER	S	15	8	11	1	12	9	9	2	2	1	5	75.00	48.00
	PARLOW, Frank		C	15.00	8.00	11.00	1.00	12.00	9.00	9.00	2.00	2.00	1.00	5.00		
8	LOVELL, John	USA	S	3	4	8	4	4	11	3	12	1	10	12	72.00	48.00
	OGLETREE, Charlie		C	3.00	4.00	8.00	4.00	4.00	11.00	3.00	12.00	1.00	10.00	12.00		
9	van TEYLINGEN, Ron	NED	S	13	6	2	17	2	6	7	9	PMS	5	6	93.00	56.00
	DERCKSEN, Herbert		C	13.00	6.00	2.00	17.00	2.00	6.00	7.00	9.00	20.00	5.00	6.00		
10	THORENS, Patrick	SUI	S	7	9	13	11	10	1	11	7	10	11	13	103.00	77.00
	WOHNLICH, Stephane		C	7.00	9.00	13.00	11.00	10.00	1.00	11.00	7.00	10.00	11.00	13.00		
11	PEERS, Marc	CAN	S	17	11	9	9	9	12	17	8	9	8	8	117.00	83.00
	JANSE, Roy		C	17.00	11.00	9.00	9.00	9.00	12.00	17.00	8.00	9.00	8.00	8.00		
12	KONOVALOV, Yuriy	RUS	S	11	10	7	12	18	3	15	10	8	17	11	122.00	87.00
	MYASNIKOV, Sergey		C	11.00	10.00	7.00	12.00	18.00	3.00	15.00	10.00	8.00	17.00	11.00		
13	WILLIAMS, David	GBR	S	5	7	12	10	13	DSQ	8	14	6	12	14	121.00	87.00
	RHODES, Ian		C	5.00	7.00	12.00	10.00	13.00	20.00	8.00	14.00	6.00	12.00	14.00		
14	KRAVTSOV, Sergey	BLR	S	9	15	PMS	16	11	10	16	6	11	16	7	137.00	101.00
	BUDANTSEV, Viktor		C	9.00	15.00	20.00	16.00	11.00	10.00	16.00	6.00	11.00	16.00	7.00		
15	SELLERS, Rex	NZL	S	14	14	10	13	17	14	12	16	12	14	4	140.00	107.00
	JONES, Brian		C	14.00	14.00	10.00	13.00	17.00	14.00	12.00	16.00	12.00	14.00	4.00		
16	NYBERG, Mats	SWE	S	10	PMS	16	14	7	16	14	15	13	9	17	151.00	114.00
	LOVDEN, Magnus		C	10.00	20.00	16.00	14.00	7.00	16.00	14.00	15.00	13.00	9.00	17.00		
17	PRYYMAK, Serhiy	UKR	S	6	13	14	15	15	13	13	17	14	15	18	153.00	118.00
	CHELOMBITKO, Yevhen		C	6.00	13.00	14.00	15.00	15.00	13.00	13.00	17.00	14.00	15.00	18.00		
18	BRODIE, Shayne	FIJ	S	18	17	15	18	16	15	18	18	15	18	15	183.00	147.00
	PATTIE, Angus		C	18.00	17.00	15.00	18.00	16.00	15.00	18.00	18.00	15.00	18.00	15.00		
19	DAVIES, Alun	CAY	S	19	18	17	19	19	18	19	19	PMS	19	16	203.00	164.00
	JOSEPH, Michael		C	19.00	18.00	17.00	19.00	19.00	18.00	19.00	19.00	20.00	19.00	16.00		

Yachting / *Yachting*

Two-Person Keelboat (Star), Mixed / *Quillard à deux places (Star), Mixte*

FINAL

Rnk	Name	Ctry	Pos	Race 1	Race 2	Race 3	Race 4	Race 5	Race 6	Race 7	Race 8	Race 9	Race 10	Race 11	Total pts	Net pts	
								RANK POINTS									
1	GRAEL, Torben Schmidt	BRA	S	1	6	2	7	1	4	9	2	6	3		41.00	25.00	G
	FERREIRA, Marcelo Bastos		C	1.00	6.00	2.00	7.00	1.00	4.00	9.00	2.00	6.00	3.00				
2	WALLEN, Hans	SWE	S	4	7	7	8	2	1	3	4	8	1		45.00	29.00	S
	LOHSE, Bobbie		C	4.00	7.00	7.00	8.00	2.00	1.00	3.00	4.00	8.00	1.00				
3	BEASHEL, Colin	AUS	S	11	1	1	1	8	3	2	7	9	PMS		69.00	32.00	B
	GILES, David		C	11.00	1.00	1.00	1.00	8.00	3.00	2.00	7.00	9.00	26.00				
4	BOUNTOURIS, Anastassios	GRE	S	6	8	14	3	6	6	1	16	4	11		75.00	45.00	
	BOUKIS, Dimitrios		C	6.00	8.00	14.00	3.00	6.00	6.00	1.00	16.00	4.00	11.00				
5	DAVIS, Roderick	NZL	S	2	4	17	11	10	9	4	6	1	10		74.00	46.00	
	COWIE, Donald		C	2.00	4.00	17.00	11.00	10.00	9.00	4.00	6.00	1.00	10.00				
6	CHIEFFI, Enrico	ITA	S	15	3	6	6	3	2	5	13	14	PMS		93.00	52.00	
	SINIBALDI, Roberto		C	15.00	3.00	6.00	6.00	3.00	2.00	5.00	13.00	14.00	26.00				
7	DORESTE, Jose Luis	ESP	S	5	5	11	13	9	11	PMS	1	15	2		98.00	57.00	
	HERMIDA, Javier		C	5.00	5.00	11.00	13.00	9.00	11.00	26.00	1.00	15.00	2.00				
8	REYNOLDS, Mark	USA	S	3	2	5	5	5	21	15	22	18	5		101.00	58.00	
	HAENEL, Hal		C	3.00	2.00	5.00	5.00	5.00	21.00	15.00	22.00	18.00	5.00				
9	HESTBAEK, Micheal	DEN	S	7	9	8	2	12	10	6	10	12	13		89.00	64.00	
	HEIJLSBERG, Martin		C	7.00	9.00	8.00	2.00	12.00	10.00	6.00	10.00	12.00	13.00				
10	BUTZMANN, Frank	GER	S	8	13	4	4	17	12	8	15	2	15		98.00	66.00	
	FALKENTHAL, Kai		C	8.00	13.00	4.00	4.00	17.00	12.00	8.00	15.00	2.00	15.00				
11	CHARLES, Glyn	GBR	S	14	14	10	17	4	7	7	3	16	9		101.00	68.00	
	SKUODAS, George		C	14.00	14.00	10.00	17.00	4.00	7.00	7.00	3.00	16.00	9.00				
12	MANSFIELD, Mark	IRL	S	22	PMS	12	9	16	13	10	8	3	4		123.00	75.00	
	BURROWS, David		C	22.00	26.00	12.00	9.00	16.00	13.00	10.00	8.00	3.00	4.00				
13	BROMBY, Peter	BER	S	9	20	9	10	11	19	14	11	11	6		120.00	81.00	
	WHITE, Lee		C	9.00	20.00	9.00	10.00	11.00	19.00	14.00	11.00	11.00	6.00				

Table continued on next page / *Tableau continué à la page suivante*

Two-Person Keelboat (Star), Mixed / Quillard à deux places (Star), Mixte

FINAL - continued from previous page / suite de la page précédente

Rnk	Name	Ctry	Pos	Race 1	Race 2	Race 3	Race 4	Race 5	Race 6	Race 7	Race 8	Race 9	Race 10	Race 11	Total pts	Net pts
14	MacDONALD, Ross	CAN	S	DSQ	PMS	3	18	7	8	11	5	23	7		134.00	82.00
	JESPERSEN, Eric		C	26.00	26.00	3.00	18.00	7.00	8.00	11.00	5.00	23.00	7.00			
15	RAUDASCHL, Hubert	AUT	S	12	12	13	19	13	5	13	20	13	8		128.00	89.00
	HANAKAMP, Andreas		C	12.00	12.00	13.00	19.00	13.00	5.00	13.00	20.00	13.00	8.00			
16	BIGANISHVILI, Guram	GEO	S	13	10	22	14	23	24	21	9	5	18		159.00	112.00
	GRUZDEV, Vladimer		C	13.00	10.00	22.00	14.00	23.00	24.00	21.00	9.00	5.00	18.00			
17	SOLOVYOV, Viktor	RUS	S	10	16	21	DNF	14	15	19	19	7	21		168.00	121.00
	MIKHAYLIN, Anatoliy		C	10.00	16.00	21.00	26.00	14.00	15.00	19.00	19.00	7.00	21.00			
18	HARANGHY, Csaba	HUN	S	21	18	20	16	20	17	17	14	10	16		169.00	128.00
	KOMM, Andras		C	21.00	18.00	20.00	16.00	20.00	17.00	17.00	14.00	10.00	16.00			
19	HOLOWESKO, Mark	BAH	S	20	11	15	20	21	18	12	23	20	12		172.00	128.00
	PRITCHARD, Myles		C	20.00	11.00	15.00	20.00	21.00	18.00	12.00	23.00	20.00	12.00			
20	GRONBLOM, Richard	FIN	S	16	19	18	12	15	16	16	DNF	17	19		174.00	129.00
	KURKI, Ville		C	16.00	19.00	18.00	12.00	15.00	16.00	16.00	26.00	17.00	19.00			
21	CAYOLLA, Diogo	POR	S	19	15	16	15	18	14	20	18	21	14		170.00	129.00
	COSTA, Raul		C	19.00	15.00	16.00	15.00	18.00	14.00	20.00	18.00	21.00	14.00			
22	CALEGARI, Guillermo	ARG	S	17	17	23	22	19	22	18	17	19	17		191.00	146.00
	MAIOLA, Mauro		C	17.00	17.00	23.00	22.00	19.00	22.00	18.00	17.00	19.00	17.00			
23	KHORETSKIY, Sergey	BLR	S	18	21	19	21	22	20	22	21	22	20		206.00	162.00
	ZUYEV, Vladimir		C	18.00	21.00	19.00	21.00	22.00	20.00	22.00	21.00	22.00	20.00			
24	LOWRANCE, Robert	ASA	S	23	23	DNF	24	25	25	23	12	25	22		228.00	177.00
	TAVUI, Fua Logo		C	23.00	23.00	26.00	24.00	25.00	25.00	23.00	12.00	25.00	22.00			
25	McLEAN, Donald	CAY	S	24	22	24	23	24	23	PMS	24	24	23		237.00	187.00
	EBANKS, Carson		C	24.00	22.00	24.00	23.00	24.00	23.00	26.00	24.00	24.00	23.00			

Yachting / Yachting

Fleet/Match Race Keelboat (Soling), Mixed / Quillard match/racing (Soling), Mixte

FINAL

Rnk	Name	Ctry	Pos	Race 1	Race 2	Race 3	Race 4	Race 5	Race 6	Race 7	Race 8	Race 9	Race 10	Total pts	Net pts	
1	SCHUEMANN, Jochen	GER	S	5	5	2	4	1	9	9	6	2	9	MATCH	RACE	G
	FLACH, Thomas		C	5.00	5.00	2.00	4.00	1.00	9.00	9.00	6.00	2.00	9.00			
	JAEKEL, Bernd		C													
2	SHAYDUKO, Georgiy	RUS	S	2	11	13	8	7	4	12	8	7	3	MATCH	RACE	S
	SHABANOV, Dmitriy		C	2.00	11.00	13.00	8.00	7.00	4.00	12.00	8.00	7.00	3.00			
	SKALIN, Igor		C													
3	MADRIGALI, Jeff	USA	S	1	4	9	2	5	19	5	9	1	12	MATCH	RACE	B
	BARTON, Jim		C	1.00	4.00	9.00	2.00	5.00	19.00	5.00	9.00	1.00	12.00			
	MASSEY, Kent		C													
4	BEADSWORTH, Andrew	GBR	S	7	1	8	7	4	1	6	PMS	12	14	MATCH	RACE	
	PARKIN, Barry		C	7.00	1.00	8.00	7.00	4.00	1.00	6.00	23.00	12.00	14.00			
	STEAD, Adrian George		C													
5	ABBOTT, William	CAN	S	9	20	16	10	2	8	1	1	8	8	MATCH	RACE	
	ABBOTT, Joanne		C	9.00	20.00	16.00	10.00	2.00	8.00	1.00	1.00	8.00	8.00			
	BOSTON, Brad		C													
6	WESTERGAARD, Stig	DEN	S	15	6	3	16	PMS	2	11	PMS	4	1	MATCH	RACE	
	ANDERSEN, Jan		C	15.00	6.00	3.00	16.00	23.00	2.00	11.00	23.00	4.00	1.00			
	BOJSEN-MOELLER, Jens		C													
7	PICHUGIN, Serhiy	URK	S	DSQ	3	1	15	6	18	18	5	9	2	100.00	59.00	
	KHAYNDRAVA, Serhiy		C	23.00	3.00	1.00	15.00	6.00	18.00	18.00	5.00	9.00	2.00			
	KOROTKOV, Volodymyr		C													
8	DORESTE, Luis	ESP	S	4	8	12	13	PMS	5	8	10	10	4	97.00	61.00	
	MANRIQUE, Domingo		C	4.00	8.00	12.00	13.00	23.00	5.00	8.00	10.00	10.00	4.00			
	VERA, David		C													
9	JOHANNESSAN, Herman Horn	NOR	S	13	15	4	PMS	12	7	4	3	16	7	104.00	65.00	
	DAVIS, Paul		C	13.00	15.00	4.00	23.00	12.00	7.00	4.00	3.00	16.00	7.00			
	STOKKELAND, Espen		C													

Table continued on next page / Tableau continué à la page suivante

Fleet/Match Race Keelboat (Soling), Mixed / *Quillard match/racing (Soling), Mixte*

FINAL - *continued from previous page* / *suite de la page précédente*

Rnk	Name	Ctry	Pos	Race 1	Race 2	Race 3	Race 4	RANK POINTS Race 5	Race 6	Race 7	Race 8	Race 9	Race 10	Total pts	Net pts
10	CELON, Mario	ITA	S	6	16	14	1	8	3	3	16	15	19	101.00	66.00
	CELON, Claudio		C	6.00	16.00	14.00	1.00	8.00	3.00	3.00	16.00	15.00	19.00		
	TORBOLI, Gianni		C												
11	BOUET, Marc	FRA	S	11	DSQ	6	17	9	13	10	7	3	10	109.00	69.00
	CHTOUNDER, Sylvain		C	11.00	23.00	6.00	17.00	9.00	13.00	10.00	7.00	3.00	10.00		
	MORVAN, Gildas		C												
12	HAYES, Matt	AUS	S	10	13	5	14	PMS	6	2	14	6	DSQ	116.00	70.00
	JARVIN, Steve		C	10.00	13.00	5.00	14.00	23.00	6.00	2.00	14.00	6.00	23.00		
	McCONAGHY, Stephen		C												
13	HOLMBERG, Magnus	SWE	S	12	9	DNC	3	13	12	14	4	13	5	108.00	71.00
	ALM, Bjorn		C	12.00	9.00	23.00	3.00	13.00	12.00	14.00	4.00	13.00	5.00		
	BARNE, Johan		C												
14	HARRAP, Kelvin	NZL	S	DSQ	18	7	5	15	11	7	15	5	15	121.00	80.00
	CLARKSON, Sean		C	23.00	18.00	7.00	5.00	15.00	11.00	7.00	15.00	5.00	15.00		
	GALE, Robert		C												
15	POTMA, Willem-Nico	NED	S	8	7	10	PMS	10	15	16	2	17	16	124.00	84.00
	HETTINGA, Frank		C	8.00	7.00	10.00	23.00	10.00	15.00	16.00	2.00	17.00	16.00		
	POTMA, Gerhard		C												
16	KING, Marshall	IRL	S	3	10	11	9	16	17	13	PMS	14	17	133.00	93.00
	CONNOLLY, Garrett		C	3.00	10.00	11.00	9.00	16.00	17.00	13.00	23.00	14.00	17.00		
	O'GRADY, Daniel		C												
17	SAVAGE, Bruce	RSA	S	17	2	17	11	11	20	15	PMS	11	18	145.00	102.00
	MAYHEW, Richard		C	17.00	2.00	17.00	11.00	11.00	20.00	15.00	23.00	11.00	18.00		
	WADE LEHMAN, Clynton		C												
18	ALEVRAS, Stavros	GRE	S	14	12	18	PMS	3	16	21	11	20	13	151.00	107.00
	ALEVRAS, Panayiotis		C	14.00	12.00	18.00	23.00	3.00	16.00	21.00	11.00	20.00	13.00		
	CHANDAKAS, Stefanos		C												
19	KOMATSU, Kazunori	JPN	S	16	19	15	6	14	21	17	12	21	11	152.00	110.00
	HAZAMA, Masatoshi		C	16.00	19.00	15.00	6.00	14.00	21.00	17.00	12.00	21.00	11.00		
	HYODO, Kazuyuki		C												
20	WOSSALA, Gyorgy	HUN	S	DSQ	14	19	12	PMS	10	20	13	18	20	172.00	126.00
	KOVACSI, Laszlo		C	23.00	14.00	19.00	12.00	23.00	10.00	20.00	13.00	18.00	20.00		
	VEZER, Karoly		C												
21	ARAUJO, Edson, Jr.	BRA	S	DSQ	17	20	PMS	17	14	19	PMS	19	6	181.00	135.00
	GLOMB, Daniel		C	23.00	17.00	20.00	23.00	17.00	14.00	19.00	23.00	19.00	6.00		
	REITZ, Marcelo		C												
22	al-BUSMAIT, Essa	BRN	S	18	21	21	DNF	18	22	22	17	22	21	205.00	160.00
	al-SADA, Khalid		C	18.00	21.00	21.00	23.00	18.00	22.00	22.00	17.00	22.00	21.00		
	al-SAIE, Ahmed		C												

VENUE MAPS
PLANS DES SITES

Aquatics—Diving, Swimming, Synchronized Swimming, Water Polo
Natation — Plongeon, Natation, Natation synchronisée, Water-polo

Georgia Tech Aquatic Center,
Atlanta, Georgia
Centre de natation de Georgia Tech, Atlanta, Géorgie

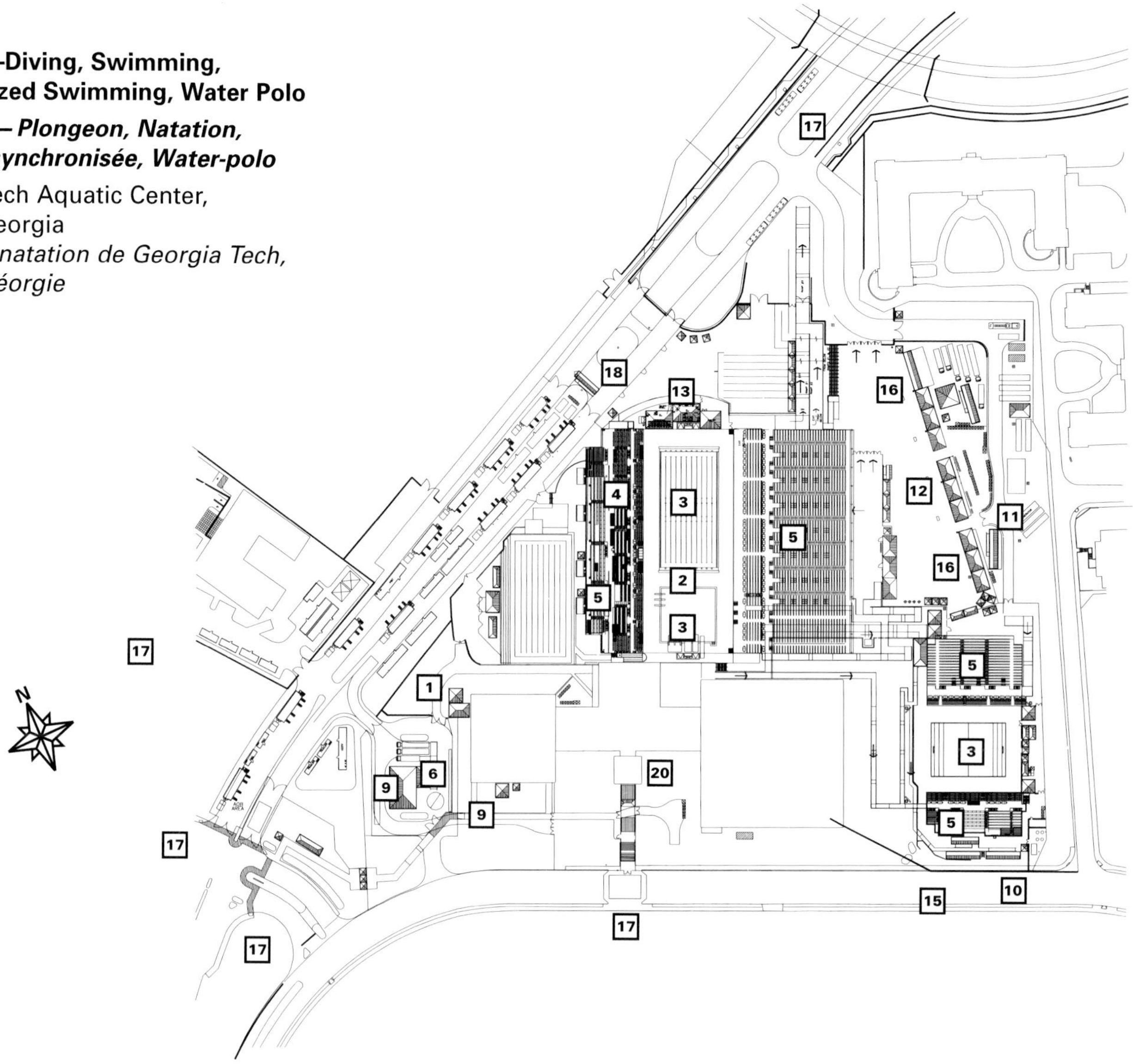

Archery / *Tir à l'arc*

Stone Mountain Park Archery Center and Velodrome
Stone Mountain, Georgia

Centre de tir à l'arc et vélodrome du parc de Stone Mountain, Stone Mountain, Géorgie

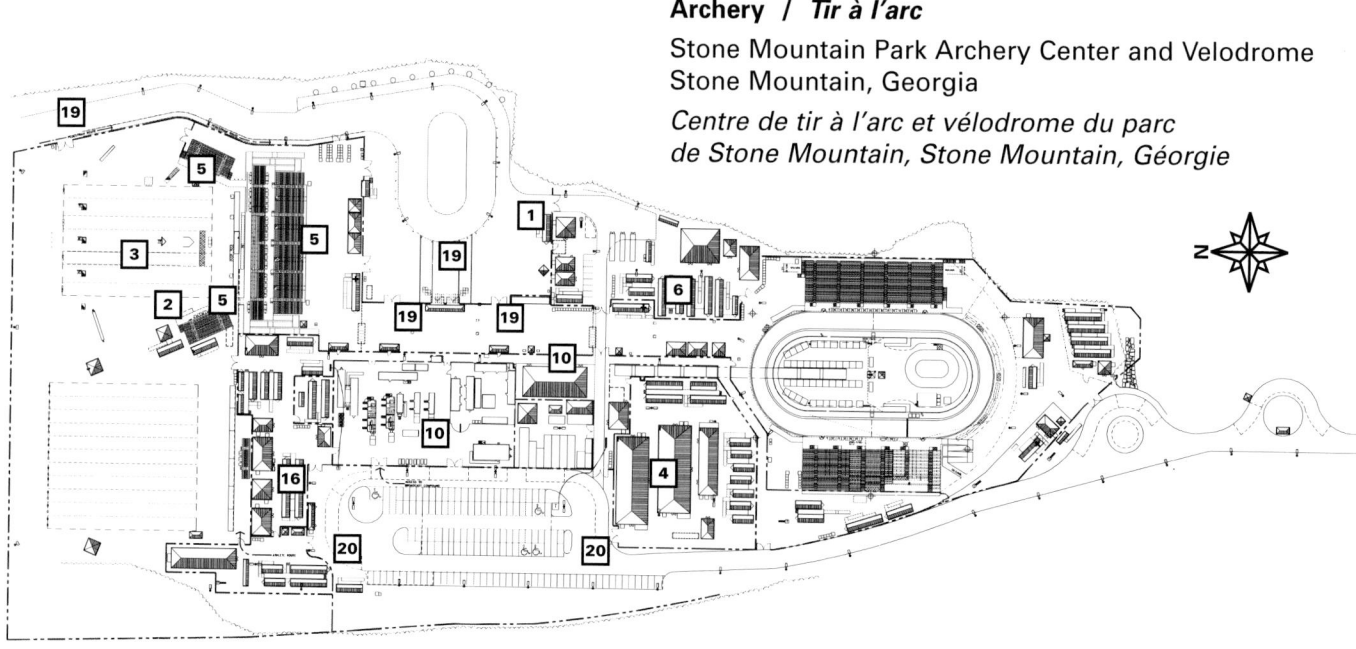

Athletics
Athlétisme
Olympic Stadium, Atlanta, Georgia
Stade olympique, Atlanta, Géorgie

LEGEND / *LEGENDE*

This legend represents the major functional areas located at each Olympic venue. The numbers below correspond to the numbers shown on the venue maps.

Les principaux domaines fonctionnels en place sur chaque site figurent dans cette légende. Les chiffres correspondent à ceux que l'on trouve sur les cartes des sites.

1 Accreditation / *Accréditation*

2 Ceremonies / *Cérémonies*

3 Competition area / *Aire de compétition*

4 Competition related area / *Aire des services liés aux compétitions*

5 Event seating / *Places*

6 ACOG management / *Direction du site*

7 Sports administration federation services / *Services administratifs des fédérations sportives*

8 Material acquisition/distribution / *Acquisition/distribution du matériel*

9 Press / *Presse*

10 Broadcasters / *Diffuseurs*

11 Health services and medical control / *Services et contrôles médicaux*

12 Spectator services / *Services aux spectateurs*

13 Olympic Family services / *Services à la Famille olympique*

14 Security / *Sécurité*

15 Technology / *Technologie*

16 Food services / *Alimentation*

17 Transportation / *Transports*

18 Ticketing / *Billetterie*

19 Spectator entrance / *Entrée réservée aux spectateurs*

20 Athlete entrance / *Entrée réservée aux athlètes*

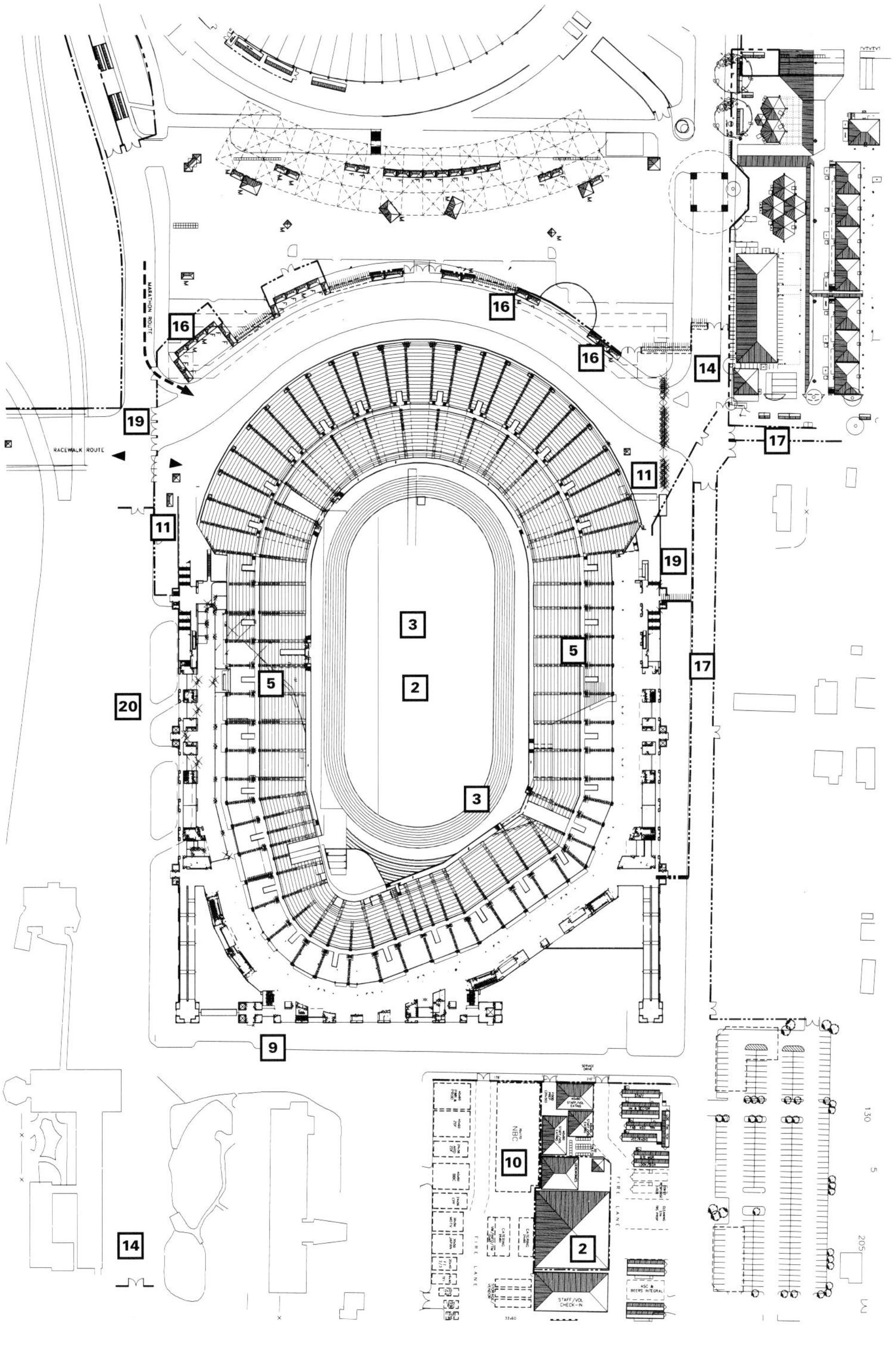

Badminton / *Badminton*

Georgia State University, Atlanta, Georgia
Université d'état de Géorgie, Atlanta, Géorgie

Note: Numbered spaces are on upper-level floors. Field of play on 3rd floor (not shown).

Remarque : Les places numérotées sont aux niveaux supérieurs. Le terrain de jeu au 2e étage n'est pas indiqué.

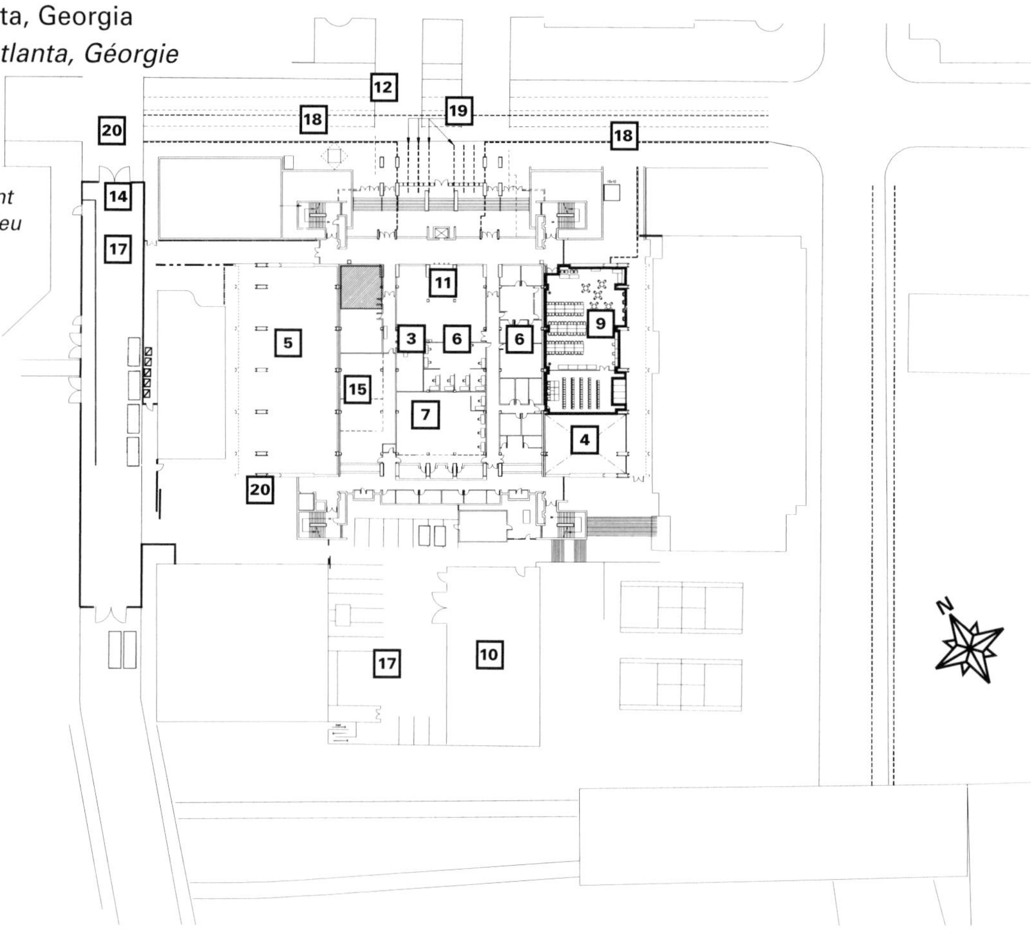

Overview
Plan du site

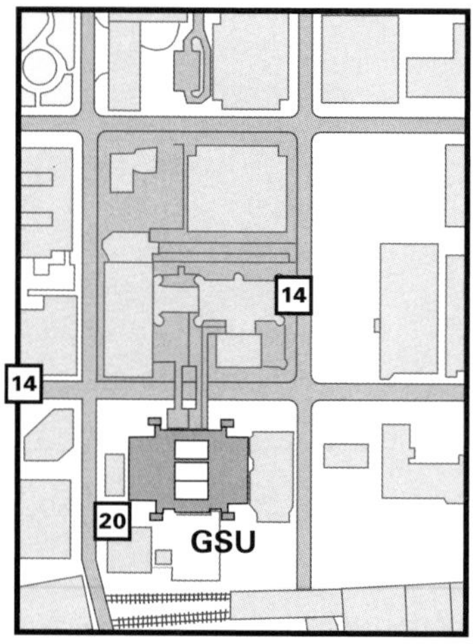

Baseball / *Baseball*

Atlanta-Fulton County Stadium, Atlanta, Georgia
Stade du comté de Fulton à Atlanta, Atlanta, Géorgie

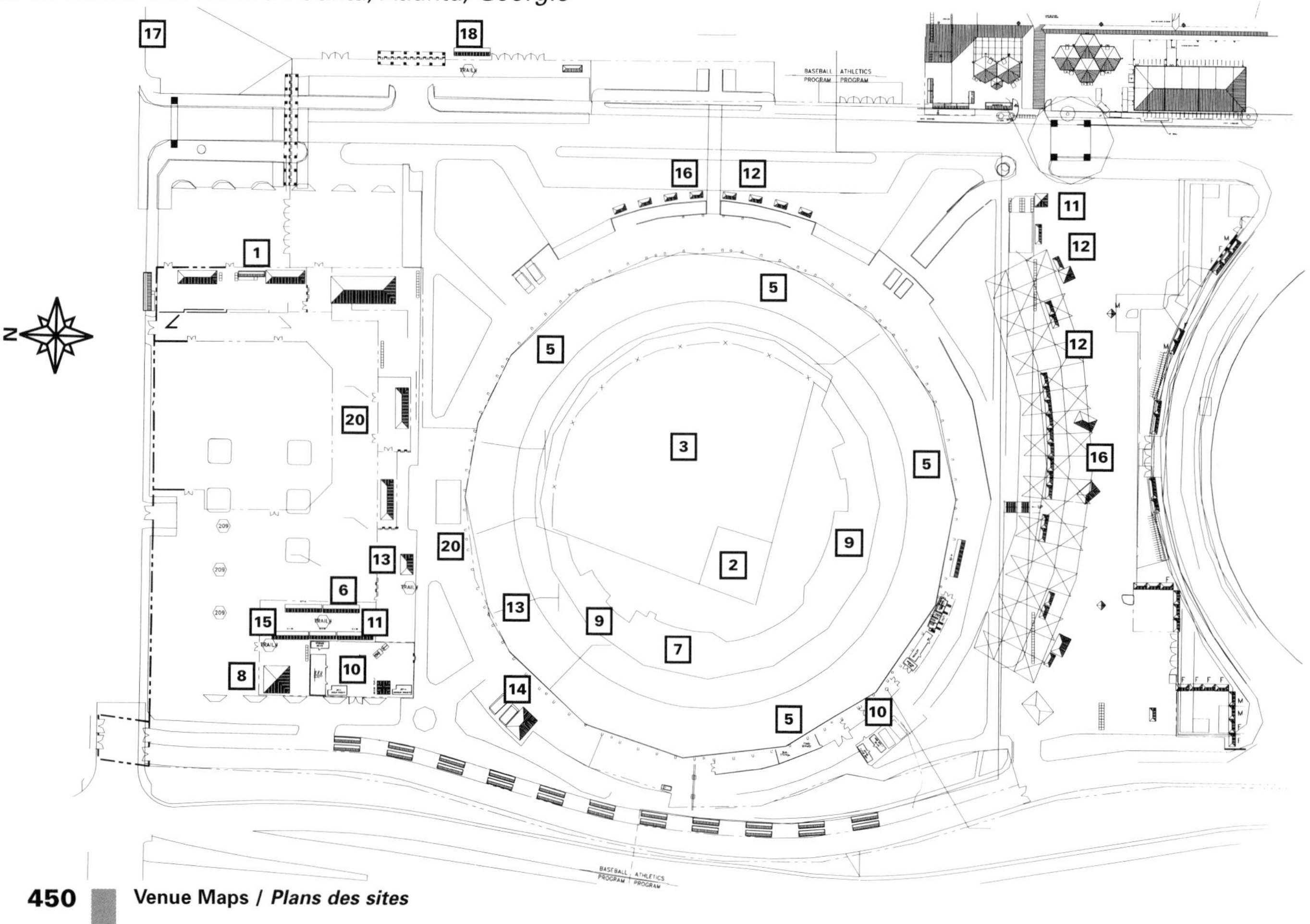

Basketball—Preliminaries
Basketball — Eliminatoires

Morehouse College Gymnasium, Atlanta, Georgia
Gymnase de Morehouse College, Atlanta, Géorgie

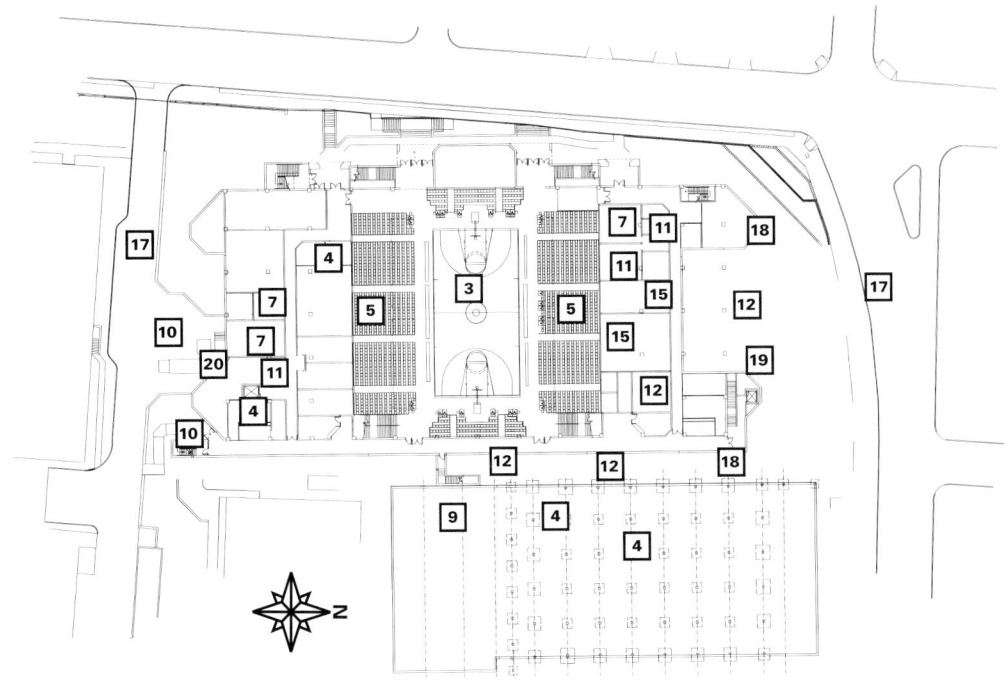

Basketball
Basketball

Georgia Dome, Atlanta, Georgia
Georgia Dome, Atlanta, Géorgie

Note: Additional seating as well as other functional areas on upper floors.

Remarque : Places supplémentaires et autres domaines fonctionnels aux niveaux supérieurs.

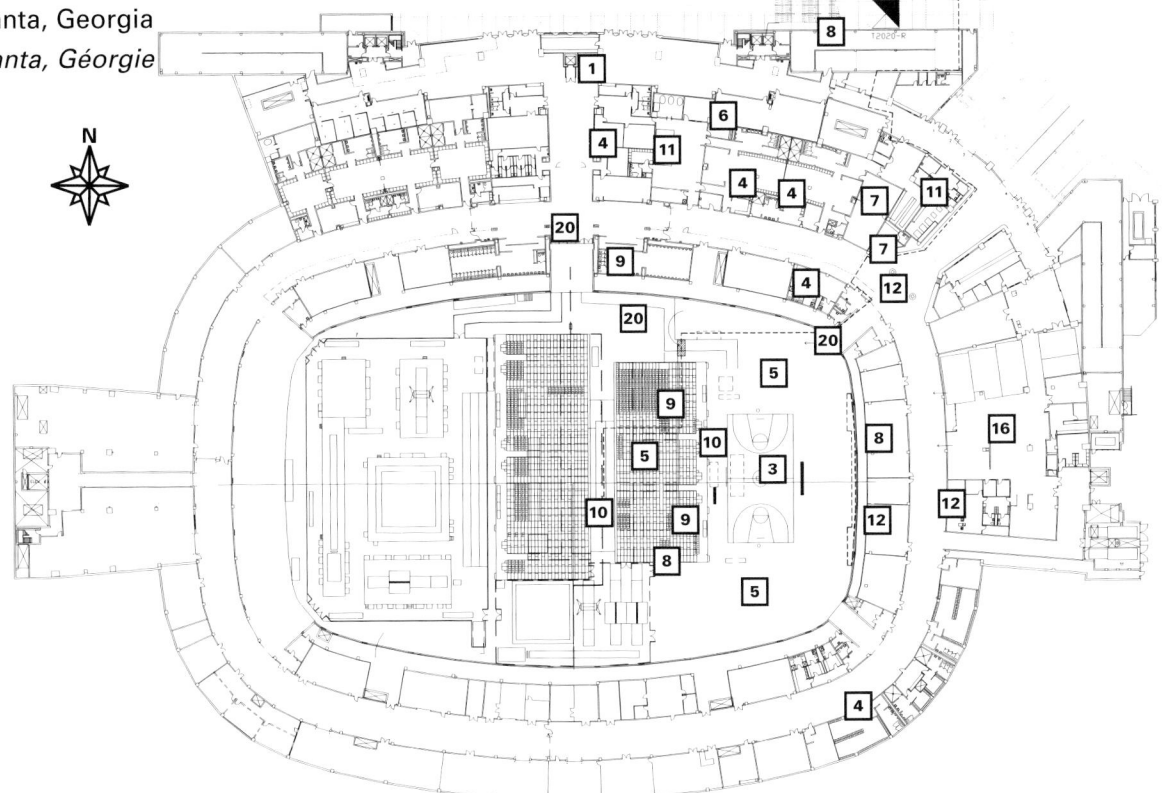

Boxing / *Boxe*

Alexander Memorial Coliseum of Georgia Tech, Atlanta, Georgia
Alexander Memorial Coliseum de Georgia Tech, Altanta, Géorgie

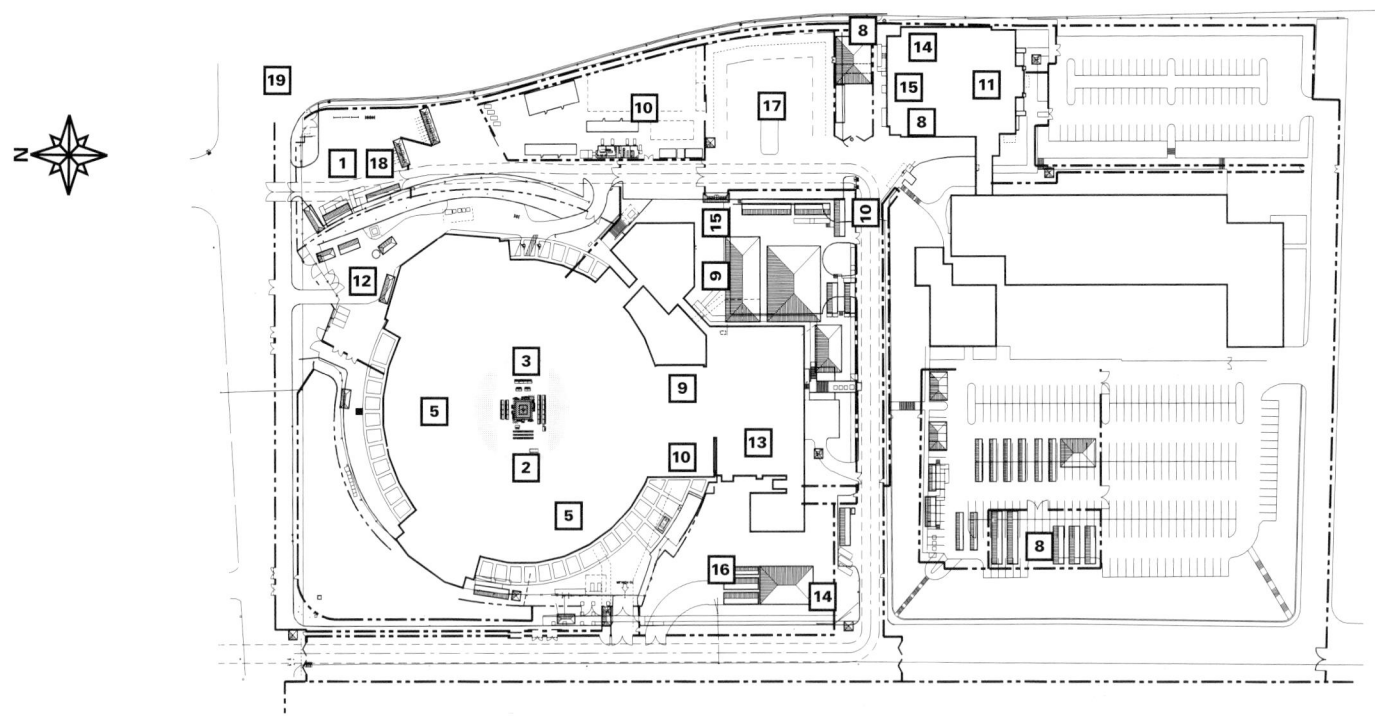

Canoe / Kayak—Slalom
Canoë / Kayak — Slalom

Ocoee Whitewater Center, Tennessee
Centre des épreuves en eaux vives de l'Ocoee, Tennessee
(See page 164 / *Voir page 164*)

Canoe / Kayak—Sprint
Canoë / Kayak — Sprint

Lake Lanier, Georgia
Lac Lanier, Géorgie

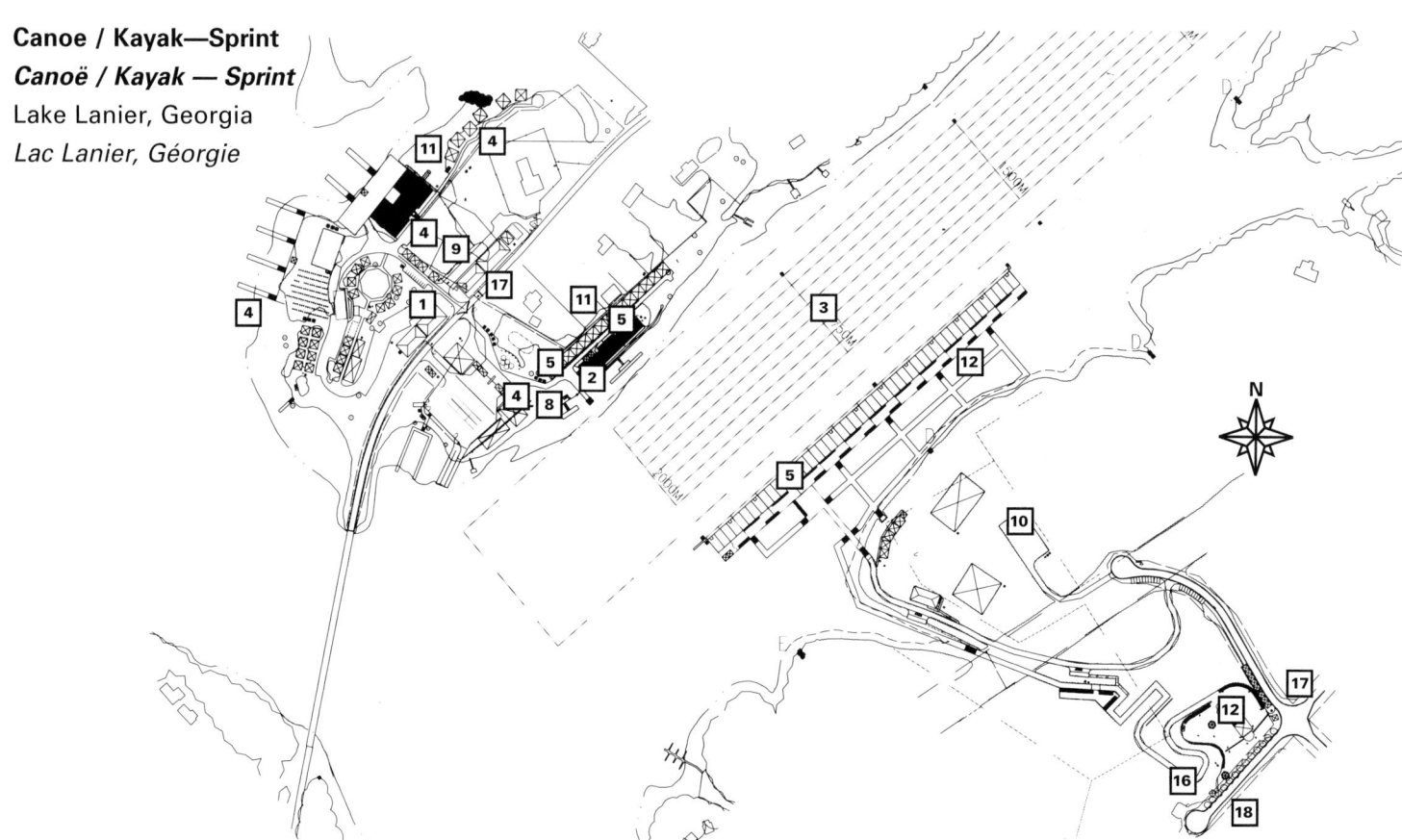

Cycling—Mountain Bike / *Cyclisme — VTT*

Georgia International Horse Park, Conyers, Georgia

Centre équestre international de Géorgie, Conyers, Géorgie

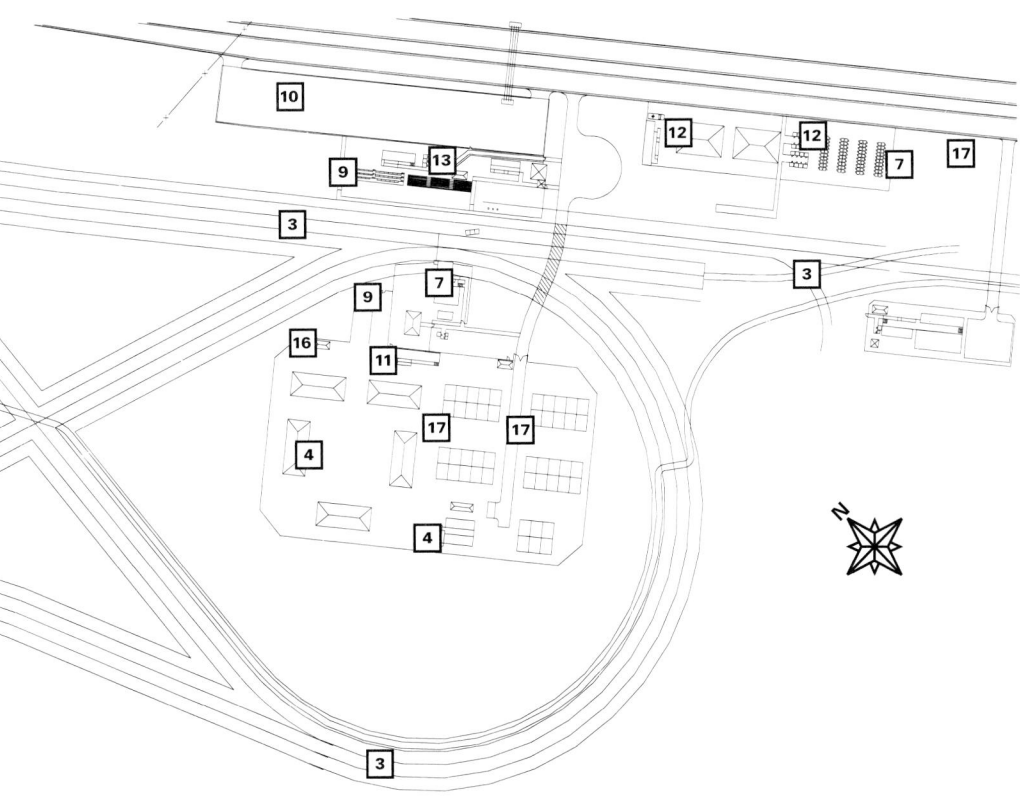

Cycling—Track / *Cyclisme — Piste*

Stone Mountain Park Archery Center and Velodrome, Stone Mountain, Georgia

Centre de tir à l'arc et vélodrome du parc de Stone Mountain, Stone Mountain, Géorgie

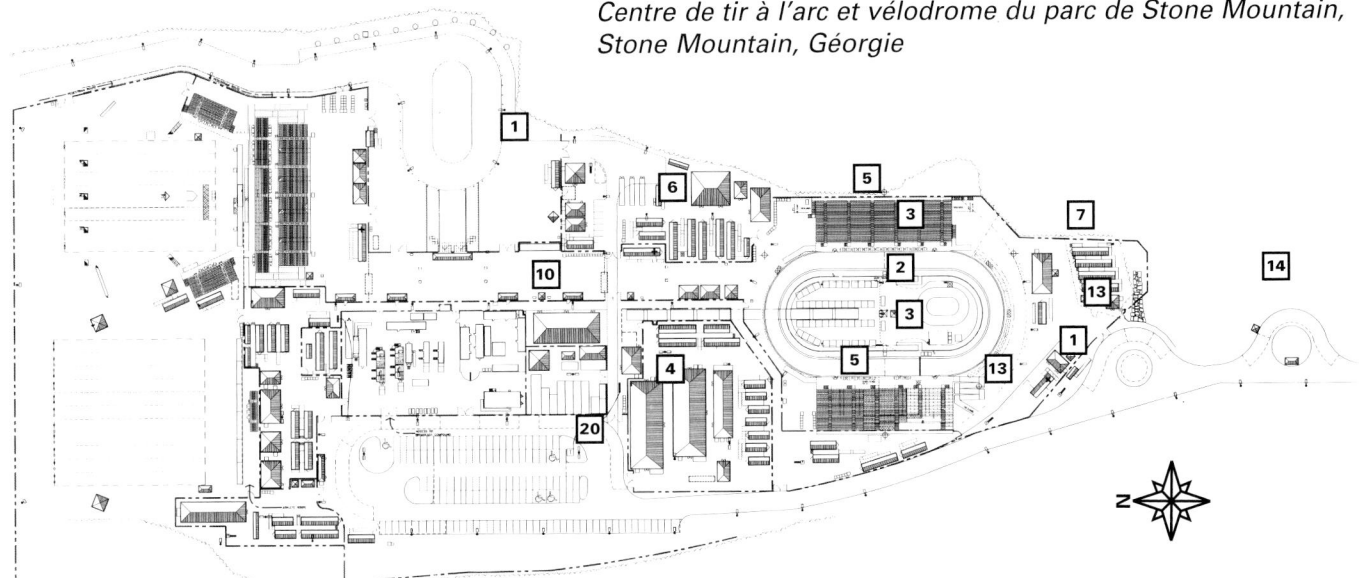

Equestrian / *Sports équestres*

Georgia International Horse Park, Conyers, Georgia

Centre équestre international de Géorgie, Conyers, Géorgie

Overview / *Plan du site*

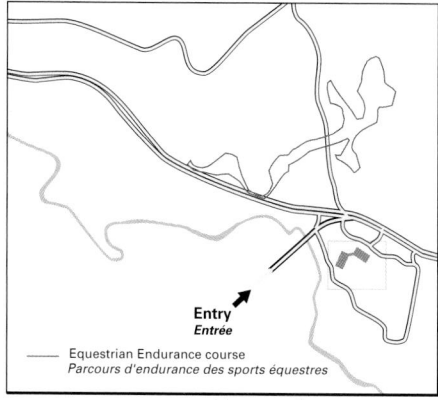

Entry
Entrée

—— Equestrian Endurance course
Parcours d'endurance des sports équestres

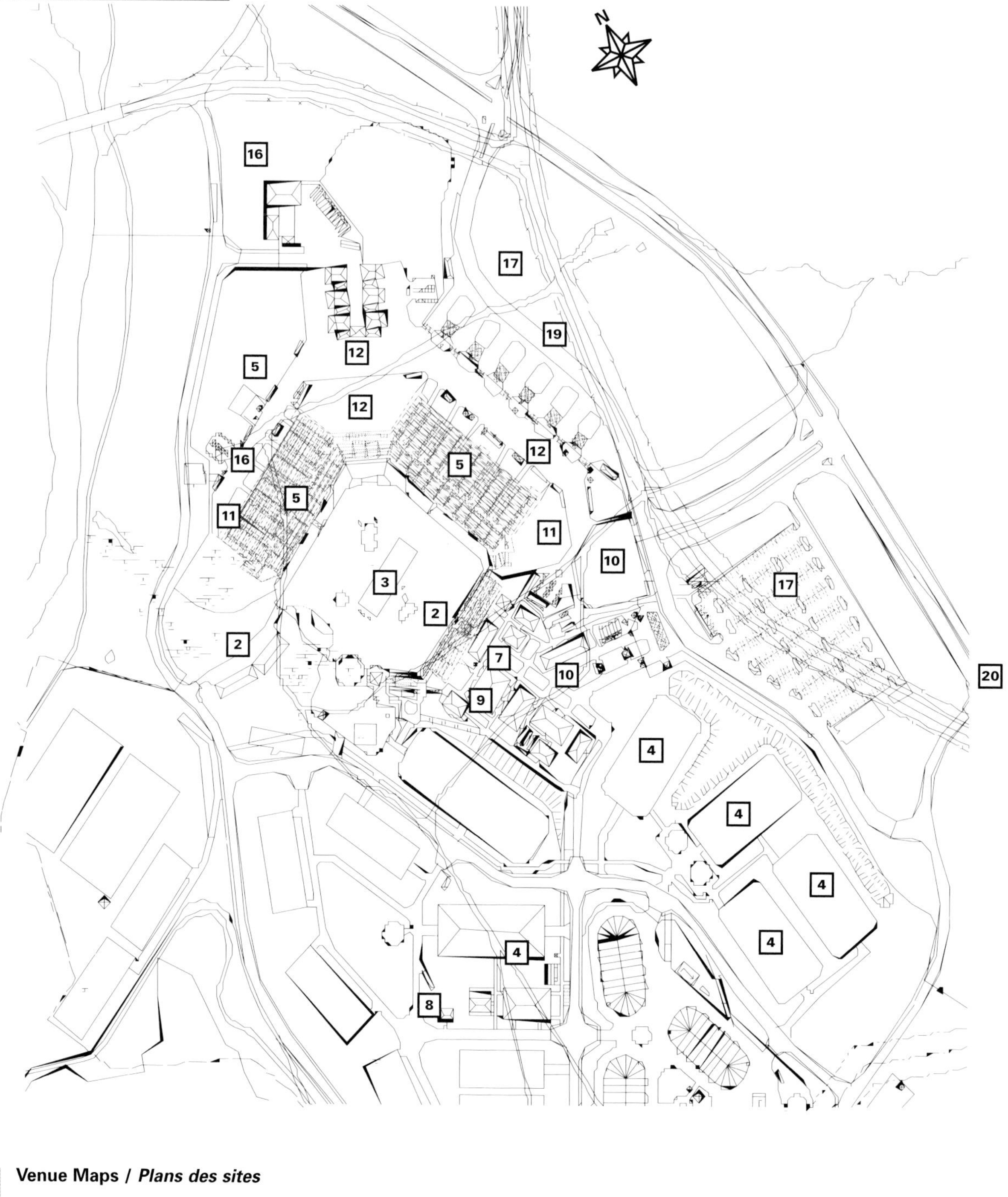

Fencing
Escrime

Georgia World Congress Center
(GWCC)—Hall F, Atlanta, Georgia

*Centre international de congrès de
Géorgie (GWCC) — Hall F,
Atlanta, Géorgie*

Note: See page 459 for overview map
of the GWCC.

*Remarque : Voir page 459 pour
le plan du GWCC.*

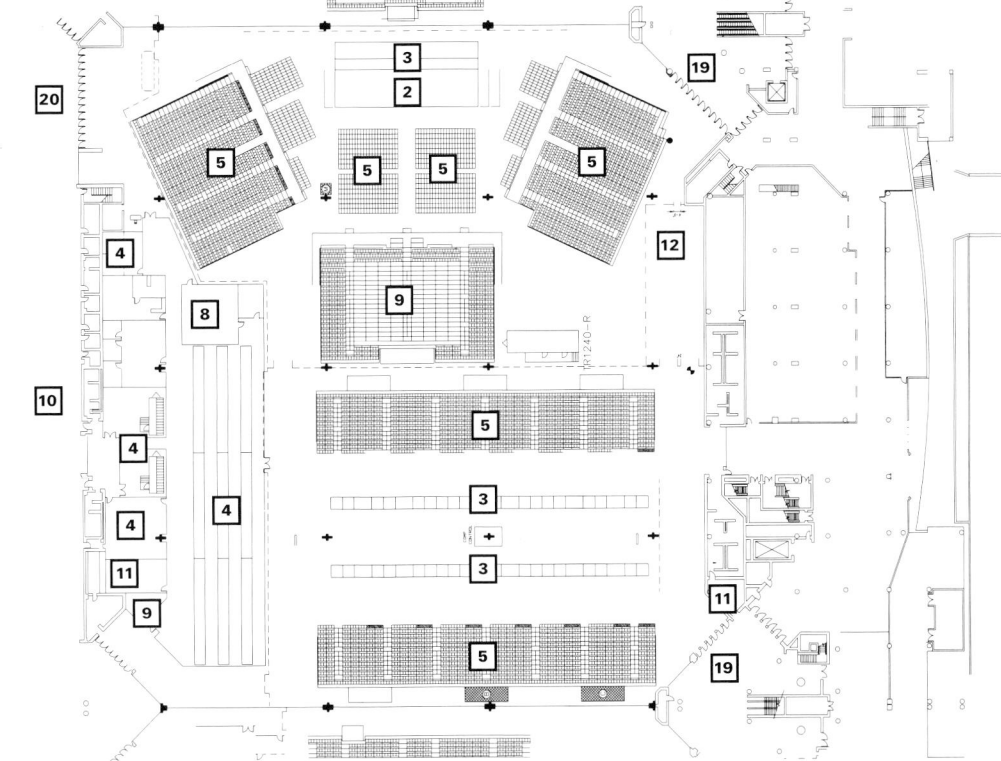

Football
Football

Sanford Stadium, University of Georgia, Athens, Georgia
Stade Sanford de l'université de Géorgie, Athens, Géorgie

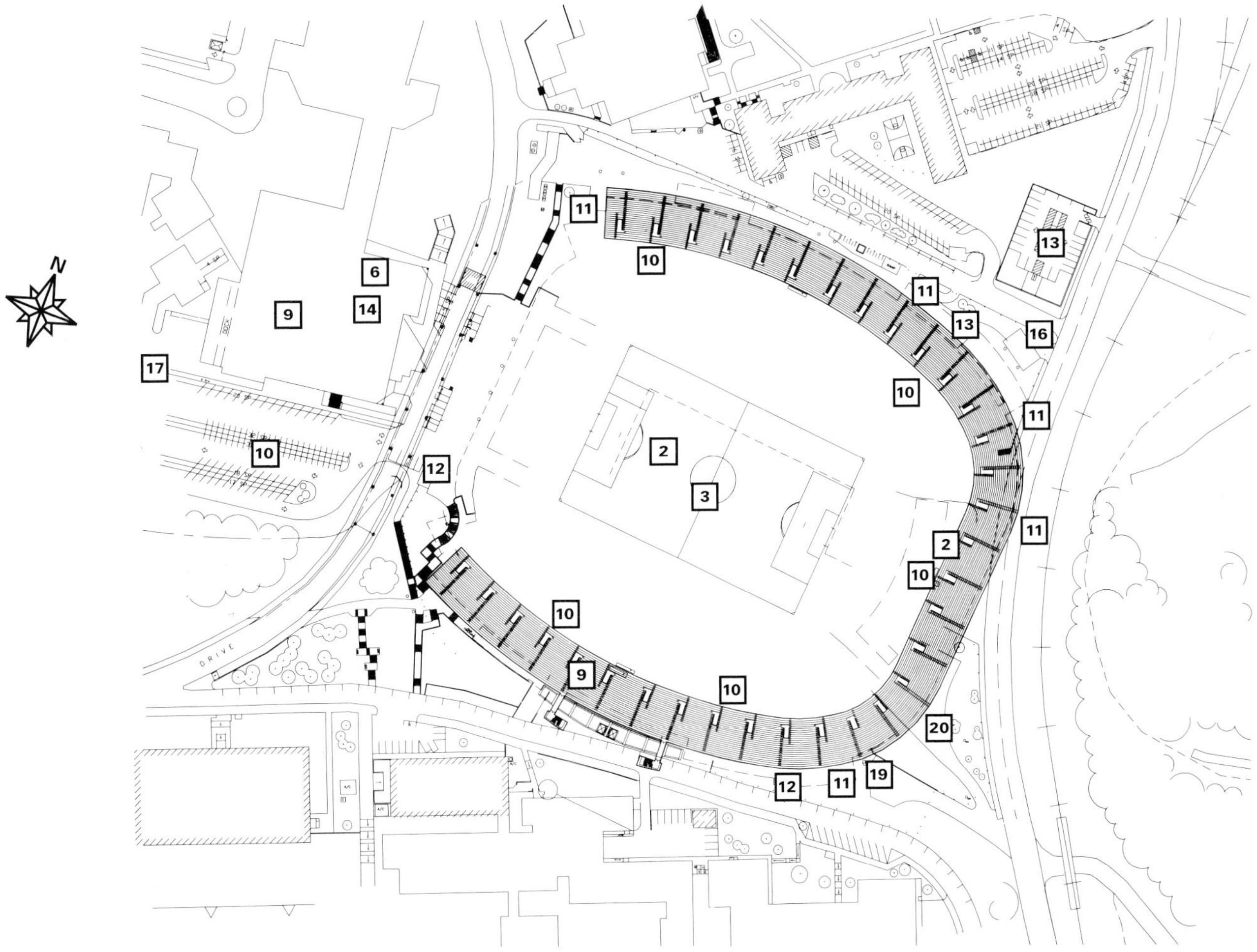

Gymnastics—Artistic

Gymnastique — Artistique

Georgia Dome, Atlanta, Georgia

Georgia Dome, Atlanta, Géorgie

Note: Additional seating as well as other functional areas on upper floors.

Remarque : Places supplémen-taires et autres domaines fonction-nels aux niveaux supérieurs.

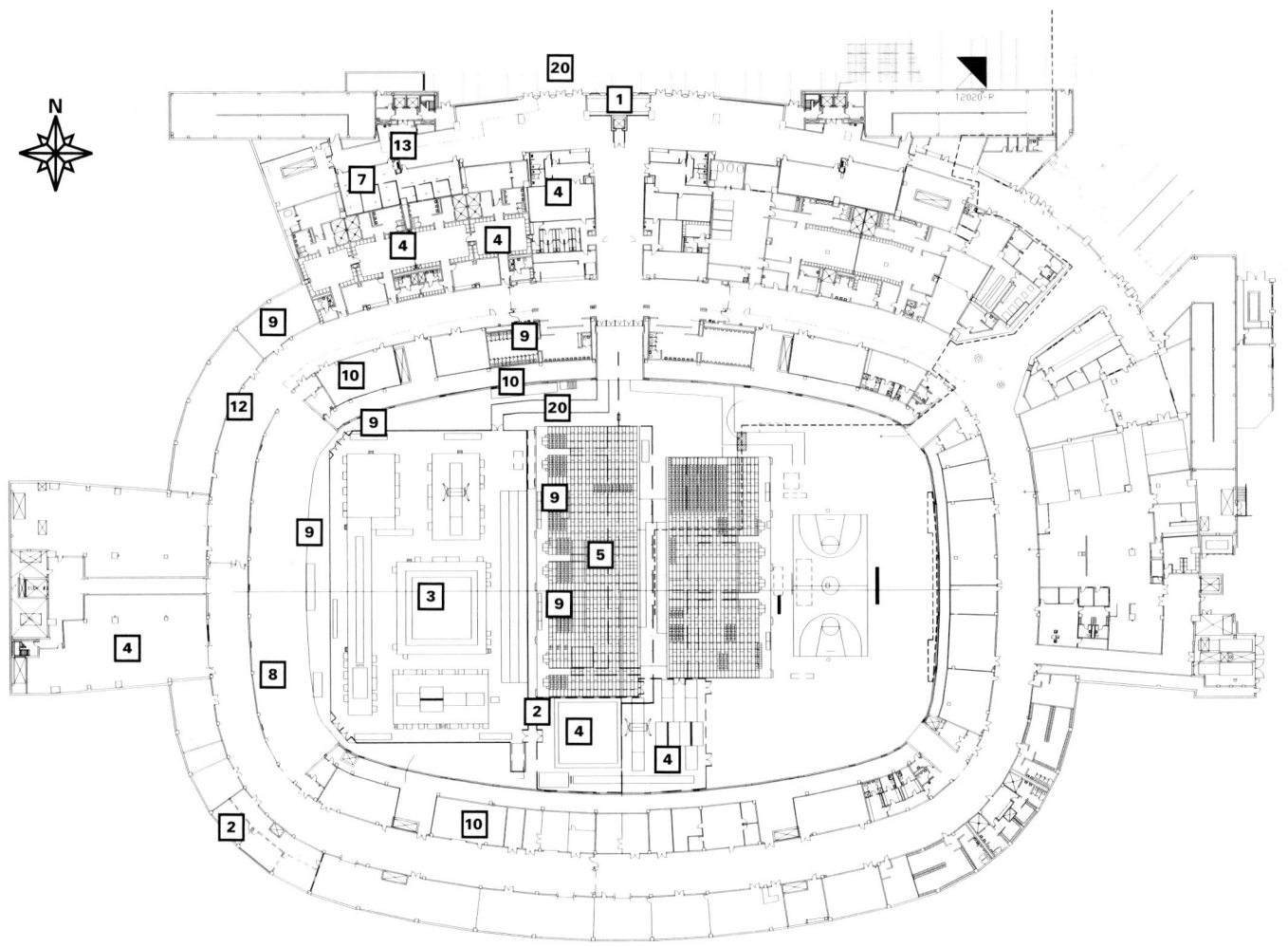

Gymnastics—Rhythmic
Gymnastique — Rythmique

University of Georgia Coliseum, Athens, Georgia

Coliseum, université de Géorgie, Athens, Géorgie

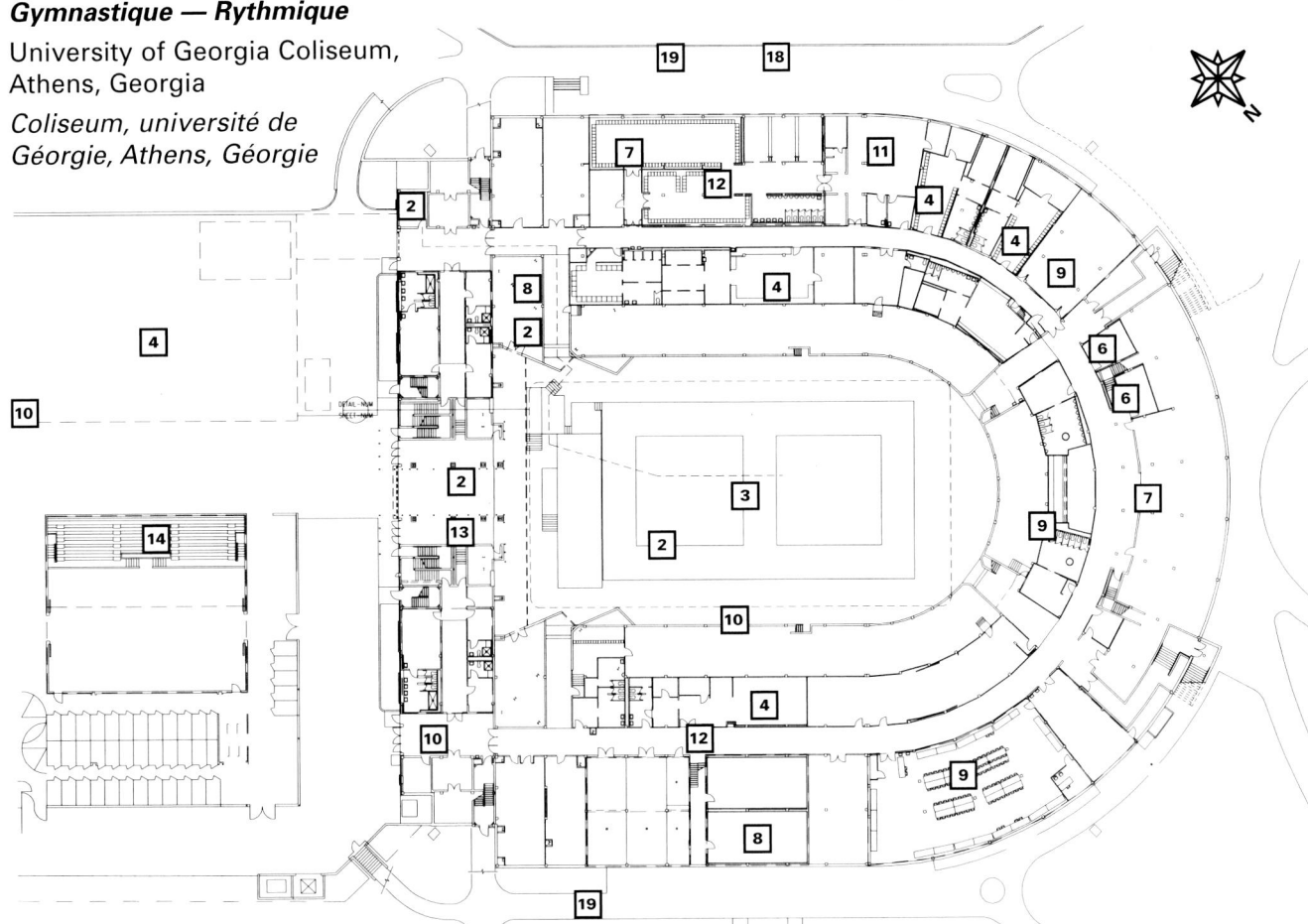

Handball
Handball

Georgia World Congress Center (also Georgia Dome on facing page), Atlanta, Georgia

Centre international de congrès de Géorgie (aussi Georgia Dome page opposée), Atlanta, Géorgie

Note: Men's handball finals were held in the same area as artistic gymnastics. See site plan on page 456.

Remarque : Les finales de handball messieurs se sont déroulées au même endroit que la gymnastique artistique. Voir page 456 pour le plan du site.

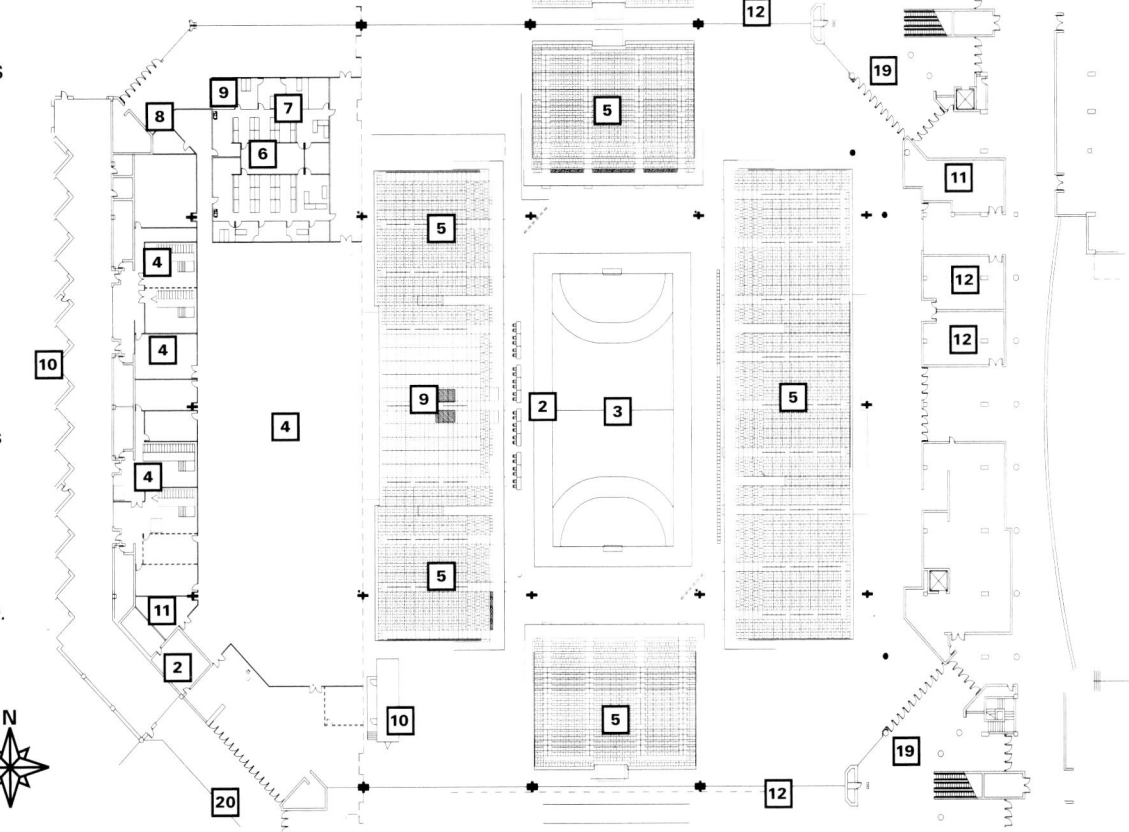

Hockey / *Hockey*

Clark Atlanta University Stadium & Morris
Brown College Stadium, Atlanta, Georgia

*Stade de l'université Clark Atlanta & stade de
Morris Brown College, Atlanta, Géorgie*

Morris Brown College Stadium
Stade de Morris Brown College

Clark Atlanta University Stadium
Stade de de l'université Clark Atlanta

Judo / *Judo*

Georgia World Congress Center (GWCC)—
Hall H, Atlanta, Georgia

*Centre international de congrès de Géorgie
(GWCC) — Hall H, Atlanta, Géorgie*

Overview map of GWCC
Plan du GWCC

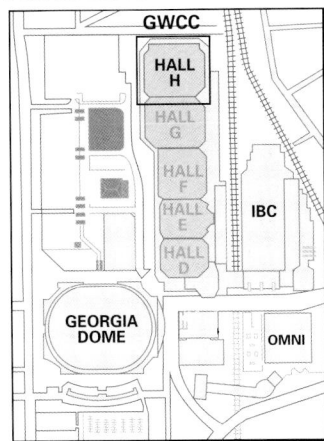

Note: Additional spaces and functional areas on upper floors.

*Remarque : Surfaces et domaines fonctionnels
supplémentaires aux niveaux supérieurs.*

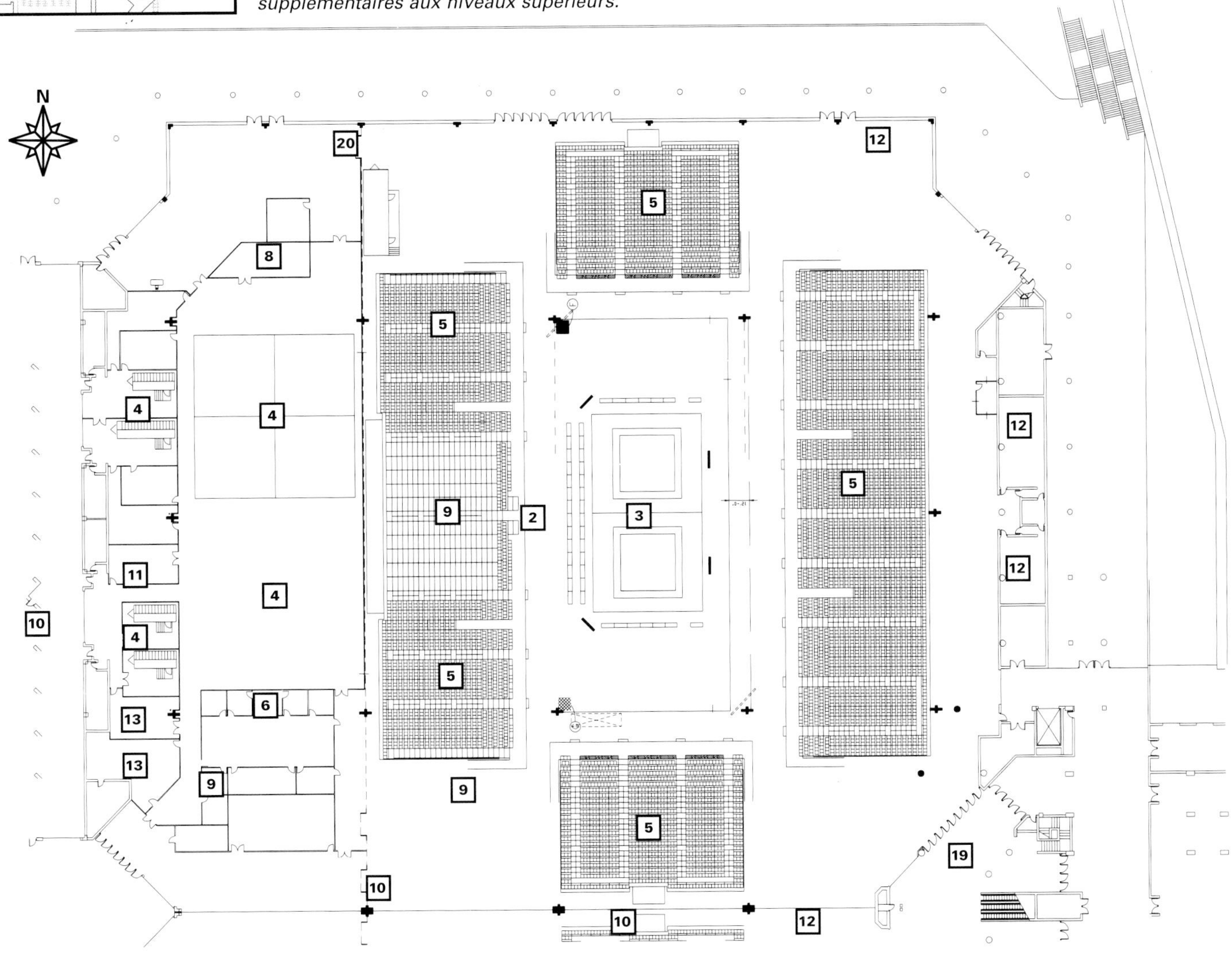

Modern Pentathlon

Pentathlon moderne

Georgia World Congress Center, Atlanta, Georgia
Centre international de congrès de Géorgie, Atlanta, Géorgie
      Fencing and shooting / *Escrime et tir*

Georgia Tech Aquatic Center, Atlanta, Georgia
Centre de natation de Georgia Tech, Atlanta, Géorgie
      Swimming / *Natation*

Georgia International Horse Park, Conyers, Georgia
Centre équestre international de Géorgie, Conyers, Géorgie
      Riding and running / *Equitation et course à pied*

Rowing / *Aviron*

Lake Lanier, Georgia
Lac Lanier, Géorgie

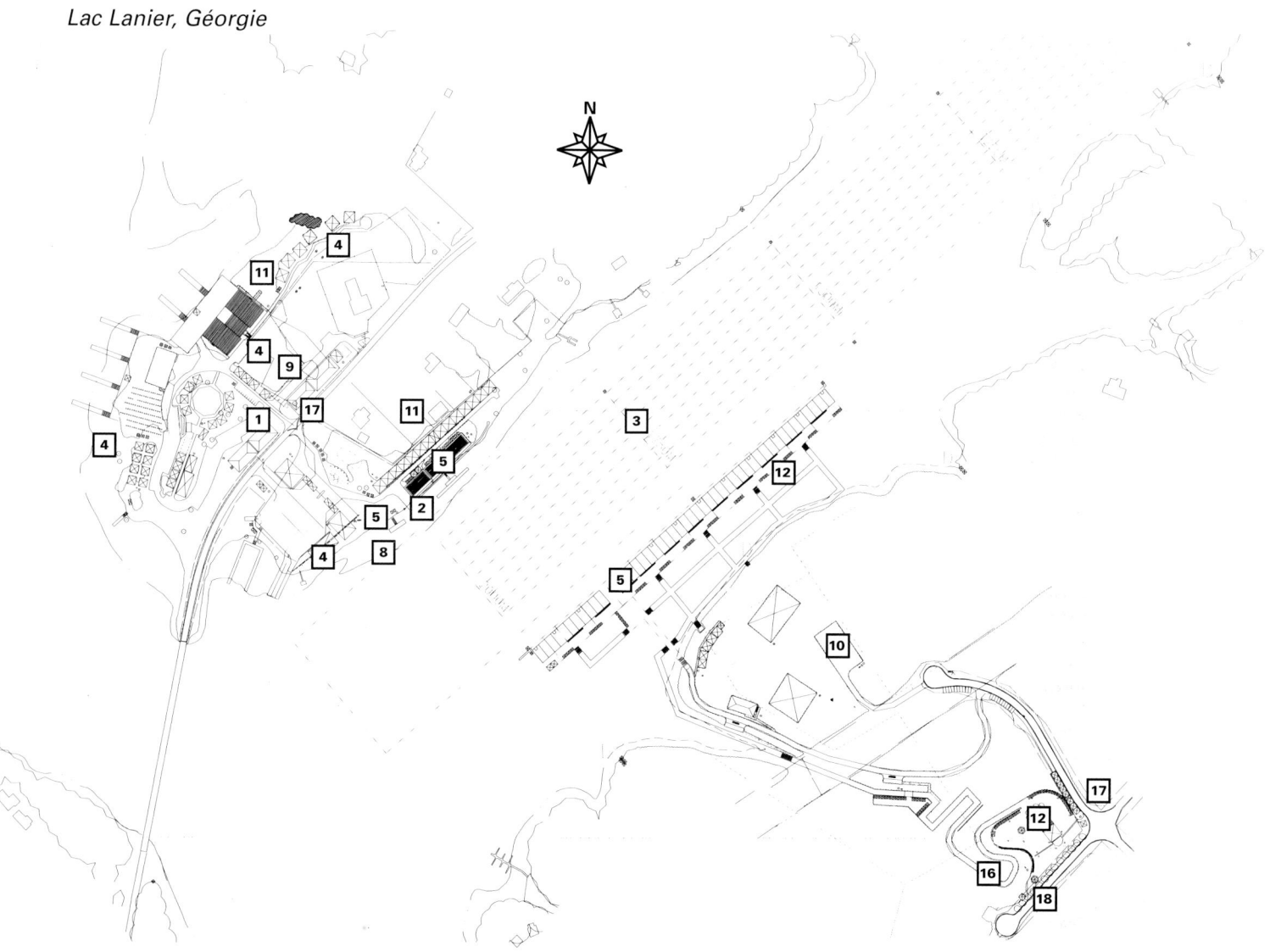

Shooting
Tir
Wolf Creek Shooting Complex, Atlanta, Georgia
Complexe de tir de Wolf Creek, Atlanta, Géorgie

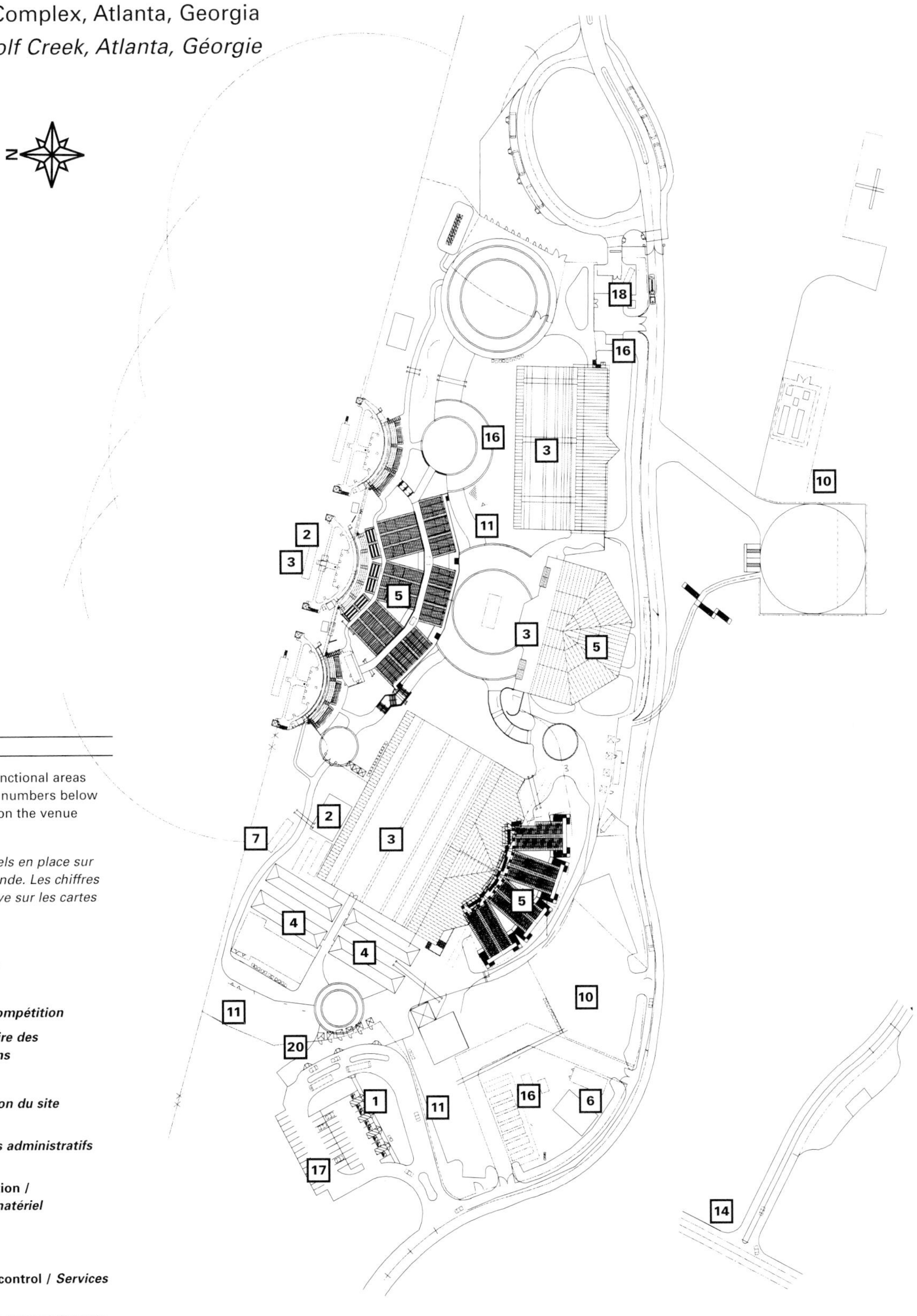

LEGEND / *LEGENDE*

This legend represents the major functional areas located at each Olympic venue. The numbers below correspond to the numbers shown on the venue maps.

Les principaux domaines fonctionnels en place sur chaque site figurent dans cette légende. Les chiffres correspondent à ceux que l'on trouve sur les cartes des sites.

1   Accreditation / *Accréditation*
2   Ceremonies / *Cérémonies*
3   Competition area / *Aire de compétition*
4   Competition related area / *Aire des services liés aux compétitions*
5   Event seating / *Places*
6   ACOG management / *Direction du site*
7   Sports administration federation services / *Services administratifs des fédérations sportives*
8   Material acquisition/distribution / *Acquisition/distribution du matériel*
9   Press / *Presse*
10 Broadcasters / *Diffuseurs*
11 Health services and medical control / *Services et contrôles médicaux*
12 Spectator services / *Services aux spectateurs*
13 Olympic Family services / *Services à la Famille olympique*
14 Security / *Sécurité*
15 Technology / *Technologie*
16 Food services / *Alimentation*
17 Transportation / *Transports*
18 Ticketing / *Billetterie*
19 Spectator entrance / *Entrée réservée aux spectateurs*
20 Athlete entrance / *Entrée réservée aux athlètes*

Softball
Softball
Golden Park, Columbus, Georgia
Golden Park, Columbus, Géorgie

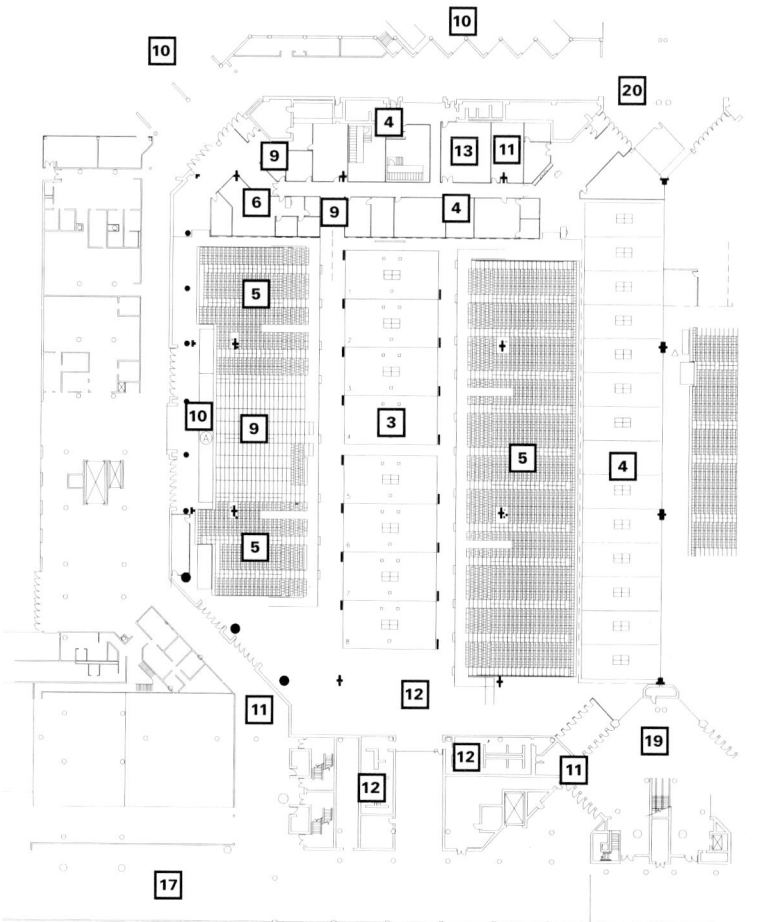

Upper level seating
Places niveau supérieur

Lower level seating
Places niveau inférieur

Section

Table Tennis
Tennis de table
Georgia World Congress Center
(GWCC)—Hall D, Atlanta, Georgia

*Centre international de congrès de
Géorgie (GWCC) — Hall D,
Atlanta, Géorgie*

Note: See page 459 for overview map of the GWCC.

Remarque : Voir page 459 pour le plan du GWCC.

Tennis

Tennis

Stone Mountain Park Tennis Center,
Stone Mountain, Georgia

*Centre de tennis du parc de Stone
Mountain, Stone Mountain, Géorgie*

LEGEND / *LEGENDE*

This legend represents the major functional areas
located at each Olympic venue. The numbers below
correspond to the numbers shown on the venue
maps.

*Les principaux domaines fonctionnels en place sur
chaque site figurent dans cette légende. Les chiffres
correspondent à ceux que l'on trouve sur les cartes
des sites.*

1   Accreditation / *Accréditation*

2   Ceremonies / *Cérémonies*

3   Competition area / *Aire de compétition*

4   Competition related area / *Aire des
    services liés aux compétitions*

5   Event seating / *Places*

6   ACOG management / *Direction du site*

7   Sports administration
    federation services / *Services administratifs
    des fédérations sportives*

8   Material acquisition/distribution /
    Acquisition/distribution du matériel

9   Press / *Presse*

10 Broadcasters / *Diffuseurs*

11 Health services and medical control / *Services
    et contrôles médicaux*

12 Spectator services / *Services aux spectateurs*

13 Olympic Family services / *Services à la Famille
    olympique*

14 Security / *Sécurité*

15 Technology / *Technologie*

16 Food services / *Alimentation*

17 Transportation / *Transports*

18 Ticketing / *Billetterie*

19 Spectator entrance / *Entrée réservée aux
    spectateurs*

20 Athlete entrance / *Entrée réservée aux
    athlètes*

Volleyball—Beach
Volleyball — De plage
Atlanta Beach, Jonesboro, Georgia
Plage d'Atlanta, Jonesboro, Géorgie

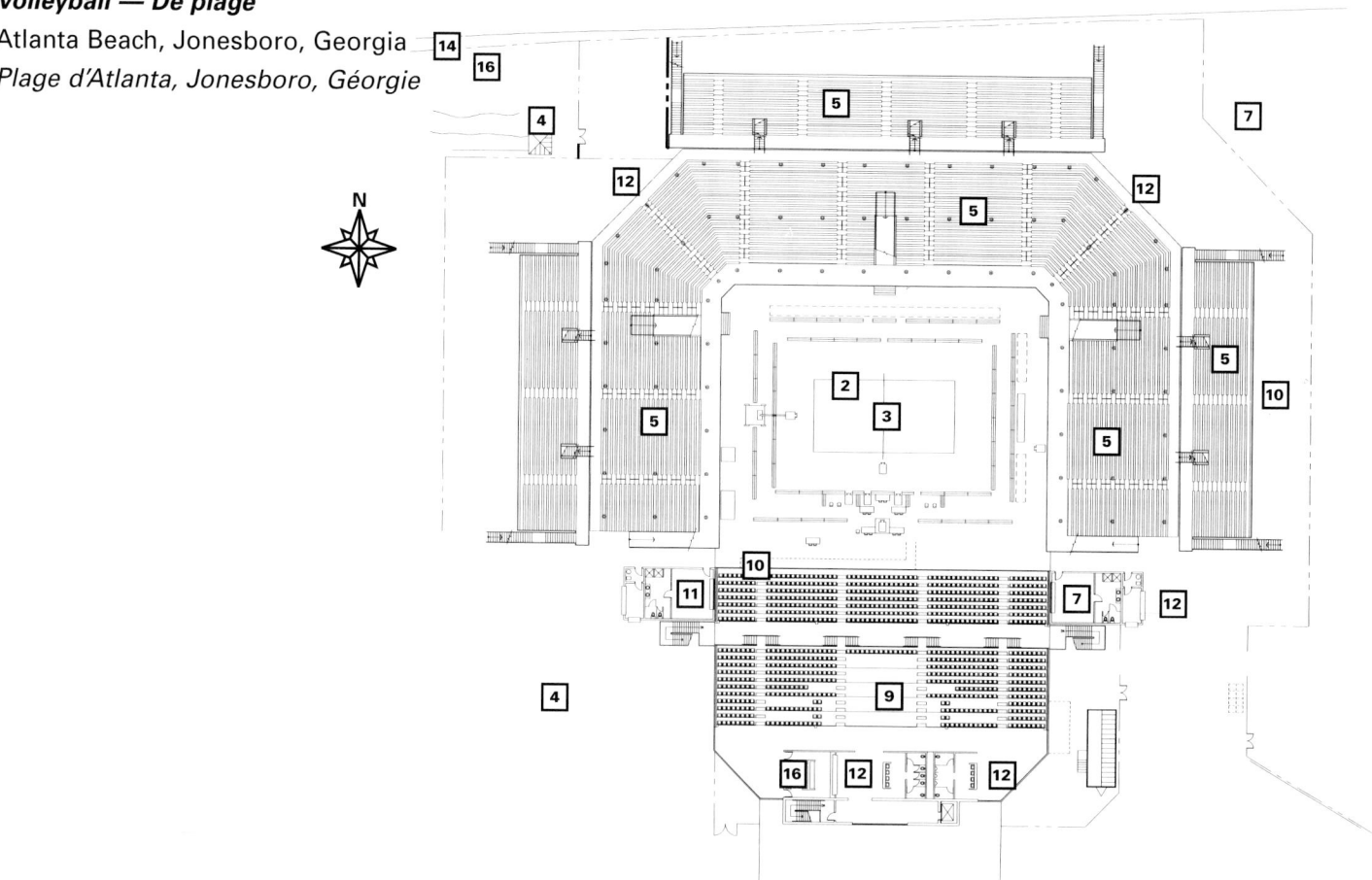

Volleyball—Indoor, Preliminaries
Volleyball — En salle, Eliminatoires
University of Georgia Coliseum, Athens, Georgia
Coliseum, université de Géorgie, Athens, Géorgie

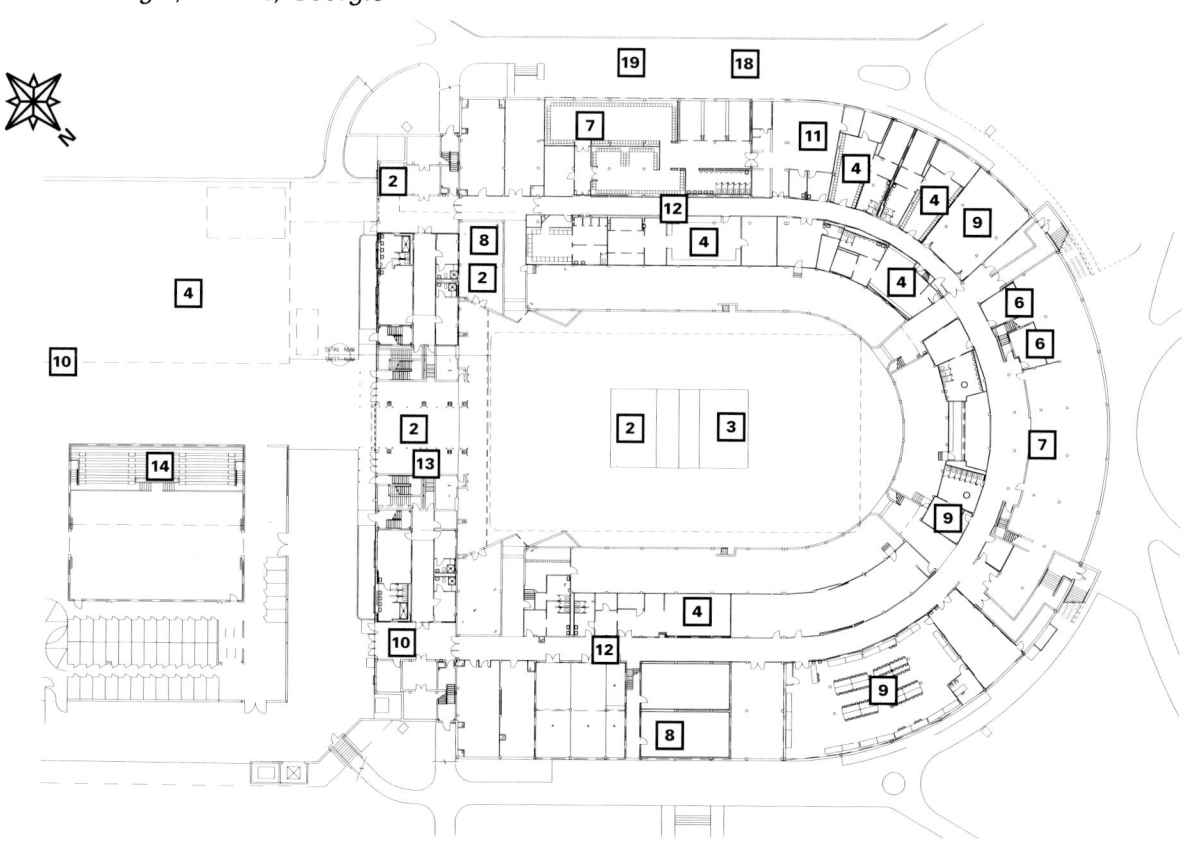

Volleyball—Indoor
Volleyball — En salle
Omni Coliseum, Atlanta, Georgia
Omni Coliseum, Atlanta, Géorgie

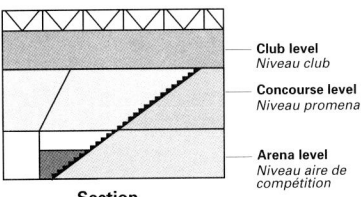

Club level
Niveau club

Concourse level
Niveau promena

Arena level
Niveau aire de compétition

Section

N

LEGEND / *LEGENDE*

This legend represents the major functional areas located at each Olympic venue. The numbers below correspond to the numbers shown on the venue maps.

Les principaux domaines fonctionnels en place sur chaque site figurent dans cette légende. Les chiffres correspondent à ceux que l'on trouve sur les cartes des sites.

1 Accreditation / *Accréditation*

2 Ceremonies / *Cérémonies*

3 Competition area / *Aire de compétition*

4 Competition related area / *Aire des services liés aux compétitions*

5 Event seating / *Places*

6 ACOG management / *Direction du site*

7 Sports administration federation services / *Services administratifs des fédérations sportives*

8 Material acquisition/distribution / *Acquisition/distribution du matériel*

9 Press / *Presse*

10 Broadcasters / *Diffuseurs*

11 Health services and medical control / *Services et contrôles médicaux*

12 Spectator services / *Services aux spectateurs*

13 Olympic Family services / *Services à la Famille olympique*

14 Security / *Sécurité*

15 Technology / *Technologie*

16 Food services / *Alimentation*

17 Transportation / *Transports*

18 Ticketing / *Billetterie*

19 Spectator entrance / *Entrée réservée aux spectateurs*

20 Athlete entrance / *Entrée réservée aux athlètes*

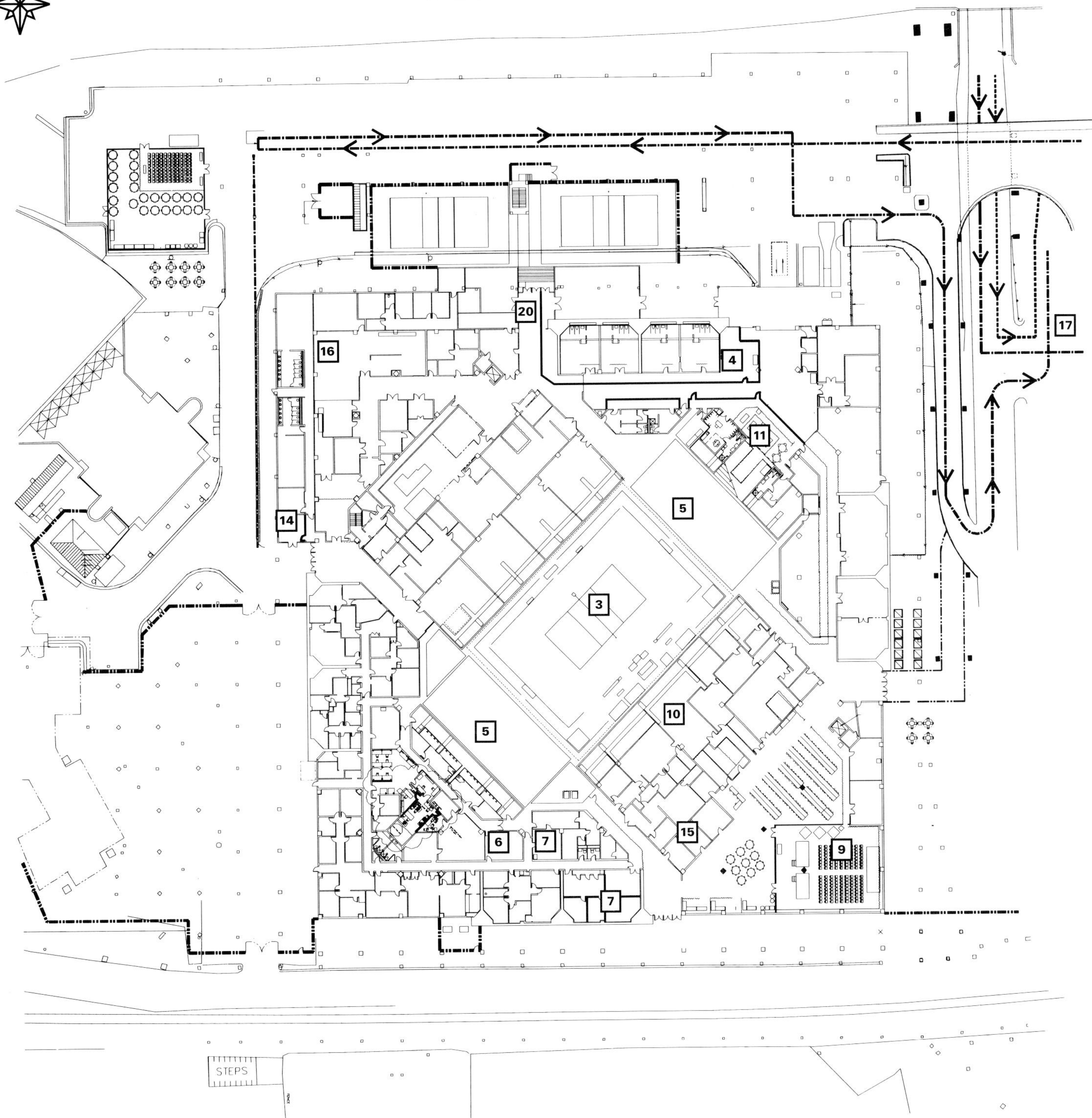

STEPS

Weightlifting / *Haltérophilie*

Georgia World Congress
Center (GWCC)—Hall E,
Atlanta, Georgia

*Centre international de
congrès de Géorgie (GWCC)
— Hall E, Atlanta, Géorgie*

Note: Additional seating as well
as other functional areas on
upper floors.

*Remarque : Places supplémentaires
et autres domaines fonctionnels
aux niveaux supérieurs.*

Wrestling / *Lutte*

Georgia World Congress Center (GWCC)—Hall G, Atlanta, Georgia

Centre international de congrès de Géorgie (GWCC) — Hall G, Atlanta, Géorgie

Note: See page 459 for overview
map of the GWCC.

*Remarque : Voir page 459 pour le
plan du GWCC.*

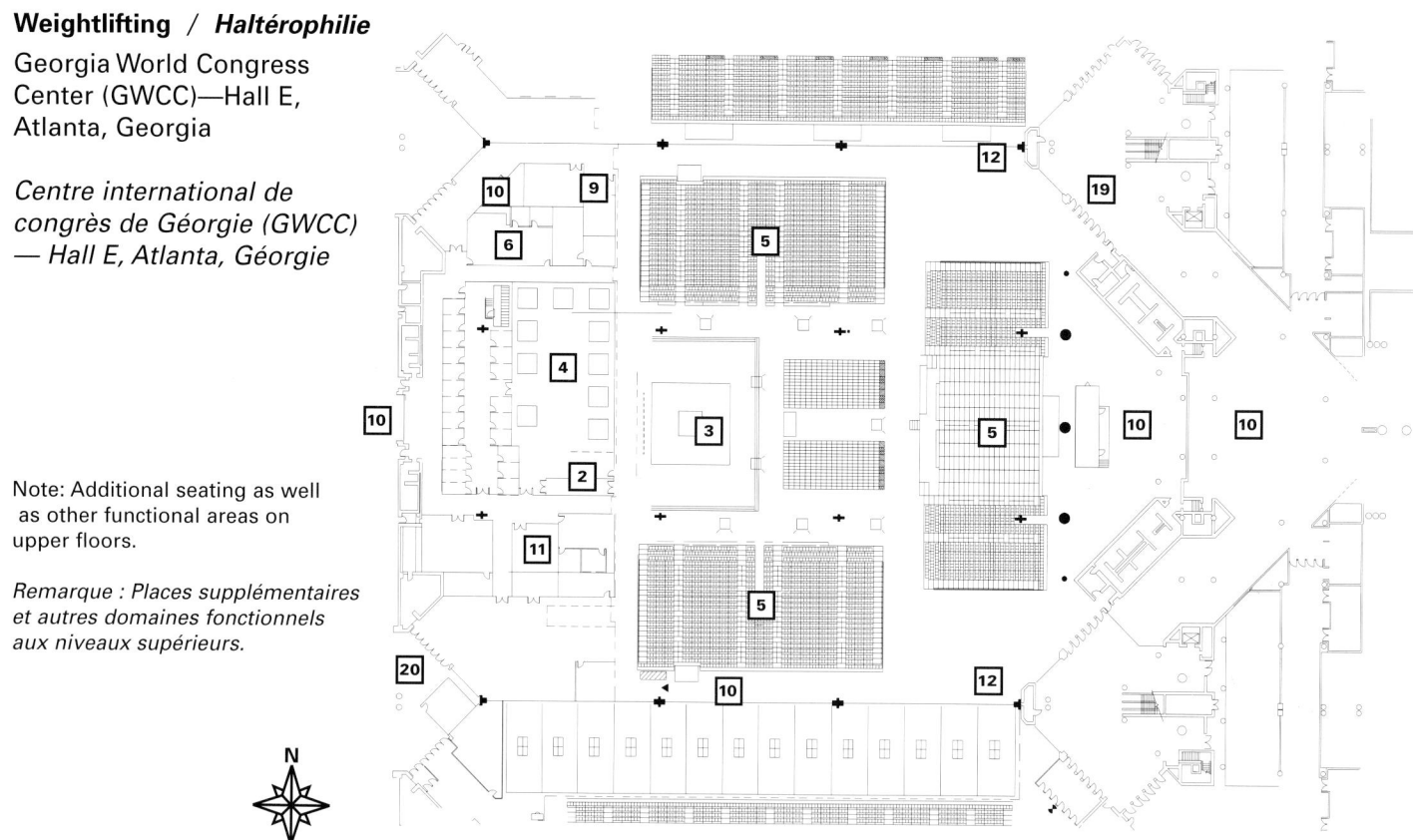

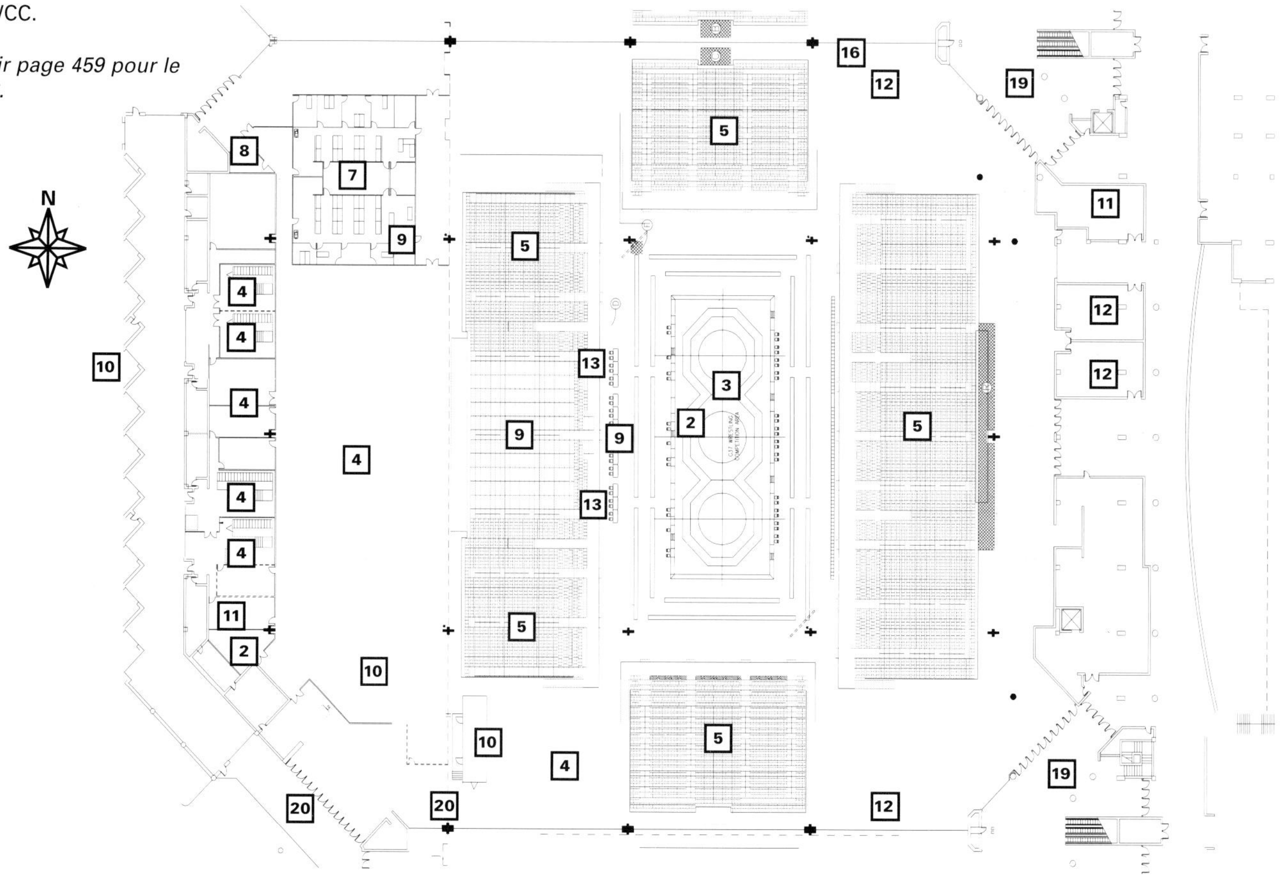

Yachting

Yachting

Wassaw Sound, Atlantic Ocean, Savannah, Georgia

Détroit de Wassaw, océan Atlantique, Savannah, Géorgie

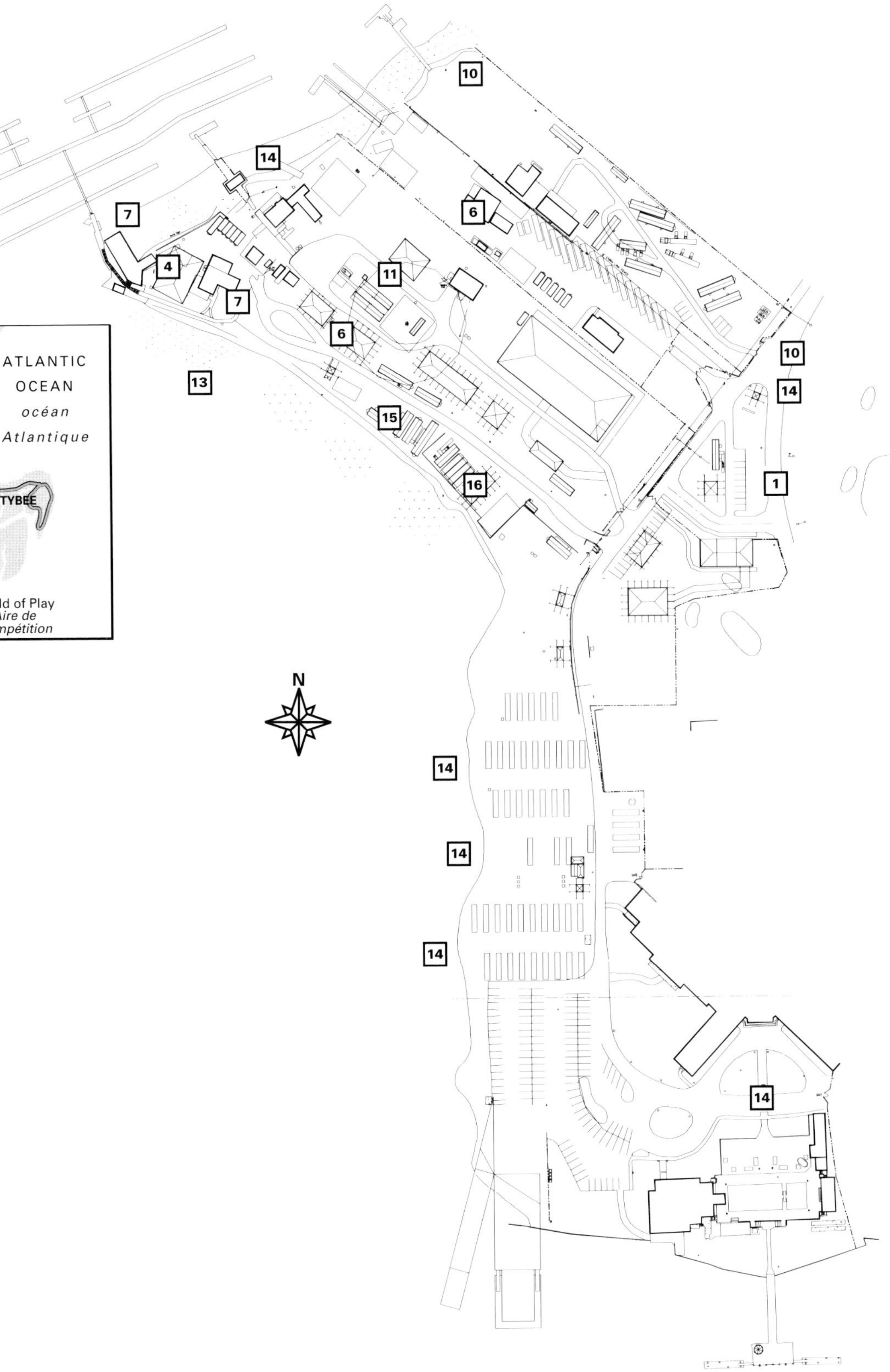

Overview / *Plan du site*

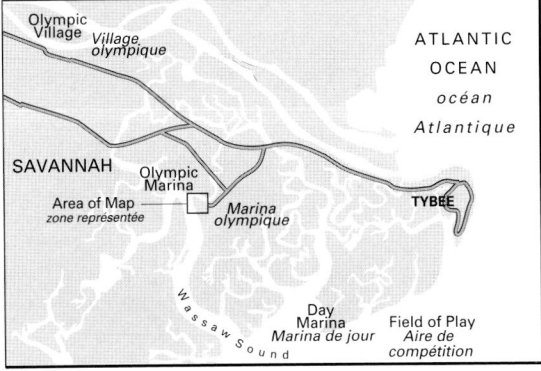

This legend represents the major functional areas located at each Olympic venue. The numbers below correspond to the numbers shown on the venue maps.

Les principaux domaines fonctionnels en place sur chaque site figurent dans cette légende. Les chiffres correspondent à ceux que l'on trouve sur les cartes des sites.

1 Accreditation / *Accréditation*
2 Ceremonies / *Cérémonies*
3 Competition area / *Aire de compétition*
4 Competition related area / *Aire des services liés aux compétitions*
5 Event seating / *Places*
6 ACOG management / *Direction du site*
7 Sports administration federation services / *Services administratifs des fédérations sportives*
8 Material acquisition/distribution / *Acquisition/distribution du matériel*
9 Press / *Presse*
10 Broadcasters / *Diffuseurs*
11 Health services and medical control / *Services et contrôles médicaux*
12 Spectator services / *Services aux spectateurs*
13 Olympic Family services / *Services à la Famille olympique*
14 Security / *Sécurité*
15 Technology / *Technologie*
16 Food services / *Alimentation*
17 Transportation / *Transports*
18 Ticketing / *Billetterie*
19 Spectator entrance / *Entrée réservée aux spectateurs*
20 Athlete entrance / *Entrée réservée aux athlètes*

ACKNOWLEDGMENTS AND CREDITS / REMERCIEMENTS

The Atlanta Committee for the Olympic Games (ACOG) acknowledges the dedicated efforts of the ACOG and Peachtree Publishers staff members who assisted in the development of this volume of the *Official Report*.

ACOG STAFF / PERSONNEL ACOG

Editor / *Rédacteur*
Ginger Watkins

Managing Editor / *Rédacteur responsable*
Paul F. Acocella

Design / *Conception*
Andrea Pavone Said
Sheri E. Thomas

Venue Drawings / *Plans des sites*
John Marshall

Editorial and Administrative / *Rédaction et administration*
Stewart Lathan

PEACHTREE PUBLISHERS STAFF / PERSONNEL PEACHTREE PUBLISHERS

Publisher / *Editeur*
Margaret M. Quinlin

Senior Editor / *Rédacteur en chef*
Maryjane Wraga

Design and Typography / *Conception et typographie*
Robin Sherman
Loraine M. Balcsik
Nicola Simmonds Carter
Melanie M. McMahon
Sara M. Stefani

Print Production / *Fabrication*
Dana L. Laurent
Simone René
  Imago, USA, Inc., NY

Editorial and Administrative / *Rédaction et administration*
Tiffany Anne Tamaroff
Alan Neely
Amy R. Sproull
Marsha McSpadden
Sherryl D. Wade

French Translation / *Traduction française*
Fabienne Boulongne-Collier
Tiffany Anne Tamaroff

PHOTO CREDITS / CRÉDITS PHOTOS

Photographs courtesy of The Atlanta Committee for the Olympic Games consisting of the following listed alphabetically by photographer / *Photos publiées avec la permission du Comité d'Atlanta pour les Jeux Olympiques. Liste des photographes par ordre alphabétique :*

Photographer, Page Number / *Photographe, Page numéro :*
Steve Dinberg—185, 365
Wingate Downs—161
Stephanie Klein-Davis—127, 241
Simon Kornblit—175
Rich Krauze—315
Jeff Najarian—109
Sandy Owens—353
Sheryl Siegel—59, 343

Photographs courtesy of the International Olympic Photographic Pool consisting of the following listed alphabetically by photographer with corresponding news agency / *Photos publiées avec la permission de l'Equipe internationale des photographes olympiques. Liste des photographes par ordre alphabétique et agence de presse correspondante :*

Photographer, Organization, Page Number / *Photographe, Organisation, Page numéro :*
John Bazemore, Associated Press—265
Al Behrman, Associated Press—115, 376
Gabriel Bouys, Agence France Presse—319
Luca Bruno, Associated Press—41
Gary Cameron, Reuters—153
Gary Caskey, Reuters—435
Robert Daemmrich, Agence France Presse—243
Don Emmert, Agence France Presse—67
John Gaps III, Associated Press—417
Karl-Heinz Kreifelts, Associated Press—193
Bruce McNamee, Reuters—423
Anja Niedringhaus, Agence France Presse—165
Denis Paquin, Associated Press—19
Jason Reed, Reuters—39
Amy Sancetta, Associated Press—15
Yoshikazu Tsuno, Agence France Presse—229
Kathy Willens, Associated Press—371
Tao-Shien Yeh, Agence France Presse—293